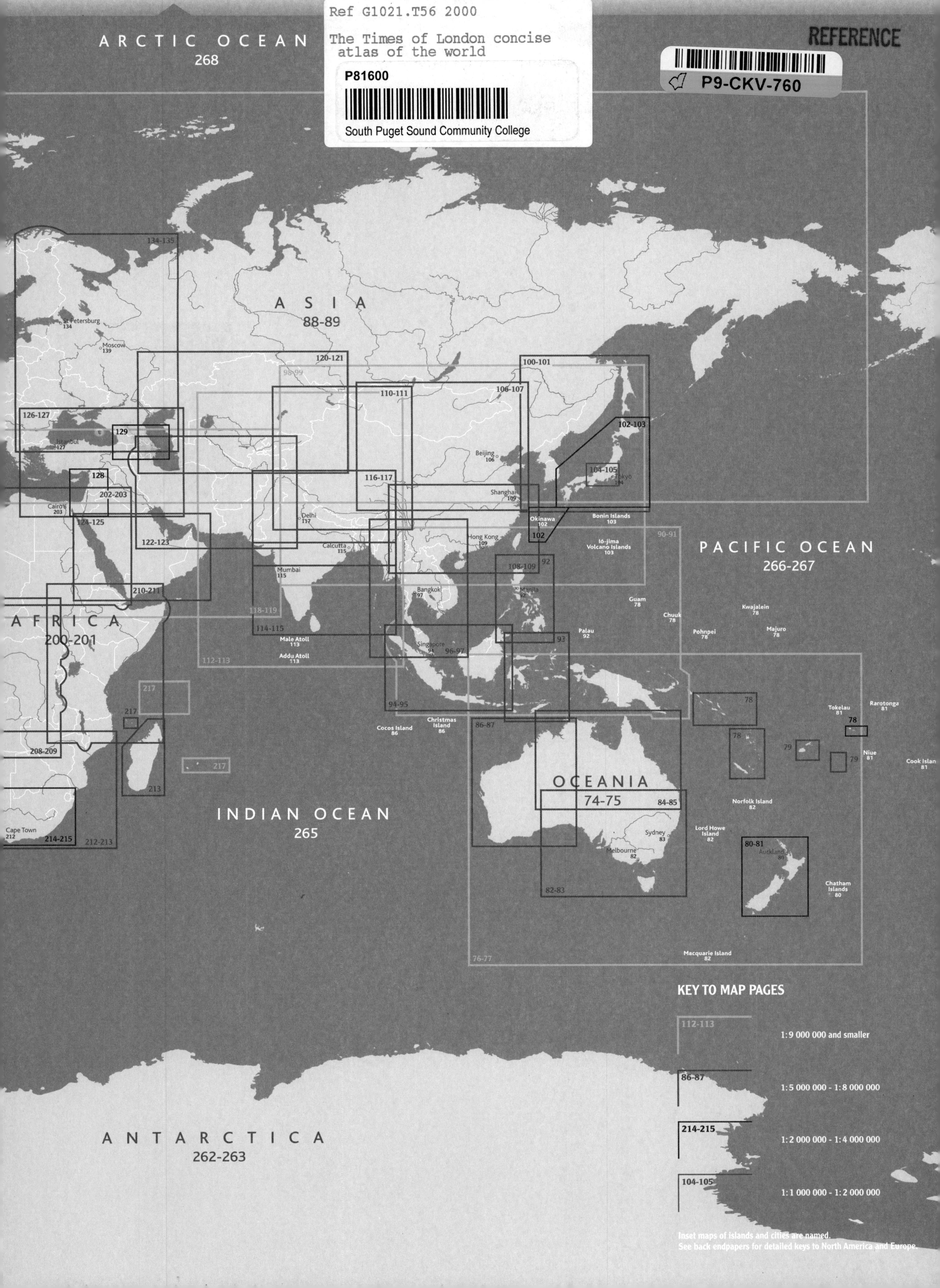
ARCTIC OCEAN
268
ASIA
88-89
St Petersburg
134
Moscow
139
134-135
120-121
98-99
100-101
110-111
106-107
126-127
129
Istanbul
127
102-103
Beijing
106
104-105
Tokyo
104
128
116-117
Shanghai
109
202-203
Cairo
203
Okinawa
102
Bonin Islands
103
124-125
Delhi
117
102
90-91
122-123
Calcutta
115
Hong Kong
109
Iō-jima
Volcano Islands
103
PACIFIC OCEAN
266-267
92
108-109
Mumbai
115
210-211
Bangkok
97
Manila
92
Guam
78
AFRICA
200-201
118-119
Kwajalein
78
Chuuk
78
114-115
Palau
92
Pohnpei
78
Majuro
78
Male Atoll
113
Singapore
94
96-97
93
112-113
Addu Atoll
113
217
94-95
78
217
Christmas Island
86
Cocos Island
86
86-87
Tokelau
81
Rarotonga
81
78
208-209
78
79
Niue
81
79
Cook Islan
81
217
OCEANIA
74-75
84-85
213
Norfolk Island
82
INDIAN OCEAN
265
Cape Town
212
214-215
212-213
Sydney
83
Lord Howe Island
82
80-81
Auckland
80
Melbourne
82
82-83
Chatham Islands
80
76-77
Macquarie Island
82
KEY TO MAP PAGES
112-113
1:9 000 000 and smaller
86-87
1:5 000 000 - 1:8 000 000
214-215
1:2 000 000 - 1:4 000 000
104-105
1:1 000 000 - 1:2 000 000
ANTARCTICA
262-263
Inset maps of islands and cities are named.
See back endpapers for detailed keys to North America and Europe.

THE TIMES

OF LONDON

CONCISE ATLAS OF THE WORLD

EIGHTH EDITION

CROWN PUBLISHERS
New York

THE TIMES OF LONDON CONCISE ATLAS OF THE WORLD
EIGHTH EDITION

First Edition 1972
Second Edition 1975
Third Edition 1978
Fourth Edition 1980
Fifth Edition 1986
Sixth Edition 1992
Seventh Edition 1995

Eighth Edition 2000

Random House, Inc. New York, London, Sydney, Auckland
www.randomhouse.com

This work published in the U.K. by Times Books Group Ltd as *The Times Concise Atlas of the World 8th Edition*.

LIBRARY OF CONGRESS CATALOGING–IN–PUBLICATION DATA IS AVAILABLE.

ISBN: 0-609-60890-8

Printed and bound in the United Kingdom

9 8 7 6 5 4 3 2 1

First U.S. Edition

THE TIMES

OF LONDON

CONCISE ATLAS OF THE WORLD

EIGHTH EDITION

CROWN PUBLISHERS
New York

CONTENTS

THE WORLD TODAY

GEOGRAPHICAL INFORMATION

ATLAS OF THE WORLD

WORLD

OCEANIA

CONTENTS

AFRICA

CONTENTS

NORTH AMERICA

SOUTH AMERICA

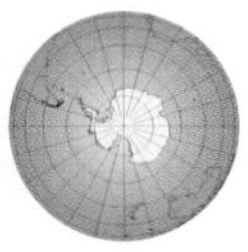

OCEANIA

Australia and the vast expanse of the Pacific Ocean dominate this satellite image of Oceania. The islands of Indonesia lie to the northwest of Australia and New Guinea lies to the north, with the islands of the Solomon Island chain, Vanuatu and New Caledonia stretching southeast from New Guinea towards New Zealand. The Hawaiian Islands appear in the top right of the image.

The different colours on these images reveal a great variety of vegetation. This is particularly evident here in the contrasts between the highlands and lowlands of New Guinea and between the east coast, the Great Dividing Range and the complex interior of Australia.

See pages 74–75 for a map of Oceania.

Data from the 1km AVHRR Global Land dataset project by ESA, CEOS, IGBP, NASA, NOAA, USGS, IONIA processed by ESA/ESRIN distributed by Eurimage S.p.A

ASIA

This image shows the continent of Asia from the Mediterranean Sea and the distinctive shape of The Gulf in the west, to Japan in the east, and from snow-covered Siberia in the north to the tropical islands of Indonesia in the south. The shapes of the Caspian and Aral Seas appear in the northwest.

The image illustrates a wide range of land cover – particularly in China, with great variation between the intricate patterns of vegetation in the southeast and the large, relatively featureless areas of the Tarim Pendi basin in the northwest, in the centre of the image. The snow covered Himalaya form a dominating feature of the image, stretching in a gentle white arc between the Indian sub-continent and China.

See pages 88–89 for a map of Asia.

Data from the 1km AVHRR Global Land dataset project by ESA, CEOS, IGBP NASA, NOAA, USGS, IONIA processed by ESA/ESRIN distributed by Eurimage S.p.A

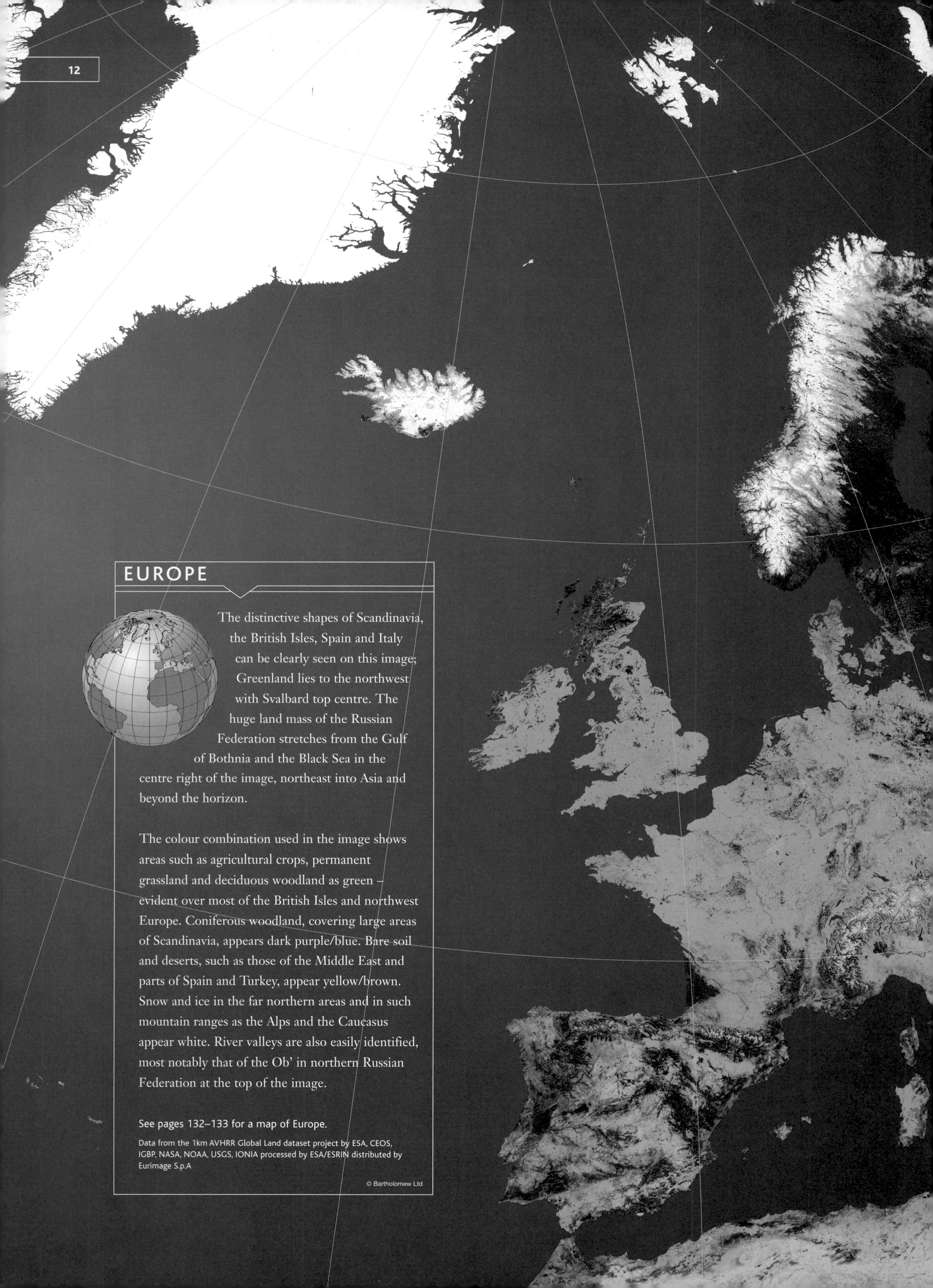

EUROPE

The distinctive shapes of Scandinavia, the British Isles, Spain and Italy can be clearly seen on this image; Greenland lies to the northwest with Svalbard top centre. The huge land mass of the Russian Federation stretches from the Gulf of Bothnia and the Black Sea in the centre right of the image, northeast into Asia and beyond the horizon.

The colour combination used in the image shows areas such as agricultural crops, permanent grassland and deciduous woodland as green – evident over most of the British Isles and northwest Europe. Coniferous woodland, covering large areas of Scandinavia, appears dark purple/blue. Bare soil and deserts, such as those of the Middle East and parts of Spain and Turkey, appear yellow/brown. Snow and ice in the far northern areas and in such mountain ranges as the Alps and the Caucasus appear white. River valleys are also easily identified, most notably that of the Ob' in northern Russian Federation at the top of the image.

See pages 132–133 for a map of Europe.

Data from the 1km AVHRR Global Land dataset project by ESA, CEOS, IGBP, NASA, NOAA, USGS, IONIA processed by ESA/ESRIN distributed by Eurimage S.p.A

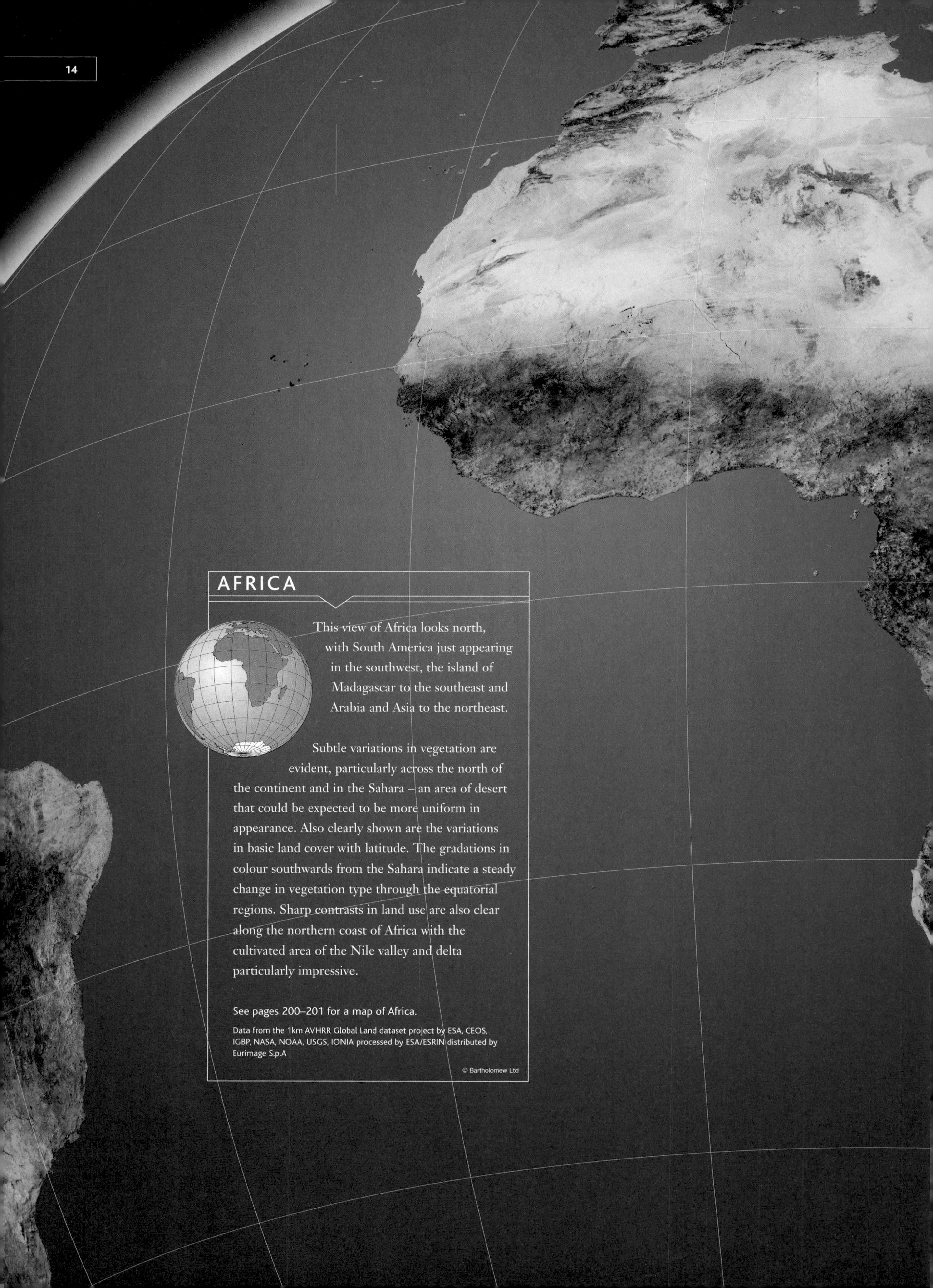

AFRICA

This view of Africa looks north, with South America just appearing in the southwest, the island of Madagascar to the southeast and Arabia and Asia to the northeast.

Subtle variations in vegetation are evident, particularly across the north of the continent and in the Sahara – an area of desert that could be expected to be more uniform in appearance. Also clearly shown are the variations in basic land cover with latitude. The gradations in colour southwards from the Sahara indicate a steady change in vegetation type through the equatorial regions. Sharp contrasts in land use are also clear along the northern coast of Africa with the cultivated area of the Nile valley and delta particularly impressive.

See pages 200–201 for a map of Africa.

Data from the 1km AVHRR Global Land dataset project by ESA, CEOS, IGBP, NASA, NOAA, USGS, IONIA processed by ESA/ESRIN distributed by Eurimage S.p.A

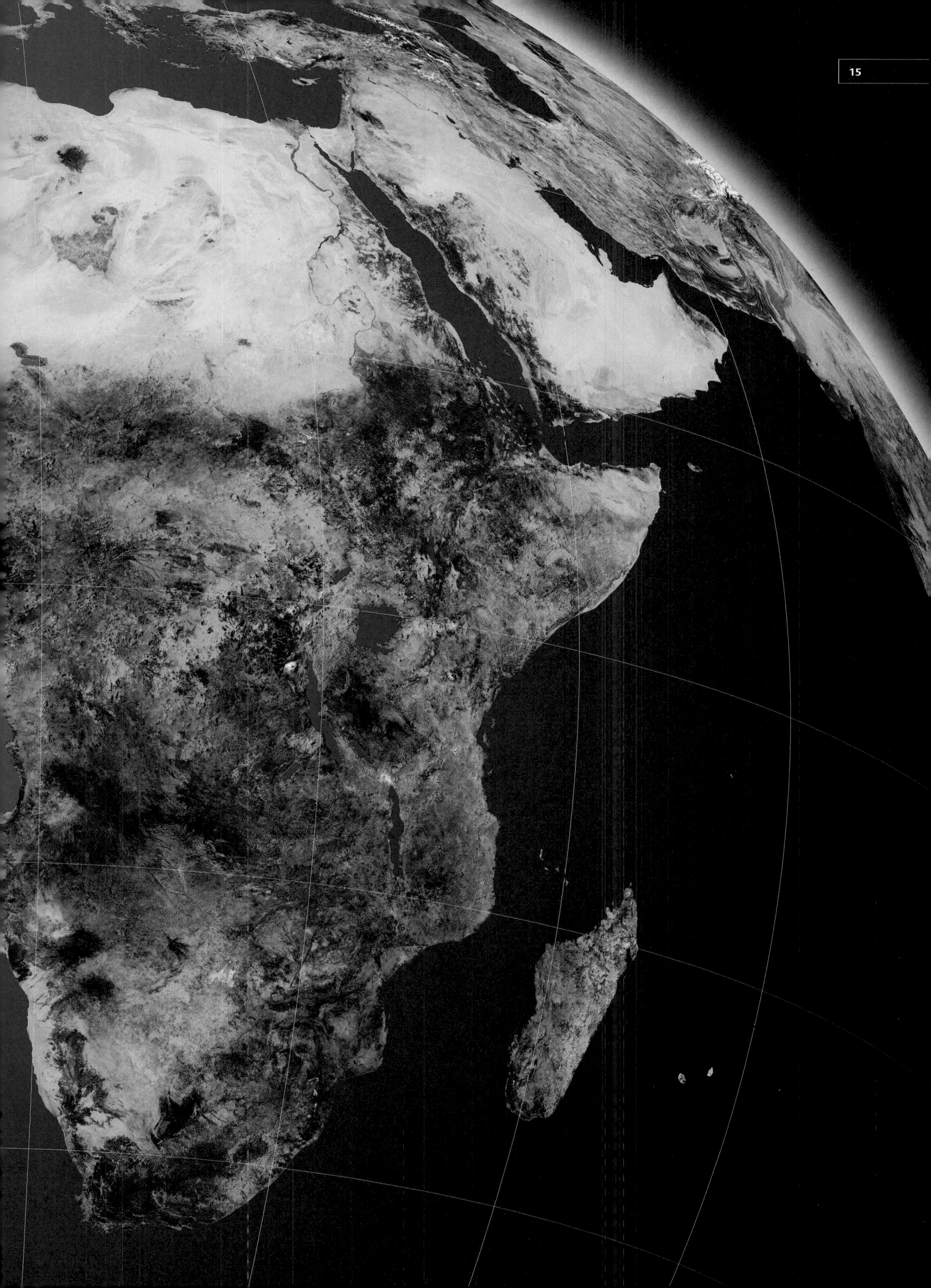

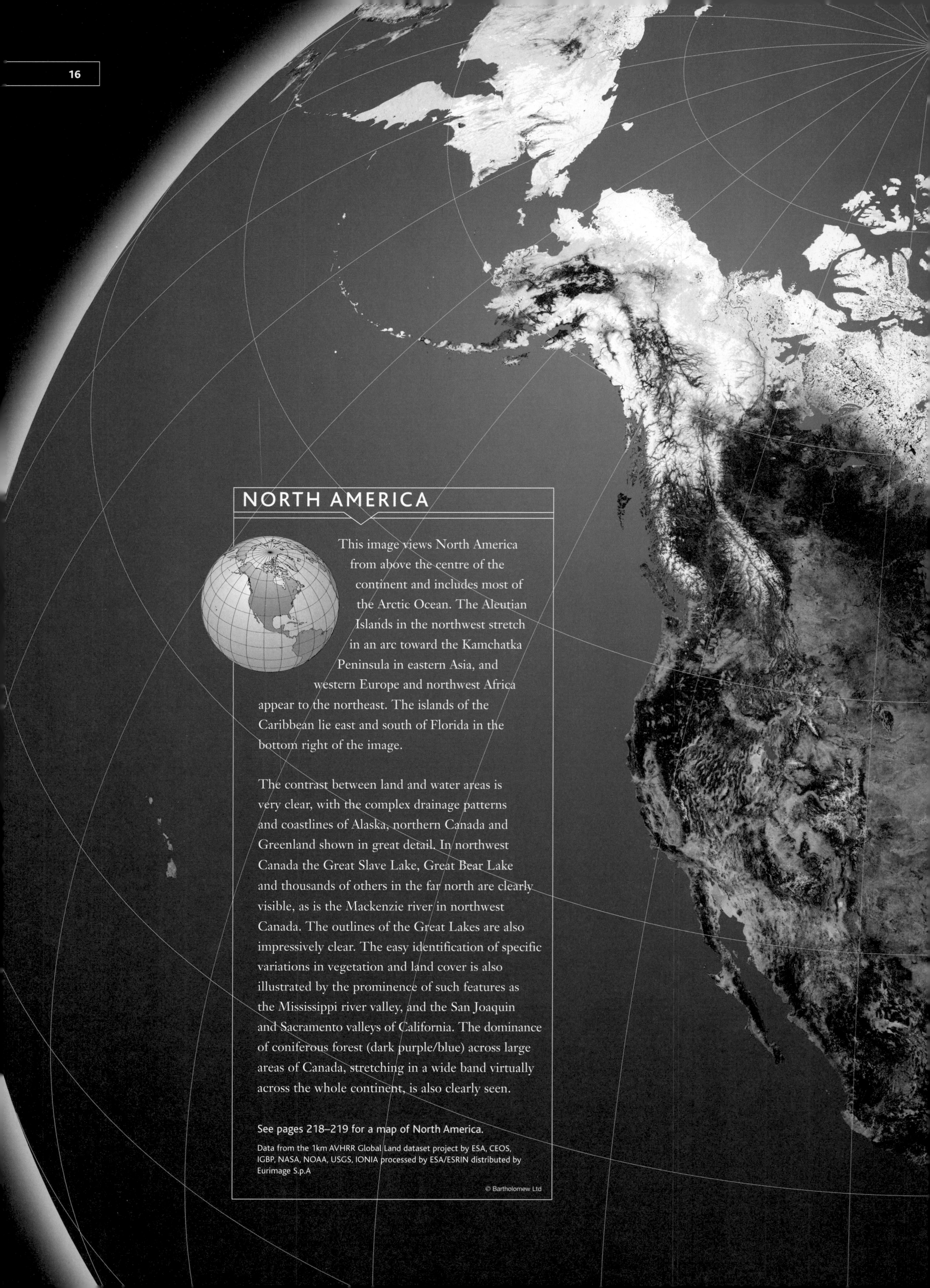

NORTH AMERICA
This image views North America from above the centre of the continent and includes most of the Arctic Ocean. The Aleutian Islands in the northwest stretch in an arc toward the Kamchatka Peninsula in eastern Asia, and western Europe and northwest Africa appear to the northeast. The islands of the Caribbean lie east and south of Florida in the bottom right of the image.

The contrast between land and water areas is very clear, with the complex drainage patterns and coastlines of Alaska, northern Canada and Greenland shown in great detail. In northwest Canada the Great Slave Lake, Great Bear Lake and thousands of others in the far north are clearly visible, as is the Mackenzie river in northwest Canada. The outlines of the Great Lakes are also impressively clear. The easy identification of specific variations in vegetation and land cover is also illustrated by the prominence of such features as the Mississippi river valley, and the San Joaquin and Sacramento valleys of California. The dominance of coniferous forest (dark purple/blue) across large areas of Canada, stretching in a wide band virtually across the whole continent, is also clearly seen.

See pages 218–219 for a map of North America.

Data from the 1km AVHRR Global Land dataset project by ESA, CEOS, IGBP, NASA, NOAA, USGS, IONIA processed by ESA/ESRIN distributed by Eurimage S.p.A

SOUTH AMERICA

South and Central America appear in the centre of this image with the Pacific Ocean to the west and the Atlantic Ocean to the east, and Africa appearing on the northeast and southeast horizons. The Galapagos Islands lie off the coast of Ecuador and the Falkland Islands, South Georgia and the Antarctic Peninsula off the southern tip of the continent.

The great range of green and blue tones represent different types and conditions of vegetation across the Amazon basin. Although the data contains no indication of surface height, it can indicate the underlying structure of the land. Here, the mountain ranges of the northern Andes and western Colombia are clearly evident. The small red areas on the east coast of Brazil, representing the major urban areas of São Paulo and Rio de Janeiro, illustrate the impressive level of detail available from this type of imagery.

See pages 248–249 for a map of South America.

Data from the 1km AVHRR Global Land dataset project by ESA, CEOS, IGBP, NASA, NOAA, USGS, IONIA processed by ESA/ESRIN distributed by Eurimage S.p.A

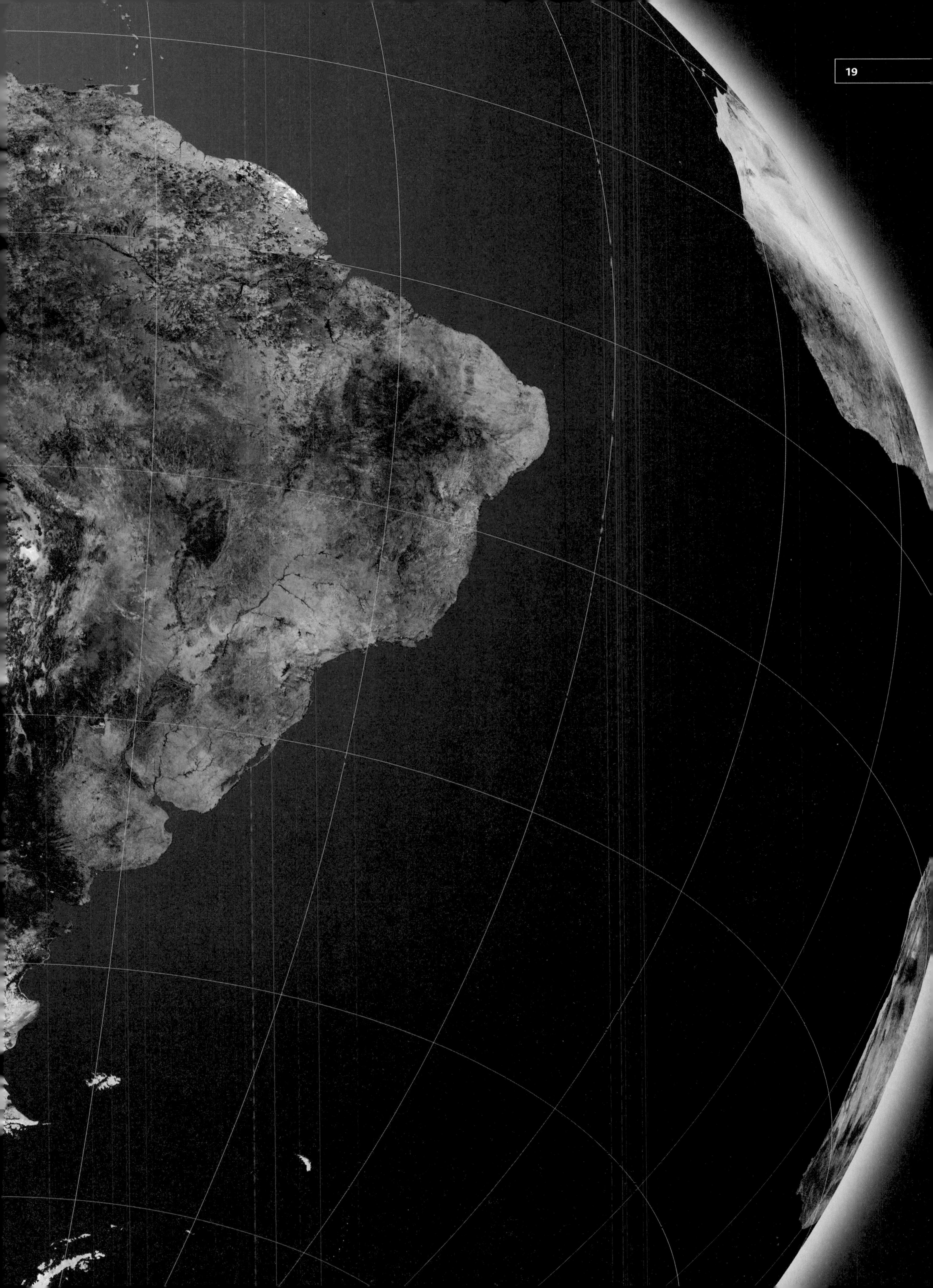

ANTARCTICA

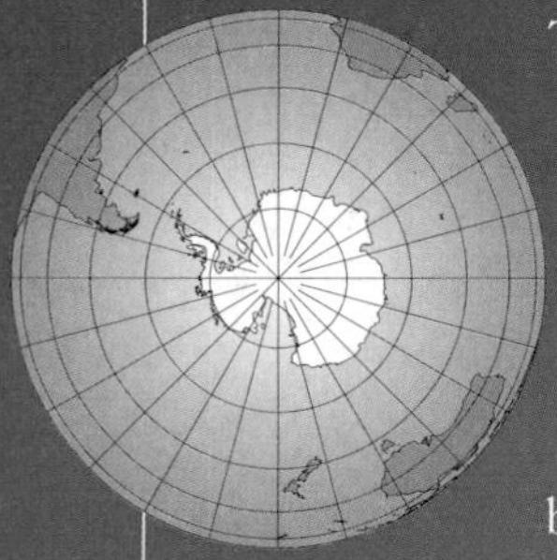

This image positions the Antarctic continent with the Greenwich meridian to the top centre. The distinctive shape of the Antarctic Peninsula lies to the top left and the prominent Ross Ice Shelf can be identified to the bottom of the image, below the Transantarctic Mountains range.

Although not completely cloud-free – there is some cloud cover in the eastern area to the right of the image – the image is impressive in its depiction of the physical features of the continent. The Ronne Ice Shelf, including Berkner Island, and the Transantarctic Mountains are particularly spectacular. Floating ice is excluded from the image, resulting in a clear definition of the extent of the continental ice sheet in an austral summer.

See pages 262–263 for a continental map of Antarctica.

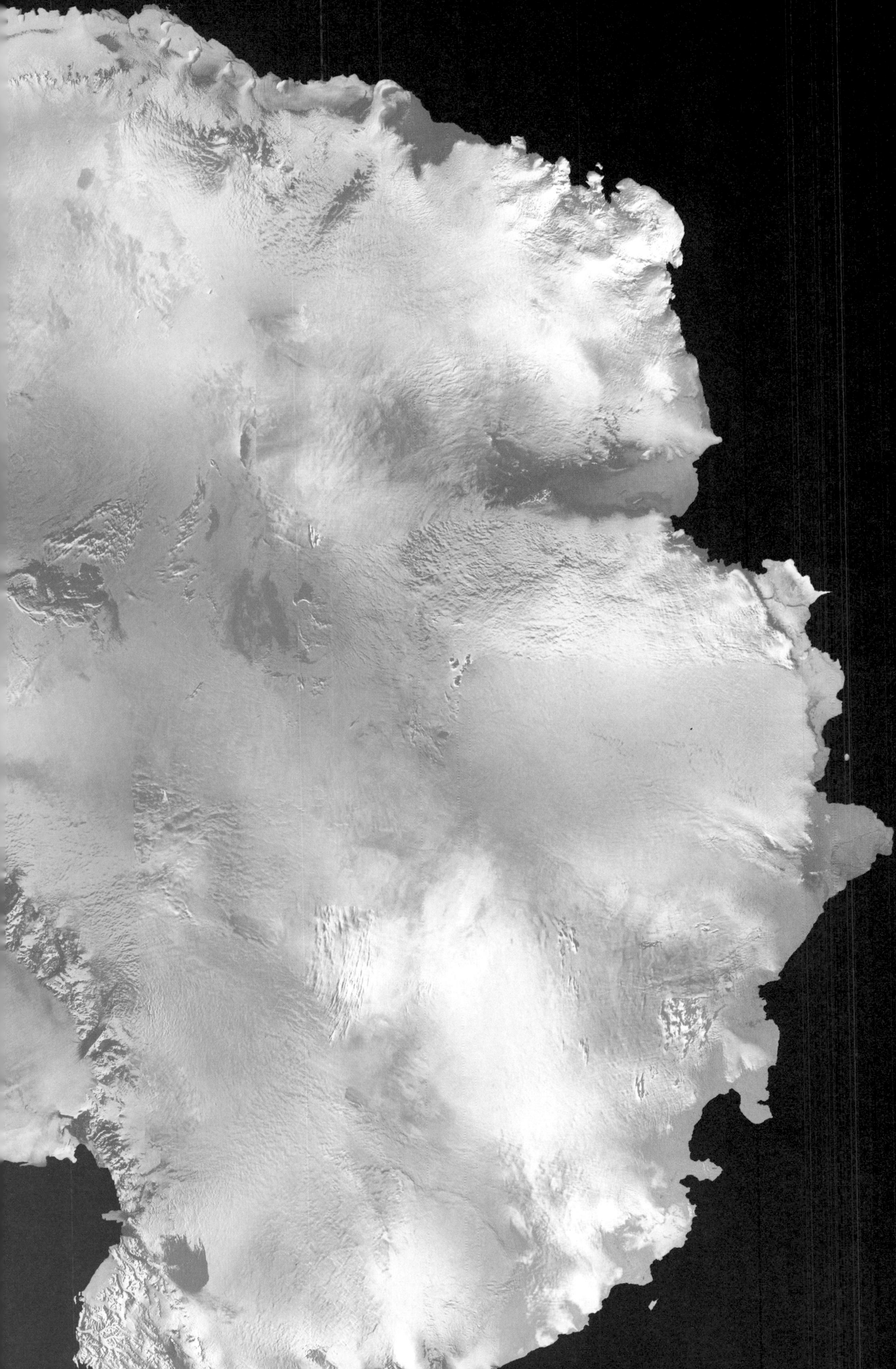

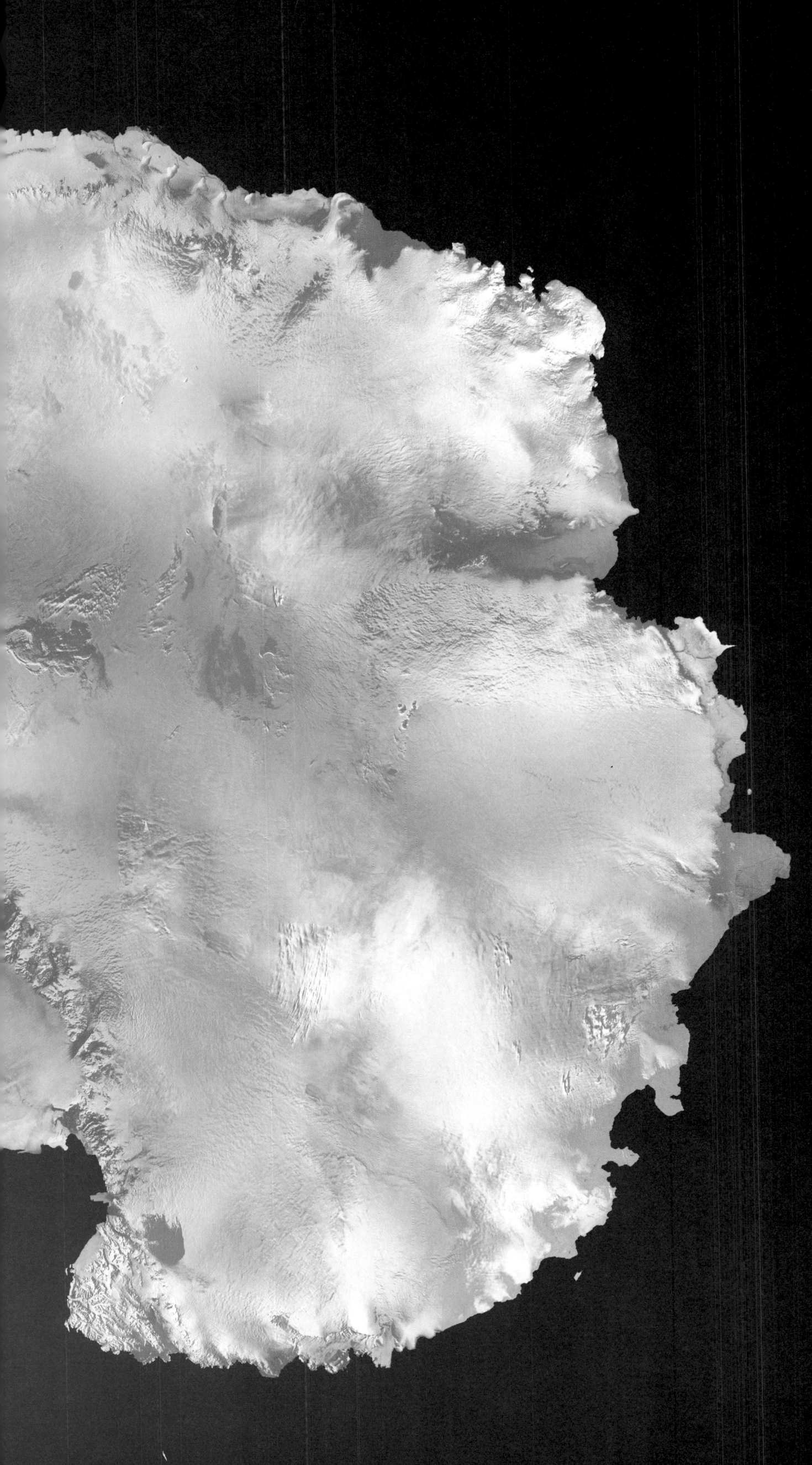

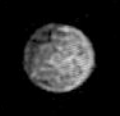

ORIGINS OF THE SOLAR SYSTEM

The nature and origin of our Solar System has been a subject of much debate. Early ideas of an Earth-centred system took many hundreds of years to be discarded in favour of Copernicus' heliocentric, or sun-centred model. More refined theories followed with Kepler's laws of orbital motion, and Newton's laws of gravity. The question of origin remained unanswered, and was regarded more as a philosophical matter.

The fact that the Sun and the planets rotate in a similar direction suggests a common formation mechanism - that of a large collapsing cloud or nebula. It is now believed that this did happen, about 4 600 million years ago. The nebula consisted of predominantly hydrogen and helium, but with a small amount of heavier elements. Over time, the cloud collapsed to form a rotating disk around a dense core. As core collapse continued and pressure in the core increased, material was heated enough to allow the nuclear fusion of hydrogen. Meanwhile as the disk cooled, the heavier elements began to condense and agglomerate. Larger bodies grew rapidly by sweeping up much of the remaining smaller material. As the core began to shine, its radiation pushed back much of the nearby volatile disk material into the outer Solar System, where it condensed and accumulated on the more distant planetary cores. This left the Inner Planets as small rocky bodies, and produced the Gas Giants of the outer system. Bombardment of the planets by a decreasing number of small bodies continued for several hundred million years, causing the craters now seen on many of the planets and moons.

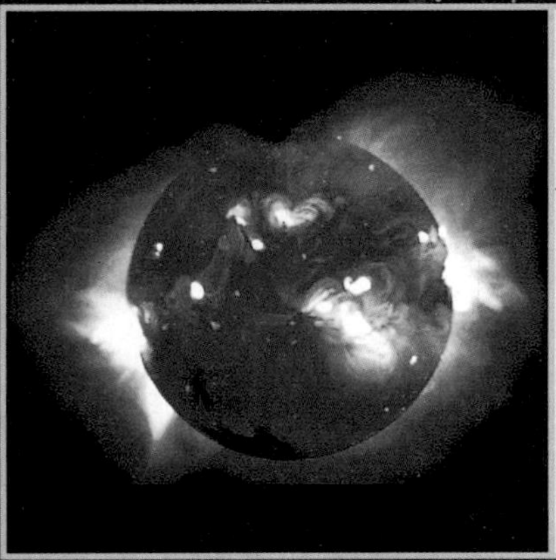

The Sun

The Sun is a typical star. It accounts for 99.85 per cent of the total mass contained within the Solar System, ensuring that it provides a dominating gravitational hold on its orbiting planets. The tremendous amount of heat and light produced by the Sun is the result of nuclear fusion reactions which occur in its core. In this process, hydrogen is converted into helium to produce a core temperature of roughly 15 million°C. Intense magnetic fields can induce cooling zones seen as dark sun spots on the Sun's surface. The Sun constantly emits a stream of charged particles which form the solar wind and cause auroral activity which can be seen on Earth.

	Sun	Mercury	Venus	Earth	Mars	Jupiter	Saturn	Uranus	Neptune	Pluto
Mass (Earth=1)	332 830	0.055	0.815	1(6 x 10^{24})	0.107	317.9	95.2	14.5	17.1	0.002
Volume (Earth=1)	1 306 000	0.06	0.89	1	0.157	1 323	752	64	54	0.006
Density (Water=1)	1.41	5.43	5.25	5.52	3.95	1.33	0.69	1.29	1.64	2.03
Equatorial diameter (km)	1 392 000	4 879	12 104	12 756	6 794	142 984	120 536	51 118	49 492	2 320
Polar flattening	0	0	0	0.003	0.005	0.065	0.108	0.03	0.021	0
Surface gravity (Earth=1)	27.5	0.38	0.902	1	0.382	0.248	1.02	0.9	1.13	0.4
Number of satellites > 100 km	-	0	0	1	0	7	13	8	6	1
Total number of satellites	-	0	0	1	2	16	20	17	8	1
Rotation period (Earth days)	25 - 36	58.65	-243	23hr 56m 4s	1.03	0.414	0.444	-0.71	0.67	-6.39
Year (Earth days/years)	-	88 days	224.7 days	365.26 days	687 days	11.86 years	29.46 years	84.01 years	164.8 years	248.6 years
Mean orbital distance (million km)	-	57.9	108.2	149.6	227.9	778.3	1 249	2 871	4 504	5 914
Orbital eccentricity	-	0.2056	0.0068	0.0167	0.0934	0.0483	0.056	0.0461	0.0097	0.2482
Mean orbital velocity (km/s)	-	47.88	35.02	29.79	24.13	13.06	9.65	6.81	5.44	4.74
Inclination of equator to orbit	7.25	0	177.3	23.45	25.19	3.12	26.73	97.86	29.56	122.46
Orbital inclination (w.r.t. ecliptic)	-	7.01	3.4	0	1.85	1.31	2.49	0.77	1.77	17.13
Mean surface temperature (°C)	5 700	427(d), -173(n)	482	15	-63	-153	-185	-215	-225	-235
Atmospheric pressure (bars)	-	10^{-15}	92	1.013	0.007	-	-	-		3 x 10^{-6}
Atmospheric composition	H_2 92.1% He 7.8% O_2 0.061%	He 42% Na 42% O_2 15%	CO_2 96% N_2 3%	N_2 77% O_2 21% Ar 1.6%	CO_2 95.3% N_2 2.7%	H_2 90% He 10%	H_2 97% He 3%	H_2 83% He 15% CH_4 2%	H_2 85% He 13% CH_4 2%	N_2 CO CH_4

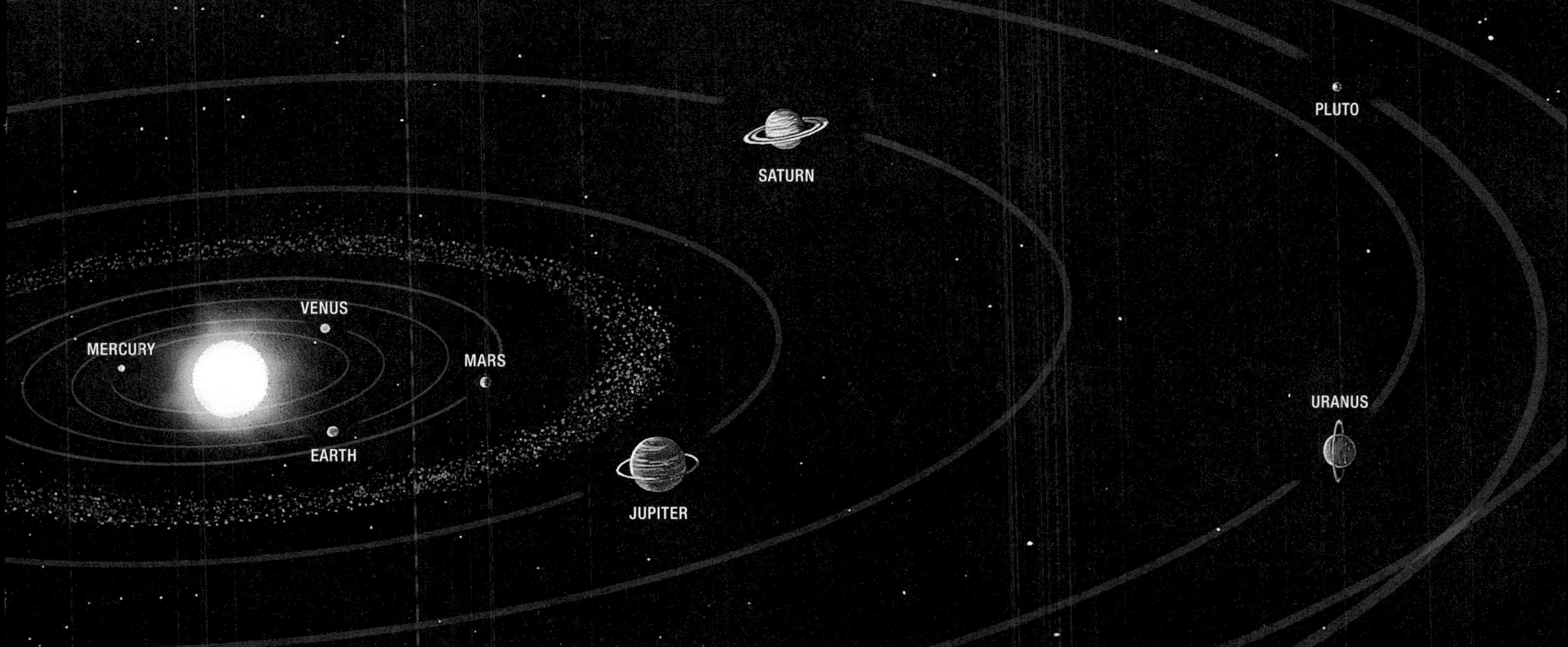
PLUTO
SATURN
VENUS
MERCURY
MARS
EARTH
JUPITER
URANUS

Mercury

Mercury's long period of rotation, close proximity to the Sun, and minimal atmosphere make its surface an extremely hostile environment with temperatures ranging from 427 to minus 173°C between its day and night side. Mercury is similar to Earth's Moon in size and appearance; its cratered surface was first photographed in detail in the mid-1970s by the Mariner 10 space probe. However the internal structure differs from the Moon; analysis of its magnetic field suggests that the core consists of molten iron, believed to be 40 per cent of the planet's volume. Mercury has a very eccentric orbit with its orbital distance varying from 46 to 70 million km.

Venus

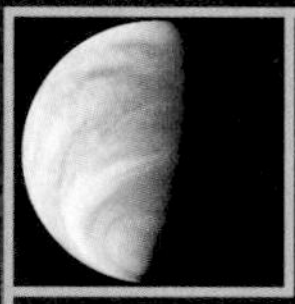

Venus' thick atmosphere of carbon dioxide and nitrogen creates not only a huge surface pressure of over ninety times that on Earth but also a greenhouse effect producing temperatures in excess of 480°C. Traces of sulphur dioxide and water vapour form clouds of dilute sulphuric acid, making the atmosphere extremely corrosive. This atmosphere reflects almost all incident visible radiation and prevents direct observation of surface features. In 1990 use of radar imaging enabled the Magellan space probe to see through the cloud. Magellan mapped 98 per cent of the planet during three years to find a surface covered in craters, volcanoes, mountains and solidified lava flows. Venus is the brightest object in the sky after the Sun and Moon and is unusual in that its year is less than its rotation period.

Earth

Earth is the largest and densest of the Inner Planets. Created some 4 500 million years ago, the core, rocky mantle and crust are similar in structure to Venus. The Earth's core is composed almost entirely of iron and oxygen compounds which exist in a molten state at temperatures of around 5 000°C. Earth is the only planet with vast quantities of life-sustaining water, with the oceans covering 70.8 per cent of its surface. The action of plate tectonics has created vast mountain ranges and is responsible for volcanic activity. The Moon is Earth's only natural satellite and with a diameter of over one quarter that of the Earth's, makes the Earth-Moon system a near double-planet.

Mars

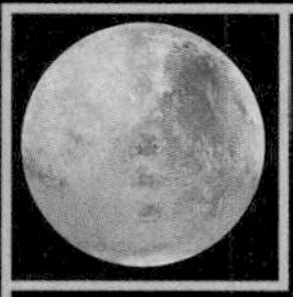

Named after the Roman god of war because of its blood-red appearance, Mars is the last of the Inner Planets. The red colour comes from the high concentration of iron-oxides on its surface. Mars has impressive surface features, including the highest known peak in the Solar System, Olympus Mons, an inactive volcano reaching a height of 23 km above the surrounding plains, and Marineris, a 2 500 km long canyon four times as deep as the Grand Canyon. The Pathfinder mission in 1997 has shown that much of the Martian surface is shaped by intense dust storms which often engulf the entire planet. Mars has polar caps composed of water and carbon dioxide ice which partially evaporate during its summer.

Jupiter

Jupiter is by far the most massive of all the planets and is the dominant body in the Solar System after the Sun. It is the innermost of the Gas Giants. The dense surface atmosphere is predominantly hydrogen, with helium, water vapour, and methane. Below this is a layer of liquid hydrogen, then an even deeper layer of metallic hydrogen. Unlike solid bodies, Jupiter's rotation period is somewhat ill-defined, with equatorial regions rotating faster than the polar caps; this, combined with convection currents in lower layers, cause intense magnetic fields and rapidly varying surface features. Most notable of these is the Great Red Spot, a giant circular storm visible since the first observations of Jupiter's surface, which shows no signs of abating.

Saturn

Although only slightly smaller that Jupiter, Saturn is a mere one third of Jupiter's mass, and the least dense of all the planets - less dense than water. The low mass, combined with a fast rotation rate, leads to the planet's significant polar flattening. Saturn exhibits a striking ring system, more than twice the diameter of the planet; the rings consist of countless small rock and ice clumps which vary in size from a grain of sand to tens of metres in diameter. It is believed that the rings were formed from a stray moon coming too close to, and being ripped apart by Saturn. Distinct bands and gaps in the rings are the result of complex interactions between Saturn and its closer moons. Recent rare opportunities to view Saturn's rings edge ways have yielded the discovery of at least two other moons.

Uranus

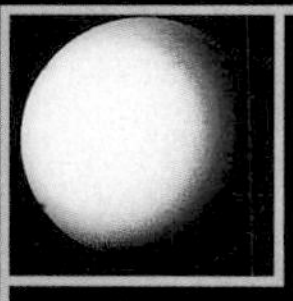

Uranus has many surprising features; the most prominent of these is the tilt of its rotation axis by over 90 degrees caused by a series of large collisions in its early history. Like the other Gas Giants, Uranus is predominantly hydrogen and helium with a small proportion of methane and other gases. However, because Uranus is colder than Jupiter and Saturn, the methane forms ice crystals which give Uranus a featureless blue-green colour. The interior is also different from that expected. Instead of having a gaseous atmosphere above liquid and metallic hydrogen layers, Uranus has a super dense gaseous atmosphere extending down to its core. Uranus' magnetic field is inclined at 60 degrees to the rotation axis, and is off centre by one third of the planet's radius, which suggests that it is not generated by the core. The system of eleven narrow rings around Uranus is prevented from spreading by the interaction of nearby 'shepherd' moons. Two new moons, Caliban and Sycorax, were discovered in 1997 although their large orbits indicate they are probably captured asteroids.

Neptune

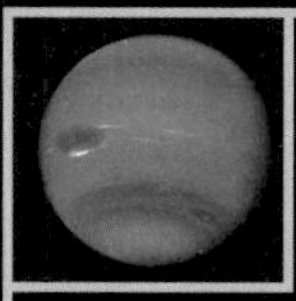

Neptune has always been associated with Uranus because of its similar size, composition and appearance, but, unexpectedly, Neptune's atmosphere is more active than that of Uranus. This was shown by Voyager 2 in 1989 with the observation of the Great Dark Spot, Neptune's equivalent to Jupiter's Great Red Spot. Voyager 2 recorded the fastest winds ever seen in the Solar System, 2 000 km per hour, around the Dark Spot. This feature disappeared in 1994, but has been replaced by a similar storm in the northern polar cap. Like Uranus, Neptune has a magnetic field highly inclined to the planet's axis of rotation and off-centre by more than half of the planet's radius. The cause of this magnetic field is convection currents in conducting fluid layers outside the core. Neptune's largest moon, Triton, is in an inclined retrograde orbit, indicating that it was captured by Neptune rather than formed alongside it. The slowly decaying orbit will one day bring Triton too close to Neptune, and it will be torn apart forming a spectacular ring.

Pluto

Pluto's existence was predicted before its discovery in 1930, from perturbations in Neptune's orbital motion. Pluto's orbit is highly eccentric and tilted with respect to the solar plane, unusually so for a planet. Its only moon, Charon, is abnormally large, and orbits Pluto at 90 degrees to the solar plane. Both Pluto and Charon have an uncharacteristically high proportion of rock, 70 per cent, with only 30 per cent water ice. All these anomalies bring Pluto's planetary status into question. It is likely that Pluto is a large planetesimal formed farther out of the Solar System, and is now in a stable orbit. Pluto, unlike Charon, possesses a methane ice surface layer, which forms a tenuous yet deep atmosphere when close to the Sun.

THE EARTH'S STRUCTURE

The interior of the Earth can be divided into three principal regions (*see 1*). The outermost region is known as the crust, which is extremely thin compared to the Earth as a whole. Under the continents the crust is about 33 km thick on average, only 0.5 per cent of the total radius of the Earth (6 370 km). Under the oceans the crust is even thinner: perhaps a third of its continental thickness. Over the course of geological time the Earth's crust has broken up into large fragments, which are known as lithospheric plates. These plates are slowly moving relative to one another at rates of a few centimetres per year – a process know as continental drift.

The next layer down is known as the mantle which is about 2 850 km thick. The distinction between the mantle and crust is made on the basis of composition and strength. There is a zone of the upper mantle, at depths between about 100 and 700 km, which behaves like a fluid when under stress. This weak zone is called the asthenosphere. The outermost 70 km or so of the mantle, together with the crust, is known as the lithosphere and is much stronger. The transition between the lithosphere and asthenosphere is due to variation in temperature, and is therefore gradual rather than being a distinct boundary.

Below the mantle is the Earth's core, which is about 3 470 km in radius, and is mainly made up of iron. The greater part of the core is completely liquid; however, there is a solid inner core, about 1 220 km in radius.

It is the dynamic processes operating in the upper parts of the Earth's interior which give rise to very dramatic and violent expressions of the huge energies involved: earthquakes and volcanoes. Both of these can be very destructive, even disastrous, in terms of both loss of life and economic impact. Consequently, study of these phenomena is very important if the natural disasters arising from them are to be mitigated.

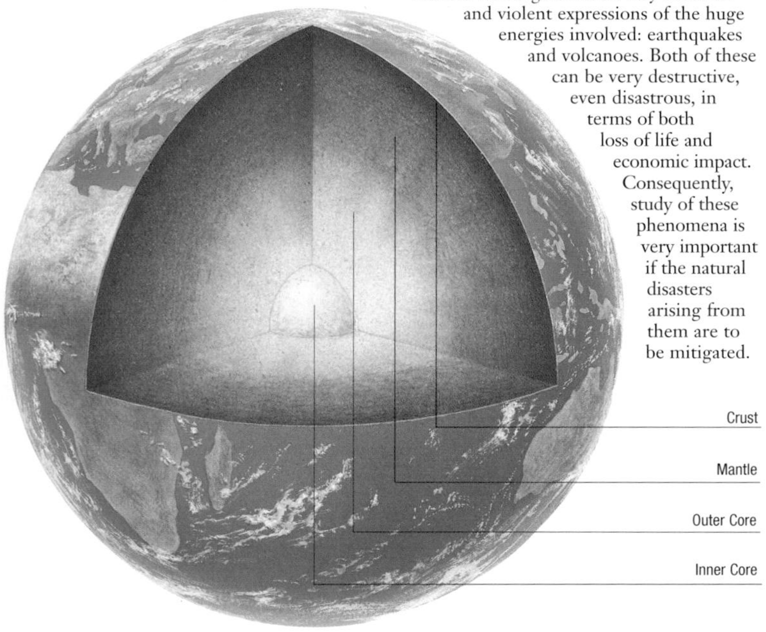
Crust
Mantle
Outer Core
Inner Core

1. THE EARTH'S INTERIOR

2. DISTRIBUTION OF MAJOR EARTHQUAKES AND VOLCANOES

Winkel Tripel Projection
scale 1:90 000 000

Key

▲	Volcanoes active between 1900 and 2000
●	Earthquakes between 1900 and 2000 causing over 10 000 deaths.

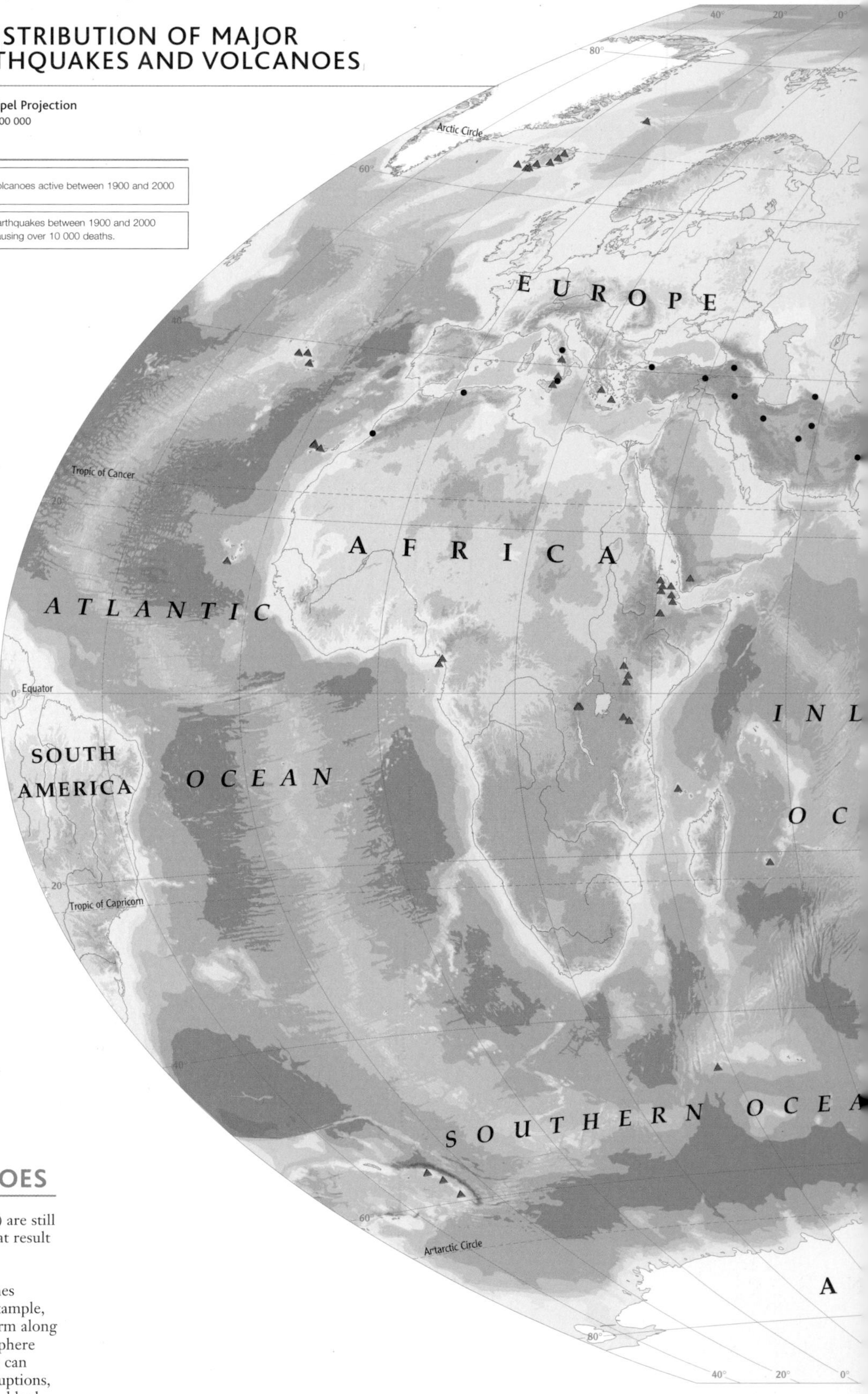
Arctic Circle
EUROPE
AFRICA
ATLANTIC
OCEAN
Tropic of Cancer
Equator
SOUTH AMERICA
Tropic of Capricorn
INDIAN
OC
SOUTHERN OCEA
Antarctic Circle
A

DISTRIBUTION OF EARTHQUAKES AND VOLCANOES

Any map showing the distribution of earthquakes and volcanoes (*see 2*) will inevitably look very similar to a map showing the boundaries of the tectonic plates (*see 3*). This is because both phenomena are largely controlled by the processes of plate tectonics. The vast majority of the world's earthquakes occur at plate boundaries as a result of one plate pushing past another along what is known as a constructive boundary, or under another at a destructive boundary, creating a subduction zone. Even those earthquakes which occur away from plate margins (intraplate earthquakes) are still mostly due to stresses in the rocks that result indirectly from plate movements.

Most major volcanoes occur along lines parallel to subduction zones, as for example, in the Andes. Other volcanoes can form along mid-ocean ridges where the asthenosphere is close to the surface; such volcanoes can produce what are known as fissure eruptions, where vast amounts of basaltic lava suddenly erupt on the surface, inundating huge areas.

3. PLATE BOUNDARIES

scale 1:270 000 000

Constructive - mid ocean ridge	Destructive	Conservative

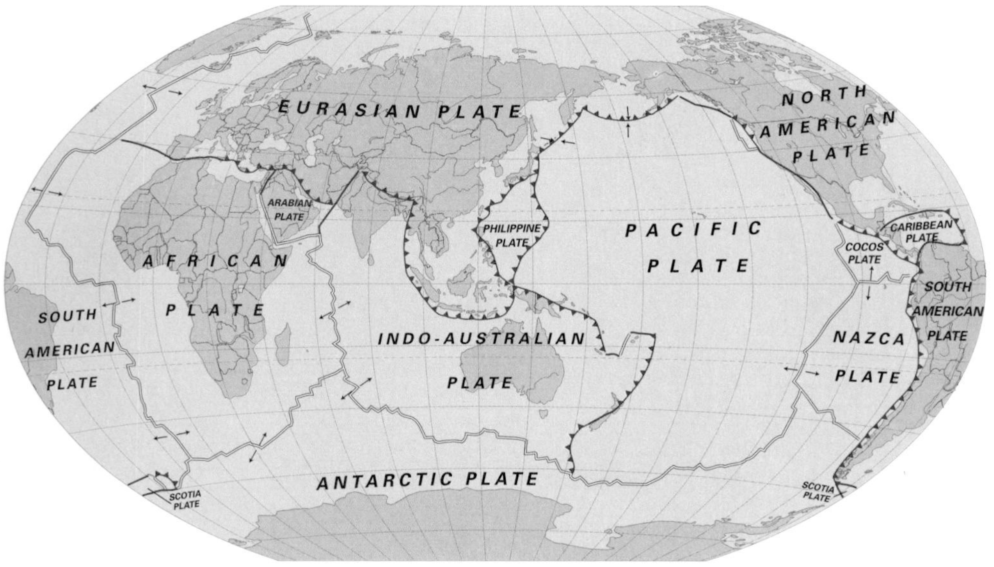
EURASIAN PLATE
NORTH AMERICAN PLATE
ARABIAN PLATE
PHILIPPINE PLATE
PACIFIC PLATE
CARIBBEAN PLATE
COCOS PLATE
AFRICAN PLATE
SOUTH AMERICAN PLATE
INDO-AUSTRALIAN PLATE
NAZCA PLATE
ANTARCTIC PLATE
SCOTIA PLATE

EARTHQUAKES

An earthquake is produced by a sudden breaking of rock in the Earth's crust as the stresses become too great for the strength of the rock to withstand. Naturally, this is most likely to happen where the rock is weakest. Where the rock breaks, a fracture line, known as a fault is left, and because there is now a break, future movements are likely to happen along the same weakness. The forces involved derive mostly from the movements of the tectonic plates; for example, between the upper surface of a subducting plate and the lower surface of the plate under which it is sliding – conditions which have caused some of the world's largest earthquakes.

The force with which the rock breaks releases a large amount of energy in the form of waves that travel through the Earth. These radiate outwards from where the fault has ruptured. The point on the fault at which the rupture begins is known as the hypocentre; this is usually at a depth of 10 to 30 km for shallow earthquakes; earthquakes in subduction zones can be as deep as 600 km below the Earth's surface. The point on the Earth's surface directly above the hypocentre is called the epicentre; this is what can be shown on a map. The magnitude of an earthquake, the so-call Richter scale, is a logarithmic approximation of the total amount of energy released. A large earthquake which may be severely damaging at the epicentre, is less strongly felt by people at greater distances. The strength of shaking at any point is known as the intensity, and this decreases with distance from the epicentre.

The earthquake off the southern coast of Honshū, Japan in January 1995 caused over 5 500 deaths and extensive damage in the Kōbe area and on Awaji-shima; the photo shows damage in Kōbe.

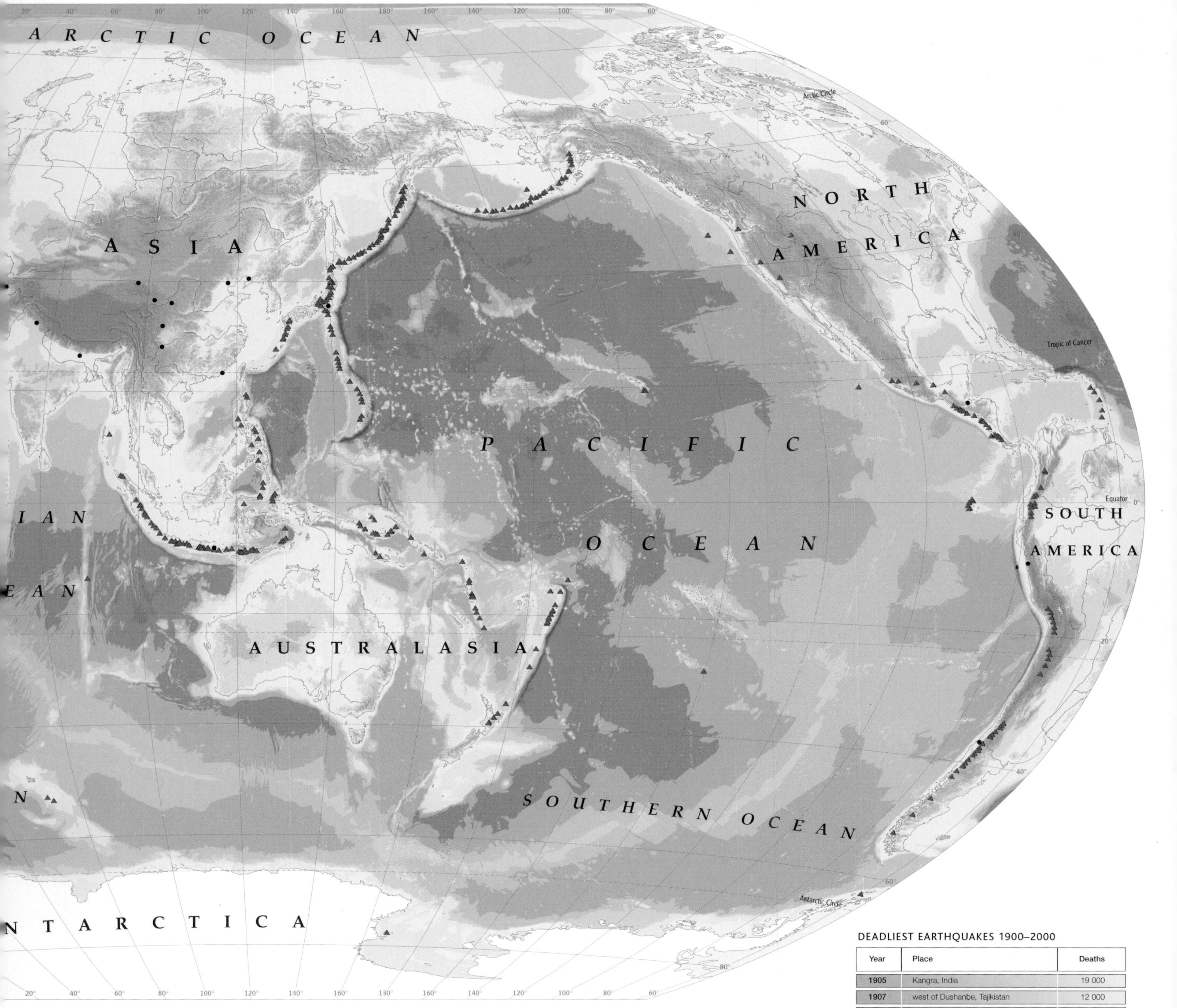
ARCTIC OCEAN
ASIA
NORTH AMERICA
Arctic Circle
Tropic of Cancer
PACIFIC
OCEAN
Equator
SOUTH AMERICA
IAN
EAN
AUSTRALASIA
SOUTHERN OCEAN
N
Antarctic Circle
NTARCTICA

VOLCANOES

In the simplest terms, a volcano is a vent at the surface of the Earth where molten rock (magma) from the interior can reach the surface. The magma originates ultimately in the Earth's mantle. It then erupts either as a stream of liquid rock (called lava when it appears at the surface) or as fine particles of ash or cinder. The erupted material builds up over time into a mountain, typically conical in shape. The exact shape of the volcano is controlled by the type of material erupted. Volcanoes in oceanic locations (such as Hawaii) tend to erupt very basic (non-acidic) lava which flows relatively easily. Because it can run quite far before cooling, this produces a very flat volcano with gentle slopes, known as a shield volcano. Continental volcanoes produce more acidic lava which flows more slowly, and they produce more ash, and therefore have steeper-sided cones. Such volcanoes also tend to erupt more explosively, because of the greater amount of steam or gas in the lava, and are generally more dangerous. They can produce what is know as a pyroclastic flow, a fast-moving cloud of super-heated ash and gases, which is what destroyed Pompeii in AD79.

Kilauea volcano, Hawaii, showing lava flows

Volcanoes can also be classified according to their eruptive history. Active volcanoes are those that are currently erupting; an eruption can go on intermittently for years, and some volcanoes, such as Stromboli in Italy, are almost permanently active. However, most volcanoes erupt much less frequently, and those that have not erupted for tens or hundreds of years, but may be expected to erupt again, are said to be dormant. Volcanoes which were once active in response to the tectonic situation as it was millions of years ago, and which cannot possibly erupt again today are said to be extinct.

DEADLIEST EARTHQUAKES 1900–2000

Year	Place	Deaths
1905	Kangra, India	19 000
1907	west of Dushanbe, Tajikistan	12 000
1908	Messina, Italy	110 000
1915	Abruzzo, Italy	35 000
1917	Bali, Indonesia	15 000
1918	Guangdong Province, China	10 000
1920	Ningxia Province, China	200 000
1923	Tokyo, Japan	142 807
1927	Qinghai Province, China	200 000
1932	Gansu Province, China	70 000
1933	Sichuan Province, China	10 000
1934	Nepal/India	10 700
1935	Quetta, Pakistan	30 000
1939	Chillán, Chile	28 000
1939	Erzincan, Turkey	32 700
1948	Ashgabat, Turkmenistan	19 800
1960	Agadir, Morocco	12 000
1962	northwest Iran	12 225
1968	Dasht-e-Bayaz, Iran	12 100
1970	Huánuco Province, Peru	66 794
1974	Yunnan and Sichuan Provinces, China	20 000
1975	Liaoning Province, China	10 000
1976	central Guatemala	22 778
1976	Hebei Province, China	242 000
1978	Khorāsan Province, Iran	20 000
1980	Ech Chélif, Algeria	11 000
1988	Spitak, Armenia	25 000
1990	Manjil, Irán	50 000
1999	Kocaeli (İzmit), Turkey	17 000

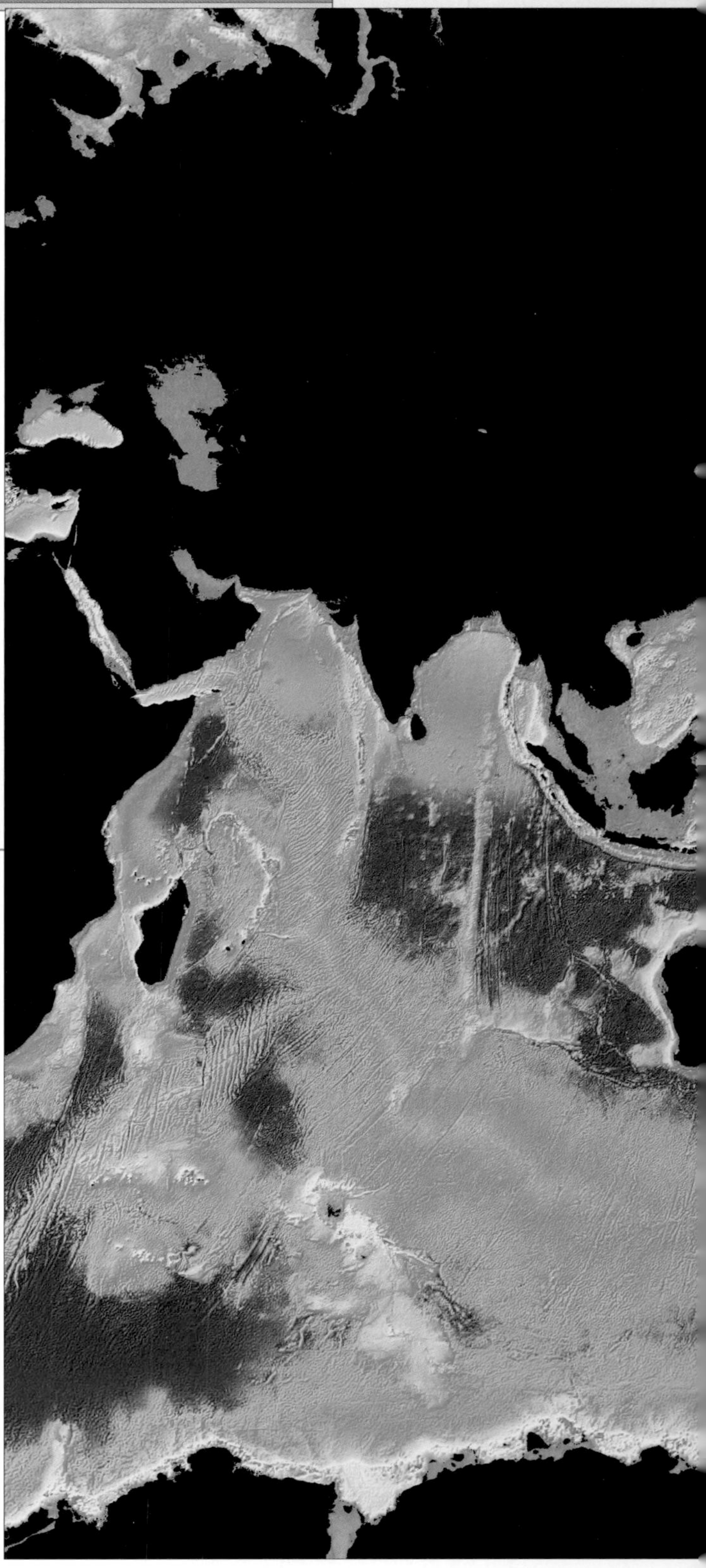

OBSERVING THE OCEANS

The oceans cover 70.8 per cent of the surface of the Earth and exert an extraordinary influence on the physical processes of the Earth and its atmosphere. The circulation of water throughout the oceans is critical to world climate and climate change. Any study of these relationships relies upon a clear understanding of the role of the oceans and of the complex processes within them. Methods of direct and indirect observation of the oceans, particularly by sampling and through the application of satellite remote sensing, have developed enormously over the last forty years and continue to provide the data required to develop this understanding.

Until the advent of Earth-observation satellites in the late 1970s all ocean observations were made from ships. The first global survey of the oceans, their bathymetry and their physical and biological characteristics, was made by HMS Challenger between 1872 and 1876. Throughout the 20th century, comprehensive descriptions of the distributions of temperature and salinity were made through numerous regional and global expeditions. Analysis of the temperature and salinity characteristics of a water sample allowed its origins to be determined, and enabled overall patterns of water circulation to be deduced.

Until the 1960s there was no means of directly measuring currents below the ocean surface. Parallel developments produced two solutions to this problem. In the USA, current-recording meters were designed which returned records of current speed and direction, and water temperature. In the UK, devices were produced which could be made to drift with the currents at a predetermined depth and which could be tracked from an attendant ship. Such floats can now be used globally, independent of ships.

Earth observation satellites have become increasingly important in observing the oceans. Radiometers allow sea surface temperatures to be monitored and radar altimeters permit ocean surface currents to be inferred from measurements of sea surface height. Such developments meant that by the early 1990s routine monitoring of ocean surface currents was possible. The combination of satellite altimetry and other observation methods has also allowed a detailed picture of the ocean floor to be established (*see 1*).

1. GLOBAL SEAFLOOR TOPOGRAPHY

This image has been produced from a combination of shipboard depth soundings and gravity data derived from satellite altimetry from the ERS-1 and Geosat satellites. The range of colours represents different depths of the ocean – from orange and yellow on the shallow continental shelves to dark blues in the deepest ocean trenches. The heavily fractured mid-ocean ridges (ranging from green to yellow) are particularly prominent.

OCEAN CIRCULATION

Most of the Earth's incoming solar radiation is absorbed in the top few tens of metres of the ocean. Thus the upper ocean is warmed, the warming being greatest around the equator. Sea water has a high thermal capacity in comparison with the atmosphere or lithosphere and as a consequence, the ocean is an extremely effective store of thermal energy. Slow ocean currents play a major role in redistributing this heat around the globe and the oceans and their circulation are thus key elements in the climate system.

Estimates of the global transport of heat by the oceans (*see 2*) show a pattern of heat flow in the Indian and North Pacific Oceans away from the equator and towards the poles. However, the Atlantic Ocean has a clear northward flow throughout, decreasing from a maximum value of 1.4 petawatts (PW) at 24ºN to effectively zero in the Arctic Ocean. This decrease is indicative of the heat loss to the atmosphere which is responsible for the temperate climate of western Europe.

Ocean currents are influenced by winds, by density gradients and by the Earth's rotation. They are also constrained by the topography of the seafloor. Surface currents are usually strong, narrow, western-boundary currents flowing towards the poles. Some of these are well known, for example the Gulf Stream in the North Atlantic Ocean, the Kuroshio Current in the northwest Pacific, and the Brazil Current (*see 3*). These poleward flows are returned towards the equator in broad, slow, interior flows which complete a gyre in each hemisphere basin. Sea surface circulation is reflected in variations in sea surface height which can vary greatly across currents (*see 4*). For example, differences in sea surface height of over 1m are evident across the Kuroshio Current. At high latitudes, winter cooling produces high density water which sinks towards the ocean floor and flows towards the equator, being constrained by the sea floor topography (*see 5*). This fills the deep ocean basins with water at temperatures close to 0ºC.

2. OCEAN TRANSPORT OF HEAT

In petawatts (PW) (10^{15} watts). 1 PW is about sixty times the global consumption of energy.

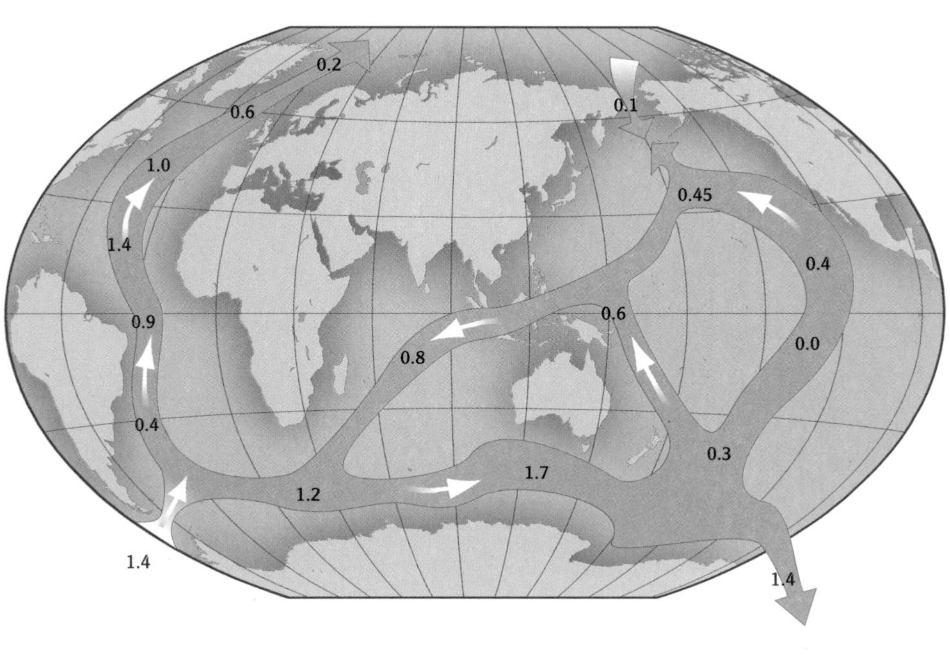

3. OCEAN SURFACE CURRENTS

scale 1 : 200 000 000

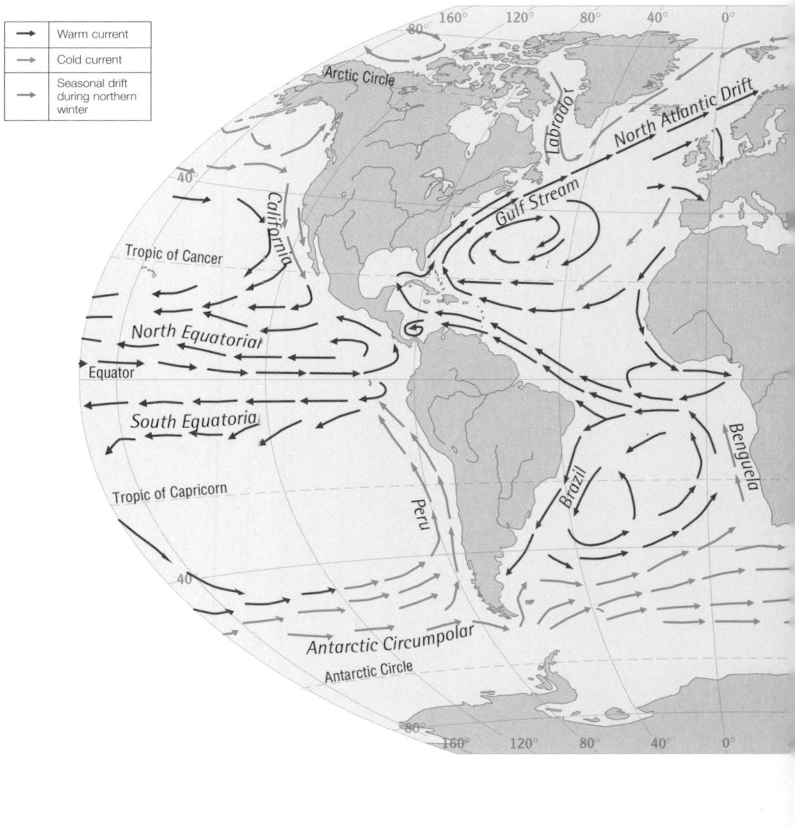

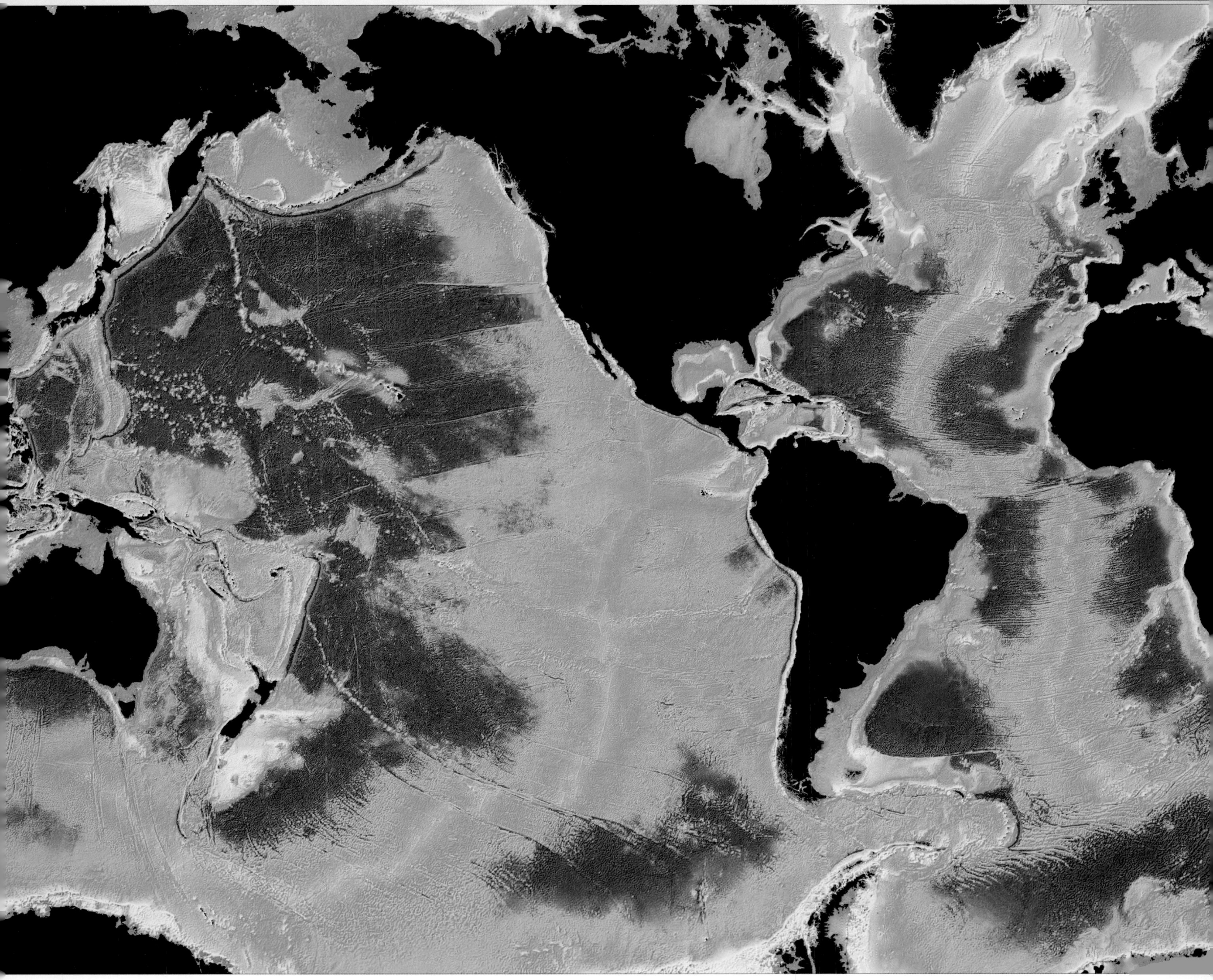

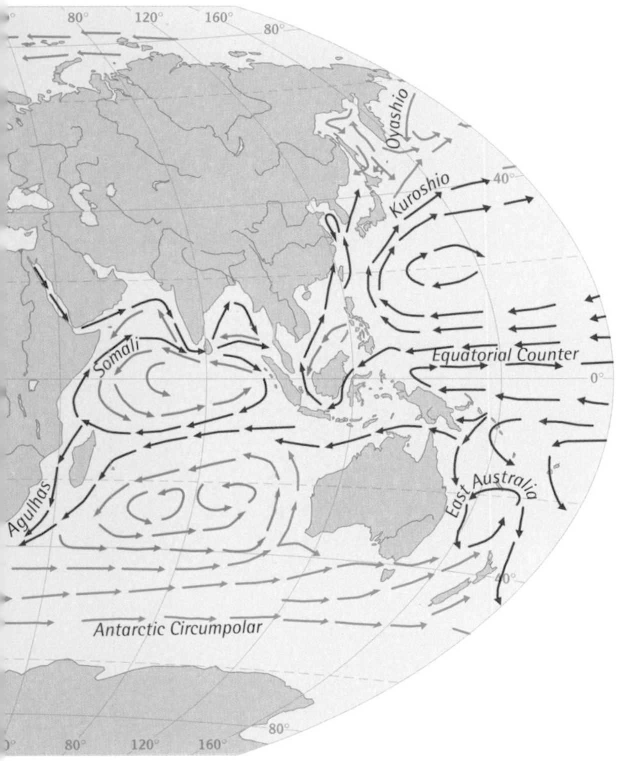

4. SEA SURFACE HEIGHT

From the TOPEX/POSEIDON satellite. Currents flow along the slopes and are strongest where the slopes are greatest.

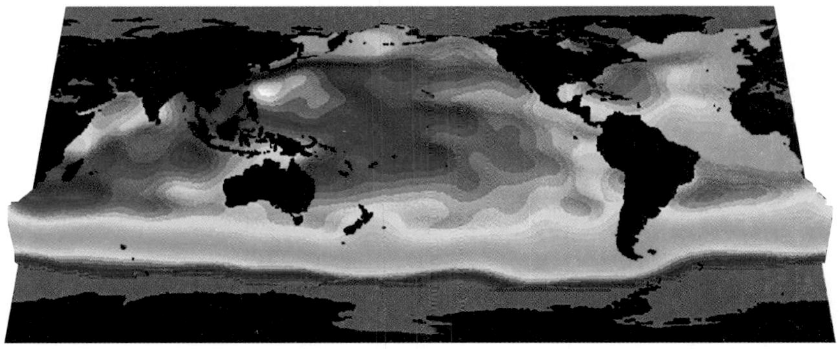

5. CROSS-SECTION OF SALINITY AND THE OCEAN FLOOR

Stretching 12 000 km across the Pacific Ocean from Antarctica (left) to Alaska (right) approximately along longitude 150°W. It shows water modified in the Antarctic descending to the ocean floor and into the ocean interior.

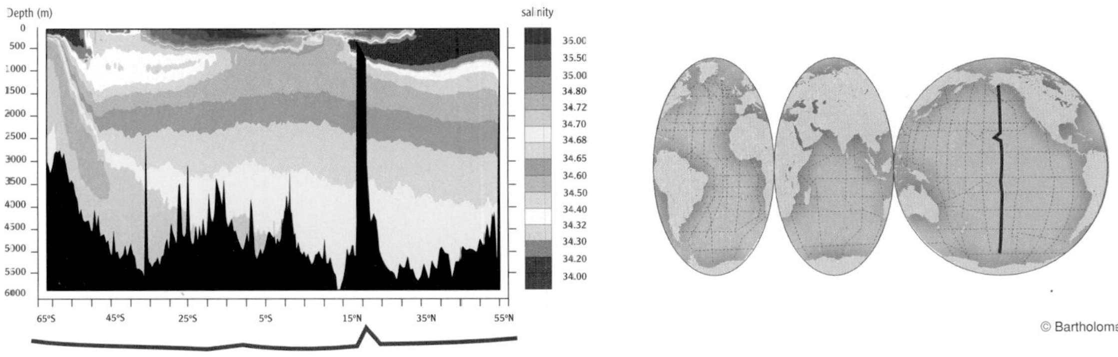

© Bartholomew Ltd

THE CLIMATE SYSTEM

The Earth's climate system is a highly complex interactive system involving the atmosphere, hydrosphere (oceans, lakes and rivers), biosphere (the Earth's living resources), cryosphere (particularly sea ice and polar ice caps) and lithosphere (the Earth's crust and upper mantle). This results in a great variety of climate types (*see 1*). Man's activities are affecting this system, and the monitoring of climate change, and of human influences upon it, is now a major issue.

Greenhouse gases such as carbon dioxide, methane and chlorofluorocarbons (CFCs) act to trap outgoing long-wave radiation, keeping the Earth's surface and lower atmosphere warmer than it would be otherwise. This is the phenomenon usually referred to as the greenhouse effect. Human activity has increased the atmospheric concentration of some of these gases and has therefore contributed to the effect. As a result of this, the world is about 0.6°C warmer than it was a hundred years ago with the three warmest years globally (in decreasing order) being 1998, 1997 and 1995 (*see 2*).

1. MAJOR CLIMATIC REGIONS AND SUB-TYPES

Köppen classification system
Winkel Tripel Projection
scale 1:110 000 000

•	Climate graph location
o	Weather extreme location

Polar		Cooler humid		Warmer humid		Dry		Tropical humid	
EF	Ice cap	Dc Dd	Subarctic	Cb Cc	Temperate	BS	Steppe	Aw As	Savanna
ET	Tundra	Db	Continental cool summer	Ca	Humid subtropical	BW	Desert	Af Am	Rain forest
		Da	Continental warm summer	Cs	Mediterranean				

A Rainy climate with no winter: coolest month above 18°C (64.4°F).

B Dry climates; limits are defined by formulae based on rainfall effectiveness:
BS Steppe or semi-arid climate.
BW Desert or arid climate.

***C** Rainy climates with mild winters: coolest month above 0°C (32°F), but below 18°C (64.4°F); warmest month above 10°C (50°F).

***D** Rainy climates with severe winters: coldest month below 0°C (32°F); warmest month above 10°C (50°F).

E Polar climates with no warm season: warmest month below 10°C (50°F).
ET Tundra climate: warmest month below 10°C (50°F) but above 0°C (32°F).
EF Perpetual frost: all months below 0°C (32°F).

* Modification of Köppen definition

a Warmest month above 22°C (71.6°F).

b Warmest month below 22°C (71.6°F).

c Less than four months over 10°C (50°F).

d As 'c', but with severe cold: coldest month below -38°C (-36.4°F).

f Constantly moist rainfall throughout the year.

***h** Warmer dry: all months above 0°C (32°F).

***k** Cooler dry: at least one month below 0°C (32°F).

m Monsoon rain: short dry season, but is compensated by heavy rains during rest of the year.

n Frequent fog.

s Dry season in summer.

w Dry season in winter.

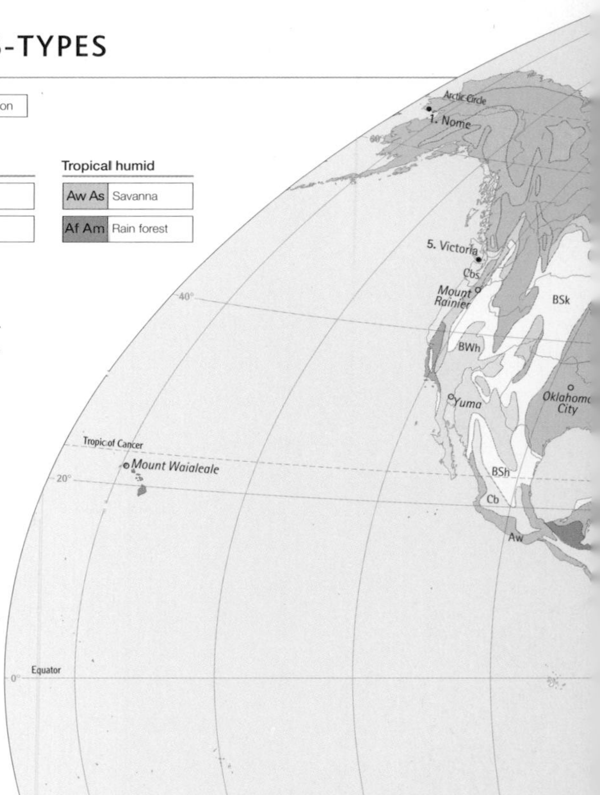

Arctic Circle
1. Nome
5. Victoria
Cbs
Mount Rainier
BSk
BWh
Yuma
Oklahoma City
Tropic of Cancer
Mount Waialeale
BSh
Cb
Aw
Equator
Tropic of Capricorn
Antarctic Circle

CLIMATE GRAPHS

These graphs relate by number, name and colour to the selected stations on the map and present mean temperature and precipitation values for each month. Red bars show average daily maximum and minimum temperatures for each month in degrees centigrade and fahrenheit. Vertical blue columns depict precipitation in millimetres and inches, with the total mean annual precipitation shown under the graph. The altitude of each station above sea level is given in metres and feet.

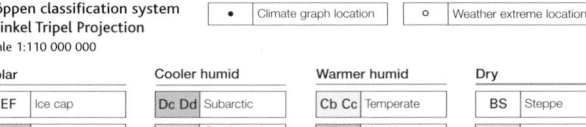

Precipitation (average monthly total)
Temperature (average daily maximum and minimum)

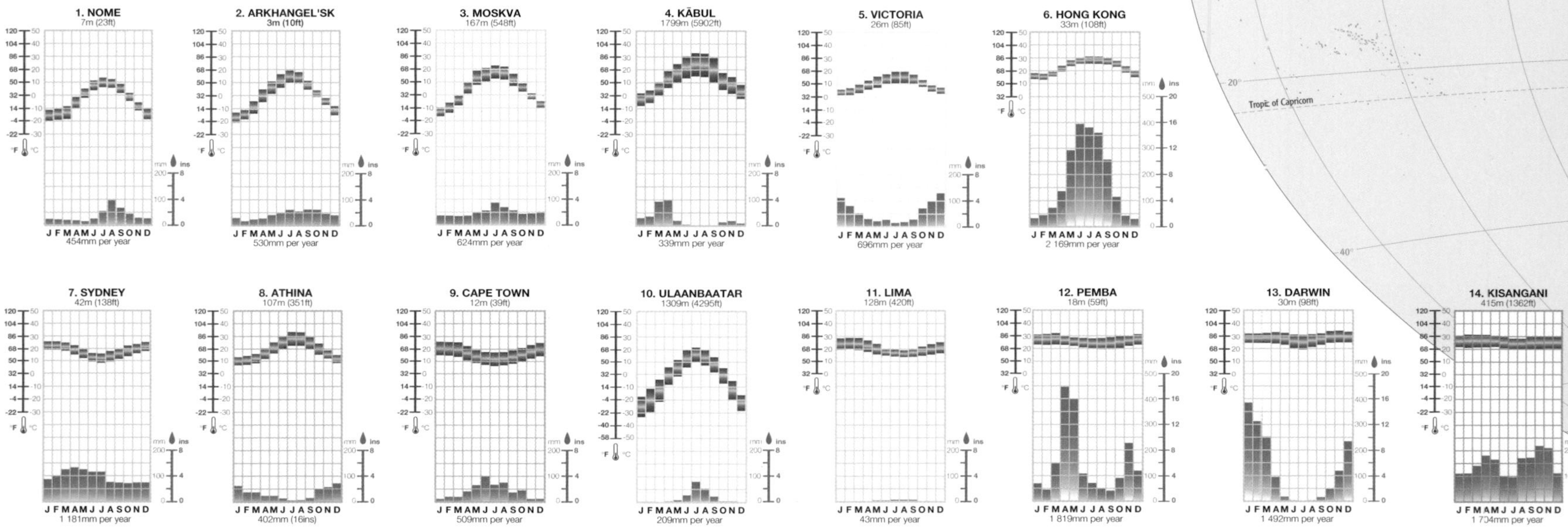

1. NOME
7m (23ft)
454mm per year
2. ARKHANGEL'SK
3m (10ft)
530mm per year
3. MOSKVA
167m (548ft)
624mm per year
4. KĀBUL
1799m (5902ft)
339mm per year
5. VICTORIA
26m (85ft)
696mm per year
6. HONG KONG
33m (108ft)
2 169mm per year
7. SYDNEY
42m (138ft)
1 181mm per year
8. ATHINA
107m (351ft)
402mm (16ins)
9. CAPE TOWN
12m (39ft)
509mm per year
10. ULAANBAATAR
1309m (4295ft)
209mm per year
11. LIMA
128m (420ft)
43mm per year
12. PEMBA
18m (59ft)
1 819mm per year
13. DARWIN
30m (98ft)
1 492mm per year
14. KISANGANI
415m (1362ft)
1 734mm per year
J F M A M J J A S O N D
°F °C
mm ins

CLIMATE CHANGE

Future climate change depends on how quickly and to what extent the concentration of greenhouse gases and aerosols in the atmosphere increases. If we assume that no action is taken to limit future greenhouse gas emissions, then a warming during the 21st century of 0.2 to 0.3°C per decade is likely. Such a rate of warming would be greater than anything that has occurred over the last 10 000 years.

The detailed climatic response to the increase in carbon dioxide and other greenhouse gases is predicted using complex mathematical models of the climate. One of the most advanced climate models in the world is that produced by the Hadley Centre of the UK Meteorological Office. This model has produced predictions of climatic change, including changes in temperature and precipitation (*see 3 and 4*). According to this model, some regions of the world will warm more quickly than others and precipitation will increase in some areas and decrease in others. Such changes are likely to have significant impacts on sea-level which could rise by as much as 50 cm over the next century. Human impacts would also be through the effects on water resources, food production and health.

2. COMBINED GLOBAL LAND, AIR AND SEA SURFACE TEMPERATURES 1860-1999

Relative to 1961-1990 average. The black line is a smoothing of the annual values to suppress sub-decadal time-scale variations.

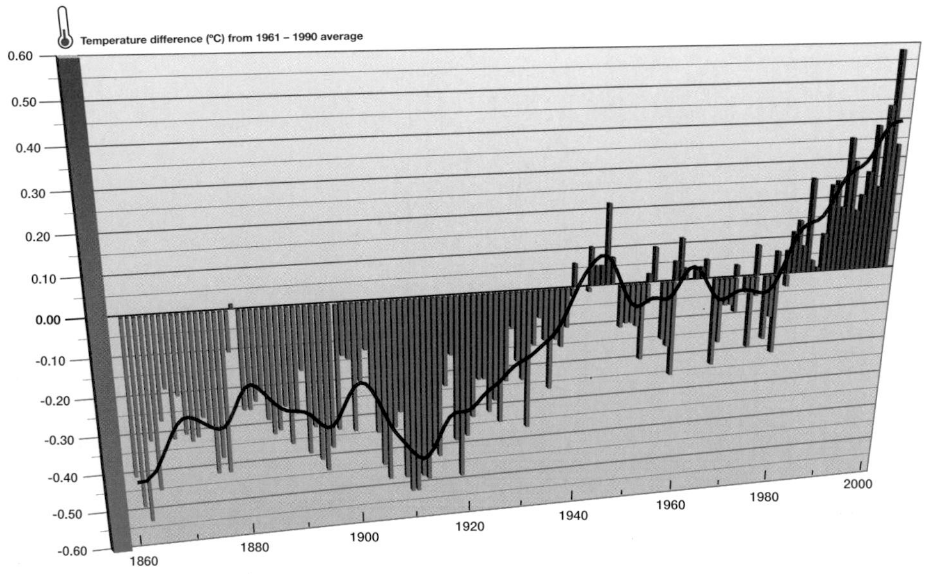

Temperature difference (°C) from 1961 – 1990 average
0.60
0.50
0.40
0.30
0.20
0.10
0.00
-0.10
-0.20
-0.30
-0.40
-0.50
-0.60
1860
1880
1900
1920
1940
1960
1980
2000

3. TEMPERATURE IN THE 2050s

Predicted annual mean temperature change

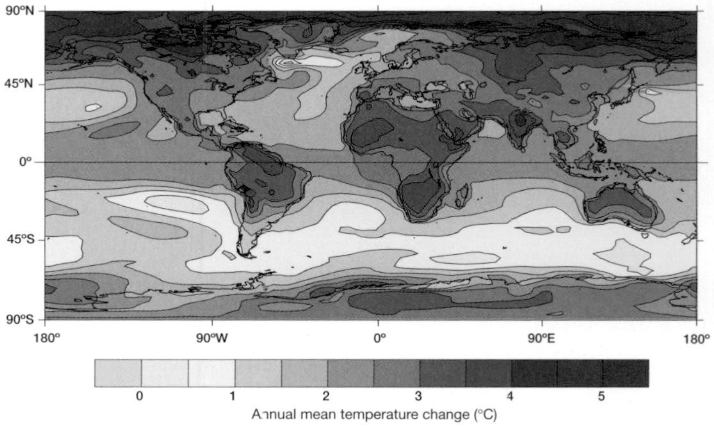

90°N
45°N
0°
45°S
90°S
180°
90°W
0°
90°E
180°
0
1
2
3
4
5
Annual mean temperature change (°C)

4. PRECIPITATION IN THE 2050s

Predicted average precipitation change

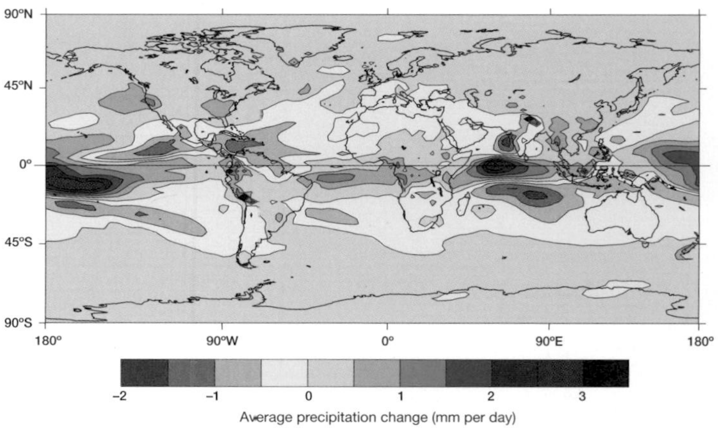

90°N
45°N
0°
45°S
90°S
180°
90°W
0°
90°E
180°
–2
–1
0
1
2
3
Average precipitation change (mm per day)

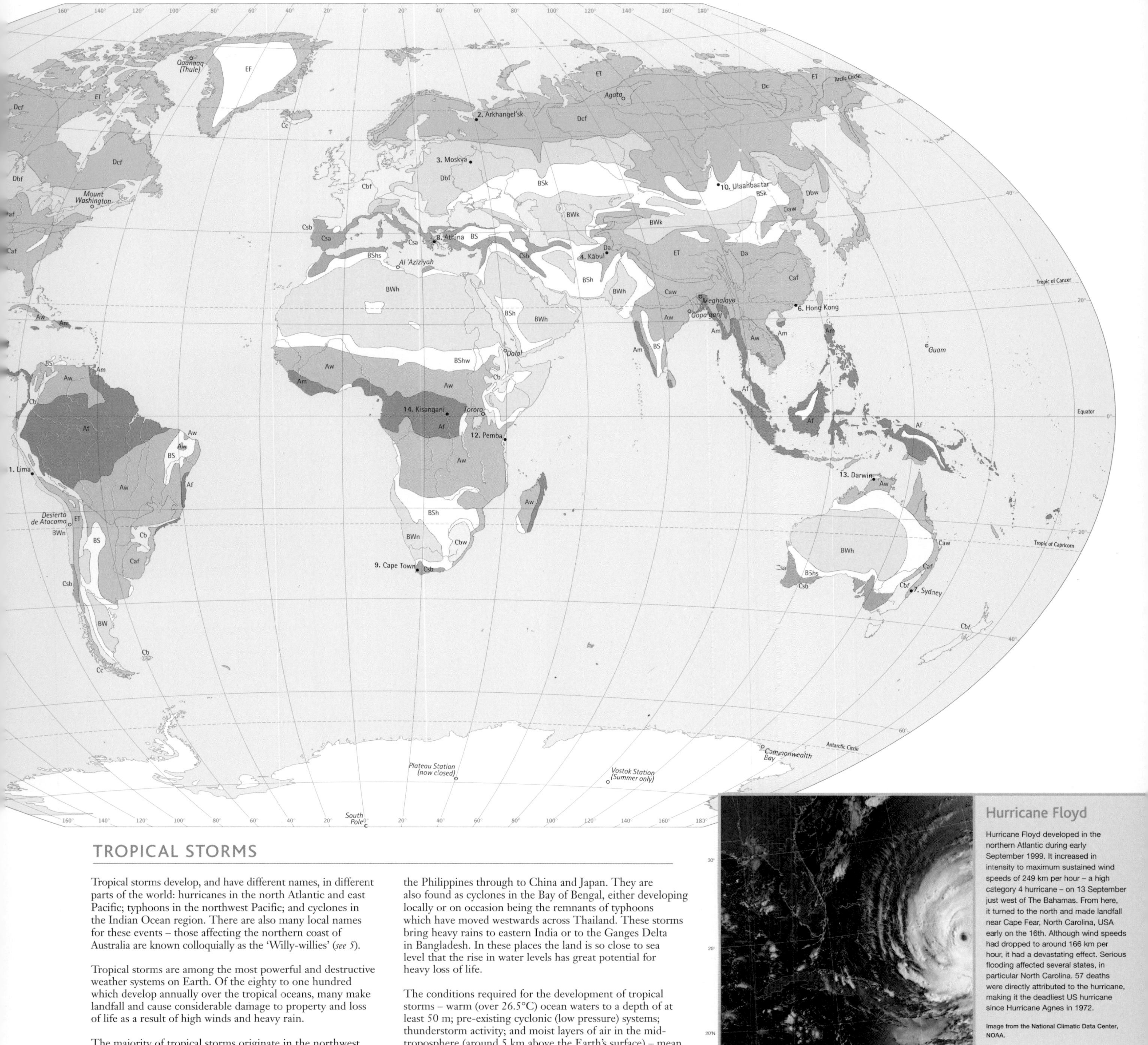

TROPICAL STORMS

Tropical storms develop, and have different names, in different parts of the world: hurricanes in the north Atlantic and east Pacific; typhoons in the northwest Pacific; and cyclones in the Indian Ocean region. There are also many local names for these events – those affecting the northern coast of Australia are known colloquially as the 'Willy-willies' (*see 5*).

Tropical storms are among the most powerful and destructive weather systems on Earth. Of the eighty to one hundred which develop annually over the tropical oceans, many make landfall and cause considerable damage to property and loss of life as a result of high winds and heavy rain.

The majority of tropical storms originate in the northwest Pacific, where as typhoons they commonly affect areas from the Philippines through to China and Japan. They are also found as cyclones in the Bay of Bengal, either developing locally or on occasion being the remnants of typhoons which have moved westwards across Thailand. These storms bring heavy rains to eastern India or to the Ganges Delta in Bangladesh. In these places the land is so close to sea level that the rise in water levels has great potential for heavy loss of life.

The conditions required for the development of tropical storms – warm (over 26.5°C) ocean waters to a depth of at least 50 m; pre-existing cyclonic (low pressure) systems; thunderstorm activity; and moist layers of air in the mid-troposphere (around 5 km above the Earth's surface) – mean that most occur in mid- to late-summer in the areas concerned.

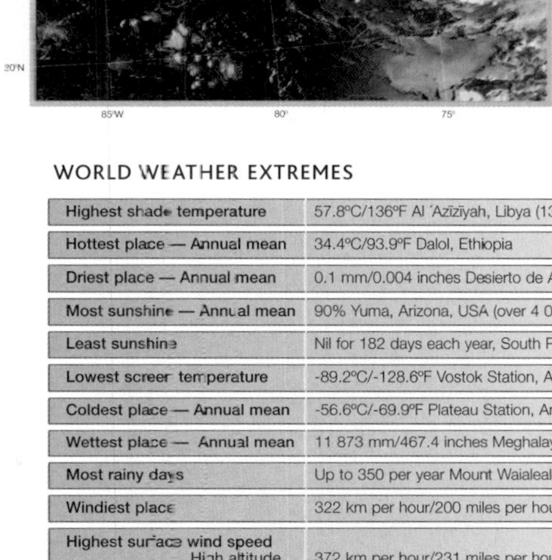

Hurricane Floyd

Hurricane Floyd developed in the northern Atlantic during early September 1999. It increased in intensity to maximum sustained wind speeds of 249 km per hour – a high category 4 hurricane – on 13 September just west of The Bahamas. From here, it turned to the north and made landfall near Cape Fear, North Carolina, USA early on the 16th. Although wind speeds had dropped to around 166 km per hour, it had a devastating effect. Serious flooding affected several states, in particular North Carolina. 57 deaths were directly attributed to the hurricane, making it the deadliest US hurricane since Hurricane Agnes in 1972.

Image from the National Climatic Data Center, NOAA.

5. TRACKS OF TROPICAL STORMS

Wind speeds often over 160 km per hour
scale 1:295 000 000

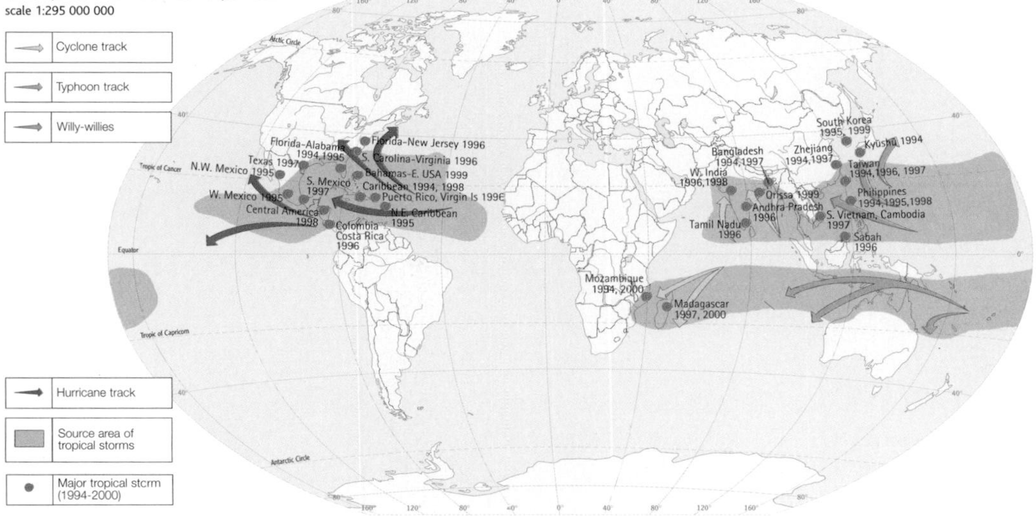

WORLD WEATHER EXTREMES

Highest shade temperature	57.8°C/136°F Al 'Azīzīyah, Libya (13th September 1922)
Hottest place — Annual mean	34.4°C/93.9°F Dalol, Ethiopia
Driest place — Annual mean	0.1 mm/0.004 inches Desierto de Atacama, Chile
Most sunshine — Annual mean	90% Yuma, Arizona, USA (over 4 000 hours)
Least sunshine	Nil for 182 days each year, South Pole
Lowest screen temperature	-89.2°C/-128.6°F Vostok Station, Antarctica (21st July 1983)
Coldest place — Annual mean	-56.6°C/-69.9°F Plateau Station, Antarctica
Wettest place — Annual mean	11 873 mm/467.4 inches Meghalaya, India
Most rainy days	Up to 350 per year Mount Waialeale, Hawaii, USA
Windiest place	322 km per hour/200 miles per hour in gales, Commonwealth Bay, Antarctica
Highest surface wind speed	
High altitude	372 km per hour/231 miles per hour Mount Washington, New Hampshire, USA, (12th April 1934)
Low altitude	333 km per hour/207 miles per hour Qaanaaq (Thule), Greenland 8th March 1972)
Tornado	512 km per hour/318 miles per hour Oklahoma City, Oklahoma, USA (3rd May 1999)
Greatest snowfall	31 102 mm/1 224.5 inches Mount Rainier, Washington, USA (19th February 1971 — 18th February 1972)
Heaviest hailstones	1 kg/2.21 lb Gopalganj, Bangladesh (14th April 1986)
Thunder-days average	251 days per year Tororo, Uganda
Highest barometric pressure	1 083.8 mb Agata, Siberia, Russian Federation (31st December 1968)
Lowest barometric pressure	870 mb 483 km/300 miles west of Guam, Pacific Ocean (12th October 1979)

© Bartholomew Ltd

THE DISCover PROJECT

Most existing global land cover maps show only a general idea of the actual conditions on the Earth's surface. They tend to be fairly coarse, of unknown accuracy, and are derived from a variety of primary data sources. Most also contain a climate element in the class definitions which leads to a mixture of potential versus actual land cover. Since 1992 the International Geosphere Biosphere Programme's (IGBP) Data and Information System (DIS) has been working towards the completion of a new global land cover data set without these shortcomings. The resulting land cover map as shown here – known as DISCover – was completed in June 1997 and shows the Earth's land cover as it was in 1992/1993 at a ground resolution of 1 km (*see 1*).

The final data set has been created from over 4.4 terabytes of data from the Advanced Very High Resolution Radiometer (AVHRR) sensor on board the polar orbiting satellites of the US National Oceanic and Atmospheric Administration (NOAA). These satellites provide images of the entire Earth's surface every day at a ground resolution of 1 km (see also the continental satellite images on pages 8-21). Development of the data set used to create DISCover was endorsed by the G7 Committee on Earth Observation Satellites, and implemented by the United States Geological Survey (USGS), the National Aeronautics and Space Administration (NASA), NOAA, and the European Space Agency (ESA).

Collecting the data involved the collaborative efforts of twenty-three satellite receiving stations around the world.

The subsequent classification of the data was performed at the USGS Earth Resources Observation Systems (EROS) Data Center in Sioux Falls, South Dakota, at the University of Nebraska–Lincoln, USA and at the European Commission's Joint Research Centre (JRC) in Italy. The accuracy of the map classification is currently being assessed by specialists in the USA, comparing it with a sample of more than 400 high resolution satellite images from the US Landsat (*see 2*) and French SPOT (*see 3*) satellites.

The land cover classes shown on the map are not the typical vegetation classes often found in world vegetation maps. For example, there are no tundra or tropical rainforest classes. This is because the philosophy for DISCover was to describe land cover in terms of structure – in particular the three components of above-ground biomass, leaf longevity and leaf type – mainly for the science community interested in global change, and not in terms of traditional climate/vegetation distinctions.

4. GLOBAL LAND COVER COMPOSITION

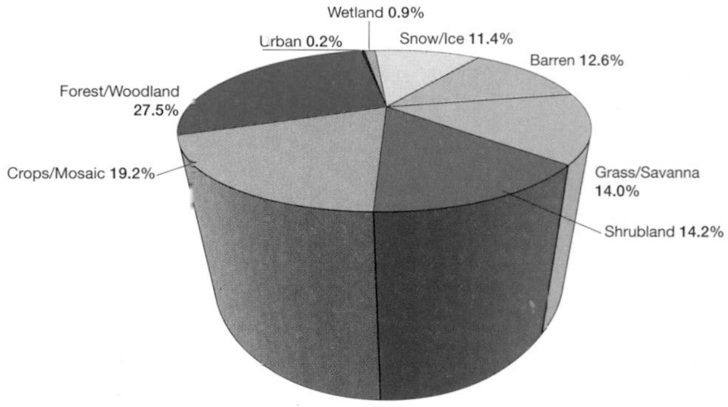

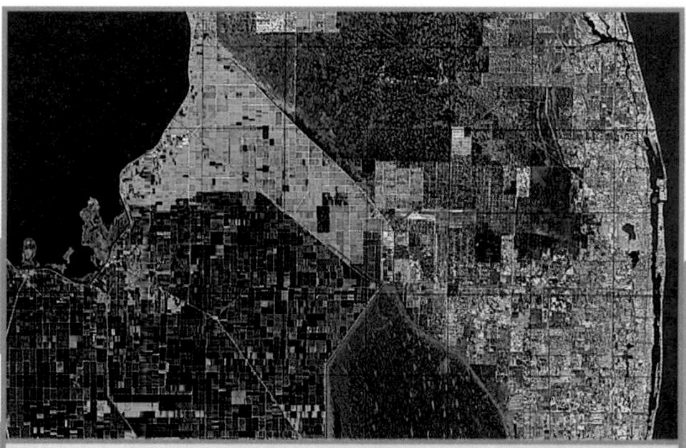

2. Agricultural land use in Florida, USA

This example of high resolution Landsat satellite imagery illustrates the level of land cover detail available from such images. It shows part of Florida, USA with Lake Okeechobee to the top left and the city of West Palm Beach to the far right. The regular field pattern shows crops at different stages of growth and the dark green, mottled areas (top centre and bottom centre) are parts of the Everglades swamp.

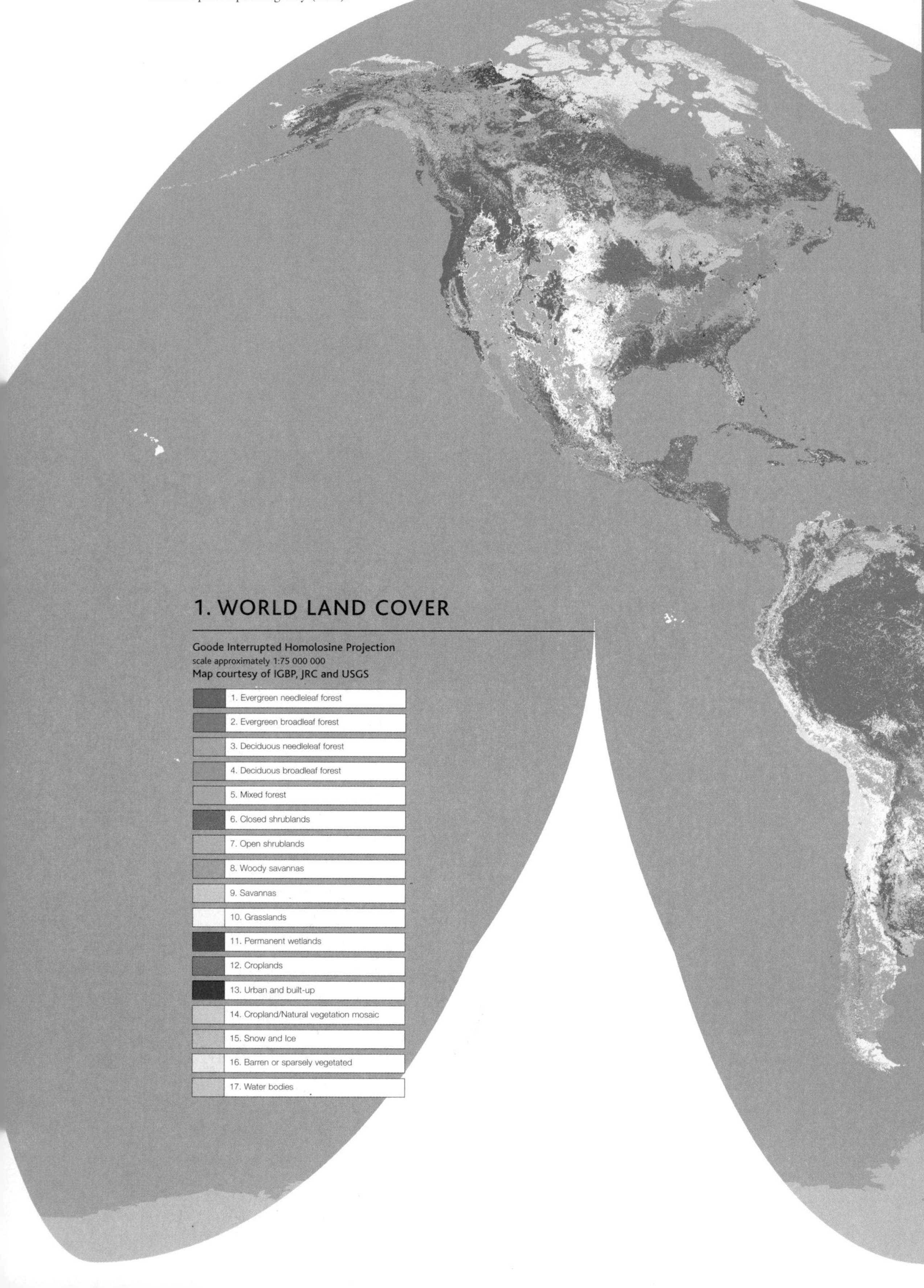

1. WORLD LAND COVER

Goode Interrupted Homolosine Projection
scale approximately 1:75 000 000
Map courtesy of IGBP, JRC and USGS

LANDCOVER GRAPHS - CLASSIFICATION

Class description	IGBP/DISCover classes
Forest/Woodland	1 Evergreen needleleaf forest 2 Evergreen broadleaf forest 3 Deciduous needleleaf forest 4 Deciduous broadleaf forest 5 Mixed forest
Shrubland	6 Closed shrublands 7 Open shrublands
Grass/Savanna	8 Woody savannas 9 Savannas 10 Grasslands
Wetland	11 Permanent wetlands
Crops/Mosaic	12 Croplands 14 Cropland/Natural vegetation mosaic
Urban	13 Urban and built-up
Snow/Ice	15 Snow and Ice
Barren	16 Barren or sparsely vegetated

5. CONTINENTAL LAND COVER COMPOSITION

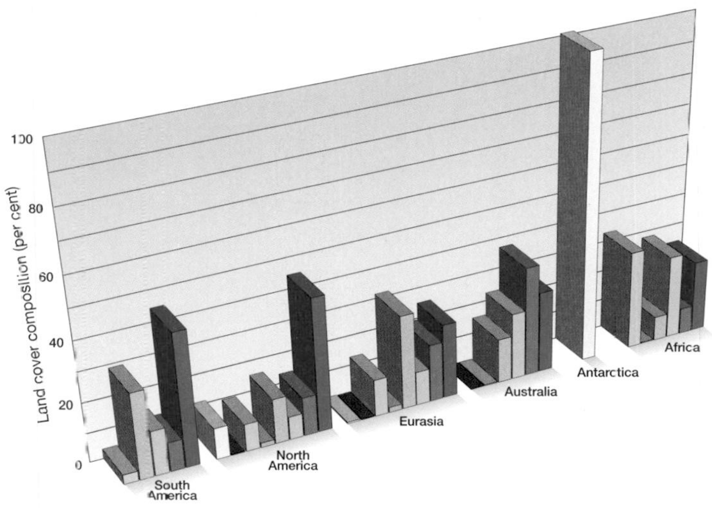
100
80
60
40
20
0
Land cover composition (per cent)
South America
North America
Eurasia
Australia
Antarctica
Africa

INTERPRETATION AND USES

The high resolution of the imagery used to compile the data set and map allows detailed interpretation of land cover patterns across the world. An additional benefit of holding the data in digital form is the ease with which land cover on global and continental scales can be extracted and analysed (*see 4 and 5*).

The small areas of permanent wetlands show just how rare these fragile ecosystems are. Apart from those in Sudan and the Okavango Delta in Botswana, only the swamp areas of Siberia are really evident on the global scale. In contrast, the concentration the world's extensive croplands in the northern hemisphere is obvious with the cereal belt in North America clearly visible. This contrasts with western Europe where the smaller field sizes and more common mixed farming lead to much of this region being classified as cropland/natural vegetation mosaics. The cereal belts of eastern Europe show the transition once again to extensive agriculture.

One of the most striking agricultural features on the Earth's surface is the heavily cultivated Nile valley and delta. In fact, humankind's influence on the Earth's vegetation is apparent throughout the map. Tropical forest cover is far from the uniform, unbroken swath so often depicted on world vegetation maps. In all areas of the world the tropical forest margins show encroachment of cropland or savanna in the wake of human activity (*see 3*), although parts of their interiors still remain largely untouched. In the light of such patterns, the global figures for tropical deforestation rates (typically around 0.5–1 per cent per year) become even more alarming. Deforestation is not uniform, so such figures hide far more rapid rates of loss in the forest margins.

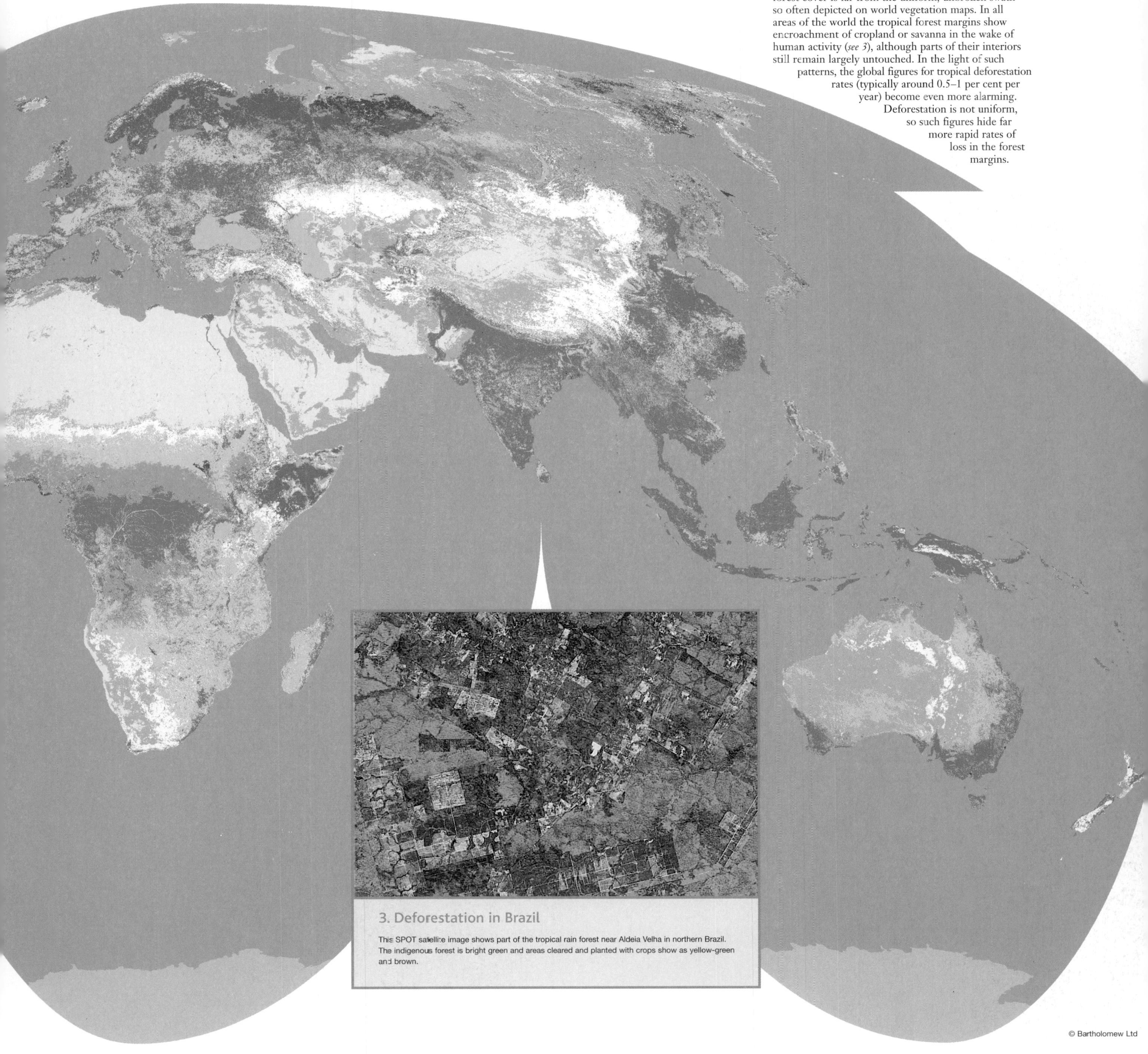

3. Deforestation in Brazil

This SPOT satellite image shows part of the tropical rain forest near Aldeia Velha in northern Brazil. The indigenous forest is bright green and areas cleared and planted with crops show as yellow-green and brown.

POPULATION DISTRIBUTION AND GROWTH

People are distributed very unevenly over the Earth. As shown on the population distribution map *(see 1)*, over a quarter of the land area is uninhabited or has extremely low population density. Barely a quarter of the land area is occupied at densities of 10 or more persons per square km, with the three largest concentrations in east Asia, the Indian subcontinent and Europe accounting for over half the world total. China and India dominate the scene, together accounting for nearly two-fifths of world population *(see 2)*.

Over the past half century world population has been growing faster than it has ever done before. Whereas world population did not pass the one billion mark until 1804 and took another 123 years to reach two billion in 1927, it then added the third billion in 33 years, the fourth in 14 years and the fifth in 13 years, with the 6 billion mark being passed only 12 years after this in 1999. It is expected that another three billion people will have been added to the world population by 2050 *(see 3)*.

Population growth since 1950 has been spread very unevenly between the continents. While overall numbers have been growing extremely rapidly since 1950, a massive 89 per cent increase has taken place in the less developed regions, especially southern and eastern Asia, while Europe's population is now almost stationary and ageing rapidly. India and China alone are responsible for over one-third of current growth, but most of the highest percentage rates of growth are to be found in Sub-Saharan Africa. The latest trends in population growth at country level *(see 4)* emphasize the continuing contrast between the more and less developed regions. Annual growth rates of 1.5 per cent or more are very common in Latin America, Africa and the southern half of Asia. A number of countries have rates in excess of 3.0 per cent, which if continued would lead to the doubling of their populations in 23 years or less.

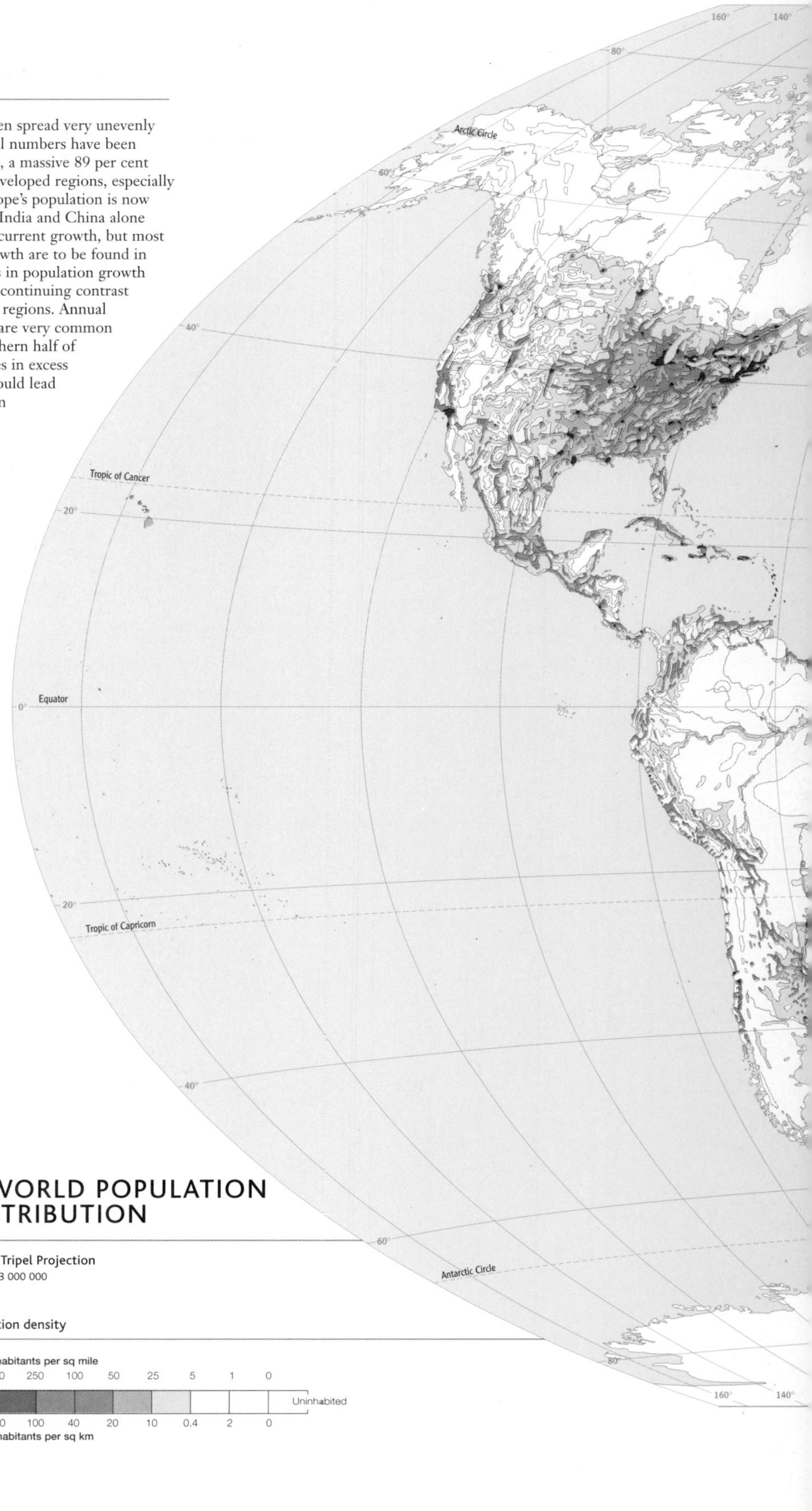

1. WORLD POPULATION DISTRIBUTION

Winkel Tripel Projection
scale 1:93 000 000

Population density

inhabitants per sq mile: 500 | 250 | 100 | 50 | 25 | 5 | 1 | 0 | Uninhabited
inhabitants per sq km: 200 | 100 | 40 | 20 | 10 | 0.4 | 2 | 0

2. TOP TEN COUNTRIES BY POPULATION AND POPULATION DENSITY

TOTAL POPULATION 1998	COUNTRY	RANK	COUNTRY	POPULATION DENSITY 1998 (countries with populations over 10 million) per sq mile	per sq km
1 262 817 000	China	1	Bangladesh	2 244	866
982 223 000	India	2	Taiwan	1 568	606
274 028 000	USA	3	South Korea	1 203	465
206 338 000	Indonesia	4	Netherlands	978	378
165 851 000	Brazil	5	Japan	866	334
148 166 000	Pakistan	6	Belgium	861	332
147 434 000	Russian Federation	7	India	830	320
126 281 000	Japan	8	Sri Lanka	729	281
124 774 000	Bangladesh	9	Philippines	630	243
106 409 000	Nigeria	10	UK	622	240

3. WORLD POPULATION GROWTH BY CONTINENT 1750–2050

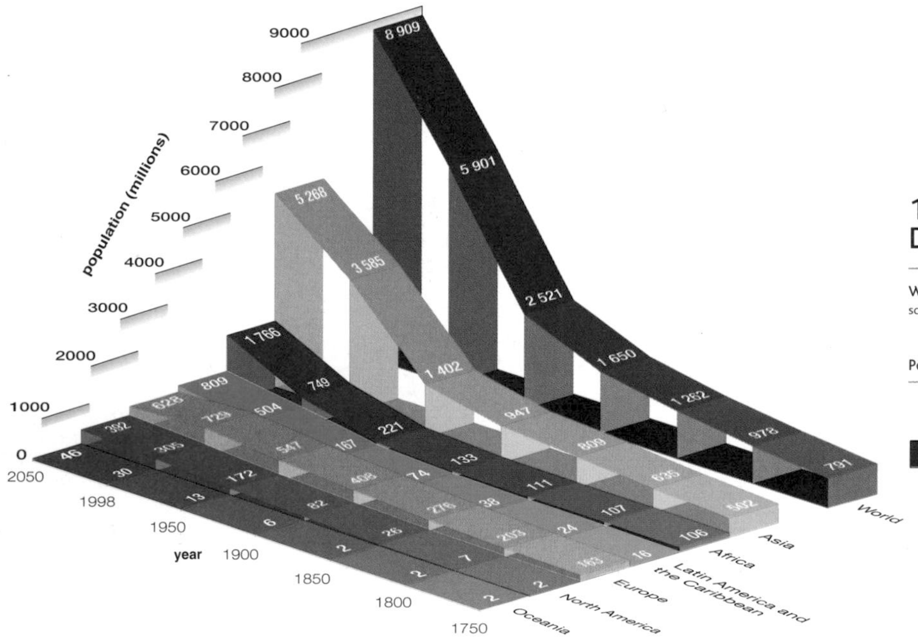

4. POPULATION CHANGE 1995–2000

Average annual rate of population change (per cent) and the top ten contributors to world population growth (net annual addition)
scale 1:255 000 000

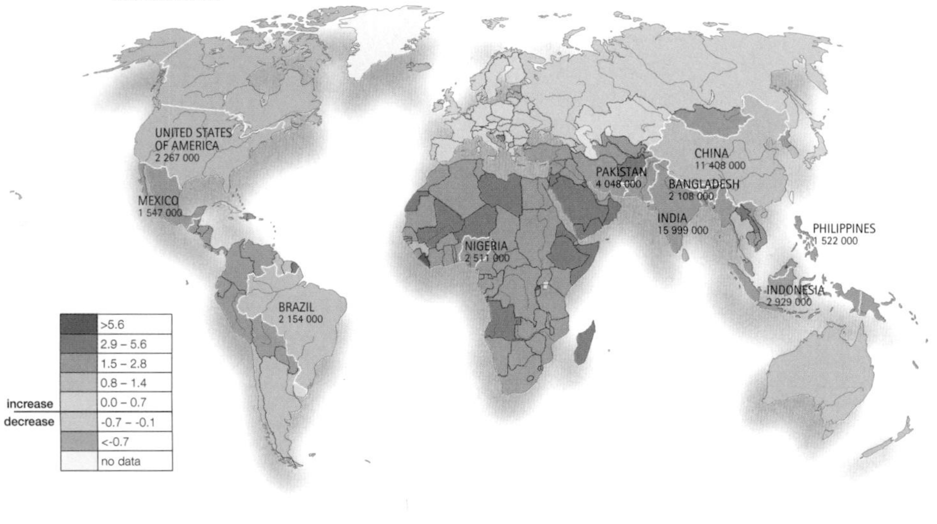

5. KEY POPULATION STATISTICS FOR MAJOR REGIONS

	Population 1998 (millions)	Growth (per cent)	Infant mortality rate	Total fertility rate	Life expectancy (years)
World	5 901	1.33	57	2.7	65
More developed regions[1]	1 182	0.28	9	1.6	75
Less developed regions[2]	4 719	1.59	63	3.0	63
Africa	749	2.37	87	5.1	51
Asia	3 585	1.38	57	2.6	66
Europe[3]	729	0.03	12	1.4	73
Latin America and the Caribbean[4]	504	1.57	36	2.7	69
North America	305	0.85	7	1.9	77
Oceania	30	1.30	24	2.4	74

Except for population (1998), the data are annual averages projected for the period 1995-2000.
1. Europe, North America, Australia, New Zealand and Japan.
2. Africa, Asia (excluding Japan), Latin America and the Caribbean, and Oceania (excluding Australia and New Zealand).
3. Includes Russian Federation.
4. South America, Central America (including Mexico) and all Caribbean Islands.

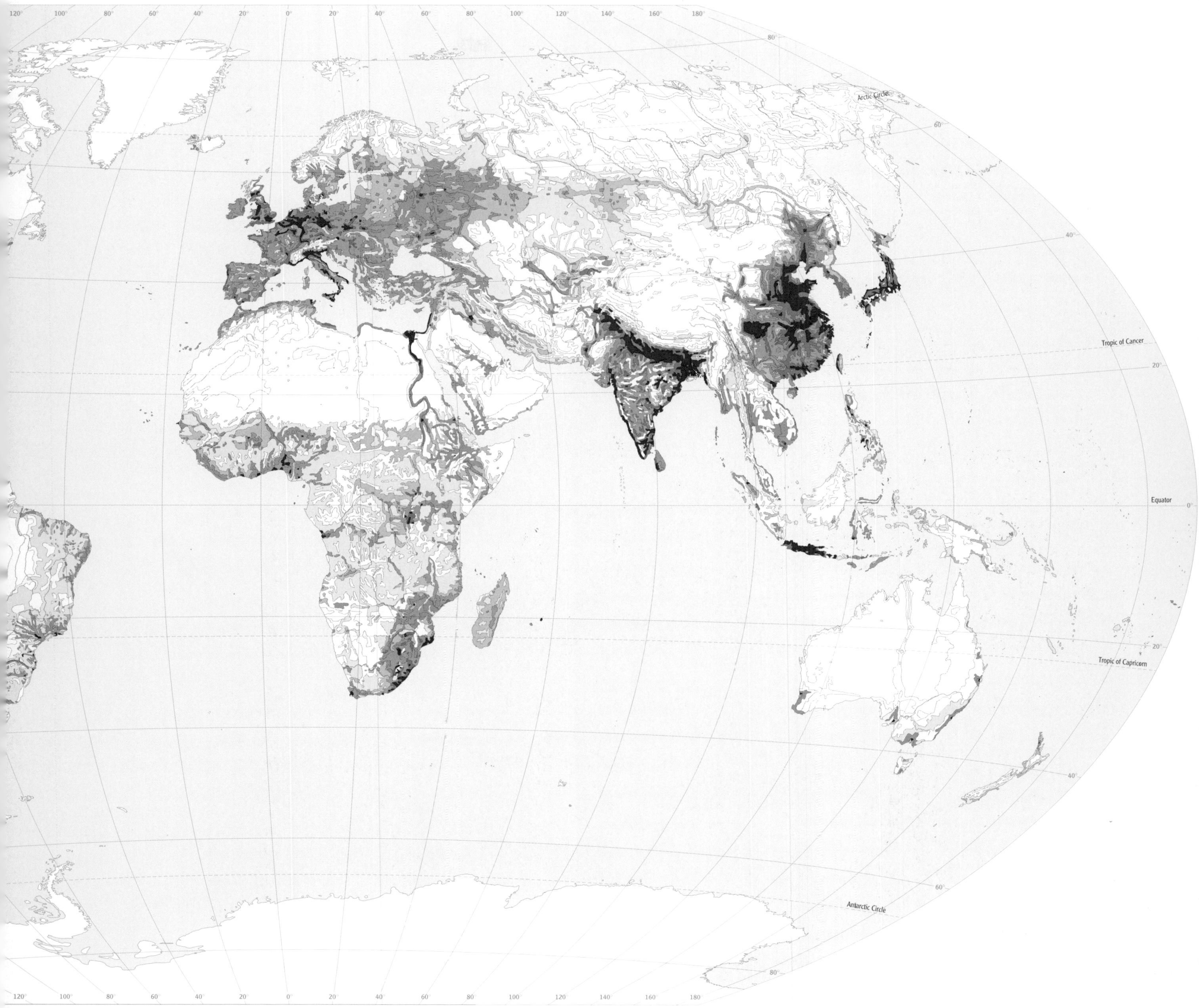
Arctic Circle
Tropic of Cancer
Equator
Tropic of Capricorn
Antarctic Circle

DEMOGRAPHIC TRANSITION

Behind patterns of population growth lies the 'demographic transition' process, where countries pass through a phase of falling death rates and then a phase of falling fertility. Most parts of the world have passed through the first phase, with the average life expectancy of 63 years in the less developed world now not far behind that of 75 years in the more developed regions *(see 5)*. Even so, infant mortality – a very good indicator of human development levels – remains a major challenge in the less developed regions *(see 6)*. Here, an average of sixty-three out of every one thousand babies die before their first birthday compared to only nine out of every one thousand in the more developed regions. Sub-Saharan Africa started this transitional phase later than most other parts of the world and has so far seen life expectancy rise to only 48 years, with progress being hampered by continuing high levels of infant mortality and by rising numbers of AIDS-related deaths.

Reductions in fertility rate *(see 7)* hold the key to the successful completion of the transition and the future stabilization of population growth. Much of the more developed world is well advanced in this process. In particular Europe's total fertility rate (broadly the average number of babies born to each woman) is now down to 1.4 – well below the 'replacement rate' of 2.1 needed to give a constant population in the long term. By contrast, the average for less developed regions, excluding China, is 3.8 and it is as high as 6.5 in Sub-Saharan Africa.

6. INFANT MORTALITY RATE 1995–2000

Deaths of infants less than one year old per 1000 live births
scale 1:315 000 000

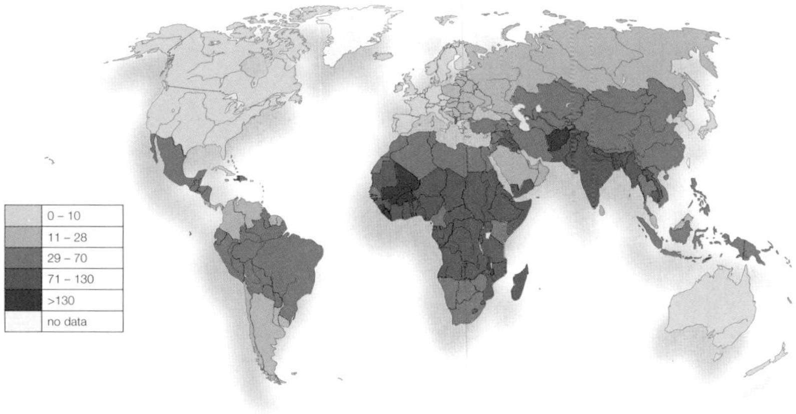
0 – 10
11 – 28
29 – 70
71 – 130
>130
no data

7. TOTAL FERTILITY RATE 1995–2000

Estimate of the number of children a woman will bear during her child-bearing years.
scale 1:315 000 000

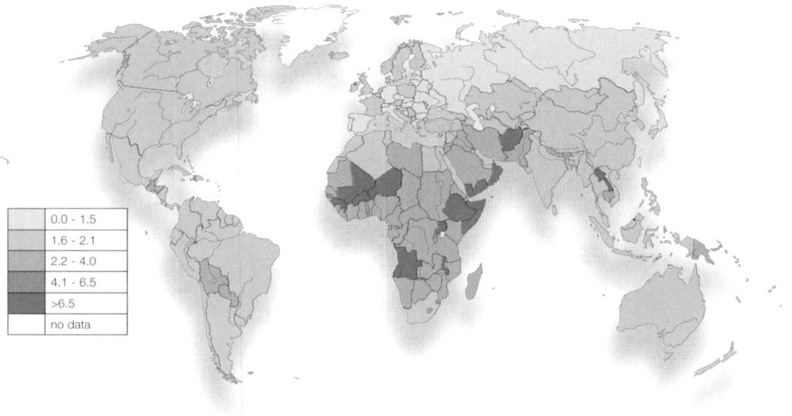
0.0 - 1.5
1.6 - 2.1
2.2 - 4.0
4.1 - 6.5
>6.5
no data

© Bartholomew Ltd

TOWARDS AN URBANIZED WORLD

World population is urbanizing rapidly but the current level of urbanization – the proportion of the population living in urban conditions – varies greatly across the world, as does its rate of increase. In the hundred years up to 1950 the greatest changes in urban population patterns took place in Europe and North America. Relatively few large cities developed elsewhere and most of these were in coastal locations with good trading connections with the imperial and industrial nations. This legacy is still highly visible on the world map of major cities (*see 1*). The main feature of the past half century has been the massive growth in the numbers of urban dwellers in the less developed regions. This process is still accelerating, posing an even greater logistical challenge during the next few decades than it did in the closing decades of the twentieth century.

The year 2006 is likely to be a momentous point in world history, when for the first time urban dwellers will outnumber those living in traditionally rural areas, according to UN projections. The annual rise in the percentage of the world's population living in cities has been accelerating steadily since the 1970s and will be running at unprecedentedly high levels for the next three decades. As a result, by 2030, 61.1 per cent of the world's population will be urbanites compared to 36.7 per cent in 1970 and 47.4 per cent in 2000 (*see 2*). In absolute terms, the global urban population more than doubled between 1970 and 2000 and is expected to grow by a further 2.2 billion by 2030 (*see 3*).

1. THE WORLD'S MAJOR CITIES

Urban agglomerations with over 1 million inhabitants
Winkel Tripel Projection
scale 1:106 000 000

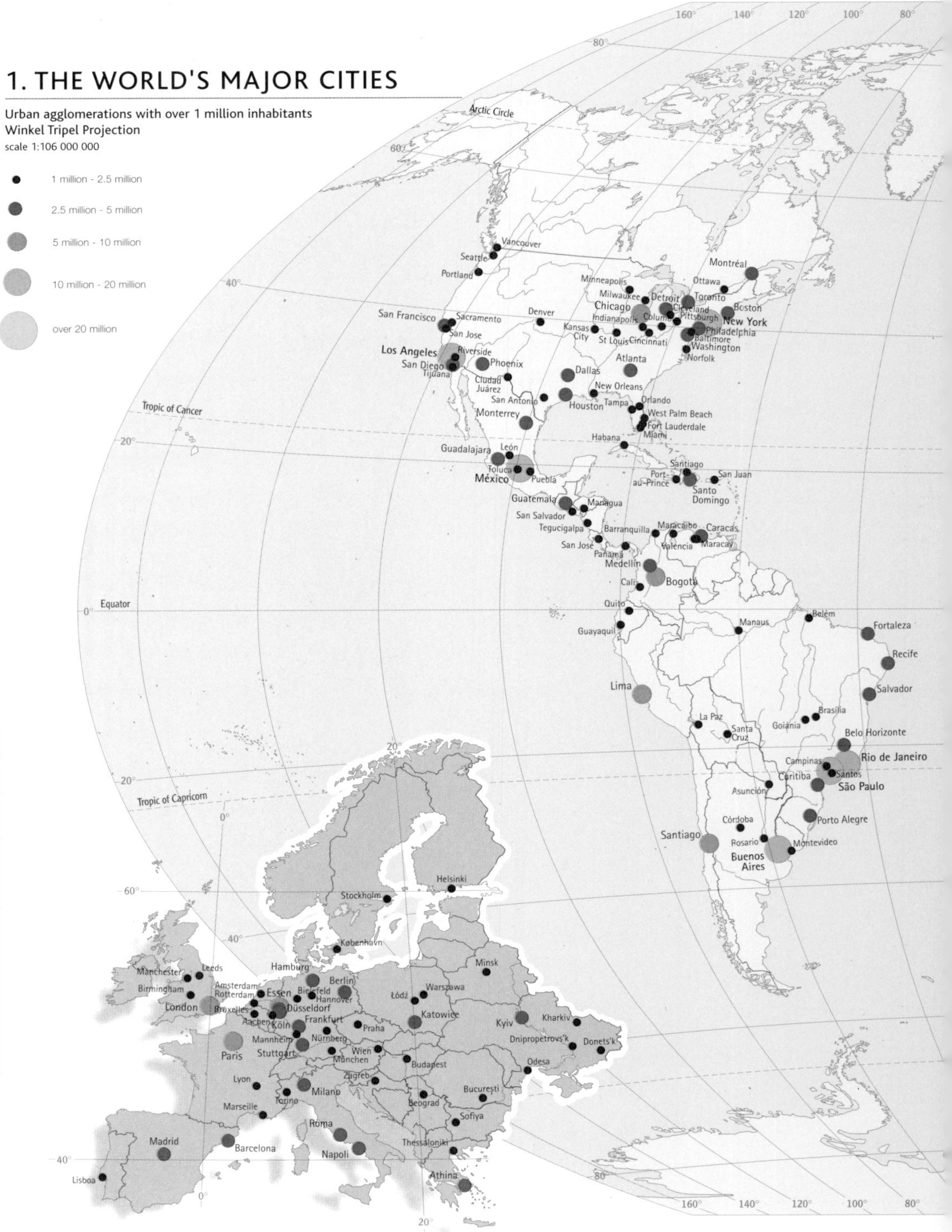

2. LEVEL OF URBANIZATION BY MAJOR REGION 1970–2030

Urban population as a percentage of total population

	1970	2000	2030
World	36.7	47.4	61.1
More developed regions[1]	67.7	76.1	83.7
Less developed regions[2]	25.1	40.5	57.3
Africa	23.0	37.8	54.4
Asia	23.4	37.6	55.2
Europe[3]	64.5	74.9	82.9
Latin America and the Caribbean[4]	57.4	75.4	83.2
North America	73.8	77.2	84.4
Oceania	70.8	70.0	74.5

1. Europe, North America, Australia, New Zealand and Japan.
2. Africa, Asia (excluding Japan), Latin America and the Caribbean, and Oceania (excluding Australia and New Zealand).
3. Includes Russian Federation.
4. South America, Central America (including Mexico) and all Caribbean Islands.

3. TOTAL URBAN POPULATION OF MAJOR REGIONS 1950–2030

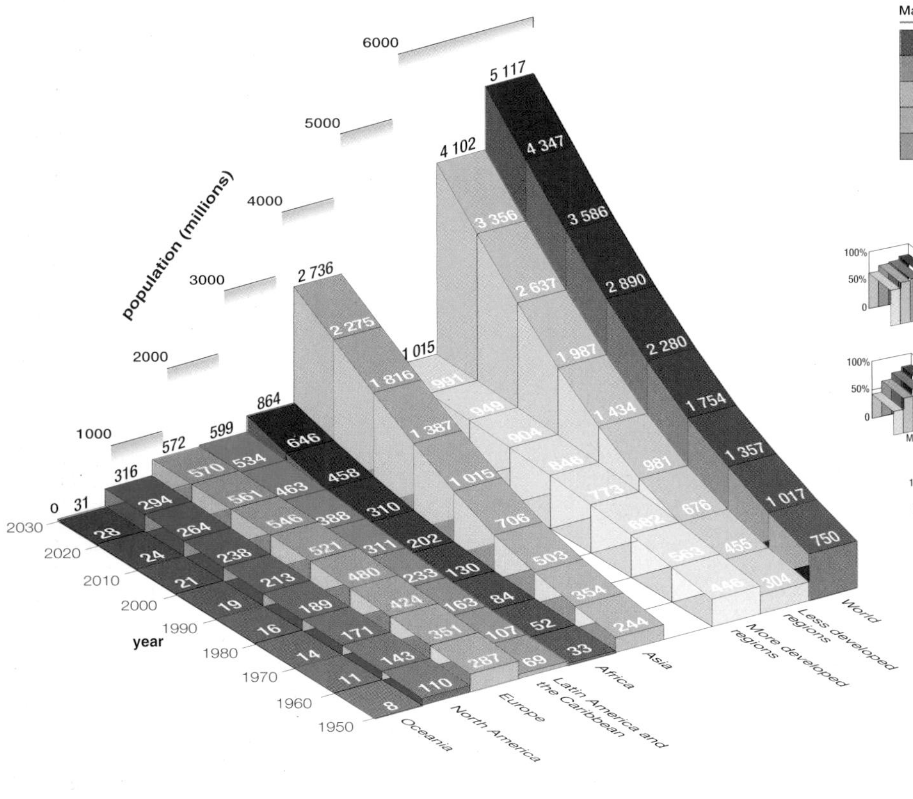

4. LEVEL OF URBANIZATION

Percentage of total population living in urban areas 2000 and growth in urbanization 1950-2025 (selected countries)
scale 1:250 000 000

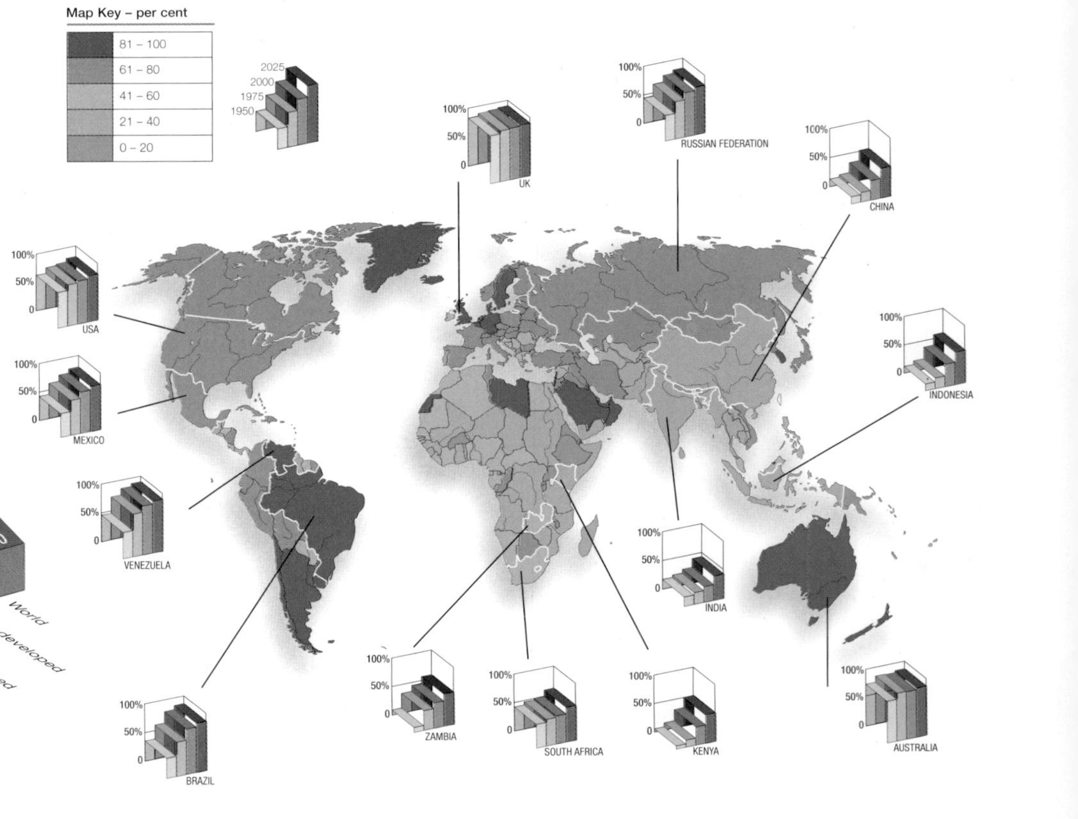

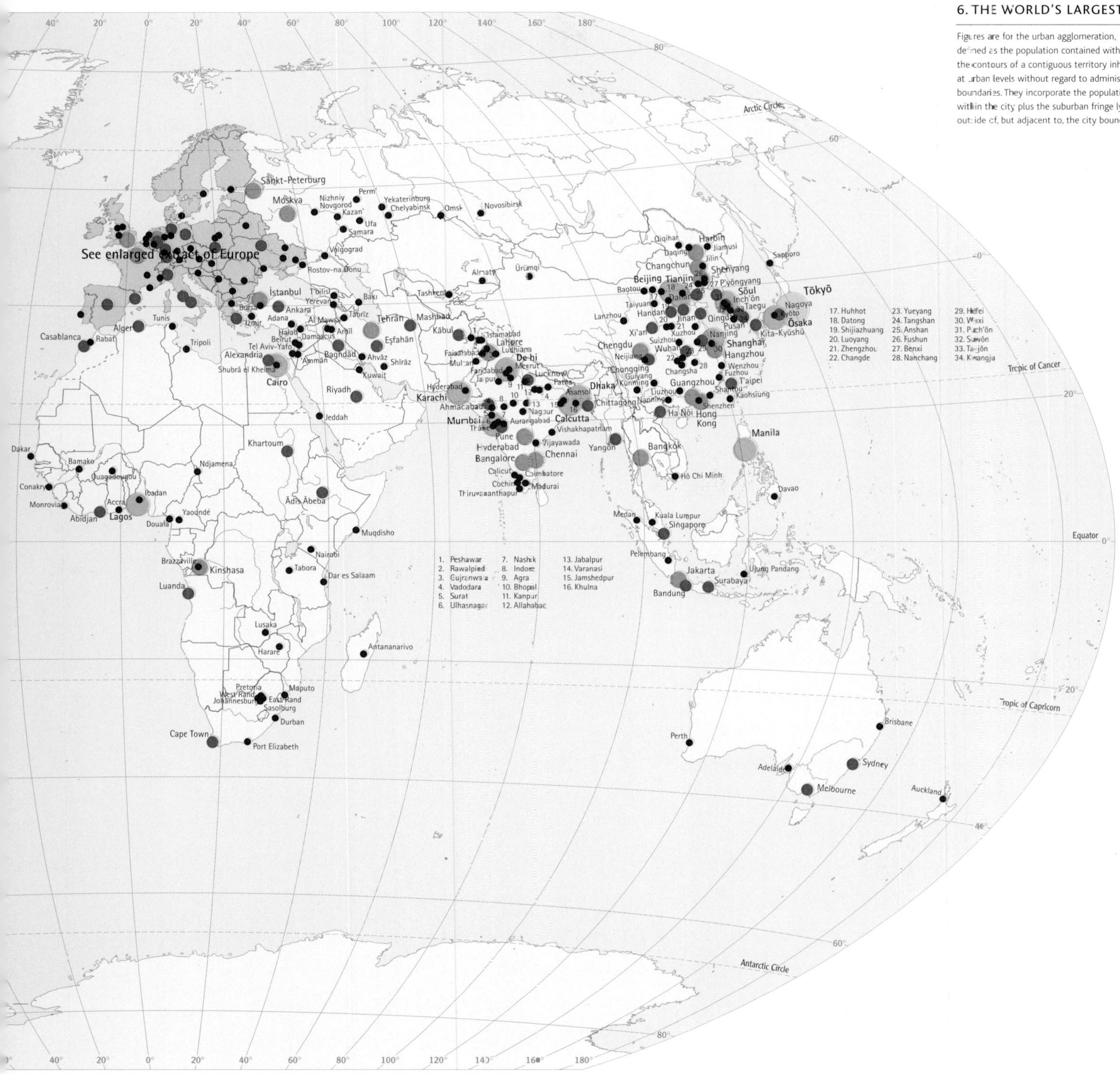

6. THE WORLD'S LARGEST CITIES 2000

Figures are for the urban agglomeration, defined as the population contained within the contours of a contiguous territory inhabited at urban levels without regard to administrative boundaries. They incorporate the population within the city plus the suburban fringe lying outside of, but adjacent to, the city boundaries.

Tōkyō Japan	28 025 000
México Mexico	18 131 000
Mumbai India	18 042 000
São Paulo Brazil	17 711 000
New York USA	16 626 000
Shanghai China	14 173 000
Lagos Nigeria	13 488 000
Los Angeles USA	13 129 000
Calcutta India	12 900 000
Buenos Aires Argentina	12 431 000
Sŏul South Korea	12 215 000
Beijing China	12 033 000
Karachi Pakistan	11 774 000
Delhi India	11 680 000
Dhaka Bangladesh	10 979 000
Manila Philippines	10 818 000
Cairo Egypt	10 772 000
Ōsaka Japan	10 609 000
Rio de Janeiro Brazil	10 556 000
Tianjin China	10 239 000
Jakarta Indonesia	9 815 000
Paris France	9 638 000
İstanbul Turkey	9 413 000
Moskva Russian Federation	9 299 000
London United Kingdom	7 640 000
Lima Peru	7 443 000
Tehrān Iran	7 380 000
Bangkok Thailand	7 221 000
Chicago USA	6 945 000
Bogotá Colombia	6 834 000
Hyderabad India	6 833 000
Chennai India	6 639 000
Essen Germany	6 559 000
Hangzhou China	6 389 000
Hong Kong China	6 097 000
Lahore Pakistan	6 030 000
Shenyang China	5 681 000
Changchun China	5 566 000
Bangalore India	5 544 000
Harbin China	5 475 000
Chengdu China	5 293 000
Santiago Chile	5 261 000
Guangzhou China	5 162 000
Sankt-Peterburg Russian Federation	5 132 000
Kinshasa Dem. Rep. Congo	5 068 000
Baghdād Iraq	4 796 000
Jinan China	4 789 000
Wuhan China	4 750 000
Toronto Canada	4 657 000
Yangôn Myanmar	4 458 000
Alger Algeria	4 447 000
Philadelphia USA	4 398 000
Qingdao China	4 376 000
Milano Italy	4 251 000
Pusan South Korea	4 239 000
Belo Horizonte Brazil	4 160 000
Ahmadabad India	4 154 000
Madrid Spain	4 072 000
San Francisco USA	4 051 000
Alexandria Egypt	3 995 000
Washington USA	3 927 000
Dallas USA	3 912 000
Guadalajara Mexico	3 908 000
Chongqing China	3 896 000
Medellín Colombia	3 831 000
Detroit USA	3 785 000
Handan China	3 763 000
Frankfurt Germany	3 700 000
Porto Alegre Brazil	3 699 000
Ha Nôi Vietnam	3 678 000
Sydney Australia	3 665 000
Santo Domingo Dominican Republic	3 601 000
Singapore Singapore	3 587 000
Casablanca Morocco	3 535 000
Katowice Poland	3 488 000
Pune India	3 485 000
Bandung Indonesia	3 420 000
Monterrey Mexico	3 416 000
Montréal Canada	3 401 000
Nagoya Japan	3 377 000
Nanjing China	3 375 000
Houston USA	3 365 000
Abidjan Côte d'Ivoire	3 359 000
Xi'an China	3 352 000
Berlin Germany	3 337 000
Riyadh Saudi Arabia	3 328 000
Recife Brazil	3 307 000
Düsseldorf Germany	3 251 000
Ankara Turkey	3 190 000
Melbourne Australia	3 188 000
Salvador Brazil	3 180 000
Dalian China	3 153 000
Caracas Venezuela	3 153 000
Ādīs Ābeba Ethiopia	3 112 000
Athina Greece	3 103 000
Cape Town South Africa	3 092 000
Köln Germany	3 067 000
Maputo Mozambique	3 017 000
Napoli Italy	3 012 000
Fortaleza Brazil	3 007 000
San Diego USA	2 983 000
Boston USA	2 915 000
Chittagong Bangladesh	2 906 000
Kita-Kyūshū Japan	2 898 000
Kyiv Ukraine	2 897 000
T'aipei Taiwan	2 880 000
Inch'ŏn South Korea	2 837 000
Barcelona Spain	2 819 000
Khartoum Sudan	2 748 000
P'yŏngyang North Korea	2 726 000
Kābul Afghanistan	2 716 000
Guatemala Guatemala	2 697 000
Atlanta USA	2 689 000
Stuttgart Germany	2 688 000
Roma Italy	2 688 000
Hamburg Germany	2 680 000
Luanda Angola	2 665 000
Eşfahān Iran	2 644 000
Phoenix USA	2 607 000
Lucknow India	2 565 000
Taegu South Korea	2 559 000
Curitiba Brazil	2 519 000
Surabaya Indonesia	2 507 000
Tashkent Uzbekistan	2 495 000
Kanpur India	2 447 000
Johannesburg South Africa	2 412 000
İzmir Turkey	2 399 000
Mashhad Iran	2 378 000
Arbīl Iraq	2 368 000
Minneapolis USA	2 363 000
Surat India	2 341 000
Damascus Syria	2 335 000
Nairobi Kenya	2 320 000
München Germany	2 306 000
Habana Cuba	2 302 000
Taiyuan China	2 280 000
Zhengzhou China	2 275 000
Birmingham United Kingdom	2 271 000
Warszawa Poland	2 269 000
Manchester United Kingdom	2 252 000
Guiyang China	2 230 000
Faisalabad Pakistan	2 228 000
Miami USA	2 210 000
Ḥalab Syria	2 173 000
Tel Aviv-Yafo Israel	2 170 000
Jaipur India	2 143 000
București Romania	2 130 000
Guayaquil Ecuador	2 127 000
Peshawar Pakistan	2 094 000
Seattle USA	2 084 000
Cali Colombia	2 082 000
Dakar Senegal	2 077 000
Wien Austria	2 072 000
St Louis USA	2 071 000
Nagpur India	2 060 000

REGIONAL PATTERNS OF URBANIZATION

There is a broad contrast in the levels of urbanization between the more and less developed regions (*see 4*). In the more developed regions as a whole, three-quarters of the population now live in urban places. Excluding city states, levels range from 97 per cent for Belgium to under 40 per cent for Albania, Bosnia-Herzegovina and Portugal. Many countries have seen very little increase in their level of urbanization over the last few decades, with some reporting renewed population growth in rural areas. Only 40.5 per cent of the population in the less developed regions are urbanites, but this represents a big jump from the 25.1 per cent figure for 1970. Africa and Asia both currently average less than this, but will be seeing the greatest changes in the future, with their urban proportions likely to pass the 50 per cent mark by 2025. Between 2000 and 2030, Africa and Asia are expected to account for 86 per cent of the world's new urbanites – around 550 and 1 350 million people in absolute terms.

Alongside the rise in the world's urban population has occurred a massive increase in the number and size of cities. In 1950, New York was the only urban agglomeration with over 10 million inhabitants, but the number of cities of this size had grown to five by 1975 and to fourteen by 1995. There are expected to be twenty-six such cities by 2015, according to UN figures (*see 5*). This increase is principally an Asian phenomenon. Asia's total of cities of this size has grown from two to seven between 1975 and 1995, and today Asia dominates any list of the world's largest cities (*see 6*). Even more impressively, eleven of the additional twelve megacities that are expected to emerge by 2015 are in Asian countries, nine of them in south and east Asia. This massive growth is due to a combination of in-migration and natural increase, together with the physical outward expansion of their built-up areas and the incorporation of nearby settlements.

5. CITIES OF OVER 10 MILLION INHABITANTS 1975–2015

Figures are for urban agglomerations as defined in Table 6.

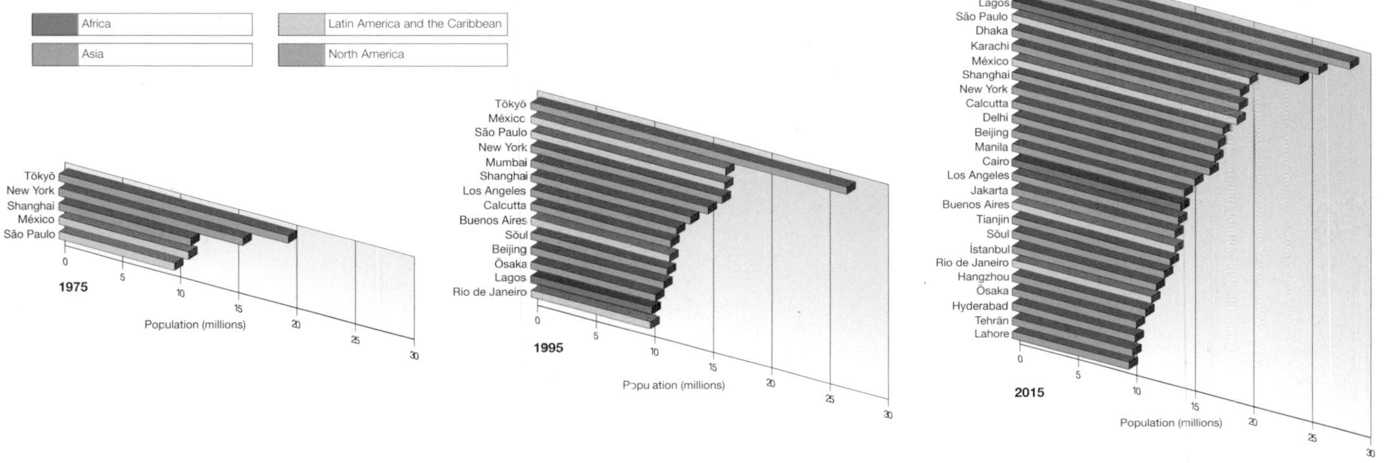

© Bartholomew Ltd

THE DISTRIBUTION OF MINERALS

Geological processes have determined the distribution of mineral resources but the location of productive mines is the result of geological, economic and political factors. The map *(see 1)* shows the locations of the most important mines producing industrial and metallic minerals. The bulk of world reserves – those resources which can be extracted economically at a particular time – are located at the mines shown.

Many aspects of the distribution of mineral resources are related to the Earth's tectonic structure. For example, the numerous large copper mines around parts of the Pacific rim are related to the destructive plate margins in these areas *(see pages 24-25)*. Most iron ore now comes from giant sedimentary deposits which have been naturally enriched by near-surface processes. These occur in ancient 'cratons' which are areas of the crust which have been internally stable for more than half a billion years and are typified by western Australia, eastern Brazil and the Canadian and Eurasian 'shields'. Output from the main iron ore producers has varied over time, with China becoming the leading world producer in the 1990s *(see 2)*.

Another striking relationship of mineral resources to geography and climate is provided by the distribution of bauxite, the main ore of aluminium. With few exceptions, major bauxite deposits are situated in the tropics, because bauxite is formed by the weathering of rocks at the Earth's surface under tropical climatic conditions *(see 3)*.

1. LOCATION OF SIGNIFICANT MINES

Producing mines or major deposits in active development, 1999
See table below for index to sites
Winkel Tripel Projection
scale 1:100 000 000

>5% of world production
1-5% of world production
Other selected deposits (<1% of world production)

METALLIC MINERALS

- Iron **Fe**
- Copper **Cu**
- Gold **Au**
- Uranium **U**
- Aluminium **Al**
- Manganese **Mn**
- Lead **Pb**, Zinc **Zn**, Cadmium **Cd**, Silver **Ag**
- Tin **Sn**, Tantalum **Ta**, Beryllium **Be**, Antimony **Sb**, Mercury **Hg**, Bismuth **Bi**, Caesium **Cs**, Rubidium **Rb**
- Nickel **Ni**, Molybdenum **Mo**, Niobium **Nb**, Cobalt **Co**, Chromium **Cr**, Platinum **Pt**, Palladium **Pd**, Vanadium **V**, Tungsten **W**

INDUSTRIAL (NON METALLIC) MINERALS

- Potash **K**, Phosphate **P**, Borates **B**, Sulphur **S**, Lithium **Li**
- Baryte **Ba**, Fluorspar **F**, Asbestos **Asb**
- Titanium minerals (ilmenite, rutile) **Ti**, Zircon **Zr**
- Diamonds **Diam.**

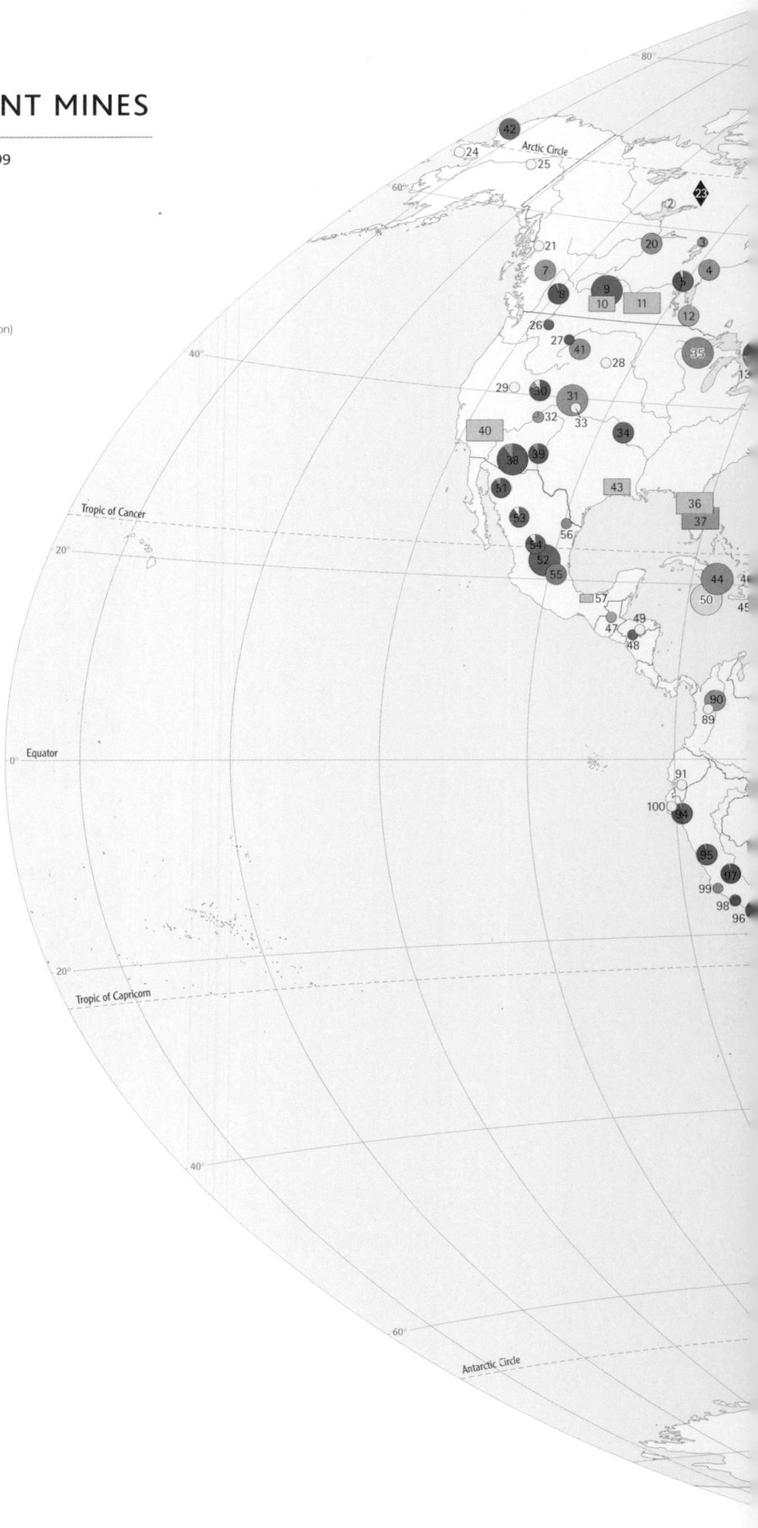

Arctic Circle
Tropic of Cancer
Equator
Tropic of Capricorn
Antarctic Circle

TYPES OF MINERAL

Minerals are usually grouped into four classes defined chiefly by their use:

Industrial minerals are minerals such as salt, fluorspar, barytes and sulphur, which are used in their natural state in industrial processes, and phosphate rock and potash which are vital constituents of fertilizers in addition to other uses. Gemstones are a special case in that, with the exception of industrial diamonds which are used as an abrasive, they are valued only for their aesthetic appearance.

Metallic minerals are mined to extract the metals they contain. Deposits of metallic minerals are evaluated chiefly on the costs of mining the ore and of extracting the metal from it.

Construction minerals such as sand, gravel, clay and gypsum, are used to make building materials. Their production costs are relatively low, but because their transport costs are high, they are normally used close to where they are produced. They are produced in most countries and are not shown on the map.

Energy minerals comprise coal, oil and natural gas, collectively known as 'fossil fuels', and uranium, the raw material for nuclear power. In terms of mass they are the most important traded minerals. Uranium is shown on the map; the others are shown on pages 38-39.

MINERAL PRODUCTION

Economies of scale have always been a strong influence on the geographic patterns of mineral production: a very large orebody is able to supply a significant proportion of world demand and can often be worked at a lower unit cost than a smaller deposit. Thus, for example, only a handful of giant mines in the Americas dominate the world supply of copper *(see 4)*. Similar geographical concentration of supply are marked also in other minerals, including chromium and nickel *(see 5 and 6)*. Production of gold *(see 7)* and diamonds was until fairly recently dominated by southern African countries but advances in exploration and processing technology have led to many new discoveries of both of these commodities in other continents, notably Australia and North America. China is the dominant producer of tungsten, antimony and fluorspar *(see 8)*, having a large number of small to medium sized mines. The absence of mines of these materials elsewhere indicates not a lack of resources, but a lack of economic reserves.

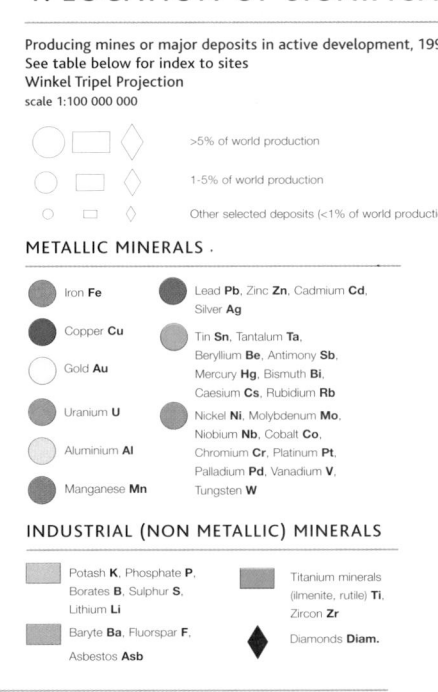

2. IRON ORE PRODUCERS 1972-1998

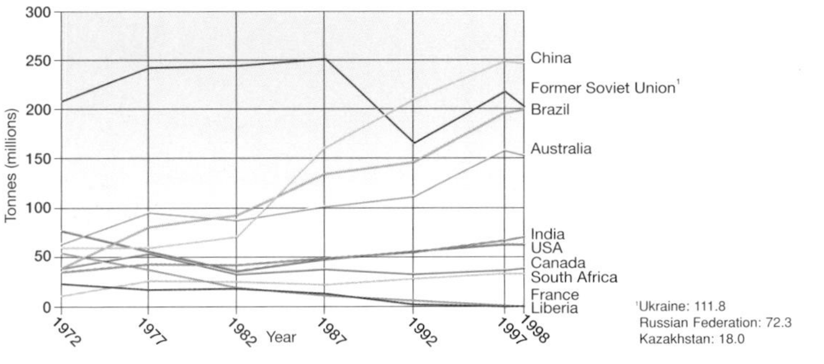

300
250
200
150
100
50
0
Tonnes (millions)
1972
1977
1982
1987
1992
1997
1998
Year
China
Former Soviet Union[1]
Brazil
Australia
India
USA
Canada
South Africa
France
Liberia

[1]Ukraine: 111.8
Russian Federation: 72.3
Kazakhstan: 18.0

3. ALUMINIUM ORE PRODUCTION 1998

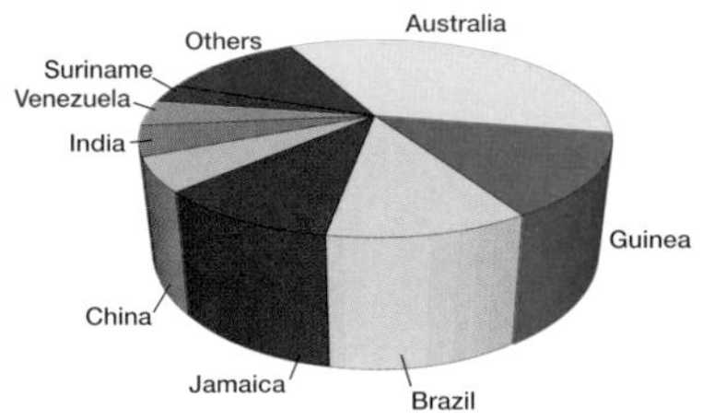

Australia
Others
Suriname
Venezuela
India
Guinea
China
Jamaica
Brazil

4. COPPER PRODUCTION 1998

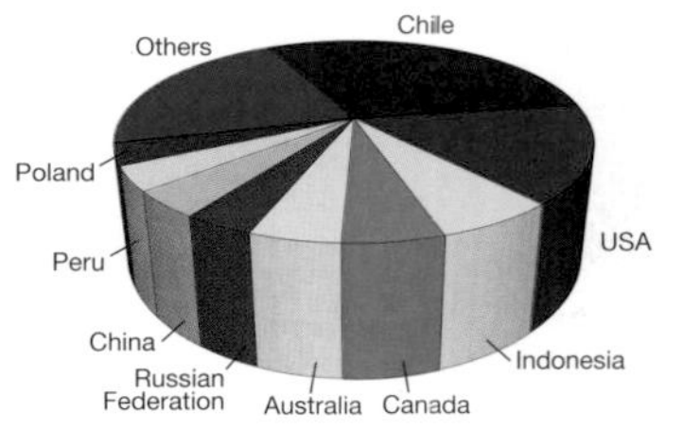

Chile
Others
Poland
Peru
USA
China
Russian Federation
Australia
Canada
Indonesia

INDEX TO SITES ON THE MAP

KEY: SITE NUMBER, MINE/*PROVINCE/DISTRICT/AREA*, **MINERALS**

NORTH AMERICA

Canada
1 Polaris, **Pb, Zn**
2 Yellowknife, **Au**
3 Wollaston Lake, **U**
4 Thompson, **Ni**
5 Flin Flon, **Cu, Zn, Ag, Au**
6 Nanisivik, Arctic Bay, **Pb, Zn, Ag**
7 Endako, **Mo**
8 Highland Valley, **Cu, Mo**
9 Sullivan, **Pb, Zn, Ag, Sb**
10 Alberta, **S**
11 Saskatchewan, **K**
12 Bernic Lake, **Ta, Li, Cs, Rb**
13 Sudbury, **Ni, Cu, Co, Pt**
14 Timmins, Noranda, **Cu, Pb, Zn, Au**
15 Asbestos, **Asb**
16 Niobec, **Nb**
17 Gaspé, **Cu**
18 Lac Allard, **Ti**
19 *Northern Québec*, **Fe**
20 *Athabasca Basin*, **U**
21 Eskay Creek, **Au, Ag**
22 Raglan, **Ni, Cu, Co, Pt**
23 Ekati (*Lac de Gras*) **Diam.**

USA
24 Nome, **Au**
25 Fairbanks, **Au**
26 Coeur d'Alene, **Pb, Zn, Ag**
27 Continental (*Butte, Montana*), **Cu**
28 Homestake, **Au**
29 Carlin, **Au**
30 Bingham Canyon, **Cu, Mo, Au**
31 Henderson, **Mo, W**
32 *Colorado Plateau*, **U, V**
33 Cresson (*Cripple Creek*), **Au**
34 *Viburnum Trend*, **Pb, Zn, Ag**
35 *Lake Superior, Minnesota*, **Fe**
36 *Florida*, **P**
37 *Florida, East Coast*, **Ti, Zr**
38 *Arizona*, **Cu, Mo**
39 *New Mexico*, **Cu, Mo**
40 Boron, Searles Lake, **B**
41 Stillwater, **Pt, Pd**
42 Red Dog, **Zn, Pb, Ag**
43 *Texas, Louisiana*, **S**

CENTRAL AMERICA

Cuba
44 *Eastern Cuba*, **Ni, Co**

Dominican Republic
45 Pueblo Viejo, **Au**
46 Bonao, **Ni**

Guatemala
47 *Ixtahuacan*, **Sb**

Honduras
48 El Mochito, **Zn, Pb, Ag**
49 San Andres, **Au**

Jamaica
50 *Jamaica*, **Al**

Mexico
51 *Sonora*, **Cu, Mo**
52 *San Luis Potosí*, **Pb, Zn, Ag, Sb**
53 Chihuahua, *Northern Durango*, **Pb, Zn, Ag, Cu, Au**
54 *Zacatecas*, **Pb, Zn, Ag, Cu, Au**
55 *Hidalgo*, **Mn**
56 Hercules, **Fe**
57 Coatzacoalcos, **S**

SOUTH AMERICA

Argentina
58 Aguilar, **Pb, Zn, Ag**
59 Bajo de la Alumbrera, **Cu, Mo, Au**
60 El Pachon, **Cu, Mo, Au**
61 *Northern Provinces*, **B**

Bolivia
62 Potosí, Oruro, **Sn, Sb, Pb, Zn, Ag, W**

Brazil
63 Trombetas, **Al**
64 *Rondônia*, **Sn**
65 Carajás,
66 Igarape Azul, Carajás, **Mn**
67 Caraiba, **Cu**
68 Campo Formoso, **Cr**
69 Cana Brava, **Cr**
70 Niquelândia, **Ni**
71 Morro do Niquel, **Ni**
72 Tocantins, **Ni**
73 Urucum, **Mn, Fe**
74 Vazante, **Pb, Zn**
75 Boquira, **Pb, Zn**
76 Jequitinhonha, **Diam.**
77 *Araxá*, **Nb, P**
78 Morro Velho, **Au**
79 *Iron Quadrilateral*, **Fe**
80 Morro da Fumaça, **F**
81 *Roraima*, **Diam.**

Chile
82 Chuquicamata, Abra, **Cu, Mo**
83 Escondida, El Salvador, **Cu, Mo, Au**
84 Disputada, Andina, Pelambres, **Cu, Mo**
85 El Teniente, **Cu, Mo**
86 Cerro Colorado, Quebrada Blanca, **Cu, Mo**
87 La Candelaria, **Cu, Mo, Au**
88 *Atacama*, **Fe**

Colombia
89 Titiribi, **Au**
90 Cerro Matoso, **Ni**

Ecuador
91 Portovelo, **Au**

Guyana
92 *Guyana*, **Al**
93 Omai, **Au**

Peru
94 *Northern Peru*, **Pb, Zn, Ag, Cu, Mo**
95 Cerro de Pasco, *central Peru*, **Pb, Zn, Ag, Cu, Mo**
96 Cuajone, Toquepala, **Cu, Mo**
97 Tintaya, **Cu, Mo**
98 Cerro Verde, **Cu, Mo**
99 Marcona, **Fe**
100 Yanacocha, **Au**

Suriname
101 *Suriname*, **Al**

Venezuela
102 Cedeno, **Al**
103 Cerro Bolivar, San Isidro, **Fe**
104 Cristinas, **Au, Cu**

EUROPE

Albania
1 *Kukës*, **Cr**

Austria
2 Mittersill, **W**

Belarus
3 Soligorsk, **K**

Belgium
4 Fleurus, **Ba**

Bulgaria
5 Chleopech, **Cu, Au**

Czech Republic
6 Erzgebirge, **U**

Finland
7 Kemi, **Cr**
8 Siilinjärvi, **P**
9 *Outokumpu Area*, **Cu, Ni, Co, Zn, Ag**

France
10 Chaillac, **Ba, F**
11 *South of Massif Central*, **F**
12 Lodève, **U**
13 Vendée, **U**
14 Salsigne, **Au, Bi, Ag, Cu**
15 Lacq, **S**
16 *Alsace*, **K**

Germany
17 *Stassfurt*, **K**
18 Mechernich, **Ba**

Greece
19 Parnasse, **Al**
20 Evvoia, **Ni**

Hungary
21 *Danube Region*, **Al**

Ireland
22 Navan, Lisheen, Galmoy, **Zn, Pb, Ag**

Italy
23 *Iglesiente*, **Pb, Zn, Ag, Ba, F**
24 Furtei, **Au**

Norway
25 Tellnes, **Ti**

Poland
26 *Lubin Region*, **Cu, Ag, Au**
27 *Upper Silesia* (*Kraków*), **Pb, Zn, Ag**
28 Tarnobrzeg, **S**

Portugal
29 Neves Corvo, **Cu, Sn, Zn**
30 *Iberian Pyrite Belt*, **Cu, Ag, Pb, Zn, S**
31 *Panasqueira*, **W, Cu, Sn**

Romania
32 *Apuseni Mountains*, **Au, Zn, Pb, Ag**

Russian Federation (in Europe)
33 Pechenga, **Ni, Cu, Pt, Co**
34 Monchegorsk, **Ni, Cu, Pt, Co**
35 Lovozero, Khibiny, **P, Nb**
36 Berezniki, Solikamsk, **K**
37 Kotshkanav, **Cr, Pt**
38 Kursk, **Fe**
39 Tyrnyauz, **W, Mo**
40 Sadan, **Pb, Zn, Ag**

Spain
30 *Iberian Pyrite Belt*, **Cu, Ag, Pb, Zn, S**
41 El Valle (Río Narcea), **Au**
42 Almaden, **Hg**
43 Reocin, **Zn, Pb, Ag**
44 La Collada, **F**

Sweden
45 Kiruna, **Fe**
46 *Skellefteå*, **Cu, Zn, Pb, Au, Ag**
47 Aitik, **Cu, Ag, Au**
48 Bjorkdal, **Au**
49 Laisvall, **Pb, Zn, Ag**
50 Falun, **Pb, Zn, Ag, Cu**
51 Zinkgruvan, **Zn, Pb, Ag**
52 Grängesberg, **Fe**
53 Malmberget, **Fe**

Ukraine
54 Kalush, **K**
55 *Krivoy Rog*, **Fe**
56 Nikopol, **Mn**

United Kingdom
57 Boulby, **K**
58 Foss, **Ba**
59 *Southern Pennines*, **F, Ba**

Yugoslavia
60 Bor, **Cu, Au**
61 Trepča, **Pb, Zn, Ag**

AFRICA

Algeria
1 *Annaba*, **Hg**
2 *Djebel Onk and Gafsa Region*, **P**

Angola
3 *Lunda Norte*, **Diam.**

Botswana
4 Orapa, **Diam.**
5 Jwaneng, **Diam.**
6 Selebi-Phikwe, **Ni, Cu**

Central African Republic
7 Berbérati, **Diam.**
8 Kotto, **Diam.**

Democratic Republic of Congo
9 Kasai, **Diam.**
10 Bakwanga, **Diam.**
11 *Copperbelt*, **Cu, Co**

Gabon
12 Mounana, **U**
13 Moanda, **Mn**

Ghana
14 Nsuta, **Mn**
15 *Ashanti, Western*, **Au**
16 Birim, **Diam.**

Guinea
17 Boké, Kindia, **Al**
18 Kono, Sanniquellie, Macenta, **Diam.**

Ivory Coast (Côte d'Ivoire)
19 Tortiya Segala, **Diam.**

Kenya
20 Kerio Valley, **F**

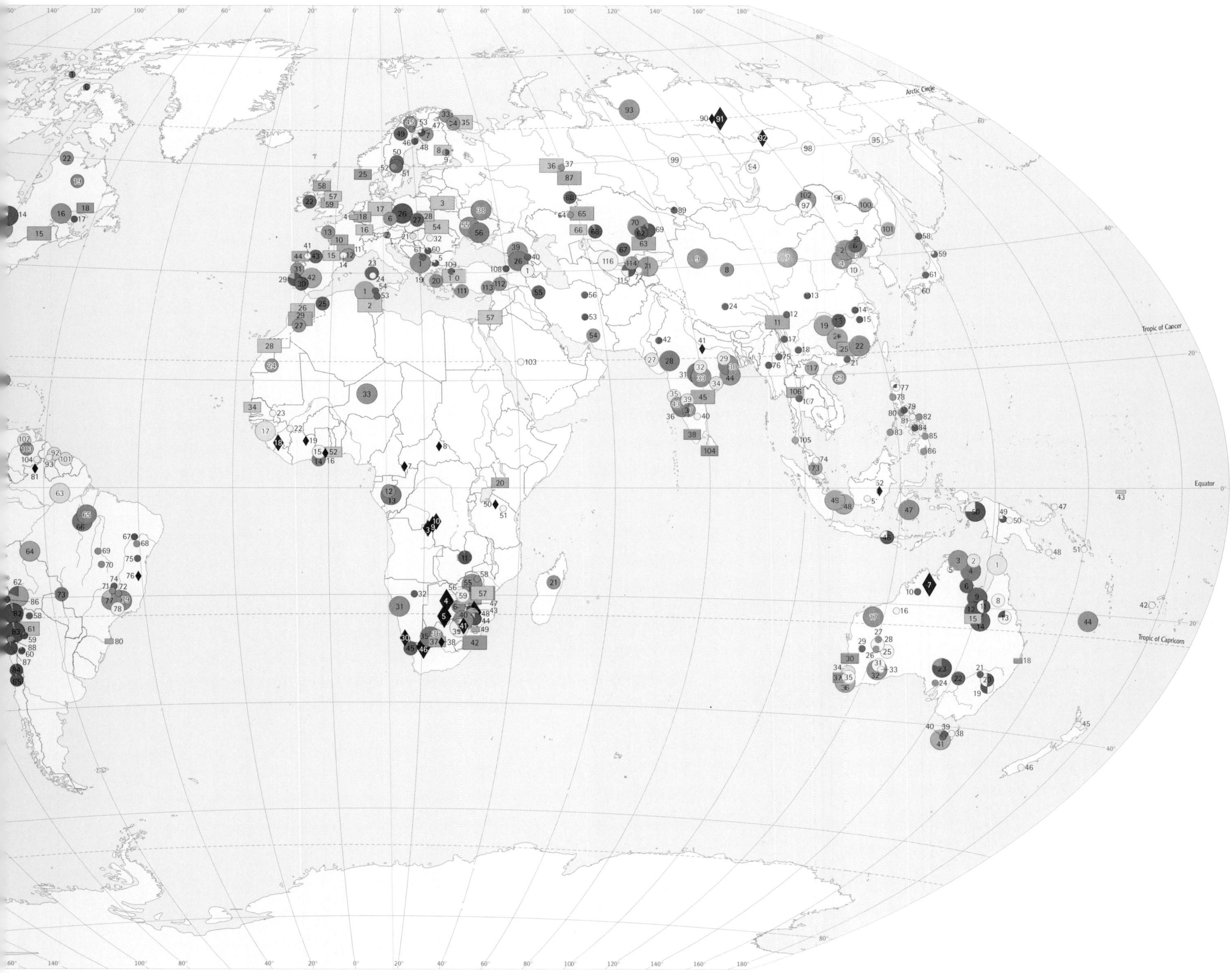
Arctic Circle
Tropic of Cancer
Equator
Tropic of Capricorn

5. CHROMIUM ORE PRODUCTION 1998

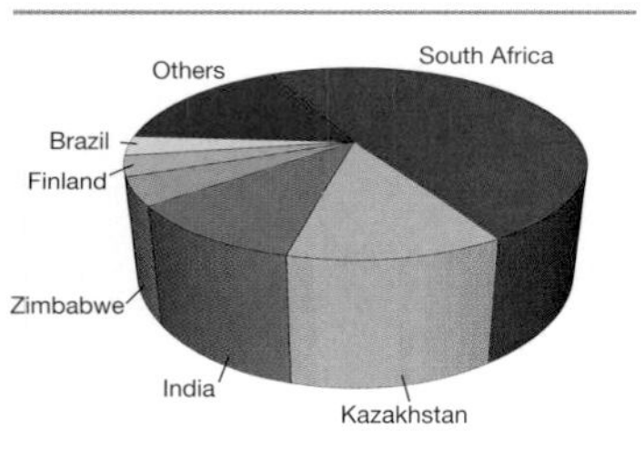
Others
South Africa
Brazil
Finland
Zimbabwe
India
Kazakhstan

6. NICKEL PRODUCTION 1998

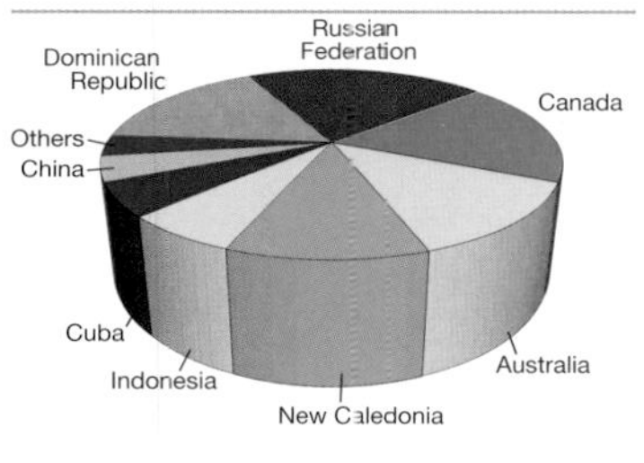
Russian Federation
Dominican Republic
Canada
Others
China
Cuba
Indonesia
Australia
New Caledonia

7. GOLD PRODUCTION 1972–1998

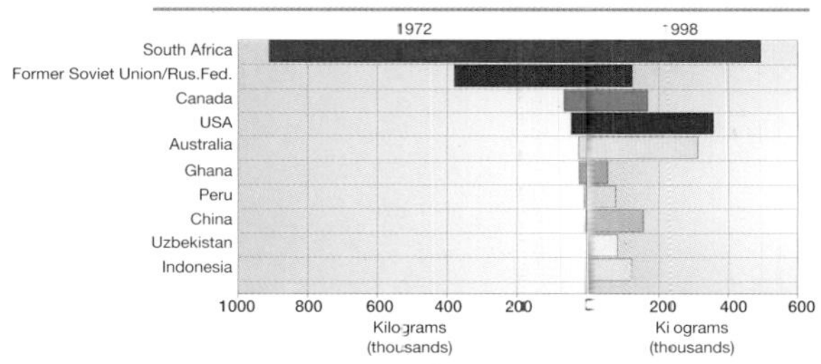
1972
1998
South Africa
Former Soviet Union/Rus.Fed.
Canada
USA
Australia
Ghana
Peru
China
Uzbekistan
Indonesia
1000
800
600
400
200
200
400
600
Kilograms (thousands)
Kilograms (thousands)

8. FLUORSPAR PRODUCTION 1998

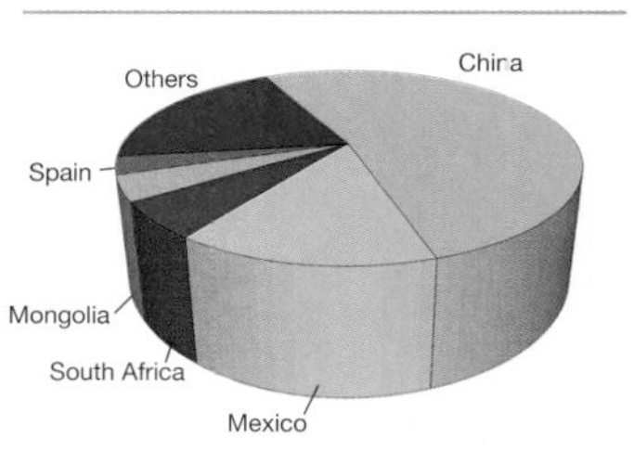
Others
China
Spain
Mongolia
South Africa
Mexico

Liberia
18 Kono, Sanniquellie, Macenta, **Diam.**
Madagascar
21 Andriamena, **Cr**
Mali
22 Syama, **Au**
23 Sadiola, **Au**
Mauritania
24 Fdérik, **Fe**
Morocco
25 *Touissit, Boubeker*, **Pb, Zn, Ag**
26 *Central Morocco*, **P**
27 Bou Azzer, **Co**
28 Boukra, **P**
29 *Jebel Irhoud, Jebel Zelmou*, **Ba, F**
Namibia
30 Oranjemund, **Diam.**
31 Rossing, **U**
32 Kombat, **Pb, Zn, Ag**
Niger
33 *Agadez*, **U**
Senegal
34 Taiba, **P**
Sierra Leone
18 Kono, Sanniquellie, Macenta, **Diam.**
South Africa, Republic of
35 *Northern Cape*, **Mn**
36 Sishen, **Fe**
37 *Griqualand*, **Asb**
38 Kimberley, **Diam.**
39 *Witwatersrand*, **Au, U**
40 *Bushveld*, **Cr, Pt, Ni, V, F**
41 Premier Mine, **Diam.**
42 Richards Bay, **Ti, Zr**
43 Murchison Range, **Sb**
44 Phalaborwa, **Cu, P**
45 Black Mountain, **Pb, Zn, Ag**
46 Finsch, **Diam.**
47 Messina, **Cu**
48 Venetia, **Diam.**
Swaziland
49 *Swaziland*, **Asb**
Tanzania
50 *Northern Tanzania*, **Diam.**
51 Golden Pride, **Au**
Togo
52 *Hahotoé, Akoumapé*, **P**
Tunisia
2 *Djebel Onk and Gafsa Region*, **P**
53 *Northern Tunisia*, **Pb, F**
54 Bou Grine, **Zn, Pb**
Zambia
11 *Copperbelt*, **Cu, Co**
Zimbabwe
55 *Great Dyke*, **Cr, Pt, Pd**
56 Zvishavane, **Asb**
57 Bikita, **Li, Be**
58 Bindura, **Ni, Cu**
59 *Bulawayo*, **Au**

ASIA

Armenia
1 *Armenia*, **Cu, Mo, Au**
China
2 Jinzhou, **Mo**
3 Hongtoushan, **Cu, Zn**
4 Shijiaying, Shuicheng, **Fe**
5 Nanfen, **Fe**
6 Chengchengtsu, **Pb, Zn**
7 Bayan Obo Kuanggu, **Fe**
8 Jinchuan, **Ni, Cu**
9 Xinjiang Uygur Zizhiqu (Sinkiang), **Fe**
10 Penglai, **Au**
11 Sichuan, **Asb**
12 Cheng Xian, **Pb, Zn**
13 Changduicheng, **Cu, Mo**
14 Shinchao, **Cu**
15 Tongshankou, **Cu**
16 Dexing, **Cu, Ag, Au**
17 Lanping, **Pb, Zn**
18 Zhehai, **Pb, Zn**
19 *Hunan-Sichuan*, **Hg, Sb**
20 *Hunan-Guangxi*, **Sn, W**
21 Fankou, **Pb, Zn**
22 *South Jiangxi, Guangdong*, **W**
23 Hainan, **Fe**
24 Xitieshan, **Pb, Zn**
25 *South China*, **Ba, F**
Georgia
26 Chiatura, **Mn**
India
27 Bhuj, **Al**
28 Panch Mahals, **Mn**
29 Ranchi, **Al**
30 Bihar, Orissa, **Fe, Mn**
31 Nagpur, Balaghat, **Mn**
32 Madhya Pradesh, **Al**
33 Rowghat, Bailadila, **Fe**
34 Koraput, **Al**
35 Maharashtra, **Al**
36 Supa, **Mn**
37 Karnataka, **Fe, Mn**
38 *Southeast Kerala* (*Travancore*), **Ti, Zr**
39 Hutti, **Al**
40 Kolar, **Au**
41 Majhgawan, **Diam.**
42 Rajasthan, **Cu, Zn, Pb, Ag**
43 Goa, **Fe**
44 *Cuttack*, **Cr**
45 Mangampet, **Ba**
Indonesia
46 Batu Hijau, **Cu, Au**
47 Pomalaa, **Ni**
48 Belitung, **Sn**
49 Bangka, **Sn**
50 Grasberg, **Cu, Au**
51 Kelian, **Au**
52 Kalimantan, **Diam.**
Iran
53 Sar Cheshmeh, **Cu, Ag, Au, Mo**
54 *Faryab Area*, **Cr**
55 Angorhan, **Pb, Zn, Ag**
56 Nakhlak, **Pb, Zn, Ag**
Israel
57 *Dead Sea Region*, **K, P**
Japan
58 Toyoha, **Pb, Zn, Ag**
59 *Hokuroko District*, **Pb, Zn, Ag, Cu**
60 Hishikari, **Au, Ag**
61 Kamioka, **Pb, Zn, Ag**
Jordan
57 *Dead Sea Region*, **K, P**
Kazakhstan
62 Balkhash, **Cu, Mo**
63 Chiganak, Baikanour, **Ba**
64 Khrom Tau, **Cr**
65 Kiembay, **Asb**
66 Kara Tau, **P**
67 Achisay, **Pb, Zn, Ag**
68 Dzhezkazgan, **Cu, Mo**
69 Kounrad, **Cu, Mo**
70 Akchatau, **W, Mo**
Kyrgystan
71 *Kyrgyzstan*, **Hg, Sb, U**
72 Kumtor, **Au**
Malaysia
73 Malaya, **Sn, Ti**
74 Penjom, **Au**
Myanmar
75 Bawdwin, **Zn, Pb, Ag**
76 Monywa, **Cu**
Philippines
77 Luzon, **Au, Cu**
78 Zambales Mountains, **Cr**
79 Marinduque, **Cu, Mo, Au**
80 Mindoro, **Ni, Co**
81 Masbate, **Au**
82 Samar, **Cr**
83 Palawan, **Ni, Co**
84 Cebu, **Cu, Mo, Au**
85 Northern Mindanao, **Ni, Co**
86 Southern Mindanao, **Ni, Co**
Russian Federation (in Asia)
87 Bazhenovskoye, **Asb**
88 *Central Urals*, **Cu, Zn, Au**
89 Altay, **Pb, Zn, Ag, Cu**
90 Alakit, **Diam.**
91 Daldyn, **Diam.**
92 Malaya Botuobiya, **Diam.**
93 Noril'sk, **Ni, Cu, Pt, Co**
94 *Lena, Vitim*, **Au**
95 *Magadan Region*, **Au**
96 *Amur*, **Au**
97 Zabaykal'sk, **Au**
98 Yakutsk, **Au**
99 Yenisey, **Au**
100 Birobidzhan, **Sn**
101 Primorskiy Kray, **Sn, W**
102 Chitinskaya, **W, Sn**
Saudi Arabia
103 Madh adh Dhahab, **Au, Ag, Cu, Zn**
Sri Lanka
104 *Southern Sri Lanka*, **Ti, Zr**
Thailand
105 *Southern Thailand, Phuket*, **Sn, W**
106 *Northern Thailand*, **Ba, F**
107 Mae Sod, **Zn, Cd**
Turkey
108 Murgul, **Cu**
109 Biga Region, **Pb, Zn, Ag, Ba**
110 Balikesir, Emet, **B**
111 Fethiye, **Cr**
112 Malatya, Guleman, **Cr, Fe**
113 Karsanti, **Cr**
Uzbekistan/Tajikistan
114 *Almalyk*, **U, F**
115 *Southeast Uzbekistan/Tajikistan*, **Cu, Au, Pb, Zn, Ag**
116 Muruntau, Zarafshan, **Au**
Vietnam
117 *Vietnam*, **Sn**

OCEANIA

Australia
1 Weipa, **Al**
2 Gove, **Al**
3 Ranger, **U**
4 Groote Eylandt, **Mn**
5 Mount Todd, **Au**
6 McArthur River, **Pb, Zn, Ag**
7 Argyll, **Diam.**
8 Kidston, **Au, Ag**
9 Century, **Zn, Pb, Ag**
10 *Lennard Shelf*, **Zn, Pb, Ag**
11 Ernest Henry, **Cu, Au**
12 *Mount Isa Region*, **Cu, Pb, Zn, Ag**
13 Mount Leyshon, **Au, Ag, Cu**
14 Cannington, **Pb, Ag, Zn**
15 Phosphate Hill, **P**
16 Telfer, **Au**
17 Hamersley Range, **Fe**
18 *Sydney, Brisbane*, **Ti, Zr**
19 Cadia, **Au, Cu**
20 North Parkes, **Cu, Au, Ag**
21 Elura, **Zn, Pb**
22 Broken Hill, **Pb, Zn, Ag**
23 Olympic Dam, **Cu, U**
24 *Middleback Ranges*, **Fe**
25 Granny Smith, **Au**
26 Leinster, **Ni, Cu**
27 Mount Keith, **Ni, Cu**
28 Agnew, **Au**
29 Golden Grove, **Zn, Ag, Au, Cu**
30 Eneabba, **Ti, Zr**
31 *Kalgoorlie Region*, **Au, Ag**
32 Kambalda, **Ni, Cu, Co, Pt**
33 St Ives, **Au**
34 *Darling Ranges*, **Al**
35 Boddington, **Au, Cu**
36 Greenbushes, **Ta, Li**
37 *Capel*, **Ti, Zr**
38 Beaconsfield, **Au**
39 Hellyer, **Zn, Pb, Ag**
40 Rosebery, **Zn, Pb, Ag**
41 Renison Bell, **Sn**
Fiji
42 Viti Levu, Emperor, **Au**
Nauru
43 *Nauru*, **P**
New Caledonia
44 *New Caledonia*, **Ni, Co**
New Zealand
45 Martha Hill, **Au, Ag**
46 Macraes, **Au, Ag**
Papua New Guinea
47 Lihir, **Au**
48 Misima, **Au, Ag**
49 Ok Tedi, **Cu, Au**
50 Porgera, **Au**
Solomon Islands
51 Gold Ridge, Au

ENERGY PRODUCTION AND CONSUMPTION

The world's energy resources are unevenly distributed (*see 1*). Similarly, the geography of energy production and consumption is highly uneven, with three countries, the USA, Russian Federation and China, dominating both the production and consumption of energy (*see 2*). Some countries – typically the oil-exporting states, such as Saudi Arabia, Nigeria, Venezuela, Mexico and Indonesia – produce much more than they consume, but many of the most advanced industrial economies, such as the USA and Japan, consume vastly more energy than they produce. The USA is the largest single energy consumer, using over a quarter of the world's energy despite having only 5 per cent of its population.

As a result of the uneven geography of production and consumption, energy sources are the largest single item in international trade (*see 3*). Taking the example of oil, some regions are net exporters, such as the Middle East and West Africa. Others rely heavily upon imported oil and so have to generate wealth by other means to be able to pay for their imports. These include the USA, Central and Western Europe and Japan (*see 4*).

1. DISTRIBUTION OF RESOURCES

Winkel Tripel Projection
scale 1:94 000 000

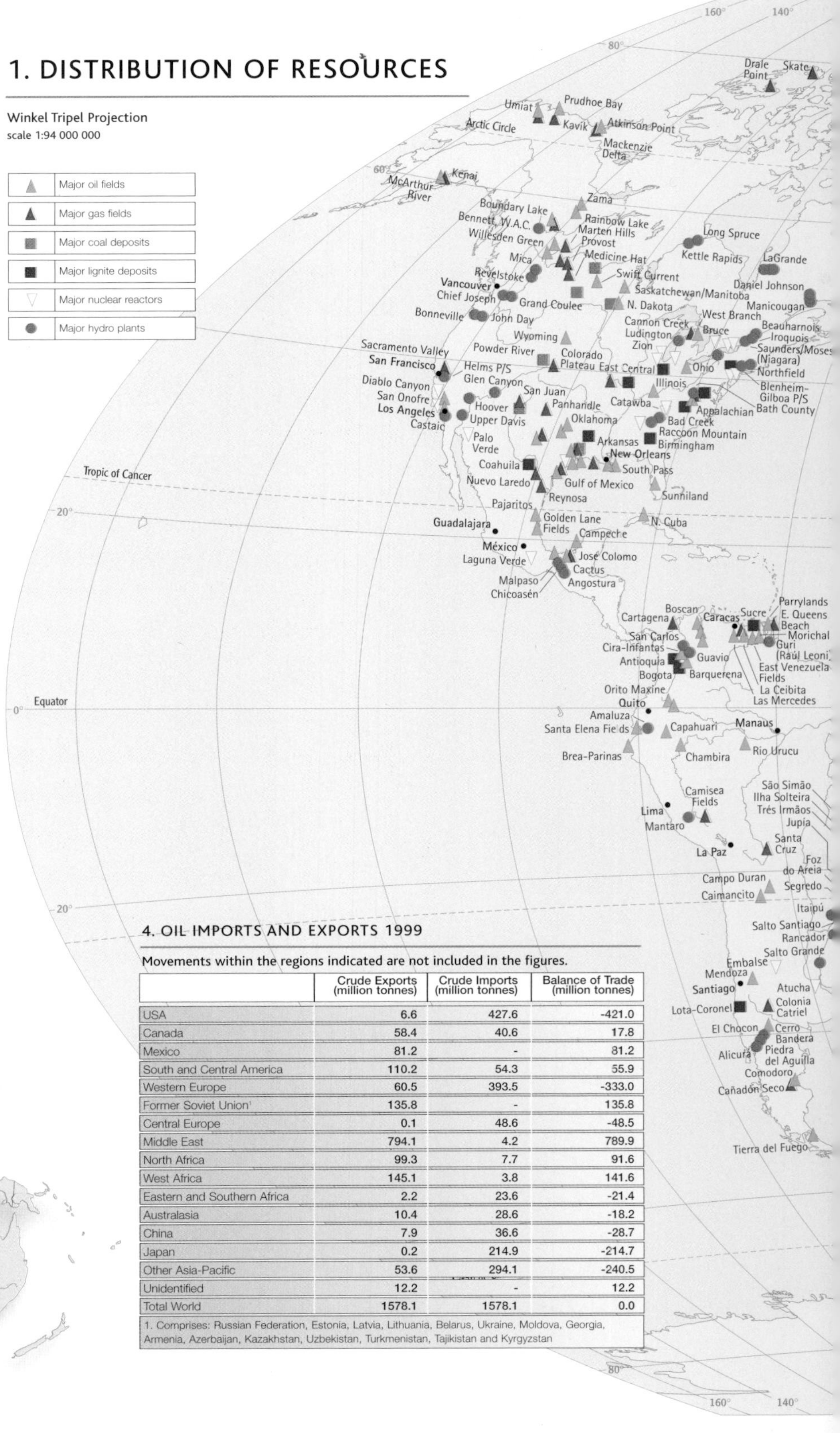

2. WORLD'S TOP 10 ENERGY PRODUCERS AND CONSUMERS 1998

Million tonnes of oil equivalent

Producers		Consumers	
USA	1 835	USA	2 389
Russian Federation	1 034	China	855
China	835	Russian Federation	655
Saudi Arabia	529	Japan	536
Canada	433	Germany	349
UK	293	India	315
India	251	Canada	299
Iran	249	France	252
Mexico	234	UK	246
Australia	209	Brazil	204
World total	9 631	World total	9 519

3. THE ENERGY TRADE

Major trade flows between trading regions 1999
scale 1:217 000 000

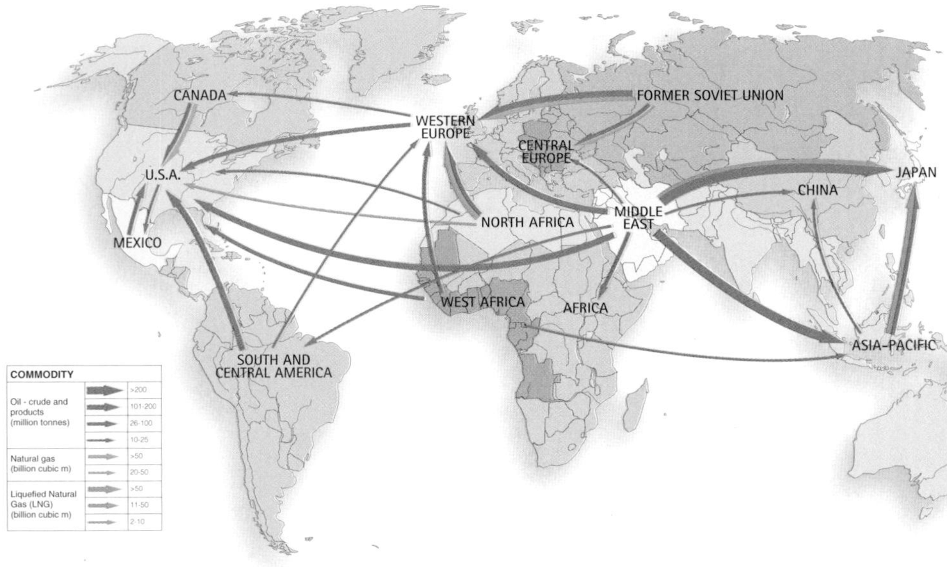

4. OIL IMPORTS AND EXPORTS 1999

Movements within the regions indicated are not included in the figures.

	Crude Exports (million tonnes)	Crude Imports (million tonnes)	Balance of Trade (million tonnes)
USA	6.6	427.6	-421.0
Canada	58.4	40.6	17.8
Mexico	81.2	-	81.2
South and Central America	110.2	54.3	55.9
Western Europe	60.5	393.5	-333.0
Former Soviet Union[1]	135.8	-	135.8
Central Europe	0.1	48.6	-48.5
Middle East	794.1	4.2	789.9
North Africa	99.3	7.7	91.6
West Africa	145.1	3.8	141.6
Eastern and Southern Africa	2.2	23.6	-21.4
Australasia	10.4	28.6	-18.2
China	7.9	36.6	-28.7
Japan	0.2	214.9	-214.7
Other Asia-Pacific	53.6	294.1	-240.5
Unidentified	12.2	-	12.2
Total World	1578.1	1578.1	0.0

1. Comprises: Russian Federation, Estonia, Latvia, Lithuania, Belarus, Ukraine, Moldova, Georgia, Armenia, Azerbaijan, Kazakhstan, Uzbekistan, Turkmenistan, Tajikistan and Kyrgyzstan

ENERGY RESERVES AND RATES OF CONSUMPTION

Proven energy reserves are also unevenly distributed (*see 5*). Nearly two-thirds of proven oil reserves are concentrated in the Middle East. Reserves in the USA and Russian Federation have declined and Europe's reserves are expected to dry up early this century. Central America and Africa are expected to cease oil exports around 2025. Proven reserves of natural gas are dominated by the Former Soviet Union and the Middle East while coal reserves are more evenly distributed between the Asia-Pacific region, North America and the Former Soviet Union.

Between 1989 and 1999 the world level of primary energy consumption increased by 11 per cent (*see 6*). This change was led by the Middle East with a 52 per cent increase, followed by South and Central America with a 38 per cent rise. Relatively costly energy in Europe depressed consumption to the comparatively low growth level of 2 per cent, while the dissolution of the Soviet Union led to the collapse in consumption there by over a third. If rates of energy consumption were to remain constant, then it has been estimated that proven oil reserves would last forty years, natural gas sixty years and coal three hundred years. However, because energy consumption rates are increasing these estimates may need revision.

5. PROVEN ENERGY RESERVES 1999

	Oil	%	Natural Gas	%	Coal	%
North America[1]	8.4	6.0	7.31	5.0	256 477	26.1
South & Central America	12.9	9.2	6.31	4.3	21 574	2.2
Europe	2.7	1.9	5.15	3.5	122 032	12.4
Former Soviet Union[2]	9.0	6.4	56.70	38.7	230 178	23.4
Middle East	91.5	65.2	49.52	33.8	193	-
Africa	10.0	7.1	11.16	7.7	61 412	6.2
Asia-Pacific	5.9	4.2	10.28	7.0	292 345	29.7
World	140.4	100	146.43	100	984.211	100

1. Canada, USA and Mexico 2. See footnote for table 4

Oil (thousand million barrels) Natural Gas (trillion cubic metres) Coal (million tonnes)

6. PRIMARY ENERGY CONSUMPTION

Million tonnes of oil equivalent

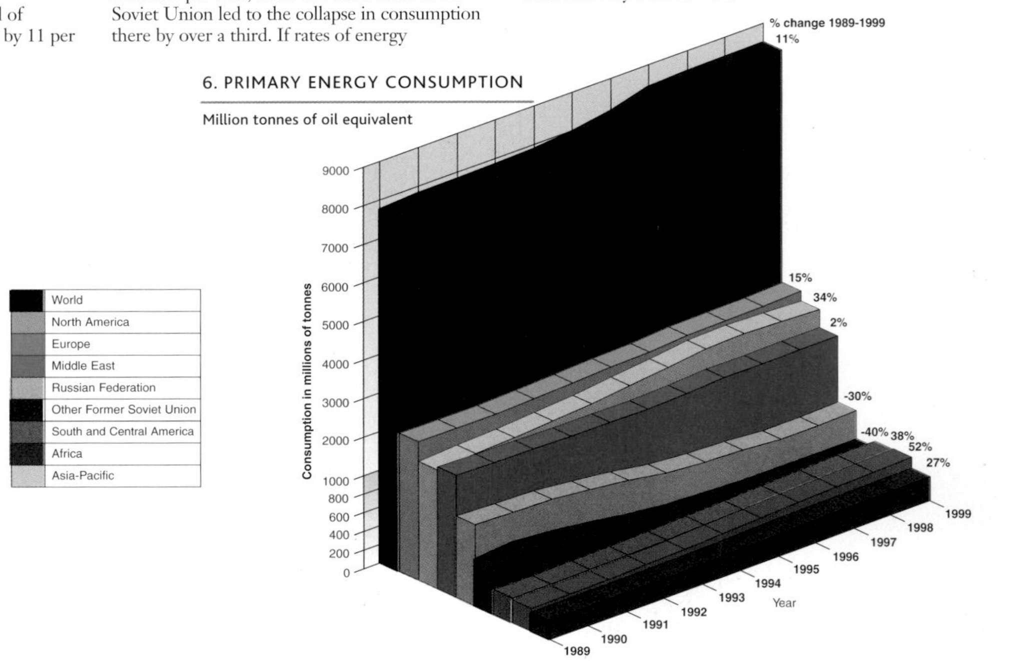

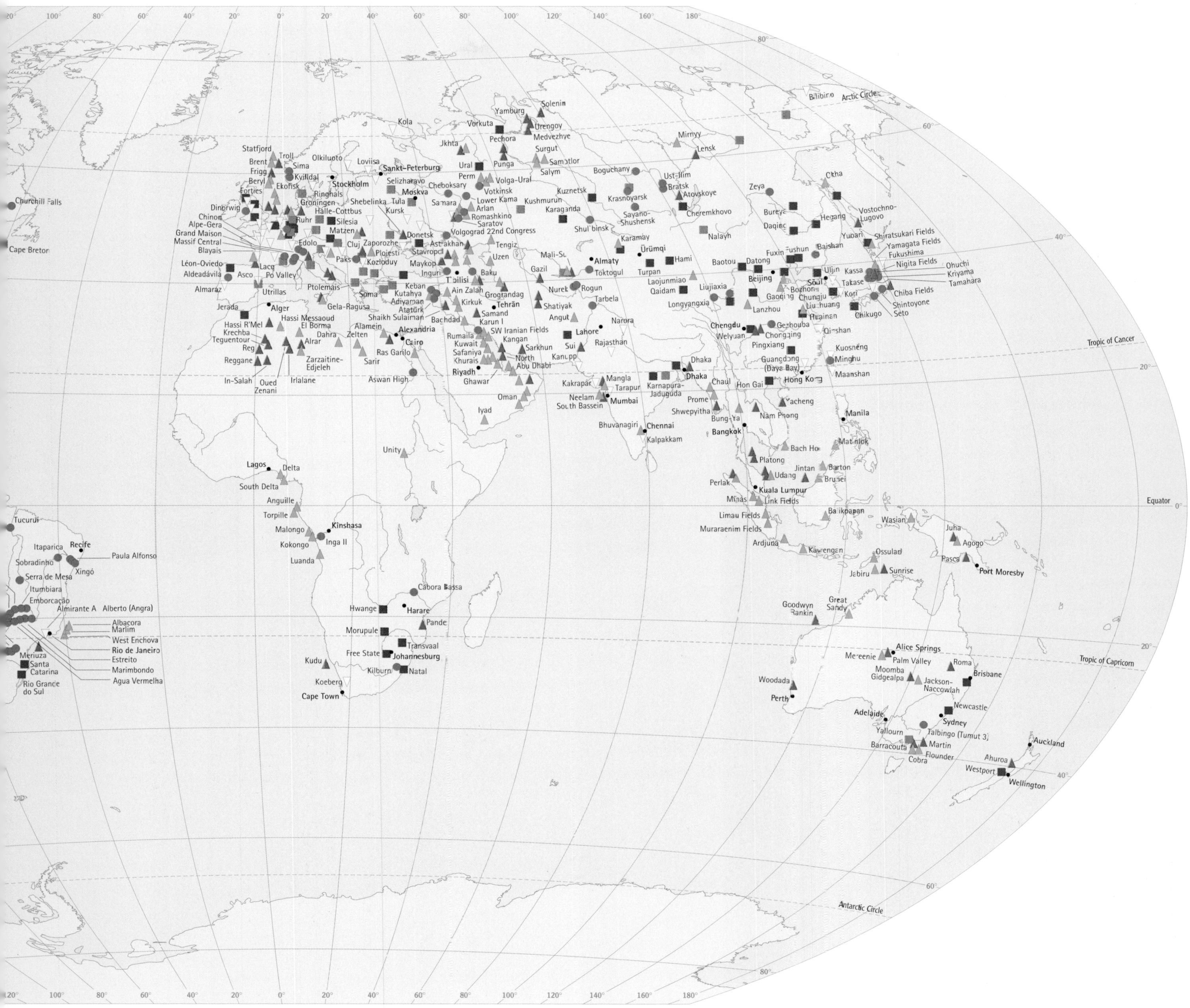
Arctic Circle
Tropic of Cancer
Equator
Tropic of Capricorn
Antarctic Circle
Churchill Falls
Cape Breton
Statfjord
Brent
Frigg
Beryl
Forties
Troll
Sima
Kvilldal
Ekofisk
Olkiluoto
Loviisa
Sankt-Peterburg
Stockholm
Ringhals
Groningen
Shebelinka
Tula
Moskva
Kursk
Halle-Cottbus
Silesia
Ruhr
Dinorwig
Chinon
Alpe-Gera
Grand Maison
Massif Central
Blayais
León-Oviedo
Aldeadávila
Almaraz
Lacq
Asco
Po Valley
Edolo
Matzen
Paks
Cluj
Zaporozhe
Ploiesti
Kozloduy
Donetsk
Volgograd 22nd Congress
Astrakhan
Stavropol
Maykop
Inguri
Tbilisi
Baku
Tengiz
Uzen
Kola
Vorkuta
Jkhta
Pechora
Yamburg
Solenin
Urengoy
Medvezhye
Surgut
Samotlor
Salym
Ural
Punga
Perm
Volga-Ural
Cheboksary
Selizharovo
Votkinsk
Lower Kama
Arlan
Romashkino
Saratov
Samara
Kushmurun
Karaganda
Kuznetsk
Boguchany
Krasnoyarsk
Sayano-Shushensk
Ust-Ilim
Bratsk
Atovskoye
Cheremkhovo
Mirnyy
Lensk
Bilibino
Zeya
Bureya
Daqing
Okha
Hegang
Vostochno-Lugovo
Yubari
Shiratsukari Fields
Yamagata Fields
Fukushima
Nigita Fields
Ohuchi
Kriyama
Tamahara
Chiba Fields
Shintoyone
Seto
Chikugo
Kori
Kassa
Takase
Ulijin
Seoul
Fuxin
Fushun
Baishan
Beijing
Datong
Baotou
Nalayh
Karamay
Shul'binsk
Ürümqi
Hami
Turpan
Laojunmiao
Qaidam
Liujiaxia
Longyangxia
Lanzhou
Gaoping
Bozhou
Chungju
Liu huang
Huainan
Qinshan
Chengdu
Weiyuan
Gezhouba
Chongqing
Pingxiang
Kuosheng
Minghu
Maanshan
Guangdong (Daya Bay)
Hong Kong
Mali-Su
Almaty
Toktogul
Gazil
Nurek
Rogun
Tarbela
Shatiyak
Angut
Narora
Lahore
Sui
Rajasthan
Kanupp
Keban
Kutahya
Adiyaman
Atatürk
Ain Zalah
Grogtandag
Kirkuk
Tehrān
Samand
Karun I
Shaikh Sulaiman
Baghdad
SW Iranian Fields
Kangan
Rumaila
Kuwait
Safaniya
Khurais
Sarkhun
North
Abu Dhabi
Riyadh
Ghawar
Oman
Iyad
Soma
Ptolemais
Gela-Ragusa
Utrillas
Jerada
Alger
Hassi R'Mel
Krechba
Teguentour
Reg
Reggane
In-Salah
Hassi Messaoud
El Borma
Dahra
Zelten
Alrar
Zarzaitine-Edjeleh
Oued Zenani
Irlalane
Alamein
Alexandria
Cairo
Ras Garilo
Sarir
Aswan High
Kakrapar
Tarapur
Mangla
Neelam
South Bassein
Mumbai
Karnapura-Jaduguda
Dhaka
Chennai
Bhuvanagiri
Kalpakkam
Chaul
Hon Gai
Prome
Shwepyitha
Bung-Ya
Bangkok
Yacheng
Nam Phong
Manila
Mat-nlok
Bach Ho
Platong
Jintan
Barton
Udang
Brunei
Perlak
Kuala Lumpur
Minas
Link Fields
Limau Fields
Muraraenim Fields
Badikpapan
Wasian
Ardjuna
Kawengan
Juha
Agogo
Pasca
Port Moresby
Ossulad
Jebiru
Sunrise
Goodwyn
Rankin
Great Sandy
Alice Springs
Mereenie
Palm Valley
Roma
Moomba
Gidgealpa
Jackson-Naccowlah
Brisbane
Woodada
Perth
Newcastle
Adelaide
Sydney
Yallourn
Talbingo (Tumut 3)
Barracouta
Martin
Flounder
Cobra
Auckland
Ahuroa
Westport
Wellington
Unity
Lagos
Delta
South Delta
Anguille
Torpille
Malongo
Kokongo
Kinshasa
Inga II
Luanda
Cabora Bassa
Hwange
Harare
Pande
Morupule
Transvaal
Free State
Johannesburg
Kudu
Kilburn
Natal
Koeberg
Cape Town
Tucuruí
Itaparica
Recife
Sobradinho
Paula Alfonso
Xingó
Serra de Mesa
Itumbiara
Emborcação
Almirante A
Alberto (Angra)
Albacora
Marlim
West Enchova
Rio de Janeiro
Estreito
Marimbondo
Agua Vermelha
Meriuza
Santa Catarina
Rio Grande do Sul

ALTERNATIVE ENERGY SOURCES

Alternatives to traditional energy sources are nuclear power and renewable resources. Consumption of nuclear power (*see 7*) has been at relatively low levels and has grown more slowly than traditional energy sources. Asia-Pacific and South and Central America have experienced the highest growth in the past decade, led by Japan, which generates two-thirds of its electricity from nuclear sources. The question of sustainability has underpinned the search for new sources of energy which are less detrimental to the environment than traditional sources and nuclear power. One proposed solution is conservation through increased energy efficiency, i.e. increasing the ratio of useful energy input to output. Other solutions lie in energy resources which are renewable, such as geothermal, wind, solar, biomass and hydropower. Around 5 per cent of total primary energy requirements in Australia, Austria, Canada, Denmark, Sweden and Switzerland are currently met by renewables. The most successful form of renewable energy has been hydroelectric power, consumption of which has risen over 20 per cent in world terms between 1989 and 1999 (*see 8*), with South and Central America showing the largest rise (52 per cent), followed by Asia-Pacific (31 per cent).

7. NUCLEAR ENERGY CONSUMPTION

Million tonnes of oil equivalent

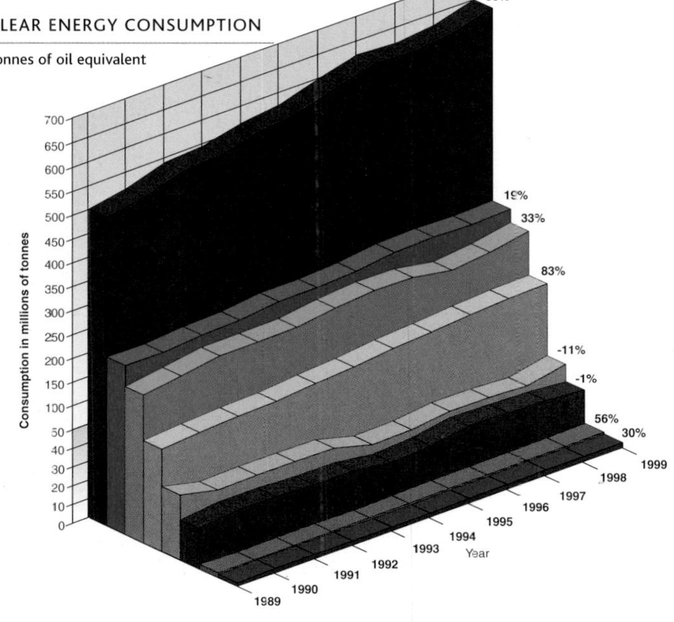
% change 1989-1999
30%
19%
33%
83%
-11%
-1%
56%
30%
Consumption in millions of tonnes
700
650
600
550
500
450
400
350
300
250
200
150
100
50
40
30
20
10
0
1989
1990
1991
1992
1993
1994
1995
1996
1997
1998
1999
Year

8. HYDROELECRICITY CONSUMPTION

Million tonnes of oil equivalent

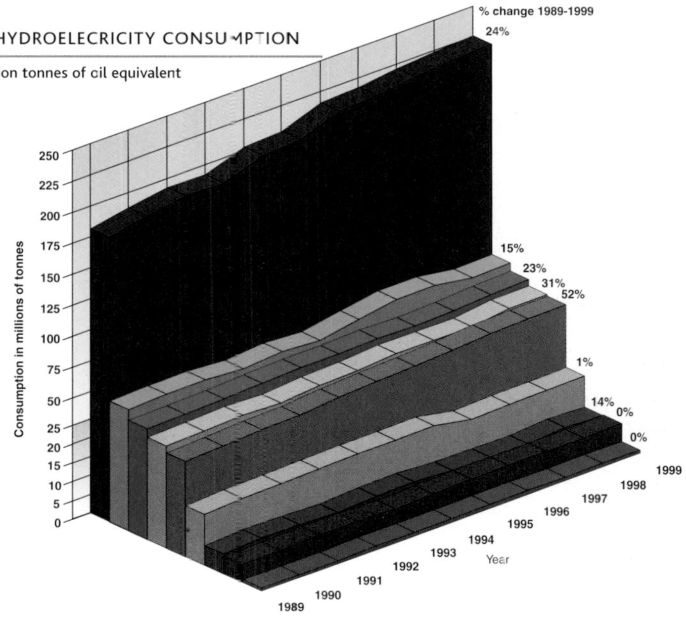
% change 1989-1999
24%
15%
23%
31%
52%
1%
14%
0%
0%
Consumption in millions of tonnes
250
225
200
175
150
125
100
75
50
25
20
15
10
5
0
1989
1990
1991
1992
1993
1994
1995
1996
1997
1998
1999
Year

© Bartholomew Ltd

GLOBAL TOURISM AND AIR TRAVEL

The globalization of the world's social, economic and financial markets, whereby physical and political boundaries are no longer obstacles to movement between countries, has been made possible by improved transport and telecommunications networks. The growth of international air travel has meant that more people can move between countries with greater frequency and more cheaply.

International tourism grew throughout the world in the latter part of the 20th century. Between 1989-1999 the average annual growth rate for international tourist arrivals worldwide was nearly 5 per cent (over 230 million people – *see 1*). This global figure masks wide regional variations, however (*see 2*). Europe contributes the most to worldwide figures in terms of volume, but the rate of growth there has slowed, due mainly to the growing accessibility of East Asian and Pacific destinations. The regional share of tourist arrivals in this region has grown significantly in the last thirty years.

Improvements in air transport technology, an increasing number of air carriers and favourable economic conditions have combined to produce large increases in worldwide air travel. Passenger and freight traffic grew steadily in the latter half of the 20th century and this pattern is expected to continue. The largest proportion of international travel today occurs between the USA and Europe, and within the East Asia and Pacific region (*see 3*). Routes between the Middle East and both Africa and Europe – carrying high numbers of passengers in the 1980s – have been overtaken by routes within the East Asia and Pacific region and by long haul flights from Europe to East Asia and western USA. The pattern is reinforced by airport statistics (*see 4*). Airports in the USA – where air travel is used as much for internal as for international travel – and Europe dominate. However, as Far Eastern economies have developed, these countries have become more popular destinations for both business and leisure travellers.

1. INTERNATIONAL TOURIST ARRIVALS 1989 – 1999

'Tourist' refers to a visitor (visiting for either leisure or business) who stays for at least one night in the country visited

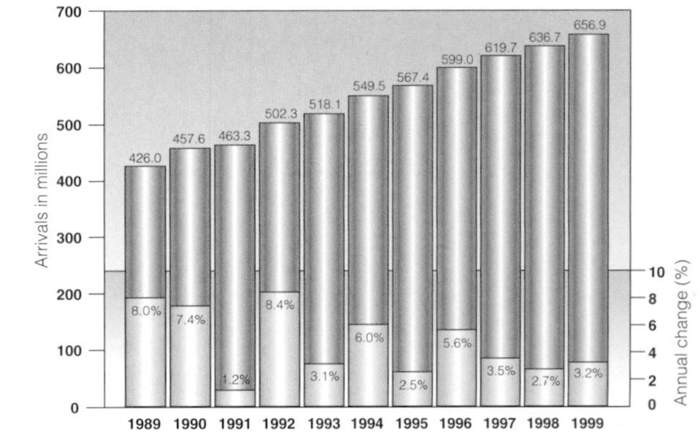

2. REGIONAL SHARE OF INTERNATIONAL TOURIST ARRIVALS 1970–1999

Height of each chart relates to total worldwide tourist arrivals

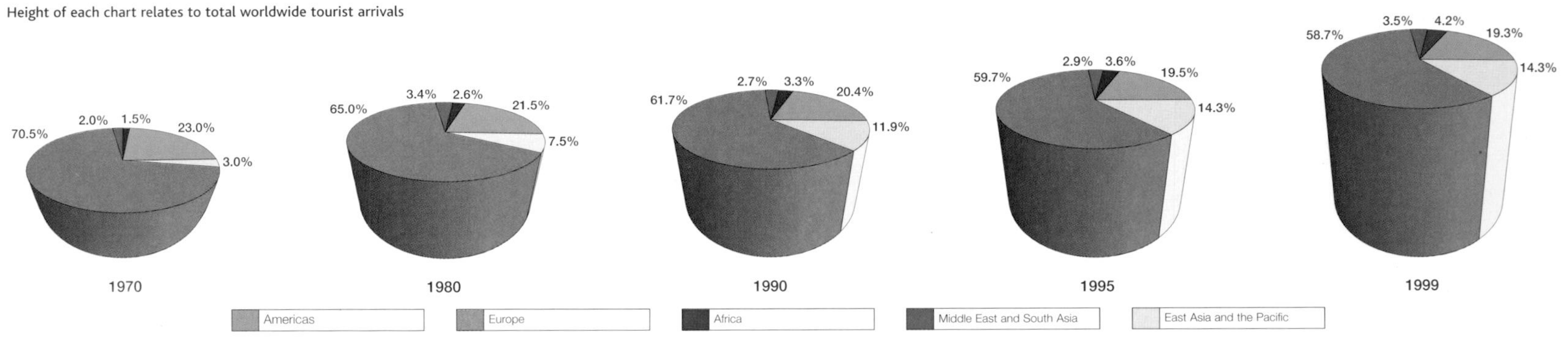

3. BUSIEST SCHEDULED INTERNATIONAL AIR PASSENGER ROUTES 1999

Figures are for scheduled international passenger traffic in both directions. Land colours represent World Tourism Organization regions
Briesemeister Projection
scale 1:129 500 000

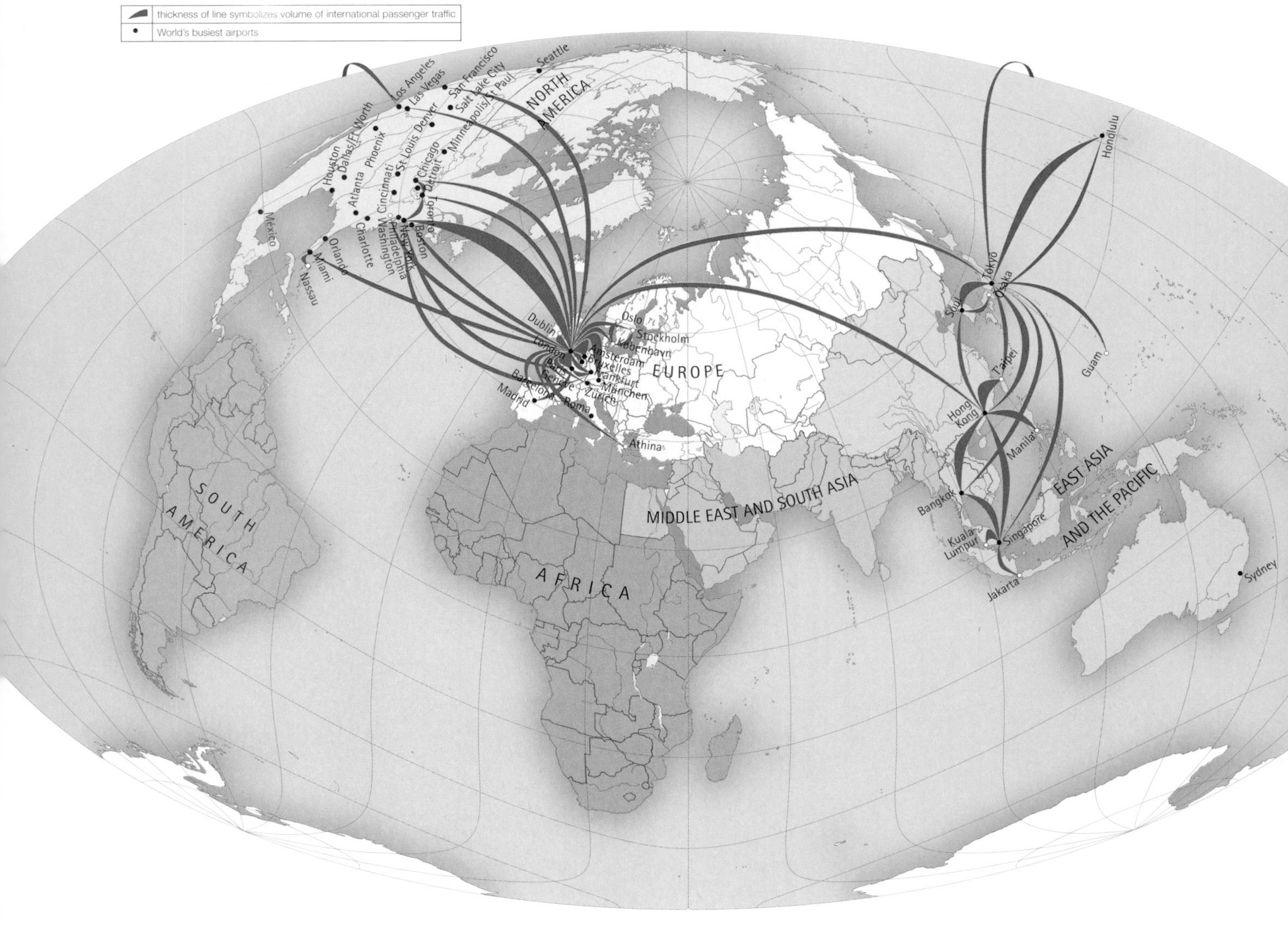

Route	Number of passengers
London–New York	3 793 405
Amsterdam–London	2 992 447
London–Paris	2 449 049
Hong Kong–T'aipei	2 381 710
Sŏul–Tōkyō	2 154 211
Kuala Lumpur–Singapore	2 073 874
Bangkok–Hong Kong	1 975 228
Frankfurt–London	1 928 209
Honolulu–Tōkyō	1 890 343
Bangkok–Singapore	1 798 607
Hong Kong–Tōkyō	1 678 542
Hong Kong–Manila	1 463 014
Hong Kong–Singapore	1 456 021
Dublin–London	1 387 477
Bangkok–Tōkyō	1 286 850
London–Madrid	1 264 659
New York–Toronto	1 262 157
New York–Paris	1 253 899
Los Angeles–London	1 244 180
Bruxelles–London	1 223 334
Jakarta–Singapore	1 181 580
Ōsaka–Sŏul	1 157 984
Hong Kong–Sŏul	1 146 669
Los Angeles–Tōkyō	1 142 747
Chicago–London	1 110 305
London–Zürich	1 083 403
Singapore–Tōkyō	1 071 597
Boston–London	1 055 978
London–Stockholm	1 055 828
Barcelona–London	1 028 320
Madrid–Paris	1 021 285
London–San Francisco	1 016 824
Chicago–Toronto	991 529
T'aipei–Tōkyō	986 424
London–München	975 606
Frankfurt–New York	965 365
Frankfurt–Paris	965 231
London–Toronto	945 283
Genève–London	945 223
London–Washington	925 487
London–Tōkyō	924 232
København–London	884 971
London–Miami	882 245
Hong Kong–London	881 924
Honolulu–Ōsaka	871 907
København–Oslo	870 994
Guam–Tōkyō	867 245
Miami–Nassau	858 866
Athina–London	850 610

4. THE WORLD'S BUSIEST AIRPORTS 1999

Figures given are total passenger arrivals and departures.
See map 3 for airport locations

Atlanta Hartsfield	USA	77 939 536
Chicago O'Hare	USA	72 568 076
Los Angeles	USA	63 876 561
London Heathrow	UK	62 263 710
Dallas/Ft Worth	USA	60 000 125
Tōkyō Haneda	Japan	54 338 212
Frankfurt	Germany	45 858 315
Paris Charles de Gaulle	France	43 596 943
San Francisco	USA	40 387 422
Denver	USA	38 034 231
Amsterdam	Netherlands	36 781 015
Minneapolis/St Paul	USA	34 216 331
Detroit Wayne County	USA	34 038 381
Miami	USA	33 899 246
New York Newark	USA	33 814 000
Las Vegas McCarran	USA	33 669 185
Phoenix Sky Harbor	USA	33 533 353
Sŏul Kimpo	South Korea	33 371 074
Houston	USA	33 089 333
New York JFK	USA	32 003 000
London Gatwick	UK	30 559 461
St Louis Lambert	USA	30 188 973

INTERNATIONAL TELECOMMUNICATIONS

Increased availability and ownership of telecommunications equipment over the last thirty years (*see 5*) has aided the globalization of the world economy. Over half of the world's fixed telephone lines have been installed since 1987, and the majority of the world's Internet hosts have come on-line since 1997. Network access is uneven, however. Over half of existing telephone lines and cellular phones are in North America and Europe, and over 70 per cent of Internet host computers are located in North America (*see 6*).

One measure of the perceived 'death of distance' is the steady rise in international telephone calls, which has increased nearly 400 per cent since 1988. The map (*see 8*) shows telephone and fax traffic between countries in different continents for routes using at least 100 million minutes of telecommunications time in 1998. In that year, these streams totalled 27.3 billion minutes, which accounted for approximately 29 per cent of global international traffic

Growing volumes of data traffic, particularly from the Internet, have boosted demand for international transmission capacity. Most traffic is routed over fibre-optic cables which encode electronic signals into beams of laser light, which are sent down fine fibres of coated glass. In 1999, the world's trans-oceanic cables could carry approximately 250 gigabits per second (Gbps), which is equivalent to 17.5 million simultaneous phone calls. By 2001, international cable capacity will have grown by close to 400 per cent, although the largest cable systems will still only link a relative handful of countries (*see 7*).

5. WORLD COMMUNICATIONS EQUIPMENT 1970–2000

Source: TeleGeography, Inc and International Telecommunications Union

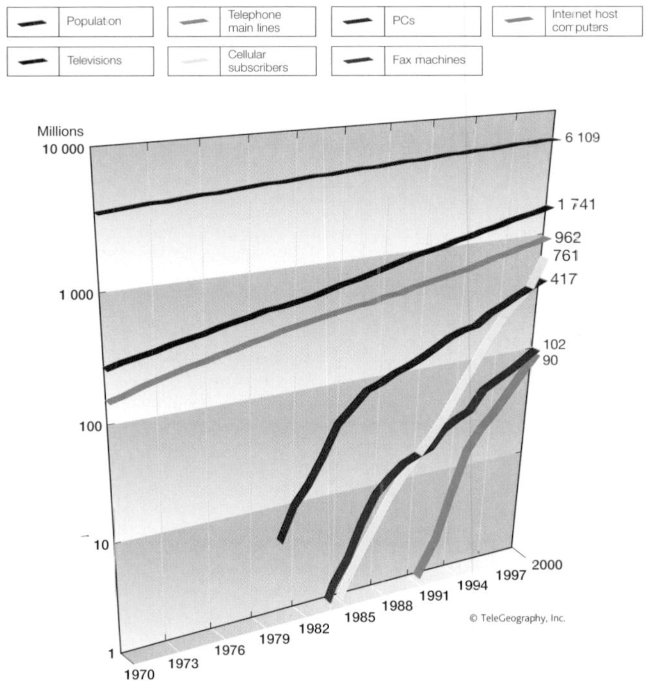

Population
Telephone main lines
PCs
Internet host computers
Televisions
Cellular subscribers
Fax machines
Millions
10 000
1 000
100
10
1
6 109
1 741
962
761
417
102
90
1970
1973
1976
1979
1982
1985
1988
1991
1994
1997
2000
© TeleGeography, Inc.

6. INTERNATIONAL TELECOMMUNICATIONS INDICATORS BY REGION 1998

Source: TeleGeography, Inc and International Telecommunications Union

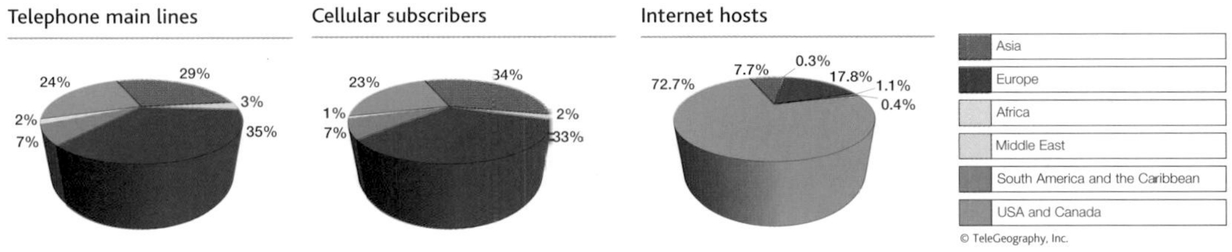

Telephone main lines
24%
29%
3%
35%
2%
7%
Cellular subscribers
23%
34%
1%
7%
2%
33%
Internet hosts
72.7%
7.7%
0.3%
17.8%
1.1%
0.4%
Asia
Europe
Africa
Middle East
South America and the Caribbean
USA and Canada
© TeleGeography, Inc.

7. CAPACITY OF MAJOR INTERNATIONAL SUBMARINE CABLES 1999 AND 2001

Each 10 Gbps of cable capacity can carry approximately 700 000 simultaneous calls

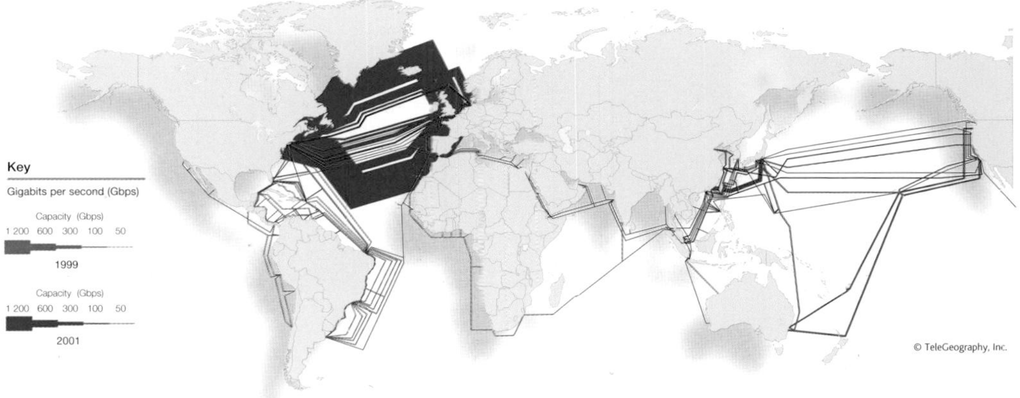

Key
Gigabits per second (Gbps)
Capacity (Gbps)
1 200 600 300 100 50
1999
Capacity (Gbps)
1 200 600 300 100 50
2001
© TeleGeography, Inc.

8. INTERNATIONAL TELECOMMUNICATIONS TRAFFIC 1998

Each band is proportional to the total annual traffic on the public telephone network in both directions between each pair of countries
Robinson Projection
scale 1:144 000 000

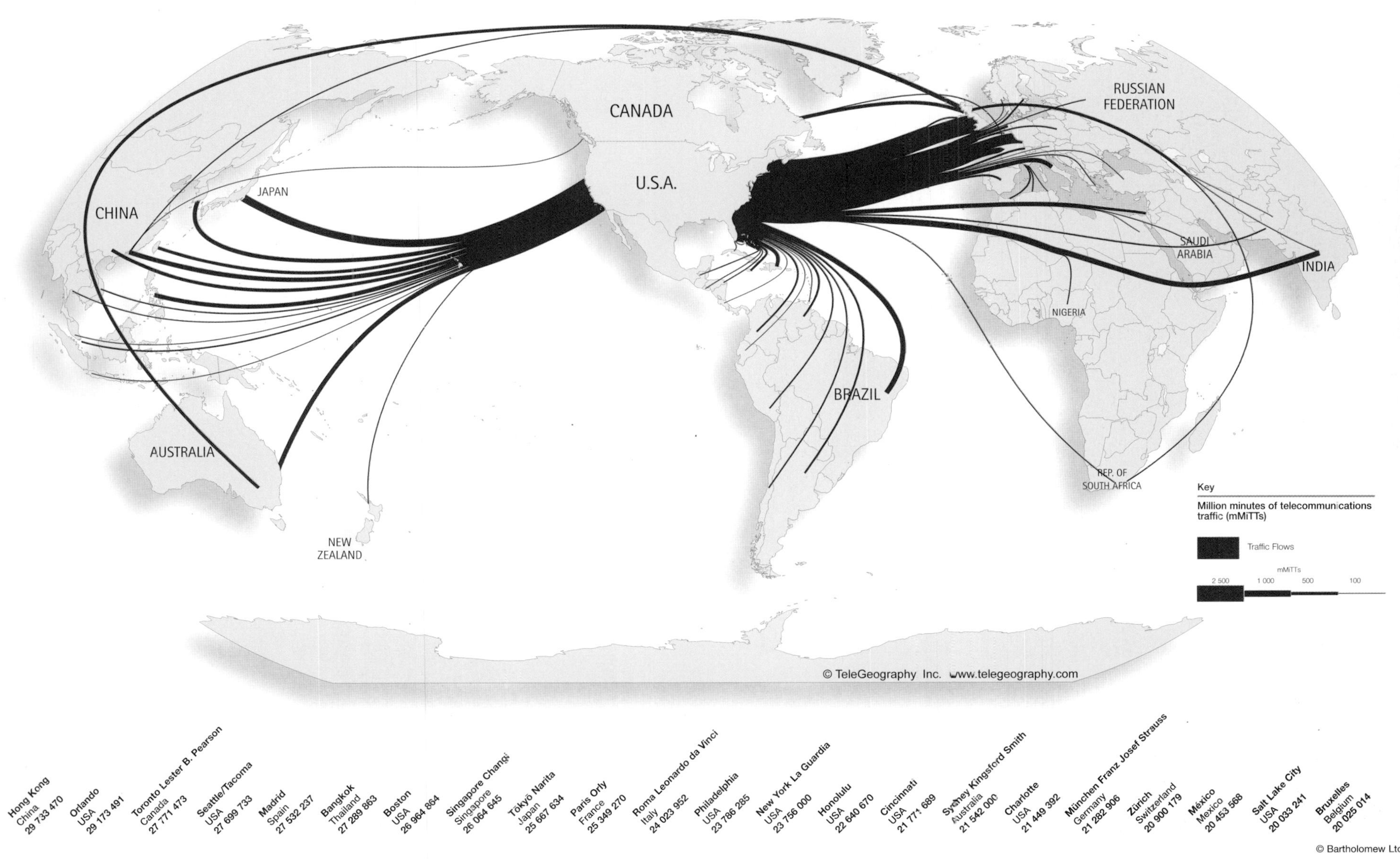

CANADA
RUSSIAN FEDERATION
U.S.A.
JAPAN
CHINA
SAUDI ARABIA
INDIA
NIGERIA
BRAZIL
AUSTRALIA
REP. OF SOUTH AFRICA
NEW ZEALAND
Key
Million minutes of telecommunications traffic (mMiTTs)
Traffic Flows
mMITTs
2 500 1 000 500 100
© TeleGeography Inc. www.telegeography.com
Hong Kong China 29 733 470
Orlando USA 29 173 491
Toronto Lester B. Pearson Canada 27 771 473
Seattle/Tacoma USA 27 699 733
Madrid Spain 27 532 237
Bangkok Thailand 27 289 863
Boston USA 26 964 864
Singapore Changi Singapore 26 064 645
Tōkyō Narita Japan 25 667 634
Paris Orly France 25 349 270
Roma Leonardo da Vinci Italy 24 023 952
Philadelphia USA 23 786 285
New York La Guardia USA 23 756 000
Honolulu USA 22 640 670
Cincinnati USA 21 771 689
Sydney Kingsford Smith Australia 21 542 000
Charlotte USA 21 449 392
München Franz Josef Strauss Germany 21 282 906
Zürich Switzerland 20 900 179
México Mexico 20 453 568
Salt Lake City USA 20 033 241
Bruxelles Belgium 20 025 014

© Bartholomew Ltd

PREHISTORIC AND CLASSICAL CARTOGRAPHY (500 BC – AD 500)

The evolution of mapping has been inextricably linked to people's knowledge of the world and to related scientific and technological developments. Mapping skills have been influenced by factors such as way of life and the nature of the physical environment, and maps can therefore provide an excellent insight into cultures and civilizations. Surviving examples of ancient maps are rare. Their limits of coverage tended to be the extent of the producers' accurate geographical knowledge. Beyond the local area, maps appeared to reflect a speculative or cosmological approach *(see 1)*.

The most significant contribution of the Greeks to cartography was theoretical rather than practical. It is primarily the work of Claudius Ptolemy, a Greek mathematician, astronomer and geographer living in the 2nd century AD, which provides us with information about the level of geographical knowledge at this time. Ptolemy's work *Geographia* included theoretical principles of cartography, lists of place names and computed co-ordinates. Later maps, based on this work, show how he believed the world to look at that time *(see 2)*.

1. MAP OF THE WORLD

Carved on a Babylonian clay tablet, c. 600 BC. Babylon is shown as a rectangle intersected by vertical lines representing the Euphrates river. Small circles show other cities and countries, and the world is encircled by an ocean – the 'Bitter River'.
British Museum, Department of Western Asiatic Antiquities, London, UK.

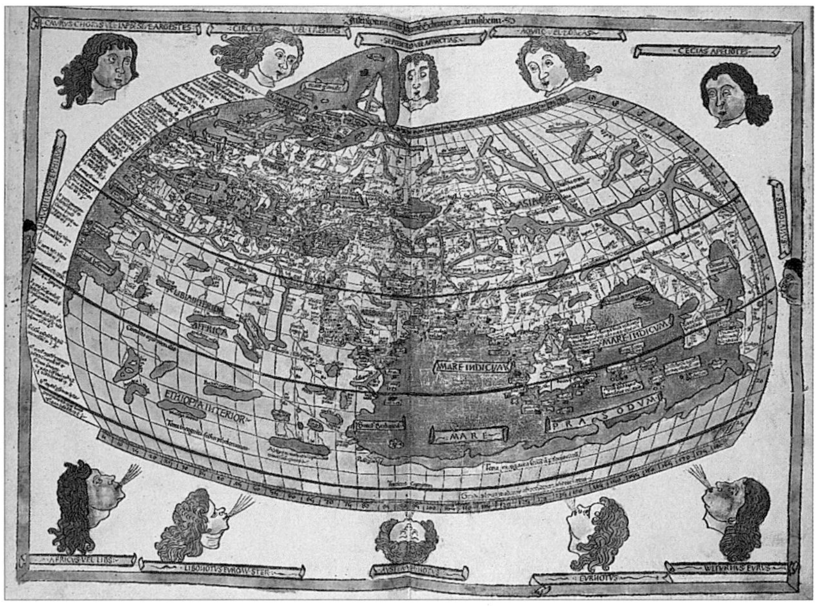

2. PTOLEMAIC WORLD MAP

Based on the work of Claudius Ptolemy, produced by Donis Nicolaus in Ulm, Germany, 1630. The map includes lines of latitude and longitude which give a sense of accuracy. The figures represent different wind directions.
British Library, London, UK.

AD 500–1600

During this period, maps originating in the classical tradition were overlain with later Christian elements. Such maps were usually oval or circular in shape, schematic in content, and centred on Jerusalem. These world maps *(mappæmundi)* conveyed a Christian perspective of the world, and their detail ranged from the virtually diagrammatic to the highly complex *(see 3)*.

Maps from the later medieval period include sea charts, town plans and local, district and route maps. Of these, portolan charts – sea charts designed primarily for navigation – were by far the most significant *(see 4)*. Providing impressively detailed and accurate information on coastlines, harbours and related navigational matters, the charts appear to have been regularly updated. Route maps, for the use of pilgrims and merchants travelling overland, also developed over this period, as exemplified by Matthew Paris's map of the route from London to Otranto, Italy produced around AD 1250 *(see 5)*.

The 15th and 16th centuries were essentially the age of exploration and discovery, a period which witnessed an explosion of global knowledge and a veritable renaissance in cartography. The period saw a great development of world maps, many of which began to include the coastal detail of the earlier portolan charts and to show the latest geographical information resulting from the voyages of discovery. Rome and Venice dominated European map production from 1550 to 1570, but later in the period dominance in mapmaking passed to the Low Countries. This 'Golden Age' of Dutch cartography is exemplified by the first printed 'atlas' of map sheets by Abraham Ortelius in 1570 – the *Theatrum Orbis Terrarum*. The term 'atlas' was coined by Gerard Mercator the Flemish cartographer – perhaps the most widely known figure in the history of cartography. His work, in particular his map projection published in 1569, make him the geographical colossus of the period.

3. THE HEREFORD MAPPAMUNDI

Produced on vellum, and attributed to Richard of Haldingham and Lafford, c. 1290. The map follows the form of a T-O map, centred on Jerusalem, with east to the top. The continents of Asia (top), Africa (lower right) and Europe (lower left) are separated by the Mediterranean Sea and the Nile and Don rivers.
Hereford Cathedral, Hereford, UK.

4. THE CARTE PISANE

The oldest surviving portolan chart, c. 1290. It shows most of Europe, with a remarkably detailed coastline of the Mediterranean Sea with Italy and Sicily in the centre.
Bibliothèque Nationale, Paris, France.

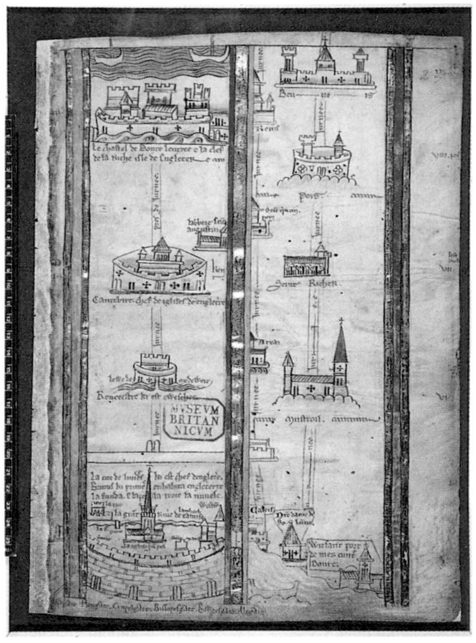

5. ITINERARY MAP OF A ROUTE FROM LONDON TO ITALY

Produced by Matthew Paris, c. 1250. This is a fine, early example of a road map in strip form. This extract includes Rochester, Canterbury and Dover.
British Library, London, UK.

1600–1900

Cartography in the earlier years of the 17th century was dominated by the Low Countries, epitomized by the Blaeu publishing house *(see 6)* but, by the late 17th century, the world centre for cartographic production had shifted from Amsterdam to Paris. France was one of the first countries to recognize the importance of establishing a national survey and mapping programme. There, the Cassini family established the national survey of France well ahead of other such surveys in western Europe *(see 7)*.

The colonial scramble for North America, and the American War of Independence (1775–1783), drove the development of cartography in North America, and it was an age, too, when the exploration of Australia, Tasmania and New Zealand resulted in their appearance on world maps. Such exploration was aided by great developments in navigation and particularly the ability to establish longitude more precisely.

During the 19th century special maps appeared in greater numbers reflecting scientific and social observation and analysis. One significant example of this development of thematic mapping was the *Physikalischer Atlas* of Heinrich Berghaus, published in two volumes in 1845 and 1848 *(see 8)*. Lithographic printing of maps was developed in the early years of the century allowing the production of multiple copies of maps very much more cheaply, stimulating a proliferation of maps for mass consumption and for educational purposes.

As the 19th century progressed, factors such as exploration and emigration were reflected in extended world coverage of maps and charts. Work on national surveys proceeded, one particularly notable national cartographic achievement being the Great Trigonometrical Survey (GTS) of India which facilitated the creation of extensive and detailed topographic maps of the sub-continent.

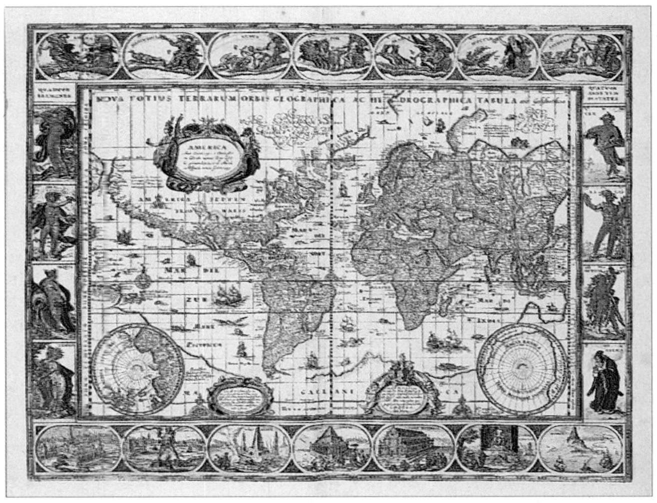

6. WORLD MAP

Produced in Amsterdam by Willem Blaeu, 1630. This is one of the finest examples of early maps on Mercator's projection. British Library, London, UK.

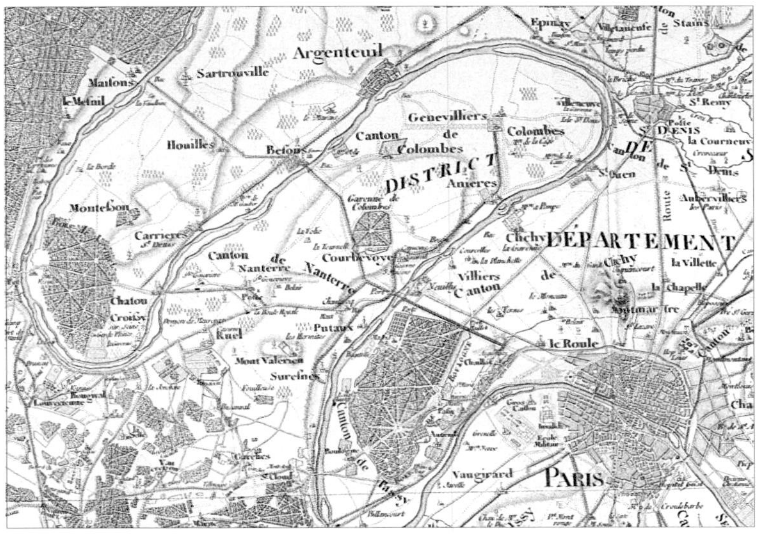

7. CARTE DE FRANCE

Detail from the first sheet – Sheet No. 1 Paris – by Cassini de Thury, 1736. Original scale 1:86 400. National Library of Scotland, Edinburgh, UK.

20TH CENTURY

War, politics and technological development were instrumental in prompting the expansion of map and chart coverage throughout the 20th century. The development of aviation and, in turn, space exploration, and photography and imagery possible through them, have been particularly significant in recent developments in cartography and have spawned a new age in cartography. The development of the computer has led to the production of digital maps and the consequent development of Geographical Information Systems (GIS) which allow users to combine and manipulate geographical data sets of many kinds.

There has been a significant increase in map coverage throughout the world, and yet the fact that comprehensive national topographic mapping has been produced, does not mean that it is readily available *(see 9)*. Many countries, particularly in Africa and Asia, impose strict restrictions on the release of their mapping. The question of national map coverage and availability is complicated by the activities of external mapping organizations. The former USSR had extensive programmes producing topographic mapping of countries throughout the world *(see 10)*. Easy access to this previously classified military mapping has recently served to extend map availability.

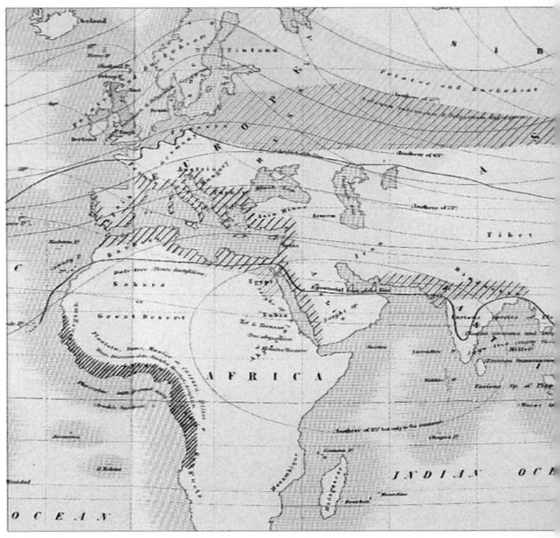

8. THEMATIC ATLAS MAP

Extract from a map of the *Survey of the geographical distribution and cultivation of the most important plants which are used as food for man: with indications of the isotheres and isokhimenes*, 1842. Published in the *Physikalischer Atlas* by Heinrich Berghaus, 1845 and 1848. This English language version appeared as Plate 44 in W & A K Johnston's *National Atlas of Historical, Commercial and Political Geography*, 1847. National Library of Scotland, Edinburgh, UK.

10. GROZNYY, RUSSIAN FEDERATION

Extract from a Russian military topographic map 1:500 000, 1988.

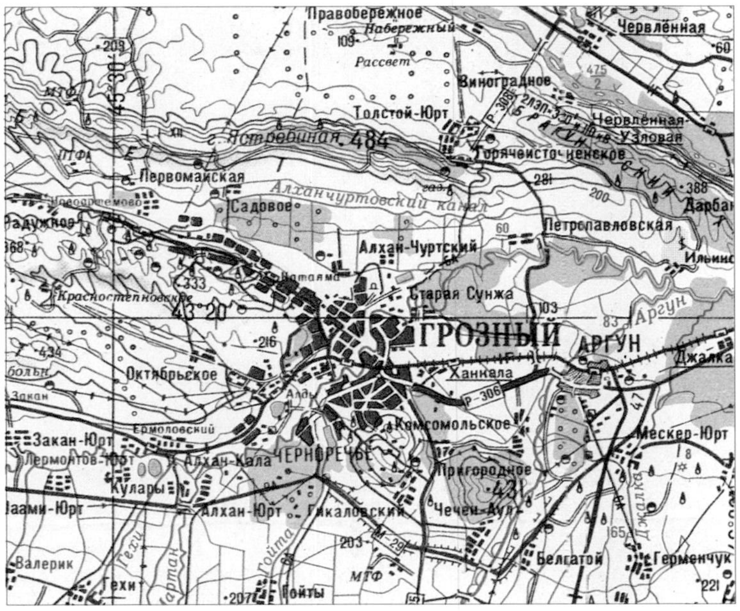

9. AVAILABILITY OF TOPOGRAPHIC MAPPING

Degree of access to topographic mapping of scales 1:100 000 or larger

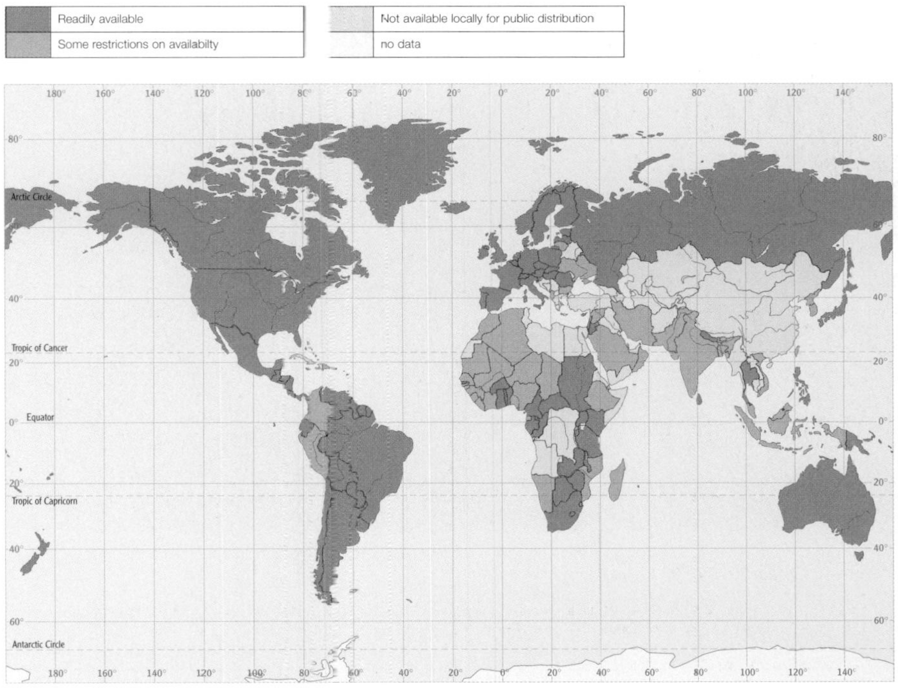

© Bartholomew Ltd

MEASURING THE EARTH

Speculation on the form of the universe and the place of the known world in it, and the attempts to express these graphically, constituted an important influence on mapmakers from earliest times. The Greeks inherited from the Babylonians such beliefs that the Earth was stationary, flat, the centre of the universe, and surrounded by water. Pythagoras in the 6th century BC and Aristotle in the 4th century BC proposed that the Earth was a sphere, revolving on its own axis. In Alexandria, Egypt, Eratosthenes (*c.* 276–194 BC) measured the circumference of the Earth using elementary geometric techniques. His value proved to be only 320 kilometres less than the true value, an error of less than 1 per cent.

One of the principal challenges of cartography is how to depict the spherical world on a flat map surface. It is essentially an impossible task without distorting the map in terms of either shape, azimuth (angles or bearings), area or distance. The problem assumed greater importance with the development of sea charts and the need to navigate in safety, preferably in straight lines (to reflect constant compass bearing) over considerable distances while simultaneously compensating for the curvature of the Earth. Mercator achieved this in the 16th century with his map projection in which the distance between the lines of latitude increases away from the equator. This projection, in modified form, still serves navigators well but has also resulted in distorted perceptions of the relative sizes of land areas, as those in high latitudes (eg Greenland) appear relatively too large, and those in low latitudes (eg India) appear relatively too small.

As far as establishing position on the Earth in terms of latitude and longitude is concerned, the concept of the tropics and the equator was established in early times through astronomical observation of the sun, moon and planets. The concept was later refined by Hipparchus and incorporated by Ptolemy into his *Geographia* (see page 42). The development of navigational instruments allowed latitude to be determined relatively easily. However, the establishment of longitude proved more problematic. In the 17th century Galileo established a method of determining longitude based on observations of the movement of Jupiter's moons, which served reasonably well on land. But the ability to establish longitude correctly at sea was believed to be so crucial that a Board of Longitude was established by the UK government in 1714 offering a prize of £20 000 for any method of defining longitude to within half a degree. In the search for a mechanical means of establishing longitude which could be used both on land and at sea, the principal difficulty was the lack of an accurate timepiece: the longitudinal value of a position being the distance reflected by the difference between local time and the time of a known position, with 15° of longitude equivalent to a time difference of one hour. The prize was eventually awarded to the Englishman John Harrison *(see 1)* whose marine chronometers, culminating in the one known as H4 which won the prize *(see 2)*, were remarkably accurate and also highly reliable at sea.

Any longitudinal position needs to be defined with reference to a standard position. Such a line of zero longitude, usually referred to as the prime meridian, could, in theory, be placed anywhere. Separate prime meridians were established in, for example, Paris, Cadiz, Naples, Pulkova and Stockholm, as well as London. The universal acceptance, in 1884, of a single prime meridian – the Greenwich Meridian – was an early example of international standardization in cartography.

1. JOHN HARRISON (1693–1776)

2. JOHN HARRISON'S FOURTH MARINE CHRONOMETER, H4.

Made c. 1760. This was the first truly accurate chronometer and won Harrison the Board of Longitude prize in 1772.

4. SPOT satellite image.

Showing Bandar Seri Begawan, Brunei. A high level of detail is visible within the built-up area and also along the coast within Brunei Bay. Variations in sediments and currents produce the variety of colours within the bay itself.

SURVEYING

Surveying is the initial data collection stage in the mapmaking process and it was the Greeks who established the first systematic approach. Astronomy underpinned its development and instruments such as the gnomon, a sundial device, and the astrolabe, a navigational instrument, were adopted by land surveyors to establish position. Major advances took place during the 16th, 17th and 18th centuries with the development of increasingly accurate surveying instruments which improved the precision of measurements and allowed the introduction of greater topographical detail into maps. The systematic surveying of entire countries, and the subsequent production of detailed, large scale maps, began in earnest in the 18th century, notably in France (see page 43). It was James Cook (1728–1779) who combined the traditional approach to marine surveying with newer land surveying techniques and laid the foundations of modern nautical charting *(see 3)*.

In the 20th century, technological developments have been reflected in related advances in surveying. The availability of aerial photography and satellite imagery allowed cartography to extend to formerly inaccessible parts of the world and have provided a vast amount of data for numerous mapping applications. Aerial photography and high resolution satellite imagery (*see 4*, and also pages 8-21) are important for the production of large-scale topographic mapping, while lower resolution imagery from a variety of sensors provides data on a global scale. The accurate coverage provided by the Global Positioning System (GPS), a satellite navigation system designed in the USA primarily for military use, is now widely used by surveyors for position fixing and also for navigation.

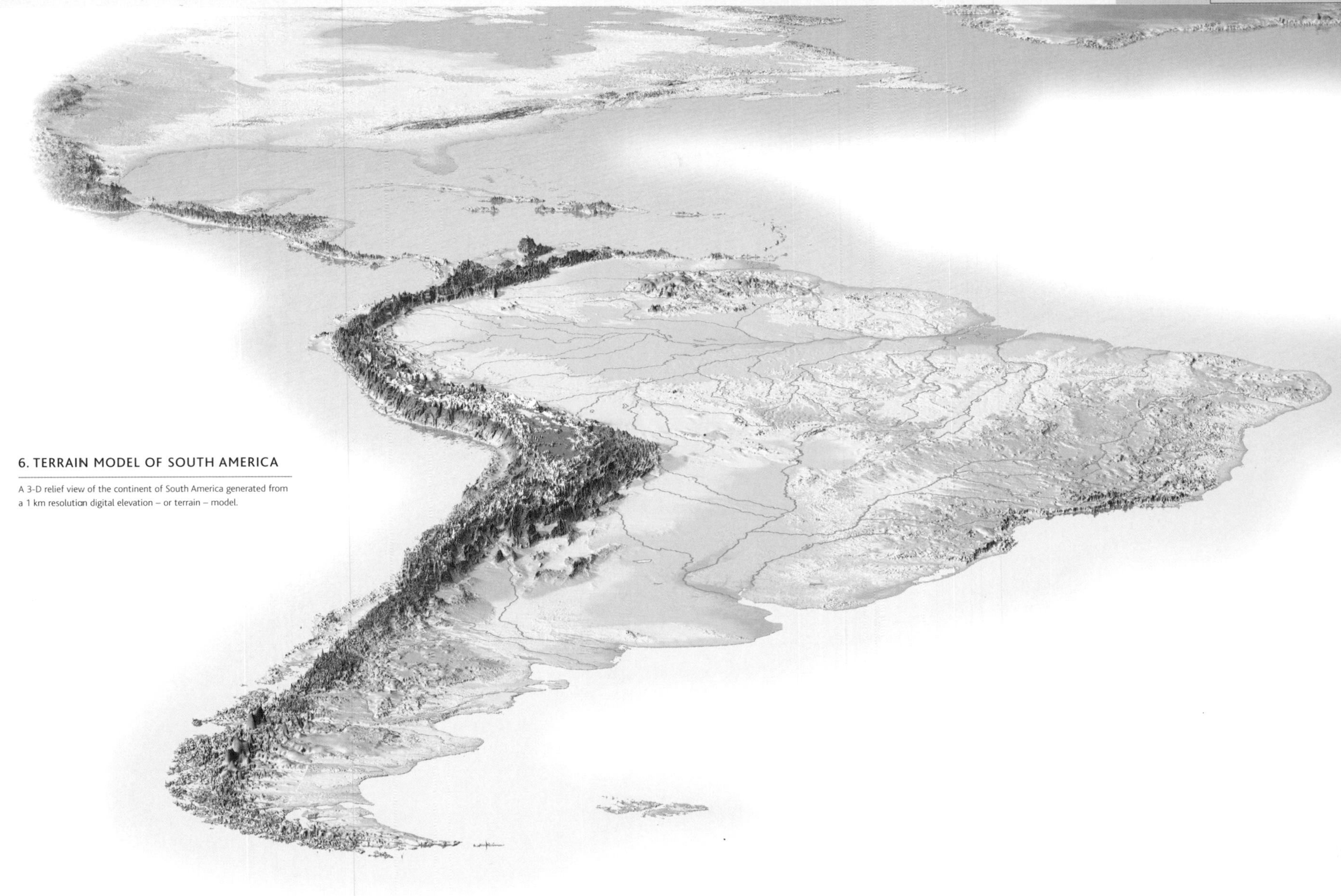

6. TERRAIN MODEL OF SOUTH AMERICA

A 3-D relief view of the continent of South America generated from a 1 km resolution digital elevation – or terrain – model.

3. CAPTAIN COOK'S CHART OF NEW ZEALAND 1772

This chart was published following Cook's explorations in 1769 and 1770. The chart is remarkably accurate in terms of the shape of the islands and in terms of latitude. However, the coloured overlays representing the coastline from a later survey in 1788 (green) and from British Admiralty charts up to 1958 (red), illustrate well the problems of establishing longitude at the time of Cook's voyages.

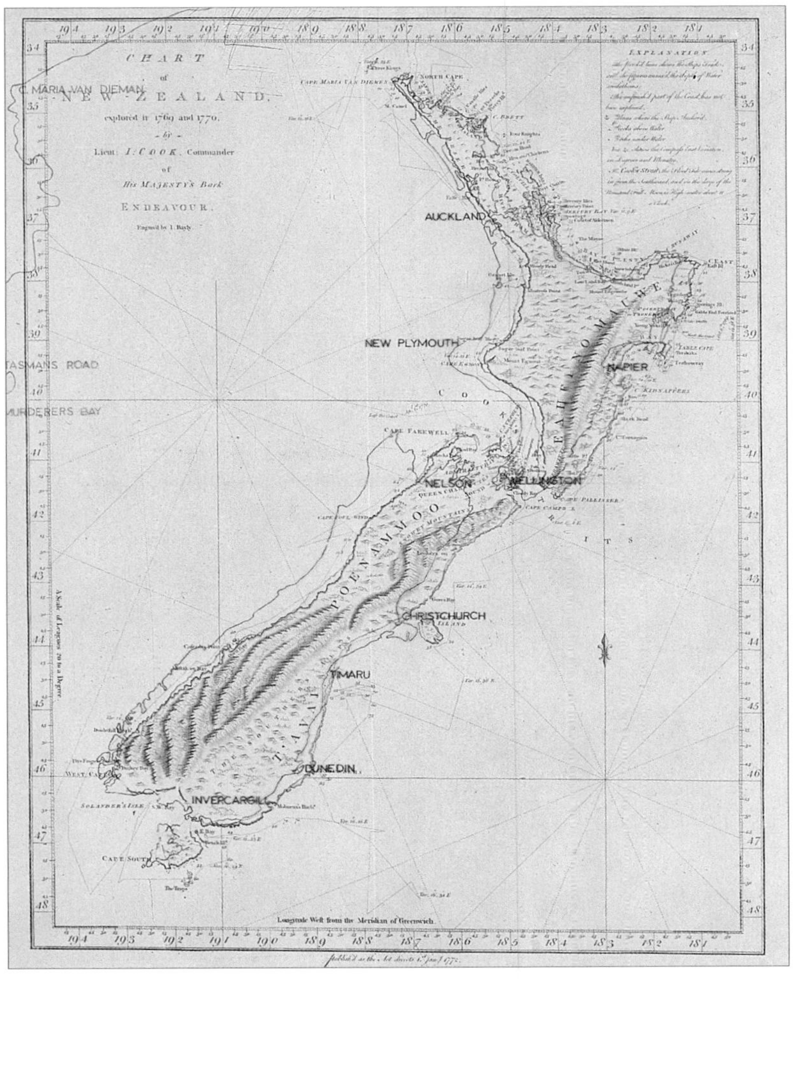

MAP PRODUCTION TECHNIQUES

For centuries, the only method of producing maps was to draw and copy them by hand. Production was, therefore, time-consuming and labour-intensive. As a result, few maps were produced and even fewer survived. In the 15th century, the invention of printing prompted a veritable revolution in mapmaking. It allowed the production of repeat copies and in a form consistent with the original, thus eliminating human error likely in hand copying. Early relief woodcut prints gave way during the 16th century to printing from engraved copper plates *(see 5)*. This allowed greater versatility and continued to be the principal method of map reproduction until the introduction of the much faster process of lithographic printing in the early 19th century. Later in the 19th century the development of photographic techniques was applied to mapmaking, eventually becoming an integral part of the process and facilitating the greater use of colour.

The most significant revolution in cartographic production, since the introduction of printing, dates from the late 1950s with the increasing use of the computer. This accelerated map production processes and allowed the generation of digital data, the manipulation of which supports new forms of output and visualization *(see 6)*. Maps can now be produced from scale-free and seamless databases, allowing individual customization of the output, and the ability to produce digital images of early maps by scanning allows their increased copying and wider dissemination. Digital maps are also now widely available on the Internet and the World Wide Web.

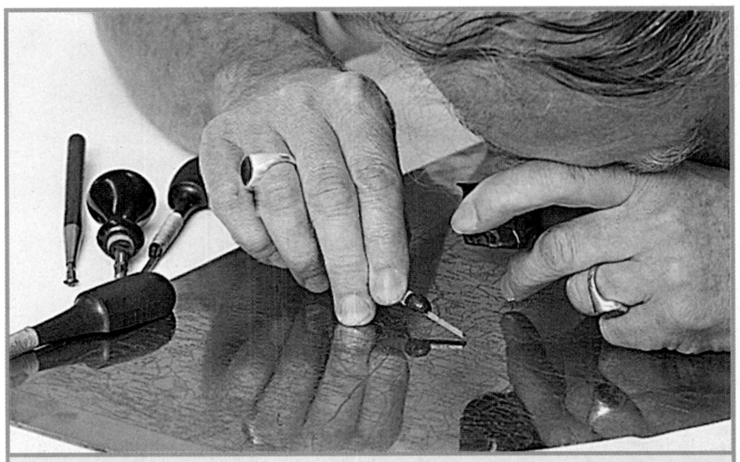

5. Copper Engraving

The highly skilled task of engraving a map on a copper plate. The image had to be drawn in reverse, for the map to appear correct when printed.

EUROPE total land area: 9 908 599 sq km / **3 825 731 sq miles**

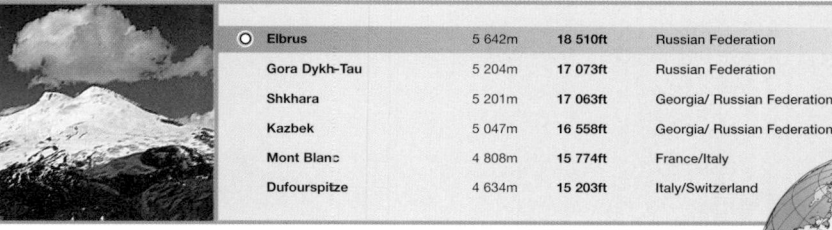

Elbrus	5 642m	**18 510ft**	Russian Federation
Gora Dykh-Tau	5 204m	**17 073ft**	Russian Federation
Shkhara	5 201m	**17 063ft**	Georgia/ Russian Federation
Kazbek	5 047m	**16 558ft**	Georgia/ Russian Federation
Mont Blanc	4 808m	**15 774ft**	France/Italy
Dufourspitze	4 634m	**15 203ft**	Italy/Switzerland

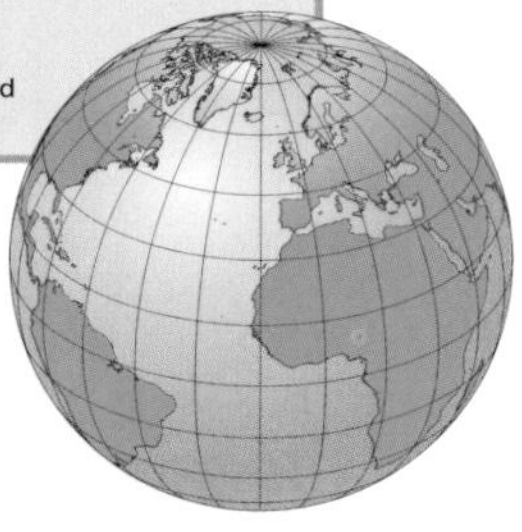

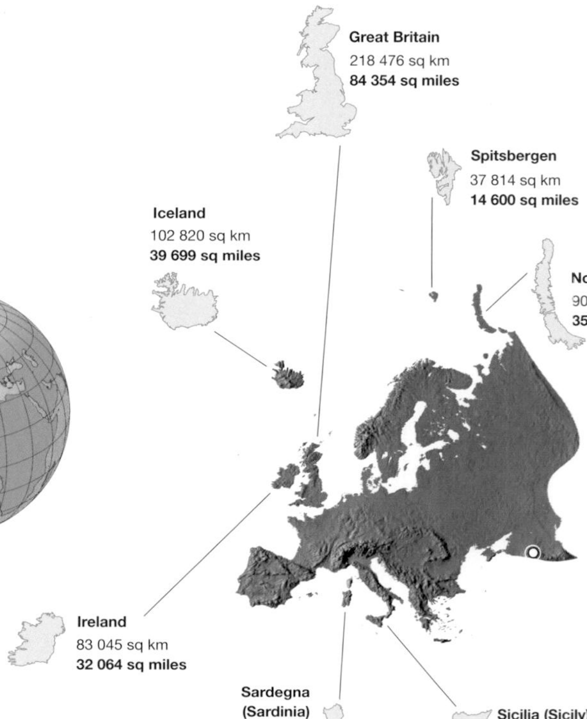
Great Britain
218 476 sq km
84 354 sq miles
Spitsbergen
37 814 sq km
14 600 sq miles
Iceland
102 820 sq km
39 699 sq miles
Novaya Zemlya
90 650 sq km
35 000 sq miles
Ireland
83 045 sq km
32 064 sq miles
Sardegna
(Sardinia)
24 090 sq km
9 301 sq miles
Sicilia (Sicily)
25 426 sq km
9 817 sq miles

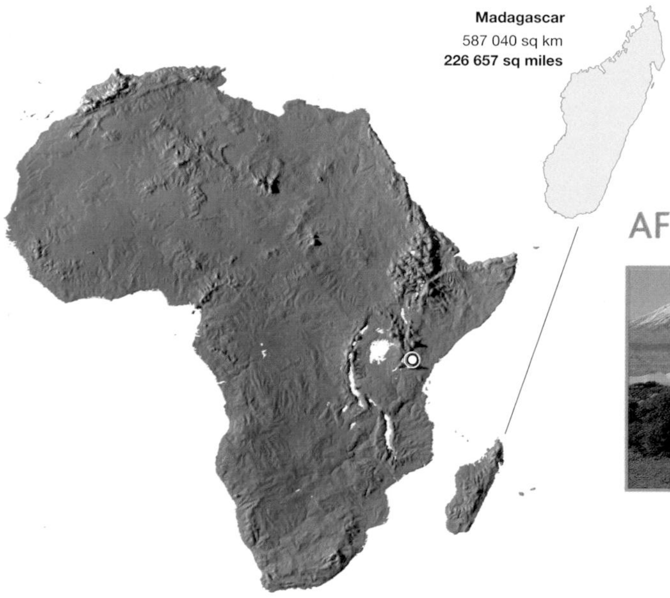
Madagascar
587 040 sq km
226 657 sq miles

AFRICA total land area: 30 343 578 sq km / **11 715 721 sq miles**

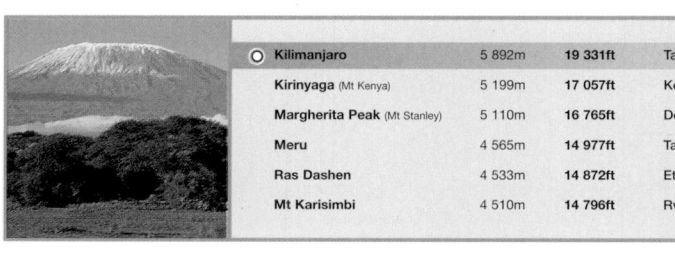

Kilimanjaro	5 892m	**19 331ft**	Tanzania
Kirinyaga (Mt Kenya)	5 199m	**17 057ft**	Kenya
Margherita Peak (Mt Stanley)	5 110m	**16 765ft**	Democratic Republic of Congo/Uganda
Meru	4 565m	**14 977ft**	Tanzania
Ras Dashen	4 533m	**14 872ft**	Ethiopia
Mt Karisimbi	4 510m	**14 796ft**	Rwanda

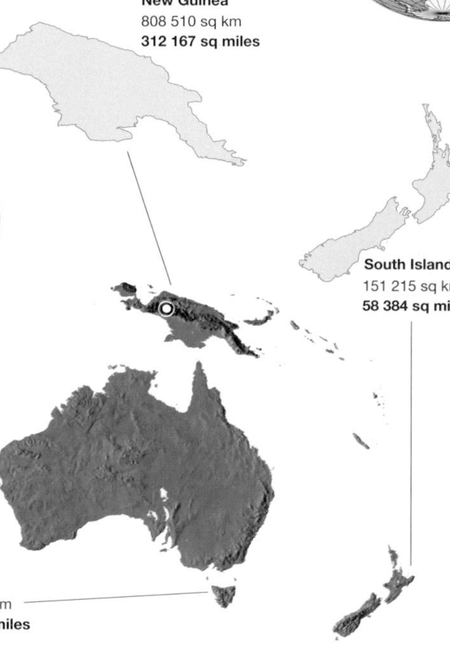
New Guinea
808 510 sq km
312 167 sq miles
North Island (New Zealand)
115 777 sq km
44 702 sq miles
South Island (New Zealand)
151 215 sq km
58 384 sq miles
Tasmania
67 800 sq km
26 178 sq miles

AUSTRALASIA total land area: 8 820 962 sq km / **3 405 792 sq miles**

Puncak Jaya	5 030m	**16 502ft**	Indonesia
Puncak Trikora	4 730m	**15 518ft**	Indonesia
Puncak Mandala	4 700m	**15 420ft**	Indonesia
Puncak Yamin	4 595m	**15 075ft**	Indonesia
Mt Wilhelm	4 509m	**14 793ft**	Papua New Guinea
Mt Kubor	4 359m	**14 301ft**	Papua New Guinea

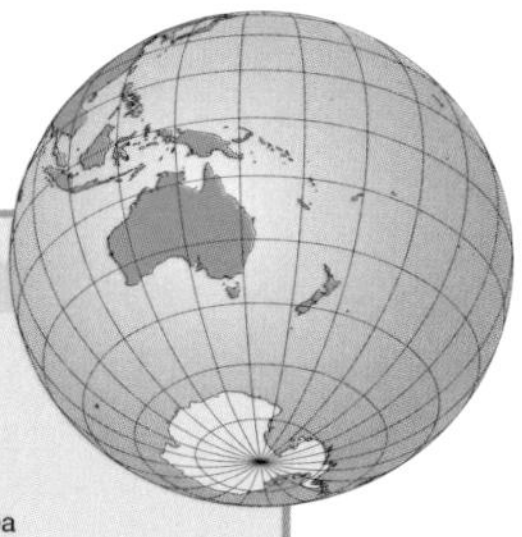

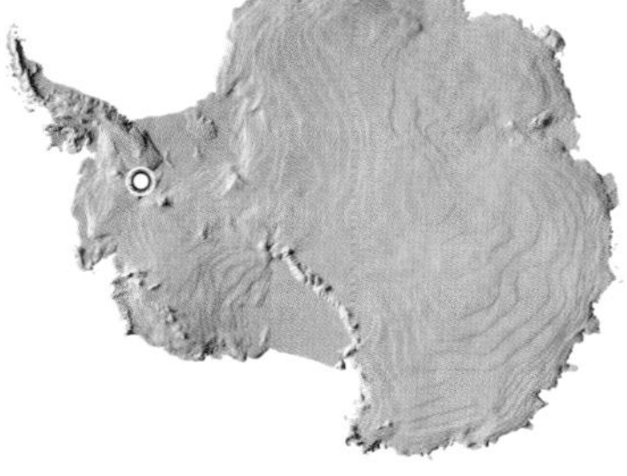

ANTARCTICA total land area: 12 093 000 sq km* / **4 669 133 sq miles***

*excluding ice shelves

Vinson Massif	4 897m	**16 066ft**
Mt Tyree	4 852m	**15 918ft**
Mt Kirkpatrick	4 528m	**14 855ft**
Mt Markham	4 351m	**14 275ft**
Mt Jackson	4 190m	**13 747ft**
Mt Sidley	4 181m	**13 717ft**

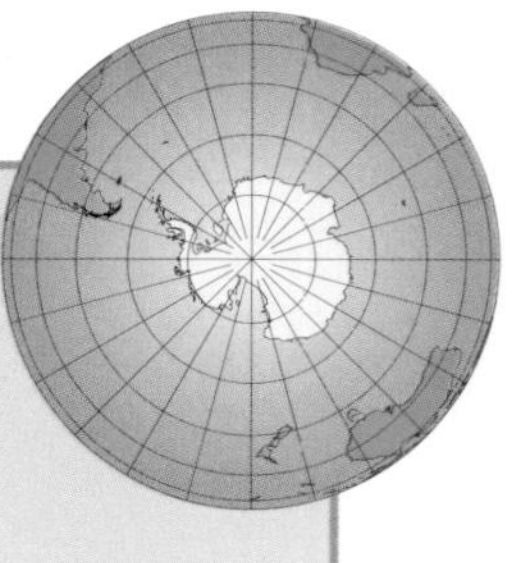

HIGHEST MOUNTAINS IN THE WORLD

Mt Everest	China/Nepal	8 848m / **29 028ft**
K2	China/Jammu and Kashmir	8 611m / **28 251ft**
Kangchenjunga	India/Nepal	8 586m / **28 169ft**
Lhotse	China/Nepal	8 516m / **27 939ft**
Makalu	China/Nepal	8 463m / **27 765ft**
Cho Oyu	China/Nepal	8 201m / **26 906ft**
Dhaulagiri	Nepal	8 167m / **26 794ft**
Manaslu	Nepal	8 163m / **26 781ft**
Nanga Parbat	Jammu and Kashmir	8 126m / **26 660ft**
Annapurna I	Nepal	8 091m / **26 545ft**
Gasherbrum I	China/Jammu and Kashmir	8 068m / **26 469ft**
Broad Peak	China/Jammu and Kashmir	8 047m / **26 401ft**
Gasherbrum II	China/Jammu and Kashmir	8 035m / **26 361ft**
Xixabangma Feng	China	8 012m / **26 286ft**
Annapurna II	Nepal	7 937m / **26 040ft**
Nuptse	Nepal	7 885m / **25 869ft**
Himalchul	Nepal	7 864m / **25 800ft**
Masherbrum	Jammu and Kashmir	7 821m / **25 659ft**
Nanda Devi	India	7 816m / **25 643ft**
Rakaposhi	Jammu and Kashmir	7 788m / **25 551ft**
Namjagbarwa Feng	China	7 756m / **25 446ft**
Kamet	China	7 756m / **25 446ft**

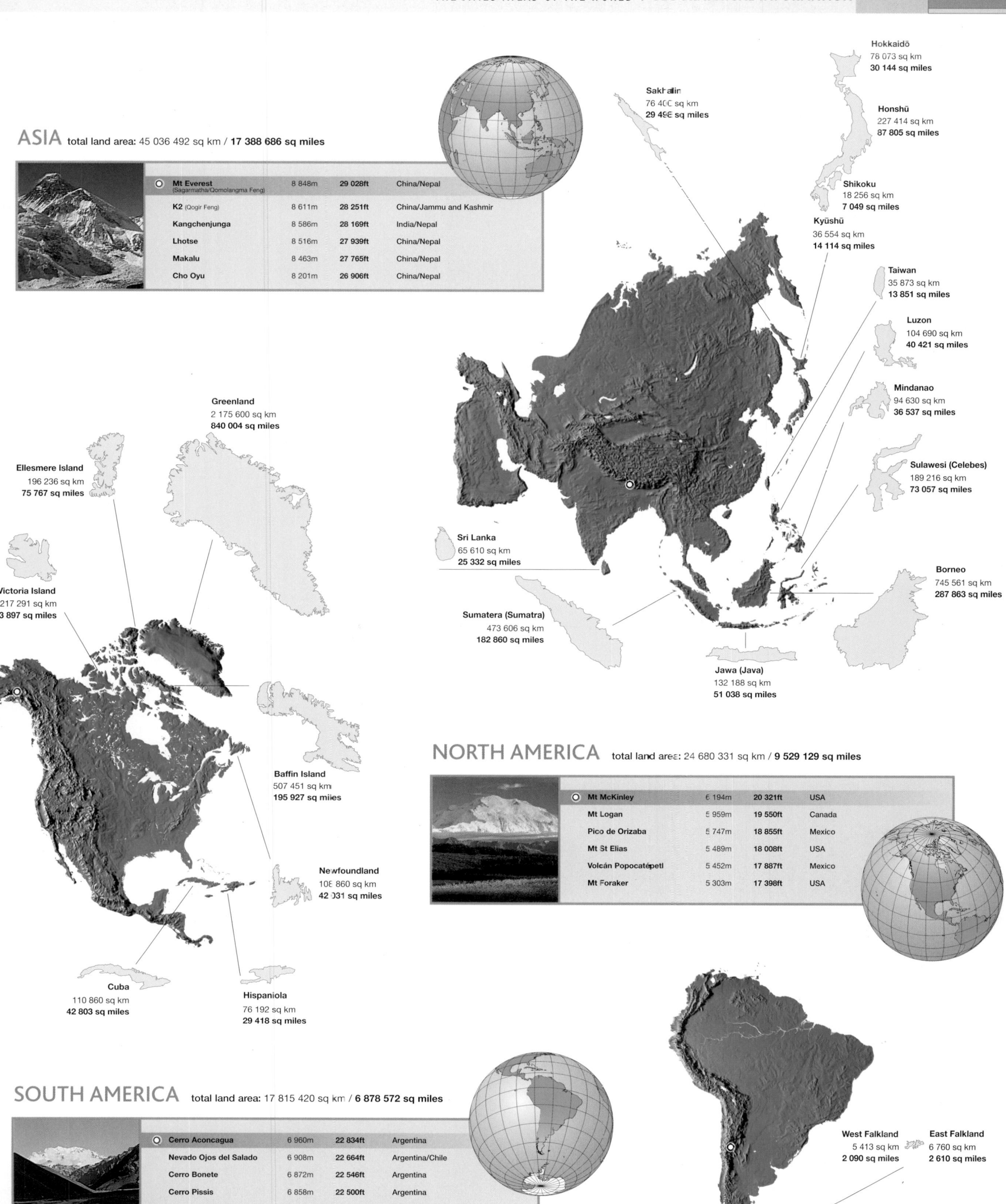

ASIA total land area: 45 036 492 sq km / **17 388 686 sq miles**

Mt Everest (Sagarmatha/Qomolangma Feng)	8 848m	**29 028ft**	China/Nepal
K2 (Qogir Feng)	8 611m	**28 251ft**	China/Jammu and Kashmir
Kangchenjunga	8 586m	**28 169ft**	India/Nepal
Lhotse	8 516m	**27 939ft**	China/Nepal
Makalu	8 463m	**27 765ft**	China/Nepal
Cho Oyu	8 201m	**26 906ft**	China/Nepal

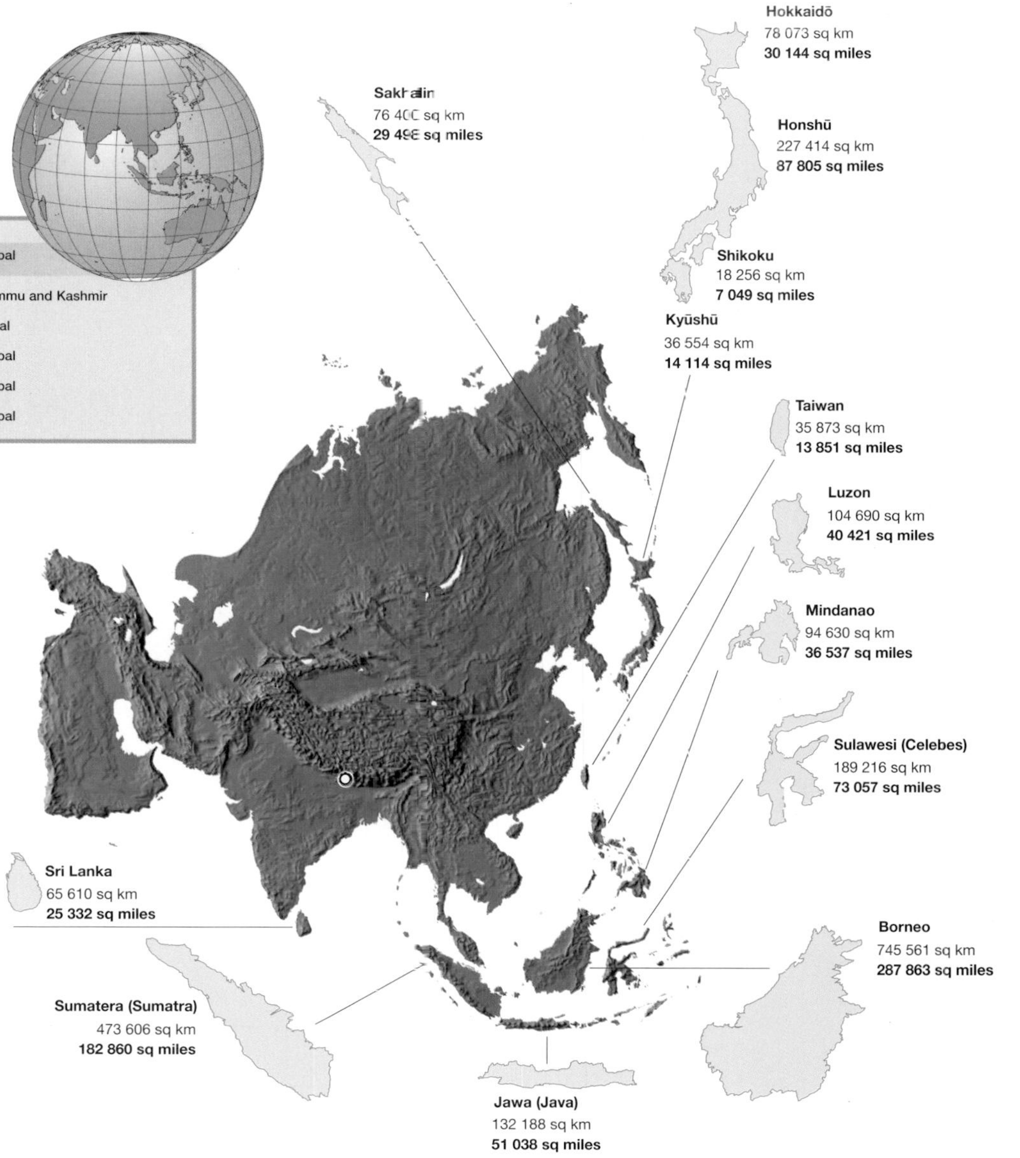
Sakhalin
76 400 sq km
29 498 sq miles
Hokkaidō
78 073 sq km
30 144 sq miles
Honshū
227 414 sq km
87 805 sq miles
Shikoku
18 256 sq km
7 049 sq miles
Kyūshū
36 554 sq km
14 114 sq miles
Taiwan
35 873 sq km
13 851 sq miles
Luzon
104 690 sq km
40 421 sq miles
Mindanao
94 630 sq km
36 537 sq miles
Sulawesi (Celebes)
189 216 sq km
73 057 sq miles
Borneo
745 561 sq km
287 863 sq miles
Sri Lanka
65 610 sq km
25 332 sq miles
Sumatera (Sumatra)
473 606 sq km
182 860 sq miles
Jawa (Java)
132 188 sq km
51 038 sq miles

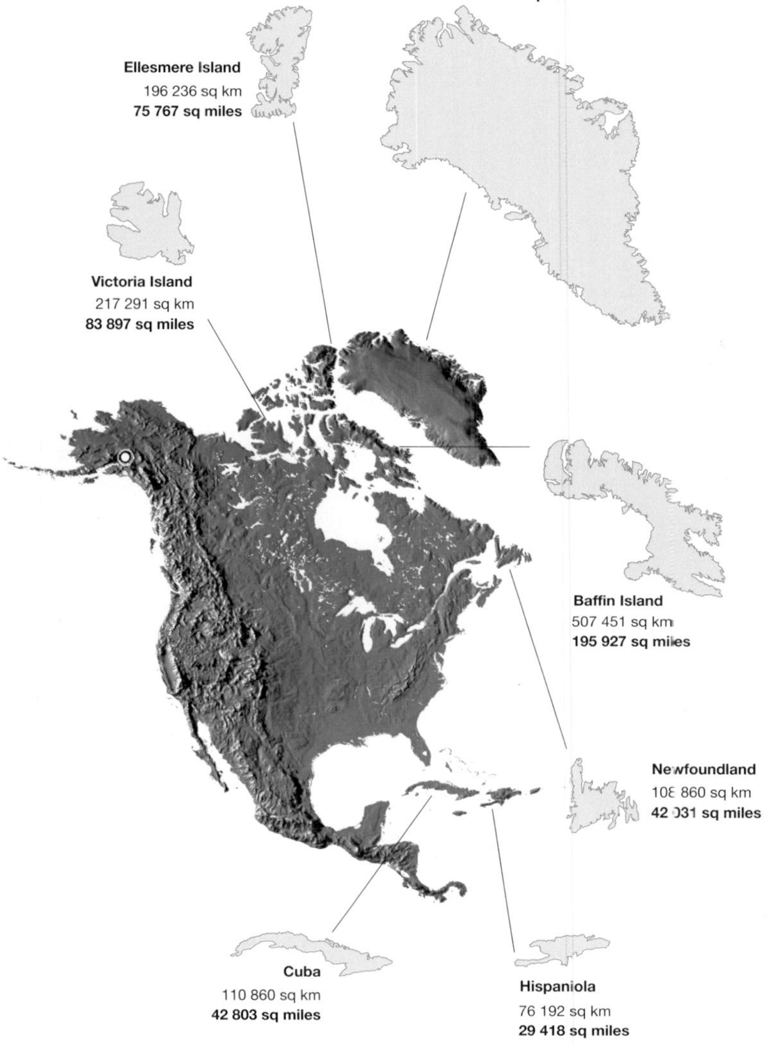
Greenland
2 175 600 sq km
840 004 sq miles
Ellesmere Island
196 236 sq km
75 767 sq miles
Victoria Island
217 291 sq km
83 897 sq miles
Baffin Island
507 451 sq km
195 927 sq miles
Newfoundland
108 860 sq km
42 031 sq miles
Cuba
110 860 sq km
42 803 sq miles
Hispaniola
76 192 sq km
29 418 sq miles

NORTH AMERICA total land area: 24 680 331 sq km / **9 529 129 sq miles**

Mt McKinley	6 194m	**20 321ft**	USA
Mt Logan	5 959m	**19 550ft**	Canada
Pico de Orizaba	5 747m	**18 855ft**	Mexico
Mt St Elias	5 489m	**18 008ft**	USA
Volcán Popocatépetl	5 452m	**17 887ft**	Mexico
Mt Foraker	5 303m	**17 398ft**	USA

SOUTH AMERICA total land area: 17 815 420 sq km / **6 878 572 sq miles**

Cerro Aconcagua	6 960m	**22 834ft**	Argentina
Nevado Ojos del Salado	6 908m	**22 664ft**	Argentina/Chile
Cerro Bonete	6 872m	**22 546ft**	Argentina
Cerro Pissis	6 858m	**22 500ft**	Argentina
Cerro Tupungato	6 800m	**22 309ft**	Argentina/Chile
Cerro Mercedario	6 770m	**22 211ft**	Argentina

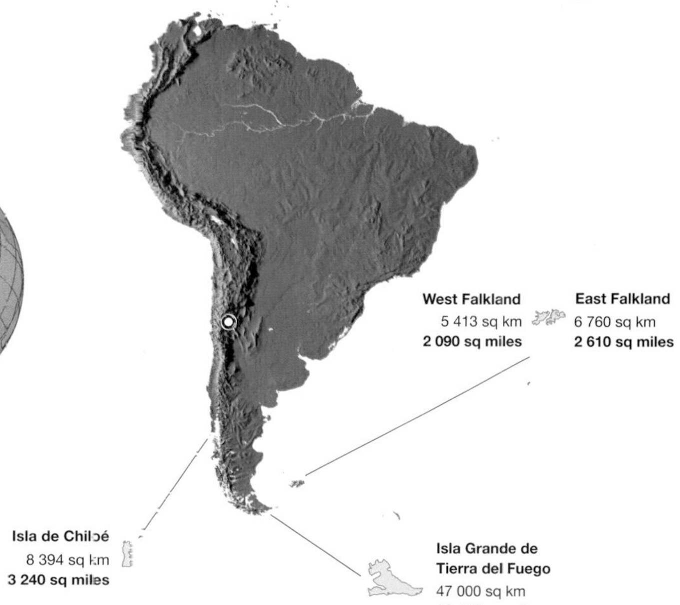
West Falkland
5 413 sq km
2 090 sq miles
East Falkland
6 760 sq km
2 610 sq miles
Isla de Chiloé
8 394 sq km
3 240 sq miles
Isla Grande de Tierra del Fuego
47 000 sq km
18 147 sq miles

Gurla Mandhata China 7 739m / **25 390ft**
Muztag China 7 723m / **25 338ft**
Kongur Shan China 7 719m / **25 324ft**
Tirich Mir Pakistan 7 690m / **25 229ft**
Kula Kangri Bhutan 7 554m / **24 783ft**
Muztagata China 7 546m / **24 757ft**
Gongga Shan China 7 514m / **24 652ft**
Qullai Garmo Tajikistan 7 495m / **24 590ft**
Jongsang India/Nepal 7 483m / **24 550ft**
Teram Kangri China/Jammu and Kashmir 7 470m / **24 508ft**
Pik Pobedy China/Kyrgyzstan 7 439m / **24 406ft**
Ganesh I China/Nepal 7 415m / **24 327ft**
Churen Himal Nepal 7 371m / **24 183ft**
Sad Istragh Afghanistan/Pakistan 7 367m / **24 170ft**
Kabru India/Nepal 7 353m / **24 124ft**
Chamlang Nepal 7 319m / **24 012ft**
Choksiam China 7 316m / **24 002ft**
Chomo Lhari Bhutan 7 313m / **23 992ft**
Muztag China 7 282m / **23 891ft**
Langtang Lirung Nepal 7 254m / **23 799ft**
Gankar Punsum Bhutan 7 239m / **23 750ft**
Nagarzê China 7 223m / **23 697ft**

© Bartholomew Ltd

OCEANS AND SEAS

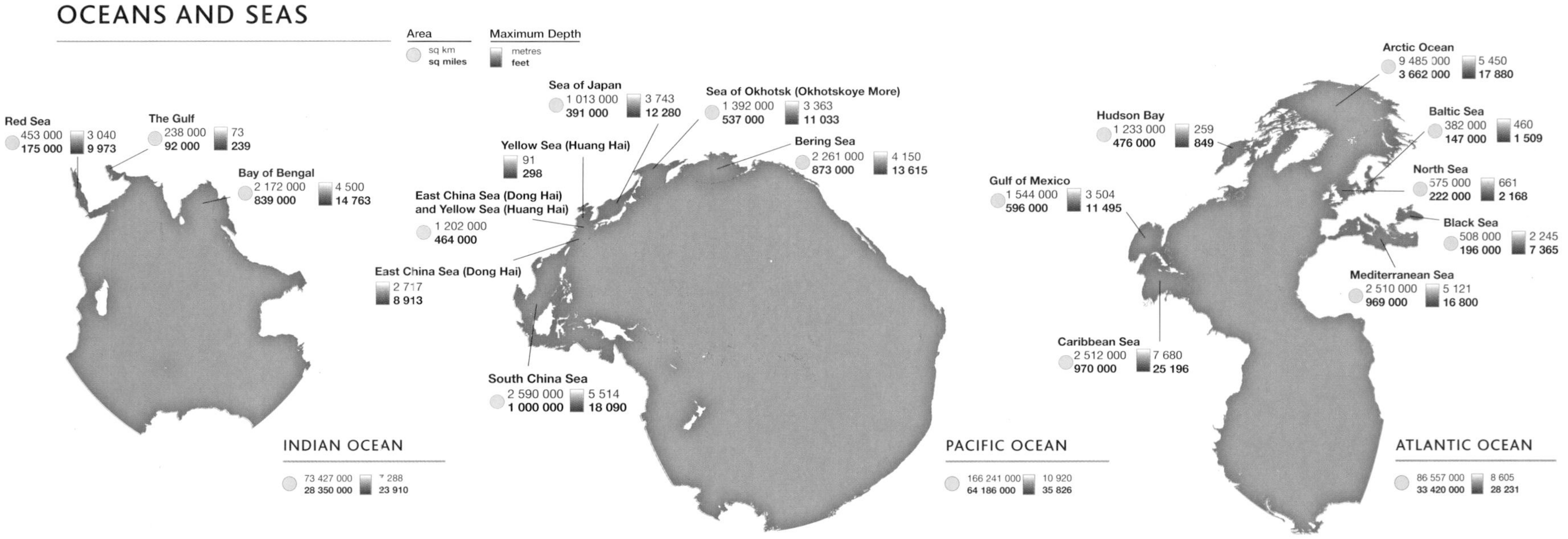
Area
sq km
sq miles
Maximum Depth
metres
feet
Red Sea
453 000 | 3 040
175 000 | 9 973
The Gulf
238 000 | 73
92 000 | 239
Bay of Bengal
2 172 000 | 4 500
839 000 | 14 763
Sea of Japan
1 013 000 | 3 743
391 000 | 12 280
Sea of Okhotsk (Okhotskoye More)
1 392 000 | 3 363
537 000 | 11 033
Yellow Sea (Huang Hai)
91
298
Bering Sea
2 261 000 | 4 150
873 000 | 13 615
East China Sea (Dong Hai) and Yellow Sea (Huang Hai)
1 202 000
464 000
East China Sea (Dong Hai)
2 717
8 913
South China Sea
2 590 000 | 5 514
1 000 000 | 18 090
INDIAN OCEAN
73 427 000 | 7 288
28 350 000 | 23 910
PACIFIC OCEAN
166 241 000 | 10 920
64 186 000 | 35 826
Hudson Bay
1 233 000 | 259
476 000 | 849
Gulf of Mexico
1 544 000 | 3 504
596 000 | 11 495
Caribbean Sea
2 512 000 | 7 680
970 000 | 25 196
Arctic Ocean
9 485 000 | 5 450
3 662 000 | 17 880
Baltic Sea
382 000 | 460
147 000 | 1 509
North Sea
575 000 | 661
222 000 | 2 168
Black Sea
508 000 | 2 245
196 000 | 7 365
Mediterranean Sea
2 510 000 | 5 121
969 000 | 16 800
ATLANTIC OCEAN
86 557 000 | 8 605
33 420 000 | 28 231

EUROPE

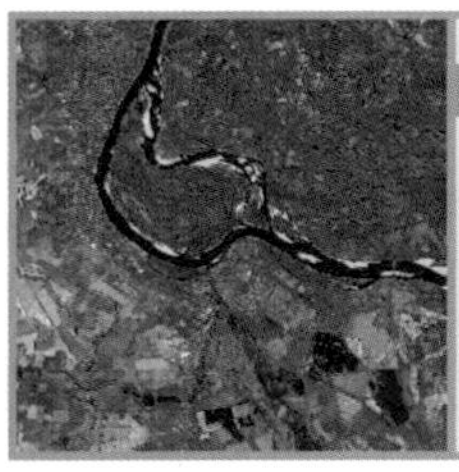

Volga	3 688 km	2 291 miles
Danube	2 850 km	1 770 miles
Dnieper	2 285 km	1 419 miles
Kama	2 028 km	1 260 miles
Don	1 931 km	1 199 miles
Pechora	1 802 km	1 119 miles

Rybinskoye Vodokhranilishche
Vyatka
Kama
Volga
Oka
Volga
Caspian Sea

Volga drainage basin
1 380 000 sq km
533 000 sq miles

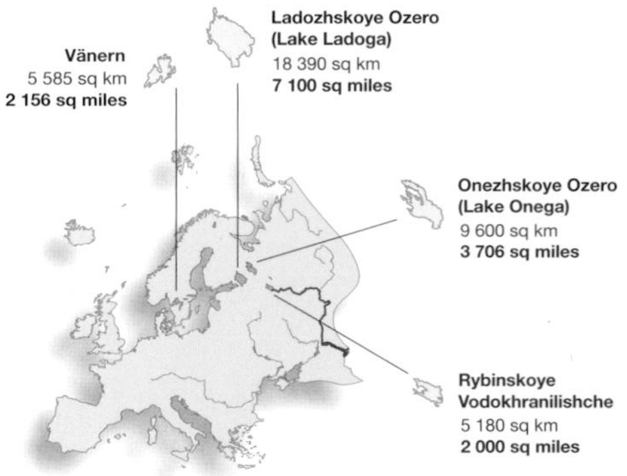
Vänern
5 585 sq km
2 156 sq miles
Ladozhskoye Ozero (Lake Ladoga)
18 390 sq km
7 100 sq miles
Onezhskoye Ozero (Lake Onega)
9 600 sq km
3 706 sq miles
Rybinskoye Vodokhranilishche
5 180 sq km
2 000 sq miles

AFRICA

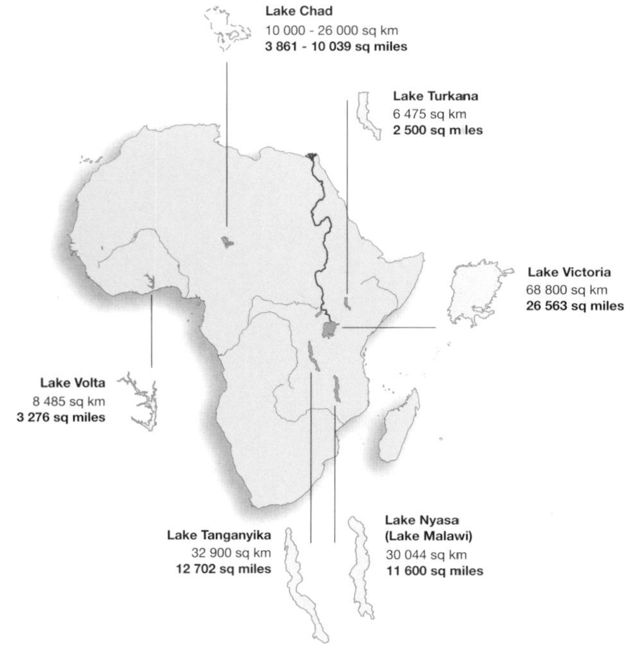
Lake Chad
10 000 - 26 000 sq km
3 861 - 10 039 sq miles
Lake Turkana
6 475 sq km
2 500 sq miles
Lake Victoria
68 800 sq km
26 563 sq miles
Lake Volta
8 485 sq km
3 276 sq miles
Lake Tanganyika
32 900 sq km
12 702 sq miles
Lake Nyasa (Lake Malawi)
30 044 sq km
11 600 sq miles

Mediterranean Sea
Nile
Atbara
Bahr el Azraq (Blue Nile)
Bahr el Abiad (White Nile)
Bahr el Jebel (White Nile)
Lake Albert
Lake Kyoga
Lake Victoria

Nile drainage basin
3 349 000 sq km
1 293 000 sq miles

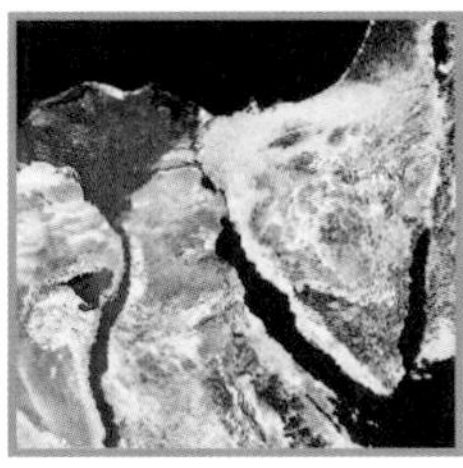

Nile	6 695 km	4 160 miles
Congo	4 667 km	2 900 miles
Niger	4 184 km	2 599 miles
Zambezi (Zambeze)	2 736 km	1 700 miles
Webi Shabeelle	2 490 km	1 547 miles
Ubangi	2 250 km	1 398 miles

Lungwebungu
Kafue
Luangwa
Lake Nyasa (Lake Malawi)
Cuando
Zambezi
Zambeze
Lake Kariba
Indian Ocean

Zambezi (Zambeze) drainage basin
1 330 000 sq km
514 000 sq miles

Ubangi
Congo
Uele
Atlantic Ocean
Congo
Kasai
Kwango
Lomami
Lualaba
Lake Tanganyika
Lake Mweru

Congo drainage basin
3 700 000 sq km
1 429 000 sq miles

Niger
Bani
Kaduna
Benue
Gulf of Guinea

Niger drainage basin
1 890 000 sq km
730 000 sq miles

AUSTRALASIA

Murray-Darling	3 750 km	2 330 miles
Darling	2 739 km	1 702 miles
Murray	2 589 km	1 608 miles
Murrumbidgee	1 690 km	1 050 miles
Lachlan	1 480 km	919 miles
Macquarie	950 km	590 miles

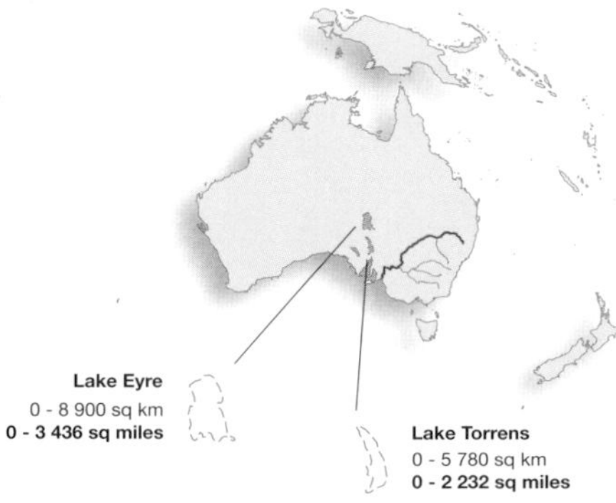
Lake Eyre
0 - 8 900 sq km
0 - 3 436 sq miles
Lake Torrens
0 - 5 780 sq km
0 - 2 232 sq miles

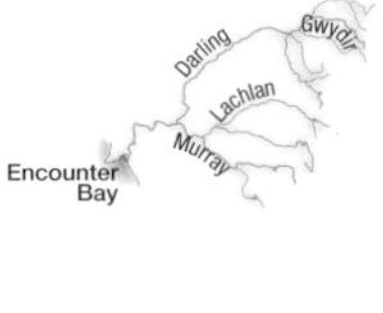
Darling
Gwydir
Lachlan
Murray
Encounter Bay

Murray-Darling drainage basin
1 058 000 sq km
408 000 sq miles

LONGEST RIVERS IN THE WORLD

- **Nile** Africa 6 695 km / **4 160 miles**
- **Amazonas (Amazon)** South America 6 516 km / **4 049 miles**
- **Chang Jiang (Yangtze)** Asia 6 380 km / **3 964 miles**
- **Mississippi-Missouri** North America 5 969 km / **3 709 miles**
- **Ob'-Irtysh** Asia 5 568 km / **3 459 miles**
- **Yenisey-Angara-Selenga** Asia 5 550 km / **3 448 miles**
- **Huang He (Yellow River)** Asia 5 464 km / **3 395 miles**
- **Congo** Africa 4 667 km / **2 900 miles**
- **Río de la Plata-Paraná** South America 4 500 km / **2 796 miles**
- **Irtysh** Asia 4 440 km / **2 759 miles**
- **Mekong** Asia 4 425 km / **2 749 miles**
- **Heilong Jiang (Amur)-Argun'** Asia 4 416 km / **2 744 miles**
- **Lena-Kirenga** Asia 4 400 km / **2 734 miles**
- **Mackenzie-Peace-Finlay** North America 4 241 km / **2 635 miles**
- **Niger** Africa 4 184 km / **2 599 miles**
- **Yenisey** Asia 4 090 km / **2 541 miles**
- **Missouri** North America 4 086 km / **2 539 miles**
- **Mississippi** North America 3 765 km / **2 339 miles**
- **Murray-Darling** Australasia 3 750 km / **2 330 miles**
- **Ob'** Asia 3 701 km / **2 300 miles**
- **Volga** Europe 3 688 km / **2 291 miles**
- **Purus** South America 3 218 km / **2 000 miles**

ASIA

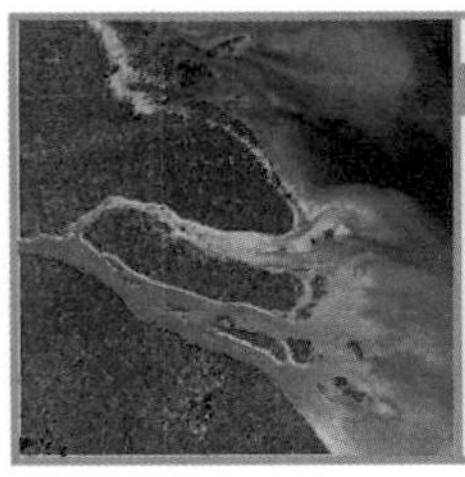

Chang Jiang (Yangtze)	6 380 km	3 964 miles
Ob'-Irtysh	5 568 km	3 459 miles
Yenisey-Angara-Selenga	5 550 km	3 448 miles
Huang He (Yellow River)	5 464 km	3 395 miles
Mekong	4 425 km	2 749 miles
Heilong Jiang (Amur)-Argun'	4 416 km	2 744 miles

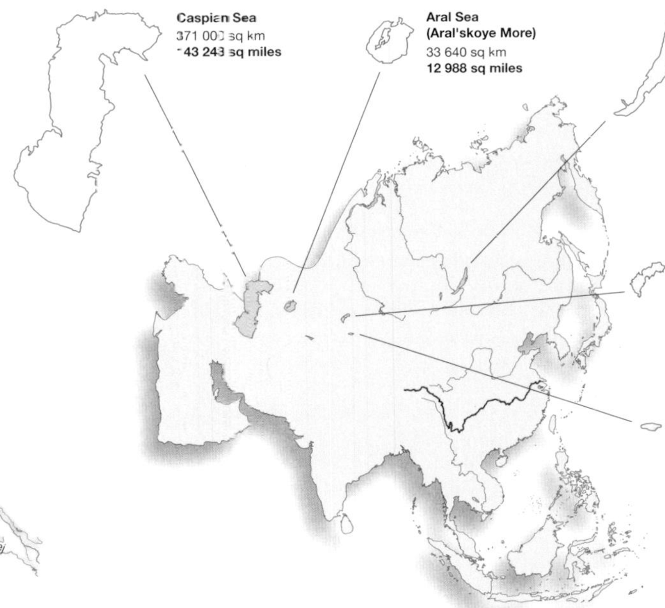

Caspian Sea
371 000 sq km
143 243 sq miles

Aral Sea (Aral'skoye More)
33 640 sq km
12 988 sq miles

Ozero Baykal (Lake Baikal)
30 500 sq km
11 776 sq miles

Ozero Balkhash
17 400 sq km
6 718 sq miles

Ysyk-Köl
6 200 sq km
2 393 sq miles

Chang Jiang (Yangtze) drainage basin
1 959 000 sq km
756 000 sq miles

Lena-Kirenga drainage basin
2 490 000 sq km
961 000 sq miles

Indus drainage basin
1 166 000 sq km
450 000 sq miles

Ganga (Ganges)-Brahmaputra drainage basin
1 621 000 sq km
626 000 sq miles

Shaṭṭ al'Arab drainage basin
1 114 000 sq km
430 000 sq miles

Heilong Jiang (Amur)-Argun' drainage basin
1 855 000 sq km
716 000 sq miles

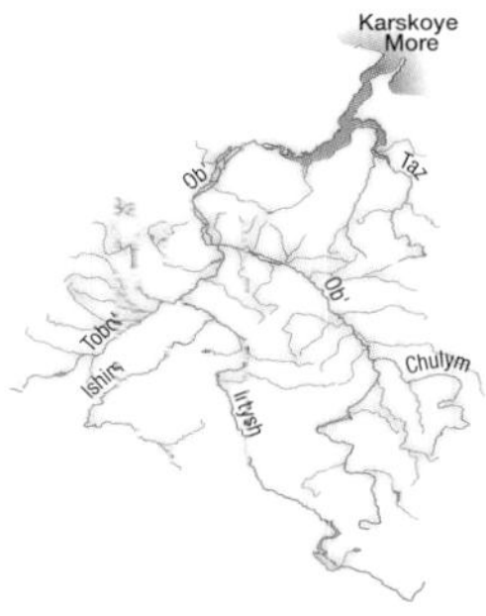

Ob'-Irtysh drainage basin
2 990 000 sq km
1 154 000 sq miles

Yenisey-Angara-Selenga drainage basin
2 580 000 sq km
996 000 sq miles

NORTH AMERICA

Great Bear Lake
31 328 sq km
12 095 sq miles

Great Slave Lake
28 568 sq km
11 030 sq miles

Lake Winnipeg
24 387 sq km
9 415 sq miles

Lake Superior
82 100 sq km
31 698 sq miles

Lake Huron
59 600 sq km
23 011 sq miles

Lake Michigan
57 800 sq km
22 316 sq miles

Lake Ontario
18 960 sq km
7 320 sq miles

Lake Erie
25 700 sq km
9 922 sq miles

Mississippi-Missouri drainage basin
3 250 000 sq km
1 255 000 sq miles

Mississippi-Missouri	5 969 km	3 709 miles
Mackenzie-Peace-Finlay	4 241 km	2 635 miles
Missouri	4 086 km	2 539 miles
Mississippi	3 765 km	2 339 miles
Yukon	3 185 km	1 979 miles
Rio Grande (Río Bravo del Norte)	3 057 km	1 899 miles

Nelson-Saskatchewan drainage basin
1 150 000 sq km
444 000 sq miles

Mackenzie-Peace-Finlay drainage basin
1 805 000 sq km
697 000 sq miles

St Lawrence-St Louis drainage basin
1 463 000 sq km
565 000 sq miles

SOUTH AMERICA

Amazonas (Amazon)	6 516 km	4 049 miles
Río de la Plata-Paraná	4 500 km	2 796 miles
Purus	3 218 km	1 999 miles
Madeira	3 200 km	1 988 miles
São Francisco	2 900 km	1 802 miles
Tocantins	2 750 km	1 708 miles

Amazonas (Amazon) drainage basin
7 050 000 sq km
2 722 000 sq miles

Río de la Plata-Paraná drainage basin
3 103 000 sq km
1 197 000 sq miles

Lago Titicaca
8 340 sq km
3 220 sq miles

- **Madeira** South America 3 200 km / 1 988 miles
- **Yukon** North America 3 185 km / 1 979 miles
- **Indus** Asia 3 180 km / 1 976 miles
- **Syrdar'ya** Asia 3 078 km / 1 913 miles
- **St Lawrence** North America 3 058 km / 1 900 miles
- **Rio Grande (Río Bravo del Norte)** North America 3 057 km / 1 899 miles
- **São Francisco** South America 2 900 km / 1 802 miles
- **Danube** Europe 2 850 km / 1 770 miles
- **Brahmaputra** Asia 2 840 km / 1 765 miles
- **Salween** Asia 2 816 km / 1 750 miles
- **Euphrates** Asia 2 815 km / 1 749 miles
- **Tocantins** South America 2 750 km / 1 708 miles
- **Tarim He** Asia 2 750 km / 1 708 miles
- **Darling** Australasia 2 739 km / 1 702 miles
- **Zambezi (Zambeze)** Africa 2 736 km / 1 700 miles
- **Araguaia** South America 2 627 km / 1 632 miles
- **Paraguay** South America 2 600 km / 1 615 miles
- **Murray** Australasia 2 589 km / 1 608 miles
- **Nelson-Saskatchewan** North America 2 570 km / 1 597 miles
- **Nizhnyaya Tunguska** Asia 2 559 km / 1 590 miles
- **Amudar'ya** Asia 2 540 km / 1 578 miles
- **Ural** Europe / Asia 2 534 km / 1 575 miles

© Bartholomew Ltd

All independent countries and populated dependent and disputed territories are included in this list of the states and territories of the world; the list is arranged in alphabetical order by the conventional name form. For independent states, the full name is given below the conventional name, if this is different; for territories, the status is given. The capital city name is given in the local form as shown on the reference maps.

The statistics used for the area and population are the latest available and include estimates. The information on languages and religions is based on the latest information on 'de facto' speakers of the language or 'de facto' adherents of the religion. The information available on languages and religions varies greatly from country to country, some countries include questions in census others do not, in which case best estimates are used. The order of the languages and religions reflect their relative importance within the country; generally, languages or religions are included when more than one per cent of the population are estimated to be speakers or adherents.

Membership of the following international organizations is shown by the abbreviations below; territories are not shown as having separate memberships of these organizations.

APEC	Asia-Pacific Economic Cooperation
ASEAN	Association of Southeast Asian Nations
CARICOM	Caribbean Community
CIS	Commonwealth of Independent States
Comm.	The Commonwealth
EU	European Union
OECD	Organization of Economic Cooperation and Development
OPEC	Organization of Petroleum Exporting Countries
SADC	Southern African Development Community
UN	United Nations

AFGHANISTAN
Islamic Emirate of Afghanistan

Area Sq Km	652 225	Currency	Afghani
Area Sq Miles	251 825	Languages	Dari, Pushtu, Uzbek, Turkmen
Population	21 354 000	Religions	Sunni Muslim, Shi'a Muslim
Capital	Kābul	Organizations	UN

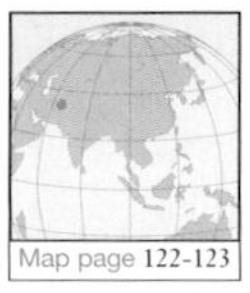
Map page 122-123

A landlocked country in central Asia, Afghanistan borders Pakistan, Iran, Turkmenistan, Uzbekistan, Tajikistan and China. The central highlands are bordered by plains in the north and southwest, and by the Hindu Kush to the northeast. The climate is dry with cold winters and hot summers. Over the last twenty years war has disrupted the economy which was highly dependent on farming and livestock rearing.

ALBANIA
Republic of Albania

Area Sq Km	28 748	Currency	Lek
Area Sq Miles	11 100	Languages	Albanian, Greek
Population	3 119 000	Religions	Sunni Muslim, Orthodox, Roman Catholic
Capital	Tiranë	Organizations	UN

Albania lies in the western Balkans in southeast Europe, on the Adriatic Sea. It is mountainous, with coastal plains where half the population lives. The economy is based on agriculture and mining, mainly chromium. The fall of communism brought foreign aid for the ailing economy, but Albania remains one of the poorest countries in Europe.

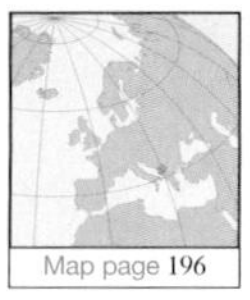
Map page 196

ALGERIA
Democratic and Popular Republic of Algeria

Area Sq Km	2 381 741	Currency	Dinar
Area Sq Miles	919 595	Languages	Arabic, French, Berber
Population	30 081 000	Religions	Sunni Muslim
Capital	Alger	Organizations	OPEC, UN

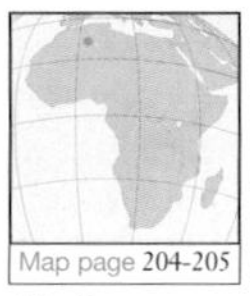
Map page 204-205

Algeria is on the Mediterranean coast of northwest Africa. The second largest country in Africa, it extends southwards from the coastal plain to the Atlas Mountains and to the Sahara which is dry sandstone plateau and desert, cut by valleys and rocky mountains, including the Hoggar in the southeast. The climate is Mediterranean on the coast, but dry inland. Most people live on the coastal plain and on the fertile northern slopes of the Atlas Mountains. Oil, natural gas and related products are the mainstay of the economy and account for over ninety five per cent of export earnings. Agriculture employs about a quarter of the workforce, producing mainly food crops; attempts are being made to diversify the economy, but unemployment remains high, as do social tensions.

American Samoa
United States Unincorporated Territory

Area Sq Km	197	Currency	US dollar
Area Sq Miles	76	Languages	Samoan, English
Population	63 000	Religions	Protestant, Roman Catholic
Capital	Fagatogo		

Lying in the south Pacific Ocean, American Samoa consists of five main islands and two coral atolls. The main island is Tutuila. The economy is strongly linked to the USA, tuna and tuna products are the main export.

Map page 78

ANDORRA
Principality of Andorra

Area Sq Km	465	Currency	French franc, Spanish peseta
Area Sq Miles	180	Languages	Spanish, Catalan, French
Population	72 000	Religions	Roman Catholic
Capital	Andorra la Vella	Organizations	UN

Map page 186

A landlocked state in southwest Europe, Andorra nestles in the Pyrenees between France and Spain. It consists of deep valleys and gorges, surrounded by mountains. Tourism (there are about ten million visitors a year) is the mainstay of the economy, banking is also important.

ANGOLA
Republic of Angola

Area Sq Km	1 246 700	Currency	Kwanza
Area Sq Miles	481 354	Languages	Portuguese, Bantu, local languages
Population	12 092 000	Religions	Roman Catholic, Protestant, traditional beliefs
Capital	Luanda	Organizations	SADC, UN

Angola lies on the Atlantic coast of southern central Africa. Its small northern province, Cabinda, is separated from the rest of the country by part of Democratic Republic of Congo. Much of Angola is high plateau, with a narrow coastal plain where most people live. The climate is equatorial in the north but desert in the south. Over eighty per cent of the population rely on subsistence agriculture. Angola is rich in minerals, and oil accounts for around seventy five per cent of exports earnings. Continued civil war for the last twenty years has restricted economic development.

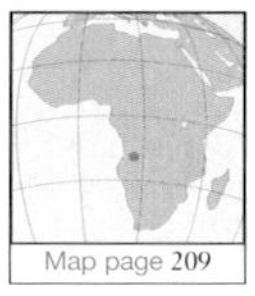
Map page 209

Anguilla
United Kingdom Overseas Territory

Area Sq Km	155	Currency	E. Carib. dollar
Area Sq Miles	60	Languages	English
Population	8 000	Religions	Protestant, Roman Catholic
Capital	The Valley		

Anguilla lies at the northern end of the Leeward Islands in the Caribbean. Tourism and fishing are the basis of the economy

Map page 247

ANTIGUA AND BARBUDA

Area Sq Km	442	Currency	E. Carib. dollar
Area Sq Miles	171	Languages	English, creole
Population	67 000	Religions	Protestant, Roman Catholic
Capital	St John's	Organizations	CARICOM, Comm., UN

Map page 247

The state comprises Antigua, Barbuda and the tiny island of Redonda, in the Leeward Islands in the eastern Caribbean. Antigua, the largest and most populous, is mainly hilly scrubland, with many beaches and a warm, dry climate. The economy relies heavily on tourism with about half the tourists coming from the USA.

ARGENTINA
Argentine Republic

Area Sq Km	2 766 889	Currency	Peso
Area Sq Miles	1 068 302	Languages	Spanish, Italian, Amerindian languages
Population	36 123 000	Religions	Roman Catholic, Protestant
Capital	Buenos Aires	Organizations	UN

Argentina occupies almost the whole of the southern part of South America, from Bolivia to Cape Horn and from the Andes to the Atlantic Ocean. The second largest South American state has four geographical regions: the subtropical forests and swampland in the northeast; the temperate fertile plains or Pampas in the centre, which support most of the farming and the bulk of the population; the wooded foothills and valleys of the Andes in the west; and the cold, semi-arid plateaus of Patagonia, in the south. The highest mountain in South America, Cerro Aconcagua is in Argentina. Nearly ninety per cent of the population live in towns and cities. Though declining as a percentage of the GDP, agricultural products still dominate exports, which include motor vehicles and crude oil. Most trade is with Brazil and the USA.

Map page 258-259

ARMENIA
Republic of Armenia

Area Sq Km	29 800	Currency	Dram
Area Sq Miles	11 506	Languages	Armenian, Azeri
Population	3 536 000	Religions	Armenian Orthodox
Capital	Yerevan	Organizations	CIS, UN

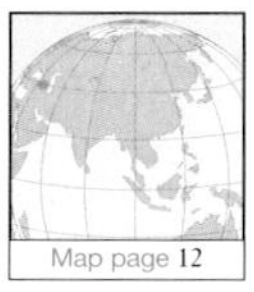
Map page 12

A landlocked state in southwest Asia, Armenia is in the south of the Lesser Caucasus and borders Georgia, Azerbaijan, Iran and Turkey. It is mountainous, with a central plateau-basin, and dry, with warm summers and cold winters. One third of the population lives in Yerevan. Armenia supports the ethnic Armenians in Nagorno-Karabkh in their separatist dispute with Azerbaijan. Economic growth has been slow; gold, jewellery and precious stones are important exports; many Armenians depend on remittances from abroad.

Aruba
Self-governing Netherlands Territory

Area Sq Km	193	Currency	Florin
Area Sq Miles	75	Languages	Papiamento, Dutch, English
Population	94 000	Religions	Roman Catholic, Protestant
Capital	Oranjestad		

The most southwesterly of the islands in the Lesser Antilles in the Caribbean, Aruba lies just off the coast of Venezuela. Tourism and offshore finance are the most important sectors of the economy.

Map page 247

Ascension Dependency of St Helena

Area Sq Km (Miles) 88 (34)	Population 1 100	Capital Georgetown

A volcanic island in the south Atlantic Ocean about 1300 kilometres (800 miles) northwest of St Helena.

Map page 216

AUSTRALIA
Commonwealth of Australia

Area Sq Km	7 682 395	Currency	Dollar
Area Sq Miles	2 966 189	Languages	English, Italian, Greek
Population	18 520 000	Religions	Protestant, Roman Catholic, Orthodox
Capital	Canberra	Organizations	APEC, Comm., OECD, UN

Australia, the world's sixth largest country, occupies the smallest, flattest and driest continent. The western half of the continent is mostly arid plateaus, ridges and vast deserts. The central-eastern area comprises the lowlands of river systems draining into Lake Eyre, while to the east is the Great Dividing Range, a belt of ridges and plateaus running from Queensland to Tasmania. Climatically more than two-thirds of the country is arid or semi-arid. The north is tropical monsoon, the east subtropical, and the southwest and southeast temperate. A majority of Australia's highly urbanized population lives in cities along on the east, southeast and southwest coasts. Australia is rich in natural resources. It has vast mineral deposits and various sources of energy. It is among the world's leading producers of iron ore, bauxite, nickel, copper and uranium, and other minerals include lead, gold, silver, zinc, manganese, tungsten and gems. It is a major producer of coal; oil and natural gas are also being exploited. Although accounting for only five per cent of the workforce, agriculture continues to be an important sector of the economy with food and agricultural raw materials making up around one third of exports by value; fuel, ores and metals, and manufactures account for the remainder of exports. Japan and the USA are Australia's main trading partners.

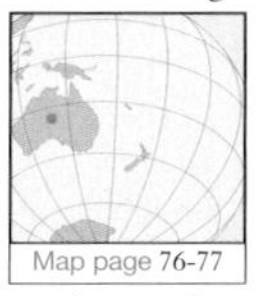
Map page 76-77

Australian Capital Territory (Federal territory)
Area Sq Km (Miles) 2 400 (927)	Population 299 243	Capital Canberra

New South Wales (State)
Area Sq Km (Miles) 801 600 (309 499)	Population 6 038 696	Capital Sydney

Northern Territory (Territory)
Area Sq Km (Miles) 1 346 200 (519 771)	Population 195 101	Capital Darwin

Queensland (State)
Area Sq Km (Miles) 1 727 200 (666 876)	Population 3 368 850	Capital Brisbane

South Australia (State)
Area Sq Km (Miles) 984 000 (379 925)	Population 1 427 936	Capital Adelaide

Tasmania (State)
Area Sq Km (Miles) 67 800 (26 178)	Population 459 659	Capital Hobart

Victoria (State)
Area Sq Km (Miles) 227 600 (87 877)	Population 4 373 520	Capital Melbourne

Western Australia (State)
Area Sq Km (Miles) 2 525 500 (975 101)	Population 1 726 095	Capital Perth

AUSTRIA
Republic of Austria

Area Sq Km	83 855	Currency	Schilling, Euro
Area Sq Miles	32 377	Languages	German, Croatian, Turkish
Population	8 140 000	Religions	Roman Catholic, Protestant
Capital	Wien (Vienna)	Organizations	EU, OECD, UN

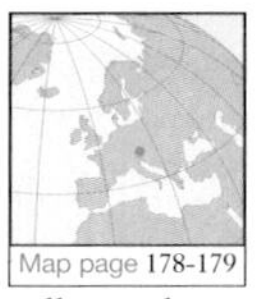
Map page 178-179

A landlocked state in central Europe, Austria borders the Czech Republic, Hungary, Slovenia, Switzerland, Italy, Germany and Liechtenstein. Two-thirds of the country, from the Swiss border to eastern Austria, lies within the Alps, with low mountains to the north. The only lowlands are in the east. The Danube river valley in the northeast contains almost all the agricultural land and most of the population. Though the climate varies with altitude, in general summers are warm and winters cold with heavy snowfalls. Manufacturing industry and tourism are the most important sectors of the economy. Exports are dominated by manufactured goods of which machinery and transport equipment make up over one third; Germany is Austria's main trading partner.

AZERBAIJAN
Azerbaijani Republic

Area Sq Km	86 600	Currency	Manat
Area Sq Miles	33 436	Languages	Azeri, Armenian, Russian, Lezgian
Population	7 669 000	Religions	Shi'a Muslim, Sunni Muslim, Orthodox
Capital	Bakı	Organizations	CIS, UN

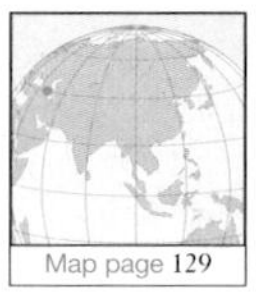
Map page 129

Azerbaijan lies to the southeast of the Caucasus, on the Caspian Sea. Its region of NaxÁivan is separated from the rest of the country by part of Armenia. It has mountains in the northeast and west, valleys in the centre and a low coastal plain. The climate is continental. It is rich in energy and mineral resources. Oil production, onshore and offshore, is the main industry and the basis of heavy industries. Agriculture is still important, with cotton and tobacco the main cash crops. War with Armenia has reduced output.

THE BAHAMAS
Commonwealth of The Bahamas

Area Sq Km	13 939	Currency	Dollar
Area Sq Miles	5 382	Languages	English, creole
Population	296 000	Religions	Protestant, Roman Catholic
Capital	Nassau	Organizations	CARICOM, Comm., UN

The Bahamas is an archipelago of about seven hundred islands and over two thousand cays, to the northeast of Cuba and east of the Florida coast of the USA. Twenty-two islands are inhabited, and two

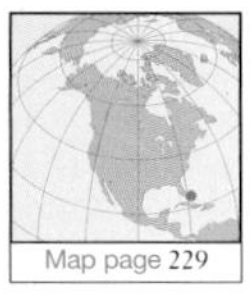

Map page 229

thirds of the population live on the main island of New Providence. The climate is warm for much of the year, with heavy rainfall in the summer. Tourism is the islands' main industry. Offshore banking, insurance and ship registration are also major foreign exchange earners.

BAHRAIN
State of Bahrain

Area Sq Km	691	Currency	Dinar
Area Sq Miles	267	Languages	Arabic, English
Population	595 000	Religions	Shi'a Muslim, Sunni Muslim, Christian
Capital	Manama	Organizations	UN

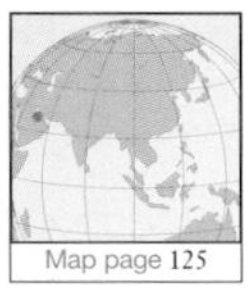

Map page 125

Bahrain consists of more than thirty islands lying in a bay in The Gulf, off the coasts of Saudi Arabia and Qatar. Bahrain Island, the largest island is connected to Muharraq and Sitrah islands by causeways. Oil production and processing are the main sectors of the economy.

BANGLADESH
People's Republic of Bangladesh

Area Sq Km	143 998	Currency	Taka
Area Sq Miles	55 598	Languages	Bengali, English
Population	124 774 000	Religions	Sunni Muslim, Hindu
Capital	Dhaka	Organizations	Comm., UN

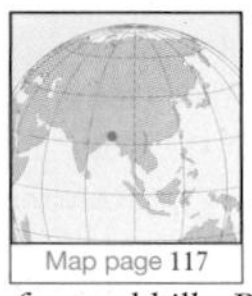

Map page 117

The south Asian state of Bangladesh is in the northeast of the Indian subcontinent, on the Bay of Bengal. It consists almost entirely of the low-lying alluvial plains and deltas of the Ganges and Brahmaputra rivers. The southwest is swampy, with mangrove forests in the delta area. The north, northeast and southeast have low forested hills. Bangladesh is one of the world's most densely populated and least developed countries. The economy is agriculture based, though the garment industry is the main export sector. Floods and cyclones during the summer monsoon season often cause devastating flooding and destroy crops. The country relies on large scale foreign aid and remittances from workers abroad.

BARBADOS

Area Sq Km	430	Currency	Dollar
Area Sq Miles	166	Languages	English, creole
Population	268 000	Religions	Protestant, Roman Catholic
Capital	Bridgetown	Organizations	CARICOM, Comm, UN

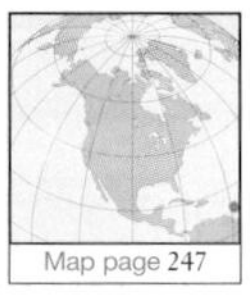

Map page 247

The most easterly of the Caribbean islands, Barbados is small and densely populated, with white-sand beaches and a tropical climate. The economy is based on tourism, financial services, light industries and sugar production.

BELARUS
Republic of Belarus

Area Sq Km	207 600	Currency	Rouble
Area Sq Miles	80 155	Languages	Belorussian, Russian
Population	10 315 000	Religions	Belorussian Orthodox, Roman Catholic
Capital	Minsk	Organizations	CIS, UN

Belarus is a landlocked state in east Europe, bounded by Lithuania, Latvia, Russia, Ukraine and Poland. Belarus consists of low hills and plains, with many lakes, rivers and, in the south, extensive marshes; forests cover around a third of the country. It has a continental climate. Agriculture contributes a third of national income, with beef cattle and grains as the major products. Manufacturing industries produce a range of items, from construction equipment to textiles. Belarus remains closely tied economically to Russia.

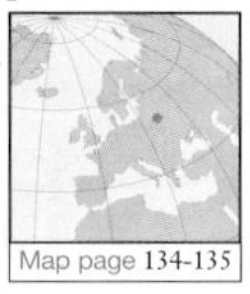

Map page 134-135

BELGIUM
Kingdom of Belgium

Area Sq Km	30 520	Currency	Franc, Euro
Area Sq Miles	11 784	Languages	Dutch (Flemish), French (Walloon), German
Population	10 141 000	Religions	Roman Catholic, Protestant
Capital	Bruxelles	Organizations	EU, OECD, UN

Belgium lies on the North Sea coast of western Europe. Beyond low sand dunes and a narrow belt of reclaimed land are fertile plains which extend to the Sambre-Meuse river valley from where the land rises to the forested Ardennes plateau in the southeast. Belgium has mild winters and cool summers. It is densely populated and has a highly urbanized population. The economy is based on trade, industry and services. With few mineral resources, Belgium imports raw materials for processing and manufacture. The agricultural sector is small, but provides for most food needs and a tenth of exports. A large services sector reflects Belgium's position as the home base for over eight hundred international institutions. The headquarters of the EU are in Bruxelles.

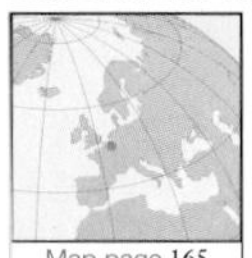

Map page 165

BELIZE

Area Sq Km	22 965	Currency	Dollar
Area Sq Miles	8 867	Languages	English, Spanish, Mayan, creole
Population	230 000	Religions	Roman Catholic, Protestant
Capital	Belmopan	Organizations	CARICOM, Comm., UN

Belize is on the Caribbean coast of central America and includes cays and a large barrier reef offshore. Belize's coastal areas are flat and swampy; the north and west are hilly, to the southwest are the Maya Mountains. Forests cover about half of the country. The climate is humid tropical, but tempered by sea breezes. A third of the population lives in the capital. The economy is based primarily on agriculture, forestry and fishing. Exports include raw sugar, orange concentrate and bananas.

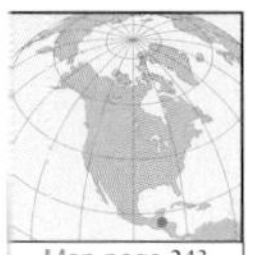

Map page 243

BENIN
Republic of Benin

Area Sq Km	112 620	Currency	CFA franc
Area Sq Miles	43 483	Languages	French, Fon, Yoruba, Adja, local languages
Population	5 781 000	Religions	Traditional beliefs, Roman Catholic, Sunni Muslim
Capital	Porto-Novo	Organizations	UN

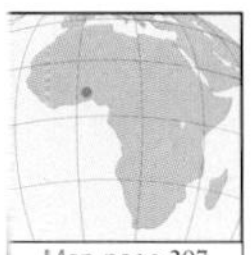

Map page 207

Benin is in west Africa, on the Gulf of Guinea. The climate is tropical in the north, but equatorial in the south. The economy is based mainly on agriculture and transit trade. Agricultural products account for two thirds of export earnings. Oil, produced offshore, is also a major export.

Bermuda
United Kingdom Overseas Territory

Area Sq Km	54	Currency	Dollar
Area Sq Miles	21	Languages	English
Population	64 000	Religions	Protestant, Roman Catholic
Capital	Hamilton		

In the Atlantic Ocean to the east of the USA, Bermuda is a group of small islands. The climate is warm and humid. The economy is based on tourism, insurance and shipping.

Map page 231

BHUTAN
Kingdom of Bhutan

Area Sq Km	46 620	Currency	Ngultrum
Area Sq Miles	18 000	Languages	Dzongkha, Nepali, Assamese
Population	2 004 000	Religions	Buddhist, Hindu
Capital	Thimphu	Organizations	UN

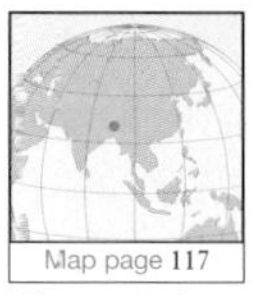

Map page 117

Bhutan is in the eastern Himalaya, between China and India. It is mountainous in the north, with fertile valleys where most people live. The climate ranges between permanently cold in the far north and subtropical in the south. Most of the population is involved in livestock raising and subsistence farming. Bhutan is the world's largest producer of cardamom. Tourism is an increasingly important foreign currency earner.

BOLIVIA
Republic of Bolivia

Area Sq Km	1 098 581	Currency	Boliviano
Area Sq Miles	424 164	Languages	Spanish, Quechua, Aymara
Population	7 957 000	Religions	Roman Catholic, Protestant, Baha'i
Capital	La Paz/Sucre	Organizations	UN

Map page 252-253

A landlocked state in central South America, Bolivia borders Brazil, Paraguay, Argentina, Chile and Peru. Most Bolivians live in the high plateau within the Andes ranges. The lowlands range between dense rainforest in the northeast and semi-arid grasslands in the southeast. Bolivia is rich in minerals (zinc, tin and silver) and sales generate around half of export income. Natural gas and timber are also exported. Subsistence farming predominates, though soya beans and, unofficially, coca are exported. USA is the main trading partner.

Bonaire part of Netherlands Antilles

Area Sq Km (Miles) 288 (111) Population 14 218

An island in the Caribbean Sea off the north coast of Venezuela; known for its fine beaches; tourism is the mainstay of the economy.

Map page 247

BOSNIA-HERZEGOVINA
Republic of Bosnia and Herzegovina

Area Sq Km	51 130	Currency	Marka
Area Sq Miles	19 741	Languages	Bosnian, Serbian, Croatian
Population	3 675 000	Religions	Sunni Muslim, Orthodox, Roman Catholic, Protestant
Capital	Sarajevo	Organizations	UN

Bosnia-Herzegovina lies in the western Balkans of southern Europe, on the Adriatic Sea. It is mountainous, with ridges running northwest-southeast. The main lowlands are around the Sava valley in the north. Summers are warm, but winters can be very cold. The Dayton Accord split the country into Republika Srpska and Federacija Bosna i Hercegovina. Much of the population relies on UN aid.

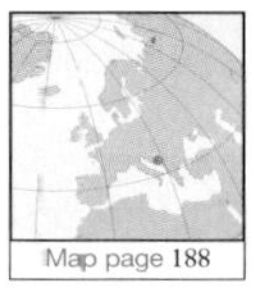

Map page 188

BOTSWANA
Republic of Botswana

Area Sq Km	581 370	Currency	Pula
Area Sq Miles	224 468	Languages	English, Setswana, Shona, local languages
Population	1 570 000	Religions	Traditional beliefs, Protestant, Roman Catholic
Capital	Gaborone	Organizations	Comm., SADC, UN

Botswana, a landlocked state in southern Africa, borders South Africa, Namibia, and Zimbabwe. Over half of the country lies within the Kalahari Desert, with swamps to the north and salt-pans to the northeast. Most people live near the eastern border. As a result of the AIDS epidemic, life expectancy has fallen by fourteen per cent since 1975. The climate is subtropical, but drought-prone. The economy was founded on cattle rearing, and though beef remains an important export, the economy is now based on mining. Diamonds account for eighty per cent of export earnings. Copper-nickel matte is also exported.

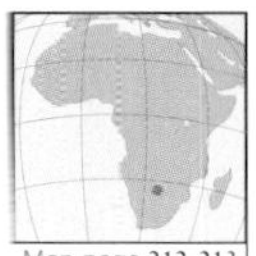

Map page 212-213

BRAZIL
Federative Republic of Brazil

Area Sq Km	8 547 379	Currency	Real
Area Sq Miles	3 300 161	Languages	Portuguese
Population	165 851 000	Religions	Roman Catholic, Protestant
Capital	Brasília	Organizations	UN

Brazil, in eastern South America, covers almost half of the continent - making it the world's fifth largest country - and borders ten countries and the Atlantic Ocean. The northwest contains the vast basin of the Amazon. The centre west is largely a vast plateau of savanna and rock escarpments. The northeast is mostly semi-arid plateaus, while to the east and south are rugged mountains, fertile valleys and narrow, fertile coastal plains. The Amazon basin is hot, humid and wet; the rest of Brazil is cooler and drier, with seasonal variations. The northeast is drought-prone. Most Brazilians live in urban areas along the coast and on the central plateau. Brazil has large and well developed agricultural, mining, and service sectors and the economy is larger than that of all other South American countries combined. Brazil is the world's largest producer of coffee, other agricultural crops include grains and sugar cane; mineral production includes iron, aluminium, and gold. Manufactured goods include food products, transport equipment, machinery and industrial chemicals. The main trading partners are USA and Argentina. Despite its natural wealth and being one of the largest economies in the world, Brazil has a large external debt and growing poverty gap.

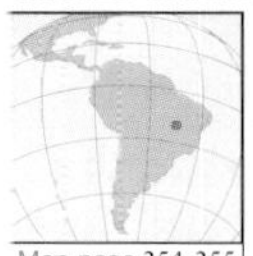

Map page 254-255

British Indian Ocean Territory
United Kingdom Overseas Territory

Area Sq Km (Miles) 60 (23) Population *uninhabited*

The territory consists of the Chagos Archipelago in central Indian Ocean. The islands are uninhabited apart from the joint British-US military base on Diego Garcia.

Map page 88

BRUNEI
State of Brunei Darussalam

Area Sq Km	5 765	Currency	Dollar
Area Sq Miles	2 226	Languages	Malay, English, Chinese
Population	315 000	Religions	Sunni Muslim, Buddhist, Christian
Capital	Bandar Seri Begawan	Organizations	APEC, ASEAN, Comm., UN

The southeast Asian state of Brunei lies on the northwest coast of the island of Borneo, on the South China Sea. Its two enclaves are surrounded inland by the Malaysian state of Sarawak. Tropical rainforest covers over two thirds of Brunei. The narrow coastal plain supports some crops and most of the population. The economy is dominated by the oil and gas industries.

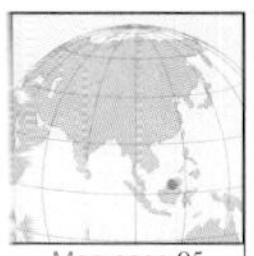

Map page 95

BULGARIA
Republic of Bulgaria

Area Sq Km	110 994	Currency	Lev
Area Sq Miles	42 855	Languages	Bulgarian, Turkish, Romany, Macedonian
Population	8 336 000	Religions	Bulgarian Orthodox, Sunni Muslim
Capital	Sofiya	Organizations	UN

Map page 197

Bulgaria, in south Europe, borders Romania, Yugoslavia, Macedonia, Greece, Turkey and the Black Sea. The Balkan Mountains separate the Danube plains in the north from the Rhodope Mountains and the lowlands in the south. The economy is based on agriculture and manufacturing, chiefly machinery, consumer goods, chemicals and metals. Recent fiscal reforms have reduced inflation and helped economic recovery. Bulgaria is negotiating to join the EU.

BURKINA
Democratic Republic of Burkina Faso

Area Sq Km	274 200	Currency	CFA franc
Area Sq Miles	105 869	Languages	French, Moore (Mossi), Fulani, local languages
Population	11 305 000	Religions	Sunni Muslim, traditional beliefs, Roman Catholic
Capital	Ouagadougou	Organizations	UN

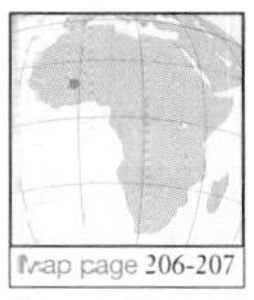

Map page 206-207

Burkina, a landlocked country in west Africa, borders Mali, Niger, Benin, Togo, Ghana and Côte d'Ivoire. The north of Burkina lies within the Sahara and is arid. The south is mainly semi-arid savanna. Rainfall is erratic and droughts are common. Livestock rearing and farming are the main activities. Cotton, livestock, groundnuts and some minerals are exported. Burkina relies heavily on aid, and is amongst the poorest and least developed countries in the world.

BURUNDI
Republic of Burundi

Area Sq Km	27 835	Currency	Franc
Area Sq Miles	10 747	Languages	Kirundi (Hutu, Tutsi), French
Population	6 457 000	Religions	Roman Catholic, traditional beliefs, Protestant
Capital	Bujumbura	Organizations	UN

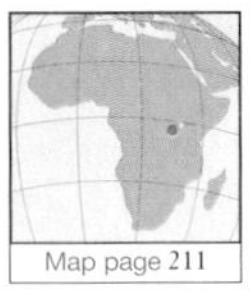
Map page 211

The densely populated east African state of Burundi borders Rwanda, Democratic Republic of Congo, Tanzania and Lake Tanganyika. It is hilly with high plateaus and a tropical climate. Burundi depends upon subsistence farming, coffee exports; ethnic violence in the mid 1990s increased dependence on foreign aid.

CAMBODIA
Kingdom of Cambodia

Area Sq Km	181 000	Currency	Riel
Area Sq Miles	69 884	Languages	Khmer, Vietnamese
Population	10 716 000	Religions	Buddhist, Roman Catholic, Sunni Muslim
Capital	Phnum Pénh	Organizations	ASEAN, UN

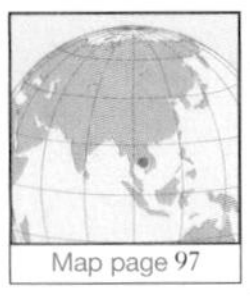
Map page 97

Cambodia lies in southeast Asia, on the Gulf of Thailand and occupies the Mekong river basin, with the Tônlé Sap at its centre; there are mountains in the southwest and north. The climate is tropical monsoon, forests cover half the land. Most people live on the plains and are engaged in farming (chiefly rice growing), fishing and forestry. Devastated by decades of civil war, continued political instability hampers development.

CAMEROON
Republic of Cameroon

Area Sq Km	475 442	Currency	CFA franc
Area Sq Miles	183 569	Languages	French, English, Fang, Bamileke, local languages
Population	14 305 000	Religions	Roman Catholic, Sunni Muslim, Protestant
Capital	Yaoundé	Organizations	Comm., UN

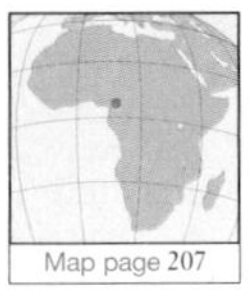
Map page 207

Cameroon is in west Africa, on the Gulf of Guinea. The coastal plains, southern and central plateaus are covered with tropical forest. Despite oil resources and favourable agricultural conditions Cameroon still faces problems of underdevelopment. Oil, timber and cocoa are the main exports. France is the main trading partner.

CANADA

Area Sq Km	9 970 610	Currency	Dollar
Area Sq Miles	3 849 674	Languages	English, French
Population	30 563 000	Religions	Roman Catholic, Protestant, Orthodox, Jewish
Capital	Ottawa	Organizations	APEC, Comm., OECD, UN

The world's second largest country, Canada covers the northern two-fifths of North America and has coastlines on the Atlantic, Arctic and Pacific Oceans. On the west coast, the mountain ranges include the Coast Mountains, interior plateaus and the Rocky Mountains. In the centre lie the fertile prairies. Further east, covering about half the total land area, is the Canadian Shield, fairly flat lowlands around the Hudson Bay extending to Labrador. The Shield is bordered to the south by the fertile Great Lakes-St Lawrence lowlands. In the far north climatic conditions are polar, the rest of Canada has a continental climate. Winters are long and cold with heavy snowfalls, while summers are hot with light to moderate rainfall. Most Canadians live in the south, chiefly in the southeast, in the urban areas of the Great Lakes-St Lawrence basin. Canada is rich in mineral and energy resources. Only five per cent of land is as arable, but that is still a large area. Canada is among the world's leading producers of wheat, a leading exporter of wood from its vast coniferous forests, and fish and seafood from its rich Atlantic and Pacific fishing grounds. It is a top producer of nickel, uranium, copper, iron ore, zinc and other minerals, as well as oil and natural gas. Its abundant raw materials are the basis for manufacturing industries. Main exports are machinery, motor vehicles, oil, timber, newsprint and paper, wood pulp and wheat. Since the 1989 free trade agreement with USA and the 1994 North America Free Trade Agreement (which includes Mexico), trade with the USA has grown and now accounts for around eighty per cent of imports and around seventy five per cent of exports.

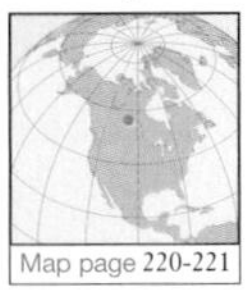
Map page 220-221

	Area Sq Km (Miles)	Population	Capital
Alberta (Province)	661 190 (255 287)	2 914 900	Edmonton
British Columbia (Province)	947 800 (365 948)	4 009 900	Victoria
Manitoba (Province)	649 950 (250 947)	1 138 000	Winnipeg
New Brunswick (Province)	73 440 (28 355)	753 000	Fredericton
Newfoundland (Province)	405 720 (156 649)	544 400	St John's
Northwest Territories (Province)	1 432 320 (553 022)	45 500	Yellowknife
Nova Scotia (Province)	55 490 (21 425)	934 600	Halifax
Nunavut (Territory)	1 994 000 (769 888)	22 000	Iqaluit
Ontario (Province)	1 068 580 (412 581)	11 411 500	Toronto
Prince Edward Island (Province)	5 660 (2 185)	136 400	Charlottetown
Québec (Province)	1 540 680 (594 860)	7 333 300	Québec
Saskatchewan (Province)	652 330 (251 866)	1 024 400	Regina
Yukon Territory (Territory)	483 450 (186 661)	31 700	Whitehorse

CAPE VERDE
Republic of Cape Verde

Area Sq Km	4 033	Currency	Escudo
Area Sq Miles	1 557	Languages	Portuguese, creole
Population	408 000	Religions	Roman Catholic, Protestant
Capital	Praia	Organizations	UN

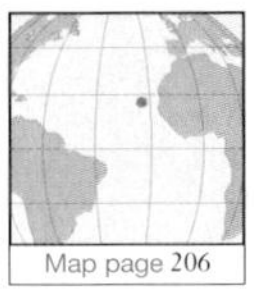
Map page 206

Cape Verde is a group of ten semi-arid volcanic islands off the coast of west Africa. The economy is based on fishing and subsistence farming, but relies on emigrant workers' remittances and foreign aid.

Cayman Islands
United Kingdom Overseas Territory

Area Sq Km	259	Currency	Dollar
Area Sq Miles	100	Languages	English
Population	36 000	Religions	Roman Catholic, Protestant
Capital	George Town	Organizations	UN

A group of islands in the Caribbean, northwest of Jamaica; there are three main islands: Grand Cayman, Little Cayman and Cayman Brac. They form one of the world's major offshore financial centres, tourism is also important and is aimed at the luxury market.

Map page 246

CENTRAL AFRICAN REPUBLIC

Area Sq Km	622 436	Currency	CFA franc
Area Sq Miles	240 324	Languages	French, Sango, Banda, Baya, local languages
Population	3 485 000	Religions	Protestant, Roman Catholic, trad. beliefs, Muslim
Capital	Bangui	Organizations	UN

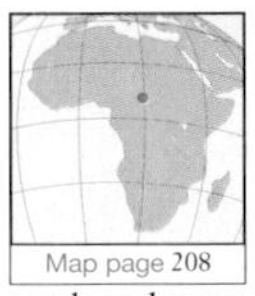
Map page 208

The landlocked Central African Republic borders Chad, Sudan, Democratic Republic of Congo, Congo and Cameroon. Most of the country is savanna plateau, drained by the Ubangi and Chari river systems, with mountains to the east and west. The climate is tropical with high rainfall. Most of the population live in the south and west, and a majority of the workforce is involved in subsistence farming. Some cotton, coffee, tobacco and timber are exported, but diamonds account for around half of export earnings.

CHAD
Republic of Chad

Area Sq Km	1 284 000	Currency	CFA franc
Area Sq Miles	495 755	Languages	Arabic, French, Sara, local languages
Population	7 270 000	Religions	Sunni Muslim, Roman Catholic, Protestant
Capital	Ndjamena	Organizations	UN

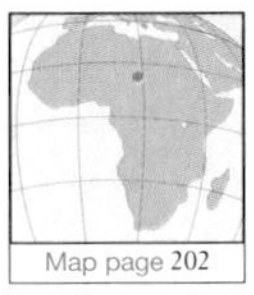
Map page 202

Chad is a landlocked state of central Africa, bordered by Libya, Sudan, Central African Republic, Niger, Nigeria and Cameroon. It consists of plateaus, the Tibesti mountains in the north and Lake Chad basin in the west. Climatic conditions range between desert in the north and tropical forest in the southwest. The largely rural population live in the south and near Lake Chad. Farming, cattle herding and fishing are the main activities; raw cotton is the main export. Chad relies heavily on foreign aid.

CHILE
Republic of Chile

Area Sq Km	756 945	Currency	Peso
Area Sq Miles	292 258	Languages	Spanish, Amerindian languages
Population	14 824 000	Religions	Roman Catholic, Protestant
Capital	Santiago	Organizations	APEC, UN

Chile lies along the Pacific coast of the southern half of South America. Between the Andes in the east and the lower coastal ranges, is a central valley, with a mild climate, where most Chileans live. To the north is the arid Atacama Desert, to the south is cold, wet forested grassland. Chile is the world's leading exporter of copper; nitrates, molybdenum, gold, iron are also important. Agriculture, forestry and fishing are important activities. Copper accounts for a third of the value of exports, other minerals, timber and fish production are also important.

Map page 258-259

CHINA
People's Republic of China

Area Sq Km	9 584 492	Currency	Yuan
Area Sq Miles	3 700 593	Languages	Mandarin, Wu, Cantonese, Hsiang, regional languages
Population	1 262 817 000	Religions	Confucian, Taoist, Buddhist, Christian, Muslim
Capital	Beijing	Organizations	APEC, UN

China, the world's most populous and third largest country, occupies almost the whole of east Asia, borders fourteen states and has coastlines on the Yellow, East China and South China Seas. It has an amazing variety of landscapes. The southwest contains the high Plateau of Tibet, flanked by the Himalaya and Kunlun Shan. The north is mountainous with arid basins and extends from the Tien Shan and Altai Mountains and vast Taklimakan Shamo in the west to the plateau and Gobi desert in the centre-east. Eastern China is predominantly lowland and is divided broadly into the basins of the Huang He (Yellow River) in the north, Chang Jiang (Yangtze) in the centre and Xi Jiang (Pearl River) in the southeast. Climatic conditions and vegetation are as diverse as the topography: much of the country experiences temperate conditions, while southwest China has an extreme mountain climate, and the southeast enjoys a moist, warm subtropical climate. Nearly seventy per cent of China's huge population live in rural areas, chiefly in the northern part of the eastern lowlands, in the Red Basin and along the coast. Agriculture employs around half of the working population. The main crops are rice, wheat, soya beans, peanuts, cotton, tobacco and hemp. China is rich in coal, oil and natural gas and has the world's largest potential in hydroelectric power; it is a major world producer of iron ore, molybdenum, copper, asbestos and gold. Economic reforms from the early 1980's onward led to an explosion in manufacturing development concentrated on the 'coastal economic open region'. The main exports are machinery, textiles, footwear, toy and sports goods. Japan and the USA are the main trading partners.

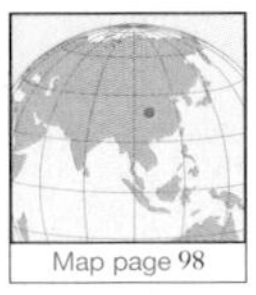
Map page 98

	Area Sq Km (Miles)	Population	Capital
Anhui (Province)	139 000 (53 668)	60 130 000	Hefei
Beijing (Municipality)	16 800 (6 487)	12 510 000	Beijing
Chongqing (Municipality)	23 000 (8 880)	14 600 000	Chongqing
Fujian (Province)	121 400 (46 873)	32 370 000	Fuzhou
Gansu (Province)	453 700 (175 175)	24 380 000	Lanzhou
Guangdong (Province)	178 000 (68 726)	68 680 000	Guangzhou
Guangxi Zhuangzu Zizhiqu (Autonomous Region)	236 000 (91 120)	45 430 000	Nanning
Guizhou (Province)	176 000 (67 954)	35 080 000	Guiyang
Hainan (Province)	34 000 (13 127)	7 240 000	Haikou
Hebei (Province)	187 700 (72 471)	64 370 000	Shijiazhuang
Heilongjiang (Province)	454 600 (175 522)	37 010 000	Harbin
Henan (Province)	167 000 (64 479)	91 000 000	Zhengzhou
Hong Kong (Special Administrative Region)	1 075 (415)	6 706 965	Hong Kong
Hubei (Province)	185 900 (71 776)	57 720 000	Wuhan
Hunan (Province)	210 000 (81 081)	63 920 000	Changsha
Jiangsu (Province)	102 600 (39 614)	70 660 000	Nanjing
Jiangxi (Province)	166 900 (64 440)	40 630 000	Nanchang
Jilin (Province)	187 000 (72 201)	25 920 000	Changchun
Liaoning (Province)	147 400 (56 911)	40 920 000	Shenyang
Macau (Special Administrative Region)	17 (7)	459 000	Macau
Nei Mongol Zizhiqu (Inner Mongolia) (Autonomous Region)	1 183 000 (456 759)	22 840 000	Huhhot
Ningxia Huizu Zizhiqu (Autonomous Region)	66 400 (25 637)	5 130 000	Yinchuan
Qinghai (Province)	721 000 (278 380)	4 810 000	Xining
Shaanxi (Province)	205 600 (79 383)	35 140 000	Xi'an
Shandong (Province)	153 300 (59 189)	87 050 000	Jinan
Shanghai (Municipality)	6 300 (2 432)	14 150 000	Shanghai
Shanxi (Province)	156 300 (60 348)	30 770 000	Taiyuan
Sichaun (Province)	569 000 (219 692)	98 650 000	Chengdu
Tianjin (Municipality)	11 300 (4 363)	9 420 000	Tianjin
Xinjiang Uygur Zizhiqu (Sinkiang) (Autonomous Region)	1 600 000 (617 763)	16 610 000	Ürümqi
Xizang Zizhiqu (Tibet) (Autonomous Region)	1 228 400 (474 288)	2 400 000	Lhasa
Yunnan (Province)	394 000 (152 124)	39 900 000	Kunming
Zhejiang (Province)	101 800 (39 305)	43 190 000	Hangzhou

Christmas Island
Australian External Territory

Area Sq Km	135	Currency	Austr. dollar
Area Sq Miles	52	Languages	English
Population	2 195	Religions	Buddhist, Sunni Muslim, Protestant, Roman Catholic
Capital	The Settlement		

The island is situated in the east of the Indian Ocean, to the south of Indonesia. The economy is based on phosphate extraction, though reserves are nearing depletion; tourism is developing and is the major employer.

Map page 86

Cocos Islands (Keeling Islands)
Australian External Territory

Area Sq Km	14	Currency	Austr. dollar
Area Sq Miles	5	Languages	English
Population	637	Religions	Sunni Muslim, Christian
Capital	West Island		

The Cocos Islands are two separate coral atolls in the east of the Indian Ocean between Sri Lanka and Australia. Most of the population live on West Island and Home Island. Coconuts are the only cash crop and the economy is based on these and on tourism.

Map page 86

COLOMBIA
Republic of Colombia

Area Sq Km	1 141 748	Currency	Peso
Area Sq Miles	440 831	Languages	Spanish, Amerindian languages
Population	40 803 000	Religions	Roman Catholic, Protestant
Capital	Bogotá	Organizations	APEC, UN

A state in northwest South America, Colombia has coastlines on the Pacific Ocean and the Caribbean Sea. Behind coastal plains lie three ranges of the Andes, separated by high valleys and plateaus where most Colombians live. To the southeast are grasslands and then the forests of the Amazon. Colombia has a tropical climate, though temperatures vary with altitude. Only five per cent of land can be cultivated, but a range of crops are grown. Coffee (Colombia is the world's second largest producer), sugar, bananas, cotton and flowers are exported. Coal, nickel, gold, silver, platinum and emeralds (Colombia

Map page 250

is the world's largest producer) are mined. Oil and its products are the main export. Industry involves processing minerals and agricultural produce. The main trade partner is the USA. In spite of government efforts to stop the drugs trade, coca growing and cocaine smuggling are rife.

COMOROS
Federal Islamic Republic of the Comoros

Area Sq Km	1 862	Currency	Franc
Area Sq Miles	719	Languages	Comorian, French, Arabic
Population	658 000	Religions	Sunni Muslim, Roman Catholic
Capital	Moroni	Organizations	UN

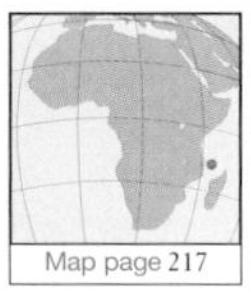

Map page 217

The state comprises three volcanic islands: Grande Comore, Anjouan and Mohéil, and some coral atolls in the Indian Ocean, off the east African coast. The tropical islands are mountainous, with poor soil. Subsistence farming predominates, but vanilla, cloves and ylang-ylang (an essential oil) are exported.

CONGO
Republic of the Congo

Area Sq Km	342 000	Currency	CFA franc
Area Sq Miles	132 047	Languages	French, Kongo, Monokutuba, local languages
Population	2 785 000	Religions	Roman Catholic, Protestant, trad. beliefs, Muslim
Capital	Brazzaville	Organizations	UN

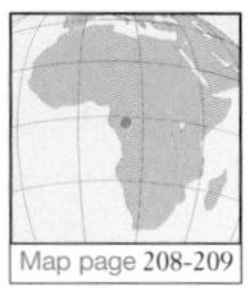

Map page 208-209

Congo, in central Africa, is mostly forest or savanna-covered plateaus drained by the Ubangi-Congo river systems. Sand dunes and lagoons line the short Atlantic coast. The climate is hot and tropical. Most Congolese live in the southern third of the country. Half of the workforce are farmers, growing food crops and cash crops including sugar, coffee, cocoa and oil palms. Oil makes up over three quarters of export revenues, hardwoods are the second biggest export earner.

CONGO, DEMOCRATIC REPUBLIC OF

Area Sq Km	2 345 410	Currency	Franc
Area Sq Miles	905 568	Languages	French, Lingala, Swahili, Kongo, local languages
Population	49 139 000	Religions	Christian, Sunni Muslim
Capital	Kinshasa	Organizations	SADC, UN

The central African state consists of the basin of the Congo river flanked by plateaus, with high mountain ranges to the east and a short Atlantic coastline to the west. The climate is tropical with rainforest

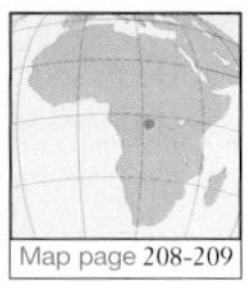

Map page 208-209

close to the Equator and savannas to the north and south. Congo has fertile land that grows a range of food crops and cash crops, chiefly coffee. It has vast mineral resources, copper, cobalt and diamonds being the most important. Continued political instability inhibits development.

Cook Islands
Self-governing New Zealand Territory

Area Sq Km	293	Currency	Dollar
Area Sq Miles	113	Languages	English, Maori
Population	19 000	Religions	Protestant, Roman Catholic
Capital	Avarua		

Groups of coral atolls and volcanic islands in the southwest Pacific Ocean. The main island is Rarotonga. Distance from foreign markets and few natural resources hinder development and there were severe economic problems in the late 1990s.

Map page 81

COSTA RICA
Republic of Costa Rica

Area Sq Km	51 100	Currency	Colón
Area Sq Miles	19 730	Languages	Spanish
Population	3 841 000	Religions	Roman Catholic, Protestant
Capital	San José	Organizations	UN

Costa Rica has coastlines on the Caribbean Sea and Pacific Ocean.

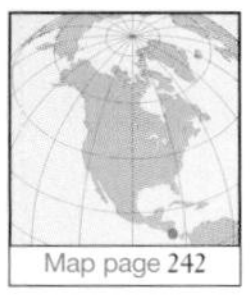

Map page 242

From the tropical coastal plains, the land rises to mountains and a temperate central plateau where most people live. The economy depends on tourism, with ecotourism becoming increasingly important, and agriculture; main exports are textiles, coffee and bananas; almost half of all trade is with USA.

CÔTE D'IVOIRE
Republic of Côte d'Ivoire

Area Sq Km	322 463	Currency	CFA franc
Area Sq Miles	124 504	Languages	French, creole, Akan, local languages
Population	14 292 000	Religions	Muslim, Roman Catholic, trad. beliefs, Protestant
Capital	Yamoussoukro	Organizations	UN

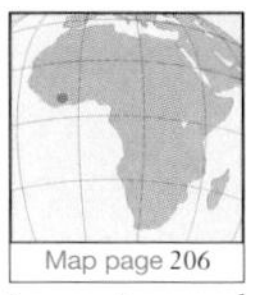

Map page 206

Côte d'Ivoire is in west Africa, on the Gulf of Guinea. In the north are plateaus and savanna, in the south are low undulating plains and rainforest, with sand-bars and lagoons on the coast. Temperatures are warm, and rainfall is heavier in the south. Most of the workforce is engaged in farming. Côte d'Ivoire is a major producer of cocoa and coffee, and agricultural products (including cotton and timber) are the main export. Oil and gas have begun to be exploited.

CROATIA
Republic of Croatia

Area Sq Km	56 538	Currency	Kuna
Area Sq Miles	21 829	Languages	Croatian, Serbian
Population	4 481 000	Religions	Roman Catholic, Serbian Orthodox, Sunni Muslim
Capital	Zagreb	Organizations	UN

The south European state of Croatia has a long coastline on the

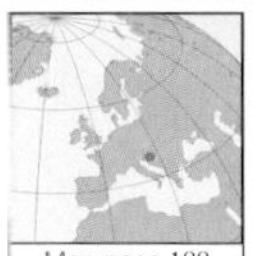

Map page 188

Adriatic Sea and many offshore islands. Coastal areas have a Mediterranean climate, inland is colder and wetter. Croatia was strong agriculturally and industrially, but conflict in 1991-1992, the loss of markets and tourist revenue have caused economic difficulties; recovery has been slow.

CUBA
Republic of Cuba

Area Sq Km	110 860	Currency	Peso
Area Sq Miles	42 803	Languages	Spanish
Population	110 860	Religions	Roman Catholic, Protestant
Capital	La Habana	Organizations	UN

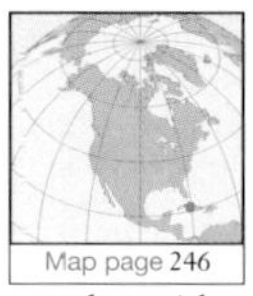

Map page 246

Cuba comprises the island of Cuba, the largest island in the Caribbean, and many islets and cays. A fifth of Cubans live in and around La Habana. Cuba is slowly recovering from the withdrawal of aid and subsidies from the former USSR. Sugar remains the basis of the economy, though tourism is developing and is, together with remittances from workers abroad, an important source of foreign currency.

Curaçao part of Netherlands Antilles

Area Sq Km (Miles) 444 (171)	Population 151 448	Capital Willemstad

An island in the Caribbean Sea off the north coast of Venezuela, it is the largest and most populous island of the Netherlands Antilles. Oil refining and tourism form the basis of the economy.

Map page 247

CYPRUS
Republic of Cyprus

Area Sq Km	9 251	Currency	Pound
Area Sq Miles	3 572	Languages	Greek, Turkish, English
Population	771 000	Religions	Greek Orthodox, Sunni Muslim
Capital	Lefkosia	Organizations	Comm., UN

The eastern Mediterranean island of Cyprus has hot dry summers

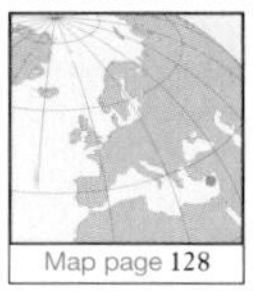

Map page 128

and mild winters. The economy of the Greek south is based mainly on specialist agriculture and tourism, though shipping and offshore banking are also major sources of income. The Turkish north depends upon agriculture, tourism and aid from Turkey. Cyprus is negotiating to join the EU.

CZECH REPUBLIC

Area Sq Km	78 864	Currency	Koruna
Area Sq Miles	30 450	Languages	Czech, Moravian, Slovak
Population	10 282 000	Religions	Roman Catholic, Protestant
Capital	Praha	Organizations	UN

Map page 176-177

The landlocked Czech Republic in central Europe consists of rolling countryside, wooded hills and fertile valleys. The climate is temperate, but winters are fairly cold. The country has substantial reserves of coal and lignite, timber and some minerals, chiefly iron ore. It is highly industrialized and major manufactures include industrial machinery, consumer goods, cars, iron and steel, chemicals and glass. Germany is the main trading partner. The Czech Republic began formal talks on EU accession in 1998.

DENMARK
Kingdom of Denmark

Area Sq Km	43 075	Currency	Krone
Area Sq Miles	16 631	Languages	Danish
Population	5 270 000	Religions	Protestant
Capital	København	Organizations	EU, OECD, UN

In north Europe, Denmark occupies the Jylland (Jutland) peninsula and nearly five hundred islands in and between the North and Baltic Seas. The country is low-lying, with long, indented coastlines. The climate is cool and temperate, with rainfall throughout the year. A fifth of the population lives around København on the largest of the islands, Sjælland (Zealand). Denmark's main natural resource is its agricultural potential; two thirds of the total area is fertile farmland or pasture. But agriculture is now high-tech and with forestry and fishing employs only around six per cent of the workforce. Denmark is self-sufficient in oil and natural gas, produced from fields in the North Sea. Manufacturing,

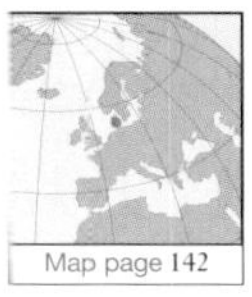

Map page 142

largely based on imported raw materials, now accounts for over half of exports which include machinery, food, furniture, and pharmaceuticals. The main trading partners are Germany and Sweden.

DJIBOUTI
Republic of Djibouti

Area Sq Km	23 200	Currency	Franc
Area Sq Miles	8 958	Languages	Somali, Afar, French, Arabic
Population	623 000	Religions	Sunni Muslim, Christian
Capital	Djibouti	Organizations	UN

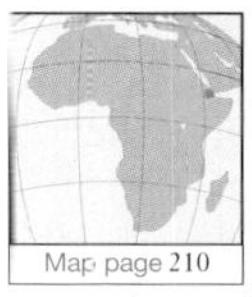

Map page 210

Djibouti lies in northeast Africa, on the Gulf of Aden at the entrance to the Red Sea. Most of the country is semi-arid desert with high temperatures and low rainfall. More than half of the population live in the capital. There is some camel, sheep and goat herding but with few natural resources, the economy is based on services and trade. The deep-water port and the railway line to Ādīs Ābeba in Ethiopia account for about two thirds of national income.

DOMINICA
Commonwealth of Dominica

Area Sq Km	750	Currency	E. Carib. dollar
Area Sq Miles	290	Languages	English, creole
Population	71 000	Religions	Roman Catholic, Protestant
Capital	Roseau	Organizations	CARICOM, Comm., UN

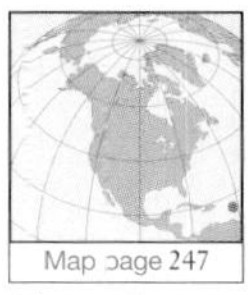

Map page 247

Dominica is the most northerly of the Windward Islands in the eastern Caribbean. It is very mountainous and forested, with a coastline of steep cliffs. The climate is tropical and rainfall abundant. Around a quarter of Dominicans live in the capital. The economy is based on agriculture, with bananas (the major export), coconuts and citrus fruits the most important crops. Tourism is developing, but is hindered by the rugged coastline and lack of sandy beaches.

DOMINICAN REPUBLIC

Area Sq Km	48 442	Currency	Peso
Area Sq Miles	18 704	Languages	Spanish, creole
Population	8 232 000	Religions	Roman Catholic, Protestant
Capital	Santo Domingo	Organizations	UN

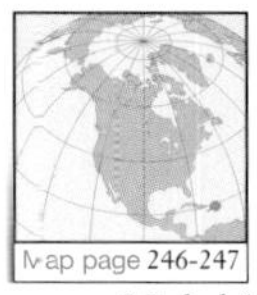

Map page 246-247

The state occupies the eastern two thirds of the Caribbean island of Hispaniola (the western third is Haiti). The frontier with Haiti is closed. It has a series of mountain ranges, fertile valleys and a large coastal plain in the east. The climate is hot tropical, with heavy rainfall. Sugar, coffee and cocoa are the main cash crops. Nickel (the main export), and gold are mined, and there is some light industry. USA is the main trading partner. Tourism is the main foreign exchange earner.

East Timor
under UN Transitional Administration

Area Sq Km	14 874	Languages	Portuguese, Tetun, English
Area Sq Miles	5 743	Religions	Roman Catholic
Population	857 000		
Capital	Dili		

The eastern part, and a small coastal enclave to the west, of the island Timor, which is part of Indonesian archipelago to the north of Western Australia. A referendum in 1999 officially ended Indonesia's occupation; East Timor is under a UN transitional administration.

Map page 93

ECUADOR
Republic of Ecuador

Area Sq Km	272 045	Currency	Sucre
Area Sq Miles	105 037	Languages	Spanish, Quechua, and other Amerindian languages
Population	12 175 000	Religions	Roman Catholic
Capital	Quito	Organizations	APEC, UN

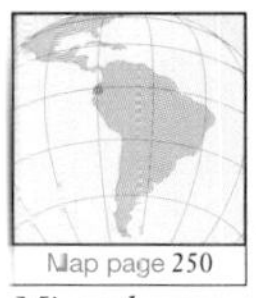

Map page 250

Ecuador is in northwest South America, on the Pacific coast. It consists of a broad coastal plain, the high ranges of the Andes and the forested upper Amazon basin to the east. The climate is tropical, moderated by altitude. Most people live on the coast or in the mountain valleys. Ecuador is one of South America's main oil producers. Mineral reserves include gold. Most of the workforce depends on agriculture; bananas, shrimps, coffee and cocoa are exported; USA is the main trading partner.

EGYPT
Arab Republic of Egypt

Area Sq Km	1 000 250	Currency	Pound
Area Sq Miles	386 199	Languages	Arabic
Population	65 978 000	Religions	Sunni Muslim, Coptic Christian
Capital	Cairo	Organizations	UN

Egypt, on the eastern Mediterranean coast of North Africa, is low-lying, with areas below sea level in the Qattâra depression, and mountain ranges along the Red Sea coast and in the Sinai peninsula. It is a land of desert and semi-desert, except for the Nile valley, where ninety nine per cent of Egyptians live, nearly half of them in towns and cities. A project for the development of Sinai aims to resettle over three million people in the area by 2017. The summers are hot, the winters mild and rainfall is negligible. Less than four per cent of land (chiefly around the Nile floodplain and delta) is cultivated, but farming employs about one third of the workforce; cotton is the main cash crop, rice, fruit and vegetables are exported, but Egypt imports

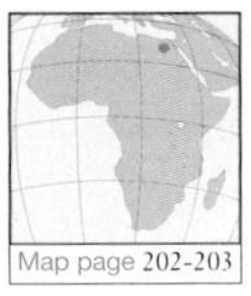
Map page 202-203

over half its food needs. There are oil and natural gas reserves, though nearly a quarter of electricity comes from hydro-electric power. Main exports are oil and oil products, cotton, textiles and clothing.

EL SALVADOR
Republic of El Salvador

Area Sq Km	21 041	Currency	Colón
Area Sq Miles	8 124	Languages	Spanish
Population	6 032 000	Religions	Roman Catholic, Protestant
Capital	San Salvador	Organizations	UN

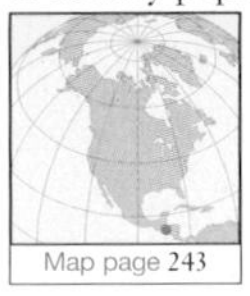
Map page 243

A densely populated state on the Pacific coast of central America, El Salvador has a coastal plain and volcanic mountain ranges that enclose a plateau where most people live. The coast is hot, with heavy summer rainfall, the highlands are cooler. Coffee (the chief export), sugar and cotton are main cash crops. The main trading partners are USA and Guatemala.

EQUATORIAL GUINEA
Republic of Equatorial Guinea

Area Sq Km	28 051	Currency	CFA franc
Area Sq Miles	10 831	Languages	Spanish, French, Fang
Population	431 000	Religions	Roman Catholic, traditional beliefs
Capital	Malabo	Organizations	UN

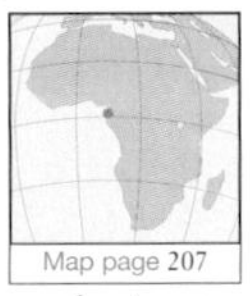
Map page 207

The state consists of Rio Muni, an enclave on the Atlantic coast of central Africa, and the islands of Bioco, Annobón and the Corisco group. Most people live on the coastal plain and upland plateau of Rio Muni; the capital is on the fertile volcanic island of Bioco. The climate is hot, humid and wet. Oil production started in 1992 and oil is now the main export along with timber, but the economy depends heavily upon foreign aid.

ERITREA
State of Eritrea

Area Sq Km	117 400	Currency	Nakfa
Area Sq Miles	45 328	Languages	Tigrinya, Tigre
Population	3 577 000	Religions	Sunni Muslim, Coptic Christian
Capital	Asmara	Organizations	UN

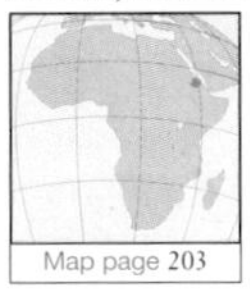
Map page 203

Eritrea, on the Red Sea coast of northeast Africa, consists of high plateau in the north and a coastal plain that widens to the south. The coast is hot, inland is cooler. Rainfall is unreliable. The agricultural-based economy has suffered from over thirty years of war and occasional poor rains. Eritrea is one of the least developed countries in the world.

ESTONIA
Republic of Estonia

Area Sq Km	45 200	Currency	Kroon
Area Sq Miles	17 452	Languages	Estonian, Russian
Population	1 429 000	Religions	Protestant, Estonian and Russian Orthodox
Capital	Tallinn	Organizations	UN

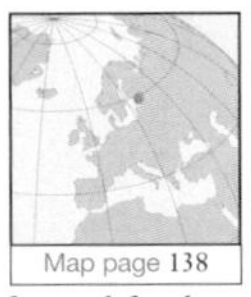
Map page 138

Estonia is in north Europe, on the Gulf of Finland and Baltic Sea. The land, over one third of which is forested, is generally low-lying, with many lakes. The climate is temperate. About one third of Estonians live in Tallinn. Industries and exported goods include timber, furniture production, shipbuilding, leather, fur and food processing. The main trading partners are Russia, Finland and Sweden. Estonia is negotiating to join the EU.

ETHIOPIA
Federal Democratic Republic of Ethiopia

Area Sq Km	1 133 880	Currency	Birr
Area Sq Miles	437 794	Languages	Oromo, Amharic, Tigrinya, local languages
Population	59 649 000	Religions	Ethiopian Orthodox, Muslim, trad. beliefs
Capital	Ādīs Ābeba	Organizations	UN

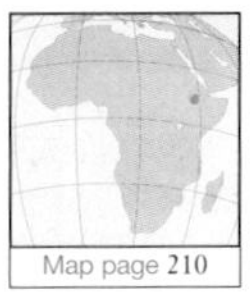
Map page 210

A landlocked country in northeast Africa, Ethiopia borders Eritrea, Djibouti, Somalia, Kenya and Sudan. The western half is a mountainous region traversed by the Great Rift Valley. To the east is mostly arid plateaus. The highlands are warm with summer rainfall, though droughts occur; the east is hot and dry. Most people live in the centre-north. Civil war, continued conflict with Eritrea and poor infrastructure hamper economic development. Subsistence farming is the main activity, though droughts have led to famine. Coffee is the main export and there is some light industry; Ethiopia remains one of the least developed countries in the world.

Falkland Islands
United Kingdom Overseas Territory

Area Sq Km	12 170	Currency	Pound
Area Sq Miles	4 699	Languages	English
Population	2 000	Religions	Protestant, Roman Catholic
Capital	Stanley		

Map page 259

Lying in the southwest Atlantic Ocean, northeast of Cape Horn, there are two main islands, West Falkland and East Falkland, where most of the population live, and many smaller islands. The economy is based on sheep farming and the sale of fishing licences, though oil has been discovered off-shore.

Faroe Islands
Self-governing Danish Territory

Area Sq Km	1 399	Currency	Danish krone
Area Sq Miles	540	Languages	Faroese, Danish
Population	43 000	Religions	Protestant
Capital	Tórshavn	Organizations	UN

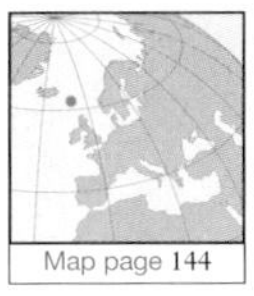
Map page 144

A self governing territory, lying in the north Atlantic Ocean between the UK and Iceland. The islands benefit from the North Atlantic Drift which has a moderating effect on the climate. The economy is based on deep-sea fishing.

FIJI
Sovereign Democratic Republic of Fiji

Area Sq Km	18 330	Currency	Dollar
Area Sq Miles	7 077	Languages	English, Fijian, Hindi
Population	796 000	Religions	Christian, Hindu, Sunni Muslim
Capital	Suva	Organizations	Comm., UN

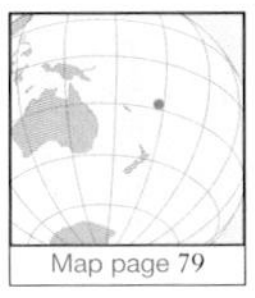
Map page 79

Fiji comprises two main islands, Vanua Levu and Viti Levu of volcanic origin and mountainous, and over three hundred smaller islands in the south Pacific Ocean. The climate is tropical and the economy is based on agriculture (chiefly sugar, the main export), fishing, forestry, gold mining and tourism.

FINLAND
Republic of Finland

Area Sq Km	338 145	Currency	Markka, Euro
Area Sq Miles	130 559	Languages	Finnish, Swedish
Population	5 154 000	Religions	Protestant, Greek Orthodox
Capital	Helsinki	Organizations	EU, OECD, UN

Finland is in north Europe, on the Gulf of Bothnia and the Gulf of Finland. It is low-lying, forests cover over seventy per cent of the land area, only about eight per cent is cultivated, though Finland is self-sufficient in cereals and dairy products. Summers are short and warm, and winters are long and severe, particularly in the north. Most people live in the southern third of the country, along the coast or near the many lakes. Timber is a major resource and there are important mineral resources, chiefly chromium. Main industries include metal working, electronics, paper and paper products, and chemicals; these account for most of the exports. The main trading partners are Germany, Sweden and the UK.

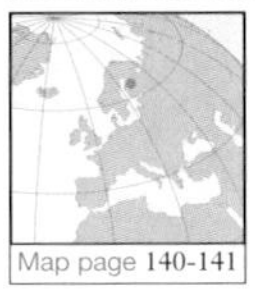
Map page 140-141

FRANCE
French Republic

Area Sq Km	543 965	Currency	Franc, Euro
Area Sq Miles	210 026	Languages	French, Arabic
Population	58 683 000	Religions	Roman Catholic, Protestant, Sunni Muslim
Capital	Paris	Organizations	EU, OECD, UN

France lies in southwest Europe, with coastlines on the Atlantic Ocean and Mediterranean Sea; it includes the Mediterranean island of Corsica. Northern and western regions consist mostly of flat or rolling countryside, and include the major lowlands of the Paris basin, the Loire valley and the Aquitaine basin, drained by the Seine, Loire and Garonne river systems respectively. The centre-south is dominated by the Massif Central. Eastwards, are the Vosges and Jura mountains and the Alps. In the southwest, the Pyrenees form a natural border with Spain. The climate is temperate with warm summers and cool winters, apart from the Mediterranean coast which has hot, dry summers and mild winters with some rainfall. Over seventy per cent of the population live in towns, but Greater Paris is the only major conurbation, with almost a sixth of the French population. Rich soil, a large cultivable area and contrasts in temperature and relief have given France a substantial and varied agricultural base; it is a major producer of both fresh and processed food. Major agricultural exports include cereals (chiefly wheat), dairy products, wines and sugar. France has relatively few mineral resources; it has coal reserves, some oil and natural gas, but it relies heavily on nuclear and hydroelectric power and imported fuels. France is one of the world's major industrial countries. Main industries include food processing, iron, steel and aluminium production, chemicals, cars, electronics and oil refining. The main exports are machinery, agricultural products, cars and other transport equipment. France has a strong services sector and tourism is a major source of revenue and employment. Trade is predominantly with other EU countries.

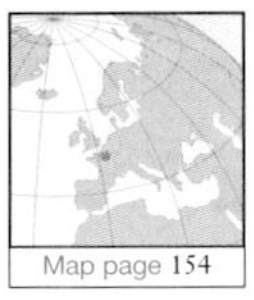
Map page 154

French Guiana
French Overseas Department

Area Sq Km	90 000	Currency	French franc
Area Sq Miles	34 749	Languages	French, creole
Population	167 000	Religions	Roman Catholic
Capital	Cayenne		

French Guiana, on the northeast coast of South America, is densely forested. The climate is tropical with high rainfall. Most people live in the coastal strip; agriculture is mostly subsistence farming; forestry and fishing are important, though timber and mineral resources are largely unexploited and industry is limited. French Guiana depends upon French aid. The European Space Agency (ESA) base is near Kourou.

Map page 251

FRENCH POLYNESIA
French Overseas Territory

Area Sq Km	3 265	Currency	Pacific franc
Area Sq Miles	1 261	Languages	French, Tahitian, Polynesian languages
Population	227 000	Religions	Protestant, Roman Catholic
Capital	Papeete		

Extending over a vast area of the southeast Pacific Ocean, French Polynesia comprises more than one hundred and thirty islands and coral atolls. The main island groups are the Marquesas Islands, the Tuamotu Archipelago and the Society Islands. The capital, Papeete, is on Tahiti in the Society Islands. The climate is subtropical and the economy is based on tourism.

Map page 79

French Southern and Antarctic Lands
French Overseas Territory

Area Sq Km (Miles) 439 580 (169 723) Population *uninhabited*

This territory includes Crozet Island, Kerguelen, Amsterdam Island and St Paul Island. All are uninhabited apart from scientific research staff. In accordance with the Antarctic Treaty, French territorial claims in Antarctica have been suspended.

Map page 73

GABON
Gabonese Republic

Area Sq Km	267 667	Currency	CFA franc
Area Sq Miles	103 347	Languages	French, Fang, local languages
Population	1 167 000	Religions	Roman Catholic, Protestant, traditional beliefs
Capital	Libreville	Organizations	UN

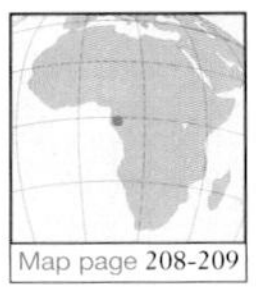
Map page 208-209

Gabon, on the Atlantic coast of central Africa consists of low plateaus, with a coastal plain lined by lagoons and mangrove swamps. The climate is tropical and rainforests cover over three quarters of the land area. Over seventy per cent of the population lives in towns. The economy is heavily dependent on oil, which accounts for around eighty per cent of exports; manganese, uranium and timber are the other exports. Agriculture is mainly at subsistence level.

THE GAMBIA
Republic of The Gambia

Area Sq Km	11 295	Currency	Dalasi
Area Sq Miles	4 361	Languages	English, Malinke, Fulani, Wolof
Population	1 229 000	Religions	Sunni Muslim, Protestant
Capital	Banjul	Organizations	Comm., UN

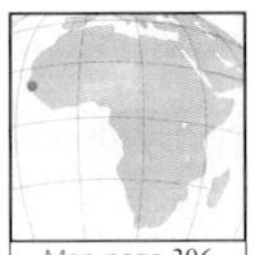
Map page 206

The Gambia, on the coast of west Africa, occupies a strip of land along the lower Gambia river. Sandy beaches are backed by mangrove swamps, beyond which is savanna. The climate is tropical, with rainfall in the summer. Over seventy per cent of Gambians are farmers, growing chiefly groundnuts (the main export) but also cotton, oil palms and food crops. Livestock rearing and fishing are important, while manufacturing is limited. Re-exports, mainly from Senegal, and tourism are major sources of income.

Gaza semi-autonomous region

Area Sq Km	363	Currency	Israeli shekel
Area Sq Miles	140	Languages	Arabic
Population	1 036 000	Religions	Sunni Muslim, Shi'a Muslim
Capital	Gaza		

Gaza is a narrow strip of land on the southeast corner of the Mediterranean Sea, between Egypt and Israel. The Palestinian territory has limited autonomy from Israel.

Map page 128

GEORGIA
Republic of Georgia

Area Sq Km	69 700	Currency	Lari
Area Sq Miles	26 911	Languages	Georgian, Russian, Armenian, Azeri, Ossetian, Abkhaz
Population	5 059 000	Religions	Georgian Orthodox, Russian Orthodox, Sunni Muslim
Capital	T'bilisi	Organizations	CIS, UN

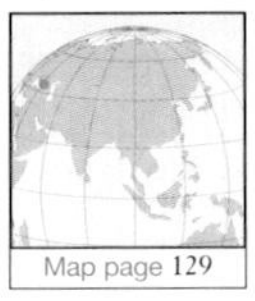
Map page 129

Georgia is in the northwest Caucasus, in southwest Asia, on the Black Sea. Mountain ranges in the north and south flank the Kura and Rioni valleys. The climate is generally mild, but subtropical along the coast. Agriculture is important, with tea, grapes, and citrus fruits the main crops. Mineral resources include manganese, coal and oil, and the main industries are steel, oil refining and machine building. Economic development remains slow.

GERMANY
Federal Republic of Germany

Area Sq Km	357 028	Currency	Mark, Euro
Area Sq Miles	137 849	Languages	German, Turkish
Population	82 133 000	Religions	Protestant, Roman Catholic
Capital	Berlin	Organizations	EU, OECD, UN

The west European state of Germany borders nine countries and has coastlines on the North and Baltic Seas. Behind the indented coastline, and covering about one third of the country, is the north German plain, a region of fertile farmland and sandy heaths drained by the country's major rivers. The central highlands are a belt of forested hills and plateaus which stretches from the Eifel region in the west to the Erzgebirge along the border with the Czech Republic. Farther south the land rises to the Schwäbische Alb, with the high rugged and forested Schwarzald (Black Forest) in the southwest and the Alps in the far south. The climate is temperate, with continental conditions in eastern areas where

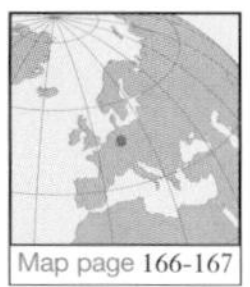
Map page 166-167

winters are colder. The population is highly urbanized with over eighty-five per cent living in cities and towns. With the exception of coal, lignite, potash and baryte, Germany lacks minerals and other industrial raw materials. It has a small agricultural base, though a few products (chiefly wines and beers) enjoy an international reputation. Germany is the world's third ranking economy after that of USA and Japan. It's industries are amongst the world's most technologically advanced, producing machinery, motor vehicles, electrical equipment, chemicals and pharmaceuticals. The majority of trade is with other countries in the EU.

State	Area Sq Km (Miles)	Population	Capital
Baden-Württemberg (State)	35 751 (13 804)	10 374 505	Stuttgart
Bayern (State)	70 552 (27 240)	12 043 869	München
Berlin(State)	891 (344)	3 467 322	Berlin
Brandenburg(State)	29 476 (11 381)	2 554 441	Potsdam
Bremen(State)	404 (156)	678 731	Bremen
Hamburg(State)	755 (292)	1 708 528	Hamburg
Hessen(State)	21 114 (8 152)	6 027 284	Wiesbaden
Mecklenburg-Vorpommern(State)	23 170 (8 946)	1 817 196	Schwerin
Niedersachsen(State)	47 612 (18 383)	7 795 149	Hannover
Nordrhein-Westfalen(State)	34 079 (13 158)	17 947 715	Düsseldorf
Rheinland-Pfalz(State)	19 853 (7 665)	4 009 753	Mainz
Saarland(State)	2 570 (992)	1 084 184	Saarbrücken
Sachsen(State)	18 413 (7 109)	4 545 702	Dresden
Sachsen-Anhalt(State)	20 446 (7 894)	2 731 463	Magdeburg
Schleswig-Holstein(State)	15 771 (6 089)	2 742 293	Kiel
Thüringen(State)	16 171 (6 244)	2 491 119	Erfurt

GHANA
Republic of Ghana

Area Sq Km	238 537	Currency	Cedi
Area Sq Miles	92 100	Languages	English, Hausa, Akan, local languages
Population	19 162 000	Religions	Christian, Sunni Muslim, traditional beliefs
Capital	Accra	Organizations	Comm., UN

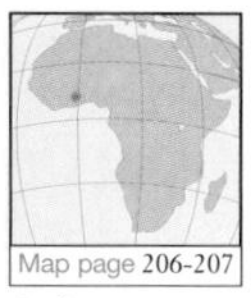
Map page 206-207

A west African state on the Gulf of Guinea, Ghana is a land of plains and low plateaus covered with savanna and rainforest. In the east is the Volta basin. The climate is tropical, with high rainfall in the south, where most people live. Agriculture employs around sixty per-cent of the workforce, main exports are gold, timber, cocoa and manganese ore.

Gibraltar
United Kingdom Overseas Territory

Area Sq Km	7	Currency	Pound
Area Sq Miles	3	Languages	English, Spanish
Population	25 000	Religions	Roman Catholic, Protestant, Sunni Muslim
Capital	Gibraltar		

Gibraltar lies on the south coast of Spain at the western entrance to the Mediterranean Sea. The economy depends on tourism, offshore banking and shipping services.

Map page 185

GREECE
Hellenic Republic

Area Sq Km	131 957	Currency	Drachma
Area Sq Miles	50 949	Languages	Greek
Population	10 600 000	Religions	Greek Orthodox, Sunni Muslim
Capital	Athina	Organizations	EU, OECD, UN

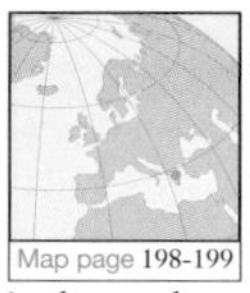
Map page 198-199

Greece occupies the southern Balkans in south Europe and many islands in the Ionian, Aegean and Mediterranean Seas. The islands make up over one fifth of its area. Mountains and hills cover much of the country. The most important lowlands are the plains of Thessalia in the centre-east and around Thessalonika in the northeast. Summers are hot and dry. Winters are mild and wet, but colder in the north with heavy snowfalls in the mountains. One third of Greeks live in the Athina area. Employment in agriculture is decreasing, but still accounts for around twenty per cent of the workforce and exports include citrus fruits, raisins, wine, olives and olive oil. Aluminium and nickel are mined and a wide range of manufactures are produced including food and tobacco, textiles, clothing, and chemicals. Tourism is an important industry and there is a large services sector. Most trade is with other EU countries.

GREENLAND
Self-governing Danish Territory

Area Sq Km	2 175 600	Currency	Danish krone
Area Sq Miles	840 004	Languages	Greenlandic, Danish
Population	56 000	Religions	Protestant
Capital	Nuuk		

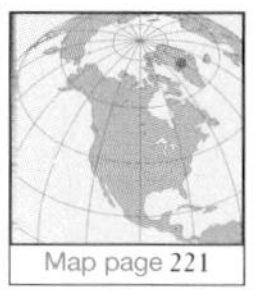
Map page 221

Situated to the northeast of North America between the Atlantic and Arctic Oceans, Greenland is the largest island in the world. It has a polar climate and over eighty per cent of the land area is permanent ice cap. The economy is based on fishing and fish processing.

GRENADA

Area Sq Km	378	Currency	E. Carib. dollar
Area Sq Miles	146	Languages	English, creole
Population	93 000	Religions	Roman Catholic, Protestant
Capital	St George's	Organizations	CARICOM, Comm., UN

The Caribbean state comprises Grenada, the most southerly of the Windward Islands, and the southern islands of The Grenadines. Grenada has wooded hills, beaches in the southwest, a warm climate and good rainfall. Agriculture is the main activity, with bananas, nutmeg and cocoa the main exports. Tourism is the main foreign exchange earner.

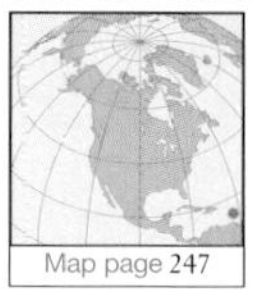
Map page 247

Guadeloupe
French Overseas Department

Area Sq Km	1 780	Currency	French franc
Area Sq Miles	687	Languages	French, creole
Population	443 000	Religions	Roman Catholic
Capital	Basse-Terre		

Guadeloupe, in the Leeward Islands in the Caribbean, consists of two main islands, Basse-Terre and Grande Terre, connected by a bridge, Marie Galante and a few outer islands. The climate is tropical, but moderated by trade winds. Bananas, sugar and rum, tourism and French aid are the main sources of foreign exchange.

Map page 247

Guam
United States Unincorporated Territory

Area Sq Km	541	Currency	US dollar
Area Sq Miles	209	Languages	Chamorro, English, Tagalog
Population	161 000	Religions	Roman Catholic
Capital	Agana		

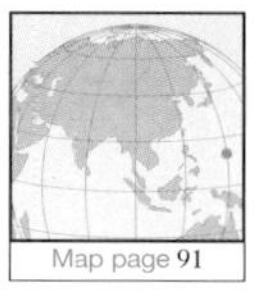
Map page 91

Lying at the south end of the North Mariana Islands in the western Pacific Ocean, Guam has a humid tropical climate. The island has a large US military base and the economy relies on that and on tourism, which has grown rapidly.

GUATEMALA
Republic of Guatemala

Area Sq Km	108 890	Currency	Quetzal
Area Sq Miles	42 043	Languages	Spanish, Mayan languages
Population	10 801 000	Religions	Roman Catholic, Protestant
Capital	Guatemala	Organizations	UN

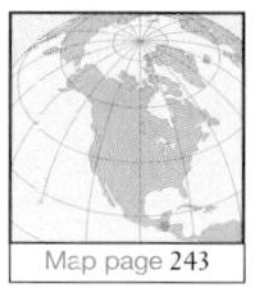
Map page 243

The most populous country in Central America after Mexico, Guatemala has a long Pacific and a short Caribbean coastline. Northern areas are lowland tropical forests. To the south lie mountain ranges with some active volcanoes, then the Pacific coastal plain. The climate is hot tropical in the lowlands, cooler in the highlands, where most people live. Farming is the main activity, coffee, sugar and bananas are the main exports. There is some manufacturing (chiefly clothing and textiles). Most trade is with USA.

GUERNSEY
United Kingdom Crown Dependency

Area Sq Km	78	Currency	Pound
Area Sq Miles	30	Languages	English, French
Population	64 555	Religions	Protestant, Roman Catholic
Capital	St Peter Port		

One of the Channel Islands lying off the west coast of the Cherbourg peninsula in northern France.

Map page 158

GUINEA
Republic of Guinea

Area Sq Km	245 857	Currency	Franc
Area Sq Miles	94 926	Languages	French, Fulani, Malinke, local languages
Population	7 337 000	Religions	Sunni Muslim, traditional beliefs, Christian
Capital	Conakry	Organizations	UN

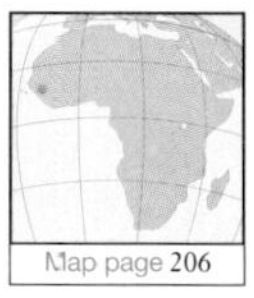
Map page 206

Guinea is in west Africa, on the Atlantic Ocean. There are mangrove swamps along the coast, inland are lowlands and then the Fouta Djallon mountains and plateaus. To the east are savanna plains drained by the upper Niger river system, while to the southeast are mountains. The climate is tropical, with high coastal rainfall. Agriculture is the main activity employing nearly eighty per cent of the workforce, with coffee, bananas and pineapples the chief cash crops. There are huge reserves of bauxite; bauxite, alumina, gold, coffee and diamonds are the main exports.

GUINEA-BISSAU
Republic of Guinea-Bissau

Area Sq Km	36 125	Currency	CFA franc
Area Sq Miles	13 948	Languages	Portuguese, crioulo, local languages
Population	1 161 000	Religions	Traditional beliefs, Sunni Muslim, Christian
Capital	Bissau	Organizations	UN

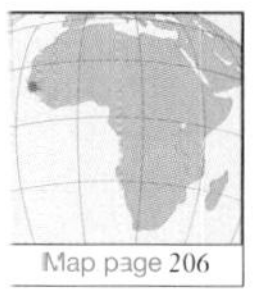
Map page 206

Guinea-Bissau, on the Atlantic coast of west Africa, includes the Bijagos Archipelago. The mainland coast is swampy and contains many estuaries. Inland are forested plains and to the east are savanna plateaus. The climate is tropical. The economy is based mainly on subsistence farming, there is little industry and timber and mineral resources are largely unexploited. Cashews make up over eighty per cent of exports. Guinea-Bissau is one of the least developed countries in the world.

GUYANA
Co-operative Republic of Guyana

Area Sq Km	214 969	Currency	Dollar
Area Sq Miles	83 000	Languages	English, creole, Amerindian languages
Population	850 000	Religions	Protestant, Hindu, Roman Catholic, Sunni Muslim
Capital	Georgetown	Organizations	CARICOM, Comm., UN

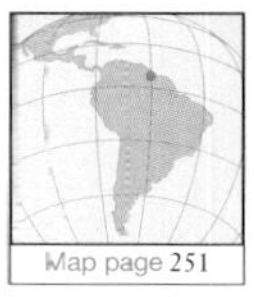
Map page 251

Guyana, on the northeast coast of South America, consists of the highlands in the west, and the savanna uplands of the southwest. Most of the country is densely forested; a lowland coastal belt supports crops and most of the population. The generally hot, humid and wet conditions are modified along the coast by sea breezes. The economy is based on agriculture, mining and forestry. Sugar, bauxite, gold, rice and timber are the main exports.

HAITI
Republic of Haiti

Area Sq Km	27 750	Currency	Gourde
Area Sq Miles	10 714	Languages	French, creole
Population	7 952 000	Religions	Roman Catholic, Protestant, Voodoo
Capital	Port-au-Prince	Organizations	CARICOM, UN

Haiti, occupying the western third of the Caribbean island of Hispaniola, is a mountainous state, with small coastal plains and a central valley. The Dominican Republic occupies the rest of the island. The climate is tropical, hottest in coastal areas. Haiti has few natural resources, is overpopulated and relies on exports of local crafts and coffee, and remittances from workers abroad.

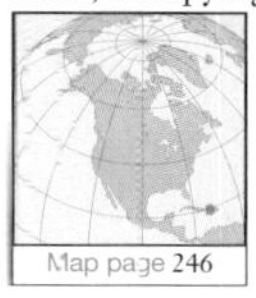
Map page 246

HONDURAS
Republic of Honduras

Area Sq Km	112 088	Currency	Lempira
Area Sq Miles	43 277	Languages	Spanish, Amerindian languages
Population	6 147 000	Religions	Roman Catholic, Protestant
Capital	Tegucigalpa	Organizations	UN

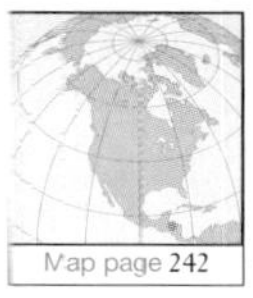
Map page 242

Honduras, in central America, is a mountainous and forested country with lowland areas along its long Caribbean and short Pacific coasts. Coastal areas are hot and humid with heavy summer rainfall, inland is cooler and drier. Most people live in the central valleys. Coffee and bananas are the main exports, along with shrimps and zinc. Industry involves mainly agricultural processing. Honduras was the country hardest hit by hurricane Mitch in 1998 but has received significant aid for reconstruction.

HUNGARY
Republic of Hungary

Area Sq Km	93 030	Currency	Forint
Area Sq Miles	35 919	Languages	Hungarian
Population	10 116 000	Religions	Roman Catholic, Protestant
Capital	Budapest	Organizations	OECD, UN

Map page 176-177

A landlocked country in central Europe, Hungary borders Austria, Slovakia, Ukraine, Romania, Yugoslavia, Croatia and Slovenia. The Danube river flows north-south through central Hungary. To the east lies a great plain, flanked by highlands in the north. To the west low mountains and Lake Balaton separate a small plain and southern uplands. The climate is continental, with warm summers and cold winters. Sixty per cent of the population live in urban areas, and one fifth lives in Budapest. Some minerals and energy resources are exploited, chiefly bauxite, coal and natural gas. Hungary has an industrial economy. The main industries produce metals, machinery, transport equipment, chemicals and food products. The main trading partners are Germany and Austria. Hungary is negotiating to join the EU.

ICELAND
Republic of Iceland

Area Sq Km	102 820	Currency	Króna
Area Sq Miles	39 699	Languages	Icelandic
Population	276 000	Religions	Protestant
Capital	Reykjavik	Organizations	OECD, UN

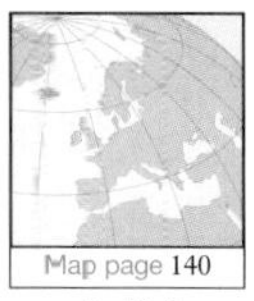
Map page 140

Iceland lies in the Atlantic Ocean, near the Arctic Circle to the northwest of Scandinavia. It consists mainly of a plateau of basalt lava flows. Some of its two hundred volcanoes are active, and there are geysers and hot springs; one tenth of the country is covered by ice caps. Only coastal lowlands can be cultivated and settled, and over half the population lives in the Reykjavik area. The climate is mild, moderated by the North Atlantic Drift and southwesterly winds. The mainstay of the economy is fishing and fish processing, which account for seventy per cent of exports. Agriculture involves mainly sheep and dairy farming. Hydro-electric and geothermal energy resources are considerable. The main industries produce aluminium, ferro-silicon and fertilizers. Tourism, including ecotourism, is growing in importance.

© Bartholomew Ltd

INDIA
Republic of India

Area Sq Km	3 065 027	Currency	Rupee
Area Sq Miles	1 183 414	Languages	Hindi, English, many regional languages
Population	982 223 000	Religions	Hindu, Sunni Muslim, Shi'a Muslim, Sikh, Christian
Capital	New Delhi	Organizations	Comm., UN

The south Asian state of India occupies a peninsula that juts out into the Indian Ocean between the Arabian Sea and Bay of Bengal. The heart of the peninsula is the Deccan plateau, bordered on either side by ranges of hills, the Western Ghats and the lower Eastern Ghats, which fall away to narrow coastal plains. To the north is a broad plain, drained by the Indus, Ganges and Brahmaputra rivers and their tributaries. The plain is intensively farmed and is the most populous region. In the west is the Thar Desert. The Himalaya form India's northern border, together with parts of the Karakoram and Hindu Kush ranges in the northwest. The climate shows marked seasonal variation: the hot season from March to June; the monsoon season from June to October; and the cold season from November to

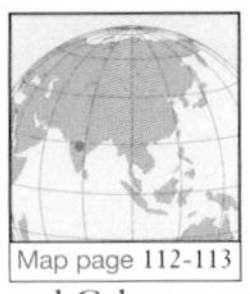

Map page 112-113

February. Rainfall ranges between very high in the northeast Assam region to negligible in the Thar Desert, while temperatures range from very cold in the Himayalas to tropical heat over much of the south. Over seventy per cent of the huge population – the second largest in the world – is rural, though Mumbai and Calcutta rank among the ten largest cities in the world. Agriculture, forestry and fishing account for a quarter of national output and two thirds of employment. Much of the farming is on a subsistence basis and involves mainly rice and wheat growing. India is a major world producer of tea, sugar, jute, cotton and tobacco. Livestock is raised mainly for dairy products and hides. India has major reserves of coal, reserves of oil and natural gas and many minerals, including iron, manganese, bauxite, diamonds and gold. The manufacturing sector is large and diverse. The main manufactures are chemicals and chemical products, textiles, iron and steel, food products, electrical goods and transport equipment; software and pharmaceuticals are also important. All the main manufactured products are exported, together with diamonds and jewellery. The USA, Germany, Japan and the UK are the main trading partners.

INDONESIA
Republic of Indonesia

Area Sq Km	1 919 445	Currency	Rupiah
Area Sq Miles	741 102	Languages	Indonesian, local languages
Population	206 338 000	Religions	Sunni Muslim, Protestant, Roman Catholic
Capital	Jakarta	Organizations	APEC, ASEAN, OPEC, UN

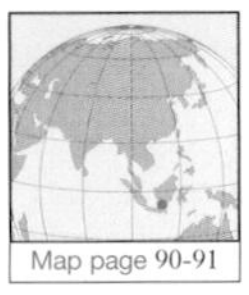

Map page 90-91

Indonesia, the largest and most populous country in southeast Asia, consists of over thirteen thousand islands extending along the equator between the Pacific and Indian Oceans. Sumatera, Jawa, Sulawesi, Kalimantan (two thirds of Borneo) and Irian Jaya (western New Guinea) make up ninety per cent of the land area. Most of Indonesia is mountainous and covered with rainforest or mangrove swamps, and there are over three hundred volcanoes, many active. Two thirds of the population live in the lowland areas of Jawa and Madura. The climate is tropical monsoon. Agriculture is the largest sector of the economy and Indonesia is among the world's top producers of rice, palm oil, tea, coffee, rubber and tobacco. It is the world's leading exporter of natural gas, a major exporter of oil and timber, and a major producer of tin. A range of goods are produced including textiles, clothing, cement, fertilizer and vehicles. Main exports are oil, natural gas, timber products and clothing. The main trading partner is Japan. However, Indonesia remains a relatively poor country, and ethnic tensions and civil unrest are hindering economic development.

IRAN
Islamic Republic of Iran

Area Sq Km	1 648 000	Currency	Rial
Area Sq Miles	636 296	Languages	Farsi, Azeri, Kurdish, regional languages
Population	65 758 000	Religions	Shi'a Muslim, Sunni Muslim
Capital	Tehrān	Organizations	OPEC, UN

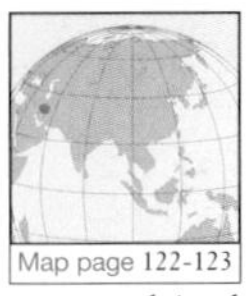

Map page 122-123

Iran is in southwest Asia, on The Gulf, the Gulf of Oman and Caspian Sea. Eastern Iran is high plateau, with large salt pans and a vast sand desert. In the west the Zagros Mountains form a series of ridges, while to the north lie the Elburz Mountains. Most farming and settlement is on the narrow plain along the Caspian Sea and the foothills of the north and west. The climate is one of extremes, with hot summers and very cold winters. Most of the light rainfall is in the winter months. Agriculture involves about a third of the workforce. Wheat is the main crop but fruit (chiefly dates) and pistachio nuts are grown for export. Petroleum (the main export) and natural gas are Iran's leading natural resources. Manufactures include carpets, clothing, food products and construction materials.

IRAQ
Republic of Iraq

Area Sq Km	438 317	Currency	Dinar
Area Sq Miles	169 235	Languages	Arabic, Kurdish, Turkmen
Population	21 800 000	Religions	Shi'a Muslim, Sunni Muslim, Christian
Capital	Baghdād	Organizations	OPEC, UN

Iraq, which lies on the northwest shores of The Gulf in southwest Asia, has at its heart the lowland valley of the Tigris and Euphrates rivers. In the southeast where the two rivers join are marshes and the Shatt al Arab waterway. Northern Iraq is hilly, while western Iraq is desert. Summers are hot and dry, while winters are mild with light, unreliable

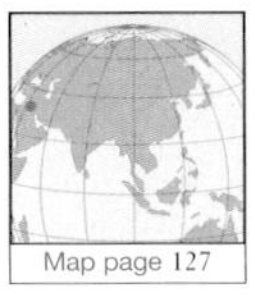

Map page 127

rainfall. The Tigris-Euphrates valley contains most of the arable land and population, including one in five who live in Baghdād. Defeat in the 1991 Gulf war and continued international sanctions have ruined the economy and caused considerable hardship. Oil is exported, almost all to Japan.

IRELAND, REPUBLIC OF

Area Sq Km	70 282	Currency	Punt, Euro
Area Sq Miles	27 136	Languages	English, Irish
Population	3 681 000	Religions	Roman Catholic, Protestant
Capital	Dublin	Organizations	EU, OECD, UN

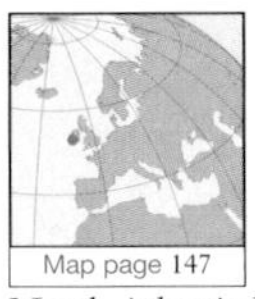

Map page 147

A state in northwest Europe, the Irish Republic occupies some eighty per cent of the island of Ireland. It is a lowland country of wide valleys, lakes and peat bogs, with isolated mountain ranges around the coast. The west coast is rugged and indented with many bays. The climate is mild due to the North Atlantic Drift and rainfall is plentiful, though highest in the west. Nearly sixty per cent of people live in urban areas, Dublin and Cork being the main cities. Resources include natural gas, peat, lead and zinc. Agriculture, the traditional mainstay, now employs less than ten per cent of the workforce, while industry employs nearly thirty per cent. The main industries are electronics, pharmaceuticals and engineering as well as food processing, brewing and textiles. Service industries are expanding, with tourism a major foreign exchange earner. The UK is the main trading partner.

Isle of Man
United Kingdom Crown Dependency

Area Sq Km	572	Currency	Pound
Area Sq Miles	221	Languages	English
Population	77 000	Religions	Protestant, Roman Catholic
Capital	Douglas		

In the Irish Sea, the island is self governing while the UK is responsible for defense and foreign affairs. The island is not part of the EU, but has a special relationship with the EU which allows for free trade.

Map page 148

ISRAEL
State of Israel

Area Sq Km	20 770	Currency	Shekel
Area Sq Miles	8 019	Languages	Hebrew, Arabic
Population	5 984 000	Religions	Jewish, Sunni Muslim, Christian, Druze
Capital	Jerusalem	Organizations	UN

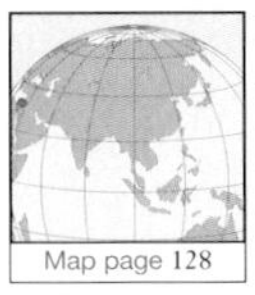

Map page 128

Israel lies on the Mediterranean coast of southwest Asia. Beyond the coastal Plain of Sharon are the hills and valleys of Samaria with the Galilee highlands to the north. In the east is the rift valley, which extends from Lake Tiberias to the Gulf of Aqaba and contains the Jordan river and Dead Sea. In the south is the Negev, a triangular semi-desert plateau. Most people live on the coastal plain or in northern and central areas. Much of Israel has warm summers and mild, wet winters. Southern Israel is hot and dry. Agricultural production was boosted by the inclusion of the West Bank in 1967. Mineral resources are few, and manufacturing makes the largest contribution to the economy. Israel exports machinery and transport equipment, diamonds, clothing, fruit and vegetables. Tourism and foreign aid are important to the economy.

ITALY
Italian Republic

Area Sq Km	301 245	Currency	Lira, Euro
Area Sq Miles	116 311	Languages	Italian
Population	57 369 000	Religions	Roman Catholic
Capital	Roma	Organizations	EU, OECD, UN

Most of the south European state of Italy occupies a peninsula that juts out into the Mediterranean Sea. It includes the islands of Sicily and Sardinia and about seventy much smaller islands in the surrounding seas. Italy is mountainous and dominated by two high ranges: the Alps, which form its northern border; and the various ranges of the Apennines, which run almost the full length of the peninsula. Many of Italy's mountains are of volcanic origin and its active volcanoes are

Map page 188-189

Vesuvio, near Naples, Etna and Stromboli. The main lowland area, the Po river valley in the northeast, is the main agricultural and industrial area and is the most populous region. Italy has a Mediterranean climate with warm, dry summers and mild winters. Northern Italy experiences colder, wetter winters, with heavy snow in the Alps. Italy's natural resources are limited. Only about twenty per cent of the land is suitable for cultivation. Some oil, natural gas and coal are produced, but most fuels and minerals used by industry must be imported. Italy has a fairly diversified economy. Agriculture is important, with cereals, vines, fruit and vegetables the main crops; Italy is the world's largest wine producer. The north is the centre of Italian industry, especially around Turin, Milan and Genoa. Italy's leading manufactures include industrial and office equipment, domestic appliances, cars, textiles, clothing, leather goods, chemicals and metal products. Italy has a strong service sector. With over twenty-five million visitors a year, tourism is a major employer and accounts for five per cent of the national income. Finance and banking are also important. Most trade is with other EU countries.

JAMAICA

Area Sq Km	10 991	Currency	Dollar
Area Sq Miles	4 244	Languages	English, creole
Population	2 538 000	Religions	Protestant, Roman Catholic
Capital	Kingston	Organizations	CARICOM, Comm., UN

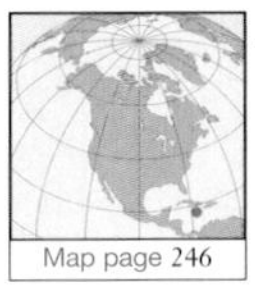

Map page 246

Jamaica, the third largest Caribbean island, has beaches and densely populated coastal plains traversed by hills and plateaus rising to the forested Blue Mountains in the east. The climate is tropical, but cooler and wetter on high ground. The economy is based on tourism, agriculture, mining and light manufacturing. Bauxite, alumina, sugar and bananas are the main exports. The USA is the main trading partner. Jamaica receives foreign aid.

Jammu and Kashmir Disputed territory (India,Pakistan)

Area Sq Km (Miles) 222 236 (85 806)	Population 13 000 000	Capital Srinagar	

A region in the north of Pakistan and India to the west of the Karakoram and Himalaya. The 'Line of control' separates the northern, Pakistani controlled area and the southern, Indian controlled area.

Map page 116

JAPAN

Area Sq Km	377 727	Currency	Yen
Area Sq Miles	145 841	Languages	Japanese
Population	126 281 000	Religions	Shintoist, Buddhist, Christian
Capital	Tōkyō	Organizations	APEC, OECD, UN

Japan, lies in the Pacific Ocean off the coast of east Asia and consists of four main islands - Hokkaidō, Honshū, Shikoku and Kyūshū - and more than three thousand smaller islands in the surrounding Sea of

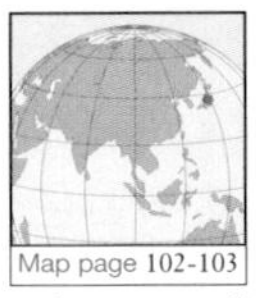

Map page 102-103

Japan, East China Sea and Pacific Ocean. The central island of Honshū accounts for sixty per cent of the total land area and contains eighty per cent of the population. Behind the long and deeply indented coastline, nearly three quarters of Japan is mountainous and heavily forested. Japan has over sixty active volcanoes, and is subject to frequent earthquakes, typhoons and tidal waves. The climate is generally temperate maritime, with warm summers and mild winters, except in western Hokkaidō and northwest Honshū, where the winters are very cold with heavy snow. Japan has few natural resources. It has a limited land area of which only fourteen per cent is suitable for cultivation, and production of its few industrial raw materials: coal, oil, natural gas, lead, zinc and copper is insufficient for its industry. Most raw materials must be imported, including about ninety per cent of energy requirements. Yet Japan is the world's second largest industrial economy, with a range of modern heavy and light industries centred mainly around the major ports of Yokohama, Ōsaka and Tōkyō. It is the world's largest manufacturer of cars, motorcycles and merchant ships, and a major producer of steel, textiles, chemicals and cement. It is a leading producer of many consumer durables, such as washing machines, and electronic equipment, chiefly office equipment and computers. Japan has a strong service sector, banking and finance are particularly important and Tōkyō is one of the world's major stock exchanges. Owing to intensive agricultural production, Japan is seventy per cent self-sufficient in food. The main food crops are rice, barley, fruit, wheat and soya beans. Livestock raising (chiefly cattle, pigs and chickens) and fishing are also important. Japan has one of the largest fishing fleets in the world. A major trading nation, Japan has trade links with many countries in southeast Asia and in Europe, though the main trading partner is USA.

Jersey
United Kingdom Crown Dependency

Area Sq Km	116	Currency	Pound
Area Sq Miles	45	Languages	English, French
Population	89 136	Religions	Protestant, Roman Catholic
Capital	St Helier		

One of the Channel Islands lying off the west coast of the Cherbourg peninsula in northern France.

Map page 148

JORDAN
Hashemite Kingdom of Jordan

Area Sq Km	89 206	Currency	Dinar
Area Sq Miles	34 443	Languages	Arabic
Population	6 304 000	Religions	Sunni Muslim, Christian
Capital	'Ammān	Organizations	UN

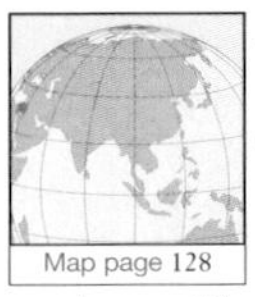

Map page 128

Jordan, in southwest Asia, is landlocked apart from a short coastline on the Gulf of Aqaba. Much of Jordan is rocky desert plateaus. To the west of the mountains, the land falls below sea level to the Dead Sea and Jordan river. Much of Jordan is hot and dry, the west is cooler and wetter; most people live in the northwest. Phosphates, potash, pharmaceuticals, fruit and vegetables are the main exports. Jordan's economy relies upon tourism, workers' remittances and foreign aid.

KAZAKHSTAN
Republic of Kazakhstan

Area Sq Km	2 717 300	Currency	Tenge
Area Sq Miles	1 049 155	Languages	Kazakh, Russian, Ukrainian, German, Uzbek, Tatar
Population	16 319 000	Religions	Sunni Muslim, Russian Orthodox, Protestant
Capital	Astana	Organizations	CIS, UN

Stretching across central Asia, Kazakhstan covers a vast area of steppe land and semi-desert. The land is flat in the west rising to mountains in

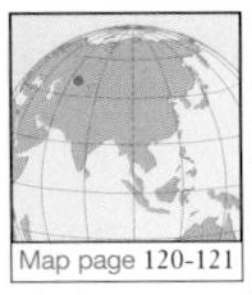
Map page 120-121

the southeast. The climate is continental and mainly dry. Agriculture and livestock rearing are important, with cotton and tobacco the main cash crops. Kazakhstan is very rich in minerals, including coal, chromium, gold, molybdenum, lead and zinc and has substantial reserves of oil and gas; oil pipelines to the Black Sea are planned. Mining, metallurgy, machine building and food processing are major industries. Oil and gas, and minerals are the main exports and Russia is the dominant trading partner.

KENYA
Republic of Kenya

Area Sq Km	582 646	Currency	Shilling
Area Sq Miles	224 961	Languages	Swahili, English, local languages
Population	29 008 000	Religions	Christian, traditional beliefs
Capital	Nairobi	Organizations	Comm., UN

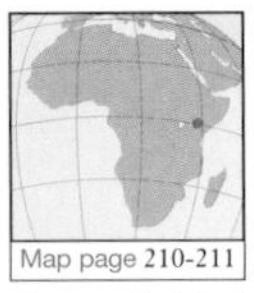
Map page 210-211

Kenya is in east Africa, on the Indian Ocean. Inland beyond the coastal plains the land rises to plateaus interrupted by volcanic mountains. The Great Rift Valley runs north-south to the west of Nairobi. Most people live in central Kenya. Conditions are tropical on the coast, semi-desert in the north and savanna in the south. Hydro-electric power from the Upper Tana river provides most of the electricity requirement. Agricultural products, mainly tea, coffee, fruit and vegetables are the main exports. Light industry is important. Tourism is the main foreign exchange earner; oil refining and re-exports for landlocked neighbours are others.

KIRIBATI
Republic of Kiribati

Area Sq Km	717	Currency	Australian dollar
Area Sq Miles	277	Languages	Gilbertese, English
Population	81 000	Religions	Roman Catholic, Protestant
Capital	Bairiki	Organizations	Comm., UN

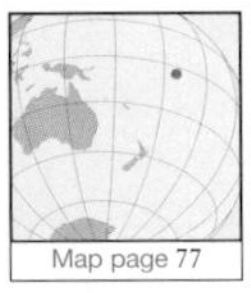
Map page 77

Kiribati comprises coral islands in the Gilbert, Phoenix and Line groups and the volcanic island of Banaba, straddling the equator in the Pacific Ocean. Most people live on the Gilbert Islands, and the capital, Bairiki, is on Tarawa, one of the Gilbert Islands. The climate is hot, wetter in the north. Copra and fish are exported, but Kiribati relies on remittances from workers abroad and foreign aid.

KUWAIT
State of Kuwait

Area Sq Km	17 818	Currency	Dinar
Area Sq Miles	6 880	Languages	Arabic
Population	1 811 000	Religions	Sunni Muslim, Shi'a Muslim, Christian, Hindu
Capital	Kuwait	Organizations	OPEC, UN

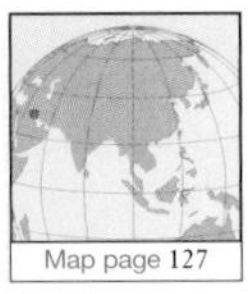
Map page 127

Kuwait lies on the northwest shores of The Gulf in southwest Asia. It is mainly low-lying desert, with irrigated areas along the bay, Kuwait Jun, where most people live. Summers are hot and dry, winters are cool with some rainfall. The oil industry, which accounts for eighty per cent of exports, has largely recovered from the damage caused by Iraq in 1991. Income is also derived from extensive overseas investments.

KYRGYZSTAN
Kyrgyz Republic

Area Sq Km	198 500	Currency	Som
Area Sq Miles	76 641	Languages	Kyrgyz, Russian, Uzbek
Population	4 643 000	Religions	Sunni Muslim, Russian Orthodox
Capital	Bishkek	Organizations	CIS, UN

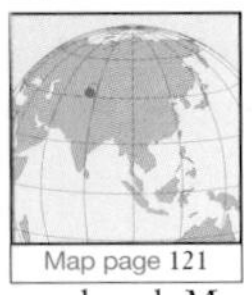
Map page 121

A landlocked central Asian state, Kyrgyzstan is rugged and mountainous, lying to the west of the Tien Shan range. Most people live in the valleys of the north and west. Summers are hot and winters cold. Agriculture (chiefly livestock farming) is the main activity. Some oil and gas, coal, gold, antimony and mercury are produced. Manufactures include machinery, metals and products, which are the main exports. Most trade is with the Russian Federation, Kazakhstan and Uzbekistan.

LAOS
Lao People's Democratic Republic

Area Sq Km	236 800	Currency	Kip
Area Sq Miles	91 429	Languages	Lao, local languages
Population	5 163 000	Religions	Buddhist, traditional beliefs
Capital	Vientiane	Organizations	ASEAN, UN

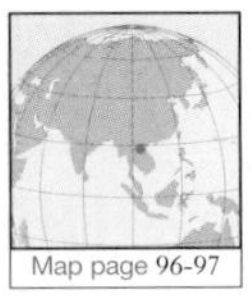
Map page 96-97

A landlocked country in southeast Asia, Laos borders Vietnam, Cambodia, Thailand, Myanmar and China. The land is mostly forested mountains and plateaus. The climate is tropical monsoon. Most people live in the Mekong valley and the low plateau in the south, and grow food crops, chiefly rice. Hydro-electricity from a plant on the Mekong, timber, coffee and tin are exported, but Laos depends on aid.

LATVIA
Republic of Latvia

Area Sq Km	63 700	Currency	Lat
Area Sq Miles	24 595	Languages	Latvian, Russian
Population	2 424 000	Religions	Protestant, Roman Catholic, Russian Orthodox
Capital	Riga	Organizations	UN

Latvia is in north Europe, on the Baltic Sea and Gulf of Riga. The land is flat near the coast but hilly with woods and lakes inland. Latvia has a modified continental climate. One third of the people live in Riga.

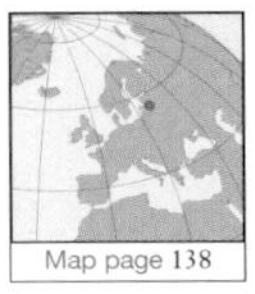
Map page 138

Crop and livestock farming are important. Latvia has few natural resources. Industries include food products, transport equipment, wood and wood products and textiles; these form most of the exports. The main trading partners are Russia and Germany. Latvia is negotiating to join the EU.

LEBANON
Republic of Lebanon

Area Sq Km	10 452	Currency	Pound
Area Sq Miles	4 036	Languages	Arabic, Armenian, French
Population	3 191 000	Religions	Shi'a Muslim, Sunni Muslim, Christian
Capital	Beirut	Organizations	UN

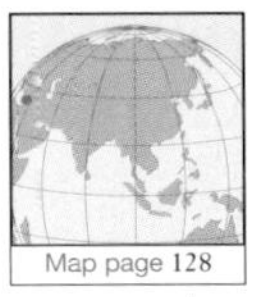
Map page 128

Lebanon lies on the Mediterranean coast of southwest Asia. Beyond the coastal strip, where most people live, are two parallel mountain ranges, separated by the El Beq'a valley. The 1975-1991 civil war crippled the traditional sectors of banking, commerce and tourism; some fruit production and light industry survived; reconstruction of the infrastructure is under way, and financial service companies are beginning to return.

LESOTHO
Kingdom of Lesotho

Area Sq Km	30 355	Currency	Loti
Area Sq Miles	11 720	Languages	Sesotho, English, Zulu
Population	2 062 000	Religions	Christian, traditional beliefs
Capital	Maseru	Organizations	Comm., SADC, UN

Map page 215

Lesotho is a landlocked state surrounded by the Republic of South Africa. It is a mountainous country lying within the Drakensberg range. Farming and herding are the main activities. Exports include livestock, vegetables, wool and mohair. The economy depends heavily on South Africa for transport links and employment; a major hydro-electric plant completed in 1998 will allow the sale of water to South Africa.

LIBERIA
Republic of Liberia

Area Sq Km	111 369	Currency	Dollar
Area Sq Miles	43 000	Languages	English, creole, local languages
Population	2 666 000	Religions	Traditional beliefs, Christian, Sunni Muslim
Capital	Monrovia	Organizations	UN

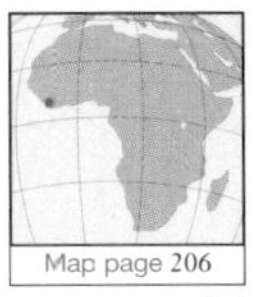
Map page 206

Liberia is on the Atlantic coast of west Africa. Beyond the coastal belt of sandy beaches and mangrove swamps the land rises to a forested plateau, with highlands along the Guinea border. A quarter of the population lives along the coast. The climate is hot with heavy rainfall. Sporadic civil war throughout the 1990's has ruined the economy and destroyed much of the infrastructure especially around Monrovia; Liberia relies on foreign aid.

LIBYA
Socialist People's Libyan Arab Jamahiriya

Area Sq Km	1 759 540	Currency	Dinar
Area Sq Miles	679 362	Languages	Arabic, Berber
Population	5 339 000	Religions	Sunni Muslim
Capital	Tripoli	Organizations	OPEC, UN

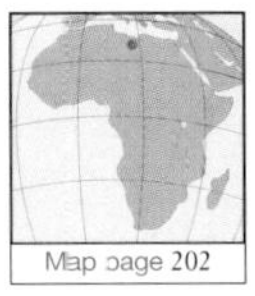
Map page 202

Libya lies on the Mediterranean coast of north Africa. The desert plains and hills of the Sahara dominate the landscape and the climate is hot and dry. Most people live in cities near the coast, where the climate is cooler with moderate rainfall. Farming and herding, chiefly in the northwest, are important but the main industry is oil. Libya is a major oil producer and oil accounts for virtually all of export earnings. Italy and Germany are the main trading partners.

LIECHTENSTEIN
Principality of Liechtenstein

Area Sq Km	160	Currency	Swiss franc
Area Sq Miles	62	Languages	German
Population	32 000	Religions	Roman Catholic, Protestant
Capital	Vaduz	Organizations	UN

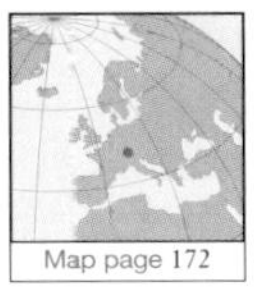
Map page 172

A landlocked state between Switzerland and Austria Liechtenstein has an industrialized, free-enterprize economy. Low business taxes have attracted companies to establish nominal offices providing about a third of state revenues. Banking is also important. Major products include precision instruments, ceramics and textiles.

LITHUANIA
Republic of Lithuania

Area Sq Km	65 200	Currency	Litas
Area Sq Miles	25 174	Languages	Lithuanian, Russian, Polish
Population	3 694 000	Religions	Roman Catholic, Protestant, Russian Orthodox
Capital	Vilnius	Organizations	UN

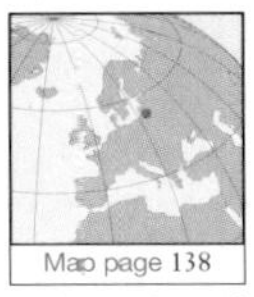
Map page 138

Lithuania is in north Europe, on the eastern shores of the Baltic Sea. It is mainly lowland with many lakes, rivers and marshes. The climate is generally temperate. Agriculture, fishing and forestry are important, but manufacturing dominates the economy. The main products are processed foods, textiles, chemicals, wood and wood products. Russia and Germany are the main trading partners. Lithuania is negotiating to join the EU.

LUXEMBOURG
Grand Duchy of Luxembourg

Area Sq Km	2 586	Currency	Franc, Euro
Area Sq Miles	998	Languages	Letzeburgish, German, French
Population	422 000	Religions	Roman Catholic
Capital	Luxembourg	Organizations	EU, OECD, UN

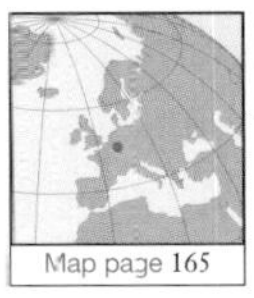
Map page 165

Luxembourg, a small landlocked country in west Europe, borders Belgium, France and Germany. The hills and forests of the Ardennes dominate the north, with rolling pasture to the south, where the main towns, farms and industries are found. The iron and steel industry is still important, but light industries (including textiles, chemicals and food products) are growing. Luxembourg is a major banking centre and the home base of key European Union institutions.

MACEDONIA (F.Y.R.O.M.)
Republic of Macedonia

Area Sq Km	25 713	Currency	Denar
Area Sq Miles	9 928	Languages	Macedonian, Albanian, Turkish
Population	1 999 000	Religions	Macedonian Orthodox, Sunni Muslim
Capital	Skopje	Organizations	UN

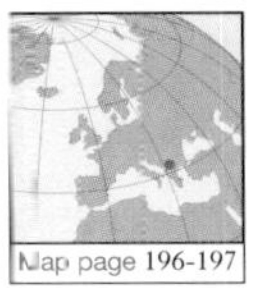
Map page 196-197

The Former Yugoslav Republic of Macedonia, is a landlocked state in southern Europe, bordered by Yugoslavia, Bulgaria, Greece and Albania. Lying within the south Balkans, it is a mountainous country, traversed northwest-southeast by the Vardar valley. It has hot summers, but very cold winters. The economy is based on industry, mining and agriculture. But the conflicts in the region have reduced trade and caused economic difficulties. Aid and loans are now assisting in modernization and development.

MADAGASCAR
Republic of Madagascar

Area Sq Km	587 041	Currency	Franc
Area Sq Miles	226 658	Languages	Malagasy, French
Population	15 057 000	Religions	Traditional beliefs, Christian, Sunni Muslim
Capital	Antananarivo	Organizations	UN

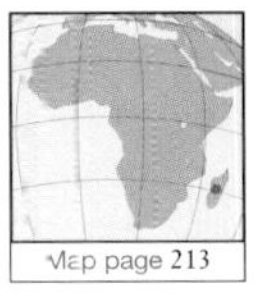
Map page 213

Madagascar lies off the east coast of southern Africa. The world's fourth largest island, it is mainly a high plateau with a coastal strip to the east and scrubby plain to the west. The climate is tropical with heavy rainfall in the north and east. Most people live on the plateau. Though the amount of arable land is limited the economy is based on agriculture. The main industries are agricultural processing, textile manufacturing and oil refining, foreign aid is important. Exports include coffee, vanilla, cloves, cloth, sugar and shrimps. France is the main trading partner.

MALAWI
Republic of Malawi

Area Sq Km	118 484	Currency	Kwacha
Area Sq Miles	45 747	Languages	Chichewa, English, local languages
Population	10 346 000	Religions	Christian, traditional beliefs, Sunni Muslim
Capital	Lilongwe	Organizations	Comm., SADC, UN

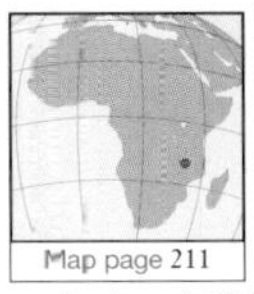
Map page 211

Landlocked Malawi in central Africa is a narrow hilly country at the southern end of the Great Rift Valley. One fifth of the country is covered by Lake Malawi, which lies above sea level. Most people live in the southern regions. The climate is mainly subtropical with varying rainfall. The economy is predominantly agricultural. Tobacco, tea and sugar are the main exports. The small manufacturing sector involves mainly chemicals, textiles and agricultural products. Malawi relies heavily on foreign aid.

MALAYSIA
Federation of Malaysia

Area Sq Km	332 965	Currency	Ringgit
Area Sq Miles	128 559	Languages	Malay, English, Chinese, Tamil, local languages
Population	21 410 000	Religions	Sunni Muslim, Buddhist, Hindu, Christian
Capital	Kuala Lumpur	Organizations	APEC, ASEAN, Comm., UN

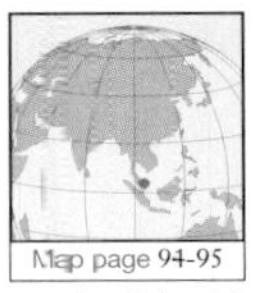
Map page 94-95

The Federation of Malaysia, in southeast Asia, comprises two regions, separated by the South China Sea. The western region occupies the southern Malay Peninsula, which has a chain of mountains dividing the eastern coastal strip from the wider plains to the west. To the east, the states of Sabah and Sarawak in the north of the island of Borneo are mainly rainforest-covered hills and mountains with mangrove swamps along the coast. Both regions have a tropical climate with heavy rainfall. About eighty per cent of the population live in the western part of the country, Peninsular Malaysia, mainly on the coasts. The country is rich in natural resources and has reserves of minerals and fuels. It is an important producer of tin, oil, natural gas and tropical hardwoods. Agriculture remains a substantial part of the economy, but industry has become the most important sector. The main exports are transport and electronic equipment, oil, palm oil, wood and rubber. The main trading partners are Japan, USA and Singapore.

MALDIVES
Republic of the Maldives

Area Sq Km	298	Currency	Rufiyaa
Area Sq Miles	115	Languages	Divehi (Maldivian)
Population	271 000	Religions	Sunni Muslim
Capital	Male	Organizations	Comm., UN

The Maldive archipelago comprises over a thousand coral atolls (around two hundred of which are inhabited), in the Indian Ocean, southwest of India. Over eighty per cent of the land area is less than one metre above sea level. The main atolls are North and South Male

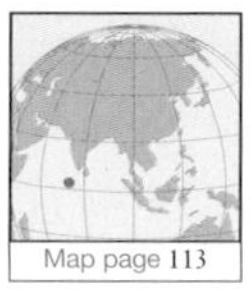
Map page 113

and Addu. The climate is hot, humid and monsoonal. There is little cultivation and almost all food is imported. Tourism has expanded rapidly and is the most important sector of the economy.

MALI
Republic of Mali

Area Sq Km	1 240 140	Currency	CFA franc
Area Sq Miles	478 821	Languages	French, Bambara, local languages
Population	10 694 000	Religions	Sunni Muslim, traditional beliefs, Christian
Capital	Bamako	Organizations	UN

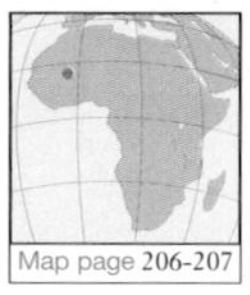
Map page 206-207

A landlocked state in west Africa, Mali is low-lying, rising to mountains in the northeast. Northern regions lie within the Sahara desert. To the south, around the Niger river, are marshes and savanna grassland. Rainfall is unreliable. Most people live along the Niger and Sénégal rivers. Exports include cotton, livestock and gold. Mali is one of the least developed countries in the world and relies heavily on foreign aid.

MALTA
Republic of Malta

Area Sq Km	316	Currency	Lira
Area Sq Miles	122	Languages	Maltese, English
Population	384 000	Religions	Roman Catholic
Capital	Valletta	Organizations	Comm., UN

Map page 195

The islands of Malta and Gozo lie in the Mediterranean Sea, off the coast of south Italy. Malta, the main island, has low hills and an indented coastline. The islands have hot, dry summers and mild winters. The main industries are tourism, ship building and repair, electronics and textiles, which are the main exports. Malta is negotiating to join the EU.

MARSHALL ISLANDS
Republic of the Marshall Islands

Area Sq Km	181	Currency	US dollar
Area Sq Miles	70	Languages	English, Marshallese
Population	60 000	Religions	Protestant, Roman Catholic
Capital	Dalap-Uliga-Darrit	Organizations	UN

The Marshall Islands consist of over a thousand atolls, islands and islets, within two chains, in the north of the Pacific Ocean. The main atolls are Majuro (home to half the population), Kwajalein, Jaluit, Enewetak and Bikini. The climate is tropical with heavy autumn rainfall. About half the workforce are employed in farming or fishing but the islands depend heavily on US aid.

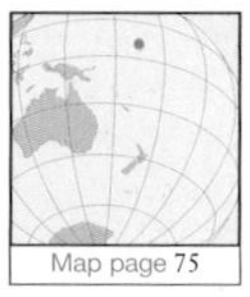
Map page 75

Martinique
French Overseas Department

Area Sq Km	1 079	Currency	French franc
Area Sq Miles	417	Languages	French, creole
Population	389 000	Religions	Roman Catholic, traditional beliefs
Capital	Fort-de-France		

Martinique, one of the Caribbean Windward Islands, has volcanic peaks in the north, a populous central plain, and hills and beaches in the south. The economy is based on sugar cane, bananas, oil refining, rum distilling, tourism and French aid.

Map page 247

MAURITANIA
Islamic Arab and African Republic of Mauritania

Area Sq Km	1 030 700	Currency	Ouguiya
Area Sq Miles	397 955	Languages	Arabic, French, local languages
Population	2 529 000	Religions	Sunni Muslim
Capital	Nouakchott	Organizations	UN

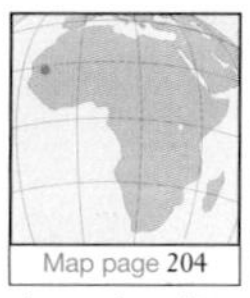
Map page 204

Mauritania is on the Atlantic coast of northwest Africa and lies almost entirely within the Sahara desert. Oases and a fertile strip along the Sénégal river to the south are the only areas suitable for cultivation. The climate is generally hot and dry. About a quarter of Mauritanians live in Nouakchott. Though most of the workforce depend on livestock rearing and subsistence farming, the economy is heavily dependent on iron ore mining and fishing, which together account for ninety per cent of export earnings, and foreign aid.

MAURITIUS
Republic of Mauritius

Area Sq Km	2 040	Currency	Rupee
Area Sq Miles	788	Languages	English, creole, Hindi, Bhojpuri, French
Population	1 141 000	Religions	Hindu, Roman Catholic, Sunni Muslim
Capital	Port Louis	Organizations	Comm., SADC, UN

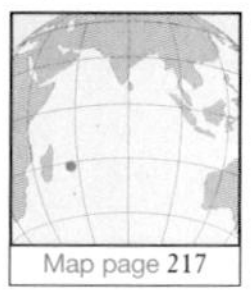
Map page 217

The state comprises Mauritius, Rodrigues and some twenty small islands in the Indian Ocean, east of Madagascar. The main island of Mauritius is volcanic in origin and has a coral coast rising to a central plateau. Most people live in the north and west side of the island. The climate is warm and humid. The economy is based on sugar production, light manufacturing (chiefly clothing) and tourism.

Mayotte
French Territorial Collectivity

Area Sq Km	373	Currency	French franc
Area Sq Miles	144	Languages	French, Mahorian
Population	144 944	Religions	Sunni Muslim, Christian
Capital	Dzaoudzi		

Lying in the Indian Ocean off the east coast of central Africa, Mayotte is geographically part of the Comoros archipelago. The economy is based on agriculture, but Mayotte depends heavily on aid from France.

Map page 217

MEXICO
United Mexican States

Area Sq Km	1 972 545	Currency	Peso
Area Sq Miles	761 604	Languages	Spanish, Amerindian languages
Population	95 831 000	Religions	Roman Catholic, Protestant
Capital	México	Organizations	APEC, OECD, UN

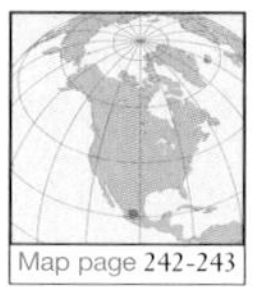
Map page 242-243

The largest country in Central America, Mexico extends south from the USA to Guatemala and Belize, and from the Pacific Ocean to the Gulf of Mexico. The greater part of the country is high plateau flanked by the western and eastern ranges of the Sierra Madre mountains. The principal lowland is the Yucatán peninsula in the southeast. The climate varies with latitude and altitude: hot and humid in the lowlands, warm on the plateau and cool with cold winters in the mountains. The north is arid, while the far south has heavy rainfall. México is one of the world's largest conurbations and the centre of trade and industry. Agriculture involves a quarter of the workforce, crops include grains, sugar cane, coffee, cotton and vegetables. Mexico is rich in minerals, including copper, zinc, lead, tin, sulphur, and silver. It is one of the world's largest producers of oil, from vast oil and gas reserves in the Gulf of Mexico. The oil and petrochemical industries still dominate, but a variety of manufactures are now produced including iron and steel, motor vehicles, textiles, chemicals and food and tobacco products. Tourism is growing in importance. Around three-quarters of all trade is with USA.

MICRONESIA, FEDERATED STATES OF

Area Sq Km	701	Currency	US dollar
Area Sq Miles	271	Languages	English, Chuukese, Pohnpeian, local languages
Population	114 000	Religions	Roman Catholic, Protestant
Capital	Palikir	Organizations	UN

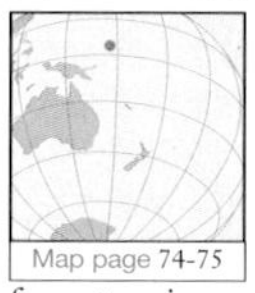
Map page 74-75

Micronesia comprises over six hundred atolls and islands of the Caroline Islands in the north Pacific Ocean. A third of the population lives on Pohnpei. The climate is tropical with heavy rainfall. Fishing and subsistence farming are the main activities. Copra and fish are the main exports. Income also derives from tourism and the licensing of foreign fishing fleets. The islands depend heavily on US aid.

MOLDOVA
Republic of Moldova

Area Sq Km	33 700	Currency	Leu
Area Sq Miles	13 012	Languages	Romanian, Ukrainian, Gagauz, Russian
Population	4 378 000	Religions	Romanian Orthodox, Russian Orthodox
Capital	Chişinău	Organizations	CIS, UN

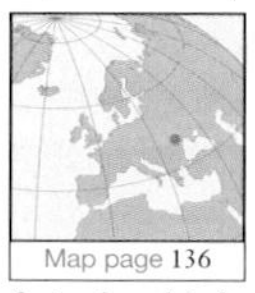
Map page 136

Moldova is in east Europe, between Romania and Ukraine. It consists of hilly steppe land, drained by the Prut and Nistru (Dniester) rivers; the latter provides access to the Black Sea through Ukrainian territory. Moldova has no mineral resources and the economy is mainly agricultural, with sugar beet, tobacco, wine and fruit the chief products. Food processing and textiles are the main industries. Russia is the main trading partner.

MONACO
Principality of Monaco

Area Sq Km	2	Currency	French franc
Area Sq Miles	1	Languages	French, Monegasque, Italian
Population	33 000	Religions	Roman Catholic
Capital	Monaco-Ville	Organizations	UN

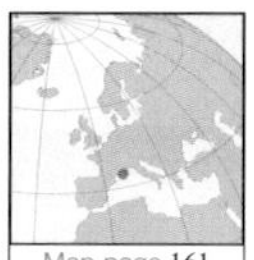
Map page 161

The principality occupies a rocky peninsula and a strip of land on France's Mediterranean coast. It depends on service industries (chiefly tourism, banking and finance) and light industry.

MONGOLIA

Area Sq Km	1 565 000	Currency	Tugrik
Area Sq Miles	604 250	Languages	Khalka (Mongolian), Kazakh, local languages
Population	2 579 000	Religions	Buddhist, Sunni Muslim
Capital	Ulaanbaatar	Organizations	UN

Mongolia is a landlocked country in east Asia between Russia and China. Much of it is high steppe land, with mountains and lakes in the west and north. In the south is the Gobi desert. Mongolia has long, cold winters and short, mild summers. A quarter of the population lives in the capital. Livestock breeding and agricultural processing are important; there are some mineral resources. Copper and textiles are the main exports.

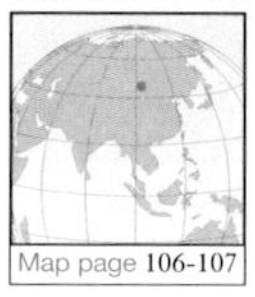
Map page 106-107

Montserrat
United Kingdom Overseas Territory

Area Sq Km	100	Currency	E. Carib. dollar
Area Sq Miles	39	Languages	English
Population	11 000	Religions	Protestant, Roman Catholic
Capital	Plymouth	Organizations	CARICOM

An island in the Leeward Island group in the Lesser Antilles in the Caribbean. From 1995 to 1997 the volcanoes in the Soufrière Hills erupted for the first time since 1630, over sixty per cent of the island was covered in volcanic ash, the capital town was destroyed, many people emigrated and the remaining population moved to the north of the island. Reconstruction, funded by aid from the UK has begun.

Map page 247

MOROCCO
Kingdom of Morocco

Area Sq Km	446 550	Currency	Dirham
Area Sq Miles	172 414	Languages	Arabic, Berber, French
Population	27 377 000	Religions	Sunni Muslim
Capital	Rabat	Organizations	UN

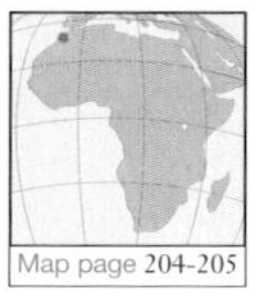
Map page 204-205

Lying in the northwest corner of Africa, Morocco has both Atlantic and Mediterranean coasts. The Atlas Mountains separate the arid south and disputed region of Western Sahara from the fertile regions of the west and north, which have a milder climate. Most Moroccans live on the Atlantic coastal plain. The economy is based mainly on agriculture, phosphate mining and tourism, the main industries are food processing, textiles and chemicals. France is the main trading partner.

MOZAMBIQUE
Republic of Mozambique

Area Sq Km	799 380	Currency	Metical
Area Sq Miles	308 642	Languages	Portuguese, Makua, Tsonga, local languages
Population	18 880 000	Religions	Traditional beliefs, Roman Catholic, Sunni Muslim
Capital	Maputo	Organizations	Comm., SADC, UN

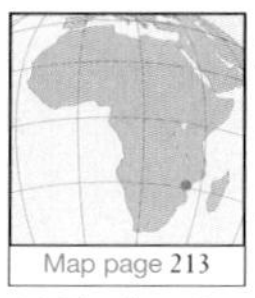
Map page 213

Mozambique lies on the east coast of southern Africa. The land is mainly a savanna plateau drained by the Zambezi and Limpopo rivers, with highlands to the north. Most people live on the coast or in the river valleys. In general the climate is tropical with winter rainfall, but droughts occur. Reconstruction began in 1992 after sixteen years of civil war. The economy is based on subsistence agriculture. Exports include shrimps, cashews, cotton and sugar, but Mozambique relies heavily on aid, and remains one of the least developed countries in the world.

MYANMAR
Union of Myanmar

Area Sq Km	676 577	Currency	Kyat
Area Sq Miles	261 228	Languages	Burmese, Shan, Karen, local languages
Population	44 497 000	Religions	Buddhist, Christian, Sunni Muslim
Capital	Yangôn	Organizations	ASEAN, UN

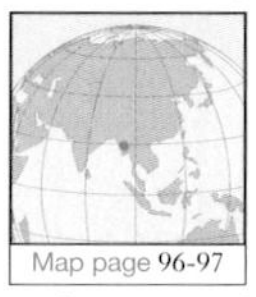
Map page 96-97

Myanmar is in southeast Asia, on the Bay of Bengal and Andaman Sea. Most people live in the valley and delta of the Irrawaddy river, which is flanked on three sides by mountains and high plateaus. The climate is hot and monsoonal, and rainforest covers much of the land. Most people are employed in agriculture. Myanmar is rich in minerals, including zinc, lead, copper and silver. Political and social unrest and lack of foreign investment have affected economic development.

NAMIBIA
Republic of Namibia

Area Sq Km	824 292	Currency	Dollar
Area Sq Miles	318 261	Languages	English, Afrikaans, German, Ovambo, local languages
Population	1 660 000	Religions	Protestant, Roman Catholic
Capital	Windhoek	Organizations	Comm., SADC, UN

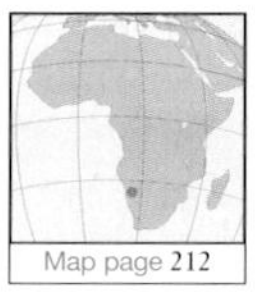
Map page 212

Namibia lies on the Atlantic coast of southern Africa. Mountain ranges separate the coastal Namib Desert from the interior plateau, bordered to the south and east by the Kalahari Desert. Namibia is hot and dry, but some summer rain falls in the north which supports crops and livestock; most of the population live in this area. Most of the workforce are employed in agriculture though the economy is based on mineral extraction, predominantly diamonds, but also uranium, lead, zinc and silver. Fishing is increasingly important. The economy is closely linked to that of South Africa.

NAURU
Republic of Nauru

Area Sq Km	21	Currency	Australian dollar
Area Sq Miles	8	Languages	Nauruan, English
Population	11 000	Religions	Protestant, Roman Catholic
Capital	Yaren	Organizations	Comm., UN

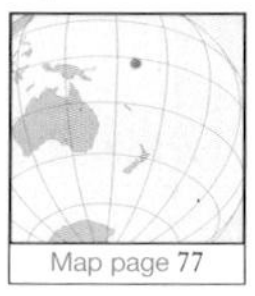
Map page 77

Nauru is a coral island near the equator in the Pacific Ocean, it has a fertile coastal strip, a barren central plateau and a tropical climate. The economy is based on phosphate mining, but reserves are near exhaustion and replacement of this income is a serious long-term problem.

NEPAL
Kingdom of Nepal

Area Sq Km	147 181	Currency	Rupee
Area Sq Miles	56 827	Languages	Nepali, Maithili, Bhojpuri, English, local languages
Population	22 847 000	Religions	Hindu, Buddhist, Sunni Muslim
Capital	Kathmandu	Organizations	UN

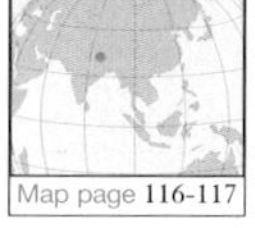
Map page 116-117

The south Asian country of Nepal lies in the eastern Himalaya between India and China. High mountains (including Everest) dominate northern Nepal. Most people live in the temperate central valleys and subtropical southern plains. The economy is based largely on agriculture and forestry; there is some manufacturing, chiefly textiles and carpets, and tourism is important. Nepal relies heavily on foreign aid.

NETHERLANDS
Kingdom of the Netherlands

Area Sq Km	41 526	Currency	Guilder, Euro
Area Sq Miles	16 033	Languages	Dutch, Frisian
Population	15 678 000	Religions	Roman Catholic, Protestant, Sunni Muslim
Capital	Amsterdam/ 's-Gravenhage	Organizations	EU, OECD, UN

The Netherlands lie on the North Sea coast of western Europe. Apart from low hills in the far southeast, the land is flat and low-lying, much of it below sea level. The coastal region includes the delta of five rivers and polders (reclaimed land), protected by sand dunes, dikes and canals. The climate is temperate, with cool summers and mild winters. Rainfall is spread evenly throughout the year. The Netherlands is a densely populated and highly urbanized country, with the majority of people living in the western Amsterdam-Rotterdam-s'Gravenhage area. Horticulture and dairy farming are important activities, though they employ less than four per cent of the workforce. The Netherlands rank as the world's third agricultural exporter, and is a leading producer and exporter of natural gas from reserves in the North Sea, but otherwise lacks raw materials. The economy is based mainly on international trade and manufacturing industry. The main industries produce food products, chemicals, machinery, electric and electronic goods and transport equipment. Germany is the main trading partner followed by other EU countries.

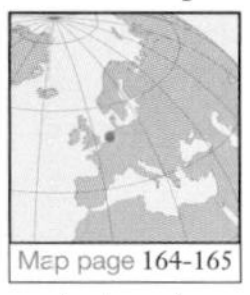
Map page 164-165

Netherlands Antilles
Self-governing NetherlandsTerritory

Area Sq Km	800	Currency	NA guilder
Area Sq Miles	309	Languages	Dutch, Papiamento, English
Population	213 000	Religions	Roman Catholic, Protestant
Capital	Willemstad		

The territory comprises two separate island groups: Curaçao and Bonaire off the northern coast of Venezuela, and Saba, Sint Eustatius and the southern part of Sint Maarten in the northern Lesser Antilles.

Map page 247

New Caledonia
French Overseas Territory

Area Sq Km	19 058	Currency	Pacific franc
Area Sq Miles	7 358	Languages	French, local languages
Population	206 000	Religions	Roman Catholic, Protestant, Sunni Muslim
Capital	Nouméa		

An island group, lying in the southwest Pacific, with a sub-tropical climate. The economy is based on nickel mining and tourism, and aid from France.

Map page 78

NEW ZEALAND

Area Sq Km	270 534	Currency	Dollar
Area Sq Miles	104 454	Languages	English, Maori
Population	3 796 000	Religions	Protestant, Roman Catholic
Capital	Wellington	Organizations	APEC, Comm., OECD, UN

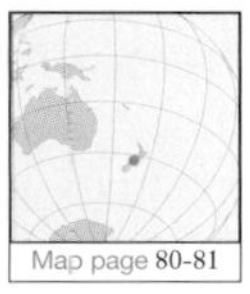
Map page 80-81

New Zealand comprises two main islands separated by the narrow Cook Strait, and a number of smaller islands. North Island, where three quarters of the population live, has mountain ranges, broad fertile valleys and a central plateau with hot springs and active volcanoes. South Island is also mountainous with the Southern Alps running its entire length. The only major lowland area is the Canterbury Plains in the centre east. The climate is generally temperate, though South Island has colder winters. Farming is the mainstay of the economy. New Zealand is one of the world's leading producers of meat (beef, lamb and mutton), wool and dairy products; fruit and fish are also important. Coal, oil and natural gas are produced, but hydroelectric and geothermal power provide much of the country's energy needs. Other industries produce timber, wood pulp, iron, aluminium, machinery and chemicals. Tourism is the fastest growing sector of the economy. The main trading partners are Australia, USA and Japan.

NICARAGUA
Republic of Nicaragua

Area Sq Km	130 000	Currency	Córdoba
Area Sq Miles	50 193	Languages	Spanish, Amerindian languages
Population	4 807 000	Religions	Roman Catholic, Protestant
Capital	Managua	Organizations	UN

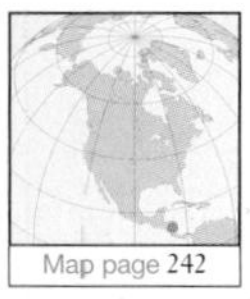
Map page 242

Nicaragua lies at the heart of Central America, with both Pacific and Caribbean coasts. Mountain ranges separate the east, which is largely rainforest, from the more developed western regions, which include Lake Nicaragua and some active volcanoes. The highest land is in the north. The climate is tropical. The economy is largely agricultural. Exports include coffee, seafood and bananas. Nicaragua relies heavily on aid and was one of the countries worse hit by hurricane Mitch in 1998; though it has received significant relief to help reconstruction, development has been seriously affected.

NIGER
Republic of Niger

Area Sq Km	1 267 000	Currency	CFA franc
Area Sq Miles	489 191	Languages	French, Hausa, Fulani, local languages
Population	10 078 000	Religions	Sunni Muslim, traditional beliefs
Capital	Niamey	Organizations	UN

A landlocked state of west Africa, Niger lies mostly within the Sahara desert, but with savanna in the south and Niger valley. The mountains of the Air massif dominate central regions. Much of the country is hot and dry. The south has some summer rainfall, though droughts occur. The economy depends on subsistence farming and herding, and uranium exports, but Niger is one of the world's least developed countries and relies heavily on foreign aid.

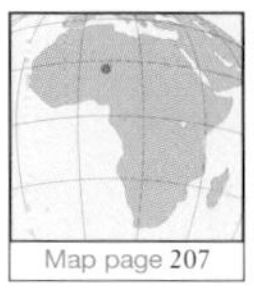
Map page 207

NIGERIA
Federal Republic of Nigeria

Area Sq Km	923 768	Currency	Naira
Area Sq Miles	356 669	Languages	English, Hausa, Yoruba, Ibo, Fulani, local languages
Population	106 409 000	Religions	Sunni Muslim, Christian, traditional beliefs
Capital	Abuja	Organizations	Comm., OPEC, UN

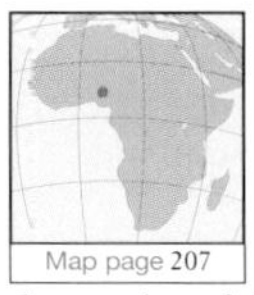
Map page 207

Nigeria is in west Africa, on the Gulf of Guinea, and is the most populous country in Africa. The Niger delta dominates coastal areas, fringed with sandy beaches, mangrove swamps and lagoons. Inland is a belt of rainforest that gives way to woodland or savanna on high plateaus. The far north is the semi-desert edge of the Sahara. The climate is tropical with heavy summer rainfall in the south but low rainfall in the north. Most people live in the coastal lowlands or in western Nigeria. About half the workforce is involved in agriculture, mainly growing subsistence crops, but agricultural production has failed to keep up with the rapid population growth and Nigeria is now a net importer of food. Cocoa and rubber are the only significant export crops. The economy is heavily dependent on vast oil resources in the Niger delta and shallow offshore waters, which account for over ninety per cent of export earnings. Nigeria also has natural gas reserves and some mineral deposits, but these are largely undeveloped. Industry involves mainly oil refining, chemicals (chiefly fertilizer), agricultural processing, textiles, steel manufacture and vehicle assembly. Political instability has left Nigeria with heavy debts, poverty and unemployment.

Niue
Self-governing New Zealand Overseas Territory

Area Sq Km	258	Currency	NZ dollar
Area Sq Miles	100	Languages	English, Polynesian
Population	2 000	Religions	Christian
Capital	Alofi		

One of the largest coral islands in the world, in the south Pacific Ocean about 500 kilometres (300 miles) east of Tonga. The economy depends on aid and remittances from New Zealand. The population is declining because of migration to New Zealand.

Map page 81

Norfolk Island
Australian External Territory

Area Sq Km	35	Currency	Australian dollar
Area Sq Miles	14	Languages	English
Population	2 000	Religions	Protestant, Roman Catholic
Capital	Kingston		

In the south Pacific Ocean, between Vanuatu and New Zealand; tourism has increased steadily and is the mainstay of the economy, providing revenues for agricultural development.

Map page 82

Northern Mariana Islands
United States Commonwealth

Area Sq Km	477	Currency	US dollar
Area Sq Miles	184	Languages	English, Chamorro, local languages
Population	70 000	Religions	Roman Catholic
Capital	Saipan		

A chain of islands in the northwest Pacific Ocean, extending over 550 kilometres (350 miles) north to south; the main island is Saipan; tourism is a major industry employing around half the workforce, the majority of tourists are from Japan.

Map page 74

NORTH KOREA
People's Democratic Republic of Korea

Area Sq Km	120 538	Currency	Won
Area Sq Miles	46 540	Languages	Korean
Population	23 348 000	Religions	Traditional beliefs, Chondoist, Buddhist
Capital	P'yŏngyang	Organizations	UN

Map page 101

Occupying the northern half of the Korean peninsula in east Asia, North Korea is a rugged and mountainous country. The principal lowlands and the main agricultural areas are the plains in the southwest. More than half the population lives in urban areas, mainly on the coastal plains. North Korea has a continental climate, with cold, dry winters and hot, wet summers. About a third of the workforce is involved in agriculture, mainly growing food crops on cooperative farms. A variety of minerals and ores, chiefly iron ore, are mined and are the basis of the country's heavy industry. Exports include minerals (lead, magnesite and zinc) and metal products (chiefly iron and steel). The economy has declined since 1991 when ties to the former USSR and eastern bloc collapsed, and there were serious food shortages between 1994 and 1998. North Korea receives some foreign aid.

NORWAY
Kingdom of Norway

Area Sq Km	323 878	Currency	Krone
Area Sq Miles	125 050	Languages	Norwegian
Population	4 419 000	Religions	Protestant, Roman Catholic
Capital	Oslo	Organizations	OECD, UN

Norway stretches along the north and west coasts of Scandinavia, from the Arctic Ocean to the southern North Sea. Its extensive coastline is indented with fjords and fringed with many islands. Inland, the terrain is mountainous, with coniferous forests and lakes in the south. The only major lowland areas are along the southern North Sea and Skagerrak coasts, where most people live. The climate is modified by the North Atlantic Drift. Norway has vast petroleum and natural gas resources in the North Sea. It is west one of Europe's leading producers of oil and gas, which account for around half of export earnings. Related industries include engineering (oil and gas platforms) and petrochemicals. More traditional industries process local raw materials: fish, timber and minerals. Agriculture is limited, but fishing and fish farming are important. Norway is the world's leading exporter of farmed salmon. Merchant shipping and tourism are major sources of foreign exchange.

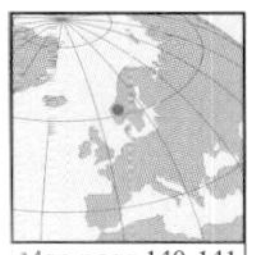
Map page 140-141

OMAN
Sultanate of Oman

Area Sq Km	309 500	Currency	Rial
Area Sq Miles	119 499	Languages	Arabic, Baluchi, Indian languages
Population	2 382 000	Religions	Ibadhi Muslim, Sunni Muslim
Capital	Muscat	Organizations	UN

In southwest Asia, Oman occupies the east and southeast coasts of the Arabian Peninsula and an enclave north of the United Arab Emirates. Most of the land is desert, with mountains in the north and south. The climate is hot and mainly dry. Most people live on the coastal strip on the Gulf of Oman. The majority depend on farming and fishing, but the oil and gas industries dominate the economy, with around eighty per cent of export revenues from oil.

Map page 125

PAKISTAN
Islamic Republic of Pakistan

Area Sq Km	803 940	Currency	Rupee
Area Sq Miles	310 403	Languages	Urdu, Punjabi, Sindhi, Pushtu, English
Population	148 166 000	Religions	Sunni Muslim, Shi'a Muslim, Christian, Hindu
Capital	Islamabad	Organizations	Comm., UN

Pakistan is in the northwest part of the Indian subcontinent in south Asia, on the Arabian Sea. Eastern and southern Pakistan are dominated by the great basin drained by the Indus river system. It is the main agricultural area and contains most of the predominantly rural population. To the north the land rises to the mountains of the Karakoram, Hindu Kush and Himalaya. The west is semi-desert plateaus and mountain ranges. The climate ranges between dry desert and tundra on the mountain tops. However, temperatures are generally warm and rainfall is monsoonal. Agriculture is the main sector of the economy, employing about half the workforce; cultivation is based on extensive irrigation schemes. Pakistan is one of the world's leading producers of cotton and an important exporter of rice. However, much of the country's food needs must be imported. Pakistan produces natural gas and has a variety of mineral deposits including coal and gold, but they are little developed. The main industries are textiles and clothing manufacture and food processing, with fabrics and ready-made clothing the leading exports. Pakistan also produces leather goods, fertilizers, chemicals, paper and precision instruments. The country depends heavily upon foreign aid and remittances from Pakistanis working abroad.

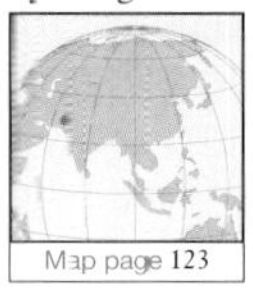
Map page 123

PALAU
Republic of Palau

Area Sq Km	497	Currency	US dollar
Area Sq Miles	192	Languages	Palauan, English
Population	19 000	Religions	Roman Catholic, Protestant, traditional beliefs
Capital	Koror	Organizations	UN

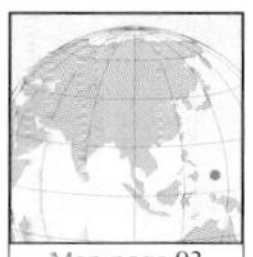
Map page 92

Palau comprises over three hundred islands in the western Caroline Islands in the west Pacific Ocean. The climate is tropical. The economy is based on farming, fishing and tourism; Palau is heavily dependent on US aid.

PANAMA
Republic of Panama

Area Sq Km	77 082	Currency	Balboa
Area Sq Miles	29 762	Languages	Spanish, English, Amerindian languages
Population	2 767 000	Religions	Roman Catholic, Protestant, Sunni Muslim
Capital	Panamá	Organizations	UN

Panama is the most southerly state in central America and has Pacific and Caribbean coasts. It is hilly, with mountains in the west and jungle near the Colombian border. The climate is tropical. Most people live on the drier Pacific side. The economy is based mainly on services related to the canal: shipping, banking and tourism. Exports include bananas, shrimps, coffee, clothing and fish products. USA is the main trading partner.

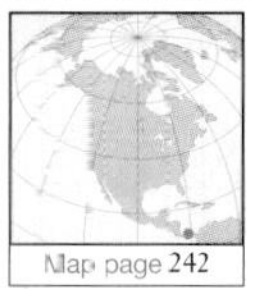
Map page 242

PAPUA NEW GUINEA
Independent State of Papua New Guinea

Area Sq Km	462 840	Currency	Kina
Area Sq Miles	178 704	Languages	English, Tok Pisin (creole), local languages
Population	4 600 000	Religions	Protestant, Roman Catholic, traditional beliefs
Capital	Port Moresby	Organizations	Comm., UN

Map page 77

Papua New Guinea, in Australasia, occupies the eastern half of the island of New Guinea and includes many island groups. Papua New Guinea has a forested and mountainous interior, bordered by swampy plains, and a tropical monsoon climate. Most of the workforce are farmers. Timber, copra, coffee and cocoa are important, but exports are dominated by minerals, chiefly gold and copper. The country depends on foreign aid. Australia and Japan are the main trading partners.

PARAGUAY
Republic of Paraguay

Area Sq Km	406 752	Currency	Guaraní
Area Sq Miles	157 048	Languages	Spanish, Guaraní
Population	5 222 000	Religions	Roman Catholic, Protestant
Capital	Asunción	Organizations	UN

Map page 253

Paraguay is a landlocked country in central South America, bordering Bolivia, Brazil and Argentina. The river Paraguay separates a sparsely populated western zone of marsh and flat alluvial plains from a more developed, hilly and forested region to the east and south. The climate is subtropical. Virtually all electricity is produced by hydro plants and surplus power is exported to Brazil and Argentina. The hydroelectric dam at Itaipu is the largest in the world. The mainstay of the economy is agriculture and agricultural industries. Exports include cotton, soya bean and edible oil products, timber and meat. Brazil and Argentina are the main trading partners.

PERU
Republic of Peru

Area Sq Km	1 285 216	Currency	Sol
Area Sq Miles	496 225	Languages	Spanish, Quechua, Aymara
Population	24 797 000	Religions	Roman Catholic, Protestant
Capital	Lima	Organizations	APEC, UN

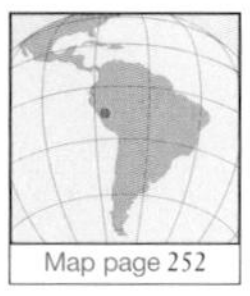
Map page 252

Peru lies on the Pacific coast of South America. Most people live on the coastal strip and the plateaus of the high Andes. East of the Andes is the Amazon rainforest. The coast is temperate with low rainfall, while the east is hot, humid and wet. Agriculture involves one third of the workforce, fishing is also important; agriculture and fishing were both disrupted by the El Nino effect in the 1990s. Sugar, cotton, coffee and, illegally, coca are the main cash crops. Copper and copper products, fishmeal, zinc products, coffee, petroleum and its products, and textiles are the main exports. America is the main trading partner.

PHILIPPINES
Republic of the Philippines

Area Sq Km	300 000	Currency	Peso
Area Sq Miles	115 831	Languages	English, Pilipino, Cebuano, local languages
Population	72 944 000	Religions	Roman Catholic, Protestant, Sunni Muslim
Capital	Manila	Organizations	APEC, ASEAN, UN

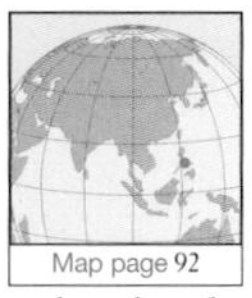
Map page 92

The Philippines, in southeast Asia, consists of over seven thousand islands and atolls lying between the South China Sea and the Pacific Ocean. The islands of Luzon and Mindanao account for two thirds of the land area. They and nine other fairly large islands are mountainous and forested. There are active volcanoes, and earthquakes are common. Most people live in the plains on the larger islands or on the coastal strips. The climate is hot and humid with heavy monsoonal rainfall. Coconuts, sugar, pineapples and bananas are the main agricultural crops; fish and timber are also important. The Philippines produces copper, gold, chromium, cobalt and nickel as well as oil, though geothermal power is also used. The main industries process raw materials and produce electrical and electronic equipment and components, footwear and clothing, textiles and furniture. These manufactured goods are the main exports. Foreign aid and remittances from workers abroad are important to the economy, which faces problems of high population growth rate and high unemployment. USA is the main trading partner.

Pitcairn Islands
United Kingdom Overseas Territory

Area Sq Km	45	Currency	NZ dollar
Area Sq Miles	17	Languages	English
Population	46	Religions	Protestant
Capital	Adamstown		

An island group in the southeast Pacific Ocean consisting of Pitcairn Island and three uninhabited islands. It was originally settled by mutineers from HMS Bounty.

Map page 75

POLAND
Polish Republic

Area Sq Km	312 683	Currency	Złoty
Area Sq Miles	120 728	Languages	Polish, German
Population	38 718 000	Religions	Roman Catholic, Polish Orthodox
Capital	Warszawa	Organizations	OECD, UN

Map page 174-175

Poland lies on the Baltic coast of central Europe. The Odra (Oder) and Wisla (Vistula) deltas dominate the coast. Inland, much of Poland is low-lying with woods and lakes. In the south the land rises to the Sudety and western part of the Carpathian Mountains which form the borders with the Czech Republic and Slovakia respectively. The climate is continental, with warm summers and cold winters. Around a quarter of the workforce is involved in agriculture, and exports include livestock products and sugar. The economy is heavily industrialized, with mining and manufacturing accounting for forty per cent of national income. Poland is one of the world's major producers of coal, and also produces copper, zinc, lead, sulphur and natural gas. The main industries are machinery and transport equipment, ship building, metal and chemical production. Germany is the main trading partner. Poland is negotiating to join the EU.

PORTUGAL
Portuguese Republic

Area Sq Km	88 940	Currency	Escudo, Euro
Area Sq Miles	34 340	Languages	Portuguese
Population	9 869 000	Religions	Roman Catholic, Protestant
Capital	Lisboa	Organizations	EU, OECD, UN

Map page 180

Portugal lies in the western part of the Iberian peninsula in southwest Europe, has an Atlantic coastline and is bordered by Spain to the north and east. The land north of the river Tejo (Tagus) is mostly highland with extensive forests of pine and cork. South of the river is undulating lowland. The climate in the north is cool and moist, the south is warmer, with dry, mild winters. Most Portuguese live near the coast, with one third of the total population in Lisbon (Lisboa) and Oporto. Agriculture, fishing and forestry involve about twelve per cent of the workforce. Mining and manufacturing are the main sectors of the economy. Portugal produces kaolin, copper, tin, zinc, tungsten and salt. Export manufactures include textiles, clothing and footwear, electrical machinery and transport equipment, cork and wood products, and chemicals. Service industries, chiefly tourism and banking, are important to the economy as are remittances from workers abroad. Most trade is with other EU countries.

PUERTO RICO
United States Commonwealth

Area Sq Km	9 104	Currency	US dollar
Area Sq Miles	3 515	Languages	Spanish, English
Population	3 810 000	Religions	Roman Catholic, Protestant
Capital	San Juan		

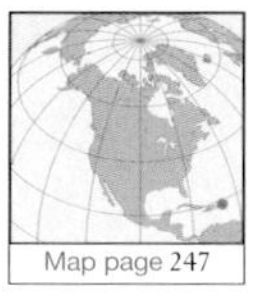
Map page 247

The Caribbean island of Puerto Rico has a forested, hilly interior, coastal plains and a tropical climate. Half the population lives in the San Juan area. The economy is based on manufacturing (chiefly chemicals, electronics and food), tourism and agriculture. USA is the predominant trading partner.

QATAR
State of Qatar

Area Sq Km	11 437	Currency	Riyal
Area Sq Miles	4 416	Languages	Arabic
Population	579 000	Religions	Sunni Muslim
Capital	Doha	Organizations	OPEC, UN

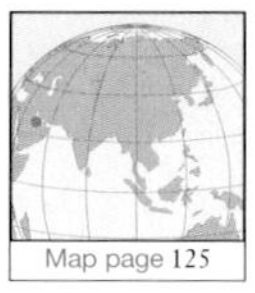
Map page 125

The emirate occupies a peninsula that extends northwards from east-central Saudi Arabia into The Gulf in southwest Asia. The land is flat and barren with sand dunes and salt pans. The climate is hot and mainly dry. Most people live in the Doha area. The economy is heavily dependent on oil and natural gas production and the oil-refining industry. Income also comes from overseas investment. Japan is the largest trading partner.

Réunion
French Overseas Department

Area Sq Km	2 551	Currency	French franc
Area Sq Miles	985	Languages	French, creole
Population	682 000	Religions	Roman Catholic
Capital	St-Denis		

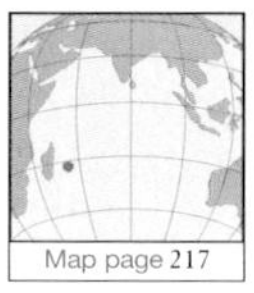
Map page 217

The Indian Ocean island of Réunion is mountainous, with coastal lowlands and a warm climate. It depends heavily on sugar, tourism and French aid. Some uninhabited islets to the east are administered from Réunion.

ROMANIA

Area Sq Km	237 500	Currency	Leu
Area Sq Miles	91 699	Languages	Romanian, Hungarian
Population	22 474 000	Religions	Romanian Orthodox, Protestant, Roman Catholic
Capital	Bucureşti	Organizations	UN

Map page 196-197

Romania lies on the Black Sea coast of east Europe. Mountains separate the Transylvanian Basin at the centre of the country from the populous plains of the east and south and the Danube delta. The climate is continental. Romania has mineral resources (zinc, lead, silver and gold), and oil and natural gas reserves. Economic reform has been slow and sporadic, but measures to accelerate change were introduced in 1999. Agriculture still employs over a quarter of the workforce. The main exports are textiles, mineral products, chemicals, machinery and footwear. The most important trading partners are Germany and Italy. Negotiations to join the EU have been started.

RUSSIAN FEDERATION

Area Sq Km	17 075 400	Currency	Rouble
Area Sq Miles	6 592 849	Languages	Russian, Tatar, Ukrainian, local languages
Population	147 434 000	Religions	Russian Orthodox, Sunni Muslim, Protestant
Capital	Moskva	Organizations	APEC, CIS, UN

Russia occupies much of east Europe and all of north Asia, and is the world's largest state, nearly twice the size of the USA. It borders thirteen countries to the west and south and has long coastlines on the Arctic and Pacific Oceans to the north and east. European Russia lies west of the Ural mountains. To the south the land rises to uplands and the Caucasus on the border with Georgia and Azerbaijan. East of the Urals lies the flat West Siberian Plain; much of central Siberia is plateau. In the south is Lake Baikal, the world's deepest lake, and the Sayan ranges on the border with Kazakhstan and Mongolia. Eastern Siberia is rugged and mountainous with many active volcanoes in the Kamchatka Peninsula. Russia's major rivers are the Volga in the west and the Ob', Yenisey, Lena and Amur in Siberia. The climate and vegetation range between arctic tundra in the north and semi-arid steppe towards the Black and Caspian Sea coasts in the south. In general, the climate is continental

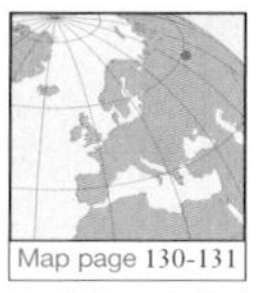
Map page 130-131

with extreme temperatures. The majority of the population (the seventh largest in the world), and industry and agriculture are concentrated in European Russia, but there has been increased migration to Siberia to exploit its vast natural resources. The economy is heavily dependent on exploitation of raw materials and on heavy industry. Russia has a wealth of mineral resources, though they are often difficult to exploit because of the climate and remote locations. It is one of the world's leading producers of petroleum, natural gas and coal as well as iron ore, nickel, copper and bauxite, and many precious and rare metals. Forests cover over forty per cent of the land area and supply an important timber, paper and pulp industry; around eight per cent of land is suitable for cultivation, but farming is generally inefficient and food, especially grains, must be imported. Fishing is important and Russia has a large fleet operating around the world. The transition to a market economy has been slow and difficult, with high unemployment and considerable underemployment. As well as mining and extractive industries there is a wide range of manufacturing industry from steel mills to aircraft and space vehicles, shipbuilding, synthetic fabrics, plastics, cotton fabrics, consumer durable, chemicals and fertilizers. Exports include fuels, metals, machinery, chemicals and forest products. The most important trading partners include Germany, Italy, USA, China and Switzerland.

RWANDA
Republic of Rwanda

Area Sq Km	26 338	Currency	Franc
Area Sq Miles	10 169	Languages	Kinyarwanda, French, English
Population	6 604 000	Religions	Roman Catholic, traditional beliefs, Protestant
Capital	Kigali	Organizations	UN

A densely populated and landlocked state in east Africa, Rwanda

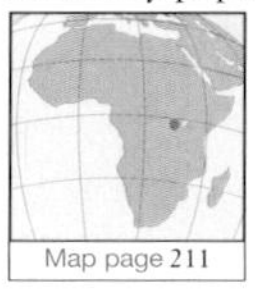
Map page 211

is situated in the mountains and plateaus to the east of the Great Rift Valley. The climate is warm with a summer dry season. Rwanda depends upon subsistence farming, coffee and tea exports, light industry and foreign aid, but in the 1990s civil war and ethnic conflict devastated the country.

Saba part of Netherlands Antilles

Area Sq Km (Miles) 13 (5)	Population 1 200	Capital Bottom

An island in the Leeward Islands in the Lesser Antilles in the Caribbean, to the south of Sint Maarten.

Map page 247

St-Barthélémy Dependency of Guadeloupe

Area Sq Km (Miles) 21 (8)	Population 5 038	Capital Gustavia

An island in the Leeward Islands in the Lesser Antilles in the Caribbean south of Sint Maarten. Tourism is the main economic activity.

Map page 247

St Helena
United Kingdom Overseas Territory

Area Sq Km	121	Currency	Pound sterling
Area Sq Miles	47	Languages	English
Population	5 644	Religions	Protestant, Roman Catholic
Capital	Jamestown		

St Helena and its dependencies, Ascension and Tristan da Cunha are isolated island groups lying in the south Atlantic Ocean. St Helena is a rugged island of volcanic origin; the main activity is fishing but the island depends on financial aid from the UK.

Map page 216

ST KITTS AND NEVIS
Federation of St Kitts and Nevis

Area Sq Km	261	Currency	E. Carib. dollar
Area Sq Miles	101	Languages	English, creole
Population	39 000	Religions	Protestant, Roman Catholic
Capital	Basseterre	Organizations	CARICOM, Comm., UN

St Kitts and Nevis are in the Leeward Islands in the Caribbean Sea.

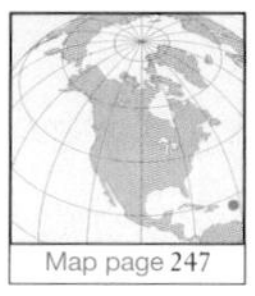
Map page 247

Both volcanic islands are mountainous and forested with sandy beaches and a warm, wet climate. About three-quarters of the population live on St Kitts. Agriculture is the main activity, with sugar the main product. Tourism and manufacturing (chiefly garments and electronic components) are important.

ST LUCIA

Area Sq Km	616	Currency	E. Carib. dollar
Area Sq Miles	238	Languages	English, creole
Population	150 000	Religions	Roman Catholic, Protestant
Capital	Castries	Organizations	CARICOM, Comm., UN

St Lucia, one of the Windward Islands in the Caribbean Sea, is a

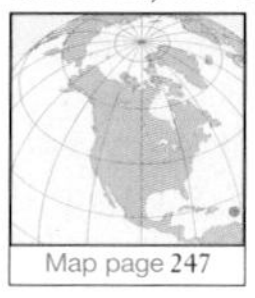
Map page 247

volcanic island with forested mountains, hot springs, sandy beaches and a wet tropical climate. Agriculture is the main activity, with bananas accounting for about forty per cent of export earnings. Tourism, agricultural processing and light manufacturing are increasingly important.

St Martin Dependency of Guadeloupe

Area Sq Km (Miles) 54 (21)	Population 28 518	Capital Marigot

The northern part of one of the Leeward Islands is in the Caribbean, the other part of the island is part of the Netherlands Antilles. Tourism is the main source of income.

Map page 247

St Pierre and Miquelon
French Territorial Collectivity

Area Sq Km	242	Currency	French franc
Area Sq Miles	93	Languages	French
Population	7 000	Religions	Roman Catholic
Capital	St-Pierre		

A group of islands off the south coast of Newfoundland in eastern Canada. The islands are unsuitable for agriculture; fishing and fish processing are still important, though the islands rely heavily on assistance from France.

Map page 225

ST VINCENT AND THE GRENADINES

Area Sq Km	389	Currency	E. Carib. dollar
Area Sq Miles	150	Languages	English, creole
Population	112 000	Religions	Protestant, Roman Catholic
Capital	Kingstown	Organizations	CARICOM, Comm., UN

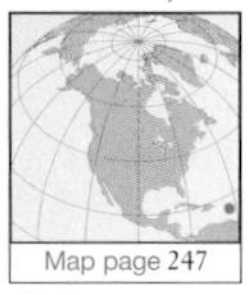
Map page 247

St Vincent, whose territory includes islets and cays in The Grenadines, is in the Windward Islands in the Caribbean Sea. St Vincent is forested and mountainous, with an active volcano, Soufrière. The climate is tropical and wet. The economy is based mainly on agriculture and tourism. Bananas account for around a third of export earnings, arrowroot is also important.

SAMOA
Independent State of Samoa

Area Sq Km	2 831	Currency	Tala
Area Sq Miles	1 093	Languages	Samoan, English
Population	174 000	Religions	Protestant, Roman Catholic
Capital	Apia	Organizations	Comm., UN

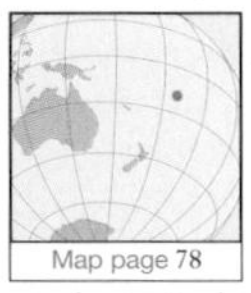
Map page 78

Samoa consists of two larger mountainous and forested islands, Savai'i and Upolu, and seven smaller islands in the south Pacific Ocean. Over half the population live on Upolu. The climate is tropical. The economy is based on agriculture, with some fishing and light manufacturing. Traditional exports are coconut products, timber, taro, cocoa and fruit. Tourism is increasing, but the islands depend upon workers' remittances and foreign aid.

SAN MARINO
Republic of San Marino

Area Sq Km	61	Currency	Ital. lira
Area Sq Miles	24	Languages	Italian
Population	26 000	Religions	Roman Catholic
Capital	San Marino	Organizations	UN

Map page 191

Landlocked San Marino lies in northeast Italy. A third of the people live in the capital. There is some agriculture and light industry, but most income comes from tourism. Most trade is with Italy.

SÃO TOMÉ AND PRÍNCIPE
Democratic Republic of São Tomé and Principe

Area Sq Km	964	Currency	Dobra
Area Sq Miles	372	Languages	Portuguese, creole
Population	141 000	Religions	Roman Catholic, Protestant
Capital	São Tomé	Organizations	UN

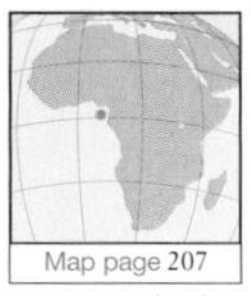
Map page 207

The two main islands and adjacent islets lie off the coast of west Africa in the Gulf of Guinea. São Tomé is the larger island with over ninety per cent of the population. Both São Tomé and Príncipe are mountainous and tree-covered, and have a hot and humid climate. The economy is heavily dependent on cocoa, which accounts for around ninety per cent of export earnings.

SAUDI ARABIA
Kingdom of Saudi Arabia

Area Sq Km	2 200 000	Currency	Riyal
Area Sq Miles	849 425	Languages	Arabic
Population	20 181 000	Religions	Sunni Muslim, Shi'a Muslim
Capital	Riyadh	Organizations	OPEC, UN

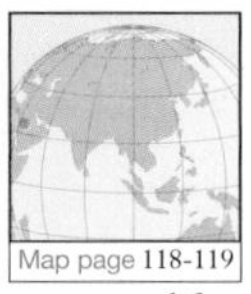
Map page 118-119

Saudi Arabia occupies most of the Arabian Peninsula in southwest Asia. The terrain is desert or semi-desert plateaus, which rise to mountains running parallel to the Red Sea in the west and slope down to plains in the southeast and along The Gulf in the east. Over eighty per cent of the population live in urban areas. There are around four million foreign workers in Saudi Arabia employed mainly in the oil and service industries. Summers are hot, winters are warm and rainfall is low. Saudi Arabia has the world's largest reserves of oil and significant natural gas reserves, located in the northeast, both onshore and in The Gulf. Crude oil and refined products account for over ninety per cent of export earnings. Other industries and irrigated agriculture are being encouraged, but most food and raw materials are imported. Saudi Arabia has important banking and commercial interests. Each year around two million pilgrims visit Islam's holiest cities, Mecca and Medina, in the west. Japan, USA, South Korea and Singapore are the main export trading partners.

SENEGAL
Republic of Senegal

Area Sq Km	196 720	Currency	CFA franc
Area Sq Miles	75 954	Languages	French, Wolof, Fulani, local languages
Population	9 003 000	Religions	Sunni Muslim, Roman Catholic, traditional beliefs
Capital	Dakar	Organizations	UN

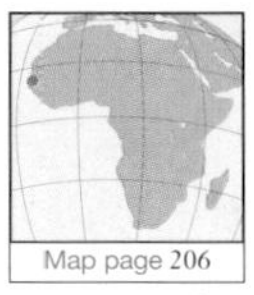
Map page 206

Senegal lies on the Atlantic coast of west Africa. The north is arid semi-desert, while the south is mainly fertile savanna bushland. The climate is tropical with summer rains, though droughts occur. One fifth of the population lives in and around Dakar. Fish, chemical products, groundnuts and phosphates are the main exports. Dakar is a major port and tourism is developing. France is the main trading partner.

SEYCHELLES
Republic of the Seychelles

Area Sq Km	455	Currency	Rupee
Area Sq Miles	176	Languages	English, French, creole
Population	76 000	Religions	Roman Catholic, Protestant
Capital	Victoria	Organizations	Comm., SADC, UN

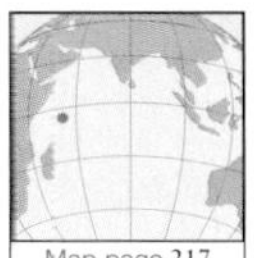
Map page 217

The Seychelles comprises an archipelago of over one hundred granitic and coral islands in the western Indian Ocean. Over ninety per cent of the population live on the main island, Mahé. The climate is hot and humid with heavy rainfall. The economy is based mainly on tourism, fishing and light manufacturing.

SIERRA LEONE
Republic of Sierra Leone

Area Sq Km	71 740	Currency	Leone
Area Sq Miles	27 699	Languages	English, creole, Mende, Temne, local languages
Population	4 568 000	Religions	Sunni Muslim, traditional beliefs
Capital	Freetown	Organizations	Comm., UN

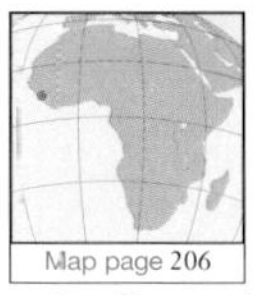
Map page 206

Sierra Leone lies on the Atlantic coast of west Africa. Its coast is heavily indented and lined with mangrove swamps. Inland is a forested area rising to savanna plateaus, with the mountains to the northeast. The climate is tropical and rainfall is heavy. Most of the workforce is involved in subsistence farming. Cocoa and coffee are the main cash crops, but diamonds and rutile (titanium ore) are the main exports, though a substantial amount of diamonds are smuggled out of the country. Civil war and economic decline have caused serious difficulties.

SINGAPORE
Republic of Singapore

Area Sq Km	639	Currency	Dollar
Area Sq Miles	247	Languages	Chinese, English, Malay, Tamil
Population	3 476 000	Religions	Buddhist, Taoist, Sunni Muslim, Christian, Hindu
Capital	Singapore	Organizations	APEC, ASEAN, Comm., UN

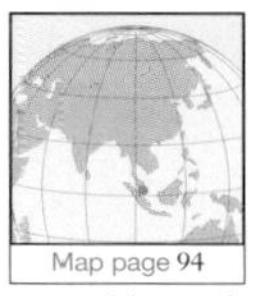
Map page 94

The state comprises the main island of Singapore and over fifty other islands, lying off the southern tip of the Malay Peninsula in southeast Asia. Singapore is generally low-lying and includes land reclaimed from swamps and the sea. It is hot and humid, with heavy rainfall throughout the year. There are fish farms and vegetable gardens in the north and east of the island, but most food needs must be imported. Singapore also lacks mineral and energy resources. Manufacturing industries and services are the main sectors of the economy. Their rapid development has fuelled the nation's impressive economic growth over the last three decades. The main industries include electronics, oil refining, chemicals, pharmaceuticals, ship repair, food processing and textiles. Singapore is a major financial centre. Its port is one of the world's largest and busiest and acts as an entrepôt for neighbouring states. Tourism is also important. Japan, USA and Malaysia are the main trading partners.

Sint Eustatius part of Netherlands Antilles

Area Sq Km (Miles) 21 (8)	Population 1 900	Capital Oranjestad

An island in the Leeward Islands in the Lesser Antilles in the Caribbean south of Sint Maarten; there is a developing tourism industry.

Map page 247

Sint Maarten part of Netherlands Antilles

Area Sq Km (Miles) 34 (13)	Population 38 567	Capital Philipsburg

The southern part of one of the Leeward Islands is in the Caribbean, the other part of the island is a dependency of Guadeloupe. Tourism and fishing are the most important industries.

Map page 247

SLOVAKIA
Slovak Republic

Area Sq Km	49 035	Currency	Koruna
Area Sq Miles	18 933	Languages	Slovak, Hungarian, Czech
Population	5 377 000	Religions	Roman Catholic, Protestant, Orthodox
Capital	Bratislava	Organizations	UN

A landlocked country in central Europe, Slovakia borders the Czech Republic, Poland, Ukraine, Hungary and Austria. Slovakia is mountainous along the border with Poland in the north, but low-lying in the southwest. The climate is continental. There are a range of manufacturing industries and the main exports are machinery and transport equipment, but during the 1990s there were continued economic difficulties and economic growth has been slow. Most trade is with EU countries and the Czech Republic and negotiations to join the EU have begun.

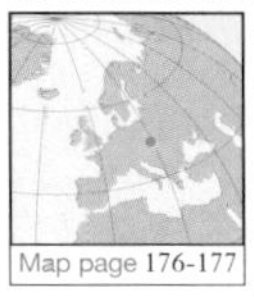
Map page 176-177

SLOVENIA
Republic of Slovenia

Area Sq Km	20 251	Currency	Tólar
Area Sq Miles	7 819	Languages	Slovene, Croatian, Serbian
Population	1 993 000	Religions	Roman Catholic, Protestant
Capital	Ljubljana	Organizations	UN

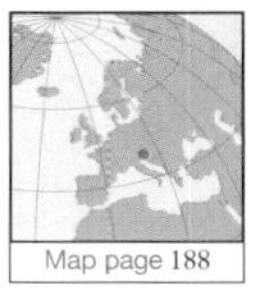
Map page 188

Slovenia lies in the northwest Balkans of south Europe and has a short coastline on the Adriatic Sea. It is mountainous and hilly, with lowlands on the coast and in the Sava and Drava river valleys. The climate is generally continental, but Mediterranean nearer the coast. The main agricultural products are potatoes, grains and sugar beet; the main industries include metal processing, electronics and consumer goods. Trade has been re-orientated towards western markets, the main trading partners are Germany and Italy. Negotiations to join the EU have begun.

SOLOMON ISLANDS

Area Sq Km	28 370	Currency	Dollar
Area Sq Miles	10 954	Languages	English, creole, local languages
Population	417 000	Religions	Protestant, Roman Catholic
Capital	Honiara	Organizations	Comm., UN

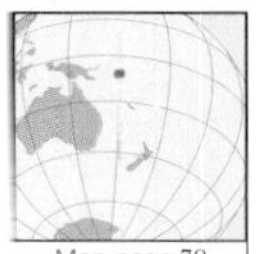
Map page 78

The state consists of the Solomon, Santa Cruz and Shortland Islands in the southwest Pacific Ocean. The six main islands are volcanic, mountainous and forested, though Guadalcanal, the most populous, has a large lowland area. The climate is generally hot and humid. Subsistence farming, forestry and fishing predominate. Exports include timber products, fish, copra and palm oil. The islands depend on foreign aid.

SOMALIA
Somali Democratic Republic

Area Sq Km	637 657	Currency	Shilling
Area Sq Miles	246 201	Languages	Somali, Arabic
Population	9 237 000	Religions	Sunni Muslim
Capital	Muqdisho	Organizations	UN

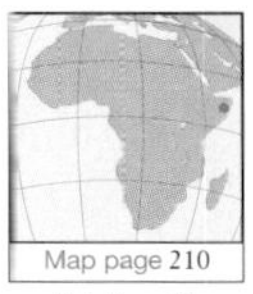
Map page 210

Somalia is in the northeast Africa, on the Gulf of Aden and Indian Ocean. It consists of a dry scrubby plateau, rising to highlands in the north. The climate is hot and dry, but coastal areas and the Jubba and Webi Shabeelle river valleys support crops and most of the population. Subsistence farming and livestock rearing are the main activities. Exports include livestock and bananas. Frequent drought and civil war have prevented economic development. Somalia is one of the poorest and least developed countries in the world.

SOUTH AFRICA, REPUBLIC OF

Area Sq Km	1 219 090	Currency	Rand
Area Sq Miles	470 693	Languages	Afrikaans, English, nine official local languages
Population	39 357 000	Religions	Protestant, Roman Catholic, Sunni Muslim, Hindu
Capital	Pretoria/ Cape Town	Organizations	Comm., SADC, UN

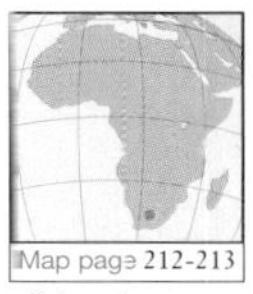
Map page 212-213

South Africa occupies most of the southern part of Africa. It borders five states, surrounds Lesotho and has a long coastline stretching from the Atlantic to the Indian Ocean. Much of the land is a vast plateau, covered with grassland or bush and drained by the Orange and Limpopo river systems. A fertile coastal plain rises to mountain ridges in the south and east, including Table Mountain near Cape Town and the Drakensberg range in the east. Gauteng is the most populous province, with Johannesburg and Pretoria its main cities. South Africa has warm summers and mild winters. Most of the country has rainfall in summer, but the coast around Cape Town has winter rains. South Africa is the largest and most developed economy in Africa, though wealth and economic control is unevenly distributed and unemployment is very high. Agriculture employs about a third of the workforce, crops include fruit, wine, wool and maize. South Africa is rich in minerals. It is the world's leading producer of gold and chromium and an important producer of diamonds; many other minerals are also mined. The main industries process minerals and agricultural produce, manufacture chemical products, electrical equipment and textiles, and assemble motor vehicles. Financial services are also important.

SOUTH KOREA
Republic of Korea

Area Sq Km	99 274	Currency	Won
Area Sq Miles	38 330	Languages	Korean
Population	46 109 000	Religions	Buddhist, Protestant, Roman Catholic
Capital	Sŏul	Organizations	APEC, UN

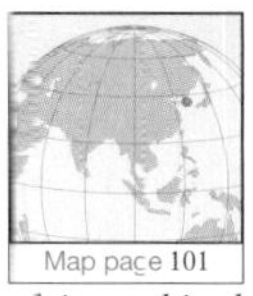
Map page 101

The state consists of the southern half of the Korean Peninsula in east Asia and many islands lying off the western and southern coasts in the Yellow Sea. The terrain is mountainous, though less rugged than that of North Korea. Population density is high and highly urbanized; most people live on the western coastal plains and in the basins of the Han-gang in the northwest and the Naktong-gang in the southeast. South Korea has a continental climate, with hot, wet summers and dry, cold winters. Arable land is limited by the mountainous terrain, but because of intensive farming South Korea is nearly self-sufficient in food. Sericulture is important as is fishing, which contributes to exports. South Korea has few mineral resources, except for coal and tungsten. It has achieved high economic growth based mainly on export manufacturing. The main manufactures are cars, electronic and electrical goods, ships, steel, chemicals, and toys as well as textiles, clothing, footwear and food products. USA and Japan are the main trading partners.

SPAIN
Kingdom of Spain

Area Sq Km	504 782	Currency	Peseta, Euro
Area Sq Miles	194 897	Languages	Castilian, Catalan, Galician, Basque
Population	39 628 000	Religions	Roman Catholic
Capital	Madrid	Organizations	EU, OECD, UN

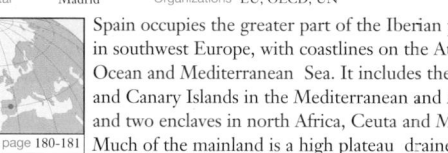

Map page 180-181

Spain occupies the greater part of the Iberian peninsula in southwest Europe, with coastlines on the Atlantic Ocean and Mediterranean Sea. It includes the Balearic and Canary Islands in the Mediterranean and Atlantic, and two enclaves in north Africa, Ceuta and Melilla. Much of the mainland is a high plateau drained by the Duero, Tagus and Guadiana rivers. The plateau is interrupted by a low mountain range and bounded to the east and north also by mountains, including the Pyrenees which form the border with France and Andorra. The main lowland areas are the Ebro basin in the northeast, the eastern coastal plains and the Guadalquivir basin in the southwest. Over three quarters of the population live in urban areas. The plateau experiences hot summers and cold winters. Conditions are cooler and wetter to the north, though warmer and drier to the south. Agriculture involves about ten per cent of the workforce and fruit, vegetables and wine are exported. Fishing is an important industry and Spain has a large fishing fleet. Mineral resources include lead, copper, mercury and fluorspar. Some oil is produced, but Spain has to import most energy needs. The economy is based on manufacturing and services. The principal products are machinery, transport equipment, and motor vehicles; other manufactures are agricultural products, chemicals, steel and other metals, paper products, wood and cork products, clothing and footwear, and textiles. With around fifty million visitors a year, tourism is a major industry, banking and commerce are also important. Around seventy per cent of trade is with other EU countries.

SRI LANKA
Democratic Socialist Republic of Sri Lanka

Area Sq Km	65 610	Currency	Rupee
Area Sq Miles	25 332	Languages	Sinhalese, Tamil, English
Population	18 455 000	Religions	Buddhist, Hindu, Sunni Muslim, Roman Catholic
Capital	Sri Jayewardenepura Kotte	Organizations	Comm., UN

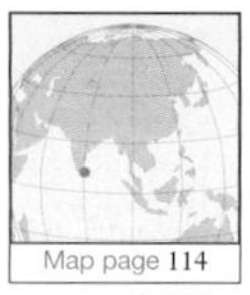

Map page 114

Sri Lanka lies in the Indian Ocean off the southeast coast of India in south Asia. It has rolling coastal plains with mountains in the centre-south. The climate is hot and monsoonal and most people live on the west coast. Manufactures (chiefly textiles and clothing), tea, rubber, copra and gems are exported. The economy relies on aid and workers' remittances. Tourism has been damaged by separatist activities.

SUDAN
Republic of the Sudan

Area Sq Km	2 505 813	Currency	Dinar
Area Sq Miles	967 500	Languages	Arabic, Dinka, Nubian, Beja, Nuer, local languages
Population	28 292 000	Religions	Sunni Muslim, traditional beliefs, Christian
Capital	Khartoum	Organizations	UN

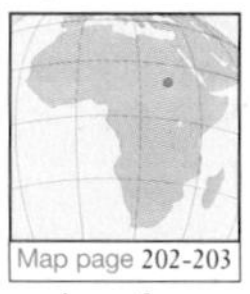

Map page 202-203

Africa's largest country, Sudan is in the northeast, on the Red Sea. It lies within the upper Nile basin, much of which is arid plain but with swamps to the south. Mountains lie to the northeast, west and south. The climate is hot and arid with light summer rainfall, though droughts occur. Most people live along the Nile and are farmers and herders. Cotton, gum arabic, livestock and other agricultural products are exported. The government is working with foreign investors to develop oil resources; but civil war in the south of Sudan continues to restrict growth of the economy.

SURINAME
Republic of Suriname

Area Sq Km	163 820	Currency	Guilder
Area Sq Miles	63 251	Languages	Dutch, Surinamese, English, Hindi
Population	414 000	Religions	Hindu, Roman Catholic, Protestant, Sunni Muslim
Capital	Paramaribo	Organizations	CARICOM, UN

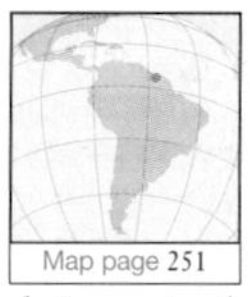

Map page 251

Suriname, on the Atlantic coast of northern South America, consists of a swampy coastal plain (where most people live), central plateaus and highlands in the south. The climate is tropical and rainforest covers much of the land. Bauxite mining is the main industry, and alumina and aluminium are the chief exports, with shrimps, rice, bananas and timber also exported. The main trading partners are The Netherlands, Norway and USA.

SWAZILAND
Kingdom of Swaziland

Area Sq Km	17 364	Currency	Lilangeni
Area Sq Miles	6 704	Languages	Swazi, English
Population	952 000	Religions	Christian, traditional beliefs
Capital	Mbabane	Organizations	Comm., SADC, UN

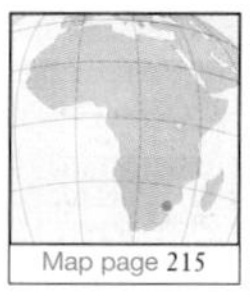

Map page 215

Landlocked Swaziland in southern Africa lies between Mozambique and South Africa. Savanna plateaus descend from mountains in the west towards hill country in the east. The climate is subtropical, but temperate in the mountains. Subsistence farming predominates. Asbestos and some diamonds are mined. Exports include sugar, fruit and wood pulp. Tourism and workers' remittances are important to the economy. Most trade is with South Africa.

SWEDEN
Kingdom of Sweden

Area Sq Km	449 964	Currency	Krona
Area Sq Miles	173 732	Languages	Swedish
Population	8 875 000	Religions	Protestant, Roman Catholic
Capital	Stockholm	Organizations	EU, OECD, UN

Map page 140-141

Sweden, the largest and most populous of the Scandinavian countries, occupies the eastern part of the peninsula in north Europe and borders the North and Baltic Seas and Gulf of Bothnia. Forested mountains cover the northern half of the country, part of which lies within the Arctic Circle. Southwards is a lowland lake region, where most of the population lives. Farther south is an upland region, and then a fertile plain at the tip of the peninsula. Sweden has warm summers and cold winters, though the latter are longer and more severe in the north. Natural resources include coniferous forests, mineral deposits and water resources. There is little agriculture, though some dairy products, meat, cereals and vegetables are produced in the south. The forests supply timber for export and for the important pulp, paper and furniture industries. Sweden is an important producer of iron ore and copper; zinc, lead, silver and gold are also mined. Machinery and transport equipment, chemicals, electrical goods and telecommunications equipment are the main industries. The majority of trade is with other EU countries.

SWITZERLAND
Swiss Confederation

Area Sq Km	41 293	Currency	Franc
Area Sq Miles	15 943	Languages	German, French, Italian, Romansch
Population	7 299 000	Religions	Roman Catholic, Protestant
Capital	Bern	Organizations	OECD

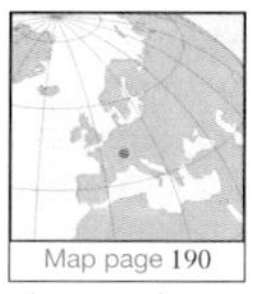

Map page 190

Switzerland is a landlocked country of west central Europe that is surrounded by France, Germany, Austria, Liechtenstein and Italy. It is also Europe's most mountainous country. The southern half lies within the Alps, while the northwest is dominated by the Jura mountains. The rest of the land is a high plateau where most people live. The climate varies greatly, depending on altitude and relief, but in general summers are mild and winters are cold with heavy snowfalls. Switzerland has one of the highest standards of living in the world. Yet it has few mineral resources and most food and industrial raw materials have to be imported. Manufacturing makes the largest contribution to the economy and though varied is specialist in certain products. Engineering is the most important industry, producing precision instruments and heavy machinery, other important industries are chemicals and pharmaceuticals. Banking and financial services are very important and Zurich is one of the world's leading banking cities. Tourism, and international organizations based in Switzerland are also major foreign currency earners. Germany is the main trading partner.

SYRIA
Syrian Arab Republic

Area Sq Km	185 180	Currency	Pound
Area Sq Miles	71 498	Languages	Arabic, Kurdish, Armenian
Population	15 333 000	Religions	Sunni Muslim, Shi'a Muslim, Christian
Capital	Damascus	Organizations	UN

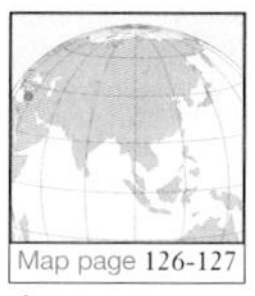

Map page 126-127

Syria is in southwest Asia, on the Mediterranean Sea. Behind the coastal plain lies a range of hills and then a plateau cut by the Euphrates river. Mountains flank the southwest borders with Lebanon and Israel, east of which is desert. The climate is Mediterranean in coastal regions, hotter and drier inland. Most Syrians live on the coast or in the river valleys. Cotton, cereals and fruit are important, but the main exports are petroleum and its products, and textiles.

TAIWAN

Area Sq Km	36 179	Currency	Dollar
Area Sq Miles	13 969	Languages	Mandarin, Min, Hakka, local languages
Population	21 908 135	Religions	Buddhist, Taoist, Confucian, Christian
Capital	T'aipei	Organizations	APEC

Map page 109

The east Asian state consists of the island of Taiwan, separated from mainland China by the Taiwan Strait, and several much smaller islands. Much of Taiwan is mountainous and forested. Densely populated coastal plains in the west contain the bulk of the population and most economic activity. Taiwan has a tropical monsoon climate, with warm, wet summers and mild winters. Agriculture is highly productive. Taiwan is virtually self-sufficient in food and exports some products. Coal, oil and natural gas are produced and a few minerals are mined but none of them are of great significance to the economy. Taiwan depends heavily on imports of raw materials and exports of manufactured goods. The main manufactures are electrical and electronic goods, including television sets, personal computers and calculators, textiles, fertilizers, clothing, footwear and toys. The main trading partners are USA, Japan and Germany.

TAJIKISTAN
Republic of Tajikistan

Area Sq Km	143 100	Currency	Rouble
Area Sq Miles	55 251	Languages	Tajik, Uzbek, Russian
Population	6 015 000	Religions	Sunni Muslim
Capital	Dushanbe	Organizations	CIS, UN

Landlocked Tajikistan in central Asia is a mountainous country, occupying the Alai Range and the Pamir. In less mountainous western areas summers are warm though winters are cold. Agriculture is the

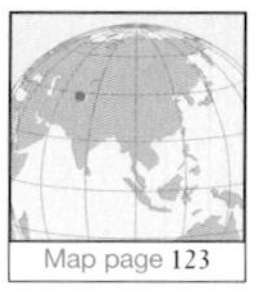

Map page 123

main sector of the economy, chiefly cotton growing and cattle breeding. Mineral deposits include lead, zinc, and uranium. Metal processing, textiles and clothing are the main manufactures; the main exports are aluminium and cotton. Russia, Kazakhstan and Uzbekistan are the main trading partners.

TANZANIA
United Republic of Tanzania

Area Sq Km	945 087	Currency	Shilling
Area Sq Miles	364 900	Languages	Swahili, English, Nyamwezi, local languages
Population	32 102 000	Religions	Muslim, traditional beliefs, Christian
Capital	Dodoma	Organizations	Comm., SADC, UN

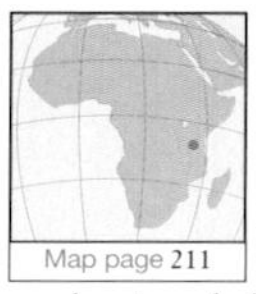

Map page 211

Tanzania lies on the coast of east Africa and includes the island of Zanzibar in the Indian Ocean. Most of the mainland is a savanna plateau lying east of the Great Rift Valley. In the north are Kilimanjaro, the highest mountain in Africa, and the Serangeti National Park. The climate is tropical. The economy is predominantly based on agriculture which employs an estimated ninety per cent of the workforce. Coffee, cotton, cashew nuts and tobacco are the main exports, with cloves from Zanzibar. Agricultural processing and gold and diamond mining are the main industries, though tourism is growing. Tanzania is one of the least developed countries in the world and depends heavily on aid.

THAILAND
Kingdom of Thailand

Area Sq Km	513 115	Currency	Baht
Area Sq Miles	198 115	Languages	Thai, Lao, Chinese, Malay, Mon-Khmer languages
Population	60 300 000	Religions	Buddhist, Sunni Muslim
Capital	Bangkok	Organizations	APEC, ASEAN, UN

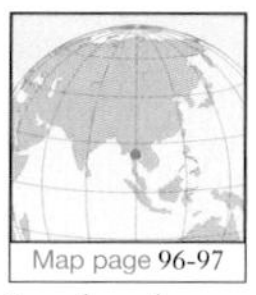

Map page 96-97

A country in southeast Asia, Thailand borders Myanmar, Laos, Cambodia and Malaysia and has coastlines on the Gulf of Thailand and Andaman Sea. Central Thailand is dominated by the Chao Phraya river basin, which contains Bangkok, the only major urban centre, and most economic activity. To the east is a dry plateau drained by tributaries of the Mekong river, while to the north, west and south, extending halfway down the Malay peninsula, are forested hills and mountains. Many small islands line the coast. The climate is hot, humid and monsoonal. About half the workforce is involved in agriculture. Thailand is one of the world's leading exporters of rice and rubber, and a major exporter of maize and tapioca. Fish and fish processing are important. Thailand produces natural gas, some oil and lignite, minerals (chiefly tin, tungsten and baryte) and gemstones. Manufacturing is the largest contributor to national income, with electronics, textiles, clothing and footwear, and food processing the main industries. With around seven million visitors a year, tourism is the major source of foreign exchange. Japan and USA are the main trading partners.

TOGO
Republic of Togo

Area Sq Km	56 785	Currency	CFA franc
Area Sq Miles	21 925	Languages	French, Ewe, Kabre, local languages
Population	4 397 000	Religions	Traditional beliefs, Christian, Sunni Muslim
Capital	Lomé	Organizations	UN

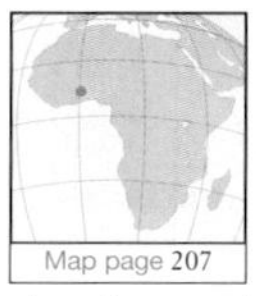

Map page 207

Togo is a long narrow country in west Africa with a short coastline on the Gulf of Guinea. The interior consists of plateaus rising to mountainous areas. The climate is tropical, drier inland. Agriculture is the mainstay of the economy. Phosphate mining and food processing are the main industries. Cotton, phosphates, coffee and cocoa are the main exports. Lomé is an entrepôt trade centre.

Tokelau New Zealand Overseas Territory

Area Sq Km (Miles) 10 (4) Population 1 000

Tokelau consists of three atolls, Atafu, Nukunonu and Fakaofa, in the Pacific Ocean north of Samoa. Subsistence agriculture is the main activity, and the islands rely on aid and remittances from New Zealand.

Map page 81

TONGA
Kingdom of Tonga

Area Sq Km	748	Currency	Pa'anga
Area Sq Miles	289	Languages	Tongan, English
Population	98 000	Religions	Protestant, Roman Catholic
Capital	Nuku'alofa	Organizations	Comm., UN

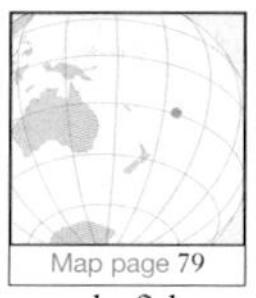

Map page 79

Tonga comprises some one hundred and seventy islands in the south Pacific Ocean, northeast of New Zealand. The three main groups are Tongatapu (where sixty per cent of Tongans live), Ha'apai and Vava'u. The climate is warm with good rainfall and the economy relies heavily on agriculture. Exports include squash, fish, vanilla beans and root crops. Tourism and light industry are increasingly important.

TRINIDAD AND TOBAGO
Republic of Trinidad and Tobago

Area Sq Km	5 130	Currency	Dollar
Area Sq Miles	1 981	Languages	English, creole, Hindi
Population	1 283 000	Religions	Roman Catholic, Hindu, Protestant, Sunni Muslim
Capital	Port of Spain	Organizations	CARICOM, Comm., UN

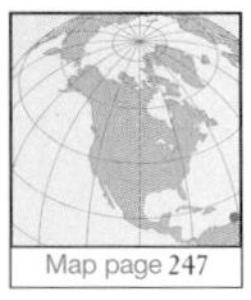

Map page 247

Trinidad, the most southerly Caribbean island, lies off the Venezuelan coast. It is hilly in the north, with a central plain. Tobago, to the northeast, is smaller more mountainous and less developed. The climate is tropical. Oil and petrochemicals industries dominate the economy. The main crops are cocoa, sugar cane, coffee and fruit and vegetables. Tourism is also important.USA is the main trading partner.

Tristan da Cunha Dependency of St Helena

Area Sq Km (Miles) 98 (38) Population 300 Capital Settlement of Edinburgh

A group of volcanic islands in the south Atlantic Ocean, the other main islands in the group are Nightingale Island and Inaccessible Island; the group is over 2000 kilometres (1250 miles) south of St Helena. The economy is based on fishing, fish processing and agriculture, and ecotourism is increasing.

Map page 216

TUNISIA
Republic of Tunisia

Area Sq Km	164 150	Currency	Dinar
Area Sq Miles	63 379	Languages	Arabic, French
Population	9 335 000	Religions	Sunni Muslim
Capital	Tunis	Organizations	UN

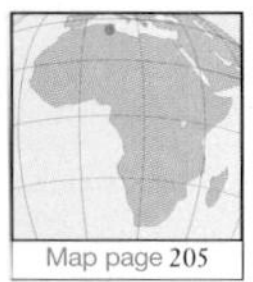

Map page 205

Tunisia is on the Mediterranean coast of north Africa. The north is mountainous with valleys and coastal plains, where most people live. The north has a Mediterranean climate, the south is hot and arid. Oil and phosphates are the main resources. The main crops are olives and citrus fruit. Exports include petroleum products, textiles, fruit and phosphorus; tourism is important with around five million visitors a year. Most trade is with EU countries; Tunisia has an agreement with the EU to create a free trade zone.

TURKEY
Republic of Turkey

Area Sq Km	779 452	Currency	Lira
Area Sq Miles	300 948	Languages	Turkish, Kurdish
Population	64 479 000	Religions	Sunni Muslim, Shi'a Muslim
Capital	Ankara	Organizations	OECD, UN

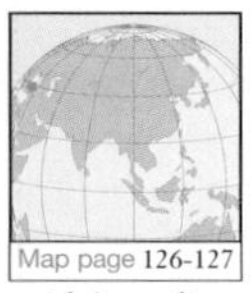

Map page 126-127

Turkey occupies the Asia Minor peninsula of southwest Asia and has coastlines on the Black, Mediterranean and Aegean Seas. It includes eastern Thrace, which is in south Europe and separated from the rest of the country by the Bosporus, Sea of Marmara and Dardanelles. The Asian mainland consists of the semi-arid Anatolian plateau, flanked to the north, south and east by mountains. Over forty per cent of Turks live in central Anatolia and the Marmara and Aegean coastal plains. The coast has a Mediterranean climate, but inland conditions are more extreme with hot, dry summers and cold, snowy winters. Agriculture involves about forty per cent of the workforce and products include cotton, grain, tobacco, fruit, nuts and livestock. Turkey is a leading producer of chrome, iron ore, lead, tin, borates, and baryte; coal is also mined. The main manufactures are textiles (the chief export), food processing, steel, vehicles and chemicals; tourism is a major industry with nine million visitors a year. Germany and USA are the main trading partners. Remittances by workers aboard are important.

TURKMENISTAN
Republic of Turkmenistan

Area Sq Km	488 100	Currency	Manat
Area Sq Miles	188 456	Languages	Turkmen, Uzbek, Russian
Population	4 309 000	Religions	Sunni Muslim, Russian Orthodox
Capital	Ashgabat	Organizations	CIS, UN

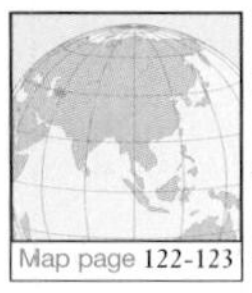

Map page 122-123

Turkmenistan, in central Asia, lies mainly within the plains of the Karakum Desert; most people live on the desert fringes: the foothills of the Kopet Dag in the south, Amudar'ya valley in the north and Caspian Sea plains in the west. The climate is dry with extreme temperatures. The economy is based mainly on irrigated agriculture, chiefly cotton growing, and the production of natural gas; there are also reserves of oil. Development of the natural gas and oil resources depend on building further pipelines. Russia is the main trading partner.

Turks and Caicos Islands
United Kingdom Overseas Territory

Area Sq Km (Miles) 430 (166) Population 16 000 Capital Grand Turk

The state consists of forty or so low-lying islands and cays in the northern Caribbean. Only eight islands are inhabited; two fifths of the people live on Grand Turk and Salt Cay. The climate is tropical. The economy is based on tourism, fishing and offshore banking.

Map page 246

TUVALU

Area Sq Km	25	Currency	Dollar
Area Sq Miles	10	Languages	Tuvaluan, English
Population	11 000	Religions	Protestant
Capital	Vaiaku	Organizations	Comm.

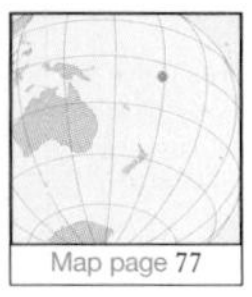

Map page 77

Tuvalu comprises nine low lying coral atolls in the south Pacific Ocean. One third of the population lives on Funafuti and most people depend on subsistence farming and fishing. The islands export copra, stamps and clothing, but rely heavily on foreign aid. Tuvalu is a special member of the Commonwealth.

UGANDA
Republic of Uganda

Area Sq Km	241 038	Currency	Shilling
Area Sq Miles	93 065	Languages	English, Swahili, Luganda, local languages
Population	20 554 000	Religions	Roman Catholic, Protestant, Muslim, trad. beliefs
Capital	Kampala	Organizations	Comm., UN

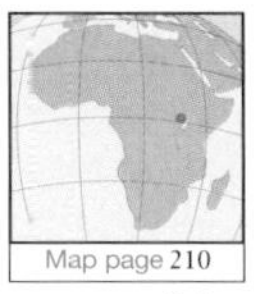

Map page 210

A landlocked country in east Africa, Uganda consists of a savanna plateau with mountains and lakes. The climate is warm and wet. Most people live in the southern half of the country; life expectancy in Uganda has fallen by fifteen per cent since 1975 because of AIDS. Agriculture employs around eighty per cent of the workforce and dominates the economy. Coffee, cotton and tea are the main exports. Uganda relies heavily on aid.

UKRAINE

Area Sq Km	603 700	Currency	Hryvnia
Area Sq Miles	233 090	Languages	Ukrainian, Russian
Population	50 861 000	Religions	Orthodox, Ukrainian Catholic, Roman Catholic
Capital	Kyiv	Organizations	CIS, UN

Map page 136-137

Ukraine lies on the Black Sea coast of east Europe. Much of the land is steppe, generally flat and treeless, but with rich black soil and drained by the river Dnieper. Along the border with Belarus are forested, marshy plains. The only uplands are the Carpathian Mountains in the west and smaller ranges on the Crimea peninsula. Summers are warm and winters are cold, with milder conditions in the Crimea. About a quarter of the population lives in the mainly industrial areas around Donets'k, Kyiv and Dnipropetrovs'k. The Ukraine is rich in natural resources: fertile soil, substantial mineral and natural gas deposits, and forests. Agriculture and livestock raising are important, but mining and manufacturing are the most important sectors of the economy. Coal, iron and manganese mining, steel and metal production, machinery, chemicals and food processing are the main industries. Russia is the main trading partner.

UNITED ARAB EMIRATES
Federation of Emirates

Area Sq Km	83 600	Currency	Dirham
Area Sq Miles	32 278	Languages	Arabic,English
Population	2 377 453	Religions	Sunni Muslim, Shi'a Muslim
Capital	Abu Dhabi	Organizations	OPEC, UN

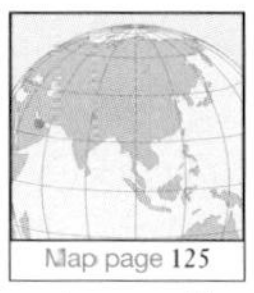

Map page 125

The UAE lies on the northeast of the Arabian Peninsula, in southwest Asia. Six emirates lie on The Gulf while the seventh, Fujairah, lies on the Gulf of Oman. Most of the land is flat desert with sand dunes and salt pans. The only hilly area is in the northeast. Over eighty per cent of the population live in three emirates - Abu Dhabi, Dubai and Sharjah. Summers are hot and winters are mild with occasional rainfall in coastal areas. Fruit and vegetables are grown in oases and irrigated areas, but the Emirates wealth is based on hydrocarbons, mainly within Abu Dhabi, but with smaller supplies in Dubai, Sharjah and Ras al Khaimah. The UAE is the third largest oil producer in the Middle East after Saudi Arabia and Iran. Dubai is an important entrepôt trade centre; tourism is increasing in importance.

Abu Dhabi (Emirate)
Area Sq Km (Miles) 73 060 (28 209) Population 928 360 Capital Abu Dhabi

Ajman (Emirate)
Area Sq Km (Miles) 260 (100) Population 118 812 Capital Ajman

Dubai (Emirate)
Area Sq Km (Miles) 3 900 (1 506) Population 674 101 Capital Dubai

Fujairah (Emirate)
Area Sq Km (Miles) 1 300 (502) Population 76 254 Capital Fujairah

Ras al Khaimah (Emirate)
Area Sq Km (Miles) 1 700 (656) Population 144 430 Capital Ras al Khaimah

Sharjah (Emirate)
Area Sq Km (Miles) 2 600 (1 004) Population 400 339 Capital Sharjah

Umm al Qaiwain (Emirate)
Area Sq Km (Miles) 780 (301) Population 35 157 Capital Umm al Qaiwain

UNITED KINGDOM
United Kingdom of Great Britain and Northern Ireland

Area Sq Km	244 082	Currency	Pound
Area Sq Miles	94 241	Languages	English, Welsh, Gaelic
Population	58 649 000	Religions	Protestant, Roman Catholic, Muslim
Capital	London	Organizations	Comm., EU, OECD, UN

A country in northwest Europe, the United Kingdom occupies the island of Great Britain, part of Ireland and many small adjacent islands. Great Britain comprises the countries of England, Scotland and Wales. England covers over half the land area and supports over four-fifths of the population, chiefly in the southeast region. The landscape is flat or rolling with some uplands, notably the Cheviot Hills on the Scottish border, the Pennines in the centre-north and the hills of the Lake District in the northwest. Scotland consists of southern uplands, central lowlands, highlands (which include the UK's highest peak) and islands. Wales is a land of mountains and river valleys. Northern Ireland contains uplands, plains and the UK's largest lake, Lough Neagh. The climate is mild, wet and variable. The UK has few mineral deposits, but has important energy resources. Over forty per cent of land is suitable for grazing, about twenty five per cent is cultivated, and ten per cent is forested. Agriculture involves mainly sheep and cattle raising and dairy farming, with crop and fruit growing in the east and southeast. Productivity is high, but about one third of food needs must be imported. The UK produces petroleum and natural gas from reserves in the North Sea and is self-sufficient in energy in net terms. It also has

Map page 144-145

reserves of coal, though the coal industry has contracted. Major manufactures are food and drinks, motor vehicles and parts, aerospace equipment, machinery, electronic and electrical equipment, and chemicals and chemical products. However, the economy is dominated by service industries, including banking, insurance, finance and business services. London is one of the world's major financial centres. Tourism is a major industry, with around twenty five million visitors a year. International trade is also important, equivalent to a third of national income; over half of trade is with other EU countries.

England (Constituent country)
Area Sq Km (Miles) 130 423 (50 357) Population 49 284 200 Capital London

Northern Ireland (Province)
Area Sq Km (Miles) 14 121 (5 452) Population 1 675 000 Capital Belfast

Scotland (Constituent country)
Area Sq Km (Miles) 78 772 (30 414) Population 5 122 500 Capital Edinburgh

Wales (Principality)
Area Sq Km (Miles) 20 766 (8 018) Population 2 926 900 Capital Cardiff

UNITED STATES OF AMERICA
Federal Republic

Area Sq Km	9 809 378	Currency	Dollar
Area Sq Miles	3 787 422	Languages	English, Spanish
Population	274 028 000	Religions	Protestant, Roman Catholic, Sunni Muslim, Jewish
Capital	Washington	Organizations	APEC, OECD, UN

Map page 228-229

The USA comprises forty eight contiguous states in North America, bounded by Canada and Mexico, and the states of Alaska, to the northwest of Canada, and Hawaii, in the Pacific Ocean. The populous eastern states consist of the Atlantic coastal plain (which includes the Florida peninsula and the Gulf of Mexico coast) and the Appalachian Mountains. The central states form a vast interior plain drained by the Mississippi-Missouri river system. To the west lie the Rocky Mountains, separated from the Pacific coastal ranges by the intermontane plateaus. The coastal ranges are prone to earthquakes. Hawaii is a group of some twenty volcanic islands. Climatic conditions range between arctic in Alaska to desert in the intermontane plateaus. Most of the USA is temperate, though the interior has continental conditions. The USA has abundant natural resources. It has major reserves minerals and energy resources. About twenty per cent of the land can be used for crops, over twenty five per cent is suitable for livestock rearing and over thirty per cent is forested. The USA has the largest and most technologically advanced economy in the world, based on manufacturing and services. Though agriculture accounts for only about two per cent national income, productivity is high and the USA is a net exporter of food, chiefly grains and fruit. Cotton is the major industrial crop; livestock rearing, forestry and fishing are also important. The USA produces iron ore, copper, lead, zinc, and many other minerals. It is a major producer of coal, petroleum and natural gas, though being the world's biggest energy user it imports significant quantities of petroleum and its products. Manufacturing is well diversified. The main industries are: petroleum, steel, motor vehicles, aerospace, telecommunications, electrics, food processing, chemicals and consumer goods. Tourism is a major foreign currency earner with around forty-five million visitors a year. Other important service industries are banking and finance, and Wall Street in New York is a major stock exchange.

Alabama (State)
Area Sq Km (Miles) 135 775 (52 423) Population 4 351 999 Capital Montgomery

Alaska (State)
Area Sq Km (Miles) 1 700 130 (656 424) Population 614 010 Capital Juneau

Arizona (State)
Area Sq Km (Miles) 295 274 (114 006) Population 4 668 631 Capital Phoenix

Arkansas (State)
Area Sq Km (Miles) 137 741 (53 182) Population 2 538 303 Capital Little Rock

California (State)
Area Sq Km (Miles) 423 999 (163 707) Population 32 666 550 Capital Sacramento

Colorado (State)
Area Sq Km (Miles) 269 618 (104 100) Population 3 970 971 Capital Denver

Connecticut (State)
Area Sq Km (Miles) 14 359 (5 544) Population 3 274 069 Capital Hartford

Delaware (State)
Area Sq Km (Miles) 6 446 (2 489) Population 743 603 Capital Dover

District of Columbia (District)
Area Sq Km (Miles) 176 (68) Population 523 124 Capital Washington

Florida (State)
Area Sq Km (Miles) 170 312 (65 758) Population 14 915 980 Capital Tallahassee

Georgia (State)
Area Sq Km (Miles) 153 951 (59 441) Population 7 642 207 Capital Atlanta

Hawaii (State)
Area Sq Km (Miles) 28 314 (10 932) Population 1 193 001 Capital Honolulu

Idaho (State)
Area Sq Km (Miles) 216 456 (83 574) Population 1 228 684 Capital Boise

Illinois (State)
Area Sq Km (Miles) 150 007 (57 918) Population 13 045 326 Capital Springfield

Indiana (State)
Area Sq Km (Miles) 94 327 (36 420) Population 5 899 195 Capital Indianapolis

Iowa (State)
Area Sq Km (Miles) 145 754 (56 276) Population 2 862 447 Capital Des Moines

Kansas (State)
Area Sq Km (Miles) 213 109 (82 282) Population 2 629 067 Capital Topeka

Kentucky (State)
Area Sq Km (Miles) 104 664 (40 411) Population 3 936 499 Capital Frankfort

Louisiana (State)
Area Sq Km (Miles) 134 273(51 843) Population 4 368 967 Capital Baton Rouge

Maine (State)
Area Sq Km (Miles) 91 652(35 387) Population 1 244 250 Capital Augusta

Maryland (State)
Area Sq Km (Miles) 32 134(12 407) Population 5 134 808 Capital Annapolis

Massachusetts (State)
Area Sq Km (Miles) 27 337 (10 555) Population 6 147 132 Capital Boston

Michigan (State)
Area Sq Km (Miles) 250 737 (96 810) Population 9 817 242 Capital Lansing

Minnesota (State)
Area Sq Km (Miles) 225 181 (86 943) Population 4 725 419 Capital St Paul

Mississippi (State)
Area Sq Km (Miles) 125 443 (48 434) Population 2 752 092 Capital Jackson

Missouri (State)
Area Sq Km (Miles) 180 545 (69 709) Population 5 438 559 Capital Jefferson City

Montana (State)
Area Sq Km (Miles) 380 847 (147 046) Population 880 453 Capital Helena

Nebraska (State)
Area Sq Km (Miles) 200 356 (77 358) Population 1 662 719 Capital Lincoln

Nevada (State)
Area Sq Km (Miles) 286 367 (110 567) Population 1 746 898 Capital Carson City

New Hampshire (State)
Area Sq Km (Miles) 24 219 (9 351) Population 1 185 048 Capital Concord

New Jersey (State)
Area Sq Km (Miles) 22 590 (8 722) Population 8 115 011 Capital Trenton

New Mexico (State)
Area Sq Km (Miles) 314 937(121 598) Population 1 736 931 Capital Santa Fe

New York (State)
Area Sq Km (Miles) 141 090 (54 475) Population 18 175 301 Capital Albany

North Carolina (State)
Area Sq Km (Miles) 139 396 (53 821) Population 7 546 493 Capital Raleigh

North Dakota (State)
Area Sq Km (Miles) 183 123 (70 704) Population 638 244 Capital Bismarck

Ohio (State)
Area Sq Km (Miles) 116 104 (44 828) Population 11 209 493 Capital Columbus

Oklahoma (State)
Area Sq Km (Miles) 181 048 (69 903) Population 3 346 713 Capital Oklahoma City

Oregon (State)
Area Sq Km (Miles) 254 819 (98 386) Population 3 281 974 Capital Salem

Pennsylvania (State)
Area Sq Km (Miles) 119 290 (46 058) Population 12 001 451 Capital Harrisburg

Rhode Island (State)
Area Sq Km (Miles) 4 002 (1 545) Population 988 480 Capital Providence

South Carolina (State)
Area Sq Km (Miles) 82 898 (32 007) Population 3 835 962 Capital Columbia

South Dakota (State)
Area Sq Km (Miles) 199 742 (77 121) Population 738 171 Capital Pierre

Tennessee (State)
Area Sq Km (Miles) 109 158 (42 146) Population 5 430 621 Capital Nashville

Texas (State)
Area Sq Km (Miles) 695 673 (268 601) Population 19 759 614 Capital Austin

Utah (State)
Area Sq Km (Miles) 219 900 (84 904) Population 2 099 758 Capital Salt Lake City

Vermont (State)
Area Sq Km (Miles) 24 903 (9 615) Population 590 883 Capital Montpelier

Virginia (State)
Area Sq Km (Miles) 110 771 (42 769) Population 6 791 345 Capital Richmond

Washington (State)
Area Sq Km (Miles) 184 674 (71 303) Population 5 689 263 Capital Olympia

West Virginia (State)
Area Sq Km (Miles) 62 758 (24 231) Population 1 811 156 Capital Charleston

Wisconsin (State)
Area Sq Km (Miles) 169 652 (65 503) Population 5 223 500 Capital Madison

Wyoming (State)
Area Sq Km (Miles) 253 347 (97 818) Population 480 907 Capital Cheyenne

URUGUAY
Oriental Republic of Uruguay

Area Sq Km 176 215 | Currency Peso
Area Sq Miles 68 037 | Languages Spanish
Population 3 289 000 | Religions Roman Catholic, Protestant, Jewish
Capital Montevideo | Organizations UN

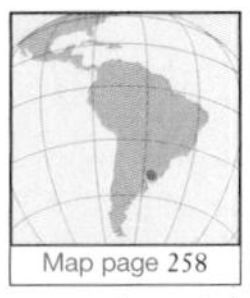
Map page 258

Uruguay, on the Atlantic coast of central South America, is a low-lying land of prairies. The coast and the River Plate estuary in the south are fringed with lagoons and sand dunes. Almost half the population lives in Montevideo. Uruguay has warm summers and mild winters. The economy is based on cattle and sheep ranching, and the main industries produce food products, textiles, and petroleum products. Meat, wool, hides, textiles and agricultural products are the main exports. Brazil and Argentina are the main trading partners.

UZBEKISTAN
Republic of Uzbekistan

Area Sq Km 447 400 | Currency Sum
Area Sq Miles 172 742 | Languages Uzbek, Russian, Tajik, Kazakh
Population 23 574 000 | Religions Sunni Muslim, Russian Orthodox
Capital Tashkent | Organizations CIS, UN

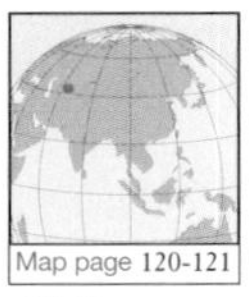
Map page 120-121

A landlocked country of central Asia, Uzbekistan borders the Aral Sea and five countries. It consists mainly of the flat Kyzylkum Desert, which rises eastwards towards the mountains. Most settlement is in the basin around Fergana. The climate is dry and arid. The economy is based mainly on irrigated agriculture, chiefly cotton production. Uzbekistan is rich in minerals including gold, copper, lead, zinc and uranium and has the largest gold mine in the world. Industry specializes in fertilizers and machinery for cotton harvesting and textile manufacture. Russia is the main trading partner.

VANUATU
Republic of Vanuatu

Area Sq Km 12 190 | Currency Vatu
Area Sq Miles 4 707 | Languages English, Bislama (creole), French
Population 182 000 | Religions Protestant, Roman Catholic, traditional beliefs
Capital Port Vila | Organizations Comm., UN

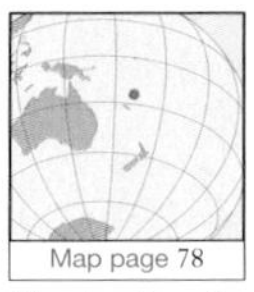
Map page 78

Vanuatu occupies an archipelago of some eighty islands in the southwest Pacific. Many of the islands are mountainous, of volcanic origin and densely forested. The climate is tropical with heavy rainfall. Half the population lives on the main islands of Éfaté and Espíritu Santo, and the majority of people live by farming. Copra, beef, timber, vegetables, and cocoa are the main exports; tourism is growing. Australia and Japan are the main trading partners.

VATICAN CITY
Vatican City State

Area Sq Km 0.5 | Currency Italian lira
Area Sq Miles 0.2 | Languages Italian
Population 480 | Religions Roman Catholic
Capital Vatican City

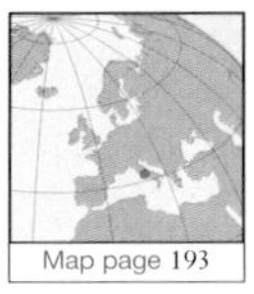
Map page 193

The world's smallest sovereign state, the Vatican City occupies a hill to the west of the river Tiber in the Italian capital, Rome. It is the headquarters of the Roman Catholic church and income comes from investments, voluntary contributions and tourism.

VENEZUELA
Republic of Venezuela

Area Sq Km 912 050 | Currency Bolívar
Area Sq Miles 352 144 | Languages Spanish, Amerindian languages
Population 23 242 000 | Religions Roman Catholic, Protestant
Capital Caracas | Organizations OPEC, UN

Map page 250-251

Venezuela is in northern South America, on the Caribbean Sea. Its coast is much indented, with the oil-rich area of Lago de Maracaibo at the western end and the swampy Orinoco Delta in the east. Mountain ranges run parallel to the coast then turn southwestwards to form the northern extension of the Andes. Central Venezuela is lowland grasslands drained by the Orinoco river system, while to the south are the Guiana Highlands which contain the Angel Falls, the world's highest waterfall. Over eighty per cent of the population live in towns, mostly in the coastal mountain areas. The climate is tropical, with summer rainfall. Temperatures are lower in the mountains. Farming is important, particularly cattle ranching and dairy farming; coffee, maize, rice and sugar cane are the main crops. Venezuela is a major oil producer, and sales account for about seventy five per cent of export earnings. Aluminium, iron ore, copper and gold are also mined and manufactures include petrochemicals, aluminium, steel, textiles and food products. USA is the dominant trading partner.

VIETNAM
Socialist Republic of Vietnam

Area Sq Km 329 565 | Currency Dong
Area Sq Miles 127 246 | Languages Vietnamese, Thai, Khmer, Chinese, local languages
Population 77 562 000 | Religions Buddhist, Taoist, Roman Catholic
Capital Ha Nôi | Organizations APEC, ASEAN, UN

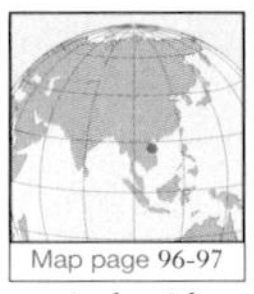
Map page 96-97

Vietnam is in southeast Asia, with the South China Sea to the east and south. The Red River delta lowlands in the north are separated from the huge Mekong delta in the south by long, narrow coastal plains backed by the mountainous and forested terrain of the Annam Plateau. Most people live in the river deltas. The climate is tropical, with summer monsoon rains. Over three quarters of the workforce is involved in agriculture, forestry and fishing. Rice is the main crop; coffee, tea and rubber are important cash crops. Vietnam is the world's third largest rice exporter, after the USA and Thailand. Oil, coal and copper are produced; the main industries are food processing, clothing and footwear, cement and fertilizers. Exports include oil, coffee, rice, clothing, fish and fish products. Japan and Singapore are the main trading partners.

Virgin Islands (U.K.)
United Kingdom Overseas Territory

Area Sq Km 153 | Currency US dollar
Area Sq Miles 59 | Languages English
Population 20 000 | Religions Protestant, Roman Catholic
Capital Road Town

The Caribbean territory comprises four main islands and over thirty islets at the eastern end of the Virgin Islands group. Apart from the flat coral atoll of Anegada, the islands are volcanic in origin and hilly. The climate is subtropical and tourism is the main industry.

Map page 247

Virgin Islands (U.S.A.)
United States Unincorporated Territory

Area Sq Km 352 | Currency US dollar
Area Sq Miles 136 | Languages English, Spanish
Population 94 000 | Religions Protestant, Roman Catholic
Capital Charlotte Amalie

The territory consists of three main islands and over fifty islets in the Caribbean's western Virgin Islands. The islands are mostly hilly and of volcanic origin and the climate is subtropical. The economy is based on tourism, with some manufacturing, including a major oil refinery, on St Croix.

Map page 247

Wallis and Futuna Islands
French Overseas Territory

Area Sq Km 274 | Currency Pacific franc
Area Sq Miles 106 | Languages French, Wallisian, Futunian
Population 14 000 | Religions Roman Catholic
Capital Matā'utu

The south Pacific territory comprises the volcanic islands of the Wallis archipelago and Hoorn Islands. The climate is tropical. The islands depend upon subsistence farming, the sale of licences to foreign fishing fleets, workers' remittances and French aid.

Map page 75

West Bank
Territory Occupied by Israel

Area Sq Km 5 860 | Languages Arabic, Hebrew
Area Sq Miles 2 263 | Religions Sunni Muslim, Jewish, Shi'a Muslim, Christian

The territory consists of the west bank of the river Jordan and parts of Judea and Samaria. The land was annexed by Israel in 1967, but the Jericho area was granted self-government under an agreement between Israel and the PLO in 1993.

Map page 128

WESTERN SAHARA
Disputed territory (Morocco)

Area Sq Km 266 000 | Currency Moroccan dirhamr
Area Sq Miles 102 703 | Languages Arabic
Population 275 000 | Religions Sunni Muslim
Capital Laâyoune

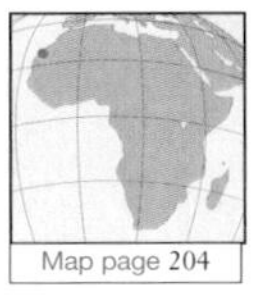
Map page 204

Situated on the northwest coast of Africa, the territory of Western Sahara is controlled by Morocco. The land is low, flat desert with higher land in the northeast. There is little cultivation and only about twenty per cent of the land is pasture. Livestock herding, fishing and phosphate mining are the main activities. All trade is controlled by Morocco.

YEMEN
Republic of Yemen

Area Sq Km 527 968 | Currency Rial
Area Sq Miles 203 850 | Languages Arabic
Population 16 887 000 | Religions Sunni Muslim, Shi'a Muslim
Capital Şan'ā' | Organizations UN

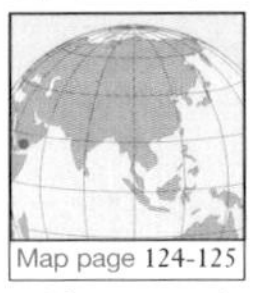
Map page 124-125

Yemen occupies the southwestern Arabian Peninsula, on the Red Sea and Gulf of Aden. Beyond the Red Sea coastal plain the land rises to a mountain range then descends to desert plateaus. Much of Yemen is hot and arid, but rainfall in the west supports crops and most settlement. Farming and fishing are the main activities, with cotton the main cash crop. The main exports are crude oil, cotton, coffee and dried fruit. Despite its oil resources Yemen is one of the poorest countries in the Arab World.

YUGOSLAVIA
Federal Republic of Yugoslavia

Area Sq Km 102 173 | Currency Dinar
Area Sq Miles 39 449 | Languages Serbian, Albanian, Hungarian
Population 10 635 000 | Religions Serbian and Montenegrin Orthodox, Muslim
Capital Beograd | Organizations UN

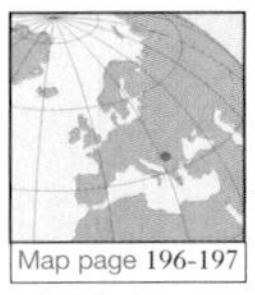
Map page 196-197

The south European state comprises two of the former Yugoslav republics: Serbia and the much smaller Montenegro. The landscape is for the most part rugged, mountainous and forested. Northern Serbia is low-lying, drained by the Danube river system. The climate is Mediterranean on the coast, continental inland. Since 1991 the economy has been seriously affected by war, trade embargoes and economic sanctions.

ZAMBIA
Republic of Zambia

Area Sq Km 752 614 | Currency Kwacha
Area Sq Miles 290 586 | Languages English, Bemba, Nyanja, Tonga, local languages
Population 8 781 000 | Religions Christian, traditional beliefs
Capital Lusaka | Organizations Comm., SADC, UN

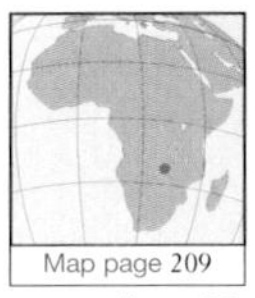
Map page 209

A landlocked state in central Africa, Zambia borders seven countries. It is dominated by high savanna plateaus and bordered by the Zambezi river in the south. Most people live in the Copperbelt area. Life expectancy has dropped by seventeen per cent because of AIDS, compared to 1975. The climate is tropical with a rainy season from November to May. Agriculture employs around eighty per cent of the workforce, but is mainly at subsistence level. Copper mining is the mainstay of the economy, though reserves are declining. Copper and cobalt are the main exports.

ZIMBABWE
Republic of Zimbabwe

Area Sq Km 390 759 | Currency Dollar
Area Sq Miles 150 873 | Languages English, Shona, Ndebele
Population 11 377 000 | Religions Christian, traditional beliefs
Capital Harare | Organizations Comm., SADC, UN

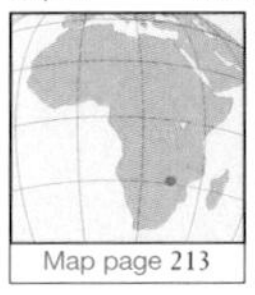
Map page 213

Zimbabwe, a landlocked state in southern central Africa, consists of high plateaus flanked by the Zambezi river valley and Lake Kariba in the north and the Limpopo in the south. Most people live in central Zimbabwe. The effect of AIDS has reduced life expectancy by seventeen per cent compared to 1975. There are significant mineral resources including gold, nickel, copper, asbestos, platinum and chromium. Agriculture is a major sector of the economy, crops include tobacco, maize, sugar cane, and cotton, and beef cattle are important. Exports include tobacco, gold, ferroalloys, nickel and cotton. South Africa is the main trading partner.

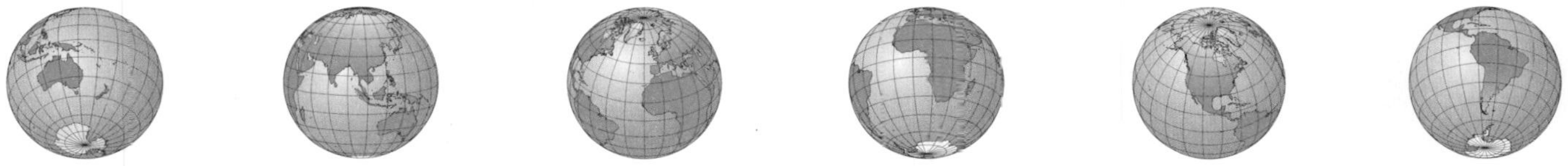

ATLAS OF THE WORLD

ATLAS MAPPING

The Atlas of the World includes a variety of styles and scales of mapping which together provide comprehensive coverage of all parts of the world; the map styles and editorial policies followed are introduced here. The area covered by each map is shown on the front and back endpapers.

Each continent is introduced by a politically coloured map followed by reference maps of sub-continental regions and then more detailed reference mapping of regions and individual countries. Scales for continental maps (*see 1*) range between 1:15 000 000 and 1:27 000 000 and regional maps (*see 2*) are in the range 1:11 000 000 to 1:13 000 000. Mapping for most countries is at scales between 1:3 000 000 and 1:7 500 000 (*see 3*) although selected, more densely populated areas of Europe, North America and Asia are mapped at larger scales, up to 1:1 000 000 (*see 4*). Large-scale city plans of a selection of the world's major cities (*see 5*), are included on the appropriate map pages. A suite of maps covering the world's oceans and poles (*see 6*) at a variety of scales, concludes the main reference map section.

The symbols and place name abbreviations used on the maps are fully explained on pages 68–69 and a glossary of geographical terms is included at the back of the atlas on pages 269–272. The alphanumeric reference system used in the index is based on latitude and longitude, and the number and letter for each graticule square are shown within each map frame, in red. The numbers of adjoining or overlapping pages are shown by arrows in the page frame and accompanying numbers in the margin.

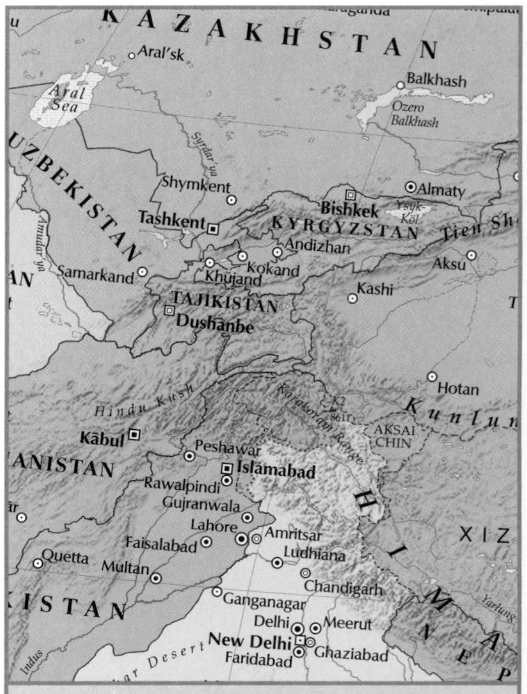

1. Continental map of Asia
(extract from pages 88–89)

BOUNDARIES

The status, names and boundaries of nations are shown in this atlas as they are at the time of going to press, as far as can be ascertained. Where an international boundary symbol appears in the sea or ocean it does not necessarily infer a legal maritime boundary, but shows which off-shore islands belong to which country.

Where international boundaries are the subject of dispute it may be that no portrayal of them will meet with the approval of any of the countries involved, but it is not seen as the function of this atlas to try to adjudicate between the rights and wrongs of political issues. The atlas aims to take a neutral viewpoint of all such cases. Although reference mapping at atlas scales is not the ideal medium for indicating territorial claims, every reasonable attempt is made to show where an active territorial dispute exists, and where there is an important difference between 'de facto' (existing in fact, on the ground) and 'de jure' (according to law) boundaries. This is done by the use of a different symbol where international boundaries are disputed, or where the alignment is unconfirmed, to that used for settled international boundaries. Cease-fire lines are also shown by a separate symbol. For clarity, disputed boundaries and areas are annotated where this is considered necessary.

The latest internal administrative division boundaries are shown on the maps for selected countries where the combination of map scale and the number of divisions permits, with recent changes to local government systems being taken into account as far as possible. Towns which are first-order and second-order administrative centres are also symbolized where scale permits.

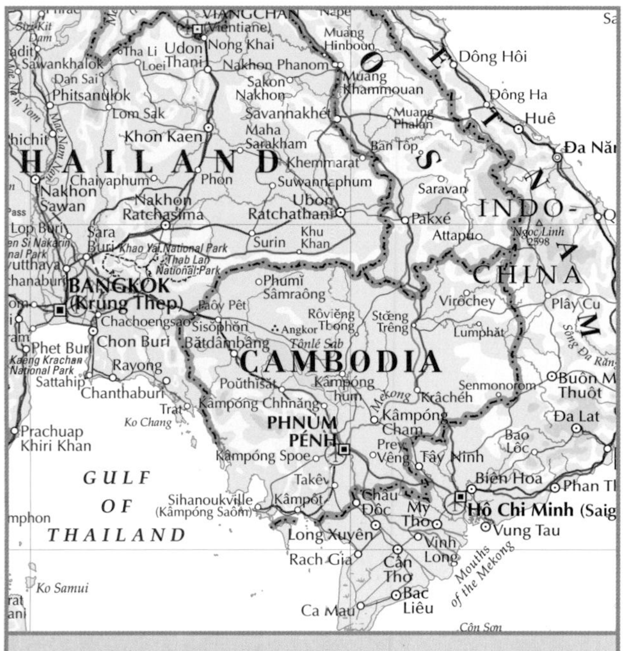

2. Southeast Asia 1:13 000 000
(extract from pages 90–91)

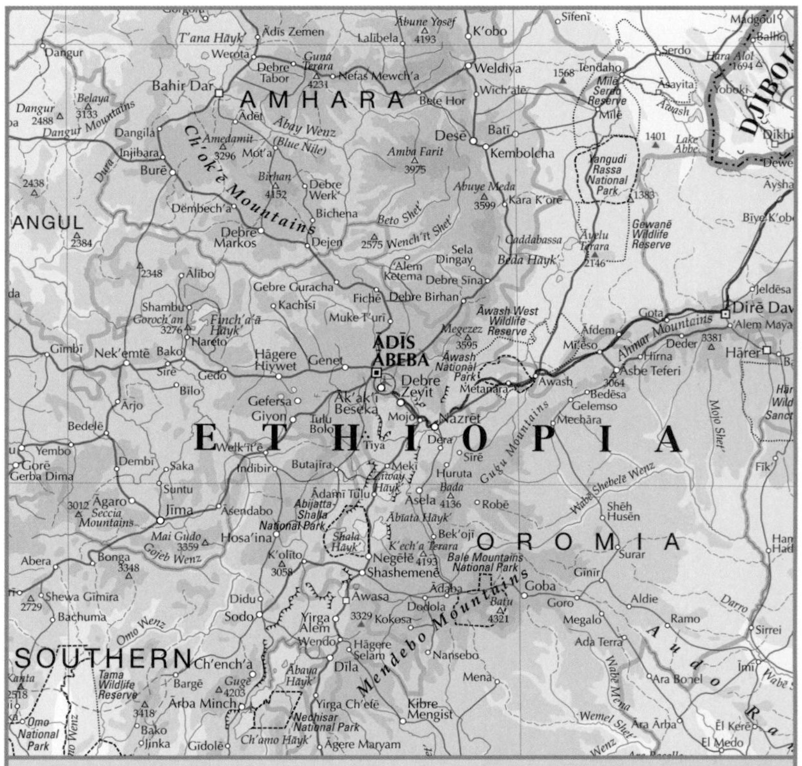

3. Africa East Central 1:7 500 000
(extract from pages 210–211)

PLACE NAMES

The spelling of place names on maps has always been a matter of great complexity, because of the variety of the world's languages and the systems used to write them down. Continuing changes in official languages, and in writing systems, also have to be taken into account. In many countries different languages are in use in different regions, or side-by-side in the same region. Sometimes the problem is dealt with by the use of a 'lingua franca' such as English to provide a mutually intelligible standard. In many cases the most spoken language takes precedence, but there is still the potential for widely varying name forms even within a single country. A worldwide trend towards national, regional and ethnic self-determination is operating at the same time as pressure towards increased international standardization of name forms.

There is no standard way of spelling names or of converting them from one alphabet, or symbol set, to another. Instead, conventional ways of spelling have evolved in each of the world's major languages, and the results often differ significantly from the name as it is spelled in the original language. Familiar examples of English conventional names include Munich (München), Florence (Firenze) and Moscow (from the transliterated form, Moskva).

In this atlas, local name forms are used where these are in the Roman alphabet. Such a policy results in mapping which is internally consistent and which closely reflects name forms found in the country itself. These local forms are those which are officially recognized by the government of the country concerned, usually as represented by its official mapping agency. This is a basic principle laid down by the United Kingdom government's Permanent Committee on Geographical Names (PCGN) and the equivalent United States Board on Geographic Names (BGN).

For languages in non-Roman alphabets and syllabaries, the atlas generally follows BGN/PCGN romanization principles. For example, Russian-language names are spelled using the standard BGN/PCGN system, which gives names such as Lipetsk and Yoshkar-Ola as opposed to a system used in eastern Europe which gives Lipeck and Joškar-Ola.

Although local forms are preferred, prominent English-language conventional names and historic names are not neglected. Together with significant superseded names and other alternate spellings, they are included in brackets on the maps where space permits, and are cross-referenced in the index. The names of continents, oceans, seas and under-water features in international waters appear in English throughout the atlas, as do those of other international features – features crossing one or more international boundary – where such an English form exists and is in common use.

Country names are shown in conventional English form, and include changes promulgated by national governments and adopted by the United Nations – Myanmar (replacing Burma), Belarus (replacing Belorussia and a variety of other versions including the traditional White Russia), Kyrgyzstan (for Kirghizia or Kirgizia), Moldova (Moldavia), and Côte d'Ivoire (Ivory Coast). In the adoption of these name forms for country names, and for certain city names, such as Beijing (replacing Peking), the gradual incorporation of local forms into common English usage can be seen at work. This atlas reflects that process.

CHANGES IN NAME FORMS

Place names are, to an extent, a mirror for the changes that continue to transform the political world. Predictably, changes of territorial control have an effect on name forms. Yet even in countries where name forms could be expected to have been standardized, there are continuing issues for the cartographer to address. In the UK, for example, the increased prominence given to the use of Gaelic and Welsh has meant that more consideration has been given to the use of Gaelic and Welsh name forms in relation to the English form. Name spelling

PROJECTIONS

The creation of computer-generated maps presents the opportunity to select projections specifically for the area and scale of each map. As the only way to show the Earth with absolute accuracy is on a globe, all map projections are compromises. Some projections seek to maintain correct area relationships (equal area projections), true distances and bearings from a point (equidistant projections) or correct angles and shapes (conformal projections); others attempt to achieve a balance between these properties. The choice of projections used in this atlas has been made on an individual continental and regional basis. Projections used, and their individual parameters, have been defined to minimize distortion and to reduce scale errors as much as possible.

For world maps, the Bartholomew version of the Winkel Tripel Projection is used. This projection combines elements of conformality with that of equal area, and shows, over the world as a whole, relatively true shapes and reasonably equal areas. The Mercator Projection (*see 7*) has been selected for the regional maps of southeast Asia along the Equator , while in higher latitudes, particularly in Europe and to some extent in North America, the Conic Equidistant Projection (*see 8*) has been used extensively for regional mapping. The Lambert Azimuthal Equal Area Projection (*see 9*) has been employed in both South America and Australia.

7. MERCATOR PROJECTION

This rectangular or cylindrical projection is constructed on the basis of a cylinder in contact with the globe, in this case around the Equator. Scale is correct along the Equator and distortion increases away from it in both directions.

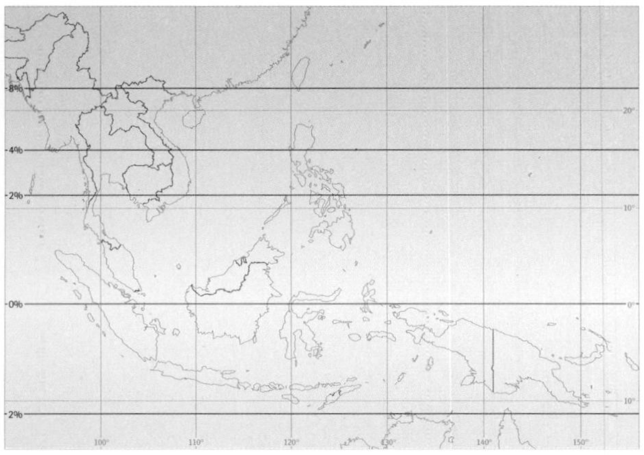

8. CONIC EQUIDISTANT PROJECTION

Constructed on the basis of a cone intersecting the globe along two standard parallels (55°N and 75°N in this illustration), along both of which scale is correct. Lines of equal scale error are parallel to the standard lines, with distortion increasing away from each.

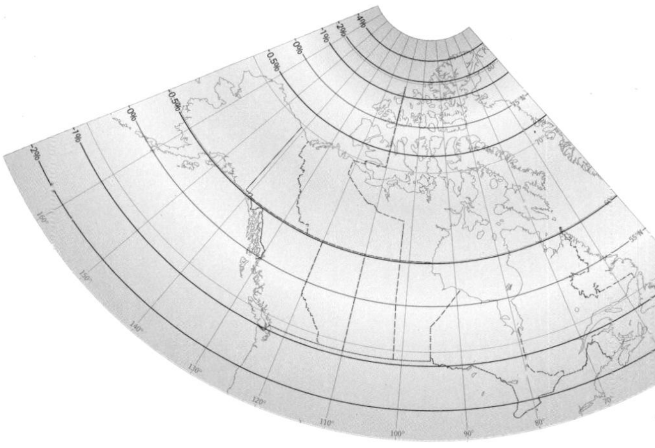

9. LAMBERT AZIMUTHAL EQUAL AREA PROJECTION

Points are projected onto a plane in contact with the globe at the centre point (25°S, 135°E in this illustration). Scale is correct at the centre, and scale errors increase in concentric circles away from it. Areas are true in relation to the corresponding areas on the globe.

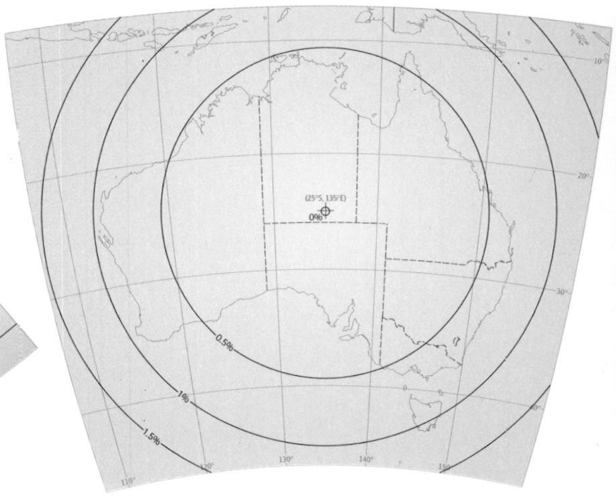

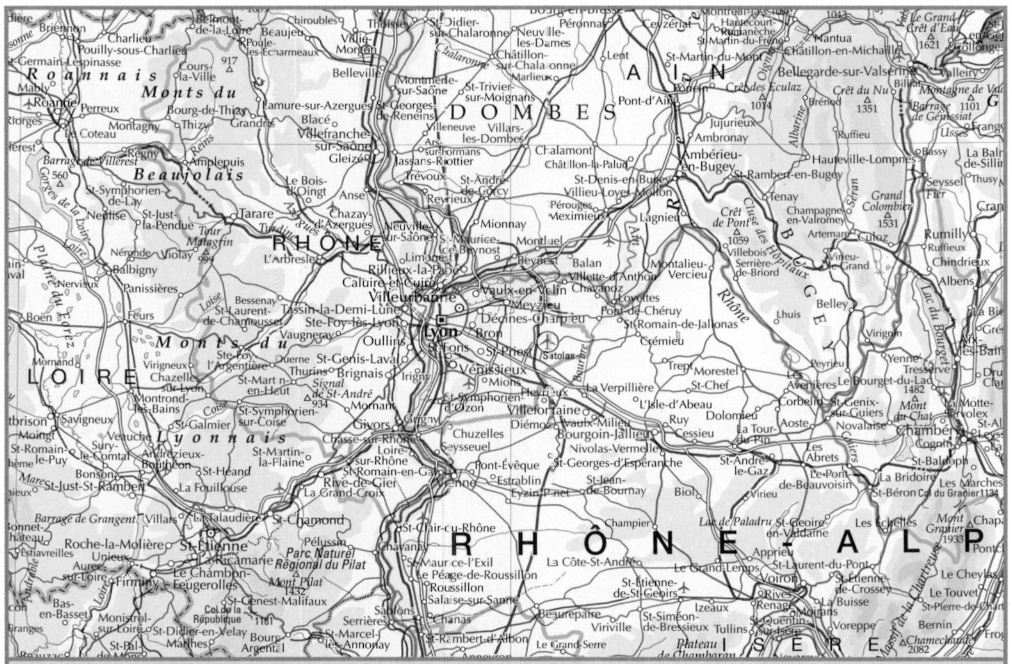

4. France Southeast 1:1 200 000
(extract from pages 160–161)

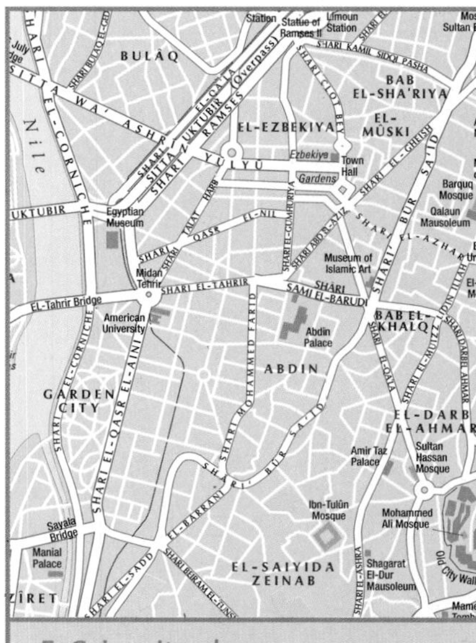

5. Cairo city plan
(extract from page 203)

issues are, in fact, likely to emerge in any part of the world. A close watch is kept on areas where changes might be expected, although sometimes they crop up in unexpected places.

The dissolution of the former USSR gave rise to many changes in name forms. Names were converted from Russian to the main national language in Belarus, Ukraine, Moldova, Armenia, Georgia, Azerbaijan, Kyrgyzstan and Tajikistan. On the maps, where space permits, the main Russian-language forms for significant places are shown as alternatives in such cases. Russian naturally continues to be used as the main form in the Russian Federation, although in Chechnia main Chechen alternative forms have been included in the index as cross-references. Russian also continues to be used as the prime language on maps of Kazakhstan, Turkmenistan and Uzbekistan. In Kazakhstan, both Russian and Kazakh are recognized as joint official languages, and Russian is maintained as the first form, while Kazakh alternatives (derived from Kazakh cyrillic), are included for main place names where space permits on the maps, with additional alternatives in the index.

In Spain, account is taken of the official prominence now given to Catalan, Galician and some Basque names, which results in name forms such as Eivissa for Ibiza; A Coruña for La Coruña; and San Sebastián amended to Donostia-San Sebastián.

Chinese name forms, which use the official Pinyin romanization system continue to change. Name forms have been brought into line with the latest official sources resulting in a more rigorous and updated use of the principle whereby numerous towns, which are the centres of administrative units such as the county or 'xian', officially take the name of the county itself. The alternative place name in common local use is shown in brackets where possible.

As well as the above-mentioned systematic changes in name forms, which mostly involve official modifications in the way all names in a country are rendered in the Roman alphabet, the atlas also aims to account for entirely new names being adopted. Such name changes can happen for a variety of reasons – one example is the move away from communist-inspired names in the former Soviet Union. Changes can be a result of official policy changes, such as those in India when Bombay was changed to Mumbai, and Madras to Chennai. Although particularly prominent, these in fact represent the continuation of a long process of name amendments in India since independence.

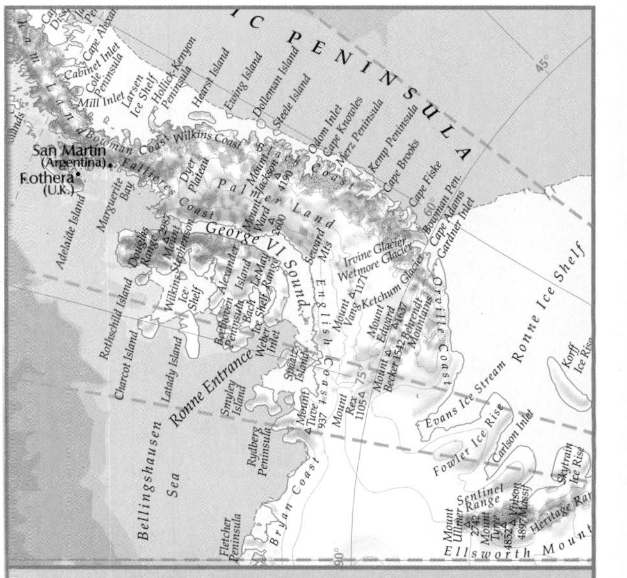

6. Antarctica 1:18 000 000
(extract from pages 262–263)

REFERENCE MAPS

CITIES AND TOWNS

Population	National Capital	Administrative Capital Shown for selected countries only		Other City or Town
		First order	Second order Scales larger than 1:9 000 000.	
over 5 million	**BEIJING** ▣	**Tianjin** ▣	Los Angeles ◉	**New York** ◉
1 million to 5 million	**KĀBUL** ▣	Sydney ▣	Tangshan ◉	**Kaohsiung** ◉
500 000 to 1 million	BANGUI ▣	Trujillo ▣	Agra ◉	Jeddah ◎
100 000 to 500 000	WELLINGTON ▣	Mansa ▣	Naogaon ◎	Apucarana ◎
50 000 to 100 000	PORT OF SPAIN ▢	Potenza ▢	Trier ○	Arecibo ○
10 000 to 50 000	MALABO ▢	Chinhoyi ▢	Willimantic ○	Ceres ○
1 000 to 10 000	VALLETTA ▢	Ati ▢	Nepalganj ○	Abla ○
under 1000 Scales 1: 4 000 000 and larger		Chhukha ▢	Carmel ○	Lopigna ○

⬭ Built-up area

MISCELLANEOUS FEATURES

---------- National park ·········· Regional park ·········· Reserve or special land area ∴ Site of specific interest ᴧᴧᴧᴧᴧᴧ Wall

RELIEF

Contour intervals used in layer-colouring for land height and sea depth

Scales 1:4 000 000 and larger	Scales 1:4 000 000 and larger (Europe only)	Scales smaller than 1:4 000 000	Oceans and Antarctica (Pages 262-268)
METRES / FEET	METRES / FEET	METRES / FEET	METRES / FEET
6000 / 19686	6000 / 19686	6000 / 19686	4000 / 13124
5000 / 16404	5000 / 16404	5000 / 16404	2000 / 6562
4000 / 13124	4000 / 13124	4000 / 13124	1000 / 3281
3000 / 9843	3000 / 9843	3000 / 9843	500 / 1640
2000 / 6562	2000 / 6562	2000 / 6562	200 / 656
1500 / 4921	1500 / 4921	1000 / 3281	0 / 0
1000 / 3281	1000 / 3281	500 / 1640	LAND BELOW SEA LEVEL
500 / 1640	500 / 1640	200 / 656	200 / 656
200 / 656	200 / 656	0 / 0	2000 / 6562
100 / 328	100 / 328	LAND BELOW SEA LEVEL	3000 / 9843
0 / 0	0 / 0	200 / 656	4000 / 13124
LAND BELOW SEA LEVEL	LAND BELOW SEA LEVEL	2000 / 6562	5000 / 16409
200 / 656	50 / 164	4000 / 13124	6000 / 19686
1000 / 3281	200 / 656	6000 / 19686	7000 / 22967
2000 / 6562	1000 / 3281		9000 / 29529
	2000 / 6562		

1234 △ Summit Height in metres

-123 ⊙ Spot height Surface height in metres for depressions and areas below sea level.

5678 Ocean deep In metres. Ocean pages only.

STYLES OF LETTERING

Cities and towns are explained separately

		Physical features	
Country	**FRANCE**		
Overseas Territory/Dependency	**Guadeloupe**	Island	*Gran Canaria*
Disputed Territory	AKSAI CHIN	Lake	*LAKE ERIE*
Administrative name, first order internal division Shown for selected countries only.	**SCOTLAND**	Mountain	*Mt Blanc*
Administrative name, second order internal division Scales 1:4 000 000 and larger. Shown for selected countries only.	MANCHE	River	*Thames*
Area name	ARTOIS	Region	*PAMPAS*

BOUNDARIES

▪-▪-▪-▪ International boundary

▪▪▪▪ Disputed international boundary or alignment unconfirmed

⬟ Undefined international boundary in the sea.
All land within this boundary is part of state or territory named.

▪-▪-▪-▪ Administrative boundary, first order internal division.
Scales 1:4 000 000 and larger.
Shown for selected countries only.

——— Administrative boundary, first order internal division.
Scales smaller than 1:4 000 000.
Shown for selected countries only.

——— Administrative boundary, second order internal division.
Scales 1:4 000 000 and larger.
Shown for selected countries only.

▪-▪-▪-▪ Disputed administrative boundary
Scales 1:4 000 000 and larger.
Shown for selected countries only.

•••••• Ceasefire line or other boundary described on the map

LAND AND SEA FEATURES

Rock desert

Sand desert / Dunes

⌣ Oasis

Lava field

1234 ▲ Volcano height in metres

Marsh

Ice cap / Glacier

Nunatak

—— Coral reef

··········· Escarpment

··········· Flood dyke

) [123 Pass height in metres

—— Ice shelf

LAKES AND RIVERS

Lake

Impermanent lake

Salt lake or lagoon

Impermanent salt lake

Dry salt lake or salt pan

123 Lake height surface height above sea level, in metres

——— River

------- Impermanent river

------- Wadi or watercourse

‖ Waterfall

— Dam

| Barrage

TRANSPORT

══ Motorway Scales 1:4 000 000 and larger.

—— Main road

—— Secondary road

═╪═ Motorway tunnel

—·—·— Road tunnel

----- Track

—— Main railway

—— Secondary railway

—•—•— Railway tunnel

------- Canal

—— Minor canal

✈ Main airport

✈ Regional airport

CITY PLANS

- Built-up area
- Cemetery
- Park
- ▪ Place of worship
- ▪ General place of interest
- ▪ Transport location
- ▪ Academic / municipal building

CONTINENTAL MAPS

BOUNDARIES

Symbol	Boundary
———	International boundary
- - - - - - -	Disputed international boundary or alignment unconfirmed
⁄‾‾‾	Undefined international boundary in the sea. All land within this boundary is part of state or territory named.
••••••••	Ceasefire line
- - - - -	Administrative boundary Shown for selected countries only.

CITIES AND TOWNS

Population	National Capital	Other City or Town
over 5 million	**Beijing** ▣	New York ◉
1 million to 5 million	**Kabul** ▣	Kaohsiung ◉
500 000 to 1 million	**Bangui** ▣	Khulna ◉
100 000 to 500 000	**Wellington** ⊡	Iquitos ⊙
50 000 to 100 000	**Port of Spain** □	Naga ○
10 000 to 50 000	**Malabo** □	Ushuaia ○
under 10 000	**Valletta** ▫	Arviat ∘

ABBREVIATIONS

A.C.T.	Australian Capital Territory		
Arch.	Archipelago		
	Archipiélago	Spanish	archipelago
B.	Bay		
	Bahia, Baía	Portuguese	bay
	Bahía	Spanish	bay
	Baie	French	bay
Bol.	Bol'shaya, Bol'shoy, Bol'shoye	Russian	big
C.	Cape		
	Cabo	Portuguese, Spanish	cape, headland
	Cap	Catalan, French	cape, headland
Cach.	Cachoeira	Portuguese	waterfall, rapids
Can.	Canal	French, Portuguese, Spanish	canal, channel
Cd	Ciudad	Spanish	city, town
Chan.	Channel		
Co	Cerro	Spanish	hill, mountain, peak
Cord.	Cordillera	Spanish	mountain range
Cr.	Creek		
Cuch.	Cuchilla	Spanish	hills, mountain range
D.	Dağ, Dağı	Turkish	mountain
	Dāgh	Farsi	mountain, mountains
	Dağları	Turkish	mountain range
	Danau	Indonesian, Malay	lake
Div.	Division		
Dr	Doctor		
E.	East, Eastern		
Emb.	Embalse	Spanish	reservoir
Est.	Estero	Spanish	estuary, inlet
	Estrecho	Spanish	strait
Fj.	Fjörður	Icelandic	fjord, inlet
Ft	Fort		
G.	Gebel	Arabic	hill, mountain
	Golfo	Italian, Spanish	gulf, bay
	Gora	Russian	mountain
	Gunung	Indonesian, Malay	hill, mountain
Gd	Grand	French	big
Gde	Grande	French, Italian, Portuguese, Spanish	big
Geb.	Gebergte	Afrikaans, Dutch	mountain range
Gen.	General		
Gl.	Glacier		
Gp	Group		
Gt	Great		
Harb.	Harbour		
Hd	Head		
I.	Island, Isle		
	Ilha	Portuguese	island
	Isla	Spanish	island
Î.	Île	French	island
im.	imeni	Russian	'in the name of'
Ind. Res.	Indian Reservation		
Ing.	Ingeniero	Spanish	engineer
Is	Islands, Isles		
	Islas	Spanish	islands
Îs	Îles	French	islands
J.	Jabal, Jebel	Arabic	mountain, mountains
Kep.	Kepulauan	Indonesian, Malay	archipelago, islands
Khr.	Khrebet	Russian	mountain range
L.	Lake		
	Loch	(Scotland)	lake
	Lough	(Ireland)	lake
	Lac	French	lake
	Lago	Portuguese, Spanish	lake
Lag.	Laguna	Spanish	lagoon
M.	Mys	Russian	cape, point
Mt	Mount		
	Mont	French	hill, mountain
Mt.	Mountain		
Mte	Monte	Portuguese, Spanish	hill, mountain

Mts	Mountains		
	Monts	French	hills, mountains
N.	North, Northern		
Nev.	Nevado	Spanish	peak
Nat.	National		
Nat. Park	National Park		
Nat. Res.	Nature Reserve		
Nizh.	Nizhniy, Nizhnyaya	Russian	lower
N.E.	Northeast, Northeastern		
N.H.S.	National Heritage Site		
N.W.	Northwest, Northwestern		
O.	Ostrov	Russian	island
O-va	Ostrova	Russian	islands
Oz.	Ozero	Russian, Ukrainian	lake
P.	Paso	Spanish	pass
	Pulau	Indonesian, Malay	island
Pass.	Passage		
Peg.	Pegunungan	Indonesian, Malay	mountain range
Pen.	Peninsula		
	Península	Spanish	peninsula
Pk	Peak		
	Puncak	Indonesian	mountain, peak
P-ov	Poluostrov	Russian	peninsula
P. P.	Pulau-pulau	Indonesian	islands
Psa	Presa	Spanish	reservoir
Pt	Point		
Pta	Punta	Italian, Spanish	cape, point
Pte	Pointe	French	cape, point
Pto	Porto	Portuguese	harbour, port
	Puerto	Spanish	harbour, port
R.	River		
	Rio	Portuguese	river
	Río	Spanish	river
	Rivière	French	river
	Rūd	Farsi	river
Ra.	Range		
Rec.	Recreation		
Res.	Reservation, Reserve		
Resr	Reservoir		
S.	South, Southern		
	Salar, Salina, Salinas	Spanish	salt pan, salt pans
Sa	Serra	Portuguese	mountain range
	Sierra	Spanish	mountain range
Sd	Sound		
S.E.	Southeast, Southeastern		
Serr.	Serranía	Spanish	mountain range
Sk.	Shuiku	Chinese	reservoir
Sr.	Sredniy, Srednyaya	Russian	middle, central
St	Saint		
	Sankt	German, Russian	saint
	Sint	Dutch	saint
Sta	Santa	Italian, Portuguese, Spanish	saint
Ste	Sainte	French	saint
Sto	Santo	Italian, Portuguese, Spanish	saint
Str.	Strait		
S.W.	Southwest, Southwestern		
Tg	Tanjong, Tanjung	Indonesian, Malay	cape, point
Tk	Teluk, Telukan	Indonesian, Malay	bay, gulf
Tte	Teniente	Spanish	lieutenant
Va	Villa	Spanish	town
Vdkhr.	Vodokhranilishche	Russian	reservoir
Verkh.	Verkhniy, Verkhnyaya	Russian	upper
Vol.	Volcano		
	Volcan	French	volcano
	Volcán	Spanish	volcano
Vozv.	Vozvyshennost'	Russian	hills, upland
W.	West, Western		
	Wadi, Wâdi, Wādī	Arabic	watercourse

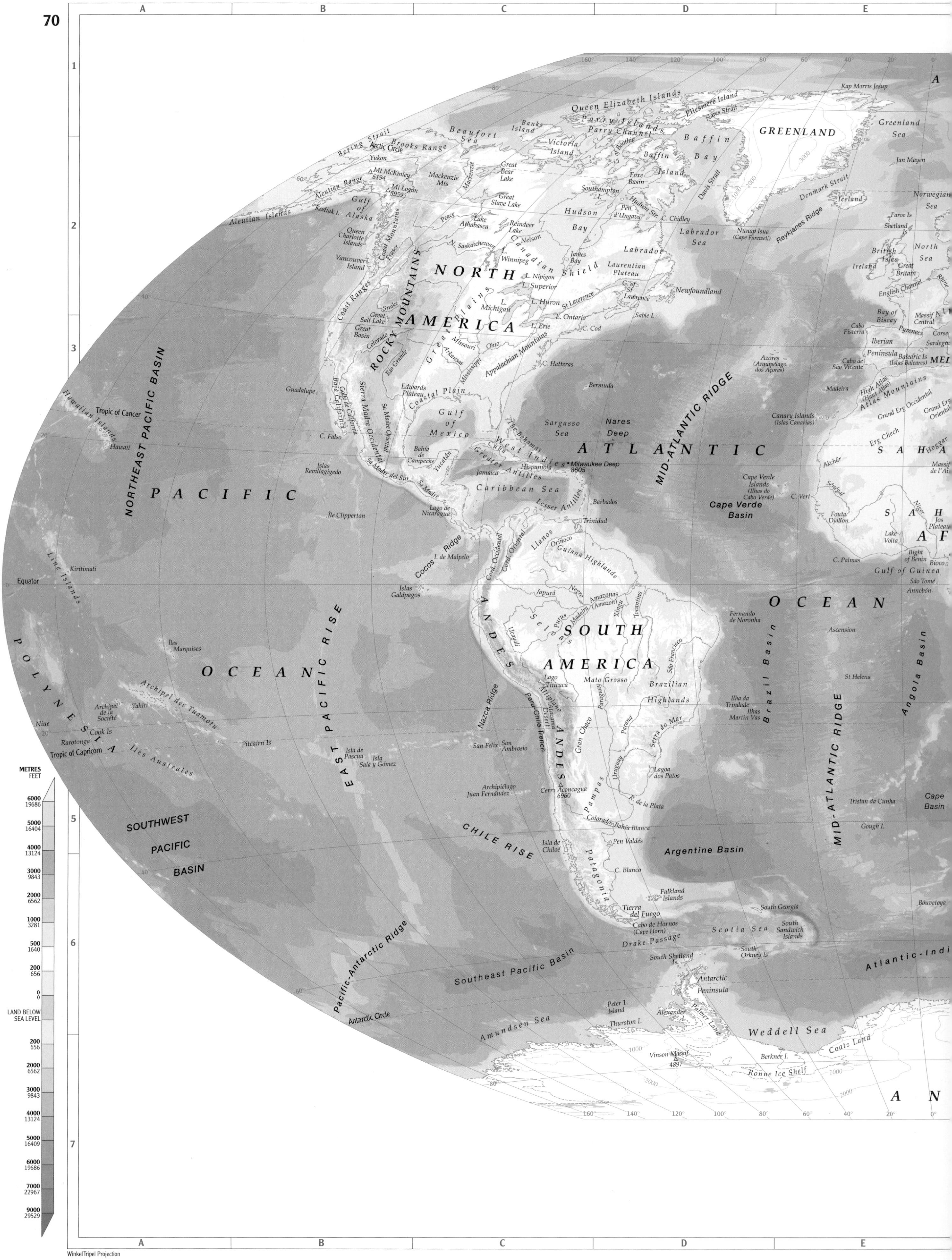
A
B
C
D
E
1
2
3
4
5
6
7
NORTH AMERICA
SOUTH AMERICA
GREENLAND
PACIFIC
OCEAN
ATLANTIC
OCEAN
POLYNESIA
Queen Elizabeth Islands
Parry Islands
Parry Channel
Ellesmere Island
Nares Strait
Kap Morris Jesup
Greenland Sea
Jan Mayen
Denmark Strait
Iceland
Norwegian Sea
Faroe Is
Shetland Is
North Sea
British Isles
Great Britain
Ireland
English Channel
Rhine
Bay of Biscay
Massif Central
Alps
Corse
Sardegna
Pyrenees
Iberian Peninsula
Cabo Fisterra
Cabo de São Vicente
Balearic Is (Islas Baleares)
Madeira
High Atlas (Haut Atlas)
Atlas Mountains
Grand Erg Occidental
Canary Islands (Islas Canarias)
Azores (Arquipélago dos Açores)
Erg Chech
SAHARA
Hoggar
Akchâr
Sénégal
Cape Verde Islands (Ilhas do Cabo Verde)
C. Vert
Cape Verde Basin
Fouta Djallon
Niger
Jos Plateau
Lake Volta
AFRICA
Bight of Benin
Bioco
C. Palmas
Gulf of Guinea
São Tomé
Annobón
Ascension
St Helena
Angola Basin
Tristan da Cunha
Cape Basin
Gough I.
Bouvetøya
Atlantic-Indian
Beaufort Sea
Banks Island
Victoria Island
Gulf of Boothia
Baffin Bay
Baffin Island
Foxe Basin
Davis Strait
Southampton I.
Hudson Strait
Pen. d'Ungava
C. Chidley
Hudson Bay
Labrador Sea
Labrador
Nunap Isua (Cape Farewell)
Reykjanes Ridge
James Bay
Canadian Shield
Laurentian Plateau
Newfoundland
G. of St Lawrence
St Lawrence
Sable I.
C. Cod
Bering Strait
Arctic Circle
Brooks Range
Yukon
Mt McKinley 6194
Mt Logan 5959
Mackenzie Mts
Mackenzie
Great Bear Lake
Great Slave Lake
Aleutian Range
Aleutian Islands
Kodiak I.
Gulf of Alaska
Queen Charlotte Islands
Coast Mountains
Fraser
Peace
Lake Athabasca
Reindeer Lake
Nelson
N. Saskatchewan
L. Winnipeg
L. Nipigon
L. Superior
L. Michigan
L. Huron
L. Ontario
L. Erie
Vancouver Island
Coast Ranges
Snake
ROCKY MOUNTAINS
Great Salt Lake
Great Basin
Colorado
Rio Grande
Great Plains
Missouri
Arkansas
Ohio
Mississippi
Appalachian Mountains
C. Hatteras
Bermuda
Edwards Plateau
Coastal Plain
Guadalupe
Baja California
Golfo de California
Sierra Madre Occidental
Sa Madre Oriental
Gulf of Mexico
Bahía de Campeche
Yucatán
Sa Madre del Sur
Sa Madre
C. Falso
Islas Revillagigedo
The Bahamas
West Indies
Cuba
Greater Antilles
Hispaniola
Jamaica
Milwaukee Deep 8605
Sargasso Sea
Nares Deep
MID-ATLANTIC RIDGE
Caribbean Sea
Lesser Antilles
Barbados
Trinidad
Lago de Nicaragua
Île Clipperton
Cocos Ridge
I. de Malpelo
Cord. Occidental
Cord. Oriental
Llanos
Orinoco
Guiana Highlands
Islas Galápagos
Japurá
Negro
Amazonas (Amazon)
Madeira
Xingu
Tocantins
Purus
Selvas
Ucayali
ANDES
Fernando de Noronha
Mato Grosso
Brazilian Highlands
São Francisco
Lago Titicaca
Altiplano
Atacama Desert
Peru-Chile Trench
Paraguay
Paraná
Gran Chaco
Serra do Mar
Uruguay
Lagoa dos Patos
Ilha da Trindade
Ilhas Martin Vas
Brazil Basin
San Felix
San Ambrosio
Cerro Aconcagua 6960
Pampas
R. de la Plata
Colorado
Bahía Blanca
Pen Valdés
Argentine Basin
Isla de Chiloé
Patagonia
C. Blanco
Falkland Islands
Tierra del Fuego
Cabo de Hornos (Cape Horn)
South Georgia
South Sandwich Islands
Scotia Sea
Drake Passage
South Orkney Is
South Shetland Is.
Antarctic Peninsula
Palmer Land
Alexander I.
Peter I. Island
Thurston I.
Amundsen Sea
Weddell Sea
Coats Land
Berkner I.
Ronne Ice Shelf
Vinson Massif 4897
AN
NORTHEAST PACIFIC BASIN
Hawaiian Islands
Hawaii
Tropic of Cancer
Equator
Kiritimati
Line Islands
Îles Marquises
EAST PACIFIC RISE
Archipel des Tuamotu
Archipel de la Société
Tahiti
Niue
Cook Is
Rarotonga
Tropic of Capricorn
Îles Australes
Pitcairn Is
Isla de Pascua
Isla Sala y Gómez
Nazca Ridge
Archipiélago Juan Fernández
CHILE RISE
SOUTHWEST PACIFIC BASIN
Pacific-Antarctic Ridge
Southeast Pacific Basin
Antarctic Circle
METRES
FEET
6000 19686
5000 16404
4000 13124
3000 9843
2000 6562
1000 3281
500 1640
200 656
0 0
LAND BELOW SEA LEVEL
200 656
2000 6562
3000 9843
4000 13124
5000 16409
6000 19686
7000 22967
9000 29529

ARCTIC OCEAN
Severnaya Zemlya
Spitsbergen
Zemlya Frantsa Iosifa
Novosibirskiye Ostrova
Laptev Sea (More Laptevykh)
Poluostrov Taymyr
Vostochno-Sibirskoye More
Ostrov Vrangelya
Bjørnøya (Bear Island)
North Cape (Nordkapp)
Barents Sea
Novaya Zemlya
Kara Sea (Karskoye More)
Poluostrov Yamal
Central Siberian Plateau (Sredne Sibirskoye Ploskogor'ye)
SIBERIA
Verkhoyanskiy Khrebet
Kolyma
Arctic Circle
Bering Sea
Lappland
Kola Peninsula (Kol'skiy Poluostrov)
White Sea (Beloye More)
Scandinavia
G. of Bothnia
Lake Onega (Oz. Onezhskoye)
Lake Ladoga (Ladozhskoye Oz.)
Rubinskoye Vdkhr.
Baltic Sea
North European Plain
Pechora
Ural Mountains (Ural'skiy Khrebet)
West Siberian Plain (Zapadno Sibirskaya Ravnina)
Ob'
Irtysh
Yenisey
Lena
Vilyuy
Angara
Eastern Sayan Mts (Vostochnyy Sayan)
Ozero Baykal
Hövsgöl Nuur
Stanovoy Khrebet
Sea of Okhotsk
Kamchatka (Poluostrov Kamchatka)
Aleutian Islands
Aleutian Trench
Sakhalin
Emperor Seamount Chain
Kuril Islands (Kuril'skiye Ostrova)
Kuril Trench
Hokkaidō
EUROPE
Carpathian Mts
Dnieper
Don
Volga
Ural
Kirghiz Steppe
Sea of Azov
Crimea
Danube
Black Sea
Caspian Sea
Aral Sea
Elbrus 5642
Caucasus
Kazakhskiy Melkosopochnik
Ozero Balkhash
Ozero Zaysan
Altai Mountains
Hangayn Nuruu
GOBI
ASIA
Da Hinggan Ling
Amur
Manchurian Plain
Sikhote Alin
Sea of Japan
Honshū
Plato Ustyurt
Turan Lowland
Syrdar'ya
Amudar'ya
Tien Shan
Tarim Pendi
Taklimakan Desert (Taklimakan Shamo)
Qilian Shan
Qaidam Pendi
Kunlun Shan
Altun Shan
Pamir
Alai Ra.
Hindu Kush
Karakoram
K2 8611
Adriatic Sea
Apennines
Sicilia
Aegean Sea
Anatolia
Taurus
Toros D.
Anadolu
Agri Dagi 5165
Elburz Mountains (Reshteh-ye Alborz)
Karakum Desert (Peski Karakumy)
Dasht-e Kavir
Dasht-e Lut
Zagros Mountains (Kuhha-ye Zagros)
MEDITERRANEAN SEA
Kriti
Cyprus
Gulf of Sirte
Tigris
Euphrates (Al Furat)
Syrian Desert (Badiyat ash Sham)
Helmand
Indus
Thar Desert
Plateau of Tibet (Qing Zang Gaoyuan)
HIMALAYA
Brahmaputra
Mt Everest 8848
Ganga
Sichuan Pendi
Gongga Shan 7514
Chang Jiang
Qin Ling
Huang He
Bo Hai
Yellow Sea
Korea Strait
Shikoku
Kyūshū
East China Sea
Nansei-shotō
Okinawa
Ogasawara-shotō (Bonin Islands)
Kazan-rettō (Volcano Islands)
Iō-jima
Japan Trench
Midway Is
Tropic of Cancer
PACIFIC
Mid-Pacific Mountains
Qattara Depression
Sinai
An Nafud
Libyan Desert
Nile
Red Sea
Arabian Peninsula
Najd
Ad Dahna'
The Gulf
G. of Oman
Ra's al Hadd
Rann of Kachchh
Deccan
Xi Jiang
Taiwan
Luzon Strait
Hainan
Gulf of Tongking
Annam Plateau
Mekong
Irrawaddy
Salween
Tibesti
Nubian Desert
Rub' al Khali
Asir
Arabian Sea
Western Ghats
Eastern Ghats
Bay of Bengal
Luzon
Philippine Sea
Philippines
Northern Mariana Islands
Guam
Challenger Deep 10920
Mariana Trench
MICRONESIA
Marshall Islands
Massif Ennedi
Bodélé
Lake Chad
Marra Plateau
Ras Dashen 4620
Danakil
Gulf of Aden
Suqutra (Socotra)
C. Guardafui (Raas Caseyr)
Ethiopian Highlands
Blue Nile
Haud
Andaman Is
Andaman Sea
Gulf of Thailand
Tônlé Sab
South China Sea
Palawan
Sulu Sea
Mindanao
Palau Is
Caroline Islands
Pohnpei
Kosrae
Sudd
White Nile
Webi Shabeelle
Lake Turkana
C. Comorin
Palk Str.
Sri Lanka
Nicobar Is
Mui Ca Mau
Malay Peninsula
Kep. Natuna
Celebes Sea
Str. of Malacca
Sumatera
Kep. Mentawai
Mt Cameroun 4100
Maldives
INDIAN
Borneo
Halmahera
Gilbert Is
Equator
Kingsmill Group
Congo
Congo Basin
Kasai
Great Rift Valley
Lake Victoria
Kirinyaga 5199
Kilimanjaro 5892
Somali Basin
Mahé
Amirante Is
Pemba I.
Zanzibar I.
Lake Tanganyika
Seychelles
Aldabra Is
Mid-indian Basin
Chagos Archipelago
Ninetyeast Ridge
Greater Sunda Islands
Java Sea
Jawa
Makassar Strait
Sulawesi
Maluku (Moluccas)
Seram
Buru
Banda Sea
New Guinea
Puncak Jaya 5030
Mt Wilhelm 4509
Bismarck Sea
New Ireland
New Britain
Bougainville I.
Solomon Sea
Solomon Is
MELANESIA
OCEAN
Phoenix Islands
Tuvalu
Tokelau
Mitumba Mts
Comoros
Great Rift Valley
Lake Nyasa
Tanjona Bobaomby
Christmas I.
Flores Sea
Lesser Sunda Islands
Sumba
Timor
Arafura Sea
C. York
Cape York Pen.
Gulf of Carpentaria
Arnhem Land
Timor Sea
Coral Sea
Sta Cruz Is
Espiritu Santo
Wallis and Futuna Is
Sava'i
Upolu
Huila Plateau
Cubango
Zambezi
Mozambique Channel
Madagascar
Cocos Is
West Australian Basin
Okavango Delta
Makgadikgadi
Limpopo
OCEAN
Rodrigues
Mauritius
Réunion
Kimberley Plateau
Barkly Tableland
Great Barrier Reef
Vanua Levu
Fiji
Viti Levu
Namib Desert
Kalahari Desert
North West C.
Great Sandy Desert
MacDonnell Ranges
AUSTRALIA
Musgrave Ranges
Nouvelle Calédonie
Tonga
Tongatapu Group
Tonga Trench
Tropic of Capricorn
Tonga Deep 10800
Madagascar Basin
Orange
Vaal
Drakensberg
Great Karoo
Cape of Good Hope
C. Agulhas
Natal Basin
Perth Basin
Great Victoria Desert
Lake Eyre
Great Dividing Range
Nullarbor Plain
C. Leeuwin
Great Australian Bight
Darling
Murray
Norfolk I.
Lord Howe I.
Kermadec Is
Île Amsterdam
Île St Paul
Crozet Basin
South Australian Basin
Mt Kosciuszko 2230
Bass Strait
Tasman Sea
North C.
Agulhas Basin
Prince Edward Is
Îles Crozet
Southeast Indian Ridge
Tasmania
New Zealand
North Island
South Island
Aoraki 3754
Chatham Is
Îles Kerguelen
Heard I.
Snares I.
Stewart I.
Bounty Is
Auckland Is
Antipodes Is
Campbell I.
Macquarie I.
SOUTHERN OCEAN
Australian-Antarctic Basin
Davis Sea
Enderby Land
Kemp Land
Amery Ice Shelf
Wilkes Land
Balleny Is.
Antarctic Circle
Antarctic Mountains
Ross Sea
ANTARCTICA
F
G
H
I
J
1
2
3
4
5
6
7

MILES
KILOMETRES
2400
1800
1200
600
0
4200
3600
3000
2400
1800
1200
600
0

1:70 000 000

© Bartholomew Ltd

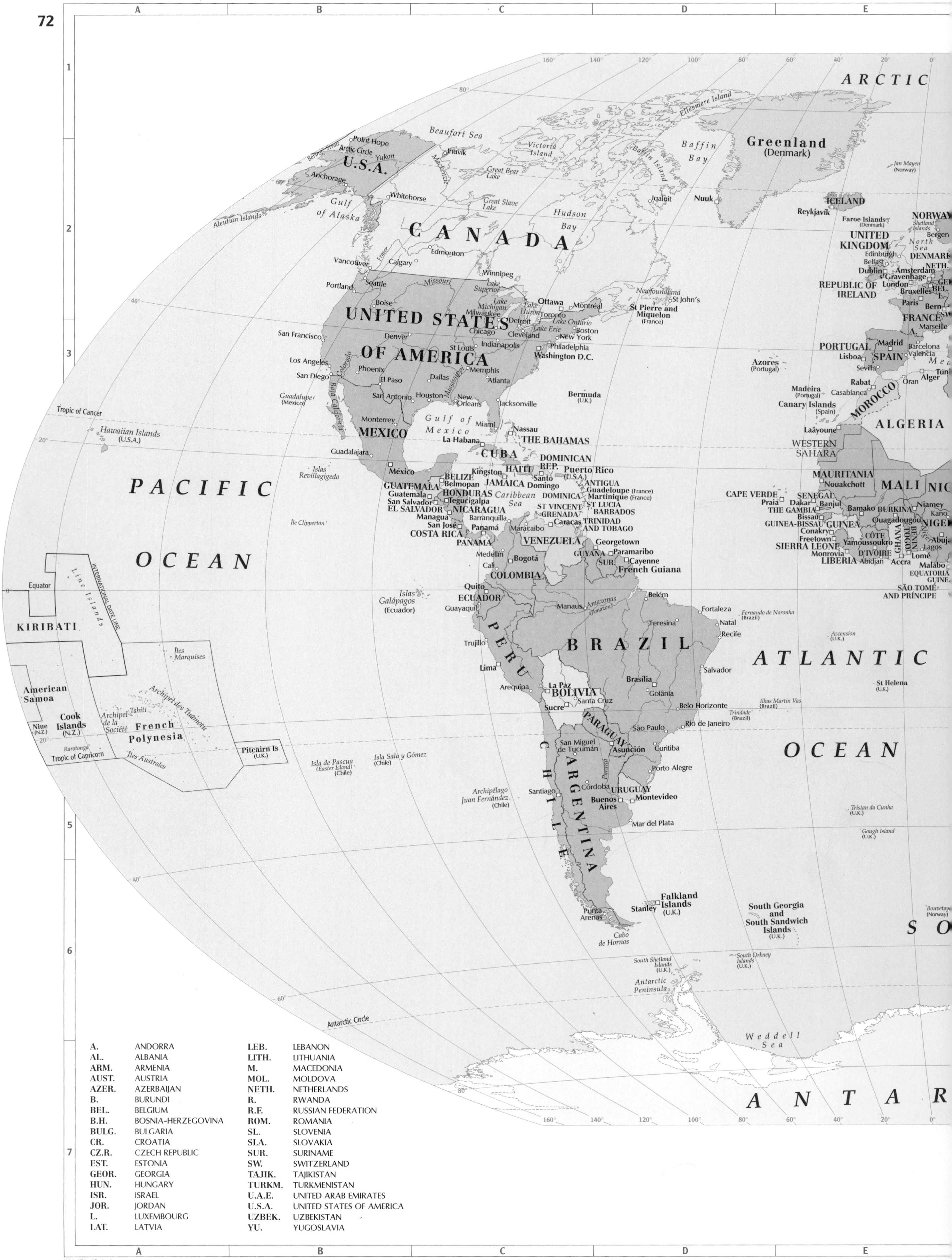
A
B
C
D
E
1
2
3
5
6
7
ARCTIC
Beaufort Sea
Ellesmere Island
Baffin Bay
Baffin Island
Greenland
(Denmark)
Jan Mayen
(Norway)
Victoria Island
Point Hope
Bering Strait
Arctic Circle
Yukon
U.S.A.
Inuvik
Mackenzie
Great Bear Lake
Anchorage
Whitehorse
Great Slave Lake
Iqaluit
Nuuk
ICELAND
Reykjavík
Faroe Islands
(Denmark)
NORWAY
Shetland Islands
Bergen
Aleutian Islands
Gulf of Alaska
Hudson Bay
CANADA
UNITED KINGDOM
North Sea
Edinburgh
Belfast
Dublin
DENMARK
NETH.
Amsterdam
's Gravenhage
REPUBLIC OF IRELAND
London
Bruxelles
BEL.
L.
Paris
Bern
FRANCE
Marseille
Edmonton
Calgary
Vancouver
Fraser
Winnipeg
Seattle
Portland
Missouri
Lake Superior
Boise
Lake Michigan
Lake Huron
Milwaukee
Ottawa
Montréal
Toronto
Lake Ontario
Newfoundland
St John's
St Pierre and Miquelon
(France)
UNITED STATES OF AMERICA
Detroit
Chicago
Cleveland
Lake Erie
Boston
New York
Philadelphia
Washington D.C.
San Francisco
Denver
St Louis
Indianapolis
Los Angeles
San Diego
Colorado
Phoenix
El Paso
Dallas
Memphis
Atlanta
Mississippi
PORTUGAL
Lisboa
Madrid
SPAIN
Barcelona
Valencia
Sevilla
Azores
(Portugal)
Rabat
Casablanca
Oran
Alger
Madeira
(Portugal)
Canary Islands
(Spain)
MOROCCO
ALGERIA
Laâyoune
WESTERN SAHARA
San Antonio
Houston
New Orleans
Jacksonville
Bermuda
(U.K.)
Guadalupe
(Mexico)
Baja California
Tropic of Cancer
Monterrey
Gulf of Mexico
Miami
Nassau
Hawaiian Islands
(U.S.A.)
MEXICO
La Habana
THE BAHAMAS
CUBA
DOMINICAN REP.
Guadalajara
Islas Revillagigedo
México
Kingston
HAITI
Santo Domingo
Puerto Rico
(U.S.A.)
BELIZE
Belmopan
JAMAICA
ANTIGUA
Guadeloupe (France)
Martinique (France)
GUATEMALA
Guatemala
HONDURAS
Caribbean Sea
DOMINICA
San Salvador
Tegucigalpa
ST LUCIA
EL SALVADOR
NICARAGUA
ST VINCENT
BARBADOS
Managua
GRENADA
Barranquilla
Caracas
TRINIDAD AND TOBAGO
San José
Panamá
Maracaibo
COSTA RICA
PANAMA
VENEZUELA
Georgetown
Paramaribo
Cayenne
French Guiana
GUYANA
SUR.
Medellín
Bogotá
Cali
COLOMBIA
PACIFIC OCEAN
Île Clipperton
MAURITANIA
Nouakchott
MALI
CAPE VERDE
Praia
SENEGAL
Dakar
Banjul
THE GAMBIA
Bissau
GUINEA-BISSAU
GUINEA
Conakry
Freetown
SIERRA LEONE
Monrovia
LIBERIA
Bamako
BURKINA
Ouagadougou
Niamey
Kano
NIGER
GHANA
TOGO
BENIN
Abuja
Lagos
CÔTE D'IVOIRE
Yamoussoukro
Abidjan
Accra
Lomé
Malabo
EQUATORIAL GUINEA
SÃO TOMÉ AND PRÍNCIPE
Equator
Line Islands
INTERNATIONAL DATE LINE
KIRIBATI
Quito
ECUADOR
Guayaquil
Islas Galápagos
(Ecuador)
Manaus
Amazonas
(Amazon)
Belém
Fortaleza
Fernando de Noronha
(Brazil)
Natal
Recife
Teresina
Trujillo
PERU
BRAZIL
Lima
Ascension
(U.K.)
ATLANTIC OCEAN
Îles Marquises
Arequipa
La Paz
BOLIVIA
Santa Cruz
Brasília
Goiânia
Salvador
St Helena
(U.K.)
American Samoa
Archipel des Tuamotu
Tahiti
Archipel de la Société
French Polynesia
Cook Islands
(N.Z.)
Niue
(N.Z.)
Rarotonga
Tropic of Capricorn
Îles Australes
Pitcairn Is
(U.K.)
Sucre
Belo Horizonte
Ilhas Martin Vas
(Brazil)
Trindade
(Brazil)
PARAGUAY
São Paulo
Rio de Janeiro
San Miguel de Tucumán
Asunción
Curitiba
Isla de Pascua
(Easter Island)
(Chile)
Isla Sala y Gómez
(Chile)
CHILE
ARGENTINA
Paraná
Porto Alegre
Córdoba
URUGUAY
Santiago
Archipiélago Juan Fernández
(Chile)
Buenos Aires
Montevideo
Tristan da Cunha
(U.K.)
Mar del Plata
Gough Island
(U.K.)
Falkland Islands
(U.K.)
Stanley
Punta Arenas
Cabo de Hornos
South Georgia and South Sandwich Islands
(U.K.)
Bouvetøya
(Norway)
South Shetland Islands
(U.K.)
South Orkney Islands
(U.K.)
Antarctic Peninsula
Antarctic Circle
Weddell Sea
ANTARCTICA

A.	ANDORRA	LEB.	LEBANON
AL.	ALBANIA	LITH.	LITHUANIA
ARM.	ARMENIA	M.	MACEDONIA
AUST.	AUSTRIA	MOL.	MOLDOVA
AZER.	AZERBAIJAN	NETH.	NETHERLANDS
B.	BURUNDI	R.	RWANDA
BEL.	BELGIUM	R.F.	RUSSIAN FEDERATION
B.H.	BOSNIA-HERZEGOVINA	ROM.	ROMANIA
BULG.	BULGARIA	SL.	SLOVENIA
CR.	CROATIA	SLA.	SLOVAKIA
CZ.R.	CZECH REPUBLIC	SUR.	SURINAME
EST.	ESTONIA	SW.	SWITZERLAND
GEOR.	GEORGIA	TAJIK.	TAJIKISTAN
HUN.	HUNGARY	TURKM.	TURKMENISTAN
ISR.	ISRAEL	U.A.E.	UNITED ARAB EMIRATES
JOR.	JORDAN	U.S.A.	UNITED STATES OF AMERICA
L.	LUXEMBOURG	UZBEK.	UZBEKISTAN
LAT.	LATVIA	YU.	YUGOSLAVIA

Winkel Tripel Projection

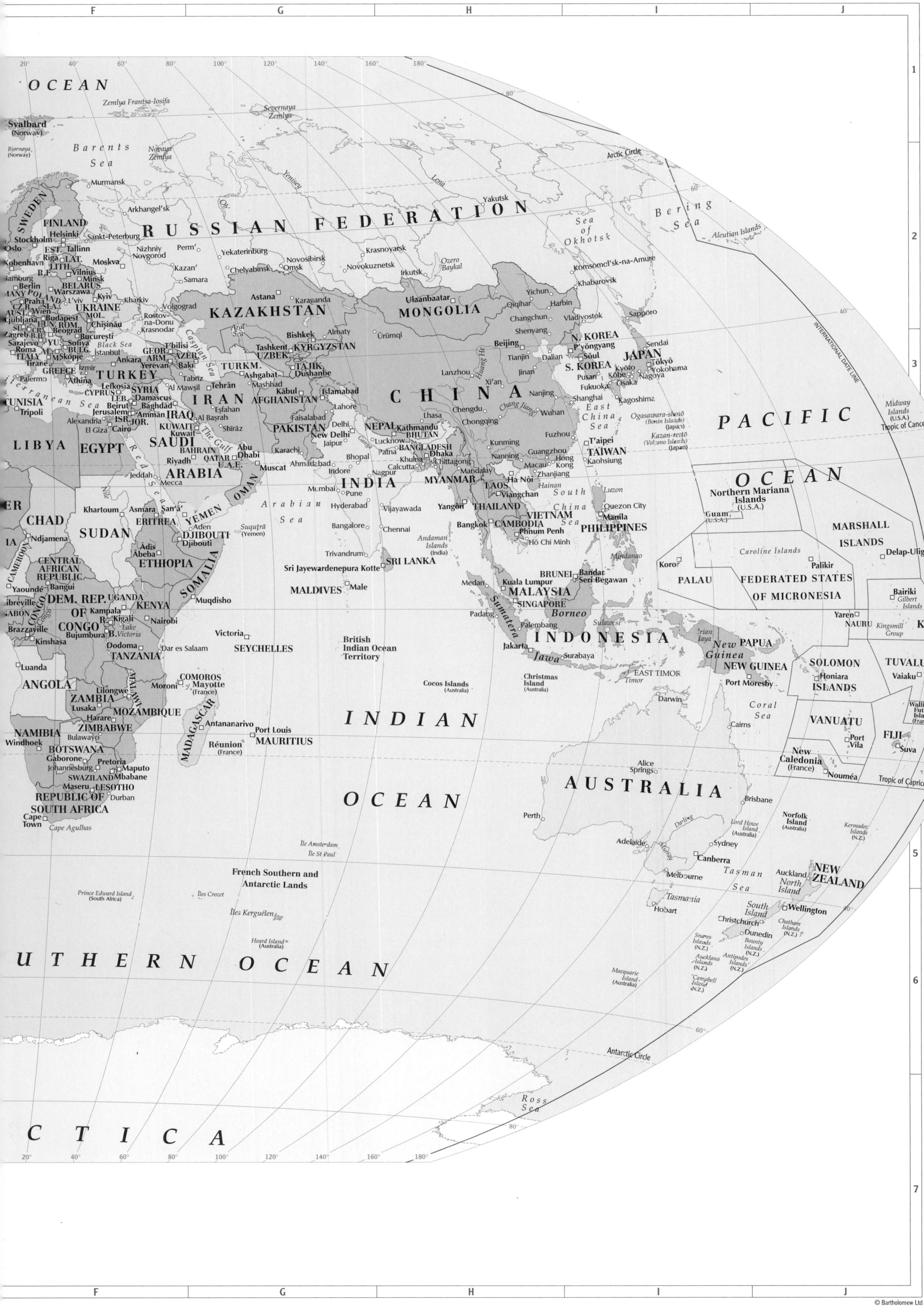
F
G
H
I
J
1
2
3
4
5
6
7
OCEAN
Svalbard (Norway)
Barents Sea
Zemlya Frantsa-Iosifa
Severnaya Zemlya
Novaya Zemlya
RUSSIAN FEDERATION
Sea of Okhotsk
Bering Sea
Aleutian Islands
Arctic Circle
FINLAND
SWEDEN
Helsinki
Stockholm
Oslo
Sankt-Peterburg
Tallinn
Riga
Moskva
Murmansk
Arkhangel'sk
Yakutsk
Yekaterinburg
Novosibirsk
Krasnoyarsk
Novokuznetsk
Omsk
Chelyabinsk
Irkutsk
Ozero Baykal
Komsomol'sk-na-Amure
Khabarovsk
Vladivostok
Sapporo
Kyiv
UKRAINE
KAZAKHSTAN
Astana
Karaganda
MONGOLIA
Ulaanbaatar
Harbin
Qiqihar
Changchun
Shenyang
Beijing
Tianjin
Dalian
N. KOREA
P'yŏngyang
Sŏul
S. KOREA
Pusan
JAPAN
Tōkyō
Yokohama
Kyōto
Kōbe
Ōsaka
Nagoya
Sendai
Fukuoka
Kagoshima
Almaty
Bishkek
KYRGYZSTAN
Tashkent
UZBEK.
TAJIK.
Dushanbe
Ürümqi
Lanzhou
Xi'an
Nanjing
Shanghai
Wuhan
Chengdu
Chongqing
CHINA
East China Sea
Black Sea
Caspian Sea
Aral Sea
TURKEY
Ankara
İstanbul
GREECE
Athina
TURKM.
Ashgabat
Tehrān
IRAN
Mashhad
AFGHANISTAN
Kābul
Islamabad
PAKISTAN
Lahore
Faisalabad
Karachi
SYRIA
Damascus
Beirut
Jerusalem
Amman
Baghdad
IRAQ
Al Başrah
Eşfahan
Shīrāz
KUWAIT
SAUDI ARABIA
Riyadh
Jeddah
Mecca
QATAR
U.A.E.
Abu Dhabi
Muscat
OMAN
YEMEN
Aden
Şan'ā'
LIBYA
EGYPT
Cairo
Alexandria
Tripoli
TUNISIA
CHAD
Ndjamena
SUDAN
Khartoum
ERITREA
Asmara
DJIBOUTI
ETHIOPIA
Ādīs Ābeba
SOMALIA
Muqdisho
CENTRAL AFRICAN REPUBLIC
Bangui
DEM. REP. OF CONGO
Kinshasa
UGANDA
Kampala
KENYA
Nairobi
TANZANIA
Dar es Salaam
Dodoma
ANGOLA
Luanda
ZAMBIA
Lusaka
MALAWI
Lilongwe
MOZAMBIQUE
ZIMBABWE
Harare
NAMIBIA
Windhoek
BOTSWANA
Gaborone
Pretoria
Johannesburg
Maputo
SWAZILAND
Mbabane
LESOTHO
Maseru
Durban
REPUBLIC OF SOUTH AFRICA
Cape Town
Cape Agulhas
MADAGASCAR
Antananarivo
COMOROS
Moroni
Mayotte (France)
Réunion (France)
Port Louis
MAURITIUS
SEYCHELLES
Victoria
Arabian Sea
INDIA
New Delhi
Delhi
Mumbai
Pune
Hyderabad
Bangalore
Chennai
Vijayawada
Kolkata
Calcutta
Nagpur
Ahmadabad
Jaipur
Lucknow
Patna
Bhopal
Indore
Trivandrum
SRI LANKA
Sri Jayewardenepura Kotte
MALDIVES
Male
NEPAL
Kathmandu
BHUTAN
BANGLADESH
Dhaka
Khulna
Chittagong
MYANMAR
Mandalay
Yangon
THAILAND
Bangkok
LAOS
Viangchan
CAMBODIA
Phnum Penh
VIETNAM
Ha Nôi
Hô Chi Minh
Kunming
Nanning
Guangzhou
Hong Kong
Macau
Zhanjiang
Hainan
Fuzhou
T'aipei
TAIWAN
Kaohsiung
South China Sea
Luzon
PHILIPPINES
Manila
Quezon City
Mindanao
Andaman Islands (India)
MALAYSIA
Kuala Lumpur
SINGAPORE
BRUNEI
Bandar Seri Begawan
Medan
Padang
Sumatera
Palembang
Borneo
Sulawesi
INDONESIA
Jakarta
Jawa
Surabaya
EAST TIMOR
Timor
New Guinea
PAPUA NEW GUINEA
Port Moresby
PALAU
Koror
Caroline Islands
FEDERATED STATES OF MICRONESIA
Palikir
MARSHALL ISLANDS
Delap-Uliga-Djarrit
Northern Mariana Islands (U.S.A.)
Guam (U.S.A.)
PACIFIC OCEAN
Midway Islands (U.S.A.)
Tropic of Cancer
INTERNATIONAL DATE LINE
Ogasawara-shotō (Bonin Islands) (Japan)
Kazan-rettō (Volcano Islands) (Japan)
NAURU
Yaren
KIRIBATI
Bairiki
Gilbert Islands
Phoenix Islands
Kingsmill Group
Equator
SOLOMON ISLANDS
Honiara
TUVALU
Vaiaku
Tokelau (N.Z.)
VANUATU
Port Vila
FIJI
Suva
SAMOA
Apia
TONGA
Wallis and Futuna Islands (France)
New Caledonia (France)
Nouméa
Tropic of Capricorn
Coral Sea
British Indian Ocean Territory
Cocos Islands (Australia)
Christmas Island (Australia)
INDIAN OCEAN
AUSTRALIA
Darwin
Cairns
Alice Springs
Brisbane
Perth
Adelaide
Sydney
Canberra
Melbourne
Tasmania
Hobart
Darling
Murray
Lord Howe Island (Australia)
Norfolk Island (Australia)
Kermadec Islands (N.Z.)
Tasman Sea
NEW ZEALAND
Auckland
North Island
Wellington
South Island
Christchurch
Dunedin
Chatham Islands (N.Z.)
Bounty Islands (N.Z.)
Antipodes Islands (N.Z.)
Snares Islands (N.Z.)
Auckland Islands (N.Z.)
Campbell Island (N.Z.)
Macquarie Island (Australia)
Île Amsterdam
Île St Paul
French Southern and Antarctic Lands
Prince Edward Island (South Africa)
Îles Crozet
Îles Kerguélen
Heard Island (Australia)
SOUTHERN OCEAN
Antarctic Circle
Ross Sea
CTICA
20°
40°
60°
80°
100°
120°
140°
160°
180°

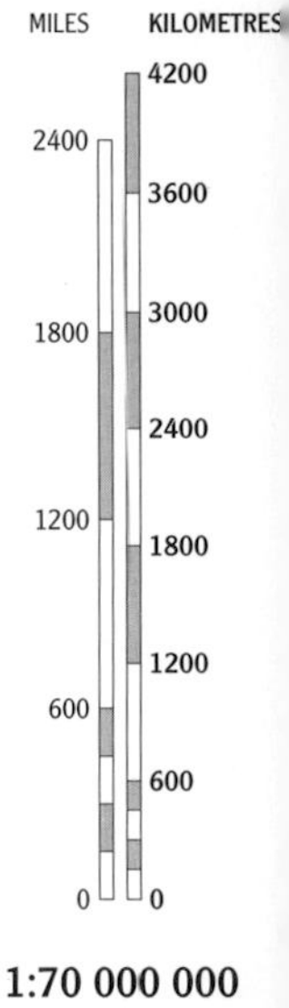
MILES
KILOMETRES
2400
1800
1200
600
0
4200
3600
3000
2400
1800
1200
600
0

1:70 000 000

© Bartholomew Ltd

A
B
C
D
E
1
2
3
4
5
6
7
Kuril'skiye Ostrova
Hokkaidō
Sea of Japan
Honshū
Shikoku
Kyūshū
Ogasawara-shotō
Kazan-rettō
East China Sea
Nansei-shotō
A S I A
Chang Jiang
Taiwan Strait
Luzon Strait
Luzon
Xun Jiang
Hainan
Tropic of Cancer
Samar
Palau Islands
Pagan
Tinian
Saipan
Rota
Northern Mariana Islands
(U.S.A.)
Guam
(U.S.A.)
Hagåtña
Ulithi
Fais
Yap
Sorol
Faraulep
Ngulu
Caroline Islands
Eauripik
Pikelot
Hall Islands
Chuuk
Mortlock Islands
FEDERATED STATES
Palawan
Panay
Negros
Mindanao
Sulu Sea
South China Sea
Mekong
Gulf of Thailand
Bay of Bengal
Celebes Sea
Molucca Sea
Halmahera
Borneo
Makassar Strait
Sulawesi
Banda Sea
Strait of Malacca
Sumatera
Kepulauan Mentawai
Java Sea
Flores Sea
Jawa (Java)
Bali
Sumbawa
Flores
Sumba
Timor
Timor Sea
Ashmore and Cartier Islands
(Australia)
Arafura Sea
Mussau Island
Admiralty Islands
New Hanover
New Ireland
Bismarck Sea
Vanimo
Wewak
Sepik
Madang
Rabaul
New Britain
Bougainville Island
New Guinea
Mt Wilhelm
Goroka
Lae
PAPUA NEW GUINEA
Kerema
Balimo
Daru
Gulf of Papua
Port Moresby
Woodlark Island
D'Entrecasteaux Islands
Louisiade Archipelago
Torres Strait
Cape York
Coral Sea Islands Territory
(Australia)
Coral Sea
Melville Island
Wessel Islands
Cape Arnhem
Gulf of Carpentaria
Cape York Peninsula
Groote Eylandt
Bathurst Island
Darwin
Arnhem Land
Cape Londonderry
Wellesley Islands
Cooktown
Mitchell
Cairns
Gilbert
Normanton
Great Barrier Reef
Townsville
Wyndham
NORTHERN TERRITORY
Mackay
Cloncurry
Mount Isa
Christmas Island
(Australia)
Cape Lévêque
Halls Creek
Broome
Great Sandy Desert
Rockhampton
Gladstone
Fraser Island
QUEENSLAND
Longreach
Great Dividing Range
Alice Springs
Mount Liebig
Lake Mackay
Port Hedland
Karratha
Lake Disappointment
Maryborough
INDIAN OCEAN
Cocos Islands
(Australia)
Equator
Barrow Island
Newman
A U S T R A L I A
Charleville
Brisbane
Toowoomba
Gold Coast
Lake Amadeus
Oodnadatta
Lake Eyre (North)
Diamantina
Cooper Creek (Barcoo Creek)
Grafton
North West Cape
Paraburdoo
WESTERN AUSTRALIA
Great Victoria Desert
SOUTH AUSTRALIA
Darling
NEW SOUTH WALES
Tamworth
Newcastle
Meekatharra
Mount Magnet
Leonora
Woomera
Port Augusta
Broken Hill
Lachlan
Orange
Lithgow
Sydney
Wollongong
Ceduna
Whyalla
Port Pirie
Geraldton
Lake Moore
Kalgoorlie
Great Australian Bight
Port Lincoln
Adelaide
Wagga Wagga
A.C.T.
Canberra
Murray
Albury
Cape Carnot
Kangaroo Island
Bendigo
VICTORIA
Melbourne
Geelong
Perth
Fremantle
Bunbury
Esperance
Mount Gambier
Bass Strait
Flinders Island
Albany
Cape Leeuwin
King Island
Launceston
Devonport
TASMANIA
Hobart
South East Cape
SOUTHERN OCEAN
Tropic of Capricorn

Orthographic Projection

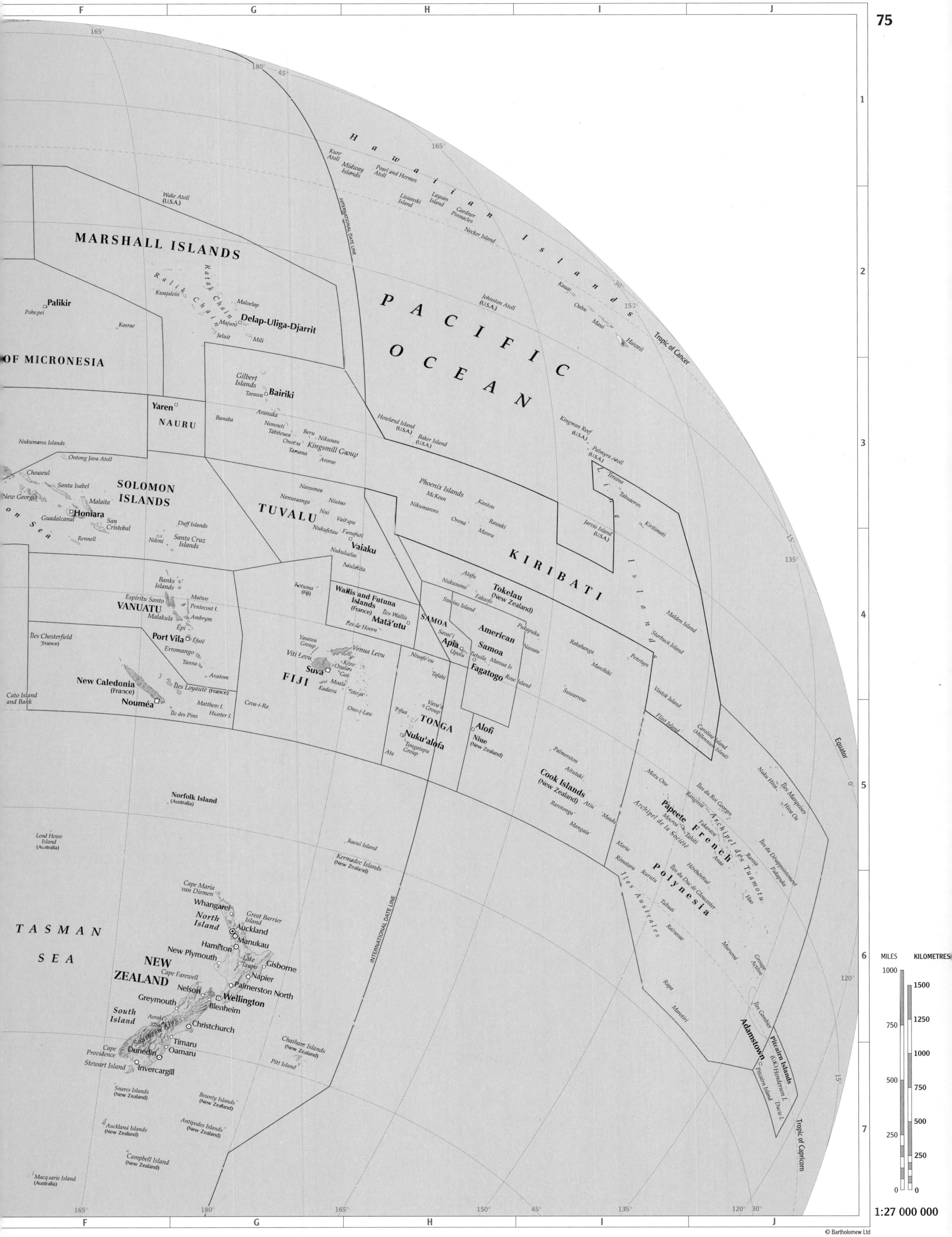
F
G
H
I
J
1
2
3
4
5
6
7
165°
180°
45°
150°
135°
120°
30°
15°
0°
Hawaiian Islands
Kure Atoll
Midway Islands
Pearl and Hermes Atoll
Lisianski Island
Laysan Island
Gardner Pinnacles
Necker Island
Kauai
Oahu
Maui
Hawaii
Tropic of Cancer
Wake Atoll (U.S.A.)
INTERNATIONAL DATE LINE
MARSHALL ISLANDS
Ratak Chain
Ralik Chain
Kwajalein
Maloelap
Majuro
Delap-Uliga-Djarrit
Jaluit
Mili
Palikir
Pohnpei
Kosrae
OF MICRONESIA
Johnston Atoll (U.S.A.)
PACIFIC OCEAN
Gilbert Islands
Tarawa
Bairiki
Yaren
NAURU
Banaba
Aranuka
Nonouti
Tabiteuea
Beru
Nikunau
Onotoa
Kingsmill Group
Tamana
Arorae
Howland Island (U.S.A.)
Baker Island (U.S.A.)
Kingman Reef (U.S.A.)
Palmyra Atoll (U.S.A.)
Teraina
Tabuaeran
Kiritimati
Line Islands
Jarvis Island (U.S.A.)
Nukumanu Islands
Ontong Java Atoll
Choiseul
Santa Isabel
New Georgia
Malaita
SOLOMON ISLANDS
Honiara
Guadalcanal
San Cristobal
Rennell
Duff Islands
Ndeni
Santa Cruz Islands
TUVALU
Nanumea
Nanumanga
Niutao
Nui
Vaitupu
Nukufetau
Funafuti
Vaiaku
Nukulaelae
Niulakita
Phoenix Islands
McKean
Nikumaroro
Kanton
Orona
Rawaki
Manra
KIRIBATI
Banks Islands
Espíritu Santo
Maéwo
VANUATU
Pentecost I.
Malakula
Ambrym
Epi
Port Vila
Éfaté
Erromango
Tanna
Aratom
Îles Chesterfield (France)
New Caledonia (France)
Îles Loyauté (France)
Nouméa
Cato Island and Bank
Matthew I.
Hunter I.
Île des Pins
Rotuma (Fiji)
Wallis and Futuna Islands (France)
Îles Wallis
Matā'utu
Îles de Hoorn
SAMOA
Savai'i
Apia
Upolu
Atafu
Nukunono
Fakaofo
Tokelau (New Zealand)
Swains Island
American Samoa
Tutuila
Manua Is
Fagatogo
Rose Island
Pukapuka
Nassau
Rakahanga
Manihiki
Penrhyn
Malden Island
Starbuck Island
Suwarrow
Vostok Island
Flint Island
Caroline Island (Millennium Island)
Yasawa Group
Vanua Levu
Viti Levu
Suva
Koro
Ovalau
Gau
Moala
Kadavu
Totoya
FIJI
Ceva-i-Ra
Ono-i-Lau
Niuafo'ou
Tafahi
Vava'u Group
Tofua
TONGA
Nuku'alofa
Tongatapu Group
Ata
Alofi
Niue (New Zealand)
Equator
Palmerston
Aitutaki
Cook Islands (New Zealand)
Rarotonga
Atiu
Mauke
Mangaia
Motu One
Îles du Roi Georges
Rangiroa
Archipel de la Société
Papeete
Moorea
Tahiti
Fakarava
Anaa
French Polynesia
Archipel des Tuamotu
Nuku Hiva
Îles Marquises
Hiva Oa
Raroia
Îles du Désappointement
Pukapuka
Hereheretue
Îles du Duc de Gloucester
Hao
Maria
Rimatara
Rurutu
Tubuai
Îles Australes
Raivavae
Mururoa
Groupe Actéon
Rapa
Marotiri
Îles Gambier
Adamstown
Pitcairn Islands (U.K.)
Henderson I.
Ducie I.
Pitcairn Island
Tropic of Capricorn
Norfolk Island (Australia)
Lord Howe Island (Australia)
Raoul Island
Kermadec Islands (New Zealand)
Cape Maria van Diemen
Whangarei
Great Barrier Island
North Island
Auckland
Manukau
Hamilton
New Plymouth
Lake Taupo
Gisborne
Napier
NEW ZEALAND
Cape Farewell
Nelson
Palmerston North
Wellington
Blenheim
Greymouth
South Island
Aoraki
Southern Alps
Christchurch
Timaru
Cape Providence
Dunedin
Oamaru
Stewart Island
Invercargill
TASMAN SEA
Chatham Islands (New Zealand)
Pitt Island
Snares Islands (New Zealand)
Bounty Islands (New Zealand)
Antipodes Islands (New Zealand)
Auckland Islands (New Zealand)
Campbell Island (New Zealand)
Macquarie Island (Australia)
MILES
KILOMETRES
1000
750
500
250
0
1500
1250
1000
750
500
250
0
1:27 000 000

© Bartholomew Ltd

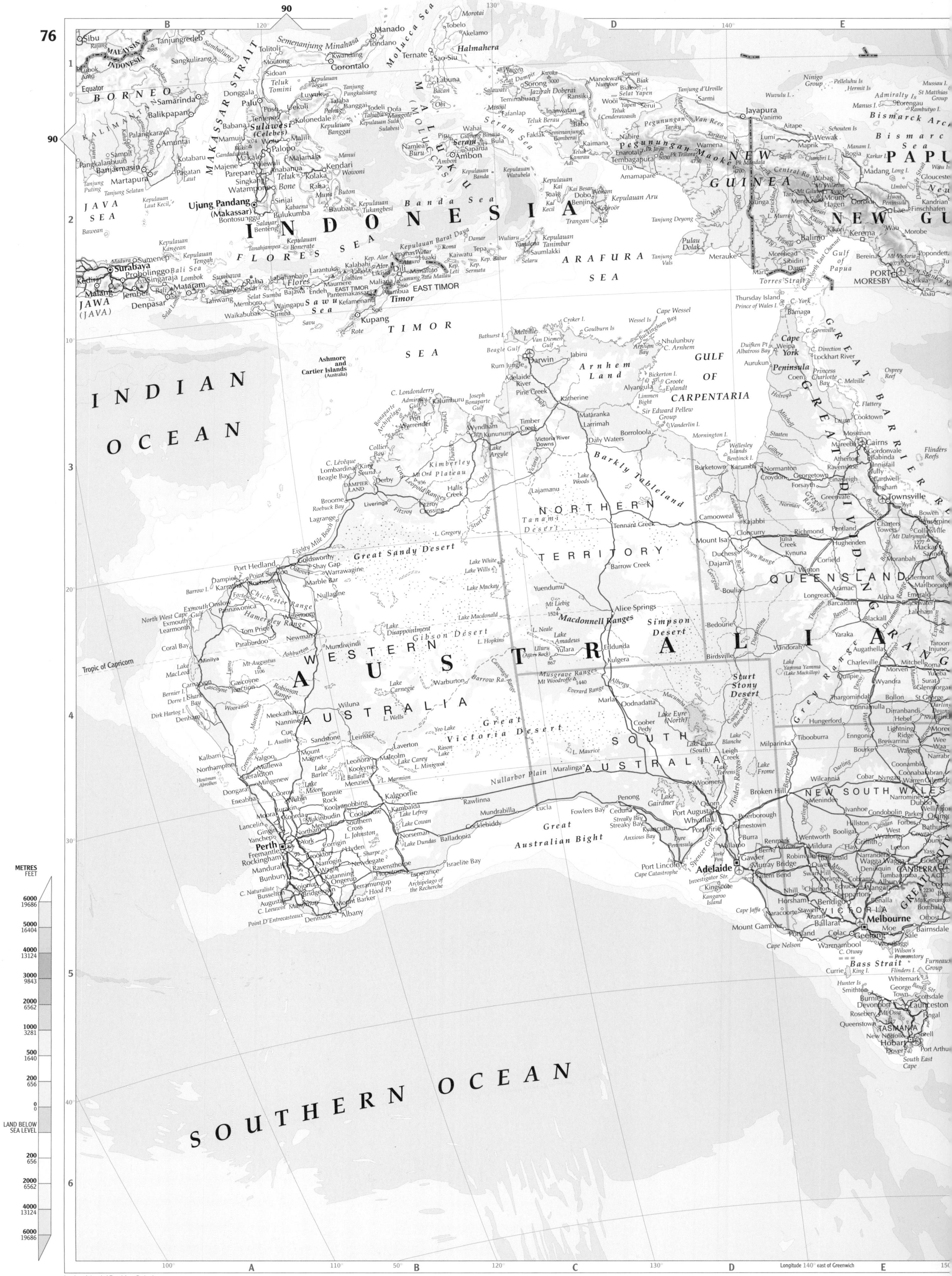
INDIAN OCEAN
SOUTHERN OCEAN
AUSTRALIA
INDONESIA
NEW GUINEA
PAPUA NEW GUINEA
WESTERN AUSTRALIA
NORTHERN TERRITORY
SOUTH AUSTRALIA
QUEENSLAND
NEW SOUTH WALES
VICTORIA
TASMANIA
EAST TIMOR
BORNEO
KALIMANTAN
Sulawesi (Celebes)
JAVA SEA
FLORES SEA
Banda Sea
ARAFURA SEA
TIMOR SEA
Sawu Sea
GULF OF CARPENTARIA
GREAT BARRIER REEF
GREAT DIVIDING RANGE
Great Australian Bight
Bass Strait
Torres Strait
Molucca Sea
Seram Sea
Halmahera
MALUKU (MOLUCCAS)
Jawa (Java)
Timor
Flores
Great Sandy Desert
Gibson Desert
Great Victoria Desert
Simpson Desert
Sturt Stony Desert
Tanami Desert
Nullarbor Plain
Barkly Tableland
Kimberley Plateau
Arnhem Land
Cape York Peninsula
Macdonnell Ranges
Musgrave Ranges
Flinders Ranges
Lake Eyre (North)
Lake Eyre (South)
Lake Torrens
Lake Gairdner
Lake Frome
Ashmore and Cartier Islands (Australia)
Tropic of Capricorn
Equator
Perth
Darwin
Adelaide
Melbourne
Canberra
Hobart
Surabaya
Ujung Pandang (Makassar)
Port Moresby
Alice Springs
Kalgoorlie
Broome
Port Hedland
Geraldton
Albany
Esperance
Katherine
Tennant Creek
Mount Isa
Townsville
Cairns
Rockhampton
Port Augusta
Whyalla
Port Lincoln
Broken Hill
Mildura
Ballarat
Bendigo
Geelong
Launceston
Kupang
Dili
Jayapura
Denpasar
Mataram
METRES
FEET
6000 19686
5000 16404
4000 13124
3000 9843
2000 6562
1000 3281
500 1640
200 656
0 0
LAND BELOW SEA LEVEL
200 656
2000 6562
4000 13124
6000 19686
90
B
C
D
E
A
1
2
3
4
5
6
100°
110°
120°
130°
140°
150°
10°
20°
30°
40°
0°
Longitude 140° east of Greenwich

Lambert Azimuthal Equal Area Projection

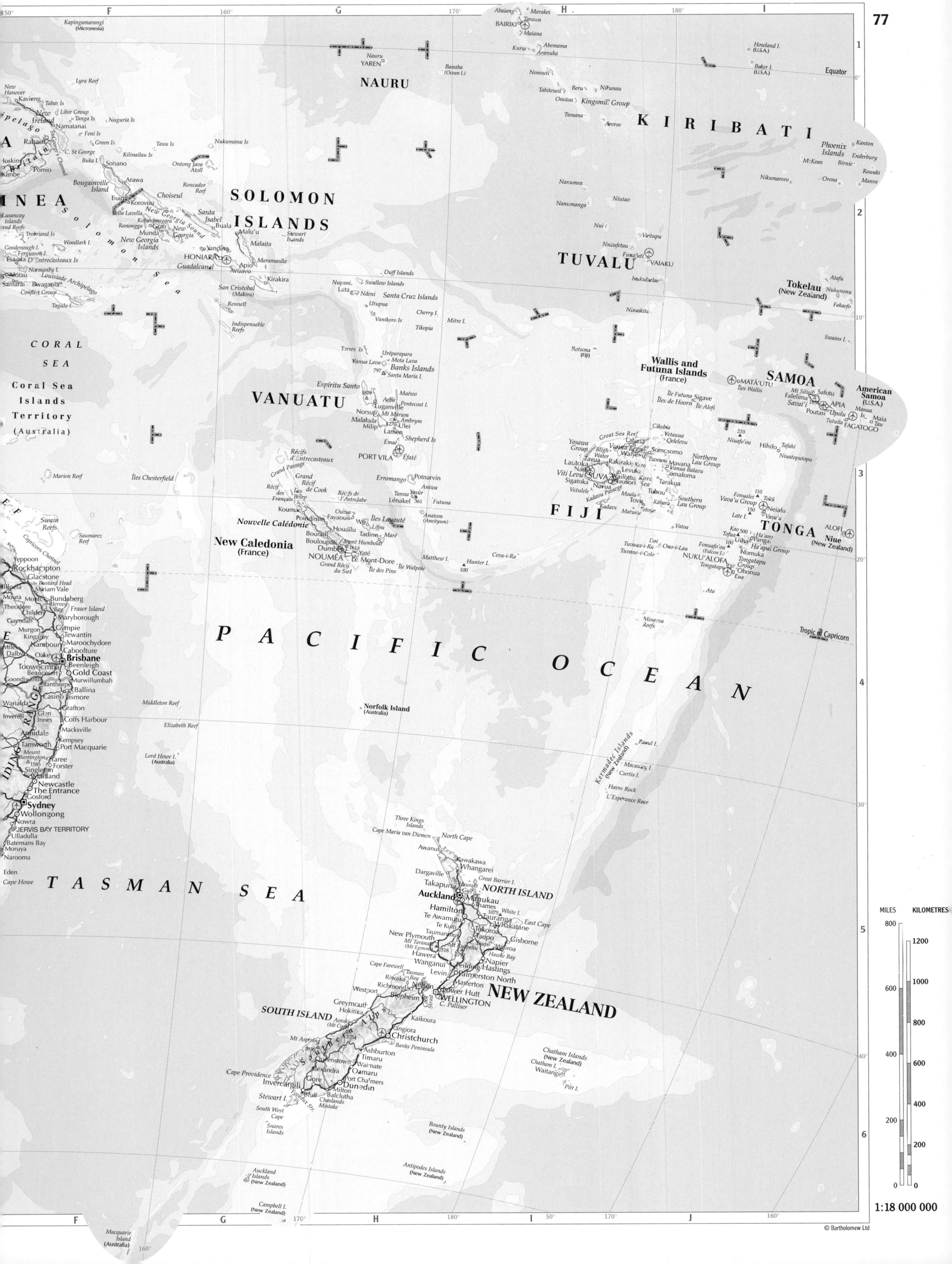
NAURU
Nauru
YAREN
Banaba (Ocean I.)
KIRIBATI
BAIRIKI
Tarawa
Abaiang
Marakei
Maiana
Kuria
Abemama
Aranuka
Nonouti
Tabiteuea
Beru
Nikunau
Onotoa
Kingsmill Group
Tamana
Arorae
Howland I. (U.S.A.)
Baker I. (U.S.A.)
Equator
Phoenix Islands
Kanton
Enderbury
McKean
Birnie
Rawaki
Manra
Orona
Nikumaroro
Kapingamarangi (Micronesia)
Lyra Reef
New Hanover
Kavieng
Tabar Is
New Ireland
Lihir Group
Tanga Is
Namatanai
Nuguria Is
Feni Is
Green Is
Rabaul
St George's Channel
C. St George
Buka I.
Kilinailau Is
Tauu Is
Nukumanu Is
Ontong Java Atoll
Sohano
Arawa
Bougainville Island
Roncador Reef
Kimbe
Hoskins
Pomio
GUINEA
SOLOMON ISLANDS
Choiseul
Buin
Korovou
Vella Lavella
Kolombangara
New Georgia Sound
Santa Isabel
Buala
Ranongga
Gizo
Munda
New Georgia Islands
Malu'u
Malaita
Stewart Islands
HONIARA
Yandina
Guadalcanal
Auki
Maramasike
Avuavu
Kirakira
San Cristobal (Makira)
Rennell
Indispensable Reefs
Solomon Sea
Lusancay Islands and Reefs
Trobriand Is
Woodlark I.
Goodenough I.
Fergusson I.
Esa'ala
D'Entrecasteaux Is
Normanby I.
Alotau
Louisiade Archipelago
Samarai
Bwagaoia
Conflict Group
Tagula I.
Duff Islands
Nupani
Lata
Swallow Islands
Ndeni
Santa Cruz Islands
Utupua
Vanikoro Is
Cherry I.
Tikopia
Mitre I.
TUVALU
Nanumea
Niutao
Nanumanga
Nui
Vaitupu
Nukufetau
Funafuti
VAIAKU
Nukulaelae
Niulakita
Tokelau (New Zealand)
Atafu
Nukunonu
Fakaofo
Swains I.
CORAL SEA
Coral Sea Islands Territory (Australia)
Torres Is
Ureparapara
Mota Lava
Vanua Lava
Banks Islands
Santa Maria I.
Espiritu Santo
VANUATU
Maewo
Aoba
Pentecost I.
Luganville
Norsup
Mt Marum
Ambrym
Malakula
Milip
Ulei
Lamen
Emaé
Shepherd Is
PORT VILA
Éfaté
Erromango
Potnarvin
Aniwa
Tanna
Yasur
Lénakel
Futuna
Anatom (Aneityum)
Wallis and Futuna Islands (France)
MATĀ'UTU
Îles Wallis
Île Futuna
Sigave
Îles de Hoorn
Île Alofi
SAMOA
Savai'i
Falelima
Mt Silisili
Safotu
APIA
Poutasi
'Upolu
American Samoa (U.S.A.)
Manua Is.
Tutuila
FAGATOGO
Maia
Tau
Rotuma (Fiji)
Cikobia
Vetauua
Qelelevu
Niuafo'ou
Hihifo
Tafahi
Niuatoputapu
Great Sea Reef
Labasa
Yasawa Group
Bligh Water
Vanua Levu
Somosomo
Taveuni
Waiyevo
Tavua
Rakiraki
Koro
Lautoka
Nadi
Levuka
Viti Levu
SUVA
Nausori
Mavana
Vanua Balavu
Lomaloma
Northern Lau Group
Sigatoka
Navua
Koro Sea
Tarakua
Vatulele
Kadavu Passage
Kadavu
Moala
Totoya
Matuku
Tubou
Kabara
Southern Lau Group
FIJI
Vatoa
Récifs d'Entrecasteaux
Grand Passage
Grand Récif de Cook
Récif des Français
Îles Belep
Récifs de l'Astrolabe
Koumac
Poindimié
Ouvéa
Fayaoué
Îles Loyauté
Wé
Lifou
Houaïlu
Bourail
Tadine
Maré
Bouloupari
Mont Humboldt
Dumbéa
NOUMÉA
Mont-Dore
Yaté
Grand Récif du Sud
Île des Pins
Nouvelle Calédonie
New Caledonia (France)
Île Walpole
Matthew I.
Hunter I.
Ceva-i-Ra
Tuvana-i-Ra
Tuvana-i-Colo
Ono-i-Lau
Fonualei
Toku
Vava'u Group
Neiafu
Vava'u
Late I.
Kao
Tofua
Ha'apai Group
Ha'ano
Uiha
Pangai
Nomuka
TONGA
ALOFI
Niue (New Zealand)
Fonuafo'ou (Falcon I.)
NUKU'ALOFA
Tongatapu
Tongatapu Group
Ohonua
'Eua
'Ata
Minerva Reefs
Tropic of Capricorn
Marion Reef
Îles Chesterfield
Swain Reefs
Saumarez Reef
Capricorn Channel
Yeppoon
Rockhampton
Gladstone
Bustard Head
Miriam Vale
Biloela
Moura
Monto
Bundaberg
Theodore
Childers
Hervey Bay
Fraser Island
Gayndah
Maryborough
Murgon
Gympie
Kingaroy
Tewantin
Nambour
Maroochydore
Miles
Dalby
Oakey
Caboolture
Brisbane
Toowoomba
Beenleigh
Beaudesert
Gold Coast
Goondiwindi
Stanthorpe
Murwillumbah
Ballina
Casino
Lismore
Warialda
Grafton
Inverell
Glen Innes
Coffs Harbour
Armidale
Macksville
Kempsey
Port Macquarie
Tamworth
Mount Barrington
Taree
Forster
Singleton
Maitland
Newcastle
The Entrance
Gosford
Sydney
Wollongong
Nowra
JERVIS BAY TERRITORY
Ulladulla
Batemans Bay
Moruya
Narooma
Eden
Cape Howe
PACIFIC OCEAN
Middleton Reef
Norfolk Island (Australia)
Elizabeth Reef
Lord Howe I. (Australia)
Kermadec Islands (New Zealand)
Raoul I.
Macauley I.
Curtis I.
Havre Rock
L'Espérance Rock
TASMAN SEA
Three Kings Islands
Cape Maria van Diemen
North Cape
Awanui
Kawakawa
Whangarei
Dargaville
Great Barrier I.
Takapuna
Hauraki Gulf
NORTH ISLAND
Auckland
Manukau
Thames
Hamilton
Te Awamutu
Tauranga
White I.
Whakatane
East Cape
Te Kuiti
Taumarunui
Rotorua
Taupo
Gisborne
New Plymouth
Mt Taranaki (Mt Egmont)
Mt Ruapehu
Wairoa
Hawera
Hawke Bay
Wanganui
Napier
Hastings
Levin
Feilding
Palmerston North
Cape Farewell
Tasman Bay
Riwaka
Richmond
Nelson
Masterton
Westport
Blenheim
Cook Strait
Lower Hutt
WELLINGTON
C. Palliser
NEW ZEALAND
Greymouth
Hokitika
SOUTH ISLAND
Aoraki (Mt Cook)
Southern Alps
Kaikoura
Rangiora
Christchurch
Banks Peninsula
Mt Aspiring
Ashburton
Queenstown
Timaru
Waimate
Alexandra
Oamaru
Cape Providence
Gore
Port Chalmers
Invercargill
Dunedin
Bluff
Milton
Balclutha
Foveaux Str.
Stewart I.
Chaslands Mistake
South West Cape
Snares Islands
Chatham Islands (New Zealand)
Chatham I.
Waitangi
Pitt I.
Bounty Islands (New Zealand)
Antipodes Islands (New Zealand)
Auckland Islands (New Zealand)
Campbell I. (New Zealand)
Macquarie Island (Australia)
MILES
KILOMETRES
1:18 000 000

© Bartholomew Ltd

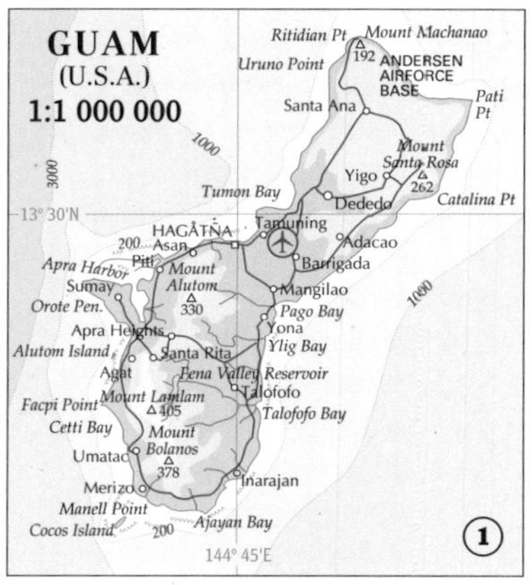
GUAM
(U.S.A.)
1:1 000 000
Ritidian Pt
Mount Machanao
Uruno Point
ANDERSEN AIRFORCE BASE
Pati Pt
Santa Ana
Mount Santa Rosa
262
Yigo
Dededo
Catalina Pt
Tumon Bay
13° 30'N
HAGÅTÑA
Tamuning
Asan
Adacao
Barrigada
Piti
Apra Harbor
Sumay
Mount Alutom
330
Mangilao
Orote Pen.
Pago Bay
Apra Heights
Yona
Alutom Island
Santa Rita
Ylig Bay
Agat
Fena Valley Reservoir
Facpi Point
Mount Lamlam
405
Talofofo
Talofofo Bay
Cetti Bay
Mount Bolanos
378
Umatac
Merizo
Inarajan
Manell Point
Cocos Island
Ajayan Bay
144° 45'E
1

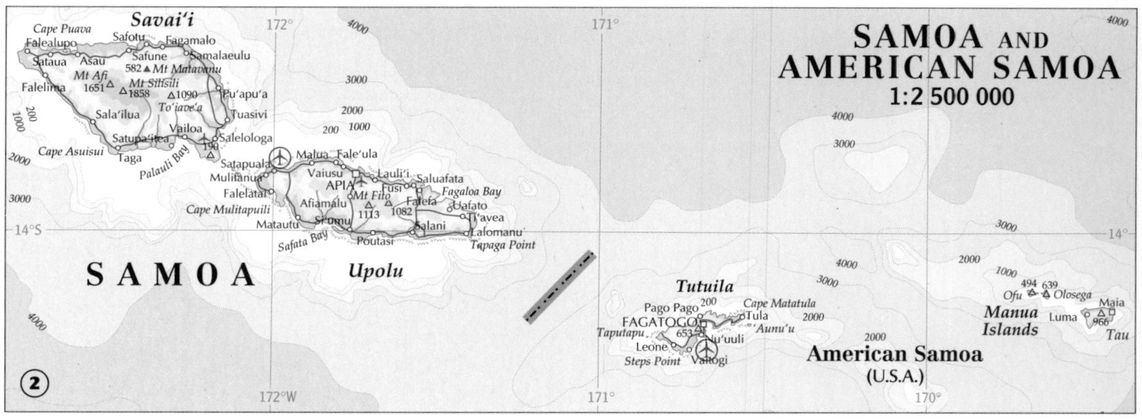
Savai'i
Cape Puava
Falealupo
Safotu
Fagamalo
Sataua
Asau
Samalaeulu
Mt Afi
1651
Mt Matavanu
Mt Silisili
1858
Pu'apu'a
Falelima
Sala'ilua
To'iave'a
Tuasivi
Satupaitea
Vailoa
Salelologa
Cape Asuisui
Taga
Palauli Bay
Satapuala
Malua
Fale'ula
Mulifanua
Vaiusu
APIA
Lauli'i
Saluafata
Falelatai
Mt Fito
Fusi
Fagaloa Bay
Afiamalu
1113
Falefa
1082
Uafato
Cape Mulitapuili
Si'umu
Salani
Ti'avea
Matautu
Safata Bay
Poutasi
Lalomanu
Tapaga Point
SAMOA
Upolu
SAMOA AND AMERICAN SAMOA
1:2 500 000
Tutuila
Pago Pago
Cape Matatula
FAGATOGO
Tula
Taputapu
Aunu'u
Leone
Faleasao
Steps Point
Vaitogi
Ofu
Olosega
Luma
Manua Islands
Tau
American Samoa
(U.S.A.)
172°W
171°
170°
14°S
2

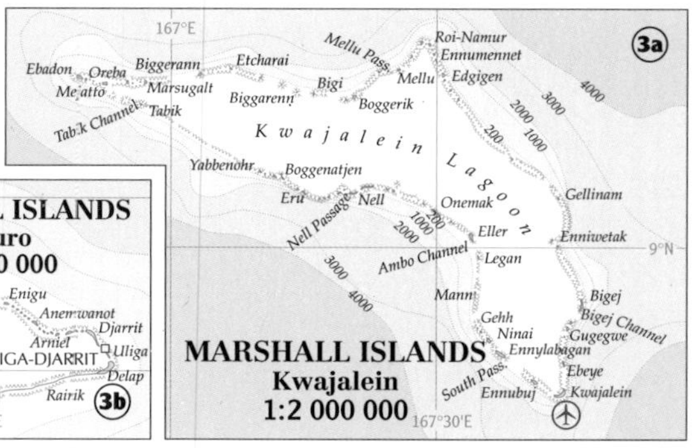
167°E
Roi-Namur
Ennumennet
Ebadon
Oreba
Biggerann
Etcharai
Mellu Pass
Mellu
Edgigen
Meatto
Marsugalt
Bigi
Biggerenn
Boggerik
Tabik
Kwajalein Lagoon
Yabbenohr
Boggenatjen
Gellinam
Eru
Nell
Onemak
Nell Passage
Eller
Enniwetak
Ambo Channel
Legan
9°N
Mann
Bigej
Gehh
Ninai
Bigej Channel
Ennylabegan
Gugegwe
Ebeye
South Pass
Ennubuj
Kwajalein
MARSHALL ISLANDS
Kwajalein
1:2 000 000
167°30'E
3a

7°15'
MARSHALL ISLANDS
Majuro
1:1 000 000
Jaloklab
Roguron
Ajokwola
Anenj
Calalin Channel
Eroj
West Landing
Calalin
Enigu
Lobikaere
Anenwanot
Djarrit
Majuro Lagoon
Arrak
DELAP-ULIGA-DJARRIT
Uliga
7°05'N
Woje
Delap
Majuro
Rairik
171°15'E
3b

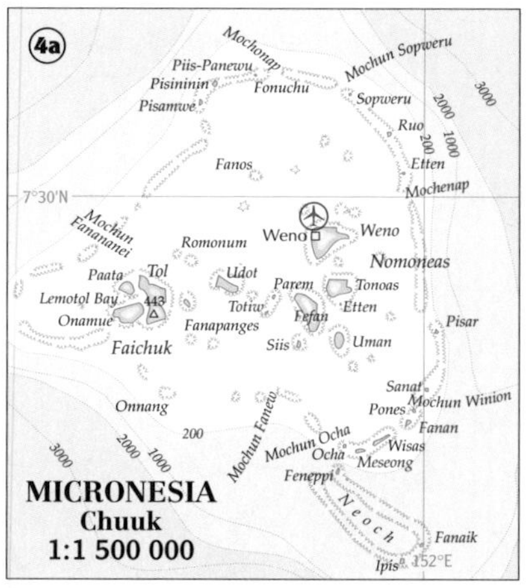
4a
Mochonap
Mochun Sopweru
Piis-Panewu
Pisininin
Fonuchu
Pisamwe
Sopweru
Ruo
Etten
Fanos
Mochenap
7°30'N
Mochun Fanananei
Romonum
Weno
Weno
Nomoneas
Udot
Paata
Tol
Parem
Tonoas
Lemotol Bay
Onamue
443
Totiw
Etten
Fefan
Fanapanges
Pisar
Faichuk
Siis
Uman
Sanat
Mochun Winion
Onnang
Pones
Fanan
Mochun Feneu
Mochun Ocha
Wisas
Ocha
Meseong
Fenepi
Neoch
MICRONESIA
Chuuk
1:1 500 000
Fanaik
Ipis
152°E

MICRONESIA
Pohnpei
1:1 000 000
4b
Parempei
7°N
Palikir Passage
Deke
Sokehs
Kolonia
PALIKIR
Dehpehk
Alohkapw
Temwetemwensekir
590
Tauak Passage
Pweil Weite
772
Nanlaud
760
Dolohmwar
Temwen
Lenwohi
Sekeren Ijap
Pwok
Kepidau en Pohnahtik
158°15'E

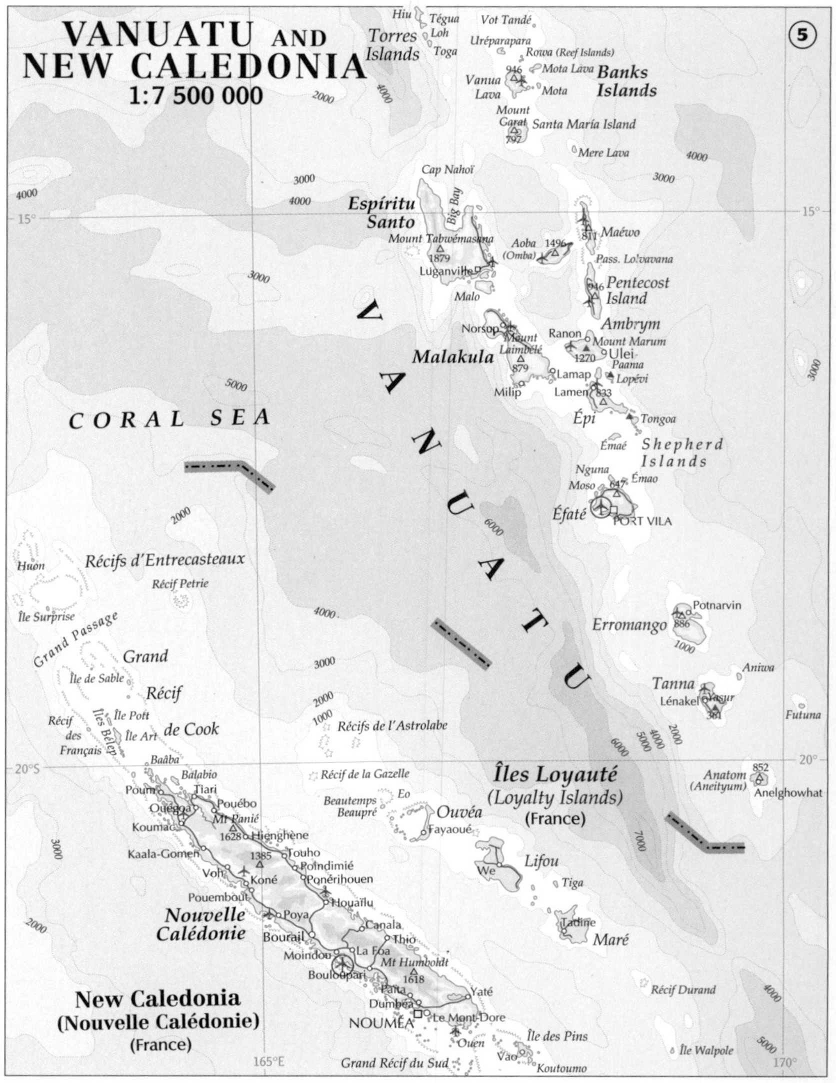
VANUATU AND NEW CALEDONIA
1:7 500 000
5
Hiu
Tégua
Torres Islands
Loh
Toga
Vot Tandé
Uréparapara
Rowa (Reef Islands)
Vanua Lava
Mota Lava
Banks Islands
Mota
Mount Garat
797
Santa Maria Island
Mere Lava
Cap Nahoï
Big Bay
Espíritu Santo
15°
Mount Tabwémasana
1879
Aoba (Omba)
1496
Maéwo
Luganville
Pass. Lolvavana
Malo
Pentecost Island
Ambrym
Malakula
Norsup
Mount Lambéré
Ranon
Mount Marum
Ulei
1270
Paama
Lopévi
Lamap
Lamen
Milip
Épi
Tongoa
Émaé
Shepherd Islands
Nguna
Moso
Émao
Éfaté
PORT VILA
CORAL SEA
VANUATU
Huon
Récifs d'Entrecasteaux
Récif Petrie
Île Surprise
Grand Passage
Potnarvin
Erromango
Grand Récif
Île de Sable
Tanna
Lénakel
Aniwa
Récif des Français
Île Pott
Île Art
Îles Belep
de Cook
Récifs de l'Astrolabe
Futuna
20°S
Baaba
Balabio
Récif de la Gazelle
Îles Loyauté
(Loyalty Islands)
(France)
Anatom (Aneityum)
852
Anelghowhat
Poum
Tiari
Beautemps Beaupré
Ouvéa
Ouégoa
Mt Panié
1628
Hienghène
Fayaoué
Koumac
Kaala-Gomen
Touho
Poindimié
Voh
Koné
Ponérihouen
Lifou
Pouembout
Houaïlou
Tiga
Nouvelle Calédonie
Poya
Bourail
Canala
Thio
Maré
Moindou
La Foa
Mt Humboldt
1618
Boulouparis
Yaté
Récif Durand
Paita
Dumbéa
Le Mont Dore
NOUMÉA
Ouen
Île des Pins
Île Walpole
Vao
New Caledonia
(Nouvelle Calédonie)
(France)
Grand Récif du Sud
Koutoumo
165°E
170°

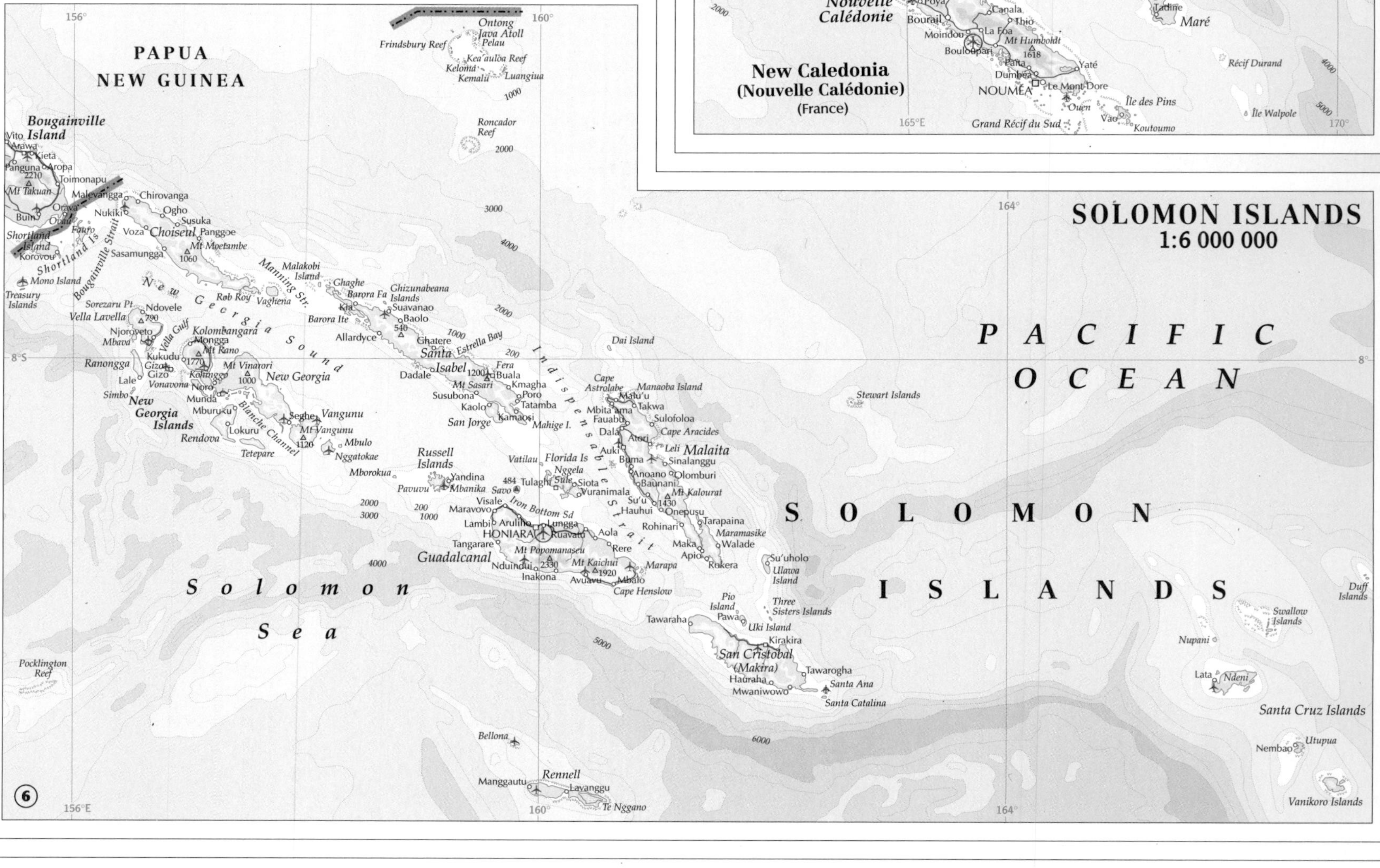
156°
160°
PAPUA NEW GUINEA
Ontong Java Atoll
Pelau
Frindsbury Reef
Kea'aulōa Reef
Kelomā
Kemalū
Luangiua
Roncador Reef
Bougainville Island
Kieta
Panguna
Aropa
Toimonapu
Mt Takuan
2210
Malevangga
Chirovanga
Buin
Ogho
Nukiki
Susuka
Shortland Island
Korovou
Voza
Choiseul
Panggoe
Mt Maetambe
Fauro
Sasamungga
Shortland Is Strait
Bougainville Strait
Mono Island
Treasury Islands
Malakobi Island
Ghaghe
Manning Str.
Chizunabeana Islands
New Georgia Sound
Barora Fa
Sorezaru Pt
Ndovele
Rob Roy
Vaghena
Suavanao
Vella Lavella
Kia
Baolo
Barora Ite
Njoroveto
Vella Gulf
Kolombangara
Allardyce
Ghatere
Mbava
Mongga
Estrella Bay
Dai Island
8°S
Ranongga
Kukudu
Mt Rano
Mt Vinatori
Santa Isabel
Fera
Buala
Lale
Gizo
Kolonggo
Vonavona
Noro
New Georgia
Dadale
Mt Sasari
Kmagha
Indispensable Strait
Cape Astrolabe
Manaoba Island
Simbo
Munda
Susubona
Poro
Maluʻu
Stewart Islands
New Georgia Islands
Mburuku
Kaolo
Tatamba
Mbita'ama
Takwa
Rendova
Lokuru
Blanche Channel
Seghe
Vangunu
San Jorge
Kamaosi
Mahige I.
Fauabu
Solofoloa
Dala
Cape Aracides
Tetepare
Mt Vangunu
Mbulo
Auki
Leli
Malaita
Nggatokae
Russell Islands
Vatilau
Florida Is
Sinalanggu
Mborokua
Yandina
Tulaghi
Nggela
Anoano
Olomburi
Pavuvu
Mbanika
Savo
Siota
Baunani
Visale
Iron Bottom Sd
Vuranimala
Mt Kalourat
Maravovo
Hauhui
Su'u
Lambi
Aruliho
Lungga
Aola
Rohinari
Onepusu
HONIARA
Ruavatu
Tarapaina
Mt Popomanaseu
Rere
Maka
Maramasike
Guadalcanal
Tangarare
Apio
Walade
Nduindui
2330
Mt Kaichui
Marapa
Rokera
Su'uholo
Inakona
Avuavu
Mbalo
Ulawa Island
Cape Henslow
Pio Island
Three Sisters Islands
Duff Islands
Swallow Islands
Tawaraha
Pawa
Uki Island
Kirakira
Nupani
San Cristobal (Makira)
Hauraha
Tawarogha
Santa Ana
Lata
Ndeni
Mwaniwowo
Santa Catalina
Santa Cruz Islands
Utupua
Nembao
Solomon Sea
SOLOMON ISLANDS
PACIFIC OCEAN
SOLOMON ISLANDS
1:6 000 000
Pocklington Reef
Bellona
Rennell
Manggautu
Lavanggu
Te Nggano
Vanikoro Islands
156°E
164°
6

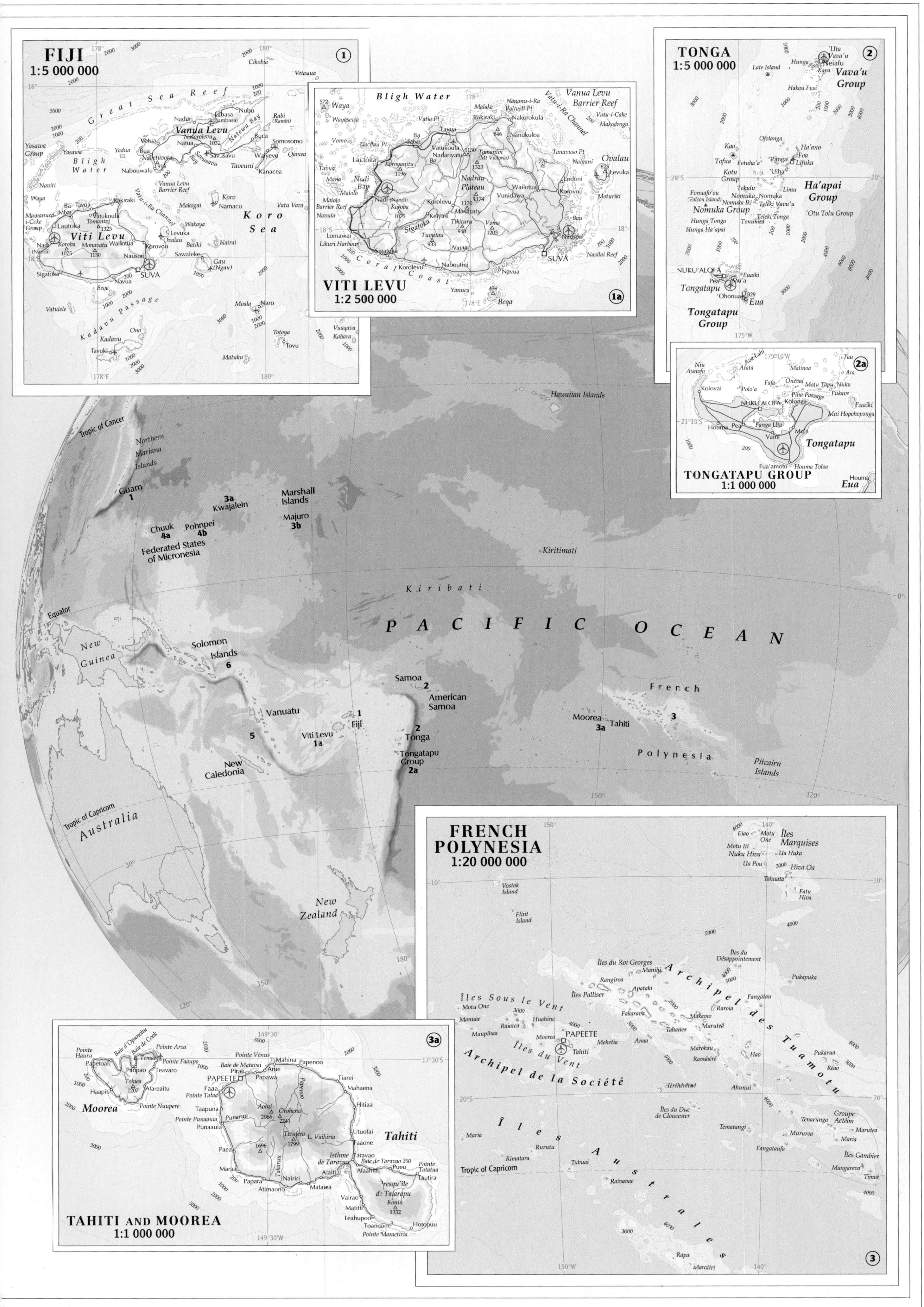
FIJI
1:5 000 000
1
Great Sea Reef
Vanua Levu
Bligh Water
Viti Levu
Koro Sea
Kadavu Passage
Yasawa Group
Taveuni
Kadavu
SUVA
VITI LEVU
1:2 500 000
1a
Bligh Water
Vanua Levu Barrier Reef
Vatu-i-Ra Channel
Nadrau Plateau
Coral Coast
Ovalau
SUVA
TONGA
1:5 000 000
2
Vava'u Group
Ha'apai Group
Nomuka Group
Tongatapu Group
NUKU'ALOFA
Tongatapu
'Eua
TONGATAPU GROUP
1:1 000 000
2a
Tongatapu
NUKU'ALOFA
Eua
Hawaiian Islands
Tropic of Cancer
Northern Mariana Islands
Guam 1
Marshall Islands
3a Kwajalein
Majuro 3b
Chuuk 4a
Pohnpei 4b
Federated States of Micronesia
Kiritimati
Kiribati
Equator
PACIFIC OCEAN
New Guinea
Solomon Islands 6
Samoa 2
American Samoa
Vanuatu
5
Viti Levu 1a
Fiji 1
Tonga 2
Tongatapu Group 2a
New Caledonia
French
Polynesia
Moorea 3a
Tahiti
3
Pitcairn Islands
Tropic of Capricorn
Australia
New Zealand
FRENCH POLYNESIA
1:20 000 000
Îles Marquises
Archipel des Tuamotu
Îles Sous le Vent
Îles du Vent
Archipel de la Société
Îles Australes
PAPEETE
Tahiti
Tropic of Capricorn
3
TAHITI AND MOOREA
1:1 000 000
3a
Moorea
Tahiti
PAPEETE
Presqu'île de Taiarapu

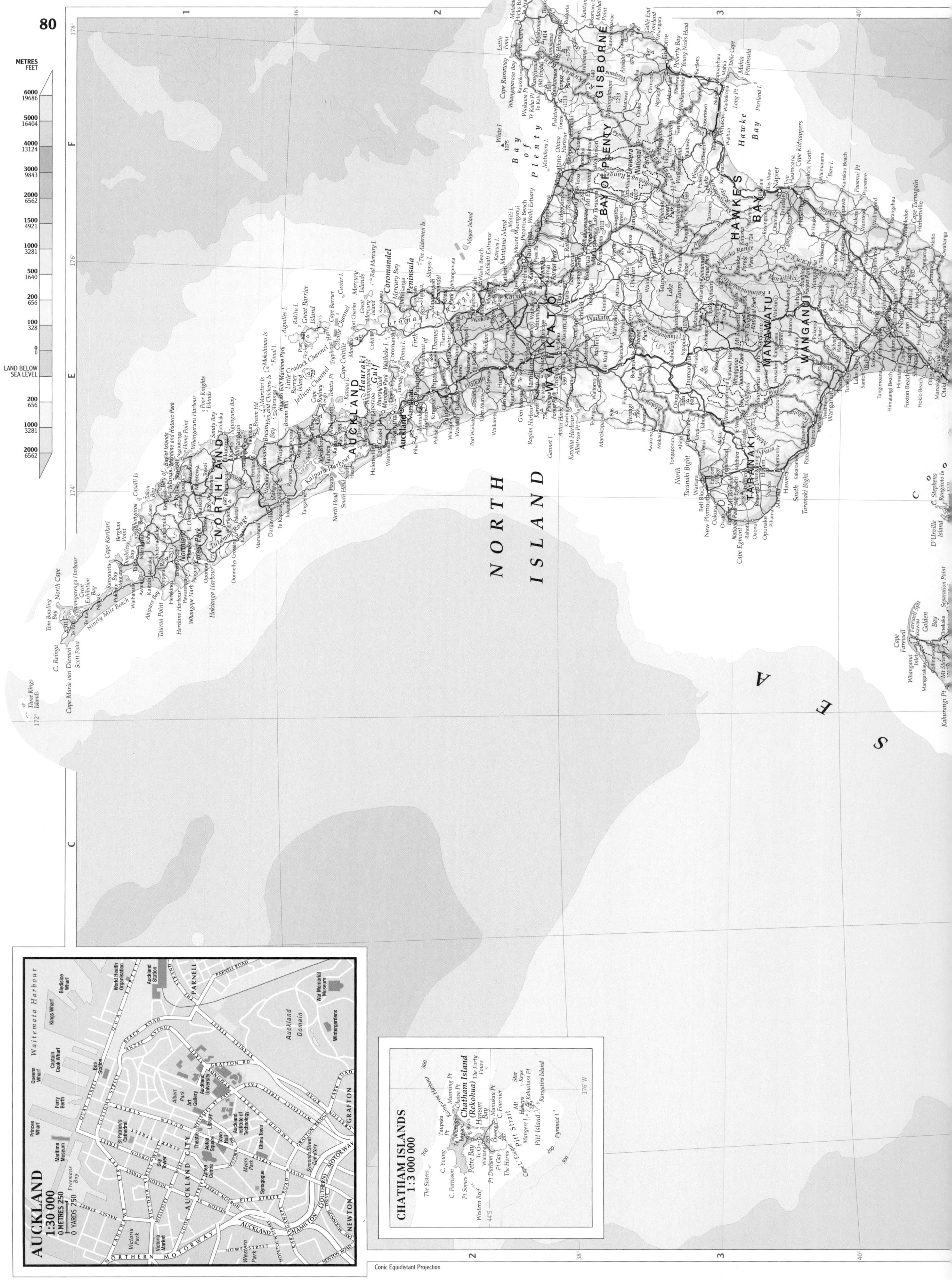

Conic Equidistant Projection

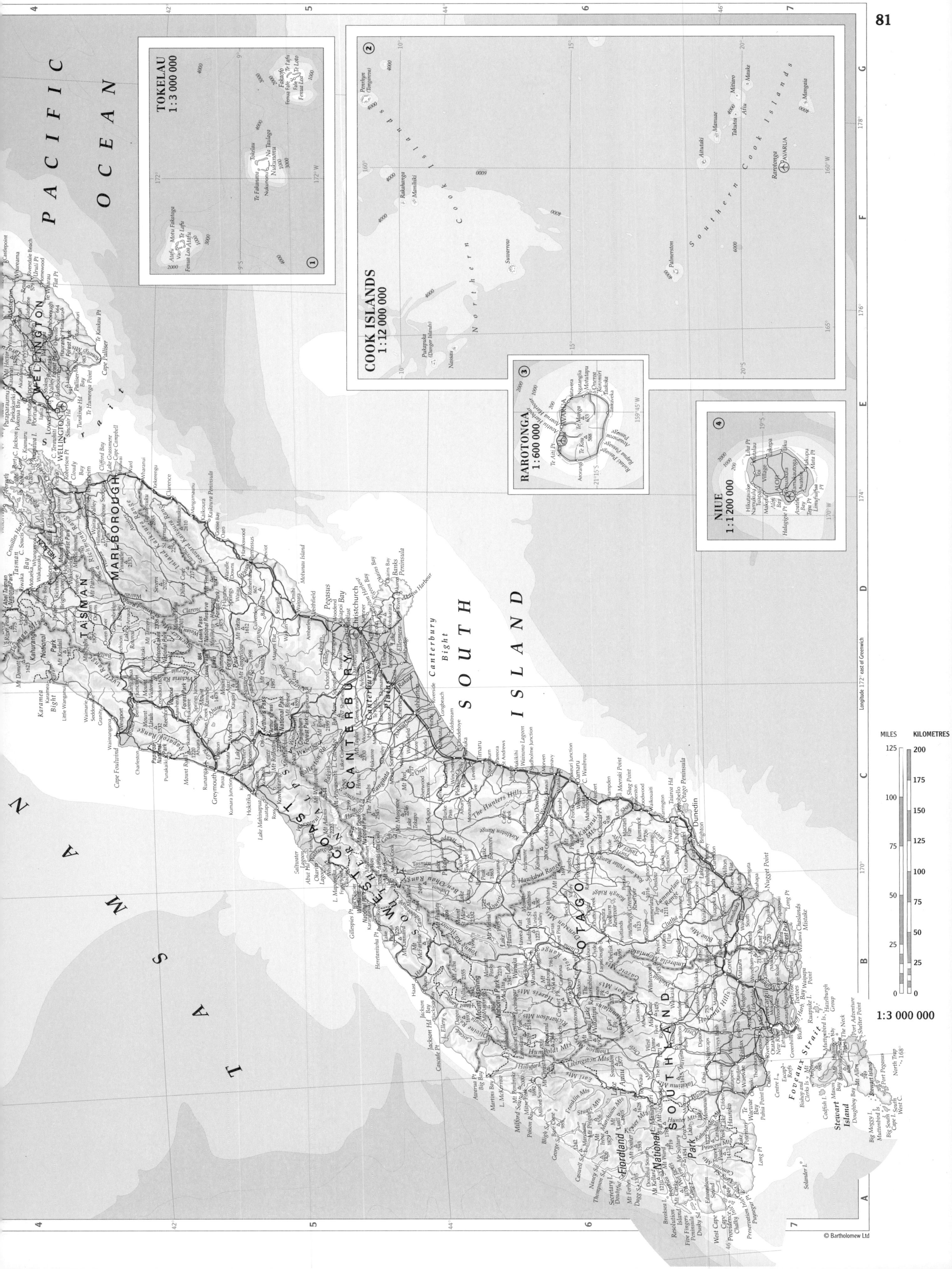
PACIFIC OCEAN
TASMAN SEA
SOUTH ISLAND
TOKELAU 1:3 000 000
COOK ISLANDS 1:12 000 000
RAROTONGA 1:600 000
NIUE 1:1 200 000
Northern Cook Islands
Southern Cook Islands
WELLINGTON
MARLBOROUGH
TASMAN
CANTERBURY
WEST COAST
OTAGO
SOUTHLAND
Christchurch
Dunedin
Canterbury Bight
Foveaux Strait
Stewart Island
MILES
KILOMETRES
1:3 000 000
Longitude 172° east of Greenwich

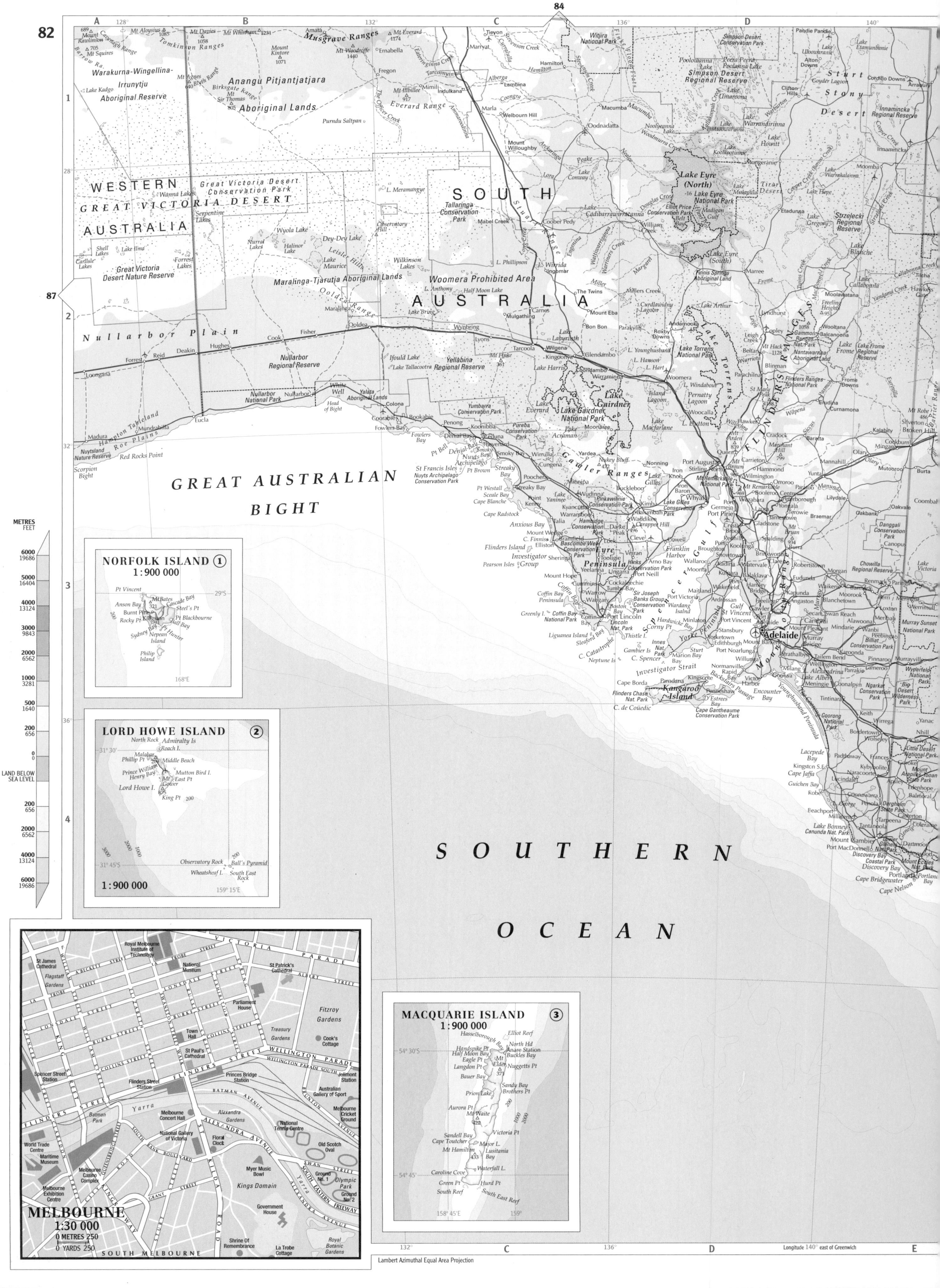
84
87
WESTERN AUSTRALIA
SOUTH AUSTRALIA
GREAT VICTORIA DESERT
Nullarbor Plain
GREAT AUSTRALIAN BIGHT
SOUTHERN OCEAN
Musgrave Ranges
Anangu Pitjantjatjara Aboriginal Lands
Warakurna-Wingellina-Irrunytju Aboriginal Reserve
Great Victoria Desert Conservation Park
Great Victoria Desert Nature Reserve
Maralinga-Tjarutja Aboriginal Lands
Woomera Prohibited Area
Nullarbor Regional Reserve
Nullarbor National Park
Yellabina Regional Reserve
Tallaringa Conservation Park
Simpson Desert
Simpson Desert Regional Reserve
Simpson Desert Conservation Park
Witjira National Park
Sturt Stony Desert
Strzelecki Desert
Tirari Desert
Lake Eyre (North)
Lake Eyre (South)
Lake Eyre National Park
Lake Torrens
Lake Torrens National Park
Lake Gairdner
Lake Gairdner National Park
Lake Frome
Lake Blanche
Lake Callabonna
FLINDERS RANGES
Flinders Ranges National Park
Gawler Ranges
Eyre Peninsula
Yorke Peninsula
Spencer Gulf
Gulf St Vincent
Investigator Strait
Kangaroo Island
Adelaide
Port Augusta
Port Pirie
Whyalla
Port Lincoln
Ceduna
Coober Pedy
Oodnadatta
Marla
Woomera
Tarcoola
Eucla
Mount Gambier
Broken Hill
Murray Bridge
Younghusband Peninsula
Coorong National Park
Lacepede Bay
Encounter Bay
NORFOLK ISLAND 1:900 000
LORD HOWE ISLAND 1:900 000
MACQUARIE ISLAND 1:900 000
MELBOURNE 1:30 000
Royal Melbourne Institute of Technology
National Museum
St Patrick's Cathedral
Parliament House
Fitzroy Gardens
Treasury Gardens
Cook's Cottage
Town Hall
St Paul's Cathedral
Flinders Street Station
Spencer Street Station
Princes Bridge Station
Jolimont Station
Australian Gallery of Sport
Melbourne Cricket Ground
National Tennis Centre
Melbourne Concert Hall
National Gallery of Victoria
Alexandra Gardens
Batman Park
World Trade Centre
Maritime Museum
Melbourne Casino Complex
Melbourne Exhibition Centre
Myer Music Bowl
Kings Domain
Government House
Shrine Of Remembrance
La Trobe Cottage
Royal Botanic Gardens
Olympic Park
SOUTH MELBOURNE
METRES FEET
LAND BELOW SEA LEVEL
Longitude 140° east of Greenwich
Lambert Azimuthal Equal Area Projection

85
E
F
G
H
144°
148°
152°
1
2
3
28°
32°
36°
QUEENSLAND
NEW SOUTH WALES
VICTORIA
TASMANIA
GREAT DIVIDING RANGE
GREY RANGE
TASMAN SEA
Darling Downs
Bass Strait
Banks Strait
Furneaux Group
Hunter Islands
King Island
Flinders Island
Cape Barren I.
Fraser Island
Moreton Island
North Stradbroke I.
Brisbane
Sydney
Canberra
Melbourne
Hobart
Newcastle
Wollongong
Gold Coast
Tweed Heads
Port Macquarie
Coffs Harbour
Toowoomba
Tamworth
Dubbo
Wagga Wagga
Albury
Bendigo
Ballarat
Geelong
Launceston
Devonport
Burnie
AUSTRALIAN CAPITAL TERRITORY
JERVIS BAY TERRITORY
Wilson's Promontory National Park
Ninety Mile Beach
Cape Howe
Cape Everard
Cape Otway
Cape Liptrap
Cape Wickham
Cape Grim
South East Cape
Tasman Hd
Maatsuyker Group
MILES
KILOMETRES
250
200
150
100
50
0
400
350
300
250
200
150
100
50
0

1:6 000 000

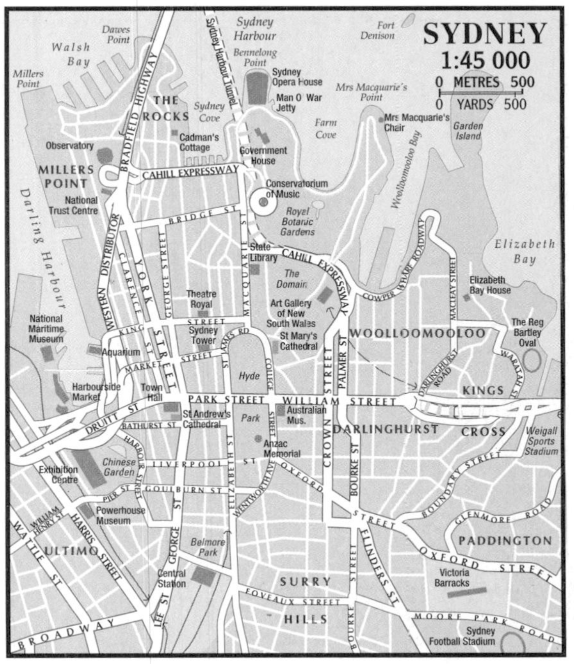
SYDNEY
1:45 000
METRES 500
YARDS 500
Walsh Bay
Dawes Point
Sydney Harbour
Fort Denison
Bennelong Point
Sydney Opera House
Millers Point
THE ROCKS
Sydney Cove
Farm Cove
Mrs Macquarie's Point
Mrs Macquarie's Chair
Garden Island
Observatory
MILLERS POINT
CAHILL EXPRESSWAY
Government House
Conservatorium of Music
Royal Botanic Gardens
Darling Harbour
State Library
The Domain
Theatre Royal
Art Gallery of New South Wales
Sydney Tower
St Mary's Cathedral
National Maritime Museum
Aquarium
WOOLLOOMOOLOO
Elizabeth Bay
Elizabeth Bay House
The Reg Bartley Oval
KINGS CROSS
Hyde Park
Harbourside Market
Town Hall
St Andrew's Cathedral
Australian Mus.
Anzac Memorial
DARLINGHURST
Weigall Sports Stadium
Chinese Garden
Exhibition Centre
Powerhouse Museum
ULTIMO
Belmore Park
Central Station
SURRY HILLS
PADDINGTON
Victoria Barracks
Sydney Football Stadium
BROADWAY
WILLIAM STREET
OXFORD STREET
MOORE PARK ROAD

© Bartholomew Ltd

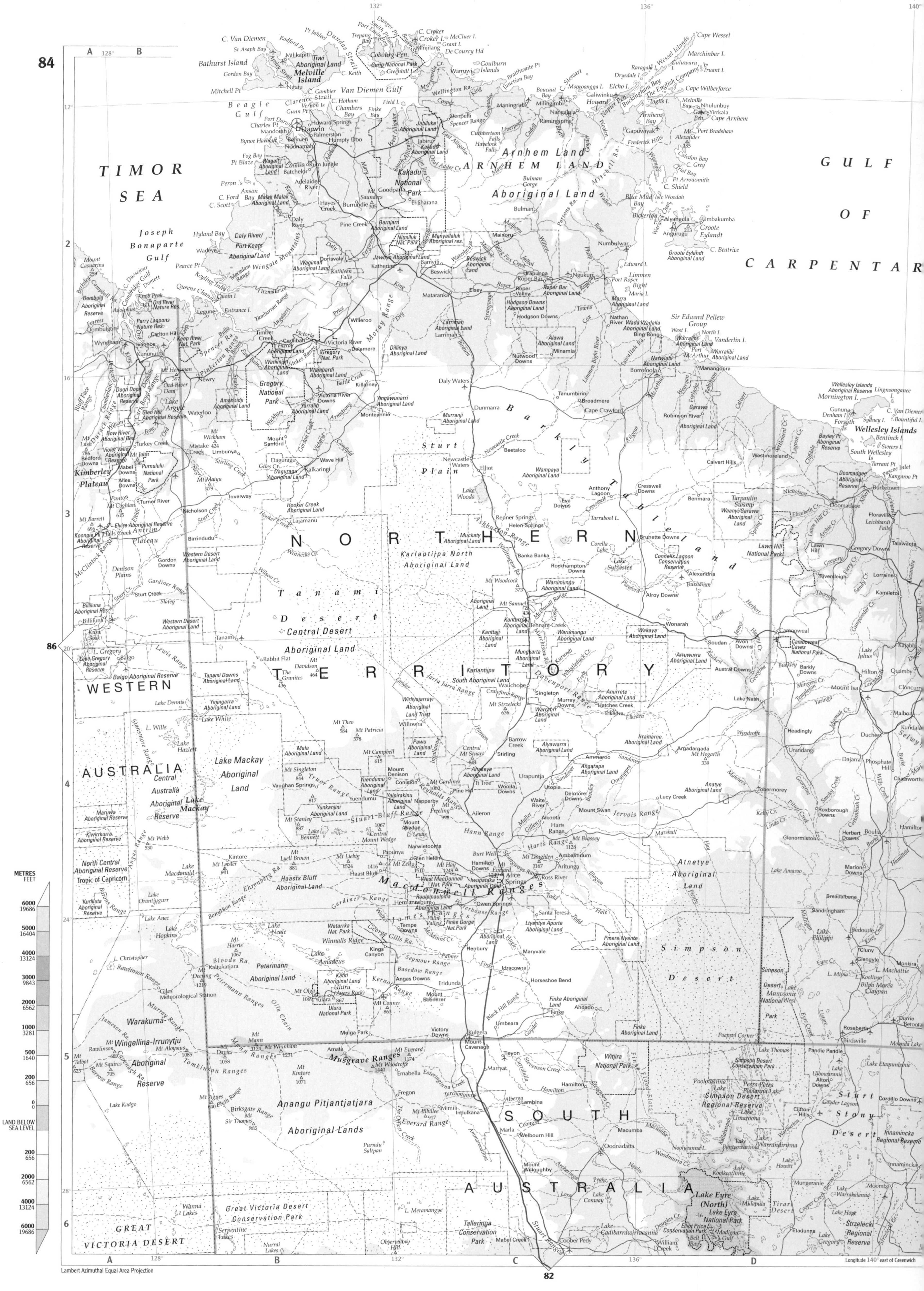
TIMOR SEA
Joseph Bonaparte Gulf
Beagle Gulf
Van Diemen Gulf
GULF OF CARPENTARIA
Bathurst Island
Melville Island
Tiwi Aboriginal Land
Cobourg Pen.
Darwin
Arnhem Land
ARNHEM LAND
Aboriginal Land
Kakadu National Park
Groote Eylandt
Sir Edward Pellew Group
Wellesley Islands
Mornington I.
Katherine
Daly Waters
Barkly Tableland
Sturt Plain
Kimberley Plateau
Gregory National Park
Lake Argyle
Wyndham
Kununurra
Halls Creek
Tanami Desert
Central Desert Aboriginal Land
NORTHERN TERRITORY
Tennant Creek
Lake Mackay Aboriginal Land
Lake Mackay
WESTERN AUSTRALIA
Mount Isa
Camooweal
Burketown
Tropic of Capricorn
Alice Springs
Macdonnell Ranges
Simpson Desert
Uluru
Ayers Rock
Petermann Aboriginal Land
Musgrave Ranges
Anangu Pitjantjatjara Aboriginal Lands
Ngaanyatjarra
Warakurna
Wingellina-Irrunytju Aboriginal Reserve
Great Victoria Desert Conservation Park
GREAT VICTORIA DESERT
Tallaringa Conservation Park
SOUTH AUSTRALIA
Witjira National Park
Simpson Desert Regional Reserve
Lake Eyre (North)
Lake Eyre National Park
Coober Pedy
Oodnadatta
Birdsville
Sturt Stony Desert
Innamincka Regional Reserve
Strzelecki Regional Reserve
Kulgera
Finke
Boulia
METRES FEET
6000 19686
5000 16404
4000 13124
3000 9843
2000 6562
1000 3281
500 1640
200 656
0 0
LAND BELOW SEA LEVEL
200 656
2000 6562
4000 13124
6000 19686
Lambert Azimuthal Equal Area Projection
Longitude 140° east of Greenwich

86

82

PAPUA NEW GUINEA
CORAL SEA
Coral Sea Islands Territory
GREAT BARRIER REEF
Great Barrier Reef Marine Park (Far North Section)
Great Barrier Reef Marine Park (Cairns Section)
Great Barrier Reef Marine Park (Central Section)
Great Barrier Reef Marine Park (Capricorn Section)
CAPE YORK PENINSULA
GREAT DIVIDING RANGE
QUEENSLAND
Darling Downs
Tropic of Capricorn
Capricorn Channel
Swain Reefs
Cape York
Thursday I.
Prince of Wales Island
Cairns
Townsville
Mackay
Rockhampton
Gladstone
Bundaberg
Brisbane
Toowoomba
Fraser Island
Whitsunday Group
Flinders Reefs
Willis Group
Magdelaine Cays
Herald Cays
Coringa Is
Diamond Islets
Lihou Reef and Cays
Osprey Reef
Bougainville Reef
Holmes Reef
Flora Reef
Marion Reef
Longreach
Charleville
Roma
Emerald
Hughenden
Winton
Mount Isa
Normanton
Karumba
Weipa
Cooktown
MILES
KILOMETRES
1:6 000 000

© Bartholomew Ltd

84
93
TIMOR SEA
INDIAN OCEAN
INDONESIA
NORTHERN TERRITORY
GREAT SANDY DESERT
Tanami Desert
Central Desert Aboriginal Land
Joseph Bonaparte Gulf
Kimberley Plateau
Beagle Gulf
Van Diemen Gulf
Melville Island
Bathurst Island
Darwin
Kakadu National Park
Wyndham
Derby
Broome
Eighty Mile Beach
Port Hedland
Dampier Land
Dampier Archipelago
Hamersley Range
Lake Mackay
Ashmore and Cartier Islands (Australia)
CHRISTMAS ISLAND 1:1 200 000
COCOS ISLANDS 1:1 200 000
METRES
FEET
6000
19686
5000
16404
4000
13124
3000
9843
2000
6562
1000
3281
500
1640
200
656
0
LAND BELOW SEA LEVEL
Lambert Azimuthal Equal Area Projection

82
WESTERN AUSTRALIA
SOUTH AUSTRALIA
GREAT AUSTRALIAN BIGHT
GIBSON DESERT
GREAT VICTORIA DESERT
Nullarbor Plain
Little Sandy Desert
Perth
Kalgoorlie
Boulder
Esperance
Geraldton
Albany
Bunbury
Carnarvon
Shark Bay
Houtman Abrolhos
Eucla
Ceduna
Tropic of Capricorn
Nullarbor Regional Reserve
Great Victoria Desert Nature Reserve
Archipelago of the Recherche
Longitude 120° east of Greenwich
MILES
KILOMETRES

1:6 000 000

© Bartholomew Ltd

EUROPE
RUSSIA
ARCTIC
Karskoye More
Nordkapp
Gulf of Bothnia
Beloye More
Arctic Circle
Baltic Sea
Ozero Onezhskoye
Rybinskoye Vodokhranilishche
Ural'skiy Khrebet (Ural Mountains)
Noril'sk
Urengoy
Surgut
Tobol'sk
Yekaterinburg
Chelyabinsk
Omsk
Novosibirsk
Tomsk
Krasnoyarsk
Novokuznetsk
Barnaul
Volga
Alps
Carpathian Mountains
Adriatic Sea
Sea of Azov
Black Sea
Ural'sk
Aktyubinsk
Astana
Pavlodar
Karaganda
Semipalatinsk
Ust'-Kamenogorsk
Kyzyl
Ulaangom
Atyrau
KAZAKHSTAN
Aral'sk
Aral Sea
Balkhash
Ozero Balkhash
Ozero Zaysan
Altay
Altai Mountains
Tacheng
Aktau
Caspian Sea
Samsun
Bursa
Ankara
TURKEY
İzmir
Sivas
Konya
Kayseri
Antalya
Erzurum
Malatya
Adana
Gaziantep
T'bilisi
GEORGIA
ARMENIA
AZERBAIJAN
Yerevan
Bakı
UZBEKISTAN
Shymkent
Tashkent
Bishkek
Almaty
KYRGYZSTAN
Yining
Ürümqi
Turpan
Turkmenbashi
TURKMENISTAN
Ashgabat
Samarkand
Kokand
Andizhan
Khujand
TAJIKISTAN
Dushanbe
Tien Shan
XINJIANG UYGUR ZIZHIQU (SINKIANG)
Korla
Aksu
Kashi
Tarim Pendi
Lop Nur
Qaidam Pendi
Golmud
Mediterranean Sea
Lefkosia
CYPRUS
LEBANON
Beirut
Halab
SYRIA
Tabrīz
Ardabīl
Al Mawşil
Arbīl
Kirkūk
Tehrān
Gorgān
Mashhad
ISRAEL
Tel Aviv-Yafo
Damascus
Gaza
'Ammān
Jerusalem
JORDAN
Baghdād
IRAQ
Kermānshāh
Qom
Dasht-e Kavīr
Borūjerd
Eşfahān
IRAN
Birjand
Herāt
AFGHANISTAN
Kābul
Kandahār
Peshawar
Islāmābād
Rawalpindi
Gujranwala
Lahore
Amritsar
Ludhiana
Chandigarh
Hotan
Kunlun Shan
Hindu Kush
AKSAI CHIN
XIZANG ZIZHIQU (TIBET)
An Najaf
Al Başrah
Ahvāz
Ābādān
Kuwait
KUWAIT
An Nafūd
Shīrāz
Kermān
Būshehr
Zāhedān
Quetta
Faisalabad
Multan
PAKISTAN
Bandar-e 'Abbās
The Gulf
Ad Dammām
BAHRAIN
Al Manāmah
Al Hufūf
QATAR
Doha
Dubai
Riyadh
Al Madīnah
Abū Dhabi
UNITED ARAB EMIRATES
Gulf of Oman
Muscat
Ibrā'
Şūr
Jeddah
Mecca
SAUDI ARABIA
Rub' al Khālī
OMAN
Maşīrah
Libyan Desert
Tropic of Cancer
Nile
Red Sea
Bayuda Desert
Pasni
Karachi
Hyderabad
Thar Desert
Jodhpur
Ganganagar
Delhi
New Delhi
Meerut
Faridabad
Ghaziabad
Jaipur
Agra
Lucknow
Kanpur
Beawar
Gwalior
Kota
Allahabad
Varanasi
Patna
Gorakhpur
Kathmandu
NEPAL
HIMALAYA
Mount Everest
Thimphu
BHUTAN
Dibrugarh
Darjiling
Lhasa
Xigazê
Guwahati
Shillong
BANGLADESH
Dhaka
Khulna
Chittagong
Ahmadabad
Vadodara
Indore
Bhopal
Jabalpur
Ranchi
Asansol
Jamshedpur
Calcutta (Kolkata)
Mouths of the Ganges
Surat
Nashik
Thane
Mumbai
Ulhasnagar
Aurangabad
Nagpur
INDIA
Cuttack
Pune
Solapur
Deccan
Hyderabad
Vishakhapatnam
Dharwad
Kurnool
Vijayawada
Nellore
Mangalore
Bangalore
Chennai
Mysore
Salem
Calicut
Coimbatore
Tiruchchirappalli
Madurai
Cochin
Jaffna
Trivandrum
Trincomalee
Gulf of Mannar
SRI LANKA
Kandy
Colombo
Sri Jayewardenepura Kotte
Laccadive Islands (India)
Male
MALDIVES
ARABIAN SEA
BAY OF BENGAL
Andaman Islands (India)
Andaman Sea
Nicobar Islands (India)
Banda Aceh
Simeulue
Mandalay
Meiktila
Sittwe
Yangon
Bassein
Pyè
Al Hudaydah
Şan'ā'
YEMEN
Şalālah
Ta'izz
Al Mukallā
Aden
Gulf of Aden
Suquţrā
AFRICA
Equator
Lake Victoria
Lake Nyasa
Mahé
Seychelles
Coëtivy
Aldabra Islands (Seychelles)
Farquhar Islands (Seychelles)
Njazidja
Comoros
Mayotte
Agalega Islands (Mauritius)
INDIAN OCEAN
British Indian Ocean Territory
Chagos Archipelago
Diego Garcia

Orthographic Projection

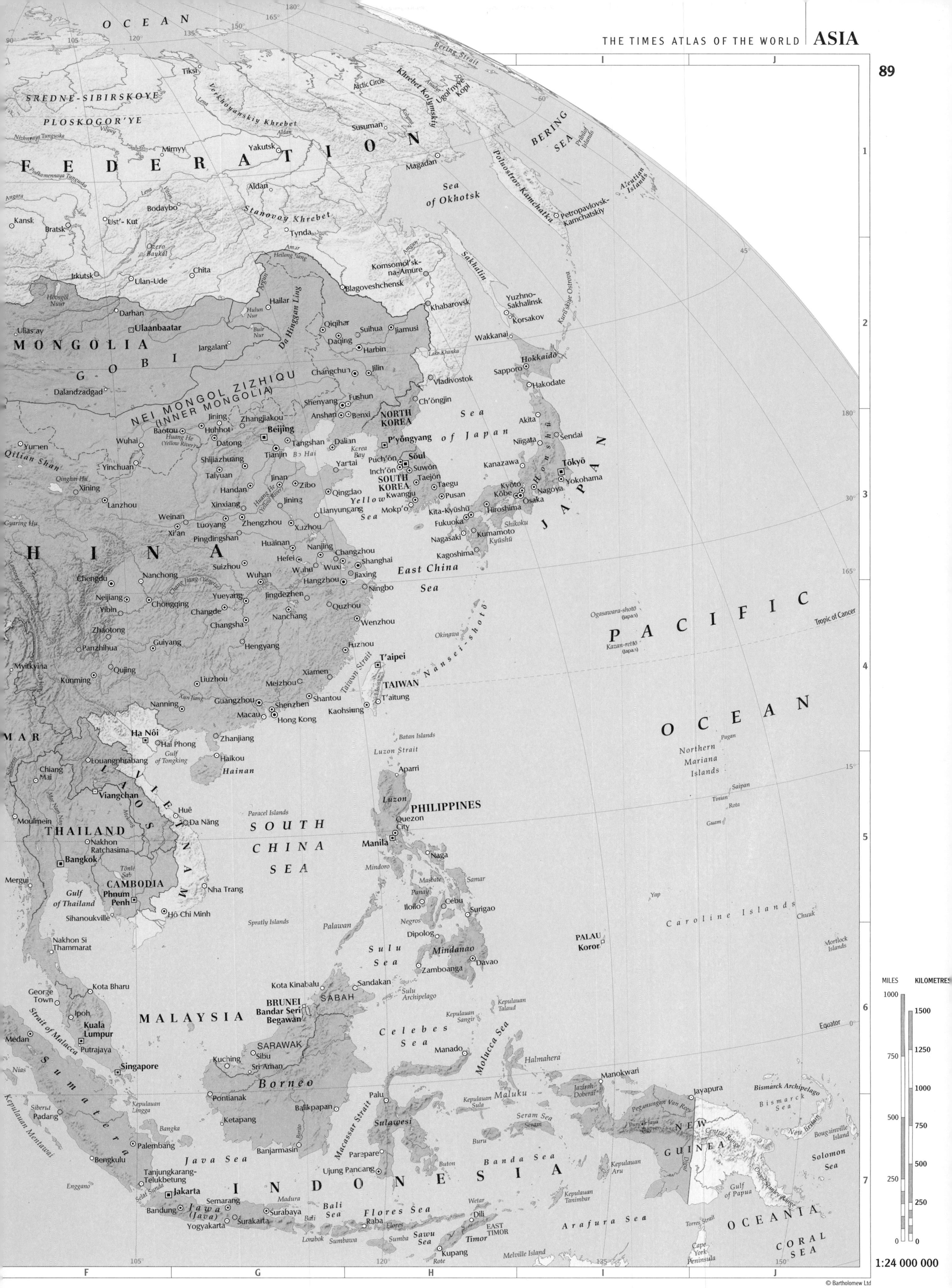
OCEAN
SREDNE-SIBIRSKOYE
PLOSKOGOR'YE
FEDERATION
Tiksi
Verkhoyanskiy Khrebet
Arctic Circle
Khrebet Kolymskiy
Ugol'nyye Kopi
Bering Strait
Susuman
Yakutsk
Mirnyy
Magadan
BERING SEA
Pribilof Islands
Aleutian Islands
Sea of Okhotsk
Poluostrov Kamchatka
Petropavlovsk-Kamchatskiy
Aldan
Bodaybo
Stanovoy Khrebet
Ust'-Kut
Kansk
Bratsk
Tynda
Ozero Baykal
Irkutsk
Ulan-Ude
Chita
Komsomol'sk-na-Amure
Blagoveshchensk
Sakhalin
Yuzhno-Sakhalinsk
Korsakov
Khabarovsk
Kuril'skiye Ostrova
Hövsgöl Nuur
Darhan
Ulaanbaatar
Hailar
Hulun Nur
Buir Nur
Da Hinggan Ling
Qiqihar
Daqing
Suihua
Jiamusi
Harbin
Uliastay
MONGOLIA
GOBI
Jargalant
Wakkanai
Lake Khanka
Hokkaidō
Sapporo
Hakodate
Changchun
Jilin
Vladivostok
NEI MONGOL ZIZHIQU (INNER MONGOLIA)
Dalandzadgad
Fushun
Shenyang
Ch'ŏngjin
Anshan
Benxi
NORTH KOREA
Sea of Japan
Akita
Sendai
Niigata
Jining
Zhangjiakou
Baotou
Hohhot
Beijing
P'yŏngyang
Wuhai
Datong
Tangshan
Dalian
Korea Bay
Yumen
Tianjin
Bo Hai
Qilian Shan
Yinchuan
Shijiazhuang
Yantai
Puch'ŏn
Sŏul
Inch'ŏn
Suwŏn
Kanazawa
Tōkyō
Yokohama
Taiyuan
Taejŏn
SOUTH KOREA
Taegu
Honshū
Qinghai Hu
Xining
Handan
Jinan
Zibo
Qingdao
Kwangju
Pusan
Kyōto
Kōbe
Nagoya
Ōsaka
JAPAN
Lanzhou
Xinxiang
Jining
Yellow Sea
Mokp'o
Kita-Kyūshū
Hiroshima
Weinan
Lianyungang
Fukuoka
Gyaring Hu
Xi'an
Luoyang
Zhengzhou
Xuzhou
Nagasaki
Kumamoto
Shikoku
Kyūshū
Pingdingshan
Huainan
Nanjing
Changzhou
Kagoshima
CHINA
Hefei
Wuxi
Shanghai
Suizhou
Wuhu
Chengdu
Nanchong
Wuhan
Hangzhou
Jiaxing
East China Sea
Ningbo
Neijiang
Chongqing
Yueyang
Jingdezhen
Yibin
Changde
Quzhou
Nanchang
Changsha
Zhaotong
Wenzhou
Ogasawara-shotō (Japan)
PACIFIC
Tropic of Cancer
Okinawa
Nansei-shotō
Panzhihua
Guiyang
Hengyang
Fuzhou
Kazan-rettō (Japan)
Myitkyina
Quiing
T'aipei
Kunming
Liuzhou
Xiamen
Taiwan Strait
TAIWAN
Meizhou
Xun Jiang
Nanning
Guangzhou
Shantou
T'aitung
OCEAN
Shenzhen
Kaohsiung
Macau
Hong Kong
Ha Nôi
Hai Phong
Zhanjiang
Batan Islands
Pagan
MAR
Luzon Strait
Northern Mariana Islands
Louangphrabang
Gulf of Tongking
Haikou
Hainan
Aparri
Chiang Mai
LAOS
VIETNAM
Viangchan
Luzon
PHILIPPINES
Saipan
Tinian
Rota
Huê
Paracel Islands
Quezon City
Guam
Moulmein
Đa Nẵng
SOUTH CHINA SEA
THAILAND
Nakhon Ratchasima
Manila
Bangkok
Naga
Tônlé Sab
Mindoro
Mergui
CAMBODIA
Masbate
Samar
Gulf of Thailand
Phnum Penh
Nha Trang
Panay
Yap
Iloilo
Cebu
Surigao
Sihanoukville
Hô Chi Minh
Spratly Islands
Palawan
Negros
Caroline Islands
Chuuk
Nakhon Si Thammarat
Dipolog
PALAU
Koror
Mortlock Islands
Sulu Sea
Mindanao
Davao
Zamboanga
Kota Bharu
Kota Kinabalu
Sandakan
George Town
SABAH
Sulu Archipelago
Kepulauan Talaud
BRUNEI
Bandar Seri Begawan
Kepulauan Sangir
Ipoh
MALAYSIA
Kuala Lumpur
Celebes Sea
Molucca Sea
Equator
Medan
Strait of Malacca
Putrajaya
SARAWAK
Sibu
Manado
Singapore
Kuching
Sri Aman
Halmahera
Nias
Sumatera
Borneo
Manokwari
Jayapura
Bismarck Archipelago
Bismarck Sea
Pontianak
Maluku
Jazirah Doberai
Kepulauan Lingga
Palu
Kepulauan Sula
Siberut
Padang
Balikpapan
Seram Sea
Seram
Pegunungan Van Rees
New Britain
Bougainville Island
Kepulauan Mentawai
Ketapang
Macassar Strait
Sulawesi
NEW GUINEA
Central Range
Bangka
Buru
Solomon Sea
Palembang
Banjarmasin
Parepare
Java Sea
Banda Sea
Bengkulu
Buton
Kepulauan Aru
Digul
Owen Stanley Range
Ujung Pandang
Tanjungkarang-Telukbetung
INDONESIA
Enggano
Selat Sunda
Jakarta
Madura
Kepulauan Tanimbar
Gulf of Papua
Semarang
Bali Sea
Flores Sea
Wetar
Bandung
Jawa (Java)
Surabaya
Dili
Arafura Sea
OCEANIA
Torres Strait
Surakarta
Bali
Raba
Flores
EAST TIMOR
Yogyakarta
Lombok
Sumbawa
Sumba
Sawu Sea
Timor
Cape York Peninsula
CORAL SEA
Kupang
Rote
Melville Island
MILES
KILOMETRES
1:24 000 000
© Bartholomew Ltd

98
112
METRES
FEET
6000
19686
5000
16404
4000
13124
3000
9843
2000
6562
1000
3281
500
1640
200
656
0
0
LAND BELOW SEA LEVEL
CHINA
YUNNAN
GUIZHOU
HUNAN
JIANGXI
FUJIAN
GUANGXI ZHUANGZU ZIZHIQU
GUANGDONG
HAINAN
TAIWAN
T'AIPEI
Kaohsiung
Kunming
Guiyang
Fuzhou
Nanning
Guangzhou (Canton)
Shenzhen
Kowloon
Hong Kong
Macau
Shantou
Xiamen (Amoy)
Haikou
Zhanjiang
Tropic of Cancer
MYANMAR
THAILAND
LAOS
VIETNAM
INDO-CHINA
CAMBODIA
HA NOI
Hai Phong
VIANGCHAN (Vientiane)
Louangphrabang
BANGKOK (Krung Thep)
PHNUM PENH
Ho Chi Minh (Saigon)
Đa Năng
Huê
Gulf of Tongking
GULF OF THAILAND
Mergui Archipelago
SOUTH CHINA SEA
Paracel Islands (Xisha Qundao)
Spratly Islands
Luzon Strait
LUZON
MANILA
Quezon City
Philippine Sea
Mindoro
Palawan
Panay
Negros
Cebu
SULU SEA
Sulu Archipelago
CELEBES SEA
MALAYSIA
Semenanjung Malaysia
KUALA LUMPUR
SINGAPORE
Strait of Malacca
SABAH
SARAWAK
BRUNEI
BANDAR SERI BEGAWAN
Kota Kinabalu
Kuching
BORNEO
KALIMANTAN
SUMATERA
Medan
Padang
Palembang
Bangka
JAVA SEA
JAKARTA
Bandung
Semarang
Surabaya
JAWA (JAVA)
Bali
Lombok
Sumbawa
Flores
Sumba
FLORES SEA
Sawu Sea
Makassar Strait
SULAWESI (CELEBES)
Ujung Pandang (Makassar)
Teluk Tomini
INDONESIA
Kepulauan Mentawai
INDIAN OCEAN
Equator
Christmas Island (Australia)
A
B
C
D
E
F
100°
105°
110°
115°
120°
25°
20°
15°
10°
5°
0°
1
2
3
4
5
6
7
8
9

Mercator Projection

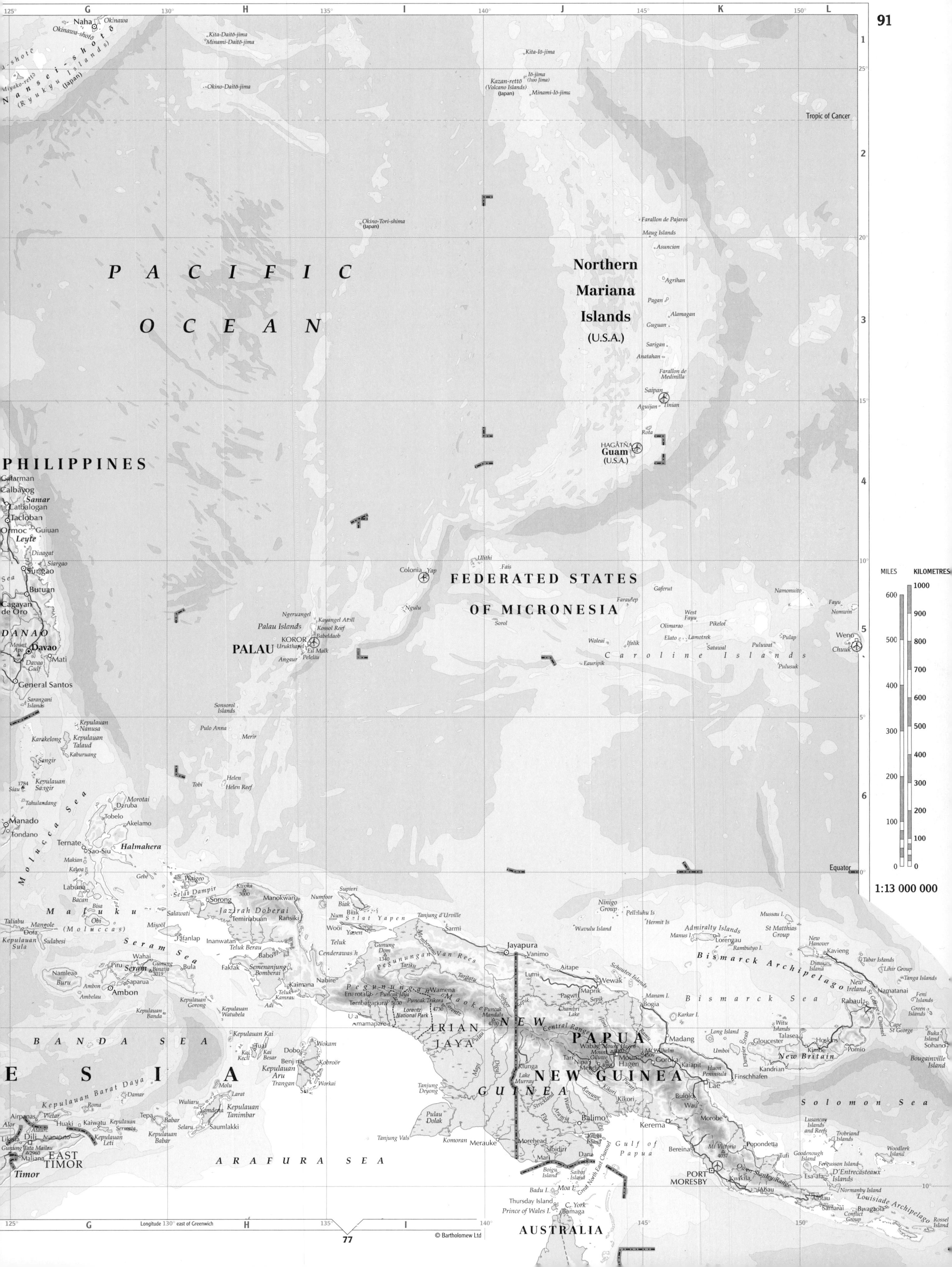
PACIFIC OCEAN
PHILIPPINES
Northern Mariana Islands (U.S.A.)
FEDERATED STATES OF MICRONESIA
PALAU
KOROR
Palau Islands
Caroline Islands
HAGÅTÑA
Guam (U.S.A.)
Tropic of Cancer
Equator
Naha
Okinawa
Okinawa-shotō
Nansei-shotō (Ryukyu Islands) (Japan)
Miyako-rettō
Kita-Daitō-jima
Minami-Daitō-jima
Oki-Daitō-jima
Kita-Iō-jima
Iō-jima (Iwo Jima)
Kazan-rettō (Volcano Islands) (Japan)
Minami-Iō-jima
Okino-Tori-shima (Japan)
Farallon de Pajaros
Maug Islands
Asuncion
Agrihan
Pagan
Alamagan
Guguan
Sarigan
Anatahan
Farallon de Medinilla
Saipan
Tinian
Aguijan
Rota
Ulithi
Fais
Colonia
Yap
Ngulu
Sorol
Faraulep
Gaferut
West Fayu
Olimarao
Pikelot
Elato
Lamotrek
Satawal
Woleai
Ifalik
Eauripik
Puluwat
Pulap
Pulusuk
Namonuito
Fayu
Nomwin
Weno
Chuuk
Ngeruangel
Kayangel Atoll
Kossol Reef
Babeldaob
Urukthapel
Eil Malk
Peleliu
Angaur
Sonsorol Islands
Pulo Anna
Merir
Tobi
Helen
Helen Reef
Catarman
Calbayog
Samar
Catbalogan
Tacloban
Ormoc
Guiuan
Leyte
Dinagat
Siargao
Surigao
Butuan
Cagayan de Oro
DANAO
Mount Apo 2954
Davao
Davao Gulf
Mati
General Santos
Sarangani Islands
Kepulauan Nanusa
Karakelong
Kepulauan Talaud
Kaburuang
Sangir
Kepulauan Sangir
Siau
Tahulandang
Manado
Tondano
Morotai
Daruba
Tobelo
Akelamo
Ternate
Sao-Siu
Halmahera
Makian
Kayoa
Molucca Sea
Gebe
Waigeo
Selat Dampir
Sorong
Kwoka 3000
Manokwari
Salawati
Jazirah Doberai
Teminabuan
Ransiki
Labuha
Bacan
Bisa
Obi
Maluku (Moluccas)
Taliabu
Mangole
Sula
Kepulauan Sula
Sulabesi
Misoöl
Seram Sea
Fakfak
Kaimana
Inanwatan
Teluk Berau
Babo
Semenanjung Bomberai
Wahai
Piru
Seram
Gunung Binaiya 3019
Bula
Namlea
Buru
Ambon
Saparua
Ambelau
Kepulauan Gorong
Kepulauan Watubela
Kepulauan Banda
Adi
Teluk Kamrau
Biak
Supiori
Numfoor
Num
Selat Yapen
Yapen
Serui
Waren
Wooi
Teluk Cenderawasih
Gunung Dom 1340
Pegunungan Van Rees
Tanjung d'Urville
Sarmi
Jayapura
Vanimo
Nabire
Pegunungan Maoke
Enarotali
Tembagapura
Puncak Jaya 5030
Wamena
Puncak Trikora 4730
Lorentz National Park
Puncak Mandala 4760
IRIAN JAYA
Amamapare
BANDA SEA
Kepulauan Kai
Kai Kecil
Kai Besar
Dobo
Wokam
Kobroor
Kepulauan Aru
Trangan
Workai
Molu
Larat
Kepulauan Tanimbar
Yamdena
Saumlakki
Wuliaru
Selaru
Damar
Roma
Kepulauan Barat Daya
Wetar
Alor
Airpanas
Huaki
Kaiwatu
Kepulauan Sermata
Kepulauan Leti
Kepulauan Babar
Babar
Tepa
Lakor
Atauro
Dili
Manatuto
Liquiçá
Gunung Tata Mailau 2960
Maliana
EAST TIMOR
Timor
ASIA
ARAFURA SEA
Tanjung Vals
Komoran
Pulau Dolak
Tanjung Dryong
Merauke
Digul
Mapi
Kolepom
NEW GUINEA
PAPUA NEW GUINEA
Ninigo Group
Pelleluhu Is
Hermit Is
Wuvulu Island
Admiralty Islands
Manus I.
Lorengau
Rambutyo I.
Mussau I.
St Matthias Group
New Hanover
Kavieng
Tabar Islands
Lihir Group
Tanga Islands
Djaul Island
New Ireland
Namatanai
Feni Islands
Green Islands
Bismarck Archipelago
Bismarck Sea
Schouten Islands
Aitape
Wewak
Lumi
Manam I.
Bogia
Karkar I.
Madang
Long Island
Umboi
Dampier Strait
Gloucester
Talasea
Hoskins
Kimbe
New Britain
Pomio
Rabaul
St George's Channel
Cape St George
Buka Island
Sohano
Bougainville Island
Kandrian
Sepik
Maprik
Pagwi
Chambri Lake
Central Range
Mount Hagen
Mount Wilhelm
Wabag
Goroka
Kainantu
Kaiapit
Huon Peninsula
Finschhafen
Lae
Tari
Nipa
Mendi
Lake Murray
Kiunga
Strickland
Fly
Kikori
Bulolo
Wau
Morobe
Kerema
Balimo
Kiwai Island
Gulf of Papua
Bereina
Mt Victoria 4037
Popondetta
Tufi
Solomon Sea
Woodlark Islands
Trobriand Islands
Lusancay Islands and Reefs
Goodenough Island
Fergusson Island
D'Entrecasteaux Islands
Esa-ala
Normanby Island
Louisiade Archipelago
Rossel Island
Misima
Conflict Group
Bwagaoia
Samarai
Alotau
Abau
Kwikila
Owen Stanley Range
PORT MORESBY
Morehead
Sibidiri
Mari
Daru
Boigu Island
Saibai Island
Great North East Channel
Badu I.
Moa I.
Thursday Island
Prince of Wales I.
C. York
Bamaga
AUSTRALIA
MILES
KILOMETRES
0 100 200 300 400 500 600
0 100 200 300 400 500 600 700 800 900 1000
1:13 000 000
Longitude 130° east of Greenwich
125° 130° 135° 140° 145° 150°
G H I J K L
1 2 3 4 5 6
25° 20° 15° 10° 5° 0° 10°

77

© Bartholomew Ltd

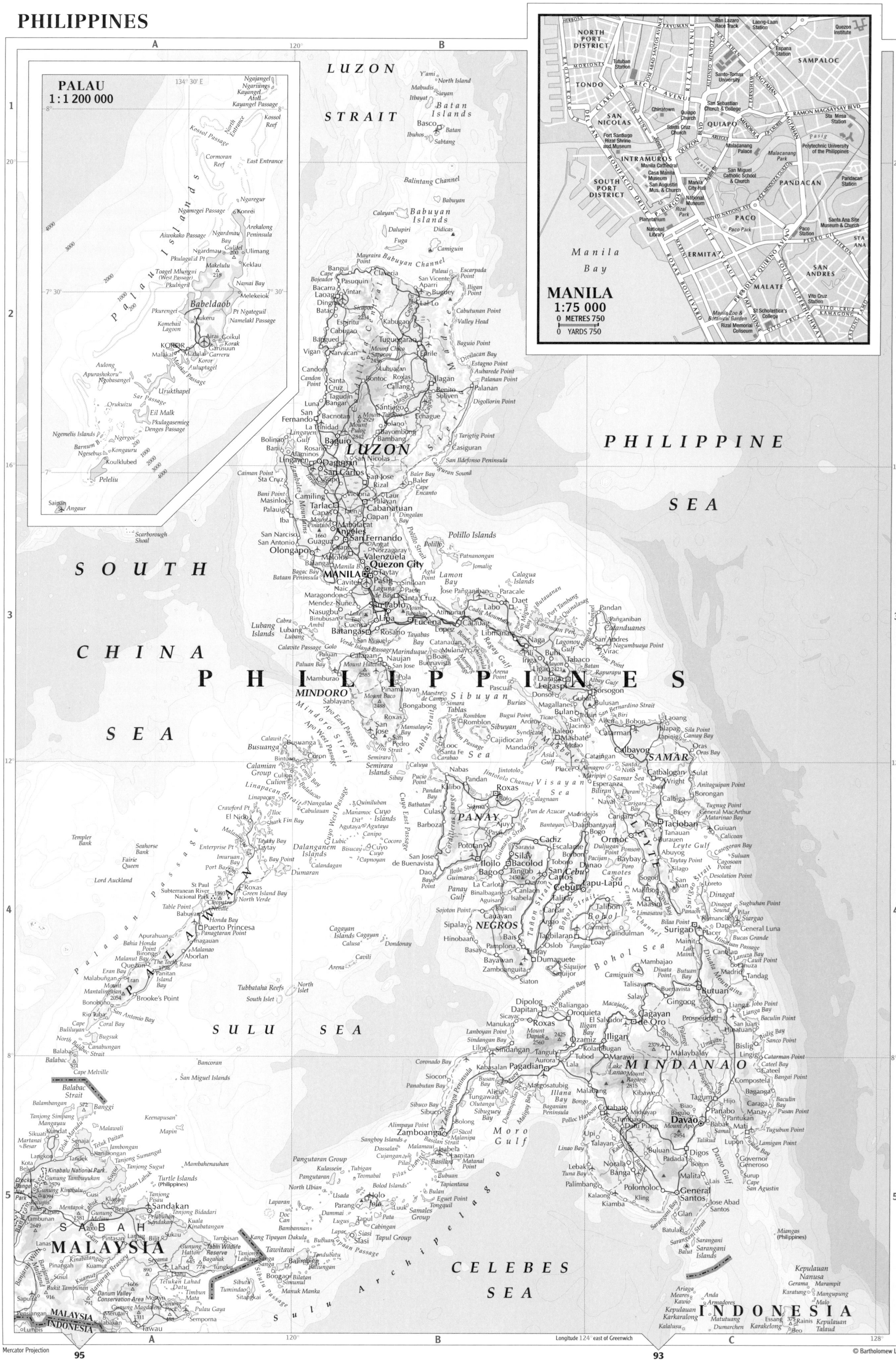
PALAU
1:1 200 000
Babeldaob
Koror
Peleliu
Angaur
MANILA
1:75 000
0 METRES 750
0 YARDS 750
NORTH PORT DISTRICT
TONDO
SAN NICOLAS
QUIAPO
SAMPALOC
INTRAMUROS
SOUTH PORT DISTRICT
PANDACAN
PACO
ERMITA
MALATE
SAN ANDRES
Manila Bay
LUZON STRAIT
Batan Islands
Babuyan Islands
Babuyan Channel
Balintang Channel
LUZON
Baguio
San Fernando
Tarlac
Angeles
Olongapo
Quezon City
MANILA
Batangas
Lucena
Naga
Legaspi
PHILIPPINE SEA
SOUTH CHINA SEA
PHILIPPINES
MINDORO
Mindoro Strait
Sibuyan Sea
Samar Sea
Visayan Sea
SAMAR
LEYTE
PANAY
NEGROS
Cebu
Bohol
Bohol Sea
Tacloban
Iloilo
Bacolod
Dumaguete
Surigao
Butuan
Cagayan de Oro
Iligan
Zamboanga
Pagadian
MINDANAO
Davao
General Santos
Moro Gulf
PALAWAN
Puerto Princesa
Palawan Passage
SULU SEA
Sulu Archipelago
Jolo
CELEBES SEA
Balabac Strait
SABAH
MALAYSIA
Sandakan
Tawau
INDONESIA
METRES
FEET
6000
19686
5000
16404
4000
13124
3000
9843
2000
6562
1000
3281
500
1640
200
656
0
0
LAND BELOW SEA LEVEL
200
656
2000
6562
4000
13124
6000
19686
Longitude 124° east of Greenwich

© Bartholomew Ltd

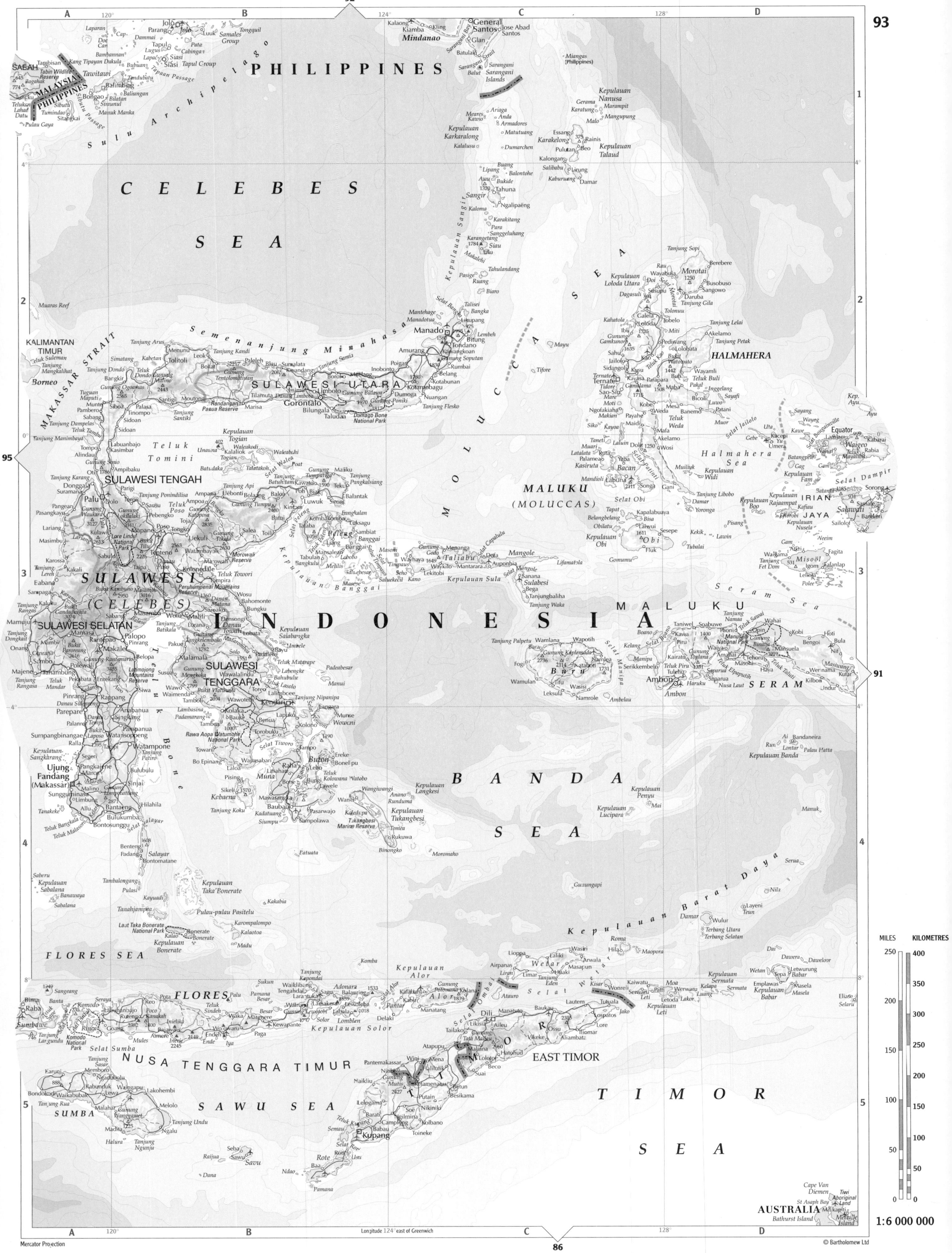
PHILIPPINES
Mindanao
Sulu Archipelago
CELEBES SEA
Semenanjung Minahasa
SULAWESI UTARA
Manado
Gorontalo
MAKASSAR STRAIT
KALIMANTAN TIMUR
Borneo
SULAWESI TENGAH
Teluk Tomini
Palu
SULAWESI (CELEBES)
SULAWESI SELATAN
SULAWESI TENGGARA
Teluk Bone
Ujung Fandang (Makassar)
INDONESIA
MOLUCCA SEA
MALUKU (MOLUCCAS)
HALMAHERA
Halmahera Sea
Ternate
Morotai
Kepulauan Sula
Kepulauan Banggai
Buru
SERAM
Seram Sea
Ambon
IRIAN JAYA
Misoöl
Waigeo
BANDA SEA
Kepulauan Banda
Kepulauan Tukangbesi
Buton
Muna
Kepulauan Barat Daya
Wetar
Alor
FLORES SEA
FLORES
NUSA TENGGARA TIMUR
SAWU SEA
SUMBA
Savu
TIMOR
Kupang
Dili
EAST TIMOR
TIMOR SEA
AUSTRALIA
Bathurst Island
Melville Island
MILES
KILOMETRES
1:6 000 000

© Bartholomew Ltd

97
THAILAND
MALAYSIA
KEDAH
PERAK
KELANTAN
TERENGGANU
PAHANG
SELANGOR
NEGERI SEMBILAN
MELAKA
JOHOR
SEMENANJUNG MALAYSIA
KUALA LUMPUR
SINGAPORE
ACEH
SUMATERA UTARA
SUMATERA BARAT
RIAU
JAMBI
BENGKULU
SUMATERA SELATAN
LAMPUNG
SUMATERA
INDO
Medan
Padang
Pekanbaru
Palembang
Jambi
Bangka
Kepulauan Riau
Kepulauan Lingga
JAKARTA
JAWA B
STRAIT OF MALACCA
PEGUNUNGAN BARISAN
Kepulauan Mentawai
Selat Mentawai
Equator
SOUTH
INDIAN OCEAN
SINGAPORE
1 : 360 000
Johor Bahru
MALAYSIA
Strait of Singapore
METRES
FEET
6000
19686
5000
16404
4000
13124
3000
9843
2000
6562
1000
3281
500
1640
200
656
0
0
LAND BELOW SEA LEVEL
200
656
2000
6562
4000
13124
6000
19686
Longitude 104° east of Greenwich
Christmas Island
(Australia)
Mercator Projection

SOUTH CHINA SEA
SULU SEA
PHILIPPINES
92
CELEBES SEA
SABAH
BRUNEI
MALAYSIA
SARAWAK
KALIMANTAN TIMUR
BORNEO
KALIMANTAN BARAT
KALIMANTAN TENGAH
KALIMANTAN SELATAN
KALIMANTAN
INDONESIA
93
MAKASSAR STRAIT
SULAWESI TENGAH
SULAWESI (CELEBES)
SULAWESI SELATAN
JAVA SEA
BALI SEA
FLORES SEA
JAWA TENGAH
JAWA TIMUR
YOGYAKARTA
BALI
NUSA TENGGARA BARAT
JAWA (JAVA)
Kota Kinabalu
Sandakan
Tawau
Kuching
Pontianak
Samarinda
Balikpapan
Banjarmasin
Palu
Ujung Pandang Makassar
Surabaya
Semarang
Bandung
Denpasar
Mataram
Lombok
Sumbawa
Madura
Selat Karimata
Selat Makassar
Equator
108°
112°
116°
120°
E
F
G
1
2
3
4
5

MILES | KILOMETRES

250 | 400
200 | 350
150 | 300
100 | 250
50 | 200
0 | 150
 | 100
 | 50
 | 0

1:6 000 000

© Bartholomew Ltd

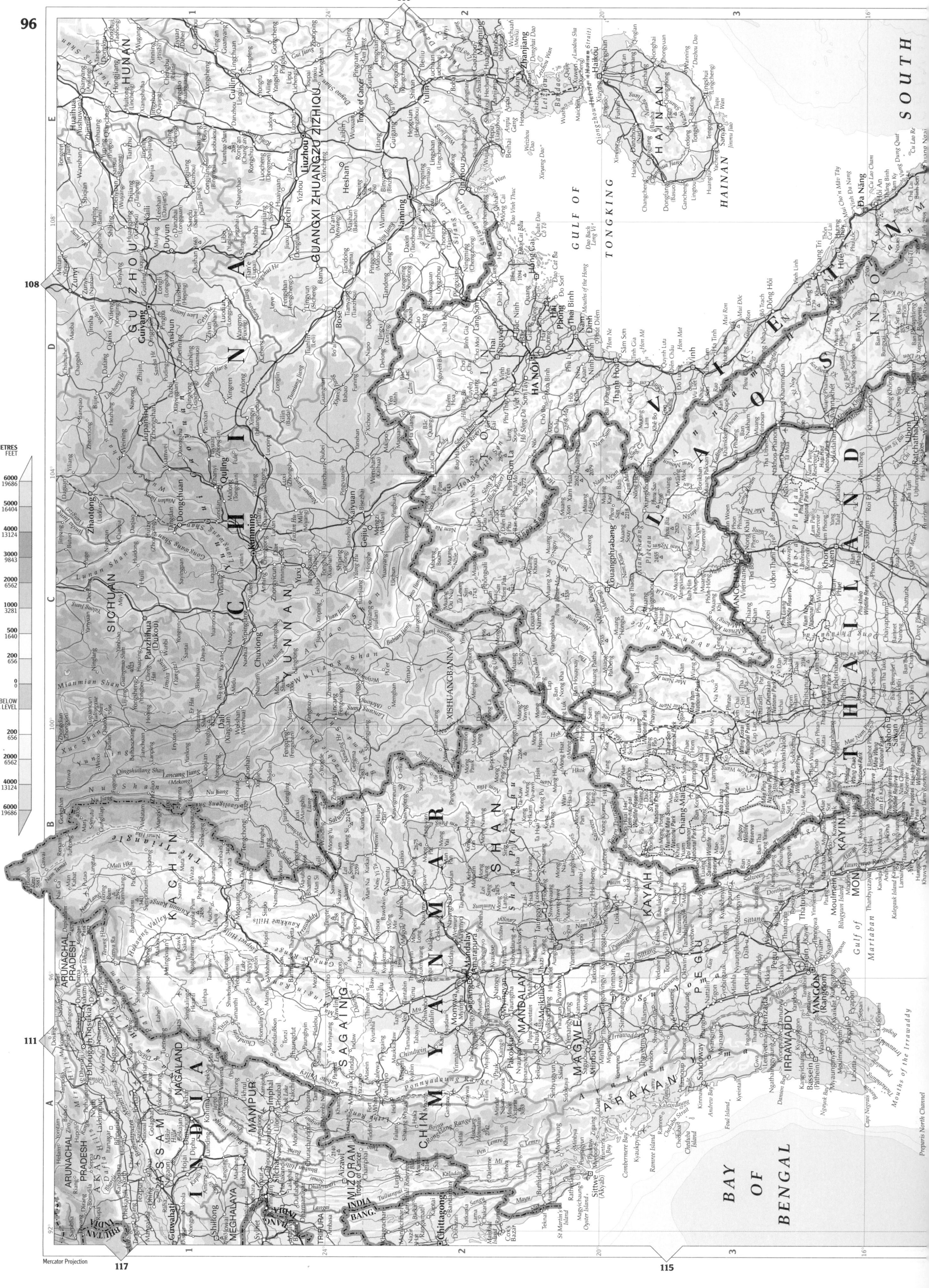

109
108
111
117
115
METRES
FEET
6000
19686
5000
16404
4000
13124
3000
9843
2000
6562
1000
3281
500
1640
200
656
0
0
LAND BELOW SEA LEVEL
200
656
2000
6562
4000
13124
6000
19686
CHINA
MYANMAR
INDIA
LAOS
THAILAND
VIETNAM
BAY OF BENGAL
GULF OF TONGKING
GULF OF Martaban
HAINAN
YUNNAN
SICHUAN
GUIZHOU
HUNAN
GUANGXI ZHUANGZU ZIZHIQU
SHAN
KACHIN
SAGAING
MANDALAY
MAGWE
ARAKAN
PEGU
IRRAWADDY
KAYAH
KAYIN
MON
CHIN
ASSAM
NAGALAND
MANIPUR
MIZORAM
MEGHALAYA
TRIPURA
ARUNACHAL PRADESH
BANG.
BHUTAN
XISHUANGBANNA
Kunming
Hanoi
Mandalay
Yangon (Rangoon)
Vientiane
Chiang Mai
Nanning
Haikou
Da Nang
Hue
Haiphong
Chittagong
Tropic of Cancer
Mouths of the Irrawaddy
Mercator Projection

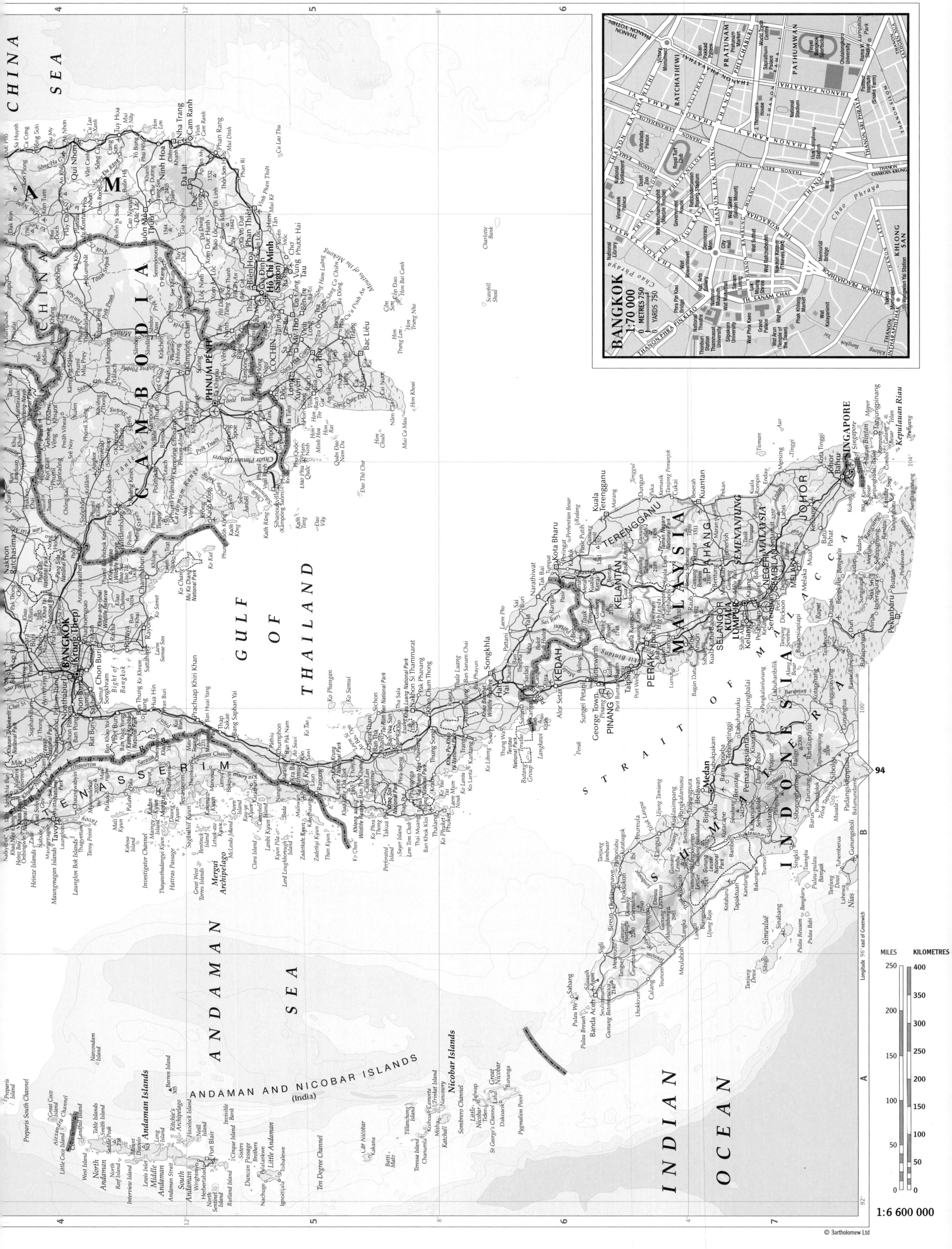

SOUTH CHINA SEA
CAMBODIA
GULF OF THAILAND
MALAYSIA
INDONESIA
STRAIT OF MALACCA
ANDAMAN SEA
INDIAN OCEAN
ANDAMAN AND NICOBAR ISLANDS
(India)
BANGKOK
(Krung Thep)
PHNUM PENH
Hô Chi Minh
(Saigon)
KUALA LUMPUR
SINGAPORE
Medan
George Town
Songkhla
Nakhon Ratchasima
Andaman Islands
Nicobar Islands
Mergui Archipelago
TENASSERIM
KEDAH
KELANTAN
TERENGGANU
PAHANG
PERAK
SELANGOR
JOHOR
MELAKA
NEGERI SEMBILAN
PINANG
BANGKOK
1:70 000
METRES 750
YARDS 750
MILES
KILOMETRES
1:6 600 000

© Bartholomew Ltd

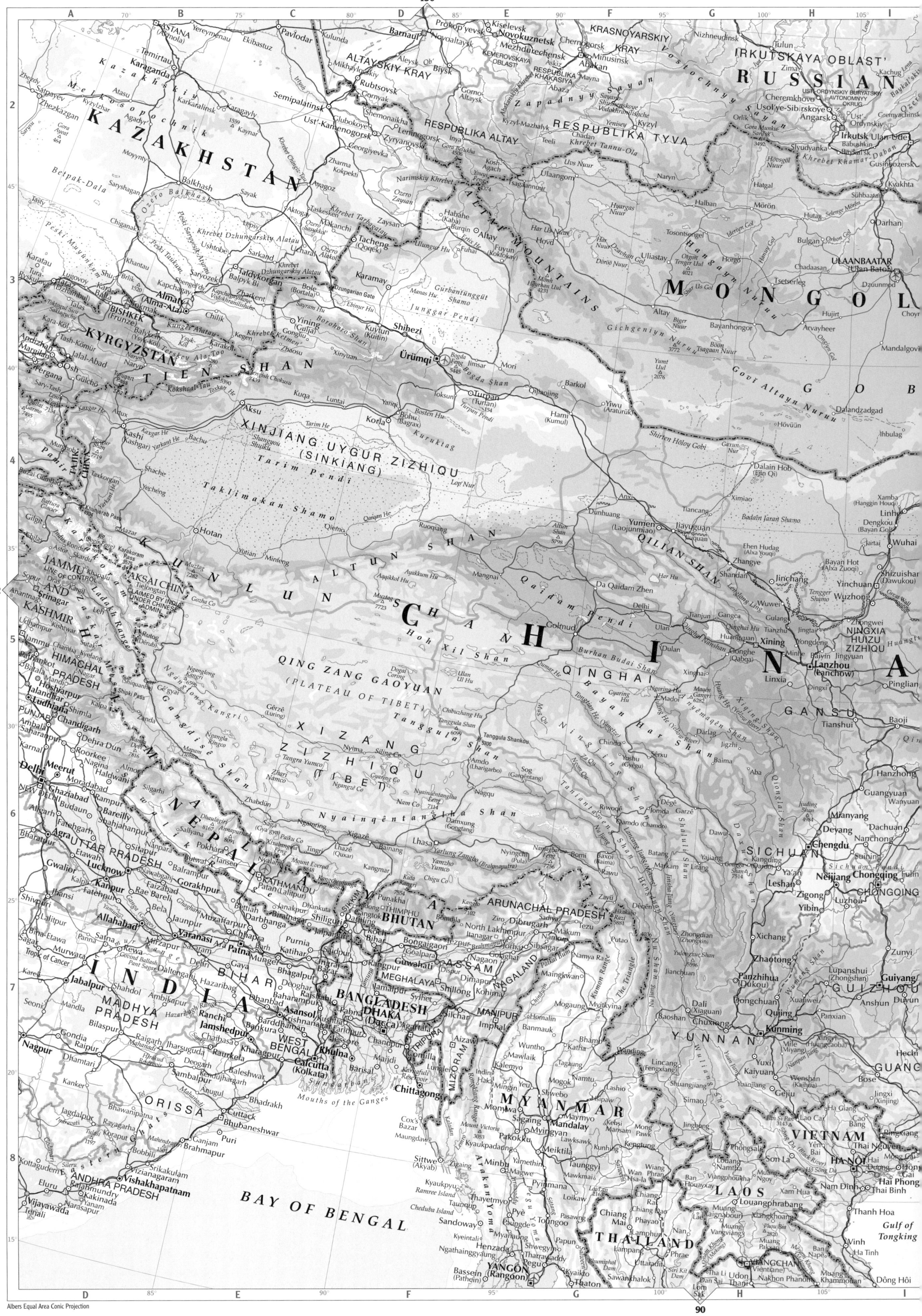
130
112
90
KAZAKHSTAN
KYRGYZSTAN
RUSSIAN
MONGOL
CHINA
XINJIANG UYGUR ZIZHIQU (SINKIANG)
Taklimakan Shamo
Tarim Pendi
TIEN SHAN
KUNLUN SHAN
ALTUN SHAN
ALTAY MOUNTAINS
QING ZANG GAOYUAN (PLATEAU OF TIBET)
XIZANG ZIZHIQU (TIBET)
QINGHAI
GANSU
SICHUAN
YUNNAN
GUIZHOU
NINGXIA HUIZU ZIZHIQU
JAMMU AND KASHMIR
HIMACHAL PRADESH
UTTAR PRADESH
MADHYA PRADESH
ANDHRA PRADESH
ORISSA
WEST BENGAL
BIHAR
INDIA
NEPAL
BHUTAN
BANGLADESH
ARUNACHAL PRADESH
ASSAM
MEGHALAYA
NAGALAND
MANIPUR
MIZORAM
TRIPURA
MYANMAR
THAILAND
LAOS
VIETNAM
BAY OF BENGAL
Gulf of Tongking
Mouths of the Ganges
Ürümqi
Lhasa
KATHMANDU
THIMPHU
DHAKA (Dacca)
Calcutta (Kolkata)
Delhi
NEW DELHI
Chengdu
Chongqing
Kunming
Lanzhou (Lanchow)
Xining
ULAANBAATAR (Ulan Bator)
Irkutsk
Almaty (Alma-Ata)
BISHKEK (Frunze)
YANGON (Rangoon)
Mandalay
HA NOI
VIANGCHAN (Vientiane)
Albers Equal Area Conic Projection

METRES / FEET

Metres	Feet
6000	19686
5000	16404
4000	13124
3000	9843
2000	6562
1000	3281
500	1640
200	656
0	0
LAND BELOW SEA LEVEL	
200	656
2000	6562
4000	13124
6000	19686

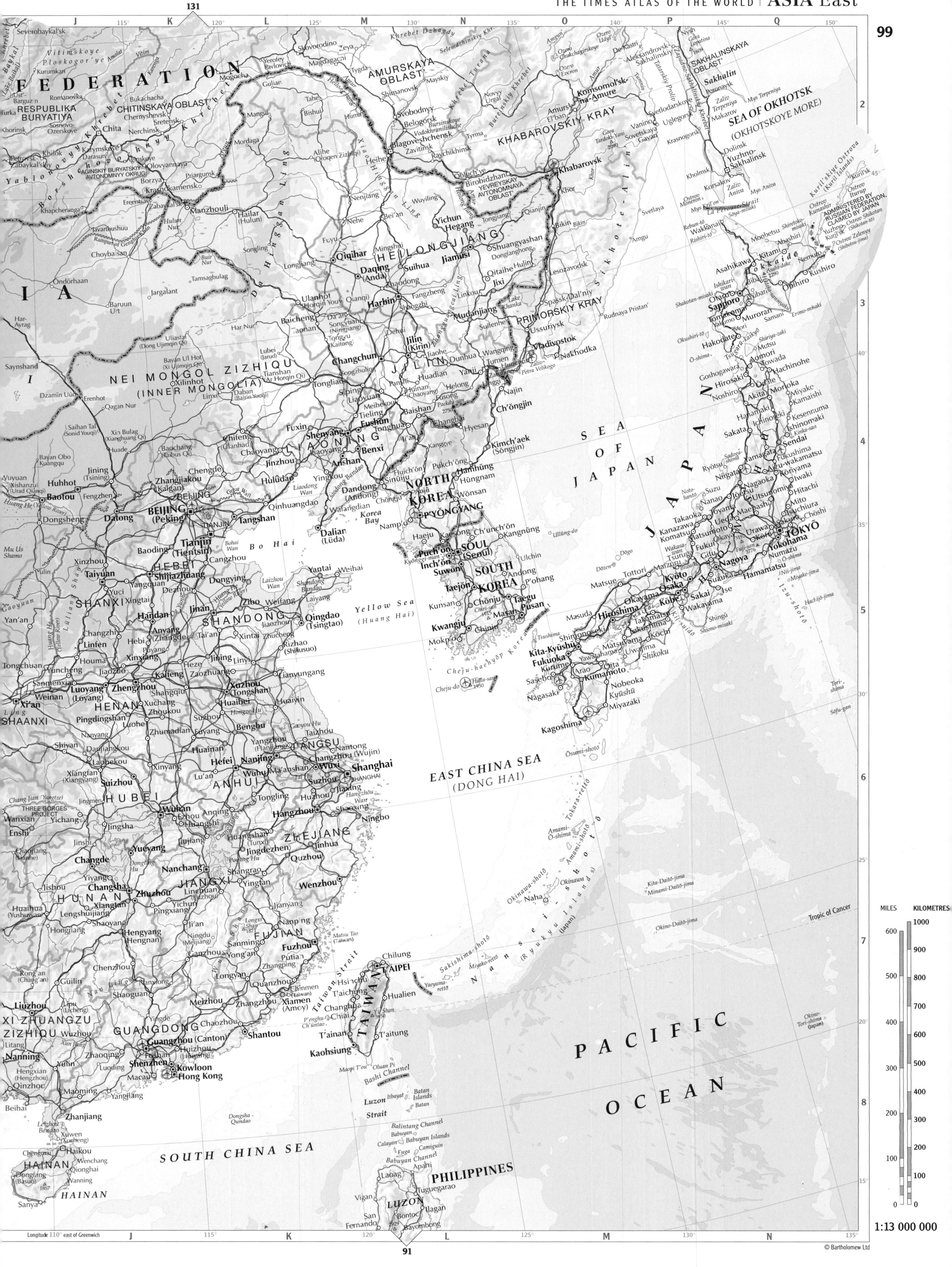
FEDERATION
RESPUBLIKA BURYATIYA
CHITINSKAYA OBLAST'
AMURSKAYA OBLAST'
KHABAROVSKIY KRAY
SAKHALINSKAYA OBLAST'
SEA OF OKHOTSK
(OKHOTSKOYE MORE)
YEVREYSKAYA AVTONOMNAYA OBLAST'
HEILONGJIANG
PRIMORSKIY KRAY
NEI MONGOL ZIZHIQU
(INNER MONGOLIA)
JILIN
LIAONING
SEA OF JAPAN
JAPAN
NORTH KOREA
P'YONGYANG
SOUTH KOREA
SOUL (Seoul)
TOKYO
BEIJING (Peking)
HEBEI
SHANXI
SHANDONG
Bo Hai
Yellow Sea
(Huang Hai)
HENAN
SHAANXI
JIANGSU
ANHUI
Shanghai
HUBEI
ZHEJIANG
JIANGXI
HUNAN
FUJIAN
EAST CHINA SEA
(DONG HAI)
TAIWAN
T'AIPEI
XI ZHUANGZU ZIZHIQU
GUANGDONG
Hong Kong
HAINAN
SOUTH CHINA SEA
PHILIPPINES
LUZON
PACIFIC OCEAN
Tropic of Cancer
Longitude 110° east of Greenwich
MILES
KILOMETRES
1:13 000 000

© Bartholomew Ltd

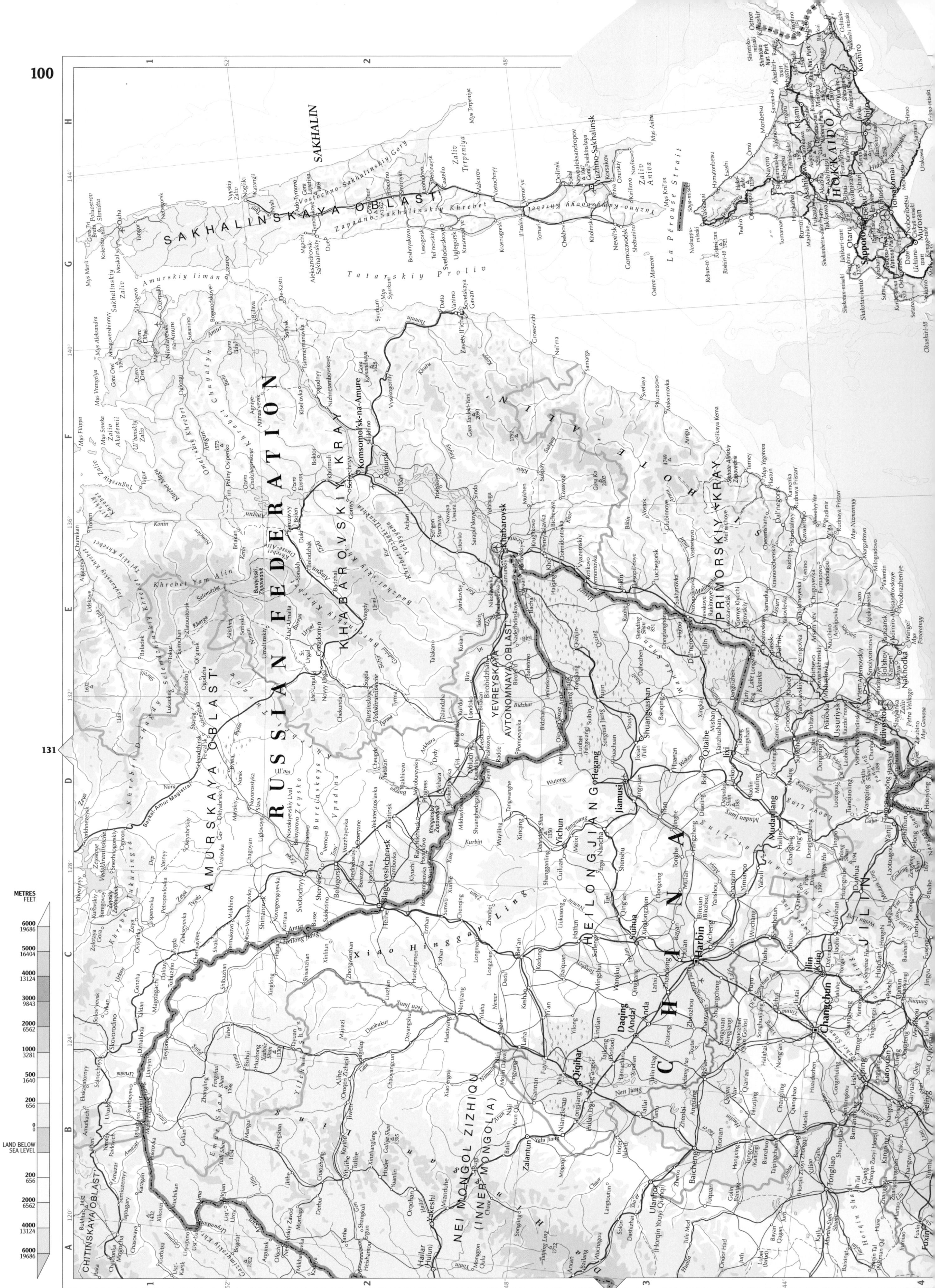

131

107

Conic Equidistant Projection

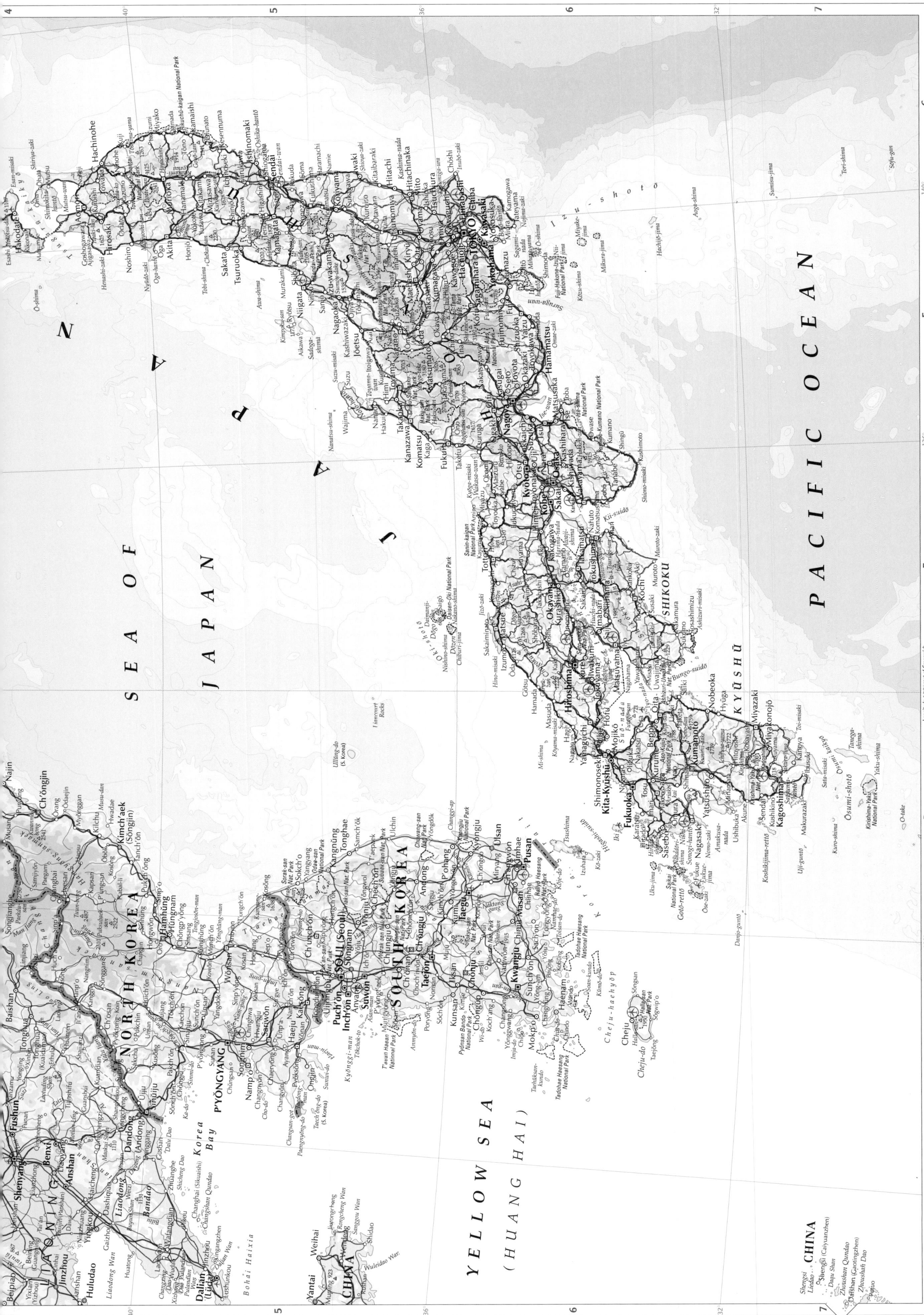

MILES KILOMETRES
250 400
350
200 300
150 250
200
100 150
50 100
50
0 0

1:6 000 000

© Bartholomew Ltd

RYUKYU ISLANDS
CONTINUATION AT THE SAME SCALE
1:1 200 000
Polyconic Projection
METRES
FEET
LAND BELOW SEA LEVEL
HOKKAIDŌ
La Pérouse Strait
Sea of Okhotsk
(Okhotskoye More)
Kuril'skiye Ostrova
(Kuril Islands)
ADMINISTERED BY RUSSIAN FEDERATION, CLAIMED BY JAPAN
EAST CHINA SEA
(DONG HAI)
NANSEI-SHOTŌ
(RYUKYU ISLANDS)
JAPAN
KAGOSHIMA
OKINAWA
AOMORI
AKITA
IWATE
YAMAGATA
MIYAGI
Okinawa
Sapporo
Asahikawa
Kushiro
Hakodate
Muroran
Aomori
Hachinohe
Akita
Morioka
Sendai
Niigata
Naha
Nago
Tokara-rettō
Amami-shotō
Amami-Ō-shima
Tokunoshima
Ōsumi-shotō
Yaku-shima
Sakishima-shotō
Yaeyama-rettō
Miyako-rettō
Senkaku-shotō
Okinawa-shotō

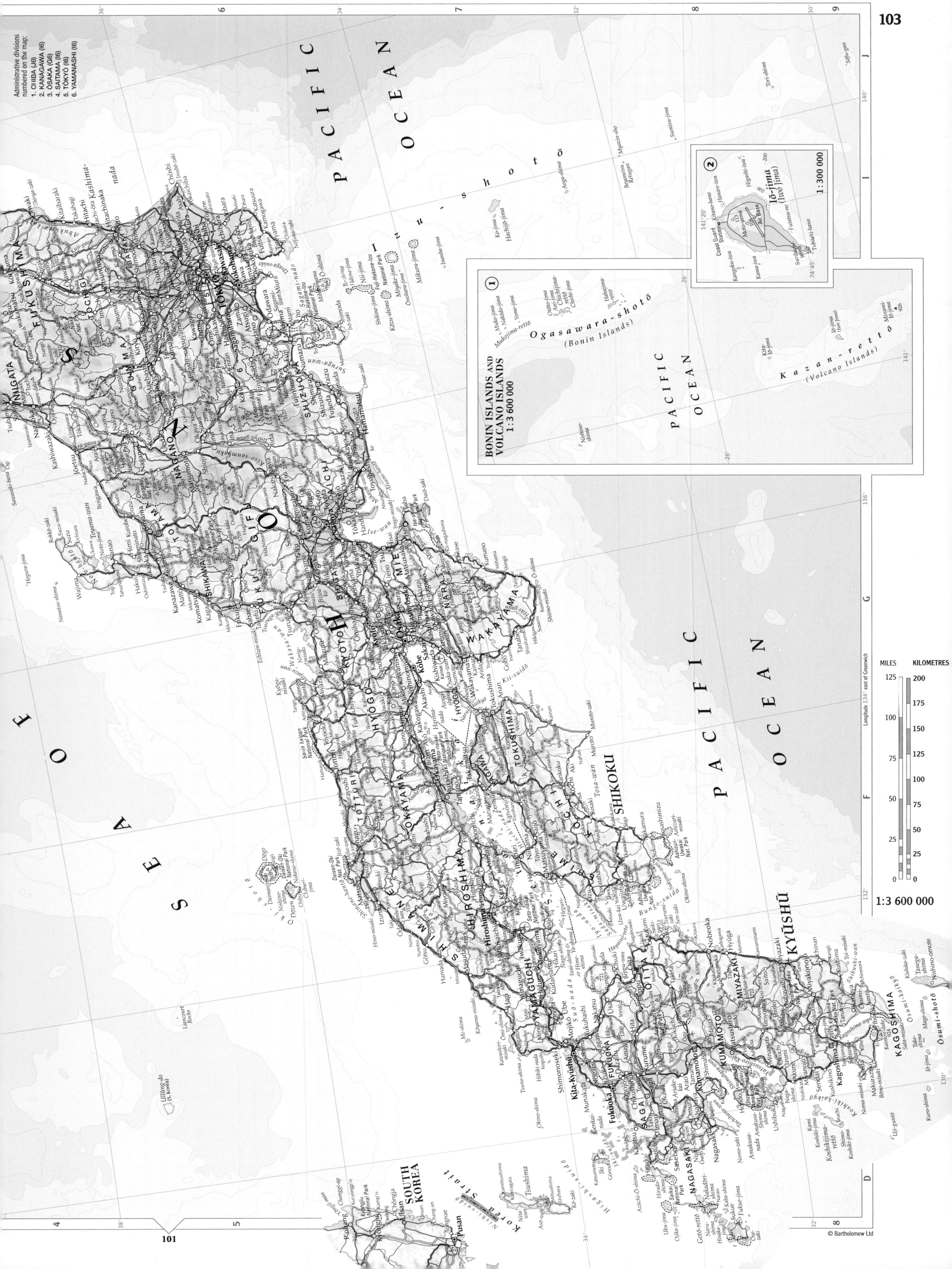
PACIFIC OCEAN
SEA OF JAPAN
HONSHŪ
SHIKOKU
KYŪSHŪ
SOUTH KOREA
Korea Strait
BONIN ISLANDS AND VOLCANO ISLANDS
1:3 600 000
Ogasawara-shotō
(Bonin Islands)
Kazan-rettō
(Volcano Islands)
Iō-jima
(Iwo Jima)
1:300 000
Administrative divisions numbered on the map:
1. CHIBA (J6)
2. KANAGAWA (I6)
3. OSAKA (G6)
4. SAITAMA (I6)
5. TOKYO (I6)
6. YAMANASHI (I6)
MILES
KILOMETRES
1:3 600 000
Longitude 134° east of Greenwich

101

© Bartholomew Ltd

SEA OF JAPAN
Toyama-wan
Wakasa-wan
Ōsaka-wan
Ise-wan
Mikawa-wan
Enshū-nada
PACIFIC OCEAN
TOYAMA
ISHIKAWA
FUKUI
GIFU
SHIGA
KYŌTO
HYŌGO
ŌSAKA
NARA
MIE
AICHI
WAKAYAMA
SHIKOKU
Kanazawa
Toyama
Takaoka
Fukui
Gifu
Nagoya
Kyōto
Ōtsu
Ōsaka
Kōbe
Nara
Tsu
Wakayama
Tokushima
Hamamatsu
Toyohashi
Okazaki
Yokkaichi
Suzuka
Matsusaka
Ise
Takayama
Noto-hantō National Park
Kii-hantō
Harima-nada
Awaji-shima
Kii-suidō
Tomogashima-suidō
Irago-suidō
Atsumi-hantō
Chita-hantō
Shima-hantō
METRES
FEET
6000
19686
5000
16404
4000
13124
3000
9843
2000
6562
1500
4921
1000
3281
500
1640
200
656
100
328
0
0
LAND BELOW SEA LEVEL
50
164
200
656
1000
3281
2000
6562
TŌKYŌ
1:125 000
0 METRES 1000
0 YARDS 1000
TOSHIMA-KU
BUNKYŌ-KU
SHINJUKU-KU
TAITŌ-KU
CHŪŌ-KU
CHIYODA-KU
MINATO-KU
Imperial Palace
Ueno Zoo
Tōkyō Station
Tōkyō Tower

Conic Equidistant Projection

103

102

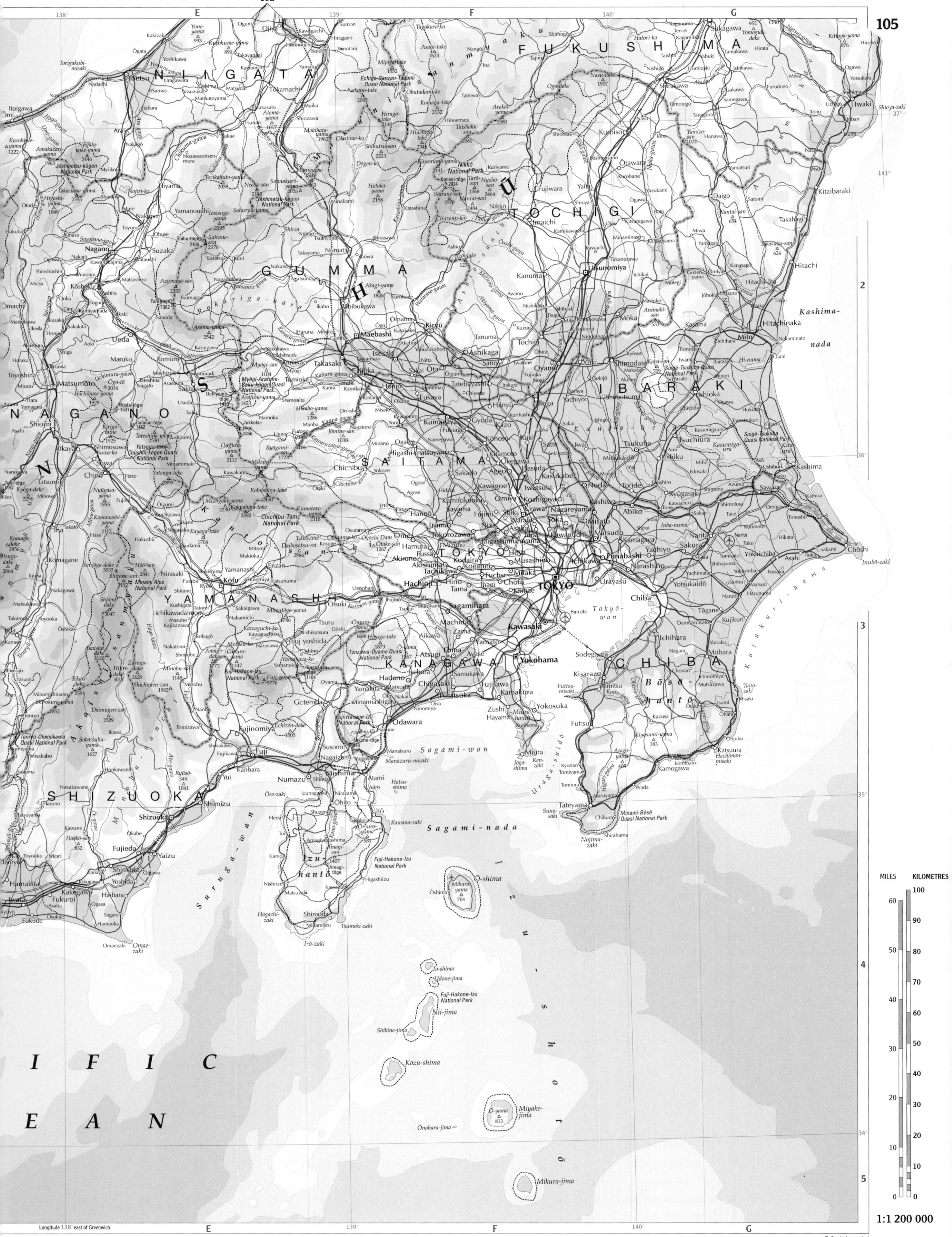
NIIGATA
FUKUSHIMA
TOCHIGI
GUMMA
IBARAKI
NAGANO
SAITAMA
TOKYO
YAMANASHI
KANAGAWA
CHIBA
SHIZUOKA
Kashima-nada
Sagami-wan
Sagami-nada
Suruga-wan
Tōkyō-wan
Kujūkuri-hama
Bōsō-hantō
Izu-hantō
Izu-shotō
PACIFIC OCEAN
TŌKYŌ
Yokohama
Kawasaki
Chiba
Maebashi
Utsunomiya
Mito
Kōfu
Shizuoka
Nagano
Niigata
Ō-shima
Nii-jima
Kōzu-shima
Miyake-jima
Mikura-jima
MILES
KILOMETRES
1:1 200 000
Longitude 138° east of Greenwich

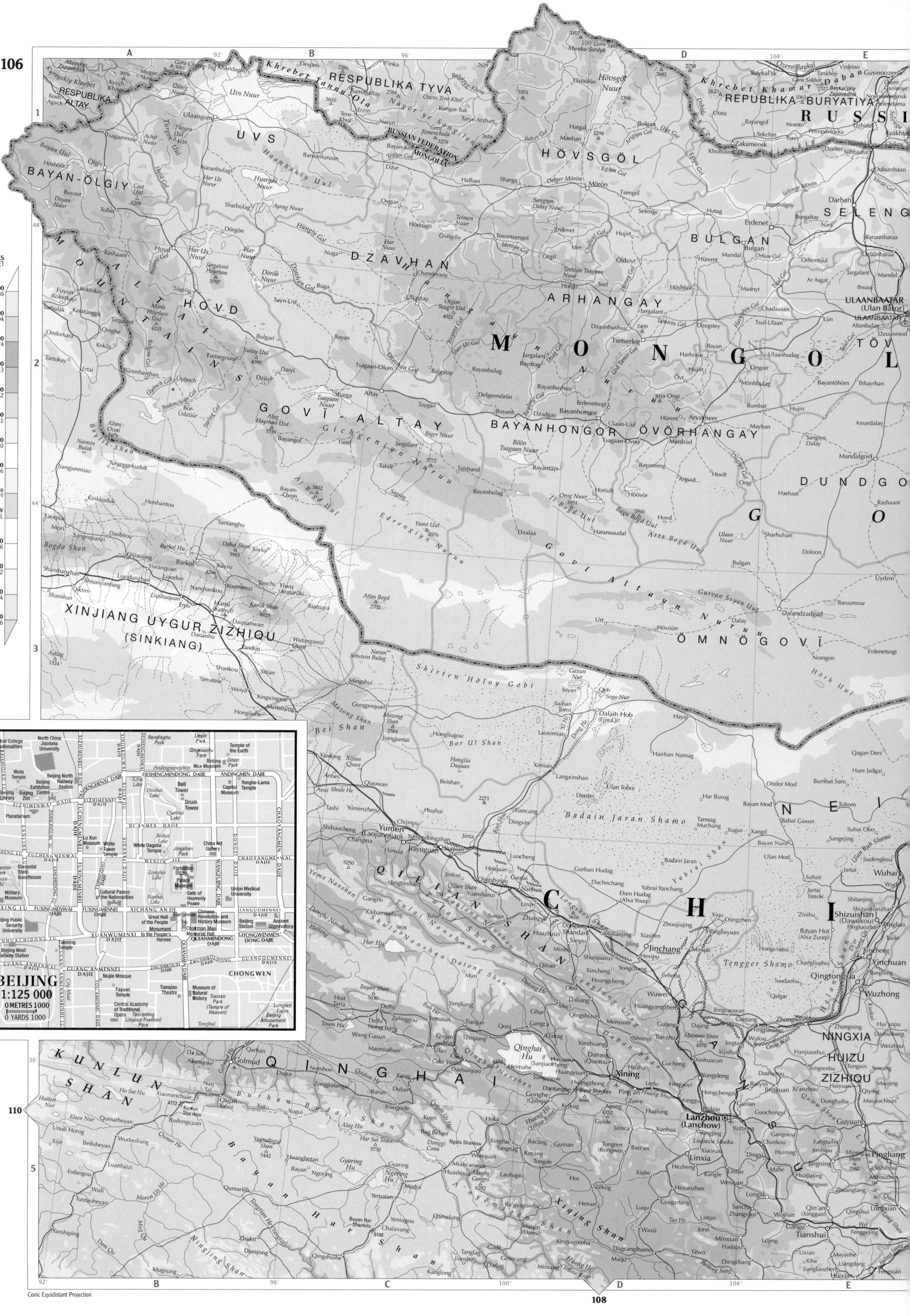
METRES
FEET
6000
19686
5000
16404
4000
13124
3000
9843
2000
6562
1000
3281
500
1640
200
656
0
0
LAND BELOW SEA LEVEL
RESPUBLIKA TYVA
RESPUBLIKA ALTAY
REPUBLIKA BURYATIYA
RUSSIAN FEDERATION
MONGOLIA
UVS
HÖVSGÖL
BAYAN-ÖLGIY
DZAVHAN
BULGAN
SELENG
ARHANGAY
HOVD
MONGOL
TÖV
GOVĬ-ALTAY
BAYANHONGOR
ÖVÖRHANGAY
DUNDGO
ÖMNÖGOVĬ
ALTAI MOUNTAINS
XINJIANG UYGUR ZIZHIQU
(SINKIANG)
QILIAN SHAN
CHINA
NEI
NINGXIA HUIZU ZIZHIQU
QINGHAI
GANSU
KUNLUN SHAN
ULAANBAATAR
(Ulan Bator)
Uvs Nuur
Hövsgöl Nuur
Ozero Baykal
Qinghai Hu
Hami
Yumen
Lanzhou
(Lanchow)
Xining
Yinchuan
Golmud
Badain Jaran Shamo
Tengger Shamo
Gobi Altay Nuruu
Bayan Har Shan
BEIJING
1:125 000
CHONGWEN
A
B
C
D
E
1
2
3
4
5
110
92°
96°
100°
104°
48°
44°
36°

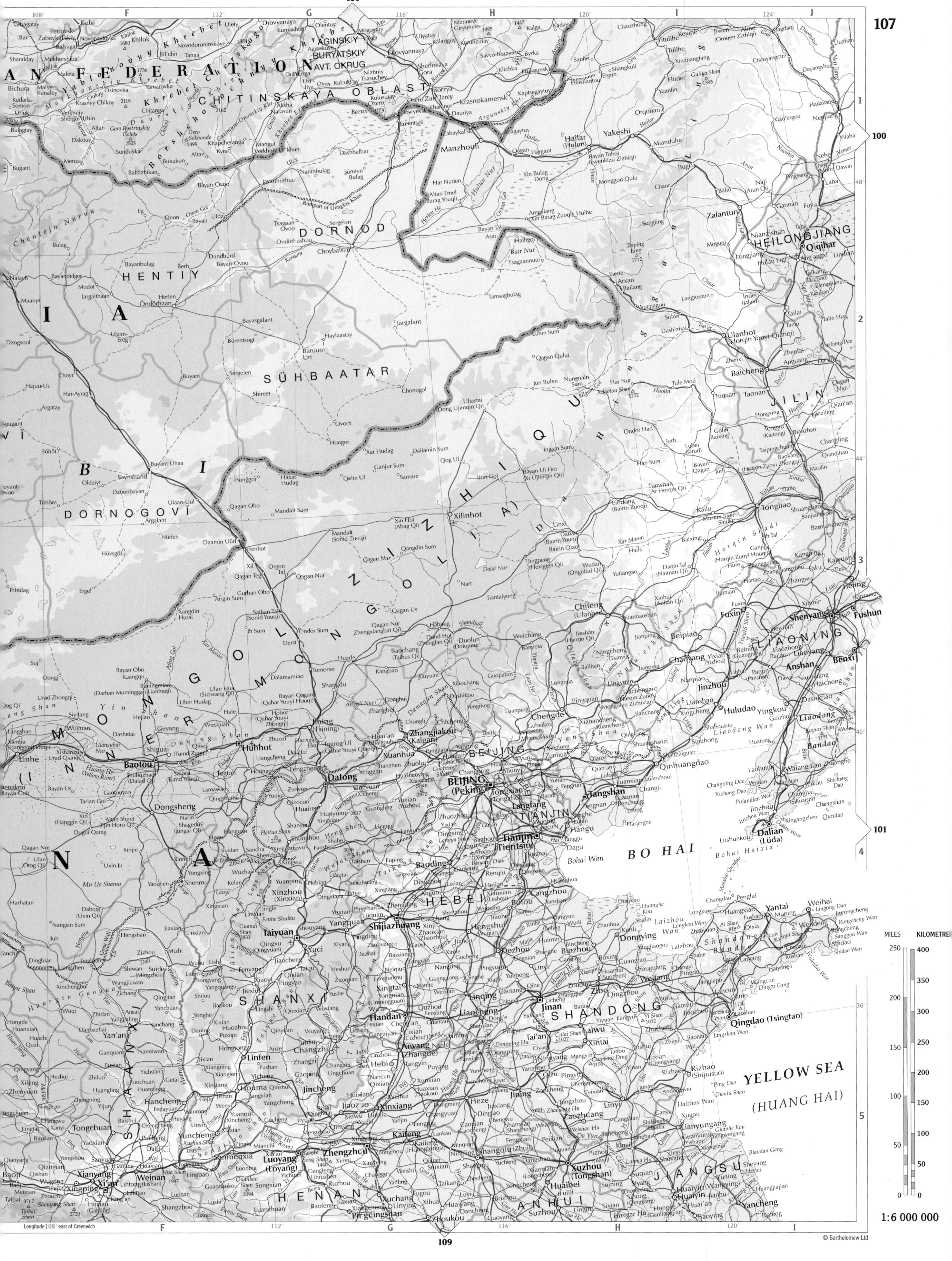
CHITINSKAYA OBLAST
AGINSKIY BURYATSKIY AVT. OKRUG
DORNOD
HENTIY
SÜHBAATAR
DORNOGOVĬ
HEILONGJIANG
JILIN
LIAONING
BEIJING
TIANJIN
HEBEI
SHANXI
SHANDONG
HENAN
ANHUI
JIANGSU
SHAANXI
NEI MONGOL ZIZHIQU (INNER MONGOLIA)
BO HAI
YELLOW SEA
(HUANG HAI)
Bohai Wan
Bohai Haixia
Liaodong Wan
Laizhou Wan
Beijing (Peking)
Tianjin (Tientsin)
Shenyang
Dalian (Lüda)
Qingdao (Tsingtao)
Taiyuan
Shijiazhuang
Jinan
Zhengzhou
Luoyang
Xi'an
Hohhot
Baotou
Datong
Zhangjiakou (Kalgan)
Qiqihar
Hailar (Hulun)
Manzhouli
Choybalsan
Erenhot
Xilinhot
Chifeng (Ulanhad)
Tongliao
Fushun
Anshan
Benxi
Tangshan
Qinhuangdao
Yantai
Weihai
Zibo
Xuzhou (Tongshan)
Kaifeng
Handan
Anyang
Baoding
Cangzhou
Lianyungang
MILES
KILOMETRES
1:6 000 000
Longitude 108° east of Greenwich

© Bartholomew Ltd

106
111
96
QINGHAI
GANSU
SHAANXI
SICHUAN
XIZANG ZIZHIQU (TIBET)
CHONGQING
GUIZHOU
YUNNAN
GUANGXI ZHUANGZU ZIZHIQU
KACHIN
MYANMAR
SHAN
THAILAND
LAOS
VIETNAM
TONKIN
HAINAN
GULF OF TONGKING
CHINA
INDIA
XISHUANGBANNA
Chengdu
Chongqing
Kunming
Guiyang
Nanning
HA NOI
VIANGCHAN (Vientiane)
Chiang Mai
Louangphrabang
Haikou
Zhanjiang
Liuzhou
Zunyi
Xichang
Panzhihua (Dukou)
Dali (Xiaguan)
Leshan
Neijiang
Zigong
Yibin
Luzhou
Mianyang
Deyang
Nanchong
Guangyuan
Hanzhong
Ankang
Baoji
Xianyang
Xi'an
Tianshui
Qujing
Zhaotong
Gejiu
Kaiyuan
Hai Phong
Vinh
Thanh Hoa
Wanxian
Fuling
THREE GREAT GORGES PROJECT
Fengtongzai Giant Panda Reserve
Wolong Reserve
Tropic of Cancer
METRES
FEET
6000
19686
5000
16404
4000
13124
3000
9843
2000
6562
1000
3281
500
1640
200
656
0
0
LAND BELOW SEA LEVEL
200
656
2000
6562
4000
13124
6000
19686
A
B
C
D
1
2
3
4
5
96°
100°
104°
108°
32°
28°
24°
20°

Conic Equidistant Projection

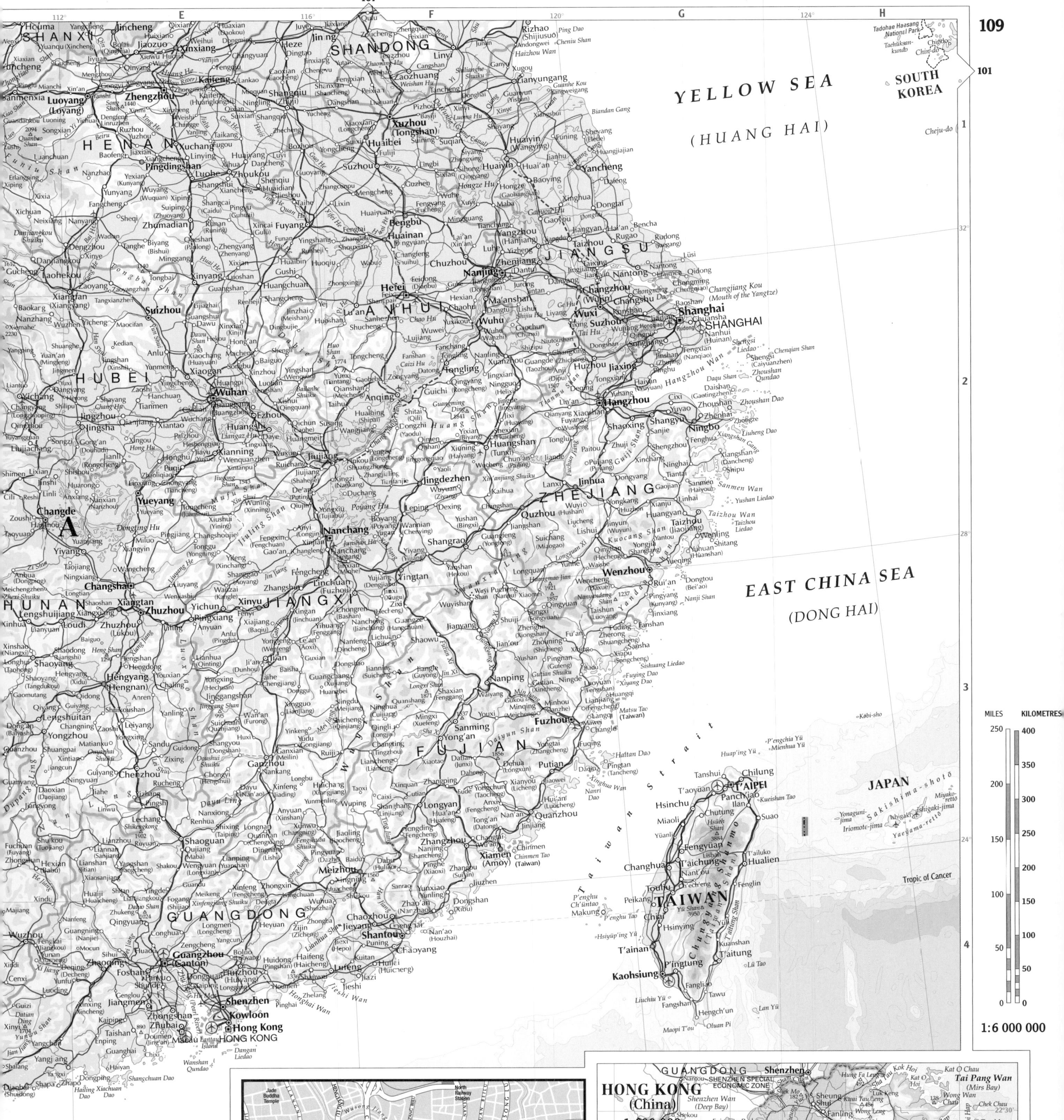
107
101
YELLOW SEA
(HUANG HAI)
EAST CHINA SEA
(DONG HAI)
SOUTH KOREA
JAPAN
SHANXI
SHANDONG
HENAN
JIANGSU
ANHUI
HUBEI
ZHEJIANG
JIANGXI
HUNAN
FUJIAN
GUANGDONG
TAIWAN
Taiwan Strait
Shanghai
Nanjing
Hangzhou
Wuhan
Changsha
Nanchang
Fuzhou
Hefei
Zhengzhou
Guangzhou (Canton)
Shenzhen
Kowloon
Hong Kong
Xiamen (Amoy)
T'AIPEI
Kaohsiung
Tropic of Cancer
MILES
KILOMETRES
1:6 000 000
Longitude 112° east of Greenwich

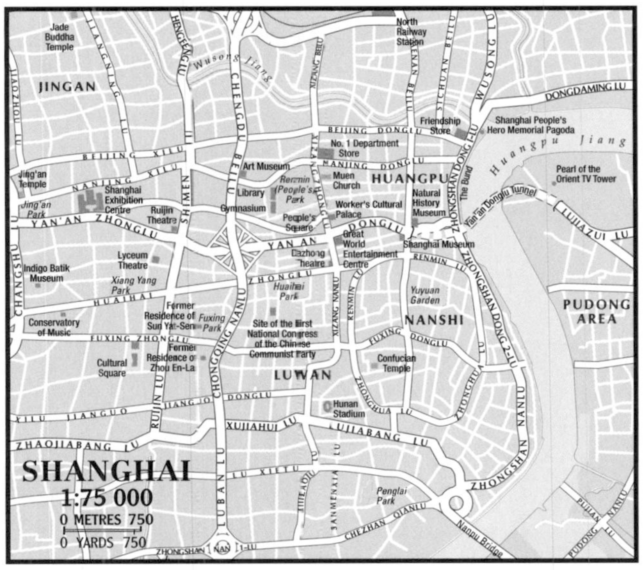
SHANGHAI
1:75 000
0 METRES 750
0 YARDS 750
JINGAN
HUANGPU
NANSHI
LUWAN
PUDONG AREA
Huangpu Jiang

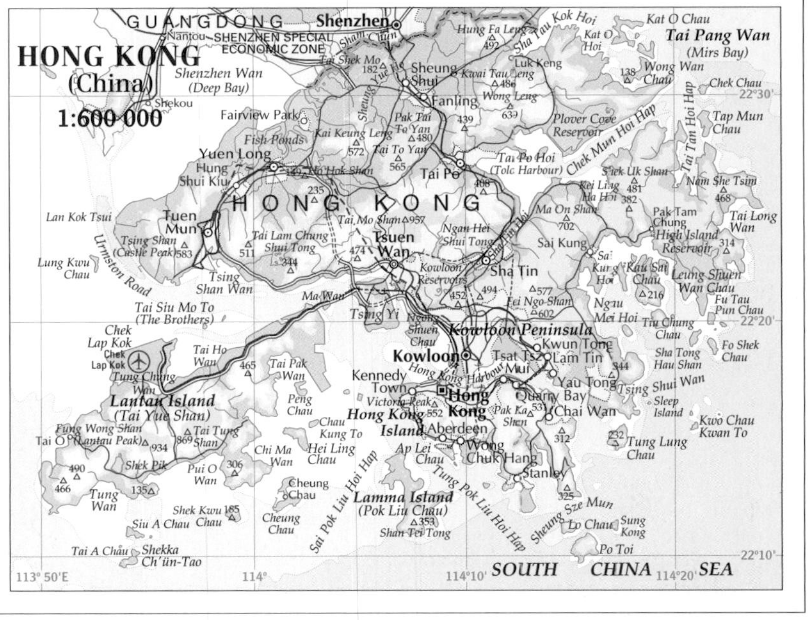
HONG KONG (China)
1:600 000
GUANGDONG
SHENZHEN SPECIAL ECONOMIC ZONE
Shenzhen
HONG KONG
Kowloon
Kowloon Peninsula
Hong Kong Island
Lantau Island (Tai Yue Shan)
Lamma Island (Pok Liu Chau)
Tai Pang Wan (Mirs Bay)
Shenzhen Wan (Deep Bay)
SOUTH CHINA SEA

© Bartholomew Ltd

106

121

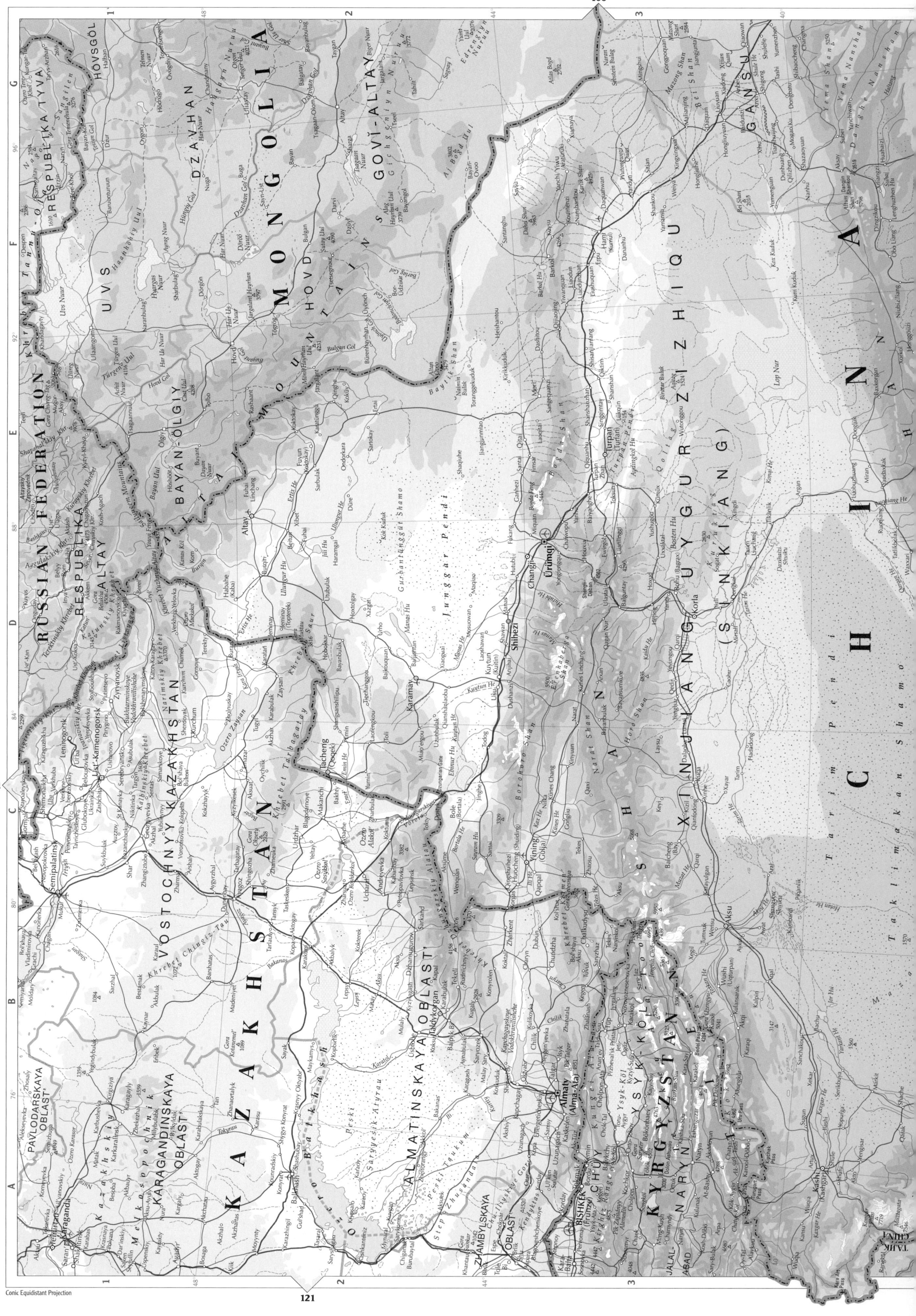
KAZAKHSTAN
MONGOLIA
CHINA
RUSSIAN FEDERATION
RESPUBLIKA ALTAY
RESPUBLIKA TYVA
KYRGYZSTAN
VOSTOCHNYY KAZAKHSTAN
KARAGANDINSKAYA OBLAST'
PAVLODARSKAYA OBLAST'
ALMATINSKAYA OBLAST'
ZHAMBYLSKAYA OBLAST
XINJIANG UYGUR ZIZHIQU (SINKIANG)
GANSU
UVS
DZAVHAN
HOVD
BAYAN-ÖLGIY
GOVĬ-ALTAY
HÖVSGÖL
ALTAY MOUNTAINS
Junggar Pendi
Tarim Pendi
Taklimakan Shamo
Ozero Balkhash
Ürümqi
Almaty (Alma-Ata)
Bishkek (Frunze)
Semipalatinsk
Ust'-Kamenogorsk
Karaganda
Turpan
Hami (Kumul)
Kashi (Kashgar)
Aksu
Karamay
Shihezi
Yining (Gulja)
Korla
Altay
Hovd
Ölgiy
Ulaangom
Tacheng (Qoqek)
Balkhash
Taldykorgan
Lop Nur
Ysyk-Köl
Uvs Nuur
Tien Shan

121

Conic Equidistant Projection

METRES
FEET

METRES	FEET
6000	19686
5000	16404
4000	13124
3000	9843
2000	6562
1000	3281
500	1640
200	656
0	0
LAND BELOW SEA LEVEL	
200	656
2000	6562
4000	13124
6000	19686

108

111

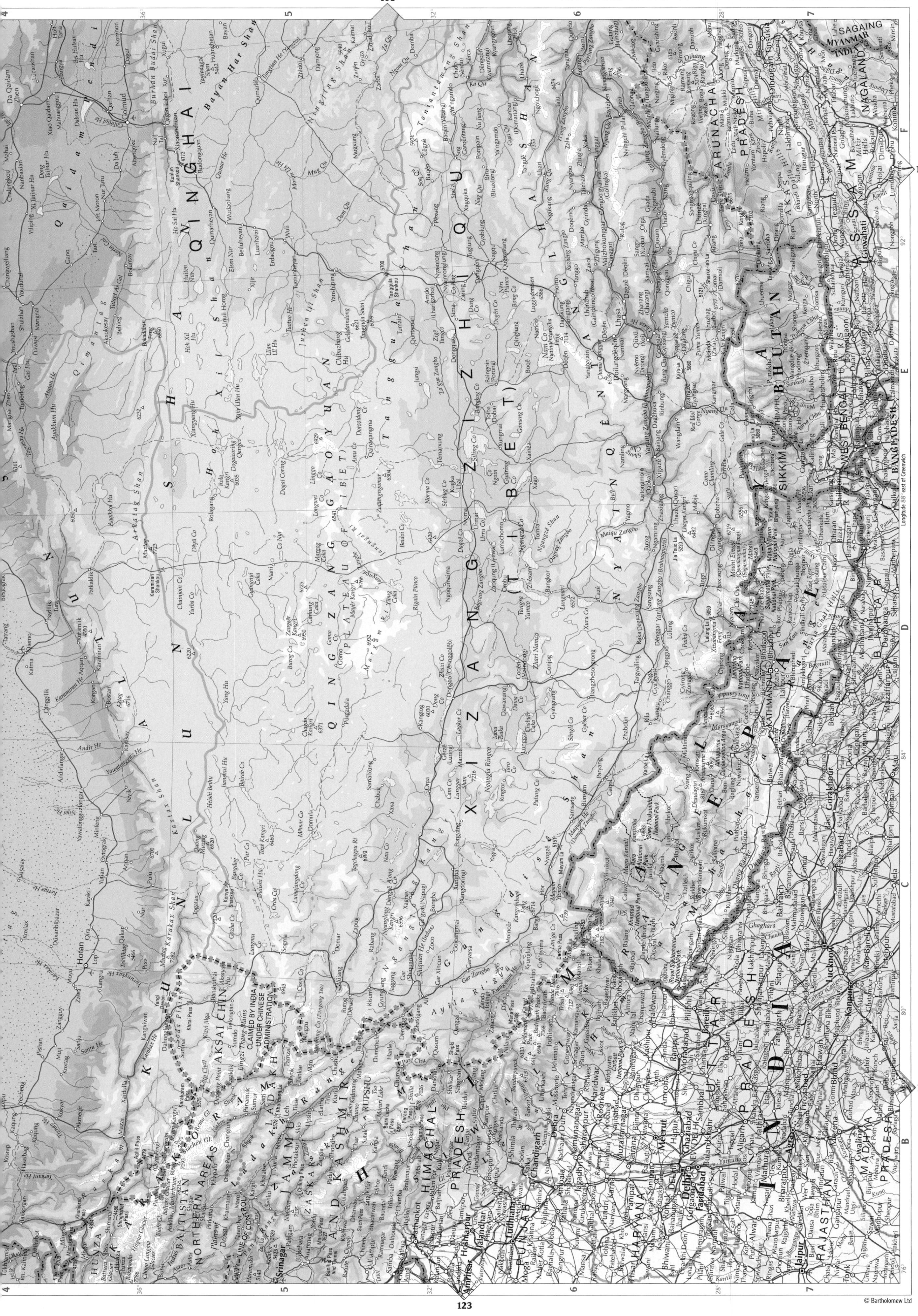
QINGHAI
XIZANG ZIZHIQU (TIBET)
QINGZANG GAOYUAN (PLATEAU OF TIBET)
KUNLUN SHAN
HIMALAYA
NEPAL
BHUTAN
SIKKIM
ARUNACHAL PRADESH
ASSAM
NAGALAND
WEST BENGAL
BANGLADESH
BIHAR
UTTAR PRADESH
HIMACHAL PRADESH
PUNJAB
HARYANA
RAJASTHAN
MADHYA PRADESH
JAMMU AND KASHMIR
AKSAI CHIN
NORTHERN AREAS
INDIA
Lhasa
Kathmandu
Delhi
Lucknow
Kanpur
Jaipur
Agra
Srinagar
Hotan
Golmud

117

116

MILES | KILOMETRES

250 200 150 100 50 0

400 350 300 250 200 150 100 50 0

1:6 000 000

123

© Bartholomew Ltd

98

130

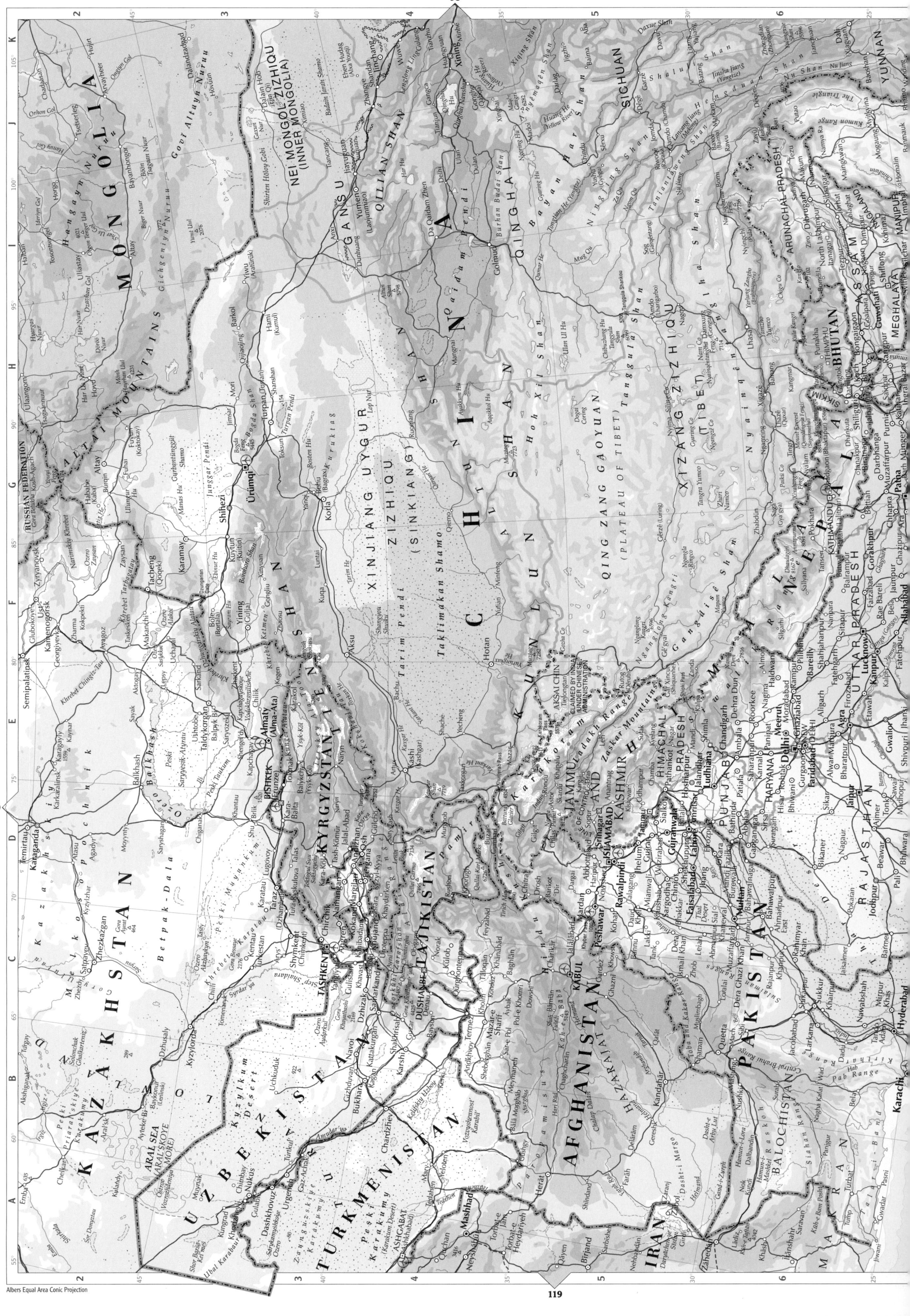
KAZAKHSTAN
UZBEKISTAN
TURKMENISTAN
KYRGYZSTAN
TAJIKISTAN
AFGHANISTAN
PAKISTAN
IRAN
MONGOLIA
CHINA
NEPAL
BHUTAN
RUSSIAN FEDERATION
XINJIANG UYGUR ZIZHIQU (SINKIANG)
XIZANG ZIZHIQU (TIBET)
QINGHAI
GANSU
NEI MONGOL ZIZHIQU (INNER MONGOLIA)
SICHUAN
YUNNAN
JAMMU AND KASHMIR
HIMACHAL PRADESH
UTTAR PRADESH
RAJASTHAN
PUNJAB
HARYANA
ARUNACHAL PRADESH
ASSAM
MEGHALAYA
SIKKIM
BALOCHISTAN
QING ZANG GAOYUAN (PLATEAU OF TIBET)
Taklimakan Shamo
Tarim Pendi
KUNLUN SHAN
TIEN SHAN
ALTAI MOUNTAINS
ARAL SEA
Ürümqi
TASHKENT
BISHKEK
DUSHANBE
ASHGABAT
KABUL
ISLAMABAD
KATHMANDU
THIMPHU
NEW DELHI
Lhasa
Almaty (Alma-Ata)
Karachi
Lahore
Peshawar
Kandahar
Herat
Mashhad
Samarkand
Bukhara
Kashi (Kashgar)
Hotan
Aksu
Xining
Golmud
Hami (Kumul)
Karamay
Semipalatinsk
Karaganda
Balkhash
Kyzylorda
Aral'sk
Ulaangom
Hovd
Altay
Uliastay
Lucknow
Kanpur
Agra
Jaipur
Jodhpur
Hyderabad
Multan
Faisalabad
Quetta
Patna

METRES
FEET
6000
19686
5000
16404
4000
13124
3000
9843
2000
6562
1000
3281
500
1640
200
656
0
0
LAND BELOW SEA LEVEL
200
656
2000
6562
4000
13124
6000
19686

Albers Equal Area Conic Projection

119

BAY OF BENGAL
ARABIAN SEA
INDIAN OCEAN
ANDAMAN SEA
INDIA
MYANMAR
BANGLADESH
SRI LANKA
MALDIVES
INDONESIA
ANDAMAN AND NICOBAR ISLANDS (India)
LAKSHADWEEP (India)
MAHARASHTRA
ANDHRA PRADESH
KARNATAKA
MADHYA PRADESH
GUJARAT
ORISSA
Mumbai (Bombay)
Chennai (Madras)
Calcutta (Kolkata)
Hyderabad
Bangalore
Colombo
YANGON (Rangoon)
DHAKA (Dacca)
Tropic of Cancer
Equator
MALE ATOLL (Maldives) 1:1 200 000
ADDU ATOLL (Maldives) 1:1 200 000
MILES
KILOMETRES

1:12 000 000

© Bartholomew Ltd

116

A
B
C
D
1
2
3
4
5
72°
76°
80°
20°
16°
12°
8°
Tropic of Cancer
Gulf of Kachchh
GUJARAT
MADHYA PRADESH
MAHARASHTRA
INDIA
DECCAN
ANDHRA PRADESH
KARNATAKA
TAMIL NADU
KERALA
GOA
ARABIAN SEA
Gulf of Khambhat
Ahmadabad
Gandhinagar
Rajkot
Jamnagar
Vadodara
(Baroda)
Surat
Bhopal
Indore
Jabalpur
Nagpur
Nashik
Aurangabad
Mumbai
(Bombay)
Thane
Ulhasnagar
Pune
(Poona)
Solapur
Hyderabad
Secunderabad
Warangal
Vijayawada
Guntur
Kolhapur
Belgaum
Hubli
Dharwad
Bellary
Kurnool
Nellore
Mangalore
Mysore
Bangalore
Chennai
(Madras)
Pondicherry
(Puducherry)
Salem
Coimbatore
Calicut
(Kozhikode)
Cochin
(Kochi)
Madurai
Tiruchchirappalli
Thanjavur
Trivandrum
(Thiruvananthapuram)
Nagercoil
Tuticorin
Direction Bank
Angria's Bank
Cora Dive
Sesostris Bank
Bassas de Pedro
Padua Bank
Cherbaniani Reef
Byramgore Reef
Laccadive Islands
Amindivi Islands
LAKSHADWEEP
(India)
Cannanore Islands
Nine Degree Channel
Minicoy
Eight Degree Channel
MALDIVES
Ihavandhippolhu Atoll
Thiladhunmathee Atoll
Makunudhoo
Miladhunmadulu Atoll
Maalhosmadulu Atoll
Faadhippolhu Atoll
Coromandel Coast
Malabar Coast
Palk Strait
Gulf of Mannar
SRI LANKA
Jaffna
Trincomalee
Colombo
SRI JAYEWARDENEPURA KOTTE
Kandy
Galle
Batticaloa
Dondra Head

METRES
FEET

METRES	FEET
6000	19686
5000	16404
4000	13124
3000	9843
2000	6562
1000	3281
500	1640
200	656
0	0
LAND BELOW SEA LEVEL	
200	656
2000	6562
4000	13124
6000	19686

Conic Equidistant Projection

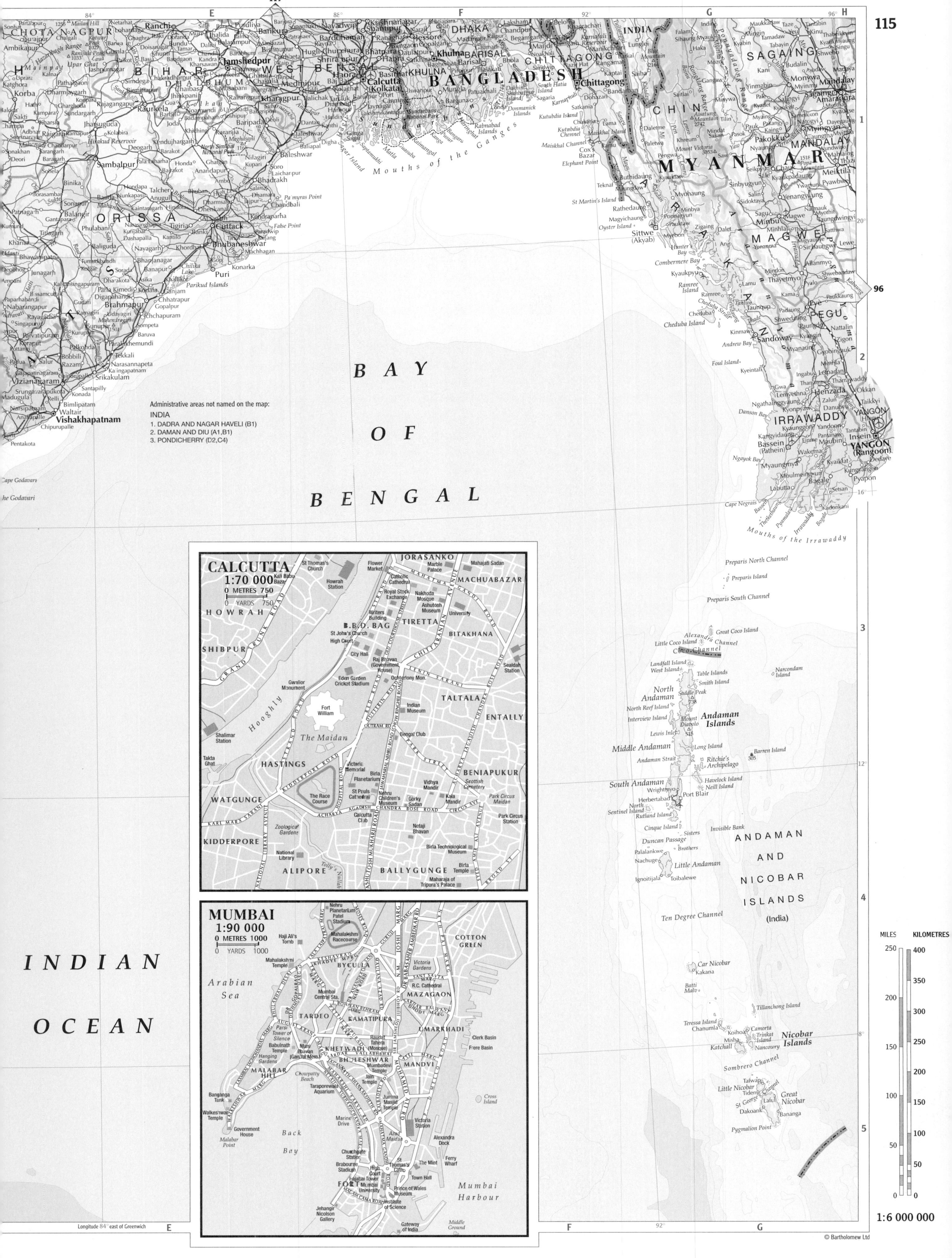
117
96
BAY OF BENGAL
INDIAN OCEAN
BANGLADESH
MYANMAR
ORISSA
WEST BENGAL
BIHAR
CHITTAGONG
KHULNA
BARISAL
DHAKA
SAGAING
CHIN
MANDALAY
MAGWE
PEGU
IRRAWADDY
YANGON
Calcutta (Kolkata)
Chittagong
Jamshedpur
Ranchi
Cuttack
Bhubaneshwar
Puri
Brahmapur
Vishakhapatnam
Sittwe (Akyab)
Yangon (Rangoon)
Bassein (Pathein)
Mouths of the Ganges
Mouths of the Irrawaddy
Administrative areas not named on the map:
INDIA
1. DADRA AND NAGAR HAVELI (B1)
2. DAMAN AND DIU (A1,B1)
3. PONDICHERRY (D2,C4)
Andaman Islands
North Andaman
Middle Andaman
South Andaman
Port Blair
Little Andaman
Ten Degree Channel
Car Nicobar
Nicobar Islands
Great Nicobar
Little Nicobar
ANDAMAN AND NICOBAR ISLANDS (India)
Preparis North Channel
Preparis South Channel
Great Coco Island
Narcondam Island
Barren Island
CALCUTTA
1:70 000
HOWRAH
SHIBPUR
B.B.D. BAG
TIRETTA
BITAKHANA
JORASANKO
MACHUABAZAR
TALTALA
ENTALLY
HASTINGS
WATGUNGE
BENIAPUKUR
KIDDERPORE
ALIPORE
BALLYGUNGE
Fort William
The Maidan
Hooghly
MUMBAI
1:90 000
Arabian Sea
BYCULLA
MAZAGAON
TARDEO
KAMATIPURA
UMARKHADI
KHETWADI
BHULESHWAR
MANDVI
MALABAR HILL
FORT
COTTON GREEN
Back Bay
Mumbai Harbour
MILES
KILOMETRES
1:6 000 000
Longitude 84° east of Greenwich

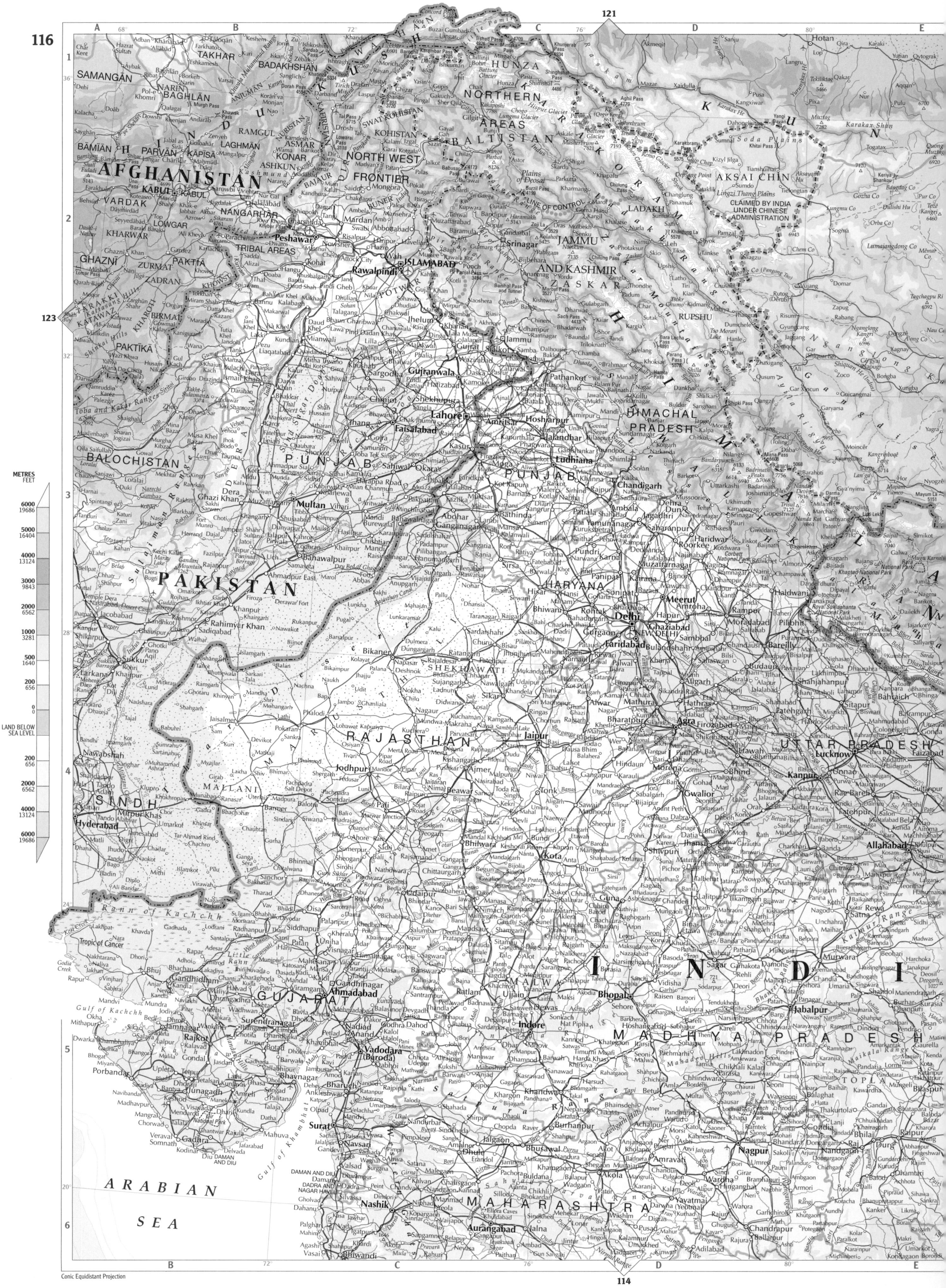

Conic Equidistant Projection

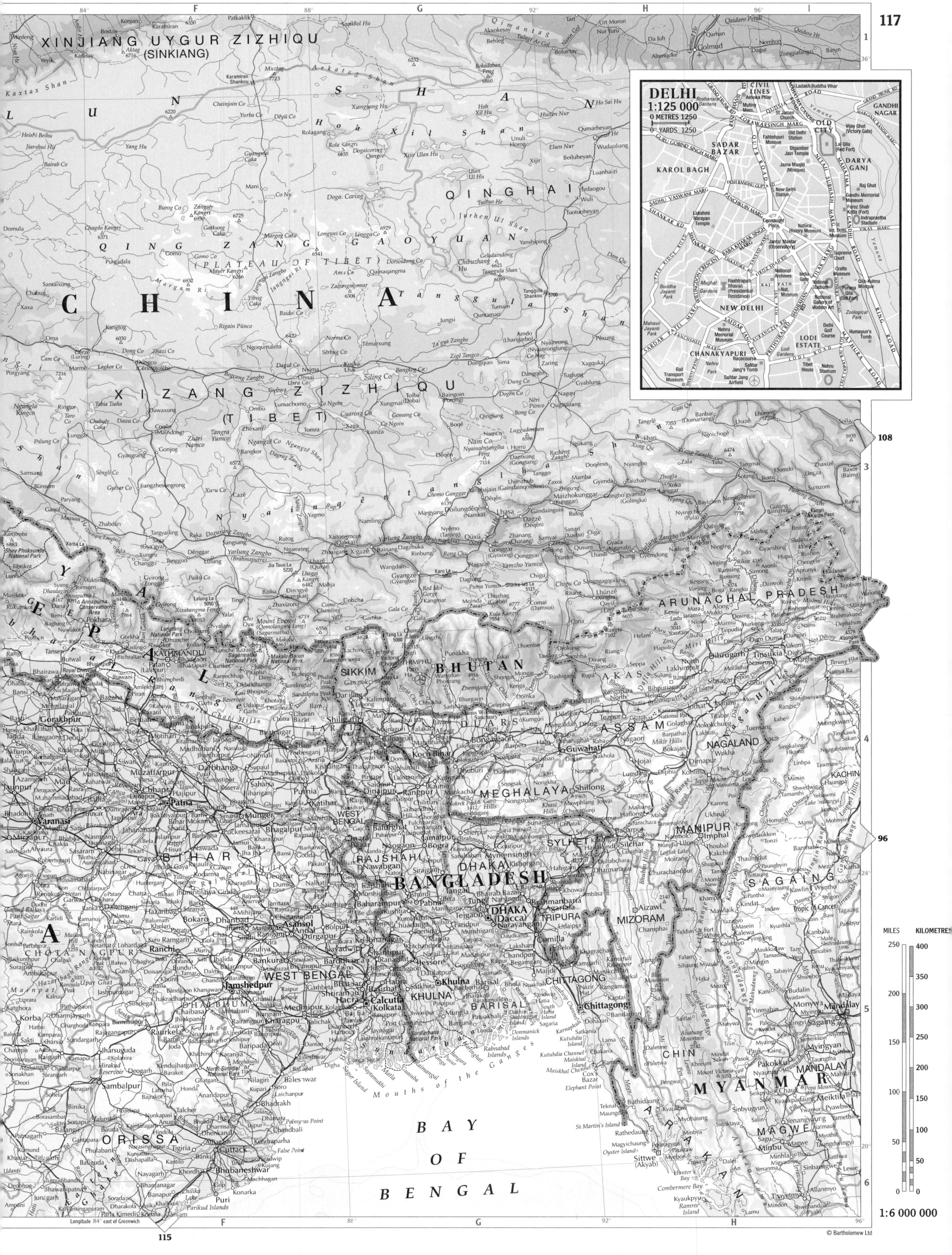
XINJIANG UYGUR ZIZHIQU
(SINKIANG)
K U N L U N S H A N
QINGHAI
Q I N G Z A N G G A O Y U A N
(PLATEAU OF TIBET)
C H I N A
XIZANG ZIZHIQU
(TIBET)
N E P A L
SIKKIM
BHUTAN
ARUNACHAL PRADESH
ASSAM
NAGALAND
MEGHALAYA
MANIPUR
MIZORAM
TRIPURA
BANGLADESH
RAJSHAHI
DHAKA
SYLHET
KHULNA
BARISAL
CHITTAGONG
BIHAR
WEST BENGAL
ORISSA
CHOTA NAGPUR
MYANMAR
SAGAING
CHIN
MAGWE
MANDALAY
ARAKAN
KACHIN
BAY OF BENGAL
Mouths of the Ganges
Lhasa
KATHMANDU
THIMPHU
Darjiling
Guwahati
Shillong
Imphal
Aizawl
Patna
Varanasi
Gorakhpur
Ranchi
Jamshedpur
Calcutta (Kolkata)
Dhaka (Dacca)
Chittagong
Cuttack
Bhubaneshwar
Puri
Sambalpur
Mandalay
Sittwe (Akyab)
Mount Everest (Qomolangma Feng)
Tropic of Cancer
DELHI
1:125 000
0 METRES 1250
0 YARDS 1250
CIVIL LINES
OLD CITY
SADAR BAZAR
KAROL BAGH
DARYA GANJ
NEW DELHI
CHANAKYAPURI
LODI ESTATE
Connaught Place
Rashtrapati Bhavan (Presidential Residence)
Jama Masjid (Mosque)
Lal Qila (Red Fort)
Purana Qila (Old Fort)
Raj Ghat
Safdar Jang's Tomb
Humayun's Tomb
MILES
KILOMETRES
1:6 000 000

135

199

202

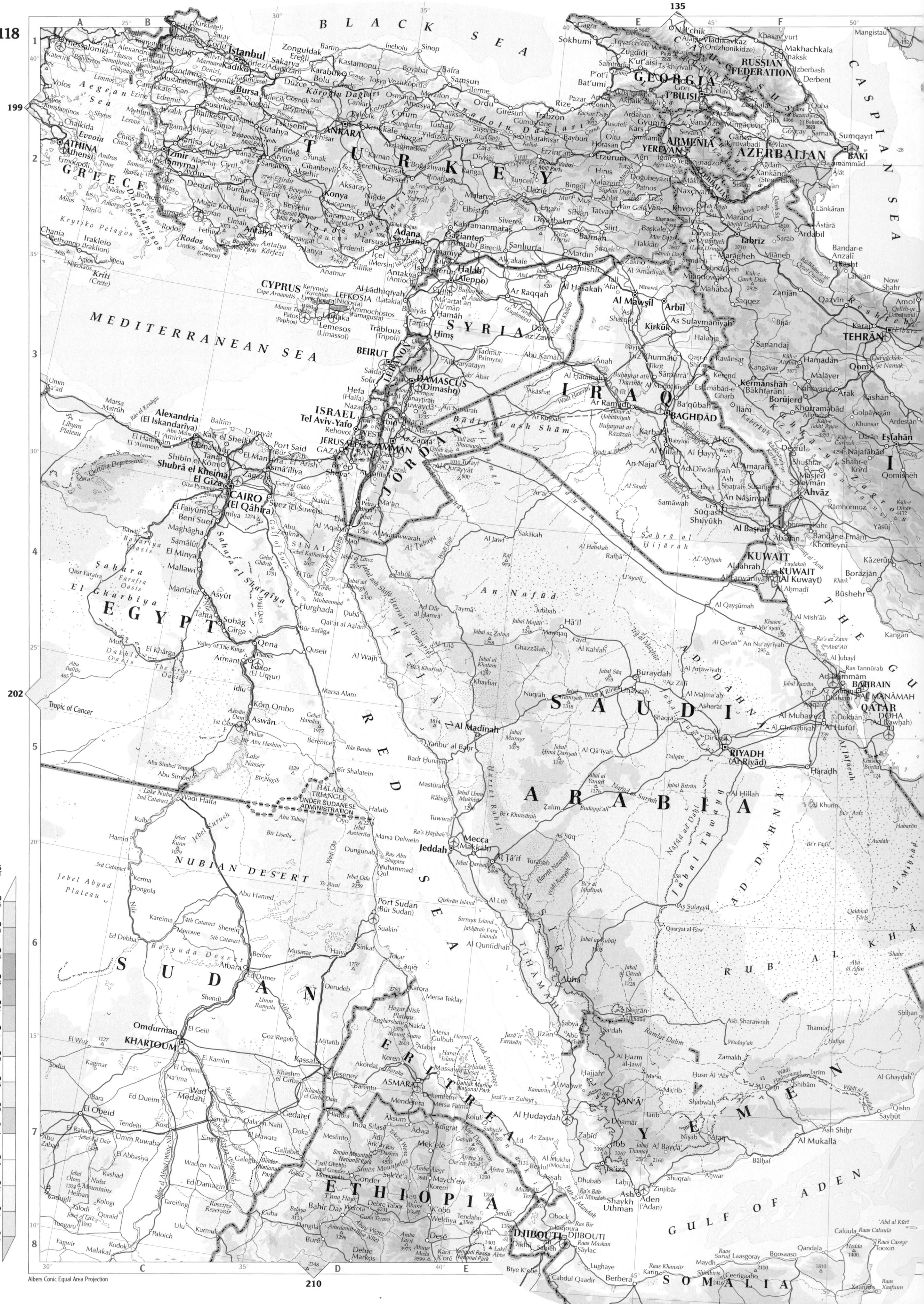
BLACK SEA
CASPIAN SEA
MEDITERRANEAN SEA
RED SEA
GULF OF ADEN
TURKEY
GREECE
GEORGIA
ARMENIA
AZERBAIJAN
RUSSIAN FEDERATION
CYPRUS
SYRIA
LEBANON
ISRAEL
JORDAN
IRAQ
KUWAIT
SAUDI ARABIA
QATAR
BAHRAIN
YEMEN
EGYPT
SUDAN
ERITREA
ETHIOPIA
DJIBOUTI
SOMALIA
İstanbul
ANKARA
İzmir (Smyrna)
Adana (Seyhan)
ATHINA (Athens)
T'BILISI
YEREVAN
BAKI
TEHRAN
BAGHDĀD
DAMASCUS (Dimashq)
BEIRUT
Tel Aviv-Yafo
JERUSALEM
AMMAN
CAIRO (El Qâhira)
Alexandria (El Iskandarîya)
KUWAIT (Al Kuwayt)
RIYADH (Ar Riyāḍ)
Mecca (Makkah)
Jeddah
Al Madīnah
DOHA (Ad Dawḥah)
AL MANĀMAH
SAN'Ā'
Aden ('Adan)
ASMARA
KHARTOUM
Omdurman
Port Sudan (Būr Sudan)
DJIBOUTI
Tropic of Cancer
NUBIAN DESERT
An Nafūd
HALAIB TRIANGLE UNDER SUDANESE ADMINISTRATION
METRES FEET
6000 19686
5000 16404
4000 13124
3000 9843
2000 6562
1000 3281
500 1640
200 656
0 0
LAND BELOW SEA LEVEL
200 656
2000 6562
4000 13124
6000 19686

Albers Conic Equal Area Projection

210

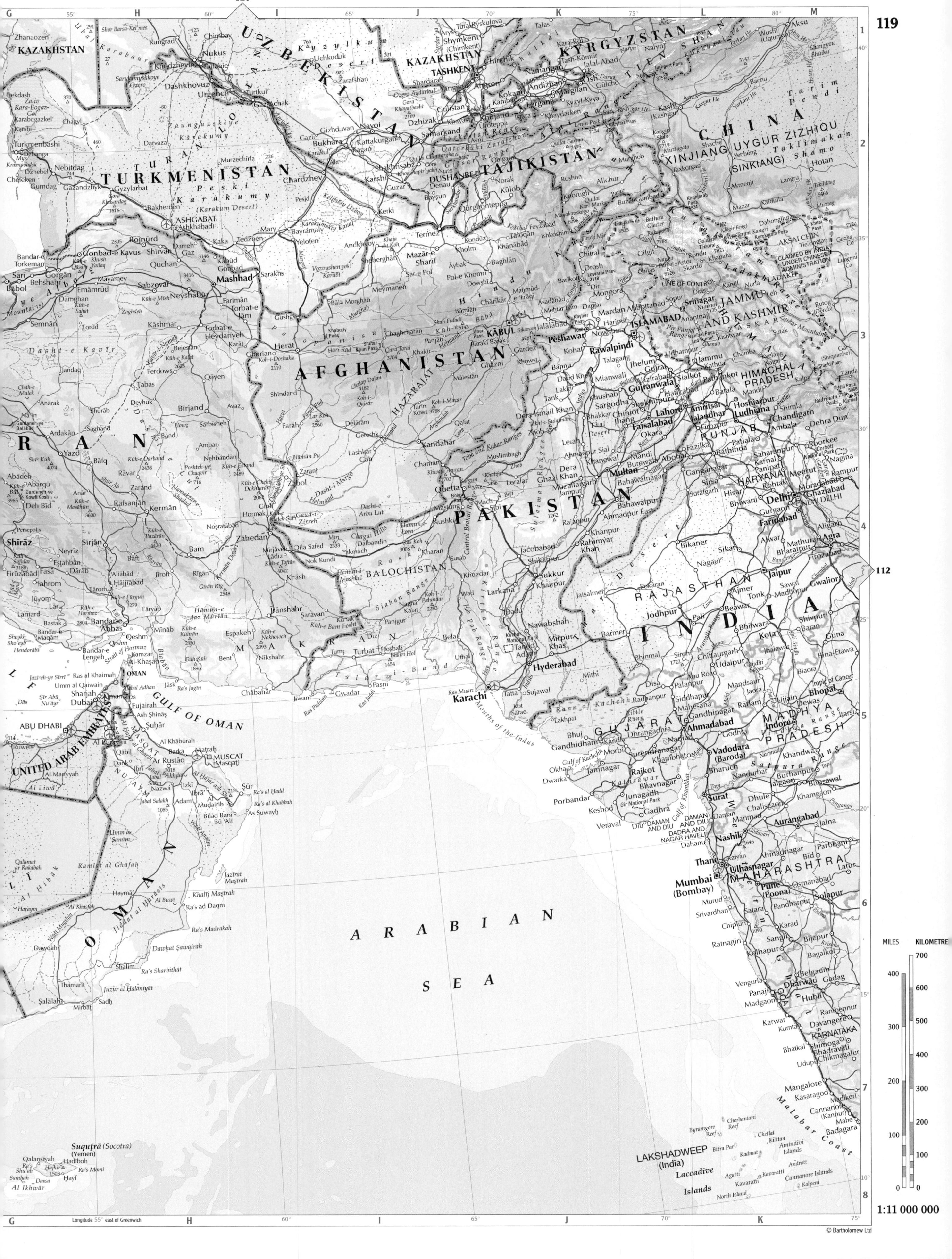
120
112
KAZAKHSTAN
UZBEKISTAN
KYRGYZSTAN
TAJIKISTAN
TURKMENISTAN
AFGHANISTAN
PAKISTAN
CHINA
XINJIANG UYGUR ZIZHIQU (SINKIANG)
JAMMU AND KASHMIR
HIMACHAL PRADESH
PUNJAB
HARYANA
RAJASTHAN
INDIA
GUJARAT
MADHYA PRADESH
MAHARASHTRA
KARNATAKA
BALOCHISTAN
IRAN
OMAN
UNITED ARAB EMIRATES
ABU DHABI
MUSCAT (Masqat)
GULF OF OMAN
ARABIAN SEA
LAKSHADWEEP (India)
Laccadive Islands
Suquṭrā (Socotra) (Yemen)
TASHKENT
DUSHANBE
ASHGABAT (Ashkhabad)
KABUL
ISLAMABAD
NEW DELHI
Karachi
Mumbai (Bombay)
Longitude 55° east of Greenwich
MILES
KILOMETRES
1:11 000 000

© Bartholomew Ltd

134

METRES
FEET
6000
19686
5000
16404
4000
13124
3000
9843
2000
6562
1000
3281
500
1640
200
656
0
0
LAND BELOW SEA LEVEL
200
656
2000
6562
4000
13124
6000
19686
RUSSIAN FEDERATION
RESPUBLIKA BASHKORTOSTAN
SAMARSKAYA OBLAST'
SARATOVSKAYA OBLAST'
ORENBURGSKAYA OBLAST'
CHELYABINSKAYA OBLAST'
KUSTANAYSKAYA OBLAST'
ZAPADNYY KAZAKHSTAN
AKTYUBINSKAYA OBLAST'
ATYRAUSKAYA OBLAST'
KAZAK
MANGISTAUSKAYA OBLAST'
KZYL-ORDINSKAYA OBLAST'
ARAL SEA
(ARAL'SKOYE MORE)
RESPUBLIKA KARAKALPAKISTAN
UZBEKISTAN
NAVOIYSKAYA OBLAST'
BUKHARSKAYA OBLAST'
DASHKHOVUZSKAYA OBLAST'
BALKANSKAYA OBLAST'
TURKMENISTAN
LEBAPSKAYA OBLAST'
AKHAL'SKAYA OBLAST'
MARYYSKAYA OBLAST'
CASPIAN SEA
RESPUBLIKA DAGESTAN
AZERBAIJAN
IRAN
GOLESTAN
KHORĀSAN
MĀZANDARĀN
SEMNĀN
KYZYLKUM DESERT
PESKI KARAKUMY (KARAKUM DESERT)
Ustyurt Plateau
Prikaspiyskaya Nizmennost' (Caspian Lowland)
Zaliv Kara-Bogaz-Gol
Samara (Kuybyshev)
Saratov
Uralsk
Orenburg
Orsk
Aktyubinsk
Magnitogorsk
Kostanay
Astrakhan'
Atyrau (Gur'yev)
Aktau (Shevchenko)
Makhachkala
Derbent
BAKI
Sumqayıt
Turkmenbashi
Nebitdag
ASHGABAT (Ashkhabad)
Nukus
Urgench
Dashkhovuz
Chardzhev
Bukhara
Navoi
Karshi
Kzyl-Orda
Aral'sk
Chelkar
Gorgan
Sari
A B C D E F
48° 52° 56° 60° 64°
1 2 3 4 5 6
Administrative regions numbered on the map:
UZBEKISTAN
1. ANDIZHANSKAYA OBLAST' (H4)
2. DZHIZAKSKAYA OBLAST' (F5)
3. FERGANSKAYA OBLAST' (G4)
4. KASHKADAR'INSKAYA OBLAST' (F5)
5. NAMANGANSKAYA OBLAST' (G4)
6. SAMARKANDSKAYA OBLAST' (F5)
7. SYRDAR'INSKAYA OBLAST' (G4)
8. TASHKENTSKAYA OBLAST' (G4)

Conic Equidistant Projection

122

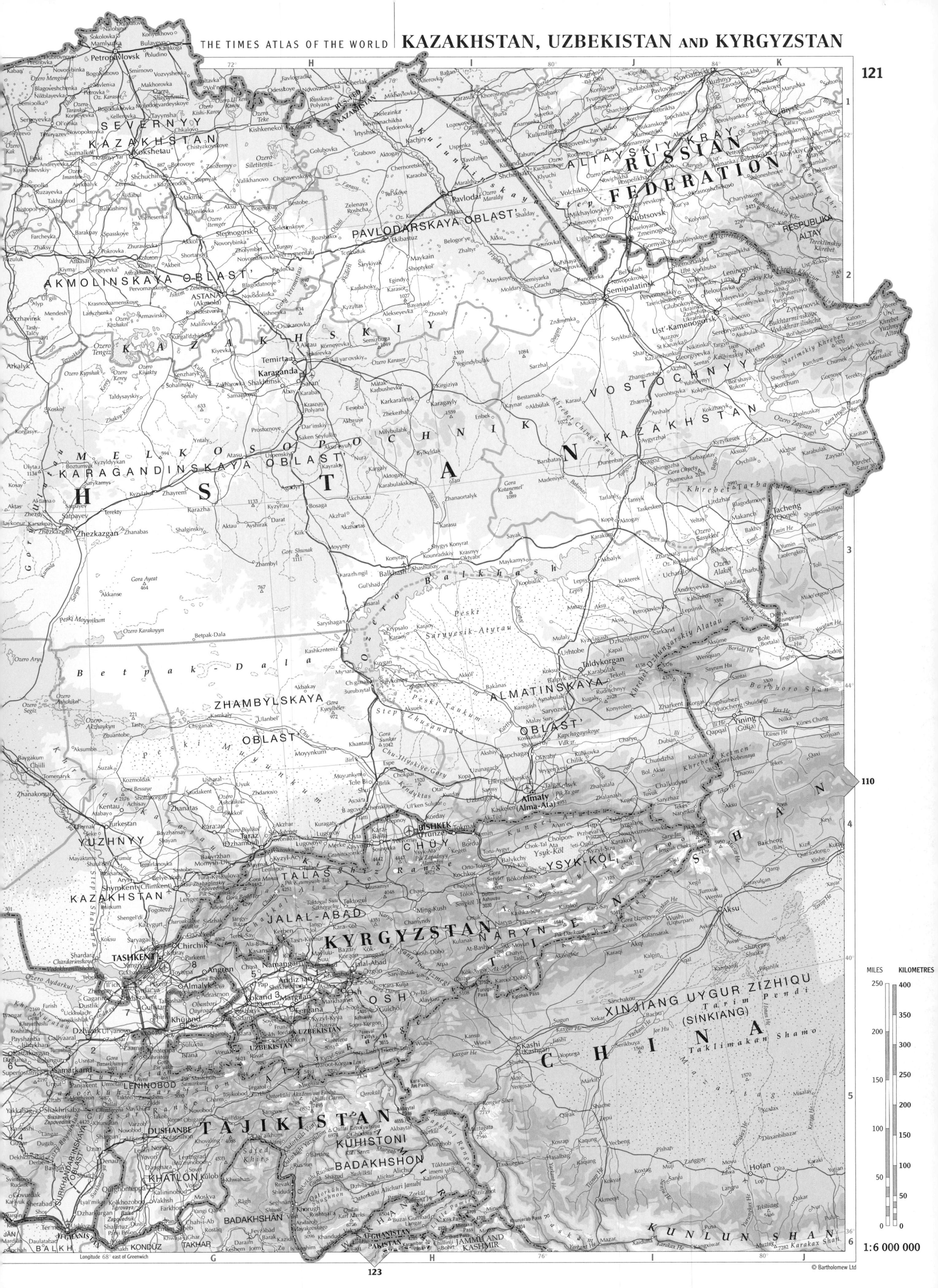
KAZAKHSTAN
SEVERNYY KAZAKHSTAN
AKMOLINSKAYA OBLAST'
PAVLODARSKAYA OBLAST'
KARAGANDINSKAYA OBLAST'
VOSTOCHNYY KAZAKHSTAN
ALMATINSKAYA OBLAST'
ZHAMBYLSKAYA OBLAST
YUZHNYY KAZAKHSTAN
RUSSIAN FEDERATION
ALTAYSKIY KRAY
RESPUBLIKA ALTAY
KYRGYZSTAN
CHUY
TALAS
YSYK-KÖL
JALAL-ABAD
NARYN
OSH
TAJIKISTAN
KUHISTONI BADAKHSHON
KHATLON
LENINOBOD
UZBEKISTAN
AFGHANISTAN
PAKISTAN
JAMMU AND KASHMIR
XINJIANG UYGUR ZIZHIQU (SINKIANG)
CHINA
Astana (Akmola)
Almaty (Alma-Ata)
Bishkek (Frunze)
TASHKENT
DUSHANBE
Karaganda
Semipalatinsk
Pavlodar
Ust'-Kamenogorsk
Ozero Balkhash
Betpak-Dala
Taklimakan Shamo
Tarim Pendi
KUNLUN SHAN
TIEN SHAN
Longitude 68° east of Greenwich
MILES
KILOMETRES
1:6 000 000
© Bartholomew Ltd
110
123

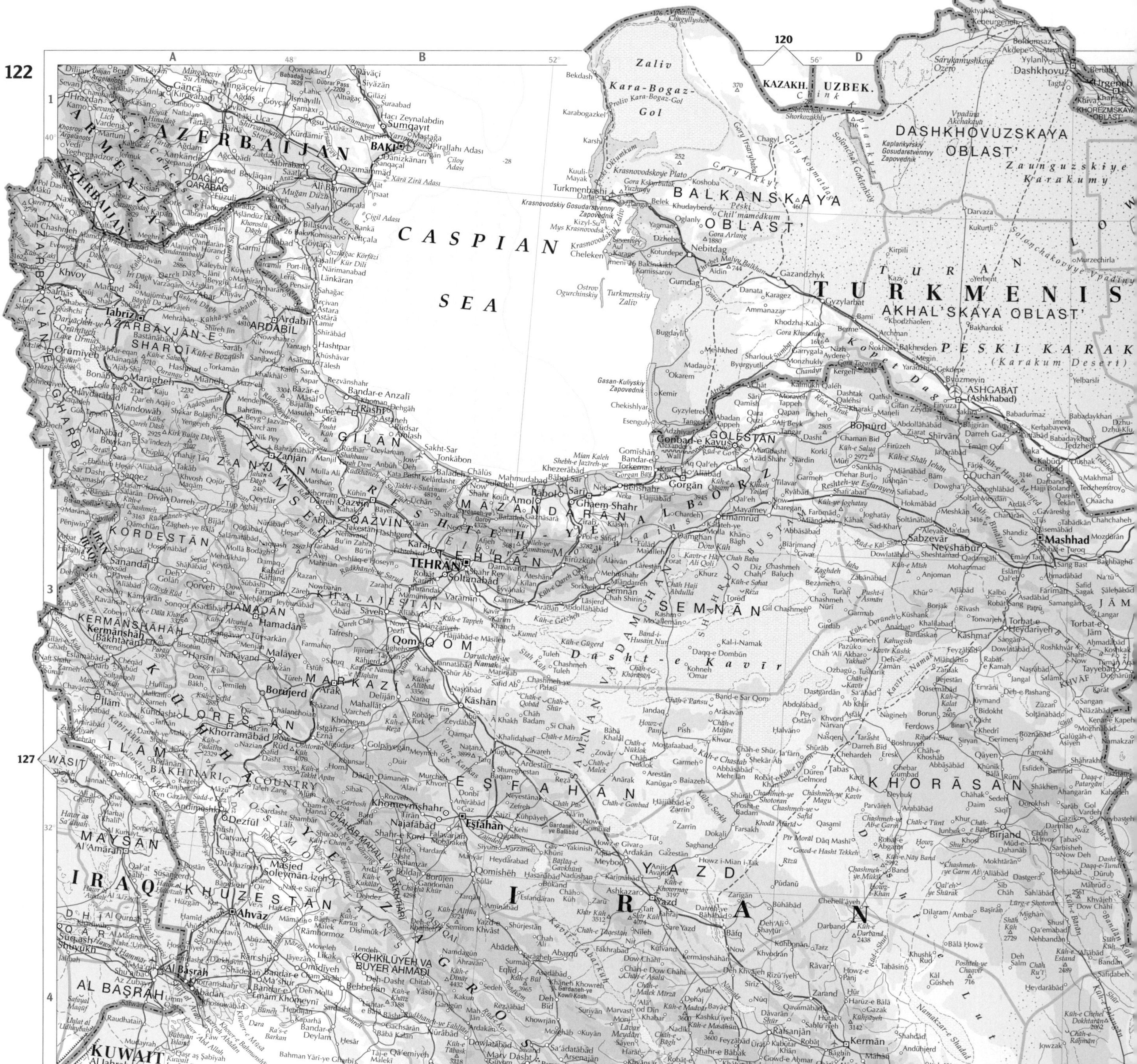

Conic Equidistant Projection

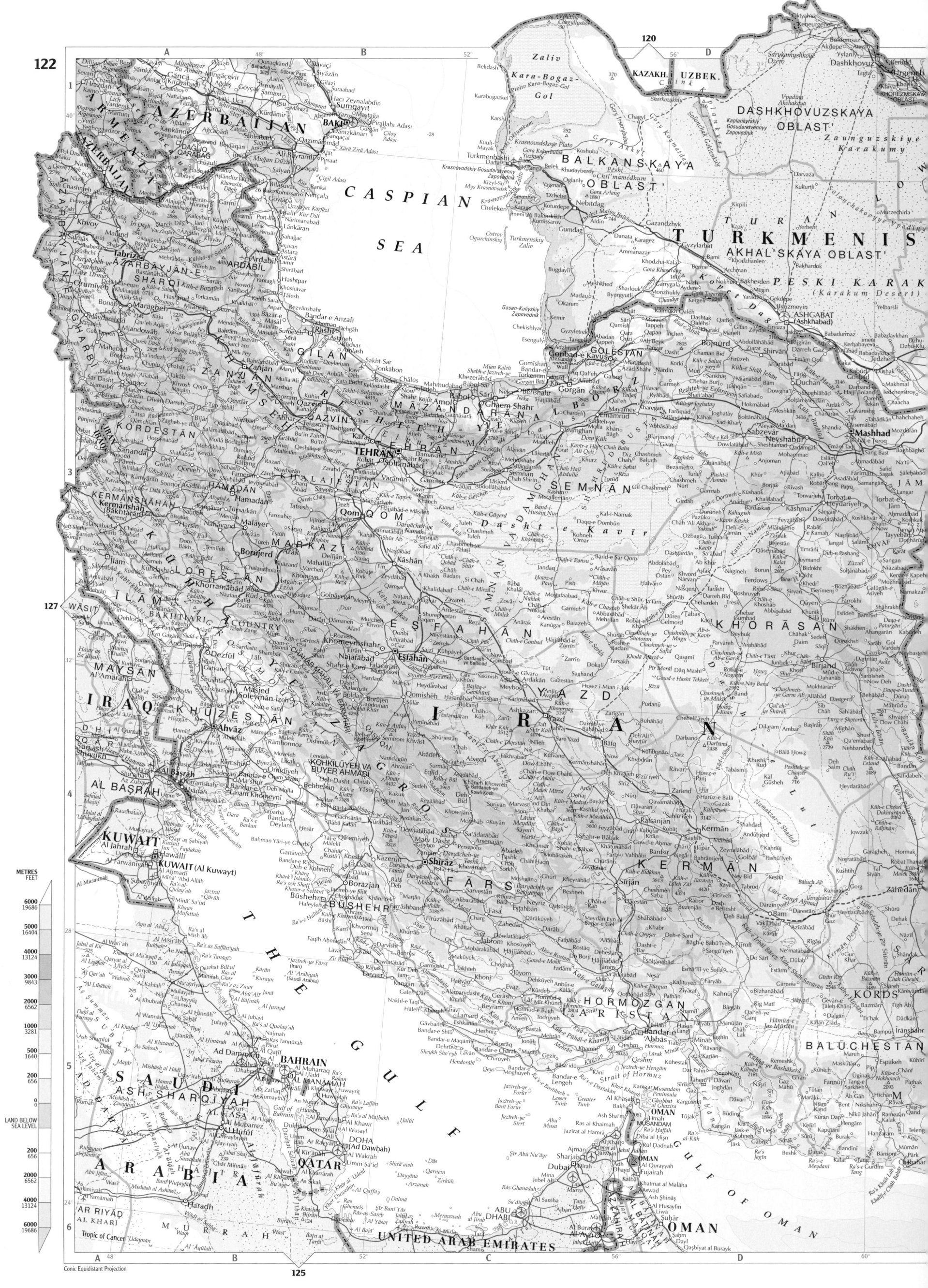

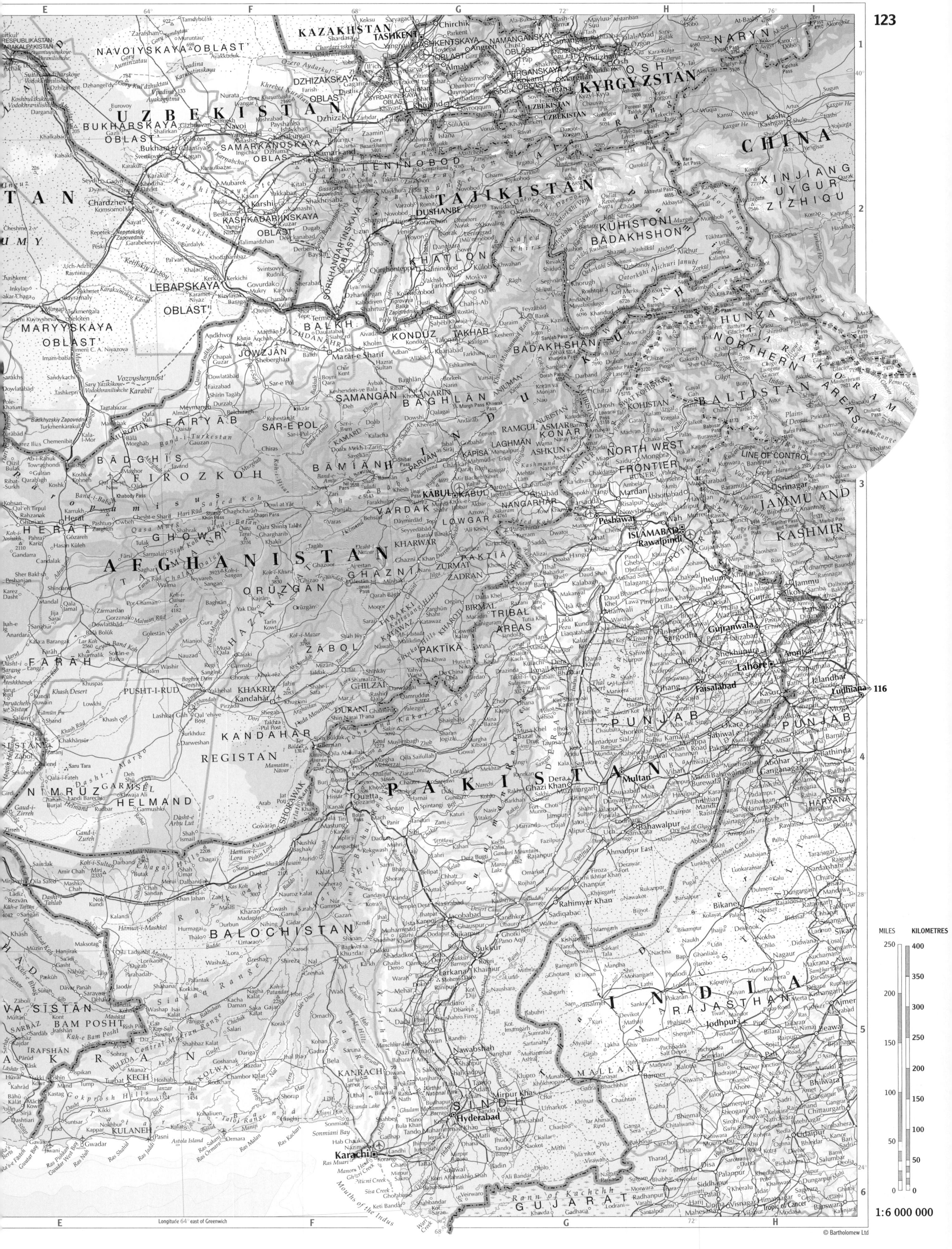
KAZAKHSTAN
UZBEKISTAN
TAJIKISTAN
KYRGYZSTAN
CHINA
XINJIANG UYGUR ZIZHIQU
AFGHANISTAN
PAKISTAN
INDIA
JAMMU AND KASHMIR
NORTHERN AREAS
NORTH WEST FRONTIER
TRIBAL AREAS
PUNJAB
SINDH
BALOCHISTAN
RAJASTHAN
GUJARAT
HARYANA
Tashkent
Dushanbe
Kabul
Islamabad
Rawalpindi
Peshawar
Lahore
Faisalabad
Multan
Quetta
Hyderabad
Karachi
Kandahār
Herat
Samarkand
Bukhara
Jodhpur
Ludhiana
116
MILES
KILOMETRES
1:6 000 000
Longitude 64° east of Greenwich

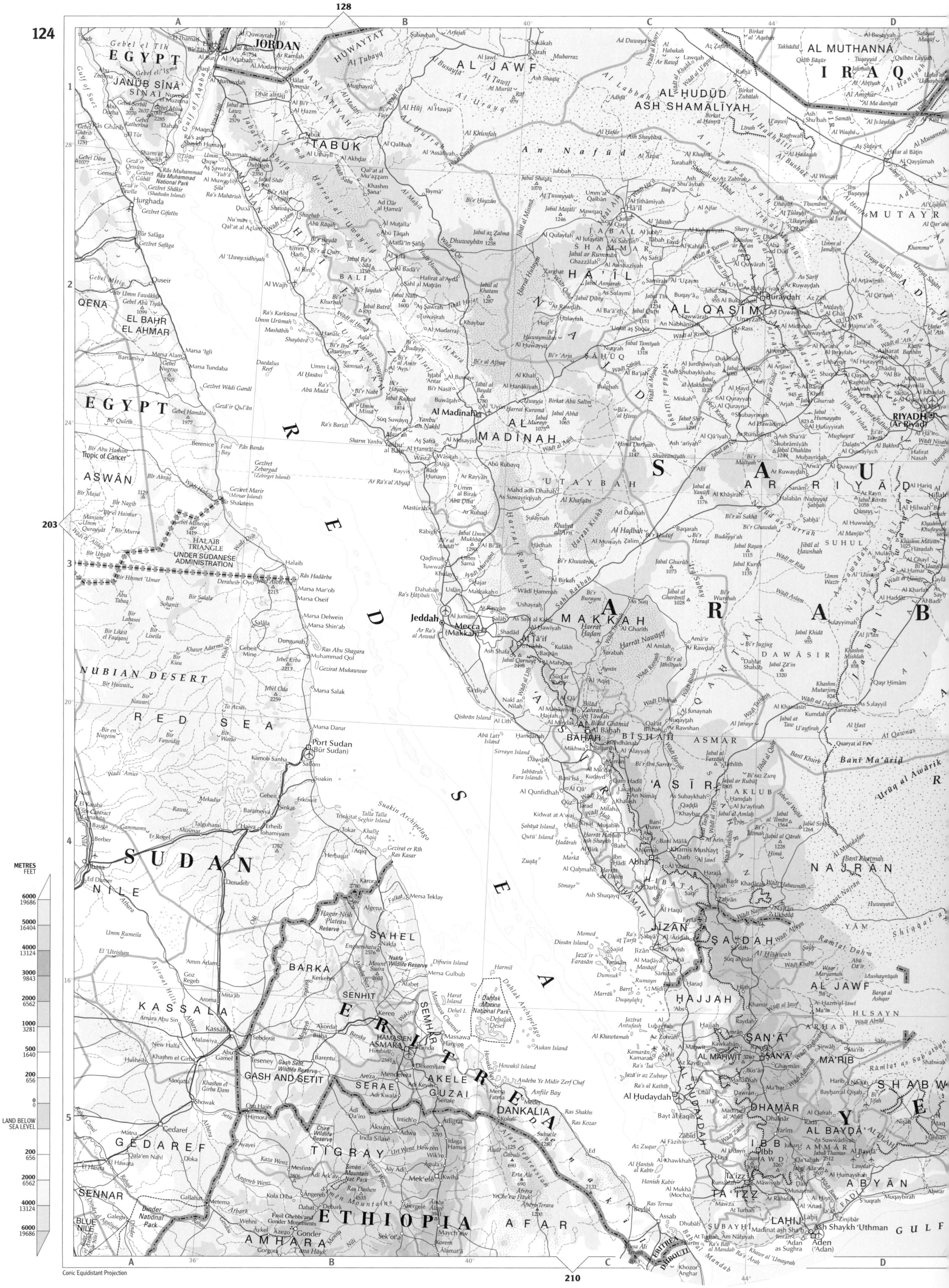
128
203
210
EGYPT
JORDAN
IRAQ
SAUDI ARABIA
SUDAN
ERITREA
ETHIOPIA
DJIBOUTI
YEMEN
RED SEA
NUBIAN DESERT
HALAIB TRIANGLE
UNDER SUDANESE ADMINISTRATION
Tropic of Cancer
Gulf of Suez
Gulf of Aqaba
JANŪB SĪNĀ'
QENA
EL BAHR EL AHMAR
ASWÂN
KASSALA
GEDAREF
SENNAR
BLUE NILE
NILE
AL JAWF
AL ḤUDŪD ASH SHAMĀLĪYAH
AL MUTHANNĀ
TABŪK
ḤĀ'IL
AL QASĪM
AL MADĪNAH
MAKKAH
AR RIYĀḌ
AL BĀḤAH
'ASĪR
JĪZĀN
NAJRĀN
ṢA'DAH
ḤAJJAH
ṢAN'Ā'
MA'RIB
AL ḤUDAYDAH
DHAMĀR
IBB
TA'IZZ
LAHIJ
ABYĀN
AL BAYḌĀ'
SHABWA
SAHEL
BARKA
SENHIT
SEMHAR
HAMASIEN
SERAE
AKELE GUZAI
DANKALIA
GASH AND SETIT
TIGRAY
AMHARA
AFAR
An Nafūd
Jeddah
Mecca (Makkah)
Al Madīnah
RIYADH (Ar Riyāḍ)
Port Sudan (Bûr Sudan)
Asmara
Aden ('Adan)
Ṣan'ā'
Hurghada
Tabūk
Ḥā'il
Buraydah
Abhā
Jīzān
Al Ḥudaydah
Ta'izz
Kassala
Gedaref
Massawa
Assab
Mek'ele
Gonder
Dahlak Archipelago
Suakin Archipelago
Bab al Mandab
GULF
METRES
FEET
6000
19686
5000
16404
4000
13124
3000
9843
2000
6562
1000
3281
500
1640
200
656
0
0
LAND BELOW SEA LEVEL
200
656
2000
6562
4000
13124
6000
19686
A
B
C
D
1
2
3
4
5
36°
40°
44°
28°
24°
20°
16°

Conic Equidistant Projection

MILES | KILOMETRES

1:6 000 000

© Bartholomew Ltd

137

BLACK SEA
Administrative divisions numbered on the map:
RUSSIAN FEDERATION
1. CHECHENSKAYA RESPUBLIKA (G2)
2. INGUSHSKAYA RESPUBLIKA (G2)
3. RESPUBLIKA SEVERNAYA OSETIYA (G2)
4. KABARDINO-BALKARSKAYA RESPUBLIKA (F2)
5. KARACHAYEVO-CHERKESSKAYA RESPUBLIKA (F2)
6. RESPUBLIKA ADYGEYA (F1)
GEORGIA
7. AP'KHAZET'I (F2)
8. SAMKHRET' OSET'I (G2)
9. ACH'ARA (F2)
ROMANIA
BULGARIA
GREECE
TURKEY
UKRAINE
KRASNODARSKIY
AEGEAN SEA
CYPRUS
SYRIA
LEBANON
ISRAEL
JORDAN
EGYPT
MEDITERRANEAN SEA
Administrative divisions numbered on the map:
EGYPT
10. EL ISKANDARÎYA (C5)
11. BEHEIRA (C5)
12. EL QÂHIRA (C5)
13. DAQAHLÎYA (C5)
14. DUMYÂT (C5)
15. GHARBÎYA (C5)
16. ISMÂ'ILÎYA (D5)
17. KAFR EL SHEIKH (C5)
18. MINÛFÎYA (C5)
19. BÛR SA'ÎD (D5)
20. QALYÛBÎYA (C5)
21. SHARQÎYA (C5)
22. EL SUWEIS (D5)
BUCUREŞTI (Bucharest)
SOFIYA
ATHINA (Athens)
İstanbul
ANKARA
BEIRUT (Beyrouth)
DAMASCUS (Dimashq)
AMMAN
JERUSALEM
CAIRO (El Qâhira)
Alexandria (El Iskandarîya)

198

METRES / FEET
6000 / 19686
5000 / 16404
4000 / 13124
3000 / 9843
2000 / 6562
1000 / 3281
500 / 1640
200 / 656
0 / 0
LAND BELOW SEA LEVEL
200 / 656
2000 / 6562
4000 / 13124
6000 / 19686

Conic Equidistant Projection

203 124

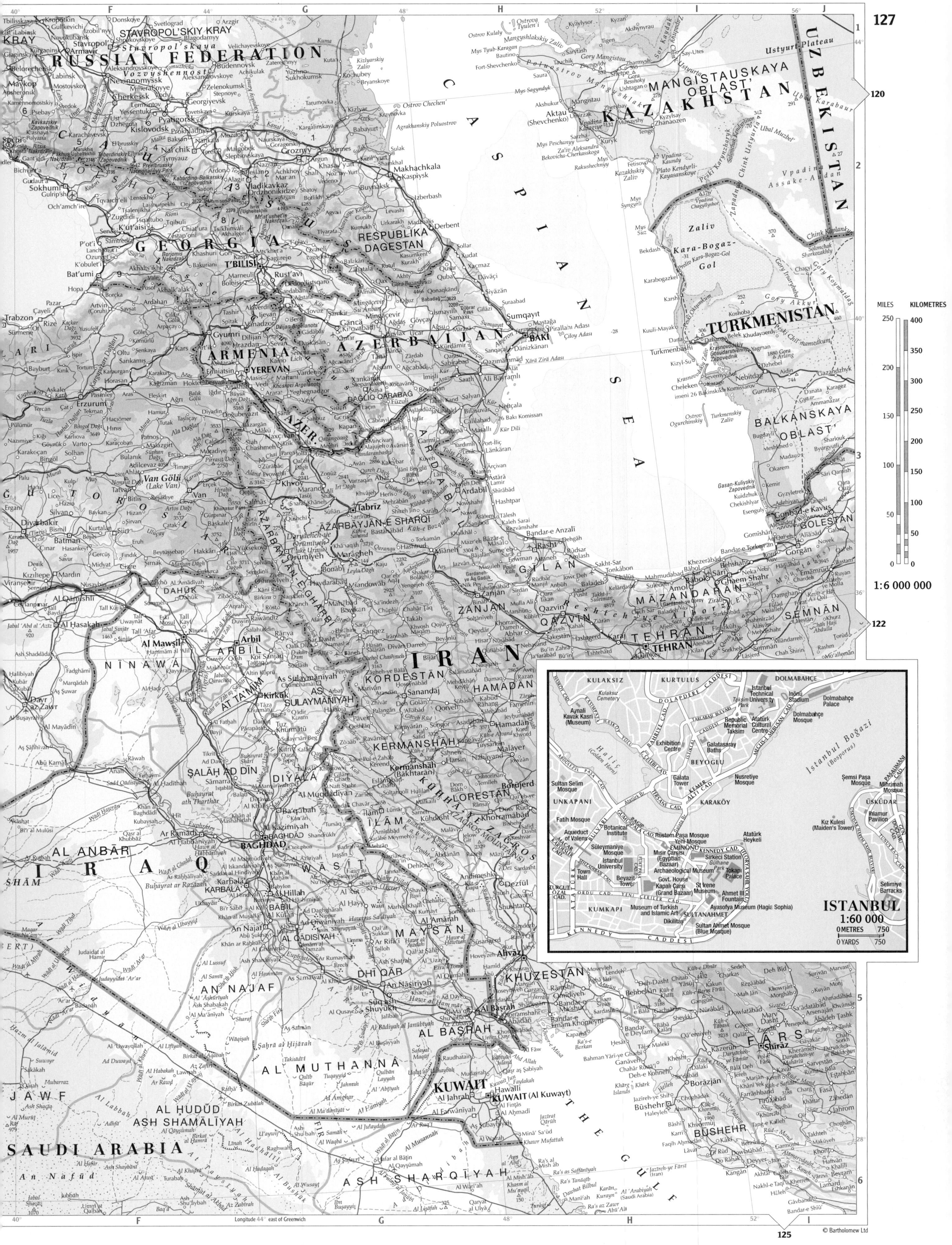
RUSSIAN FEDERATION
STAVROPOL'SKIY KRAY
KRAY
GEORGIA
T'BILISI
ARMENIA
YEREVAN
AZERBAIJAN
BAKI
RESPUBLIKA DAGESTAN
CASPIAN SEA
KAZAKHSTAN
MANGISTAUSKAYA OBLAST'
UZBEKISTAN
TURKMENISTAN
BALKANSKAYA OBLAST'
Kara-Bogaz-Gol
Ustyurt Plateau
IRAN
TEHRAN
GOLESTAN
MAZANDARAN
SEMNAN
QAZVIN
ZANJAN
GILAN
ARDABIL
ĀZARBAYJĀN-E SHARQĪ
ĀZARBAYJĀN-E GHARBĪ
KORDESTĀN
HAMADĀN
KERMĀNSHĀH
LORESTĀN
ĪLĀM
KHŪZESTĀN
BŪSHEHR
FĀRS
Shīrāz
Tabrīz
IRAQ
BAGHDĀD
Al Mawşil
Arbīl
Kirkūk
Al Başrah
NĪNAWĀ
DAHŪK
ARBĪL
AT TA'MĪM
AS SULAYMĀNĪYAH
ŞALĀḨ AD DĪN
DIYĀLĀ
AL ANBĀR
WĀSIŢ
BĀBIL
KARBALĀ'
AL QĀDISĪYAH
MAYSĀN
DHĪ QĀR
AL BAŞRAH
AN NAJAF
AL MUTHANNÁ
KUWAIT
KUWAIT (Al Kuwayt)
SAUDI ARABIA
AL ḨUDŪD ASH SHAMĀLĪYAH
ASH SHARQĪYAH
JAWF
THE GULF
Van Gölü (Lake Van)
Daryācheh-ye Orūmīyeh
Erzurum
Diyarbakır
Trabzon
MILES
KILOMETRES
1:6 000 000
ISTANBUL
1:60 000
0 METRES 750
0 YARDS 750
İstanbul Boğazi (Bosporus)
Haliç (Golden Horn)
BEYOĞLU
ÜSKÜDAR
SULTANAHMET
Longitude 44° east of Greenwich

© Bartholomew Ltd
120
122
125

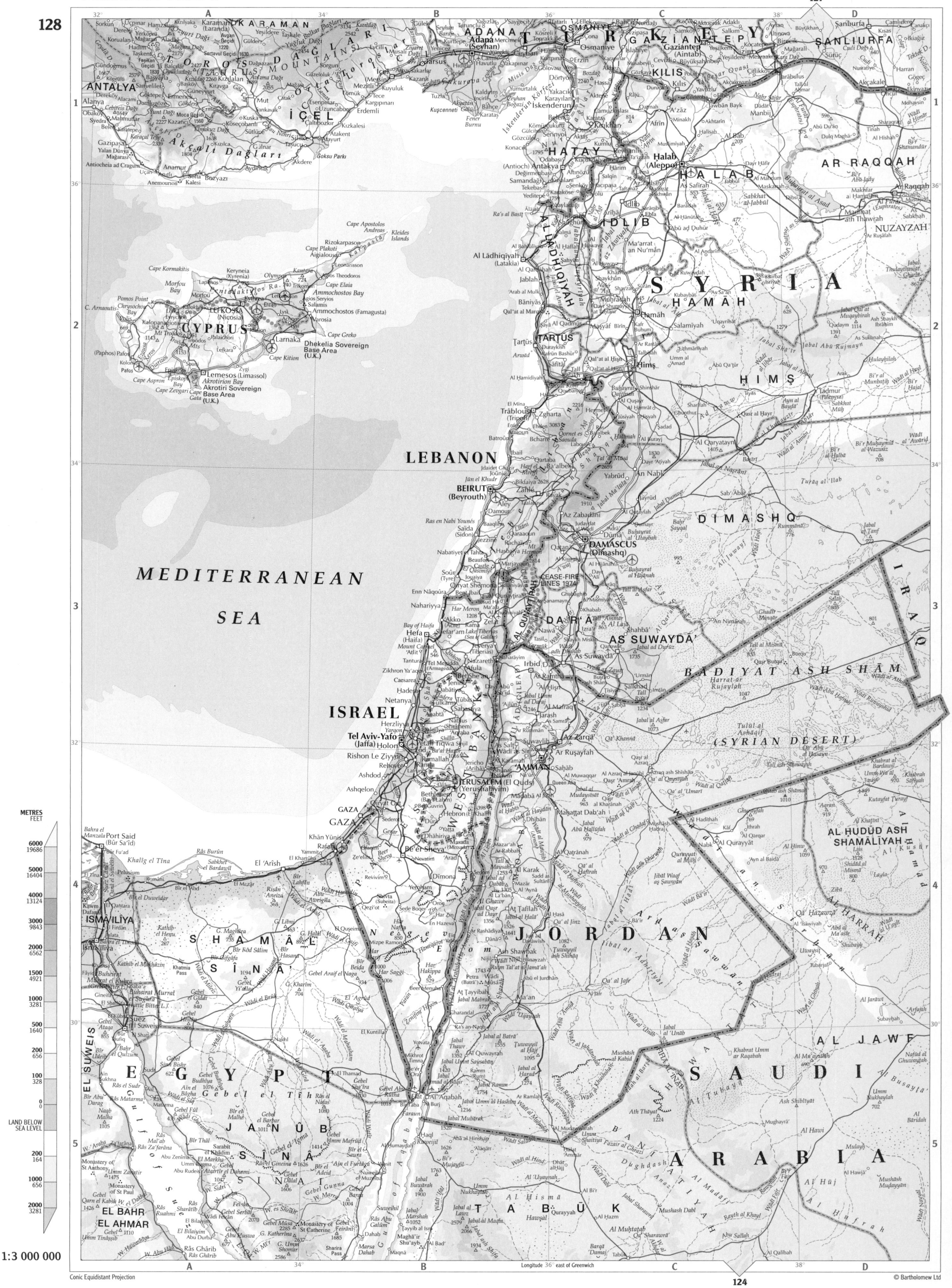
127
124
MEDITERRANEAN SEA
CYPRUS
LEBANON
ISRAEL
SYRIA
JORDAN
SAUDI ARABIA
EGYPT
IRAQ
TURKEY
GAZA
WEST BANK
BEIRUT (Beyrouth)
DAMASCUS (Dimashq)
JERUSALEM (El Quds) (Yerushalayim)
'AMMAN
Tel Aviv-Yafo (Jaffa)
LEFKOSIA (Nicosia)
Halab (Aleppo)
Port Said (Bûr Sa'îd)
Suez (El Suweis)
Al 'Aqabah
Elat
Hims
Hamah
Tarabulus
Trablous (Tripoli)
Sayda (Sidon)
Sour (Tyre)
Hefa (Haifa)
Gulf of Suez
Gulf of Aqaba
SHAMÂL SÎNÂ'
JANÛB SÎNÂ'
BĀDIYAT ASH SHĀM (SYRIAN DESERT)
AL ḤUDŪD ASH SHAMĀLĪYAH
AL JAWF
TABŪK
DIMASHQ
HIMS
HAMĀH
IDLIB
HALAB
AR RAQQAH
HATAY
ADANA
İÇEL
ANTALYA
KILIS
GAZIANTEP
SANLIURFA
AL LĀDHIQĪYAH
TARTUS
DAR'Ā
AS SUWAYDĀ'
AL QUNAYTIRAH
CEASE-FIRE LINES 1974
Dhekelia Sovereign Base Area (U.K.)
Akrotiri Sovereign Base Area (U.K.)
METRES
FEET
6000 19686
5000 16404
4000 13124
3000 9843
2000 6562
1500 4921
1000 3281
500 1640
200 656
100 328
0 0
LAND BELOW SEA LEVEL
200 164
1000 656
2000 3281
Longitude 36° east of Greenwich

1:3 000 000

Conic Equidistant Projection

© Bartholomew Ltd

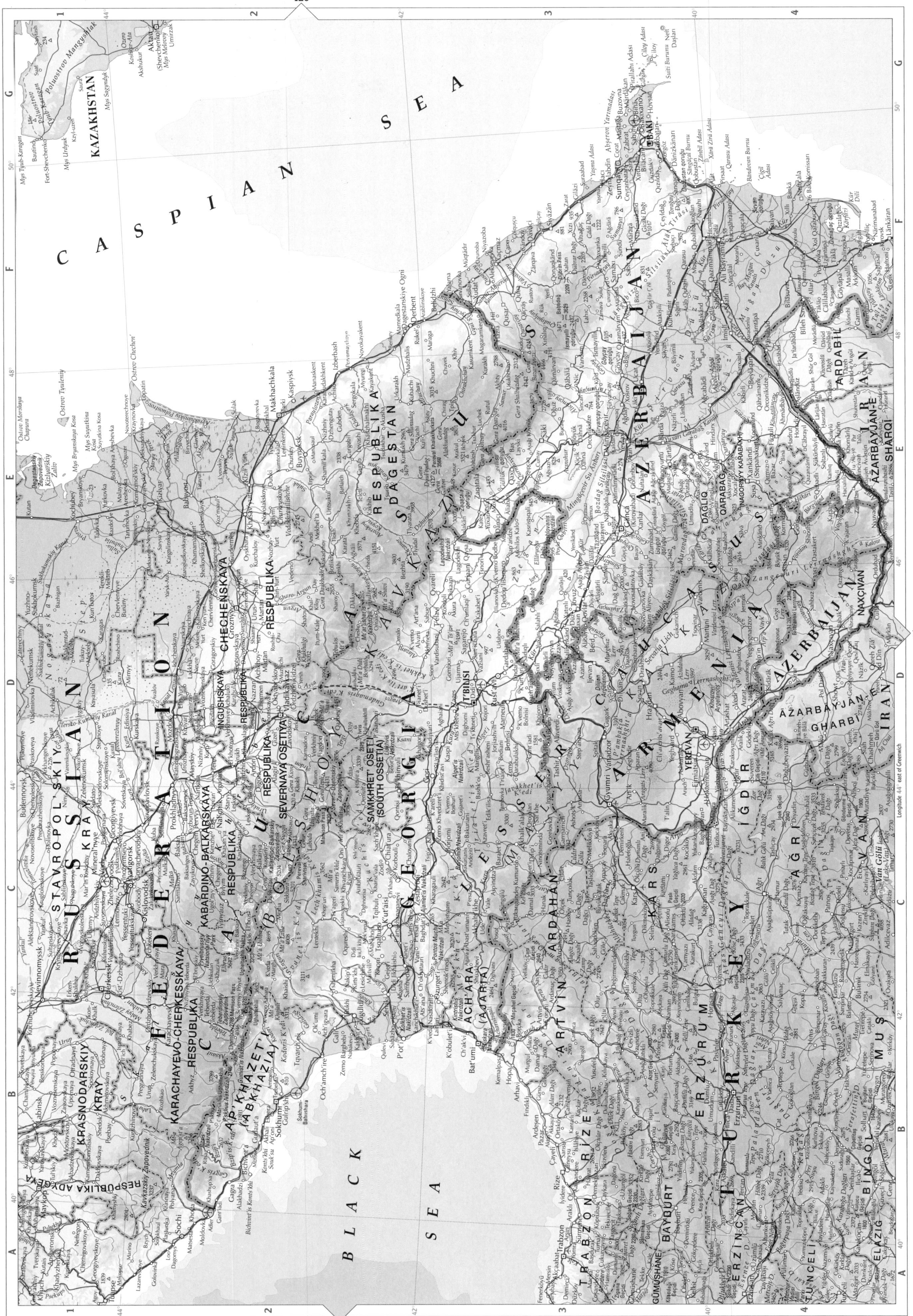
120
127
126
CASPIAN SEA
BLACK SEA
RUSSIAN FEDERATION
GEORGIA
ARMENIA
AZERBAIJAN
TURKEY
IRAN
KAZAKHSTAN
STAVROPOL'SKIY KRAY
KRASNODARSKIY KRAY
RESPUBLIKA DAGESTAN
CHECHENSKAYA RESPUBLIKA
INGUSHSKAYA RESPUBLIKA
RESPUBLIKA SEVERNAYA OSETIYA
KABARDINO-BALKARSKAYA RESPUBLIKA
KARACHAYEVO-CHERKESSKAYA RESPUBLIKA
RESPUBLIKA ADYGEYA
AP'KHAZET'I (ABKHAZIA)
SAMKHRET OSET'I (SOUTH OSSETIA)
ACH'ARA (AJARIA)
NAGORNYY KARABAKH
NAXÇIVAN
ARDABIL
ÄZARBAYJAN-E SHARQI
ÄZARBAYJAN-E GHARBI
TBILISI
YEREVAN
BAKI
Makhachkala
Groznyy
Vladikavkaz
Sokhumi
Bat'umi
Trabzon
Erzurum
Kars
Gäncä
Longitude 44° east of Greenwich

MILES | KILOMETRES

1:3 000 000

© Bartholomew Ltd

Conic Equidistant Projection

167

112

RUSSIAN FEDERATION
MILES
KILOMETRES
1:18 000 000
Longitude 100° east of Greenwich
Laptevykh More (Laptev Sea)
Vostochno-Sibirskoye More (East Siberian Sea)
Chukchi Sea
BERING SEA
SEA OF OKHOTSK (OKHOTSKOYE MORE)
SEA OF JAPAN
EAST CHINA SEA (DONG HAI)
Yellow Sea (Huang Hai)
Bo Hai
Korea Strait
Novosibirskiye Ostrova (New Siberia Islands)
Severnaya Zemlya (North Land)
Poluostrov Taymyr
Severo-Sibirskaya Nizmennost'
SREDNE-SIBIRSKOYE PLOSKOGOR'YE (CENTRAL SIBERIAN PLATEAU)
Verkhoyanskiy Khrebet
Khrebet Cherskogo
Kolymskoye Nagor'ye
Koryakskiy Khrebet
POLUOSTROV KAMCHATKA (KAMCHATKA PENINSULA)
Kuril'skiye Ostrova (Kuril Islands)
Stanovoy Khrebet
Sakhalin
U.S.A.
MONGOLIA
GOBI
CHINA
NORTH KOREA
SOUTH KOREA
JAPAN
Hokkaidō
Honshū
ULAANBAATAR (Ulan Bator)
BEIJING (Peking)
P'YONGYANG
SOUL (Seoul)
TŌKYŌ
Krasnoyarsk
Irkutsk
Yakutsk
Magadan
Khabarovsk
Vladivostok
Harbin
Shenyang
Shanghai
Lanzhou (Lanchow)
Tianjin (Tientsin)
Dalian (Lüda)
Qingdao (Tsingtao)
Sapporo
Sendai
Nagoya
Osaka
Hiroshima
Fukuoka
Petropavlovsk-Kamchatskiy
Yuzhno-Sakhalinsk
Komsomol'sk-na-Amure
Petropavlovsk-Kamchatskiy

© Bartholomew Ltd

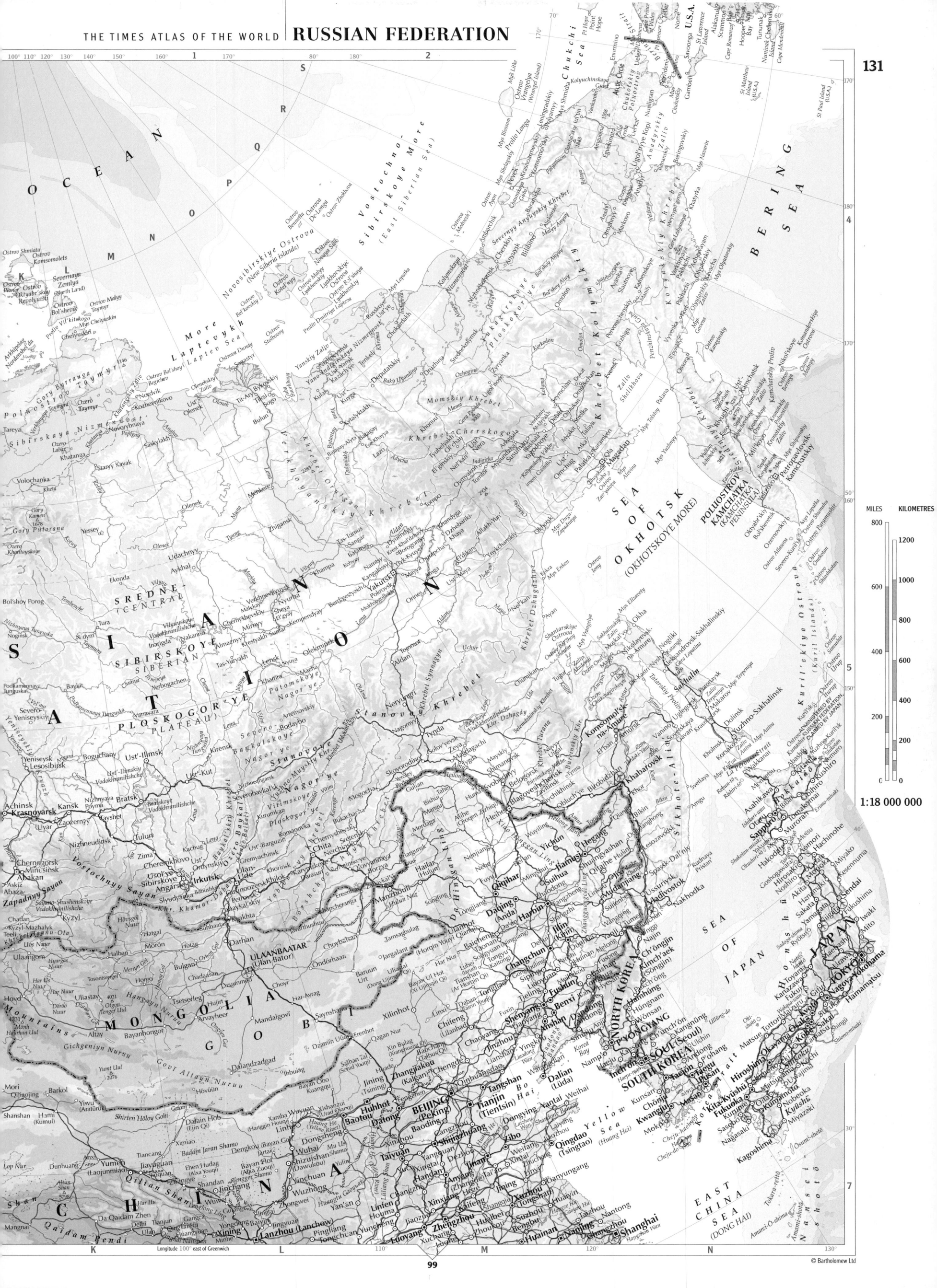

NORTH AMERICA
Greenland
Baffin Bay
Arctic Circle
Greenland Sea
Svalbard
(Norway)
Spitsbergen
Nordaustlandet
Longyearbyen
Zemlya Frantsa-Iosifa
BARENTS SEA
Bjørnøya
(Norway)
Jan Mayen
(Norway)
Denmark Strait
ICELAND
Reykjavík
NORWEGIAN SEA
Nordkapp
NORWAY
SWEDEN
Gulf of Bothnia
Trondheim
Faroe Islands
(Denmark)
Tórshavn
Shetland Islands
Bergen
Oslo
Stockholm
Vänern
Vättern
Orkney Islands
Outer Hebrides
Skagerrak
Kattegat
Göteborg
Ålborg
SCOTLAND
DENMARK
København
Malmö
Odense
Bornholm
Glasgow
Edinburgh
NORTH SEA
NORTHERN IRELAND
Belfast
UNITED KINGDOM
Dublin
REPUBLIC OF IRELAND
Manchester
Liverpool
Leeds
WALES
Birmingham
ENGLAND
Cardiff
London
Hamburg
Bremen
Berlin
Hannover
Bielefeld
NETHERLANDS
Amsterdam
's-Gravenhage
Rotterdam
GERMANY
Essen
Düsseldorf
Köln
Leipzig
Aachen
Bonn
Frankfurt am Main
Bruxelles
Lille
BELGIUM
LUXEMBOURG
Luxembourg
Nürnberg
Mannheim
Stuttgart
München
ATLANTIC OCEAN
English Channel
Channel Islands
Seine
Paris
Strasbourg
Brest
Rennes
Orléans
Loire
Dijon
Zürich
LIECHTENSTEIN
Bern
Innsbruck
SWITZERLAND
Nantes
FRANCE
Genève
Lyon
Milano
Torino
Genova
Bay of Biscay
Bordeaux
Rhône
MONACO
Nice
Toulouse
Marseille
A Coruña
Bilbao
Pyrenees
Andorra la Vella
ANDORRA
Ebro
Corse
Zaragoza
Barcelona
Porto
Salamanca
Madrid
Tajo
SPAIN
PORTUGAL
Menorca
Sardegna
Islas Baleares
Mallorca
Valencia
Eivissa
Lisboa
MEDI
Córdoba
Sevilla
Cartagena
Cádiz
Málaga
Gibraltar (U.K.)
Ceuta (Spain)
Melilla
(Spain)
AF
Corvo
Flores
Arquipélago dos Açores
São Jorge
Faial
Pico
Terceira
Azores
(Portugal)
São Miguel
Ponta Delgada
Santa Maria
Arquipélago da Madeira
Madeira
(Portugal)
Funchal
Ilha de Porto Santo

Orthographic Projection

F
G
H
I
J
1
2
3
4
5
6
7
Karskoye More
Novaya Zemlya
Arctic Circle
Yenisey
Ostrov Kolguyev
Vorkuta
Ural'skiy Khrebet
(Ural Mountains)
Pechora
Ob'
Irtysh
Murmansk
Beloye More
Arkhangel'sk
Severnaya Dvina
Syktyvkar
Perm'
Kirov
Izhevsk
Naberezhnyye Chelny
Ufa
Petrozavodsk
Onezhskoye Ozero
Ladozhskoye Ozero
FINLAND
Tampere
Turku
Helsinki
Sankt-Peterburg
Vologda
Rybinskoye Vodokhranilishche
Volga
Yaroslavl'
Nizhniy Novgorod
Kazan'
Tallinn
Lake Peipus
ESTONIA
Ul'yanovsk
Samara
Orenburg
RUSSIAN FEDERATION
Moskva
Gotland
LATVIA
Riga
Tula
Penza
Öland
Baltic Sea
Smolensk
Saratov
LITHUANIA
Vitsyebsk
Vilnius
Mahilyow
Kaliningrad
RUS. FED.
Minsk
Voronezh
Gdańsk
Hrodna
BELARUS
Homyel'
Belgorod
Don
Volgograd
Białystok
Brest
Chernihiv
Sumy
Kharkiv
Bydgoszcz
POLAND
Wisła
Warszawa
Kyiv
Volga
Astrakhan'
Poznań
Łódź
Rivne
UKRAINE
Dnipropetrovs'k
Donets'k
Rostov-na-Donu
Odra
Wrocław
Katowice
Kraków
L'viv
Dniester (Dnister)
Kirovohrad
Praha
CZECH REPUBLIC
Brno
SLOVAKIA
Košice
Carpathian Mountains
MOLDOVA
Mykolayiv
Dnipro (Dnieper)
Sea of Azov
Stavropol'
Krasnodar
Groznyy
Bratislava
Iaşi
Chişinău
Odesa
Donau (Danube)
Wien
Budapest
Debrecen
Salzburg
AUSTRIA
HUNGARY
Oradea
ROMANIA
Simferopol'
Novorossiysk
Caucasus
Szeged
Braşov
SLOVENIA
Ljubljana
Zagreb
Timişoara
Trieste
CROATIA
Bucureşti
Craiova
Black Sea
Caspian Sea
Zaliv Kara-Bogaz-Gol
Venezia
BOSNIA-HERZEGOVINA
Beograd
Pleven
Varna
Bologna
Sarajevo
Niš
BULGARIA
Burgas
SAN MARINO
Firenze
Split
YUGOSLAVIA
Sofiya
Podgorica
Edirne
İstanbul
Marmara Denizi
Adriatic Sea
Skopje
MACEDONIA
ALBANIA
Tiranë
Thessaloniki
VATICAN CITY
Roma
ITALY
Bari
Napoli
Larisa
Aegean Sea
TURKEY
Tyrrhenian Sea
Cosenza
Ionian Sea
GREECE
Athina
Dodekanisos
Rodos
Palermo
Messina
Sicilia
Siracusa
Cyprus
Kriti
Valletta
MALTA
MEDITERRANEAN SEA
AFRICA
Aral Sea
Ozero Balkhash
Altai Mountains
Tien Shan
Hindu Kush
Nahr Dijlah (Tigris)
Al Furāt (Euphrates)
Kūhhā-ye Zagros (Zagros Mountains)
The Gulf
ASIA
15°
30°
45°
60°
75°
90°
105°

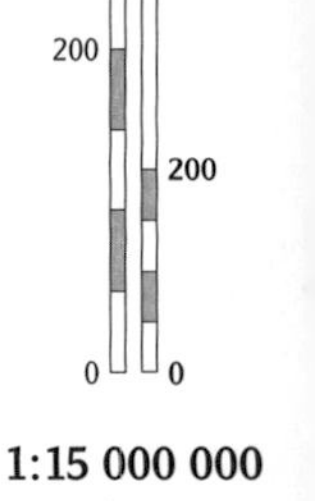
MILES
KILOMETRES
600
400
200
0
1000
800
600
400
200
0

1:15 000 000

© Bartholomew Ltd

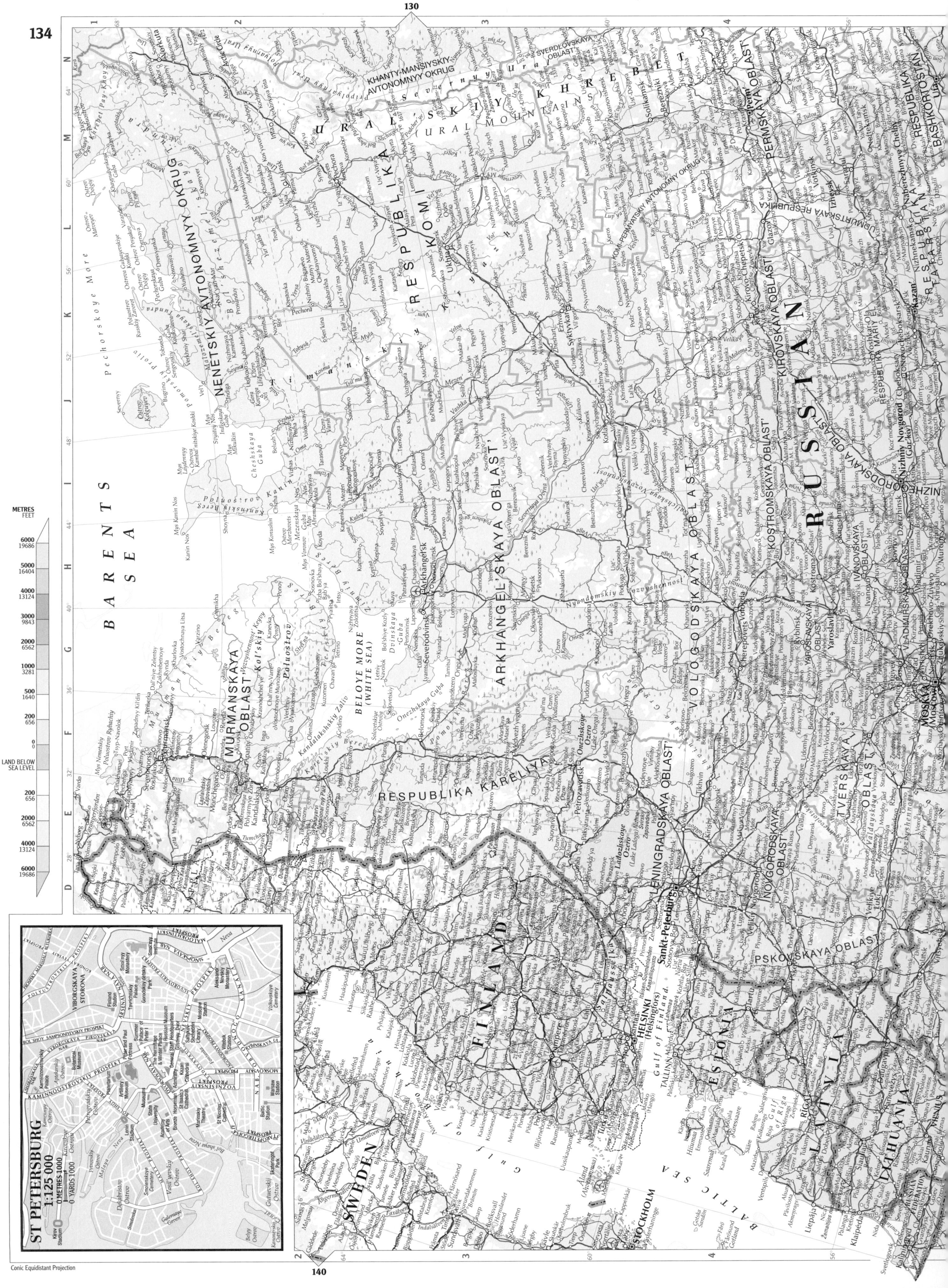
130
140
BARENTS SEA
PECHORSKOYE MORE
BELOYE MORE (WHITE SEA)
BALTIC SEA
Gulf of Finland
Gulf of Riga
RUSSIA
FINLAND
SWEDEN
ESTONIA
LATVIA
LITHUANIA
RESPUBLIKA KOMI
RESPUBLIKA KARELIYA
NENETSKIY AVTONOMNYY OKRUG
KHANTY-MANSIYSKIY AVTONOMNYY OKRUG
KOMI-PERMYATSKIY AVTONOMNYY OKRUG
ARKHANGEL'SKAYA OBLAST'
MURMANSKAYA OBLAST'
VOLOGODSKAYA OBLAST'
LENINGRADSKAYA OBLAST'
NOVGORODSKAYA OBLAST'
PSKOVSKAYA OBLAST'
TVERSKAYA OBLAST'
YAROSLAVSKAYA OBLAST'
KOSTROMSKAYA OBLAST'
KIROVSKAYA OBLAST'
PERMSKAYA OBLAST'
UDMURTSKAYA RESPUBLIKA
RESPUBLIKA TATARSTAN
RESPUBLIKA BASHKORTOSTAN
URAL'SKIY KHREBET (URAL MOUNTAINS)
Timanskiy Kryazh
Sankt-Peterburg
HELSINKI (Helsingfors)
TALLINN
STOCKHOLM
MOSKVA
Arkhangel'sk
Murmansk
Vologda
Petrozavodsk
Syktyvkar
Nizhniy Novgorod (Gor'kiy)
Kazan'
Perm'
METRES
FEET
6000 19686
5000 16404
4000 13124
3000 9843
2000 6562
1000 3281
500 1640
200 656
0 0
LAND BELOW SEA LEVEL
200 656
2000 6562
4000 13124
6000 19686
ST PETERSBURG
1:125 000
0 METRES 1000
0 YARDS 1000

Conic Equidistant Projection

RUSSIAN FEDERATION
KAZAKHSTAN
UKRAINE
BELARUS
POLAND
ROMANIA
MOLDOVA
BULGARIA
TURKEY
GEORGIA
ARMENIA
AZERBAIJAN
TURKMENISTAN
CASPIAN SEA
BLACK SEA
Sea of Azov
Volgograd (Stalingrad)
Rostov-na-Donu
Astrakhan'
Samara (Kuybyshev)
Saratov
Voronezh
Kharkiv
Dnipropetrovs'k
Kyyiv (Kiev)
Odesa
Chişinău
Bucureşti (Bucharest)
İstanbul
Krasnodar
Stavropol'
Makhachkala
T'bilisi
Baki
Administrative divisions in Russian Federation numbered on the map:
1. INGUSHSKAYA RESPUBLIKA (18)
2. RESPUBLIKA SEVERNAYA OSETIYA (18)
Longitude 40° east of Greenwich
120
122
126
175

MILES | KILOMETRES

1:7 200 000

© Bartholomew Ltd

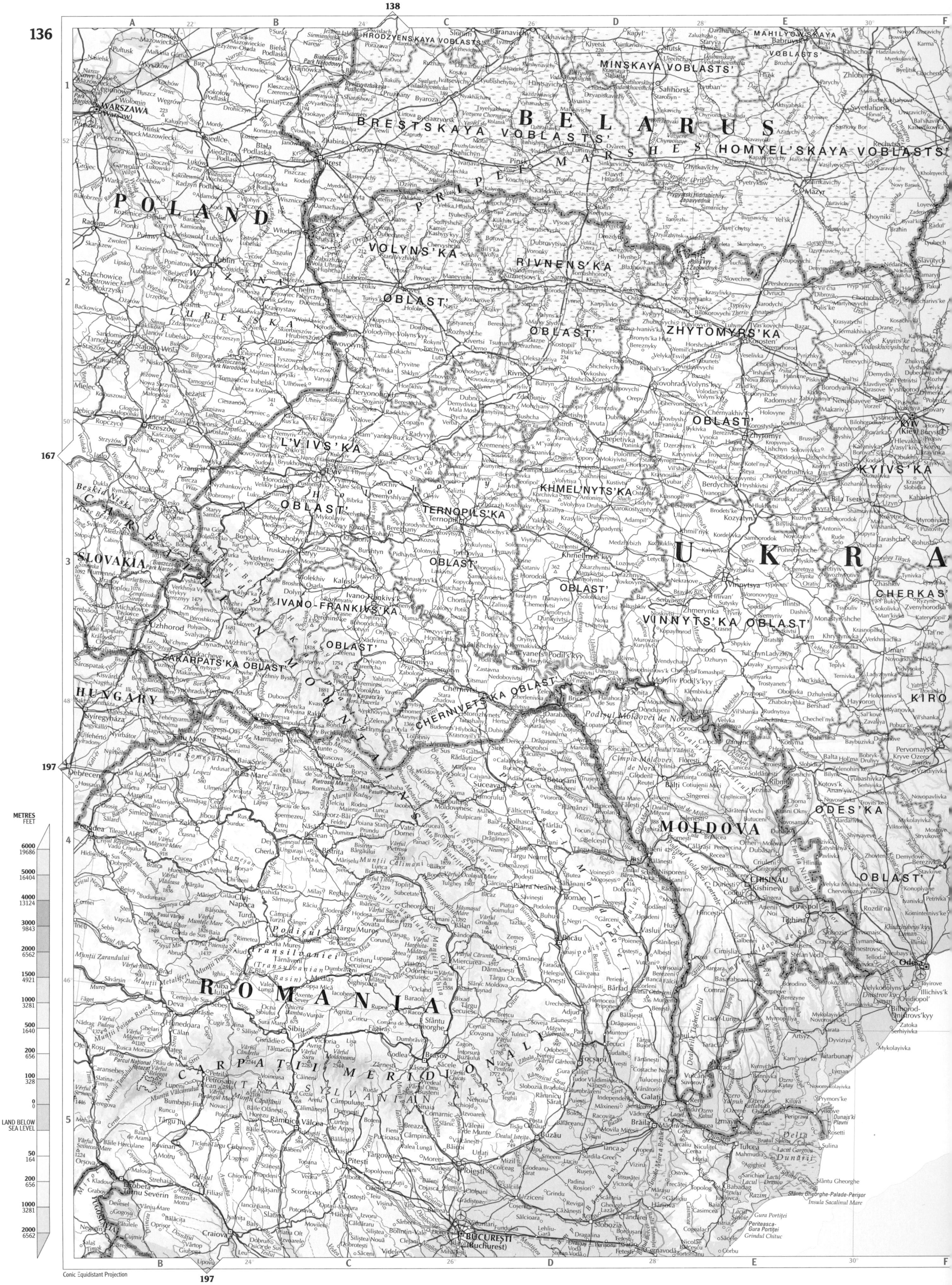
138
POLAND
BELARUS
UKRA
SLOVAKIA
HUNGARY
ROMANIA
MOLDOVA
HRODZYENSKAYA VOBLASTS'
MINSKAYA VOBLASTS'
MAHILYOWSKAYA VOBLASTS'
BRESTSKAYA VOBLASTS'
HOMYEL'SKAYA VOBLASTS'
PRIPET MARSHES
VOLYNS'KA OBLAST'
RIVNENS'KA OBLAST'
ZHYTOMYRS'KA OBLAST'
KYIVS'KA
L'VIVS'KA OBLAST'
TERNOPILS'KA OBLAST'
KHMEL'NYTS'KA OBLAST'
IVANO-FRANKIVS'KA OBLAST'
ZAKARPATS'KA OBLAST'
CHERNIVETS'KA OBLAST'
VINNYTS'KA OBLAST'
CHERKAS'
KIRO
ODES'KA OBLAST'
CARPATHIAN MOUNTAINS
CARPAŢII MERIDIONALI
WARSZAWA (Warsaw)
KYIV (Kiev)
CHIŞINĂU (Kishinev)
BUCUREŞTI (Bucharest)
Odesa
167
197
METRES FEET
6000 19686
5000 16404
4000 13124
3000 9843
2000 6562
1500 4921
1000 3281
500 1640
200 656
100 328
0 0
LAND BELOW SEA LEVEL
50 164
200 656
1000 3281
2000 6562
Conic Equidistant Projection
197

139
135
RUSSIAN FEDERATION
BRYANSKAYA OBLAST'
ORLOVSKAYA OBLAST'
LIPETSKAYA OBLAST'
TAMBOVSKAYA OBLAST'
KURSKAYA OBLAST'
VORONEZHSKAYA OBLAST'
BELGORODSKAYA OBLAST'
CHERNIHIVS'KA OBLAST'
SUMS'KA OBLAST'
POLTAVS'KA OBLAST'
KHARKIVS'KA OBLAST'
LUHANS'KA OBLAST'
DONETS'KA OBLAST'
DNIPROPETROVS'KA OBLAST'
ZAPORIZ'KA OBLAST'
KHERSONS'KA OBLAST'
MYKOLAYIVS'KA OBLAST'
ROSTOVSKAYA OBLAST'
KRASNODARSKIY KRAY
RESPUBLIKA KRYM
Krymskyy Pivostriv
Sea of Azov
Gulf of Taganrog
BLACK SEA
Kyiv
Kharkiv
Dnipropetrovs'k
Zaporizhzhya
Donets'k
Luhans'k
Mariupol'
Rostov-na-Donu
Krasnodar
Simferopol'
Sevastopol'
Kherson
Mykolayiv
Kirovohrad
Poltava
Sumy
Belgorod
Kursk
Voronezh
Orel
Lipetsk
Kerch
Novorossiysk
Longitude 32° east of Greenwich

MILES | KILOMETRES

1:3 000 000

© Bartholomew Ltd

141
GULF OF BOTHNIA
FINLAND
LÄNSI-SUOMI
ETELÄ-SUOMI
HELSINKI (Helsingfors)
GULF OF FINLAND
SWEDEN
UPPSALA
STOCKHOLM
143
GOTLAND
Gotland (Sweden)
BALTIC SEA
Hiiumaa
Saaremaa
ESTONIA
TALLINN
Lake Peipus
Lake Pskov
GULF OF RIGA
LATVIA
RIGA
PSKOVSKAYA OBL
LITHUANIA
VILNIUS
Gulf of Gdańsk
RUSSIAN FEDERATION
KALININGRADSKAYA OBLAST'
VITSYEBSKAYA VOBLASTS
MINSKAYA VOBLASTS'
MINSK
BELARUS
HRODZYENSKAYA VOBLASTS'
BRESTSKAYA VOBLASTS
POLAND
POJEZIERZE MAZURSKIE
NIZINA MAZOWIECKA
WARSZAWA (Warsaw)
167
136
METRES
FEET
6000 19686
5000 16404
4000 13124
3000 9843
2000 6562
1500 4921
1000 3281
500 1640
200 656
100 328
0 0
LAND BELOW SEA LEVEL
50 164
200 656
1000 3281
2000 6562

Conic Equidistant Projection

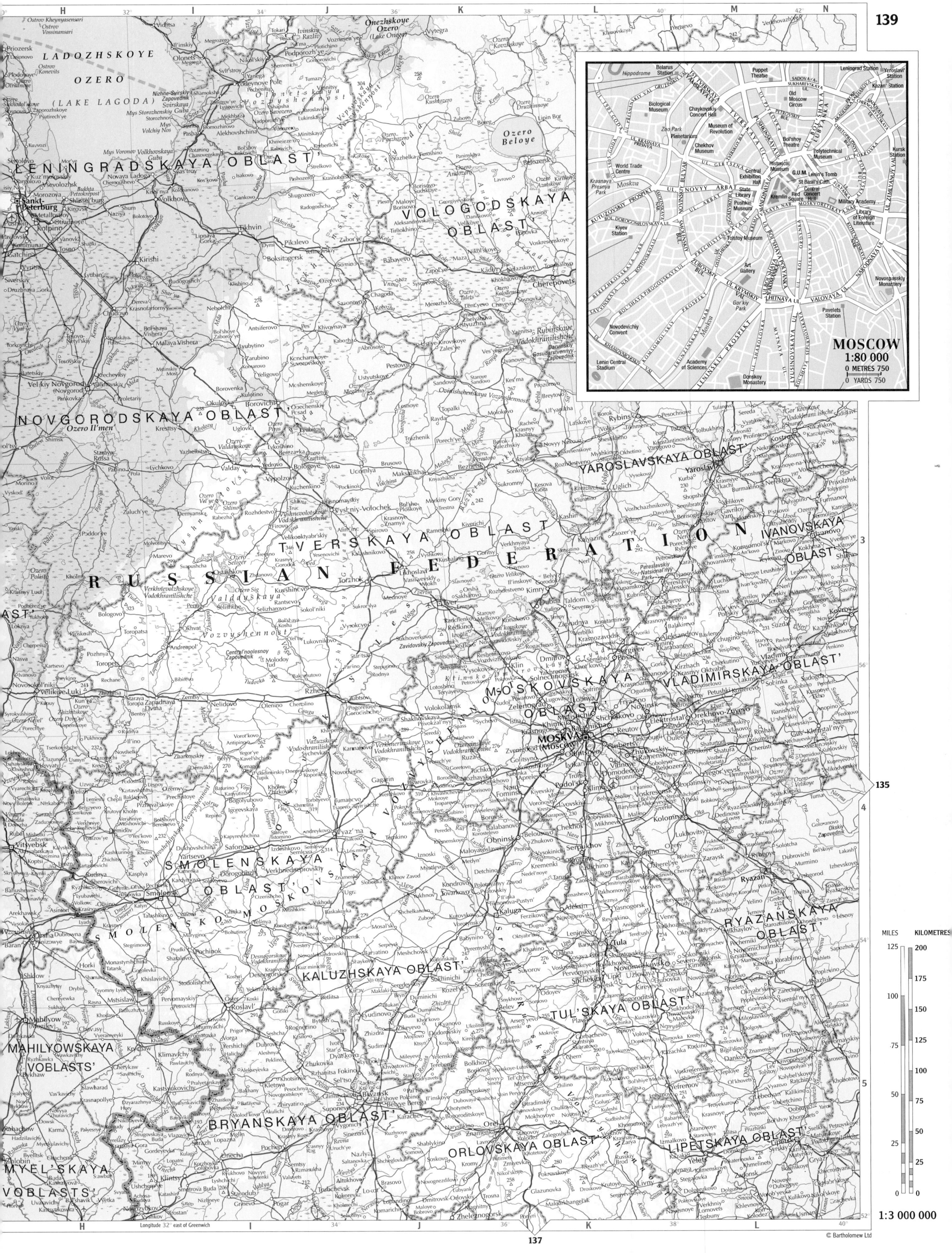
MOSCOW
1:80 000
0 METRES 750
0 YARDS 750
RUSSIAN FEDERATION
LENINGRADSKAYA OBLAST'
VOLOGODSKAYA OBLAST'
NOVGORODSKAYA OBLAST'
TVERSKAYA OBLAST
YAROSLAVSKAYA OBLAST'
IVANOVSKAYA OBLAST'
VLADIMIRSKAYA OBLAST'
MOSKOVSKAYA OBLAST'
SMOLENSKAYA OBLAST'
KALUZHSKAYA OBLAST'
TUL'SKAYA OBLAST'
RYAZANSKAYA OBLAST'
BRYANSKAYA OBLAST'
ORLOVSKAYA OBLAST'
LIPETSKAYA OBLAST'
MAHILYOWSKAYA VOBLASTS'
LADOZHSKOYE OZERO (LAKE LAGODA)
Onezhskoye Ozero (Lake Onega)
Ozero Beloye
Ozero Il'men
MOSKVA (Moscow)
Sankt-Peterburg
MILES
KILOMETRES
1:3 000 000
Longitude 32° east of Greenwich

135

137

© Bartholomew Ltd

138

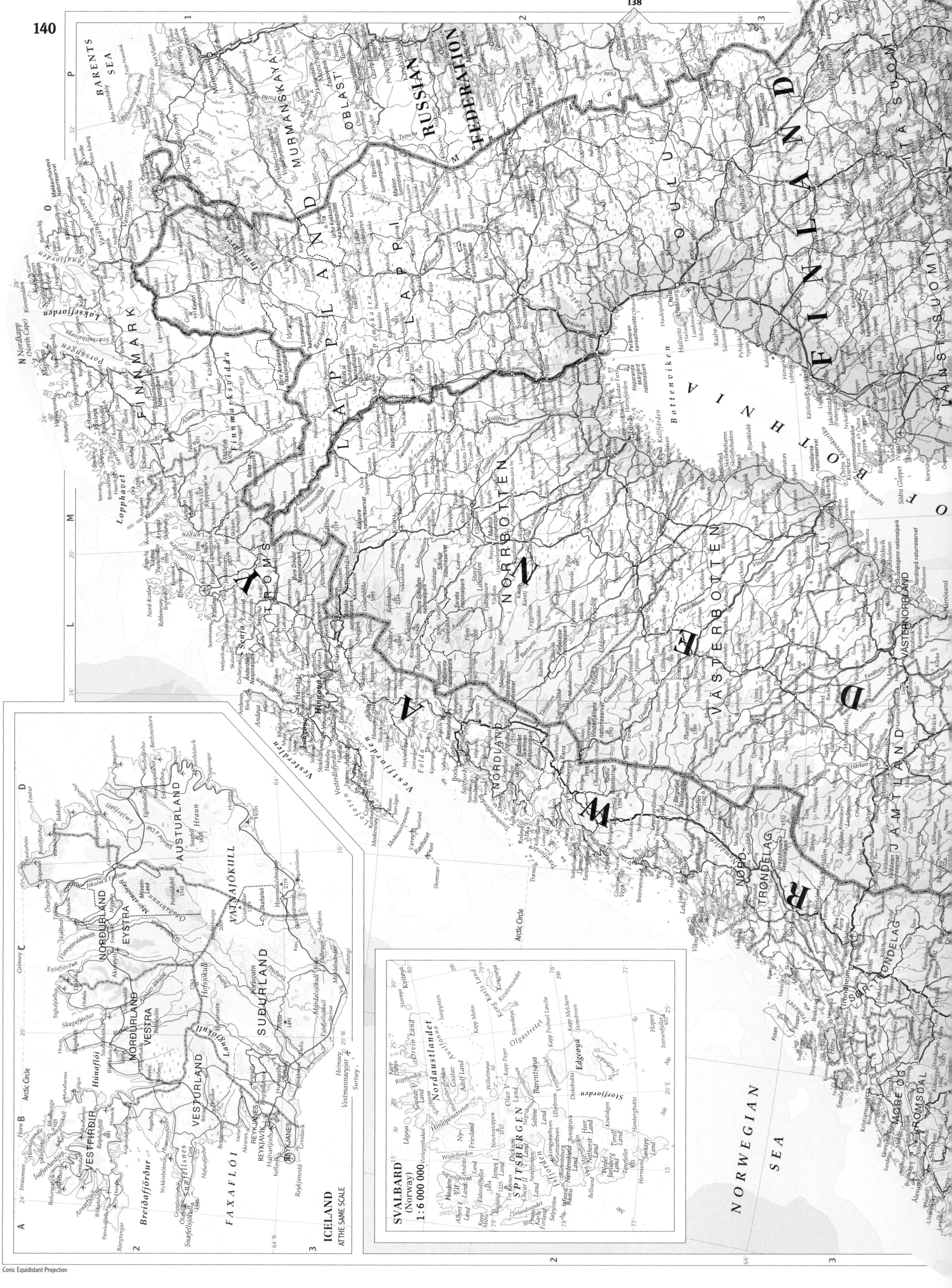
BARENTS SEA
NORWEGIAN SEA
FINNMARK
TROMS
NORDLAND
NORRBOTTEN
VÄSTERBOTTEN
JÄMTLAND
VÄSTERNORRLAND
NORD-TRØNDELAG
SØR-TRØNDELAG
MØRE OG ROMSDAL
LAPPI
OULU
MURMANSKAYA OBLAST'
RUSSIAN FEDERATION
FINLAND
SUOMI
Bottenviken
Arctic Circle
Lofoten
Vesterålen
ICELAND
AT THE SAME SCALE
VESTFIRÐIR
NORÐURLAND VESTRA
NORÐURLAND EYSTRA
AUSTURLAND
SUÐURLAND
VESTURLAND
REYKJANES
REYKJAVÍK
VATNAJÖKULL
FAXAFLÓI
Breiðafjörður
Húnaflói
SVALBARD
(Norway)
1:6 000 000
Nordaustlandet
SPITSBERGEN
Edgeøya
Barentsøya
Storfjorden
Longyearbyen

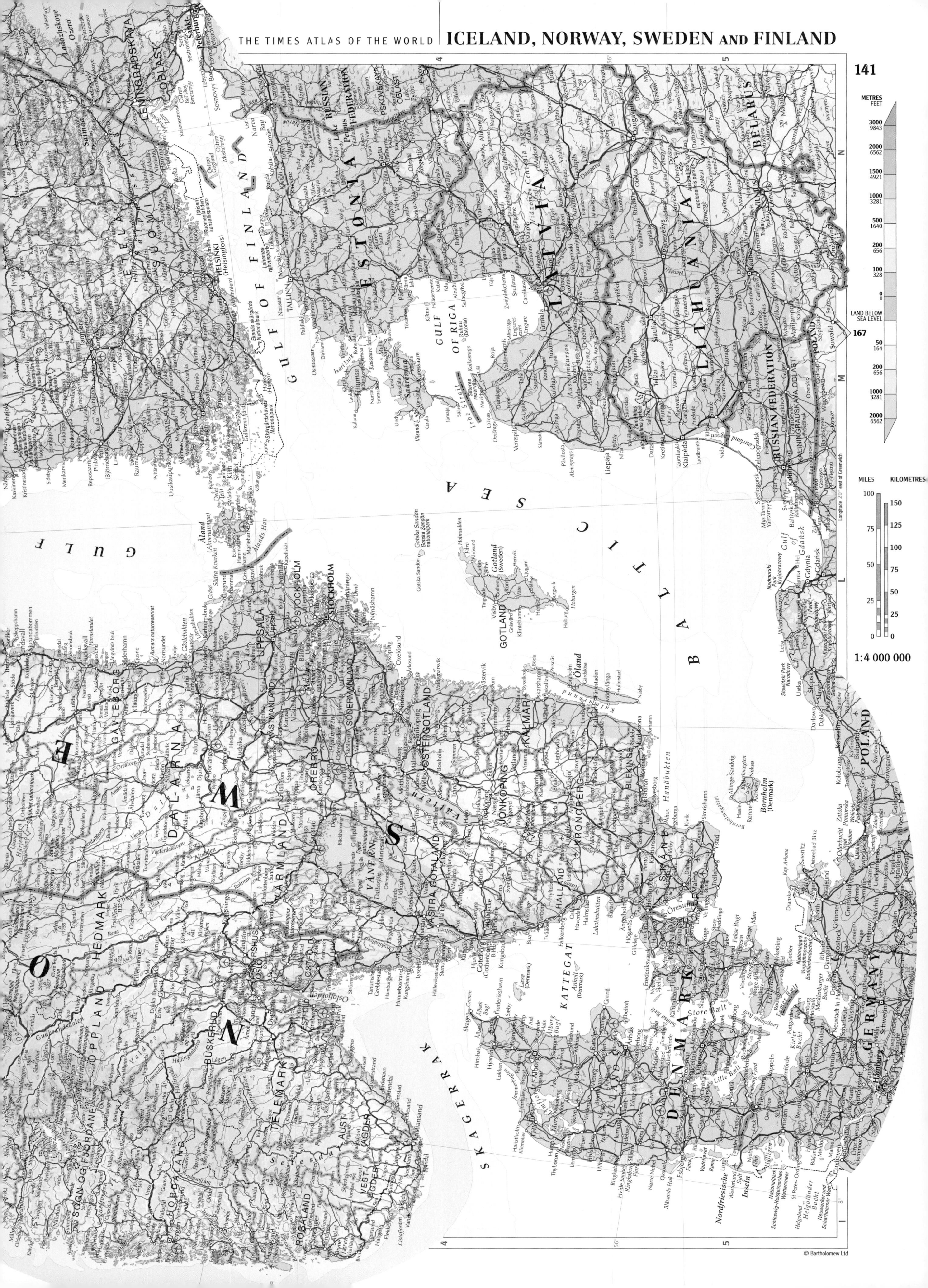
GULF OF FINLAND
GULF OF RIGA
BALTIC SEA
SKAGERRAK
KATTEGAT
ESTONIA
LATVIA
LITHUANIA
RUSSIAN FEDERATION
BELARUS
POLAND
GERMANY
DENMARK
SWEDEN
NORWAY
SUOMI
HELSINKI (Helsingfors)
TALLINN
STOCKHOLM
OSLO
KØBENHAVN
METRES
FEET
3000 9843
2000 6562
1500 4921
1000 3281
500 1640
200 656
100 328
0 0
LAND BELOW SEA LEVEL
50 164
200 656
1000 3281
2000 6562
167
MILES
KILOMETRES
1:4 000 000

© Bartholomew Ltd

Conic Equidistant Projection

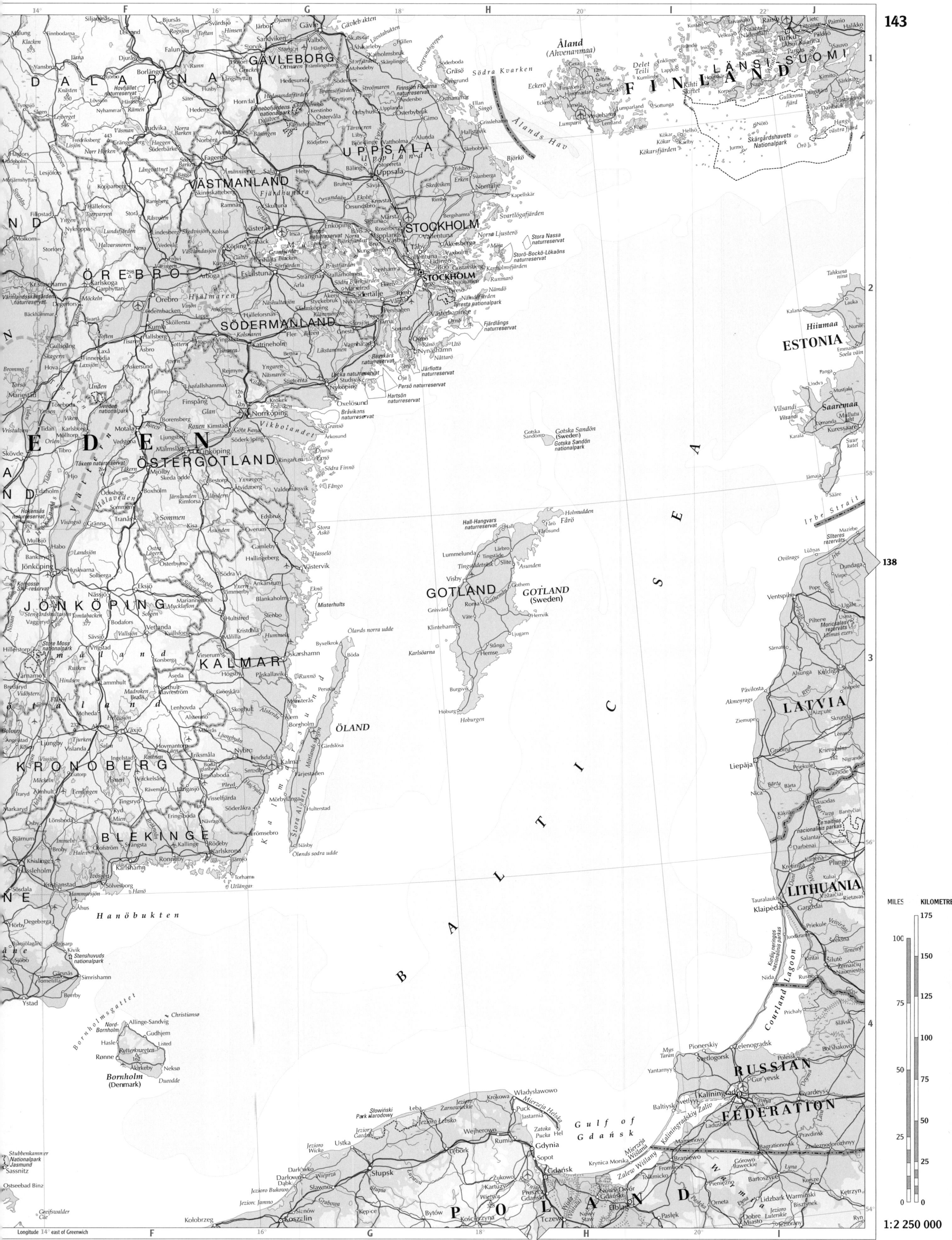
GÄVLEBORG
DALARNA
UPPSALA
VÄSTMANLAND
ÖREBRO
SÖDERMANLAND
STOCKHOLM
ÖSTERGÖTLAND
JÖNKÖPING
KALMAR
KRONOBERG
BLEKINGE
GOTLAND
GOTLAND (Sweden)
ÖLAND
Åland (Ahvenanmaa)
LÄNSI-SUOMI
FINLAND
Hiiumaa
ESTONIA
Saaremaa
LATVIA
LITHUANIA
RUSSIAN FEDERATION
POLAND
Bornholm (Denmark)
BALTIC SEA
Ålands Hav
Södra Kvarken
Gulf of Gdańsk
Hanöbukten
Irbe Strait
Courland Lagoon
Gotska Sandön (Sweden)
Gävle
Uppsala
Västerås
Örebro
Norrköping
Linköping
Jönköping
Växjö
Kalmar
Karlskrona
Nyköping
Visby
Stockholm
Kaliningrad
Klaipėda
Liepāja
Ventspils
Gdańsk
Gdynia
Sopot
Elbląg
Słupsk
Rønne
Ystad
Simrishamn
Kristianstad
Mariehamn
Turku (Åbo)
Miles
Kilometres
1:2 250 000
138
175
Longitude 14° east of Greenwich

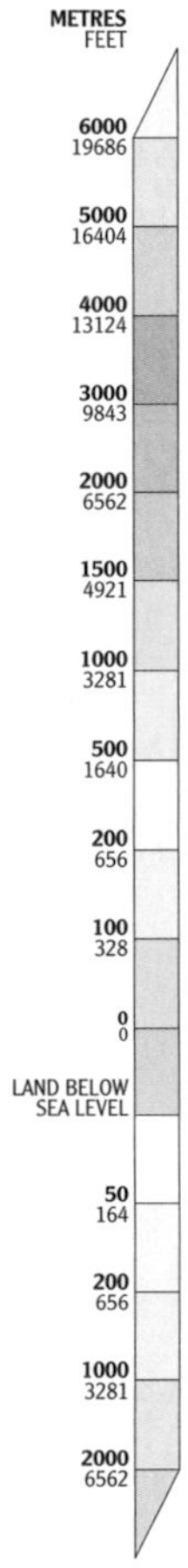
METRES
FEET
6000
19686
5000
16404
4000
13124
3000
9843
2000
6562
1500
4921
1000
3281
500
1640
200
656
100
328
0
0
LAND BELOW SEA LEVEL
50
164
200
656
1000
3281
2000
6562

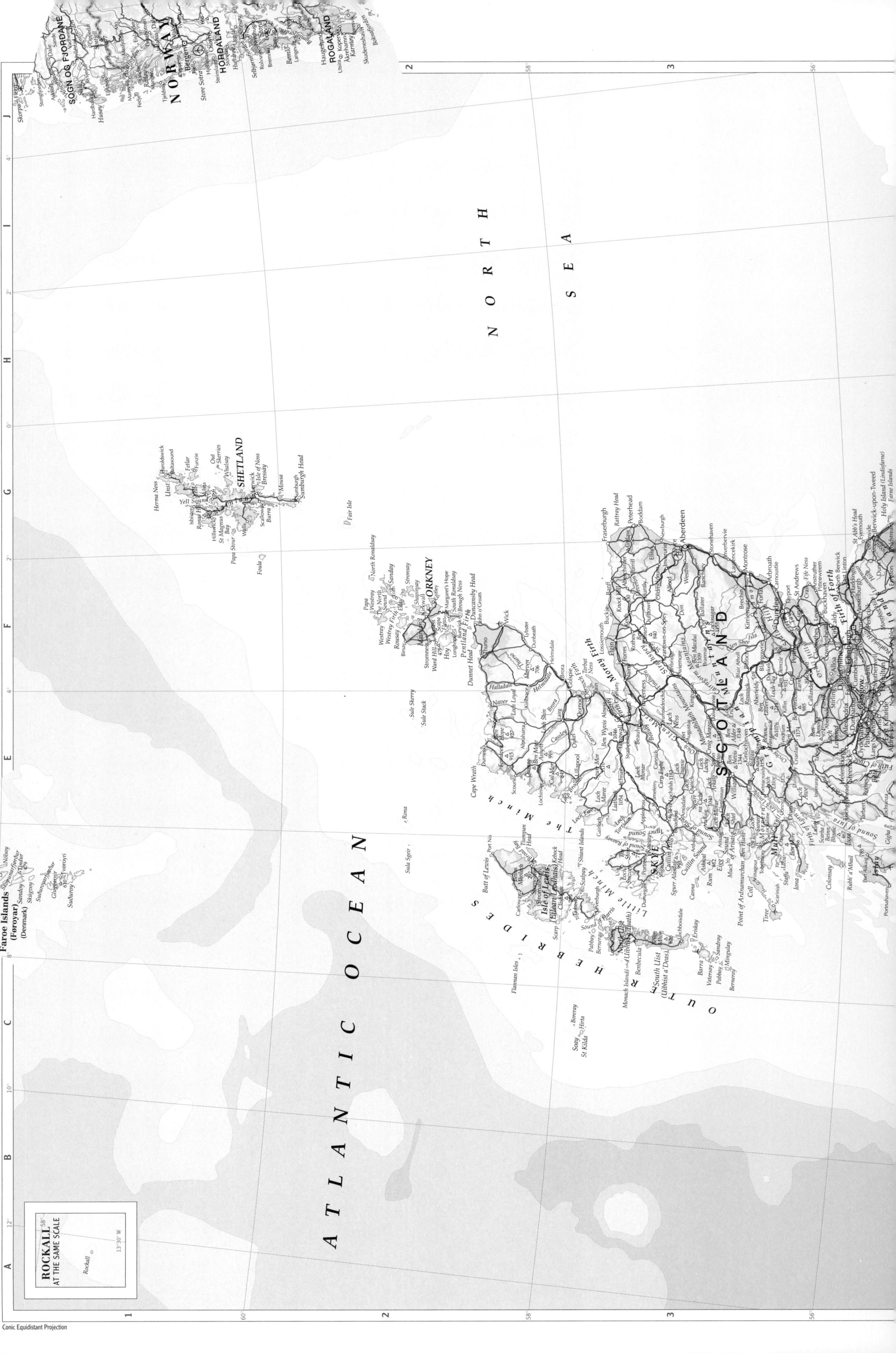
ATLANTIC OCEAN
NORTH SEA
NORWAY
SOGN OG FJORDANE
HORDALAND
ROGALAND
Bergen
Haugesund
SHETLAND
Unst
Yell Sound
Fair Isle
Foula
ORKNEY
Kirkwall
Stromness
Pentland Firth
Sule Skerry
Sule Stack
Rona
Sula Sgeir
Faroe Islands (Føroyar) (Denmark)
TÓRSHAVN
Suðuroy
SCOTLAND
Aberdeen
Dundee
Edinburgh
Glasgow
Inverness
Moray Firth
Firth of Forth
Cape Wrath
Butt of Lewis
The Minch
Little Minch
Isle of Lewis (Eilean Leodhais)
SKYE
Mull
Islay
OUTER HEBRIDES
South Uist (Uibhist a'Deas)
Barra
Flannan Isles
St Kilda
Hirta
Soay
Boreray
ROCKALL AT THE SAME SCALE
Rockall
13°30' W

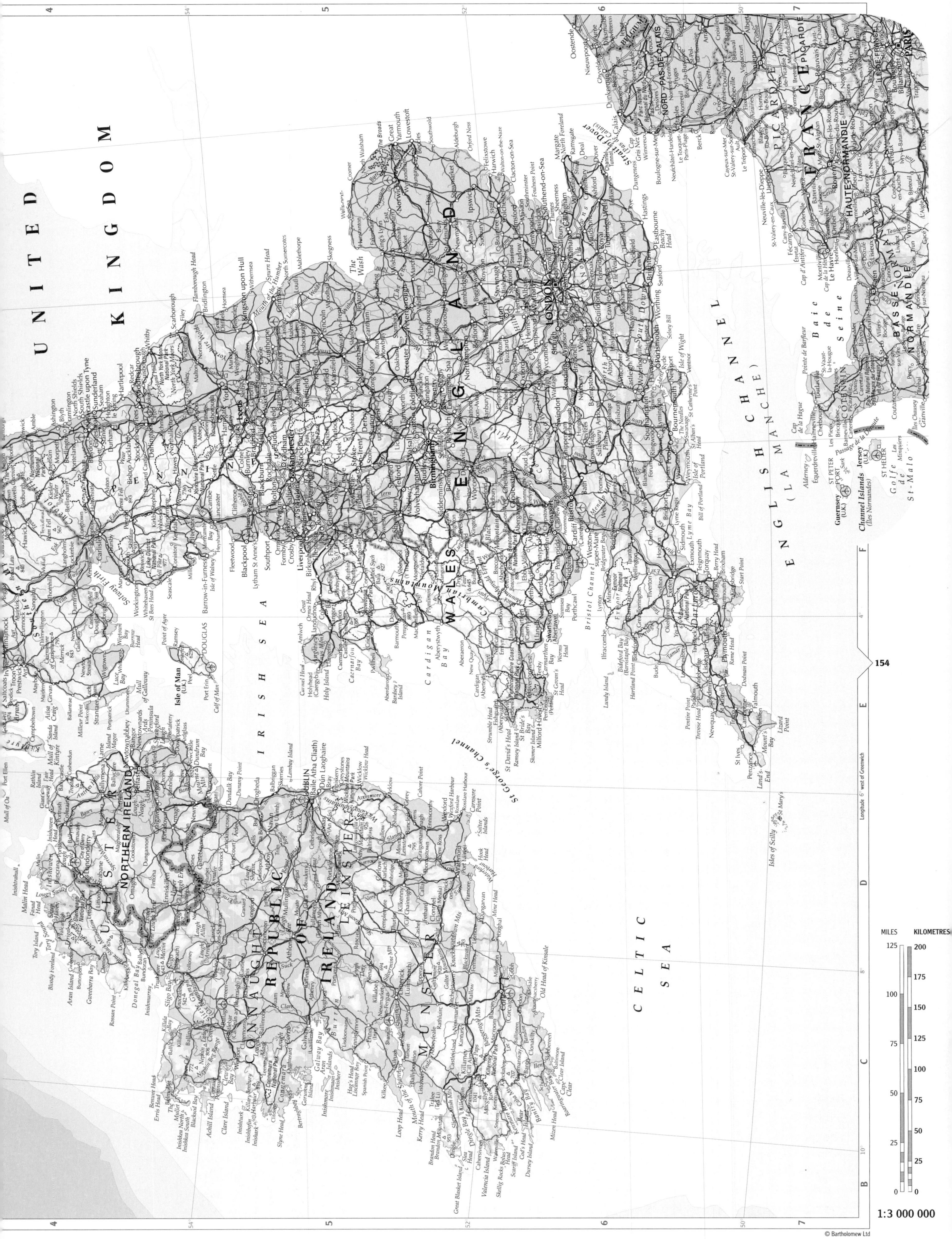
UNITED KINGDOM
IRISH SEA
CELTIC SEA
ENGLISH CHANNEL
(LA MANCHE)
ENGLAND
WALES
NORTHERN IRELAND
REPUBLIC OF IRELAND
ULSTER
CONNAUGHT
LEINSTER
MUNSTER
FRANCE
LONDON
DUBLIN
154
MILES
KILOMETRES
1:3 000 000

© Bartholomew Ltd

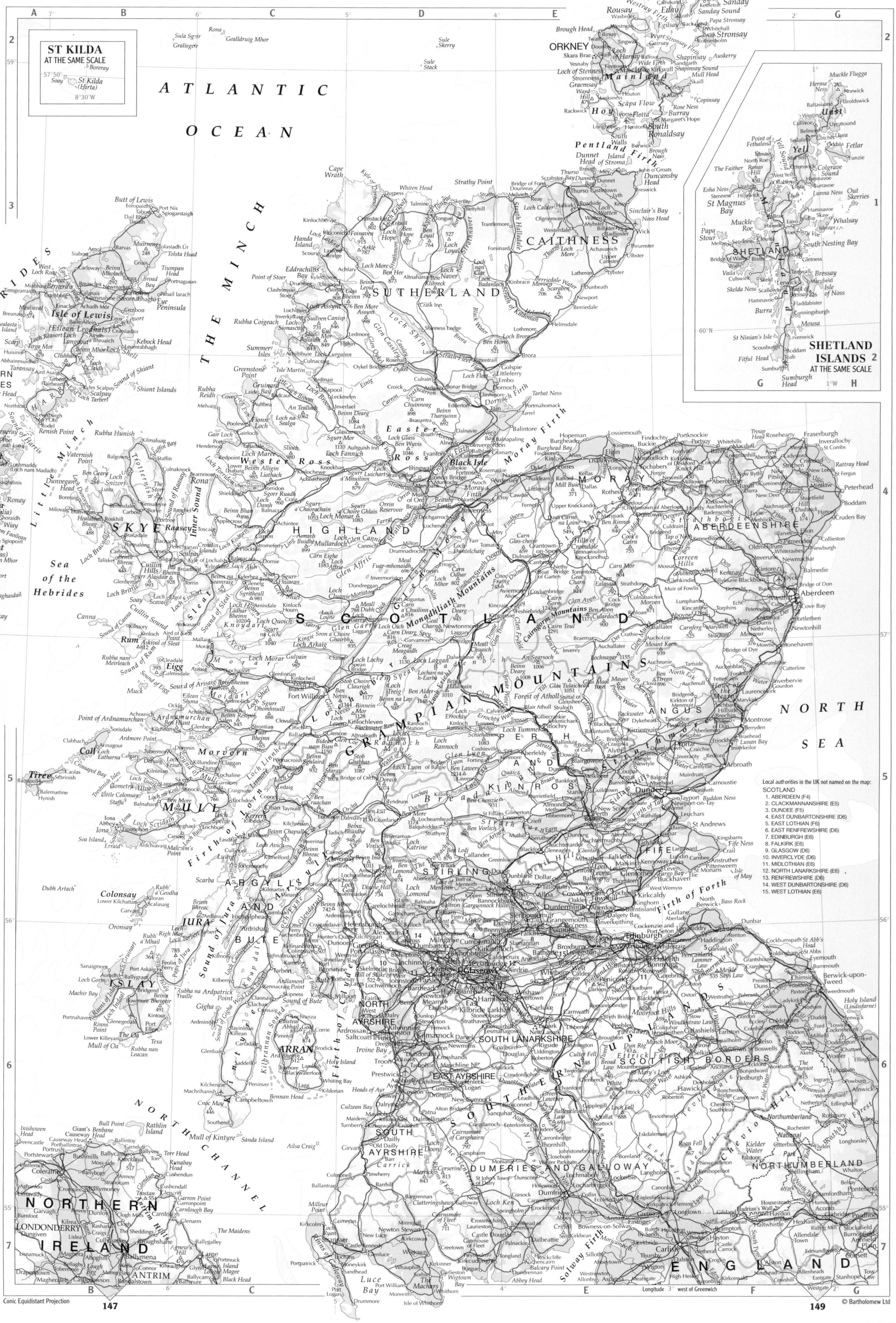
ST KILDA
AT THE SAME SCALE
ATLANTIC OCEAN
ORKNEY
Mainland
Pentland Firth
THE MINCH
OUTER HEBRIDES
WESTERN ISLES
Isle of Lewis
CAITHNESS
SUTHERLAND
SHETLAND ISLANDS
AT THE SAME SCALE
SHETLAND
Unst
Yell
HIGHLAND
SKYE
Sea of the Hebrides
Little Minch
Moray Firth
MORAY
ABERDEENSHIRE
SCOTLAND
GRAMPIAN MOUNTAINS
Cairngorm Mountains
Monadhliath Mountains
ANGUS
NORTH SEA
PERTH AND KINROSS
MULL
ARGYLL AND BUTE
JURA
ISLAY
ARRAN
FIFE
Firth of Forth
STIRLING
SOUTH LANARKSHIRE
NORTH AYRSHIRE
EAST AYRSHIRE
SOUTH AYRSHIRE
SCOTTISH BORDERS
SOUTHERN UPLANDS
DUMFRIES AND GALLOWAY
Solway Firth
NORTHUMBERLAND
ENGLAND
NORTHERN IRELAND
NORTH CHANNEL
Mull of Kintyre
ANTRIM
LONDONDERRY
Edinburgh
Glasgow
Aberdeen
Dundee
Inverness
Carlisle
METRES
FEET
6000 19686
5000 16404
4000 13124
3000 9843
2000 6562
1500 4921
1000 3281
500 1640
200 656
100 328
0 0
LAND BELOW SEA LEVEL
50 164
200 656
1000 3281
2000 6562
Local authorities in the UK not named on the map:
SCOTLAND
1. ABERDEEN (F4)
2. CLACKMANNANSHIRE (E5)
3. DUNDEE (F5)
4. EAST DUNBARTONSHIRE (D6)
5. EAST LOTHIAN (F6)
6. EAST RENFREWSHIRE (D6)
7. EDINBURGH (E6)
8. FALKIRK (E6)
9. GLASGOW (D6)
10. INVERCLYDE (D6)
11. MIDLOTHIAN (E6)
12. NORTH LANARKSHIRE (E6)
13. RENFREWSHIRE (D6)
14. WEST DUNBARTONSHIRE (D6)
15. WEST LOTHIAN (E6)
Longitude 3° west of Greenwich

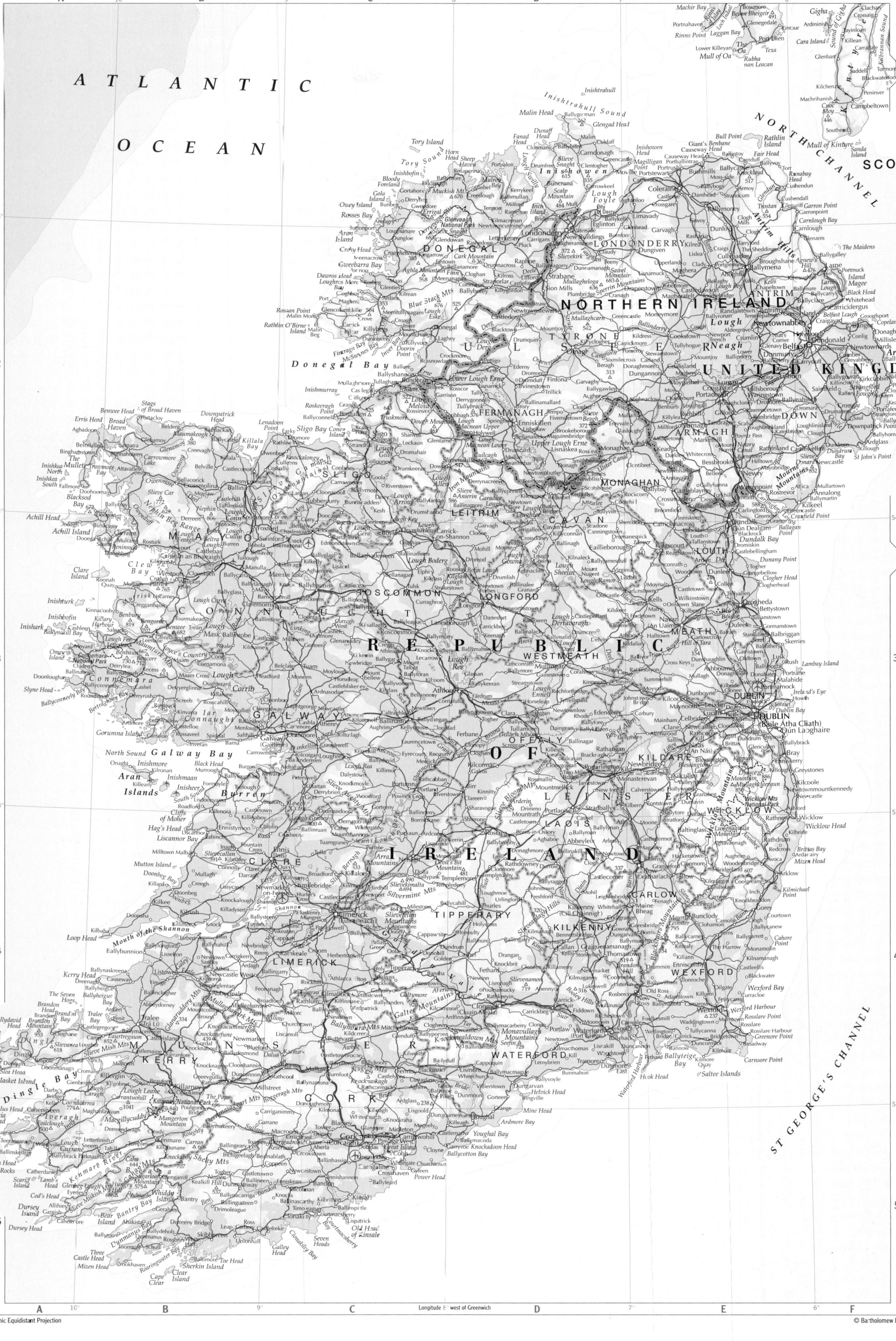
ATLANTIC
OCEAN
NORTH CHANNEL
SCOTLAND
ST GEORGE'S CHANNEL
NORTHERN IRELAND
UNITED KINGDOM
REPUBLIC
OF
IRELAND
ULSTER
CONNAUGHT
LEINSTER
MUNSTER
DONEGAL
LONDONDERRY
ANTRIM
TYRONE
FERMANAGH
ARMAGH
DOWN
MONAGHAN
CAVAN
LEITRIM
SLIGO
MAYO
ROSCOMMON
LONGFORD
LOUTH
MEATH
WESTMEATH
GALWAY
OFFALY
KILDARE
DUBLIN
WICKLOW
LAOIS
CARLOW
KILKENNY
WEXFORD
TIPPERARY
CLARE
LIMERICK
KERRY
CORK
WATERFORD
Donegal Bay
Galway Bay
Dingle Bay
Aran Islands
Ards Peninsula
Mull of Kintyre
Mull of Galloway
Longitude 8° west of Greenwich
146
148
MILES
KILOMETRES
1:1 500 000

© Bartholomew Ltd

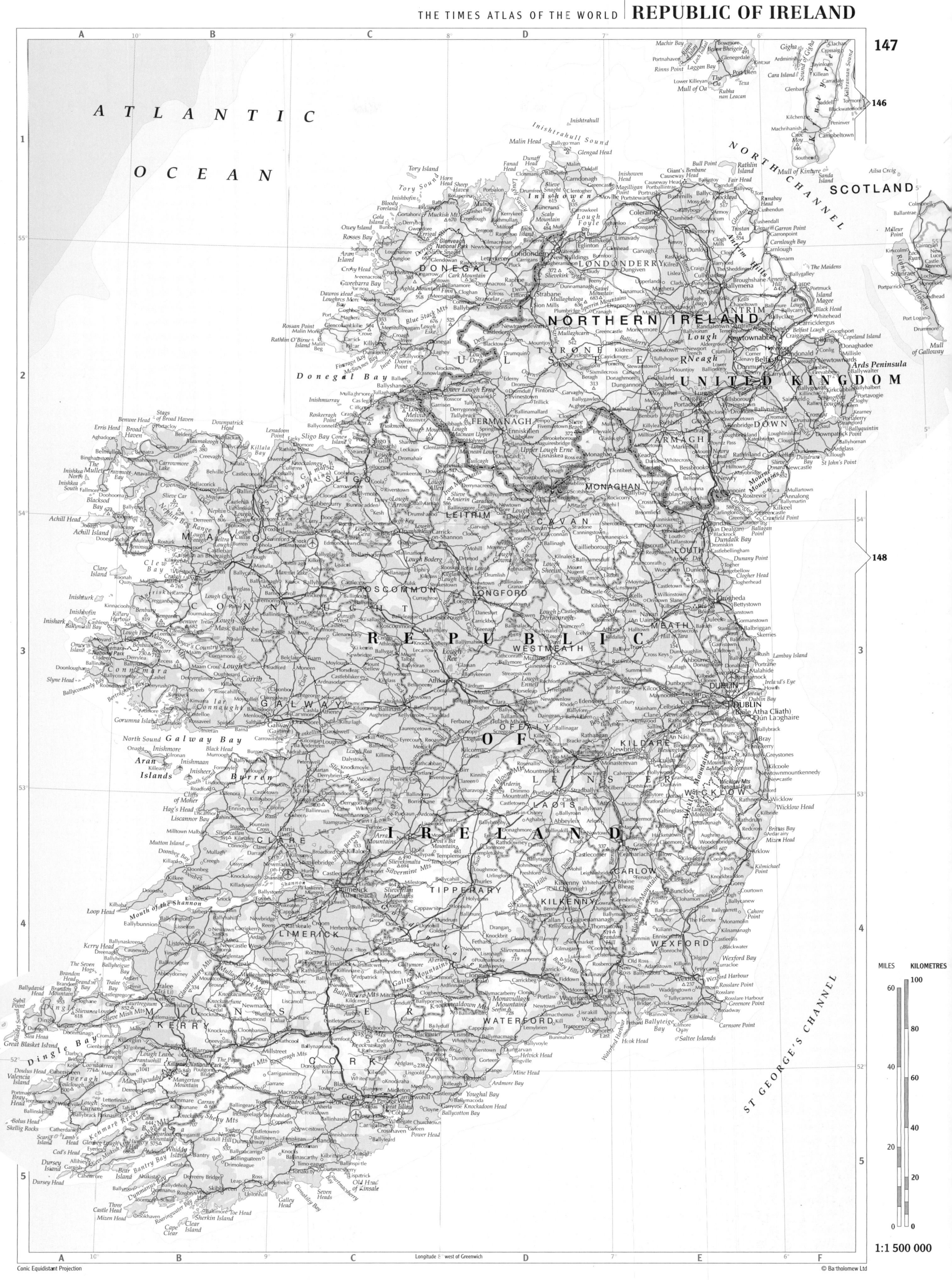

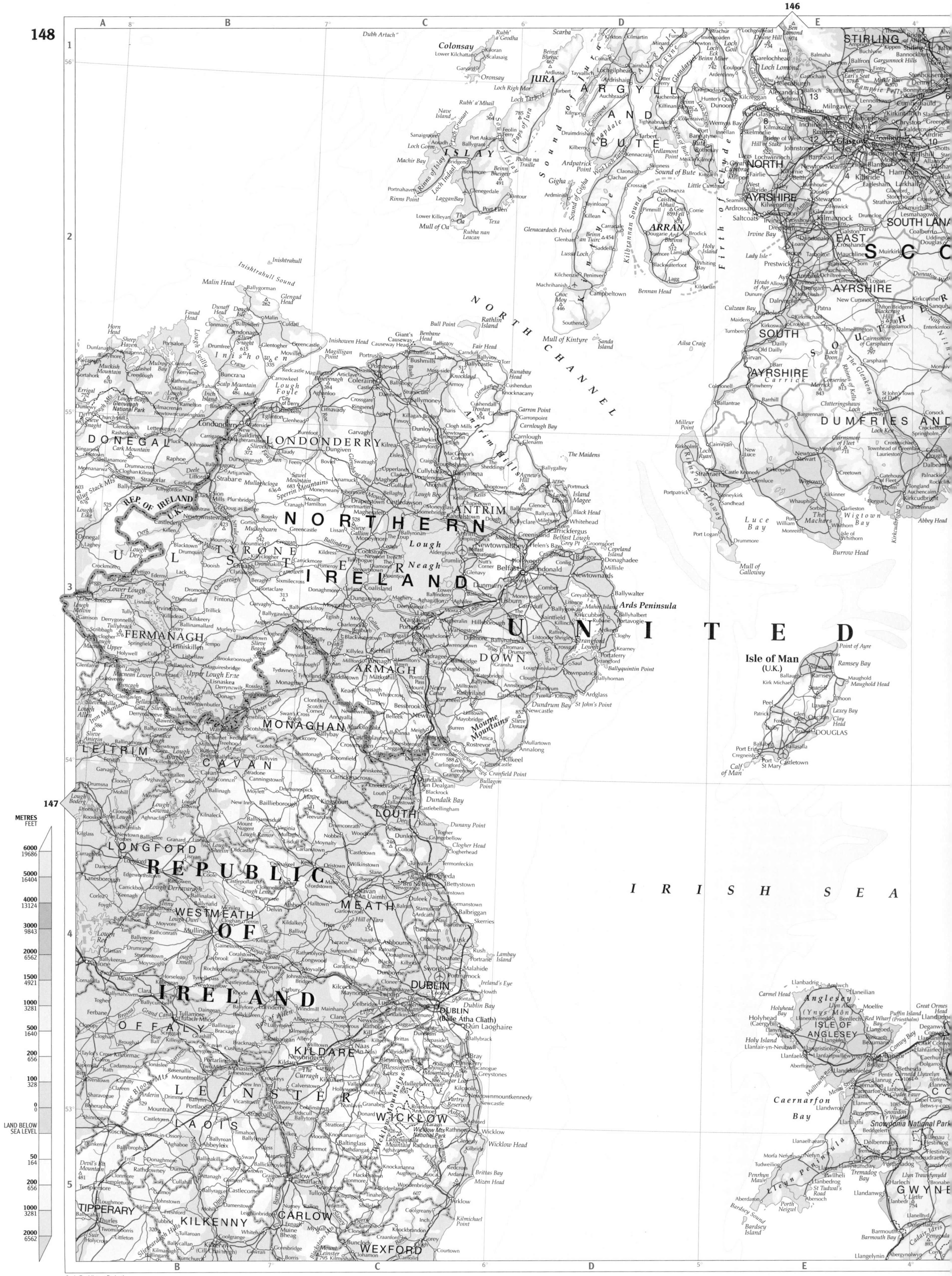

Conic Equidistant Projection

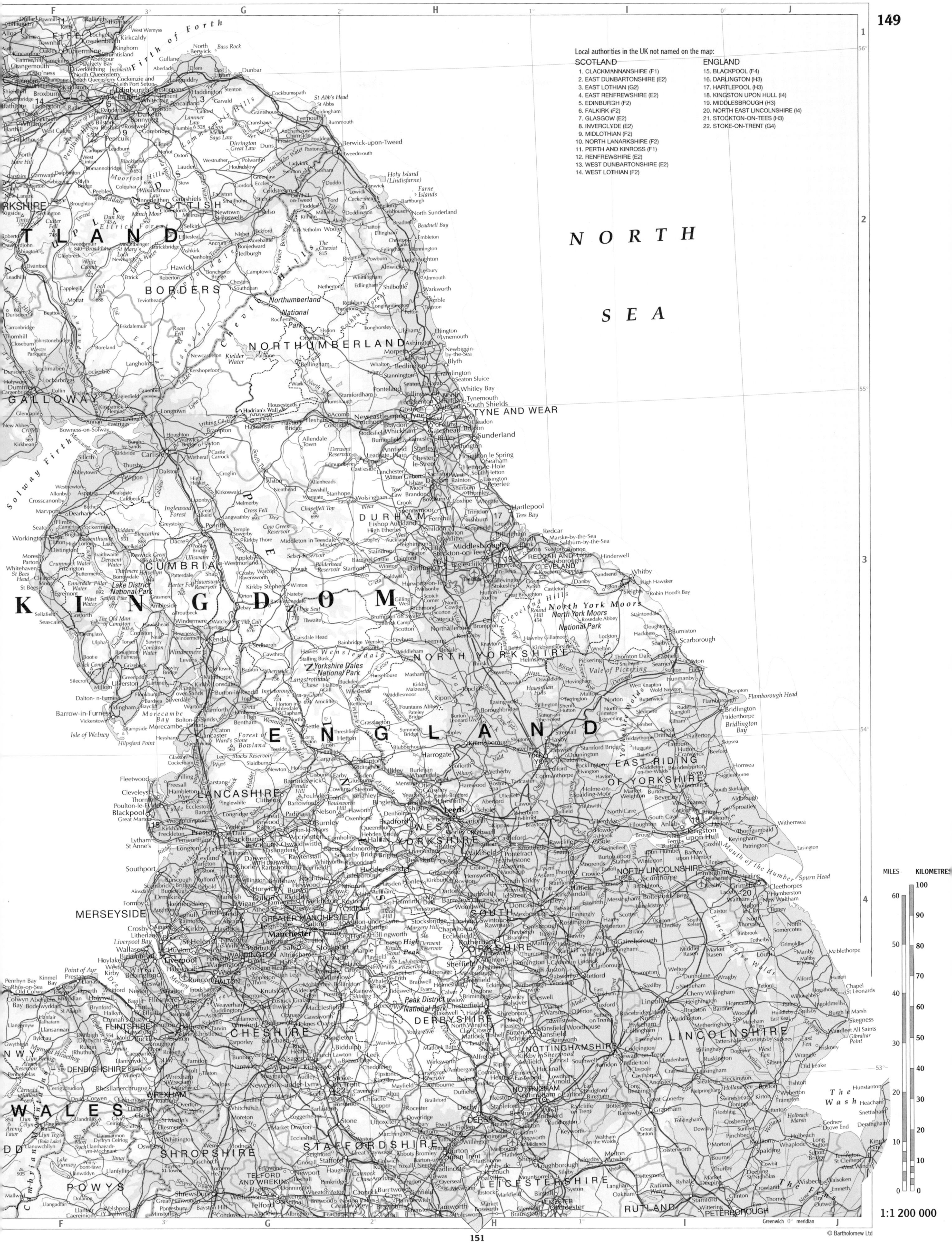
Local authorities in the UK not named on the map:
SCOTLAND
1. CLACKMANNANSHIRE (F1)
2. EAST DUNBARTONSHIRE (E2)
3. EAST LOTHIAN (G2)
4. EAST RENFREWSHIRE (E2)
5. EDINBURGH (F2)
6. FALKIRK (F2)
7. GLASGOW (E2)
8. INVERCLYDE (E2)
9. MIDLOTHIAN (F2)
10. NORTH LANARKSHIRE (F2)
11. PERTH AND KINROSS (F1)
12. RENFREWSHIRE (E2)
13. WEST DUNBARTONSHIRE (E2)
14. WEST LOTHIAN (F2)
ENGLAND
15. BLACKPOOL (F4)
16. DARLINGTON (H3)
17. HARTLEPOOL (H3)
18. KINGSTON UPON HULL (I4)
19. MIDDLESBROUGH (H3)
20. NORTH EAST LINCOLNSHIRE (I4)
21. STOCKTON-ON-TEES (H3)
22. STOKE-ON-TRENT (G4)
NORTH SEA
UNITED KINGDOM
ENGLAND
WALES
SCOTTISH BORDERS
NORTHUMBERLAND
TYNE AND WEAR
DURHAM
CUMBRIA
NORTH YORKSHIRE
EAST RIDING OF YORKSHIRE
LANCASHIRE
WEST YORKSHIRE
SOUTH YORKSHIRE
GREATER MANCHESTER
MERSEYSIDE
CHESHIRE
DERBYSHIRE
NOTTINGHAMSHIRE
LINCOLNSHIRE
NORTH LINCOLNSHIRE
STAFFORDSHIRE
SHROPSHIRE
LEICESTERSHIRE
RUTLAND
POWYS
DENBIGHSHIRE
FLINTSHIRE
WREXHAM
DUMFRIES AND GALLOWAY
Edinburgh
Newcastle upon Tyne
Sunderland
Middlesbrough
York
Leeds
Bradford
Manchester
Liverpool
Sheffield
Kingston upon Hull
Nottingham
Derby
Lincoln
Carlisle
Blackpool
Preston
Firth of Forth
Solway Firth
Morecambe Bay
Mouth of the Humber
The Wash
Lake District National Park
Yorkshire Dales National Park
North York Moors National Park
Peak District National Park
Northumberland National Park
Greenwich 0° meridian
MILES
KILOMETRES

1:1 200 000

© Bartholomew Ltd

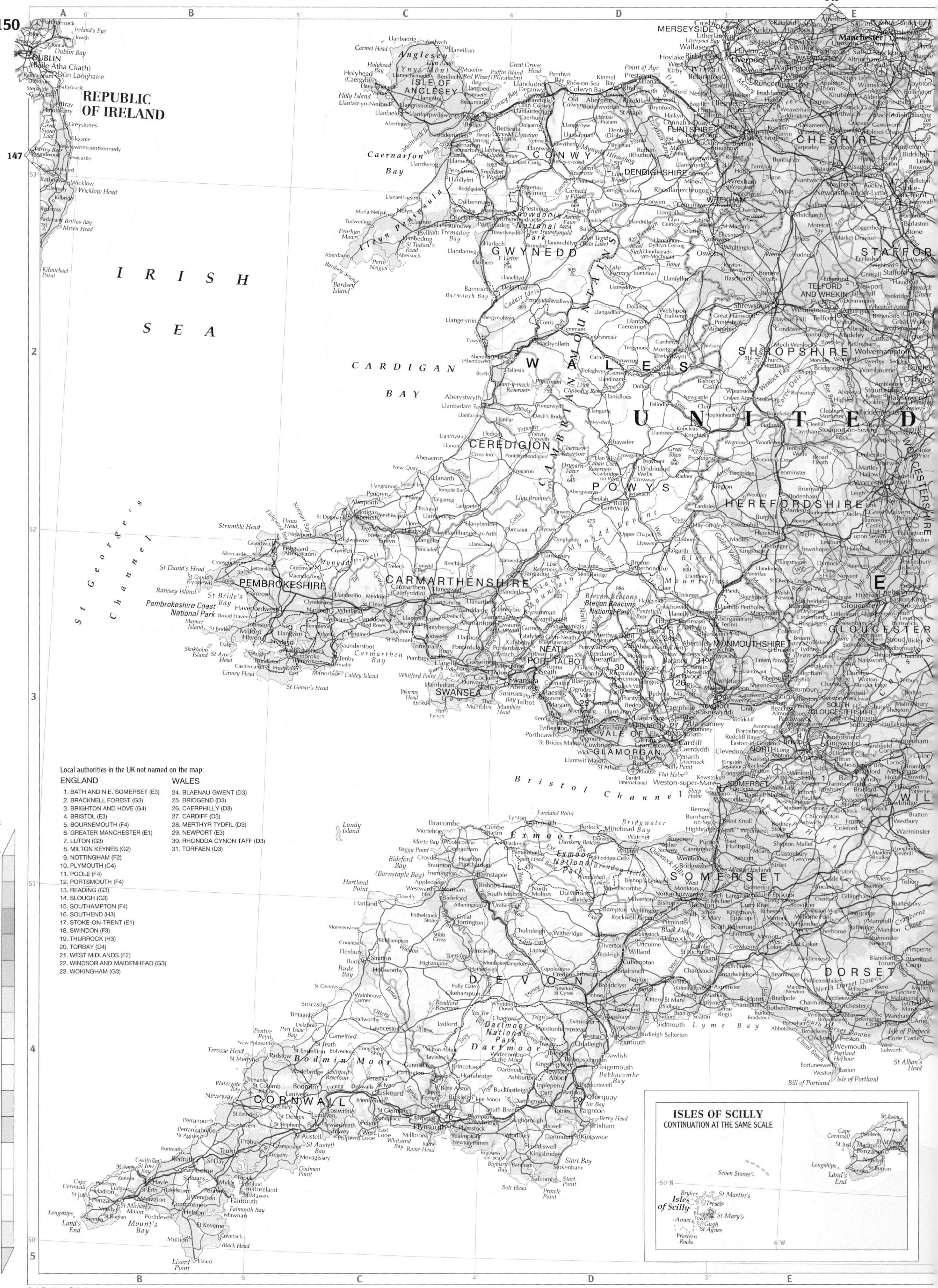

Local authorities in the UK not named on the map:

ENGLAND

1. BATH AND N.E. SOMERSET (E3)
2. BRACKNELL FOREST (G3)
3. BRIGHTON AND HOVE (G4)
4. BRISTOL (E3)
5. BOURNEMOUTH (F4)
6. GREATER MANCHESTER (E1)
7. LUTON (G3)
8. MILTON KEYNES (G2)
9. NOTTINGHAM (F2)
10. PLYMOUTH (C4)
11. POOLE (F4)
12. PORTSMOUTH (F4)
13. READING (G3)
14. SLOUGH (G3)
15. SOUTHAMPTON (F4)
16. SOUTHEND (H3)
17. STOKE-ON-TRENT (E1)
18. SWINDON (F3)
19. THURROCK (H3)
20. TORBAY (D4)
21. WEST MIDLANDS (F2)
22. WINDSOR AND MAIDENHEAD (G3)
23. WOKINGHAM (G3)

WALES

24. BLAENAU GWENT (D3)
25. BRIDGEND (D3)
26. CAERPHILLY (D3)
27. CARDIFF (D3)
28. MERTHYR TYDFIL (D3)
29. NEWPORT (E3)
30. RHONDDA CYNON TAFF (D3)
31. TORFAEN (D3)

Conic Equidistant Projection

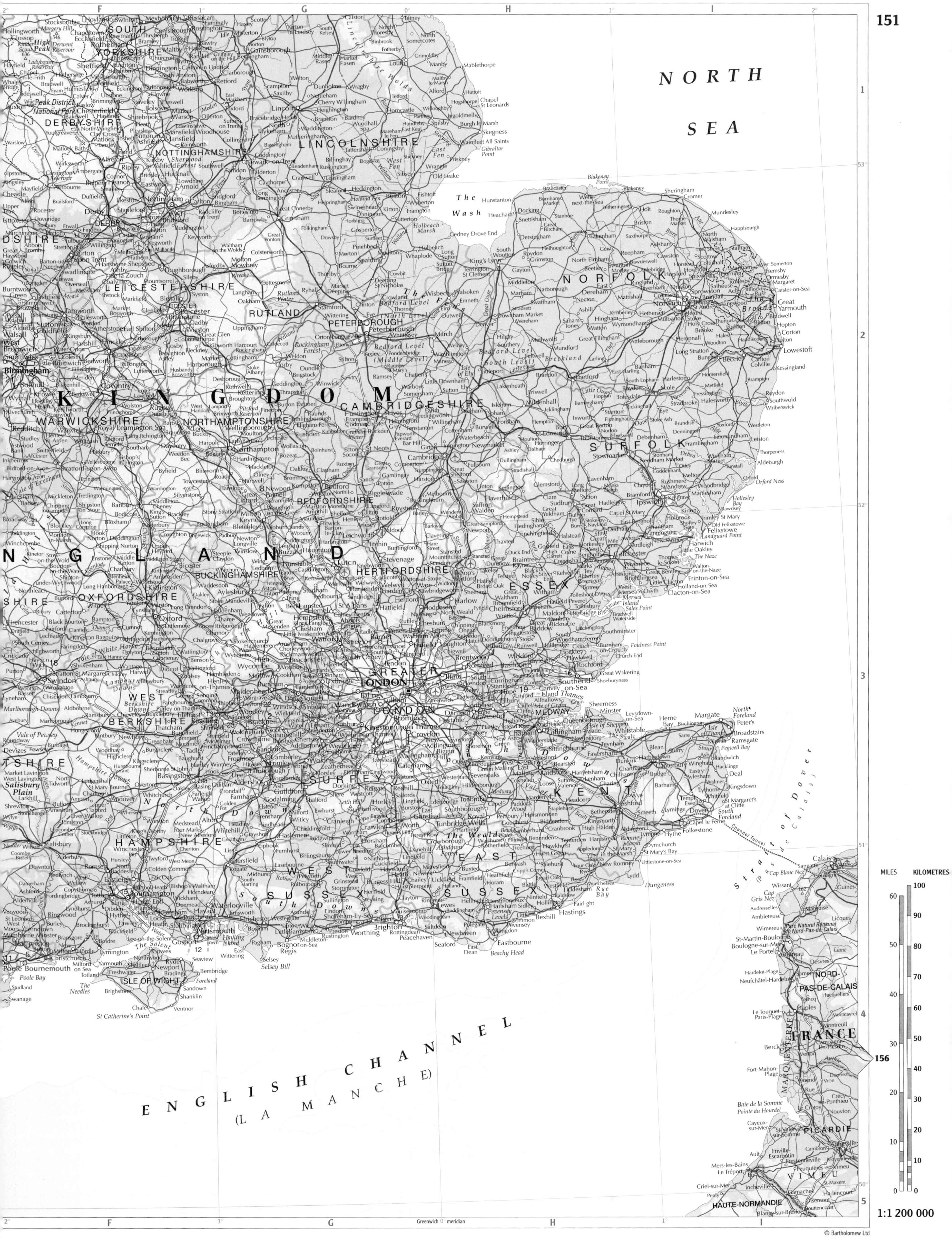
NORTH SEA
The Wash
ENGLISH CHANNEL
(LA MANCHE)
Strait of Dover
(Pas de Calais)
KINGDOM
ENGLAND
SOUTH YORKSHIRE
DERBYSHIRE
NOTTINGHAMSHIRE
LINCOLNSHIRE
LEICESTERSHIRE
RUTLAND
NORFOLK
SUFFOLK
CAMBRIDGESHIRE
NORTHAMPTONSHIRE
WARWICKSHIRE
BEDFORDSHIRE
BUCKINGHAMSHIRE
HERTFORDSHIRE
OXFORDSHIRE
ESSEX
GREATER LONDON
LONDON
MEDWAY
KENT
SURREY
WEST BERKSHIRE
BERKSHIRE
HAMPSHIRE
WEST SUSSEX
EAST SUSSEX
ISLE OF WIGHT
NORD-PAS-DE-CALAIS
FRANCE
PICARDIE
HAUTE-NORMANDIE
Birmingham
Peterborough
Cambridge
Norwich
Ipswich
Southampton
Portsmouth
Brighton
Dover
Calais
MILES
KILOMETRES
1:1 200 000
156
Greenwich 0° meridian
© Bartholomew Ltd

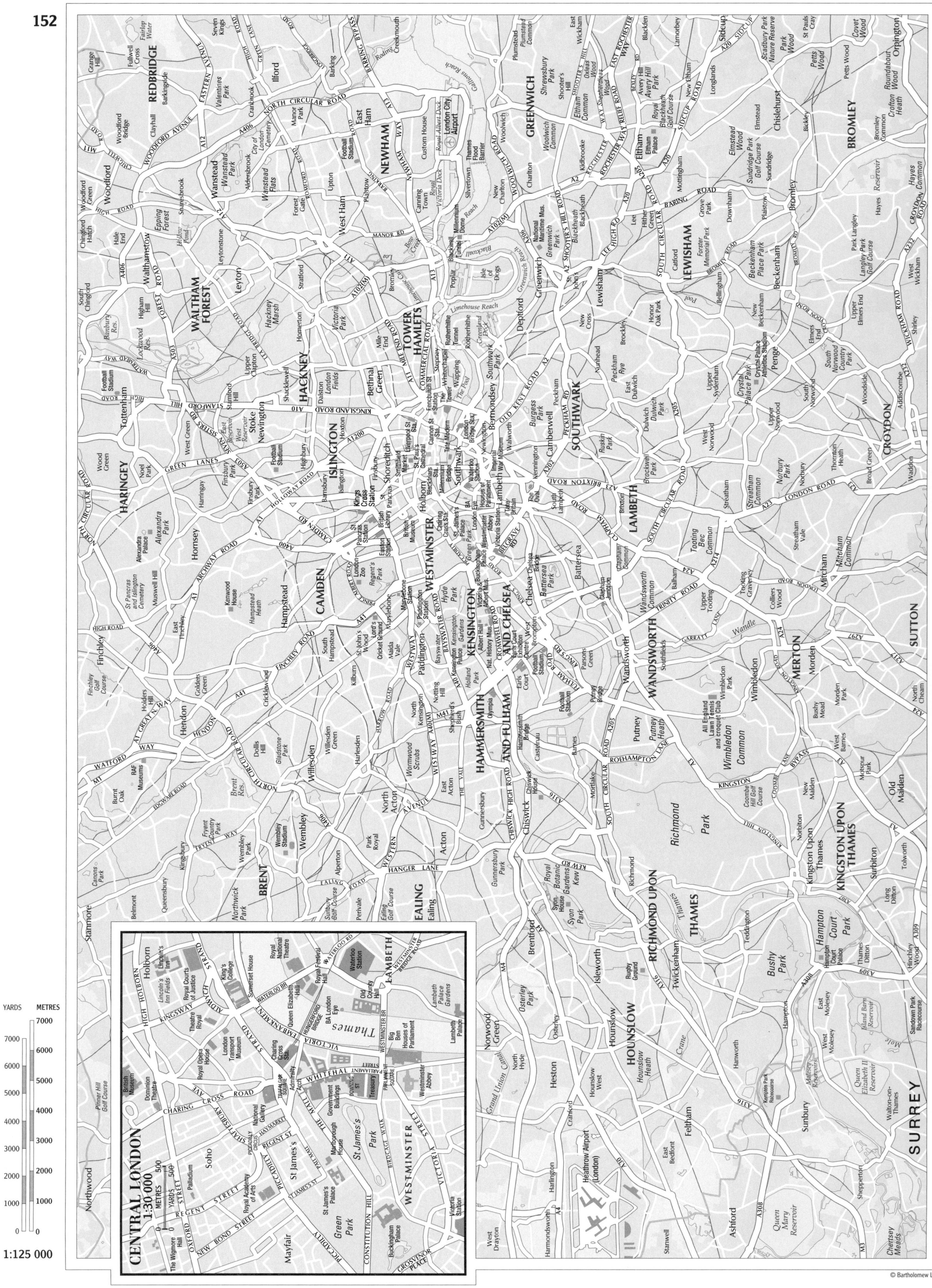
REDBRIDGE
WALTHAM FOREST
HARINGEY
HACKNEY
ISLINGTON
CAMDEN
NEWHAM
TOWER HAMLETS
GREENWICH
LEWISHAM
SOUTHWARK
LAMBETH
WESTMINSTER
KENSINGTON AND CHELSEA
HAMMERSMITH AND FULHAM
WANDSWORTH
MERTON
SUTTON
CROYDON
BROMLEY
BRENT
EALING
HOUNSLOW
RICHMOND UPON THAMES
KINGSTON UPON THAMES
SURREY
Ilford
Barking
East Ham
West Ham
Stratford
Leyton
Walthamstow
Woodford
Wanstead
Tottenham
Wood Green
Hornsey
Stoke Newington
Hampstead
Finchley
Hendon
Willesden
Wembley
Acton
Paddington
Holborn
Shoreditch
Bethnal Green
Poplar
Deptford
Greenwich
Eltham
Lewisham
Camberwell
Peckham
Brixton
Battersea
Wandsworth
Putney
Wimbledon
Mitcham
Beckenham
Penge
Norwood
Streatham
Chiswick
Brentford
Isleworth
Twickenham
Richmond Park
Hounslow
Feltham
Heathrow Airport (London)
Hampton Court Park
Bushy Park
Kingston Upon Thames
Surbiton
Sidcup
Orpington
London City Airport
Thames
CENTRAL LONDON
1:30 000
METRES 0 500
YARDS 0 500
Soho
Mayfair
St James's
Green Park
St James's Park
Buckingham Palace
Westminster Abbey
Houses of Parliament
Big Ben
Waterloo Station
Victoria Station
Trafalgar Square
National Gallery
British Museum
Royal Festival Hall
Somerset House
King's College
YARDS
METRES
7000
6000
5000
4000
3000
2000
1000
0
1:125 000

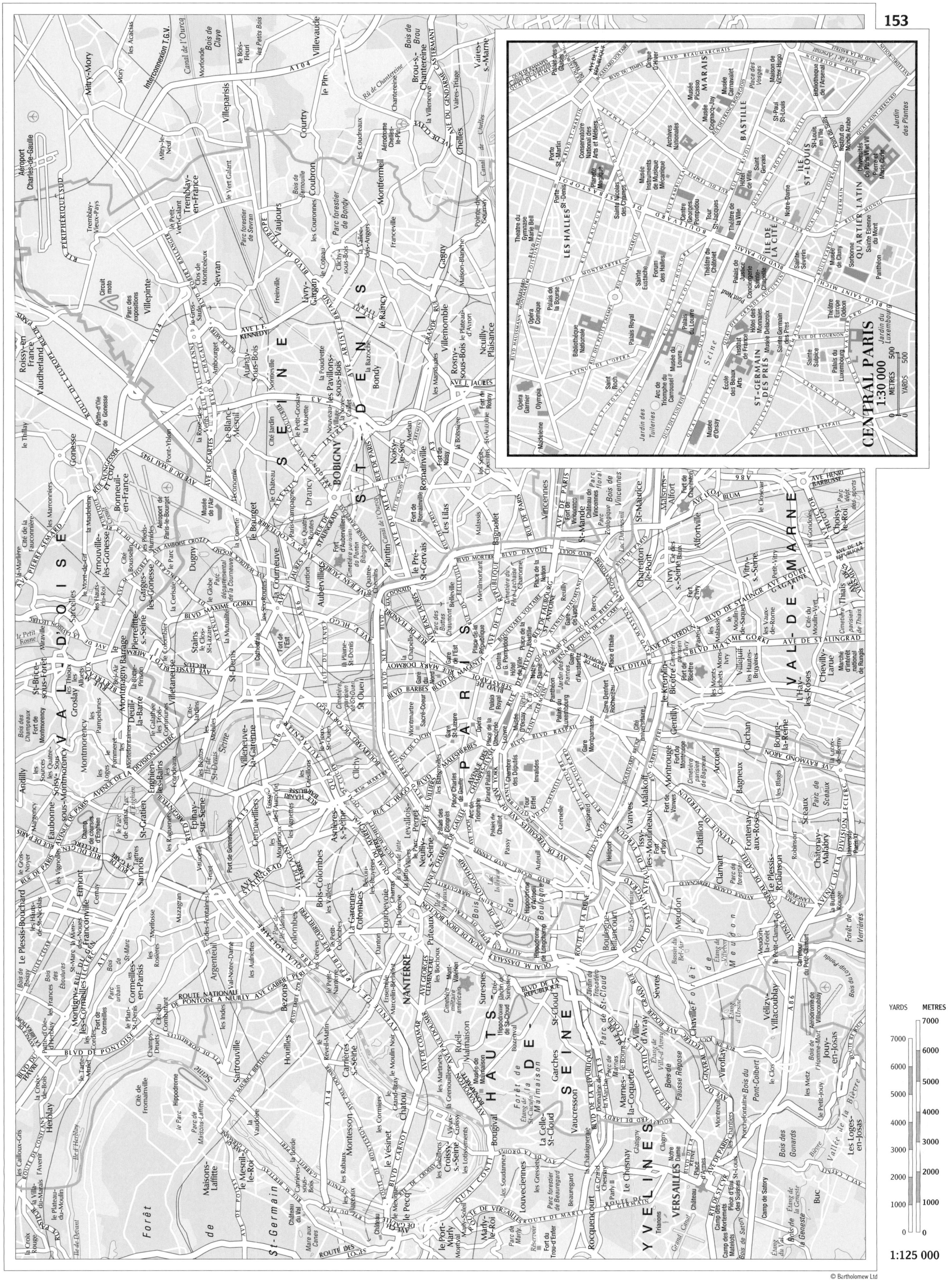
CENTRAL PARIS
1:30 000
METRES 500
YARDS 500
PARIS
SEINE-ST-DENIS
VAL-D'OISE
VAL-DE-MARNE
HAUTS-DE-SEINE
YVELINES
VERSAILLES
NANTERRE
BOBIGNY
ST-GERMAIN DES PRÉS
QUARTIER LATIN
ÎLE DE LA CITÉ
ÎLE ST-LOUIS
LES HALLES
MARAIS
BASTILLE
Seine
YARDS
METRES
7000
6000
5000
4000
3000
2000
1000
0
1:125 000

© Bartholomew Ltd

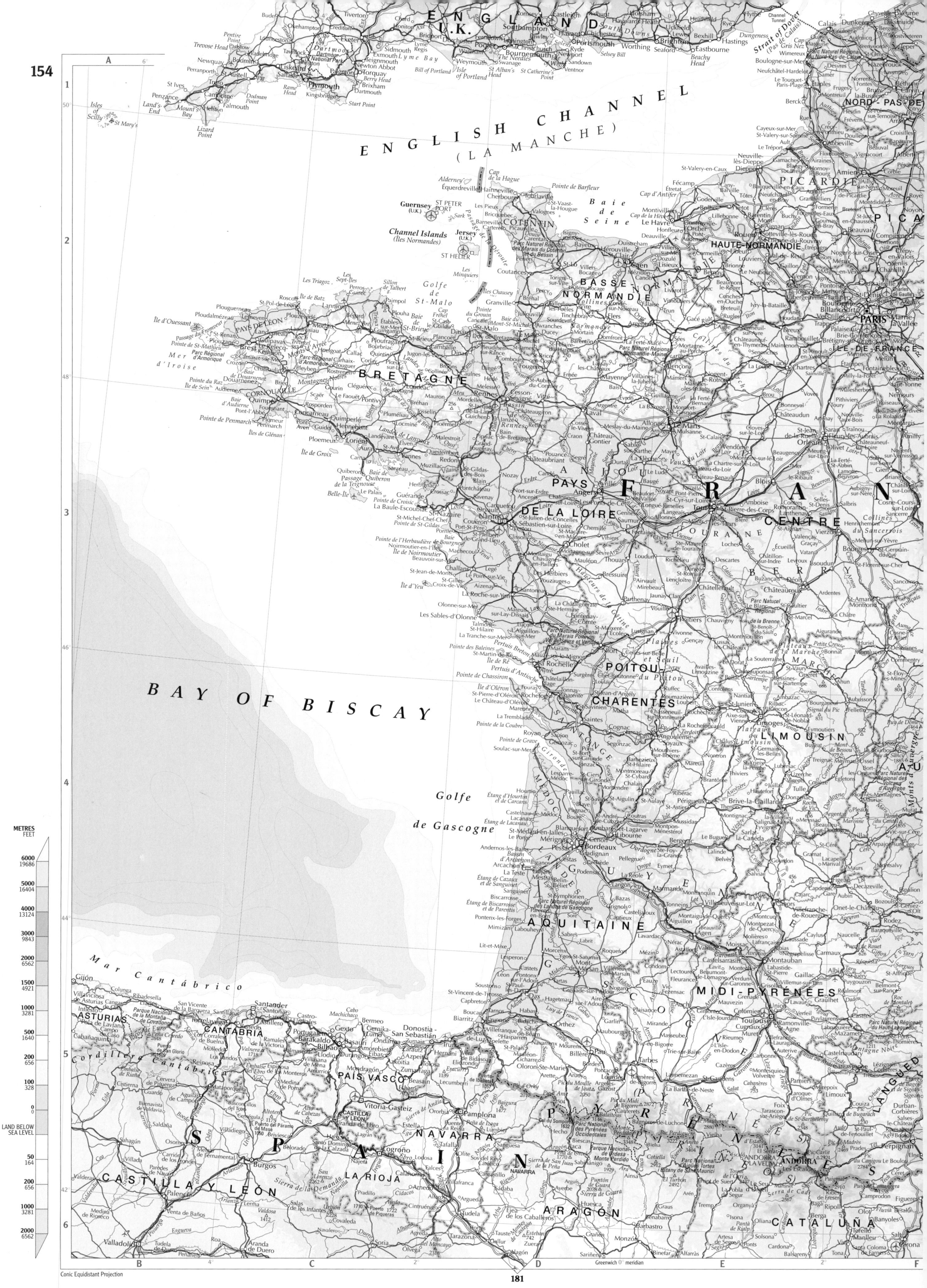
ENGLAND
U.K.
ENGLISH CHANNEL
(LA MANCHE)
Channel Islands
(Îles Normandes)
Guernsey (U.K.)
Jersey (U.K.)
Alderney
Baie de Seine
COTENTIN
Golfe de St-Malo
BASSE-NORMANDIE
HAUTE-NORMANDIE
PICARDIE
NORD - PAS-DE
ÎLE-DE-FRANCE
PARIS
BRETAGNE
PAYS DE LA LOIRE
CENTRE
FRANCE
ANJOU
TOURAINE
BERRY
POITOU-CHARENTES
LIMOUSIN
AQUITAINE
MIDI-PYRÉNÉES
LANGUEDOC
PYRÉNÉES
BAY OF BISCAY
Golfe de Gascogne
Mar Cantábrico
Cordillera Cantábrica
ASTURIAS
CANTABRIA
PAÍS VASCO
NAVARRA
LA RIOJA
CASTILLA Y LEÓN
ARAGÓN
CATALUÑA
ANDORRA
SPAIN
METRES
FEET
6000 19686
5000 16404
4000 13124
3000 9843
2000 6562
1500 4921
1000 3281
500 1640
200 656
100 328
0 0
LAND BELOW SEA LEVEL
50 164
200 656
1000 3281
2000 6562
A B C D E F
1 2 3 4 5 6
Greenwich 0° meridian

Conic Equidistant Projection

181

166

BELGIUM
BRUXELLES (Brussels)
LUXEMBOURG
GERMANY
RHEINLAND-PFALZ
SAARLAND
HESSEN
BADEN-WÜRTTEMBERG
BAYERN
NORDRHEIN-WESTFALEN
Frankfurt am Main
Mannheim
Stuttgart
Nürnberg
München (Munich)
CZECH REPUBLIC
AUSTRIA
LIECHTENSTEIN
SWITZERLAND
BERN
Zürich
Genève
LORRAINE
ALSACE
CHAMPAGNE-ARDENNE
FRANCHE-COMTÉ
BOURGOGNE
RHÔNE-ALPES
PROVENCE-ALPES-CÔTE-D'AZUR
MASSIF CENTRAL
Lyon
Marseille
Nice
MONACO
Strasbourg
Dijon
Reims
Metz
Nancy
ITALY
PIEMONTE
VALLE D'AOSTA
LOMBARDIA
TRENTINO-ALTO ADIGE
VENETO
EMILIA-ROMAGNA
LIGURIA
TOSCANA
Milano (Milan)
Torino (Turin)
Genova (Genoa)
Bologna
Firenze (Florence)
CORSE (CORSICA) (France)
Bastia
Ajaccio
LIGURIAN SEA
Golfo di Genova
GOLFE DU LION
MEDITERRANEAN SEA
Isola d'Elba
Arcipelago Toscano

188

MILES | KILOMETRES

1:3 000 000

© Bartholomew Ltd

165

151

159

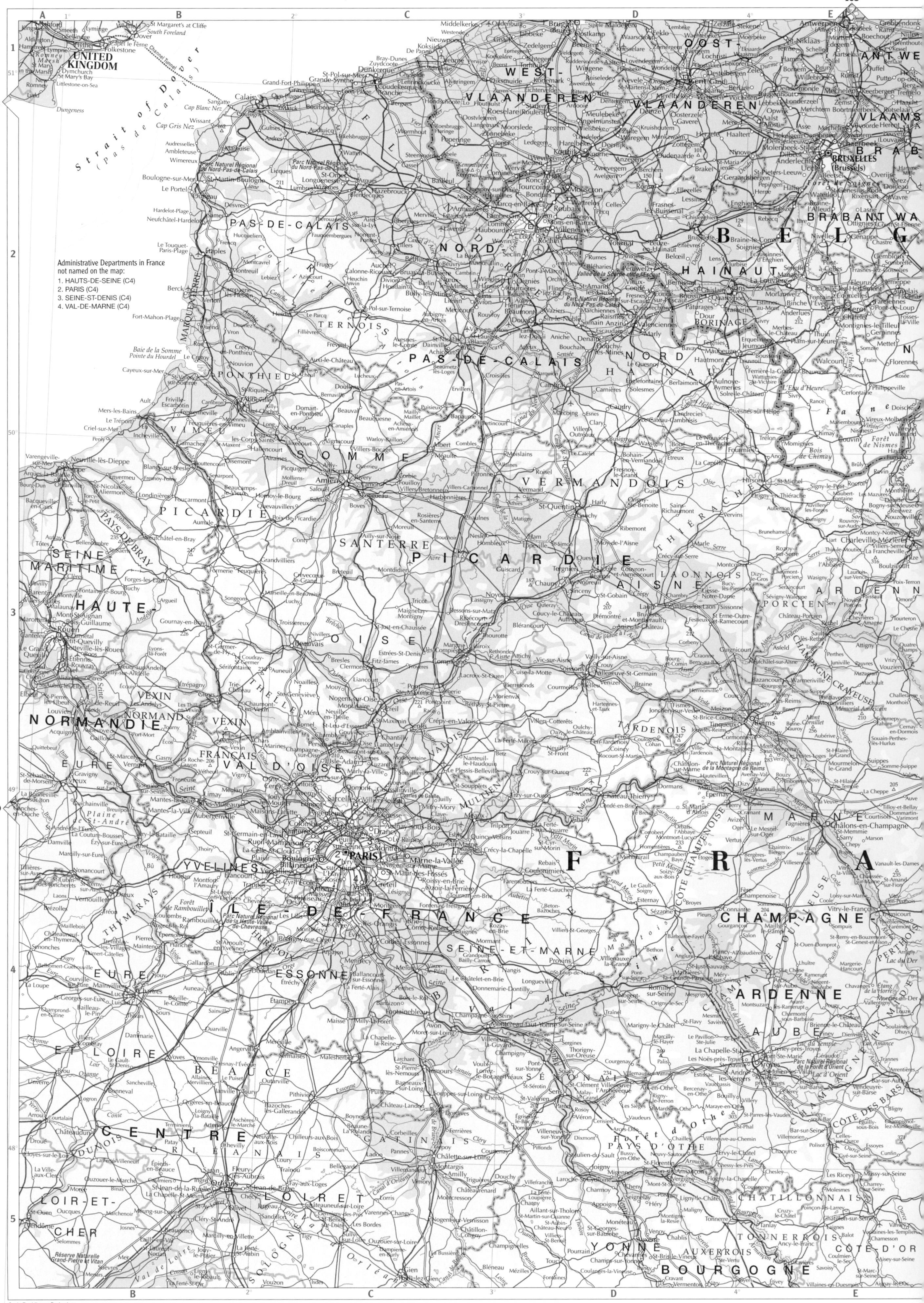
Administrative Departments in France not named on the map:
1. HAUTS-DE-SEINE (C4)
2. PARIS (C4)
3. SEINE-ST-DENIS (C4)
4. VAL-DE-MARNE (C4)
UNITED KINGDOM
Strait of Dover (pas de Calais)
WEST-VLAANDEREN
OOST-VLAANDEREN
ANTWERPEN
VLAAMS BRABANT
BRABANT WALLON
HAINAUT
BELGIUM
NORD
PAS-DE-CALAIS
SOMME
PICARDIE
AISNE
OISE
SEINE-MARITIME
HAUTE-NORMANDIE
EURE
VAL D'OISE
YVELINES
ILE-DE-FRANCE
ESSONNE
SEINE-ET-MARNE
MARNE
CHAMPAGNE-ARDENNE
AUBE
EURE-ET-LOIR
CENTRE
LOIRET
LOIR-ET-CHER
YONNE
BOURGOGNE
CÔTE-D'OR
FRANCE
PARIS
BRUXELLES (Brussels)
Reims
Amiens
Rouen
Orléans
Troyes
Lille
Calais
Dunkerque
Boulogne-sur-Mer
Beauvais
Chartres
Châlons-en-Champagne
Conic Equidistant Projection

METRES / FEET

METRES	FEET
6000	19686
5000	16404
4000	13124
3000	9843
2000	6562
1500	4921
1000	3281
500	1640
200	656
100	328
0	0
LAND BELOW SEA LEVEL	
50	164
200	656
1000	3281
2000	6562

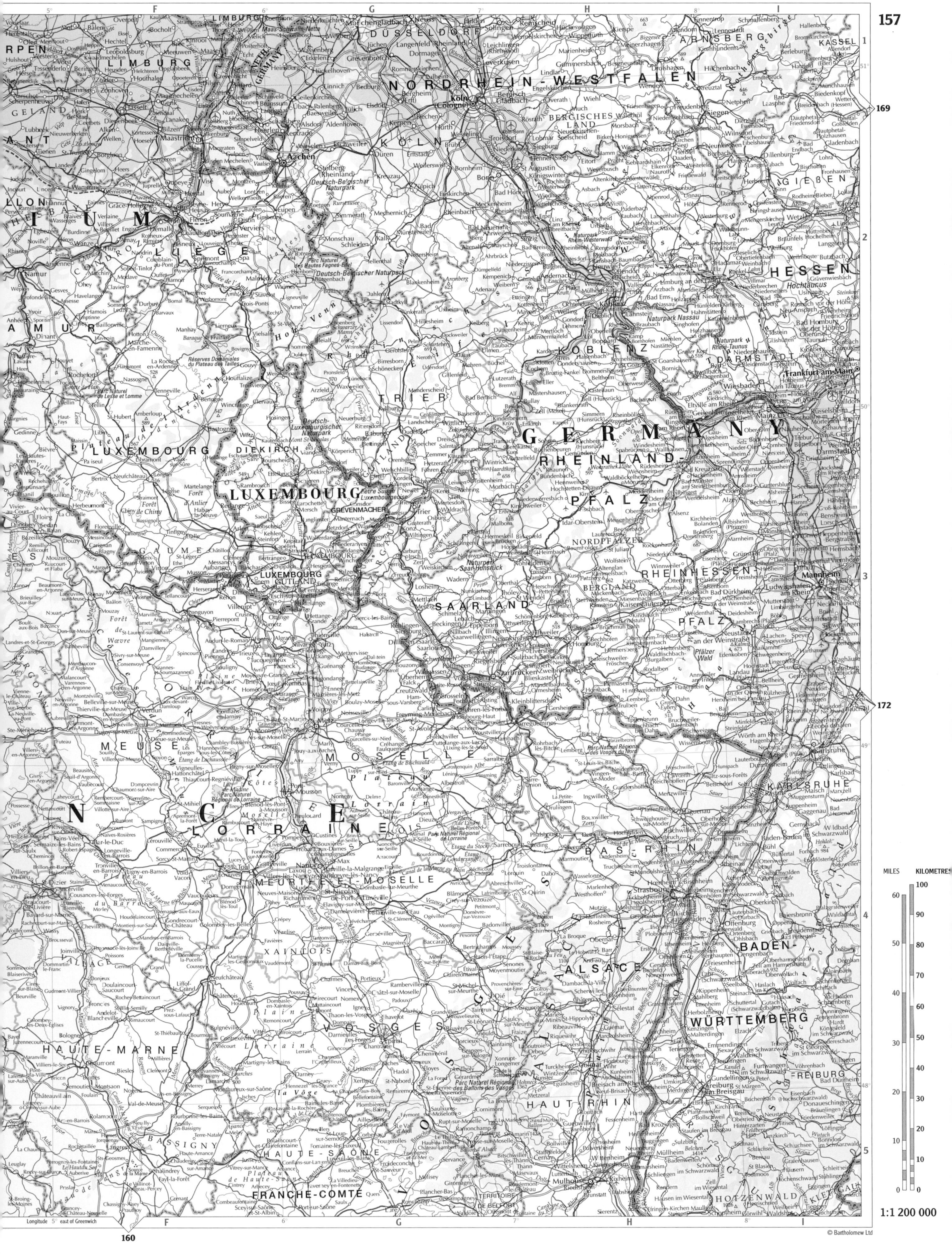
NORDRHEIN-WESTFALEN
DÜSSELDORF
KÖLN
ARNSBERG
LIMBURG
LIÈGE
NAMUR
LUXEMBOURG
KOBLENZ
TRIER
HESSEN
DARMSTADT
GERMANY
RHEINLAND-PFALZ
RHEINHESSEN-PFALZ
SAARLAND
KARLSRUHE
MOSELLE
LORRAINE
MEUSE
MEURTHE-ET-MOSELLE
BAS-RHIN
ALSACE
VOSGES
HAUT-RHIN
HAUTE-MARNE
HAUTE-SAÔNE
FRANCHE-COMTÉ
BADEN-WÜRTTEMBERG
FREIBURG
Frankfurt am Main
Mannheim
Strasbourg
Metz
Nancy
Luxembourg
Aachen
Köln
Mulhouse
MILES
KILOMETRES
1:1 200 000
Longitude 5° east of Greenwich
169
172
160

© Bartholomew Ltd

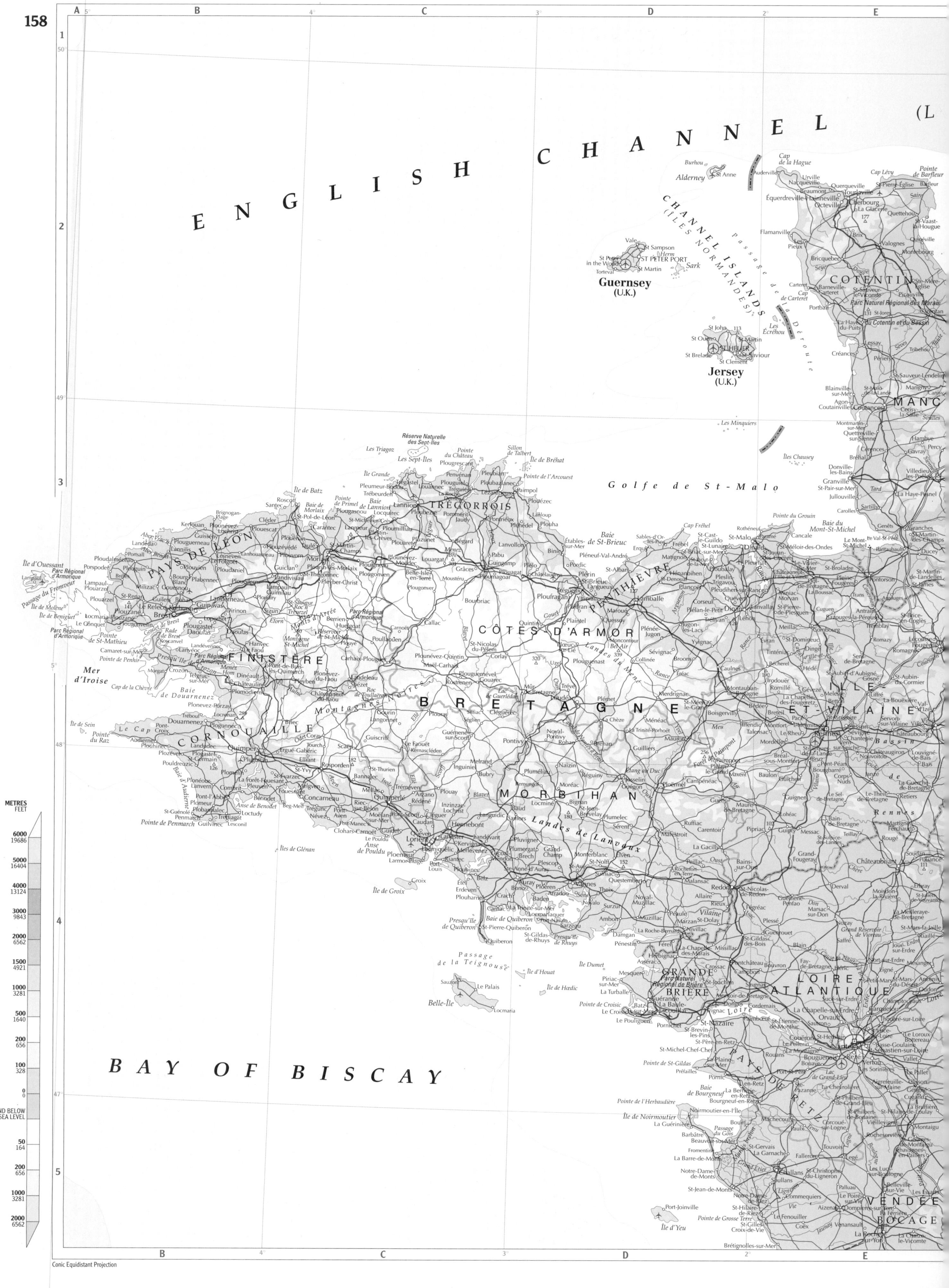

Conic Equidistant Projection

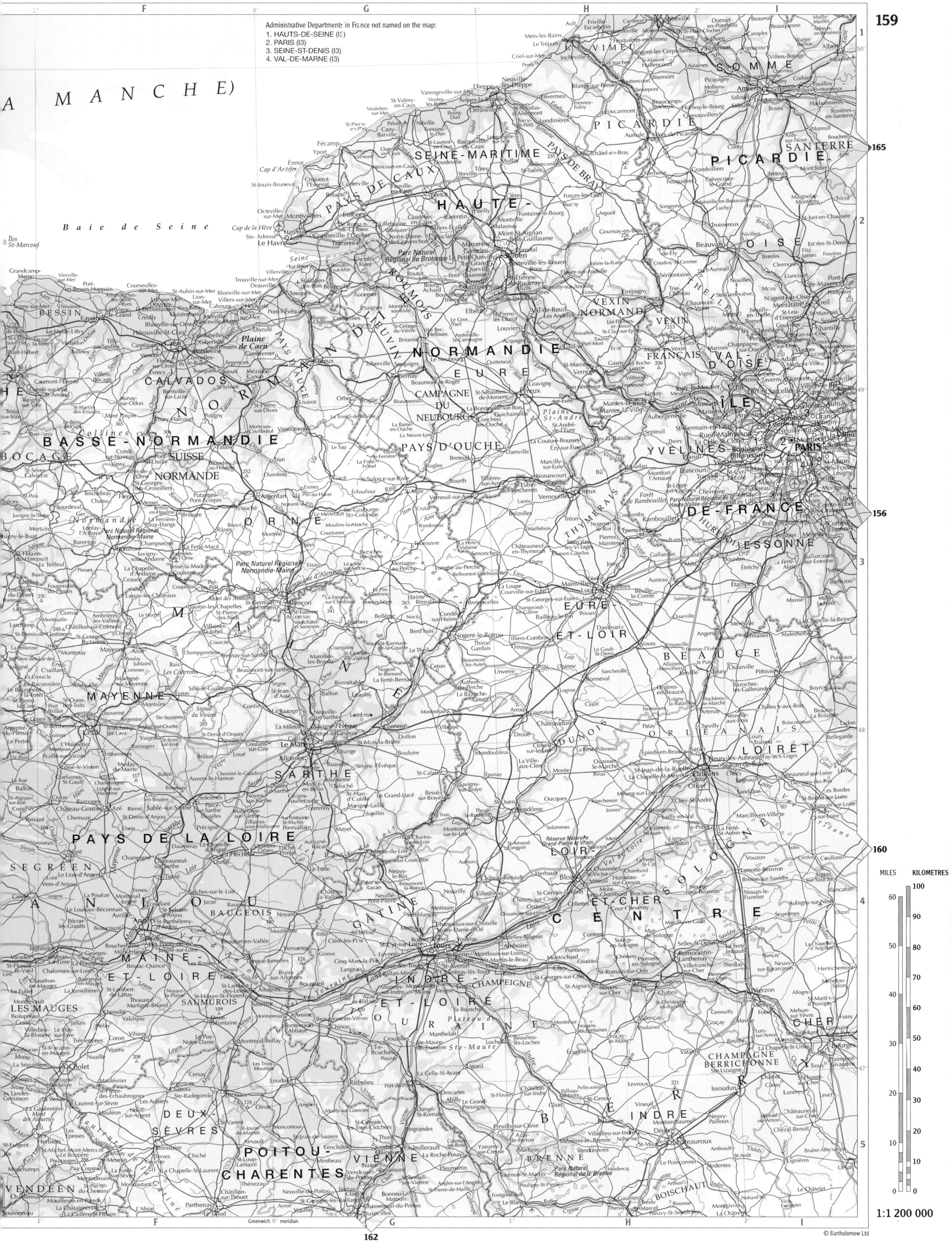
Administrative Departments in France not named on the map:
1. HAUTS-DE-SEINE (I3)
2. PARIS (I3)
3. SEINE-ST-DENIS (I3)
4. VAL-DE-MARNE (I3)
F
G
H
I
1
2
3
4
5
165
156
160
162
(LA MANCHE)
Baie de Seine
SOMME
PICARDIE
SANTERRE
SEINE-MARITIME
PAYS DE CAUX
PAYS DE BRAY
HAUTE-NORMANDIE
OISE
VEXIN NORMAND
VEXIN FRANÇAIS
VAL-D'OISE
ÎLE-DE-FRANCE
YVELINES
ESSONNE
PARIS
EURE
CAMPAGNE DU NEUBOURG
PAYS D'OUCHE
BASSE-NORMANDIE
CALVADOS
BESSIN
SUISSE NORMANDE
ORNE
MAYENNE
MAINE
SARTHE
EURE-ET-LOIR
BEAUCE
LOIRET
ORLÉANAIS
LOIR-ET-CHER
CENTRE
SOLOGNE
PAYS DE LA LOIRE
ANJOU
MAINE-ET-LOIRE
SAUMUROIS
INDRE-ET-LOIRE
TOURAINE
CHAMPEIGNE
CHER
INDRE
BERRY
BRENNE
BOISCHAUT
CHAMPAGNE BERRICHONNE
DEUX-SÈVRES
POITOU-CHARENTES
VIENNE
LES MAUGES
VENDÉEN
Le Havre
Rouen
Caen
Alençon
Le Mans
Chartres
Orléans
Tours
Angers
Blois
Bourges
Châteauroux
Amiens
Beauvais
Évreux
Laval
Poitiers
Greenwich 0° meridian
MILES
KILOMETRES

1:1 200 000

© Bartholomew Ltd

172

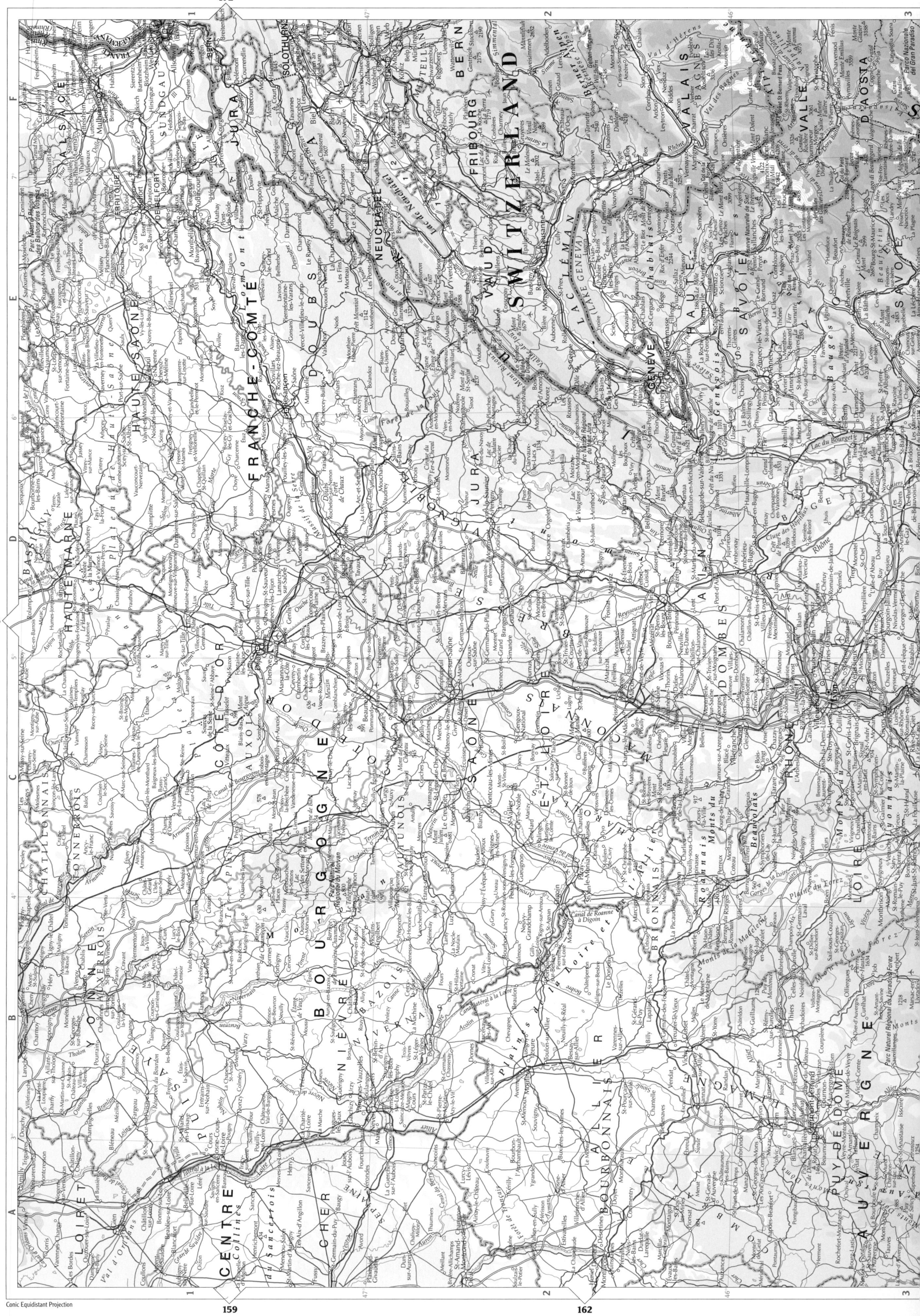
ALSACE
SUNDGAU
JURA
BERN
SOLOTHURN
NEUCHÂTEL
FRIBOURG
VAUD
SWITZERLAND
VALAIS
LAC LÉMAN
(LAKE GENEVA)
GENÈVE
HAUTE-SAVOIE
SAVOIE
VALLE D'AOSTA
HAUTE-SAÔNE
DOUBS
FRANCHE-COMTÉ
HAUTE-MARNE
CÔTE-D'OR
JURA
AIN
DOMBES
BRESSE
SAÔNE-ET-LOIRE
RHÔNE
LOIRE
BOURGOGNE
YONNE
NIÈVRE
ALLIER
BOURBONNAIS
PUY-DE-DÔME
AUVERGNE
CHER
LOIRET
CENTRE

156

METRES
FEET
6000 19686
5000 16404
4000 13124
3000 9843
2000 6562
1500 4921
1000 3281
500 1640
200 656
100 328
0 0
LAND BELOW SEA LEVEL
50 164
200 656
1000 3281
2000 6562

Conic Equidistant Projection

159

162

190

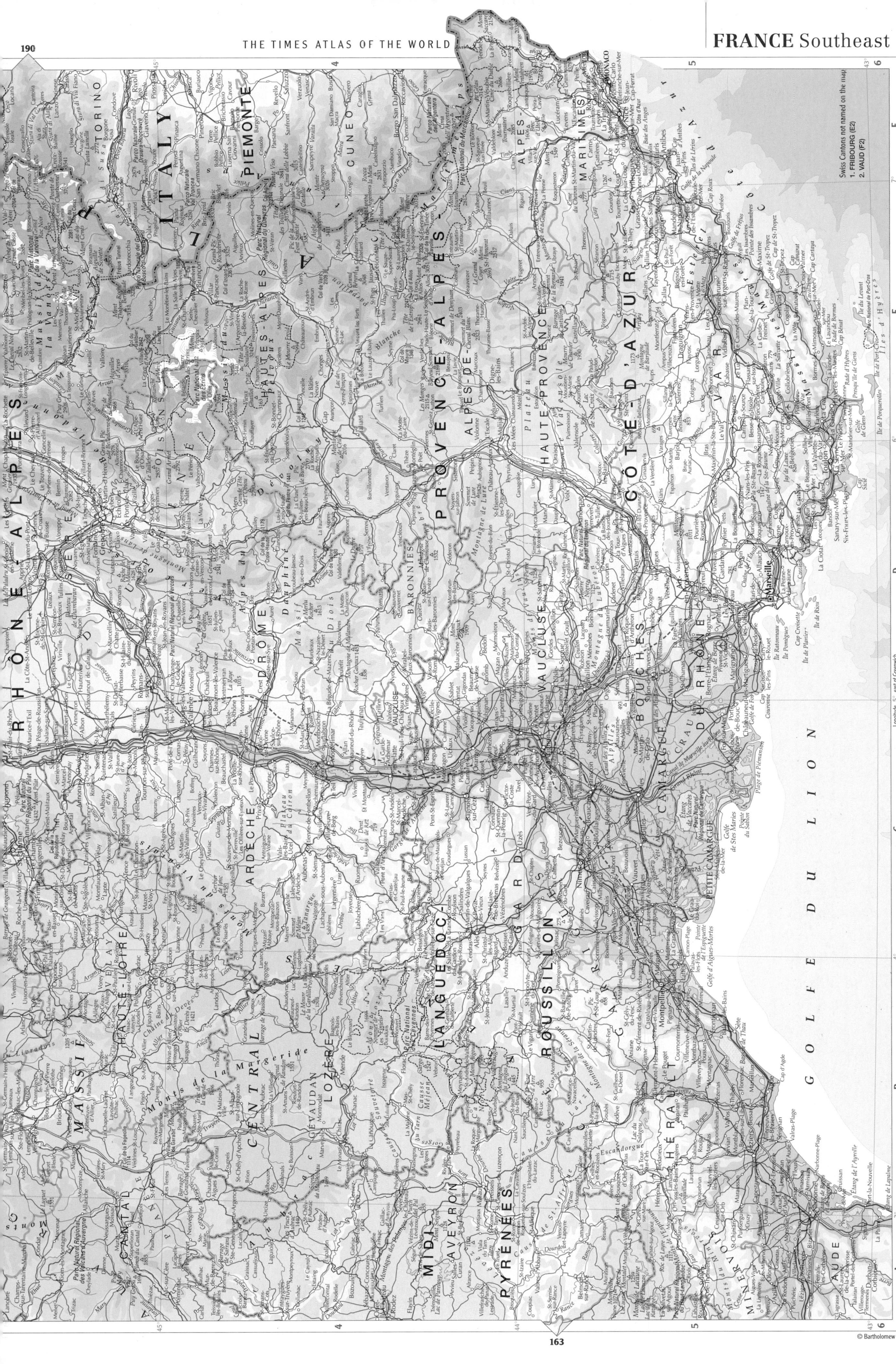

MILES KILOMETRES

1:1 200 000

163

160

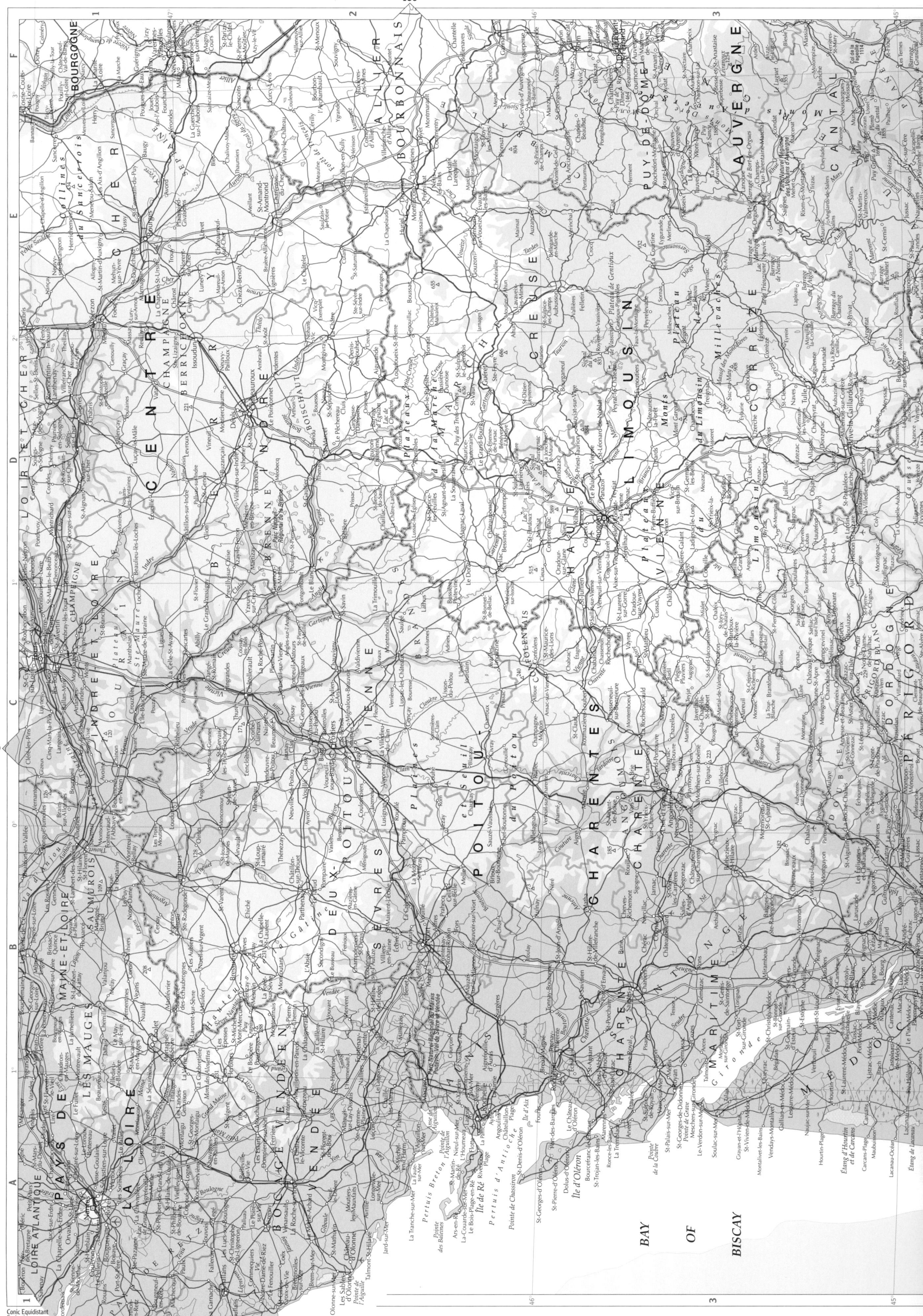
PAYS DE LA LOIRE
LOIRE ATLANTIQUE
MAINE-ET-LOIRE
LES MAUGES
SAUMUROIS
BOCAGE VENDÉEN
VENDÉE
DEUX-SÈVRES
POITOU
VIENNE
CHARENTES
CHARENTE
CHARENTE-MARITIME
SAINTONGE
ANGOUMOIS
LIMOUSIN
HAUTE-VIENNE
CREUSE
CORRÈZE
PÉRIGORD
DORDOGNE
AUVERGNE
PUY-DE-DÔME
CANTAL
ALLIER
BOURBONNAIS
CHER
CENTRE
INDRE
INDRE-ET-LOIRE
LOIR-ET-CHER
BOURGOGNE
CHAMPAGNE BERRICHONNE
BRENNE
Plateau de Millevaches
BAY OF BISCAY
Île de Ré
Île d'Oléron
Gironde

159

METRES
FEET
6000 19686
5000 16404
4000 13124
3000 9843
2000 6562
1500 4921
1000 3281
500 1640
200 656
100 328
0 0
LAND BELOW SEA LEVEL
50 164
200 656
1000 3281
2000 6562

Conic Equidistant Projection

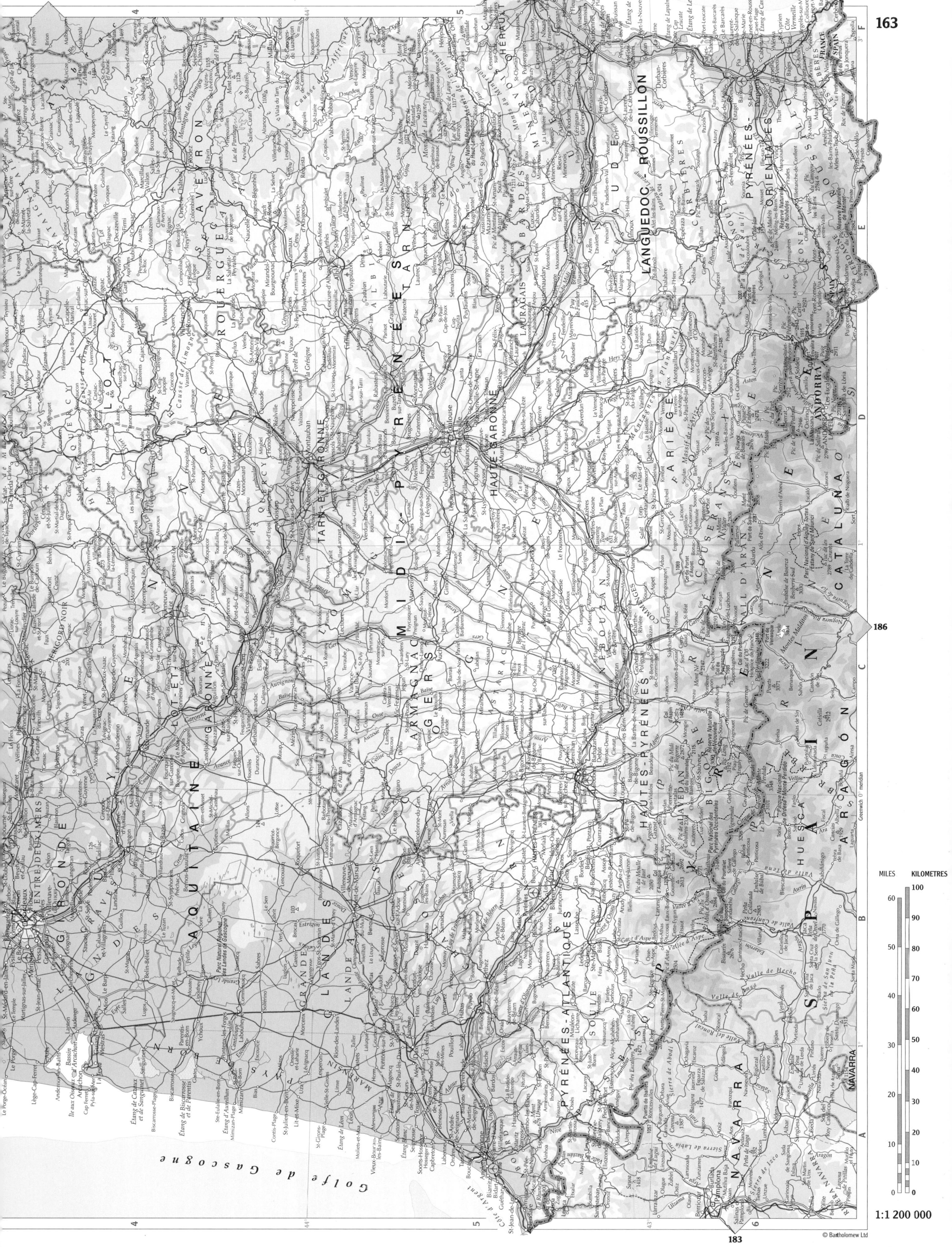
Golfe du Lion
Golfe de Gascogne
AQUITAINE
MIDI-PYRÉNÉES
LANGUEDOC-ROUSSILLON
PYRÉNÉES-ATLANTIQUES
HAUTES-PYRÉNÉES
HAUTE-GARONNE
TARN-ET-GARONNE
LOT-ET-GARONNE
GIRONDE
LANDES
GERS
ARIÈGE
AUDE
TARN
AVEYRON
LOT
PYRÉNÉES-ORIENTALES
ANDORRA
CATALUÑA
ARAGÓN
NAVARRA
HUESCA
Toulouse
Montauban
Pamplona
MILES
KILOMETRES
1:1 200 000

163
186
183

© Bartholomew Ltd

168

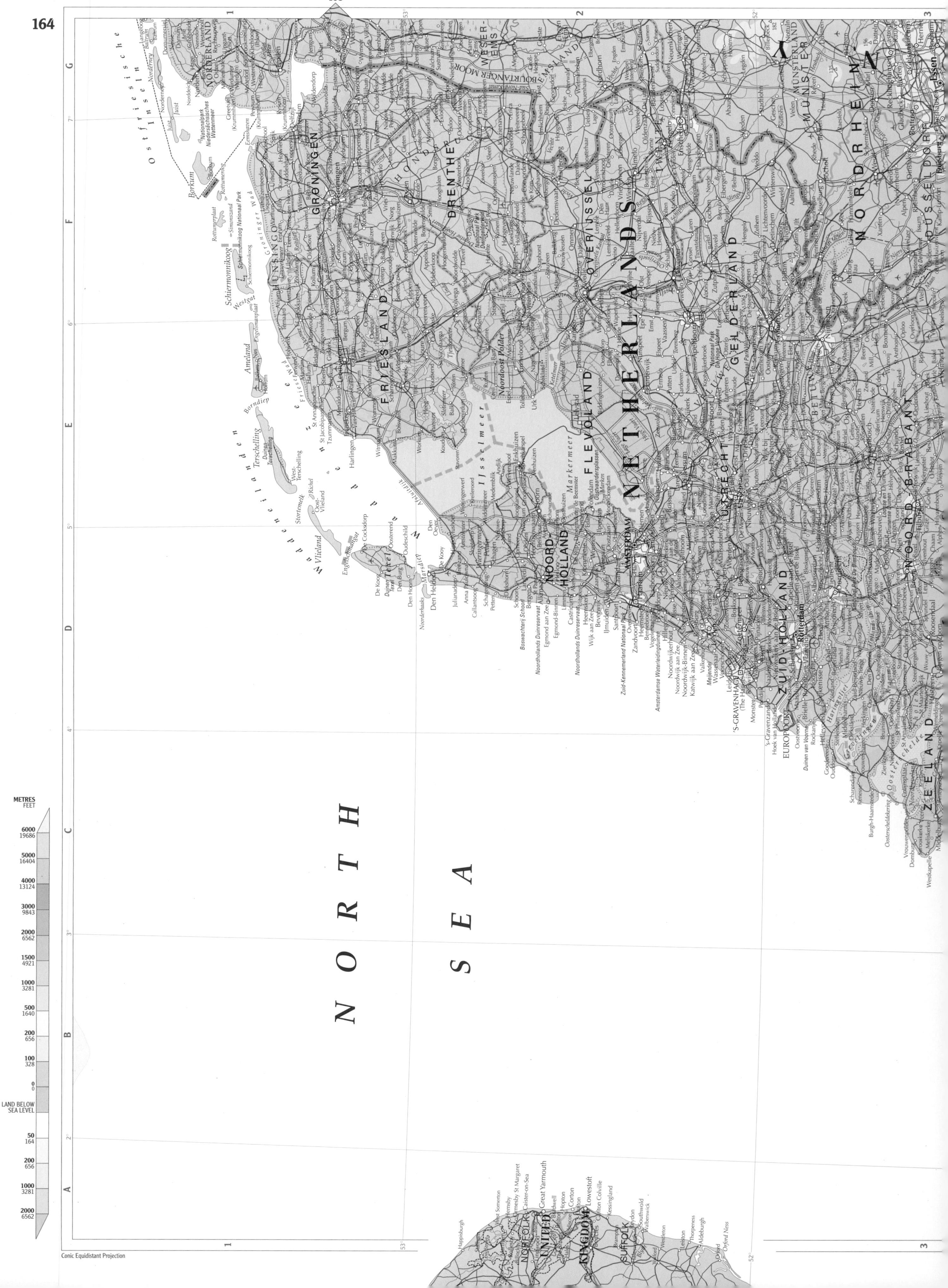
NORTH SEA
NETHERLANDS
GRONINGEN
FRIESLAND
DRENTHE
OVERIJSSEL
FLEVOLAND
GELDERLAND
UTRECHT
NOORD-HOLLAND
ZUID-HOLLAND
NOORD-BRABANT
ZEELAND
AMSTERDAM
Rotterdam
'S-GRAVENHAGE (The Hague)
IJsselmeer
Markermeer
Waddenzee
Ostfriesische Inseln
Texel
Vlieland
Terschelling
Ameland
Schiermonnikoog
Borkum
UNITED KINGDOM
NORFOLK
SUFFOLK
Great Yarmouth
Lowestoft
METRES
FEET
6000
19686
5000
16404
4000
13124
3000
9843
2000
6562
1500
4921
1000
3281
500
1640
200
656
100
328
0
0
LAND BELOW SEA LEVEL
50
164
200
656
1000
3281
2000
6562

Conic Equidistant Projection

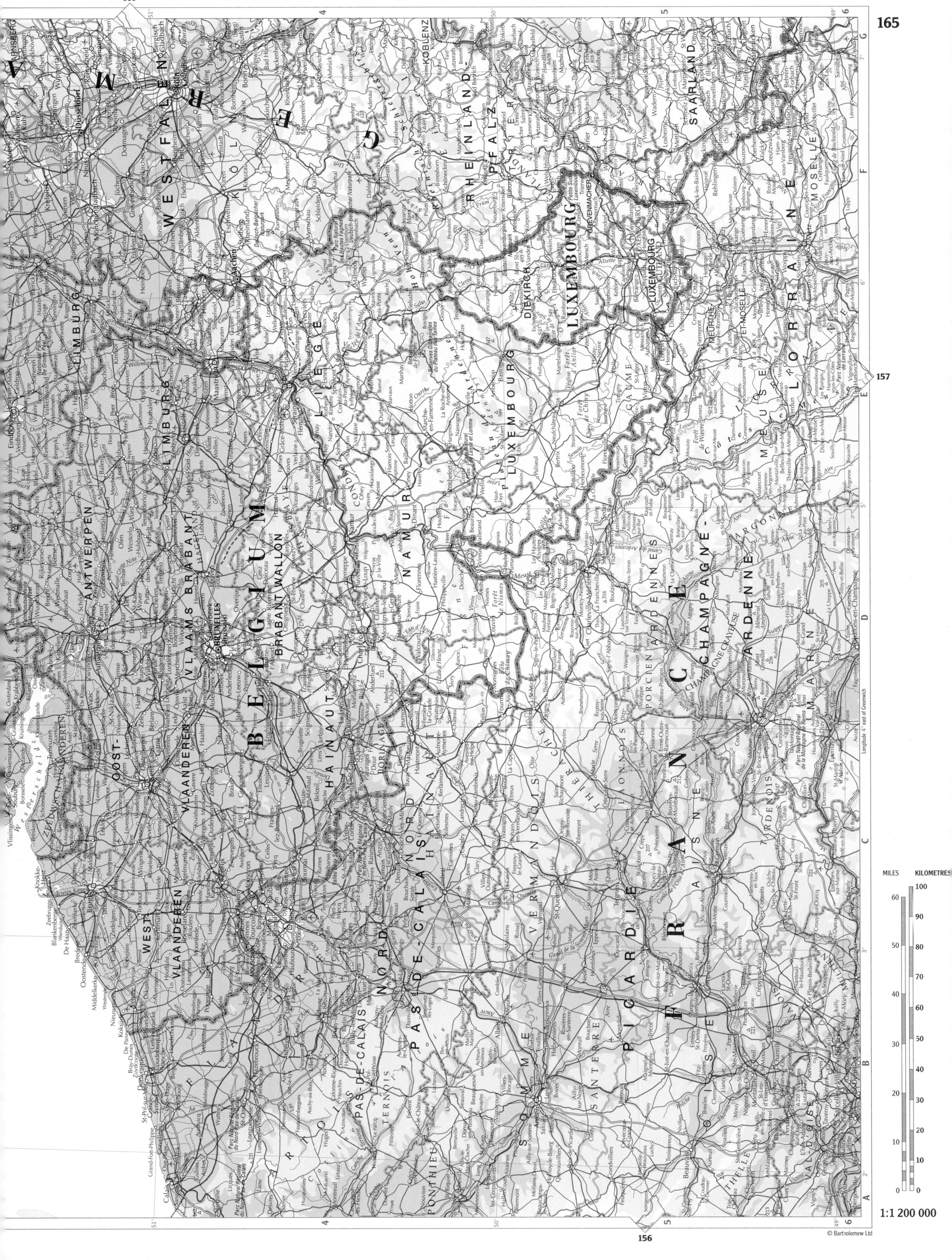
BELGIUM
LUXEMBOURG
FRANCE
GERMANY
NORD
PAS-DE-CALAIS
PICARDIE
CHAMPAGNE-ARDENNE
LORRAINE
RHEINLAND-PFALZ
SAARLAND
NORDRHEIN-WESTFALEN
LIMBURG
ANTWERPEN
OOST-VLAANDEREN
WEST-VLAANDEREN
VLAAMS BRABANT
BRABANT WALLON
HAINAUT
NAMUR
LIÈGE
BRUXELLES
MILES
KILOMETRES
1:1 200 000
Longitude 4° east of Greenwich
169
157
156
© Bartholomew Ltd

142
155
188
A
B
C
D
E
F
1
2
3
4
5
6
NORTH SEA
DENMARK
NETHERLANDS
BELGIUM
GERMANY
FRANCE
SWITZERLAND
AUSTRIA
ITALY
LUXEMBOURG
LIECHTENSTEIN
SCHLESWIG-HOLSTEIN
MECKLENBURG-VORPOMMERN
NIEDERSACHSEN
NORDRHEIN-WESTFALEN
HESSEN
THÜRINGEN
RHEINLAND-PFALZ
SAARLAND
BADEN-WÜRTTEMBERG
BAYERN
LORRAINE
ALSACE
CHAMPAGNE-ARDENNE
BOURGOGNE
FRANCHE-COMTÉ
RHÔNE-ALPES
PICARDIE
NORD-PAS-DE-CALAIS
TRENTINO ALTO ADIGE
VENETO
FRIULI VENEZIA GIULIA
LOMBARDIA
PIEMONTE
ALPS
VOSGES
JURA
AMSTERDAM
Rotterdam
'S-GRAVENHAGE (The Hague)
BRUXELLES
Hamburg
Bremen
Hannover
Düsseldorf
Köln (Cologne)
Frankfurt am Main
Stuttgart
München (Munich)
Nürnberg
Leipzig
Strasbourg
Zürich
BERN
Genève
Lyon
METRES
FEET
6000 19686
5000 16404
4000 13124
3000 9843
2000 6562
1500 4921
1000 3281
500 1640
200 656
100 328
0 0
LAND BELOW SEA LEVEL
50 164
200 656
1000 3281
2000 6562

Conic Equidistant Projection

188

BALTIC SEA
Gulf of Gdańsk
RUSSIAN FEDERATION
LITHUANIA
POLAND
BELARUS
UKRAINE
CZECH REPUBLIC
SLOVAKIA
HUNGARY
ROMANIA
SLOVENIA
CROATIA
YUGOSLAVIA
CARPATHIAN MOUNTAINS
WARSZAWA
PRAHA (Prague)
WIEN (Vienna)
BRATISLAVA
BUDAPEST
Longitude 14° east of Greenwich
© Bartholomew Ltd

134

136

196

MILES KILOMETRES

1:3 000 000

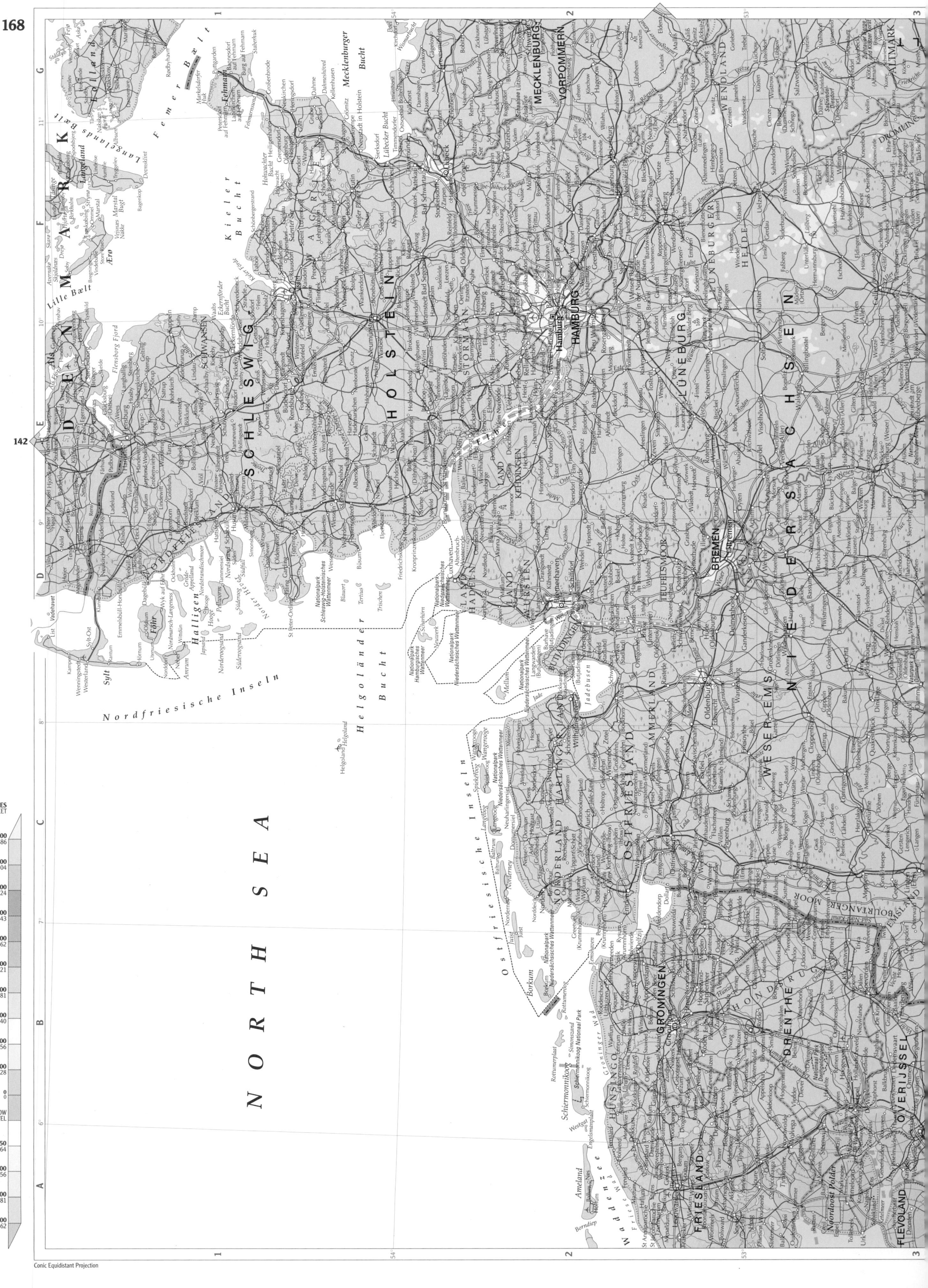
170
142
NORTH SEA
DENMARK
SCHLESWIG-HOLSTEIN
MECKLENBURG-VORPOMMERN
HAMBURG
BREMEN
NIEDERSACHSEN
GRONINGEN
DRENTHE
FRIESLAND
OVERIJSSEL
FLEVOLAND
ALTMARK
Nordfriesische Inseln
Ostfriesische Inseln
Helgoländer Bucht
Kieler Bucht
Mecklenburger Bucht
Lübecker Bucht
Fehmarn
Langeland
Lolland
Ærø
Sylt
Föhr
Amrum
Helgoland
Borkum
Juist
Norderney
Ameland
Schiermonnikoog
Waddenzee
Lille Bælt
Femer Bælt
Langelands Bælt
Flensborg Fjord
Elbe
Weser
Jadebusen
Dollart
Lüneburger Heide
Kiel
Lübeck
Hamburg
Bremen
Bremerhaven
Cuxhaven
Oldenburg
Emden
Wilhelmshaven
Groningen
Lüneburg
Neumünster
Flensburg
Schwerin
Nationalpark Schleswig-Holsteinisches Wattenmeer
Nationalpark Niedersächsisches Wattenmeer
Nationalpark Hamburgisches Wattenmeer
METRES
FEET
6000
19686
5000
16404
4000
13124
3000
9843
2000
6562
1500
4921
1000
3281
500
1640
200
656
100
328
0
0
LAND BELOW SEA LEVEL
50
164
200
656
1000
3281
2000
6562

Conic Equidistant Projection

171

GERMANY
NETHERLANDS
BELGIUM
LUXEMBOURG
NORDRHEIN-WESTFALEN
HESSEN
THÜRINGEN
RHEINLAND-PFALZ
BAYERN
Bielefeld
Düsseldorf
Köln
Essen
Dortmund
Kassel
Göttingen
Frankfurt am Main
Wiesbaden
Koblenz
Aachen
Hannover

173

172

MILES KILOMETRES

1:1 200 000

164

157

© Bartholomew Ltd

Conic Equidistant Projection

174

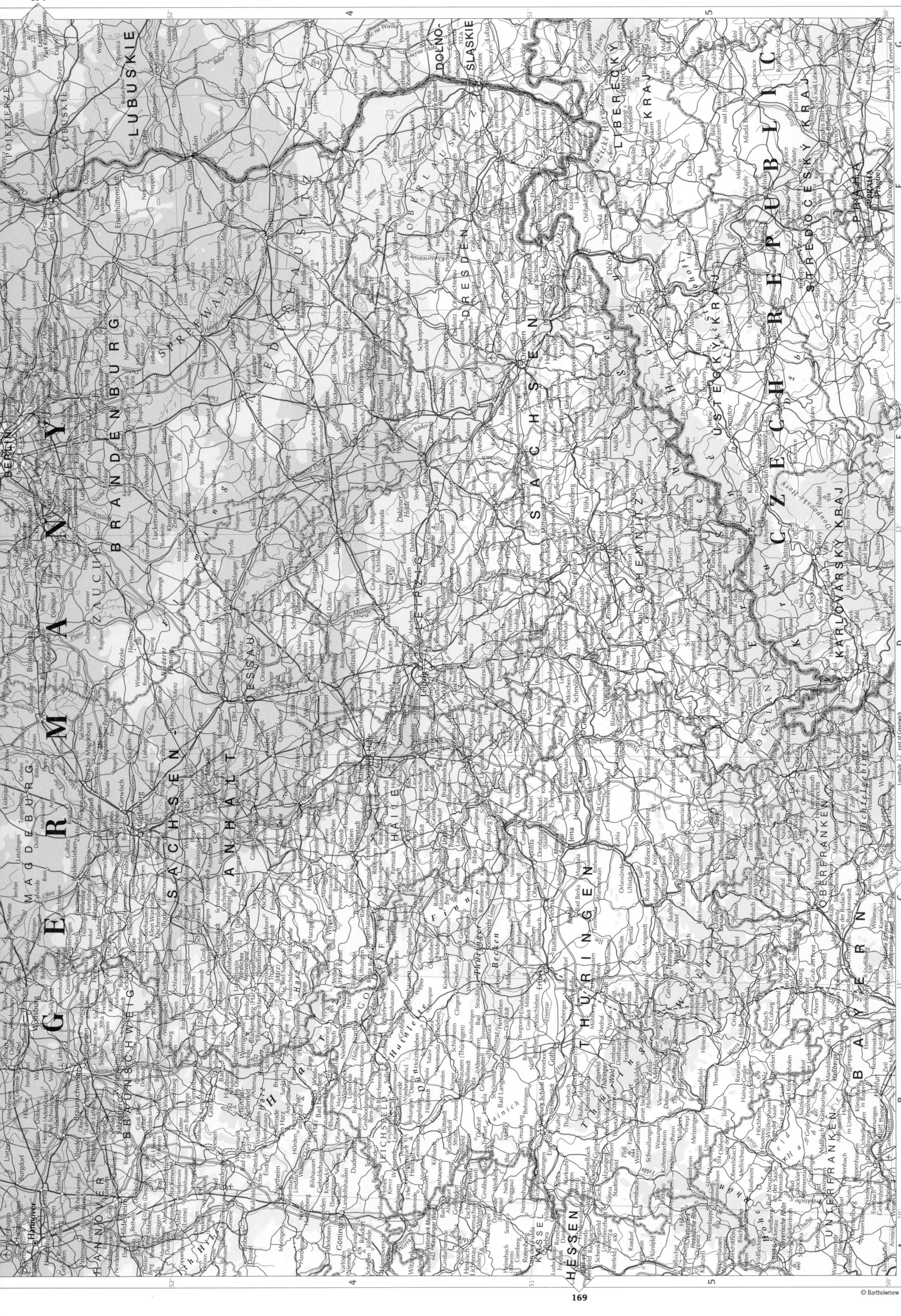
BERLIN
BRANDENBURG
SACHSEN
SACHSEN-ANHALT
THÜRINGEN
HESSEN
BAYERN
LUBUSKIE
DOLNOŚLĄSKIE
LIBERECKÝ KRAJ
ÚSTECKÝ KRAJ
STŘEDOČESKÝ KRAJ
KARLOVARSKÝ KRAJ
CZECH REPUBLIC
GERMANY
PRAHA (Prague)
Dresden
Leipzig
Magdeburg
Chemnitz
Erfurt
Halle
Dessau
Kassel
Göttingen
Hannover
Braunschweig
Wolfsburg
Jena
Cottbus
SPREEWALD
OBERLAUSITZ
NIEDERLAUSITZ
Harz
Thüringer Wald
Erzgebirge
VOGTLAND
OBERFRANKEN
UNTERFRANKEN
EICHSFELD
Longitude 12° east of Greenwich

176

173

MILES | KILOMETRES

0 10 20 30 40 50 60 (miles)

0 10 20 30 40 50 60 70 80 90 100 (kilometres)

1:1 200 000

169

© Bartholomew Ltd

169

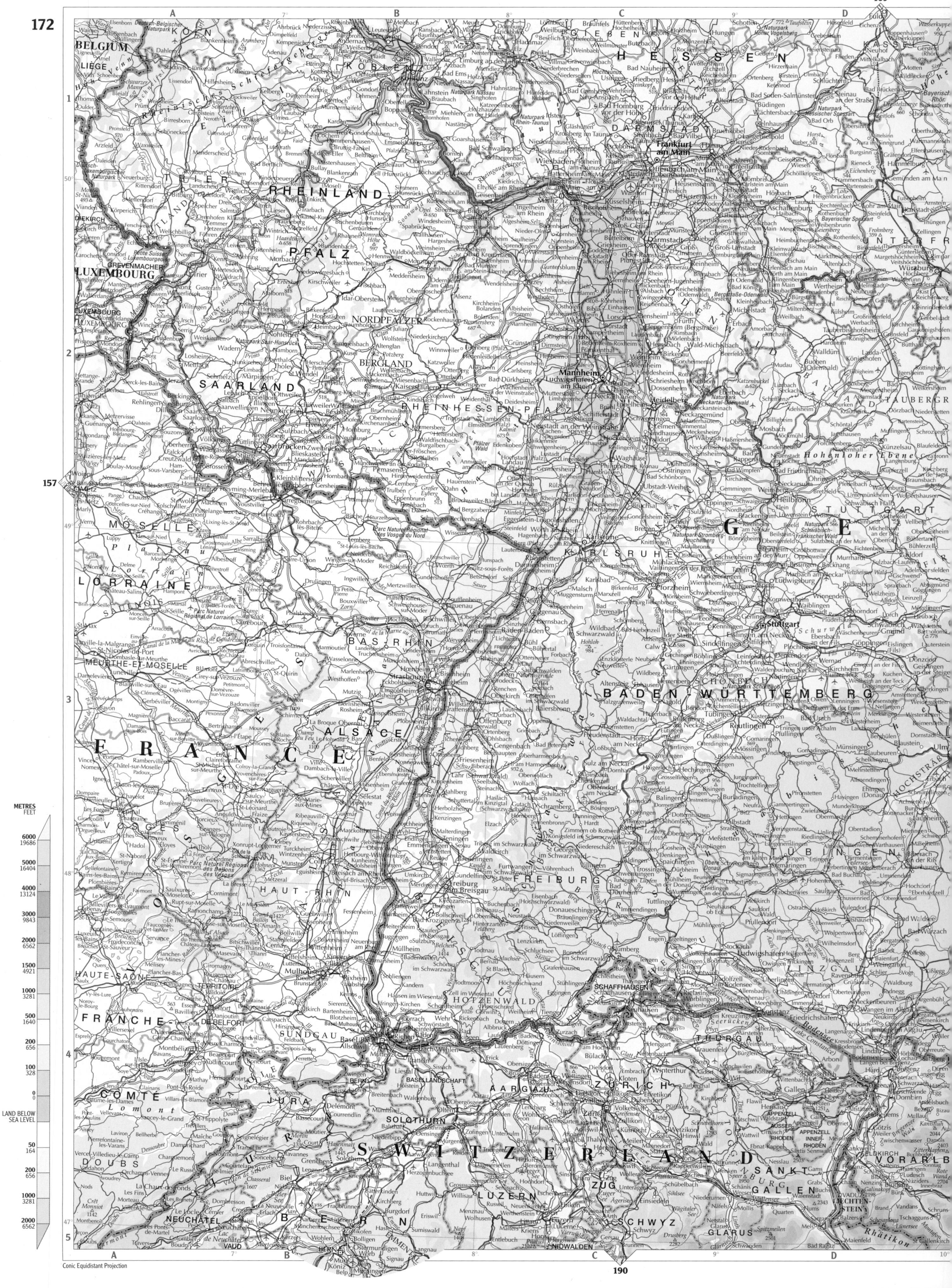
BELGIUM
LUXEMBOURG
HESSEN
RHEINLAND-PFALZ
SAARLAND
NORDPFÄLZER BERGLAND
MOSELLE
LORRAINE
BAS-RHIN
ALSACE
FRANCE
VOSGES
HAUT-RHIN
HAUTE-SAÔNE
FRANCHE-COMTÉ
DOUBS
JURA
SUNDGAU
BADEN-WÜRTTEMBERG
KARLSRUHE
STUTTGART
FREIBURG
TÜBINGEN
HOTZENWALD
SCHAFFHAUSEN
AARGAU
ZÜRICH
SOLOTHURN
BASELLANDSCHAFT
SWITZERLAND
LUZERN
BERN
ZUG
SCHWYZ
GLARUS
NIDWALDEN
SANKT GALLEN
APPENZELL AUSSER-RHODEN
APPENZELL INNER-RHODEN
NEUCHÂTEL
VAUD
LIECHTENSTEIN
VORARLBERG
THURGAU
DARMSTADT
Frankfurt am Main
Wiesbaden
Mainz
Koblenz
Trier
Saarbrücken
Mannheim
Ludwigshafen am Rhein
Heidelberg
Heilbronn
Stuttgart
Karlsruhe
Strasbourg
Freiburg im Breisgau
Mulhouse
Basel
Zürich
Bern
Ulm
Würzburg
Konstanz
METRES
FEET
6000 19686
5000 16404
4000 13124
3000 9843
2000 6562
1500 4921
1000 3281
500 1640
200 656
100 328
0 0
LAND BELOW SEA LEVEL
50 164
200 656
1000 3281
2000 6562

Conic Equidistant Projection

157

190

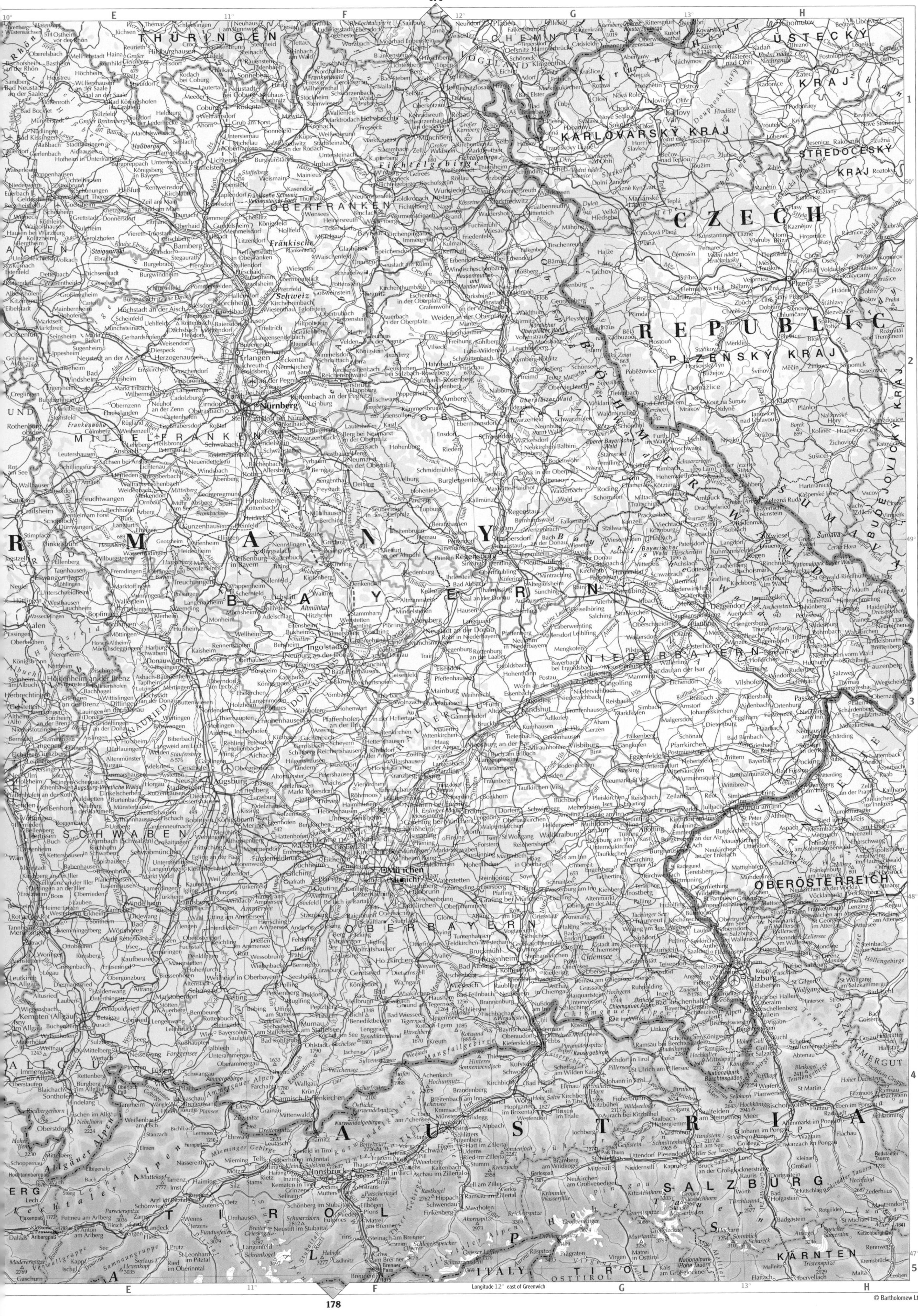
THÜRINGEN
CHEMNITZ
ÚSTECKÝ KRAJ
KARLOVARSKÝ KRAJ
STŘEDOČESKÝ KRAJ
CZECH REPUBLIC
PLZEŇSKÝ KRAJ
JIHOČESKÝ KRAJ
OBERFRANKEN
OBERPFALZ
MITTELFRANKEN
GERMANY
BAYERN
NIEDERBAYERN
SCHWABEN
OBERBAYERN
OBERÖSTERREICH
AUSTRIA
SALZBURG
TIROL
KÄRNTEN
ITALY
OSTTIROL
Nürnberg
Regensburg
Augsburg
München (Munich)
Ingolstadt
Salzburg
Innsbruck
Plzeň
Erlangen
Bamberg
Landshut
Passau
Fichtelgebirge
Böhmerwald
Bayerischer Wald
Šumava
Chiemsee
Ammersee
171
174
176
178
Longitude 12° east of Greenwich

MILES | KILOMETRES

1:1 200 000

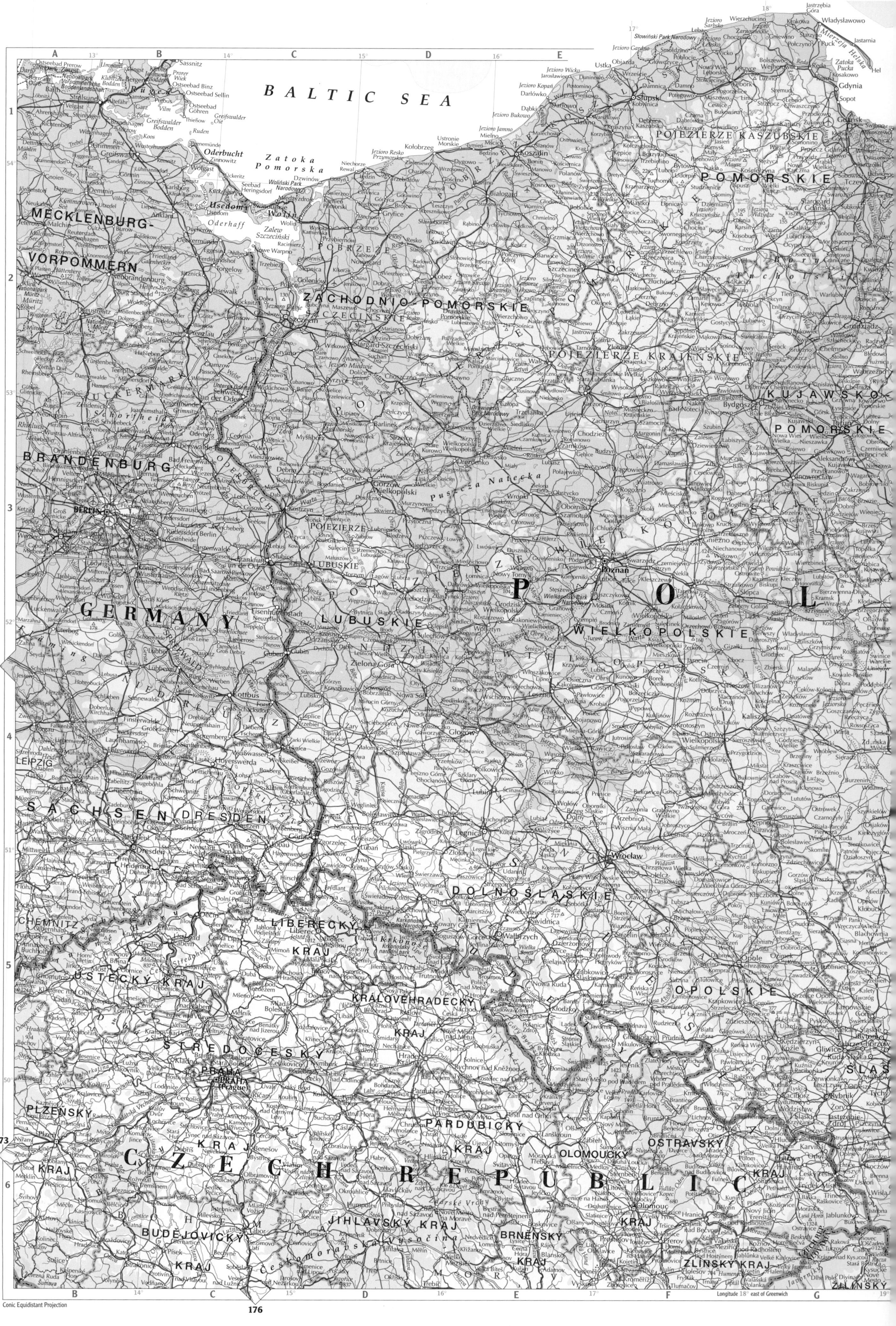
BALTIC SEA
Zatoka Pomorska
Oderbucht
MECKLENBURG-VORPOMMERN
BRANDENBURG
GERMANY
SACHSEN
DRESDEN
LEIPZIG
CHEMNITZ
BERLIN
ZACHODNIO-POMORSKIE
POMORSKIE
POJEZIERZE KASZUBSKIE
POJEZIERZE KRAJEŃSKIE
KUJAWSKO-POMORSKIE
WIELKOPOLSKIE
LUBUSKIE
DOLNOŚLĄSKIE
OPOLSKIE
POL
Poznań
Wrocław
Szczecin
Gdańsk
Bydgoszcz
LIBERECKÝ KRAJ
ÚSTECKÝ KRAJ
KRÁLOVEHRADECKÝ KRAJ
STŘEDOČESKÝ
PRAHA
PLZEŇSKÝ KRAJ
BUDĚJOVICKÝ KRAJ
PARDUBICKÝ KRAJ
JIHLAVSKÝ KRAJ
OLOMOUCKÝ KRAJ
OSTRAVSKÝ KRAJ
BRNĚNSKÝ KRAJ
ZLÍNSKÝ KRAJ
CZECH REPUBLIC
METRES FEET
6000 19686
5000 16404
4000 13124
3000 9843
2000 6562
1500 4921
1000 3281
500 1640
200 656
100 328
0 0
LAND BELOW SEA LEVEL
50 164
200 656
1000 3281
2000 6562
Longitude 18° east of Greenwich

171
173
176

Conic Equidistant Projection

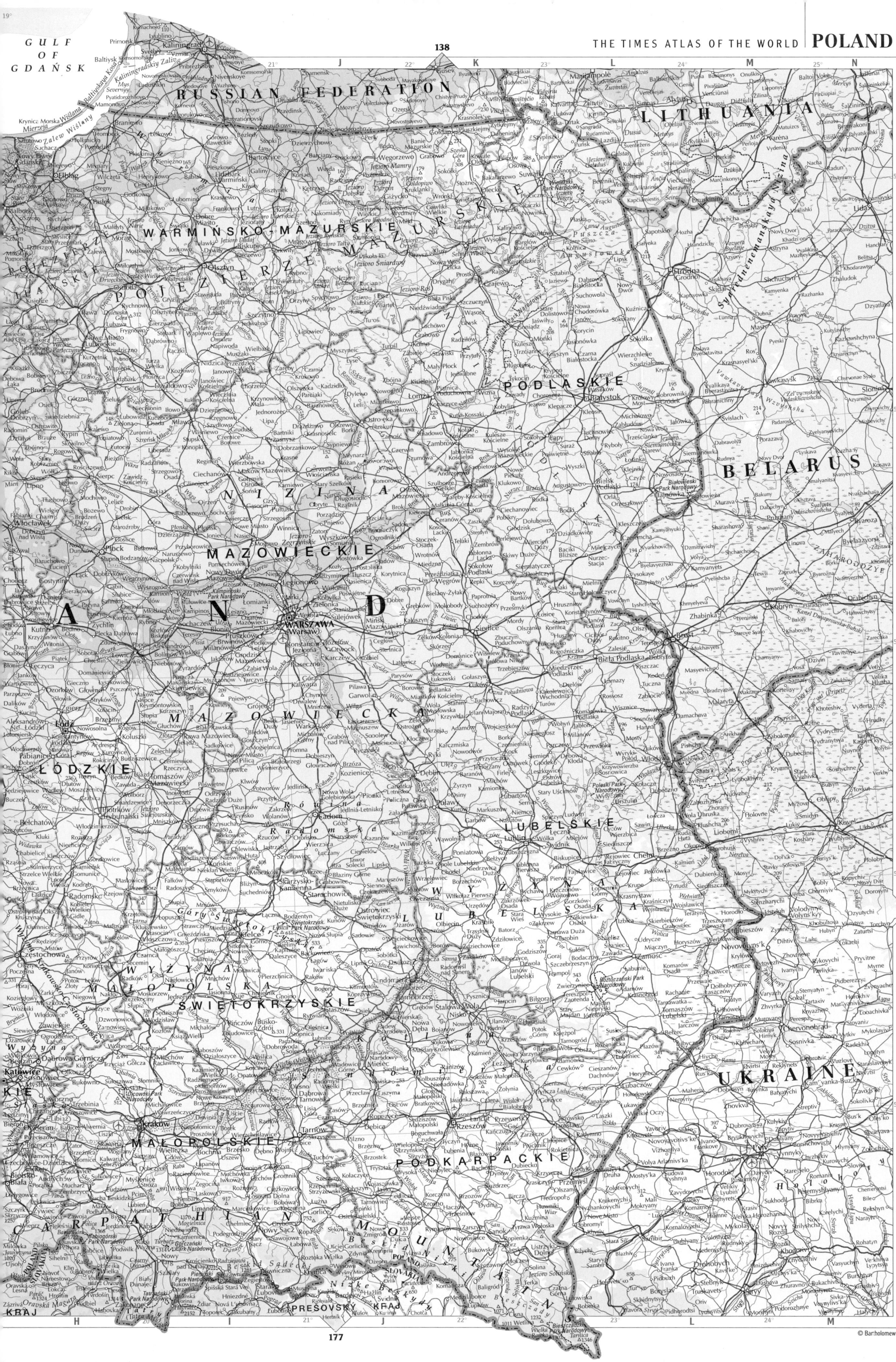
GULF OF GDAŃSK
RUSSIAN FEDERATION
LITHUANIA
BELARUS
UKRAINE
WARMIŃSKO-MAZURSKIE
PODLASKIE
MAZOWIECKIE
ŁÓDZKIE
LUBELSKIE
ŚWIĘTOKRZYSKIE
MAŁOPOLSKIE
PODKARPACKIE
WARSZAWA (Warsaw)
Kaliningrad
Elbląg
Olsztyn
Białystok
Łódź
Lublin
Kielce
Kraków
Rzeszów
Hrodna
Brest
L'viv
CARPATHIAN MOUNTAINS
PREŠOVSKÝ KRAJ

MILES KILOMETRES

1:1 800 000

© Bartholomew Ltd

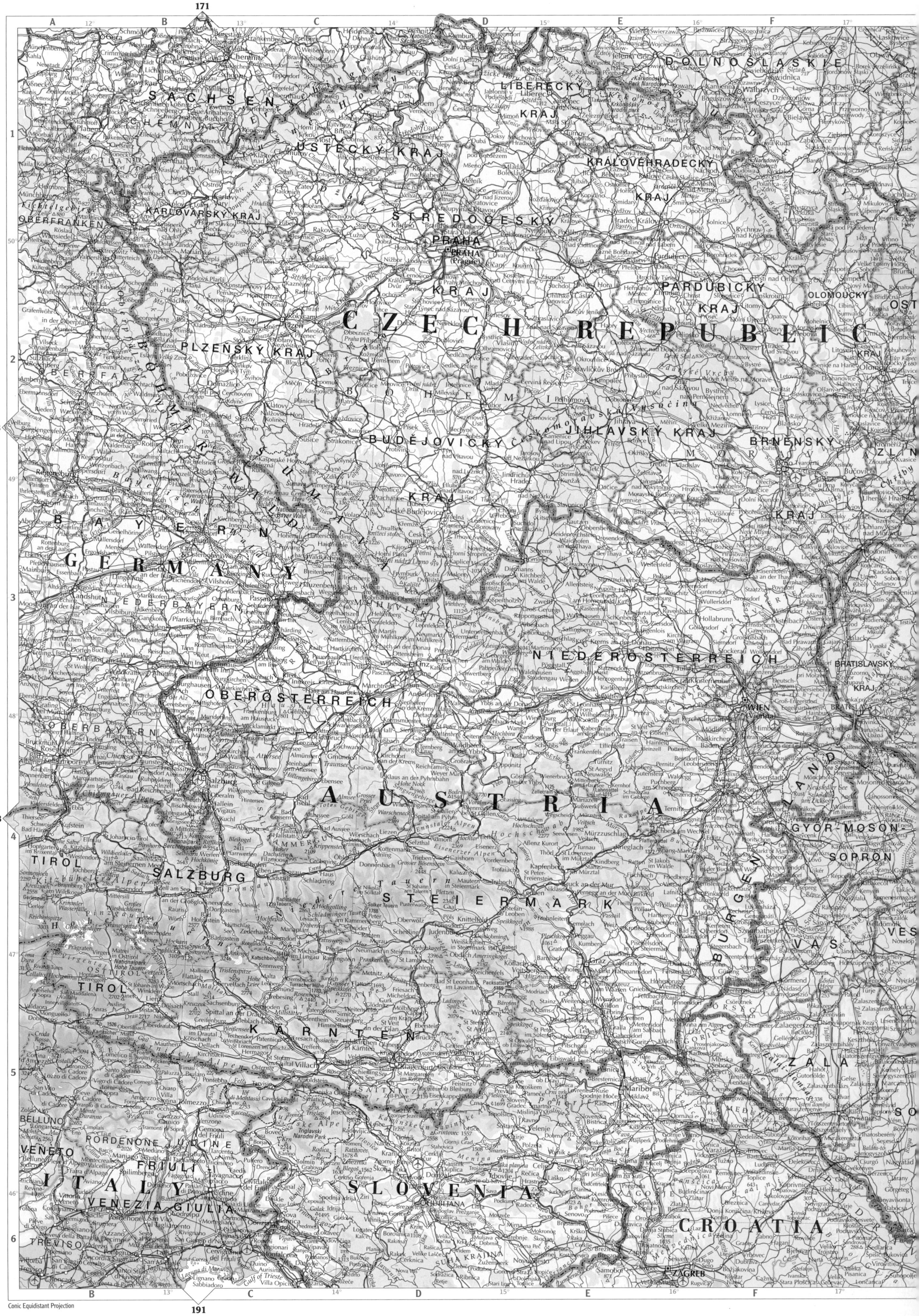

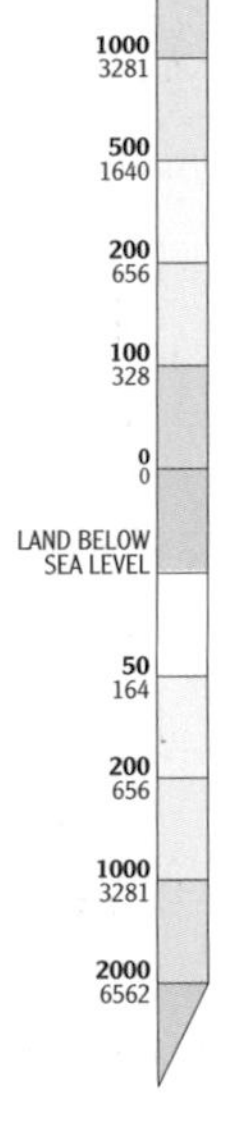

171
173
178
191

POLAND
SLOVAKIA
HUNGARY
ROMANIA
UKRAINE
YUGOSLAVIA
OPOLSKIE
ŚLĄSKIE
MAŁOPOLSKIE
ŚWIĘTOKRZYSKIE
PODKARPACKIE
LUBELSKIE
CARPATHIAN MOUNTAINS
ŽILINSKÝ KRAJ
PREŠOVSKÝ KRAJ
TRENČIANSKY KRAJ
BANSKOBYSTRICKÝ KRAJ
KOŠICKÝ KRAJ
NITRIANSKY KRAJ
TRNAVSKÝ
BORSOD-ABAÚJ-ZEMPLÉN
SZABOLCS-SZATMÁR-BEREG
NÓGRÁD
HEVES
KOMÁROM-ESZTERGOM
PEST
FEJÉR
JÁSZ-NAGYKUN-SZOLNOK
HAJDÚ-BIHAR
BÁCS-KISKUN
BÉKÉS
CSONGRÁD
TOLNA
BARANYA
SATU MARE
SĂLAJ
BIHOR
ARAD
TIMIŞ
VOJVODINA
BUDAPEST
MILES
KILOMETRES
1:1 800 000
Longitude 18° east of Greenwich
© Bartholomew Ltd

174
136
197
196

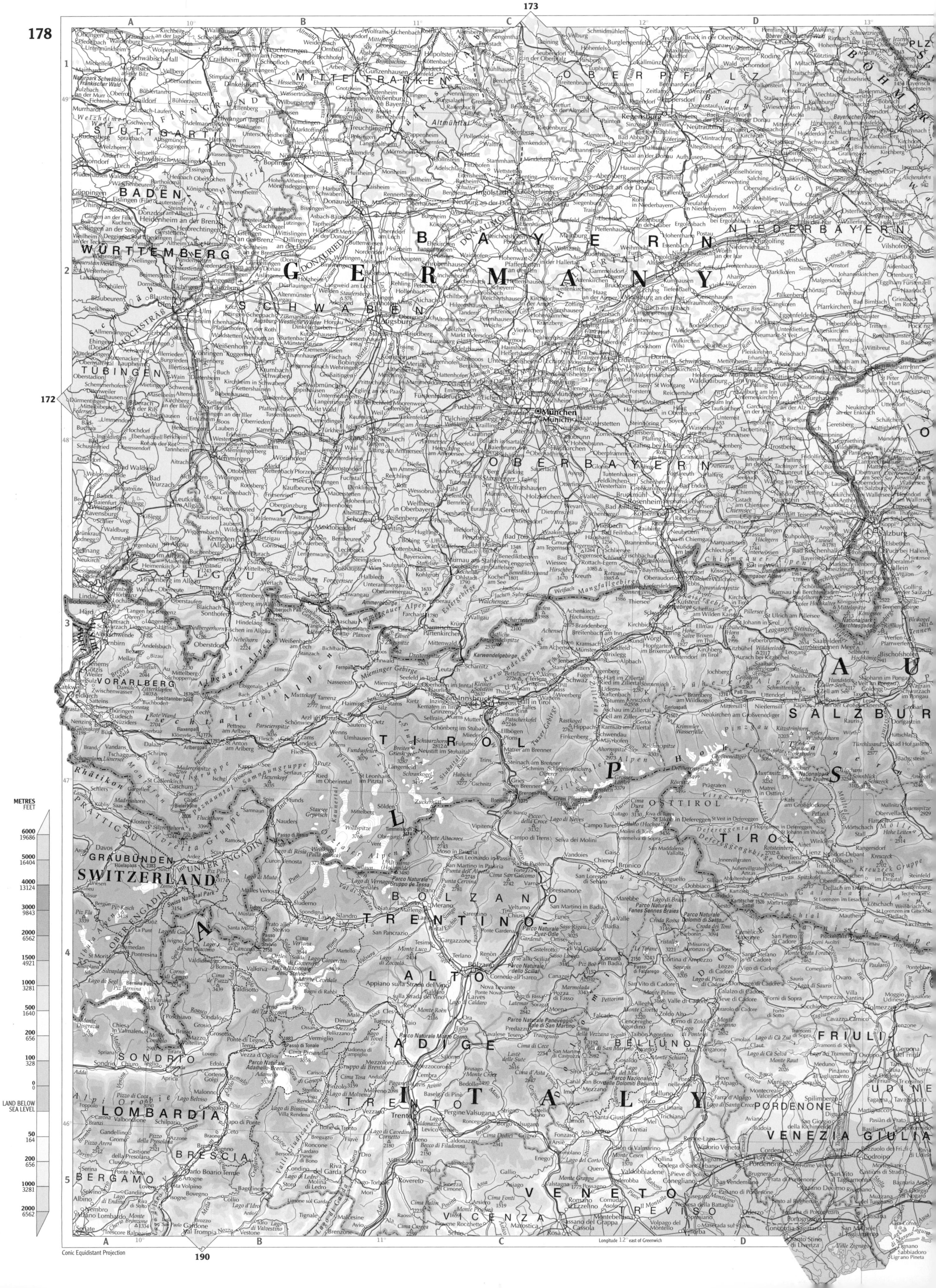
173
172
190
GERMANY
AUSTRIA
ITALY
SWITZERLAND
BAYERN
BADEN-WÜRTTEMBERG
MITTELFRANKEN
OBERPFALZ
NIEDERBAYERN
SCHWABEN
OBERBAYERN
TIROL
OSTTIROL
SALZBURG
VORARLBERG
GRAUBÜNDEN
LOMBARDIA
TRENTINO-ALTO ADIGE
BOLZANO
TRENTO
VENETO
FRIULI-VENEZIA GIULIA
UDINE
PORDENONE
BELLUNO
TREVISO
VICENZA
BRESCIA
BERGAMO
SONDRIO
STUTTGART
TÜBINGEN
ALLGÄU
München (Munich)
Augsburg
Regensburg
Ingolstadt
Innsbruck
Salzburg
Bolzano
Trento
Lindau
Bodensee
Kempten (Allgäu)
Memmingen
Ulm
Landshut
Rosenheim
ALPEN
METRES
FEET
6000
19686
5000
16404
4000
13124
3000
9843
2000
6562
1500
4921
1000
3281
500
1640
200
656
100
328
0
0
LAND BELOW SEA LEVEL
50
164
200
656
1000
3281
2000
6562
Longitude 12° east of Greenwich

Conic Equidistant Projection

174
CZECH REPUBLIC
JIHLAVSKÝ KRAJ
BUDĚJOVICKÝ KRAJ
BRNĚNSKÝ KRAJ
NIEDERÖSTERREICH
WIEN (Vienna)
SLOVAKIA
BURGENLAND
GYŐR-MOSON-SOPRON
177
STEIERMARK
KÄRNTEN
VAS
HUNGARY
ZALA
SLOVENIA
CROATIA
ZAGREB
LJUBLJANA
GORIZIA
Gulf of Trieste
Graz
Linz
Salzburg
MILES
KILOMETRES
1:1 200 000
191
© Bartholomew Ltd

METRES
FEET
6000
19686
5000
16404
4000
13124
3000
9843
2000
6562
1500
4921
1000
3281
500
1640
200
656
100
328
0
0
LAND BELOW SEA LEVEL
50
164
200
656
1000
3281
2000
6562
A T L A N T I C O C E A N
BAY OF
Mar Cantábrico
Costa Verde
GALICIA
ASTURIAS
CANTABRIA
CORDILLERA CANTÁBRICA
CASTILLA Y LEÓN
PORTUGAL
S P A
EXTREMADURA
ANDALUCÍA
SIERRA MORENA
GOLFO DE CÁDIZ
Costa de la Luz
Costa del Sol
MEDITE
MOROCCO
Strait of Gibraltar
MADRID
LISBOA (Lisbon)
Porto
Sevilla
Córdoba
Málaga
Granada
Gibraltar (U.K.)
Longitude 8° west of Greenwich

Conic Equidistant Projection

204

154

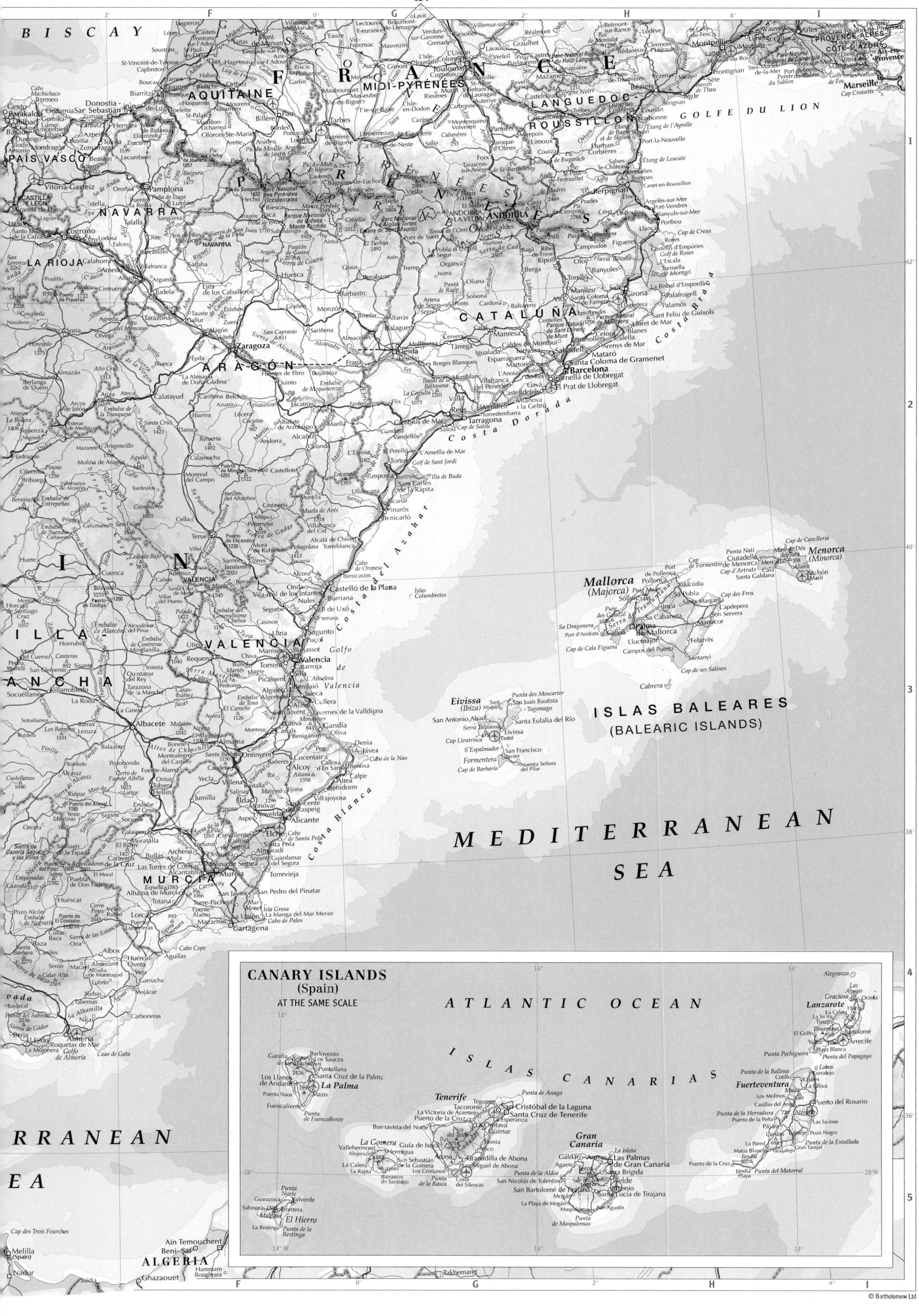

MILES | KILOMETRES

1:3 000 000

© Bartholomew Ltd

A
B
C
D
9°
8°
7°
6°
1
2
3
4
5
43°
42°
41°
40°
Mar Ca
Costa Ver
ATLANTIC OCEAN
GALICIA
A CORUÑA
LUGO
PONTEVEDRA
OURENSE
ASTURI
CORDILLERA
PORTUGAL
VIANA DO CASTELO
MINHO
BRAGA
VILA REAL
BRAGANÇA
PORTO
DOURO
AVEIRO
VISEU
BEIRA ALTA
GUARDA
COIMBRA
CASTELO BRANCO
BEIRA BAIXA
LEIRIA
SALAMANC
ZAMORA
CÁCERES
EXTREMADURA
A Coruña
Ferrol
Santiago de Compostela
Lugo
Ourense
Pontevedra
Vigo
Oviedo
Gijón
Porto
Braga
Bragança
Viseu
Aveiro
Coimbra
Guarda
Castelo Branco
Leiria
Zamora
Salamanca
Cáceres
METRES
FEET
6000
19686
5000
16404
4000
13124
3000
9843
2000
6562
1500
4921
1000
3281
500
1640
200
656
100
328
0
0
LAND BELOW
SEA LEVEL
50
164
200
656
1000
3281
2000
6562

Conic Equidistant Projection

184

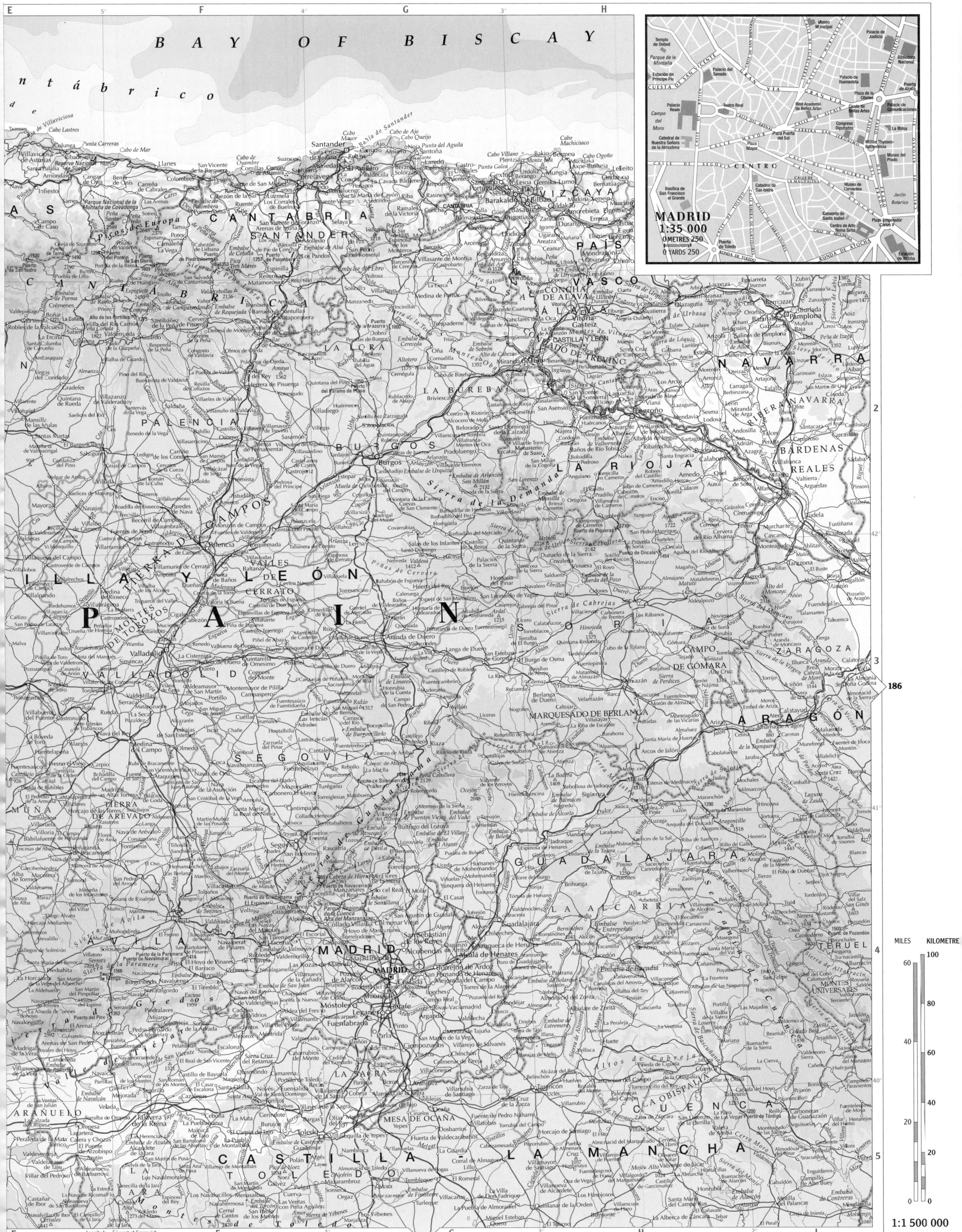
BAY OF BISCAY
MADRID
1:35 000
0 METRES 250
0 YARDS 250
CANTABRIA
PAÍS VASCO
NAVARRA
LA RIOJA
BARDENAS REALES
CASTILLA Y LEÓN
SPAIN
ARAGÓN
ZARAGOZA
GUADALAJARA
LA ALCARRIA
CUENCA
CASTILLA - LA MANCHA
TOLEDO
MESA DE OCAÑA
LA SAGRA
TERUEL
SORIA
BURGOS
PALENCIA
VALLADOLID
SEGOVIA
ÁVILA
MADRID
VIZCAYA
TIERRA DE CAMPOS
MARQUESADO DE BERLANGA
CAMPO DE GÓMARA
Longitude 5° west of Greenwich
185
186
MILES
KILOMETRES
1:1 500 000

© Bartholomew Ltd

182

PORTUGAL
LEIRIA
CASTELO BRANCO
BEIRA BAIXA
SANTARÉM
RIBATEJO
PORTALEGRE
LISBOA
LISBOA (Lisbon)
ÉVORA
SETÚBAL
Baía de Setúbal
BEJA
FARO
ALGARVE
CÁCERES
EXTREMADURA
BADAJOZ
TIERRA DE BARROS
LLANOS DE OLIVENZA
EL ANDEVALO
HUELVA
CONDADO DE NIEBLA
EL ALJARAFE
SEVILLA
CÁDIZ
Costa de la Luz
Playa de Castilla
GOLFO DE CÁDIZ
Las Marismas
Sierra de Aracena
Sierra de San Pedro
Strait of
MOROC
TANGER
MADEIRA
(Portugal)
1:1 250 000
Arquipélago da Madeira
Ilha da Madeira
Ilha de Porto Santo
Ilhas Desertas
FUNCHAL

Conic Equidistant Projection

METRES / FEET

METRES	FEET
6000	19686
5000	16404
4000	13124
3000	9843
2000	6562
1500	4921
1000	3281
500	1640
200	656
100	328
0	0
LAND BELOW SEA LEVEL	
50	164
200	656
1000	3281
2000	6562

183

187

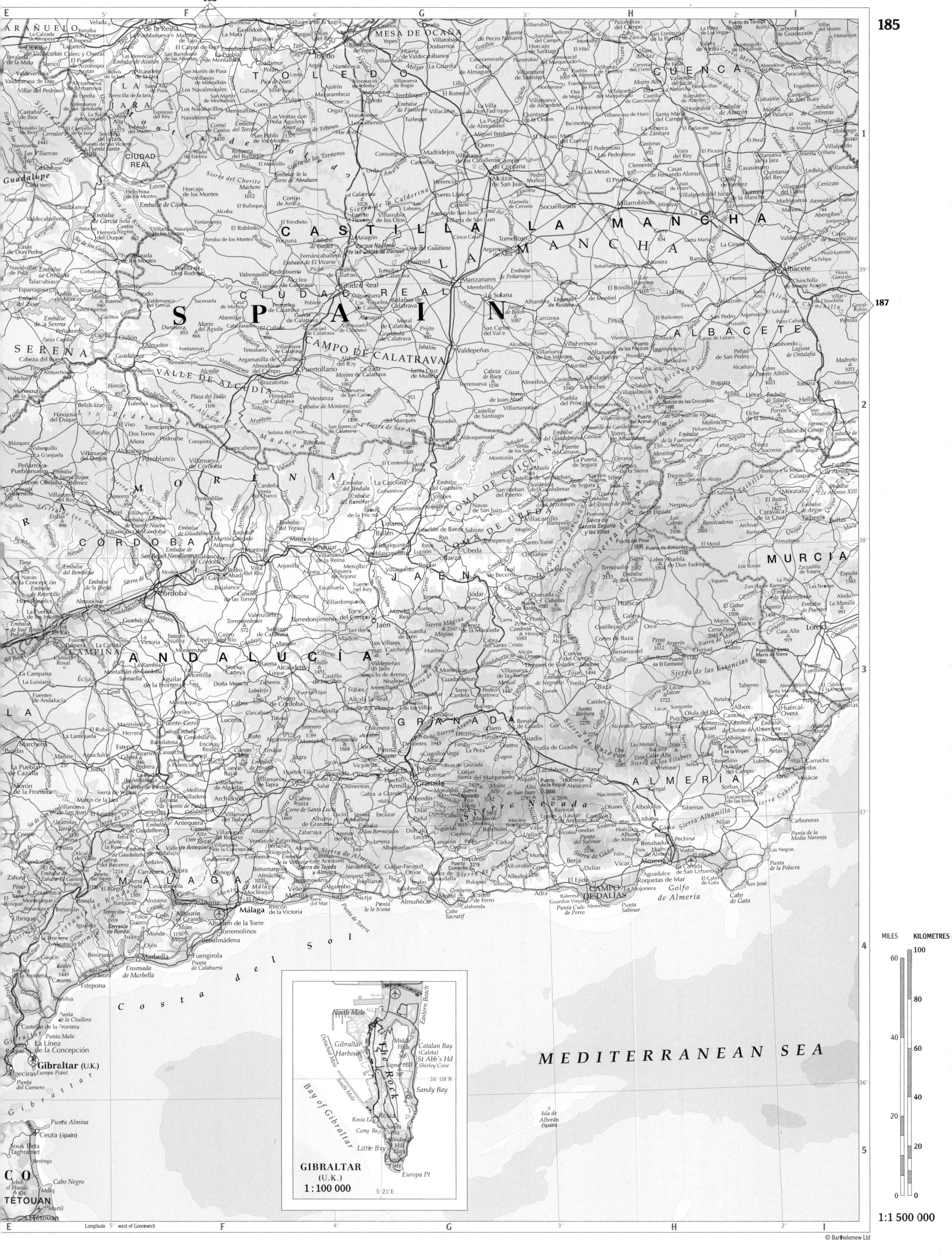

MILES KILOMETRES

1:1 500 000

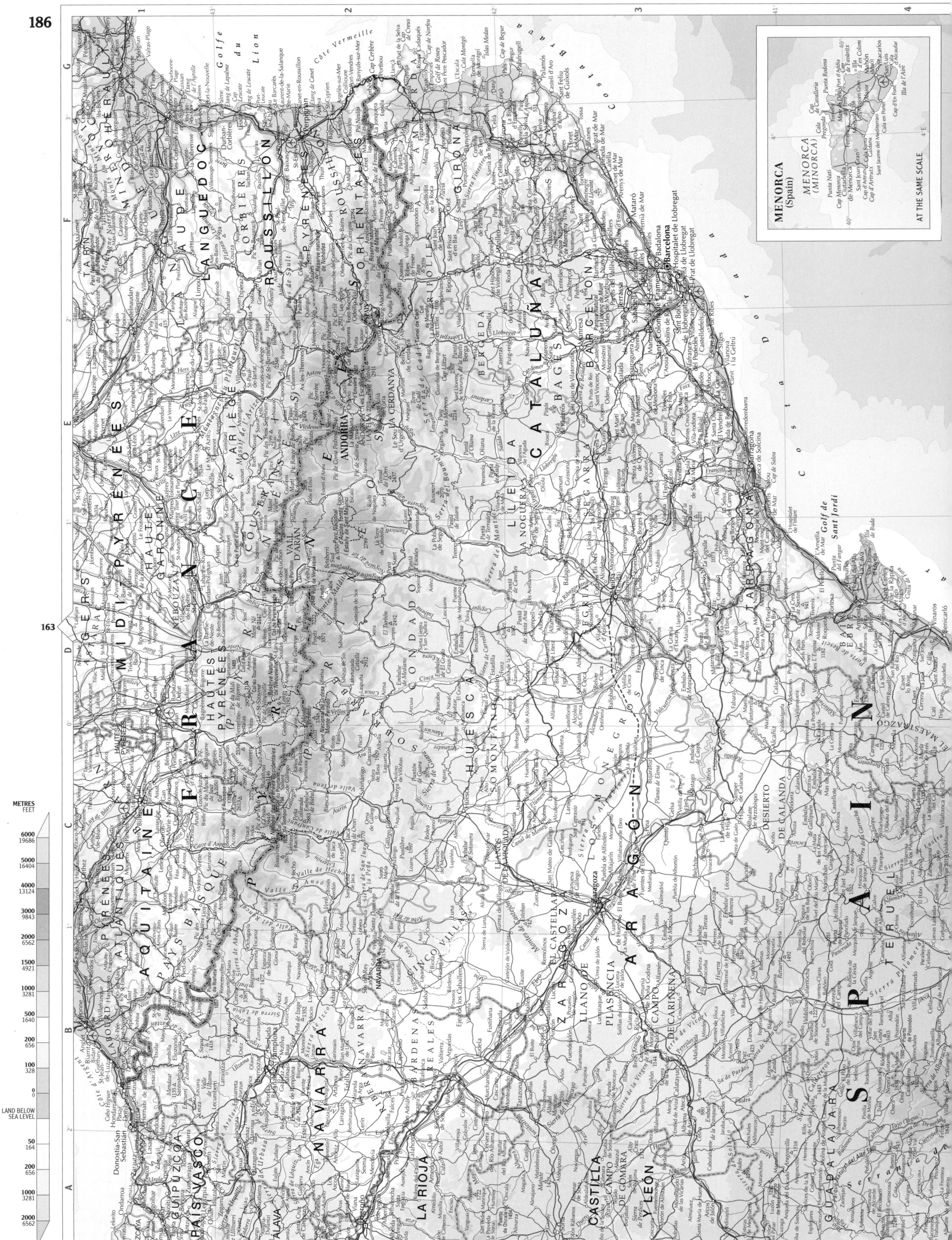

163

Conic Equidistant Projection

183

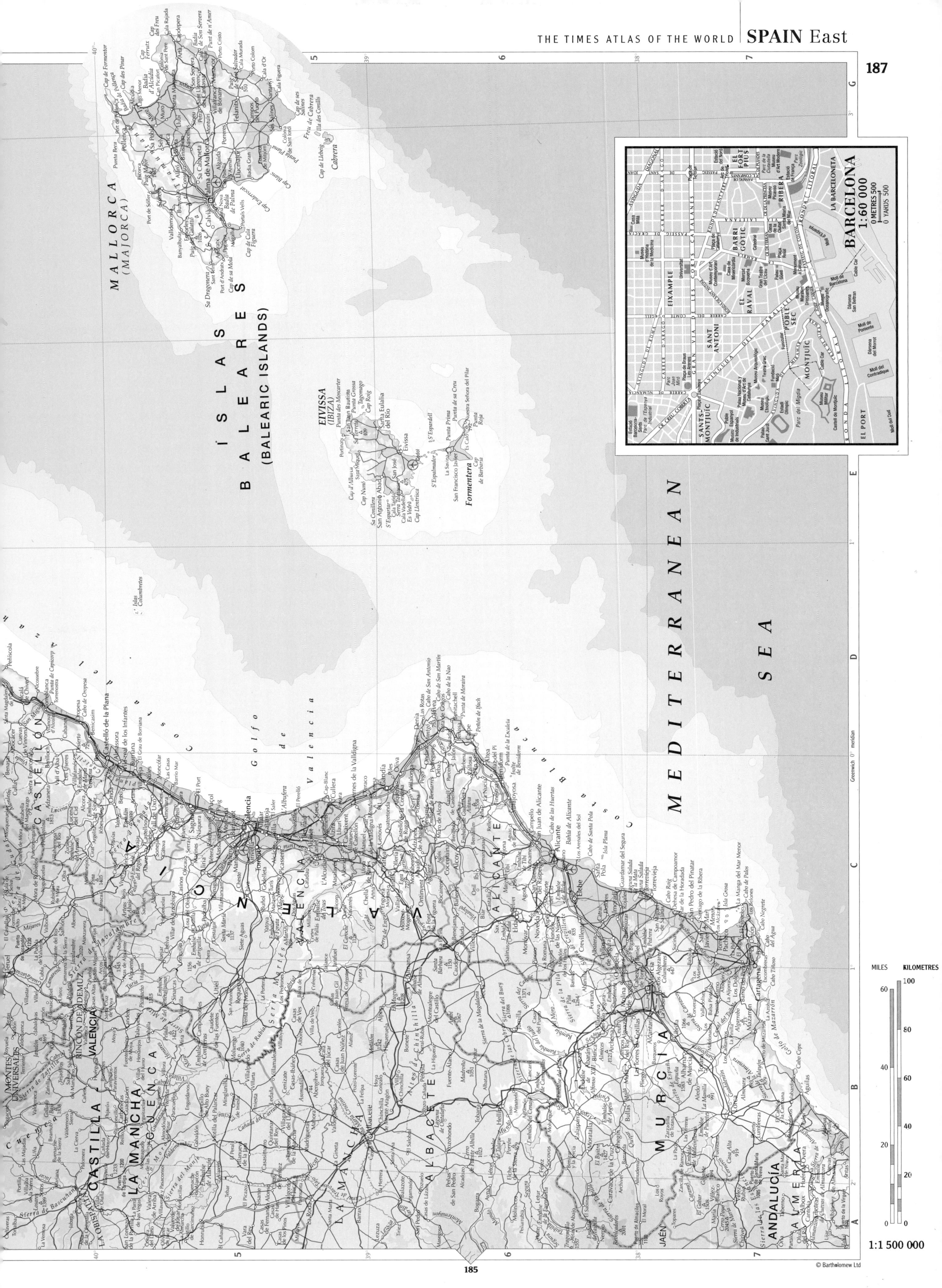
ISLAS BALEARES
(BALEARIC ISLANDS)
MALLORCA
(MAJORCA)
Palma de Mallorca
Cabrera
EIVISSA
(IBIZA)
Eivissa
Formentera
MEDITERRANEAN
SEA
Golfo de Valencia
Costa del Azahar
Costa Blanca
BARCELONA
1:60 000
CASTELLÓN
Castelló de la Plana
VALENCIA
Valencia
ALICANTE
Alicante
MURCIA
Cartagena
ALBACETE
Albacete
CUENCA
CASTILLA - LA MANCHA
ANDALUCÍA
ALMERÍA
Greenwich 0° meridian
MILES
KILOMETRES
1:1 500 000

185

196
167
166
155

METRES	FEET
6000	19686
5000	16404
4000	13124
3000	9843
2000	6562
1500	4921
1000	3281
500	1640
200	656
100	328
0	0
LAND BELOW SEA LEVEL	
50	164
200	656
1000	3281
2000	6562

Conic Equidistant Projection

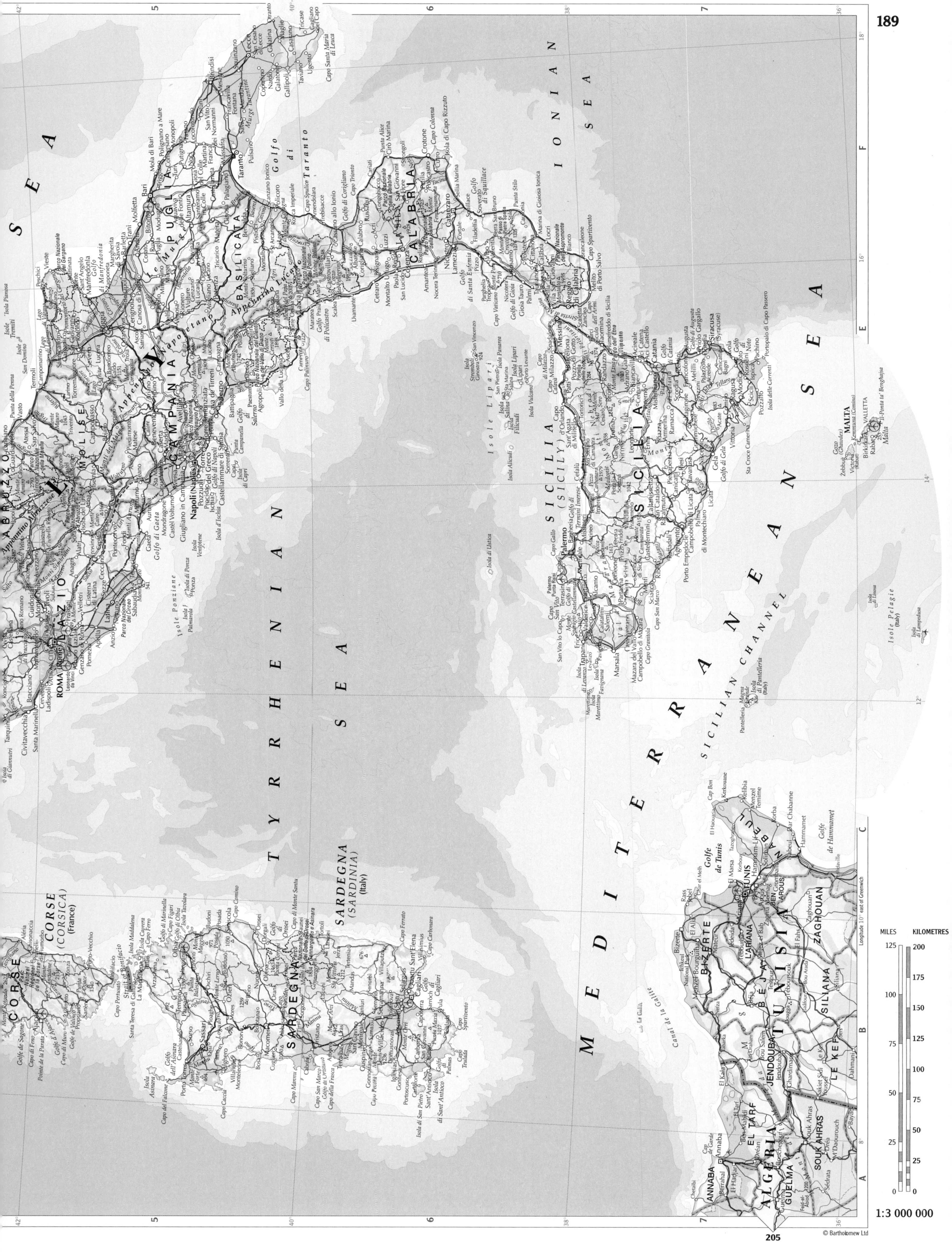
TYRRHENIAN SEA
MEDITERRANEAN SEA
IONIAN SEA
SICILIAN CHANNEL
SICILIA (SICILY)
SARDEGNA (SARDINIA) (Italy)
CORSE (CORSICA) (France)
MALTA
VALLETTA
TUNISIA
ALGERIA
TUNIS
ROMA (Rome)
Napoli (Naples)
Palermo
Catania
Messina
Cagliari
Sassari
Bari
Taranto
Lecce
Brindisi
Reggio di Calabria
Siracusa (Syracuse)
LAZIO
CAMPANIA
MOLISE
PUGLIA
BASILICATA
CALABRIA
Golfo di Taranto
Isole Eolie o Lipari
Isole Pelagie (Italy)
Golfe de Tunis
Golfe de Hammamet
Longitude 10° east of Greenwich
MILES
KILOMETRES

1:3 000 000

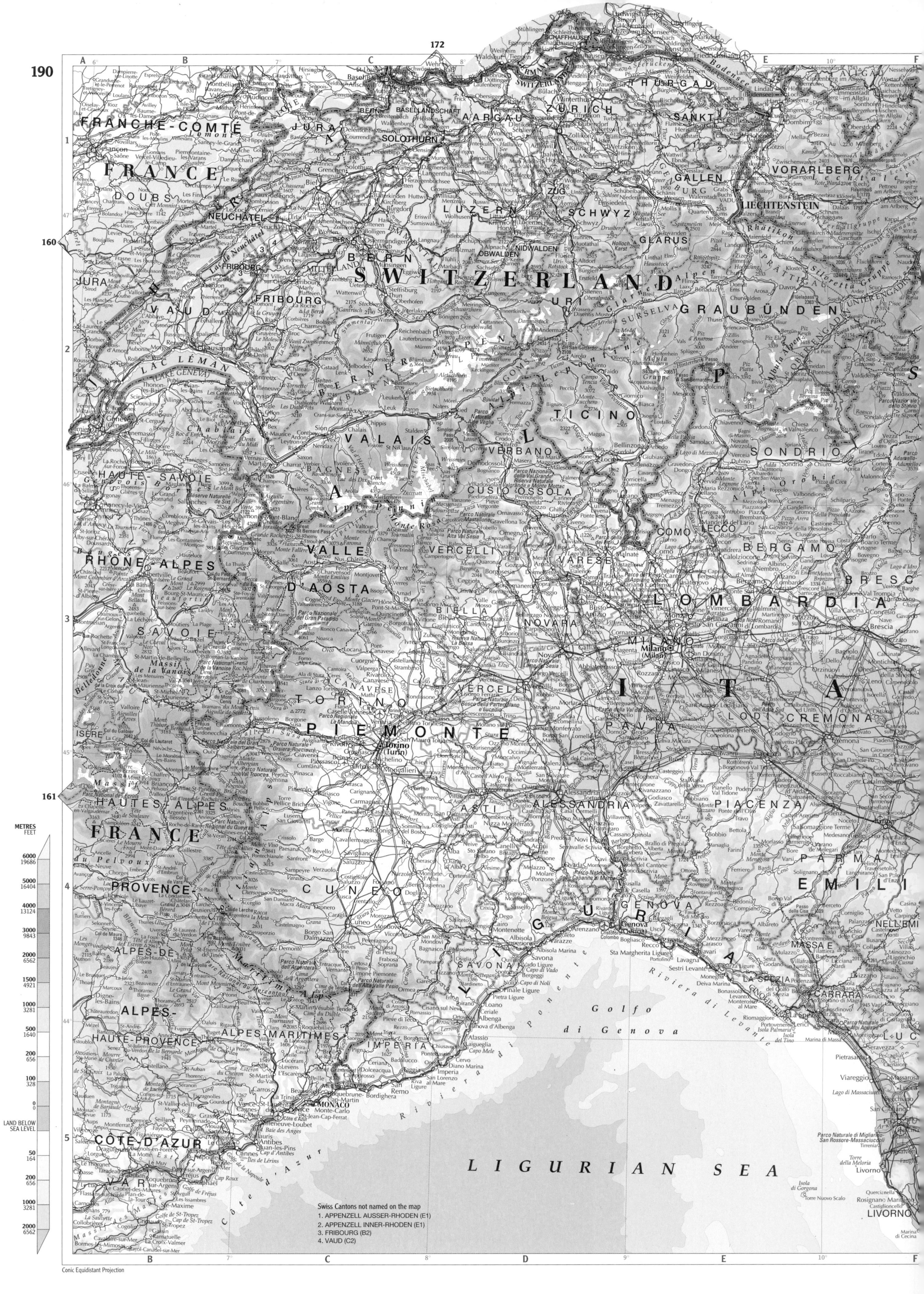
172
160
161
METRES
FEET
6000 19686
5000 16404
4000 13124
3000 9843
2000 6562
1500 4921
1000 3281
500 1640
200 656
100 328
0
LAND BELOW SEA LEVEL
50 164
200 656
1000 3281
2000 6562
FRANCHE-COMTÉ
FRANCE
DOUBS
JURA
VAUD
RHÔNE-ALPES
SAVOIE
HAUTE-SAVOIE
ISÈRE
HAUTES-ALPES
PROVENCE-
ALPES-DE-HAUTE-PROVENCE
ALPES-MARITIMES
CÔTE-D'AZUR
VAR
MONACO
SWITZERLAND
SCHAFFHAUSEN
BASELLANDSCHAFT
AARGAU
ZÜRICH
THURGAU
SANKT GALLEN
SOLOTHURN
NEUCHÂTEL
BERN
LUZERN
SCHWYZ
ZUG
GLARUS
OBWALDEN
NIDWALDEN
URI
FRIBOURG
VALAIS
TICINO
GRAUBÜNDEN
LIECHTENSTEIN
VORARLBERG
LAC LÉMAN
(LAKE GENEVA)
Genève
Lausanne
Bern
Zürich
Basel
Luzern
ITALIA
VALLE D'AOSTA
PIEMONTE
LOMBARDIA
LIGURIA
EMILIA
SONDRIO
BERGAMO
COMO
LECCO
VARESE
VERBANO-CUSIO-OSSOLA
VERCELLI
BIELLA
NOVARA
MILANO
Milano (Milan)
TORINO
Torino (Turin)
ALESSANDRIA
ASTI
CUNEO
SAVONA
GENOVA
Genova
IMPERIA
PAVIA
LODI
CREMONA
PIACENZA
PARMA
MASSA E CARRARA
LA SPEZIA
LIVORNO
Golfo di Genova
Riviera di Ponente
Riviera di Levante
Côte d'Azur
LIGURIAN SEA
Swiss Cantons not named on the map
1. APPENZELL AUSSER-RHODEN (E1)
2. APPENZELL INNER-RHODEN (E1)
3. FRIBOURG (B2)
4. VAUD (C2)

Conic Equidistant Projection

178
176
196
193
GERMANY
BAYERN
AUSTRIA
TIROL
SALZBURG
STEIERMARK
OSTTIROL
KÄRNTEN
BOLZANO
TRENTINO-
ALTO ADIGE
TRENTO
BELLUNO
FRIULI-
UDINE
PORDENONE
VENEZIA GIULIA
GORIZIA
SLOVENIA
CROATIA
GORSKI KOTAR
VICENZA
TREVISO
VENETO
VERONA
PADOVA
VENEZIA
ROVIGO
FERRARA
MANTOVA
EMILIA-ROMAGNA
MODENA
BOLOGNA
RAVENNA
FORLÌ
RIMINI
SAN MARINO
PESARO
E URBINO
ANCONA
MARCHE
MACERATA
PERUGIA
UMBRIA
AREZZO
SIENA
FIRENZE
PRATO
PISTOIA
PISA
TOSCANA
Gulf of Trieste
Trieste
Gulf of Venice
ADRIATIC SEA
Ljubljana
Rijeka
Ancona
Pula
Krk
Cres
Lošinj
MILES
KILOMETRES
0
20
40
60
80
100
1:1 500 000
Longitude 11° east of Greenwich

© Bartholomew Ltd

191

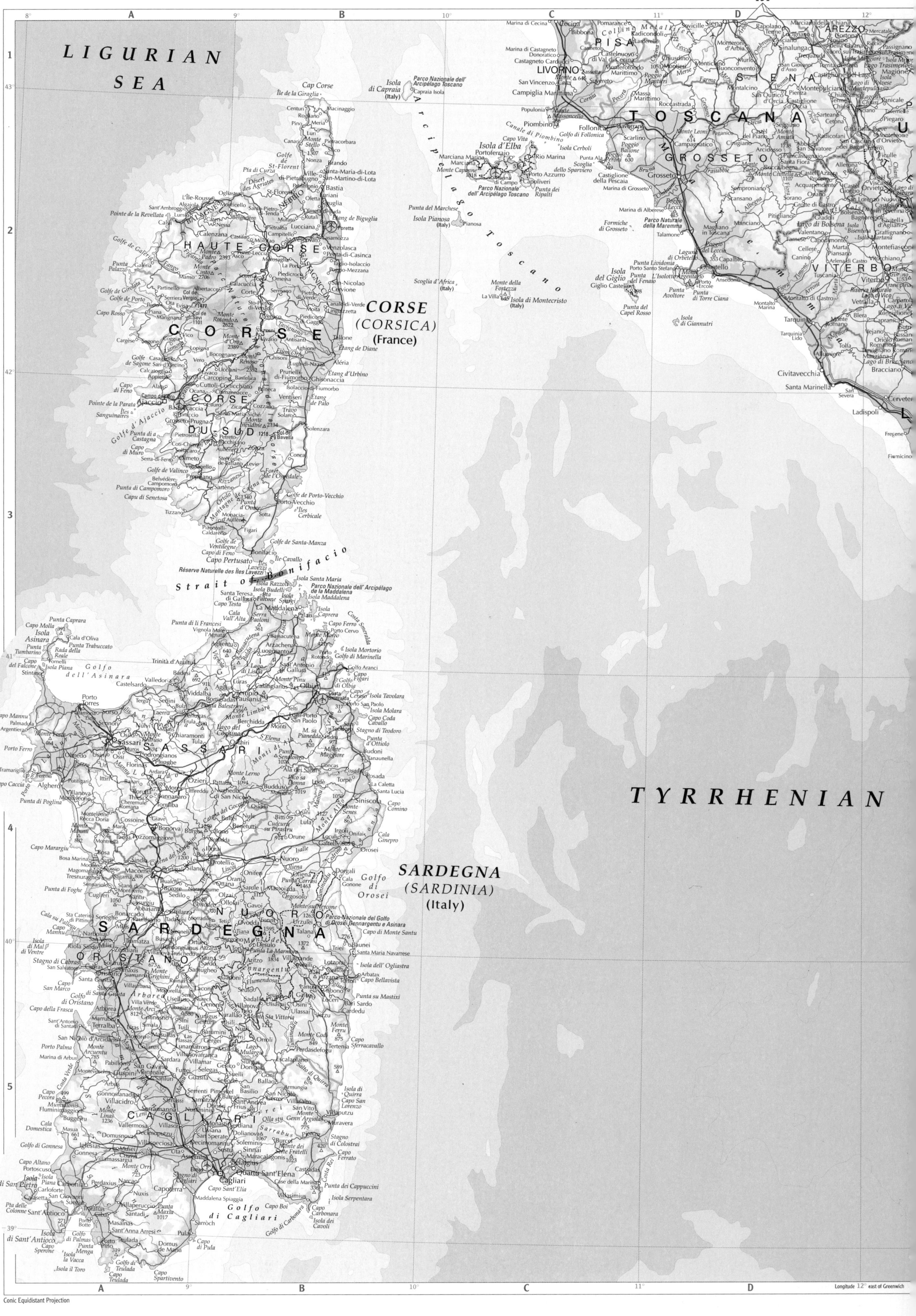

LIGURIAN SEA
TYRRHENIAN
CORSE (CORSICA) (France)
SARDEGNA (SARDINIA) (Italy)
TOSCANA
Strait of Bonifacio
HAUTE-CORSE
CORSE-DU-SUD
SASSARI
NUORO
ORISTANO
CAGLIARI
GROSSETO
LIVORNO
PISA
SIENA
AREZZO
VITERBO
Ajaccio
Bastia
Sassari
Cagliari
Isola d'Elba
Isola di Capraia (Italy)
Isola Pianosa (Italy)
Isola del Giglio
Isola di Montecristo (Italy)
Golfo di Cagliari
Golfo di Orosei
Golfo dell'Asinara
Civitavecchia
Longitude 12° east of Greenwich

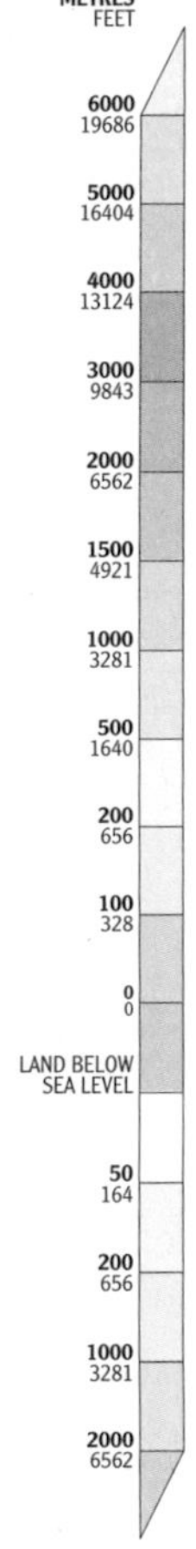

METRES
FEET
6000
19686
5000
16404
4000
13124
3000
9843
2000
6562
1500
4921
1000
3281
500
1640
200
656
100
328
0
0
LAND BELOW SEA LEVEL
50
164
200
656
1000
3281
2000
6562

ADRIATIC SEA
CROATIA
SEA
MARCHE
ABRUZZO
MOLISE
PUGLIA
CAMPANIA
BASILICATA
CALABRIA
LAZIO
UMBRIA
ITALY
MACERATA
ASCOLI PICENO
TERAMO
PESCARA
CHIETI
L'AQUILA
RIETI
ROMA
FROSINONE
LATINA
CASERTA
BENEVENTO
ISERNIA
CAMPOBASSO
FOGGIA
AVELLINO
NAPOLI
SALERNO
POTENZA
MATERA
BARI
COSENZA
Golfo di Gaeta
Golfo di Napoli
Golfo di Salerno
Golfo di Policastro
Golfo di Manfredonia
Isole Tremiti (Italy)
Isole Ponziane
Isola d'Ischia
Isola di Capri
Palagruža (Croatia)
Jabuka (Croatia)
ROME
1:50 000
VATICAN CITY
TRASTEVERE
SALARIO
TRIONFALE
Villa Borghese
MILES
KILOMETRES
1:1 500 000
195

193
TYRRHENIAN SEA
SICILIAN CHANNEL
SICILIA
(SICILY)
TUNISIA
Isole Ponziane
Isola Palmarola
Isola Zannone
Isola di Gavi
Isola di Ponza
Ponza
Isola Ventotene
Isola di Ustica
Ustica
Isole Lipari
Isola Alicudi
Isola Filicudi
Isola Salina
Isola Lipari
Lipari
Isola Vulcano
Golfo di Napoli
Golfo di Salerno
Isola d'Ischia
Isola di Capri
Napoli
(Naples)
CASERTA
BENEVENTO
NAPOLI
CAMPANIA
Salerno
Agropoli
Isola Licosa
Capo San Vito
Capo Gallo
Golfo di Castellammare
Golfo di Palermo
Palermo
Capo Zafferano
Golfo di Termini Imerese
Trapani
Isola Marettimo
Isola di Levanzo
Isola Favignana
Marsala
Mazara del Vallo
Capo Granitola
Capo San Marco
TRAPANI
PALERMO
AGRIGENTO
CALTANISSETTA
ENNA
CATANIA
RAGUSA
Agrigento
Licata
Gela
Golfo di Gela
Vittoria
Ragusa
Pantelleria
Isola di Pantelleria
(Italy)
Cap Bon
Kelibia
METRES
FEET
6000 19686
5000 16404
4000 13124
3000 9843
2000 6562
1500 4921
1000 3281
500 1640
200 656
100 328
0 0
LAND BELOW SEA LEVEL
50 164
200 656
1000 3281
2000 6562

Conic Equidistant Projection

ADRIATIC SEA
Strait of Otranto
GOLFO DI TARANTO
IONIAN SEA
PUGLIA
BASILICATA
CALABRIA
BARI
BRINDISI
TARANTO
LECCE
MATERA
POTENZA
COSENZA
CROTONE
CATANZARO
VIBO VALENTIA
REGGIO DI CALABRIA
SALERNO
FOGGIA
SIRACUSA
Golfo di Policastro
Golfo di Santa Eufemia
Golfo di Squillace
Golfo di Gioia
Golfo di Milazzo
Golfo di Catania
Golfo di Noto
Golfo di Augusta
Golfo di Corigliano
Capo Santa Maria di Leuca
Capo Colonna
Capo Rizzuto
Capo Spartivento
Capo Vaticano
Punta Alice
Isola Stromboli
Isola Panarea
Isola Capo Passero
Parco Nazionale del Pollino
Parco Nazionale della Calabria
Parco Nazionale dell'Aspromonte
Parco Nazionale del Cilento e del Vallo di Diano
LA SILA
Bari
Taranto
Brindisi
Lecce
Matera
Potenza
Cosenza
Crotone
Catanzaro
Reggio di Calabria
Messina
Catania
Siracusa
Gallipoli
Otranto
Monopoli
Altamura
Barletta
Andria
Trani
Molfetta
Lamezia Terme
Paola
Rossano
Locri
Siderno
Taormina
Acireale
Augusta
Avola
Milazzo
MALTA
1:500 000
Gozo (Ghawdex)
Kemmuna (Comino)
Kemmunett (Cominotto)
Malta
Valletta
Sliema
Rabat
Mdina
Filfla
Marsaxlokk
14°10'
14°20'
14°30'
36°00'
35°50'
MILES
KILOMETRES
Longitude 16° east of Greenwich
1:1 500 000

© Bartholomew Ltd

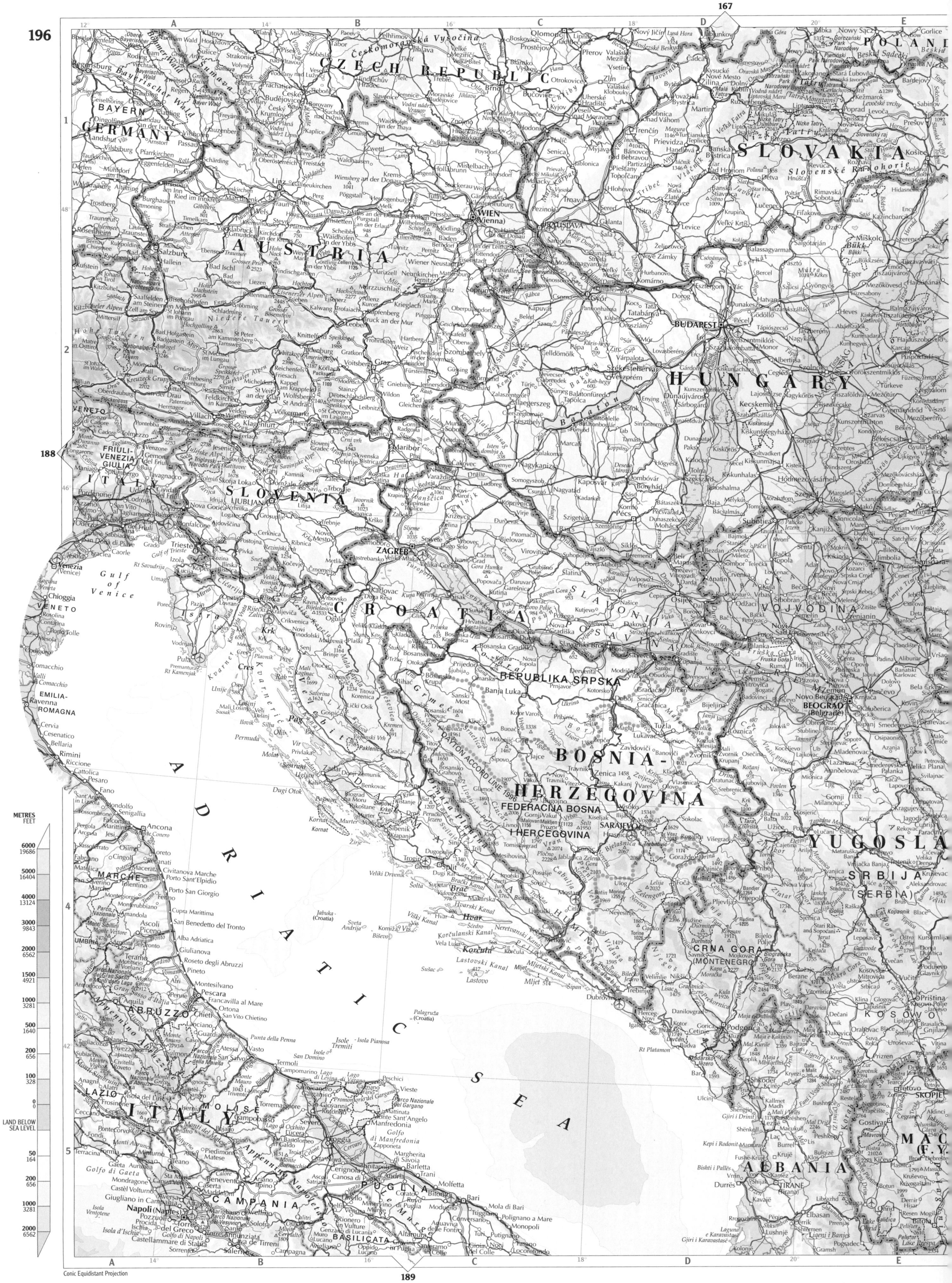
167
188
189
CZECH REPUBLIC
SLOVAKIA
POLAND
GERMANY
BAYERN
AUSTRIA
HUNGARY
SLOVENIA
CROATIA
BOSNIA-HERZEGOVINA
REPUBLIKA SRPSKA
FEDERACNA BOSNA I HERCEGOVINA
YUGOSLA
SRBIJA (SERBIA)
CRNA GORA (MONTENEGRO)
VOJVODINA
KOSOVO
ALBANIA
MAC (F.Y.
ITALY
VENETO
FRIULI-VENEZIA GIULIA
EMILIA-ROMAGNA
MARCHE
UMBRIA
ABRUZZO
LAZIO
MOLISE
CAMPANIA
PUGLIA
BASILICATA
SLAVONIJA
POSAVINA
ADRIATIC SEA
Gulf of Venice
Gulf of Trieste
WIEN (Vienna)
BRATISLAVA
BUDAPEST
LJUBLJANA
ZAGREB
SARAJEVO
BEOGRAD (Belgrade)
TIRANË
SKOPJE
Venezia (Venice)
Trieste
Rijeka
Split
Dubrovnik
Napoli (Naples)
Bari
Ancona
Pescara
Foggia
Graz
Linz
Salzburg
Brno
Olomouc
Košice
Miskolc
Debrecen
Szeged
Pécs
Osijek
Novi Sad
Banja Luka
Tuzla
Mostar
Podgorica
Durrës
Shkodër
DAYTON ACCORD LINE 1995
METRES
FEET
6000
19686
5000
16404
4000
13124
3000
9843
2000
6562
1500
4921
1000
3281
500
1640
200
656
100
328
0
0
LAND BELOW SEA LEVEL
50
164
200
656
1000
3281
2000
6562
Conic Equidistant Projection

UKRAINE
MOLDOVA
ROMANIA
BULGARIA
GREECE
TURKEY
MACEDONIA
BLACK SEA
Marmara Denizi
BUCUREŞTI (Bucharest)
SOFIYA
CHIŞINĂU (Kishinev)
Odesa
İstanbul
CARPAŢII MERIDIONALI
STARA PLANINA (BALKAN MOUNTAINS)
RHODOPE MOUNTAINS
L'VIVS'KA OBLAST'
TERNOPIL'S'KA OBLAST'
KHMEL'NYTS'KA OBLAST'
VINNYTS'KA OBLAST'
CHERKAS'KA OBLAST'
KIROVOHRADS'KA OBLAST'
MYKOLAYIVS'KA OBLAST'
ODES'KA OBLAST'
IVANO-FRANKIVS'KA OBLAST'
ZAKARPATS'KA OBLAST'
CHERNIVETS'KA OBLAST'
ANATOLIKI MAKEDONIA KAI THRAKI
KENTRIKI MAKEDONIA
EDİRNE
KIRKLARELİ
TEKİRDAĞ
KOCAELİ
136
198
MILES
KILOMETRES
1:3 000 000
Longitude 22° east of Greenwich

© Bartholomew Ltd

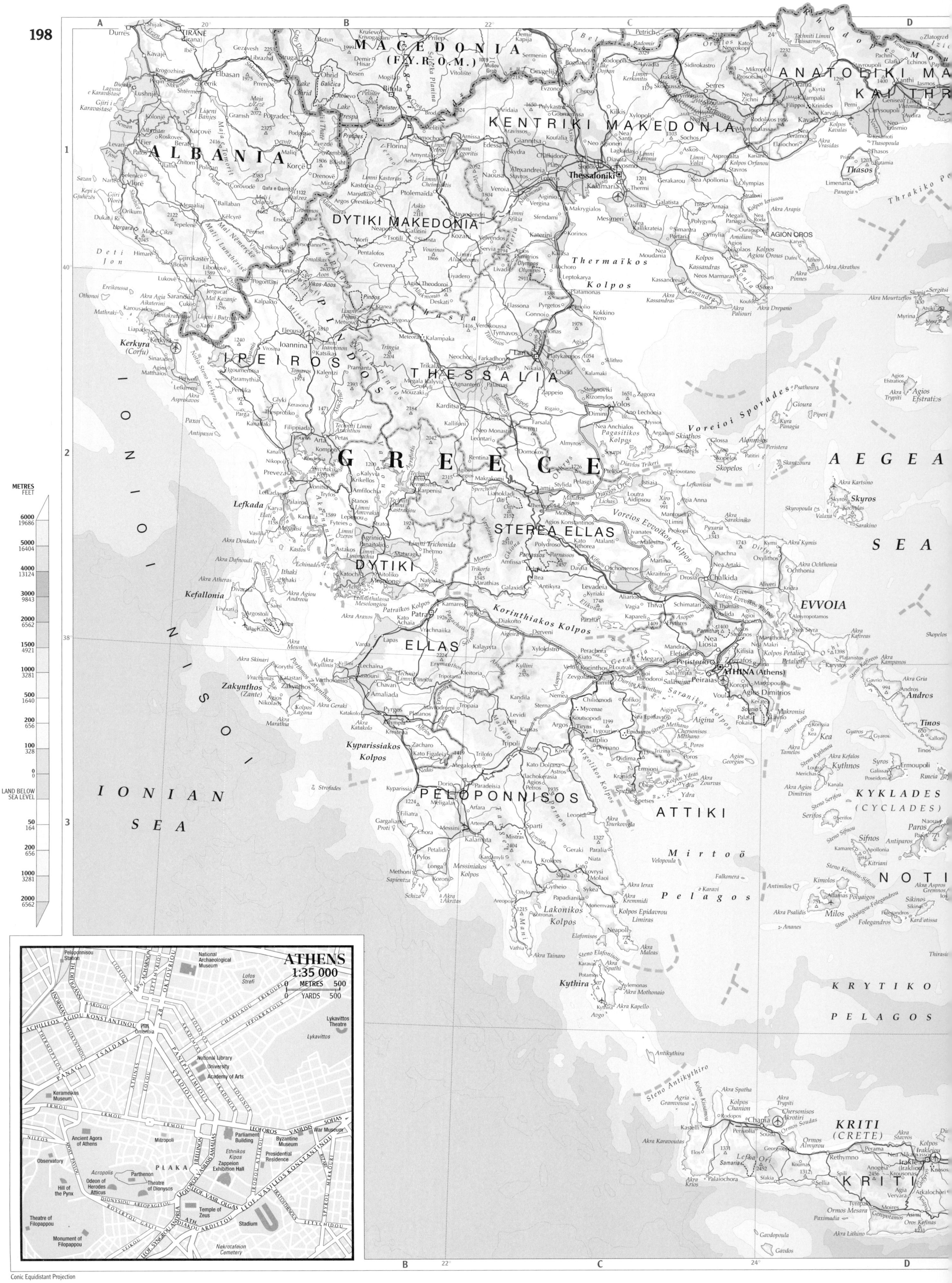
ALBANIA
MACEDONIA (F.Y.R.O.M.)
GREECE
KENTRIKI MAKEDONIA
DYTIKI MAKEDONIA
ANATOLIKI MAKEDONIA KAI THRAKI
IPEIROS
THESSALIA
STEREA ELLAS
DYTIKI ELLAS
PELOPONNISOS
ATTIKI
NOTIO AIGAIO
KRITI
IONIAN SEA
IONIOI NISOI
AEGEAN SEA
KYKLADES (CYCLADES)
KRITI (CRETE)
Mirtoö Pelagos
Krytiko Pelagos
Thermaïkos Kolpos
Voreioi Sporades
EVVOIA
Korinthiakos Kolpos
Saronikos Kolpos
Argolikos Kolpos
Lakonikos Kolpos
Messiniakos Kolpos
Kyparissiakos Kolpos
Patraïkos Kolpos
Deti Jon
Tiranë (Tirana)
Durrës
Thessaloniki
Athina (Athens)
Peiraias
Larisa
Volos
Ioannina
Patra
Kerkyra (Corfu)
Kefallonia
Zakynthos (Zante)
Lefkada
Kythira
Chania
Irakleio (Iraklion)
Rethymno
Thasos
Skyros
Andros
Tinos
Milos
Paros
Sifnos
Serifos
Kythnos
Aigina
A B C D
1 2 3
20° 22° 24°
38° 40°
METRES FEET
6000 19686
5000 16404
4000 13124
3000 9843
2000 6562
1500 4921
1000 3281
500 1640
200 656
100 328
0 0
LAND BELOW SEA LEVEL
50 164
200 656
1000 3281
2000 6562
ATHENS
1:35 000
METRES 0 500
YARDS 0 500
National Archaeological Museum
Peloponnisou Station
Lofos Strefi
Lykavittos Theatre
Lykavittos
Plat. Omonoia
National Library
University
Academy of Arts
Kerameikos Museum
Ancient Agora of Athens
Mitropoli
Parliament Building
Byzantine Museum
War Museum
Ethnikos Kipos
Zappeion Exhibition Hall
Presidential Residence
Observatory
Acropolis
Parthenon
Odeon of Herodes Atticus
Theatre of Dionysos
PLAKA
Hill of the Pynx
Temple of Zeus
Stadium
Theatre of Filopappou
Monument of Filopappou
Nekrotafeion Cemetery

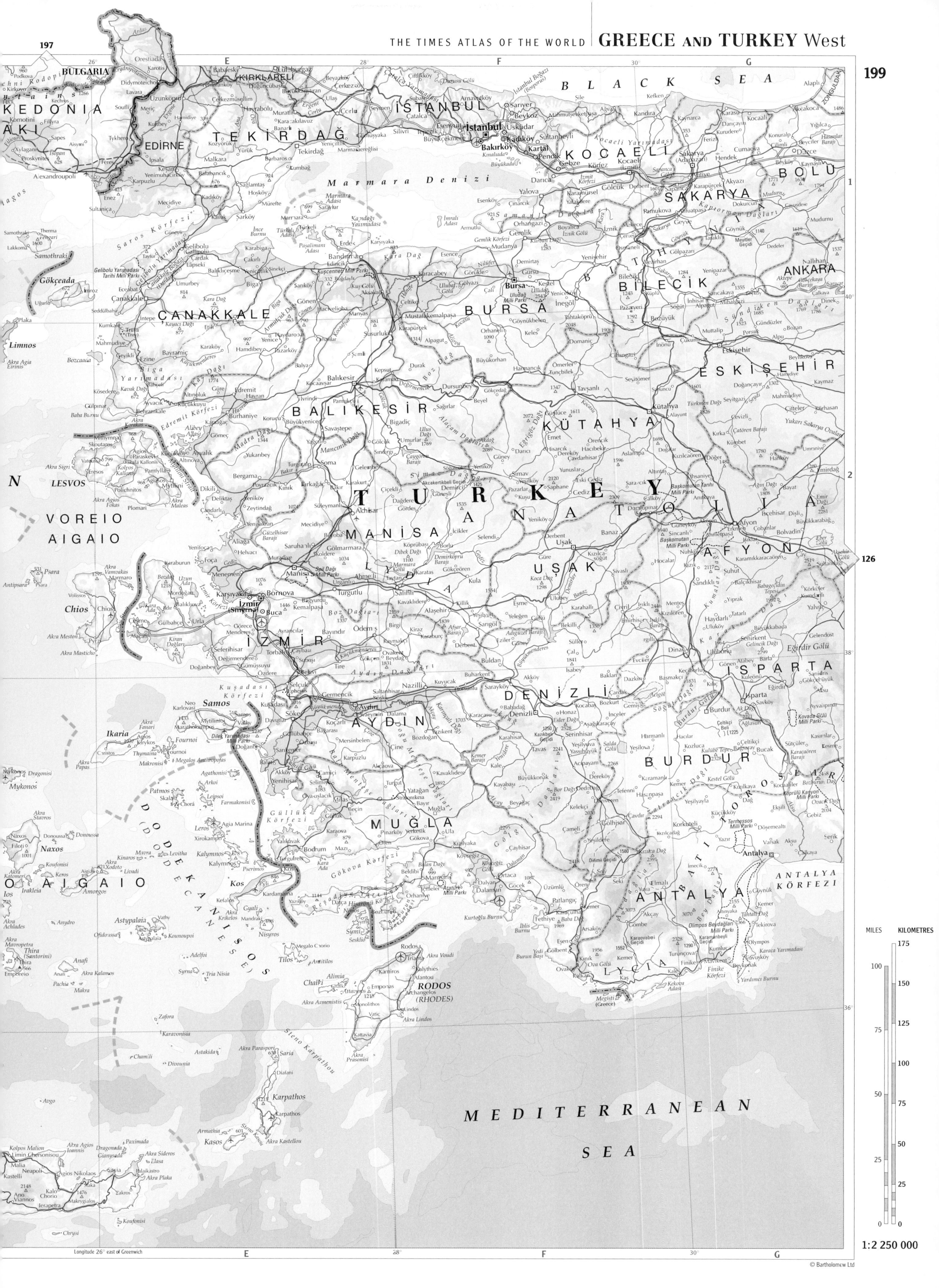
197
126
BLACK SEA
MEDITERRANEAN SEA
TURKEY
ANATOLIA
BULGARIA
VOREIO AIGAIO
DODEKANISOS
LYCIA
LYDIA
BITHYNIA
Marmara Denizi
Saros Körfezi
Edremit Körfezi
Kuşadası Körfezi
Güllük Körfezi
Gökova Körfezi
ANTALYA KÖRFEZI
EDİRNE
TEKİRDAĞ
İSTANBUL
KOCAELİ
SAKARYA
BOLU
BİLECİK
BURSA
ÇANAKKALE
BALIKESİR
KÜTAHYA
ESKİŞEHİR
ANKARA
MANİSA
İZMİR
UŞAK
AFYON
AYDIN
DENİZLİ
MUĞLA
BURDUR
ISPARTA
ANTALYA
İstanbul
Bursa
İzmir
Manisa
Balıkesir
Kütahya
Eskişehir
Afyon
Uşak
Denizli
Aydın
Muğla
Burdur
Isparta
Antalya
Lesvos
Chios
Samos
Ikaria
Kos
Rodos (RHODES)
Karpathos
Limnos
Gökçeada
Naxos
Mykonos
Astypalaia
Kasos
Longitude 26° east of Greenwich
MILES
KILOMETRES
1:2 250 000

© Bartholomew Ltd

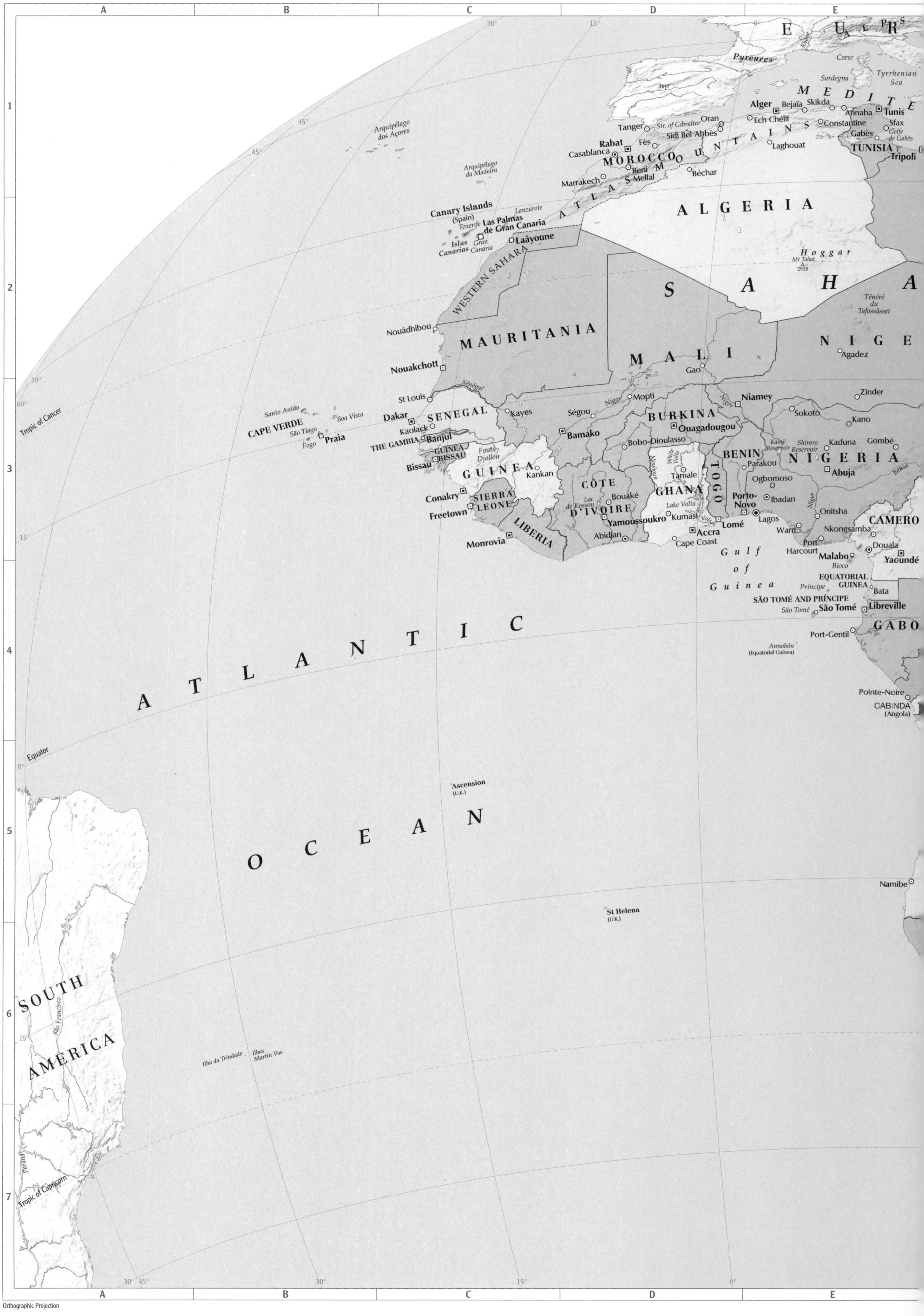
A
B
C
D
E
1
2
3
4
5
6
7
E U R
ALPS
Pyrenees
Corse
Sardegna
Tyrrhenian Sea
Tajo
M E D I T E
Alger
Bejaïa
Skikda
Annaba
Tunis
Ech Chélif
Oran
Constantine
Sfax
Str. of Gibraltar
Tanger
Sidi Bel Abbès
Gabès
Golfe de Gabès
Laghouat
TUNISIA
Tripoli
Rabat
Fès
Casablanca
MOROCCO
Beni Mellal
Marrakech
Béchar
A T L A S M O U N T A I N S
Arquipélago dos Açores
Arquipélago da Madeira
Canary Islands (Spain)
Lanzarote
Tenerife
Las Palmas de Gran Canaria
Islas Canarias
Gran Canaria
Laâyoune
A L G E R I A
Hoggar
Mt Tahat 2918
WESTERN SAHARA
S A H A
Ténéré du Tafassâsset
Nouâdhibou
MAURITANIA
M A L I
N I G E
Agadez
Nouakchott
Gao
St Louis
Sénégal
Niger
Mopti
Niamey
Zinder
Santo Antão
Boa Vista
CAPE VERDE
São Tiago
Fogo
Praia
Dakar
SENEGAL
Kayes
Ségou
BURKINA
Ouagadougou
Sokoto
Kano
Kaolack
THE GAMBIA
Banjul
Bamako
Bobo-Dioulasso
Kainji Reservoir
Shiroro Reservoir
Kaduna
Gombé
GUINEA-BISSAU
Bissau
Fouta Djallon
GUINEA
Kankan
BENIN
NIGERIA
Parakou
Abuja
Benue
White Volta
Mouhoun
Tamale
TOGO
Ogbomoso
CÔTE D'IVOIRE
Bouaké
GHANA
Conakry
SIERRA LEONE
Freetown
Lac de Kossou
Lake Volta
Porto-Novo
Ibadan
Yamoussoukro
Kumasi
Volta
Lomé
Lagos
Onitsha
Niger
LIBERIA
Monrovia
Abidjan
Accra
Cape Coast
Warri
Nkongsamba
CAMERO
Port Harcourt
Douala
Malabo
Bioco
Yaoundé
Gulf of Guinea
EQUATORIAL GUINEA
Príncipe
Bata
SÃO TOMÉ AND PRÍNCIPE
São Tomé
Libreville
GABO
Port-Gentil
Annobón (Equatorial Guinea)
Pointe-Noire
CABINDA (Angola)
Tropic of Cancer
A T L A N T I C
O C E A N
Equator
Ascension (U.K.)
St Helena (U.K.)
Namibe
SOUTH AMERICA
São Francisco
Ilha da Trindade
Ilhas Martin Vas
Paraná
Tropic of Capricorn
30°
15°
0°
45°
60°

Orthographic Projection

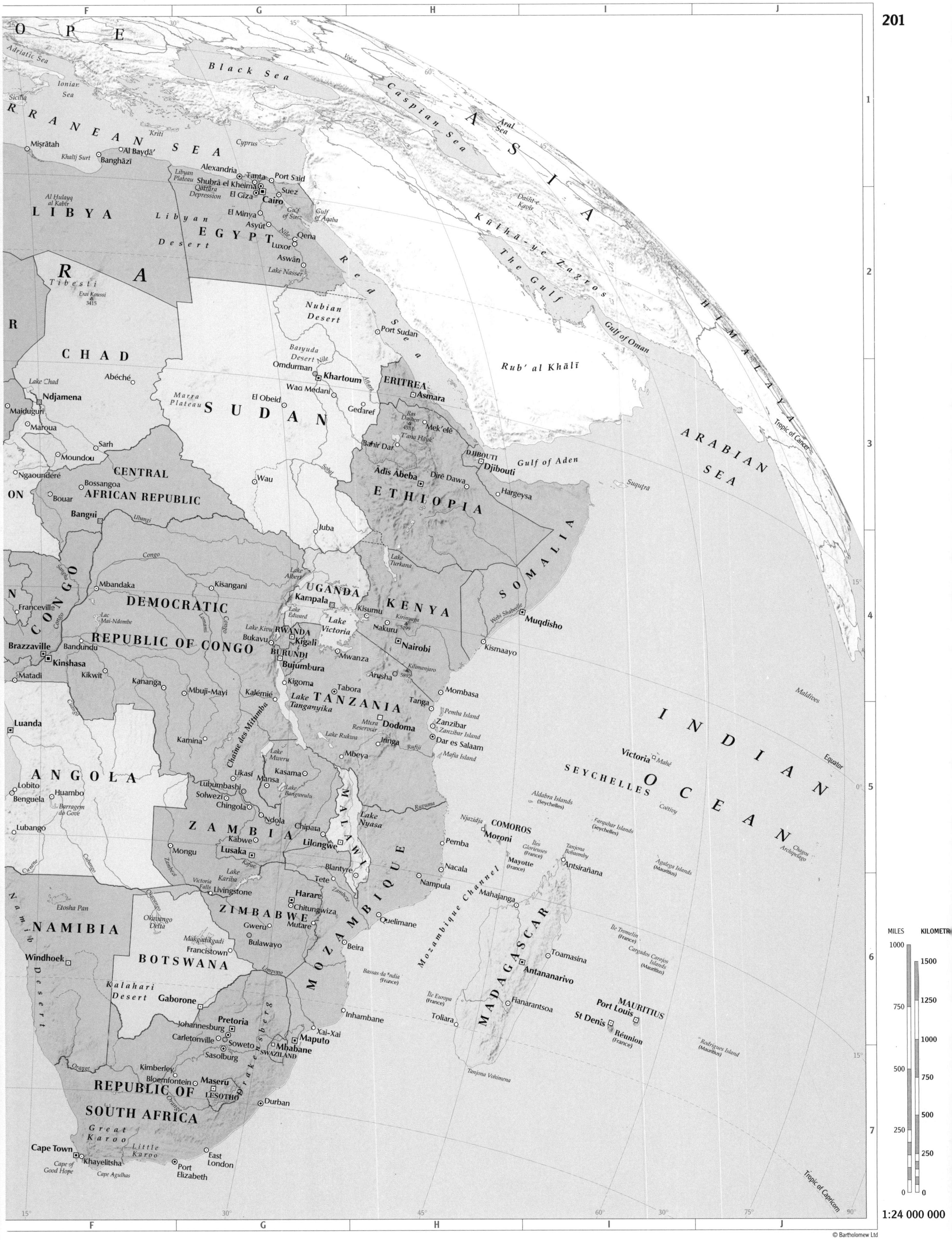
E U R O P E
Adriatic Sea
Ionian Sea
Sicilia
M E D I T E R R A N E A N S E A
Black Sea
Caspian Sea
Volga
Aral Sea
A S I A
Kriti
Cyprus
Miṣrātah
Khalīj Surt
Al Bayḍā'
Banghāzī
Alexandria
Ṭanṭa
Port Said
Shubrâ el Kheima
Suez
Libyan Plateau
Qattâra Depression
El Gîza
Cairo
Gulf of Suez
Gulf of Aqaba
Al Hulayq al Kabīr
L I B Y A
Libyan Desert
E G Y P T
El Minya
Asyûṭ
Nile
Qena
Luxor
Aswân
Lake Nasser
S A H A R A
Tibesti
Emi Koussi 3415
Dasht-e Kavīr
Kūhhā-ye Zagros
The Gulf
Gulf of Oman
H I M A L A Y A
Red Sea
Nubian Desert
Port Sudan
Bayuda Desert
Omdurman
Khartoum
Wad Medani
Rub' al Khālī
C H A D
Abéché
Lake Chad
Ndjamena
Maiduguri
Maroua
Marra Plateau
El Obeid
S U D A N
ERITREA
Asmara
Gedaref
Ras Dashen 4533
Mek'elē
T'ana Hāyk'
Bahir Dar
Sarh
Moundou
Ngaoundéré
CENTRAL AFRICAN REPUBLIC
Bossangoa
Bouar
Bangui
Ubangi
Wau
Sobat
DJIBOUTI
Djibouti
Gulf of Aden
Ādīs Ābeba
Dirē Dawa
E T H I O P I A
Hargeysa
Suquṭra
ARABIAN SEA
Tropic of Cancer
Juba
Lake Turkana
S O M A L I A
Congo
Sangha
Lake Albert
UGANDA
Kampala
Lake Edward
Mbandaka
Kisangani
DEMOCRATIC REPUBLIC OF CONGO
Lac Mai-Ndombe
Lomami
Franceville
CONGO
Brazzaville
Kinshasa
Bandundu
Kikwit
Matadi
Kananga
Mbuji-Mayi
Kalémié
Lake Kivu
RWANDA
Kigali
Bukavu
BURUNDI
Bujumbura
Kigoma
Lake Victoria
Kisumu
K E N Y A
Kirinyaga 5199
Nakuru
Nairobi
Mwanza
Arusha
Kilimanjaro 5892
Webi Shabeelle
Muqdisho
Kismaayo
Tabora
Lake Tanganyika
T A N Z A N I A
Tanga
Mombasa
Pemba Island
Zanzibar
Zanzibar Island
Dar es Salaam
Mafia Island
Dodoma
Mtera Reservoir
Iringa
Rufiji
Lake Rukwa
Mbeya
Chaîne des Mitumba
Kamina
Luanda
Cuanza
A N G O L A
Lobito
Benguela
Huambo
Barragem do Gove
Lubango
Cunene
Cubango
Lake Mweru
Kasama
Likasi
Lubumbashi
Mansa
Lake Bangweulu
Solwezi
Chingola
Ndola
Z A M B I A
Kabwe
Lusaka
Mongu
Zambeze
Kafue
Lake Kariba
Victoria Falls
Livingstone
Chipata
Lilongwe
MALAWI
Lake Nyasa
Ruvuma
Blantyre
Tete
Zambezi
Harare
Chitungwiza
ZIMBABWE
Gweru
Mutare
Bulawayo
Maldives
I N D I A N O C E A N
Equator
Victoria
Mahé
SEYCHELLES
Aldabra Islands (Seychelles)
Coëtivy
Farquhar Islands (Seychelles)
Chagos Archipelago
Njazidja
COMOROS
Moroni
Îles Glorieuses (France)
Mayotte (France)
Tanjona Bobaomby
Antsirañana
Agalega Islands (Mauritius)
Pemba
Nacala
Nampula
MOZAMBIQUE
Quelimane
Beira
Mozambique Channel
Mahajanga
MADAGASCAR
Île Tromelin (France)
Cargados Carajos Islands (Mauritius)
Toamasina
Antananarivo
Fianarantsoa
Toliara
Bassas da India (France)
Île Europa (France)
Inhambane
Port Louis
MAURITIUS
St Denis
Réunion (France)
Rodrigues Island (Mauritius)
Tanjona Vohimena
Etosha Pan
Okavango
Okavango Delta
NAMIBIA
Namib Desert
Windhoek
Makgadikgadi
Francistown
BOTSWANA
Limpopo
Kalahari Desert
Gaborone
Pretoria
Johannesburg
Carletonville
Soweto
Sasolburg
Drakensberg
SWAZILAND
Mbabane
Maputo
Xai-Xai
Orange
Kimberley
Bloemfontein
Maseru
LESOTHO
REPUBLIC OF SOUTH AFRICA
Durban
Great Karoo
Little Karoo
Cape Town
Khayelitsha
Cape of Good Hope
Cape Agulhas
East London
Port Elizabeth
Tropic of Capricorn
MILES
KILOMETRES
1:24 000 000

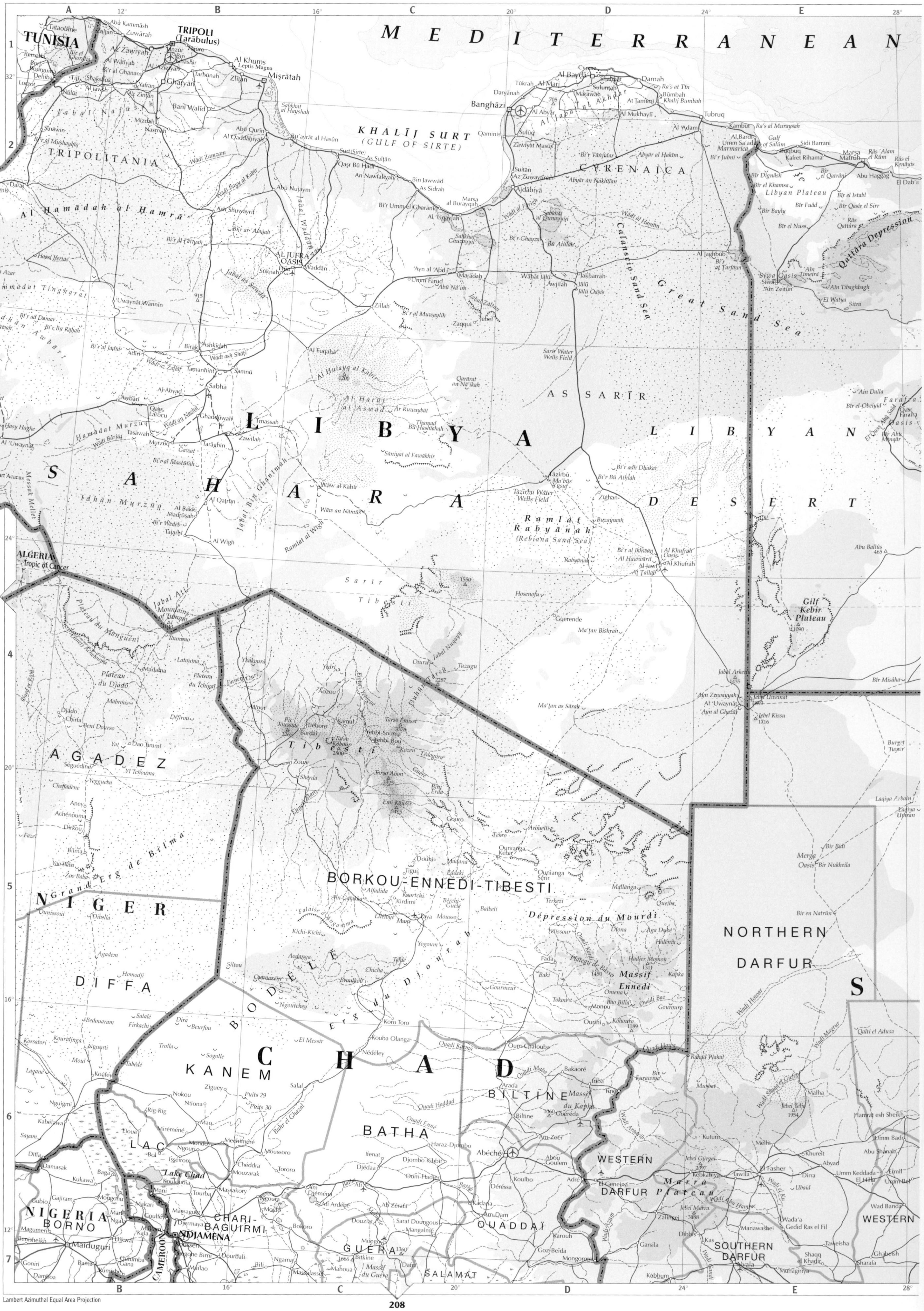

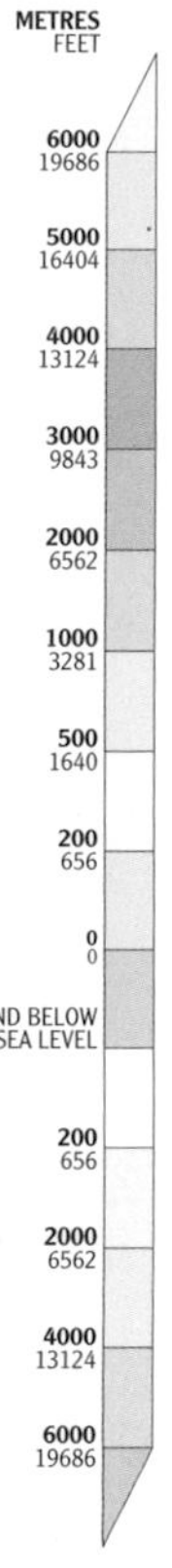

Lambert Azimuthal Equal Area Projection

205

208

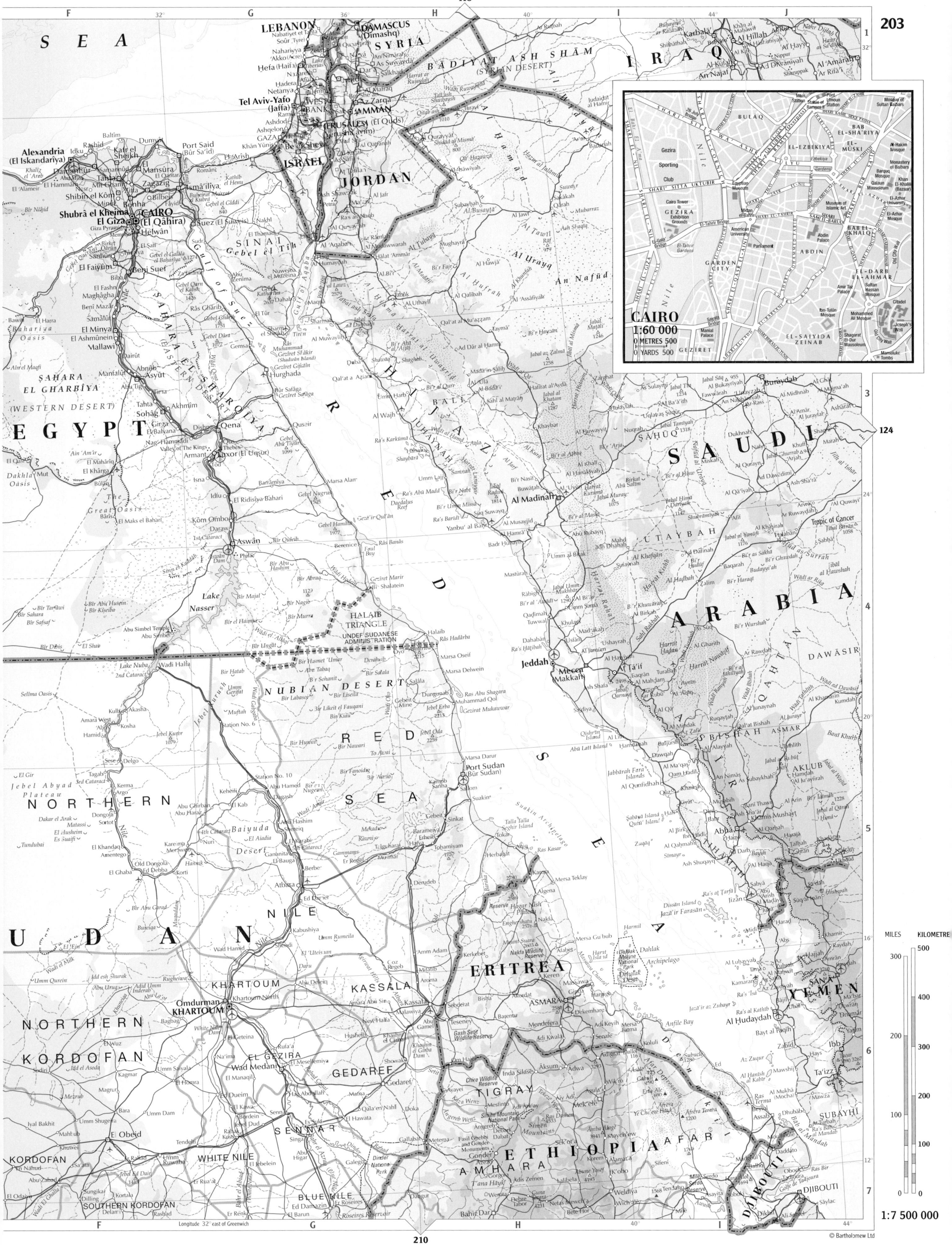
SEA
LEBANON
SYRIA
DAMASCUS (Dimashq)
BADIYAT ASH SHAM (SYRIAN DESERT)
IRAQ
Tel Aviv-Yafo (Jaffa)
AMMAN
ISRAEL
JORDAN
Alexandria (El Iskandarîya)
Port Said (Bûr Sa'îd)
Shubra el Kheima
CAIRO (El Qâhira)
El Giza
Suez (El Suweis)
SINAI
Gulf of Suez
Gulf of Aqaba
Al Nafud
EGYPT
SAHARA EL GHARBÎYA (WESTERN DESERT)
SAHARA EL SHARQÎYA (EASTERN DESERT)
Luxor (El Uqsur)
Aswân
Lake Nasser
HALAIB TRIANGLE
UNDEF. SUDANESE ADMINISTRATION
NUBIAN DESERT
RED SEA
HIJAZ
SAUDI ARABIA
Al Madinah
Jeddah
Mecca Makkah
Tropic of Cancer
UTAYBAH
DAWASIR
ASIR
Port Sudan (Bûr Sudan)
NORTHERN
SUDAN
NILE
KHARTOUM
Omdurman
KASSALA
NORTHERN KORDOFAN
EL GEZIRA
GEDAREF
SENNAR
WHITE NILE
BLUE NILE
SOUTHERN KORDOFAN
KORDOFAN
ERITREA
ASMARA
Dahlak Archipelago
TIGRAY
AMHARA
ETHIOPIA
AFAR
YEMEN
SAN'A
DJIBOUTI
CAIRO 1:60 000
METRES 500
YARDS 500
Nile
Gezira
EL-EZBEKIYA
ABDIN
GARDEN CITY
MILES
KILOMETRES
1:7 500 000
Longitude 32° east of Greenwich

180

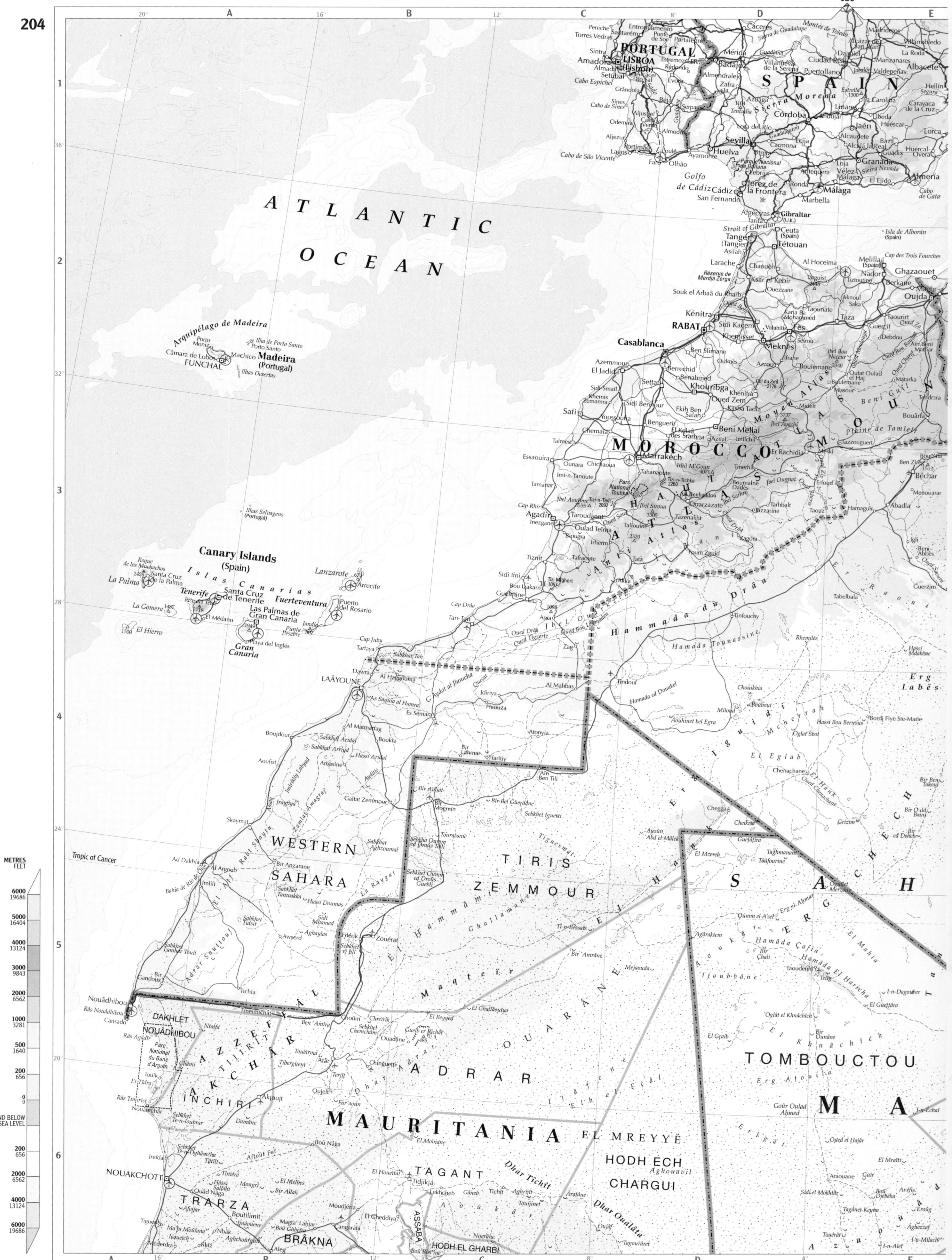

ATLANTIC OCEAN
PORTUGAL
LISBOA (Lisbon)
SPAIN
MOROCCO
RABAT
Casablanca
Marrakech
Fès
Meknès
Tanger (Tangier)
Ceuta (Spain)
Gibraltar (U.K.)
Strait of Gibraltar
Golfo de Cádiz
Sevilla
Córdoba
Granada
Málaga
Almería
Oujda
Agadir
Safi
Essaouira
Kénitra
Tétouan
Arquipélago de Madeira
Madeira (Portugal)
FUNCHAL
Ilhas Selvagens (Portugal)
Canary Islands (Spain)
Islas Canarias
Lanzarote
Fuerteventura
Gran Canaria
Tenerife
La Palma
La Gomera
El Hierro
Santa Cruz de Tenerife
Las Palmas de Gran Canaria
LAÂYOUNE
WESTERN SAHARA
Ad Dakhla
Tropic of Cancer
Nouâdhibou
DAKHLET NOUÂDHIBOU
Parc National du Banc d'Arguin
MAURITANIA
NOUAKCHOTT
TRARZA
INCHIRI
ADRAR
TAGANT
BRÂKNA
ASSABA
HODH EL GHARBI
HODH ECH CHARGUI
TIRIS ZEMMOUR
TOMBOUCTOU
Tindouf
Hammada du Drâa
Anti Atlas
Haut Atlas
Moyen Atlas
El Mreyyé
Erg Iguidi
Lambert Azimuthal Equal Area Projection
METRES FEET
6000 19686
5000 16404
4000 13124
3000 9843
2000 6562
1000 3281
500 1640
200 656
0 0
LAND BELOW SEA LEVEL
200 656
2000 6562
4000 13124
6000 19686

206

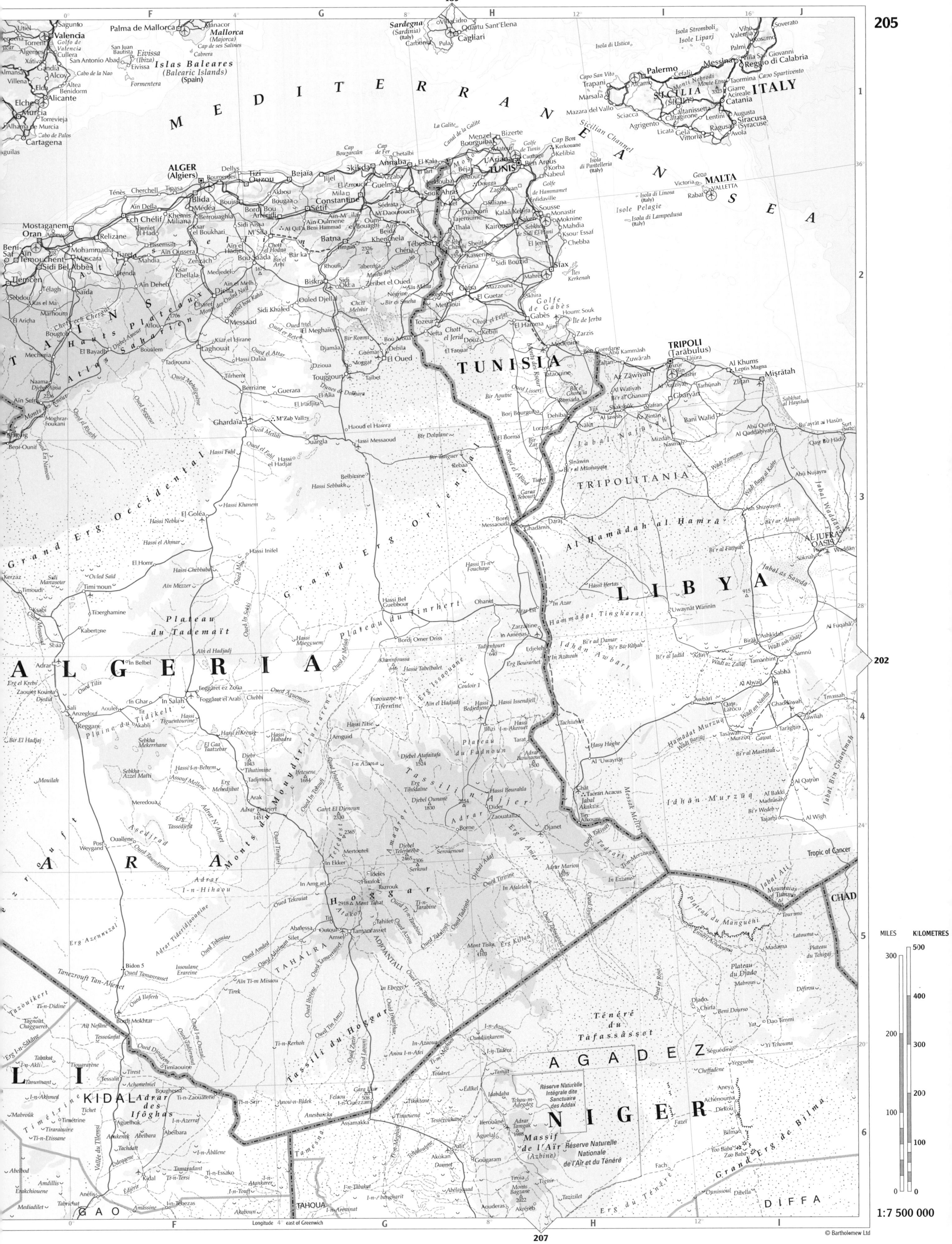
MEDITERRANEAN SEA
ALGERIA
TUNISIA
LIBYA
NIGER
MALI
CHAD
ITALY
MALTA
VALLETTA
ALGER (Algiers)
TUNIS
TRIPOLI (Țarābulus)
Islas Baleares (Balearic Islands) (Spain)
Mallorca (Majorca)
Eivissa (Ibiza)
Palma de Mallorca
Valencia
Alicante
Murcia
Cartagena
Sardegna (Sardinia) (Italy)
Cagliari
Sicilia (Sicily)
Palermo
Messina
Catania
Siracusa (Syracuse)
Reggio di Calabria
Sicilian Channel
Isole Pelagie
Oran
Mostaganem
Tlemcen
Sidi Bel Abbès
Constantine
Annaba
Skikda
Bejaïa
Sétif
Batna
Biskra
Blida
Médéa
Tébessa
Sfax
Sousse
Kairouan
Gabès
Gafsa
Tozeur
Bizerte
Golfe de Gabès
Île de Jerba
Chott el Jerid
Chott Melrhir
Touggourt
Ouargla
Ghardaïa
Laghouat
Djelfa
Hassi Messaoud
El Oued
El Goléa
Timimoun
Adrar
In Salah
Reggane
Tamanrasset
Djanet
In Aménas
Bordj Mokhtar
Kidal
Gao
Agadez
Arlit
Tahoua
Diffa
Bilma
Ghadāmis
Misrātah
Al Khums
Sabhā
Awbārī
Murzūq
Ghāt
Tropic of Cancer
Atlas Saharien
Hauts Plateaux
Tell Atlas
Grand Erg Occidental
Grand Erg Oriental
Plateau du Tademaït
Plateau du Tinrhert
Tassili n'Ajjer
Hoggar
Ahaggar
Tassili du Hoggar
Tanezrouft
Adrar des Ifôghas
Massif de l'Aïr (Azbine)
Ténéré du Tafassâsset
Plateau du Djado
Plateau du Manguéni
Grand Erg de Bilma
Erg du Ténéré
Tripolitania
Jabal Nafūsah
Al Ḥamādah al Ḥamrā'
Idhān Awbārī
Idhān Murzūq
Ḥamādat Murzuq
Ḥammādat Tingharat
Messak Mellet
Réserve Naturelle Nationale de l'Aïr et du Ténéré
Réserve Naturelle Intégrale dite Sanctuaire des Addax
MILES
KILOMETRES

1:7 500 000

© Bartholomew Ltd

204

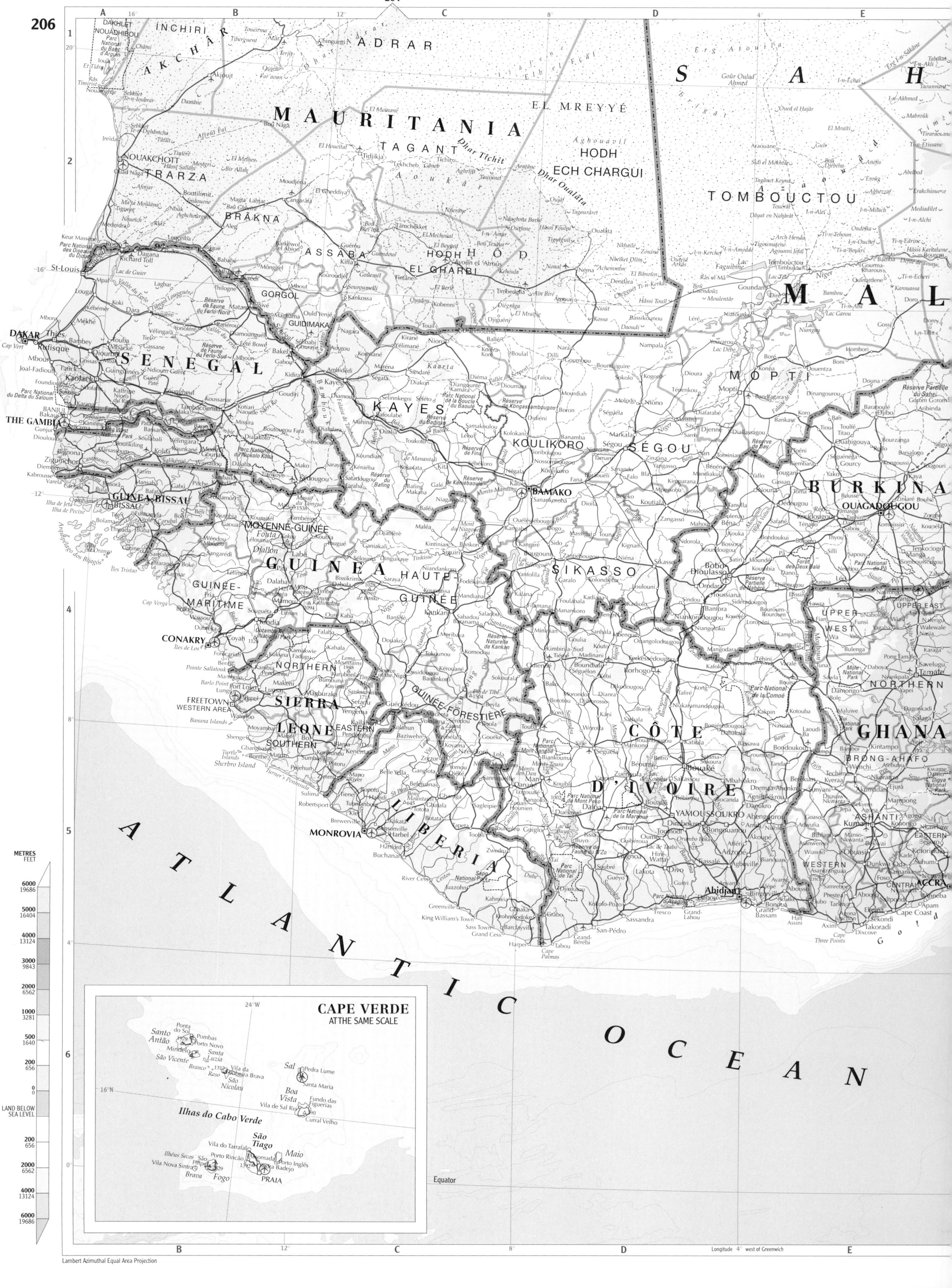
MAURITANIA
SENEGAL
THE GAMBIA
GUINEA-BISSAU
GUINEA
SIERRA LEONE
LIBERIA
CÔTE D'IVOIRE
GHANA
BURKINA
MALI
SAHARA
ATLANTIC OCEAN
NOUAKCHOTT
DAKAR
BANJUL
BISSAU
CONAKRY
FREETOWN
MONROVIA
BAMAKO
OUAGADOUGOU
YAMOUSSOUKRO
ACCRA
Abidjan
ADRAR
INCHIRI
TAGANT
TRARZA
BRÂKNA
ASSABA
GORGOL
GUIDIMAKA
HODH ECH CHARGUI
HODH EL GHARBI
TOMBOUCTOU
MOPTI
KAYES
KOULIKORO
SÉGOU
SIKASSO
MOYENNE-GUINÉE
HAUTE-GUINÉE
GUINÉE-MARITIME
GUINÉE-FORESTIÈRE
NORTHERN
SOUTHERN
EASTERN
WESTERN AREA
UPPER WEST
UPPER EAST
BRONG-AHAFO
ASHANTI
METRES
FEET
6000
19686
5000
16404
4000
13124
3000
9843
2000
6562
1000
3281
500
1640
200
656
0
0
LAND BELOW SEA LEVEL
200
656
2000
6562
4000
13124
6000
19686
CAPE VERDE
AT THE SAME SCALE
Ilhas do Cabo Verde
Santo Antão
São Vicente
São Nicolau
Sal
Boa Vista
Maio
São Tiago
Fogo
Brava
PRAIA
Equator
Longitude 4° west of Greenwich
Lambert Azimuthal Equal Area Projection

205

ALGERIA
ARA
Tassili du Hoggar
Ténéré du Tafassâsset
Adrar des Ifôghas
KIDAL
AGADEZ
Massif de l'Aïr (Azbine)
Réserve Naturelle Intégrale dite Sanctuaire des Addax
Réserve Naturelle Nationale de l'Aïr et du Ténéré
Grand Erg de Bilma
Erg du Ténéré
BORKOU-ENNEDI-TIBESTI
GAO
NIGER
DIFFA
TAHOUA
ZINDER
KANEM
TILLABÉRI
MARADI
CHAD
LAC
Lake Chad
NIAMEY
DOSSO
SOKOTO
N'DJAMENA
CHARI-BAGUIRMI
JIGAWA
YOBE
ZAMFARA
KATSINA
KANO
BORNO
KEBBI
EXTRÊME-NORD
BAUCHI
GOMBE
KADUNA
MAYO-KEBBI
NIGER
PLATEAU
ADAMAWA
BENIN
NIGERIA
ABUJA
FEDERAL CAPITAL TERRITORY
TOGO
KWARA
NASSARAWA
NORD
OYO
TARABA
EKITI
KOGI
OSUN
BENUE
ADAMAOUA
OGUN
ONDO
EDO
ENUGU
EBONYI
NORD OUEST
Lagos
LAGOS
PORTO NOVO
Cotonou
LOMÉ
ACCRA
Slave Coast
Bight of Benin
DELTA
IMO
ABIA
CROSS RIVER
AKWA IBOM
RIVERS
BAYELSA
Mouths of the Niger
OUEST
SUD OUEST
CAMEROON
CENTRE
LITTORAL
Douala
YAOUNDÉ
EST
CENTRAL AFRICAN REPUBLIC
MALABO
Bioco
SUD
EQUATORIAL GUINEA
RÍO MUNI
WOLEU-NTEM
SANGHA
GULF OF GUINEA
SÃO TOMÉ AND PRÍNCIPE
Príncipe
SÃO TOMÉ
São Tomé
LIBREVILLE
ESTUAIRE
OGOOUÉ-IVINDO
CONGO
CUVETTE
GABON
MOYEN-OGOOUÉ
OGOOUÉ-LOLO
HAUT-OGOOUÉ
Port-Gentil
OGOOUÉ MARITIME
NGOUNIÉ
Annobón (Equatorial Guinea)

202

MILES | KILOMETRES

1:7 500 000

208

208

210

202

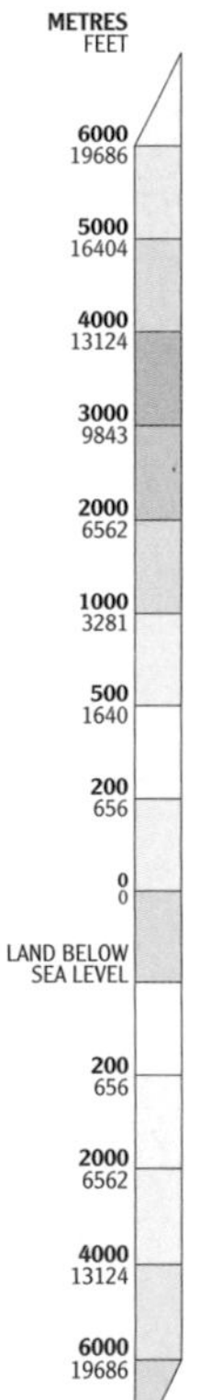
METRES
FEET
6000
19686
5000
16404
4000
13124
3000
9843
2000
6562
1000
3281
500
1640
200
656
0
LAND BELOW SEA LEVEL
200
656
2000
6562
4000
13124
6000
19686

SUDAN
CHAD
CENTRAL AFRICAN REPUBLIC
CAMEROON
NIGERIA
GABON
CONGO
DEMOCRATIC REPUBLIC
EQUATORIAL GUINEA
NDJAMENA
BANGUI
YAOUNDÉ
LIBREVILLE
MALABO
Douala
Kisangani
Mbandaka
ORIENTALE
ÉQUATEUR
NORD-KIVU
MANIEMA
RWANDA
UGANDA
Equator

Lambert Azimuthal Equal Area Projection

207

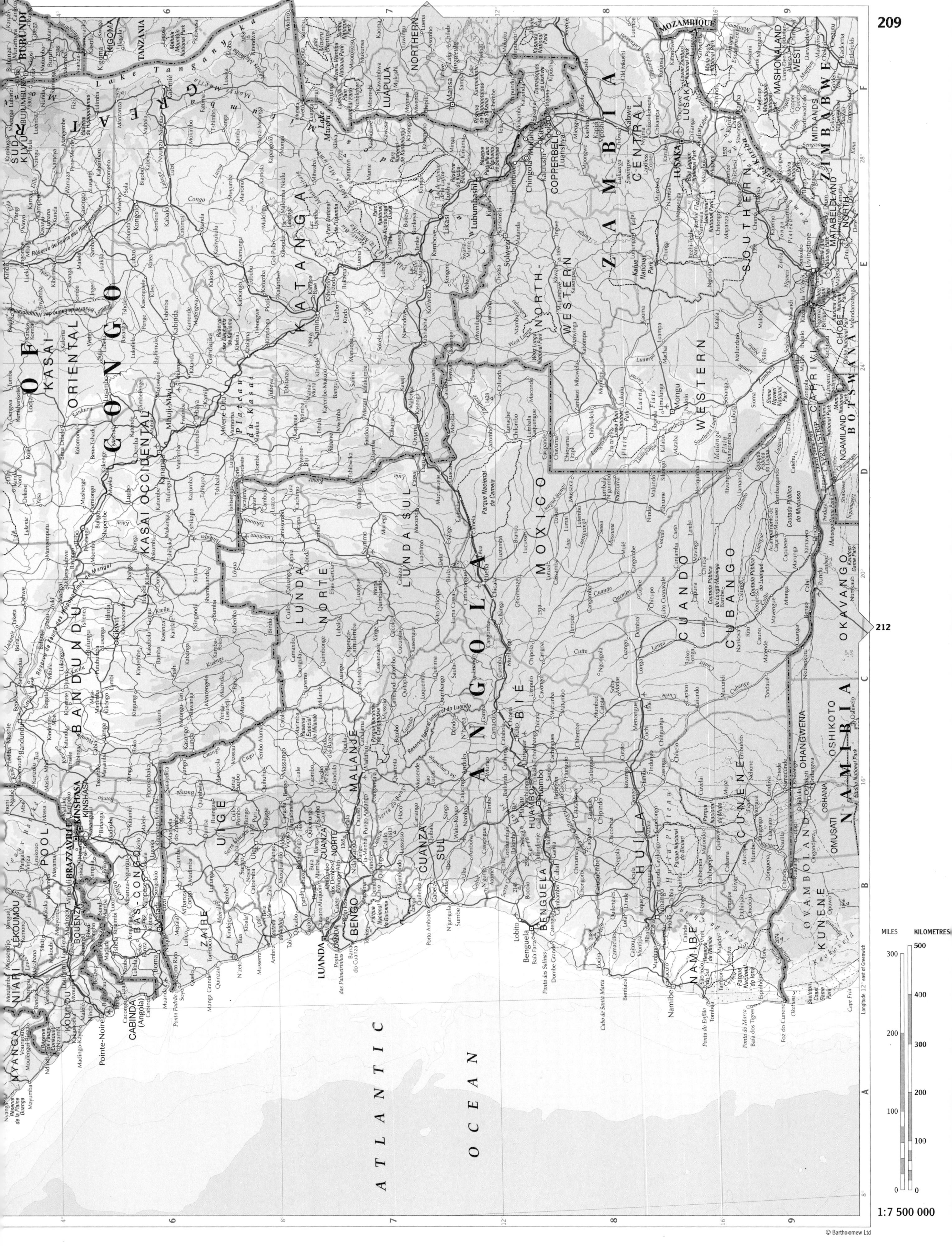
ANGOLA
CONGO
ZAMBIA
NAMIBIA
BOTSWANA
ZIMBABWE
MOZAMBIQUE
TANZANIA
BURUNDI
ATLANTIC OCEAN
KATANGA
KASAI ORIENTAL
KASAI OCCIDENTAL
BANDUNDU
BAS-CONGO
KINSHASA
BRAZZAVILLE
POOL
LUANDA
BENGO
UIGE
ZAIRE
MALANJE
CUANZA NORTE
CUANZA SUL
LUNDA NORTE
LUNDA SUL
MOXICO
BIÉ
HUAMBO
BENGUELA
HUÍLA
NAMIBE
CUNENE
CUANDO CUBANGO
NORTH-WESTERN
WESTERN
SOUTHERN
CENTRAL
COPPERBELT
LUAPULA
NORTHERN
LUSAKA
CABINDA (Angola)
KOUILOU
NIARI
LÉKOUMOU
BOUENZA
NYANGA
CAPRIVI
OKAVANGO
OHANGWENA
OSHIKOTO
OSHANA
OMUSATI
KUNENE
OVAMBOLAND
NGAMILAND
CHOBE
MATABELELAND NORTH
MIDLANDS
MASHONALAND WEST
Lake Tanganyika
MILES
KILOMETRES
0
100
200
300
400
500
1:7 500 000

© Bartholomew Ltd

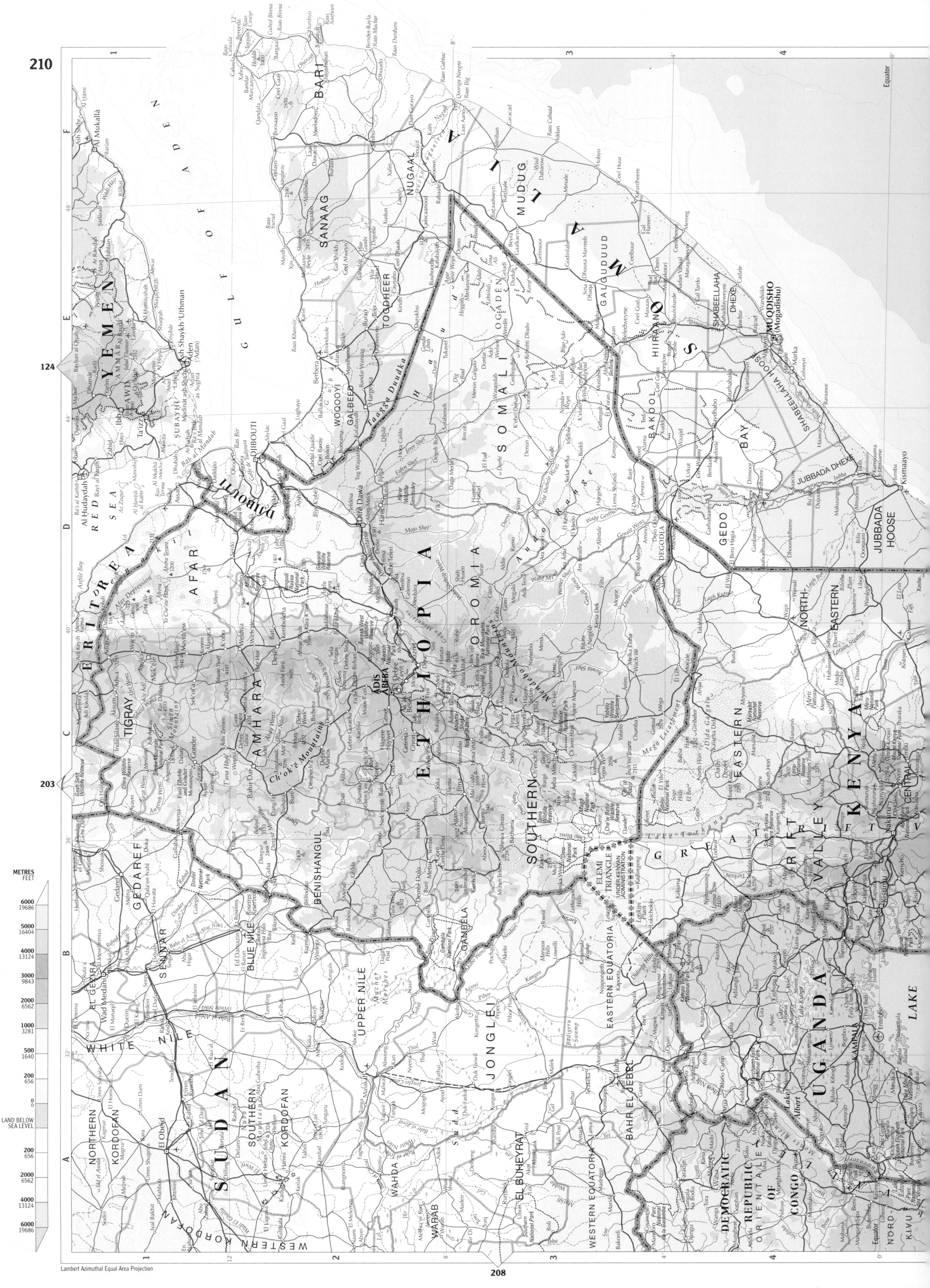

Lambert Azimuthal Equal Area Projection

208
124
203

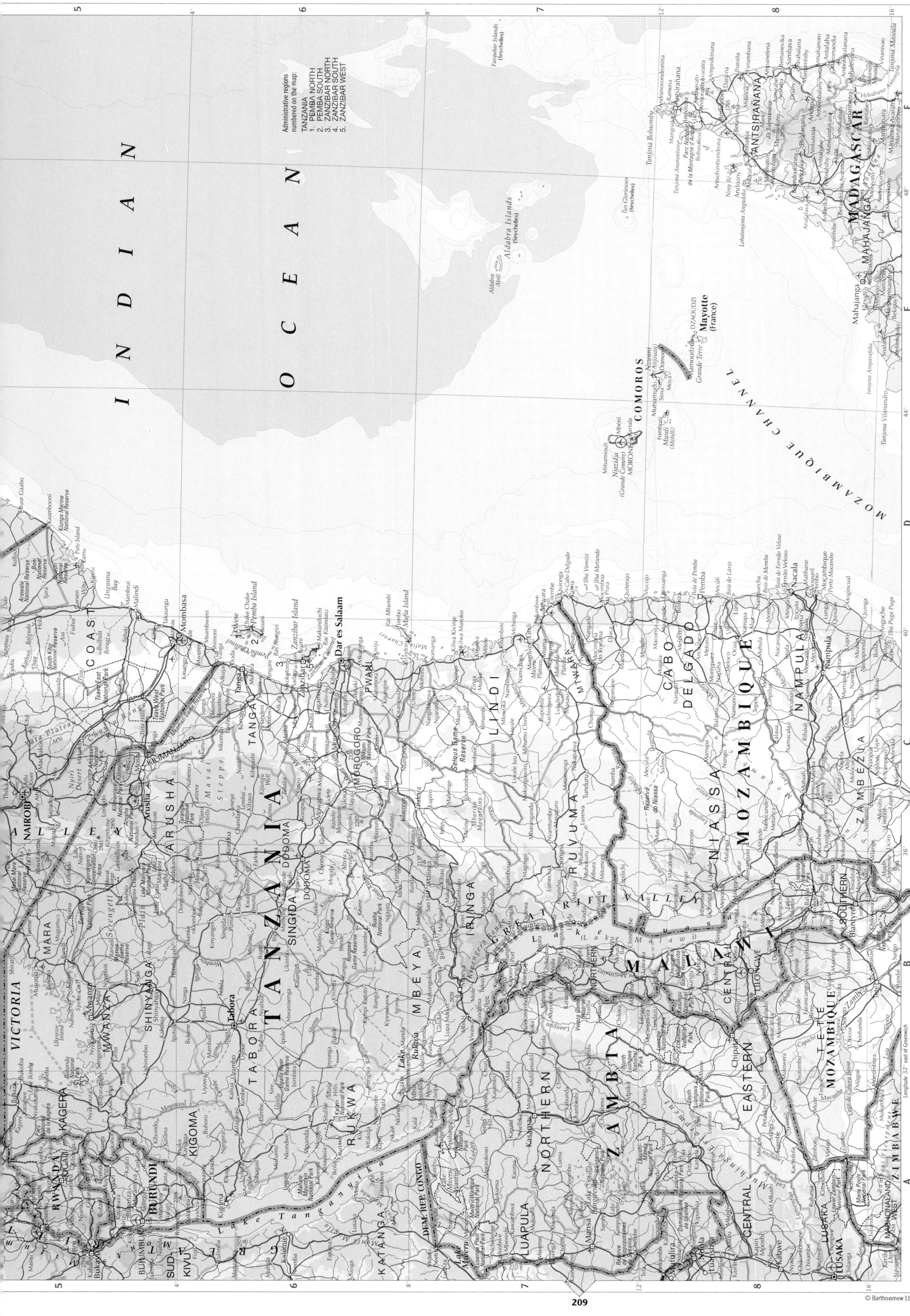

213

MILES KILOMETRES

1:7 500 000

© Bartholomew Ltd

209

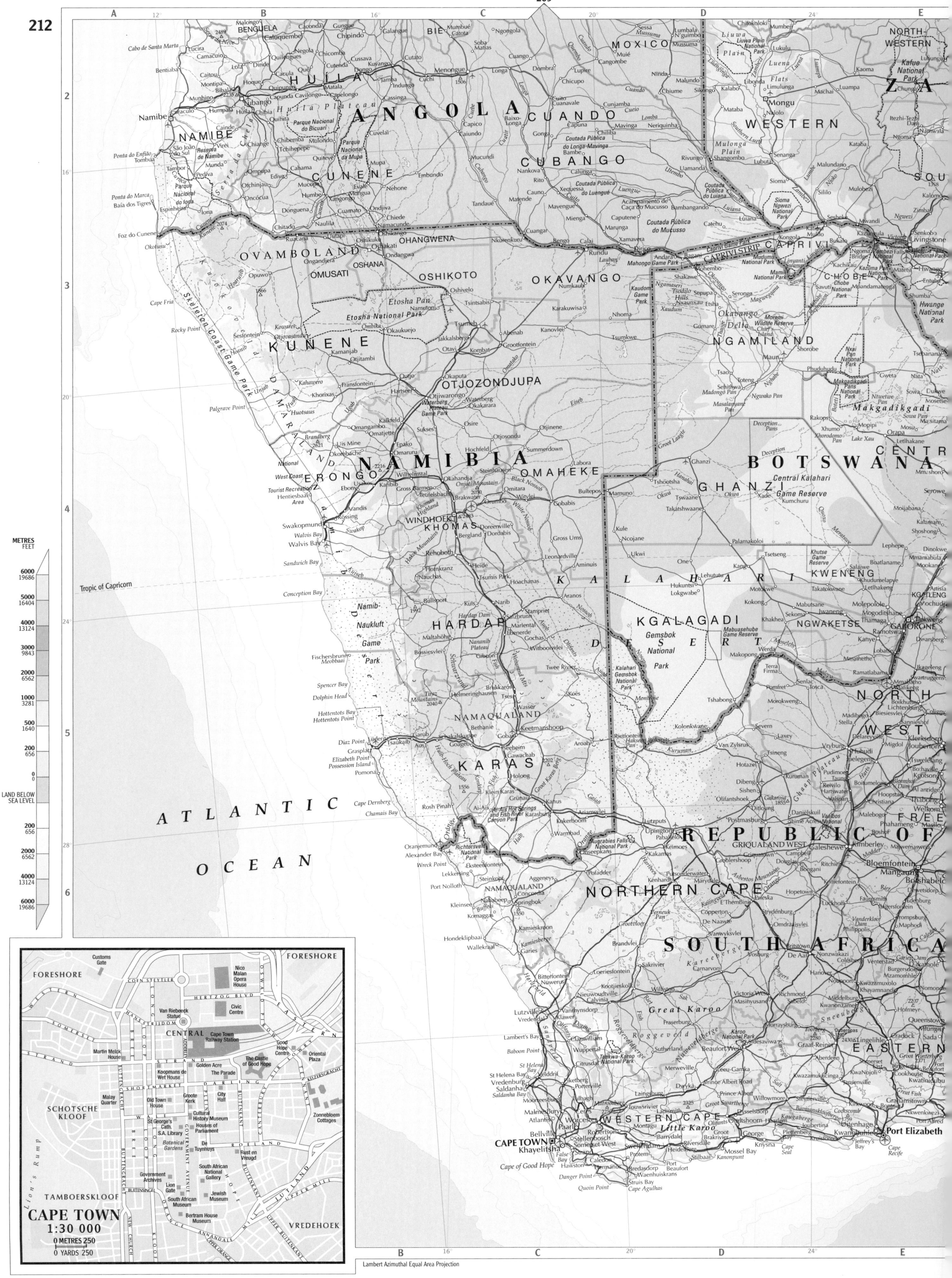
ANGOLA
NAMIBIA
BOTSWANA
REPUBLIC OF SOUTH AFRICA
ZA
ATLANTIC OCEAN
HUILA
NAMIBE
CUNENE
CUANDO CUBANGO
MOXICO
BIE
OVAMBOLAND
OMUSATI
OSHANA
OHANGWENA
OSHIKOTO
OKAVANGO
KUNENE
OTJOZONDJUPA
ERONGO
OMAHEKE
KHOMAS
HARDAP
KARAS
NAMAQUALAND
GHANZI
NGAMILAND
CHOBE
KWENENG
KGALAGADI
NGWAKETSE
NORTH WEST
NORTHERN CAPE
WESTERN CAPE
EASTERN
WESTERN
NORTH-WESTERN
CAPRIVI STRIP
CAPRIVI
KALAHARI DESERT
Namib-Naukluft Game Park
Skeleton Coast Game Park
Etosha Pan
Etosha National Park
Central Kalahari Game Reserve
Kalahari Gemsbok National Park
Gemsbok National Park
Great Karoo
Little Karoo
Tropic of Capricorn
Namibe
Lubango
Windhoek
Walvis Bay
Swakopmund
Lüderitz
Keetmanshoop
Rundu
Maun
Ghanzi
Gaborone
Kimberley
Bloemfontein
Upington
Springbok
CAPE TOWN
Khayelitsha
Port Elizabeth
Cape of Good Hope
Cape Agulhas
Livingstone
Mongu
METRES
FEET
6000
19686
5000
16404
4000
13124
3000
9843
2000
6562
1000
3281
500
1640
200
656
0
0
LAND BELOW SEA LEVEL
200
656
2000
6562
4000
13124
6000
19686
CAPE TOWN
1:30 000
0 METRES 250
0 YARDS 250
FORESHORE
SCHOTSCHE KLOOF
TAMBOERSKLOOF
VREDEHOEK
CENTRAL
Cape Town Railway Station
The Castle of Good Hope
Civic Centre
Nico Malan Opera House
City Hall
Houses of Parliament
South African National Gallery
South African Museum
Lion's Rump
Lambert Azimuthal Equal Area Projection

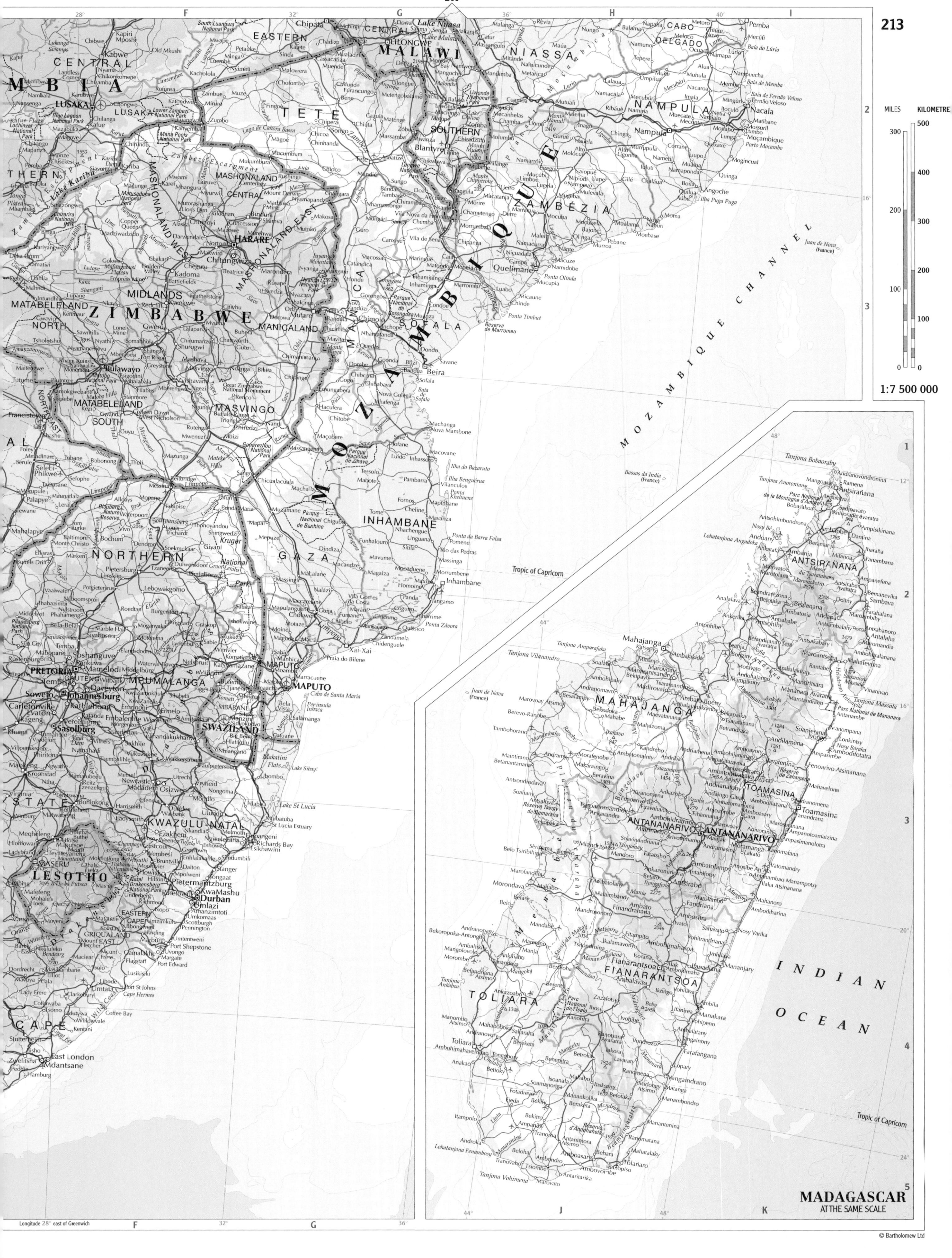
ZAMBIA
MALAWI
MOZAMBIQUE
ZIMBABWE
SWAZILAND
LESOTHO
MADAGASCAR
MOZAMBIQUE CHANNEL
INDIAN OCEAN
Tropic of Capricorn
LUSAKA
HARARE
LILONGWE
MAPUTO
MBABANE
MASERU
ANTANANARIVO
Bulawayo
Beira
Quelimane
Nampula
Nacala
Blantyre
Inhambane
Durban
Pietermaritzburg
Johannesburg
Soweto
PRETORIA
East London
Toamasina
Mahajanga
Antsiranana
Fianarantsoa
Toliara
Antsirabe
CABO DELGADO
NIASSA
NAMPULA
TETE
ZAMBÉZIA
SOFALA
MANICA
INHAMBANE
GAZA
MASHONALAND CENTRAL
MASHONALAND EAST
MASHONALAND WEST
MIDLANDS
MANICALAND
MASVINGO
MATABELELAND NORTH
MATABELELAND SOUTH
NORTHERN
MPUMALANGA
KWAZULU NATAL
EASTERN CAPE
GAUTENG
MAHAJANGA
ANTSIRAÑANA
TOAMASINA
ANTANANARIVO
FIANARANTSOA
TOLIARA
Juan de Nova (France)
Bassas da India (France)
MILES
KILOMETRES
1:7 500 000
MADAGASCAR AT THE SAME SCALE
Longitude 28° east of Greenwich

© Bartholomew Ltd

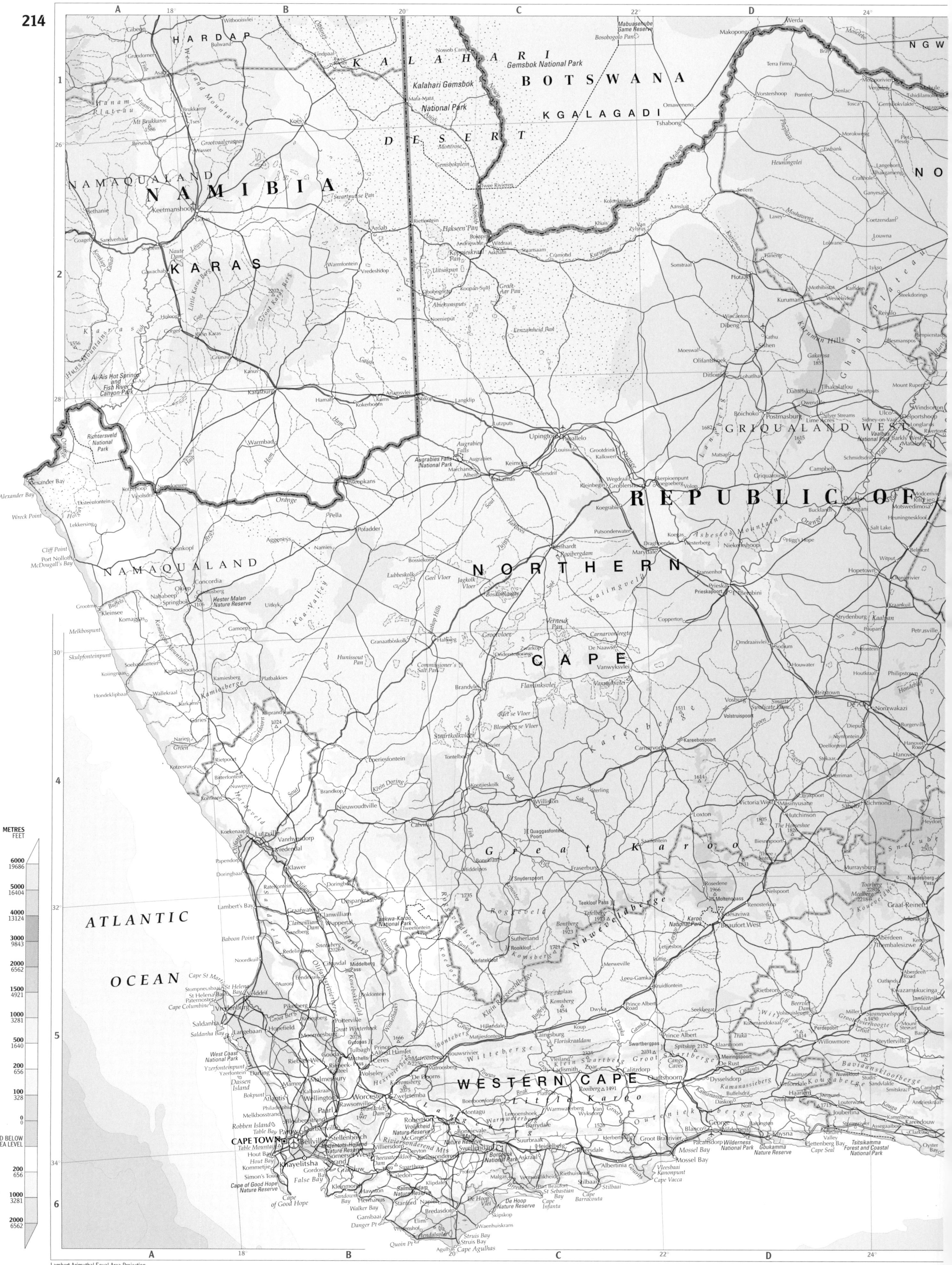

Lambert Azimuthal Equal Area Projection

215
SOUTH AFRICA
NORTH WEST
FREE STATE
GAUTENG
MPUMALANGA
KWAZULU-NATAL
EASTERN CAPE
LESOTHO
SWAZILAND
MOZAMBIQUE
HHOHHO
MANZINI
LUBOMBO
SHISELWENI
GRIQUALAND EAST
INDIAN OCEAN
PRETORIA
Johannesburg
Maputo
Maseru
Mbabane
Bloemfontein
Mangaung
Kimberley
Pietermaritzburg
Durban
East London
Port Elizabeth
Richards Bay
Port Shepstone
Umtata
Queenstown
Grahamstown
Uitenhage
Welkom
Kroonstad
Bethlehem
Harrismith
Ladysmith
Newcastle
Vryheid
Ulundi
Sasolburg
Soweto
Vereeniging
Vanderbijlpark
Drakensberg
Maluti Mountains
Kruger National Park
Hluhluwe Game Reserve
St Lucia Game Reserve
Addo Elephant National Park
Algoa Bay
St Francis Bay
Cape St Francis
Seal Point
MILES
KILOMETRES
1:3 300 000
Longitude 26° east of Greenwich
E
F
G
H
I
26°
28°
30°
32°
1
2
3
4
5
6

© Bartholomew Ltd

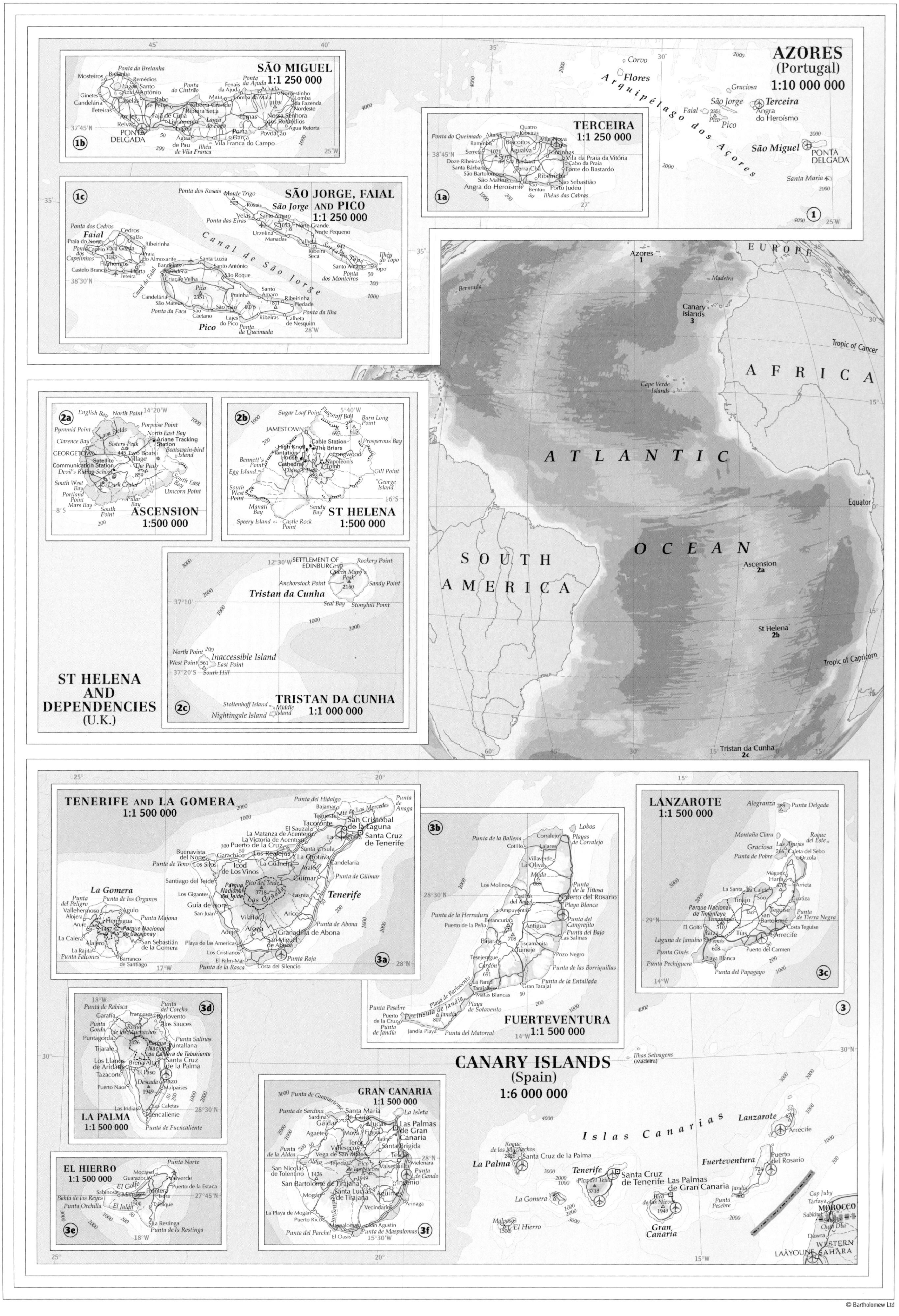
AZORES
(Portugal)
1:10 000 000
Arquipélago dos Açores
Corvo
Flores
Graciosa
São Jorge
Terceira
Angra do Heroísmo
Faial
Pico
São Miguel
PONTA DELGADA
Santa Maria
SÃO MIGUEL
1:1 250 000
Ponta da Bretanha
Mosteiros
Remédios
Lagoa Santo António
Ginetes
Candelária
Feteiras
Capelas
Rabo de Peixe
Ribeira Grande
Ribeira Seca
Maia
Lomba da Maia
Achada
Nordestinho
Lomba da Fazenda
Nordeste
Fenais da Ajuda
Ponta da Ajuda
Arrifes
Relva
Fajã de Cima
Livramento
Lagoa
Lagoa do Fogo
Furnas
Nossa Senhora dos Remédios
Povoação
Água Retorta
PONTA DELGADA
Água de Pau
Ilhéu de Vila Franca
Vila Franca do Campo
TERCEIRA
1:1 250 000
Ponta do Queimado
Altares
Quatro Ribeiras
Raminho
Biscoitos
Vila Nova
Lajes
Serreta
Agualva
Fontinhas
Doze Ribeiras
Santa Bárbara
São Bartolomeu
Terra Chã
Vila da Praia da Vitória
Cabo da Praia
Fonte do Bastardo
São Mateus
Ribeirinha
São Sebastião
Angra do Heroísmo
São Bento
Porto Judeu
Ilhéus das Cabras
SÃO JORGE, FAIAL AND PICO
1:1 250 000
Ponta dos Rosais
Monte Trigo
Rosais
São Jorge
Velas
Santo Amaro
Ponta das Eiras
Urzelina
Manadas
Norte Grande
Norte Pequeno
Calheta
Serra do Topo
Ribeira Seca
Ilhéu do Topo
Topo
Santo Antão
Ponta dos Monteiros
Canal de São Jorge
Ponta dos Cedros
Faial
Cedros
Salão
Praia do Norte
Ribeirinha
Ponta do Capelo
Pico Gordo
Capelinhos
Praia do Almoxarife
Flamengos
Horta
Castelo Branco
Feteira
Bandeiras
Madalena
Criação Velha
Santa Luzia
Santo António
São Roque
Canal do Faial
Candelária
São Mateus
Prainha
Santo Amaro
Ribeirinha
Piedade
São João
Ponta da Faca
São Caetano
Lajes do Pico
Ribeiras
Calheta de Nesquim
Ponta da Ilha
Pico
Ponta da Queimada
ST HELENA AND DEPENDENCIES
(U.K.)
ASCENSION
1:500 000
English Bay
North Point
Porpoise Point
North East Bay
Ariane Tracking Station
Pyramid Point
Clarence Bay
Sisters Peak
Two Boats
Boatswain-bird Island
GEORGETOWN
Communication Station
Devil's Riding School
The Peak
South West Bay
Dark Crater
South East Bay
Unicorn Point
Portland Point
Mars Bay
Pillar Bay
South Point
ST HELENA
1:500 000
Sugar Loaf Point
Flagstaff Bay
Barn Long Point
JAMESTOWN
Cable Station
The Briars
High Knoll
Plantation House
Prosperous Bay
Longwood
Bennett's Point
Egg Island
Cathedral
Diana's Peak
Napoleon's Tomb
Gill Point
George Island
South West Point
Manati Bay
Sandy Bay
Speery Island
Castle Rock Point
TRISTAN DA CUNHA
1:1 000 000
SETTLEMENT OF EDINBURGH
Rookery Point
Queen Mary's Peak
Anchorstock Point
Sandy Point
Tristan da Cunha
Seal Bay
Stonyhill Point
North Point
West Point
Inaccessible Island
East Point
South Hill
Stoltenhoff Island
Middle Island
Nightingale Island
EUROPE
Azores
Madeira
Bermuda
Canary Islands
Tropic of Cancer
AFRICA
Cape Verde Islands
ATLANTIC OCEAN
Equator
SOUTH AMERICA
Ascension
St Helena
Tropic of Capricorn
Tristan da Cunha
TENERIFE AND LA GOMERA
1:1 500 000
Punta del Hidalgo
Bajamar
Punta de Anaga
Tegueste
Mte de las Mercedes
San Cristóbal de la Laguna
Santa Cruz de Tenerife
Tacoronte
El Sauzal
La Matanza de Acentejo
La Victoria de Acentejo
Puerto de la Cruz
Los Realejos
Santa Úrsula
La Orotava
Buenavista del Norte
Garachico
Punta de Teno
Los Silos
Icod de Los Vinos
La Guancha
Candelaria
Arafo
Santiago del Teide
Güímar
Punta de Güímar
Parque Nacional del Teide
Pico del Teide
Las Cañadas
Los Gigantes
Fasnia
Tenerife
Guía de Isora
San Juan
Arico
Vilaflor
Arona
Adeje
Granadilla de Abona
Punta de Abona
San Miguel de Abona
Playa de las Americas
Los Cristianos
El Palm-Mar
Punta de la Rasca
Punta Roja
Costa del Silencio
La Gomera
Punta del Peligro
Punta de los Órganos
Vallehermoso
Agulo
Alojera
Hermigua
Punta Majona
Arure
Parque Nacional de Garajonay
La Calera
Alajeró
San Sebastián de la Gomera
La Rajita
Punta Falcones
Barranco de Santiago
LANZAROTE
1:1 500 000
Alegranza
Punta Delgada
Montaña Clara
Roque del Este
Graciosa
Las Agujas
Caleta del Sebo
Punta de Pobre
Orzola
Máguez
Haría
Arrieta
La Santa
Tinajo
Soo
Guatiza
Parque Nacional de Timanfaya
Teguise
San Bartolomé
Punta de Tierra Negra
El Golfo
Tías
Arrecife
Costa Teguise
Laguna de Janubio
Yaiza
Femés
Puerto del Carmen
Punta Ginés
Punta Pechiguera
Playa Blanca
Punta del Papagayo
FUERTEVENTURA
1:1 500 000
Lobos
Punta de la Ballena
Corralejo
Playas de Corralejo
Cotillo
Lajares
Villaverde
La Oliva
Tindaya
Los Molinos
Punta de la Tiñosa
Casillas del Ángel
Puerto del Rosario
La Ampuyenta
Punta de la Herradura
Betancuria
Punta del Cangrejito
Puerto de la Peña
Antigua
Punta del Bajo
Las Salinas
Pájara
Tiscamanita
Tuineje
Pozo Negro
Tesejerague
Cardón
Punta de las Borriquillas
La Pared
Tarajalejo
Gran Tarajal
Punta de la Entallada
Matas Blancas
Playa de Barlovento
Península de Jandía
Jandía
Playa de Sotavento
Punta Pesebre
Puerto de la Cruz
Punta de Jandía
Jandía Playa
Punta del Matorral
LA PALMA
1:1 500 000
Punta de Rabisca
Punta del Corcho
Garafía
Franceses
Barlovento
Los Sauces
Punta Gorda
Roque de los Muchachos
Puntagorda
Punta Salinas
Tijarafe
Puntallana
Parque Nacional de la Caldera de Taburiente
Santa Cruz de la Palma
Los Llanos de Aridane
Breña Alta
El Paso
Tazacorte
Puerto Naos
Deseada
Mazo
Malpaises
Las Indias
Las Caletas
Fuencaliente
Punta de Fuencaliente
EL HIERRO
1:1 500 000
Punta Norte
Mocanal
Guarazoca
Valverde
El Golfo
Puerto de la Estaca
Sabinosa
Frontera
Malpaso
Bahía de los Reyes
Punta Orchilla
El Julán
Tiñor
Taibique
La Restinga
Punta de la Restinga
GRAN CANARIA
1:1 500 000
Punta de Guanarteme
Punta de Sardina
Santa María de Guía
La Isleta
Sardina
Gáldar
Arucas
Las Palmas de Gran Canaria
Agaete
Moya
Firgas
Teror
Tafira
Valleseco
Vega de San Mateo
Santa Brígida
Telde
Punta de la Aldea
Aldea
Tejeda
Pico de las Nieves
Valsequillo
Melenara
San Nicolás de Tolentino
Punta de Gando
Ingenio
San Bartolomé de Tirajana
Santa Lucía de Tirajana
Agüimes
Mogán
Vecindario
Arinaga
La Playa de Mogán
Puerto Rico
Maspalomas
San Agustín
Punta del Parchel
El Oasis
Punta de Maspalomas
CANARY ISLANDS
(Spain)
1:6 000 000
Ilhas Selvagens (Madeira)
Islas Canarias
Lanzarote
Arrecife
Roque de los Muchachos
Santa Cruz de la Palma
La Palma
Fuerteventura
Puerto del Rosario
Tenerife
Pico del Teide
Santa Cruz de Tenerife
Las Palmas de Gran Canaria
La Gomera
Pico de las Nieves
Punta Pesebre
Jandía
El Hierro
Malpaso
Gran Canaria
Cap Juby
Tarfaya
MOROCCO
WESTERN SAHARA
LAÂYOUNE

© Bartholomew Ltd

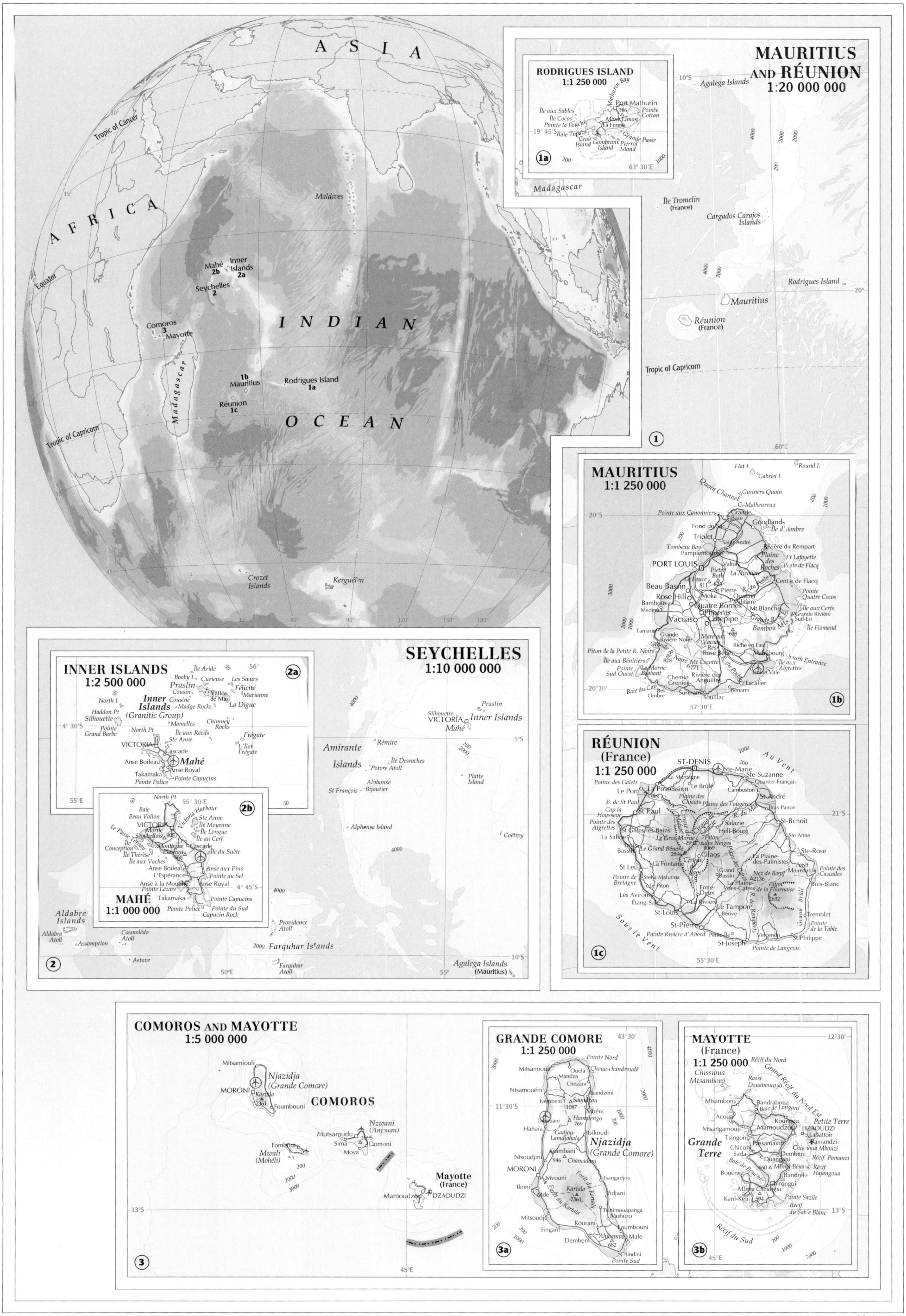
ASIA
AFRICA
INDIAN OCEAN
Tropic of Cancer
Equator
Tropic of Capricorn
Maldives
Mahé 2b
Inner Islands 2a
Seychelles 2
Comoros 3
Mayotte
Madagascar
1b Mauritius
Rodrigues Island 1a
Réunion 1c
Crozet Islands
Kerguelen
MAURITIUS AND RÉUNION
1:20 000 000
Agalega Islands
Île Tromelin (France)
Cargados Carajos Islands
Rodrigues Island
Mauritius
Réunion (France)
Tropic of Capricorn
RODRIGUES ISLAND
1:1 250 000
Mathurin Bay
Port Mathurin
Pointe Cotton
Île aux Sables
Île Cocos
Pointe la Fouche
Baie Topaze
Mont Limon
La Ferme
Grande Passe
Crab Island
Gombrani Island
Pierrot Island
Madagascar
MAURITIUS
1:1 250 000
Flat I.
Round I.
Gabriel I.
Quoin Channel
Gunners Quoin
C. Malheureux
Pointe aux Canonniers
Grande Baie
Goodlands
Île d'Ambre
Fond du Sac
Triolet
Tombeau Bay
Pamplemousses
Rivière du Rempart
Plaine des Roches
Poste de Flacq
PORT LOUIS
Beau Bassin
Rose Hill
Moka
Centre de Flacq
Pointe Quatre Cocos
Bambous
Quatre Bornes
Phoenix
Vacoas
Curepipe
Mt Blanche
Île aux Cerfs
Grande Rivière Sud-Est
Bambou Mts
Île Flamand
Tamarin
Grande Rivière Noire
Mare aux Vacoas
Rose Belle
Mahébourg
South Entrance
Piton de la Petite R. Noire
Île aux Bénitiers
Pointe Sud Ouest
Le Morne Brabant
Chemin Grenier
Rivière des Anguilles
Plaine Magnien
Île aux Aigrettes
Baie du Cap
Bel Ombre
Surinam
Souillac
L'Escalier
Benares
57°30'E
RÉUNION (France)
1:1 250 000
ST-DENIS
Ste-Marie
Ste-Suzanne
Au Vent
Pointe des Galets
Le Port
La Possession
Le Brûlé
St-André
B. de St Paul
Cap la Houssaye
St-Paul
Plaine des Chicots
Plaine des Fougères
Salazie
Hell-Bourg
St-Benoit
Pointe des Aigrettes
St Gilles-les-Bains
Le Gros Morne
Piton des Neiges
3069
Ste Anne
La Saline
Le Grand Bénare
Cilaos
Ste-Rose
St Leu
La Fontaine
La Plaine-des-Palmistes
Pointe de Bretagne
Grand Bassin
Piton de la Fournaise
2632
Les Avirons
Étang-Salé
Entre-Deux
Le Tampon
Bois-Blanc
St-Louis
St-Pierre
Tremblet
Pointe de la Table
Pointe Rivière d'Abord
St-Joseph
Vincendo
St-Philippe
Pointe de Langevin
Sous le Vent
55°30'E
SEYCHELLES
1:10 000 000
INNER ISLANDS
1:2 500 000
Île Aride
Praslin
Curieuse
Les Sœurs
Félicité
Marianne
Cousin
Cousine
La Digue
North I.
Inner Islands (Granitic Group)
Madge Rocks
Silhouette
Mamelles
Chimney Rocks
Pointe Grand Barbe
North Pt
Île aux Récifs
Frégate
VICTORIA
Cascade
Mahé
Anse Boileau
Anse Royal
Takamaka
Pointe Police
Pointe Capucins
MAHÉ
1:1 000 000
Baie Beau Vallon
Victoria Harbour
Ste Anne
Île Moyenne
Île Longue
Île au Cerf
Conception
Île Thérèse
Île aux Vaches
Île du Suète
Anse Boileau
Anse aux Pins
L'Espérance
Pointe au Sel
Anse à la Mouche
Anse Royal
Pointe Lazare
Pointe Capucins
Pointe du Sud
Capucin Rock
Praslin
Silhouette
VICTORIA
Inner Islands
Mahé
Amirante Islands
Rémire
Île Desroches
Poivre Atoll
Alphonse
Bijoutier
St François
Platte Island
Alphonse Island
Coëtivy
Aldabra Islands
Aldabra Atoll
Assomption
Cosmolédo Atoll
Astove
Providence Atoll
Farquhar Islands
Farquhar Atoll
Agalega Islands (Mauritius)
COMOROS AND MAYOTTE
1:5 000 000
Mitsamiouli
Njazidja (Grande Comore)
MORONI
Kartala
Foumbouni
COMOROS
Nzwani (Anjouan)
Mutsamudu
Sima
Domoni
Moya
Fomboni
Mwali (Mohéli)
Mayotte (France)
Mamoudzou
DZAOUDZI
GRANDE COMORE
1:1 250 000
Pointe Nord
Mitsamiouli
Ouela
Choua-chandroudé
Mandza
Chezani
Ntsamouéni
Bandzéni
Ivembeni
Saoudjou
Mbéni
Hamalengo
Hahaia
Itsikoudi
Lamdjahala
Njazidja (Grande Comore)
Ntsoudjini
Koimbani
Chamadjani
MORONI
Mvouni
Tsangadjou
Ikoni
Kartala
2361
Pidjani
Mitsoudjé
Mohoro
Kourani
Singani
Foumbouni
Dembeni
Male
Chindini
Pointe Sud
MAYOTTE (France)
1:1 250 000
Récif du Nord
Chissioua Mtsamboro
Grand Récif du Nord Est
Rassi Douamougno
Mtsamboro
Bandraboua
Baie de Longoni
Acoua
Koungou
Petite Terre
Mamoudzou
DZAOUDZI
Labattoir
Pamandzi
Mtsangamouji
Grande Terre
Tsingoni
Passamainti
Chissioua Mbouzi
Chiconi
Dembeni
Sada
Récif Pamanzi
Mt Bénara
Récif Hajangoua
Bandrélé
Bouéni
Chirongui
Mlima Choungui
Kani-Kéli
Pointe Saziley
Récif du Sable Blanc
Récif du Sud

© Bartholomew Ltd

A
B
C
D
E
1
2
3
4
5
6
7
ASIA
ARCTIC OCEAN
Arctic Circle
Chukchi Sea
BERING SEA
Bering Strait
Point Hope
Barrow
BEAUFORT SEA
Nome
Norton Sound
St Lawrence Island
St Matthew Island
Nunivak Island
Pribilof Islands
Attu Island
Aleutian Islands
Andreanof Islands
Fox Islands
Bristol Bay
Aleutian Range
Kodiak Island
ALASKA
Brooks Range
Kuskokwim Mts
Alaska Range
Anchorage
Yukon
Gulf of Alaska
Wrangell Mountains
Juneau
Alexander Archipelago
YUKON TERRITORY
Whitehorse
Watson Lake
NORTHWEST TERRITORIES
Inuvik
Great Bear Lake
Deline
Yellowknife
Great Slave Lake
Fort Simpson
Fort Nelson
Mackenzie Mountains
Ogilvie Mountains
Sachs Harbour
Banks Island
Victoria Island
Prince Patrick Island
Melville Island
Queen Elizabeth Islands
Amundsen Gulf
Bathurst Inlet
NUN
CANADA
BRITISH COLUMBIA
ALBERTA
SASKATCHEWAN
COAST MOUNTAINS
ROCKY MOUNTAINS
Prince Rupert
Queen Charlotte Islands
Hecate Str.
Queen Charlotte Sound
Dawson Creek
Williston Lake
Grande Prairie
Fort McMurray
Lake Athabasca
Uranium City
Lesser Slave Lake
Prince George
Edmonton
Jasper
Lloydminster
Prince Albert
Saskatoon
Kamloops
Calgary
Medicine Hat
Lethbridge
Regina
Lynn Lake
Lake Winnipegosis
Vancouver Island
Vancouver
Victoria
Seattle
Olympia
Spokane
WASHINGTON
Portland
Salem
Eugene
OREGON
IDAHO
Boise
Twin Falls
Bitterroot Range
Cascade Range
Coast Ranges
MONTANA
Great Falls
Helena
Billings
NOR DAK
Bismarck
SOU DAK
Pierre
Rapid City
Casper
WYOMING
Bighorn Mountains
Cheyenne
NEBR
North Platte
Great Salt Lake
Salt Lake City
Uinta Mountains
UTAH
NEVADA
Reno
Carson City
Great Basin
Sierra Nevada
Mount Whitney
Sacramento
San Francisco
San Jose
COLORADO
Denver
Colorado Springs
Colorado Plateau
UNITED STAT
CALIFORNIA
Las Vegas
Los Angeles
San Diego
Tijuana
Ensenada
Mexicali
ARIZONA
Phoenix
Tucson
NEW MEXICO
Albuquerque
Santa Fe
Amarillo
Lubbock
El Paso
Ciudad Juárez
Sacramento Mts
TE
Edwards Plateau
Hermosillo
Chihuahua
Golfo de California
Baja California
Guadalupe (Mexico)
Villa Insurgentes
La Paz
Los Mochis
Sierra Madre Occidental
Torreón
Monterrey
Durango
MEXIC
Mazatlán
San Luis Potosí
Tepic
León
Guadalajara
Morelia
Islas Revillagigedo (Mexico)
Île Clipperton (France)
PACIFIC OCEAN
Tropic of Cancer
Midway Islands (U.S.A.)
Kauai
Oahu
Honolulu
Maui
HAWAII
Hawaii
Hawaiian Islands (U.S.A.)
Equator
Line Islands
Administrative regions abbreviated on the map:
U.S.A.
CONN. CONNECTICUT
DEL. DELAWARE
MD MARYLAND
MASS. MASSACHUSETTS
N.H. NEW HAMPSHIRE
N.J. NEW JERSEY
R.I. RHODE ISLAND
VER. VERMONT
W. VIRG. WEST VIRGINIA
CANADA
P.E.I. PRINCE EDWARD ISLAND

Orthographic Projection

E U R O P E
Alps
Iceland
Greenland (Kalaallit Nunaat) (Denmark)
Greenland Sea
Denmark Strait
Station Nord
Daneborg
Kong Oscars Fjord
Uummannaq
Nuussuaq
Ilulissat
Ammassalik
Nuuk
Nanortalik
Baffin Bay
Davis Strait
Baffin Island
Ellesmere Island
Devon Island
Lancaster Sd
Clyde River
Cumberland Peninsula
Cumberland Sound
Cape Mercy
Iqaluit
Frobisher Bay
Resolution I.
Labrador Sea
Foxe Basin
Melville Peninsula
Repulse Bay
Southampton Island
Cape Dorset
Coral Harbour
Hudson Strait
Hudson Bay
Péninsule d'Ungava
Ungava Bay
Nain
Labrador
NEWFOUNDLAND
Strait of Belle Isle
Gander
St John's
Cape Race
Belcher Islands
James Bay
Fort George
MANITOBA
Thompson
Lake Winnipeg
ONTARIO
Moosonee
QUÉBEC
Sept-Îles
Île d'Anticosti
Gulf of St Lawrence
Cabot Str.
St Pierre and Miquelon (France)
Lac Mistassini
Chicoutimi
Québec
Montréal
Ottawa
Timmins
Rouyn
North Bay
Lake Nipigon
Thunder Bay
International Falls
Winnipeg
Lake Superior
Sault Ste Marie
NEW BRUNSWICK
P.E.I.
Charlottetown
Fredericton
NOVA SCOTIA
Halifax
Sable Island
Cape Sable
MAINE
Augusta
Montpelier
Concord
Boston
Providence
Cape Cod
NEW YORK
Albany
Hartford
New York
Trenton
Philadelphia
Dover
Annapolis
Baltimore
Washington
Richmond
VIRGINIA
NORTH CAROLINA
Raleigh
Cape Hatteras
SOUTH CAROLINA
Columbia
Charlotte
GEORGIA
Atlanta
Savannah
Macon
Jacksonville
Tallahassee
FLORIDA
Orlando
Tampa
Cape Canaveral
West Palm Beach
Miami
Straits of Florida
THE BAHAMAS
Nassau
Grand Bahama
Great Abaco
Andros
Bermuda (U.K.)
Toronto
Lake Ontario
Lake Erie
Lake Huron
Lake Michigan
Detroit
Buffalo
Erie
Cleveland
Pittsburgh
Harrisburg
PENNSYLVANIA
OHIO
Columbus
Toledo
Lansing
Grand Rapids
MICHIGAN
Milwaukee
Madison
Chicago
WISCONSIN
MINNESOTA
Duluth
Minneapolis
St Paul
Rochester
Sioux Falls
IOWA
Des Moines
Omaha
Lincoln
ILLINOIS
INDIANA
Indianapolis
Fort Wayne
Cincinnati
Frankfort
Charleston
W. VIRG.
KENTUCKY
Knoxville
Nashville
TENNESSEE
Chattanooga
Huntsville
Memphis
ARKANSAS
Little Rock
MISSOURI
Springfield
St Louis
Jefferson City
Kansas City
Topeka
Wichita
Tulsa
Oklahoma City
OKLAHOMA
Ozark Plateau
Appalachian Mountains
UNITED STATES OF AMERICA
MISSISSIPPI
Jackson
ALABAMA
Montgomery
Mobile
LOUISIANA
Baton Rouge
New Orleans
Shreveport
Dallas
Fort Worth
TEXAS
Austin
San Antonio
Houston
Corpus Christi
Apalachee Bay
GULF OF MEXICO
Matamoros
Ciudad Victoria
Tampico
Poza Rica
México
Puebla
Veracruz
Toluca
Acapulco
Oaxaca
Sierra Madre del Sur
Golfo de Tehuantepec
Bahía de Campeche
Mérida
Yucatán
Yucatan Channel
Villahermosa
BELIZE
Belmopan
San Pedro Sula
GUATEMALA
Guatemala
HONDURAS
Tegucigalpa
San Salvador
EL SALVADOR
NICARAGUA
Managua
Lago de Nicaragua
COSTA RICA
San José
PANAMA
Panamá
Colón
Golfo de Panamá
La Habana
Santa Clara
CUBA
Holguín
Turks and Caicos Is (U.K.)
Acklins Island
Great Inagua
Hispaniola
HAITI
Port-au-Prince
DOMINICAN REPUBLIC
Santiago
Santo Domingo
San Juan
Puerto Rico (U.S.A.)
Cayman Is (U.K.)
Montego Bay
JAMAICA
Kingston
Greater Antilles
Leeward Islands
Virgin Is (U.K.)
Virgin Is (U.S.A.)
Anguilla (U.K.)
ANTIGUA AND BARBUDA
ST KITTS AND NEVIS
Montserrat (U.K.)
Guadeloupe (France)
DOMINICA
Martinique (France)
ST LUCIA
BARBADOS
ST VINCENT AND THE GRENADINES
GRENADA
TRINIDAD AND TOBAGO
Port of Spain
Windward Islands
Lesser Antilles
Aruba (Neth.)
Netherlands Antilles
Bonaire
Curaçao
CARIBBEAN SEA
SOUTH AMERICA
Cordillera Oriental
Amazonas (Amazon)
ATLANTIC OCEAN
Arquipélago dos Açores
Arquipélago da Madeira
Islas Canarias
Tropic of Cancer
Ilhas do Cabo Verde
Equator
AFRICA
Arctic Circle
F G H I J
1 2 3 4 5 6 7
MILES
KILOMETRES
1000
750
500
250
0
1500
1250
1000
750
500
250
0

1:27 000 000

131

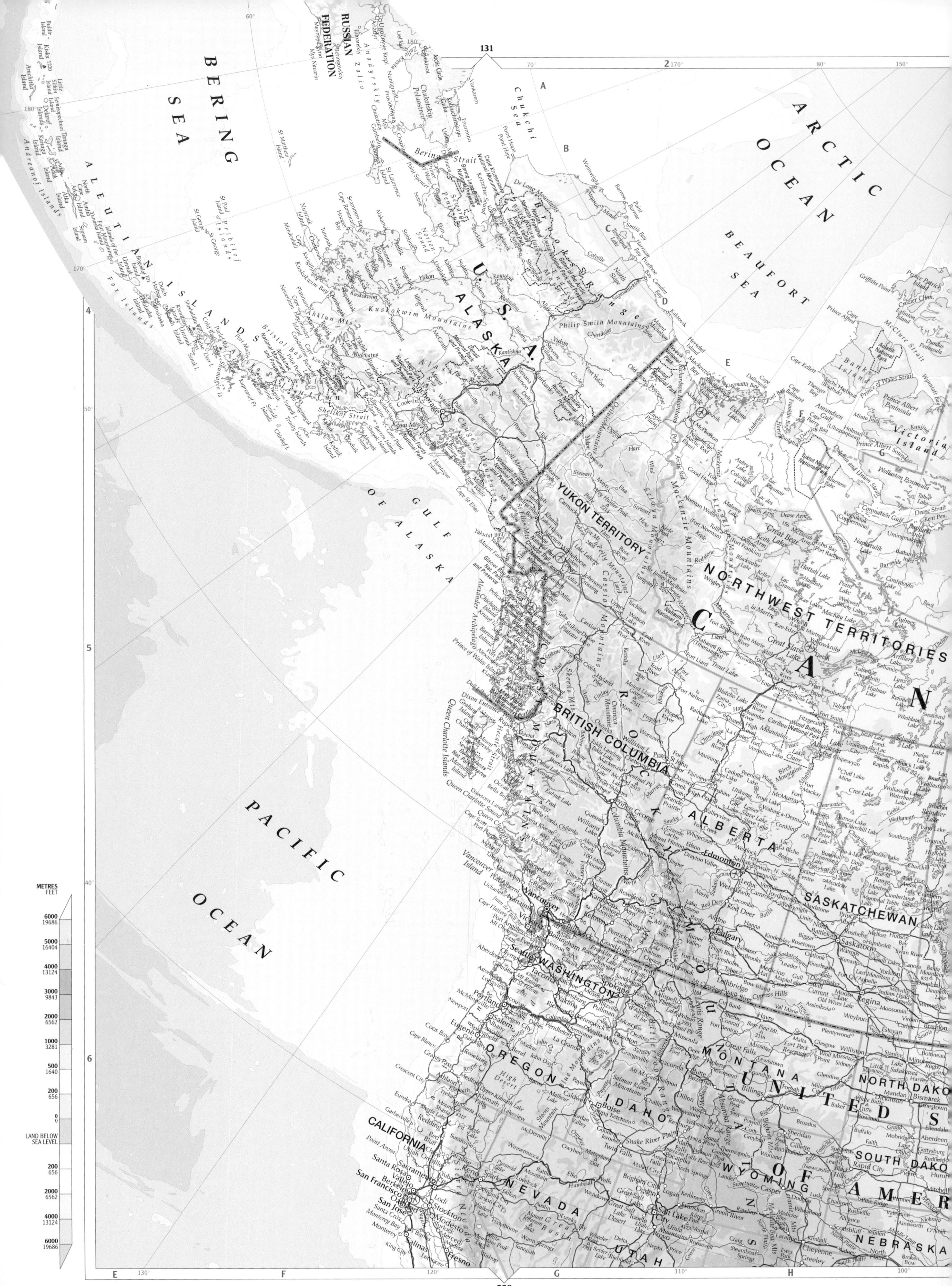
BERING SEA
ARCTIC OCEAN
BEAUFORT SEA
Chukchi Sea
RUSSIAN FEDERATION
ALEUTIAN ISLANDS
U.S.A.
ALASKA
Brooks Range
Alaska Range
GULF OF ALASKA
PACIFIC OCEAN
YUKON TERRITORY
NORTHWEST TERRITORIES
BRITISH COLUMBIA
ALBERTA
SASKATCHEWAN
ROCKY MOUNTAINS
COAST MOUNTAINS
WASHINGTON
OREGON
IDAHO
MONTANA
WYOMING
NEVADA
UTAH
CALIFORNIA
NORTH DAKO
SOUTH DAKO
NEBRASKA
UNITED STATES OF AMER
CAN
Victoria Island
Banks Island
Anchorage
Vancouver
Seattle
Portland
Edmonton
Calgary
San Francisco
METRES
FEET
6000
19686
5000
16404
4000
13124
3000
9843
2000
6562
1000
3281
500
1640
200
656
0
0
LAND BELOW SEA LEVEL
200
656
2000
6562
4000
13124
6000
19686

228

Greenland
(Kalaallit Nunaat)
(Denmark)
GREENLAND SEA
ICELAND
REYKJAVIK
BAFFIN BAY
Davis Strait
Denmark Strait
LABRADOR SEA
ATLANTIC OCEAN
HUDSON BAY
NUNAVUT
CANADA
MANITOBA
ONTARIO
QUÉBEC
NEWFOUNDLAND
NEW BRUNSWICK
NOVA SCOTIA
PRINCE EDWARD ISLAND
QUEEN ELIZABETH ISLANDS
Ellesmere Island
Devon Island
Baffin Island
Southampton Island
Labrador
Ungava Bay
Hudson Strait
Foxe Basin
James Bay
Gulf of St Lawrence
Cabot Strait
St Pierre and Miquelon (France)
Lake Superior
Lake Michigan
Lake Huron
Lake Erie
Lake Winnipeg
MINNESOTA
WISCONSIN
MICHIGAN
IOWA
NEW YORK
PENNSYLVANIA
VERMONT
NEW HAMPSHIRE
MAINE
Winnipeg
Thunder Bay
Montréal
OTTAWA
Québec
Toronto
Halifax
St John's
Boston
New York
Philadelphia
Chicago
Detroit
Minneapolis
Milwaukee
Longitude 70° west of Greenwich
MILES
KILOMETRES
1:15 000 000

© Bartholomew Ltd

220

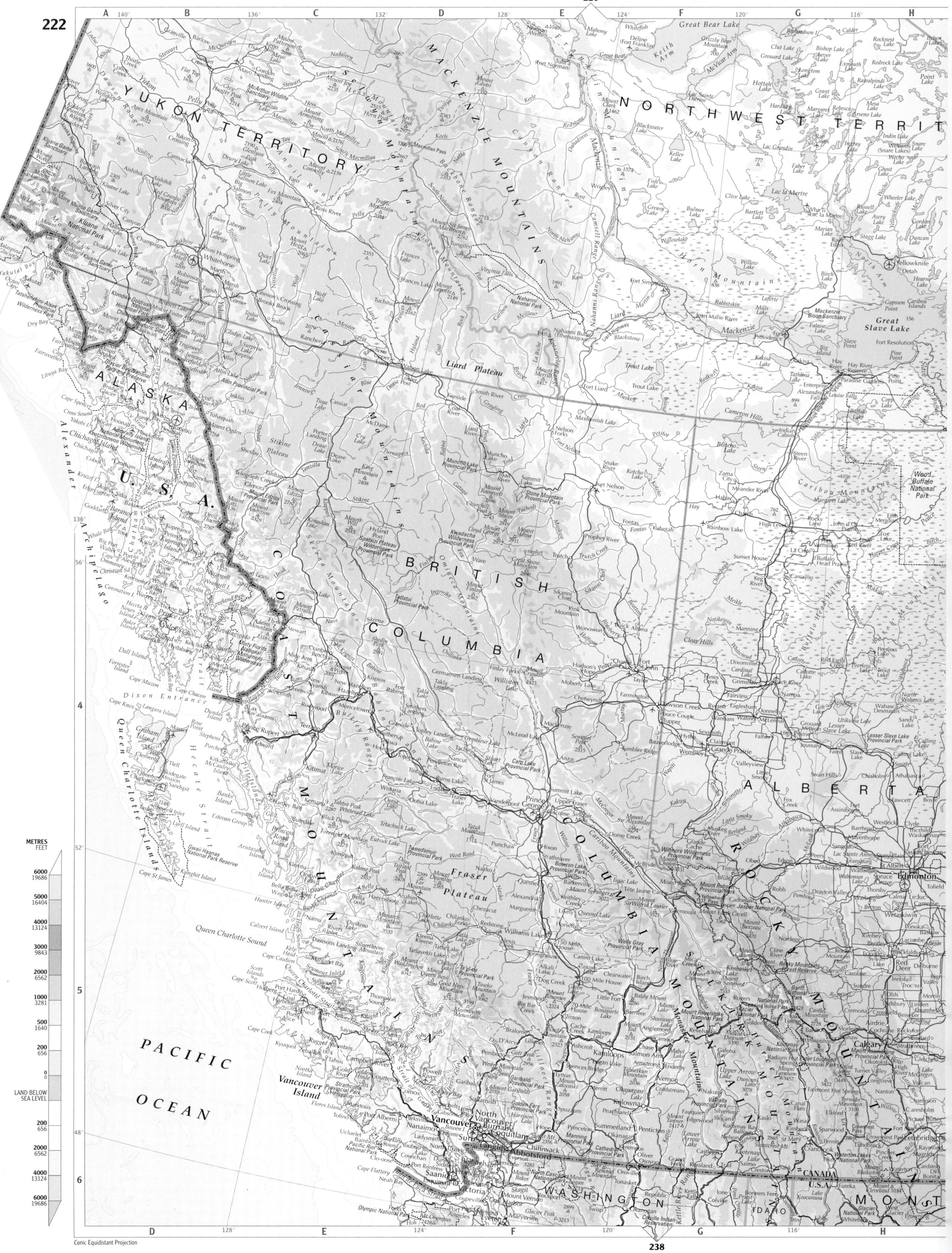

Conic Equidistant Projection

238

221

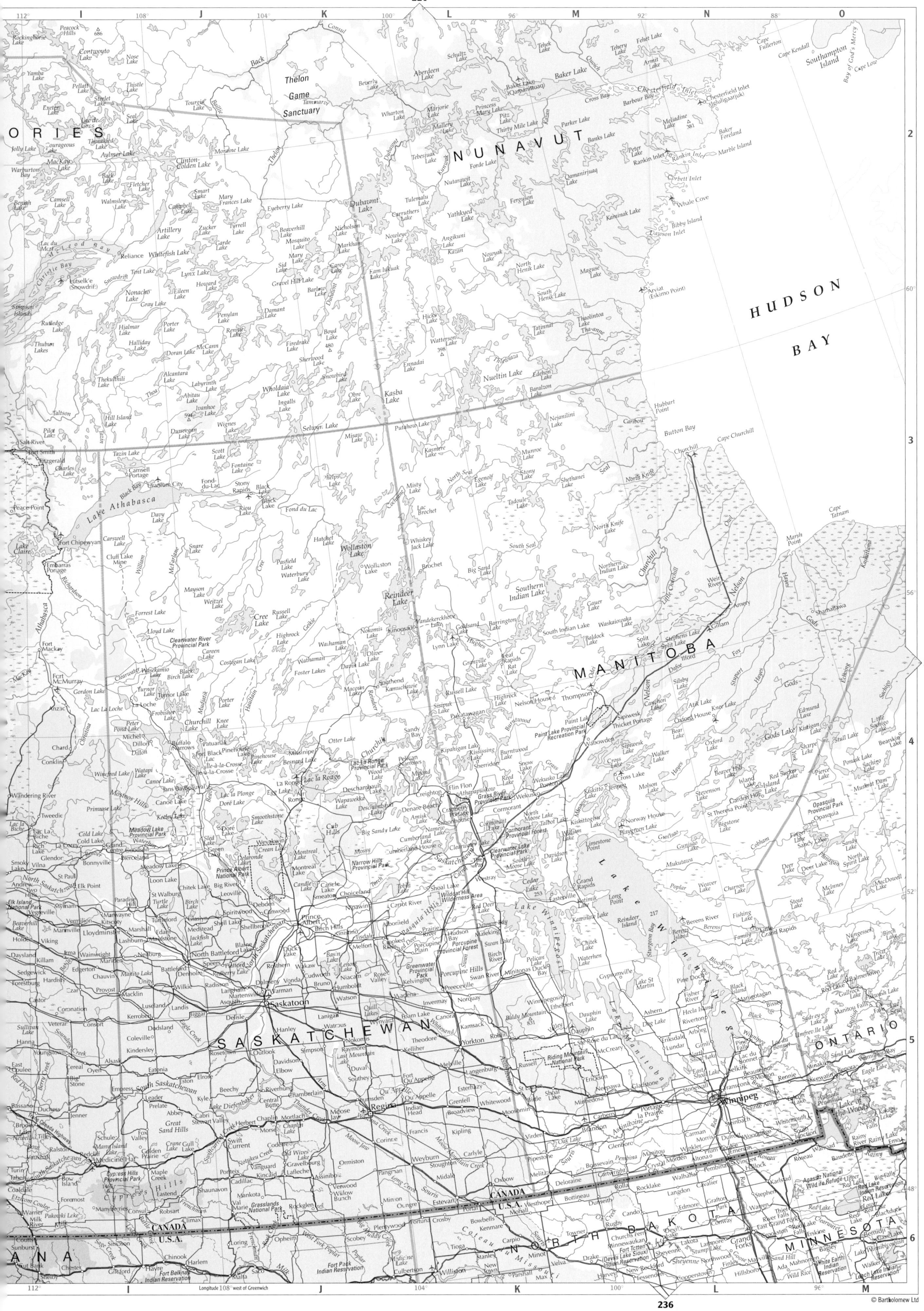

224

236

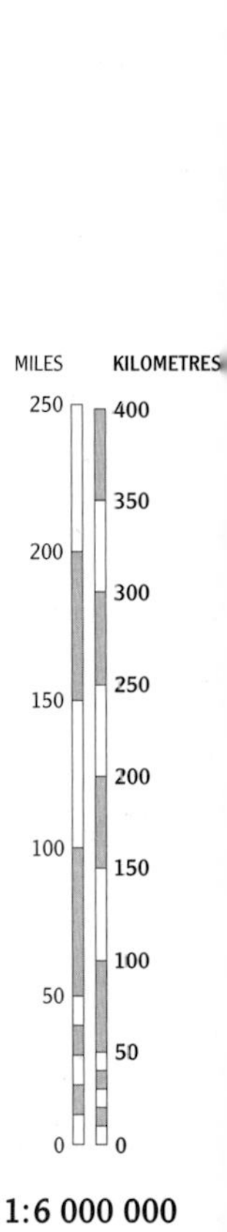

1:6 000 000

© Bartholomew Ltd

Conic Equidistant Projection

236

230

Ungava Bay
LABRADOR SEA
Torngat Mountains
LABRADOR
NEWFOUNDLAND
QUÉBEC
Smallwood Reservoir
Lake Melville
Mealy Mountains
Hope Mountains
Strait of Belle Isle
Long Range Mountains
GULF OF ST LAWRENCE
Détroit d'Honguedo
Île d'Anticosti
Cabot Strait
Péninsule de Gaspé
Monts Notre Dame
St Lawrence
NEW BRUNSWICK
PRINCE EDWARD ISLAND
NOVA SCOTIA
Cape Breton Island
Northumberland Strait
Bay of Fundy
Gulf of Maine
MAINE
VERMONT
NEW HAMPSHIRE
White Mountains
CANADA
USA
St Pierre and Miquelon (France)
ATLANTIC OCEAN
Sable Island
Québec
Halifax
St John's
Boston
Portland
Saint John
Fredericton
Charlottetown
Moncton
Sydney
Corner Brook
Gander
Sept-Îles
Chicoutimi
Rimouski
Gaspé
Happy Valley-Goose Bay
Labrador City
Schefferville
Kuujjuaq (Fort Chimo)
Nain
Hopedale
Cartwright
Bangor
Augusta
Manchester
Concord
Longitude 72° west of Greenwich
© Bartholomew Ltd

MILES | KILOMETRES

1:6 000 000

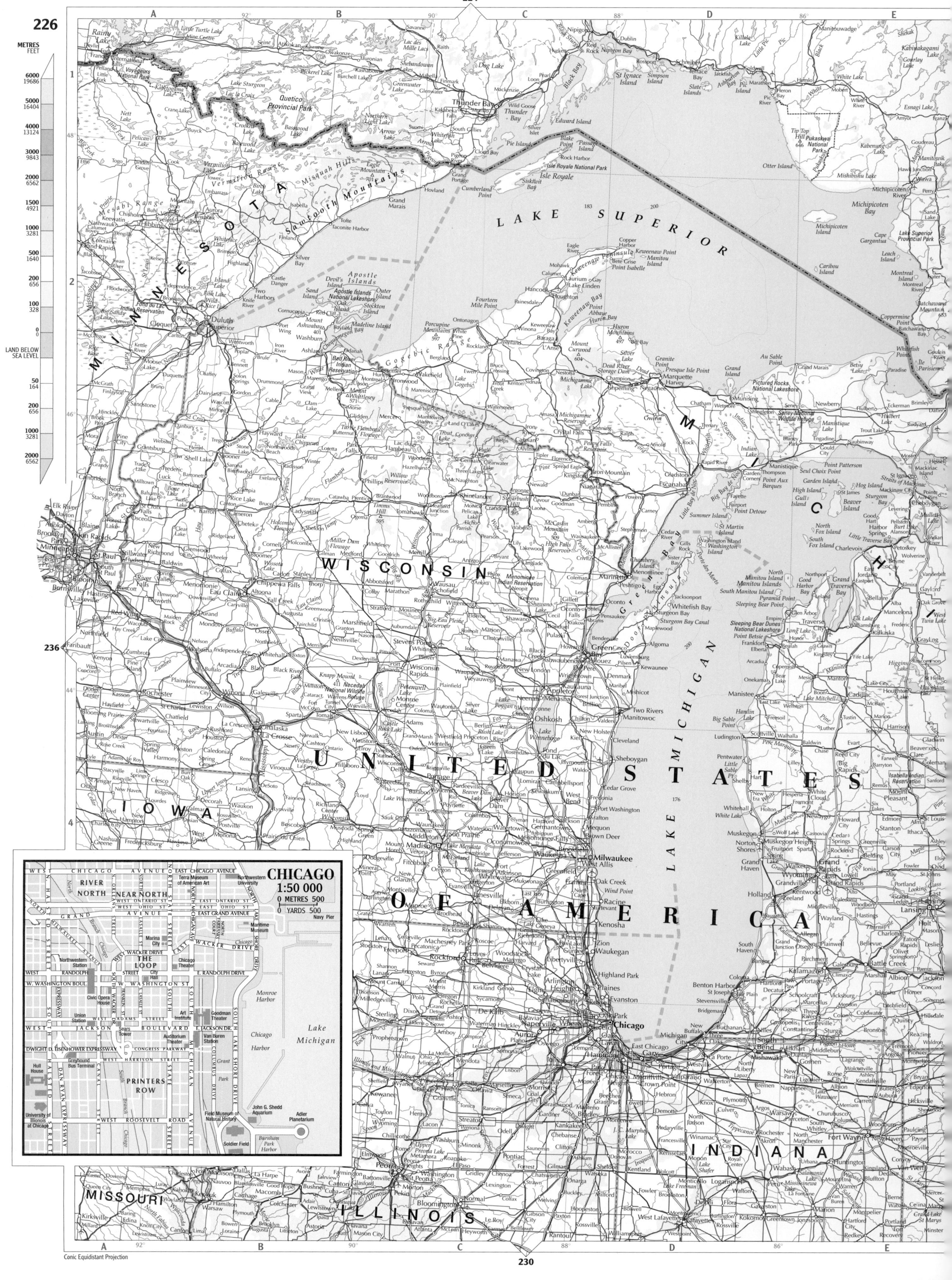
224
230
236
METRES
FEET
6000 19686
5000 16404
4000 13124
3000 9843
2000 6562
1500 4921
1000 3281
500 1640
200 656
100 328
0 0
LAND BELOW SEA LEVEL
50 164
200 656
1000 3281
2000 6562
LAKE SUPERIOR
LAKE MICHIGAN
MINNESOTA
WISCONSIN
MICHIGAN
IOWA
MISSOURI
ILLINOIS
INDIANA
UNITED STATES OF AMERICA
CHICAGO
1:50 000
0 METRES 500
0 YARDS 500
Lake Michigan
Conic Equidistant Projection

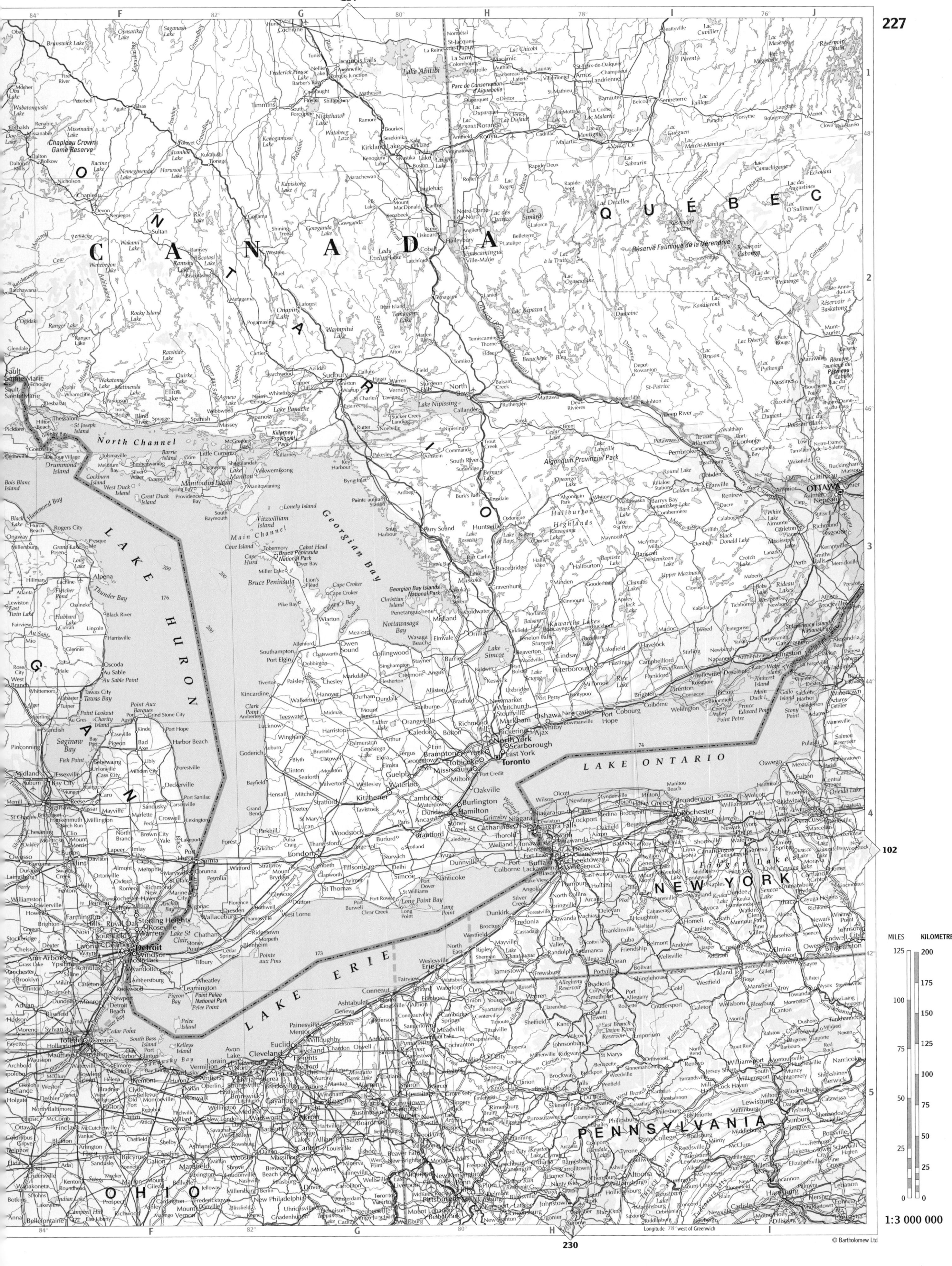
224
CANADA
ONTARIO
QUÉBEC
LAKE HURON
LAKE ONTARIO
LAKE ERIE
MICHIGAN
NEW YORK
PENNSYLVANIA
OHIO
Georgian Bay
North Channel
Main Channel
Manitoulin Island
Bruce Peninsula
Lake Nipissing
Lake Simcoe
Algonquin Provincial Park
Toronto
OTTAWA
Detroit
Cleveland
Buffalo
Rochester
Syracuse
Pittsburgh
Sudbury
Hamilton
Kingston
Toledo
Akron
Erie
Saginaw Bay
Thunder Bay
Long Point Bay
Finger Lakes
102
230
MILES
KILOMETRES
1:3 000 000
Longitude 78° west of Greenwich

220

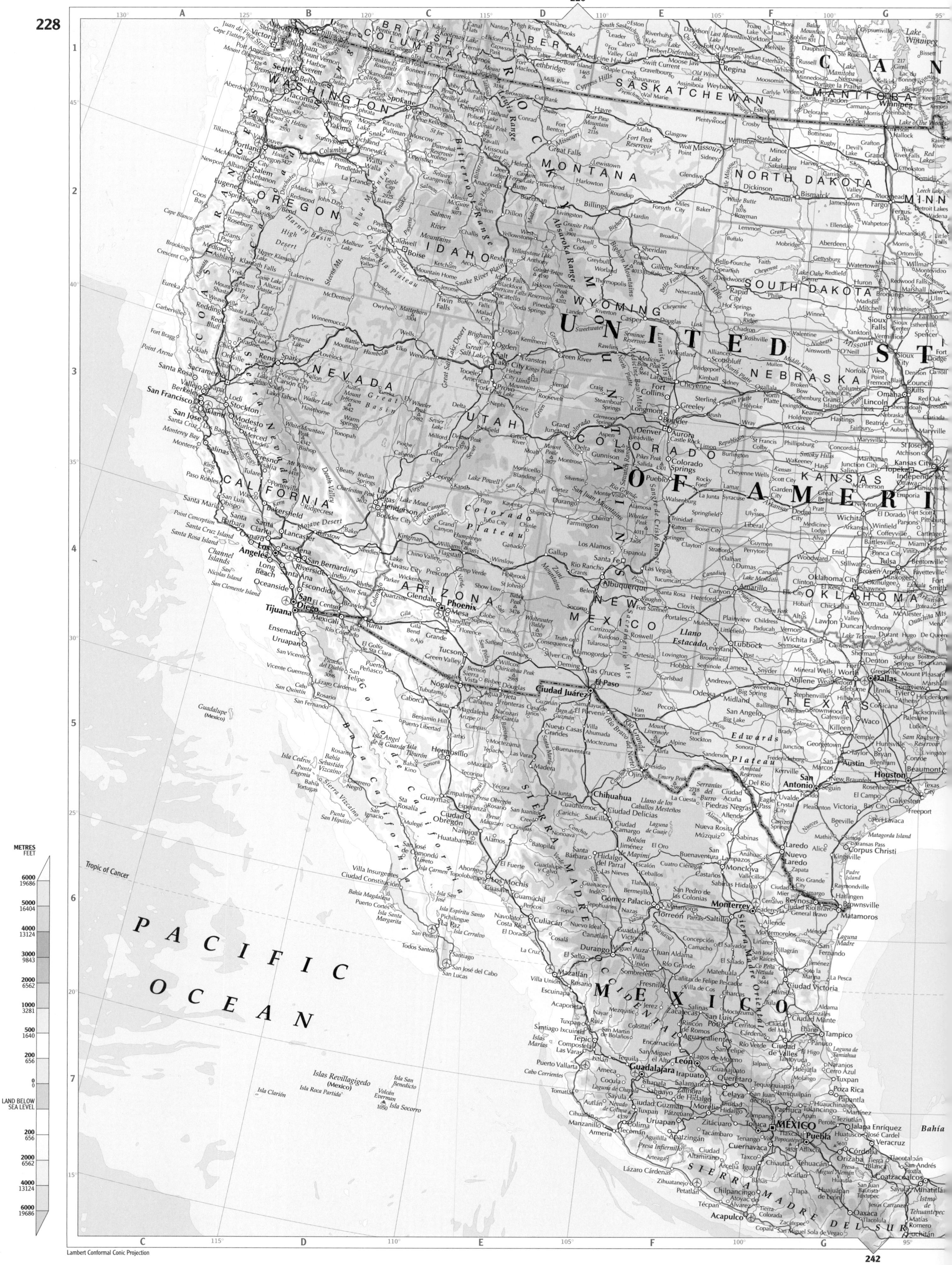

Lambert Conformal Conic Projection

242

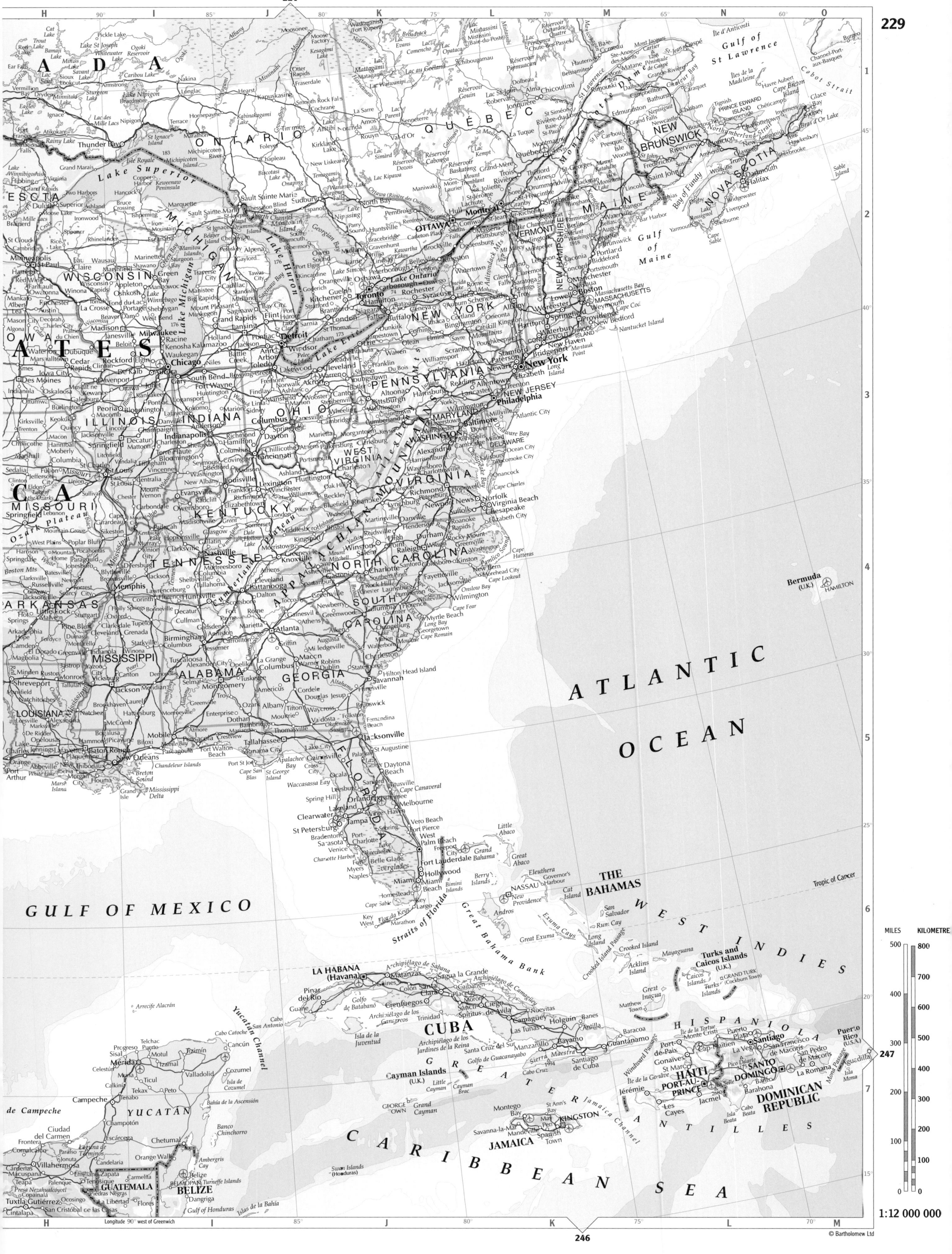
ATLANTIC OCEAN
GULF OF MEXICO
CARIBBEAN SEA
Gulf of St Lawrence
Gulf of Maine
QUÉBEC
ONTARIO
NEW BRUNSWICK
NOVA SCOTIA
PRINCE EDWARD ISLAND
MAINE
VERMONT
NEW HAMPSHIRE
NEW YORK
MASSACHUSETTS
CONNECTICUT
RHODE ISLAND
PENNSYLVANIA
NEW JERSEY
MARYLAND
DELAWARE
WEST VIRGINIA
VIRGINIA
NORTH CAROLINA
SOUTH CAROLINA
GEORGIA
FLORIDA
ALABAMA
MISSISSIPPI
LOUISIANA
ARKANSAS
MISSOURI
TENNESSEE
KENTUCKY
OHIO
INDIANA
ILLINOIS
MICHIGAN
WISCONSIN
Lake Superior
Lake Michigan
Lake Huron
Lake Erie
Lake Ontario
APPALACHIAN MOUNTAINS
Ozark Plateau
New York
Philadelphia
Washington
Chicago
Detroit
Toronto
Montréal
OTTAWA
Québec
Boston
Atlanta
Jacksonville
Miami
New Orleans
Memphis
Nashville
Pittsburgh
Cleveland
Baltimore
Bermuda (U.K.)
HAMILTON
THE BAHAMAS
NASSAU
WEST INDIES
Tropic of Cancer
Straits of Florida
Great Bahama Bank
Turks and Caicos Islands (U.K.)
LA HABANA (Havana)
CUBA
Cayman Islands (U.K.)
JAMAICA
KINGSTON
HISPANIOLA
HAITI
PORT-AU-PRINCE
DOMINICAN REPUBLIC
SANTO DOMINGO
Puerto Rico (U.S.A.)
GREATER ANTILLES
Jamaica Channel
Windward Passage
Yucatan Channel
YUCATÁN
BELIZE
BELMOPAN
GUATEMALA
Gulf of Honduras
de Campeche
Longitude 90° west of Greenwich
221
246
247
MILES
KILOMETRES
1:12 000 000

© Bartholomew Ltd

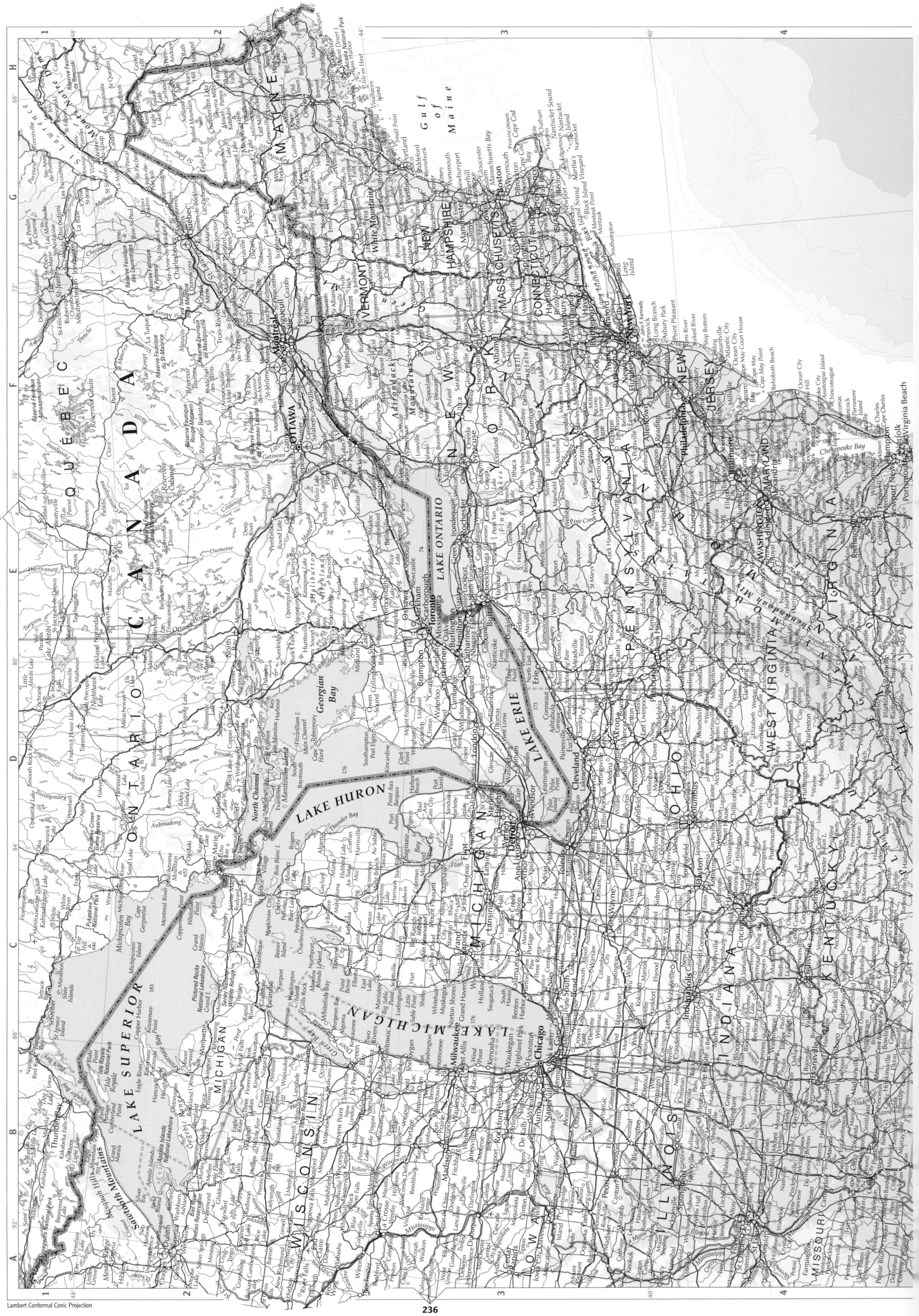

METRES / FEET

6000 / 19686
5000 / 16404
4000 / 13124
3000 / 9843
2000 / 6562
1000 / 3281
500 / 1640
200 / 656
0 / 0
LAND BELOW SEA LEVEL
200 / 656
2000 / 6562
4000 / 13124
6000 / 19686

224

236

Lambert Conformal Conic Projection

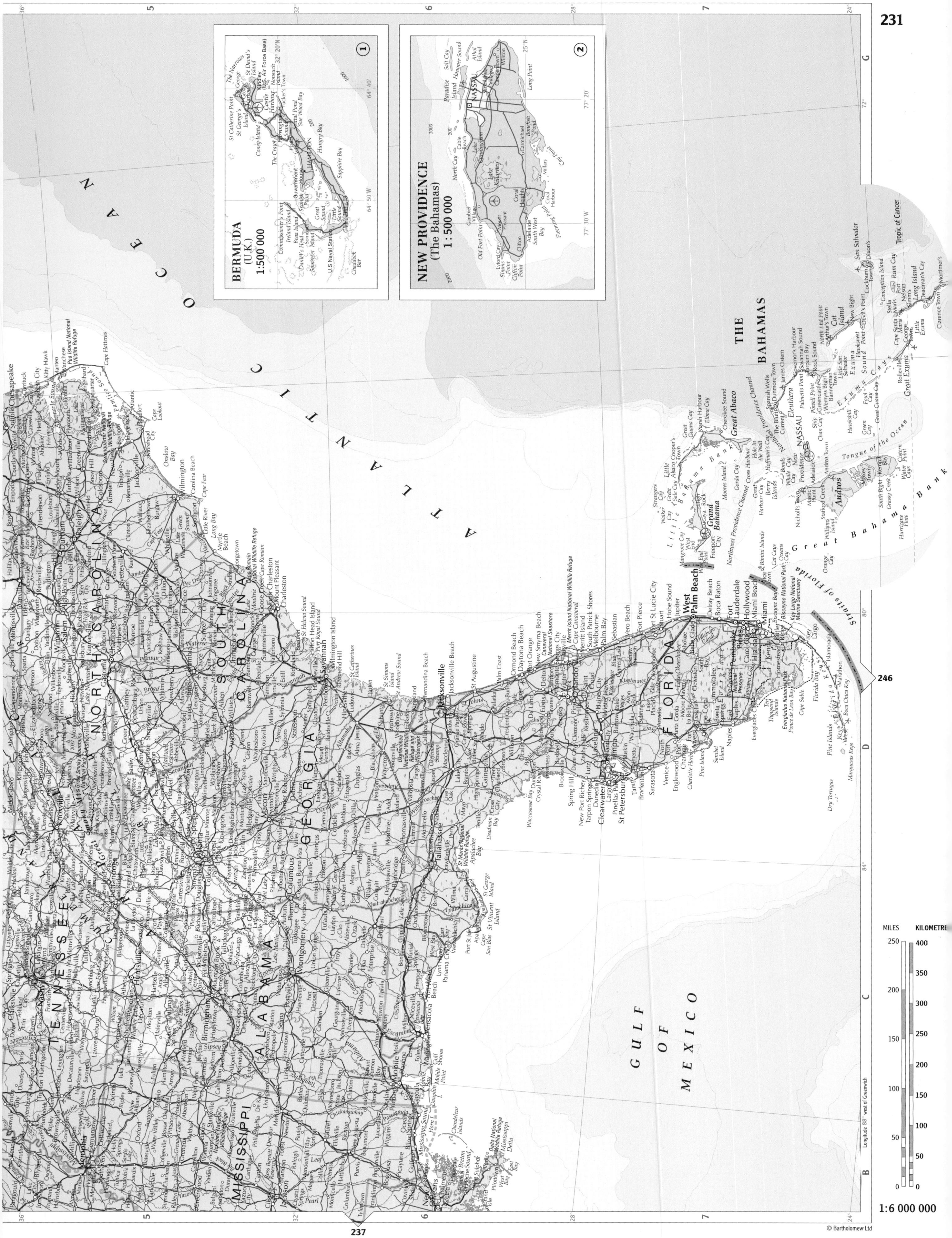
BERMUDA
(U.K.)
1:500 000
NEW PROVIDENCE
(The Bahamas)
1:500 000
ATLANTIC OCEAN
GULF OF MEXICO
THE BAHAMAS
TENNESSEE
NORTH CAROLINA
SOUTH CAROLINA
GEORGIA
ALABAMA
MISSISSIPPI
FLORIDA
Straits of Florida
Great Bahama Bank
Tropic of Cancer
MILES
KILOMETRES
1:6 000 000

246

237

© Bartholomew Ltd

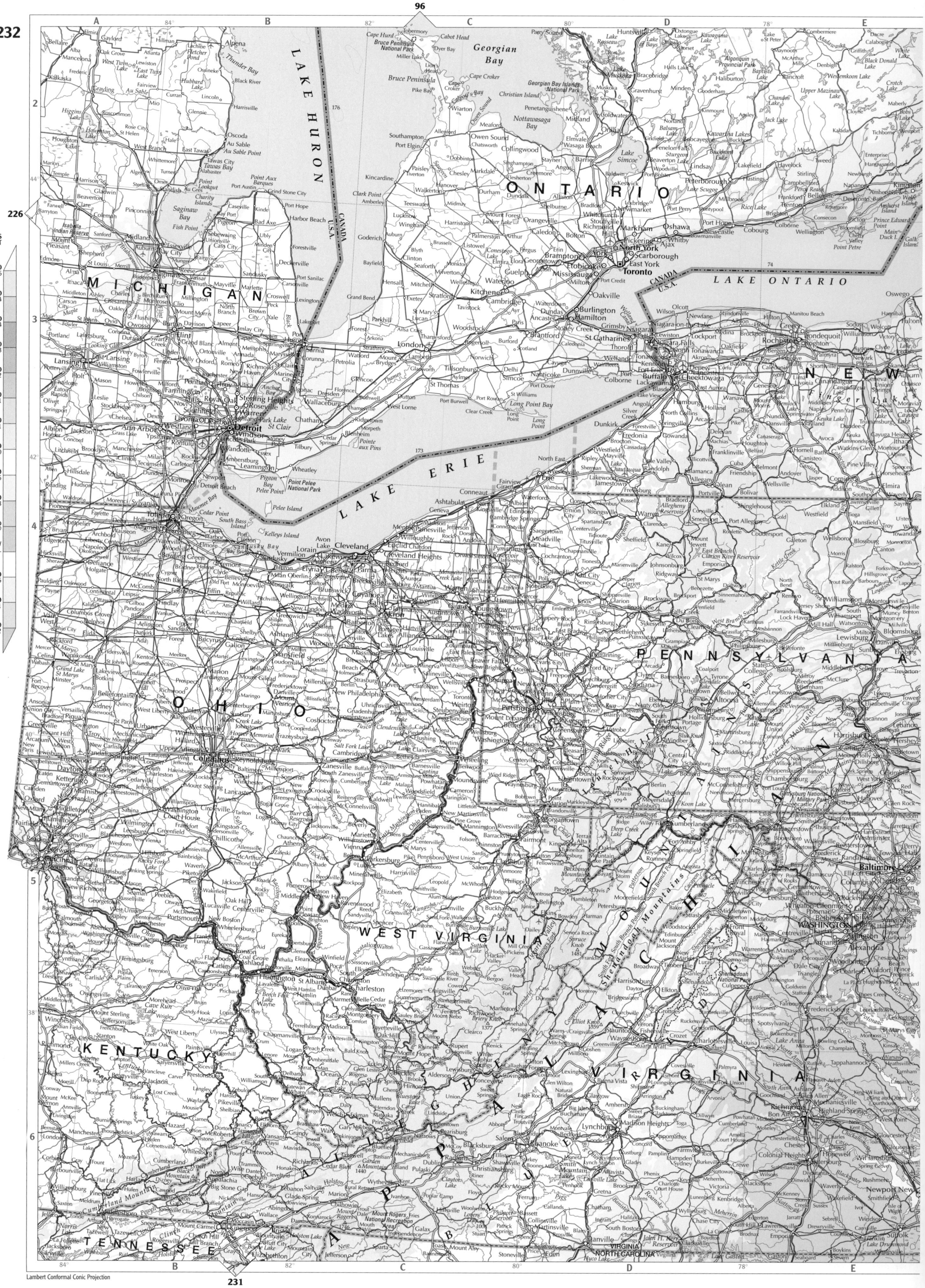
96
226
231
METRES
FEET
6000
19686
5000
16404
4000
13124
3000
9843
2000
6562
1500
4921
1000
3281
500
1640
200
656
100
328
0
0
LAND BELOW SEA LEVEL
200
656
1000
3281
2000
6562
LAKE HURON
Georgian Bay
ONTARIO
LAKE ONTARIO
LAKE ERIE
MICHIGAN
OHIO
PENNSYLVANIA
NEW
WEST VIRGINIA
VIRGINIA
KENTUCKY
TENNESSEE
NORTH CAROLINA
CANADA
U.S.A.
Detroit
Toronto
Cleveland
Pittsburgh
Columbus
Baltimore
WASHINGTON
Richmond
Buffalo

Lambert Conformal Conic Projection

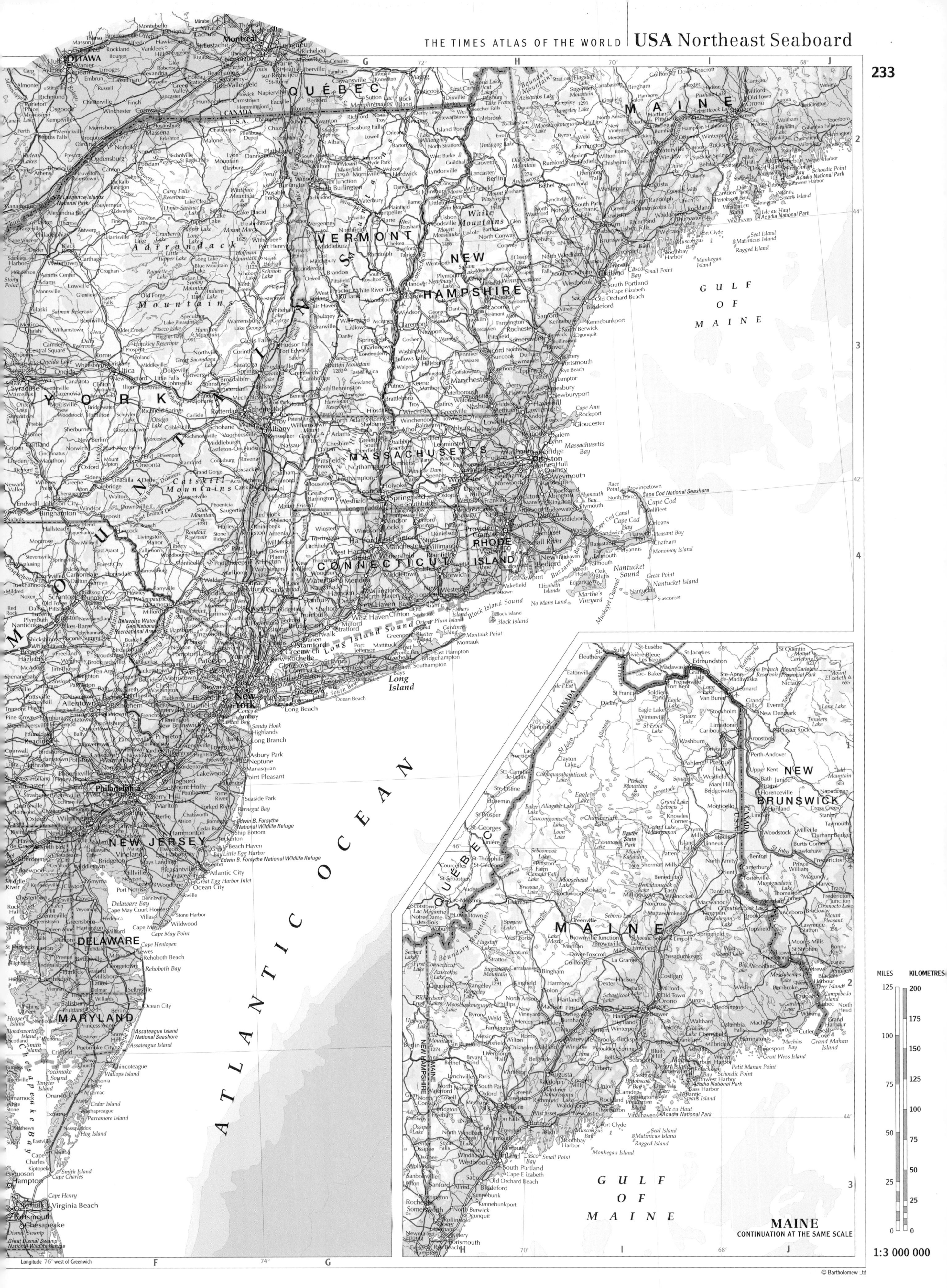
QUÉBEC
MAINE
VERMONT
NEW HAMPSHIRE
NEW YORK
MASSACHUSETTS
RHODE ISLAND
CONNECTICUT
NEW JERSEY
DELAWARE
MARYLAND
NEW BRUNSWICK
ATLANTIC OCEAN
GULF OF MAINE
Adirondack Mountains
Catskill Mountains
White Mountains
Long Island Sound
Cape Cod
Chesapeake Bay
Ottawa
Montréal
Boston
New York
Philadelphia
MAINE
CONTINUATION AT THE SAME SCALE
MILES
KILOMETRES
Longitude 76° west of Greenwich

1:3 000 000

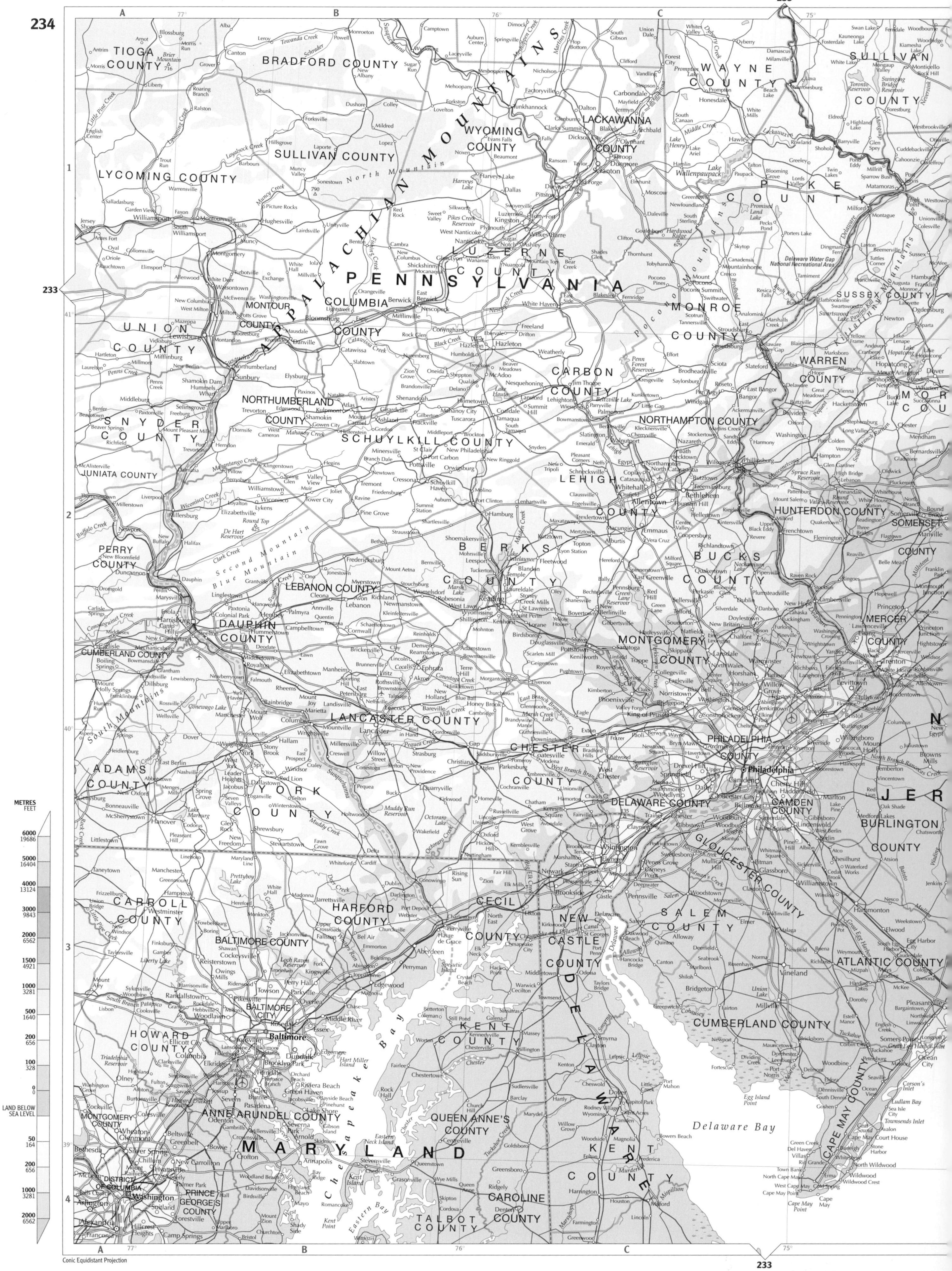
233
A
B
C
77°
76°
75°
41°
40°
39°
1
2
3
4
PENNSYLVANIA
MARYLAND
DELAWARE
APPALACHIAN MOUNTAINS
North Mountain
Second Mountain
Blue Mountain
South Mountains
Pocono Mountains
Kittatinny Mountains
TIOGA COUNTY
BRADFORD COUNTY
SULLIVAN COUNTY
LYCOMING COUNTY
WYOMING COUNTY
LACKAWANNA COUNTY
WAYNE COUNTY
PIKE COUNTY
SULLIVAN COUNTY
LUZERNE COUNTY
COLUMBIA COUNTY
MONTOUR COUNTY
UNION COUNTY
SNYDER COUNTY
NORTHUMBERLAND COUNTY
SCHUYLKILL COUNTY
CARBON COUNTY
MONROE COUNTY
SUSSEX COUNTY
WARREN COUNTY
NORTHAMPTON COUNTY
LEHIGH COUNTY
JUNIATA COUNTY
PERRY COUNTY
DAUPHIN COUNTY
LEBANON COUNTY
BERKS COUNTY
BUCKS COUNTY
HUNTERDON COUNTY
SOMERSET COUNTY
MERCER COUNTY
MONTGOMERY COUNTY
CUMBERLAND COUNTY
LANCASTER COUNTY
CHESTER COUNTY
PHILADELPHIA COUNTY
DELAWARE COUNTY
CAMDEN COUNTY
BURLINGTON COUNTY
GLOUCESTER COUNTY
ADAMS COUNTY
YORK COUNTY
SALEM COUNTY
ATLANTIC COUNTY
CUMBERLAND COUNTY
CAPE MAY COUNTY
CARROLL COUNTY
HARFORD COUNTY
CECIL COUNTY
NEW CASTLE COUNTY
BALTIMORE COUNTY
BALTIMORE CITY
HOWARD COUNTY
KENT COUNTY
ANNE ARUNDEL COUNTY
QUEEN ANNE'S COUNTY
MONTGOMERY COUNTY
PRINCE GEORGE'S COUNTY
DISTRICT OF COLUMBIA
CAROLINE COUNTY
TALBOT COUNTY
KENT COUNTY
Philadelphia
Baltimore
Washington
Harrisburg
Allentown
Reading
Lancaster
Scranton
Wilkes-Barre
Trenton
Wilmington
Dover
Annapolis
Chesapeake Bay
Delaware Bay
Eastern Bay
Lake Wallenpaupack
Delaware Water Gap National Recreational Area
METRES
FEET
6000
19686
5000
16404
4000
13124
3000
9843
2000
6562
1500
4921
1000
3281
500
1640
200
656
100
328
0
0
LAND BELOW SEA LEVEL
50
164
200
656
1000
3281
2000
6562

Conic Equidistant Projection

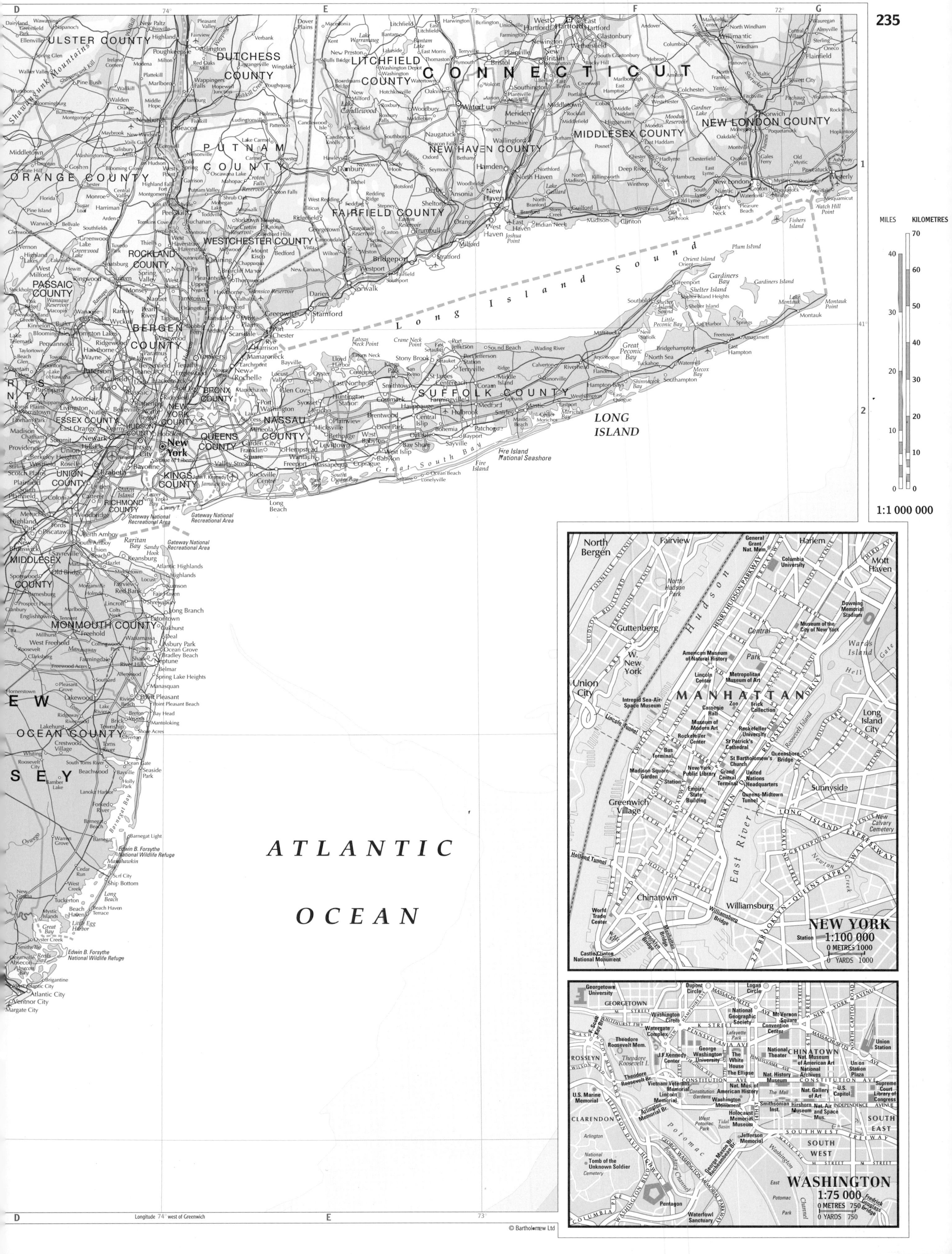
ULSTER COUNTY
DUTCHESS COUNTY
LITCHFIELD COUNTY
CONNECTICUT
MIDDLESEX COUNTY
NEW LONDON COUNTY
NEW HAVEN COUNTY
PUTNAM COUNTY
ORANGE COUNTY
FAIRFIELD COUNTY
WESTCHESTER COUNTY
ROCKLAND COUNTY
PASSAIC COUNTY
BERGEN COUNTY
BRONX COUNTY
NEW YORK COUNTY
SUFFOLK COUNTY
NASSAU COUNTY
QUEENS COUNTY
ESSEX COUNTY
HUDSON COUNTY
UNION COUNTY
KINGS COUNTY
RICHMOND COUNTY
MIDDLESEX COUNTY
MONMOUTH COUNTY
OCEAN COUNTY
Long Island Sound
LONG ISLAND
New York
Hartford
New Haven
Bridgeport
Stamford
Newark
Fire Island National Seashore
Gateway National Recreational Area
Edwin B. Forsythe National Wildlife Refuge
Atlantic City
ATLANTIC OCEAN
MILES
KILOMETRES
1:1 000 000
Longitude 74° west of Greenwich
MANHATTAN
Central Park
Hudson
East River
NEW YORK
1:100 000
0 METRES 1000
0 YARDS 1000
GEORGETOWN
CHINATOWN
ROSSLYN
CLARENDON
Potomac
WASHINGTON
1:75 000
0 METRES 750
0 YARDS 750
© Bartholomew Ltd

230

223

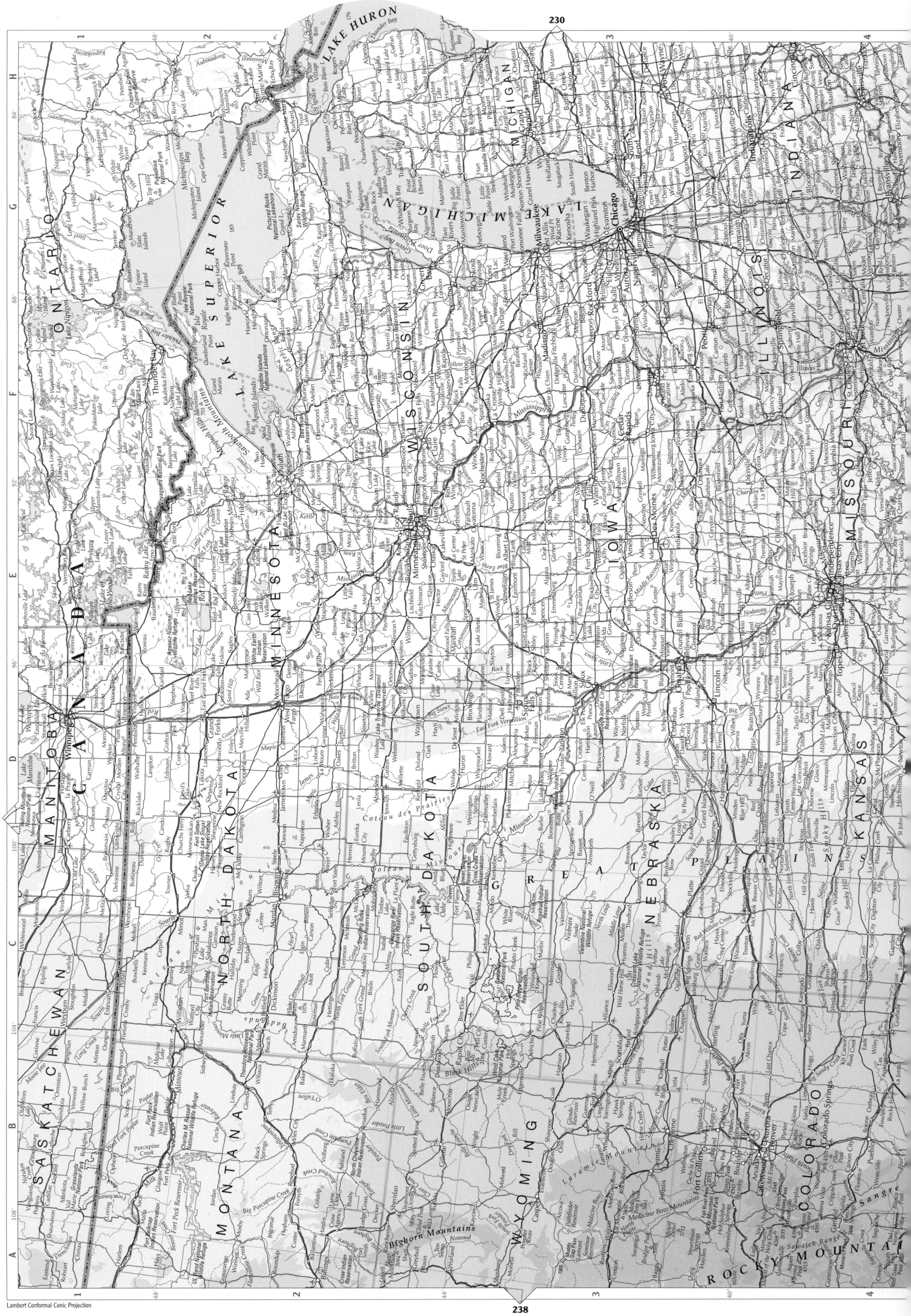
LAKE HURON
LAKE SUPERIOR
LAKE MICHIGAN
ONTARIO
MANITOBA
CANADA
SASKATCHEWAN
MICHIGAN
WISCONSIN
MINNESOTA
NORTH DAKOTA
SOUTH DAKOTA
MONTANA
WYOMING
IOWA
NEBRASKA
ILLINOIS
INDIANA
MISSOURI
KANSAS
COLORADO
GREAT PLAINS
ROCKY MOUNTAI

METRES
FEET

6000
19686

5000
16404

4000
13124

3000
9843

2000
6562

1000
3281

500
1640

200
656

0
0

LAND BELOW
SEA LEVEL

200
656

2000
6562

4000
13124

6000
19686

Lambert Conformal Conic Projection

238

231

243

239

MILES | KILOMETRES
250 200 150 100 50 0
400 350 300 250 200 150 100 50 0

1:6 000 000

© Bartholomew Ltd

236

222

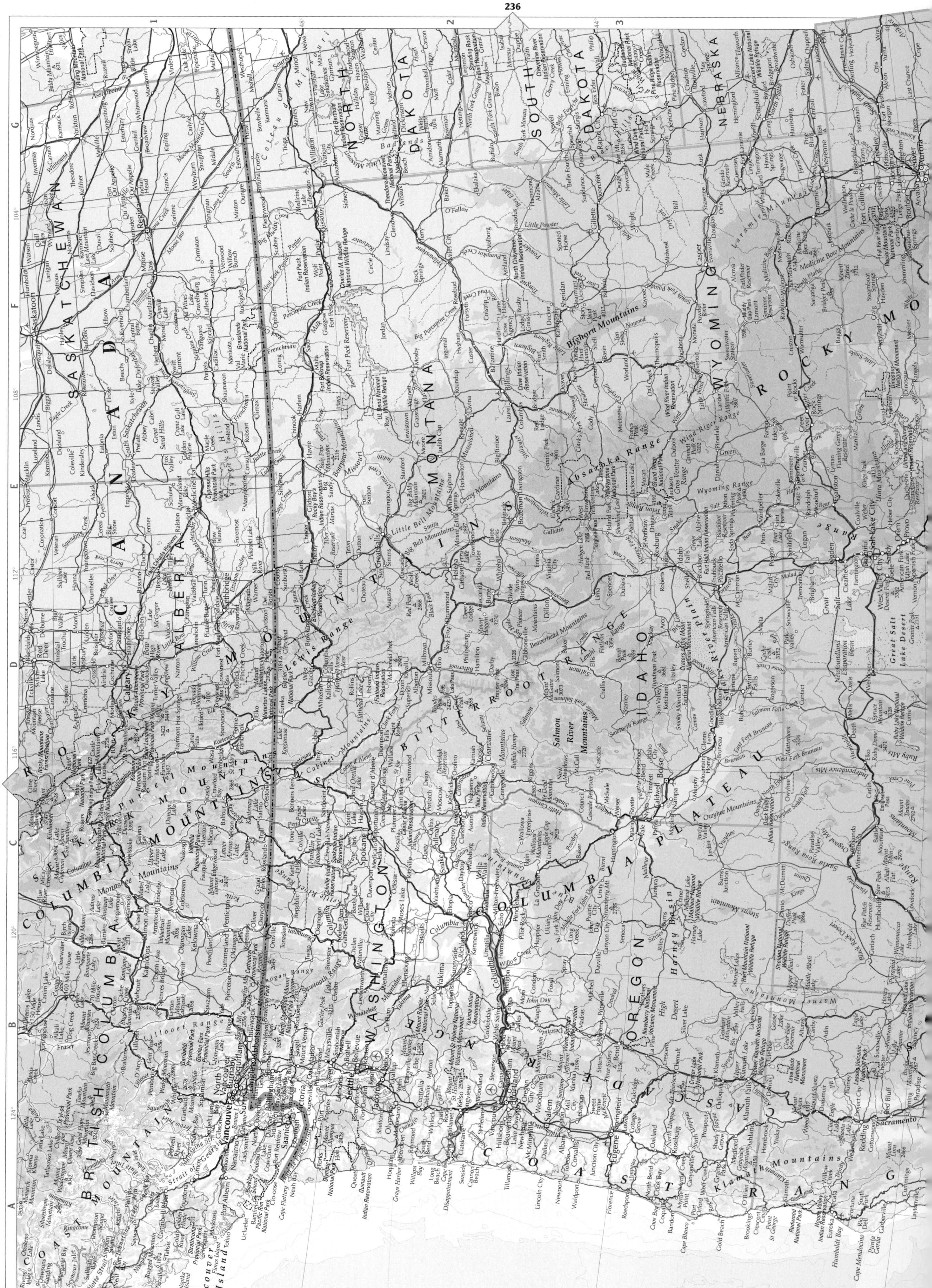
SASKATCHEWAN
CANADA
ALBERTA
BRITISH COLUMBIA
NORTH DAKOTA
SOUTH DAKOTA
NEBRASKA
MONTANA
WYOMING
IDAHO
WASHINGTON
OREGON
ROCKY MOUNTAINS
BITTERROOT RANGE
COLUMBIA PLATEAU
CASCADE RANGE
COAST MOUNTAINS
COAST RANGES
Vancouver Island
Great Salt Lake Desert

METRES FEET
6000 19686
5000 16404
4000 13124
3000 9843
2000 6562
1000 3281
500 1640
200 656
0 0
LAND BELOW SEA LEVEL
200 656
2000 6562
4000 13124
6000 19686

Lambert Conformal Conic Projection

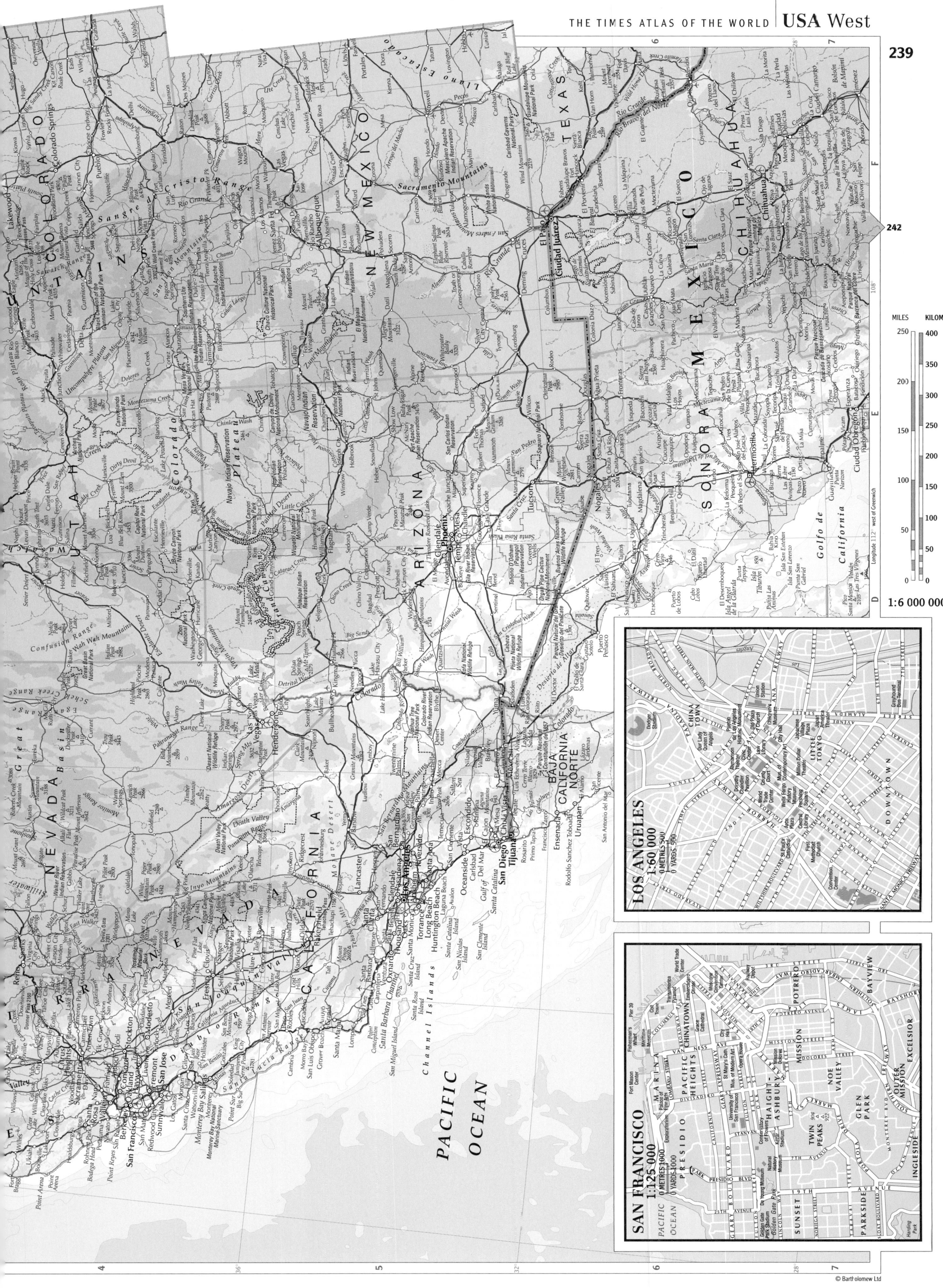
PACIFIC OCEAN
NEVADA
CALIFORNIA
UTAH
ARIZONA
NEW MEXICO
COLORADO
TEXAS
BAJA CALIFORNIA NORTE
SONORA
CHIHUAHUA
MEXICO
Golfo de California
LOS ANGELES
1:60 000
SAN FRANCISCO
1:125 000
MILES
KILOMETRES
1:6 000 000
242

© Bartholomew Ltd

238

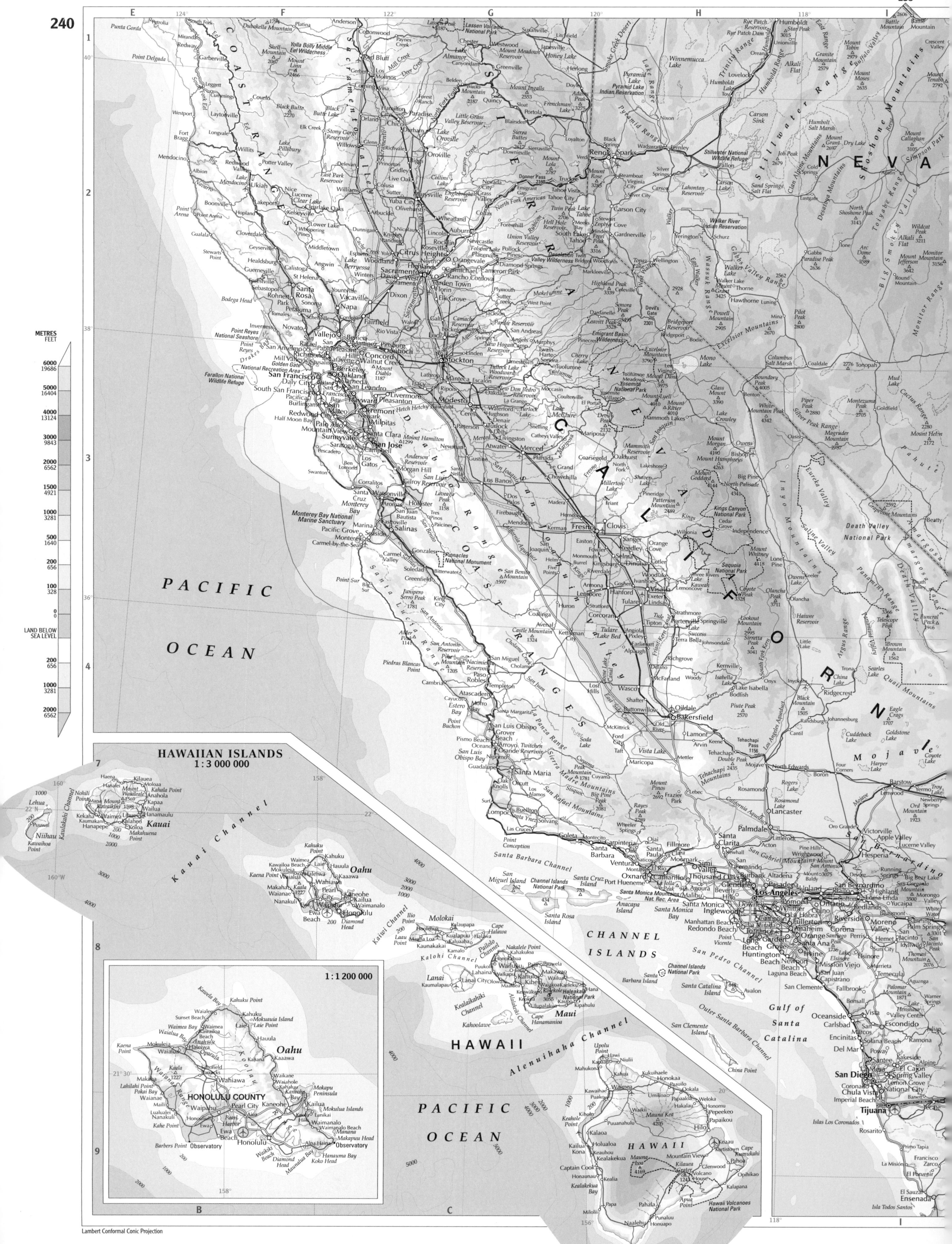
METRES
FEET
6000
19686
5000
16404
4000
13124
3000
9843
2000
6562
1500
4921
1000
3281
500
1640
200
656
100
328
0
0
LAND BELOW
SEA LEVEL
200
656
1000
3281
2000
6562
PACIFIC
OCEAN
HAWAIIAN ISLANDS
1 : 3 000 000
1 : 1 200 000
HONOLULU COUNTY
HAWAII
PACIFIC
OCEAN
Kauai Channel
Alenuihaha Channel
Kauai
Niihau
Oahu
Molokai
Lanai
Maui
HAWAII
Honolulu
COAST RANGES
SIERRA NEVADA
CALIFORNIA
NEVADA
Sacramento Valley
Diablo Range
San Joaquin Valley
Santa Lucia Range
Mojave
CHANNEL
ISLANDS
Santa Barbara Channel
San Pedro Channel
Gulf of Santa Catalina
Monterey Bay National Marine Sanctuary
Farallon National Wildlife Refuge
Point Reyes National Seashore
Golden Gate National Recreation Area
Lassen Volcanic National Park
Yosemite National Park
Kings Canyon National Park
Sequoia National Park
Death Valley National Park
Channel Islands National Park
Hawaii Volcanoes National Park
Haleakala National Park
Sacramento
San Francisco
Oakland
San Jose
Fresno
Stockton
Modesto
Bakersfield
Santa Barbara
Los Angeles
Long Beach
Anaheim
Santa Ana
Riverside
San Bernardino
San Diego
Tijuana
Ensenada
Reno
Carson City
E
F
G
H
I
B
C
1
2
3
4
7
8
9

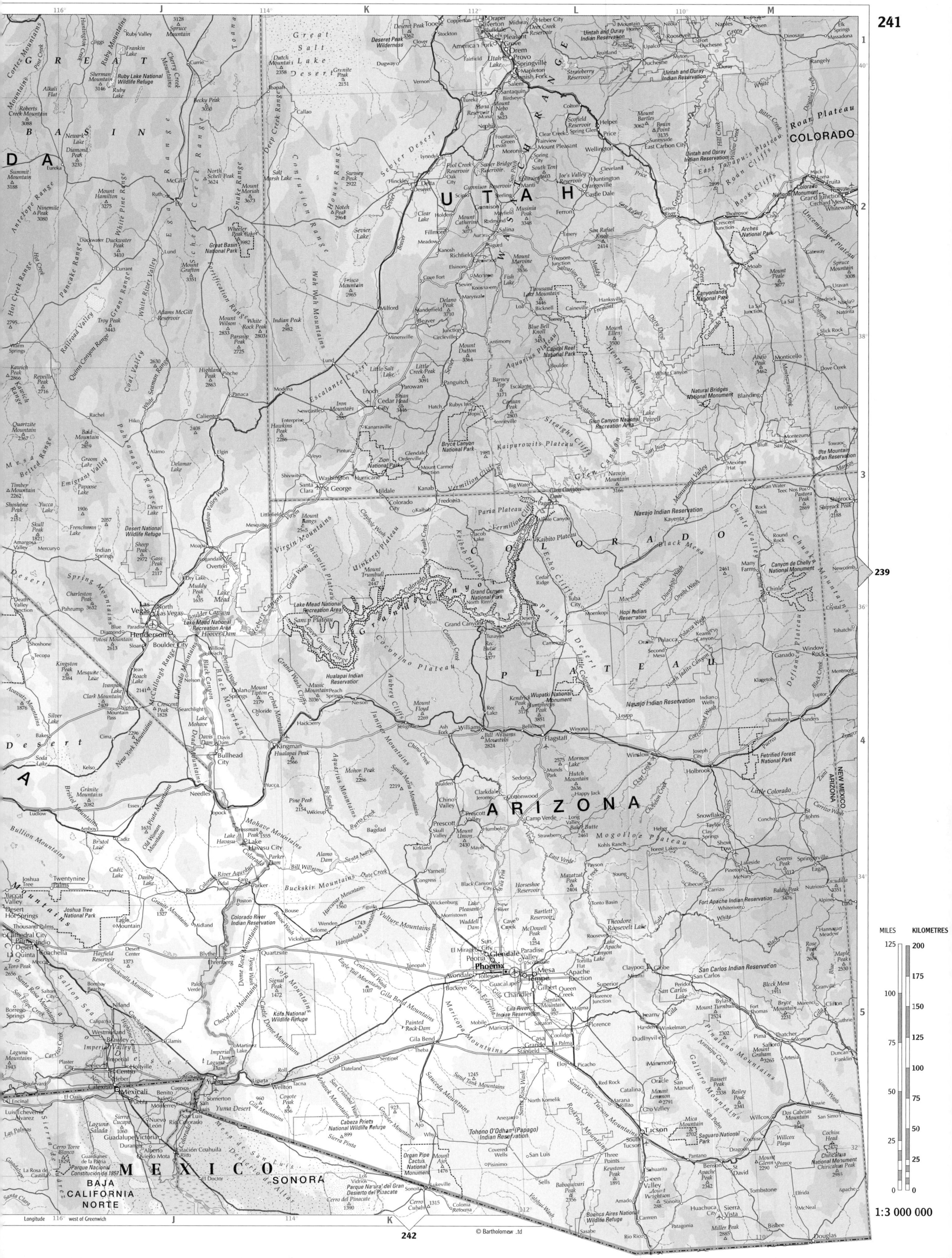
UTAH
ARIZONA
COLORADO
NEW MEXICO
ARIZONA
MEXICO
SONORA
BAJA CALIFORNIA NORTE
GREAT BASIN
COLORADO PLATEAU
WASATCH RANGE
Great Salt Lake Desert
Phoenix
Tucson
Las Vegas
Henderson
Flagstaff
Provo
Orem
Mexicali
Yuma
Kingman
Moab
Grand Junction
Grand Canyon National Park
Lake Mead National Recreation Area
Glen Canyon National Recreation Area
Canyonlands National Park
Capitol Reef National Park
Bryce Canyon National Park
Zion National Park
Great Basin National Park
Arches National Park
Petrified Forest National Park
Canyon de Chelly National Monument
Navajo Indian Reservation
Hopi Indian Reservation
Fort Apache Indian Reservation
San Carlos Indian Reservation
Tohono O'Odham (Papago) Indian Reservation
Joshua Tree National Park
Organ Pipe Cactus National Monument
Saguaro National Park
Lake Powell
Lake Mead
239
242
MILES
KILOMETRES
1:3 000 000
Longitude 116° west of Greenwich
© Bartholomew Ltd

239

ARIZONA
NEW MEXICO
UNITED
BAJA CALIFORNIA NORTE
BAJA CALIFORNIA SUR
SONORA
CHIHUAHUA
SINALOA
DURANGO
COAH
ZACATECAS
NAYARIT
JALISCO
COLIMA
AGUASCALIENTES
MEX
SIERRA MADRE OCCIDENTAL
Golfo de California
Tropic of Cancer
PACIF
Tijuana
Mexicali
Ensenada
Tucson
Nogales
El Paso
Ciudad Juárez
Hermosillo
Chihuahua
Ciudad Obregón
Los Mochis
Culiacán
Mazatlán
Durango
Torreón
Tepic
Guadalajara
La Paz
HONDURAS
EL SALVADOR
NICARAGUA
COSTA RICA
PANAMA
COLOMBIA
BELIZE
GUATEMALA
TEGUCIGALPA
MANAGUA
SAN JOSÉ
PANAMÁ
CARIBBEAN SEA
PACIFIC OCEAN
Gulf of Honduras
MOSQUITIA
METRES
FEET
6000 19686
5000 16404
4000 13124
3000 9843
2000 6562
1000 3281
500 1640
200 656
0
LAND BELOW SEA LEVEL
200 656
2000 6562
4000 13124
6000 19686
CENTRAL AMERICA
CONTINUATION AT THE SAME SCALE

250

237
E
F
G
H
I
100°
96°
92°
88°
STATES OF AMERICA
TEXAS
LOUISIANA
MISSISSIPPI
ALABAMA
FLORIDA
Edwards Plateau
Dallas
Fort Worth
Abilene
Waco
Austin
San Antonio
Houston
Galveston
Corpus Christi
Laredo
Brownsville
Shreveport
Jackson
Baton Rouge
New Orleans
Mobile
Pensacola
Montgomery
GULF OF MEXICO
Tropic of Cancer
Bahía de Campeche
Yucatan Channel
Arrecife Alacrán
Cayo Nuevo
Cayos Arcas
NUEVO LEÓN
Monterrey
Saltillo
Nuevo Laredo
Matamoros
Reynosa
TAMAULIPAS
Ciudad Victoria
Tampico
Ciudad Madero
SAN LUIS POTOSÍ
San Luis Potosí
VERACRUZ
Poza Rica
Jalapa Enríquez
Veracruz
Córdoba
Orizaba
Coatzacoalcos
Minatitlán
GUANAJUATO
León
Guanajuato
QUERÉTARO
Querétaro
HIDALGO
Pachuca
MICHOACÁN
Morelia
MÉXICO
Toluca
Tlalnepantla
TLAXCALA
PUEBLA
Puebla
MORELOS
Cuernavaca
GUERRERO
Chilpancingo
Acapulco
SIERRA MADRE DEL SUR
OAXACA
Oaxaca
Istmo de Tehuantepec
Golfo de Tehuantepec
Salina Cruz
Juchitán
TABASCO
Villahermosa
CHIAPAS
Tuxtla Gutiérrez
Tapachula
CAMPECHE
Campeche
Ciudad del Carmen
Laguna de Términos
YUCATÁN
Mérida
Progreso
QUINTANA ROO
Cancún
Cozumel
Chetumal
BELIZE
Belize
Belmopan
Gulf of Honduras
GUATEMALA
Guatemala
HONDURAS
San Pedro Sula
EL SALVADOR
San Salvador
Santa Ana
San Miguel
PACIFIC OCEAN
Longitude 100° west of Greenwich
MILES
KILOMETRES
250
200
150
100
50
0
400
350
300
250
200
150
100
50
0
1:6 600 000

242

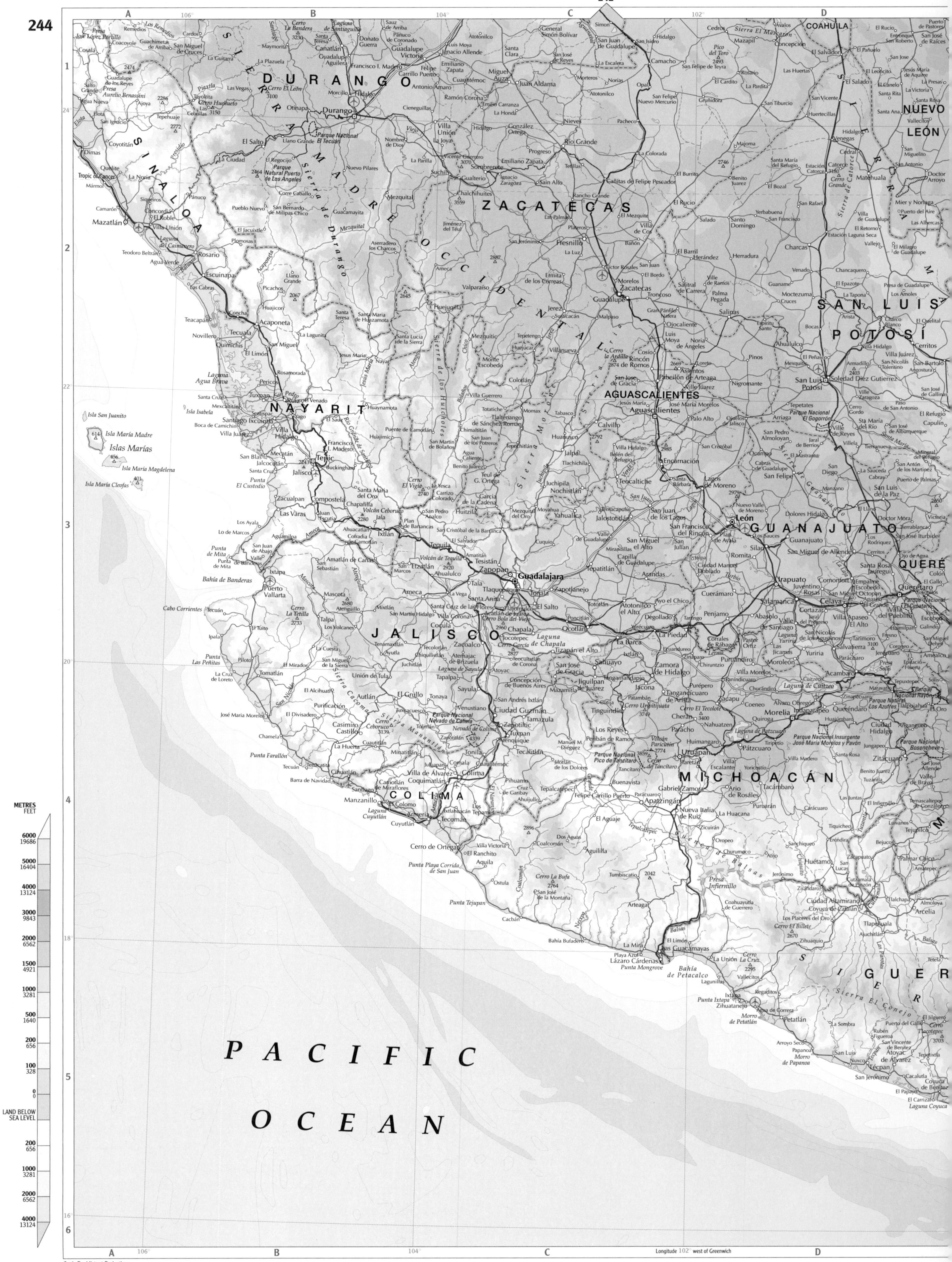

DURANGO
SINALOA
ZACATECAS
NAYARIT
AGUASCALIENTES
SAN LUIS POTOSÍ
GUANAJUATO
JALISCO
COLIMA
MICHOACÁN
COAHUILA
NUEVO LEÓN
SIERRA MADRE OCCIDENTAL
PACIFIC OCEAN
Durango
Mazatlán
Zacatecas
Aguascalientes
San Luis Potosí
León
Guadalajara
Tepic
Colima
Morelia
Querétaro
Puerto Vallarta
Manzanillo
Lázaro Cárdenas
Islas Marías
Tropic of Cancer
METRES
FEET
6000
19686
5000
16404
4000
13124
3000
9843
2000
6562
1500
4921
1000
3281
500
1640
200
656
100
328
0
0
LAND BELOW SEA LEVEL
200
656
1000
3281
2000
6562
4000
13124
Longitude 102° west of Greenwich

Conic Equidistant Projection

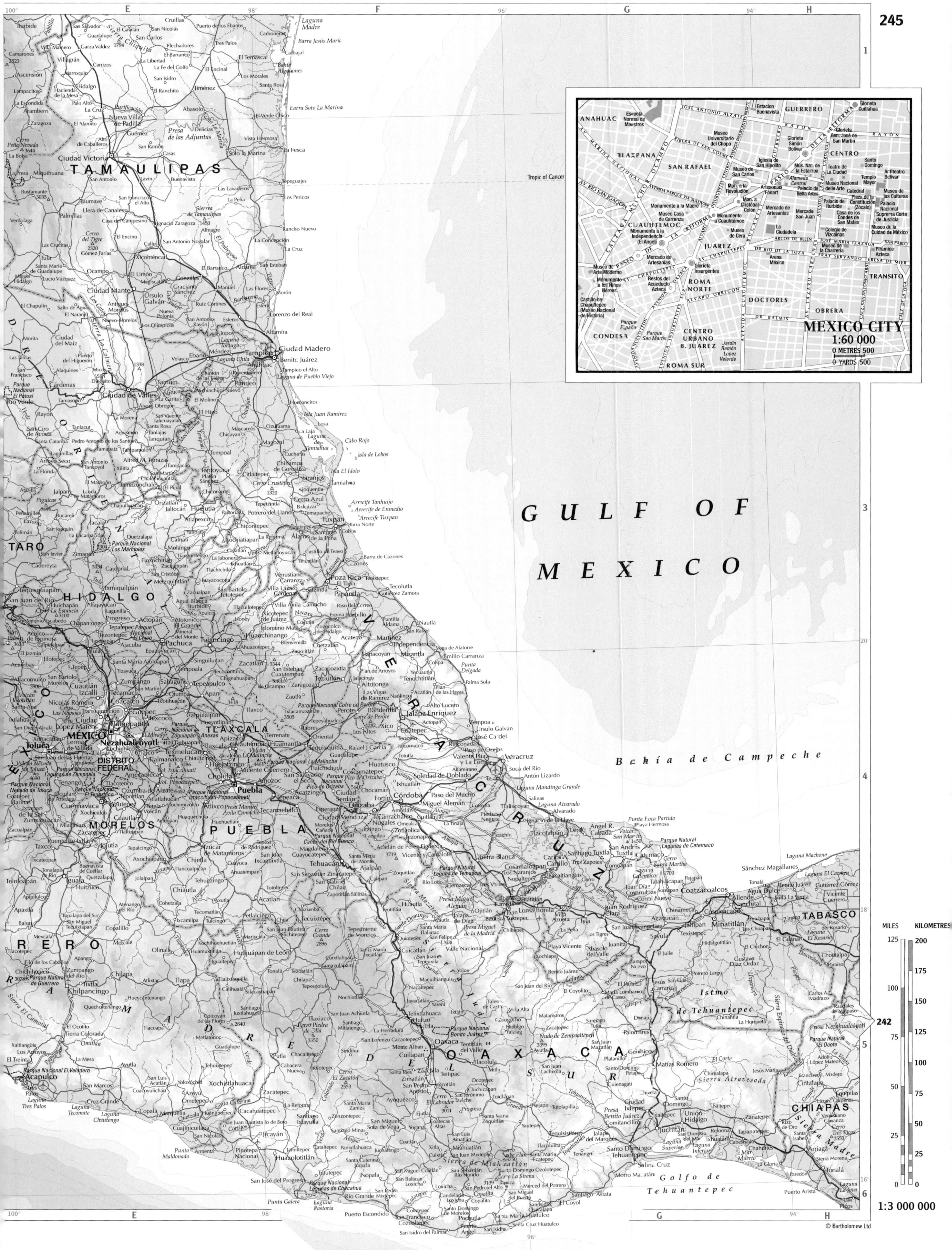
GULF OF MEXICO
Bahía de Campeche
Golfo de Tehuantepec
Tropic of Cancer
TAMAULIPAS
HIDALGO
TLAXCALA
DISTRITO FEDERAL
MORELOS
PUEBLA
VERACRUZ
OAXACA
TABASCO
CHIAPAS
Istmo de Tehuantepec
Sierra Madre del Sur
MEXICO CITY
1:60 000
0 METRES 500
0 YARDS 500
MILES
KILOMETRES
1:3 000 000
242
© Bartholomew Ltd

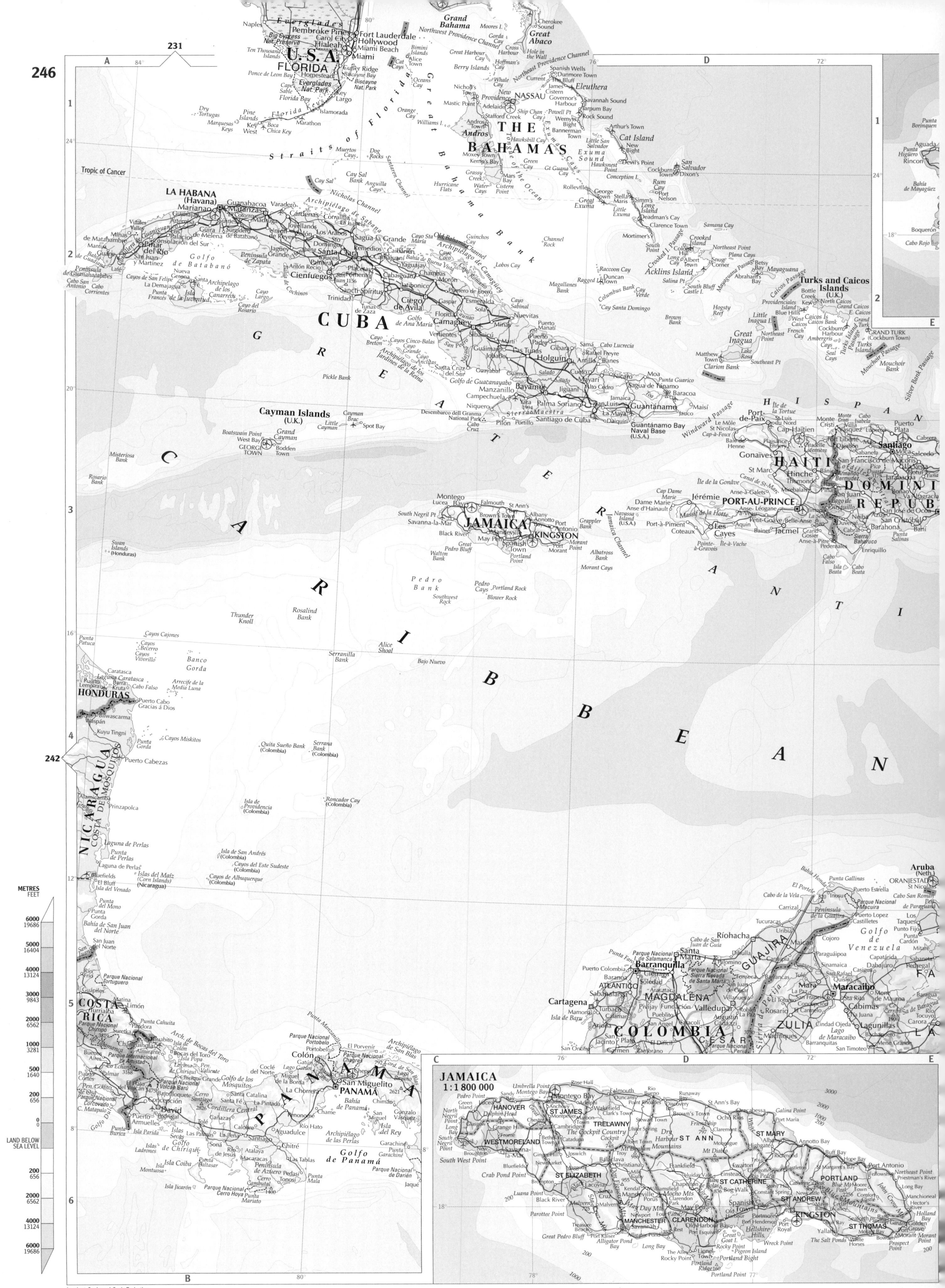

231
242
U.S.A.
FLORIDA
Naples
Everglades
Pembroke Pines
Fort Lauderdale
Hollywood
Carol City
Hialeah
Miami Beach
Miami
Big Cypress Nat. Preserve
Ten Thousand Islands
Homestead
Biscayne Bay
Biscayne Nat. Park
Everglades Nat. Park
Key Largo
Florida Bay
Florida Keys
Islamorada
Marathon
Dry Tortugas
Marquesas Keys
Key West
Straits of Florida
Grand Bahama
Great Abaco
Northwest Providence Channel
Northeast Providence Channel
Andros
New Providence
NASSAU
Eleuthera
THE BAHAMAS
Great Bahama Bank
Tongue of the Ocean
Exuma Sound
Cat Island
San Salvador
Long Island
Great Exuma
Crooked Island
Acklins Island
Mayaguana
Great Inagua
Little Inagua I.
Turks and Caicos Islands (U.K.)
GRAND TURK (Cockburn Town)
Tropic of Cancer
LA HABANA (Havana)
Marianao
Guanabacoa
Matanzas
Cárdenas
Varadero
Pinar del Río
Golfo de Batabanó
Isla de la Juventud
Nueva Gerona
Cienfuegos
Santa Clara
Sancti Spíritus
Trinidad
Ciego de Avila
Camagüey
Nuevitas
Las Tunas
Holguín
Bayamo
Manzanillo
Palma Soriano
Santiago de Cuba
Guantánamo
Guantánamo Bay Naval Base (U.S.A.)
Baracoa
CUBA
Windward Passage
Cayman Islands (U.K.)
Grand Cayman
GEORGE TOWN
Little Cayman
Cayman Brac
HAITI
Port-de-Paix
Cap-Haïtien
Gonaïves
PORT-AU-PRINCE
Jérémie
Les Cayes
Jacmel
Santiago
DOMINICAN REPUBLIC
JAMAICA
KINGSTON
Montego Bay
Navassa Island (U.S.A.)
GREATER ANTILLES
CARIBBEAN
Pedro Bank
Rosalind Bank
Serranilla Bank
Thunder Knoll
Alice Shoal
Bajo Nuevo
Swan Islands (Honduras)
Cayos Cajones
Banco Gorda
HONDURAS
Puerto Cabezas
Cayos Miskitos
NICARAGUA
COSTA DE MOSQUITOS
Quita Sueño Bank (Colombia)
Serrana Bank (Colombia)
Roncador Cay (Colombia)
Isla de Providencia (Colombia)
Isla de San Andrés (Colombia)
Islas del Maíz (Corn Islands) (Nicaragua)
Laguna de Perlas
Bluefields
San Juan del Norte
COSTA RICA
Limón
Parque Nacional Tortuguero
PANAMA
Colón
PANAMÁ
Golfo de Panamá
Golfo de los Mosquitos
Golfo de Chiriquí
David
Isla Coiba
Península de Azuero
Archipiélago de las Perlas
Archipiélago de San Blas
Aruba (Neth.)
ORANJESTAD
Península de la Guajira
Golfo de Venezuela
Maracaibo
Lago de Maracaibo
ZULIA
Ríohacha
Santa Marta
Barranquilla
Cartagena
ATLÁNTICO
MAGDALENA
Valledupar
COLOMBIA
CESAR
METRES
FEET
6000
19686
5000
16404
4000
13124
3000
9843
2000
6562
1000
3281
500
1640
200
656
0
0
LAND BELOW SEA LEVEL
200
656
2000
6562
4000
13124
6000
19686
JAMAICA
1:1 800 000
HANOVER
ST JAMES
TRELAWNY
WESTMORELAND
ST ELIZABETH
MANCHESTER
CLARENDON
ST ANN
ST MARY
ST CATHERINE
ST ANDREW
PORTLAND
ST THOMAS
KINGSTON
Montego Bay
Negril Point
Savanna-la-Mar
Black River
Mandeville
May Pen
Spanish Town
Port Antonio
Morant Point
Blue Mountains
The Cockpit Country
Portland Point

Lambert Conformal Conic Projection

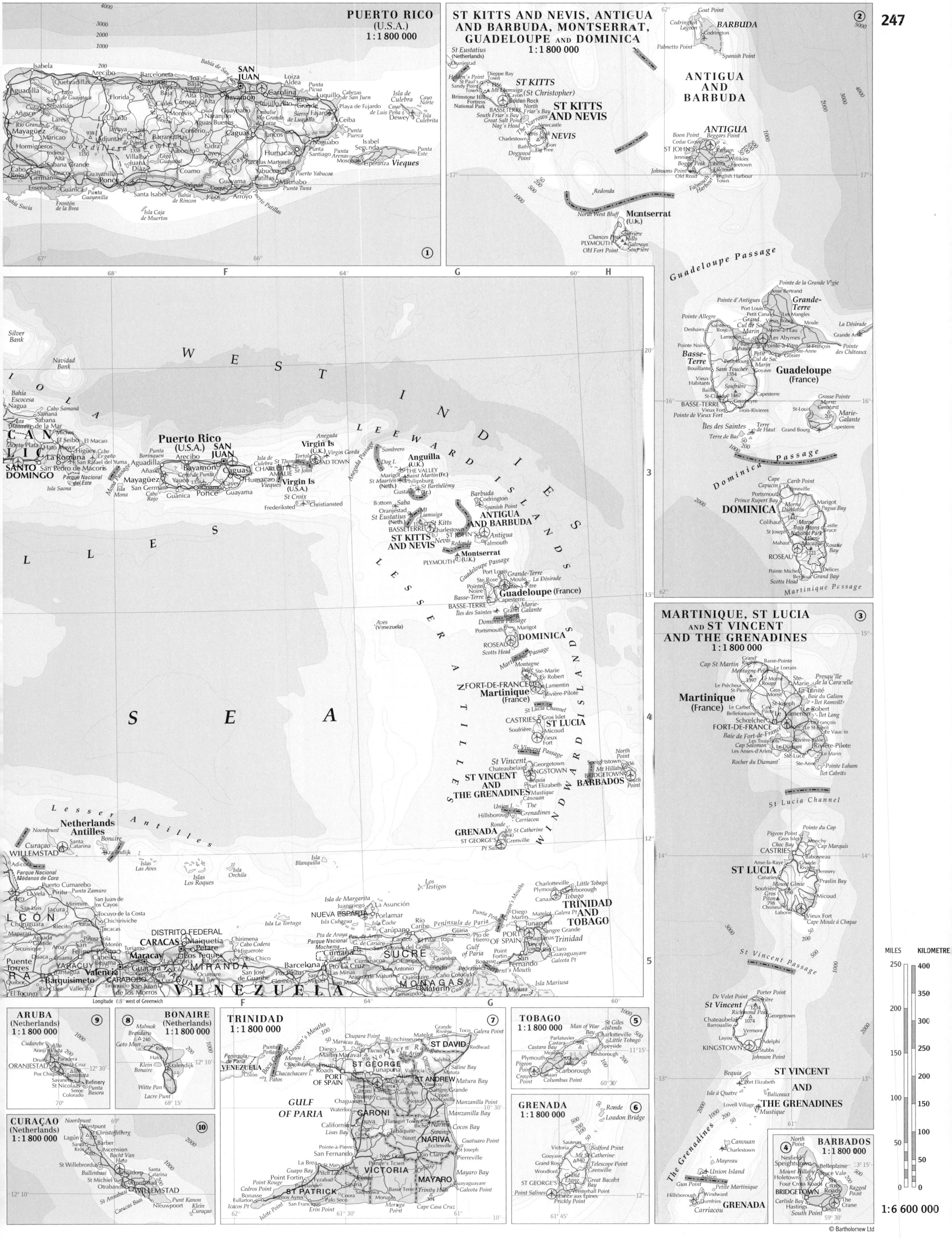
PUERTO RICO
(U.S.A.)
1:1 800 000
SAN JUAN
Bayamón
Carolina
Caguas
Mayagüez
Ponce
Humacao
Arecibo
Aguadilla
Cordillera Central
Vieques
Isla de Culebra
ST KITTS AND NEVIS, ANTIGUA AND BARBUDA, MONTSERRAT, GUADELOUPE AND DOMINICA
1:1 800 000
ST KITTS (St Christopher)
ST KITTS AND NEVIS
NEVIS
BASSETERRE
Charlestown
ANTIGUA AND BARBUDA
BARBUDA
ANTIGUA
ST JOHN'S
Montserrat (U.K.)
PLYMOUTH
Redonda
Guadeloupe Passage
Grande-Terre
Basse-Terre
Guadeloupe (France)
Marie-Galante
Îles des Saintes
La Désirade
Dominica Passage
DOMINICA
ROSEAU
Martinique Passage
WEST INDIES
LEEWARD ISLANDS
LESSER ANTILLES
WINDWARD ISLANDS
Lesser Antilles
Netherlands Antilles
SEA
Puerto Rico (U.S.A.)
Virgin Is (U.K.)
Virgin Is (U.S.A.)
ROAD TOWN
CHARLOTTE AMALIE
Anguilla (U.K.)
THE VALLEY
SANTO DOMINGO
FORT-DE-FRANCE
Martinique (France)
CASTRIES
ST LUCIA
KINGSTOWN
ST VINCENT AND THE GRENADINES
BRIDGETOWN
BARBADOS
GRENADA
ST GEORGE'S
PORT OF SPAIN
TRINIDAD AND TOBAGO
CARACAS
Maracay
Valencia
Barquisimeto
Barcelona
Cumaná
VENEZUELA
WILLEMSTAD
Isla de Margarita
NUEVA ESPARTA
Longitude 68° west of Greenwich
MARTINIQUE, ST LUCIA AND ST VINCENT AND THE GRENADINES
1:1 800 000
St Lucia Channel
St Vincent Passage
The Grenadines
Carriacou
ARUBA (Netherlands) 1:1 800 000
ORANJESTAD
BONAIRE (Netherlands) 1:1 800 000
Kralendijk
CURAÇAO (Netherlands) 1:1 800 000
TRINIDAD 1:1 800 000
GULF OF PARIA
ST GEORGE
ST ANDREW
ST DAVID
CARONI
NARIVA
VICTORIA
MAYARO
ST PATRICK
TOBAGO 1:1 800 000
Scarborough
GRENADA 1:1 800 000
BARBADOS 1:1 800 000
MILES
KILOMETRES
1:6 600 000

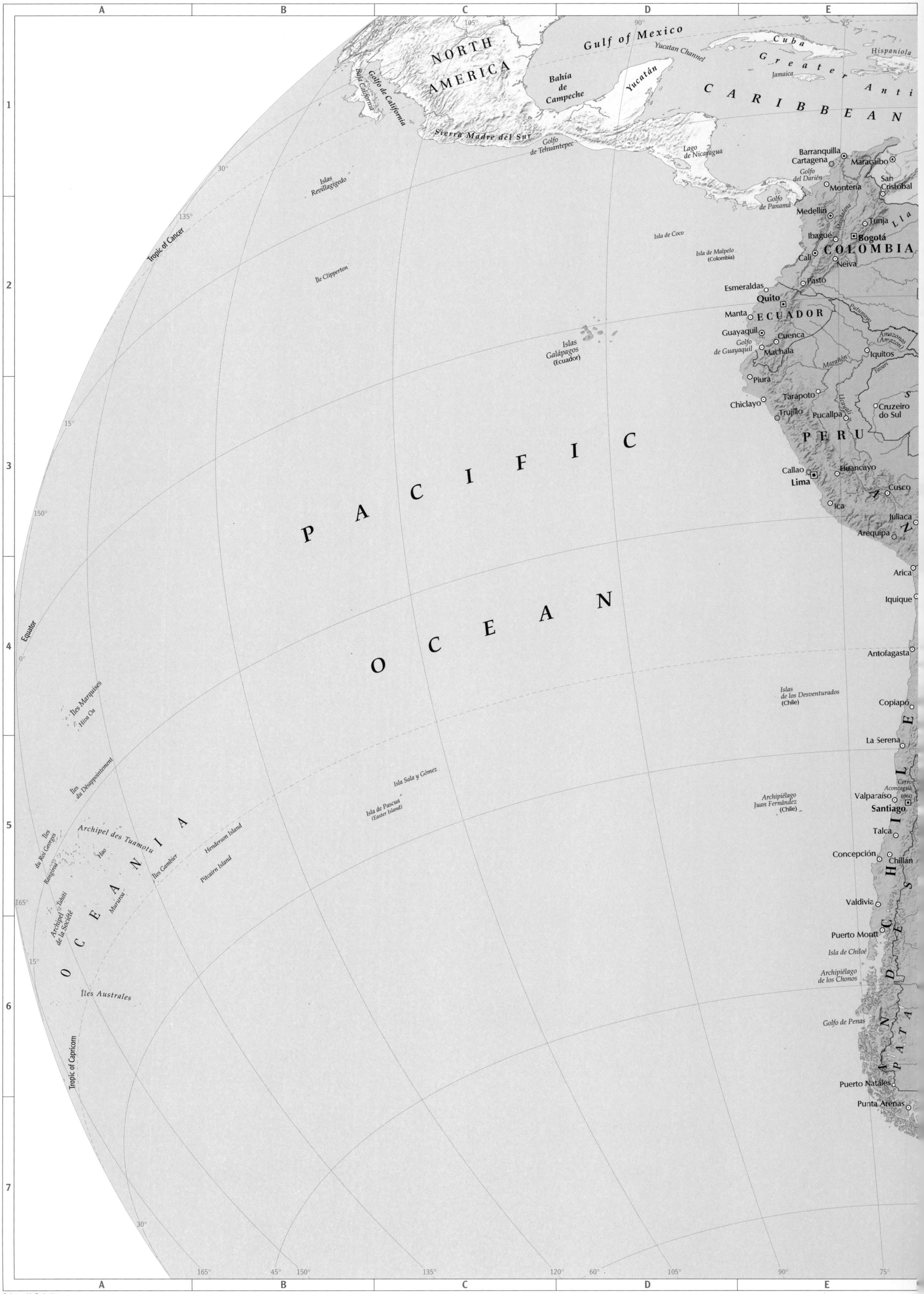

NORTH AMERICA
Gulf of Mexico
Yucatan Channel
Cuba
Hispaniola
Greater Antilles
Jamaica
Bahía de Campeche
Yucatán
CARIBBEAN
Golfo de California
Baja California
Sierra Madre del Sur
Golfo de Tehuantepec
Lago de Nicaragua
Barranquilla
Cartagena
Maracaibo
Golfo del Darién
Montería
San Cristóbal
Golfo de Panamá
Medellín
Tunja
Ibagué
Bogotá
Cali
COLOMBIA
Neiva
Pasto
Islas Revillagigedo
Tropic of Cancer
Île Clipperton
Isla de Coco
Isla de Malpelo (Colombia)
Esmeraldas
Quito
Manta
ECUADOR
Guayaquil
Cuenca
Golfo de Guayaquil
Machala
Iquitos
Islas Galápagos (Ecuador)
Piura
Chiclayo
Tarapoto
Trujillo
Pucallpa
Cruzeiro do Sul
PERU
Callao
Lima
Huancayo
Cusco
Ica
Juliaca
Arequipa
PACIFIC
OCEAN
Arica
Iquique
Antofagasta
Equator
Islas de los Desventurados (Chile)
Copiapó
La Serena
Îles Marquises
Hiva Oa
Îles du Désappointement
Isla Sala y Gómez
Isla de Pascua (Easter Island)
Archipiélago Juan Fernández (Chile)
Valparaíso
Santiago
Talca
Concepción
Chillán
Îles du Roi Georges
Archipel des Tuamotu
Hao
Rangiroa
Îles Gambier
Henderson Island
Pitcairn Island
Tahiti
Mururoa
Archipel de la Société
OCEANIA
Valdivia
Puerto Montt
Isla de Chiloé
Archipiélago de los Chonos
Îles Australes
Golfo de Penas
Tropic of Capricorn
Puerto Natales
Punta Arenas
CHILE
ANDES

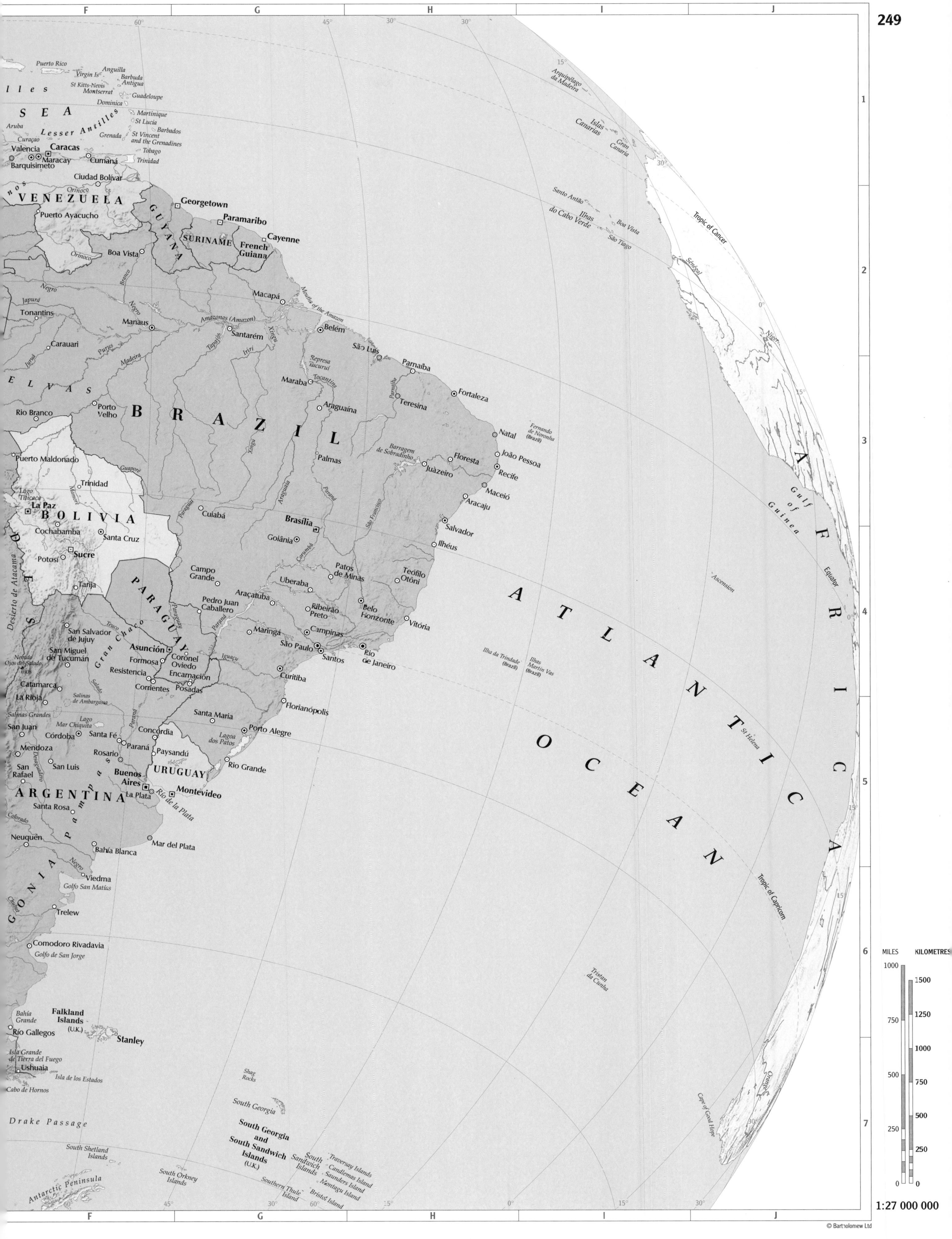
F
G
H
I
J
1
2
3
4
5
6
7
Puerto Rico
Anguilla
Virgin Is
Barbuda
St Kitts-Nevis
Antigua
Montserrat
Guadeloupe
Dominica
SEA
Martinique
St Lucia
Lesser Antilles
Barbados
Aruba
Curaçao
Grenada
St Vincent and the Grenadines
Tobago
Trinidad
Valencia
Caracas
Maracay
Cumaná
Barquisimeto
Ciudad Bolívar
Orinoco
VENEZUELA
Georgetown
GUYANA
Paramaribo
Puerto Ayacucho
SURINAME
French Guiana
Cayenne
Boa Vista
Orinoco
Branco
Negro
Japurá
Macapá
Mouths of the Amazon
Tonantins
Manaus
Amazonas (Amazon)
Santarém
Xingu
Belém
Carauari
Purus
Tapajós
Iriri
Represa Tucuruí
São Luís
Parnaíba
Juruá
Madeira
Marabá
Tocantins
Parnaíba
Teresina
Fortaleza
Rio Branco
Porto Velho
BRAZIL
Araguaína
Natal
Fernando de Noronha (Brazil)
Puerto Maldonado
Barragem de Sobradinho
Floresta
João Pessoa
Palmas
Juàzeiro
Recife
Guaporé
Trinidad
Xingu
Maceió
Lago Titicaca
La Paz
Mamoré
Araguaia
Paraná
São Francisco
Aracaju
BOLIVIA
Cuiabá
Brasília
Salvador
Cochabamba
Santa Cruz
Goiânia
Ilhéus
Potosí
Sucre
Paraguai
Corumbá
Campo Grande
Patos de Minas
Teófilo Otôni
Tarija
PARAGUAY
Uberaba
Desierto de Atacama
Aracatuba
Pedro Juan Caballero
Belo Horizonte
Ribeirão Preto
Vitória
ATLANTIC OCEAN
San Salvador de Jujuy
Teuco
Gran Chaco
Maringá
Campinas
Asunción
São Paulo
Rio de Janeiro
Santos
San Miguel de Tucumán
Coronel Oviedo
Iguaçu
Formosa
Ilha da Trindade (Brazil)
Ilhas Martin Vas (Brazil)
Resistencia
Encarnación
Curitiba
Catamarca
Corrientes
Posadas
Salado
La Rioja
Salinas de Ambargasta
Florianópolis
Salinas Grandes
Santa Maria
Lago Mar Chiquita
San Juan
Córdoba
Santa Fé
Concórdia
Porto Alegre
Lagoa dos Patos
St Helena
Mendoza
Paraná
Rosario
Paysandú
San Rafael
San Luis
Buenos Aires
URUGUAY
Rio Grande
Montevideo
ARGENTINA
La Plata
Río de la Plata
Santa Rosa
Colorado
Pampas
Neuquén
Mar del Plata
Bahía Blanca
Negro
Viedma
Golfo San Matías
Trelew
Chubut
Comodoro Rivadavia
Golfo de San Jorge
Tristan da Cunha
Bahía Grande
Falkland Islands (U.K.)
Río Gallegos
Stanley
Isla Grande de Tierra del Fuego
Ushuaia
Isla de los Estados
Shag Rocks
Cabo de Hornos
South Georgia
Drake Passage
South Georgia and South Sandwich Islands (U.K.)
South Shetland Islands
South Sandwich Islands
Traversay Islands
Candlemas Island
Saunders Island
Montagu Island
South Orkney Islands
Antarctic Peninsula
Southern Thule Island
Bristol Island
Arquipélago da Madeira
Islas Canarias
Gran Canaria
Santo Antão
Ilhas do Cabo Verde
Boa Vista
São Tiago
Tropic of Cancer
Sénégal
Niger
AFRICA
Gulf of Guinea
Equator
Ascension
Tropic of Capricorn
Orange
Cape of Good Hope
MILES
KILOMETRES
1:27 000 000

246

242

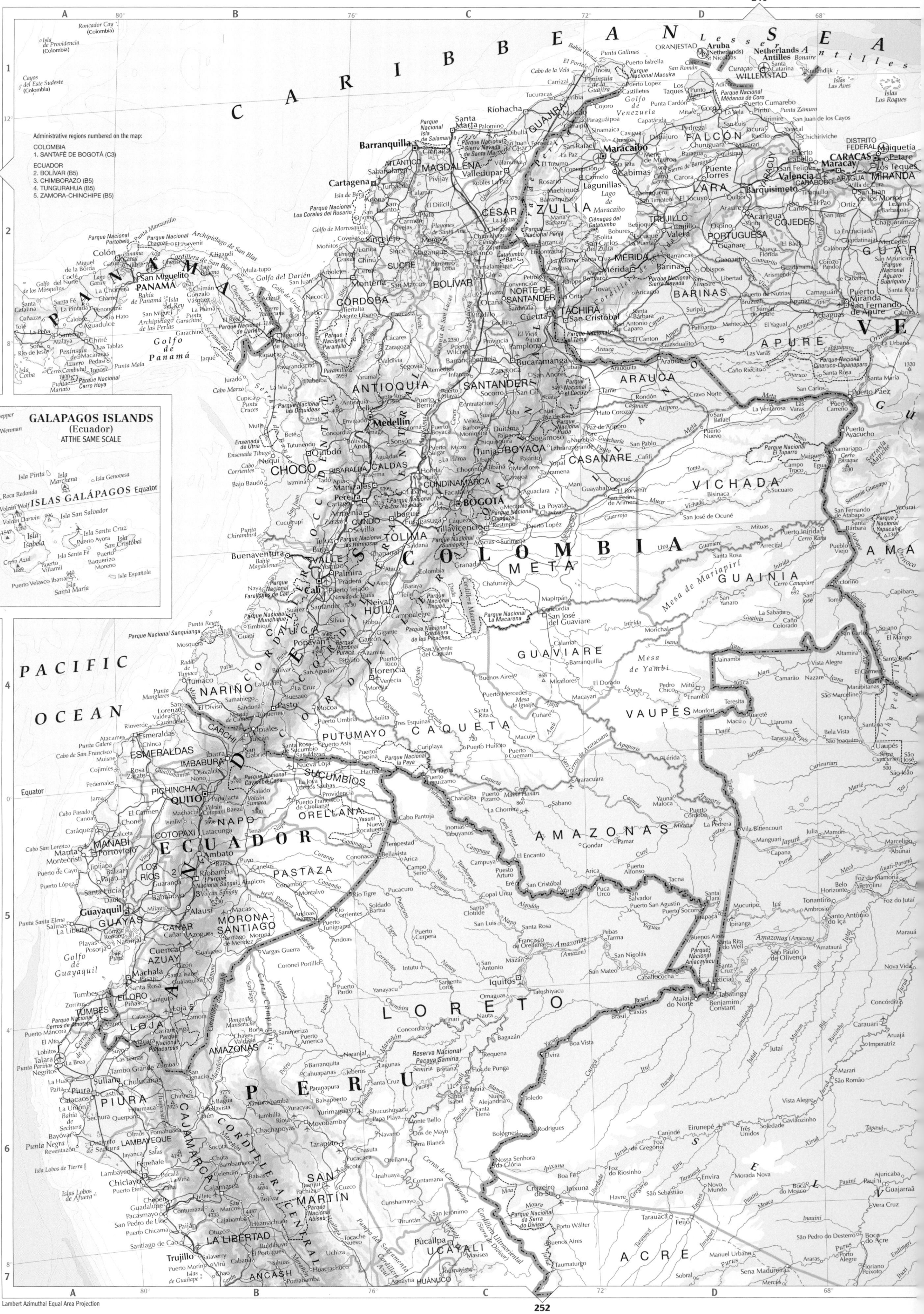
CARIBBEAN SEA
PACIFIC OCEAN
COLOMBIA
ECUADOR
PERU
PANAMA
Administrative regions numbered on the map:
COLOMBIA
1. SANTAFÉ DE BOGOTÁ (C3)
ECUADOR
2. BOLÍVAR (B5)
3. CHIMBORAZO (B5)
4. TUNGURAHUA (B5)
5. ZAMORA-CHINCHIPE (B5)
GALAPAGOS ISLANDS
(Ecuador)
AT THE SAME SCALE
ISLAS GALÁPAGOS
Equator
METRES
FEET
6000
19686
5000
16404
4000
13124
3000
9843
2000
6562
1000
3281
500
1640
200
656
0
0
LAND BELOW SEA LEVEL
200
656
2000
6562
4000
13124
6000
19686
BOGOTÁ
QUITO
CARACAS
Medellín
Cali
Barranquilla
Cartagena
Maracaibo
Guayaquil
Iquitos
Trujillo
Lesser Antilles
Golfo de Venezuela
Golfo de Panamá
Golfo de Guayaquil
AMAZONAS
LORETO
VICHADA
GUAINÍA
VAUPÉS
CAQUETÁ
GUAVIARE
META
PUTUMAYO
NARIÑO
ACRE

Lambert Azimuthal Equal Area Projection

252

247

ATLANTIC
OCEAN
MILES
KILOMETRES
1:7 500 000
GRENADA
ST GEORGE'S
The Grenadines
Tobago
TRINIDAD
AND
TOBAGO
PORT OF SPAIN
Trinidad
NUEVA ESPARTA
SUCRE
MONAGAS
DELTA
AMACURO
ANZOÁTEGUI
Ciudad Guayana
Ciudad Bolívar
Barcelona
Cumaná
Maturín
NEZUELA
BOLÍVAR
GUYANA
GEORGETOWN
New Amsterdam
Linden
Bartica
Lethem
Kaieteur Falls
Pakaraima Mountains
Kanuku Mountains
Salto del Angel (Angel Falls)
Auyán Tepui
Parque Nacional Canaima
La Gran Sabana
SURINAME
PARAMARIBO
Nieuw Nickerie
Wilhelmina Gebergte
French
Guiana
CAYENNE
Kourou
St-Laurent-du-Maroni
Parque Nacional de Cabo Orange
Cabo Orange
Serra Tumucumaque
AMAPÁ
Macapá
Equator
Mouths of the Amazon
Ilha de Marajó
Belém
RORAIMA
Boa Vista
Serra Parima
Serra Pacaraima
Parque Nacional Parima-Tapirapecó
Parque Nacional Serranía de la Neblina
Parque Nacional do Pico da Neblina
ZONAS
AMAZONAS
Amazonas (Amazon)
Manaus
Parque Nacional do Jaú
Negro
Branco
Barcelos
Manacapuru
Itacoatiara
Parintins
Óbidos
Santarém
Alenquer
Monte Alegre
Almeirim
Altamira
Tucuruí
Itaituba
Parque Nacional Amazônia
LITIGATED AREA
BRAZIL
PARÁ
Coari
Tefé
Borba
Manicoré
Humaitá
Porto Velho
RONDÔNIA
MATO GROSSO
Serra do Cachimbo
Serra dos Carajás
São Félix
Jacareacanga
Planalto Maracanaquará
Longitude 64° west of Greenwich

254
253

© Bartholomew Ltd

250

PERU
ANDES
CORDILLERA OCCIDENTAL
CORDILLERA ORIENTAL
CHILE
BOLIV
AMAZON
SELVAS
ACRE
LORETO
SAN MARTÍN
AMAZONAS
CAJAMARCA
LA LIBERTAD
ANCASH
HUÁNUCO
PASCO
UCAYALI
JUNÍN
LIMA
HUANCAVELICA
AYACUCHO
APURÍMAC
CUSCO
MADRE DE DIOS
ICA
AREQUIPA
PUNO
MOQUEGUA
TACNA
PANDO
LA PAZ
BENI
COCHABAMBA
ORURO
POTOSÍ
CHUQUISACA
TARIJA
TARAPACÁ
ANTOFAGASTA
ATACAMA
JUJUY
SALTA
TUCUMÁN
CATAMARCA
LA RIOJA
SANTIAGO DEL ESTERO
PACIFIC OCEAN
Tropic of Capricorn
Lago Titicaca
Salar de Uyuni
Lima
Callao
Trujillo
Arequipa
Cusco
La Paz
Sucre
Arica
Iquique
Antofagasta
JUAN FERNÁNDEZ ISLANDS (Chile)
AT THE SAME SCALE
Archipiélago Juan Fernández
Isla Robinson Crusoe
Alejandro Selkirk
Islas de los Desventurados
Isla San Félix
San Ambrosio
80° W

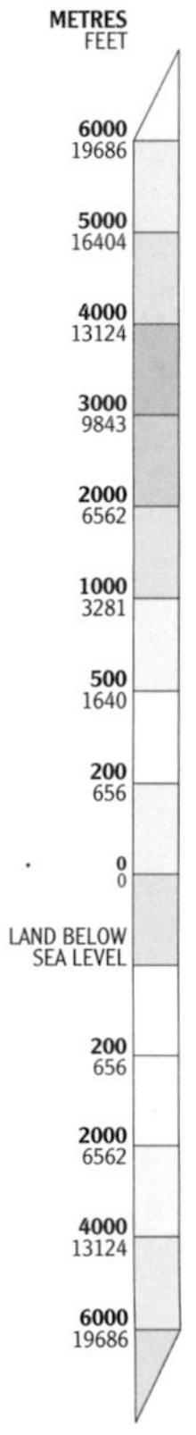
METRES
FEET
6000
19686
5000
16404
4000
13124
3000
9843
2000
6562
1000
3281
500
1640
200
656
0
0
LAND BELOW SEA LEVEL
200
656
2000
6562
4000
13124
6000
19686

Lambert Azimuthal Equal Area Projection

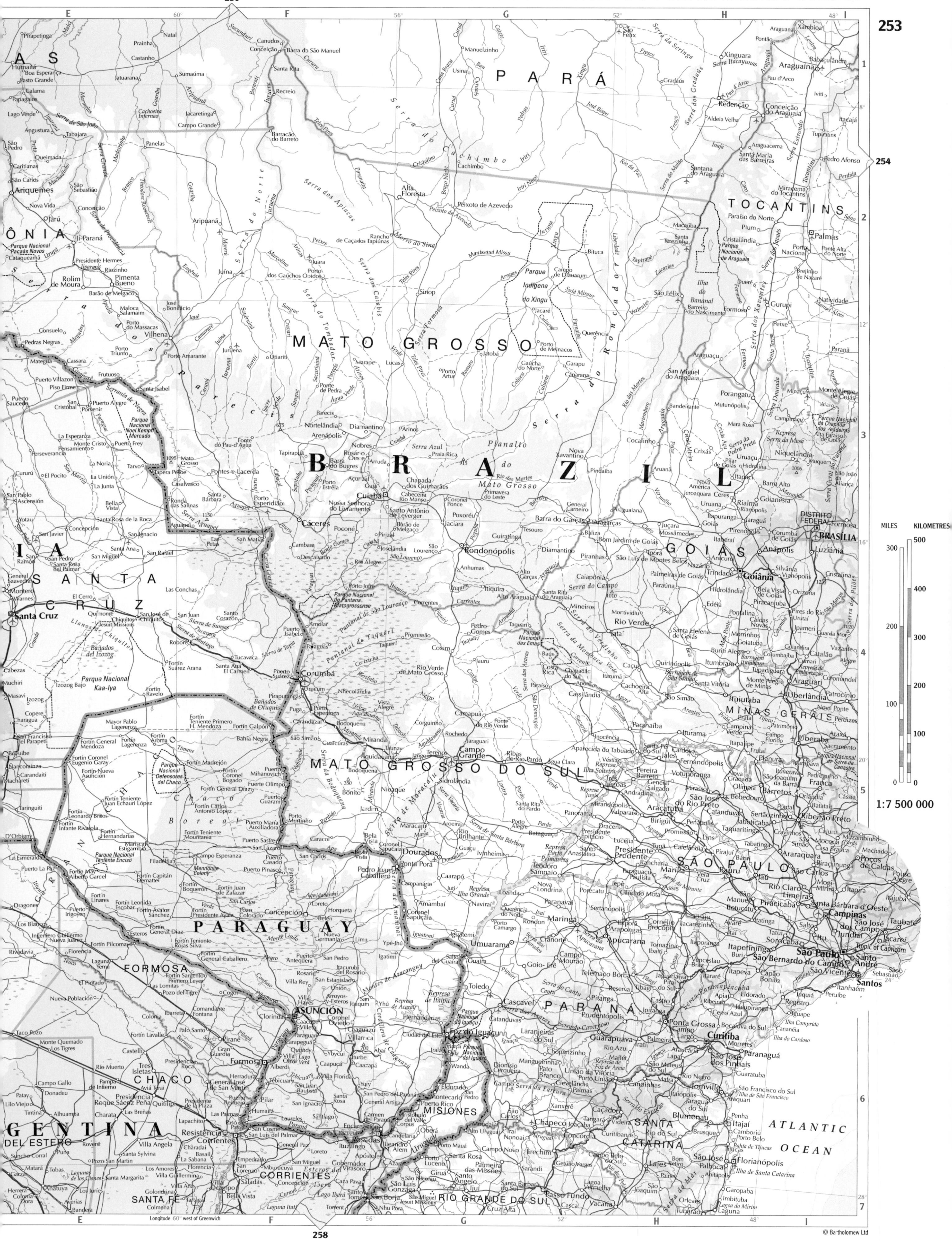
251
254
258
PARÁ
TOCANTINS
MATO GROSSO
BRAZIL
GOIÁS
DISTRITO FEDERAL
BRASÍLIA
MINAS GERAIS
MATO GROSSO DO SUL
SÃO PAULO
PARANÁ
SANTA CATARINA
RIO GRANDE DO SUL
PARAGUAY
ASUNCIÓN
SANTA CRUZ
CHACO
FORMOSA
CORRIENTES
MISIONES
SANTA FE
ATLANTIC OCEAN
MILES
KILOMETRES
1:7 500 000
Longitude 60° west of Greenwich

© Bartholomew Ltd

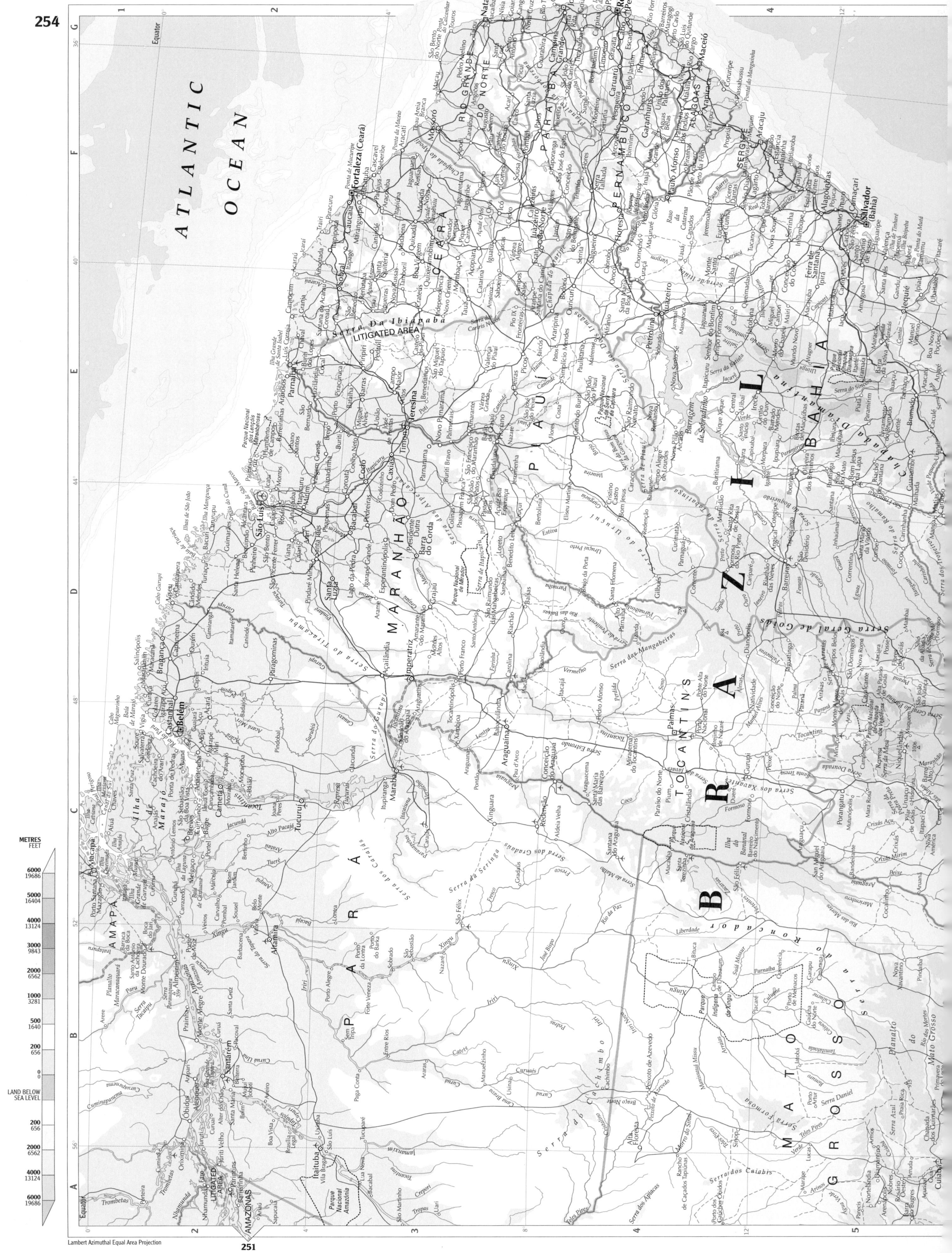
ATLANTIC OCEAN
BRAZIL
PARÁ
MARANHÃO
PIAUÍ
CEARÁ
RIO GRANDE DO NORTE
PARAÍBA
PERNAMBUCO
ALAGOAS
SERGIPE
BAHIA
TOCANTINS
MATO GROSSO
AMAPÁ
AMAZONAS
LITIGATED AREA
Belém
São Luís
Teresina
Fortaleza (Ceará)
Natal
João Pessoa
Recife (Pernambuco)
Maceió
Aracaju
Salvador (Bahia)
Palmas
Macapá
Santarém
Cuiabá
Serra da Ibiapaba
Serra Geral de Goiás
Serra do Roncador
Equator
METRES
FEET
6000 19686
5000 16404
4000 13124
3000 9843
2000 6562
1000 3281
500 1640
200 656
0 0
LAND BELOW SEA LEVEL
200 656
2000 6562
4000 13124
6000 19686

Lambert Azimuthal Equal Area Projection

251

ATLANTIC
OCEAN
Tropic of Capricorn
RIO DE JANEIRO
1:125 000
ATLANTIC OCEAN
Baía de Guanabara
COPACABANA
BOTAFOGO
IPANEMA
LEBLON
FLAMENGO
LARANJEIRAS
URCA
LEME
COSME VELHO
Parque Nacional da Tijuca
MINAS GERAIS
SÃO PAULO
PARANÁ
SANTA CATARINA
RIO GRANDE DO SUL
MATO GROSSO DO SUL
GOIÁS
DISTRITO FEDERAL
ESPÍRITO SANTO
RIO DE JANEIRO
PARAGUAY
ARGENTINA
MISIONES
CORRIENTES
URUGUAY
BRASÍLIA
Belo Horizonte
Rio de Janeiro
São Paulo
Curitiba
Porto Alegre
Goiânia
Campo Grande
Vitória
Florianópolis
Santos
Campinas
Tropic of Capricorn
MILES
KILOMETRES
Longitude 52° west of Greenwich
1:7 500 000

253

258

© Bartholomew Ltd

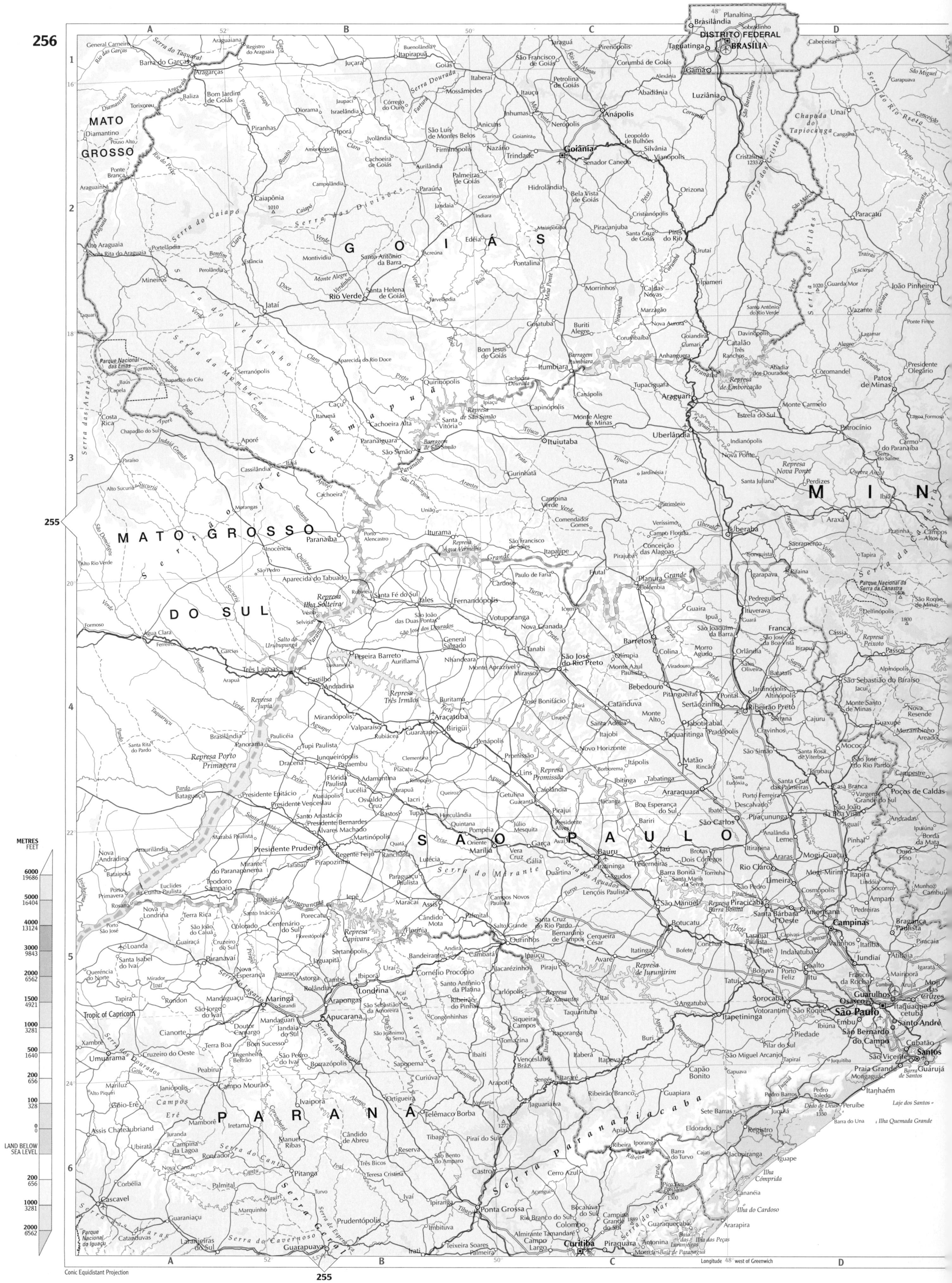
DISTRITO FEDERAL
BRASÍLIA
Brasilândia
Planaltina
Sobradinho
Taguatinga
Gama
MATO GROSSO
GOIÁS
MATO GROSSO DO SUL
SÃO PAULO
PARANÁ
MIN
Goiânia
Anápolis
Luziânia
Rio Verde
Jataí
Itumbiara
Uberlândia
Uberaba
Araguari
Catalão
Ituiutaba
Paranaíba
Três Lagoas
Araçatuba
Presidente Prudente
Marília
Bauru
São José do Rio Preto
Ribeirão Preto
Franca
Araraquara
São Carlos
Campinas
Piracicaba
Sorocaba
São Paulo
Guarulhos
Santo André
São Bernardo do Campo
Santos
São Vicente
Guarujá
Londrina
Maringá
Apucarana
Campo Mourão
Umuarama
Cascavel
Guarapuava
Ponta Grossa
Curitiba
Paranaguá
Tropic of Capricorn
Parque Nacional das Emas
Parque Nacional da Serra da Canastra
Parque Nacional do Iguaçu
Represa Ilha Solteira
Represa Três Irmãos
Represa Porto Primavera
Represa Capivara
Represa de Xavantes
Represa de Jurumirim
Represa Nova Ponte
Represa de Emborcação
Represa de São Simão
Represa Água Vermelha
Represa Promissão
Serra do Caiapó
Serra dos Divisões
Serra da Mantiqueira
Serra do Mar
Serra de Paranapiacaba
Serra Geral
Serra do Mirante
Serra dos Agudos
Serra dos Pilões
Chapada do Tapiocanga
METRES
FEET
6000 19686
5000 16404
4000 13124
3000 9843
2000 6562
1500 4921
1000 3281
500 1640
200 656
100 328
0 0
LAND BELOW SEA LEVEL
200 656
1000 3281
2000 6562
Longitude 48° west of Greenwich
A
B
C
D
1
2
3
4
5
6
52°
50°
48°
16°
18°
20°
22°
24°
255

Conic Equidistant Projection

255

254

257

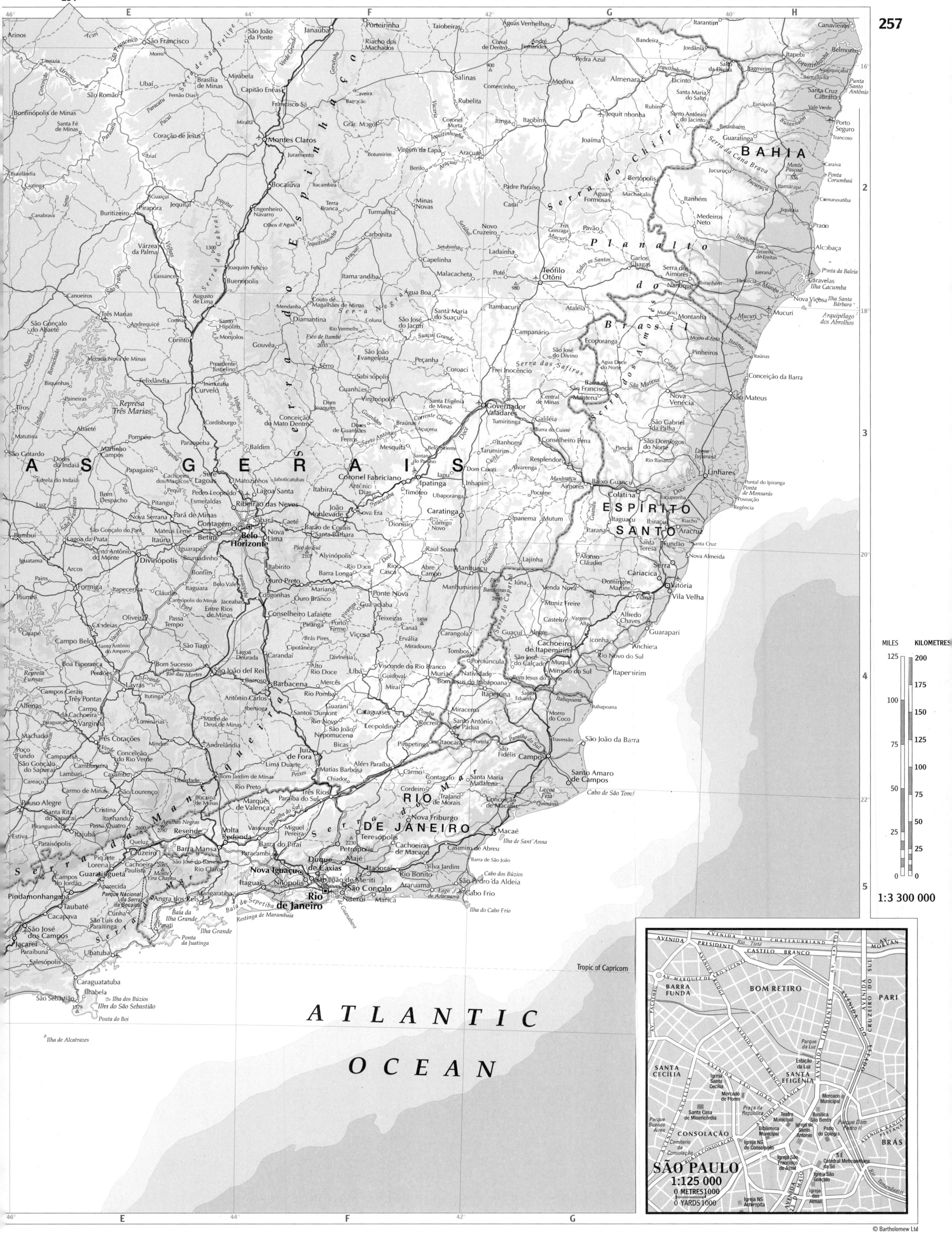
BAHIA
MINAS GERAIS
ESPIRITO SANTO
RIO DE JANEIRO
ATLANTIC
OCEAN
Tropic of Capricorn
Serra do Espinhaço
Planalto do Brasil
Serra da Mantiqueira
Serra do Mar
Belo Horizonte
Rio de Janeiro
Vitória
Nova Iguaçu
Duque de Caxias
Niterói
São Gonçalo
Governador Valadares
Montes Claros
Juiz de Fora
Teófilo Otôni
Ipatinga
Campos
Linhares
Colatina
Cachoeiro de Itapemirim
Petrópolis
Volta Redonda
Barra Mansa
Taubaté
São José dos Campos
Represa Três Marias
Represa Furnas
Baía da Ilha Grande
Baía de Guanabara
Cabo Frio
Cabo de São Tomé
Arquipélago dos Abrolhos
Ilha de São Sebastião
MILES
KILOMETRES
1:3 300 000
SÃO PAULO
1:125 000
0 METRES 1000
0 YARDS 1000
BOM RETIRO
BARRA FUNDA
PARI
SANTA CECÍLIA
SANTA EFIGÊNIA
CONSOLAÇÃO
BRÁS
SÉ
Estação da Luz
Catedral Metropolitana da Sé
Teatro Municipal
Mercado Municipal
Parque Dom Pedro II

© Bartholomew Ltd

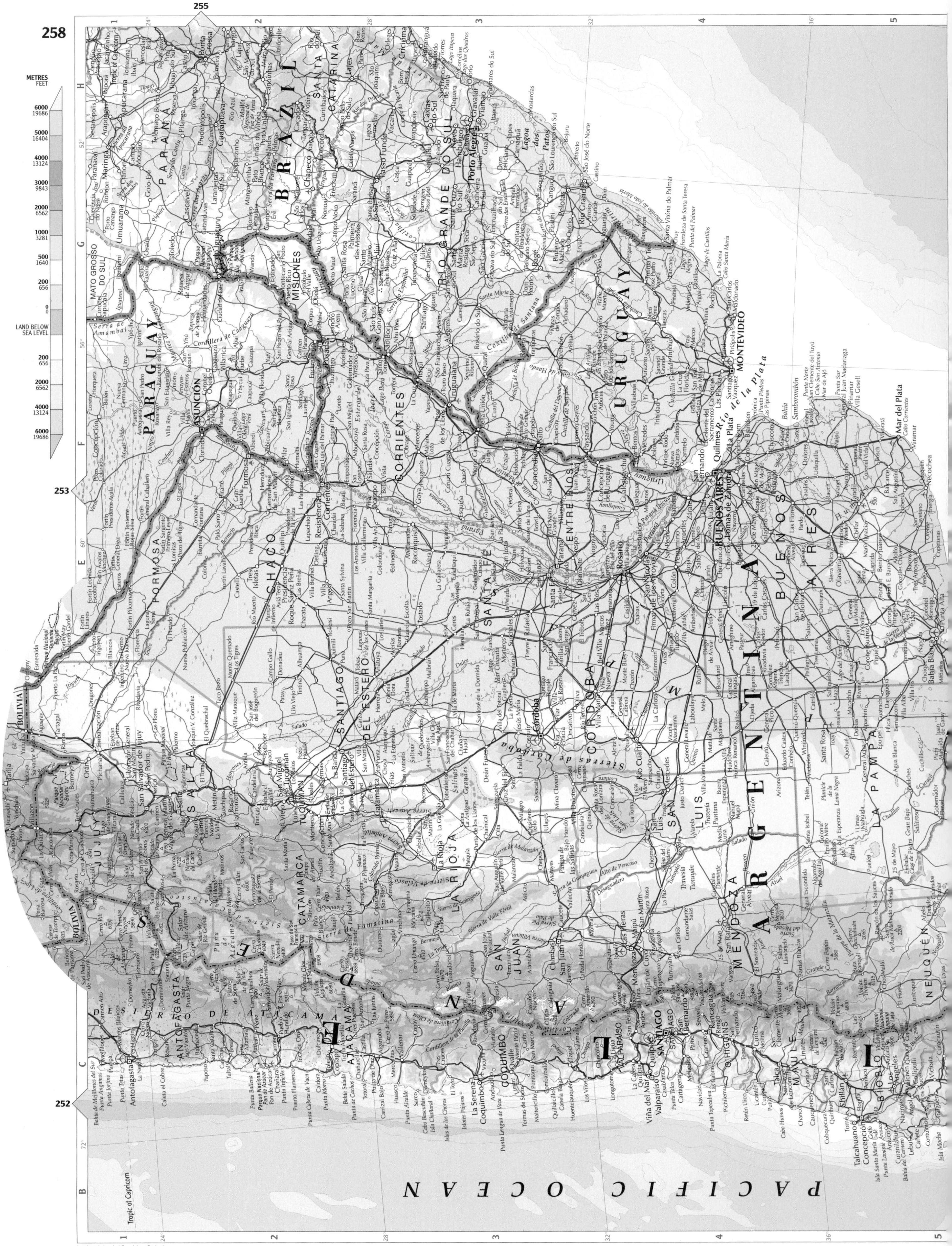
METRES
FEET
6000
19686
5000
16404
4000
13124
3000
9843
2000
6562
1000
3281
500
1640
200
656
0
0
LAND BELOW SEA LEVEL
PACIFIC OCEAN
ARGENTINA
CHILE
URUGUAY
PARAGUAY
BRAZIL
BOLIVIA
BUENOS AIRES
MONTEVIDEO
SANTIAGO
ASUNCIÓN
Tropic of Capricorn
255
253
252

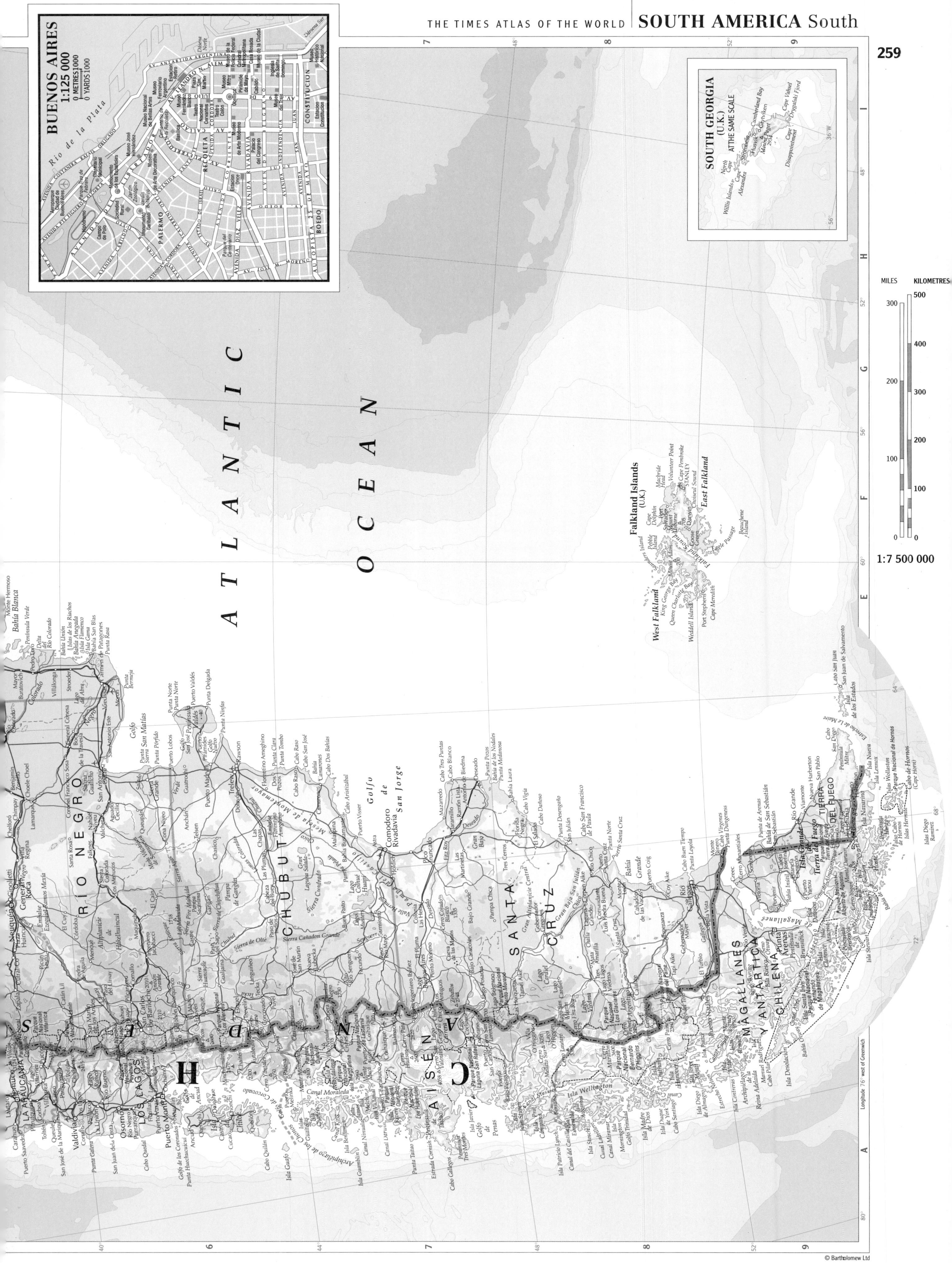
BUENOS AIRES
1:125 000
Río de la Plata
SOUTH GEORGIA
(U.K.)
AT THE SAME SCALE
ATLANTIC
OCEAN
Falkland Islands
(U.K.)
West Falkland
East Falkland
STANLEY
RÍO NEGRO
CHUBUT
SANTA CRUZ
TIERRA DEL FUEGO
MAGALLANES Y ANTÁRTICA CHILENA
AISÉN
LOS LAGOS
LA ARAUCANÍA
CHILE
Golfo San Matías
Golfo San Jorge
Comodoro Rivadavia
Punta Arenas
Cabo de Hornos
(Cape Horn)
MILES
KILOMETRES
1:7 500 000
Longitude 76° west of Greenwich

© Bartholomew Ltd

258

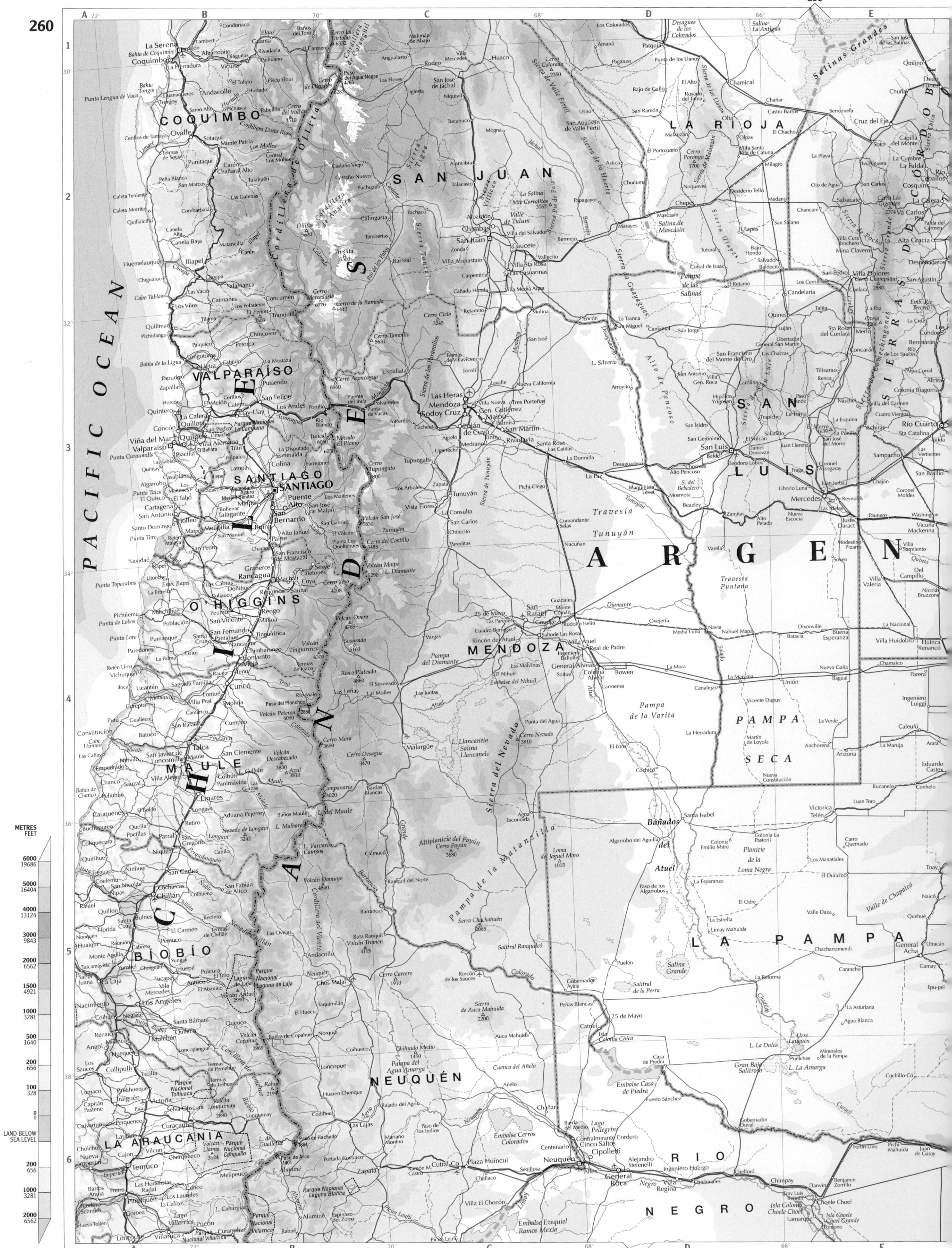
PACIFIC OCEAN
ANDES
CHILE
ARGEN
COQUIMBO
VALPARAÍSO
SANTIAGO
O'HIGGINS
MAULE
BÍOBÍO
LA ARAUCANIA
SAN JUAN
LA RIOJA
SAN LUIS
MENDOZA
LA PAMPA
NEUQUÉN
RIO NEGRO
SIERRAS DE CÓRDOBA
PAMPA SECA
Travesia Tunuyán
Travesia Puntana
Salinas Grandes
Bañados del Atuel
La Serena
Coquimbo
Ovalle
Illapel
Valparaíso
Viña del Mar
Santiago
Rancagua
Talca
Curicó
Linares
Chillán
Concepción
Los Angeles
Temuco
San Juan
Mendoza
San Rafael
San Luis
Mercedes
Río Cuarto
Neuquén
General Roca
General Acha
Cerro Aconcagua 6960
Volcán Maipú 5290
METRES
FEET
6000 19686
5000 16404
4000 13124
3000 9843
2000 6562
1500 4921
1000 3281
500 1640
200 656
100 328
0 0
LAND BELOW SEA LEVEL
200 656
1000 3281
2000 6562

Conic Equidistant Projection

259

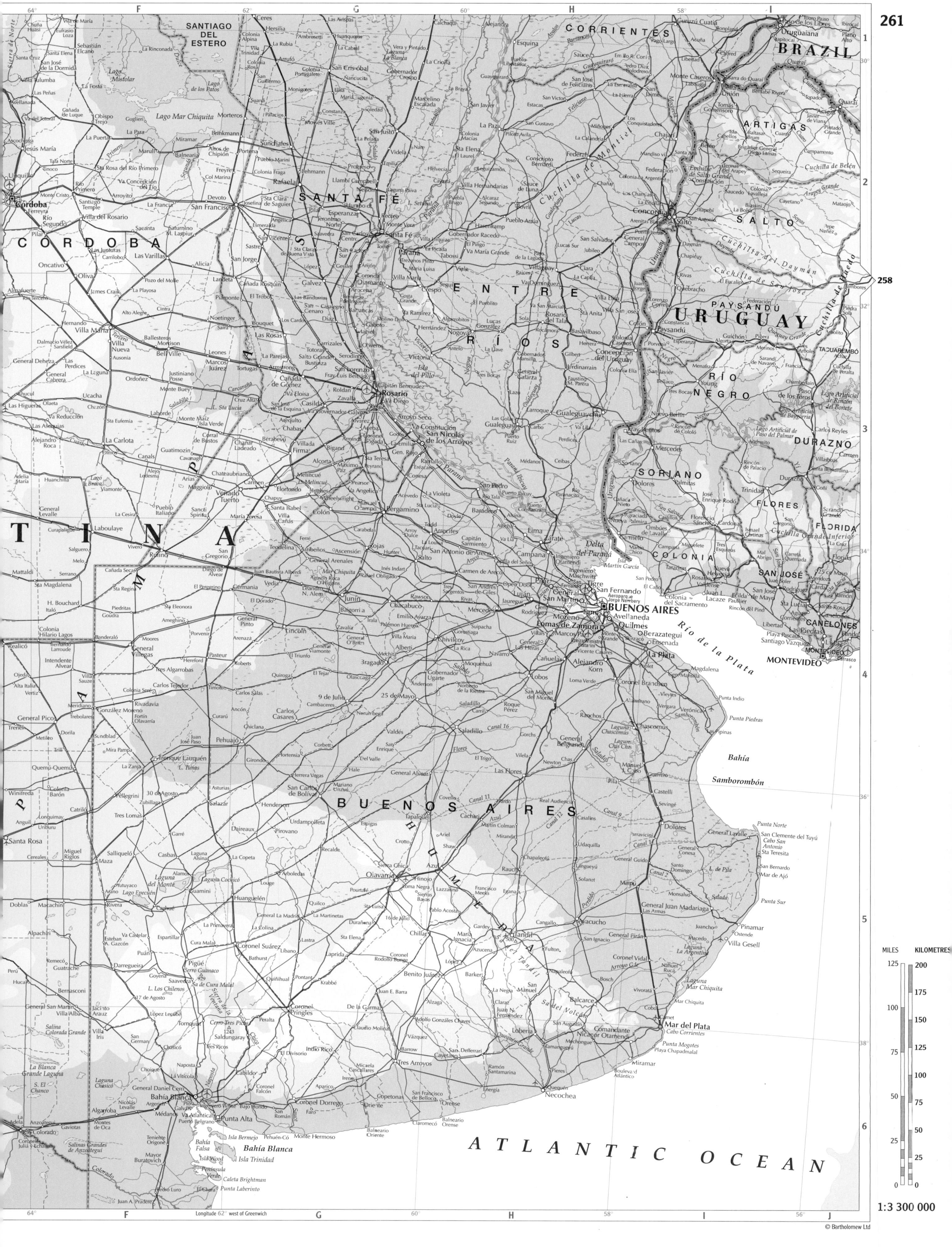
SANTIAGO DEL ESTERO
CORRIENTES
BRAZIL
ARTIGAS
SALTO
SANTA FÉ
CÓRDOBA
ENTRE RÍOS
PAYSANDÚ
URUGUAY
RÍO NEGRO
TACUAREMBÓ
DURAZNO
SORIANO
FLORES
FLORIDA
COLONIA
SAN JOSÉ
CANELONES
MONTEVIDEO
BUENOS AIRES
Río de la Plata
Bahía Samborombón
ATLANTIC OCEAN
Córdoba
Rosario
Santa Fé
Paraná
Concordia
Salto
Paysandú
Mar del Plata
Bahía Blanca
Bahía Blanca
Lago Mar Chiquita
Laguna Mar Chiquita
Cuchilla de Montiel
Cuchilla Grande Inferior
Delta del Paraná
La Plata
Tandil
Olavarría
Necochea
Tres Arroyos
Junín
Pergamino
San Nicolás de los Arroyos
Gualeguaychú
Mercedes
Fray Bentos
Colonia del Sacramento
258
MILES
KILOMETRES
125
100
75
50
25
0
200
175
150
125
100
75
50
25
0
1:3 300 000
Longitude 62° west of Greenwich
64°
62°
60°
58°
56°
F
G
H
I
J
1
2
3
4
5
6

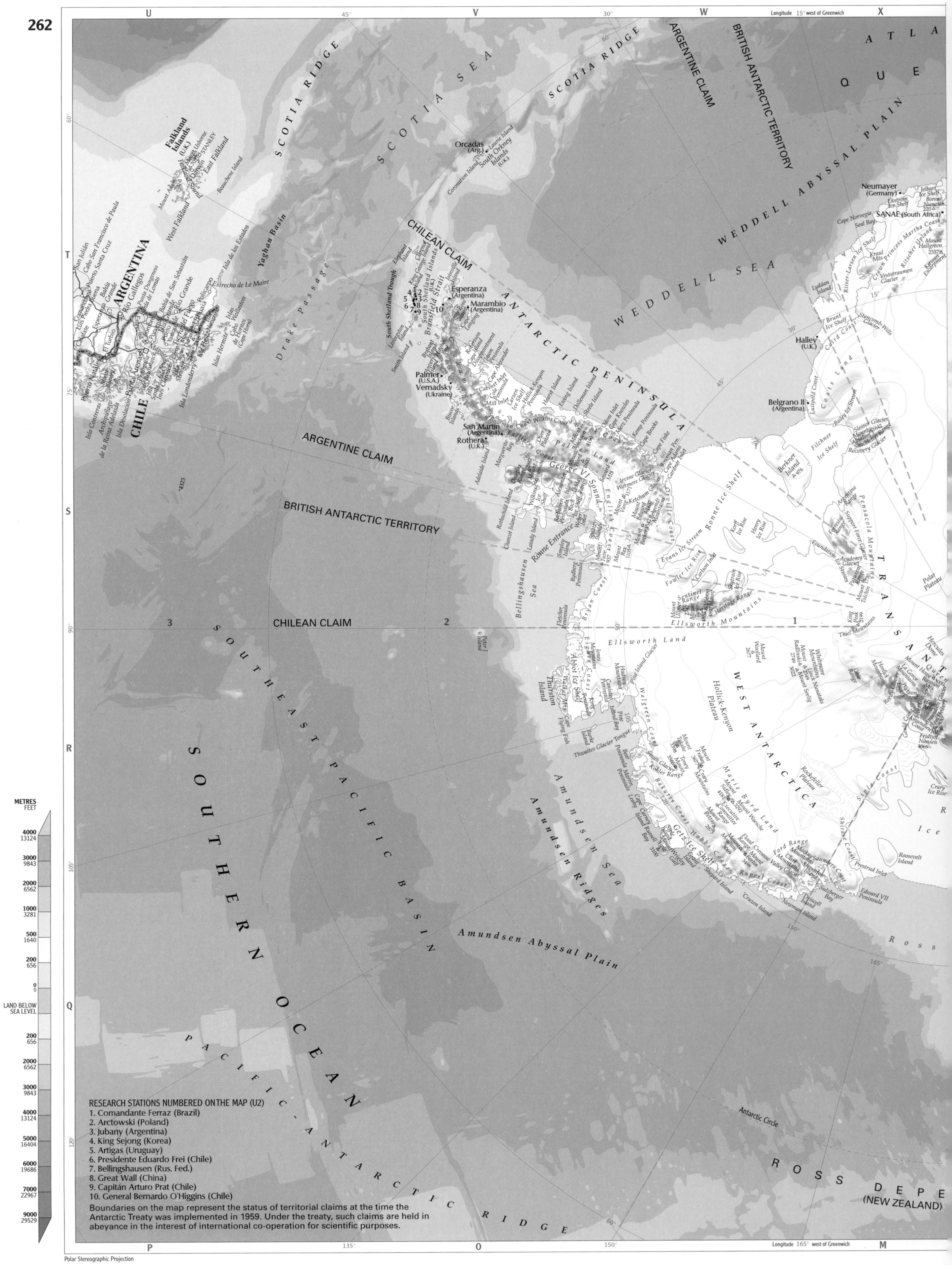
METRES
FEET
4000
13124
3000
9843
2000
6562
1000
3281
500
1640
200
656
0
0
LAND BELOW SEA LEVEL
200
656
2000
6562
3000
9843
4000
13124
5000
16404
6000
19686
7000
22967
9000
29529
Longitude 15° west of Greenwich
Longitude 165° west of Greenwich
SCOTIA SEA
SCOTIA RIDGE
ARGENTINE CLAIM
BRITISH ANTARCTIC TERRITORY
CHILEAN CLAIM
WEDDELL SEA
WEDDELL ABYSSAL PLAIN
ANTARCTIC PENINSULA
ARGENTINA
CHILE
Falkland Islands (U.K.)
Drake Passage
Yaghan Basin
South Shetland Trough
Orcadas (Arg.)
South Orkney Islands (U.K.)
Esperanza (Argentina)
Marambio (Argentina)
Palmer (U.S.A.)
Vernadsky (Ukraine)
San Martín (Argentina)
Rothera (U.K.)
Halley (U.K.)
Belgrano II (Argentina)
Neumayer (Germany)
SANAE (South Africa)
Ronne Ice Shelf
Filchner Ice Shelf
Ellsworth Mountains
Ellsworth Land
WEST ANTARCTICA
Hollick-Kenyon Plateau
Marie Byrd Land
Bellingshausen Sea
Amundsen Sea
Amundsen Ridges
Amundsen Abyssal Plain
SOUTHEAST PACIFIC BASIN
SOUTHERN OCEAN
PACIFIC-ANTARCTIC RIDGE
Peter I Island
Thurston Island
Getz Ice Shelf
Antarctic Circle
ROSS DEPENDENCY (NEW ZEALAND)
Pensacola Mountains
Thiel Mountains
RESEARCH STATIONS NUMBERED ON THE MAP (U2)
1. Comandante Ferraz (Brazil)
2. Arctowski (Poland)
3. Jubany (Argentina)
4. King Sejong (Korea)
5. Artigas (Uruguay)
6. Presidente Eduardo Frei (Chile)
7. Bellingshausen (Rus. Fed.)
8. Great Wall (China)
9. Capitán Arturo Prat (Chile)
10. General Bernardo O'Higgins (Chile)
Boundaries on the map represent the status of territorial claims at the time the Antarctic Treaty was implemented in 1959. Under the treaty, such claims are held in abeyance in the interest of international co-operation for scientific purposes.

Polar Stereographic Projection

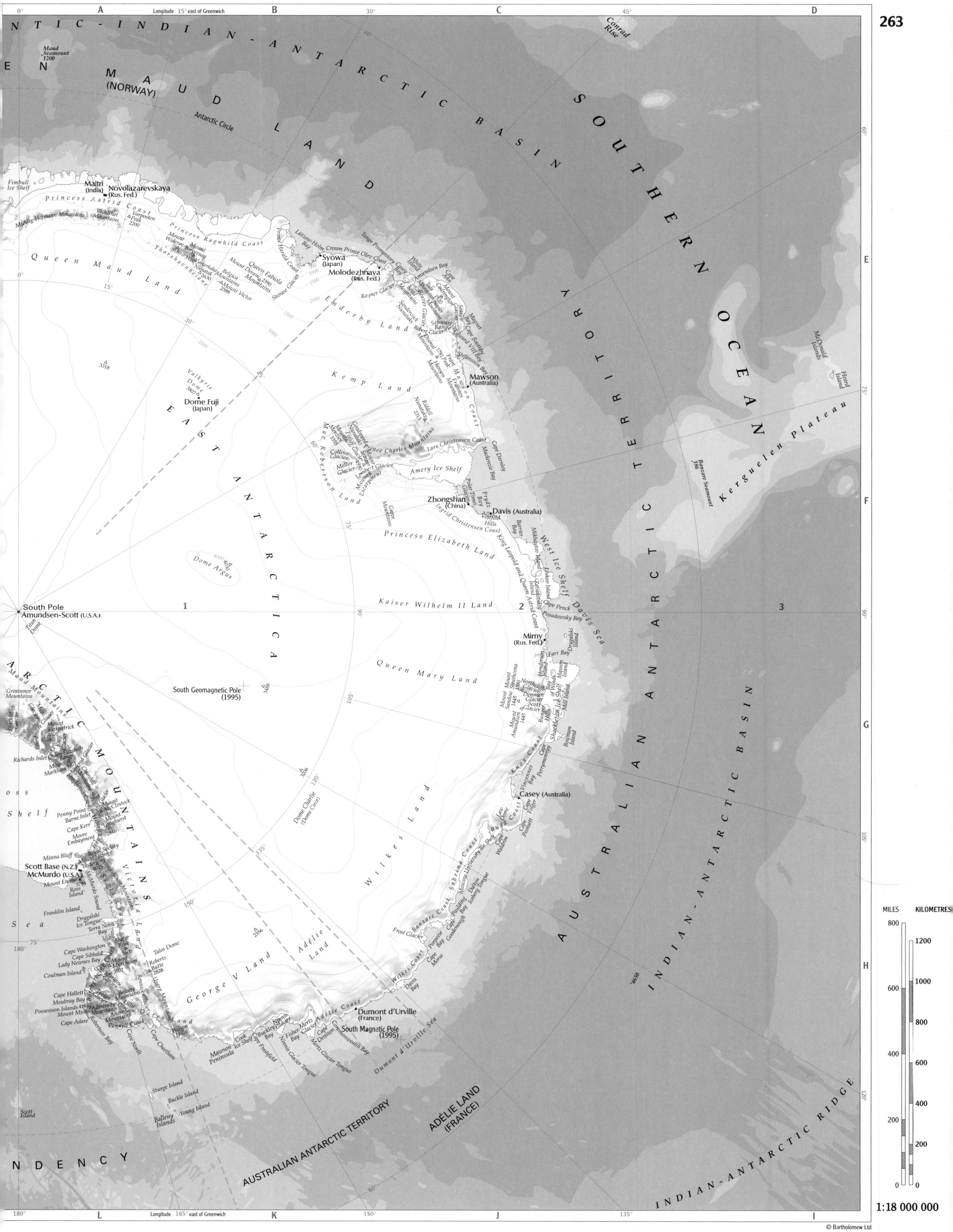
Longitude 15° east of Greenwich
Longitude 165° east of Greenwich
SOUTHERN OCEAN
EAST ANTARCTICA
TRANSANTARCTIC MOUNTAINS
AUSTRALIAN ANTARCTIC TERRITORY
ADÉLIE LAND (FRANCE)
DRONNING MAUD LAND (NORWAY)
ATLANTIC-INDIAN-ANTARCTIC BASIN
AUSTRALIAN-ANTARCTIC BASIN
INDIAN-ANTARCTIC BASIN
INDIAN-ANTARCTIC RIDGE
Kerguelen Plateau
Conrad Rise
Antarctic Circle
Maud Seamount 1200
Fimbull Ice Shelf
Maitri (India)
Novolazarevskaya (Rus. Fed.)
Princess Astrid Coast
Princess Ragnhild Coast
Queen Maud Land
Syowa (Japan)
Molodezhnaya (Rus. Fed.)
Enderby Land
Kemp Land
Mawson (Australia)
Mawson Coast
Dome Fuji (Japan)
Valkyrie Dome
Prince Charles Mountains
Amery Ice Shelf
Lars Christensen Coast
Zhongshan (China)
Davis (Australia)
Ingrid Christensen Coast
Princess Elizabeth Land
Dome Argus
West Ice Shelf
Davis Sea
Kaiser Wilhelm II Land
Mirny (Rus. Fed.)
Queen Mary Land
South Geomagnetic Pole (1995)
South Pole
Amundsen-Scott (U.S.A.)
Casey (Australia)
Knox Coast
Budd Coast
Sabrina Coast
Banzare Coast
Wilkes Land
Dome Charlie (Dome Circe)
Wilkes Coast
Adélie Land
George V Land
Adélie Coast
Dumont d'Urville (France)
South Magnetic Pole (1995)
Dumont d'Urville Sea
Mawson Peninsula
Cook Ice Shelf
Scott Base (N.Z.)
McMurdo (U.S.A.)
Mount Erebus
Ross Island
Victoria Land
Franklin Island
Cape Adare
Balleny Islands
Sturge Island
Buckle Island
Young Island
Scott Island
McDonald Islands
Heard Island
Banzare Seamount
MILES
KILOMETRES
1:18 000 000

© Bartholomew Ltd

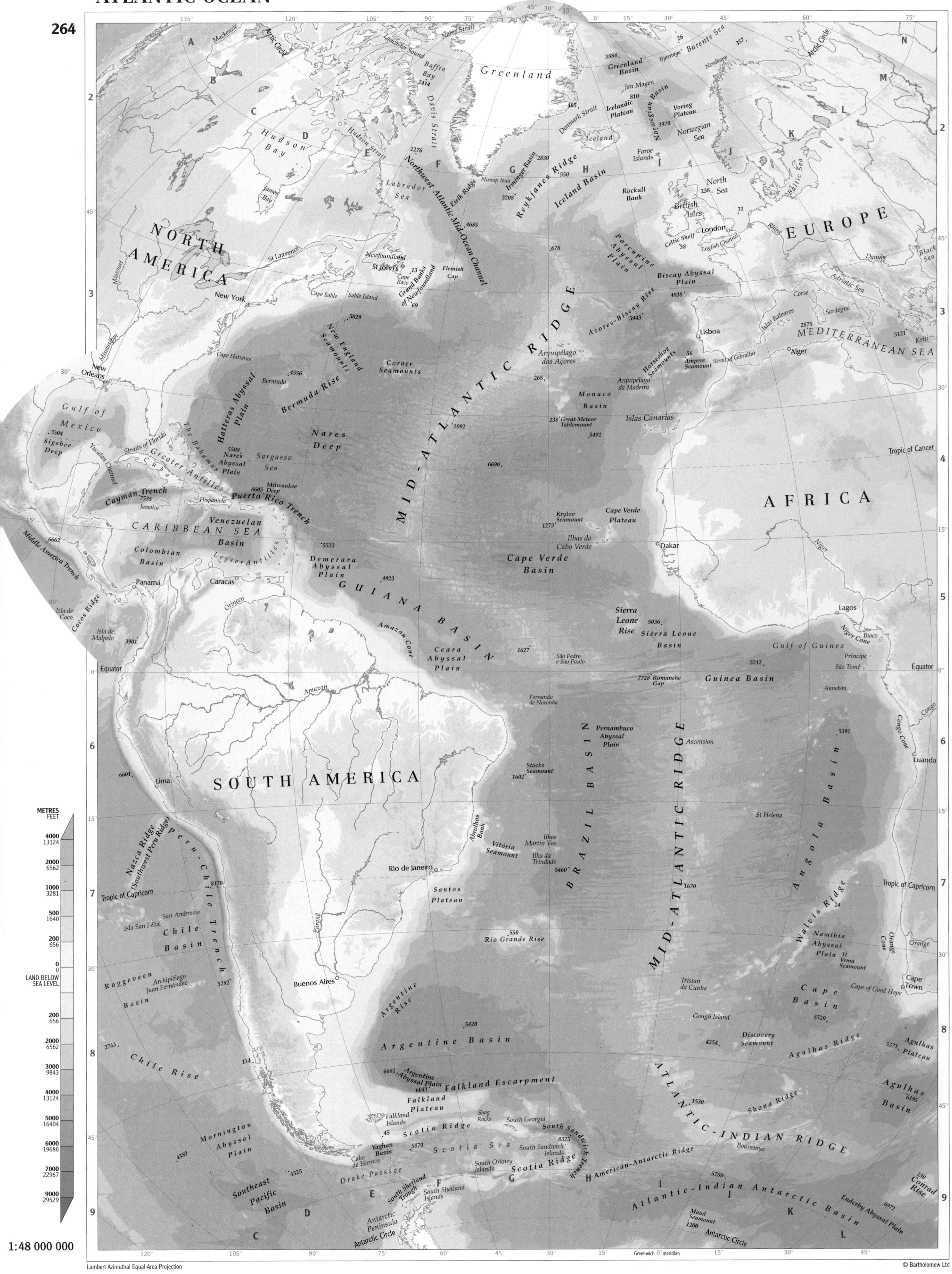
Greenland
Baffin Bay
Davis Strait
Hudson Bay
James Bay
Hudson Strait
Labrador Sea
Northwest Atlantic Mid-Ocean Channel
Irminger Basin
Reykjanes Ridge
Iceland Basin
Iceland
Denmark Strait
Icelandic Plateau
Jan Mayen
Greenland Basin
Norwegian Basin
Voring Plateau
Norwegian Sea
Barents Sea
Bjørnøya
Nordkapp
Faroe Islands
Rockall Bank
North Sea
British Isles
London
English Channel
Celtic Shelf
Porcupine Abyssal Plain
Biscay Abyssal Plain
Azores-Biscay Rise
EUROPE
Baltic Sea
Rhine
Danube
Black Sea
Adriatic Sea
Corse
Sardegna
Islas Baleares
MEDITERRANEAN SEA
Kriti
Lisboa
Strait of Gibraltar
Alger
Horseshoe Seamounts
Ampere Seamount
Arquipélago dos Açores
Arquipélago da Madeira
Monaco Basin
Great Meteor Tablemount
Islas Canarias
Tropic of Cancer
AFRICA
Niger
Dakar
Cape Verde Plateau
Krylov Seamount
Ilhas do Cabo Verde
Cape Verde Basin
Sierra Leone Rise
Sierra Leone Basin
Lagos
Niger Cone
Bioco
Gulf of Guinea
Príncipe
São Tomé
Equator
Annobón
Guinea Basin
Romanche Gap
São Pedro e São Paulo
Congo
Congo Cone
Luanda
Angola Basin
Ascension
St Helena
Walvis Ridge
Tropic of Capricorn
Namibia Abyssal Plain
Vema Seamount
Orange Cone
Orange
Cape Town
Cape of Good Hope
Cape Basin
Agulhas Ridge
Agulhas Plateau
Agulhas Basin
Discovery Seamount
Gough Island
Tristan da Cunha
Shona Ridge
Bouvetøya
ATLANTIC-INDIAN RIDGE
American-Antarctic Ridge
Atlantic-Indian Antarctic Basin
Enderby Abyssal Plain
Conrad Rise
Maud Seamount
Antarctic Circle
NORTH AMERICA
Mackenzie
Arctic Circle
Lancaster Sound
Nares Strait
St Lawrence
Missouri
Mississippi
New York
Newfoundland
St John's
Cape Race
Grand Banks of Newfoundland
Flemish Cap
Eirik Ridge
Nunap Isua
Cape Sable
Sable Island
New England Seamounts
Corner Seamounts
Cape Hatteras
Bermuda
Bermuda Rise
Hatteras Abyssal Plain
New Orleans
Gulf of Mexico
Sigsbee Deep
Yucatan Channel
Straits of Florida
The Bahamas
Greater Antilles
Cuba
Nares Abyssal Plain
Sargasso Sea
Nares Deep
Milwaukee Deep
Puerto Rico Trench
Cayman Trench
Jamaica
Hispaniola
Venezuelan Basin
CARIBBEAN SEA
Colombian Basin
Lesser Antilles
Middle America Trench
Panamá
Caracas
Orinoco
Cocos Ridge
Isla de Coco
Isla de Malpelo
Demerara Abyssal Plain
GUIANA BASIN
Amazon Cone
Ceara Abyssal Plain
MID-ATLANTIC RIDGE
Amazon
Fernando de Noronha
Pernambuco Abyssal Plain
Stocks Seamount
BRAZIL BASIN
SOUTH AMERICA
Lima
Nazca Ridge (Southwest Peru Ridge)
Peru-Chile Trench
Abrolhos Bank
Vitória Seamount
Ilhas Martin Vas
Ilha da Trindade
Rio de Janeiro
Santos Plateau
Paraná
Rio Grande Rise
San Ambrosio
Isla San Félix
Chile Basin
Chile Trench
Archipiélago Juan Fernández
Roggeveen Basin
Buenos Aires
Argentine Rise
Argentine Basin
Argentine Abyssal Plain
Falkland Escarpment
Falkland Plateau
Falkland Islands
Chile Rise
Scotia Ridge
Shag Rocks
South Georgia
South Sandwich Trench
South Sandwich Islands
Scotia Sea
Yaghan Basin
Cabo de Hornos
Drake Passage
South Orkney Islands
South Shetland Trough
South Shetland Islands
Antarctic Peninsula
Mornington Abyssal Plain
Southeast Pacific Basin
METRES
FEET
4000 13124
2000 6562
1000 3281
500 1640
200 656
0 0
LAND BELOW SEA LEVEL
200 656
2000 6562
3000 9843
4000 13124
5000 16404
6000 19686
7000 22967
9000 29529
1:48 000 000
Greenwich 0° meridian

© Bartholomew Ltd

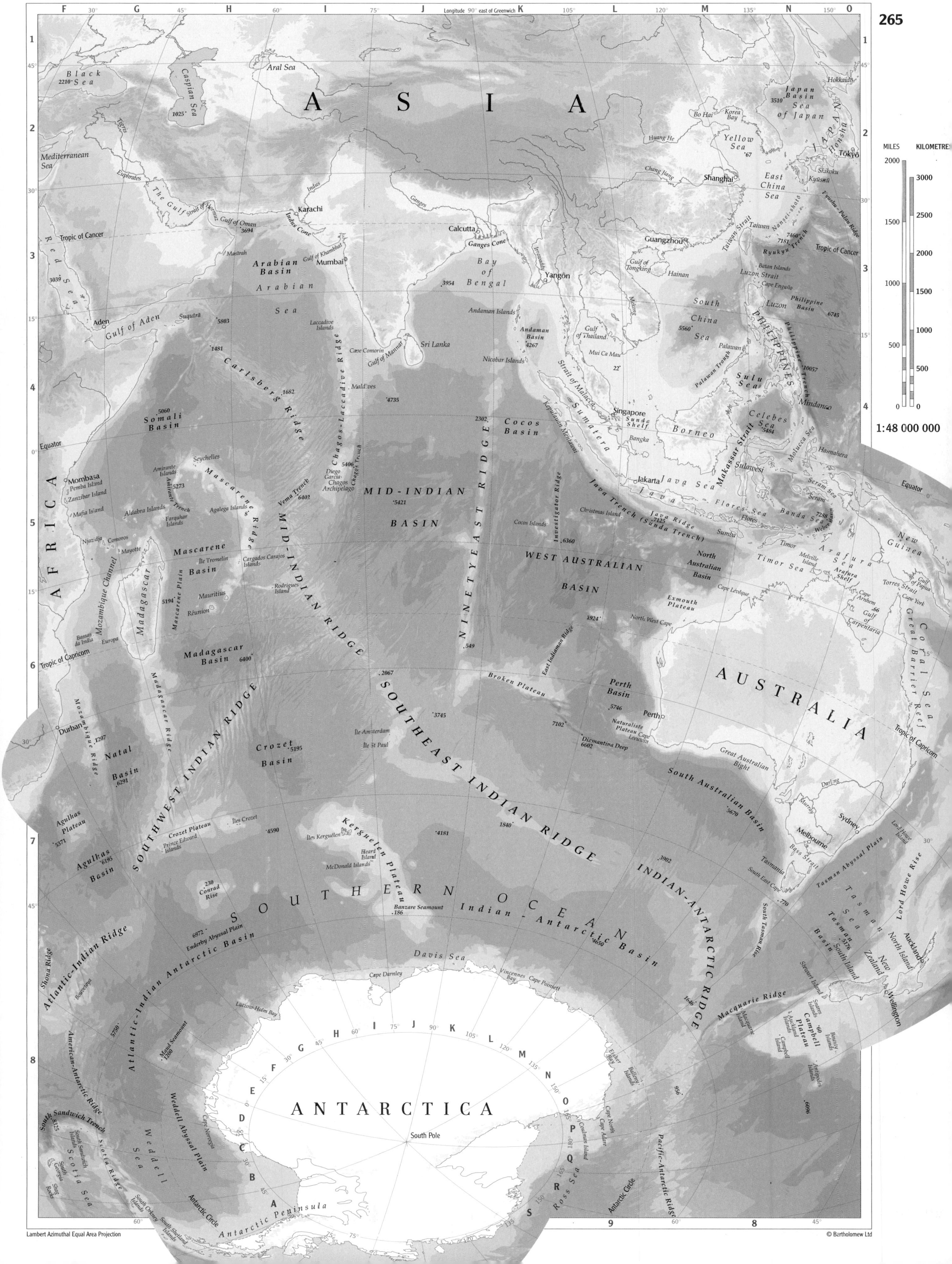

Lambert Azimuthal Equal Area Projection

© Bartholomew Ltd

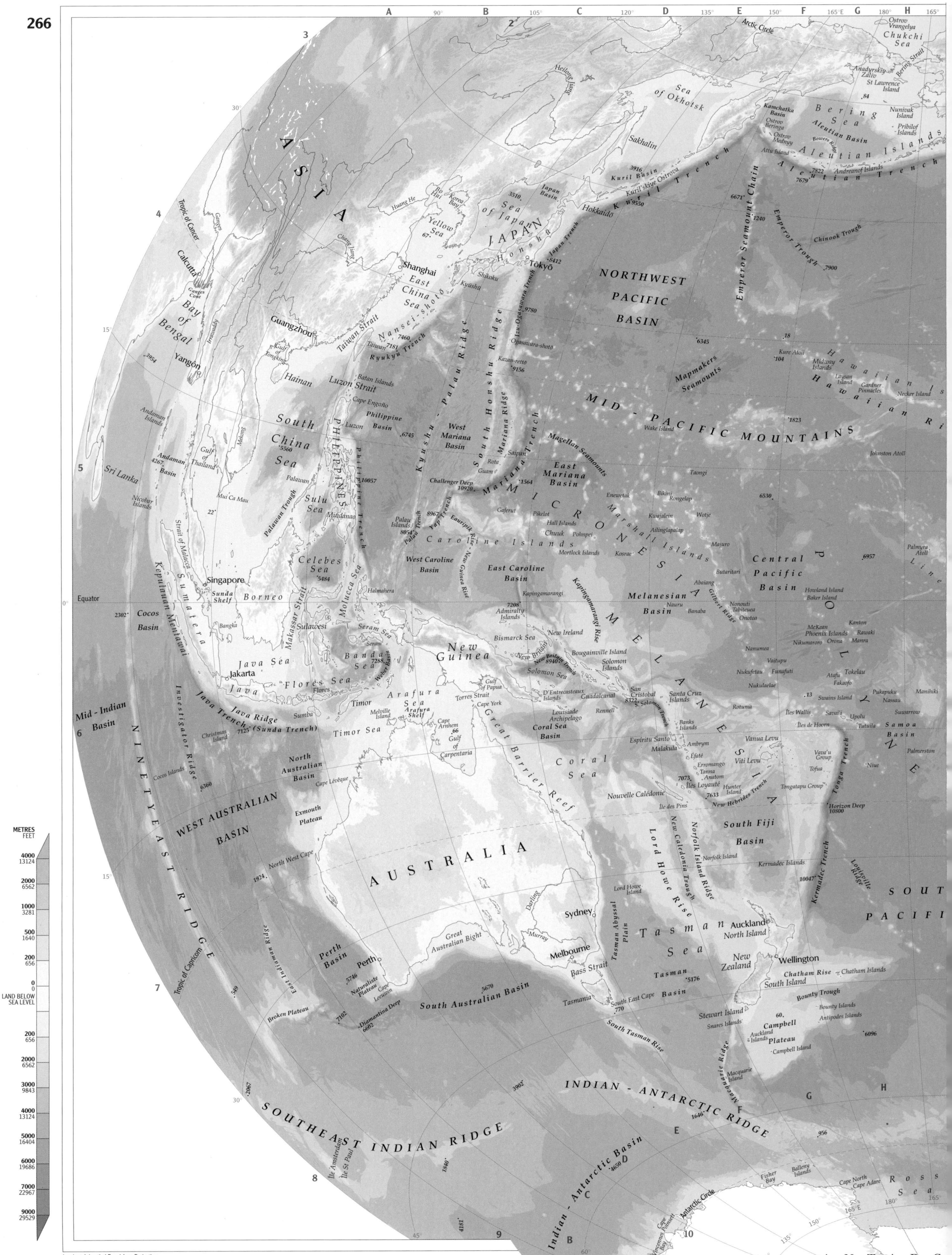

METRES
FEET
4000
13124
2000
6562
1000
3281
500
1640
200
656
0
0
LAND BELOW SEA LEVEL
200
656
2000
6562
3000
9843
4000
13124
5000
16404
6000
19686
7000
22967
9000
29529
ASIA
AUSTRALIA
ANTARC
Equator
Tropic of Cancer
Tropic of Capricorn
Arctic Circle
Antarctic Circle
Chukchi Sea
Ostrov Vrangelya
Bering Strait
Anadyrskiy Zaliv
St Lawrence Island
Nunivak Island
Pribilof Islands
Bering Sea
Kamchatka Basin
Ostrov Beringa
Ostrov Mednyy
Aleutian Basin
Bowers Ridge
Aleutian Islands
Andreanof Islands
Aleutian Trench
Attu Island
Sea of Okhotsk
Sakhalin
Heilong Jiang
Kuril Basin
Kuril'skiye Ostrova
Kuril Trench
Japan Basin
Sea of Japan
Hokkaido
Honshu
JAPAN
Japan Trench
Tokyo
Shikoku
Kyushu
Korea Bay
Bo Hai
Huang He
Yellow Sea
Chang Jiang
Shanghai
East China Sea
Nansei-shoto
Taiwan
Taiwan Strait
Ryukyu Trench
Guangzhou
Gulf of Tongking
Hainan
Luzon Strait
Batan Islands
Cape Engaño
Luzon
Philippine Basin
PHILIPPINES
Philippine Trench
Mindanao
Sulu Sea
Palawan
Palawan Trough
South China Sea
Mekong
Gulf of Thailand
Mui Ca Mau
Irrawaddy
Yangon
Bay of Bengal
Calcutta
Ganges
Ganges Cone
Andaman Islands
Andaman Basin
Sri Lanka
Nicobar Islands
Strait of Malacca
Sumatera
Kepulauan Mentawai
Singapore
Sunda Shelf
Borneo
Celebes Sea
Molucca Sea
Halmahera
Makassar Strait
Sulawesi
Bangka
Java Sea
Jakarta
Java
Flores Sea
Flores
Sumba
Timor
Timor Sea
Seram
Seram Sea
Banda Sea
Weber Basin
Java Ridge
Java Trench (Sunda Trench)
Investigator Ridge
Christmas Island
Cocos Islands
Cocos Basin
Mid-Indian Basin
NINETYEAST RIDGE
North Australian Basin
WEST AUSTRALIAN BASIN
Exmouth Plateau
Cape Lévêque
North West Cape
Perth Basin
Perth
Naturaliste Plateau
Cape Leeuwin
East Indiaman Ridge
Broken Plateau
Diamantina Deep
South Australian Basin
Great Australian Bight
Murray
Darling
Sydney
Melbourne
Bass Strait
Tasmania
South East Cape
South Tasman Rise
New Guinea
Gulf of Papua
Torres Strait
Cape York
Arafura Sea
Arafura Shelf
Melville Island
Cape Arnhem
Gulf of Carpentaria
Great Barrier Reef
Coral Sea
Coral Sea Basin
Louisiade Archipelago
D'Entrecasteaux Islands
Solomon Sea
New Britain
New Britain Trench
Bismarck Sea
New Ireland
Admiralty Islands
Bougainville Island
Solomon Islands
Guadalcanal
Rennell
San Cristobal
S. Solomon Trench
Santa Cruz Islands
Banks Islands
Espíritu Santo
Malakula
Ambrym
Éfaté
Erromango
Tanna
Anatom
Îles Loyauté
Hunter Island
New Hebrides Trench
Nouvelle Calédonie
Île des Pins
New Caledonia Trough
Norfolk Island Ridge
Norfolk Island
Lord Howe Rise
Lord Howe Island
Tasman Abyssal Plain
Tasman Sea
Tasman Basin
South Fiji Basin
Vanua Levu
Viti Levu
Kermadec Islands
Kermadec Trench
Tonga Trench
Horizon Deep
Tongatapu Group
Auckland
North Island
New Zealand
Wellington
Chatham Rise
Chatham Islands
South Island
Bounty Trough
Bounty Islands
Antipodes Islands
Stewart Island
Snares Islands
Campbell Plateau
Auckland Islands
Campbell Island
Macquarie Ridge
Macquarie Island
INDIAN - ANTARCTIC RIDGE
SOUTHEAST INDIAN RIDGE
Indian - Antarctic Basin
Île Amsterdam
Île St Paul
Fisher Bay
Balleny Islands
Cape North
Cape Adare
Ross Sea
Cape Poinsett
Vincennes Bay
NORTHWEST PACIFIC BASIN
Emperor Seamount Chain
Emperor Trough
Chinook Trough
Izu-Ogasawara Trench
Ogasawara-shoto
Kazan-retto
South Honshu Ridge
Kyushu - Palau Ridge
West Mariana Basin
Mariana Ridge
Mariana Trench
Saipan
Rota
Guam
Challenger Deep
East Mariana Basin
Magellan Seamounts
Mapmakers Seamounts
MID - PACIFIC MOUNTAINS
Wake Island
Hawaiian Islands
Hawaiian Ridge
Midway Islands
Kure Atoll
Laysan Island
Gardner Pinnacles
Necker Island
Johnston Atoll
MICRONESIA
Palau Islands
Palau Trench
Yap Trench
Eauripik Rise
Caroline Islands
Gaferut
Pikelot
Hall Islands
Chuuk
Pohnpei
Mortlock Islands
Kosrae
West Caroline Basin
East Caroline Basin
Eauripik - New Guinea Rise
Kapingamarangi
Kapingamarangi Rise
Marshall Islands
Enewetak
Bikini
Rongelap
Kwajalein
Ailinglapalap
Wotje
Majuro
Taongi
Melanesian Basin
MELANESIA
Nauru
Banaba
Butaritari
Abaiang
Gilbert Ridge
Nonouti
Tabiteuea
Onotoa
Central Pacific Basin
POLYNESIA
Howland Island
Baker Island
Palmyra Atoll
Line Islands
McKean
Phoenix Islands
Kanton
Rawaki
Nikumaroro
Orona
Manra
Nanumea
Vaitupu
Nukufetau
Funafuti
Nukulaelae
Tokelau
Atafu
Fakaofo
Swains Island
Pukapuka
Nassau
Manihiki
Suwarrow
Rotuma
Îles Wallis
Îles de Hoorn
Savai'i
Upolu
Tutuila
Samoa Basin
Palmerston
Niue
Vava'u Group
Tofua
Louisville Ridge
SOUTH PACIFIC

Lambert Azimuthal Equal Area Projection

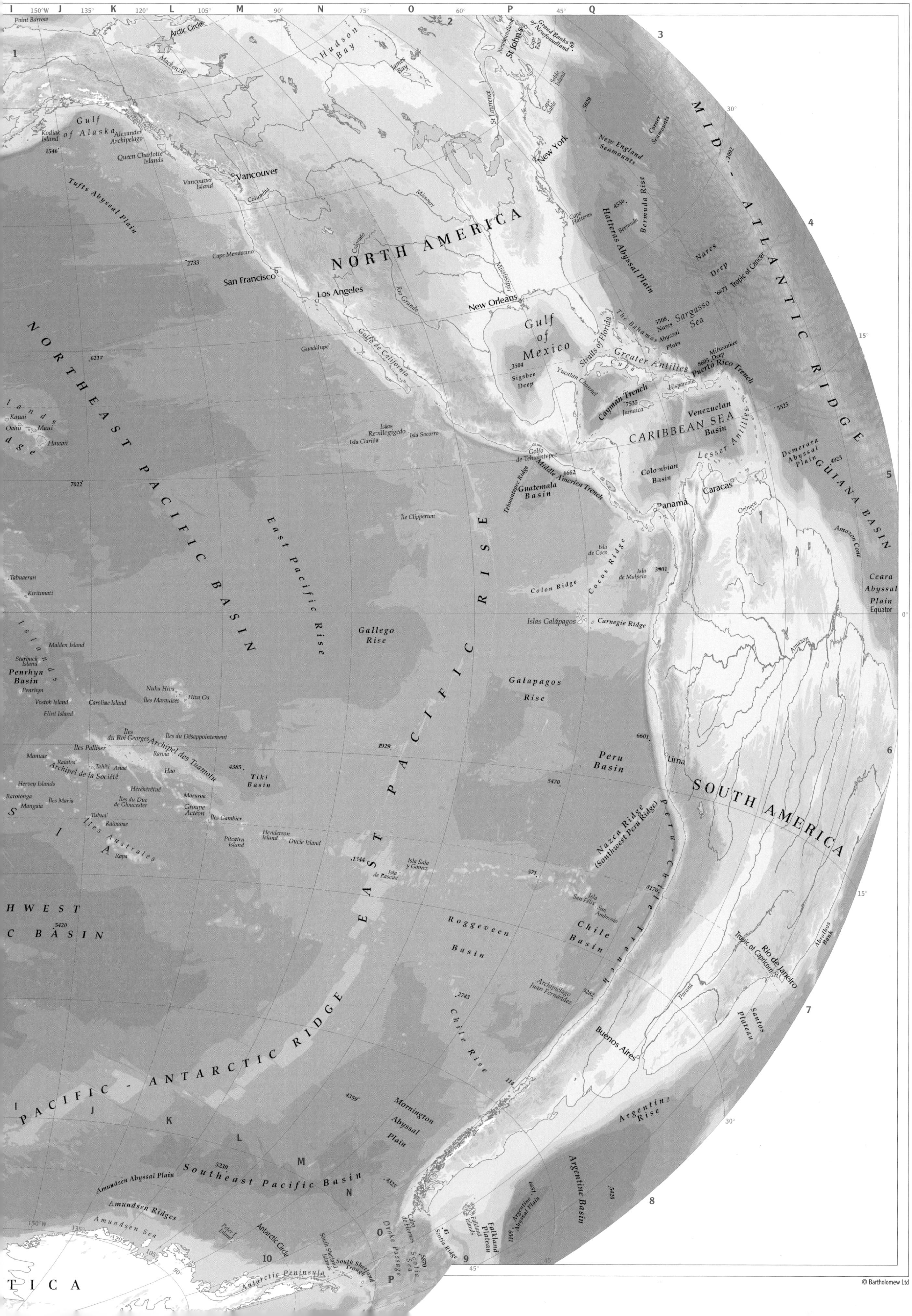
NORTH AMERICA
SOUTH AMERICA
NORTHEAST PACIFIC BASIN
EAST PACIFIC RISE
PACIFIC - ANTARCTIC RIDGE
MID - ATLANTIC RIDGE
GUIANA BASIN
Hudson Bay
James Bay
Gulf of Alaska
Kodiak Island
Alexander Archipelago
Queen Charlotte Islands
Vancouver Island
Vancouver
Columbia
Tufts Abyssal Plain
Cape Mendocino
San Francisco
Los Angeles
Colorado
Rio Grande
Missouri
Mississippi
New Orleans
Golfo de California
Guadalupe
Gulf of Mexico
Sigsbee Deep
Yucatan Channel
Straits of Florida
The Bahamas
Cuba
Greater Antilles
Hispaniola
Jamaica
Cayman Trench
Puerto Rico Trench
Milwaukee Deep
Nares Abyssal Plain
Sargasso Sea
Nares Deep
Tropic of Cancer
Hatteras Abyssal Plain
Cape Hatteras
Bermuda
Bermuda Rise
New England Seamounts
Corner Seamounts
New York
St Lawrence
St John's
Grand Banks of Newfoundland
Cape Sable
Sable Island
Arctic Circle
Mackenzie
Point Barrow
Venezuelan Basin
CARIBBEAN SEA
Lesser Antilles
Colombian Basin
Caracas
Panamá
Orinoco
Demerara Abyssal Plain
Amazon Cone
Ceara Abyssal Plain
Equator
Amazon
Golfo de Tehuantepec
Middle America Trench
Tehuantepec Ridge
Guatemala Basin
Isla de Coco
Cocos Ridge
Isla de Malpelo
Colon Ridge
Islas Galápagos
Carnegie Ridge
Islas Revillagigedo
Isla Clarión
Isla Socorro
Île Clipperton
Gallego Rise
Galapagos Rise
Kauai
Oahu
Maui
Hawaii
Tabuaeran
Kiritimati
Malden Island
Starbuck Island
Penrhyn Basin
Penrhyn
Vostok Island
Caroline Island
Flint Island
Nuku Hiva
Hiva Oa
Îles Marquises
Îles du Roi Georges
Îles du Désappointement
Îles Palliser
Archipel des Tuamotu
Raroia
Hao
Manuae
Raiatea
Tahiti
Anaa
Archipel de la Société
Hervey Islands
Rarotonga
Mangaia
Îles Maria
Hérêhérêtue
Îles du Duc de Gloucester
Moruroa
Groupe Actéon
Îles Gambier
Tubuai
Raivavae
Îles Australes
Rapa
Pitcairn Island
Henderson Island
Ducie Island
Tiki Basin
Isla Sala y Gómez
Isla de Pascua
Peru Basin
Lima
Nazca Ridge (Southwest Peru Ridge)
Peru-Chile Trench
Isla San Félix
San Ambrosio
Chile Basin
Roggeveen Basin
Archipiélago Juan Fernández
Chile Rise
Buenos Aires
Paraná
Rio de Janeiro
Tropic of Capricorn
Abrolhos Bank
Santos Plateau
Argentine Rise
Argentine Basin
Argentine Abyssal Plain
Falkland Plateau
Falkland Islands
Scotia Ridge
Scotia Sea
Drake Passage
Cabo de Hornos
South Shetland Islands
South Shetland Trough
Antarctic Peninsula
Antarctic Circle
Peter I Island
Amundsen Sea
Amundsen Ridges
Amundsen Abyssal Plain
Southeast Pacific Basin
Mornington Abyssal Plain
HWEST
C BASIN
TICA
© Bartholomew Ltd

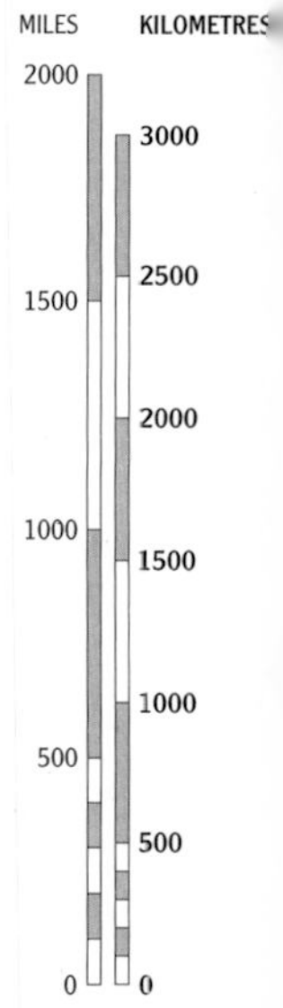
MILES
KILOMETRES
2000
1500
1000
500
0
3000
2500
2000
1500
1000
500
0

1:48 000 000

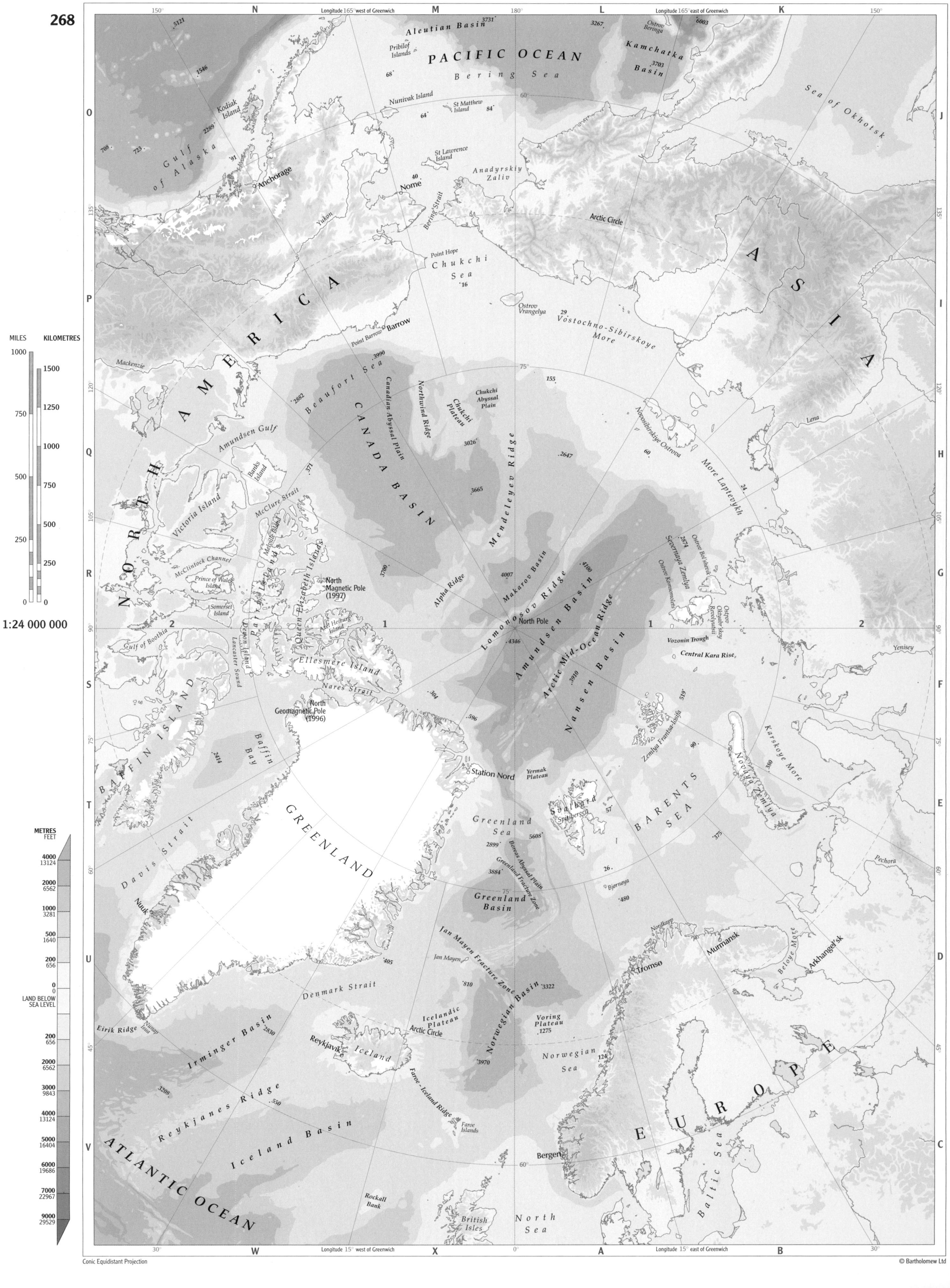

Longitude 165° west of Greenwich
Longitude 165° east of Greenwich
Longitude 15° west of Greenwich
Longitude 15° east of Greenwich
PACIFIC OCEAN
Bering Sea
Aleutian Basin
Pribilof Islands
Kamchatka Basin
Ostrov Beringa
Sea of Okhotsk
Nunivak Island
St Matthew Island
St Lawrence Island
Anadyrskiy Zaliv
Kodiak Island
Gulf of Alaska
Anchorage
Nome
Bering Strait
Yukon
Arctic Circle
Point Hope
Chukchi Sea
Ostrov Vrangelya
Vostochno-Sibirskoye More
ASIA
NORTH AMERICA
Point Barrow
Barrow
Mackenzie
Beaufort Sea
Canadian Abyssal Plain
Northwind Ridge
Chukchi Plateau
Chukchi Abyssal Plain
CANADA BASIN
Mendeleyev Ridge
Novosibirskiye Ostrova
More Laptevykh
Lena
Amundsen Gulf
Banks Island
Victoria Island
McClure Strait
McClintock Channel
Prince of Wales Island
Somerset Island
Melville Island
Queen Elizabeth Islands
North Magnetic Pole (1997)
Alpha Ridge
Makarov Basin
Lomonosov Ridge
North Pole
Amundsen Basin
Arctic Mid-Ocean Ridge
Nansen Basin
Severnaya Zemlya
Ostrov Bol'shevik
Ostrov Komsomolets
Ostrov Oktyabr'skoy Revolyutsii
Vozonin Trough
Central Kara Rise
Yenisey
Gulf of Boothia
Devon Island
Lancaster Sound
Axel Heiberg Island
Ellesmere Island
Nares Strait
North Geomagnetic Pole (1996)
BAFFIN ISLAND
Baffin Bay
Station Nord
Yermak Plateau
Zemlya Frantsa-Iosifa
Novaya Zemlya
Karskoye More
Svalbard
Spitsbergen
BARENTS SEA
GREENLAND
Greenland Sea
Boreas Abyssal Plain
Greenland Fracture Zone
Greenland Basin
Bjørnøya
Pechora
Davis Strait
Nuuk
Jan Mayen Fracture Zone
Jan Mayen
Nordkapp
Murmansk
Tromsø
Beloye More
Arkhangel'sk
Denmark Strait
Norwegian Basin
Voring Plateau
Icelandic Plateau
Arctic Circle
Eirik Ridge
Irminger Basin
Reykjavík
Iceland
Norwegian Sea
EUROPE
Faroe-Iceland Ridge
Faroe Islands
Reykjanes Ridge
Iceland Basin
ATLANTIC OCEAN
Bergen
Baltic Sea
Rockall Bank
British Isles
North Sea
MILES
KILOMETRES
1:24 000 000
METRES
FEET
LAND BELOW SEA LEVEL

GLOSSARY

A

Geographical term	Language	Meaning
-á	Icelandic	river
-å	Danish	river
Āb	Farsi	river
Abajo	Spanish	lower
Abbaye	French	abbey
Abhainn	Gaelic	river
Abyār	Arabic	wells
Açude	Portuguese	reservoir
Adası	Azeri, Turkish	island
Adrar	Berber	hills, mountains
Agia, Agios	Greek	saint
Agioi	Greek	saints
Aiguille	French	peak
Aïn, 'Aïn, 'Aîn, Aïn, 'Aïn	Arabic	spring, well
Akra	Greek	cape, point
Ala-	Finnish	lower
Allt	Gaelic	river
Alpi	Italian	mountain range
Alpe	Slovene	mountain range
Alpen	German	mountain range
Alpes	French	mountain range
Alt-	German	old
Alta	Italian, Portuguese, Spanish	upper
Altiplanicie	Spanish	high plain
Alto	Italian, Portuguese, Spanish	upper
Alto	Spanish	summit
-älv, -älven	Swedish	river
Ano	Greek	upper
Anou, Ânou	Berber	well
Anse	French	bay
Ao	Thai	bay
Archipel	French	archipelago
Archipiélago	Spanish	archipelago
Arenas	Spanish	sands
Argelancts'	Armenian	reserve
Arkhipelag	Russian	archipelago
Arquipélago	Portuguese	archipelago
Arrecife	Spanish	reef
Arriba	Spanish	upper
Arroio	Portuguese	watercourse
Arroyo	Spanish	watercourse
Augstiene	Latvian	hill region
Aust-	Norwegian	east, eastern
Austur-	Icelandic	east, eastern
Avtonomnaya, Avtonomnyy	Russian	autonomous
Āw	Kurdish	river
'Ayn	Arabic	spring, waterhole, well

B

Geographical term	Language	Meaning
Baai, -baai	Afrikaans, Dutch	bay
Bāb	Arabic	strait
Bad	German	spa
Badia	Catalan	bay
Bādiyah	Arabic	desert
Bælt	Danish	strait
Bagh	Gaelic	bay
Bahia	Portuguese	bay
Bahía	Spanish	bay
Bahr, Baḩr, Baḩr	Arabic	bay, lake, canal, river, watercourse
Bahra, Baḩra	Arabic	lagoon, lake
Baía	Portuguese	bay
Baie	French	bay
Baixa, Baixo	Portuguese	lower
Baja	Spanish	lower
Bajja	Maltese	bay
Bajo	Spanish	depression, lower
Bālā	Farsi	upper
Ban	Laotian, Thai	village
Banc	Welsh	hill
Banco	Spanish	shoal
Bandao	Chinese	peninsula
Bandar	Arabic, Farsi, Somali	anchorage, inlet, port, harbour
Bandar	Malay	port, town
Banī	Arabic	desert
Banjaran	Malay	mountain range
Baraj, Barajı	Turkish	dam
Barat	Indonesian, Malay	west, western
Barra	Portuguese, Spanish	sandbank, sandbar, spit
Barrage	French	dam
Barragem	Portuguese	dam, reservoir
Barranco	Spanish	gorge, ravine
Baruun	Mongolian	west, western
Bas, Basse	French	lower
Bassin	French	basin
Bāţin, Baţn	Arabic	depression
-beek	Afrikaans, Dutch	river
Beg, Beag	Gaelic, Irish	small
Bei	Chinese	north, northern
bei	German	at, near
Beinn	Gaelic	mountain
Belogor'ye	Russian	mountain range
Ben	Gaelic	mountain
Bereg	Russian	coastal area
-berg, -berge	German, Norwegian, Swedish, Afrikaans	mountain, mountains
Besar	Indonesian, Malay	big
Bi'ār	Arabic	wells
Bir, Bi'r, Bîr	Arabic	waterhole, well
Birkat	Arabic	waterhole, well
-bjerg	Danish	hill
Boca	Portuguese, Spanish	mouth
Bodden	German	bay
Boğazı	Turkish	strait, pass
Bois	French	forest, wood
Boloto	Russian	marsh
Bol'shaya, Bol'shiye, Bol'shoy, Bol'shoye	Russian	big
-bong	Korean	mountain
Boquerón	Spanish	pass
Bory	Polish	woods
-botn	Norwegian	valley floor
-botten	Swedish	valley floor
Böyük	Azeri	big
Braţul	Romanian	arm, branch
-bre, -breen	Norwegian	glacier
Bredning	Danish	bay
Breg	Croatian, Serbian	hill
-bron	Afrikaans	spring, well
Brücke	German	bridge
Bucht	German	bay
Bugt	Danish	bay
-bugten	Danish	bay
Bukhta	Russian	bay
Bukit	Indonesian, Malay	hill, mountain
-bukt, -bukta	Norwegian	bay
-bukten	Swedish	bay
Bulag	Mongolian	spring
Bulak	Russian, Uighur	spring
Bum	Burmese	mountain
Burnu, Burun	Turkish	cape, point
Büyük	Turkish	big
Bwlch	Welsh	pass

C

Geographical term	Language	Meaning
Cabo	Portuguese, Spanish	cape, point
Cachoeira	Portuguese	waterfall
Caka	Tibetan	salt lake
Cala	Catalan, Italian	bay
Caleta	Spanish	inlet
Câmpia	Romanian	plain
Campo	Italian, Spanish	plain
Cañada, Cañadón	Spanish	ravine, gorge
Canal	French, Portuguese, Spanish	canal, channel
Caño	Spanish	river
Cañon	Spanish	canyon
Caol	Gaelic	hill
Cap	Catalan, French	cape, point
Capo	Italian	cape, point
Carn	Welsh	hill
Castell	Catalan	castle
Causse	French	limestone plateau
Çay, -çay, Çayı, -çayı	Azeri, Turkish	river
Cayo	Spanish	island
Cefn	Welsh	hill, ridge
Cerro	Spanish	hill, mountain, peak
Česká, České, Český	Czech	Czech
Chaco	Spanish	plain
Chāh	Farsi	river
Chaîne	French	mountain range
Cham	Kurdish	river
Chapada	Portuguese	hills, uplands
Château	French	castle, palace
Chau	Chinese	island
Chaung	Burmese	river
Chāy	Kurdish	river
Chhu	Dzongkha (Bhutan)	river
Chiang	Thai	town
Chink	Russian	hill range
Chiyā	Kurdish	mountain, hill range
Chott	Arabic	salt lake
Chuan	Chinese	river
Chuŏr Phnum	Cambodian	mountain range
Ci	Indonesian	river
Ciénaga	Spanish	marshy lake
Cima	Italian	peak
Cime	French	peak
Città	Italian	city
Ciudad	Spanish	town, city
Cnoc	Gaelic	hill
Co	Tibetan	lake
Col	French	pass
Collado	Spanish	mountain
Colle	Italian	pass
Colline	French	hill
Cona	Tibetan	lake
Cordillera	Spanish	mountain range
Corno	Italian	peak
Coronel	Spanish	colonel
Costa	Catalan, Italian, Portuguese, Spanish	coastal area
Côte	French	coast, hill region, slope
Coutada	Portuguese	reserve
Coxilha	Portuguese	mountain pasture
Cratère	French	crater
Creag	Gaelic	mountain
Cruz	Spanish	cross
Cu Lao	Vietnamese	island
Cuchilla	Spanish	mountain range
Cuenca	Spanish	deep valley, river basin
Cueva	Spanish	cave
Cumbre	Spanish	mountain
-cun	Chinese	village

D

Geographical term	Language	Meaning
Da	Chinese	big
Da	Vietnamese	river
Dağ, Dağı	Azeri, Turkish	hill(s), mountain(s)
Dāgh	Farsi	mountain(s)
Dağları	Turkish	mountains
-dake	Japanese	hill, mountain
-dal	Afrikaans, Danish, Swedish	valley
-dal, -dalen	Norwegian	valley
-dalur	Icelandic	valley
-dan	Korean	cape, point
Danau	Indonesian, Malay	lake
Dao	Chinese	island
Đao	Vietnamese	island
Daqq	Farsi	salt flat, salt lake
-dara	Tajik	river
Darreh	Farsi	valley
Dar'ya	Russian	river
Daryācheh	Farsi	lake
Dashan	Chinese	mountain
Dasht	Farsi	desert
Dataran Tinggi	Malay	plateau
Davan	Kazakh	pass
Dawḩat	Arabic	bay
Dayr	Arabic	monastery
Dealul	Romanian	hill, mountain
Dealurile	Romanian	hills
Deh	Farsi	village
Deir	Arabic	monastery
Denizi	Turkish	sea
Deresi	Turkish	river
Desierto	Spanish	desert
Détroit	French	channel
-diep	Dutch	channel
Dingzi	Chinese	hill, small mountain
Djebel	Arabic	mountain
-do	Korean	island
Dolna, Dolni	Bulgarian	lower
Dolna, Dolne, Dolny	Polish	lower
Dolní	Czech	lower
Dong	Chinese	east, eastern
-dong	Korean	village
Donja, Donji	Croatian, Serbian	lower
Dorf	German	village
-dorp	Afrikaans, Dutch	village
Druim	Gaelic	hill, mountain
Dund	Mongolian	middle, central
Düzü	Azeri	plain
-dyngja	Icelandic	hill, mountain
Dzüün	Mongolian	east, eastern

E

Geographical term	Language	Meaning
Eilean	Gaelic	island
-elv, -elva	Norwegian	river
Embalse	Spanish	reservoir
'Emeq	Hebrew	plain
Ensenada	Spanish	bay
Erg, 'Erg, 'Erg	Arabic	sand dunes
Eski	Turkish	old
Estany	Catalan	pond
Estero	Spanish	estuary, inlet, lagoon
Estrada	Spanish	bay
Estrecho	Spanish	strait
Étang	French	lagoon, lake
-ey, -eyjar	Icelandic	island, islands
-eyri	Icelandic	sandbar
ežeras	Lithuanian	lake
ezers	Latvian	lake

F

Geographical term	Language	Meaning
Falaise	French	cliff, escarpment
Farihy	Malagasy	lake
Fayḑat	Arabic	waterhole
-fell	Icelandic	hill, mountain
Fels	German	rock
Feng	Chinese	mountain
Fiume	Italian	river

Geographical term	Language	Meaning
-fjäll, -fjällen, -fjället	Swedish	hill(s), mountain(s)
-fjallgarður	Icelandic	mountains
-fjara	Icelandic	beach
-fjell, -fjellet	Norwegian	mountain
-fjöll	Icelandic	hill(s), mountain(s)
Fjord, -fjord, -fjorden	Danish, Norwegian, Swedish	fjord
-fjörður	Icelandic	fjord
Fliegu	Maltese	channel
-fljót	Icelandic	river
-flói	Icelandic	bay
-főcsatorna	Hungarian	canal
Foel	Welsh	hill
Förde	German	inlet
Forêt	French	forest
Forst	German	forest
-foss	Icelandic	waterfall
-foss, -fossen	Norwegian	rapids, waterfall
Fuente	Spanish	source, well
Fulayj	Arabic	watercourse

G

Geographical term	Language	Meaning
-gan	Japanese	rock
Gang	Dzongkha (Bhutan)	mountain
Gang	Chinese	bay, river
-gang	Korean	river
Gaoyuan	Chinese	plateau
Gardaneh	Farsi	pass
-gat	Dutch	channel
-gata	Japanese	inlet, lagoon, lake
Gau	German	district
Gave	French	torrent
-gawa	Japanese	river
Gebel	Arabic	mountain
Gebergte	Dutch	mountain range
Gebiet	German	district, region
Gebirge	German	mountains
Geodha	Gaelic	inlet
Gezâ'ir	Arabic	islands
Gezirat	Arabic	island
Ghard	Arabic	sand dunes
Ghubba	Arabic	bay
Gjiri	Albanian	bay
Gletscher	German	glacier
Gobernador	Spanish	governor
Gobi	Mongolian	desert
Gol	Mongolian	river
Göl	Azeri	lake
Golets	Russian	mountain
Golf	Catalan	gulf
Golfe	French	bay, gulf
Golfo	Italian, Spanish	bay, gulf
Gölü	Azeri, Turkish	lake
Gora	Bulgarian, Croatian, Russian, Serbian	mountain(s)
Gorges	French	gorge
Górka	Polish	hill
Gornja, Gornje, Gornji	Croatian, Serbian	upper
Gorno-	Russian	mountainous
Gory	Russian	mountains
Góry	Polish	mountains
Gou	Chinese	river
Graben	German	trench
-grad	Bulgarian, Croatian, Russian, Serbian	town
Grand, Grande	French	big
-gród	Polish	town
Groot	Afrikaans, Dutch	big
Gross, Grosse, Grossen, Grosser (also Groß-)	German	big
Grotta	Italian	cave
Grotte	French	cave
Grotte	Italian	caves
Groupe	French	group
Grund	German	ground, valley
Gruppo	Italian	group
Gryada	Russian	mountains
Guan	Chinese	pass
Guba	Russian	bay, gulf
Gubed	Somali	bay
-guntō	Japanese	islands
Gunung	Indonesian, Malay	mountain
Guri	Albanian	peak

H

Geographical term	Language	Meaning
Ḩafar	Arabic	wells
Hafen	German	port, harbour
Haff	German	bay
Hai	Chinese	lake, sea
Haixia	Chinese	channel, strait
-háls	Icelandic	ridge
-halvøya	Norwegian	peninsula
Hamada, Hammada	Arabic	plateau
-hamn	Norwegian, Swedish	port, harbour
-hamrar	Icelandic	cliffs
Hāmūn	Farsi	marsh, salt pan
-hantō	Japanese	peninsula
Har	Hebrew	mountain
Hara	Belorussian	hill
Hardt	German	wooded hills
Ḩarrat, Ḩarrāt	Arabic	lava field
Hassi	Arabic	well
-haug, -haugen	Norwegian	hill
-havn	Danish, Faroese, Norwegian	bay, harbour, port
Hawr	Arabic	lake, impermanent lake, marsh
Häyk'	Amharic	lake
He	Chinese	river
-hegység	Hungarian	hills, mountains
-hei	Norwegian	heath, moor
-heide	Dutch	heath, marsh
Heide	German	heath, moor
-heiði	Icelandic	heath
Helodrano	Malagasy	bay
Higashi-	Japanese	east, eastern
-hisar	Turkish	castle
Ḩişn	Arabic	fort
Hka	Burmese	river
-hnjúkur	Icelandic	hill
-ho	Korean	lake
-hø	Norwegian	peak
Hoch	German	high
Hoek	Dutch	cape, point
-höfði	Icelandic	hill, mountain
-höfn	Icelandic	cove
Hög	Swedish	height, high
-högda	Norwegian	height
Höhe	German	height
Hohen-	German	high
Hoi, Hoi Hap	Chinese	bay, channel, harbour, inlet
-høj, -høje	Danish	hill, hills
Hon	Vietnamese	island
Hoog	Dutch	high
Hora, Hory	Czech, Ukrainian	mountain(s)
-horn	Icelandic	cape, point, peak
Horn, -horn	German	mountain, peak
Horná, Horné, Horní, Horný	Czech	upper
Ḩorvot	Hebrew	ruins
-hot	Mongolian	town
-hrad	Czech	town
-hraun	Icelandic	lava field
Hu	Chinese	lake

I

Geographical term	Language	Meaning
Idd	Arabic	well
Île	French	island
Ilha, Ilhéu	Portuguese	island
Illa	Catalan	island
im	German	in
imeni	Russian	in the name of
Inish	Irish	island
Insel, Inseln	German	island, islands
Insula	Romanian	island
Irq, 'Irq	Arabic	hill, sand dune, sand dunes
Isla	Spanish	island
Iso-	Finnish	big
Isola, Isole	Italian	island, islands
Isolte	Catalan	island
Isthme	French	isthmus
Istmo	Spanish	isthmus
-iwa	Japanese	island

J

Geographical term	Language	Meaning
Jabal	Arabic	mountain
järv	Estonian	lake
-järvi	Finnish	lake
Jasiired	Somali	island
Jaun-	Latvian	new
-jaure	Lappish	lake
Jazīrah, Jazīreh, Jazīrat	Arabic	island
Jbel, Jebel	Arabic	mountain
Jezero, jezero	Croatian, Serbian, Slovene	lake
Jezioro	Polish	lake
Jiang	Chinese	river
Jiao	Chinese	cape, point
Jibāl	Arabic	mountains
-jima	Japanese	island
Jing	Chinese	well
-jõgi	Estonian	river
-joki	Finnish	river
-jokka	Lappish	river
-jökull, jökullen	Icelandic, Norwegian	glacier, ice cap

K

Geographical term	Language	Meaning
Kaap	Afrikaans	cape, point
-kai	Japanese	bay, channel
-kaigan	Japanese	coastal area
-kaikyō	Japanese	channel, strait
Kali	Indonesian, Malay	river
kalnas, kalnis	Lithuanian	hill
Kalns	Latvian	hill
Kamen'	Russian	rock
Kamm	German	ridge, crest
Kâmpóng	Cambodian	town, village
-kanaal	Dutch	canal
Kanal	German, Russian	canal
Kanał	Polish	canal
Kanalı	Azeri	canal
Kaôh	Cambodian	island
Kap	Danish	cape, point
Kapp	Norwegian	cape, point
Karang	Indonesian, Malay	reef
Kato	Greek	lower
Kavīr	Farsi	salt desert
-kawa	Japanese	river
Kecil	Indonesian, Malay	small
K'edi	Georgian	hills
Kefar	Hebrew	village
Kepi	Albanian	cape, point
Kepulauan	Indonesian	islands
Keski-	Finnish	middle, central
Khabrah, Khabrat	Arabic	impermanent lake
Khalīg, Khalīj	Arabic	bay, gulf
Khao	Thai	peak
Khashm	Arabic	hill
Khawr	Arabic	bay, channel
Khor, Khōr	Arabic	bay
Khowr	Farsi	bay, inlet
Khrebet	Russian	mountain range
Kis-	Hungarian	small
Kita-	Japanese	north, northern
Klein	Afrikaans	small
Klein, Kleine, Kleiner	German	small
Klint	Danish	cliff
-kloof	Afrikaans	pass
Knock	Irish	hill
-ko	Japanese	lake
Ko	Thai	island
-kōchi, -kōgen	Japanese	plateau
Koh	Farsi	mountain
Kok	Chinese	cape, point
Köl	Kazakh, Kyrgyz	lake
Kolpos	Greek	gulf
Koog	German	polder (reclaimed land)
-kop	Afrikaans	hill, mountain
Kopf	German	hill
Körfezi	Turkish	bay, gulf
kõrgustik	Estonian	upland
Kosa	Russian, Ukrainian	spit
Kou	Chinese	river mouth
-köy	Turkish	village
Kraj	Croatian, Czech, Polish, Serbian	region
Krajobrazowy	Polish	regional
Kray	Russian	territory
Kryazh	Russian	hills, ridge
Kuala	Malay	river mouth
Küçük	Turkish	small
Kuduk	Uighur	well
Kūh	Farsi	mountain
Kūhhā	Farsi	mountain range
Kul'	Russian	lake
-kŭl	Tajik	lake
-küla	Estonian	village
Kum	Russian	sandy desert
-kundo	Korean	islands
Kuppe	German	hill top
kurk	Estonian	channel, strait
K'vemo	Georgian	upper
-kvísl, kvíslar	Icelandic	river, rivers
-kylä	Finnish	village
Kyun	Burmese	island

L

Geographical term	Language	Meaning
La	Tibetan	pass
Lac	French	lake
Lacul	Romanian	lake
Laem	Thai	cape, point
Lago	Italian, Portuguese, Spanish	lake
Lagoa	Portuguese	lagoon
Laguna	Spanish	lagoon, lake
Lagune	French	lagoon
laht	Estonian	bay
-laid	Estonian	island
Lam	Thai	river
Län	Swedish	county
Land	German	province
Lande	French	heath, sandy moor
Las	Polish	wood, forest
Laut	Indonesian, Malay	sea
Lerr	Armenian	mountain
Lerrnashght'a	Armenian	mountains
Lich	Armenian	lake
Liedao	Chinese	islands
Liel-	Latvian	big
Lille	Danish, Norwegian	small
Liman	Russian	bay, lagoon, lake
Limni	Greek	lagoon, lake
Limnothalassa	Greek	inlet, lagoon
Ling	Chinese	mountain range
Liqeni	Albanian	lake
Llano	Spanish	plain, prairie
Llyn	Welsh	lake
Loch, Lochan	Gaelic	lake, small lake
Lohatanjona	Malagasy	cape, point
Loi	Burmese	mountain
looduskaitseala	Estonian	reserve
Luonnonpuisto	Finnish	nature reserve
-luoto	Finnish	rocky island
Lyman	Ukrainian	bay, lake

M

Geographical term	Language	Meaning
Macizo	Spanish	mountain range
Madh	Albanian	big
Madīnat	Arabic	town
Mae, Mae Nam	Thai	river
mägi	Estonian	hill
Măgura	Romanian	hill, mountain
Maḩaţţat	Arabic	station
Maja	Albanian	mountain
Mal	Albanian	mountain(s)
Mala	Croatian, Serbian	small
Malá	Czech, Slovak	small
Mali	Albanian	mountain
Mali	Croatian, Serbian, Ukrainian	small
Malo	Croatian, Serbian	small
Maloye	Russian	small
Maly, Malyya	Belorussian	small
-man	Korean	bay
Mar	Spanish	lagoon, lake
Marais	French	marsh, swamp
Mare	Italian	sea
Mare	Romanian	big
marios	Lithuanian	lake
Marsa	Arabic	anchorage, bay, inlet
Marsch	German	fen, marsh
Masabb	Arabic	estuary
Massif	French	mountains, upland
Ma'ţan	Arabic	well
Mayor	Spanish	higher, larger
Maz-	Latvian	small
Meall	Gaelic	hill, mountain
Meer	Dutch, German	lake
Mega, Megalo-	Greek	big
Men	Chinese	gate

Geographical term	Language	Meaning
Menor	Portuguese, Spanish	smaller, lesser
Mersa	Arabic	anchorage, inlet
Mesa, Meseta	Spanish	tableland
Mesto	Croatian, Serbian	town
Město	Czech	town
Mets	Armenian	big
Mezzo	Italian	middle, central
Miao	Chinese	temple
Miasto	Polish	town
Mic, Mica	Romanian	small
Mikra, Mikri	Greek	small
Mīnā'	Arabic	port, harbour
Minami-	Japanese	south, southern
-mine	Japanese	mountain
-misaki	Japanese	cape, point
Mishāsh	Arabic	well
Mittel-, Mitten-	German	middle, central
Moel	Welsh	hill
Monasterio	Spanish	monastery
Moni	Greek	monastery
Mont	French	hill, mountain
Montagna	Italian	mountain
Montagne	French	mountain
Monte	Italian, Portuguese, Spanish	hill, mountain
Monti	Italian	mountains
Moor	German	marsh, moor, swamp
Moos	German	marsh, moss
More	Russian	sea
Mörön	Mongolian	river
Morro	Portuguese	hill
Morro	Spanish	cape, point
-mose	Danish	marsh, moor
Moyen	French	middle, central
Mt'a	Georgian	mountain
Muang	Laotian, Thai	town
Muara	Indonesian, Malay	estuary
Mui	Vietnamese	cape, point
Mun	Chinese	channel
Munții	Romanian	mountains
Mynydd	Welsh	mountain
-mýri	Icelandic	marsh
Mys	Russian	cape, point

N

Geographical term	Language	Meaning
na	Croatian, Czech, Russian, Serbian, Slovak, Slovene	on
Nacional	Portuguese, Spanish	national
nacionalinis	Lithuanian	national
nad	Czech, Polish, Slovak	above, over
-nada	Japanese	bay, gulf
Nafūd	Arabic	desert, sand dunes
Nagor'ye	Russian	mountains, plateau
Nagy-	Hungarian	big
Nahr	Arabic	river
Nakhon	Thai	town
Nakrdzali	Georgian	reserve
Nam	Burmese, Laotian	river
Nam	Korean, Vietnamese	south, southern
Nan	Chinese	south, southern
Nanshan	Chinese	mountain range
Narodowy	Polish	national
Nationaal	Dutch	national
Naturreservat	Norwegian, Swedish	nature reserve
Natuurreservaat	Dutch	nature reserve
Naviglio	Italian	canal
Nawa-	Urdu	new
Nazionale	Italian	national
Neder-	Dutch	lower
Nehri	Turkish	river
Nei	Chinese	inner
Nek	Afrikaans	pass
-nes	Icelandic	cape, point
Neu-	German	new
Neuf, Neuve	French	new
Nevado, Nevada	Spanish	snow-covered mountain(s)
Nieder-	German	lower
Nieuw, Nieuwe, Nieuwer	Dutch	new
nina	Estonian	cape, point
Nishi-	Japanese	west, western
Nizhneye, Nizhniy, Nizhniye, Nizhnyaya	Russian	lower
Nizina	Belorussian	lowland
Nízke	Slovak	low
Nizmennost'	Russian	lowland
Nižní	Czech	lower
Nižný	Slovak	lower
Noguera	Catalan	river
Noord	Dutch	north, northern
Nord	French, German	north, northern
Nord-, Nordre	Danish	north, northern
Norður	Icelandic	north, northern
Norra	Swedish	north, northern
Nørre	Danish	north, northern
Norte	Portuguese, Spanish	north, northern
Nos	Bulgarian, Russian	cape, point, spit
Nosy	Malagasy	island
Nou	Romanian	new
Nouveau, Nouvelle	French	new
Nova	Bulgarian, Croatian, Portuguese, Serbian, Slovene, Ukrainian	new
Nová	Czech	new
Novaya	Russian	new
Nové	Czech, Slovak	new
Novi	Bulgarian, Croatian, Serbian, Ukrainian	new
Novo	Portuguese, Slovene	new
Novo-, Novoye	Russian	new
Novy	Belorussian	new
Nový	Czech	new
Novyy, Novyye	Russian, Ukrainian	new
Novyya	Belorussian	new
Nowa, Nowe, Nowy	Polish	new
Nueva, Nuevo	Spanish	new
-numa	Japanese	lake

Geographical term	Language	Meaning
-núpur	Icelandic	hill
Nur	Chinese, Mongolian	lake
Nuruu	Mongolian	mountain range
Nuur	Mongolian	lake
Ny-	Danish, Norwegian, Swedish	new

O

Geographical term	Language	Meaning
-ø	Danish	island
-ö	Swedish	island
oaivi, oaivve	Lappish	hill, mountain
Obanbari	Tajik	reservoir
Ober-	German	upper
Oblast'	Russian, Ukrainian	administrative division
-odde	Danish, Norwegian	cape, point
Oeste	Spanish	west, western
Okrug	Russian	administrative district
-ön	Swedish	island
Öndör-	Mongolian	upper
-oog	German	island
Oost, Ooster	Dutch	east, eastern
-öræfi	Icelandic	lava field
Oriental	Spanish	east, eastern
Ormos	Greek	bay
Oros	Greek	mountain
-ós	Icelandic	river mouth
Ost-	German	east, eastern
Øster-	Danish, Norwegian	east, eastern
Östra-	Swedish	east, eastern
Ostriv	Ukrainian	island
Ostrov, Ostrova	Russian	island, islands
Oud, Oude, Ouden, Ouder	Dutch	old
Oued	Arabic	watercourse
Ovası	Turkish	plain
Over-	Danish, Dutch	upper
Över-, Övre-	Norwegian, Swedish	upper
-oy	Faroese	island
Ozero	Russian, Ukrainian	lake

P

Geographical term	Language	Meaning
-pää	Finnish	hill
Pampa	Spanish	plain
Pantà	Catalan	reservoir
Pantanal	Portuguese	marsh
Pao	Chinese	small lake
Parbat	Urdu	mountain
Parc	French	park
Parc Naturel	French	nature reserve
Parco	Italian	park
parkas	Lithuanian	park
Parque	Portuguese, Spanish	park
-pas	Afrikaans	pass
Paso	Spanish	pass
Paß	German	pass
Passage	French	channel
Passe	French	channel
Passo	Italian	pass
Pasul	Romanian	pass
Pegunungan	Indonesian, Malay	mountain range
Pelabuhan	Malay	port, harbour
Pen	Welsh	hill
Peña	Spanish	cliff, rock
Pendi	Chinese	basin
Península	Spanish	peninsula
Péninsule	French	peninsula
Penisola	Italian	peninsula
Pereval	Russian	pass
Pervo-, Pervyy	Russian	first
Peski	Russian	desert
Petit, Petite	French	small
Phou	Laotian	mountain
Phu	Thai, Vietnamese	mountain
Phumĭ	Cambodian	town, village
Pic	Catalan, French	peak
Picacho	Spanish	peak
Pico	Spanish	peak
Pik	Russian	peak
Pingyuan	Chinese	plain
Pivostriv	Ukrainian	peninsula
Pizzo	Italian	peak
-plaat	Dutch	flat, sandbank, shoal
Plage	French	beach
Plaine	French	plain
Planalto	Portuguese	plateau
Planina	Bulgarian, Croatian, Serbian	mountain(s)
Platforma	Romanian	plateau
Plato	Bulgarian, Russian	plateau
Playa	Spanish	beach
Plaza	Spanish	market-place, square
Ploskogor'ye	Russian	plateau
Po	Chinese	lake
pod	Czech, Russian, Slovak	under, sub-, near
Podişul	Romanian	plateau
Pointe	French	cape, point
Pojezierze	Polish	area of lakes
Polje	Croatian, Serbian	plain
Poluostrov	Russian	peninsula
Pont	French	bridge
Ponta	Maltese, Portuguese	cape, point
Ponte	Portuguese	bridge
poolsaar	Estonian	peninsula
Porogi	Russian	rapids
Port	Catalan, French, Maltese, Russian	port, harbour
Portella	Italian	pass
Portillo	Spanish	gap, pass
Porto	Italian, Portuguese, Spanish	bay, port, harbour, pass
Pradesh	Hindi	state

Geographical term	Language	Meaning
Praia	Portuguese	beach, shore
Prêk	Cambodian	lake, river
près	French	near, beside
Presa	Spanish	reservoir
Presqu'île	French	peninsula
Pri-	Russian	near, by
Proliv	Russian	channel, strait
Protoka	Russian	channel, watercourse
Pueblo	Spanish	village
Puente	Spanish	bridge
Puerta	Spanish	narrow pass
Puerto	Spanish	pass, port, harbour
Puig	Catalan	hill, mountain
Puk-	Korean	north, northern
Pulau	Indonesian, Malay	island
Pulau-pulau	Indonesian, Malay	islands
Puncak	Indonesian, Malay	hill, mountain, summit
Punta	Italian, Spanish	cape, point
Punta	Italian	hill, mountain
Puntan	Marshallese	cape, point
Puy	French	peak

Q

Geographical term	Language	Meaning
Qā'	Arabic	depression, salt flat, impermanent lake
Qabr	Arabic	tomb
Qafa	Albanian	pass
Qala	Maltese	bay
Qalamat	Arabic	well
Qalti	Arabic	well
Qāret	Arabic	hill
Qatorkŭhi	Tajik	mountain range
Qi	Chinese	banner (administrative division)
Qiao	Chinese	bridge
Qiryat	Hebrew	town
Qolleh	Farsi	mountain
Qoor, Qooriga	Somali	bay
qoruğu	Azeri	reserve
Qu	Tibetan	river
Quan	Chinese	spring, well
Quebrada	Spanish	ravine, river
Qullai	Tajik	mountain
Qundao	Chinese	islands

R

Geographical term	Language	Meaning
Raas	Somali	cape, point
Rade	French	harbour
rags	Latvian	cape, point
Rambla	Catalan	river
Ramla	Maltese	bay, harbour
Ramlat	Arabic	sandy desert
-rani	Icelandic	spur
Ras	Arabic, Maltese	cape, point
Ra's	Arabic, Farsi	cape, point
Râs, Rās	Arabic	cape, point
Ravnina	Russian	plain
Récif	French	reef
Represa	Portuguese, Spanish	reservoir
Reserva	Portuguese, Spanish	reserve
Réserve de Faune, Réserve Faunique	French	wildlife reserve
Réserve Naturelle	French	nature reserve
Reshteh	Farsi	mountain range
Respublika	Russian	republic
-rettō	Japanese	island chain, island group
rezervatas	Lithuanian	reserve
-ri	Korean	village
Ri	Tibetan	mountain
Ría	Spanish	estuary, inlet, river mouth
Ribeirão, Ribeiro	Portuguese	river
Rio	Portuguese	river
Río	Spanish	river
Riserva	Italian	reserve
-rivier	Afrikaans	river
Riviera	Italian	coastal area
Rivière	French	river
Roca	Spanish	rock
Rocher	French	rock
Rt	Croatian, Serbian	cape, point
Rū, Rūbār	Kurdish	river
Rubh', Rubha	Gaelic	cape, point
Rūd, Rūdkhāneh	Farsi	river
Rujm	Arabic	hill

S

Geographical term	Language	Meaning
-saar	Estonian	island
-saari	Finnish	island
Sabkhat, Sabkhet	Arabic	impermanent lake, salt flat, salt marsh
Sadd, Saddat	Arabic	dam
Sagar, Sagara	Hindi	lake
Şaghīr, Şaghīr	Arabic	small
Şaḩrā'	Arabic	desert
-saki	Japanese	cape, point
Salar, Salina	Spanish	salt pan
Salto	Portuguese, Spanish	waterfall
San	Italian, Maltese, Portuguese, Spanish	saint
San	Laotian	mountain
-san	Japanese, Korean	mountain
-sanchi	Japanese	mountain range
-sandur	Icelandic	sandy area
Sankt	German, Russian	saint
-sanmaek	Korean	mountain range
-sanmyaku	Japanese	mountain range
Sant	Catalan	saint
Sant'	Italian	saint

Geographical term	Language	Meaning
Santa	Italian, Portuguese, Spanish	saint
Santo	Italian, Portuguese, Spanish	saint
São	Portuguese	saint
Sar	Kurdish	mountain
Sarīr	Arabic	desert
Satu	Romanian	village
Say	Kyrgyz	river
Schloß	German	castle, mansion
Şcoglio	Italian	reef, rock
Sebkha, Sebkhet	Arabic	salt flat, salt marsh
See, -see	German	lake
-şehir	Turkish	town
Selat	Indonesian, Malay	channel, strait
Selatan	Indonesian, Malay	south, southern
-selkä	Finnish	lake, open water, ridge
Selo	Croatian, Russian, Serbian	village
Selva	Portuguese, Spanish	forest
Semenanjung	Indonesian, Malay	peninsula
Seno	Spanish	bay, sound
Serra	Catalan, Portuguese	hills, mountains
Serranía	Spanish	mountain range
-seter	Norwegian	mountain pasture
-seto	Japanese	channel, strait
Severnaya, Severnoye, Severnyy, Severo-	Russian	north, northern
Sfântu	Romanian	saint
Sgeir	Gaelic	island
Sgor, Sgorach, Sgorr, Sgurr	Gaelic	hill
Shahr	Farsi	town
Sha'īb, Sha'īān	Arabic	watercourse
Shamo	Chinese	desert
Shan	Chinese	hill(s), mountain(s)
Shang	Chinese	next to, upper
Shankou	Chinese	pass
Sharm	Arabic	bay
Shaṭṭ	Arabic	estuary, river mouth, watercourse
Shën-	Albanian	saint
Shet'	Amharic	watercourse
Shi	Chinese	city
-shima	Japanese	island
-sho	Japanese	island
-shotō	Japanese	islands
Shui	Chinese	river
Shui Tong	Chinese	reservoir
Shuiku	Chinese	reservoir
Sierra	Spanish	mountain range
Silsiläsi	Azeri	hills
-sjø	Norwegian	lake
-sjö, -sjön	Swedish	lake
-sjór	Icelandic	lake
-sker	Icelandic	island
-skog	Norwegian	wood
Slieau	Manx	hill, mountain
Slieve	Irish	hill, mountain
Sloboda	Russian	large village
Sø	Danish, Norwegian	lake
Söder, Södra	Swedish	south, southern
Solonchak	Russian	salt lake
Sommet	French	peak, summit
Sønder-, Søndre	Danish	south, southern
Sông	Vietnamese	river
Sopka	Russian	hill, mountain, volcano
Sør-	Norwegian	south, southern
Sor	Russian	salt pan
sous	French	under
Sovkhoz	Russian	state farm
Spitze	German	peak
Sredna, Sredno	Bulgarian	middle, central
Sredne-, Sredneye, Sredniy, Srednyaya	Russian	middle, central
Sron	Gaelic	hill
Stac	Gaelic	hill, stack
-stad	Afrikaans, Norwegian, Swedish	town
-stadt	German	town
-staður	Icelandic	town
Stagno	Italian	lagoon, lake
Stara, Stari	Croatian, Serbian, Ukrainian	old
Stará, Staré, Starý	Czech	old
Staraya, Stary, Staryya	Belorussian	old
Staraya, Staroye, Staryy, Staryye	Russian	old
Stare, Staro-, Staryy	Ukrainian	old
Stausee	German	reservoir
Steno	Greek	strait
Step'	Russian	plain, steppe
Stob	Gaelic	hill, mountain
Stœng	Cambodian	river
Stór-, Stóra, Stóri	Icelandic	big
Stor, Stora	Swedish	big
Store	Danish	big
Strand	Danish, German	beach
-strand	Norwegian, Swedish	beach
Straße	German	street
Stretta	Italian	strait
-strönd	Icelandic	beach
Sud	French	south, southern
Süd-, Süder-	German	south, southern
Suður-	Icelandic	south, southern
Suid	Afrikaans	south, southern
-suidō	Japanese	channel, strait
Sul	Portuguese	south, southern
sul, sull'	Italian	on
Sund	Swedish	strait, sound
Sungai	Indonesian, Malay	river
-suo	Finnish	marsh, swamp
Superior	Spanish	upper
Sūq	Arabic	market
Sur	Spanish	south, southern
sur	French	on
Suur	Estonian	big
Sveti	Croatian, Serbian	saint
Syðra, Syðri	Icelandic	south, southern
sýsla	Icelandic	county
Szent-	Hungarian	saint
-sziget	Hungarian	island

T

Geographical term	Language	Meaning
-tag	Uighur	mountain
-take	Japanese	hill, mountain
Tal	German	valley
Tall	Arabic	hill
Tanjona	Malagasy	cape, point
Tanjong, Tanjung	Indonesian, Malay	cape, point
Tao	Chinese	island
Tassili	Berber	plateau
Tau	Russian	mountain(s)
Taung	Burmese	mountain
Tba	Georgian	lake
Techniti Limni	Greek	reservoir
tekojärvi	Finnish	reservoir
Tell	Arabic	hill, mountain
Teluk, Telukan	Indonesian, Malay	bay, gulf
Tengah	Indonesian, Malay	middle, central
Teniente	Spanish	lieutenant
Tepe, Tepesi	Turkish	hill, mountain
Terara	Amharic	mountain
Terre	French	land
Thale	Thai	lake
Thamad	Arabic	well
Tierra	Spanish	land
Timur	Indonesian, Malay	east, eastern
-tind, -tinden	Norwegian	peak
-tindar	Icelandic	peak
-tindur	Faroese, Icelandic	peak
Tir'at	Arabic	canal, river, watercourse
Tizi	Berber	pass
-tjåkkå	Lappish	mountain
-tjärro	Lappish	mountain
-tó	Hungarian	lake
-tō	Japanese	island
-to	Korean	island
-tōge	Japanese	pass
-tong	Korean	village
Tônlé	Cambodian	lake, river
Too	Kyrgyz	mountain range
-topp, -toppen	Norwegian	peak
T'ou	Chinese	cape, point
Tsentral'nyy	Russian	central
Tso	Tibetan	lake
Tsqalsats'avi	Georgian	reservoir
Tsui	Chinese	cape, point
Túnel	Spanish	tunnel
-tunturi	Finnish	treeless mountain

U

Geographical term	Language	Meaning
Über-	German	upper
-udden	Swedish	cape, point
Ugheltekhili	Georgian	pass
Új-	Hungarian	new
Ujung	Indonesian	cape, point
Unter-, unter	German	below, lower
'Uqlat	Arabic	well
-ura	Japanese	inlet
'Urayq, 'Urūq	Arabic	sand dunes
Ust'-, Ust'ye	Russian	river mouth
Utara	Indonesian, Malay	north, northern
Uttar	Hindi	north, northern
Uul	Mongolian	mountain range
Uval	Russian	hills
'Uyūn	Arabic	springs

V

Geographical term	Language	Meaning
v	Czech	in
-vaara, -vaarat	Finnish	hill(s), mountain(s)
Vaart, -vaart	Dutch	canal
-vaðall	Icelandic	inlet
-våg	Norwegian	bay
-vágur	Faroese	bay
Väike-	Estonian	small
väin	Estonian	bay, channel, strait
Val	French, Portuguese, Spanish	valley
Vale	Portuguese, Romanian	valley
Vall	Catalan, Spanish	valley
Valle	Italian, Spanish	valley
Vallée	French	valley
Valli	Italian	valleys
Vallon	French	small valley
Vârful	Romanian	hill, mountain
-város	Hungarian	town
-varre	Norwegian	mountain
Väster, Västra	Swedish	west, western
-vatn	Icelandic	lake
-vatn, -vatnet	Norwegian	lake
-vatten, -vattnet	Swedish	lake
Vaux	French	valleys
Vechi	Romanian	old
veehoidla	Estonian	lake
-veld	Afrikaans	field
Velha, Velho	Portuguese	old
Velika	Croatian, Slovene, Serbian	big
Velikaya, Velikiy, Velikiye	Russian	big
Velike	Slovene	big
Veliki	Croatian, Serbian	big
Velká, Velké, Velký	Czech	big
Veľká, Veľké, Veľký	Slovak	big
-vellir	Icelandic	plain
Velyka	Ukrainian	big
Verkhne-, Verkhneye, Verkhniy, Verkhnyaya	Russian	upper
-vesi	Finnish	lake, water
Viaduc	French	viaduct
-vidda	Norwegian	plateau
Vieja, Viejo	Spanish	old
Vieux	French	old
Vig	Danish	bay
-vík	Icelandic	bay
-vik	Norwegian	bay, inlet
Vila	Portuguese	small town
Ville	French	town
Vinh	Vietnamese	bay
-víz	Hungarian	river
-víztároló	Hungarian	reservoir
-vlei	Afrikaans	lake, salt pan
-vloer	Afrikaans	salt pan
Voblasts'	Belorussian	province
Vodaskhovishcha	Belorussian	reservoir
Vodná nádrž	Slovak	reservoir
Vodní nádrž	Czech	reservoir
Vodokhranilishche	Russian	reservoir
Vodoskhovyshche	Ukrainian	reservoir
-vogur	Icelandic	bay
Volcán	Spanish	volcano
Vostochno-, Vostochnyy	Russian	east, eastern
-vötn	Icelandic	lakes
Vozvyshennost'	Russian	hills, upland
Vozyera	Belorussian	lake
Vpadina	Russian	depression
Vrchovina	Czech	hills, mountain region
Vrŭkh	Bulgarian	hill, mountain
Vulkan	Russian	volcano
Vyalikaya, Vyalikaye, Vyaliki, Vyalikiya	Belorussian	big
Vyerkhnya	Belorussian	upper
Vysokaya, Vysokoye	Russian	upper

W

Geographical term	Language	Meaning
-waard	Dutch	polder (reclaimed land)
Wad	Dutch	sandflat
Wadi, Wâdi, Wādī	Arabic	watercourse
Wai	Chinese	outer
Wald	German	forest
Wan	Chinese	bay
-wan	Japanese	bay
Wand	German	cliff
Wasser	German	water
Wāw	Arabic	well
Webi	Somali	river
Wenz	Amharic	river, watercourse
Wielka, Wielki, Wielkie, Wielko-	Polish	big
-woud	Dutch	wood, forest
Wysoka, Wysoki, Wysokie	Polish	upper
Wyżna	Polish	lowland
Wzvyshsha	Belorussian	upland

X

Geographical term	Language	Meaning
Xé	Vietnamese	river
Xi	Chinese	river, west, western
Xia	Chinese	gorge, lower
Xian	Chinese	county
Xiao	Chinese	small

Y

Geographical term	Language	Meaning
Yam	Hebrew	lake, sea
-yama	Japanese	mountain
Yang	Chinese	channel
Yangi	Russian	new
Yarımadası	Azeri, Turkish	peninsula
Yazovir	Bulgarian	reservoir
Ye	Burmese	island
Yeni	Turkish	new
Yli-	Finnish	upper
Ynys	Welsh	island
Yoma	Burmese	mountain range
You	Chinese	right
Ytra-, Ytri-	Icelandic	outer
Ytre-	Norwegian	outer
Ytter-	Norwegian, Swedish	outer
Yuan	Chinese	spring
Yumco	Tibetan	lake
Yunhe	Chinese	canal
Yuzhno-, Yuzhnyy	Russian	south, southern

Z

Geographical term	Language	Meaning
Za-	Russian	behind, beyond
-zaki	Japanese	cape, point
Zalew	Polish	bay
Zaliv	Russian	bay, gulf, inlet
-zan	Japanese	mountain
Zand	Dutch	sandbank, sandhill
Zangbo	Tibetan	river
Zapadnaya, Zapadno-, Zapadnyy	Russian	west, western
Zapavyednik	Belorussian	reserve
Zapovednik	Russian	reserve
Zapovidnyk	Ukrainian	reserve
Zatoka	Polish, Ukrainian	bay, gulf, lagoon
-zee	Dutch	lake, sea
Zemlya	Russian	land
Zemo	Georgian	upper
Zhen	Chinese	town
Zhong	Chinese	middle, central
Zhou	Chinese	island
Zizhiqu	Chinese	autonomous region
Zuid, Zuider	Dutch	south, southern
Zuo	Chinese	left

INTRODUCTION TO THE INDEX

The index includes names shown on the maps in the Atlas of the World. Each entry includes the country or geographical area in which the feature is located, a page number and an alphanumeric reference. Additional details within the entries are explained below. Abbreviations used in the index are explained in the table below.

REFERENCING

Names are referenced by page number, the first element of each entry, and by a grid reference. The grid reference correlates to the alphanumeric values which appear within each map frame. These reflect the graticule on the map – the letter relates to longitude divisions, the number to latitude divisions.

Names are generally referenced to the largest scale map page on which they appear. For large geographical features, including countries, the reference is to the largest scale map on which the feature appears in its entirety, or on which the majority of it appears.

Rivers are referenced to their lowest downstream point – either their mouth or their confluence with another river. The river name will generally be positioned as close to this point as possible, but may not necessarily be in the same grid square.

ALTERNATIVE NAMES

Alternative names or name forms appear as cross-references and refer the user to the entry for the map form of the name.

For rivers with multiple names – for example those which flow through several countries – all alternative name forms are included within the main index entries, with details of the countries in which each form applies. Different types of name used are: alternative forms or spellings currently in use (alt.); English conventional name forms normally used in English-language contexts (conv.); and long names – full forms of names which are most commonly used in the abbreviated form.

ADMINISTRATIVE QUALIFIERS

Entries within the following countries include the main administrative division in which they occur: Australia, Canada, China, India, U.K., U.S.A. and Yugoslavia. Administrative divisions are also included to differentiate duplicate names – entries of exactly the same name and feature type within the one country – where these division names are shown on the maps. In such cases, duplicate names are alphabetized in the order of the administrative division names.

Additional qualifiers are included for names within selected geographical areas, to indicate more clearly their location. In particular, this has been applied to island nations to indicate the island group, or individual island, on which a feature occurs.

DESCRIPTORS

Entries, other than those for towns and cities, include a descriptor indicating the type of geographical feature. Descriptors are not included where the type of feature is implicit in the name itself, unless there is a town or city of exactly the same name.

INSETS

Entries relating to names appearing on insets are indicated by a small box symbol: ▫, followed by an index number if there is more than one inset on the page, or by a grid reference if the inset has its own alphanumeric values.

NAME FORMS AND ALPHABETICAL ORDER

Name forms are as they appear on the maps, with additional alternative forms included as cross-references. Names appear in full in the index, although they may appear in abbreviated form on the maps.

The Icelandic characters Þ and þ are transliterated and alphabetized as 'Th' and 'th'. The German character ß is alphabetized as 'ss'. Names beginning with Mac or Mc are alphabetized exactly as they appear. The terms Saint, Sainte, etc, are abbreviated to St, Ste, etc, but alphabetized as if in the full form.

Name form policies are explained in the Introduction to the Atlas (pp 66-67).

NUMERICAL ENTRIES

Entries beginning with numerals appear at the beginning of the index, in numerical order. Elsewhere, numerals appear before 'a'.

PERMUTED TERMS

Names beginning with generic, geographical terms are permuted – the descriptive term is placed after, and the index alphabetized by, the main part of the name. For example, Lake Superior is indexed as Superior, Lake; Mount Everest as Everest, Mount. This policy is applied to all languages. Permuting has not been applied to names of towns, cities or administrative divisions beginning with such geographical terms. These remain in their full form, for example, Lake Isabella, California, USA.

The definite article is not permuted in any language.

INDEX ABBREVIATIONS

A.C.T.	Australian Capital Territory
admin. dist.	administrative district
admin. div.	administrative division
admin. reg.	administrative region
Afgh.	Afghanistan
AK	Alaska
AL	Alabama
Alg.	Algeria
alt.	alternative name form
Alta	Alberta
Andhra Prad.	Andhra Pradesh
AR	Arkansas
Arg.	Argentina
Arun. Prad.	Arunachal Pradesh
Austr.	Australia
aut. comm.	autonomous community
aut. div.	autonomous division
aut. prov.	autonomous province
aut. reg.	autonomous region
aut. rep.	autonomous republic
AZ	Arizona
Azer.	Azerbaijan
b.	bay
Bangl.	Bangladesh
B.C.	British Columbia
B.I.O.T.	British Indian Ocean Territory
Bol.	Bolivia
Bos.-Herz.	Bosnia-Herzegovina
Bulg.	Bulgaria
c.	cape
CA	California
Can.	Canada
C.A.R.	Central African Republic
CO	Colorado
Col.	Colombia
conv.	conventional name form
CT	Connecticut
Czech Rep.	Czech Republic
DC	District of Columbia
DE	Delaware
Dem. Rep. Congo	Democratic Republic of Congo
depr.	depression
dept	department
des.	desert
Dom. Rep.	Dominican Republic
E.	East, Eastern
Equat. Guinea	Equatorial Guinea
esc.	escarpment
est.	estuary
Eth.	Ethiopia
Fin.	Finland
FL	Florida
for.	forest
Fr. Guiana	French Guiana
Fr. Polynesia	French Polynesia
g.	gulf
GA	Georgia
Gd Bahama	Grand Bahama
Ger	Germany
Guat.	Guatemala
hd	headland
Heilong.	Heilongjiang
HI	Hawaii
Hima. Prad.	Himachal Pradesh
H.K.	Hong Kong
Hond.	Honduras
i.	island
is	islands
IA	Iowa
ID	Idaho
IL	Illinois
imp. l.	impermanent lake
IN	Indiana
Indon.	Indonesia
isth	isthmus
Kazakh.	Kazakhstan
KS	Kansas
KY	Kentucky
Kyrg.	Kyrgyzstan
l.	lake
LA	Louisiana
lag.	lagoon
Lith	Lithuania
Lux.	Luxembourg
MA	Massachusetts
Madag.	Madagascar
Mach. Prad.	Madhya Pradesh
Mahar.	Maharashtra
Man.	Manitoba
Maur.	Mauritania
MD	Maryland
ME	Maine
Mex.	Mexico
MI	Michigan
MN	Minnesota
MO	Missouri
Moz.	Mozambique
MS	Mississippi
MT	Montana
mt.	mountain
mts	mountains
mun.	municipality
N.	North
N.B.	New Brunswick
NC	North Carolina
ND	North Dakota
NE	Nebraska
Neth.	Netherlands
Nfld.	Newfoundland
NH	New Hampshire
Nic.	Nicaragua
NJ	New Jersey
NM	New Mexico
N.S.	Nova Scotia
N.S.W.	New South Wales
N.T.	Northern Territory
NV	Nevada
N.W.T.	Northwest Territories
NY	New York
N.Z.	New Zealand
OH	Ohio
OK	Oklahoma
Ont.	Ontario
OR	Oregon
PA	Pennsylvania
Pak.	Pakistan
Para.	Paraguay
P.E.I.	Prince Edward Island
pen.	peninsula
Phil.	Philippines
plat.	plateau
P.N.G.	Papua New Guinea
Pol.	Poland
Port.	Portugal
pref.	prefecture
prov.	province
Qld	Queensland
Que.	Québec
r.	river
r. mouth	river mouth
reg.	region
Rep.	Republic
research stn	research station
resr	reservoir
rf	reef
RI	Rhode Island
Rus. Fed.	Russian Federation
S.	South
S.A.	South Australia
Sask.	Saskatchewan
SC	South Carolina
SD	South Dakota
sea chan.	sea channel
Sing.	Singapore
str.	strait
Switz.	Switzerland
Tajik.	Tajikistan
Tanz.	Tanzania
Tas.	Tasmania
terr.	territory
Thai.	Thailand
TN	Tennessee
Trin. and Tob.	Trinidad and Tobago
tun.	tunnel
Turkm.	Turkmenistan
TX	Texas
U.A.E.	United Arab Emirates
U.K.	United Kingdom
Ukr.	Ukraine
Uru.	Uruguay
U.S.A.	United States of America
UT	Utah
Uttar Prad.	Uttar Pradesh
Uzbek.	Uzbekistan
VA	Virginia
val.	valley
Venez.	Venezuela
Vic.	Victoria
vol.	volcano
vol. crater	volcanic crater
VT	Vermont
W.	West, Western
W.A.	Western Australia
WA	Washington
WI	Wisconsin
WV	West Virginia
WY	Wyoming
Y.T.	Yukon Territory
Yugo.	Yugoslavia

1

A

169 C3 Ahaus Ger.
168 E2 Ahausen Ger.
147 D4 Ahenny Rep. of Ireland
147 C5 Aherla Rep. of Ireland
147 D4 Aherlow r. Rep. of Ireland
217 □3a Ahibambo mt. Njazidja Comoros
182 D4 Ahigal Spain
182 D3 Ahigal de Villarino Spain
185 F3 Ahillo mt. Spain
184 E2 Ahillones Spain
80 F3 Ahimanawa Range mts North I. N.Z.
80 D1 Ahipara North I. N.Z.
114 D2 Ahiri Mahar. India
80 E3 Ahititi North I. N.Z.
138 F2 Ahja r. Estonia
220 B4 Ahklun Mountains AK U.S.A.
127 F3 Ahlat Turkey
170 F2 Ahlbeck Ger.
168 E3 Ahlden (Aller) Ger.
169 C4 Ahlen Ger.
168 E2 Ahlerstedt Ger.
168 D3 Ahlhorn Ger.
171 C4 Ahlsdorf Ger.
116 C5 Ahmadabad Gujarat India
128 B5 Aḥmad al Bāqir, Jabal mt. Jordan
129 E4 Āhmādbäyli Azer.
114 B2 Ahmadnagar Mahar. India
114 C2 Ahmadpur Mahar. India
123 G4 Ahmadpur East Pak.
123 G4 Ahmadpur Sial Pak.
210 D2 Ahmar Mountains Eth.
Ahmedabad Gujarat India see Ahmadabad
Ahmednagar Mahar. India see Ahmadnagar
199 E2 Ahmetli Turkey
199 G2 Ahmetpaşa Turkey
168 F3 Ahnsbeck Ger.
207 G5 Ahoada Nigeria
147 E2 Ahoghill Northern Ireland U.K.
242 C3 Ahome Mex.
116 C4 Ahore Rajasthan India
169 F5 Ahorn Ger.
178 C3 Ahornspitze mt. Austria
231 E4 Ahoskie NC U.S.A.
169 C5 Ahr r. Ger.
122 B4 Ahram Iran
Ahrâmât el Jîzah tourist site Egypt see Giza Pyramids
137 H5 Ahrarne Ukr.
117 E4 Ahraura Uttar Prad. India
169 B5 Ahrbrück Ger.
168 F1 Ahrensbök Ger.
168 F2 Ahrensburg Ger.
170 E3 Ahrensfelde Ger.
170 D1 Ahrenshagen Ger.
169 C4 Ahse r. Ger.
134 D3 Ähtäri Fin.
138 F2 Ahtme Estonia
243 H6 Ahuachapán El Salvador
244 C3 Ahualulco Jalisco Mex.
244 D2 Ahualulco San Luis Potosí Mex.
162 E2 Ahun France
79 □3 Ahunui atoll Arch. des Tuamotu Fr. Polynesia
81 C6 Ahuriri r. South I. N.Z.
143 F4 Åhus Sweden
122 B4 Ahvāz Iran
Ahvenanmaa is Fin. see Åland
116 C5 Ahwa Gujarat India
124 D5 Aḥwar Yemen
Ahwāz Iran see Ahvāz
101 C4 Ai r. China
250 D4 Aiari r. Brazil
107 F3 Aibag Gol r. China
183 I2 Aibar Spain
179 G4 Aibl Austria
247 □1 Aibonito Puerto Rico
173 F3 Aichach Ger.
172 C3 Aichhalden Ger.
104 D4 Aichi pref. Japan
173 E4 Aichstetten Ger.
232 B5 Aid OH U.S.A.
173 H3 Aidenbach Ger.
169 F5 Aidhausen Ger.
194 D5 Aidone Sicilia Italy
240 □ Aiea HI U.S.A.
193 I5 Aiello Calabro Italy
193 H5 Aieta Italy
162 B2 Aiffres France
198 C2 Aigeira Greece
179 F3 Aigen im Ennstal Austria
179 E2 Aigen im Mühlkreis Austria
128 B2 Aigialousa Cyprus
198 C3 Aigina Greece
198 C3 Aigina i. Greece
198 C1 Aiginio Greece
198 C2 Aigio Greece
190 B2 Aigle Switz.
161 E4 Aigle de Chambeyron mt. France
161 E4 Aiglun France
163 C5 Aignan France
156 E5 Aignay-le-Duc France
161 B4 Aigoual, Mont mt. France
162 C3 Aigre France
162 B2 Aigrefeuille-d'Aunis France
158 E4 Aigrefeuille-sur-Maine France
258 G4 Aiguá Uru.
160 C1 Aigue, Mont hill France
160 E3 Aiguebelle France
160 E3 Aigueblanche France
160 B2 Aigueperse France
161 C4 Aigues r. France
161 C5 Aigues-Mortes France
161 B5 Aigues-Mortes, Golfe d' b. France
161 A5 Aigues-Vives France
161 C5 Aigues-Vives France
163 D6 Aigues-Vives France
161 D4 Aiguille, Mont mt. France
160 F3 Aiguille d'Argentière mt. France/Switz.
160 F3 Aiguille de la Grande Sassière mt. France
161 E3 Aiguille de Péclet mt. France
161 E3 Aiguille de Scolette mt. France/Italy
160 E3 Aiguille du Midi mt. France
161 E4 Aiguilles France
161 E3 Aiguilles d'Arves mts France
160 E3 Aiguilles des Glaciers mts France
160 E3 Aiguille Verte mt. France
163 C4 Aiguillon France
162 D2 Aigurande France
Aihua Yunnan China see Yunxian
Aihui Heilong. China see Heihe
252 A2 Aija Peru
Aijal Mizoram India see Aizawl
105 F3 Aikawa Japan
231 D5 Aiken SC U.S.A.
108 B3 Ailao Shan mts Yunnan China
84 C4 Aileron N.T. Austr.
108 D3 Ailing Guangxi China
Ailinglabelab atoll Marshall Is see Ailinglapalap
266 G6 Ailinglapalap atoll Marshall Is
156 D5 Aillant-sur-Tholon France
163 B4 Aillas France
161 E5 Aille r. France
157 G5 Aillevillers-et-Lyaumont France
156 B2 Ailly-le-Haut-Clocher France
156 C3 Ailly-sur-Noye France
156 C3 Ailly-sur-Somme France
227 G4 Ailsa Craig Ont. Can.
146 C6 Ailsa Craig i. Scotland U.K.
161 C5 Aimargues France
160 E3 Aime France
Aimeo i. Fr. Polynesia see Moorea
258 D3 Aimogasta Arg.
257 G3 Aimorés Brazil
257 G2 Aimorés, Serra dos hills Brazil
160 D2 Ain dept Rhône-Alpes France
160 D3 Ain r. France
160 A2 Ainay-le-Château France
138 E3 Ainaži Latvia
205 G2 Aïn Beïda Alg.
204 E2 Aïn Beni Mathar Morocco
204 C4 'Aïn Ben Tili Maur.
205 F1 Aïn Defla Alg.
205 F2 Aïn Deheb Alg.
173 E3 Aindling Ger.
205 F2 Aïn el Hadjel Alg.
205 G2 Aïn el Melh Alg.
178 D4 Ainet Austria
163 A5 Ainhoa France
205 G1 Aïn-M'Lila Alg.
Aïn Mokra Alg. see Berrahal
205 G2 Aïn Oulmene Alg.
205 F2 Aïn Oussera Alg.
173 G4 Ainring Ger.
186 D2 Ainsa Spain
Ain Salah Alg. see In Salah
149 F4 Ainsdale Merseyside, England U.K.
205 E2 Aïn Sefra Alg.
236 D3 Ainsworth NE U.S.A.
Aintab Turkey see Gaziantep
205 E2 Aïn Temouchent Alg.
149 G4 Aintree Merseyside, England U.K.
183 I3 Ainzón Spain
103 G6 Aioi Japan
250 C4 Aipe Col.
252 D4 Aiquile Bol.
156 B3 Airaines France
190 C4 Airasca Italy
94 B2 Airbangis Sumatera Indon.
146 B4 Aird Asaig Western Isles, Scotland U.K.
146 C4 Aird of Sleat Highland, Scotland U.K.
222 H5 Airdrie Alta Can.
146 E6 Airdrie North Lanarkshire, Scotland U.K.
157 E3 Aire r. France
149 H4 Airedale val. England U.K.
163 B5 Aire-sur-l'Adour France
156 C2 Aire-sur-la-Lys France
95 E3 Airhitam r. Indon.
146 B3 Airidh a'Bhruaich Western Isles, Scotland U.K.
85 G4 Airlie Beach Qld Austr.
86 B4 Airlie Island W.A. Austr.
193 G3 Airola Italy
190 D2 Airolo Switz.
223 J4 Air Ronge Sask. Can.
146 E5 Airth Falkirk, Scotland U.K.
149 G3 Airton North Yorkshire, England U.K.
162 B2 Airvault France
96 A2 Aisatung Mountain Myanmar
173 F2 Aisch r. Ger.
259 B7 Aisén admin. reg. Chile
156 E5 Aisey-sur-Seine France
107 I4 Ai Shan hill Shandong China
222 B2 Aishihik Y.T. Can.
173 E3 Aislingen Ger.
156 D3 Aisne dept Picardie France
157 C3 Aisne r. France
205 E2 Aïssa, Djebel mt. Alg.
160 E1 Aïssey France
160 C1 Aisy-sur-Armançon France
187 C6 Aitana mt. Spain
204 D3 Aït Benhaddou tourist site Morocco
173 G3 Aiterach r. Ger.
173 G3 Aiterhofen Ger.
146 F2 Aith Orkney, Scotland U.K.
236 E2 Aitkin MN U.S.A.
198 B2 Aitoliko Greece
186 D3 Aitona Spain
120 C1 Aitova Rus. Fed.
173 E4 Aitrach Ger.
173 E4 Aitrang Ger.
81 □2 Aitutaki i. Cook Is
197 F2 Aiud Romania
138 E3 Aiviekste r. Latvia
Aix France see Aix-en-Provence
160 C3 Aix r. France
156 D4 Aix-en-Othe France
161 D5 Aix-en-Provence France
162 D3 Aixe-sur-Vienne France
Aix-la-Chapelle Ger. see Aachen
160 D3 Aix-les-Bains France
210 C1 Āīy Ādī Eth.
Aíyina i. Greece see Aigina
Aiyínion Greece see Aiginio
Aíyion Greece see Aigio
Aíyira Greece see Aigeira
117 H5 Aizawl Mizoram India
158 E5 Aizenay France
138 E3 Aizkraukle Latvia
183 I2 Aizpun Spain
138 C3 Aizpute Latvia
103 I5 Aizu-wakamatsu Japan
124 C2 Ajā, Jibāl mts Saudi Arabia
192 A3 Ajaccio Corse France
Ajaccio airport Corse France see Campo dell'Oro
192 A3 Ajaccio, Golfe d' b. Corse France
245 E3 Ajacuba Mex.
116 E4 Ajaigarh Madh. Prad. India
250 C4 Ajajú r. Col.
177 L3 Ajak Hungary
245 F4 Ajalpán Mex.
116 C5 Ajanta Mahar. India
Ajanta Range hills India see Sahyadriparvat Range
207 G5 Ajaokuta Nigeria
Ajaria aut. rep. Georgia see Ach'ara
207 G4 Ajasse Nigeria
162 D3 Ajat France
227 H4 Ajax Ont. Can.
81 D5 Ajax, Mount South I. N.Z.
Ajayameru Rajasthan India see Ajmer
106 B2 Aj Bogd Uul mts Mongolia
202 D2 Ajdābiyā Libya
188 D3 Ajdovščina Slovenia
a-Jiddét des. Oman see Ḥarāsīs, Jiddat al
117 G4 Ajimganj W. Bengal India
177 G4 Ajka Hungary
128 B3 'Ajlūn Jordan
125 F2 Ajman U.A.E.
116 C4 Ajmer Rajasthan India
Ajmer-Merwara Rajasthan India see Ajmer
183 G1 Ajo Spain
241 K5 Ajo AZ U.S.A.
241 K5 Ajo, Mount AZ U.S.A.
183 G5 Ajofrín Spain
78 □3b Ajokwola i. Majuro Marshall Is
114 B2 Ajra Mahar. India
92 B4 Ajuy Phil.
102 K2 Akabira Japan
Akademii Nauk, Khrebet mt. Tajik. see Akademiyai Fanho, Qatorkŭhi
123 G2 Akademiyai Fanho, Qatorkŭhi mt. Tajik.
102 I4 Aka-gawa r. Japan
103 F6 Akagi Japan
105 F2 Akagi-yama vol. Japan
105 E3 Akaishi-dake mt. Japan
105 D4 Akaishi-sanmyaku mts Japan
210 C2 Āk'ak'ī Beseka Eth.
202 A3 Akakus, Jabal mts Libya
114 C2 Akalkot Mahar. India
Akamagaseki Japan see Shimonoseki
207 H5 Akamkpa Nigeria
198 B2 Akarnanika mts Greece
81 D5 Akaroa South I. N.Z.
81 D5 Akaroa Harbour South I. N.Z.
127 E4 Akāshat Iraq
104 A4 Akashi Japan
215 G1 Akasia S. Africa
140 M2 Äkäsjoki r. Fin.
177 I5 Akasztó Hungary
81 E4 Akatarawa North I. N.Z.
121 H3 Akbakay Kazakh.
116 E4 Akbarpur Uttar Prad. India
117 E4 Akbarpur Uttar Prad. India
121 G2 Akbeit Kazakh.
128 C1 Akbez Turkey
205 G1 Akbou Alg.
120 C2 Akbulak Rus. Fed.
129 A3 Akçaabat Turkey
126 E3 Akçadağ Turkey
129 C4 Akça Dağ mt. Turkey
126 E3 Akçakale Turkey
199 G1 Akçakoca Turkey
128 A1 Akçalı Dağları mts Turkey
199 E3 Akçaova Turkey
199 F3 Akçay Antalya Turkey
199 F3 Akçay r. Turkey
122 D1 Akchakaya, Vpadina depr. Turkm.
206 B2 Akchâr reg. Maur.
121 H3 Akchatau Kazakh.
Akchi Kazakh. see Akshiy
129 B4 Akdağ mt. Turkey
199 F2 Akdağ mt. Turkey
199 F3 Akdağ mts Turkey
199 G3 Ak Dağı mt. Turkey
199 F3 Akdağlar mts Turkey
126 D3 Akdağmadeni Turkey
129 C3 Akdam Turkey
122 D1 Akdepe Turkm.
128 A1 Akdere Turkey
129 B4 Akdoğan Dağı mts Turkey
149 G2 Akeld Northumberland, England U.K.
124 B5 Akele Guzai prov. Eritrea
171 D4 Aken Ger.
143 H2 Åkersberga Sweden
142 D1 Akershus county Norway
164 D2 Akersloot Neth.
143 G2 Åkers styckebruk Sweden
208 D4 Aketi Dem. Rep. Congo
Akgyr Erezi hills Turkm. see Akkyr, Gory
129 D2 Akhalgori Georgia
Akhali-Afoni Georgia see Akhali Ap'oni
129 B2 Akhali Ap'oni Georgia
129 C3 Akhalk'alak'i Georgia
Akhal Oblast admin. div. Turkm. see Akhal'skaya Oblast'
122 D2 Akhal'skaya Oblast' admin. div. Turkm.
129 C3 Akhalts'ikhe Georgia
202 D2 Akhḍar, Al Jabal al mts Libya
125 G3 Akhḍar, Jabal mts Oman
Akhelóös r. Greece see Acheloös
197 H4 Akheloy Bulg.
199 E2 Akhisar Turkey
129 D3 Akhk'erp'i Georgia
129 D2 Akhmeta Georgia
129 B1 Akhmetovskaya Rus. Fed.
203 F3 Akhmîm Egypt
116 C2 Akhnoor Jammu and Kashmir
Akhsu Azer. see Ağsu
Akhta Armenia see Hrazdan
127 I6 Akhtar Iran
128 C1 Akhtarīn Syria
135 I6 Akhtubinsk Rus. Fed.
129 E3 Akhty Rus. Fed.
Akhtyrka Ukr. see Okhtyrka
137 J5 Akhtyrskiy Rus. Fed.
120 D1 Akhunovo Rus. Fed.
129 E3 Akhvay, Gora mt. Azer./Rus. Fed.
103 F7 Aki Japan
208 B5 Akiéni Gabon
Akıncılar Turkey see Selçuk
126 E2 Akıncılar Turkey
113 □1 Akinfushi i. N. Male Maldives
143 F4 Åkirkeby Bornholm Denmark
105 F3 Akiruno Japan
105 F3 Akishima Japan
100 E1 Akishma r. Rus. Fed.
102 J4 Akita Japan
102 J4 Akita pref. Japan
80 F4 Akitio North I. N.Z.
105 F2 Akiyama-gawa r. Japan
206 B2 Akjoujt Maur.
204 C3 Akka Morocco
140 L2 Akkajaure l. Sweden
Akkerman Ukr. see Bilhorod-Dnistrovs'kyy
120 D2 Akkermanovka Rus. Fed.
128 B3 'Akko Israel
121 G1 Akkol' Akmolinskaya Oblast' Kazakh.
135 J7 Akkol' Kazakh.
121 G4 Akkol' Kazakh.
199 E3 Akköy Turkey
199 F3 Akköy Turkey
164 E1 Akkrum Neth.
121 I2 Akku Kazakh.
Akkul' Kazakh. see Akkol'
120 F3 Akkum Kazakh.
126 E2 Akkuş Turkey
122 C1 Akkyr, Gory hills Turkm.
120 B3 Akkystau Kazakh.
207 F4 Aklampa Benin
220 E3 Aklavik N.W.T. Can.
116 D4 Aklera Rajasthan India
Ak-Mechet Kazakh. see Kyzylorda
138 D4 Akmena r. Lith.
138 D3 Akmenė Lith.
Akmola Kazakh. see Astana
Akmola Oblast admin. div. Kazakh. see Akmolinskaya Oblast'
Akmolinsk Kazakh. see Astana
121 G2 Akmolinskaya Oblast' admin. div. Kazakh.
138 E3 Aknīste Latvia
204 E2 Aknoul Morocco
103 G6 Akō Japan
210 B3 Akobo Wenz r. Eth./Sudan
116 D5 Akodia Madh. Prad. India
114 B2 Akola Mahar. India
116 D5 Akola Mahar. India
207 H6 Akom II Cameroon
207 I6 Akonolinga Cameroon
203 H6 Akordat Eritrea
199 G2 Akören Afyon Turkey
126 D3 Akören Turkey
116 D5 Akot Mahar. India
206 E5 Akoupé Côte d'Ivoire
221 L3 Akpatok Island Nunavut Can.
110 B3 Akqi Xinjiang China
198 C2 Akraifnio Greece
140 □B2 Akranes Iceland
142 A2 Åkrehamn Norway
236 C3 Akron CO U.S.A.
226 D5 Akron IN U.S.A.
232 D3 Akron NY U.S.A.
232 C4 Akron OH U.S.A.
234 B2 Akron PA U.S.A.
Akrotiri Bay Cyprus see Akrotirion Bay
128 A2 Akrotirion Bay Cyprus
Akrotiriou, Kolpos b. Cyprus see Akrotirion Bay
128 A2 Akrotiri Sovereign Base Area military base Cyprus
111 B5 Aksai Chin terr. Asia
199 F1 Aksakal Turkey
197 H4 Aksakovo Bulg.
135 K5 Aksakovo Rus. Fed.
126 D3 Aksaray Turkey
130 H3 Aksarka Rus. Fed.
129 B2 Aksaut r. Rus. Fed.
110 F4 Aksay Gansu China
120 C2 Aksay Kazakh.
121 H4 Ak-Say r. Kyrg.
135 G7 Aksay Rostovskaya Oblast' Rus. Fed.
135 I7 Aksay Volgogradskaya Oblast' Rus. Fed.
137 J4 Aksay r. Rus. Fed.
126 C3 Akşehir Turkey
199 G2 Akşehir Gölü l. Turkey
126 C3 Akseki Turkey
120 C1 Aksenovo Rus. Fed.
122 C4 Aks-e Rostam r. Iran
107 G1 Aksha Rus. Fed.
120 C2 Akshatau Kazakh.
120 E2 Akshiganak Kazakh.
121 I4 Akshiy Kazakh.
120 B4 Akshukur Kazakh.
110 C3 Aksu Xinjiang China
121 I3 Aksu Almatinskaya Oblast' Kazakh.
121 I1 Aksu Pavlodarskaya Oblast' Kazakh.
121 G1 Aksu Severnyy Kazakhstan Kazakh.
120 C2 Aksu Zapadnyy Kazakhstan Kazakh.
121 I3 Aksu r. Kazakh.
Aksu r. Tajik. see Oksu
199 G3 Aksu Antalya Turkey
199 G3 Aksu Isparta Turkey
199 G3 Aksu r. Turkey
120 F2 Aksuat Kustanayskaya Oblast' Kazakh.
121 J3 Aksuat Vostochnyy Kazakhstan Kazakh.
121 H2 Aksu-Ayuly Kazakh.
135 J5 Aksubayevo Rus. Fed.
121 H3 Aksuek Kazakh.
110 C3 Aksu He r. China
210 C1 Āksum Eth.
111 D4 Aktag mt. Xinjiang China
134 K5 Aktanysh Rus. Fed.
128 C1 Aktaş Turkey
127 G3 Aktas Dağı mt. Turkey
129 E2 Aktash r. Rus. Fed.
120 F5 Aktash Uzbek.
121 G3 Aktau Karagandinskaya Oblast' Kazakh.
121 H2 Aktau Karagandinskaya Oblast' Kazakh.
120 B4 Aktau Mangistauskaya Oblast' Kazakh.
128 C1 Aktepe Turkey
199 G1 Aktepe hill Turkey
110 B4 Akto Xinjiang China
121 H2 Aktogay Karagandinskaya Oblast' Kazakh.
121 H1 Aktogay Pavlodarskaya Oblast' Kazakh.
121 I3 Aktogay Vostochnyy Kazakhstan Kazakh.
128 C1 Aktoprak Turkey
139 H4 Aktsyabrskaya Belarus
138 G5 Aktsyabrski Homyel'skaya Voblasts' Belarus
138 G4 Aktsyabrski Vitsyebskaya Voblasts' Belarus
121 H4 Ak-Tüz Kyrg.
120 D2 Aktyubinsk Kazakh.
120 D2 Aktyubinskaya Oblast' admin. div. Kazakh.
Aktyubinsk Oblast admin. div. Kazakh. see Aktyubinskaya Oblast'
Aktyuz Kyrg. see Ak-Tüz
221 K3 Akulivik Que. Can.
206 E5 Akumadan Ghana
103 E7 Akune Japan
210 B4 Akur mt. Uganda
129 D3 Akura Georgia
207 G5 Akure Nigeria
140 □C2 Akureyri Iceland
80 E2 Akuroa North I. N.Z.
102 □1 Akuseki-jima i. Japan
129 E2 Akusha Rus. Fed.
220 B4 Akutan AK U.S.A.
207 G5 Akwa Ibom state Nigeria
207 H4 Akwanga Nigeria
207 H5 Akwaya Cameroon
Akyab Myanmar see Sittwe
129 C3 Akyaka Turkey
120 D2 Ak"yar Rus. Fed.
199 G1 Akyazı Turkey
121 H3 Akzhal Karagandinskaya Oblast' Kazakh.
121 J2 Akzhal Vostochnyy Kazakhstan Kazakh.
120 F3 Akzhar Kzyl-Ordinskaya Oblast' Kazakh.
121 J3 Akzhar Vostochnyy Kazakhstan Kazakh.
121 G4 Akzhar Zhambylskaya Oblast' Kazakh.
121 F3 Akzhaykyn, Ozero salt l. Kazakh.
142 C1 Ål Norway
138 G5 Ala r. Belarus
191 G3 Ala Italy
231 C6 Alabama r. AL U.S.A.
231 C5 Alabama state U.S.A.
231 C5 Alabaster AL U.S.A.
227 F3 Alabaster MI U.S.A.
121 G4 Ala-Buka Kyrg.
202 D1 Al Abyār Libya
195 F4 Alaca r. Italy
126 D2 Alaca Turkey
129 B3 Alaca Dağı mt. Turkey
126 E3 Alacahan Turkey
126 D2 Alaçam Turkey
199 F2 Alaçam Dağları mts Turkey
Alacant Spain see Alicante
199 E2 Alaçatı Turkey
243 H4 Alacrán, Arrecife rf Mex.
197 G5 Aladag mt. Bulg.
126 D3 Aladağ Turkey
129 C3 Aladağ mt. Turkey
127 F3 Ala Dağlar mts Turkey
126 D3 Ala Dağları mts Turkey
192 B4 Alà dei Sardi Sardegna Italy
190 C3 Ala di Stura Italy
183 E3 Alaejos Spain
114 C4 Alagapuram Tamil Nadu India
Alagez mt. Armenia see Aragats Lerr
106 B2 Alag Hayrhan Uul mt. Mongolia
129 D2 Alagir Rus. Fed.
190 C3 Alagna Valsesia Italy
161 B3 Alagnon r. France
254 F4 Alagoas state Brazil
254 F5 Alagoinhas Brazil
186 B3 Alagón Spain
182 D5 Alagón r. Spain
129 C3 Alagöz Dağı mt. Turkey
92 C5 Alah r. Phil.
94 C3 Alahanpanjang Sumatera Indon.
140 M3 Alahärmä Fin.
127 H5 Al Aḥmadī Kuwait
163 E5 Alaigne France
186 □ Alaior Spain
123 G2 Alai Range mts Asia
122 C3 Ālaivān Iran
184 D3 Alájar Spain
140 M3 Alajärvi Fin.
216 □3a Alajero La Gomera Canary Is
124 C2 Al Ajfar Saudi Arabia
138 F2 Alajõgi r. Estonia
242 □I7 Alajuela Costa Rica
213 □J4 Alak Ambohimaha Madag.
220 B3 Alakanuk AK U.S.A.
129 B2 Alakhadzi Georgia
129 E3 Alakhundag, Gora mt. Rus. Fed.
116 D3 Alaknanda r. India
121 J3 Alakol', Ozero salt l. Kazakh.
Ala Kul salt l. Kazakh. see Alakol', Ozero
140 O2 Alakurtti Rus. Fed.
251 F5 Alalaú r. Brazil
124 C4 Al 'Alayyah Saudi Arabia
Alalia Corse France see Aléria
182 B2 A Lama Spain
127 F3 Al 'Amādīyah Iraq
91 K3 Alamagan i. N. Mariana Is
Alamaguan i. N. Mariana Is see Alamagan
127 G5 Al 'Amārah Iraq
210 C1 Ālamat'ā Eth.
185 F3 Alameda Spain
240 F3 Alameda CA U.S.A.
185 G1 Alameda de Cervera Spain
183 G4 Alameda de la Sagra Spain
127 G5 Al Amghar waterhole Iraq
185 F2 Alamillo Spain
92 A2 Alaminos Phil.
239 F6 Alamito Creek r. TX U.S.A.
124 C3 Al Amlah Saudi Arabia
245 F3 Álamo Mex.
184 C2 Álamo r. Port.
184 E4 Alamo r. Spain
231 D5 Alamo GA U.S.A.
241 J3 Alamo NV U.S.A.
237 F5 Alamo TN U.S.A.
239 F5 Alamogordo NM U.S.A.
237 D6 Alamo Heights TX U.S.A.
250 A6 Alamor Ecuador
242 C2 Alamos Sonora Mex.
242 C3 Alamos Sonora Mex.
243 E3 Alamos r. Mex.
242 C3 Alamos, Sierra mts Mex.
239 F4 Alamosa CO U.S.A.
239 F5 Alamosa Creek r. NM U.S.A.
114 C3 Alampur Andhra Prad. India
124 D5 Al 'Anad Yemen
140 K2 Alanäs Sweden
127 F4 Al Anbār governorate Iraq
141 L3 Åland is Fin.
170 C2 Aland r. Ger.
114 C2 Aland Karnataka India
122 A2 Aland r. Iran
129 B3 Alan Dağı mt. Turkey
Åland Islands Fin. see Åland
184 C2 Alandroal Port.
141 L4 Ålands Hav sea chan. Fin./Sweden
114 D3 Alandur Tamil Nadu India
184 D2 Alange Spain
184 D2 Alange, Embalse de resr Spain
Alania aut. reg. Georgia see Samkhret' Oset'i
184 E2 Alanís Spain
226 E3 Alanson MI U.S.A.
126 D3 Alanya Turkey
177 H5 Alap Hungary
231 D6 Alapaha r. GA U.S.A.
114 C4 Alapakam Tamil Nadu India
199 G1 Alaplı Turkey
Alappuzha Kerala India see Alleppey
116 D4 Alapur Uttar Prad. India
128 B5 Al 'Aqabah Jordan
124 C3 Al 'Aqīq Saudi Arabia
125 E2 Al 'Arabīyah i. Saudi Arabia
Al 'Arabīyah as Sa'ūdīyah country Asia see Saudi Arabia
183 E4 Alaraz Spain
183 H5 Alarcón Spain
183 H5 Alarcón, Embalse de resr Spain
183 F2 Alar del Rey Spain
187 F5 Alaró Spain
124 D2 Al Arṭāwīyah Saudi Arabia
95 G5 Alas, Selat sea chan. Indon.
199 F2 Alaşehir Turkey
129 D3 Äläsgärli Azer.
Alashiya country Asia see Cyprus
220 D3 Alaska state U.S.A.
213 F3 Alaska Zimbabwe
220 D4 Alaska, Gulf of AK U.S.A.
222 A2 Alaska Highway Can./U.S.A.
220 B4 Alaska Peninsula AK U.S.A.
220 D3 Alaska Range mts AK U.S.A.
190 D4 Alassio Italy
141 M3 Alastaro Fin.
129 F4 Älät Azer.
120 E5 Alat Uzbek.
192 A3 Alata Corse France
187 B5 Alatoz Spain
193 F3 Alatri Italy
129 F3 Älät Tiräsi plat. Azer.
177 J4 Alattyán Hungary
135 I5 Alatyr' Rus. Fed.
135 I5 Alatyr' r. Rus. Fed.
250 B5 Alausí Ecuador
183 H2 Álava prov. País Vasco Spain
129 D3 Alaverdi Armenia
140 N2 Alavieska Fin.
140 M3 Alavus Fin.
125 G3 Al Awābī Oman
82 E3 Alawoona S.A. Austr.
Alay Kyrka Toosu mts Asia see Alai Range
125 F2 Al 'Ayn U.A.E.
Alayskiy Khrebet mts Asia see Alai Range
129 E3 Alazani r. Azer./Georgia
131 Q2 Alazeya r. Rus. Fed.
202 B1 Al 'Azīzīyah Libya
172 C4 Alb r. Ger.
190 D4 Alba Italy
186 B4 Alba Spain
226 E3 Alba MI U.S.A.
234 B1 Alba PA U.S.A.
81 B6 Alba, Mount South I. N.Z.
193 F2 Alba Adriatica Italy
128 C1 Al Bāb Syria
185 I1 Albacete Spain
185 I2 Albacete prov. Castilla - La Mancha Spain
124 B2 Al Badā'i' Saudi Arabia
183 E4 Alba de Tormes Spain
124 D3 Al Badī' Saudi Arabia
127 G5 Al Bādiyah al Janūbīyah hill Iraq
142 D3 Ålbæk Denmark
142 D3 Ålbæk Bugt b. Denmark
192 A5 Albagiara Sardegna Italy
124 C3 Al Bāḥah Egypt
124 C3 Al Bāḥah prov. Saudi Arabia
128 B2 Al Bahlūlīyah Syria
Al Bahrayn country Asia see Bahrain
187 C6 Albaida Spain
197 F2 Alba Iulia Romania
185 H2 Albaladejo Spain
184 D1 Albalá del Caudillo Spain
161 C4 Alba-la-Romaine France
186 C3 Albalate de Arzobispo Spain
186 D3 Albalate de Cinca Spain
183 H4 Albalate de las Nogueras Spain
183 H4 Albalate de Zorita Spain
186 C3 Albalatillo Spain
163 E5 Alban France
185 H3 Albánchez Spain
193 H4 Albanella Italy
196 D5 Albania country Europe
193 I4 Albano di Lucania Italy
193 E3 Albano Laziale Italy
87 C7 Albany W.A. Austr.
224 D2 Albany r. Ont. Can.
246 □ Albany Jamaica
231 C6 Albany GA U.S.A.
236 E3 Albany MO U.S.A.
233 G3 Albany NY U.S.A.
232 B5 Albany OH U.S.A.
238 B2 Albany OR U.S.A.
237 D5 Albany TX U.S.A.
186 F2 Albanyà Spain
85 G5 Albany Downs Qld Austr.
258 G4 Albardão do João Maria coastal area Brazil
202 E2 Al Bardī Libya
260 C2 Albardón Arg.
190 E2 Albaredo per San Marco Italy
161 B4 Albaret-le-Comtal France
190 E4 Albareto Italy
161 B4 Albaret-Ste-Marie France
160 D3 Albarine r. France
161 C5 Albaron France
183 I4 Albarracín Spain
184 D1 Albarragena r. Spain
137 J4 Albasi r. Rus. Fed.
127 G5 Al Başrah Iraq
127 G5 Al Başrah governorate Iraq
150 C4 Albaston Cornwall, England U.K.
185 I2 Albatana Spain
186 D3 Albatàrrec Spain
187 C6 Albatera Spain
125 G3 Al Bāṭinah admin. reg. Oman
85 E2 Albatross Bay Qld Austr.
83 F5 Albatross Island Tas. Austr.
202 D1 Al Bayḍā' Libya
124 D5 Al Bayḍā' Yemen
124 D5 Al Bayḍā' governorate Yemen
172 C4 Albbruck Ger.
157 H4 Albe r. France
192 D2 Albegna r. Italy
186 D3 Albelda Spain
183 H2 Albelda de Iregua Spain
186 C2 Albella Spain
231 D5 Albemarle NC U.S.A.
Albemarle Island Islas Galápagos Ecuador see Isabela, Isla
231 E5 Albemarle Sound sea chan. NC U.S.A.
183 H4 Albendea Spain
185 F3 Albendín Spain
190 D4 Albenga Italy
160 D3 Albens France
187 C4 Albentosa Spain
183 F5 Alberche r. Spain
253 F6 Alberdi Para.
182 B4 Albergaria-a-Velha Port.
182 B5 Albergaria dos Doze Port.
190 B3 Albergian, Monte mt. Italy
187 C5 Alberic Spain
183 H2 Alberite Spain
179 F2 Alberndorf in der Riedmark Austria
184 C3 Albernoa Port.
186 C2 Albero Alto Spain
195 G2 Alberobello Italy
191 H3 Alberoni Italy
178 A3 Alberschwende Austria
168 E1 Albersdorf Ger.
83 F3 Albert N.S.W. Austr.
84 D3 Albert r. Qld Austr.
156 C3 Albert France
82 D3 Albert, Lake S.A. Austr.
210 A4 Albert, Lake Dem. Rep. Congo/Uganda
222 H4 Alberta prov. Can.
232 E6 Alberta VA U.S.A.
192 A2 Albertacce Corse France
190 E4 Alberta Ligure Italy
261 G4 Alberti Arg.
140 □ Albert I Land reg. Svalbard
214 C6 Albertinia S. Africa
177 I4 Albertirsa Hungary
236 E3 Albert Lea MN U.S.A.
210 B4 Albert Nile r. Sudan/Uganda
225 H4 Alberton P.E.I. Can.
215 G2 Alberton S. Africa
238 D2 Alberton MT U.S.A.
241 J5 Alberto Oviedo Mota Mex.
215 E2 Albertshoek S. Africa
173 E2 Albertshofen Ger.
246 □ Albert Town Jamaica
81 B6 Albert Town South I. N.Z.
Albertville Dem. Rep. Congo see Kalémié
160 E3 Albertville France
231 C5 Albertville AL U.S.A.
186 C3 Alberuela de Tubo Spain
186 D3 Albesa Spain
197 H2 Albeşti Romania
197 H2 Albeşti Romania
157 G4 Albestroff France
163 E5 Albi France
236 E3 Albia IA U.S.A.
163 D4 Albias France
125 E2 Al Bīḍah des. Saudi Arabia
195 F3 Albidona Italy
191 G3 Albignasego Italy
251 H3 Albina Suriname
190 E3 Albino Italy
240 F2 Albion CA U.S.A.
230 C3 Albion IN U.S.A.
226 E4 Albion MI U.S.A.
236 D3 Albion NE U.S.A.
234 D3 Albion NJ U.S.A.
232 D3 Albion NY U.S.A.
232 C4 Albion PA U.S.A.
183 E2 Albires Spain
124 C4 Al Birk Saudi Arabia
172 C2 Albisheim (Pfrimm) Ger.
190 D4 Albisola Marina Italy
190 D4 Albisola Superiore Italy
124 D3 Al Biyāḍh reg. Saudi Arabia
164 D3 Alblasserdam Neth.
187 D4 Albocácer Spain
185 H3 Alboloduy Spain
161 C3 Albon France
185 G4 Albondón Spain
187 B5 Alborea Spain
142 C3 Ålborg Denmark
142 D3 Ålborg Bugt b. Denmark
122 B2 Alborz, Reshteh-ye mts Iran
197 G3 Albota Romania
185 H3 Albox Spain
177 H2 Albrechtice Czech Rep.
150 E2 Albrighton Shropshire, England U.K.
85 F4 Albro Qld Austr.
172 D3 Albstadt Ger.
173 D3 Albuch hills Ger.
125 E2 Al Budayyi Bahrain
184 B3 Albufeira Port.
187 B7 Albujón Spain
124 C2 Al Bukayrīyah Saudi Arabia
190 E2 Albula r. Switz.
190 E2 Albula Alpen mts Switz.
185 G4 Albuñol Spain
185 G4 Albuñuelas Spain
239 F5 Albuquerque NM U.S.A.
246 B4 Albuquerque, Cayos de is Caribbean Sea
125 F2 Al Buraymī Oman
233 G2 Alburg VT U.S.A.
128 B5 Al Burj Jordan
193 H4 Alburno, Monte mt. Italy
184 D1 Alburquerque Spain
234 C2 Alburtis PA U.S.A.
83 F4 Albury N.S.W. Austr.
81 C6 Albury South I. N.Z.
127 F4 Al Buşayrah Syria
128 D4 Al Busayṭā' plain Saudi Arabia
126 E5 Al Busayṭā' plain Saudi Arabia
124 D1 Al Bushūk well Saudi Arabia
160 E3 Alby-sur-Chéran France
252 B3 Alca Peru
184 A2 Alcabideche Port.
187 C5 Alcácer Spain
184 B2 Alcácer do Sal Port.
184 B2 Alcáçovas Port.
184 B2 Alcáçovas r. Port.
185 I2 Alcadozo Spain
186 C4 Alcaine Spain
182 C5 Alcains Port.
187 D4 Alcalá de Chivert Spain
184 E3 Alcalá de Guadaira Spain
186 C2 Alcalá de Gurrea Spain
183 G4 Alcalá de Henares Spain
187 C4 Alcalá de la Selva Spain
187 B5 Alcalá del Júcar Spain
184 E4 Alcalá de los Gazules Spain
184 E3 Alcalá del Río Spain
185 E4 Alcalá del Valle Spain
185 G3 Alcalá la Real Spain
194 B5 Alcamo Sicilia Italy
186 D3 Alcampell Spain
186 D3 Alcanadre r. Spain
186 D4 Alcanar Spain
184 B1 Alcanede Port.
184 B1 Alcanena Port.
184 B1 Alcanhões Port.
182 D3 Alcañices Spain
186 C3 Alcañiz Spain
254 D2 Alcântara Brazil
182 D5 Alcántara Spain
182 D5 Alcántara, Embalse de resr Spain
187 B7 Alcantarilla Spain
183 H4 Alcantud Spain
185 F2 Alcaracejos Spain
194 D4 Alcara li Fusi Sicilia Italy
185 H2 Alcaraz Spain
184 C3 Alcaria do Cume hill Port.
184 C3 Alcaria Ruiva Port.
180 C4 Alcaria Ruiva hill Port.
184 C2 Alcarrache r. Port./Spain
186 D3 Alcarràs Spain
185 F4 Alcaucín Spain
185 F3 Alcaudete Spain
183 F5 Alcaudete de la Jara Spain
163 B5 Alçay-Alçabéhéty-Sunharette France
184 D2 Alcazaba r. Spain
183 H4 Alcázar del Rey Spain
185 G1 Alcázar de San Juan Spain
183 F3 Alcazarén Spain
Alcazarquivir Morocco see Ksar el Kebir
151 F2 Alcester Warwickshire, England U.K.
137 J3 Alchevs'k Ukr.
260 E3 Alcira Arg.
Alcira Spain see Alzira
185 F1 Alcoba Spain
257 H2 Alcobaça Brazil
182 B5 Alcobaça Port.
183 G4 Alcobendas Spain
184 B1 Alcobertas Port.
Alcocebre Spain see Alcossebre
183 H4 Alcocer Spain
183 G2 Alcocero de Mola Spain
184 B2 Alcochete Port.
184 B1 Alcoentre Port.
182 B4 Alcofra Port.
185 F3 Alcolea Andalucía Spain
185 H4 Alcolea Andalucía Spain
185 F2 Alcolea de Calatrava Spain
186 D3 Alcolea de Cinca Spain
183 H3 Alcolea del Pinar Spain
184 E3 Alcolea del Río Spain
186 D3 Alcoletge Spain
184 E1 Alcollarín Spain
184 C2 Alconchel Spain
184 D2 Alconera Spain
185 H3 Alcóntar Spain
84 C4 Alcoota N.T. Austr.
187 C4 Alcora Spain
183 G4 Alcorcón Spain
186 C4 Alcorisa Spain
184 D1 Alcorneo r. Port./Spain
183 I4 Alcoroches Spain
261 G3 Alcorta Arg.
187 D4 Alcossebre Spain
184 C3 Alcoutim Port.
238 F3 Alcova WY U.S.A.
186 E3 Alcover Spain
187 C6 Alcoy Spain
177 H4 Alcsútdobos Hungary
186 C3 Alcubierre Spain
183 G3 Alcubilla de Avellaneda Spain
185 G2 Alcubillas Spain
187 C5 Alcublas Spain
187 G5 Alcúdia Spain
185 F2 Alcudia r. Spain
Alcudia de Carlet Spain see L'Alcudia
185 G3 Alcudia de Guadix Spain
181 E4 Alcudia de Monteagud Spain
184 D1 Alcuéscar Spain
217 □2 Aldabra Atoll Aldabra Is Seychelles
217 □2 Aldabra Islands Seychelles
242 D2 Aldama Chihuahua Mex.
245 E2 Aldama Tamaulipas Mex.
131 N4 Aldan Rus. Fed.
131 N3 Aldan r. Rus. Fed.
151 F3 Aldbourne Wiltshire, England U.K.
149 I4 Aldbrough East Riding of Yorkshire, England U.K.
151 I2 Alde r. England U.K.
216 □3f Aldea r. Gran Canaria Canary Is
184 E1 Aldeacentenera Spain
182 D3 Aldeadávila de la Ribera Spain
184 D1 Aldea del Cano Spain
183 F4 Aldea del Fresno Spain
182 D4 Aldea del Obispo Spain
185 G2 Aldea del Rey Spain
182 E5 Aldea de Trujillo Spain
183 H3 Aldealafuente Spain
183 H3 Aldealpozo Spain
183 F3 Aldeamayor de San Martín Spain
183 E5 Aldeanueva de Barbarroya Spain
182 E3 Aldeanueva de Figueroa Spain
182 E4 Aldeanueva del Camino Spain
183 E5 Aldeanueva de San Bartolomé Spain
185 G2 Aldeaquemada Spain
182 E3 Aldearrodrigo Spain
183 F3 Aldeaseca Spain
182 E4 Aldeatejada Spain
183 F4 Aldeavieja Spain
151 I2 Aldeburgh Suffolk, England U.K.
182 D4 Aldehuela de la Bóveda Spain
182 D4 Aldehuela de Yeltes Spain
184 C1 Aldeia da Mata Port.
182 D4 Aldeia da Ponte Port.
184 C2 Aldeia de Ferreira Port.
182 C4 Aldeia do Bispo Port.
184 B3 Aldeia dos Elvas Port.
184 B3 Aldeia dos Palheiros Port.
182 D4 Aldeia Velha Guarda Port.
184 B1 Aldeia Velha Portalegre Port.
234 B1 Alden PA U.S.A.
151 G3 Aldenham Hertfordshire, England U.K.
169 B5 Aldenhoven Ger.
191 G3 Aldeno Italy
151 F3 Alderbury Wiltshire, England U.K.
233 F3 Alder Creek NY U.S.A.
147 E2 Aldergrove Northern Ireland U.K.
151 F4 Alderholt Dorset, England U.K.
149 G4 Alderley Edge Cheshire, England U.K.
158 D2 Alderney i. Channel Is
240 G4 Alder Peak CA U.S.A.
173 H3 Aldersbach Ger.
151 G3 Aldershot Hampshire, England U.K.
232 C6 Alderson WV U.S.A.
196 E5 Aldinci Macedonia
172 C3 Aldingen Ger.
149 F3 Aldingham Cumbria, England U.K.
151 H3 Aldington Kent, England U.K.
215 H3 Aldinville S. Africa
186 D4 Aldover Spain
151 F2 Aldridge West Midlands, England U.K.
163 A5 Aldudes France
142 E3 Åled Sweden
185 I3 Aledo Spain
236 F3 Aledo IL U.S.A.
206 B2 Aleg Maur.
216 □3c Alegranza i. Canary Is
257 G4 Alegre Espírito Santo Brazil
256 D3 Alegre Minas Gerais Brazil
255 B9 Alegrete Brazil
184 C1 Alegrete Port.
183 H2 Alegría-Dulantzi Spain
239 E5 Alegros Mountain NM U.S.A.
261 H1 Alejandra Arg.
261 H4 Alejandro Korn Arg.
261 F3 Alejandro Roca Arg.
252 □ Alejandro Selkirk, Isla i. S. Pacific Ocean
260 D6 Alejandro Stefenelli Arg.
139 I1 Alekhovshchina Rus. Fed.
Aleksandriya Kirovohrads'ka Oblast' Ukr. see Oleksandriya
139 M5 Aleksandro-Nevskiy Rus. Fed.
Aleksandropol Armenia see Gyumri
139 L3 Aleksandrov Rus. Fed.
196 E4 Aleksandrovac Srbija Yugo.
Aleksandrov Dar Ukr. see Rakhmanivka
120 B2 Aleksandrov Gay Rus. Fed.
135 K5 Aleksandrovka Orenburgskaya Oblast' Rus. Fed.
137 J4 Aleksandrovka Rostovskaya Oblast' Rus. Fed.
197 G4 Aleksandrovo Khaskovo Bulg.
197 G4 Aleksandrovo Lovech Bulg.
134 L4 Aleksandrovsk Rus. Fed.
Aleksandrovsk Ukr. see Zaporizhzhya
Aleksandrovskiy Rus. Fed. see Aleksandrovsk
129 C1 Aleksandrovskoye Stavropol'skiy Kray Rus. Fed.
127 G1 Aleksandrovskoye Stavropol'skiy Kray Rus. Fed.
130 I3 Aleksandrovskoye Tomskaya Oblast' Rus. Fed.
100 G2 Aleksandrovsk-Sakhalinskiy Sakhalin Rus. Fed.
175 I3 Aleksandrów Pol.
174 G3 Aleksandrów Kujawski Pol.
175 H4 Aleksandrów Łódzki Pol.
177 I6 Aleksa Šantić Vojvodina, Srbija Yugo.
129 F3 Alekseyevka Azer.
Alekseyevka Akmolinskaya Oblast' Kazakh. see Akkol'
121 H2 Alekseyevka Pavlodarskaya Oblast' Kazakh.
Alekseyevka Vostochnyy Kazakhstan Kazakh. see Terekty
135 G6 Alekseyevka Belgorodskaya Oblast' Rus. Fed.
135 G6 Alekseyevka Belgorodskaya Oblast' Rus. Fed.
137 K3 Alekseyevo-Lozovskoye Rus. Fed.
135 H6 Alekseyevskaya Rus. Fed.
139 K4 Aleksin Rus. Fed.
197 E4 Aleksinac Srbija Yugo.
143 G3 Ålem Sweden
208 A5 Alèmbé Gabon
210 D2 'Alem Maya Eth.
257 F4 Além Paraíba Brazil
140 J3 Ålen Norway
159 G3 Alençon France
160 B2 Alène r. France
251 H5 Alenquer Brazil
184 B1 Alenquer Port.
184 B1 Alenquer r. Port.
240 □C9 Alenuihaha Channel HI U.S.A.
163 E6 Alénya France
Alep Syria see Ḥalab
206 E5 Alépé Côte d'Ivoire
Aleppo Syria see Ḥalab
114 C2 Aler r. India
173 E3 Alerheim Ger.
192 B2 Aléria Corse France
186 C2 Alerre Spain
221 L1 Alert Nunavut Can.
222 E5 Alert Bay B.C. Can.
161 C4 Alès France
192 A5 Ales Sardegna Italy
197 F2 Aleşd Romania
Aleshki Ukr. see Tsyurupyns'k

103 D7 Amakusa-nada *b.* Japan
125 F4 Amal Oman
142 E2 Åmal Sweden
114 D2 Amalapuram *Andhra Prad.* India
99 K1 Amalat *r.* Rus. Fed.
193 G4 Amalfi Italy
215 E2 Amalia S. Africa
198 B3 Amaliada Greece
116 C5 Amalner *Mahar.* India
253 G5 Amambaí Brazil
253 G5 Amambaí, Serra de *hills* Brazil/Para.
102 □1 Amami-Ō-shima *i.* Japan
102 □1 Amami-shotō *is* Japan
141 K3 Åmån *r.* Sweden
157 G5 Amance France
157 F5 Amance *r.* France
160 E1 Amancey France
232 B5 Amanda *OH* U.S.A.
193 F2 Amandola Italy
120 D2 Amangel'dy *Aktyubinskaya Oblast'* Kazakh.
120 F2 Amangel'dy *Kustanayskaya Oblast'* Kazakh.
120 F1 Amankaragay Kazakh.
Amankeldi *Aktyubinskaya Oblast'* Kazakh. *see* Amangel'dy
Amankeldi *Kustanayskaya Oblast'* Kazakh. *see* Amangel'dy
120 E3 Amanotkel' Kazakh.
Amanqaraghay Kazakh. *see* Amankaragay
193 I5 Amantea Italy
215 H4 Amanzimtoti S. Africa
251 I4 Amapá Brazil
251 I4 Amapá *state* Brazil
245 F4 Amapa *r.* Mex.
242 □I6 Amapala Hond.
251 I4 Amapari *r.* Brazil
197 I3 Amaradia *r.* Romania
255 B9 Amaral Ferrador Brazil
254 E3 Amarante Brazil
182 B3 Amarante Port.
254 D3 Amarante do Maranhão Brazil
96 B2 Amarapura Myanmar
114 C4 Amaravati *r.* India
106 E2 Amardalay Mongolia
182 B3 Amarela, Serra *mts* Port.
184 C2 Amareleja Port.
182 B3 Amares Port.
254 F5 Amargosa Brazil
241 I3 Amargosa Desert *NV* U.S.A.
240 I3 Amargosa Range *mts CA* U.S.A.
241 I3 Amargosa Valley *NV* U.S.A.
185 G1 Amarguillo *r.* Spain
Amargura Island Tonga *see* Fonualei
237 C5 Amarillo *TX* U.S.A.
258 C4 Amarillo, Cerro *mt.* Arg.
116 E5 Amarkantak *Madh. Prad.* India
193 G2 Amaro, Monte *mt.* Italy
195 F4 Amaroni Italy
84 D4 Amaroo, Lake *salt flat Qld* Austr.
117 G5 Amarpur *Tripura* India
116 D5 Amarwara *Madh. Prad.* India
226 C2 Amasa *MI* U.S.A.
193 F5 Amaseno Italy
193 F3 Amaseno *r.* Italy
129 C3 Amasia Armenia
Amasia Turkey *see* Amasya
204 B4 Amasine Western Sahara
126 D2 Amasra Turkey
126 D2 Amasya Turkey
82 B1 Amata *S.A.* Austr.
250 D5 Amataurá Brazil
243 G5 Amatenango Mex.
215 H3 Amatikulu S. Africa
245 F4 Amatlán Mex.
244 D3 Amatlán de Cañas Mex.
195 F4 Amato *r.* Italy
193 F2 Amatrice Italy
235 E1 Amawalk *NY* U.S.A.
165 E4 Amay Belgium
183 F2 Amaya *mt.* Spain
100 B1 Amazar Rus. Fed.
100 B1 Amazar *r.* Rus. Fed.
251 I4 Amazon *r.* S. America *alt.* Amazonas
251 I4 Amazon, Mouths of the Brazil
252 C3 Amazon, Source of the Peru
251 E6 Amazonas *state* Brazil
250 D5 Amazonas *dept* Col.
250 B6 Amazonas *dept* Peru
251 I4 Amazonas *r.* S. America *conv.* Amazon
251 E4 Amazonas *state* Venez.
264 F5 Amazon Cone *sea feature* S. Atlantic Ocean
210 C1 Āmba Ālagē *mt.* Eth.
114 B2 Ambad *Mahar.* India
210 C2 Amba Farit *mt.* Eth.
213 □I4 Ambahikily Madag.
114 C2 Ambajogai *Mahar.* India
116 D3 Ambala *Haryana* India
213 □J3 Ambalajanakomby Madag.
114 D5 Ambalangoda Sri Lanka
213 □J4 Ambalatany Madag.
213 □J4 Ambalavao Madag.
84 C4 Ambalindum *N.T.* Austr.
207 H6 Ambam Cameroon
213 □K2 Ambanja Madag.
162 B4 Ambarès-et-Lagarve France
258 D3 Ambargasta, Salinas de *salt pan* Arg.
134 F2 Ambarnyy Rus. Fed.
117 G5 Ambasa *Tripura* India
183 E2 Ambasaguas Spain
114 C4 Ambasamudram *Tamil Nadu* India
85 F5 Ambathala *Qld* Austr.
250 B5 Ambato Ecuador
258 D3 Ambato, Sierra *mts* Arg.
213 □J3 Ambato Boeny Madag.
213 □J4 Ambato Finandrahana Madag.
213 □J3 Ambatolampy Madag.
213 □J3 Ambatomainty Madag.
213 □J3 Ambatomanoina Madag.
213 □K3 Ambatondrazaka Madag.
213 □K2 Ambatosia Madag.
213 □K3 Ambatosoratra Madag.
162 D3 Ambazac France
Ambejogai *Mahar.* India *see* Ambajogai
Ambelón Greece *see* Ampelonas
Amber *Rajasthan* India *see* Amer
173 F2 Amberg Ger.
226 D3 Amberg *WI* U.S.A.
149 H4 Ambergate *Derbyshire, England* U.K.
246 E2 Ambergris Cays *is* Turks and Caicos Is
160 D3 Ambérieu-en-Bugey France
227 G3 Amberley *Ont.* Can.
81 D5 Amberley *South I.* N.Z.
165 E4 Amberloup Belgium
160 B3 Ambert France
162 B3 Ambès France
116 E5 Ambgaon *Mahar.* India
163 E5 Ambialet France
Ambianum France *see* Amiens
206 C3 Ambidédi Mali
160 B2 Ambierle France
116 C5 Ambika *r.* India
117 E5 Ambikapur *Madh. Prad.* India
213 □J4 Ambila Madag.
159 G4 Ambillou France
213 □K2 Ambilobe Madag.
222 D3 Ambition, Mount *B.C.* Can.
156 C3 Amblainville France
149 H2 Amble *Northumberland, England* U.K.
150 E2 Amblecote *West Midlands, England* U.K.
220 C3 Ambler *AK* U.S.A.
234 C2 Ambler *PA* U.S.A.
149 G3 Ambleside *Cumbria, England* U.K.
156 B2 Ambleteuse France
165 E4 Amblève *r.* Belgium
117 F5 Ambo *Orissa* India
252 A2 Ambo Peru
213 □J5 Amboasary Madag.
213 □K3 Amboasary Gara Madag.
213 □K3 Amboavory Madag.
213 □K3 Ambodifotatra Madag.
213 □K4 Ambodiharina Madag.
213 □J3 Ambohidratrimo Madag.
213 □K3 Ambohijanahary Madag.
213 □J4 Ambohimahasoa Madag.
213 □I4 Ambohimahavelona Madag.
213 □K2 Ambohitra *mt.* Madag.
213 □K2 Ambohitralanana Madag.
Amboina *Maluku* Indon. *see* Ambon
162 C1 Amboise France
158 D4 Ambon France
93 D3 Ambon *Maluku* Indon.
93 C3 Ambon *i. Maluku* Indon.
213 □J5 Ambondro Madag.
156 E3 Ambonnay France
211 C5 Amboseli National Park Kenya
213 □J4 Ambositra Madag.
213 □J5 Ambovombe Madag.
241 J4 Amboy *CA* U.S.A.
226 C5 Amboy *IL* U.S.A.
159 H5 Ambrault France
Ambre, Cap d' *c.* Madag. *see* Bobaomby, Tanjona
159 F3 Ambrières-les-Vallées France
Ambrim *i.* Vanuatu *see* Ambrym
209 B6 Ambriz Angola
Ambrizete Angola *see* N'zeto
129 C2 Ambrolauri Georgia
160 D2 Ambronay France
151 F3 Ambrosden *Oxfordshire, England* U.K.
78 □5 Ambrym *i.* Vanuatu
95 F4 Ambunten *Jawa Timur* Indon.
114 C3 Ambur *Tamil Nadu* India
85 G5 Amby *Qld* Austr.
220 A4 Amchitka Island *AK* U.S.A.
202 D6 Am-Dam Chad
130 H3 Amderma Rus. Fed.
111 E5 Amdo *Xizang* China
244 D3 Amealco Mex.
244 B3 Ameca Mex.
244 B3 Ameca *r.* Mex.
245 E4 Amecameca Mex.
210 C2 Amedamit *mt.* Eth.
190 E4 Ameglia Italy
179 E2 Ameisberg *hill* Austria
184 C3 Ameixial Port.
165 F4 Amel Belgium
164 E1 Ameland *i.* Neth.
193 E2 Amelia Italy
232 E6 Amelia Court House *VA* U.S.A.
163 E6 Amélie-les-Bains-Palalda France
168 F2 Amelinghausen Ger.
116 E4 Amellu *Uttar Prad.* India
182 B5 Amêndoa Port.
184 C3 Amendoeira Port.
195 F3 Amendolara Italy
195 E5 Amendolea *r.* Italy
233 G4 Amenia *NY* U.S.A.
111 A7 Amer *Rajasthan* India
186 F2 Amer Spain
173 G4 Amerang Ger.
182 C2 A Merca Spain
240 G2 American, North Fork *r. CA* U.S.A.
256 D5 Americana Brazil
264 H9 American-Antarctic Ridge *sea feature* S. Atlantic Ocean
238 D3 American Falls *ID* U.S.A.
241 L1 American Fork *UT* U.S.A.
78 □2 American Samoa *terr.* S. Pacific Ocean
231 C5 Americus *GA* U.S.A.
179 F3 Ameringkogel *mt.* Austria
164 E3 Amerongen Neth.
164 E2 Amersfoort Neth.
215 G2 Amersfoort S. Africa
151 G3 Amersham *Buckinghamshire, England* U.K.
223 M3 Amery *Man.* Can.
236 E3 Ames *IA* U.S.A.
151 F3 Amesbury *Wiltshire, England* U.K.
233 H3 Amesbury *MA* U.S.A.
116 C4 Amet *Rajasthan* India
116 E4 Amethi *Uttar Prad.* India
186 A1 Amezketa Spain
182 C2 A Mezquita Spain
198 B2 Amfilochia Greece
198 C2 Amfissa Greece
159 G2 Amfreville-la-Campagne France
131 O3 Amga Rus. Fed.
107 H1 Amgalang *Nei Mongol* China
131 T3 Amguema Rus. Fed.
99 O1 Amgun' *r.* Rus. Fed.
210 C2 Amhara *admin. reg.* Eth.
225 H4 Amherst *N.S.* Can.
233 G3 Amherst *MA* U.S.A.
232 B4 Amherst *OH* U.S.A.
232 D6 Amherst *VA* U.S.A.
86 E3 Amherst, Mount *hill W.A.* Austr.
227 F4 Amherstburg *Ont.* Can.
232 C6 Amherstdale *WV* U.S.A.
227 I3 Amherstview *Ont.* Can.
184 B1 Amiais de Baixo Port.
192 D2 Amiata, Monte *mt.* Italy
Amida Turkey *see* Diyarbakır
236 C2 Amidon *ND* U.S.A.
184 C2 Amieira Port.
182 C5 Amieira do Tejo Port.
156 C3 Amiens France
126 E3 Amik Ovası *marsh* Turkey
125 F4 Amilḩayt, Wādī al *r.* Oman
156 C5 Amilly France
Amíndhaion Greece *see* Amyntaio
114 B4 Amindivi Islands *Lakshadweep* India
128 B2 Amioun Lebanon
116 D3 Amipshahr *Uttar Prad.* India
Amirabad Iran *see* Fūlād Maïalleh
217 □2 Amirante Islands Seychelles
265 H5 Amirante Trench *sea feature* Indian Ocean
Amistad, Represa de *resr* Mex./U.S.A. *see* Amistad Reservoir
243 E2 Amistad Reservoir Mex./U.S.A.
Amisus Turkey *see* Samsun
237 F6 Amite *LA* U.S.A.
237 F6 Amite Creek *r. MS* U.S.A.
85 H5 Amity Point *Qld* Austr.
116 D5 Amla *Madh. Prad.* India
124 C4 Amlaḩ, Jabal al *hill* Saudi Arabia
207 F5 Amlamé Togo
122 B2 Amlash Iran
142 C2 Åmli Norway
220 A4 Amlia Island *AK* U.S.A.
150 C1 Amlwch *Isle of Anglesey, Wales* U.K.
128 B4 'Ammān Jordan
150 D3 Ammanford *Carmarthenshire, Wales* U.K.
134 E2 Ämmänsaari Fin.
128 C3 'Ammār, Tall *hill* Syria
140 L2 Ammarnäs Sweden
84 C4 Ammaroo *N.T.* Austr.
221 O3 Ammassalik Greenland
173 F4 Ammer *r.* Ger.
140 L3 Ammerån *r.* Sweden
172 C3 Ammerbuch Ger.
178 B3 Ammergauer Alpen *mts* Austria/Ger.
169 F4 Ammern Ger.
168 F2 Ammersbek Ger.
157 H4 Ammerschwihr France
173 F4 Ammersee *l.* Ger.
198 B1 Ammochori *Dytiki Makedonia* Greece
128 A2 Ammochostos Cyprus
128 B2 Ammochostos Bay Cyprus
124 C5 Am Nābiyah Yemen
Amne Machin Range *mts* China *see* A'nyêmaqên Shan
157 G3 Amnéville France
Amnok-kang *r.* China/N. Korea *see* Yalu Jiang
116 C5 Amod *Gujarat* India
182 C2 Amoeiro Spain
108 B4 Amo Jiang *r. Yunnan* China
122 C2 Amol Iran
137 H2 Amon' Rus. Fed.
182 B3 Amonde Port.
169 D5 Amöneburg Ger.
254 F2 Amontada Brazil
183 F5 Amor *mt.* Spain
172 D2 Amorbach Ger.
183 H1 Amorebieta Spain
258 F3 Amores *r.* Arg.
199 D3 Amorgos *i.* Greece
256 B2 Amorinópolis Brazil
237 F5 Amory *MS* U.S.A.
224 E3 Amos *Que.* Can.
142 D4 Åmose *r.* Denmark
142 C2 Åmot *Buskerud* Norway
142 B2 Åmot *Telemark* Norway
141 L3 Åmot Sweden
Amota *i.* Vanuatu *see* Mota
250 A6 Amotape, Cerros de *mts* Peru
142 E2 Åmotfors Sweden
163 B5 Amou France
205 F2 Amour, Djebel *mts* Alg.
206 D2 Amourj Maur.
Amoy *Fujian* China *see* Xiamen
245 E4 Amozoc Mex.
213 □K2 Ampanefena Madag.
115 D2 Ampani *Orissa* India
213 □J5 Ampanihy Madag.
213 □K3 Amparafaravola Madag.
114 D5 Amparai Sri Lanka
256 D5 Amparo Brazil
213 □K3 Ampasimanolotra Madag.
213 □K3 Ampasimbe Madag.
178 C3 Ampass Austria
198 C2 Ampelonas Greece
95 G5 Ampenan *Lombok* Indon.
173 F3 Amper *r.* Ger.
207 H4 Amper Nigeria
264 I3 Ampere Seamount *sea feature* N. Atlantic Ocean
191 H2 Ampezzo Italy
173 G3 Ampfing Ger.
173 H3 Ampflwang im Hausruckwald Austria
90 D3 Amphitrite Group *is* Paracel Is
160 C3 Amplepuis France
151 F3 Amport *Hampshire, England* U.K.
186 D4 Amposta Spain
151 G2 Ampthill *Bedfordshire, England* U.K.
183 F3 Ampudia Spain
183 G1 Ampuero Spain
161 E5 Ampus France
225 H3 Amqui *Que.* Can.
114 C2 Amrabad *Andhra Prad.* India
124 C2 'Amrah, Jabal *hill* Saudi Arabia
124 C5 'Amrān Yemen
Amraoti *Mahar.* India *see* Amravati
116 D5 Amravati *Mahar.* India
116 B5 Amreli *Gujarat* India
190 E1 Amriswil Switz.
116 C3 Amritsar *Punjab* India
116 D3 Amroha *Uttar Prad.* India
168 D1 Amrum *i.* Ger.
140 L2 Åmsele Sweden
Amselfeld *prov.* Yugo. *see* Kosovo
164 D2 Amstelveen Neth.
164 D2 Amsterdam Neth.
215 H2 Amsterdam S. Africa
233 F3 Amsterdam *NY* U.S.A.
232 C4 Amsterdam *OH* U.S.A.
265 J7 Amsterdam, Île *i.* Indian Ocean
179 F2 Amstetten Austria
172 D3 Amstetten Ger.
235 F1 Amston *CT* U.S.A.
208 D2 Am Timan Chad
172 D4 Amtzell Ger.
250 C4 Amú *r.* Col.
120 D3 Amudar'ya *r.* Asia
Amudaryo *r.* Asia *see* Amudar'ya
221 I2 Amund Ringnes Island *Nunavut* Can.
263 G2 Amundsen, Mount Antarctica
267 K10 Amundsen Abyssal Plain *sea feature* Southern Ocean
268 B1 Amundsen Basin *sea feature* Arctic Ocean
262 O1 Amundsen Coast Antarctica
220 F2 Amundsen Gulf *N.W.T.* Can.
267 K10 Amundsen Ridge *sea feature* Southern Ocean
263 A1 Amundsen-Scott *research stn* Antarctica
95 F3 Amuntai *Kalimantan Selatan* Indon.
100 E2 Amur *r.* China/Rus. Fed. *alt.* Heilong Jiang
93 C2 Amurang *Sulawesi Utara* Indon.
Amur Oblast *admin. div.* Rus. Fed. *see* Amurskaya Oblast'
183 H1 Amurrio Spain
100 F2 Amursk Rus. Fed.
100 D1 Amurskaya Oblast' *admin. div.* Rus. Fed.
100 D3 Amurzet Rus. Fed.
195 F4 Amusa *r.* Italy
183 F2 Amusco Spain
198 B2 Amvrakia, Limni *l.* Greece
198 B2 Amvrakikos Kolpos *b.* Greece
137 J4 Amvrosiyivka Ukr.
Amyderya *r.* Asia *see* Amudar'ya
198 B1 Amyntaio Greece
226 E1 Amyot *Ont.* Can.
197 I4 Amzacea Romania
202 D6 Am-Zoer Chad
199 E1 Ana *r.* Turkey
79 □3 Anaa *atoll Arch. des Tuamotu* Fr. Polynesia
93 B3 Anabanua *Sulawesi Selatan* Indon.
131 M2 Anabar *r.* Rus. Fed.
83 E3 Ana Branch *r. N.S.W.* Austr.
128 B3 'Anabtā West Bank
240 H4 Anacapa Islands *CA* U.S.A.
193 G4 Anacapri Italy
251 E2 Anaco Venez.
238 D2 Anaconda *MT* U.S.A.
238 B1 Anacortes *WA* U.S.A.
237 D5 Anadarko *OK* U.S.A.
182 B4 Anadia Port.
126 E2 Anadolu Dağları *mts* Turkey
131 S3 Anadyr' Rus. Fed.
131 S3 Anadyr' *r.* Rus. Fed.
Anadyr, Gulf of Rus. Fed. *see* Anadyrskiy Zaliv
131 T3 Anadyrskiy Zaliv *b.* Rus. Fed.
199 D3 Anafi *i.* Greece
254 E5 Anagé Brazil
193 F3 Anagni Italy
Anagnia Italy *see* Anagni
127 F4 'Ānah Iraq
240 I5 Anaheim *CA* U.S.A.
222 E4 Anahim Lake *B.C.* Can.
240 □B7 Anahola *HI* U.S.A.
243 E3 Anáhuac Mex.
245 F2 Anáhuac Mex.
237 E6 Anahuac *TX* U.S.A.
114 C4 Anaimalai Hills India
114 C4 Anai Mudi Peak *Kerala* India
Anaiteum *i.* Vanuatu *see* Anatom
251 I5 Anajás Brazil
251 I5 Anajás, Ilha *i.* Brazil
254 D2 Anajatuba Brazil
213 □I4 Anakao Madag.
115 D2 Anakapalle *Andhra Prad.* India
85 F4 Anakie *Qld* Austr.
213 □J2 Analalava Madag.
256 D5 Analândia Brazil
213 □I4 Analavelona *mts* Madag.
234 C1 Analomink *PA* U.S.A.
251 F5 Anamã Brazil
94 D2 Anambas, Kepulauan *is* Indon.
207 G5 Anambra *state* Nigeria
Anamooka *i.* Tonga *see* Nomuka
236 F3 Anamosa *IA* U.S.A.
251 G4 Anamu *r.* Brazil
126 D3 Anamur Turkey
104 A5 Anan Japan
116 C5 Anand *Gujarat* India
117 F5 Anandapur *Orissa* India
116 D3 Anandpur *Punjab* India
117 F5 Anandpur *r. W. Bengal* India
121 I4 Anan'ev Kyrg.
114 C3 Anantapur *Andhra Prad.* India
116 C2 Anantnag Jammu and Kashmir
116 D4 Anant Peth *Madh. Prad.* India
Ananyev Ukr. *see* Anan'yiv
Anan'yevo Kyrg. *see* Anan'ev
136 E4 Anan'yiv Ukr.
135 G7 Anapa Rus. Fed.
195 E5 Anapo *r. Sicilia* Italy
198 D4 Anapodaris *r. Kriti* Greece
256 C2 Anápolis Brazil
251 I5 Anapú *r.* Brazil
Anár Fin. *see* Inari
122 C4 Anār Iran
122 C3 Anārak Iran
122 B3 Anarbar *r.* Iran
177 L3 Anarcs Hungary
263 L2 Anare Mountains Antarctica
147 A4 Anascaul Rep. of Ireland
247 □1 Añasco Puerto Rico
247 □1 Añasco, Río Grande de *r.* Puerto Rico
140 M2 Ånäset Sweden
137 J4 Anastasiyevka Rus. Fed.
137 I5 Anastasiyevskaya Rus. Fed.
91 K3 Anatahan *i.* N. Mariana Is
Anatajan *i.* N. Mariana Is *see* Anatahan
199 G2 Anatolia *reg.* Turkey
198 D1 Anatoliki Makedonia kai Thraki *admin. reg.* Greece
78 □5 Anatom *i.* Vanuatu
258 E3 Añatuya Arg.
251 F4 Anauá *r.* Brazil
256 A5 Anaurilândia Brazil
251 F5 Anavilhanas, Arquipélago das *is* Brazil
183 E4 Anaya de Alba Spain
Anaypazari Turkey *see* Gülnar
106 C3 Anbei *Gansu* China
101 C5 Anbyon N. Korea
182 B4 Ançã Port.
182 C2 Ancares, Serra dos *mts* Spain
252 A2 Ancash *dept* Peru
227 H4 Ancaster *Ont.* Can.
151 G2 Ancaster *Lincolnshire, England* U.K.
258 D3 Ancasti, Sierra *mts* Arg.
161 B4 Ance *r.* France
161 E4 Ancelle France
158 E4 Ancenis France
157 F4 Ancerville France
Anchang *Sichuan* China *see* Anxian
207 H4 Anchau Nigeria
257 G4 Anchieta Brazil
220 D3 Anchorage *AK* U.S.A.
Anchorage Island *atoll* Cook Is *see* Suwarrow
Anchuthengu *Kerala* India *see* Anjengo
Anci *Hebei* China *see* Langfang
138 D4 Ančia *r.* Lith.
183 H2 Ancín Spain
An Cóbh Rep. of Ireland *see* Cóbh
252 A2 Ancón Peru
191 I5 Ancona Italy
191 H5 Ancona *prov. Marche* Italy
156 C3 Ancre *r.* France
146 F6 Ancrum *Scottish Borders, Scotland* U.K.
211 C8 Ancuabe Moz.
259 B6 Ancud Chile
259 B6 Ancud, Golfo de *g.* Chile
156 E5 Ancy-le-Franc France
Ancyra Turkey *see* Ankara
Anda *Heilong.* China *see* Daqing
100 C3 Anda *Heilong.* China
260 B5 Andacollo Arg.
260 B2 Andacollo Chile
84 C5 Andado *N.T.* Austr.
252 B3 Andahuaylas Peru
213 □K3 Andaingo Gara Madag.
117 F5 Andal *W. Bengal* India
Andalaly Rus. Fed. *see* Nozhay-Yurt
258 D2 Andalgalá Arg.
191 G2 Andalo Italy
140 I3 Åndalsnes Norway
185 F3 Andalucía *aut. comm.* Spain
Andalusia S. Africa *see* Jan Kempdorp
Andalusia *aut. comm.* Spain *see* Andalucía
231 C6 Andalusia *AL* U.S.A.
125 G3 Andām, Wādī *r.* Oman
97 A5 Andaman and Nicobar Islands *union terr.* India
265 K4 Andaman Basin *sea feature* Indian Ocean
115 G3 Andaman Islands *Andaman & Nicobar Is* India
97 A5 Andaman Sea Indian Ocean
82 D2 Andamooka *S.A.* Austr.
161 C3 Andance France
213 □K2 Andapa Madag.
185 H4 Andarax *r.* Spain
179 I3 Andau Austria
182 E3 Andavías Spain
173 F4 Andechs Ger.
190 E2 Andeer Switz.
Andegavum France *see* Angers
190 D1 Andelfingen Switz.
156 B3 Andelle *r.* France
157 F4 Andelot-Blancheville France
160 D2 Andelot-en-Montagne France
178 A3 Andelsbuch Austria
164 E3 Andelst Neth.
140 L1 Andenes Norway
165 E4 Andenne Belgium
207 F3 Andéramboukane Mali
165 D4 Anderlecht Belgium
165 D4 Anderlues Belgium
190 D2 Andermatt Switz.
169 C5 Andernach Ger.
163 A4 Andernos-les-Bains France
143 G1 Andersbo Sweden
220 F3 Anderson *r. N.W.T.* Can.
220 D3 Anderson *AK* U.S.A.
240 F1 Anderson *CA* U.S.A.
230 C3 Anderson *IN* U.S.A.
237 E4 Anderson *MO* U.S.A.
231 D5 Anderson *SC* U.S.A.
83 F5 Anderson Bay *Tas.* Austr.
232 B5 Andersonville *OH* U.S.A.
169 C3 Andervenne Ger.
250 C3 Andes Col.
252 B3 Andes *mts* S. America
140 L1 Andfjorden *sea chan.* Norway
Andhíparos *i.* Greece *see* Antiparos
114 C2 Andhra Pradesh *state* India
164 E2 Andijk Neth.
Andijon Uzbek. *see* Andizhan
Andijon Wiloyati *admin. div.* Uzbek. *see* Andizhanskaya Oblast'
Andikíra Greece *see* Antikyra
213 □K3 Andilamena Madag.
213 □K3 Andilanatoby Madag.
157 F5 Andilly-en-Bassigny France
122 B3 Andīmeshk Iran
Andímilos *i.* Greece *see* Antimilos
Andípsara *i.* Greece *see* Antipsara
256 B5 Andirá Brazil
111 C4 Andir He *r.* China
126 E3 Andırın Turkey
129 E2 Andiyskoye Koysu *r.* Rus. Fed.
114 C4 Andiyur *Tamil Nadu* India
121 H4 Andizhan Uzbek.
Andizhan Oblast *admin. div.* Uzbek. *see* Andizhanskaya Oblast'
121 H4 Andizhanskaya Oblast' *admin. div.* Uzbek.
123 F2 Andkhui *r.* Afgh.
123 F2 Andkhvoy Afgh.
157 H4 Andlau France
157 H4 Andlau *r.* France
186 A1 Andoain Spain
213 □K2 Andoany Madag.
250 B5 Andoas Peru
177 G5 Andocs Hungary
139 K2 Andoga *r.* Rus. Fed.
139 K2 Andogskaya Gryada *hills* Rus. Fed.
213 □K2 Andohajango Madag.
114 C2 Andol *Andhra Prad.* India
114 C2 Andola *Karnataka* India
157 H4 Andolsheim France
Andong *Liaoning* China *see* Dandong
101 D5 Andong S. Korea
85 E2 Andoom *Qld* Austr.
179 E2 Andorf Austria
177 J4 Andornaktálya Hungary
190 D3 Andorno Micca Italy
186 E2 Andorra *country* Europe
186 C4 Andorra Spain
186 E2 Andorra la Vella Andorra
Andorra la Vieja Andorra *see* Andorra la Vella
183 I2 Andosilla Spain
159 F3 Andouillé France
177 H4 Andovce Slovakia
151 F3 Andover *Hampshire, England* U.K.
235 F1 Andover *CT* U.S.A.
233 H3 Andover *MA* U.S.A.
233 H3 Andover *NH* U.S.A.
234 D2 Andover *NJ* U.S.A.
232 E3 Andover *NY* U.S.A.
232 C4 Andover *OH* U.S.A.
140 K1 Andøya *i.* Norway
139 K2 Andozero, Ozero *l.* Rus. Fed.
161 C3 Andrable *r.* France
256 D5 Andradas Brazil
241 J5 Andrade *CA* U.S.A.
256 B4 Andradina Brazil
Andraitx Spain *see* Andratx
213 □J3 Andramasina Madag.
195 H3 Andrano Italy
213 □I4 Andranopasy Madag.
187 F5 Andratx Spain
220 A4 Andreanof Islands *AK* U.S.A.
139 I3 Andreapol' Rus. Fed.
140 □ Andrée Land *reg.* Svalbard
257 G1 André Fernandes Brazil
257 E4 Andrelândia Brazil
257 E3 Andrequicé Brazil
175 H4 Andrespol Pol.
163 C5 Andrest France
223 H4 Andrew *Alta* Can.
231 E5 Andrews *SC* U.S.A.
237 C5 Andrews *TX* U.S.A.
121 J3 Andreyevka *Almatinskaya Oblast'* Kazakh.
121 F1 Andreyevka *Severnyy Kazakhstan* Kazakh.
120 B1 Andreyevka Rus. Fed.
137 G1 Andreykovichi Rus. Fed.
160 C3 Andrézieux-Bouthéon France
193 I3 Andria Italy
213 □J3 Andriamena Madag.
213 □J3 Andriba Madag.
177 L4 Andrid Romania
214 E5 Andrieskraal S. Africa
214 C2 Andriesvale S. Africa
213 □J4 Andringitra *mts* Madag.
137 I4 Andrivka Ukr.
136 D2 Andriyevychi Ukr.
137 I4 Andriyivka *Donets'ka Oblast'* Ukr.
137 I3 Andriyivka *Kharkivs'ka Oblast'* Ukr.
137 G5 Andriyivka *Respublika Krym* Ukr.
137 I4 Andriyivka *Zaporiz'ka Oblast'* Ukr.
213 □J5 Androka Madag.
213 □K2 Androna *reg.* Madag.
Andropov Rus. Fed. *see* Rybinsk
246 C1 Andros *i.* Bahamas
198 D3 Andros *Notio Aigaio* Greece
198 D3 Andros *i.* Greece
233 I3 Androscoggin *r. ME/NH* U.S.A.
120 B1 Androsovka Rus. Fed.
246 C1 Andros Town *Andros* Bahamas
Andrushevka Ukr. *see* Andrushivka
136 E2 Andrushivka Ukr.
136 E3 Andrushky Ukr.
175 H6 Andrychów Pol.
175 K3 Andrzejewo Pol.
140 L1 Andselv Norway
185 F2 Andújar Spain
209 C7 Andulo Angola
161 B4 Anduze France
129 C1 Andzhiyevskiy Rus. Fed.
87 F4 Anec, Lake *salt flat W.A.* Austr.
259 C6 Anecón Grande *mt.* Arg.
Āneen-Kio N. Pacific Ocean *see* Wake Atoll
247 F3 Anegada *i.* Virgin Is (U.K.)
259 E6 Anegada, Bahía *b.* Arg.
247 G3 Anegada Passage Virgin Is (U.K.)
241 K5 Anegam *AZ* U.S.A.
207 F5 Aného Togo
Aneityum *i.* Vanuatu *see* Anatom
'Aneiza, Jabal *hill* Iraq *see* 'Unayzah, Jabal
78 □3b Aneju *i. Majuro* Marshall Is
114 C3 Anekal *Karnataka* India
128 A1 Anemourion *tourist site* Turkey
78 □3b Anemwanot *i. Majuro* Marshall Is
136 E4 Anenii Noi Moldova
156 B4 Anet France
Anetchom, Île *i.* Vanuatu *see* Anatom
186 D2 Aneto *mt.* Spain
Ānewetak *atoll* Marshall Is *see* Enewetak
Aneytioum, Île *i.* Vanuatu *see* Anatom
203 I6 Anfile Bay Eritrea
178 B5 Anfo Italy
109 E3 Anfu *Jiangxi* China
114 C4 Angadippuram *Kerala* India
84 B2 Angalarri *r. N.T.* Austr.
244 D4 Angangueo Mex.
107 I2 Ang'angxi *Heilong.* China
98 H1 Angara *r.* Rus. Fed.
207 F4 Angaradébou Benin
98 H1 Angarsk Rus. Fed.
84 C5 Angas Downs *N.T.* Austr.
86 F4 Angas Range *hills W.A.* Austr.
82 D3 Angaston *S.A.* Austr.
92 B3 Angat Phil.
Angatau *atoll Arch. des Tuamotu* Fr. Polynesia *see* Fangatau
256 C5 Angatuba Brazil
92 □ Angaur *i.* Palau
141 K3 Ånge Sweden
182 B4 Angeja Port.
251 F3 Angel, Salto del *waterfall* Venez.
242 B2 Angel de la Guarda, Isla *i.* Mex.
92 B3 Angeles Phil.
Angel Falls Venez. *see* Angel, Salto del
142 E3 Ängelholm Sweden
237 E6 Angelina *r. TX* U.S.A.
85 F5 Angellala Creek *r. Qld* Austr.
87 C4 Angelo *r. W.A.* Austr.
245 G4 Angel R. Cabada Mex.
240 G2 Angels Camp *CA* U.S.A.
143 E3 Angelstad Sweden
160 C1 Angely France
173 G4 Anger Ger.
210 C1 Āngereb Wenz *r.* Eth.
140 L3 Ångermanälven *r.* Sweden
170 F2 Angermünde Ger.
171 C3 Angern Ger.
179 H2 Angern an der March Austria
159 F4 Angers France
156 C4 Angerville France
191 H5 Anghiari Italy
254 D4 Angical Brazil
254 F3 Angicos Brazil
240 H4 Angiola *CA* U.S.A.
198 C1 Angitis *r.* Greece
97 C4 Angkor *tourist site* Cambodia
162 B3 Anglade France
162 E3 Anglards-de-Salers France
150 B3 Angle *Pembrokeshire, Wales* U.K.
81 A7 Anglem, Mount *hill Stewart I.* N.Z.
222 G5 Anglemont *B.C.* Can.
163 E5 Anglès France
186 F3 Anglès Spain
150 C1 Anglesey *i. Wales* U.K.
186 E3 Anglesona Spain
159 G5 Angles-sur-l'Anglin France
163 A5 Anglet France
237 E6 Angleton *TX* U.S.A.
227 H2 Angliers *Que.* Can.
159 G5 Angliers France
162 C2 Anglin *r.* France
Anglo-Egyptian Sudan *country* Africa *see* Sudan
192 A4 Anglona *reg. Sardegna* Italy
156 D4 Anglure France
Angmagssalik Greenland *see* Ammassalik
213 H3 Angoche Moz.
122 D5 Angohrān Iran
162 D3 Angoisse France
260 A5 Angol Chile
209 C7 Angola *country* Africa
230 C3 Angola *IN* U.S.A.
232 D3 Angola *NY* U.S.A.
264 I7 Angola Basin *sea feature* S. Atlantic Ocean
220 E4 Angoon *AK* U.S.A.
Angora Turkey *see* Ankara
242 C3 Angostura Mex.
162 C3 Angoulême France
162 A2 Angoulins France
216 □1a Angra do Heroísmo *Terceira* Azores
257 E5 Angra dos Reis Brazil
121 G4 Angren Uzbek.
193 G4 Angri Italy
159 F4 Angrie France
97 C4 Ang Thong Thai.
107 I2 Anguang *Jilin* China
186 C2 Angüés Spain
183 H2 Anguiano Spain
247 G3 Anguilla *terr.* West Indies
246 C2 Anguilla Cays *is* Bahamas
193 E2 Anguillara Sabazia Italy
191 G3 Anguillara Veneta Italy
183 H3 Anguita Spain
107 G4 Anguo *Hebei* China
84 D2 Angurugu *N.T.* Austr.
227 H3 Angus *Ont.* Can.
146 F5 Angus *admin. div. Scotland* U.K.
240 F2 Angwin *CA* U.S.A.
256 C3 Anhanguera Brazil
165 D4 Anhée Belgium
142 D3 Anholt *i.* Denmark
109 D2 Anhua *Hunan* China
109 F1 Anhui *prov.* China
Anhwei *prov.* China *see* Anhui
129 C3 Ani *tourist site* Turkey
191 F4 Ania *r.* Italy
220 C3 Aniak *AK* U.S.A.
161 B5 Aniane France
156 D2 Aniche France
256 C2 Anicuns Brazil
207 F5 Anié Togo
163 B6 Anie, Pic d' *mt.* France
193 E3 Aniene *r.* Italy
178 E3 Anif Austria
103 □3 Ani-jima *i.* Japan
120 E2 Anikhovka Rus. Fed.
134 H4 Anikovo Rus. Fed.
105 G2 Animaki-san *hill* Japan
239 E4 Animas *r. CO* U.S.A.
197 E3 Anina Romania
183 I3 Aniñón Spain
207 H6 Añisoc Equat. Guinea
255 C8 Anitápolis Brazil
199 G2 Anıtkaya *Afyon* Turkey
128 A1 Anıtlı Turkey
100 G3 Aniva *Sakhalin* Rus. Fed.
100 G3 Aniva, Zaliv *b. Sakhalin* Rus. Fed.
213 □K3 Anivorano Madag.
213 □K2 Anivorano Avaratra Madag.
226 C3 Aniwa *WI* U.S.A.
78 □5 Aniwa *i.* Vanuatu
156 D3 Anizy-le-Château France
116 C5 Anjad *Madh. Prad.* India
213 □J3 Anjafy *mt.* Madag.
141 N3 Anjalankoski Fin.
116 D5 Anjangaon *Mahar.* India
116 B5 Anjar *Gujarat* India
114 C4 Anjengo *Kerala* India
109 F2 Anji *Zhejiang* China
116 D5 Anji *Mahar.* India
Anjiang *Hunan* China *see* Qianyang
104 D4 Anjō Japan
122 D3 Anjoman Iran
162 B1 Anjou, Val d' *val.* France
Anjouan *i.* Comoros *see* Nzwani
213 □J3 Anjozorobe Madag.
99 M4 Anjŭ N. Korea
164 F1 Anjum Neth.
207 G3 Anka Nigeria
213 □I4 Ankaboa, Tanjona *pt* Madag.
108 D1 Ankang *Shaanxi* China
126 D3 Ankara Turkey
199 G1 Ankara *prov.* Turkey
191 I3 Ankaran Slovenia
143 G3 Ankarsrum Sweden
140 L2 Ankarsund Sweden
213 □K2 Ankatafa Madag.
213 □J3 Ankavandra Madag.
213 □J4 Ankazoabo Madag.
213 □J3 Ankazobe Madag.
213 □J3 Ankazomiriotra Madag.
236 E3 Ankeny *IA* U.S.A.
170 D2 Ankershagen Ger.
213 □I4 Ankiliabo Madag.
170 E2 Anklam Ger.
116 C5 Ankleshwar *Gujarat* India
Anklesvar *Gujarat* India *see* Ankleshwar
213 □K3 Ankofa *mt.* Madag.
178 E3 Ankogel *mt.* Austria
114 B3 Ankola *Karnataka* India
207 G5 Ankpa Nigeria
168 C3 Ankum Ger.
149 I4 Anlaby *East Riding of Yorkshire, England* U.K.
173 F3 Anlauter *r.* Ger.
160 B2 Anlezy France
165 E5 Anlier, Forêt d' *for.* Belgium
Anling *Henan* China *see* Yanling
207 F5 Anloga Ghana
108 C3 Anlong *Guizhou* China
97 D4 Ânlong Vêng Cambodia
109 E2 Anlu *Hubei* China
232 C5 Anmoore *WV* U.S.A.
An Muileann gCearr Rep. of Ireland *see* Mullingar
263 D2 Ann, Cape Antarctica
135 H6 Anna Rus. Fed.
187 C5 Anna Spain
232 A4 Anna *OH* U.S.A.
205 G1 Annaba Alg.
189 A7 Annaba *prov.* Alg.
171 E5 Annaberg-Buchholtz Ger.
128 C4 An Nabk Saudi Arabia
128 C2 An Nabk Syria
171 E4 Annaburg Ger.
147 C4 Annacotty Rep. of Ireland
124 C1 An Nafūd *des.* Saudi Arabia
147 C1 Annagry Rep. of Ireland
171 E4 Annahütte Ger.
251 G4 Annai Guyana
127 G5 An Najaf Iraq
127 F5 An Najaf *governorate* Iraq
105 E2 Annaka Japan
147 D2 Annalee *r.* Rep. of Ireland
147 F2 Annalong *Northern Ireland* U.K.
96 D3 Annam Highlands *mts* Laos/Vietnam
148 C4 Annamoe Rep. of Ireland
146 E7 Annan *Dumfries and Galloway, Scotland* U.K.
146 E7 Annan *r. Scotland* U.K.
234 D2 Annandale *NJ* U.S.A.
232 E5 Annandale *VA* U.S.A.
164 D2 Anna Paulowna Neth.
86 D3 Anna Plains *W.A.* Austr.
234 B4 Annapolis *MD* U.S.A.
225 H4 Annapolis Royal *N.S.* Can.
117 E3 Annapurna I *mt.* Nepal
227 F4 Ann Arbor *MI* U.S.A.
251 G3 Anna Regina Guyana
171 C4 Annarode Ger.
An Nás Rep. of Ireland *see* Naas
127 G5 An Nāşirīyah Iraq
147 E2 Annayalla Rep. of Ireland
146 D6 Annbank *South Ayrshire, Scotland* U.K.
193 I5 Annea *r.* Italy
87 C5 Annean, Lake *salt flat W.A.* Austr.
234 B4 Anne Arundel County *county MD* U.S.A.
Anne Arundel Town *MD* U.S.A. *see* Annapolis
160 E3 Annecy France
160 E3 Annecy, Lac d' *l.* France
160 E3 Annecy-le-Vieux France
160 E2 Annemasse France
164 F1 Annen Neth.
162 C3 Annesse-et-Beaulieu France
161 C3 Anneyron France
149 H3 Annfield Plain *Durham, England* U.K.
148 E2 Annick *r. Scotland* U.K.
85 E2 Annie *r. Qld* Austr.
128 C3 An Nimārah Syria
124 C4 An Nimāş Saudi Arabia
108 B3 Anning *Yunnan* China
108 B3 Anning He *r. Sichuan* China
139 M5 Annino Rus. Fed.
231 C5 Anniston *AL* U.S.A.
207 G7 Annobón *i.* Equat. Guinea
156 C2 Annœullin France
161 C3 Annonay France
161 E5 Annot France
246 □ Annotto Bay Jamaica
148 D3 Annsborough *Northern Ireland* U.K.
125 E2 An Nu'ayrīyah Saudi Arabia
125 E2 An Nuqay'ah Qatar
232 B6 Annville *KY* U.S.A.
234 B2 Annville *PA* U.S.A.
172 B2 Annweiler am Trifels Ger.
186 A1 Anoeta Spain
198 D4 Anogeia *Kriti* Greece
226 A3 Anoka *MN* U.S.A.
198 C2 Ano Lechonia *Thessalia* Greece
183 I3 Añón Spain
Anonima *atoll* Micronesia *see* Namonuito
139 M4 Anopino Rus. Fed.
156 E3 Anor France
185 F2 Añora Spain
251 F5 Anori Brazil
213 □K3 Anosibe An'Ala Madag.
157 G4 Anould France
183 G5 Añover de Tajo Spain
199 D4 Ano Viannos *Kriti* Greece
Anóyia *Kriti* Greece *see* Anogeia
108 D4 Anpu *Guangdong* China
108 D4 Anpu Gang *b.* China
109 F2 Anqing *Anhui* China
107 H4 Anqiu *Shandong* China
183 H4 Anquela del Ducado Spain
178 D4 Anras Austria
109 E3 Anren *Hunan* China
169 D4 Anröchte Ger.
An Rubha *pen. Scotland* U.K. *see* Eye Peninsula
165 E4 Ans Belgium
142 C3 Ans Denmark
162 C3 Ansac-sur-Vienne France
107 F4 Ansai *Shaanxi* China
173 E2 Ansbach Ger.
160 C3 Anse France
246 D3 Anse-à-Galets Haiti
246 E3 Anse-à-Pitre Haiti
246 D3 Anse-à-Veau Haiti
247 □2 Anse Bertrand Guadeloupe
192 D2 Ansedonia Italy
165 D4 Anseremme Belgium
83 F4 Anser Group *is Tas.* Austr.
179 F2 Ansfelden Austria
146 E5 An Sgarsoch *mt. Scotland* U.K.
107 I3 Anshan *Liaoning* China
108 C3 Anshun *Guizhou* China
108 B2 Anshunchang *Sichuan* China
182 B5 Ansião Port.
191 H2 Ansiei *r.* Italy
260 C2 Ansilta *mt.* Arg.
260 C2 Ansilta, Cordillera de *mts* Arg.
258 G3 Ansina Uru.
126 E5 An Sirhān, Wādī *watercourse* Saudi Arabia
140 L3 Ansjö Sweden
236 D3 Ansley *NE* U.S.A.
186 C2 Ansó Spain
237 D5 Anson *TX* U.S.A.
84 B2 Anson Bay *N.T.* Austr.
207 F3 Ansongo Mali
235 E1 Ansonia *CT* U.S.A.
232 A4 Ansonia *OH* U.S.A.
224 D3 Ansonville *Ont.* Can.
171 E5 Ansprung Ger.
232 C5 Ansted *WV* U.S.A.
146 F5 Anstruther *Fife, Scotland* U.K.
Ansu *Hebei* China *see* Xushui
151 I2 Ant *r. England* U.K.
116 D4 Anta *Rajasthan* India
252 B3 Anta Peru
252 B3 Antabamba Peru
126 E3 Antakya Turkey
213 □K2 Antalaha Madag.
199 G3 Antalya Turkey
199 G3 Antalya *prov.* Turkey
199 G3 Antalya Körfezi *g.* Turkey
213 □K3 Antanambao Manampotsy Madag.
213 □J3 Antananarivo Madag.
213 □J3 Antananarivo *prov.* Madag.
213 □J3 Antanifotsy Madag.
213 □J5 Antanimora Atsimo Madag.
An tAonach Rep. of Ireland *see* Nenagh
262 Antarctica *continent*
262 T2 Antarctic Peninsula Antarctica
182 C4 Antas Port.
185 I3 Antas Spain
185 I3 Antas *r.* Spain
182 C2 Antas de Ulla Spain
146 C4 An Teallach *mt. Scotland* U.K.
241 I2 Antelope Range *mts NV* U.S.A.
162 B3 Antenne *r.* France
185 F3 Antequera Spain
178 D4 Anterselva di Sopra Italy
234 A1 Antes Fort *PA* U.S.A.
161 E5 Anthéor France
178 E3 Anthering Austria
160 B1 Anthien France
237 D4 Anthony *KS* U.S.A.
239 F5 Anthony *NM* U.S.A.
82 C2 Anthony, Lake *salt flat S.A.* Austr.
84 C3 Anthony Lagoon *N.T.* Austr.
204 C3 Anti Atlas *mts* Morocco
161 F5 Antibes France
225 I3 Anticosti, Île d' *i. Que.* Can.
Anticosti Island *Que.* Can. *see* Anticosti, Île d'
159 G2 Antifer, Cap d' *c.* France
226 C3 Antigo *WI* U.S.A.
225 I4 Antigonish *N.S.* Can.
247 □2 Antigua *i.* Antigua and Barbuda
216 □3b Antigua *Fuerteventura* Canary Is
243 H6 Antigua Guat.
Antigua *country* West Indies *see* Antigua and Barbuda
247 □2 Antigua and Barbuda *country* West Indies
Antigua Guatemala Guat. *see* Antigua
245 E2 Antiguo-Morelos Mex.
198 C2 Antikyra Greece
198 C4 Antikythiro, Steno *sea chan.* Greece
Anti Lebanon *mts* Lebanon/Syria *see* Sharqī, Jabal ash
246 D2 Antilla Cuba
195 E5 Antillo *Sicilia* Italy
198 D3 Antimilos *i.* Greece
241 L2 Antimony *UT* U.S.A.
An tInbhear Mór Rep. of Ireland *see* Arklow
Antioch Turkey *see* Antakya
240 G2 Antioch *CA* U.S.A.
226 C4 Antioch *IL* U.S.A.
128 A1 Antiocheia ad Cragum *tourist site* Turkey
Antiochia Turkey *see* Antakya
250 C3 Antioquia Col.
250 C3 Antioquia *dept* Col.
198 D3 Antiparos *i.* Greece
77 H6 Antipodes Islands N.Z.
199 D2 Antipsara *i.* Greece
192 B2 Antisanti *Corse* France
Antium Italy *see* Anzio
237 E5 Antlers *OK* U.S.A.

An t-Ob Western Isles, Scotland U.K. see Leverburgh
252 C5 Antofagasta Chile
252 C5 Antofagasta admin. reg. Chile
165 C4 Antoing Belgium
177 H3 Antol Slovakia
190 E4 Antola, Monte mt. Italy
213 □J2 Antonhibe Madag.
256 C6 Antonina Brazil
136 D3 Antoniny Ukr.
195 F3 Antonio r. Italy
244 B1 Antonio Amaro Mex.
257 F4 Antônio Carlos Brazil
257 F3 Antônio Dias Brazil
António Enes Moz. see Angoche
136 E3 Antoniv Ukr.
137 G2 Antonivka Chernihivs'ka Oblast' Ukr.
137 G4 Antonivka Khersons'ka Oblast' Ukr.
177 L3 Antonivka Zakarpats'ka Oblast' Ukr.
245 G4 Antón Lizardo Mex.
162 C3 Antonne-et-Trigonant France
246 B2 Antón Recio Cuba
156 C4 Antony France
136 C1 Antopal' Belarus
161 C4 Antraigues-sur-Volane France
158 E3 Antrain France
137 J3 Antratsyt Ukr.
147 E2 Antrim Northern Ireland U.K.
147 E2 Antrim county Northern Ireland U.K.
234 A1 Antrim PA U.S.A.
147 E1 Antrim Hills Northern Ireland U.K.
86 F3 Antrim Plateau W.A. Austr.
193 F2 Antrodoco Italy
134 H4 Antropovo Rus. Fed.
213 □K2 Antsahanoro Madag.
213 □K2 Antsakabary Madag.
213 □J3 Antsalova Madag.
213 □K2 Antsambalahy Madag.
Antseranana Madag. see Antsirañana
139 I2 Antsiferovo Rus. Fed.
213 □J3 Antsirabe Madag.
213 □K2 Antsirabe Avaratra Madag.
213 □K2 Antsirañana Madag.
213 □K2 Antsirañana prov. Madag.
138 F3 Antsla Estonia
213 □J2 Antsohihy Madag.
140 M2 Anttis Sweden
141 N3 Anttola Fin.
Antu Jilin China see Songjiang
260 B5 Antuco Chile
260 B5 Antuco, Volcán vol. Chile
160 C2 Antully France
Antunnacum Ger. see Andernach
Antwerp Belgium see Antwerpen
233 F2 Antwerp NY U.S.A.
165 D3 Antwerpen Belgium
165 D3 Antwerpen prov. Belgium
186 A1 Antzuola Spain
An Uaimh Rep. of Ireland see Navan
100 E4 Anuchino Rus. Fed.
259 C6 Anueque, Sierra mts Arg.
117 F5 Anugul Orissa India
116 C3 Anupgarh Rajasthan India
114 D4 Anuradhapura Sri Lanka
Anvers Belgium see Antwerpen
262 T2 Anvers Island Antarctica
222 C2 Anvil Range mts Y.T. Can.
156 C2 Anvin France
109 F3 Anxi Fujian China
106 B3 Anxi Gansu China
108 C2 Anxian Sichuan China
109 E2 Anxiang Hunan China
107 G4 Anxin Hebei China
82 C3 Anxious Bay S.A. Austr.
Anxur Italy see Terracina
206 D5 Anyama Côte d'Ivoire
Anyang Guangxi China see Du'an
107 G4 Anyang Henan China
101 C5 Anyang S. Korea
94 D4 Anyar Jawa Barat Indon.
106 C5 A'nyêmaqên Shan mts China
109 E2 Anyi Jiangxi China
138 E4 Anykščiai Lith.
215 H2 Anysspruit S. Africa
109 E3 Anyuan Jiangxi China
109 E3 Anyuan Jiangxi China
108 C2 Anyue Sichuan China
100 F2 Anyuy r. Rus. Fed.
131 R3 Anyuysk Rus. Fed.
190 D2 Anza r. Italy
223 I3 Anzac Alta Can.
222 F4 Anzac B.C. Can.
186 C2 Anzánigo Spain
193 H3 Anzano di Puglia Italy
161 B3 Anzat-le-Luguet France
107 G4 Anze Shanxi China
165 C4 Anzegem Belgium
173 F2 Anzelberg hill Ger.
130 J4 Anzhero-Sudzhensk Rus. Fed.
193 H4 Anzi Italy
156 D2 Anzin France
176 A3 Anzing Ger.
193 E3 Anzio Italy
251 E2 Anzoátegui state Venez.
185 F3 Anzur r. Spain
78 □5 Aoba i. Vanuatu
104 B3 Aoba-yama hill Japan
103 I7 Aoga-shima i. Japan
Aohan Qi Nei Mongol China see Xinhui
183 I2 Aoiz Spain
78 □6 Aola Guadalcanal Solomon Is
Aomen Macau China see Macau
102 J3 Aomori Japan
102 J3 Aomori pref. Japan
146 C4 Aonach Buidhe hill Scotland U.K.
198 B1 Aoos r. Greece
146 B6 Aoradh Argyll and Bute, Scotland U.K.
81 C5 Aoraki mt. South I. N.Z.
97 D4 Aôral, Phnum mt. Cambodia
Aorangi mt. South I. N.Z. see Aoraki
81 C5 Aoraki mt. South I. N.Z.
81 E4 Aorangi Mountains North I. N.Z.
81 D4 Aorere r. South I. N.Z.
183 I2 Aos Spain
190 C3 Aosta Italy
160 D3 Aoste France
Aotearoa country Oceania see New Zealand
208 C2 Aouk, Bahr r. C.A.R./Chad
208 D2 Aoukalé r. C.A.R./Chad
204 D5 Aoukâr reg. Mali/Maur.
205 F4 Aoulef Alg.
204 C3 Aoulime, Jbel mt. Morocco
206 C3 Aourou Mali
161 D4 Aouste-sur-Sye France
Aoxi Jiangxi China see Le'an
Aoyang Jiangxi China see Shanggao
253 F5 Apa r. Brazil
197 F2 Apa Romania
210 B4 Apac Uganda
241 M6 Apache AZ U.S.A.
237 D5 Apache OK U.S.A.
241 L5 Apache Junction AZ U.S.A.
241 L6 Apache Peak AZ U.S.A.
252 D5 Apagado, Volcán vol. Bol.
177 K4 Apagy Hungary
197 F2 Apahida Romania
256 C5 Apaiaí r. Brazil
Apaiang atoll Kiribati see Abaiang
177 I4 Apaj Hungary
231 C6 Apalachee Bay FL U.S.A.
231 C6 Apalachicola FL U.S.A.
231 C6 Apalachicola r. FL U.S.A.
206 E5 Apam Ghana
Apamama atoll Gilbert Is Kiribati see Abemama
Apamea Turkey see Dinar
245 E4 Apan Mex.
157 G5 Apance r. France
250 D5 Apaporis r. Col.
129 D3 Aparan Armenia
257 E5 Áparecida Brazil
256 B4 Aparecida do Tabuado Brazil
177 H5 Aparhant Hungary
Aparima South I. N.Z. see Riverton
81 B7 Aparima r. South I. N.Z.
92 B2 Aparri Phil.
138 E3 Apaščia r. Lith.
244 D3 Apaseo El Grande Mex.
79 □3 Apataki atoll Arch. des Tuamotu Fr. Polynesia
177 K5 Apateu Romania
177 J5 Apátfalva Hungary
196 D3 Apatin Vojvodina, Srbija Yugo.
134 F2 Apatity Rus. Fed.
251 H3 Apatou Fr. Guiana
244 C4 Apatzingán Mex.
245 E4 Apaxtla Mex.
138 F3 Ape Latvia
191 H5 Apecchio Italy
253 E2 Apediá r. Brazil
164 E2 Apeldoorn Neth.
169 E3 Apelern Ger.
168 C2 Apen Ger.
170 C3 Apenburg Ger.
168 E2 Apensen Ger.
252 D3 Apere r. Bol.
182 C2 A Peroxa Spain
222 B2 Apex Mountain Y.T. Can.
116 E3 Api mt. Nepal
Api i. Vanuatu see Épi
Apia atoll Kiribati see Abaiang
78 □2 Apia Samoa
253 F2 Apiacas, Serra dos hills Brazil
256 C6 Apiaí Brazil
251 F4 Apiaú, Serra do mts Brazil
193 G3 Apice Italy
182 B2 A Picota Spain
191 I5 Apiro Italy
237 C4 Apishapa r. CO U.S.A.
80 E3 Apiti North I. N.Z.
245 E4 Apizaco Mex.
129 B2 Ap'khazet'i aut. rep. Georgia
252 B4 Aplao Peru
92 C5 Apo, Mount vol. Mindanao Phil.
137 I2 Apochka r. Rus. Fed.
254 F3 Apodi Brazil
254 F3 Apodi, Chapada do hills Brazil
92 B3 Apo East Passage Phil.
171 C4 Apolda Ger.
Apollinopolis Magna Egypt see Idfu
83 E4 Apollo Bay Vic. Austr.
Apollonia Bulg. see Sozopol
182 C1 A Pontenova Spain
231 D6 Apopka FL U.S.A.
255 B6 Aporé Brazil
256 B3 Aporé Brazil
256 B3 Aporé r. Brazil
177 H5 Apostag Hungary
221 N3 Apostolens Tommelfinger mt. Greenland
258 G2 Apóstoles Arg.
137 G4 Apostolove Ukr.
251 G3 Apoteri Guyana
Apoucaroua atoll Arch. des Tuamotu Fr. Polynesia see Pukarua
92 B3 Apo West Passage Phil.
232 B6 Appalachia VA U.S.A.
232 B6 Appalachian Mountains U.S.A.
Appalla i. Fiji see Kabara
164 F2 Appelscha Neth.
193 F2 Appennino Abruzzese mts Italy
193 H4 Appennino Lucano mts Italy
193 H3 Appennino Napoletano mts Italy
191 F5 Appennino Tosco-Emiliano mts Italy
191 H5 Appennino Umbro-Marchigiano mts Italy
172 B3 Appenweier Ger.
190 E1 Appenzell Switz.
190 E1 Appenzell Ausser-Rhoden canton Switz.
190 E1 Appenzell Inner-Rhoden canton Switz.
191 G2 Appiano sulla Strada del Vino Italy
192 A2 Appietto Corse France
191 I5 Appignano Italy
164 F1 Appingedam Neth.
149 G3 Appleby-in-Westmorland Cumbria, England U.K.
146 C4 Applecross Highland, Scotland U.K.
150 C3 Appledore Devon, England U.K.
151 H3 Appledore Kent, England U.K.
236 D2 Appleton MN U.S.A.
226 C3 Appleton WI U.S.A.
149 G4 Appleton Thorn Warrington, England U.K.
240 I4 Apple Valley CA U.S.A.
156 D5 Appoigny France
232 D6 Appomattox VA U.S.A.
161 D3 Apprieu France
139 K4 Aprelevka Rus. Fed.
160 D1 Apremont France
157 F4 Apremont-la-Forêt France
190 F2 Aprica Italy
193 H3 Apricena Italy
195 F3 Aprigliano Italy
193 E3 Aprilia Italy
129 A1 Apsheronsk Rus. Fed.
Apsheronskaya Rus. Fed. see Apsheronsk
Apsheronskiy Poluostrov pen. Azer. see Abşeron Yarımadası
82 E4 Apsley Vic. Austr.
227 H3 Apsley Ont. Can.
161 D5 Apt France
256 B5 Apucarana Brazil
256 B5 Apucarana, Serra da hills Brazil
182 B3 Apúlia Port.
Apulum Romania see Alba Iulia
92 A4 Apurahuan Phil.
250 E3 Apure r. Venez.
250 D3 Apure state Venez.
252 B3 Apurímac dept Peru
252 B3 Apurimac r. Peru
Aq"a Georgia see Sokhumi
'Aqaba Jordan see Al 'Aqabah
124 A1 Aqaba, Gulf of Asia
Aqadyr Kazakh. see Agadyr'
110 B3 Aqal Xinjiang China
Aqbeyit Kazakh. see Akbeit
123 F2 Āqchah Afgh.
127 G3 Aq Chai r. Iran
122 C3 Áqdā Iran
122 A2 Aqdoghmish r. Iran
106 A3 Aqitag mt. Xinjiang China
Aqköl Akmolinskaya Oblast' Kazakh. see Akkol'
Aqköl Kazakh. see Akkol'
Aqmola Kazakh. see Astana
Aqmola Oblysy admin. div. Kazakh. see Akmolinskaya Oblast'
Aqqystaū Kazakh. see Akkystau
128 B3 'Aqraba West Bank
127 F3 'Aqrah Iraq
128 D4 'Aqran hill Saudi Arabia
Aqsay Kazakh. see Aksay
Aqsayqin Hit terr. Asia see Aksai Chin
Aqshataū Kazakh. see Akchatau
Aqshī Kazakh. see Akshiy
Aqshuqyr Kazakh. see Akshukur
Aqsū Almatinskaya Oblast' Kazakh. see Aksu
Aqsū Pavlodarskaya Oblast' Kazakh. see Aksu
Aqsū Severnyy Kazakhstan Kazakh. see Aksu
Aqsūat Vostochnyy Kazakhstan Kazakh. see Aksuat
Aqsū-Ayuly Kazakh. see Aksu-Ayuly
Aqtaū Mangistauskaya Oblast' Kazakh. see Aktau
Aqtöbe Kazakh. see Aktyubinsk
Aqtöbe Oblysy admin. div. Kazakh. see Aktyubinskaya Oblast'
Aqtoghay Karagandinskaya Oblast' Kazakh. see Aktogay
Aqtoghay Pavlodarskaya Oblast' Kazakh. see Aktogay
Aquae Grani Ger. see Aachen
Aquae Gratianae France see Aix-les-Bains
Aquae Mortuae France see Aigues-Mortes
Aquae Sextiae France see Aix-en-Provence
Aquae Statiellae Italy see Acqui Terme
241 K4 Aquarius Mountains AZ U.S.A.
241 L3 Aquarius Plateau UT U.S.A.
195 F2 Aquaviva delle Fonti Italy
235 F2 Aquebogue NY U.S.A.
253 F5 Aquidabánmi r. Para.
253 G5 Aquidauana Brazil
253 F4 Aquidauana r. Brazil
244 C4 Aquila Mex.
242 D2 Aquiles Mex.
193 H4 Aquilonia Italy
186 C2 Aquilué Spain
246 D3 Aquin Haiti
Aquincum Hungary see Budapest
193 F3 Aquino Italy
Aquinum Italy see Aquino
Aquiry r. Brazil see Acre
Aquisgranum Ger. see Aachen
163 B4 Aquitaine admin. reg. France
Aqzhal Vostochnyy Kazakhstan Kazakh. see Akzhal
Aqzhar Vostochnyy Kazakhstan Kazakh. see Akzhar
Aqzhayqyn Köli salt l. Kazakh. see Akzhaykyn, Ozero
117 F4 Ara Bihar India
186 D2 Ara r. Spain
231 C5 Arab AL U.S.A.
208 F2 Arab, Bahr el watercourse Sudan
125 E4 'Arabah, Wādī r. Yemen
128 B5 'Arabah, Wādī al watercourse Israel/Jordan
137 H5 Arabats'ka Strilka, Kosa spit Ukr.
Arabatskaya Strelka spit Ukr. see Arabats'ka Strilka, Kosa
187 B6 Arabí mt. Spain
265 I4 Arabian Basin sea feature Indian Ocean
Arabian Gulf Asia see The Gulf
125 G4 Arabian Oryx Sanctuary tourist site Saudi Arabia
119 J6 Arabian Sea Indian Ocean
129 F3 Äräb Qubalı Azer.
163 D6 Arac r. France
126 D2 Araç Turkey
251 F5 Araça r. Brazil
254 F4 Aracaju Brazil
253 G6 Aracanguy, Montes de hills Para.
258 D2 Aracar, Volcán vol. Arg.
246 D5 Aracataca Col.
254 F3 Aracati Brazil
254 E5 Aracatu Brazil
256 B4 Araçatuba Brazil
184 D3 Aracena Spain
259 C9 Aracena, Isla i. Chile
184 C3 Aracena, Sierra de hills Spain
198 B2 Arachthos r. Greece
198 B2 Arachthos, Techniti Limni resr Greece
197 E4 Aračinovo Macedonia
254 F3 Aracoiaba Brazil
257 G3 Aracruz Brazil
257 F2 Araçuaí Brazil
257 F2 Araçuaí r. Brazil
128 B4 'Arad Israel
196 E2 Arad Romania
177 K5 Arad county Romania
202 D6 Arada Chad
182 B4 Arada, Serra de mts Port.
125 F3 'Arādah U.A.E.
122 C3 Arādān Iran
184 B3 Arade r. Port.
195 H2 Aradeo Italy
177 J5 Aradului, Câmpia plain Romania
216 □3a Arafo Tenerife Canary Is
105 E2 Arafune-yama mt. Japan
76 D2 Arafura Sea Austr./Indon.
266 D6 Arafura Shelf sea feature Austr./Indon.
256 A1 Aragarças Brazil
129 D3 Aragats Lerr mt. Armenia
105 E1 Ara-gawa r. Japan
105 F3 Ara-gawa r. Japan
163 C6 Aragnouet France
183 3 Aragón aut. comm. Spain
183 I2 Aragón r. Spain
194 C5 Aragona Sicilia Italy
183 H4 Aragoncillo Spain
183 H4 Aragoncillo mt. Spain
250 E2 Aragua state Venez.
254 C4 Araguacema Brazil
254 C5 Araguaçu Brazil
251 E2 Aragua de Barcelona Venez.
256 C Araguaia r. Brazil
256 B1 Araguaiana Brazil
254 C3 Araguaína Brazil
256 A2 Araguainha Brazil
251 F2 Araguao, Boca r. mouth Venez.
256 C3 Araguari Brazil
256 C3 Araguari r. Minas Gerais Brazil
251 I4 Araguari r. Amápa Brazil
254 C3 Araguatins Brazil
129 D3 Aragvi r. Georgia
125 F4 'Ārah, Wādī r. Oman
105 E2 Arai Japan
183 H2 Araia Spain
128 B4 Araif el Naga, Gebel hill Egypt
254 E2 Araiosos Brazil
205 F4 Arak Alg.
122 B3 Arāk Iran
105 F1 Arakai-yama mt. Japan
96 A2 Arakan state Myanmar
96 A2 Arakan Yoma mts Myanmar
Arakhthos r. Greece see Arachthos
104 D2 Araki-gawa r. Japan
80 G3 Arakihi hill North I. N.Z.
114 C3 Arakkonam Tamil Nadu India
129 B3 Araklı Turkey
129 D4 Araks r. Armenia/Turkey alt. Aras (Turkey), alt. Araz (Azerbaijan)
110 C3 Aral Xinjiang China
Aral Kazakh. see Aral'sk
Aral Tajik. see Vose
129 D4 Aralık Turkey
120 E3 Aral Sea salt l. Kazakh./Uzbek.
120 E3 Aral'sk Kazakh.
120 B2 Aralsor, Ozero l. Kazakh.
120 E3 Aralsul'fat Kazakh.
Aral Tengizi salt l. Kazakh./Uzbek. see Aral Sea
85 F4 Aramac Qld Austr.
124 D2 Aramah plat. Saudi Arabia
182 B2 A Ramallosa Spain
245 E1 Aramberri Mex.
254 D3 Arame Brazil
91 J8 Aramia r. P.N.G.
163 B5 Aramits France
161 C5 Aramon France
129 E3 Aran Azer.
114 C2 Aran r. India
183 I3 Aranda r. Spain
183 G3 Aranda de Duero Spain
183 I3 Aranda de Moncayo Spain
244 C3 Arandas Mex.
196 E3 Aranđelovac Srbija Yugo.
116 E5 Arang Madh. Prad. India
182 C4 Aranhas Port.
114 C3 Arani Tamil Nadu India
147 C2 Aran Island Rep. of Ireland
147 B3 Aran Islands Rep. of Ireland
183 G4 Aranjuez Spain
212 C5 Aranos Namibia
237 D7 Aransas Pass TX U.S.A.
114 C4 Arantangi Tamil Nadu India
256 B3 Arantes r. Brazil
77 H1 Aranuka atoll Gilbert Is Kiribati
97 C4 Aranyaprathet Thai.
177 L3 Aranyosapáti Hungary
183 G4 Aranzueque Spain
103 E7 Arao Japan
237 D5 Arapaho OK U.S.A.
236 D3 Arapahoe NE U.S.A.
81 E4 Arapawa Island South I. N.Z.
261 I2 Arapey Grande r. Uru.
182 E4 Arapiles Spain
254 F4 Arapiraca Brazil
126 E3 Arapkir Turkey
256 B5 Arapongas Brazil
256 C6 Arapoti Brazil
Arapsun Turkey see Gülşehir
80 E3 Arapuni North I. N.Z.
255 C8 Araquari Brazil
127 F5 'Ar'ar Saudi Arabia
251 F5 Arara r. Brazil
250 C5 Araracuara Col.
250 C5 Araracuara, Cerros de hills Col.
255 C9 Araranguá Brazil
256 C6 Ararapira Brazil
256 C4 Araraquara Brazil
256 D5 Araras Brazil
254 E3 Araras, Açude resr Brazil
256 A3 Araras, Serra das hills Brazil
256 A6 Araras, Serra das mts Brazil
129 D4 Ararat Armenia
83 E4 Ararat Vic. Austr.
Ararat, Mount Turkey see Ağrı Dağı
254 D2 Arari Brazil
117 F4 Araria Bihar India
254 E3 Araripe Brazil
254 E3 Araripe, Chapada do hills Brazil
254 E3 Araripina Brazil
257 F5 Araruama Brazil
183 H2 Aras Spain
127 F3 Aras Turkey
127 G3 Aras r. Turkey alt. Araks (Armenia/Turkey), alt. Araz (Azerbaijan)
187 B5 Aras de Alpuente Spain
106 E1 Ar Asgat Mongolia
129 C4 Aras Güneyi Dağları mts Turkey
104 C3 Arashima-dake mt. Japan
129 B4 Aras Nehri r. Turkey
255 F5 Arataca Brazil
251 I5 Arataú r. Brazil
Aratürük Xinjiang China see Yiwu
252 D2 Arauã r. Brazil
251 F6 Arauá r. Brazil
251 F6 Arauá r. Brazil
250 D3 Arauca Col.
250 D3 Arauca dept Col.
250 E3 Arauca r. Venez.
255 C8 Araucária Brazil
258 B5 Arauco Chile
258 B5 Arauco, Golfo de b. Chile
161 C3 Araules France
250 D3 Arauquita Col.
250 D2 Araure Venez.
116 C4 Aravalli Range mts India
138 E2 Aravete Estonia
183 H3 Araviana r. Spain
160 E3 Aravis mts France
198 C1 Aravissos Greece
78 □6 Arawa P.N.G.
81 B6 Arawata r. South I. N.Z.
80 F3 Arawhana mt. North I. N.Z.
Arawhata r. South I. N.Z. see Arawata
256 D3 Araxá Brazil
Araya Spain see Araia
251 E2 Araya, Península de pen. Venez.
126 C3 Arayıt Dağı mt. Turkey
129 F3 Araz r. Azer. alt. Araks (Armenia/Turkey), alt. Aras (Turkey)
182 B4 Arazede Port.
186 B3 Arba r. Spain
186 B2 Arba de Biel r. Spain
186 B2 Arba de Luesia r. Spain
Arbailu Iraq see Arbīl
210 C3 Ārba Minch Eth.
163 C6 Arbas France
192 B5 Arbatax Sardegna Italy
134 J4 Arbazh Rus. Fed.
186 D3 Arbeca Spain
157 F5 Arbecey France
190 E2 Arbedo Switz.
Arbela Iraq see Arbīl
160 D2 Arbent France
163 B6 Arbéost France
173 E2 Arberg Ger.
Arberth Pembrokeshire, Wales U.K. see Narberth
179 F2 Arbesbach Austria
183 H4 Arbeteta Spain
191 G5 Arbia r. Italy
127 G3 Arbīl Iraq
127 F4 Arbīl governorate Iraq
183 H2 Arbizu Spain
143 F2 Arboga Sweden
160 D2 Arbois France
185 H3 Arboleas Spain
250 B2 Arboletes Col.
190 E1 Arbon Switz.
192 A5 Arborea Sardegna Italy
192 A5 Arborea reg. Sardegna Italy
223 K4 Arborfield Sask. Can.
223 L5 Arborg Man. Can.
190 D3 Arborio Italy
141 L3 Arbrå Sweden
146 F5 Arbroath Angus, Scotland U.K.
186 F3 Arbúcies Spain
240 F2 Arbuckle CA U.S.A.
123 E4 Arbu Lut, Dasht-e des. Afgh.
163 B5 Arbus France
192 A5 Arbus Sardegna Italy
137 F4 Arbuzynka Ukr.
161 D5 Arc r. France
161 E3 Arc r. France
163 A4 Arcachon France
163 A4 Arcachon, Bassin d' inlet France
232 D3 Arcade NY U.S.A.
231 D7 Arcadia FL U.S.A.
237 E5 Arcadia LA U.S.A.
226 D3 Arcadia MI U.S.A.
232 D4 Arcadia PA U.S.A.
226 B3 Arcadia WI U.S.A.
160 E3 Arcalod, Pointe d' mt. France
232 A5 Arcanum OH U.S.A.
243 H4 Arcas, Cayos is Mex.
238 A3 Arcata CA U.S.A.
240 I2 Arc Dome mt. NV U.S.A.
193 F3 Arce Italy
244 D4 Arcelia Mex.
164 F3 Arcen Neth.
157 F5 Arc-en-Barrois France
183 G1 Arceniega Spain
162 B3 Arces France
156 D4 Arces-Dilo France
160 D1 Arc-et-Senans France
191 H5 Arcevia Italy
Archangel Rus. Fed. see Arkhangel'sk
Archangel Oblast admin. div. Rus. Fed. see Arkhangel'skaya Oblast'
199 F3 Archangelos Notio Aigaio Greece
197 F4 Archar r. Bulg.
234 C1 Archbald PA U.S.A.
232 A4 Archbold OH U.S.A.
187 B6 Archena Spain
85 E2 Archer r. Qld Austr.
237 D5 Archer City TX U.S.A.
157 G4 Arches France
162 B3 Archiac France
185 F3 Archidona Spain
84 D3 Archie Creek r. Qld Austr.
177 L5 Archiş Romania
185 I2 Archivel Spain
122 D2 Archman Turkm.
192 A5 Arci, Monte hill Sardegna Italy
192 D2 Arcidosso Italy
156 E4 Arcis-sur-Aube France
122 B2 Ärçivan Azer.
160 D1 Arc-lès-Gray France
191 F3 Arco Italy
238 D3 Arco ID U.S.A.
184 □ Arco da Calheta Madeira
182 C3 Arco de Baúlhe Port.
190 E4 Arcola Italy
232 E5 Arcola VA U.S.A.
160 E2 Arçon France
160 B2 Arconce r. France
159 G3 Arconnay France
257 E4 Arcos Brazil
184 C2 Arcos Port.
183 G2 Arcos Spain
183 H3 Arcos de Jalón Spain
184 E4 Arcos de la Frontera Spain
187 B5 Arcos de las Salinas Spain
182 B3 Arcos de Valdevez Port.
114 C3 Arcot Tamil Nadu India
254 F4 Arcoverde Brazil
182 B3 Arcozelo Braga Port.
182 C4 Arcozelo Guarda Port.
182 B3 Arcozelo Porto Port.
182 B3 Arcozelo Viana do Castelo Port.
160 D1 Arc-sur-Tille France
221 J2 Arctic Bay Nunavut Can.
268 B1 Arctic Mid-Ocean Ridge sea feature Arctic Ocean
268 Arctic Ocean
220 E3 Arctic Red r. N.W.T. Can.
Arctic Red River N.W.T. Can. see Tsiigehtchic
262 N8 Arctowski research stn Antarctica
192 A5 Arcuentu, Monte hill Sardegna Italy
186 D2 Arcusa Spain
160 B1 Arcy-sur-Cure France
126 B2 Arda r. Bulg. alt. Ardas (Greece)
190 F3 Arda r. Italy
122 B2 Ardabīl Iran
122 A2 Ardabīl prov. Iran
179 F2 Ardagger Markt Austria
147 B4 Ardagh Rep. of Ireland
127 F2 Ardahan Turkey
129 C3 Ardahan prov. Turkey
122 D2 Ardāk Iran
122 C4 Ardakān Iran
122 C3 Ardakān Iran
122 B4 Ardal Iran
141 I3 Årdal Norway
183 G3 Ardal mt. Spain
185 F4 Ardales Spain
142 B2 Ardalsknapen hill Norway
141 I3 Årdalstangen Norway
147 E4 Ardanairy Rep. of Ireland
163 A6 Ardanaz Spain
129 C3 Ardanuç Turkey
192 A4 Ardara Sardegna Italy
147 C2 Ardara Rep. of Ireland
126 B2 Ardas r. Greece alt. Arda (Bulgaria)
128 C4 Arḑ aş Şawwān plain Jordan
135 H5 Ardatov Nizhegorodskaya Oblast' Rus. Fed.
135 I5 Ardatov Respublika Mordoviya Rus. Fed.
148 C5 Ardattin Rep. of Ireland
227 G3 Ardbeg Ont. Can.
146 C6 Ard Bheinn hill Scotland U.K.
148 C4 Ardcath Rep. of Ireland
146 B5 Ardchiavaig Argyll and Bute, Scotland U.K.
147 C4 Ardconry Rep. of Ireland
193 E3 Ardea Italy
161 C4 Ardèche dept Rhône-Alpes France
161 C4 Ardèche r. France
147 E3 Ardee Rep. of Ireland
146 D5 Arden Argyll and Bute, Scotland U.K.
235 D1 Arden NY U.S.A.
82 D3 Arden, Mount hill S.A. Austr.
156 E3 Ardennes dept Champagne-Ardenne France
156 E3 Ardennes r. France
162 D2 Ardentes France
146 D5 Ardentinny Argyll and Bute, Scotland U.K.
240 G2 Arden Town CA U.S.A.
147 D3 Arderin hill Rep. of Ireland
146 D4 Ardersier Highland, Scotland U.K.
161 B3 Ardes France
129 B3 Ardeşen Turkey
122 C3 Ardestān Iran
190 F2 Ardez Switz.
147 B4 Ardfert Rep. of Ireland
147 D4 Ardfinnan Rep. of Ireland
146 D4 Ardgay Highland, Scotland U.K.
147 C4 Ardglass Rep. of Ireland
147 F2 Ardglass Northern Ireland U.K.
129 B4 Ardıcın Dağı mt. Turkey
184 C2 Ardila r. Port.
197 G5 Ardino Bulg.
80 F3 Ardkeen North I. N.Z.
147 F2 Ardkeen Northern Ireland U.K.
151 H3 Ardleigh Essex, England U.K.
83 F3 Ardlethan N.S.W. Austr.
146 D5 Ardlui Argyll and Bute, Scotland U.K.
146 C5 Ardlussa Argyll and Bute, Scotland U.K.
146 C4 Ardmair Highland, Scotland U.K.
146 C6 Ardminish Argyll and Bute, Scotland U.K.
146 C5 Ardmolich Highland, Scotland U.K.
147 B3 Ardmore Rep. of Ireland
237 D5 Ardmore OK U.S.A.
234 C2 Ardmore PA U.S.A.
147 C4 Ardnacrusha Rep. of Ireland
146 B5 Ardnamurchan pen. Scotland U.K.
146 B5 Ardnamurchan, Point of Scotland U.K.
147 C3 Ardnasodan Rep. of Ireland
137 G1 Ardon' Rus. Fed.
129 D2 Ardon Respublika Severnaya Osetiya Rus. Fed.
129 D2 Ardon r. Rus. Fed.
190 C2 Ardon Switz.
165 C4 Ardooie Belgium
195 F4 Ardore Italy
147 C4 Ardpatrick Rep. of Ireland
146 C6 Ardpatrick Point Scotland U.K.
147 C3 Ardrahan Rep. of Ireland
156 B2 Ardres France
146 C5 Ardrishaig Argyll and Bute, Scotland U.K.
82 D3 Ardrossan S.A. Austr.
146 D6 Ardrossan North Ayrshire, Scotland U.K.
148 C4 Ardscull Rep. of Ireland
235 E1 Ardsley NY U.S.A.
147 F2 Ards Peninsula Northern Ireland U.K.
147 D2 Ardstraw Northern Ireland U.K.
197 F2 Ardusat Romania
146 C4 Ardvasar Highland, Scotland U.K.
140 K3 Åre Sweden
256 D4 Areado Brazil
183 H1 Areatza Spain
160 E3 Arèches France
247 □1 Arecibo Puerto Rico
261 H3 Areco r. Arg.
197 G3 Arefu Romania
254 F3 Areia Branca Brazil
182 B5 Areias Port.
139 H4 Arekhawsk Belarus
Arel Belgium see Arlon
Arelas France see Arles
Arelate France see Arles
142 D2 Aremark Norway
169 B5 Aremberg hill Ger.
186 D2 Arén Spain
240 F2 Arena, Point CA U.S.A.
258 D2 Arenal, Campo del plain Arg.
242 □I7 Arenal, Volcán vol. Costa Rica
253 F3 Arenápolis Brazil
183 F1 Arenas de Iguña Spain
185 G4 Arenas del Rey Spain
185 G1 Arenas de San Juan Spain
183 E4 Arenas de San Pedro Spain
142 C2 Arendal Norway
165 E3 Arendonk Belgium
170 C3 Arendsee l. Ger.
170 C3 Arendsee (Altmark) Ger.
163 B4 Arengosse France
150 D2 Arenig Fawr hill Wales U.K.
183 H3 Arenillas Spain
185 F2 Arenosillo r. Spain
185 F2 Arenoso r. Spain
169 E4 Arenshausen Ger.
195 F3 Arente r. Italy
186 F3 Arenys de Mar Spain
190 D4 Arenzano Italy
182 B3 Areosa Port.
252 C4 Arequipa Peru
252 B3 Arequipa dept Peru
261 G3 Arequlto Arg.
163 A4 Arès France
182 B1 Ares Spain
138 G5 Aresa r. Belarus
173 F3 Aresing Ger.
163 B5 Arette France
163 B6 Arette-Pierre-St-Martin France
183 E4 Arevalillo Spain
183 F3 Arevalillo r. Spain
183 F3 Arévalo Spain
184 C1 Arez Port.
191 G5 Arezzo Italy
191 G5 Arezzo prov. Toscana Italy
198 C3 Arfara Greece
163 E5 Arfons France
183 I2 Arga r. Spain
84 D4 Argadargada N.T. Austr.
198 C2 Argalasti Greece
185 E2 Argallón Spain
185 G1 Argamasilla de Alba Spain
185 F2 Argamasilla de Calatrava Spain
185 H2 Argamasón Spain
110 E3 Argan Xinjiang China
183 G4 Arganda Spain
182 B4 Arganil Port.
182 D2 Arganza Spain
92 B4 Argao Phil.
193 F3 Argatone, Monte mt. Italy
190 E3 Argegno Italy
Argel Alg. see Alger
163 B5 Argelès-Gazost France
163 F6 Argelès-sur-Mer France
161 A5 Argeliers France
187 C4 Argelita Spain
172 D4 Argen r. Ger.
172 D4 Argenbühl Ger.
159 F2 Argences France
161 E5 Argens r. France
191 G4 Argenta Italy
159 F3 Argentan France
192 D2 Argentario, Monte hill Italy
162 D3 Argentat France
186 B4 Argente Spain
190 B4 Argentera Italy
190 C4 Argentera, Cima dell' mt. Italy
156 C4 Argenteuil France
172 B2 Argenthal Ger.
192 A4 Argentiera Sardegna Italy
160 E3 Argentière France
190 C5 Argentina r. Italy
258 D4 Argentina country S. America
262 V1 Argentina Range mts Antarctica
160 E3 Argentine France
264 F9 Argentine Abyssal Plain sea feature S. Atlantic Ocean
264 G8 Argentine Basin sea feature S. Atlantic Ocean
Argentine Republic country S. America see Argentina
264 F8 Argentine Rise sea feature S. Atlantic Ocean
259 B8 Argentino, Lago l. Arg.
162 B1 Argenton r. France
159 F5 Argenton-Château France
Argentoratum France see Strasbourg
159 F3 Argentre France
159 E3 Argentré-du-Plessis France
159 I4 Argent-sur-Sauldre France
185 H3 Argerín mt. Spain
197 H3 Argeş r. Romania
183 F5 Argés Spain
197 G3 Argeşel r. Romania
123 F4 Arghandab r. Afgh.
123 F4 Arghastan r. Afgh.
148 B4 Arghavas Rep. of Ireland
198 C3 Argolikos Kolpos b. Greece
160 E3 Argonay France
226 C3 Argonne WI U.S.A.
198 C3 Argos Greece
185 I2 Argos r. Spain
226 D5 Argos IN U.S.A.
198 B1 Argos Orestiko Greece
198 B2 Argostoli Ionioi Nisoi Greece
158 E3 Argouges France
Argovie canton Switz. see Aargau
129 C2 Argudan Rus. Fed.
183 I2 Arguedas Spain
156 B3 Argueil France
185 H2 Arguellite Spain
158 D3 Arguenon r. France
186 C2 Arguís Spain
183 I5 Arguisuelas Spain
182 E3 Argujillo Spain
100 B1 Argun' r. China/Rus. Fed.
129 E2 Argun r. Georgia/Rus. Fed.
129 D2 Argun Rus. Fed.
207 G3 Argungu Nigeria
240 I4 Argus Range mts CA U.S.A.
106 D2 Arguut Mongolia
225 H5 Argyle N.S. Can.
226 B5 Argyle IA U.S.A.
226 C4 Argyle WI U.S.A.
86 F3 Argyle, Lake W.A. Austr.
146 C5 Argyll reg. Scotland U.K.
146 C6 Argyll and Bute admin. div. Scotland U.K.
Argyrokastron Albania see Gjirokastër
106 D2 Arhangay prov. Mongolia
129 B3 Arhavi Turkey
Ar Horqin Qi Nei Mongol China see Tianshan
142 D3 Århus Denmark
142 D3 Århus county Denmark
142 D3 Århus Bugt b. Denmark
142 D3 Århus-Tirstrup airport Denmark
80 E3 Aria North I. N.Z.
195 D4 Ária, Monte hill Isole Lipari Italy
83 F3 Ariah Park N.S.W. Austr.
103 E7 Ariake-kai b. Japan
193 H3 Ariano Irpino Italy
191 H4 Ariano nel Polesine Italy
261 F3 Arias Arg.
113 D11 Ari Atoll Maldives
251 F2 Aribí r. Venez.
206 E3 Aribinda Burkina
252 C4 Arica Chile
250 D2 Aricagua Venez.
193 E3 Ariccia Italy
216 □3a Arico Tenerife Canary Is
87 D7 Arid, Cape W.A. Austr.
104 B4 Arida Japan
104 B4 Arida-gawa r. Japan
129 C4 Arı Dağı mt. Turkey
198 C1 Aridaia Greece
163 D6 Ariège dept Midi-Pyrénées France
163 D5 Ariège r. France
197 F2 Arieş r. Romania
177 L5 Arieşeni Romania
197 F2 Arieşul Mic r. Romania
199 G1 Arifiye Turkey
106 D1 Arigiyn Gol r. Mongolia
128 C2 Arīḩā Syria
Arīhā West Bank see Jericho
183 G2 Arija Spain
236 C3 Arikaree r. CO U.S.A.
196 E4 Arilje Srbija Yugo.
247 □7 Arima Trin. and Tob.
Ariminum Italy see Rimini
146 B5 Arinagour Argyll and Bute, Scotland U.K.
186 C3 Ariño Spain
257 D1 Arinos Brazil
253 F2 Arinos r. Brazil
160 D2 Arinthod France
244 D4 Ario de Rosáles Mex.
138 D4 Ariogala Lith.
250 D3 Ariporo r. Col.
253 F2 Aripuanã Brazil
251 F6 Aripuanã r. Brazil
253 E2 Ariquemes Brazil
255 B6 Ariranhá r. Brazil
146 C5 Arisaig Highland, Scotland U.K.
146 C5 Arisaig, Sound of sea chan. Scotland U.K.
234 B2 Aristes PA U.S.A.
258 G2 Aristóbulo del Valle Arg.
123 H4 Aritwala Pak.
192 B5 Aritzo Sardegna Italy
186 B2 Arive Spain
213 □J3 Arivonimamo Madag.
Arixang Xinjiang China see Wenquan
114 C4 Ariyalur Tamil Nadu India
182 C4 Ariz Port.
183 H3 Ariza Spain
258 D2 Arizaro, Salar de salt flat Arg.
163 D5 Arize r. France
183 I2 Arizola Spain
260 E4 Arizona Arg.
241 L4 Arizona state U.S.A.
242 C2 Arizpe Mex.
124 D2 'Arjah Saudi Arabia
142 E2 Årjäng Sweden
140 L2 Arjeplog Sweden
250 C2 Arjona Col.
185 F3 Arjona Spain
185 F3 Arjonilla Spain
116 E5 Arjuni Mahar. India
135 H6 Arkadak Rus. Fed.
237 E5 Arkadelphia AR U.S.A.
137 I3 Arkadivka Ukr.
146 C5 Arkaig, Loch l. Scotland U.K.
114 C3 Arkalgud Karnataka India
198 D4 Arkalochori Kriti Greece
121 F2 Arkalyk Kazakh.
237 F5 Arkansas r. AR U.S.A.
237 E5 Arkansas state U.S.A.
237 F5 Arkansas City AR U.S.A.
237 D4 Arkansas City KS U.S.A.
197 F4 Arkata r. Bulg.
111 E4 Arkatag Shan mts China
222 C2 Arkell, Mount Y.T. Can.
202 E4 Arkenu, Jabal mt. Libya
134 H2 Arkhangel'sk Rus. Fed.
134 H3 Arkhangel'skaya Oblast' admin. div. Rus. Fed.
135 L5 Arkhangel'skoye Rus. Fed.
129 D1 Arkhangel'skoye Rus. Fed.
139 K5 Arkhangel'skoye Rus. Fed.
137 K2 Arkhangel'skoye Rus. Fed.
137 G4 Arkhanhel's'ke Ukr.
100 D2 Arkhara Rus. Fed.
100 D2 Arkhara r. Rus. Fed.
129 E3 Arkhilos Kalo Georgia
137 J5 Arkhipo-Osipovka Rus. Fed.
139 M3 Arkhipovka Rus. Fed.
129 D2 Arkhonskaya Rus. Fed.
129 B2 Arkhyz Rus. Fed.
Árki i. Greece see Arkoi
129 F4 Ärkivan Azer.
146 D3 Arkle hill Scotland U.K.
147 E4 Arklow Rep. of Ireland
199 E3 Arkoi i. Greece
227 G4 Arkona Ont. Can.
Arkonam Tamil Nadu India see Arakkonam
143 G2 Årkosund Sweden
134 J4 Arkul' Rus. Fed.
143 G2 Ärla Sweden
161 B3 Arlanc France
122 C2 Arlang, Gora mt. Turkm.
183 F2 Arlanza r. Spain
183 G2 Arlanzón Spain
183 F2 Arlanzón r. Spain
183 H4 Arlas r. Spain
168 C2 Arle (Großheide) Ger.
161 B4 Arlempdes France
192 D2 Arlena di Castro Italy
161 C5 Arles France
151 G2 Arlesey Bedfordshire, England U.K.
147 D4 Arless Rep. of Ireland
163 E6 Arles-sur-Tech France
160 C1 Arleuf France
156 D2 Arleux France
226 C5 Arlington IL U.S.A.
235 E1 Arlington NY U.S.A.
232 B4 Arlington OH U.S.A.
238 B2 Arlington OR U.S.A.
236 D2 Arlington SD U.S.A.
234 A4 Arlington VA U.S.A.
226 C4 Arlington WI U.S.A.
226 C4 Arlington Heights IL U.S.A.
207 G2 Arlit Niger
165 E5 Arlon Belgium
84 C4 Arltunga N.T. Austr.
190 D3 Arluno Italy
160 E3 Arly r. France
223 J5 Arm r. Sask. Can.
184 B3 Armação de Pêra Port.
182 B1 Armada Spain
232 B3 Armada MI U.S.A.
87 B7 Armadale W.A. Austr.
146 E6 Armadale West Lothian, Scotland U.K.
Armageddon tourist site Israel see Tel Megiddo
147 E2 Armagh Northern Ireland U.K.
147 E2 Armagh county Northern Ireland U.K.
125 E4 Armah, Wādī r. Yemen
183 H4 Armallones Spain
182 C3 Armamar Port.
156 D5 Armance r. France
156 D5 Armançon r. France
203 G3 Armant Egypt
140 M2 Armasjärvi Sweden
135 H7 Armavir Rus. Fed.
163 A5 Armendarits France
129 D3 Armenia country Asia
250 C3 Armenia Col.
190 D3 Armeno Italy
Armenopolis Romania see Gherla
183 E4 Armenteros Spain
156 C2 Armentières France
193 I4 Armento Italy
244 C4 Armeria Mex.
244 C4 Armería r. Mex.
83 G2 Armidale N.S.W. Austr.
185 G3 Armilla Spain
238 E2 Armington MT U.S.A.
161 B5 Armissan France
149 H5 Armitage Staffordshire, England U.K.
240 H3 Armona CA U.S.A.
116 E5 Armori Mahar. India
236 D3 Armour SD U.S.A.
147 E1 Armoy Northern Ireland U.K.
172 C2 Armsheim Ger.
261 G3 Armstrong Arg.
84 B3 Armstrong r. N.T. Austr.
222 G5 Armstrong B.C. Can.
224 B3 Armstrong Ont. Can.
222 C2 Armstrong, Mount Y.T. Can.
Armstrong Island Cook Is see Rarotonga
232 C5 Armstrong Mills OH U.S.A.
100 F3 Armu r. Rus. Fed.
183 F3 Armuña Spain
192 B5 Armungia Sardegna Italy
182 E2 Armunia Spain
114 C2 Armur Andhra Prad. India
199 E2 Armutçuk Dağı mts Turkey
199 F1 Armutlu Turkey
Armutova Turkey see Gömeç
137 G4 Armyans'k Ukr.
Armyanskaya S.S.R. country Asia see Armenia
142 C4 Arnå r. Denmark
162 D3 Arnac-Pompadour France
190 C3 Arnad Italy
144 D1 Árnafjall hill Faroe Is
159 G4 Arnage France
198 C1 Arnaia Greece
140 □B2 Arnarfjörður inlet Iceland
225 G1 Arnaud r. Que. Can.
199 F1 Arnavutköy Turkey
160 C1 Arnay-le-Duc France
173 G2 Arnbruck Ger.
149 G3 Arncliffe North Yorkshire, England U.K.
150 E4 Arne Dorset, England U.K.
170 D3 Arneburg Ger.
183 H2 Arnedillo Spain
183 H2 Arnedo Spain
182 B2 Arnego r. Spain
163 A5 Arnéguy France
254 E3 Arneiroz Brazil
140 M2 Arnemark Sweden
164 C3 Arnemuiden Neth.
142 D1 Årnes Norway
186 D4 Arnes Spain
237 D4 Arnett OK U.S.A.
179 G4 Arnfels Austria
164 E3 Arnhem Neth.
84 D2 Arnhem, Cape N.T. Austr.
84 D2 Arnhem Bay N.T. Austr.
84 C2 Arnhem Land reg. N.T. Austr.
78 □3b Arniel i. Majuro Marshall Is
146 C4 Arnisdale Highland, Scotland U.K.
198 B1 Arnissa Greece

191 F5 Arno r. Italy
82 D3 Arno Bay S.A. Austr.
182 B2 Arnoia r. Spain
146 B3 Arnol Western Isles, Scotland U.K.
149 H4 Arnold Nottinghamshire, England U.K.
234 B3 Arnold MD U.S.A.
226 D2 Arnold MI U.S.A.
236 F4 Arnold MO U.S.A.
225 K4 Arnold's Cove Nfld. Can.
179 E4 Arnoldstein Austria
162 E1 Arnon r. France
Arnon r. Jordan see Mawjib, Wādī al
177 J3 Arnót Hungary
234 A1 Arnot PA U.S.A.
140 M1 Arnøya i. Norway
Arnoya r. Spain see Arnoia
224 E4 Arnprior Ont. Can.
148 E1 Arnprior Stirling, Scotland U.K.
169 D4 Arnsberg Ger.
169 D4 Arnsberg admin. reg. Nordrhein-Westfalen Ger.
169 D4 Arnsberger Wald hills Ger.
173 G2 Arnschwang Ger.
171 E4 Arnsdorf bei Dresden Ger.
169 F5 Arnstadt Ger.
227 H3 Arnstein Ont. Can.
171 A5 Arnstein Ger.
173 G3 Arnstorf Ger.
227 H1 Arntfield Que. Can.
183 G1 Arnuero Spain
251 E3 Aro r. Venez.
212 C5 Aroab Namibia
261 G3 Arocena Arg.
184 D3 Aroche Spain
182 B4 Arões Port.
182 B3 Arões Port.
177 J4 Ároktő Hungary
224 C3 Aroland Ont. Can.
169 E4 Arolsen Ger.
203 H6 Aroma Sudan
240 G3 Aromas CA U.S.A.
159 F3 Aron France
160 B2 Aron r. France
159 F3 Aron r. France
116 D4 Aron Madh. Prad. India
216 □3a Arona Tenerife Canary Is
190 D3 Arona Italy
233 □J1 Aroostook N.B. Can.
233 □J1 Aroostook r. ME U.S.A.
77 H2 Arorae i. Gilbert Is Kiribati
Arore i. Gilbert Is Kiribati see Arorae
92 B3 Aroroy Phil.
242 C2 Aros r. Mex.
182 B3 Arosa Port.
190 E2 Arosa Switz.
Arossi i. Solomon Is see San Cristobal
182 B4 Arouca Port.
129 D4 Arp'a r. Armenia
129 C3 Arpa r. Armenia/Turkey
127 F2 Arpaçay Turkey
128 B1 Arpaçsakarlar Turkey
156 C4 Arpajon France
163 E4 Arpajon-sur-Cère France
193 F3 Arpino Italy
Arpinum Italy see Arpino
Arqalyq Kazakh. see Arkalyk
193 F2 Arquata del Tronto Italy
190 D4 Arquata Scrivia Italy
163 E6 Arques Languedoc-Roussillon France
156 C2 Arques Nord - Pas-de-Calais France
156 B3 Arques-la-Bataille France
185 G2 Arquillos Spain
123 F5 Arra r. Pak.
182 B2 Arrabal Spain
85 E5 Arrabury Qld Austr.
173 G2 Arrach Ger.
157 G4 Arracourt France
158 D4 Arradon France
206 E5 Arrah Côte d'Ivoire
Arrah Bihar India see Ara
124 D5 Ar Rāhidah Yemen
254 D5 Arraias Brazil
254 B4 Arraias r. Brazil
254 D5 Arraias, Serra de hills Brazil
184 C2 Arraiolos Port.
127 F4 Ar Ramādī Iraq
147 C4 Arra Mountains hills Rep. of Ireland
128 C3 Ar Ramthā Jordan
146 C6 Arran i. Scotland U.K.
157 F3 Arrancy-sur-Crusne France
184 A2 Arranhó Port.
128 D2 Ar Raqqah Syria
128 D1 Ar Raqqah governorate Syria
156 C2 Arras France
Arrasate Spain see Mondragón
163 B6 Arras-en-Lavedan France
124 C2 Ar-Rass Saudi Arabia
163 C4 Arrats r. France
163 A5 Arraute-Charritte France
124 C3 Ar Rawḑah Saudi Arabia
125 D5 Ar Rawḑah Yemen
124 D3 Ar Rayn Saudi Arabia
125 E2 Ar Rayyān Qatar
163 C6 Arreau France
250 D4 Arrecifal Col.
216 □3c Arrecife Lanzarote Canary Is
261 G4 Arrecifes Arg.
183 G1 Arredondo Spain
158 B3 Arrée, Monts d' hills France
156 E4 Arrentières France
Arretium Italy see Arezzo
179 E4 Arriach Austria
245 H5 Arriagá Mex.
244 D3 Arriaga San Luis Potosí Mex.
185 E4 Arriate Spain
261 G4 Arribeños Arg.
127 G5 Ar Rifā'ī Iraq
182 B4 Arrifana Aveiro Port.
182 B4 Arrifana Coimbra Port.
182 C4 Arrifana Guarda Port.
216 □1b Arrifes São Miguel Azores
156 E4 Arrigny France
183 H1 Arrigorriaga Spain
127 G5 Ar Rihāb salt flat Iraq
125 F3 Ar Rimāl des. Saudi Arabia
232 D6 Arrington VA U.S.A.
87 B6 Arrino W.A. Austr.
183 E1 Arriondas Spain
Ar Riyāḑ Saudi Arabia see Riyadh
124 D2 Ar Riyāḑ prov. Saudi Arabia
185 F1 Arroba de los Montes Spain
182 D4 Arrobuey mt. Spain
146 D5 Arrochar Argyll and Bute, Scotland U.K.
258 G4 Arroio Grande Brazil
159 F2 Arromanches-les-Bains France
184 C1 Arronches Port.
193 E2 Arrone Italy
192 D2 Arrone r. Italy
193 E3 Arrone r. Italy
183 H2 Arroniz Spain
163 B5 Arros r. France
190 D4 Arroscia r. Italy
156 B4 Arrou France
160 B2 Arroux r. France
226 C1 Arrow r. Ont. Can.
150 E2 Arrow r. England U.K.
147 C2 Arrow, Lough l. Rep. of Ireland
238 E2 Arrow Creek r. MT U.S.A.
81 C5 Arrowsmith, Mount South I. N.Z.
81 B6 Arrowtown South I. N.Z.
183 F2 Arroyal Spain
261 F2 Arroyito Arg.
247 □1 Arroyo Puerto Rico
184 D1 Arroyo de la Luz Spain
184 D2 Arroyo de San Serván Spain
261 I5 Arroyo Grande r. Arg.
240 G4 Arroyo Grande CA U.S.A.
184 D2 Arroyomolinos de León Spain
261 G3 Arroyo Seco Arg.
245 E3 Arroyo Seco Mex.
184 A2 Arruda dos Vinhos Port.
261 G2 Arrufó Arg.
127 G5 Ar Rumaythah Iraq
128 C3 Ar Ruşayfah Jordan
125 G3 Ar Rustāq Oman
127 F4 Ar Ruţbah Iraq
124 D3 Ar Ruwayḑah Saudi Arabia
157 G3 Arry France
142 C3 Års Denmark
122 A2 Ars Iran
199 F3 Arsaköy Turkey
Ărsarybaba Erezi hills Turkm. see Irsarybaba, Gory
186 E2 Arsèguel Spain
122 C4 Arsenajān Iran
162 A2 Ars-en-Ré France
100 E3 Arsen'yev Rus. Fed.
139 K5 Arsen'yevo Rus. Fed.
138 G4 Arshanskaye Wzvyshsha hills Belarus
191 G3 Arsiè Italy
191 G3 Arsiero Italy
114 C3 Arsikere Karnataka India
129 A3 Arsin Turkey
134 J4 Arsk Rus. Fed.
193 F2 Arsoli Italy
160 C3 Ars-sur-Formans France
157 G3 Ars-sur-Moselle France
78 □5 Art, Île i. New Caledonia
198 B2 Arta Greece
187 G5 Artà Spain
183 I2 Artajona Spain
129 D2 Art'ana Georgia
187 C5 Artana Spain
190 C3 Artanavaz r. Italy
159 G4 Artannes-sur-Indre France
129 D4 Artashat Armenia
243 E3 Arteaga Coahuila Mex.
244 C4 Arteaga Michoacán Mex.
187 C5 Arteas de Abajo mt. Spain
100 E4 Artem Rus. Fed.
160 D3 Artemare France
246 B2 Artemisa Cuba
137 I3 Artemivka Kharkivs'ka Oblast' Ukr.
137 H3 Artemivka Poltavs'ka Oblast' Ukr.
137 J3 Artemivs'k Ukr.
137 J3 Artemivs'k Ukr.
Artemovsk Ukr. see Artemivs'k
131 M4 Artemovskiy Irkutskaya Oblast' Rus. Fed.
100 E4 Artemovskiy Primorskiy Kray Rus. Fed.
191 G2 Artèn Italy
193 E3 Artena Italy
156 B4 Artenay France
171 C4 Artern (Unstrut) Ger.
186 E3 Artés Spain
186 E3 Artesa de Segre Spain
241 M5 Artesia AZ U.S.A.
239 F5 Artesia NM U.S.A.
190 D1 Arth Switz.
163 E5 Arthès France
163 B5 Arthez-d'Asson France
163 B5 Arthez-de-Béarn France
159 H5 Arthon France
158 E4 Arthon-en-Retz France
87 B5 Arthur r. W.A. Austr.
227 G4 Arthur Ont. Can.
236 C3 Arthur NE U.S.A.
232 B6 Arthur TN U.S.A.
82 D2 Arthur, Lake salt flat S.A. Austr.
232 C4 Arthur, Lake PA U.S.A.
83 F5 Arthur Lake Tas. Austr.
85 G4 Arthur Point Qld Austr.
81 C5 Arthur's Pass South I. N.Z.
246 D1 Arthur's Town Cat I. Bahamas
148 C2 Articlave Northern Ireland U.K.
186 C2 Artieda Spain
186 D2 Arties Spain
148 B3 Artigarvan Northern Ireland U.K.
262 U2 Artigas research stn Antarctica
261 I2 Artigas Uru.
261 I2 Artigas dept Uru.
163 D5 Artigat France
129 C3 Art'ik Armenia
223 I2 Artillery Lake N.W.T. Can.
163 B5 Artix France
138 F1 Artjärvi Fin.
168 F2 Artlenburg Ger.
190 F3 Artogne Italy
127 F3 Artos Dağı mt. Turkey
126 E2 Artova Turkey
Artsakh aut. reg. Azer. see Dağlıq Qarabağ
106 D2 Arts Bogd Uul mts Mongolia
Artsiz Ukr. see Artsyz
136 E5 Artsyz Ukr.
161 E5 Artuby r. France
Artur de Paiva Angola see Kuvango
110 B4 Artux Xinjiang China
127 F2 Artvin Turkey
129 B3 Artvin prov. Turkey
91 H8 Aru, Kepulauan is Indon.
182 C2 A Rúa Spain
210 A4 Arua Uganda
254 C5 Aruanã Brazil
247 □9 Aruba terr. West Indies
216 □3f Arucas Gran Canaria Canary Is
163 B5 Arudy France
256 D5 Arujá Brazil
107 J2 Arun r. China
117 F4 Arun r. Nepal
117 H4 Arunachal Pradesh state India
81 C5 Arundel South I. N.Z.
151 G4 Arundel West Sussex, England U.K.
Arun Qi Nei Mongol China see Naji
142 D4 Årup Denmark
114 C4 Aruppukkottai Tamil Nadu India
211 C5 Arusha Tanz.
211 C5 Arusha admin. reg. Tanz.
211 C5 Arusha National Park Tanz.
95 E3 Arut r. Indon.
208 D4 Aruwimi r. Dem. Rep. Congo
236 B4 Arvada CO U.S.A.
147 D3 Arvagh Rep. of Ireland
161 E3 Arvan r. France
106 D2 Arvayheer Mongolia
160 E2 Arve r. France
162 A3 Arvert France
163 B4 Arveyres France
116 D5 Arvi Mahar. India
223 M2 Arviat Nunavut Can.
230 G1 Arvida Que. Can.
140 L2 Arvidsjaur Sweden
161 A4 Arvieu France
161 E4 Arvieux France
142 E2 Arvika Sweden
240 H4 Arvin CA U.S.A.
195 F3 Arvo, Lago l. Italy
232 D6 Arvonia VA U.S.A.
124 D3 Arwā' Saudi Arabia
107 H2 Arxan Nei Mongol China
Aryanah Tunisia see L'Ariana
134 K4 Aryazh Rus. Fed.
121 G1 Arykbalyk Kazakh.
Aryqbayq Kazakh. see Arykbalyk
121 G4 Arys' Kazakh.
121 G4 Arys' r. Kazakh.
192 B3 Arzachena Sardegna Italy
163 B5 Arzacq-Arraziguet France
135 H5 Arzamas Rus. Fed.
192 B5 Arzana Sardegna Italy
158 C4 Arzano France
169 C5 Arzbach Ger.
171 D5 Arzberg Bayern Ger.
171 E4 Arzberg Sachsen Ger.
163 E5 Arzens France
205 E2 Arzew Alg.
169 B5 Arzfeld Ger.
135 I7 Arzgir Rus. Fed.
191 G3 Arzignano Italy
Arzila Morocco see Asilah
178 B3 Arzl im Pitztal Austria
161 B3 Arzon r. France
182 B2 Arzúa Spain
165 E3 As Belgium
176 B1 Aš Czech Rep.
142 D3 Aså Denmark
142 E3 Åsa Sweden
207 G5 Asaba Nigeria
128 D1 Asad, Buḩayrat al resr Syria
123 G3 Asadābād Afgh.
122 B3 Asadābād Iran
129 E3 Aşağı Ağcakänd Azer.
129 D3 Aşağı Äskipara Azer.
129 D3 Aşağı Ayıblı Azer.
129 C3 Aşağı Dağ mt. Turkey
199 F3 Aşağıkaraçay Turkey
129 B3 Aşağıkatıklı Turkey
129 C4 Aşağıküpkıran Turkey
129 E3 Aşağı Oratağ Azer.
129 D4 Aşağısağmallı Turkey
129 B4 Aşağısöylemez Turkey
94 B2 Asahan r. Indon.
105 G3 Asahi Japan
102 I4 Asahi-dake mt. Japan
102 K2 Asahi-dake vol. Japan
103 F6 Asahi-gawa r. Japan
102 K2 Asahikawa Japan
105 F1 Asahi-take mt. Japan
105 F3 Asaka Japan
121 H4 Asaka Uzbek.
104 C3 Asake-gawa r. Japan
104 C4 Asamaga-take hill Japan
206 E5 Asamankese Ghana
105 E2 Asama-yama vol. Japan
206 E5 Asankranguaa Ghana
117 F5 Asansol W. Bengal India
206 E5 Asanwenso Ghana
163 B5 Asasp-Arros France
Asava i. Fiji see Yasawa
210 D2 Āsayita Eth.
169 C5 Asbach Ger.
173 E3 Asbach-Bäumenheim Ger.
230 G2 Asbestos Que. Can.
Asbestos Hill Que. Can. see Purtuniq
214 D3 Asbestos Mountains S. Africa
210 D2 Āsbe Teferi Eth.
143 F2 Åsbro Sweden
233 F4 Asbury Park NJ U.S.A.
163 A5 Ascain France
Ascalon Israel see Ashqelon
193 H4 Ascea Italy
261 G4 Ascensión Arg.
253 E3 Ascensión Bol.
245 E1 Ascensión Mex.
Ascension atoll Micronesia see Pohnpei
216 □2a Ascension i. S. Atlantic Ocean
173 G2 Ascha Ger.
173 G2 Ascha r. Ger.
179 F2 Aschach an der Donau Austria
172 D2 Aschaffenburg Ger.
178 C3 Aschau im Zillertal Austria
173 G4 Aschau in Chiemgau Ger.
179 F2 Aschbach Markt Austria
169 C4 Ascheberg Ger.
168 F1 Ascheberg (Holstein) Ger.
173 H3 Aschenstein hill Ger.
156 C4 Aschères-le-Marché France
171 C4 Aschersleben Ger.
173 F3 Aschheim Ger.
191 G5 Asciano Italy
192 B2 Asco Corse France
193 F2 Ascoli Piceno Italy
193 F2 Ascoli Piceno prov. Marche Italy
193 H3 Ascoli Satriano Italy
190 D2 Ascona Switz.
151 G3 Ascot Windsor and Maidenhead, England U.K.
252 C5 Ascotán, Salar de salt flat Chile
163 D6 Ascou France
182 B2 As Covas Spain
Asculum Italy see Ascoli Piceno
Asculum Picenum Italy see Ascoli Piceno
233 G3 Ascutney VT U.S.A.
113 □1 Asdhu i. N. Male Maldives
Asdu i. N. Male Maldives see Asdhu
Āseb Eritrea see Assab
143 F3 Åseda Sweden
205 F4 Asedjrad plat. Alg.
120 C1 Asekeyevo Rus. Fed.
210 C3 Āsela Eth.
140 L2 Åsele Sweden
141 K3 Åsen Sweden
168 E2 Asendorf Niedersachsen Ger.
168 E3 Asendorf Niedersachsen Ger.
197 G4 Asenovgrad Bulg.
142 B2 Åseral Norway
138 F2 Aseri Estonia
122 D3 Aşfāk Iran
128 C3 Aşfar, Jabal al mt. Jordan
128 C3 Aşfar, Tall al hill Syria
156 E3 Asfeld France
151 G2 Asfordby Leicestershire, England U.K.
151 I3 Ash Kent, England U.K.
151 G3 Ash Surrey, England U.K.
134 L5 Asha Rus. Fed.
104 D2 Ashahi-dake mt. Japan
206 E5 Ashanti admin. reg. Ghana
134 L4 Ashap Rus. Fed.
124 D2 Asharat Saudi Arabia
235 G1 Ashaway RI U.S.A.
147 E3 Ashbourne Rep. of Ireland
149 H4 Ashbourne Derbyshire, England U.K.
231 D6 Ashburn GA U.S.A.
87 B4 Ashburton watercourse W.A. Austr.
81 C5 Ashburton South I. N.Z.
81 C6 Ashburton r. South I. N.Z.
150 D4 Ashburton Devon, England U.K.
84 C3 Ashburton Range hills N.T. Austr.
151 F3 Ashbury Oxfordshire, England U.K.
151 F2 Ashby de la Zouch Leicestershire, England U.K.
150 E3 Ashchurch Gloucestershire, England U.K.
Ashchysay Kazakh. see Achisay
150 E3 Ashcott Somerset, England U.K.
222 F5 Ashcroft B.C. Can.
128 B4 Ashdod Israel
237 E5 Ashdown AR U.S.A.
151 H3 Ashdown Forest reg. England U.K.
231 E5 Asheboro NC U.S.A.
237 D5 Asher OK U.S.A.
223 L5 Ashern Man. Can.
231 D5 Asheville NC U.S.A.
224 C2 Asheweig r. Ont. Can.
83 G2 Ashford N.S.W. Austr.
147 E3 Ashford Rep. of Ireland
148 C5 Ashford r. Rep. of Ireland
151 F4 Ashford Hampshire, England U.K.
151 H3 Ashford Kent, England U.K.
151 G3 Ashford Surrey, England U.K.
241 K4 Ash Fork AZ U.S.A.
122 D2 Ashgabat Turkm.
80 E4 Ashhurst North I. N.Z.
102 K2 Ashibetsu Japan
105 F2 Ashikaga Japan
151 H2 Ashill Norfolk, England U.K.
149 H2 Ashington Northumberland, England U.K.
226 C4 Ashippun WI U.S.A.
104 B4 Ashiya Japan
122 C4 Ashkazar Iran
Ashkelon Israel see Ashqelon
Ashkhabad Turkm. see Ashgabat
Ashkhabadskaya Oblast' admin. div. Turkm. see Akhal'skaya Oblast'
146 F6 Ashkirk Scottish Borders, Scotland U.K.
226 D5 Ashkum IL U.S.A.
231 C5 Ashland AL U.S.A.
237 D4 Ashland KS U.S.A.
232 B5 Ashland KY U.S.A.
233 □I1 Ashland ME U.S.A.
237 F5 Ashland MS U.S.A.
238 F2 Ashland MT U.S.A.
236 D3 Ashland NE U.S.A.
233 H3 Ashland NH U.S.A.
232 B4 Ashland OH U.S.A.
238 B3 Ashland OR U.S.A.
234 B2 Ashland PA U.S.A.
232 E6 Ashland VA U.S.A.
226 B2 Ashland WI U.S.A.
231 C4 Ashland City TN U.S.A.
83 G2 Ashley N.S.W. Austr.
81 D5 Ashley r. South I. N.Z.
151 H2 Ashley Cambridgeshire, England U.K.
226 E5 Ashley IN U.S.A.
226 E4 Ashley MI U.S.A.
236 D2 Ashley ND U.S.A.
232 B4 Ashley OH U.S.A.
234 C1 Ashley PA U.S.A.
86 D2 Ashmore and Cartier Islands terr. Austr.
86 D2 Ashmore Reef Ashmore & Cartier Is Austr.
138 E4 Ashmyanskaye Wzvyshsha hills Belarus
138 E4 Ashmyany Hrodzyenskaya Voblasts' Belarus
138 F4 Ashmyany Hrodzyenskaya Voblasts' Belarus
116 D4 Ashoknagar Madh. Prad. India
129 C3 Ashots'k' Armenia
128 B4 Ashqelon Israel
127 F5 Ash Shabakah Iraq
127 F3 Ash Shaddādah Syria
124 C3 Ash Shafa Saudi Arabia
Ash Sham Syria see Damascus
125 G2 Ash Sha'm U.A.E.
127 G5 Ash Shanāfīyah Iraq
124 D2 Ash Sha'rā' Saudi Arabia
125 D4 Ash Sharawrah Saudi Arabia
Ash Shāriqah U.A.E. see Sharjah
127 F4 Ash Sharqāţ Iraq
125 G3 Ash Sharqīyah admin. reg. Oman
125 G3 Ash Sharqīyah reg. Oman
125 E3 Ash Sharqīyah prov. Saudi Arabia
127 G5 Ash Shaţrah Iraq
128 B4 Ash Shawbak Jordan
124 D5 Ash Shaykh 'Uthman Yemen
128 C5 Ash Shiblīyāt hill Saudi Arabia
125 E5 Ash Shiḩr Yemen
125 G2 Ash Shināş Oman
124 C2 Ash Shubaykīyah Saudi Arabia
125 D2 Ash Shumlūl Saudi Arabia
124 C4 Ash Shuqayq Saudi Arabia
Ash Shurayf Saudi Arabia see Khaybar
116 D5 Ashta Madh. Prad. India
114 B2 Ashta Mahar. India
232 C4 Ashtabula OH U.S.A.
129 D3 Ashtarak Armenia
114 B2 Ashti Mahar. India
114 C2 Ashti Mahar. India
116 D5 Ashti Mahar. India
214 C5 Ashton S. Africa
149 G4 Ashton Cheshire, England U.K.
238 E2 Ashton ID U.S.A.
226 C5 Ashton IL U.S.A.
234 A3 Ashton MD U.S.A.
215 E6 Ashton Bay S. Africa
149 G4 Ashton-under-Lyne Greater Manchester, England U.K.
225 H2 Ashuanipi r. Nfld. Can.
230 F1 Ashuapmushuan r. Que. Can.
Ashur Iraq see Ash Sharqāţ
151 F4 Ashurst Hampshire, England U.K.
151 H3 Ashurst Kent, England U.K.
231 C5 Ashville AL U.S.A.
233 □I2 Ashville ME U.S.A.
232 D4 Ashville PA U.S.A.
226 B2 Ashwabay, Mount hill WI U.S.A.
226 C3 Ashwaubenon WI U.S.A.
150 E3 Ashwick Somerset, England U.K.
128 C2 'Āşī r. Lebanon/Syria
128 C1 Asi r. Turkey alt. 'Āşī, Nahr al (Asia), conv. Orontes (Lebanon/Syria)
128 C1 'Āşī, Nahr al r. Asia alt. Asi (Turkey), conv. Orontes (Lebanon/Syria)
88 Asia continent
191 G3 Asiago Italy
244 C2 Asientos Mex.
114 C2 Asifabad Andhra Prad. India
115 E2 Asika Orissa India
141 N3 Asikkala Fin.
204 D2 Asilah Morocco
252 C3 Asillo Peru
198 D4 Asimi Kriti Greece
186 B2 Asín Spain
192 A4 Asinara, Golfo dell' b. Sardegna Italy
192 A3 Asinara, Isola i. Sardegna Italy
116 C4 Asind Rajasthan India
130 J4 Asino Rus. Fed.
139 H4 Asintorf Belarus
138 G5 Asipovichy Belarus
124 C4 'Asīr prov. Saudi Arabia
124 C3 'Asīr reg. Saudi Arabia
Asisium Italy see Assisi
138 C1 Askainen Fin.
127 F3 Aşkale Turkey
137 G4 Askaniya Nova Ukr.
120 D1 Askarovo Rus. Fed.
147 C4 Askeaton Rep. of Ireland
215 F4 Askeaton S. Africa
142 D2 Asker Norway
129 A4 Asker Dağı mt. Turkey
149 H4 Askern South Yorkshire, England U.K.
143 F2 Askersund Sweden
214 C2 Askham S. Africa
147 C2 Askill Rep. of Ireland
142 D2 Askim Norway
134 L4 Askino Rus. Fed.
198 B1 Askio mt. Greece
207 I4 Askira Nigeria
146 B5 Askival hill Scotland U.K.
98 F1 Askiz Rus. Fed.
141 N3 Askola Fin.
143 G2 Äsköping Sweden
198 C1 Askos Kentriki Makedonia Greece
116 E3 Askot Uttar Prad. India
142 A1 Askøy i. Norway
214 C6 Askraal S. Africa
141 I3 Askvoll Norway
129 E4 Askyaran Azer.
199 F2 Aslanapa Turkey
122 A2 Aşlāndūz Iran
138 G5 Aslik r. Belarus
Aslóközpont Hungary see Mórahalom
203 H6 Asmara Eritrea
Āsmera Eritrea see Asmara
143 F3 Åsnen l. Sweden
182 B1 As Neves Galicia Spain
182 B2 As Neves Galicia Spain
182 C2 As Nogais Spain
193 F1 Aso r. Italy
190 F3 Asola Italy
191 G3 Asolo Italy
185 I1 Asomadilla hill Spain
198 C2 Asopos r. Greece
198 C3 Asopos r. Greece
210 B2 Āsosa Eth.
103 E7 Aso-san vol. Japan
203 H4 Asoteriba, Jebel mt. Sudan
238 C2 Asotin WA U.S.A.
177 I5 Ásotthalom Hungary
134 L4 Aspa Rus. Fed.
179 E2 Aspach Austria
179 H3 Aspang-Markt Austria
122 B2 Aspar Iran
121 H4 Aspara Kazakh.
179 H2 Asparn an der Zaya Austria
197 H4 Asparukhovo Bulg.
140 K3 Aspås Sweden
149 F3 Aspatria Cumbria, England U.K.
187 C6 Aspe Spain
140 L3 Äspea Sweden
239 F4 Aspen CO U.S.A.
164 E3 Asperen Neth.
172 D3 Asperg Ger.
237 C5 Aspermont TX U.S.A.
234 A3 Aspers PA U.S.A.
163 C5 Aspet France
129 C3 Aspindza Georgia
161 B5 Aspiran France
81 B6 Aspiring, Mount South I. N.Z.
182 C1 As Pontes de García Rodríguez Spain
161 D4 Aspremont France
161 D4 Aspres-sur-Buëch France
163 E4 Asprières France
Aspropotamos r. Greece see Acheloös
198 C1 Asprovalta Greece
116 C5 Aspur Rajasthan India
223 J4 Asquith Sask. Can.
191 G3 Assa r. Italy
204 C3 Assa Morocco
129 D2 Assa r. Rus. Fed.
128 C2 As Sa'an Syria
203 I6 Assab Eritrea
206 C2 Assaba admin. reg. Maur.
124 C2 Aš Sab'ān Saudi Arabia
128 D2 As Sabkhah Syria
128 C3 Aş Şafā lava field Syria
Aş Şafāqis Tunisia see Sfax
128 B4 Aş Şāfī Jordan
128 C1 As Safīrah Syria
124 C5 Aş Şahīf Yemen
Assake Uzbek. see Asaka
120 D4 Assake-Audan, Vpadina depr. Uzbek.
125 D2 As Salamiyah Saudi Arabia
127 F4 Aş Şālihīyah Syria
128 B3 As Salţ Jordan
117 G4 Assam state India
127 G5 As Samāwah Iraq
172 D2 Assamstadt Ger.
125 E3 Aş Şanām reg. Saudi Arabia
163 B5 Assat France
124 D3 As Sawādah reg. Saudi Arabia
165 D4 Asse Belgium
161 D5 Asse r. France
214 E5 Assegaaibos S. Africa
192 B5 Assemini Sardegna Italy
164 F1 Assen Neth.
164 D2 Assendelft Neth.
165 C3 Assenede Belgium
142 C4 Assens Denmark
158 D4 Assérac France
193 F2 Assergi Italy
165 E4 Assesse Belgium
163 D4 Assier France
223 J5 Assiniboia Sask. Can.
223 L5 Assiniboine r. Man./Sask. Can.
222 H5 Assiniboine, Mount Alta/B.C. Can.
256 B5 Assis Brazil
256 A6 Assis Chateaubriand Brazil
193 E1 Assisi Italy
169 D5 Aßlar Ger.
178 D4 Assling Austria
173 G4 Aßling Ger.
190 E3 Asso Italy
206 □ Assomada São Tiago Cape Verde
217 □2 Assomption i. Seychelles
163 B5 Asson France
194 D5 Assoro Sicilia Italy
127 G5 Aş Şubayḩīyah Kuwait
124 C4 As Subaykhah Saudi Arabia
125 E5 As Sufāl Yemen
127 G4 As Sulaymānīyah Iraq
127 G4 As Sulaymānīyah governorate Iraq
124 C2 As Sulaymī Saudi Arabia
124 D3 As Sulayyil Saudi Arabia
125 E2 Aş Şulb reg. Saudi Arabia
184 C1 Assumar Port.
124 D2 Aş Şummān plat. Saudi Arabia
125 E3 Aş Şummān plat. Saudi Arabia
As Sūrīyah country Asia see Syria
127 F4 Aş Şuwar Syria
128 C3 As Suwaydā' Syria
128 C3 As Suwaydā' governorate Syria
125 G3 As Suwayḩ Oman
125 G3 As Suwayq Oman
124 C3 As Suwayriqīyah Saudi Arabia
As Suways Egypt see El Suweis
124 D5 As Suwwādīyah Yemen
146 C3 Assynt, Loch l. Scotland U.K.
141 J3 Asta r. Norway
191 G2 Asta, Cima d' mt. Italy
Astacus Turkey see Kocaeli
163 C4 Astaffort France
198 B2 Astakos Greece
121 G2 Astana Kazakh.
122 B2 Astaneh Iran
122 B2 Āstārā Iran
142 E1 Åsteby Sweden
179 F2 Asten Austria
165 E3 Asten Neth.
Asterabad Iran see Gorgān
190 D4 Asti Italy
190 D4 Asti prov. Piemonte Italy
191 G3 Astico r. Italy
177 L4 Aştileu Romania
252 C3 Astillero Peru
Astin Tag mts China see Altun Shan
Astipálaia i. Greece see Astypalaia
163 D6 Aston r. France
151 G3 Aston Clinton Buckinghamshire, England U.K.
116 C2 Astor Jammu and Kashmir
123 H3 Astor r. Pak.
256 B5 Astorga Brazil
182 D2 Astorga Spain
226 B5 Astoria IL U.S.A.
238 B2 Astoria OR U.S.A.
142 E3 Åstorp Sweden
217 □2 Astove i. Seychelles
Astrabad Iran see Gorgān
Astrakhan' Kazakh. see Astrakhanka
120 B3 Astrakhan' Rus. Fed.
Astrakhan' Bazar Azer. see Cälilabad
121 G2 Astrakhanka Kazakh.
137 H4 Astrakhanka Ukr.
Astrakhan Oblast admin. div. Rus. Fed. see Astrakhanskaya Oblast'
120 A3 Astrakhanskaya Oblast' admin. div. Rus. Fed.
138 E4 Astravyets Belarus
129 F3 Astraxanka Azer.
Astrida Rwanda see Butare
78 □5 Astrolabe, Récifs de l' rf New Caledonia
198 C3 Astros Greece
138 E5 Astryna Belarus
139 H5 Astsyer r. Belarus
183 F2 Astudillo Spain
193 E3 Astura r. Italy
182 D1 Asturias airport Spain
182 D1 Asturias aut. comm. Spain
Asturica Augusta Spain see Astorga
151 F2 Astwood Bank Worcestershire, England U.K.
199 E3 Astypalaia i. Greece
121 J2 Asubulak Kazakh.
Asūbulaq Kazakh. see Asubulak
239 D6 Asunción r. Mex.
91 K3 Asuncion i. N. Mariana Is
253 F6 Asunción Para.
243 H6 Asunción Mita Guat.
192 A5 Asuni Sardegna Italy
104 C2 Asuwa-gawa r. Japan
138 G3 Asvyeya Belarus
138 G3 Asvyeyskaye, Vozyera l. Belarus
210 A4 Aswa r. Uganda
125 G2 Aswad Oman
203 G3 Aswân Egypt
124 A2 Aswân governorate Egypt
203 F3 Asyût Egypt
126 C6 Asyût governorate Egypt
177 J3 Aszaló Hungary
79 □2a Ata i. Tonga
250 E3 Atabapo r. Col./Venez.
121 G4 Atabay Kazakh.
199 G3 Atabey Turkey
258 C2 Atacama admin. reg. Chile
258 C2 Atacama, Desierto de des. Chile
252 C5 Atacama, Salar de salt flat Chile
250 B4 Atacames Ecuador
205 G4 Atafaitafa, Djebel mt. Alg.
81 □1 Atafu atoll Tokelau
81 □1 Atafu i. Tokelau
104 B3 Atago-san hill Japan
105 F3 Atago-yama hill Japan
128 A5 Atairtîr el Dahami, Gebel mt. Egypt
128 B1 Atakent Turkey
129 F3 Atakişili Azer.
205 G5 Atakor mts Alg.
207 F5 Atakpamé Togo
254 G4 Atalaia Brazil
184 B2 Atalaia hill Port.
250 D6 Atalaia do Norte Brazil
Atalándi Greece see Atalanti
198 C2 Atalanti Greece
242 □J7 Atalaya Panama
252 B2 Atalaya Peru
185 I3 Atalaya Arabe hill Spain
257 G3 Ataléia Brazil
105 F3 Atami Japan
Ataniya Turkey see Adana
177 J4 Átány Hungary
124 D5 'Ataq Yemen
128 A5 'Ataqa, Gebel hill Egypt
183 F3 Ataquines Spain
204 B5 Atâr Maur.
96 B3 Ataran r. Myanmar
Atas i. Cocos Is see South Island
240 G4 Atascadero CA U.S.A.
121 G2 Atasu Kazakh.
111 E4 Atatan He r. China
Atáviros mt. Notio Aigaio Greece see Attavyros
122 D1 Atayab Turkm.
128 A1 Atayurt Turkey
203 G5 Atbara Sudan
203 G5 Atbara r. Sudan
121 G2 Atbasar Kazakh.
121 H4 At-Bashy Kyrg.
236 E4 Atchison KS U.S.A.
234 D3 Atco NJ U.S.A.
183 I3 Atea Spain
206 E5 Atebubu Ghana
183 I3 Ateca Spain
182 C3 Atei Port.
182 C2 A Teixeira Spain
193 G3 Ateleta Italy
193 H4 Atella Italy
193 H4 Atella r. Italy
244 C3 Atemajac de Brizuela Mex.
105 E1 Atema-yama mt. Japan
252 C3 Aten Bol.
193 H4 Atena Lucana Italy
244 B3 Atengo r. Mex.
244 B3 Atenguillo r. Mex.
244 C4 Atenquique Mex.
Ateransk Kazakh. see Atyrau
193 F2 Aterno r. Italy
123 E3 Āteshkhāneh, Kūh-e hill Afgh.
193 G2 Atessa Italy
234 C3 Atglen PA U.S.A.
165 C4 Ath Belgium
222 H4 Athabasca Alta Can.
222 I3 Athabasca r. Alta Can.
223 I3 Athabasca, Lake Alberta/Saskatchewan Can.
117 F5 Athagarh Orissa India
232 B5 Athalia OH U.S.A.
147 E3 Athboy Rep. of Ireland
147 B4 Athea Rep. of Ireland
Athenae Greece see Athina
147 C3 Athenry Rep. of Ireland
227 J3 Athens Ont. Can.
Athens Greece see Athina
231 C5 Athens AL U.S.A.
231 D5 Athens GA U.S.A.
233 G3 Athens NY U.S.A.
232 B5 Athens OH U.S.A.
232 E4 Athens PA U.S.A.
231 C5 Athens TN U.S.A.
237 E5 Athens TX U.S.A.
169 F4 Athenstedt Ger.
150 C4 Atherington Devon, England U.K.
151 F2 Atherstone Warwickshire, England U.K.
85 F3 Atherton Qld Austr.
149 G4 Atherton Greater Manchester, England U.K.
211 C5 Athi r. Kenya
156 C3 Athies France
156 D3 Athies-sous-Laon France
198 C3 Athina Greece
Athínai Greece see Athina
211 C5 Athi River Kenya
159 F3 Athis-de-l'Orne France
156 C4 Athis-Mons France
147 C4 Athlacca Rep. of Ireland
147 C3 Athleague Rep. of Ireland
147 D3 Athlone Rep. of Ireland
114 B2 Athni Karnataka India
81 B6 Athol South I. N.Z.
233 G3 Athol MA U.S.A.
146 D5 Atholl, Forest of reg. Scotland U.K.
198 D1 Athos mt. Greece
Athos, Mount admin. div. Greece see Agion Oros
127 F4 Ath Tharthār, Wādī r. Iraq
128 C5 Ath Thāyat mt. Saudi Arabia
147 E4 Athy Rep. of Ireland
202 C6 Ati Chad
202 B4 Ati, Jabal mts Libya
80 F3 Atiamuri North I. N.Z.
256 D5 Atibaia Brazil
252 B4 Atico Peru
183 H3 Atienza Spain
222 H4 Atikameg Alta Can.
224 D2 Atikameg r. Ont. Can.
224 B3 Atikokan Ont. Can.
92 B3 Atimonan Phil.
193 F3 Atina Italy
114 C4 Atirampattinam Tamil Nadu India
243 H6 Atitlán Guat.
81 □2 Atiu i. Cook Is
Atjeh admin. dist. Indon. see Aceh
131 Q3 Atka Rus. Fed.
220 A4 Atka AK U.S.A.
220 A4 Atka Island AK U.S.A.
177 I4 Atkár Hungary
135 I6 Atkarsk Rus. Fed.
237 E5 Atkins AR U.S.A.
245 E4 Atlacomulco Mex.
215 F1 Atlanta S. Africa
231 C5 Atlanta GA U.S.A.
226 C5 Atlanta IL U.S.A.
227 E3 Atlanta MI U.S.A.
237 E5 Atlanta TX U.S.A.
126 D3 Atlantı Turkey
236 E3 Atlantic IA U.S.A.
233 □I2 Atlantic ME U.S.A.
231 E5 Atlantic NC U.S.A.
233 F5 Atlantic City NJ U.S.A.
234 D3 Atlantic County county NJ U.S.A.
235 D2 Atlantic Highlands NJ U.S.A.
263 H3 Atlantic-Indian-Antarctic Basin sea feature S. Atlantic Ocean
265 D8 Atlantic-Indian Ridge sea feature Southern Ocean
250 C2 Atlántico dept Col.
264 Atlantic Ocean
238 E3 Atlantic Peak WY U.S.A.
214 B5 Atlantis S. Africa
245 E3 Atlapexco Mex.
234 B2 Atlas PA U.S.A.
106 C3 Atlas Bogd mt. Mongolia
Atlas Méditerranéen mts Alg. see Atlas Tellien
204 D3 Atlas Mountains Africa
205 F2 Atlas Saharien mts Alg.
205 F2 Atlas Tellien mts Alg.
245 E4 Atlatlahucan Mex.
222 C3 Atlin B.C. Can.
128 B3 'Atlit Israel
245 E4 Atlixco Mex.
114 C3 Atmakur Andhra Prad. India
114 C3 Atmakur Andhra Prad. India
231 C6 Atmore AL U.S.A.
116 D5 Atner Madh. Prad. India
114 C2 Atnur Karnataka India
252 D5 Atocha Bol.
237 D5 Atoka OK U.S.A.
245 E3 Atotonico El Grande Mex.
244 C3 Atotonilco el Alto Mex.
96 D3 Atouat mt. Laos
184 A1 Atouguia da Baleia Port.
244 C3 Atoyac Mex.
245 F5 Atoyac r. Oaxaca Mex.
245 E4 Atoyac r. Puebla Mex.
245 F4 Atoyac r. Veracruz Mex.
244 D5 Atoyac de Álvarez Mex.
114 B2 Atpadi Mahar. India
220 C2 Atqasuk AK U.S.A.
117 G4 Atrai r. India
122 C2 Atrak, Rūd-e r. Iran/Turkm. alt. Atrek, alt. Etrek
142 E3 Ätran r. Sweden
116 D4 Atranh Uttar Prad. India
250 B2 Atrato r. Col.
245 G5 Atravesada, Sierra mts Mex.
122 C2 Atrek r. Iran/Turkm. alt. Atrak, Rūd-e, alt. Etrek
193 F2 Atri Italy
Atria Italy see Adria
193 G4 Atripalda Italy
Atropatene country Asia see Azerbaijan
129 C2 Ats'ana Georgia
234 D3 Atsion NJ U.S.A.
105 F3 Atsugi Japan
128 B4 Aţ Ţafīlah Jordan
124 C3 Aţ Ţā'if Saudi Arabia
177 H5 Attala Hungary
Attalea Turkey see Antalya
Attalia Turkey see Antalya
231 C5 Attalla AL U.S.A.
127 F4 At Ta'mīm governorate Iraq
202 D1 At Tamīmī Libya
148 B5 Attanagh Rep. of Ireland
97 D4 Attapu Laos
147 B2 Attavalley Rep. of Ireland
199 E3 Attavyros mt. Notio Aigaio Greece
224 D2 Attawapiskat Ont. Can.
224 D2 Attawapiskat r. Ont. Can.
203 H2 Aţ Ţawīl mts Saudi Arabia
124 C1 At Taysīyah plat. Saudi Arabia
128 B4 Aţ Ţayyibah Jordan
80 D4 Attempt Hill hill South I. N.Z.
169 C4 Attendorn Ger.
173 F3 Attenkirchen Ger.
215 G1 Atteridgeville S. Africa
179 E3 Attersee Austria
179 E3 Attersee l. Austria
165 E5 Attert Belgium
165 F5 Attert r. Lux.
147 E2 Attica Northern Ireland U.K.
230 C3 Attica IN U.S.A.
232 D3 Attica NY U.S.A.
232 B4 Attica OH U.S.A.
156 D3 Attichy France
193 E2 Attigliano Italy
160 D2 Attignat France
156 E3 Attigny France
198 C3 Attiki admin. reg. Greece
114 C4 Attingal Kerala India
233 H4 Attleboro MA U.S.A.
151 I2 Attleborough Norfolk, England U.K.
151 I2 Attlebridge Norfolk, England U.K.
179 E2 Attnang Austria
123 H3 Attock City Pak.
Attopeu Laos see Attapu
126 E5 Aţ Ţubayq reg. Saudi Arabia
266 G2 Attu Island AK U.S.A.
83 G2 Attunga N.S.W. Austr.
At Tūnisīyah country Africa see Tunisia
114 C4 Attur Tamil Nadu India
114 C4 Attur Tamil Nadu India
124 C5 At Turbah Yemen
124 D5 At Turbah Yemen
147 C3 Attymon Rep. of Ireland
125 E5 Atūd Yemen
260 D5 Atuel r. Arg.
162 C3 Atur France
143 F2 Åtvidaberg Sweden
117 G4 Atwari Bangl.
240 G3 Atwater CA U.S.A.
236 C4 Atwood KS U.S.A.
135 I5 Atyashevo Rus. Fed.
120 B3 Atyrau Kazakh.
Atyrau Oblast admin. div. Kazakh. see Atyrauskaya Oblast'
Atyraū Oblysy admin. div. Kazakh. see Atyrauskaya Oblast'
120 B3 Atyrauskaya Oblast' admin. div. Kazakh.
135 H5 Atyur'yevo Rus. Fed.
137 G2 Atyusha Ukr.
192 B5 Atzara Sardegna Italy
179 G2 Atzenbrugg Austria
171 C4 Atzendorf Ger.
178 A3 Au Austria
190 E1 Au Switz.
250 E5 Auati-Paraná r. Brazil
173 E2 Aub Ger.
169 E5 Aubach r. Ger.
161 D5 Aubagne France
161 C5 Aubais France
165 E5 Aubange Belgium
162 D3 Aubazines France
159 G3 Aube France
156 E4 Aube dept Champagne-Ardenne France
156 D4 Aube r. France
213 H3 Aúbe Moz.
165 E4 Aubel Belgium
161 C4 Aubenas France
156 E3 Aubenton France
156 B4 Aubergenville France
156 E3 Aubérive France
157 F5 Auberive Champagne-Ardenne France
162 C3 Aubeterre-sur-Dronne France
156 D4 Aubetin r. France
156 B3 Aubevoye France
163 C5 Aubiet France
161 D4 Aubignan France
159 G4 Aubigné-Racan France
161 D4 Aubignosc France
156 C2 Aubigny-en-Artois France
159 I4 Aubigny-sur-Nère France
163 E4 Aubin France
224 D4 Aubinadong r. Ont. Can.
190 B2 Aubonne Switz.
161 C5 Aubord France
157 F3 Auboué France
161 A4 Aubrac mts France
157 F3 Aubreville France
241 K4 Aubrey Cliffs mts AZ U.S.A.
220 F3 Aubry Lake N.W.T. Can.
85 G5 Auburn r. Qld Austr.
227 G4 Auburn Ont. Can.
231 C5 Auburn AL U.S.A.
240 G2 Auburn CA U.S.A.
236 F4 Auburn IL U.S.A.
230 C3 Auburn IN U.S.A.
233 H3 Auburn MA U.S.A.
233 □H2 Auburn ME U.S.A.
227 E4 Auburn MI U.S.A.
236 E3 Auburn NE U.S.A.
232 E3 Auburn NY U.S.A.
234 B2 Auburn PA U.S.A.
238 B2 Auburn WA U.S.A.
234 B1 Auburn Center PA U.S.A.
226 B3 Auburndale WI U.S.A.
85 G5 Auburn Range hills Qld Austr.
162 E3 Aubusson France
156 D2 Auby France
260 C5 Auca Mahuida, Sierra de mt. Arg.
163 D5 Aucamville France
138 D3 Auce Latvia
163 C5 Auch France
146 E5 Auchallater Aberdeenshire, Scotland U.K.
148 D2 Auchbraad Argyll and Bute, Scotland U.K.
156 C2 Auchel France
146 F5 Auchenblae Aberdeenshire, Scotland U.K.
146 C6 Auchenbreck Argyll and Bute, Scotland U.K.
146 E7 Auchencairn Dumfries and Galloway, Scotland U.K.
146 F6 Auchencrow Scottish Borders, Scotland U.K.
207 G5 Auchi Nigeria
146 D6 Auchinleck East Ayrshire, Scotland U.K.
146 F5 Auchmull Angus, Scotland U.K.
146 F4 Auchnagatt Aberdeenshire, Scotland U.K.
146 E4 Aucholzie Aberdeenshire, Scotland U.K.
146 F5 Auchronie Angus, Scotland U.K.
146 E5 Auchterarder Perth and Kinross, Scotland U.K.
146 E5 Auchtermuchty Fife, Scotland U.K.
156 C2 Auchy-au-Bois France
80 E2 Auckland North I. N.Z.
80 E2 Auckland admin. reg. North I. N.Z.
77 G6 Auckland Islands N.Z.

163 B6 Aucun France
161 A5 Aude dept Languedoc-Roussillon France
161 B5 Aude r. France
224 C3 Auden Ont. Can.
Audenarde Belgium see Oudenaarde
163 A4 Audenge France
158 E2 Auderville France
233 □H2 Audet Que. Can.
160 D1 Audeux France
158 B3 Audierne France
160 E1 Audincourt France
150 E2 Audlem Cheshire, England U.K.
149 G4 Audley Staffordshire, England U.K.
163 B5 Audon France
210 D3 Audo Range mts Eth.
156 B2 Audresselles France
138 E2 Audru Estonia
156 C2 Audruicq France
236 E3 Audubon IA U.S.A.
234 C3 Audubon NJ U.S.A.
157 F3 Audun-le-Roman France
171 D5 Aue Ger.
168 C2 Aue r. Ger.
169 E3 Aue r. Ger.
169 F3 Aue r. Ger.
173 H3 Auerbach Bayern Ger.
171 D5 Auerbach Sachsen Ger.
171 D5 Auerbach Sachsen Ger.
173 F2 Auerbach in der Oberpfalz Ger.
171 D5 Auersberg mt. Ger.
179 H2 Auersthal Austria
171 D5 Auerswalde Ger.
156 B3 Auffay France
173 G3 Aufhausen Ger.
85 F5 Augathella Qld Austr.
147 D2 Augher Northern Ireland U.K.
147 E2 Aughnacloy Northern Ireland U.K.
147 C3 Aughrim Galway Rep. of Ireland
147 E4 Aughrim Wicklow Rep. of Ireland
149 G4 Aughton Lancashire, England U.K.
149 H4 Aughton South Yorkshire, England U.K.
162 C3 Augignac France
214 C3 Augrabies S. Africa
214 C3 Augrabies Falls S. Africa
227 F3 Au Gres MI U.S.A.
173 E3 Augsburg Ger.
178 B2 Augsburg airport Ger.
138 E3 Augšlīgatne Latvia
138 F3 Augšzemes augstiene hills Latvia
87 B7 Augusta W.A. Austr.
195 E5 Augusta Sicilia Italy
237 F5 Augusta AR U.S.A.
231 D5 Augusta GA U.S.A.
226 B5 Augusta IL U.S.A.
237 D4 Augusta KS U.S.A.
232 A5 Augusta KY U.S.A.
233 □I2 Augusta ME U.S.A.
238 D2 Augusta MT U.S.A.
234 D1 Augusta NJ U.S.A.
226 B3 Augusta WI U.S.A.
232 D5 Augusta WV U.S.A.
195 E5 Augusta, Golfo di b. Sicilia Italy
Augusta Auscorum France see Auch
Augusta Taurinorum Italy see Torino
Augusta Treverorum Ger. see Trier
Augusta Vindelicorum Ger. see Augsburg
168 E1 Augustenborg Denmark
246 D5 Augustin Cadazzi Col.
Augusto Cardosa Moz. see Metangula
257 E3 Augusto de Lima Brazil
Augustodunum France see Autun
254 F3 Augusto Severo Brazil
175 K2 Augustów Pol.
175 L3 Augustowo Pol.
87 C5 Augustus, Mount W.A. Austr.
171 E5 Augustusburg Ger.
86 E2 Augustus Island W.A. Austr.
169 E3 Auhagen Ger.
173 F3 Au in der Hallertau Ger.
157 E4 Aujon r. France
222 C3 Auke Bay AK U.S.A.
78 □6 Auki Malaita Solomon Is
168 E1 Aukrug Ger.
138 D4 Aukštelkai Lith.
140 L2 Auktsjaur Sweden
86 D4 Auld, Lake salt flat W.A. Austr.
146 E4 Auldearn Highland, Scotland U.K.
169 F4 Auleben Ger.
190 E4 Aulella r. Italy
172 D4 Aulendorf Ger.
193 H4 Auletta Italy
Auliye Ata Zhambylskaya Oblast' Kazakh. see Taraz
190 E4 Aulla Italy
192 B3 Aullène Corse France
160 B3 Aulnat France
160 B3 Aulnat airport France
162 B2 Aulnay France
156 C4 Aulnay-sous-Bois France
158 B3 Aulne r. France
157 G4 Aulnois sur-Seille France
156 D2 Aulnoye-Aymeries France
Aulon Albania see Vlorë
163 C5 Aulon France
170 C3 Aulosen Ger.
156 B2 Ault France
146 C4 Aultbea Highland, Scotland U.K.
146 D4 Aultguish Inn Highland, Scotland U.K.
163 D6 Aulus-les-Bains France
171 C5 Auma Ger.
156 B3 Aumale France
160 A2 Aumance r. France
157 F3 Aumetz France
120 E4 Auminzatau, Gory hills Uzbek.
160 D2 Aumont France
161 B4 Aumont-Aubrac France
168 F2 Aumühle Ger.
207 G4 Auna Nigeria
160 B1 Aunay-en-Bazois France
159 F2 Aunay-sur-Odon France
156 B4 Auneau France
156 C3 Auneuil France
142 D3 Auning Denmark
183 H4 Auñón Spain
191 I2 Aupa r. Italy
225 G1 Aupaluk Que. Can.
161 E5 Aups France
141 M3 Aura Fin.
173 E2 Aurach Ger.
178 D3 Aurach bei Kitzbühel Austria
114 C2 Aurad Karnataka India
163 D5 Auradé France
169 E5 Aura im Sinngrund Ger.
116 D4 Auraiya Uttar Prad. India
138 D1 Aurajoki r. Fin.
117 F4 Aurangabad Bihar India
114 B2 Aurangabad Mahar. India
158 D4 Auray France
159 E2 Aure r. France
140 J3 Aure Norway
161 C3 Aurec-sur-Loire France
163 C5 Aureilhan France
161 C5 Aureille France
161 D4 Aurel Provence-Alpes-Côte-d'Azur France
161 D4 Aurel Rhône-Alpes France
244 A1 Aurelio Benassini, Presa resr Mex.
163 B5 Aurensan France
168 C2 Aurich Ger.
256 B4 Auriflama Brazil
163 C5 Aurignac France
Aurigny i. Channel Is see Alderney
256 B2 Aurilândia Brazil
162 E4 Aurillac France
186 C2 Aurín r. Spain
191 G2 Aurino r. Italy
161 D5 Auriol France
191 I3 Aurisina Italy
80 E3 Auroa North I. N.Z.
179 E2 Aurolzmünster Austria
161 E4 Auron France
160 A1 Auron r. France
191 H2 Auronzo di Cadore Italy
92 B5 Aurora Phil.
214 B5 Aurora S. Africa
238 F4 Aurora CO U.S.A.
226 C5 Aurora IL U.S.A.
233 □I2 Aurora ME U.S.A.
226 A2 Aurora MN U.S.A.
237 E4 Aurora MO U.S.A.
236 D3 Aurora NE U.S.A.
232 C4 Aurora OH U.S.A.
241 L2 Aurora UT U.S.A.
Aurora Island Vanuatu see Maéwo
163 B4 Auros France
161 B4 Auroux France
85 E2 Aurukun Qld Austr.
193 F3 Aurunci, Monti mts Italy
114 C2 Ausa Mahar. India
191 I3 Ausa r. Italy
227 F3 Au Sable MI U.S.A.
227 F3 Au Sable r. MI U.S.A.
233 G2 Ausable r. NY U.S.A.
233 G2 Ausable Forks NY U.S.A.
191 I3 Ausa-Corno Italy
Auschwitz Pol. see Oświęcim
Ausculum Italy see Ascoli Satriano
Ausculum Apulum Italy see Ascoli Satriano
183 H2 Ausejo Spain
193 F3 Ausente r. Italy
177 L4 Auşeu Romania
146 F2 Auskerry i. Scotland U.K.
171 C3 Ausleben Ger.
193 F3 Ausoni, Monti mts Italy
193 F3 Ausonia Italy
163 D5 Ausseing Tour hill France
163 E5 Aussillon France
161 E3 Aussois France
163 D5 Aussonne France
163 B5 Aussurucq France
142 C2 Aust-Agder county Norway
140 □C2 Austari-Jökulsá r. Iceland
140 □ Austfonna ice cap Svalbard
226 A4 Austin MN U.S.A.
240 I2 Austin NV U.S.A.
237 D6 Austin TX U.S.A.
87 C5 Austin, Lake salt flat W.A. Austr.
232 C4 Austintown OH U.S.A.
192 B4 Austis Sardegna Italy
84 D4 Austral Downs N.T. Austr.
79 □3 Australes, Îles is Fr. Polynesia
76 C4 Australia country Oceania
263 J2 Australian Antarctic Territory Antarctica
83 G3 Australian Capital Territory admin. div. Austr.
87 B7 Australind W.A. Austr.
179 E3 Austria country Europe
138 D3 Austrumkursas augstiene hills Latvia
140 □D2 Austurland constituency Iceland
140 K1 Austvågøy i. Norway
251 G5 Autazes Brazil
163 D5 Auterive France
Autesiodorum France see Auxerre
160 D1 Autet France
156 B2 Authie r. France
227 H1 Authier Que. Can.
159 F4 Authion r. France
159 G4 Authon Centre France
161 E4 Authon Provence-Alpes-Côte-d'Azur France
159 G3 Authon-du-Perche France
244 B4 Autlán Mex.
183 H2 Autol Spain
161 D3 Autrans France
157 F4 Autreville France
160 D1 Autrey-lès-Gray France
157 E3 Autry France
160 C2 Autun France
156 E3 Auve France
165 D4 Auvelais Belgium
160 B3 Auvergne admin. reg. France
161 A4 Auvergne reg. France
160 A3 Auvergne, Monts d' mts France
159 F4 Auvers-le-Hamon France
156 C3 Auvers-sur-Oise France
162 C3 Auvézère r. France
163 C4 Auvignon r. France
163 C4 Auvillar France
156 E3 Auvillers-les-Forges France
156 D5 Auxerre France
156 C2 Auxi-le-Château France
160 D1 Auxonne France
160 C2 Auxy France
251 F3 Auyan Tepuí plat. Venez.
160 A2 Auzances France
163 D6 Auzat France
161 B3 Auzat-sur-Allier France
162 E3 Auze r. France
163 E4 Auzits France
161 B3 Auzon France
163 C4 Auzoue r. France
121 J2 Auzzov Kazakh.
96 A2 Ava Myanmar
237 E4 Ava MO U.S.A.
233 F3 Ava NY U.S.A.
256 C5 Avaí Brazil
162 C2 Availles-Limouzine France
160 B1 Avallon France
159 F3 Avaloirs, Mont des hill France
240 H5 Avalon CA U.S.A.
234 D3 Avalon NJ U.S.A.
225 K4 Avalon Peninsula Nfld. Can.
261 H2 Avalos r. Arg.
122 A2 Avān Iran
114 C4 Avanashi Tamil Nadu India
182 B4 Avanca Port.
163 C4 Avance r. France
161 E4 Avançon France
251 G3 Avanganna mt. Guyana
114 D2 Avanigadda Andhra Prad. India
126 D3 Avanos Turkey
156 E4 Avant-lès-Ramerupt France
Avarau atoll Cook Is see Palmerston
256 C5 Avaré Brazil
Avaricum France see Bourges
127 G3 Āvārsin Iran
129 E2 Avarskoye Koysu r. Rus. Fed.
81 □3 Avarua Rarotonga Cook Is
140 L2 Avaträsk Sweden
140 L2 Avaviken Sweden
232 B6 Avawam KY U.S.A.
Avdeyevka Ukr. see Avdiyivka
198 D1 Avdira Anatoliki Makedonia kai Thraki Greece
137 I3 Avdiyivka Ukr.
182 B3 Ave r. Port.
151 F3 Avebury Wiltshire, England U.K.
182 D2 A Veiga Galicia Spain
184 B1 Aveiras de Cima Port.
182 B4 Aveiro Port.
182 B4 Aveiro admin. dist. Port.
182 B4 Aveiro, Ria de est. Port.
182 B5 Avelar Port.
182 B3 Aveleda Braga Port.
182 D3 Aveleda Bragança Port.
151 H3 Aveley Thurrock, England U.K.
165 C4 Avelgem Belgium
261 H4 Avellaneda Buenos Aires Arg.
258 F3 Avellaneda Santa Fé Arg.
193 G4 Avellino Italy
193 H4 Avellino prov. Campania Italy
158 C4 Aven r. France
240 G3 Avenal CA U.S.A.
156 E3 Avenay-Val-d'Or France
190 C2 Avenches Switz.
161 B5 Avène France
164 D2 Avenhorn Neth.
182 B1 Avenida do Marqués de Figueroa Spain
Avenio France see Avignon
Aventicum Switz. see Avenches
160 B2 Avermes France
146 D4 Averon r. Scotland U.K.
140 I3 Averøya i. Norway
190 E2 Avers Switz.
193 G4 Aversa Italy
247 G4 Aves i. West Indies
Aves is West Indies see Las Aves, Islas
156 C2 Avesnes-le-Comte France
156 D2 Avesnes-sur-Helpe France
143 G1 Avesta Sweden
190 E4 Aveto r. Italy
195 G2 Avetrano Italy
161 A4 Aveyron dept Midi-Pyrénées France
163 D4 Aveyron r. France
193 F2 Avezzano Italy
186 E2 Avia Spain
182 B2 Avia r. Spain
191 H2 Aviano Italy
258 E2 Aviá Terai Arg.
146 E4 Aviemore Highland, Scotland U.K.
81 C6 Aviemore, Lake South I. N.Z.
190 C3 Avigliana Italy
193 H4 Avigliano Italy
193 E2 Avigliano Umbro Italy
161 C5 Avignon France
163 D5 Avignonet-Lauragais France
183 F4 Ávila Spain
183 F4 Ávila prov. Castilla y León Spain
183 E4 Ávila, Sierra de mts Spain
182 E1 Avilés Spain
160 E1 Avilley France
137 J4 Avilo-Uspenka Rus. Fed.
182 B1 Aviño Spain
182 B3 Avintes Port.
186 E3 Avinyó Spain
191 F3 Avio Italy
156 C2 Avion France
182 B2 Avión mt. Spain
157 F3 Avioth France
184 C1 Avis Port.
191 G2 Avisio r. Italy
156 E4 Avize France
128 A1 Avlama Dağı mt. Turkey
198 C2 Avlida Greece
Avlona Albania see Vlorë
142 C3 Avlum Denmark
134 I3 Avnyugskiy Rus. Fed.
83 F5 Avoca Tas. Austr.
83 E4 Avoca Vic. Austr.
83 E3 Avoca r. Vic. Austr.
147 E4 Avoca Rep. of Ireland
215 H1 Avoca S. Africa
236 E3 Avoca IA U.S.A.
232 E3 Avoca NY U.S.A.
146 D4 Avoch Highland, Scotland U.K.
159 G4 Avoine France
195 E6 Avola Sicilia Italy
87 C6 Avon r. W.A. Austr.
156 C4 Avon France
150 D4 Avon r. Devon, England U.K.
150 E3 Avon r. England U.K.
151 E2 Avon r. England U.K.
151 F4 Avon r. England U.K.
226 B5 Avon IL U.S.A.
232 E3 Avon NY U.S.A.
234 B2 Avon PA U.S.A.
147 E4 Avonbeg r. Rep. of Ireland
149 F2 Avonbridge Falkirk, Scotland U.K.
241 K5 Avondale AZ U.S.A.
234 C3 Avondale PA U.S.A.
235 G1 Avondale RI U.S.A.
84 D4 Avon Downs N.T. Austr.
85 F4 Avon Downs Qld Austr.
232 B4 Avon Lake OH U.S.A.
147 E4 Avonmore r. Rep. of Ireland
150 E3 Avonmouth Bristol, England U.K.
231 D7 Avon Park FL U.S.A.
214 D5 Avontuur S. Africa
160 A1 Avord France
160 E2 Avoriaz France
138 E3 Avoti Latvia
160 E1 Avoudrey France
197 H1 Avrămeni Romania
197 E2 Avram Iancu Romania
158 E3 Avranches France
156 C3 Avre r. France
159 H3 Avre r. France
157 G4 Avricourt France
197 G3 Avrig Romania
157 F3 Avril France
162 A2 Avrillé France
159 F4 Avrillé France
129 B3 Avsek Dağı mt. Turkey
Avveel Fin. see Ivalo
Avvil Fin. see Ivalo
128 B3 A'waj r. Syria
104 A4 Awaji-shima i. Japan
80 F3 Awakeri North I. N.Z.
80 E3 Awakino North I. N.Z.
125 E2 Awālī Bahrain
165 E4 Awans Belgium
80 D1 Awanui North I. N.Z.
210 E2 Āwarē Eth.
81 B7 Awarua South I. N.Z.
210 C3 Āwasa Eth.
210 D2 Āwash Eth.
210 D2 Āwash r. Eth.
110 C3 Awat Xinjiang China
210 C3 Āwatā Shet' r. Eth.
81 E4 Awatere r. South I. N.Z.
202 B3 Awbārī Libya
147 C4 Awbeg r. Rep. of Ireland
146 C5 Awe, Loch l. Scotland U.K.
208 E2 Aweil Sudan
207 G5 Awgu Nigeria
207 G5 Awka Nigeria
204 B4 Awlitis watercourse Western Sahara
93 B3 Awo r. Indon.
150 E3 Awre Gloucestershire, England U.K.
93 C2 Awu vol. Indon.
178 C3 Axams Austria
163 E6 Axat France
150 D4 Axe r. Devon/Dorset, England U.K.
150 E3 Axe r. North Somerset/Somerset, England U.K.
83 F4 Axedale Vic. Austr.
165 C3 Axel Neth.
221 I2 Axel Heiberg Island Nunavut Can.
197 G2 Axente Sever Romania
206 E5 Axim Ghana
198 C1 Axios r. Greece
163 D6 Ax-les-Thermes France
150 E4 Axminster Devon, England U.K.
245 E4 Axochiapan Mex.
183 H1 Axpe-Busturia Spain
168 D2 Axstedt Ger.
Axum Eth. see Āksum
156 E3 Ay France
104 B3 Ayabe Japan
204 D2 Ayachi, Jbel mt. Morocco
261 H5 Ayacucho Arg.
252 B3 Ayacucho Peru
252 B3 Ayacucho dept Peru
121 J3 Ayagoz Kazakh.
Ayaguz Kazakh. see Ayagoz
120 F4 Ayakagytma, Vpadina depr. Uzbek.
120 F4 Ayakkuduk Uzbek.
Ayaköz Kazakh. see Ayagoz
206 E5 Ayamé Côte d'Ivoire
184 C3 Ayamonte Spain
131 O4 Ayan Rus. Fed.
126 D2 Ayancık Turkey
101 C5 Ayang N. Korea
207 G5 Ayangba Nigeria
250 C3 Ayapel, Serranía de mts Col.
126 D2 Ayaş Turkey
105 F3 Ayase Japan
252 C3 Ayaviri Peru
210 C1 Ayayei Eth.
123 G2 Āybak Afgh.
149 H3 Aycliffe Durham, England U.K.
121 G1 Aydabul Kazakh.
137 J2 Aydar Rus. Fed.
137 J3 Aydar r. Ukr.
121 F4 Aydarkul', Ozero l. Uzbek.
120 F3 Aydarly Kazakh.
160 A3 Aydat France
125 F4 'Aydim, Wādī r. Oman
199 E3 Aydın Turkey
199 F3 Aydın prov. Turkey
128 A1 Aydıncık Turkey
199 E2 Aydın Dağları mts Turkey
129 C4 Aydınlar Turkey
129 B3 Aydıntepe Turkey
121 G3 Ayeat, Gora hill Kazakh.
183 H2 Ayedo mt. Spain
210 D2 Āyelu Terara vol. Eth.
162 D3 Ayen France
233 H3 Ayer MA U.S.A.
186 C2 Ayerbe Spain
Ayers Rock hill N.T. Austr. see Uluru
Ayeyarwady r. Myanmar see Irrawaddy
110 D1 Aygulakskiy Khrebet mts Rus. Fed.
Ayiá Greece see Agia
Ayiásos Voreio Aigaio Greece see Agiasos
173 F4 Aying Ger.
Áyion Óros admin. div. Greece see Agion Oros
Áyios Dhimítrios Attiki Greece see Agios Dimitrios
Áyios Evstrátios i. Greece see Agios Efstratios
Áyios Nikólaos Kriti Greece see Agios Nikolaos
210 C1 Āykel Eth.
131 M3 Aykhal Rus. Fed.
134 J3 Aykino Rus. Fed.
81 D5 Aylesbury South I. N.Z.
151 G3 Aylesbury Buckinghamshire, England U.K.
151 H3 Aylesford Kent, England U.K.
151 I3 Aylesham Kent, England U.K.
232 E6 Aylett VA U.S.A.
183 G3 Ayllón Spain
227 G4 Aylmer Ont. Can.
227 J3 Aylmer Que. Can.
223 I1 Aylmer Lake N.W.T. Can.
151 I2 Aylsham Norfolk, England U.K.
120 E2 Aymagambetov Kazakh.
190 C3 Aymavilles Italy
252 B3 Ayna Peru
185 H2 Ayna Spain
121 I3 Aynabulak Kazakh.
163 D4 Aynac France
125 D5 'Ayn Ba Ma'bad Yemen
123 G2 Aynī Tajik.
126 E3 'Ayn 'Īsá Syria
244 C3 Ayo el Chico Mex.
131 R3 Ayon, Ostrov i. Rus. Fed.
182 D2 Ayoo de Vidriales Spain
245 F5 Ayoquezco Mex.
187 B5 Ayora Spain
207 F3 Ayorou Niger
207 I6 Ayos Cameroon
206 C2 'Ayoûn el 'Atroûs Maur.
85 F3 Ayr Qld Austr.
227 G4 Ayr Ont. Can.
146 D6 Ayr South Ayrshire, Scotland U.K.
146 D6 Ayr r. Scotland U.K.
150 D1 Ayr, Point of Wales U.K.
128 C1 Ayran Turkey
126 D3 Ayrancı Turkey
199 E2 Ayrancılar Turkey
129 E3 Äyriçay r. Azer.
159 G5 Ayron France
129 D3 Ayrum Armenia
149 H3 Aysgarth North Yorkshire, England U.K.
210 D2 Āysha Eth.
173 E3 Aystetten Ger.
120 E3 Ayteke Bi Kazakh.
197 H4 Aytos Bulg.
197 H4 Aytoska Reka r. Bulg.
162 A2 Aytré France
93 D2 Ayu, Kepulauan atoll Irian Jaya Indon.
183 H2 Ayuda r. Spain
184 D1 Ayuela r. Spain
125 F4 Ayun Oman
Ayuthia Thai. see Ayutthaya
137 K4 Ayutinskiy Rus. Fed.
245 E5 Ayutla Mex.
97 C4 Ayutthaya Thai.
199 E2 Ayvacık Turkey
126 E3 Ayvalı Turkey
199 E2 Ayvalık Turkey
199 G3 Ayvalıpınar Turkey
165 E4 Aywaille Belgium
125 E4 Aywat al Manāhīl, Wādī r. Yemen
125 E4 Aywat aş Şay'ar, Wādī r. Yemen
242 □I6 Azacualpa Hond.
183 I2 Azagra Spain
186 C3 Azaila Spain
Azak Rus. Fed. see Azov
184 B1 Azambuja Port.
184 C2 Azambuja r. Port.
117 E4 Azamgarh Uttar Prad. India
252 C3 Azangaro Peru
196 E3 Azanja Srbija Yugo.
157 F3 Azannes-et-Soumazannes France
186 D3 Azanúy Spain
206 E2 Azaouâd reg. Mali
207 F2 Azaouagh, Vallée de watercourse Mali/Niger
252 C4 Azapa Chile
258 G3 Azara Arg.
Azaran Iran see Hashtrud
Azärbayjan country Asia see Azerbaijan
122 A2 Āžarbāyjān-e Gharbī prov. Iran
122 A2 Āžarbāyjān-e Sharqī prov. Iran
207 H4 Azare Nigeria
184 C2 Azaruja Port.
138 G5 Azarychy Belarus
129 D3 Azatamut Armenia
139 K2 Azatskoye, Ozero l. Rus. Fed.
129 C3 Azavret'i Georgia
159 H5 Azay-le-Ferron France
159 G4 Azay-le-Rideau France
128 C1 A'zāz Syria
Azbine mts Niger see L'Aïr, Massif de
126 D2 Azdavay Turkey
159 F4 Azé France
204 C2 Azemmour Morocco
162 D2 Azerables France
129 F3 Azerbaijan country Asia
Azerbaydzhanskaya S.S.R. country Asia see Azerbaijan
160 C3 Azergues r. France
184 C2 Azevel r. Port.
210 C1 Āzezo Eth.
129 D3 Azhdahak Lerr mt. Armenia
204 D2 Azilal Morocco
227 G2 Azilda Ont. Can.
161 A5 Azille France
156 C2 Azincourt France
184 B1 Azinhaga Port.
184 C3 Azinhal Port.
182 D3 Azinhoso Port.
Azizbekov Armenia see Vayk'
Aziziye Turkey see Pınarbaşı
186 A1 Azkoitia Spain
135 K5 Aznakayevo Rus. Fed.
184 D3 Aznalcázar Spain
184 D3 Aznalcóllar Spain
250 B5 Azogues Ecuador
184 A2 Azóia Port.
216 □1 Azores aut. reg. N. Atlantic Ocean
264 H3 Azores-Biscay Rise sea feature N. Atlantic Ocean
Azotus Israel see Ashdod
135 G7 Azov Rus. Fed.
137 I4 Azov, Sea of Rus. Fed./Ukr.
Azovs'ke More sea Rus. Fed./Ukr. see Azov, Sea of
Azovskoye More sea Rus. Fed./Ukr. see Azov, Sea of
245 E5 Azoyú Mex.
186 A1 Azpeitia Spain
203 G6 Azraq, Bahr el r. Sudan alt. Abay Wenz (Ethiopia), conv. Blue Nile
204 D2 Azrou Morocco
239 E4 Aztec NM U.S.A.
246 E3 Azua Dom. Rep.
184 E2 Azuaga Spain
186 C3 Azuara Spain
250 B5 Azuay prov. Ecuador
258 C2 Azúcar r. Chile
185 F2 Azuel Spain
183 H2 Azuelo Spain
185 G1 Azuer r. Spain
242 □J8 Azuero, Península de pen. Panama
258 C2 Azufre, Cerro del mt. Chile
261 H5 Azul Arg.
261 H5 Azul r. Arg.
260 B4 Azul vol. Chile
243 H5 Azul r. Mex.
250 □ Azul, Cerro vol. Islas Galápagos Ecuador
252 B2 Azul, Cordillera mts Peru
253 G3 Azul, Serra hills Brazil
102 J5 Azuma-san vol. Japan
105 E2 Azumaya-san mt. Japan
183 G4 Azuqueca de Henares Spain
163 A5 Azur France
182 B3 Azurara Port.
252 D5 Azurduy Bol.
183 E5 Azután Spain
160 B2 Azy-le-Vif France
'Azza Gaza see Gaza
205 G1 Azzaba Alg.
128 C3 Az Zabadānī Syria
125 G3 Az Zāhirah admin. reg. Oman
125 E2 Az Zahrān Saudi Arabia
125 E2 Az Zallāq Bahrain
191 H3 Azzano Decimo Italy
Az Zaqāzīq Egypt see Zagazig
128 C1 Az Zarbah Syria
128 C3 Az Zarqā' Jordan
202 B1 Az Zāwīyah Libya
124 C5 Az Zaydīyah Yemen
204 B5 Azzeffâl hills Maur./W. Sahara
124 D2 Az Zilfī Saudi Arabia
190 F3 Azzone Italy
127 G5 Az Zubayr Iraq
124 C5 Az Zuhrah Yemen
124 C5 Az Zuqur i. Yemen

B

79 □1a Ba Viti Levu Fiji
78 □5 Baâba i. New Caledonia
95 G2 Baai r. Indon.
128 C2 Ba'albek Lebanon
171 C4 Baalberge Ger.
164 F2 Baalder Neth.
128 B4 Ba'al Hazor mt. West Bank
157 F3 Baâlon France
190 D1 Baar Switz.
210 D4 Baardheere Somalia
173 F3 Baar-Ebenhausen Ger.
165 D3 Baarle-Hertog Belgium
165 D3 Baarle-Nassau Neth.
164 E2 Baarn Neth.
116 D4 Bab Uttar Prad. India
197 F4 Baba mt. Bulg.
179 F1 Baba hill Czech Rep.
123 G3 Bābā, Kūh-e mts Afgh.
206 B2 Bababé Maur.
254 D3 Babaçulândia Brazil
197 I3 Babadag Romania
199 F3 Babadağ Turkey
199 F3 Baba Dağ mt. Turkey
197 I3 Babadagului, Podişul plat. Romania
122 E2 Babadaykhan Akhal'skaya Oblast' Turkm.
122 E2 Babadaykhan Akhal'skaya Oblast' Turkm.
199 E1 Babaeski Turkey
199 G2 Babageçidin Tepesi mt. Turkey
250 B5 Babahoyo Ecuador
116 E3 Babai r. Nepal
106 E3 Babai Gaxun Nei Mongol China
127 G3 Bābā Jān Iran
129 D4 Babāk Azer.
92 C5 Babak Phil.
203 I6 Bāb al Mandab str. Africa/Asia
124 C5 Bāb al Mandab, Ra's c. Yemen
93 A3 Babana Sulawesi Selatan Indon.
215 H3 Babanango S. Africa
215 G3 Babangiboni mt. S. Africa
207 H5 Babanki Cameroon
208 E2 Babanusa Sudan
Babao Qinghai China see Qilian
108 C4 Babao Yunnan China
95 F4 Babat Jawa Timur Indon.
211 B6 Babati Tanz.
139 J2 Babayevo Rus. Fed.
137 H3 Babaykivka Ukr.
129 E2 Babayurt Rus. Fed.
150 D4 Babbacombe Bay England U.K.
87 B5 Babbage Island W.A. Austr.
164 F3 Babberich Neth.
92 □ Babeldaob i. Palau
215 G1 Babelegi S. Africa
Babelthuap i. Palau see Babeldaob
173 E3 Babenhausen Bayern Ger.
172 C2 Babenhausen Hessen Ger.
197 G3 Băbeni Romania
116 E4 Baberu Uttar Prad. India
175 H6 Babia Góra mt. Pol.
175 I1 Babiak Warmińsko-Mazurskie Pol.
174 G3 Babiak Wielkopolskie Pol.
108 B4 Babian Jiang r. Yunnan China
176 G2 Babice Czech Rep.
175 H5 Babice Pol.
127 G4 Bābil governorate Iraq
183 E4 Babilafuente Spain
174 D3 Babimost Pol.
85 F3 Babinda Qld Austr.
220 F4 Babine r. B.C. Can.
222 E4 Babine r. B.C. Can.
222 E4 Babine Range mts B.C. Can.
176 G5 Babócsa Hungary
122 C2 Bābol Iran
177 G4 Bábolna Hungary
122 C2 Bābol Sar Iran
214 B5 Baboon Point S. Africa
241 L6 Baboquivari Peak AZ U.S.A.
174 F5 Baborów Pol.
175 I3 Baboszewo Pol.
208 B3 Baboua C.A.R.
138 G5 Babruysk Belarus
138 D4 Babtai Lith.
Babu Guangxi China see Hexian
197 E5 Babuna Planina mts Macedonia
98 I1 Babushkin Rus. Fed.
197 F4 Babušnica Srbija Yugo.
92 A4 Babuyan Phil.
92 B2 Babuyan Channel Phil.
92 B2 Babuyan Islands Phil.
149 I4 Babworth Nottinghamshire, England U.K.
127 G4 Babylon tourist site Iraq
235 E2 Babylon NY U.S.A.
139 J4 Babynino Rus. Fed.
196 D3 Bač Vojvodina, Srbija Yugo.
210 E3 Bacaadweyn Somalia
250 D5 Bacaba r. Brazil
242 C3 Bacabáchi Mex.
254 D3 Bacabal Brazil
251 I5 Bacajá r. Brazil
126 C2 Bacakliyayla Tepesi mt. Turkey
243 H5 Bacalar Mex.
93 C3 Bacan i. Maluku Indon.
163 C6 Bacanère, Pic de mt. France
185 H3 Bacares Spain
92 B2 Bacarra Phil.
197 H2 Bacău Romania
157 G4 Baccarat France
191 H3 Bacchiglione r. Italy
190 D2 Baceno Italy
96 D2 Băc Giang Vietnam
173 G2 Bach an der Donau Ger.
169 C5 Bacharach Ger.
138 G4 Bacheykava Belarus
173 E3 Bachhagel Ger.
239 F6 Bachiniva Mex.
175 K6 Bachórz Pol.
110 B4 Bachu Xinjiang China
175 K3 Baciki Bliższe Pol.
85 E3 Back r. Qld Austr.
223 M1 Back r. N.W.T./Nunavut Can.
146 F2 Backaland Orkney, Scotland U.K.
196 D3 Bačka Palanka Vojvodina, Srbija Yugo.
196 D3 Bačka Topola Vojvodina, Srbija Yugo.
232 D5 Backbone Mountain MD U.S.A.
222 D2 Backbone Ranges mts N.W.T. Can.
140 L3 Backe Sweden
142 E2 Bäckefors Sweden
143 F2 Bäckhammar Sweden
177 H6 Bački Breg Vojvodina, Srbija Yugo.
177 H6 Bački Monoštor Vojvodina, Srbija Yugo.
196 D3 Bački Petrovac Vojvodina, Srbija Yugo.
172 D3 Backnang Ger.
196 E3 Bačko Gradište Vojvodina, Srbija Yugo.
175 J5 Baćkowice Pol.
82 D3 Backstairs Passage S.A. Austr.
150 E3 Backwell North Somerset, England U.K.
97 D5 Bac Liêu Vietnam
96 D2 Băc Ninh Vietnam
92 B2 Bacnotan Phil.
92 B3 Baco, Mount Mindoro Phil.
242 C2 Bacoachi Mex.
242 C3 Bacobampo Mex.
193 G4 Bacoli Italy
92 B4 Bacolod Phil.
Bacou, Pic de mt. France see Guerreys, Pic de
156 A3 Bacqueville-en-Caux France
177 I5 Bácsalmás Hungary
177 I5 Bácsbokod Hungary
177 I5 Bácsborsód Hungary
177 I5 Bács-Kiskun county Hungary
Bactra Afgh. see Balkh
177 I3 Bacúch Slovakia
149 G4 Bacup Lancashire, England U.K.
254 D2 Bacuri Brazil
236 C2 Bad r. SD U.S.A.
Bada Guangxi China see Xilin
210 C3 Bada mt. Eth.
173 G3 Bad Abbach Ger.
114 B4 Badagara Kerala India
173 G4 Bad Aibling Ger.
106 D3 Badain Jaran Shamo des. Nei Mongol China
251 F5 Badajós, Lago l. Brazil
184 D2 Badajoz Spain
184 D2 Badajoz prov. Extremadura Spain
123 G2 Badakhshān prov. Afgh.
Badakhshan aut. rep. Tajik. see Kūhistoni Badakhshon
Badakhshoni Kūhī aut. rep. Tajik. see Kūhistoni Badakhshon
186 F3 Badalona Spain
190 C5 Badalucco Italy
183 G1 Bádames Spain
114 B3 Badami Karnataka India
127 F5 Badanah Saudi Arabia
Badaojiang Jilin China see Baishan
183 H2 Badarán Spain
Badarinath mts India see Badrinath Peaks
117 H4 Badarpur Assam India
179 E3 Bad Aussee Austria
227 F4 Bad Axe MI U.S.A.
169 C3 Bad Bentheim Ger.
168 C3 Badbergen Ger.
172 B2 Bad Bergzabern Ger.
171 C5 Bad Berka Ger.
169 D4 Bad Berleburg Ger.
171 C5 Bad Berneck im Fichtelgebirge Ger.
169 C5 Bad Bertrich Ger.
168 F2 Bad Bevensen Ger.
171 C4 Bad Bibra Ger.
173 H3 Bad Birnbach Ger.
171 C5 Bad Blankenburg Ger.
179 E4 Bad Bleiberg Austria
169 F5 Bad Bocklet Ger.
171 D5 Bad Brambach Ger.
168 E2 Bad Bramstedt Ger.
169 C5 Bad Breisig Ger.
169 E5 Bad Brückenau Ger.
172 D3 Bad Buchau Ger.
169 D5 Bad Camberg Ger.
146 C4 Badcaul Highland, Scotland U.K.
225 I4 Baddeck N.S. Can.
169 F3 Baddeckenstedt Ger.
123 F4 Baddo r. Pak.
170 C1 Bad Doberan Ger.
169 E4 Bad Driburg Ger.
171 D4 Bad Düben Ger.
172 C2 Bad Dürkheim Ger.
171 D4 Bad Dürrenberg Ger.
172 C3 Bad Dürrheim Ger.
171 C4 Badeborn Ger.
162 D3 Badefols-d'Ans France
169 E3 Bad Eilsen Ger.
171 D5 Bad Elster Ger.
Bademli Turkey see Aladağ
169 C5 Bad Ems Ger.
179 H2 Baden Austria
158 D4 Baden France
190 D1 Baden Switz.
186 B3 Badenas Spain
172 C3 Baden-Baden Ger.
169 D5 Bad Endbach Ger.
173 G4 Bad Endorf Ger.
169 F4 Badenhausen Ger.
146 D5 Badenoch reg. Scotland U.K.
146 F4 Badenscoth Aberdeenshire, Scotland U.K.
172 B4 Badenweiler Ger.
172 C3 Baden-Württemberg land Ger.
207 G3 Badér Niger
169 F4 Badersleben Ger.
192 A4 Badesi Sardegna Italy
169 D3 Bad Essen Ger.
173 G4 Bad Feilnbach Ger.
170 F3 Bad Freienwalde Ger.
172 D2 Bad Friedrichshall Ger.
173 H3 Bad Füssing Ger.
179 G4 Bad Gams Austria
169 F4 Bad Gandersheim Ger.
178 E3 Badgastein Austria
225 K3 Badger Nfld. Can.
123 E3 Bādghīs prov. Afgh.
179 G4 Bad Gleichenberg Austria
179 E3 Bad Goisern Austria
179 F2 Bad Großpertholz Austria
169 F4 Bad Grund (Harz) Ger.
179 F2 Bad Hall Austria
178 D3 Bad Häring Austria
169 F4 Bad Harzburg Ger.
173 F4 Bad Heilbrunn Ger.
172 C3 Bad Herrenalb Ger.
169 E5 Bad Hersfeld Ger.
164 D2 Badhoevedorp Neth.
178 E3 Bad Hofgastein Austria
169 D5 Bad Homburg vor der Höhe Ger.
169 C5 Bad Honnef Ger.
206 B4 Badi r. Guinea
191 G2 Badia Italy
191 G3 Badia Calavena Italy
187 F5 Badia Gran Spain
191 G3 Badia Polesine Italy
191 H5 Badia Tedalda Italy
169 D3 Bad Iburg Ger.
183 G4 Badiel r. Spain
210 B3 Badigeru Swamp Sudan
123 G5 Badin Pak.
177 I3 Badín Slovakia
242 D3 Badiraguato Mex.
179 E3 Bad Ischl Austria
126 E4 Bādiyat ash Shām des. Asia
Badje-Sohppar Sweden see Övre Soppero
169 E4 Bad Karlshafen Ger.
169 F5 Bad Kissingen Ger.
170 C2 Bad Kleinen Ger.
179 E4 Bad Kleinkirchheim Austria
171 C5 Bad Klosterlausnitz Ger.
173 F4 Bad Kohlgrub Ger.
172 D2 Bad König Ger.
Bad Königsdorff Pol. see Jastrzębie-Zdrój
169 F5 Bad Königshofen im Grabfeld Ger.
171 C4 Bad Kösen Ger.
179 F2 Bad Kreuzen Austria
172 B2 Bad Kreuznach Ger.
172 B4 Bad Krozingen Ger.
169 D5 Bad Laasphe Ger.
169 D3 Bad Laer Ger.
236 C2 Badlands reg. ND U.S.A.
236 C3 Badlands reg. SD U.S.A.
169 F4 Bad Langensalza Ger.
171 C4 Bad Lauchstädt Ger.
171 D4 Bad Lausick Ger.
169 F4 Bad Lauterberg im Harz Ger.
179 F2 Bad Leonfelden Austria
171 E4 Bad Liebenwerda Ger.
172 C3 Bad Liebenzell Ger.
169 D4 Bad Lippspringe Ger.
146 E3 Badlipster Highland, Scotland U.K.
172 D2 Bad Mergentheim Ger.
179 E3 Bad Mitterndorf Austria
169 E3 Bad Münder am Deister Ger.
172 B2 Bad Münster am Stein-Ebernburg Ger.
169 B5 Bad Münstereifel Ger.
171 F4 Bad Muskau Ger.
169 D5 Bad Nauheim Ger.
116 C5 Badnawar Madh. Prad. India
169 E3 Bad Nenndorf Ger.
169 C5 Bad Neuenahr-Ahrweiler Ger.
169 F5 Bad Neustadt an der Saale Ger.
169 D3 Bad Oeynhausen Ger.
195 F4 Badolato Italy
185 F3 Badolatosa Spain
168 F2 Bad Oldesloe Ger.
108 D2 Badong Hubei China
157 G4 Badonviller France
169 E5 Bad Orb Ger.
207 F5 Badou Togo
196 D3 Badovinci Srbija Yugo.
172 C3 Bad Peterstal Ger.
179 H2 Bad Pirawarth Austria
215 H1 Badplaas S. Africa
169 E4 Bad Pyrmont Ger.
179 G4 Bad Radkersburg Austria
190 E1 Bad Ragaz Switz.
172 D2 Bad Rappenau Ger.
173 G4 Bad Reichenhall Ger.
124 B3 Badr Ḩunayn Saudi Arabia
116 D3 Badrinath Peaks India
169 D3 Bad Rothenfelde Ger.
171 F3 Bad Saarow-Pieskow Ger.
169 F4 Bad Sachsa Ger.
172 B4 Bad Säckingen Ger.
179 F4 Bad St Leonhard im Lavanttal Austria
169 F3 Bad Salzdetfurth Ger.
169 E5 Bad Salzschlirf Ger.
169 D3 Bad Salzuflen Ger.
169 F5 Bad Salzungen Ger.
169 D4 Bad Sassendorf Ger.
179 E2 Bad Schallerbach Austria
171 F5 Bad Schandau Ger.
171 D4 Bad Schmiedeberg Ger.
172 C2 Bad Schönborn Ger.
172 D3 Bad Schussenried Ger.
169 D5 Bad Schwalbach Ger.
168 F2 Bad Schwartau Ger.
168 F2 Bad Segeberg Ger.
151 F2 Badsey Worcestershire, England U.K.
169 E5 Bad Soden-Salmünster Ger.
169 E4 Bad Sooden-Allendorf Ger.
171 C5 Bad Steben Ger.
171 C4 Bad Suderode Ger.
171 C4 Bad Sulza Ger.
170 D1 Bad Sülze Ger.
169 F4 Bad Tennstedt Ger.
173 F4 Bad Tölz Ger.
109 F3 Badu Fujian China
172 D3 Bad Überkingen Ger.
91 J9 Badu Island Qld Austr.
186 B3 Badules Spain
114 D5 Badulla Sri Lanka
172 D3 Bad Urach Ger.
114 C3 Badvel Andhra Prad. India
169 D5 Bad Vilbel Ger.
179 H3 Bad Vöslau Austria
172 D4 Bad Waldsee Ger.
179 H3 Bad Waltersdorf Austria
173 F4 Bad Wiessee Ger.
169 E4 Bad Wildungen Ger.
170 C3 Bad Wilsnack Ger.
172 D2 Bad Wimpfen Ger.
179 E2 Bad Wimsbach-Neydharting Austria
173 E2 Bad Windsheim Ger.
173 E4 Bad Wörishofen Ger.
172 D4 Bad Wurzach Ger.
179 F2 Bad Zell Austria
169 E4 Bad Zwesten Ger.
168 D2 Bad Zwischenahn Ger.
Bae Cinmel Conwy, Wales U.K. see Kinmel Bay
Bae Colwyn Conwy, Wales U.K. see Colwyn Bay
170 C2 Baek Ger.
142 C4 Bække Denmark
142 C3 Bækmarksbro Denmark
165 E4 Baelen Belgium
185 F3 Baena Spain
Bae Penrhyn Conwy, Wales U.K. see Penrhyn Bay
169 B5 Baesweiler Ger.
185 G3 Baeza Spain
207 H5 Bafang Cameroon
206 B3 Bafatá Guinea-Bissau
123 H3 Baffa Pak.
221 L2 Baffin Bay sea Can./Greenland
221 L3 Baffin Island Nunavut Can.
207 H5 Bafia Cameroon
207 F4 Bafilo Togo
206 C3 Bafing r. Guinea/Mali
164 F1 Baflo Neth.
206 C3 Bafoulabé Mali
207 H5 Bafoussam Cameroon
122 C4 Bāfq Iran
126 D2 Bafra Turkey
122 D4 Bāft Iran
208 E4 Bafwasende Dem. Rep. Congo
177 I4 Bag Hungary
186 E2 Bagà Spain
106 D2 Baga Bogd Uul mts Mongolia
117 F4 Bagaha Bihar India
95 G1 Bagahak hill Sabah Malaysia
195 E4 Bagaladi Italy
114 B2 Bagalkot Karnataka India
177 K4 Bagamér Hungary
211 C6 Bagamoyo Tanz.
121 I1 Bagan Rus. Fed.
92 C5 Baganga Phil.
94 C2 Bagansiapiapi Sumatera Indon.
190 F4 Baganza r. Italy
199 E3 Bağarası Turkey
161 C4 Bagard France
207 G3 Bagaroua Niger
209 C5 Bagata Dem. Rep. Congo
241 K4 Bagdad AZ U.S.A.
Bagdadi Georgia see Baghdat'i
258 G3 Bagé Brazil
160 C2 Bâgé-le-Châtel France
168 F1 Bagenkop Denmark
114 C3 Bagepalli Karnataka India
Bagerhat Bangl. see Bagherhat
163 E6 Bages France
116 D3 Bageshwar Uttar Prad. India
114 C2 Bagevadi Karnataka India
143 F2 Baggå Sweden
238 F3 Baggs WY U.S.A.
116 C5 Bagh Madh. Prad. India
Bagh a'Chaisteil Western Isles, Scotland U.K. see Castlebay
122 E2 Baghbaghū Iran
127 G4 Baghdād Iraq
127 G4 Baghdād governorate Iraq
129 C2 Baghdat'i Georgia
117 G5 Bagherhat Bangl.
194 C4 Bagheria Sicilia Italy
122 D4 Bāghīn Iran
123 G2 Baghlān Afgh.
123 G3 Baghlān prov. Afgh.
122 A2 Bāghlī Da hill Iran
129 C3 Baghramyan Armenia
150 D1 Bagillt Flintshire, Wales U.K.
129 A4 Bağırpaşa Dağı mts Turkey
Bağırsak Deresi r. Syria/Turkey see Sājūr, Nahr
129 B4 Bağlar Turkey
236 E2 Bagley MN U.S.A.
117 E3 Baglung Nepal
141 J3 Bagn Norway
191 G4 Bagnacavallo Italy
163 E4 Bagnac-sur-Célé France
195 E4 Bagnara Calabra Italy
190 E4 Bagnaria Italy
191 I3 Bagnaria Arsa Italy
190 D4 Bagnasco Italy
156 C4 Bagneaux-sur-Loing France
163 C5 Bagnères-de-Bigorre France
163 C6 Bagnères-de-Luchon France
190 E2 Bagni di Masino Italy
191 F2 Bagni di Rabbi Italy

121 F3 Baygakum Kazakh.
120 C2 Bayganin Kazakh.
120 E1 Baygora Kazakh.
137 J1 Baygora r. Rus. Fed.
261 I3 Baygorria, Lago Artificial de resr Uru.
124 D5 Bayḥan al Qiṣab Yemen
235 D2 Bay Head NJ U.S.A.
123 E3 Bāyimlī Azer.
199 E2 Bayındır Turkey
199 F3 Bayır Turkey
Bay Islands is Hond. see La Bahía, Islas de
111 F6 Bayizhen Xizang China
127 F4 Bayjī Iraq
Baykadam Kazakh. see Saudakent
106 E1 Baykal, Ozero l. Rus. Fed.
100 D1 Baykal-Amur Magistral Rus. Fed.
Baykal Range mts Rus. Fed. see Baykal'skiy Khrebet
106 E1 Baykal'sk Rus. Fed.
98 I1 Baykal'skiy Khrebet mts Rus. Fed.
127 F3 Baykan Turkey
134 L5 Baykibashevo Rus. Fed.
131 K3 Baykit Rus. Fed.
120 D1 Baymak Rus. Fed.
231 C6 Bay Minette AL U.S.A.
125 F3 Baynūna'h reg. U.A.E.
Bayo Spain see Baio Grande
80 F2 Bay of Plenty admin. reg. North I. N.Z.
92 B2 Bayombong Phil.
157 G4 Bayon France
Bayona Spain see Baiona
163 A5 Bayonne France
235 D2 Bayonne NJ U.S.A.
250 A6 Bayóvar Peru
227 F4 Bay Port MI U.S.A.
235 E2 Bayport NY U.S.A.
Bayqadam Kazakh. see Saudakent
129 C3 Bayraktutan Turkey
123 E2 Bayramaly Turkm.
199 E2 Bayramiç Turkey
173 F2 Bayreuth Ger.
234 B4 Bay Ridge MD U.S.A.
173 G4 Bayrischzell Ger.
Bayrūt Lebanon see Beirut
237 F6 Bay St Louis MS U.S.A.
Bayshonas Kazakh. see Baychunas
235 E2 Bay Shore NY U.S.A.
234 B3 Bayside Beach MD U.S.A.
237 F6 Bay Springs MS U.S.A.
150 E2 Bayston Hill Shropshire, England U.K.
121 F5 Baysun Uzbek.
121 F5 Baysuntau, Gory mts Uzbek.
124 C5 Bayt al Faqīh Yemen
106 A2 Baytik-Shan mts China
Bayt Lahm West Bank see Bethlehem
237 E6 Baytown TX U.S.A.
183 H3 Bayubas de Abajo Spain
80 F3 Bay View North I. N.Z.
235 D3 Bayville NJ U.S.A.
235 E2 Bayville NY U.S.A.
Bayyrqum Kazakh. see Bairkum
121 G4 Bayzhansay Kazakh.
185 H3 Baza Spain
185 H3 Baza r. Spain
185 H3 Baza, Sierra de mts Spain
179 F5 Bázakerettye Hungary
136 D3 Bazaliya Ukr.
156 E3 Bazancourt France
136 E2 Bazar Ukr.
120 B2 Bazarchulan Kazakh.
129 E3 Bazardyuzi, Gora mt. Azer./Rus. Fed.
122 B2 Bāzār-e Māsāl Iran
127 G3 Bāzārgān Iran
121 G5 Bazarkhanym, Gora mt. Uzbek.
121 H4 Bazar-Korgon Kyrg.
Bazar Kurgan Kyrg. see Bazar-Korgon
120 A1 Bazarnyy Karabulak Rus. Fed.
135 I5 Bazarnyy Syzgan Rus. Fed.
Bazarshulan Kazakh. see Bazarchulan
120 B2 Bazartobe Kazakh.
163 B4 Bazas France
137 H4 Bazavluk r. Ukr.
157 E3 Bazeilles France
163 C5 Bazet France
108 C2 Bazhong Sichuan China
107 H4 Bazhou Hebei China
163 D5 Baziège France
163 C5 Bazillac France
224 F4 Bazin r. Que. Can.
206 C4 Baziwehn Liberia
122 E5 Bazmān Iran
122 E5 Bazmān, Kūh-e mt. Iran
160 E1 Bazoches France
159 F5 Bazoches-au-Houlme France
156 C4 Bazoches-les-Gallerandes France
159 G3 Bazoches-sur-Hoëne France
159 F5 Bazougers France
159 F3 Bazouges France
158 E3 Bazouges-la-Pérouse France
128 C2 Bcharre Lebanon
97 D5 Be r. Vietnam
236 C2 Beach ND U.S.A.
227 I3 Beachburg Ont. Can.
232 C3 Beach City OH U.S.A.
235 D2 Beach Glen NJ U.S.A.
235 D3 Beach Haven NJ U.S.A.
235 D3 Beach Haven Terrace NJ U.S.A.
234 C1 Beach Lake PA U.S.A.
82 E4 Beachport S.A. Austr.
235 D3 Beachwood NJ U.S.A.
151 H4 Beachy Head hd England U.K.
87 C3 Beacon W.A. Austr.
233 G4 Beacon NY U.S.A.
215 F5 Beacon Bay S. Africa
235 E3 Beacon Falls CT U.S.A.
83 F5 Beaconsfield Tas. Austr.
151 G3 Beaconsfield Buckinghamshire, England U.K.
149 H2 Beadnell Northumberland, England U.K.
259 C9 Beagle, Canal sea chan. Arg.
86 C2 Beagle Bank rf W.A. Austr.
86 C3 Beagle Bay W.A. Austr.
84 B2 Beagle Gulf N.T. Austr.
87 E6 Beagle Island W.A. Austr.
213 □K2 Bealanana Madag.
Béal an Átha Rep. of Ireland see Ballina
Béal Átha na Sluaighe Rep. of Ireland see Ballinasloe
147 C5 Bealnablath Rep. of Ireland
237 C5 Beals Creek r. TX U.S.A.
150 E4 Beaminster Dorset, England U.K.
213 □J5 Beampingaratra mts Madag.
183 I3 Beamud Spain
213 □K2 Beandrarezona Madag.
238 D3 Bear r. ID U.S.A.
147 B5 Beara reg. Rep. of Ireland
Bearalváhki Norway see Berlevåg
234 C1 Bear Creek PA U.S.A.
237 C4 Bear Creek r. KS U.S.A.
224 C3 Beardmore Ont. Can.
236 F3 Beardstown IL U.S.A.
Bear Island i. Arctic Ocean see Bjørnøya
227 G2 Bear Island Ont. Can.
147 B5 Bear Island i. Rep. of Ireland
182 B2 Beariz Spain
226 D3 Bear Lake MI U.S.A.
238 E3 Bear Lake l. ID U.S.A.
116 D4 Bearma r. Madh. Prad. India
236 C3 Bear Mountain SD U.S.A.
Bearnaraigh i. Western Isles, Scotland U.K. see Berneray
238 E1 Bear Paw Mountain MT U.S.A.
238 E1 Bearpaw Mountains MT U.S.A.
262 Q2 Bear Peninsula Antarctica
146 D6 Bearsden East Dunbartonshire, Scotland U.K.
223 N4 Bearskin Lake Ont. Can.
151 I3 Bearsted Kent, England U.K.
116 C3 Beas r. India
184 D3 Beas Spain
186 A1 Beasain Spain
185 G3 Beas de Granada Spain
185 H2 Beas de Segura Spain
236 D3 Beatrice NE U.S.A.
213 F3 Beatrice Zimbabwe
84 D2 Beatrice, Cape N.T. Austr.
146 E6 Beattock Dumfries and Galloway, Scotland U.K.
222 F3 Beatton r. B.C. Can.
240 I3 Beatty NV U.S.A.
224 E3 Beattyville Que. Can.
232 B6 Beattyville KY U.S.A.
161 F5 Beaucaire France
156 B3 Beaucamps-le-Vieux France
161 C4 Beauchastel France
160 E1 Beaucourt France
159 F4 Beaucouzé France
163 C5 Beaudéan France
85 H5 Beaudesert Qld Austr.
Beauduc, Golfe de b. France see Stes Maries, Golfe des
159 G3 Beaufay France
83 E4 Beaufort Vic. Austr.
160 D2 Beaufort Franche-Comté France
160 E3 Beaufort Rhône-Alpes France
147 B4 Beaufort Rep. of Ireland
231 E5 Beaufort NC U.S.A.
231 D5 Beaufort SC U.S.A.
128 B3 Beaufort Castle tourist site Lebanon
162 B1 Beaufort-en-Vallée France
163 E3 Beaufortin mts France
220 E2 Beaufort Sea Can./U.S.A.
214 D5 Beaufort West S. Africa
156 B5 Beaugency France
233 G2 Beauharnois Que. Can.
161 E4 Beaujeu Provence-Alpes-Côte-d'Azur France
160 C2 Beaujeu Rhône-Alpes France
160 C2 Beaujolais, Monts du hills France
161 C5 Beaulieu France
159 H4 Beaulieu-lès-Loches France
162 D4 Beaulieu-sur-Dordogne France
160 A1 Beaulieu-sur-Loire France
160 B2 Beaulon France
146 D4 Beauly Highland, Scotland U.K.
146 D4 Beauly r. Scotland U.K.
146 D4 Beauly Firth est. Scotland U.K.
163 C5 Beaumarchés France
150 C1 Beaumaris Isle of Anglesey, Wales U.K.
161 D4 Beaumes-de-Venise France
159 G2 Beaumesnil France
156 C2 Beaumetz-lès-Loges France
165 D4 Beaumont Belgium
163 C4 Beaumont Aquitaine France
160 B3 Beaumont Auvergne France
158 E2 Beaumont Basse-Normandie France
159 G5 Beaumont Poitou-Charentes France
81 B6 Beaumont South I. N.Z.
240 I5 Beaumont CA U.S.A.
237 F6 Beaumont MS U.S.A.
234 C1 Beaumont PA U.S.A.
237 E6 Beaumont TX U.S.A.
163 C5 Beaumont-de-Lomagne France
161 D5 Beaumont-de-Pertuis France
157 F3 Beaumont-en-Argonne France
159 G4 Beaumont-en-Véron France
159 G4 Beaumont-la-Ronce France
159 F2 Beaumont-le-Roger France
159 G3 Beaumont-les-Autels France
161 C4 Beaumont-lès-Valence France
156 C3 Beaumont-sur-Oise France
159 G3 Beaumont-sur-Sarthe France
160 C1 Beaune France
156 C4 Beaune-la-Rolande France
159 F4 Beaupréau France
156 C2 Beauquesne France
165 D4 Beauraing Belgium
161 D3 Beaurepaire France
160 D2 Beaurepaire-en-Bresse France
161 D4 Beaurières France
223 L5 Beauséjour Man. Can.
157 F4 Beausite France
161 F5 Beausoleil France
156 D3 Beautor France
156 B3 Beauvais France
223 J4 Beauval Sask. Can.
156 C2 Beauval France
161 E4 Beauvezer France
163 C4 Beauville France
158 D5 Beauvoir-sur-Mer France
162 B2 Beauvoir-sur-Niort France
161 C5 Beauvoisin France
161 C3 Beauzac France
163 C5 Beauzelle France
223 J4 Beaver r. Alberta/Saskatchewan Can.
224 C2 Beaver r. Ont. Can.
222 C2 Beaver r. Y.T. Can.
222 E3 Beaver r. Y.T. Can.
237 C4 Beaver OK U.S.A.
241 K2 Beaver UT U.S.A.
237 C4 Beaver r. OK U.S.A.
241 K2 Beaver r. UT U.S.A.
236 C3 Beaver City NE U.S.A.
222 A2 Beaver Creek Y.T. Can.
237 E4 Beaver Creek r. MO U.S.A.
238 F1 Beaver Creek r. MT U.S.A.
236 C2 Beaver Creek r. ND U.S.A.
236 D3 Beaver Creek r. NE U.S.A.
232 B6 Beaver Dam KY U.S.A.
226 C4 Beaver Dam WI U.S.A.
232 C4 Beaver Falls PA U.S.A.
262 D2 Beaver Glacier Antarctica
238 D2 Beaverhead r. MT U.S.A.
238 D2 Beaverhead Mountains MT U.S.A.
237 E4 Beaver Lake resr AR U.S.A.
222 G4 Beaverlodge Alta Can.
234 C2 Beaver Meadows PA U.S.A.
234 A2 Beaver Springs PA U.S.A.
224 E4 Beaverton Ont. Can.
226 E3 Beaverton MI U.S.A.
238 B2 Beaverton OR U.S.A.
234 A2 Beavertown PA U.S.A.
116 C4 Beawar Rajasthan India
177 J5 Beba Veche Romania
208 C2 Bébédjia Chad
256 C4 Bebedouro Brazil
253 F4 Beberibe Brazil
171 C3 Bebertal Ger.
149 F4 Bebington Merseyside, England U.K.
208 C2 Béboto Chad
201 E5 Bebra Ger.
108 A2 Bêca Qinghai China
160 E3 Becca du Lac mt. France
151 I2 Beccles Suffolk, England U.K.
191 G2 Becco di Filadonna mt. Italy
182 E4 Becedas Spain
183 G3 Beceite Spain
196 E3 Bečej Vojvodina, Srbija Yugo.
182 C2 Becerreá Spain
182 F3 Becerrero hill Spain
183 F2 Becerril de Campos Spain
204 E3 Béchar Alg.
172 B2 Becherbach Ger.
158 E3 Becherel France
134 G4 Bechevinka Rus. Fed.
173 E2 Bechhofen Bayern Ger.
172 E3 Bechhofen Rheinland-Pfalz Ger.
171 F5 Bechlín Czech Rep.
234 C2 Bechtelsville PA U.S.A.
172 C2 Bechtheim Ger.
Bechuanaland country Africa see Botswana
176 D2 Bechyně Czech Rep.
177 K6 Becicherecu Mic Romania
183 E2 Becilla de Valderaduey Spain
199 E3 Beçin Turkey
168 E2 Beckdorf Ger.
169 E3 Beckedorf Ger.
166 D3 Beckeln Ger.
262 T1 Becker, Mount Antarctica
172 A2 Beckingen Ger.
149 I4 Beckingham Nottinghamshire, England U.K.
232 C6 Beckley WV U.S.A.
177 G3 Becko Slovakia
81 B6 Becks South I. N.Z.
168 D2 Beckum Ger.
241 J2 Becky Peak NV U.S.A.
197 G2 Beclean Romania
159 F4 Bécon-les-Granits France
171 E5 Bečov Czech Rep.
176 B1 Bečov nad Teplou Czech Rep.
176 F5 Becsehely Hungary
176 F5 Becsvölgye Hungary
177 G2 Bečva r. Czech Rep.
210 D2 Beda Hāyk' l. Eth.
149 H3 Bedale North Yorkshire, England U.K.
161 B5 Bédarieux France
161 C4 Bédarrides France
169 B5 Bedburg Ger.
169 B4 Bedburg-Hau Ger.
150 D3 Beddau Rhondda Cynon Taff, Wales U.K.
150 C1 Beddgelert Gwynedd, Wales U.K.
151 H4 Beddingham East Sussex, England U.K.
233 □I2 Beddington ME U.S.A.
158 E3 Bédée France
179 G4 Bedekovčina Croatia
210 C2 Bedelē Eth.
168 D2 Bederkesa Ger.
210 D2 Bedēsa Eth.
134 L5 Bedeyeva Polyana Rus. Fed.
225 I4 Bedford N.S. Can.
233 G2 Bedford Que. Can.
215 F5 Bedford E. Cape S. Africa
215 H3 Bedford Kwazulu-Natal S. Africa
151 G2 Bedford Bedfordshire, England U.K.
236 E3 Bedford IA U.S.A.
230 C4 Bedford IN U.S.A.
230 C4 Bedford KY U.S.A.
235 E1 Bedford NY U.S.A.
232 D4 Bedford PA U.S.A.
232 D6 Bedford VA U.S.A.
85 F2 Bedford, Cape Qld Austr.
86 E3 Bedford Downs W.A. Austr.
232 C4 Bedford Heights OH U.S.A.
235 E1 Bedford Hills NY U.S.A.
151 G2 Bedford Level (Middle Level) lowland England U.K.
151 G2 Bedford Level (North Level) lowland England U.K.
151 H2 Bedford Level (South Level) lowland England U.K.
151 G2 Bedfordshire admin. div. England U.K.
83 F3 Bedgerebong N.S.W. Austr.
116 B5 Bedi Gujarat India
129 D3 Bediani Georgia
175 H4 Będków Pol.
149 H2 Bedlington Northumberland, England U.K.
175 H3 Bedlno Pol.
185 G3 Bedmar Spain
188 F2 Bednja r. Croatia
135 H5 Bednodem'yanovsk Rus. Fed.
161 D4 Bédoin France
191 G2 Bedollo Italy
190 E4 Bedonia Italy
84 D5 Bedourie Qld Austr.
163 B5 Bedous France
241 M2 Bedrock CO U.S.A.
163 D4 Béduer France
164 F1 Bedum Neth.
150 D3 Bedwas Caerphilly, Wales U.K.
151 F2 Bedworth Warwickshire, England U.K.
175 H5 Będzin Pol.
174 D1 Będzino Pol.
226 D5 Beecher IL U.S.A.
233 H2 Beecher Falls VT U.S.A.
83 F4 Beechworth Vic. Austr.
223 J5 Beechy Sask. Can.
168 F3 Beedenbostel Ger.
149 I4 Beeford East Riding of Yorkshire, England U.K.
164 E3 Beek Gelderland Neth.
166 E3 Beek Noord-Brabant Neth.
164 E2 Beekbergen Neth.
172 C3 Beelitz Ger.
234 D1 Beemerville NJ U.S.A.
171 C3 Beendorf Ger.
85 H5 Beenleigh Qld Austr.
170 E2 Beenz Ger.
150 D4 Beer Devon, England U.K.
172 C2 Beerfelden Ger.
87 C6 Beeringgnurding, Mount hill W.A. Austr.
165 C3 Beernem Belgium
164 E3 Beers Neth.
165 D3 Beerse Belgium
165 D4 Beersel Belgium
Beersheba Israel see Be'ér Sheva'
128 B4 Be'ér Sheva' Israel
165 B3 Beerst Belgium
168 F4 Beesenlaublingen Ger.
171 C4 Beesenstedt Ger.
171 F3 Beeskow Ger.
215 F1 Beestekraal S. Africa
169 C3 Beesten Ger.
151 F1 Beeston Nottinghamshire, England U.K.
84 C3 Beetaloo N.T. Austr.
262 T2 Beethoven Peninsula Antarctica
151 H2 Beetley Norfolk, England U.K.
164 F1 Beetsterzwaag Neth.
168 F2 Beetzendorf Ger.
237 D6 Beeville TX U.S.A.
213 □K3 Befandriana Atsimo Madag.
213 □K2 Befandriana Avaratra Madag.
213 □J4 Befasy Madag.
213 □J4 Befotaka Madag.
83 G4 Bega N.S.W. Austr.
197 E3 Bega r. Romania
163 E5 Bégaar France
162 B3 Bégadan France
117 G5 Begamganj Bangl.
158 C3 Bégard France
123 G4 Begari r. Pak.
Begichev, Ostrov i. Rus. Fed. see Bol'shoy Begichev, Ostrov
185 G3 Begíjar Spain
165 D3 Begijnendijk Belgium
163 B4 Bègles France
158 C4 Beg-Meil France
94 D2 Begna r. Norway
182 D1 Begonte Spain
206 E5 Begoro Ghana
Begovat Uzbek. see Bekabad
116 C4 Begun Rajasthan India
186 G3 Begur Spain
117 F4 Begusarai Bihar India
213 □J5 Behara Madag.
125 F5 Behbehān Iran
126 C5 Beheira governorate Egypt
168 F2 Behlendorf Ger.
262 T2 Behrendt Mountains Antarctica
157 G3 Behren-lès-Forbach France
170 D1 Behren-Lübchin Ger.
170 D4 Behringen Ger.
122 C2 Behshahr Iran
215 E5 Behulpsaam S. Africa
100 C2 Bei'an Heilong. China
Bei'ao Zhejiang China see Dongtou
108 C1 Beiba Shaanxi China
108 C2 Beibei Chongqing China
108 C2 Beichuan Sichuan China
Beida Libya see Al Bayḍā'
171 D5 Beierfeld Ger.
Beigang Taiwan see Peikang
149 H4 Beighton South Yorkshire, England U.K.
190 D4 Beigua, Monte mt. Italy
108 C3 Beihai Guangxi China
104 E3 Bei Jiang r. China
107 H4 Beijing Beijing China
107 H3 Beijing mun. China
164 F2 Beilen Neth.
108 D4 Beiliu Guangxi China
173 F2 Beilngries Ger.
171 E4 Beilrode Ger.
172 D2 Beilstein Ger.
172 D3 Beimerstetten Ger.
208 B2 Béinamar Chad
190 C3 Beinasco Italy
156 E3 Beine-Nauroy France
190 E3 Beinette Italy
107 I3 Beining Liaoning China
146 C4 Beinn Alligin hill Scotland U.K.
148 D2 Beinn an Tuirc hill Scotland U.K.
146 B6 Beinn Bheigeir hill Scotland U.K.
146 C5 Beinn Bhreac hill Argyll and Bute, Scotland U.K.
146 C5 Beinn Bhreac hill Argyll and Bute, Scotland U.K.
146 C6 Beinn Bhreac hill Argyll and Bute, Scotland U.K.
146 B4 Beinn Bhreac hill Highland, Scotland U.K.
146 D5 Beinn Bhuidhe hill Scotland U.K.
146 C5 Beinn Chapull hill Scotland U.K.
146 D4 Beinn Dearg mt. Highland, Scotland U.K.
146 E5 Beinn Dearg mt. Perth and Kinross, Scotland U.K.
146 D5 Beinn Dorain mt. Scotland U.K.
144 E3 Beinn Heasgarnich mt. Scotland U.K.
146 D5 Beinn Ime mt. Scotland U.K.
146 D3 Beinn Leoid hill Scotland U.K.
146 B3 Beinn Mholach hill Scotland U.K.
146 C5 Beinn Mhòr hill Scotland U.K.
146 A4 Beinn Mhòr hill Western Isles, Scotland U.K.
146 B4 Beinn Mhòr hill Western Isles, Scotland U.K.
Beinn na Faoghlia i. Scotland U.K. see Benbecula
146 D5 Beinn na Lap hill Scotland U.K.
146 C4 Beinn na Seamraig hill Scotland U.K.
146 C5 Beinn Resipol hill Scotland U.K.
146 C4 Beinn Sgritheall hill Scotland U.K.
146 C5 Beinn Sgulaird hill Scotland U.K.
146 D4 Beinn Tharsuinn hill Scotland U.K.
146 D5 Beinn Udlamain mt. Scotland U.K.
190 D1 Beinwil Switz.
107 I3 Beipiao Liaoning China
213 G3 Beira Moz.
Beira prov. Moz. see Sofala
184 C1 Beira Alta reg. Port.
183 I2 Beire Spain
109 E1 Beiru r. China
128 B3 Beirut Lebanon
222 H5 Beiseker Alta Can.
106 C3 Beishan Nei Mongol China
110 F3 Bei Shan mts Gansu China
106 B3 Bei Shan mts China
213 F4 Beitbridge Zimbabwe
146 D6 Beith North Ayrshire, Scotland U.K.
128 B4 Beit Jālā West Bank
197 F2 Beiuș Romania
Beizhen Liaoning China see Beining
184 C2 Beja Port.
184 B3 Beja admin. dist. Port.
205 H1 Béja Tunisia
189 B7 Béja admin. div. Tunisia
205 G1 Bejaïa Alg.
182 E4 Béjar Spain
122 D3 Bejestān Iran
123 G4 Beji r. Pak.
187 C5 Bejís Spain
247 E5 Bejuma Venez.
207 I6 Bek r. Cameroon
119 J1 Bekabad Uzbek.
213 □J3 Bekapaika Madag.
94 D4 Bekasi Jawa Barat Indon.
122 C1 Bekdash Turkm.
177 K5 Békés Hungary
177 K5 Békés county Hungary
177 K5 Békéscsaba Hungary
177 J5 Békéssámson Hungary
177 J5 Békésszentandrás Hungary
137 G4 Bekhtery Ukr.
199 F2 Bekilli Turkey
213 □J5 Bekily Madag.
Bekobod Uzbek. see Bekabad
213 □I4 Bekoropoka-Antongo Madag.
135 H5 Bekovo Rus. Fed.
206 E5 Bekwai Ghana
206 E5 Bekyem Ghana
117 F4 Bela Bihar India
116 E4 Bela Uttar Prad. India
123 F5 Bela Pak.
177 H2 Belá Slovakia
123 G4 Belab r. Pak.
213 F5 Bela-Bela S. Africa
207 I5 Bélabo Cameroon
162 D2 Bélâbre France
196 E3 Bela Crkva Vojvodina, Srbija Yugo.
177 H3 Beladice Slovakia
177 H2 Belá-Dulice Slovakia
121 J2 Bel'agash Kazakh.
158 D3 Bel Air hill France
234 B3 Bel Air MD U.S.A.
185 E2 Belalcázar Spain
176 B2 Bělá nad Radbuzou Czech Rep.
197 F4 Bela Palanka Srbija Yugo.
177 J3 Bélapátfalva Hungary
176 D1 Bělá pod Bezdězem Czech Rep.
176 G1 Bělá pod Pradědem Czech Rep.
114 B2 Belapur Mahar. India
135 E5 Belarus country Europe
183 I2 Belascoáin Spain
197 F5 Belasica mts Bulg./Macedonia
Belasitsa mts Bulg./Macedonia see Belasica
Belau country N. Pacific Ocean see Palau
209 B6 Bela Vista Bengo Angola
Bela Vista Huambo Angola see Katchiungo
253 F5 Bela Vista Brazil
213 G5 Bela Vista Moz.
256 C2 Bela Vista de Goiás Brazil
94 B2 Belawan Sumatera Indon.
210 C2 Belaya mt. Eth.
137 H2 Belaya Rus. Fed.
137 J5 Belaya r. Rus. Fed.
131 S3 Belaya r. Rus. Fed.
137 G1 Belaya Berezka Rus. Fed.
137 I1 Belaya Glina Rus. Fed.
135 H6 Belaya Kalitva Rus. Fed.
134 J4 Belaya Kholunitsa Rus. Fed.
95 G3 Belayan r. Indon.
95 F2 Belayan, Gunung mt. Indon.
139 L3 Belaya Rechka Rus. Fed.
Belaya Tserkva Ukr. see Bila Tserkva
182 B4 Belazaima do Chão Port.
190 D2 Belbo r. Italy
163 D6 Belcaire France
163 E3 Belcastel France
197 H2 Belcești Romania
175 H4 Bełchatów Pol.
172 B4 Belchen mt. Ger.
232 B6 Belcher KY U.S.A.
224 E1 Belcher Islands Nunavut Can.
183 G3 Belchite Spain
176 C2 Bělčice Czech Rep.
147 C3 Belclare Rep. of Ireland
227 I1 Belcourt Que. Can.
117 G5 Beldanga W. Bengal India
240 G1 Belden CA U.S.A.
147 B2 Belderg Rep. of Ireland
226 E4 Belding MI U.S.A.
120 C1 Belebey Rus. Fed.
176 G4 Beled Hungary
210 E3 Beledweyne Somalia
206 C5 Belefuanai Liberia
122 C2 Belek Turkm.
206 D3 Béléko Mali
207 I5 Bélel Cameroon
207 I4 Bélel Nigeria
254 C2 Belém Brazil
258 D2 Belén Arg.
126 A1 Belen Antalya Turkey
128 C1 Belen Hatay Turkey
261 I2 Belén Uru.
239 F5 Belen NM U.S.A.
261 I2 Belén, Cuchilla de hills Uru.
197 G4 Belene Bulg.
78 □5 Bélep, Îles is New Caledonia
163 D6 Bélesta France
139 K5 Belev Rus. Fed.
199 E2 Belevi Turkey
176 F5 Belezna Hungary
81 D5 Belfast South I. N.Z.
215 H1 Belfast S. Africa
147 F2 Belfast Northern Ireland U.K.
233 □I2 Belfast ME U.S.A.
232 D3 Belfast NY U.S.A.
148 C3 Belfast International airport Northern Ireland U.K.
147 F2 Belfast Lough inlet Northern Ireland U.K.
165 F3 Belfeld Neth.
236 C2 Belfield ND U.S.A.
210 B2 Bēlfodiyo Eth.
149 H2 Belford Northumberland, England U.K.
160 E1 Belfort France
163 D4 Belfort-du-Quercy France
193 F1 Belforte del Chienti Italy
114 B3 Belgaum Karnataka India
161 E5 Belgentier France
171 E4 Belgern Ger.
171 D4 Belgershain Ger.
Belgian Congo country Africa see Congo, Democratic Republic of
Belgicafjella mts Antarctica see Belgica Mountains
263 C2 Belgica Mountains Antarctica
België country Europe see Belgium
190 E3 Belgioioso Italy
Belgique country Europe see Belgium
165 D4 Belgium country Europe
192 B2 Belgodère Corse France
135 G6 Belgorod Rus. Fed.
Belgorod-Dnestrovskyy Ukr. see Bilhorod-Dnistrovs'kyy
Belgorod Oblast admin. div. Rus. Fed. see Belgorodskaya Oblast'
135 G6 Belgorodskaya Oblast' admin. div. Rus. Fed.
233 □I2 Belgrade ME U.S.A.
238 E2 Belgrade MT U.S.A.
Belgrade Srbija Yugo. see Beograd
262 V1 Belgrano II research stn Antarctica
81 D4 Belgrove South I. N.Z.
163 B4 Belhade France
156 B4 Belhomert-Guéhouville France
206 B4 Béli Guinea-Bissau
207 H5 Beli Nigeria
186 E3 Belianes Spain
179 H4 Belica Croatia
194 B5 Belice r. Sicilia Italy
184 C3 Beliche r. Port.
194 C5 Belici r. Sicilia Italy
196 E4 Beli Drim r. Yugo.
129 F3 Belidzhi Rus. Fed.
Beliliou i. Palau see Peleliu
197 H4 Beli Lom r. Bulg.
188 G3 Beli Manastir Croatia
163 B4 Belin-Béliet France
183 G4 Belinchón Spain
232 D5 Belington WV U.S.A.
Belingwe Zimbabwe see Mberengwa
135 H5 Belinskiy Rus. Fed.
197 E3 Belinț Romania
94 D3 Belinyu Indon.
197 F3 Beli Timok r. Yugo.
197 F5 Belitsa Bulg.
137 H2 Belitsa Rus. Fed.
95 E3 Belitung i. Indon.
177 L5 Beliu Romania
209 B6 Belize Angola
243 H5 Belize Belize
243 H5 Belize country Central America
251 H3 Bélizon Fr. Guiana
Beljak Austria see Villach
197 E3 Beljanica mt. Yugo.
85 G5 Bell Qld Austr.
83 G3 Bell r. N.S.W. Austr.
224 E3 Bell r. Que. Can.
169 C5 Bell Ger.
215 F5 Bell S. Africa
169 C5 Bell (Hunsrück) Ger.
82 C3 Bell, Point S.A. Austr.
193 H4 Bella Italy
222 D4 Bella Bella B.C. Can.
162 D2 Bellac France
160 E3 Bellacha, Mont mt. France
222 E4 Bella Coola B.C. Can.
222 E4 Bella Coola r. B.C. Can.
147 B2 Bellacorick Rep. of Ireland
147 E2 Bellaghy Northern Ireland U.K.
190 E3 Bellagio Italy
147 C3 Bellahy Rep. of Ireland
226 E3 Bellaire MI U.S.A.
237 E6 Bellaire TX U.S.A.
147 C3 Bellanagare Rep. of Ireland
147 D2 Bellanaleck Northern Ireland U.K.
147 C2 Bellanamore Rep. of Ireland
147 C3 Bellaneeny Rep. of Ireland
190 E2 Bellano Italy
193 F2 Bellante Italy
191 H4 Bellaria Italy
114 C3 Bellary Karnataka India
83 G2 Bellata N.S.W. Austr.
261 I2 Bella Unión Uru.
147 B3 Bellavary Rep. of Ireland
258 F3 Bella Vista Arg.
253 F5 Bella Vista Para.
250 B6 Bellavista Peru
80 E3 Bell Block North I. N.Z.
85 G4 Bell Cay rf Qld Austr.
186 D3 Bellclaire d'Urgell Spain
232 C5 Belle WV U.S.A.
246 D3 Belle-Anse Haiti
171 C4 Belleben Ger.
161 D3 Belledonne mts France
147 C2 Belleek Northern Ireland U.K.
147 E2 Belleek Northern Ireland U.K.
157 G4 Bellefontaine France
247 □3 Bellefontaine Martinique
232 B4 Bellefontaine OH U.S.A.
232 E4 Bellefonte PA U.S.A.
236 C2 Belle Fourche SD U.S.A.
236 C2 Belle Fourche r. SD U.S.A.
156 C5 Bellegarde Centre France
161 C5 Bellegarde Languedoc-Roussillon France
162 E3 Bellegarde-en-Marche France
160 D2 Bellegarde-sur-Valserine France
231 D7 Belle Glade FL U.S.A.
158 C4 Belle-Île i. France
225 K3 Belle Isle i. Nfld. Can.
225 J3 Belle Isle, Strait of Nfld. Can.
158 C3 Belle-Isle-en-Terre France
159 G3 Bellême France
234 D2 Belle Mead NJ U.S.A.
241 L4 Bellemont AZ U.S.A.
160 B2 Bellenaves France
173 E3 Bellenberg Ger.
156 B3 Bellencombre France
160 B2 Bellerive-sur-Allier France
157 G4 Belles-Forêts France
224 E4 Belleterre Que. Can.
156 D3 Belleu France
160 E2 Bellevaux France
160 D2 Bellevesvre France
224 E4 Belleville Ont. Can.
160 C2 Belleville France
236 D4 Belleville KS U.S.A.
235 D2 Belleville NJ U.S.A.
160 A1 Belleville-sur-Loire France
157 F3 Belleville-sur-Meuse France
158 E5 Belleville-sur-Vie France
230 B3 Bellevue IA U.S.A.
226 E4 Bellevue MI U.S.A.
236 E3 Bellevue NE U.S.A.
232 B4 Bellevue OH U.S.A.
238 B2 Bellevue WA U.S.A.
161 B3 Bellevue-la-Montagne France
160 D3 Belley France
226 C5 Bellflower IL U.S.A.
172 C2 Bellheim Ger.
160 E1 Bellherbe France
160 D2 Bellignat France
Bellin Que. Can. see Kangirsuk
83 H2 Bellingen N.S.W. Austr.
149 G2 Bellingham Northumberland, England U.K.
238 B1 Bellingham WA U.S.A.
262 U2 Bellingshausen research stn Antarctica
Bellingshausen Island atoll Arch. de la Société Fr. Polynesia see Motu One
164 G1 Bellingwolde Neth.
190 D3 Bellinzago Novarese Italy
190 E2 Bellinzona Switz.
222 D4 Bell Island Hot Springs AK U.S.A.
193 G4 Bellizzi Italy
234 C3 Bellmawr NJ U.S.A.
250 C3 Bello Col.
183 I4 Bello Spain
163 B5 Bellocq France
78 □6 Bellona i. Solomon Is
159 F3 Bellou-en-Houlme France
233 G3 Bellows Falls VT U.S.A.
186 E3 Bellpuig d'Urgell Spain
146 D6 Bellshill North Lanarkshire, Scotland U.K.
191 H2 Belluno Italy
191 H2 Belluno prov. Veneto Italy
114 C3 Belluru Karnataka India
235 D1 Bellvale NY U.S.A.
186 E2 Bellver de Cerdanya Spain
261 F3 Bell Ville Arg.
214 B5 Bellville S. Africa
232 B4 Bellville OH U.S.A.
237 D6 Bellville TX U.S.A.
232 D4 Bellwood PA U.S.A.
222 H5 Belly r. Alta Can.
169 D3 Belm Ger.
235 D2 Belmar NJ U.S.A.
177 K5 Bélmegyer Hungary
185 E2 Bélmez Spain
185 G3 Bélmez de la Moraleda Spain
83 G3 Belmont N.S.W. Austr.
163 C5 Belmont France
214 E3 Belmont S. Africa
146 □H1 Belmont Shetland, Scotland U.K.
233 H3 Belmont NH U.S.A.
232 D3 Belmont NY U.S.A.
160 C2 Belmont-de-la-Loire France
257 H1 Belmonte Brazil
182 C4 Belmonte Port.
182 D1 Belmonte Asturias Spain
183 H5 Belmonte Castilla - La Mancha Spain
193 I5 Belmonte Calabro Italy
193 G3 Belmonte del Sannio Italy
193 E2 Belmonte in Sabina Italy
194 C4 Belmonte Mezzagno Sicilia Italy
161 A5 Belmont-sur-Rance France
243 H5 Belmopan Belize
85 E3 Belmore Creek r. Qld Austr.
147 B2 Belmullet Rep. of Ireland
213 □J4 Belo Madag.
255 E5 Belo Campo Brazil
165 C4 Belœil Belgium
Beloe More sea Rus. Fed. see Beloye More
Beloevo Rus. Fed. see Beloyevo
100 E2 Belogorsk Rus. Fed.
Belogorsk Ukr. see Bilohirs'k
121 I2 Belogor'ye Kazakh.
137 K2 Belogor'ye Rus. Fed.
197 F4 Belogradchik Bulg.
213 □J5 Beloha Madag.
257 F3 Belo Horizonte Brazil
236 D4 Beloit KS U.S.A.
226 C4 Beloit WI U.S.A.
254 F4 Belo Jardim Brazil
Belokamensk Ukr. see Inkerman
121 K2 Belokurikha Rus. Fed.
Belo Monte Brazil see Batalha
134 F2 Belomorsk Rus. Fed.
117 G5 Belonia Tripura India
139 L4 Beloomut Rus. Fed.
257 F3 Belo Oriente Brazil
Beloozersk Belarus see Byelaazyorsk
139 L4 Beloozerskiy Rus. Fed.
Belopol'ye Ukr. see Bilopillya
183 G2 Belorado Spain
135 G7 Belorechensk Rus. Fed.
Belorechenskaya Rus. Fed. see Belorechensk
126 E3 Belören Turkey
126 D3 Belören Turkey
120 D1 Beloretsk Rus. Fed.
Belorussia country Europe see Belarus
Belorusskaya S.S.R. country Europe see Belarus
197 H4 Beloslav Bulg.
Belostok Pol. see Białystok
177 G2 Bělotín Czech Rep.
197 F4 Belotintsi Bulg.
213 □J3 Belo Tsiribihina Madag.
121 J2 Belousovka Kazakh.
139 K4 Belousovo Rus. Fed.
257 E4 Belo Vale Brazil
197 G4 Belovo Bulg.
100 D2 Beloyarovo Rus. Fed.
139 K1 Beloye, Ozero l. Rus. Fed.
134 G2 Beloye More sea Rus. Fed.
134 K4 Beloyevo Rus. Fed.
120 C1 Belozerka Rus. Fed.
139 K1 Belozersk Rus. Fed.
Belozerskoye Ukr. see Bilozers'ke
190 C2 Belp Switz.
172 B5 Belp airport Switz.
194 D5 Belpasso Sicilia Italy
163 D5 Belpech France
149 H4 Belper Derbyshire, England U.K.
232 C5 Belpre OH U.S.A.
149 H2 Belsay Northumberland, England U.K.
175 I4 Belsk Duży Pol.
82 D2 Beltana S.A. Austr.
82 D2 Belt Bay salt flat S.A. Austr.
241 I3 Belted Range mts NV U.S.A.
106 C1 Beltes Gol r. Mongolia
169 C5 Beltheim Ger.
179 H4 Beltinci Slovenia
177 L4 Beltiug Romania
151 I2 Belton Norfolk, England U.K.
236 E4 Belton MO U.S.A.
237 D6 Belton TX U.S.A.
147 B3 Beltra Mayo Rep. of Ireland
147 C2 Beltra Sligo Rep. of Ireland
164 F2 Beltrum Neth.
Bel'ts' Moldova see Bălți
234 B3 Beltsville MD U.S.A.
Bel'tsy Moldova see Bălți
147 D2 Belturbet Rep. of Ireland
192 A5 Belu r. Sardegna Italy
112 G2 Belukha, Gora mt. Kazakh./Rus. Fed.
114 B3 Belur Karnataka India
177 H2 Beluša Slovakia
232 C5 Belva WV U.S.A.
192 A3 Belvédère-Campomoro Corse France
193 H5 Belvedere Marittimo Italy
184 C1 Belver Port.
186 D3 Belver de Cinca Spain
163 D4 Belvès France
163 E5 Belvèze-du-Razès France
161 C4 Belvézet France
226 C4 Belvidere IL U.S.A.
234 C2 Belvidere NJ U.S.A.
147 B2 Belville Rep. of Ireland
183 F5 Belvís de la Jara Spain
85 F4 Belyando r. Qld Austr.
85 F4 Belyando Crossing Qld Austr.
120 D2 Belyayevka Rus. Fed.
Belyayevka Ukr. see Bilyayivka
121 G4 Belye Vody Kazakh.
84 B2 Belyuen N.T. Austr.
139 I4 Belyy Rus. Fed.
130 I2 Belyy, Ostrov i. Rus. Fed.
139 J5 Belyye Berega Rus. Fed.
139 K4 Belyye Stolby Rus. Fed.
139 K3 Belyy Gorodok Rus. Fed.
137 J2 Belyy Kolodez' Rus. Fed.
130 J4 Belyy Yar Rus. Fed.
158 C4 Belz France
136 C2 Belz Ukr.
175 L5 Bełżec Pol.
171 D3 Belzig Ger.
237 F5 Belzoni MS U.S.A.
175 K4 Bełżyce Pol.
213 □J3 Bemaraha, Plateau du Madag.
209 B6 Bembe Angola
207 F4 Bembèrèkè Benin
185 E3 Bembézar r. Spain
182 D2 Bembibre Castilla y León Spain
182 B1 Bembibre Galicia Spain
151 F4 Bembridge Isle of Wight, England U.K.
236 E2 Bemidji MN U.S.A.
237 F5 Bemis TN U.S.A.
164 E3 Bemmel Neth.
182 D3 Bemposta Bragança Port.
184 B1 Bemposta Santarém Port.
149 I3 Bempton East Riding of Yorkshire, England U.K.
206 D3 Béna Burkina
186 D2 Benabarre Spain
209 D6 Bena Dibele Dem. Rep. Congo
187 C5 Benaguasil Spain
185 H4 Benahadux Spain
185 E4 Benahavís Spain
204 D2 Benahmed Morocco
146 E4 Ben Aigan hill Scotland U.K.
185 E2 Benajarafe r. Spain
146 D5 Ben Alder mt. Scotland U.K.
83 F4 Benalla Vic. Austr.
185 F4 Benalmádena Spain
185 G3 Benalúa de Guadix Spain
185 G3 Benalúa de las Villas Spain
184 E4 Benalup de Sidonia Spain
185 F4 Benamargosa Spain
185 H3 Benamaurel Spain
185 F3 Benamejí Spain
185 F4 Benamocarra Spain
185 E4 Benaocaz Spain
185 E4 Benaoján Spain
Benares Uttar Prad. India see Varanasi
205 H1 Ben Arous Tunisia
189 B7 Ben Arous admin. div. Tunisia
187 C4 Benasal Spain
187 C6 Benasau Spain
186 D2 Benasque Spain
162 C2 Benassay France
176 D1 Benátky nad Jizerou Czech Rep.
184 B2 Benavente Port.
182 E2 Benavente Spain
252 D3 Benavides Bol.
182 E2 Benavides de Orbigo Spain
184 C1 Benavila Port.
146 E4 Ben Avon mt. Scotland U.K.
147 B3 Benbaun hill Rep. of Ireland
146 A4 Benbecula i. Scotland U.K.
147 C2 Benbulben hill Rep. of Ireland
147 E2 Benburb Northern Ireland U.K.
147 B3 Benbury hill Rep. of Ireland
184 C2 Bencatel Port.
109 G1 Bencha Jiangsu China
Bencheng Hebei China see Luannan
146 E5 Ben Chonzie hill Scotland U.K.
147 B3 Bencorr hill Rep. of Ireland
146 C5 Ben Cruachan mt. Scotland U.K.
87 C6 Bencubbin W.A. Austr.
238 B2 Bend OR U.S.A.
215 F4 Bendearg mt. S. Africa
209 C5 Bendela Dem. Rep. Congo
83 G2 Bendemeer N.S.W. Austr.
Bender Moldova see Tighina
210 F2 Bender-Bayla Somalia
226 D3 Benderville WI U.S.A.
Bendery Moldova see Tighina
168 E2 Bendestorf Ger.
83 F4 Bendigo Vic. Austr.
83 G4 Bendoc Vic. Austr.
169 C5 Bendorf Ger.
Bendzin Pol. see Będzin
138 D3 Bēne Latvia
164 E3 Beneden-Leeuwen Neth.
225 J2 Benedict, Mount hill Nfld. Can.
233 □I2 Benedicta ME U.S.A.
173 F4 Benediktbeuren Ger.
173 F4 Benediktenwand mt. Ger.
184 B1 Benedita Port.
254 E3 Beneditinos Brazil
254 D3 Benedito Leite Brazil
182 E3 Benegiles Spain
163 B5 Bénéjacq France
187 C6 Benejama Spain
187 C6 Benejúzar Spain
151 H3 Benenden Kent, England U.K.
213 □J4 Benenitra Madag.
176 D2 Benešov Czech Rep.
179 F2 Benešov nad Černou Czech Rep.
176 D1 Benešov nad Ploučnicí Czech Rep.
163 A5 Bénesse-Maremne France
195 F4 Benestare Italy
157 G4 Bénestroff France
162 B2 Benet France
192 B4 Benetutti Sardegna Italy
190 C4 Bene Vagienna Italy
162 D2 Bénévent-l'Abbaye France
193 G3 Benevento Italy
193 G3 Benevento prov. Campania Italy
Beneventum Italy see Benevento
232 D4 Benezette PA U.S.A.
157 H4 Benfeld France
234 A2 Benfer PA U.S.A.
184 B1 Benfica do Ribatejo Port.
107 H5 Beng r. China
96 C3 Beng, Nam r. Laos
Benga i. Fiji see Beqa
113 G8 Bengal, Bay of sea Indian Ocean
207 I6 Bengbis Cameroon
109 F1 Bengbu Anhui China
146 B4 Ben Geary hill Scotland U.K.
Benghazi Libya see Banghāzī
94 C2 Bengkalis Sumatera Indon.
94 C3 Bengkulu Sumatera Indon.
94 C3 Bengkulu prov. Indon.
209 B7 Bengo prov. Angola
147 B3 Bengorm hill Rep. of Ireland
142 E2 Bengtsfors Sweden
209 B8 Benguela Angola
209 B8 Benguela prov. Angola
204 D2 Benguerir Morocco
203 F2 Benha Egypt
146 D3 Ben Hee hill Scotland U.K.
146 B5 Ben Hiant hill Scotland U.K.
146 D3 Ben Hope hill Scotland U.K.
146 D3 Ben Horn hill Scotland U.K.
252 D3 Beni dept Bol.
252 D2 Beni r. Bol.
208 F4 Beni Dem. Rep. Congo
204 E3 Beni-Abbès Alg.
183 F1 Benia de Onís Spain
187 C6 Beniarrés Spain
180 D5 Beni Boufrah Morocco
186 D4 Benicarló Spain
187 D4 Benicasim Spain
240 F2 Benicia CA U.S.A.
187 C6 Benidorm Spain
187 C6 Beniel Spain
187 C5 Benifaió Spain
186 D4 Benifallet Spain
187 C6 Benifallim Spain
Benifayo Spain see Benifaió
181 F3 Benigánim Spain
204 E2 Beni Guil reg. Morocco
187 C6 Benilloba Spain
203 F2 Benî Mazâr Egypt
204 D2 Beni Mellal Morocco
207 F4 Benin country Africa
207 G5 Benin r. Nigeria
207 F5 Benin, Bight of g. Africa
207 G5 Benin City Nigeria
205 E3 Beni-Ounif Alg.
205 E2 Beni-Saf Alg.
210 E2 Benishangul admin. reg. Eth.
207 I4 Benisheikh Nigeria
187 D6 Benissa Spain
186 D3 Benissanet Spain
203 F2 Beni Suef Egypt
126 C5 Beni Suef governorate Egypt
187 D6 Benitachell Spain
114 C2 Benithora r. India
Benito r. Equat. Guinea see Mbini
261 H5 Benito Juárez Arg.
241 J5 Benito Juárez Mex.

245 H4 Benito Juárez Mex.
245 F2 Benito Juárez Mex.
245 G5 Benito Juárez, Presa resr Mex.
92 B2 Benito Soliven Phil.
185 H3 Benizalón Spain
185 I2 Benizar y la Tercia Spain
250 D6 Benjamim Constant Brazil
237 D5 Benjamin TX U.S.A.
259 B7 Benjamin, Isla i. Chile
242 C2 Benjamín Hill Mex.
236 C3 Benkelman NE U.S.A.
190 E1 Benken Switz.
146 D3 Ben Klibreck hill Scotland U.K.
188 E3 Benkovac Croatia
197 H4 Benkovski Bulg.
146 D5 Ben Lawers mt. Scotland U.K.
146 D5 Ben Ledi hill Scotland U.K.
150 C1 Benllech Isle of Anglesey, Wales U.K.
187 D4 Benlloch Spain
83 G2 Ben Lomond mt. N.S.W. Austr.
146 D5 Ben Lomond hill Scotland U.K.
240 F3 Ben Lomond CA U.S.A.
146 D3 Ben Loyal hill Scotland U.K.
146 D5 Ben Lui mt. Scotland U.K.
215 F4 Ben Macdhui mt. Lesotho
144 F3 Ben Macdui mt. Scotland U.K.
189 A7 Ben Mahidi Alg.
84 D3 Benmara N.T. Austr.
81 C5 Ben More mt. South I. N.Z.
146 B5 Ben More hill Scotland U.K.
146 D5 Ben More mt. Scotland U.K.
81 C6 Benmore, Lake South I. N.Z.
146 D3 Ben More Assynt hill Scotland U.K.
81 C6 Benmore Peak South I. N.Z.
171 C4 Benndorf Ger.
164 D2 Bennebroek Neth.
169 F4 Benneckenstein (Harz) Ger.
164 E2 Bennekom Neth.
222 C3 Bennett B.C. Can.
226 B2 Bennett WI U.S.A.
147 D4 Bennettsbridge Rep. of Ireland
231 E5 Bennettsville SC U.S.A.
146 C5 Ben Nevis mt. Scotland U.K.
80 E3 Benneydale North I. N.Z.
233 H3 Bennington NH U.S.A.
233 G3 Bennington VT U.S.A.
171 C4 Bennstedt Ger.
171 C4 Bennungen Ger.
158 B4 Bénodet France
81 B6 Ben Ohau Range mts South I. N.Z.
215 G2 Benoni S. Africa
207 I4 Bénoué r. Cameroon
208 C2 Bénoy Chad
182 C4 Benquerença Port.
163 B5 Benquet France
146 E4 Ben Rinnes hill Scotland U.K.
184 B3 Bensafrim Port.
171 D3 Bensdorf Ger.
169 F5 Benshausen Ger.
172 C2 Bensheim Ger.
204 D2 Ben Slimane Morocco
151 F3 Benson Oxfordshire, England U.K.
241 L6 Benson AZ U.S.A.
236 E2 Benson MN U.S.A.
206 C5 Bensonville Liberia
232 C5 Bens Run WV U.S.A.
146 C5 Ben Starav mt. Scotland U.K.
122 D5 Bent Iran
164 F2 Bentelo Neth.
206 B4 Benti Guinea
209 B8 Bentiaba Angola
180 E5 Ben Tieb Morocco
84 D3 Bentinck Island Qld Austr.
97 B5 Bentinck Island Myanmar
146 E5 Ben Tirran hill Scotland U.K.
208 F2 Bentiu Sudan
128 B3 Bent Jbail Lebanon
222 H4 Bentley Alta Can.
149 H4 Bentley South Yorkshire, England U.K.
232 C4 Bentleyville PA U.S.A.
253 F4 Bento Gomes r. Brazil
233 □J2 Benton N.B. Can.
237 E5 Benton AR U.S.A.
240 H3 Benton CA U.S.A.
236 F4 Benton IL U.S.A.
237 F4 Benton KY U.S.A.
237 E5 Benton LA U.S.A.
237 F4 Benton MO U.S.A.
234 B1 Benton PA U.S.A.
231 C5 Benton TN U.S.A.
Bentong Malaysia see Bentung
226 D4 Benton Harbor MI U.S.A.
237 E4 Bentonville AR U.S.A.
232 B5 Bentonville OH U.S.A.
97 D5 Bên Tre Vietnam
94 C2 Bentung Malaysia
170 D1 Bentwisch Ger.
170 E2 Bentzin Ger.
207 G5 Benue r. Nigeria
207 H5 Benue state Nigeria
94 C2 Benum, Gunung mt. Malaysia
177 I3 Beňuš Slovakia
146 D5 Ben Vorlich hill Argyll and Bute, Scotland U.K.
146 D5 Ben Vorlich hill Perth and Kinross/Stirling, Scotland U.K.
147 B3 Benwee hill Rep. of Ireland
232 C4 Benwood WV U.S.A.
146 D4 Ben Wyvis mt. Scotland U.K.
107 I3 Benxi Liaoning China
196 E3 Beograd Srbija Yugo.
116 E4 Beohari Madh. Prad. India
206 D5 Béoumi Côte d'Ivoire
94 C4 Bepagut, Gunung mt. Indon.
108 C3 Bepian Jiang r. Guizhou China
103 E7 Beppu Japan
79 □1a Beqa i. Fiji
247 □3 Bequia i. St Vincent
254 D2 Bequimão Brazil
117 G4 Bera Bangl.
261 G3 Berabevú Arg.
116 C4 Berach r. India
147 D2 Beragh Northern Ireland U.K.
213 □K2 Beramanja Madag.
196 D4 Berane Crna Gora Yugo.
183 G1 Beranga Spain
183 H1 Berango Spain
183 H2 Berantevilla Spain
116 D5 Berasia Madh. Prad. India
94 B2 Berastagi Sumatera Indon.
198 A1 Berat Albania
163 D5 Bérat France
95 G3 Beratus, Gunung mt. Indon.
173 F2 Beratzhausen Ger.
95 G2 Berau r. Indon.
91 H7 Berau, Teluk b. Indon.
261 H4 Berazategui Arg.
186 C3 Berbegal Spain
203 G5 Berber Sudan
210 E2 Berbera Somalia
208 B3 Berbérati C.A.R.
215 H2 Berbice S. Africa
183 I2 Berbinzana Spain
183 G1 Bercedo Spain
177 I4 Bercel Hungary
156 D4 Bercenay-en-Othe France
183 E3 Bercero Spain
190 E4 Berceto Italy
165 C4 Berchem Belgium
192 B4 Berchidda Sardegna Italy
173 F2 Berching Ger.
120 D2 Berchogur Kazakh.
173 H4 Berchtesgaden Ger.
173 G4 Berchtesgadener Alpen mts Ger.
185 G4 Bérchules Spain
182 E2 Bercianos del Páramo Spain
156 B2 Berck France
129 D3 Berd Armenia
137 I4 Berda r. Ukr.
159 G3 Berd'huis France
Berdichev Ukr. see Berdychiv
131 N3 Berdigestyakh Rus. Fed.
130 J4 Berdsk Rus. Fed.
182 D1 Berducedo Spain
186 C2 Berdún Spain
137 I4 Berdyans'k Ukr.
136 E3 Berdychiv Ukr.
208 C2 Béré Chad
232 A6 Berea KY U.S.A.
232 C4 Berea OH U.S.A.
150 C4 Bere Alston Devon, England U.K.
Béréby Côte d'Ivoire see Grand-Bérébi
210 F2 Bereeda Somalia
150 C4 Bere Ferrers Devon, England U.K.
139 K1 Bereg Rus. Fed.
177 L3 Beregdaróc Hungary
Beregovo Ukr. see Berehove
190 E3 Bereguardo Italy
136 C3 Berehomet Ukr.
136 B3 Berehove Ukr.
179 H5 Berek Croatia
137 I3 Bereka Ukr.
137 I3 Bereka r. Ukr.
177 K4 Berekböszörmény Hungary
213 □J4 Bereketa Madag.
177 J4 Berekfürdő Hungary
211 B6 Bereku Tanz.
206 E5 Berekum Ghana
177 H6 Beremend Hungary
139 L3 Berendeyevo Rus. Fed.
252 C4 Berenguela Bol.
203 G4 Berenice Egypt
Berenice Libya see Banghāzī
223 L4 Berens r. Man. Can.
223 L4 Berens River Man. Can.
213 □J4 Berenty Madag.
150 E4 Bere Regis Dorset, England U.K.
225 H4 Beresford N.B. Can.
236 D3 Beresford SD U.S.A.
136 C2 Berestechko Ukr.
197 H2 Bereşti Romania
137 G2 Berestivka Ukr.
137 H3 Berestova r. Ukr.
137 I4 Berestove Ukr.
137 H3 Berestoven'ka Ukr.
137 G2 Berestovets' Ukr.
136 C2 Berestyane Ukr.
177 K4 Berettyó r. Hungary
177 K4 Berettyóújfalu Hungary
213 □J3 Berevo Madag.
Bereza Belarus see Byaroza
137 F2 Berezan' Ukr.
137 F4 Berezanka Ukr.
137 J5 Berezanskaya Rus. Fed.
139 I3 Berezayka Rus. Fed.
136 D2 Berezdiv Ukr.
197 I2 Berezeni Romania
136 C3 Berezhany Ukr.
Berezino Belarus see Byerazino
137 G2 Berezivka Chernihivs'ka Oblast' Ukr.
137 G4 Berezivka Kirovohrads'ka Oblast' Ukr.
136 F4 Berezivka Odes'ka Oblast' Ukr.
136 D3 Berezivka Zhytomyrs'ka Oblast' Ukr.
136 E2 Berezivka Zhytomyrs'ka Oblast' Ukr.
137 F2 Berezna Ukr.
136 D2 Berezne Ukr.
137 G4 Bereznehuvate Ukr.
134 H3 Bereznik Arkhangel'skaya Oblast' Rus. Fed.
134 L4 Berezniki Rus. Fed.
136 D2 Bereznyky Ukr.
Berezov Rus. Fed. see Berezovo
134 L3 Berezovaya r. Rus. Fed.
136 D2 Berezove Ukr.
Berezovka Belarus see Byarozawka
100 C2 Berezovka Amurskaya Oblast' Rus. Fed.
120 D1 Berezovka Orenburgskaya Oblast' Rus. Fed.
134 L4 Berezovka Permskaya Oblast' Rus. Fed.
Berezovka Odes'ka Oblast' Ukr. see Berezivka
130 H3 Berezovo Rus. Fed.
100 E2 Berezovyy Rus. Fed.
136 E4 Berezyne Ukr.
172 D4 Berg Baden-Württemberg Ger.
171 C5 Berg Bayern Ger.
173 F4 Berg Bayern Ger.
169 B5 Berg Rheinland-Pfalz Ger.
165 F5 Berg Lux.
172 C3 Berg (Pfalz) Ger.
171 C4 Berga Sachsen-Anhalt Ger.
171 D5 Berga Thüringen Ger.
186 E2 Berga Spain
199 E2 Bergama Turkey
190 E3 Bergamo Italy
190 E3 Bergamo prov. Lombardia Italy
186 C4 Bergantes r. Spain
183 H1 Bergara Spain
172 D4 Bergatreute Ger.
173 F2 Berg bei Neumarkt in der Oberpfalz Ger.
179 E2 Berg bei Rohrbach Austria
141 L3 Bergby Sweden
170 C2 Berge Brandenburg Ger.
168 C3 Berge Niedersachsen Ger.
186 C4 Berge Spain
190 D4 Bergeggi Italy
173 G4 Bergen Bayern Ger.
170 E1 Bergen Mecklenburg-Vorpommern Ger.
168 E3 Bergen Niedersachsen Ger.
164 D2 Bergen Neth.
142 A1 Bergen Norway
215 H2 Bergen S. Africa
232 E3 Bergen NY U.S.A.
168 F3 Bergen (Dumme) Ger.
235 D2 Bergen County county NJ U.S.A.
235 E2 Bergenfield NJ U.S.A.
164 D3 Bergen op Zoom Neth.
164 F2 Bergentheim Neth.
163 C4 Bergerac France
156 E4 Bergères-lès-Vertus France
263 B2 Bergerson, Mount Antarctica
160 C2 Bergesserin France
165 E3 Bergeyk Neth.
170 E3 Bergfelde Ger.
164 E3 Bergharen Neth.
172 B3 Berghaupten Ger.
178 E3 Bergheim Austria
173 F3 Bergheim Ger.
169 E4 Bergheim (Edertal) Ger.
169 B5 Bergheim (Erft) Ger.
164 E3 Berghem Neth.
171 E3 Bergholz-Rehbrücke Ger.
172 D3 Berghülen Ger.
178 E4 Berg im Drautal Austria
169 C5 Bergisch Gladbach Ger.
169 C4 Bergkamen Ger.
173 F3 Bergkirchen Ger.
226 C2 Bergland MI U.S.A.
140 L2 Bergnäs Sweden
140 L2 Bergnäsviken Sweden
169 C4 Bergneustadt Ger.
Bergomum Italy see Bergamo
232 C5 Bergoo WV U.S.A.
169 F5 Bergrheinfeld Ger.
143 H2 Bergshamra Sweden
141 L3 Bergsjö Sweden
140 M2 Bergsviken Sweden
173 E2 Bergtheim Ger.
183 G2 Bergüenda Spain
156 C2 Bergues France
164 F1 Bergum Neth.
190 E2 Bergün Switz.
215 G3 Bergville S. Africa
171 D4 Bergwitz Ger.
107 F2 Berh Mongolia
94 C3 Berhala, Selat sea chan. Indon.
Berhampur W. Bengal India see Baharampur
197 H2 Berheci r. Romania
177 H4 Berhida Hungary
257 F2 Berilo Brazil
131 R4 Beringa, Ostrov i. Rus. Fed.
87 C5 Beringarra W.A. Austr.
165 E3 Beringe Neth.
184 C2 Beringel Port.
165 E3 Beringen Belgium
131 S3 Beringovskiy Chukotskiy Avtonomnyy Okrug Rus. Fed.
220 A4 Bering Sea N. Pacific Ocean
220 B3 Bering Strait Rus. Fed./U.S.A.
151 F3 Berinsfield Oxfordshire, England U.K.
Berislav Ukr. see Beryslav
136 F4 Berizky Ukr.
185 H4 Berja Spain
169 F5 Berka Ger.
140 J3 Berkåk Norway
204 E2 Berkane Morocco
164 D3 Berkel Neth.
164 F2 Berkel r. Neth.
86 E2 Berkeley r. W.A. Austr.
150 E3 Berkeley Gloucestershire, England U.K.
240 F3 Berkeley CA U.S.A.
235 D2 Berkeley Heights NJ U.S.A.
232 D5 Berkeley Springs WV U.S.A.
168 F2 Berkenthin Ger.
151 G3 Berkhamsted Hertfordshire, England U.K.
173 E3 Berkheim Ger.
164 E2 Berkhout Neth.
262 U1 Berkner Island Antarctica
197 F4 Berkovitsa Bulg.
234 C2 Berks County county PA U.S.A.
233 G3 Berkshire Hills MA U.S.A.
151 F2 Berkswell West Midlands, England U.K.
164 F2 Berkum Neth.
165 D3 Berlaar Belgium
156 D2 Berlaimont France
222 G4 Berland r. Alta Can.
184 E2 Berlanga Spain
183 H3 Berlanga de Duero Spain
165 D3 Berlare Belgium
140 O1 Berlevåg Norway
164 E3 Berlicum Neth.
164 E1 Berlikum Neth.
170 E3 Berlin Ger.
171 E3 Berlin land Ger.
235 F1 Berlin CT U.S.A.
233 F5 Berlin MD U.S.A.
233 □H2 Berlin NH U.S.A.
234 D3 Berlin NJ U.S.A.
232 C4 Berlin OH U.S.A.
232 D5 Berlin PA U.S.A.
226 C4 Berlin WI U.S.A.
262 O1 Berlin, Mount Antarctica
169 F4 Berlingerode Ger.
81 C4 Berlins South I. N.Z.
234 C2 Berlinsville PA U.S.A.
196 E3 Berlişte Romania
171 C4 Berlstedt Ger.
83 G4 Bermagui N.S.W. Austr.
172 D4 Bermatingen Ger.
122 D2 Berme Turkm.
242 E3 Bermejíllo Mex.
260 D3 Bermejo r. Arg.
258 F2 Bermejo r. Arg./Bol.
252 D5 Bermejo Bol.
261 G6 Bermejo, Isla i. Arg.
183 H1 Bermeo Spain
182 D3 Bermillo de Sayago Spain
231 □1 Bermuda terr. N. Atlantic Ocean
264 E4 Bermuda Rise sea feature N. Atlantic Ocean
190 C2 Bern Switz.
190 C2 Bern canton Switz.
163 C5 Bernac-Dessus France
195 F2 Bernalda Italy
239 F5 Bernalillo NM U.S.A.
256 C5 Bernardino de Campos Brazil
183 F3 Bernardos Spain
234 D2 Bernardsville NJ U.S.A.
176 D2 Bernartice Czech Rep.
261 F5 Bernasconi Arg.
172 C4 Bernau Baden-Württemberg Ger.
170 E3 Bernau Brandenburg Ger.
173 G4 Bernau am Chiemsee Ger.
156 C2 Bernaville France
159 G2 Bernay France
173 E4 Bernbeuren Ger.
171 C4 Bernburg (Saale) Ger.
179 H3 Berndorf Austria
168 D2 Berne Ger.
Berne Switz. see Bern
226 E5 Berne IN U.S.A.
177 H3 Bernecebaráti Hungary
183 H2 Bernedo Spain
190 C2 Berner Alpen mts Switz.
146 A4 Berneray i. Western Isles, Scotland U.K.
146 A5 Berneray i. Western Isles, Scotland U.K.
Bernese Alps mts Switz. see Berner Alpen
182 E2 Bernesga r. Spain
160 E2 Bernex France
173 F2 Berngau Ger.
179 H2 Bernhardsthal Austria
173 G2 Bernhardswald Ger.
87 B5 Bernier Island W.A. Austr.
161 D3 Bernin France
183 H4 Berninches mt. Spain
146 B4 Bernisdale Highland, Scotland U.K.
165 C4 Bernissart Belgium
170 C2 Bernitt Ger.
172 B2 Bernkastel-Kues Ger.
163 B4 Bernos-Beaulac France
173 F4 Bernried Bayern Ger.
173 G3 Bernried Bayern Ger.
171 F4 Bernsdorf Ger.
173 E3 Bernstadt Baden-Württemberg Ger.
171 F4 Bernstadt Sachsen Ger.
232 A6 Bernstadt KY U.S.A.
179 H3 Bernstein Austria
234 B2 Bernville PA U.S.A.
Beroea Greece see Veroia
Beroea Syria see Ḩalab
190 D1 Beromünster Switz.
213 □J4 Beroroha Madag.
176 D2 Beroun Czech Rep.
176 D2 Berounka r. Czech Rep.
197 F5 Berovo Macedonia
191 G4 Berra Italy
189 A7 Berrahal Alg.
161 A5 Berre r. France
161 D5 Berre, Étang de lag. France
204 D2 Berrechid Morocco
161 D5 Berre-l'Étang France
82 E3 Berri S.A. Austr.
205 F2 Berriane Alg.
161 C4 Berrias-et-Casteljau France
183 H1 Berriatúa Spain
83 G4 Berridale N.S.W. Austr.
146 E3 Berriedale Highland, Scotland U.K.
146 E3 Berriedale Water r. Scotland U.K.
158 C3 Berrien France
83 F3 Berrigan N.S.W. Austr.
183 I2 Berriozar Spain
184 D3 Berrocal Spain
260 E3 Berrotarán Arg.
205 F1 Berrouaghia Alg.
150 D3 Berrow Somerset, England U.K.
156 E3 Berru France
83 G3 Berry N.S.W. Austr.
156 D3 Berry-au-Bac France
223 I5 Berry Creek r. Alta Can.
246 C1 Berry Islands Bahamas
234 B2 Berrysburg PA U.S.A.
237 E4 Berryville AR U.S.A.
232 E5 Berryville VA U.S.A.
168 C3 Bersenbrück Ger.
136 E3 Bershad' Ukr.
162 B3 Berson France
191 F3 Bersone Italy
120 E1 Bersuat Rus. Fed.
129 B3 Berta r. Turkey
182 B2 Bertamirans Spain
171 F4 Berthelsdorf Ger.
161 A4 Bertholène France
156 C2 Bertincourt France
191 H4 Bertinoro Italy
165 E4 Bertogne Belgium
254 E3 Bertolínia Brazil
257 G2 Bertópolis Brazil
207 I5 Bertoua Cameroon
165 F5 Bertrange Lux.
157 G4 Bertrichamps France
165 E5 Bertrix Belgium
77 H2 Beru atoll Gilbert Is Kiribati
168 C2 Berumbur Ger.
120 E4 Beruni Uzbek.
251 F5 Beruri Brazil
114 C5 Beruwala Sri Lanka
197 F2 Berveni Romania
146 F5 Bervie Water r. Scotland U.K.
159 G2 Berville-sur-Mer France
83 F4 Berwick Vic. Austr.
233 H3 Berwick ME U.S.A.
227 I5 Berwick PA U.S.A.
149 G2 Berwick-upon-Tweed Northumberland, England U.K.
150 D2 Berwyn hills Wales U.K.
234 C2 Berwyn PA U.S.A.
137 G4 Beryslav Ukr.
Berytus Lebanon see Beirut
197 E3 Berzasca Romania
138 F3 Bērzaune Latvia
138 D4 Beržė r. Lith.
176 G5 Berzence Hungary
175 L1 Berźniki Pol.
185 E1 Berzocana Spain
161 B4 Bès r. France
213 □J3 Besalampy Madag.
186 F2 Besalú Spain
160 E1 Besançon France
183 F2 Besande Spain
95 F3 Besar, Gunung mt. Indon.
94 C1 Besar, Gunung mt. Malaysia
183 F1 Besaya r. Spain
160 B2 Besbre r. France
186 F3 Bescanó Spain
139 H5 Besed' r. Rus. Fed.
169 D5 Beselich-Obertiefenbach Ger.
177 H3 Beše ňov Slovakia
177 J4 Besenyőtelek Hungary
177 J4 Besenyszög Hungary
Beshariq Uzbek. see Besharyk
121 G4 Besharyk Uzbek.
120 F5 Beshkent Uzbek.
122 C4 Beshneh Iran
129 D3 Besht'asheni Georgia
121 G4 Besh-Ter, Gora mt. Kyrg./Uzbek.
Besh-Ter Toosu mt. Kyrg./Uzbek. see Besh-Ter, Gora
Beshtor Toghi mt. Kyrg./Uzbek. see Besh-Ter, Gora
186 D2 Besiberri Sud mt. Spain
127 F3 Beşiri Turkey
175 J6 Beskid Niski hills Pol.
175 I6 Beskid Sądecki mts Pol.
Beskra Alg. see Biskra
129 D2 Beslan Rus. Fed.
197 F5 Beslet mt. Bulg.
197 F4 Besna Kobila mt. Yugo.
126 E3 Besni Turkey
190 D3 Besozzo Italy
Beşparmak Dağları mts Cyprus see Pentadaktylos Range
139 K4 Besputa r. Rus. Fed.
149 H4 Bessacarr South Yorkshire, England U.K.
161 B5 Bessan France
208 B3 Béssao Chad
Bessarabka Moldova see Basarabeasca
121 G4 Bessaye, Gora mt. Kazakh.
160 B2 Bessay-sur-Allier France
147 E2 Bessbrook Northern Ireland U.K.
161 E3 Besse France
160 A3 Besse-et-St-Anastaise France
161 C4 Bessèges France
231 C5 Bessemer AL U.S.A.
226 B2 Bessemer MI U.S.A.
232 C4 Bessemer PA U.S.A.
160 C3 Bessenay France
172 D2 Bessenbach Ger.
159 G4 Bessé-sur-Braye France
161 E5 Besse-sur-Issole France
120 C3 Besshoky, Gora hill Kazakh.
163 D5 Bessières France
162 D2 Bessines-sur-Gartempe France
129 B1 Besskorbnaya Rus. Fed.
135 I5 Bessonovka Rus. Fed.
162 E3 Bessou, Mont de hill France
164 E3 Best Neth.
120 C2 Bestamak Aktyubinskaya Oblast' Kazakh.
121 I2 Bestamak Vostochnyy Kazakhstan Kazakh.
171 E3 Bestensee Ger.
215 G3 Besters S. Africa
121 H1 Bestobe Kazakh.
143 F2 Bestorp Sweden
169 D4 Bestwig Ger.
84 C2 Beswick N.T. Austr.
213 □J3 Betafo Madag.
213 □J3 Betanantanana Madag.
252 D4 Betanzos Bol.
182 B1 Betanzos Spain
207 I5 Bétaré Oya Cameroon
226 D2 Bete Grise MI U.S.A.
186 B1 Betelu Spain
187 C5 Bétera Spain
207 F4 Bétérou Benin
183 H4 Beteta Spain
204 D2 Beth, Oued r. Morocco
215 G2 Bethal S. Africa
212 C5 Bethanie Namibia
235 F1 Bethany CT U.S.A.
236 E3 Bethany MO U.S.A.
237 D5 Bethany OK U.S.A.
177 K6 Bethausen Romania
220 B3 Bethel AK U.S.A.
235 E1 Bethel CT U.S.A.
233 □H2 Bethel ME U.S.A.
232 A5 Bethel OH U.S.A.
234 B2 Bethel PA U.S.A.
169 E3 Betheln Ger.
232 C4 Bethel Park PA U.S.A.
246 □ Bethel Town Jamaica
156 E3 Bétheny France
151 H3 Bethersden Kent, England U.K.
150 C1 Bethesda Gwynedd, Wales U.K.
234 A4 Bethesda MD U.S.A.
232 C4 Bethesda OH U.S.A.
215 E4 Bethesdaweg S. Africa
156 C3 Béthisy-St-Pierre France
80 F2 Bethlehem North I. N.Z.
215 G3 Bethlehem S. Africa
234 C2 Bethlehem PA U.S.A.
128 B4 Bethlehem West Bank
215 E5 Bethlesdorp S. Africa
163 D6 Bethmale France
156 D4 Bethon France
235 E2 Bethpage NY U.S.A.
215 E4 Bethulie S. Africa
156 C2 Béthune France
156 B3 Béthune r. France
257 E3 Betim Brazil
213 □J4 Betioky Madag.
95 F5 Betiri, Gunung mt. Indon.
Bet Lehem West Bank see Bethlehem
139 I4 Betlitsa Rus. Fed.
116 C5 Betma Madh. Prad. India
156 D4 Beton-Bazoches France
97 C6 Betong Thai.
84 E5 Betoota Qld Austr.
210 C2 Beto Shet' r. Eth.
208 C4 Bétou Congo
121 G3 Betpak-Dala plain Kazakh.
213 □J3 Betrandraka Madag.
213 □J4 Betroka Madag.
157 H4 Betschdorf France
128 B3 Bet She'an Israel
225 G3 Betsiamites Que. Can.
225 G3 Betsiamites r. Que. Can.
213 □J2 Betsiboka r. Madag.
104 C2 Betsu-zan mt. Japan
246 D2 Betsy Bay Mayaguana Bahamas
157 G3 Bettelainville France
178 C3 Bettelwurf mt. Austria
165 F5 Bettembourg Lux.
165 F5 Bettendorf Lux.
234 B3 Betterton MD U.S.A.
117 F4 Bettiah Bihar India
215 G2 Bettiesdam S. Africa
172 A2 Bettingen Ger.
143 G2 Bettna Sweden
190 E4 Bettola Italy
158 E3 Betton France
193 E1 Bettona Italy
146 D3 Bettyhill Highland, Scotland U.K.
147 E3 Bettystown Rep. of Ireland
116 D5 Betul Madh. Prad. India
116 D4 Betwa r. India
150 D1 Betws-y-coed Conwy, Wales U.K.
187 C5 Betxi Spain
156 C3 Betz France
169 C5 Betzdorf Ger.
165 F5 Betzdorf Lux.
173 F2 Betzenstein Ger.
173 E4 Betzigau Ger.
209 B6 Béu Angola
161 E4 Beuil France
83 E3 Beulah Vic. Austr.
150 D2 Beulah Powys, Wales U.K.
226 D3 Beulah MI U.S.A.
236 C2 Beulah ND U.S.A.
151 H3 Beult r. England U.K.
164 E3 Beuningen Neth.
169 F4 Beuren Ger.
172 C3 Beuron Ger.
157 E4 Beurville France
Beuthen Pol. see Bytom
160 C2 Beuvray, Mont hill France
160 B1 Beuvron r. France
159 H4 Beuvron r. France
156 C2 Beuvry France
159 G2 Beuzeville France
193 E2 Bevagna Italy
190 B2 Bevaix Switz.
169 C3 Bever r. Ger.
161 F5 Bévéra r. France
87 C7 Beverley W.A. Austr.
149 I4 Beverley East Riding of Yorkshire, England U.K.
233 H3 Beverly MA U.S.A.
234 D2 Beverly NJ U.S.A.
232 C5 Beverly OH U.S.A.
240 H4 Beverly Hills CA U.S.A.
169 E4 Bevern Ger.
168 D2 Beverstedt Ger.
169 E4 Beverungen Ger.
164 D2 Beverwijk Neth.
156 B4 Béville-le-Comte France
150 E2 Bewdley Worcestershire, England U.K.
190 C2 Bex Switz.
172 B2 Bexbach Ger.
151 H4 Bexhill East Sussex, England U.K.
111 D4 Bextograk Xinjiang China
199 F3 Beyağaç Turkey
199 E1 Beyazköy Turkey
Beyce Turkey see Orhaneli
163 B4 Beychac-et-Caillau France
199 G1 Beyciler Bolu Turkey
199 F2 Beydağ Turkey
199 G3 Bey Dağları mts Turkey
171 C3 Beyendorf Ger.
199 G3 Beykonak Turkey
199 G1 Beyköy Turkey
199 F1 Beykoz Turkey
206 C4 Beyla Guinea
Beylagan Azer. see Beyläqan
129 E4 Beyläqan Azer.
199 G2 Beylikova Turkey
203 I6 Beylul Eritrea
163 D4 Beynac-et-Cazenac France
162 D3 Beynat France
165 E4 Beyne-Heusay Belgium
120 C3 Beyneu Kazakh.
160 D3 Beynost France
199 E2 Beyoba Manisa Turkey
103 I8 Beyoneisu Retugan i. Japan
126 C2 Beypazarı Turkey
126 E3 Beypınarı Turkey
114 B4 Beypore Kerala India
122 C5 Beyram Iran
Beyrouth Lebanon see Beirut
126 C3 Beyşehir Turkey
126 C3 Beyşehir Gölü l. Turkey
137 J5 Beysug Rus. Fed.
137 J4 Beysug r. Rus. Fed.
137 J5 Beysuzhek r. Rus. Fed.
127 F3 Beytüşşebap Turkey
161 D4 Bez r. France
187 B4 Bezas Spain
178 A3 Bezau Austria
134 J4 Bezbozhnik Rus. Fed.
196 D3 Bezdan Vojvodina, Srbija Yugo.
160 D1 Bèze France
129 C2 Bezengi Rus. Fed.
176 G4 Bezenye Hungary
138 G3 Bezhanitskaya Vozvyshennost' hills Rus. Fed.
138 G3 Bezhanitsy Rus. Fed.
197 G4 Bezhanovo Bulg.
139 K3 Bezhetsk Rus. Fed.
139 K3 Bezhetskiy Verkh reg. Rus. Fed.
129 E2 Bezhta Rus. Fed.
161 B5 Béziers France
175 I1 Bezledy Pol.
Bezmein Turkm. see Byuzmeyin
161 C5 Bezouce France
177 L3 Bežovce Slovakia
Bezwada Andhra Prad. India see Vijayawada
116 B4 Bhabhar Gujarat India
116 C5 Bhabra Madh. Prad. India
117 E4 Bhabua Bihar India
116 B5 Bhachau Gujarat India
116 B5 Bhadar r. India
116 C2 Bhadarwah Jammu and Kashmir
123 H4 Bhadaur Punjab India
117 F4 Bhadgaon Nepal
117 E4 Bhadohi Uttar Prad. India
116 C3 Bhadra Rajasthan India
114 D2 Bhadrachalam Andhra Prad. India
Bhadrachalam Road Station Andhra Prad. India see Kottagudem
117 F5 Bhadrakh Orissa India
114 B3 Bhadravati Karnataka India
123 F4 Bhag Pak.
111 B5 Bhaga r. India
117 F4 Bhagalpur Bihar India
117 G5 Bhagirathi r. India
114 C2 Bhainsa Andhra Prad. India
116 D5 Bhainsdehi Madh. Prad. India
117 G4 Bhairab Bazar Bangl.
117 E4 Bhairawa Nepal
Bhairawaha Nepal see Bhairawa
119 I4 Bhairi Hol mt. Pak.
123 G4 Bhakkar Pak.
Bhaktapur Nepal see Bhadgaon
114 C2 Bhalki Karnataka India
123 H3 Bhalwal Pak.
116 D5 Bhamgarh Madh. Prad. India
96 B1 Bhamo Myanmar
116 D5 Bhandara Mahar. India
116 D4 Bhander Madh. Prad. India
115 E2 Bhanjanagar Orissa India
116 C4 Bhanpura Madh. Prad. India
116 D5 Bhanrer Range hills Madh. Prad. India
Bharat country Asia see India
116 D4 Bharatpur Rajasthan India
117 H4 Bhareli r. India
123 E5 Bhari r. Pak.
116 D4 Bharthana Uttar Prad. India
116 C5 Bharuch Gujarat India
116 E5 Bhatapara Madh. Prad. India
Bhatinda Punjab India see Bathinda
114 B3 Bhatkal Karnataka India
Bhatnair Rajasthan India see Hanumangarh
117 G5 Bhatpara W. Bengal India
123 H3 Bhaun Gharibwal Pak.
114 C4 Bhavani Tamil Nadu India
114 C4 Bhavani r. India
116 C5 Bhavnagar Gujarat India
123 H4 Bhawana Pak.
115 D2 Bhawanipatna Orissa India
Bhearnaraigh, Eilean i. Western Isles, Scotland U.K. see Berneray
Bheemavaram Andhra Prad. India see Bhimavaram
215 H2 Bhekuzulu S. Africa
123 H3 Bhera Pak.
116 E3 Bheri r. Nepal
116 E5 Bhilai Madh. Prad. India
116 C4 Bhildi Gujarat India
116 C4 Bhilwara Rajasthan India
114 C2 Bhima r. India
114 D2 Bhimavaram Andhra Prad. India
123 H3 Bhimbar Pak.
117 F4 Bhimnagar Bihar India
116 D4 Bhind Madh. Prad. India
116 C4 Bhindar Rajasthan India
116 E4 Bhinga Uttar Prad. India
114 B2 Bhingar Mahar. India
116 C4 Bhinmal Rajasthan India
114 B2 Bhiwandi Mahar. India
116 D3 Bhiwani Haryana India
116 B5 Bhogat Gujarat India
116 C5 Bhokardan Mahar. India
117 G5 Bhola Bangl.
116 D4 Bhongaon Uttar Prad. India
114 C2 Bhongir Andhra Prad. India
215 G4 Bhongweni S. Africa
116 D5 Bhopal Madh. Prad. India
114 D2 Bhopalpatnam Madh. Prad. India
114 B2 Bhor Mahar. India
Bhrigukaccha Gujarat India see Bharuch
117 F5 Bhuban Orissa India
117 F5 Bhubaneshwar Orissa India
Bhubaneswar Orissa India see Bhubaneshwar
116 B5 Bhuj Gujarat India
96 B3 Bhumiphol Dam Thai.
215 H2 Bhunya Swaziland
116 C5 Bhusawal Mahar. India
117 G4 Bhutan country Asia
116 B4 Bhuttewala Rajasthan India
114 C4 Bhuvanagiri Tamil Nadu India
250 E5 Biá r. Brazil
209 E7 Bia, Monts mts Dem. Rep. Congo
96 C3 Bia, Phou mt. Laos
122 D5 Bīabān mts Iran
174 F4 Biadki Pol.
Biafra, Bight of g. Africa see Benin, Bight of
174 F5 Biała Pol.
175 I5 Biała r. Pol.
174 F5 Biała r. Pol.
174 G4 Biała-Parcela Pierwsza Pol.
175 K2 Biała Piska Pol.
175 L3 Biała Podlaska Pol.
175 I4 Biała Rawska Pol.
174 F2 Białe Błota Pol.
175 K4 Białka r. Pol.
175 I4 Białobrzegi Pol.
175 K5 Białobrzegi Pol.
174 D2 Białogard Pol.
174 F2 Białośliwie Pol.
175 L3 Białowieża Pol.
174 E2 Biały Bór Pol.
175 I6 Biały Dunajec Pol.
175 L2 Białystok Pol.
194 D5 Biancavilla Sicilia Italy
195 F4 Bianco Italy
190 C3 Bianco, Corno mt. Italy
Bianco, Monte mt. France/Italy see Mont Blanc
107 I5 Biandan Gang r. mouth China
190 D3 Biandrate Italy
208 D3 Bianga C.A.R.
206 D5 Biankouma Côte d'Ivoire
206 E5 Bianouan Côte d'Ivoire
160 E2 Bians-les-Usiers France
190 D3 Bianzè Italy
Bianzhuang Shandong China see Cangshan
92 C5 Biao Phil.
116 D5 Biaora Madh. Prad. India
187 C6 Biar Spain
122 C2 Bīārjmand Iran
163 A5 Biarritz France
Biarritz airport France see Parme
163 A5 Biarrotte France
162 D4 Biars-sur-Cère France
163 A4 Bias Aquitaine France
163 C4 Bias Aquitaine France
190 D2 Biasca Switz.
177 H4 Biatorbágy Hungary
203 F2 Biba Egypt
102 J2 Bibai Japan
209 B8 Bibala Angola
83 G4 Bibbenluke N.S.W. Austr.
191 G5 Bibbiena Italy
191 F5 Bibbona Italy
207 I4 Bibémi Cameroon
172 C3 Biberach Ger.
172 D3 Biberach an der Riß Ger.
173 E3 Biberbach Ger.
173 E2 Bibert r. Ger.
206 E5 Bibiani Ghana
191 I3 Bibione Italy
117 G4 Bibiyana r. Bangl.
172 C2 Biblis Ger.
Biblos Lebanon see Jbail
136 C3 Bibrka Ukr.
151 F3 Bibury Gloucestershire, England U.K.
257 F4 Bicas Brazil
177 M4 Bicaz Maramureș Romania
197 H2 Bicaz Neamț Romania
193 H3 Biccari Italy
151 F3 Bicester Oxfordshire, England U.K.
210 C2 Bichena Eth.
Bicheng Chongqing China see Bishan
83 G5 Bicheno Tas. Austr.
100 E3 Bichevaya Rus. Fed.
207 H3 Bichi Nigeria
100 F1 Bichi r. Rus. Fed.
173 F4 Bichl Ger.
114 B3 Bicholim Goa India
107 E1 Bichura Rus. Fed.
129 B2 Bichvint'a Georgia
172 C2 Bickenbach Ger.
151 F2 Bickenhill West Midlands, England U.K.
84 D2 Bickerton Island N.T. Austr.
150 C4 Bickleigh Devon, England U.K.
150 D4 Bickleigh Devon, England U.K.
151 H3 Bicknacre Essex, England U.K.
241 L2 Bicknell UT U.S.A.
129 F3 Bico Azer.
187 C5 Bicorp Spain
184 B3 Bicos Port.
177 H4 Bicske Hungary
150 E2 Bicton Shropshire, England U.K.
114 B2 Bid Mahar. India
207 G4 Bida Nigeria
163 A5 Bidache France
114 C2 Bidar Karnataka India
163 A5 Bidart France
116 C4 Bidasar Rajasthan India
125 G3 Bidbid Oman
233 □H3 Biddeford ME U.S.A.
151 H3 Biddenden Kent, England U.K.
164 E2 Biddinghuizen Neth.
149 G4 Biddulph Staffordshire, England U.K.
146 C5 Bidean nam Bian mt. Scotland U.K.
150 C3 Bideford Devon, England U.K.
150 C3 Bideford Bay England U.K.
191 H4 Bidente r. Italy
151 F2 Bidford-on-Avon Warwickshire, England U.K.
122 D4 Bīdkhan, Kūh-e mt. Iran
205 F5 Bidon 5 tourist site Alg.
163 B5 Bidos France
163 A5 Bidouze r. France
177 K3 Bidovce Slovakia
100 E3 Bidzhar r. Rus. Fed.
Bié Angola see Kuito
209 C8 Bié prov. Angola
169 E5 Bieber Ger.
172 C2 Biebesheim am Rhein Ger.
175 K2 Biebrza r. Pol.
175 J6 Biecz Pol.
169 D5 Biedenkopf Ger.
171 C3 Biederitz Ger.
186 C2 Biel Spain
190 C1 Biel Switz.
175 K3 Bielany-Żyłaki Pol.
174 E5 Bielawa Pol.
169 D3 Bielefeld Ger.
174 C2 Bielice Pol.
175 I5 Bieliny Kapitulne Pol.
Bielitz Pol. see Bielsko-Biała
190 D3 Biella Italy
190 D3 Biella prov. Piemonte Italy
163 B5 Bielle France
186 D2 Bielsa Spain
175 H3 Bielsk Pol.
175 H6 Bielsko-Biała Pol.
175 L3 Bielsk Podlaski Pol.
169 E4 Bielstein hill Ger.
168 F2 Bienenbüttel Ger.
97 D5 Biên Hoa Vietnam
160 D2 Bienne r. France
Bienne Switz. see Biel
190 F3 Bienno Italy
185 H2 Bienservida Spain
184 D2 Bienvenida Spain
184 D2 Bienvenida hill Spain
183 H4 Bienvenida mt. Spain
251 H4 Bienvenue Fr. Guiana
209 B8 Bié Plateau Angola
177 H1 Bierawa Pol.
174 G5 Bierawka r. Pol.
85 F5 Bierbank Qld Austr.
174 G5 Bierdzany Pol.
171 C4 Biere Ger.
190 B2 Bière Switz.
186 C2 Bierge Spain
159 F4 Bierné France
163 D6 Biert France
175 H5 Bieruń Pol.
174 F4 Bierutów Pol.
174 G3 Bierzwienna-Długa Pol.
174 D2 Bierzwnik Pol.
186 C2 Biescas Spain
170 C3 Biese r. Ger.
170 E3 Biesenthal Ger.
174 E1 Biesiekierz Pol.
215 E2 Biesiesvlei S. Africa
157 F4 Biesles France
214 D4 Biesrespoort S. Africa
173 E4 Biessenhofen Ger.
175 K6 Bieszczady mts Pol.
172 C3 Bietigheim Ger.
172 D3 Bietigheim-Bissingen Ger.
170 E2 Bietikow Ger.
190 C2 Bietschhorn mt. Switz.
165 E5 Bièvre Belgium
175 H3 Bieżuń Pol.
193 H3 Biferno r. Italy
208 A5 Bifoun Gabon
240 F2 Big r. CA U.S.A.
199 E1 Biga Turkey
199 E1 Biga r. Turkey
199 F2 Bigadiç Turkey
261 G3 Bigand Arg.
163 B4 Biganos France
187 C6 Bigastro Spain
199 E2 Biga Yarımadası pen. Turkey
238 E2 Big Baldy Mountain MT U.S.A.
222 F5 Big Bar Creek B.C. Can.
226 D2 Big Bay MI U.S.A.
78 □5 Big Bay b. Vanuatu
226 D3 Big Bay de Noc MI U.S.A.
240 I4 Big Bear Lake CA U.S.A.
238 E2 Big Belt Mountains MT U.S.A.
215 H2 Big Bend Swaziland
237 F5 Big Black r. MS U.S.A.
236 D4 Big Blue r. NE U.S.A.
150 D4 Bigbury-on-Sea Devon, England U.K.
78 □3a Bigej i. Kwajalein Marshall Is
234 C3 Big Elk Creek r. MD U.S.A.
106 C2 Biger Nuur salt l. Mongolia
236 E1 Big Falls MN U.S.A.
226 A1 Big Fork r. MN U.S.A.
223 J4 Biggar Sask. Can.
146 E6 Biggar South Lanarkshire, Scotland U.K.
78 □3a Biggarenn i. Kwajalein Marshall Is
215 G3 Biggarsberg S. Africa
86 E2 Bigge Island W.A. Austr.
85 H5 Biggenden Qld Austr.
222 B3 Bigger, Mount B.C. Can.
78 □3a Biggerann i. Kwajalein Marshall Is
151 H3 Biggin Hill Greater London, England U.K.
151 G2 Biggleswade Bedfordshire, England U.K.
240 G2 Biggs CA U.S.A.
238 B2 Biggs OR U.S.A.
238 D2 Big Hole r. MT U.S.A.
238 F2 Bighorn r. Montana/Wyoming U.S.A.
238 F2 Bighorn Mountains WY U.S.A.
78 □3a Bigi i. Kwajalein Marshall Is
139 L5 Bigil'dino Rus. Fed.
129 E3 Bığır Azer.
232 D6 Big Island VA U.S.A.
237 C6 Big Lake TX U.S.A.
238 D3 Big Lost r. ID U.S.A.
238 F1 Big Muddy Creek r. MT U.S.A.
158 D4 Bignan France
190 D2 Bignasco Switz.
206 A3 Bignona Senegal
209 E6 Bigobo Dem. Rep. Congo
232 D6 Big Otter r. VA U.S.A.
240 H3 Big Pine CA U.S.A.
240 H4 Big Pine Peak CA U.S.A.
238 F2 Big Porcupine Creek r. MT U.S.A.
222 C3 Big Port Walter AK U.S.A.
226 E4 Big Rapids MI U.S.A.
226 C3 Big Rib r. WI U.S.A.
223 J4 Big River Sask. Can.
222 C2 Big Salmon Y.T. Can.
222 C2 Big Salmon r. Y.T. Can.
238 E1 Big Sandy MT U.S.A.
238 E3 Big Sandy r. WY U.S.A.
236 C4 Big Sandy Creek r. CO U.S.A.
236 D3 Big Sioux r. SD U.S.A.
240 I2 Big Smokey Valley NV U.S.A.
237 C5 Big Spring TX U.S.A.
236 C3 Big Springs NE U.S.A.
223 I5 Big Stone Alta Can.
236 D2 Big Stone City SD U.S.A.
232 B6 Big Stone Gap VA U.S.A.
237 F5 Big Sunflower r. MS U.S.A.
240 G3 Big Sur CA U.S.A.
238 E2 Big Timber MT U.S.A.
224 B2 Big Trout Lake Ont. Can.
186 B2 Bigüezal Spain
192 B2 Biguglia Corse France
222 H4 Big Valley Alta Can.
241 L3 Big Water UT U.S.A.
227 H3 Bigwin Ont. Can.
188 E3 Bihać Bos.-Herz.
117 F4 Bihar state India
177 K4 Biharia Romania
117 F4 Bihariganj Bihar India
177 K4 Biharkeresztes Hungary
177 K4 Biharnagybajom Hungary
117 F4 Bihar Sharif Bihar India
177 K5 Biharugra Hungary
177 L5 Bihor county Romania
197 F2 Bihor, Vârful mt. Romania
177 L5 Bihorului, Munții mts Romania
117 H4 Bihpuriagaon Assam India
206 A4 Bijagós, Arquipélago dos is Guinea-Bissau
116 C4 Bijainagar Rajasthan India
116 D4 Bijaipur Madh. Prad. India
114 B2 Bijapur Karnataka India
122 A3 Bījār Iran
114 D2 Bijarpur Madh. Prad. India
116 D4 Bijawar Madh. Prad. India
116 C2 Bijbehara Jammu and Kashmir
188 G3 Bijeljina Bos.-Herz.
188 E3 Bijelolasica mt. Croatia
196 D4 Bijelo Polje Crna Gora Yugo.
108 C3 Bijie Guizhou China
117 G4 Bijni Assam India
116 D3 Bijnor Uttar Prad. India
116 C4 Bijolia Rajasthan India
217 □2 Bijoutier i. Seychelles
125 E2 Bijrān, Khashm hill Saudi Arabia
116 C4 Bikampur Rajasthan India
116 C3 Bikaner Rajasthan India
120 E3 Bikbauli Kazakh.
128 B3 Bikfaiya Lebanon
100 E3 Bikin Rus. Fed.
100 E3 Bikin r. Rus. Fed.
213 F4 Bikita Zimbabwe
208 C5 Bikoro Dem. Rep. Congo
108 C1 Bikou Gansu China
177 I6 Bikovo Vojvodina, Srbija Yugo.
117 F4 Bikramganj Bihar India
137 J3 Bila r. Ukr.
137 J3 Bila r. Ukr.
129 F3 Biläcarı Azer.
125 G3 Bilād Banī Bū 'Alī Oman
125 G3 Bilād Banī Bū Ḩasan Oman
124 C3 Bilād Ghāmid reg. Saudi Arabia
124 C3 Bilād Zahran reg. Saudi Arabia
137 G4 Bila Krynytsya Ukr.
207 E3 Bilanga Burkina
116 C4 Bilara Rajasthan India
116 D3 Bilari Uttar Prad. India
116 D3 Bilaspur Hima. Prad. India
116 E5 Bilaspur Madh. Prad. India
129 F4 Biläsuvar Azer.
136 F3 Bila Tserkva Ukr.
97 B4 Bilauktaung Range mts Myanmar/Thai.

183 H1 Bilbao Spain
203 F2 Bilbeis Egypt
Bilbo Spain see Bilbao
197 G2 Bilbor Romania
146 E3 Bilbster Highland, Scotland U.K.
188 G4 Bileća Bos.-Herz.
199 F1 Bilecik Turkey
199 G1 Bilecik prov. Turkey
196 E3 Biled Romania
129 F4 Bīleh Savār Iran
137 I3 Bilen'ke Ukr.
137 H4 Bilen'ke Ukr.
175 K5 Biłgoraj Pol.
211 A5 Bilharamulo Tanz.
116 E4 Bilhaur Uttar Prad. India
136 F4 Bilhorod-Dnistrovs'kyy Ukr.
208 D3 Bili r. Dem. Rep. Congo
131 R3 Bilibino Rus. Fed.
96 B3 Bilin Myanmar
176 C1 Bílina Czech Rep.
193 I4 Bilioso r. Italy
92 C4 Biliran i. Phil.
198 B1 Bilisht Albania
107 I4 Biliu r. China
177 M3 Bilky Ukr.
238 F3 Bill WY U.S.A.
87 B5 Billabalong W.A. Austr.
Billabong Creek r. N.S.W. Austr. see Moulamein Creek
87 B5 Billabong Roadhouse W.A. Austr.
142 D3 Billdal Sweden
168 F2 Bille r. Ger.
169 C4 Billerbeck Ger.
163 B5 Billère France
151 H3 Billericay Essex, England U.K.
160 D2 Billiat France
172 D2 Billigheim Ger.
86 E3 Billiluna W.A. Austr.
264 J2 Billingford Norfolk, England U.K.
149 H3 Billingham Stockton-on-Tees, England U.K.
149 I4 Billinghay Lincolnshire, England U.K.
238 E2 Billings MT U.S.A.
151 G3 Billingshurst West Sussex, England U.K.
Billiton i. Indon. see Belitung
151 I2 Billockby Norfolk, England U.K.
150 E4 Bill of Portland hd England U.K.
160 B3 Billom France
142 C4 Billund Denmark
141 J5 Billund airport Denmark
241 J4 Bill Williams r. AZ U.S.A.
241 K4 Bill Williams Mountain AZ U.S.A.
160 B2 Billy France
207 I2 Bilma Niger
85 G5 Biloela Qld Austr.
176 F5 Bilo Gora hills Croatia
137 H5 Bilohirs'k Ukr.
136 D2 Bilohir"ya Ukr.
136 D3 Bilohorodka Khmel'nyts'ka Oblast' Ukr.
136 F2 Bilohorodka Kyivs'ka Oblast' Ukr.
251 G4 Biloku Guyana
137 J3 Bilokurakyne Ukr.
114 C2 Biloli Mahar. India
137 J3 Biloluts'k Ukr.
137 H2 Bilopillya Ukr.
136 D2 Bilotyn Ukr.
177 H2 Bílovec Czech Rep.
177 G2 Bílovice Czech Rep.
137 J3 Bilovods'k Ukr.
237 F6 Biloxi MS U.S.A.
137 G4 Bilozerka Ukr.
137 I3 Bilozers'ke Ukr.
169 F4 Bilshausen Ger.
136 C3 Bil'shivtsi Ukr.
116 D3 Bilsi Uttar Prad. India
137 H2 Bil's'k Ukr.
136 C2 Bil's'ka Volya Ukr.
146 E6 Bilston Midlothian, Scotland U.K.
164 E2 Bilthoven Neth.
202 D6 Biltine Chad
202 D6 Biltine pref. Chad
149 I4 Bilton East Riding of Yorkshire, England U.K.
96 B3 Bilugyun Island Myanmar
137 H3 Bilukhivka Ukr.
93 B2 Bilungala Sulawesi Utara Indon.
136 F4 Bilyayivka Ukr.
175 K6 Bilychi Ukr.
137 H3 Bilyky Ukr.
136 E3 Bilylivka Ukr.
136 E4 Bilyne Ukr.
137 I3 Bilyts'ke Ukr.
136 C3 Bilyy Cheremosh r. Ukr.
137 I2 Bilyy Kolodyaz' Ukr.
165 E4 Bilzen Belgium
208 E4 Bima r. Dem. Rep. Congo
95 G5 Bima Sumbawa Indon.
207 F4 Bimbila Ghana
246 C1 Bimini Islands Bahamas
115 D2 Bimlipatam Andhra Prad. India
129 G3 Binä Azer.
173 G3 Bina r. Ger.
177 H4 Bíňa Slovakia
186 D3 Binaced Spain
116 D4 Bina-Etawa Madh. Prad. India
93 D3 Binaija, Gunung mt. Seram Indon.
92 B4 Binalbagan Phil.
122 D2 Bīnālūd, Kūh-e mts Iran
156 B5 Binas France
190 E3 Binasco Italy
85 F4 Binbee Qld Austr.
126 E3 Binboğa Daği mt. Turkey
149 I4 Binbrook Lincolnshire, England U.K.
165 D4 Binche Belgium
107 H4 Bincheng Shandong China
108 B3 Binchuan Yunnan China
208 B2 Binder Chad
116 E4 Bindki Uttar Prad. India
173 F2 Bindlach Ger.
85 G5 Bindle Qld Austr.
Bindloe Island Islas Galápagos Ecuador see Marchena, Isla
213 F3 Bindura Zimbabwe
186 D3 Binefar Spain
148 C2 Binevenagh hill Northern Ireland U.K.
213 E3 Binga Zimbabwe
213 G3 Binga, Monte mt. Moz.
83 G2 Bingara N.S.W. Austr.
84 D2 Bing Bong N.T. Austr.
106 D4 Bingcaowan Gansu China
172 D3 Bingen Ger.
172 B2 Bingen am Rhein Ger.
164 F3 Bingerden Neth.
206 E5 Bingerville Côte d'Ivoire
151 G2 Bingham Nottinghamshire, England U.K.
233 □I2 Bingham ME U.S.A.
147 A2 Binghamstown Rep. of Ireland
233 F3 Binghamton NY U.S.A.
202 B3 Bin Ghanīmah, Jabal hills Libya
149 H4 Bingley West Yorkshire, England U.K.
Bingmei Guizhou China see Congjiang
127 F3 Bingöl Turkey
129 B4 Bingöl prov. Turkey
127 F3 Bingol Dağı mt. Turkey
129 B4 Bingöl Dağları mts Turkey
Bingxi Jiangxi China see Yushan
108 A2 Bingzhongluo Yunnan China
158 D3 Binic France
92 B4 Binicuil Phil.
186 C2 Biniés Spain
117 E5 Binika Orissa India
187 F5 Binisalem Spain
94 B2 Binjai Sumatera Indon.
83 G2 Binnaway N.S.W. Austr.
146 D5 Binnein Mor mt. Scotland U.K.
168 E3 Binnen Ger.
129 C4 Binpınar Turkey
117 F5 Binpur W. Bengal India
81 C5 Binser, Mount South I. N.Z.
173 E3 Binswangen Ger.
94 D2 Bintan i. Indon.
94 C1 Bintang, Bukit mts Malaysia
92 B3 Bintuan Phil.
94 C4 Bintuhan Sumatera Indon.
95 F2 Bintulu Sarawak Malaysia
92 B3 Binubusan Phil.
100 C3 Binxian Heilong. China
107 F5 Binxian Shaanxi China
Binxian Shandong China see Bincheng
108 D4 Binyang Guangxi China
207 G4 Bin-Yauri Nigeria
172 B4 Binzen Ger.
Binzhou Guangxi China see Binyang
Binzhou Heilong. China see Binxian
107 H4 Binzhou Shandong China
260 A5 Bíobío admin. reg. Chile
260 A5 Bíobío r. Chile
207 H6 Bioco i. Equat. Guinea
188 E4 Biograd na Moru Croatia
Bioko i. Equat. Guinea see Bioco
160 D3 Biol France
190 C3 Bionaz Italy
186 E3 Biosca Spain
161 F5 Biot France
186 B2 Biota Spain
204 C3 Biougra Morocco
168 C3 Bippen Ger.
257 E3 Biquinhas Brazil
Bir Mahar. India see Bid
210 D2 Bir, Ras pt Djibouti
100 E2 Bira Rus. Fed.
100 E2 Bira r. Rus. Fed.
123 E5 Bīrag, Kūh-e mts Iran
202 B3 Birāk Libya
100 D2 Birakan Rus. Fed.
127 F4 Bi'r al Mulūsi Iraq
134 G3 Birandozero Rus. Fed.
208 D2 Birao C.A.R.
117 F4 Biratnagar Nepal
222 H3 Birch r. Alta Can.
223 J4 Birch Hills Sask. Can.
151 I3 Birchington Kent, England U.K.
83 E3 Birchip Vic. Austr.
177 L6 Birchiş Romania
222 G5 Birch Island B.C. Can.
222 H3 Birch Mountains Y.T. Can.
223 K4 Birch River Man. Can.
232 C5 Birch River WV U.S.A.
227 F4 Birch Run MI U.S.A.
226 B3 Birchwood WI U.S.A.
210 D3 Bircot Eth.
175 K6 Bircza Pol.
164 E1 Birdaard Neth.
147 C4 Birdhill Rep. of Ireland
234 B2 Bird in Hand PA U.S.A.
Bird Island N. Mariana Is see Farallon de Medinilla
234 C2 Birdsboro PA U.S.A.
241 L2 Birdseye UT U.S.A.
84 D5 Birdsville Qld Austr.
234 B4 Birdsville MD U.S.A.
84 C2 Birdum r. N.T. Austr.
126 E3 Birecik Turkey
Birendranagar Nepal see Surkhet
211 A5 Birenga Rwanda
202 E5 Bir en Natrûn well Sudan
94 B1 Bireun Sumatera Indon.
199 F2 Birgi İzmir Turkey
210 C2 Birhan mt. Eth.
256 B4 Birigüi Brazil
129 D3 Birinci Şıxlı Azer.
122 D3 Bīrjand Iran
142 C2 Birkeland Norway
172 C2 Birkenau Ger.
172 C3 Birkenfeld Baden-Württemberg Ger.
172 D2 Birkenfeld Bayern Ger.
172 B2 Birkenfeld Rheinland-Pfalz Ger.
149 F4 Birkenhead Merseyside, England U.K.
169 C5 Birken-Honigsessen Ger.
170 E3 Birkenwerder Berlin Ger.
168 G1 Birket Denmark
203 F2 Birket Qârûn l. Egypt
179 G3 Birkfeld Austria
195 □ Birkirkara Malta
82 B1 Birksgate Range hills S.A. Austr.
169 F4 Birkungen Ger.
137 H2 Birky Ukr.
Bîrlad Romania see Bârlad
121 H3 Birlik Zhambylskaya Oblast' Kazakh.
Birlik Zhambylskaya Oblast' Kazakh. see Brlik
151 F2 Birmingham West Midlands, England U.K.
231 C5 Birmingham AL U.S.A.
117 F5 Birmitrapur Orissa India
204 C4 Bîr Mogreïn Maur.
178 D3 Birnhorn mt. Austria
207 F4 Birni Benin
78 □5 Birnie i. Kiribati
207 F3 Birnin-Gaouré Niger
207 G4 Birnin-Gwari Nigeria
207 G3 Birnin-Kebbi Nigeria
207 G3 Birnin Konni Niger
207 H4 Birnin Kudu Nigeria
207 H3 Birniwa Nigeria
100 E2 Birobidzhan Rus. Fed.
163 C4 Biron France
92 A4 Birong Phil.
117 F4 Birpur Bihar India
147 D3 Birr Rep. of Ireland
169 B5 Birresborn Ger.
83 F2 Birrie r. N.S.W. Austr.
84 B3 Birrindudu N.T. Austr.
Bîrsana Romania see Bârsana
146 E2 Birsay Orkney, Scotland U.K.
190 C1 Birse r. Switz.
Birshoghyr Kazakh. see Berchogur
134 K5 Birsk Rus. Fed.
151 F2 Birstall Leicestershire, England U.K.
169 E5 Birstein Ger.
138 E4 Birštonas Lith.
85 E2 Birthday Mountain hill Qld Austr.
223 K5 Birtle Man. Can.
149 H3 Birtley Tyne and Wear, England U.K.
111 F6 Biru Xizang China
136 E4 Biruinţa Moldova
Biruinţsa Moldova see Ştefan Vodă
Biruni Uzbek. see Beruni
114 B3 Birur Karnataka India
Biruxiong Xizang China see Biru
138 E3 Biržai Lith.
195 □ Birżebbuġa Malta
193 H3 Bisaccia Italy
194 C5 Bisacquino Sicilia Italy
104 C3 Bisai Japan
116 D3 Bisalpur Uttar Prad. India
116 C3 Bisau Rajasthan India
186 C2 Bisaurín mt. Spain
241 M6 Bisbee AZ U.S.A.
Biscari Sicilia Italy see Acate
163 A4 Biscarrosse France
163 A4 Biscarrosse et de Parentis, Étang de l. France
163 A4 Biscarrosse-Plage France
154 B4 Biscay, Bay of sea France/Spain
264 I3 Biscay Abyssal Plain sea feature N. Atlantic Ocean
193 I3 Bisceglie Italy
173 E2 Bischberg Ger.
172 D2 Bischbrunn Ger.
157 H4 Bischheim France
169 D5 Bischoffen Ger.
169 F4 Bischofferode Ger.
173 F1 Bischofsgrün Ger.
172 C2 Bischofsheim Ger.
169 F5 Bischofsheim an der Rhön Ger.
178 E3 Bischofshofen Austria
173 H3 Bischofsmais Ger.
171 F4 Bischofswerda Ger.
173 G4 Bischofswiesen Ger.
190 E1 Bischofszell Switz.
157 H4 Bischwiller France
262 T2 Biscoe Islands Antarctica
216 □1a Biscoitos Terceira Azores
224 D4 Biscotasing Ont. Can.
193 F2 Bisenti Italy
134 L4 Biser Rus. Fed.
134 L4 Bisert' r. Rus. Fed.
197 H4 Bisertsi Bulg.
108 B4 Bisezhai Yunnan China
203 H6 Bisha Eritrea
108 C2 Bishan Chongqing China
Bishbek Kyrg. see Bishkek
127 H4 Bīsheh Iran
121 H4 Bishkek Kyrg.
117 F5 Bishnupur W. Bengal India
215 F5 Bisho S. Africa
240 H3 Bishop CA U.S.A.
149 H3 Bishop Auckland Durham, England U.K.
146 D6 Bishopbriggs East Dunbartonshire, Scotland U.K.
150 E2 Bishop's Castle Shropshire, England U.K.
150 E3 Bishop's Cleeve Gloucestershire, England U.K.
150 D3 Bishop's Hull Somerset, England U.K.
151 F2 Bishop's Itchington Warwickshire, England U.K.
150 D3 Bishop's Lydeard Somerset, England U.K.
151 H3 Bishop's Stortford Hertfordshire, England U.K.
150 C3 Bishop's Tawton Devon, England U.K.
150 D4 Bishopsteignton Devon, England U.K.
151 F4 Bishop's Waltham Hampshire, England U.K.
146 D6 Bishopton Renfrewshire, Scotland U.K.
231 D5 Bishopville SC U.S.A.
126 E4 Bishrī, Jabal hills Syria
196 D5 Bishti i Pallës pt Albania
100 B1 Bishui Heilong. China
Bishui Henan China see Biyang
215 G4 Bisi S. Africa
193 I5 Bisignano Italy
172 C3 Bisingen Ger.
205 G2 Biskra Alg.
175 K4 Biskupice Lubelskie Pol.
174 G4 Biskupice Opolskie Pol.
177 I3 Biskupice Slovakia
175 H2 Biskupiec Warmińsko-Mazurskie Pol.
175 I2 Biskupiec Warmińsko-Mazurskie Pol.
150 E3 Bisley Gloucestershire, England U.K.
92 C4 Bislig Phil.
236 C2 Bismarck ND U.S.A.
91 K7 Bismarck Archipelago is P.N.G.
76 E2 Bismarck Range mts P.N.G.
91 K7 Bismarck Sea P.N.G.
170 C3 Bismark (Altmark) Ger.
127 F3 Bismil Turkey
141 J3 Bismo Norway
236 C2 Bison SD U.S.A.
122 A3 Bīsotūn Iran
140 L3 Bispgården Sweden
168 F2 Bispingen Ger.
115 D2 Bissamcuttak Orissa India
206 B4 Bissau Guinea-Bissau
207 H5 Bissaula Nigeria
165 F5 Bissen Lux.
169 D3 Bissendorf Ger.
168 E3 Bissendorf (Wedemark) Ger.
223 M5 Bissett Man. Can.
206 C4 Bissikrima Guinea
173 E3 Bissingen Ger.
206 B3 Bissorã Guinea-Bissau
190 D4 Bistagno Italy
222 G3 Bistcho Lake Alta Can.
196 E5 Bistra mt. Macedonia
197 F3 Bistra r. Romania
196 E4 Bistra mt. Yugo.
197 F4 Bistreţ Romania
179 F4 Bistrica Slovenia
197 G2 Bistriţa Romania
197 G2 Bistriţa r. Romania
197 H2 Bistriţa r. Romania
197 G2 Bistriţa Bârgăului Romania
197 G2 Bistriţei, Munţii mts Romania
197 F5 Bistritsa r. Bulg.
116 E4 Biswan Uttar Prad. India
143 I4 Bisztynek Pol.
Bitadoo i. S. Male Maldives see Biyadhoo
208 A4 Bitam Gabon
172 A2 Bitburg Ger.
157 H3 Bitche France
195 F1 Bitetto Italy
116 E4 Bithur Uttar Prad. India
208 C2 Bitkine Chad
127 F3 Bitlis Turkey
196 E5 Bitola Macedonia
Bitolj Macedonia see Bitola
195 F1 Bitonto Italy
124 D3 Bitrān, Jabal hill Saudi Arabia
157 H5 Bitschwiller-lès-Thann France
241 M2 Bitter Creek r. UT U.S.A.
238 E3 Bitter Creek r. WY U.S.A.
171 D4 Bitterfeld Ger.
214 B4 Bitterfontein S. Africa
238 D2 Bitterroot r. MT U.S.A.
238 D2 Bitterroot Range mts ID U.S.A.
240 G3 Bitterwater CA U.S.A.
192 B4 Bitti Sardegna Italy
171 C3 Bittkau Ger.
150 E3 Bitton South Gloucestershire, England U.K.
207 E4 Bittou Burkina
93 C2 Bitung Sulawesi Utara Indon.
215 G4 Bityi S. Africa
135 G6 Bityug r. Rus. Fed.
172 D3 Bitz Ger.
207 I4 Biu Nigeria
183 I2 Biurrun Spain
215 H2 Bivane r. S. Africa
190 E2 Bivio Switz.
197 H2 Bivolari Romania
194 C5 Bivona Sicilia Italy
226 A2 Biwabik MN U.S.A.
104 B3 Biwa-ko l. Japan
197 G2 Bixad Romania
146 □G1 Bixter Shetland, Scotland U.K.
121 K1 Biya r. Rus. Fed.
113 □1 Biyadhoo i. S. Male Maldives
Biyang Anhui China see Yixian
109 E1 Biyang Henan China
121 K1 Biysk Rus. Fed.
215 G4 Bizana S. Africa
161 A5 Bizanet France
163 B5 Bizanos France
161 A5 Bize-Minervois France
103 G6 Bizen Japan
Bizerta Tunisia see Bizerte
205 H1 Bizerte Tunisia
189 B7 Bizerte admin. div. Tunisia
140 □A2 Bjargtangar hd Iceland
140 L1 Bjarkøy Norway
143 E3 Bjärnum Sweden
143 E4 Bjärsjölagård Sweden
140 L3 Bjästa Sweden
196 D4 Bjelasica mts Yugo.
188 G4 Bjelašnica mts Bos.-Herz.
188 F3 Bjelovar Croatia
140 L1 Bjerkvik Norway
168 F1 Bjerreby Denmark
142 C3 Bjerringbro Denmark
143 F1 Björbo Sweden
142 D2 Bjørkelangen Norway
140 L2 Björkfjället mts Sweden
140 L1 Björkliden Sweden
143 G1 Björklinge Sweden
142 D3 Björkö Sweden
140 L2 Björksele Sweden
140 L3 Björna Sweden
142 A1 Bjørnafjorden b. Norway
142 B2 Bjørnanuten mt. Norway
Björneborg Fin. see Pori
268 B2 Bjørnøya i. Arctic Ocean
142 E1 Bjurberget Sweden
140 L3 Bjurholm Sweden
143 F1 Bjursås Sweden
206 D3 Bla Mali
146 B4 Bla Bheinn hill Scotland U.K.
160 C2 Blacé France
196 E4 Blace Kosovo, Srbija Yugo.
196 E4 Blace Srbija Yugo.
174 G5 Blachownia Pol.
223 L5 Black r. Man. Can.
226 D1 Black r. Ont. Can.
224 D3 Black r. Ont. Can.
229 H3 Black r. AR U.S.A.
237 F5 Black r. AR U.S.A.
241 L5 Black r. AZ U.S.A.
227 F4 Black r. MI U.S.A.
231 E5 Black r. SC U.S.A.
226 B3 Black r. WI U.S.A.
146 F6 Blackadder Water r. Scotland U.K.
85 F5 Blackall Qld Austr.
224 B2 Blackbear r. Ont. Can.
226 A2 Blackberry MN U.S.A.
151 F3 Black Bourton Oxfordshire, England U.K.
85 E3 Blackbull Qld Austr.
148 C4 Black Bull Rep. of Ireland
146 F4 Blackburn Aberdeenshire, Scotland U.K.
149 G4 Blackburn Blackburn with Darwen, England U.K.
146 E6 Blackburn West Lothian, Scotland U.K.
149 G4 Blackburn with Darwen admin. div. England U.K.
85 H5 Blackbutt Qld Austr.
240 F2 Black Butte mt. CA U.S.A.
240 F2 Black Butte Lake CA U.S.A.
241 J4 Black Canyon gorge AZ U.S.A.
241 K4 Black Canyon City AZ U.S.A.
262 T2 Black Coast Antarctica
149 F3 Black Combe hill England U.K.
148 E2 Blackcraig Hill hill Scotland U.K.
226 C3 Black Creek WI U.S.A.
234 B1 Black Creek r. PA U.S.A.
222 E4 Black Dome mt. B.C. Can.
150 D4 Black Down Hills England U.K.
236 E2 Blackduck MN U.S.A.
222 H4 Blackfalds Alta Can.
151 F4 Blackfield Hampshire, England U.K.
238 D3 Blackfoot ID U.S.A.
238 D2 Black Foot r. MT U.S.A.
146 E5 Blackford Perth and Kinross, Scotland U.K.
Black Forest mts Ger. see Schwarzwald
149 H4 Black Hill hill England U.K.
238 F2 Black Hills SD U.S.A.
146 E6 Blackhope Scar hill Scotland U.K.
146 D4 Black Isle pen. Scotland U.K.
223 J3 Black Lake Sask. Can.
148 B3 Blacklion Rep. of Ireland
146 E5 Blacklunans Perth and Kinross, Scotland U.K.
241 M5 Black Mesa mt. AZ U.S.A.
241 L3 Black Mesa ridge AZ U.S.A.
150 D3 Blackmoor Gate Devon, England U.K.
151 H3 Blackmore Essex, England U.K.
150 D3 Black Mountain hill Wales U.K.
240 I4 Black Mountain CA U.S.A.
232 B6 Black Mountain KY U.S.A.
150 D3 Black Mountains hills Wales U.K.
241 J4 Black Mountains AZ U.S.A.
212 C4 Black Nossob watercourse Namibia
151 H3 Black Notley Essex, England U.K.
Black Pagoda Orissa India see Konarka
149 F4 Blackpool Blackpool, England U.K.
246 □ Black River Jamaica
227 F3 Black River MI U.S.A.
233 F2 Black River NY U.S.A.
Black River r. Vietnam see Đa, Sông
226 B3 Black River Falls WI U.S.A.
Black Rock hill Jordan see 'Unāb, Jabal al
147 E3 Blackrock Rep. of Ireland
238 C3 Black Rock Desert NV U.S.A.
232 C6 Blacksburg VA U.S.A.
135 G8 Black Sea Asia/Europe
238 E3 Blacks Fork r. WY U.S.A.
233 □J2 Blacks Harbour N.B. Can.
231 D6 Blackshear GA U.S.A.
147 A2 Blacksod Bay Rep. of Ireland
240 H2 Black Springs NV U.S.A.
147 E4 Blackstairs Mountains hills Rep. of Ireland
222 F2 Blackstone r. N.W.T. Can.
232 D6 Blackstone VA U.S.A.
226 C1 Black Sturgeon r. Ont. Can.
83 G2 Black Sugarloaf mt. N.S.W. Austr.
225 K2 Black Tickle Nfld. Can.
147 D2 Blacktown Northern Ireland U.K.
215 H3 Black Umfolozi r. S. Africa
83 G2 Blackville N.S.W. Austr.
206 E4 Black Volta r. Africa alt. Mouhoun, alt. Volta Noire
85 G4 Blackwater Qld Austr.
222 E2 Blackwater r. N.W.T. Can.
147 E2 Blackwater r. N. Ireland/Rep. of Ireland
147 E4 Blackwater Rep. of Ireland
147 E3 Blackwater r. Cavan/Meath Rep. of Ireland
147 D4 Blackwater r. Rep. of Ireland
151 H3 Blackwater r. England U.K.
146 D3 Black Water r. Highland, Scotland U.K.
146 D4 Black Water r. Highland, Scotland U.K.
232 E6 Blackwater r. VA U.S.A.
146 C6 Blackwaterfoot North Ayrshire, Scotland U.K.
146 D5 Blackwater Reservoir Scotland U.K.
148 C3 Blackwatertown Northern Ireland U.K.
87 B7 Blackwood r. W.A. Austr.
150 D3 Blackwood Caerphilly, Wales U.K.
165 E3 Bladel Neth.
150 D2 Blaenau Ffestiniog Gwynedd, Wales U.K.
150 D3 Blaenau Gwent admin. div. Wales U.K.
150 D3 Blaenavon Torfaen, Wales U.K.
150 D3 Blaengarw Bridgend, Wales U.K.
150 D3 Blaengwrach Neath Port Talbot, Wales U.K.
140 K2 Blåfjellshatten mt. Norway
150 E3 Blagdon North Somerset, England U.K.
163 D5 Blagnac France
157 F3 Blagny France
135 H7 Blagodarnyy Rus. Fed.
121 H2 Blagodatnoye Kazakh.
137 H2 Blagodatnoye Rus. Fed.
197 F4 Blagoevgrad Bulg.
121 F1 Blagoveshchenka Severnyy Kazakhstan Kazakh.
121 I1 Blagoveshchenka Rus. Fed.
100 C2 Blagoveshchensk Amurskaya Oblast' Rus. Fed.
134 L5 Blagoveshchensk Respublika Bashkortostan Rus. Fed.
Blagoveshchenskoye Severnyy Kazakhstan Kazakh. see Blagoveshchenka
121 H4 Blagoveshchenskoye Zhambylskaya Oblast' Kazakh.
137 H4 Blahodatne Khersons'ka Oblast' Ukr.
137 F4 Blahodatne Mykolayivs'ka Oblast' Ukr.
137 H4 Blahovishchenka Zaporiz'ka Oblast' Ukr.
137 I4 Blahovishchenka Zaporiz'ka Oblast' Ukr.
173 G2 Blaibach Ger.
146 C5 Blaich Highland, Scotland U.K.
173 E4 Blaichach Ger.
222 H5 Blaikiston, Mount B.C. Can.
158 E4 Blain France
232 E4 Blain PA U.S.A.
226 A3 Blaine MN U.S.A.
238 B1 Blaine WA U.S.A.
223 J4 Blaine Lake Sask. Can.
157 G4 Blainville-sur-l'Eau France
158 E2 Blainville-sur-Mer France
159 F2 Blainville-sur-Orne France
236 D3 Blair NE U.S.A.
226 B3 Blair WI U.S.A.
85 F4 Blair Athol Qld Austr.
146 E5 Blair Atholl Perth and Kinross, Scotland U.K.
215 F1 Blairbeth S. Africa
146 E5 Blairgowrie Perth and Kinross, Scotland U.K.
232 D6 Blairs VA U.S.A.
240 G2 Blairsden CA U.S.A.
234 D2 Blairstown NJ U.S.A.
231 D5 Blairsville GA U.S.A.
232 D4 Blairsville PA U.S.A.
157 E4 Blaise r. France
157 E4 Blaiserives France
160 C1 Blaisy-Bas France
197 F2 Blaj Romania
163 C5 Blajan France
177 L5 Blăjeni Romania
120 E2 Blak Rus. Fed.
Blakang Mati, Pulau i. Sing. see Sentosa
231 C6 Blakely GA U.S.A.
234 C1 Blakely PA U.S.A.
150 E3 Blakeney Gloucestershire, England U.K.
151 I2 Blakeney Norfolk, England U.K.
234 C1 Blakeslee PA U.S.A.
206 C5 Blama Sierra Leone
157 G4 Blâmont France
163 E5 Blan France
187 B6 Blanca Spain
261 G6 Blanca, Bahía b. Arg.
252 A2 Blanca, Cordillera mts Peru
239 F5 Blanca, Sierra mt. NM U.S.A.
159 I4 Blancafort France
239 F4 Blanca Peak CO U.S.A.
183 I4 Blancas Spain
148 C4 Blanchardstown Rep. of Ireland
161 E4 Blanche r. France
161 E4 Blanche ridge France
82 C3 Blanche, Cape S.A. Austr.
82 D2 Blanche, Lake salt flat S.A. Austr.
86 D4 Blanche, Lake salt flat W.A. Austr.
232 B5 Blanchester OH U.S.A.
82 D3 Blanchetown S.A. Austr.
247 □7 Blanchisseuse Trin. and Tob.
258 C3 Blanco r. Arg.
252 D3 Blanco r. Bol.
250 C6 Blanco r. Peru
214 D5 Blanco S. Africa
185 E3 Blanco r. Spain
182 C2 Blancos Spain
225 J3 Blanc-Sablon Que. Can.
83 F3 Bland r. N.S.W. Austr.
232 C6 Bland VA U.S.A.
140 □B2 Blanda r. Iceland
150 E4 Blandford Camp Dorset, England U.K.
150 E4 Blandford Forum Dorset, England U.K.
241 M3 Blanding UT U.S.A.
226 B5 Blandinsville IL U.S.A.
234 C2 Blandon PA U.S.A.
186 F3 Blanes Spain
226 E2 Blaney Park MI U.S.A.
94 B2 Blangkejeren Sumatera Indon.
159 G2 Blangy-le-Château France
156 B3 Blangy-sur-Bresle France
176 D2 Blanice r. Czech Rep.
176 D2 Blanice r. Czech Rep.
143 G3 Blankaholm Sweden
170 C2 Blankenberg Ger.
165 C3 Blankenberge Belgium
169 F4 Blankenburg (Harz) Ger.
171 E3 Blankenfelde Ger.
171 D5 Blankenhain Sachsen Ger.
171 C5 Blankenhain Thüringen Ger.
169 B5 Blankenheim Nordrhein-Westfalen Ger.
171 C4 Blankenheim Sachsen-Anhalt Ger.
169 C5 Blankenrath Ger.
170 E2 Blankensee Ger.
171 C5 Blankenstein Ger.
163 B4 Blanquefort France
251 E2 Blanquilla, Isla i. Venez.
185 H2 Blanquillo mt. Spain
176 F2 Blansko Czech Rep.
211 B8 Blantyre Malawi
162 C3 Blanzac-Porcheresse France
160 B3 Blanzat France
162 C2 Blanzay France
160 C2 Blanzy France
164 E2 Blaricum Neth.
147 C5 Blarney Rep. of Ireland
232 D3 Blasdell NY U.S.A.
163 B4 Blasimon France
141 I3 Blaskavlen mt. Norway
140 K3 Blåstöten mt. Sweden
174 G4 Błaszki Pol.
176 C2 Blatná Czech Rep.
176 G3 Blatné Slovakia
165 C4 Blaton Belgium
140 L2 Blattniksele Sweden
172 D3 Blaubeuren Ger.
172 D2 Blaufelden Ger.
172 D3 Blaustein Ger.
Blaven hill Scotland U.K. see Bla Bheinn
158 C4 Blavet r. France
134 B2 Blåviksjön Sweden
161 B3 Blavozy France
149 H3 Blaydon Tyne and Wear, England U.K.
162 B3 Blaye France
163 E4 Blaye-les-Mines France
161 E4 Blayeul Sommet mt. France
83 G3 Blayney N.S.W. Austr.
84 B2 Blaze, Point N.T. Austr.
136 D2 Blazhove Ukr.
175 J4 Błaziny Górne Pol.
179 H1 Blažovice Czech Rep.
175 K6 Błażowa Pol.
185 E2 Blázquez Spain
151 I3 Blean Kent, England U.K.
168 F2 Bleckede Ger.
186 C2 Blecua Spain
179 F4 Bled Slovenia
175 I4 Błędów Pol.
174 G2 Błędowo Pol.
174 D3 Bledzew Pol.
95 F4 Blega Jawa Timur Indon.
179 F4 Blegoš mt. Slovenia
165 C4 Bléharies Belgium
169 B5 Bleialf Ger.
179 F4 Bleiburg Austria
169 F4 Bleicherode Ger.
169 D5 Bleidenstadt Ger.
178 E3 Bleikogel mt. Austria
164 D2 Bleiswijk Neth.
168 F1 Blekendorf Ger.
143 F3 Blekinge county Sweden
149 F3 Blencathra hill England U.K.
156 C2 Blendecques France
168 E3 Blender Ger.
156 C5 Bléneau France
224 D5 Blenheim Ont. Can.
81 D4 Blenheim South I. N.Z.
151 F3 Blenheim Palace tourist site England U.K.
157 G4 Blénod-lès-Pont-à-Mousson France
157 F4 Blénod-lès-Toul France
161 D4 Bléone r. France
192 E2 Blera Italy
156 D3 Blérancourt France
162 C1 Bléré France
165 F3 Blerick Neth.
186 C3 Blesa Spain
164 D3 Bleskensgraaf Neth.
161 B3 Blesle France
214 E2 Blesmanspos S. Africa
147 E3 Blessington Rep. of Ireland
147 E3 Blessington Lakes Rep. of Ireland
160 A2 Blet France
151 G2 Bletchley Milton Keynes, England U.K.
142 C2 Bletoppen mt. Norway
160 D2 Bletterans France
208 F4 Bleus, Monts mts Dem. Rep. Congo
151 F3 Blewbury Oxfordshire, England U.K.
168 D2 Blexen (Nordenham) Ger.
177 J3 Blh r. Slovakia
205 F1 Blida Alg.
168 E2 Bliedersdorf Ger.
172 B2 Blies r. Ger.
172 B2 Blieskastel Ger.
156 E4 Bligny France
160 C1 Bligny-sur-Ouche France
164 G1 Blijham Neth.
182 E1 Blimea Spain
179 F2 Blindenmarkt Austria
170 E2 Blindow Ger.
224 D4 Blind River Ont. Can.
215 F5 Blinkwater S. Africa
82 D2 Blinman S.A. Austr.
190 D2 Blinnenhorn mt. Italy/Switz.
238 D3 Bliss ID U.S.A.
227 F5 Blissfield MI U.S.A.
232 C4 Blissfield OH U.S.A.
151 G2 Blisworth Northamptonshire, England U.K.
95 F5 Blitar Jawa Timur Indon.
174 G4 Blizanów Pol.
173 G2 Blížejov Czech Rep.
176 E3 Blížkovice Czech Rep.
Bliznetsy Ukr. see Blyznyuky
Bliznyuki Ukr. see Blyznyuky
175 I4 Bliżyn Pol.
233 H4 Block Island RI U.S.A.
233 H4 Block Island i. RI U.S.A.
233 H4 Block Island Sound sea chan. RI U.S.A.
151 F2 Blockley Gloucestershire, England U.K.
215 H2 Bloedrivier S. Africa
215 F3 Bloemfontein S. Africa
215 E2 Bloemhof S. Africa
215 E2 Bloemhof Dam S. Africa
159 H4 Blois France
164 E2 Blokzijl Neth.
169 E4 Blomberg Ger.
214 C4 Blomberg se Vloer salt pan S. Africa
142 A1 Blomøy i. Norway
140 □C2 Blöndulón l. Iceland
140 □B2 Blönduós Iceland
175 H3 Błonie Pol.
175 I3 Błonie Pol.
171 D4 Blönsdorf Ger.
159 G2 Blonville-sur-Mer France
84 B5 Bloods Range mts N.T. Austr.
223 L5 Bloodvein r. Man. Can.
147 C1 Bloody Foreland pt Rep. of Ireland
226 B3 Bloomer WI U.S.A.
227 I4 Bloomfield Ont. Can.
236 E3 Bloomfield IA U.S.A.
230 C4 Bloomfield IN U.S.A.
237 F4 Bloomfield MO U.S.A.
239 F4 Bloomfield NM U.S.A.
85 F2 Bloomfield River Qld Austr.
235 D1 Bloomingburg NY U.S.A.
235 D1 Bloomingdale NJ U.S.A.
234 C2 Blooming Glen PA U.S.A.
235 D1 Blooming Grove NY U.S.A.
234 C1 Blooming Grove PA U.S.A.
226 A4 Blooming Prairie MN U.S.A.
226 C5 Bloomington IL U.S.A.
230 C4 Bloomington IN U.S.A.
226 A3 Bloomington MN U.S.A.
227 I5 Bloomsburg PA U.S.A.
85 G4 Bloomsbury Qld Austr.
234 C2 Bloomsbury NJ U.S.A.
95 E4 Blora Jawa Tengah Indon.
227 I5 Blossburg PA U.S.A.
221 P3 Blosseville Kyst coastal area Greenland
160 F1 Blotzheim France
214 B5 Bloubergstrand S. Africa
215 F3 Bloudrif S. Africa
231 C6 Blountstown FL U.S.A.
232 B6 Blountville TN U.S.A.
163 C5 Blousson-Sérian France
176 C2 Blovice Czech Rep.
170 C2 Blowatz Ger.
151 F2 Bloxham Oxfordshire, England U.K.
149 H4 Blubberhouses North Yorkshire, England U.K.
178 A3 Bludenz Austria
178 A3 Bludesch Austria
222 D3 Blue r. B.C. Can.
237 E5 Blue r. OK U.S.A.
148 B4 Blue Ball Rep. of Ireland
234 B2 Blue Ball PA U.S.A.
234 C2 Blue Bell PA U.S.A.
241 L2 Blue Bell Knoll mt. UT U.S.A.
222 F3 Blueberry r. B.C. Can.
215 E5 Blue Cliff S. Africa
Blue Creek r. Mex. see Azul
241 J3 Blue Diamond NV U.S.A.
236 E3 Blue Earth MN U.S.A.
236 E2 Blue Earth r. MN U.S.A.
232 C6 Bluefield VA U.S.A.
232 C6 Bluefield WV U.S.A.
246 □ Bluefields Jamaica
242 □J6 Bluefields Nic.
147 B4 Blueford Rep. of Ireland
215 F4 Bluegums S. Africa
233 □I2 Blue Hill ME U.S.A.
236 D3 Blue Hill NE U.S.A.
232 D4 Blue Knob hill PA U.S.A.
225 J3 Blue Mountain hill Nfld. Can.
117 H5 Blue Mountain Mizoram India
234 B2 Blue Mountain ridge PA U.S.A.
233 F3 Blue Mountain Lake NY U.S.A.
246 □ Blue Mountain Peak Jamaica
83 G3 Blue Mountains N.S.W. Austr.
246 □ Blue Mountains Jamaica
81 B7 Blue Mountains South I. N.Z.
238 C2 Blue Mountains OR U.S.A.
84 D2 Blue Mud Bay N.T. Austr.
210 B2 Blue Nile r. Eth. alt. Ābay Wenz (Ethiopia), alt. Azraq, Bahr el (Sudan)
210 B2 Blue Nile state Sudan
236 D4 Blue Rapids KS U.S.A.
231 C5 Blue Ridge GA U.S.A.
232 D6 Blue Ridge VA U.S.A.
232 C6 Blue Ridge mts VA U.S.A.
222 G4 Blue River B.C. Can.
147 C2 Blue Stack Mountains hills Rep. of Ireland
85 G4 Bluff Qld Austr.
81 B7 Bluff South I. N.Z.
241 M3 Bluff UT U.S.A.
232 B6 Bluff City TN U.S.A.
241 L1 Bluffdale UT U.S.A.
86 E3 Bluff Face Range hills W.A. Austr.
87 C7 Bluff Knoll mt. W.A. Austr.
87 B5 Bluff Point W.A. Austr.
230 C3 Bluffton IN U.S.A.
232 B4 Bluffton OH U.S.A.
179 H3 Blumau in Steiermark Austria
172 C4 Blumberg Baden-Württemberg Ger.
170 E3 Blumberg Brandenburg Ger.
255 C8 Blumenau Brazil
170 E2 Blumenhagen Ger.
170 E2 Blumenholz Ger.
170 D2 Blumenthal Ger.
190 C2 Blümlisalp mt. Switz.
236 C2 Blunt SD U.S.A.
222 F5 Blustry Mountain B.C. Can.
238 B3 Bly OR U.S.A.
137 F2 Blystova Ukr.
84 C2 Blyth r. N.T. Austr.
227 G4 Blyth Ont. Can.
149 H2 Blyth Northumberland, England U.K.
149 H4 Blyth Nottinghamshire, England U.K.
151 I2 Blyth r. England U.K.
146 E6 Blyth Bridge Scottish Borders, Scotland U.K.
215 H3 Blythdale Beach S. Africa
241 J5 Blythe CA U.S.A.
237 F5 Blytheville AR U.S.A.
87 F5 Blyth Range hills W.A. Austr.
149 I4 Blyton Lincolnshire, England U.K.
137 I3 Blyznyuky Ukr.
142 C2 Bø Norway
206 C5 Bo Sierra Leone
92 B3 Boac Phil.
242 □I6 Boaco Nic.
182 D4 Boada Spain
183 G4 Boadilla del Monte Spain
183 F2 Boadilla de Rioseco Spain
257 E4 Boa Esperança Brazil
256 C4 Boa Esperança do Sul Brazil
107 G5 Bo'ai Henan China
108 C4 Bo'ai Yunnan China
182 D1 Boal Spain
182 B3 Boalhosa Port.
208 C3 Boali C.A.R.
232 E4 Boalsburg PA U.S.A.
254 E5 Boa Nova Brazil
191 G3 Boara Pisani Italy
232 C4 Boardman OH U.S.A.
235 E1 Boardmans Bridge CT U.S.A.
146 D4 Boath Highland, Scotland U.K.
85 F5 Boatman Qld Austr.
146 E4 Boat of Garten Highland, Scotland U.K.
184 □ Boaventura Madeira
254 F3 Boa Viagem Brazil
251 F4 Boa Vista Brazil
206 □ Boa Vista i. Cape Verde
182 B5 Boa Vista Port.
83 F3 Bobadah N.S.W. Austr.
185 F3 Bobadilla Andalucía Spain
183 H2 Bobadilla La Rioja Spain
183 E3 Bobadilla del Campo Spain
108 D4 Bobai Guangxi China
213 □K1 Bobaomby, Tanjona c. Madag.
171 D4 Bobbau Ger.
115 D2 Bobbili Andhra Prad. India
190 E4 Bobbio Italy
190 C4 Bobbio Pellice Italy
227 H3 Bobcaygeon Ont. Can.
172 C2 Bobenheim-Roxheim Ger.
136 D2 Bober r. Ukr.
136 B3 Boberka Ukr.
182 D1 Bobia mt. Spain
156 C4 Bobigny France
173 F4 Böbing Ger.
173 E3 Bobingen Ger.
170 C2 Bobitz Ger.
172 D3 Böblingen Ger.
175 M4 Bobly Ukr.
206 D4 Bobo-Dioulasso Burkina
174 E2 Bobolice Pol.
92 C3 Bobon Phil.
213 F4 Bobonong Botswana
182 B2 Boborás Spain
177 L4 Bobota Romania
Bobotov Kuk mt. Yugo. see Durmitor
197 F4 Bobovdol Bulg.
177 L3 Bobove Ukr.
175 I6 Bobowa Pol.
174 G2 Bobowo Pol.
121 G4 Boboyob, Gora mt. Uzbek.
138 G4 Bobr Belarus
138 G4 Bobr r. Belarus
174 D3 Bóbr r. Pol.
173 H2 Böbrach Ger.
Bobriki Rus. Fed. see Novomoskovsk
Bobrinets Ukr. see Bobrynets'
135 H6 Bobrov Rus. Fed.
177 I2 Bobrov Slovakia
177 I2 Bobrovec Slovakia
Bobrovitsa Ukr. see Bobrovytsya
137 I2 Bobrovo-Dvorskoye Rus. Fed.
137 F2 Bobrovytsya Ukr.
171 G4 Bobrowice Pol.
174 G3 Bobrowniki Kujawsko-Pomorskie Pol.
175 L2 Bobrowniki Podlaskie Pol.
175 H2 Bobrowo Pol.
Bobruysk Belarus see Babruysk
138 F5 Bobryk r. Belarus
136 F4 Bobryk-Druhyy Ukr.
137 G3 Bobrynets' Ukr.
137 I2 Bobryshevo Rus. Fed.
108 B1 Bobso Sichuan China
232 D5 Bobtown PA U.S.A.
213 □J4 Boby mt. Madag.
179 G4 Boč hill Slovenia
182 D4 Bocacara Spain
183 F2 Boca de Huérgano Spain
245 F4 Boca del Río Mex.
252 D2 Boca do Acre Brazil
247 □7 Boca Grande r. mouth Trin. and Tob./Venez.
257 E5 Bocaina de Minas Brazil
187 C6 Bocairent Spain
257 F2 Bocaiúva Brazil
256 C6 Bocaiúva do Sul Brazil
206 D5 Bocanda Côte d'Ivoire
177 J6 Bočar Vojvodina, Srbija Yugo.
208 B3 Bocaranga C.A.R.
231 D7 Boca Raton FL U.S.A.
242 □J7 Bocas del Toro Panama
242 □J7 Bocas del Toro, Archipiélago del is Panama
195 F3 Bocchigliero Italy
183 G3 Boceguillas Spain
176 F5 Bocfölde Hungary
175 I6 Bochnia Pol.
165 E3 Bocholt Belgium
169 B4 Bocholt Ger.
176 C1 Bochov Czech Rep.
169 C4 Bochum Ger.
213 F4 Bochum S. Africa
169 F3 Bockenem Ger.
173 F3 Bockhorn Bayern Ger.
168 D2 Bockhorn Niedersachsen Ger.
168 C2 Bockhorst Ger.
175 L3 Boćki Pol.
192 B2 Bocognano Corse France
209 B8 Bocoio Angola
177 J4 Boconád Hungary
165 D4 Bocq r. Belgium
177 J3 Bőcs Hungary
177 I5 Bócsa Hungary
197 E3 Bocşa Romania
177 L4 Bocşa Romania
177 K5 Bocsig Romania
208 C3 Boda C.A.R.
141 K3 Boda Dalarna Sweden
143 G3 Böda Kalmar Sweden
175 L5 Bodaczów Pol.
143 F3 Bodafors Sweden
143 F3 Boda glasbruk Sweden
177 H4 Bodajk Hungary
83 G4 Bodalla N.S.W. Austr.
87 C6 Bodallin W.A. Austr.
131 M4 Bodaybo Rus. Fed.
146 G4 Boddam Aberdeenshire, Scotland U.K.
146 □G2 Boddam Shetland, Scotland U.K.
246 B3 Bodden Town Cayman Is
170 C2 Boddin Ger.
87 C7 Boddington W.A. Austr.
171 C4 Bode r. Ger.
240 F2 Bodega Head hd CA U.S.A.
164 D2 Bodegraven Neth.
172 C3 Bodelshausen Ger.
150 D1 Bodelwyddan Denbighshire, Wales U.K.
140 M2 Boden Sweden
169 E4 Bodenfelde Ger.
150 E2 Bodenham Herefordshire, England U.K.
172 C2 Bodenheim Ger.
173 G3 Bodenkirchen Ger.
173 H2 Bodenmais Ger.
172 D4 Bodensee l. Ger./Switz.
168 F3 Bodenteich Ger.
169 E4 Bodenwerder Ger.
179 F3 Bodenwies mt. Austria
173 G2 Bodenwöhr Ger.
147 D3 Boderg, Lough l. Rep. of Ireland
207 G4 Bode-Sadu Nigeria
197 H2 Bodeşti Romania
240 H4 Bodfish CA U.S.A.
114 C2 Bodhan Andhra Prad. India
117 F4 Bodh Gaya Bihar India
151 F2 Bodicote Oxfordshire, England U.K.
240 H2 Bodie CA U.S.A.
114 C4 Bodinayakkanur Tamil Nadu India
184 D2 Bodión r. Spain
172 D4 Bodman Ger.
150 C4 Bodmin Cornwall, England U.K.
150 C4 Bodmin Moor moorland England U.K.
172 D4 Bodnegg Ger.
140 K2 Bodø Norway
254 F3 Bodocó Brazil
172 D4 Bodolz Ger.
184 D2 Bodonal de la Sierra Spain
253 F4 Bodoquena Brazil
253 F5 Bodoquena, Serra da hills Brazil
177 K3 Bodrog r. Hungary
177 K3 Bodroghalom Hungary

199 E3 **Bodrum** Turkey
140 K3 **Bodsjö** Sweden
140 M2 **Bodträskfors** Sweden
113 □1 **Boduhali** *i. N. Male* Maldives
177 J3 **Bódva** *r.* Hungary
177 J3 **Bodva** *r.* Slovakia
177 J3 **Bódvaszilas** Hungary
175 I3 **Bodzanów** Pol.
175 I5 **Bodzentyn** Pol.
163 C4 **Boé** France
165 D3 **Boechout** Belgium
183 F3 **Boecillo** Spain
183 F2 **Boedo** *r.* Spain
160 E2 **Boëge** France
214 D3 **Boegoeberg** S. Africa
164 E3 **Boekel** Neth.
165 C3 **Boekhoute** Belgium
160 C3 **Boën** France
208 D5 **Boende** Dem. Rep. Congo
214 C5 **Boerboonfontein** S. Africa
237 D6 **Boerne** *TX* U.S.A.
215 F5 **Boesmans** *r.* S. Africa
237 F6 **Boeuf** *r. LA* U.S.A.
182 D2 **Boeza** Spain
182 D2 **Boeza** *r.* Spain
256 C5 **Bofete** Brazil
206 B4 **Boffa** Guinea
161 C4 **Boffres** France
169 E4 **Boffzen** Ger.
142 C2 **Bøfjell** *hill* Norway
177 J4 **Bogács** Hungary
182 D4 **Bogajo** Spain
96 A3 **Bogale** Myanmar
96 A4 **Bogale** *r.* Myanmar
237 F6 **Bogalusa** *LA* U.S.A.
83 F2 **Bogan** *r. N.S.W.* Austr.
207 E3 **Bogandé** Burkina
83 F3 **Bogan Gate** *N.S.W.* Austr.
85 F4 **Bogantungan** *Qld* Austr.
185 H2 **Bogarra** Spain
196 D3 **Bogatić** *Srbija* Yugo.
134 J4 **Bogatye Saby** Rus. Fed.
174 C5 **Bogatynia** Pol.
126 D3 **Boğazlıyan** Turkey
111 D6 **Bogcang Zangbo** *r. Xizang* China
177 K6 **Bogda** Romania
110 E3 **Bogda Feng** *mt. Xinjiang* China
197 G4 **Bogdan** *mt.* Bulg.
197 G4 **Bogdana** Romania
197 F5 **Bogdanci** Macedonia
177 L4 **Bogdand** Romania
174 D3 **Bogdaniec** Pol.
Bogdanovka Georgia *see* **Ninotsminda**
120 C1 **Bogdanovka** Rus. Fed.
106 A3 **Bogda Shan** *mts* China
121 H1 **Bogembay** Kazakh.
173 G3 **Bogen** Ger.
140 L1 **Bogen** Norway
142 D4 **Bogense** Denmark
83 G2 **Boggabilla** *Qld* Austr.
83 G2 **Boggabri** *N.S.W.* Austr.
78 □3a **Boggenatjen** *i. Kwajalein* Marshall Is
147 B4 **Boggeragh Mountains** *hills* Rep. of Ireland
78 □3a **Boggerik** *i. Kwajalein* Marshall Is
87 C4 **Boggola** *hill W.A.* Austr.
247 □2 **Boggy Peak** *hill Antigua* Antigua and Barbuda
Boghari Alg. *see* **Ksar el Boukhari**
85 F4 **Bogie** *r. Qld* Austr.
146 F4 **Bogie** *r. Scotland* U.K.
190 E4 **Bogliasco** Italy
190 D2 **Bognanco** Italy
146 F4 **Bogniebrae** *Aberdeenshire, Scotland* U.K.
151 G4 **Bognor Regis** *West Sussex, England* U.K.
156 E3 **Bogny-sur-Meuse** France
207 I4 **Bogo** Cameroon
170 D1 **Bogø** Denmark
170 D1 **Bogo** *i.* Denmark
92 C4 **Bogo** Phil.
Bogodukhov Ukr. *see* **Bohodukhiv**
121 G1 **Bogodukhovka** Kazakh.
147 D3 **Bog of Allen** *reg.* Rep. of Ireland
121 G1 **Bogolyubovo** Kazakh.
139 I4 **Bogolyubovo** *Smolenskaya Oblast'* Rus. Fed.
139 M3 **Bogolyubovo** *Vladimirskaya Oblast'* Rus. Fed.
83 F4 **Bogong, Mount** *Vic.* Austr.
94 D4 **Bogor** *Jawa Barat* Indon.
175 J5 **Bogoria** Pol.
139 L5 **Bogoroditsk** Rus. Fed.
139 J5 **Bogoroditskoye** Rus. Fed.
134 H4 **Bogorodsk** Rus. Fed.
100 G1 **Bogorodskoye** *Khabarovskiy Kray* Rus. Fed.
134 J4 **Bogorodskoye** *Kirovskaya Oblast'* Rus. Fed.
250 C3 **Bogotá** Col.
177 K3 **Bogota** *hill* Slovakia
130 J4 **Bogotol** Rus. Fed.
134 I4 **Bogovarovo** Rus. Fed.
Bogoyavlenskoye *Tambovskaya Oblast'* Rus. Fed. *see* **Pervomayskiy**
117 G4 **Bogra** Bangl.
131 K4 **Boguchany** Rus. Fed.
135 H6 **Boguchar** Rus. Fed.
137 K3 **Boguchar** *r.* Rus. Fed.
175 J6 **Boguchwała** Pol.
206 B2 **Bogué** Maur.
237 F6 **Bogue Chitto** *r. MS* U.S.A.
Boguslav Ukr. *see* **Bohuslav**
174 E5 **Boguszów-Gorce** Pol.
246 □ **Bog Walk** Jamaica
177 H5 **Bogyiszló** Hungary
95 F2 **Boh** *r.* Indon.
107 H4 **Bo Hai** *g.* China
107 I4 **Bohai Haixia** *sea chan.* China
156 D3 **Bohain-en-Vermandois** France
107 H4 **Bohai Wan** *b.* China
158 B3 **Bohars** France
136 C3 **Bohdan** Ukr.
137 H4 **Bohdanivka** Ukr.
179 G2 **Böheimkirchen** Austria
176 D1 **Bohemia** *reg.* Czech Rep.
235 E2 **Bohemia** *NY* U.S.A.
86 E3 **Bohemia Downs** *W.A.* Austr.
Bohemian Forest *mts* Ger. *see* **Böhmer Wald**
147 C4 **Boher** Rep. of Ireland
148 B4 **Boheraphuca** Rep. of Ireland
207 F5 **Bohicon** Benin
179 E4 **Bohinjska Bistrica** Slovenia
179 E4 **Bohinjsko jezero** *l.* Slovenia
172 C2 **Böhl** Ger.
171 D4 **Böhlen** Ger.
171 D4 **Böhlitz-Ehrenberg** Ger.
215 G3 **Bohlokong** S. Africa
168 E3 **Böhme** Ger.
168 E3 **Böhme** *r.* Ger.
Böhmen *reg.* Czech Rep. *see* **Bohemia**
173 G2 **Böhmer Wald** *mts* Ger.
169 D3 **Bohmte** Ger.
170 D3 **Böhne** Ger.
137 H2 **Bohodukhiv** Ukr.
137 G3 **Bohodukhivka** Ukr.
92 C4 **Bohol** *i.* Phil.
147 B3 **Bohola** Rep. of Ireland
92 C4 **Bohol Sea** Phil.
92 B4 **Bohol Strait** Phil.
176 G5 **Böhönye** Hungary
179 G4 **Bohor** *mt.* Slovenia
136 C3 **Bohorodchany** Ukr.
183 E4 **Bohoyo** Spain
110 D3 **Bohu** *Xinjiang* China
177 H2 **Bohumín** Czech Rep.
176 G2 **Bohuňovice** Czech Rep.
136 F3 **Bohuslav** Ukr.
176 C2 **Bohutín** Czech Rep.
177 L4 **Boianu Mare** Romania
214 D3 **Boichoko** S. Africa
215 F2 **Boikhutso** S. Africa
86 D3 **Boileau, Cape** *W.A.* Austr.
234 A2 **Boiling Springs** *PA* U.S.A.
96 A2 **Boinu** *r.* Myanmar
254 F5 **Boipeba, Ilha** *i.* Brazil
182 B2 **Boiro** Spain
256 B3 **Bois** *r.* Brazil
156 C4 **Boiscommun** France
160 E2 **Bois-d'Amont** France
236 D2 **Bois de Sioux** *r. MN* U.S.A.
238 C3 **Boise** *ID* U.S.A.
238 C3 **Boise** *r. ID* U.S.A.
237 C4 **Boise City** *OK* U.S.A.
158 D3 **Boisgervilly** France
156 B3 **Bois-Guillaume** France
156 C4 **Bois-le-Roi** France
161 C5 **Boisseron** France
163 E4 **Boisset** France
161 C4 **Boisset-et-Gaujac** France
223 K5 **Boissevain** *Man.* Can.
163 E5 **Boissezon** France
191 H2 **Boite** *r.* Italy
215 E2 **Boitumelong** S. Africa
256 D5 **Boituva** Brazil
170 E2 **Boitzenburg** Ger.
162 C2 **Boivre** *r.* France
168 F2 **Boize** *r.* Ger.
168 F2 **Boizenburg** Ger.
174 D4 **Bojadła** Pol.
193 G3 **Bojano** Italy
175 J5 **Bojanów** Pol.
174 E4 **Bojanowo** Pol.
92 B2 **Bojeador, Cape** Phil.
177 H3 **Bojná** Slovakia
177 H3 **Bojnice** Slovakia
197 E4 **Bojnik** *Srbija* Yugo.
122 D2 **Bojnūrd** Iran
95 E4 **Bojonegoro** *Jawa Timur* Indon.
207 H5 **Boju-Ega** Nigeria
Bokaak *atoll* Marshall Is *see* **Majuro**
111 E4 **Bokadaban Feng** *mt. Qinghai/Xinjiang* China
117 H4 **Bokajan** *Assam* India
117 F5 **Bokaro** *Bihar* India
206 B4 **Boké** Guinea
168 D2 **Bokel** Ger.
214 B5 **Bokfontein** S. Africa
83 F2 **Bokhara** *r. N.S.W.* Austr.
207 H5 **Bokito** Cameroon
168 E1 **Böklund** Ger.
209 B6 **Boko** Congo
177 H4 **Bokod** Hungary
Bokombayevskoye Kyrg. *see* **Bökönbaev**
121 I4 **Bökönbaev** Kyrg.
Bokonbayevo Kyrg. *see* **Bökönbaev**
177 K4 **Bököny** Hungary
202 C6 **Bokoro** Chad
209 B6 **Boko-Songho** Congo
Bokovo-Antratsit Ukr. *see* **Antratsyt**
135 H6 **Bokovskaya** Rus. Fed.
215 G2 **Boksburg** S. Africa
139 I2 **Boksitogorsk** Rus. Fed.
214 C2 **Bokspits** S. Africa
100 F2 **Boktor** Rus. Fed.
208 D5 **Bokungu** Dem. Rep. Congo
Bokurdak Turkm. *see* **Bakhardok**
202 B6 **Bol** Chad
244 C3 **Bola del Viejo, Cerro** *mt.* Mex.
206 B4 **Bolama** Guinea-Bissau
123 F4 **Bolan** *r.* Pak.
208 E3 **Bolanda, Jebel** *mt.* Sudan
172 C2 **Bolanden** Ger.
160 E1 **Bolandoz** France
190 E4 **Bolano** Italy
244 B3 **Bolaños** *r.* Mex.
185 G2 **Bolaños de Calatrava** Spain
159 G2 **Bolbec** France
177 H5 **Bölcske** Hungary
122 B4 **Boldajī** Iran
170 E2 **Boldekow** Ger.
168 E1 **Bolderslev** Denmark
177 K3 **Boldogkőváralja** Hungary
149 H3 **Boldon** *Tyne and Wear, England* U.K.
151 F4 **Boldre** *Hampshire, England* U.K.
197 H3 **Boldu** Romania
122 D1 **Boldumsaz** Turkm.
177 K6 **Böldur** Romania
177 J3 **Boldva** Hungary
110 C2 **Bole** *Xinjiang* China
206 E4 **Bole** Ghana
186 C2 **Bolea** Spain
136 B3 **Bolekhiv** Ukr.
177 G3 **Boleráz** Slovakia
175 I5 **Bolesław** Pol.
174 D4 **Bolesławiec** Pol.
174 G4 **Bolesławiec** Pol.
174 C3 **Boleszkowice** Pol.
135 J5 **Bolgar** *Respublika Tatarstan* Rus. Fed.
206 E4 **Bolgatanga** Ghana
Bolgrad Ukr. *see* **Bolhrad**
136 E5 **Bolhrad** Ukr.
100 D3 **Boli** *Heilong.* China
140 M2 **Boliden** Sweden
Bolifuri *i. S. Male* Maldives *see* **Bolifushi**
113 □1 **Bolifushi** *i. S. Male* Maldives
175 I3 **Bolimów** Pol.
92 A2 **Bolinao** Phil.
197 G3 **Bolintin-Vale** Romania
250 C2 **Bolívar** *dept* Col.
252 A1 **Bolívar** Peru
237 E4 **Bolivar** *MO* U.S.A.
232 D3 **Bolivar** *NY* U.S.A.
237 F5 **Bolivar** *TN* U.S.A.
251 F3 **Bolívar** *state* Venez.
252 D4 **Bolivia** *country* S. America
197 E4 **Boljevac** *Srbija* Yugo.
128 A1 **Bolkar Dağları** *mts* Turkey
139 K5 **Bolkhov** Rus. Fed.
227 F1 **Bolkow** *Ont.* Can.
170 C1 **Bölkow** Ger.
174 E5 **Bolków** Pol.
172 D3 **Boll** Ger.
142 E3 **Bollebygd** Sweden
161 C4 **Bollène** France
190 C3 **Bollengo** Italy
190 C2 **Bolligen** Switz.
168 E1 **Bollingstedt** Ger.
149 G4 **Bollington** *Cheshire, England* U.K.
141 L3 **Bollnäs** Sweden
83 F2 **Bollon** *Qld* Austr.
142 E2 **Bollsbyn** Sweden
172 B4 **Bollschweil** Ger.
140 L3 **Bollstabruk** Sweden
166 E3 **Bollstedt** Ger.
184 D3 **Bollullos Par del Condado** Spain
157 H5 **Bollwiller** France
143 E3 **Bolmen** *l.* Sweden
151 G2 **Bolnhurst** *Bedfordshire, England* U.K.
129 D3 **Bolnisi** Georgia
208 C5 **Bolobo** Dem. Rep. Congo
92 B5 **Bolod Islands** Phil.
191 G4 **Bologna** Italy
191 G4 **Bologna** *prov. Emilia-Romagna* Italy
157 F4 **Bologne** France
250 C6 **Bolognesi** *Loreto* Peru
252 B2 **Bolognesi** *Ucayali* Peru
194 C5 **Bolognetta** *Sicilia* Italy
193 F2 **Bolognola** Italy
139 H3 **Bologovo** Rus. Fed.
139 J3 **Bologoye** Rus. Fed.
215 E3 **Bolokanang** S. Africa
139 K4 **Bolokhovo** Rus. Fed.
208 D4 **Bolombo** *r.* Dem. Rep. Congo
Bolon' Rus. Fed. *see* **Achan**
243 H4 **Bolonchén de Rejón** Mex.
207 H6 **Bolondo** Equat. Guinea
92 B5 **Bolong** Phil.
209 B7 **Bolongongo** Angola
192 A4 **Bolotana** *Sardegna* Italy
215 F4 **Bolotwa** S. Africa
96 D4 **Bolovens, Phouphieng** *plat.* Laos
117 F5 **Bolpur** *W. Bengal* India
129 F4 **Bolqarçay** *r.* Azer.
258 C3 **Bolsa, Cerro** *mt.* Arg.
192 D2 **Bolsena** Italy
192 D2 **Bolsena, Lago di** *l.* Italy
138 C4 **Bol'shakovo** Rus. Fed.
129 E1 **Bol'shaya Areshevka** Rus. Fed.
134 J4 **Bol'shaya Atnya** Rus. Fed.
137 J1 **Bol'shaya Bereyka** Rus. Fed.
120 B1 **Bol'shaya Chernigovka** Rus. Fed.
120 F1 **Bol'shaya Churakovka** Kazakh.
120 B1 **Bol'shaya Glushitsa** Rus. Fed.
134 F2 **Bol'shaya Imandra, Ozero** *l.* Rus. Fed.
137 I2 **Bol'shaya Khalan'** Rus. Fed.
134 I4 **Bol'shaya Kokshaga** *r.* Rus. Fed.
137 K1 **Bol'shaya Lipovitsa** Rus. Fed.
135 H7 **Bol'shaya Martinovka** Rus. Fed.
Bol'shaya Novoselka Ukr. *see* **Velyka Novosilka**
134 M1 **Bol'shaya Oyu** *r.* Rus. Fed.
134 M2 **Bol'shaya Rogovaya** *r.* Rus. Fed.
134 L2 **Bol'shaya Synya** *r.* Rus. Fed.
Bol'shaya Tsarevshchina *Samarskaya Oblast'* Rus. Fed. *see* **Volzhskiy**
134 K4 **Bol'shaya Usa** Rus. Fed.
139 I2 **Bol'shaya Vishera** Rus. Fed.
121 I2 **Bol'shaya Vladimirovka** Kazakh.
137 J2 **Bol'she Bykovo** Rus. Fed.
137 J4 **Bol'shekrepinskaya** Rus. Fed.
121 K2 **Bol'shenarymskoye** Kazakh.
139 J3 **Bol'she-Ploskoye** Rus. Fed.
137 I2 **Bol'shetroitskoye** Rus. Fed.
131 L2 **Bol'shevik, Ostrov** *i. Severnaya Zemlya* Rus. Fed.
134 K2 **Bol'shezemel'skaya Tundra** *lowland* Rus. Fed.
120 D3 **Bol'shiye Barsuki, Peski** *des.* Kazakh.
137 J4 **Bol'shiye Saly** Rus. Fed.
121 I4 **Bol'shoy Aksu** Kazakh.
131 Q3 **Bol'shoy Aluy** *r.* Rus. Fed.
131 R3 **Bol'shoy Anyuy** *r.* Rus. Fed.
131 M2 **Bol'shoy Begichev, Ostrov** *i.* Rus. Fed.
138 G1 **Bol'shoy Berezovyy, Ostrov** *i.* Rus. Fed.
121 J2 **Bol'shoy Bukon'** Kazakh.
137 I2 **Bol'shoye Gorodishche** Rus. Fed.
135 I5 **Bol'shoye Ignatovo** Rus. Fed.
134 I5 **Bol'shoye Murashkino** Rus. Fed.
139 J5 **Bol'shoye Polpino** Rus. Fed.
134 G4 **Bol'shoye Selo** Rus. Fed.
137 H2 **Bol'shoye Soldatskoye** Rus. Fed.
120 C2 **Bol'shoy Ik** *r.* Rus. Fed.
120 A2 **Bol'shoy Irgiz** *r.* Rus. Fed.
100 E4 **Bol'shoy Kamen'** Rus. Fed.
Bol'shoy Kavkaz *mts* Asia/Europe *see* **Caucasus**
139 L5 **Bol'shoy Khomutets** Rus. Fed.
134 L2 **Bol'shoy Patok** *r.* Rus. Fed.
131 O4 **Bol'shoy Shantar, Ostrov** *i.* Rus. Fed.
Bol'shoy Tokmak Kyrg. *see* **Tokmak**
Bol'shoy Tokmak Ukr. *see* **Tokmak**
139 H3 **Bol'shoy Tuder** *r.* Rus. Fed.
120 B2 **Bol'shoy Uzen'** *r.* Kazakh./Rus. Fed.
129 B1 **Bol'shoy Zelenchuk** *r.* Rus. Fed.
149 H4 **Bolsover** *Derbyshire, England* U.K.
164 E1 **Bolsward** Neth.
174 G1 **Bolszewo** Pol.
186 D2 **Boltañá** Spain
149 H3 **Boltby** *North Yorkshire, England* U.K.
190 C2 **Boltigen** Switz.
227 H4 **Bolton** *Ont.* Can.
92 C5 **Bolton** Phil.
149 G4 **Bolton** *Greater Manchester, England* U.K.
149 G3 **Bolton-le-Sands** *Lancashire, England* U.K.
137 H3 **Boltyshka** Ukr.
126 C2 **Bolu** Turkey
199 G1 **Bolu** *prov.* Turkey
140 □B2 **Bolungarvík** Iceland
111 F4 **Boluntay** *Qinghai* China
109 E4 **Boluo** *Guangdong* China
139 J5 **Bolva** *r.* Rus. Fed.
199 G2 **Bolvadin** Turkey
150 C4 **Bolventor** *Cornwall, England* U.K.
177 H6 **Bóly** Hungary
197 H4 **Bolyarovo** Bulg.
191 G2 **Bolzano** Italy
191 G2 **Bolzano** *prov. Trentino - Alto Adige* Italy
209 B6 **Boma** Dem. Rep. Congo
83 G3 **Bomaderry** *N.S.W.* Austr.
207 G5 **Bomadi** Nigeria
108 A2 **Bomai** *Sichuan* China
165 E4 **Bomal** Belgium
193 G2 **Bomba** Italy
83 G4 **Bombala** *N.S.W.* Austr.
184 A1 **Bombarral** Port.
Bombay *Mahar.* India *see* **Mumbai**
80 E2 **Bombay** *North I.* N.Z.
241 J5 **Bombay Beach** *CA* U.S.A.
91 H7 **Bomberai, Semenanjung** *pen.* Indon.
209 B5 **Bombo** *r.* Dem. Rep. Congo
257 E3 **Bom Despacho** Brazil
117 H4 **Bomdila** *Arun. Prad.* India
150 E2 **Bomere Heath** *Shropshire, England* U.K.
111 F6 **Bomi** *Xizang* China
254 G3 **Bom Jardim** Brazil
256 A2 **Bom Jardim de Goiás** Brazil
257 E4 **Bom Jardim de Minas** Brazil
254 D4 **Bom Jesus** *Piauí* Brazil
255 C9 **Bom Jesus** *Rio Grande do Sul* Brazil
254 E4 **Bom Jesus da Gurgueia, Serra do** *hills* Brazil
254 E5 **Bom Jesus da Lapa** Brazil
256 C3 **Bom Jesus de Goiás** Brazil
257 G4 **Bom Jesus do Itabapoana** Brazil
257 G4 **Bom Jesus do Norte** Brazil
168 E3 **Bomlitz** Ger.
142 A2 **Bømlo** *i.* Norway
208 E4 **Bomokandi** *r.* Dem. Rep. Congo
208 C4 **Bomongo** Dem. Rep. Congo
163 E6 **Bompas** France
194 C5 **Bompensiere** *Sicilia* Italy
194 D5 **Bompietro** *Sicilia* Italy
255 C8 **Bom Retiro** Brazil
257 E4 **Bom Sucesso** *Minas Gerais* Brazil
256 B5 **Bom Sucesso** *Paraná* Brazil
Bona Alg. *see* **Annaba**
160 B1 **Bona** France
122 A2 **Bonāb** Iran
163 C6 **Bonac-Irazein** France
190 E2 **Bonaduz** Switz.
232 E6 **Bon Air** *VA* U.S.A.
247 □8 **Bonaire** *i.* Neth. Antilles
83 H2 **Bonalbo** *N.S.W.* Austr.
195 F4 **Bonamico** *r.* Italy
242 □I6 **Bonanza** Nic.
184 D4 **Bonanza** Spain
246 E3 **Bonao** Dom. Rep.
86 E2 **Bonaparte Archipelago** *is W.A.* Austr.
183 E2 **Boñar** Spain
146 D4 **Bonar Bridge** *Highland, Scotland* U.K.
192 A4 **Bonarcado** *Sardegna* Italy
247 □7 **Bonasse** Trin. and Tob.
190 E4 **Bonassola** Italy
225 K3 **Bonavista** *Nfld.* Can.
160 D1 **Bonboillon** France
82 C2 **Bon Bon** *S.A.* Austr.
159 F3 **Bonchamp-lès-Laval** France
146 F6 **Bonchester Bridge** *Scottish Borders, Scotland* U.K.
190 C1 **Boncourt** Switz.
137 J3 **Bondarevo** Rus. Fed.
135 H5 **Bondari** Rus. Fed.
191 G4 **Bondeno** Italy
208 D4 **Bondo** Dem. Rep. Congo
92 B3 **Bondoc Peninsula** Phil.
172 C3 **Bondorf** Ger.
206 E4 **Bondoukou** Côte d'Ivoire
206 E4 **Bondoukui** Burkina
95 F4 **Bondowoso** *Jawa Timur* Indon.
231 E7 **Bonds Cay** *i.* Bahamas
226 C3 **Bonduel** *WI* U.S.A.
156 D2 **Bondues** France
Bondyuzhskiy Rus. Fed. *see* **Mendeleyevsk**
Bône Alg. *see* **Annaba**
93 B4 **Bone, Teluk** *b.* Indon.
168 F1 **Bönebüttel** Ger.
193 G3 **Bonefro** Italy
214 C4 **Bonekraal** S. Africa
169 C4 **Bönen** Ger.
163 C4 **Bon-Encontre** France
93 B4 **Bonerate, Kepulauan** *is* Indon.
146 E5 **Bo'ness** *Falkirk, Scotland* U.K.
236 D3 **Bonesteel** *SD* U.S.A.
187 B6 **Bonete** Spain
257 E4 **Bonfim** Brazil
256 A2 **Bonfim** *r.* Brazil
257 E2 **Bonfinópolis de Minas** Brazil
210 C3 **Bonga** Eth.
92 B3 **Bongabong** Phil.
117 G4 **Bongaigaon** *Assam* India
208 D4 **Bongandanga** Dem. Rep. Congo
214 D3 **Bongani** S. Africa
92 A5 **Bongao** Phil.
85 H5 **Bongaree** *Qld* Austr.
93 B3 **Bongka** *r.* Indon.
206 C5 **Bong Mountains** *hills* Liberia
209 B7 **Bongo, Serra do** *mts* Angola
213 □J3 **Bongolava** *mts* Madag.
208 B2 **Bongor** Chad
206 D5 **Bongouanou** Côte d'Ivoire
208 B5 **Bongoville** Gabon
97 E4 **Bông Sơn** Vietnam
237 D5 **Bonham** *TX* U.S.A.
140 L3 **Bönhamn** Sweden
206 E3 **Boni** Mali
183 I5 **Boniches** Spain
206 D4 **Boniéredougou** Côte d'Ivoire
174 G3 **Boniewo** Pol.
192 B3 **Bonifacio** *Corse* France
Bonifacio, Bocche di *str.* France/Italy *see* **Bonifacio, Strait of**
Bonifacio, Bouches de *str.* France/Italy *see* **Bonifacio, Strait of**
192 A3 **Bonifacio, Strait of** France/Italy
193 H5 **Bonifati** Italy
231 C6 **Bonifay** *FL* U.S.A.
190 C2 **Bönigen** Switz.
174 E1 **Bonin** Pol.
Bonin Islands N. Pacific Ocean *see* **Ogasawara-shotō**
231 D7 **Bonita Springs** *FL* U.S.A.
253 F5 **Bonito** Brazil
256 B2 **Bonito** *r.* Brazil
146 F6 **Bonjedward** *Scottish Borders, Scotland* U.K.
207 F3 **Bonkoukou** Niger
169 C5 **Bonn** Ger.
Bonna Ger. *see* **Bonn**
163 D5 **Bonnac** France
192 A4 **Bonnanaro** *Sardegna* Italy
162 D2 **Bonnat** France
160 C2 **Bonnay** France
172 C4 **Bonndorf im Schwarzwald** Ger.
161 D4 **Bonne** *r.* France
234 A3 **Bonneauville** *PA* U.S.A.
163 C5 **Bonnefont** France
238 C1 **Bonners Ferry** *ID* U.S.A.
159 G3 **Bonnétable** France
159 G5 **Bonneuil-Matours** France
156 B4 **Bonneval** *Centre* France
160 E3 **Bonneval** *Rhône-Alpes* France
161 F3 **Bonneval-sur-Arc** France
160 E2 **Bonnevaux** France
160 E2 **Bonneville** France
82 E4 **Bonney, Lake** *S.A.* Austr.
156 B3 **Bonnières-sur-Seine** France
87 C6 **Bonnie Rock** *W.A.* Austr.
161 D5 **Bonnieux** France
214 C5 **Bonnievale** S. Africa
172 D2 **Bönnigheim** Ger.
168 E2 **Bönningstedt** Ger.
163 B5 **Bonnut** France
207 G5 **Bonny** Nigeria
146 E5 **Bonnybridge** *Falkirk, Scotland* U.K.
215 G4 **Bonny Ridge** S. Africa
146 E6 **Bonnyrigg** *Midlothian, Scotland* U.K.
233 □J2 **Bonny River** *N.B.* Can.
160 A1 **Bonny-sur-Loire** France
223 I4 **Bonnyville** *Alta* Can.
158 D4 **Bono** France
192 B4 **Bono** *Sardegna* Italy
92 A4 **Bonobono** Phil.
97 D5 **Bonom Mhai** *mt.* Vietnam
Bononia Italy *see* **Bologna**
192 A4 **Bonorva** *Sardegna* Italy
206 E5 **Bonoua** Côte d'Ivoire
81 B6 **Bonpland, Mount** *South I.* N.Z.
240 I5 **Bonsall** *CA* U.S.A.
160 E2 **Bons-en-Chablais** France
83 G2 **Bonshaw** *N.S.W.* Austr.
160 C3 **Bonson** France
214 C5 **Bontberg** *mt.* S. Africa
206 B5 **Bonthe** Sierra Leone
92 B2 **Bontoc** Phil.
93 A4 **Bontosunggu** *Sulawesi Selatan* Indon.
215 G4 **Bontrand** S. Africa
215 E5 **Bontrug** S. Africa
177 G4 **Bőny** Hungary
177 H5 **Bonyhád** Hungary
84 B4 **Bonython Range** *hills N.T.* Austr.
143 H2 **Boo** Sweden
93 D3 **Boo, Kepulauan** *is Irian Jaya* Indon.
170 F2 **Boock** Ger.
82 C2 **Bookabie** *S.A.* Austr.
241 M2 **Book Cliffs** *ridge UT* U.S.A.
237 C4 **Booker** *TX* U.S.A.
206 C4 **Boola** Guinea
83 G2 **Boolba** *Qld* Austr.
82 D3 **Booleroo Centre** *S.A.* Austr.
147 D4 **Booley Hills** Rep. of Ireland
83 F3 **Booligal** *N.S.W.* Austr.
87 B5 **Boologooro** *W.A.* Austr.
83 G2 **Boomi** *N.S.W.* Austr.
226 E3 **Boon** *MI* U.S.A.
85 H5 **Boonah** *Qld* Austr.
239 F4 **Boone** *CO* U.S.A.
236 E3 **Boone** *IA* U.S.A.
231 D4 **Boone** *NC* U.S.A.
232 D6 **Boones Mill** *VA* U.S.A.
237 E5 **Booneville** *AR* U.S.A.
232 B6 **Booneville** *KY* U.S.A.
237 F5 **Booneville** *MS* U.S.A.
215 F1 **Boons** S. Africa
232 E5 **Boonsboro** *MD* U.S.A.
235 D2 **Boonton** *NJ* U.S.A.
106 C2 **Böön Tsagaan Nuur** *salt l.* Mongolia
240 F2 **Boonville** *CA* U.S.A.
230 C4 **Boonville** *IN* U.S.A.
236 E4 **Boonville** *MO* U.S.A.
233 F3 **Boonville** *NY* U.S.A.
252 D3 **Boopi** *r.* Bol.
210 D2 **Boorama** Somalia
83 F3 **Booroorban** *N.S.W.* Austr.
83 G3 **Boorowa** *N.S.W.* Austr.
83 E4 **Boort** *Vic.* Austr.
165 D4 **Boortmeerbeek** Belgium
156 B3 **Boos** France
173 E3 **Boos** Ger.
210 F2 **Boosaaso** Somalia
168 F1 **Boostedt** Ger.
233 □I3 **Boothbay Harbor** *ME* U.S.A.
263 D2 **Boothby, Cape** Antarctica
221 J3 **Boothia, Gulf of** *Nunavut* Can.
221 I2 **Boothia Peninsula** *Nunavut* Can.
149 F3 **Bootle** *Cumbria, England* U.K.
149 G4 **Bootle** *Merseyside, England* U.K.
208 A5 **Booué** Gabon
173 E3 **Bopfingen** Ger.
206 C5 **Bopolu** Liberia
169 C5 **Boppard** Ger.
258 G3 **Boqueirão** Brazil
254 D5 **Boqueirão, Serra do** *hills* Brazil
247 □1 **Boquerón** Puerto Rico
176 B2 **Bor** Czech Rep.
134 I4 **Bor** Rus. Fed.
210 A3 **Bor** Sudan
126 D3 **Bor** Turkey
197 F3 **Bor** *Srbija* Yugo.
129 F4 **Boradigah** Azer.
213 □K3 **Boraha, Nosy** *i.* Madag.
238 D2 **Borah Peak** *ID* U.S.A.
Boran Kazakh. *see* **Buran**
156 C3 **Boran-sur-Oise** France
Boraraigh *i. Western Isles, Scotland* U.K. *see* **Boreray**
142 E3 **Borås** Sweden
117 E5 **Borasambar** *Orissa* India
122 B4 **Borāzjān** Iran
251 G6 **Borba** Brazil
184 C2 **Borba** Port.
190 D4 **Borbera** *r.* Italy
92 C4 **Borbon** Phil.
190 D4 **Borbore** *r.* Italy
256 C4 **Borborema** Brazil
254 F3 **Borborema, Planalto da** *plat.* Brazil
197 G2 **Borca** Romania
Borchalo Georgia *see* **Marneuli**
169 D4 **Borchen** Ger.
263 K2 **Borchgrevink Coast** Antarctica
127 F2 **Borçka** Turkey
164 F2 **Borculo** Neth.
86 D3 **Borda, Cape** *W.A.* Austr.
256 D5 **Borda da Mata** Brazil
199 F3 **Bor Dağı** *mt.* Turkey
183 H3 **Bordalba** Spain
177 I5 **Bordány** Hungary
163 B4 **Bordeaux** France
116 D5 **Bordehi** *Madh. Prad.* India
184 B3 **Bordeira** Port.
168 D1 **Bordelum** Ger.
87 C7 **Borden** *W.A.* Austr.
225 I4 **Borden** *P.E.I.* Can.
221 G2 **Borden Island** *N.W.T.* Can.
221 J2 **Borden Peninsula** *Nunavut* Can.
234 D2 **Bordentown** *NJ* U.S.A.
163 C6 **Bordères-Louron** France
163 C5 **Bordères-sur-l'Échez** France
Borders *admin. div. Scotland* U.K. *see* **Scottish Borders**
82 E4 **Bordertown** *S.A.* Austr.
163 B5 **Bordes** *Aquitaine* France
163 C5 **Bordes** *Midi-Pyrénées* France
168 F1 **Bordesholm** Ger.
190 C5 **Bordighera** Italy
186 F2 **Bordils** Spain
194 B5 **Bordino** *r. Sicilia* Italy
205 G1 **Bordj Bou Arréridj** Alg.
186 C4 **Bordón** Spain
144 D1 **Borðoy** *i.* Faroe Is
121 H4 **Bordu** Kyrg.
Bordunskiy Kyrg. *see* **Bordu**
197 H3 **Bordușani** Romania
190 E4 **Bore** Italy
206 E3 **Boré** Mali
262 X2 **Boreas Nunatak** Antarctica
151 H3 **Boreham** *Essex, England* U.K.
151 G3 **Borehamwood** *Hertfordshire, England* U.K.
173 H2 **Borek** *hill* Czech Rep.
175 I5 **Borek** Pol.
174 F5 **Borek Strzeliński** Pol.
174 F4 **Borek Wielkopolski** Pol.
225 G1 **Borel** *r. Que.* Can.
146 E6 **Boreland** *Dumfries and Galloway, Scotland* U.K.
136 C2 **Boremel'** Ukr.
143 F2 **Boren** *l.* Sweden
143 F2 **Borensberg** Sweden
146 B4 **Boreraig** *Highland, Scotland* U.K.
146 A4 **Boreray** *i. Western Isles, Scotland* U.K.
146 □ **Boreray** *i. Western Isles, Scotland* U.K.
179 H2 **Bořetice** Czech Rep.
172 A2 **Borg** Ger.
Borgå Fin. *see* **Porvoo**
140 K2 **Borgafjäll** Sweden
140 □B2 **Borgarnes** Iceland
169 E4 **Borgentreich** Ger.
168 C3 **Börger** Ger.
164 F2 **Borger** Neth.
237 C5 **Borger** *TX* U.S.A.
187 G5 **Borges** *r.* Spain
190 D4 **Borghetto di Borbera** Italy
143 G3 **Borgholm** *Kalmar* Sweden
169 D3 **Borgholzhausen** Ger.
195 F4 **Borgia** Italy
146 D3 **Borgie** *r. Scotland* U.K.
165 E4 **Borgloon** Belgium
192 B2 **Borgo** *Corse* France
191 F5 **Borgo a Mozzano** Italy
190 D3 **Borgo d'Ale** Italy
191 F3 **Borgoforte** Italy
190 C3 **Borgofranco d'Ivrea** Italy
195 H2 **Borgo Grappa** Italy
190 D3 **Borgo-lavezzaro** Italy
190 D3 **Borgomanero** Italy
190 C5 **Borgomaro** Italy
190 C3 **Borgone Susa** Italy
190 E3 **Borgonovo Val Tidone** Italy
191 G4 **Borgo Panigale** *airport* Italy
193 F2 **Borgorose** Italy
190 C4 **Borgo San Dalmazzo** Italy
191 G5 **Borgo San Lorenzo** Italy
190 D3 **Borgo San Martino** Italy
190 D3 **Borgosesia** Italy
191 G4 **Borgo Tossignano** Italy
190 E4 **Borgo Val di Taro** Italy
191 G2 **Borgo Valsugana** Italy
193 F2 **Borgo Velino** Italy
190 D3 **Borgo Vercelli** Italy
170 E3 **Borgsdorf** Ger.
142 C1 **Borgsjåbrotet** *mt.* Norway
168 E1 **Borgstedt** Ger.
146 D7 **Borgue** *Dumfries and Galloway, Scotland* U.K.
116 D5 **Bori** *Mahar.* India
116 C5 **Bori** *r.* India
207 G5 **Bori** Nigeria
Börili Kazakh. *see* **Burli**
139 J5 **Borilovo** Rus. Fed.
234 B3 **Boring** *MD* U.S.A.
197 G5 **Borino** Bulg.
139 L5 **Borinskoye** Rus. Fed.
Borislav Ukr. *see* **Boryslav**
135 H6 **Borisoglebsk** Rus. Fed.
139 L3 **Borisoglebskiy** Rus. Fed.
Borisov Belarus *see* **Barysaw**
135 G6 **Borisovka** Rus. Fed.
139 K2 **Borisovo-Sudskoye** Rus. Fed.
Borispol' Ukr. *see* **Boryspil'**
213 □J2 **Boriziny** Madag.
188 F3 **Borja** *mts* Bos.-Herz.
250 B6 **Borja** Peru
183 I3 **Borja** Spain
183 H3 **Borjabad** Spain
Borjas Blancas Spain *see* **Les Borges Blanques**
129 C3 **Borjomi** Georgia
138 G4 **Borkavichy** Belarus
169 B4 **Borken** Ger.
169 E4 **Borken (Hessen)** Ger.
140 L1 **Borkenes** Norway
171 D3 **Borkheide** Ger.
175 K4 **Borki** Pol.
202 C5 **Borkou-Ennedi-Tibesti** *pref.* Chad
175 I4 **Borkowice** Pol.
168 B2 **Borkum** Ger.
168 B2 **Borkum** *i.* Ger.
143 F1 **Borlänge** Sweden
199 F2 **Borlu** Turkey
161 E5 **Bormes-les-Mimosas** France
190 D4 **Bormida** *r.* Italy
190 F2 **Bormio** Italy
171 C3 **Born** Ger.
171 D4 **Borna** *Sachsen* Ger.
171 E4 **Borna** *Sachsen* Ger.
170 D1 **Born am Darß** Ger.
169 F4 **Born-Berge** *hill* Ger.
164 E1 **Borndiep** *sea chan.* Neth.
160 E2 **Borne** *r.* France
164 F2 **Borne** Neth.
156 C3 **Bornel** France
165 D3 **Bornem** Belgium
90 D6 **Borneo** *i.* Asia
164 F2 **Bornerbroek** Neth.
160 E3 **Bornes** *mts* France
182 D3 **Bornes** Port.
182 C3 **Bornes de Aguiar** Port.
174 E2 **Borne Sulinowo** Pol.
169 B5 **Bornheim** Ger.
169 C5 **Bornhofen** Ger.
143 F4 **Bornholm** *county* Denmark
141 K5 **Bornholm** *i.* Denmark
168 F1 **Bornhöved** Ger.
169 C5 **Bornich** Ger.
207 I4 **Borno** *state* Nigeria
184 E4 **Bornos** Spain
183 H4 **Bornova** *r.* Spain
199 E2 **Bornova** Turkey
168 F2 **Börnsen** Ger.
171 C4 **Bornstedt** Ger.
183 I3 **Borobia** Spain
95 E4 **Borobudur** *tourist site* Indon.
177 L5 **Borod** Romania
137 H3 **Borodayivka** Ukr.
136 E4 **Borodino** Ukr.
138 G1 **Borodinskoye** Rus. Fed.
136 E2 **Borodyanka** Ukr.
131 O3 **Borogontsy** Rus. Fed.
110 C2 **Borohoro Shan** *mts* China
176 F1 **Borohrádek** Czech Rep.
139 L2 **Borok** Rus. Fed.
139 K3 **Borok-Sulezhskiy** Rus. Fed.
137 H2 **Boromlya** Ukr.
137 H2 **Boromlya** *r.* Ukr.
206 E4 **Boromo** Burkina
206 D3 **Boron** Mali
240 I4 **Boron** *CA* U.S.A.
92 C4 **Borongan** Phil.
174 G5 **Boronów** Pol.
192 A4 **Borore** *Sardegna* Italy
85 G5 **Bororen** *Qld* Austr.
174 G5 **Boroszów** Pol.
177 I5 **Borota** Hungary
206 D4 **Borotou** Côte d'Ivoire
149 H3 **Boroughbridge** *North Yorkshire, England* U.K.
151 H3 **Borough Green** *Kent, England* U.K.
137 I3 **Borova** *Kharkivs'ka Oblast'* Ukr.
136 F2 **Borova** *Kyivs'ka Oblast'* Ukr.
137 J3 **Borova** *r.* Ukr.
197 F4 **Borovan** Bulg.
176 D3 **Borovany** Czech Rep.
136 C2 **Borove** *Rivnens'ka Oblast'* Ukr.
136 D2 **Borove** *Rivnens'ka Oblast'* Ukr.
139 I2 **Borovenka** Rus. Fed.
139 I2 **Borovichi** Rus. Fed.
121 K1 **Borovlyanka** Rus. Fed.
179 F5 **Borovnica** Slovenia
188 G3 **Borovo Selo** Croatia
134 J4 **Borovoy** *Kirovskaya Oblast'* Rus. Fed.
134 F2 **Borovoy** *Respublika Kareliya* Rus. Fed.
134 K3 **Borovoy** *Respublika Komi* Rus. Fed.
121 G1 **Borovoye** Kazakh.
139 K4 **Borovsk** Rus. Fed.
120 F1 **Borovskoy** Kazakh.
175 J5 **Borów** Pol.
175 J5 **Borowa** Pol.
175 J4 **Borowie** Pol.
183 G4 **Borox** Spain
257 E3 **Borrachudo** *r.* Brazil
256 B5 **Borrazópolis** Brazil
143 F4 **Borrby** Sweden
170 D1 **Borre** Denmark
241 I5 **Borrego Springs** *CA* U.S.A.
170 D2 **Borrentin** Ger.
162 D4 **Borrèze** France
187 C4 **Borriol** Spain
147 E4 **Borris** Rep. of Ireland
147 D4 **Borris-in-Ossory** Rep. of Ireland
147 C4 **Borrisokane** Rep. of Ireland
84 D3 **Borroloola** *N.T.* Austr.
149 F3 **Borrowdale** *Cumbria, England* U.K.
177 K4 **Borș** Romania
140 J3 **Børsa** Norway
197 F2 **Borșa** Romania
197 G2 **Borșa** Romania
177 K3 **Borša** Slovakia
116 C5 **Borsad** *Gujarat* India
165 D3 **Borsbeek** Belgium
171 D4 **Borsdorf** Ger.
197 G2 **Borsec** Romania
198 A1 **Borsh** Albania
137 K2 **Borshchevskiye Peski** Rus. Fed.
136 E4 **Borshchi** Ukr.
136 D3 **Borshchiv** Ukr.
136 C3 **Borshchivka** Ukr.
107 F1 **Borshchovochnyy Khrebet** *mts* Rus. Fed.
175 M6 **Borshchovychi** Ukr.
127 G4 **Borsippa** *tourist site* Iraq
120 B1 **Borskoye** Rus. Fed.
Borský Jur Slovakia *see* **Borský Svätý Jur**
179 I2 **Borský Svätý Jur** Slovakia
177 K3 **Borsod-Abaúj-Zemplén** *county* Hungary
177 J3 **Borsodbóta** Hungary
177 J3 **Borsodnádasd** Hungary
177 J3 **Borsodszentgyörgy** Hungary
165 C3 **Borssele** Neth.
169 F3 **Börßum** Ger.
168 D3 **Borstel** Ger.
171 E5 **Borstendorf** Ger.
Bortala *Xinjiang* China *see* **Bole**
110 C2 **Bortala He** *r.* China
150 C2 **Borth** *Ceredigion, Wales* U.K.
192 A4 **Bortigali** *Sardegna* Italy
192 B4 **Bortigiadas** *Sardegna* Italy
162 E3 **Bort-les-Orgues** France
106 B2 **Bor-Üdzüür** Mongolia
122 B4 **Borūjen** Iran
122 B3 **Borūjerd** Iran
106 C3 **Bor Ul Shan** *mts* China
197 G4 **Borushtitsa** Bulg.
192 A4 **Borutta** *Sardegna* Italy
146 B4 **Borve** *Highland, Scotland* U.K.
136 B3 **Borynya** Ukr.
136 B3 **Boryslav** Ukr.
136 F2 **Boryspil'** Ukr.
174 G2 **Bory Tucholskie** *for.* Pol.
175 K4 **Borzechów** Pol.
174 F4 **Borzęciczki** Pol.
137 G2 **Borzenka** *r.* Ukr.
136 B3 **Borzhava** *r.* Ukr.
Borzhomi Georgia *see* **Borjomi**
137 G2 **Borzna** Ukr.
190 E4 **Borzonasca** Italy
177 H4 **Börzsöny** *hills* Hungary
107 H1 **Borzya** Rus. Fed.
107 G1 **Borzya** *r.* Rus. Fed.
174 F1 **Borzytuchom** Pol.
192 A4 **Bosa** *Sardegna* Italy
177 G3 **Bošáca** Slovakia
121 H3 **Bosaga** Kazakh.
Bosagha Kazakh. *see* **Bosaga**
Bosaginskiy Kazakh. *see* **Bosaga**
192 A4 **Bosa Marina** *Sardegna* Italy
197 H2 **Bosanci** Romania
188 F3 **Bosanska Dubica** Bos.-Herz.
188 F3 **Bosanska Gradiška** Bos.-Herz.
188 F3 **Bosanska Kostajnica** Bos.-Herz.
188 F3 **Bosanska Krupa** Bos.-Herz.
188 G3 **Bosanski Brod** Bos.-Herz.
188 F3 **Bosanski Novi** Bos.-Herz.
188 F3 **Bosanski Petrovac** Bos.-Herz.
188 G3 **Bosanski Šamac** Bos.-Herz.
188 F3 **Bosansko Grahovo** Bos.-Herz.
177 H3 **Bošany** Slovakia
176 G4 **Bősárkány** Hungary
168 F1 **Bosau** Ger.
215 F3 **Bosberg** *mt.* S. Africa
150 E2 **Bosbury** *Herefordshire, England* U.K.
150 C4 **Boscastle** *Cornwall, England* U.K.
233 H3 **Boscawen** *NH* U.S.A.
Boscawen Island Tonga *see* **Niuatoputopu**
193 E1 **Bosco** Italy
226 B4 **Boscobel** *WI* U.S.A.
191 G3 **Bosco Chiesanuova** Italy
190 D4 **Bosco Marengo** Italy
193 G4 **Boscotrecase** Italy
168 F1 **Bösdorf** Ger.
108 C4 **Bose** *Guangxi* China
168 C2 **Bösel** Ger.
151 G4 **Bosham** *West Sussex, England* U.K.
Boshchakul' Kazakh. *see* **Bozshakol'**
100 G2 **Boshnyakovo** *Sakhalin* Rus. Fed.
215 F1 **Boshoek** S. Africa
215 E3 **Boshof** S. Africa
197 F4 **Bosilegrad** *Srbija* Yugo.
Bosiljgrad *Srbija* Yugo. *see* **Bosilegrad**
172 C3 **Bösingen** Ger.
120 E1 **Boskol'** Kazakh.
164 D2 **Boskoop** Neth.
176 F2 **Boskovice** Czech Rep.
188 G3 **Bosna** *r.* Bos.-Herz.
197 H4 **Bosna** *hills* Bulg.
Bosna i Hercegovina *country* Europe *see* **Bosnia-Herzegovina**
Bosna Saray Bos.-Herz. *see* **Sarajevo**
Bosnia and Herzegovina, Federation of *aut. div.* Bos.-Herz. *see* **Federacija Bosna i Hercegovina**
188 F3 **Bosnia-Herzegovina** *country* Europe
208 C3 **Bosobolo** Dem. Rep. Congo
105 G3 **Bōsō-hantō** *pen.* Japan
Bosost Spain *see* **Bòssost**
179 H1 **Bošovice** Czech Rep.
215 F2 **Bospoort** S. Africa
Bosporus *str.* Turkey *see* **İstanbul Boğazı**
182 B1 **Bosque** Spain
208 C3 **Bossangoa** C.A.R.
141 K3 **Bössbod** Sweden
208 C3 **Bossembélé** C.A.R.
162 C4 **Bosset** France
214 C3 **Bossiekom** S. Africa
237 E5 **Bossier City** *LA* U.S.A.
206 D4 **Bossora** Burkina
186 D2 **Bòssost** Spain
215 F1 **Bosspruit** S. Africa
86 D3 **Bossut, Cape** *W.A.* Austr.
111 D4 **Bostan** *Xinjiang* China
122 A4 **Bostān** Iran
110 D3 **Bosten Hu** *l.* China
147 C3 **Boston** Rep. of Ireland
151 G2 **Boston** *Lincolnshire, England* U.K.
233 H3 **Boston** *MA* U.S.A.
82 C3 **Boston Bay** *S.A.* Austr.
227 H1 **Boston Creek** *Ont.* Can.
237 E5 **Boston Mountains** *AR* U.S.A.
149 H4 **Boston Spa** *West Yorkshire, England* U.K.
188 G3 **Bosut** *r.* Croatia
226 D5 **Boswell** *IN* U.S.A.
232 D4 **Boswell** *PA* U.S.A.
116 B5 **Botad** *Gujarat* India
206 C5 **Botata** Liberia
140 L3 **Boteå** Sweden
197 G3 **Boteni** Romania
151 I2 **Botesdale** *Suffolk, England* U.K.
212 E4 **Boteti** *r.* Botswana
135 D8 **Botev** *mt.* Bulg.
197 F4 **Botevgrad** Bulg.
215 F2 **Bothaville** S. Africa
168 E2 **Bothel** Ger.
149 F3 **Bothel** *Cumbria, England* U.K.
238 B2 **Bothell** *WA* U.S.A.
150 E4 **Bothenhampton** *Dorset, England* U.K.
141 L3 **Bothnia, Gulf of** Fin./Sweden
83 F5 **Bothwell** *Tas.* Austr.
227 G4 **Bothwell** *Ont.* Can.
182 C3 **Boticas** Port.
188 G4 **Botin** *mt.* Bos.-Herz.
179 G5 **Botinec Stupnički** Croatia
137 H4 **Botiyeve** Ukr.
177 L4 **Botiz** Romania
232 A4 **Botkins** *OH* U.S.A.
135 I6 **Botkul', Ozero** *l.* Kazakh./Rus. Fed.
129 E2 **Botlikh** Rus. Fed.
207 H6 **Bot Makak** Cameroon
136 E4 **Botna** *r.* Moldova
186 B3 **Botorrita** Spain
197 H2 **Botoșani** Romania
107 H4 **Botou** *Hebei* China
195 F4 **Botricello** Italy
206 D5 **Botro** Côte d'Ivoire
235 E1 **Botsford** *CT* U.S.A.
215 F3 **Botshabelo** S. Africa
140 M2 **Botsmark** Sweden
212 D5 **Botswana** *country* Africa
195 F3 **Botte Donato, Monte** *mt.* Italy
169 D4 **Bottendorf (Burgwald)** Ger.
168 F3 **Bottendorf (Obernholz)** Ger.
140 M2 **Bottenviken** *g.* Fin./Sweden
151 G2 **Bottesford** *Leicestershire, England* U.K.
149 I4 **Bottesford** *North Lincolnshire, England* U.K.
192 B4 **Bottidda** *Sardegna* Italy
236 C1 **Bottineau** *ND* U.S.A.
247 G3 **Bottom** *Saba* Neth. Antilles
169 B4 **Bottrop** Ger.
256 C5 **Botucatu** Brazil
257 F2 **Botumirim** Brazil
196 E5 **Botun** Macedonia
Botushany Moldova *see* **Butuceni**
225 K3 **Botwood** *Nfld.* Can.
172 B3 **Bötzingen** Ger.
206 D5 **Bouaflé** Côte d'Ivoire
156 B3 **Bouafles** France
206 D5 **Bouaké** Côte d'Ivoire
205 F2 **Boualem** Alg.
206 D4 **Bouandougou** Côte d'Ivoire
208 B3 **Bouar** C.A.R.
204 E2 **Bouârfa** Morocco
158 E4 **Bouaye** France
176 C2 **Boubín** *mt.* Czech Rep.
208 C3 **Bouca** C.A.R.
163 A5 **Boucau** France
84 C2 **Boucaut Bay** *N.T.* Austr.
161 D5 **Bouc-Bel-Air** France
159 F3 **Boucé** France
156 D2 **Bouchain** France
189 A7 **Bouchegouf** Alg.
159 F4 **Bouchemaine** France
Boucher, Île *i. Î. Loyauté* New Caledonia *see* **Tiga**
233 G2 **Boucherville** *Que.* Can.
161 D5 **Bouches-du-Rhône** *dept Provence-Alpes-Côte-d'Azur* France
227 J2 **Bouchette** *Que.* Can.
156 C3 **Bouchoir** France
225 H4 **Bouctouche** *N.B.* Can.
180 E5 **Boudinar** Morocco
190 B2 **Boudry** Switz.
156 D2 **Boué** France
217 □3b **Bouéni** Mayotte
209 B6 **Bouenza** *admin. reg.* Congo
209 B6 **Bouenza** *r.* Congo
159 F4 **Bouessay** France
159 H5 **Bouesse** France
205 G1 **Bougaa** Alg.
86 E2 **Bougainville, Cape** *W.A.* Austr.
91 L8 **Bougainville Island** P.N.G.
85 F2 **Bougainville Reef** *Coral Sea Is Terr.* Austr.
78 □6 **Bougainville Strait** Solomon Is
Bougie Alg. *see* **Bejaïa**
163 C4 **Bouglon** France
206 D4 **Bougouni** Mali
205 F2 **Bougtob** Alg.
158 E4 **Bouguenais** France
163 D5 **Bouillac** France
247 □2 **Bouillante** Guadeloupe
161 C5 **Bouillargues** France
165 E5 **Bouillon** Belgium
156 D4 **Bouilly** France
158 D5 **Bouin** France
205 F1 **Bouira** Alg.
204 C3 **Bou Izakarn** Morocco
160 E2 **Boujailles** France
161 B5 **Boujan-sur-Libron** France
204 B4 **Boujdour** Western Sahara
205 F2 **Bou Kahil, Djebel** *mts* Alg.
207 F4 **Boukoumbé** Benin
208 C2 **Boukta** Chad
157 G3 **Boulay-Moselle** France
162 C3 **Boulazac** France
161 C5 **Boulbon** France
87 D6 **Boulder** *W.A.* Austr.
238 F3 **Boulder** *CO* U.S.A.
238 D2 **Boulder** *MT* U.S.A.
241 L3 **Boulder** *UT* U.S.A.
241 J3 **Boulder Canyon** *gorge NV* U.S.A.
241 J4 **Boulder City** *NV* U.S.A.
204 D2 **Boulemane** *Boulemane* Morocco

146 C6 **Brodick** North Ayrshire, Scotland U.K.
232 D6 **Brodnax** VA U.S.A.
175 H2 **Brodnica** Kujawsko-Pomorskie Pol.
174 E3 **Brodnica** Wielkopolskie Pol.
176 G3 **Brodské** Slovakia
174 C4 **Brody** Pol.
136 C2 **Brody** Ukr.
215 E2 **Broedersput** S. Africa
164 F3 **Broekhuizenvorst** Neth.
215 E4 **Broekpoort** r. S. Africa
159 G2 **Broglie** France
169 C5 **Brohl** Ger.
170 E2 **Brohm** Ger.
160 D1 **Broin** France
174 D2 **Brojce** Pol.
175 J3 **Brok** Pol.
175 J3 **Brok** r. Pol.
168 E2 **Brokdorf** Ger.
142 C2 **Brokefjell** mt. Norway
87 C7 **Broke Inlet** W.A. Austr.
237 E4 **Broken Arrow** OK U.S.A.
83 G3 **Broken Bay** N.S.W. Austr.
236 D3 **Broken Bow** NE U.S.A.
237 E5 **Broken Bow** OK U.S.A.
232 E5 **Brokenburg** VA U.S.A.
223 L5 **Brokenhead** r. Man. Can.
82 E2 **Broken Hill** N.S.W. Austr.
Broken Hill Zambia see **Kabwe**
265 K7 **Broken Plateau** sea feature Indian Ocean
251 H3 **Brokopondo** Suriname
Brokopondo Stuwmeer resr Suriname see **Professor van Blommestein Meer**
168 E2 **Brokstedt** Ger.
194 D4 **Brolo** Sicilia Italy
173 E2 **Brombachsee** l. Ger.
Bromberg Pol. see **Bydgoszcz**
168 F3 **Brome** Ger.
150 E2 **Bromfield** Shropshire, England U.K.
151 G2 **Bromham** Bedfordshire, England U.K.
150 E3 **Bromham** Wiltshire, England U.K.
151 G3 **Bromley** Greater London, England U.K.
161 A4 **Brommat** France
149 H3 **Brompton** North Yorkshire, England U.K.
149 H3 **Brompton on Swale** North Yorkshire, England U.K.
143 G3 **Brömsebro** Sweden
150 E2 **Bromsgrove** Worcestershire, England U.K.
169 D4 **Bromskirchen** Ger.
150 E2 **Bromyard** Herefordshire, England U.K.
160 C3 **Bron** France
150 D2 **Bronaber** Gwynedd, Wales U.K.
183 I4 **Bronchales** Spain
142 C3 **Brønderslev** Denmark
206 E5 **Brong-Ahafo** admin. reg. Ghana
190 E3 **Broni** Italy
215 G1 **Bronkhorstspruit** S. Africa
139 L4 **Bronnitsy** Rus. Fed.
140 K2 **Brønnøysund** Norway
231 D6 **Bronson** FL U.S.A.
226 E5 **Bronson** MI U.S.A.
194 D5 **Bronte** Sicilia Italy
235 E2 **Bronx County** county NY U.S.A.
136 D2 **Bronyts'ka Huta** Ukr.
190 E3 **Bronzone, Monte** mt. Italy
151 I2 **Brooke** Norfolk, England U.K.
232 E5 **Brooke** VA U.S.A.
147 D2 **Brookeborough** Northern Ireland U.K.
92 A4 **Brooke's Point** Phil.
235 E1 **Brookfield** CT U.S.A.
236 E4 **Brookfield** MO U.S.A.
226 C4 **Brookfield** WI U.S.A.
237 F6 **Brookhaven** MS U.S.A.
238 A3 **Brookings** OR U.S.A.
236 D2 **Brookings** SD U.S.A.
234 C3 **Brookland Terrace** DE U.S.A.
233 H3 **Brookline** MA U.S.A.
226 B5 **Brooklyn** IL U.S.A.
227 E4 **Brooklyn** MI U.S.A.
234 B3 **Brooklyn Park** MD U.S.A.
226 A3 **Brooklyn Park** MN U.S.A.
232 D6 **Brookneal** VA U.S.A.
226 A3 **Brook Park** MN U.S.A.
223 I5 **Brooks** Alta Can.
233 □I2 **Brooks** ME U.S.A.
232 C6 **Brooks** WV U.S.A.
262 T2 **Brooks, Cape** Antarctica
222 C2 **Brooks Brook** Y.T. Can.
234 C3 **Brookside** DE U.S.A.
220 D3 **Brooks Range** mts AK U.S.A.
226 D5 **Brookston** IN U.S.A.
226 A2 **Brookston** MN U.S.A.
231 D6 **Brooksville** FL U.S.A.
232 A5 **Brooksville** KY U.S.A.
87 C7 **Brookton** W.A. Austr.
233 □J2 **Brookton** ME U.S.A.
230 C4 **Brookville** IN U.S.A.
232 D4 **Brookville** PA U.S.A.
146 C4 **Broom, Loch** inlet Scotland U.K.
86 D3 **Broome** W.A. Austr.
87 C7 **Broomehill** W.A. Austr.
147 E2 **Broomfield** Rep. of Ireland
151 H3 **Broomfield** Essex, England U.K.
158 D3 **Broons** France
161 A4 **Broquiès** France
146 E3 **Brora** Highland, Scotland U.K.
146 E3 **Brora** r. Scotland U.K.
143 F4 **Brösarp** Sweden
150 E2 **Broseley** Shropshire, England U.K.
136 C3 **Broshniv Osada** Ukr.
147 B4 **Brosna** Rep. of Ireland
147 D3 **Brosna** r. Rep. of Ireland
162 B3 **Brossac** France
140 L1 **Brøstadbotn** Norway
197 G2 **Broșteni** Romania
232 D6 **Brosville** VA U.S.A.
256 C5 **Brotas** Brazil
184 B2 **Brotas** Port.
254 E5 **Brotas de Macaúbas** Brazil
238 B3 **Brothers** OR U.S.A.
186 C2 **Broto** Spain
157 F4 **Brottes** France
149 I3 **Brotton** Redcar and Cleveland, England U.K.
156 B4 **Brou** France
149 G3 **Brough** Cumbria, England U.K.
149 I4 **Brough** East Riding of Yorkshire, England U.K.
146 E3 **Brough** Highland, Scotland U.K.
148 B4 **Broughal** Rep. of Ireland
146 E2 **Brough Head** hd Scotland U.K.
147 E2 **Broughshane** Northern Ireland U.K.
150 E1 **Broughton** Flintshire, Wales U.K.
151 G2 **Broughton** Northamptonshire, England U.K.
149 I4 **Broughton** North Lincolnshire, England U.K.
146 E6 **Broughton** Scottish Borders, Scotland U.K.
151 F2 **Broughton Astley** Leicestershire, England U.K.
149 F3 **Broughton in Furness** Cumbria, England U.K.
Broughton Island Nunavut Can. see **Qikiqtarjuaq**
146 F2 **Broughtown** Orkney, Scotland U.K.
176 F1 **Broumov** Czech Rep.
157 E4 **Brousseval** France
157 G4 **Brouvelieures** France
164 C3 **Brouwershaven** Neth.
136 F2 **Brovary** Ukr.
85 G5 **Brovinia** Qld Austr.
142 C3 **Brovst** Denmark
236 E2 **Browerville** MN U.S.A.
87 C6 **Brown, Lake** salt flat W.A. Austr.
82 D3 **Brown, Mount** hill S.A. Austr.
82 C3 **Brown, Point** S.A. Austr.
227 F4 **Brown City** MI U.S.A.
85 E3 **Brown Creek** r. Qld Austr.
226 D4 **Brown Deer** WI U.S.A.
149 G4 **Brown Edge** Staffordshire, England U.K.
87 E5 **Browne Range** hills W.A. Austr.
237 C5 **Brownfield** TX U.S.A.
151 F2 **Brownhills** West Midlands, England U.K.
238 D1 **Browning** MT U.S.A.
240 I4 **Brown Mountain** CA U.S.A.
226 A4 **Brownsdale** MN U.S.A.
234 D3 **Browns Mills** NJ U.S.A.
246 □ **Brown's Town** Jamaica
230 C4 **Brownstown** IN U.S.A.
234 B2 **Brownstown** PA U.S.A.
236 D2 **Browns Valley** MN U.S.A.
230 C4 **Brownsville** KY U.S.A.
232 D4 **Brownsville** PA U.S.A.
237 F5 **Brownsville** TN U.S.A.
237 D7 **Brownsville** TX U.S.A.
251 H3 **Brownsweg** Suriname
233 □I2 **Brownville** ME U.S.A.
233 □I2 **Brownville Junction** ME U.S.A.
237 D6 **Brownwood** TX U.S.A.
86 D2 **Browse Island** W.A. Austr.
146 E6 **Broxburn** West Lothian, Scotland U.K.
190 C2 **Broye** r. Switz.
156 D4 **Broyes** France
171 F5 **Brozany** Czech Rep.
182 D5 **Brozas** Spain
138 G5 **Brozha** Belarus
190 F3 **Brozzo** Italy
176 E2 **Brtnice** Czech Rep.
146 E5 **Bruar Water** r. Scotland U.K.
156 C2 **Bruay-la-Bussière** France
237 F5 **Bruce** MS U.S.A.
226 B3 **Bruce** WI U.S.A.
86 C4 **Bruce, Mount** W.A. Austr.
226 C2 **Bruce Crossing** MI U.S.A.
227 G3 **Bruce Peninsula** Ont. Can.
87 C6 **Bruce Rock** W.A. Austr.
157 H4 **Bruche** r. France
168 E3 **Bruchhausen-Vilsen** Ger.
169 D5 **Bruchköbel** Ger.
172 B2 **Bruchmühlbach** Ger.
172 C2 **Bruchsal** Ger.
172 B2 **Bruchweiler-Bärenbach** Ger.
171 D3 **Brück** Ger.
178 D3 **Bruck an der Großglocknerstraße** Austria
179 H2 **Bruck an der Leitha** Austria
179 G3 **Bruck an der Mur** Austria
173 F3 **Bruckberg** Ger.
172 B2 **Brücken** Ger.
172 B2 **Brücken (Pfalz)** Ger.
173 G2 **Bruck in der Oberpfalz** Ger.
179 F4 **Brückl** Austria
173 F4 **Bruckmühl** Ger.
195 E5 **Brucoli** Sicilia Italy
175 H3 **Brudzeń Duży** Pol.
174 G3 **Brudzew** Pol.
150 E3 **Brue** r. England U.K.
161 D5 **Brue-Auriac** France
170 C2 **Brüel** Ger.
159 I5 **Bruère-Allichamps** France
165 C4 **Brugelette** Belgium
Bruges Belgium see **Brugge**
190 D1 **Brugg** Switz.
165 C3 **Brugge** Belgium
169 E3 **Brüggen** Ger.
169 B4 **Brüggen** Ger.
190 E4 **Brugnato** Italy
191 H3 **Brugnera** Italy
163 D5 **Bruguières** France
140 I3 **Bruhagen** Norway
172 C2 **Brühl** Ger.
169 B5 **Brühl** Ger.
232 B5 **Bruin** KY U.S.A.
232 D4 **Bruin** PA U.S.A.
164 D3 **Bruinisse** Neth.
241 L2 **Bruin Point** mt. UT U.S.A.
214 A1 **Brukkaros, Mount** Namibia
222 G4 **Brûlé** Alta Can.
226 B2 **Brule** WI U.S.A.
159 F4 **Brûlon** France
165 D5 **Brûly** Belgium
257 E4 **Brumadinho** Brazil
254 E5 **Brumado** Brazil
157 H4 **Brumath** France
164 F2 **Brummen** Neth.
177 H2 **Brumov-Bylnice** Czech Rep.
177 G1 **Brumovice** Czech Rep.
141 J3 **Brumunddal** Norway
192 C2 **Bruna** r. Italy
147 E3 **Brú Na Bóinne** tourist site Meath Rep. of Ireland
170 C3 **Brunau** Ger.
151 I2 **Brundall** Norfolk, England U.K.
151 I2 **Brundish** Suffolk, England U.K.
Brundisium Italy see **Brindisi**
238 D3 **Bruneau** ID U.S.A.
238 D3 **Bruneau** r. ID U.S.A.
238 D3 **Bruneau, East Fork** r. Idaho/Nevada U.S.A.
238 D3 **Bruneau, West Fork** r. Idaho/Nevada U.S.A.
156 E3 **Brunehamel** France
95 F1 **Brunei** country Asia
Brunei Brunei see **Bandar Seri Begawan**
95 F1 **Brunei Bay** Malaysia
183 G4 **Brunete** Spain
84 C3 **Brunette Downs** N.T. Austr.
140 K3 **Brunflo** Sweden
191 G2 **Brunico** Italy
163 D4 **Bruniquel** France
179 G4 **Brunn** Austria
Brünn Czech Rep. see **Brno**
170 E2 **Brunn** Ger.
143 G2 **Brunna** Sweden
179 H2 **Brunn am Gebirge** Austria
190 D1 **Brunnen** Switz.
81 C5 **Brunner, Lake** South I. N.Z.
234 B2 **Brunnerville** PA U.S.A.
223 J4 **Bruno** Sask. Can.
226 A2 **Bruno** MN U.S.A.
168 E2 **Brunsbüttel** Ger.
165 E4 **Brunssum** Neth.
157 H5 **Brunstatt** France
Brunswick Ger. see **Braunschweig**
231 D6 **Brunswick** GA U.S.A.
232 E5 **Brunswick** MD U.S.A.
233 □I3 **Brunswick** ME U.S.A.
236 E4 **Brunswick** MO U.S.A.
232 C4 **Brunswick** OH U.S.A.
259 C9 **Brunswick, Península de** pen. Chile
86 E2 **Brunswick Bay** W.A. Austr.
83 H2 **Brunswick Head** N.S.W. Austr.
87 B7 **Brunswick Junction** W.A. Austr.
176 G2 **Bruntál** Czech Rep.
215 H3 **Bruntville** S. Africa
83 F5 **Bruny Island** Tas. Austr.
196 E4 **Brus** Srbija Yugo.
Brusa Turkey see **Bursa**
178 C4 **Brusago** Italy
170 C2 **Brüsewitz** Ger.
236 C3 **Brush** CO U.S.A.
233 F2 **Brushton** NY U.S.A.
190 F2 **Brusio** Switz.
177 I3 **Brusno** Slovakia
139 J3 **Brusovo** Rus. Fed.
255 C8 **Brusque** Brazil
161 A5 **Brusque** France
Brussel Belgium see **Bruxelles**
Brussels Belgium see **Bruxelles**
227 G4 **Brussels** Ont. Can.
170 F2 **Brüssow** Ger.
177 L4 **Brusturi** Romania
197 H2 **Brusturi-Drăgănești** Romania
174 F2 **Brusy** Pol.
136 E2 **Brusyliv** Ukr.
83 F4 **Bruthen** Vic. Austr.
150 E3 **Bruton** Somerset, England U.K.
169 C5 **Bruttig-Fankel** Ger.
165 D4 **Bruxelles** Belgium
157 G4 **Bruyères** France
156 D3 **Bruyères-et-Montbérault** France
158 E3 **Bruz** France
177 H2 **Brvnište** Slovakia
175 I3 **Brwinów** Pol.
236 G3 **Bryan** OH U.S.A.
237 D6 **Bryan** TX U.S.A.
82 D3 **Bryan, Mount** hill S.A. Austr.
262 S2 **Bryan Coast** Antarctica
137 J3 **Bryanka** Ukr.
139 J5 **Bryansk** Rus. Fed.
139 I5 **Bryanskaya Oblast'** admin. div. Rus. Fed.
Bryansk Oblast admin. div. Rus. Fed. see **Bryanskaya Oblast'**
129 E1 **Bryanskoye** Rus. Fed.
237 E5 **Bryant** AR U.S.A.
226 C3 **Bryant** WI U.S.A.
237 E4 **Bryant Creek** r. MO U.S.A.
233 □H2 **Bryant Pond** ME U.S.A.
241 M5 **Bryce Mountains** AZ U.S.A.
150 □ **Bryher** i. England U.K.
137 G4 **Brylivka** Ukr.
150 D1 **Brymbo** Wrexham, Wales U.K.
150 D3 **Brynamman** Carmarthenshire, Wales U.K.
142 A2 **Bryne** Norway
150 D1 **Brynford** Flintshire, Wales U.K.
175 H5 **Brynica** r. Pol.
135 G7 **Bryn'kovskaya** Rus. Fed.
150 D3 **Brynmawr** Blaenau Gwent, Wales U.K.
234 C2 **Bryn Mawr** PA U.S.A.
231 D5 **Bryson City** NC U.S.A.
135 G7 **Bryukhovetskaya** Rus. Fed.
136 B3 **Bryukhovychi** Ukr.
196 E3 **Brzava** r. Yugo.
174 F5 **Brzeg** Pol.
174 E4 **Brzeg Dolny** Pol.
174 G3 **Brześć Kujawski** Pol.
Brześć nad Bugiem Belarus see **Brest**
175 I6 **Brzesko** Pol.
175 H6 **Brzeszcze** Pol.
174 G3 **Brzezie** Pol.
175 H4 **Brzeziny** Łódzkie Pol.
175 J6 **Brzeziny** Podkarpackie Pol.
174 G4 **Brzeziny** Wielkopolskie Pol.
175 H6 **Brzeźnica** Pol.
175 J5 **Brzeźnica** Pol.
174 G4 **Brzeźnio** Pol.
175 L4 **Brzeźno** Pol.
174 G3 **Brzeźno** Pol.
174 D2 **Brzeźno** Pol.
175 J6 **Brzostek** Pol.
177 J3 **Brzotín** Slovakia
175 J4 **Brzóza** Pol.
175 K6 **Brzozów** Pol.
175 K2 **Brzozówka** r. Pol.
175 H2 **Brzuze** Pol.
175 K5 **Brzyska Wola** Pol.
156 B4 **Bû** France
124 D4 **Bū** well Yemen
142 E3 **Bua** Sweden
159 F3 **Buais** France
78 □6 **Buala** Sta Isabel Solomon Is
Buandougou Côte d'Ivoire see **Bouandougou**
182 B4 **Buarcos** Port.
94 C2 **Buatan** Sumatera Indon.
206 B4 **Buba** Guinea-Bissau
211 A5 **Bubanza** Burundi
173 F2 **Bubenreuth** Ger.
213 F4 **Bubi** r. Zimbabwe
158 C4 **Bubry** France
149 I4 **Bubwith** East Riding of Yorkshire, England U.K.
199 E2 **Buca** Turkey
199 G3 **Bucak** Turkey
177 G3 **Bučany** Slovakia
250 C3 **Bucaramanga** Col.
92 C4 **Bucas Grande** i. Phil.
86 D3 **Buccaneer Archipelago** is W.A. Austr.
194 D5 **Buccheri** Sicilia Italy
193 G2 **Bucchianico** Italy
191 G4 **Bucciana, Monte** mt. Italy
190 E3 **Buccinasco** Italy
193 H4 **Buccino** Italy
197 H2 **Bucecea** Romania
197 G3 **Bucegi, Munții** mts Romania
184 A2 **Bucelas** Port.
160 D1 **Bucey-lès-Gy** France
173 E3 **Buch** Ger.
136 C3 **Buchach** Ukr.
173 G3 **Buch am Erlbach** Ger.
83 G4 **Buchan** Vic. Austr.
206 C5 **Buchanan** Liberia
231 C5 **Buchanan** GA U.S.A.
226 D5 **Buchanan** MI U.S.A.
235 E1 **Buchanan** NY U.S.A.
232 D6 **Buchanan** VA U.S.A.
85 F4 **Buchanan, Lake** salt flat Qld Austr.
87 D5 **Buchanan, Lake** salt flat W.A. Austr.
225 J3 **Buchans** Nfld. Can.
Bucharest Romania see **București**
173 G3 **Buchbach** Ger.
169 C5 **Büchel** Ger.
168 F2 **Büchen** Ger.
172 D2 **Buchen (Odenwald)** Ger.
172 C4 **Buchenbach** Baden-Württemberg Ger.
173 F2 **Büchenbach** Ger.
173 E4 **Buchenberg** Ger.
172 B2 **Büchenbeuren** Ger.
170 D2 **Buchholz** Ger.
168 E3 **Buchholz (Aller)** Ger.
169 C5 **Buchholz (Westerwald)** Ger.
179 F2 **Buchkirchen** Austria
173 H3 **Büchlberg** Ger.
173 E3 **Buchloe** Ger.
176 G2 **Buchlovice** Czech Rep.
146 D5 **Buchlyvie** Stirling, Scotland U.K.
168 E2 **Bucholz in der Nordheide** Ger.
190 E1 **Buchs** Switz.
260 A5 **Buchupureo** Chile
156 B3 **Buchy** France
191 G5 **Bucine** Italy
234 B3 **Buck** PA U.S.A.
151 G2 **Buckden** Cambridgeshire, England U.K.
149 G3 **Buckden** North Yorkshire, England U.K.
169 E3 **Bückeburg** Ger.
168 E3 **Bücken** Ger.
241 K5 **Buckeye** AZ U.S.A.
150 D4 **Buckfastleigh** Devon, England U.K.
232 C5 **Buckhannon** WV U.S.A.
232 D5 **Buckhannon** r. WV U.S.A.
146 E5 **Buckhaven** Fife, Scotland U.K.
227 H3 **Buckhorn** Ont. Can.
146 F4 **Buckie** Moray, Scotland U.K.
227 J3 **Buckingham** Que. Can.
151 G2 **Buckingham** Buckinghamshire, England U.K.
234 C2 **Buckingham** PA U.S.A.
232 D6 **Buckingham** VA U.S.A.
84 C2 **Buckingham Bay** N.T. Austr.
151 G3 **Buckinghamshire** admin. div. England U.K.
220 B3 **Buckland** AK U.S.A.
214 D3 **Bucklands** S. Africa
85 G5 **Buckland Tableland** reg. Qld Austr.
82 D3 **Buckleboo** S.A. Austr.
151 F3 **Bucklebury** West Berkshire, England U.K.
263 K2 **Buckle Island** Antarctica
150 D1 **Buckley** Flintshire, Wales U.K.
226 C5 **Buckley** IL U.S.A.
237 D4 **Bucklin** KS U.S.A.
170 F3 **Buckow Märkische Schweiz** Ger.
146 F4 **Bucksburn** Aberdeen, Scotland U.K.
234 C2 **Bucks County** county PA U.S.A.
241 K4 **Buckskin Mountains** AZ U.S.A.
240 G2 **Bucks Mountain** CA U.S.A.
233 □I2 **Bucksport** ME U.S.A.
170 D3 **Bückwitz** Ger.
176 G2 **Bučovice** Czech Rep.
209 B6 **Buco-Zau** Angola
177 K4 **Bucsa** Hungary
197 G3 **Bucșani** Romania
197 H3 **București** Romania
156 D3 **Bucy-lès-Pierrepont** France
232 B4 **Bucyrus** OH U.S.A.
175 H4 **Buczek** Pol.
186 D4 **Buda, Illa de** i. Spain
139 H5 **Buda-Kashalyova** Belarus
177 H4 **Budakeszi** Hungary
96 A2 **Budalin** Myanmar
177 H4 **Budaörs** Hungary
177 I4 **Budapest** Hungary
116 D3 **Budaun** Uttar Prad. India
87 B6 **Budd, Mount** hill W.A. Austr.
83 F2 **Budda** N.S.W. Austr.
263 H2 **Budd Coast** Antarctica
171 C3 **Büddenstedt** Ger.
234 D2 **Budd Lake** NJ U.S.A.
192 B4 **Buddusò** Sardegna Italy
150 C4 **Bude** Cornwall, England U.K.
237 F6 **Bude** MS U.S.A.
150 C4 **Bude Bay** England U.K.
176 D2 **Budějovický kraj** admin. reg. Czech Rep.
165 E3 **Budel** Neth.
168 E1 **Büdelsdorf** Ger.
136 C3 **Budenets'** Ukr.
169 D5 **Budenheim** Ger.
129 D1 **Budennovsk** Rus. Fed.
Budennoye Belgorodskaya Oblast' Rus. Fed. see **Krasnogvardeyskoye**
184 B3 **Budens** Port.
85 H5 **Buderim** Qld Austr.
197 H3 **Budești** Romania
128 A5 **Budhiya, Gebel** mt. Egypt
123 H4 **Budhlada** Punjab India
183 H4 **Budia** Spain
169 E5 **Büdingen** Ger.
179 H4 **Budinšćina** Croatia
177 G2 **Budišov nad Budišovkou** Czech Rep.
174 F5 **Budkowiczanka** r. Pol.
150 D4 **Budleigh Salterton** Devon, England U.K.
139 I2 **Budogoshch'** Rus. Fed.
191 H2 **Budoia** Italy
106 B5 **Budongquan** Qinghai China
192 B4 **Budoni** Sardegna Italy
191 G4 **Budrio** Italy
175 J1 **Budry** Pol.
Büdszentmihály Hungary see **Tiszavasvári**
125 E3 **Budū', Sabkhat al** salt pan Saudi Arabia
197 F2 **Budureasa** Romania
177 L4 **Buduslău** Romania
196 D4 **Budva** Crna Gora Yugo.
Budweis Czech Rep. see **České Budějovice**
171 F5 **Budyně nad Ohří** Czech Rep.
175 H4 **Budziszewice** Pol.
175 H6 **Budzów** Pol.
174 E3 **Budzyń** Pol.
207 H5 **Buea** Cameroon
161 D4 **Buëch** r. France
240 G4 **Buellton** CA U.S.A.
186 B4 **Bueña** Spain
234 D3 **Buena** NJ U.S.A.
183 H5 **Buenache de Alarcón** Spain
183 H4 **Buenache de la Sierra** Spain
260 E4 **Buena Esperanza** Arg.
250 B4 **Buenaventura** Col.
242 D2 **Buenaventura** Mex.
183 F4 **Buenaventura** Spain
244 C4 **Buenavista** Mex.
Buena Vista i. N. Mariana Is see **Tinian**
92 B3 **Buenavista** Phil.
239 F4 **Buena Vista** CO U.S.A.
231 C5 **Buena Vista** GA U.S.A.
232 D6 **Buena Vista** VA U.S.A.
216 □3a **Buenavista del Norte** Tenerife Canary Is
183 F2 **Buenavista de Valdavia** Spain
183 H4 **Buendía** Spain
183 H4 **Buendia, Embalse de** resr Spain
209 B6 **Buenga** r. Angola
209 B6 **Buengas** Angola
257 E2 **Buenópolis** Brazil
261 H4 **Buenos Aires** Arg.
261 G5 **Buenos Aires** prov. Arg.
250 D5 **Buenos Aires** Col.
259 B7 **Buenos Aires, Lago** l. Arg./Chile
255 F5 **Buerarema** Brazil
250 B4 **Buesaco** Col.
160 E2 **Buet, Le Mont** mt. France
182 B2 **Bueu** Spain
185 G2 **Buey, Cabeza de** mt. Spain
242 D3 **Búfalo** Mex.
222 H2 **Buffalo** r. Alta/N.W.T. Can.
236 E2 **Buffalo** MN U.S.A.
237 E4 **Buffalo** MO U.S.A.
232 D3 **Buffalo** NY U.S.A.
232 C5 **Buffalo** OH U.S.A.
237 D4 **Buffalo** OK U.S.A.
236 C2 **Buffalo** SD U.S.A.
237 D6 **Buffalo** TX U.S.A.
226 B3 **Buffalo** WI U.S.A.
238 F2 **Buffalo** WY U.S.A.
237 E4 **Buffalo** r. AR U.S.A.
231 C5 **Buffalo** r. TN U.S.A.
226 B3 **Buffalo** r. WI U.S.A.
234 A2 **Buffalo Creek** r. PA U.S.A.
222 G3 **Buffalo Head Hills** Y.T. Can.
222 G3 **Buffalo Head Prairie** Alta Can.
238 D2 **Buffalo Hump** mt. ID U.S.A.
223 I4 **Buffalo Narrows** Sask. Can.
213 F4 **Buffalo Range** Zimbabwe
246 □ **Buff Bay** Jamaica
215 H3 **Buffels** r. Kwazulu-Natal S. Africa
214 C5 **Buffels** r. W. Cape S. Africa
214 D5 **Buffelsdrif** S. Africa
213 E4 **Buffels Drift** S. Africa
160 C2 **Buffières** France
169 F4 **Bufleben** Ger.
231 C5 **Buford** GA U.S.A.
197 G3 **Buftea** Romania
175 L4 **Bug** r. Pol.
250 B4 **Buga** Col.
106 B2 **Buga** Mongolia
Buga Buga i. Vanuatu see **Toga**
177 I5 **Bugac** Hungary
210 B5 **Bugala Island** Uganda
83 G2 **Bugaldie** N.S.W. Austr.
207 G5 **Bugana** Nigeria
107 E1 **Bugant** Mongolia
163 E6 **Bugarach, Pic de** mt. France
Bugaz Ukr. see **Zatoka**
151 F2 **Bugbrooke** Northamptonshire, England U.K.
199 E1 **Buğdaylı** Balıkesir Turkey
122 C2 **Bugdayli** Turkm.
162 D3 **Bugeat** France
165 D3 **Buggenhout** Belgium
192 A5 **Buggerru** Sardegna Italy
172 B4 **Buggingen** Ger.
184 □ **Bugio** i. Madeira
193 F2 **Bugnara** Italy
163 B5 **Bugnein** France
188 F3 **Bugojno** Bos.-Herz.
107 I1 **Bugt** Nei Mongol China
92 B2 **Buguey** Phil.
135 K5 **Bugul'ma** Rus. Fed.
120 E3 **Bugun'** Kazakh.
Bügür Xinjiang China see **Luntai**
120 C1 **Buguruslan** Rus. Fed.
177 I4 **Bugyi** Hungary
122 C4 **Būhābād** Iran
199 F3 **Buharkent** Turkey
213 F3 **Buhera** Zimbabwe
106 C4 **Buh He** r. China
92 B3 **Buhi** Phil.
172 C3 **Bühl** Ger.
238 D3 **Buhl** ID U.S.A.
226 A2 **Buhl** MN U.S.A.
172 C3 **Bühlertal** Ger.
172 D2 **Bühlertann** Ger.
172 D2 **Bühlerzell** Ger.
169 F3 **Bühne** Ger.
136 D2 **Buhryn** Ukr.
127 F3 **Bühtan** r. Turkey
211 B6 **Buhu** r. Tanz.
197 H2 **Buhuși** Romania
191 I2 **Buia** Italy
222 F3 **Buick** B.C. Can.
146 C5 **Buie, Loch** b. Scotland U.K.
150 D2 **Builth Wells** Powys, Wales U.K.
260 B3 **Buin** Chile
135 J5 **Buinsk** Rus. Fed.
107 H2 **Buir Nur** l. Mongolia
161 D4 **Buis-les-Baronnies** France
164 F1 **Buitenpost** Neth.
183 G4 **Buitrago del Lozoya** Spain
185 F3 **Bujalance** Spain
197 E4 **Bujanovac** Srbija Yugo.
186 C3 **Bujaraloz** Spain
197 G4 **Bujoru** Romania
211 A5 **Bujumbura** Burundi
179 H3 **Bük** Hungary
174 E3 **Buk** Pol.
99 K1 **Bukachacha** Rus. Fed.
175 M6 **Bukachivtsi** Ukr.
209 E7 **Bukama** Dem. Rep. Congo
121 J1 **Bukanskoye** Rus. Fed.
120 E4 **Bukantau, Gory** hills Uzbek.
208 F5 **Bukavu** Dem. Rep. Congo
211 B6 **Bukene** Tanz.
120 F5 **Bukhara** Uzbek.
Bukhara Oblast admin. div. Uzbek. see **Bukharskaya Oblast'**
120 E4 **Bukharskaya Oblast'** admin. div. Uzbek.
Bukhoro Uzbek. see **Bukhara**
Bukhoro Wiloyati admin. div. Uzbek. see **Bukharskaya Oblast'**
121 K2 **Bukhtarminskoye Vodokhranilishche** resr Kazakh.
94 □ **Bukit Timah** hill Sing.
94 C3 **Bukittinggi** Sumatera Indon.
177 J3 **Bükk** mts Hungary
177 J4 **Bükkábrány** Hungary
177 J4 **Bükkalja** hills Hungary
114 C3 **Bukkapatnam** Andhra Prad. India
177 G5 **Bükkösd** Hungary
177 J4 **Bükkzsérc** Hungary
171 D4 **Buko** Ger.
211 A5 **Bukoba** Tanz.
177 H2 **Bukovec** Czech Rep.
177 L2 **Bukovské vrchy** hills Slovakia
175 K5 **Bukowa** r. Pol.
174 F3 **Bukowe** Pol.
174 F4 **Bukowice** Pol.
174 G2 **Bukowiec** Pol.
171 G3 **Bukowiec** hill Pol.
174 F1 **Bukowina** Pol.
175 I6 **Bukowina Tatrzańska** Pol.
174 G4 **Bukownica** Pol.
175 H5 **Bukowno** Pol.
175 K6 **Bukowsko** Pol.
Bükreș Romania see **București**
136 F3 **Buky** Ukr.
122 C4 **Būl, Kūh-e** mt. Iran
206 B3 **Bula** Guinea-Bissau
209 B7 **Bula Atumba** Angola
190 D1 **Bülach** Switz.
107 F1 **Bulag** Mongolia
107 E1 **Bulagtay** Mongolia
83 H3 **Bulahdelal** N.S.W. Austr.
92 B3 **Bulan** Phil.
126 E2 **Bulancak** Turkey
116 D3 **Bulandshahr** Uttar Prad. India
127 F3 **Bulanık** Turkey
120 C1 **Bulanovo** Rus. Fed.
93 B2 **Bulawa, Gunung** mt. Indon.
213 F4 **Bulawayo** Zimbabwe
121 G1 **Bulayevo** Kazakh.
126 E3 **Bulbul** Syria
199 F2 **Buldan** Turkey
116 D5 **Buldana** Mahar. India
252 A2 **Buldibuyo** Peru
120 C2 **Buldurta** Kazakh.
Buldyrty Kazakh. see **Buldurta**
210 E3 **Bulei** well Eth.
215 H1 **Bulembu** Swaziland
151 F3 **Bulford** Wiltshire, England U.K.
106 D1 **Bulgan** Bulgan Mongolia
Bulgan Hovd Mongolia see **Bürenhayrhan**
106 B2 **Bulgan** Hovd Mongolia
106 D1 **Bulgan** Hövsgöl Mongolia
106 D2 **Bulgan** Ömnögovĭ Mongolia
106 D1 **Bulgan** prov. Mongolia
106 A2 **Bulgan Gol** r. Mongolia
Bulgar Respublika Tatarstan Rus. Fed. see **Bolgar**
197 I4 **Bŭlgarevo** Bulg.
197 G4 **Bulgaria** country Europe
Bŭlgariya country Europe see **Bulgaria**
193 H4 **Bulgheria, Monte** mt. Italy
157 F4 **Bulgnéville** France
129 C3 **Bulgurlu** Turkey
137 G5 **Bulhanak** r. Ukr.
168 D2 **Bülkau** Ger.
151 F2 **Bulkington** Warwickshire, England U.K.
222 D4 **Bulkley Ranges** mts B.C. Can.
175 I3 **Bulkowo** Pol.
185 F2 **Bullaque** r. Spain
185 I2 **Bullas** Spain
85 E5 **Bullawarra, Lake** salt flat Qld Austr.
169 C5 **Bullay** Ger.
190 C2 **Bulle** Switz.
83 E2 **Bullea, Lake** salt flat N.S.W. Austr.
81 C4 **Buller** r. South I. N.Z.
87 C6 **Bullfinch** W.A. Austr.
241 J4 **Bullhead City** AZ U.S.A.
83 G3 **Bulli** N.S.W. Austr.
165 F4 **Büllingen** Belgium
241 I4 **Bullion Mountains** CA U.S.A.
140 M2 **Bullmark** Sweden
84 B2 **Bullo** r. N.T. Austr.
183 H4 **Bullones** r. Spain
83 E2 **Bulloo Downs** Qld Austr.
83 E2 **Bulloo Lake** salt flat Qld Austr.
80 E4 **Bulls** North I. N.Z.
235 E1 **Bulls Bridge** CT U.S.A.
235 D1 **Bullville** NY U.S.A.
156 C2 **Bully-les-Mines** France
84 C2 **Bulman** N.T. Austr.
84 C2 **Bulman Gorge** N.T. Austr.
151 H2 **Bulmer Tye** Essex, England U.K.
260 A5 **Bulnes** Chile
83 E4 **Buloke, Lake** dry lake Vic. Austr.
196 E5 **Bulqizë** Albania
192 B4 **Bultei** Sardegna Italy
215 F3 **Bultfontein** S. Africa
95 G2 **Bulu, Gunung** mt. Indon.
92 C5 **Buluan** Phil.
93 B4 **Bulukumba** Sulawesi Selatan Indon.
209 C6 **Bulungu** Bandundu Dem. Rep. Congo
209 D6 **Bulungu** Kasai Occidental Dem. Rep. Congo
121 F5 **Bulungur** Uzbek.
92 C3 **Bulusan** Phil.
215 G3 **Bulwer** S. Africa
177 L5 **Bulz** Romania
192 A4 **Bulzi** Sardegna Italy
78 □6 **Buma** Malaita Solomon Is
209 C6 **Bumba** Bandundu Dem. Rep. Congo
208 D4 **Bumba** Équateur Dem. Rep. Congo
106 E2 **Bumbat** Mongolia
197 F3 **Bumbești-Jiu** Romania
206 C4 **Bumbuna** Sierra Leone
96 B1 **Bumpha Bum** mt. Myanmar
147 B3 **Bunacurry** Rep. of Ireland
147 C1 **Bunbeg** Rep. of Ireland
87 B7 **Bunbury** W.A. Austr.
149 G4 **Bunbury** Cheshire, England U.K.
147 E4 **Bunclody** Rep. of Ireland
147 D1 **Buncrana** Rep. of Ireland
211 B5 **Bunda** Tanz.
85 H5 **Bundaberg** Qld Austr.
83 F2 **Bundaleer** Qld Austr.
83 G2 **Bundarra** N.S.W. Austr.
168 C2 **Bunde** Niedersachsen Ger.
169 D3 **Bünde** Ger.
172 B2 **Bundenbach** Ger.
168 C2 **Bunderhee** Ger.
116 C4 **Bundi** Rajasthan India
210 A4 **Bundibugyo** Uganda
147 C2 **Bundoran** Rep. of Ireland
117 F5 **Bundu** Bihar India
196 D5 **Bunë** r. Albania/Yugo.
207 H3 **Bunga** r. Nigeria
104 B3 **Bunga-dake** mt. Japan
94 B3 **Bungalaut, Selat** sea chan. Indon.
151 I2 **Bungay** Suffolk, England U.K.
96 C4 **Bung Boraphet** l. Thai.
83 G3 **Bungendore** N.S.W. Austr.
263 G2 **Bunger Hills** Antarctica
85 G5 **Bungil Creek** r. Qld Austr.
209 B6 **Bungo** Angola
210 B4 **Bungoma** Kenya
103 F7 **Bungo-suidō** sea chan. Japan
103 E7 **Bungo-takada** Japan
Bunguran, Kepulauan is Indon. see **Natuna, Kepulauan**
Bunguran, Pulau i. Indon. see **Natuna Besar**
208 F4 **Bunia** Dem. Rep. Congo
183 G2 **Buniel** Spain
177 L6 **Bunila** Romania
87 D6 **Buningonia** well W.A. Austr.
207 I4 **Buni-Yadi** Nigeria
116 C2 **Bunji** Jammu and Kashmir
237 F4 **Bunker** MO U.S.A.
85 H4 **Bunker Group** atolls Qld Austr.
209 E7 **Bunkeya** Dem. Rep. Congo
237 E6 **Bunkie** LA U.S.A.
141 K3 **Bunkris** Sweden
147 D4 **Bunmahon** Rep. of Ireland
147 B2 **Bunnahowen** Rep. of Ireland
147 C2 **Bunnanadden** Rep. of Ireland
231 D6 **Bunnell** FL U.S.A.
164 E2 **Bunnik** Neth.
147 B2 **Bunnyconnellan** Rep. of Ireland
80 E4 **Bunnythorpe** North I. N.Z.
187 C5 **Buñol** Spain
164 E2 **Bunschoten-Spakenburg** Neth.
177 L5 **Buntești** Romania
87 C6 **Buntine** W.A. Austr.
151 G3 **Buntingford** Hertfordshire, England U.K.
183 I3 **Buñuel** Spain
207 H4 **Bununu** Nigeria
126 D3 **Bünyan** Turkey
187 F5 **Bunyola** Spain
207 G3 **Bunza** Nigeria
188 F3 **Buoač** Bos.-Herz.
193 H4 **Buonabitacolo** Italy
193 G3 **Buonalbergo** Italy
192 D1 **Buonconvento** Italy
97 E4 **Buôn Mê Thuột** Vietnam
193 H5 **Buonvicino** Italy
111 D6 **Bup** r. China
Buqayq Saudi Arabia see **Abqaiq**
Buqtyrma Bögeni resr Kazakh. see **Bukhtarminskoye Vodokhranilishche**
210 F2 **Buraan** Somalia
87 C6 **Burakin** W.A. Austr.
121 K2 **Buran** Kazakh.
257 H2 **Buranhaém** r. Brazil
120 C2 **Burannoye** Rus. Fed.
191 H5 **Burano** r. Italy
210 E2 **Burao** Somalia
92 C4 **Burauen** Phil.
116 C5 **Buray** r. India
124 C2 **Buraydah** Saudi Arabia
134 K5 **Burayevo** Rus. Fed.
169 D5 **Burbach** Ger.
151 F3 **Burbage** Wiltshire, England U.K.
186 B3 **Burbáguena** Spain
240 H4 **Burbank** CA U.S.A.
192 B5 **Burcei** Sardegna Italy
137 H4 **Burchak** Ukr.
226 B1 **Burchell Lake** Ont. Can.
83 F3 **Burcher** N.S.W. Austr.
85 F3 **Burdekin** r. Qld Austr.
85 F4 **Burdekin Falls** Qld Austr.
160 D2 **Burdet, Mont** mt. France
Burdigala France see **Bordeaux**
165 E4 **Burdinne** Belgium
199 G3 **Burdur** Turkey
199 G3 **Burdur** prov. Turkey
199 G3 **Burdur Gölü** l. Turkey
Burdwan W. Bengal India see **Barddhaman**
210 C2 **Burē** Amhara Eth.
210 B2 **Burē** Oromia Eth.
151 I2 **Bure** r. England U.K.
161 D4 **Bure, Pic de** mt. France
140 M2 **Bureå** Sweden
100 E2 **Bureinskiy Khrebet** mts Rus. Fed.
183 F2 **Burejo** r. Spain
169 D4 **Büren** Ger.
164 E3 **Buren** Neth.
190 C1 **Büren an der Aare** Switz.
106 A2 **Bürenhayrhan** Hovd Mongolia
107 F2 **Bürentsogt** Mongolia
260 A5 **Bureo** r. Chile
151 H3 **Bures** Suffolk, England U.K.
100 D2 **Bureya** r. Rus. Fed.
Bureya-Pristan' Rus. Fed. see **Novobureyskiy**
Bureya Range mts Rus. Fed. see **Bureinskiy Khrebet**
227 G4 **Burford** Ont. Can.
151 F3 **Burford** Oxfordshire, England U.K.
163 C5 **Burg** France
171 F4 **Burg** Ger.
168 E2 **Burg (Dithmarschen)** Ger.
106 E1 **Burgaltay** Mongolia
182 E3 **Burganes de Valverde** Spain
197 H4 **Burgas** Bulg.
179 H3 **Burgau** Austria
173 E3 **Burgau** Ger.
184 B3 **Burgau** Port.
170 C1 **Burg auf Fehmarn** Ger.
231 E5 **Burgaw** NC U.S.A.
171 C3 **Burg bei Magdeburg** Ger.
173 E4 **Burgberg im Allgäu** Ger.
173 E2 **Burgbernheim** Ger.
169 C5 **Burgbrohl** Ger.
169 F3 **Burgdorf** Niedersachsen Ger.
169 F3 **Burgdorf** Niedersachsen Ger.
190 C1 **Burgdorf** Switz.
173 E2 **Burgebrach** Ger.
171 C5 **Bürgel** Ger.
179 H3 **Burgenland** land Austria
225 J4 **Burgeo** Nfld. Can.
215 F4 **Burgersdorp** S. Africa
213 F5 **Burgersfort** S. Africa
214 E4 **Burgerville** S. Africa
87 D6 **Burges, Mount** hill W.A. Austr.
233 E6 **Burgess** VA U.S.A.
151 G4 **Burgess Hill** West Sussex, England U.K.
173 E2 **Burghaslach** Ger.
169 E5 **Burghaun** Ger.
173 G3 **Burghausen** Ger.
149 F3 **Burgh by Sands** Cumbria, England U.K.
151 F3 **Burghclere** Hampshire, England U.K.
146 E4 **Burghead** Moray, Scotland U.K.
173 F3 **Burgheim** Ger.
151 F3 **Burghfield Common** West Berkshire, England U.K.
164 C3 **Burgh-Haamstede** Neth.
150 E2 **Burghill** Herefordshire, England U.K.
149 J4 **Burgh le Marsh** Lincolnshire, England U.K.
194 C5 **Burgio** Sicilia Italy
194 D5 **Burgio, Serra di** hill Sicilia Italy
178 E2 **Burgkirchen** Austria
173 G3 **Burgkirchen an der Alz** Ger.
171 C5 **Burgkunstadt** Ger.
190 E1 **Bürglen** Thurgau Switz.
190 D2 **Bürglen** Uri Switz.
173 G2 **Burglengenfeld** Ger.
173 E2 **Burgoberbach** Ger.
183 F4 **Burgohondo** Spain
192 A4 **Burgos** Sardegna Italy
243 F3 **Burgos** Mex.
183 G2 **Burgos** Spain
183 G2 **Burgos** prov. Castilla y León Spain
169 F5 **Burgpreppach** Ger.
172 D3 **Burgrieden** Ger.
173 F2 **Burgsalach** Ger.
169 E5 **Burgsinn** Ger.
172 D2 **Bürgstadt** Ger.
171 D5 **Burgstädt** Ger.
170 E2 **Burg Stargand** Ger.
143 H3 **Burgsvik** Gotland Sweden
173 F2 **Burgthann** Ger.
169 F4 **Burgtonna** Ger.
186 B2 **Burguete** Spain
186 B2 **Burgui** Spain
184 E3 **Burguillos** Spain
184 D2 **Burguillos del Cerro** Spain
173 E2 **Burgwindheim** Ger.
117 F5 **Burhabalanga** r. India
106 B5 **Burhan Budai Shan** mts China
199 E2 **Burhaniye** Turkey
116 D5 **Burhanpur** Madh. Prad. India
116 E5 **Burhar-Dhanpuri** Madh. Prad. India
168 D2 **Burhave (Butjadingen)** Ger.
117 F4 **Burhi Gandak** r. India
158 D2 **Burhou** i. Channel Is
256 C5 **Buri** Brazil
92 B3 **Burias** i. Phil.
190 C4 **Buriasco** Italy
Buriat-Mongol Republic aut. rep. Rus. Fed. see **Buryatiya, Respublika**
120 D2 **Buribay** Rus. Fed.
162 B3 **Burie** France
117 E4 **Buri Gandak** r. Nepal
225 K4 **Burin** Nfld. Can.
225 K4 **Burin Peninsula** Nfld. Can.
96 C4 **Buriram** Thai.
256 B4 **Buritama** Brazil
254 E2 **Buriti** Brazil
253 F3 **Buriti** r. Brazil
256 C3 **Buriti Alegre** Brazil
254 E3 **Buriti Bravo** Brazil
254 E2 **Buriti dos Lopes** Brazil
254 E4 **Buritirama** Brazil
255 D5 **Buritis** Brazil
257 E2 **Buritizeiro** Brazil
187 C5 **Burjassot** Spain
177 L6 **Burjuc** Romania
173 E2 **Burk** Ger.
121 I4 **Burkan-Suu** r. Kyrg.
169 E5 **Burkardroth** Ger.
237 D5 **Burkburnett** TX U.S.A.
84 D4 **Burke** watercourse Qld Austr.
236 D3 **Burke** SD U.S.A.
262 Q2 **Burke Island** Antarctica
81 C6 **Burke Pass** South I. N.Z.
230 C4 **Burkesville** KY U.S.A.
84 D3 **Burketown** Qld Austr.
232 D6 **Burkeville** VA U.S.A.
131 P3 **Burkhala** Rus. Fed.
206 E4 **Burkina** country Africa
Burkina Faso country Africa see **Burkina**
224 E4 **Burk's Falls** Ont. Can.
121 I1 **Burla** Rus. Fed.
121 I1 **Burla** r. Rus. Fed.
183 I2 **Burlada** Spain
172 D3 **Burladingen** Ger.
163 E5 **Burlats** France
85 E4 **Burleigh** Qld Austr.
234 D3 **Burleigh** NJ U.S.A.
151 F4 **Burley** Hampshire, England U.K.
238 D3 **Burley** ID U.S.A.
150 E2 **Burley Gate** Herefordshire, England U.K.
149 H4 **Burley in Wharfedale** West Yorkshire, England U.K.
120 E1 **Burli** Kazakh.
120 C2 **Burlin** Kazakh.
240 F3 **Burlingame** CA U.S.A.
224 E5 **Burlington** Ont. Can.
236 C4 **Burlington** CO U.S.A.
235 F1 **Burlington** CT U.S.A.
230 B3 **Burlington** IA U.S.A.
226 D5 **Burlington** IN U.S.A.
236 E4 **Burlington** KS U.S.A.
236 G4 **Burlington** KY U.S.A.
231 E4 **Burlington** NC U.S.A.
234 D2 **Burlington** NJ U.S.A.
233 G2 **Burlington** VT U.S.A.
238 B1 **Burlington** WA U.S.A.
226 C4 **Burlington** WI U.S.A.
234 D3 **Burlington County** county NJ U.S.A.
120 D1 **Burly** Rus. Fed.
Burma country Asia see **Myanmar**
134 J4 **Burmakino** Kirovskaya Oblast' Rus. Fed.
139 M3 **Burmakino** Yaroslavskaya Oblast' Rus. Fed.
178 D3 **Bürmoos** Austria
222 F5 **Burnaby** B.C. Can.
148 B5 **Burnchurch** Rep. of Ireland
146 F2 **Burness** Orkney, Scotland U.K.
237 D6 **Burnet** TX U.S.A.
85 H5 **Burnett** r. Qld Austr.
85 H5 **Burnett Heads** Qld Austr.
238 B3 **Burney** CA U.S.A.
259 B9 **Burney, Monte** vol. Chile
147 C4 **Burnfoot** Rep. of Ireland
147 E2 **Burnfoot** Northern Ireland U.K.
81 D5 **Burnham** South I. N.Z.
151 G3 **Burnham** Buckinghamshire, England U.K.
233 □I2 **Burnham** ME U.S.A.
232 E4 **Burnham** PA U.S.A.
151 H2 **Burnham Market** Norfolk, England U.K.
151 H3 **Burnham-on-Crouch** Essex, England U.K.
150 E3 **Burnham-on-Sea** Somerset, England U.K.
148 E2 **Burnhouse** North Ayrshire, Scotland U.K.
83 F5 **Burnie** Tas. Austr.
232 B6 **Burning Springs** KY U.S.A.
149 I3 **Burniston** North Yorkshire, England U.K.
149 G4 **Burnley** Lancashire, England U.K.
146 F6 **Burnmouth** Scottish Borders, Scotland U.K.
149 H3 **Burnopfield** Durham, England U.K.
Burnoye Kazakh. see **Bauyrzhan Momysh-Uly**
238 C3 **Burns** OR U.S.A.
220 H3 **Burnside** r. Nunavut Can.
87 D5 **Burnside, Lake** salt flat W.A. Austr.
238 C3 **Burns Junction** OR U.S.A.
222 E4 **Burns Lake** B.C. Can.
226 A3 **Burnsville** MN U.S.A.
232 C5 **Burnsville** WV U.S.A.
238 C2 **Burnt** r. OR U.S.A.
146 E5 **Burntisland** Fife, Scotland U.K.
223 L4 **Burntwood** r. Man. Can.
151 F2 **Burntwood Green** Staffordshire, England U.K.
225 G1 **Buron** r. Que. Can.
183 E1 **Burón** Spain
190 D3 **Buronzo** Italy
163 B5 **Buros** France
120 E4 **Burovoy** Uzbek.
170 E2 **Burow** Ger.
110 D2 **Burqin** Xinjiang China
110 D2 **Burqin** r. China
128 D3 **Burqu'** Jordan
82 D3 **Burra** S.A. Austr.
146 □G1 **Burra** i. Scotland U.K.
146 □G1 **Burravoe** Shetland, Scotland U.K.
146 F3 **Burray** i. Scotland U.K.
196 E5 **Burrel** Albania
240 H3 **Burrel** CA U.S.A.
146 E5 **Burrelton** Perth and Kinross, Scotland U.K.
147 B3 **Burren** Rep. of Ireland
147 B3 **Burren** reg. Rep. of Ireland
148 C3 **Burren** Northern Ireland U.K.
83 G3 **Burrendong Reservoir** N.S.W. Austr.
83 G2 **Burren Junction** N.S.W. Austr.
83 G3 **Burrewarra Point** N.S.W. Austr.
187 C5 **Burriana** Spain
83 G3 **Burrinjuck Reservoir** N.S.W. Austr.
226 B4 **Burr Oak** IA U.S.A.
147 B3 **Burron** Rep. of Ireland
148 E3 **Burrow Head** hd Scotland U.K.
84 B2 **Burrundie** N.T. Austr.
150 C3 **Burry Port** Carmarthenshire, Wales U.K.
178 A3 **Bürs** Austria
199 F1 **Bursa** Turkey
199 F1 **Bursa** prov. Turkey
203 G3 **Bûr Safâga** Egypt
203 G2 **Bûr Sa'îd** Egypt
126 D5 **Bûr Sa'îd** governorate Egypt
149 G4 **Burscough** Lancashire, England U.K.
149 G4 **Burscough Bridge** Lancashire, England U.K.
169 E4 **Bursfelde** Ger.
136 C3 **Burshtyn** Ukr.
172 C2 **Bürstadt** Ger.
151 G3 **Burstow** Surrey, England U.K.

Būr Sudan Sudan see Port Sudan
82 E3 Burta N.S.W. Austr.
173 E3 Burtenbach Ger.
138 E3 Burtnieku ezers l. Latvia
151 F4 Burton Dorset, England U.K.
227 F4 Burton MI U.S.A.
150 E4 Burton Bradstock Dorset, England U.K.
149 G3 Burton-in-Kendal Cumbria, England U.K.
151 G2 Burton Latimer Northamptonshire, England U.K.
149 H3 Burton Leonard North Yorkshire, England U.K.
147 C2 Burtonport Rep. of Ireland
234 B3 Burtonsville MD U.S.A.
149 I4 Burton upon Stather North Lincolnshire, England U.K.
151 F2 Burton upon Trent Staffordshire, England U.K.
140 M2 Burträsk Sweden
233 □J1 Burtts Corner N.B. Can.
83 E3 Burtundy N.S.W. Austr.
84 C4 Burt Well N.T. Austr.
93 C3 Buru i. Maluku Indon.
183 F5 Burujón Spain
137 H5 Burul'cha r. Ukr.
126 C5 Burullus, Bahra el lag. Egypt
Burullus, Lake lag. Egypt see Burullus, Bahra el
Burultokay Xinjiang China see Fuhai
211 A5 Burundi country Africa
Burunniy Rus. Fed. see Tsagan Aman
211 A5 Bururi Burundi
150 E2 Burwarton Shropshire, England U.K.
151 H4 Burwash East Sussex, England U.K.
222 B2 Burwash Landing Y.T. Can.
151 H2 Burwell Cambridgeshire, England U.K.
236 D3 Burwell NE U.S.A.
146 F3 Burwick Orkney, Scotland U.K.
149 G4 Bury Greater Manchester, England U.K.
Buryatia aut. rep. Rus. Fed. see Buryatiya, Respublika
106 G1 Buryatiya, Respublika aut. rep. Rus. Fed.
Buryatskaya Mongolskaya A.S.S.R. aut. rep. Rus. Fed. see Buryatiya, Respublika
137 G2 Buryn' Ukr.
151 H2 Bury St Edmunds Suffolk, England U.K.
174 G4 Burzenin Pol.
161 C4 Burzet France
192 A4 Busachi Sardegna Italy
190 D4 Busalla Italy
Busan S. Korea see Pusan
190 F4 Busana Italy
238 F2 Busby MT U.S.A.
190 C4 Busca Italy
179 H2 Buschberg hill Austria
170 D3 Buschow Ger.
168 E1 Busdorf Ger.
Buseire Syria see Al Buşayrah
194 B4 Buseto Palizzolo Sicilia Italy
148 C2 Bush r. Northern Ireland U.K.
136 E3 Busha Ukr.
136 D2 Bushcha Ukr.
122 B4 Būshehr Iran
122 B4 Būshehr prov. Iran
210 A5 Bushenyi Uganda
151 G3 Bushey Hertfordshire, England U.K.
Bushire Iran see Būshehr
234 C1 Bushkill PA U.S.A.
234 D1 Bush Kill r. PA U.S.A.
147 E1 Bushmills Northern Ireland U.K.
231 D6 Bushnell FL U.S.A.
226 B5 Bushnell IL U.S.A.
196 E5 Bushtricë Albania
210 B4 Busia Kenya
156 D2 Busigny France
177 I3 Bušince Slovakia
208 D4 Businga Dem. Rep. Congo
208 C5 Busira r. Dem. Rep. Congo
136 C3 Bus'k Ukr.
142 C1 Buskerud county Norway
175 I5 Busko-Zdrój Pol.
Buskul' Kazakh. see Boskol'
157 G5 Bussang France
87 B7 Busselton W.A. Austr.
193 H4 Bussento r. Italy
190 F3 Busseto Italy
162 C3 Bussière-Badil France
162 D2 Bussière-Dunoise France
162 D3 Bussière-Galant France
162 C2 Bussière-Poitevine France
190 B2 Bussigny Switz.
193 F2 Bussi sul Tirino Italy
171 C5 Büßleben Ger.
191 F3 Bussolengo Italy
190 C3 Bussoleno Italy
164 E2 Bussum Neth.
156 D4 Bussy-en-Othe France
160 C1 Bussy-le-Grand France
243 E3 Bustamante Mex.
197 G3 Buşteni Romania
261 G3 Bustinza Arg.
190 D3 Busto Arsizio Italy
92 A3 Busuanga Phil.
92 A3 Busuanga i. Phil.
168 D1 Büsum Ger.
191 I2 But r. Italy
208 E4 Buta Dem. Rep. Congo
210 C2 Butajīra Eth.
197 F4 Butan Bulg.
97 B6 Butang Group is Thai.
211 A5 Butare Rwanda
266 G6 Butaritari atoll Kiribati
146 C6 Bute i. Scotland U.K.
146 C6 Bute, Sound of sea chan. Scotland U.K.
197 H2 Butea Romania
222 D4 Butedale B.C. Can.
208 F4 Butembo Dem. Rep. Congo
177 L5 Buteni Romania
194 D5 Butera Sicilia Italy
165 F4 Bütgenbach Belgium
215 G3 Butha Buthe Lesotho
Butha Qi Nei Mongol China see Zalantun
96 A2 Buthidaung Myanmar
160 F3 Buthier di Valpelline r. Italy
255 C9 Butiá Brazil
210 A4 Butiaba Uganda
237 F5 Butler AL U.S.A.
231 C5 Butler GA U.S.A.
226 E5 Butler IN U.S.A.
232 A5 Butler KY U.S.A.
236 E4 Butler MO U.S.A.
235 D1 Butler NJ U.S.A.
232 D4 Butler PA U.S.A.
147 D2 Butlers Bridge Rep. of Ireland
93 B4 Buton i. Indon.
136 E4 Butor Moldova
137 I2 Butovo Rus. Fed.
170 D2 Bütow Ger.
184 D2 Butrera mt. Spain
198 B2 Butrintit, Liqeni i l. Albania
175 I2 Butryny Pol.
190 E1 Bütschwil Switz.
175 M4 Butsyn Ukr.
237 F5 Buttahatchee r. MS U.S.A.
238 D2 Butte MT U.S.A.
236 D3 Butte NE U.S.A.
172 C2 Büttelborn Ger.
171 C4 Buttelstedt Ger.
173 F2 Buttenheim Ger.
173 E3 Buttenwiesen Ger.
149 F3 Buttermere Cumbria, England U.K.
226 B2 Butternut WI U.S.A.
149 I3 Butterwick North Yorkshire, England U.K.
94 C1 Butterworth Malaysia
215 G5 Butterworth S. Africa
240 G2 Buttes, Sierra mt. CA U.S.A.
147 C4 Buttevant Rep. of Ireland
172 D2 Bütthard Ger.
146 B3 Butt of Lewis hd Scotland U.K.
240 H4 Buttonwillow CA U.S.A.
171 C4 Buttstädt Ger.
169 F4 Büttstedt Ger.
87 D7 Butty Head hd W.A. Austr.
234 C2 Buttzville NJ U.S.A.
92 C4 Butuan Phil.
136 E4 Butuceni Moldova
108 B3 Butuo Sichuan China
135 H6 Buturlinovka Rus. Fed.
117 E4 Butwal Nepal
Butysh Rus. Fed. see Kama
169 D5 Butzbach Ger.
170 C2 Bützow Ger.
234 C2 Butztown PA U.S.A.
210 E4 Buulobarde Somalia
Buurakan r. Kyrg. see Burkan-Suu
211 D5 Buur Gaabo Somalia
210 E4 Buurhabaka Somalia
164 F2 Buurse Neth.
210 B4 Buvuma Island Uganda
128 B5 Buwārah, Jabal mt. Saudi Arabia
124 B2 Buwāṭah Saudi Arabia
117 F4 Buxar Bihar India
159 G5 Buxerolles France
173 F3 Buxheim Ger.
160 A2 Buxières-les-Mines France
151 H4 Buxted East Sussex, England U.K.
168 E2 Buxtehude Ger.
149 H4 Buxton Derbyshire, England U.K.
160 C2 Buxy France
134 H4 Buy Rus. Fed.
134 K4 Buy r. Rus. Fed.
106 C2 Buyant Bayanhongor Mongolia
106 A1 Buyant Bayan-Ölgiy Mongolia
107 F2 Buyant Hentiy Mongolia
106 A1 Buyant Gol r. Mongolia
106 C2 Buyant Gol r. Mongolia
107 F2 Buyant-Uhaa Mongolia
226 A1 Buyck MN U.S.A.
129 E2 Buynaksk Rus. Fed.
206 D5 Buyo Côte d'Ivoire
108 B4 Buyuan Jiang r. Yunnan China
127 G3 Büyük Ağrı Dağı mt. Turkey
129 C3 Büyükçatak Turkey
199 F1 Büyükçekmece Turkey
199 G2 Büyükkabaca Turkey
199 G2 Büyükkarabağ Turkey
199 E1 Büyükkarıştıran Turkey
199 F3 Büyükkonak Turkey
199 E3 Büyükmenderes r. Turkey
199 F2 Büyükorhan Turkey
128 C1 Büyükşahinbey Turkey
199 E2 Büyükyenice Balıkesir Turkey
107 I3 Buyun Shan mt. Liaoning China
120 B3 Buzachi, Poluostrov pen. Kazakh.
162 D2 Buzançais France
157 E3 Buzancy France
197 H3 Buzău Romania
197 H3 Buzău r. Romania
197 H3 Buzău r. Romania
135 K5 Buzdyak Rus. Fed.
191 I3 Buzet Croatia
163 C4 Buzet-sur-Baïse France
163 D5 Buzet-sur-Tarn France
139 M4 Buzha r. Rus. Fed.
213 G3 Búzi Moz.
213 G3 Búzi r. Moz.
197 E3 Buziaş Romania
177 K3 Buzica Slovakia
Büzmeyin Turkm. see Byuzmeyin
129 G3 Buzovna Azer.
120 C1 Buzuluk Rus. Fed.
135 H6 Buzuluk r. Rus. Fed.
163 B5 Buzy France
233 H4 Buzzards Bay MA U.S.A.
Bwcle Flintshire, Wales U.K. see Buckley
114 B3 Byadgi Karnataka India
138 G4 Byahoml' Belarus
197 G4 Byala Ruse Bulg.
197 H4 Byala Varna Bulg.
199 E1 Byala Reka r. Bulg.
197 F4 Byala Slatina Bulg.
138 G5 Byalynichy Belarus
Byam Martin atoll Arch. des Tuamotu Fr. Polynesia see Ahunui
138 E5 Byarezina r. Belarus
138 H5 Byarezina r. Belarus
138 E5 Byaroza Belarus
138 E5 Byarozawka Belarus
175 K4 Bychawa Pol.
174 G5 Bycina Pol.
174 G4 Byczyna Pol.
174 G2 Bydgoszcz Pol.
138 E5 Byelaazyorsk Belarus
136 D2 Byelavusha Belarus
139 H5 Byelitsk Belarus
Byelorussia country Europe see Belarus
175 N1 Byenyakoni Belarus
Byerastavitsa Belarus see Pahranichny
138 G5 Byerazino Belarus
238 F4 Byers CO U.S.A.
138 G4 Byeshankovichy Belarus
232 C5 Byesville OH U.S.A.
139 H5 Byesyedz' r. Belarus
85 G4 Byfield Qld Austr.
151 F2 Byfield Northamptonshire, England U.K.
151 G3 Byfleet Surrey, England U.K.
140 M2 Bygdeå Sweden
140 M2 Bygdsiljum Sweden
142 B2 Bygland Norway
171 F4 Byhleguhre Ger.
137 I3 Byk r. Ukr.
139 H5 Bykhaw Belarus
Bykhov Belarus see Bykhaw
136 D2 Bykivka Ukr.
142 B2 Bykle Norway
135 I6 Bykovo Rus. Fed.
241 L5 Bylas AZ U.S.A.
150 D1 Bylchau Conwy, Wales U.K.
168 E1 Bylderup-Bov Denmark
221 K2 Bylot Island Nunavut Can.
129 C2 Bylym Rus. Fed.
227 G3 Byng Inlet Ont. Can.
85 E3 Bynoe r. Qld Austr.
84 B2 Bynoe Harbour N.T. Austr.
107 H1 Byrka Rus. Fed.
137 G2 Byrlivka Ukr.
83 F2 Byrock N.S.W. Austr.
226 C4 Byron IL U.S.A.
233 □H2 Byron ME U.S.A.
232 B3 Byron MI U.S.A.
83 H2 Byron, Cape N.S.W. Austr.
83 H2 Byron Bay N.S.W. Austr.
Byron Island Gilbert Is Kiribati see Nikunau
131 K2 Byrranga, Gory mts Rus. Fed.
137 G1 Byryne Ukr.
136 E2 Byshiv Ukr.
176 D1 Byšice Czech Rep.
140 M2 Byske Sweden
140 M2 Byskeälven r. Sweden
100 D1 Byssa r. Rus. Fed.
175 H6 Bystra Pol.
177 I2 Bystrá mt. Slovakia
176 F2 Bystré Czech Rep.
177 K2 Bystré Slovakia
177 H3 Bystričany Slovakia
177 H2 Bystřice Czech Rep.
176 D2 Bystřice Czech Rep.
176 E1 Bystřice r. Czech Rep.
176 F2 Bystřice nad Pernštejnem Czech Rep.
177 G2 Bystřice pod Hostýnem Czech Rep.
107 F1 Bystrinskiy Golets, Gora mt. Rus. Fed.
Bystrovka Kyrg. see Kemin
136 C3 Bystrytsya Ukr.
136 B3 Bystrytsya r. Ukr.
121 K1 Bystryy Istok Rus. Fed.
134 K5 Bystryy Tanyp r. Rus. Fed.
174 F5 Bystrzyca Pol.
174 E4 Bystrzyca r. Pol.
175 K4 Bystrzyca r. Pol.
174 E5 Bystrzyca Kłodzka Pol.
176 F1 Bystrzyckie, Góry mts Czech Rep./Pol.
131 O3 Bytantay r. Rus. Fed.
177 H2 Bytča Slovakia
174 D3 Bytnica Pol.
174 G5 Bytom Pol.
174 D4 Bytom Odrzański Pol.
139 J5 Bytosh' Rus. Fed.
143 G4 Bytów Pol.
211 A5 Byumba Rwanda
122 D2 Byuzmeyin Turkm.
143 G3 Byxelkrok Kalmar Sweden
Byzantium Turkey see İstanbul
176 G3 Bzenec Czech Rep.
129 B2 Bzip'i r. Georgia
129 B2 Bzip'is K'edi hills Georgia
175 I3 Bzura r. Pol.

C

96 D3 Ca, Sông r. Vietnam
253 F6 Caacupé Para.
253 F6 Caaguazú Para.
253 G6 Caaguazú, Cordillera de hills Para.
209 B8 Caála Angola
251 F5 Caapiranga Brazil
255 B7 Caarapó Brazil
253 F6 Caazapá Para.
253 F3 Cabaçal r. Brazil
246 C2 Cabaiguán Cuba
163 B6 Cabaliros, Pic de mt. France
252 B3 Caballas Peru
185 G3 Caballo mt. Spain
250 D5 Caballococha Peru
252 A2 Cabana Peru
163 C5 Cabanac France
163 B4 Cabanac-et-Villagrains France
252 C3 Cabanaconde Peru
182 B3 Cabana Maior Port.
182 E1 Cabañaquinta Spain
184 C3 Cabanas Port.
185 H3 Cabañas mt. Spain
182 E5 Cabañas del Castillo Spain
182 C4 Cabanas de Viriato Port.
182 D2 Cabañas Raras Spain
92 B3 Cabanatuan Phil.
163 D5 Cabanères hill France
187 D4 Cabanes Spain
161 C5 Cabannes France
225 G4 Cabano Que. Can.
188 E3 Čabar Croatia
161 E5 Cabasse France
186 D3 Cabassers Spain
182 C2 Cabe r. Spain
184 C3 Cabeça Gorda Port.
184 B2 Cabeção Port.
256 D1 Cabeceiras Brazil
182 C3 Cabeceiras de Basto Port.
184 C1 Cabeço de Vide Port.
182 C5 Cabeço Rainha mt. Port.
254 G3 Cabedelo Brazil
163 E6 Cabestany France
177 L5 Căbeşti Romania
182 D3 Cabeza de Framontanos Spain
185 E2 Cabeza del Buey Spain
182 D3 Cabeza del Caballo Spain
184 D2 Cabeza la Vaca Spain
183 G5 Cabezamesada Spain
185 F2 Cabezarados Spain
253 E4 Cabezas Bol.
183 E4 Cabezas del Villar Spain
247 □1 Cabezas de San Juan pt Puerto Rico
184 C3 Cabezas Rubias Spain
183 I3 Cabezo de Morés mt. Spain
187 B6 Cabezo de Torres Spain
184 C3 Cabezo Gordo hill Spain
183 F3 Cabezón Spain
183 H2 Cabezón de Cameros Spain
183 F1 Cabezón de la Sal Spain
183 F1 Cabezón de Liébana Spain
182 E4 Cabezuela del Valle Spain
261 G6 Cabildo Arg.
250 D2 Cabimas Venez.
209 B6 Cabinda Angola
209 B6 Cabinda prov. Angola
238 D1 Cabinet Mountains MT U.S.A.
Cabistra Turkey see Ereğli
226 B2 Cable WI U.S.A.
254 G4 Cabo Brazil
216 □1a Cabo da Praia Terceira Azores
213 H2 Cabo Delgado prov. Moz.
257 F5 Cabo Frio Brazil
183 H3 Cabolafuente Spain
237 E4 Cabool MO U.S.A.
85 H5 Caboolture Qld Austr.
242 B2 Caborca Mex.
225 I4 Cabot Strait Nfld./N.S. Can.
159 F2 Cabourg France
Cabo Verde country N. Atlantic Ocean see Cape Verde
206 □ Cabo Verde, Ilhas do is N. Atlantic Ocean
Cabo Yubi Morocco see Tarfaya
185 F3 Cabra Spain
185 F3 Cabra r. Spain
182 B3 Cabração Port.
186 E3 Cabra del Camp Spain
185 G3 Cabra del Santo Cristo Spain
187 C4 Cabra de Mora Spain
246 E3 Cabral Dom. Rep.
257 E2 Cabral, Serra do mts Brazil
192 A5 Cabras Sardegna Italy
185 F3 Cabras mt. Spain
192 A5 Cabras, Stagno di l. Sardegna Italy
129 E4 Căbrayıl Azer.
183 H3 Cabrejas, Sierra de mts Spain
183 H3 Cabrejas del Pinar Spain
184 B2 Cabrela Port.
184 B2 Cabrela r. Port.
246 E3 Cabrera Dom. Rep.
187 F5 Cabrera i. Spain
185 F2 Cabrera r. Spain
163 D4 Cabrerets France
223 I5 Cabri Sask. Can.
183 I5 Cabriel r. Spain
161 D5 Cabrières-d'Aigues France
182 C4 Cabril Port.
182 D2 Cabrillanes Spain
182 D4 Cabrillas Spain
183 H4 Cabrillas r. Spain
254 F4 Cabrobó Brazil
92 B2 Cabugao Phil.
188 F4 Čabulja mt. Bos.-Herz.
182 D2 Cacabelos Spain
255 C8 Caçador Brazil
Cacagoin Sichuan China see Qagca
245 E5 Cacahuatepec Mex.
196 E4 Čačak Srbija Yugo.
257 E5 Caçapava Brazil
255 B9 Caçapava do Sul Brazil
232 D5 Cacapon r. WV U.S.A.
182 D3 Caçarelhos Port.
250 C3 Cácares Col.
194 C5 Caccamo Sicilia Italy
193 I3 Caccia, Monte hill Italy
195 F3 Caccuri Italy
184 A2 Cacém Port.
255 B9 Cacequi Brazil
253 F4 Cáceres Brazil
184 D1 Cáceres Spain
182 D5 Cáceres prov. Extremadura Spain
261 H5 Cachari Arg.
237 F4 Cache r. IL U.S.A.
206 A3 Cacheau r. Guinea-Bissau
222 F5 Cache Creek B.C. Can.
240 G2 Cache Creek r. CA U.S.A.
238 F3 Cache la Poudre r. CO U.S.A.
238 D3 Cache Peak ID U.S.A.
206 A3 Cacheu Guinea-Bissau
258 D2 Cachi Arg.
258 D2 Cachi, Nevados de mts Arg.
254 B4 Cachimbo, Serra do hills Brazil
209 D7 Cachimo Angola
258 C2 Cachina r. Chile
209 C8 Cachingues Angola
254 F5 Cachoeira Bahia Brazil
256 B3 Cachoeira Mato Grosso do Sul Brazil
256 B3 Cachoeira Alta Brazil
256 B2 Cachoeira de Goiás Brazil
254 C2 Cachoeira do Arari Brazil
257 E3 Cachoeira dos Macacos Brazil
255 B9 Cachoeira do Sul Brazil
257 E5 Cachoeira Paulista Brazil
257 F5 Cachoeiras de Macacu Brazil
257 G4 Cachoeiro de Itapemirim Brazil
184 C3 Cachopo Port.
177 G3 Čachtice Slovakia
182 B4 Cacia Port.
185 G3 Cacín Spain
185 F3 Cacín r. Spain
206 B4 Cacine Guinea-Bissau
209 C7 Cacolo Angola
244 B3 Cacoma, Sierra mts Mex.
209 B8 Caconda Angola
209 B6 Cacongo Angola
237 C4 Cactus TX U.S.A.
240 I3 Cactus Range mts NV U.S.A.
256 B3 Caçu Brazil
209 B7 Cacuaco Angola
209 C7 Caculama Angola
254 E5 Caculé Brazil
257 H2 Cacumba, Ilha i. Brazil
209 B7 Cacuso Angola
184 A1 Cadafais Port.
150 D2 Cadair Idris hills Wales U.K.
163 D5 Cadalen France
183 F4 Cadalso de los Vidrios Spain
148 B4 Cadamstown Rep. of Ireland
186 G2 Cadaqués Spain
184 A1 Cadaval Port.
177 H2 Čadca Slovakia
210 D2 Caddabassa i. Eth.
151 G3 Caddington Bedfordshire, England U.K.
191 F4 Cadelbosco di Sopra Italy
84 C2 Cadell r. N.T. Austr.
190 D2 Cadenazzo Switz.
168 E2 Cadenberge Ger.
161 D5 Cadenet France
190 E4 Cadeo Italy
243 E3 Cadereyta Nuevo León Mex.
245 E3 Cadereyta Querétaro Mex.
Cader Idris hills Wales U.K. see Cadair Idris
161 C4 Caderousse France
Cadí mt. Spain see Torre de Cadí
186 E2 Cadí, Túnel de tun. Spain
185 G4 Cádiar Spain
82 C2 Cadibarrawirracanna, Lake salt flat S.A. Austr.
92 B3 Cadig Mountains Phil.
227 H1 Cadillac Que. Can.
223 J5 Cadillac Sask. Can.
163 B4 Cadillac France
226 E3 Cadillac MI U.S.A.
129 C3 Çadır Dağı mt. Turkey
129 B4 Çadırkaya Turkey
92 B4 Cadiz Phil.
184 D4 Cádiz Spain
184 E4 Cádiz prov. Andalucía Spain
241 J4 Cadiz CA U.S.A.
230 C4 Cadiz KY U.S.A.
232 C4 Cadiz OH U.S.A.
184 C4 Cádiz, Golfo de g. Spain
173 E2 Cadolzburg Ger.
222 G4 Cadomin Alta Can.
191 G3 Cadoneghe Italy
226 B3 Cadott WI U.S.A.
222 G3 Cadotte r. Alta Can.
222 G3 Cadotte Lake Alta Can.
163 D5 Cadours France
87 C6 Cadoux W.A. Austr.
254 E4 Caém Brazil
159 F2 Caen France
159 F2 Caen, Plaine de plain France
150 D3 Caerau Cardiff, Wales U.K.
Caerdydd Cardiff, Wales U.K. see Cardiff
Caere Italy see Cerveteri
Caerffili Caerphilly, Wales U.K. see Caerphilly
Caerfyrddin Carmarthenshire, Wales U.K. see Carmarthen
150 D1 Caergwrle Flintshire, Wales U.K.
Caergybi Isle of Anglesey, Wales U.K. see Holyhead
150 D1 Caerhun Conwy, Wales U.K.
150 E3 Caerleon Newport, Wales U.K.
150 C1 Caernarfon Gwynedd, Wales U.K.
150 C1 Caernarfon Bay Wales U.K.
150 C1 Caernarfon Castle tourist site Wales U.K.
Caernarvon Gwynedd, Wales U.K. see Caernarfon
150 D3 Caerphilly Caerphilly, Wales U.K.
150 D3 Caerphilly admin. div. Wales U.K.
150 D2 Caersws Powys, Wales U.K.
150 E3 Caerwent Monmouthshire, Wales U.K.
Caesaraugusta Spain see Zaragoza
Caesarea Alg. see Cherchell
128 B3 Caesarea tourist site Israel
Caesarea Cappadociae Turkey see Kayseri
Caesarea Philippi Syria see Bāniyās
Caesarodunum France see Tours
Caesaromagus Essex, England U.K. see Chelmsford
257 F3 Caeté Brazil
252 C2 Caeté r. Brazil
254 E5 Caetité Brazil
190 C3 Cafasse Italy
258 D2 Cafayate Arg.
256 C4 Cafelândia Brazil
Caffa Ukr. see Feodosiya
251 G4 Cafuini r. Brazil
92 B2 Cagayan r. Phil.
92 C4 Cagayan de Oro Phil.
92 B4 Cagayan Islands Phil.
193 H4 Caggiano Italy
191 H5 Cagli Italy
192 B5 Cagliari Sardegna Italy
192 B5 Cagliari prov. Sardegna Italy
192 B5 Cagliari, Golfo di b. Sardegna Italy
163 E5 Cagnac-les-Mines France
193 H3 Cagnano Varano Italy
161 F5 Cagnes-sur-Mer France
250 C5 Caguán r. Col.
247 □1 Caguas Puerto Rico
147 B5 Caha hill Rep. of Ireland
231 C5 Cahaba r. AL U.S.A.
209 B9 Cahama Angola
147 B5 Caha Mountains hills Rep. of Ireland
147 C4 Caher Rep. of Ireland
147 A5 Cahermore Rep. of Ireland
147 A5 Cahersiveen Rep. of Ireland
147 D4 Cahir Rep. of Ireland
Cahirciveen Rep. of Ireland see Cahersiveen
234 D1 Cahoonzie NY U.S.A.
163 D4 Cahors France
250 B6 Cahuapanas Peru
136 E5 Cahul Moldova
163 D5 Cahuzac-sur-Vère France
213 G3 Caia Moz.
184 C2 Caia Port.
184 C2 Caia r. Port.
184 C1 Caia, Barragem do resr Port.
253 F3 Caiabis, Serra dos hills Brazil
256 B1 Caiapó r. Brazil
256 A2 Caiapó, Serra do mts Brazil
256 B2 Caiapônia Brazil
193 G3 Caiazzo Italy
246 C2 Caibarién Cuba
96 D2 Cai Bâu, Đao i. Vietnam
97 D5 Cai Be Vietnam
254 F3 Caicó Brazil
246 E2 Caicos Islands Turks and Caicos Is
246 D2 Caicos Passage Bahamas/Turks and Caicos Is
109 E2 Caidian Hubei China
Caidu Henan China see Shangcai
87 E7 Caiguna W.A. Austr.
108 D2 Caihua Hubei China
252 C3 Cailloma Peru
244 A2 Caimanero, Laguna del lag. Mex.
260 B2 Caimanes Chile
209 B8 Caimbambo Angola
183 I4 Caimodorro mt. Spain
136 E4 Căinar r. Moldova
209 B8 Cainde Angola
197 G3 Câineni Romania
241 L2 Caineville UT U.S.A.
108 B1 Cainnyigoin Sichuan China
182 B1 Caión Spain
161 C4 Cairanne France
262 W1 Caird Coast Antarctica
146 A4 Cairinis Western Isles, Scotland U.K.
146 C5 Cairnbaan Argyll and Bute, Scotland U.K.
146 D5 Cairndow Argyll and Bute, Scotland U.K.
146 E5 Cairneyhill Fife, Scotland U.K.
146 E4 Cairn Gorm mt. Scotland U.K.
146 E4 Cairngorm Mountains Scotland U.K.
146 C7 Cairnryan Dumfries and Galloway, Scotland U.K.
85 F3 Cairns Qld Austr.
146 D6 Cairnsmore of Carsphairn hill Scotland U.K.
146 D7 Cairnsmore of Fleet hill Scotland U.K.
146 E4 Cairn Toul mt. Scotland U.K.
203 F2 Cairo Egypt
231 C6 Cairo GA U.S.A.
237 F4 Cairo IL U.S.A.
193 F3 Cairo, Monte mt. Italy
190 D4 Cairo Montenotte Italy
Caisleán an Bharraigh Rep. of Ireland see Castlebar
161 C5 Caissargues France
146 C6 Caisteal Abhail hill Scotland U.K.
151 I2 Caister-on-Sea Norfolk, England U.K.
149 I4 Caistor Lincolnshire, England U.K.
146 E3 Caithness reg. Scotland U.K.
209 B8 Caitou Angola
209 C8 Caiundo Angola
83 F2 Caiwarro Qld Austr.
109 F3 Caixi Fujian China
Caiyuanzhen Zhejiang China see Shengsi
252 D5 Caiza Bol.
109 F2 Caizi Hu l. China
252 A1 Cajabamba Peru
252 A1 Cajamarca Peru
250 B6 Cajamarca dept Peru
254 D2 Cajapió Brazil
163 D4 Cajarc France
254 D2 Cajari Brazil
252 A2 Cajatambo Peru
254 F3 Cajàzeiras Brazil
196 D4 Čajetina Srbija Yugo.
92 B3 Cajidiocan Phil.
177 H3 Čajkov Slovakia
188 G4 Čajniče Bos.-Herz.
260 A6 Cajon Chile
245 G5 Cajonos r. Mex.
252 D4 Cajuata Bol.
256 D4 Cajuru Brazil
197 G2 Cajvana Romania
106 C4 Caka Qinghai China
177 H3 Čakajovce Slovakia
Caka'lho Xizang China see Yanjing
129 A4 Çakırkaş Turkey
129 C3 Çakmak Turkey
129 C4 Çakmak Dağı mts Turkey
188 F2 Čakovec Croatia
199 F2 Çal Turkey
Çal Turkey see Çukurca
215 F4 Cala S. Africa
184 D3 Cala Spain
184 D3 Cala r. Spain
207 H5 Calabar Nigeria
187 B7 Calabardina Spain
227 I3 Calabogie Ont. Can.
193 I6 Calabria admin. reg. Italy
186 D3 Calaceite Spain
192 B2 Calacuccia Corse France
186 □ Cala d'Alcaufar Spain
192 A3 Cala d'Oliva Sardegna Italy
187 G5 Cala d'Or Spain
186 □ Cala en Porter Spain
186 E3 Calaf Spain
197 F4 Calafat Romania
259 B8 Calafate Arg.
186 E3 Calafell Spain
187 G5 Cala Figuera Spain
197 H2 Calafindeşti Romania
193 H3 Calaggio r. Italy
192 B4 Cala Gonone Sardegna Italy
92 B3 Calagua Islands Phil.
Calagurris Spain see Calahorra
185 G4 Calahonda Spain
183 I2 Calahorra Spain
209 C9 Calai Angola
156 B2 Calais France
233 □J2 Calais ME U.S.A.
258 D2 Calalasteo, Sierra de mts Arg.
78 □3b Calalin i. Majuro Marshall Is
191 H2 Calalzo di Cadore Italy
252 C5 Calama Chile
190 D4 Calamandrana Italy
250 C2 Calamar Col.
92 A4 Calamian Group is Phil.
187 G5 Cala Millor Spain
186 B4 Calamocha Spain
184 D2 Calamonte Spain
187 G5 Cala Murada Spain
197 F3 Călan Romania
146 B3 Calanais Western Isles, Scotland U.K.
184 D3 Calañas Spain
190 E2 Calancasca r. Switz.
186 C4 Calanda Spain
209 C7 Calandula Angola
94 A1 Calang Sumatera Indon.
192 B4 Calangianus Sardegna Italy
195 E4 Calanna Italy
202 D2 Calanscio Sand Sea des. Libya
92 B3 Calapan Phil.
187 G5 Cala Rajada Spain
185 H3 Calar Alta mt. Spain
136 E4 Călăraşi Moldova
197 H3 Călăraşi Romania
186 □ Cala Santa Galdana Spain
194 D5 Calascibetta Sicilia Italy
192 A5 Calasetta Sardegna Italy
185 I2 Calasparra Spain
194 B5 Calatafimi Sicilia Italy
183 H3 Calatañazor Spain
187 E6 Cala Tarida Spain
183 I3 Calatayud Spain
183 I3 Calatorao Spain
171 E4 Calau Ger.
92 B3 Calauag Phil.
187 E6 Cala Vadella Spain
185 E2 Calaveruela hill Spain
92 C3 Calbayog Phil.
171 C4 Calbe (Saale) Ger.
169 F3 Calberlah Ger.
92 C4 Calbiga Phil.
252 C3 Calca Peru
243 G2 Calcasieu r. LA U.S.A.
192 A2 Calcatoggio Corse France
190 F5 Calci Italy
193 I4 Calciano Italy
190 F3 Calcinato Italy
190 E3 Calcio Italy
251 I4 Calçoene Brazil
117 G5 Calcutta W. Bengal India
197 G3 Căldăraru Romania
193 F1 Caldarola Italy
191 G2 Caldaro sulla Strada del Vino Italy
250 C3 Caldas dept Col.
184 A1 Caldas da Rainha Port.
Caldas de Mombuy Spain see Caldes de Montbui
184 B3 Caldas de Monchique Port.
182 B2 Caldas de Reis Spain
182 B3 Caldas de Vizela Port.
256 C2 Caldas Novas Brazil
149 F3 Caldbeck Cumbria, England U.K.
186 C2 Caldearenas Spain
151 G2 Caldecott Rutland, England U.K.
182 B3 Caldelas Port.
182 B3 Caldelas Taipas Port.
169 E4 Calden Ger.
222 G1 Calder r. N.W.T. Can.
258 C2 Caldera Chile
146 E6 Caldercruix North Lanarkshire, Scotland U.K.
183 I4 Caldereros, Sierra de mts Spain
85 F5 Caldervale Qld Austr.
186 F3 Caldes de Montbui Spain
186 F3 Caldes d'Estrac Spain
149 G3 Caldew r. England U.K.
150 C3 Caldey Island Wales U.K.
150 E3 Caldicot Monmouthshire, Wales U.K.
129 C4 Çaldıran Van Turkey
127 F3 Çaldıran Van Turkey
191 G3 Caldogno Italy
191 G2 Caldonazzo Italy
149 H3 Caldwell North Yorkshire, England U.K.
238 C3 Caldwell ID U.S.A.
237 D4 Caldwell KS U.S.A.
232 C5 Caldwell OH U.S.A.
237 D6 Caldwell TX U.S.A.
227 H4 Caledon Ont. Can.
215 F4 Caledon r. Lesotho/S. Africa
214 B6 Caledon S. Africa
148 C3 Caledon Northern Ireland U.K.
84 D2 Caledon Bay N.T. Austr.
225 H4 Caledonia N.S. Can.
227 H4 Caledonia Ont. Can.
Caledonia admin. div. U.K. see Scotland
226 E4 Caledonia MI U.S.A.
226 B4 Caledonia MN U.S.A.
232 E3 Caledonia NY U.S.A.
186 F3 Calella Spain
85 G4 Calen Qld Austr.
182 B3 Calendário Port.
192 A2 Calenzana Corse France
191 G5 Calenzano Italy
231 C5 Calera AL U.S.A.
184 D2 Calera de León Spain
183 E5 Calera y Chozas Spain
183 G3 Caleruega Spain
260 B4 Caletones Chile
260 E4 Caleufú Arg.
241 J5 Calexico CA U.S.A.
148 E3 Calf of Man i. Isle of Man
146 F2 Calfsound Orkney, Scotland U.K.
222 H5 Calgary Alta Can.
146 B5 Calgary Argyll and Bute, Scotland U.K.
216 □1c Calheta São Jorge Azores
184 □ Calheta Madeira
216 □1c Calheta de Nesquim Pico Azores
231 C5 Calhoun GA U.S.A.
230 C4 Calhoun KY U.S.A.
250 B4 Cali Col.
199 F1 Çalı Turkey
114 B4 Calicut Kerala India
241 J3 Caliente NV U.S.A.
236 E4 California MO U.S.A.
240 F1 California state U.S.A.
242 B2 California, Golfo de g. Mex.
186 D4 Cálig Spain
163 C4 Calignac France
129 F4 Călilabad Azer.
258 D1 Calilegua Arg.
197 G3 Călimăneşti Romania
197 G2 Călimani, Munţii mts Romania
195 H2 Calimera Italy
260 C2 Calingasta Arg.
Calininsc Moldova see Cupcina
241 J5 Calipatria CA U.S.A.
240 F2 Calistoga CA U.S.A.
193 H4 Calitri Italy
214 C5 Calitzdorp S. Africa
190 D4 Calizzano Italy
199 G3 Çalkaya Turkey
243 H4 Calkiní Mex.
199 G2 Çalköy Turkey
82 E2 Callabonna, Lake salt flat S.A. Austr.
158 C3 Callac France
232 C6 Callaghan VA U.S.A.
240 I2 Callaghan, Mount NV U.S.A.
231 D6 Callahan FL U.S.A.
147 D4 Callan Rep. of Ireland
148 C3 Callan r. Northern Ireland U.K.
224 E4 Callander Ont. Can.
146 D5 Callander Stirling, Scotland U.K.
232 D6 Callands VA U.S.A.
92 B2 Callang Phil.
Callanish Western Isles, Scotland U.K. see Calanais
164 D2 Callantsoog Neth.
252 A3 Callao Peru
241 K2 Callao UT U.S.A.
161 E5 Callas France
163 B4 Callen France
182 E1 Callezuela Spain
161 E5 Callian France
190 D3 Calliano Italy
233 F4 Callicoon NY U.S.A.
85 G5 Callide Qld Austr.
222 H4 Calling Lake Alta Can.
150 C4 Callington Cornwall, England U.K.
85 G5 Calliope Qld Austr.
Callipolis Turkey see Gelibolu
187 C6 Callosa d'En Sarrià Spain
187 C6 Callosa de Segura Spain
227 G2 Callum Ont. Can.
87 B5 Callyharra Springs W.A. Austr.
222 H4 Calmar Alta Can.
226 B4 Calmar IA U.S.A.
197 G4 Călmăţui r. Romania
163 D5 Calmont Midi-Pyrénées France
163 E4 Calmont Midi-Pyrénées France
245 E3 Calnali Mex.
150 E3 Calne Wiltshire, England U.K.
197 G3 Câlniştea r. Romania
190 E3 Calolziocorte Italy
183 I4 Calomarde Spain
186 G3 Calonge Spain
163 C4 Calonges France
156 C2 Calonne-Ricouart France
231 D7 Caloosahatchee r. FL U.S.A.
193 G3 Calore Italy
193 G3 Calore r. Italy
193 H4 Calore r. Italy
243 H4 Calotmul Mex.
85 H5 Caloundra Qld Austr.
177 G4 Čalovec Slovakia
Čalovo Slovakia see Veľký Meder
187 D6 Calpe Spain
245 E4 Calpulálpan Mex.
224 C3 Calstock Ont. Can.
194 C5 Caltabellotta Sicilia Italy
194 D5 Caltagirone Sicilia Italy
194 D5 Caltagirone r. Sicilia Italy
194 D5 Caltanissetta Sicilia Italy
194 C5 Caltanissetta prov. Sicilia Italy
194 C5 Caltavuturo Sicilia Italy
128 A1 Çaltıbozkır Turkey
190 D3 Caltignaga Italy
183 H3 Caltojar Spain
147 C3 Caltraghlea Rep. of Ireland
160 C3 Caluire-et-Cuire France
209 B7 Calulo Angola
226 C2 Calumet MI U.S.A.
226 A2 Calumet MN U.S.A.
209 D8 Calunda Angola
209 B8 Caluquembe Angola
190 C3 Caluso Italy
210 F2 Caluula Somalia
159 F2 Calvados dept Basse-Normandie France
182 B4 Calvão Port.
182 B3 Calvario Spain
182 E4 Calvarrasa de Abajo Spain
182 E4 Calvarrasa de Arriba Spain
193 H4 Calvello Italy
149 H4 Calver Derbyshire, England U.K.
147 E3 Calverstown Rep. of Ireland
84 D3 Calvert r. N.T. Austr.
84 D3 Calvert Hills N.T. Austr.
235 F2 Calverton NY U.S.A.
87 D4 Calvert Range hills W.A. Austr.
192 A2 Calvi Corse France
192 C1 Calvi, Monte hill Italy
187 F5 Calvià Spain
193 E2 Calvi dell'Umbria Italy
163 D4 Calvignac France
244 C3 Calvillo Mex.
146 E5 Calvine Perth and Kinross, Scotland U.K.
163 E4 Calvinet France
214 B4 Calvinia S. Africa
193 G3 Calvi Risorta Italy
161 C5 Calvisson France
182 E4 Calvitero mt. Spain
194 D6 Calvo, Monte hill Sicilia Italy
193 H3 Calvo, Monte mt. Italy
171 C3 Calvörde Ger.
182 C3 Calvos Spain
172 C3 Calw Ger.
185 G2 Calzada de Calatrava Spain
182 E3 Calzada de Valdunciel Spain
182 D4 Calzadilla Spain
151 H2 Cam r. England U.K.
209 B7 Camabatela Angola
254 F5 Camaçari Brazil
184 □ Camacha Madeira
224 E4 Camachigama r. Que. Can.
244 C1 Camacho Mex.
209 B8 Camacuio Angola
209 C8 Camacupa Angola
250 E2 Camaguán Venez.
246 C2 Camagüey Cuba
246 C2 Camagüey, Archipiélago de is Cuba
94 C1 Camah, Gunung mt. Malaysia
190 F5 Camaiore Italy
251 G6 Camaiú r. Brazil
246 C2 Camajuaní Cuba
Çamalan Turkey see Gülek
191 G5 Camaldoli Italy
183 F1 Camaleño Spain
254 F5 Camamu Brazil
252 B4 Camana Peru
252 B4 Camaná r. Peru
186 B4 Camañas Spain
209 D7 Camanongue Angola
255 B6 Camapuã Brazil
255 C9 Camaquã Brazil
255 C9 Camaquã r. Brazil
197 F2 Camăr Romania
184 □ Câmara de Lobos Madeira
253 F3 Camararé r. Brazil
186 D3 Camarasa Spain
183 F4 Camarena Spain
187 B4 Camarena r. Spain
187 B4 Camarena de la Sierra Spain
161 A5 Camarès France
161 C4 Camaret-sur-Aigues France
158 B3 Camaret-sur-Mer France
243 F3 Camargo Mex.
161 C5 Camargue reg. France
240 H4 Camarillo CA U.S.A.
182 A1 Camariñas Spain
186 D4 Camarles Spain
259 D7 Camarones, Bahía b. Arg.
147 E4 Camaross Rep. of Ireland
182 D2 Camarzana de Tera Spain
184 D3 Camas Spain
238 B2 Camas WA U.S.A.
238 D3 Camas r. ID U.S.A.
238 D3 Camas Creek r. ID U.S.A.
146 C5 Camasnacroise Highland, Scotland U.K.
194 C5 Camastra Sicilia Italy
97 D5 Ca Mau Vietnam
209 C7 Camaxilo Angola
182 B2 Cambados Spain
256 B5 Cambará Brazil
Cambay Gujarat India see Khambhat
Cambay, Gulf of India see Khambhat, Gulf of
256 B5 Cambé Brazil
151 G3 Camberley Surrey, England U.K.
163 B4 Cambes France
97 D4 Cambodia country Asia
163 A5 Cambo-les-Bains France
163 E5 Cambon France
255 C8 Camboriú Brazil
150 B4 Camborne Cornwall, England U.K.
234 B1 Cambra PA U.S.A.
82 D3 Cambrai S.A. Austr.
156 D2 Cambrai France
182 B1 Cambre Spain
159 G2 Cambremer France
182 C3 Cambres Port.
214 E5 Cambria S. Africa
Cambria admin. div. U.K. see Wales
240 G4 Cambria CA U.S.A.
150 D2 Cambrian Mountains hills Wales U.K.
224 D5 Cambridge Ont. Can.
246 □ Cambridge Jamaica
80 E2 Cambridge North I. N.Z.
151 H2 Cambridge Cambridgeshire, England U.K.
236 F3 Cambridge IL U.S.A.
233 H3 Cambridge MA U.S.A.
233 E5 Cambridge MD U.S.A.
226 A3 Cambridge MN U.S.A.
233 G3 Cambridge NY U.S.A.
232 C4 Cambridge OH U.S.A.
234 C2 Cambridge PA U.S.A.
233 G2 Cambridge VT U.S.A.
226 C4 Cambridge WI U.S.A.
221 H3 Cambridge Bay Nunavut Can.
86 F2 Cambridge Gulf W.A. Austr.
151 H2 Cambridgeshire admin. div. England U.K.
232 C4 Cambridge Springs PA U.S.A.
186 E3 Cambrils de Mar Spain
156 C2 Cambrin France
156 B2 Cambron France
170 C2 Cambs Ger.
256 D5 Cambuí Brazil
209 D6 Cambulo Angola
209 C7 Cambundi-Catembo Angola
257 E4 Cambuquira Brazil
171 C4 Camburg Ger.
250 A3 Cambutal, Cerro mt. Panama
83 G3 Camden N.S.W. Austr.
231 C5 Camden AL U.S.A.
237 E5 Camden AR U.S.A.
234 C3 Camden DE U.S.A.
233 □I2 Camden ME U.S.A.
231 E4 Camden NC U.S.A.
234 C3 Camden NJ U.S.A.
233 F3 Camden NY U.S.A.
232 A5 Camden OH U.S.A.
231 D5 Camden SC U.S.A.
237 F4 Camden TN U.S.A.
234 C3 Camden County county NJ U.S.A.
86 E2 Camden Sound sea chan. W.A. Austr.
236 E4 Camdenton MO U.S.A.
209 D7 Cameia Angola
150 C4 Camelford Cornwall, England U.K.
199 F3 Çameli Turkey
136 E3 Camenca Moldova
191 I5 Camerano Italy
193 F1 Camerino Italy
Camerinum Italy see Camerino
241 L4 Cameron AZ U.S.A.
237 E6 Cameron LA U.S.A.
236 E4 Cameron MO U.S.A.
237 D6 Cameron TX U.S.A.
226 B3 Cameron WI U.S.A.
232 C5 Cameron WV U.S.A.
94 C1 Cameron Highlands Malaysia
94 C1 Cameron Highlands mts Malaysia
222 G3 Cameron Hills Y.T. Can.
81 A7 Cameron Mountains South I. N.Z.
240 G2 Cameron Park CA U.S.A.
207 I5 Cameroon country Africa
193 H4 Camerota Italy
Cameroun country Africa see Cameroon
207 H5 Cameroun, Mont vol. Cameroon
149 F3 Camerton Cumbria, England U.K.
251 I5 Cametá Brazil
84 B3 Camfield r. N.T. Austr.
199 E3 Çamiçi Muğla Turkey
193 F2 Camicia, Monte mt. Italy
92 B2 Camiguin i. Phil.
128 B1 Camili Turkey
92 B3 Camiling Phil.
231 C6 Camilla GA U.S.A.
168 F2 Camin Ger.
252 C4 Camiña Chile
182 B3 Caminha Port.
182 D4 Caminomorisco Spain
186 B4 Caminreal Spain
252 E5 Camiri Bol.
252 B2 Camisea r. Peru

209 D7 **Camissombo** Angola
128 D1 **Çamlıdere** Turkey
129 B3 **Çamlıhemşin** Turkey
129 B3 **Çamlıkaya** Turkey
87 C7 **Camm, Lake** *salt flat* *W.A.* Austr.
194 C5 **Cammarata** *Sicilia* Italy
194 C5 **Cammarata, Monte** *mt.* *Sicilia* Italy
171 D3 **Cammer** Ger.
170 D2 **Cammin** Ger.
Cammin Pol. *see* **Kamień Pomorski**
254 E2 **Camocim** Brazil
147 E4 **Camolin** Rep. of Ireland
156 C3 **Camon** France
190 F3 **Camonica, Val** *val.* Italy
84 D3 **Camooweal** *Qld* Austr.
185 F4 **Camorro Alto** *mt.* Spain
158 D4 **Camors** France
92 C4 **Camotes Sea** *g.* Phil.
244 B4 **Camotlán de Miraflores** Mex.
147 D2 **Camowen** *r.* *Northern Ireland* U.K.
147 B4 **Camp** Rep. of Ireland
193 H4 **Campagna** Italy
161 B4 **Campagnac** France
192 D2 **Campagnatico** Italy
163 B5 **Campagne** *Aquitaine* France
163 C4 **Campagne** *Aquitaine* France
156 B2 **Campagne-lès-Hesdin** France
261 H4 **Campana** Arg.
195 F3 **Campana** Italy
259 B8 **Campana, Isla** *i.* Chile
260 B4 **Campanario** *mt.* Arg./Chile
257 G3 **Campanário** Brazil
184 □ **Campanario** Madeira
184 E2 **Campanario** Spain
257 E4 **Campanha** Brazil
193 G3 **Campania** *admin. reg.* Italy
184 D4 **Campano** Spain
85 F4 **Campaspe** *r.* *Qld* Austr.
183 F3 **Campaspero** Spain
214 D3 **Campbell** S. Africa
240 G3 **Campbell** *CA* U.S.A.
232 C4 **Campbell** *OH* U.S.A.
84 B4 **Campbell, Mount** *hill* *N.T.* Austr.
224 E4 **Campbellford** *Ont.* Can.
232 B4 **Campbell Hill** *hill* *OH* U.S.A.
77 G6 **Campbell Island** N.Z.
266 G9 **Campbell Plateau** *sea feature* S. Pacific Ocean
86 E2 **Campbell Range** *hills* *W.A.* Austr.
222 E5 **Campbell River** *B.C.* Can.
227 I3 **Campbells Bay** *Que.* Can.
226 C4 **Campbellsport** *WI* U.S.A.
232 A5 **Campbellstown** *OH* U.S.A.
230 C4 **Campbellsville** *KY* U.S.A.
225 H4 **Campbellton** *N.B.* Can.
83 G3 **Campbelltown** *N.S.W.* Austr.
83 F5 **Campbell Town** *Tas.* Austr.
234 B2 **Campbelltown** *PA* U.S.A.
146 C6 **Campbeltown** *Argyll and Bute, Scotland* U.K.
158 E4 **Campbon** France
232 C6 **Camp Creek** *WV* U.S.A.
186 F2 **Campdevànol** Spain
182 C3 **Campeã** Port.
243 H5 **Campeche** Mex.
243 H5 **Campeche** *state* Mex.
245 H4 **Campeche, Bahía de** *g.* Mex.
246 C2 **Campechuela** Cuba
187 C6 **Campello** Spain
193 E2 **Campello sul Clitunne** Italy
182 B5 **Campelo** Port.
184 A1 **Campelos** Port.
158 D4 **Campénéac** France
197 F2 **Câmpeni** Romania
83 E4 **Camperdown** *Vic.* Austr.
215 H3 **Camperdown** S. Africa
190 D3 **Campertogno** Italy
256 D4 **Campestre** Brazil
161 B5 **Campestre-et-Luc** France
234 B2 **Camp Hill** *PA* U.S.A.
226 B3 **Campia** *WI* U.S.A.
197 F2 **Câmpia Turzii** Romania
191 G5 **Campi Bisenzio** Italy
192 A5 **Campidano** *reg.* *Sardegna* Italy
192 C1 **Campiglia Marittima** Italy
190 C3 **Campiglia Soana** Italy
147 E4 **Campile** Rep. of Ireland
184 B3 **Campilhas** *r.* Port.
183 I5 **Campillo de Alto Buey** Spain
185 G3 **Campillo de Arenas** Spain
183 I4 **Campillo de Dueñas** Spain
184 E2 **Campillo de Llerena** Spain
185 F3 **Campillos** Spain
183 I5 **Campillos-Paravientos** Spain
197 G3 **Câmpina** Romania
256 A6 **Campina da Lagoa** Brazil
254 G3 **Campina Grande** Brazil
256 C6 **Campina Grande do Sul** Brazil
256 D5 **Campinas** Brazil
256 C3 **Campina Verde** Brazil
184 C2 **Campinho** Port.
183 G3 **Campisábalos** Spain
195 H2 **Campi Salentina** Italy
192 B2 **Campitello** *Corse* France
193 F2 **Campli** Italy
207 H6 **Campo** Cameroon
Campo *r.* Cameroon *see* **Ntem**
213 H3 **Campo** Moz.
182 B3 **Campo** Port.
186 D2 **Campo** Spain
250 C4 **Campoalegre** Col.
254 E4 **Campo Alegre de Lourdes** Brazil
193 G3 **Campobasso** Italy
193 G3 **Campobasso** *prov.* *Molise* Italy
194 C5 **Campobello di Licata** *Sicilia* Italy
194 B5 **Campobello di Mazara** *Sicilia* Italy
257 E4 **Campo Belo** Brazil
255 C8 **Campo Belo do Sul** Brazil
182 B1 **Campo da Feira** Spain
191 G3 **Campodarsego** Italy
183 E1 **Campo de Caso** Spain
185 G1 **Campo de Criptana** Spain
192 A3 **Campo dell'Oro** *airport* *Corse* France
183 G3 **Campo de San Pedro** Spain
193 F3 **Campodimele** Italy
191 G2 **Campo di Trens** Italy
190 E2 **Campodolcino** Italy
255 B8 **Campo Erê** Brazil
194 C5 **Campofelice di Roccella** *Sicilia* Italy
256 C3 **Campo Florido** Brazil
191 I2 **Campoformido** Italy
254 E4 **Campo Formoso** Brazil
194 C5 **Campofranco** *Sicilia* Italy
184 D3 **Campofrío** Spain
258 E2 **Campo Gallo** Arg.
255 B7 **Campo Grande** Brazil
182 B2 **Campo Lameiro** Spain
256 C6 **Campo Largo** Brazil
193 F3 **Campoli Appennino** Italy
190 D4 **Campo Ligure** Italy
191 H3 **Campolongo Maggiore** Italy
184 E1 **Campo Lugar** Spain
254 E3 **Campo Maior** Brazil
184 C1 **Campo Maior** Port.
193 H3 **Campomarino** *Molise* Italy
195 G2 **Campomarino** *Puglia* Italy
190 D4 **Campomorone** Italy
256 A6 **Campo Mourão** Brazil
182 D2 **Camponaraya** Spain
255 B8 **Campo Novo** Brazil
193 I5 **Campora San Giovanni** Italy
183 G4 **Campo Real** Spain
194 C5 **Camporeale** *Sicilia* Italy
184 B3 **Campo Redondo** Port.
190 F4 **Camporgiano** Italy
190 C5 **Camporosso** Italy
187 B5 **Camporrobles** Spain
257 G4 **Campos** Brazil
182 C3 **Campos** Port.
256 D3 **Campos Altos** Brazil
191 G4 **Camposanto** Italy
254 D5 **Campos Belos** Brazil
187 G5 **Campos del Puerto** Spain
187 B6 **Campos del Río** Spain
257 E5 **Campos do Jordão** Brazil
257 E4 **Campos Gerais** Brazil
256 C5 **Campos Novos Paulista** Brazil
254 E3 **Campos Sales** Brazil
185 G3 **Campotéjar** Spain
190 D2 **Campo Tencia** *mt.* Switz.
193 F2 **Campotosto** Italy
193 F2 **Campotosto, Lago di** *l.* Italy
191 G2 **Campo Tures** Italy
236 F3 **Camp Point** *IL* U.S.A.
186 F2 **Camprodon** Spain
148 E1 **Campsie Fells** *hills* *Scotland* U.K.
161 E5 **Camps-la-Source** France
234 B4 **Camp Springs** *MD* U.S.A.
232 B6 **Campton** *KY* U.S.A.
146 F6 **Camptown** *Scottish Borders, Scotland* U.K.
234 B1 **Camptown** *PA* U.S.A.
197 G3 **Câmpulung** Romania
197 F2 **Câmpulung la Tisa** Romania
197 G2 **Câmpulung Moldovenesc** Romania
250 C5 **Campuya** *r.* Peru
241 L4 **Camp Verde** *AZ* U.S.A.
97 E5 **Cam Ranh** Vietnam
222 H4 **Camrose** *Alta* Can.
150 B3 **Camrose** *Pembrokeshire, Wales* U.K.
223 I3 **Camsell Portage** *Sask.* Can.
222 F2 **Camsell Range** *mts* *N.W.T.* Can.
191 G4 **Camugnano** Italy
Camulodunum *Essex, England* U.K. *see* **Colchester**
185 G1 **Camuñas** Spain
129 C3 **Çamurlu Dağ** *mt.* Turkey
128 C1 **Çamuzkışlası** Turkey
129 C3 **Çamyazı** Turkey
199 E1 **Çan** Turkey
177 K3 **Čaňa** Slovakia
257 F4 **Canaã** Brazil
225 H4 **Canaan** *r.* *N.S.* Can.
233 G3 **Canaan** *CT* U.S.A.
241 L3 **Canaan Peak** *UT* U.S.A.
254 B3 **Cana Brava** *r.* Brazil
257 H2 **Cana Brava, Serra da** *hills* Brazil
114 B3 **Canacona** *Goa* India
220 J5 **Canada** *country* N. America
187 C6 **Cañada** Spain
268 O1 **Canada Basin** *sea feature* Arctic Ocean
186 C4 **Cañada de Benatanduz** Spain
261 G3 **Cañada de Gómez** Arg.
185 I1 **Cañada del Carrascal** *r.* Spain
183 I5 **Cañada del Hoyo** Spain
185 E3 **Cañada Rosal** Spain
261 G3 **Cañada Rosquin** Arg.
234 C1 **Canadensis** *PA* U.S.A.
237 C5 **Canadian** *TX* U.S.A.
237 E5 **Canadian** *r.* U.S.A.
259 C7 **Cañadon Grande, Sierra** *mts* Arg.
233 F3 **Canajoharie** *NY* U.S.A.
199 E1 **Çanakkale** Turkey
199 E1 **Çanakkale** *prov.* Turkey
78 □5 **Canala** New Caledonia
192 B2 **Canale-di-Verde** *Corse* France
183 H4 **Canalejas del Arroyo** Spain
183 F3 **Canalejas de Peñafiel** Spain
222 H5 **Canal Flats** *B.C.* Can.
182 D4 **Canalizo** *hill* Spain
261 F3 **Canals** Arg.
163 D5 **Canals** France
187 C6 **Canals** Spain
191 G2 **Canàl San Bovo** Italy
232 B5 **Canal Winchester** *OH* U.S.A.
183 H4 **Cañamares** Spain
185 G2 **Cañamares** *r.* Spain
183 H4 **Cañamares** *r.* Spain
185 E1 **Cañamero** Spain
232 E3 **Canandaigua** *NY* U.S.A.
242 C2 **Cananea** Mex.
256 D6 **Cananéia** Brazil
250 D4 **Canapiare, Cerro** *hill* Col.
156 C2 **Canaples** France
256 C3 **Canápolis** Brazil
250 B5 **Cañar** Ecuador
250 B5 **Cañar** *prov.* Ecuador
254 B5 **Canarana** Brazil
192 B2 **Canari** *Corse* France
216 □3 **Canarias, Islas** *is* N. Atlantic Ocean
Canarias, Islas *terr.* N. Atlantic Ocean *see* **Canary Islands**
191 G4 **Canaro** Italy
216 □3 **Canary Islands** *terr.* N. Atlantic Ocean
182 C4 **Canas de Senhorim** Port.
232 E3 **Canaseraga** *NY* U.S.A.
233 F3 **Canastota** *NY* U.S.A.
256 D3 **Canastra, Serra da** *mts* Brazil
244 B1 **Canatlán** Mex.
182 D5 **Cañaveral** Spain
231 D6 **Canaveral, Cape** *FL* U.S.A.
184 D2 **Cañaveral de León** Spain
183 H4 **Cañaveras** Spain
183 H4 **Cañaveruelas** Spain
257 H1 **Canavieiras** Brazil
242 □J7 **Cañazas** Panama
191 G2 **Canazei** Italy
83 F2 **Canbelego** *N.S.W.* Austr.
83 G3 **Canberra** *A.C.T.* Austr.
238 B3 **Canby** *CA* U.S.A.
236 D2 **Canby** *MN* U.S.A.
158 E3 **Cancale** France
185 I2 **Cancarix** Spain
161 C3 **Cance** *r.* France
193 H4 **Cancellara** Italy
193 G3 **Cancello ed Arnone** Italy
156 B2 **Canche** *r.* France
250 C6 **Canchyuaya, Cerros de** *hills* Peru
186 C2 **Cancias** *mt.* Spain
163 C4 **Cancon** France
243 I4 **Cancún** Mex.
163 B6 **Candanchú** Spain
Çandar Turkey *see* **Kastamonu**
252 C4 **Candarave** Peru
199 E2 **Çandarlı** Turkey
182 E1 **Candás** Spain
186 D3 **Candasnos** Spain
159 E4 **Candé** France
257 E4 **Candeias** Brazil
252 E2 **Candeias** *r.* Brazil
193 H3 **Candela** Italy
237 C7 **Candela** *r.* Mex.
258 G2 **Candelaria** *Misiones* Arg.
260 E3 **Candelaria** *San Luis* Arg.
216 □1c **Candelária** *Pico* Azores
216 □1b **Candelária** *São Miguel* Azores
216 □3a **Candelaria** *Tenerife* Canary Is
243 H5 **Candelaria** Mex.
182 E4 **Candelario** Spain
182 E4 **Candelario, Sierra de** *mts* Spain
193 H3 **Candelaro** *r.* Italy
183 E4 **Candeleda** Spain
83 G4 **Candelo** *N.S.W.* Austr.
190 D3 **Candelo** Italy
182 B3 **Candemil** Port.
Candia *Kriti* Greece *see* **Irakleio**
190 D3 **Candia Lomellina** Italy
256 B6 **Cândido de Abreu** Brazil
254 D2 **Cândido Mendes** Brazil
256 B5 **Cândido Mota** Brazil
191 H5 **Candigliano** *r.* Italy
182 D2 **Candín** Spain
126 D2 **Çandır** Turkey
223 J4 **Candle Lake** *Sask.* Can.
235 E1 **Candlewood Isle** *CT* U.S.A.
235 E1 **Candlewood Knolls** *CT* U.S.A.
236 D1 **Cando** *ND* U.S.A.
92 B2 **Candon** Phil.
215 H2 **Candover** S. Africa
197 F3 **Cândrelu, Vârful** *mt.* Romania
86 B4 **Cane** *r.* *W.A.* Austr.
194 D5 **Cane, Monte** *hill* *Sicilia* Italy
Canea *Kriti* Greece *see* **Chania**
184 A2 **Caneças** Port.
182 B3 **Canedo** Port.
186 D2 **Canejan** Spain
163 B4 **Canéjean** France
260 B2 **Canela Baja** Chile
190 D4 **Canelli** Italy
261 I4 **Canelones** Uru.
261 J4 **Canelones** *dept* Uru.
192 E2 **Canepina** Italy
182 D1 **Canero** Spain
161 A5 **Canet** *Languedoc-Roussillon* France
161 B5 **Canet** *Languedoc-Roussillon* France
163 F6 **Canet, Étang de** *lag.* France
186 F3 **Canet de Mar** Spain
258 B5 **Cañete** Chile
183 I4 **Cañete** Spain
185 F3 **Cañete de las Torres** Spain
185 E4 **Cañete la Real** Spain
163 F6 **Canet-en-Roussillon** France
186 D4 **Canet lo Roig** Spain
163 F6 **Canet-Plage** France
237 E4 **Caney** *KS* U.S.A.
237 E4 **Caney** *r.* *KS* U.S.A.
186 C2 **Canfranc-Estación** Spain
252 B3 **Cangallo** Peru
209 C8 **Cangamba** Angola
209 C7 **Cangandala** Angola
182 B2 **Cangas** Spain
182 D1 **Cangas del Narcea** Spain
183 E1 **Cangas de Onís** Spain
209 B7 **Cangola** Angola
209 D8 **Cangombe** Angola
107 H5 **Cangshan** *Shandong* China
254 G3 **Canguaretama** Brazil
258 G3 **Canguçu** Brazil
258 G3 **Canguçu, Serra do** *hills* Brazil
107 H4 **Cangzhou** *Hebei* China
184 B2 **Canha** Port.
184 B2 **Canha** *r.* Port.
184 □ **Canhas** Madeira
184 B2 **Canhestros** Port.
163 D4 **Caniac-du-Causse** France
225 G2 **Caniapiscau** *Que.* Can.
225 G1 **Caniapiscau** *r.* *Que.* Can.
225 G2 **Caniapiscau, Lac** *l.* *Que.* Can.
Caniçado Moz. *see* **Guija**
184 □ **Caniçal** Madeira
194 C5 **Canicattì** *Sicilia* Italy
195 E5 **Canicattini Bagni** *Sicilia* Italy
184 □ **Caniço** Madeira
183 G3 **Canicosa de la Sierra** Spain
163 E6 **Canigou, Pic du** *mt.* France
185 H3 **Caniles** Spain
185 F4 **Canillas de Aceituno** Spain
186 E2 **Canillo** Andorra
222 F5 **Canim Lake** *B.C.* Can.
254 F3 **Canindé** Brazil
192 D2 **Canino** Italy
146 C3 **Canisp** *hill* *Scotland* U.K.
232 E3 **Canisteo** *NY* U.S.A.
232 E3 **Canisteo** *r.* *NY* U.S.A.
262 R2 **Canisteo Peninsula** Antarctica
158 E2 **Canisy** France
244 C2 **Cañitas de Felipe Pescador** Mex.
183 E3 **Cañizal** Spain
183 H4 **Cañizares** Spain
183 E3 **Cañizo** Spain
185 H3 **Canjáyar** Spain
239 F4 **Canjilon** *NM* U.S.A.
126 D2 **Çankırı** Turkey
211 A5 **Cankuzo** Burundi
92 B4 **Canlaon** Phil.
87 B6 **Canna** *W.A.* Austr.
195 F2 **Canna** *r.* Italy
146 B4 **Canna** *i.* *Scotland* U.K.
146 B4 **Canna, Sound of** *sea chan.* *Scotland* U.K.
114 B4 **Cannanore** *Kerala* India
114 B4 **Cannanore Islands** *Lakshadweep* India
193 E2 **Cannara** Italy
160 B2 **Canne** *r.* France
194 C5 **Canne** *r.* *Sicilia* Italy
190 D2 **Cannero Riviera** Italy
161 F5 **Cannes** France
194 D4 **Canneto** *Isole Lipari* Italy
192 C1 **Canneto** *Toscana* Italy
190 F3 **Canneto sull'Oglio** Italy
146 D4 **Cannich** *Highland, Scotland* U.K.
87 C6 **Canning Hill** *hill* *W.A.* Austr.
147 D3 **Canningstown** Rep. of Ireland
150 D3 **Cannington** *Somerset, England* U.K.
190 D2 **Cannobio** Italy
150 E2 **Cannock** *Staffordshire, England* U.K.
150 E2 **Cannock Chase** *reg.* *England* U.K.
226 A3 **Cannon** *r.* *MN* U.S.A.
236 C2 **Cannonball** *r.* *ND* U.S.A.
238 B2 **Cannon Beach** *OR* U.S.A.
235 E1 **Cannondale** *CT* U.S.A.
215 F5 **Cannon Rocks** S. Africa
232 B5 **Cannonsburg** *KY* U.S.A.
85 G4 **Cannonvale** *Qld* Austr.
83 G4 **Cann River** *Vic.* Austr.
184 C2 **Cano** Port.
250 A5 **Canoa** Ecuador
255 C9 **Canoas** Brazil
257 E3 **Canoeiros** Brazil
223 I4 **Canoe Lake** *Sask.* Can.
163 E6 **Canohès** France
255 C8 **Canoinhas** Brazil
195 F4 **Canolo** Italy
146 F6 **Canonbie** *Dumfries and Galloway, Scotland* U.K.
239 F4 **Canon City** *CO* U.S.A.
231 D6 **Canoochia** *r.* *GA* U.S.A.
85 G4 **Canoona** *Qld* Austr.
82 E3 **Canopus** *S.A.* Austr.
223 K5 **Canora** *Sask.* Can.
193 I3 **Canosa di Puglia** Italy
247 □3 **Canouan** *i.* St Vincent
83 G3 **Canowindra** *N.S.W.* Austr.
187 F5 **Can Pastilla** Spain
187 G5 **Can Picafort** Spain
183 H4 **Canredondo** Spain
193 G3 **Cansano** Italy
225 I4 **Canso** *N.S.* Can.
252 A2 **Canta** Peru
183 F1 **Cantabria** *aut. comm.* Spain
Cantabrian Mountains Spain *see* **Cantábrica, Cordillera**
Cantabrian Sea Spain *see* **Cantábrico, Mar**
182 F1 **Cantábrica, Cordillera** *mts* Spain
182 D1 **Cantábrico, Mar** *sea* Spain
191 G4 **Cantagallo** Italy
161 A3 **Cantal** *dept* *Auvergne* France
183 E3 **Cantalapiedra** Spain
183 G3 **Cantalejo** Spain
193 E2 **Cantalice** Italy
183 G3 **Cantalojas** Spain
183 E3 **Cantalpino** Spain
182 B4 **Cantanhede** Port.
186 C4 **Cantavieja** Spain
177 I6 **Čantavir** *Vojvodina, Srbija* Yugo.
156 B3 **Canteleu** France
163 A4 **Canteloupe** *r.* France
162 B3 **Cantenac** France
187 B7 **Canteras** Spain
185 H1 **Canteras** *hill* Spain
225 H4 **Canterbury** *N.B.* Can.
81 D5 **Canterbury** *admin. reg.* *South I.* N.Z.
151 I3 **Canterbury** *Kent, England* U.K.
81 C6 **Canterbury Bight** *b.* *South I.* N.Z.
81 C5 **Canterbury Plains** *South I.* N.Z.
97 D5 **Cần Thơ** Vietnam
191 H5 **Cantiano** Italy
240 I4 **Cantil** *CA* U.S.A.
92 C4 **Cantilan** Phil.
184 E3 **Cantillana** Spain
183 F3 **Cantimpalos** Spain
254 E4 **Canto do Buriti** Brazil
190 C3 **Cantoira** Italy
Canton *Guangdong* China *see* **Guangzhou**
150 D3 **Canton** *Cardiff, Wales* U.K.
231 C5 **Canton** *GA* U.S.A.
226 B5 **Canton** *IL* U.S.A.
236 F3 **Canton** *MO* U.S.A.
237 F5 **Canton** *MS* U.S.A.
234 C3 **Canton** *NJ* U.S.A.
233 F2 **Canton** *NY* U.S.A.
232 C4 **Canton** *OH* U.S.A.
227 I5 **Canton** *PA* U.S.A.
236 D3 **Canton** *SD* U.S.A.
237 E5 **Canton** *TX* U.S.A.
226 B3 **Canton** *WI* U.S.A.
Canton Island *Phoenix Is* Kiribati *see* **Kanton**
185 H3 **Cantoria** Spain
185 F1 **Cantos Negros** *hill* Spain
256 A6 **Cantu** *r.* Brazil
190 E3 **Cantù** Italy
256 B6 **Cantu, Serra do** *hills* Brazil
Cantuaria *Kent, England* U.K. *see* **Canterbury**
254 F4 **Canudos** Brazil
261 H4 **Cañuelas** Arg.
Canusium Italy *see* **Canosa di Puglia**
251 E6 **Canutama** Brazil
81 D4 **Canvastown** *South I.* N.Z.
151 H3 **Canvey Island** *Essex, England* U.K.
223 J4 **Canwood** *Sask.* Can.
213 G3 **Canxixe** Moz.
159 G2 **Cany-Barville** France
187 C5 **Cànyoles** *r.* Spain
222 B2 **Canyon** *Y.T.* Can.
237 C5 **Canyon** *TX* U.S.A.
238 C2 **Canyon City** *OR* U.S.A.
240 G2 **Canyon Creek** *r.* *CA* U.S.A.
240 G1 **Canyondam** *CA* U.S.A.
238 E2 **Canyon Ferry Lake** *MT* U.S.A.
222 E2 **Canyon Ranges** *mts* *N.W.T.* Can.
238 B3 **Canyonville** *OR* U.S.A.
209 D6 **Canzar** Angola
101 C4 **Cao** *r.* China
96 D2 **Cao Băng** Vietnam
Caocheng *Shandong* China *see* **Caoxian**
Caohe *Hubei* China *see* **Qichun**
110 D3 **Caohu** *Xinjiang* China
Caojiahe *Hubei* China *see* **Qichun**
108 A3 **Caojian** *Yunnan* China
146 B5 **Caolas** *Argyll and Bute, Scotland* U.K.
Caolas Scalpaigh *Western Isles, Scotland* U.K. *see* **Kyles Scalpay**
146 C6 **Caolisport, Loch** *inlet* *Scotland* U.K.
209 C7 **Caombo** Angola
97 E4 **Cao Nguyên Đắc Lắc** *plat.* Vietnam
191 G2 **Caorame** *r.* Italy
191 H3 **Caorle** Italy
107 G5 **Caoxian** *Shandong* China
Caozhou *Shandong* China *see* **Heze**
227 F4 **Capac** *MI* U.S.A.
193 H4 **Capaccio** Italy
194 C4 **Capaci** *Sicilia* Italy
209 D7 **Capaia** Angola
Çapakçur Turkey *see* **Bingöl**
192 D2 **Capalbio** Italy
177 L5 **Căpâlna** Romania
250 E3 **Capanaparo** *r.* Venez.
254 D2 **Capanema** Brazil
192 C2 **Capanne, Monte** *mt.* Italy
191 F5 **Capannoli** Italy
191 F5 **Capannori** Italy
256 C6 **Capão Bonito** Brazil
257 G4 **Caparaó, Serra do** *mts* Brazil
184 A2 **Caparica** Port.
250 D3 **Caparo** *r.* Venez.
182 B4 **Caparrosa** Port.
183 I2 **Caparroso** Spain
92 B3 **Capas** Phil.
197 F3 **Căpățânii, Munții** *mts* Romania
225 I4 **Cap-aux-Meules** *Que.* Can.
187 C5 **Cap-Blanc** Spain
163 A5 **Capbreton** France
225 H3 **Cap-Chat** *Que.* Can.
161 B5 **Cap d'Agde** France
186 □ **Cap d'Artrutx** Spain
225 F4 **Cap-de-la-Madeleine** *Que.* Can.
163 E4 **Capdenac** France
163 E4 **Capdenac-Gare** France
186 □ **Cap d'En Font** Spain
187 G5 **Capdepera** Spain
85 F4 **Cape** *r.* *Qld* Austr.
Cape Bald *N.B.* Can. *see* **Cap-Pelé**
83 G5 **Cape Barren Island** *Tas.* Austr.
264 J8 **Cape Basin** *sea feature* S. Atlantic Ocean
82 D3 **Cape Borda** *S.A.* Austr.
225 I4 **Cape Breton Island** *N.S.* Can.
225 K2 **Cape Charles** *Nfld.* Can.
233 E6 **Cape Charles** *VA* U.S.A.
206 E5 **Cape Coast** Ghana
Cape Coast Castle Ghana *see* **Cape Coast**
233 H4 **Cape Cod Bay** *MA* U.S.A.
231 D7 **Cape Coral** *FL* U.S.A.
84 C3 **Cape Crawford** *N.T.* Austr.
227 G3 **Cape Croker** *Ont.* Can.
221 K3 **Cape Dorset** *Nunavut* Can.
233 □H3 **Cape Elizabeth** *ME* U.S.A.
222 C3 **Cape Fanshaw** *AK* U.S.A.
231 E5 **Cape Fear** *r.* *NC* U.S.A.
225 I4 **Cape George** *N.S.* Can.
237 F4 **Cape Girardeau** *MO* U.S.A.
Cape Juby Morocco *see* **Tarfaya**
87 B7 **Capel** *W.A.* Austr.
151 H3 **Capel** *Kent, England* U.K.
151 G3 **Capel** *Surrey, England* U.K.
216 □1b **Capelas** *São Miguel* Azores
150 D1 **Capel Curig** *Conwy, Wales* U.K.
257 F2 **Capelinha** Brazil
85 G4 **Capella** *Qld* Austr.
164 D3 **Capelle aan de IJssel** Neth.
151 I3 **Capel le Ferne** *Kent, England* U.K.
165 F5 **Capellen** Lux.
216 □1c **Capelo** *Faial* Azores
209 B8 **Capelongo** *Huíla* Angola
Capelongo *Huíla* Angola *see* **Kuvango**
151 I2 **Capel St Mary** *Suffolk, England* U.K.
234 D4 **Cape May** *NJ* U.S.A.
234 D3 **Cape May County** *county* *NJ* U.S.A.
234 D3 **Cape May Court House** *NJ* U.S.A.
234 D4 **Cape May Point** *NJ* U.S.A.
209 C7 **Capenda-Camulemba** Angola
163 E5 **Capendu** France
225 H5 **Cape Sable Island** *N.S.* Can.
225 J3 **Cape St George** *Nfld.* Can.
161 B5 **Capestang** France
247 □2 **Capesterre** Guadeloupe
193 F2 **Capestrano** Italy
214 B5 **Cape Town** S. Africa
206 □ **Cape Verde** *country* N. Atlantic Ocean
264 G5 **Cape Verde Basin** *sea feature* N. Atlantic Ocean
264 G4 **Cape Verde Plateau** *sea feature* N. Atlantic Ocean
233 E2 **Cape Vincent** *NY* U.S.A.
225 H4 **Cape Wolfe** *P.E.I.* Can.
85 E2 **Cape York Peninsula** *Qld* Austr.
163 A4 **Cap Ferret** France
246 D3 **Cap-Haïtien** Haiti
185 G4 **Capileira** Spain
185 E2 **Capilla** Spain
244 C3 **Capilla de Guadalupe** Mex.
260 E2 **Capilla del Monte** Arg.
254 C2 **Capim** *r.* Brazil
182 C4 **Capinha** Port.
256 C3 **Capinópolis** Brazil
252 D4 **Capinota** Bol.
193 F3 **Capistrello** Italy
239 F5 **Capitan** *NM* U.S.A.
262 U2 **Capitán Arturo Prat** *research stn* Antarctica
261 G3 **Capitán Bermudez** Arg.
260 A6 **Capitán Pastene** Chile
261 H4 **Capitán Sarmiento** Arg.
257 F2 **Capitão Enéas** Brazil
234 C3 **Capitol Park** *DE* U.S.A.
256 B5 **Capivara, Represa** *resr* Brazil
256 D5 **Capivari** Brazil
254 F5 **Capivari** *r.* *Bahia* Brazil
256 D5 **Capivari** *r.* *São Paulo* Brazil
194 D5 **Capizzi** *Sicilia* Italy
177 L4 **Căpleni** Romania
188 F4 **Čapljina** Bos.-Herz.
186 E2 **Cap Llitzet** *mt.* Spain
213 G2 **Capoche** *r.* Moz./Zambia
192 D2 **Capodimonte** Italy
190 F2 **Capo di Ponte** Italy
193 G4 **Capodochino** *airport* Italy
194 D4 **Capo d'Orlando** *Sicilia* Italy
192 C2 **Capoliveri** Italy
191 G5 **Capolona** Italy
193 H4 **Caposele** Italy
192 A5 **Capoterra** *Sardegna* Italy
163 D6 **Capoulet** France
193 F2 **Cappadocia** Italy
147 C4 **Cappagh** Rep. of Ireland
147 C4 **Cappamore** Rep. of Ireland
147 C4 **Cappawhite** Rep. of Ireland
168 D2 **Cappel** Ger.
225 H4 **Cap-Pelé** *N.B.* Can.
193 G2 **Cappelle sul Tavo** Italy
168 D3 **Cappeln (Oldenburg)** Ger.
146 E6 **Capplegill** *Dumfries and Galloway, Scotland* U.K.
147 D4 **Cappoquin** Rep. of Ireland
193 G3 **Capracotta** Italy
192 B1 **Capraia, Isola di** *i.* Italy
192 B1 **Capraia Isola** Italy
192 E2 **Capranica** Italy
193 G4 **Capri** Italy
193 G4 **Capri, Isola di** *i.* Italy
193 G3 **Capriati a Volturno** Italy
85 G4 **Capricorn, Cape** *Qld* Austr.
85 G4 **Capricorn Channel** *Qld* Austr.
85 H4 **Capricorn Group** *atolls* *Qld* Austr.
190 E3 **Caprino Bergamasco** Italy
191 F3 **Caprino Veronese** Italy
212 D3 **Caprivi** *admin. reg.* Namibia
Capsa Tunisia *see* **Gafsa**
240 □D9 **Captain Cook** *HI* U.S.A.
163 B4 **Captieux** France
232 C5 **Captina** *r.* *OH* U.S.A.
193 G3 **Capua** Italy
244 D3 **Capulín** Mex.
209 B8 **Capunda Cavilongo** Angola
171 D3 **Caputh** Ger.
146 E5 **Caputh** *Perth and Kinross, Scotland* U.K.
163 C5 **Capvern-les-Bains** France
250 C4 **Caqueta** *dept* Col.
250 D5 **Caquetá** *r.* Col.
250 C3 **Cáqueza** Col.
183 G4 **Carabaña** Spain
252 C3 **Carabaya, Cordillera de** *mts* Peru
251 F5 **Carabinani** *r.* Brazil
250 E2 **Carabobo** *state* Venez.
197 G3 **Caracal** Romania
251 F4 **Caracarai** Brazil
250 E2 **Caracas** Venez.
253 F5 **Caracol** *Mato Grosso do Sul* Brazil
254 E4 **Caracol** *Piauí* Brazil
252 D4 **Caracollo** Bol.
185 F2 **Caracuel de Calatrava** Spain
92 C5 **Caraga** Phil.
83 F3 **Caragabal** *N.S.W.* Austr.
190 C4 **Caraglio** Italy
257 E5 **Caraguatatuba** Brazil
259 B5 **Carahue** Chile
257 G2 **Caraí** Brazil
147 F1 **Cara Island** *Scotland* U.K.
257 H2 **Caraiva** Brazil
251 I6 **Carajás, Serra dos** *hills* Brazil
Carales *Sardegna* Italy *see* **Cagliari**
Caralis *Sardegna* Italy *see* **Cagliari**
Caralps Spain *see* **Queralbs**
163 D5 **Caraman** France
193 G2 **Caramanico Terme** Italy
185 I3 **Caramel** *r.* Spain
92 B3 **Caramoan Peninsula** Phil.
182 B4 **Caramulo** Port.
182 B4 **Caramulo** *mt.* Port.
182 B4 **Caramulo, Serra do** *mts* Port.
253 F3 **Caraná** *r.* Brazil
252 D3 **Caranavi** Bol.
177 L5 **Cărand** Romania
257 F4 **Carandaí** Brazil
253 E5 **Carandaiti** Bol.
182 D1 **Caranga** Spain
257 F4 **Carangola** Brazil
182 B5 **Caranguejeira** Port.
197 F3 **Caransebeş** Romania
158 C3 **Carantec** France
250 C5 **Cara Paraná** *r.* Col.
193 H3 **Carapelle** Italy
193 H3 **Carapelle** *r.* Italy
193 H3 **Carapellotto** *r.* Italy
82 D3 **Carappee Hill** *hill* *S.A.* Austr.
225 H4 **Caraquet** *N.B.* Can.
250 A5 **Caráquez** Ecuador
250 C3 **Carare** *r.* Col.
190 E4 **Carasco** Italy
197 E3 **Caraşova** Romania
177 L4 **Carastelec** Romania
242 □J6 **Caratasca** Hond.
242 □J6 **Caratasca, Laguna** *lag.* Hond.
257 F3 **Caratinga** Brazil
250 D5 **Caratué** *r.* Col.
233 □I2 **Caratunk** *ME* U.S.A.
250 E6 **Carauari** Brazil
254 F3 **Caraúbas** Brazil
Carauná *mt.* Brazil *see* **Grande, Serra**
185 I2 **Caravaca de la Cruz** Spain
190 E3 **Caravaggio** Italy
257 H2 **Caravelas** Brazil
252 B3 **Caravelí** Peru
182 E3 **Carbajales de Alba** Spain
182 B2 **Carballeda de Avia** Spain
182 B2 **Carballiño** Spain
182 B1 **Carballo** *Galicia* Spain
182 C2 **Carballo** *Galicia* Spain
182 D3 **Carbellino** Spain
223 L5 **Carberry** *Man.* Can.
242 C2 **Carbó** Mex.
194 B5 **Carboi** *r.* *Sicilia* Italy
163 B4 **Carbon-Blanc** France
234 C2 **Carbon County** *county* *PA* U.S.A.
239 F4 **Carbondale** *CO* U.S.A.
237 F4 **Carbondale** *IL* U.S.A.
234 C1 **Carbondale** *PA* U.S.A.
225 K4 **Carbonear** *Nfld.* Can.
183 H3 **Carbonera de Frentes** Spain
185 I4 **Carboneras** Spain
183 I5 **Carboneras de Guadazaón** Spain
183 F3 **Carbonero El Mayor** Spain
185 G2 **Carboneros** Spain
192 A5 **Carbonia** *Sardegna* Italy
191 H2 **Carbonìn** Italy
257 F2 **Carbonita** Brazil
163 D5 **Carbonne** France
146 B4 **Carbost** *Highland, Scotland* U.K.
146 B4 **Carbost** *Highland, Scotland* U.K.
147 E3 **Carbury** Rep. of Ireland
182 D4 **Carcaboso** Spain
185 F3 **Carcabuey** Spain
187 C5 **Carcaixent** Spain
222 G3 **Carcajou** *Alta* Can.
222 D1 **Carcajou** *r.* *N.W.T.* Can.
197 I3 **Carcaliu** Romania
162 A3 **Carcans** France
162 A3 **Carcans-Plage** France
182 D3 **Carção** Port.
92 B4 **Carcar** Phil.
261 G3 **Carcaraña** *r.* Arg.
190 D4 **Carcare** Italy
163 E5 **Carcassonne** France
183 I2 **Carcastillo** Spain
187 B5 **Carcelén** Spain
161 E5 **Carcès** France
185 G3 **Carchelejo** Spain
250 B4 **Carchi** *prov.* Ecuador
190 D3 **Carcoforo** Italy
149 H4 **Carcroft** *South Yorkshire, England* U.K.
222 C2 **Carcross** *Y.T.* Can.
163 D4 **Cardaillac** France
199 E1 **Çardak** *anakkale* Turkey
199 F3 **Çardak** Turkey
261 I4 **Cardal** Uru.
Cardamomes, Chaîne des *mts* Cambodia *see* **Cardomom Range**
114 C4 **Cardamon Hills** India
186 F3 **Cardedeu** Spain
192 B5 **Cardedu** *Sardegna* Italy
185 F2 **Cardeña** Spain
183 G2 **Cardeñadijo** Spain
246 B2 **Cárdenas** Cuba
245 E2 **Cárdenas** Mex.
243 G5 **Cárdenas** Mex.
183 I5 **Cardenete** Spain
183 F4 **Cardeñosa** Spain
195 E4 **Cardeto** Italy
Çardi Turkey *see* **Harmancık**
259 C8 **Cardiel, Lago** *l.* Arg.
150 D3 **Cardiff** *Cardiff, Wales* U.K.
150 D3 **Cardiff** *admin. div.* *Wales* U.K.
234 B3 **Cardiff** *MD* U.S.A.
150 D3 **Cardiff International** *airport* *Wales* U.K.
150 C2 **Cardigan** *Ceredigion, Wales* U.K.
150 C2 **Cardigan Bay** *Wales* U.K.
182 B5 **Cardigos** Port.
233 F2 **Cardinal** *Ont.* Can.
195 F4 **Cardinale** Italy
232 B4 **Cardington** *OH* U.S.A.
193 F3 **Cardito** Italy
96 C4 **Cardomom Range** *mts* Cambodia
216 □3b **Cardón** *hill* *Fuerteventura* Canary Is
242 B3 **Cardón, Cerro** *hill* Mex.
186 E3 **Cardona** Spain
261 I3 **Cardona** Uru.
245 E3 **Cardonal** Mex.
186 E3 **Cardoner** *r.* Spain
256 C4 **Cardoso** Brazil
256 D6 **Cardoso, Ilha do** *i.* Brazil
81 B6 **Cardrona** *South I.* N.Z.
81 B6 **Cardrona, Mount** *South I.* N.Z.
146 D6 **Cardross** *Argyll and Bute, Scotland* U.K.
222 H5 **Cardston** *Alta* Can.
85 F3 **Cardwell** *Qld* Austr.
257 E5 **Careaçu** Brazil
191 G3 **Carega, Cima** *mt.* Italy
197 F2 **Carei** Romania
177 L4 **Careilor, Câmpia** *plain* Romania
251 G5 **Careiro** Brazil
251 F5 **Careiro do Castanho** Brazil
260 B2 **Carén** Chile
183 I3 **Carenas** Spain
158 E2 **Carentan** France
158 D4 **Carentoir** France
183 F1 **Cares** *r.* Spain
232 B4 **Carey** *OH* U.S.A.
87 D6 **Carey, Lake** *salt flat* *W.A.* Austr.
87 B5 **Carey Downs** *W.A.* Austr.
217 □1 **Cargados Carajos Islands** Mauritius
146 E6 **Cargenbridge** *Dumfries and Galloway, Scotland* U.K.
192 A2 **Cargèse** *Corse* France
158 C3 **Carhaix-Plouguer** France
252 A2 **Carhuamayo** Peru
261 F5 **Carhué** Arg.
182 C4 **Caria** Port.
254 F4 **Cariacá** *r.* Brazil
257 G4 **Cariacica** Brazil
250 B6 **Cariamanga** Ecuador
209 B7 **Cariango** Angola
195 F3 **Cariati** Italy
246 B3 **Caribbean Sea** N. Atlantic Ocean
222 F4 **Cariboo Mountains** *B.C.* Can.
223 M3 **Caribou** *r.* *Man.* Can.
222 E2 **Caribou** *r.* *N.W.T.* Can.
233 □I1 **Caribou** *ME* U.S.A.
226 E2 **Caribou Island** *Ont.* Can.
222 H2 **Caribou Islands** *N.W.T.* Can.
224 B3 **Caribou Lake** *Ont.* Can.
222 H3 **Caribou Mountains** *Alta* Can.
242 D3 **Carichic** Mex.
92 C4 **Carigara** Phil.
157 F3 **Carignan** France
190 C4 **Carignano** Italy
83 F2 **Carinda** *N.S.W.* Austr.
186 B3 **Cariñena** Spain
254 E5 **Carinhanha** Brazil
254 E5 **Carinhanha** *r.* Brazil
194 C4 **Carini** *Sicilia* Italy
182 C1 **Cariño** Spain
193 F3 **Carinola** Italy
Carinthia *land* Austria *see* **Kärnten**
209 D8 **Caripande** Angola
251 F2 **Caripe** Venez.
251 F2 **Caripito** Venez.
254 E3 **Cariris Novos, Serra dos** *hills* Brazil
251 F2 **Caris** *r.* Venez.
190 D3 **Carisio** Italy
191 F2 **Carisolo** Italy
177 L6 **Cârjiţi** Romania
147 D2 **Cark Mountain** *hill* Rep. of Ireland
163 D5 **Carla-Bayle** France
Carlabhagh *Western Isles, Scotland* U.K. *see* **Carloway**
147 E2 **Carland** *Northern Ireland* U.K.
147 E3 **Carlanstown** Rep. of Ireland
193 G3 **Carlantino** Italy
161 A4 **Carlat** France
195 E5 **Carlentini** *Sicilia* Italy
187 C5 **Carlet** Spain
227 F4 **Carleton** *MI* U.S.A.
225 H4 **Carleton, Mount** *hill* *N.B.* Can.
224 E4 **Carleton Place** *Ont.* Can.
215 F2 **Carletonville** S. Africa
197 G2 **Cârlibaba** Romania
238 C3 **Carlin** *NV* U.S.A.
157 G3 **Carling** France
147 E2 **Carlingford** Rep. of Ireland
147 E2 **Carlingford Lough** *inlet* Rep. of Ireland/U.K.
236 F4 **Carlinville** *IL* U.S.A.
149 G3 **Carlisle** *Cumbria, England* U.K.
232 A5 **Carlisle** *KY* U.S.A.
233 F3 **Carlisle** *NY* U.S.A.
227 I5 **Carlisle** *PA* U.S.A.
215 F5 **Carlisle Bridge** S. Africa
87 E6 **Carlisle Lakes** *salt flat* *W.A.* Austr.
234 A2 **Carlisle Springs** *PA* U.S.A.
163 D6 **Carlit, Pic** *mt.* France
192 A5 **Carloforte** *Sardegna* Italy
195 F3 **Carlopoli** Italy
256 C5 **Carlópolis** Brazil
146 E6 **Carlops** *Scottish Borders, Scotland* U.K.
245 G4 **Carlos A. Carrillo** Mex.
261 G4 **Carlos Casares** Arg.
257 G2 **Carlos Chagas** Brazil
261 I3 **Carlos Reyles** Uru.
261 F4 **Carlos Tejedor** Arg.
168 F2 **Carlow** Ger.
147 E4 **Carlow** Rep. of Ireland
147 E4 **Carlow** *county* Rep. of Ireland
146 B3 **Carloway** *Western Isles, Scotland* U.K.
Carlsbad Czech Rep. *see* **Karlovy Vary**
240 I5 **Carlsbad** *CA* U.S.A.
239 F5 **Carlsbad** *NM* U.S.A.
237 C6 **Carlsbad** *TX* U.S.A.
172 C2 **Carlsberg** Ger.
265 H4 **Carlsberg Ridge** *sea feature* Indian Ocean
171 D5 **Carlsfeld** Ger.
215 E4 **Carlton** S. Africa
151 F2 **Carlton** *Nottinghamshire, England* U.K.
226 A2 **Carlton** *MN* U.S.A.
151 I2 **Carlton Colville** *Suffolk, England* U.K.
86 F2 **Carlton Hill** *W.A.* Austr.
149 H4 **Carlton in Lindrick** *Nottinghamshire, England* U.K.
146 E6 **Carluke** *South Lanarkshire, Scotland* U.K.
163 D4 **Carlux** France
223 K5 **Carlyle** *Sask.* Can.
236 F4 **Carlyle** *IL* U.S.A.
222 B2 **Carmacks** *Y.T.* Can.
190 C4 **Carmagnola** Italy
223 L5 **Carman** *Man.* Can.
Carmana Iran *see* **Kermān**
150 C3 **Carmarthen** *Carmarthenshire, Wales* U.K.
150 C3 **Carmarthen Bay** *Wales* U.K.
150 C3 **Carmarthenshire** *admin. div.* *Wales* U.K.
163 E4 **Carmaux** France
230 C4 **Carmel** *IN* U.S.A.
233 □I2 **Carmel** *ME* U.S.A.
233 G4 **Carmel** *NY* U.S.A.
128 B3 **Carmel, Mount** *hill* Israel
240 G3 **Carmel-by-the-Sea** *CA* U.S.A.
243 H5 **Carmelita** Guat.
261 H3 **Carmelo** Uru.
240 G3 **Carmel Valley** *CA* U.S.A.
261 G3 **Carmen** Arg.
250 C2 **Carmen** Col.
242 D2 **Carmen** *r.* Mex.
92 C4 **Carmen** Phil.
261 I3 **Carmen** Uru.
241 L6 **Carmen** *AZ* U.S.A.
183 F5 **Carmena** Spain
261 H4 **Carmen de Areco** Arg.
259 E6 **Carmen de Patagones** Arg.
182 E2 **Cármenes** Spain
236 F4 **Carmi** *IL* U.S.A.
195 H2 **Carmiano** Italy
240 G2 **Carmichael** *CA* U.S.A.
85 G4 **Carmila** *Qld* Austr.
257 F4 **Carmo** Brazil
257 E4 **Carmo da Cachoeira** Brazil
257 E5 **Carmo de Minas** Brazil
256 D3 **Carmo do Paranaíba** Brazil
87 C7 **Carmody, Lake** *salt flat* *W.A.* Austr.
Carmona Angola *see* **Uíge**
184 E3 **Carmona** Spain
184 D1 **Carmonita** Spain
257 E4 **Carmópolis do Minas** Brazil
146 F5 **Carmyllie** *Angus, Scotland* U.K.
158 C4 **Carnac** France
146 D4 **Carn a'Chuilinn** *hill* *Scotland* U.K.
147 E2 **Carnagh** *Northern Ireland* U.K.
87 B6 **Carnamah** *W.A.* Austr.
87 B5 **Carnarvon** *W.A.* Austr.
214 D4 **Carnarvon** S. Africa
87 D5 **Carnarvon Range** *hills* *W.A.* Austr.
85 G5 **Carnarvon Range** *mts* *Qld* Austr.
146 F5 **Carnbee** *Fife, Scotland* U.K.
146 D4 **Carn Chuinneag** *hill* *Scotland* U.K.
146 D4 **Carn Dearg** *hill* *Highland, Scotland* U.K.
146 D4 **Carn Dearg** *hill* *Highland, Scotland* U.K.
147 D1 **Carndonagh** Rep. of Ireland
147 E1 **Carnduff** *Northern Ireland* U.K.
146 E4 **Carn Ealasaid** *hill* *Scotland* U.K.
150 D1 **Carnedd Llywelyn** *mt.* *Wales* U.K.
150 D2 **Carnedd y Filiast** *hill* *Wales* U.K.
87 D5 **Carnegie** *W.A.* Austr.
87 D5 **Carnegie, Lake** *salt flat* *W.A.* Austr.
267 N6 **Carnegie Ridge** *sea feature* S. Pacific Ocean
146 C4 **Carn Eighe** *mt.* *Scotland* U.K.
146 E4 **Carne na Loine** *hill* *Scotland* U.K.
258 B5 **Carnero, Bahía del** *b.* Chile
82 C2 **Carnes** *S.A.* Austr.
231 D5 **Carnesville** *GA* U.S.A.
147 E4 **Carnew** Rep. of Ireland
226 D3 **Carney** *MI* U.S.A.
262 P2 **Carney Island** Antarctica
234 C3 **Carneys Point** *NJ* U.S.A.
146 F4 **Carnferg** *hill* *Scotland* U.K.
149 G3 **Carnforth** *Lancashire, England* U.K.
146 E4 **Carn Glas-choire** *hill* *Scotland* U.K.
115 G4 **Car Nicobar** *i.* *Andaman & Nicobar Is* India
156 D2 **Carnières** France
138 E3 **Carnikava** Latvia
147 F2 **Carnlough** *Northern Ireland* U.K.
146 E4 **Carn Mor** *hill* *Scotland* U.K.
147 C3 **Carnmore** Rep. of Ireland
150 D2 **Carno** *Powys, Wales* U.K.
146 D4 **Carn Odhar** *hill* *Scotland* U.K.
158 C3 **Carnoët** France
161 B5 **Carnon-Plage** France
208 B3 **Carnot** C.A.R.
76 D5 **Carnot, Cape** *S.A.* Austr.
182 A2 **Carnota** Spain
86 D3 **Carnot Bay** *W.A.* Austr.
161 E5 **Carnoules** France
146 F5 **Carnoustie** *Angus, Scotland* U.K.
161 D5 **Carnoux-en-Provence** France
147 E4 **Carnsore Point** Rep. of Ireland
148 C3 **Carnteel** *Northern Ireland* U.K.
146 E6 **Carnwath** *South Lanarkshire, Scotland* U.K.
227 F4 **Caro** *MI* U.S.A.
251 F4 **Caroaebe** *r.* Brazil
Caroch *mt.* Spain *see* **El Caroche**
85 H3 **Carola Cay** *rf* *Coral Sea Is Terr.* Austr.
231 D7 **Carol City** *FL* U.S.A.
193 I5 **Carolei** Italy
254 D3 **Carolina** Brazil
247 □1 **Carolina** Puerto Rico
215 H2 **Carolina** S. Africa
231 E5 **Carolina Beach** *NC* U.S.A.
222 H4 **Caroline** *Alta* Can.
234 C4 **Caroline County** *county* *MD* U.S.A.
267 I6 **Caroline Island** Kiribati
266 E5 **Caroline Islands** N. Pacific Ocean
81 A6 **Caroline Peak** *South I.* N.Z.
158 E3 **Carolles** France
214 A3 **Carolusberg** S. Africa
161 D4 **Caromb** France
190 E2 **Carona** Italy
251 F2 **Caroní** *r.* Venez.
194 D4 **Caronia** *Sicilia* Italy
250 D2 **Carora** Venez.
197 I3 **C. A. Rosetti** Romania
195 G2 **Carosino** Italy
195 G2 **Carovigno** Italy
193 G3 **Carovilli** Italy
227 I3 **Carp** *Ont.* Can.
190 E4 **Carpaneto Piacentino** Italy
192 E2 **Carparola** Italy
177 I2 **Carpathian Mountains** Europe
Carpaţii *mts* Europe *see* **Carpathian Mountains**
197 F3 **Carpaţii Meridionali** *mts* Romania
191 H5 **Carpegna** Italy
190 F3 **Carpenedolo** Italy
84 D2 **Carpentaria, Gulf of** *N.T./Qld* Austr.
85 F3 **Carpentaria Downs** *Qld* Austr.
161 D4 **Carpentras** France
191 F4 **Carpi** Italy
195 H2 **Carpignano Salentino** Italy
190 D3 **Carpignano Sesia** Italy
254 G3 **Carpina** Brazil
191 H5 **Carpina** *r.* Italy
177 L5 **Cărpinet** Romania
190 F4 **Carpineti** Italy
193 F3 **Carpineto Romano** Italy
196 E3 **Cărpiniş** Romania
193 H3 **Carpino** Italy
193 G3 **Carpinone** Italy
240 H4 **Carpinteria** *CA* U.S.A.
183 E3 **Carpio** Spain
236 C1 **Carpio** *ND* U.S.A.
159 F2 **Carpiquet** France
158 E4 **Carquefou** France
161 E5 **Carqueiranne** France
184 D1 **Carquesa** *hill* Spain
147 B3 **Carra, Lough** *l.* Rep. of Ireland
233 □H2 **Carrabassett** *ME* U.S.A.
231 C6 **Carrabelle** *FL* U.S.A.
147 C3 **Carracastle** Rep. of Ireland
182 D2 **Carracedelo** Spain
146 C6 **Carradale** *Argyll and Bute, Scotland* U.K.
Carraig na Siuire Rep. of Ireland *see* **Carrick-on-Suir**
250 C2 **Carraipía** Col.
182 B1 **Carral** Spain
147 B3 **Carraloe** Rep. of Ireland
147 B5 **Carran** *hill* Rep. of Ireland
183 G4 **Carranque** Spain
147 B5 **Carrantuohill** *mt.* Rep. of Ireland
184 B3 **Carrapateira** Port.
182 C4 **Carrapichana** Port.
190 F4 **Carrara** Italy
186 C4 **Carrascal** *mt.* Spain
182 E4 **Carrascal del Obispo** Spain
183 G3 **Carrascal del Río** Spain
183 H4 **Carrascosa** Spain
183 H4 **Carrascosa del Campo** Spain
83 F3 **Carrathool** *N.S.W.* Austr.
185 F4 **Carratraca** Spain
182 C3 **Carrazeda de Ansiães** Port.

182 C3 Carrazedo de Montenegro Port.
86 F3 Carr Boyd Range hills W.A. Austr.
146 E4 Carrbridge Highland, Scotland U.K.
182 B3 Carreço Port.
184 B1 Carregado Port.
182 C4 Carregal do Sal Port.
182 B5 Carregueiros Port.
182 B1 Carreira Spain
184 C3 Carreiros r. Port.
183 F1 Carreña de Cabrales Spain
260 C5 Carrero, Cerro mt. Arg.
163 B5 Carresse-Cassaber France
Carrhae Turkey see Harran
183 G1 Carriazo Spain
147 C2 Carrick Donegal Rep. of Ireland
147 E4 Carrick Wexford Rep. of Ireland
146 D6 Carrick reg. Scotland U.K.
147 D4 Carrickbeg Rep. of Ireland
147 D3 Carrickboy Rep. of Ireland
147 F2 Carrickfergus Northern Ireland U.K.
147 E3 Carrickmacross Rep. of Ireland
147 D2 Carrickmore Northern Ireland U.K.
147 C3 Carrick-on-Shannon Rep. of Ireland
147 D4 Carrick-on-Suir Rep. of Ireland
182 B5 Carriço Port.
82 D3 Carrieton S.A. Austr.
147 C5 Carrigaline Rep. of Ireland
147 D3 Carrigallen Rep. of Ireland
147 B5 Carriganimmy Rep. of Ireland
147 D2 Carrigans Rep. of Ireland
147 B4 Carrigkerry Rep. of Ireland
147 C5 Carrigtwohill Rep. of Ireland
242 E3 Carrillo Mex.
236 D2 Carrington ND U.S.A.
182 B1 Carrio Spain
183 F2 Carrion r. Spain
185 G1 Carrión de Calatrava Spain
184 D3 Carrión de los Céspedes Spain
183 F2 Carrión de los Condes Spain
261 G3 Carrizales Arg.
241 L4 Carrizo AZ U.S.A.
237 C4 Carrizo Creek r. TX U.S.A.
182 E2 Carrizo de la Ribera Spain
185 H2 Carrizosa Spain
237 D6 Carrizo Springs TX U.S.A.
239 F5 Carrizozo NM U.S.A.
185 H1 Carro hill Spain
236 E3 Carroll IA U.S.A.
234 A3 Carroll County county MD U.S.A.
237 F5 Carrollton AL U.S.A.
231 C5 Carrollton GA U.S.A.
236 F4 Carrollton IL U.S.A.
230 C4 Carrollton KY U.S.A.
236 E4 Carrollton MO U.S.A.
237 F5 Carrollton MS U.S.A.
232 C4 Carrollton OH U.S.A.
232 D4 Carrolltown PA U.S.A.
85 E3 Carron r. Qld Austr.
146 D4 Carron r. Highland, Scotland U.K.
146 C4 Carron, Loch inlet Scotland U.K.
146 E6 Carronbridge Dumfries and Galloway, Scotland U.K.
161 F5 Carros France
223 K4 Carrot r. Sask. Can.
223 K4 Carrot River Sask. Can.
159 F3 Carrouges France
147 D1 Carrowkeel Rep. of Ireland
147 C3 Carrowmore Rep. of Ireland
147 C2 Carrowneden Rep. of Ireland
232 E6 Carrsville VA U.S.A.
190 C4 Carrù Italy
237 F4 Carruthersville MO U.S.A.
147 F2 Carryduff Northern Ireland U.K.
161 D5 Carry-le-Rouet France
162 B3 Cars France
163 D4 Carsac-Aillac France
146 C5 Carsaig Argyll and Bute, Scotland U.K.
126 E2 Çarşamba Turkey
129 A3 Çarşıbaşı Turkey
193 F2 Carsoli Italy
86 E2 Carson r. W.A. Austr.
236 C2 Carson ND U.S.A.
240 H2 Carson r. NV U.S.A.
226 E4 Carson City MI U.S.A.
240 H2 Carson City NV U.S.A.
86 E2 Carson Escarpment W.A. Austr.
240 H2 Carson Lake NV U.S.A.
227 F4 Carsonville MI U.S.A.
160 F1 Carspach France
146 D6 Carsphairn Dumfries and Galloway, Scotland U.K.
146 E6 Carstairs South Lanarkshire, Scotland U.K.
Carstensz-top mt. Indon. see Jaya, Puncak
260 B3 Cartagena Chile
250 C2 Cartagena Col.
187 C7 Cartagena Spain
250 C3 Cartago Col.
242 □J7 Cartago Costa Rica
185 F4 Cártama Spain
184 B1 Cartaxo Port.
184 C3 Cartaya Spain
162 B3 Cartelègue France
85 E2 Carter, Mount hill Qld Austr.
158 E2 Carteret France
235 D2 Carteret NJ U.S.A.
Carteret Island Solomon Is see Malaita
231 C5 Cartersville GA U.S.A.
81 E4 Carterton North I. N.Z.
151 F3 Carterton Oxfordshire, England U.K.
183 F1 Cartes Spain
205 H1 Carthage tourist site Tunisia
226 B5 Carthage IL U.S.A.
237 E4 Carthage MO U.S.A.
231 B5 Carthage MS U.S.A.
231 E5 Carthage NC U.S.A.
233 F3 Carthage NY U.S.A.
231 C4 Carthage TN U.S.A.
237 E5 Carthage TX U.S.A.
Carthago tourist site Tunisia see Carthage
Carthago Nova Spain see Cartagena
227 G2 Cartier Ont. Can.
86 D2 Cartier Island Ashmore & Cartier Is Austr.
149 G3 Cartmel Cumbria, England U.K.
191 H5 Cartoceto Italy
223 L5 Cartwright Man. Can.
225 J2 Cartwright Nfld. Can.
254 G4 Caruarú Brazil
182 D2 Carucedo Spain
193 G3 Carunchio Italy
197 H2 Cărunta, Vârful mt. Romania
251 F2 Carúpano Venez.
254 D2 Carutapera Brazil
182 B5 Carvalhal Santarém Port.
184 B2 Carvalhal Setúbal Port.
182 C3 Carvalho de Egas Port.
232 B6 Carver KY U.S.A.
182 D3 Carviçais Port.
156 C2 Carvin France
184 A1 Carvoeira Port.
184 B3 Carvoeiro Port.
184 A1 Carvoeiro, Cabo c. Port.
85 F5 Carwell Qld Austr.
129 F3 Çarxı Azer.
231 E5 Cary NC U.S.A.
83 E2 Caryapundy Swamp Qld Austr.
232 A6 Caryville TN U.S.A.
226 B3 Caryville WI U.S.A.
185 I3 Casa Alta hill Spain
185 F4 Casabermeja Spain
258 D1 Casabindo, Cerro de mt. Arg.
260 B3 Casablanca Chile
204 D2 Casablanca Morocco
256 D4 Casa Branca Brazil
184 B2 Casa Branca Évora Port.
184 C2 Casa Branca Portalegre Port.
193 G3 Casacalenda Italy
242 C2 Casa de Janos Mex.
185 F2 Casa de Michos Spain
260 D6 Casa de Piedra, Embalse resr Arg.
193 G3 Casagiove Italy
192 A2 Casaglione Corse France
241 L5 Casa Grande AZ U.S.A.
195 H2 Casa l'Abate Italy
193 G2 Casalanguida Italy
183 H2 Casalarreina Spain
193 G2 Casalbordino Italy
193 H3 Casalbore Italy
193 H4 Casalbuono Italy
190 E3 Casalbuttano ed Uniti Italy
190 D4 Casàl Cermelli Italy
191 G4 Casalecchio di Reno Italy
190 D3 Casale Monferrato Italy
193 H4 Casaletto Spartano Italy
191 G4 Casalfiumanese Italy
191 F4 Casalgrande Italy
190 C4 Casalgrasso Italy
184 B1 Casalinho Port.
190 F4 Casalmaggiore Italy
193 H3 Casalnuovo Monterotaro Italy
190 E3 Casalpusterlengo Italy
193 H3 Casalvecchio di Puglia Italy
193 H4 Casàl Velino Italy
206 A3 Casamance r. Senegal
195 F2 Casamassima Italy
192 B2 Casamozza Corse France
250 D3 Casanare dept Col.
250 D3 Casanare r. Col.
185 F4 Casarabonela Spain
195 H2 Casarano Italy
182 D5 Casar de Cáceres Spain
182 D4 Casar de Palomero Spain
183 G3 Casarejos Spain
185 E4 Casares Spain
182 D4 Casares de las Hurdes Spain
185 F3 Casariche Spain
183 F4 Casarrubios del Monte Spain
191 H3 Casarsa della Delizia Italy
190 E4 Casarza Ligure Italy
187 B4 Casas Altas Spain
185 H1 Casas de Benitez Spain
185 E1 Casas de Don Pedro Spain
185 H1 Casas de Fernando Alonso Spain
185 H1 Casas de Haro Spain
187 B5 Casas de Juan Gil Spain
185 I1 Casas de Juan Núñez Spain
185 H2 Casas de Lázaro Spain
182 E4 Casas del Monte Spain
185 H1 Casas de los Pinos Spain
187 B6 Casas del Puerto Spain
182 D5 Casas de Millán Spain
187 B5 Casas de Ves Spain
242 D2 Casas Grandes Mex.
242 D2 Casas Grandes r. Mex.
185 I1 Casas-Ibáñez Spain
185 H1 Casasimarro Spain
184 C2 Casas Novas de Mares Port.
183 E3 Casasola de Arión Spain
182 E5 Casatejada Spain
190 E3 Casatenovo Italy
183 F4 Casavieja Spain
261 F5 Casbas Arg.
255 B9 Casca Brazil
87 D7 Cascade W.A. Austr.
81 B6 Cascade r. South I. N.Z.
236 F3 Cascade IA U.S.A.
238 C2 Cascade ID U.S.A.
238 E2 Cascade MT U.S.A.
228 B2 Cascade Range mts Can./U.S.A.
184 A2 Cascais Port.
242 □I7 Cascal, Paso del pass Nic.
183 I2 Cascante Spain
187 B4 Cascante del Río Spain
225 H3 Cascapédia r. Que. Can.
254 F3 Cascavel Ceará Brazil
256 A6 Cascavel Paraná Brazil
193 F2 Cascia Italy
191 F5 Casciana Terme Italy
190 F5 Cascina Italy
197 H3 Căscioarele Romania
226 D3 Casco WI U.S.A.
233 □I3 Casco Bay ME U.S.A.
184 B2 Casebres Port.
183 I2 Cáseda Spain
192 B5 Case della Marina Sardegna Italy
190 D3 Casei Gerola Italy
170 F2 Casekow Ger.
190 D4 Casella Italy
193 H4 Caselle in Pittari Italy
190 C3 Caselle Torinese Italy
195 F2 Case Perrone Italy
186 E2 Caserras Spain
193 G3 Caserta Italy
193 G3 Caserta prov. Campania Italy
184 B3 Casével Port.
227 F4 Caseville MI U.S.A.
263 H2 Casey research stn Antarctica
210 F2 Caseyr, Raas c. Somalia
147 D1 Cashel Donegal Rep. of Ireland
147 C3 Cashel Galway Rep. of Ireland
147 B3 Cashel Galway Rep. of Ireland
147 D4 Cashel Laois Rep. of Ireland
147 D4 Cashel Tipperary Rep. of Ireland
147 C3 Cashla Rep. of Ireland
147 A3 Cashleen Rep. of Ireland
85 G5 Cashmere Qld Austr.
226 B4 Cashton WI U.S.A.
92 B2 Casiguran Phil.
261 G3 Casilda Arg.
183 F4 Casillas Spain
182 D4 Casillas de Flores Spain
197 I3 Casimcea Romania
197 I3 Casimcea r. Romania
244 B4 Casimiro Castillo Mex.
257 F5 Casimiro de Abreu Brazil
190 F4 Casina Italy
83 H2 Casino N.S.W. Austr.
187 C5 Casinos Spain
176 E2 Čáslav Czech Rep.
252 A2 Casma Peru
Casnewydd Newport, Wales U.K. see Newport
226 E4 Casnovia MI U.S.A.
182 D2 Casoio r. Spain
190 F4 Casola in Lunigiana Italy
191 G4 Casola Valsenio Italy
191 G5 Casole d'Elsa Italy
193 G2 Casoli Italy
193 G4 Casoria Italy
186 C3 Caspe Spain
238 F3 Casper WY U.S.A.
226 C2 Caspian MI U.S.A.
Caspian Lowland Kazakh./Rus. Fed. see Prikaspiyskaya Nizmennost'
120 B3 Caspian Sea Asia/Europe
232 D5 Cass WV U.S.A.
227 F4 Cass r. MI U.S.A.
213 G2 Cassacatiza Moz.
232 D3 Cassadaga NY U.S.A.
186 F3 Cassà de la Selva Spain
163 C5 Cassagnabère-Tournas France
163 E4 Cassagnes-Bégonhès France
209 D7 Cassai Angola
209 D8 Cassamba Angola
163 E4 Cassaniouze France
193 I5 Cassano allo Ionio Italy
195 F2 Cassano delle Murge Italy
190 D3 Cassano Magnano Italy
190 D4 Cassano Spinola Italy
194 D5 Cassaro Sicilia Italy
227 F4 Cass City MI U.S.A.
156 C2 Cassel France
224 F4 Casselman Ont. Can.
236 D2 Casselton ND U.S.A.
163 C4 Casseneuil France
256 D4 Cássia Brazil
222 D3 Cassiar B.C. Can.
222 D3 Cassiar Mountains B.C. Can.
195 E6 Cassibile Sicilia Italy
195 E6 Cassibile r. Sicilia Italy
256 B3 Cassilândia Brazil
83 G3 Cassilis N.S.W. Austr.
190 D4 Cassine Italy
193 F3 Cassino Italy
161 D5 Cassis France
236 E2 Cass Lake MN U.S.A.
146 D4 Cassley r. Scotland U.K.
191 G3 Cassola Italy
209 B7 Cassongue Angola
226 D5 Cassopolis MI U.S.A.
161 A4 Cassuéjouls France
237 E4 Cassville MO U.S.A.
176 G3 Častá Slovakia
190 D3 Castagliona Olona Italy
191 G3 Castagnaro Italy
192 C1 Castagneto Carducci Italy
190 D4 Castagnole delle Lanze Italy
190 D4 Castagnole Monferrato Italy
187 C6 Castalla Spain
183 E5 Castañar de Ibor Spain
183 H2 Castañares de Rioja Spain
163 D5 Castanet-Tolosan France
254 D2 Castanhal Brazil
182 C4 Castanheira Port.
182 B4 Castanheira de Pêra Port.
260 C2 Castaño r. Arg.
190 D3 Castano Primo Italy
243 E3 Castaños Mex.
190 E2 Castasegna Switz.
190 E3 Casteggio Italy
183 I2 Castejón Spain
186 D3 Castejón del Puente Spain
186 C3 Castejón de Monegros Spain
186 D2 Castejón de Sos Spain
186 C3 Castejón de Valdejasa Spain
193 H3 Castèl Baronia Italy
191 I5 Castelbellino Italy
191 G4 Castèl Bolognese Italy
194 D5 Castelbuono Sicilia Italy
193 H4 Castelcivita Italy
194 C4 Casteldaccia Sicilia Italy
191 F3 Castèl d'Ario Italy
190 C4 Casteldelfino Italy
193 F2 Castèl del Monte Italy
192 D2 Castèl del Piano Italy
191 G4 Castèl del Rio Italy
194 D5 Castèl di Iudica Sicilia Italy
193 F2 Castèl di Lama Italy
194 D5 Castèl di Lucio Sicilia Italy
193 G3 Castèl di Sangro Italy
182 C4 Casteleiro Port.
191 I5 Castelfidardo Italy
191 F5 Castelfiorentino Italy
186 C3 Castelflorite Spain
191 G5 Castèl Focognano Italy
193 F3 Castelforte Italy
193 H4 Castelfranci Italy
191 G5 Castelfranco di Sopra Italy
191 F5 Castelfranco di Sotto Italy
191 G4 Castelfranco Emilia Italy
193 H3 Castelfranco in Miscano Italy
191 G3 Castelfranco Veneto Italy
193 G2 Castèl Frentano Italy
192 D2 Castèl Giorgio Italy
190 F3 Castèl Goffredo Italy
193 H4 Castelgrande Italy
163 C4 Casteljaloux France
173 E2 Castell Ger.
190 D4 Castell'Alfero Italy
193 F2 Castellalto Italy
194 B4 Castellammare, Golfo di b. Sicilia Italy
194 B4 Castellammare del Golfo Sicilia Italy
193 G4 Castellammare di Stabia Italy
190 C3 Castellamonte Italy
195 G2 Castellana Grotte Italy
161 E5 Castellane France
195 F2 Castellaneta Italy
195 F2 Castellaneta Marina Italy
185 H2 Castellanos mt. Spain
183 F2 Castellanos de Castro Spain
185 E4 Castellar de la Frontera Spain
183 I4 Castellar de la Muela Spain
186 E2 Castellar de la Ribera Spain
185 G2 Castellar de Santiago Spain
185 G2 Castellar de Santisteban Spain
190 E4 Castell'Arquato Italy
192 D2 Castell'Azzara Italy
190 D4 Castellazzo Bormida Italy
186 D3 Castelldans Spain
186 G3 Castell d'Aro Spain
186 D4 Castell de Cabres Spain
187 C6 Castell de Castells Spain
186 E3 Castelldefels Spain
185 G4 Castell de Ferro Spain
190 E3 Castelleone Italy
190 D3 Castelletto sopra Ticino Italy
186 F2 Castellfollit de la Roca Spain
186 C4 Castellfort Spain
261 I5 Castelli Buenos Aires Arg.
258 E2 Castelli Chaco Arg.
191 G5 Castellina in Chianti Italy
191 F5 Castellina Marittima Italy
193 F3 Castelliri Italy
Castell-nedd Neath Port Talbot, Wales U.K. see Neath
Castell Newydd Emlyn Ceredigion, Wales U.K. see Newcastle Emlyn
187 C5 Castellnovo Spain
191 G4 Castello d'Argile Italy
Castello de Ampurias Spain see Castelló d'Empúries
187 C5 Castelló de la Plana Spain
186 G2 Castelló d'Empúries Spain
187 C6 Castelló de Rugat Spain
190 D4 Castello di Annone Italy
187 C4 Castellón prov. Valencia Spain
Castellón de la Plana Spain see Castelló de la Plana
186 C4 Castellote Spain
191 G2 Castello Tesino Italy
186 D3 Castellserà Spain
186 F3 Castellterçol Spain
191 F3 Castellucchio Italy
193 H3 Castelluccio dei Sauri Italy
193 H4 Castelluccio Inferiore Italy
193 H3 Castellucio Valmaggiore Italy
194 D4 Castell'Umberto Sicilia Italy
194 B4 Castelluzzo Sicilia Italy
193 E3 Castèl Madama Italy
191 G4 Castèl Maggiore Italy
190 C4 Castelmagno Italy
191 G3 Castelmassa Italy
163 C4 Castelmoron-sur-Lot France
194 D1 Castel Morrone Italy
163 D5 Castelnau France
163 C5 Castelnau-Barbarens France
163 D5 Castelnaudary France
163 C5 Castelnau-d'Auzan France
163 C4 Castelnaud-de-Gratecambe France
163 E5 Castelnau-de-Brassac France
162 B3 Castelnau-de-Médoc France
163 D5 Castelnau-de-Montmiral France
163 D5 Castelnau d'Estréfonds France
161 B5 Castelnau-le-Lez France
163 C5 Castelnau-Magnoac France
163 D4 Castelnau-Montratier France
163 B5 Castelnau-Rivière-Basse France
191 F4 Castelnovo di Sotto Italy
190 F4 Castelnovo ne'Monti Italy
191 G5 Castelnuovo Berardenga Italy
193 H3 Castelnuovo della Daunia Italy
190 F4 Castelnuovo di Garfagnana Italy
192 C1 Castelnuovo di Val di Cecina Italy
190 C3 Castelnuovo Don Bosco Italy
190 D4 Castelnuovo Scrivia Italy
257 G4 Castelo Brazil
182 D4 Castelo Bom Port.
216 □1c Castelo Branco Faial Azores
182 D3 Castelo Branco Bragança Port.
182 C5 Castelo Branco Castelo Branco Port.
182 C4 Castelo Branco admin. dist. Port.
182 B5 Castelo de Bode, Barragem do resr Port.
182 B3 Castelo de Paiva Port.
184 C1 Castelo de Vide Port.
182 B3 Castelo do Neiva Port.
254 E3 Castelo do Piauí Brazil
182 B3 Castelões Port.
182 C3 Castelo Melhor Port.
182 D4 Castelo Mendo Port.
182 D4 Castelo Rodrigo Port.
191 I5 Castelplanio Italy
191 I5 Castelraimondo Italy
193 E2 Castèl Ritaldi Italy
191 G2 Castelrotto Italy
163 C4 Castelsagrat France
190 E3 Castèl San Giovanni Italy
191 G5 Castèl San Niccolò Italy
191 G4 Castèl San Pietro Terme Italy
193 F2 Castèl Sant'Angelo Italy
193 F2 Castelsantangelo sul Nera Italy
193 H4 Castelsaraceno Italy
192 A4 Castelsardo Sardegna Italy
163 D4 Castelsarrasin France
186 C4 Castelseras Spain
194 C5 Casteltermini Sicilia Italy
190 E3 Castelverde Italy
193 G3 Castelvetere in Val Fortore Italy
194 B5 Castelvetrano Sicilia Italy
190 E3 Castelvetro Placentino Italy
192 E2 Castèl Viscardo Italy
193 F3 Castèl Volturno Italy
191 G4 Castenaso Italy
163 C5 Castéra-Verduzan France
82 E4 Casterton Vic. Austr.
163 B5 Castetnau-Camblong France
163 A5 Castets France
192 B5 Castiadas Sardegna Italy
187 B4 Castielfabib Spain
186 C2 Castiello de Jaca Spain
192 B2 Castifao Corse France
190 F5 Castiglioncello Italy
191 G4 Castiglione dei Pepoli Italy
192 E1 Castiglione del Lago Italy
192 C2 Castiglione della Pescaia Italy
190 F3 Castiglione della Stiviere Italy
192 D1 Castiglione d'Orcia Italy
192 E2 Castiglione in Teverina Italy
193 G3 Castiglione Messer Marino Italy
191 G5 Castiglion Fiorentino Italy
193 F2 Castignano Italy
185 E1 Castilblanco Spain
184 E3 Castilblanco de los Arroyos Spain
232 D3 Castile NY U.S.A.
256 B4 Castilho Brazil
183 I2 Castiliscar Spain
250 A6 Castilla Peru
183 G5 Castilla - La Mancha aut. comm. Spain
183 F3 Castilla y León aut. comm. Spain
184 D3 Castilleja de la Cuesta Spain
185 H3 Castillejar Spain
183 E3 Castillejo hill Spain
182 D4 Castillejo de Martin Viejo Spain
183 G3 Castillejo de Mesleón Spain
183 G3 Castillejo de Robledo Spain
250 D2 Castilletes Col.
260 C3 Castillo, Cerro del mt. Arg.
259 C7 Castillo, Pampa del hills Arg.
183 F4 Castillo de Bayuela Spain
183 H5 Castillo de Garcimuñoz Spain
185 G3 Castillo de Locubín Spain
163 D6 Castillon-en-Couserans France
163 B4 Castillon-la-Bataille France
163 C4 Castillonnès France
186 B2 Castillo-Nuevo Spain
258 G4 Castillos Uru.
258 G4 Castillos, Lago de l. Uru.
183 H3 Castilruiz Spain
190 F3 Castione della Presolana Italy
178 E5 Castiòns di Strada Italy
147 B3 Castlebar Rep. of Ireland
146 A5 Castlebay Western Isles, Scotland U.K.
147 E3 Castlebellingham Rep. of Ireland
147 C3 Castleblakeney Rep. of Ireland
147 E2 Castleblayney Rep. of Ireland
151 F2 Castle Bromwich West Midlands, England U.K.
149 G3 Castle Carrock Cumbria, England U.K.
150 E3 Castle Cary Somerset, England U.K.
147 D4 Castlecomer Rep. of Ireland
147 C4 Castleconnell Rep. of Ireland
147 B2 Castleconor Rep. of Ireland
241 L2 Castle Dale UT U.S.A.
226 B2 Castle Danger MN U.S.A.
147 E2 Castledawson Northern Ireland U.K.
147 D2 Castlederg Northern Ireland U.K.
147 E4 Castledermot Rep. of Ireland
241 J5 Castle Dome Mountains AZ U.S.A.
151 F2 Castle Donington Leicestershire, England U.K.
146 E7 Castle Douglas Dumfries and Galloway, Scotland U.K.
147 E4 Castleellis Rep. of Ireland
147 D2 Castlefinn Rep. of Ireland
149 H4 Castleford West Yorkshire, England U.K.
147 C5 Castlefreke Rep. of Ireland
147 C2 Castlegal Rep. of Ireland
222 G5 Castlegar B.C. Can.
147 A4 Castlegregory Rep. of Ireland
147 B2 Castlehill Rep. of Ireland
246 D2 Castle Island Bahamas
147 B4 Castleisland Rep. of Ireland
148 B4 Castlejordan Rep. of Ireland
146 D7 Castle Kennedy Dumfries and Galloway, Scotland U.K.
147 C4 Castlelyons Rep. of Ireland
83 F4 Castlemaine Vic. Austr.
147 B4 Castlemaine Rep. of Ireland
150 B3 Castlemartin Pembrokeshire, Wales U.K.
147 C5 Castlemartyr Rep. of Ireland
222 H5 Castle Mountain Alta Can.
240 G4 Castle Mountain CA U.S.A.
81 F4 Castlepoint North I. N.Z.
147 D3 Castlepollard Rep. of Ireland
147 C3 Castlerea Rep. of Ireland
83 F2 Castlereagh r. N.S.W. Austr.
147 F2 Castlereagh Northern Ireland U.K.
147 E1 Castlerock Northern Ireland U.K.
239 F4 Castle Rock CO U.S.A.
238 B2 Castle Rock WA U.S.A.
147 E1 Castleroe Northern Ireland U.K.
149 H3 Castleside Durham, England U.K.
246 □ Castleton Jamaica
149 I3 Castleton North Yorkshire, England U.K.
233 G3 Castleton-On-Hudson NY U.S.A.
148 E3 Castletown Isle of Man
147 B3 Castletown Clare Rep. of Ireland
147 C5 Castletown Cork Rep. of Ireland
147 D4 Castletown Laois Rep. of Ireland
147 E3 Castletown Meath Rep. of Ireland
146 E3 Castletown Highland, Scotland U.K.
147 C4 Castletownroche Rep. of Ireland
147 B3 Castleville Rep. of Ireland
147 F2 Castlewellan Northern Ireland U.K.
223 I4 Castor Alta Can.
224 E2 Castor, Rivière du r. Que. Can.
237 E6 Castor Creek r. LA U.S.A.
Castra Regina Ger. see Regensburg
183 F2 Castrejón de la Peña Spain
182 C3 Castrelo do Val Spain
163 E5 Castres France
164 D2 Castricum Neth.
161 B5 Castries France
247 □3 Castries St Lucia
195 H3 Castrignano del Capo Italy
185 H3 Castril Spain
185 H3 Castril r. Spain
183 F3 Castrillo de Don Juan Spain
183 F3 Castrillo de Duero Spain
183 G3 Castrillo de la Reina Spain
183 G3 Castrillo de la Vega Spain
183 F2 Castrillo de Villavega Spain
183 F3 Castrillo Tejeriego Spain
256 C6 Castro Brazil
259 B6 Castro Chile
195 H2 Castro Italy
182 C2 Castro Spain
182 A1 Castro r. Spain
254 F5 Castro Alves Brazil
183 G1 Castrobarto Spain
182 E2 Castrocalbón Spain
182 C2 Castro Caldelas Spain
191 G4 Castrocaro Terme Italy
182 D2 Castrocontrigo Spain
182 C4 Castro Daire Port.
193 F3 Castro dei Volsci Italy
185 F3 Castro del Río Spain
182 C1 Castro de Ouro Spain
182 C1 Castro de Rei Spain
194 C5 Castrofilippo Sicilia Italy
182 E3 Castrogonzalo Spain
183 F2 Castrojeriz Spain
182 B2 Castro Laboreiro Port.
184 C3 Castro Marim Port.
183 F2 Castromocho Spain
183 E3 Castromonte Spain
182 E3 Castronuevo Spain
183 E3 Castronuño Spain
194 C5 Castronuovo di Sicilia Sicilia Italy
193 G3 Castropignano Italy
182 D2 Castropodame Spain
182 C1 Castropol Spain
169 C4 Castrop-Rauxel Ger.
195 E4 Castroreale Sicilia Italy
183 G1 Castro-Urdiales Spain
182 B2 Castrove hill Spain
184 B3 Castro Verde Port.
182 C1 Castroverde Spain
183 E3 Castroverde de Campos Spain
193 I5 Castrovillari Italy
240 G3 Castroville CA U.S.A.
252 B3 Castrovirreyna Peru
184 E2 Castuera Spain
106 A1 Cast Uul mt. Mongolia
86 E2 Casuarina, Mount hill W.A. Austr.
127 F3 Çat Turkey
209 C8 Catabola Angola
242 □I6 Catacamas Hond.
250 A6 Catacaos Peru
250 B6 Catacocha Ecuador
187 C5 Catadau Spain
257 F4 Cataguases Brazil
92 B3 Catainğan Phil.
127 F3 Çatak Turkey
256 D3 Catalão Brazil
199 F1 Çatalca Turkey
199 F1 Çatalca Yarımadası pen. Turkey
241 L5 Catalina AZ U.S.A.
Catalonia aut. comm. Spain see Cataluña
186 E3 Cataluña aut. comm. Spain
Catalunya aut. comm. Spain see Cataluña
126 D2 Çatalzeytin Turkey
258 D3 Catamarca Arg.
258 D2 Catamarca prov. Arg.
Catambia Moz. see Catandica
Catana Sicilia Italy see Catania
92 B3 Catanauan Phil.
213 G3 Catandica Moz.
92 C3 Catanduanes i. Phil.
256 C4 Catanduva Brazil
256 A6 Catanduvas Brazil
195 E5 Catania Sicilia Italy
194 D5 Catania prov. Sicilia Italy
195 E5 Catania, Golfo di g. Sicilia Italy
195 F4 Catanzaro Italy
195 F4 Catanzaro prov. Calabria Italy
195 F4 Catanzaro Marina Italy
226 B3 Cataract WI U.S.A.
254 F3 Catarina Brazil
237 D6 Catarina TX U.S.A.
92 C3 Catarman Phil.
187 C5 Catarroja Spain
234 C2 Catasauqua PA U.S.A.
82 C3 Catastrophe, Cape S.A. Austr.
226 B3 Catawba WI U.S.A.
231 D5 Catawba r. SC U.S.A.
227 I5 Catawissa PA U.S.A.
234 B2 Catawissa Creek r. PA U.S.A.
96 D2 Cat Ba, Đao i. Vietnam
92 C4 Catbalogan Phil.
246 C1 Cat Cays is Bahamas
92 C5 Cateel Phil.
245 G4 Catemaco Mex.
245 G4 Catemaco, Laguna l. Mex.
260 B3 Catemu Chile
194 D5 Catenanuova Sicilia Italy
209 B8 Catengue Angola
151 G3 Caterham Surrey, England U.K.
192 A2 Cateri Corse France
209 B7 Catete Angola
251 H6 Catete r. Brazil
83 G4 Cathcart N.S.W. Austr.
215 F5 Cathcart S. Africa
241 I5 Cathedral City CA U.S.A.
215 G3 Cathedral Peak Lesotho
147 A5 Catherdaniel Rep. of Ireland
231 C5 Catherine AL U.S.A.
241 K2 Catherine, Mount UT U.S.A.
240 G3 Catheys Valley CA U.S.A.
238 B2 Cathlamet WA U.S.A.
186 D4 Catí Spain
193 F2 Catignano Italy
206 B4 Catió Guinea-Bissau
246 D1 Cat Island Bahamas
182 C4 Cativelos Port.
232 B5 Catlettsburg KY U.S.A.
243 I4 Catoche, Cabo c. Mex.
182 B2 Catoira Spain
254 F3 Catolé do Rocha Brazil
149 G3 Caton Lancashire, England U.K.
195 E4 Catona r. Italy
234 B3 Catonsville MD U.S.A.
244 D2 Catorce Mex.
244 D2 Catorce, Sierra de mts Mex.
182 D2 Catoute mt. Spain
187 C6 Catral Spain
191 H5 Catria, Monte mt. Italy
260 D5 Catriel Arg.
261 F5 Catriló Arg.
251 F4 Catrimani r. Brazil
146 D6 Catrine East Ayrshire, Scotland U.K.
150 E2 Catshill Worcestershire, England U.K.
233 G3 Catskill NY U.S.A.
233 F3 Catskill Mountains NY U.S.A.
157 G3 Cattenom France
169 F5 Catterfeld Ger.
149 H3 Catterick North Yorkshire, England U.K.
149 H3 Catterick Camp North Yorkshire, England U.K.
146 F5 Catterline Aberdeenshire, Scotland U.K.
81 C6 Cattle Creek South I. N.Z.
191 H5 Cattolica Italy
194 C5 Cattolica Eraclea Sicilia Italy
213 G2 Catur Moz.
163 D4 Catus France
194 C5 Catuso, Monte mt. Sicilia Italy
177 L4 Căuaș Romania
254 C2 Cauaxi r. Brazil
92 B4 Cauayan Phil.
225 I1 Caubvick, Mount Nfld. Can.
250 B4 Cauca dept Col.
250 C2 Cauca r. Col.
254 F2 Caucaia Brazil
250 C3 Caucasia Col.
129 B2 Caucasus mts Asia/Europe
260 C2 Caucete Arg.
158 C4 Caudan France
162 C4 Caudau r. France
159 G2 Caudebec-en-Caux France
163 C4 Caudecoste France
187 C6 Caudete Spain
187 B5 Caudete de las Fuentes Spain
187 C5 Caudiel Spain
163 E6 Caudiès de-Fenouillèdes France
156 D2 Caudry France
163 D5 Caujac France
158 D3 Caulnes France
195 F4 Caulonia Italy
163 D4 Caumont Midi-Pyrénées France
163 D5 Caumont Midi-Pyrénées France
159 F2 Caumont-l'Éventé France
161 C5 Caumont-sur-Durance France
246 C2 Caunao r. Cuba
163 E5 Caunes-Minervois France
209 C7 Caungula Angola
260 A4 Cauquenes Chile
251 E3 Caura r. Venez.
251 F5 Caurés r. Brazil
192 A3 Cauro Corse France
225 H3 Causapscal Que. Can.
136 E4 Căușeni Moldova
147 B4 Causeway Rep. of Ireland
147 E1 Causeway Head Northern Ireland U.K.
163 D4 Caussade France
252 D3 Cautário r. Brazil
163 B6 Cauterets France
246 C2 Cauto r. Cuba
129 F3 Cavad Azer.
193 G4 Cava de'Tirreni Italy
182 B3 Cávado r. Port.
190 D3 Cavaglià Italy
161 D5 Cavaillon France
161 E5 Cavalaire-sur-Mer France
254 D5 Cavalcante Brazil
184 B3 Cavaleiro Port.
191 G2 Cavalese Italy
236 D1 Cavalier ND U.S.A.
190 C4 Cavallermaggiore Italy
191 H3 Cavallino Italy
206 D5 Cavally r. Côte d'Ivoire
190 E3 Cava Manara Italy
147 D3 Cavan Rep. of Ireland
147 D3 Cavan county Rep. of Ireland
190 E2 Cavargna Italy
191 H3 Cavarzere Italy
191 I2 Cavazzo Carnico Italy
199 F2 Çavdarhisar Turkey
199 F3 Çavdır Turkey
81 C6 Cave South I. N.Z.
237 F4 Cave City AR U.S.A.
230 C4 Cave City KY U.S.A.
241 L5 Cave Creek AZ U.S.A.
191 I2 Cave del Predil Italy
161 C5 Caveirac France
87 F5 Cavenagh Range hills W.A. Austr.
83 E4 Cavendish Vic. Austr.
255 B9 Cavera, Serra do hills Brazil
256 A6 Cavernoso, Serra do mts Brazil
150 E2 Caverswall Staffordshire, England U.K.
182 C3 Cavês Port.
191 G4 Cavezzo Italy
251 I4 Caviana, Ilha i. Brazil
162 B3 Cavignac France
92 B3 Cavite Phil.
191 J3 Čavle Croatia
197 F2 Cavnic Romania
193 E3 Cavo, Monte hill Italy
195 F2 Cavone r. Italy
190 C4 Cavour Italy
226 C3 Cavour WI U.S.A.
191 F4 Cavriago Italy
191 G5 Cavriglia Italy
126 C3 Çavuşçu Turkey
199 G3 Çavuşköy Turkey
146 E4 Cawdor Highland, Scotland U.K.
83 E3 Cawndilla Lake imp. l. N.S.W. Austr.
Cawnpore Uttar Prad. India see Kanpur
149 H4 Cawood North Yorkshire, England U.K.
232 B6 Cawood KY U.S.A.
151 I2 Cawston Norfolk, England U.K.
257 E4 Caxambu Brazil
182 B5 Caxarias Port.
254 E3 Caxias Brazil
255 C9 Caxias do Sul Brazil
209 B7 Caxito Angola
251 I5 Caxiuana, Baía de l. Brazil
199 G2 Çay Turkey
129 C3 Çayarası Turkey
199 E2 Çaybaşı İzmir Turkey
Çaybaşı Turkey see Çayeli
231 D5 Cayce SC U.S.A.
126 D2 Çaycuma Turkey
127 F2 Çayeli Turkey
251 H3 Cayenne Fr. Guiana
156 B2 Cayeux-sur-Mer France
247 □1 Cayey Puerto Rico
126 D3 Çayhan Turkey
199 F3 Çayhisar Turkey
126 C2 Çayırhan Turkey
129 B4 Çayırlı Turkey
129 B3 Çaykara Turkey
163 D4 Caylus France
246 C3 Cayman Brac i. Cayman Is
246 B3 Cayman Islands terr. West Indies
264 D4 Cayman Trench sea feature Caribbean Sea
210 E2 Caynabo Somalia
150 E2 Caynham Shropshire, England U.K.
161 B4 Cayres France
246 B2 Cay Sal i. Bahamas
246 B2 Cay Sal Bank sea feature Bahamas
246 D2 Cay Santa Domingo i. Bahamas
149 I4 Caythorpe Lincolnshire, England U.K.
149 I3 Cayton North Yorkshire, England U.K.
240 G4 Cayucos CA U.S.A.
227 H4 Cayuga Ont. Can.
232 E3 Cayuga Heights NY U.S.A.
246 D2 Cay Verde i. Bahamas
209 D7 Cazage Angola
Cazaje Angola see Cazage
183 F4 Cazalegas Spain
184 E3 Cazalla de la Sierra Spain
163 D4 Cazals Midi-Pyrénées France
163 D4 Cazals Midi-Pyrénées France
197 H3 Căzănești Romania
163 B5 Cazaubon France
163 A4 Cazaux et de Sanguinet, Étang de l. France
233 F3 Cazenovia NY U.S.A.
163 D5 Cazères France
163 D4 Cazes-Mondenard France
163 E5 Cazilhac France
188 F3 Čažma Croatia
209 D7 Cazombo Angola
245 F3 Cazones Mex.
245 F3 Cazones r. Mex.
185 H3 Cazorla Spain
185 G3 Cazorla, Sierra de mts Spain
163 D4 Cazoulès France
213 G2 Cazula Moz.
183 F2 Cea Castilla y León Spain
182 C2 Cea Galicia Spain
183 E2 Cea r. Spain
Ceadâr-Lunga Moldova see Ciadîr-Lunga
Ceanannus Mór Meath Rep. of Ireland see Kells
146 A4 Ceann a'Bháigh Western Isles, Scotland U.K.
183 H1 Ceanuri Spain
Ceará Brazil see Fortaleza
254 F3 Ceará state Brazil
264 G6 Ceara Abyssal Plain sea feature S. Atlantic Ocean
146 B3 Cearsiadair Western Isles, Scotland U.K.
197 I3 Ceatalchioi Romania
Ceatharlach Rep. of Ireland see Carlow
159 F3 Ceaucé France
161 B3 Céaux-d'Allègre France
242 D3 Ceballos Mex.
128 A1 Cebireis Dağı mt. Turkey
182 C5 Cebolais de Cima Port.
183 F5 Cebolla Spain
244 B4 Ceboruco, Cerro mt. Mex.
244 B3 Ceboruco, Volcán vol. Mex.
177 I3 Čebovce Slovakia
183 F4 Cebreros Spain
92 B4 Cebu Phil.
92 B4 Cebu i. Phil.
193 F3 Ceccano Italy
177 H5 Cece Hungary
178 C4 Cece, Cima di mt. Italy
177 K3 Čečejovce Slovakia
176 E2 Čechtice Czech Rep.
177 H3 Čechynce Slovakia
226 C3 Cecil WI U.S.A.
234 C3 Cecil County county MD U.S.A.
85 G5 Cecil Plains Qld Austr.
87 D5 Cecil Rhodes, Mount hill W.A. Austr.
234 C3 Cecilton MD U.S.A.
191 F5 Cecina Italy
191 F5 Cecina r. Italy
195 F3 Cecita, Lago di l. Italy
182 D5 Ceclavín Spain
182 C3 Cedães Port.
226 E4 Cedar r. MI U.S.A.
236 C2 Cedar r. ND U.S.A.
236 D3 Cedar r. NE U.S.A.
214 B5 Cedarberg mts S. Africa
232 C6 Cedar Bluff VA U.S.A.
234 D3 Cedar Brook NJ U.S.A.
241 K3 Cedar City UT U.S.A.
239 F4 Cedaredge CO U.S.A.
236 E3 Cedar Falls IA U.S.A.
240 H3 Cedar Grove CA U.S.A.
226 D4 Cedar Grove WI U.S.A.
232 C5 Cedar Grove WV U.S.A.
223 K4 Cedar Lake Man. Can.
230 B3 Cedar Rapids IA U.S.A.
241 L3 Cedar Ridge AZ U.S.A.
226 D3 Cedar River MI U.S.A.
235 D3 Cedar Run NJ U.S.A.
227 F4 Cedar Springs Ont. Can.
226 E4 Cedar Springs MI U.S.A.
231 C5 Cedartown GA U.S.A.
215 G4 Cedarville S. Africa
226 C4 Cedarville IL U.S.A.
227 E3 Cedarville MI U.S.A.
232 B5 Cedarville OH U.S.A.
190 F2 Cedegolo Italy
182 B1 Cedeira Spain
182 B1 Cedeira hill Spain
183 F5 Cedena r. Spain
182 C5 Cedillo Spain
183 G4 Cedillo del Condado Spain
244 D2 Cedral Mex.
186 C4 Cedrillas Spain
192 B4 Cedrino r. Sardegna Italy
254 F3 Cedro Brazil
216 □1c Cedros Faial Azores
244 D1 Cedros Mex.
242 B2 Cedros, Isla i. Mex.
174 G1 Cedry Wielkie Pol.
82 C3 Ceduna S.A. Austr.
174 C3 Cedynia Pol.
182 A2 Cée Spain
210 E3 Ceelbuur Somalia
210 E2 Ceerigaabo Somalia
177 K5 Cefa Romania
194 D4 Cefalù Sicilia Italy
Cefn Bychan Caerphilly, Wales U.K. see Newbridge
150 D2 Cefn-mawr Wrexham, Wales U.K.
183 F3 Cega r. Spain
191 H3 Ceggia Italy
177 I4 Cegléd Hungary
177 I4 Ceglédbercel Hungary
195 G2 Ceglie Messapica Italy
175 J3 Cegłów Pol.
196 E5 Čegrane Macedonia
177 L4 Cehal Romania
185 I2 Cehegín Spain
108 C3 Ceheng Guizhou China
196 D4 Čehotina r. Yugo.
197 F2 Cehu Silvaniei Romania
247 □1 Ceiba Puerto Rico
177 L5 Ceica Romania
161 B5 Ceilhes-et-Rocozels France
Ceinewydd Ceredigion, Wales U.K. see New Quay
183 E2 Ceinos de Campos Spain
157 G4 Ceintrey France
182 B4 Ceira Port.
182 B4 Ceira r. Port.
176 F3 Čejč Czech Rep.
177 K3 Cejkov Slovakia
179 H2 Čejkovice Czech Rep.
174 G2 Cekcyn Pol.
126 D2 Çekerek Turkey
174 G4 Ceków-Kolonia Pol.
186 B4 Celadas Spain
94 C1 Celah, Gunung mt. Malaysia
176 D1 Čelákovice Czech Rep.
193 F2 Celano Italy
182 C2 Celanova Spain
244 D3 Celaya Mex.
147 E3 Celbridge Rep. of Ireland
163 D4 Célé r. France
Celebes i. Indon. see Sulawesi
93 B2 Celebes Sea Indon./Phil.
129 C4 Çelebibağı Turkey
182 B3 Celeiros Port.
250 B6 Celendín Peru
193 G3 Celenza Valfortore Italy
195 F3 Celico Italy
236 G3 Celina OH U.S.A.
231 C4 Celina TN U.S.A.
188 E2 Celje Slovenia
186 B4 Cella Spain
176 G4 Celldömölk Hungary
168 F3 Celle Ger.
192 D2 Cellere Italy
165 C4 Celles Belgium
163 D6 Celles France
162 B2 Celles-sur-Belle France
160 B3 Celles-sur-Durolle France
156 E4 Celles-sur-Ource France
159 H4 Cellettes France
191 H2 Cellina r. Italy
193 F2 Cellino Attanasio Italy
195 G2 Cellino San Marco Italy
193 F3 Cellole Italy
193 H3 Celone r. Italy
182 C4 Celorico da Beira Port.
182 C3 Celorico de Basto Port.
Celovec Austria see Klagenfurt
186 F2 Celrà Spain
145 D6 Celtic Sea Rep. of Ireland/U.K.
264 I2 Celtic Shelf sea feature N. Atlantic Ocean
199 G3 Çeltikçi Turkey
199 F1 Çeltikçi Turkey
129 C4 Çem r. Turkey
95 F2 Cemaru, Gunung mt. Indon.
191 G2 Cembra Italy
126 D2 Cemilbey Turkey
126 E3 Çemişgezek Turkey
150 D2 Cemmaes Powys, Wales U.K.
179 F4 Čemšeniška planina mt. Slovenia
163 D4 Cénac-et-St-Julien France
196 E2 Cenad Romania
191 G2 Cencenighe Agordino Italy
161 C4 Cendras France
162 C4 Cendrieux France
196 E3 Cenei Romania
191 G3 Ceneselli Italy
190 D4 Cengio Italy
183 H2 Cenicero Spain
183 F4 Ceniclentos Spain
185 I1 Cenizate Spain
190 F4 Ceno r. Italy
163 B4 Cenon France
196 E3 Čenta Vojvodina, Srbija Yugo.
190 C4 Centallo Italy
Centane S. Africa see Kentani
81 B6 Centaur Peak South I. N.Z.
Centellas Spain see Centelles
186 F3 Centelles Spain
260 C6 Centenario Arg.
256 B5 Centenário do Sul Brazil
213 F3 Centenary Zimbabwe
236 C2 Center ND U.S.A.
236 D3 Center NE U.S.A.
237 E6 Center TX U.S.A.
232 B4 Centerburg OH U.S.A.
235 E2 Centereach NY U.S.A.
235 F2 Center Moriches NY U.S.A.
233 □H3 Center Ossipee NH U.S.A.
231 C5 Center Point AL U.S.A.
235 E2 Centerport NY U.S.A.
234 C2 Center Square PA U.S.A.
234 C2 Center Valley PA U.S.A.
231 C5 Centerville AL U.S.A.
236 E3 Centerville IA U.S.A.
237 F4 Centerville MO U.S.A.
232 B5 Centerville OH U.S.A.
232 D4 Centerville PA U.S.A.
232 D4 Centerville PA U.S.A.
231 C5 Centerville TN U.S.A.
237 E6 Centerville TX U.S.A.
232 C5 Centerville WV U.S.A.
191 G4 Cento Italy
193 H4 Centola Italy
Centrafricaine, République country Africa see Central African Republic
212 E4 Central admin. dist. Botswana
254 E4 Central Brazil
206 E5 Central admin. reg. Ghana
210 C5 Central prov. Kenya
211 B3 Central admin. reg. Malawi
239 E5 Central NM U.S.A.
209 F8 Central prov. Zambia
252 D4 Central, Cordillera mts Bol.
250 B4 Central, Cordillera mts Col.
246 E3 Central, Cordillera mts Dom. Rep.
242 □J7 Central, Cordillera mts Panama

252 A2 Central, Cordillera mts Peru
92 B2 Central, Cordillera mts Phil.
247 □1 Central, Cordillera mts Puerto Rico
Central African Empire country Africa see Central African Republic
208 D3 Central African Republic country Africa
123 F4 Central Brahui Range mts Pak.
223 J5 Central Butte Sask. Can.
236 F3 Central City IA U.S.A.
236 D3 Central City NE U.S.A.
232 D4 Central City PA U.S.A.
257 G3 Central de Minas Brazil
233 H4 Central Falls RI U.S.A.
236 F4 Centralia IL U.S.A.
238 B2 Centralia WA U.S.A.
235 E2 Central Islip NY U.S.A.
123 F5 Central Makran Range mts Pak.
84 C4 Central Mount Stuart hill N.T. Austr.
84 B4 Central Mount Wedge N.T. Austr.
266 G5 Central Pacific Basin sea feature Pacific Ocean
Central Provinces state India see Madhya Pradesh
215 G3 Central Range mts Lesotho
91 J7 Central Range mts P.N.G.
Central Russian Upland hills Rus. Fed. see Sredne-Russkaya Vozvyshennost'
Central Siberian Plateau Rus. Fed. see Sredne-Sibirskoye Ploskogor'ye
233 E3 Central Square NY U.S.A.
235 D1 Central Valley NY U.S.A.
235 G1 Central Village CT U.S.A.
207 H5 Centre prov. Cameroon
162 D1 Centre admin. reg. France
231 C5 Centre AL U.S.A.
234 B3 Centreville MD U.S.A.
226 E5 Centreville MI U.S.A.
232 E5 Centreville VA U.S.A.
192 B2 Centuri Corse France
213 G1 Centurion S. Africa
194 D5 Centuripe Sicilia Italy
231 C6 Century FL U.S.A.
109 D4 Cenxi Guangxi China
Ceos i. Greece see Kea
146 B3 Ceos Western Isles, Scotland U.K.
163 D4 Céou r. France
193 G2 Cepagatti Italy
Cephaloedium Sicilia Italy see Cefalù
Cephalonia i. Greece see Kefallonia
188 G3 Čepin Croatia
182 C4 Cepões Port.
156 C4 Cepoy France
191 D4 Ceppaloni Italy
193 F3 Ceprano Italy
95 E4 Cepu Jawa Tengah Indon.
196 D3 Cer hills Yugo.
Ceram i. Maluku Indon. see Seram
194 D5 Cerami Sicilia Italy
194 D5 Cerami r. Sicilia Italy
Ceram Sea Indon. see Seram Sea
190 D3 Cerano Italy
175 K3 Ceranów Pol.
159 G4 Cérans-Foulletourte France
195 E4 Cerasi Italy
193 H4 Ceraso Italy
177 L6 Cerbăl Romania
241 J4 Cerbat Mountains AZ U.S.A.
163 F6 Cerbère France
186 G2 Cerbère, Cap c. France/Spain
Cerbol r. Spain see Servol
184 B1 Cercal Lisboa Port.
184 B3 Cercal Setúbal Port.
184 B3 Cercal hill Port.
176 D2 Čerčany Czech Rep.
183 F4 Cercedilla Spain
182 B2 Cercedo Spain
193 G2 Cercemaggiore Italy
193 F2 Cerchio Italy
176 B2 Čerchov mt. Czech Rep.
160 B2 Cercy-la-Tour France
194 C5 Cerda Sicilia Italy
186 F3 Cerdanyola del Vallès Spain
182 C4 Cerdeira Port.
159 I4 Cerdon France
163 D4 Cère r. France
191 G3 Cerea Italy
223 I5 Cereal Alta Can.
177 I3 Cered Hungary
150 D2 Ceredigion admin. div. Wales U.K.
191 G3 Ceregnano Italy
174 F3 Cerekwica Pol.
158 E3 Cérences France
195 F3 Cerenzia Italy
261 G1 Ceres Arg.
254 C5 Ceres Brazil
190 C3 Ceres Italy
214 B5 Ceres S. Africa
240 G3 Ceres CA U.S.A.
190 C3 Ceresole Reale Italy
193 G3 Ceresone r. Italy
161 D5 Céreste France
163 E6 Céret France
250 C2 Cereté Col.
183 G3 Cerezo de Abajo Spain
183 G3 Cerezo de Arriba Spain
183 G2 Cerezo de Riotirón Spain
165 D4 Cerfontaine Belgium
177 K2 Čergov mts Slovakia
156 C3 Cergy France
171 G5 Cerhenice Czech Rep.
190 D4 Ceriale Italy
190 C5 Ceriana Italy
193 H3 Cerignola Italy
Cerigo i. Greece see Kythira
126 D3 Çerikli Turkey
160 A2 Cérilly France
156 D4 Cerisiers France
159 F2 Cerisy-la-Forêt France
158 E2 Cerisy-la-Salle France
159 F5 Cerizay France
191 J3 Cerk mt. Slovenia
126 D2 Çerkeş Turkey
199 F1 Çerkezköy Turkey
199 E1 Çerkezmüsellim Turkey
179 F4 Cerklje Slovenia
188 E3 Cerknica Slovenia
179 E4 Cerkno Slovenia
129 C3 Çerme Turkey
197 E2 Cermei Romania
193 F2 Cermignano Italy
126 E3 Çermik Turkey
197 I3 Cerna Romania
197 F3 Cerna r. Romania
197 F3 Cerna r. Romania
197 G3 Cerna r. Romania
182 B5 Cernache do Bonjardim Port.
176 F2 Černá Hora Czech Rep.
176 C3 Černá Hora mt. Czech Rep.
197 H3 Cernat Romania
Cernăuţi Chernivets'ka Oblast' Ukr. see Chernivtsi
197 I3 Cernavodă Romania
157 H5 Cernay France
156 E5 Cernay-en-Dormois France
176 C1 Černčice Czech Rep.
183 G2 Cernégula Spain
179 H4 Černelavci Slovenia
190 B1 Cernier Switz.
177 H3 Černík Slovakia
177 L2 Černiny hill Slovakia
190 E3 Cernobbio Italy
176 D2 Černošice Czech Rep.
176 B2 Černošín Czech Rep.
176 D2 Černovice Czech Rep.
176 B2 Cérou r. France
256 C5 Cerqueira César Brazil
182 D4 Cerralbo Spain
243 F3 Cerralvo Mex.
191 H5 Cerreto d'Esi Italy
193 E2 Cerreto di Spoleto Italy
193 G3 Cerreto Sannita Italy
150 D1 Cerrigydrudion Conwy, Wales U.K.
196 D5 Cërrik Albania
258 D2 Cerrillos Arg.
244 D2 Cerritos Mex.
193 G3 Cerro al Volturno Italy
256 C6 Cerro Azul Brazil
245 E3 Cerro Azul Mex.
252 A3 Cerro Azul Peru
258 C2 Cerro Bonete mt. Arg.
184 E3 Cerro del Hierro Spain
244 C4 Cerro de Ortega Mex.
252 A2 Cerro de Pasco Peru
185 G4 Cerrón mt. Spain
250 C1 Cerrón, Cerro mt. Venez.
260 C6 Cerros Colorados, Embalse resr Arg.
159 F4 Cersay France
193 I4 Cersosimo Italy
191 G5 Certaldo Italy
197 F3 Certeju de Sus Romania
190 E3 Certosa di Pavia Italy
190 C4 Certosa di Pesio Italy
182 C3 Cerva Port.
182 B3 Cervães Port.
183 E5 Cervales mt. Spain
87 B6 Cervantes W.A. Austr.
259 B8 Cervantes, Cerro mt. Arg.
193 F3 Cervaro Italy
193 H3 Cervaro r. Italy
193 H4 Cervati, Monte mt. Italy
183 F2 Cervatos de la Cueza Spain
176 F1 Červená Voda Czech Rep.
171 G5 Červené Pečky Czech Rep.
197 G4 Cervenia Romania
176 G2 Červenka Czech Rep.
186 E3 Cervera Spain
186 D4 Cervera r. Spain
184 C3 Cervera de la Cañada Spain
183 H5 Cervera del Llano Spain
183 F4 Cervera de los Montes Spain
183 I2 Cervera del Río Alhama Spain
183 F2 Cervera de Pisuerga Spain
192 E3 Cerveteri Italy
191 H4 Cervia Italy
193 H4 Cervialto, Monte mt. Italy
191 I3 Cervignano del Friuli Italy
191 G2 Cervina, Punta mt. Italy
193 G3 Cervinara Italy
176 E2 Červiná Řečice Czech Rep.
192 B2 Cervione Corse France
190 D3 Cervo Italy
190 C3 Cervo r. Italy
182 C1 Cervo Spain
160 B1 Cervon France
193 I5 Cerzeto Italy
191 I5 Cesano r. Italy
250 C2 César dept Col.
250 C2 César r. Col.
194 D5 Cesarò Sicilia Italy
178 D5 Cesen, Monte mt. Italy
191 H4 Cesena Italy
191 H4 Cesenatico Italy
190 C4 Cesio Italy
138 E3 Cēsis Latvia
176 D1 Česká Kamenice Czech Rep.
176 D1 Česká Lípa Czech Rep.
Česká Republika country Europe see Czech Republic
176 F1 Česká Skalice Czech Rep.
177 I3 České Brezovo Slovakia
176 D3 České Budějovice Czech Rep.
176 C1 České Středohoří hills Czech Rep.
179 F2 České Velenice Austria
176 D2 Českomoravská Vysočina hills Czech Rep.
176 D1 Český Brod Czech Rep.
171 F5 Český Dub Czech Rep.
176 D3 Český Krumlov Czech Rep.
176 B2 Český Les mts Czech Rep./Ger.
179 G1 Český Rudolec Czech Rep.
177 H2 Český Těšín Czech Rep.
188 F3 Česma r. Croatia
199 F2 Çeşme Turkey
188 E2 Cespedosa Spain
191 H3 Cessalto Italy
161 A5 Cesse r. France
161 B5 Cessenon-sur-Orb France
160 D3 Cessieu France
83 G3 Cessnock N.S.W. Austr.
158 E3 Cesson-Sévigné France
163 B4 Cestas France
206 C5 Cestos r. Liberia
182 B1 Cesuras Spain
138 F3 Cesvaine Latvia
177 L4 Cetariu Romania
197 F3 Cetate Romania
Cetatea Albă Ukr. see Bilhorod-Dnistrovs'kyy
188 F4 Cetina r. Croatia
183 I3 Cetina Spain
196 D4 Cetinje Crna Gora Yugo.
190 F2 Ceto Italy
159 G3 Ceton France
193 G2 Cetona Italy
193 H5 Cetraro Italy
163 B6 Cette-Eygun France
161 D4 Céüse France
161 D4 Céüse, Montagne de mt. France
180 D5 Ceuta N. Africa
187 B6 Ceutí Spain
190 D4 Ceva Italy
77 H4 Ceva-i-Ra rf Fiji
191 F2 Cevedale, Monte mt. Italy
161 B5 Cévennes mts France
183 F3 Cevico de la Torre Spain
183 F3 Cevico Navero Spain
160 E3 Cevins France
190 D2 Cevio Switz.
129 B3 Cevizli Erzurum Turkey
199 G2 Cevizli Eskişehir Turkey
128 C1 Cevizli Gaziantep Turkey
Cevizlik Turkey see Maçka
174 F1 Cewice Pol.
175 K5 Cewków Pol.
126 D3 Ceyhan Turkey
128 B1 Ceyhan r. Turkey
127 F3 Ceylanpınar Turkey
129 F3 Ceyläq Azer.
Ceylon country Asia see Sri Lanka
129 F3 Ceyranbatan Azer.
161 D5 Ceyreste France
160 D2 Ceyzériat France
162 B3 Cézac France
161 C4 Cèze r. France
182 C3 Chã Port.
164 D3 Chaam Neth.
122 E5 Chābahār Iran
162 G3 Chabanais France
261 G5 Chabas Arg.
161 D4 Chabestan France
160 D4 Chabeuil France
175 H4 Chabielice Pol.
161 D2 Chablais mts France
243 H5 Chablé Mex.
156 D5 Chablis France
162 C3 Chabrac France
161 D4 Chabre ridge France
160 B3 Chabreloche France
159 H4 Chabris France
Chabrol i. Îles Loyauté New Caledonia see Lifou
111 F7 Chabua Assam India
261 G4 Chacabuco Arg.
245 G4 Chacaltianguis Mex.
260 C5 Chachahuén, Sierra mt. Arg.
250 B6 Chachapoyas Peru
116 D4 Chachaura-Binaganj Madh. Prad. India
139 H5 Chachersk Belarus
97 C4 Chachoengsao Thai.
182 D3 Chacim Port.
258 E2 Chaco prov. Arg.
253 F5 Chaco Boreal reg. Para.
251 G6 Chacorão, Cachoeira da waterfall Brazil
202 C6 Chad country Africa
202 B6 Chad, Lake Africa
98 F1 Chadan Rus. Fed.
234 C3 Chadds Ford PA U.S.A.
213 G2 Chadiza Zambia
161 B3 Chadrac France
236 C3 Chadron NE U.S.A.
Chadyr-Lunga Moldova see Ciadîr-Lunga
96 B3 Chae Hom Thai.
101 C5 Chaeryŏng N. Korea
237 F4 Chaffee MO U.S.A.
259 B7 Chaffers, Isla i. Chile
226 A2 Chaffey WI U.S.A.
250 C4 Chafurray Col.
123 E4 Chagai Hills Afgh./Pak.
114 C3 Chagallamarri Andhra Prad. India
120 F3 Chagan Kzyl-Ordinskaya Oblast' Kazakh.
121 I2 Chagan Vostochnyy Kazakhstan Kazakh.
150 D4 Chagford Devon, England U.K.
122 B4 Chagha Khūr mt. Iran
123 F3 Chaghcharān Afgh.
121 G1 Chaglinka r. Kazakh.
160 C2 Chagny France
139 J2 Chagoda Rus. Fed.
139 J2 Chagoda r. Rus. Fed.
139 K2 Chagodoshcha r. Rus. Fed.
265 I5 Chagos Archipelago is B.I.O.T.
265 I5 Chagos-Laccadive Ridge sea feature Indian Ocean
265 I5 Chagos Trench sea feature Indian Ocean
120 B1 Chagra r. Rus. Fed.
Chagrayskoye Plato plat. Kazakh. see Shagyray, Plato
247 □7 Chaguanas Trin. and Tob.
250 E2 Chaguaramas Venez.
122 C1 Chagyllyshor, Vpadina depr. Turkm.
136 E5 Chaha r. Ukr.
122 B3 Chahār Maḩāll vā Bakhtīārī prov. Iran
122 C4 Chāh Ḩaqq Iran
123 G3 Chah-i-Ab Afgh.
245 G5 Chahuites Mex.
100 B4 Chai r. China
117 F5 Chaibasa Bihar India
Chaigoubu Hebei China see Huai'an
151 G4 Chailey East Sussex, England U.K.
162 D2 Chaillac France
159 F3 Chailland France
162 A2 Chaillé-les-Marais France
156 D4 Chailley France
96 C4 Chainat Thai.
161 B3 Chaîne du Devès mts France
156 E4 Chaintrix-Bierges France
97 C4 Chai Si r. Thai.
259 B6 Chaitén Chile
109 □ Chai Wan H.K. China
110 D3 Chaiwopu Xinjiang China
96 B5 Chaiya Thai.
96 C4 Chaiyaphum Thai.
261 I2 Chajarí Arg.
117 F4 Chakai Bihar India
123 G4 Chakar r. Pak.
213 F3 Chakari Zimbabwe
211 C6 Chake Chake Tanz.
117 E4 Chakia Uttar Prad. India
123 H4 Chak Jhumra Pak.
117 F5 Chakradharpur Bihar India
117 F5 Chakulia Bihar India
129 B3 Ch'ak'vi Georgia
123 H3 Chakwal Pak.
252 B3 Chala Peru
163 E6 Chalabre France
Chaladidi Georgia see Sabazho
162 C3 Chalais France
190 C2 Chalais Switz.
162 C2 Chalamont France
123 F3 Chalap Dalan mts Afgh.
160 C2 Chalaronne r. France
242 □H6 Chalatenango El Salvador
213 H3 Chaláua Moz.
Chalcedon Turkey see Kadıköy
244 C2 Chalchihuites Mex.
245 E4 Chalco Mex.
151 F4 Chale Isle of Wight, England U.K.
162 C3 Chaleix France
161 C4 Chalencon France
111 F4 Chalengkou Qinghai China
156 C4 Chalette-sur-Loing France
225 H3 Chaleur Bay inlet N.B./Que. Can.
Chaleurs, Baie de inlet N.B./Que. Can. see Chaleur Bay
234 C2 Chalfont PA U.S.A.
150 E3 Chalford Gloucestershire, England U.K.
151 F3 Chalgrove Oxfordshire, England U.K.
259 C8 Chalía r. Arg.
175 H3 Chalin Pol.
157 F5 Chalindrey France
109 E3 Chaling Hunan China
116 C5 Chalisgaon Mahar. India
114 C4 Chalisseri Kerala India
160 A2 Chalivoy-Milon France
Chalkar, Ozero salt l. Kazakh. see Shalkar, Ozero
198 C2 Chalki Thessalia Greece
199 E3 Chalki i. Greece
198 C2 Chalkida Greece
198 C1 Chalkidona Kentriki Makedonia Greece
121 I4 Chalkudysu Kazakh.
114 C3 Challakere Karnataka India
158 F5 Challans France
252 D4 Challapata Bol.
266 E5 Challenger Deep sea feature N. Pacific Ocean
156 E3 Challerange France
160 D3 Challes-les-Eaux France
238 D2 Challis ID U.S.A.
237 F6 Chalmette LA U.S.A.
160 B2 Chalmoux France
162 C2 Chaloire r. France
158 F4 Chalonnes-sur-Loire France
156 E4 Châlons-en-Champagne France
Châlons-sur-Marne France see Châlons-en-Champagne
160 C2 Chalon-sur-Saône France
129 D3 Chalovani Georgia
116 C1 Chalt Jammu and Kashmir
137 J4 Chaltyr' Rus. Fed.
215 F5 Chalumna S. Africa
162 C3 Châlus France
122 B2 Chālūs Iran
122 B2 Chālūs, Rūd-e r. Iran
173 G2 Cham Ger.
190 D1 Cham Switz.
122 B3 Cham, Kūh-e hill Iran
239 F4 Chama NM U.S.A.
239 F4 Chama r. NM U.S.A.
211 B7 Chama Zambia
217 □3a Chamadani mt. Njazidja Comoros
212 B5 Chamais Bay Namibia
160 B3 Chamalières France
161 D4 Chamaloc France
123 F4 Chaman Pak.
97 C4 Chaman Bak, Khao mt. Thai.
173 G2 Chamb r. Ger.
116 D2 Chamba Hima. Prad. India
211 C7 Chamba Tanz.
116 D4 Chambal r. India
129 D3 Chambarak Armenia
161 D3 Chambaran, Plateau de France
246 C2 Chambas Cuba
162 D3 Chamberet France
160 D2 Chambéria France
86 E3 Chamberlain r. W.A. Austr.
223 J5 Chamberlain Sask. Can.
236 D3 Chamberlain SD U.S.A.
233 □I1 Chamberlain Lake ME U.S.A.
241 M4 Chambers AZ U.S.A.
84 B2 Chambers Bay N.T. Austr.
232 E5 Chambersburg PA U.S.A.
160 D3 Chambéry France
211 A7 Chambeshi Zambia
205 H2 Chambi, Jebel mt. Tunisia
250 C6 Chambira r. Peru
157 F3 Chambley-Bussières France
156 C3 Chambly France
159 G3 Chambois France
160 C1 Chambolle-Musigny France
160 A3 Chambon-sur-Lac France
162 E2 Chambon-sur-Voueize France
225 F3 Chambord Que. Can.
159 H4 Chambord France
162 D3 Chamboulive France
159 G4 Chambray-lès-Tours France
91 J7 Chambri Lake P.N.G.
156 D3 Chambry France
Chamdo Xizang China see Qamdo
161 D3 Chamechaude mt. France
173 G2 Chamerau Ger.
156 E5 Chamesson France
162 D3 Chameyrat France
260 D2 Chamical Arg.
129 B1 Chamlyk-Svyatskaya Rus. Fed.
210 C3 Ch'amo Hāyk' l. Eth.
190 C3 Chamois Italy
Chamoli Uttar Prad. India see Gopeshwar
160 E3 Chamonix-Mont-Blanc France
Chamouchouane r. Que. Can. see Ashuapmushuan
161 D4 Chamouse, Montagne de mt. France
160 E3 Chamoux-sur-Gelon France
117 E5 Champa Madh. Prad. India
162 E3 Champagnac France
162 C3 Champagnac-de-Belair France
161 B3 Champagnac-le-Vieux France
222 B2 Champagne Y.T. Can.
159 G3 Champagné France
156 E4 Champagne-Ardenne admin. reg. France
215 G3 Champagne Castle mt. S. Africa
160 D3 Champagne-en-Valromey France
162 C3 Champagne-Mouton France
156 C3 Champagne-sur-Oise France
156 C4 Champagne-sur-Seine France
157 G5 Champagney France
160 D2 Champagnole France
86 E2 Champagny Islands W.A. Austr.
230 B3 Champaign IL U.S.A.
149 F2 Champany Falkirk, Scotland U.K.
260 E2 Champaquí, Cerro mt. Arg.
252 A2 Champara mt. Peru
97 D4 Champasak Laos
156 D4 Champaubert France
162 C3 Champcevinel France
162 B2 Champdeniers-St-Denis France
160 C1 Champ-d'Oiseau France
157 H4 Champ du Feu mt. France
160 B3 Champeix France
190 B2 Champéry Switz.
160 C2 Champforgeuil France
159 F3 Champgenéteux France
117 H5 Champhai Mizoram India
161 D3 Champier France
159 F4 Champigné France
156 D5 Champignelles France
157 G4 Champigneulles France
156 E4 Champignol-lez-Mondeville France
156 D4 Champigny France
222 H5 Champion Alta Can.
226 D2 Champion MI U.S.A.
233 G2 Champlain NY U.S.A.
232 E5 Champlain VA U.S.A.
224 F4 Champlain, Lake Can./U.S.A.
160 B1 Champlemy France
156 E5 Champlitte France
227 I1 Champneuf Que. Can.
162 C3 Champniers France
161 E4 Champoléon France
160 B3 Champoly France
243 H5 Champotón Mex.
156 B4 Champrond-en-Gâtine France
159 F3 Champsecret France
161 A3 Champs-sur-Tarentaine-Marchal France
156 D5 Champs-sur-Yonne France
161 D3 Champ-sur-Drac France
161 E4 Champtercier France
158 E4 Champtoceaux France
160 D1 Champvans France
114 C4 Chamrajnagar Karnataka India
161 D3 Chamrousse France
184 B1 Chamusca Port.
135 I5 Chamzinka Rus. Fed.
97 C6 Chana Thai.
161 B4 Chanac France
Chanak Turkey see Çanakkale
243 G5 Chanal Mex.
260 C6 Chañar Arg.
258 C2 Chañaral Chile
260 B2 Chañaral Alto Chile
122 D2 Chanārān Iran
261 F3 Chañar Ladeado Arg.
251 E3 Chanaro, Cerro mt. Venez.
161 C3 Chanas France
184 C1 Chança Port.
Chança r. Port./Spain see Chanza
160 C1 Chanceaux France
159 G4 Chanceaux-sur-Choisille France
162 C3 Chancelade France
182 B5 Chancelaria Port.
247 □2 Chances Peak vol. Montserrat
260 A4 Chanco Chile
Chanda Mahar. India see Chandrapur
220 D3 Chandalar r. AK U.S.A.
116 D3 Chandausi Uttar Prad. India
117 F5 Chandbali Orissa India
116 D4 Chanderi Madh. Prad. India
116 D5 Chandia Madh. Prad. India
116 D3 Chandigarh Chandigarh India
117 F5 Chandil Bihar India
225 H3 Chandler Que. Can.
241 L5 Chandler AZ U.S.A.
237 D5 Chandler OK U.S.A.
252 C2 Chandless r. Brazil
117 G5 Chandpur Bangl.
116 D3 Chandpur Uttar Prad. India
114 D2 Chandragiri Andhra Prad. India
114 C2 Chandrapur Mahar. India
116 D5 Chandur Mahar. India
116 C5 Chandvad Mahar. India
122 E2 Chandyr r. Turkm.
183 F3 Chañe Spain
97 C4 Chang, Ko i. Thai.
Chang'an Guangxi China see Rong'an
107 F5 Chang'an Shaanxi China
213 G5 Changane r. Moz.
213 G3 Changara Moz.
101 D4 Changbai Jilin China
101 C4 Changbai Shan mts China/N. Korea
Chang Cheng research stn Antarctica see Great Wall
Changchow Fujian China see Zhangzhou
Changchow Jiangsu China see Changzhou
100 C4 Changchun Jilin China
107 I4 Changdao Shandong China
109 D2 Changde Hunan China
159 F3 Changé France
159 G4 Changé France
109 F1 Changfeng Anhui China
107 G5 Changge Henan China
101 E6 Changgi-ap pt S. Korea
100 C4 Changhai Liaoning China
109 E2 Chang Hu l. China
109 G3 Changhua Taiwan
108 D5 Changhua Jiang r. China
101 D6 Changhŭng S. Korea
94 □ Changi Sing.
110 D3 Changji Xinjiang China
108 D5 Changjiang Hainan China
99 L5 Chang Jiang r. China alt. Jinsha Jiang, alt. Tongtian He, alt. Zhi Qu, conv. Yangtze, long Yangtze Kiang
109 G2 Changjiang Kou r. mouth China
101 C4 Changjin N. Korea
101 C4 Changjin-gang r. N. Korea
Changkiang Guangdong China see Zhanjiang
109 F3 Changle Fujian China
Changleng Jiangxi China see Xinjian
107 H4 Changli Hebei China
107 I2 Changling Jilin China
106 E4 Changliushui Nei Mongol China
109 E3 Changning Hunan China
Changning Jiangxi China see Xunwu
108 C2 Changning Sichuan China
101 C5 Changnyŏn N. Korea
Ch'ang-pai Shan mts China/N. Korea see Changbai Shan
107 H3 Changping Beijing China
Changpu Hunan China see Suining
109 E2 Changsha Hunan China
109 F2 Changshan Zhejiang China
107 I4 Changshan Qundao is China
108 C3 Changshi Guizhou China
108 C2 Changshou Chongqing China
109 E2 Changshoujie Hunan China
109 G2 Changshu Jiangsu China
101 C6 Changsŏng S. Korea
109 F3 Changtai Fujian China
Changteh Hunan China see Changde
109 F3 Changting Fujian China
100 D3 Changting Heilong. China
100 C4 Changtu Liaoning China
242 □J7 Changuinola Panama
101 D6 Ch'angwŏn S. Korea
107 E5 Changwu Shaanxi China
109 F2 Changxing Zhejiang China
160 C2 Changy France
109 D2 Changyang Hubei China
107 H4 Changyi Shandong China
101 C5 Changyŏn N. Korea
Changyuan Chongqing China see Rongchang
107 G5 Changyuan Henan China
107 G4 Changzhi Shanxi China
107 G5 Changzhi Shanxi China
109 G2 Changzhou Jiangsu China
258 D2 Chañi, Nevado de mt. Arg.
198 D4 Chania Kriti Greece
162 B3 Chaniers France
198 C4 Chanion, Kolpos b. Kriti Greece
106 E5 Chankou Gansu China
114 B3 Channagiri Karnataka India
114 C3 Channapatna Karnataka India
158 D2 Channel Islands English Chan.
240 H5 Channel Islands CA U.S.A.
225 J4 Channel-Port-aux-Basques Nfld. Can.
246 C2 Channel Rock i. Bahamas
145 H6 Channel Tunnel France/U.K.
226 C2 Channing MI U.S.A.
237 C5 Channing TX U.S.A.
182 C2 Chantada Spain
131 S3 Chantal'skiy mt. Rus. Fed.
160 B2 Chantelle France
158 E3 Chantepie France
97 C4 Chanthaburi Thai.
156 C3 Chantilly France
162 A2 Chantonnay France
157 G4 Chantraine France
160 E1 Chantrans France
159 F3 Chanu France
237 E4 Chanute KS U.S.A.
130 I4 Chany, Ozero salt l. Rus. Fed.
184 C3 Chanza r. Port./Spain
252 A2 Chao Peru
182 B2 Chao Spain
107 H4 Chaobai Xinhe r. China
109 F2 Chaohu Anhui China
109 F2 Chao Hu l. China
97 C4 Chao Phraya r. Thai.
107 I1 Chaor Nei Mongol China
107 I2 Chaor r. China
204 D2 Chaouèn Morocco
180 D5 Chaouèn prov. Morocco
156 E4 Chaource France
109 F4 Chaoyang Guangdong China
Chaoyang Heilong. China see Jiayin
Chaoyang Jilin China see Huinan
107 I3 Chaoyang Liaoning China
107 I1 Chaozhong Nei Mongol China
109 F4 Chaozhou Guangdong China
253 G3 Chapada dos Guimarães Brazil
255 B6 Chapadão do Sul Brazil
254 E2 Chapadinha Brazil
224 F3 Chapais Que. Can.
244 C3 Chapala Mex.
244 C3 Chapala, Laguna de l. Mex.
260 E5 Chapaleofú, Valle de val. Arg.
244 C3 Chapalilla Mex.
245 E3 Chapantongo Mex.
252 D3 Chapare r. Bol.
161 D3 Chapareillan France
250 C4 Chaparral Col.
137 H3 Chapayeve Ukr.
137 G3 Chapayevka Ukr.
120 B2 Chapayevo Kazakh.
120 B1 Chapayevsk Rus. Fed.
121 H1 Chapayevskoye Kazakh.
161 C3 Chapdes-Beaufort France
255 B8 Chapecó Brazil
255 B8 Chapecó r. Brazil
149 H4 Chapel-en-le-Frith Derbyshire, England U.K.
149 G3 Chapelfell Top hill England U.K.
231 E5 Chapel Hill NC U.S.A.
165 D4 Chapelle-lez-Herlaimont Belgium
149 J4 Chapel St Leonards Lincolnshire, England U.K.
246 □ Chapelton Jamaica
147 E2 Chapeltown Northern Ireland U.K.
149 H4 Chapeltown South Yorkshire, England U.K.
183 F4 Chapinería Spain
224 D4 Chapleau Ont. Can.
223 J5 Chaplin Sask. Can.
Chaplinka Ukr. see Chaplynka
131 T3 Chaplino Rus. Fed.
137 G2 Chapliyivka Ukr.
139 L5 Chaplygin Rus. Fed.
137 I3 Chaplyne Ukr.
137 G4 Chaplynka Ukr.
222 G5 Chapman, Mount B.C. Can.
232 D4 Chapmanville PA U.S.A.
232 B6 Chapmanville WV U.S.A.
235 E1 Chappaqua NY U.S.A.
236 C3 Chappell NE U.S.A.
83 F5 Chappell Islands Tas. Austr.
Chapra Bihar India see Chhapra
258 F2 Charadai Arg.
253 E4 Charagua Bol.
252 C4 Charaña Bol.
261 G4 Charata Arg.
160 C2 Charbonnat France
161 F3 Charbonnel, Pointe de mt. France
244 D2 Charcas Mex.
160 D1 Charcenne France
160 D2 Charchilla France
262 S2 Charcot Island Antarctica
223 I4 Chard Alta Can.
150 E4 Chard Somerset, England U.K.
Chardara Kazakh. see Shardara
121 G4 Chardarinskoye Vodokhranilishche resr Kazakh./Uzbek.
232 C4 Chardon OH U.S.A.
150 E4 Chardstock Devon, England U.K.
123 E2 Chardzhev Turkm.
Chardzhou Turkm. see Chardzhev
Chardzhouskaya Oblast' admin. div. Turkm. see Lebapskaya Oblast'
205 F2 Charef Alg.
162 C3 Charente dept Poitou-Charentes France
162 B3 Charente r. France
162 B3 Charente-Maritime dept Poitou-Charentes France
160 A2 Charenton-du-Cher France
158 G3 Charentonne r. France
129 D3 Ch'arents'avan Armenia
150 E3 Charfield South Gloucestershire, England U.K.
160 D1 Chargey-lès-Gray France
208 B1 Chari r. Cameroon/Chad
208 C2 Chari-Baguirmi pref. Chad
123 G3 Chārīkār Afgh.
151 H3 Charing Kent, England U.K.
236 E3 Chariton IA U.S.A.
236 E4 Chariton r. U.S.A.
Chärjew Turkm. see Chardzhev
116 D4 Charkhari Uttar Prad. India
116 D3 Charkhi Dadri Haryana India
Charkhlik Xinjiang China see Ruoqiang
151 F3 Charlbury Oxfordshire, England U.K.
215 G2 Charl Cilliers S. Africa
147 E2 Charlemont Northern Ireland U.K.
165 D4 Charleroi Belgium
225 G4 Charlesbourg Que. Can.
226 A4 Charles City IA U.S.A.
232 E6 Charles City VA U.S.A.
156 C3 Charles de Gaulle airport France
Charles Island Islas Galápagos Ecuador see Santa María, Isla
84 B2 Charles Point N.T. Austr.
81 C4 Charleston South I. N.Z.
237 E5 Charleston AR U.S.A.
226 B5 Charleston IA U.S.A.
236 F4 Charleston IL U.S.A.
237 F4 Charleston MO U.S.A.
237 F5 Charleston MS U.S.A.
231 E5 Charleston SC U.S.A.
232 C5 Charleston WV U.S.A.
241 J3 Charleston Peak NV U.S.A.
147 C3 Charlestown Rep. of Ireland
215 G2 Charlestown S. Africa
247 □2 Charlestown St Kitts and Nevis
234 C3 Charlestown MD U.S.A.
233 G3 Charlestown NH U.S.A.
233 H4 Charlestown RI U.S.A.
232 E5 Charles Town WV U.S.A.
Charlestown of Aberlour Moray, Scotland U.K. see Aberlour
85 F5 Charleville Qld Austr.
Charleville Rep. of Ireland see Rathluirc
156 E3 Charleville-Mézières France
226 E3 Charlevoix MI U.S.A.
222 F3 Charlie Lake B.C. Can.
160 C2 Charlieu France
226 E4 Charlotte MI U.S.A.
231 D5 Charlotte NC U.S.A.
247 F3 Charlotte Amalie Virgin Is (U.S.A.)
232 D6 Charlotte Court House VA U.S.A.
142 E2 Charlottenberg Sweden
232 D5 Charlottesville VA U.S.A.
225 I4 Charlottetown P.E.I. Can.
247 □5 Charlotteville Trin. and Tob.
83 E4 Charlton Vic. Austr.
151 F3 Charlton Hampshire, England U.K.
150 E3 Charlton Wiltshire, England U.K.
150 E3 Charlton Kings Gloucestershire, England U.K.
151 G3 Charlwood Surrey, England U.K.
156 D4 Charly France
162 C3 Charmé France
157 G4 Charmes France
161 C4 Charmes-sur-Rhône France
190 C2 Charmey Switz.
150 E4 Charminster Dorset, England U.K.
157 G4 Charmois-l'Orgueilleux France
156 E4 Charmont-sous-Barbuise France
150 E4 Charmouth Dorset, England U.K.
156 D5 Charmoy France
160 C2 Charnay-lès-Mâcon France
184 A2 Charneca Port.
139 H4 Charnitsa r. Belarus
86 E3 Charnley r. W.A. Austr.
156 D5 Charny France
157 F3 Charny-sur-Meuse France
160 C2 Charolles France
159 I5 Chârost France
160 E1 Charquemont France
190 C2 Charrat Switz.
156 E5 Charrey-sur-Seine France
160 B2 Charrin France
162 C2 Charroux France
156 B3 Chars France
123 G3 Charsadda Pak.
123 F2 Charshanga Turkm.
Charsk Kazakh. see Shar
175 H5 Charsznica Pol.
232 B5 Charters KY U.S.A.
85 F4 Charters Towers Qld Austr.
151 I3 Chartham Kent, England U.K.
156 B4 Chartres France
121 G4 Charvakskoye Vodokhranilishche resr Kazakh./Uzbek.
190 C3 Charvensod Italy
160 E2 Charvonnex France
121 I4 Charyn r. Kazakh.
121 J1 Charysh r. Rus. Fed.
121 J2 Charyshskoye Rus. Fed.
174 F2 Charzykowy Pol.
116 F5 Chas Bihar India
182 B4 Chãs mt. Port.
261 H4 Chascomús Arg.
222 G5 Chase B.C. Can.
234 B3 Chase MD U.S.A.
226 E4 Chase MI U.S.A.
236 E4 Chase City VA U.S.A.
138 G4 Chashniki Belarus
198 B2 Chasia reg. Greece
137 I3 Chasiv Yar Ukr.
236 E2 Chaska MN U.S.A.
81 B7 Chaslands Mistake c. South I. N.Z.
101 C4 Chasŏng N. Korea
159 G5 Chasseneuil-du-Poitou France
162 C3 Chasseneuil-sur-Bonnieure France
162 C3 Chassenon France
161 B4 Chasseradès France
190 C1 Chasseral mt. Switz.
160 C3 Chasse-sur-Rhône France
161 C4 Chassezac r. France
157 F5 Chassigny-Aisey France
159 F3 Chassillé France
162 A2 Chassiron, Pointe de pt France
122 C3 Chastab, Kūh-e mts Iran
165 D4 Chastre Belgium
134 K4 Chastyye Rus. Fed.
122 C2 Chat Iran
160 D3 Chat, Mont du mt. France
Chatang Xizang China see Zhanang
161 D4 Château-Arnoux France
247 □3 Châteaubelair St Vincent
162 B3 Châteaubernard France
158 E3 Châteaubourg France
261 G3 Chateaubriand Arg.
158 E4 Châteaubriant France
160 B1 Château-Chinon France
190 C2 Château-d'Oex Switz.
162 A2 Château-d'Olonne France
159 G4 Château-du-Loir France
156 B4 Châteaudun France
160 B3 Châteaugay France
233 F2 Chateaugay NY U.S.A.
158 E3 Châteaugiron France
159 F4 Château-Gontier France
233 G2 Châteauguay Que. Can.
225 G1 Châteauguay r. Que. Can.
156 C4 Château-Landon France
159 G4 Château-la-Vallière France
162 C3 Château-l'Évêque France
158 B3 Châteaulin France
161 C5 Châteauneuf-de-Gadagne France
161 C3 Châteauneuf-de-Galaure France
161 B4 Châteauneuf-de-Randon France
158 E3 Châteauneuf-d'Ille-et-Vilaine France
158 C3 Châteauneuf-du-Faou France
161 C4 Châteauneuf-du-Pape France
161 C4 Châteauneuf-du-Rhône France
156 B4 Châteauneuf-en-Thymerais France
162 D3 Châteauneuf-la-Forêt France
160 A2 Châteauneuf-les-Bains France
161 D5 Châteauneuf-les-Martigues France
162 B3 Châteauneuf-sur-Charente France
159 I5 Châteauneuf-sur-Cher France
156 C5 Châteauneuf-sur-Loire France
159 F4 Châteauneuf-sur-Sarthe France
160 B1 Châteauneuf-Val-de-Bargis France
162 D2 Châteauponsac France
156 E3 Château-Porcien France
161 E4 Châteauredon France
156 C5 Châteaurenard France
159 G4 Château-Renault France
162 D2 Châteauroux France
161 E4 Châteauroux France
157 G4 Château-Salins France
156 D3 Château-Thierry France
157 E4 Châteauvillain France
222 G3 Chateh Alta Can.
160 E2 Châtel France
162 A2 Châtelaillon-Plage France
158 D3 Châtelaudren France
160 B1 Châtel-Censoir France
160 B3 Châteldon France
165 D4 Châtelet Belgium
160 C1 Châtel-Gérard France
160 B3 Châtelguyon France
162 C2 Châtellerault France
160 B2 Châtel-Montagne France
160 B2 Châtelperron France
190 B2 Châtel-St-Denis Switz.
157 G4 Châtel-sur-Moselle France
162 E2 Châtelus-Malvaleix France
157 H4 Châtenois France
157 F4 Châtenois France
160 E1 Châtenois-les-Forges France
160 C2 Châtenoy-le-Royal France
226 A4 Chatfield MN U.S.A.
232 B4 Chatfield OH U.S.A.
225 H4 Chatham N.B. Can.
224 D5 Chatham Ont. Can.
151 H3 Chatham Medway, England U.K.
222 C3 Chatham AK U.S.A.
233 I4 Chatham MA U.S.A.
226 D2 Chatham MI U.S.A.
235 D2 Chatham NJ U.S.A.
233 G3 Chatham NY U.S.A.
234 C3 Chatham PA U.S.A.
232 D6 Chatham VA U.S.A.
259 B8 Chatham, Isla i. Chile
Chatham Island Islas Galápagos Ecuador see San Cristóbal, Isla
Chatham Island Samoa see Savai'i
80 □ Chatham Islands S. Pacific Ocean
266 H8 Chatham Rise sea feature S. Pacific Ocean
222 C3 Chatham Strait AK U.S.A.
165 E5 Châtillon Belgium
190 C3 Châtillon Italy
156 C5 Châtillon-Coligny France
160 B1 Châtillon-en-Bazois France
161 D4 Châtillon-en-Diois France
160 D2 Châtillon-en-Michaille France
160 D3 Châtillon-la-Palud France
160 C2 Châtillon-sur-Chalaronne France
159 F3 Châtillon-sur-Colmont France
162 D2 Châtillon-sur-Indre France
160 A1 Châtillon-sur-Loire France
156 D3 Châtillon-sur-Marne France
156 E5 Châtillon-sur-Seine France
159 F5 Châtillon-sur-Thouet France
121 G4 Chatkal mts Kyrg.
121 G4 Chatkal r. Kyrg.
237 F6 Chatom AL U.S.A.
117 F4 Chatra Bihar India
116 C4 Chatsu Rajasthan India
84 E4 Chatsworth Qld Austr.
227 G3 Chatsworth Ont. Can.
231 C5 Chatsworth GA U.S.A.
226 C5 Chatsworth IL U.S.A.
234 D3 Chatsworth NJ U.S.A.
Chattagam Bangl. see Chittagong
231 C6 Chattahoochee FL U.S.A.
231 C6 Chattahoochee r. GA U.S.A.
231 C5 Chattanooga TN U.S.A.
161 D3 Chatte France
151 H2 Chatteris Cambridgeshire, England U.K.
81 B6 Chatto Creek South I. N.Z.
149 H2 Chatton Northumberland, England U.K.
96 C4 Chatturat Thai.
161 D4 Chatuzange-le-Goubet France
234 C3 Chatwood PA U.S.A.
Chatyrkël', Ozero l. Kyrg. see Chatyr-Köl
121 H4 Chatyr-Köl l. Kyrg.
185 G3 Chauchina Spain
157 F5 Chaudenay France
161 B4 Chaudes-Aigues France
161 B4 Chaudeyrac France
165 E4 Chaudfontaine Belgium
97 D5 Châu Đốc Vietnam
159 F4 Chaudron-en-Mauges France
160 C2 Chauffailles France
157 F4 Chauffayer France
116 B4 Chauhtan Rajasthan India
96 A2 Chauk Myanmar
116 E4 Chauka r. India
Chaukhamba mts India see Badrinath Peaks
156 C3 Chaulnes France
160 D2 Chaumergy France
157 F4 Chaumont France
156 B3 Chaumont-en-Vexin France
156 E3 Chaumont-Porcien France
157 F4 Chaumont-sur-Aire France
159 H4 Chaumont-sur-Loire France
162 C2 Chaunay France
232 B5 Chauncey OH U.S.A.
156 D3 Chauny France
Chau Phu Vietnam see Châu Đốc
116 D5 Chaurai Madh. Prad. India
162 B2 Chauray France
160 D2 Chaussin France
104 D3 Chausu-yama mt. Japan
Chausy Belarus see Chavusy
121 H4 Chauvay Kyrg.
162 C2 Chauvigny France
223 I4 Chauvin Alta Can.
160 D1 Chaux, Forêt de for. France
158 E5 Chavagnes-en-Paillers France
114 D4 Chavakachcheri Sri Lanka
254 E2 Chaval Brazil
161 C3 Chavanay France
156 E4 Chavanges France
161 B3 Chavaniac-Lafayette France
160 D3 Chavanoz France
122 A3 Chavār Iran
198 B3 Chavari Dytiki Ellas Greece
157 G4 Chavelot France
256 F5 Chaves Brazil
182 C3 Chaves Port.
139 H5 Chavusy Belarus
123 F4 Chawal r. Pak.
96 D2 Chây r. Vietnam
Chayan Kazakh. see Shayan
252 D4 Chayanta r. Bol.
Chayek Kyrg. see Chaek
139 K2 Chayevo Rus. Fed.
134 K4 Chaykovskiy Rus. Fed.
160 C3 Chazay-d'Azergues France
162 C3 Chazelles France
160 C3 Chazelles-sur-Lyon France
233 G2 Chazy NY U.S.A.
149 G4 Cheadle Greater Manchester, England U.K.
151 F2 Cheadle Staffordshire, England U.K.
232 D5 Cheat r. WV U.S.A.
176 B1 Cheb Czech Rep.
226 D5 Chebanse IL U.S.A.
205 H2 Chebba Tunisia
134 I5 Cheboksary Rus. Fed.
226 E3 Cheboygan MI U.S.A.
183 J2 Checa Spain
136 E3 Chechel'nyk Ukr.
129 E2 Chechen', Ostrov i. Rus. Fed.
109 G4 Ch'ech'eng Taiwan
129 D2 Chechenskaya Respublika aut. rep. Rus. Fed.

Chechnya aut. rep. Rus. Fed. see Chechenskaya Respublika
101 D5 Chech'ŏn S. Korea
136 C3 Chechva r. Ukr.
175 I5 Chęciny Pol.
237 E5 Checotah OK U.S.A.
156 C4 Chécy France
151 H2 Chedburgh Suffolk, England U.K.
150 E3 Cheddar Somerset, England U.K.
149 G4 Cheddleton Staffordshire, England U.K.
96 A3 Cheduba Island Myanmar
157 E4 Chée r. France
147 E4 Cheekpoint Rep. of Ireland
232 D3 Cheektowaga NY U.S.A.
224 D3 Cheepash r. Ont. Can.
85 F5 Cheepie Qld Austr.
263 K2 Cheetham, Cape Antarctica
157 F4 Chef-Boutonne France
Chefoo Shandong China see Yantai
220 B3 Chefornak AK U.S.A.
100 E2 Chegdomyn Rus. Fed.
Chegem 1 Rus. Fed. see Chegem Pervyy
129 C2 Chegem r. Rus. Fed.
129 C2 Chegem Pervyy Rus. Fed.
204 D4 Chegga Maur.
213 F3 Chegutu Zimbabwe
238 B2 Chehalis WA U.S.A.
238 B2 Chehalis r. WA U.S.A.
127 G4 Chehariz tourist site Iraq
122 A3 Chehel Chashmeh, Kūh-e hill Iran
122 E4 Chehel Dokhtarān, Kūh-e mt. Iran
198 B1 Cheimaditis, Limni l. Greece
161 E5 Cheiron, Cime du mt. France
101 C6 Cheju S. Korea
101 C6 Cheju-do i. S. Korea
101 C6 Cheju-haehyŏp sea chan. S. Korea
139 K4 Chekalin Rus. Fed.
134 K5 Chekan Rus. Fed.
Chek Chue H.K. China see Stanley
139 K4 Chekhov Moskovskaya Oblast' Rus. Fed.
100 G3 Chekhov Sakhalin Rus. Fed.
Chekiang prov. China see Zhejiang
109 □ Chek Lap Kok i. H.K. China
134 F4 Chekshino Rus. Fed.
209 B9 Chela, Serra da mts Angola
156 C5 Chélan France
238 B2 Chelan WA U.S.A.
238 B1 Chelan, Lake WA U.S.A.
137 J4 Chelbas r. Rus. Fed.
137 J5 Chelbasskaya Rus. Fed.
156 B4 Cheleiros Port.
184 A2 Cheleiros r. Port.
122 C2 Cheleken Turkm.
184 C2 Cheles Spain
120 D5 Chelkar Kazakh.
108 C2 Chella Spain
175 L4 Chełm Pol.
175 H5 Chełmek Pol.
151 H3 Chelmer r. England U.K.
175 I6 Chełmiec Pol.
174 G2 Chełmno Pol.
174 G3 Chełmno Pol.
151 H3 Chelmsford Essex, England U.K.
233 H3 Chelmsford MA U.S.A.
174 G2 Chełmża Pol.
227 E4 Chelsea MI U.S.A.
233 G3 Chelsea VT U.S.A.
80 E4 Cheltenham North I. N.Z.
150 E3 Cheltenham Gloucestershire, England U.K.
234 C2 Cheltenham PA U.S.A.
187 C5 Chelva Spain
130 H4 Chelyabinsk Rus. Fed.
120 E1 Chelyabinskaya Oblast' admin. div. Rus. Fed.
Chelyabinsk Oblast admin. div. Rus. Fed. see Chelyabinskaya Oblast'
232 C5 Chelyan WV U.S.A.
131 L2 Chelyuskin, Mys c. Rus. Fed.
204 C3 Chemaïa Morocco
243 I4 Chemax Mex.
159 F4 Chemazé France
213 G3 Chemba Moz.
209 F7 Chembe Zambia
136 C3 Chemerivtsi Ukr.
159 H4 Chémery France
157 E3 Chémery-sur-Bar France
162 B1 Chemillé France
160 D2 Chemin France
157 E4 Cheminon France
159 F4 Chemiré-le-Gaudin France
Chemmis Egypt see Akhmīm
171 D5 Chemnitz Ger.
171 D5 Chemnitz admin. reg. Sachsen Ger.
Chemulpo S. Korea see Inch'ŏn
238 B3 Chemult OR U.S.A.
227 I5 Chemung r. NY U.S.A.
116 B3 Chenab r. India/Pak.
233 F3 Chenango r. NY U.S.A.
233 F3 Chenango Bridge NY U.S.A.
160 C2 Chênas France
210 C3 Ch'ench'a Eth.
Chendir r. Turkm. see Chandyr
160 D1 Chenecey-Buillon France
162 E2 Chénérailles France
114 D3 Chengalpattu Tamil Nadu India
114 C3 Chengam Tamil Nadu India
107 G4 Cheng'an Hebei China
108 D3 Chengbu Hunan China
107 F5 Chengcheng Shaanxi China
Chengchow Henan China see Zhengzhou
107 H3 Chengde Hebei China
108 C2 Chengdu Sichuan China
108 B3 Chenggong Yunnan China
109 F4 Chenghai Guangdong China
Chengjiang Jiangxi China see Taihe
108 B3 Chengjiang Yunnan China
108 D2 Chengkou Chongqing China
108 D5 Chengmai Hainan China
Chengqiao Shanghai China see Chongming
Chengshou Sichuan China see Yingshan
Chengtu Sichuan China see Chengdu
107 G5 Chengwu Shandong China
108 C1 Chengxian Gansu China
Chengxian Guizhou China see Fuquan
Chengxiang Chongqing China see Wuxi
Chengxiang Jiangxi China see Quannan
Chengxiang Sichuan China see Mianning
Chengxiang Sichuan China see Tianquan
Chengxiang Sichuan China see Qingshen
Chengyang Shandong China see Juxian
Chengzhong Guangxi China see Ningming
Chengzi Yunnan China see Longchuan
157 G4 Cheniménil France
114 D3 Chennai Tamil Nadu India
120 C5 Chenoa IL U.S.A.
159 H4 Chenonceaux France
160 D1 Chenôve France
Chenstokhov Pol. see Częstochowa
107 E1 Chentejn Nuruu mts Mongolia
108 D3 Chenxi Hunan China
156 D5 Cheny France
Chenyang Hunan China see Chenxi
Chenying Jiangxi China see Wannian
109 E3 Chenzhou Hunan China
Chenzhou Kam Cambodia see Chŏâm Khsant
197 G5 Chepelare Bulg.
250 B6 Chepén Peru
260 D2 Chepes Arg.
137 I3 Chepil' Ukr.
242 □K7 Chepo Panama
150 E3 Chepstow Monmouthshire, Wales U.K.
134 J4 Cheptsa r. Rus. Fed.
156 E4 Chepy France
159 I4 Cher dept Centre France
162 C1 Cher r. France
Chera state India see Kerala
187 C5 Chera Spain
162 B3 Chérac France
160 D3 Chéran r. France
244 D4 Cherán Mex.
190 C4 Cherasco Italy
163 B5 Chéraute France
231 E5 Cheraw SC U.S.A.
158 E2 Cherbourg France
205 F1 Cherchell Alg.
Cherchen Xinjiang China see Qiemo
135 J5 Cherdakly Rus. Fed.
134 L3 Cherdyn' Rus. Fed.
158 E4 Chère r. France
177 L4 Cherechiu Romania
129 D2 Cherek r. Rus. Fed.
138 G3 Cherekha r. Rus. Fed.
135 G6 Cheremisinovo Rus. Fed.
98 H1 Cheremkhovo Rus. Fed.
121 J1 Cheremnoye Rus. Fed.
100 E3 Cheremshany Rus. Fed.
134 J4 Cheremukhovka Rus. Fed.
192 A4 Cheremule Sardegna Italy
130 J4 Cherepanovo Rus. Fed.
Cherepkovo Moldova see Ciripcău
139 K2 Cherepovets Rus. Fed.
134 I3 Cherevkovo Rus. Fed.
205 E2 Chergui, Chott ech imp. l. Alg.
205 G2 Chéria Alg.
114 C2 Cherial Andhra Prad. India
190 E3 Cherio r. Italy
151 F3 Cheriton Hampshire, England U.K.
233 F6 Cheriton VA U.S.A.
136 F3 Cherkas'ka Oblast' admin. div. Ukr.
137 H3 Cherkas'ke Ukr.
137 I3 Cherkas'ke Ukr.
Cherkas'ke Ukr. see Zymohir"ya
Cherkasskaya Oblast' admin. div. Ukr. see Cherkas'ka Oblast'
Cherkasskoye Ukr. see Zymohir"ya
Cherkassy Ukr. see Cherkasy
137 G3 Cherkasy Ukr.
Cherkasy Oblast admin. div. Ukr. see Cherkas'ka Oblast'
129 C1 Cherkessk Rus. Fed.
139 L3 Cherkutino Rus. Fed.
114 D2 Cherla Andhra Prad. India
121 H1 Cherlak Rus. Fed.
136 D3 Cherlenivka Ukr.
129 D2 Chermen Rus. Fed.
134 L4 Chermoz Rus. Fed.
139 K5 Chern' Rus. Fed.
139 K5 Chern' r. Rus. Fed.
121 G4 Chernak Kazakh.
139 L5 Chernava Lipetskaya Oblast' Rus. Fed.
139 L5 Chernava Ryazanskaya Oblast' Rus. Fed.
134 L1 Chernaya r. Rus. Fed.
138 F2 Chernaya r. Rus. Fed.
137 K2 Chernaya Kalitva r. Rus. Fed.
134 J4 Chernaya Kholunitsa Rus. Fed.
137 G2 Chernecha Sloboda Ukr.
Chernenko Moldova see Şoldăneşti
137 H3 Cherneshchyna Ukr.
Chernigov Ukr. see Chernihiv
100 E3 Chernigovka Rus. Fed.
Chernigov Oblast admin. div. Ukr. see Chernihivs'ka Oblast'
129 A1 Chernigovskaya Rus. Fed.
Chernigovskaya Oblast' admin. div. Ukr. see Chernihivs'ka Oblast'
129 A1 Chernigovskoye Rus. Fed.
137 F2 Chernihiv Ukr.
Chernihiv Oblast admin. div. Ukr. see Chernihivs'ka Oblast'
137 G2 Chernihivs'ka Oblast' admin. div. Ukr.
197 G4 Cherni Lom r. Bulg.
137 I4 Cherninivka Ukr.
136 D3 Chernivets'ka Oblast' admin. div. Ukr.
Chernivetskaya Oblast' admin. div. Ukr. see Chernivets'ka Oblast'
197 F4 Cherni Vrŭkh mt. Bulg.
136 C3 Chernivtsi Chernivets'ka Oblast' Ukr.
136 E3 Chernivtsi Vinnyts'ka Oblast' Ukr.
Chernivtsi Oblast admin. div. Ukr. see Chernivets'ka Oblast'
136 C3 Cherniyiv Ukr.
Chernobyl' Ukr. see Chornobyl'
98 F1 Chernogorsk Rus. Fed.
129 C1 Chernolesskoye Rus. Fed.
134 K3 Chernorechenskiy Rus. Fed.
121 I1 Chernoretskoye Kazakh.
134 I4 Chernovskoye Rus. Fed.
Chernovtsy Chernivets'ka Oblast' Ukr. see Chernivtsi
Chernovtsy Oblast admin. div. Ukr. see Chernivets'ka Oblast'
Chernoye More sea Asia/Europe see Black Sea
134 L4 Chernushka Rus. Fed.
136 E2 Chernyakhiv Ukr.
138 C4 Chernyakhovsk Rus. Fed.
135 G6 Chernyanka Rus. Fed.
99 K1 Chernyshevsk Rus. Fed.
131 M3 Chernyshevskiy Rus. Fed.
135 H6 Chernyshkovskiy Rus. Fed.
135 I7 Chernyye Zemli reg. Rus. Fed.
Chernyy Irtysh r. China/Kazakh. see Ertix He
120 C2 Chernyy Otrog Rus. Fed.
134 F3 Chernyy Porog Rus. Fed.
Chernyy Rynok Rus. Fed. see Kochubey
135 I6 Chernyy Yar Rus. Fed.
236 E3 Cherokee IA U.S.A.
237 D4 Cherokee OK U.S.A.
231 D4 Cherokee Lake TN U.S.A.
237 E4 Cherokees, Lake o' the OK U.S.A.
246 C1 Cherokee Sound Gt Abaco Bahamas
156 D4 Chéroy France
260 A6 Cherquenco Chile
117 G4 Cherrapunji Meghalaya India
149 I4 Cherry Burton East Riding of Yorkshire, England U.K.
236 C2 Cherry Creek r. SD U.S.A.
241 J1 Cherry Creek Mountains NV U.S.A.
233 □J2 Cherryfield ME U.S.A.
234 C3 Cherry Hill NJ U.S.A.
77 G3 Cherry Island Solomon Is
227 I4 Cherry Valley Ont. Can.
234 C2 Cherryville PA U.S.A.
149 I4 Cherry Willingham Lincolnshire, England U.K.
131 R3 Cherskiy Rus. Fed.
Cherskiy Range mts Chitinskaya Oblast' Rus. Fed. see Cherskogo, Khrebet
107 F1 Cherskogo, Khrebet mts Chitinskaya Oblast' Rus. Fed.
131 P3 Cherskogo, Khrebet mts Respublika Sakha (Yakutiya) Rus. Fed.
198 C1 Cherso Kentriki Makedonia Greece
190 C4 Chersogno, Monte mt. Italy
186 D4 Chert Spain
Cherta Spain see Xerta
Cherthala Kerala India see Shertally
Chertkov Ukr. see Chortkiv
135 H6 Chertkovo Rus. Fed.
81 C5 Chertsey South I. N.Z.
151 G3 Chertsey Surrey, England U.K.
139 M4 Cherusti Rus. Fed.
162 D3 Cherveix-Cubas France
197 G4 Cherven Bryag Bulg.
162 B3 Cherves-Richemont France
129 D2 Chervlennaya Rus. Fed.
129 D1 Chervlennyye Buruny Rus. Fed.
137 G3 Chervona Kam"yanka Ukr.
137 H2 Chervone Sums'ka Oblast' Ukr.
136 E3 Chervone Zhytomyrs'ka Oblast' Ukr.
137 I4 Chervone Pole Ukr.
137 F2 Chervoni Partyzany Ukr.
Chervonoarmeyskoye Ukr. see Vil'nyans'k
Chervonoarmiys'k Ukr. see Krasnoarmiys'k
Chervonoarmiys'k Ukr. see Radyvyliv
136 E2 Chervonoarmiys'k Ukr.
Chervonograd Ukr. see Chervonohrad
136 C2 Chervonohrad Ukr.
137 H4 Chervonohryhorivka Ukr.
137 I3 Chervonooskil's'ke Vodoskhovyshche resr Ukr.
Chervonopartizansk Ukr. see Chervonopartyzans'k
137 J3 Chervonopartyzans'k Ukr.
137 G2 Chervonozavods'ke Ukr.
136 F4 Chervonoznam"yanka Ukr.
137 I3 Chervonyy Donets' Ukr.
137 G4 Chervonyy Mayak Ukr.
138 G5 Chervyen' Belarus
151 F3 Cherwell r. England U.K.
139 H5 Cherykaw Belarus
227 E4 Chesaning MI U.S.A.
233 E6 Chesapeake VA U.S.A.
234 B4 Chesapeake Bay MD/VA U.S.A.
232 E5 Chesapeake Beach MD U.S.A.
234 C3 Chesapeake City MD U.S.A.
151 G3 Chesham Buckinghamshire, England U.K.
149 G4 Cheshire admin. div. England U.K.
235 F1 Cheshire CT U.S.A.
233 G3 Cheshire MA U.S.A.
149 G4 Cheshire Plain England U.K.
134 I2 Cheshskaya Guba b. Rus. Fed.
151 G3 Cheshunt Hertfordshire, England U.K.
150 E4 Chesil Beach England U.K.
234 D3 Chesilhurst NJ U.S.A.
227 G3 Chesley Ont. Can.
156 E5 Chesley France
120 E1 Chesma Rus. Fed.
Chesnokovka Rus. Fed. see Novoaltaysk
156 D4 Chessy-les-Pres France
187 C5 Cheste Spain
225 H4 Chester N.S. Can.
149 G4 Chester Cheshire, England U.K.
240 G1 Chester CA U.S.A.
235 F1 Chester CT U.S.A.
236 F4 Chester IL U.S.A.
234 B4 Chester MD U.S.A.
238 E1 Chester MT U.S.A.
234 D2 Chester NJ U.S.A.
235 D1 Chester NY U.S.A.
232 C5 Chester OH U.S.A.
234 C3 Chester PA U.S.A.
231 D5 Chester SC U.S.A.
232 E6 Chester VA U.S.A.
234 B4 Chester r. MD U.S.A.
246 □ Chester Castle Jamaica
234 C2 Chester County county PA U.S.A.
149 H4 Chesterfield Derbyshire, England U.K.
235 F1 Chesterfield CT U.S.A.
236 F4 Chesterfield MO U.S.A.
231 D5 Chesterfield SC U.S.A.
232 E6 Chesterfield VA U.S.A.
77 F3 Chesterfield, Îles is New Caledonia
223 N2 Chesterfield Inlet Nunavut Can.
223 M2 Chesterfield Inlet inlet Nunavut Can.
149 H3 Chester-le-Street Durham, England U.K.
146 F6 Chesters Scottish Borders, Scotland U.K.
234 B3 Chestertown MD U.S.A.
233 G3 Chestertown NY U.S.A.
233 F2 Chesterville Ont. Can.
234 C3 Chesterville MD U.S.A.
232 D4 Chestnut Ridge PA U.S.A.
234 C3 Cheswold DE U.S.A.
226 B3 Chetek WI U.S.A.
225 I4 Chéticamp N.S. Can.
237 E4 Chetopa KS U.S.A.
243 H5 Chetumal Mex.
222 F4 Chetwynd B.C. Can.
109 □ Cheung Chau H.K. China
109 □ Cheung Chau H.K. China
161 E4 Cheval Blanc, Sommet du mt. France
162 B3 Chevanceaux France
156 D5 Chevannes France
241 L4 Chevelon Creek r. AZ U.S.A.
177 K6 Chevereşu Mare Romania
234 B4 Cheverly MD U.S.A.
160 D1 Chevigny-St-Sauveur France
157 F4 Chevillon France
156 B4 Chevilly France
81 D5 Cheviot South I. N.Z.
232 A5 Cheviot OH U.S.A.
149 G2 Cheviot Hills England U.K.
85 E5 Cheviot Range hills Qld Austr.
224 F2 Chevreulx r. Que. Can.
156 C4 Chevreuse France
210 C3 Che'w Bahir salt l. Eth.
238 C1 Chewelah WA U.S.A.
150 E3 Chew Magna Bath and North East Somerset, England U.K.
237 D5 Cheyenne OK U.S.A.
238 F3 Cheyenne WY U.S.A.
236 C2 Cheyenne r. SD U.S.A.
236 C4 Cheyenne Wells CO U.S.A.
161 A3 Cheylade France
87 C7 Cheyne Bay W.A. Austr.
114 D3 Cheyur Tamil Nadu India
114 C3 Cheyyar r. India
222 E4 Chezacut B.C. Can.
159 I5 Chezal-Benoît France
163 B6 Chèze France
116 D4 Chhabra Rajasthan India
116 C4 Chhapar Rajasthan India
117 F4 Chhapra Bihar India
116 D4 Chhata Uttar Prad. India
117 G4 Chhatak Bangl.
117 F4 Chhatarpur Bihar India
116 D4 Chhatarpur Madh. Prad. India
115 E2 Chhatrapur Orissa India
97 C5 Chhay Arêng, Stœng r. Cambodia
116 D4 Chhibramau Uttar Prad. India
116 D5 Chhindwara Madh. Prad. India
116 D4 Chhipa Barod Rajasthan India
97 D4 Chhlong, Prêk r. Cambodia
116 D5 Chhota Chhindwara Madh. Prad. India
116 C5 Chhota Udepur Gujarat India
116 E5 Chhuikhadan Madh. Prad. India
Chhuk Cambodia see Phumĭ Chhuk
117 G4 Chhukha Bhutan
257 F4 Chiador Brazil
109 G4 Chiai Taiwan
191 G3 Chiampo Italy
191 G3 Chiampo r. Italy
192 D1 Chianciano Terme Italy
209 B8 Chiange Angola
96 C3 Chiang Kham Thai.
96 C3 Chiang Khan Thai.
96 B3 Chiang Mai Thai.
96 B3 Chiang Rai Thai.
192 E2 Chiani r. Italy
191 F5 Chianni Italy
243 G5 Chiapa Mex.
245 H5 Chiapas state Mex.
194 D5 Chiaramonte Gulfi Sicilia Italy
192 A4 Chiaramonti Sardegna Italy
191 I5 Chiaravalle Italy
195 F4 Chiaravalle Centrale Italy
190 E3 Chiari Italy
193 I4 Chiaromonte Italy
191 I2 Chiarso r. Italy
191 H5 Chiascio r. Italy
190 E3 Chiasso Italy
129 C2 Chiat'ura Georgia
245 E4 Chiautempan Mex.
245 E4 Chiautla Mex.
245 E4 Chiautzingo Mex.
190 E4 Chiavari Italy
190 E3 Chiavenna r. Italy
190 E2 Chiavenno Italy
105 G3 Chiba Japan
105 G3 Chiba pref. Japan
213 G4 Chibabava Moz.
209 B8 Chibemba Angola
Chibi Zimbabwe see Chivi
209 B8 Chibia Angola
Chibizovka Rus. Fed. see Zherdevka
213 G4 Chiboma Moz.
224 F3 Chibougamau Que. Can.
224 F3 Chibougamau r. Que. Can.
213 G5 Chibuto Moz.
209 F8 Chibwe Zambia
Chicacole Andhra Prad. India see Srikakulam
226 D5 Chicago IL U.S.A.
226 D5 Chicago Heights IL U.S.A.
209 D6 Chicapa r. Angola
245 E2 Chicayán r. Mex.
225 H3 Chic-Chocs, Monts mts Que. Can.
197 G3 Chicera Hamba hill Romania
222 B3 Chichagof AK U.S.A.
220 E4 Chichagof Island AK U.S.A.
123 F5 Chichak r. Pak.
204 C3 Chichaoua Morocco
252 D5 Chichas, Cordillera de mts Bol.
159 F5 Chiché France
107 G3 Chicheng Hebei China
Chicheng Sichuan China see Pengxi
243 H4 Chichén Itzá tourist site Mex.
151 G4 Chichester West Sussex, England U.K.
86 C4 Chichester Range mts W.A. Austr.
116 E5 Chichgarh Mahar. India
105 F3 Chichibu Japan
105 F2 Chichibu-gawa r. Japan
245 E5 Chichihualco Mex.
103 □3 Chichi-jima i. Japan
103 □3 Chichijima-rettō is Japan
116 D5 Chicholi Madh. Prad. India
232 E6 Chickahominy r. VA U.S.A.
231 C5 Chickamauga Lake TN U.S.A.
237 F6 Chickasawhay r. MS U.S.A.
237 D5 Chickasha OK U.S.A.
150 E4 Chickerell Dorset, England U.K.
184 D4 Chiclana de la Frontera Spain
250 B6 Chiclayo Peru
261 G6 Chico r. Buenos Aires Arg.
259 C6 Chico r. Chubut Arg.
259 D7 Chico r. Chubut Arg.
259 C8 Chico r. Santa Cruz Arg.
244 C2 Chico r. Mex.
240 G2 Chico CA U.S.A.
Chicobea i. Fiji see Cikobia
209 B8 Chicomba Angola
243 G6 Chicomucelo Mex.
217 □3b Chiconi Mayotte
211 B8 Chicono Moz.
245 E3 Chicontepec Mex.
233 G3 Chicopee MA U.S.A.
92 B2 Chico Sapocoy, Mount Luzon Phil.
225 G3 Chicoutimi Que. Can.
225 G3 Chicoutimi r. Que. Can.
209 C8 Chicupo Angola
114 C4 Chidambaram Tamil Nadu India
151 G3 Chiddingfold Surrey, England U.K.
111 F6 Chido Xizang China
101 C6 Chido S. Korea
209 C9 Chiede Angola
231 D6 Chiefland FL U.S.A.
212 D3 Chief's Island Botswana
173 G4 Chiemgauer Alpen mts Ger.
173 G4 Chieming Ger.
173 G4 Chiemsee l. Ger.
191 G2 Chienes Italy
209 F7 Chiengi Zambia
Chiengmai Thai. see Chiang Mai
191 I5 Chienti r. Italy
190 C3 Chieri Italy
157 F3 Chiers r. France
190 E2 Chiesa in Valmalenco Italy
177 L4 Chieşd Romania
191 F3 Chiese r. Italy
193 G2 Chieti Italy
193 G2 Chieti prov. Abruzzo Italy
193 H3 Chieuti Italy
151 F3 Chieveley West Berkshire, England U.K.
165 C4 Chièvres Belgium
107 H3 Chifeng Nei Mongol China
257 G2 Chifre, Serra do mts Brazil
213 G2 Chifunde Moz.
121 H3 Chiganak Kazakh.
105 F3 Chigasaki Japan
220 C4 Chiginagak Volcano, Mount AK U.S.A.
137 K2 Chigla r. Rus. Fed.
220 C4 Chignik AK U.S.A.
160 E3 Chignin France
250 B3 Chigorodó Col.
252 D5 Chiguana Bol.
111 E6 Chigu Co l. China
151 H3 Chigwell Essex, England U.K.
242 D2 Chihuahua Mex.
242 D2 Chihuahua state Mex.
260 C6 Chihuido Medio mt. Arg.
121 F3 Chiili Kazakh.
106 C3 Chijinpu Gansu China
129 D3 Chikaani Georgia
116 D5 Chikalda Mahar. India
108 D4 Chikan Guangdong China
237 D4 Chikaskia r. KS U.S.A.
114 C3 Chik Ballapur Karnataka India
138 G3 Chikhachevo Rus. Fed.
116 D5 Chikhali Kalan Parasia Madh. Prad. India
116 D5 Chikhli Mahar. India
114 B3 Chikmagalur Karnataka India
114 B2 Chikodi Karnataka India
114 B2 Chikodi Road Karnataka India
129 C2 Chikola Rus. Fed.
106 E1 Chikoy Rus. Fed.
107 E1 Chikoy r. Rus. Fed.
103 E7 Chikugo Japan
105 E1 Chikuma-gawa r. Japan
103 E7 Chikushino Japan
211 B8 Chikwawa Malawi
245 E2 Chila, Laguna l. Mex.
222 F4 Chilanko r. B.C. Can.
222 E4 Chilanko Forks B.C. Can.
245 E5 Chilapa Mex.
116 C2 Chilas Jammu and Kashmir
114 C5 Chilaw Sri Lanka
252 A3 Chilca Peru
187 C5 Chilches Spain
150 E3 Chilcompton Somerset, England U.K.
222 F5 Chilcotin r. B.C. Can.
85 G3 Chilcott Island Coral Sea Is Terr. Austr.
85 H5 Childers Qld Austr.
237 C5 Childress TX U.S.A.
151 F3 Childrey Oxfordshire, England U.K.
259 B7 Chile country S. America
267 N8 Chile Basin sea feature S. Pacific Ocean
259 C7 Chile Chico Chile
258 D3 Chilecito Arg.
209 B8 Chilengue, Serra do mts Angola
267 N8 Chile Rise sea feature S. Pacific Ocean
252 A1 Chilete Peru
135 I7 Chilgir Rus. Fed.
151 H3 Chilham Kent, England U.K.
232 C6 Chilhowie VA U.S.A.
Chilia-Nouă Ukr. see Kiliya
197 I3 Chilia Veche Romania
121 I4 Chilik Kazakh.
121 I4 Chilik r. Kazakh.
115 E2 Chilika Lake India
209 E8 Chililabombwe Zambia
198 C3 Chiliomodi Greece
222 C3 Chilkat r. Can./U.S.A.
222 F4 Chilko r. B.C. Can.
85 F3 Chillagoe Qld Austr.
260 A5 Chillán Chile
260 A5 Chillán r. Chile
260 B5 Chillán, Nevado mts Chile
261 H5 Chillar Arg.
156 C4 Chilleurs-aux-Bois France
226 C5 Chillicothe IL U.S.A.
236 E4 Chillicothe MO U.S.A.
232 B5 Chillicothe OH U.S.A.
116 C1 Chillinji Jammu and Kashmir
222 F5 Chilliwack B.C. Can.
185 F2 Chillón Spain
185 G2 Chilluévar Spain
234 B4 Chillum MD U.S.A.
122 C1 Chil'mamedkum, Peski des. Turkm.
117 G4 Chilmari Bangl.
259 B6 Chiloé, Isla de i. Chile
Chiloé, Isla Grande de i. Chile see Chiloé, Isla de
183 G4 Chiloeches Spain
238 B3 Chiloquin OR U.S.A.
245 E5 Chilpancingo Mex.
232 B3 Chilson MI U.S.A.
83 F4 Chiltern Vic. Austr.
151 G3 Chiltern Hills England U.K.
226 C3 Chilton WI U.S.A.
209 D7 Chiluage Angola
209 F7 Chilubi Zambia
211 B7 Chilumba Malawi
109 G3 Chilung Taiwan
211 B7 Chimala Tanz.
243 H6 Chimaltenango Guat.
213 G3 Chimanimani Zimbabwe
165 D4 Chimay Belgium
165 D4 Chimay, Bois de for. Belgium
260 B4 Chimbarongo Chile
260 C2 Chimbas Arg.
120 D4 Chimbay Uzbek.
252 A2 Chimbote Peru
Chimboy Uzbek. see Chimbay
185 G3 Chimeneas Spain
123 H4 Chimian Pak.
250 C2 Chimichaguá Col.
121 G4 Chimion Uzbek.
Chimishliya Moldova see Cimişlia
Chimkent Kazakh. see Shymkent
Chimkentskaya Oblast' admin. div. Kazakh. see Yuzhnyy Kazakhstan
213 G3 Chimoio Moz.
185 F2 Chimorra hill Spain
260 D6 Chimpay Arg.
123 G2 Chimtargha, Qullai mt. Tajik.
Chimtorga, Gora mt. Tajik. see Chimtargha, Qullai
96 A2 Chin state Myanmar
98 E4 China country Asia
243 F3 China Mex.
China, Republic of country Asia see Taiwan
China Bakir r. Myanmar see To
245 G4 Chinameca Mex.
245 F3 Chinampa de Gorostiza Mex.
190 C4 Chinanale Italy
242 □I6 Chinandega Nic.
239 F6 Chinati Peak TX U.S.A.
121 G4 Chinaz Uzbek.
252 A3 Chincha Alta Peru
222 G3 Chinchaga r. Alta Can.
85 G5 Chinchilla Qld Austr.
185 I2 Chinchilla de Monte Aragón Spain
114 C2 Chincholi Karnataka India
183 G4 Chinchón Spain
243 I5 Chinchorro, Banco sea feature Mex.
260 B3 Chincolco Chile
233 F6 Chincoteague VA U.S.A.
233 F6 Chincoteague Bay MD/VA U.S.A.
213 H3 Chinde Moz.
101 C6 Chindo S. Korea
101 C6 Chin-do i. S. Korea
160 D3 Chindrieux France
108 A1 Chindu Qinghai China
96 A2 Chindwin r. Myanmar
116 C2 Chineni Jammu and Kashmir
Chinese Turkestan aut. reg. China see Xinjiang Uygur Zizhiqu
151 G3 Chingford Greater London, England U.K.
Chinghai prov. China see Qinghai
101 C5 Chinghwa N. Korea
120 C2 Chingirlau Kazakh.
121 I2 Chingiz-Tau, Khrebet mts Kazakh.
Chingleput Tamil Nadu India see Chengalpattu
209 E8 Chingola Zambia
209 C8 Chinguar Angola
204 B5 Chinguetti Maur.
101 D6 Chinhae S. Korea
213 F3 Chinhoyi Zimbabwe
Chini Hima. Prad. India see Kalpa
252 C3 Chiñijo Bol.
Chining Shandong China see Jining
123 H4 Chiniot Pak.
242 C3 Chinipas Mex.
97 D4 Chinit, Stœng r. Cambodia
101 D6 Chinju S. Korea
208 D3 Chinko r. C.A.R.
241 M3 Chinle AZ U.S.A.
109 F3 Chinmen Taiwan
109 F3 Chinmen Tao i. Taiwan
114 D3 Chinna Ganjam Andhra Prad. India
114 C4 Chinnamanur Tamil Nadu India
Chinnamp'o N. Korea see Namp'o
114 C4 Chinna Salem Tamil Nadu India
151 G3 Chinnor Oxfordshire, England U.K.
114 C2 Chinnur Andhra Prad. India
105 E3 Chino Japan
240 I4 Chino CA U.S.A.
87 C7 Chinocup, Lake salt flat W.A. Austr.
162 C1 Chinon France
238 E1 Chinook MT U.S.A.
266 H3 Chinook Trough sea feature N. Pacific Ocean
241 K4 Chino Valley AZ U.S.A.
Chinoz Uzbek. see Chinaz
211 B7 Chinsali Zambia
114 D2 Chintalnar Madh. Prad. India
114 C3 Chintamani Karnataka India
197 F2 Chinteni Romania
211 B7 Chintheche Malawi
250 C2 Chinú Col.
165 E5 Chiny Belgium
165 E5 Chiny, Forêt de for. Belgium
213 G3 Chioco Moz.
191 H3 Chioggia Italy
190 B3 Chiomonte Italy
199 E2 Chios Voreio Aigaio Greece
199 D2 Chios i. Greece
211 B8 Chipata Zambia
111 B5 Chip Chap r. China/India
259 C6 Chipchihua, Sierra de mts Arg.
209 F7 Chipili Zambia
209 B8 Chipindo Angola
107 H4 Chiping Shandong China
Chipinga Zimbabwe see Chipinge
213 G4 Chipinge Zimbabwe
184 D4 Chipiona Spain
231 C6 Chipley FL U.S.A.
114 B2 Chiplun Mahar. India
225 H4 Chipman N.B. Can.
150 E3 Chippenham Wiltshire, England U.K.
213 G3 Chipperone, Monte mt. Moz.
236 E2 Chippewa r. MN U.S.A.
226 A3 Chippewa r. WI U.S.A.
226 B3 Chippewa Falls WI U.S.A.
151 F2 Chipping Campden Gloucestershire, England U.K.
151 F3 Chipping Norton Oxfordshire, England U.K.
151 H3 Chipping Ongar Essex, England U.K.
150 E3 Chipping Sodbury South Gloucestershire, England U.K.
190 C2 Chippis Switz.
186 C3 Chiprana Spain
197 F4 Chiprovtsi Bulg.
Chipuriro Zimbabwe see Guruve
115 D2 Chipurupalle Andhra Prad. India
115 D2 Chipurupalle Andhra Prad. India
243 H6 Chiquimula Guat.
250 C3 Chiquinquira Col.
261 G4 Chiquita, Mar l. Arg.
245 E1 Chiquita, Sierra mts Mex.
244 D4 Chiquito r. Mex.
253 E4 Chiquitos Jesuit Missions tourist site Brazil
135 H6 Chir r. Rus. Fed.
161 B4 Chirac France
114 D3 Chirada Andhra Prad. India
211 B8 Chiradzulu Malawi
129 F3 Chirakhchay r. Rus. Fed.
114 B4 Chirakkal Kerala India
114 D3 Chirala Andhra Prad. India
213 G3 Chiramba Moz.
111 A6 Chirawa Rajasthan India
150 D2 Chirbury Shropshire, England U.K.
121 G4 Chirchik Uzbek.
121 G4 Chirchik r. Uzbek.
213 F4 Chiredzi Zimbabwe
250 E2 Chirgua r. Venez.
241 M6 Chiricahua Peak AZ U.S.A.
250 C2 Chiriguaná Col.
250 B6 Chirinos Peru
242 □J7 Chiriquí, Golfo de b. Panama
242 □J7 Chiriquí, Laguna de b. Panama
242 □J7 Chiriquí Grande Panama
101 C6 Chiri-san mt. S. Korea
185 H3 Chirivel Spain
129 D2 Chiri-Yurt Rus. Fed.
150 D2 Chirk Wrexham, Wales U.K.
146 F6 Chirnside Scottish Borders, Scotland U.K.
217 □3b Chirongui Mayotte
160 C2 Chiroubles France
197 G4 Chirpan Bulg.
104 D3 Chiryū Japan
209 F8 Chisamba Zambia
209 E8 Chisasa Zambia
224 E2 Chisasibi Que. Can.
243 H6 Chisec Guat.
151 F3 Chiseldon Swindon, England U.K.
197 H3 Chiselet Romania
Chishima-retto is Rus. Fed. see Kuril Islands
135 K5 Chishmy Rus. Fed.
222 H4 Chisholm Alta Can.
233 □H2 Chisholm ME U.S.A.
226 A2 Chisholm MN U.S.A.
123 H4 Chishtian Mandi Pak.
108 C2 Chishui Guizhou China
108 C3 Chishuihe Sichuan China
108 C2 Chishui He r. China
Chisimaio Somalia see Kismaayo
136 E4 Chişinău Moldova
177 L5 Chişindia Romania
197 E2 Chişineu-Criş Romania
177 L4 Chişlaz Romania
190 C4 Chisola r. Italy
190 C4 Chisone r. Italy
134 J5 Chistopol' Rus. Fed.
121 F1 Chistopol'ye Kazakh.
Chistyakovo Ukr. see Torez
121 G1 Chistyakovskoye Kazakh.
252 D5 Chita Bol.
104 C4 Chita Japan
99 J1 Chita Rus. Fed.
104 C4 Chita-hantō pen. Japan
Chitaldrug Karnataka India see Chitradurga
116 B4 Chitalwana Rajasthan India
Chita Oblast admin. div. Rus. Fed. see Chitinskaya Oblast'
209 D6 Chitato Angola
223 J4 Chitek Lake Sask. Can.
209 C8 Chitembo Angola
191 G5 Chitignano Italy
100 A2 Chitinskaya Oblast' admin. div. Rus. Fed.
211 B7 Chitipa Malawi
213 G4 Chitobe Moz.
209 D8 Chitokoloki Zambia
Chitor Rajasthan India see Chittaurgarh
102 J2 Chitose Japan
114 C3 Chitradurga Karnataka India
116 E4 Chitrakut Uttar Prad. India
123 G3 Chitral Pak.
123 G3 Chitral r. Pak.
114 C3 Chitravati r. India
242 □J8 Chitré Panama
116 B5 Chitrod Gujarat India
117 G5 Chittagong Bangl.
117 G5 Chittagong admin. div. Bangl.
117 F5 Chittaranjan W. Bengal India
116 C4 Chittaurgarh Rajasthan India
114 C3 Chittoor Andhra Prad. India
Chittorgarh Rajasthan India see Chittaurgarh
114 C4 Chittur Kerala India
213 F3 Chitungwiza Zimbabwe
211 C7 Chiulezi r. Moz.
Chiu Lung H.K. China see Kowloon
209 D8 Chiume Angola
213 H2 Chiúre Novo Moz.
190 E2 Chiuro Italy
191 G2 Chiusa Italy
190 C4 Chiusa di Pesio Italy
191 I2 Chiusaforte Italy
194 C5 Chiusa Sclafani Sicilia Italy
190 C5 Chiusavecchia Italy
192 D1 Chiusdino Italy
190 C3 Chiusella r. Italy
192 D1 Chiusi Italy
191 G5 Chiusi della Verna Italy
213 G2 Chiúta Moz.
187 C5 Chiva Spain
190 C3 Chivasso Italy
252 C3 Chivay Peru
252 C3 Chive Bol.
213 F3 Chivhu Zimbabwe
213 F4 Chivi Zimbabwe
261 G4 Chivilcoy Arg.
162 B2 Chizé France
120 B2 Chizha Vtoraya Kazakh.
Chkalov Rus. Fed. see Orenburg
137 H4 Chkalove Ukr.
121 G1 Chkalovo Kazakh.
Chkalovo Rus. Fed. see Kurchaloy
134 H4 Chkalovsk Rus. Fed.
Chkalovskaya Oblast' admin. div. Rus. Fed. see Orenburgskaya Oblast'
137 I3 Chkalovs'ke Ukr.
100 E3 Chkalovskoye Rus. Fed.
177 G2 Chlebičov Czech Rep.
177 I2 Chlebnice Slovakia
Chlef Alg. see Ech Chélif
175 I4 Chlewiska Pol.
177 K3 Chlmec r. Slovakia
175 K6 Chłopice Pol.
241 J4 Chloride AZ U.S.A.
174 E3 Chludowo Pol.
173 H2 Chlumčany Czech Rep.
176 C1 Chlumec Czech Rep.
176 E1 Chlumec nad Cidlinou Czech Rep.
176 D3 Chlum u Třeboně Czech Rep.
177 H2 Chmeľová hill Slovakia
175 I5 Chmielnik Pol.
175 K4 Chmiel Pierwszy Pol.
97 D4 Chŏâm Khsant Cambodia
260 B2 Choapa r. Chile
212 E3 Chobe admin. dist. Botswana
174 D3 Chobienice Pol.
245 F4 Chocamán Mex.
247 □3 Choc Bay St Lucia
176 F1 Choceň Czech Rep.
175 H3 Choceń Pol.
101 C5 Choch'iwŏn S. Korea
177 G3 Chocholná-Velčice Slovakia
174 D4 Chocianów Pol.
174 D2 Chociwel Pol.
250 B3 Choco dept Col.
241 J5 Chocolate Mountains AZ/CA U.S.A.
250 C3 Chocontá Col.
231 C6 Choctawhatchee r. FL U.S.A.
174 F4 Chocz Pol.
174 F1 Choczewo Pol.
114 D2 Chodavaram Andhra Prad. India
175 H3 Chodecz Pol.
175 K4 Chodel Pol.
175 J4 Chodelka r. Pol.
176 B1 Chodov Czech Rep.
176 B2 Chodová Planá Czech Rep.
175 K3 Chodów Pol.
175 H3 Chodów Pol.
174 E3 Chodzież Pol.
260 E6 Choele Choel Arg.
105 F3 Chōfu Japan
223 J4 Choiceland Sask. Can.
78 □6 Choiseul i. Solomon Is
259 F8 Choiseul Sound sea chan. Falkland Is
160 E3 Choisy France
242 C3 Choix Mex.
174 C3 Chojna Pol.
174 F2 Chojnice Pol.
174 D4 Chojnów Pol.
102 J4 Chōkai-san vol. Japan
210 C2 Ch'ok'ē Mountains Eth.
129 C2 Ch'okhatauri Georgia
121 H4 Chokpar Kazakh.
Chokue Moz. see Chókwé
131 P2 Chokurdakh Rus. Fed.
213 G5 Chókwé Moz.
240 G4 Cholame CA U.S.A.
240 G4 Cholame Creek r. CA U.S.A.
108 A1 Chola Shan mts Sichuan China
260 A6 Cholchol Chile
162 B1 Cholet France
242 □I6 Choloma Hond.
121 I4 Cholpon-Ata Kyrg.
151 F3 Cholsey Oxfordshire, England U.K.
245 E4 Cholula Mex.
242 □I6 Choluteca Hond.
209 E9 Choma Zambia
101 D5 Chŏmch'ŏn S. Korea
161 B3 Chomelix France
161 C4 Chomérac France
Chomo Xizang China see Yadong
111 E6 Chomo Ganggar mt. Xizang China
117 G4 Chomo Lhari mt. Bhutan
116 C4 Chomun Rajasthan India
176 C1 Chomutov Czech Rep.
176 C1 Chomutovka r. Czech Rep.
131 L3 Chona r. Rus. Fed.
101 C5 Ch'ŏnan S. Korea
97 C4 Chon Buri Thai.
259 B6 Chonchi Chile
250 A5 Chone Ecuador
Chong'an Fujian China see Wuyishan
101 C5 Ch'ŏngch'ŏn-gang r. N. Korea
101 D6 Ch'ongdo S. Korea
Chonggye Xizang China see Qonggyai
103 D6 Chŏngja S. Korea
101 D4 Ch'ŏngjin N. Korea
101 C5 Chŏngju N. Korea
101 C5 Ch'ŏngju S. Korea
108 A2 Chongkü Xizang China
107 G3 Chongli Hebei China
Chonglong Sichuan China see Zizhong
109 G2 Chongming Shanghai China
109 G2 Chongming Dao i. China
209 B8 Chongoroi Angola
101 C5 Chŏngp'yŏng N. Korea
108 C2 Chongqing Chongqing China
Chongqing Sichuan China see Chongzhou
108 C2 Chongqing mun. China
109 E3 Chongren Jiangxi China
101 C6 Chŏngŭp S. Korea
209 F8 Chongwe Zambia
109 E2 Chongyang Hubei China
109 F3 Chongyang Xi r. China
109 E3 Chongyi Jiangxi China
108 B2 Chongzhou Sichuan China
108 C4 Chongzuo Guangxi China
101 C6 Chŏnju S. Korea
245 H5 Chontalpa Mex.
117 F3 Cho Oyu mt. China/Nepal
157 E2 Chooz France
136 B3 Chop Ukr.
117 E4 Chopan Uttar Prad. India
116 C5 Chopda Mahar. India
97 D5 Chơ Phước Hai Vietnam
255 B8 Chopimzinho Brazil
136 E2 Chopovychi Ukr.
233 E5 Choptank r. MD U.S.A.
252 D4 Choquecamata Bol.
198 B3 Chora Greece
199 E3 Chorá tourist site Greece
161 E4 Chorges France
149 G4 Chorley Lancashire, England U.K.
151 G3 Chorleywood Hertfordshire, England U.K.
136 E4 Chorna Ukr.
137 G5 Chorna r. Ukr.
136 C3 Chorna Tysa Ukr.
175 M5 Chorniyiv Ukr.
137 G3 Chornobay Ukr.
136 F2 Chornobyl' Ukr.
177 L3 Chornoholova Ukr.
137 F4 Chornomors'ke Ukr.
135 F7 Chornomors'ke Ukr.
136 E3 Chornorudka Ukr.
137 G2 Chornukhy Ukr.
137 F3 Chornyy Tashlyk r. Ukr.
129 B3 Chorokhi r. Georgia/Turkey
175 K2 Choroszcz Pol.
85 E4 Chorregon Qld Austr.
254 F4 Chorrochó Brazil
136 C3 Chortkiv Ukr.
116 B5 Chorwad Gujarat India
101 C5 Ch'ŏrwŏn S. Korea
175 I2 Chorzele Pol.
174 G5 Chorzów Pol.
101 C4 Ch'osan N. Korea
105 G3 Chōshi Japan
259 B5 Choshuenco, Volcán vol. Chile
260 B5 Chos Malal Arg.
174 D2 Choszczno Pol.
250 B6 Chota Peru
238 D2 Choteau MT U.S.A.
176 E2 Chotěboř Czech Rep.
173 H2 Chotěšov Czech Rep.
116 B5 Chotila Gujarat India
177 H4 Chotín Slovakia
217 □3a Choua-chandroudé i. Comoros
156 E3 Chouilly France
204 B5 Choûm Maur.
184 B1 Chouto Port.
159 H4 Chouzy-sur-Cisse France
240 G3 Chowchilla CA U.S.A.
114 B4 Chowghat Kerala India
222 G4 Chown, Mount Alta Can.
121 K2 Choya Rus. Fed.
107 G2 Choybalsan Mongolia
160 D1 Choye France
107 F2 Choyr Mongolia
182 E2 Chozas de Abajo Spain
Chozas de la Sierra Spain see Soto del Real
176 E2 Chrast Pardubický kraj Czech Rep.
176 C2 Chrást Czech Rep.
176 D1 Chrastava Czech Rep.
171 F5 Chřibská Czech Rep.
176 G2 Chřiby hills Czech Rep.
236 G4 Chrisman IL U.S.A.
215 H2 Chrissiesmeer S. Africa
81 D5 Christchurch South I. N.Z.
151 F4 Christchurch Dorset, England U.K.
246 □ Christiana Jamaica
215 E2 Christiana S. Africa
234 C3 Christiana PA U.S.A.
Christiania Norway see Oslo
232 C6 Christiansburg VA U.S.A.
142 C4 Christiansfeld Denmark
Christianshåb Greenland see Qasigiannguit

247 F3 Christiansted Virgin Is (U.S.A.)
226 B3 Christie WI U.S.A.
223 I3 Christina r. Alta Can.
81 B6 Christina, Mount South I. N.Z.
149 G4 Christleton Cheshire, England U.K.
86 E3 Christmas Creek W.A. Austr.
86 E3 Christmas Creek r. W.A. Austr.
86 □1 Christmas Island terr. Indian Ocean
149 H2 Christon Bank Northumberland, England U.K.
87 E5 Christopher, Lake salt flat W.A. Austr.
176 E2 Chrudim Czech Rep.
175 H3 Chruślin Pol.
198 D1 Chrysoupoli Greece
148 E2 Chryston North Lanarkshire, Scotland U.K.
175 H5 Chrzanów Pol.
174 F4 Chrząstowa Wielka Pol.
174 G5 Chrząstowice Pol.
174 E3 Chrzypsko Wielkie Pol.
Chu Kazakh. see Shu
121 F3 Chu r. Kazakh.
117 G5 Chuadanga Bangl.
109 G2 Chuansha Shanghai China
108 A2 Chubalung Sichuan China
137 I4 Chubarivka Ukr.
Chubarovka Ukr. see Polohy
Chubartau Kazakh. see Barshatas
238 D3 Chubbuck ID U.S.A.
137 J4 Chuburka r. Rus. Fed.
259 C6 Chubut prov. Arg.
259 D6 Chubut r. Arg.
177 H2 Chuchelná Czech Rep.
135 H5 Chuchkovo Rus. Fed.
241 J5 Chuckwalla Mountains CA U.S.A.
242 □K7 Chucunaque r. Panama
150 D4 Chudleigh Devon, England U.K.
136 E2 Chudniv Ukr.
174 G5 Chudoba Pol.
139 H2 Chudovo Rus. Fed.
Chudskoye, Ozero l. Estonia/Rus. Fed. see Peipus, Lake
220 D3 Chugach Mountains AK U.S.A.
103 F6 Chūgoku-sanchi mts Japan
Chuggênsumdo Qinghai China see Jigzhi
Chuguchak Xinjiang China see Tacheng
Chuguyev Ukr. see Chuhuyiv
100 E3 Chuguyevka Rus. Fed.
238 F3 Chugwater WY U.S.A.
Chuhai Guangdong China see Zhuhai
137 I3 Chuhuyiv Ukr.
121 H3 Chu-Iliyskiye Gory mts Kazakh.
108 A2 Chuka Xizang China
Chukai Malaysia see Cukai
Chukchi Peninsula Rus. Fed. see Chukotskiy Poluostrov
268 M1 Chukchi Plateau sea feature Arctic Ocean
220 A3 Chukchi Sea Rus. Fed./U.S.A.
134 H4 Chukhloma Rus. Fed.
131 T3 Chukotskiy Poluostrov pen. Rus. Fed.
137 G4 Chulakivka Ukr.
Chulakkurgan Kazakh. see Shollakorgan
Chulaktau Kazakh. see Karatau
240 I5 Chula Vista CA U.S.A.
187 C5 Chulilla Spain
150 D4 Chulmleigh Devon, England U.K.
250 A6 Chulucanas Peru
123 I3 Chulung Pass Pak.
106 D1 Chuluut Gol r. Mongolia
130 J4 Chulym Rus. Fed.
110 D1 Chulyshman r. Rus. Fed.
252 C3 Chuma Bol.
137 H4 Chumaky Ukr.
258 D3 Chumbicha Arg.
108 A1 Chumda Qinghai China
197 G4 Chumerna mt. Bulg.
100 E1 Chumikan Rus. Fed.
129 D3 Ch'umlaqi Georgia
116 C3 Chumphae Thai.
97 B5 Chumphon Thai.
96 C4 Chum Saeng Thai.
260 E2 Chuña Arg.
131 K4 Chuna r. Rus. Fed.
109 F2 Chun'an Zhejiang China
140 P2 Chuna-Tundra plain Rus. Fed.
101 C5 Ch'unch'ŏn S. Korea
121 I4 Chundzha Kazakh.
209 E8 Chunga Zambia
Chung-hua Jen-min Kung-ho-kuo country Asia see China
Chung-hua Min-kuo country Asia see Taiwan
101 C5 Ch'ungju S. Korea
Chungking Chongqing China see Chongqing
Ch'ungmu S. Korea see T'ongyŏng
101 C5 Chŭngsan N. Korea
109 G4 Chungyang Shanmo mts Taiwan
100 D4 Chunhua Jilin China
243 H5 Chunhuhux Mex.
Chunxi Jiangsu China see Gaochun
131 K3 Chunya r. Rus. Fed.
211 B7 Chunya Tanz.
97 D4 Chuŏr Phnum Dângrêk mts Cambodia/Thai.
Chuosijia Sichuan China see Guanyinqiao
134 F2 Chupa Rus. Fed.
137 H2 Chupakhivka Ukr.
122 A2 Chūplū Iran
136 F3 Chupyra Ukr.
258 C5 Chuquicamata Chile
252 D5 Chuquisaca dept Bol.
Chuqung Qinghai China see Chindu
134 K4 Chur Rus. Fed.
190 E2 Chur Switz.
117 H4 Churachandpur Manipur India
131 O3 Churapcha Rus. Fed.
134 K5 Churayevo Rus. Fed.
151 H2 Church End Essex, England U.K.
148 B3 Church Hill Rep. of Ireland
234 C3 Church Hill MD U.S.A.
232 B6 Church Hill TN U.S.A.
223 M3 Churchill Man. Can.
223 M3 Churchill r. Man. Can.
225 I2 Churchill r. Nfld. Can.
225 I2 Churchill Falls Nfld. Can.
263 K1 Churchill Mountains Antarctica
222 E3 Churchill Peak B.C. Can.
149 G4 Church Lawton Cheshire, England U.K.
236 D1 Churchs Ferry ND U.S.A.
150 E2 Church Stretton Shropshire, England U.K.
234 B4 Churchton MD U.S.A.
147 C4 Churchtown Cork Rep. of Ireland
147 C5 Churchtown Cork Rep. of Ireland
234 C2 Churchtown PA U.S.A.
234 B3 Churchville MD U.S.A.
232 D5 Churchville VA U.S.A.
106 A1 Chureg-Tag, Gora mt. Rus. Fed.
117 F4 Churia Ghati Hills Nepal
252 A2 Churin Peru
129 E2 Churkey Rus. Fed.
129 E2 Churkeyskoye Vodokhranilishche resr Rus. Fed.
134 I4 Churov Rus. Fed.
137 G1 Churovichi Rus. Fed.
116 C3 Churu Rajasthan India
Churubay Nura Karagandinskaya Oblast' Kazakh. see Abay
226 E5 Churubusco IN U.S.A.
250 D2 Churuguara Venez.
190 E2 Churwalden Switz.
116 D2 Chushul Jammu and Kashmir
241 M3 Chuska Mountains NM U.S.A.
134 L4 Chusovaya r. Rus. Fed.
134 L4 Chusovoy Rus. Fed.
Chust Ukr. see Khust
121 G4 Chust Uzbek.
225 G3 Chute-des-Passes Que. Can.
227 I2 Chute-Rouge Que. Can.
137 H3 Chutove Ukr.
109 G3 Chutung Taiwan
78 □4a Chuuk is Micronesia
Chuvashia aut. rep. Rus. Fed. see Chuvashskaya Respublika
Chuvashskaya A.S.S.R. aut. rep. Rus. Fed. see Chuvashskaya Respublika
135 I5 Chuvashskaya Respublika aut. rep. Rus. Fed.
108 B3 Chuxiong Yunnan China
121 H4 Chüy admin. div. Kyrg.
258 G4 Chuy Uru.
97 E4 Chư Yang Sin mt. Vietnam
Chuyskaya Oblast' admin. div. Kyrg. see Chüy
160 C3 Chuzelles France
109 F1 Chuzhou Anhui China
176 D3 Chvalšiny Czech Rep.
127 G4 Chwārtā Iraq
174 G1 Chwaszczyno Pol.
Chwitffordd Flintshire, Wales U.K. see Whitford
174 G6 Chybie Pol.
136 F4 Chychykliya r. Ukr.
121 G3 Chyganak Kazakh.
137 G3 Chyhyryn Ukr.
Chymyshliya Moldova see Cimişlia
136 B3 Chynadiyeve Ukr.
171 F5 Chýňava Czech Rep.
175 J4 Chynów Pol.
Chystyakove Ukr. see Torez
211 C5 Chyulu Range mts Kenya
175 M6 Chyzhykiv Ukr.
196 E3 Ciacova Romania
Ciadâr-Lunga Moldova see Ciadîr-Lunga
136 E4 Ciadîr-Lunga Moldova
163 C5 Ciadoux France
193 H5 Ciagola, Monte mt. Italy
247 □1 Ciales Puerto Rico
192 B3 Ciamannacce Corse France
95 E4 Ciamis Jawa Barat Indon.
193 E3 Ciampino Italy
193 E3 Ciampino airport Italy
193 C5 Cianciana Sicilia Italy
94 D4 Cianjur Jawa Barat Indon.
256 A5 Cianorte Brazil
161 F5 Cians r. France
174 G5 Ciasna Pol.
175 H4 Ciążeń Pol.
94 D4 Cibadak Jawa Barat Indon.
177 J5 Cibakháza Hungary
95 E4 Cibatu Jawa Barat Indon.
241 L4 Cibecue AZ U.S.A.
94 D4 Cibinong Jawa Barat Indon.
211 A5 Cibitoke Burundi
237 D6 Cibolo Creek r. TX U.S.A.
184 B2 Ciborro Port.
94 D4 Ci Buni r. Indon.
242 C2 Cibuta, Sierra mt. Mex.
190 E4 Cicagna Italy
188 D3 Čičarija mts Croatia
193 G4 Cicciano Italy
126 D3 Çiçekdağı Turkey
128 B1 Çiçekli Turkey
199 F2 Çiçekli Turkey
193 H4 Cicerale Italy
226 D5 Cicero IL U.S.A.
254 F4 Cicero Dantas Brazil
196 E4 Ćićevac Srbija Yugo.
174 E4 Cicha Woda r. Pol.
175 L3 Cicibór Duży Pol.
177 G4 Čičov Slovakia
183 I2 Cidacos r. Spain
126 D2 Cide Turkey
176 E1 Cidlina r. Czech Rep.
183 H3 Cidones Spain
247 □1 Cidra Puerto Rico
175 I3 Ciechanów Pol.
175 K3 Ciechanowiec Pol.
174 G3 Ciechocinek Pol.
246 C2 Ciego de Avila Cuba
175 I4 Ciełądz Pol.
260 C3 Cielo, Cerro mt. Arg.
183 G4 Ciempozuelos Spain
250 C2 Ciénaga Col.
246 B2 Cienfuegos Cuba
174 F3 Cienin Zaborny Pol.
174 F5 Ciepielów Pol.
174 E5 Ciepłowody Pol.
163 C6 Cier-de-Luchon France
177 G3 Čierna Voda Slovakia
177 I3 Čierna voda r. Slovakia
177 K3 Čierne Kľačany Slovakia
177 I3 Čierny Balog Slovakia
163 C6 Cierp-Gaud France
174 F2 Cierznie Pol.
175 L5 Cieszanów Pol.
174 F4 Cieszków Pol.
174 G6 Cieszyn Śląskie Pol.
174 F4 Cieszyn Wielkopolskie Pol.
163 C5 Cieutat France
162 D3 Cieux France
187 B6 Cieza Spain
175 I6 Ciężkowice Pol.
128 C1 Çiflikköy Turkey
199 G2 Çifteler Turkey
Çiftlik Turkey see Kelkit
129 B4 Çiftlikköy Turkey
199 F1 Çiftlikköy Turkey
183 F3 Cifuentes Spain
183 F3 Cigales Spain
177 J4 Cigánd Hungary
190 D3 Cigliano Italy
183 G5 Cigüela r. Spain
126 D3 Cihanbeyli Turkey
199 F2 Cihangazi Turkey
244 B4 Cihuatlán Mex.
185 F1 Cijara, Embalse de resr Spain
177 J6 Čik r. Yugo.
Cikai Yunnan China see Gongshan
198 A1 Çikes, Maja e mt. Albania
79 □1 Cikobia i. Fiji
188 F4 Čikola r. Croatia
95 E4 Cilacap Jawa Tengah Indon.
127 F2 Çıldır Turkey
127 F2 Çıldır Gölü l. Turkey
95 E4 Ciledug Jawa Barat Indon.
109 D2 Cili Hunan China
197 G4 Cilieni Romania
199 G1 Çilimli Turkey
Cill Airne Rep. of Ireland see Killarney
183 I4 Cillas Spain
Cill Chainnigh Rep. of Ireland see Kilkenny
146 A4 Cille Bhrighde Western Isles, Scotland U.K.
182 D4 Cilleros Spain
Cill Mhantáin Rep. of Ireland see Wicklow
127 G3 Çilo Dağı mt. Turkey
129 G3 Çiloy Azer.
150 D3 Cilybebyll Neath Port Talbot, Wales U.K.
150 D2 Cilycwm Carmarthenshire, Wales U.K.
241 J4 Cima CA U.S.A.
94 D4 Cimahi Jawa Barat Indon.
182 E2 Cimanes del Tejar Spain
237 C4 Cimarron KS U.S.A.
239 F4 Cimarron NM U.S.A.
237 D4 Cimarron r. OK U.S.A.
239 F4 Cimarron Creek r. CO U.S.A.
183 I3 Cimballa Spain
194 C5 Ciminna Sicilia Italy
192 E2 Cimino, Monte mt. Italy
136 E4 Cimişlia Moldova
191 H2 Cimolais Italy
191 F4 Cimone, Monte mt. Italy
Cîmpeni Romania see Câmpeni
Cîmpia Turzii Romania see Câmpia Turzii
Cîmpina Romania see Câmpina
Cîmpulung Romania see Câmpulung
Cîmpulung la Tisa Romania see Câmpulung la Tisa
Cîmpulung Moldovenesc Romania see Câmpulung Moldovenesc
127 F3 Çınar Turkey
199 F1 Çınarcık Turkey
250 E3 Cinaruco r. Venez.
186 D3 Cinca r. Spain
186 D2 Cinca, Canal de r. Spain
188 F4 Cincar mt. Bos.-Herz.
236 G4 Cincinnati OH U.S.A.
233 F3 Cincinnatus NY U.S.A.
185 G1 Cinco Casas Spain
Cinco de Outubro Angola see Xá-Muteba
260 C6 Cinco Saltos Arg.
186 C4 Cinctorres Spain
197 G3 Cincu Romania
150 E3 Cinderford Gloucestershire, England U.K.
199 F3 Çine Turkey
199 E3 Çine r. Turkey
182 E2 Ciñera Spain
165 E4 Ciney Belgium
182 B3 Cinfães Port.
191 I5 Cingoli Italy
192 D2 Cinigiano Italy
190 E3 Cinisello Balsamo Italy
194 C4 Cinisi Sicilia Italy
177 I3 Činobaňa Slovakia
159 G4 Cinq-Mars-la-Pile France
195 F4 Cinquefrondi Italy
190 E4 Cinque Terre reg. Italy
245 H5 Cintalapa Mex.
163 D5 Cintegabelle France
192 A2 Cinto, Monte mt. France
185 F1 Cintrey France
183 I2 Cintruénigo Spain
215 G5 Cintsa S. Africa
256 B5 Cinzas r. Brazil
197 H3 Ciolpani Romania
177 L6 Ciordan, Dealul hill Romania
188 F4 Čiovo i. Croatia
Ciping Jiangxi China see Jinggangshan
254 F4 Cipó Brazil
257 E3 Cipó r. Brazil
260 D6 Cipolletti Arg.
257 F4 Cipotânea Brazil
187 C4 Cirat Spain
182 E2 Cirbanal mt. Spain
193 G3 Circello Italy
193 F3 Circeo, Monte hill Italy
220 D3 Circle AK U.S.A.
238 F2 Circle MT U.S.A.
232 B5 Circleville OH U.S.A.
241 K2 Circleville UT U.S.A.
95 E4 Cirebon Jawa Barat Indon.
151 F3 Cirencester Gloucestershire, England U.K.
Cirene tourist site Libya see Cyrene
157 E4 Cirey-sur-Blaise France
157 G4 Cirey-sur-Vezouze France
183 I3 Ciria Spain
190 C3 Ciriè Italy
193 I4 Cirigliano Italy
136 D4 Ciripcău Moldova
159 G3 Cirò Italy
177 K3 Cirocha r. Slovakia
195 G3 Cirò Marina Italy
163 B4 Ciron r. France
225 I1 Cirque Mountain Nfld. Can.
Cirta Alg. see Constantine
183 G5 Ciruelos Spain
160 C2 Ciry-le-Noble France
190 D4 Cisano sul Neva Italy
241 M2 Cisco UT U.S.A.
178 C4 Cismòn r. Italy
175 K6 Cisna Pol.
196 F3 Cisnădie Romania
183 F2 Cisneros Spain
191 H3 Cisòn di Valmarino Italy
159 G5 Cissé France
193 E3 Cisterna di Latina Italy
195 G2 Cisternino Italy
182 E2 Cistierna Spain
246 D3 Citadelle Laferrière tourist site Haiti
191 H5 Citerna Italy
245 F3 Citlaltépec Mex.
Citlaltépetl vol. Mex. see Orizaba, Pico de
188 F4 Čitluk Bos.-Herz.
163 E5 Citou France
237 F6 Citronelle AL U.S.A.
214 B5 Citrusdal S. Africa
240 C2 Citrus Heights CA U.S.A.
191 G3 Cittadella Italy
192 E2 Città della Pieve Italy
191 H5 Città di Castello Italy
190 C3 Città di Torino airport Italy
193 E2 Cittaducale Italy
195 F4 Cittanova Italy
193 E2 Cittareale Italy
193 G2 Città Sant'Angelo Italy
190 D3 Cittiglio Italy
147 D1 City of Derry airport Northern Ireland U.K.
197 G3 Ciucaș, Vârful mt. Romania
197 F2 Ciucea Romania
243 E2 Ciudad Acuña Mex.
244 D4 Ciudad Altamirano Mex.
251 F2 Ciudad Bolívar Venez.
242 D3 Ciudad Camargo Mex.
243 E5 Ciudad Constitución Mex.
242 D3 Ciudad Cuauhtémoc Mex.
243 H5 Ciudad del Carmen Mex.
253 G6 Ciudad del Este Para.
242 D2 Ciudad Delicias Mex.
245 E2 Ciudad del Maíz Mex.
245 E3 Ciudad de Valles Mex.
251 F2 Ciudad Guayana Venez.
242 C4 Ciudad Guzmán Mex.
244 D4 Ciudad Hidalgo Mex.
245 G5 Ciudad Ixtepec Mex.
242 D2 Ciudad Juárez Mex.
242 D3 Ciudad Lerdo Mex.
245 E4 Ciudad López Mateos Mex.
245 F2 Ciudad Madero Mex.
245 E2 Ciudad Mante Mex.
244 D3 Ciudad Manuel Doblado Mex.
245 F4 Ciudad Mendoza Mex.
243 F3 Ciudad Mier Mex.
242 C3 Ciudad Obregón Mex.
185 G2 Ciudad Real Spain
185 G2 Ciudad Real prov. Castilla - La Mancha Spain
243 F3 Ciudad Río Bravo Mex.
182 D4 Ciudad Rodrigo Spain
245 F4 Ciudad Serdán Mex.
Ciudad Trujillo Dom. Rep. see Santo Domingo
245 E2 Ciudad Victoria Mex.
197 E3 Ciudanovița Romania
177 L4 Ciuhoi Romania
136 D4 Ciuhur r. Moldova
136 D4 Ciulucul de Mijloc r. Moldova
197 G2 Ciumani Romania
177 K5 Ciumeghiu Romania
186 □ Ciutadella de Menorca Spain
162 C2 Civaux France
191 H2 Cividale del Friuli Italy
191 I2 Civita Italy
193 E2 Civita Castellana Italy
193 F3 Civita d'Antino Italy
191 I5 Civitanova Marche Italy
193 F2 Civitaquana Italy
192 D2 Civitavecchia Italy
192 D2 Civitella, Monte mt. Italy
193 F2 Civitella Casanova Italy
193 F2 Civitella d'Agliano Italy
191 G4 Civitella di Romagna Italy
191 G5 Civitella in Val di Chiana Italy
193 F3 Civitella Roveto Italy
159 I5 Civray Centre France
162 C2 Civray Poitou-Charentes France
199 F2 Çivril Turkey
192 B5 Cixerri r. Sardegna Italy
109 G2 Cixi Zhejiang China
108 E1 Cixian Hebei China
177 L4 Cizer Romania
Cizhou Hebei China see Cixian
171 F5 Čížkovice Czech Rep.
127 F3 Cizre Turkey
176 C2 Čkyně Czech Rep.
146 B5 Clabhach Argyll and Bute, Scotland U.K.
146 C6 Clachan Argyll and Bute, Scotland U.K.
146 B4 Clachan Highland, Scotland U.K.
238 B2 Clackamas r. OR U.S.A.
146 E5 Clackmannanshire admin. div. Scotland U.K.
151 I3 Clacton-on-Sea Essex, England U.K.
146 C5 Cladich Argyll and Bute, Scotland U.K.
147 B3 Clady Northern Ireland U.K.
147 E2 Clady Northern Ireland U.K.
146 C5 Claggan Highland, Scotland U.K.
162 C2 Clain r. France
163 C4 Clairac France
223 H3 Claire, Lake Alta Can.
222 G4 Clairmont Alta Can.
156 C3 Clairoix France
163 E4 Clairvaux-d'Aveyron France
160 D2 Clairvaux-les-Lacs France
162 C2 Claise r. France
161 D3 Claix France
160 B1 Clamecy France
226 B2 Clam Lake WI U.S.A.
148 B3 Clanabogan Northern Ireland U.K.
240 I2 Clan Alpine Mountains NV U.S.A.
81 C6 Clandeboye South I. N.Z.
147 E3 Clane Rep. of Ireland
151 F3 Clanfield Oxfordshire, England U.K.
161 F4 Clans France
231 C5 Clanton AL U.S.A.
215 F4 Clanville S. Africa
214 B5 Clanwilliam S. Africa
146 C6 Claonaig Argyll and Bute, Scotland U.K.
151 G2 Clapham Bedfordshire, England U.K.
149 G3 Clapham North Yorkshire, England U.K.
261 H2 Clara Arg.
85 E3 Clara r. Qld Austr.
147 D3 Clara Rep. of Ireland
85 E3 Claraville Qld Austr.
149 I4 Clarborough Nottinghamshire, England U.K.
83 E3 Clare N.S.W. Austr.
82 D3 Clare S.A. Austr.
147 C4 Clare county Rep. of Ireland
147 B3 Clare r. Rep. of Ireland
151 H2 Clare Suffolk, England U.K.
226 E4 Clare MI U.S.A.
147 C4 Clarecastle Rep. of Ireland
147 D3 Clareen Rep. of Ireland
147 C3 Claregalway Rep. of Ireland
147 A3 Clare Island Rep. of Ireland
246 □ Claremont Jamaica
233 G3 Claremont NH U.S.A.
85 E2 Claremont Isles Qld Austr.
237 E4 Claremore OK U.S.A.
147 C3 Claremorris Rep. of Ireland
83 H2 Clarence r. N.S.W. Austr.
81 D5 Clarence South I. N.Z.
81 D5 Clarence r. South I. N.Z.
259 C9 Clarence, Isla i. Chile
263 A2 Clarence Island Antarctica
84 B1 Clarence Strait N.T. Austr.
222 C3 Clarence Strait AK U.S.A.
246 D2 Clarence Town Long I. Bahamas
246 □ Clarendon parish Jamaica
81 C7 Clarendon South I. N.Z.
237 F5 Clarendon AR U.S.A.
232 D4 Clarendon PA U.S.A.
237 C5 Clarendon TX U.S.A.
246 □ Clarendon Park Jamaica
215 G3 Clarens S. Africa
225 K3 Clarenville Nfld. Can.
222 H5 Claresholm Alta Can.
161 B5 Claret Languedoc-Roussillon France
161 D4 Claret Provence-Alpes-Côte-d'Azur France
187 C5 Clariano r. Spain
85 E3 Clarina Creek r. Qld Austr.
236 E3 Clarinda IA U.S.A.
232 C5 Clarington OH U.S.A.
236 E3 Clarion IA U.S.A.
232 D4 Clarion PA U.S.A.
232 D4 Clarion r. PA U.S.A.
246 D2 Clarion Bank sea feature Bahamas
80 E2 Claris North I. N.Z.
236 D2 Clark SD U.S.A.
223 M1 Clark, Point N.W.T. Can.
234 B2 Clark Creek r. PA U.S.A.
241 K4 Clarkdale AZ U.S.A.
85 F3 Clarke r. Qld Austr.
215 G4 Clarkebury S. Africa
85 F4 Clarke Range mts Qld Austr.
85 F3 Clarke River Qld Austr.
85 E3 Clarkes Creek r. Qld Austr.
225 K3 Clarke's Head Nfld. Can.
231 D5 Clarkesville GA U.S.A.
238 C1 Clark Fork r. ID U.S.A.
238 C1 Clark Fork r. MT U.S.A.
231 D5 Clark Hill Reservoir Georgia/S. Carolina U.S.A.
241 J4 Clark Mountain CA U.S.A.
262 O1 Clark Mountains Antarctica
235 D2 Clarksburg NJ U.S.A.
232 C5 Clarksburg WV U.S.A.
237 F5 Clarksdale MS U.S.A.
238 E2 Clark's Fork Yellowstone r. MT U.S.A.
81 C6 Clarks Junction South I. N.Z.
214 E6 Clarkson S. Africa
234 C1 Clarks Summit PA U.S.A.
238 C2 Clarkston WA U.S.A.
246 □ Clark's Town Jamaica
237 E5 Clarksville AR U.S.A.
234 B3 Clarksville MD U.S.A.
231 C4 Clarksville TN U.S.A.
237 E5 Clarksville TX U.S.A.
232 D6 Clarksville VA U.S.A.
256 B1 Claro r. Mato Grosso Brazil
256 B3 Claro r. Goiás Brazil
190 E2 Claro Switz.
156 D2 Clary France
146 D4 Clashmore Highland, Scotland U.K.
146 C3 Clashnessie Highland, Scotland U.K.
238 B2 Clatskanie OR U.S.A.
237 C5 Claude TX U.S.A.
257 E4 Cláudio Brazil
147 D2 Claudy Northern Ireland U.K.
171 J2 Clausnitz Ger.
234 C2 Claussville PA U.S.A.
169 F4 Clausthal-Zellerfeld Ger.
191 H2 Claut Italy
191 H2 Clauzetto Italy
92 B2 Claveria Phil.
151 H3 Clavering Essex, England U.K.
150 E2 Claverley Shropshire, England U.K.
165 E4 Clavier Belgium
231 D5 Claxton GA U.S.A.
234 B2 Clay PA U.S.A.
232 C5 Clay WV U.S.A.
233 G2 Clayburg NY U.S.A.
236 D4 Clay Center KS U.S.A.
236 D3 Clay Center NE U.S.A.
232 B6 Clay City KY U.S.A.
149 H4 Clay Cross Derbyshire, England U.K.
151 I2 Claydon Suffolk, England U.K.
156 C4 Claye-Souilly France
234 C3 Claymont DE U.S.A.
149 I4 Claypole Lincolnshire, England U.K.
241 L5 Claypool AZ U.S.A.
241 L4 Clay Springs AZ U.S.A.
151 G4 Clayton West Sussex, England U.K.
231 C6 Clayton AL U.S.A.
234 C3 Clayton DE U.S.A.
231 D5 Clayton GA U.S.A.
234 C3 Clayton NJ U.S.A.
237 C4 Clayton NM U.S.A.
233 E2 Clayton NY U.S.A.
237 E5 Clayton OK U.S.A.
233 □I1 Clayton Lake ME U.S.A.
149 G4 Clayton-le-Moors Lancashire, England U.K.
261 H3 Clé r. Arg.
146 B5 Cleadale Highland, Scotland U.K.
149 H3 Cleadon Tyne and Wear, England U.K.
147 B5 Cleady Rep. of Ireland
147 B5 Clear, Cape Rep. of Ireland
232 C5 Clearco WV U.S.A.
227 G4 Clear Creek Ont. Can.
241 L2 Clear Creek UT U.S.A.
241 L4 Clear Creek r. AZ U.S.A.
238 F2 Clear Creek r. WY U.S.A.
232 D4 Clearfield PA U.S.A.
238 D3 Clearfield UT U.S.A.
237 D5 Clear Fork Brazos r. TX U.S.A.
222 G3 Clear Hills Y.T. Can.
147 B5 Clear Island Rep. of Ireland
236 E3 Clear Lake IA U.S.A.
236 D2 Clear Lake SD U.S.A.
226 A3 Clear Lake WI U.S.A.
240 F2 Clearlake Oaks CA U.S.A.
238 F2 Clearmont WY U.S.A.
232 E5 Clear Spring MD U.S.A.
222 G5 Clearwater B.C. Can.
223 I3 Clearwater r. Alberta/Saskatchewan Can.
222 H4 Clearwater r. Alta Can.
231 D7 Clearwater FL U.S.A.
238 C2 Clearwater r. ID U.S.A.
236 E2 Clearwater r. MN U.S.A.
226 C3 Clearwater Lake WI U.S.A.
238 D2 Clearwater Mountains ID U.S.A.
149 F3 Cleator Moor Cumbria, England U.K.
237 D5 Cleburne TX U.S.A.
159 F3 Clécy France
158 C3 Cléder France
150 E2 Cleehill Shropshire, England U.K.
238 B2 Cle Elum WA U.S.A.
149 I4 Cleethorpes North East Lincolnshire, England U.K.
157 F4 Clefmont France
158 C4 Cléguer France
158 C3 Cléguérec France
150 E2 Clehonger Herefordshire, England U.K.
197 G3 Clejani Romania
161 D4 Clelles France
155 E5 Clémency Lux.
256 B4 Clementina Brazil
231 D5 Clemson SC U.S.A.
232 C5 Clendenin WV U.S.A.
168 F3 Clenze Ger.
150 E2 Cleobury Mortimer Shropshire, England U.K.
156 B3 Cléon France
234 B2 Cleona PA U.S.A.
161 C4 Cléon-d'Andran France
92 A4 Cleopatra Needle mt. Palawan Phil.
159 G4 Cléré-les-Pins France
156 B3 Clères France
156 E4 Clérey France
Clerf Lux. see Clervaux
227 H1 Cléricy Que. Can.
161 C3 Clérieux France
81 B6 Clerke, Mount South I. N.Z.
86 B3 Clerke Reef W.A. Austr.
160 C2 Clermain France
85 F4 Clermont Qld Austr.
163 D5 Clermont Midi-Pyrénées France
156 C3 Clermont Picardie France
215 H3 Clermont S. Africa
231 D6 Clermont FL U.S.A.
159 F4 Clermont-Créans France
162 C4 Clermont-de-Beauregard France
Clermont de Tonnère atoll Arch. des Tuamotu Fr. Polynesia see Reao
157 F3 Clermont-en-Argonne France
160 B3 Clermont-Ferrand France
161 B5 Clermont-l'Hérault France
160 E1 Clerval France
155 E4 Clervaux Lux.
165 F5 Clervé r. Lux.
164 C4 Cléry r. France
156 B5 Cléry-St-André France
191 G2 Cles Italy
82 D3 Cleve S.A. Austr.
150 E3 Clevedon North Somerset, England U.K.
231 D5 Cleveland GA U.S.A.
237 F5 Cleveland MS U.S.A.
232 C4 Cleveland OH U.S.A.
231 C5 Cleveland TN U.S.A.
237 E6 Cleveland TX U.S.A.
241 L2 Cleveland UT U.S.A.
232 B6 Cleveland VA U.S.A.
226 D4 Cleveland WI U.S.A.
85 F3 Cleveland, Cape Qld Austr.
238 D1 Cleveland, Mount MT U.S.A.
85 F3 Cleveland Bay Qld Austr.
232 C4 Cleveland Heights OH U.S.A.
149 H3 Cleveland Hills England U.K.
255 B8 Clevelândia Brazil
149 F4 Cleveleys Lancashire, England U.K.
Cleves Ger. see Kleve
147 B3 Clew Bay Rep. of Ireland
215 G1 Clewer S. Africa
231 D7 Clewiston FL U.S.A.
81 A7 Clifden South I. N.Z.
147 A3 Clifden Rep. of Ireland
84 D3 Cliffdale r. Qld Austr.
151 H3 Cliffe Medway, England U.K.
151 H3 Cliffe Woods Medway, England U.K.
147 C2 Cliffoney Rep. of Ireland
215 F4 Clifford S. Africa
234 C1 Clifford PA U.S.A.
234 C5 Clifford VA U.S.A.
85 G5 Clifton Qld Austr.
151 G2 Clifton Bedfordshire, England U.K.
241 M5 Clifton AZ U.S.A.
226 D5 Clifton IL U.S.A.
236 D4 Clifton KS U.S.A.
235 D2 Clifton NJ U.S.A.
237 D6 Clifton TX U.S.A.
234 C1 Clifton VA U.S.A.
85 F3 Clifton Beach Qld Austr.
232 D6 Clifton Forge VA U.S.A.
82 D1 Clifton Hills S.A. Austr.
233 G3 Clifton Park NY U.S.A.
223 I5 Climax Sask. Can.
226 E4 Climax MI U.S.A.
232 B6 Clinch r. TN U.S.A.
232 B6 Clinchco VA U.S.A.
232 B6 Clinch Mountain mts TN/VA U.S.A.
232 B6 Clinchport VA U.S.A.
222 G4 Cline River Alta Can.
165 D3 Clinge Neth.
169 F4 Clingen Ger.
222 F5 Clinton B.C. Can.
224 D5 Clinton Ont. Can.
81 B7 Clinton South I. N.Z.
237 E5 Clinton AR U.S.A.
235 F1 Clinton CT U.S.A.
230 B3 Clinton IA U.S.A.
236 F3 Clinton IL U.S.A.
237 F4 Clinton KY U.S.A.
237 F6 Clinton LA U.S.A.
233 □I2 Clinton ME U.S.A.
227 F4 Clinton MI U.S.A.
236 E4 Clinton MO U.S.A.
237 F5 Clinton MS U.S.A.
231 E5 Clinton NC U.S.A.
233 F3 Clinton NY U.S.A.
232 C4 Clinton OH U.S.A.
237 D5 Clinton OK U.S.A.
231 D5 Clinton SC U.S.A.
231 C4 Clinton TN U.S.A.
223 J1 Clinton-Colden Lake N.W.T. Can.
226 C3 Clintonville WI U.S.A.
232 C6 Clintonville WV U.S.A.
232 B6 Clintwood VA U.S.A.
231 C6 Clio AL U.S.A.
227 F4 Clio MI U.S.A.
159 H5 Clion France
218 E7 Clipperton, Île terr. N. Pacific Ocean
146 B4 Clisham hill Scotland U.K.
158 E4 Clisson France
149 G4 Clitheroe Lancashire, England U.K.
80 F3 Clive North I. N.Z.
252 D4 Cliza Bol.
87 B4 Cloates, Point W.A. Austr.
215 F3 Clocolan S. Africa
147 D4 Clogh Kilkenny Rep. of Ireland
147 E4 Clogh Wexford Rep. of Ireland
147 E2 Clogh Northern Ireland U.K.
147 D2 Cloghan Donegal Rep. of Ireland
147 D3 Cloghan Offaly Rep. of Ireland
148 B4 Cloghan Westmeath Rep. of Ireland
147 A4 Cloghane Rep. of Ireland
147 F2 Cloghboy Rep. of Ireland
147 D4 Clogheen Rep. of Ireland
147 B3 Clogher Rep. of Ireland
147 D2 Clogher Northern Ireland U.K.
147 E3 Clogherhead Rep. of Ireland
147 E1 Clogh Mills Northern Ireland U.K.
147 F2 Cloghy Northern Ireland U.K.
147 E4 Clohamon Rep. of Ireland
158 C4 Clohars-Carnoët France
85 E4 Clonagh Qld Austr.
147 C5 Clonakilty Rep. of Ireland
147 D3 Clonard Rep. of Ireland
147 D3 Clonaslee Rep. of Ireland
84 E4 Cloncurry Qld Austr.
85 E3 Cloncurry r. Qld Austr.
147 E3 Clondalkin Rep. of Ireland
147 D4 Clonea Rep. of Ireland
147 E3 Clonee Rep. of Ireland
147 D4 Cloneen Rep. of Ireland
147 E4 Clonegal Rep. of Ireland
147 D2 Clones Rep. of Ireland
147 D1 Clonmany Rep. of Ireland
147 D4 Clonmel Rep. of Ireland
147 D3 Clonmellon Rep. of Ireland
147 E4 Clonmore Carlow Rep. of Ireland
147 D4 Clonmore Tipperary Rep. of Ireland
147 D3 Clonopy Rep. of Ireland
147 D4 Clonoulty Rep. of Ireland
147 E4 Clonroche Rep. of Ireland
147 E3 Clontarf Rep. of Ireland
147 E2 Clontibret Rep. of Ireland
147 D3 Clonygowan Rep. of Ireland
147 C2 Cloonacool Rep. of Ireland
147 B4 Cloonbannin Rep. of Ireland
147 B3 Cloonboo Rep. of Ireland
147 D3 Cloone Rep. of Ireland
148 B4 Clooneagh Rep. of Ireland
147 C3 Cloonfad Roscommon Rep. of Ireland
147 C3 Cloonfad Roscommon Rep. of Ireland
147 B3 Cloonkeen Rep. of Ireland
147 C3 Cloontia Rep. of Ireland
222 E5 Clo-oose B.C. Can.
168 D3 Cloppenburg Ger.
226 A2 Cloquet MN U.S.A.
226 A2 Cloquet r. MN U.S.A.
258 F2 Clorinda Arg.
146 E6 Closeburn Dumfries and Galloway, Scotland U.K.
226 C1 Cloud Bay Ont. Can.
238 F2 Cloud Peak WY U.S.A.
81 E4 Cloudy Bay South I. N.Z.
162 C2 Clouère r. France
147 F2 Clough Northern Ireland U.K.
149 I3 Cloughton North Yorkshire, England U.K.
146 □G1 Clousta Shetland, Scotland U.K.
227 F3 Clova Que. Can.
146 E5 Clova Angus, Scotland U.K.
150 C3 Clovelly Devon, England U.K.
146 F6 Clovenfords Scottish Borders, Scotland U.K.
241 K1 Clover UT U.S.A.
240 F2 Cloverdale CA U.S.A.
240 H3 Clovis CA U.S.A.
237 C5 Clovis NM U.S.A.
146 C5 Clovullin Highland, Scotland U.K.
149 H4 Clowne Derbyshire, England U.K.
156 B5 Cloyes-sur-le-Loir France
227 I3 Cloyne Ont. Can.
147 C5 Cloyne Rep. of Ireland
Cluain Meala Rep. of Ireland see Clonmel
146 C4 Cluanie, Loch l. Scotland U.K.
223 I3 Cluff Lake Mine Sask. Can.
162 D2 Cluis France
197 F2 Cluj-Napoca Romania
161 E4 Clumanc France
150 D2 Clun Shropshire, England U.K.
150 D2 Clun r. England U.K.
146 D5 Clunes Highland, Scotland U.K.
84 D5 Cluny Qld Austr.
160 C2 Cluny France
160 E2 Cluses France
Clusium Italy see Chiusi
190 E3 Clusone Italy
232 D6 Cluster Springs VA U.S.A.
81 B7 Clutha r. South I. N.Z.
87 E5 Clutterbuck Hills hill W.A. Austr.
150 E3 Clutton Bath and North East Somerset, England U.K.
150 D1 Clwydian Range hills Wales U.K.
150 D3 Clydach Swansea, Wales U.K.
150 D3 Clydach Vale Rhondda Cynon Taff, Wales U.K.
222 H4 Clyde Alta Can.
81 B6 Clyde South I. N.Z.
146 D6 Clyde r. Scotland U.K.
232 E3 Clyde NY U.S.A.
232 B4 Clyde OH U.S.A.
146 D6 Clyde, Firth of est. Scotland U.K.
146 D6 Clydebank West Dunbartonshire, Scotland U.K.
221 L2 Clyde River Nunavut Can.
146 E6 Clydesdale val. Scotland U.K.
81 B7 Clydevale South I. N.Z.
226 C4 Clyman WI U.S.A.
232 D4 Clymer PA U.S.A.
150 C3 Clynderwen Carmarthenshire, Wales U.K.
150 D2 Clyro Powys, Wales U.K.
175 J5 Ćmielów Pol.
146 E4 Cnoc Fraing hill Scotland U.K.
146 C6 Cnoc Moy hill Scotland U.K.
Cnossus tourist site Greece see Knosos
182 C3 Côa r. Port.
245 E4 Coacalco Mex.
241 I5 Coachella CA U.S.A.
147 C5 Coachford Rep. of Ireland
147 E2 Coagh Northern Ireland U.K.
242 E3 Coahuila state Mex.
222 E3 Coal r. Y.T. Can.
146 E6 Coalburn South Lanarkshire, Scotland U.K.
226 C5 Coal City IL U.S.A.
244 C4 Coalcomán r. Mex.
223 H5 Coaldale Alta Can.
240 I2 Coaldale NV U.S.A.
234 C2 Coaldale PA U.S.A.
237 D5 Coalgate OK U.S.A.
232 B5 Coal Grove OH U.S.A.
222 E5 Coal Harbour B.C. Can.
240 G3 Coalinga CA U.S.A.
147 E2 Coalisland Northern Ireland U.K.
232 D4 Coalport PA U.S.A.
222 E3 Coal River B.C. Can.
215 G2 Coalville S. Africa
151 F2 Coalville Leicestershire, England U.K.
238 E3 Coalville UT U.S.A.
247 □1 Coamo Puerto Rico
182 D1 Coaña Spain
251 F6 Coari Brazil
251 F6 Coari r. Brazil
251 F6 Coari, Lago l. Brazil
163 E5 Coarraze France
240 H3 Coarsegold CA U.S.A.
252 C3 Coasa Peru
211 D5 Coast prov. Kenya
Coast admin. reg. Tanz. see Pwani
197 H1 Coasta Ibăneștilor ridge Romania
237 E6 Coastal Plain U.S.A.
222 E4 Coast Mountains B.C. Can.
85 G5 Coast Range hills Qld Austr.
240 F1 Coast Ranges mts CA U.S.A.
146 D6 Coatbridge North Lanarkshire, Scotland U.K.
245 F4 Coatepec Mex.
245 E4 Coatepec Harinas Mex.
243 H6 Coatepeque Guat.
234 C3 Coatesville PA U.S.A.
225 G4 Coaticook Que. Can.
221 J3 Coats Island Nunavut Can.
262 V1 Coats Land reg. Antarctica
245 G4 Coatzacoalcos Mex.
245 G4 Coatzacoalcos r. Mex.
245 F3 Coatzintla Mex.
197 I3 Cobadin Romania
227 H2 Cobalt Ont. Can.
235 F1 Cobalt CT U.S.A.
243 H6 Cobán Guat.
129 D3 Çobandağ hill Azer./Georgia
199 G2 Çobanlar Turkey
83 F2 Cobar N.S.W. Austr.
83 G4 Cobargo N.S.W. Austr.
87 E5 Cobb, Lake salt flat W.A. Austr.
83 E4 Cobden Vic. Austr.
227 I3 Cobden Ont. Can.
183 G4 Cobeja Spain
183 H4 Cobeta Spain
147 C5 Cobh Rep. of Ireland
223 M4 Cobham r. Man./Ont. Can.
151 G3 Cobham Surrey, England U.K.
252 C2 Cobija Bol.
Coblenz Ger. see Koblenz
233 F3 Cobleskill NY U.S.A.
148 C4 Coblinstown Rep. of Ireland
222 C3 Cobol AK U.S.A.
224 E5 Cobourg Ont. Can.
84 C1 Cobourg Peninsula N.T. Austr.
260 A5 Cobquecura Chile
87 C5 Cobra W.A. Austr.
83 F3 Cobram Vic. Austr.
184 C3 Cobres r. Port.
211 B8 Cóbuè Moz.
169 F5 Coburg Ger.
183 F3 Coca Spain
252 C4 Cocachacra Peru
254 E2 Cocal Brazil
234 B2 Cocalico Creek r. PA U.S.A.
254 C5 Cocalinho Brazil
Cocanada Andhra Prad. India see Kakinada
252 D4 Cocapata Bol.
193 H4 Coccovello, Monte mt. Italy
187 C6 Cocentaina Spain
252 D4 Cochabamba Bol.
252 D4 Cochabamba dept Bol.
259 B6 Cochamó Chile
260 A5 Cocharcas Chile
169 C5 Cochem Ger.
114 C4 Cochin Kerala India
241 M5 Cochise AZ U.S.A.
241 M5 Cochise Head mt. AZ U.S.A.
231 D5 Cochran GA U.S.A.
222 H5 Cochrane Alta Can.
224 D4 Cochrane Ont. Can.
223 K3 Cochrane r. Sask. Can.
232 C4 Cochranton PA U.S.A.
234 C3 Cochranville PA U.S.A.
171 C4 Cochstedt Ger.
177 L5 Cociuba Mare Romania
82 C3 Cockaleechie S.A. Austr.
146 E4 Cock Bridge Aberdeenshire, Scotland U.K.
82 E3 Cockburn S.A. Austr.
246 E2 Cockburn Harbour Turks and Caicos Is
146 F6 Cockburnspath Scottish Borders, Scotland U.K.
246 D1 Cockburn Town San Salvador Bahamas
Cockburn Town Turks and Caicos Is see Grand Turk
149 H2 Cockenheugh hill England U.K.
146 F6 Cockenzie and Port Seton East Lothian, Scotland U.K.
149 F3 Cocker r. England U.K.
149 G4 Cockerham Lancashire, England U.K.
149 F3 Cockermouth Cumbria, England U.K.
150 D3 Cockett Swansea, Wales U.K.
234 B3 Cockeysville MD U.S.A.
87 E7 Cocklebiddy W.A. Austr.
215 E5 Cockscomb mt. S. Africa
254 C4 Coco r. Brazil
242 □J6 Coco r. Hond./Nic.
267 N5 Coco, Isla de i. N. Pacific Ocean
208 A4 Cocobeach Gabon
115 G3 Coco Channel India
241 K4 Coconino Plateau AZ U.S.A.
83 F3 Cocoparra Range hills N.S.W. Austr.
250 C3 Cocorná Col.
254 D5 Cocos Brazil
265 K4 Cocos Basin sea feature Indian Ocean
86 □2 Cocos Islands terr. Indian Ocean
267 N5 Cocos Ridge sea feature N. Pacific Ocean
244 C3 Cocula Mex.
163 C4 Cocumont France
233 H4 Cod, Cape MA U.S.A.
197 H2 Codăești Romania
251 F5 Codajás Brazil
149 H3 Cod Beck r. England U.K.
151 I2 Coddenham Suffolk, England U.K.
149 I4 Coddington Nottinghamshire, England U.K.
223 J5 Coderre Sask. Can.
191 H3 Codevigo Italy
81 A7 Codfish Island Stewart I. N.Z.
192 B5 Codi, Monte hill Sardegna Italy
151 G3 Codicote Hertfordshire, England U.K.
191 H4 Codigoro Italy
197 G3 Codlea Romania
149 H4 Codnor Derbyshire, England U.K.
254 E3 Codó Brazil
190 E3 Codogno Italy
187 E6 Codolar airport Spain
234 B3 Codorus PA U.S.A.
183 I3 Codos Spain
263 D2 Codrington, Mount Antarctica
191 H3 Codroipo Italy
192 A4 Codrongianos Sardegna Italy
136 E4 Codru Moldova
177 L5 Codru-Moma, Munții mts Romania
150 E2 Codsall Staffordshire, England U.K.
238 E2 Cody WY U.S.A.
232 B6 Coeburn VA U.S.A.
215 E5 Coega S. Africa
260 A5 Coelemu Chile
254 E3 Coelho Neto Brazil
85 E2 Coen Qld Austr.
85 E2 Coen r. Qld Austr.
244 D4 Coeneo Mex.
215 E5 Coerney S. Africa
251 G3 Coeroeni r. Suriname
169 C4 Coesfeld Ger.
217 □2 Coëtivy i. Seychelles
214 E2 Coetzersdam S. Africa
238 C2 Coeur d'Alene ID U.S.A.
238 C2 Coeur d'Alene r. ID U.S.A.
164 F2 Coevorden Neth.
158 E5 Coëx France
215 G4 Coffee Bay S. Africa
222 B2 Coffee Creek Y.T. Can.
237 F5 Coffeeville MS U.S.A.
237 E4 Coffeyville KS U.S.A.
82 C3 Coffin Bay S.A. Austr.
82 C3 Coffin Bay b. S.A. Austr.
83 H2 Coffs Harbour N.S.W. Austr.
215 F5 Cofimvaba S. Africa
245 F4 Cofre de Perote mt. Mex.
187 B5 Cofrentes Spain
Cogâlniceanu airport Romania see Kogălniceanu
197 I3 Cogealac Romania
183 F3 Cogeces del Monte Spain
151 H3 Coggeshall Essex, England U.K.
192 A2 Coggia Corse France
190 D3 Coggiola Italy
192 A4 Coghinas r. Sardegna Italy
192 B4 Coghinas, Lago del l. Sardegna Italy
215 G4 Coghlan S. Africa
86 E3 Coghlan, Mount hill W.A. Austr.
186 D2 Cogigar r. Spain
162 B3 Cognac France
162 D3 Cognac-la-Forêt France
190 C3 Cogne Italy
160 D3 Cognin France

207 H6 Cogo Equat. Guinea
190 D4 Cogoleto Italy
161 E5 Cogolin France
183 G2 Cogollos Spain
183 F2 Cogollos r. Spain
185 G3 Cogollos Vega Spain
183 G4 Cogolludo Spain
182 C4 Cogula Port.
234 C3 Cohansey r. NJ U.S.A.
Čohkkiras Sweden see Jukkasjärvi
232 E3 Cohocton r. NY U.S.A.
233 G3 Cohoes NY U.S.A.
83 F3 Cohuna Vic. Austr.
242 □J8 Coiba, Isla i. Panama
262 T3 Coig r. Arg.
146 C3 Coigeach, Rubha pt Scotland U.K.
259 B7 Coihaique Chile
260 A5 Coihüe Chile
114 C4 Coimbatore Tamil Nadu India
182 B4 Coimbra Port.
182 B4 Coimbra admin. dist. Port.
185 F4 Coín Spain
156 D3 Coincy France
252 C4 Coipasa, Salar de salt flat Bol.
Coire Switz. see Chur
160 C3 Coise r. France
182 C4 Coja Port.
197 G3 Cojasca Romania
250 D2 Cojedes state Venez.
259 C7 Cojudo Blanco, Cerro mt. Arg.
177 J6 Čoka Vojvodina, Srbija Yugo.
238 E3 Cokeville WY U.S.A.
83 E4 Colac Vic. Austr.
81 A7 Colac South I. N.Z.
260 C1 Colangüil, Cordillera de mts Arg.
254 C2 Colares Brazil
257 G3 Colatina Brazil
163 C4 Colayrac-St-Cirq France
169 D5 Cölbe Ger.
Colbert Alg. see Aïn Oulmene
171 C3 Colbitz Ger.
191 H5 Colbordola Italy
227 I4 Colborne Ont. Can.
260 B4 Colbún Chile
236 C4 Colby KS U.S.A.
226 B3 Colby WI U.S.A.
252 B3 Colca r. Peru
197 H3 Colceag Romania
215 E5 Colchester S. Africa
151 H3 Colchester Essex, England U.K.
235 F1 Colchester CT U.S.A.
226 B5 Colchester IL U.S.A.
220 B4 Cold Bay AK U.S.A.
151 F4 Colden Common Hampshire, England U.K.
146 F6 Coldingham Scottish Borders, Scotland U.K.
171 D4 Colditz Ger.
223 I4 Cold Lake Alta Can.
234 D4 Cold Spring NJ U.S.A.
235 E1 Cold Spring NY U.S.A.
237 E6 Coldspring TX U.S.A.
240 I2 Cold Springs NV U.S.A.
222 G5 Coldstream B.C. Can.
81 C6 Coldstream South I. N.Z.
146 F6 Coldstream Scottish Borders, Scotland U.K.
227 H3 Coldwater Ont. Can.
237 D4 Coldwater KS U.S.A.
226 E5 Coldwater MI U.S.A.
237 F5 Coldwater r. MS U.S.A.
237 C4 Coldwater Creek r. OK U.S.A.
226 D1 Coldwell Ont. Can.
233 H2 Colebrook NH U.S.A.
215 G3 Coleford S. Africa
150 E3 Coleford Gloucestershire, England U.K.
150 E3 Coleford Somerset, England U.K.
85 E2 Coleman r. Qld Austr.
234 B3 Coleman MD U.S.A.
226 E4 Coleman MI U.S.A.
237 D6 Coleman TX U.S.A.
226 C3 Coleman WI U.S.A.
Çölemerik Turkey see Hakkâri
215 G3 Colenso S. Africa
197 G3 Colentina r. Romania
262 T2 Cole Peninsula Antarctica
82 E4 Coleraine Vic. Austr.
147 E1 Coleraine Northern Ireland U.K.
226 A2 Coleraine MN U.S.A.
81 C5 Coleridge, Lake South I. N.Z.
150 E3 Colerne Wiltshire, England U.K.
114 C4 Coleroon r. India
252 C4 Coles, Punta de pt Peru
83 G5 Coles Bay Tas. Austr.
215 E4 Colesberg S. Africa
151 F2 Coleshill Warwickshire, England U.K.
234 A3 Colesville MD U.S.A.
234 D1 Colesville NJ U.S.A.
223 I5 Coleville Sask. Can.
240 H2 Coleville CA U.S.A.
240 G2 Colfax CA U.S.A.
226 C5 Colfax IL U.S.A.
237 E6 Colfax LA U.S.A.
238 C2 Colfax WA U.S.A.
226 B3 Colfax WI U.S.A.
146 □H1 Colgrave Sound str. Scotland U.K.
259 C7 Colhué Huapí, Lago l. Arg.
197 G3 Colibași Romania
190 E2 Colico Italy
160 D2 Coligny France
215 F2 Coligny S. Africa
247 □2 Colihaut Dominica
164 C3 Colijnsplaat Neth.
244 C4 Colima Mex.
244 C4 Colima state Mex.
244 C4 Colima, Nevado de vol. Mex.
256 C4 Colina Brazil
260 B3 Colina Chile
254 D3 Colinas Brazil
183 G1 Colindres Spain
146 C6 Colintraive Argyll and Bute, Scotland U.K.
254 B5 Coliseu r. Brazil
146 B5 Coll i. Scotland U.K.
183 I4 Collado Bajo mt. Spain
183 G3 Collado Hermoso Spain
183 G4 Collado Villalba Spain
190 F4 Collagna Italy
178 D4 Collalto mt. Austria/Italy
182 E1 Collanzo Spain
83 G2 Collarenebri N.S.W. Austr.
193 F2 Collarmele Italy
193 E2 Collazzone Italy
190 F4 Collecchio Italy
193 F2 Colledara Italy
191 G5 Colle di Val d'Elsa Italy
213 F4 Colleen Bawn Zimbabwe
193 F3 Colleferro Italy
231 C5 College Park GA U.S.A.
237 D6 College Station TX U.S.A.
234 C2 Collegeville PA U.S.A.
190 C3 Collegno Italy
191 G2 Colle Isarco Italy
193 F3 Collelongo Italy
193 F3 Collepardo Italy
195 H2 Collepasso Italy
83 F2 Collerina N.S.W. Austr.
190 F5 Collesalvetti Italy
193 G3 Colle Sannita Italy
194 C5 Collesano Sicilia Italy
193 G3 Colletorto Italy
234 B1 Colley PA U.S.A.
193 H4 Colliano Italy
193 G3 Colli a Volturno Italy
83 G2 Collie N.S.W. Austr.
87 C7 Collie W.A. Austr.
86 E3 Collier Bay W.A. Austr.
87 C5 Collier Range hills W.A. Austr.
237 F5 Collierville TN U.S.A.
146 G4 Collieston Aberdeenshire, Scotland U.K.
146 E6 Collin Dumfries and Galloway, Scotland U.K.
192 A5 Collinas Sardegna Italy
158 D3 Collinée France
149 I4 Collingham Nottinghamshire, England U.K.
168 C2 Collinghorst (Rhauderfehn) Ger.
224 D4 Collingwood Ont. Can.
80 D4 Collingwood South I. N.Z.
235 D2 Collingwood Park NJ U.S.A.
237 F6 Collins MS U.S.A.
221 H2 Collinson Peninsula Nunavut Can.
85 F4 Collinsville Qld Austr.
231 C5 Collinsville AL U.S.A.
237 E4 Collinsville OK U.S.A.
232 D6 Collinsville VA U.S.A.
178 B5 Collio Italy
163 F6 Collioure France
260 A5 Collipulli Chile
171 E4 Collmberg hill Ger.
161 E5 Collobrières France
190 B2 Collombey Switz.
234 A1 Collomsville PA U.S.A.
147 E3 Collon Rep. of Ireland
160 D2 Collonges France
162 D3 Collonges-la-Rouge France
147 C2 Collooney Rep. of Ireland
157 H4 Colmar France
161 E4 Colmars France
173 E2 Colmberg Ger.
182 C4 Colmeal Port.
185 F4 Colmenar Spain
182 E4 Colmenar de Montemayor Spain
183 G4 Colmenar de Oreja Spain
183 G4 Colmenar Viejo Spain
160 B1 Colméry France
146 D6 Colmonell South Ayrshire, Scotland U.K.
151 F3 Coln r. England U.K.
146 E4 Colnabaichin Aberdeenshire, Scotland U.K.
151 G3 Colnbrook Windsor and Maidenhead, England U.K.
149 G4 Colne Lancashire, England U.K.
151 H3 Colne r. England U.K.
151 G3 Colney Heath Hertfordshire, England U.K.
168 D3 Colnrade Ger.
83 G3 Colo r. N.S.W. Austr.
195 F2 Colobraro Italy
191 G3 Cologna Veneta Italy
163 C5 Cologne France
Cologne Ger. see Köln
234 D3 Cologne NJ U.S.A.
226 D4 Coloma MI U.S.A.
226 C3 Coloma WI U.S.A.
Colomb-Béchar Alg. see Béchar
159 F2 Colombelles France
156 C4 Colombes France
157 F4 Colombey-les-Belles France
157 E4 Colombey-les-Deux-Églises France
256 C4 Colômbia Brazil
250 C4 Colombia Col.
243 F3 Colombia Mex.
250 C4 Colombia country S. America
264 D5 Colombian Basin sea feature S. Atlantic Ocean
190 B2 Colombier Switz.
160 E3 Colombier, Mont mt. France
163 E4 Colombiès France
256 C6 Colombo Brazil
114 C5 Colombo Sri Lanka
227 H1 Colombourg Que. Can.
183 F1 Colombres Spain
185 G3 Colomera Spain
185 G3 Colomera r. Spain
186 F2 Colomers Spain
163 D5 Colomiers France
261 G3 Colón Buenos Aires Arg.
261 H3 Colón Entre Ríos Arg.
246 B2 Colón Cuba
244 D3 Colón Mex.
242 □K7 Colón Panama
226 E5 Colon MI U.S.A.
Colón, Archipiélago de is Pacific Ocean see Galápagos, Islas
82 C2 Colona S.A. Austr.
116 E4 Colonelganj Uttar Prad. India
246 D2 Colonel Hill Bahamas
258 E2 Colonia Arg.
91 I5 Colonia Yap Micronesia
261 I4 Colonia dept Uru.
235 D2 Colonia NJ U.S.A.
Colonia Agrippina Ger. see Köln
260 D4 Colonia Alvear Arg.
261 F5 Colonia Barón Arg.
260 E3 Colonia Biagorria Arg.
261 H3 Colonia Caseros Arg.
260 E6 Colonia Choele Choel, Isla i. Arg.
261 I4 Colonia del Sacramento Uru.
187 G5 Colònia de Sant Jordi Spain
187 G5 Colònia de Sant Pere Spain
258 E3 Colonia Dora Arg.
261 F4 Colonia Hilario Lagos Arg.
Colonia Julia Fenestris Italy see Fano
259 C7 Colonia Las Heras Arg.
232 E6 Colonial Heights VA U.S.A.
234 B2 Colonial Park PA U.S.A.
195 G3 Colonna, Capo c. Italy
193 F2 Colonnella Italy
267 M5 Colon Ridge sea feature Pacific Ocean
146 B5 Colonsay i. Scotland U.K.
260 F6 Colorado r. Arg.
258 D3 Colorado r. La Rioja Arg.
260 C2 Colorado r. San Juan Arg.
256 B5 Colorado Brazil
260 B4 Colorado r. Chile
245 F5 Colorado r. Mex.
242 B2 Colorado r. Mex./U.S.A.
237 D6 Colorado r. TX U.S.A.
241 M2 Colorado state U.S.A.
260 D2 Colorado, Cerro mt. Arg.
259 E5 Colorado, Delta del Río Arg.
241 K3 Colorado City AZ U.S.A.
237 C5 Colorado City TX U.S.A.
241 I5 Colorado Desert CA U.S.A.
241 M3 Colorado Plateau CO U.S.A.
258 C2 Colorados, Cerro mt. Arg.
239 F4 Colorado Springs CO U.S.A.
190 F4 Colorno Italy
184 B3 Colos Port.
Colossae Turkey see Honaz
161 D5 Colostre r. France
245 F6 Colotepec r. Mex.
244 C2 Colotlán Mex.
170 E2 Cölpin Ger.
252 D4 Colquechaca Bol.
146 E6 Colquhar Scottish Borders, Scotland U.K.
252 D4 Colquiri Bol.
231 C6 Colquitt GA U.S.A.
157 H4 Colroy-la-Grande France
232 B6 Colson KY U.S.A.
151 G2 Colsterworth Lincolnshire, England U.K.
238 F2 Colstrip MT U.S.A.
151 I2 Coltishall Norfolk, England U.K.
240 I4 Colton CA U.S.A.
233 F2 Colton NY U.S.A.
241 L2 Colton UT U.S.A.
235 D2 Colts Neck NJ U.S.A.
187 B7 Columbares hill Spain
235 F1 Columbia CT U.S.A.
230 C4 Columbia KY U.S.A.
237 E5 Columbia LA U.S.A.
234 B3 Columbia MD U.S.A.
236 E4 Columbia MO U.S.A.
237 F6 Columbia MS U.S.A.
231 E5 Columbia NC U.S.A.
234 C2 Columbia NJ U.S.A.
234 B2 Columbia PA U.S.A.
231 D5 Columbia SC U.S.A.
231 C5 Columbia TN U.S.A.
238 B2 Columbia r. WA U.S.A.
221 K1 Columbia, Cape Nunavut Can.
234 A4 Columbia, District of admin. dist. U.S.A.
222 G4 Columbia, Mount Alta/B.C. Can.
242 B2 Columbia, Sierra mts Mex.
230 C3 Columbia City IN U.S.A.
234 B1 Columbia County county PA U.S.A.
233 □J2 Columbia Falls ME U.S.A.
238 D1 Columbia Falls MT U.S.A.
222 F4 Columbia Mountains B.C. Can.
231 C5 Columbiana AL U.S.A.
232 C4 Columbiana OH U.S.A.
238 C2 Columbia Plateau U.S.A.
214 A5 Columbine, Cape S. Africa
231 C5 Columbus GA U.S.A.
230 C4 Columbus IN U.S.A.
237 E4 Columbus KS U.S.A.
237 F5 Columbus MS U.S.A.
238 E2 Columbus MT U.S.A.
231 D5 Columbus NC U.S.A.
236 D3 Columbus NE U.S.A.
234 D2 Columbus NJ U.S.A.
239 F6 Columbus NM U.S.A.
232 B5 Columbus OH U.S.A.
232 D4 Columbus PA U.S.A.
237 D6 Columbus TX U.S.A.
226 C4 Columbus WI U.S.A.
232 A4 Columbus Grove OH U.S.A.
257 F3 Coluna Brazil
183 E1 Colunga Spain
240 F2 Colusa CA U.S.A.
80 E2 Colville North I. N.Z.
238 C1 Colville WA U.S.A.
220 C2 Colville r. AK U.S.A.
80 E2 Colville, Cape North I. N.Z.
87 E6 Colville, Lake salt flat W.A. Austr.
80 E2 Colville Channel North I. N.Z.
220 F3 Colville Lake N.W.T. Can.
151 F2 Colwich Staffordshire, England U.K.
150 D1 Colwyn Bay Conwy, Wales U.K.
162 D3 Coly France
150 D4 Colyton Devon, England U.K.
191 H4 Comacchio Italy
191 H4 Comacchio, Valli di lag. Italy
111 E6 Comai Xizang China
244 C4 Comala Mex.
243 G5 Comalcalco Mex.
245 E3 Comales r. Mex.
197 H3 Comana Romania
237 D6 Comanche TX U.S.A.
262 U2 Comandante Ferraz research stn Antarctica
258 F2 Comandante Fontana Arg.
259 C8 Comandante Luis Piedra Buena Arg.
261 I6 Comandante Nicanor Otamendi Arg.
197 H2 Comănești Romania
186 E2 Coma Pedrosa, Pic de mt. Andorra
197 G3 Comarnic Romania
242 □I6 Comayagua Hond.
231 D5 Combahee r. SC U.S.A.
157 F5 Combeaufontaine France
160 E3 Combe de Savoie val. France
150 C3 Combe Martin Devon, England U.K.
147 F2 Comber Northern Ireland U.K.
227 I3 Combermere Ont. Can.
96 A3 Combermere Bay Myanmar
151 H2 Comberton Cambridgeshire, England U.K.
150 E4 Combe St Nicholas Somerset, England U.K.
165 E4 Comblain-au-Pont Belgium
160 C1 Comblanchien France
156 C2 Combles France
160 E3 Combloux France
190 F2 Combolo, Monte mt. Italy/Switz.
158 E3 Combourg France
158 B4 Combrit France
160 B3 Combronde France
260 E3 Comechingones, Sierra de mts Arg.
191 H2 Comeglians Italy
191 H2 Comèlico Superiore Italy
184 C1 Comenda Port.
256 C3 Comendador Gomes Brazil
257 G2 Comercinho Brazil
247 □1 Comerio Puerto Rico
191 H5 Comero, Monte mt. Italy
85 G4 Comet Qld Austr.
85 G4 Comet r. Qld Austr.
237 D6 Comfort TX U.S.A.
232 C5 Comfort WV U.S.A.
117 G5 Comilla Bangl.
183 F1 Comillas Spain
165 B4 Comines Belgium
Comino i. Malta see Kemmuna
Cominotto i. Malta see Kemmunett
194 D6 Comiso Sicilia Italy
245 G5 Comitancillo Mex.
243 G5 Comitán de Domínguez Mex.
194 C5 Comitini Sicilia Italy
177 J6 Comloșu Mare Romania
235 E2 Commack NY U.S.A.
227 H3 Commanda Ont. Can.
147 D2 Commeen Rep. of Ireland
160 D2 Commenailles France
163 B4 Commensacq France
160 A2 Commentry France
158 E5 Commequiers France
159 F3 Commer France
157 F4 Commercy France
214 B4 Commissioner's Salt Pan S. Africa
221 J3 Committee Bay Nunavut Can.
215 H2 Commondale S. Africa
Commonwealth Territory admin. div. Austr. see Jervis Bay Territory
190 E3 Como Italy
190 E3 Como prov. Lombardia Italy
190 E3 Como, Lago di l. Italy
Como, Lake Italy see Como, Lago di
245 G4 Comoapan Mex.
260 B3 Comodoro Arturo Merino Benitez airport Chile
259 D7 Comodoro Rivadavia Arg.
Comoé r. Côte d'Ivoire see Komoé
244 D3 Comonfort Mex.
Comores country Africa see Comoros
217 □3 Comoros country Africa
222 E5 Comox B.C. Can.
185 G4 Cómpeta Spain
190 E4 Compiano Italy
156 C3 Compiègne France
163 E4 Compolibat France
184 B2 Comporta Port.
244 B3 Compostela Mex.
92 C5 Compostela Phil.
162 D3 Compreignac France
256 D6 Comprida, Ilha i. Brazil
161 E5 Comps-sur-Artuby France
240 H5 Compton CA U.S.A.
226 C5 Compton IL U.S.A.
136 E4 Comrat Moldova
146 E5 Comrie Perth and Kinross, Scotland U.K.
237 C6 Comstock TX U.S.A.
193 F2 Comunanza Italy
194 D5 Comunelli r. Sicilia Italy
96 D3 Con, Sông r. Vietnam
111 E7 Cona Xizang China
191 H3 Cona Italy
128 C1 Çona Turkey
206 B4 Conakry Guinea
250 B5 Conambo r. Ecuador
83 F5 Conara Junction Tas. Austr.
192 B3 Conca Corse France
191 H5 Conca r. Italy
260 E3 Concarán Arg.
158 C4 Concarneau France
192 B4 Concas Sardegna Italy
254 F3 Conceição Brazil
256 E2 Conceição r. Brazil
184 C3 Conceição Port.
257 H3 Conceição da Barra Brazil
256 C3 Conceição das Alagoas Brazil
257 G5 Conceição de Macabu Brazil
254 C4 Conceição do Araguaia Brazil
254 F4 Conceição do Coité Brazil
257 F3 Conceição do Mato Dentro Brazil
257 E4 Conceição do Rio Verde Brazil
258 F3 Concepción Arg.
258 D2 Concepción Arg.
253 E4 Concepción Bol.
258 B5 Concepción Chile
244 D1 Concepción Mex.
242 B2 Concepción r. Mex.
242 □J7 Concepción Panama
253 F5 Concepción Para.
244 C4 Concepción de Buenos Aires Mex.
261 H3 Concepción del Uruguay Arg.
212 B4 Conception Bay Namibia
246 D2 Conception Island Bahamas
190 F3 Concesio Italy
213 F3 Concession Zimbabwe
183 G1 Concha Spain
256 C5 Conchas Brazil
239 F5 Conchas NM U.S.A.
156 A4 Conches-en-Ouche France
241 M4 Concho AZ U.S.A.
237 D6 Concho r. TX U.S.A.
242 D2 Conchos r. Chihuahua Mex.
243 F3 Conchos r. Nuevo León/Tamaulipas Mex.
260 B3 Concón Chile
240 F3 Concord CA U.S.A.
226 E4 Concord MI U.S.A.
231 D5 Concord NC U.S.A.
233 H3 Concord NH U.S.A.
232 E4 Concord PA U.S.A.
232 D6 Concord VA U.S.A.
233 H2 Concord VT U.S.A.
261 I2 Concordia Arg.
255 B8 Concórdia Brazil
244 A2 Concordiá Mex.
250 C6 Concordia Peru
214 A3 Concordia S. Africa
236 D4 Concordia KS U.S.A.
191 H3 Concordia Sagittaria Italy
123 H2 Concord Peak Afgh.
163 D4 Concorès France
163 D4 Concots France
260 B2 Concumén Chile
209 B7 Conda Angola
85 G5 Condamine Qld Austr.
85 G5 Condamine r. Qld Austr.
161 A3 Condat France
162 D3 Condat-sur-Vienne France
156 D3 Condé-en-Brie France
242 □I6 Condega Nic.
182 B4 Condeixa-a-Nova Port.
159 G3 Condé-sur-Huisne France
156 D2 Condé-sur-l'Escaut France
159 F3 Condé-sur-Noireau France
159 E2 Condé-sur-Vire France
255 E5 Condeúba Brazil
191 F3 Condino Italy
83 F3 Condobolin N.S.W. Austr.
195 E4 Condofuri Italy
163 C5 Condom France
238 B2 Condon OR U.S.A.
250 B6 Condor, Cordillera del mts Ecuador/Peru
190 C3 Condove Italy
150 E2 Condover Shropshire, England U.K.
231 C6 Conecuh r. AL U.S.A.
191 H3 Conegliano Italy
239 F4 Conejos CO U.S.A.
239 F4 Conejos r. Colorado/New Mexico U.S.A.
227 H5 Conemaugh r. PA U.S.A.
191 I5 Conero, Monte hill Italy
261 G3 Conesa Arg.
234 B3 Conestoga PA U.S.A.
234 B2 Conestoga Creek r. PA U.S.A.
232 C4 Conesville OH U.S.A.
234 B2 Conewago Creek r. PA U.S.A.
157 G5 Coney r. France
235 E2 Coney Island NY U.S.A.
157 F3 Conflans-en-Jarnisy France
157 G5 Conflans-sur-Lanterne France
193 I5 Conflenti Italy
91 L9 Conflict Group is P.N.G.
232 D5 Confluence PA U.S.A.
Confoederatio Helvetica country Europe see Switzerland
162 C2 Confolens France
241 K2 Confusion Range mts UT U.S.A.
253 F6 Confuso r. Para.
147 B3 Cong Rep. of Ireland
150 C4 Congdon's Shop Cornwall, England U.K.
Congdü Xizang China see Nyalam
109 E4 Conghua Guangdong China
108 D3 Congjiang Guizhou China
149 G4 Congleton Cheshire, England U.K.
208 B5 Congo country Africa
209 B6 Congo r. Congo/Dem. Rep. Congo
Congo (Brazzaville) country Africa see Congo
Congo (Kinshasa) country Africa see Congo, Democratic Republic of
208 D5 Congo, Democratic Republic of country Africa
Congo, Republic of country Africa see Congo
208 D5 Congo Basin Dem. Rep. Congo
264 J6 Congo Cone sea feature S. Atlantic Ocean
Congo Free State country Africa see Congo, Democratic Republic of
257 F4 Congonhas Brazil
256 B5 Congonhinhas Brazil
182 D2 Congosto Spain
183 F2 Congosto de Valdavia Spain
150 E3 Congresbury North Somerset, England U.K.
241 K4 Congress AZ U.S.A.
159 E4 Congrier France
243 H5 Conhuas Mex.
81 C6 Conical Peak hill South I. N.Z.
259 C6 Cónico, Cerro mt. Arg.
156 B4 Conie r. France
184 D4 Conil de la Frontera Spain
149 I4 Coningsby Lincolnshire, England U.K.
149 H4 Conisbrough South Yorkshire, England U.K.
84 C4 Coniston N.T. Austr.
224 D4 Coniston Ont. Can.
149 F3 Coniston Cumbria, England U.K.
85 F3 Conjuboy Qld Austr.
185 G4 Conjuros hill Spain
243 H4 Conkal Mex.
223 I4 Conklin Alta Can.
260 E3 Conlara r. Arg.
159 F3 Conlie France
160 D2 Conliège France
147 F2 Conlig Northern Ireland U.K.
224 E2 Conn r. Que. Can.
147 B2 Conn, Lough l. Rep. of Ireland
Connacht reg. Rep. of Ireland see Connaught
150 D1 Connah's Quay Flintshire, Wales U.K.
156 D4 Connantre France
227 G1 Connaught Ont. Can.
147 B3 Connaught reg. Rep. of Ireland
161 C4 Connaux France
232 C4 Conneaut OH U.S.A.
232 C4 Conneaut Lake PA U.S.A.
232 C4 Conneautville PA U.S.A.
235 F1 Connecticut r. CT U.S.A.
233 G4 Connecticut state U.S.A.
146 C5 Connel Argyll and Bute, Scotland U.K.
232 D4 Connellsville PA U.S.A.
85 E5 Connemara Qld Austr.
147 B3 Connemara reg. Rep. of Ireland
84 B5 Conner, Mount hill N.T. Austr.
159 G3 Connerré France
230 C4 Connersville IN U.S.A.
147 B4 Connolly Rep. of Ireland
222 C2 Connolly, Mount Y.T. Can.
146 B7 Connor Northern Ireland U.K.
85 G4 Connors Range hills Qld Austr.
83 F3 Conoble N.S.W. Austr.
234 B2 Conodoguinet Creek r. PA U.S.A.
250 C5 Cononaco r. Ecuador
146 D4 Conon Bridge Highland, Scotland U.K.
177 K5 Conop Romania
177 I6 Čonoplja Vojvodina, Srbija Yugo.
226 C2 Conover WI U.S.A.
170 E2 Conow Ger.
234 B3 Conowingo MD U.S.A.
163 E4 Conques France
163 E5 Conques-sur-Orbiel France
256 D3 Conquista Brazil
185 F2 Conquista Spain
238 E1 Conrad MT U.S.A.
264 L9 Conrad Rise sea feature Southern Ocean
237 E6 Conroe TX U.S.A.
191 G4 Consandolo Italy
261 H2 Conscripto Bernardi Arg.
165 F5 Consdorf Lux.
227 I3 Consecon Ont. Can.
257 F4 Conselheiro Lafaiete Brazil
257 G3 Conselheiro Pena Brazil
191 G4 Conselice Italy
187 F5 Consell Spain
157 F3 Consenvoye France
149 H3 Consett Durham, England U.K.
234 C2 Conshohocken PA U.S.A.
182 B2 Consistorio Spain
246 B2 Consolación del Sur Cuba
97 D5 Côn Son i. Vietnam
223 I4 Consort Alta Can.
Constance Ger. see Konstanz
Constance, Lake Ger./Switz. see Bodensee
184 B1 Constância Port.
197 I3 Constanța Romania
Constanța airport Romania see Kogălniceanu
186 E3 Constantí Spain
Constantia tourist site Cyprus see Salamis
Constantia Ger. see Konstanz
182 D3 Constantim Bragança Port.
182 C3 Constantim Vila Real Port.
184 E3 Constantina Spain
205 G1 Constantine Alg.
150 B4 Constantine Cornwall, England U.K.
226 E5 Constantine MI U.S.A.
Constantinople Turkey see İstanbul
183 F4 Constanzana Spain
260 A4 Constitución Chile
261 I2 Constitución Uru.
185 G1 Consuegra Spain
85 G5 Consuelo Qld Austr.
223 I5 Consul Sask. Can.
223 K1 Consul r. Nunavut Can.
238 D3 Contact NV U.S.A.
257 F4 Contagalo Brazil
257 E3 Contagem Brazil
252 B1 Contamana Peru
191 H3 Contarina Italy
254 F5 Contas r. Brazil
215 E3 Content S. Africa
194 C5 Contessa Entellina Sicilia Italy
190 C2 Conthey Switz.
193 E2 Contigliano Italy
146 D4 Contin Highland, Scotland U.K.
232 A4 Continental OH U.S.A.
163 A4 Contis-Plage France
233 H3 Contoocook r. NH U.S.A.
260 C6 Contralmirante Cordero Arg.
250 C3 Contratacion Col.
259 B8 Contreras, Isla i. Chile
162 D1 Contres France
157 F4 Contrexéville France
193 H4 Controne Italy
258 B5 Contulmo Chile
252 A1 Contumazá Peru
193 H4 Contursi Terme Italy
223 I1 Contwoyto Lake N.W.T./Nunavut Can.
156 C3 Conty France
237 F6 Convent LA U.S.A.
260 B4 Convento Viejo Chile
195 G2 Conversano Italy
232 A4 Convoy OH U.S.A.
215 E4 Conway S. Africa
Conway Conwy, Wales U.K. see Conwy
237 E5 Conway AR U.S.A.
232 A6 Conway KY U.S.A.
236 D1 Conway ND U.S.A.
233 □H3 Conway NH U.S.A.
231 E5 Conway SC U.S.A.
85 G4 Conway, Cape Qld Austr.
82 C2 Conway, Lake salt flat S.A. Austr.
237 D4 Conway Springs KS U.S.A.
150 D1 Conwy Conwy, Wales U.K.
150 D1 Conwy admin. div. Wales U.K.
150 D1 Conwy r. Wales U.K.
150 C1 Conwy Bay Wales U.K.
234 B2 Conyngham PA U.S.A.
82 C2 Coober Pedy S.A. Austr.
Cooch Behar W. Bengal India see Koch Bihar
85 G5 Coogoon r. Qld Austr.
82 B2 Cook S.A. Austr.
226 A2 Cook MN U.S.A.
222 B2 Cook, Mount Can./U.S.A.
Cook, Mount South I. N.Z. see Aoraki
Cook Atoll Kiribati see Tarawa
239 F5 Cookes Peak NM U.S.A.
231 C4 Cookeville TN U.S.A.
151 G3 Cookham Windsor and Maidenhead, England U.K.
215 E5 Cookhouse S. Africa
220 C3 Cook Inlet sea chan. AK U.S.A.
81 □2 Cook Islands S. Pacific Ocean
150 E2 Cookley Worcestershire, England U.K.
233 F3 Cooksburg NY U.S.A.
146 E4 Cook's Cairn hill Scotland U.K.
225 K3 Cook's Harbour Nfld. Can.
85 F2 Cooks Passage Qld Austr.
147 E2 Cookstown Northern Ireland U.K.
81 E4 Cook Strait South I. N.Z.
234 A3 Cooksville MD U.S.A.
85 F2 Cooktown Qld Austr.
147 C2 Coola Rep. of Ireland
83 F2 Coolabah N.S.W. Austr.
85 F5 Cooladdi Qld Austr.
83 G2 Coolah N.S.W. Austr.
83 F3 Coolamon N.S.W. Austr.
147 C2 Coolaney Rep. of Ireland
156 E4 Coole France
156 E4 Coole r. France
148 B4 Coole Rep. of Ireland
87 D6 Coolgardie W.A. Austr.
147 D4 Coolgrange Rep. of Ireland
147 E4 Coolgreany Rep. of Ireland
84 B2 Coolibah N.T. Austr.
241 L5 Coolidge AZ U.S.A.
87 B6 Coolimba W.A. Austr.
147 E3 Coolock Rep. of Ireland
147 D4 Coolroebeg Rep. of Ireland
85 H5 Coolum Beach Qld Austr.
83 G4 Cooma N.S.W. Austr.
147 A5 Coomacarrea hill Rep. of Ireland
82 E3 Coombah N.S.W. Austr.
150 C4 Coombe Cornwall, England U.K.
151 F3 Coombe Bissett Wiltshire, England U.K.
83 G2 Coonabarabran N.S.W. Austr.
82 D3 Coonalpyn S.A. Austr.
83 G2 Coonamble N.S.W. Austr.
87 D6 Coonana W.A. Austr.
82 E4 Coonawarra S.A. Austr.
82 C2 Coondambo S.A. Austr.
Coondapoor Karnataka India see Kundapura
86 C4 Coongan r. W.A. Austr.
85 F5 Coongoola Qld Austr.
226 A3 Coon Rapids MN U.S.A.
84 C2 Cooper r. N.T. Austr.
237 E5 Cooper TX U.S.A.
82 D2 Cooper Creek watercourse Qld/S.A. Austr.
232 B4 Cooperdale OH U.S.A.
83 H2 Coopernook N.S.W. Austr.
234 C2 Coopersburg PA U.S.A.
233 □I2 Coopers Mills ME U.S.A.
231 E7 Cooper's Town Bahamas
236 D2 Cooperstown ND U.S.A.
233 F3 Cooperstown NY U.S.A.
82 C2 Coorabie S.A. Austr.
87 C5 Coor-de-Wandy hill W.A. Austr.
87 C6 Coorow W.A. Austr.
85 H5 Cooroy Qld Austr.
231 C5 Coosa r. AL U.S.A.
238 A3 Coos Bay OR U.S.A.
83 G3 Cootamundra N.S.W. Austr.
147 D2 Cootehill Rep. of Ireland
114 D3 Cooum r. India
85 G5 Cooyar Qld Austr.
177 L5 Copăcel Romania
260 B5 Copahue, Volcán vol. Chile
243 G5 Copainalá Mex.
245 E5 Copala Mex.
245 E4 Copalillo Mex.
245 F6 Copalita r. Mex.
242 □H6 Copán tourist site Hond.
195 F4 Copanello Italy
236 C4 Cope CO U.S.A.
226 E3 Copemish MI U.S.A.
Copenhagen Denmark see København
195 H2 Copertino Italy
261 G6 Copetonas Arg.
96 D3 Cô Pi, Phou mt. Laos/Vietnam
235 E2 Copiague NY U.S.A.
258 C2 Copiapó Chile
258 C2 Copiapo, Volcán vol. Chile
146 F3 Copinsay i. Scotland U.K.
234 C2 Coplay PA U.S.A.
82 D2 Copley S.A. Austr.
149 H3 Copley Durham, England U.K.
149 H4 Copmanthorpe York, England U.K.
186 E3 Copons Spain
190 E3 Coppa r. Italy
191 G4 Copparo Italy
147 C5 Coppeen Rep. of Ireland
251 G3 Coppename r. Suriname
169 E3 Coppenbrügge Ger.
169 E4 Coppengrave Ger.
209 E8 Copperbelt prov. Zambia
224 D4 Copper Cliff Ont. Can.
85 E3 Copperfield r. Qld Austr.
226 D2 Copper Harbor MI U.S.A.
Coppermine Nunavut Can. see Kugluktuk
220 G3 Coppermine r. Nunavut Can.
214 D3 Copperton S. Africa
241 K1 Copperton UT U.S.A.
150 D4 Copplestone Devon, England U.K.
197 G2 Copșa Mică Romania
151 G3 Copthorne Surrey, England U.K.
151 F4 Copythorne Hampshire, England U.K.
111 D6 Coqên Xizang China
247 □1 Coqui Puerto Rico
Coquilhatville Dem. Rep. Congo see Mbandaka
Coquille i. Micronesia see Pikelot
238 A3 Coquille OR U.S.A.
244 C4 Coquimatlán Mex.
260 B1 Coquimbo Chile
260 B2 Coquimbo admin. reg. Chile
260 B1 Coquimbo, Bahía de b. Chile
222 F5 Coquitlam B.C. Can.
197 G4 Corabia Romania
257 E2 Coração de Jesus Brazil
195 F4 Corace r. Italy
Coracesium Turkey see Alanya
252 B3 Coracora Peru
83 H2 Coraki N.S.W. Austr.
87 B4 Coral Bay W.A. Austr.
79 □1a Coral Coast Fiji
221 J3 Coral Harbour Nunavut Can.
231 □2 Coral Heights Bahamas
78 □5 Coral Sea S. Pacific Ocean
266 F6 Coral Sea Basin S. Pacific Ocean
77 F3 Coral Sea Islands Territory terr. Austr.
147 D3 Coralstown Rep. of Ireland
235 E2 Coram NY U.S.A.
83 E4 Corangamite, Lake Vic. Austr.
232 C4 Coraopolis PA U.S.A.
129 F3 Corat Azer.
193 I3 Corato Italy
158 C3 Coray France
186 C4 Corbalán Spain
147 B2 Corbally Rep. of Ireland
156 C4 Corbeil-Essonnes France
156 C4 Corbeilles France
256 A6 Corbélia Brazil
160 D3 Corbelin France
157 G5 Corbenay France
156 D3 Corbeny France
186 D3 Corbera de Terra Alta Spain
156 C3 Corbie France
190 C2 Corbières Switz.
160 B1 Corbigny France
232 A6 Corbin KY U.S.A.
234 D3 Corbin City NJ U.S.A.
186 D3 Corbins Spain
191 H3 Corbola Italy
185 E3 Corbones r. Spain
149 G3 Corbridge Northumberland, England U.K.
197 I3 Corbu Romania
151 G2 Corby Northamptonshire, England U.K.
186 G3 Corçà Spain
Corcaigh Rep. of Ireland see Cork
160 D1 Corcelles-lès-Cîteaux France
193 E2 Corchiano Italy
193 E1 Corciano Italy
157 G4 Corcieux France
185 G1 Córcoles r. Spain
240 H3 Corcoran CA U.S.A.
158 E5 Corcoué-sur-Logne France
259 C6 Corcovado Arg.
259 B6 Corcovado, Golfo de sea chan. Chile
182 A2 Corcubión Spain
Corcyra i. Greece see Kerkyra
147 B4 Cordal Rep. of Ireland
85 H5 Cordalba Qld Austr.
257 F5 Cordeiro Brazil
231 D6 Cordele GA U.S.A.
240 F2 Cordelia CA U.S.A.
237 D5 Cordell OK U.S.A.
158 E4 Cordemais France
191 H3 Cordenòns Italy
163 D4 Cordes France
191 H2 Cordevole r. Italy
191 H3 Cordignano Italy
92 B4 Cordilleras Range mts Phil.
82 E1 Cordillo Downs S.A. Austr.
182 B4 Cordinhã Port.
257 E3 Cordisburgo Brazil
261 E2 Córdoba Arg.
261 F3 Córdoba prov. Arg.
250 C2 Córdoba dept Col.
245 F4 Córdoba Mex.
185 F3 Córdoba Spain
185 F2 Córdoba prov. Andalucía Spain
260 E3 Córdoba, Sierras de mts Arg.
184 D1 Cordobilla de Lácara Spain
252 B3 Cordova Peru
Cordova Spain see Córdoba
220 D3 Cordova AK U.S.A.
234 C4 Cordova MD U.S.A.
183 H2 Cordovín Spain
Corduba Spain see Córdoba
183 I4 Corduente Spain
254 E2 Coreaú Brazil
191 F4 Coreglia Antelminelli Italy
85 E3 Corella r. Qld Austr.
183 I2 Corella Spain
84 C3 Corella Lake salt flat N.T. Austr.
182 E3 Coreses Spain
150 E4 Corfe Castle Dorset, England U.K.
150 E4 Corfe Mullen Dorset, England U.K.
85 E4 Corfield Qld Austr.
193 F2 Corfinio Italy
232 D3 Corfu NY U.S.A.
182 C3 Corgo r. Port.
255 B6 Corguinho Brazil
193 E3 Cori Italy
182 D5 Coria Spain
184 D3 Coria del Río Spain
191 H5 Coriano Italy
254 D5 Coribe Brazil
83 G3 Coricudgy mt. N.S.W. Austr.
195 F3 Corigliano, Golfo di b. Italy
195 F3 Corigliano Calabro Italy
191 I5 Corinaldo Italy
85 G3 Coringa Islands Coral Sea Is Terr. Austr.
Corinium Gloucestershire, England U.K. see Cirencester
83 F5 Corinna Tas. Austr.
223 J5 Corinne Sask. Can.
Corinth Greece see Korinthos
237 F5 Corinth MS U.S.A.
233 G3 Corinth NY U.S.A.
Corinth, Gulf of sea chan. Greece see Korinthiakos Kolpos
Corinthus Greece see Korinthos
257 E3 Corinto Brazil
242 □I6 Corinto Nic.
185 E4 Coripe Spain
253 F4 Corixa Grande r. Bol./Brazil
253 F4 Corixinha r. Brazil
147 C5 Cork Rep. of Ireland
147 C4 Cork county Rep. of Ireland
158 C3 Corlay France
148 B4 Corlea Rep. of Ireland
147 B2 Corlee Rep. of Ireland
194 C5 Corleone Sicilia Italy
193 I4 Corleto Perticara Italy
199 E1 Çorlu Turkey
199 E1 Çorlu r. Turkey
160 C2 Cormatin France
159 G2 Cormeilles France
159 F2 Cormelles-le-Royal France
182 B1 Corme-Porto Spain
162 B3 Corme-Royal France
156 D3 Cormicy France
191 I3 Cormons Italy
156 E3 Cormontreuil France
191 I3 Cormor r. Italy
223 K4 Cormorant Man. Can.
193 H3 Cornacchia, Monte mt. Italy
147 D3 Cornafulla Rep. of Ireland
183 H2 Cornago Spain
147 B3 Cornamona Rep. of Ireland
190 E3 Cornaredo Italy
161 C4 Cornas France
168 D3 Cornau Ger.
169 E4 Cornberg Ger.
159 F4 Corné France
191 G2 Cornedo all'Isarco Italy
163 E6 Corneilla-del-Vercol France
215 G2 Cornelia S. Africa
256 B5 Cornélio Procópio Brazil
226 B3 Cornell WI U.S.A.
186 F3 Cornellá de Llobregat Spain
186 F2 Cornellà de Terri Spain
182 D1 Cornellana Spain
225 J3 Corner Brook Nfld. Can.
83 F4 Corner Inlet b. Vic. Austr.
185 I3 Corneros r. Spain
264 F3 Corner Seamounts sea feature N. Atlantic Ocean
136 E4 Cornești Moldova
Corneto Italy see Tarquinia
191 G3 Cornetto mt. Italy
232 B6 Cornettsville KY U.S.A.
177 L6 Cornetu, Vârful hill Romania
146 F4 Cornhill Aberdeenshire, Scotland U.K.
149 G2 Cornhill-on-Tweed Northumberland, England U.K.
149 G4 Cornholme West Yorkshire, England U.K.
197 H2 Corni Romania
192 C2 Cornia r. Italy
190 F4 Corniglio Italy
156 E3 Cornillet, Mont hill France
157 G5 Cornimont France
237 F4 Corning AR U.S.A.
240 F2 Corning CA U.S.A.
236 E3 Corning IA U.S.A.
232 E3 Corning NY U.S.A.
232 B5 Corning OH U.S.A.
Corn Islands is Nic. see Maíz, Islas del
193 E2 Corno r. Italy
193 F2 Corno, Monte mt. Italy
190 F2 Corno di Campo mt. Italy/Switz.
226 B2 Cornucopia WI U.S.A.
191 H3 Cornuda Italy
183 G2 Cornudilla Spain
161 B5 Cornus France
224 F4 Cornwall Ont. Can.
225 I4 Cornwall P.E.I. Can.
150 C4 Cornwall admin. div. England U.K.
235 D1 Cornwall NY U.S.A.
234 B2 Cornwall PA U.S.A.
221 I2 Cornwallis Island Nunavut Can.
221 I2 Cornwall Island Nunavut Can.
235 D1 Cornwall on Hudson NY U.S.A.
82 D3 Corny Point S.A. Austr.
250 D2 Coro Venez.
257 F3 Coroaci Brazil
254 D3 Coroatá Brazil
252 C4 Corocoro Bol.
251 F2 Corocoro, Isla i. Venez.
147 B4 Corofin Rep. of Ireland
80 E2 Coroglen North I. N.Z.
252 D4 Coroico Bol.
256 D3 Coromandel Brazil
80 E2 Coromandel North I. N.Z.
114 D4 Coromandel Coast India
80 E2 Coromandel Peninsula North I. N.Z.
80 E2 Coromandel Range hills North I. N.Z.
159 F4 Coron France
92 B3 Coron Phil.
184 B2 Corona r. Port.
183 I2 Corona mt. Spain
240 I5 Corona CA U.S.A.
239 F5 Corona NM U.S.A.
182 B3 Coronado Port.
240 I5 Coronado CA U.S.A.
242 □J7 Coronado, Bahiá de b. Costa Rica
223 I4 Coronation Alta Can.
220 G3 Coronation Gulf Nunavut Can.
262 U2 Coronation Island S. Orkney Is Atlantic Ocean
86 E2 Coronation Islands W.A. Austr.
261 G2 Coronda Arg.
261 G3 Coronel Bogada Arg.
261 H4 Coronel Brandsen Arg.
261 G6 Coronel Dorrego Arg.
257 F3 Coronel Fabriciano Brazil
258 D2 Coronel Moldes Arg.
257 F2 Coronel Murta Brazil
253 F6 Coronel Oviedo Para.
261 G5 Coronel Pringles Arg.
253 G5 Coronel Sapucaia Mato Grosso do Sul Brazil
253 G5 Coronel Sapucaia Mato Grosso do Sul Brazil
261 G5 Coronel Suárez Arg.
261 I5 Coronel Vidal Arg.
81 B6 Coronet Peak South I. N.Z.
198 B1 Çorovodë Albania
83 F3 Corowa N.S.W. Austr.
243 H5 Corozal Belize
247 □1 Corozal Puerto Rico
161 D4 Corps France
158 E4 Corps-Nuds France
258 G2 Corpus Arg.
237 D7 Corpus Christi TX U.S.A.
252 D4 Corque Bol.
259 B5 Corral Chile
182 E4 Corral mt. Spain
183 G5 Corral de Almaguer Spain
261 F3 Corral de Bustos Arg.
185 F2 Corral de Calatrava Spain
183 F5 Corral de Cantos mt. Spain
182 E3 Corrales Spain
244 D3 Corrales de Rábago Mex.
246 B2 Corralilla Cuba
240 G3 Corralitos CA U.S.A.
260 D2 Corralitos, Monte mt. Arg.
245 G4 Corral Nuevo Mex.
185 I2 Corral-Rubio Spain
87 B5 Corrandibby Range hills W.A. Austr.
213 H2 Corrane Moz.
192 B4 Corrasi, Punta mt. Sardegna Italy
147 B3 Corraun Peninsula Rep. of Ireland
157 G5 Corre France
146 F4 Correen Hills Scotland U.K.
191 F4 Correggio Italy
256 B2 Córrego do Ouro Brazil
257 F3 Córrego Novo Brazil
254 D4 Corrente Brazil
254 E5 Corrente r. Bahia Brazil
256 B3 Corrente r. Minas Gerais Brazil
257 F3 Corrente Grande r. Brazil
253 G4 Correntes r. Brazil
254 D5 Correntina Brazil
Correntina r. Brazil see Éguas

162 D3 Corrèze France
162 D3 Corrèze dept Limousin France
162 D3 Corrèze r. France
147 B3 Corrib, Lough l. Rep. of Ireland
191 I5 Corridonia Italy
146 C6 Corrie North Ayrshire, Scotland U.K.
258 F2 Corrientes Arg.
261 H1 Corrientes prov. Arg.
258 F3 Corrientes r. Arg.
250 C5 Corrientes r. Peru
244 B3 Corrientes, Cabo c. Mex.
237 E6 Corrigan TX U.S.A.
87 C7 Corrigin W.A. Austr.
151 H3 Corringham Thurrock, England U.K.
150 D2 Corris Gwynedd, Wales U.K.
156 D4 Corrobert France
232 D4 Corry PA U.S.A.
83 F4 Corryong Vic. Austr.
190 C4 Corsaglia r. Italy
195 H3 Corsano Italy
192 B2 Corse admin. reg. France
192 A2 Corse i. France
192 B1 Corse, Cap c. Corse France
192 A3 Corse-du-Sud dept Corse France
146 D6 Corserine hill Scotland U.K.
158 D3 Corseul France
150 E3 Corsham Wiltshire, England U.K.
Corsica i. France see Corse
237 D5 Corsicana TX U.S.A.
190 E3 Corsico Italy
146 E6 Corsock Dumfries and Galloway, Scotland U.K.
195 F4 Cortale Italy
244 D3 Cortazar Mex.
192 B2 Corte Corse France
184 D2 Corte de Peleas Spain
182 B2 Cortegada Spain
184 D3 Cortegana Spain
190 D4 Cortemilia Italy
190 F2 Corteno Golgi Italy
190 E3 Corteolona Italy
183 I3 Cortes Spain
Cortes, Sea of g. Mex. see California, Golfo de
186 C4 Cortes de Aragón Spain
185 H3 Cortes de Baza Spain
185 E4 Cortes de la Frontera Spain
187 C5 Cortes de Pallás Spain
239 E4 Cortez CO U.S.A.
241 I1 Cortez Mountains NV U.S.A.
184 B2 Cortiçadas do Lavre Port.
186 D3 Cortiella r. Spain
185 F1 Cortijo de Arriba Spain
245 E5 Cortijos r. Mex.
185 H2 Cortijos Nuevos Spain
191 H2 Cortina d'Ampezzo Italy
233 E3 Cortland NY U.S.A.
232 C4 Cortland OH U.S.A.
151 I2 Corton Suffolk, England U.K.
191 G5 Cortona Italy
206 B4 Corubal r. Guinea-Bissau
184 B2 Coruche Port.
Çoruh Turkey see Artvin
129 B3 Çoruh r. Turkey
127 F2 Çoruh r. Turkey
182 D2 Corullón Spain
126 D2 Çorum Turkey
253 F4 Corumbá Brazil
256 C3 Corumbá r. Brazil
256 C1 Corumbá de Goiás Brazil
256 C3 Corumbaíba Brazil
256 B5 Corumbataí r. Brazil
197 G2 Corund Romania
177 L4 Corund r. Romania
232 B3 Corunna Ont. Can.
Corunna Spain see A Coruña
227 E4 Corunna MI U.S.A.
254 F4 Coruripe Brazil
238 B2 Corvallis OR U.S.A.
191 G2 Corvara in Badia Italy
150 E2 Corve Dale val. England U.K.
187 B7 Corvera Spain
193 E3 Corvia, Colle hill Italy
216 □1 Corvo i. Azores
150 D2 Corwen Denbighshire, Wales U.K.
236 E3 Corydon IA U.S.A.
230 C4 Corydon IN U.S.A.
151 H3 Coryton Thurrock, England U.K.
232 D4 Coryville PA U.S.A.
Cos i. Greece see Kos
186 B4 Cosa Spain
244 A1 Cosalá Mex.
245 G4 Cosamaloapan Mex.
129 A3 Coşandere Turkey
151 F2 Cosby Leicestershire, England U.K.
193 E2 Coscerno, Monte mt. Italy
195 F3 Coscile r. Italy
245 F4 Coscomatepec Mex.
183 H3 Coscurita Spain
Cosentia Italy see Cosenza
193 I5 Cosenza Italy
193 I5 Cosenza prov. Calabria Italy
197 H3 Coşereni Romania
195 F3 Coserie r. Italy
146 E5 Coshieville Perth and Kinross, Scotland U.K.
232 C4 Coshocton OH U.S.A.
244 C2 Cosío Mex.
190 C4 Cosio di Arroscia Italy
183 G4 Coslada Spain
217 □2 Cosmolédo Atoll Seychelles
256 D5 Cosmópolis Brazil
160 A1 Cosne-Cours-sur-Loire France
160 A2 Cosne-d'Allier France
245 G5 Cosoleacaque Mex.
195 E4 Cosoleto Italy
260 E2 Cosquín Arg.
190 D3 Cossato Italy
171 E4 Cossebaude Ger.
159 F4 Cossé-le-Vivien France
192 A4 Cossoine Sardegna Italy
156 B5 Cosson r. France
190 B2 Cossonay Switz.
184 A2 Costa Bela coastal area Port.
187 C6 Costa Blanca coastal area Spain
186 G3 Costa Brava coastal area Spain
191 H5 Costacciaro Italy
197 H3 Costache Negri Romania
184 A2 Costa da Caparica Port.
184 B2 Costa da Galé coastal area Port.
184 C3 Costa de la Luz coastal area Spain
187 C5 Costa del Azahar coastal area Spain
185 E4 Costa del Sol coastal area Spain
242 □J6 Costa de Mosquitos coastal area Nic.
184 A2 Costa do Estoril coastal area Port.
186 F3 Costa Dorada coastal area Spain
184 A2 Costa do Sol coastal area Port.
252 D3 Costa Marques Brazil
256 A3 Costa Rica Brazil
246 A5 Costa Rica country Central America
242 D3 Costa Rica Mex.
182 D1 Costa Verde coastal area Spain
190 F3 Costa Volpino Italy
177 K6 Coşteiu Romania
147 B3 Costelloe Rep. of Ireland
Costermansville Dem. Rep. Congo see Bukavu
151 I2 Costessey Norfolk, England U.K.
136 D4 Costeşti Moldova
197 G3 Costeşti Romania
197 H2 Costeşti Romania
233 □I2 Costigan ME U.S.A.
190 D4 Costigliole d'Asti Italy
190 C4 Costigliole Saluzzo Italy
186 B3 Cosuenda Spain
197 F3 Coşuştea r. Romania
171 E4 Coswig Sachsen Ger.
171 D4 Coswig Sachsen-Anhalt Ger.
252 B3 Cotabambas Peru
92 C5 Cotabato Phil.
252 D4 Cotacajes r. Bol.
252 D5 Cotagaita Bol.
252 B3 Cotahuasi Peru
257 G3 Cotaxé r. Brazil
222 D3 Cote, Mount AK U.S.A.
236 D2 Coteau des Prairies slope SD U.S.A.
236 C1 Coteau du Missouri slope ND U.S.A.
236 C2 Coteau du Missouri slope SD U.S.A.
233 F2 Coteau Station Que. Can.
246 D3 Coteaux Haiti
156 D4 Côte Champenoise reg. France
163 A5 Côte d'Argent coastal area France
161 F5 Côte d'Azur airport France
161 F5 Côte d'Azur coastal area France
156 E4 Côte des Bars reg. France
206 D5 Côte d'Ivoire country Africa
156 E5 Côte-d'Or dept Bourgogne France
160 C2 Côte d'Or reg. France
Côte Française de Somalis country Africa see Djibouti
254 D4 Cotegipe Brazil
158 D3 Côtes-d'Armor dept Bretagne France
157 E3 Côtes de Meuse ridge France
157 F4 Côtes de Moselle hills France
Côtes-du-Nord dept Bretagne France see Côtes-d'Armor
163 F6 Côte Vermeille coastal area France
150 C3 Cothi r. Wales U.K.
252 D2 Coti r. Brazil
Cotiaeum Turkey see Kütahya
192 A3 Coti-Chiavari Corse France
186 D2 Cotiella mt. Spain
161 E5 Cotignac France
191 G4 Cotignola Italy
251 F4 Cotingo r. Brazil
136 E4 Cotiujeni Moldova
136 E4 Cotiujenii Mici Moldova
197 G3 Cotmeana r. Romania
207 F5 Cotonou Benin
250 B5 Cotopaxi prov. Ecuador
250 B5 Cotopaxi, Volcán vol. Ecuador
Cotovsc Moldova see Hînceşti
195 F3 Cotronei Italy
150 E3 Cotswold Hills England U.K.
238 B3 Cottage Grove OR U.S.A.
193 E2 Cottanello Italy
171 F4 Cottbus Ger.
114 D3 Cotteliar r. India
151 H2 Cottenham Cambridgeshire, England U.K.
151 G2 Cottesmore Rutland, England U.K.
161 E4 Cottian Alps mts France/Italy
251 H4 Cottica Suriname
Cottiennes, Alpes mts France/Italy see Cottian Alps
149 I4 Cottingham East Riding of Yorkshire, England U.K.
151 G2 Cottingham Northamptonshire, England U.K.
226 A2 Cotton MN U.S.A.
241 K4 Cottonwood AZ U.S.A.
240 F1 Cottonwood CA U.S.A.
238 C2 Cottonwood ID U.S.A.
236 D4 Cottonwood r. KS U.S.A.
236 E2 Cottonwood r. MN U.S.A.
236 D4 Cottonwood Falls KS U.S.A.
246 E3 Cotuí Dom. Rep.
237 D6 Cotulla TX U.S.A.
197 H1 Coţuşca Romania
161 B3 Coubon France
160 C2 Couches France
184 B2 Couço Port.
161 B4 Coucouron France
156 D3 Coucy-le-Château-Auffrique France
159 H4 Couddes France
156 C1 Coudekerque-Branche France
232 D4 Coudersport PA U.S.A.
82 D4 Couëdic, Cape de S.A. Austr.
158 E4 Couëron France
158 E3 Couesnon r. France
163 D6 Couflens France
163 D5 Coufouleux France
162 C2 Couhé France
163 E6 Couiza France
159 G3 Coulaines France
156 D5 Coulanges-la-Vineuse France
160 B1 Coulanges-lès-Nevers France
160 B1 Coulanges-sur-Yonne France
159 G3 Coulans-sur-Gée France
162 C3 Coulaures France
238 C2 Coulee City WA U.S.A.
238 C2 Coulee Dam WA U.S.A.
160 A2 Couleuvre France
159 I4 Coullons France
263 L2 Coulman Island Antarctica
156 E5 Coulmier-le-Sec France
156 B5 Coulmiers France
156 B2 Coulogne France
156 D3 Coulognes-Cohan France
162 C2 Coulombiers France
156 B4 Coulombs France
156 D4 Coulommiers France
161 C5 Coulon r. France
224 E4 Coulonge r. Que. Can.
162 B2 Coulonges-sur-l'Autize France
162 C3 Coulounieix-Chamiers France
146 D5 Coulport Argyll and Bute, Scotland U.K.
240 G3 Coulterville CA U.S.A.
238 C2 Council ID U.S.A.
236 E3 Council Bluffs IA U.S.A.
236 D4 Council Grove KS U.S.A.
151 F2 Countesthorpe Leicestershire, England U.K.
146 E5 Coupar Angus Perth and Kinross, Scotland U.K.
238 B1 Coupeville WA U.S.A.
161 A5 Coupiac France
159 F3 Couptrain France
182 B3 Coura Port.
251 G3 Courantyne r. Guyana
165 D4 Courcelles Belgium
233 □H2 Courcelles Que. Can.
157 G3 Courcelles-Chaussy France
157 G3 Courcelles-sur-Nied France
160 E1 Courchaton France
161 E3 Courchevel France
159 H4 Cour-Cheverny France
159 F3 Courcité France
162 B2 Courçon France
156 E3 Courcy France
182 C2 Courel, Serra do mts Spain
159 G3 Courgains France
156 D4 Courgenay France
190 C1 Courgenay Switz.
138 C4 Courland Lagoon b. Lith./Rus. Fed.
160 D2 Courlaoux France
159 F5 Courlay France
156 D4 Courlon-sur-Yonne France
190 B3 Courmayeur Italy
156 D3 Courmelles France
160 B3 Cournon-d'Auvergne France
161 B5 Cournonterral France
160 B3 Courpière France
190 C1 Courrendlin Switz.
163 C5 Courrensan France
156 C2 Courrières France
160 A1 Cours France
162 C3 Coursac France
161 B5 Coursan France
161 F5 Coursegoules France
159 F2 Courseulles-sur-Mer France
160 C2 Cours-la-Ville France
160 B1 Courson-les-Carrières France
190 C1 Court Switz.
156 B4 Courtalain France
190 C1 Courtelary Switz.
160 F1 Courtelevant France
222 E5 Courtenay B.C. Can.
156 D4 Courtenay France
161 C4 Courthézon France
156 E4 Courtisols France
232 E6 Courtland VA U.S.A.
147 C5 Courtmacsherry Rep. of Ireland
159 G3 Courtomer France
147 E4 Courtown Rep. of Ireland
Courtrai Belgium see Kortrijk
165 D4 Court-St-Etienne Belgium
156 B4 Courville-sur-Eure France
160 D2 Cousance France
157 F4 Cousances-les-Forges France
237 E5 Coushatta LA U.S.A.
160 B1 Cousin r. France
217 □2a Cousin i. Inner Islands Seychelles
162 D3 Coussac-Bonneval France
159 G5 Coussay-les-Bois France
156 E5 Coussegrey France
157 F4 Coussey France
161 D5 Coustellet France
163 E6 Coustouges France
158 E2 Coutances France
159 F3 Couterne France
Coutinho Moz. see Ulongue
257 F3 Couto de Magalhães de Minas Brazil
162 B3 Coutras France
223 I5 Coutts Alta Can.
162 C3 Couture r. France
247 □7 Couva Trin. and Tob.
190 B2 Couvet Switz.
165 D4 Couvin Belgium
156 D3 Couvron-et-Aumencourt France
163 C4 Couze r. France
163 C4 Couze-et-St-Front France
162 D3 Couzeix France
182 E4 Covacha del Losar mt. Spain
182 C2 Cova da Serpe, Sierra da mts Spain
183 H3 Covaleda Spain
183 G2 Covarrubias Spain
177 K5 Covăsinţ Romania
197 H3 Covasna Romania
146 C4 Cove Highland, Scotland U.K.
146 F4 Cove Bay Aberdeen, Scotland U.K.
241 K2 Cove Fort UT U.S.A.
182 B2 Covelo Spain
240 F2 Covelo CA U.S.A.
232 D5 Cove Mountains hills PA U.S.A.
252 D3 Covendo Bol.
151 F2 Coventry West Midlands, England U.K.
149 H3 Cover r. England U.K.
150 B4 Coverack Cornwall, England U.K.
241 K5 Covered Wells AZ U.S.A.
232 D6 Covesville VA U.S.A.
182 C4 Covilhã Port.
231 D5 Covington GA U.S.A.
230 C3 Covington IN U.S.A.
232 A5 Covington KY U.S.A.
237 F6 Covington LA U.S.A.
226 C2 Covington MI U.S.A.
232 A4 Covington OH U.S.A.
237 F5 Covington TN U.S.A.
232 C6 Covington VA U.S.A.
227 F2 Cow r. Ont. Can.
83 F3 Cowal, Lake dry lake N.S.W. Austr.
232 B5 Cowan KY U.S.A.
87 D6 Cowan, Lake salt flat W.A. Austr.
225 F4 Cowansville Que. Can.
151 G2 Cowbit Lincolnshire, England U.K.
150 D3 Cowbridge Vale of Glamorgan, Wales U.K.
87 C6 Cowcowing Lakes salt flat W.A. Austr.
146 E5 Cowdenbeath Fife, Scotland U.K.
82 D3 Cowell S.A. Austr.
232 C5 Cowen WV U.S.A.
83 F4 Cowes Vic. Austr.
151 F4 Cowes Isle of Wight, England U.K.
151 G4 Cowfold West Sussex, England U.K.
146 E5 Cowie Stirling, Scotland U.K.
85 F5 Cowley Qld Austr.
149 G4 Cowling North Yorkshire, England U.K.
238 B2 Cowlitz r. WA U.S.A.
232 D6 Cowpasture r. VA U.S.A.
83 G3 Cowra N.S.W. Austr.
149 G3 Cowshill Durham, England U.K.
84 C2 Cox r. N.T. Austr.
163 D5 Cox France
Coxen Hole Hond. see Roatán
151 H3 Coxheath Kent, England U.K.
149 H3 Coxhoe Durham, England U.K.
258 G3 Coxilha de Santana hills Brazil/Uru.
255 B9 Coxilha Grande hills Brazil
255 B6 Coxim Brazil
255 B6 Coxim r. Brazil
233 G3 Coxsackie NY U.S.A.
117 G5 Cox's Bazar Bangl.
149 H3 Coxwold North Yorkshire, England U.K.
260 B4 Coya Chile
206 B4 Coyah Guinea
150 D3 Coychurch Bridgend, Wales U.K.
146 D6 Coylton South Ayrshire, Scotland U.K.
146 E4 Coylumbridge Highland, Scotland U.K.
239 D6 Coyote r. Mex.
241 J5 Coyote Peak hill AZ U.S.A.
240 H3 Coyote Peak CA U.S.A.
244 A2 Coyotitán Mex.
244 D5 Coyuca de Benitez Mex.
244 D4 Coyuca de Catalán Mex.
236 D3 Cozad NE U.S.A.
185 G2 Cózar Spain
162 B3 Cozes France
197 G3 Cozia, Vârful mt. Romania
Cozie, Alpi mts France/Italy see Cottian Alps
243 I4 Cozumel Mex.
192 B3 Cozzano Corse France
193 I5 Cozzo del Pellegrino mt. Italy
148 C5 Craanford Rep. of Ireland
85 E1 Crab Island Qld Austr.
158 C4 Crach France
193 I4 Craco Italy
Cracovia Pol. see Kraków
85 G5 Cracow Qld Austr.
Cracow Pol. see Kraków
150 E2 Cradley Herefordshire, England U.K.
82 D2 Cradock S.A. Austr.
215 E5 Cradock S. Africa
80 E2 Cradock Channel North I. N.Z.
190 F3 Craffaro r. Italy
214 E2 Crafthole S. Africa
146 F5 Craichie Angus, Scotland U.K.
177 L4 Craidorolţ Romania
146 C4 Craig Highland, Scotland U.K.
222 C4 Craig AK U.S.A.
238 F3 Craig CO U.S.A.
146 C6 Craigandaive Argyll and Bute, Scotland U.K.
147 F2 Craigavad Northern Ireland U.K.
147 E2 Craigavon Northern Ireland U.K.
146 D6 Craigdarroch East Ayrshire, Scotland U.K.
83 F4 Craigieburn Vic. Austr.
81 C5 Craigieburn South I. N.Z.
146 C5 Craignure Argyll and Bute, Scotland U.K.
147 E2 Craigs Northern Ireland U.K.
232 D5 Craigsville VA U.S.A.
232 C5 Craigsville WV U.S.A.
146 F5 Crail Fife, Scotland U.K.
173 E2 Crailsheim Ger.
197 F3 Craiova Romania
177 K5 Craiva Romania
234 B3 Craley PA U.S.A.
156 D4 Cramant France
149 H2 Cramlington Northumberland, England U.K.
214 C2 Cramond S. Africa
163 D5 Crampagna France
148 B2 Crana r. Rep. of Ireland
149 G4 Cranage Cheshire, England U.K.
147 D2 Cranagh Northern Ireland U.K.
222 D4 Cranberry Junction B.C. Can.
234 D2 Cranberry Lake NJ U.S.A.
223 K4 Cranberry Portage Man. Can.
150 E4 Cranborne Chase for. England U.K.
83 F4 Cranbourne Vic. Austr.
87 C7 Cranbrook W.A. Austr.
222 H5 Cranbrook B.C. Can.
151 H3 Cranbrook Kent, England U.K.
235 D2 Cranbury NJ U.S.A.
226 C3 Crandon WI U.S.A.
238 C3 Crane OR U.S.A.
237 C6 Crane TX U.S.A.
226 A1 Crane Lake MN U.S.A.
151 G2 Cranfield Bedfordshire, England U.K.
148 B2 Cranford Rep. of Ireland
160 E3 Cran-Gevrier France
151 G3 Cranleigh Surrey, England U.K.
163 E4 Cransac France
146 F6 Cranshaws Scottish Borders, Scotland U.K.
146 D3 Cranstackie hill Scotland U.K.
232 B5 Cranston KY U.S.A.
233 H4 Cranston RI U.S.A.
149 I4 Cranwell Lincolnshire, England U.K.
Cranz Rus. Fed. see Zelenogradsk
159 F4 Craon France
156 D3 Craonne France
161 B3 Craponne-sur-Arzon France
262 P1 Crary Mountains Antarctica
146 D3 Crask Inn Highland, Scotland U.K.
197 F2 Crasna Romania
197 F2 Crasna r. Romania
136 E4 Crasnoe Moldova
254 E3 Crateús Brazil
146 E4 Crathie Aberdeenshire, Scotland U.K.
193 I5 Crati r. Italy
254 F3 Crato Brazil
184 C1 Crato Port.
147 C3 Craughwell Rep. of Ireland
190 D3 Cravagliana Italy
160 E1 Cravanche France
156 D5 Cravant France
253 F3 Cravari r. Brazil
150 E2 Craven Arms Shropshire, England U.K.
256 D4 Cravinhos Brazil
236 C3 Crawford NE U.S.A.
238 C1 Crawford Bay B.C. Can.
146 E6 Crawfordjohn South Lanarkshire, Scotland U.K.
81 C5 Crawford Range mts South I. N.Z.
230 C3 Crawfordsville IN U.S.A.
231 C6 Crawfordville FL U.S.A.
231 D5 Crawfordville GA U.S.A.
169 F5 Crawinkel Ger.
151 G3 Crawley West Sussex, England U.K.
238 E2 Crazy Mountains MT U.S.A.
146 A4 Creag Ghoraidh Western Isles, Scotland U.K.
146 D5 Creag Meagaidh mt. Scotland U.K.
158 E2 Créances France
160 C1 Créancey France
182 B2 Crecente Spain
160 C2 Crêches-sur-Saône France
156 B2 Crécy-en-Ponthieu France
156 C4 Crécy-la-Chapelle France
156 D3 Crécy-sur-Serre France
150 E2 Credenhill Herefordshire, England U.K.
150 D4 Crediton Devon, England U.K.
223 J3 Cree r. Sask. Can.
150 D3 Creech St Michael Somerset, England U.K.
239 F4 Creede CO U.S.A.
147 B4 Creegh Rep. of Ireland
242 D3 Creel Mex.
223 J3 Cree Lake Sask. Can.
227 G3 Creemore Ont. Can.
147 D1 Creeslough Rep. of Ireland
146 D7 Creetown Dumfries and Galloway, Scotland U.K.
147 B2 Creevagh Rep. of Ireland
147 D2 Creggan Northern Ireland U.K.
147 E2 Creggan Northern Ireland U.K.
147 B3 Cregganbaun Rep. of Ireland
147 C3 Creggs Rep. of Ireland
173 E2 Creglingen Ger.
157 G3 Créhange France
223 K4 Creighton Sask. Can.
215 G4 Creighton S. Africa
156 C3 Creil France
164 E2 Creil Neth.
161 B4 Creissels France
190 E3 Crema Italy
160 B3 Cremeaux France
183 E2 Crémenes Spain
160 D3 Crémieu France
169 F3 Cremlingen Ger.
222 H5 Cremona Alta Can.
190 F3 Cremona Italy
190 F3 Cremona prov. Lombardia Italy
156 E4 Creney-près-Troyes France
179 H4 Črenšovci Slovenia
163 B4 Créon France
157 F4 Crépey France
251 G6 Crepori r. Brazil
156 D3 Crépy France
156 C3 Crépy-en-Valois France
188 E3 Cres Croatia
188 E3 Cres i. Croatia
238 B3 Crescent OR U.S.A.
238 A3 Crescent City CA U.S.A.
231 D6 Crescent City FL U.S.A.
90 D3 Crescent Group is Paracel Is
83 H2 Crescent Head N.S.W. Austr.
190 D3 Crescentino Italy
241 M2 Crescent Junction UT U.S.A.
241 J4 Crescent Peak NV U.S.A.
240 I1 Crescent Valley NV U.S.A.
226 A4 Cresco IA U.S.A.
234 C1 Cresco PA U.S.A.
191 G4 Crespino Italy
261 G3 Crespo Arg.
183 F4 Crespos Spain
162 D3 Cressensac France
172 B4 Cressier Switz.
234 B2 Cressona PA U.S.A.
84 C3 Cresswell Downs N.T. Austr.
83 E4 Cressy Vic. Austr.
161 D4 Crest France
232 B4 Crestline OH U.S.A.
222 G5 Creston B.C. Can.
236 E3 Creston IA U.S.A.
238 F3 Creston WY U.S.A.
231 C6 Crestview FL U.S.A.
160 E3 Crest-Voland France
235 D3 Crestwood Village NJ U.S.A.
149 H4 Creswell Derbyshire, England U.K.
234 B3 Creswell PA U.S.A.
83 E4 Creswick Vic. Austr.
Creta i. Greece see Kriti
191 H2 Creta Forata, Monte mt. Italy
186 D4 Cretas Spain
160 D2 Crêt de la Neige mt. France
160 D3 Crêt de Pont mt. France
160 D2 Crêt des Eculaz mt. France
160 D2 Crêt du Nu mt. France
236 D3 Crete NE U.S.A.
156 C4 Créteil France
160 E1 Crêt Monniot mt. France
159 F2 Creully France
186 G2 Creus, Cap de c. Spain
162 E2 Creuse dept Limousin France
162 C1 Creuse r. France
173 F2 Creußen Ger.
173 F2 Creußen r. Ger.
157 G3 Creutzwald France
169 F4 Creuzburg Ger.
160 B2 Creuzier-le-Vieux France
191 G4 Crevalcore Italy
162 D2 Crevant France
157 G4 Crévéchamps France
156 C3 Crèvecœur-le-Grand France
187 C6 Crevillente Spain
149 G4 Crewe Cheshire, England U.K.
232 D6 Crewe VA U.S.A.
150 E4 Crewkerne Somerset, England U.K.
163 C4 Creysse France
216 □1c Criação Velha Pico Azores
146 D5 Crianlarich Stirling, Scotland U.K.
150 C2 Criccieth Gwynedd, Wales U.K.
255 C9 Criciúma Brazil
150 D3 Crickhowell Powys, Wales U.K.
151 F3 Cricklade Wiltshire, England U.K.
136 E4 Cricova Moldova
197 H3 Cricovu Sărat r. Romania
232 A4 Cridersville OH U.S.A.
146 E5 Crieff Perth and Kinross, Scotland U.K.
156 B2 Criel-sur-Mer France
146 E7 Criffell hill Scotland U.K.
149 H4 Crigglestone West Yorkshire, England U.K.
188 E3 Crikvenica Croatia
222 B3 Crillon, Mount AK U.S.A.
148 C3 Crilly Northern Ireland U.K.
Crimea pen. Ukr. see Kryms'kyy Pivostriv
Crimean Republic aut. rep. Ukr. see Krym, Respublika
171 D5 Crimmitschau Ger.
146 G4 Crimond Aberdeenshire, Scotland U.K.
146 C5 Crinan Argyll and Bute, Scotland U.K.
151 I2 Cringleford Norfolk, England U.K.
171 E4 Crinitz Ger.
239 F4 Cripple Creek CO U.S.A.
151 H4 Cripp's Corner East Sussex, England U.K.
159 G2 Criquetot-l'Esneval France
197 I3 Crişan Romania
233 F6 Crisfield MD U.S.A.
195 G2 Crispiano Italy
190 C4 Crissolo Italy
256 D2 Cristais, Serra dos mts Brazil
208 A4 Cristal, Monts de mts Equat. Guinea/Gabon
254 C4 Cristalândia Brazil
256 D2 Cristalina Brazil
Cristalino r. Brazil see Mariembero
253 G2 Cristalino r. Brazil
191 H2 Cristallo mt. Italy
256 C2 Cristianópolis Brazil
257 E5 Cristina Brazil
254 D4 Cristino Castro Brazil
177 L5 Criştioru de Jos Romania
182 E4 Cristóbal Spain
190 D4 Cristoforo Colombo airport Italy
197 G2 Cristuru Secuiesc Romania
197 E2 Crişul Alb r. Romania
197 E2 Crişul Negru r. Romania
197 E2 Crişul Repede r. Romania
197 E2 Crişurilor, Câmpia plain Romania
252 B3 Criterion mt. Peru
136 E4 Criuleni Moldova
170 C2 Crivitz Ger.
226 C3 Crivitz WI U.S.A.
254 C5 Crixás Brazil
254 C5 Crixás Açu r. Brazil
254 C5 Crixás Mirim r. Brazil
197 E5 Crna r. Macedonia
179 F4 Črna Slovenia
196 D4 Crna Glava mt. Yugo.
196 E4 Crna Gora mts Macedonia/Yugo.
196 D4 Crna Gora aut. rep. Yugo.
197 F4 Crna Trava Srbija Yugo.
196 E5 Crni Drim r. Macedonia
197 F4 Crni Timok r. Yugo.
188 E2 Črni vrh mt. Slovenia
188 E3 Črnomelj Slovenia
197 F4 Crnook mt. Yugo.
147 C2 Croagh Rep. of Ireland
147 C2 Croagheheen hill Rep. of Ireland
147 B3 Croagh Patrick hill Rep. of Ireland
188 E3 Croatia country Europe
195 F4 Crocchio r. Italy
195 F4 Crocco, Monte mt. Italy
191 G2 Croce, Monte mt. Italy
193 E2 Croce di Serra, Monte hill Italy
169 F5 Crock Ger.
95 F1 Crocker, Banjaran mts Malaysia
146 E6 Crocketford Dumfries and Galloway, Scotland U.K.
237 E6 Crockett TX U.S.A.
147 D2 Crockmore Rep. of Ireland
162 E3 Crocq France
191 H2 Croda dei Toni mt. Italy
191 H2 Croda Rossa mt. Italy
190 D2 Crodo Italy
150 D3 Croeserw Neath Port Talbot, Wales U.K.
150 B3 Croesgoch Pembrokeshire, Wales U.K.
149 H4 Crofton West Yorkshire, England U.K.
234 B3 Crofton MD U.S.A.
236 D3 Crofton NE U.S.A.
150 C3 Crofty Swansea, Wales U.K.
147 C3 Croghan Rep. of Ireland
233 F3 Croghan NY U.S.A.
149 G3 Croglin Cumbria, England U.K.
193 F2 Crognaleto Italy
146 D4 Croick Highland, Scotland U.K.
156 C2 Croisilles France
190 C3 Croix-Rousse mt. Italy
84 C1 Croker, Cape N.T. Austr.
84 C1 Croker Island N.T. Austr.
147 B4 Cromane Rep. of Ireland
146 D4 Cromarty Highland, Scotland U.K.
146 D4 Cromarty Firth est. Scotland U.K.
146 E4 Cromdale, Hills of Scotland U.K.
151 I2 Cromer Norfolk, England U.K.
150 E3 Cromhall South Gloucestershire, England U.K.
81 B6 Cromwell South I. N.Z.
235 F1 Cromwell CT U.S.A.
226 A2 Cromwell MN U.S.A.
81 C5 Cronadun South I. N.Z.
160 B2 Cronat France
161 B3 Cronce r. France
151 G3 Crondall Hampshire, England U.K.
149 H3 Crook Durham, England U.K.
238 B2 Crooked r. OR U.S.A.
246 D2 Crooked Island Bahamas
246 D2 Crooked Island Passage Bahamas
223 K4 Crooked River Sask. Can.
147 B5 Crookhaven Rep. of Ireland
236 D2 Crookston MN U.S.A.
147 C5 Crookstown Rep. of Ireland
232 B5 Crooksville OH U.S.A.
83 G3 Crookwell N.S.W. Austr.
147 C4 Croom Rep. of Ireland
195 F3 Cropalati Italy
195 F4 Cropani Italy
83 G2 Croppa Creek N.S.W. Austr.
85 E2 Crosbie r. Qld Austr.
146 B3 Crosbost Western Isles, Scotland U.K.
149 F4 Crosby Merseyside, England U.K.
149 I4 Crosby North Lincolnshire, England U.K.
236 E2 Crosby MN U.S.A.
236 C1 Crosby ND U.S.A.
149 G3 Crosby Ravensworth Cumbria, England U.K.
237 C5 Crosbyton TX U.S.A.
195 F3 Crosia Italy
207 H5 Cross r. Nigeria
158 D4 Crossac France
146 C6 Crossaig Argyll and Bute, Scotland U.K.
148 B4 Crossakeel Rep. of Ireland
149 F3 Crosscanonby Cumbria, England U.K.
231 D6 Cross City FL U.S.A.
233 □J1 Cross Creek N.B. Can.
147 D3 Crossdoney Rep. of Ireland
237 E5 Crossett AR U.S.A.
149 G3 Cross Fell hill England U.K.
222 H5 Crossfield Alta Can.
146 E6 Crossford South Lanarkshire, Scotland U.K.
147 F2 Crossgar Northern Ireland U.K.
147 E1 Crossgare Northern Ireland U.K.
150 D2 Crossgates Powys, Wales U.K.
146 D6 Crosshands East Ayrshire, Scotland U.K.
147 C5 Crosshaven Rep. of Ireland
146 D6 Crosshill South Ayrshire, Scotland U.K.
148 E2 Crosshouse East Ayrshire, Scotland U.K.
150 C2 Cross Inn Ceredigion, Wales U.K.
148 B4 Crosskeys Rep. of Ireland
147 E3 Cross Keys Rep. of Ireland
223 L4 Cross Lake Man. Can.
81 D5 Crossley, Mount South I. N.Z.
147 E2 Crossmaglen Northern Ireland U.K.
241 J4 Crossman Peak AZ U.S.A.
146 E7 Crossmichael Dumfries and Galloway, Scotland U.K.
147 B2 Crossmolina Rep. of Ireland
207 H5 Cross River state Nigeria
231 C5 Crossville TN U.S.A.
150 D2 Crossway Powys, Wales U.K.
191 F4 Crostolo r. Italy
149 G4 Croston Lancashire, England U.K.
227 F4 Croswell MI U.S.A.
Croton Italy see Crotone
195 G3 Crotone Italy
195 F3 Crotone prov. Calabria Italy
235 E1 Croton Falls NY U.S.A.
235 E1 Crotonville NY U.S.A.
161 E4 Crots France
171 D5 Crottendorf Ger.
151 H3 Crouch r. England U.K.
151 F3 Croughton Northamptonshire, England U.K.
162 C2 Croutelle France
156 D3 Crouy France
156 D3 Crouy-sur-Ourcq France
159 G4 Crouzilles France
147 C2 Crove Rep. of Ireland
222 E3 Crow r. B.C. Can.
238 F2 Crow Agency MT U.S.A.
151 H3 Crowborough East Sussex, England U.K.
238 F3 Crow Creek r. CO U.S.A.
237 D5 Crowell TX U.S.A.
150 E3 Crow Hill Herefordshire, England U.K.
151 G2 Crowland Lincolnshire, England U.K.
149 I4 Crowle North Lincolnshire, England U.K.
237 E6 Crowley LA U.S.A.
146 C4 Crowlin Islands Scotland U.K.
230 C3 Crown Point IN U.S.A.
239 E5 Crownpoint NM U.S.A.
233 G3 Crown Point NY U.S.A.
263 C2 Crown Prince Olav Coast Antarctica
262 W1 Crown Princess Martha Coast Antarctica
234 B3 Crownsville MD U.S.A.
85 H5 Crows Nest Qld Austr.
222 H5 Crowsnest Pass Alta Can.
151 G3 Crowthorne Bracknell Forest, England U.K.
236 E2 Crow Wing r. MN U.S.A.
146 D4 Croy Highland, Scotland U.K.
150 C3 Croyde Devon, England U.K.
85 E3 Croydon Qld Austr.
151 G3 Croydon Greater London, England U.K.
234 D2 Croydon PA U.S.A.
162 D2 Crozant France
232 D5 Crozet VA U.S.A.
265 H8 Crozet, Îles is Indian Ocean
217 □1 Crozet Basin sea feature Indian Ocean
265 G7 Crozet Plateau sea feature Indian Ocean
220 F2 Crozier Channel N.W.T. Can.
158 B3 Crozon France
161 C4 Cruas France
197 G2 Crucea Romania
252 C3 Crucero Peru
246 B2 Cruces Cuba
195 F3 Crucoli Italy
146 G4 Cruden Bay Aberdeenshire, Scotland U.K.
245 E1 Cruillas Mex.
146 B3 Crulabhig Western Isles, Scotland U.K.
159 G3 Crulai France
232 B6 Crum WV U.S.A.
150 D3 Crumlin Caerphilly, Wales U.K.
147 E2 Crumlin Northern Ireland U.K.
160 E2 Cruseilles France
147 C4 Crusheen Rep. of Ireland
157 F3 Crusnes France
157 F3 Crusnes r. France
245 F3 Crustepec, Cerro mt. Mex.
183 H5 Cruz mt. Spain
255 B9 Cruz Alta Brazil
260 E2 Cruz del Eje Arg.
257 E5 Cruzeiro Brazil
256 A5 Cruzeiro do Oeste Brazil
252 B1 Cruzeiro do Sul Acre Brazil
256 A5 Cruzeiro do Sul Paraná Brazil
262 O2 Cruzen Island Antarctica
245 E5 Cruz Grande Mex.
161 A5 Cruzy France
156 E5 Cruzy-le-Châtel France
196 D3 Crvenka Vojvodina, Srbija Yugo.
150 C3 Crymych Pembrokeshire, Wales U.K.
222 F4 Crysdale, Mount B.C. Can.
241 M3 Crystal NM U.S.A.
234 C3 Crystal Beach MD U.S.A.
82 D3 Crystal Brook S.A. Austr.
223 L5 Crystal City Man. Can.
236 F4 Crystal City MO U.S.A.
237 D6 Crystal City TX U.S.A.
226 C2 Crystal Falls MI U.S.A.
226 C4 Crystal Lake IL U.S.A.
231 D6 Crystal River FL U.S.A.
237 F6 Crystal Springs MS U.S.A.
177 J5 Csabacsűd Hungary
176 G4 Csabrendek Hungary
176 F5 Csákánydoroszló Hungary
177 H4 Csákvár Hungary
177 J5 Csanádapáca Hungary
177 J5 Csanádi-hát hills Hungary
177 J5 Csanádpalota Hungary
177 J5 Csanytelek Hungary
177 H4 Császár Hungary
177 I5 Császártöltés Hungary
177 H5 Csátalja Hungary
177 I5 Csávoly Hungary
177 I4 Csécse Hungary
177 I4 Csemő Hungary
177 I5 Csengele Hungary
177 L4 Csenger Hungary
177 J5 Csépa Hungary
176 F4 Csepreg Hungary
177 J3 Cserehát mts Hungary
177 I4 Cserhát hills Hungary
177 I4 Cserhátsurány Hungary
177 J5 Cserkeszőlő Hungary
177 J3 Csernely Hungary
176 G5 Cserszegtomaj Hungary
179 H4 Cserta r. Hungary
176 F5 Csesztreg Hungary
177 G4 Csetény Hungary
Csév Hungary see Piliscsév
177 I5 Csikéria Hungary
177 H4 Csókakő Hungary
177 K4 Csökmő Hungary
177 G5 Csököly Hungary
176 G5 Csokonyavisonta Hungary
177 J3 Csokvaomány Hungary
177 H4 Csolnok Hungary
177 I5 Csólyospálos Hungary
177 I4 Csömör Hungary
177 J5 Csongrád Hungary
177 J5 Csongrád county Hungary
177 G5 Csopak Hungary
177 H4 Csór Hungary
176 G4 Csorna Hungary
176 F5 Csörnyeföld Hungary
176 F5 Csörötnek Hungary
177 J5 Csorvás Hungary
177 H4 Csősz Hungary
177 G4 Csót Hungary
177 H4 Csóványos hill Hungary
176 G5 Csurgó Hungary
127 G4 Ctesiphon tourist site Iraq
182 D2 Cua r. Spain
182 E4 Cuacos de Yuste Spain
97 D5 Cu'a Đinh An r. mouth Vietnam
259 C7 Cuadrada, Sierra hills Arg.
182 E2 Cuadros Spain
245 E5 Cuajinicuilapa Mex.
182 C3 Cualedro Spain
213 H2 Cuamba Moz.
209 D9 Cuando r. Angola/Zambia
209 C8 Cuando Cubango prov. Angola
209 C9 Cuangar Angola
209 C7 Cuango Angola
209 C6 Cuango r. Angola/Dem. Rep. Congo
209 B7 Cuanza r. Angola
209 B7 Cuanza Norte prov. Angola
209 B7 Cuanza Sul prov. Angola
261 I2 Cuareim r. Uru.
261 I2 Cuaro r. Uru.
186 C3 Cuarte de Huerva Spain
261 F3 Cuarto r. Arg.
209 C9 Cuatir r. Angola
Cuatretonda Spain see Quatretonda
242 E3 Cuatro Ciénegas Mex.
252 E4 Cuatro Ojos Bol.
242 D2 Cuauhtémoc Mex.
244 C4 Cuauhtémoc Mex.
244 C1 Cuauhtémoc Mex.
245 E4 Cuautla Mex.
245 E4 Cuautlán Izcalli Mex.
184 C2 Cuba Port.
226 B5 Cuba IL U.S.A.
239 F4 Cuba NM U.S.A.
232 D3 Cuba NY U.S.A.
232 B5 Cuba OH U.S.A.
246 B2 Cuba country West Indies
241 K6 Cubabi, Cerro mt. Mex.
209 B8 Cubal Angola
209 B7 Cubal r. Angola
182 B2 Cubalhão Port.
209 D9 Cubango r. Angola/Namibia
256 D5 Cubatão Brazil
186 D3 Cubells Spain
223 J4 Cub Hills Sask. Can.
182 D1 Cubia r. Spain
185 G3 Cubillas r. Spain
183 G2 Cubillo r. Spain
162 C3 Cubjac France
187 B4 Cubla Spain
183 G2 Cubo de Bureba Spain
183 H3 Cubo de la Solana Spain
136 E4 Cubolta r. Moldova
126 D2 Çubuk Turkey
162 B4 Cubzac-les-Ponts France
186 B3 Cucalón Spain
259 B6 Cucao Chile
241 J5 Cucapa, Sierra mts Mex.
191 H5 Cucco, Monte mt. Italy
192 B4 Cuccuru su Pirastru hill Sardegna Italy
209 C8 Cuchi Angola
258 G4 Cuchilla Grande hills Uru.
261 I3 Cuchilla Grande Inferior hills Uru.
151 G3 Cuckfield West Sussex, England U.K.
151 H4 Cuckmere r. England U.K.
197 G2 Cucu, Vârful mt. Romania
250 E4 Cucuí Amazonas Brazil
209 C7 Cucumbi Angola
161 D5 Cucuron France
250 C3 Cúcuta Col.
186 C3 Cucutas hill Spain
197 H3 Cudalbi Romania
114 C4 Cuddalore Tamil Nadu India
114 C3 Cuddapah Andhra Prad. India
85 E5 Cuddapan, Lake salt flat Qld Austr.
234 D1 Cuddebackville NY U.S.A.
194 B5 Cuddia r. Sicilia Italy
149 G4 Cuddington Cheshire, England U.K.
128 D1 Cudi Dağı hill Turkey
182 D1 Cudillero Spain
163 B4 Cudos France
223 J4 Cudworth Sask. Can.
149 H4 Cudworth South Yorkshire, England U.K.
87 C5 Cue W.A. Austr.
209 C8 Cuebe r. Angola
209 D8 Cueio r. Angola
183 F3 Cuéllar Spain
209 C8 Cuemba Angola
250 B5 Cuenca Ecuador
92 B3 Cuenca Phil.
183 H4 Cuenca Spain
183 H5 Cuenca prov. Castilla - La Mancha Spain
183 H4 Cuenca, Serranía de mts Spain
183 E2 Cuenca de Campos Spain
244 D3 Cuerámaro Mex.
245 E4 Cuernavaca Mex.
237 D6 Cuero TX U.S.A.
161 E5 Cuers France
183 F5 Cuerva Spain
183 H4 Cuervo r. Spain
246 D2 Cueto Cuba
245 F3 Cuetzalán Mex.
259 C7 Cueva de las Manos tourist site Santa Cruz Arg.
187 D4 Cuevas r. Spain
185 F3 Cuevas Altas hill Spain
185 F3 Cuevas Bajas Spain
185 I3 Cuevas de Almanzora Spain
185 E4 Cuevas del Becerro Spain
185 H3 Cuevas del Campo Spain
183 G2 Cuevas de San Clemente Spain
187 D4 Cuevas de Vinromá Spain
186 B4 Cuevas Labradas Spain
252 E5 Cuevo Bol.
183 F2 Cueza r. Spain
151 G3 Cuffley Hertfordshire, England U.K.
158 E4 Cugand France
161 D5 Cuges-les-Pins France
197 F3 Cugir Romania
197 F3 Cugir r. Romania
192 A4 Cuglieri Sardegna Italy
163 D5 Cugnaux France
209 C6 Cugo r. Angola
158 E3 Cuguen France
253 F3 Cuiabá Brazil
253 F4 Cuiabá r. Brazil
245 F5 Cuicatlan Mex.
Cuihua Yunnan China see Daguan
Cuijiang Fujian China see Ninghua
164 E3 Cuijk Neth.
243 H6 Cuilapa Guat.
245 F5 Cuilapan Mex.
147 D2 Cuilcagh hill Rep. of Ireland/U.K.
146 B4 Cuillin Hills Scotland U.K.
146 B4 Cuillin Sound sea chan. Scotland U.K.
209 C7 Cuilo Angola
209 B6 Cuilo Pombo Angola
100 D3 Cuiluan Heilong. China
209 B6 Cuimba Angola
160 D2 Cuiseaux France
156 D3 Cuise-la-Motte France
160 C2 Cuisery France
257 G3 Cuité r. Brazil
245 F4 Cuitláhuac Mex.
209 D9 Cuito r. Angola
209 C8 Cuito Cuanavale Angola
244 D4 Cuitzeo, Laguna de l. Mex.
251 F5 Cuiuni r. Brazil
236 F4 Cuivre r. MO U.S.A.
197 F3 Cujmir Romania
94 C1 Cukai Malaysia
198 B2 Çukë Albania
129 C4 Çukurbağ Turkey
127 F3 Çukurca Turkey
129 A3 Çukurçayır Turkey
199 G2 Çukurhisar Eskişehir Turkey
128 B1 Çukurova plat. Turkey
136 E4 Cula r. Moldova
107 H4 Culai Shan mt. Shandong China
162 E2 Culan France
146 E4 Culardoch hill Scotland U.K.
92 B4 Culasi Phil.
238 F1 Culbertson MT U.S.A.
236 C3 Culbertson NE U.S.A.
146 D4 Culbokie Highland, Scotland U.K.
83 F3 Culcairn N.S.W. Austr.
177 M4 Culciu Romania
147 D1 Culdaff Rep. of Ireland
146 F4 Culdrain Aberdeenshire, Scotland U.K.
247 □1 Culebra, Isla de i. Puerto Rico

252 A2 Culebras Peru
247 □1 Culebrinas r. Puerto Rico
164 E3 Culemborg Neth.
129 D4 Culfa Azer.
242 D3 Culiacán Mex.
92 A4 Culion Phil.
92 A4 Culion i. Phil.
148 B3 Culkey Northern Ireland U.K.
187 C4 Culla Spain
148 B5 Cullahill Rep. of Ireland
185 H3 Cullar r. Spain
185 H3 Cúllar-Baza Spain
147 E2 Cullaville Northern Ireland U.K.
147 B2 Culleens Rep. of Ireland
146 F4 Cullen Moray, Scotland U.K.
237 E5 Cullen LA U.S.A.
85 E1 Cullen Point Qld Austr.
187 C5 Cullera Spain
146 D4 Cullicudden Highland, Scotland U.K.
147 B3 Cullin Rep. of Ireland
215 G1 Cullinan S. Africa
146 C5 Cullipool Argyll and Bute, Scotland U.K.
146 □G1 Cullivoe Shetland, Scotland U.K.
231 C5 Cullman AL U.S.A.
150 D4 Cullompton Devon, England U.K.
190 B2 Cully Switz.
147 E2 Cullybackey Northern Ireland U.K.
147 E2 Cullyhanna Northern Ireland U.K.
146 C3 Cul Mor hill Scotland U.K.
147 D1 Culmore Northern Ireland U.K.
150 D4 Culmstock Devon, England U.K.
146 C4 Culnacraig Highland, Scotland U.K.
146 B4 Culnaknock Highland, Scotland U.K.
160 D3 Culoz France
232 E5 Culpeper VA U.S.A.
250 □ Culpepper, Isla i. Islas Galápagos Ecuador
146 D4 Culrain Highland, Scotland U.K.
146 □G1 Culswick Shetland, Scotland U.K.
146 E6 Culter Fell hill Scotland U.K.
146 F4 Cults Aberdeen, Scotland U.K.
254 B4 Culuene r. Brazil
226 D5 Culver IN U.S.A.
87 E7 Culver, Point W.A. Austr.
81 D5 Culverden South I. N.Z.
146 D6 Culzean Bay Scotland U.K.
254 D2 Cumã, Baía do inlet Brazil
129 C4 Cumaçay Turkey
251 E2 Cumaná Venez.
199 G1 Cumaova Turkey
256 C3 Cumari Brazil
250 B4 Cumbal, Nevado de vol. Col.
232 B6 Cumberland KY U.S.A.
232 D5 Cumberland MD U.S.A.
232 C5 Cumberland OH U.S.A.
232 D6 Cumberland VA U.S.A.
226 A3 Cumberland WI U.S.A.
232 A6 Cumberland r. KY U.S.A.
259 □ Cumberland Bay S. Georgia
234 C3 Cumberland County county NJ U.S.A.
234 A2 Cumberland County county PA U.S.A.
223 K4 Cumberland House Sask. Can.
85 G4 Cumberland Islands Qld Austr.
232 B6 Cumberland Mountain mts KY/TN U.S.A.
221 L3 Cumberland Peninsula Nunavut Can.
231 C5 Cumberland Plateau Kentucky/Tennessee U.S.A.
221 L3 Cumberland Sound sea chan. Nunavut Can.
146 E6 Cumbernauld North Lanarkshire, Scotland U.K.
256 D5 Cumbica airport São Paulo Brazil
183 F5 Cumbre Alta mt. Spain
259 C7 Cumbre Negro mt. Arg.
184 D2 Cumbres de San Bartolomé Spain
184 D2 Cumbres Mayores Spain
149 F3 Cumbria admin. div. England U.K.
114 C3 Cumbum Andhra Prad. India
184 B3 Cumeada Port.
190 C4 Cumiana Italy
182 C3 Cumieira Port.
251 H5 Cuminapanema r. Brazil
146 F4 Cuminestown Aberdeenshire, Scotland U.K.
170 C2 Cumlosen Ger.
231 C5 Cumming GA U.S.A.
240 F2 Cummings CA U.S.A.
82 C3 Cummins S.A. Austr.
86 E3 Cummins Range hills W.A. Austr.
83 G3 Cumnock N.S.W. Austr.
146 D6 Cumnock East Ayrshire, Scotland U.K.
151 F3 Cumnor Oxfordshire, England U.K.
242 C2 Cumpas Mex.
260 B4 Cumpeo Chile
126 D3 Çumra Turkey
159 F4 Cunault France
260 A6 Cunco Chile
87 C6 Cunderdin W.A. Austr.
250 C3 Cundinamarca dept Col.
215 G3 Cundycleugh S. Africa
163 C4 Cunegès France
209 B9 Cunene prov. Angola
209 B9 Cunene r. Angola/Namibia alt. Kunene
190 C4 Cuneo Italy
190 C4 Cuneo prov. Piemonte Italy
171 F4 Cunewalde Ger.
156 E4 Cunfin France
82 C3 Cungena S.A. Austr.
97 E4 Cung Son Vietnam
126 E3 Çüngüş Turkey
257 E5 Cunha Brazil
182 C4 Cunha Port.
209 C8 Cunhinga Angola
136 E4 Cunicea Moldova
186 E3 Cunit Spain
160 B3 Cunlhat France
83 F2 Cunnamulla Qld Austr.
146 □G1 Cunningsburgh Shetland, Scotland U.K.
182 B2 Cuntis Spain
197 E3 Cununa mt. Romania
140 N1 Čuokkaraš'ša mt. Norway
190 C3 Cuorgnè Italy
146 E5 Cupar Fife, Scotland U.K.
251 H5 Cupari r. Brazil
177 L4 Cupari, Dealul hill Romania
136 D3 Cupcina Moldova
193 G2 Cupello Italy
193 F1 Cupra Marittima Italy
191 I5 Cupramontana Italy
196 E4 Ćuprija Srbija Yugo.
242 C3 Cupula, Pico mt. Mex.
163 D5 Cuq-Toulza France
254 F4 Curaçá Brazil
250 D6 Curaçá r. Brazil
247 □10 Curaçao i. Neth. Antilles
260 B6 Curacautín Chile
260 E6 Curacó r. Arg.
258 B5 Curanilahue Chile
252 C2 Curanja r. Peru
250 C5 Curaray r. Ecuador
260 B6 Curarrehue Chile
177 L5 Curăţele Romania
258 F3 Curaya r. Arg.
82 D2 Curdlawidny Lagoon salt flat S.A. Austr.
250 D5 Curé r. Col.
160 B1 Cure r. France
190 D3 Cureggio Italy
260 A4 Curepto Chile
160 C2 Curgy France
Curia Switz. see Chur
260 B4 Curicó Chile
250 E5 Curicuriari, Serra hill Brazil
250 E5 Curieuriari r. Brazil
254 D4 Curimata Brazil
195 F4 Curinga Italy
256 C6 Curitiba Brazil
255 C8 Curitibanos Brazil
256 B6 Curiúva Brazil
83 G2 Curlewis N.S.W. Austr.
82 D2 Curnamona S.A. Austr.
209 A8 Curoca r. Angola
190 D3 Curone r. Italy
191 F2 Curon Venosta Italy
182 C3 Curopos Port.
83 G2 Currabubula N.S.W. Austr.
147 E4 Curracloe Rep. of Ireland
147 E3 Curragh Rep. of Ireland
147 C3 Curraghroe Rep. of Ireland
147 C3 Curragh West Rep. of Ireland
147 C4 Curraglass Rep. of Ireland
184 □ Curral das Freiras Madeira
251 I5 Curralinho Brazil
227 F3 Curran MI U.S.A.
241 J2 Currant NV U.S.A.
83 F2 Curranyalpa N.S.W. Austr.
182 B2 Currás Spain
85 E5 Currawilla Qld Austr.
237 F4 Current r. MO U.S.A.
83 E4 Currie Tas. Austr.
241 J1 Currie NV U.S.A.
231 E4 Currituck NC U.S.A.
147 C3 Curry Rep. of Ireland
150 E3 Curry Rivel Somerset, England U.K.
195 H2 Cursi Italy
177 L6 Curtea Romania
197 G3 Curtea de Argeș Romania
196 E2 Curtici Romania
87 D6 Curtin W.A. Austr.
85 H5 Curtis Channel Qld Austr.
83 F4 Curtis Group is Tas. Austr.
85 G4 Curtis Island Qld Austr.
77 I5 Curtis Island N.Z.
177 L4 Curtuișeni Romania
251 H6 Curuá r. Brazil
251 I4 Curuá, Ilha i. Brazil
254 B3 Curuaés r. Brazil
251 H5 Curuapanema r. Brazil
251 H5 Curuá Una r. Brazil
254 D2 Curuçá Brazil
94 C3 Curup Sumatera Indon.
251 E4 Curupira, Serra mts Brazil/Venez.
253 E3 Cururú Bol.
253 F1 Cururu r. Brazil
254 D2 Cururupu Brazil
251 F3 Curutú, Cerro mt. Venez.
261 H1 Curuzú Cuatiá Arg.
257 E3 Curvelo Brazil
226 C2 Curwood, Mount hill MI U.S.A.
193 G3 Cusano Mutri Italy
252 C3 Cusco Peru
252 B3 Cusco dept Peru
147 E1 Cushendall Northern Ireland U.K.
147 E1 Cushendun Northern Ireland U.K.
148 B4 Cushina Rep. of Ireland
237 D4 Cushing OK U.S.A.
190 F4 Cusna, Monte mt. Italy
162 C3 Cussac France
162 B3 Cussac-Fort-Médoc France
161 B4 Cussac-sur-Loire France
160 B2 Cusset France
231 C5 Cusseta GA U.S.A.
160 C1 Cussy-les-Forges France
238 F2 Custer MT U.S.A.
236 C3 Custer SD U.S.A.
157 G4 Custines France
194 B4 Custonaci Sicilia Italy
238 D1 Cut Bank MT U.S.A.
238 D1 Cut Bank Creek r. MT U.S.A.
231 C6 Cuthbert GA U.S.A.
84 C2 Cuthbertson Falls N.T. Austr.
191 F4 Cutigliano Italy
240 H3 Cutler CA U.S.A.
233 □J2 Cutler ME U.S.A.
231 D7 Cutler Ridge FL U.S.A.
194 D5 Cutò r. Sicilia Italy
237 F6 Cut Off LA U.S.A.
260 C6 Cutral-Co Arg.
195 F3 Cutro Italy
195 H2 Cutrofiano Italy
83 F2 Cuttaburra Creek r. Qld Austr.
117 F5 Cuttack Orissa India
192 A3 Cuttoli-Corticchiato Corse France
244 D4 Cutzamala r. Mex.
209 B8 Cuvelai Angola
208 B5 Cuvette admin. reg. Congo
87 B5 Cuvier, Cape W.A. Austr.
163 E5 Cuxac-Cabardès France
161 A5 Cuxac-d'Aude France
129 F4 Çuxanlı Azer.
168 D2 Cuxhaven Ger.
232 C4 Cuyahoga Falls OH U.S.A.
240 H4 Cuyama CA U.S.A.
240 G4 Cuyama r. CA U.S.A.
92 B3 Cuyapo Phil.
92 B4 Cuyo Phil.
92 B4 Cuyo East Passage Phil.
92 B4 Cuyo Islands Phil.
92 B4 Cuyo West Passage Phil.
251 G3 Cuyuni r. Guyana
244 B4 Cuyutlán Mex.
162 D4 Cuzance France
Cuzco Peru see Cusco
185 F2 Cuzna r. Spain
163 C4 Cuzorn France
171 F5 Cvikov Czech Rep.
150 D3 Cwm Blaenau Gwent, Wales U.K.
150 D3 Cwmafan Neath Port Talbot, Wales U.K.
150 D2 Cwmbach Powys, Wales U.K.
150 D3 Cwmbran Torfaen, Wales U.K.
150 D3 Cwmllynfell Neath Port Talbot, Wales U.K.
211 A5 Cyangugu Rwanda
174 C3 Cybinka Pol.
Cyclades dept Greece see Kyklades
Cyclades is Greece see Kyklades
175 L4 Cyców Pol.
Cydonia Kriti Greece see Chania
Cydweli Carmarthenshire, Wales U.K. see Kidwelly
83 F5 Cygnet Tas. Austr.
232 B4 Cygnet OH U.S.A.
Cymru admin. div. U.K. see Wales
150 D2 Cynghordy Carmarthenshire, Wales U.K.
150 C3 Cynin r. Wales U.K.
232 A5 Cynthiana KY U.S.A.
150 C3 Cynwyl Elfed Carmarthenshire, Wales U.K.
223 I5 Cypress Hills Sask. Can.
128 A2 Cyprus country Asia
202 D3 Cyrenaica reg. Libya
202 D1 Cyrene tourist site Libya
156 D2 Cysoing France
Cythera i. Greece see Kythira
150 C3 Cywyn r. Wales U.K.
174 E3 Czacz Pol.
174 G4 Czajków Pol.
174 E2 Czaplinek Pol.
223 I4 Czar Alta Can.
175 J5 Czarna Podkarpackie Pol.
175 K5 Czarna Podkarpackie Pol.
175 H4 Czarna r. Pol.
175 H5 Czarna r. Pol.
175 J5 Czarna r. Pol.
175 L2 Czarna Białostocka Pol.
174 F1 Czarna Dąbrówka Pol.
175 K6 Czarna Górna Pol.
175 L2 Czarna Hańcza r. Pol.
175 I5 Czarna Nida r. Pol.
174 G3 Czarna Struga r. Pol.
174 G2 Czarna Woda Pol.
175 H5 Czarnca Pol.
174 E2 Czarne Pol.
175 J2 Czarnia Pol.
174 E3 Czarnków Pol.
174 G4 Czarnożyły Pol.
175 H6 Czarny Dunajec Pol.
177 I2 Czarny Dunajec r. Pol.
174 G4 Czastary Pol.
175 I6 Czchów Pol.
175 H6 Czechowice-Dziedzice Pol.
176 E2 Czech Republic country Europe
175 J4 Czekarzewice Pol.
175 K4 Czemierniki Pol.
174 E3 Czempiń Pol.
175 L3 Czeremcha Pol.
174 F4 Czermin Pol.
174 D4 Czerna Mała r. Pol.
174 D4 Czerna Wielka r. Pol.
174 F4 Czernica Pol.
174 E2 Czernica r. Pol.
175 I2 Czernice Borowe Pol.
174 F3 Czerniejewo Pol.
175 I4 Czerniewice Pol.
174 G3 Czernikowo Pol.
174 E4 Czernina Pol.
Czernowitz Chernivets'ka Oblast' Ukr. see Chernivtsi
174 F2 Czersk Pol.
174 D3 Czerwieńsk Pol.
175 J3 Czerwin Pol.
175 I3 Czerwińsk nad Wisłą Pol.
174 G5 Czerwionka-Leszczyny Pol.
174 E3 Czerwonak Pol.
171 G4 Czerwona Woda Pol.
175 J3 Czerwonka Włościańska Pol.
175 H4 Czestków Pol.
175 H5 Częstochowa Pol.
174 F4 Czeszów Pol.
174 E2 Człopa Pol.
174 F2 Człuchów Pol.
174 F3 Czmoń Pol.
171 F4 Czorneboh hill Ger.
175 I3 Czosnów Pol.
175 J6 Czudec Pol.
175 L3 Czyże Pol.
175 K3 Czyżew-Osada Pol.

D

96 D2 Đa, Sông r. Vietnam
169 C5 Daaden Ger.
107 J2 Da'an Jilin China
92 B4 Daanbantayan Phil.
164 F2 Daarle Neth.
128 B4 Dabāb, Jabal aḑ mt. Jordan
211 B7 Dabaga Tanz.
250 D2 Dabajuro Venez.
206 D4 Dabakala Côte d'Ivoire
107 H3 Daban Nei Mongol China
106 D4 Daban Shan mts China
108 B2 Dabao Sichuan China
177 I4 Dabas Hungary
108 D1 Daba Shan mts China
210 C1 Dabat Eth.
Dabba Sichuan China see Daocheng
250 B3 Dabeiba Col.
96 B3 Dabein Myanmar
170 C2 Dabel Ger.
116 C5 Dabhoi Gujarat India
114 B2 Dabhol Mahar. India
174 D3 Dąbie Pol.
174 G3 Dąbie Pol.
174 C2 Dąbie, Jezioro l. Pol.
109 E2 Dabie Shan mts China
143 G4 Dąbki Pol.
157 H4 Dabo France
116 D4 Daboh Madh. Prad. India
206 C4 Dabola Guinea
206 D5 Dabou Côte d'Ivoire
206 E4 Daboya Ghana
107 F4 Dabqig Nei Mongol China
116 D4 Dabra Madh. Prad. India
174 G3 Dąbroszyn Pol.
174 F3 Dąbrowa Kujawsko-Pomorskie Pol.
174 F5 Dąbrowa Opolskie Pol.
174 F5 Dąbrowa Opolskie Pol.
175 L2 Dąbrowa Białostocka Pol.
174 G3 Dąbrowa Biskupia Pol.
174 G2 Dąbrowa Chełmińska Pol.
175 H5 Dąbrowa Górnicza Pol.
175 I5 Dąbrowa Tarnowska Pol.
175 H3 Dąbrowice Pol.
174 D3 Dąbrówka Wielkopolska Pol.
175 I2 Dąbrówno Pol.
109 F3 Dabu Guangdong China
197 G4 Dăbuleni Romania
Dacca Bangl. see Dhaka
173 F3 Dachau Ger.
173 F3 Dachauer Moos marsh Ger.
106 D4 Dachechang Nei Mongol China
107 H3 Dachengzi Liaoning China
114 C2 Dachepalle Andhra Prad. India
175 L5 Dachnów Pol.
169 F4 Dachrieden Ger.
173 E2 Dachsbach Ger.
108 C2 Dachuan Sichuan China
176 E2 Dačice Czech Rep.
227 I3 Dacre Ont. Can.
149 G3 Dacre Cumbria, England U.K.
177 H4 Dad Hungary
129 B4 Dadaş Turkey
126 D2 Daday Turkey
210 D1 Daddato Djibouti
231 D6 Dade City FL U.S.A.
231 C5 Dadeville AL U.S.A.
Dadong Liaoning China see Donggang
163 D5 Dadou r. France
116 C5 Dadra Dadra India
Dadra Mahar. India see Achalpur
116 C5 Dadra and Nagar Haveli union terr. India
123 F5 Dadu Pak.
108 B2 Dadu He r. Sichuan China
97 D5 Đa Dung r. Vietnam
92 B3 Daet Phil.
108 C3 Dafang Guizhou China
109 G1 Dafeng Jiangsu China
117 H4 Dafla Hills India
198 C3 Dafni Dytiki Ellas Greece
223 M4 Dafoe r. Man. Can.
226 E2 Dafter MI U.S.A.
177 H4 Dág Hungary
116 C5 Dag Rajasthan India
199 G3 Dağ Antalya Turkey
210 D3 Daga Medo Eth.
206 B2 Dagana Senegal
183 G4 Daganzo de Arriba Spain
106 D5 Dagcanglhamo Gansu China
129 D3 Dağ Cäyir Azer.
129 C3 Dağcı Turkey
138 F3 Dagda Latvia
199 F2 Dağdere Manisa Turkey
Dage Hebei China see Fengning
168 D1 Dagebüll Ger.
Dagenraad atoll Arch. des Tuamotu Fr. Polynesia see Manihi
129 E2 Dagestan, Respublika aut. rep. Rus. Fed.
Dagestanskaya A.S.S.R. aut. rep. Rus. Fed. see Dagestan, Respublika
129 F2 Dagestanskiye Ogni Rus. Fed.
Dagezhen Hebei China see Fengning
215 E5 Daggaboersnek S. Africa
Daghestan aut. rep. Rus. Fed. see Dagestan, Respublika
163 D4 Daglan France
129 E4 Dağlıq Qarabağ aut. reg. Azer.
190 C1 Dagmersellen Switz.
Dagö i. Estonia see Hiiumaa
Dagon Myanmar see Yangôn
81 B6 Dagon mt. South I. N.Z.
129 C3 Dağpınar Turkey
111 D6 Dagrag Zangbo r. Xizang China
107 H4 Dagu Tianjin China
107 I4 Dagu r. China
108 B3 Daguan Yunnan China
100 D3 Daguokui Shan hill Heilong. China
92 B2 Dagupan Phil.
84 B3 Daguragu N.T. Austr.
Dagxoi Sichuan China see Sowa
Dagxoi Sichuan China see Yidun
111 E6 Dagzê Xizang China
124 B3 Dahabān Saudi Arabia
222 E2 Dahadinni r. N.W.T. Can.
Dahalach, Isole is Eritrea see Dahlak Archipelago
Dahana des. Saudi Arabia see Ad Dahnā'
114 B2 Dahanu Mahar. India
Dahe Guangxi China see Ziyuan
107 F3 Dahei r. China
100 D3 Daheiding Shan mt. China
106 B3 Dahei Shan mt. Xinjiang China
109 F3 Daheng Fujian China
Daheyan Xinjiang China see Turpan Zhan
100 E3 Dahezhen Heilong. China
107 H3 Da Hinggan Ling mts China
114 B2 Dahivadi Mahar. India
203 I6 Dahlak Archipelago is Eritrea
169 B5 Dahlem Ger.
171 E4 Dahlen Ger.
168 F2 Dahlenburg Ger.
171 E4 Dahlener Heide reg. Ger.
171 C3 Dahlenwarsleben Ger.
231 D5 Dahlonega GA U.S.A.
171 E3 Dahlwitz-Hoppegarten Ger.
205 H2 Dahmani Tunisia
171 E4 Dahme Brandenburg Ger.
170 C1 Dahme Schleswig-Holstein Ger.
171 E3 Dahme r. Ger.
172 B2 Dahn Ger.
116 C5 Dahod Gujarat India
Dahomey country Africa see Benin
Dahra Senegal see Dara
168 F3 Dähre Ger.
127 F3 Dahūk Iraq
127 F3 Dahūk governorate Iraq
125 E4 Dahyah, Wādī r. Yemen
105 E3 Daibosatsu-rei mt. Japan
107 H4 Daicheng Hebei China
Daido r. N. Korea see Taedong-gang
105 G2 Daigo Japan
78 □6 Dai Island Solomon Is
140 L2 Daikanvik Sweden
96 B3 Daik-u Myanmar
146 B3 Dail Bho Thuath Western Isles, Scotland U.K.
232 D5 Dailey WV U.S.A.
146 D6 Dailly South Ayrshire, Scotland U.K.
122 D3 Daim Iran
103 F5 Daimanji-san hill Japan
185 G1 Daimiel Spain
105 E3 Daimugen-zan mt. Japan
147 D3 Daingean Rep. of Ireland
237 E5 Daingerfield TX U.S.A.
104 C2 Dainichiga-take vol. Japan
104 C2 Dainichi-gawa r. Japan
104 C2 Dainichi-zan mt. Japan
108 A1 Dainkog Sichuan China
85 F3 Daintree Qld Austr.
156 C2 Dainville France
157 F4 Dainville-Bertheléville France
261 G5 Daireaux Arg.
Dairen Liaoning China see Dalian
146 F5 Dairsie Fife, Scotland U.K.
203 F3 Dairût Egypt
235 D1 Dairyland NY U.S.A.
226 A2 Dairyland WI U.S.A.
103 F6 Dai-sen vol. Japan
109 G2 Daishan Zhejiang China
104 B4 Daitō Japan
105 F2 Daiya-gawa r. Japan
Daiyue Shanxi China see Shanyin
109 F3 Daiyun Shan mts China
246 E3 Dajabón Dom. Rep.
84 D4 Dajarra Qld Austr.
Dajie Yunnan China see Jiangchuan
108 B2 Dajin Chuan r. Sichuan China
106 D4 Dajing Gansu China
106 B4 Da Juh Qinghai China
206 A3 Dakar Senegal
Dakhla Western Sahara see Ad Dakhla
203 F3 Dakhla Oasis Egypt
204 A5 Dakhlet Nouâdhibou admin. reg. Maur.
129 B1 Dakhovskaya Rus. Fed.
97 D4 Đak Nghe r. Vietnam
138 G5 Dakol'ka r. Belarus
116 C5 Dakor Gujarat India
207 G3 Dakoro Niger
236 E3 Dakota City IA U.S.A.
236 D3 Dakota City NE U.S.A.
196 E4 Đakovica Kosovo, Srbija Yugo.
188 G3 Đakovo Croatia
209 D7 Dala Angola
177 J5 Đala Vojvodina, Srbija Yugo.
178 B3 Dalaas Austria
206 B4 Dalaba Guinea
146 A4 Dalabrog Western Isles, Scotland U.K.
Dalad Qi Nei Mongol China see Shulinzhao
Dalai Jilin China see Da'an
106 D3 Dalain Hob Nei Mongol China
122 A3 Dālā Khānī, Kūh-e mt. Iran
122 B4 Dālakī Iran
122 B4 Dalaki, Rūd-e r. Iran
128 A5 Dalal, Gebel mt. Egypt
143 G1 Dalälven r. Sweden
199 F3 Dalama Aydın Turkey
107 G3 Dalamamiao Nei Mongol China
199 F3 Dalaman Turkey
199 F3 Dalaman r. Turkey
106 E3 Dalandzadgad Mongolia
92 B4 Dalanganem Islands Phil.
110 C3 Dalaoba Xinjiang China
Dalap-Uliga-Darrit Majuro Marshall Is see Delap-Uliga-Djarrit
143 F1 Dalarna county Sweden
141 K3 Dalarna reg. Sweden
97 E5 Đa Lat Vietnam
Dalatando Angola see N'dalatando
106 D3 Dalay Mongolia
146 E7 Dalbeattie Dumfries and Galloway, Scotland U.K.
85 F4 Dalbeg Qld Austr.
170 C2 Dalberg-Wendelstorf Ger.
226 A3 Dalbo MN U.S.A.
142 E2 Dalbosjön l. Sweden
85 G5 Dalby Qld Austr.
142 E4 Dalby Sweden
259 B6 Dalcahue Chile
142 A1 Dale Hordaland Norway
141 I3 Dale Sogn og Fjordane Norway
150 B3 Dale Pembrokeshire, Wales U.K.
232 E5 Dale City VA U.S.A.
169 B5 Daleiden Ger.
164 F2 Dalen Neth.
215 G2 Daleside S. Africa
175 I5 Daleszyce Pol.
231 C6 Daleville AL U.S.A.
234 C1 Daleville PA U.S.A.
141 K3 Dalfors Sweden
164 F2 Dalfsen Neth.
87 C5 Dalgaranger, Mount hill W.A. Austr.
83 G4 Dalgety N.S.W. Austr.
87 B5 Dalgety r. W.A. Austr.
146 E5 Dalgety Bay Fife, Scotland U.K.
151 H2 Dalham Suffolk, England U.K.
237 C4 Dalhart TX U.S.A.
225 H3 Dalhousie N.B. Can.
116 D2 Dalhousie Hima. Prad. India
107 F5 Dali Shaanxi China
108 B3 Dali Yunnan China
107 F4 Dali r. China
107 I4 Dalian Liaoning China
Daliang Guangdong China see Shunde
106 D4 Daliang Qinghai China
108 B2 Daliang Shan mts Sichuan China
185 H4 Dalías Spain
Daliburgh Western Isles, Scotland U.K. see Dalabrog
129 E4 Dälidağ mt. Azer.
175 H4 Dalików Pol.
129 E3 Dälilär Azer.
129 E3 Dälimämmädli Azer.
107 I3 Dalin Nei Mongol China
107 I3 Daling r. China
Dalinghe Liaoning China see Linhai
101 C4 Dalizi Jilin China
188 G3 Dalj Croatia
146 E6 Dalkeith Midlothian, Scotland U.K.
117 F4 Dalkola W. Bengal India
85 H5 Dallarnil Qld Austr.
146 E4 Dallas Moray, Scotland U.K.
238 B2 Dallas OR U.S.A.
234 C1 Dallas PA U.S.A.
237 D5 Dallas TX U.S.A.
226 B5 Dallas City IL U.S.A.
234 B3 Dallastown PA U.S.A.
Dalles City OR U.S.A. see The Dalles
170 E3 Dallgow Ger.
220 E4 Dall Island AK U.S.A.
210 D1 Dallol vol. Eth.
188 E3 Dalmacija reg. Croatia
146 D5 Dalmally Argyll and Bute, Scotland U.K.
116 E4 Dalman Uttar Prad. India
177 H5 Dalmand Hungary
Dalmatia reg. Croatia see Dalmacija
234 B2 Dalmatia PA U.S.A.
146 D6 Dalmellington East Ayrshire, Scotland U.K.
223 J4 Dalmeny Sask. Can.
190 E3 Dalmine Italy
146 D4 Dalnavie Highland, Scotland U.K.
100 E3 Dal'negorsk Rus. Fed.
100 E3 Dal'nerechensk Rus. Fed.
134 I5 Dal'neye Konstantinovo Rus. Fed.
Dalny Liaoning China see Dalian
206 D5 Daloa Côte d'Ivoire
85 G1 Daloloia Group is P.N.G.
108 C3 Dalou Shan mts China
171 D5 Dalovice Czech Rep.
146 D6 Dalry North Ayrshire, Scotland U.K.
146 D6 Dalrymple East Ayrshire, Scotland U.K.
85 F4 Dalrymple, Lake Qld Austr.
85 G4 Dalrymple, Mount Qld Austr.
138 D1 Dalsbruk Fin.
142 E2 Dals Långed Sweden
157 G3 Dalstein France
149 G3 Dalston Cumbria, England U.K.
117 F4 Daltenganj Bihar India
224 C3 Dalton Ont. Can.
215 H3 Dalton S. Africa
231 C5 Dalton GA U.S.A.
233 G3 Dalton MA U.S.A.
232 C4 Dalton OH U.S.A.
234 C1 Dalton PA U.S.A.
Daltonganj Bihar India see Daltenganj
149 F3 Dalton-in-Furness Cumbria, England U.K.
227 E1 Dalton Mills Ont. Can.
147 C4 Dalua r. Rep. of Ireland
94 C2 Daludalu Sumatera Indon.
161 E4 Daluis France
109 E4 Daluo Shan mt. Guangdong China
140 □C2 Dalvík Iceland
87 C6 Dalwallinu W.A. Austr.
146 D5 Dalwhinnie Highland, Scotland U.K.
84 B2 Daly r. N.T. Austr.
199 F3 Dalyan Turkey
240 F3 Daly City CA U.S.A.
84 B2 Daly River N.T. Austr.
147 C3 Dalystown Rep. of Ireland
84 C3 Daly Waters N.T. Austr.
136 B2 Damachava Belarus
207 H3 Damagaram Takaya Niger
129 C3 Damal Turkey
116 C5 Daman Daman India
116 B5 Daman and Diu union terr. India
138 E5 Damanava Belarus
122 B3 Dāmaneh Iran
203 F2 Damanhûr Egypt
Damão Daman India see Daman
122 B3 Damaq Iran
129 B3 Damar Turkey
208 C3 Damara C.A.R.
212 C4 Damaraland reg. Namibia
Damas Syria see Damascus
207 I3 Damasak Nigeria
157 G4 Damas-aux-Bois France
128 C3 Damascus Syria
232 E5 Damascus MD U.S.A.
234 C1 Damascus PA U.S.A.
232 C6 Damascus VA U.S.A.
174 F3 Damasławek Pol.
207 H4 Damaturu Nigeria
122 C3 Damāvand Iran
122 C3 Damāvand, Qolleh-ye mt. Iran
163 C4 Damazan France
209 B6 Damba Angola
157 H4 Dambach-la-Ville France
207 F4 Dambai Ghana
207 H3 Dambatta Nigeria
170 C2 Dambeck Ger.
207 I4 Damboa Nigeria
179 H1 Dambořice Czech Rep.
197 G3 Dâmbovița r. Romania
117 H4 Damchara Assam India
120 F2 Damdy Kustanayskaya Oblast' Kazakh.
157 G4 Damelevières France
246 D3 Dame Marie Haiti
151 F4 Damerham Hampshire, England U.K.
148 B5 Damerstown Rep. of Ireland
156 D3 Damery France
158 D4 Damgan France
122 C2 Damghan Iran
147 E1 Damhead Northern Ireland U.K.
163 D5 Damiatte France
Damietta Egypt see Dumyât
159 G3 Damigny France
107 G4 Daming Hebei China
108 D4 Daming Shan mt. Guangxi China
108 A1 Damjong Qinghai China
Dammam Saudi Arabia see Ad Dammām
156 B4 Dammarie France
190 D2 Dammastock mt. Switz.
165 C3 Damme Belgium
168 D3 Damme Ger.
174 F1 Damnica Pol.
174 F1 Damno Pol.
116 D5 Damoh Madh. Prad. India
206 E4 Damongo Ghana
128 B3 Damour Lebanon
168 E1 Damp Ger.
94 C2 Dampar, Tasik l. Malaysia
160 D1 Damparis France
86 C4 Dampier W.A. Austr.
86 C4 Dampier Archipelago is W.A. Austr.
160 D1 Dampierre France
156 C5 Dampierre-en-Burly France
160 E1 Dampierre-sur-Linotte France
160 D1 Dampierre-sur-Salon France
93 D3 Dampir, Selat sea chan. Irian Jaya Indon.
160 E1 Damprichard France
Damqoq Zangbo r. Xizang China see Maquan He
111 F5 Dam Qu r. Qinghai China
97 D5 Dâmrei, Chuŏr Phnum mts Cambodia
117 H3 Damroh Arun. Prad. India
171 D3 Damsdorf Ger.
170 C2 Damshagen Ger.
170 D1 Damsholte Denmark
190 B1 Damvant Switz.
156 B4 Damville France
157 F3 Damvillers France
164 F1 Damwoude Neth.
Damxoi Xizang China see Comai
111 E6 Damxung Xizang China
231 E4 Dan r. NC U.S.A.
240 H3 Dana, Mount CA U.S.A.
129 E3 Danaçı Azer.
185 G2 Dañador r. Spain
Danakil reg. Eritrea/Eth. see Denakil
206 C5 Danané Côte d'Ivoire
96 E3 Đa Năng Vietnam
106 B3 Dananhu Xinjiang China
92 C4 Danao Phil.
108 B2 Danba Sichuan China
234 C2 Danboro PA U.S.A.
151 H3 Danbury Essex, England U.K.
233 G4 Danbury CT U.S.A.
231 D4 Danbury NC U.S.A.
233 H3 Danbury NH U.S.A.
226 A2 Danbury WI U.S.A.
149 I3 Danby North Yorkshire, England U.K.
233 G3 Danby VT U.S.A.
109 E1 Dancheng Henan China
Dancheng Zhejiang China see Xiangshan
87 B6 Dandaragan W.A. Austr.
209 B7 Dande r. Angola
116 E3 Dandel'dhura Nepal
114 B3 Dandeli Karnataka India
149 F2 Danderhall Midlothian, Scotland U.K.
101 C4 Dandong Liaoning China
104 D3 Dando-san mt. Japan
231 D4 Dandridge TN U.S.A.
138 C4 Danė r. Lith.
149 G4 Dane r. England U.K.
151 H3 Danehill East Sussex, England U.K.
147 D3 Danesfort Rep. of Ireland
197 G4 Daneți Romania
Dänew Turkm. see Dyanev
108 D1 Danfeng Shaanxi China
Danfeng Yunnan China see Shizong
233 □J2 Danforth ME U.S.A.
Dangara Tajik. see Danghara
100 D3 Dangbizhen Rus. Fed.
106 E5 Dangchang Gansu China
Dangchengwan Gansu China see Subei
209 B6 Dange Angola
Danger Islands atoll Cook Is see Pukapuka
84 B1 Danger Point N.T. Austr.
214 B6 Danger Point S. Africa
162 C2 Dangé-St-Romain France
123 G2 Danghara Tajik.
106 B4 Danghe Nanshan mts China
210 C2 Dangila Eth.
Dangla Shan mts Xizang China see Tanggula Shan
117 H4 Dangori Assam India
111 E6 Dangqên Xizang China
243 H5 Dangriga Belize
107 H5 Dangshan Anhui China
109 F2 Dangtu Anhui China
207 G4 Dan-Gulbi Nigeria
210 B2 Dangur mt. Eth.
109 D2 Dangyang Hubei China
174 G5 Daniec Pol.
238 E3 Daniel WY U.S.A.
254 B5 Daniel, Serra hills Brazil
225 J3 Daniel's Harbour Nfld. Can.
214 D3 Daniëlskuil S. Africa
233 H4 Danielson CT U.S.A.
215 G2 Danielsrus S. Africa
231 D5 Danielsville GA U.S.A.
134 H4 Danilov Rus. Fed.
196 D4 Danilovgrad Crna Gora Yugo.
121 G1 Danilovka Kazakh.
135 I6 Danilovka Rus. Fed.
134 G4 Danilovskaya Vozvyshennost' hills Rus. Fed.
107 F4 Daning Shanxi China
129 F3 Dänizkänarı Azer.
Danjiang Guizhou China see Leishan
109 D1 Danjiangkou Hubei China
160 E1 Danjoutin France
125 G3 Ḑank Oman
124 C5 Dankalia prov. Eritrea
171 C4 Dankerode Ger.
169 F5 Dankmarshausen Ger.
139 L5 Dankov Rus. Fed.
121 I4 Dankova, Pik mt. Kyrg.
108 B2 Danleng Sichuan China
242 □I6 Danlí Hond.
221 P1 Danmark Fjord inlet Greenland
169 F3 Danndorf Ger.
168 G1 Dannemare Denmark
160 F1 Dannemarie France
233 G2 Dannemora NY U.S.A.
170 C2 Dannenberg (Elbe) Ger.
170 E2 Dannenwalde Ger.
80 F4 Dannevirke North I. N.Z.
168 E1 Dannewerk Ger.
215 H3 Dannhauser S. Africa
206 E4 Dano Burkina
Danshui Taiwan see Tanshui
232 E3 Dansville NY U.S.A.
116 C4 Danta Gujarat India
232 B6 Dante VA U.S.A.
114 D2 Dantewara Madh. Prad. India
Dantu Jiangsu China see Zhenjiang
197 I3 Danube r. Europe alt. Donau (Austria/Germany), alt. Duna (Hungary), alt. Dunaj (Slovakia), alt. Dunărea (Romania), alt. Dunav (Yugoslavia)
Danube Delta Romania see Dunării, Delta
96 A3 Danubyu Myanmar
237 E5 Danville AR U.S.A.
230 C3 Danville IL U.S.A.
230 C4 Danville IN U.S.A.
230 C4 Danville KY U.S.A.
232 B4 Danville OH U.S.A.
227 I5 Danville PA U.S.A.
232 D6 Danville VA U.S.A.
233 G2 Danville VT U.S.A.
Danxian Hainan China see Danzhou
109 F2 Danyang Jiangsu China
108 C3 Danzhai Guizhou China
108 D3 Danzhou Guangxi China
108 D5 Danzhou Hainan China
Danzhou Shaanxi China see Yichuan
Danzig Pol. see Gdańsk
Danzig, Gulf of Pol./Rus. Fed. see Gdańsk, Gulf of
92 B4 Dao Phil.
182 B4 Dão r. Port.
108 B2 Daocheng Sichuan China
Daojiang Hunan China see Daoxian
Daokou Henan China see Huaxian
159 F4 Daon France
108 D2 Daoshiping Hubei China
106 D4 Daotanghe Qinghai China
Dao Tay Sa is S. China Sea see Paracel Islands
Daoud Alg. see Aïn Beïda
206 E5 Daoukro Côte d'Ivoire
158 B3 Daoulas France
109 D3 Daoxian Hunan China
108 C2 Daozhen Guizhou China
92 C4 Dapa Phil.
207 F4 Dapaong Togo
117 I4 Daphabum mt. Arun. Prad. India
Daphnae tourist site Egypt see Kawm Dafanah
231 C6 Daphne AL U.S.A.
92 B4 Dapiak, Mount Mindanao Phil.
Dapingdi Sichuan China see Yanbian
92 B4 Dapitan Phil.
Dapu Guangxi China see Liucheng
126 C5 Daqahlîya governorate Egypt
111 F4 Da Qaidam Zhen Qinghai China
108 B3 Daqiao Yunnan China
100 C3 Daqing Heilong. China
107 I3 Daqin Tal Nei Mongol China
109 F3 Daqiu Fujian China
110 F3 Daquan Gansu China
106 B3 Daquanwan Xinjiang China
127 G4 Dāqūq Iraq
206 B3 Dara Senegal
128 C3 Dar'ā Syria
128 C3 Dar'ā governorate Syria
203 G3 Dâra, Gebel mt. Egypt
251 E5 Daraá r. Brazil
122 C4 Dārāb Iran
197 H1 Darabani Romania
92 B3 Daraga Phil.
138 G5 Darahanava Belarus
122 B3 Dārān Iran
97 E4 Đa Răng, Sông r. Vietnam
177 G6 Darány Hungary
99 J1 Darasun Rus. Fed.
Daraut-Kurgan Kyrg. see Daroot-Korgan
196 E4 Đaravica mt. Yugo.
203 G3 Daraw Egypt
207 H4 Darazo Nigeria
Darband Uzbek. see Derbent
122 D4 Darband, Kūh-e mt. Iran
138 C3 Darbėnai Lith.
180 D5 Dar Ben Karricha el Behri Morocco
117 F4 Darbhanga Bihar India
238 D2 Darby MT U.S.A.
234 C3 Darby PA U.S.A.
147 A4 Darby's Bridge Rep. of Ireland
108 A1 Darcang Sichuan China
189 C7 Dar Chabanne Tunisia
180 D5 Dar Chaoui Morocco
222 F5 D'Arcy B.C. Can.
188 G3 Darda Croatia
237 E5 Dardanelle AR U.S.A.
240 H2 Dardanelle CA U.S.A.
169 F4 Dardesheim Ger.
Dardo Sichuan China see Kangding
191 F2 Darè Italy
Dar el Beida Morocco see Casablanca
126 E3 Darende Turkey
211 C6 Dar es Salaam Tanz.
83 E3 Dareton N.S.W. Austr.
81 D5 Darfield South I. N.Z.
190 F3 Darfo Boario Terme Italy
123 E1 Darganata Turkm.
80 D1 Dargaville North I. N.Z.
175 J1 Dargin, Jezioro l. Pol.
83 F4 Dargo Vic. Austr.
207 F3 Dargol Niger
170 D2 Dargun Ger.
106 E1 Darhan Mongolia
Darhan Muminggan Lianheqi Nei Mongol China see Bailingmiao
199 F1 Darıca Turkey
199 G1 Darıçayırı Sakarya Turkey
199 F2 Darıcı Turkey
235 E1 Darien CT U.S.A.
231 D6 Darien GA U.S.A.
250 B2 Darién, Golfo del g. Col.
242 □K7 Darién, Serranía del mts Panama
129 A4 Darıkent Turkey
121 H2 Dar'inskiy Kazakh.
120 B2 Dar'inskoye Kazakh.
242 □I6 Darío Nic.
199 F3 Darıveren Denizli Turkey
Darīya Kazakh. see Dar'inskiy
Darjeeling W. Bengal India see Darjiling
117 G4 Darjiling W. Bengal India
87 C7 Darkan W.A. Austr.
82 D3 Darke Peak S.A. Austr.
147 E2 Darkley Northern Ireland U.K.
108 A1 Darlag Qinghai China
83 E3 Darling r. N.S.W. Austr.
214 B5 Darling S. Africa
85 G5 Darling Downs hills Qld Austr.
169 F4 Darlingerode Ger.
87 B7 Darling Range hills W.A. Austr.
149 H3 Darlington Darlington, England U.K.
149 H3 Darlington admin. div. England U.K.
234 B3 Darlington MD U.S.A.
231 E5 Darlington SC U.S.A.
226 B4 Darlington WI U.S.A.
83 F3 Darlington Point N.S.W. Austr.
87 D5 Darlot, Lake salt flat W.A. Austr.
143 G4 Darłówko Pol.
143 G4 Darłowo Pol.
197 H2 Dărmănești Romania
114 C2 Darmaraopet Andhra Prad. India
172 C2 Darmstadt Ger.
169 D6 Darmstadt admin. reg. Hessen Ger.
116 C5 Darna r. India
202 D1 Darnah Libya
215 H3 Darnall S. Africa
156 B3 Darnétal France
157 G4 Darney France
83 E3 Darnick N.S.W. Austr.
157 G4 Darnieulles France
186 F2 Darnius Spain
263 E2 Darnley, Cape Antarctica
186 G2 Daró r. Spain
183 I3 Daroca Spain
121 H5 Daroot-Korgan Kyrg.
134 I4 Darovskoy Rus. Fed.
182 B3 Darque Port.
146 F4 Darra Aberdeenshire, Scotland U.K.
147 B4 Darragh Rep. of Ireland
261 F5 Darregueira Arg.
122 D2 Darreh Gaz Iran
Darreh Gozaru r. Iran see Gīzeh Rūd
122 C4 Darreh-ye Bāhābād Iran
123 G3 Darreh-ye Shekārī r. Afgh.
123 G3 Darreh-ye Shekārī r. Afgh.
185 G3 Darro Spain
114 C3 Darsi Andhra Prad. India
170 D1 Darß pen. Ger.
150 D4 Dart r. England U.K.
128 C1 Dār Ta'izzah Syria
Dartang Xizang China see Baqên
151 H3 Dartford Kent, England U.K.
150 D4 Dartington Devon, England U.K.
150 D4 Dartmeet Devon, England U.K.
82 E4 Dartmoor Vic. Austr.
150 C4 Dartmoor hills England U.K.
150 D4 Dartmoor National Park England U.K.
225 I4 Dartmouth N.S. Can.
150 D4 Dartmouth Devon, England U.K.
85 F5 Dartmouth, Lake salt flat Qld Austr.
83 F4 Dartmouth Reservoir Vic. Austr.
149 H4 Darton South Yorkshire, England U.K.
91 J8 Daru P.N.G.
206 C5 Daru Sierra Leone
104 A3 Daruga-mine mt. Japan
188 F3 Daruvar Croatia
122 D1 Darvaza Turkm.
146 D6 Darvel East Ayrshire, Scotland U.K.
Darvi Hovd Mongolia see Bulgan
123 G2 Darvoz, Qatorkŭhi mts Tajik.
149 G4 Darwen Blackburn with Darwen, England U.K.
213 F3 Darwendale Zimbabwe
116 D5 Darwha Mahar. India
84 B2 Darwin N.T. Austr.
259 F8 Darwin Falkland Is
259 C9 Darwin, Monte mt. Chile
250 □ Darwin, Volcán vol. Islas Galápagos Ecuador
Darwin Island Islas Galápagos Ecuador see Culpepper, Isla
123 G4 Darya Khan Pak.
120 F3 Dar'yalyktakyr, Ravnina plain Kazakh.
202 D1 Daryānah Libya
Dar"yoi Amu r. Asia see Amudar'ya
Dar"yoi Sir r. Asia see Syrdar'ya
122 D4 Dārzīn Iran
116 B5 Dasada Gujarat India
107 G4 Dasha r. China
175 M6 Dashava Ukr.
107 G1 Dashbalbar Mongolia
Dashhowuz Turkm. see Dashkhovuz
107 I3 Dashiqiao Liaoning China
106 A3 Dashitou Xinjiang China
136 E3 Dashiv Ukr.
107 I2 Dashizhai Nei Mongol China
Dashkesan Azer. see Daşkäsän
122 D1 Dashkhovuz Turkm.
Dashkhovuz Oblast admin. div. Turkm. see Dashkhovuzskaya Oblast'
122 D1 Dashkhovuzskaya Oblast' admin. div. Turkm.
Dashköpri Turkm. see Tashkepri

122 D2 **Dasht** Iran
123 E5 **Dasht** *r.* Pak.
122 C4 **Dasht-e Palang** *r.* Iran
176 E1 **Dašice** Czech Rep.
173 F3 **Dasing** Ger.
123 H3 **Daska** Pak.
129 E3 **Daşkäsän** Azer.
214 D5 **Daskop** S. Africa
170 D1 **Daskow** Ger.
108 C3 **Dasongshu** *Yunnan* China
123 H2 **Daspar** *mt.* Pak.
207 F5 **Dassa** Benin
169 E4 **Dassel** Ger.
168 F2 **Dassendorf** Ger.
214 B5 **Dassen Island** S. Africa
168 F2 **Dassow** Ger.
129 E4 **Dastakert** Armenia
100 D4 **Da Suifen He** *r.* China
116 C3 **Dasuya** *Punjab* India
215 G2 **Dasville** S. Africa
175 H3 **Daszyna** Pol.
199 E3 **Datça** Turkey
102 J2 **Date** Japan
241 K5 **Dateland** *AZ* U.S.A.
116 C5 **Datha** *Gujarat* India
116 D4 **Datia** *Madh. Prad.* India
109 F3 **Datian** *Fujian* China
109 D4 **Datian Ding** *mt. Guangdong* China
239 F5 **Datil** *NM* U.S.A.
Datong *Fujian* China *see* **Tong'an**
100 C3 **Datong** *Heilong.* China
106 D4 **Datong** *Qinghai* China
107 G3 **Datong** *Shanxi* China
106 D4 **Datong He** *r.* China
106 C4 **Datong Shan** *mts* China
169 C4 **Datteln** Ger.
169 F4 **Datterode (Ringgau)** Ger.
92 C5 **Datu Piang** Phil.
123 G3 **Daud Khel** Pak.
117 F4 **Daudnagar** *Bihar* India
138 E4 **Daugai** Lith.
138 E3 **Daugava** *r.* Latvia *alt.* **Zakhodnyaya Dzvina,** *alt.* **Zapadnaya Dvina,** *conv.* **Western Dvina**
138 F4 **Daugavpils** Latvia
138 D3 **Daugyvenė** *r.* Lith.
123 F2 **Daulatabad** Afgh.
Daulatabad Iran *see* **Malāyer**
117 G5 **Daulatpur** Bangl.
250 B5 **Daule** Ecuador
163 D5 **Daumazan-sur-Arize** France
159 F4 **Daumeray** France
169 B5 **Daun** Ger.
114 B2 **Daund** *Mahar.* India
96 A2 **Daungyu** *r.* Myanmar
223 K5 **Dauphin** *Man.* Can.
161 D5 **Dauphin** France
234 B2 **Dauphin** *PA* U.S.A.
234 B2 **Dauphin County** *county* *PA* U.S.A.
161 D4 **Dauphiné, Alpes du** *mts* France
207 H3 **Daura** Nigeria
87 B5 **Daurie Creek** *r. W.A.* Austr.
107 H1 **Dauriya** Rus. Fed.
116 D4 **Dausa** *Rajasthan* India
169 D5 **Dautphetal-Friedensdorf** Ger.
169 D5 **Dautphetal-Holzhausen** Ger.
146 E4 **Dava** *Moray, Scotland* U.K.
129 F3 **Däväçi** Azer.
114 B3 **Davangere** *Karnataka* India
92 C5 **Davao** Phil.
92 C5 **Davao Gulf** Phil.
123 E5 **Dāvar Panāh** Iran
215 G2 **Davel** S. Africa
230 B3 **Davenport** *IA* U.S.A.
233 F3 **Davenport** *NY* U.S.A.
238 C2 **Davenport** *WA* U.S.A.
85 E5 **Davenport Downs** *Qld* Austr.
84 C4 **Davenport Range** *hills* *N.T.* Austr.
151 F2 **Daventry** *Northamptonshire, England* U.K.
215 G2 **Daveyton** S. Africa
161 C3 **Davézieux** France
242 □J7 **David** Panama
236 D3 **David City** *NE* U.S.A.
223 J5 **Davidson** *Sask.* Can.
84 B4 **Davidson, Mount** *hill* *N.T.* Austr.
234 B4 **Davidsonville** *MD* U.S.A.
82 B1 **Davies, Mount** *S.A.* Austr.
256 D3 **Davinópolis** Brazil
146 D4 **Daviot** *Highland, Scotland* U.K.
263 F2 **Davis** *research stn* Antarctica
86 D4 **Davis** *r. W.A.* Austr.
240 G2 **Davis** *CA* U.S.A.
232 D5 **Davis** *WV* U.S.A.
232 D5 **Davis, Mount** *hill PA* U.S.A.
241 J4 **Davis Dam** *AZ* U.S.A.
225 I2 **Davis Inlet** *Nfld.* Can.
227 F4 **Davison** *MI* U.S.A.
263 G2 **Davis Sea** Antarctica
221 M3 **Davis Strait** Can./Greenland
135 K5 **Davlekanovo** Rus. Fed.
198 C2 **Davlia** Greece
177 H5 **Dávod** Hungary
195 F4 **Davoli** Italy
190 E2 **Davos** Switz.
199 E3 **Davutlar** Turkey
232 C6 **Davy** *WV* U.S.A.
136 D1 **Davyd-Haradok** Belarus
175 M6 **Davydiv** Ukr.
137 G4 **Davydiv Brid** Ukr.
137 H4 **Davydivka** Ukr.
Davydkovo Rus. Fed. *see* **Tolbukhino**
137 J2 **Davydovka** Rus. Fed.
107 I3 **Dawa** *Liaoning* China
Dawahaidy *atoll Arch. des Tuamotu* Fr. Polynesia *see* **Ravahéré**
210 D3 **Dawa Wenz** *r.* Eth.
111 D6 **Dawaxung** *Xizang* China
108 B2 **Dawê** *Sichuan* China
Dawei Myanmar *see* **Tavoy**
Dawei *b.* Myanmar *see* **Tavoy**
107 H5 **Dawen** *r.* China
150 D4 **Dawlish** *Devon, England* U.K.
96 B3 **Dawna Range** *mts* Myanmar/Thai.
125 F4 **Dawqah** Oman
124 D5 **Ḍawrān** Yemen
85 G4 **Dawson** *r. Qld* Austr.
220 E3 **Dawson** *Y.T.* Can.
231 C6 **Dawson** *GA* U.S.A.
236 D2 **Dawson** *ND* U.S.A.
259 C9 **Dawson, Isla** *i.* Chile
222 G5 **Dawson, Mount** *B.C.* Can.
222 F4 **Dawson Creek** *B.C.* Can.
222 A2 **Dawson Range** *mts Y.T.* Can.
222 E5 **Dawsons Landing** *B.C.* Can.
231 C5 **Dawsonville** *GA* U.S.A.
109 E2 **Dawu** *Hubei* China
Dawu *Qinghai* China *see* **Maqên**
108 B2 **Dawu** *Sichuan* China
Dawu Taiwan *see* **Tawu**
Dawukou *Ningxia* China *see* **Shizuishan**
109 E2 **Dawu Shan** *hill Hubei* China
125 G3 **Dawwah** Oman
163 A5 **Dax** France
Daxian *Sichuan* China *see* **Dachuan**
108 C4 **Daxin** *Guangdong* China
Daxing *Yunnan* China *see* **Ninglang**
Daxing *Yunnan* China *see* **Lüchun**
Daxue *Zhejiang* China *see* **Wencheng**
108 B2 **Daxue Shan** *mts Sichuan* China
Dayan *Yunnan* China *see* **Lijiang**
107 I4 **Dayang** *r.* China
111 F7 **Dayang** *r.* India
107 J1 **Dayangshu** *Nei Mongol* China
108 B3 **Dayao** *Yunnan* China
109 E2 **Daye** *Hubei* China
108 B2 **Dayi** *Sichuan* China
108 A3 **Daying Jiang** *r.* China
Dayishan *Jiangsu* China *see* **Guanyun**
129 D2 **Daykhokh, Gora** *mt.* Rus. Fed.
83 F4 **Daylesford** *Vic.* Austr.
261 H2 **Daymán** *r.* Uru.
261 I2 **Daymán, Cuchilla del** *hills* Uru.
108 D2 **Dayong** *Hunan* China
128 B3 **Dayr Abū Sa'īd** Jordan
127 F4 **Dayr az Zawr** Syria
128 C1 **Dayr Ḥāfir** Syria
223 H4 **Daysland** *Alta* Can.
226 A3 **Dayton** *MN* U.S.A.
232 A5 **Dayton** *OH* U.S.A.
231 C5 **Dayton** *TN* U.S.A.
237 E6 **Dayton** *TX* U.S.A.
232 D5 **Dayton** *VA* U.S.A.
238 C2 **Dayton** *WA* U.S.A.
231 D6 **Daytona Beach** *FL* U.S.A.
109 E3 **Dayu** *Jiangxi* China
109 E3 **Dayu Ling** *mts* China
107 H5 **Da Yunhe** *canal* China
238 C2 **Dayville** *OR* U.S.A.
103 E7 **Dazaifu** Japan
122 A2 **Dazgir** Iran
Dazhe *Guangdong* China *see* **Pingyuan**
Dazhongji *Jiangsu* China *see* **Dafeng**
108 C2 **Dazhu** *Sichuan* China
199 F3 **Dazkırı** Turkey
108 C2 **Dazu** *Chongqing* China
108 C2 **Dazu Rock Carvings** *tourist site Chongqing* China
214 E4 **De Aar** S. Africa
147 C4 **Dead** *r.* Rep. of Ireland
233 □H2 **Dead** *r. ME* U.S.A.
226 D2 **Dead** *r. MI* U.S.A.
246 D2 **Deadman's Cay** *Long I.* Bahamas
241 J4 **Dead Mountains** *NV* U.S.A.
128 B4 **Dead Sea** *salt l.* Asia
236 C2 **Deadwood** *SD* U.S.A.
84 C2 **Deaf Adder Creek** *r. N.T.* Austr.
87 F6 **Deakin** *W.A.* Austr.
151 I3 **Deal** *Kent, England* U.K.
235 D2 **Deal** *NJ* U.S.A.
215 E3 **Dealesville** S. Africa
222 E4 **Dean** *r. B.C.* Can.
109 E2 **De'an** *Jiangxi* China
150 E3 **Dean, Forest of** *England* U.K.
260 E2 **Deán Funes** Arg.
Deanuvuotna *inlet* Norway *see* **Tanafjorden**
146 E5 **Dean Water** *r. Scotland* U.K.
227 F4 **Dearborn** *MI* U.S.A.
149 F3 **Dearham** *Cumbria, England* U.K.
149 H4 **Dearne** *r. England* U.K.
238 C2 **Deary** *ID* U.S.A.
222 D3 **Dease** *r. B.C.* Can.
220 F3 **Dease Arm** *b. N.W.T.* Can.
222 D3 **Dease Lake** *B.C.* Can.
220 H3 **Dease Strait** *Nunavut* Can.
240 I3 **Death Valley** *CA* U.S.A.
240 I3 **Death Valley** *depr. CA* U.S.A.
241 I3 **Death Valley Junction** *CA* U.S.A.
159 G2 **Deauville** France
238 E2 **Deaver** *WY* U.S.A.
129 E3 **Deavgay, Gora** *mt.* Rus. Fed.
117 G5 **Debagram** *W. Bengal* India
137 J3 **Debal'tseve** Ukr.
Debal'tsovo Ukr. *see* **Debal'tseve**
108 C4 **Debao** *Guangxi* China
196 E5 **Debar** Macedonia
210 C1 **Debark** Eth.
223 J4 **Debden** *Sask.* Can.
204 E2 **Debdou** Morocco
129 D3 **Debed** *r.* Armenia
151 I2 **Deben** *r. England* U.K.
151 I2 **Debenham** *Suffolk, England* U.K.
225 I4 **Debert** *N.S.* Can.
134 K4 **Debesy** Rus. Fed.
175 J5 **Dębica** Pol.
164 E2 **De Bilt** Neth.
131 Q3 **Debin** Rus. Fed.
175 J4 **Dęblin** Pol.
174 F1 **Dębnica Kaszubska** Pol.
175 I6 **Dębno** Pol.
174 C3 **Dębno** Pol.
206 D3 **Débo, Lac** *l.* Mali
87 C6 **Deborah East, Lake** *salt flat W.A.* Austr.
87 C6 **Deborah West, Lake** *salt flat W.A.* Austr.
175 I4 **Dęborzeczka** Pol.
175 L4 **Dębowa Kłoda** Pol.
175 H2 **Dębowa Łąka** Pol.
210 C2 **Debre Birhan** Eth.
177 K4 **Debrecen** Hungary
210 C2 **Debre Markos** Eth.
210 C2 **Debre Sīna** Eth.
196 E5 **Debrešte** Macedonia
210 C2 **Debre Tabor** Eth.
210 C2 **Debre Werk'** Eth.
210 C2 **Debre Zeyit** Eth.
174 F2 **Debrzno** Pol.
Deçan *Kosovo, Srbija* Yugo. *see* **Dečani**
196 E4 **Dečani** *Kosovo, Srbija* Yugo.
231 C5 **Decatur** *AL* U.S.A.
231 C5 **Decatur** *GA* U.S.A.
230 B4 **Decatur** *IL* U.S.A.
230 C3 **Decatur** *IN* U.S.A.
226 E4 **Decatur** *MI* U.S.A.
237 F5 **Decatur** *MS* U.S.A.
231 C5 **Decatur** *TN* U.S.A.
237 D5 **Decatur** *TX* U.S.A.
237 F5 **Decaturville** *TN* U.S.A.
163 E4 **Decazeville** France
114 C2 **Deccan** *plat.* India
85 H5 **Deception Bay** *Qld* Austr.
Deception Island Vanuatu *see* **Moso**
212 D4 **Deception Pans** *salt pan* Botswana
108 B3 **Dechang** *Sichuan* China
Decheng *Guangdong* China *see* **Deqing**
177 G3 **Dechtice** Slovakia
192 A5 **Decimomannu** *Sardegna* Italy
192 A5 **Decimoputzu** *Sardegna* Italy
176 D1 **Děčín** Czech Rep.
160 C3 **Décines-Charpieu** France
160 B2 **Decize** France
238 F2 **Decker** *MT* U.S.A.
227 F4 **Deckerville** *MI* U.S.A.
164 D1 **De Cocksdorp** Neth.
195 F3 **Decollatura** Italy
226 B4 **Decorah** *IA* U.S.A.
84 C1 **De Courcy Head** *hd N.T.* Austr.
177 H5 **Decs** Hungary
Dedang *Yunnan* China *see* **Yongde**
96 A3 **Dedaye** Myanmar
151 F3 **Deddington** *Oxfordshire, England* U.K.
199 F3 **Dedebağı** Turkey
126 C3 **Dedegöl Dağları** *mts* Turkey
169 F3 **Dedeleben** Ger.
129 C4 **Dedeli** Turkey
170 E2 **Dedelow** Ger.
168 F3 **Dedelstorf** Ger.
164 F2 **Dedemsvaart** Neth.
210 D2 **Deder** Eth.
177 J3 **Dédestapolcsány** Hungary
151 H3 **Dedham** *Essex, England* U.K.
139 L4 **Dedinovo** Rus. Fed.
256 D6 **Dedo de Deus** *mt.* Brazil
214 B5 **De Doorns** S. Africa
129 E3 **Dedop'listsqaro** Georgia
206 E3 **Dédougou** Burkina
138 G3 **Dedovichi** Rus. Fed.
100 C2 **Dedu** *Heilong.* China
120 C2 **Dedurovka** Rus. Fed.
211 B8 **Dedza** Malawi
213 G2 **Dedza Mountain** Malawi
147 E3 **Dee** *r.* Rep. of Ireland
150 D1 **Dee** *est. Wales* U.K.
149 F4 **Dee** *r. England/Wales* U.K.
146 F4 **Dee** *r. Scotland* U.K.
116 D4 **Deeg** *Rajasthan* India
147 C4 **Deel** *r. Cork/Limerick* Rep. of Ireland
147 B2 **Deel** *r. Mayo* Rep. of Ireland
147 E3 **Deel** *r. Meath/Westmeath* Rep. of Ireland
147 D2 **Deele** *r.* Rep. of Ireland
214 D4 **Deelfontein** S. Africa
169 E4 **Deensen** Ger.
241 K2 **Deep Creek Range** *mts UT* U.S.A.
151 G2 **Deeping St Nicholas** *Lincolnshire, England* U.K.
224 E4 **Deep River** *Ont.* Can.
235 F1 **Deep River** *CT* U.S.A.
83 G2 **Deepwater** *N.S.W.* Austr.
234 C3 **Deepwater** *NJ* U.S.A.
240 F2 **Deer Creek** *r. CA* U.S.A.
234 B3 **Deer Creek** *r. MD* U.S.A.
234 C3 **Deerfield** *NJ* U.S.A.
232 C4 **Deerfield** *OH* U.S.A.
210 E3 **Deeri** Somalia
87 F5 **Deering, Mount** *W.A.* Austr.
233 □I2 **Deer Isle** *ME* U.S.A.
225 J3 **Deer Lake** *Nfld.* Can.
223 M4 **Deer Lake** *Ont.* Can.
165 C4 **Deerlijk** Belgium
238 D2 **Deer Lodge** *MT* U.S.A.
235 E2 **Deer Park** *NY* U.S.A.
238 C2 **Deer Park** *WA* U.S.A.
Deesa *Gujarat* India *see* **Disa**
238 D3 **Deeth** *NV* U.S.A.
171 D3 **Deetz** Ger.
137 J5 **Defanovka** Rus. Fed.
Defeng *Guizhou* China *see* **Liping**
236 G3 **Defiance** *OH* U.S.A.
241 M4 **Defiance Plateau** *AZ* U.S.A.
231 C6 **De Funiak Springs** *FL* U.S.A.
163 D4 **Dégagnac** France
116 C4 **Degana** *Rajasthan* India
182 D2 **Degaña** Spain
191 H2 **Degano** *r.* Italy
150 D1 **Deganwy** *Conwy, Wales* U.K.
108 A2 **Dêgê** *Sichuan* China
184 C2 **Degebe** *r.* Port.
143 F4 **Degeberga** Sweden
210 D2 **Degeh Bur** Eth.
225 G4 **Dégelis** *Que.* Can.
207 G5 **Degema** Nigeria
143 F2 **Degerfors** Sweden
173 G3 **Deggendorf** Ger.
172 D3 **Deggingen** Ger.
123 H4 **Degh** *r.* Pak.
128 C1 **Değirmenbaşı** Turkey
199 F2 **Değirmencik** *r.* Turkey
199 E2 **Değirmendere** Turkey
129 C3 **Değirmenlidere** Turkey
Değirmenlik Cyprus *see* **Kythrea**
190 D4 **Dego** Italy
244 C3 **Degollado** Mex.
86 C4 **De Grey** *W.A.* Austr.
86 C4 **De Grey** *r. W.A.* Austr.
135 H6 **Degtevo** Rus. Fed.
165 C3 **De Haan** Belgium
203 I6 **Dehalak Deset** *i.* Eritrea
122 C4 **Deh Bīd** Iran
122 B4 **Deh-Dasht** Iran
122 B4 **Deh-e Kohneh** Iran
187 C7 **Dehesa de Campoamor** Spain
183 F2 **Dehesa de Montejo** Spain
185 G3 **Dehesas de Guadix** Spain
122 A3 **Deh Golān** Iran
122 A3 **Dehlorān** Iran
78 □4b **Dehpehk** *i. Pohnpei* Micronesia
Dehqonobod Uzbek. *see* **Dekhkanabad**
116 D3 **Dehra Dun** *Uttar Prad.* India
117 F4 **Dehri** *Bihar* India
109 F3 **Dehua** *Fujian* China
100 C3 **Dehui** *Jilin* China
172 C2 **Deidesheim** Ger.
185 G3 **Deifontes** Spain
182 D3 **Deilão** Port.
173 F2 **Deining** Ger.
173 E3 **Deiningen** Ger.
165 C4 **Deinze** Belgium
126 D4 **Deïr el Qamar** Lebanon
Deir-ez-Zor Syria *see* **Dayr az Zawr**
172 C3 **Deißlingen** Ger.
190 E4 **Deiva Marina** Italy
197 F2 **Dej** Romania
196 E5 **Dejë, Mal** *mt.* Albania
210 C2 **Dejen** Eth.
175 J1 **Dejguny, Jezioro** *l.* Pol.
Deji *Xizang* China *see* **Rinbung**
108 D2 **Dejiang** *Guizhou* China
226 C5 **De Kalb** *IL* U.S.A.
237 F5 **De Kalb** *MS* U.S.A.
237 E5 **De Kalb** *TX* U.S.A.
233 F2 **De Kalb Junction** *NY* U.S.A.
191 I3 **Dekani** Slovenia
203 H6 **Dekemhare** Eritrea
78 □4b **Deke Sokehs** *i. Pohnpei* Micronesia
121 F5 **Dekhkanabad** Uzbek.
207 G5 **Dekina** Nigeria
165 D3 **De Klinge** Belgium
208 C3 **Dékoa** C.A.R.
164 D1 **De Koog** Neth.
164 D2 **De Kooy** Neth.
164 F2 **De Krim** Neth.
150 C4 **Delabole** *Cornwall, England* U.K.
261 G5 **De la Garma** Arg.
84 B2 **Delamere** *N.T.* Austr.
149 G4 **Delamere** *Cheshire, England* U.K.
234 D2 **Delanco** *NJ* U.S.A.
231 D6 **De Land** *FL* U.S.A.
240 H4 **Delano** *CA* U.S.A.
234 B2 **Delano** *PA* U.S.A.
241 K2 **Delano Peak** *UT* U.S.A.
78 □3b **Delap** *i. Majuro* Marshall Is
78 □3b **Delap-Uliga-Djarrit** *Majuro* Marshall Is
215 E2 **Delareyville** S. Africa
220 A4 **Delarof Islands** *AK* U.S.A.
226 C5 **Delavan** *IL* U.S.A.
226 C4 **Delavan** *WI* U.S.A.
234 C2 **Delaware** *NJ* U.S.A.
232 B4 **Delaware** *OH* U.S.A.
236 E4 **Delaware** *r. KS* U.S.A.
234 C3 **Delaware** *r. NJ/PA* U.S.A.
233 F5 **Delaware** *state* U.S.A.
233 F4 **Delaware, East Branch** *r. NY* U.S.A.
233 F4 **Delaware, West Branch** *r. NY* U.S.A.
233 F5 **Delaware Bay** *DE/NJ* U.S.A.
234 C3 **Delaware City** *DE* U.S.A.
234 C3 **Delaware County** *county PA* U.S.A.
234 C2 **Delaware Water Gap** *PA* U.S.A.
225 G1 **Delay** *r. Que.* Can.
232 B6 **Delbarton** *WV* U.S.A.
222 H5 **Del Bonita** *Alta* Can.
169 D4 **Delbrück** Ger.
222 H4 **Delburne** *Alta* Can.
260 E4 **Del Campillo** Arg.
197 F5 **Delčevo** Macedonia
164 F2 **Delden** Neth.
83 G4 **Delegate** *N.S.W.* Austr.
182 E5 **Deleitosa** Spain
179 H4 **Đelekovec** Croatia
190 C1 **Delémont** Switz.
141 M3 **Delet Teili** *b.* Fin.
240 F2 **Delevan** *CA* U.S.A.
232 D3 **Delevan** *NY* U.S.A.
256 D4 **Delfinópolis** Brazil
164 D2 **Delft** Neth.
164 F1 **Delfzijl** Neth.
240 E1 **Delgada, Point** *CA* U.S.A.
106 D1 **Delger Mörön** *r.* Mongolia
234 D3 **Del Haven** *NJ* U.S.A.
227 G4 **Delhi** *Ont.* Can.
106 C4 **Delhi** *Qinghai* China
116 D3 **Delhi** *Delhi* India
111 B6 **Delhi** *admin. div.* India
240 G3 **Delhi** *CA* U.S.A.
239 F4 **Delhi** *CO* U.S.A.
237 F5 **Delhi** *LA* U.S.A.
233 F3 **Delhi** *NY* U.S.A.
127 F3 **Deli** *r.* Turkey
194 C5 **Delia** *Sicilia* Italy
194 B5 **Delia** *r. Sicilia* Italy
195 E4 **Delianuova** Italy
126 D3 **Delice** Turkey
126 D2 **Delice** *r.* Turkey
247 □2 **Delices** Dominica
251 H3 **Délices** Fr. Guiana
193 H3 **Deliceto** Italy
122 B3 **Delījān** Iran
199 E2 **Deliktaş** Turkey
222 F1 **Déline** *N.W.T.* Can.
Delingha *Qinghai* China *see* **Delhi**
168 F2 **Delingsdorf** Ger.
223 J5 **Delisle** *Sask.* Can.
171 D4 **Delitzsch** Ger.
178 E4 **Dellach** Austria
178 E4 **Dellach im Drautal** Austria
160 F1 **Delle** France
169 E4 **Delligsen** Ger.
190 F3 **Dello** Italy
236 D3 **Dell Rapids** *SD* U.S.A.
205 F1 **Dellys** Alg.
240 I5 **Del Mar** *CA* U.S.A.
233 F5 **Delmar** *DE* U.S.A.
215 G2 **Delmas** S. Africa
157 G4 **Delme** France
168 D2 **Delmenhorst** Ger.
234 D3 **Delmont** *NJ* U.S.A.
232 D4 **Delmont** *PA* U.S.A.
84 C4 **Delmore Downs** *N.T.* Austr.
188 E3 **Delnice** Croatia
239 F4 **Del Norte** *CO* U.S.A.
108 C4 **Delong** *Guangxi* China
131 Q2 **De-Longa, Ostrova** *is Novosibirskiye O-va* Rus. Fed.
De Long Islands *Novosibirskiye O-va* Rus. Fed. *see* **De-Longa, Ostrova**
220 B3 **De Long Mountains** *AK* U.S.A.
De Long Strait Rus. Fed. *see* **Longa, Proliv**
83 F5 **Deloraine** *Tas.* Austr.
223 K5 **Deloraine** *Man.* Can.
149 G4 **Delph** *Greater Manchester, England* U.K.
198 C2 **Delphi** *tourist site* Greece
230 C3 **Delphi** *IN* U.S.A.
232 A4 **Delphos** *OH* U.S.A.
214 E3 **Delportshoop** S. Africa
231 D7 **Delray Beach** *FL* U.S.A.
242 C2 **Del Río** Mex.
237 C6 **Del Rio** *TX* U.S.A.
141 L3 **Delsbo** Sweden
207 G5 **Delta** *state* Nigeria
239 E4 **Delta** *CO* U.S.A.
232 A4 **Delta** *OH* U.S.A.
234 B3 **Delta** *PA* U.S.A.
241 K2 **Delta** *UT* U.S.A.
251 F2 **Delta Amacuro** *state* Venez.
85 E3 **Delta Downs** *Qld* Austr.
220 D3 **Delta Junction** *AK* U.S.A.
231 D6 **Deltona** *FL* U.S.A.
83 G2 **Delungra** *N.S.W.* Austr.
164 G2 **De Lutte** Neth.
116 B5 **Delvada** *Gujarat* India
168 E1 **Delve** Ger.
147 D3 **Delvin** Rep. of Ireland
198 B2 **Delvinë** Albania
136 C3 **Delyatyn** Ukr.
120 C1 **Dema** *r.* Rus. Fed.
95 E4 **Demak** *Jawa Tengah* Indon.
157 F4 **Demange-aux-Eaux** France
Demavend *mt.* Iran *see* **Damāvand, Qolleh-ye**
209 D6 **Demba** Dem. Rep. Congo
209 B7 **Demba Chio** Angola
138 E4 **Dembava** Lith.
210 C2 **Dembech'a** Eth.
217 □3a **Dembeni** *Njazidja* Comoros
217 □3b **Dembeni** Mayotte
210 B2 **Dembī Dolo** Eth.
177 K3 **Demecser** Hungary
164 E2 **De Meern** Neth.
170 C2 **Demen** Ger.
165 D3 **Demer** *r.* Belgium
Demerara Guyana *see* **Georgetown**
264 F5 **Demerara Abyssal Plain** *sea feature* S. Atlantic Ocean
137 H5 **Demerdzhi** *mt.* Ukr.
139 H4 **Demidov** Rus. Fed.
160 C2 **Demigny** France
239 F5 **Deming** *NM* U.S.A.
251 F5 **Demini** *r.* Brazil
251 F4 **Demini, Serras do** *mts* Brazil
199 F2 **Demirci** *Manisa* Turkey
129 A3 **Demirci** *Trabzon* Turkey
196 E5 **Demir Hisar** Macedonia
197 F5 **Demir Kapija** Macedonia
129 C3 **Demirkent** Turkey
197 H5 **Demirköy** Turkey
199 F2 **Demirler** *r.* Turkey
129 A3 **Demirözü** Turkey
199 F1 **Demirtaş** Turkey
215 E5 **Demistkraal** S. Africa
170 E2 **Demmin** Ger.
190 C4 **Demonte** Italy
231 C5 **Demopolis** *AL* U.S.A.
230 C3 **Demotte** *IN* U.S.A.
94 C4 **Dempo, Gunung** *vol.* Indon.
87 D7 **Dempster, Point** *W.A.* Austr.
163 C5 **Dému** France
137 I3 **Demuryne** Ukr.
Dem'yanovka *Kustanayskaya Oblast'* Kazakh. *see* **Leninskoye**
134 I3 **Dem'yanovo** Rus. Fed.
139 I3 **Demyansk** Rus. Fed.
136 F2 **Demydiv** Ukr.
136 C2 **Demydivka** Ukr.
136 F4 **Demydove** Ukr.
214 C4 **De Naawte** S. Africa
156 D2 **Denain** France
240 G3 **Denair** *CA* U.S.A.
203 I6 **Denakil** *reg.* Eritrea/Eth.
223 K4 **Denare Beach** *Sask.* Can.
163 E5 **Dénat** France
121 F5 **Denau** Uzbek.
224 E4 **Denbigh** *Ont.* Can.
150 D1 **Denbigh** *Denbighshire, Wales* U.K.
150 D1 **Denbighshire** *admin. div. Wales* U.K.
164 D3 **Den Bommel** Neth.
Den Bosch Neth. *see* **'s-Hertogenbosch**
164 D1 **Den Burg** Neth.
149 H4 **Denby Dale** *West Yorkshire, England* U.K.
96 C3 **Den Chai** Thai.
206 D2 **Dendâra** Maur.
165 D4 **Denderleeuw** Belgium
165 D3 **Dendermonde** Belgium
164 E2 **Den Dolder** Neth.
165 D3 **Dendre** *r.* Belgium
213 F4 **Dendron** S. Africa
164 E3 **Den Dungen** Neth.
164 G2 **Denekamp** Neth.
196 E4 **Đeneral Jankovič** *Kosovo, Srbija* Yugo.
134 L3 **Denezhkin Kamen', Gora** *mt.* Rus. Fed.
207 H3 **Dengas** Niger
207 G3 **Denge** Nigeria
107 G5 **Dengfeng** *Henan* China
207 H4 **Dengi** Nigeria
Dengjiabu *Jiangxi* China *see* **Yujiang**
Dêngka *Gansu* China *see* **Têwo**
Dêngkagoin *Gansu* China *see* **Têwo**
107 E3 **Dengkou** *Nei Mongol* China
111 F6 **Dêngqên** *Xizang* China
109 E4 **Dengta** *Guangdong* China
163 B5 **Denguin** France
Dengxian *Henan* China *see* **Dengzhou**
109 E1 **Dengzhou** *Henan* China
Dengzhou *Shandong* China *see* **Penglai**
Den Haag Neth. *see* **'s-Gravenhage**
87 B5 **Denham** *W.A.* Austr.
86 F2 **Denham** *r. W.A.* Austr.
164 F2 **Den Ham** Neth.
151 G3 **Denham** *Buckinghamshire, England* U.K.
246 □ **Denham, Mount** *hill* Jamaica
84 D3 **Denham Island** *Qld* Austr.
85 G4 **Denham Range** *mts Qld* Austr.
87 B5 **Denham Sound** *sea chan. W.A.* Austr.
164 D2 **Den Helder** Neth.
223 I4 **Denholm** *Sask.* Can.
146 F6 **Denholm** *Scottish Borders, Scotland* U.K.
149 H4 **Denholme** *West Yorkshire, England* U.K.
164 D1 **Den Hoorn** Neth.
187 D6 **Denia** Spain
82 C3 **Denial Bay** *S.A.* Austr.
82 C3 **Denial Bay** *b. S.A.* Austr.
83 F3 **Deniliquin** *N.S.W.* Austr.
238 C3 **Denio** *NV* U.S.A.
236 E3 **Denison** *IA* U.S.A.
237 D5 **Denison** *TX* U.S.A.
263 J2 **Denison, Cape** Antarctica
86 F3 **Denison Plains** *W.A.* Austr.
Denisovka Kazakh. *see* **Ordzhonikidze**
199 F3 **Denizli** Turkey
199 F3 **Denizli** *prov.* Turkey
161 E4 **Denjuan, Sommet de** *mt.* France
172 D3 **Denkendorf** *Baden-Württemberg* Ger.
173 F3 **Denkendorf** *Bayern* Ger.
172 C3 **Denkingen** *Baden-Württemberg* Ger.
172 D4 **Denkingen** *Baden-Württemberg* Ger.
173 E4 **Denklingen** Ger.
169 F3 **Denkte** Ger.
83 G3 **Denman** *N.S.W.* Austr.
87 C7 **Denmark** *W.A.* Austr.
142 D3 **Denmark** *country* Europe
226 D3 **Denmark** *WI* U.S.A.
Denmark Fjord *inlet* Greenland *see* **Danmark Fjord**
221 P3 **Denmark Strait** Greenland/Iceland
151 F4 **Denmead** *Hampshire, England* U.K.
171 E4 **Dennewitz** Ger.
215 G1 **Dennilton** S. Africa
151 I2 **Dennington** *Suffolk, England* U.K.
86 F4 **Dennis, Lake** *salt flat W.A.* Austr.
232 C4 **Dennison** *OH* U.S.A.
234 D3 **Dennisville** *NJ* U.S.A.
146 E5 **Denny** *Falkirk, Scotland* U.K.
164 E2 **Den Oever** Neth.
Denow Uzbek. *see* **Denau**
95 F5 **Denpasar** *Bali* Indon.
170 E2 **Densow** Ger.
190 C2 **Dent Blanche** *mt.* Switz.
161 C4 **Dent de Rez** *hill* France
165 C4 **Dentergem** Belgium
173 E2 **Dentlein am Forst** Ger.
149 G4 **Denton** *Greater Manchester, England* U.K.
234 C4 **Denton** *MD* U.S.A.
237 D5 **Denton** *TX* U.S.A.
161 E3 **Dent Parrachée** *mt.* France
87 B7 **D'Entrecasteaux, Point** *W.A.* Austr.
77 G3 **D'Entrecasteaux, Récifs** *rf* New Caledonia
91 L8 **D'Entrecasteaux Islands** P.N.G.
190 B2 **Dents du Midi** *mt.* Switz.
151 H2 **Denver** *Norfolk, England* U.K.
238 F4 **Denver** *CO* U.S.A.
234 B2 **Denver** *PA* U.S.A.
224 E2 **Denys** *r. Que.* Can.
172 B3 **Denzlingen** Ger.
117 F4 **Deo** *Bihar* India
116 D3 **Deoband** *Uttar Prad.* India
115 D2 **Deobhog** *Madh. Prad.* India
234 B2 **Deodate** *PA* U.S.A.
117 F5 **Deogarh** *Orissa* India
116 C4 **Deogarh** *Rajasthan* India
116 E5 **Deogarh** *mt. Madh. Prad.* India
117 F4 **Deoghar** *Bihar* India
116 D5 **Deoli** *Mahar.* India
162 D2 **Déols** France
116 D5 **Deori** *Madh. Prad.* India
117 E4 **Deoria** *Uttar Prad.* India
116 C2 **Deosai, Plains of** Jammu and Kashmir
100 C1 **Dep** *r.* Rus. Fed.
116 C5 **Depalpur** *Madh. Prad.* India
165 B3 **De Panne** Belgium
225 H2 **De Pas, Rivière** *r. Que.* Can.
226 C3 **De Pere** *WI* U.S.A.
232 D3 **Depew** *NY* U.S.A.
233 F3 **Deposit** *NY* U.S.A.
227 I2 **Depot-Forbes** *Que.* Can.
227 I2 **Depot-Rowanton** *Que.* Can.
111 B5 **Depsang Point** *hill* Aksai Chin
226 C5 **Depue** *IL* U.S.A.
131 O3 **Deputatskiy** Rus. Fed.
Dêqên *Xizang* China *see* **Dagzê**
111 E6 **Dêqên** *Xizang* China
108 A2 **Dêqên** *Yunnan* China
109 D4 **Deqing** *Guangdong* China
109 G2 **Deqing** *Zhejiang* China
237 E5 **De Queen** *AR* U.S.A.
237 E6 **De Quincy** *LA* U.S.A.
156 E4 **Der, Lac du** *l.* France
123 G4 **Dera Ghazi Khan** Pak.
123 G4 **Dera Ismail Khan** Pak.
263 C2 **Deram, Mount** Antarctica
136 D2 **Derazhne** Ukr.
136 D3 **Derazhnya** Ukr.
171 C3 **Derben** Ger.
129 F2 **Derbent** Rus. Fed.
199 G1 **Derbent** *Kocaeli* Turkey
199 F2 **Derbent** *Manisa* Turkey
199 F2 **Derbent** *Uşak* Turkey
121 F5 **Derbent** Uzbek.
Derbesiye Turkey *see* **Şenyurt**
100 B2 **Derbur** *Nei Mongol* China
83 F5 **Derby** *Tas.* Austr.
86 D3 **Derby** *W.A.* Austr.
215 F1 **Derby** S. Africa
151 F2 **Derby** *Derby, England* U.K.
151 F2 **Derby** *admin. div. England* U.K.
235 E1 **Derby** *CT* U.S.A.
237 D4 **Derby** *KS* U.S.A.
233 G2 **Derby Line** *VT* U.S.A.
149 H4 **Derbyshire** *admin. div. England* U.K.
177 K4 **Derecske** Hungary
128 A1 **Dereiçi** Turkey
177 J5 **Derekegyház** Hungary
128 A1 **Dereköy** Turkey
199 F3 **Dereköy** Turkey
199 F2 **Dereköy** *Kütahya* Turkey
169 F4 **Derenburg** Ger.
169 E4 **Derental** Ger.
137 H3 **Derezuvate** Ukr.
147 D2 **Derg** *r.* Rep. of Ireland/U.K.
147 D2 **Derg, Lough** *l.* Rep. of Ireland
147 C4 **Derg, Lough** *l.* Rep. of Ireland
120 B2 **Dergachi** Rus. Fed.
Dergachi Ukr. *see* **Derhachi**
137 I2 **Derhachi** Ukr.
237 E6 **De Ridder** *LA* U.S.A.
164 D2 **De Rijp** Neth.
127 F3 **Derik** Turkey
126 D3 **Derinkuyu** Turkey
137 G3 **Deriyivka** Ukr.
137 J3 **Derkul** *r.* Rus. Fed./Ukr.
169 F5 **Dermbach** Ger.
Derna Libya *see* **Darnah**
177 L4 **Derna** Romania
129 B3 **Dernekpazarı** Turkey
136 C2 **Derno** Ukr.
108 A2 **Dêrong** *Sichuan* China
120 B5 **Derow** Iran
147 D3 **Derravaragh, Lough** *l.* Rep. of Ireland
213 H3 **Derre** Moz.
147 B2 **Derreen** Rep. of Ireland
147 B5 **Derreendaragh** Rep. of Ireland
147 B5 **Derreeny Bridge** Rep. of Ireland
147 C2 **Derry** Rep. of Ireland
147 E4 **Derry** *r.* Rep. of Ireland
Derry *Northern Ireland* U.K. *see* **Londonderry**
233 H3 **Derry** *NH* U.S.A.
147 C1 **Derrybeg** Rep. of Ireland
147 C3 **Derrybrien** Rep. of Ireland
147 B3 **Derryerglinna** Rep. of Ireland
147 D2 **Derrygonnelly** *Northern Ireland* U.K.
147 C4 **Derrygoolin** Rep. of Ireland
147 B3 **Derrylea** Rep. of Ireland
148 B3 **Derrylin** *Northern Ireland* U.K.
147 D2 **Derrynacreeve** Rep. of Ireland
147 B5 **Derrynasaggart Mountains** *hills* Rep. of Ireland
148 B3 **Derrynawilt** *Northern Ireland* U.K.
147 B3 **Derryrush** Rep. of Ireland
148 C3 **Derrytrasna** *Northern Ireland* U.K.
147 C2 **Derryveagh Mountains** *hills* Rep. of Ireland
197 H2 **Dersca** Romania
151 H2 **Dersingham** *Norfolk, England* U.K.
106 D3 **Derstei** *Nei Mongol* China
168 C3 **Dersum** Ger.
Dêrub *Xizang* China *see* **Rutog**
203 H5 **Derudeb** Sudan
214 D5 **De Rust** S. Africa
193 E2 **Deruta** Italy
146 B5 **Dervaig** *Argyll and Bute, Scotland* U.K.
158 E4 **Derval** France
198 C2 **Derveni** *Peloponnisos* Greece
188 F3 **Derventa** Bos.-Herz.
190 E2 **Dervio** Italy
83 F5 **Derwent** *r. Tas.* Austr.
151 F2 **Derwent** *r. Derbyshire, England* U.K.
149 I4 **Derwent** *r. England* U.K.
149 F3 **Derwent Water** *l. England* U.K.
Derweze Turkm. *see* **Darvaza**
139 J3 **Derza** *r.* Rus. Fed.
120 C1 **Derzhavino** Rus. Fed.
121 F2 **Derzhavinsk** Kazakh.
Derzhavinskiy Kazakh. *see* **Derzhavinsk**
197 F4 **Desa** Romania
260 D4 **Desaguadero** *r.* Arg.
252 C4 **Desaguadero** *r.* Bol.
260 C4 **Desague, Cerro** *mt.* Arg.
161 C4 **Désaignes** France
190 D3 **Desana** Italy
79 □3 **Désappointement, Îles du** *is Arch. des Tuamotu* Fr. Polynesia
237 F5 **Des Arc** *AR* U.S.A.
240 I2 **Desatoya Mountains** *NV* U.S.A.
227 F2 **Desbarats** *Ont.* Can.
151 G2 **Desborough** *Northamptonshire, England* U.K.
260 B4 **Descabezado, Volcán** *vol.* Chile
256 D4 **Descalvado** Brazil
182 D4 **Descargamaría** Spain
162 C2 **Descartes** France
223 K4 **Deschambault Lake** *Sask.* Can.
238 B2 **Deschutes** *r. OR* U.S.A.
210 C2 **Desē** Eth.
216 □3d **Deseada** *vol. La Palma* Canary Is
259 D7 **Deseado** Arg.
259 D7 **Deseado** *r.* Arg.
246 C3 **Desembarco del Granma National Park** *tourist site Granma* Cuba
242 B2 **Desemboque** Mex.
191 F3 **Desenzano del Garda** Italy
241 K2 **Deseret** *UT* U.S.A.
241 K1 **Deseret Peak** *UT* U.S.A.
227 I3 **Deseronto** *Ont.* Can.
184 □ **Deserta Grande** *i.* Madeira
184 □ **Desertas, Ilhas** *is* Madeira
241 J5 **Desert Center** *CA* U.S.A.
241 I5 **Desert Hot Springs** *CA* U.S.A.
160 A2 **Désertines** France
148 C3 **Desertmartin** *Northern Ireland* U.K.
241 L3 **Desert View** *AZ* U.S.A.
185 G2 **Desesperada** *mt.* Spain
161 B3 **Desges** France
247 □2 **Deshaies** *i.* Guadeloupe
232 B4 **Deshler** *OH* U.S.A.
116 C4 **Deshnok** *Rajasthan* India
187 D4 **Desierto** *hill* Spain
250 A6 **Desíerto de Sechura** *des.* Peru
190 E3 **Desio** Italy
198 B2 **Deskati** Greece
179 E4 **Deskle** Slovenia
236 D2 **De Smet** *SD* U.S.A.
236 E3 **Des Moines** *IA* U.S.A.
237 C4 **Des Moines** *NM* U.S.A.
228 H2 **Des Moines** *r. IA* U.S.A.
136 E3 **Desna** *r.* Rus. Fed./Ukr.
137 F2 **Desna** *r.* Rus. Fed./Ukr.
136 F2 **Desna** Ukr.
197 F4 **Desnățui** *r.* Romania
139 I4 **Desnogorsk** Rus. Fed.
259 C7 **Desnudo, Cerro** *mt.* Arg.
259 B9 **Desolación, Isla** *i.* Chile
226 B4 **DeSoto** *WI* U.S.A.
215 E5 **Despatch** S. Africa
106 B1 **Despen** Rus. Fed.
260 E2 **Despeñaderos** Arg.
226 D4 **Des Plaines** *IL* U.S.A.
196 E3 **Despotovac** *Srbija* Yugo.
217 □2 **Desroches, Île** *i.* Seychelles
171 D4 **Dessau** Ger.
171 D4 **Dessau** *admin. reg. Sachsen-Anhalt* Ger.
165 E3 **Dessel** Belgium
160 E1 **Dessoubre** *r.* France
Dessye Eth. *see* **Desē**
164 F2 **De Steeg** Neth.
165 C3 **Destelbergen** Belgium
227 H1 **Destor** *Que.* Can.
82 D3 **D'Estrees Bay** *S.A.* Austr.
182 D2 **Destriana** Spain
222 B2 **Destruction Bay** *Y.T.* Can.
192 B4 **Desulo** *Sardegna* Italy
156 B2 **Desvres** France
174 D3 **Deszczno** Pol.
177 J5 **Deszk** Hungary
196 E3 **Deta** Romania
222 H2 **Detah** *N.W.T.* Can.
139 K4 **Detchino** Rus. Fed.
213 E3 **Dete** Zimbabwe
168 C2 **Detern** Ger.
198 A1 **Deti Jon** *b.* Albania/Greece
196 E4 **Đetinja** *r.* Yugo.
177 J4 **Detk** Hungary
169 D4 **Detmold** Ger.
169 D4 **Detmold** *admin. reg. Nordrhein-Westfalen* Ger.
227 F3 **De Tour Village** *MI* U.S.A.
227 F4 **Detroit** *MI* U.S.A.
227 F5 **Detroit Beach** *MI* U.S.A.
236 E2 **Detroit Lakes** *MN* U.S.A.
Dett Zimbabwe *see* **Dete**
173 E2 **Dettelbach** Ger.
172 D3 **Dettingen an der Erms** Ger.
173 E3 **Dettingen an der Iller** Ger.
170 D1 **Dettmannsdorf** Ger.
169 F3 **Dettum** Ger.
157 H4 **Dettwiller** France
97 D4 **Det Udom** Thai.
177 I3 **Detva** Slovakia
171 D4 **Deuben** Ger.
156 C2 **Deûle** *r.* France
169 F4 **Deuna** Ger.
165 E3 **Deurne** Neth.
168 F2 **Deutsch Evern** Ger.
179 G3 **Deutschfeistritz** Austria
179 G4 **Deutsch Goritz** Austria
179 F4 **Deutsch-Griffen** Austria
170 D3 **Deutschhof** Ger.
179 H3 **Deutsch Kaltenbrunn** Austria
179 H3 **Deutschkreutz** Austria
Deutschland *country* Europe *see* **Germany**
179 G4 **Deutschlandsberg** Austria
171 E5 **Deutschneudorf** Ger.
179 H2 **Deutsch-Wagram** Austria
171 D4 **Deutzen** Ger.
227 H2 **Deux-Rivières** *Ont.* Can.
159 F5 **Deux-Sèvres** *dept Poitou-Charentes* France
197 F3 **Deva** Romania
183 F1 **Deva** *r.* Spain
Deva *Cheshire, England* U.K. *see* **Chester**
114 C2 **Devadurga** *Karnataka* India
114 C4 **Devakottai** *Tamil Nadu* India
237 F5 **De Valls Bluff** *AR* U.S.A.
Devana *Aberdeen, Scotland* U.K. *see* **Aberdeen**
114 C3 **Devanhalli** *Karnataka* India
114 C2 **Devarkonda** *Andhra Prad.* India
177 J4 **Dévaványa** Hungary
176 G4 **Devecser** Hungary
126 D3 **Develi** Turkey
164 F2 **Deventer** Neth.
190 D2 **Devero** *r.* Italy
146 F4 **Deveron** *r. Scotland* U.K.
197 F3 **Devesel** Romania
129 C4 **Devetaş** Turkey
176 E2 **Devét Skal** *hill* Czech Rep.
116 C5 **Devgadh Bariya** *Gujarat* India
Devghar *Bihar* India *see* **Deoghar**
116 B4 **Devikot** *Rajasthan* India
156 E3 **Deville** France
81 D4 **Devil River Peak** *South I.* N.Z.
237 C6 **Devils** *r. TX* U.S.A.
81 D4 **Devil's Backbone** *mt. South I.* N.Z.
147 D4 **Devil's Bit Mountain** *hill* Rep. of Ireland
150 D2 **Devil's Bridge** *Ceredigion, Wales* U.K.
236 D1 **Devil's Lake** *ND* U.S.A.
220 E4 **Devil's Paw** *mt. AK* U.S.A.
240 H3 **Devil's Peak** *CA* U.S.A.
246 D1 **Devil's Point** *Cat I.* Bahamas
222 C3 **Devil's Thumb** *mt. Alaska/B.C.* Can./U.S.A.
197 G5 **Devin** Bulg.
237 D6 **Devine** *TX* U.S.A.
137 J2 **Devitsa** *r.* Rus. Fed.
151 F3 **Devizes** *Wiltshire, England* U.K.
116 C4 **Devli** *Rajasthan* India
226 A1 **Devlin** *Ont.* Can.
197 H4 **Devnya** Bulg.
196 D5 **Devoll** *r.* Albania
161 D4 **Dévoluy** *mts* France
227 F2 **Devon** *Ont.* Can.
215 G2 **Devon** S. Africa
150 D4 **Devon** *admin. div. England* U.K.
149 I4 **Devon** *r. England* U.K.
146 E5 **Devon** *r. Scotland* U.K.
221 I2 **Devon Island** *Nunavut* Can.
83 F5 **Devonport** *Tas.* Austr.
240 I4 **Devore** *CA* U.S.A.
261 F2 **Devoto** Arg.
126 C2 **Devrek** Turkey
135 F8 **Devrekâni** Turkey
126 D2 **Devrez** *r.* Turkey
114 B2 **Devrukh** *Mahar.* India
117 G4 **Dewanganj** Bangl.
116 D5 **Dewas** *Madh. Prad.* India
215 F3 **Dewetsdorp** S. Africa
247 □1 **Dewey** Puerto Rico
164 F2 **De Wijk** Neth.
237 F5 **De Witt** *AR* U.S.A.
236 F3 **De Witt** *IA* U.S.A.
233 E3 **DeWitt** *NY* U.S.A.
149 H4 **Dewsbury** *West Yorkshire, England* U.K.
109 F2 **Dexing** *Jiangxi* China
233 □I2 **Dexter** *ME* U.S.A.
227 F4 **Dexter** *MI* U.S.A.
226 A4 **Dexter** *MN* U.S.A.
237 F4 **Dexter** *MO* U.S.A.
239 F5 **Dexter** *NM* U.S.A.
233 E2 **Dexter** *NY* U.S.A.
226 B3 **Dexterville** *WI* U.S.A.
108 C2 **Deyang** *Sichuan* China
82 B2 **Dey-Dey Lake** *salt flat S.A.* Austr.
137 H2 **Deykalivka** Ukr.
143 I4 **Deyma** *r.* Rus. Fed.
Deynau Turkm. *see* **Dyanev**
122 B5 **Deyyer** Iran
122 B4 **Dez** *r.* Iran
183 H3 **Deza** Spain
182 B2 **Deza** *r.* Spain
222 B2 **Dezadeash** *Y.T.* Can.
122 B3 **Dezfūl** Iran
107 H4 **Dezhou** *Shandong* China
Dezhou *Sichuan* China *see* **Dechang**
Dezh Shāhpūr Iran *see* **Marīvān**
177 L5 **Dezna** Romania
190 F3 **Dezzo** *r.* Italy
128 B3 **Dhahab, Wādī adh** *r.* Syria
128 B4 **Dhāhiriya** West Bank
124 D2 **Dhahlān, Jabal** *hill* Saudi Arabia
Dhahran Saudi Arabia *see* **Aẓ Ẓahrān**
117 G5 **Dhaka** Bangl.
117 G5 **Dhaka** *admin. div.* Bangl.
117 G5 **Dhaleswari** *r.* Bangl.
117 H4 **Dhaleswari** *r.* India
114 B2 **Dhalgaon** *Mahar.* India
124 D5 **Dhamār** Yemen
124 D5 **Dhamār** *governorate* Yemen
116 C5 **Dhamnod** *Madh. Prad.* India
116 D3 **Dhampur** *Uttar Prad.* India
116 E5 **Dhamtari** *Madh. Prad.* India
117 F5 **Dhanbad** *Bihar* India
116 C5 **Dhandhuka** *Gujarat* India
116 C4 **Dhanera** *Gujarat* India
116 E3 **Dhang Range** *mts* Nepal
117 F4 **Dhankuta** Nepal
116 C5 **Dhar** *Madh. Prad.* India
206 B2 **Ḍhar Adrar** *hills* Maur.
116 C5 **Dharampur** *Gujarat* India
117 F4 **Dharan Bazar** Nepal
114 C4 **Dharapuram** *Tamil Nadu* India
116 B5 **Dhari** *Gujarat* India
117 H4 **Dharmanagar** *Tripura* India
114 C3 **Dharmapuri** *Tamil Nadu* India
114 C3 **Dharmavaram** *Andhra Prad.* India
117 E5 **Dharmjaygarh** *Madh. Prad.* India
116 C3 **Dharmkot** *Punjab* India
206 D2 **Ḍhar Oualâta** *hills* Maur.
206 C2 **Ḍhar Tîchît** *hills* Maur.
114 C2 **Dharur** *Mahar.* India
114 B3 **Dharwad** *Karnataka* India
Dharwar *Karnataka* India *see* **Dharwad**
116 B5 **Dhasa** *Gujarat* India
116 D4 **Dhasan** *r. Madh. Prad.* India
117 E3 **Dhaulagiri** *mt.* Nepal
116 D4 **Dhaulpur** *Rajasthan* India
116 E4 **Dhaurahra** *Uttar Prad.* India
Dhávlia Greece *see* **Davlia**
Dhawlagiri *mt.* Nepal *see* **Dhaulagiri**
116 C4 **Dhebar Lake** India
128 A2 **Dhekelia Sovereign Base Area** *military base* Cyprus
117 H4 **Dhekiajuli** *Assam* India
117 F5 **Dhenkanal** *Orissa* India
Dheskáti Greece *see* **Deskati**
Dhiakoptón Greece *see* **Diakofto**
128 B4 **Dhībān** Jordan
Dhídhima Greece *see* **Didima**
Dhidhimótikhon Greece *see* **Didymoteicho**
113 □1 **Dhiffushi** *i. N. Male* Maldives
113 □1 **Dhigufinolhu** *i. S. Male* Maldives
117 H4 **Dhing** *Assam* India
127 G5 **Dhī Qār** *governorate* Iraq
Dhodhekánisos *is* Greece *see* **Dodekanisos**
Dhofar *admin. reg.* Oman *see* **Ẓufār**
116 B5 **Dhola** *Gujarat* India
116 C5 **Dholka** *Gujarat* India
Dhomokós Greece *see* **Domokos**
114 C3 **Dhone** *Andhra Prad.* India
116 B5 **Dhoraji** *Gujarat* India
116 B5 **Dhori** *Gujarat* India
116 B5 **Dhrangadhra** *Gujarat* India
116 B5 **Dhrol** *Gujarat* India
172 A2 **Dhron** Ger.
Dhrosiá Greece *see* **Drosia**
Dhubri *Assam* India *see* **Dhuburi**
117 G4 **Dhuburi** *Assam* India
116 C5 **Dhule** *Mahar.* India
Dhulia *Mahar.* India *see* **Dhule**
117 F4 **Dhulian** *Bihar* India
116 D5 **Dhuma** *Madh. Prad.* India
210 F2 **Dhuudo** Somalia
210 E3 **Dhuusa Marreeb** Somalia
124 B2 **Dhuwaybān** *basin* Saudi Arabia
Dhytikí Ellás *admin. reg.* Greece *see* **Dytiki Ellas**
Dhytikí Makedhonía *admin. reg.* Greece *see* **Dytiki Makedonia**
198 D4 **Dia** *i.* Greece
161 F4 **Diable, Cime du** *mt.* France
240 G3 **Diablo, Mount** *CA* U.S.A.
242 B2 **Diablo, Picacho del** *mt.* Mex.
240 G3 **Diablo Range** *mts CA* U.S.A.
211 C7 **Diaca** Moz.
206 D3 **Diafarabé** Mali
206 D3 **Diaka** *r.* Mali
198 C2 **Diakofto** Greece
206 C3 **Diakon** Mali
177 G3 **Diakovce** Slovakia
206 C3 **Dialafara** Mali
206 B3 **Dialakoto** Senegal
206 E3 **Diallassagou** Mali
261 G3 **Diamante** Arg.
260 D4 **Diamante** *r.* Arg.
193 H5 **Diamante** Italy

260 C4 Diamante, Pampa del plain Arg.
85 D5 Diamantina watercourse Qld Austr.
257 F3 Diamantina Brazil
254 E5 Diamantina, Chapada plat. Brazil
265 K7 Diamantina Deep sea feature Indian Ocean
85 E4 Diamantina Lakes Qld Austr.
256 A2 Diamantino Mato Grosso Brazil
253 F3 Diamantino Mato Grosso Brazil
256 A2 Diamantino r. Brazil
117 G5 Diamond Harbour W. Bengal India
85 G3 Diamond Islets Coral Sea Is Terr. Austr.
241 J2 Diamond Peak NV U.S.A.
240 G2 Diamond Springs CA U.S.A.
238 E3 Diamondville WY U.S.A.
206 C3 Diamou Mali
206 B3 Diamounguél Senegal
109 D4 Dianbai Guangdong China
Dianbu Anhui China see Feidong
108 B3 Diancang Shan mt. Yunnan China
85 G2 Diane Bank sea feature Coral Sea Is Terr. Austr.
206 C3 Diangounté Kamara Mali
206 C5 Diani r. Guinea
108 C2 Dianjiang Chongqing China
190 D4 Diano d'Alba Italy
190 D5 Diano Marina Italy
257 D4 Dianópolis Brazil
206 D4 Dianra Côte d'Ivoire
Dianyang Yunnan China see Shidian
Diaobingshan Liaoning China see Tiefa
100 D3 Diaoling Heilong. China
207 F3 Diapaga Burkina
128 A2 Diarizos r. Cyprus
206 C4 Diatifère Guinea
198 C1 Diavata Kentriki Makedonia Greece
115 G3 Diavolo, Mount hill Andaman & Nicobar Is India
261 G3 Diaz Arg.
125 G2 Dibā al Ḥiṣn U.A.E.
125 G3 Dibab Oman
Dibang r. India see Dingba Qu
209 D6 Dibaya Dem. Rep. Congo
209 C6 Dibaya-Lubwe Dem. Rep. Congo
151 F4 Dibden Hampshire, England U.K.
199 F2 Dibek Dağı mt. Turkey
214 D2 Dibeng S. Africa
136 E2 Dibrova Kyivs'ka Oblast' Ukr.
136 D2 Dibrova Zhytomyrs'ka Oblast' Ukr.
117 H4 Dibrugarh Assam India
182 B2 Dices Spain
168 D3 Dickel Ger.
237 C5 Dickens TX U.S.A.
233 □I1 Dickey ME U.S.A.
236 C2 Dickinson ND U.S.A.
231 C4 Dickson TN U.S.A.
234 C1 Dickson City PA U.S.A.
140 □ Dickson Land reg. Svalbard
127 F3 Dicle r. Turkey alt. Dijlah, Nahr (Iraq/Syria), conv. Tigris
191 G5 Dicomano Italy
164 F3 Didam Neth.
151 F3 Didcot Oxfordshire, England U.K.
169 F3 Didderse Ger.
129 D2 Didi Borbalo, Mt'a Georgia
206 C3 Didiéni Mali
129 C2 Didi Jikhaishi Georgia
129 D3 Didi Lilo Georgia
198 C3 Didima Greece
136 E2 Didivshchyna Ukr.
222 H5 Didsbury Alta Can.
116 C4 Didwana Rajasthan India
213 □K3 Didy Madag.
199 E1 Didymoteicho Greece
138 F4 Didžiasalis Lith.
161 D4 Die France
215 H1 Die Berg mt. S. Africa
215 H1 Die Berg mt. S. Africa
169 C5 Dieblich Ger.
206 E4 Diébougou Burkina
172 C2 Dieburg Ger.
177 L5 Dieci Romania
Diedenhofen France see Thionville
173 E3 Diedorf Bayern Ger.
169 F4 Diedorf Thüringen Ger.
223 I5 Diefenbaker, Lake Sask. Can.
162 E3 Diège r. France
183 E4 Diego Alvaro Spain
259 B8 Diego de Almagro, Isla i. Chile
265 I5 Diego Garcia i. B.I.O.T.
247 □7 Diego Martin Trin. and Tob.
259 C9 Diego Ramírez, Islas is Chile
Diégo Suarez Madag. see Antsirañana
206 C5 Diéké Guinea
170 D2 Diekhof Ger.
169 D3 Diekholzen Ger.
165 F5 Diekirch Lux.
165 E5 Diekirch admin. dist. Lux.
190 D1 Dielsdorf Switz.
206 C3 Diéma Mali
206 A3 Diembéreng Senegal
169 E4 Diemel r. Ger.
164 D2 Diemen Neth.
160 D3 Diémoz France
172 C2 Dienheim Ger.
161 A3 Dienne France
138 E3 Dienvidsusēja r. Latvia
156 E4 Dienville France
169 D3 Diepenau Ger.
165 E5 Diepenbeek Belgium
164 F2 Diepenheim Neth.
164 F2 Diepenveen Neth.
168 D3 Diepholz Ger.
158 B3 Dieppe France
247 □2 Dieppe Bay Town St Kitts and Nevis
214 D4 Dieput S. Africa
169 C5 Dierdorf Ger.
164 F2 Dieren Neth.
237 E5 Dierks AR U.S.A.
108 E4 Di'er Nonchang Qu r. China
100 C3 Di'er Songhua Jiang r. China
168 F3 Diesdorf Ger.
171 D4 Dieskau Ger.
173 E2 Diespeck Ger.
164 E3 Diessen Neth.
173 F4 Dießen am Ammersee Ger.
190 D1 Diessenhofen Switz.
165 E4 Diest Belgium
179 F2 Dietachdorf Austria
173 E3 Dietenheim Ger.
173 E2 Dietenhofen Ger.
173 G3 Dietersburg Ger.
173 F2 Dietfurt an der Altmühl Ger.
190 D1 Dietikon Switz.
172 C3 Dietingen Ger.
179 F2 Dietmanns Niederösterreich Austria
179 G2 Dietmanns Niederösterreich Austria
173 E4 Dietmannsried Ger.
173 F4 Dietramszell Ger.
173 E2 Dietzenbach Ger.
169 D5 Dietzhölztal-Ewersbach Ger.
157 F3 Dieue-sur-Meuse France
161 C3 Dieulefit France
157 G4 Dieulouard France
157 G4 Dieuze France
164 F2 Diever Neth.
169 D5 Diez Ger.
185 G3 Diezma Spain
207 I3 Diffa Niger
207 I2 Diffa dept Niger
165 E5 Differdange Lux.
115 E2 Digapahandi Orissa India
117 H4 Digboi Assam India
225 H4 Digby N.S. Can.
141 K3 Digerbergen hill Sweden
142 E4 Digerberget hill Sweden
116 C4 Diggi Rajasthan India
129 D3 Dighomi Georgia
236 C4 Dighton KS U.S.A.
114 C2 Diglur Mahar. India
162 C3 Dignac France
191 H2 Dignano Italy
161 E4 Digne-les-Bains France
156 B4 Digny France
160 B2 Digoin France
191 H2 Digòn r. Italy
129 C3 Digor Turkey
129 D2 Digora Rus. Fed.
92 C5 Digos Phil.
116 D5 Digras Mahar. India
123 G5 Digri Pak.
91 I8 Digul r. Indon.
111 F7 Dihang r. India alt. Yarlung Zangbo (China), conv. Brahmaputra
175 M5 Dihtiv Ukr.
137 G2 Dihtyari Ukr.
210 D4 Diinsoor Somalia
127 G5 Dijlah, Nahr r. Iraq/Syria alt. Dicle (Turkey), conv. Tigris
165 D4 Dijle r. Belgium
160 D1 Dijon France
Dijon airport France see Longvic
140 L2 Dikanäs Sweden
116 C4 Diken Madh. Prad. India
210 D2 Dikhil Djibouti
117 H4 Dikho r. India
199 E2 Dikili Turkey
165 B4 Dikkebus Belgium
129 D2 Diklosmta mt. Rus. Fed.
129 C3 Dikmeköyü Turkey
206 D4 Dikodougou Côte d'Ivoire
114 B2 Diksal Mahar. India
165 B3 Diksmuide Belgium
130 J2 Dikson Rus. Fed.
207 I3 Dikwa Nigeria
210 C3 Dīla Eth.
185 G3 Dilar Spain
185 G3 Dilar r. Spain
122 D4 Dilaram Iran
165 D4 Dilbeek Belgium
129 B3 Dilek Dağı mt. Turkey
93 C5 Dili East Timor
129 D3 Dilijan Armenia
81 D5 Dilion Cone mt. South I. N.Z.
129 C3 Dilip'i Georgia
Dilizhan Armenia see Dilijan
169 D5 Dillenburg Ger.
237 D6 Dilley TX U.S.A.
206 D3 Dilli Mali
142 D2 Dilling Norway
203 F6 Dilling Sudan
172 A2 Dillingen (Saar) Ger.
173 E3 Dillingen an der Donau Ger.
220 C4 Dillingham AK U.S.A.
223 I4 Dillon Sask. Can.
223 I4 Dillon r. Alberta/Saskatchewan Can.
238 D2 Dillon MT U.S.A.
231 E5 Dillon SC U.S.A.
227 I5 Dillsburg PA U.S.A.
232 D6 Dillwyn VA U.S.A.
209 D7 Dilolo Dem. Rep. Congo
165 E3 Dilsen Belgium
127 G4 Diltāwa Iraq
207 I5 Dimako Cameroon
117 H4 Dimapur Nagaland India
191 F2 Dimaro Italy
244 A2 Dimas Mex.
Dimashq Syria see Damascus
128 C3 Dimashq governorate Syria
209 D6 Dimbelenge Dem. Rep. Congo
206 D5 Dimbokro Côte d'Ivoire
83 E4 Dimboola Vic. Austr.
85 F3 Dimbulah Qld Austr.
198 C2 Dimini Thessalia Greece
Dimitrov Ukr. see Dymytrov
197 G4 Dimitrovgrad Bulg.
135 J5 Dimitrovgrad Rus. Fed.
197 F4 Dimitrovgrad Srbija Yugo.
Dimitrovo Bulg. see Pernik
237 C5 Dimmitt TX U.S.A.
234 C1 Dimock PA U.S.A.
128 B4 Dīmona Israel
92 C4 Dinagat i. Phil.
117 G4 Dinajpur Bangl.
195 F4 Dinami Italy
158 D3 Dinan France
116 C2 Dinanagar Punjab India
165 D4 Dinant Belgium
117 F4 Dinapur Bihar India
199 G2 Dinar Turkey
122 B4 Dīnār, Kūh-e mt. Iran
188 F3 Dinara mt. Bos.-Herz.
188 F3 Dinara Planina mts Bos.-Herz./Croatia
158 D3 Dinard France
Dinaric Alps mts Bos.-Herz./Croatia see Dinara Planina
150 D3 Dinas Powys Vale of Glamorgan, Wales U.K.
Dinbych Denbighshire, Wales U.K. see Denbigh
Dinbych-y-Pysgod Pembrokeshire, Wales U.K. see Tenby
209 B8 Dinde Angola
210 D2 Dinder r. Sudan
124 A5 Dinder el Agaliyin r. Sudan
114 C2 Dindi r. India
114 C4 Dindigul Tamil Nadu India
207 H4 Dindima Nigeria
116 E5 Dindori Madh. Prad. India
116 C5 Dindori Mahar. India
158 B3 Dinéault France
199 G2 Dinek Eskişehir Turkey
126 D3 Dinek Konya Turkey
209 C6 Dinga Dem. Rep. Congo
123 H3 Dinga Pak.
108 D5 Ding'an Hainan China
117 F4 Dingba Qu r. India
117 G4 Dingbian Shaanxi China
109 E2 Dingbujie Anhui China
Dingcheng Hainan China see Ding'an
158 E3 Dingé France
169 F4 Dingelstädt Ger.
94 C3 Dingin, Bukit mt. Indon.
147 A4 Dingle Rep. of Ireland
147 A4 Dingle pen. Rep. of Ireland
147 A4 Dingle Bay Rep. of Ireland
234 D1 Dingmans Ferry PA U.S.A.
109 E3 Dingnan Jiangxi China
85 G4 Dingo Qld Austr.
173 G3 Dingolfing Ger.
Dingping Sichuan China see Linshui
92 B2 Dingras Phil.
107 G5 Dingtao Shandong China
206 C4 Dinguiraye Guinea
225 I4 Dingwall N.S. Can.
146 D4 Dingwall Highland, Scotland U.K.
106 E5 Dingxi Gansu China
Dingxian Hebei China see Dingzhou
107 G4 Dingxiang Shanxi China
106 C3 Dingxin Gansu China
107 G4 Dingxing Hebei China
107 F1 Dingyuan Anhui China
107 G3 Dingzhou Hebei China
110 F4 Dingzikou Qinghai China
116 F5 Dinhata W. Bengal India
96 D2 Dinh Lâp Vietnam
147 D4 Dinin r. Rep. of Ireland
164 F2 Dinkel r. Neth.
173 E2 Dinkelsbühl Ger.
173 E2 Dinkelscherben Ger.
168 D3 Dinklage Ger.
146 F4 Dinnet Aberdeenshire, Scotland U.K.
111 D6 Dinngyê Xizang China
149 F4 Dinnington South Yorkshire, England U.K.
241 M1 Dinosaur CO U.S.A.
137 J5 Dinskaya Rus. Fed.
169 B4 Dinslaken Ger.
164 E3 Dinteloord Neth.
164 F3 Dinther Neth.
240 H3 Dinuba CA U.S.A.
232 E6 Dinwiddie VA U.S.A.
164 E3 Dinxperlo Neth.
206 D3 Dioïla Mali
161 D4 Diois, Massif du mts France
206 C4 Dion r. Guinea
257 F3 Dionísio Brazil
255 B8 Dionísio Cerqueira Brazil
161 C5 Dions France
256 B2 Diorama Brazil
Dioscurias Georgia see Sokhumi
177 H4 Diósd Hungary
197 F2 Diosig Romania
177 I4 Diósjenő Hungary
Diospolis Magna tourist site Egypt see Thebes
160 B2 Diou France
206 A3 Diouloulou Senegal
207 F3 Dioundiou Niger
206 D3 Dioura Mali
206 A3 Diourbel Senegal
123 H4 Dipalpur Pak.
116 E3 Dipayal Nepal
117 H4 Diphu Assam India
193 I5 Dipignano Italy
Dipkarpaz Cyprus see Rizokarpason
123 G5 Diplo Pak.
92 B4 Dipolog Phil.
165 F5 Dippach Lux.
169 E5 Dipperz Ger.
171 E5 Dippoldiswalde Ger.
81 B6 Dipton South I. N.Z.
Dipu Zhejiang China see Anji
117 H4 Dirang Arun. Prad. India
206 E2 Diré Mali
85 E2 Direction, Cape Qld Austr.
210 D2 Dirē Dawa Eth.
242 □I7 Diriamba Nic.
209 D9 Dirico Angola
194 D5 Dirillo r. Sicilia Italy
158 B3 Dirinon France
87 B5 Dirk Hartog Island W.A. Austr.
164 D2 Dirkshorn Neth.
164 D3 Dirksland Neth.
173 E3 Dirlewang Ger.
172 C2 Dirmstein Ger.
83 G2 Dirranbandi Qld Austr.
149 G2 Dirrington Great Law hill Scotland U.K.
124 C4 Dirs Saudi Arabia
Dirschau Pol. see Tczew
241 L3 Dirty Devil r. UT U.S.A.
116 C4 Disa Gujarat India
117 H4 Disang r. India
262 T2 Disappointment, Cape Antarctica
259 □ Disappointment, Cape S. Georgia
87 D4 Disappointment, Lake salt flat W.A. Austr.
Disappointment Islands Arch. des Tuamotu Fr. Polynesia see Désappointement, Îles du
173 E3 Dischingen Ger.
82 E4 Discovery Bay Vic. Austr.
264 J8 Discovery Seamounts sea feature S. Atlantic Ocean
190 D2 Disentis Muster Switz.
190 E2 Disgrazia, Monte mt. Italy
203 G3 Dishna Egypt
Disko i. Greenland see Qeqertarsuaq
Disko Bugt b. Greenland see Qeqertarsuup Tunua
199 G2 Dişli Turkey
84 E3 Dismal Creek r. Qld Austr.
263 D2 Dismal Mountains Antarctica
156 C4 Disneyland Paris tourist site France
195 H2 Diso Italy
165 E4 Dison Belgium
112 H6 Dispur Assam India
232 E6 Disputanta VA U.S.A.
225 G4 Disraëli Que. Can.
151 I2 Diss Norfolk, England U.K.
159 G5 Dissay France
159 G4 Dissay-sous-Courcillon France
169 D3 Dissen am Teutoburger Wald Ger.
206 E4 Dissin Burkina
149 F3 Distington Cumbria, England U.K.
256 D1 Distrito Federal admin. dist. Brazil
245 E4 Distrito Federal admin. dist. Mex.
250 E2 Distrito Federal admin. dist. Venez.
126 C5 Disûq Egypt
171 C4 Ditfurt Ger.
214 D3 Ditloung S. Africa
194 E5 Dittaino r. Sicilia Italy
169 F5 Dittelbrunn Ger.
173 E2 Dittenheim Ger.
151 H3 Ditton Kent, England U.K.
172 D3 Ditzingen Ger.
116 B5 Diu Daman India
92 C4 Diuata Mountains Phil.
179 E5 Divača Slovenia
122 A3 Dīvān Darreh Iran
Divehi country Indian Ocean see Maldives
208 B5 Divénié Congo
190 D2 Diveria r. Italy
159 F2 Dives r. France
159 F2 Dives-sur-Mer France
135 H5 Diveyevo Rus. Fed.
Divichi Azer. see Däväçi
238 D2 Divide MT U.S.A.
234 C3 Dividing Creek NJ U.S.A.
195 E4 Divieto Sicilia Italy
177 I3 Divín Slovakia
177 H2 Divina Slovakia
257 F4 Divinésia Brazil
257 E4 Divinópolis Brazil
156 C2 Divion France
256 B2 Divisões, Serra das mts Brazil
Divisor, Sierra de mts Peru see Ultraoriental, Cordillera
135 H7 Divnoye Rus. Fed.
206 D5 Divo Côte d'Ivoire
160 E2 Divonne-les-Bains France
184 B2 Divor r. Port.
126 E3 Divriği Turkey
134 L4 Div'ya Rus. Fed.
Diwaniyah Iraq see Ad Dīwānīyah
206 E5 Dixcove Ghana
233 □H2 Dixfield ME U.S.A.
156 D4 Dixmont France
233 □I2 Dixmont ME U.S.A.
240 G2 Dixon CA U.S.A.
226 C5 Dixon IL U.S.A.
238 D2 Dixon MT U.S.A.
220 E4 Dixon Entrance sea chan. Can./U.S.A.
222 G3 Dixonville Alta Can.
233 H2 Dixville Que. Can.
127 F3 Diyadin Turkey
127 G4 Diyālá governorate Iraq
127 G4 Diyālá, Nahr r. Iraq
127 F3 Diyarbakır Turkey
116 B4 Diyodar Gujarat India
Dizak Iran see Dāvar Panāh
207 H6 Dizangué Cameroon
Dize Turkey see Yüksekova
232 B6 Dizney KY U.S.A.
156 D3 Dizy France
156 E3 Dizy-le-Gros France
207 I6 Dja r. Cameroon
202 B4 Djado, Plateau du Niger
Djakarta Indon. see Jakarta
Djakovica Kosovo, Srbija Yugo. see Đakovica
205 G2 Djamâa Alg.
208 B5 Djambala Congo
205 H4 Djanet Alg.
78 □3b Djarrit i. Majuro Marshall Is
Djarrit-Uliga-Dalap Majuro Marshall Is see Delap-Uliga-Djarrit
205 F4 Djebr mt. Alg.
202 C6 Djédaa Chad
205 F2 Djelfa Alg.
208 E3 Djéma C.A.R.
Djeneral Jankovič Kosovo, Srbija Yugo. see Đeneral Jankovič
206 D3 Djenné Mali
202 B6 Djermaya Chad
206 E3 Djibo Burkina
206 D4 Djiborosso Côte d'Ivoire
210 D2 Djibouti country Africa
210 D2 Djibouti Djibouti
Djidjelli Alg. see Jijel
206 C3 Djiguéni Maur.
207 I5 Djohong Cameroon
208 B4 Djoua r. Congo/Gabon
147 E3 Djouce Mountain hill Rep. of Ireland
207 F4 Djougou Benin
207 I6 Djoum Cameroon
143 F1 Djurås Sweden
116 C3 Dlairi Punjab India
177 K3 Dlhé Klčovo Slovakia
177 H2 Dlhé Pole Slovakia
176 G2 Dlouhá Loučka Czech Rep.
174 G5 Dłubnia r. Pol.
174 F4 Długołęka Pol.
175 K2 Długołęka Pol.
175 J3 Długosiodło Pol.
175 H4 Dłutów Pol.
120 B1 Dmitriyevka Samarskaya Oblast' Rus. Fed.
135 H5 Dmitriyevka Tambovskaya Oblast' Rus. Fed.
135 F5 Dmitriyev-L'govskiy Rus. Fed.
Dmitriyevsk Donets'ka Oblast' Ukr. see Makiyivka
139 K3 Dmitrov Rus. Fed.
139 L4 Dmitrovskiy Pogost Rus. Fed.
139 J5 Dmitrovsk-Orlovskiy Rus. Fed.
137 J1 Dmitryashevka Rus. Fed.
137 G2 Dmytrivka Chernihivs'ka Oblast' Ukr.
137 H4 Dmytrivka Dnipropetrovs'ka Oblast' Ukr.
137 I3 Dmytrivka Dnipropetrovs'ka Oblast' Ukr.
137 G3 Dmytrivka Kirovohrads'ka Oblast' Ukr.
137 F4 Dmytrivka Mykolayivs'ka Oblast' Ukr.
137 I4 Dmytrivka Zaporiz'ka Oblast' Ukr.
Dmytriyevs'k Donets'ka Oblast' Ukr. see Makiyivka
139 H4 Dnepr r. Rus. Fed. alt. Dnipro (Ukraine), alt. Dnyapro (Belarus), conv. Dnieper
Dneprodzerzhinsk Ukr. see Dniprodzerzhyns'k
Dnepropetrovsk Ukr. see Dnipropetrovs'k
Dnepropetrovskaya Oblast' admin. div. Ukr. see Dnipropetrovs'ka Oblast'
Dnepropetrovsk Oblast admin. div. Ukr. see Dnipropetrovs'ka Oblast'
Dneprorudnoye Ukr. see Dniprorudne
136 E4 Dnestrovsc Moldova
135 F7 Dnieper r. Europe alt. Dnepr (Rus. Fed.), alt. Dnipro (Ukraine), alt. Dnyapro (Belarus)
136 E3 Dniester r. Ukr. alt. Dnister (Ukraine), alt. Nistru (Moldova)
137 G4 Dnipro r. Ukr. alt. Dnepr (Rus. Fed.), alt. Dnyapro (Belarus), conv. Dnieper
137 H3 Dniprodzerzhyns'k Ukr.
137 G3 Dniprodzerzhyns'ke Vodoskhovyshche resr Ukr.
137 H3 Dnipropetrovs'k Ukr.
137 H3 Dnipropetrovs'ka Oblast' admin. div. Ukr.
Dnipropetrovsk Oblast admin. div. Ukr. see Dnipropetrovs'ka Oblast'
137 H4 Dniprorudne Ukr.
137 H4 Dniprovka Ukr.
137 H3 Dniprovs'ke Vodoskhovyshche resr Ukr.
137 G4 Dnipryany Ukr.
136 E3 Dnister r. Ukr. alt. Nistru (Moldova), conv. Dniester
136 F4 Dnistrov'ky Lyman l. Ukr.
138 G3 Dno Rus. Fed.
139 H5 Dnyapro r. Belarus alt. Dnepr (Rus. Fed.), alt. Dnipro (Ukraine), conv. Dnieper
213 G3 Doa Moz.
147 E2 Doagh Northern Ireland U.K.
225 H4 Doaktown N.B. Can.
213 □K2 Doany Madag.
163 B5 Doazit France
208 C2 Doba Chad
Doba Xizang China see Toiba
177 L4 Doba Romania
138 H5 Dobasna r. Belarus
170 D2 Dobbertin Ger.
191 H2 Dobbiaco Italy
227 G3 Dobbinton Ont. Can.
235 E1 Dobbs Ferry NY U.S.A.
175 I6 Dobczyce Pol.
138 D3 Dobele Latvia
171 E4 Döbeln Ger.
91 H7 Doberai, Jazirah pen. Indon.
Doberai Peninsula Indon. see Doberai, Jazirah
171 E4 Doberlug-Kirchhain Ger.
171 F4 Döbern Ger.
179 G2 Dobersberg Austria
168 F1 Dobersdorf Ger.
171 F4 Dobershau Ger.
174 D3 Dobiegniew Pol.
175 J4 Dobieszyn Pol.
179 G4 Dobl Austria
261 E5 Doblas Arg.
188 G3 Doboj Bos.-Herz.
122 C4 Do Borjī Iran
177 K5 Doboz Hungary
175 I6 Dobra Małopolskie Pol.
174 G4 Dobra Wielkopolskie Pol.
174 C2 Dobra Zachodniopomorskie Pol.
174 D2 Dobra Zachodniopomorskie Pol.
177 L6 Dobra Romania
171 C5 Döbraberg hill Ger.
177 I3 Dobrá Niva Slovakia
176 C2 Dobřany Czech Rep.
179 F2 Dobrá Voda Czech Rep.
174 G3 Dobre Kujawsko-Pomorskie Pol.
175 J3 Dobre Mazowieckie Pol.
137 G4 Dobre Ukr.
143 I4 Dobre Miasto Pol.
197 F2 Dobrești Romania
197 H4 Dobrich Bulg.
135 H5 Dobrinka Rus. Fed.
176 D2 Dobříš Czech Rep.
171 D3 Dobritz Ger.
173 H2 Dobřív Czech Rep.
183 G2 Dobro Spain
174 G5 Dobrodzień Pol.
177 H5 Döbrököz Hungary
174 E5 Dobromierz Pol.
136 B3 Dobromyl' Ukr.
175 H4 Dobroń Pol.
177 L3 Dobron' Ukr.
176 E2 Dobronín Czech Rep.
137 I3 Dobropillya Ukr.
Dobropol'ye Ukr. see Dobropillya
175 L5 Dobrosyn Ukr.
174 F4 Dobroszyce Pol.
197 G3 Dobrotești Romania
175 M5 Dobrotvir Ukr.
197 H2 Dobrovăț Romania
171 F5 Dobrovice Czech Rep.
179 H4 Dobrovnik Slovenia
175 I5 Dobrowoda Pol.
139 L5 Dobroye Rus. Fed.
197 H4 Dobrudzhansko Plato plat. Bulg.
197 G3 Dobrun Romania
137 F1 Dobrush Belarus
176 F1 Dobruška Czech Rep.
134 L4 Dobryanka Rus. Fed.
137 F1 Dobryanka Ukr.
139 K4 Dobrynikha Rus. Fed.
175 I3 Dobrzankowo Pol.
174 D2 Dobrzany Pol.
174 F5 Dobrzeń Wielki Pol.
174 F4 Dobrzyca Pol.
174 E2 Dobrzyca r. Pol.
175 H3 Dobrzyków Pol.
175 H3 Dobrzyń nad Wisłą Pol.
177 J3 Dobšiná Slovakia
175 J1 Dobskie, Jezioro l. Pol.
81 C5 Dobson South I. N.Z.
81 B6 Dobson r. South I. N.Z.
231 D4 Dobson NC U.S.A.
150 C4 Dobwalls Cornwall, England U.K.
177 J5 Dóc Hungary
257 H3 Doce r. Espírito Santo Brazil
256 B3 Doce r. Goiás Brazil
146 D5 Dochart r. Scotland U.K.
146 D4 Dochgarroch Highland, Scotland U.K.
151 H2 Docking Norfolk, England U.K.
169 B5 Dockweiler Ger.
Doc Penfro Pembrokeshire, Wales U.K. see Pembroke Dock
244 D2 Doctor Arroyo Mex.
242 D2 Doctor Belisario Domínguez Mex.
87 E6 Doctor Hicks Range hills W.A. Austr.
244 D3 Doctor Mora Mex.
Doctor Petru Groza Romania see Ștei
114 C3 Dod Ballapur Karnataka India
151 H3 Doddinghurst Essex, England U.K.
149 G2 Doddington Northumberland, England U.K.
Dodecanese is Greece see Dodekanisos
199 E4 Dodekanisos is Greece
164 E3 Dodewaard Neth.
226 A3 Dodge Center MN U.S.A.
237 C4 Dodge City KS U.S.A.
226 B4 Dodgeville WI U.S.A.
191 G3 Dodici, Cima mt. Italy
211 B6 Dodoma Tanz.
211 B6 Dodoma admin. reg. Tanz.
223 I5 Dodsland Sask. Can.
232 B5 Dodsonville OH U.S.A.
164 F2 Doesburg Neth.
164 F3 Doetinchem Neth.
197 G3 Doftana r. Romania
224 B3 Dog r. Ont. Can.
111 E5 Dogai Coring salt l. China
111 E5 Dogaicoring Qangco salt l. China
199 E3 Doğanbey Turkey
199 E2 Doğanbey Turkey
199 G2 Doğançayır Eskişehir Turkey
126 E3 Doğanşehir Turkey
129 C4 Doğansu Turkey
222 F5 Dog Creek B.C. Can.
149 I4 Dogdyke Lincolnshire, England U.K.
199 G2 Döğer Turkey
172 C4 Dogern Ger.
224 B3 Dog Lake Ont. Can.
190 C4 Dogliani Italy
197 E3 Dognecea Romania
103 F5 Dōgo i. Japan
206 D4 Dogo Mali
207 G3 Dogondoutchi Niger
103 F6 Dōgo-yama mt. Japan
246 C1 Dog Rocks is Bahamas
127 G3 Doğubeyazıt Turkey
129 B3 Doğu Karadeniz Dağları mts Turkey
199 F3 Doğu Menteşe Dağları mts Turkey
111 D6 Dogxung Zangbo r. Xizang China
125 E2 Doha Qatar
Dohad Gujarat India see Dahod
171 C5 Döhlau Ger.
171 E5 Dohna Ger.
215 F5 Dohne S. Africa
168 C3 Dohren Ger.
111 C7 Dohrighat Uttar Prad. India
77 I4 Doi i. Fiji
111 E6 Doilungdêqên Xizang China
Doïranis, Limni l. Greece/Macedonia see Dojran, Lake
Doire Northern Ireland U.K. see Londonderry
96 B3 Doi Saket Thai.
117 F5 Doisanagar Bihar India
165 D4 Doische Belgium
256 C5 Dois Córregos Brazil
254 E4 Dois Irmãos, Serra dos hills Brazil
184 A1 Dois Portos Port.
176 G3 Dojč Slovakia
197 F5 Dojran, Lake Greece/Macedonia
Dojransko Ezero l. Greece/Macedonia see Dojran, Lake
205 G2 Dokhara, Dunes de des. Alg.
141 J3 Dokka Norway
140 M2 Dokkas Sweden
164 E1 Dokkum Neth.
164 E1 Dokkumer Ee r. Neth.
123 G5 Dokri Pak.
Dokshukino Rus. Fed. see Nartkala
138 F4 Dokshytsy Belarus
176 D1 Doksy Liberecký kraj Czech Rep.
171 F5 Doksy Středočeský kraj Czech Rep.
120 F2 Dokuchayevka Kazakh.
137 I4 Dokuchayevs'k Ukr.
199 G1 Dokurcun Sakarya Turkey
236 D2 Doland SD U.S.A.
150 D2 Dolanog Powys, Wales U.K.
241 J4 Dolan Springs AZ U.S.A.
259 D6 Dolavón Arg.
225 F3 Dolbeau Que. Can.
150 C2 Dolbenmaen Gwynedd, Wales U.K.
190 C5 Dolceacqua Italy
158 E3 Dol-de-Bretagne France
160 D1 Dole France
160 F3 Dolent, Mont mt. France/Italy
150 D2 Dolfor Powys, Wales U.K.
150 D1 Dolgarrog Conwy, Wales U.K.
150 D2 Dolgellau Gwynedd, Wales U.K.
170 E2 Dolgen Ger.
233 F3 Dolgeville NY U.S.A.
137 H2 Dolgiye Budy Rus. Fed.
175 I1 Dolgorukovo Kaliningradskaya Oblast' Rus. Fed.
139 L5 Dolgorukovo Lipetskaya Oblast' Rus. Fed.
135 G5 Dolgoye Rus. Fed.
197 H2 Dolhasca Romania
175 M5 Dołhobyczów Pol.
192 B5 Dolianova Sardegna Italy
174 D2 Dolice Pol.
Dolina Ukr. see Dolyna
129 C1 Dolinovka Rus. Fed.
100 G3 Dolinsk Sakhalin Rus. Fed.
Dolisie Congo see Loubomo
197 E4 Doljevac Srbija Yugo.
147 C4 Dolla Rep. of Ireland
146 E5 Dollar Clackmannanshire, Scotland U.K.
168 C2 Dollart Ger.
171 C3 Dolle Ger.
262 T2 Dolleman Island Antarctica
157 H5 Doller r. France
168 E2 Dollern Ger.
171 D4 Döllnitz Ger.
173 F3 Dollnstein Ger.
159 G3 Dollon France
169 F4 Döllstädt Ger.
169 F5 Dolmar hill Ger.
121 G1 Dolmatovo Kazakh.
197 G4 Dolna Lipnitska Bulg.
177 H3 Dolné Vestenice Slovakia
177 H2 Dolní Benešov Czech Rep.
171 F5 Dolní Beřkovice Czech Rep.
179 I2 Dolní Bojanovice Czech Rep.
176 E1 Dolní Bousov Czech Rep.
179 F1 Dolní Bukovsko Czech Rep.
197 H4 Dolni Chiflik Bulg.
197 G4 Dolni Dŭbnik Bulg.
179 H2 Dolní Dunajovice Czech Rep.
176 D3 Dolní Dvořiště Czech Rep.
176 F2 Dolní Kounice Czech Rep.
177 G3 Dolní Němčí Czech Rep.
176 D1 Dolní Podluží Czech Rep.
171 F5 Dolní Poustevna Czech Rep.
176 F2 Dolní Újezd Czech Rep.
176 B1 Dolní Žandov Czech Rep.
197 F4 Dolno Kamartsi Bulg.
197 G4 Dolno Levski Bulg.
174 E4 Dolnośląskie prov. Pol.
177 I2 Dolný Kubín Slovakia
Dolný Peter Slovakia see Svätý Peter
177 H3 Dolný Pial Slovakia
177 G4 Dolný Štál Slovakia
191 H3 Dolo Italy
190 F4 Dolo r. Italy
78 □4b Dolohmwar hill Pohnpei Micronesia
160 D3 Dolomieu France
Dolomites mts Italy see Dolomiti
191 G3 Dolomiti mts Italy
Dolonnur Nei Mongol China see Duolun
210 D3 Dolo Odo Eth.
261 I5 Dolores Arg.
243 H5 Dolores Guat.
242 C3 Dolores Mex.
187 C6 Dolores Spain
261 H3 Dolores Uru.
241 M2 Dolores r. CO U.S.A.
244 D3 Dolores Hidalgo Mex.
196 E3 Dolovo Vojvodina, Srbija Yugo.
220 G3 Dolphin and Union Strait Nunavut Can.
149 F2 Dolphinton South Lanarkshire, Scotland U.K.
178 D4 Dölsach Austria
174 F4 Dolsk Pol.
175 K3 Dołubowo Pol.
162 A3 Dolus-d'Oléron France
136 B3 Dolyna Ukr.
137 G3 Dolyns'ka Ukr.
137 I4 Dolzhanskaya Rus. Fed.
137 H2 Dolzhenkovo Rus. Fed.
91 I7 Dom, Gunung mt. Indon.
177 J3 Domaháza Hungary
199 F2 Domaniç Turkey
175 K3 Domanice Pol.
193 I5 Domanico Italy
175 H3 Domaniewice Łódzkie Pol.
175 I4 Domaniewice Mazowieckie Pol.
177 H2 Domaniža Slovakia
117 G4 Domar Bangl.
Domartang Xizang China see Banbar
156 C2 Domart-en-Ponthieu France
179 H4 Domašinec Croatia
177 J5 Domaszek Hungary
174 E5 Domaszków Pol.
174 F4 Domaszowice Pol.
190 E2 Domat Ems Switz.
156 D4 Domats France
176 B2 Domažlice Czech Rep.
111 F5 Domba Qinghai China
120 D2 Dombarovskiy Rus. Fed.
141 J3 Dombås Norway
157 F3 Dombasle-en-Argonne France
157 F4 Dombasle-en-Xaintois France
157 G4 Dombasle-sur-Meurthe France
129 B2 Dombay Rus. Fed.
213 G3 Dombe Moz.
209 B8 Dombe Grande Angola
177 K5 Dombegyház Hungary
177 H5 Dombóvár Hungary
177 K3 Dombrád Hungary
Dombrau Pol. see Dąbrowa Górnicza
190 B1 Dombresson Switz.
Dombrovitsa Rivnens'ka Oblast' Ukr. see Dubrovytsya
Dombrowa Pol. see Dąbrowa Górnicza
164 C3 Domburg Neth.
257 F3 Dom Cavati Brazil
Domda Qinghai China see Qingshuihe
160 A3 Dôme, Monts mts France
263 F1 Dome Argus ice feature Antarctica
263 H2 Dome Charlie ice feature Antarctica
Dome Circe ice feature Antarctica see Dome Charlie
222 F4 Dome Creek B.C. Can.
263 C2 Dome Fuji research stn Antarctica
178 D4 Domegge di Cadore Italy
138 D4 Domeikava Lith.
161 D3 Domène France
160 A2 Domérat France
241 J5 Dome Rock Mountains AZ U.S.A.
171 C3 Domersleben Ger.
86 F2 Domett, Cape W.A. Austr.
81 D4 Domett, Mount South I. N.Z.
157 F4 Domèvre-en-Haye France
157 G4 Domèvre-sur-Vezouze France
258 C3 Domeyko Chile
163 B5 Domezaine-Berraute France
255 B9 Dom Feliciano Brazil
159 F3 Domfront France
157 F4 Domgermain France
257 G4 Domingos Martins Brazil
182 C4 Dominguiso Port.
247 □2 Dominica country West Indies
242 □J7 Dominical Costa Rica
Dominicana, República country West Indies see Dominican Republic
246 E3 Dominican Republic country West Indies
247 □2 Dominica Passage Dominica/Guadeloupe
Dominique i. Fr. Polynesia see Hiva Oa
170 C2 Dömitz Ger.
257 F3 Dom Joaquim Brazil
157 E4 Dommartin-le-Franc France
156 E4 Dommartin-Varimont France
163 D4 Domme France
164 E3 Dommel r. Neth.
169 C5 Dommershausen Ger.
171 D4 Dommitzsch Ger.
197 G3 Domnești Romania
197 G3 Domnești Romania
170 C3 Dömnitz r. Ger.
210 E3 Domo Eth.
139 K4 Domodedovo Rus. Fed.
190 D2 Domodossola Italy
198 C2 Domokos Greece
217 □3 Domoni Comoros
156 C3 Domont France
177 H4 Dömös Hungary
157 G4 Dompaire France
157 F4 Dompcevrin France
255 B9 Dom Pedrito Brazil
254 D3 Dom Pedro Brazil
160 C2 Dompierre-les-Ormes France
160 B2 Dompierre-sur-Besbre France
162 A2 Dompierre-sur-Mer France
158 E5 Dompierre-sur-Yon France
95 G5 Dompu Sumbawa Indon.
157 F4 Domrémy-la-Pucelle France
177 I4 Dömsöd Hungary
170 C2 Domsühl Ger.
192 A6 Domus de Maria Sardegna Italy
192 A5 Domusnovas Sardegna Italy
260 B5 Domuyo, Volcán vol. Arg.
137 H4 Domuzla r. Ukr.
83 G2 Domville, Mount hill Qld Austr.
188 E2 Domžale Slovenia
85 G3 Don r. Qld Austr.
158 E4 Don r. France
114 C2 Don r. India
242 C3 Don Mex.
139 L5 Don r. Rus. Fed.
146 F4 Don r. Scotland U.K.
96 D4 Don, Xé r. Laos
147 E3 Donabate Rep. of Ireland
191 H3 Donada Italy
147 D2 Donagh Northern Ireland U.K.
147 F2 Donaghadee Northern Ireland U.K.
147 E2 Donaghcloney Northern Ireland U.K.
147 D4 Donaghmore Laois Rep. of Ireland
147 E3 Donaghmore Meath Rep. of Ireland
147 E2 Donaghmore Northern Ireland U.K.
83 E4 Donald Vic. Austr.
237 F6 Donaldsonville LA U.S.A.
258 C2 Donalnes, Cerro mt. Chile
231 C6 Donalsonville GA U.S.A.
184 D2 Don Álvaro Spain
185 F3 Doña Mencía Spain
147 E3 Donard Rep. of Ireland
260 B2 Doña Rosa, Cordillera mts Chile
244 B1 Donato Guerra Mex.
178 I2 Donau r. Austria/Ger. alt. Duna (Hungary), alt. Dunaj (Slovakia), alt. Dunărea (Romania), alt. Dunav (Yugoslavia), conv. Danube
172 C4 Donaueschingen Ger.
173 G2 Donaustauf Ger.
173 E3 Donauwörth Ger.
184 E2 Don Benito Spain
149 H4 Doncaster South Yorkshire England U.K.
157 E3 Donchery France
209 B7 Dondo Angola
136 D3 Donduşeni Moldova
Dondyushany Moldova see Donduşeni
147 C2 Donegal Rep. of Ireland
147 C2 Donegal county Rep. of Ireland
147 C2 Donegal Bay Rep. of Ireland
Dönenbay Kazakh. see Dunenbay
137 J3 Donetsk Rus. Fed.
137 I4 Donets'k Ukr.
137 I3 Donets'ka Oblast' admin. div. Ukr.
Donetskaya Oblast' admin. div. Ukr. see Donets'ka Oblast'
137 I2 Donetskaya Seymitsa r. Rus. Fed.
Donetsko-Amrovsiyevka Ukr. see Amvrosiyivka
Donetsk Oblast admin. div. Ukr. see Donets'ka Oblast'
137 J3 Donets'kyy Ukr.
137 J3 Donets'kyy Kryazh hills Rus. Fed./Ukr.
207 H4 Donga r. Cameroon/Nigeria
207 H5 Donga Nigeria
109 D3 Dong'an Hunan China
87 B6 Dongara W.A. Austr.
116 E5 Dongargaon Madh. Prad. India
116 E5 Dongargarh Madh. Prad. India
110 F3 Dongbatu Gansu China
Dongbo Xizang China see Mêdog
Dongchuan Yunnan China see Yao'an
108 B3 Dongchuan Yunnan China
Dongcun Shandong China see Haiyang
Dongcun Shanxi China see Lanxian
107 H4 Dong'e Shandong China
164 D3 Dongen Neth.
158 D4 Donges France
108 D5 Dongfang Hainan China
100 E3 Dongfanghong Heilong. China
100 C4 Dongfeng Jilin China
93 A3 Donggala Sulawesi Tengah Indon.
101 C5 Donggang Liaoning China
Donggou Liaoning China see Donggang
109 E3 Donggu Jiangxi China
109 E4 Dongguan Guangdong China
96 D3 Đông Ha Vietnam
107 H5 Donghai Jiangsu China
Dong Hai sea N. Pacific Ocean see East China Sea
108 C2 Dong He r. China
96 D3 Đông Hôi Vietnam
109 E4 Dong Jiang r. China
100 D3 Dongjingcheng Heilong. China
108 D3 Dongkou Hunan China
108 C3 Donglan Guangxi China
106 D4 Dongle Gansu China
107 I3 Dongliao r. China
110 E4 Donglük Xinjiang China
Dongmen Guangxi China see Luocheng
107 G5 Dongming Shandong China
100 D3 Dongning Heilong. China
209 B8 Dongo Angola
190 E2 Dongo Italy
203 F5 Dongola Sudan
210 B3 Dongotona Mountains Sudan
208 C4 Dongou Congo
96 C3 Dong Phraya Fai mts Thai.
96 C4 Dong Phraya Yen esc. Thai.
109 E4 Dongping Guangdong China
Dongping Hunan China see Anhua
107 H5 Dongping Shandong China
107 H4 Dongping Hu l. China
Dongpo Sichuan China see Meishan
111 E6 Dongqiao Xizang China
109 F4 Dongshan Fujian China
Dongshan Jiangsu China see Jiangning
109 G2 Dongshan Jiangsu China
Dongshan Jiangxi China see Shangyou
109 E3 Dongshao Jiangxi China
107 F4 Dongsheng Nei Mongol China
Dongshuan Yunnan China see Tangdan
109 G1 Dongtai Jiangsu China
109 G1 Dongtai r. China
109 E2 Dongting Hu l. China
109 G3 Dongtou Zhejiang China
Dong Ujimqin Qi Nei Mongol China see Uliastai
Dongxiang Sichuan China see Xuanhan
108 C4 Dongxing Guangxi China
100 C3 Dongxing Heilong. China
109 G2 Dongyang Zhejiang China
107 H4 Dongying Shandong China
106 D4 Dongzhen Gansu China
109 F2 Dongzhi Anhui China
260 B4 Doñihue Chile
151 G2 Donington Lincolnshire, England U.K.
237 F4 Doniphan MO U.S.A.
196 E4 Donja Dubnica Kosovo, Srbija Yugo.
179 H4 Donja Dubrava Croatia
179 H4 Donja Konjšćina Croatia
179 G5 Donja Stubica Croatia
179 H4 Donja Višnjica Croatia
222 A2 Donjek r. Y.T. Can.
157 F4 Donjeux France
188 G3 Donji Miholjac Croatia
197 F3 Donji Milanovac Srbija Yugo.
188 F3 Donji Vakuf Bos.-Herz.
188 E3 Donji Zemunik Croatia
164 F1 Donkerbroek Neth.
215 E4 Donkerpoort S. Africa
140 K2 Dønna i. Norway
225 G4 Donnacona Que. Can.
194 D6 Donnalucata Sicilia Italy
190 C3 Donnas Italy
222 G4 Donnelly Alta Can.
80 D1 Donnellys Crossing North I. N.Z.
156 D4 Donnemarie-Dontilly France
179 F3 Donnersbach Austria
172 B2 Donnersberg hill Ger.
173 E2 Donnersdorf Ger.
150 E2 Donnington Telford and Wrekin, England U.K.
87 B7 Donnybrook W.A. Austr.
147 C4 Donohill Rep. of Ireland
157 H4 Donon mt. France
192 B5 Donori Sardegna Italy
186 B1 Donostia - San Sebastián Spain
147 C5 Donoughmore Rep. of Ireland
199 D3 Donoussa i. Greece
226 D5 Donovan IL U.S.A.
137 I4 Dons'ke Ukr.
137 K4 Donskoy Rostovskaya Oblast' Rus. Fed.
139 L5 Donskoy Tul'skaya Oblast' Rus. Fed.
139 L5 Donskoye Lipetskaya Oblast' Rus. Fed.
135 H7 Donskoye Stavropol'skiy Kray Rus. Fed.

137 J2 **Donskoye Belogor'ye** *hills* Rus. Fed.
92 B3 **Donsol** Phil.
96 B3 **Donthami** *r.* Myanmar
158 E3 **Donville-les-Bains** France
163 C4 **Donzac** France
172 D3 **Donzdorf** Ger.
162 D3 **Donzenac** France
161 C4 **Donzère** France
160 B1 **Donzy** France
147 A3 **Dooagh** Rep. of Ireland
147 C2 **Doocastle** Rep. of Ireland
147 A3 **Dooega** Rep. of Ireland
147 B3 **Dooghbeg** Rep. of Ireland
147 A2 **Doogort** Rep. of Ireland
147 B2 **Doohooma** Rep. of Ireland
148 B3 **Dooish** *Northern Ireland* U.K.
86 C4 **Dooleena** *hill W.A.* Austr.
84 D3 **Doomadgee** *Qld* Austr.
147 C4 **Doon** Rep. of Ireland
146 D6 **Doon** *r. Scotland* U.K.
146 D6 **Doon, Loch** *l. Scotland* U.K.
147 B4 **Doonaha** Rep. of Ireland
147 B4 **Doonbeg** Rep. of Ireland
147 B4 **Doonbeg** *r.* Rep. of Ireland
147 A3 **Doonloughan** Rep. of Ireland
147 A4 **Doonmanagh** Rep. of Ireland
164 E2 **Doorn** Neth.
164 E2 **Doornspijk** Neth.
226 D3 **Door Peninsula** *WI* U.S.A.
174 E3 **Dopiewo** Pol.
108 B2 **Do Qu** *r. Sichuan* China
237 C5 **Dora** *NM* U.S.A.
86 D4 **Dora, Lake** *salt flat W.A.* Austr.
190 D3 **Dora Baltea** *r.* Italy
160 E3 **Dora di Ferret** *r.* Italy
160 F3 **Dora di Veny** *r.* Italy
190 C3 **Dora Riparia** *r.* Italy
Dorbiljin *Xinjiang* China *see* **Emin**
Dorbod *Heilong.* China *see* **Taikang**
Dorbod Qi *Nei Mongol* China *see* **Ulan Hua**
196 E4 **Đorče Petrov** Macedonia
150 E4 **Dorchester** *Dorset, England* U.K.
234 D3 **Dorchester** *NJ* U.S.A.
156 C4 **Dordives** France
162 C3 **Dordogne** *dept Aquitaine* France
160 A3 **Dordogne** *r.* France
151 F2 **Dordon** *Warwickshire, England* U.K.
164 D3 **Dordrecht** Neth.
215 F4 **Dordrecht** S. Africa
160 B2 **Dore** *r.* France
160 A3 **Dore, Monts** *mts* France
223 J4 **Doré Lake** *Sask.* Can.
161 B3 **Dore-l'Église** France
178 A3 **Doren** Austria
169 E3 **Dörentrup** Ger.
146 D4 **Dores** *Highland, Scotland* U.K.
257 F3 **Dores de Guanhães** Brazil
257 E3 **Dores do Indaiá** Brazil
173 G3 **Dorfen** Ger.
178 E3 **Dorfgastein** Austria
168 E3 **Dorfmark** Ger.
170 C2 **Dorf Mecklenburg** Ger.
192 B4 **Dorgali** *Sardegna* Italy
106 B1 **Dörgön** Mongolia
177 K5 **Dorgoş** Romania
123 F4 **Dori** *r.* Afgh.
207 E3 **Dori** Burkina
214 B4 **Doring** *r.* S. Africa
214 B5 **Doring** *r.* S. Africa
214 B4 **Doringbaai** S. Africa
214 B4 **Doringbos** S. Africa
198 B3 **Dorio** *Peloponnisos* Greece
84 B2 **Dorisvale** *N.T.* Austr.
151 G3 **Dorking** *Surrey, England* U.K.
157 H4 **Dorlisheim** France
206 E5 **Dormaa-Ahenkro** Ghana
169 B4 **Dormagen** Ger.
177 J4 **Dormánd** Hungary
156 D3 **Dormans** France
190 D3 **Dormelletto** Italy
172 C3 **Dormettingen** Ger.
100 E3 **Dormidontovka** Rus. Fed.
114 D2 **Dornakal** *Andhra Prad.* India
179 G4 **Dornava** Slovenia
169 E4 **Dörnberg (Habichtswald)** Ger.
178 A3 **Dornbirn** Austria
171 C4 **Dornburg (Saale)** Ger.
169 D5 **Dornburg-Frickhofen** Ger.
168 E2 **Dornbusch** Ger.
169 F5 **Dorndorf** Ger.
171 C4 **Dorndorf-Steudnitz** Ger.
182 C3 **Dornelas** Port.
160 B2 **Dornes** France
169 E4 **Dörnhagen (Fuldabrück)** Ger.
172 C3 **Dornhan** Ger.
146 C4 **Dornie** *Highland, Scotland* U.K.
171 D3 **Dörnitz** Ger.
190 D3 **Dorno** Italy
146 D4 **Dornoch** *Highland, Scotland* U.K.
146 D4 **Dornoch Firth** *est. Scotland* U.K.
107 G1 **Dornod** *prov.* Mongolia
107 F2 **Dornogovĭ** *prov.* Mongolia
234 B2 **Dornsife** *PA* U.S.A.
172 D3 **Dornstadt** Ger.
172 C3 **Dornstetten** Ger.
168 C2 **Dornum** Ger.
168 C2 **Dornumersiel** Ger.
206 E2 **Doro** Mali
197 H3 **Dorobanţu** Romania
177 H4 **Dorog** Hungary
177 I4 **Dorogháza** Hungary
139 I4 **Dorogobuzh** Rus. Fed.
197 H2 **Dorohoi** Romania
175 L4 **Dorohusk** Pol.
139 K4 **Dorokhovo** Rus. Fed.
177 L4 **Dorolţ** Romania
137 F4 **Doroshivka** Ukr.
Dorostol Bulg. *see* **Silistra**
136 C2 **Dorosyni** Ukr.
140 L2 **Dorotea** Sweden
234 D3 **Dorothy** *NJ* U.S.A.
Dorpat Estonia *see* **Tartu**
168 C3 **Dörpen** Ger.
87 B5 **Dorre Island** *W.A.* Austr.
83 H2 **Dorrigo** *N.S.W.* Austr.
238 B3 **Dorris** *CA* U.S.A.
207 H5 **Dorsale Camerounaise** *slope* Cameroon/Nigeria
227 H3 **Dorset** *Ont.* Can.
150 E4 **Dorset** *admin. div. England* U.K.
232 C4 **Dorset** *OH* U.S.A.
169 F3 **Dorstadt** Ger.
169 B4 **Dorsten** Ger.
160 D2 **Dortan** France
169 C4 **Dortmund** Ger.
232 B6 **Dorton** *KY* U.S.A.
126 E3 **Dörtyol** Turkey
174 G4 **Doruchów** Pol.
129 C4 **Dorukdibi** Turkey
168 D2 **Dorum** Ger.
168 E3 **Dörverden** Ger.
Dorylaeum Turkey *see* **Eskişehir**
172 D2 **Dörzbach** Ger.
187 C5 **Dos Aguas** Spain
122 D4 **Do Sārī** Iran
183 G5 **Dosbarrios** Spain
241 M5 **Dos Cabezas Mountains** *AZ* U.S.A.
250 C6 **Dos de Mayo** Peru
199 G3 **Döşemealtı** Turkey
123 E3 **Doshakh, Koh-i-** *mt.* Afgh.
184 E3 **Dos Hermanas** Spain
243 H5 **Dos Lagunos** Guat.
96 D2 **Đo Son** Vietnam
240 G3 **Dos Palos** *CA* U.S.A.
197 G5 **Dospat** Bulg.
197 G5 **Dospat** *r.* Bulg.
185 H3 **Dos Picos** *mt.* Spain
170 D3 **Dosse** *r.* Ger.
172 C2 **Dossenheim** Ger.
208 C2 **Dosséo, Bahr** *r.* Chad
207 F3 **Dosso** Niger
207 F3 **Dosso** *dept* Niger
190 D2 **Dossola, Val** *val.* Italy
120 C3 **Dossor** Kazakh.
185 F2 **Dos Torres** Spain
121 J3 **Dostyk** Kazakh.
Dostyq Kazakh. *see* **Dostyk**
231 C6 **Dothan** *AL* U.S.A.
168 D3 **Dötlingen** Ger.
172 C3 **Dotternhausen** Ger.
190 D1 **Döttingen** Switz.
156 D2 **Douai** France
207 H5 **Douala** Cameroon
158 B3 **Douarnenez** France
85 H5 **Double Island Point** *Qld* Austr.
237 C5 **Double Mountain Fork** *r. TX* U.S.A.
240 H4 **Double Peak** *CA* U.S.A.
85 F3 **Double Point** *Qld* Austr.
231 C5 **Double Springs** *AL* U.S.A.
176 E2 **Doubrava** *r.* Czech Rep.
160 E2 **Doubs** France
160 E1 **Doubs** *dept Franche-Comté* France
160 D2 **Doubs** *r.* France/Switz.
86 E2 **Doubtful Bay** *W.A.* Austr.
87 C7 **Doubtful Island Bay** *W.A.* Austr.
81 A6 **Doubtful Sound** *South I.* N.Z.
81 A6 **Doubtful Sound** *inlet South I.* N.Z.
156 D5 **Douchy** France
156 D2 **Douchy-les-Mines** France
160 D2 **Doucier** France
159 G2 **Doudeville** France
162 B1 **Doué-la Fontaine** France
206 E3 **Douentza** Mali
148 D2 **Dougarie** *North Ayrshire, Scotland* U.K.
205 H1 **Dougga** *tourist site* Tunisia
147 C2 **Dough Mountain** *hill* Rep. of Ireland
145 E4 **Douglas** Isle of Man
80 E3 **Douglas** *North I.* N.Z.
147 C5 **Douglas** Rep. of Ireland
214 D3 **Douglas** S. Africa
146 E6 **Douglas** *South Lanarkshire, Scotland* U.K.
222 C3 **Douglas** *AK* U.S.A.
241 M6 **Douglas** *AZ* U.S.A.
231 D6 **Douglas** *GA* U.S.A.
238 F3 **Douglas** *WY* U.S.A.
148 B3 **Douglas Bridge** *Northern Ireland* U.K.
241 M1 **Douglas Creek** *r. CO* U.S.A.
262 T2 **Douglas Range** *mts* Antarctica
234 C2 **Douglassville** *PA* U.S.A.
146 F5 **Douglastown** *Angus, Scotland* U.K.
231 C5 **Douglasville** *GA* U.S.A.
Douhudi *Hubei* China *see* **Gong'an**
157 F4 **Doulaincourt-Saucourt** France
Douliu Taiwan *see* **Touliu**
156 C2 **Doullens** France
207 F4 **Doumè** Benin
207 I5 **Doumé** Cameroon
207 I5 **Doumé** *r.* Cameroon
109 E4 **Doumen** *Guangdong* China
146 E2 **Dounby** *Orkney, Scotland* U.K.
146 D5 **Doune** *Stirling, Scotland* U.K.
146 D5 **Doune Hill** *hill Scotland* U.K.
207 F4 **Dounkassa** Benin
146 E3 **Dounreay** *Highland, Scotland* U.K.
176 C1 **Doupovské Hory** *mts* Czech Rep.
165 C4 **Dour** Belgium
256 C3 **Dourada, Cachoeira** *waterfall* Brazil
256 B2 **Dourada, Serra** *hills* Brazil
254 C5 **Dourada, Serra** *mts* Brazil
255 B7 **Dourados** Brazil
255 B7 **Dourados** *r.* Brazil
208 B2 **Dourbali** Chad
161 B4 **Dourbie** *r.* France
161 B4 **Dourbies** France
156 C4 **Dourdan** France
161 A4 **Dourdou** *r.* France
161 A5 **Dourdou** *r.* France
163 E5 **Dourgne** France
156 B2 **Douriez** France
182 B3 **Douro** *r.* Port. *alt.* **Duero (Spain)**
Doushi *Hubei* China *see* **Gong'an**
160 E3 **Doussard** France
256 A5 **Doutor Camargo** Brazil
160 E2 **Douvaine** France
158 E2 **Douve** *r.* France
159 F2 **Douvres-la-Déliverande** France
161 C3 **Doux** *r.* France
205 H2 **Douz** Tunisia
163 B5 **Douze** *r.* France
162 C3 **Douzillac** France
157 F3 **Douzy** France
191 G4 **Dovadola** Italy
136 E2 **Dovbysh** Ukr.
151 F2 **Dove** *r. Derbyshire/Staffordshire, England* U.K.
149 I3 **Dove** *r. North Yorkshire, England* U.K.
151 I2 **Dove** *r. Suffolk, England* U.K.
225 J2 **Dove Brook** *Nfld.* Can.
221 P2 **Dove Bugt** *b.* Greenland
241 M3 **Dove Creek** *CO* U.S.A.
83 F5 **Dover** *Tas.* Austr.
151 I3 **Dover** *Kent, England* U.K.
234 C3 **Dover** *DE* U.S.A.
233 □H3 **Dover** *NH* U.S.A.
234 D2 **Dover** *NJ* U.S.A.
232 C4 **Dover** *OH* U.S.A.
234 B3 **Dover** *PA* U.S.A.
231 C4 **Dover** *TN* U.S.A.
87 E7 **Dover, Point** *W.A.* Austr.
145 H6 **Dover, Strait of** France/U.K.
233 □I2 **Dover-Foxcroft** *ME* U.S.A.
151 F2 **Doveridge** *Derbyshire, England* U.K.
235 E1 **Dover Plains** *NY* U.S.A.
Dovey *r. Wales* U.K. *see* **Dyfi**
122 B4 **Doveyrīch, Rūd-e** *r.* Iran/Iraq
136 B3 **Dovhe** Ukr.
136 C2 **Dovhoshyyi** Ukr.
175 L1 **Dovinė** *r.* Lith.
141 J3 **Dovrefjell** *mts* Norway
137 H2 **Dovzhyk** Ukr.
Dow, Lake Botswana *see* **Xau, Lake**
211 B8 **Dowa** Malawi
226 D5 **Dowagiac** *MI* U.S.A.
146 E5 **Dowally** *Perth and Kinross, Scotland* U.K.
123 F2 **Dowlatābād** Afgh.
122 B4 **Dowlatābād** Iran
123 E2 **Dowlatābād** Iran
147 F2 **Down** *county Northern Ireland* U.K.
240 H5 **Downey** *CA* U.S.A.
151 H2 **Downham Market** *Norfolk, England* U.K.
240 G2 **Downieville** *CA* U.S.A.
226 A5 **Downing** *MO* U.S.A.
234 C2 **Downingtown** *PA* U.S.A.
147 F2 **Downpatrick** *Northern Ireland* U.K.
236 D4 **Downs** *KS* U.S.A.
233 F3 **Downsville** *NY* U.S.A.
226 B3 **Downsville** *WI* U.S.A.
151 F4 **Downton** *Wiltshire, England* U.K.
222 E4 **Downton, Mount** *B.C.* Can.
147 C2 **Dowra** Rep. of Ireland
122 B3 **Dow Rūd** Iran
122 A3 **Dow Sar** Iran
151 G2 **Dowsby** *Lincolnshire, England* U.K.
160 A2 **Doyet** France
240 G1 **Doyle** *CA* U.S.A.
225 J4 **Doyles** *Nfld.* Can.
234 C2 **Doylestown** *PA* U.S.A.
197 G4 **Doyrentsi** Bulg.
122 D5 **Dozdān** *r.* Iran
103 F5 **Dōzen** *is* Japan
216 □1a **Doze Ribeiras** *Terceira* Azores
159 F2 **Dozulé** France
137 G3 **Drabiv** Ukr.
137 F3 **Drabivka** Ukr.
161 D3 **Drac** *r.* France
256 B4 **Dracena** Brazil
197 E5 **Dračevo** Macedonia
171 F4 **Drachhausen** Ger.
173 H2 **Drachselsried** Ger.
164 F1 **Drachten** Neth.
174 G2 **Dragacz** Pol.
197 H3 **Dragalina** Romania
177 L5 **Drăgan** *r.* Romania
177 L5 **Drăgăneşti** Romania
197 G3 **Drăgăneşti-Olt** Romania
197 G3 **Drăgăneşti-Vlaşca** Romania
197 G3 **Drăgăşani** Romania
168 F2 **Drage** Ger.
177 L5 **Drăgeşti** Romania
214 D3 **Draghoender** S. Africa
197 F4 **Dragoman** Bulg.
Dragonera, Isla *i.* Spain *see* **Sa Dragonera**
193 G3 **Dragoni** Italy
247 □7 **Dragon's Mouths** *str.* Trin. and Tob./Venez.
241 L5 **Dragoon** *AZ* U.S.A.
142 E4 **Dragør** Denmark
197 H3 **Dragoş Vodă** Romania
141 M3 **Dragsfjärd** Fin.
161 E5 **Draguignan** France
197 H1 **Drăguşeni** Romania
197 H3 **Drăguşeni** Romania
176 G2 **Drahanovice** Czech Rep.
136 C1 **Drahichyn** Belarus
171 E4 **Drahnsdorf** Ger.
83 H2 **Drake** *N.S.W.* Austr.
236 C2 **Drake** *ND* U.S.A.
168 E3 **Drakenburg** Ger.
215 G3 **Drakensberg** *mts* Lesotho/S. Africa
213 F5 **Drakensberg** *mts* S. Africa
215 G3 **Drakensberg Garden** S. Africa
215 G4 **Draken's Rock** *mt.* S. Africa
264 E9 **Drake Passage** S. Atlantic Ocean
240 F3 **Drakes Bay** *CA* U.S.A.
129 D3 **Drakhtik** Armenia
136 E5 **Drakulya** *r.* Ukr.
198 D1 **Drama** Greece
142 D2 **Drammen** Norway
156 C4 **Drancy** France
97 D4 **Drang, Prêk** *r.* Cambodia
140 □B2 **Drangajökull** *ice cap* Iceland
147 D4 **Drangan** Rep. of Ireland
142 C2 **Drangedal** Norway
116 G4 **Drangme Chhu** *r.* Bhutan
168 D2 **Drangstedt** Ger.
160 E2 **Dranse** *r.* France
170 D2 **Dranse** Ger.
169 E4 **Dransfeld** Ger.
170 E1 **Dranske** Ger.
241 L1 **Draper** *UT* U.S.A.
222 B3 **Draper, Mount** *AK* U.S.A.
147 E2 **Draperstown** *Northern Ireland* U.K.
Drapsaca Afgh. *see* **Kondūz**
116 C2 **Dras** Jammu and Kashmir
179 H2 **Drasenhofen** Austria
179 H3 **Draßmarkt** Austria
178 F4 **Drau** *r.* Austria *alt.* **Drava (Croatia),** *alt.* **Dráva (Hungary)**
188 G3 **Drava** *r.* Croatia/Slovenia *alt.* **Drau (Austria),** *alt.* **Dráva (Hungary)**
188 G3 **Dráva** *r.* Hungary *alt.* **Drau (Austria),** *alt.* **Drava (Croatia)**
177 G6 **Drávafok** Hungary
188 E2 **Dravinja** *r.* Slovenia
188 E2 **Dravograd** Slovenia
174 D3 **Drawa** *r.* Pol.
174 D2 **Drawno** Pol.
174 E3 **Drawsko** Pol.
174 D2 **Drawsko Pomorskie** Pol.
151 I2 **Drayton** *Norfolk, England* U.K.
151 F3 **Drayton** *Oxfordshire, England* U.K.
222 H4 **Drayton Valley** *Alta* Can.
175 J2 **Drążdżewo** Pol.
189 A7 **Dréa** Alg.
189 A7 **Dréan** Alg.
168 D3 **Drebber** Ger.
171 F4 **Drebkau** Ger.
160 C2 **Drée** *r.* France
147 B4 **Dreenagh** Rep. of Ireland
170 D3 **Dreetz** Ger.
150 C3 **Drefach** *Carmarthenshire, Wales* U.K.
177 I3 **Drégelypalánk** Hungary
146 D6 **Dreghorn** *North Ayrshire, Scotland* U.K.
169 D5 **Dreieich** Ger.
178 D3 **Dreiherrnspitze** *mt.* Austria
171 C3 **Dreileben** Ger.
172 A2 **Dreis** Ger.
172 B3 **Dreisam** *r.* Ger.
173 H3 **Dreisesselberg** *mt.* Ger.
169 E5 **Dreistelzberge** *hill* Ger.
173 F4 **Dreitorspitze** *mt.* Ger.
175 K4 **Drelów** Pol.
168 E1 **Drelsdorf** Ger.
149 G1 **Drem** *East Lothian, Scotland* U.K.
191 I2 **Drenchia** Italy
188 G3 **Drenovci** Croatia
198 B1 **Drenovë** *Korçë* Albania
197 F4 **Drenovets** Bulg.
170 E2 **Drense** Ger.
169 C4 **Drensteinfurt** Ger.
164 F2 **Drenthe** *prov.* Neth.
168 D3 **Drentwede** Ger.
198 C3 **Drepano** *Peloponnisos* Greece
227 F4 **Dresden** *Ont.* Can.
171 E4 **Dresden** Ger.
171 F4 **Dresden** *admin. reg. Sachsen* Ger.
237 F4 **Dresden** *TN* U.S.A.
164 E3 **Dreumel** Neth.
156 B4 **Dreux** France
177 G2 **Dřevnice** *r.* Czech Rep.
171 D3 **Drewitz** Ger.
174 G1 **Drewnica** Pol.
232 E6 **Drewryville** *VA* U.S.A.
234 C3 **Drexel Hill** *PA* U.S.A.
174 D3 **Drezdenko** Pol.
164 E2 **Driebergen** Neth.
183 G4 **Driebes** Spain
169 D5 **Driedorf** Ger.
177 K3 **Drienov** Slovakia
164 F1 **Driesum** Neth.
151 F3 **Driffield** *Gloucestershire, England* U.K.
234 C2 **Drifton** *PA* U.S.A.
232 D4 **Driftwood** *PA* U.S.A.
238 E3 **Driggs** *ID* U.S.A.
85 G5 **Drillham** *Qld* Austr.
137 F2 **Drimaylivka** Ukr.
147 D3 **Drimmo** Rep. of Ireland
146 C5 **Drimnin** *Highland, Scotland* U.K.
147 B5 **Drimoleague** Rep. of Ireland
196 D4 **Drin** *r.* Albania
188 G3 **Drina** *r.* Bos.-Herz./Yugo.
197 F3 **Drincea** *r.* Romania
196 E4 **Drini i Zi** *r.* Albania
196 D5 **Drinit, Gjiri i** *b.* Albania
198 B1 **Drino** *r.* Albania
232 B6 **Drip Rock** *KY* U.S.A.
147 C5 **Dripsey** Rep. of Ireland
262 O1 **Driscoll Island** Antarctica
Drissa Belarus *see* **Vyerkhnyadzvinsk**
179 F1 **Dříteň** Czech Rep.
176 F3 **Drnholec** Czech Rep.
188 F4 **Drniš** Croatia
179 H4 **Drnje** Croatia
191 F3 **Dro** Italy
142 D2 **Drøbak** Norway
197 F3 **Drobeta - Turnu Severin** Romania
161 C4 **Drobie** *r.* France
175 H3 **Drobin** Pol.
137 I3 **Drobysheve** Ukr.
177 L5 **Drocea, Vârful** *hill* Romania
136 D3 **Drochia** Moldova
168 E2 **Drochtersen** Ger.
164 F1 **Drogeham** Neth.
147 E3 **Drogheda** Rep. of Ireland
Drogichin Belarus *see* **Drahichyn**
Drogobych Ukr. *see* **Drohobych**
175 K3 **Drohiczyn** Pol.
136 B3 **Drohobych** Ukr.
Droichead Átha Rep. of Ireland *see* **Drogheda**
Droichead Nua *Kildare* Rep. of Ireland *see* **Newbridge**
150 E2 **Droitwich** *Worcestershire, England* U.K.
Drokiya Moldova *see* **Drochia**
169 C4 **Drolshagen** Ger.
147 C2 **Dromahair** Rep. of Ireland
83 F4 **Dromana** *Vic.* Austr.
147 E2 **Dromara** *Northern Ireland* U.K.
161 D4 **Drôme** *dept Rhône-Alpes* France
161 C4 **Drôme** *r.* France
159 F2 **Drôme** *r.* France
234 A2 **Dromgold** *PA* U.S.A.
147 E3 **Dromiskin** Rep. of Ireland
147 D3 **Dromod** Rep. of Ireland
147 D2 **Dromore** *Northern Ireland* U.K.
147 E2 **Dromore** *Northern Ireland* U.K.
147 C2 **Dromore West** Rep. of Ireland
190 C4 **Dronero** Italy
149 H4 **Dronfield** *Derbyshire, England* U.K.
146 D6 **Drongan** *East Ayrshire, Scotland* U.K.
165 C3 **Drongen** Belgium
162 B3 **Dronne** *r.* France
221 N3 **Dronning Ingrid Land** *reg.* Greenland
221 P2 **Dronning Louise Land** *reg.* Greenland
Dronning Maud Land *reg.* Antarctica *see* **Queen Maud Land**
164 E2 **Dronten** Neth.
164 D2 **Droogmakerij de Beemster** *tourist site* Neth.
163 B4 **Dropt** *r.* France
179 G2 **Drosendorf** Austria
123 G3 **Drosh** Pak.
198 C2 **Drosia** Greece
179 H2 **Drösing** Austria
156 B4 **Droué** France
107 G1 **Drovyanaya** Rus. Fed.
224 C3 **Drowning** *r. Ont.* Can.
171 D4 **Droyßig** Ger.
136 D2 **Drozdyn'** Ukr.
150 D2 **Druid** *Denbighshire, Wales* U.K.
148 D2 **Druimdrishaig** *Argyll and Bute, Scotland* U.K.
Druk-Yul *country* Asia *see* **Bhutan**
157 H4 **Drulingen** France
147 C4 **Drumandoora** Rep. of Ireland
147 D3 **Drumanespick** Rep. of Ireland
147 F2 **Drumaness** *Northern Ireland* U.K.
146 C3 **Drumbeg** *Highland, Scotland* U.K.
147 E2 **Drumbilla** Rep. of Ireland
147 D2 **Drumcard** *Northern Ireland* U.K.
148 E2 **Drumclog** *South Lanarkshire, Scotland* U.K.
147 E3 **Drumcondra** Rep. of Ireland
147 E3 **Drumconrath** Rep. of Ireland
147 D3 **Drumcree** Rep. of Ireland
147 D2 **Drumduff** *Northern Ireland* U.K.
160 D3 **Drumettaz-Clarafond** France
147 D1 **Drumfree** Rep. of Ireland
223 H5 **Drumheller** *Alta* Can.
147 C2 **Drumkeeran** Rep. of Ireland
148 B3 **Drumlea** Rep. of Ireland
147 D3 **Drumlish** Rep. of Ireland
146 F5 **Drumlithie** *Aberdeenshire, Scotland* U.K.
147 E4 **Drummin** Rep. of Ireland
Drummond *atoll Gilbert Is* Kiribati *see* **Tabiteuea**
238 D2 **Drummond** *MT* U.S.A.
226 B2 **Drummond** *WI* U.S.A.
Drummond Island *Phoenix Is* Kiribati *see* **McKean**
85 F5 **Drummond Range** *hills Qld* Austr.
225 F4 **Drummondville** *Que.* Can.
146 D7 **Drummore** *Dumfries and Galloway, Scotland* U.K.
147 D2 **Drumnacross** Rep. of Ireland
146 D4 **Drumnadrochit** *Highland, Scotland* U.K.
148 B3 **Drumnakilly** *Northern Ireland* U.K.
147 D2 **Drumquin** *Northern Ireland* U.K.
148 B4 **Drumraney** Rep. of Ireland
147 C2 **Drumshanbo** Rep. of Ireland
148 B4 **Drumsna** Rep. of Ireland
164 E3 **Drunen** Neth.
148 B3 **Drung** Rep. of Ireland
190 D1 **Drusberg** *mt.* Switz.
157 H4 **Drusenheim** France
Druskieniki Lith. *see* **Druskininkai**
138 E5 **Druskininkai** Lith.
164 E3 **Druten** Neth.
138 H5 **Druts'** *r.* Belarus
138 F4 **Druya** Belarus
160 B1 **Druyes-les-Belles-Fontaines** France
175 H4 **Drużbice** Pol.
Druzhba Kazakh. *see* **Dostyk**
137 G1 **Druzhba** Ukr.
137 H4 **Druzhbivka** Ukr.
137 I3 **Druzhkivka** *Donets'ka Oblast'* Ukr.
Druzhkovka *Donets'ka Oblast'* Ukr. *see* **Druzhkivka**
Druzhkovka *Kharkivs'ka Oblast'* Ukr. *see* **Lozova**
139 H2 **Druzhnaya Gorka** Rus. Fed.
177 K3 **Družstevná pri Hornáde** Slovakia
175 J4 **Drwalew** Pol.
175 G2 **Drwęca** *r.* Pol.
175 I5 **Drwinia** Pol.
84 C2 **Dry** *r. N.T.* Austr.
197 G4 **Dryanovo** Bulg.
137 J1 **Dryazgi** Rus. Fed.
139 H4 **Drybin** Belarus
150 E3 **Drybrook** *Gloucestershire, England* U.K.
237 C4 **Dry Cimarron** *r. KS* U.S.A.
224 A3 **Dryden** *Ont.* Can.
233 E3 **Dryden** *NY* U.S.A.
232 B6 **Dryden** *VA* U.S.A.
238 F3 **Dry Fork** *r. WY* U.S.A.
263 G2 **Drygalski Island** Antarctica
175 K2 **Drygały** Pol.
150 D2 **Drygarn Fawr** *hill Wales* U.K.
215 E2 **Dry Harts** *r.* S. Africa
241 J3 **Dry Lake** *NV* U.S.A.
146 D5 **Drymen** *Stirling, Scotland* U.K.
138 F4 **Drysa** *r.* Belarus
86 E2 **Drysdale** *r. W.A.* Austr.
84 C1 **Drysdale Island** *N.T.* Austr.
174 G3 **Drzewce** Pol.
175 I4 **Drzewica** Pol.
174 G2 **Drzycim** Pol.
207 H5 **Dschang** Cameroon
208 D4 **Dua** *r.* Dem. Rep. Congo
122 B3 **Dūāb** *r.* Iran
192 A4 **Dualchi** *Sardegna* Italy
108 D4 **Du'an** *Guangxi* China
Duancun *Shanxi* China *see* **Wuxiang**
217 □3b **Duangani** Mayotte
85 G4 **Duaringa** *Qld* Austr.
246 E3 **Duarte, Pico** *mt.* Dom. Rep.
256 C5 **Duartina** Brazil
182 D3 **Duas Igrejas** Port.
206 E5 **Duayaw-Nkwanta** Ghana
176 D1 **Dubá** Czech Rep.
124 A2 **Ḍubā** Saudi Arabia
125 F2 **Dubai** U.A.E.
240 F1 **Dubakella Mountain** *CA* U.S.A.
136 E4 **Dubăsari** Moldova
136 E4 **Dubău** Moldova
223 L2 **Dubawnt** *r. Nunavut* Can.
223 K2 **Dubawnt Lake** *N.W.T./Nunavut* Can.
Dubayy U.A.E. *see* **Dubai**
124 A2 **Dubbagh, Jabal ad** *mt.* Saudi Arabia
83 G3 **Dubbo** *N.S.W.* Austr.
206 D5 **Dube** *r.* Liberia
136 C2 **Dubechne** Ukr.
175 L4 **Dubeczno** Pol.
171 E4 **Duben** *Brandenburg* Ger.
171 D4 **Düben** Ger.
190 D1 **Dübendorf** Switz.
171 D4 **Dübener Heide** *reg.* Ger.
175 K1 **Dubeninki** Pol.
135 I5 **Dubenki** Rus. Fed.
Dubesar' Moldova *see* **Dubăsari**
171 E5 **Dubí** Czech Rep.
175 K6 **Dubiecko** Pol.
175 L4 **Dubienka** Pol.
196 D4 **Dubinës, Maja e** *mt.* Albania
190 E2 **Dubino** Italy
136 D3 **Dubivka** Ukr.
137 F3 **Dubiyivka** Ukr.
129 E2 **Dubki** Rus. Fed.
226 D1 **Dublin** *Ont.* Can.
147 E3 **Dublin** Rep. of Ireland
147 E3 **Dublin** *county* Rep. of Ireland
231 D5 **Dublin** *GA* U.S.A.
234 B3 **Dublin** *MD* U.S.A.
234 C2 **Dublin** *PA* U.S.A.
232 C6 **Dublin** *VA* U.S.A.
147 E3 **Dublin Bay** Rep. of Ireland
176 D2 **Dublovice** Czech Rep.
136 B3 **Dublyany** *L'vivs'ka Oblast'* Ukr.
136 C3 **Dublyany** *L'vivs'ka Oblast'* Ukr.
138 F3 **Dubna** *r.* Latvia
139 K3 **Dubna** *Moskovskaya Oblast'* Rus. Fed.
139 K4 **Dubna** *Tul'skaya Oblast'* Rus. Fed.
176 G3 **Dubňany** Czech Rep.
176 D3 **Dubné** Czech Rep.
177 H3 **Dubnica nad Váhom** Slovakia
136 C2 **Dubno** Ukr.
238 D2 **Dubois** *ID* U.S.A.
232 D4 **Du Bois** *PA* U.S.A.
238 E3 **Dubois** *WY* U.S.A.
Dubossary Moldova *see* **Dubăsari**
136 B3 **Dubove** Ukr.
177 J2 **Dubovica** Slovakia
139 L5 **Dubovka** *Tul'skaya Oblast'* Rus. Fed.
135 I6 **Dubovka** *Volgogradskaya Oblast'* Rus. Fed.
Dubovo Moldova *see* **Dubău**
139 M4 **Dubovoye, Ozero** *l.* Rus. Fed.
135 H7 **Dubovskoye** Rus. Fed.
137 G2 **Dubov"yazivka** Ukr.
129 F3 **Dübrar Dağı** *mt.* Azer.
179 H5 **Dubrava** Croatia
177 I2 **Dúbrava** Slovakia
179 G5 **Dubravica** Croatia
177 I3 **Dúbravy** Slovakia
206 B4 **Dubréka** Guinea
Dubris *Kent, England* U.K. *see* **Dover**
136 D2 **Dubrivka** Ukr.
139 L4 **Dubrovichi** Rus. Fed.
139 I5 **Dubrovka** Rus. Fed.
188 G4 **Dubrovnik** Croatia
121 G1 **Dubrovnoye** Kazakh.
175 L6 **Dubrovytsya** *L'vivs'ka Oblast'* Ukr.
136 D2 **Dubrovytsya** *Rivnens'ka Oblast'* Ukr.
139 H4 **Dubrowna** Belarus
121 J4 **Dubun** Kazakh.
230 B3 **Dubuque** *IA* U.S.A.
136 F3 **Dubynove** Ukr.
138 D4 **Dubysa** *r.* Lith.
79 □3 **Duc de Gloucester, Îles du** *is Arch. des Tuamotu* Fr. Polynesia
158 E3 **Ducey** France
109 F2 **Duchang** *Jiangxi* China
170 E2 **Ducherow** Ger.
241 L1 **Duchesne** *UT* U.S.A.
241 M1 **Duchesne** *r. UT* U.S.A.
84 D4 **Duchess** *Qld* Austr.
223 I5 **Duchess** *Alta* Can.
171 E5 **Duchov** Czech Rep.
85 E2 **Ducie** *r. Qld* Austr.
267 K7 **Ducie Island** Pitcairn Is
231 C4 **Duck** *r. TN* U.S.A.
223 K4 **Duck Bay** *Man.* Can.
86 C4 **Duck Creek** *r. W.A.* Austr.
151 H3 **Duck End** *Essex, England* U.K.
223 J4 **Duck Lake** *Sask.* Can.
241 J2 **Duckwater** *NV* U.S.A.
241 J2 **Duckwater Peak** *NV* U.S.A.
159 G2 **Duclair** France
97 E5 **Đưc Trong** Vietnam
250 C4 **Duda** *r.* Col.
177 G4 **Dudar** Hungary
137 G4 **Dudchany** Ukr.
149 G2 **Duddo** *Northumberland, England* U.K.
149 F3 **Duddon** *r. England* U.K.
165 F5 **Dudelange** Lux.
169 B6 **Dudeldorf** Ger.
169 F4 **Duderstadt** Ger.
196 E2 **Dudestii Vechi** Romania
117 E4 **Dudhi** *Uttar Prad.* India
177 H3 **Dudince** Slovakia
190 C2 **Düdingen** Switz.
130 J3 **Dudinka** Rus. Fed.
150 E2 **Dudley** *West Midlands, England* U.K.
241 L5 **Dudleyville** *AZ* U.S.A.
114 C2 **Dudna** *r.* India
139 J5 **Dudorovskiy** Rus. Fed.
116 C4 **Dudu** *Rajasthan* India
215 G2 **Duduza** S. Africa
188 F2 **Dudváh** *r.* Slovakia
146 F4 **Dudwick, Hill of** *hill Scotland* U.K.
206 D5 **Duékoué** Côte d'Ivoire
94 C3 **Duen, Bukit** *vol.* Indon.
183 F3 **Dueñas** Spain
254 C4 **Dueré** Brazil
182 E2 **Duerna** *r.* Spain
160 C3 **Duerne** France
182 D3 **Duero** *r.* Spain *alt.* **Douro (Portugal)**
191 G3 **Dueville** Italy
165 D3 **Duffel** Belgium
238 C3 **Duffer Peak** *NV* U.S.A.
151 F2 **Duffield** *Derbyshire, England* U.K.
232 B6 **Duffield** *VA* U.S.A.
78 □6 **Duff Islands** Solomon Is
146 E4 **Dufftown** *Moray, Scotland* U.K.
190 C3 **Dufourspitze** *mt.* Italy/Switz.
223 L5 **Dufrost** *Man.* Can.
121 F5 **Dugab** Uzbek.
84 E3 **Dugald** *r. Qld* Austr.
188 E3 **Duga Resa** Croatia
128 C5 **Dughdash** *mts* Saudi Arabia
Dughoba Uzbek. *see* **Dugab**
188 E3 **Dugi Otok** *i.* Croatia
188 F4 **Dugi Rat** Croatia
157 F3 **Dugny-sur-Meuse** France
188 F4 **Dugopolje** Croatia
188 F3 **Dugo Selo** Croatia
199 E1 **Düğüncübaşı** Turkey
241 K1 **Dugway** *UT* U.S.A.
108 D1 **Du He** *r.* China
163 B5 **Duhort-Bachen** France
202 C4 **Duhūn Tārsū** *mts* Chad/Libya
85 E2 **Duifken Point** *Qld* Austr.
169 E3 **Duingen** Ger.
191 I3 **Duino** Italy
169 B4 **Duisburg** Ger.
250 C3 **Duitama** Col.
164 F3 **Duiven** Neth.
213 F4 **Duiwelskloof** S. Africa
108 B2 **Dujiangyan** *Sichuan* China
127 G4 **Dukān Dam** Iraq
131 Q3 **Dukat** Rus. Fed.
197 F4 **Dukat** *mt.* Yugo.
215 F4 **Dukathole** S. Africa
198 A1 **Dukat i Ri** Albania
Duke of Clarence *atoll* Tokelau *see* **Nukunonu**
Duke of Gloucester Islands *Arch. des Tuamotu* Fr. Polynesia *see* **Duc de Gloucester, Îles du**
Duke of York *atoll* Tokelau *see* **Atafu**
125 E2 **Dukhān** Qatar
124 C2 **Dukhnah** Saudi Arabia
120 B1 **Dukhovnitskoye** Rus. Fed.
139 I4 **Dukhovshchina** Rus. Fed.
139 H4 **Dukhovshehinskaya Vozvyshennost'** *hills* Rus. Fed.
100 E2 **Duki** Rus. Fed.
100 E2 **Duki** *r.* Rus. Fed.
207 H4 **Dukku** Nigeria
175 J6 **Dukla** Pol.
Dukou *Sichuan* China *see* **Panzhihua**
138 F4 **Dūkštas** Lith.
212 E4 **Dukwe** Botswana
106 E1 **Dulaanhaan** Mongolia
237 F6 **Dulac** *LA* U.S.A.
106 C4 **Dulan** *Qinghai* China
Dulawan Phil. *see* **Datu Piang**
261 F2 **Dulce** *r.* Arg.
183 H4 **Dulce** *r.* Spain
239 F4 **Dulce** *NM* U.S.A.
242 □I6 **Dulce Nombre de Culmí** Hond.
107 G1 **Dul'durga** Rus. Fed.
147 E3 **Duleek** Rep. of Ireland
131 O3 **Dulgalakh** *r.* Rus. Fed.
197 H4 **Dŭlgopol** Bulg.
85 E1 **Dulhunty** *r. Qld* Austr.
95 F2 **Dulit, Pegunungan** *mts Sarawak* Malaysia
108 D3 **Duliu Jiang** *r.* China
117 H4 **Dullabchara** *Assam* India
151 H2 **Dullingham** *Cambridgeshire, England* U.K.
215 H1 **Dullstroom** S. Africa
169 C4 **Dülmen** Ger.
146 E4 **Dulnain** *r. Scotland* U.K.
146 E4 **Dulnain Bridge** *Highland, Scotland* U.K.
197 H4 **Dulovo** Bulg.
226 A2 **Duluth** *MN* U.S.A.
236 E2 **Duluth/Superior** *airport MN* U.S.A.
150 D3 **Dulverton** *Somerset, England* U.K.
139 M3 **Dulyapino** Rus. Fed.
128 C3 **Dūmā** Syria
92 B4 **Dumaguete** Phil.
94 C2 **Dumai** *Sumatera* Indon.
129 C3 **Dumanlı Dağı** *mt.* Turkey
129 B4 **Dumanlı Tepe** *mt.* Turkey
83 G2 **Dumaresq** *r. N.S.W.* Austr.
237 F5 **Dumas** *AR* U.S.A.
237 C5 **Dumas** *TX* U.S.A.
146 D6 **Dumbarton** *West Dunbartonshire, Scotland* U.K.
215 H2 **Dumbe** S. Africa
78 □5 **Dumbéa** New Caledonia
177 I3 **Ďumbier** *mt.* Slovakia
87 C7 **Dumbleyung** *W.A.* Austr.
87 C7 **Dumbleyung, Lake** *salt flat W.A.* Austr.
177 L6 **Dumbrava** Romania
197 G2 **Dumbrăveni** Romania
197 H3 **Dumbrăveni** Romania
197 G3 **Dumbrăviţa** Romania
177 K6 **Dumbrăviţa** Romania
182 A1 **Dumbría** Spain
117 H4 **Dum Duma** *Assam* India
197 H2 **Dumeşti** Romania
146 E6 **Dumfries** *Dumfries and Galloway, Scotland* U.K.
146 E6 **Dumfries and Galloway** *admin. div. Scotland* U.K.
139 J5 **Duminichi** Rus. Fed.
197 G2 **Dumitra** Romania
117 F4 **Dumka** *Bihar* India
129 B3 **Dumlu** Turkey
129 B3 **Dumlu Dağı** *mt.* Turkey
128 A1 **Dumlugöze** Turkey
199 F2 **Dumlupınar** Turkey
114 D2 **Dummagudem** *Andhra Prad.* India
170 D2 **Dummerstorf** Ger.
224 E4 **Dumoine** *r. Que.* Can.
263 J2 **Dumont d'Urville** *research stn* Antarctica
169 B5 **Dümpelfeld** Ger.
117 F4 **Dumraon** *Bihar* India
203 F2 **Dumyât** Egypt
126 C5 **Dumyât** *governorate* Egypt
163 D5 **Dun** France
169 F4 **Dün** *ridge* Ger.
188 G3 **Duna** *r.* Hungary *alt.* **Donau (Austria/Germany),** *alt.* **Dunaj (Slovakia),** *alt.* **Dunărea (Romania),** *alt.* **Dunav (Yugoslavia),** *conv.* **Danube**
177 H4 **Dunaalmás** Hungary
Dünaburg Latvia *see* **Daugavpils**
177 H5 **Dunaegyháza** Hungary
177 H5 **Dunafalva** Hungary
177 H5 **Dunaföldvár** Hungary
177 I4 **Dunaharaszti** Hungary
188 F2 **Dunaj** *r.* Slovakia *alt.* **Donau (Austria/Germany),** *alt.* **Duna (Hungary),** *alt.* **Dunărea (Romania),** *alt.* **Dunav (Yugoslavia),** *conv.* **Danube**
175 I5 **Dunajec** *r.* Pol.
176 G3 **Dunajská Lužná** Slovakia
177 G4 **Dunajská Streda** Slovakia
177 I4 **Dunakeszi** Hungary
176 G4 **Dunakiliti** Hungary
83 F5 **Dunalley** *Tas.* Austr.
Dunanbay Kazakh. *see* **Dunenbay**
177 I5 **Dunapataj** Hungary
197 I3 **Dunărea** *r.* Romania *alt.* **Donau (Austria/Germany),** *alt.* **Duna (Hungary),** *alt.* **Dunaj (Slovakia),** *alt.* **Dunav (Yugoslavia),** *conv.* **Danube**
197 I3 **Dunării, Delta** Romania
177 G4 **Dunaszeg** Hungary
177 H5 **Dunaszekcső** Hungary
177 H5 **Dunaszentgyörgy** Hungary
176 G4 **Dunasziget** Hungary
177 I5 **Dunatetétlen** Hungary
177 H5 **Dunaújváros** Hungary
197 H3 **Dunav** *r.* Yugo. *alt.* **Donau (Austria/Germany),** *alt.* **Duna (Hungary),** *alt.* **Dunaj (Slovakia),** *alt.* **Dunărea (Romania),** *conv.* **Danube**
177 I4 **Dunavarsány** Hungary
177 H5 **Dunavecse** Hungary
197 F4 **Dunavtsi** Bulg.
136 D3 **Dunayivtsi** *Khmel'nyts'ka Oblast'* Ukr.
136 D3 **Dunayivtsi** *Khmel'nyts'ka Oblast'* Ukr.
81 C6 **Dunback** *South I.* N.Z.
85 E3 **Dunbar** *Qld* Austr.
146 F5 **Dunbar** *East Lothian, Scotland* U.K.
232 D5 **Dunbar** *PA* U.S.A.
226 C3 **Dunbar** *WI* U.S.A.
232 C5 **Dunbar** *WV* U.S.A.
146 E3 **Dunbeath** *Highland, Scotland* U.K.
146 E5 **Dunblane** *Stirling, Scotland* U.K.
147 E3 **Dunboyne** Rep. of Ireland
222 F5 **Duncan** *B.C.* Can.
241 M5 **Duncan** *AZ* U.S.A.
237 D5 **Duncan** *OK* U.S.A.
147 E4 **Duncannon** Rep. of Ireland
227 I5 **Duncannon** *PA* U.S.A.
147 B4 **Duncannon Bridge** Rep. of Ireland
115 G4 **Duncan Passage** *Andaman & Nicobar Is* India
246 □ **Duncans** Jamaica
146 E3 **Duncansby Head** *hd Scotland* U.K.
246 D2 **Duncan Town** Bahamas
151 F2 **Dunchurch** *Warwickshire, England* U.K.
147 E4 **Duncormick** Rep. of Ireland
138 D3 **Dundaga** Latvia
146 C5 **Dun da Ghaoithe** *hill Scotland* U.K.
227 G3 **Dundalk** *Ont.* Can.
147 E2 **Dundalk** Rep. of Ireland
234 B3 **Dundalk** *MD* U.S.A.
147 E3 **Dundalk Bay** Rep. of Ireland
224 E5 **Dundas** *Ont.* Can.
87 D7 **Dundas, Lake** *salt flat W.A.* Austr.
84 B1 **Dundas Strait** *N.T.* Austr.
107 F2 **Dundbürd** Mongolia
Dún Dealgan Rep. of Ireland *see* **Dundalk**
215 H3 **Dundee** S. Africa
146 F5 **Dundee** *Dundee, Scotland* U.K.
146 F5 **Dundee** *admin. div. Scotland* U.K.
227 F5 **Dundee** *MI* U.S.A.
232 E3 **Dundee** *NY* U.S.A.
106 E2 **Dundgovĭ** *prov.* Mongolia
107 H3 **Dund Hot** *Nei Mongol* China
147 F2 **Dundonald** *Northern Ireland* U.K.
146 D6 **Dundonald** *South Ayrshire, Scotland* U.K.
85 F5 **Dundoo** *Qld* Austr.
146 D4 **Dundreggan** *Highland, Scotland* U.K.
146 E7 **Dundrennan** *Dumfries and Galloway, Scotland* U.K.
147 E3 **Dundrum** *Dublin* Rep. of Ireland
147 C4 **Dundrum** *Tipperary* Rep. of Ireland
147 F2 **Dundrum** *Northern Ireland* U.K.
147 F2 **Dundrum Bay** *Northern Ireland* U.K.
116 E4 **Dundwa Range** *mts* India/Nepal
146 E6 **Duneaton Water** *r. Scotland* U.K.
146 F4 **Dunecht** *Aberdeenshire, Scotland* U.K.
81 C6 **Dunedin** *South I.* N.Z.
231 D6 **Dunedin** *FL* U.S.A.
83 G3 **Dunedoo** *N.S.W.* Austr.
121 J2 **Dunenbay** Kazakh.
163 C4 **Dunes** France
148 B2 **Dunfanaghy** Rep. of Ireland
146 E5 **Dunfermline** *Fife, Scotland* U.K.
147 E2 **Dungannon** *Northern Ireland* U.K.
Dún Garbhán *Waterford* Rep. of Ireland *see* **Dungarvan**
116 C3 **Dungargarh** *Rajasthan* India
116 C5 **Dungarpur** *Rajasthan* India
147 D4 **Dungarvan** *Kilkenny* Rep. of Ireland
147 D4 **Dungarvan** *Waterford* Rep. of Ireland
151 H4 **Dungeness** *hd England* U.K.
169 C5 **Düngenheim** Ger.
147 E2 **Dungiven** *Northern Ireland* U.K.
147 C2 **Dungloe** Rep. of Ireland
83 G3 **Dungog** *N.S.W.* Austr.
147 C5 **Dungourney** Rep. of Ireland
208 F4 **Dungu** Dem. Rep. Congo
94 C1 **Dungun** Malaysia
149 I4 **Dunholme** *Lincolnshire, England* U.K.
Dunhou *Jiangxi* China *see* **Ji'an**
100 D4 **Dunhua** *Jilin* China
110 F3 **Dunhuang** *Gansu* China
161 C3 **Dunières** France
85 G5 **Dunkeld** *Qld* Austr.
83 E4 **Dunkeld** *Vic.* Austr.
146 E5 **Dunkeld** *Perth and Kinross, Scotland* U.K.
147 C3 **Dunkellin** *r.* Rep. of Ireland
179 G2 **Dunkelsteiner Wald** *for.* Austria
156 C1 **Dunkerque** France
147 D4 **Dunkerrin** Rep. of Ireland
150 D3 **Dunkery Beacon** *hill England* U.K.
147 C2 **Dunkineely** Rep. of Ireland
Dunkirk France *see* **Dunkerque**
151 H3 **Dunkirk** *Kent, England* U.K.
232 D3 **Dunkirk** *NY* U.S.A.
232 B4 **Dunkirk** *OH* U.S.A.
206 E5 **Dunkwa** Ghana
147 E3 **Dún Laoghaire** Rep. of Ireland
236 E3 **Dunlap** *IA* U.S.A.
226 E5 **Dunlap** *IN* U.S.A.
231 C5 **Dunlap** *TN* U.S.A.
147 E3 **Dunlavin** Rep. of Ireland
147 E3 **Dunleer** Rep. of Ireland
162 D2 **Dun-le-Palestel** France
160 C1 **Dun-les-Places** France
148 A2 **Dunlewy** Rep. of Ireland
146 D6 **Dunlop** *East Ayrshire, Scotland* U.K.
147 E1 **Dunloy** *Northern Ireland* U.K.
145 D4 **Dunluce** *tourist site Northern Ireland* U.K.
147 B5 **Dunmanus** Rep. of Ireland
147 B5 **Dunmanus Bay** Rep. of Ireland
147 B5 **Dunmanway** Rep. of Ireland
84 C3 **Dunmarra** *N.T.* Austr.
147 D4 **Dunmoon** Rep. of Ireland
147 C3 **Dunmore** Rep. of Ireland
234 C1 **Dunmore** *PA* U.S.A.
232 D5 **Dunmore** *WV* U.S.A.
147 E4 **Dunmore East** Rep. of Ireland
246 C1 **Dunmore Town** *Eleuthera* Bahamas
147 F2 **Dunmurry** *Northern Ireland* U.K.
231 E5 **Dunn** *NC* U.S.A.
147 D2 **Dunnamanagh** *Northern Ireland* U.K.
231 D6 **Dunnellon** *FL* U.S.A.
146 E3 **Dunnet** *Highland, Scotland* U.K.
146 E3 **Dunnet Head** *hd Scotland* U.K.
240 G2 **Dunnigan** *CA* U.S.A.
146 E5 **Dunning** *Perth and Kinross, Scotland* U.K.
236 C3 **Dunning** *NE* U.S.A.
172 C3 **Dunningen** Ger.
149 I4 **Dunnington** *York, England* U.K.
87 C5 **Dunns Range** *hills W.A.* Austr.
227 H4 **Dunnville** *Ont.* Can.
83 E4 **Dunolly** *Vic.* Austr.
146 D6 **Dunoon** *Argyll and Bute, Scotland* U.K.
147 A4 **Dunquin** Rep. of Ireland
146 E6 **Dun Rig** *hill Scotland* U.K.
146 F6 **Duns** *Scottish Borders, Scotland* U.K.
81 D5 **Dunsandel** *South I.* N.Z.
87 B7 **Dunsborough** *W.A.* Austr.
146 E6 **Dunscore** *Dumfries and Galloway, Scotland* U.K.
236 C1 **Dunseith** *ND* U.S.A.
168 D3 **Dünsen** Ger.
147 E3 **Dunshaughlin** Rep. of Ireland
238 B3 **Dunsmuir** *CA* U.S.A.
151 G3 **Dunstable** *Bedfordshire, England* U.K.
81 B6 **Dunstan Mountains** *South I.* N.Z.
150 D3 **Dunster** *Somerset, England* U.K.
160 A2 **Dun-sur-Auron** France
157 F3 **Dun-sur-Meuse** France
81 C6 **Duntroon** *South I.* N.Z.
168 C2 **Dunum** Ger.
148 E2 **Dunure** *South Ayrshire, Scotland* U.K.
150 C3 **Dunvant** *Swansea, Wales* U.K.
146 B4 **Dunvegan** *Highland, Scotland* U.K.
146 B4 **Dunvegan, Loch** *b. Scotland* U.K.
146 B4 **Dunvegan Head** *hd Scotland* U.K.
123 G4 **Dunyapur** Pak.
107 J1 **Duobukur** *r.* China
107 H3 **Duolun** *Nei Mongol* China
114 C3 **Dupadu** *Andhra Prad.* India
109 D3 **Dupang Ling** *mts* China
227 H1 **Duparquet** *Que.* Can.
Duperré Alg. *see* **Aïn Defla**
179 F4 **Duplica** Slovenia
197 F4 **Dupnitsa** Bulg.
236 C2 **Dupree** *SD* U.S.A.
86 B4 **Dupuy, Cape** *W.A.* Austr.
Duque de Bragança Angola *see* **Calandula**
257 F5 **Duque de Caxias** Brazil
259 B8 **Duque de York, Isla** *i.* Chile
226 A2 **Duquette** *MN* U.S.A.
230 B4 **Du Quoin** *IL* U.S.A.
210 C2 **Dura** *r.* Eth.
128 B4 **Dūrā** West Bank
191 H2 **Dura, Cima** *mt.* Italy
173 E4 **Durach** Ger.
76 C3 **Durack** *r. W.A.* Austr.
86 E3 **Durack Range** *hills W.A.* Austr.
Dura Europos Syria *see* **Aş Şāliḩīyah**
126 D2 **Durağan** Turkey
199 F2 **Durak** Turkey
183 H2 **Durana** Spain
163 C4 **Durance** France
161 C5 **Durance** *r.* France
227 F4 **Durand** *MI* U.S.A.
226 B3 **Durand** *WI* U.S.A.
185 F2 **Duranes** *hill* Spain
241 J5 **Durango** *Baja California Norte* Mex.
244 B1 **Durango** *Durango* Mex.
244 B1 **Durango** *state* Mex.
183 H1 **Durango** Spain
239 F4 **Durango** *CO* U.S.A.
244 B2 **Durango, Sierra de** *mts* Mex.
197 I4 **Durankulak** Bulg.
191 H2 **Duranno, Monte** *mt.* Italy
237 F5 **Durant** *MS* U.S.A.
237 D5 **Durant** *OK* U.S.A.
163 C4 **Duras** France
183 F3 **Duratón** *r.* Spain

163 D4 Duravel France
261 I3 Durazno Uru.
261 I3 Durazno dept Uru.
Durazzo Albania see Durrës
172 C3 Durbach Ger.
163 D5 Durban France
215 H3 Durban S. Africa
161 A6 Durban-Corbières France
214 B5 Durbanville S. Africa
172 C3 Dürbheim Ger.
232 D5 Durbin WV U.S.A.
157 G4 Durbion r. France
165 E4 Durbuy Belgium
185 G4 Dúrcal Spain
185 G4 Dúrcal r. Spain
177 H2 Ďurčiná Slovakia
160 A2 Durdat-Larequille France
159 G2 Durdent r. France
188 F2 Đurđevac Croatia
110 E2 Düre Xinjiang China
169 B5 Düren Ger.
122 D3 Düren Iran
161 B5 Durfort France
116 E5 Durg Madh. Prad. India
117 G4 Durgapur Bangl.
117 F5 Durgapur W. Bengal India
227 G3 Durham Ont. Can.
149 H3 Durham Durham, England U.K.
149 G3 Durham admin. div. England U.K.
240 G2 Durham CA U.S.A.
235 F1 Durham CT U.S.A.
231 E5 Durham NC U.S.A.
233 □H3 Durham NH U.S.A.
233 □J1 Durham Bridge N.B. Can.
85 E5 Durham Downs Qld Austr.
94 C2 Duri Sumatera Indon.
146 E6 Durisdeer Dumfries and Galloway, Scotland U.K.
Durlas Rep. of Ireland see Thurles
136 E4 Durleşti Moldova
156 D1 Durme r. Belgium
172 D3 Dürmentingen Ger.
172 C3 Durmersheim Ger.
196 D4 Durmitor mt. Yugo.
146 D3 Durness Highland, Scotland U.K.
179 H2 Dürnkrut Austria
Durocortorum France see Reims
85 G5 Durong South Qld Austr.
Durostorum Bulg. see Silistra
Durovernum Kent, England U.K. see Canterbury
196 D5 Durrës Albania
84 E5 Durrie Qld Austr.
173 E3 Dürrlauingen Ger.
171 F4 Dürröhrsdorf-Dittersbach Ger.
147 D4 Durrow Rep. of Ireland
173 E2 Dürrwangen Ger.
147 A5 Dursey Island Rep. of Ireland
150 E3 Dursley Gloucestershire, England U.K.
199 F2 Dursunbey Turkey
159 F4 Durtal France
Duru Guizhou China see Wuchuan
208 F4 Duru r. Dem. Rep. Congo
183 H3 Duruelo de la Sierra Spain
122 E3 Dūruḩ Iran
210 E2 Durukhsi Somalia
128 C3 Durūz, Jabal ad mt. Syria
80 D4 D'Urville Island South I. N.Z.
234 C1 Duryea PA U.S.A.
146 □G1 Dury Voe inlet Scotland U.K.
138 E4 Dusetos Lith.
122 D2 Dushak Turkm.
108 C3 Dushan Guizhou China
123 G2 Dushanbe Tajik.
110 D2 Dushanzi Xinjiang China
129 D2 Dushet'i Georgia
227 I5 Dushore PA U.S.A.
138 D4 Dusia l. Lith.
177 H5 Dusnok Hungary
174 G2 Dusocin Pol.
86 F2 Dussejour, Cape W.A. Austr.
169 B4 Düsseldorf Ger.
169 B4 Düsseldorf admin. reg. Nordrhein-Westfalen Ger.
164 D3 Dussen Neth.
172 D3 Dußlingen Ger.
171 D4 Düßnitz Ger.
123 G2 Dusti Tajik.
121 G4 Dustlik Uzbek.
238 C2 Dusty WA U.S.A.
174 E3 Duszniki Pol.
174 E5 Duszniki-Zdrój Pol.
Dutch East Indies country Asia see Indonesia
234 E1 Dutchess County county NY U.S.A.
Dutch Guiana country S. America see Suriname
220 B4 Dutch Harbor AK U.S.A.
241 K1 Dutch Mountain UT U.S.A.
Dutch New Guinea prov. Indon. see Irian Jaya
Dutch West Indies terr. West Indies see Netherlands Antilles
179 E5 Dutovlje Slovenia
207 H4 Dutsan-Wai Nigeria
207 H4 Dutse Nigeria
207 G3 Dutsin-Ma Nigeria
85 E4 Dutton r. Qld Austr.
227 G4 Dutton Ont. Can.
238 E2 Dutton MT U.S.A.
82 D2 Dutton, Lake salt flat S.A. Austr.
241 K2 Dutton, Mount UT U.S.A.
223 J5 Duval Sask. Can.
134 L5 Duvan Rus. Fed.
137 J3 Duvanka r. Ukr.
Duvannyy Azer. see Qobustan
140 K3 Duved Sweden
246 E3 Duvergé Dom. Rep.
Duvno Bos.-Herz. see Tomislavgrad
127 G3 Duwin Iraq
108 C3 Duyun Guizhou China
199 G1 Düzce Turkey
129 D3 Düz Cırdaxan Azer.
Duzdab Iran see Zāhedān
129 A3 Düzköy Turkey
136 D1 Dvarets Belarus
197 G4 Dve Mogili Bulg.
Dvinsk Latvia see Daugavpils
134 G2 Dvinskaya Guba g. Rus. Fed.
139 H3 Dvin'ye, Ozero l. Rus. Fed.
136 D2 Dvirets' Ukr.
175 M5 Dvirtsi Ukr.
188 F3 Dvor Croatia
177 G2 Dvorce Czech Rep.
137 I3 Dvorichna Ukr.
177 H4 Dvory nad Žitavou Slovakia
176 E1 Dvůr Králové Czech Rep.
211 B8 Dwangwa Malawi
116 B5 Dwarka Gujarat India
212 E5 Dwarsberg S. Africa
87 C7 Dwellingup W.A. Austr.
215 H4 Dweshula S. Africa
226 C5 Dwight IL U.S.A.
175 J5 Dwikozy Pol.
164 F2 Dwingeloo Neth.
214 C5 Dwyka S. Africa
214 C5 Dwyka r. S. Africa
137 K3 D'yachenkovo Rus. Fed.
134 H4 D'yakonovo Rus. Fed.
137 J4 Dyakove Ukr.
148 D3 Dyan Northern Ireland U.K.
123 E2 Dyanev Turkm.
197 H4 Dyankovo Bulg.
139 J5 Dyat'kovo Rus. Fed.
234 C1 Dyberry PA U.S.A.
234 C1 Dyberry Creek r. PA U.S.A.
146 F4 Dyce Aberdeen, Scotland U.K.
175 K6 Dydnia Pol.
221 L3 Dyer, Cape Nunavut Can.
227 G3 Dyer Bay Ont. Can.
262 T2 Dyer Plateau Antarctica
237 F4 Dyersburg TN U.S.A.
81 E4 Dyeville North I. N.Z.
Dyffryn Isle of Anglesey, Wales U.K. see Valley
150 D2 Dyfi r. Wales U.K.
174 D1 Dygowo Pol.
176 H4 Dyje r. Austria/Czech Rep.
137 H3 Dykan'ka Ukr.
146 E4 Dyke Moray, Scotland U.K.
146 E5 Dykehead Angus, Scotland U.K.
129 C2 Dykh-Tau, Gora mt. Rus. Fed.
165 D4 Dyle r. Belgium
176 B2 Dyleň hill Czech Rep.
175 J2 Dylewo Pol.
175 H2 Dylewska Góra hill Pol.
129 E2 Dylym Rus. Fed.
151 H3 Dymchurch Kent, England U.K.
136 F2 Dymer Ukr.
150 E3 Dymock Gloucestershire, England U.K.
138 G1 Dymovka r. Rus. Fed.
137 I3 Dymytrov Ukr.
137 G3 Dymytrove Ukr.
142 C1 Dyna mt. Norway
83 F2 Dynevor Downs Qld Austr.
175 K6 Dynów Pol.
160 C2 Dyo France
215 G4 Dyoki S. Africa
Dyrrhachium Albania see Durrës
85 G4 Dysart Qld Austr.
150 D1 Dyserth Denbighshire, Wales U.K.
173 H2 Dýšina Czech Rep.
138 F4 Dysna r. Lith.
138 F4 Dysnų ežeras l. Lith.
214 D5 Dysselsdorp S. Africa
198 B2 Dytiki Ellas admin. reg. Greece
198 B1 Dytiki Makedonia admin. reg. Greece
197 H4 Dyulino Bulg.
129 E3 Dyul'tydag, Gora mt. Rus. Fed.
134 K5 Dyurtyuli Rus. Fed.
136 E5 Dyviziya Ukr.
175 I2 Dywity Pol.
106 D2 Dzaanhushuu Mongolia
106 C2 Dzag Gol r. Mongolia
217 □3b Dzaoudzi Mayotte
Dzaudzhikau Rus. Fed. see Vladikavkaz
106 B1 Dzavhan prov. Mongolia
106 B1 Dzavhan Gol r. Mongolia
176 C1 Džbán mts Czech Rep.
106 D2 Dzegstey Mongolia
136 D3 Dzelentsi Ukr.
106 E1 Dzelter Mongolia
Dzerzhinsk Belarus see Dzyarzhynsk
134 H4 Dzerzhinsk Rus. Fed.
Dzerzhinskoye Kazakh. see Kabanbay
137 I3 Dzerzhyns'k Ukr.
136 D2 Dzerzhyns'k Ukr.
100 D1 Dzhagdy, Khrebet mts Rus. Fed.
Dzhaksy Kazakh. see Zhaksy
120 F3 Dzhalagash Kazakh.
Dzhalalabad Azer. see Cälilabad
Dzhalal-Abad Kyrg. see Jalal-Abad
Dzhalal-Abadskaya Oblast' admin. div. Kyrg. see Jalal-Abad
134 K5 Dzhalil' Rus. Fed.
100 B1 Dzhalinda Rus. Fed.
Dzhaltyr Kazakh. see Zhaltyr
Dzhambeyty Zapadnyy Kazakhstan Kazakh. see Zhympity
Dzhambul Zhambylskaya Oblast' Kazakh. see Taraz
Dzhambulskaya Oblast' admin. div. Kazakh. see Zhambylskaya Oblast'
Dzhandari Georgia see Jandari
122 C1 Dzhanga Turkm.
120 B2 Dzhangala Kazakh.
120 E4 Dzhangel'dy Uzbek.
Dzhankel'dy Uzbek. see Dzhangel'dy
137 H5 Dzhankoy Ukr.
121 I3 Dzhansugurov Kazakh.
120 A2 Dzhanybek Kazakh.
Dzhaparidze Georgia see Jap'aridze
Dzharkent Kazakh. see Zharkent
121 F5 Dzharkurgan Uzbek.
131 O3 Dzhebariki-Khaya Rus. Fed.
197 G5 Dzhebel Bulg.
122 C2 Dzhebel Turkm.
Dzhergalan Kyrg. see Jyrgalang
Dzhermuk Armenia see Jermuk
Dzhetygara Kazakh. see Zhitikara
120 F4 Dzhetymtau, Gory hills Uzbek.
Dzhetysay Kazakh. see Zhetysay
120 E5 Dzheykhun Turkm.
Dzhezdy Kazakh. see Zhezdy
Dzhezkazgan Karagandinskaya Oblast' Kazakh. see Zhezkazgan
106 E1 Dzhida Rus. Fed.
106 E1 Dzhida r. Rus. Fed.
106 D1 Dzhidinskiy, Khrebet mts Mongolia/Rus. Fed.
Dzhingil'dy Uzbek. see Dzhangel'dy
Dzhirgatal' Tajik. see Jirgatol
121 F4 Dzhizak Uzbek.
Dzhizak Oblast admin. div. Uzbek. see Dzhizakskaya Oblast'
121 F4 Dzhizakskaya Oblast' admin. div. Uzbek.
Dzhokhar Ghala Rus. Fed. see Groznyy
Dzhordzhiashvili Georgia see Jorjiashvili
135 G7 Dzhubga Rus. Fed.
131 O4 Dzhugdzhur, Khrebet mts Rus. Fed.
Dzhul'fa Azer. see Culfa
136 E3 Dzhulynka Ukr.
121 F5 Dzhuma Uzbek.
121 I3 Dzhungarskiy Alatau, Khrebet mts China/Kazakh.
129 E2 Dzhurmut r. Rus. Fed.
Dzhurun Kazakh. see Zhuryn
136 E3 Dzhuryn Ukr.
120 F3 Dzhusaly Kzyl-Ordinskaya Oblast' Kazakh.
175 K3 Dziadkowice Pol.
174 F4 Dziadowa Kłoda Pol.
175 H2 Działdówka r. Pol.
175 I2 Działdowo Pol.
175 I5 Działoszyce Pol.
174 G4 Działoszyn Pol.
175 H2 Działyń Pol.
243 H5 Dzibalchén Mex.
174 F1 Dziemiany Pol.
174 G5 Dziergowice Pol.
175 I3 Dzierzążnia Pol.
175 H2 Dzierzgoń Pol.
175 I2 Dzierzgowo Pol.
174 E5 Dzierżoniów Pol.
175 J1 Dzietrzychowo Pol.
174 F3 Dziewierzewo Pol.
243 H4 Dzilam de Bravo Mex.
138 G4 Dzisna Belarus
243 H4 Dzitás Mex.
138 E5 Dzitva r. Belarus
136 C2 Dzivin Belarus
174 C2 Dziwna r. Pol.
207 F5 Dzodze Ghana
107 E2 Dzogsool Mongolia
106 C1 Dzöölön Mongolia
129 D3 Dzoraget r. Armenia
Dzungarian Basin China see Junggar Pendi
106 B1 Dzur Mongolia
107 F2 Dzüünbayan Mongolia
106 E2 Dzuunmod Mongolia
106 B2 Dzüyl Mongolia
175 I2 Dźwierzuty Pol.
174 C1 Dzwinów Pol.
175 K5 Dzwola Pol.
175 H5 Dzwonowice Pol.
138 F5 Dzyaniskavichy Belarus
139 I5 Dzyarazhnya r. Belarus
138 F5 Dzyarzhynsk Belarus
138 E5 Dzyatlava Belarus
136 D1 Dzyatlavichy Belarus
138 F4 Dzyerkawshchyna Belarus

E

236 C4 Eads CO U.S.A.
241 M4 Eagar AZ U.S.A.
225 J2 Eagle r. Nfld. Can.
220 D3 Eagle AK U.S.A.
239 F4 Eagle CO U.S.A.
234 C2 Eagle PA U.S.A.
236 C2 Eagle Butte SD U.S.A.
238 C2 Eagle Cap mt. OR U.S.A.
240 I4 Eagle Crags mt. CA U.S.A.
223 J4 Eagle Creek r. Sask. Can.
233 □I1 Eagle Lake ME U.S.A.
241 J5 Eagle Mountain CA U.S.A.
226 B2 Eagle Mountain hill MN U.S.A.
237 C6 Eagle Pass TX U.S.A.
259 F9 Eagle Passage Falkland Is
239 F6 Eagle Peak TX U.S.A.
220 E3 Eagle Plain Y.T. Can.
226 C2 Eagle River MI U.S.A.
226 C3 Eagle River WI U.S.A.
232 D6 Eagle Rock VA U.S.A.
149 H3 Eaglescliffe Stockton-on-Tees, England U.K.
146 E6 Eaglesfield Dumfries and Galloway, Scotland U.K.
222 G4 Eaglesham Alta Can.
146 D6 Eaglesham East Renfrewshire, Scotland U.K.
241 K5 Eagle Tail Mountains AZ U.S.A.
234 C2 Eagleville PA U.S.A.
151 G3 Ealing Greater London, England U.K.
Eap i. Micronesia see Yap
87 D5 Earaheedy W.A. Austr.
149 G4 Earby Lancashire, England U.K.
150 D2 Eardisley Herefordshire, England U.K.
223 M5 Ear Falls Ont. Can.
151 H2 Earith Cambridgeshire, England U.K.
240 H4 Earlimart CA U.S.A.
81 A6 Earl Mountains South I. N.Z.
151 G2 Earls Barton Northamptonshire, England U.K.
151 H3 Earls Colne Essex, England U.K.
151 F2 Earl Shilton Leicestershire, England U.K.
146 D5 Earl's Seat hill Scotland U.K.
146 F6 Earlston Scottish Borders, Scotland U.K.
151 I2 Earl Stonham Suffolk, England U.K.
227 H2 Earlton Ont. Can.
146 E5 Earn r. Scotland U.K.
81 B6 Earnscleugh South I. N.Z.
81 B6 Earnslaw, Mount South I. N.Z.
241 J4 Earp CA U.S.A.
146 A5 Earsairidh Western Isles, Scotland U.K.
237 C5 Earth TX U.S.A.
146 C5 Easdale Argyll and Bute, Scotland U.K.
151 G4 Easebourne West Sussex, England U.K.
149 H3 Easington Durham, England U.K.
149 J4 Easington East Riding of Yorkshire, England U.K.
149 H3 Easingwold North Yorkshire, England U.K.
147 C2 Easky Rep. of Ireland
231 D5 Easley SC U.S.A.
87 D6 East, Mount hill W.A. Austr.
84 C2 East Alligator r. N.T. Austr.
263 H1 East Antarctica reg. Antarctica
233 F4 East Ararat PA U.S.A.
232 D3 East Aurora NY U.S.A.
146 D6 East Ayrshire admin. div. Scotland U.K.
84 B2 East Baines r. N.T. Austr.
234 C2 East Bangor PA U.S.A.
East Bengal country Asia see Bangladesh
151 I3 East Bergholt Suffolk, England U.K.
235 F1 East Berlin CT U.S.A.
234 B3 East Berlin PA U.S.A.
234 B1 East Berwick PA U.S.A.
81 E4 Eastbourne North I. N.Z.
151 H4 Eastbourne East Sussex, England U.K.
232 D4 East Brady PA U.S.A.
233 F4 East Branch NY U.S.A.
151 G2 East Bridgford Nottinghamshire, England U.K.
149 I4 Eastburn East Riding of Yorkshire, England U.K.
246 E2 East Caicos i. Turks and Caicos Is
80 G2 East Cape North I. N.Z.
241 L2 East Carbon City UT U.S.A.
266 E5 East Caroline Basin sea feature N. Pacific Ocean
226 D5 East Chicago IN U.S.A.
99 M5 East China Sea N. Pacific Ocean
80 E2 East Coast Bays North I. N.Z.
150 E4 East Coker Somerset, England U.K.
223 H5 East Coulee Alta Can.
151 H4 East Dean East Sussex, England U.K.
151 H2 East Dereham Norfolk, England U.K.
146 D6 East Dunbartonshire admin. div. Scotland U.K.
223 I5 Eastend Sask. Can.
87 B6 Easter Group is W.A. Austr.
Easter Island S. Pacific Ocean see Pascua, Isla de
206 E5 Eastern admin. reg. Ghana
210 C5 Eastern prov. Kenya
206 C4 Eastern prov. Sierra Leone
211 A8 Eastern prov. Zambia
215 F4 Eastern Cape prov. S. Africa
85 E4 Eastern Creek r. Qld Austr.
Eastern Desert Egypt see Şaḩara el Sharqîya
210 B3 Eastern Equatoria state Sudan
114 C4 Eastern Ghats mts India
Eastern Lesser Sunda Islands prov. Indon. see Nusa Tenggara Timur
Eastern Samoa terr. S. Pacific Ocean see American Samoa
Eastern Sayan Mountains Rus. Fed. see Vostochnyy Sayan
Eastern Taurus plat. Turkey see Güneydoğu Toroslar
Eastern Transvaal prov. S. Africa see Mpumalanga
146 □G1 Easter Quarff Shetland, Scotland U.K.
146 D4 Easter Ross reg. Scotland U.K.
223 L4 Easterville Man. Can.
259 F9 East Falkland i. Falkland Is
233 H4 East Falmouth MA U.S.A.
149 J4 East Fen reg. England U.K.
149 I3 Eastfield North Yorkshire, England U.K.
East Flanders prov. Belgium see Oost-Vlaanderen
East Frisian Islands Ger. see Ostfriesische Inseln
149 G3 Eastgate Durham, England U.K.
240 I2 Eastgate NV U.S.A.
236 D2 East Grand Forks MN U.S.A.
226 E4 East Grand Rapids MI U.S.A.
234 C2 East Greenville PA U.S.A.
151 G3 East Grinstead West Sussex, England U.K.
235 F1 East Haddam CT U.S.A.
235 F1 East Hampton CT U.S.A.
233 G3 Easthampton MA U.S.A.
235 F2 East Hampton NY U.S.A.
151 F3 East Hanney Oxfordshire, England U.K.
151 H2 East Harling Norfolk, England U.K.
235 F1 East Hartford CT U.S.A.
235 F1 East Haven CT U.S.A.
85 E3 East Haydon Qld Austr.
233 □I2 East Holden ME U.S.A.
151 G3 East Horsley Surrey, England U.K.
150 E3 East Huntspill Somerset, England U.K.
265 K6 East Indiaman Ridge sea feature Indian Ocean
233 G3 East Jamaica VT U.S.A.
226 E3 East Jordan MI U.S.A.
East Kazakhstan Oblast admin. div. Kazakh. see Vostochnyy Kazakhstan
149 J4 East Keal Lincolnshire, England U.K.
146 D6 East Kilbride South Lanarkshire, Scotland U.K.
226 D3 East Lake MI U.S.A.
237 D5 Eastland TX U.S.A.
226 E4 East Lansing MI U.S.A.
151 F4 Eastleigh Hampshire, England U.K.
232 B4 East Liberty OH U.S.A.
146 F6 East Linton East Lothian, Scotland U.K.
235 E1 East Litchfield CT U.S.A.
232 C4 East Liverpool OH U.S.A.
146 B3 East Loch Roag inlet Scotland U.K.
146 B4 East Loch Tarbert inlet Scotland U.K.
215 F5 East London S. Africa
233 G3 East Longmeadow MA U.S.A.
150 C4 East Looe Cornwall, England U.K.
146 F6 East Lothian admin. div. Scotland U.K.
235 F1 East Lyme CT U.S.A.
224 E2 Eastmain Que. Can.
224 E2 Eastmain r. Que. Can.
151 H3 East Malling Kent, England U.K.
233 G2 Eastman Que. Can.
231 D5 Eastman GA U.S.A.
266 F5 East Mariana Basin sea feature Pacific Ocean
149 I4 East Markham Nottinghamshire, England U.K.
85 F4 Eastmere Qld Austr.
233 G3 East Middlebury VT U.S.A.
151 F2 East Midlands airport England U.K.
233 □I2 East Millinocket ME U.S.A.
235 E1 East Morris CT U.S.A.
231 D7 East Naples FL U.S.A.
235 E2 East Northport NY U.S.A.
149 I4 Eastoft North Lincolnshire, England U.K.
150 E4 Easton Dorset, England U.K.
240 H3 Easton CA U.S.A.
235 E1 Easton CT U.S.A.
233 E5 Easton MD U.S.A.
234 C2 Easton PA U.S.A.
150 E3 Easton-in-Gordano North Somerset, England U.K.
235 D2 East Orange NJ U.S.A.
267 L8 East Pacific Ridge S. Pacific Ocean
267 L4 East Pacific Rise sea feature N. Pacific Ocean
East Pakistan country Asia see Bangladesh
232 C4 East Palestine OH U.S.A.
226 C5 East Peoria IL U.S.A.
234 B2 East Petersburg PA U.S.A.
233 □J2 Eastport ME U.S.A.
226 E3 Eastport MI U.S.A.
235 F2 Eastport NY U.S.A.
151 G4 East Preston West Sussex, England U.K.
234 B3 East Prospect PA U.S.A.
235 F2 East Quogue NY U.S.A.
240 I1 East Range mts NV U.S.A.
146 D6 East Renfrewshire admin. div. Scotland U.K.
East Retford Nottinghamshire, England U.K. see Retford
231 C5 East Ridge TN U.S.A.
149 I4 East Riding of Yorkshire admin. div. England U.K.
146 E7 Eastriggs Dumfries and Galloway, Scotland U.K.
151 I3 Eastry Kent, England U.K.
230 B4 East St Louis IL U.S.A.
East Sea N. Pacific Ocean see Japan, Sea of
235 E2 East Setauket NY U.S.A.
234 C1 East Side PA U.S.A.
240 H4 East Side Canal r. CA U.S.A.
83 G4 East Sister Island Tas. Austr.
234 C1 East Stroudsburg PA U.S.A.
151 H4 East Sussex admin. div. England U.K.
232 B2 East Tawas MI U.S.A.
93 C5 East Timor terr. Asia
117 F4 East Tons r. India
83 F2 East Toorale N.S.W. Austr.
226 C4 East Troy WI U.S.A.
241 L4 East Verde r. AZ U.S.A.
Eastview Ont. Can. see Vanier
233 F6 Eastville VA U.S.A.
240 H2 East Walker r. NV U.S.A.
151 G4 East Wittering West Sussex, England U.K.
149 H4 Eastwood Nottinghamshire, England U.K.
151 F3 East Woodhay Hampshire, England U.K.
227 H4 East York Ont. Can.
87 B7 Eaton W.A. Austr.
238 F3 Eaton CO U.S.A.
230 C4 Eaton OH U.S.A.
151 G3 Eaton Bray Bedfordshire, England U.K.
223 I5 Eatonia Sask. Can.
226 E4 Eaton Rapids MI U.S.A.
235 E2 Eatons Neck NY U.S.A.
151 G2 Eaton Socon Cambridgeshire, England U.K.
231 D5 Eatonton GA U.S.A.
235 D2 Eatontown NJ U.S.A.
233 □I1 Eatonville Que. Can.
238 B2 Eatonville WA U.S.A.
226 B3 Eau Claire WI U.S.A.
226 B3 Eau Claire r. WI U.S.A.
156 B3 Eaulne r. France
163 D5 Eaunes France
91 J5 Eauripik atoll Micronesia
266 E5 Eauripik Rise-New Guinea Rise sea feature N. Pacific Ocean
Eaurypyg atoll Micronesia see Eauripik
163 B6 Eaux-Bonnes France
163 C5 Eauze France
78 □3a Ebadon i. Kwajalein Marshall Is
85 E2 Ebagoola Qld Austr.
207 G4 Eban Nigeria
245 E2 Ebano Mex.
178 D3 Ebbs Austria
150 D3 Ebbw Vale Blaenau Gwent, Wales U.K.
207 H6 Ebebiyin Equat. Guinea
169 F4 Ebeleben Ger.
142 D3 Ebeltoft Denmark
178 C3 Eben am Achensee Austria
215 G5 Ebende S. Africa
179 E4 Ebene Reichenau Austria
179 H3 Ebenfurth Austria
179 E3 Eben im Pongau Austria
232 D4 Ebensburg PA U.S.A.
179 E3 Ebensee Austria
169 F5 Ebensfeld Ger.
179 F4 Ebenthal Austria
172 D4 Ebenweiler Ger.
179 H3 Eberau Austria
172 C2 Eberbach Ger.
169 F4 Ebergötzen Ger.
172 D3 Eberhardzell Ger.
173 F2 Ebermannsdorf Ger.
173 F2 Ebermannstadt Ger.
169 F5 Ebern Ger.
179 F4 Eberndorf Austria
171 E4 Ebersbach Sachsen Ger.
171 F4 Ebersbach Sachsen Ger.
172 D3 Ebersbach an der Fils Ger.
173 F3 Ebersberg Ger.
179 E2 Eberschwang Austria
179 G3 Ebersdorf Austria
168 E2 Ebersdorf Niedersachsen Ger.
171 C5 Ebersdorf Thüringen Ger.
157 H4 Ebersmunster France
179 F4 Eberstein Austria
170 E3 Eberswalde-Finow Ger.
234 C2 Ebervale PA U.S.A.
177 K4 Ebes Hungary
102 J2 Ebetsu Japan
78 □3a Ebeye Kwajalein Marshall Is
172 C3 Ebhausen Ger.
108 B2 Ebian Sichuan China
190 D1 Ebikon Switz.
105 F3 Ebina Japan
103 E7 Ebino Japan
Ebi Nor salt l. China see Ebinur Hu
110 C2 Ebinur Hu salt l. China
128 C2 Ebla tourist site Syria
190 E1 Ebnat-Kappel Switz.
209 B7 Ebo Angola
208 D4 Ebola r. Dem. Rep. Congo
193 H4 Eboli Italy
207 H6 Ebolowa Cameroon
207 H5 Ebonyi state Nigeria
173 E2 Ebrach Ger.
Ebre r. Spain see Ebro
179 H3 Ebreichsdorf Austria
160 B2 Ébreuil France
183 H3 Ebrillos r. Spain
172 B4 Ebringen Ger.
183 4 Ebro r. Spain
183 G1 Ebro, Embalse del resr Spain
187 B4 Ebrón r. Spain
169 D5 Ebsdorfergrund-Dreihausen Ger.
169 D5 Ebsdorfergrund-Rauischholzhausen Ger.
168 F2 Ebstorf Ger.
Eburacum York, England U.K. see York
Eburodunum France see Embrun
Ebusus i. Spain see Eivissa
245 E4 Ecatepec Mex.
165 D4 Écaussinnes-d'Enghien Belgium
Ecbatana Iran see Hamadān
146 E6 Ecclefechan Dumfries and Galloway, Scotland U.K.
149 G4 Eccles Greater Manchester, England U.K.
146 F6 Eccles Scottish Borders, Scotland U.K.
232 C6 Eccles WV U.S.A.
149 H4 Ecclesfield South Yorkshire, England U.K.
150 E2 Eccleshall Staffordshire, England U.K.
149 G4 Eccleston Lancashire, England U.K.
199 E1 Eceabat Turkey
92 B2 Echague Phil.
190 B2 Echallens Switz.
246 B5 Echandi, Cerro mt. Costa Rica
183 I2 Echarri Spain
183 H2 Echarri-Aranaz Spain
159 G3 Échauffour France
205 F1 Ech Chélif Alg.
Echeng Hubei China see Ezhou
160 E1 Échenoz-la-Méline France
242 B2 Echeverria, Pico mt. Mex.
162 B3 Échillais France
198 B2 Echinades i. Greece
173 F3 Eching Bayern Ger.
173 G3 Eching Bayern Ger.
198 D1 Echinos Greece
162 B2 Échiré France
161 D3 Échirolles France
105 E3 Echizen-dake mt. Japan
Echmiadzin Armenia see Ejmiatsin
238 C2 Echo OR U.S.A.
83 F5 Echo, Lake Tas. Austr.
220 G3 Echo Bay N.W.T. Can.
224 C4 Echo Bay Ont. Can.
241 L3 Echo Cliffs esc. AZ U.S.A.
223 M4 Echoing r. Man./Ont. Can.
162 C3 Échourgnac France
179 G2 Echsenbach Austria
165 E3 Echt Neth.
146 F4 Echt Aberdeenshire, Scotland U.K.
169 F4 Echte Ger.
165 F5 Echternach Lux.
83 F4 Echuca Vic. Austr.
169 D5 Echzell Ger.
185 E3 Écija Spain
261 I4 Ecilda Paullier Uru.
148 E1 Eck, Loch l. Scotland U.K.
196 E3 Ečka Vojvodina, Srbija Yugo.
171 C4 Eckartsberga Ger.
157 H4 Eckbolsheim France
173 F2 Eckental Ger.
226 E2 Eckerman MI U.S.A.
168 E1 Eckernförde Ger.
141 L3 Eckerö Åland Fin.
173 F2 Eckersdorf Ger.
146 F6 Eckford Scottish Borders, Scotland U.K.
149 H4 Eckington Derbyshire, England U.K.
150 E2 Eckington Worcestershire, England U.K.
232 C6 Eckman WV U.S.A.
222 H4 Eckville Alta Can.
168 D2 Eckwarden (Butjadingen) Ger.
157 E4 Éclaron-Braucourt-Ste-Livière France
159 G4 Écommoy France
257 G3 Ecoporanga Brazil
156 B3 Écos France
159 F3 Écouché France
159 F4 Écouflant France
156 B3 Écouis France
157 F4 Écrouves France
177 G4 Ecs Hungary
177 I4 Ecséd Hungary
177 I4 Ecseg Hungary
177 J4 Ecsegfalva Hungary
177 I4 Ecser Hungary
250 B5 Ecuador country S. America
162 D1 Écueillé France
160 C2 Écuisses France
156 E4 Écury-sur-Coole France
203 I6 Ed Eritrea
142 D2 Ed Sweden
223 I4 Edam Sask. Can.
164 E2 Edam Neth.
146 F2 Eday i. Scotland U.K.
203 F6 Ed Dair, Jebel mt. Sudan
210 B2 Ed Damazin Sudan
203 G5 Ed Damer Sudan
203 F5 Ed Debba Sudan
168 E2 Eddelak Ger.
171 C4 Edderitz Ger.
146 D4 Edderton Highland, Scotland U.K.
225 J3 Eddies Cove Nfld. Can.
203 G6 Ed Dueim Sudan
83 G5 Eddystone Point Tas. Austr.
237 F4 Eddyville KY U.S.A.
164 E2 Ede Neth.
207 G5 Ede Nigeria
207 H6 Edéa Cameroon
165 D3 Edegem Belgium
256 C2 Edéia Brazil
177 J3 Edelény Hungary
179 G3 Edelschrott Austria
169 F3 Edemissen Ger.
83 G4 Eden N.S.W. Austr.
148 D3 Eden Northern Ireland U.K.
149 F3 Eden r. England U.K.
232 D6 Eden NC U.S.A.
237 D6 Eden TX U.S.A.
238 E3 Eden WY U.S.A.
151 H3 Edenbridge Kent, England U.K.
215 E3 Edenburg S. Africa
81 B7 Edendale South I. N.Z.
215 H3 Edendale S. Africa
147 D3 Edenderry Rep. of Ireland
149 G4 Edenfield Lancashire, England U.K.
82 E4 Edenhope Vic. Austr.
172 C2 Edenkoben Ger.
226 A3 Eden Prairie MN U.S.A.
231 E4 Edenton NC U.S.A.
215 G2 Edenvale S. Africa
215 F2 Edenville S. Africa
169 E4 Eder r. Ger.
169 E4 Edermünde Ger.
147 D2 Ederny Northern Ireland U.K.
198 C1 Edessa Greece
Edessa Turkey see Şanlıurfa
140 K3 Edevik Sweden
168 C2 Edewecht Ger.
168 C2 Edewechterdamm Ger.
Edfu Egypt see Idfu
236 D3 Edgar NE U.S.A.
86 D4 Edgar, Mount hill W.A. Austr.
86 D3 Edgar Ranges hills W.A. Austr.
233 H4 Edgartown MA U.S.A.
80 F2 Edgecumbe North I. N.Z.
80 F3 Edgecumbe, Mount hill North I. N.Z.
Edgecumbe Island Solomon Is see Utupua
231 D5 Edgefield SC U.S.A.
Edge Island Svalbard see Edgeøya
236 D2 Edgeley ND U.S.A.
234 B3 Edgemere MD U.S.A.
236 C3 Edgemont SD U.S.A.
140 □ Edgeøya i. Svalbard
223 I4 Edgerton Alta Can.
232 A4 Edgerton OH U.S.A.
232 E6 Edgerton VA U.S.A.
226 C4 Edgerton WI U.S.A.
222 G5 Edgewood B.C. Can.
234 B3 Edgewood MD U.S.A.
234 B2 Edgewood PA U.S.A.
147 D3 Edgeworthstown Rep. of Ireland
78 □3a Edgigen i. Kwajalein Marshall Is
150 E2 Edgmond Telford and Wrekin, England U.K.
Édhessa Greece see Edessa
81 B6 Edievale South I. N.Z.
169 C5 Ediger-Eller Ger.
129 C3 Edik'ilisa Georgia
236 E3 Edina MO U.S.A.
232 C4 Edinboro PA U.S.A.
237 D7 Edinburg TX U.S.A.
232 D5 Edinburg VA U.S.A.
146 E6 Edinburgh Edinburgh, Scotland U.K.
146 E6 Edinburgh admin. div. Scotland U.K.
199 E1 Edincik Turkey
136 D3 Edineţ Moldova
172 C2 Edingen-Neckarhausen Ger.
126 B2 Edirne Turkey
199 E1 Edirne prov. Turkey
234 C2 Edison PA U.S.A.
129 D1 Edissiya Rus. Fed.
231 D5 Edisto r. SC U.S.A.
238 E2 Edith, Mount MT U.S.A.
82 D3 Edithburgh S.A. Austr.
222 G4 Edith Cavell, Mount Alta Can.
87 D5 Edith Withnell, Lake salt flat W.A. Austr.
87 D6 Edjudina W.A. Austr.
173 G3 Edling Ger.
149 H2 Edlingham Northumberland, England U.K.
179 H3 Edlitz Austria
237 D5 Edmond OK U.S.A.
238 B2 Edmonds WA U.S.A.
147 C3 Edmondstown Rep. of Ireland
85 F3 Edmonton Qld Austr.
222 H4 Edmonton Alta Can.
230 C4 Edmonton KY U.S.A.
226 E4 Edmore MI U.S.A.
236 D1 Edmore ND U.S.A.
149 H3 Edmundbyres Durham, England U.K.
225 G4 Edmundston N.B. Can.
237 D6 Edna TX U.S.A.
222 C4 Edna Bay AK U.S.A.
Edo Japan see Tōkyō
207 G5 Edo state Nigeria
105 F3 Edo-gawa r. Japan
190 F2 Edolo Italy
128 B4 Edom reg. Israel/Jordan
199 E2 Edremit Turkey
199 E2 Edremit Körfezi b. Turkey
106 C2 Edrengiyn Nuruu mts Mongolia
182 D3 Edrosa Port.
182 D3 Edroso Port.
143 H2 Edsbro Sweden
143 G2 Edsbruk Sweden
141 K3 Edsbyn Sweden
140 L3 Edsele Sweden
222 G4 Edson Alta Can.
260 E4 Eduardo Castex Arg.
222 D1 Eduni, Mount N.W.T. Can.
83 F3 Edward r. N.S.W. Austr.
85 E2 Edward r. Qld Austr.
208 F5 Edward, Lake Dem. Rep. Congo/Uganda
262 T1 Edward, Mount Antarctica
86 F4 Edward, Mount N.T. Austr.
Edwardesabad Pak. see Bannu
84 C2 Edward Island N.T. Austr.
233 F2 Edwards NY U.S.A.
237 C6 Edwards Plateau TX U.S.A.
236 F4 Edwardsville IL U.S.A.
262 N1 Edward VII Peninsula Antarctica
149 H4 Edwinstowe Nottinghamshire, England U.K.
222 D3 Edziza, Mount B.C. Can.
Edzo N.W.T. Can. see Rae-Edzo
164 F2 Eefde Neth.
165 C3 Eeklo Belgium
240 E1 Eel r. CA U.S.A.
240 F1 Eel, South Fork r. CA U.S.A.
164 F1 Eelde-Paterswolde Neth.
164 E2 Eem r. Neth.
164 E2 Eemnes Neth.
214 B5 Eendekuil S. Africa
164 F1 Eenrum Neth.
164 F2 Eerbeek Neth.
165 C3 Eernegem Belgium
165 E3 Eersel Neth.
Eesti country Europe see Estonia
78 □5 Éfaté i. Vanuatu
179 F2 Eferding Austria
Efes tourist site Turkey see Ephesus
173 F2 Effeltrich Ger.
226 A2 Effie MN U.S.A.
151 G3 Effingham Surrey, England U.K.
236 F4 Effingham IL U.S.A.
234 C2 Effort PA U.S.A.
190 D1 Effretikon Switz.
126 D2 Eflâni Turkey
172 B4 Efringen-Kirchen Ger.
Efsus Turkey see Afşin
197 F3 Eftimie Murgu Romania
107 F1 Eg Mongolia
183 I2 Ega r. Spain
241 J2 Egan Range mts NV U.S.A.
227 I3 Eganville Ont. Can.
187 C6 Egea hill Spain
Egedesminde Greenland see Aasiaat
171 C4 Egeln Ger.
173 F3 Egenhofen Ger.
171 D5 Eger r. Ger.
173 E3 Eger r. Ger.
177 J4 Eger Hungary
177 J4 Egerbakta Hungary
177 J3 Egercsehi Hungary
168 E1 Egernsund Denmark
142 B2 Egersund Norway
87 C5 Egerton, Mount hill W.A. Austr.
176 F5 Egervár Hungary
168 F2 Egestorf Ger.
178 A3 Egg Austria
168 E1 Eggebek Ger.
142 C2 Eggedøla r. Norway
169 D4 Eggegebirge hills Ger.
179 G2 Eggenburg Austria
173 G3 Eggenfelden Ger.
172 C2 Eggenstein-Leopoldshafen Ger.
168 C3 Eggermühlen Ger.
171 C4 Eggersdorf Ger.
179 G3 Eggersdorf bei Graz Austria
170 E3 Eggersdorf bei Strausberg Ger.
170 F2 Eggesin Ger.
226 D3 Egg Harbor WI U.S.A.
234 D3 Egg Harbor City NJ U.S.A.
172 C4 Eggingen Ger.
190 C2 Eggiwil Switz.
173 H3 Egglham Ger.
173 F2 Eggolsheim Ger.
173 G4 Eggstätt Ger.
151 G3 Egham Surrey, England U.K.
165 D4 Eghezée Belgium
Egiarreta Spain see Eguiarreta
146 F2 Egilsay i. Scotland U.K.
140 □D2 Egilsstaðir Iceland
Eğin Turkey see Kemaliye
86 C4 Eginbah W.A. Austr.
Egindibulaq Kazakh. see Yegindybulak
173 H3 Eging am See Ger.
199 G3 Eğirdir Turkey
199 G3 Eğirdir Gölü l. Turkey
106 D1 Egiyn Gol r. Mongolia
162 E3 Égletons France
173 F4 Egling Ger.
173 E3 Egling an der Paar Ger.
149 H2 Eglingham Northumberland, England U.K.
147 D1 Eglinton Northern Ireland U.K.
172 C4 Eglisau Switz.
148 C3 Eglish Northern Ireland U.K.
173 F2 Egloffstein Ger.
150 D2 Eglwys Fach Ceredigion, Wales U.K.
150 C2 Eglwyswrw Pembrokeshire, Wales U.K.
164 D2 Egmond aan Zee Neth.
164 D2 Egmond-Binnen Neth.
80 D3 Egmont, Cape North I. N.Z.
Egmont, Mount vol. North I. N.Z. see Taranaki, Mount
80 E3 Egmont Village North I. N.Z.
191 G2 Egna Italy
149 F3 Egremont Cumbria, England U.K.
199 F2 Eğrigöz Dağı mts Turkey
156 D4 Égriselles-le-Bocage France
149 I3 Egton North Yorkshire, England U.K.
142 C4 Egtved Denmark
254 D5 Éguas r. Brazil
183 I2 Eguiarreta Spain
161 D5 Éguilles France
156 E4 Éguilly-sous-Bois France
157 H4 Eguisheim France
162 D2 Éguzon-Chantôme France
131 T3 Egvekinot Rus. Fed.
177 J4 Egyek Hungary
179 H3 Egyházasfalu Hungary
177 H5 Egyházaskozár Hungary
176 F4 Egyházasrádóc Hungary
203 F2 Egypt country Africa
234 C2 Egypt PA U.S.A.
173 E2 Ehebach r. Ger.
173 F3 Ehekirchen Ger.
106 D4 Ehen Hudag Nei Mongol China
103 F7 Ehime pref. Japan
173 E2 Ehingen Ger.
172 D3 Ehingen (Donau) Ger.
171 C3 Ehle r. Ger.
169 E4 Ehlen (Habichtswald) Ger.
172 C3 Ehningen Ger.
168 F3 Ehra-Lessien Ger.
241 J5 Ehrenberg AZ U.S.A.
84 B4 Ehrenberg Range hills N.T. Austr.
169 F5 Ehrenberg-Wüstensachsen Ger.
168 D3 Ehrenburg Ger.
179 G4 Ehrenhausen Austria
169 D5 Ehringshausen Ger.
178 B3 Ehrwald Austria
79 □3 Eiao i. Fr. Polynesia
183 H1 Eibar Spain
173 E2 Eibelstadt Ger.
171 D5 Eibenstock Ger.
164 F2 Eibergen Neth.
179 G4 Eibiswald Austria
172 C2 Eich Ger.
173 F3 Eichenau Ger.
171 C3 Eichenbarleben Ger.
169 E5 Eichenberg hill Ger.
172 D2 Eichenbühl Ger.
173 G3 Eichendorf Ger.
169 E5 Eichenzell Ger.
179 G2 Eichgraben Austria
171 D5 Eichigt Ger.
173 F3 Eichstätt Ger.
172 B3 Eichstetten Ger.
171 E3 Eichwalde Ger.
171 C4 Eickendorf Ger.
168 F3 Eicklingen Ger.
140 I3 Eide Norway
168 D1 Eider r. Ger.
142 B1 Eidfjord Norway
140 J3 Eidsvåg Norway
85 G5 Eidsvold Qld Austr.
142 D1 Eidsvoll Norway
140 □ Eidsvollfjellet mt. Svalbard
169 B5 Eifel hills Ger.
172 C4 Eigeltingen Ger.
190 D2 Eiger mt. Switz.
142 A2 Eigerøya i. Norway
146 B5 Eigg i. Scotland U.K.
146 B5 Eigg, Sound of sea chan. Scotland U.K.
114 B5 Eight Degree Channel India/Maldives
262 R2 Eights Coast Antarctica
86 D3 Eighty Mile Beach W.A. Austr.
165 E4 Eijsden Neth.
142 A1 Eikelandsosen Norway
142 B2 Eiken Norway
146 C5 Eil, Loch inlet Scotland U.K.
Eilat Israel see Elat
83 F4 Eildon Vic. Austr.
83 F4 Eildon, Lake Vic. Austr.
171 D4 Eilenburg Ger.
171 C4 Eilenstedt Ger.
251 G4 Eilerts de Haan Gebergte mts Suriname
92 □ Eil Malk i. Palau
171 C3 Eilsleben Ger.
169 E3 Eime Ger.
169 E4 Eimen Ger.
Eimeo i. Fr. Polynesia see Moorea
168 F3 Eimke Ger.
146 B3 Einacleit Western Isles, Scotland U.K.
85 F3 Einasleigh Qld Austr.
85 E3 Einasleigh r. Qld Austr.
169 E4 Einbeck Ger.
165 E3 Eindhoven Neth.
171 C4 Eine r. Ger.
172 C2 Einhausen Ger.
146 D4 Einig r. Scotland U.K.
171 D5 Einsiedel Ger.
190 D1 Einsiedeln Switz.
157 G4 Einville-au-Jard France
Éire country Europe see Ireland, Republic of
264 G2 Eirik Ridge sea feature N. Atlantic Ocean
Eiriosgaigh i. Scotland U.K. see Eriskay
250 D6 Eiru r. Brazil
250 D6 Eirunepé Brazil
169 E4 Eisberg hill Ger.
165 F5 Eisch r. Lux.
165 E4 Eisden Belgium
169 F4 Eisdorf Ger.
173 G3 Eiselfing Ger.
169 F5 Eisenach Ger.
172 C4 Eisenbach (Hochschwarzwald) Ger.
171 C5 Eisenberg Ger.
172 C2 Eisenberg (Pfalz) Ger.
179 F3 Eisenerz Austria
Eisenhower, Mount Alta Can. see Castle Mountain
179 E4 Eisenhut mt. Austria
171 F3 Eisenhüttenstadt Ger.
179 F4 Eisenkappel Austria
179 H3 Eisenstadt Austria
169 F5 Eisfeld Ger.
146 C4 Eishort, Loch inlet Scotland U.K.
138 E4 Eišiškės Lith.
171 C4 Eisleben Lutherstadt Ger.
172 D3 Eislingen (Fils) Ger.
80 E2 Eistow North I. N.Z.
173 F3 Eitensheim Ger.
169 E5 Eiterfeld Ger.
169 C5 Eitorf Ger.
169 E3 Eitzum (Despetal) Ger.
141 I3 Eivinvik Norway
187 E6 Eivissa Spain
187 E5 Eivissa i. Spain
182 C2 Eixe, Serra do mts Spain
182 B4 Eixo Port.
182 B3 Eja Port.
186 B2 Ejea de los Caballeros Spain
213 □J5 Ejeda Madag.

Ejin Horo Qi Nei Mongol China see Altan Shiret
Ejin Qi Nei Mongol China see Dalain Hob
Ejmiadzin Armenia see Ejmiatsin
129 D3 Ejmiatsin Armenia
186 C4 Ejulve Spain
206 E5 Ejura Ghana
238 F2 Ekalaka MT U.S.A.
207 H5 Ekang Nigeria
215 G1 Ekangala S. Africa
141 M4 Ekenäs Fin.
142 E2 Ekenäs Sweden
165 D3 Ekeren Belgium
143 G2 Ekerö Sweden
207 G5 Eket Nigeria
80 E4 Eketahuna North I. N.Z.
Ekhínos Greece see Echinos
Ekhmîm Egypt see Akhmîm
121 H2 Ekibastuz Kazakh.
100 E1 Ekimchan Rus. Fed.
128 D1 Ekinyazı Turkey
207 G5 Ekiti state Nigeria
207 H5 Ekondo Titi Cameroon
140 P2 Ekostrovskaya Imandra, Ozero l. Rus. Fed.
207 G5 Ekpoma Nigeria
165 C3 Eksaarde Belgium
165 E3 Eksel Belgium
Eksere Turkey see Gündoğmuş
142 E1 Ekshärad Sweden
199 G3 Ekşili Turkey
143 F3 Eksjö Sweden
214 A3 Eksteenfontein S. Africa
140 L2 Ekträsk Sweden
224 D2 Ekwan r. Ont. Can.
96 B3 Ela Myanmar
El Aaiún Western Sahara see Laâyoune
244 C4 El Aguaje Mex.
198 D1 Elaiochori Anatoliki Makedonia kai Thraki Greece
187 C7 El Algar Spain
189 B7 El Alia Tunisia
184 C3 El Almendro Spain
185 H4 El Alquián Spain
250 A6 El Alto Peru
126 C5 El 'Amirîya Egypt
156 B4 Élancourt France
215 H1 Elands r. S. Africa
213 F5 Elands r. S. Africa
215 F5 Elandsberg mt. S. Africa
215 G1 Elandsdoorn S. Africa
215 E5 Elandsdrif S. Africa
215 H3 Elandskraal S. Africa
215 G3 Elandslaagte S. Africa
215 F1 Elandsputte S. Africa
150 D2 Elan Village Powys, Wales U.K.
Elar Armenia see Abovyan
184 E3 El Arahal Spain
El Araïche Morocco see Larache
242 B2 El Arco Mex.
183 E4 El Arenal Castilla y León Spain
El Arenal Islas Baleares Spain see S'Arenal
85 F3 El Arish Qld Austr.
203 G2 El 'Arîsh Egypt
205 G1 El Arrouch Alg.
203 F3 El Ashmûnein Egypt
El Asnam Alg. see Ech Chélif
198 C2 Elassona Greece
183 G1 El Astillero Spain
128 B5 Elat Israel
204 B5 El 'Aţf reg. Western Sahara
198 B2 Elati mt. Ionioi Nisoi Greece
91 K5 Elato atoll Micronesia
126 E3 Elazığ Turkey
129 A4 Elazığ prov. Turkey
231 C6 Elba AL U.S.A.
192 C2 Elba, Isola d' i. Italy
128 A5 El Bahr El Ahmar governorate Egypt
185 H2 El Ballestero Spain
203 F3 El Balyana Egypt
100 F2 El'ban Rus. Fed.
250 C2 El Banco Col.
182 E4 El Barco de Ávila Spain
El Barco de Valdeorras Spain see O Barco
183 F4 El Barraco Spain
242 D2 El Barreal salt l. Mex.
244 C2 El Barril Mex.
196 E5 Elbasan Albania
126 D3 Elbaşı Turkey
205 F2 El Bayadh Alg.
168 E2 Elbe r. Ger.
alt. Labe (Czech Rep.)
238 B2 Elbe WA U.S.A.
206 C2 'Elb el Fçâl des. Maur.
260 B3 El Belloto airport Valparaíso Chile
169 C3 Elbergen Ger.
183 G4 El Berrueco Spain
226 D3 Elberta MI U.S.A.
241 L2 Elberta UT U.S.A.
231 D5 Elberton GA U.S.A.
156 B3 Elbeuf France
128 C1 Elbeyli Turkey
244 D4 El Billete, Cerro mt. Mex.
Elbing Pol. see Elbląg
169 F4 Elbingerode (Harz) Ger.
126 E3 Elbistan Turkey
143 H4 Elbląg Pol.
242 □J6 El Bluff Nic.
182 D4 El Bodón Spain
El Bollo Spain see O Bolo
259 C6 El Bolsón Arg.
185 H2 El Bonillo Spain
185 E4 El Bosque Spain
El Boulaïda Alg. see Blida
223 J5 Elbow Sask. Can.
231 E7 Elbow Cay i. Bahamas
236 D2 Elbow Lake MN U.S.A.
129 C2 El'brus Rus. Fed.
129 C2 Elbrus mt. Rus. Fed.
208 F3 El Buheyrat state Sudan
185 I2 El Buitre mt. Spain
185 F1 El Bullaque Spain
164 E2 Elburg Neth.
185 F4 El Burgo Spain
183 H2 Elburgo Spain
186 C3 El Burgo de Ebro Spain
183 G3 El Burgo de Osma Spain
183 E2 El Burgo Ranero Spain
Elburz Mountains Iran see Alborz, Reshteh-ye
183 I3 El Buste Spain
137 J4 El'buzd r. Rus. Fed.
182 D4 El Cabaco Spain
185 I3 El Cabildo y la Campana Spain
185 H4 El Cabo de Gata Spain
240 I5 El Cajon CA U.S.A.
251 F3 El Callao Venez.
El Caló Spain see Es Caló
245 D5 El Camotal, Sierra mts Mex.
183 E5 El Campillo de la Jara Spain
El Campo Spain see Campo Lugar
237 D6 El Campo TX U.S.A.
183 E4 El Campo de Peñaranda Spain
183 H5 El Cañavate Spain
237 C7 El Capulín r. Mex.
258 D2 El Carmen Arg.
252 E3 El Carmen Bol.
260 B5 El Carmen Chile
250 B5 El Carmen Ecuador
187 C5 El Caroche mt. Spain
185 F3 El Carpio Spain
183 F5 El Carpio de Tajo Spain
183 G4 El Casar Spain
183 F4 El Casar de Escalona Spain
187 C4 El Castellar Spain
184 D3 El Castillo de las Guardas Spain
243 G6 El Cebú, Cerro mt. Mex.
185 G2 El Centenillo Spain
241 J5 El Centro CA U.S.A.
253 E4 El Cerro Bol.
184 D3 El Cerro de Andévalo Spain
187 C6 Elche Spain
185 H2 Elche de la Sierra Spain
243 G5 El Chichónal vol. Mex.
173 E3 Elchingen Ger.
226 C3 Elcho WI U.S.A.
84 C1 Elcho Island N.T. Austr.
183 H2 Elciego Spain
El Coca Ecuador see Puerto Francisco de Orellana
185 F2 El Collado hill Spain
244 B4 El Colomo Mex.
244 D5 El Conejo, Sierra mts Mex.
186 F3 El Congost r. Spain
184 E3 El Coronil Spain
245 G5 El Corte r. Mex.
246 B2 El Cotorro Cuba
245 G6 El Coyol Mex.
182 D4 El Cubo de Don Sancho Spain
182 E3 El Cubo de Tierra del Vino Spain
184 D4 El Cuervo Spain
187 C6 Elda Spain
210 B4 Eldama Ravine Kenya
170 C2 Elde r. Ger.
227 H2 Eldee Ont. Can.
170 C2 Eldena Ger.
226 C5 Eldena IL U.S.A.
226 C3 Elderon WI U.S.A.
140 □C3 Eldhraun lava field Iceland
250 C2 El Difícil Col.
131 O3 El'dikan Rus. Fed.
168 F3 Eldingen Ger.
El Djezair Alg. see Alger
236 E4 Eldon MO U.S.A.
236 E3 Eldora IA U.S.A.
234 D3 Eldora NJ U.S.A.
258 G2 Eldorado Arg.
256 C6 Eldorado Brazil
242 D3 El Dorado Mex.
237 E5 El Dorado AR U.S.A.
237 D4 El Dorado KS U.S.A.
237 C6 Eldorado TX U.S.A.
241 J4 Eldorado Mountains NV U.S.A.
210 B4 Eldoret Kenya
234 D1 Eldred NY U.S.A.
232 C5 Eleanor WV U.S.A.
238 E2 Electric Peak MT U.S.A.
198 C2 Elefsina Greece
204 D4 El Eglab plat. Alg.
138 D3 Eleja Latvia
185 H4 El Ejido Spain
177 K5 Elek Hungary
Elek r. Rus. Fed. see Ilek
138 E4 Elektrėnai Lith.
139 L4 Elektrogorsk Rus. Fed.
139 L4 Elektrostal' Rus. Fed.
139 L4 Elektrougli Rus. Fed.
207 G5 Elele Nigeria
210 B3 Elemi Triangle terr. Africa
197 G4 Elena Bulg.
169 F4 Elend Ger.
198 B2 Eleousa Ipeiros Greece
114 B2 Elephanta Caves tourist site Mahar. India
239 F5 Elephant Butte Reservoir NM U.S.A.
262 U2 Elephant Island Antarctica
183 F4 El Escorial Spain
197 F5 Eleshnitsa Bulg.
127 F3 Eleşkirt Turkey
183 F4 El Espinar Spain
243 H6 El Estor Guat.
187 C7 El Estrecho Spain
246 C1 Eleuthera i. Bahamas
226 B3 Eleva WI U.S.A.
237 F4 Eleven Point r. MO U.S.A.
189 B7 El Fahs Tunisia
203 F2 El Faiyûm Egypt
126 C5 El Faiyûm governorate Egypt
202 E6 El Fasher Sudan
203 F2 El Fashn Egypt
180 D5 El Fendek Morocco
El Ferrol Spain see Ferrol
El Ferrol del Caudillo Spain see Ferrol
169 E5 Elfershausen Ger.
183 F4 El Fresno Spain
241 M6 Elfrida AZ U.S.A.
210 D3 El Fud Eth.
242 C3 El Fuerte Mex.
208 F2 El Fula Sudan
185 H3 El Gabar mt. Spain
184 D3 El Garrobo Spain
185 E4 El Gastor Spain
202 D6 El Geneina Sudan
169 E4 Elgershausen (Schauenburg) Ger.
183 H1 Elgeta Spain
203 G6 El Geteina Sudan
203 G6 El Gezira state Sudan
206 C2 El Gheddiya Maur.
142 D2 Elgheia hill Norway
El Ghor plain Jordan/West Bank see Al Ghawr
146 E4 Elgin Moray, Scotland U.K.
226 C4 Elgin IL U.S.A.
236 C2 Elgin ND U.S.A.
241 J3 Elgin NV U.S.A.
238 C2 Elgin OR U.S.A.
237 D6 Elgin TX U.S.A.
85 F4 Elgin Down Qld Austr.
131 P3 El'ginskiy Rus. Fed.
203 F2 El Gîza Egypt
126 C5 El Gîza governorate Egypt
183 H1 Elgoibar Spain
146 B4 Elgol Highland, Scotland U.K.
205 F3 El Goléa Alg.
216 □3e El Golfo b. El Hierro Canary Is
210 B4 Elgon, Mount Uganda
140 O1 Elgoras, Gora hill Rus. Fed.
141 J3 Elgpiggen mt. Norway
186 D2 El Grado Spain
184 C3 El Granado Spain
187 C5 El Grau de Borriana Spain
244 B4 El Grullo Mex.
245 H5 El Guanal Mex.
205 H2 El Guetar Tunisia
131 M3 El'gyay Rus. Fed.
189 A7 El Hadjar Alg.
205 H2 El Hamma Tunisia
203 F2 El Hammâm Egypt
204 C5 El Ḩammâmi reg. Maur.
204 D4 El Hank reg. Alg.
204 C5 El Ḩank esc. Mali/Maur.
203 F2 El Harra Egypt
242 □J7 El Hato del Volcán Panama
203 G6 El Hawata Sudan
126 C5 El Heiz Egypt
216 □3e El Hierro i. Canary Is
245 E3 El Higo Mex.
183 H5 El Hito Spain
183 F4 El Hoyo de Pinares Spain
246 E3 Elías Piña Dom. Rep.
193 F2 Elice Italy
Elichpur Mahar. India see Achalpur
232 A4 Elida OH U.S.A.
146 F5 Elie Fife, Scotland U.K.
209 E5 Elila r. Dem. Rep. Congo
214 B6 Elim S. Africa
220 B3 Elim AK U.S.A.
138 F1 Elimäki Fin.
Elimberrum France see Auch
234 A1 Elimsport PA U.S.A.
151 F4 Eling Hampshire, England U.K.
197 F4 Elin Pelin Bulg.
129 D2 Elin-Yurt Rus. Fed.
193 H3 Elio, Monte d' hill Italy
225 I1 Eliot, Mount Nfld. Can.
186 B1 Eliozondo Spain
Élisabethville Dem. Rep. Congo see Lubumbashi
254 E4 Eliseu Martins Brazil
El Iskandarîya Egypt see Alexandria
126 C5 El Iskandarîya governorate Egypt
135 I7 Elista Rus. Fed.
178 E3 Elixhausen Austria
233 F4 Elizabeth NJ U.S.A.
232 C5 Elizabeth WV U.S.A.
86 E3 Elizabeth, Mount hill W.A. Austr.
233 □J1 Elizabeth, Mount hill N.B. Can.
231 E4 Elizabeth City NC U.S.A.
84 D3 Elizabeth Creek r. Qld Austr.
Elizabeth Island Pitcairn Is see Henderson Island
77 F4 Elizabeth Reef Austr.
232 B6 Elizabethton TN U.S.A.
237 F4 Elizabethtown IL U.S.A.
230 C4 Elizabethtown KY U.S.A.
231 E5 Elizabethtown NC U.S.A.
233 G2 Elizabethtown NY U.S.A.
234 B2 Elizabethtown PA U.S.A.
227 I5 Elizabethville PA U.S.A.
204 C2 El Jadida Morocco
242 D3 El Jaralito Mex.
182 D4 Eljas Spain
205 H2 El Jem Tunisia
222 H5 Elk r. B.C. Can.
175 K2 Ełk Pol.
175 K2 Ełk r. Pol.
234 C3 Elk r. MD U.S.A.
231 C5 Elk r. TN U.S.A.
El Kaa Lebanon see Qaa
236 F3 Elkader IA U.S.A.
205 H1 El Kala Alg.
138 E3 Elkas kalns hill Latvia
232 B6 Elkatawa KY U.S.A.
237 D5 Elk City OK U.S.A.
240 F2 Elk Creek CA U.S.A.
84 C4 Elkedra N.T. Austr.
204 D2 El Kelaâ des Srarhna Morocco
169 C5 Elkenroth Ger.
210 D3 Ēl Kerē Eth.
222 H5 Elkford B.C. Can.
240 G2 Elk Grove CA U.S.A.
El Khalil West Bank see Hebron
203 F5 El Khandaq Sudan
203 F3 El Khârga Egypt
230 C3 Elkhart IN U.S.A.
237 C4 Elkhart KS U.S.A.
El Khartûm Sudan see Khartoum
El Khenachich esc. Mali see El Khnâchîch
204 D5 El Khnâchîch esc. Mali
226 C4 Elkhorn WI U.S.A.
236 D3 Elkhorn r. NE U.S.A.
232 B6 Elkhorn City KY U.S.A.
129 D2 El'khotovo Rus. Fed.
197 H4 Elkhovo Bulg.
Elki Turkey see Beytüşşebap
231 D4 Elkin NC U.S.A.
232 D5 Elkins WV U.S.A.
234 C2 Elkins Park PA U.S.A.
224 D4 Elk Lake Ont. Can.
232 E4 Elkland PA U.S.A.
234 C3 Elk Mills MD U.S.A.
238 F3 Elk Mountain WY U.S.A.
234 C3 Elk Neck MD U.S.A.
222 H5 Elko B.C. Can.
238 D3 Elko NV U.S.A.
223 I4 Elk Point Alta Can.
236 D3 Elk Point SD U.S.A.
234 B3 Elkridge MD U.S.A.
226 A3 Elk River MN U.S.A.
241 M1 Elk Springs CO U.S.A.
230 C4 Elkton KY U.S.A.
234 C3 Elkton MD U.S.A.
232 D5 Elkton VA U.S.A.
232 C5 Elkview WV U.S.A.
245 F5 El Labrador, Cerro mt. Mex.
143 H1 Ellan Sweden
129 E3 Elläryoğu Dağı hill Azer.
Ellas country Europe see Greece
87 B5 Ellavalla W.A. Austr.
231 C5 Ellaville GA U.S.A.
178 C3 Ellbögen Austria
158 C4 Ellé r. France
171 D5 Ellefeld Ger.
221 H2 Ellef Ringnes Island Nunavut Can.
128 C1 Ellek Turkey
87 C7 Elleker W.A. Austr.
241 L2 Ellen, Mount UT U.S.A.
116 C3 Ellenabad Haryana India
173 E2 Ellenberg Ger.
232 C5 Ellenboro WV U.S.A.
233 G2 Ellenburg Depot NY U.S.A.
233 F5 Ellendale DE U.S.A.
236 D2 Ellendale ND U.S.A.
238 B2 Ellensburg WA U.S.A.
235 D1 Ellenville NY U.S.A.
244 B1 El León, Cerro mt. Mex.
78 □3a Eller i. Kwajalein Marshall Is
168 E2 Ellerau Ger.
168 E2 Ellerbek Ger.
168 E2 Ellerhoop Ger.
81 D5 Ellesmere South I. N.Z.
150 E2 Ellesmere Shropshire, England U.K.
81 D5 Ellesmere, Lake South I. N.Z.
221 J2 Ellesmere Island Nunavut Can.
149 G4 Ellesmere Port Cheshire, England U.K.
262 S1 Ellesworth Mountains Antarctica
165 C4 Ellezelles Belgium
158 C4 Elliant France
221 H3 Ellice r. Nunavut Can.
Ellice Island atoll Tuvalu see Funafuti
Ellice Islands country S. Pacific Ocean see Tuvalu
234 B3 Ellicott City MD U.S.A.
232 D3 Ellicottville NY U.S.A.
231 C5 Ellijay GA U.S.A.
244 B2 El Limón Mex.
245 E2 El Limón Mex.
173 E2 Ellingen Ger.
149 H2 Ellingham Northumberland, England U.K.
149 H2 Ellington Northumberland, England U.K.
84 C3 Elliot N.T. Austr.
215 F4 Elliot S. Africa
85 F3 Elliot, Mount Qld Austr.
215 G4 Elliotdale S. Africa
232 D5 Elliot Knob mt. VA U.S.A.
224 D4 Elliot Lake Ont. Can.
238 D2 Ellis ID U.S.A.
236 D4 Ellis KS U.S.A.
213 E4 Ellisras S. Africa
82 C3 Elliston S.A. Austr.
232 C6 Elliston VA U.S.A.
237 F6 Ellisville MS U.S.A.
182 C1 El Llano Spain
178 D3 Ellmau Austria
146 F4 Ellon Aberdeenshire, Scotland U.K.
116 C5 Ellora Caves tourist site Mahar. India
142 D2 Ellös Sweden
182 E4 El Losar del Barco Spain
149 I4 Elloughton East Riding of Yorkshire, England U.K.
169 F4 Ellrich Ger.
236 D4 Ellsworth KS U.S.A.
233 □I2 Ellsworth ME U.S.A.
236 C3 Ellsworth NE U.S.A.
226 A3 Ellsworth WI U.S.A.
262 R1 Ellsworth Land reg. Antarctica
173 E3 Ellwangen (Jagst) Ger.
232 C4 Ellwood City PA U.S.A.
168 D2 Ellwürden Ger.
168 E2 Elm Ger.
190 E2 Elm Switz.
151 H2 Elm Cambridgeshire, England U.K.
175 I1 Elma r. Pol.
247 E3 El Macao Dom. Rep.
204 E5 El Mahia reg. Mali
259 C6 El Maitén Arg.
129 C4 Elmakaya Turkey
128 A1 Elmakuz Dağı mt. Turkey
199 F3 Elmalı Turkey
203 G6 El Manaqil Sudan
203 F2 El Mansûra Egypt
180 D5 El Manzla Morocco
189 C7 El Marsa Tunisia
186 D3 El Masroig Spain
205 G2 El Meghaïer Alg.
260 B3 El Melón Chile
170 C2 Elmenhorst Mecklenburg-Vorpommern Ger.
170 D1 Elmenhorst Mecklenburg-Vorpommern Ger.
170 E1 Elmenhorst Mecklenburg-Vorpommern Ger.
168 F2 Elmenhorst Schleswig-Holstein Ger.
168 F2 Elmenhorst Schleswig-Holstein Ger.
234 C3 Elmer NJ U.S.A.
234 C1 Elmhurst PA U.S.A.
206 E5 Elmina Ghana
128 B2 El Mīna Lebanon
203 F2 El Minya Egypt
126 C5 El Minya governorate Egypt
227 G4 Elmira Ont. Can.
225 I4 Elmira P.E.I. Can.
226 E3 Elmira MI U.S.A.
227 I4 Elmira NY U.S.A.
245 E4 El Mirador, Cerro mt. Mex.
241 K5 El Mirage AZ U.S.A.
183 G4 El Molar Spain
185 F1 El Molinillo Spain
185 H3 El Moral Spain
83 F4 Elmore Vic. Austr.
232 B4 Elmore OH U.S.A.
186 E3 El Morell Spain
260 E3 El Morro mt. Arg.
235 E1 Elmsford NY U.S.A.
168 E2 Elmshorn Ger.
172 B2 Elmstein Ger.
151 H2 Elmswell Suffolk, England U.K.
208 E2 El Muglad Sudan
187 B6 El Mugrón mt. Spain
227 H3 Elmvale Ont. Can.
226 C5 Elmwood IL U.S.A.
226 A3 Elmwood WI U.S.A.
244 C4 El Naranjo r. Mex.
163 E6 Elne France
140 I3 Elnesvågen Norway
92 A4 El Nido Phil.
203 F6 El Obeid Sudan
227 G4 Elora Ont. Can.
158 B3 Elorn r. France
250 B5 El Oro prov. Ecuador
242 E3 El Oro Coahuila Mex.
244 D4 El Oro México Mex.
183 H1 Elorrio Spain
261 G3 Elortondo Arg.
183 I2 Elorz Spain
183 F4 El Oso Spain
177 H5 Előszállás Hungary
244 A2 Elota r. Mex.
205 G2 El Oued Alg.
245 E3 Eloxochitlán Mex.
241 L5 Eloy AZ U.S.A.
157 G4 Éloyes France
185 F4 El Palo Spain
250 D2 El Pao Venez.
242 □I6 El Paraiso Hond.
245 G5 El Paraíso Mex.
216 □3d El Paso La Palma Canary Is
226 C5 El Paso IL U.S.A.
El Paso KS U.S.A. see Derby
239 F6 El Paso TX U.S.A.
182 D4 El Payo Spain
185 H1 El Pedernoso Spain
245 E2 El Pedregoso r. Mex.
184 E3 El Pedroso Spain
183 E3 El Pedroso de la Armuña Spain
260 B3 El Peñón mt. Chile
183 I5 El Peral Spain
182 E3 El Perdigón Spain
186 D4 El Perelló Spain
187 C5 El Perelló Spain
168 E1 Elpersbüttel Ger.
147 C3 Elphin Rep. of Ireland
146 C3 Elphin Highland, Scotland U.K.
185 H1 El Picazo Spain
Elpin Armenia see Yelp'in
186 D3 El Pinell de Bray Spain
182 E3 El Piñero Spain
186 E3 El pla de Santa Maria Spain
260 B3 El Plomo, Nevado mt. Chile
186 C4 El Pobo Spain
183 I4 El Pobo de Dueñas Spain
187 C5 El Port Spain
240 H3 El Portal CA U.S.A.
186 G2 El Port de la Selva Spain
240 I5 El Porvenir Baja California Norte Mex.
242 D2 El Porvenír Mex.
242 □K7 El Porvenír Panama
186 F3 El Prat de Llobregat Spain
243 H6 El Progreso Guat.
185 H1 El Provencio Spain
183 G1 El Puente Spain
183 E5 El Puente de Arzobispo Spain
El Puerto de Andraitx Spain see Port d'Andratx
184 D4 El Puerto de Santa María Spain
128 A5 El Qâ' val. Egypt
El Qâhira Egypt see Cairo
126 C5 El Qâhira governorate Egypt
128 B3 El Qasimiye r. Lebanon
203 F3 El Qasr Egypt
El Quds Israel/West Bank see Jerusalem
258 D2 El Quebrachal Arg.
260 B1 Elqui r. Chile
260 B3 El Quisco Chile
244 C4 El Ranchito Mex.
183 H2 El Rasillo Spain
184 D3 El Real de la Jara Spain
183 F4 El Real de San Vicente Spain
183 H4 El Recuenco Spain
244 D3 El Refugio Mex.
237 D5 El Reno OK U.S.A.
203 G3 El Ridisîya Bahari Egypt
240 H4 El Rio CA U.S.A.
244 A2 El Roble Mex.
185 F1 El Robledo Spain
184 D3 El Rocío Spain
183 G5 El Romeral Spain
184 C3 El Rompido Spain
184 D3 El Ronquillo Spain
223 I5 Elrose Sask. Can.
226 B4 Elroy WI U.S.A.
183 H3 El Royo Spain
185 F3 El Rubio Spain
244 C2 El Rucio Mex.
222 C2 Elsa Y.T. Can.
194 D5 Elsa r. Sicilia Italy
191 F5 Elsa r. Italy
186 B2 El Sabinar Aragón Spain
185 H2 El Sabinar Murcia Spain
203 F2 El Saff Egypt
242 B2 El Sahuaro Mex.
244 D1 El Salado Mex.
187 C5 El Saler Spain
126 D5 El Sâlhîya Egypt
185 I2 El Salobral Spain
244 B2 El Salto Durango Mex.
244 C3 El Salto Jalisco Mex.
243 H6 El Salvador country Central America
258 C2 El Salvador Chile
244 D1 El Salvador Mex.
92 C4 El Salvador Phil.
186 D3 Els Arcs Spain
227 F1 Elsas Ont. Can.
Elsass reg. France see Alsace
185 E3 El Saucejo Spain
182 D4 El Saugo Spain
242 D2 El Sauz Mex.
216 □3a El Sauzal Tenerife Canary Is
240 I6 El Sauzal Mex.
172 D2 Elsava r. Ger.
178 E3 Elsbethen Austria
149 G2 Elsdon Northumberland, England U.K.
168 E2 Elsdorf Niedersachsen Ger.
169 B5 Elsdorf Nordrhein-Westfalen Ger.
168 E1 Elsdorf-Westermühlen Ger.
169 D3 Else r. Ger.
247 E3 El Seibo Dom. Rep.
165 F4 Elsenborn Belgium
173 F3 Elsendorf Ger.
172 D2 Elsenfeld Ger.
172 C2 Elsenz r. Ger.
186 E2 El Serrat Andorra
84 C2 Elsey N.T. Austr.
168 D2 Elsfleth Ger.
84 C2 El Sharana N.T. Austr.
226 E4 Elsie MI U.S.A.
Elsinore Denmark see Helsingør
240 I5 Elsinore CA U.S.A.
241 K2 Elsinore UT U.S.A.
165 E4 Elsloo Neth.
234 C3 Elsmere DE U.S.A.
171 D4 Elsnig Ger.
171 D4 Elsnigk Ger.
186 D3 El Soleràs Spain
164 E2 Elspeet Neth.
186 E3 Els Prats de Rei Spain
164 E3 Elst Gelderland Neth.
164 E3 Elst Utrecht Neth.
151 G3 Elstead Surrey, England U.K.
171 D4 Elster Ger.
171 D5 Elsterberg Ger.
171 E4 Elsterwerda Ger.
151 G3 Elstree Hertfordshire, England U.K.
242 D2 El Sueco Mex.
203 G2 El Suweis Egypt
128 A5 El Suweis governorate Egypt
260 B3 El Tabo Chile
245 F3 El Tajín tourist site Mex.
205 H1 El Tarf Alg.
189 B7 El Tarf prov. Alg.
244 D4 El Tecolote, Cerro mt. Mex.
182 D2 El Teleno mt. Spain
245 E1 El Temascal Mex.
179 H3 Eltendorf Austria
171 D5 Elterlein Ger.
80 E3 Eltham North I. N.Z.
183 F4 El Tiemblo Spain
251 E2 El Tigre Venez.
173 E2 Eltmann Ger.
183 H5 El Toboso Spain
250 D2 El Tocuyo Venez.
147 C4 Elton Rep. of Ireland
120 A2 El'ton Rus. Fed.
151 G2 Elton Cambridgeshire, England U.K.
149 G4 Elton Cheshire, England U.K.
120 A2 El'ton, Ozero l. Rus. Fed.
238 C2 Eltopia WA U.S.A.
182 E4 El Torno Spain
261 G3 El Trébol Arg.
245 E5 El Treinta Mex.
185 F1 El Trincheto Spain
242 C4 El Triunfo Mex.
184 D3 El Tumbalejo Spain
203 G2 El Tûr Egypt
186 D2 El Turbón mt. Spain
169 D5 Eltville am Rhein Ger.
203 G3 El Uqşur Egypt
114 D2 Eluru Andhra Prad. India
138 F2 Elva Estonia
146 E6 Elvanfoot South Lanarkshire, Scotland U.K.
Elvanlı Turkey see Tömük
184 C2 Elvas Port.
158 D4 Elven France
186 E3 El Vendrell Spain
234 C2 Elverson PA U.S.A.
141 J3 Elverum Norway
250 C3 El Viejo mt. Col.
242 □I6 El Viejo Nic.
244 B3 El Vigía, Cerro mt. Mex.
149 I4 Elvington York, England U.K.
86 F3 Elvire r. W.A. Austr.
185 F2 El Viso Spain
184 E3 El Viso del Alcor Spain
190 D3 Elvo r. Italy
126 B6 El Wâdi El Jadid governorate Egypt
226 C5 Elwood IL U.S.A.
230 C3 Elwood IN U.S.A.
236 D3 Elwood NE U.S.A.
234 D3 Elwood NJ U.S.A.
169 F4 Elxleben Ger.
151 H2 Ely Cambridgeshire, England U.K.
150 D3 Ely Cardiff, Wales U.K.
226 B2 Ely MN U.S.A.
241 J2 Ely NV U.S.A.
232 B4 Elyria OH U.S.A.
227 I5 Elysburg PA U.S.A.
169 D5 Elz Ger.
172 B3 Elz r. Ger.
245 F5 El Zacatón, Cerro mt. Mex.
172 C3 Elzach Ger.
169 E3 Elze Ger.
168 E3 Elze (Wedemark) Ger.
78 □5 Émaé i. Vanuatu
160 D1 Émagny France
138 F2 Emajõgi r. Estonia
122 D2 Emām Qolī Iran
122 C2 Emāmrūd Iran
123 G2 Emām Şaḩēb Afgh.
143 G3 Emån r. Sweden
215 I2 Emangusi S. Africa
78 □5 Émao i. Vanuatu
121 J3 Emazar Kazakh.
120 D2 Emba Kazakh.
120 C3 Emba r. Kazakh.
215 G2 Embalenhle S. Africa
258 D1 Embarcación Arg.
223 I3 Embarras Portage Alta Can.
226 A2 Embarrass MN U.S.A.
Embi Kazakh. see Emba
183 I4 Embid Spain
183 I3 Embid de Ariza Spain
Embira r. Brazil see Envira
149 H2 Embleton Northumberland, England U.K.
146 E4 Embo Highland, Scotland U.K.
Émbonas Notio Aigaio Greece see Emponas
256 D3 Emborcação, Represa de resr Brazil
Emborion Greece see Emporeio
172 C4 Embrach Switz.
234 C3 Embreeville PA U.S.A.
233 F2 Embrun Ont. Can.
161 E4 Embrun France
168 F2 Embsen Ger.
256 D5 Embu Brazil
210 C5 Embu Kenya
113 □1 Embudhu i. S. Male Maldives
113 □1 Embudhu Finolhu i. S. Male Maldives
168 C2 Emden Ger.
199 E3 Emecik Turkey
Emei Sichuan China see Emeishan
108 B2 Emeishan Sichuan China
108 B2 Emei Shan mt. Sichuan China
121 J3 Emel' r. Kazakh.
85 G4 Emerald Qld Austr.
83 F4 Emerald Vic. Austr.
234 C2 Emerald PA U.S.A.
225 H2 Emeril Nfld. Can.
Emerita Augusta Spain see Mérida
252 D3 Emero r. Bol.
223 L5 Emerson Man. Can.
232 B5 Emerson KY U.S.A.
241 L2 Emery UT U.S.A.
Emesa Syria see Ḩimş
199 F2 Emet Turkey
215 H1 eMgwenya S. Africa
240 G2 Emigrant Gap CA U.S.A.
241 J3 Emigrant Valley NV U.S.A.
215 H1 eMijindini S. Africa
202 C5 Emi Koussi mt. Chad
222 G2 Emile r. N.W.T. Can.
243 H5 Emiliano Zapata Chiapas Mex.
244 C1 Emiliano Zapata Durango Mex.
244 C2 Emiliano Zapata Zacatecas Mex.
190 G4 Emilia-Romagna admin. reg. Italy
261 G4 Emilio Ayarza Arg.
245 F4 Emilio Carranza Mex.
190 C3 Emilius, Monte mt. Italy
110 C2 Emin Xinjiang China
237 F4 Eminence MO U.S.A.
110 C2 Emin He r. China
197 H4 Eminska Planina hills Bulg.
199 G2 Emirdağ Turkey
199 G2 Emir Dağı mt. Turkey
199 F2 Emirhisar Turkey
83 F5 Emita Tas. Austr.
168 E1 Emkendorf Ger.
232 D4 Emlenton PA U.S.A.
168 B3 Emlichheim Ger.
147 C4 Emly Rep. of Ireland
143 F3 Emmaboda Sweden
Emmahaven Sumatera Indon. see Telukbayur
139 K3 Emmaus Rus. Fed.
234 C2 Emmaus PA U.S.A.
83 G2 Emmaville N.S.W. Austr.
190 C1 Emme r. Switz.
164 E2 Emmeloord Neth.
168 D1 Emmelsbüll-Horsbüll Ger.
169 C5 Emmelshausen Ger.
164 F2 Emmen Neth.
172 C4 Emmen Switz.
172 B3 Emmendingen Ger.
169 E3 Emmer r. Ger.
164 G2 Emmer-Compascuum Neth.
164 F2 Emmer-Erfscheidenveen Neth.
169 B4 Emmerich Ger.
173 F3 Emmering Ger.
173 G3 Emmerting Ger.
85 F5 Emmet Qld Austr.
236 E3 Emmetsburg IA U.S.A.
238 C3 Emmett ID U.S.A.
232 B3 Emmett MI U.S.A.
114 C3 Emmiganuru Andhra Prad. India
232 E5 Emmitsburg MD U.S.A.
234 B3 Emmorton MD U.S.A.
151 H2 Emneth Norfolk, England U.K.
223 M5 Emo Ont. Can.
177 J4 Emőd Hungary
Emona Slovenia see Ljubljana
237 E5 Emory TX U.S.A.
237 C6 Emory Peak TX U.S.A.
206 B4 Empada Guinea-Bissau
242 C3 Empalme Mex.
244 D3 Empalme Escobedo Mex.
181 E4 Empanadas mt. Spain
215 H3 Empangeni S. Africa
258 F2 Empedrado Arg.
260 A4 Empedrado Chile
164 E3 Empel Neth.
266 G2 Emperor Seamount Chain sea feature N. Pacific Ocean
266 G2 Emperor Trough sea feature N. Pacific Ocean
172 C3 Empfingen Ger.
Empingham Reservoir England U.K. see Rutland Water
226 D3 Empire MI U.S.A.
191 F5 Empoli Italy
199 E3 Emponas Notio Aigaio Greece
199 D3 Emporeio Greece
236 D4 Emporia KS U.S.A.
232 E6 Emporia VA U.S.A.
232 D4 Emporium PA U.S.A.
223 I5 Empress Alta Can.
213 F3 Empress Mine Zimbabwe
165 E4 Emptinne Belgium
Empty Quarter des. Saudi Arabia see Rub' al Khālī
161 C3 Empurany France
168 C2 Ems r. Ger.
169 C3 Emsbüren Ger.
227 H3 Emsdale Ont. Can.
169 C3 Emsdetten Ger.
173 E2 Emskirchen Ger.
164 E2 Emst Neth.
168 D3 Emstek Ger.
151 G4 Emsworth Hampshire, England U.K.
215 H1 Emthonjeni S. Africa
168 D3 Emtinghausen Ger.
85 E3 Emu Creek r. Qld Austr.
138 F2 Emumägi hill Estonia
85 G4 Emu Park Qld Austr.
100 C1 Emur r. China
147 E2 Emyvale Rep. of Ireland
215 G2 Emzinoni S. Africa
104 D3 Ena Japan
140 K3 Enafors Sweden
250 D4 Enambú Col.
141 L3 Enånger Sweden
104 D3 Ena-san mt. Japan
186 D4 Encanadé mt. Spain
255 B9 Encantadas, Serra das hills Brazil
245 H5 Encantado r. Mex.
92 B3 Encanto, Cape Phil.
244 C3 Encarnación Mex.
253 G6 Encarnación Para.
206 E5 Enchi Ghana
185 I1 Encina r. Spain
186 B3 Encinacorba Spain
237 D6 Encinal TX U.S.A.
185 G2 Encinas mt. Spain
183 E4 Encinas de Abajo Spain
184 D2 Encinasola Spain
185 F3 Encinas Reales Spain
182 D2 Encinedo Spain
240 I5 Encinitas CA U.S.A.
239 F5 Encino NM U.S.A.
183 H2 Enciso Spain
82 D3 Encounter Bay S.A. Austr.
255 E5 Encruzilhada Brazil
255 B9 Encruzilhada do Sul Brazil
177 K3 Encs Hungary
177 L4 Encsencs Hungary
222 E4 Endako B.C. Can.
94 C2 Endau r. Malaysia
85 E1 Endeavour Strait Qld Austr.
142 D4 Endelave i. Denmark
77 I2 Enderbury i. Kiribati
222 G5 Enderby B.C. Can.
Enderby atoll Micronesia see Puluwat
151 F2 Enderby Leicestershire, England U.K.
264 L9 Enderby Abyssal Plain sea feature Southern Ocean
86 C4 Enderby Island W.A. Austr.
263 D2 Enderby Land reg. Antarctica
220 C3 Endicott Mountains AK U.S.A.
252 D2 Endimari r. Brazil
172 B3 Endingen Ger.
207 I6 Endom Cameroon
177 I3 Endrefalva Hungary
182 E4 Endrinal Spain
163 D6 Endron, Pique d' mt. France
227 I4 Endwell NY U.S.A.
252 B2 Ene r. Peru
87 B6 Eneabba W.A. Austr.
142 D2 Enebakk Norway
191 G3 Enego Italy
137 J5 Enem Rus. Fed.
EnenKio N. Pacific Ocean see Wake Atoll
121 I4 Energeticheskiy Kazakh.
120 D2 Energetik Rus. Fed.
Energodar Ukr. see Enerhodar
137 H4 Enerhodar Ukr.
176 G4 Enese Hungary
266 G6 Enewetak atoll Marshall Is
199 E1 Enez Turkey
182 B2 Enfesta Spain
225 I4 Enfield N.S. Can.
151 G3 Enfield Greater London, England U.K.
231 E4 Enfield NC U.S.A.
226 E2 Engadine MI U.S.A.
140 J3 Engan Norway
265 M3 Engaño, Cape Phil.
Engaños, Río de los r. Col. see Yari
215 F4 Engcobo S. Africa
169 C3 Engden Ger.
190 D2 Engelberg Switz.
231 F5 Engelhard NC U.S.A.
179 H2 Engelhartstetten Austria
179 E2 Engelhartszell Austria
168 D3 Engeln Ger.
120 A2 Engel's Saratovskaya Oblast' Rus. Fed.
173 G3 Engelsberg Ger.
164 D1 Engelschmangat sea chan. Neth.
171 D4 Engelsdorf Ger.
169 C5 Engelskirchen Ger.
172 C4 Engen Ger.
256 A5 Engenheiro Beltrão Brazil
257 F2 Engenheiro Navarro Brazil
169 D3 Enger Ger.
141 J3 Engerdal Norway
170 C3 Engersen Ger.
168 D1 Enge-Sande Ger.
94 C4 Enggano i. Indon.
203 H5 Enghershatu mt. Eritrea
165 D4 Enghien Belgium
222 C3 Engineer B.C. Can.
165 E4 Engis Belgium
149 H5 England admin. div. U.K.
225 K3 Englee Nfld. Can.
156 D2 Englefontaine France
224 E4 Englehart Ont. Can.
231 D7 Englewood FL U.S.A.
235 E2 Englewood NJ U.S.A.
232 A5 Englewood OH U.S.A.
223 M5 English r. Ont. Can.
230 C4 English IN U.S.A.
English Bazar W. Bengal India see Ingraj Bazar
234 A1 English Center PA U.S.A.
145 G7 English Channel France/U.K.
262 S2 English Coast Antarctica
234 D3 English Creek NJ U.S.A.
247 □2 English Harbour Town Antigua and Barbuda
235 D2 Englishtown NJ U.S.A.
163 D6 Engomer France
134 F2 Engozero Rus. Fed.
172 D3 Engstingen Ger.
187 C6 Enguera Spain
183 I5 Enguidanos Spain
138 D3 Engure Latvia
129 B2 Enguri r. Georgia
215 H3 Enhlalakahle S. Africa
237 D4 Enid OK U.S.A.
78 □3b Enigu i. Majuro Marshall Is
172 D3 Eningen unter Achalm Ger.
198 C2 Enipefs r. Greece
102 J2 Eniwa Japan
Eniwetok atoll Marshall Is see Enewetak
185 H4 Enix Spain
Enkeldoorn Zimbabwe see Chivhu
157 H3 Enkenbach Ger.
164 E2 Enkhuizen Neth.
172 B2 Enkirch Ger.
143 G2 Enköping Sweden
Enle Yunnan China see Zhenyuan
194 D5 Enna Sicilia Italy
194 D5 Enna prov. Sicilia Italy
190 E3 Enna r. Italy
203 F6 En Nahud Sudan
202 D5 Ennedi, Massif mts Chad
147 D3 Ennell, Lough l. Rep. of Ireland
169 C4 Ennepetal Ger.
215 F2 Ennerdale S. Africa
157 G3 Ennery France
246 D3 Ennery Haiti
160 B3 Ennezat France
83 F2 Enngonia N.S.W. Austr.
169 D4 Ennigerloh Ger.
123 H3 Enninabad Pak.
236 C2 Enning SD U.S.A.
147 C4 Ennis Rep. of Ireland
238 E2 Ennis MT U.S.A.
237 D5 Ennis TX U.S.A.
147 E4 Enniscorthy Rep. of Ireland
147 C5 Enniskean Rep. of Ireland
147 E3 Enniskerry Rep. of Ireland
147 D2 Enniskillen Northern Ireland U.K.
147 B4 Ennistymon Rep. of Ireland
78 □3a Enniwetak i. Kwajalein Marshall Is
128 B3 Enn Nâqoûra Lebanon
179 F2 Enns Austria
179 F2 Enns r. Austria
78 □3a Ennubuj i. Kwajalein Marshall Is
78 □3a Ennumennet i. Kwajalein Marshall Is
78 □3a Ennylabagan i. Kwajalein Marshall Is
140 O3 Eno Fin.
241 K3 Enoch UT U.S.A.
234 B2 Enola PA U.S.A.
140 O3 Enonkoski Fin.
140 M1 Enontekiö Fin.
231 D5 Enoree r. SC U.S.A.
233 G2 Enosburg Falls VT U.S.A.
109 E4 Enping Guangdong China
92 B2 Enrile Phil.
246 E3 Enriquillo Dom. Rep.
164 E2 Ens Neth.
83 F4 Ensay Vic. Austr.
164 F2 Enschede Neth.
173 F2 Ensdorf Ger.
169 D4 Ense Ger.
261 I4 Ensenada Arg.
242 A2 Ensenada Baja California Norte Mex.
242 C4 Ensenada Baja California Sur Mex.
247 □1 Ensenada Puerto Rico
172 B2 Ensheim Ger.
108 D2 Enshi Hubei China
104 D4 Enshū-nada g. Japan
157 H5 Ensisheim France
231 C6 Ensley FL U.S.A.
151 F3 Enstone Oxfordshire, England U.K.
161 D5 Ensuès-la-Redonne France
210 B4 Entebbe Uganda
164 F2 Enter Neth.
146 E6 Enterkinfoot Dumfries and Galloway, Scotland U.K.
222 G2 Enterprise N.W.T. Can.
227 I3 Enterprise Ont. Can.
231 C6 Enterprise AL U.S.A.
238 C2 Enterprise OR U.S.A.
241 K3 Enterprise UT U.S.A.
95 F2 Entimau, Bukit hill Sarawak Malaysia
190 D2 Entlebuch Switz.
190 C4 Entracque Italy
184 B3 Entradas Port.
161 C4 Entraigues-sur-Sorgues France
160 B1 Entrains-sur-Nohain France
159 F4 Entrammes France
222 G4 Entrance Alta Can.
84 B2 Entrance Island N.T. Austr.
161 E4 Entraunes France
161 A4 Entraygues-sur-Truyère France
261 H3 Entre Ríos prov. Arg.
252 D5 Entre Ríos Bol.
254 F4 Entre Rios Brazil
Entre Rios Moz. see Malema
257 E4 Entre Rios de Minas Brazil
161 E5 Entrevaux France
184 B1 Entroncamento Port.
215 H3 Entumeni S. Africa
207 G5 Enugu Nigeria
207 G5 Enugu state Nigeria
131 T3 Enurmino Rus. Fed.
182 C5 Envendos Port.
156 B3 Envermeu France
250 C3 Envigado Col.
252 C1 Envira Brazil
252 C1 Envira r. Brazil
177 H5 Enying Hungary
81 C5 Enys, Mount South I. N.Z.
172 D2 Enz r. Ger.
190 F4 Enza r. Italy
105 E3 Enzan Japan
179 H2 Enzersdorf an der Fischa Austria
172 C3 Enzklösterle Ger.
182 C1 Eo r. Spain
Eochaill Rep. of Ireland see Youghal
232 B6 Eolia KY U.S.A.
Eooa i. Tonga see Eua
146 B3 Eoropaidh Western Isles, Scotland U.K.
159 G2 Épaignes France
190 B2 Epalignes Switz.
245 E3 Epazoyucan Mex.
164 E2 Epe Neth.
207 F5 Epe Nigeria
208 C4 Epéna Congo
177 J5 Eperjes Hungary
156 D3 Épernay France
156 B4 Épernon France
172 C3 Epfendorf Ger.
199 E3 Ephesus tourist site Turkey
241 L2 Ephraim UT U.S.A.
234 B2 Ephrata PA U.S.A.
238 C2 Ephrata WA U.S.A.
78 □5 Épi i. Vanuatu
Epidamnus Albania see Durrës
198 C3 Epidavros tourist site Greece
156 B5 Épieds-en-Beauce France
161 E3 Épierre France
181 F2 Épila Spain
160 C2 Épinac France
157 G4 Épinal France
Epirus admin. reg. Greece see Ipeiros
160 B1 Epiry France
128 A2 Episkopi Cyprus
160 C1 Époisses France
193 F4 Epomeo, Monte hill Italy
172 A2 Eppelborn Ger.
172 C2 Eppelheim Ger.
172 B2 Eppenbrunn Ger.
171 E5 Eppendorf Ger.
172 C2 Eppertshausen Ger.
156 D3 Eppeville France
151 H3 Epping Essex, England U.K.
233 □H3 Epping NH U.S.A.
172 C2 Eppingen Ger.
173 E3 Eppishausen Ger.
169 D5 Eppstein Ger.
150 D2 Eppynt, Mynydd hills Wales U.K.
151 G3 Epsom Surrey, England U.K.
156 B3 Epte r. France
159 G4 Épuisay France
149 I4 Epworth North Lincolnshire, England U.K.

122 C4 Eqlīd Iran
208 D4 Équateur admin. reg. Dem. Rep. Congo
207 H6 Equatorial Guinea country Africa
158 E2 Équerdreville-Hainneville France
191 F5 Era r. Italy
191 H3 Eraclea Italy
191 H3 Eraclea Mare Italy
186 B1 Eracurri mt. Spain
92 A4 Eran Phil.
183 H1 Erandio Spain
116 C5 Erandol Mahar. India
215 G1 Erasmia S. Africa
Erawadi r. Myanmar see Irrawaddy
190 E3 Erba Italy
203 H4 Erba, Jebel mt. Sudan
126 E2 Erbaa Turkey
172 D3 Erbach Baden-Württemberg Ger.
172 D2 Erbach Hessen Ger.
172 E3 Erbendorf Ger.
172 B2 Erbeskopf hill Ger.
190 D3 Erbognone r. Italy
158 E4 Erbray France
128 A2 Ercan airport Cyprus
163 D6 Ercé France
127 F3 Erçek Turkey
260 A6 Ercilla Chile
127 F3 Erciş Turkey
126 D3 Erciyes Dağı mt. Turkey
177 H4 Ercsi Hungary
177 H4 Erd Hungary
140 N1 Erdalsfjellet hill Norway
Erdaobaihe Jilin China see Baihe
106 B5 Erdaogou Qinghai China
106 C4 Erdao Jiang r. China
171 C4 Erdeborn Ger.
199 E1 Erdek Turkey
126 D3 Erdemli Turkey
106 C1 Erdenet Hövsgöl Mongolia
106 E1 Erdenet Orhon Mongolia
106 D2 Erdenetsogt Bayanhongor Mongolia
106 E3 Erdenetsogt Ömnögovi Mongolia
158 C4 Erdeven France
173 F3 Erding Ger.
171 E5 Erdmannsdorf Ger.
135 I7 Erdniyevskiy Rus. Fed.
158 E4 Erdre r. France
173 F3 Erdweg Ger.
256 A6 Eré, Campos hills Brazil
158 D3 Éréac France
251 E3 Erebato r. Venez.
263 L1 Erebus, Mount vol. Antarctica
127 G5 Erech tourist site Iraq
255 B8 Erechim Brazil
127 G1 Ereentsav Mongolia
126 D3 Ereğli Turkey
126 C2 Ereğli Turkey
Erego Moz. see Errego
194 D5 Erei, Monti mts Sicilia Italy
Erementaū Kazakh. see Yereymentau
110 D3 Erenhaberga Shan mts China
107 G3 Erenhot Nei Mongol China
197 E4 Erenik r. Yugo.
129 C4 Erentepe Turkey
122 D3 Eresk Iran
183 F3 Eresma r. Spain
199 D2 Eresos Voreio Aigaio Greece
198 C2 Eretria Greece
Erevan Armenia see Yerevan
168 E1 Erfde Ger.
204 D3 Erfoud Morocco
169 B5 Erftstadt Ger.
171 C5 Erfurt Ger.
127 E3 Ergani Turkey
204 D5 Erg Atouila des. Mali
205 D4 'Erg Chech des. Alg./Mali
207 C6 Erg du Djourab des. Chad
207 H2 Erg du Ténéré des. Niger
107 F3 Ergel Mongolia
199 E1 Ergene r. Turkey
173 E2 Ergersheim Ger.
204 E4 Erg Iabès des. Alg.
204 D4 Erg Iguidi des. Alg./Maur.
205 E5 'Erg I-n-Sâkâne des. Mali
205 G4 Erg Issaouane des. Alg.
138 E3 Ērgļi Latvia
172 D4 Ergolding Ger.
173 G3 Ergoldsbach Ger.
163 E3 Ergué-Gabéric France
208 B2 Erguig r. Chad
107 I1 Ergun Nei Mongol China
Ergun He r. China/Rus. Fed. see Argun'
Ergun Youqi Nei Mongol China see Ergun
173 G3 Erharting Ger.
182 E2 Eria r. Spain
146 D3 Eriboll Highland, Scotland U.K.
146 D3 Eriboll, Loch inlet Scotland U.K.
164 F2 Erica Neth.
194 B4 Erice Sicilia Italy
183 I2 Erice Spain
184 A2 Ericeira Port.
146 E5 Ericht r. Scotland U.K.
146 D5 Ericht, Loch l. Scotland U.K.
223 L5 Erickson Man. Can.
231 E5 Erie KS U.S.A.
232 C3 Erie PA U.S.A.
227 G4 Erie, Lake Can./U.S.A.
Erieddu i. N. Male Maldives see Eriyadhu
206 D2 'Erîgât des. Mali
130 D2 Erik Eriksenstretet sea chan. Svalbard
223 L5 Eriksdale Man. Can.
143 F3 Eriksmåla Sweden
185 E2 Erillas hill Spain
227 G4 Erin Ont. Can.
231 C4 Erin TN U.S.A.
173 H3 Ering Ger.
143 F3 Eringsboda Sweden
146 A4 Eriskay i. Scotland U.K.
172 D4 Eriskirch Ger.
151 H2 Eriswell Suffolk, England U.K.
190 C1 Eriswil Switz.
Erithraí Greece see Erythres
Erithropótamos r. Greece see Erydropotamos
203 H6 Eritrea country Africa
113 □1 Eriyadhu i. N. Male Maldives
Eriyadu i. N. Male Maldives see Eriyadhu
169 B4 Erkelenz Ger.
156 C2 Erkelsbrugge France
129 B1 Erken-Shakhar Rus. Fed.
157 E3 Erkheim Ger.
129 G2 Erkmen Afyon Turkey
171 E3 Erkner Ger.
178 D3 Erl Austria
186 C2 Erla Spain
150 C1 Erlach Switz.
173 F2 Erlangen Ger.
109 D1 Erlangping Henan China
173 H3 Erlau r. Ger.
179 G2 Erlauf Austria
179 G2 Erlauf r. Austria
171 D5 Erlbach Ger.
84 C5 Erldunda N.T. Austr.
172 D2 Erlenbach am Main Ger.
169 D5 Erlensee Ger.
190 D4 Erli Italy
100 D4 Erlong Shan mt. China
234 D4 Erma NJ U.S.A.
Ermak Pavlodarskaya Oblast' Kazakh. see Aksu
164 E2 Ermelo Neth.
123 E3 Ermelo Port.
215 G2 Ermelo S. Africa
126 D3 Ermenek Turkey
128 A1 Ermenek r. Turkey
182 B3 Ermesinde Port.
187 D3 Ermidas de Sado Port.
198 C3 Ermioni Greece
244 C2 Ermita de los Correas Mex.
156 C4 Ermont France
198 D3 Ermoupoli Notio Aigaio Greece
172 D3 Erms r. Ger.
171 C4 Ermsleben Ger.
183 H1 Ermua Spain
82 C1 Ernabella S.A. Austr.
114 C4 Ernakulam Kerala India
169 D5 Erndtebrück Ger.
147 C2 Erne r. Rep. of Ireland/U.K.
159 F3 Ernée France
159 F3 Ernée r. France
87 D5 Ernest Giles Range hills W.A. Austr.
179 H2 Ernstbrunn Austria
172 A2 Ernz Noire r. Lux.
114 C4 Erode Tamil Nadu India
78 □3b Eroj i. Majuro Marshall Is
173 E3 Erolzheim Ger.
85 E5 Eromanga Qld Austr.
212 B4 Erongo admin. reg. Namibia
164 E3 Erp Neth.
177 K4 Érpatak Hungary
169 C5 Erpel Ger.
106 B3 Erpu Xinjiang China
Erqu Shaanxi China see Zhouzhi
165 D4 Erquelinnes Belgium
163 D3 Erquy France
87 B5 Errabiddy Hills W.A. Austr.
204 D3 Er Rachidia Morocco
203 F6 Er Rahad Sudan
146 B5 Erraid i. Scotland U.K.
204 E3 Er Raoui des. Alg.
186 B1 Errazu Spain
213 H3 Errego Moz.
147 C1 Errigal hill Rep. of Ireland
147 D4 Errill Rep. of Ireland
170 C1 Errindlev Denmark
190 D4 Erro r. Italy
186 B2 Erro r. Spain
146 E5 Errochty Water r. Scotland U.K.
146 D4 Errogie Highland, Scotland U.K.
233 □H2 Errol NH U.S.A.
78 □5 Erromango i. Vanuatu
Erronan i. Vanuatu see Futuna
210 B2 Er Roseires Sudan
177 H5 Érsekcsanád Hungary
198 B1 Ersekë Albania
177 I3 Érsekvadkert Hungary
169 F4 Ershausen Ger.
Ersis Turkey see Kılıçkaya
236 D2 Erskine MN U.S.A.
157 H4 Erstein France
190 D2 Erstfeld Switz.
210 D1 Erta Ale vol. Eth.
110 D4 Ertai Xinjiang China
135 H6 Ertil' Rus. Fed.
172 D3 Ertingen Ger.
Ertis Kazakh. see Irtyshsk
Ertis r. Kazakh./Rus. Fed. see Irtysh
110 D1 Ertix He r. China/Kazakh.
191 H2 Erto Italy
78 □3a Eru i. Kwajalein Marshall Is
92 D2 Erudina S.A. Austr.
207 G4 Erufu Nigeria
127 F3 Eruh Turkey
192 A4 Erula Sardegna Italy
207 F5 Eruwa Nigeria
258 G4 Erval Brazil
257 F4 Ervália Brazil
159 F4 Erve r. France
182 C3 Ervedosa do Douro Port.
183 B3 Ervidel Port.
156 C2 Ervillers France
182 C3 Ervões Port.
156 D4 Ervy-le-Châtel France
231 D4 Erwin TN U.S.A.
169 D4 Erwitte Ger.
170 C3 Erxleben Sachsen-Anhalt Ger.
171 C4 Erxleben Sachsen-Anhalt Ger.
199 E1 Erydropotamos r. Greece
199 D3 Erymanthos r. Greece
198 C2 Erythres Greece
108 A3 Eryuan Yunnan China
196 D5 Erzen r. Albania
Erzerum Turkey see Erzurum
171 E5 Erzgebirge mts Czech Rep./Ger.
100 C2 Erzhan Heilong. China
172 C2 Erzhausen Ger.
106 B1 Erzin Rus. Fed.
126 E3 Erzin Turkey
126 E3 Erzincan Turkey
129 A4 Erzincan prov. Turkey
127 F3 Erzurum Turkey
129 B3 Erzurum prov. Turkey
191 H5 Esanatoglia Italy
193 G5 Esaro r. Italy
193 I5 Esaro r. Italy
102 J4 Esashi Japan
142 C4 Esbjerg Denmark
142 C4 Esbjerg airport Denmark
156 C4 Esbly France
Esbo Fin. see Espoo
254 G4 Escada Brazil
182 C3 Escairón Spain
92 B4 Escalante Phil.
183 G1 Escalante Spain
241 L3 Escalante UT U.S.A.
241 L3 Escalante r. UT U.S.A.
241 K3 Escalante Desert UT U.S.A.
192 B5 Escalaplano Sardegna Italy
182 D4 Escalhão Port.
163 A5 Escalles, Pic des mt. France
186 E2 Escaló Spain
187 E6 Es Caló Spain
244 D2 Escalón Mex.
240 G3 Escalon CA U.S.A.
183 F4 Escalona Spain
183 F3 Escalona del Prado Spain
182 C5 Escalos de Baixo Port.
182 C5 Escalos de Cima Port.
183 H3 Escalote r. Spain
231 C6 Escambia r. FL U.S.A.
183 F4 Escamilla Spain
226 D3 Escanaba MI U.S.A.
185 B3 Escandorgue ridge France
185 F3 Escañuela Spain
183 B3 Escárcega Mex.
183 G4 Escariche Spain
182 C4 Escarigo Port.
186 B2 Escaroz Spain
163 D5 Escatalens France
186 C3 Escatrón Spain
156 D2 Escaudain France
164 C4 Escaut r. Belgium
165 C3 Esch Neth.
173 E4 Eschach r. Ger.
156 D4 Eschau France
172 D2 Eschau Ger.
168 C3 Eschborn Ger.
168 B3 Esche Ger.
168 F2 Escheburg Ger.
168 C3 Eschede Ger.
190 D1 Eschenbach Switz.
173 F2 Eschenbach in der Oberpfalz Ger.
169 D5 Eschenburg-Eibelshausen Ger.
169 E4 Eschenstruth (Helsa) Ger.
169 E4 Eschershausen Ger.
178 C4 Escholzmatt Switz.
172 E3 Eschlkam Ger.
190 C2 Escholzmatt Switz.
165 E5 Esch-sur-Alzette Lux.
165 E5 Esch-sur-Sûre Lux.
169 F4 Eschwege Ger.
169 B5 Eschweiler Ger.
247 E3 Escocesa, Bahía b. Dom. Rep.
252 C3 Escoma Bol.
252 C7 Escombreras Spain
237 C6 Escondido r. Mex.
242 □J6 Escondido r. Nic.
240 I5 Escondido CA U.S.A.
187 F5 Escorca Spain
186 D2 Escorihuela Spain
163 A5 Escos France
163 E6 Escouloubre France
163 A4 Escource France
163 A4 Escource r. France
165 E4 Escragnolles France
186 C4 Escucha Spain
241 M5 Escudilla mt. AZ U.S.A.
244 B2 Escuinapa Mex.
243 H6 Escuintla Guat.
243 G6 Escuintla Mex.
250 D2 Escuque Venez.
184 E1 Escurial Spain
183 E6 Escuriza r. Spain
160 B2 Escurolles France
256 D2 Escurso r. Brazil
182 B2 Escusa Spain
183 F4 Escusa mt. Spain
183 F5 Escúzar Spain
207 H6 Eséka Cameroon
131 O3 Esen-Khayya Rus. Fed.
199 F3 Eşen Turkey
199 F3 Eşen r. Turkey
199 F1 Esence Turkey
129 A4 Esence Dağları mts Turkey
129 D4 Eşengöl Dağı mt. Iran/Turkey
122 C2 Esenguly Turkm.
199 F1 Esenköy Turkey
128 B1 Esenpınar Turkey
168 C2 Esens Ger.
199 F1 Esenyurt Turkey
186 D2 Esera r. Spain
122 B3 Esfahān Iran
122 C3 Eşfahān prov. Iran
122 D2 Esfarayen, Reshteh-ye mts Iran
182 B2 Esfarrapada Spain
182 C2 Esgos Spain
183 F3 Esgueva r. Spain
183 F3 Esguevillas de Esgueva Spain
108 B3 Eshan Yunnan China
151 G3 Esher Surrey, England U.K.
129 B2 Eshera Georgia
215 H3 Eshowe S. Africa
213 F4 Esigodini Zimbabwe
215 I3 Esikhawini S. Africa
Esil Kazakh. see Yesil'
Esil r. Kazakh./Rus. Fed. see Ishim
191 I5 Esino r. Italy
128 B3 Eskiçöllü Tepe mt. Turkey
215 H2 eSizameleni S. Africa
85 H5 Esk Qld Austr.
83 F5 Esk r. Tas. Austr.
149 F3 Esk r. Cumbria, England U.K.
149 F3 Esk r. England/Scotland U.K.
80 F3 Eskdale North I. N.Z.
148 E2 Eskdalemuir Dumfries and Galloway, Scotland U.K.
225 H2 Esker Nfld. Can.
137 I3 Eskhar Ukr.
140 □D2 Eskifjörður Iceland
199 F2 Eski Gediz Turkey
142 D3 Eskilstrup Denmark
143 G2 Eskilstuna Sweden
220 E3 Eskimo Lakes N.W.T. Can.
Eskimo Point Nunavut Can. see Arviat
127 F3 Eski Mosul Iraq
121 H4 Eski-Nookat Kyrg.
126 D2 Eskipazar Turkey
199 G2 Eskişehir Turkey
199 G2 Eskişehir prov. Turkey
183 D3 Esla r. Spain
Eslāmābād Iran see Rīcobayo, Embalse de
122 A3 Eslāmābād-e Gharb Iran
173 G2 Eslarn Ger.
183 I2 Eslava Spain
129 B3 Esler Dağı mt. Turkey
169 D4 Eslohe (Sauerland) Ger.
142 E4 Eslöv Sweden
129 F2 Eşme Turkey
129 C3 Eşmeçayır Turkey
246 C3 Esmeralda Chile
246 C2 Esmeralda Cuba
259 B8 Esmeralda, Isla i. Chile
257 E3 Esmeraldas Brazil
250 B4 Esmeraldas Ecuador
250 B4 Esmeraldas prov. Ecuador
252 D3 Esmeraldo r. Bol.
186 □ Es Migjorn Gran Spain
232 D6 Esmont VA U.S.A.
182 B4 Esmoriz Port.
156 D2 Esnes France
165 E4 Esneux Belgium
187 C5 Espadán mt. Spain
183 D3 Espadañedo Spain
122 E5 Espakeh Iran
Espalha r. Brazil see São Francisco
161 A4 Espalion France
161 B3 Espaly-St-Marcel France
España country Europe see Spain
227 G2 Espanola Ont. Can.
239 F4 Espanola NM U.S.A.
250 □ Española, Isla i. Islas Galápagos Ecuador
182 C3 Esparragalejo Spain
185 E2 Esparragosa Spain
186 E3 Esparraguera Spain
161 D5 Esparron France
127 H3 Esparto Hond
240 F2 Esparto CA U.S.A.
186 B2 Esparza de Salazar Spain
121 H4 Espe Kazakh.
182 D4 Espeja Spain
183 G3 Espeja de San Marcelino Spain
185 F3 Espejo Spain
183 G3 Espejón Spain
164 E2 Espel Neth.
163 A5 Espelette France
169 D3 Espelkamp Ger.
169 E4 Espenau Ger.
169 E4 Espenau Ger.
184 C1 Esperança Port.
256 B6 Esperança, Serra da mts Brazil
87 D7 Esperance W.A. Austr.
87 D7 Esperance Bay W.A. Austr.
197 D1 Esperantinópolis Brazil
254 D2 Esperanza research stn Antarctica
261 G2 Esperanza Arg.
245 F4 Esperanza Puebla Mex.
242 C3 Esperanza Sonora Mex.
252 C3 Esperanza Peru
92 C4 Esperanza Phil.
247 □1 Esperanza Puerto Rico
163 E6 Espéraza France
193 F3 Esperia Italy
163 E6 Espezel France
186 B2 Espichel, Cabo c. Port.
185 F2 Espiel Spain
255 C8 Espigão, Serra do mts Brazil
183 F2 Espigüete mt. Spain
183 F1 Espinama Spain
161 E4 Espinasses France
243 E5 Espinazo Mex.
245 G5 Espinazo del Diablo, Sierra mts Mex.
257 F2 Espinhaço, Serra do mts Brazil
182 B4 Espinhal Port.
184 C2 Espinheira hill Port.
182 B3 Espinho Port.
255 B9 Espinilho, Serra do hills Brazil
183 F1 Espinilla Spain
255 E5 Espinosa Brazil
183 G3 Espinosa de Cerrato Spain
183 G3 Espinosa de Henares Spain
183 G1 Espinosa de los Monteros Spain
183 F5 Espinoso del Rey Spain
163 E6 Espira-de-l'Agly France
Espírito Santo Brazil see Vila Velha
257 G3 Espírito Santo state Brazil
184 C3 Espírito Santo Port.
92 B2 Espiritu Phil.
78 □5 Espiritu Santo i. Vanuatu
243 I5 Espíritu Santo, Bahía del b. Mex.
243 H4 Espita Mex.
182 B5 Espite Port.
254 F4 Esplanada Brazil
183 H4 Esplegares Spain
186 F3 Esplugues de Llobregat Spain
186 D3 Esplús Spain
186 G2 Espolla Spain
186 B2 Espondeilham France
186 F2 Esponellà Spain
141 N3 Espoo Fin.
187 F5 Esporles Spain
182 B3 Esposende Port.
186 E2 Espot Spain
160 E1 Esprels France
245 F5 Espuña mt. Spain
213 G4 Espungabera Moz.
234 B1 Espy PA U.S.A.
259 C6 Esquel Arg.
222 F5 Esquimalt B.C. Can.
261 H2 Esquina Arg.
243 H6 Esquipulas Guat.
183 G4 Esquivias Spain
140 M2 Esrange Sweden
204 C3 Essaouira Morocco
156 C3 Essay France
205 E5 Essé Cameroon
168 E3 Essel Ger.
204 C4 Es Semara Western Sahara
165 D3 Essen Belgium
169 C4 Essen Ger.
168 C3 Essen (Oldenburg) Ger.
173 G3 Essenbach Ger.
87 D5 Essendon, Mount hill W.A. Austr.
160 E1 Essert France
227 F4 Essex Ont. Can.
151 H3 Essex admin. div. England U.K.
241 J4 Essex CA U.S.A.
233 □ Essex CT U.S.A.
233 H3 Essex MA U.S.A.
234 B3 Essex MD U.S.A.
233 G2 Essex NY U.S.A.
235 D2 Essex County county NJ U.S.A.
233 G2 Essex Junction VT U.S.A.
Essexvale Zimbabwe see Esigodini
227 F4 Essexville MI U.S.A.
173 E3 Essingen Ger.
150 E2 Essington Staffordshire, England U.K.
172 D3 Esslingen am Neckar Ger.
131 Q4 Esso Rus. Fed.
156 D3 Essômes-sur-Marne France
156 C4 Essonne dept Île-de-France France
156 C4 Essonne r. France
156 E4 Essoyes France
207 H5 Essu Cameroon
138 F2 Essu Estonia
203 G6 Es Suki Sudan
207 I5 Est prov. Cameroon
182 C1 Estaca de Bares, Punta da pt Spain
241 J5 Estación Coahuila Mex.
185 G2 Estación de Baeza Spain
186 D2 Estadilla Spain
163 E6 Estagel France
122 C4 Eşţahbān Iran
161 A4 Estaing France
227 G2 Estaire Ont. Can.
156 C2 Estaires France
254 F4 Estância Brazil
239 F5 Estancia NM U.S.A.
122 E4 Estand, Kūh-e mt. Iran
163 B5 Estang France
185 F5 Estany de Mitjorn Spain
182 B4 Estarreja Port.
186 C2 Estarrón r. Spain
186 E2 Estats, Pic d' mt. France/Spain
190 B2 Estavayer-le-Lac Switz.
215 G3 Estcourt S. Africa
182 E2 Este r. Ger.
191 G3 Este Italy
247 □1 Este, Punta pt Puerto Rico
182 D3 Esteban hill Spain
170 C3 Estedt Ger.
246 B3 Esteli Nic.
183 H2 Estella Spain
234 D3 Estell Manor NJ U.S.A.
184 D1 Estena hill Spain
185 F1 Estena r. Spain
173 E2 Estenfeld Ger.
185 F3 Estepa Spain
182 C3 Estepar Spain
185 E4 Estepona Spain
185 F2 Esteras r. Spain
183 H3 Esteras de Medinaceli Spain
186 C4 Estercuel Spain
161 E4 Esterel reg. France
163 A5 Estérençuby France
173 F4 Estergebirge mts Ger.
223 K5 Esterhazy Sask. Can.
156 D4 Esternay France
179 E2 Esternberg Austria
240 C4 Estero Bay CA U.S.A.
190 C5 Esteron r. Italy
186 E2 Esterri d'Àneu Spain
168 C3 Esterwegen Ger.
238 F3 Estes Park CO U.S.A.
250 A1 Este Sudeste, Cayos del is Col.
223 K5 Estevan Sask. Can.
236 E3 Estherville IA U.S.A.
161 C3 Estiavreilles France
231 D5 Estill SC U.S.A.
163 C4 Estillac France
156 D4 Estinnes-au-Mont Belgium
156 D4 Estissac France
156 D5 Estiva Brazil
254 D3 Estiva r. Brazil
160 A2 Estivareilles France
187 C5 Estivella Spain
182 B4 Estiz Port.
182 B3 Estômbar Port.
223 I5 Eston Sask. Can.
149 H3 Eston Redcar and Cleveland, England U.K.
138 E2 Estonia country Europe
Estonskaya S.S.R. country Europe see Estonia
168 E2 Estorf Niedersachsen Ger.
168 E3 Estorf Niedersachsen Ger.
184 A2 Estoril Port.
163 E5 Estoublon France
160 C3 Estrablin France
156 C3 Estrées-St-Denis France
182 C5 Estreito Port.
184 □ Estreito da Calheta Madeira
184 C2 Estrela Port.
182 C4 Estrela, Serra da mts Port.
257 E3 Estrela do Indaiá Brazil
256 D3 Estrela do Sul Brazil
185 G2 Estrella mt. Spain
241 K5 Estrella, Sierra mts AZ U.S.A.
183 G4 Estremera Spain
184 C2 Estremoz Port.
183 H3 Estriégala Spain
226 C4 Estrigon r. France
224 D4 Estrondo, Serra hills Brazil
206 A4 Estuaire prov. Gabon
122 B3 Estūh Iran
Esu Cameroon see Essu
159 G4 Esvres France
177 K4 Esztár Hungary
177 H4 Esztergom Hungary
156 D3 Étables-sur-Mer France
82 D2 Etadunna S.A. Austr.
156 D2 Étagnac France
116 D4 Etah Uttar Prad. India
157 F3 Étain France
160 B1 Étais-la-Sauvin France
156 C3 Étalante France
165 D5 Étalle Belgium
225 J3 Étamamiou Que. Can.
156 C4 Étampes France
156 C3 Etamunbanie, Lake salt flat S.A. Austr.
160 C2 Étang-sur-Arroux France
156 B2 Étaples France
162 A3 Étaules France
162 B3 Étauliers France
116 D4 Etawah Uttar Prad. India
116 D4 Etawah Rajasthan India
78 □3a Etchojoa Mex.
158 C4 Étel France
141 N3 Etelä-Suomi prov. Fin.
160 E1 Eternoz France
215 H2 eThandakukhanya S. Africa
165 E5 Ethe Belgium
223 K5 Ethelbert Man. Can.
86 D4 Ethel Creek W.A. Austr.
85 E2 Ethel Creek r. Qld Austr.
214 D3 E'Thembini S. Africa
85 E3 Etheridge r. Qld Austr.
210 C3 Ethiopia country Africa
199 E2 Etili Turkey
126 D3 Etimesğut Turkey
157 F3 Étival France
157 G4 Étival-Clairefontaine France
146 C5 Etive, Loch inlet Scotland U.K.
156 E5 Étivey France
245 F5 Etla Mex.
141 J3 Etna r. Norway
195 E5 Etna, Monte vol. Sicilia Italy
Etna, Mount vol. Sicilia Italy see Etna, Monte
142 A2 Etne Norway
227 H4 Etobicoke Ont. Can.
160 B4 Étoges France
161 C4 Étoile-sur-Rhône France
85 G4 Eton Qld Austr.
151 G3 Eton Windsor and Maidenhead, England U.K.
Etorofu-tō i. Kuril'skiye O-va Rus. Fed. see Iturup, Ostrov
212 C3 Etosha Pan salt pan Namibia
208 B4 Etoumbi Congo
235 D2 Etra NJ U.S.A.
156 C4 Étréchy France
Etrek r. Iran/Turkm. see Atrek
156 B3 Étrépagny France
159 G2 Étretat France
159 F3 Étreux France
190 G4 Etropole Bulg.
190 C3 Etroubles Italy
163 B6 Etsaut France
165 F5 Ettelbruck Lux.
78 □4a Etten i. Chuuk Micronesia
78 □4a Etten i. Chuuk Micronesia
172 B3 Ettenheim Ger.
164 D3 Etten-Leur Neth.
146 D4 Etteridge Highland, Scotland U.K.
171 C4 Ettersburg Ger.
151 F2 Ettington Warwickshire, England U.K.
172 C3 Ettlingen Ger.
146 E6 Ettrick Scottish Borders, Scotland U.K.
149 G2 Ettrickbridge Scottish Borders, Scotland U.K.
146 E6 Ettrick Forest reg. Scotland U.K.
146 F6 Ettrick Water r. Scotland U.K.
169 C5 Ettringen Ger.
114 C4 Ettumanur Kerala India
160 D1 Étuz France
151 F2 Etwall Derbyshire, England U.K.
186 B1 Etxalar Spain
Etxarri Spain see Echarri
Etxarri-Aranatz Spain see Echarri-Aranaz
244 B3 Etzatlán Mex.
223 I5 Eucalypt Coulee r. Alta Can.
156 B2 Eu France
79 □2a Eua i. Tonga
83 F3 Euabalong N.S.W. Austr.
172 D2 Eubigheim Ger.
Euboea i. Greece see Evvoia
87 F6 Eucla W.A. Austr.
232 C4 Euclid OH U.S.A.
254 F4 Euclides da Cunha Brazil
256 A5 Euclides da Cunha Paulista Brazil
83 G4 Eucumbene, Lake N.S.W. Austr.
237 F5 Eudora AR U.S.A.
82 D3 Eudunda S.A. Austr.
169 F5 Euerbach Ger.
169 F5 Euerdorf Ger.
231 C6 Eufaula AL U.S.A.
237 E5 Eufaula OK U.S.A.
237 E5 Eufaula Lake resr OK U.S.A.
178 E3 Eugendorf Austria
238 B2 Eugene OR U.S.A.
253 F2 Eugênia r. Brazil
163 B5 Eugénie-les-Bains France
83 G3 Eugowra N.S.W. Austr.
183 H2 Eulate Spain
83 F2 Eulo Qld Austr.
182 C1 Eume r. Spain
85 G4 Eungella Qld Austr.
237 E6 Eunice LA U.S.A.
237 C5 Eunice NM U.S.A.
165 F4 Eupen Belgium
171 D4 Euper Ger.
118 D2 Euphrates r. Asia
alt. Al Furāt (Iraq/Syria),
alt. Fırat (Turkey)
237 F5 Eupora MS U.S.A.
141 M3 Eura Fin.
141 M3 Eurajoki Fin.
173 F3 Eurasburg Bayern Ger.
173 F4 Eurasburg Bayern Ger.
179 F2 Euratsfeld Austria
156 B3 Eure dept Haute-Normandie France
156 B3 Eure r. France
156 B4 Eure-et-Loir dept Centre France
238 A3 Eureka CA U.S.A.
237 D4 Eureka KS U.S.A.
238 D1 Eureka MT U.S.A.
241 J2 Eureka NV U.S.A.
232 B5 Eureka OH U.S.A.
236 D2 Eureka SD U.S.A.
241 L2 Eureka UT U.S.A.
221 J2 Eureka Sound sea chan. Nunavut Can.
237 E4 Eureka Springs AR U.S.A.
240 I3 Eureka Valley CA U.S.A.
83 E2 Euriowie N.S.W. Austr.
83 F4 Euroa Vic. Austr.
85 E4 Eurombah Qld Austr.
85 G5 Eurombah Creek r. Qld Austr.
201 H6 Europa, Île i. Indian Ocean
183 E1 Europa, Picos de mts Spain
132 Europe continent
164 D3 Europoort reg. Neth.
157 F4 Eurville-Bienville France
169 B5 Euskirchen Ger.
169 E5 Eußenheim Ger.
231 D6 Eustis FL U.S.A.
83 E3 Euston N.S.W. Austr.
231 C5 Eutaw AL U.S.A.
168 F1 Eutin Ger.
171 D4 Eutingen im Gäu Ger.
223 G4 Eutsuk Lake B.C. Can.
157 F4 Euville France
84 C3 Eva Downs N.T. Austr.
190 C3 Evançon r. Italy
215 G2 Evander S. Africa
222 H4 Evansburg Alta Can.
232 C4 Evans City PA U.S.A.
234 B1 Evans Falls PA U.S.A.
221 J3 Evans Strait Nunavut Can.
226 D4 Evanston IL U.S.A.
238 E3 Evanston WY U.S.A.
224 D4 Evansville Ont. Can.
230 C4 Evansville IN U.S.A.
226 C4 Evansville WI U.S.A.
238 F3 Evansville WY U.S.A.
237 D6 Evant TX U.S.A.
146 D4 Evanton Highland, Scotland U.K.
Eva Perón Arg. see La Plata
Eva Perón prov. Arg. see La Pampa
226 E4 Evart MI U.S.A.
215 F2 Evaton S. Africa
160 A2 Évaux-les-Bains France
122 C5 Evaz Iran
129 D4 Evci Turkey
199 F2 Eveiler Turkey
172 C3 Evcili Turkey
236 E2 Eveleth MN U.S.A.
237 F4 Evening Shade AR U.S.A.
131 R3 Evensk Rus. Fed.
140 L1 Evenskjær Norway
82 C2 Everard, Lake salt flat S.A. Austr.
84 C4 Everard, Mount N.T. Austr.
82 C1 Everard, Mount S.A. Austr.
82 C1 Everard Range hills S.A. Austr.
150 E3 Evercreech Somerset, England U.K.
164 E2 Everdingen Neth.
Everek Turkey see Develi
117 F4 Everest, Mount China/Nepal
233 □J1 Everett N.B. Can.
232 D4 Everett PA U.S.A.
238 B1 Everett WA U.S.A.
165 C3 Evergem Belgium
231 D7 Everglades swamp FL U.S.A.
231 D7 Everglades City FL U.S.A.
231 C6 Evergreen AL U.S.A.
228 D7 Everman, Volcán vol. Mex.
238 B1 Everson WA U.S.A.
251 G3 Everton Guyana
143 E2 Evertsberg Sweden
85 E4 Evesham Qld Austr.
151 F2 Evesham Worcestershire, England U.K.
151 F2 Evesham, Vale of val. England U.K.
169 F3 Evessen Ger.
160 E2 Évian-les-Bains France
140 M3 Evijärvi Fin.
207 H6 Evinayong Equat. Guinea
203 G6 Evington VA U.S.A.
198 B2 Evinos r. Greece
163 E5 Evisa Corse France
142 B2 Evje Norway
190 C2 Evolène Switz.
184 C2 Évora Port.
184 C2 Évora admin. dist. Port.
184 C2 Évora-Monte Port.
198 C1 Evosmo Greece
122 A2 Evowghlī Iran
158 E3 Évran France
159 E4 Évre r. France
159 F2 Évrecy France
156 B3 Évreux France
159 F3 Évron France
199 E1 Evros r. Greece/Turkey
198 C3 Evrotas r. Greece
156 C4 Évry France
198 D2 Evvoia i. Greece
198 C1 Evzonoi Kentriki Makedonia Greece
240 □ Ewa HI U.S.A.
240 □ Ewa Beach HI U.S.A.
85 F3 Ewan Qld Austr.
246 □ Ewarton Jamaica
210 D4 Ewaso Ngiro r. Kenya
214 D2 Ewbank S. Africa
146 C4 Ewe, Loch b. Scotland U.K.
151 G3 Ewell Surrey, England U.K.
226 C2 Ewen MI U.S.A.
Ewenkizu Zizhiqi Nei Mongol China see Bayan Tohoi
151 G3 Ewhurst Surrey, England U.K.
234 D2 Ewing NJ U.S.A.
262 T2 Ewing Island Antarctica
208 B5 Ewo Congo
198 C3 Examilia Peloponnisos Greece
215 F3 Excelsior S. Africa
240 H2 Excelsior Mountain CA U.S.A.
240 H2 Excelsior Mountains NV U.S.A.
236 E4 Excelsior Springs MO U.S.A.
234 B1 Exchange PA U.S.A.
162 D3 Excideuil France
150 D4 Exe r. England U.K.
150 D3 Exebridge Somerset, England U.K.
262 P1 Executive Committee Range mts Antarctica
226 B3 Exeland WI U.S.A.
83 G3 Exeter N.S.W. Austr.
227 G4 Exeter Ont. Can.
150 D4 Exeter Devon, England U.K.
240 H3 Exeter CA U.S.A.
233 □H3 Exeter NH U.S.A.
161 E3 Exilles Italy
164 F2 Exloo Neth.
159 G3 Exmes France
150 D4 Exminster Devon, England U.K.
150 D3 Exmoor hills England U.K.
150 D3 Exmoor National Park England U.K.
233 F6 Exmore VA U.S.A.
86 B4 Exmouth W.A. Austr.
150 D4 Exmouth Devon, England U.K.
83 G2 Exmouth, Mount N.S.W. Austr.
86 B4 Exmouth Gulf W.A. Austr.
265 L6 Exmouth Plateau sea feature Indian Ocean
85 G5 Expedition Range mts Qld Austr.
225 K3 Exploits r. Nfld. Can.
222 H5 Exshaw Alta Can.
234 C2 Exton PA U.S.A.
237 E5 Extoraz r. Mex.
182 G5 Extremadura aut. comm. Spain
207 I4 Extrême-Nord prov. Cameroon
182 B3 Extremo Port.
246 C1 Exuma Cays is Bahamas
246 C1 Exuma Sound sea chan. Bahamas
135 G7 Eya r. Rus. Fed.
149 H4 Eyam Derbyshire, England U.K.
211 B5 Eyasi, Lake salt l. Tanz.
Eyawadi r. Myanmar see Irrawaddy
161 D3 Eybens France
162 D3 Eyburie France
163 D6 Eycheil France
142 C2 Eydehavn Norway
168 D3 Eydelstedt Ger.
151 G2 Eye Peterborough, England U.K.
151 I2 Eye Suffolk, England U.K.
134 M2 Eyelenoborsk Rus. Fed.
146 F6 Eyemouth Scottish Borders, Scotland U.K.
146 B3 Eye Peninsula Scotland U.K.
147 B5 Eyeries Rep. of Ireland
161 D4 Eygues r. France
161 D4 Eyguians France
161 D5 Eyguières France
162 D3 Eygurande France
162 C3 Eygurande-et-Gardedeuil France
140 □C3 Eyjafjallajökull ice cap Iceland
140 □C2 Eyjafjörður inlet Iceland
210 F3 Eyl Somalia
Eylau Rus. Fed. see Bagrationovsk
163 C4 Eymet France
162 D3 Eymoutiers France
151 H3 Eynsford Kent, England U.K.
151 F3 Eynsham Oxfordshire, England U.K.
161 C5 Eyragues France
162 B3 Eyrans France
163 A4 Eyre r. France
82 D2 Eyre, Lake salt flat S.A. Austr.
147 C3 Eyrecourt Rep. of Ireland
84 D5 Eyre Creek watercourse Qld Austr.
162 D3 Eyrein France
81 B6 Eyre Mountains South I. N.Z.
81 B6 Eyre Peak South I. N.Z.
82 C3 Eyre Peninsula S.A. Austr.
161 C4 Eyrieux r. France
163 B4 Eysines France
157 F3 Eysturoy i. Faroe Is
130 A3 Eysturoy i. Faroe Is
144 D1 Eysturoy i. Faroe Is
151 I3 Eythorne Kent, England U.K.
207 H5 Eyumojok Cameroon
122 C3 Eyvānakī Iran
160 C3 Eyzin-Pinet France
215 H3 Ezakheni S. Africa
215 G2 eZamokuhle S. Africa
183 H2 Ezcaray Spain
186 B1 Ezcurra Spain
161 F5 Èze France
186 B6 Ezel KY U.S.A.
215 G2 Ezenzeleni S. Africa
260 C6 Ezequiel Ramos Mexía, Embalse resr Arg.
109 E2 Ezhou Hubei China
134 J3 Ezhva Respublika Komi Rus. Fed.
199 F2 Ezine Denizli Turkey
199 E2 Ezine Turkey
126 E2 Ezinepazar Turkey
Ezo i. Japan see Hokkaidō
128 A2 Ezousa r. Cyprus
127 G5 Ezra's Tomb tourist site Iraq
156 B4 Ézy-sur-Eure France

F

114 B5 Faadhippolhu Atoll Maldives
113 D10 Faadhippolhu Atoll Maldives
210 D4 Faafxadhuun Somalia
Faaraava atoll Arch. des Tuamotu Fr. Polynesia see Fakarava
186 D3 Fabara Spain
163 D5 Fabas France
239 F6 Fabens TX U.S.A.
182 D2 Fabero Spain
177 I4 Fábiánháza Hungary
175 H3 Fabianki Pol.
177 J5 Fábiánsebestyén Hungary
142 D4 Fåborg Denmark
177 I3 Fabova hoľa mt. Slovakia
161 B5 Fabrègues France
191 H5 Fabriano Italy
193 E2 Fabrica di Roma Italy
185 H2 Fábricas de San Juan de Alcaraz Spain
195 F4 Fabrizia Italy
192 E2 Fabro Italy
250 C3 Facatativá Col.
182 B3 Facha Port.
184 E4 Facinas Spain
85 G4 Facing Island Qld Austr.
234 C1 Factoryville PA U.S.A.
184 C1 Fadagosa Port.
207 F3 Fada-Ngourma Burkina
177 H5 Fadd Hungary
205 H4 Fadnoun, Plateau du Alg.
191 I2 Faedis Italy
191 G4 Faenza Italy
Færoerne terr. N. Atlantic Ocean see Faroe Islands
Faeroes terr. N. Atlantic Ocean see Faroe Islands
Faesulae Italy see Fiesole
192 D2 Faete, Monte hill Italy
208 C3 Fafa r. C.A.R.
182 B3 Fafe Port.
191 I2 Fagagna Italy
197 G3 Făgăraş Romania
Fagatau atoll Arch. des Tuamotu Fr. Polynesia see Fangatau
78 □2 Fagatogo American Samoa
141 J3 Fagernes Norway
143 F2 Fagersta Sweden
197 F3 Făget Romania
193 I5 Fagnano Castello Italy
165 D4 Fagne reg. Belgium
156 E4 Fagnières France
206 D2 Faguibine, Lac l. Mali
147 B4 Fahan Rep. of Ireland
168 E1 Fahrdorf Ger.
168 F2 Fahrenkrug Ger.
173 F2 Fahrenzhausen Ger.
171 E3 Fahrland Ger.
125 G3 Fahūd, Jabal hill Oman
210 E4 Faial i. Azores
184 □ Faial Madeira
216 □1c Faial, Canal do sea chan. Azores
193 G3 Faicchio Italy
78 □4a Faichuk is Chuuk Micronesia
169 C5 Faid Ger.
190 D2 Faido Switz.
182 D3 Failde Port.
165 E4 Faimes Belgium
160 C1 Fain-lès-Montbard France
157 F4 Fains-Véel France
220 D3 Fairbanks AK U.S.A.
232 A5 Fairborn OH U.S.A.
236 D3 Fairbury NE U.S.A.
226 B3 Fairchild WI U.S.A.
81 B7 Fairfax South I. N.Z.
232 E5 Fairfax VA U.S.A.
233 G2 Fairfax VT U.S.A.
81 C6 Fairfield South I. N.Z.
240 F2 Fairfield CA U.S.A.
235 E1 Fairfield CT U.S.A.
236 F3 Fairfield IA U.S.A.
238 D3 Fairfield ID U.S.A.
236 F4 Fairfield IL U.S.A.
232 A5 Fairfield OH U.S.A.
237 D6 Fairfield TX U.S.A.
241 K1 Fairfield UT U.S.A.
232 D6 Fairfield VA U.S.A.
235 E1 Fairfield County county CT U.S.A.
151 F3 Fairford Gloucestershire, England U.K.
227 F4 Fairgrove MI U.S.A.
233 H4 Fairhaven MA U.S.A.
233 G2 Fair Haven NJ U.S.A.
233 G3 Fair Haven VT U.S.A.
234 C3 Fair Hill MD U.S.A.
146 □G2 Fair Isle i. Scotland U.K.
235 D2 Fair Lawn NJ U.S.A.
234 B3 Fairlee MD U.S.A.
233 G3 Fairlee VT U.S.A.
234 D2 Fairless Hills PA U.S.A.
81 C6 Fairlie South I. N.Z.
146 D6 Fairlie North Ayrshire, Scotland U.K.
85 F2 Fairlight Qld Austr.
151 H4 Fairlight East Sussex, England U.K.
236 E3 Fairmont MN U.S.A.
232 C5 Fairmont WV U.S.A.
222 H5 Fairmont Hot Springs B.C. Can.
151 F4 Fair Oak Hampshire, England U.K.
237 F5 Fair Oaks AR U.S.A.
226 D4 Fair Plain MI U.S.A.
237 F4 Fairplay CO U.S.A.
238 D3 Fairport MI U.S.A.
234 C3 Fairton NJ U.S.A.
85 F2 Fairview Qld Austr.
222 G3 Fairview Alta Can.
226 B5 Fairview IL U.S.A.
232 B5 Fairview KY U.S.A.
227 E3 Fairview MI U.S.A.
235 D2 Fairview NJ U.S.A.
235 E1 Fairview NY U.S.A.
237 D4 Fairview OK U.S.A.
232 C3 Fairview PA U.S.A.
241 L2 Fairview UT U.S.A.
226 B4 Fairview WI U.S.A.
234 C3 Fairville PA U.S.A.
220 E4 Fairweather, Mount Alaska/B.C. Can./U.S.A.
148 B3 Fairy Water r. Northern Ireland U.K.
91 J5 Fais i. Micronesia
123 H4 Faisalabad Pak.
156 E3 Faissault France
236 C2 Faith SD U.S.A.
193 G4 Faito, Monte mt. Italy
Faizabad Afgh. see Feyzābād
116 E4 Faizabad Uttar Prad. India
184 □ Fajã da Ovelha Madeira
216 □1b Fajã de Cima São Miguel Azores
182 B4 Fajão Port.
182 B3 Fajarda Port.
247 □1 Fajardo Puerto Rico
175 K4 Fajsławice Pol.
177 H5 Fajsz Hungary
81 □1 Fakaofo atoll Tokelau
Fakaofu atoll Tokelau see Fakaofo
79 □3 Fakarava atoll Arch. des Tuamotu Fr. Polynesia
134 K4 Fakel Rus. Fed.
151 H2 Fakenham Norfolk, England U.K.
140 K3 Fåker Sweden
117 G4 Fakiragram Assam India
197 H4 Fakiyska Reka r. Bulg.
142 E4 Fakse Denmark
142 E4 Fakse Bugt b. Denmark
107 I3 Faku Liaoning China
150 C4 Fal r. England U.K.
206 C4 Falaba Sierra Leone
171 D5 Faladoira, Serra da mts Spain
207 F3 Falagountou Burkina
159 F3 Falaise France
117 G5 Falakata W. Bengal India
96 A2 Falam Myanmar
122 C3 Falavarjan Iran
191 G2 Falcade Italy
147 C1 Falcarragh Rep. of Ireland
183 I2 Falces Spain
197 H2 Fălciu Romania
161 F5 Falck France
191 G5 Falco, Monte mt. Italy
250 D2 Falcón state Venez.
194 D5 Falconara Sicilia Italy
193 I5 Falconara Albanese Italy
191 I5 Falconara Marittima Italy
195 E4 Falcone Sicilia Italy
Falcon Island Tonga see Fonuafo'ou
223 M5 Falcon Lake Man. Can.
243 F3 Falcon Lake l. Mex./U.S.A.
206 B3 Falémé r. Mali/Senegal
135 H4 Falenki Rus. Fed.
193 E2 Falerià Italy
Falerii Italy see Civita Castellana
193 I5 Falerna Italy
193 F1 Falerone Italy
Faleshty Moldova see Făleşti
136 D4 Făleşti Moldova
237 D7 Falfurrias TX U.S.A.
222 G4 Falher Alta Can.
169 F4 Falken Ger.
173 G2 Falkenberg Bayern Ger.
173 G2 Falkenberg Bayern Ger.
170 E3 Falkenberg Brandenburg Ger.
171 E4 Falkenberg Brandenburg Ger.
142 E3 Falkenberg Sweden

170 D2 Falkenhagen Ger.
171 D4 Falkenhain Ger.
170 E3 Falkensee Ger.
173 G2 Falkenstein Bayern Ger.
171 D5 Falkenstein Sachsen Ger.
170 E3 Falkenthal Ger.
146 E6 Falkirk Falkirk, Scotland U.K.
146 E6 Falkirk admin. div. Scotland U.K.
146 E5 Falkland Fife, Scotland U.K.
264 F9 Falkland Escarpment sea feature S. Atlantic Ocean
259 F8 Falkland Islands terr. S. Atlantic Ocean
264 F9 Falkland Plateau sea feature S. Atlantic Ocean
259 E9 Falkland Sound sea chan. Falkland Is
142 E2 Falköping Sweden
175 I4 Fałków Pol.
237 E4 Fall r. KS U.S.A.
232 B6 Fall Branch TN U.S.A.
240 I5 Fallbrook CA U.S.A.
226 B3 Fall Creek WI U.S.A.
190 C3 Fallère, Monte mt. Italy
158 E5 Falleron France
140 M2 Fällfors Sweden
262 T2 Fallieres Coast Antarctica
146 E5 Fallin Stirling, Scotland U.K.
168 E3 Fallingbostel Ger.
147 A2 Fallmore Rep. of Ireland
215 F5 Fallodon S. Africa
240 H2 Fallon NV U.S.A.
233 H4 Fall River MA U.S.A.
234 C1 Falls PA U.S.A.
234 A4 Falls Church VA U.S.A.
236 E3 Falls City NE U.S.A.
232 D4 Falls Creek PA U.S.A.
234 D2 Fallsington PA U.S.A.
234 B3 Fallston MD U.S.A.
190 D2 Falmenta Italy
246 □ Falmouth Jamaica
150 B4 Falmouth Cornwall, England U.K.
232 A5 Falmouth KY U.S.A.
233 H4 Falmouth MA U.S.A.
233 □H3 Falmouth ME U.S.A.
234 B2 Falmouth PA U.S.A.
232 E5 Falmouth VA U.S.A.
150 B4 Falmouth Bay England U.K.
247 □2 Falmouth Harbour Antigua and Barbuda
206 D3 Falo Mali
206 D3 Falou Mali
261 F6 Falsa, Bahía b. Arg.
225 G1 False r. Que. Can.
214 B6 False Bay S. Africa
220 B4 False Pass AK U.S.A.
117 F5 False Point India
186 D3 Falset Spain
259 C9 Falso Cabo de Hornos c. Chile
142 D4 Falster i. Denmark
149 G2 Falstone Northumberland, England U.K.
197 H2 Fălticeni Romania
143 F1 Falun Sweden
93 D3 Fam, Kepulauan is Irian Jaya Indon.
Famagusta Cyprus see Ammochostos
Famagusta Bay Cyprus see Ammochostos Bay
182 C4 Famalicão Port.
258 D3 Famatina Arg.
258 C3 Famatina, Sierra de mts Arg.
169 F5 Fambach Ger.
157 G3 Fameck France
122 B3 Famenin Iran
165 D4 Famenne val. Belgium
87 D5 Fame Range hills W.A. Austr.
86 E4 Family Well W.A. Austr.
206 D3 Fana Mali
78 □4a Fanaik i. Chuuk Micronesia
78 □4a Fanan i. Chuuk Micronesia
191 F4 Fanano Italy
78 □4a Fanapanges i. Chuuk Micronesia
109 F2 Fanchang Anhui China
213 □J4 Fandriana Madag.
147 E3 Fane r. Rep. of Ireland
96 B3 Fang Thai.
79 □3 Fangatau atoll Arch. des Tuamotu Fr. Polynesia
79 □3 Fangataufa atoll Arch. des Tuamotu Fr. Polynesia
Fangcheng Guangxi China see Fangchenggang
109 E1 Fangcheng Henan China
108 D4 Fangchenggang Guangxi China
108 D2 Fangdou Shan mts China
109 G4 Fangliao Taiwan
192 A2 Fango r. Corse France
109 G4 Fangshan Taiwan
108 D1 Fangxian Hubei China
100 D3 Fangzheng Heilong. China
196 D5 Fani i Vogël r. Albania
138 F5 Fanipal' Belarus
163 E5 Fanjeaux France
108 D2 Fankuai Sichuan China
Fankuaidian Sichuan China see Fankuai
109 □ Fanling H.K. China
186 C2 Fanlo Spain
146 C4 Fannich, Loch l. Scotland U.K.
140 J3 Fannrem Norway
122 D5 Fannūj Iran
142 C4 Fanø i. Denmark
191 I5 Fano Italy
142 C4 Fanø Bugt b. Denmark
78 □4a Fanos i. Chuuk Micronesia
Fanoualie i. Tonga see Fonualei
109 F2 Fanshan Anhui China
109 G3 Fanshan Zhejiang China
107 G4 Fanshi Shanxi China
96 C2 Fan Si Pan mt. Vietnam
177 K5 Fântâna Rece hill Romania
177 K5 Fântânele Romania
Fanum Fortunae Italy see Fano
107 G5 Fanxian Henan China
182 B3 Fão Port.
Farab Turkm. see Farap
206 C3 Faraba Mali
Farab-Pristan' Turkm. see Dzheykhun
208 F4 Faradje Dem. Rep. Congo
Faradofay Madag. see Tôlañaro
213 □J4 Farafangana Madag.
206 B3 Farafenni Gambia
193 G2 Fara Filiorum Petri Italy
202 F3 Farafra Oasis Egypt
123 E3 Farāh Afgh.
123 E3 Farāh prov. Afgh.
Faraḩābād Iran see Khezerābād
213 □K2 Farahalana Madag.
193 E2 Fara in Sabina Italy
91 K3 Farallon de Medinilla i. N. Mariana Is
91 J2 Farallon de Pajaros vol. N. Mariana Is
182 E3 Faramontanos de Tábara Spain
206 C4 Faranah Guinea
197 H2 Faraoani Romania
123 E2 Farap Turkm.
125 F4 Fararah Oman
124 C4 Farasān, Jazā'ir is Saudi Arabia
193 G2 Fara San Martino Italy
186 B2 Farasdues Spain
213 □J3 Faratsiho Madag.
91 J5 Faraulep atoll Micronesia
197 G2 Farcău, Vârful mt. Romania
173 F4 Farchant Ger.
165 D4 Farciennes Belgium
177 L6 Fârdea Romania
185 H3 Fardes r. Spain
147 D3 Fardrum Rep. of Ireland
157 G3 Farébersviller France
151 F4 Fareham Hampshire, England U.K.
156 D4 Faremoutiers France
Farewell, Cape Greenland see Nunap Isua
80 D4 Farewell, Cape South I. N.Z.
80 D4 Farewell Spit South I. N.Z.
193 E2 Farfa r. Italy
142 E2 Färgelanda Sweden
Farghona Uzbek. see Fergana
Farghona Wiloyati admin. div. Uzbek. see Ferganskaya Oblast'
231 D6 Fargo GA U.S.A.
236 D2 Fargo ND U.S.A.
163 B4 Fargues France
163 C4 Fargues-sur-Ourbise France
168 E1 Fårhus Denmark
236 E2 Faribault MN U.S.A.
116 D3 Faridabad Haryana India
116 C3 Faridkot Punjab India
117 G5 Faridpur Bangl.
116 D3 Faridpur Uttar Prad. India
122 D2 Fārīg Iran
141 K3 Färila Sweden
206 B3 Farim Guinea-Bissau
122 D3 Farīmān Iran
151 F3 Faringdon Oxfordshire, England U.K.
149 G4 Farington Lancashire, England U.K.
254 D3 Farinha r. Brazil
190 E4 Farini Italy
182 D3 Fariza de Sayago Spain
143 G3 Färjestaden Kalmar Sweden
198 C2 Farkadhon Greece
Farkhar Afgh. see Farkhato
123 G2 Farkhato Afgh.
123 G2 Farkhor Tajik.
211 B6 Farkwa Tanz.
85 G4 Farleigh Qld Austr.
151 F3 Farleigh Wallop Hampshire, England U.K.
186 C3 Farlete Spain
192 D1 Farma r. Italy
199 E3 Farmakonisi i. Greece
150 E3 Farmborough Bath and North East Somerset, England U.K.
226 C5 Farmer City IL U.S.A.
237 E5 Farmerville LA U.S.A.
235 D2 Farmingdale NJ U.S.A.
222 F4 Farmington B.C. Can.
235 F1 Farmington CT U.S.A.
234 C4 Farmington DE U.S.A.
226 B5 Farmington IL U.S.A.
233 □H2 Farmington ME U.S.A.
237 F4 Farmington MO U.S.A.
233 □H3 Farmington NH U.S.A.
239 E4 Farmington NM U.S.A.
238 E3 Farmington UT U.S.A.
232 B3 Farmington Hills MI U.S.A.
235 E2 Farmingville NY U.S.A.
177 I4 Farmos Hungary
222 E4 Far Mountain B.C. Can.
232 D6 Farmville VA U.S.A.
177 H3 Farná Slovakia
151 G3 Farnborough Hampshire, England U.K.
149 G4 Farndon Cheshire, England U.K.
149 I4 Farndon Nottinghamshire, England U.K.
149 H2 Farne Islands England U.K.
192 D2 Farnese Italy
233 G2 Farnham Que. Can.
151 G3 Farnham Surrey, England U.K.
232 E6 Farnham VA U.S.A.
87 E5 Farnham, Lake salt flat W.A. Austr.
222 G5 Farnham, Mount B.C. Can.
151 G3 Farnham Royal Buckinghamshire, England U.K.
171 C4 Farnstädt Ger.
149 G4 Farnworth Greater Manchester, England U.K.
251 G5 Faro Brazil
207 I4 Faro r. Cameroon
222 C2 Faro Y.T. Can.
184 C3 Faro Port.
184 B3 Faro admin. dist. Port.
182 C2 Faro mt. Spain
143 H3 Fårö Gotland Sweden
182 C2 Faro, Serra do mts Spain
144 D1 Faroe Islands terr. N. Atlantic Ocean
190 C3 Faroma, Monte mt. Italy
143 H3 Fårösund Gotland Sweden
217 □2 Farquhar Atoll Seychelles
217 □2 Farquhar Islands Seychelles
87 D5 Farquharson Tableland hills W.A. Austr.
146 D4 Farr Highland, Scotland U.K.
191 H2 Farra d'Alpago Italy
232 E4 Farrandsville PA U.S.A.
147 B4 Farranfore Rep. of Ireland
146 D4 Farrar r. Scotland U.K.
124 C4 Farrāsh, Jabal al hill Saudi Arabia
122 C4 Farrāshband Iran
227 J3 Farrellton Que. Can.
122 D3 Farrokhī Iran
Farrukhabad Uttar Prad. India see Fatehgarh
122 C4 Fārs prov. Iran
129 B1 Fars r. Rus. Fed.
122 C3 Farsakh Iran
198 C2 Farsala Greece
198 C2 Farsaliotis r. Greece
127 H6 Fārsī, Jazīreh-ye i. Iran
142 C3 Farsø Denmark
238 E3 Farson WY U.S.A.
142 B2 Farsund Norway
197 H3 Fărţăneşti Romania
256 B2 Fartura r. Brazil
255 B8 Fartura, Serra da mts Brazil
142 C3 Fårvang Denmark
Farvel, Kap c. Greenland see Nunap Isua
226 E4 Farwell MI U.S.A.
237 C5 Farwell TX U.S.A.
123 F2 Fāryāb prov. Afgh.
122 D4 Fāryāb Iran
138 G4 Farynava Belarus
122 C4 Fasā Iran
195 G2 Fasano Italy
137 J3 Fashchivka Ukr.
210 C1 Fasil Ghebbi and Gonder Monuments tourist site Eth.
216 □3a Fasnia Tenerife Canary Is
168 F3 Faßberg Ger.
136 E2 Fastiv Ukr.
Fastov Ukr. see Fastiv
208 F4 Fataki Dem. Rep. Congo
193 F3 Fate, Monte delle mt. Italy
116 C3 Fatehabad Haryana India
116 D4 Fatehgarh Madh. Prad. India
116 D4 Fatehgarh Uttar Prad. India
116 C4 Fatehnagar Rajasthan India
116 C4 Fatehpur Rajasthan India
116 E4 Fatehpur Uttar Prad. India
116 D4 Fatehpur Sikri Uttar Prad. India
182 C4 Fatela Port.
215 F3 Fateng Tse Ntsho S. Africa
137 H1 Fatezh Rus. Fed.
122 C4 Fatḩābād Iran
206 A3 Fatick Senegal
182 B5 Fátima Port.
Fattoilep atoll Micronesia see Faraulep
Fatuhiva i. Fr. Polynesia see Fatu Hiva
79 □3 Fatu Hiva i. Fr. Polynesia
78 □6 Fauabu Malaita Solomon Is
157 G5 Faucogney-et-la-Mer France
161 B5 Faugères France
147 D1 Faughan r. Northern Ireland U.K.
190 F5 Fauglia Italy
163 C4 Fauguerolles France
172 D2 Faulbach Ger.
146 E6 Fauldhouse West Lothian, Scotland U.K.
170 D2 Faulenrost Ger.
236 D2 Faulkton SD U.S.A.
157 G3 Faulquemont France
156 C2 Fauquembergues France
222 G5 Fauquier B.C. Can.
187 C5 Faura Spain
87 B5 Faure Island W.A. Austr.
215 E3 Fauresmith S. Africa
78 □6 Fauro i. Solomon Is
140 K2 Fauske Norway
222 H4 Faust Alta Can.
159 G2 Fauville-en-Caux France
163 C4 Faux France
162 D3 Faux-la-Montagne France
182 C3 Favaios Port.
190 E4 Favale di Malvaro Italy
191 H5 Favalto, Monte mt. Italy
194 C5 Favara Sicilia Italy
187 C5 Favara Spain
160 E3 Faverges France
157 G5 Faverney France
161 B4 Faverolles France
151 H3 Faversham Kent, England U.K.
157 F4 Favières France
194 B5 Favignana Sicilia Italy
194 B5 Favignana, Isola i. Sicilia Italy
222 H4 Fawcett Alta Can.
151 F4 Fawley Hampshire, England U.K.
224 B2 Fawn r. Ont. Can.
234 B3 Fawn Grove PA U.S.A.
215 H3 Fawnleas S. Africa
124 C2 Fawwārah Saudi Arabia
140 □B2 Faxaflói b. Iceland
140 L3 Faxälven r. Sweden
234 B1 Faxon PA U.S.A.
202 C5 Faya Chad
78 □5 Fayaoué Î. Loyauté New Caledonia
156 C5 Fay-aux-Loges France
163 D4 Faycelles France
158 E4 Fay-de-Bretagne France
161 E5 Fayence France
231 C5 Fayette AL U.S.A.
226 D3 Fayette MI U.S.A.
236 E4 Fayette MO U.S.A.
237 F6 Fayette MS U.S.A.
232 A4 Fayette OH U.S.A.
237 E4 Fayetteville AR U.S.A.
231 C5 Fayetteville GA U.S.A.
231 E5 Fayetteville NC U.S.A.
233 E3 Fayetteville NY U.S.A.
232 E5 Fayetteville PA U.S.A.
231 C5 Fayetteville TN U.S.A.
232 C5 Fayetteville WV U.S.A.
127 H5 Faylakah i. Kuwait
157 F5 Fayl-la-Forêt France
157 G5 Faymont France
186 D3 Fayón Spain
161 C4 Fay-sur-Lignon France
91 L5 Fayu i. Micronesia
191 I4 Fažana Croatia
151 F2 Fazeley Staffordshire, England U.K.
116 C3 Fazilka Punjab India
125 E2 Fazrān, Jabal hill Saudi Arabia
204 B5 Fdérik Maur.
147 B4 Feale r. Rep. of Ireland
146 C4 Fearnmore Highland, Scotland U.K.
163 B5 Féas France
234 C2 Feasterville PA U.S.A.
240 G2 Feather r. CA U.S.A.
240 G2 Feather, North Fork r. CA U.S.A.
81 E4 Featherston North I. N.Z.
150 E2 Featherstone Staffordshire, England U.K.
149 H4 Featherstone West Yorkshire, England U.K.
159 G2 Fécamp France
192 D1 Feccia r. Italy
157 H4 Fecht r. France
188 G3 Federacija Bosna i Hercegovina aut. div. Bos.-Herz.
261 I2 Federación Arg.
261 H2 Federal Arg.
207 G4 Federal Capital Territory admin. div. Nigeria
Federal District admin. dist. Brazil see Distrito Federal
Federal District admin. dist. Mex. see Distrito Federal
Federal District admin. dist. Venez. see Distrito Federal
233 F5 Federalsburg MD U.S.A.
Federated Malay States country Asia see Malaysia
144 J1 Fedje Norway
137 H4 Fedorivka Ukr.
Fedorov Zapadnyy Kazakhstan Kazakh. see Fedorovka
120 E1 Fedorovka Kustanayskaya Oblast' Kazakh.
121 I1 Fedorovka Pavlodarskaya Oblast' Kazakh.
120 B2 Fedorovka Zapadnyy Kazakhstan Kazakh.
120 C1 Fedorovka Respublika Bashkortostan Rus. Fed.
137 J4 Fedorovka Rostovskaya Oblast' Rus. Fed.
120 B1 Fedorovka Samarskaya Oblast' Rus. Fed.
135 I6 Fedorovka Saratovskaya Oblast' Rus. Fed.
137 J5 Fedorovskaya Rus. Fed.
146 D4 Feehlin r. Scotland U.K.
147 D2 Feeny Northern Ireland U.K.
78 □4a Fefan i. Chuuk Micronesia
158 D4 Fégréac France
177 J4 Fegyvernek Hungary
177 L4 Fehérgyarmat Hungary
177 K5 Fehér-Körös r. Hungary
177 H4 Fehérvárcsurgó Hungary
170 C1 Fehmarn i. Ger.
Fehmarn Belt str. Denmark/Ger. see Femer Bælt
170 D3 Fehrbellin Ger.
179 H4 Fehring Austria
257 G4 Feia, Lagoa lag. Brazil
Feicheng Shandong China see Feixian
109 F2 Feidong Anhui China
156 D2 Feignies France
252 C2 Feijó Brazil
184 A2 Feijó Port.
172 B2 Feilbingert Ger.
80 E4 Feilding North I. N.Z.
171 C5 Feilitzsch Ger.
160 C2 Feillens France
Feio r. Brazil see Aguapeí
Feira Zambia see Luangwa
254 F5 Feira de Santana Brazil
182 C1 Feira do Monte Spain
128 B5 Feirâni, Gebel mt. Egypt
160 E3 Feissons-sur-Isère France
179 F4 Feistritz im Rosental Austria
179 F4 Feistritz ob Bleiburg Austria
184 C3 Feiteira Port.
109 F2 Feixi Anhui China
107 H5 Feixian Shandong China
107 G4 Feixiang Hebei China
177 H4 Fejér county Hungary
142 D4 Fejø i. Denmark
126 D3 Feke Turkey
177 K5 Fekete-Körös r. Hungary
187 G5 Felanitx Spain
170 F2 Felchow Ger.
169 F5 Felda r. Ger.
173 F4 Feldafing Ger.
179 E4 Feld am See Austria
179 G4 Feldbach Austria
160 F1 Feldbach France
170 E2 Feldberg Ger.
172 C4 Feldberg mt. Ger.
168 E1 Felde Ger.
177 J4 Feldebrő Hungary
178 A3 Feldkirch Austria
172 D4 Feldkirch admin. reg. Austria
173 F3 Feldkirchen Ger.
179 G3 Feldkirchen bei Graz Austria
179 F4 Feldkirchen in Kärnten Austria
173 F4 Feldkirchen-Westerham Ger.
197 G2 Feldru Romania
182 D3 Felgar Port.
182 B3 Felgueiras Port.
177 J5 Felgyő Hungary
261 H2 Feliciano r. Arg.
232 A5 Felicity OH U.S.A.
113 D11 Felidhu Atoll Maldives
150 D2 Felindre Powys, Wales U.K.
161 B3 Félines France
190 F4 Felino Italy
244 B1 Felipe Carrillo Puerto Durango Mex.
244 C4 Felipe Carrillo Puerto Michoacán Mex.
243 H5 Felipe C. Puerto Mex.
193 H4 Felitto Italy
185 H4 Félix Spain
179 H3 Felixdorf Austria
257 E3 Felixlândia Brazil
151 I3 Felixstowe Suffolk, England U.K.
215 H3 Felixton S. Africa
190 D4 Felizzano Italy
172 A2 Fell Ger.
146 E6 Fell, Loch hill Scotland U.K.
191 I2 Fella r. Italy
172 D3 Fellbach Ger.
162 E3 Felletin France
149 H3 Felling Tyne and Wear, England U.K.
246 □ Fellowship Jamaica
232 D5 Fellowsville WV U.S.A.
168 F1 Felm Ger.
177 K5 Felnac Romania
Fels Lux. see Larochette
169 E4 Felsberg Ger.
Felsina Italy see Bologna
177 K3 Felsődobsza Hungary
177 I4 Felsőlajos Hungary
177 H5 Felsőnyék Hungary
177 G6 Felsőszentmárton Hungary
177 J4 Felsőtárkány Hungary
179 H4 Felső-Válicka r. Hungary
177 J3 Felsőzsolca Hungary
168 E1 Felsted Denmark
151 H3 Felsted Essex, England U.K.
149 H2 Felton Northumberland, England U.K.
234 C3 Felton DE U.S.A.
234 B3 Felton PA U.S.A.
191 G2 Feltre Italy
151 H2 Feltwell Norfolk, England U.K.
193 F2 Fema, Monte mt. Italy
254 D5 Femeas r. Brazil
168 F1 Femer Bælt str. Denmark/Ger.
216 □3c Femés hill Lanzarote Canary Is
195 F3 Femminamorta, Monte mt. Italy
142 D4 Femø i. Denmark
107 F5 Fen r. China
147 E4 Fenagh Carlow Rep. of Ireland
148 B3 Fenagh Leitrim Rep. of Ireland
216 □1b Fenais da Ajuda São Miguel Azores
160 D1 Fénay France
163 D5 Fendeille France
227 H3 Fenelon Falls Ont. Can.
78 □4a Feneppi i. Chuuk Micronesia
Fénérive Madag. see Fenoarivo Atsinanana
129 A3 Fenerköyü Turkey
190 C3 Fenestrelle Italy
157 H4 Fénétrange France
159 F4 Feneu France
136 F2 Fenevychi Ukr.
199 D1 Fengari mt. Anatoliki Makedonia kai Thraki Greece
Fengcheng Fujian China see Anxi
Fengcheng Fujian China see Lianjiang
Fengcheng Fujian China see Yongding
Fengcheng Guangdong China see Xinfeng
Fengcheng Guangxi China see Fengshan
109 E2 Fengcheng Jiangxi China
101 C4 Fengcheng Liaoning China
Fengchuan Jiangxi China see Fengxin
108 C2 Fengdu Chongqing China
Fenggang Fujian China see Shaxian
108 C3 Fenggang Guizhou China
Fenggang Jiangxi China see Yihuang
109 G2 Fenghua Zhejiang China
108 D3 Fenghuang Hunan China
Fengjiaba Sichuan China see Wangcang
108 D2 Fengjie Chongqing China
109 D4 Fengkai Guangdong China
109 G4 Fenglin Taiwan
Fengming Shaanxi China see Qishan
107 H4 Fengnan Hebei China
107 H3 Fengning Hebei China
Fengqi Shaanxi China see Luochuan
108 A3 Fengqing Yunnan China
107 G5 Fengqiu Henan China
107 H4 Fengrun Hebei China
Fengshan Fujian China see Luoyuan
108 C3 Fengshan Guangxi China
Fengshan Hubei China see Luotian
Fengshan Yunnan China see Fengqing
100 B1 Fengshui Shan mt. Heilong. China
109 F1 Fengtai Anhui China
Fengwei Yunnan China see Zhenkang
Fengweiba Yunnan China see Zhenkang
107 H5 Fengxian Jiangsu China
108 C1 Fengxian Shaanxi China
109 G2 Fengxian Shanghai China
Fengxiang Heilong. China see Luobei
Fengxiang Yunnan China see Lincang
109 E2 Fengxin Jiangxi China
109 F1 Fengyang Anhui China
Fengyi Guizhou China see Zheng'an
Fengyi Sichuan China see Maoxian
109 G3 Fengyüan Taiwan
107 G3 Fengzhen Nei Mongol China
117 G5 Feni Bangl.
162 B2 Fenioux France
190 C3 Fenis Italy
147 B4 Fenit Rep. of Ireland
150 D4 Feniton Devon, England U.K.
117 G5 Fenny r. Bangl./India
213 □K3 Fenoarivo Atsinanana Madag.
213 □J3 Fenoarivo Be Madag.
163 D5 Fenouillet France
151 G2 Fenstanton Cambridgeshire, England U.K.
173 G2 Fensterbach r. Ger.
227 F4 Fenton MI U.S.A.
81 □1 Fenua Loa i. Tokelau
81 □1 Fenua Loa i. Tokelau
Fenua Ura atoll Arch. de la Société Fr. Polynesia see Manuae
146 D6 Fenwick East Ayrshire, Scotland U.K.
149 H2 Fenwick Northumberland, England U.K.
232 C5 Fenwick WV U.S.A.
107 F4 Fenyang Shanxi China
177 L3 Fényeslitke Hungary
109 E3 Fenyi Jiangxi China
150 B4 Feock Cornwall, England U.K.
137 H5 Feodosiya Ukr.
146 B6 Feolin Ferry Argyll and Bute, Scotland U.K.
147 C4 Feonanagh Rep. of Ireland
78 □6 Fera i. Solomon Is
Férai Greece see Feres
147 D3 Ferbane Rep. of Ireland
171 D3 Ferchland Ger.
195 F4 Ferdinandea Italy
170 E2 Ferdinandshof Ger.
122 D3 Ferdows Iran
156 D4 Fère-Champenoise France
156 D3 Fère-en-Tardenois France
158 D4 Férel France
193 E2 Ferentillo Italy
193 F3 Ferentino Italy
199 E1 Feres Greece
185 I2 Férez Spain
121 G4 Fergana Uzbek.
Fergana Oblast admin. div. Uzbek. see Ferganskaya Oblast'
Fergana Range mts Kyrg. see Fergana Too Tizmegi
121 H4 Fergana Too Tizmegi mts Kyrg.
121 G4 Ferganskaya Oblast' admin. div. Uzbek.
Ferganskiy Khrebet mts Kyrg. see Fergana Too Tizmegi
227 G4 Fergus Ont. Can.
147 C4 Fergus r. Rep. of Ireland
236 D2 Fergus Falls MN U.S.A.
84 B2 Fergusson r. N.T. Austr.
205 H2 Fériana Tunisia
199 G1 Ferizli Turkey
206 D4 Ferkessédougou Côte d'Ivoire
194 D5 Ferla Sicilia Italy
179 F4 Ferlach Austria
147 D2 Fermanagh county Northern Ireland U.K.
182 B4 Fermelã Port.
182 B4 Fermentelos Port.
191 H5 Fermignano Italy
193 F1 Fermo Italy
225 H2 Fermont Que. Can.
182 D3 Fermoselle Spain
147 C4 Fermoy Rep. of Ireland
185 G1 Fernáncaballero Spain
250 □ Fernandina, Isla i. Islas Galápagos Ecuador
231 D6 Fernandina Beach FL U.S.A.
264 G6 Fernando de Noronha i. Brazil
256 B4 Fernandópolis Brazil
Fernando Poó i. Equat. Guinea see Bioco
185 F3 Fernán Núñez Spain
213 I2 Fernão Veloso Moz.
234 B3 Ferndale MD U.S.A.
234 D1 Ferndale NY U.S.A.
238 B1 Ferndale WA U.S.A.
179 E4 Ferndorf Austria
151 F4 Ferndown Dorset, England U.K.
146 E4 Ferness Highland, Scotland U.K.
160 E2 Ferney-Voltaire France
80 F3 Fernhill North I. N.Z.
150 E2 Fernhill Heath Worcestershire, England U.K.
151 G3 Fernhurst West Sussex, England U.K.
222 H5 Fernie B.C. Can.
179 G4 Fernitz Austria
83 F2 Fernlee Qld Austr.
240 H2 Fernley NV U.S.A.
234 C1 Fernridge PA U.S.A.
147 E4 Ferns Rep. of Ireland
238 C2 Fernwood ID U.S.A.
195 F4 Feroleto Antico Italy
Ferozepore Punjab India see Firozpur
161 A5 Ferrals-les-Corbières France
195 F2 Ferrandina Italy
191 G4 Ferrara Italy
191 G4 Ferrara prov. Emilia-Romagna Italy
191 H4 Ferrarese r. Italy
193 G3 Ferrazzano Italy
182 C1 Ferreira Spain
184 B2 Ferreira do Alentejo Port.
182 B5 Ferreira do Zêzere Port.
251 I4 Ferreira-Gomes Brazil
184 A1 Ferrel Port.
232 B5 Ferrellsburg WV U.S.A.
250 B6 Ferreñafe Peru
182 D3 Ferreras de Abajo Spain
182 D3 Ferreras de Arriba Spain
190 C4 Ferrere Italy
186 □ Ferreries Spain
186 B3 Ferreruela de Huerva Spain
182 D3 Ferreruela de Tábara Spain
160 F1 Ferrette France
261 E2 Ferreyra Arg.
237 F6 Ferriday LA U.S.A.
190 E4 Ferriere Italy
156 E2 Ferrière-la-Grande France
165 E4 Ferrières Belgium
156 C4 Ferrières France
161 B3 Ferrières-St-Mary France
163 D6 Ferrières-sur-Ariège France
194 D5 Ferro r. Sicilia Italy
195 F3 Ferro r. Italy
182 B1 Ferrol Spain
241 L2 Ferron UT U.S.A.
257 F3 Ferros Brazil
192 B5 Ferru, Monte hill Sardegna Italy
232 C6 Ferrum VA U.S.A.
147 E4 Ferrycarrig Rep. of Ireland
146 F5 Ferryden Angus, Scotland U.K.
149 H3 Ferryhill Durham, England U.K.
225 K4 Ferryland Nfld. Can.
Ferryville Tunisia see Menzel Bourguiba
172 A2 Ferschweiler Ger.
120 D1 Fershampenuaz Rus. Fed.
192 A4 Fertilia Sardegna Italy
179 H3 Fertő l. Austria/Hungary
179 H3 Fertőd Hungary
176 F4 Fertőrákos Hungary
176 F4 Fertőszentmiklós Hungary
179 H3 Fertőszéplak Hungary
182 B3 Fervença Port.
164 E1 Ferwerd Neth.
139 K4 Ferzikovo Rus. Fed.
204 D2 Fès Morocco
209 C6 Feshi Dem. Rep. Congo
146 E4 Feshiebridge Highland, Scotland U.K.
236 D2 Fessenden ND U.S.A.
157 H5 Fessenheim France
156 D3 Festieux France
216 □1c Feteira Faial Azores
216 □1b Feteiras São Miguel Azores
197 H3 Feteşti Romania
197 H3 Feteşti-Gară Romania
147 D4 Fethard Tipperary Rep. of Ireland
147 E4 Fethard Wexford Rep. of Ireland
Fethiye Malatya Turkey see Yazıhan
199 F3 Fethiye Muğla Turkey
146 □H1 Fetlar i. Scotland U.K.
146 F5 Fettercairn Aberdeenshire, Scotland U.K.
173 F2 Feucht Ger.
173 E2 Feuchtwangen Ger.
163 C4 Feugarolles France
225 G1 Feuilles, Rivière aux r. Que. Can.
156 B3 Feuquières France
156 B2 Feuquières-en-Vimeu France
160 C3 Feurs France
100 D1 Fevral'sk Rus. Fed.
126 E3 Fevzipaşa Turkey
162 D3 Feytiat France
123 G2 Feyzābād Afgh.
Fez Morocco see Fès
150 D2 Ffestiniog Gwynedd, Wales U.K.
150 C2 Ffostrasol Ceredigion, Wales U.K.
163 D5 Fiac France
258 D2 Fiambalá Arg.
258 D2 Fiambala r. Arg.
193 F2 Fiamignano Italy
206 E4 Fian Ghana
213 □J4 Fianarantsoa Madag.
213 □J4 Fianarantsoa prov. Madag.
208 B2 Fianga Chad
190 C3 Fiano Italy
193 E2 Fiano Romano Italy
191 I5 Fiastra r. Italy
191 F3 Fiavè Italy
184 C3 Ficalho hill Port.
194 C4 Ficarazzi Sicilia Italy
191 G4 Ficarolo Italy
210 C2 Fichē Eth.
173 F2 Fichtelberg Ger.
171 D5 Fichtelgebirge hills Ger.
173 G2 Fichtelnaab r. Ger.
172 D3 Fichtenberg Ger.
215 F3 Ficksburg S. Africa
192 E2 Ficulle Italy
194 D5 Ficuzza r. Sicilia Italy
146 E4 Fiddich r. Scotland U.K.
147 D4 Fiddown Rep. of Ireland
190 F4 Fidenza Italy
176 G2 Fidlův Kopec hill Czech Rep.
206 C4 Fié r. Guinea
178 C4 Fiè allo Sciliar Italy
178 D3 Fieberbrunn Austria
193 F1 Fiegni, Monte mt. Italy
222 G5 Field B.C. Can.
227 G2 Field Ont. Can.
232 B6 Field KY U.S.A.
84 C2 Field Island N.T. Austr.
138 F3 Fiemanka r. Latvia
197 G3 Fieni Romania
198 A1 Fier Albania
160 D3 Fier r. France
178 C4 Fiera di Primiero Italy
84 D3 Fiery Creek r. Qld Austr.
196 E4 Fierzes, Liqeni i resr Albania
190 D2 Fiesch Switz.
191 G5 Fiesole Italy
191 G4 Fiesso Umbertiano Italy
146 F5 Fife admin. div. Scotland U.K.
226 E3 Fife Lake MI U.S.A.
146 F5 Fife Ness pt Scotland U.K.
83 F3 Fifield N.S.W. Austr.
226 B3 Fifield WI U.S.A.
203 G5 Fifth Cataract rapids Sudan
222 H3 Fifth Meridian Alta Can.
161 E5 Figaniéres France
192 A2 Figarella r. Corse France
192 B3 Figari Corse France
163 E4 Figeac France
191 G5 Figline Valdarno Italy
184 B2 Figueira r. Port.
182 B4 Figueira da Foz Port.
182 D4 Figueira de Castelo Rodrigo Port.
184 B2 Figueira dos Cavaleiros Port.
184 C1 Figueira e Barros Port.
182 C4 Figueiredo de Alva Port.
184 C1 Figueiró r. Port.
182 C4 Figueiró da Granja Port.
182 B5 Figueiró dos Vinhos Port.
Figueras Spain see Figueres
186 F2 Figueres Spain
182 D3 Figueruela de Arriba Spain
205 E2 Figuig Morocco
207 I4 Figuil Cameroon
213 □J3 Fihaonana Madag.
79 □1 Fiji country S. Pacific Ocean
164 D3 Fijnaart Neth.
213 F4 Filabusi Zimbabwe
242 □I7 Filadelfia Costa Rica
195 F4 Filadelfia Italy
253 E5 Filadélfia Para.
177 I3 Fil'akovo Slovakia
206 D4 Filamana Mali
190 E4 Filattiera Italy
262 V1 Filchner Ice Shelf Antarctica
193 F3 Filettino Italy
149 I3 Filey North Yorkshire, England U.K.
193 H4 Filiano Italy
197 F3 Filiaşi Romania
198 B2 Filiates Greece
198 B3 Filiatra Greece
Filibe Bulg. see Plovdiv
194 D4 Filicudi, Isola i. Isole Lipari Italy
194 D4 Filicudi Porto Isole Lipari Italy
207 F3 Filingué Niger
199 D1 Filiouri r. Greece
Filipinas country Asia see Philippines
175 K1 Filipów Pol.
198 B2 Filippiada Greece
198 D1 Filippoi tourist site Greece
143 F2 Filipstad Sweden
190 E2 Filisur Switz.
140 J3 Fillan Norway
156 C2 Fillièvres France
160 E2 Fillinges France
Fillíra Greece see Fillyra
240 H4 Fillmore CA U.S.A.
241 K2 Fillmore UT U.S.A.
151 F2 Fillongley Warwickshire, England U.K.
199 D1 Fillyra Greece
245 F3 Filomeno Mata Mex.
199 D3 Filoti Notio Aigaio Greece
191 I5 Filottrano Italy
172 D3 Fils r. Ger.
168 C2 Filsum Ger.
150 E3 Filton South Gloucestershire, England U.K.
210 D3 Filtu Eth.
179 E3 Filzmoos Austria
149 I3 Fimber East Riding of Yorkshire, England U.K.
194 D4 Finale Sicilia Italy
191 G4 Finale Emilia Italy
190 D4 Finale Ligure Italy
185 H3 Fiñana Spain
146 F5 Finavon Angus, Scotland U.K.
232 D6 Fincastle VA U.S.A.
233 F2 Finch Ont. Can.
210 C2 Finch'a'ā Hāyk' l. Eth.
151 G3 Finchampstead Wokingham, England U.K.
85 G4 Finch Hatton Qld Austr.
151 H3 Finchingfield Essex, England U.K.
151 F2 Findern Derbyshire, England U.K.
146 E4 Findhorn Moray, Scotland U.K.
146 E4 Findhorn r. Scotland U.K.
127 F3 Fındık Turkey
129 B3 Fındıklı Turkey
232 B4 Findlay OH U.S.A.
146 F4 Findochty Moray, Scotland U.K.
151 G4 Findon West Sussex, England U.K.
233 F2 Fine NY U.S.A.
151 G2 Finedon Northamptonshire, England U.K.
195 F2 Finese, Monte hill Italy
187 C6 Finestrat Spain
83 G5 Fingal Tas. Austr.
232 E3 Finger Lakes NY U.S.A.
116 E5 Fingeshwar Madh. Prad. India
213 F2 Fingoè Moz.
163 D5 Finhan France
161 B4 Finiels, Sommet de mt. France
199 G3 Finike Turkey
199 G3 Finike Körfezi b. Turkey
177 L5 Finiş Romania
158 C3 Finistère dept Bretagne France
Finisterre Spain see Fisterra
Finisterre, Cabo c. Spain see Fisterra, Cabo
Finisterre, Cape Spain see Fisterra, Cabo
84 C5 Finke N.T. Austr.
84 C5 Finke watercourse N.T. Austr.
82 C2 Finke, Mount hill S.A. Austr.
84 B2 Finke Bay N.T. Austr.
178 C3 Finkenberg Austria
179 E4 Finkenstein Austria
234 B3 Finksburg MD U.S.A.
140 N3 Finland country Europe
226 B2 Finland MN U.S.A.
138 D2 Finland, Gulf of Europe
222 E3 Finlay r. B.C. Can.
222 E3 Finlay, Mount B.C. Can.
222 F4 Finlay Forks B.C. Can.
226 A2 Finlayson MN U.S.A.
83 F3 Finley N.S.W. Austr.
236 D2 Finley ND U.S.A.
226 C1 Finmark Ont. Can.
147 D2 Finn r. Rep. of Ireland
143 F1 Finnbodarna Sweden
171 C4 Finne ridge Ger.
147 D3 Finnea Rep. of Ireland
169 C4 Finnentrop Ger.
143 F2 Finnerödja Sweden
85 F2 Finnigan, Mount Qld Austr.
151 I2 Finningham Suffolk, England U.K.
149 I4 Finningly South Yorkshire, England U.K.
84 B2 Finniss r. N.T. Austr.
82 C3 Finniss, Cape S.A. Austr.
140 N1 Finnmark county Norway
140 M1 Finnmarksvidda reg. Norway
140 L1 Finnsnes Norway
170 E3 Finowfurt Ger.
173 F3 Finsing Ger.
143 F2 Finspång Sweden
190 D2 Finsteraarhorn mt. Switz.
171 E4 Finsterwalde Ger.
164 G1 Finsterwolde Neth.
146 E2 Finstown Orkney, Scotland U.K.
141 L3 Finström Åland Fin.
168 E2 Fintel Ger.
177 K2 Fintice Slovakia
Fîntînele Romania see Fântânele
147 D2 Fintona Northern Ireland U.K.
147 C2 Fintown Rep. of Ireland
146 D5 Fintry Stirling, Scotland U.K.
85 E4 Finucane Range hills Qld Austr.
147 B4 Finuge Rep. of Ireland
147 E1 Finvoy Northern Ireland U.K.
193 E2 Fionchi, Monte mt. Italy
146 C4 Fionn Loch l. Scotland U.K.
146 B5 Fionnphort Argyll and Bute, Scotland U.K.
192 D2 Fiora r. Italy
191 F4 Fiorano Modense Italy
190 E4 Fiorenzuola d'Arda Italy
193 F2 Fiori, Montagna dei mt. Italy
118 D2 Fırat r. Turkey alt. Al Furāt (Iraq/Syria), conv. Euphrates
129 A4 Fırat Nehri r. Turkey
240 G3 Firebaugh CA U.S.A.
235 E2 Fire Island NY U.S.A.
191 G5 Firenze Italy
191 G5 Firenze prov. Toscana Italy
191 G4 Firenzuola Italy
227 F1 Fire River Ont. Can.
222 E3 Fireside B.C. Can.
236 D3 Firesteel Creek r. SD U.S.A.
216 □3f Firgas Gran Canaria Canary Is
175 K4 Firlej Pol.
261 G3 Firmat Arg.
163 E4 Firmi France
256 B2 Firminópolis Brazil
161 C3 Firminy France
193 I5 Firmo Italy
Firmum Italy see Fermo
Firmum Picenum Italy see Fermo
139 I3 Firovo Rus. Fed.
116 D4 Firozabad Uttar Prad. India
116 D4 Firozpur Haryana India
116 C3 Firozpur Punjab India
168 C2 Firrel Ger.
203 G3 First Cataract rapids Egypt
85 F2 First Three Mile Opening sea chan. Qld Austr.
146 □G1 Firth Shetland, Scotland U.K.
Firuzabad Balūchestān va Sīstān Iran see Rāsk
122 C4 Fīrūzābād Iran
122 D2 Fīrūzeh Iran
122 C3 Fīrūzkūh Iran
122 D2 Firyuza Turkm.
186 C2 Fiscal Spain
173 E3 Fischach Ger.
179 H2 Fischamend Markt Austria
179 G3 Fischbach Austria
172 B2 Fischbach Ger.
173 F4 Fischbachau Ger.
172 B2 Fischbach bei Dahn Ger.
170 D3 Fischbeck Ger.
173 E4 Fischen im Allgäu Ger.
212 C6 Fish watercourse Namibia
214 C4 Fish r. S. Africa
149 H3 Fishburn Durham, England U.K.
82 B2 Fisher S.A. Austr.
223 L5 Fisher River Man. Can.
221 J3 Fisher Strait Nunavut Can.
232 D5 Fishersville VA U.S.A.
150 C3 Fishguard Pembrokeshire, Wales U.K.
150 C2 Fishguard Bay Wales U.K.
233 E5 Fishing Creek MD U.S.A.
234 B2 Fishing Creek r. PA U.S.A.
235 E1 Fishkill NY U.S.A.
235 E1 Fishkill Creek r. NY U.S.A.
151 H2 Fishtoft Lincolnshire, England U.K.
141 I3 Fiskå Norway
262 T2 Fiske, Cape Antarctica
156 D3 Fismes France
182 A2 Fisterra Spain
182 A2 Fisterra, Cabo c. Spain
233 H3 Fitchburg MA U.S.A.
226 C4 Fitchburg WI U.S.A.
235 F1 Fitchville CT U.S.A.
232 B4 Fitchville OH U.S.A.
183 I2 Fitero Spain
146 □G2 Fitful Head hd Scotland U.K.
Fitíai Greece see Fyteies
142 A2 Fitjar Norway
78 □2 Fito, Mount vol. Samoa
163 E6 Fitou France
252 B2 Fitzcarrald Peru
223 I3 Fitzgerald Alta Can.
231 D6 Fitzgerald GA U.S.A.
156 C3 Fitz-James France
84 B2 Fitzmaurice r. N.T. Austr.
85 G4 Fitzroy r. Qld Austr.
86 D3 Fitzroy r. W.A. Austr.
259 B8 Fitz Roy, Cerro mt. Arg.
86 E3 Fitzroy Crossing W.A. Austr.
193 F3 Fiuggi Italy
191 F4 Fiumalbo Italy
193 H3 Fiumarella r. Italy
Fiume Croatia see Rijeka
193 I5 Fiumefreddo Bruzio Italy
195 E5 Fiumefreddo di Sicilia Sicilia Italy
191 H3 Fiume Veneto Italy
192 E3 Fiumicino Italy
192 B3 Fium'Orbo r. Corse France
146 C5 Fiunary Highland, Scotland U.K.
81 C6 Five Forks South I. N.Z.
147 D2 Fivemiletown Northern Ireland U.K.
240 G3 Five Points CA U.S.A.
81 B6 Five Rivers South I. N.Z.
190 F4 Fivizzano Italy
161 B3 Fix-St-Geneys France
209 F6 Fizi Dem. Rep. Congo
Fizuli Azer. see Füzuli
140 L2 Fjällsjönäs Sweden
143 G2 Fjärdhundra reg. Sweden
142 A1 Fjell Norway
142 C3 Fjerritslev Denmark
204 D2 Fkih Ben Salah Morocco
142 C1 Flå Norway
179 E3 Flachau Austria
173 E2 Flachslanden Ger.
168 C2 Flachsmeer Ger.
146 □G1 Fladdabister Shetland, Scotland U.K.
142 C4 Fladså r. Denmark
169 F5 Fladungen Ger.
163 E4 Flagnac France
215 G4 Flagstaff S. Africa
241 L4 Flagstaff AZ U.S.A.
233 □H2 Flagstaff Lake ME U.S.A.
234 D2 Flagtown NJ U.S.A.
224 E1 Flaherty Island Nunavut Can.
160 E2 Flaine France
140 M2 Flakaberg Sweden
158 E2 Flamanville France
197 H2 Flămânzi Romania
226 B3 Flambeau r. WI U.S.A.
149 I3 Flamborough East Riding of Yorkshire, England U.K.
149 I3 Flamborough Head hd England U.K.
259 E6 Flamenco, Isla i. Arg.
216 □1c Flamengos Faial Azores
186 D2 Flamicell r. Spain
171 D3 Fläming hills Ger.
223 M4 Flanagan r. Ont. Can.
235 F2 Flanders NY U.S.A.
156 C2 Flandre reg. France
236 D2 Flandreau SD U.S.A.
146 A3 Flannan Isles Scotland U.K.
140 K2 Flåsjön l. Sweden
161 E5 Flassans-sur-Issole France
222 E2 Flat r. N.W.T. Can.
226 E4 Flat r. MI U.S.A.
234 D1 Flatbrookville NJ U.S.A.
140 □C2 Flateyjardalsheiði reg. Iceland
220 G5 Flathead r. MT U.S.A.
238 D2 Flatiron mt. ID U.S.A.
90 E4 Flat Island S. China Sea
232 B6 Flat Lick KY U.S.A.
81 A6 Flat Mountain South I. N.Z.
178 E4 Flattach Austria
85 F2 Flattery, Cape Qld Austr.
179 F4 Flattnitz Austria
222 B2 Flat Top mt. Y.T. Can.
238 F2 Flatwillow Creek r. MT U.S.A.
232 B5 Flatwoods KY U.S.A.
232 C5 Flatwoods WV U.S.A.
178 C3 Flaurling Austria
157 G4 Flavigny-sur-Moselle France
160 C1 Flavigny-sur-Ozerain France
161 A4 Flavin France
190 E1 Flawil Switz.
161 E5 Flayosc France
171 C3 Flechtingen Ger.
168 E1 Fleckeby Ger.
170 D2 Flecken Zechlin Ger.
151 F2 Fleckney Leicestershire, England U.K.
151 G3 Fleet Hampshire, England U.K.
146 D4 Fleet r. Scotland U.K.
170 C3 Fleetmark Ger.
85 F4 Fleetwood Qld Austr.
149 F4 Fleetwood Lancashire, England U.K.
234 C2 Fleetwood PA U.S.A.
172 D2 Flein Ger.
142 B2 Flekkefjord Norway
142 C2 Flekkerøy i. Norway

165 E4 Flémalle Belgium
232 B5 Flemingsburg KY U.S.A.
234 D2 Flemington NJ U.S.A.
264 G2 Flemish Cap sea feature N. Atlantic Ocean
151 H2 Flempton Suffolk, England U.K.
143 G2 Flen Sweden
168 E1 Flensborg Fjord inlet Denmark/Ger.
168 E1 Flensburg Ger.
Flensburger Förde inlet Denmark/Ger. see Flensborg Fjord
165 E4 Fléron Belgium
159 F3 Flers France
227 G3 Flesherton Ont. Can.
170 C3 Flessau Ger.
262 S2 Fletcher Peninsula Antarctica
163 C5 Fleurance France
225 J3 Fleur de Lys Nfld. Can.
162 C2 Fleuré France
160 C2 Fleurie France
190 B2 Fleurier Switz.
165 D4 Fleurus Belgium
161 B5 Fleury France
156 B5 Fleury-les-Aubrais France
156 B3 Fleury-sur-Andelle France
159 F2 Fleury-sur-Orne France
157 F3 Fléville-Lixières France
164 E2 Flevoland prov. Neth.
150 C4 Flexbury Cornwall, England U.K.
169 E5 Flieden Ger.
178 B3 Fließ Austria
149 F3 Flimby Cumbria, England U.K.
190 E2 Flims Switz.
151 H3 Flimwell East Sussex, England U.K.
85 E3 Flinders r. Qld Austr.
87 B7 Flinders Bay W.A. Austr.
85 F2 Flinders Group is Qld Austr.
82 C3 Flinders Island S.A. Austr.
83 G4 Flinders Island Tas. Austr.
85 G3 Flinders Passage Qld Austr.
82 D3 Flinders Ranges mts S.A. Austr.
85 G3 Flinders Reefs Coral Sea Is Terr. Austr.
156 D2 Flines-lez-Raches France
223 K4 Flin Flon Man. Can.
150 D1 Flint Flintshire, Wales U.K.
227 F4 Flint MI U.S.A.
231 C6 Flint r. GA U.S.A.
227 F4 Flint r. MI U.S.A.
168 F1 Flintbek Ger.
267 I6 Flint Island Kiribati
85 G5 Flinton Qld Austr.
150 D1 Flintshire admin. div. Wales U.K.
232 D5 Flintstone MD U.S.A.
157 F4 Flirey France
142 E1 Flisa Norway
141 K3 Flisa r. Norway
142 B2 Fliseggi mt. Norway
151 G2 Flitwick Bedfordshire, England U.K.
186 D3 Flix Spain
156 C2 Flixecourt France
156 E3 Flize France
142 E3 Floda Sweden
149 G2 Flodden Northumberland, England U.K.
156 D5 Flogny-la-Chapelle France
171 E5 Flöha Ger.
171 E5 Flöha r. Ger.
157 E3 Floing France
163 B4 Floirac France
262 P1 Flood Range mts Antarctica
226 A2 Floodwood MN U.S.A.
149 G3 Flookburgh Cumbria, England U.K.
84 B2 Flora r. N.T. Austr.
226 D5 Flora IN U.S.A.
161 B4 Florac France
231 C6 Florala AL U.S.A.
157 G3 Florange France
85 F3 Flora Reef Coral Sea Is Terr. Austr.
84 D3 Floraville Qld Austr.
165 D4 Floreffe Belgium
227 F4 Florence Ont. Can.
Florence Italy see Firenze
231 C5 Florence AL U.S.A.
241 L5 Florence AZ U.S.A.
239 F4 Florence CO U.S.A.
236 D4 Florence KS U.S.A.
234 D2 Florence NJ U.S.A.
238 A3 Florence OR U.S.A.
231 E5 Florence SC U.S.A.
226 C3 Florence WI U.S.A.
241 L5 Florence Junction AZ U.S.A.
233 □J1 Florenceville N.B. Can.
250 C4 Florencia Col.
261 I3 Florencio Sánchez Uru.
165 D4 Florennes Belgium
161 B5 Florensac France
Florentia Italy see Firenze
165 E5 Florenville Belgium
261 H4 Flores r. Arg.
216 □1 Flores i. Azores
254 F3 Flores Pernambuco Brazil
254 E3 Flores Piauí Brazil
243 H5 Flores Guat.
93 B5 Flores i. Indon.
261 I3 Flores dept Uru.
183 E4 Flores de Ávila Spain
254 D5 Flores de Goiás Brazil
Floreshty Moldova see Florești
93 A4 Flores Sea Indon.
254 F4 Floresta Brazil
194 D5 Floresta Sicilia Italy
136 E4 Florești Moldova
256 B5 Florestópolis Brazil
237 D6 Floresville TX U.S.A.
235 D2 Florham Park NJ U.S.A.
254 E3 Floriano Brazil
255 C8 Florianópolis Brazil
252 E4 Florida Bol.
260 A5 Florida Chile
246 C2 Florida Cuba
247 □1 Florida Puerto Rico
261 I4 Florida Uru.
261 I4 Florida dept Uru.
235 D1 Florida NY U.S.A.
231 D6 Florida state U.S.A.
231 D7 Florida, Straits of Bahamas/U.S.A.
231 D7 Florida Bay FL U.S.A.
182 E3 Florida de Liébana Spain
78 □6 Florida Islands Solomon Is
231 D7 Florida Keys is FL U.S.A.
256 B4 Flórida Paulista Brazil
195 E5 Floridia Sicilia Italy
237 B7 Florido r. Mex.
197 F2 Florii, Vârful hill Romania
240 G2 Florin CA U.S.A.
198 B1 Florina Greece
192 A4 Florinas Sardegna Italy
256 B5 Florínia Brazil
236 F4 Florissant MO U.S.A.
141 I3 Florø Norway
169 E5 Flörsbach Ger.
169 D5 Flörsheim am Main Ger.
172 C2 Flörsheim-Dalsheim Ger.
169 D5 Florstadt Ger.
173 G2 Floß Ger.
173 G2 Flossenbürg Ger.
146 E3 Flotta i. Scotland U.K.
163 E5 Floure France
226 A4 Floyd IA U.S.A.
232 C6 Floyd VA U.S.A.
241 K4 Floyd, Mount AZ U.S.A.
237 C5 Floydada TX U.S.A.
178 B4 Fluchthorn mt. Austria/Switz.
190 D2 Flüelen Switz.
190 D2 Flühli Switz.
186 C3 Flúmen r. Spain
192 B5 Flumendosa r. Sardegna Italy
193 H3 Flumeri Italy
160 E3 Flumet France
192 B4 Flumineddu r. Sardegna Italy
192 B5 Flumineddu r. Sardegna Italy
192 A5 Fluminimaggiore Sardegna Italy
190 E1 Flums Switz.
Flushing Neth. see Vlissingen
232 B3 Flushing MI U.S.A.
232 C4 Flushing OH U.S.A.
192 A4 Flussio Sardegna Italy
186 G2 Fluvià r. Spain
91 J8 Fly r. P.N.G.
262 R2 Flying Fish, Cape Antarctica
86 □1 Flying Fish Cove Christmas I.
84 C2 Flying Fox Creek r. N.T. Austr.
79 □2 Foa i. Tonga
223 K5 Foam Lake Sask. Can.
190 D3 Fobello Italy
188 G4 Foča Bos.-Herz.
199 E2 Foça Turkey
165 E4 Focant Belgium
191 H3 Focce dell'Adige r. mouth Italy
146 E4 Fochabers Moray, Scotland U.K.
215 F2 Fochville S. Africa
168 E1 Fockbek Ger.
197 H3 Focșani Romania
197 H2 Focuri Romania
159 I4 Foëcy France
84 D2 Foelsche r. N.T. Austr.
109 E4 Fogang Guangdong China
84 B2 Fog Bay N.T. Austr.
234 C2 Fogelsville PA U.S.A.
193 H3 Foggia Italy
193 H3 Foggia prov. Puglia Italy
191 H5 Foglia r. Italy
141 M3 Föglö Åland Fin.
206 □ Fogo i. Cape Verde
121 G4 Fogoleva Kazakh.
179 F3 Fohnsdorf Austria
168 D1 Föhr i. Ger.
171 D3 Fohrde Ger.
172 A2 Föhren Ger.
184 B3 Fóia hill Port.
191 G5 Foiano della Chiana Italy
177 L4 Foieni Romania
147 A5 Foilclough hill Rep. of Ireland
146 D3 Foinaven hill Scotland U.K.
163 D6 Foix France
186 E3 Foix r. Spain
139 J5 Fokino Rus. Fed.
207 G4 Fokku Nigeria
177 H5 Foktő Hungary
142 B1 Folarskarnuten mt. Norway
140 K2 Folda sea chan. Norway
177 J5 Földeák Hungary
177 K4 Földes Hungary
140 J2 Foldfjorden sea chan. Norway
198 D3 Folegandros i. Greece
231 C6 Foley AL U.S.A.
236 E2 Foley MN U.S.A.
224 D3 Foleyet Ont. Can.
85 G4 Foleyvale Qld Austr.
Folgares Angola see Capelongo
191 G3 Folgaria Italy
263 H2 Folger, Cape Antarctica
182 C2 Folgoso de Courel Spain
182 D2 Folgoso de la Ribera Spain
193 F2 Folignano Italy
193 E2 Foligno Italy
151 I3 Folkestone Kent, England U.K.
151 G2 Folkingham Lincolnshire, England U.K.
231 D6 Folkston GA U.S.A.
141 J3 Folldal Norway
191 H3 Follina Italy
140 K3 Föllinge Sweden
192 C2 Follonica Italy
150 C4 Folly Gate Devon, England U.K.
157 G3 Folschviller France
232 C5 Folsom WV U.S.A.
217 □3 Fomboni Comoros
246 C2 Fómento Cuba
135 H7 Fomin Rus. Fed.
134 H5 Fominki Rus. Fed.
134 H4 Fominskoye Rus. Fed.
183 G2 Foncea hill Spain
233 F3 Fonda NY U.S.A.
223 J3 Fond-du-Lac Sask. Can.
223 J3 Fond du Lac r. Sask. Can.
226 C4 Fond du Lac WI U.S.A.
232 B6 Fonde KY U.S.A.
182 B3 Fondevila Spain
193 F3 Fondi Italy
185 H4 Fondón Spain
185 G3 Fonelas Spain
186 B3 Fonfría Spain
182 D3 Fonfría Spain
206 C4 Fon Going ridge Guinea
192 B4 Fonni Sardegna Italy
163 C4 Fonroque France
Fonsagrada Spain see A Fonsagrada
250 C2 Fonseca Col.
163 D5 Fonsorbes France
157 G5 Fontaine Franche-Comté France
161 D3 Fontaine Rhône-Alpes France
156 C4 Fontainebleau France
160 D1 Fontaine-Française France
156 B3 Fontaine-le-Bourg France
159 G2 Fontaine-le-Dun France
160 D1 Fontaine-lès-Dijon France
157 G5 Fontaine-lès-Luxeuil France
165 D4 Fontaine-l'Évêque Belgium
160 C2 Fontaines Bourgogne France
156 D5 Fontaines Bourgogne France
161 F4 Fontan France
234 B2 Fontana PA U.S.A.
183 G4 Fontanar Spain
185 F1 Fontanarejo Spain
190 F4 Fontanellato Italy
193 F3 Fontanelle r. Italy
161 C5 Fontanès France
225 G2 Fontanges Que. Can.
190 E4 Fontanigorda Italy
161 B3 Fontannes France
185 F2 Fontanosas Spain
222 F3 Fontas B.C. Can.
222 F3 Fontas r. B.C. Can.
Font Blanca, Pic de mt. France/Spain see Port, Pic du
251 E5 Fonte Boa Brazil
193 F2 Fontecchio Italy
193 F2 Fontecellese, Monte mt. Italy
216 □1a Fonte do Bastardo Terceira Azores
207 H5 Fontem Cameroon
162 B2 Fontenay-le-Comte France
156 C4 Fontenay-Trésigny France
160 B1 Fontenoy France
157 G5 Fontenoy-le-Château France
157 F4 Fontenoy-sur-Moselle France
182 B5 Fontes Port.
159 G4 Fontevraud-l'Abbaye France
159 G5 Fontgombault France
191 G3 Fonti, Cima mt. Italy
216 □1a Fontinhas Terceira Azores
183 F4 Fontiveros Spain
157 F3 Fontoy France
163 E6 Font-Romeu-Odeillo-Via France
147 E3 Fontstown Rep. of Ireland
140 □D2 Fontur pt Iceland
161 C5 Fontvieille France
79 □2 Fonuafo'ou i. Tonga
Fonuafu'u i. Tonga see Fonuafo'ou
77 I3 Fonualei i. Tonga
78 □4a Fonuchu i. Chuuk Micronesia
177 G5 Fonyód Hungary
186 D2 Fonz Spain
191 G2 Fonzaso Italy
Foochow Fujian China see Fuzhou
227 H3 Foot's Bay Ont. Can.
108 D1 Foping Shaanxi China
190 E2 Foppolo Italy
193 E2 Forano Italy
122 C3 Forat Iran
Foraulep atoll Micronesia see Faraulep
157 G3 Forbach France
172 C3 Forbach Ger.
83 G3 Forbes N.S.W. Austr.
222 G4 Forbes, Mount Alta Can.
81 A6 Forbes, Mount South I. N.Z.
117 F4 Forbesganj Bihar India
161 E5 Forcalcueiret France
186 C4 Forcall Spain
161 D5 Forcalquier France
182 B2 Forcarei Spain
Forcary Spain see Forcarei
193 F2 Force Italy
172 B3 Forchheim Baden-Württemberg Ger.
173 F2 Forchheim Bayern Ger.
172 D2 Forchtenberg Ger.
179 H3 Forchtenstein Austria
225 H1 Ford r. Que. Can.
146 C5 Ford Argyll and Bute, Scotland U.K.
149 G2 Ford Northumberland, England U.K.
226 D3 Ford r. MI U.S.A.
84 B2 Ford, Cape N.T. Austr.
240 H4 Ford City CA U.S.A.
232 D4 Ford City PA U.S.A.
141 I3 Førde Norway
80 E3 Fordell North I. N.Z.
171 C4 Förderstedt Ger.
151 H2 Fordham Cambridgeshire, England U.K.
151 F4 Fordingbridge Hampshire, England U.K.
192 A5 Fordongianus Sardegna Italy
146 F5 Fordoun Aberdeenshire, Scotland U.K.
262 O1 Ford Range mts Antarctica
235 D2 Fords NJ U.S.A.
83 F2 Fords Bridge N.S.W. Austr.
147 E3 Fordstown Rep. of Ireland
146 F4 Fordyce Aberdeenshire, Scotland U.K.
237 E5 Fordyce AR U.S.A.
206 B4 Forécariah Guinea
221 O3 Forel, Mont mt. Greenland
151 F4 Foreland hd England U.K.
237 E5 Foreman AR U.S.A.
223 I5 Foremost Alta Can.
193 H4 Forenza Italy
222 E4 Foresight Mountain B.C. Can.
224 D5 Forest Ont. Can.
237 F5 Forest MS U.S.A.
232 B4 Forest OH U.S.A.
232 D6 Forest VA U.S.A.
223 H4 Forestburg Alta Can.
234 D1 Forestburg NY U.S.A.
234 C1 Forest City PA U.S.A.
85 E3 Forest Creek r. Qld Austr.
83 F3 Forest Hill N.S.W. Austr.
85 F5 Forest Hill Qld Austr.
240 G2 Foresthill CA U.S.A.
83 G5 Forestier Peninsula Tas. Austr.
226 C3 Forest Junction WI U.S.A.
226 A3 Forest Lake MN U.S.A.
241 L4 Forest Lakes AZ U.S.A.
231 C5 Forest Park GA U.S.A.
240 G2 Forest Ranch CA U.S.A.
151 H3 Forest Row East Sussex, England U.K.
225 G3 Forestville Que. Can.
240 F2 Forestville CA U.S.A.
234 B4 Forestville MD U.S.A.
227 F4 Forestville MI U.S.A.
232 D3 Forestville NY U.S.A.
142 A2 Føresvik Norway
160 B3 Forez, Monts du mts France
160 B3 Forez, Plaine du plain France
146 F5 Forfar Angus, Scotland U.K.
237 C4 Forgan OK U.S.A.
156 B3 Forges-les-Eaux France
173 E4 Forggensee l. Ger.
146 E4 Forgie Moray, Scotland U.K.
193 G4 Forino Italy
193 F4 Forio Italy
171 C5 Föritz Ger.
182 B3 Forjães Port.
234 B3 Fork MD U.S.A.
237 F5 Forked Deer r. TN U.S.A.
233 F5 Forked River NJ U.S.A.
147 E2 Forkhill Northern Ireland U.K.
238 A2 Forks WA U.S.A.
234 B1 Forkston PA U.S.A.
234 B1 Forksville PA U.S.A.
232 D6 Fork Union VA U.S.A.
191 H4 Forlì Italy
191 H5 Forlì prov. Emilia-Romagna Italy
191 H4 Forlimpopoli Italy
236 D2 Forman ND U.S.A.
190 D2 Formazza Italy
149 F4 Formby Merseyside, England U.K.
187 E6 Formentera i. Spain
187 G5 Formentor, Cap de c. Spain
156 B3 Formerie France
Former Yugoslav Republic of Macedonia country Europe see Macedonia
193 F3 Formia Italy
187 C4 Formiche Alte Spain
193 G3 Formicola Italy
257 E4 Formiga Brazil
191 F4 Formigine Italy
191 G4 Formignana Italy
163 E6 Formiguères France
258 F2 Formosa Arg.
258 F2 Formosa prov. Arg.
Formosa country Asia see Taiwan
255 D5 Formosa Brazil
253 G3 Formosa, Serra hills Brazil
254 D4 Formosa do Rio Preto Brazil
Formosa Strait China/Taiwan see Taiwan Strait
182 B4 Formoselha Port.
254 D5 Formoso Minas Gerais Brazil
254 C4 Formoso Tocantins Brazil
254 D5 Formoso r. Bahia Brazil
256 A3 Formoso r. Goiás Brazil
254 C4 Formoso r. Tocantins Brazil
147 B3 Formoyle Rep. of Ireland
192 A3 Fornelli Sardegna Italy
186 □ Fornells Spain
186 F3 Fornells de la Selva Spain
191 H2 Forni Avoltri Italy
191 H2 Forni di Sopra Italy
191 H2 Forni di Sotto Italy
190 C3 Forno Alpi Graie Italy
178 D4 Forno di Zoldo Italy
182 D3 Fornos Port.
182 C4 Fornos de Algodres Port.
190 F4 Fornovo di Taro Italy
193 G2 Foro r. Italy
140 J3 Forolshogna mt. Norway
137 G5 Foros Ukr.
184 B2 Foros de Vale Figueira Port.
184 B1 Foros do Arrão Port.
Føroyar terr. N. Atlantic Ocean see Faroe Islands
177 I5 Forráskút Hungary
146 E4 Forres Moray, Scotland U.K.
87 F6 Forrest W.A. Austr.
86 F2 Forrest r. W.A. Austr.
226 C5 Forrest IL U.S.A.
262 U1 Forrestal Range mts Antarctica
237 F5 Forrest City AR U.S.A.
87 F6 Forrest Lakes salt flat W.A. Austr.
226 C4 Forreston IL U.S.A.
Forrest River Mission W.A. Austr. see Oombulgurri
177 K3 Forró Hungary
162 B2 Fors France
142 B2 Forsand Norway
85 E3 Forsayth Qld Austr.
150 E2 Forsbrook Staffordshire, England U.K.
142 E2 Forshaga Sweden
146 E3 Forsinard Highland, Scotland U.K.
140 L2 Forsnäs Sweden
141 M3 Forssa Fin.
172 C2 Forst Baden-Württemberg Ger.
171 F4 Forst Brandenburg Ger.
83 H3 Forster N.S.W. Austr.
173 F3 Forstern Ger.
173 F3 Forstinning Ger.
231 D5 Forsyth GA U.S.A.
237 E4 Forsyth MO U.S.A.
238 F2 Forsyth MT U.S.A.
227 I1 Forsythe Que. Can.
84 D3 Forsyth Islands Qld Austr.
85 E4 Forsyth Range hills Qld Austr.
123 H4 Fort Abbas Pak.
224 D2 Fort Albany Ont. Can.
252 D2 Fortaleza Bol.
254 F2 Fortaleza Brazil
186 C4 Fortanete Spain
Fort Archambault Chad see Sarh
232 D5 Fort Ashby WV U.S.A.
222 H4 Fort Assiniboine Alta Can.
226 C4 Fort Atkinson WI U.S.A.
146 D4 Fort Augustus Highland, Scotland U.K.
222 E4 Fort Babine B.C. Can.
215 F5 Fort Beaufort S. Africa
238 E2 Fort Benton MT U.S.A.
223 J4 Fort Black Sask. Can.
Fort Brabant N.W.T. Can. see Tuktoyaktuk
240 F2 Fort Bragg CA U.S.A.
Fort Carillon NY U.S.A. see Ticonderoga
Fort Carnot Madag. see Ikongo
Fort Charlet Alg. see Djanet
Fort Chimo Que. Can. see Kuujjuaq
223 I3 Fort Chipewyan Alta Can.
238 F3 Fort Collins CO U.S.A.
85 E4 Fort Constantine Qld Austr.
224 E4 Fort-Coulonge Que. Can.
233 F2 Fort Covington NY U.S.A.
Fort Crampel C.A.R. see Kaga Bandoro
Fort-Dauphin Madag. see Tôlañaro
237 C6 Fort Davis TX U.S.A.
247 □3 Fort-de-France Martinique
Fort de Kock Sumatera Indon. see Bukittinggi
Fort de Polignac Alg. see Illizi
231 C5 Fort Deposit AL U.S.A.
236 E3 Fort Dodge IA U.S.A.
215 G4 Fort Donald S. Africa
241 M1 Fort Duchesne UT U.S.A.
182 B2 Forte Spain
192 A4 Forte, Monte hill Sardegna Italy
233 G3 Fort Edward NY U.S.A.
227 H4 Fort Erie Ont. Can.
86 C4 Fortescue r. W.A. Austr.
234 C3 Fortescue NJ U.S.A.
191 G2 Fortezza Italy
192 C2 Fortezza, Monte della hill Italy
233 □J1 Fort Fairfield ME U.S.A.
Fort Foureau Cameroon see Kousséri
226 A1 Fort Frances Ont. Can.
Fort Franklin N.W.T. Can. see Déljne
231 C6 Fort Gaines GA U.S.A.
239 F4 Fort Garland CO U.S.A.
232 B5 Fort Gay WV U.S.A.
Fort George Que. Can. see Chisasibi
220 F3 Fort Good Hope N.W.T. Can.
Fort Gouraud Maur. see Fdérik
146 E6 Forth South Lanarkshire, Scotland U.K.
144 F3 Forth r. Scotland U.K.
146 E5 Forth, Firth of est. Scotland U.K.
Fort Hall Kenya see Muranga
239 F6 Fort Hancock TX U.S.A.
215 F5 Fort Hare S. Africa
241 J2 Fortification Range mts NV U.S.A.
245 F4 Fortín Mex.
253 E5 Fortín Ávalos Sánchez Para.
253 F5 Fortín Carlos Antonio López Para.
253 F5 Fortín Coronel Bogado Para.
253 E5 Fortín Coronel Eugenio Garay Para.
146 D5 Fortingall Perth and Kinross, Scotland U.K.
253 E5 Fortín General Mendoza Para.
253 E5 Fortín Hernandarías Para.
253 E5 Fortín Infante Rivarola Para.
253 F5 Fortín Juan de Zalazar Para.
253 F5 Fortín Presidente Ayala Para.
253 E5 Fortín Teniente Juan Echauri López Para.
184 C1 Fortios Port.
Fort Jameson Zambia see Chipata
Fort Johnston Malawi see Mangochi
233 □I1 Fort Kent ME U.S.A.
238 B3 Fort Klamath OR U.S.A.
Fort Lamy Chad see Ndjamena
Fort Laperrine Alg. see Tamanrasset
238 F3 Fort Laramie WY U.S.A.
231 D7 Fort Lauderdale FL U.S.A.
235 E2 Fort Lee NJ U.S.A.
222 F2 Fort Liard N.W.T. Can.
246 E3 Fort Liberté Haiti
232 E5 Fort Loudon PA U.S.A.
223 I3 Fort Mackay Alta Can.
222 H5 Fort Macleod Alta Can.
226 B5 Fort Madison IA U.S.A.
156 B2 Fort-Mahon-Plage France
Fort Manning Malawi see Mchinji
226 B3 Fort McCoy WI U.S.A.
223 I3 Fort McMurray Alta Can.
220 E3 Fort McPherson N.W.T. Can.
235 E1 Fort Montgomery NY U.S.A.
236 C3 Fort Morgan CO U.S.A.
215 H3 Fort Mtombeni S. Africa
231 D7 Fort Myers FL U.S.A.
222 F3 Fort Nelson B.C. Can.
222 F3 Fort Nelson r. B.C. Can.
Fort Norman N.W.T. Can. see Tulít'a
Fort Orange NY U.S.A. see Albany
193 H3 Fortore r. Italy
231 C5 Fort Payne AL U.S.A.
238 F1 Fort Peck MT U.S.A.
238 F2 Fort Peck Reservoir MT U.S.A.
231 D7 Fort Pierce FL U.S.A.
236 C2 Fort Pierre SD U.S.A.
210 A4 Fort Portal Uganda
222 G2 Fort Providence N.W.T. Can.
223 K5 Fort Qu'Appelle Sask. Can.
Fort Randall AK U.S.A. see Cold Bay
232 A4 Fort Recovery OH U.S.A.
222 H2 Fort Resolution N.W.T. Can.
213 F3 Fort Rixon Zimbabwe
81 B7 Fortrose South I. N.Z.
146 D4 Fortrose Highland, Scotland U.K.
Fort Rosebery Zambia see Mansa
Fort Rousset Congo see Owando
Fort Rupert Que. Can. see Waskaganish
222 E4 Fort St James B.C. Can.
222 F3 Fort St John B.C. Can.
Fort Sandeman Pak. see Zhob
222 H4 Fort Saskatchewan Alta Can.
237 E4 Fort Scott KS U.S.A.
224 C1 Fort Severn Ont. Can.
120 B3 Fort-Shevchenko Kazakh.
222 F2 Fort Simpson N.W.T. Can.
223 H2 Fort Smith N.W.T. Can.
237 E5 Fort Smith AR U.S.A.
238 F2 Fort Smith MT U.S.A.
237 C6 Fort Stockton TX U.S.A.
239 F5 Fort Sumner NM U.S.A.
237 D4 Fort Supply OK U.S.A.
241 M5 Fort Thomas AZ U.S.A.
Fort Trinquet Maur. see Bîr Mogreïn
187 B6 Fortuna Spain
238 A3 Fortuna CA U.S.A.
236 C1 Fortuna ND U.S.A.
225 K4 Fortune Bay Nfld. Can.
150 E4 Fortuneswell Dorset, England U.K.
231 D5 Fort Valley GA U.S.A.
222 G3 Fort Vermilion Alta Can.
Fort Victoria Zimbabwe see Masvingo
Fort Walton FL U.S.A. see Fort Walton Beach
231 C6 Fort Walton Beach FL U.S.A.
Fort Ware B.C. Can. see Ware
234 C2 Fort Washington PA U.S.A.
230 C3 Fort Wayne IN U.S.A.
251 G3 Fort Wellington Guyana
146 C5 Fort William Highland, Scotland U.K.
239 E5 Fort Wingate NM U.S.A.
237 D5 Fort Worth TX U.S.A.
236 C2 Fort Yates ND U.S.A.
234 C1 Forty Fort PA U.S.A.
Forty-Second Hill S. Africa see 42nd Hill
220 D3 Fort Yukon AK U.S.A.
Forum Iulii France see Fréjus
122 C5 Forūr, Jazīreh-ye i. Iran
140 K2 Forvik Norway
195 E5 Forza d'Agrò Sicilia Italy
163 C6 Fos France
190 F4 Fosdinovo Italy
109 E4 Foshan Guangdong China
141 K3 Foskvallen Sweden
140 J3 Fosna pen. Norway
206 E5 Foso Ghana
193 G2 Fossacesia Italy
178 D5 Fossalta di Portogruaro Italy
190 C4 Fossano Italy
191 H5 Fossato di Vico Italy
162 C3 Fossemagne France
165 D4 Fosses-la-Ville Belgium
160 D2 Fossiat France
238 B2 Fossil OR U.S.A.
86 E3 Fossil Downs W.A. Austr.
191 H5 Fossombrone Italy
161 C5 Fos-sur-Mer France
83 F4 Foster Vic. Austr.
232 A5 Foster KY U.S.A.
222 C3 Foster, Mount Alaska/B.C. Can./U.S.A.
221 P2 Foster Bugt b. Greenland
234 D1 Fosterdale NY U.S.A.
233 □J2 Fosterville N.B. Can.
232 B4 Fostoria OH U.S.A.
177 I4 Fót Hungary
213 □J5 Fotadrevo Madag.
149 I4 Fotherby Lincolnshire, England U.K.
Fotuna i. Vanuatu see Futuna
156 B3 Foucarmont France
160 D1 Foucherans France
158 B4 Fouesnant France
157 F4 Foug France
208 A5 Fougamou Gabon
158 E3 Fougères France
157 G5 Fougerolles France
159 F3 Fougerolles-du-Plessis France
156 C3 Fouilloy France
146 □F1 Foula i. Scotland U.K.
157 F4 Foulain France
206 B3 Foulamôri Guinea
163 C4 Foulayronnes France
146 F6 Foulden Scottish Borders, Scotland U.K.
208 A5 Foulenzem Gabon
147 E4 Foulkesmill Rep. of Ireland
149 G4 Foulridge Lancashire, England U.K.
81 C4 Foulwind, Cape South I. N.Z.
207 H5 Foumban Cameroon
207 H5 Foumbot Cameroon
217 □3a Foumbouni Njazidja Comoros
204 D3 Foum Zguid Morocco
206 A3 Foundiougne Senegal
232 B6 Fount KY U.S.A.
226 A4 Fountain MN U.S.A.
147 B4 Fountain Cross Rep. of Ireland
241 L2 Fountain Green UT U.S.A.
234 C2 Fountain Hill PA U.S.A.
149 H3 Fountains Abbey tourist site England U.K.
184 C3 Foupana r. Port.
162 A3 Fouras France
163 C5 Fourcès France
160 B1 Fourchambault France
157 F4 Fourches, Mont des hill France
240 I4 Four Corners CA U.S.A.
151 H3 Four Elms Kent, England U.K.
215 G3 Fouriesburg S. Africa
151 F3 Four Marks Hampshire, England U.K.
156 E2 Fourmies France
161 B4 Fournels France
199 E3 Fournoi Greece
199 E3 Fournoi i. Greece
151 H4 Four Oaks East Sussex, England U.K.
161 C5 Fourques Languedoc-Roussillon France
163 E6 Fourques Languedoc-Roussillon France
163 C4 Fourques-sur-Garonne France
160 B2 Fours France
203 G5 Fourth Cataract rapids Sudan
206 B4 Fouta Djallon reg. Guinea
81 A7 Foveaux Strait South I. N.Z.
234 B3 Fowbelsburg MD U.S.A.
150 C4 Fowey Cornwall, England U.K.
150 C4 Fowey r. England U.K.
231 E7 Fowl Cay i. Bahamas
240 H3 Fowler CA U.S.A.
239 F4 Fowler CO U.S.A.
230 C3 Fowler IN U.S.A.
226 E4 Fowler MI U.S.A.
82 C2 Fowlers Bay S.A. Austr.
82 C3 Fowlers Bay b. S.A. Austr.
227 E4 Fowlerville MI U.S.A.
127 H3 Fowman Iran
150 E2 Fownhope Herefordshire, England U.K.
222 E3 Fox r. B.C. Can.
223 M3 Fox r. Man. Can.
226 C5 Fox r. IL U.S.A.
226 C4 Fox r. WI U.S.A.
182 B1 Foxas Spain
85 F4 Fox Creek r. Qld Austr.
222 G4 Fox Creek Alta Can.
221 K3 Foxe Basin g. Nunavut Can.
221 J3 Foxe Channel Nunavut Can.
221 K3 Foxe Peninsula Nunavut Can.
147 B3 Foxford Rep. of Ireland
81 C5 Fox Glacier South I. N.Z.
220 B4 Fox Islands AK U.S.A.
222 H3 Fox Lake Alta Can.
226 C4 Fox Lake IL U.S.A.
222 C2 Fox Mountain Y.T. Can.
238 F3 Foxpark WY U.S.A.
80 E4 Foxton North I. N.Z.
80 E4 Foxton Beach North I. N.Z.
223 I5 Fox Valley Sask. Can.
146 D4 Foyers Highland, Scotland U.K.
148 B4 Foygh Rep. of Ireland
147 D2 Foyle r. Rep. of Ireland/U.K.
147 D1 Foyle, Lough b. Rep. of Ireland/U.K.
147 B4 Foynes Rep. of Ireland
184 B1 Foz Port.
182 C1 Foz Spain
184 A1 Foz do Arelho Port.
209 A9 Foz do Cunene Angola
255 B8 Foz do Iguaçu Brazil
182 C5 Foz Giraldo Port.
190 C4 Frabosa Soprana Italy
175 L2 Frącki Pol.
227 I5 Frackville PA U.S.A.
182 E4 Frades de la Sierra Spain
186 D3 Fraga Spain
195 G2 Fragagnano Italy
179 F2 Fraham Austria
258 G4 Fraile Muerto Uru.
185 G3 Frailes Spain
165 D4 Fraire Belgium
160 D1 Fraisans France
161 A5 Fraisse-sur-Agout France
157 H4 Fraize France
262 Q1 Frakes, Mount Antarctica
165 C4 Frameries Belgium
151 H4 Framfield East Sussex, England U.K.
233 H3 Framingham MA U.S.A.
151 I2 Framlingham Suffolk, England U.K.
143 G1 Främlingshem Sweden
169 E5 Frammersbach Ger.
263 E2 Framnes Mountains Antarctica
263 D2 Fram Peak Antarctica
175 K5 Frampol Pol.
151 G2 Frampton Lincolnshire, England U.K.
150 E3 Frampton on Severn Gloucestershire, England U.K.
256 D4 Franca Brazil
193 G2 Francavilla al Mare Italy
195 E5 Francavilla di Sicilia Sicilia Italy
195 G2 Francavilla Fontana Italy
193 I4 Francavilla in Sinni Italy
154 F3 France country Europe
82 E4 Frances S.A. Austr.
222 D2 Frances r. Y.T. Can.
163 C4 Francescas France
222 D2 Frances Lake Y.T. Can.
226 D5 Francesville IN U.S.A.
208 B5 Franceville Gabon
157 G5 Franche-Comté admin. reg. France
223 K5 Francis Sask. Can.
Francis atoll Gilbert Is Kiribati see Beru
Francisco de Orellana Ecuador see Puerto Francisco de Orellana
250 C5 Francisco de Orellana Peru
242 E3 Francisco I. Madero Mex.
244 B1 Francisco I. Madero Mex.
244 B3 Francisco I. Madero Mex.
257 F2 Francisco Sá Brazil
242 A1 Francisco Zarco Mex.
213 E4 Francistown Botswana
182 C3 Franco Port.
256 D5 Franco da Rocha Brazil
194 D5 Francofonte Sicilia Italy
225 J4 Francois Nfld. Can.
186 E3 Francolí r. Spain
234 A4 Franconia VA U.S.A.
165 E4 Francorchamps Belgium
163 D4 Francoulès France
238 E3 Francs Peak WY U.S.A.
164 E1 Franeker Neth.
160 D2 Frangy France
169 D4 Frankenau Ger.
171 E5 Frankenberg Ger.
169 D4 Frankenberg (Eder) Ger.
179 E2 Frankenburg am Hausruck Austria
179 G3 Frankenfels Austria
169 F5 Frankenhain Ger.
169 F5 Frankenheim Ger.
179 E3 Frankenmarkt Austria
227 F4 Frankenmuth MI U.S.A.
172 C2 Frankenthal (Pfalz) Ger.
171 C5 Frankenwald mts Ger.
246 □ Frankfield Jamaica
227 I3 Frankford Ont. Can.
215 G2 Frankfort S. Africa
230 C3 Frankfort IN U.S.A.
230 C4 Frankfort KY U.S.A.
226 D3 Frankfort MI U.S.A.
232 B5 Frankfort OH U.S.A.
169 D5 Frankfurt am Main Ger.
171 F3 Frankfurt an der Oder Ger.
173 E3 Fränkische Alb hills Ger.
173 F2 Fränkische Rezat r. Ger.
169 E5 Fränkische Saale r. Ger.
173 F2 Fränkische Schweiz reg. Ger.
87 C7 Frankland r. W.A. Austr.
83 F4 Frankland, Cape Tas. Austr.
150 E2 Frankley Worcestershire, England U.K.
215 G4 Franklin S. Africa
241 M5 Franklin AZ U.S.A.
231 C5 Franklin GA U.S.A.
230 C4 Franklin IN U.S.A.
230 C4 Franklin KY U.S.A.
237 F6 Franklin LA U.S.A.
233 H3 Franklin MA U.S.A.
233 □I2 Franklin ME U.S.A.
231 D5 Franklin NC U.S.A.
236 D3 Franklin NE U.S.A.
233 H3 Franklin NH U.S.A.
234 D1 Franklin NJ U.S.A.
232 A5 Franklin OH U.S.A.
232 D4 Franklin PA U.S.A.
231 C5 Franklin TN U.S.A.
237 D6 Franklin TX U.S.A.
232 E6 Franklin VA U.S.A.
226 C4 Franklin WI U.S.A.
232 D5 Franklin WV U.S.A.
234 A2 Franklinburg PA U.S.A.
228 C1 Franklin D. Roosevelt Lake WA U.S.A.
232 B5 Franklin Furnace OH U.S.A.
226 C5 Franklin Grove IL U.S.A.
82 D3 Franklin Harbor b. S.A. Austr.
263 L1 Franklin Island Antarctica
222 F2 Franklin Mountains N.W.T. Can.
81 A6 Franklin Mountains South I. N.Z.
234 D2 Franklin Park NJ U.S.A.
83 F5 Franklin Sound sea chan. Tas. Austr.
235 E2 Franklin Square NY U.S.A.
221 I2 Franklin Strait Nunavut Can.
237 F6 Franklinton LA U.S.A.
234 C3 Franklinville NJ U.S.A.
232 D3 Franklinville NY U.S.A.
175 I1 Frankowo Pol.
140 K3 Frankrike Sweden
83 F4 Frankston Vic. Austr.
81 B6 Frankton South I. N.Z.
160 D1 Franois France
214 D3 Fransenhof S. Africa
141 L3 Fränsta Sweden
176 B1 Františkovy Lázně Czech Rep.
224 C3 Franz Ont. Can.
170 D1 Franzburg Ger.
81 C5 Franz Josef Glacier South I. N.Z.
Franz Josef Land is Rus. Fed. see Zemlya Frantsa-Iosifa
173 F3 Franz Josef Strauss airport Ger.
194 D5 Frasca, Monte hill Sicilia Italy
193 E3 Frascati Italy
193 I5 Frascineto Italy
173 G4 Frasdorf Ger.
86 D3 Fraser r. W.A. Austr.
222 F5 Fraser r. B.C. Can.
225 I1 Fraser r. Nfld. Can.
87 C5 Fraser, Mount hill W.A. Austr.
214 C4 Fraserburg S. Africa
146 F4 Fraserburgh Aberdeenshire, Scotland U.K.
224 D3 Fraserdale Ont. Can.
85 H5 Fraser Island Qld Austr.
87 B4 Fraser Island W.A. Austr.
222 E4 Fraser Lake B.C. Can.
222 E4 Fraser Plateau B.C. Can.
87 D7 Fraser Range W.A. Austr.
87 D7 Fraser Range hills W.A. Austr.
80 F3 Frasertown North I. N.Z.
160 E2 Frasne France
165 C4 Frasnes-lez-Buissenal Belgium
165 D4 Frasnes-lez-Gosselies Belgium
191 F4 Frassinoro Italy
193 G3 Frasso Telesino Italy
178 A3 Frastanz Austria
182 C5 Fratel Port.
194 D4 Fratello r. Sicilia Italy
226 E2 Frater Ont. Can.
197 G4 Frătești Romania
191 G3 Fratta r. Italy
191 G3 Fratta Polesine Italy
193 E2 Fratta Todina Italy
190 C1 Fraubrunnen Switz.
173 H3 Frauenau Ger.
190 D1 Frauenfeld Switz.
179 H3 Frauenkirchen Austria
171 E5 Frauenstein Ger.
179 G4 Frauental an der Laßnitz Austria
169 F5 Frauenwald Ger.
173 F3 Fraunberg Ger.
171 D5 Fraureuth Ger.
261 H3 Fray Bentos Uru.
261 G3 Fray Luis Beltrán Arg.
258 G4 Fray Marcos Uru.
163 D4 Frayssinet-le-Gélat France
234 C2 Frazer PA U.S.A.
232 B4 Frazeysburg OH U.S.A.
240 H4 Frazier Park CA U.S.A.
182 B3 Freamunde Port.
197 I3 Frecăței Romania
161 B5 Frech, Mont mt. France
182 C3 Frechas Port.
169 B5 Frechen Ger.
183 F2 Frechilla Spain
149 G4 Freckleton Lancashire, England U.K.
169 E4 Freden (Leine) Ger.
168 E2 Fredenbeck Ger.
226 E3 Frederic MI U.S.A.
226 A3 Frederic WI U.S.A.
234 C3 Frederica DE U.S.A.
142 C4 Fredericia Denmark
87 C5 Frederick r. W.A. Austr.
232 E5 Frederick MD U.S.A.
237 D5 Frederick OK U.S.A.
226 A4 Fredericksburg IA U.S.A.
234 B2 Fredericksburg PA U.S.A.
237 D6 Fredericksburg TX U.S.A.
232 E5 Fredericksburg VA U.S.A.
237 F4 Fredericktown MO U.S.A.
232 B4 Fredericktown OH U.S.A.
225 H4 Fredericton N.B. Can.
233 □J2 Fredericton Junction N.B. Can.
142 E4 Frederiksborg county Denmark
Frederikshåb Greenland see Paamiut
142 D3 Frederikshavn Denmark
142 E4 Frederikssund Denmark
247 F3 Frederiksted Virgin Is (U.S.A.)
142 E4 Frederiksværk Denmark
170 E3 Fredersdorf Ger.
241 K3 Fredonia AZ U.S.A.
237 E4 Fredonia KS U.S.A.
232 D3 Fredonia NY U.S.A.
232 C4 Fredonia PA U.S.A.
226 D4 Fredonia WI U.S.A.
140 L2 Fredrika Sweden
143 F1 Fredriksberg Sweden
Fredrikshamn Fin. see Hamina
142 D2 Fredrikstad Norway
Fredriksvern Norway see Stavern
175 K6 Fredropol Pol.
234 B2 Freeburg PA U.S.A.
233 F4 Freehold NJ U.S.A.
234 C1 Freeland PA U.S.A.
82 D3 Freeling S.A. Austr.
84 C4 Freeling, Mount hill N.T. Austr.
82 D2 Freeling Heights hill S.A. Austr.
240 H2 Freel Peak CA U.S.A.
236 D3 Freeman SD U.S.A.
234 C2 Freemansburg PA U.S.A.
231 C6 Freeport FL U.S.A.
226 C4 Freeport IL U.S.A.
233 □H3 Freeport ME U.S.A.
235 E2 Freeport NY U.S.A.
232 D4 Freeport PA U.S.A.
237 E6 Freeport TX U.S.A.
231 E7 Freeport City Bahamas
237 D7 Freer TX U.S.A.
226 D3 Freesoil MI U.S.A.
215 F3 Free State prov. S. Africa
206 B4 Freetown Sierra Leone
235 F2 Freetown NY U.S.A.
235 D2 Freewood Acres NJ U.S.A.
217 □2a Frégate i. Inner Islands Seychelles
184 D2 Fregenal de la Sierra Spain
192 E3 Fregene Italy
186 D4 Freginals Spain
82 C1 Fregon S.A. Austr.
158 D3 Fréhel France
171 E5 Freiberg Ger.
171 D4 Freiberger Mulde r. Ger.
172 C4 Freiburg admin. reg. Baden-Württemberg Ger.
Freiburg Switz. see Fribourg
168 E2 Freiburg (Elbe) Ger.
172 B3 Freiburg im Breisgau Ger.
169 E5 Freiensteinau Ger.
168 E1 Freienwill Ger.
257 G2 Frei Gonzaga Brazil
173 F2 Freihung Ger.
257 G3 Frei Inocêncio Brazil
185 H3 Freila Spain
173 G4 Freilassing Ger.
172 C2 Freinsheim Ger.
260 A6 Freire Chile
172 B2 Freisen Ger.
173 F3 Freising Ger.
161 E4 Freissinières France
179 F2 Freistadt Austria
157 G3 Freistroff France
171 E5 Freital Ger.
182 C4 Freixedas Port.
182 B5 Freixianda Port.
182 C3 Freixiel Port.
182 C4 Freixiosa Port.
182 B3 Freixo Port.
182 D3 Freixo de Espada à Cinta Port.
163 E5 Fréjairolles France
161 E5 Fréjus France
161 E5 Fréjus, Golfe de b. France
161 E3 Fréjus Tunnel France/Italy
142 A1 Frekhaug Norway
169 F3 Frellstedt Ger.
87 B7 Fremantle W.A. Austr.
173 E3 Fremdingen Ger.
150 C3 Fremington Devon, England U.K.
240 G3 Fremont CA U.S.A.
226 E5 Fremont IN U.S.A.
226 E4 Fremont MI U.S.A.
236 D3 Fremont NE U.S.A.
232 B4 Fremont OH U.S.A.
226 C3 Fremont WI U.S.A.
241 L2 Fremont r. UT U.S.A.
241 L2 Fremont Junction UT U.S.A.
232 B6 Frenchburg KY U.S.A.
246 D2 French Cay i. Turks and Caicos Is
French Congo country Africa see Congo
232 D4 French Creek r. PA U.S.A.
251 H4 French Guiana terr. S. America
French Guinea country Africa see Guinea
83 F4 French Island Vic. Austr.
238 F1 Frenchman r. MT U.S.A.
233 □I2 Frenchman Bay ME U.S.A.
236 C3 Frenchman Creek r. NE U.S.A.
81 D4 French Pass South I. N.Z.
79 □3 French Polynesia terr. S. Pacific Ocean
French Somaliland country Africa see Djibouti
73 G6 French Southern and Antarctic Lands terr. Indian Ocean
French Sudan country Africa see Mali
French Territory of the Afars and Issas country Africa see Djibouti
234 C2 Frenchtown NJ U.S.A.
233 □I1 Frenchville ME U.S.A.
156 B2 Frencq France
205 F2 Frenda Alg.
156 B3 Freneuse France
173 E2 Frensdorf Ger.
151 G3 Frensham Surrey, England U.K.
177 H2 Frenštát pod Radhoštěm Czech Rep.
193 G3 Frentani, Monti dei mts Italy
215 G3 Frere S. Africa
169 C3 Freren Ger.
179 E4 Fresach Austria
193 G3 Fresagrandinaria Italy
251 I6 Fresco r. Brazil
206 D5 Fresco Côte d'Ivoire
263 K2 Freshfield, Cape Antarctica
147 D4 Freshford Rep. of Ireland
151 F4 Freshwater Isle of Wight, England U.K.
150 C3 Freshwater East Pembrokeshire, Wales U.K.
156 B4 Fresnay-l'Evêque France
159 G3 Fresnay-sur-Sarthe France
185 G2 Fresnedas r. Spain
185 F2 Fresnedillas hill Spain
160 D1 Fresne-St-Mamès France
157 F3 Fresnes-en-Woëvre France
157 F5 Fresnes-sur-Apance France
156 D2 Fresnes-sur-Escaut France
244 C2 Fresnillo Mex.
240 H3 Fresno CA U.S.A.
240 G3 Fresno r. CA U.S.A.
182 E4 Fresno Alhándiga Spain
182 E3 Fresno de la Ribera Spain
182 E3 Fresno de Sayago Spain
183 E3 Fresno el Viejo Spain
156 B3 Fresnoy-Folny France
156 D3 Fresnoy-le-Grand France
156 B2 Fressenneville France
157 G5 Fresse-sur-Moselle France
151 I2 Fressingfield Suffolk, England U.K.
141 I3 Fresvikbreen glacier Norway
146 E3 Freswick Highland, Scotland U.K.
160 D1 Fretigney-et-Velloreille France
172 D2 Freudenberg Baden-Württemberg Ger.
173 F2 Freudenberg Bayern Ger.
169 C5 Freudenberg Nordrhein-Westfalen Ger.
172 A2 Freudenburg Ger.
172 C3 Freudenstadt Ger.
156 C2 Frévent France
232 D3 Frewsburg NY U.S.A.
171 C4 Freyburg (Unstrut) Ger.

255 C9 Garopaba Brazil
116 C4 Garoth Madh. Prad. India
206 E2 Garou, Lac l. Mali
207 I4 Garoua Cameroon
207 I5 Garoua Boulai Cameroon
143 F2 Garphyttan Sweden
Garqêntang Xizang China see Sog
182 E2 Garrafe de Torio Spain
163 A6 Garralda Spain
147 B5 Garrane Rep. of Ireland
183 H3 Garray Spain
168 D3 Garrel Ger.
226 E5 Garrett IN U.S.A.
147 C2 Garrison Northern Ireland U.K.
232 B5 Garrison KY U.S.A.
236 E2 Garrison MN U.S.A.
236 C2 Garrison ND U.S.A.
235 E1 Garrison NY U.S.A.
147 E3 Garristown Rep. of Ireland
129 C3 Garrnarrich Armenia
147 F1 Garronpoint Northern Ireland U.K.
182 D5 Garrovillas Spain
185 I3 Garrucha Spain
146 D4 Garry r. Scotland U.K.
146 D4 Garry, Loch l. Highland, Scotland U.K.
122 D2 Garrygala Turkm.
146 B3 Garrynahine Western Isles, Scotland U.K.
215 F4 Garryowen S. Africa
147 C5 Garryvoe Rep. of Ireland
173 G3 Gars am Inn Ger.
179 G2 Gars am Kamp Austria
149 G3 Garsdale Head Cumbria, England U.K.
143 F4 Gärsnäs Sweden
149 G4 Garstang Lancashire, England U.K.
168 F2 Garstedt Ger.
179 F2 Garsten Austria
81 B6 Garston South I. N.Z.
Gartar Sichuan China see Qianning
162 C2 Gartempe r. France
150 D2 Garth Powys, Wales U.K.
150 D2 Garthmyl Powys, Wales U.K.
146 D5 Gartocharn West Dunbartonshire, Scotland U.K.
Gartog Xizang China see Markam
170 C2 Gartow Ger.
172 C3 Gärtringen Ger.
170 F2 Gartz Ger.
95 D4 Garut Jawa Barat Indon.
147 D3 Garvagh Rep. of Ireland
147 E2 Garvagh Northern Ireland U.K.
147 D2 Garvaghy Northern Ireland U.K.
146 F6 Garvald East Lothian, Scotland U.K.
146 D4 Garvamore Highland, Scotland U.K.
184 B3 Garvão Port.
146 B5 Garvard Argyll and Bute, Scotland U.K.
146 D4 Garve Highland, Scotland U.K.
81 B6 Garvie Mountains South I. N.Z.
116 E4 Garwa Bihar India
175 J4 Garwolin Pol.
230 C3 Gary IN U.S.A.
232 C6 Gary WV U.S.A.
108 A2 Garyi Sichuan China
103 F6 Garyū-zan mt. Japan
170 E1 Garz Ger.
258 E3 Garza Arg.
111 B5 Gar Zangbo r. China
108 A2 Garzê Sichuan China
250 C4 Garzón Col.
Gasan-Kuli Turkm. see Esenguly
174 F3 Gąsawa Pol.
178 B4 Gaschurn Austria
171 D4 Gaschwitz Ger.
163 B5 Gascogne reg. France
154 C5 Gascogne, Golfe de g. France/Spain
236 F4 Gasconade r. MO U.S.A.
Gascony reg. France see Gascogne
Gascony, Gulf of France/Spain see Gascogne, Golfe de
87 B5 Gascoyne r. W.A. Austr.
87 C5 Gascoyne, Mount hill W.A. Austr.
87 B5 Gascoyne Junction W.A. Austr.
183 H4 Gascueña Spain
Gascuña, Golfo de g. France/Spain see Gascogne, Golfe de
113 □1 Gasfinolhu i. N. Male Maldives
124 B5 Gash and Setit prov. Eritrea
116 D2 Gasherbrum mt. Jammu and Kashmir
123 E5 Gasht Iran
207 H3 Gashua Nigeria
175 K2 Gąski Pol.
156 B3 Gasny France
175 I3 Gąsocin Pol.
246 C2 Gaspar Cuba
94 D3 Gaspar, Selat sea chan. Indon.
225 H3 Gaspé Que. Can.
225 H3 Gaspé, Péninsule de pen. Que. Can.
195 F4 Gasperina Italy
179 E2 Gaspoltshofen Austria
206 E3 Gassan Burkina
102 J4 Gassan vol. Japan
206 B3 Gassane Senegal
232 C5 Gassaway WV U.S.A.
164 F2 Gasselte Neth.
164 F2 Gasselternijveen Neth.
151 F5 Gassin France
207 H4 Gassol Nigeria
241 J3 Gass Peak NV U.S.A.
Gasteiz Spain see Vitoria-Gasteiz
100 G2 Gastello Sakhalin Rus. Fed.
179 G2 Gastern Austria
163 A4 Gastes France
232 E6 Gaston NC U.S.A.
231 D5 Gastonia NC U.S.A.
198 B3 Gastouni Greece
182 D4 Gata Spain
185 H4 Gata, Cabo de c. Spain
182 D4 Gata, Sierra de mts Spain
187 D6 Gata de Gorgos Spain
225 E3 Gataga r. B.C. Can.
196 E3 Gătaia Romania
139 H2 Gatchina Rus. Fed.
232 B6 Gate City VA U.S.A.
146 D7 Gatehouse of Fleet Dumfries and Galloway, Scotland U.K.
177 I5 Gátér Hungary
171 C4 Gatersleben Ger.
149 H3 Gateshead Tyne and Wear, England U.K.
231 E4 Gatesville NC U.S.A.
237 D6 Gatesville TX U.S.A.
241 M2 Gateway CO U.S.A.
224 F4 Gatineau Que. Can.
224 F4 Gatineau r. Que. Can.
185 F2 Gato r. Spain
Gatong Xizang China see Jomda
Gatooma Zimbabwe see Kadoma
187 C5 Gátova Spain
179 H2 Gattendorf Austria
191 H4 Gatteo a Mare Italy
151 F5 Gattières France
190 D3 Gattinara Italy
85 H5 Gatton Qld Austr.
242 □J7 Gatún, Lago l. Panama
182 B3 Gatvand Iran
151 G3 Gatwick airport England U.K.
79 □I Gau i. Fiji
172 C2 Gau-Algesheim Ger.
156 D3 Gauchy France
185 E4 Gaucín Spain
123 E4 Gaud-i-Zirreh depr. Afgh.
Gauhati Assam India see Guwahati
138 E3 Gauja r. Latvia
138 E4 Gauja r. Lith.
172 D2 Gaukönigshofen Ger.
Gaul country Europe see France
184 □ Gaula Madeira
140 J3 Gaula r. Norway
232 C5 Gauley Bridge WV U.S.A.
172 C2 Gau-Odernheim Ger.
141 I3 Gaupne Norway
Gaurdak Turkm. see Govurdak
116 E5 Gaurella Madh. Prad. India
114 C3 Gauribidanur Karnataka India
117 G5 Gaurnadi Bangl.
142 C2 Gausta mt. Norway
215 G2 Gauteng prov. S. Africa
173 F3 Gauting Ger.
186 C3 Gautizalema r. Spain
186 F3 Gavà Spain
190 F3 Gavardo Italy
163 B6 Gavarnie France
Gavarr Armenia see Kamo
123 E5 Gavāter Iran
177 K3 Gávavencsellő Hungary
122 C5 Gāvbandī Iran
122 C5 Gāvbūs, Kūh-e mts Iran
163 A5 Gave r. France
182 B2 Gave Port.
163 B5 Gave d'Arrens r. France
163 B5 Gave d'Aspe r. France
163 A5 Gave d'Oloron r. France
163 B5 Gave d'Ossau r. France
122 A3 Gāveh Rūd r. Iran
165 C4 Gavere Belgium
190 D4 Gavi Italy
255 E5 Gavião r. Brazil
184 C1 Gavião Port.
190 D3 Gavirate Italy
143 G1 Gävle Sweden
143 F1 Gävleborg county Sweden
143 G1 Gävlebukten b. Sweden
192 B4 Gavoi Sardegna Italy
192 C2 Gavorrano Italy
158 E3 Gavray France
135 H5 Gavrilovka Vtoraya Rus. Fed.
139 M3 Gavrilov Posad Rus. Fed.
139 L3 Gavrilov-Yam Rus. Fed.
117 F4 Gawan Bihar India
179 H2 Gaweinstal Austria
116 D5 Gawilgarh Hills India
82 D3 Gawler S.A. Austr.
82 C3 Gawler Ranges hills S.A. Austr.
175 K1 Gawliki Wielkie Pol.
174 D4 Gaworzyce Pol.
149 G4 Gawsworth Cheshire, England U.K.
149 G3 Gawthrop Cumbria, England U.K.
207 G4 Gawu Nigeria
120 D2 Gay Rus. Fed.
226 C2 Gay MI U.S.A.
100 D4 Gaya r. China
117 F4 Gaya Bihar India
207 F4 Gaya Niger
Gayá r. Spain see Gaià
148 B4 Gaybrook Rep. of Ireland
204 C4 G'Aydat al Jhoucha ridge Western Sahara
137 I5 Gayduk Rus. Fed.
207 F3 Gayéri Burkina
226 E3 Gaylord MI U.S.A.
236 E2 Gaylord MN U.S.A.
85 G5 Gayndah Qld Austr.
134 K3 Gayny Rus. Fed.
Gaysin Ukr. see Haysyn
151 H2 Gayton Norfolk, England U.K.
134 G4 Gayutino Rus. Fed.
Gayvoron Ukr. see Hayvoron
128 B4 Gaza terr. Asia
128 B4 Gaza Gaza
213 G4 Gaza prov. Moz.
123 E1 Gaz-Achak Turkm.
121 G4 Gazalkent Uzbek.
122 C2 Gazandzhyk Turkm.
207 I4 Gazawa Cameroon
126 E3 Gaziantep Turkey
128 C1 Gaziantep prov. Turkey
Gazibenli Turkey see Yahyalı
129 C3 Gaziler Turkey
Gazimağusa Cyprus see Ammochostos
100 B1 Gazimur r. Rus. Fed.
100 A2 Gazimurskiy Khrebet mts Rus. Fed.
126 D3 Gazipaşa Turkey
120 E4 Gazli Uzbek.
Gazojak Turkm. see Gaz-Achak
183 I2 Gazolaz Spain
191 F3 Gazoldo degli Ippoliti Italy
191 G3 Gazzo Veronese Italy
191 F3 Gazzuolo Italy
206 D5 Gbaaka Liberia
206 B5 Gbangbatok Sierra Leone
206 C5 Gbarnga Liberia
206 C5 Gbatala Liberia
177 H4 Gbelce Slovakia
176 G3 Gbely Slovakia
207 F4 Gbéroubouè Benin
207 H5 Gboko Nigeria
143 H4 Gdańsk Pol.
175 H1 Gdańsk, Gulf of Pol./Rus. Fed.
Gdańska, Zatoka g. Pol./Rus. Fed. see Gdańsk, Gulf of
Gdingen Pol. see Gdynia
138 F2 Gdov Rus. Fed.
175 I6 Gdów Pol.
143 H4 Gdynia Pol.
146 D4 Geal Charn hill Highland, Scotland U.K.
146 E4 Geal Charn hill Highland, Scotland U.K.
163 E6 Géant, Pic du mt. France
238 B3 Gearhart Mountain OR U.S.A.
Gearraidh na h-Aibhne Western Isles, Scotland U.K. see Garrynahine
148 B4 Geashill Rep. of Ireland
163 B5 Geaune France
169 F4 Gebesee Ger.
165 F4 Gebhardshain Ger.
199 G3 Gebiz Turkey
210 C2 Gebre Guracha Eth.
199 F1 Gebze Turkey
Gecheng Chongqing China see Chengkou
172 C3 Gechingen Ger.
94 C3 Gedang, Gunung mt. Indon.
138 E4 Gedanonių kalnas hill Lith.
203 G6 Gedaref Sudan
203 G6 Gedaref state Sudan
151 G2 Geddington Northamptonshire, England U.K.
177 H5 Gedeliak Hungary
169 E5 Gedern Ger.
165 D5 Gedinne Belgium
199 F2 Gediz Turkey
199 E2 Gediz r. Turkey
151 H2 Gedney Drove End Lincolnshire, England U.K.
210 D4 Gedo admin. reg. Somalia
163 C6 Gèdre France
142 D4 Gedser Denmark
142 C3 Gedsted Denmark
Gedzheti Georgia see Gejet'i
165 E3 Geel Belgium
83 F4 Geelong Vic. Austr.
87 B6 Geelvink Channel W.A. Austr.
165 E4 Geer r. Belgium
164 D3 Geertruidenberg Neth.
168 C3 Geeste Ger.
168 D2 Geeste r. Ger.
164 F2 Geesteren Neth.
170 C3 Geestgottberg Ger.
168 F2 Geesthacht Ger.
165 E4 Geetbets Belgium
171 C5 Gefell Ger.
210 C2 Gefersa Eth.
164 E3 Geffen Neth.
171 C5 Gefrees Ger.
138 C4 Gėgė r. Lith.
Gegechkori Georgia see Martvili
177 K3 Gégény Hungary
129 D3 Geghadir Armenia
129 D3 Geghama Lerrnashght'a mts Armenia
111 C5 Gê'gyai Xizang China
78 □3a Gehh i. Kwajalein Marshall Is
168 D3 Gehrde Ger.
169 E3 Gehrden Ger.
171 C5 Gehren Ger.
109 F2 Ge Hu l. China
207 H3 Geidam Nigeria
172 D2 Geiersberg hill Ger.
173 G2 Geiersthal Ger.
234 C2 Geigertown PA U.S.A.
223 K3 Geikie r. Sask. Can.
85 E2 Geikie Range hills Qld Austr.
169 B5 Geilenkirchen Ger.
142 C1 Geilo Norway
169 E5 Geisa Ger.
169 E5 Geiselbach Ger.
173 G3 Geiselhöring Ger.
173 E2 Geiselwind Ger.
173 F3 Geisenfeld Ger.
173 G3 Geisenhausen Ger.
172 B2 Geisenheim Ger.
171 E5 Geising Ger.
172 C4 Geisingen Ger.
169 F4 Geisleden Ger.
172 C3 Geislingen Ger.
172 D3 Geislingen an der Steige Ger.
169 F4 Geismar Ger.
157 H4 Geispolsheim France
178 D3 Geißstein mt. Austria
179 G3 Geistthal Austria
211 B5 Geita Tanz.
171 D4 Geithain Ger.
140 K2 Geittind mt. Norway
129 C2 Gejet'i Georgia
108 A4 Gejiu Yunnan China
122 D2 Gekdepe Turkm.
210 A3 Gel r. Sudan
194 D5 Gela Sicilia Italy
194 D5 Gela r. Sicilia Italy
194 D5 Gela, Golfo di g. Sicilia Italy
111 E5 Geladaindong mt. Qinghai China
210 E3 Geladi Eth.
211 C5 Gelai vol. Tanz.
161 F4 Gélas, Cime du mt. France/Italy
170 D1 Gelbensande Ger.
173 E2 Gelchsheim Ger.
164 F2 Gelderland prov. Neth.
164 E3 Geldermalsen Neth.
169 B4 Geldern Ger.
169 F5 Geldersheim Ger.
165 E3 Geldrop Neth.
165 E4 Geleen Neth.
199 E2 Gelembe Turkey
210 D2 Gelemso Eth.
171 D5 Gelenau Ger.
199 G2 Gelendost Turkey
135 G7 Gelendzhik Rus. Fed.
117 G4 Gelephu Bhutan
199 E1 Gelibolu Turkey
199 E1 Gelibolu Yarımadası pen. Turkey
199 G2 Gelincik Dağı mt. Turkey
163 C4 Gelise r. France
176 F5 Gelléniháza Hungary
150 D3 Gelligaer Caerphilly Wales U.K.
78 □3a Gellinam i. Kwajalein Marshall Is
169 E5 Gelnhausen Ger.
177 J3 Gelnica Slovakia
163 B5 Gelos France
142 C4 Gels r. Denmark
186 C3 Gelsa Spain
176 F5 Gelse Hungary
169 C4 Gelsenkirchen Ger.
173 F3 Geltendorf Ger.
168 E1 Gelting Ger.
171 D3 Geltow Ger.
165 D4 Gembloux Belgium
207 H5 Gembu Nigeria
160 D1 Gemeaux France
208 C4 Gemena Dem. Rep. Congo
161 D5 Gémenos France
126 E3 Gemerek Turkey
177 J3 Gemerská Hôrka Slovakia
177 J3 Gemerská Poloma Slovakia
164 E3 Gemert Neth.
199 F3 Gemiş Turkey
199 F1 Gemlik Turkey
172 C2 Gemmingen Ger.
191 I2 Gemona del Friuli Italy
162 B3 Gémozac France
203 G3 Gemsa Egypt
212 D5 Gemsbok National Park Botswana
214 E1 Gemsbokvlakte S. Africa
172 B2 Gemünden Ger.
169 D5 Gemünden (Wohra) Ger.
169 E5 Gemünden am Main Ger.
107 H1 Gen r. China
185 E4 Genal r. Spain
210 D3 Genalē Wenz r. Eth.
165 D4 Genappe Belgium
185 H2 Génave Spain
193 E3 Genazzano Italy
129 B4 Genç Turkey
162 C2 Gençay France
176 F5 Gencsapáti Hungary
124 B5 Gendoa r. Eth.
160 D1 Gendrey France
164 F3 Gendringen Neth.
164 E3 Gendt Neth.
160 C2 Générand France
164 F2 Genemuiden Neth.
260 E5 General Acha Arg.
261 G5 General Alvear Buenos Aires Arg.
260 D4 General Alvear Mendoza Arg.
261 G4 General Arenales Arg.
253 F6 General Artigas Para.
261 H4 General Belgrano Arg.
General Belgrano II research stn Antarctica see Belgrano II
262 U2 General Bernardo O'Higgins research stn Antarctica
261 F3 General Cabrera Arg.
261 H3 General Campos Arg.
256 A1 General Carneiro Brazil
259 B7 General Carrera, Lago l. Arg./Chile
261 F6 General Daniel Cerri Arg.
261 F3 General Deheza Arg.
General Freire Angola see Muxaluando
261 H3 General Galarza Arg.
260 C3 General Gutiérrez Arg.
258 F2 General José de San Martín Arg.
261 I5 General Juan Madariaga Arg.
252 C4 General Lagos Chile
261 H4 General Las Heras Arg.
261 I5 General Lavalle Arg.
261 F4 General Levalle Arg.
92 C4 General Luna Phil.
92 C4 General MacArthur Phil.
General Machado Angola see Camacupa
258 D2 General Martín Miguel de Güemes Arg.
261 F4 General Pico Arg.
261 G4 General Pinto Arg.
261 I5 General Pirán Arg.
260 D6 General Roca Arg.
261 H4 General Rodríguez Arg.
261 G4 General Rojo Arg.
253 E4 General Saavedra Bol.
256 B4 General Salgado Brazil
General San Martín research stn Antarctica see San Martín
261 H4 General San Martín Arg.
261 F5 General San Martín Arg.
92 C5 General Santos Phil.
244 C1 General Simón Bolívar Mex.
243 F3 General Terán Mex.
197 I4 General Toshevo Bulg.
261 F4 General Villegas Arg.
232 E4 Genesee PA U.S.A.
232 E3 Genesee r. NY U.S.A.
232 E3 Geneseo NY U.S.A.
182 D1 Genestoso Spain
210 C2 Genet Eth.
158 E3 Genêts France
215 F2 Geneva S. Africa
Geneva Switz. see Genève
231 C6 Geneva AL U.S.A.
226 C5 Geneva IL U.S.A.
236 D3 Geneva NE U.S.A.
232 E3 Geneva NY U.S.A.
232 C4 Geneva OH U.S.A.
Geneva, Lake France/Switz. see Léman, Lac
190 B2 Genève Switz.
160 E2 Genève canton Switz.
183 H2 Genevilla Spain
160 E2 Genevois mts France
Genf Switz. see Genève
191 H5 Genga Italy
108 B1 Gengda Sichuan China
172 C3 Gengenbach Ger.
109 E4 Genglou Guangdong China
108 A4 Gengma Yunnan China
Gengqing Sichuan China see Dêgê
Gengxuan Yunnan China see Gengma
210 B3 Geni r. Sudan
Genichesk Ukr. see Heniches'k
185 E3 Genil r. Spain
198 D1 Genisea Greece
163 B4 Génissac France
165 E4 Genk Belgium
160 D1 Genlis France
192 B5 Gennargentu, Monti del mts Sardegna Italy
192 B5 Genn'Argiolas, Monte hill Sardegna Italy
164 E3 Gennep Neth.
162 B1 Gennes France
83 G4 Genoa Vic. Austr.
Genoa Italy see Genova
226 C4 Genoa IL U.S.A.
161 B4 Génolhac France
192 B5 Genoni Sardegna Italy
162 D2 Genouillac France
162 C2 Genouillé France
159 H4 Genouilly France
190 D4 Genova Italy
190 E4 Genova prov. Liguria Italy
190 D4 Genova, Golfo di g. Italy
187 C6 Genovés Spain
250 □ Genovesa, Isla i. Islas Galápagos Ecuador
163 C4 Gensac France
165 C3 Gent Belgium
171 D3 Genthin Ger.
254 E4 Gentio do Ouro Brazil
162 E3 Gentioux, Plateau de France
162 D3 Gentioux-Pigerolles France
Genua Italy see Genova
193 I4 Genzano di Lucania Italy
193 E3 Genzano di Roma Italy
197 F2 Geoagiu r. Romania
87 B7 Geographe Bay W.A. Austr.
87 B5 Geographe Channel W.A. Austr.
Geok-Tepe Turkm. see Gekdepe
86 C4 George r. W.A. Austr.
225 H1 George r. Que. Can.
214 D5 George S. Africa
83 G3 George, Lake N.S.W. Austr.
82 D4 George, Lake S.A. Austr.
86 D4 George, Lake salt flat W.A. Austr.
210 A4 George, Lake Uganda
233 G3 George, Lake NY U.S.A.
84 B4 George Gills Range mts N.T. Austr.
150 C3 Georgeham Devon, England U.K.
George Land i. Zemlya Frantsa-Iosifa Rus. Fed. see Zemlya Georga
173 G2 Georgenberg Ger.
173 F2 Georgensgmünd Ger.
233 G3 Georges Mills NH U.S.A.
85 E3 Georgetown Qld Austr.
83 F5 George Town Tas. Austr.
246 D2 George Town Gt Exuma Bahamas
224 E5 Georgetown Ont. Can.
246 B3 George Town Cayman Is
206 B3 Georgetown Gambia
251 G3 Georgetown Guyana
94 C1 George Town Malaysia
235 E1 Georgetown CT U.S.A.
233 F5 Georgetown DE U.S.A.
231 C6 Georgetown GA U.S.A.
230 C4 Georgetown KY U.S.A.
232 B5 Georgetown OH U.S.A.
231 E5 Georgetown SC U.S.A.
237 D6 Georgetown TX U.S.A.
262 T2 George VI Sound sea chan. Antarctica
263 K2 George V Land reg. Antarctica
237 D6 George West TX U.S.A.
129 C3 Georgia country Asia
231 D5 Georgia state U.S.A.
222 E5 Georgia, Strait of B.C. Can.
231 C6 Georgiana AL U.S.A.
224 D4 Georgian Bay Ont. Can.
Georgi Traykov Bulg. see Dolni Chiflik
Georgiu-Dezh Rus. Fed. see Liski
120 D2 Georgiyevka Aktyubinskaya Oblast' Kazakh.
121 J2 Georgiyevka Vostochnyy Kazakhstan Kazakh.
Georgiyevka Zhambylskaya Oblast' Kazakh. see Korday
129 C1 Georgiyevsk Rus. Fed.
134 I4 Georgiyevskoye Kostromskaya Oblast' Rus. Fed.
129 A1 Georgiyevskoye Krasnodarskiy Kray Rus. Fed.
168 C3 Georgsdorf Ger.
168 C2 Georgsheil Ger.
169 D3 Georgsmarienhütte Ger.
Georg von Neumayer research stn Antarctica see Neumayer
163 B5 Ger Aquitaine France
159 F3 Ger Basse-Normandie France
186 E2 Ger Spain
171 C4 Gera Ger.
165 C4 Geraardsbergen Belgium
169 F5 Geraberg Ger.
172 D2 Gerabronn Ger.
195 F4 Gerace Italy
195 E4 Gerace r. Italy
195 E5 Geraci Siculo Sicilia Italy
147 B5 Gerahies Rep. of Ireland
197 J5 Gerakarou Greece
198 C3 Geraki Greece
255 B6 Geral, Serra mts Brazil
254 D4 Geral de Goiás, Serra hills Brazil
81 D6 Geraldine South I. N.Z.
255 C5 Geral do Paraná, Serra hills Brazil
87 B6 Geraldton W.A. Austr.
157 G4 Gérardmer France
179 G2 Geras Austria
179 H2 Gerasdorf bei Wien Austria
122 C5 Gerash Iran
156 E4 Géraudot France
240 F1 Gerber CA U.S.A.
157 G4 Gerbéviller France
161 C4 Gerbier de Jonc mt. France
171 C4 Gerbstedt Ger.
176 G4 Gérce Hungary
172 D2 Gerchsheim Ger.
127 F3 Gercüş Turkey
168 F3 Gerdau Ger.
215 F2 Gerdau S. Africa
Gerdauen Kaliningradskaya Oblast' Rus. Fed. see Zheleznodorozhnyy
126 D2 Gerede Turkey
126 D2 Gerede r. Turkey
184 D3 Gerena Spain
177 J5 Geréndás Hungary
182 B3 Gerês, Serra do mts Port.
177 H5 Geresdlak Hungary
123 F4 Gereshk Afgh.
178 D2 Geretsberg Austria
173 F4 Geretsried Ger.
185 H3 Gérgal Spain
129 E2 Gergebil' Rus. Fed.
192 B5 Gergei Sardegna Italy
177 K3 Gergely-hegy hill Hungary
160 C2 Gergy France
173 E2 Gerhardshofen Ger.
122 D3 Gerīmenj Iran
183 F5 Gerindote Spain
236 C3 Gering NE U.S.A.
171 D4 Geringswalde Ger.
177 J4 Gerje r. Hungary
177 H5 Gerjen Hungary
238 C3 Gerlach NV U.S.A.
177 J2 Gerlachovský štít mt. Slovakia
172 D3 Gerlingen Ger.
261 F4 Germania Arg.
Germania country Europe see Germany
Germanicea Turkey see Kahramanmaraş
222 E4 Germansen Landing B.C. Can.
German South-West Africa country Africa see Namibia
232 E5 Germantown MD U.S.A.
232 A5 Germantown OH U.S.A.
237 F5 Germantown TN U.S.A.
226 C4 Germantown WI U.S.A.
166 E3 Germany country Europe
173 E4 Germaringen Ger.
157 F4 Germay France
199 E3 Germencik Turkey
173 F3 Germering Ger.
172 C2 Germersheim Ger.
156 C5 Germigny-des-Prés France
183 H1 Gernika-Lumo Spain
171 C4 Gernrode Sachsen-Anhalt Ger.
169 F4 Gernrode Thüringen Ger.
172 C3 Gernsbach Ger.
172 C2 Gernsheim Ger.
190 E2 Gerola Alta Italy
171 C5 Geroldsgrün Ger.
173 F3 Gerolsbach Ger.
169 B5 Gerolstein Ger.
173 E2 Gerolzhofen Ger.
Gerona Spain see Girona
198 D4 Geropotamos r. Kriti Greece
191 J3 Gerovo Croatia
165 D4 Gerpinnes Belgium
151 G3 Gerrards Cross Buckinghamshire, England U.K.
192 B5 Gerrei reg. Sardegna Italy
Gerri Spain see Guerri de la Sal
163 C5 Gers dept Midi-Pyrénées France
163 C4 Gers r. France
190 D2 Gersau Switz.
169 E5 Gersfeld (Rhön) Ger.
172 B2 Gersheim Ger.
114 B3 Gersoppa Karnataka India
171 E4 Gerste r. Ger.
168 C3 Gersten Ger.
173 E3 Gerstetten Ger.
157 H4 Gerstheim France
173 E3 Gersthofen Ger.
169 F5 Gerstungen Ger.
170 E2 Gerswalde Ger.
161 D4 Gervanne r. France
171 C3 Gerwisch Ger.
Géryville Alg. see El Bayadh
160 B3 Gerzat France
111 D5 Gêrzê Xizang China
126 D2 Gerze Turkey
173 G3 Gerzen Ger.
169 C4 Gescher Ger.
179 H3 Geschriebenstein hill Austria
169 F5 Geschwenda Ger.
169 D4 Geseke Ger.
192 B5 Gesico Sardegna Italy
Gesoriacum France see Boulogne-sur-Mer
157 E3 Gespunsart France
173 E3 Gessertshausen Ger.
190 C4 Gesso r. Italy
187 C5 Gestalgar Spain
159 E4 Gesté France
192 B5 Gesturi Sardegna Italy
193 H3 Gesualdo Italy
165 E4 Gesves Belgium
177 K5 Geszt Hungary
177 K4 Geszteréd Hungary
141 L3 Geta Åland Fin.
183 G4 Getafe Spain
165 E4 Gete r. Belgium
197 F3 Getic, Podişul plat. Romania
158 E4 Gétigné France
129 D3 Getik r. Armenia
168 E1 Gettorf Ger.
234 A3 Gettysburg PA U.S.A.
236 D2 Gettysburg SD U.S.A.
108 C3 Getu He r. China
256 C4 Getulina Brazil
262 P2 Getz Ice Shelf Antarctica
165 E4 Geul r. Neth.
94 B2 Geumapang r. Indon.
94 B1 Geureudong, Gunung vol. Indon.
83 G3 Geurie N.S.W. Austr.
127 F3 Gevaş Turkey
169 C4 Gevelsberg Ger.
158 E3 Gévezé France
197 F5 Gevgelija Macedonia
184 C1 Gévora r. Spain
114 B2 Gevrai Mahar. India
160 C1 Gevrey-Chambertin France
160 E2 Gex France
Gexianzhuang Hebei China see Qinghe
183 H1 Gexto Spain
Gey Iran see Nīkshahr
171 D5 Geyer Ger.
199 E2 Geyikli Turkey
215 E2 Geysdorp S. Africa
240 F2 Geyserville CA U.S.A.
199 G1 Geyve Turkey
256 C2 Gezarina Brazil
198 B1 Gezavesh Albania
179 G2 Gföhl Austria
214 D2 Ghaap Plateau S. Africa
127 F4 Ghadaf, Wādī al watercourse Iraq
Ghadamés Libya see Ghadāmis
202 A2 Ghadāmis Libya
122 C2 Ghaem Shahr Iran
117 F4 Ghaghara r. India
78 □6 Ghaghe i. Solomon Is
117 F5 Ghaghra Bihar India
120 E2 Ghalkarteniz, Solonchak salt marsh Kazakh.
Ghallaorol Uzbek. see Gallyaaral
206 E4 Ghana country Africa
116 C4 Ghanliala Rajasthan India
116 B5 Ghantwar Gujarat India
212 D4 Ghanzi Botswana
212 D4 Ghanzi admin. dist. Botswana
Ghap'an Armenia see Kapan
124 C3 Gharāmīl, Jabal al hill Saudi Arabia
126 C5 Gharbîya governorate Egypt
205 F2 Ghardaïa Alg.
189 B7 Ghardimaou Tunisia
117 E5 Gharghoda Madh. Prad. India
203 G2 Ghârib, Gebel mt. Egypt
123 G2 Gharm Tajik.
125 G4 Gharm, Wādī r. Oman
123 F5 Gharo Pak.
202 B1 Gharyān Libya
202 A3 Ghāt Libya
116 E4 Ghatampur Uttar Prad. India
117 F5 Ghatgan Orissa India
116 C5 Ghatol Rajasthan India
117 F5 Ghatsila Bihar India
123 G4 Ghauspur Pak.
Ghawdex i. Malta see Gozo
202 C6 Ghazal, Bahr el watercourse Chad
208 F2 Ghazal, Bahr el r. Sudan
Ghazalkent Uzbek. see Gazalkent
204 E2 Ghazaouet Alg.
116 D3 Ghaziabad Uttar Prad. India
117 E4 Ghazipur Uttar Prad. India
Ghazna Afgh. see Ghaznī
123 G3 Ghaznī Afgh.
123 F3 Ghaznī prov. Afgh.
123 F3 Ghazni r. Afgh.
124 C2 Ghazzālah Saudi Arabia
190 F3 Ghedi Italy
197 F3 Ghelari Romania
197 H3 Ghelinţa Romania
Ghent Belgium see Gent
232 C6 Ghent WV U.S.A.
Gheorghe Gheorghiu-Dej Romania see Oneşti
197 H3 Gheorghe Lazăr Romania
197 G2 Gheorgheni Romania
114 B2 Gherdi Mahar. India
197 F2 Gherla Romania
190 D3 Ghiffa Italy
Ghijduwon Uzbek. see Gizhduvan
192 A4 Ghilarza Sardegna Italy
177 K5 Ghioroc Romania
197 F3 Ghioroiu Romania
177 K6 Ghiroda Romania
165 C4 Ghislenghien Belgium
192 B2 Ghisonaccia Corse France
192 B2 Ghisoni Corse France
116 C1 Ghizar Jammu and Kashmir
177 K6 Ghizela Romania
78 □6 Ghizunabeana Islands Solomon Is
114 B2 Ghod Mahar. India
114 B2 Ghod r. India
116 C5 Gholvad Mahar. India
123 G3 Ghorband r. Afgh.
116 B4 Ghotaru Rajasthan India
123 G5 Ghotki Pak.
123 F3 Ghowr prov. Afgh.
117 F4 Ghuari r. India
Ghudamis Libya see Ghadāmis
114 C2 Ghugus Mahar. India
Ghukasyan Armenia see Ashots'k'
128 C4 Ghurayfah hill Saudi Arabia
123 E3 Ghurian Afgh.
124 D2 Ghurrab, Jabal hill Saudi Arabia
124 C3 Ghurūb, Jabal hill Saudi Arabia
202 C2 Ghuzayyil, Sabkhat salt marsh Libya
Ghuzor Uzbek. see Guzar
156 C1 Ghyvelde France
97 D5 Gia Đinh Vietnam
135 H7 Giaginskaya Rus. Fed.
128 A2 Gialias r. Cyprus
96 D3 Giang r. Vietnam
198 C1 Giannitsa Greece
192 D2 Giannutri, Isola di i. Italy
193 E2 Giano dell'Umbria Italy
215 G3 Giant's Castle mt. S. Africa
147 E1 Giant's Causeway lava field Northern Ireland U.K.
235 F1 Giant's Neck CT U.S.A.
95 F5 Gianyar Bali Indon.
195 E5 Giardini-Naxos Sicilia Italy
196 E3 Giarmata Romania
194 D5 Giarratana Sicilia Italy
195 E5 Giarre Sicilia Italy
162 E3 Giat France
192 A4 Giave Sardegna Italy
190 C3 Giaveno Italy
190 C3 Giavino, Monte mt. Italy
192 A5 Giba Sardegna Italy
184 E4 Gibalbín hill Spain
246 C2 Gibara Cuba
184 E3 Gibarrayo hill Spain
86 E2 Gibb r. W.A. Austr.
236 D3 Gibbon NE U.S.A.
238 D2 Gibbonsville ID U.S.A.
86 E3 Gibb River W.A. Austr.
234 D3 Gibbsboro NJ U.S.A.
234 C3 Gibbstown NJ U.S.A.
194 B5 Gibellina Nuova Sicilia Italy
212 C5 Gibeon Namibia
159 F2 Giberville France
162 A2 Giboule r. France
184 D3 Gibraleón Spain
185 E4 Gibraltar Europe
185 □ Gibraltar, Bay of Gibraltar/Spain
184 E4 Gibraltar, Campo de reg. Spain
204 D2 Gibraltar, Strait of Morocco/Spain
87 D7 Gibson W.A. Austr.
231 D5 Gibson GA U.S.A.
226 C5 Gibson City IL U.S.A.
87 D5 Gibson Desert W.A. Austr.
234 B3 Gibson Island MD U.S.A.
222 F5 Gibsons B.C. Can.
175 L1 Giby Pol.
129 F3 Gicăki Dağı mt. Azer.
106 B2 Gichgeniyn Nuruu mts Mongolia
210 B2 Gidda Eth.
114 C3 Giddalur Andhra Prad. India
203 G2 Gîddi, Gebel el hill Egypt
237 D6 Giddings TX U.S.A.
Giddi Pass hill Egypt see Gîddi, Gebel el
140 L3 Gideälven r. Sweden
175 H5 Gidle Pol.
210 C3 Gīdolē Eth.
172 D2 Giebelstadt Ger.
169 F4 Gieboldehausen Ger.
175 H4 Gieczno Pol.
168 F1 Giekau Ger.
164 E1 Giekerk Neth.
167 K3 Giełczew r. Pol.
175 I4 Gielniów Pol.
170 D2 Gielow Ger.
156 C5 Gien France
173 E3 Giengen an der Brenz Ger.
161 D3 Gières France
165 D3 Gierle Belgium
171 C4 Giersleben Ger.
169 F4 Gierstädt Ger.
175 I2 Gierzwałd Pol.
169 E4 Gieselwerder (Oberweser) Ger.
169 D5 Gießen Ger.
169 D5 Gießen admin. reg. Hessen Ger.
164 F1 Gieten Neth.
175 I2 Gietrzwałd Pol.
159 H4 Gièvres France
122 D2 Gīfan Iran
149 G2 Gifford East Lothian, Scotland U.K.
163 E4 Giffou r. France
160 E2 Giffre r. France
169 F3 Gifhorn Ger.
222 H4 Gift Lake Alta Can.
104 C3 Gifu Japan
104 C3 Gifu pref. Japan
135 H7 Gigant Rus. Fed.
242 C3 Giganta, Cerro mt. Mex.
250 C4 Gigante Col.
185 I3 Gigante mt. Spain
161 B5 Gigean France
146 C6 Gigha i. Scotland U.K.
146 C6 Gigha, Sound of sea chan. Scotland U.K.
197 F4 Gighera Romania
192 C2 Giglio, Isola del i. Italy
192 C2 Giglio Castello Italy
161 B5 Gignac Languedoc-Roussillon France
161 D5 Gignac Provence-Alpes-Côte-d'Azur France
190 C3 Gignod Italy
161 D4 Gigondas France
182 E1 Gijón Spain
163 E5 Gijou r. France
211 A5 Gikongoro Rwanda
241 J5 Gila r. AZ U.S.A.
241 K5 Gila Bend AZ U.S.A.
241 K5 Gila Bend Mountains AZ U.S.A.
241 J5 Gila Mountains AZ U.S.A.
122 B2 Gīlān prov. Iran
122 A3 Gīlān-e Gharb Iran
197 F2 Gilău Romania
129 F3 Giläzi Azer.
149 I4 Gilberdyke East Riding of Yorkshire, England U.K.
85 E3 Gilbert r. Qld Austr.
241 L5 Gilbert AZ U.S.A.
226 A2 Gilbert MN U.S.A.
232 C6 Gilbert WV U.S.A.
Gilbert Islands country Pacific Ocean see Kiribati
234 B2 Gilberton PA U.S.A.
85 E3 Gilbert Range mts Qld Austr.
266 G6 Gilbert Ridge sea feature Pacific Ocean
85 E3 Gilbert River Qld Austr.
234 C2 Gilbertsville PA U.S.A.
232 B4 Gilboa OH U.S.A.
254 D4 Gilbués Brazil
173 F3 Gilching Ger.
238 E1 Gildford MT U.S.A.
213 H3 Gilé Moz.
185 F3 Gilena Spain
87 C6 Giles, Lake salt flat W.A. Austr.
84 B3 Giles Creek r. N.T. Austr.
87 F5 Giles Meteorological Station W.A. Austr.
84 B4 Giles Range mts N.T. Austr.
161 F5 Gilette France
202 E4 Gilf Kebir Plateau Egypt
147 E2 Gilford Northern Ireland U.K.
83 G2 Gilgai N.S.W. Austr.
83 G2 Gilgandra N.S.W. Austr.
83 G2 Gil Gil Creek r. N.S.W. Austr.
116 C2 Gilgit Jammu and Kashmir
116 C2 Gilgit r. Jammu and Kashmir
83 F3 Gilgunnia N.S.W. Austr.
95 F5 Gilimanuk Bali Indon.
Gılındire Turkey see Aydıncık
147 C2 Gill, Lough l. Rep. of Ireland
223 M3 Gillam Man. Can.
149 I3 Gillamoor North Yorkshire, England U.K.
142 E3 Gilleleje Denmark
87 E5 Gillen, Lake salt flat W.A. Austr.
169 B5 Gillenfeld Ger.
82 D3 Gilles, Lake salt flat S.A. Austr.
232 E4 Gillett PA U.S.A.
226 C3 Gillett WI U.S.A.
238 F2 Gillette WY U.S.A.
140 K3 Gillhov Sweden
85 E4 Gilliat Qld Austr.
85 E4 Gilliat r. Qld Austr.
150 E3 Gillingham Dorset, England U.K.
151 H3 Gillingham Medway, England U.K.
149 H3 Gilling West North Yorkshire, England U.K.
146 E3 Gills Highland, Scotland U.K.
226 D3 Gills Rock WI U.S.A.
160 E3 Gilly-sur-Isère France
160 B2 Gilly-sur-Loire France
235 F1 Gilman CT U.S.A.
226 D5 Gilman IL U.S.A.
226 B3 Gilman WI U.S.A.
237 E5 Gilmer TX U.S.A.
146 E5 Gilmerton Perth and Kinross, Scotland U.K.
197 F3 Gilort r. Romania
240 G3 Gilroy CA U.S.A.
169 E5 Gilserberg Ger.
149 G3 Gilsland Northumberland, England U.K.
146 F6 Gilston Scottish Borders, Scotland U.K.
168 E3 Gilten Ger.
91 J8 Giluwe, Mount P.N.G.
150 D3 Gilwern Monmouthshire, Wales U.K.
164 D3 Gilze Neth.
210 B2 Gīmbī Eth.
247 □3 Gimie, Mount vol. St Lucia
195 F4 Gimigliano Italy
223 L5 Gimli Man. Can.
143 H1 Gimo Sweden
163 D5 Gimone r. France
163 C5 Gimont France
160 B2 Gimouille France
161 D5 Ginasservis France
203 H6 Ginda Eritrea
85 G4 Gindie Qld Austr.
252 D3 Ginebra, Laguna l. Bol.
128 A5 Gineina, Râs el mt. Egypt
161 A5 Ginestas France
216 □1b Ginetes São Miguel Azores
114 D5 Gin Ganga r. Sri Lanka
114 C3 Gingee Tamil Nadu India
165 E4 Gingelom Belgium
172 D3 Gingen an der Fils Ger.
85 G5 Gin Gin Qld Austr.
87 B6 Gingin W.A. Austr.
215 H3 Gingindlovu S. Africa
92 C4 Gingoog Phil.
170 E1 Gingst Ger.
210 D3 Gīnīr Eth.
138 D4 Ginkūnai Lith.
163 E6 Ginoles France
195 F2 Ginosa Italy
195 E4 Ginostra Isole Lipari Italy
Ginzo de Limia Spain see Xinzo de Limia
184 C3 Giões Port.
198 D4 Giofyros r. Kriti Greece
193 H4 Gioi Italy
195 E4 Gioia, Golfo di b. Italy
193 F3 Gioia dei Marsi Italy
195 F2 Gioia del Colle Italy
193 G3 Gioia Sannitica Italy
195 E4 Gioia Tauro Italy
195 F4 Gioiosa Ionica Italy
194 D4 Gioiosa Marea Sicilia Italy
190 D2 Giornico Switz.
198 D2 Gioura i. Greece
193 F2 Giovenco r. Italy
191 F2 Gioveretto mt. Italy
191 G5 Giovi, Monte hill Italy
193 I3 Giovinazzo Italy
224 F2 Gipouloux r. Que. Can.
83 F4 Gippsland reg. Vic. Austr.
113 □1 Giraavaru i. N. Male Maldives
116 B4 Girab Rajasthan India
177 K2 Giraltovce Slovakia
157 G4 Girancourt France
122 D4 Gīrān Rīg mt. Iran
116 D5 Girar Mahar. India
237 E4 Girard KS U.S.A.
232 C4 Girard OH U.S.A.
232 C3 Girard PA U.S.A.
234 B2 Girardville PA U.S.A.
192 B5 Girasole Sardegna Italy
Giravaru i. N. Male Maldives see Giraavaru
123 F5 Girdar Dhor r. Pak.
123 E4 Girdi Iran
207 I4 Girei Nigeria
126 E2 Giresun Turkey
203 F3 Girga Egypt
Girgenti Sicilia Italy see Agrigento
208 C4 Giri r. Dem. Rep. Congo
117 F4 Giridih Bihar India
195 F4 Girifalco Italy
83 F2 Girilambone N.S.W. Austr.
177 K4 Girişu de Criş Romania
136 D4 Gîrla Mare r. Moldova
116 C5 Girna r. India
Girne Cyprus see Keryneia
177 K6 Giroc Romania
169 C5 Girod Ger.
157 G5 Giromagny France
250 B5 Girón Ecuador
Giron Sweden see Kiruna
186 F3 Girona Spain
186 F2 Girona prov. Cataluña Spain
163 B4 Gironde dept Aquitaine France
162 B3 Gironde est. France
163 B4 Gironde-sur-Dropt France
186 E2 Gironella Spain
163 D5 Girou r. France
163 D5 Giroussens France
151 H2 Girton Cambridgeshire, England U.K.
255 B9 Giruá Brazil
146 D6 Girvan South Ayrshire, Scotland U.K.
134 F3 Girvas Rus. Fed.
80 G3 Gisborne North I. N.Z.
80 G3 Gisborne admin. reg. North I. N.Z.
149 G4 Gisburn Lancashire, England U.K.
222 F4 Giscome B.C. Can.
211 A5 Gisenyi Rwanda
142 E3 Gislaved Sweden
156 B3 Gisors France
Gissar Tajik. see Hisor
123 F2 Gissar Range mts Tajik./Uzbek.
Gissarskiy Khrebet mts Tajik./Uzbek. see Gissar Range
193 G2 Gissi Italy
165 B3 Gistel Belgium
190 D2 Giswil Switz.
211 A5 Gitarama Rwanda
211 A5 Gitega Burundi
169 F4 Gittelde Ger.
Giuba r. Somalia see Jubba
197 F3 Giubega Romania
190 E2 Giubiasco Switz.
191 F3 Giudicarie, Valli val. Italy
193 G4 Giugliano in Campania Italy
193 F3 Giuliano di Roma Italy
193 F2 Giulianova Italy
190 F4 Giuncugnano Italy
197 G2 Giurgeului, Munţii mts Romania
197 G4 Giurgiu Romania
122 D2 Givar Iran
142 C4 Give Denmark
156 B3 Giverny France
157 E2 Givet France
160 C3 Givors France
165 D4 Givry Belgium
160 C2 Givry France
157 E4 Givry-en-Argonne France
213 F4 Giyani S. Africa
210 C2 Giyon Eth.
Giza Egypt see El Gîza

174 F3 Gizałki Pol.
126 C5 Giza Pyramids tourist site Egypt
122 A3 Gīzeh Rūd r. Iran
129 D2 Gizel' Rus. Fed.
159 G4 Gizeux France
120 F4 Gizhduvan Uzbek.
193 F2 Gizio r. Italy
78 □6 Gizo New Georgia Is Solomon Is
78 □6 Gizo i. New Georgia Is Solomon Is
175 J1 Giżycko Pol.
193 I6 Gizzeria Italy
196 E4 Gjalicë e Lumës, Mal mt. Albania
142 C2 Gjerstad Norway
198 B1 Gjirokastër Albania
221 I3 Gjoa Haven Nunavut Can.
141 J3 Gjøvik Norway
198 A1 Gjuhëzës, Kepi i pt Albania
225 J4 Glace Bay N.S. Can.
190 C3 Glacier, Monte mt. Italy
222 C3 Glacier Bay AK U.S.A.
238 B1 Glacier Peak vol. WA U.S.A.
169 B4 Gladbeck Ger.
169 D5 Gladenbach Ger.
232 C6 Glade Spring VA U.S.A.
140 J2 Gladstad Norway
85 G4 Gladstone Qld Austr.
82 D3 Gladstone S.A. Austr.
83 G5 Gladstone Tas. Austr.
223 L5 Gladstone Man. Can.
81 E4 Gladstone North I. N.Z.
226 D3 Gladstone MI U.S.A.
234 D2 Gladstone NJ U.S.A.
232 D6 Gladstone VA U.S.A.
226 E4 Gladwin MI U.S.A.
232 D6 Gladys VA U.S.A.
198 D1 Glafki Anatoliki Makedonia kai Thraki Greece
160 E1 Glainans France
146 E5 Glamis Angus, Scotland U.K.
241 J5 Glamis CA U.S.A.
188 F3 Glamoč Bos.-Herz.
179 F4 Glan r. Austria
172 B2 Glan r. Ger.
92 C5 Glan Phil.
150 D3 Glanaman Carmarthenshire, Wales U.K.
147 B4 Glanaruddery Mountains hills Rep. of Ireland
161 D4 Glandage France
162 D3 Glandon France
161 E3 Glandon r. France
169 D3 Glandorf Ger.
162 C3 Glane r. France
169 C3 Glane r. Ger.
179 F4 Glanegg Austria
164 F2 Glanerbrug Neth.
147 C5 Glanmire Rep. of Ireland
227 G4 Glanworth Ont. Can.
190 D2 Glarner Alpen mts Switz.
147 E2 Glarryford Northern Ireland U.K.
190 E1 Glarus Switz.
190 E2 Glarus canton Switz.
146 D3 Glas Bheinn hill Scotland U.K.
150 D2 Glasbury Powys, Wales U.K.
236 D4 Glasco KS U.S.A.
226 C5 Glasford IL U.S.A.
146 D6 Glasgow Glasgow, Scotland U.K.
146 D6 Glasgow admin. div. Scotland U.K.
234 C3 Glasgow DE U.S.A.
230 C4 Glasgow KY U.S.A.
238 F1 Glasgow MT U.S.A.
232 D6 Glasgow VA U.S.A.
171 E5 Glashütte Ger.
173 F2 Glashütten Ger.
169 D5 Gläshütten Ger.
147 E2 Glaslough Rep. of Ireland
223 I4 Glaslyn Sask. Can.
146 E5 Glas Maol mt. Scotland U.K.
147 D3 Glassan Rep. of Ireland
234 C3 Glassboro NJ U.S.A.
148 E2 Glassford South Lanarkshire, Scotland U.K.
240 H3 Glass Mountain CA U.S.A.
149 F3 Glasson Cumbria, England U.K.
150 E3 Glastonbury Somerset, England U.K.
235 F1 Glastonbury CT U.S.A.
146 E5 Glas Tulaichean mt. Scotland U.K.
190 D1 Glatt r. Switz.
171 E4 Glaubitz Ger.
171 D5 Glauchau Ger.
197 G3 Glavacioc r. Romania
197 H4 Glavan Bulg.
197 H2 Glăvăneşti Romania
197 H4 Glavinitsa Bulg.
196 E4 Glavnik Kosovo, Srbija Yugo.
207 F5 Glazoué Benin
134 K4 Glazov Rus. Fed.
139 K5 Glazunovka Rus. Fed.
226 C3 Gleason WI U.S.A.
222 H5 Gleichen Alta Can.
171 C4 Gleina Ger.
179 G3 Gleisdorf Austria
Gleiwitz Pol. see Gliwice
160 C3 Gleizé France
151 H2 Glemsford Suffolk, England U.K.
140 K3 Glen Sweden
233 □H2 Glen NH U.S.A.
146 C4 Glen Affric val. Scotland U.K.
227 G2 Glen Afton Ont. Can.
80 E2 Glen Afton North I. N.Z.
232 E6 Glen Allen VA U.S.A.
147 C3 Glenamaddy Rep. of Ireland
147 B2 Glenamoy Rep. of Ireland
147 B2 Glenamoy r. Rep. of Ireland
226 E3 Glen Arbor MI U.S.A.
147 E1 Glenariff Northern Ireland U.K.
147 F2 Glenarm Northern Ireland U.K.
146 D5 Glen Artney val. Scotland U.K.
146 E4 Glen Avon val. Scotland U.K.
81 C6 Glenavy South I. N.Z.
147 E2 Glenavy Northern Ireland U.K.
146 C6 Glenbarr Argyll and Bute, Scotland U.K.
146 C5 Glenbeg Highland, Scotland U.K.
147 B4 Glenbeigh Rep. of Ireland
223 L5 Glenboro Man. Can.
146 E6 Glenbreck Scottish Borders, Scotland U.K.
146 B4 Glenbrittle Highland, Scotland U.K.
234 C1 Glenburn PA U.S.A.
234 B3 Glen Burnie MD U.S.A.
146 C4 Glen Cannich val. Scotland U.K.
241 L3 Glen Canyon gorge UT U.S.A.
146 E6 Glencaple Dumfries and Galloway, Scotland U.K.
146 E5 Glencarse Perth and Kinross, Scotland U.K.
146 D3 Glen Cassley val. Scotland U.K.
146 E5 Glen Clova val. Scotland U.K.
224 D5 Glencoe Ont. Can.
215 H3 Glencoe S. Africa
146 C5 Glencoe Highland, Scotland U.K.
146 C5 Glen Coe val. Scotland U.K.
236 E2 Glencoe MN U.S.A.
147 C2 Glencolumbkille Rep. of Ireland
215 E5 Glenconnor S. Africa
235 E2 Glen Cove NY U.S.A.
147 E3 Glencullen Rep. of Ireland
227 E2 Glendale Ont. Can.
241 K5 Glendale AZ U.S.A.
240 H4 Glendale CA U.S.A.
241 K3 Glendale UT U.S.A.
82 C2 Glendambo S.A. Austr.
146 C5 Glendaruel val. Scotland U.K.
146 E4 Glen Dee val. Scotland U.K.
85 G4 Glenden Qld Austr.
238 F2 Glendive MT U.S.A.
223 I4 Glendon Alta Can.
234 C2 Glendon PA U.S.A.
147 D2 Glendowan Rep. of Ireland
147 C4 Glenduff Rep. of Ireland
147 E1 Glendun r. Northern Ireland U.K.
146 E5 Gleneagles Perth and Kinross, Scotland U.K.
148 C5 Glenealy Rep. of Ireland
146 B6 Glenegedale Argyll and Bute, Scotland U.K.
82 E4 Glenelg r. Vic. Austr.
146 C4 Glenelg Highland, Scotland U.K.
146 E5 Glenfarg Perth and Kinross, Scotland U.K.
147 D2 Glenfarne Rep. of Ireland
146 E4 Glen Feshie val. Scotland U.K.
151 F2 Glenfield Leicester, England U.K.
233 F3 Glenfield NY U.S.A.
146 C5 Glenfinnan Highland, Scotland U.K.
234 D2 Glen Gardner NJ U.S.A.
147 B5 Glengarriff Rep. of Ireland
146 C4 Glen Garry val. Highland, Scotland U.K.
146 D5 Glen Garry val. Perth and Kinross, Scotland U.K.
87 C5 Glengarry Range hills W.A. Austr.
148 B3 Glengavlen Rep. of Ireland
84 D5 Glengyle Qld Austr.
81 B7 Glenham South I. N.Z.
147 D1 Glenhead Northern Ireland U.K.
84 C4 Glen Helen N.T. Austr.
83 G2 Glen Innes N.S.W. Austr.
146 F4 Glenkindie Aberdeenshire, Scotland U.K.
146 D7 Glenluce Dumfries and Galloway, Scotland U.K.
146 D5 Glen Lyon val. Scotland U.K.
234 B1 Glen Lyon PA U.S.A.
222 C2 Glenlyon Peak Y.T. Can.
80 E2 Glen Massey North I. N.Z.
234 C2 Glenmoore PA U.S.A.
146 D4 Glen More val. Scotland U.K.
85 G5 Glenmorgan Qld Austr.
146 E5 Glen Muick val. Scotland U.K.
80 E2 Glen Murray North I. N.Z.
240 F2 Glenn CA U.S.A.
241 L6 Glenn, Mount AZ U.S.A.
147 B3 Glennagevlagh Rep. of Ireland
220 D3 Glennallen AK U.S.A.
146 C5 Glen Nevis val. Scotland U.K.
227 F3 Glennie MI U.S.A.
232 E6 Glenns VA U.S.A.
238 D3 Glenns Ferry ID U.S.A.
148 D3 Glenoe Northern Ireland U.K.
222 D3 Glenora B.C. Can.
85 E3 Glenore Qld Austr.
84 D4 Glenormiston Qld Austr.
146 D3 Glen Oykel val. Scotland U.K.
83 H2 Glenreagh N.S.W. Austr.
233 F2 Glen Robertson Ont. Can.
234 B3 Glen Rock PA U.S.A.
232 C6 Glen Rogers WV U.S.A.
237 D5 Glen Rose TX U.S.A.
146 E5 Glenrothes Fife, Scotland U.K.
86 E3 Glenroy W.A. Austr.
233 G3 Glens Falls NY U.S.A.
146 E5 Glen Shee val. Scotland U.K.
146 C4 Glen Shiel val. Scotland U.K.
234 C2 Glenside PA U.S.A.
146 D5 Glen Spean val. Scotland U.K.
234 D1 Glen Spey PA U.S.A.
147 C2 Glenties Rep. of Ireland
147 D1 Glentogher Rep. of Ireland
146 D4 Glen Tromie val. Scotland U.K.
81 C5 Glentunnel South I. N.Z.
232 C5 Glenville WV U.S.A.
226 C1 Glenwater Ont. Can.
232 D6 Glen Wilton VA U.S.A.
237 E5 Glenwood AR U.S.A.
240 □D9 Glenwood HI U.S.A.
236 E3 Glenwood IA U.S.A.
236 E2 Glenwood MN U.S.A.
235 D1 Glenwood NJ U.S.A.
239 E5 Glenwood NM U.S.A.
241 L2 Glenwood UT U.S.A.
232 B5 Glenwood WV U.S.A.
226 A3 Glenwood City WI U.S.A.
239 F4 Glenwood Springs CO U.S.A.
160 E1 Glère France
171 D4 Glesien Ger.
146 □G1 Gletness Shetland, Scotland U.K.
Glevum Gloucestershire, England U.K. see Gloucester
170 D1 Glewitz Ger.
226 B2 Glidden WI U.S.A.
171 F3 Glienicke Ger.
147 B4 Glin Rep. of Ireland
188 F3 Glina r. Bos.-Herz./Croatia
188 F3 Glina Croatia
168 F2 Glinde Ger.
171 D3 Glindow Ger.
139 J5 Glinishchevo Rus. Fed.
136 D4 Glinjeni Moldova
139 I4 Glinka Rus. Fed.
175 I3 Glinojeck Pol.
151 G2 Glinton Peterborough, England U.K.
141 J3 Glittertinden mt. Norway
174 G5 Gliwice Pol.
179 F4 Globasnitz Austria
241 L5 Globe AZ U.S.A.
177 L6 Glodea, Vârful hill Romania
197 H3 Glodeanu-Sărat Romania
136 D4 Glodeni Moldova
197 G2 Glodeni Romania
179 F4 Glödnitz Austria
Glodyany Moldova see Glodeni
Glogau Pol. see Głogów
179 G3 Gloggnitz Austria
190 E2 Glogn r. Switz.
196 E4 Glogovac Kosovo, Srbija Yugo.
174 E4 Głogów Pol.
174 F5 Głogówek Pol.
175 J5 Głogów Małopolski Pol.
174 G2 Głogowo Pol.
140 K2 Glomfjord Norway
140 L2 Glommersträsk Sweden
173 F4 Glonn Ger.
173 F3 Glonn r. Ger.
178 B4 Glorenza Italy
254 F4 Glória Brazil
184 B1 Glória do Ribatejo Port.
217 □2 Glorieuses, Îles is Indian Ocean
Glorioso Islands Indian Ocean see Glorieuses, Îles
159 G3 Glos-la-Ferrière France
198 C2 Glossa Thessalia Greece
149 H4 Glossop Derbyshire, England U.K.
171 C4 Glöthe Ger.
135 I5 Glotovka Rus. Fed.
83 G2 Gloucester N.S.W. Austr.
150 E3 Gloucester Gloucestershire, England U.K.
233 H3 Gloucester MA U.S.A.
232 E6 Gloucester VA U.S.A.
150 E3 Gloucester, Vale of val. England U.K.
234 C3 Gloucester City NJ U.S.A.
234 C3 Gloucester County county NJ U.S.A.
85 G4 Gloucester Island Qld Austr.
232 E6 Gloucester Point VA U.S.A.
150 E3 Gloucestershire admin. div. England U.K.
147 C5 Glounthaune Rep. of Ireland
233 F3 Gloversville NY U.S.A.
225 K3 Glovertown Nfld. Can.
175 J4 Głowaczów Pol.
174 F1 Główczyce Pol.
170 E1 Glowe Ger.
170 D3 Glöwen Ger.
175 H4 Głowno Pol.
174 F5 Głubczyce Pol.
137 K3 Glubokaya r. Rus. Fed.
135 H6 Glubokiy Rus. Fed.
Glubokoye Belarus see Hlybokaye
121 J2 Glubokoye Kazakh.
174 F5 Głuchołazy Pol.
175 I4 Głuchów Pol.
168 E1 Glücksburg (Ostsee) Ger.
168 E2 Glückstadt Ger.
144 D1 Gluggarnir hill Faroe Is
161 C4 Gluiras France
Glukhov Ukr. see Hlukhiv
149 H4 Glusburn North Yorkshire, England U.K.
137 H2 Glushkovo Rus. Fed.
174 E5 Głuszyca Pol.
150 C1 Glyder Fawr hill Wales U.K.
150 D2 Glyn Ceiriog Wrexham, Wales U.K.
150 D3 Glyncorrwg Neath Port Talbot, Wales U.K.
142 C3 Glyngøre Denmark
147 F2 Glynn Northern Ireland U.K.
150 D3 Glyn-Neath Neath Port Talbot, Wales U.K.
179 E4 Gmünd Austria
179 F2 Gmünd Austria
173 F4 Gmund am Tegernsee Ger.
179 E3 Gmunden Austria
232 C4 Gnadenhutten OH U.S.A.
141 L3 Gnarp Sweden
168 E2 Gnarrenburg Ger.
179 G4 Gnas Austria
147 B4 Gneevgullia Rep. of Ireland
171 D4 Gneisenaustadt Schildau Ger.
179 E4 Gnesau Austria
Gnesen Pol. see Gniezno
143 G2 Gnesta Sweden
179 G4 Gniebing Austria
174 G2 Gniew Pol.
174 G1 Gniewino Pol.
174 G3 Gniewkowo Pol.
175 I5 Gnieździska Pol.
174 F3 Gniezno Pol.
143 H3 Gnisvärd Gotland Sweden
196 E4 Gnjilane Kosovo, Srbija Yugo.
191 H4 Gnocchetta Italy
170 D2 Gnoien Ger.
174 F5 Gnojna Pol.
175 I6 Gnojnik Pol.
175 I5 Gnojno Pol.
150 E2 Gnosall Staffordshire, England U.K.
173 E2 Gnotzheim Ger.
87 C7 Gnowangerup W.A. Austr.
87 C6 Gnows Nest Range hills W.A. Austr.
168 E1 Gnutz Ger.
114 B3 Goa state India
83 G4 Goalen Head hd N.S.W. Austr.
117 G4 Goalpara Assam India
206 E5 Goaso Ghana
146 C6 Goat Fell hill Scotland U.K.
210 D3 Goba Eth.
212 C4 Gobabis Namibia
Gobannium Monmouthshire, Wales U.K. see Abergavenny
261 G2 Gobernador Crespo Arg.
259 C8 Gobernador Gregores Arg.
261 G2 Gobernador Racedo Arg.
261 G4 Gobernador Ugarte Arg.
258 F3 Gobernador Virasoro Arg.
106 E2 Gobi des. China/Mongolia
179 E2 Göblberg hill Austria
104 B5 Gobō Japan
150 D2 Gobowen Shropshire, England U.K.
Gobustan Azer. see Qobustan
199 F3 Göcek Muğla Turkey
169 B4 Goch Ger.
212 C5 Gochas Namibia
169 F5 Gochsheim Ger.
97 D5 Go Công Vietnam
179 H4 Göcsej hills Hungary
177 I4 Göd Hungary
171 F4 Göda Ger.
117 G4 Godagari Bangl.
151 G3 Godalming Surrey, England U.K.
114 D2 Godavari r. India
114 D2 Godavari, Mouths of the India
225 H3 Godbout Que. Can.
225 H3 Godbout r. Que. Can.
117 F4 Godda Bihar India
222 C3 Goddard AK U.S.A.
240 H3 Goddard, Mount CA U.S.A.
172 C2 Goddelau Ger.
169 D4 Goddelsheim (Lichtenfels) Ger.
210 D3 Godē Eth.
184 B2 Godeal hill Port.
197 F4 Godech Bulg.
234 D1 Godeffroy NY U.S.A.
178 D5 Godega di Sant'Urbano Italy
129 D4 Gödeklı Turkey
187 C5 Godelleta Spain
224 D5 Goderich Ont. Can.
159 G2 Goderville France
Godhavn Greenland see Qeqertarsuaq
116 C5 Godhra Gujarat India
116 B5 Godia Creek b. Gujarat India
190 E4 Godiasco Italy
182 C3 Godim Port.
210 E3 Godinlabe Somalia
175 H1 Godkowo Pol.
81 C5 Godley r. South I. N.Z.
151 G2 Godmanchester Cambridgeshire, England U.K.
93 C3 Godo, Gunung mt. Indon.
184 C2 Godolín r. Port./Spain
177 I4 Gödöllő Hungary
260 C3 Godoy Cruz Arg.
177 G5 Gödre Hungary
223 M3 Gods r. Man. Can.
223 M4 Gods Lake Man. Can.
151 G3 Godstone Surrey, England U.K.
Godthåb Greenland see Nuuk
140 L1 Godučohkka mt. Sweden
Godwin-Austen, Mount China/Jammu and Kashmir see K2
174 G4 Godziesze Wielkie Pol.
175 K5 Godziszów Pol.
215 F4 Goedemoed S. Africa
164 C3 Goedereede Neth.
Goedgegun Swaziland see Nhlangano
224 E3 Goéland, Lac au l. Que. Can.
164 C3 Goes Neth.
227 E2 Goetzville MI U.S.A.
233 H3 Goffstown NH U.S.A.
179 G2 Göfritz an der Wild Austria
224 D4 Gogama Ont. Can.
103 F6 Gō-gawa r. Japan
226 C2 Gogebic Range hills MI U.S.A.
128 D1 Gögeç Turkey
172 D3 Göggingen Ger.
129 D4 Gogi Lerr mt. Armenia/Azer.
174 G5 Gogolin Pol.
197 F3 Gogoşu Romania
207 F4 Gogounou Benin
Gogra Bihar India see Ghaghra
Gogra r. India see Ghaghara
116 C4 Gogunda Rajasthan India
116 D4 Gohad Madh. Prad. India
116 D3 Gohana Haryana India
116 D5 Goharganj Madh. Prad. India
168 F1 Göhl Ger.
171 D4 Gohrau Ger.
168 F2 Göhrde Ger.
170 D2 Göhren-Lebbin Ger.
254 G3 Goiana Brazil
256 C3 Goiandira Brazil
255 C5 Goianésia Brazil
256 C2 Goiânia Brazil
254 G3 Goianinha Brazil
256 C2 Goianira Brazil
256 B1 Goiás Brazil
256 B2 Goiás state Brazil
256 C3 Goiatuba Brazil
146 D5 Goil, Loch inlet Scotland U.K.
108 B1 Goincang Qinghai China
256 A6 Goio r. Brazil
256 A6 Goio-Erê Brazil
164 E3 Goirle Neth.
182 B4 Góis Port.
191 F3 Goito Italy
186 B1 Goizueta Spain
210 C3 Gojeb Wenz r. Eth.
104 B4 Gojō Japan
123 H4 Gojra Pak.
175 H4 Gojść Pol.
114 B2 Gokak Karnataka India
114 B3 Gokarn Karnataka India
128 A1 Gök Çay r. Turkey
199 D1 Gökçeada i. Turkey
199 F2 Gökçedağ Turkey
129 A3 Gökçedere Turkey
199 G3 Gökçehüyük Isparta Turkey
199 E2 Gökçen Turkey
199 F2 Gökçeören Turkey
Gökdepe Turkm. see Gekdepe
128 A1 Gökdere r. Turkey
168 E1 Gokels Ger.
126 D2 Gökirmak r. Turkey
122 D1 Goklenkuy, Solonchak salt l. Turkm.
129 B4 Gököğlan Turkey
Gökova Turkey see Ula
199 F3 Gökova Muğla Turkey
199 E3 Gökova Körfezi b. Turkey
123 E5 Gokprosh Hills Pak.
129 C4 Göksu r. Turkey
126 E3 Göksun Turkey
126 D3 Göksu Nehri r. Turkey
128 A1 Göktepe Turkey
213 F3 Gokwe Zimbabwe
142 C1 Gol Norway
176 G5 Gola Croatia
117 F5 Gola Bihar India
116 E3 Gola Uttar Prad. India
175 J4 Gołąb Pol.
Golada Spain see A Golada
117 H4 Golaghat Assam India
179 E5 Golak mt. Slovenia
117 G4 Golakganj Assam India
128 B3 Golan hills Syria
174 F3 Gołańcz Pol.
175 K4 Gołaszyn Pol.
122 D4 Golbāf Iran
126 E3 Gölbaşı Turkey
199 F3 Gölbent Muğla Turkey
157 G4 Golbey France
114 C2 Golconda Andhra Prad. India
237 F4 Golconda IL U.S.A.
238 C3 Golconda NV U.S.A.
199 E2 Gölcük Turkey
Gölçük Turkey see Etili
199 F1 Gölcük Turkey
199 F2 Gölcük r. Turkey
176 E2 Golčův Jeníkov Czech Rep.
175 H5 Gołcza Pol.
174 C2 Golczewo Pol.
232 E4 Gold PA U.S.A.
172 D4 Goldach Switz.
175 K1 Gołdap Pol.
175 J1 Gołdapa r. Pol.
169 E5 Goldbach Ger.
238 A3 Gold Beach OR U.S.A.
170 C3 Goldbeck Ger.
170 D2 Goldberg Ger.
150 E3 Goldcliff Newport, Wales U.K.
Gold Coast country Africa see Ghana
83 H2 Gold Coast Qld Austr.
206 E5 Gold Coast coastal area Ghana
179 E4 Goldeck mt. Austria
178 E3 Goldegg Austria
168 E1 Goldelund Ger.
222 G5 Golden B.C. Can.
147 D4 Golden Rep. of Ireland
80 D4 Golden Bay South I. N.Z.
238 B2 Goldendale WA U.S.A.
81 D4 Golden Downs South I. N.Z.
246 □ Golden Grove Jamaica
222 E5 Golden Hinde mt. B.C. Can.
237 F6 Golden Meadow LA U.S.A.
151 G3 Golden Pot Hampshire, England U.K.
223 I5 Golden Prairie Sask. Can.
168 D3 Goldenstedt Ger.
119 L2 Golden Throne mt. Jammu and Kashmir
147 C4 Golden Vale lowland Rep. of Ireland
215 E5 Golden Valley S. Africa
150 E2 Golden Valley val. England U.K.
213 F3 Golden Valley Zimbabwe
240 I3 Goldfield NV U.S.A.
173 F1 Goldkronach Ger.
222 E5 Gold River B.C. Can.
234 C3 Goldsboro MD U.S.A.
231 E5 Goldsboro NC U.S.A.
86 C4 Goldsworthy W.A. Austr.
237 D6 Goldthwaite TX U.S.A.
129 C4 Göldüzü Turkey
232 E5 Goldvein VA U.S.A.
127 F2 Göle Turkey
184 B1 Golegã Port.
170 F3 Golenice Pol.
174 C2 Goleniów Pol.
122 C2 Golestān prov. Iran
174 G6 Goleszów Pol.
240 H4 Goleta CA U.S.A.
242 □J7 Golfito Costa Rica
192 B4 Golfo Aranci Sardegna Italy
199 F3 Gölgeli Dağları mts Turkey
199 F3 Gölhisar Turkey
191 J3 Goli hill Croatia
237 D6 Goliad TX U.S.A.
196 E4 Golija Planina mts Yugo.
174 G3 Golina Pol.
Golingka Xizang China see Gongbo'gyamda
161 A4 Golinhac France
139 K4 Golitsyno Rus. Fed.
126 E2 Gölköy Turkey
173 E2 Gollach r. Ger.
179 H2 Göllersdorf Austria
172 C2 Göllheim Ger.
170 E2 Gollin Brandenburg Ger.
170 C2 Göllin Ger.
178 E3 Golling an der Salzach Austria
171 C4 Göllingen Ger.
170 E2 Gollmitz Ger.
171 D3 Golm Ger.
199 E2 Gölmarmara Turkey
169 E4 Golmbach Ger.
171 E3 Golmberg hill Ger.
186 D3 Golmes Spain
106 B4 Golmud Qinghai China
106 B4 Golmud He r. China
179 F4 Golnik Slovenia
192 B2 Golo r. Corse France
139 M4 Golobino Rus. Fed.
Gologory hills Ukr. see Holohory
128 B1 Gölovası Turkey
137 H2 Golovchino Rus. Fed.
122 B3 Golpāyegān Iran
199 G1 Gölpazarı Turkey
182 E3 Golpejas Spain
179 H3 Gols Austria
179 G2 Gölsen r. Austria
146 E4 Golspie Highland, Scotland U.K.
171 E4 Golßen Ger.
171 D5 Göltzsch r. Ger.
175 H2 Golub-Dobrzyń Pol.
137 I5 Golubitskaya Rus. Fed.
121 H1 Golubovka Kazakh.
174 F4 Gołuchów Pol.
209 B7 Golungo Alto Angola
122 E3 Gol Vardeh Iran
197 G5 Golyama Syutkya mt. Bulg.
197 G4 Golyama Zhelyazna Bulg.
197 G5 Golyam Perelik mt. Bulg.
197 G5 Golyam Persenk mt. Bulg.
Golyashi Belarus see Sasnovy Bor
199 F1 Gölyazı Turkey
175 I3 Gołymin-Ośrodek Pol.
139 H4 Golynki Rus. Fed.
Golyshi Kostromskaya Oblast' Rus. Fed. see Vetluzhskiy
170 F3 Golzow Brandenburg Ger.
171 D3 Golzow Brandenburg Ger.
208 F5 Goma Dem. Rep. Congo
172 D3 Gomadingen Ger.
104 B4 Gomanodan-zan mt. Japan
183 H3 Gómara Spain
172 D3 Gomaringen Ger.
116 E4 Gomati r. India
207 H4 Gombe Nigeria
207 H4 Gombe state Nigeria
211 A6 Gombe r. Tanz.
199 F3 Gömbe Turkey
211 A6 Gombe National Park Tanz.
207 I4 Gombi Nigeria
129 D3 Gombori Georgia
206 E4 Gomboussougou Burkina
Gombroon Iran see Bandar-e 'Abbās
199 E2 Gömeç Turkey
182 E3 Gomecello Spain
Gomel' Belarus see Homyel'
Gomel Oblast admin. div. Belarus see Homyel'skaya Voblasts'
Gomel'skaya Oblast' admin. div. Belarus see Homyel'skaya Voblasts'
184 B3 Gomes Aires Port.
146 B5 Gometra i. Scotland U.K.
242 E3 Gómez Palacio Mex.
250 A5 Gómez Rendón Ecuador
122 C2 Gomīshān Iran
171 C3 Gommern Ger.
111 D5 Gomo Xizang China
175 H4 Gomunice Pol.
Gonabad Iran see Jūymand
246 D3 Gonaïves Haiti
122 C2 Gonbad-e Kavus Iran
177 K3 Gönc Hungary
182 C4 Gonçalo Port.
161 D3 Goncelin France
116 E4 Gonda Uttar Prad. India
116 B5 Gondal Gujarat India
250 C5 Gondar Col.
Gondar Eth. see Gonder
182 B3 Gondar Braga Port.
182 B3 Gondar Porto Port.
172 C2 Gondelsheim Ger.
210 C1 Gonder Eth.
169 C5 Gondershausen Ger.
182 D3 Gondesende Port.
116 E5 Gondia Mahar. India
182 B3 Gondomar Port.
182 B2 Gondomar Spain
169 C5 Gondorf Ger.
182 B3 Gondoriz Port.
157 F4 Gondrecourt-le-Château France
157 F4 Gondreville France
163 C5 Gondrin France
199 E1 Gönen Turkey
199 G3 Gönen Turkey
199 E1 Gönen r. Turkey
161 E5 Gonfaron France
159 G2 Gonfreville-l'Orcher France
109 E2 Gong'an Hubei China
Gongbalou Xizang China see Gamba
111 F6 Gongbo'gyamda Xizang China
108 D3 Gongcheng Guangxi China
111 E6 Gonggar Xizang China
108 B2 Gongga Shan mt. Sichuan China
106 D4 Gonghe Qinghai China
Gonghe Yunnan China see Mouding
Gongjiang Jiangxi China see Yudu
110 C3 Gongliu Xinjiang China
207 I4 Gongola r. Nigeria
83 F2 Gongolgon N.S.W. Austr.
106 C3 Gongpoquan Gansu China
Gongquan Sichuan China see Gongxian
108 A3 Gongshan Yunnan China
Gongtang Xizang China see Damxung
108 B3 Gongwang Shan mts Yunnan China
Gongxian Henan China see Gongyi
108 C2 Gongxian Sichuan China
107 G5 Gongyi Henan China
100 C4 Gongzhuling Jilin China
192 B5 Goni Sardegna Italy
175 K2 Goniądz Pol.
108 A2 Gonjo Xizang China
192 A5 Gonnesa Sardegna Italy
198 C2 Gonnoi Greece
192 A5 Gonnosfanadiga Sardegna Italy
192 A5 Gonnosnò Sardegna Italy
160 E1 Gonsans France
215 G5 Gonubie S. Africa
177 G4 Gönyű Hungary
191 F4 Gonzaga Italy
245 E2 Gonzáles Mex.
240 G3 Gonzales CA U.S.A.
237 D6 Gonzales TX U.S.A.
261 F4 González Moreno Arg.
244 C2 González Ortega Mex.
232 E6 Goochland VA U.S.A.
232 D6 Goode VA U.S.A.
263 I2 Goodenough, Cape Antarctica
227 H3 Gooderham Ont. Can.
226 E3 Good Hart MI U.S.A.
226 B5 Good Hope IL U.S.A.
214 B6 Good Hope, Cape of S. Africa
222 E5 Good Hope Mountain B.C. Can.
238 D3 Gooding ID U.S.A.
236 C4 Goodland KS U.S.A.
226 C3 Goodman WI U.S.A.
83 F2 Goodooga N.S.W. Austr.
84 C2 Goodparla N.T. Austr.
226 B3 Goodrich WI U.S.A.
223 I4 Goodsoil Sask. Can.
263 E2 Goodspeed Nunataks nunataks Antarctica
150 C2 Goodwick Pembrokeshire, Wales U.K.
225 G2 Goodwood r. Que. Can.
81 C6 Goodwood South I. N.Z.
149 I4 Goole East Riding of Yorkshire, England U.K.
83 F3 Goolgowi N.S.W. Austr.
82 D3 Goolwa S.A. Austr.
84 C1 Goomadeer r. N.T. Austr.
87 C6 Goomalling W.A. Austr.
83 F2 Goombalie N.S.W. Austr.
85 H5 Goomeri Qld Austr.
83 G2 Goondiwindi Qld Austr.
87 D6 Goongarrie, Lake salt flat W.A. Austr.
150 B4 Goonhavern Cornwall, England U.K.
85 F4 Goonyella Qld Austr.
164 F2 Goor Neth.
87 C6 Goorly, Lake salt flat W.A. Austr.
225 I2 Goose r. Nfld. Can.
236 D2 Goose r. ND U.S.A.
Goose Bay Nfld. Can. see Happy Valley - Goose Bay
81 D5 Goose Bay South I. N.Z.
231 D5 Goose Creek SC U.S.A.
238 D3 Goose Creek r. Idaho/Nevada U.S.A.
259 F8 Goose Green Falkland Is
238 B3 Goose Lake CA U.S.A.
240 H4 Goose Lake Canal r. CA U.S.A.
114 C3 Gooty Andhra Prad. India
115 E2 Gop Orissa India
117 G5 Gopalganj Bangl.
117 F4 Gopalganj Bihar India
183 H2 Gopegui Spain
116 D3 Gopeshwar Uttar Prad. India
114 C4 Gopichettipalayam Tamil Nadu India
116 E4 Gopiganj Uttar Prad. India
172 D3 Göppingen Ger.
185 H3 Gor Spain
185 G3 Gor r. Spain
174 E4 Góra Pol.
175 I3 Góra Pol.
Goradiz Azer. see Horadiz
185 G3 Gorafe Spain
129 D2 Goragorskiy Rus. Fed.
175 K5 Goraj Pol.
175 J4 Góra Kalwaria Pol.
117 E4 Gorakhpur Uttar Prad. India
129 E3 Goranboy Azer.
175 J4 Góra Puławska Pol.
188 G4 Goražde Bos.-Herz.
139 K5 Gorbachevo Rus. Fed.
260 A6 Gorbea Chile
177 K4 Görbeháza Hungary
100 A1 Gorbitsa Rus. Fed.
134 H4 Gorchukha Rus. Fed.
177 H6 Görcsöny Hungary
246 B4 Gorda, Banco sea feature Hond.
240 E1 Gorda, Punta pt CA U.S.A.
246 C1 Gorda Cay i. Bahamas
141 K3 Gördalen Sweden
183 E2 Gordaliza del Pino Spain
190 E4 Gordana r. Italy
161 D5 Gordes France
199 F2 Gördes Turkey
183 G1 Gordexola Spain
139 H5 Gordeyevka Rus. Fed.
190 D2 Gordola Switz.
87 C7 Gordon r. W.A. Austr.
146 F6 Gordon Scottish Borders, Scotland U.K.
236 C3 Gordon NE U.S.A.
234 B2 Gordon PA U.S.A.
226 B2 Gordon WI U.S.A.
83 F5 Gordon, Lake Tas. Austr.
190 E2 Gordona Italy
84 B1 Gordon Bay N.T. Austr.
84 B3 Gordon Creek r. N.T. Austr.
86 F3 Gordon Downs W.A. Austr.
222 C2 Gordon Landing Y.T. Can.
214 B6 Gordon's Bay S. Africa
232 D5 Gordonsville VA U.S.A.
85 F3 Gordonvale Qld Austr.
234 B2 Gordonville PA U.S.A.
208 C3 Goré Chad
210 B2 Gorē Eth.
81 B7 Gore South I. N.Z.
232 D5 Gore VA U.S.A.
227 F3 Gore Bay Ont. Can.
146 E6 Gorebridge Midlothian, Scotland U.K.
199 E2 Görece İzmir Turkey
139 K4 Gorelki Rus. Fed.
129 C3 Gorelovka Georgia
135 H5 Goreloye Rus. Fed.
179 G5 Gorenja Straža Slovenia
147 E4 Goresbridge Rep. of Ireland
147 E4 Gorey Rep. of Ireland
122 C2 Gorgān Iran
122 C2 Gorgān, Rūd-e r. Iran
122 C2 Gorgan Bay Iran
Gorgany mts Ukr. see Horhany
86 C4 Gorge Range hills W.A. Austr.
85 F3 Gorge Range mts Qld Austr.
81 B7 Gorge Road South I. N.Z.
176 G5 Gőrgeteg Hungary
193 I4 Gorgoglione Italy
206 B2 Gorgol admin. reg. Maur.
190 E5 Gorgona, Isola di i. Italy
190 E3 Gorgonzola Italy
210 C1 Gorgora Eth.
207 H3 Gorgoram Nigeria
187 D6 Gorgos r. Spain
233 H2 Gorham NH U.S.A.
129 D3 Gori Georgia
196 D4 Gorica Crna Gora Yugo.
179 H4 Goričan Croatia
164 D3 Gorinchem Neth.
151 F3 Goring Oxfordshire, England U.K.
191 H4 Gorino Italy
129 E4 Goris Armenia
173 E4 Görisried Ger.
197 H4 Goritsa Bulg.
139 K3 Goritsy Rus. Fed.
170 E2 Göritz Ger.
191 I3 Gorizia Italy
191 I3 Gorizia prov. Friuli - Venezia Giulia Italy
139 L3 Gorka Rus. Fed.
129 D1 Gor'kaya Balka r. Rus. Fed.
Gorki Belarus see Horki
Gor'kiy Rus. Fed. see Nizhniy Novgorod
Gor'kovskaya Oblast' admin. div. Rus. Fed. see Nizhegorodskaya Oblast'
139 M3 Gor'kovskoye Vodokhranilishche resr Rus. Fed.
170 C2 Gorleben Ger.
142 D4 Gørlev Denmark
175 J6 Gorlice Pol.
171 F4 Görlitz Ger.
170 C2 Gorlosen Ger.
Gorlovka Ukr. see Horlivka
139 L5 Gorlovo Rus. Fed.
171 E4 Görlsdorf Ger.
147 E3 Gormanstown Rep. of Ireland
183 H3 Gormaz Spain
116 D4 Gormi Madh. Prad. India
170 E2 Görmin Ger.
Gorna Dzhumaya Bulg. see Blagoevgrad
194 E5 Gornalunga r. Sicilia Italy
197 G4 Gorna Oryakhovitsa Bulg.
171 E5 Gornau Ger.
197 G4 Gorni Dŭbnik Bulg.
188 E2 Gornja Radgona Slovenia
197 E4 Gornja Toponica Srbija Yugo.
191 J3 Gornje Jelenje Croatia
179 H4 Gornje Vratno Croatia
177 J6 Gornji Breg Vojvodina, Srbija Yugo.
197 E4 Gornji Matejevac Srbija Yugo.
196 E3 Gornji Milanovac Srbija Yugo.
188 F4 Gornji Vakuf Bos.-Herz.
175 I5 Górno Pol.
197 G4 Gorno Ablanovo Bulg.
121 K2 Gorno-Altaysk Rus. Fed.
Gorno-Altayskaya Avtonomnaya Oblast' aut. rep. Rus. Fed. see Altay, Respublika
Gorno-Badakhshan aut. rep. Tajik. see Kŭhistoni Badakhshon
130 H3 Gornopravdinsk Rus. Fed.
197 G4 Gornotrakiyska Nizina lowland Bulg.
134 L4 Gornozavodsk Permskaya Oblast' Rus. Fed.
100 G3 Gornozavodsk Sakhalin Rus. Fed.
110 C1 Gornyak Rus. Fed.
Gornyak Donets'ka Oblast' Ukr. see Hirnyk
100 E3 Gornye Klyuchi Rus. Fed.
100 F2 Gornyy Khabarovskiy Kray Rus. Fed.
137 K4 Gornyy Rostovskaya Oblast' Rus. Fed.
120 B2 Gornyy Saratovskaya Oblast' Rus. Fed.
Gornyy Altay aut. rep. Rus. Fed. see Altay, Respublika
Gornyy Badakhshan aut. rep. Tajik. see Kŭhistoni Badakhshon
135 I6 Gornyy Balykley Rus. Fed.
Goro i. Fiji see Koro
191 H4 Goro Italy
210 C2 Goroch'an mt. Eth.
Gorodenka Ukr. see Horodenka
134 H4 Gorodets Rus. Fed.
137 J2 Gorodishche Belgorodskaya Oblast' Rus. Fed.
135 I5 Gorodishche Penzenskaya Oblast' Rus. Fed.
135 I6 Gorodishche Volgogradskaya Oblast' Rus. Fed.
Gorodishche Cherkas'ka Oblast' Ukr. see Horodyshche
Gorodok Belarus see Haradok
Gorodok Rus. Fed. see Zakamensk
Gorodok Khmel'nyts'ka Oblast' Ukr. see Horodok
Gorodok L'vivs'ka Oblast' Ukr. see Horodok
135 H7 Gorodovikovsk Rus. Fed.
91 K8 Goroka P.N.G.
82 E4 Goroke Vic. Austr.
134 H4 Gorokhovets Rus. Fed.
206 E3 Gorom Gorom Burkina
91 H7 Gorong, Kepulauan is Indon.
213 G3 Gorongosa Moz.
213 G3 Gorongosa mt. Moz.
93 B2 Gorontalo Sulawesi Utara Indon.
207 G3 Goronyo Nigeria
207 F3 Gorouol r. Burkina/Niger
143 I4 Górowo Iławeckie Pol.
164 F1 Gorredijk Neth.
190 E4 Gorreto Italy
159 F3 Gorron France
169 F4 Görsbach Ger.
150 C3 Gorseinon Swansea, Wales U.K.
135 G6 Gorshechnoye Rus. Fed.
174 G2 Górsk Pol.
Gorskoye Ukr. see Hirs'ke
164 F2 Gorssel Neth.
147 C3 Gort Rep. of Ireland
148 B3 Gortaclare Northern Ireland U.K.
147 C1 Gortahork Rep. of Ireland
147 C3 Gorteen Galway Rep. of Ireland
148 B5 Gorteen Kilkenny Rep. of Ireland
147 C3 Gorteen Sligo Rep. of Ireland
147 D4 Gorteen Waterford Rep. of Ireland
147 C3 Gorteeny Rep. of Ireland
147 D2 Gortin Northern Ireland U.K.
197 H3 Goru, Vârful mt. Romania
199 F1 Görükle Turkey
257 F1 Gorutuba r. Brazil
172 C4 Görwihl Ger.
172 C2 Gorxheimertal Ger.
Goryacheistochnenskaya Rus. Fed. see Goryachevodskiy
129 C1 Goryachevodskiy Rus. Fed.
129 A1 Goryachiy Klyuch Rus. Fed.
Goryn' r. Ukr. see Horyn'
193 F2 Gorzano, Monte mt. Italy
157 G3 Gorze France
171 C4 Görzig Ger.
171 D3 Görzke Ger.
175 H4 Gorzkowice Pol.
175 L5 Gorzków-Osada Pol.
175 H2 Górzno Pol.
174 G4 Gorzów Śląski Pol.
174 D3 Gorzów Wielkopolski Pol.
174 C3 Górzyca Pol.
175 J5 Gorzyce Podkarpackie Pol.
175 K5 Gorzyce Podkarpackie Pol.
174 G6 Gorzyce Śląskie Pol.
Gosainthan mt. Xizang China see Xixabangma Feng
191 G2 Gosaldo Italy
179 E3 Gosau Austria
151 G2 Gosberton Lincolnshire, England U.K.
174 D1 Gościno Pol.
174 D4 Gósciszów Pol.
179 G4 Gosdorf Austria
104 B4 Gose Japan
171 C4 Goseck Ger.
176 F5 Gősfai Hegy hill Hungary
151 H3 Gosfield Essex, England U.K.
83 G3 Gosford N.S.W. Austr.
149 F3 Gosforth Cumbria, England U.K.
149 H2 Gosforth Tyne and Wear, England U.K.
172 C3 Gosheim Ger.
240 H3 Goshen CA U.S.A.
230 C3 Goshen IN U.S.A.
233 G3 Goshen NH U.S.A.
234 D3 Goshen NJ U.S.A.
233 F4 Goshen NY U.S.A.
232 D6 Goshen VA U.S.A.
102 J3 Goshogawara Japan
169 F4 Goslar Ger.
175 H3 Goślice Pol.
158 E3 Gosné France
188 E3 Gospić Croatia
151 F4 Gosport Hampshire, England U.K.
206 A3 Gossas Senegal
190 E1 Gossau Sankt Gallen Switz.
172 C4 Gossau Zürich Switz.
179 G4 Gössendorf Austria
206 E3 Gossi Mali
171 D5 Gößnitz Ger.
173 F2 Gößweinstein Ger.
137 I5 Gostagayevskaya Rus. Fed.
137 I2 Gostishchevo Rus. Fed.
196 E5 Gostivar Macedonia
179 F3 Göstling an der Ybbs Austria
174 F2 Gostycyn Pol.
174 F4 Gostyń Pol.
175 H3 Gostynin Pol.
108 A1 Gosu Sichuan China
174 F4 Goszcz Pol.
174 G4 Goszczanów Pol.
175 I4 Goszczyn Pol.
210 D2 Gota Eth.
142 D3 Götaälven r. Sweden
143 F3 Götaland reg. Sweden
142 D3 Göteborg Sweden
142 E3 Göteborg-Landvetter airport Sweden
105 E3 Gotemba Shizuoka Japan
Gotenba Shizuoka Japan see Gotemba
142 E2 Götene Sweden
Gotenhafen Pol. see Gdynia
169 F5 Gotha Ger.
151 F2 Gotham Nottinghamshire, England U.K.
143 H3 Gothem Gotland Sweden
143 H3 Gothemån r. Gotland Sweden
Gothenburg Sweden see Göteborg
236 C3 Gothenburg NE U.S.A.
207 F3 Gothèye Niger
143 H3 Gotland county Sweden
143 H3 Gotland i. Sweden
103 D7 Gotō-rettō is Japan
197 F5 Gotse Delchev Bulg.
143 H2 Gotska Sandön Sweden
143 H2 Gotska Sandön i. Sweden
103 F6 Gōtsu Japan
190 E4 Gottero, Monte mt. Italy
173 G3 Gotteszell Ger.
173 G3 Gottfrieding Ger.
169 E4 Göttingen Ger.
172 C4 Gottmadingen Ger.
140 L3 Gottne Sweden
222 F5 Gott Peak B.C. Can.
Gottwaldow Czech Rep. see Zlín
Goturdepe Turkm. see Koturdepe
Gotval'd Ukr. see Zmiyiv
179 H2 Götzendorf an der Leitha Austria
178 A3 Götzis Austria
158 C3 Gouarec France
164 D2 Gouda Neth.
214 B5 Gouda S. Africa
161 C4 Goudargues France
260 C4 Goudge Arg.
151 H3 Goudhurst Kent, England U.K.
206 B3 Goudiri Senegal
207 H3 Goudoumaria Niger
226 E1 Goudreau Ont. Can.
206 C4 Gouéké Guinea
158 B3 Gouesnou France
158 D3 Gouet r. France
264 I8 Gough Island S. Atlantic Ocean
160 E1 Gouhenans France
224 F3 Gouin, Réservoir resr Que. Can.
161 A4 Goul r. France
226 E2 Goulais River Ont. Can.
83 G3 Goulburn N.S.W. Austr.
83 F4 Goulburn r. Vic. Austr.
84 C1 Goulburn Islands N.T. Austr.
87 C5 Gould, Mount hill W.A. Austr.
226 E2 Gould City MI U.S.A.
262 O1 Gould Coast Antarctica
234 C1 Gouldsboro PA U.S.A.
207 I3 Goulféy Cameroon
Goulou atoll Micronesia see Ngulu
161 D5 Goult France
206 D3 Goumbou Mali
198 C1 Goumenissa Greece
160 E1 Goumois France
207 I4 Gouna Cameroon
206 E2 Goundam Mali
208 C2 Goundi Chad
208 B2 Gounou-Gaya Chad
206 B3 Gouraye Maur.
163 A5 Gourbera France
206 E3 Gourcy Burkina
163 C5 Gourdan-Polignan France
163 D4 Gourdon Midi-Pyrénées France
161 E5 Gourdon Provence-Alpes-Côte-d'Azur France
146 F5 Gourdon Aberdeenshire, Scotland U.K.
207 H3 Gouré Niger
163 B6 Gourette France
156 E4 Gourgançon France
158 C3 Gourin France
117 G4 Gouripur Bangl.
214 C6 Gourits r. S. Africa
206 E2 Gourma-Rharous Mali
156 B3 Gournay-en-Bray France
204 D5 Goûr Oulad Aḥmed reg. Mali
156 C3 Goussainville France
162 C3 Gout-Rossignol France
164 E1 Goutum Neth.
257 F3 Gouvêa Brazil
182 C4 Gouveia Port.
233 F2 Gouverneur NY U.S.A.
156 C3 Gouvieux France
165 E4 Gouvy Belgium
247 □6 Gouyave Grenada
162 E2 Gouzon France
182 B3 Gove Port.
236 C4 Gove KS U.S.A.
197 F4 Govedartsi Bulg.
84 D2 Gove Peninsula N.T. Austr.
Goverla, Gora mt. Ukr. see Hoverla, Hora
257 G3 Governador Valadares Brazil
92 C5 Governor Generoso Phil.
246 C1 Governor's Harbour Eleuthera Bahamas
106 B2 Govĭ-Altay prov. Mongolia

106 C2 Govĭ Altayn Nuruu mts Mongolia
116 E4 Govindgarh Madh. Prad. India
123 F2 Govurdak Turkm.
81 D4 Gowanbridge South I. N.Z.
232 D3 Gowanda NY U.S.A.
85 F5 Gowan Range hills Qld Austr.
175 I4 Gowarczów Pol.
234 B2 Gowen City PA U.S.A.
150 C3 Gower pen. Wales U.K.
227 G2 Gowganda Ont. Can.
174 F1 Gowidlino Pol.
174 C2 Gowienica r. Pol.
147 D3 Gowna, Lough l. Rep. of Ireland
175 J3 Goworowo Pol.
147 D4 Gowran Rep. of Ireland
Gowurdak Turkm. see Govurdak
149 G4 Gowy r. England U.K.
149 I4 Goxhill North Lincolnshire, England U.K.
258 F3 Goya Arg.
247 □2 Goyave Guadeloupe
129 E3 Göyçay Azer.
129 E3 Göyçay r. Azer.
84 C2 Goyder r. N.T. Austr.
84 C5 Goyder watercourse N.T. Austr.
82 D1 Goyder Lagoon salt flat S.A. Austr.
Goymatdag hills Turkm. see Koymatdag, Gory
199 G3 Göynük Turkey
127 F3 Göynük Turkey
199 G1 Göynük Turkey
199 G1 Göynük r. Turkey
199 F2 Göynükbelen Turkey
102 J4 Goyō-zan mt. Japan
129 F4 Göytäpä Azer.
202 D6 Goz-Beïda Chad
128 B1 Gözcüler Turkey
175 J4 Gózd Pol.
174 D4 Gozdnica Pol.
126 E3 Gözene Turkey
111 C5 Gozha Co salt l. China
195 □ Gozo i. Malta
190 D3 Gozzano Italy
214 E5 Graaf-Reinet S. Africa
214 B5 Graafwater S. Africa
172 C2 Graben-Neudorf Ger.
173 G4 Grabenstätt Ger.
169 F5 Grabfeld plain Ger.
175 G4 Grabia r. Pol.
175 H4 Grabica Pol.
206 D5 Grabo Côte d'Ivoire
214 B6 Grabouw S. Africa
197 F3 Grabovica Srbija Yugo.
121 H1 Grabovo Kazakh.
170 C2 Grabow Mecklenburg-Vorpommern Ger.
171 C3 Grabow Sachsen-Anhalt Ger.
175 H3 Grabów Pol.
143 G4 Grabowa r. Pol.
170 D2 Grabowhöfe Ger.
175 L5 Grabowiec Lubelskie Pol.
175 J4 Grabowiec Mazowieckie Pol.
175 J4 Grabów nad Pilicą Pol.
174 G4 Grabów nad Prosną Pol.
174 F2 Grabówno Pol.
174 F4 Grabowno Wielkie Pol.
175 K2 Grabowo Podlaskie Pol.
175 K1 Grabowo Warmińsko-Mazurskie Pol.
190 E1 Grabs Switz.
188 E3 Gračac Croatia
188 G3 Gračanica Bos.-Herz.
162 D1 Graçay France
87 C7 Grace, Lake salt flat W.A. Austr.
224 E4 Gracefield Que. Can.
165 E4 Grâce-Hollogne Belgium
85 G4 Gracemere Qld Austr.
158 C3 Grâces France
139 M5 Grachevka Lipetskaya Oblast' Rus. Fed.
120 C1 Grachevka Orenburgskaya Oblast' Rus. Fed.
121 I2 Grachi Kazakh.
245 E2 Graciano Sánchez Mex.
242 □H6 Gracías Hond.
216 □1c Graciosa i. Azores
216 □3c Graciosa i. Canary Is
188 G3 Gradačac Bos.-Herz.
191 H5 Gradara Italy
254 C4 Gradaús, Serra dos hills Brazil
183 E2 Gradefes Spain
197 H4 Gradets Bulg.
163 B4 Gradignan France
197 H4 Gradishte hill Bulg.
Gradiška Bos.-Herz. see Bosanska Gradiška
188 G3 Gradište Croatia
197 H3 Grădiştea Romania
191 I3 Grado Italy
182 D1 Grado Spain
192 D2 Gradoli Italy
237 C5 Grady NM U.S.A.
146 E3 Graemsay i. Scotland U.K.
185 G3 Graena Spain
173 F3 Gräfelfing Ger.
173 F2 Gräfenberg Ger.
169 E5 Gräfendorf Ger.
179 G3 Grafendorf bei Hartberg Austria
171 D4 Gräfenhainichen Ger.
172 C4 Grafenhausen Ger.
169 F5 Gräfenroda Ger.
179 F4 Grafenstein Austria
171 C5 Gräfenthal Ger.
169 F4 Gräfentonna Ger.
173 F2 Grafenwöhr Ger.
179 G2 Grafenworth Austria
192 E2 Graffignano Italy
169 F3 Grafhorst Ger.
171 C5 Gräfinau-Angstedt Ger.
173 F3 Grafing bei München Ger.
142 C1 Gråfjell mt. Norway
173 G3 Grafling Ger.
173 F3 Grafrath Ger.
140 K3 Gräftåvallen Sweden
83 H2 Grafton N.S.W. Austr.
236 D1 Grafton ND U.S.A.
232 B4 Grafton OH U.S.A.
226 D4 Grafton WI U.S.A.
232 C5 Grafton WV U.S.A.
85 F3 Grafton, Cape Qld Austr.
241 J2 Grafton, Mount NV U.S.A.
85 F3 Grafton Passage Qld Austr.
142 C1 Grågalten hill Norway
193 G4 Gragnano Italy
231 E4 Graham NC U.S.A.
237 D5 Graham TX U.S.A.
241 M5 Graham, Mount AZ U.S.A.
Graham Bell Island Zemlya Frantsa-Iosifa Rus. Fed. see Greem-Bell, Ostrov
222 C4 Graham Island B.C. Can.
221 I2 Graham Island Nunavut Can.
262 T2 Graham Land reg. Antarctica
215 F5 Grahamstown S. Africa
Grahovo Bos.-Herz. see Bosansko Grahovo
148 C5 Graigue Rep. of Ireland
147 E4 Graiguenamanagh Rep. of Ireland
151 H3 Grain Medway, England U.K.
151 H3 Grain, Isle of pen. England U.K.
173 F4 Grainau Ger.
173 H3 Grainet Ger.
161 A4 Graissac France
161 B5 Graissessac France
183 I5 Graja de Iniesta Spain
183 E2 Grajal de Campos Spain
254 D3 Grajaú Brazil
254 D2 Grajaú r. Brazil
175 K2 Grajewo Pol.
134 J4 Grakhovo Rus. Fed.
179 G4 Gralla Austria
142 C4 Gram Denmark
197 F4 Gramada mt. Yugo.
179 F2 Gramastettan Austria
163 D4 Gramat France
163 D4 Gramat, Causse de hills France
197 H4 Gramatikovo Bulg.
179 H2 Gramatneusiedl Austria
161 D5 Grambois France
170 F2 Grambow Ger.
170 C2 Gramkow Ger.
170 D1 Grammendorf Ger.
194 D5 Grammichele Sicilia Italy
Grammont Belgium see Geraardsbergen
190 C5 Grammont, Mont mt. Italy
198 B1 Grámmos mt. Greece
232 D4 Grampian PA U.S.A.
146 D5 Grampian Mountains Scotland U.K.
83 E4 Grampians, The mts Vic. Austr.
150 C4 Grampound Cornwall, England U.K.
164 F2 Gramsbergen Neth.
196 E5 Gramsh Albania
170 F2 Gramzow Ger.
Gran Hungary see Esztergom
190 C4 Grana r. Italy
190 D3 Grana r. Italy
214 B4 Granaatboskolk S. Africa
147 E3 Granabeg Rep. of Ireland
250 C4 Granada Col.
242 □I7 Granada Nic.
185 G3 Granada Spain
185 G3 Granada prov. Andalucía Spain
236 C4 Granada CO U.S.A.
216 □3a Granadilla de Abona Tenerife Canary Is
184 C3 Granado hill Spain
147 D3 Granard Rep. of Ireland
191 G4 Granarolo dell'Emilia Italy
178 D3 Granatspitze mt. Austria
185 G2 Granátula de Calatrava Spain
259 D7 Gran Bajo depr. Arg.
260 D6 Gran Bajo Salitroso salt flat Arg.
237 D5 Granbury TX U.S.A.
225 F4 Granby Que. Can.
238 F3 Granby CO U.S.A.
216 □3f Gran Canaria i. Canary Is
157 F5 Grancey-le-Château-Neuvelle France
253 E6 Gran Chaco reg. Arg./Para.
157 F4 Grand France
230 C3 Grand r. MO U.S.A.
236 C2 Grand r. SD U.S.A.
236 C2 Grand, North Fork r. SD U.S.A.
236 C2 Grand, South Fork r. SD U.S.A.
161 D4 Grand Armet mt. France
182 D1 Grandas de Salime Spain
Grand Atlas mts Morocco see Haut Atlas
246 C1 Grand Bahama i. Bahamas
157 H5 Grand Ballon mt. France
225 K4 Grand Bank Nfld. Can.
264 F3 Grand Banks of Newfoundland sea feature N. Atlantic Ocean
206 E5 Grand-Bassam Côte d'Ivoire
225 H4 Grand Bay N.B. Can.
237 F6 Grand Bay AL U.S.A.
217 □1c Grand Bénare mt. Réunion
224 D5 Grand Bend Ont. Can.
161 E4 Grand Bérard mt. France
206 D5 Grand-Bérébi Côte d'Ivoire
232 B3 Grand Blanc MI U.S.A.
246 E2 Grand Caicos i. Turks and Caicos Is
159 E2 Grandcamp-Maisy France
Grand Canal China see Da Yunhe
Grand Canary i. Canary Is see Gran Canaria
241 K3 Grand Canyon AZ U.S.A.
241 K3 Grand Canyon gorge AZ U.S.A.
246 B3 Grand Cayman i. Cayman Is
223 I4 Grand Centre Alta Can.
206 C5 Grand Cess Liberia
158 D4 Grand-Champ France
160 E1 Grand-Charmont France
160 D3 Grand Colombier mt. France
190 C3 Grand Combin mt. Switz.
238 C2 Grand Coulee WA U.S.A.
156 B3 Grand-Couronne France
226 C5 Grand Detour IL U.S.A.
260 C5 Grande r. Arg.
252 E4 Grande r. Santa Cruz Bol.
253 E4 Grande r. Santa Cruz Bol.
254 E4 Grande r. Bahia Brazil
256 B3 Grande r. São Paulo Brazil
194 C5 Grande r. Sicilia Italy
245 H5 Grande r. Chiapas Mex.
244 C4 Grande r. Jalisco/Michoacán Mex.
245 F5 Grande r. Oaxaca Mex.
245 G5 Grande r. Oaxaca Mex.
242 □J6 Grande r. Nic.
252 B3 Grande r. Peru
187 C5 Grande r. Spain
185 F4 Grande r. Spain
185 G2 Grande r. Spain
259 C8 Grande, Bahía b. Arg.
245 F5 Grande, Cerro mt. Oaxaca Mex.
244 D2 Grande, Cerro mt. San Luis Potosí Mex.
257 E5 Grande, Ilha i. Brazil
194 B5 Grande, Montagna hill Sicilia Italy
260 D5 Grande, Salina salt flat Arg.
253 E2 Grande, Serra hills Brazil
251 F4 Grande, Serra mt. Brazil
260 E2 Grande, Sierra mts Arg.
247 □2 Grande Anse Guadeloupe
217 □1b Grande Baie Mauritius
222 G4 Grande Cache Alta Can.
Grande Comore i. Comoros see Njazidja
225 I4 Grande-Entree Que. Can.
163 B4 Grande Leyre r. France
222 G4 Grande Prairie Alta Can.
207 I2 Grand Erg de Bilma des. Niger
205 E3 Grand Erg Occidental des. Alg.
205 G3 Grand Erg Oriental des. Alg.
225 H3 Grande-Rivière Que. Can.
217 □1b Grande Rivière Noire r. Mauritius
217 □1b Grande Rivière South East r. Mauritius
217 □1b Grande Rivière Sud-Est r. Mauritius
190 C3 Grande Rochère mt. Italy
238 C2 Grande Ronde r. OR U.S.A.
260 E2 Grandes, Salinas salt marsh Arg.
160 A1 Grande Sauldre r. France
160 F3 Grandes Jorasses mts France/Italy
156 C1 Grande-Synthe France
247 □2 Grande-Terre i. Guadeloupe
217 □3b Grande Terre i. Mayotte
161 D4 Grande Tête de l'Obiou mt. France
158 D5 Grand Etier r. France
190 C3 Grande Tournalin mt. Italy
163 E4 Grande-Vabre France
225 H3 Grande-Vallée Que. Can.
190 C3 Grand Eyvia r. Italy
225 H4 Grand Falls N.B. Can.
225 K3 Grand Falls Nfld. Can.
222 G5 Grand Forks B.C. Can.
236 D2 Grand Forks ND U.S.A.
156 C1 Grand-Fort-Philippe France
158 E4 Grand-Fougeray France
163 B6 Grand Gabizos mt. France
233 F3 Grand Gorge NY U.S.A.
246 E3 Grand Gosier Haiti
225 H4 Grand Harbour N.B. Can.
226 D4 Grand Haven MI U.S.A.
236 D3 Grand Island NE U.S.A.
237 F6 Grand Isle LA U.S.A.
233 □I1 Grand Isle ME U.S.A.
241 M2 Grand Junction CO U.S.A.
226 D4 Grand Junction MI U.S.A.
206 D5 Grand-Lahou Côte d'Ivoire
159 E5 Grand Lay r. France
226 E4 Grand Ledge MI U.S.A.
158 E4 Grand-Lieu, Lac de l. France
159 E5 Grand Maine r. France
225 H4 Grand Manan Island N.B. Can.
226 E2 Grand Marais MI U.S.A.
226 B2 Grand Marais MN U.S.A.
226 C4 Grand Marsh WI U.S.A.
225 F4 Grand-Mère Que. Can.
156 C4 Grand Morin r. France
184 B2 Grândola Port.
184 B2 Grândola r. Port.
184 B2 Grândola, Serra de mts Port.
161 D3 Grand Pic de Belledonne mt. France
226 C2 Grand Portage MN U.S.A.
157 E3 Grandpré France
156 C4 Grandpuits-Bailly-Carrois France
223 L4 Grand Rapids Man. Can.
226 E4 Grand Rapids MI U.S.A.
226 A2 Grand Rapids MN U.S.A.
78 □5 Grand Récif de Cook rf New Caledonia
161 C5 Grand Rhône r. France
161 B4 Grandrieu France
160 C2 Grandris France
161 E3 Grand Roc Noir mt. France
Grand St Bernard, Col du pass Italy/Switz. see Great St Bernard Pass
251 H3 Grand Santi Fr. Guiana
190 B2 Grandson Switz.
238 E3 Grand Teton mt. WY U.S.A.
226 E3 Grand Traverse Bay MI U.S.A.
246 E2 Grand Turk Turks and Caicos Is
246 E2 Grand Turk i. Turks and Caicos Is
160 E1 Grandvelle-et-le-Perrenot France
226 B2 Grand View WI U.S.A.
160 E1 Grandvillars France
226 E4 Grandville MI U.S.A.
157 G4 Grandvillers France
156 B3 Grandvilliers France
241 J4 Grand Wash Cliffs mts AZ U.S.A.
226 A3 Grandy MN U.S.A.
161 C4 Grane France
186 C3 Grañén Spain
260 B4 Graneros Chile
147 E3 Grange Louth Rep. of Ireland
147 C2 Grange Sligo Rep. of Ireland
147 D5 Grange Waterford Rep. of Ireland
160 E2 Grange, Mont de mt. France
147 E3 Grangebellow Rep. of Ireland
147 E4 Grangeford Rep. of Ireland
246 □ Grange Hill Jamaica
146 E5 Grangemouth Falkirk, Scotland U.K.
149 G3 Grange-over-Sands Cumbria England U.K.
238 E3 Granger WY U.S.A.
143 F1 Grängesberg Sweden
157 G4 Granges-sur-Vologne France
150 D3 Grangetown Cardiff, Wales U.K.
238 C2 Grangeville ID U.S.A.
140 M2 Granhult Sweden
161 D3 Granier, Mont mt. France
222 E4 Granisle B.C. Can.
234 B3 Granite MD U.S.A.
236 F4 Granite City IL U.S.A.
236 E2 Granite Falls MN U.S.A.
240 I1 Granite Mountain NV U.S.A.
241 J4 Granite Mountains CA U.S.A.
241 J5 Granite Mountains CA U.S.A.
238 E2 Granite Peak MT U.S.A.
241 K1 Granite Peak UT U.S.A.
Granitic Group is Seychelles see Inner Islands
121 H4 Granitogorsk Kazakh.
194 B5 Granitola, Capo c. Sicilia Italy
194 B5 Granitola-Torretta Sicilia Italy
81 C4 Granity South I. N.Z.
254 E2 Granja Brazil
184 C2 Granja Port.
182 E3 Granja de Moreruela Spain
184 E2 Granja de Torrehermosa Spain
182 B4 Granja do Ulmeiro Port.
259 D7 Gran Laguna Salada l. Arg
143 F2 Gränna Sweden
186 F3 Granollers Spain
174 E3 Granowo Pol.
252 B2 Gran Pajonal plain Peru
190 C3 Gran Paradiso mt. Italy
178 C4 Gran Pilastro mt. Austria/Italy
Gran San Bernardo, Colle del pass Italy/Switz. see Great St Bernard Pass
193 F2 Gran Sasso d'Italia mts Italy
171 D4 Granschütz Ger.
170 E2 Gransee Ger.
148 C3 Gransha Northern Ireland U.K.
236 C3 Grant NE U.S.A.
240 H2 Grant, Mount NV U.S.A.
240 I2 Grant, Mount NV U.S.A.
236 E3 Grant City MO U.S.A.
151 G2 Grantham Lincolnshire, England U.K.
234 B2 Grantham PA U.S.A.
262 P2 Grant Island Antarctica
84 C1 Grant Island N.T. Austr.
226 B3 Granton WI U.S.A.
146 E4 Grantown-on-Spey Highland, Scotland U.K.
226 D5 Grant Park IL U.S.A.
241 J2 Grant Range mts NV U.S.A.
239 F5 Grants NM U.S.A.
226 A3 Grantsburg WI U.S.A.
146 F6 Grantshouse Scottish Borders, Scotland U.K.
238 B3 Grants Pass OR U.S.A.
232 C5 Grantsville WV U.S.A.
234 B2 Grantville PA U.S.A.
222 B2 Granville Y.T. Can.
158 E3 Granville France
241 M5 Granville AZ U.S.A.
226 C5 Granville IL U.S.A.
233 G3 Granville NY U.S.A.
232 B4 Granville OH U.S.A.
142 B1 Granvin Norway
170 C2 Granzin Ger.
257 F2 Grão Mogol Brazil
240 I3 Grapevine Mountains NV U.S.A.
191 G3 Grappa, Monte mt. Italy
223 I1 Gras, Lac de l. N.W.T. Can.
168 D2 Grasberg Ger.
213 F5 Graskop S. Africa
171 C3 Grasleben Ger.
142 E1 Gräsmarken Sweden
149 F3 Grasmere Cumbria, England U.K.
234 B4 Grasonville MD U.S.A.
223 L3 Grass r. Man. Can.
233 F2 Grass r. NY U.S.A.
193 I4 Grassano Italy
173 G4 Grassau Ger.
161 E5 Grasse France
232 D4 Grassflat PA U.S.A.
149 H3 Grassington North Yorkshire, England U.K.
227 E4 Grass Lake MI U.S.A.
87 D7 Grass Patch W.A. Austr.
238 E2 Grassrange MT U.S.A.
240 G2 Grass Valley CA U.S.A.
83 F5 Grassy Tas. Austr.
236 C2 Grassy Butte ND U.S.A.
246 C2 Grassy Creek r. Andros Bahamas
168 E1 Gråsten Denmark
142 E2 Grästorp Sweden
186 D3 Gratallops Spain
163 D5 Graters France
163 D5 Gratertour France
226 B4 Gratiot WI U.S.A.
179 G3 Gratkorn Austria
140 L2 Gråträsk Sweden
194 C5 Gratteri Sicilia Italy
179 G3 Gratwein Austria
190 E2 Graubünden canton Switz.
Graudenz Pol. see Grudziądz
169 C5 Grauer Kopf hill Ger.
163 D5 Graulhet France
171 E4 Graupa Ger.
186 D2 Graus Spain
183 I2 Grávalos Spain
254 G4 Gravatá Brazil
255 C9 Gravataí Brazil
140 K1 Gravdal Norway
164 E3 Grave Neth.
190 E2 Gravedona Italy
223 J5 Gravelbourg Sask. Can.
156 C2 Gravelines France
190 D3 Gravellona Toce Italy
157 G3 Gravelotte France
224 E4 Gravenhurst Ont. Can.
169 D5 Grävenwiesbach Ger.
238 D2 Grave Peak ID U.S.A.
83 G2 Gravesend N.S.W. Austr.
151 H3 Gravesend Kent, England U.K.
237 E4 Gravette AR U.S.A.
156 B3 Gravigny France
193 I4 Gravina r. Italy
195 F2 Gravina di Matera r. Italy
193 I4 Gravina in Puglia Italy
192 A3 Gravona r. Corse France
226 E3 Grawn MI U.S.A.
160 D1 Gray France
231 D5 Gray GA U.S.A.
232 A6 Gray KY U.S.A.
233 □H3 Gray ME U.S.A.
232 B6 Gray TN U.S.A.
162 A3 Grayan-et-l'Hôpital France
238 B3 Grayback Mountain OR U.S.A.
222 E3 Grayling r. B.C. Can.
226 E3 Grayling MI U.S.A.
149 G3 Grayrigg Cumbria, England U.K.
151 H3 Grays Thurrock, England U.K.
151 G3 Grayshott Hampshire, England U.K.
232 B5 Grayson KY U.S.A.
230 C4 Grayville IL U.S.A.
137 H2 Grayvoron Rus. Fed.
179 G3 Graz Austria
161 C3 Grazac France
185 E4 Grazalema Spain
175 H2 Grązawy Pol.
194 D1 Grazzanise Italy
197 F4 Grdelica Srbija Yugo.
186 B4 Grea de Albarracín Spain
163 D4 Gréalou France
246 □ Great r. Jamaica
246 C1 Great Abaco i. Bahamas
76 C5 Great Australian Bight g. Austr.
149 H3 Great Ayton North Yorkshire, England U.K.
151 H3 Great Baddow Essex, England U.K.
246 C1 Great Bahama Bank sea feature Bahamas
80 E2 Great Barrier Island North I. N.Z.
85 F1 Great Barrier Reef Qld Austr.
233 G3 Great Barrington MA U.S.A.
151 H2 Great Barton Suffolk, England U.K.
241 I2 Great Basin NV U.S.A.
222 E1 Great Bear r. N.W.T. Can.
222 G1 Great Bear Lake N.W.T. Can.
Great Belt sea chan. Denmark see Store Bælt
236 D4 Great Bend KS U.S.A.
233 F4 Great Bend PA U.S.A.
151 I3 Great Bentley Essex, England U.K.
146 B3 Great Bernera i. Scotland U.K.
151 H2 Great Bircham Norfolk, England U.K.
147 A4 Great Blasket Island Rep. of Ireland
149 H3 Great Broughton North Yorkshire, England U.K.
149 F3 Great Clifton Cumbria, England U.K.
97 A4 Great Coco Island Cocos Is
151 H2 Great Cornard Suffolk, England U.K.
148 E2 Great Cumbrae i. Scotland U.K.
76 E5 Great Dividing Range mts Austr.
149 F3 Great Dodd hill England U.K.
149 I3 Great Driffield East Riding of Yorkshire, England U.K.
227 F3 Great Duck Island Ont. Can.
151 H3 Great Dunmow Essex, England U.K.
Great Eastern Erg des. Alg. see Grand Erg Oriental
149 G4 Great Eccleston Lancashire, England U.K.
234 D3 Great Egg Harbor r. NJ U.S.A.
151 H2 Great Ellingham Norfolk, England U.K.
246 B2 Greater Antilles is Caribbean Sea
Greater Khingan Mountains China see Da Hinggan Ling
151 G3 Greater London admin. div. England U.K.
149 G4 Greater Manchester admin. div. England U.K.
125 F2 Greater Tunb i. The Gulf
246 D2 Great Exuma i. Bahamas
238 E2 Great Falls MT U.S.A.
215 F5 Great Fish r. S. Africa
213 E7 Great Fish Point S. Africa
80 E4 Greatford North I. N.Z.
117 F4 Great Gandak r. India
Great Ganges atoll Cook Is see Manihiki
151 F2 Great Glen Leicestershire, England U.K.
151 G2 Great Gonerby Lincolnshire, England U.K.
151 G2 Great Gransden Cambridgeshire, England U.K.
246 C1 Great Guana Cay i. Bahamas
231 E7 Great Guana Cay i. Bahamas
151 G3 Greatham Hampshire, England U.K.
149 H3 Greatham Hartlepool, England U.K.
150 E2 Great Hanwood Shropshire, England U.K.
246 C1 Great Harbour Cay i. Bahamas
149 G4 Great Harwood Lancashire, England U.K.
151 F2 Great Haywood Staffordshire, England U.K.
151 H3 Great Horkesley Essex, England U.K.
246 D2 Great Inagua i. Bahamas
147 C5 Great Island Rep. of Ireland
214 D5 Great Karoo plat. S. Africa
215 G5 Great Kei r. S. Africa
85 G4 Great Keppel Island Qld Austr.
83 F5 Great Lake Tas. Austr.
151 G2 Great Linford Milton Keynes, England U.K.
150 E2 Great Malvern Worcestershire, England U.K.
149 F4 Great Marton Blackpool, England U.K.
234 D2 Great Meadows NJ U.S.A.
264 H4 Great Meteor Tablemount sea feature N. Atlantic Ocean
232 A5 Great Miami r. OH U.S.A.
151 G3 Great Missenden Buckinghamshire, England U.K.
115 G5 Great Nicobar i. Andaman & Nicobar Is India
150 D1 Great Ormes Head hd Wales U.K.
151 H2 Great Ouse r. England U.K.
83 G5 Great Oyster Bay Tas. Austr.
85 F3 Great Palm Island Qld Austr.
221 K3 Great Plain of the Koukdjuak Nunavut Can.
236 C3 Great Plains NE U.S.A.
151 G2 Great Ponton Lincolnshire, England U.K.
Great Rann of Kachchh marsh India see Rann of Kachchh
150 D2 Great Rhos hill Wales U.K.
210 B5 Great Rift Valley Africa
211 C6 Great Ruaha r. Tanz.
160 F3 Great St Bernard Pass Italy/Switz.
231 E7 Great Sale Cay i. Bahamas
149 G3 Great Salkeld Cumbria, England U.K.
238 D3 Great Salt Lake UT U.S.A.
241 K1 Great Salt Lake Desert UT U.S.A.
247 □2 Great Salt Pond l. St Kitts and Nevis
151 H3 Great Sampford Essex, England U.K.
223 I5 Great Sand Hills Sask. Can.
202 E2 Great Sand Sea des. Egypt/Libya
86 D4 Great Sandy Desert W.A. Austr.
Great Sandy Island Qld Austr. see Fraser Island
151 H2 Great Shelford Cambridgeshire, England U.K.
222 H2 Great Slave Lake N.W.T. Can.
231 C5 Great Smoky Mountains N. Carolina/Tennessee U.S.A.
222 E3 Great Snow Mountain B.C. Can.
151 I3 Great Stour r. England U.K.
148 C4 Great Sugar Loaf hill Rep. of Ireland
150 C4 Great Torrington Devon, England U.K.
Great Usutu r. Africa see Usutu
87 F6 Great Victoria Desert W.A. Austr.
151 H3 Great Wakering Essex, England U.K.
262 U2 Great Wall research stn Antarctica
107 H3 Great Wall tourist site China
151 H3 Great Waltham Essex, England U.K.
Great Western Erg des. Alg. see Grand Erg Occidental
83 F5 Great Western Tiers mts Tas. Austr.
149 H3 Great Whernside hill England U.K.
214 B5 Great Winterhoek mt. S. Africa
150 E2 Great Wyrley Staffordshire, England U.K.
151 I2 Great Yarmouth Norfolk, England U.K.
151 H2 Great Yeldham Essex, England U.K.
Great Zab r. Iraq see Zāb al Kabīr, Nahr az
213 F4 Great Zimbabwe National Monument tourist site Zimbabwe
142 D2 Grebbestad Sweden
169 E5 Grebenau Ger.
169 F4 Grebendorf (Meinhard) Ger.
169 E5 Grebenhain Ger.
Grebenkovskiy Ukr. see Hrebinka
129 E2 Grebenskaya Rus. Fed.
Grebenski Rus. Fed. see Grebenskaya
169 E4 Grebenstein Ger.
168 F1 Grebin Ger.
175 J3 Grębków Pol.
174 E4 Grębocice Pol.
174 G2 Grębocin Pol.
175 J5 Grębów Pol.
Grebyonka Ukr. see Hrebinka
193 E2 Greccio Italy
193 H3 Greci Italy
197 I3 Greci, Vârful hill Romania
189 D5 Greco, Monte mt. Italy
173 F2 Greding Ger.
182 E4 Gredos, Sierra de mts Spain
198 B2 Greece country Europe
232 E3 Greece NY U.S.A.
238 F3 Greeley CO U.S.A.
234 D1 Greeley PA U.S.A.
236 D3 Greely Center NE U.S.A.
221 J1 Greely Fiord inlet Nunavut Can.
130 H1 Greem-Bell, Ostrov i. Zemlya Frantsa-Iosifa Rus. Fed.
229 M1 Green r. N.B. Can.
230 C4 Green r. KY U.S.A.
236 C2 Green r. ND U.S.A.
241 M2 Green r. WY U.S.A.
226 C3 Green Bay WI U.S.A.
226 D3 Green Bay b. WI U.S.A.
234 B3 Greenbelt MD U.S.A.
232 C6 Greenbrier r. WV U.S.A.
87 C7 Greenbushes W.A. Austr.
83 G4 Green Cape N.S.W. Austr.
231 E7 Greencastle Bahamas
147 E1 Greencastle Rep. of Ireland
147 D2 Greencastle Northern Ireland U.K.
147 E2 Greencastle Northern Ireland U.K.
230 C4 Greencastle IN U.S.A.
232 E5 Greencastle PA U.S.A.
246 C1 Green Cay i. Bahamas
231 D6 Green Cove Springs FL U.S.A.
234 D3 Green Creek NJ U.S.A.
169 E4 Greene Ger.
226 A4 Greene IA U.S.A.
233 □H2 Greene ME U.S.A.
233 F3 Greene NY U.S.A.
231 D4 Greeneville TN U.S.A.
240 G3 Greenfield CA U.S.A.
236 E3 Greenfield IA U.S.A.
230 C4 Greenfield IN U.S.A.
233 G3 Greenfield MA U.S.A.
237 E4 Greenfield MO U.S.A.
232 B5 Greenfield OH U.S.A.
226 C4 Greenfield WI U.S.A.
235 D1 Greenfield Park NY U.S.A.
148 F2 Greengairs North Lanarkshire, Scotland U.K.
151 F3 Greenham West Berkshire, England U.K.
234 B3 Green Haven MD U.S.A.
87 B6 Green Head W.A. Austr.
87 B6 Green Head hd W.A. Austr.
149 G3 Greenhead Northumberland, England U.K.
84 C1 Greenhill Island N.T. Austr.
81 B7 Greenhills South I. N.Z.
147 F2 Greenisland Northern Ireland U.K.
223 J4 Green Lake Sask. Can.
226 C4 Green Lake WI U.S.A.
221 N2 Greenland terr. N. America
226 C2 Greenland MI U.S.A.
268 X2 Greenland Basin sea feature Arctic Ocean
218 G1 Greenland Sea Greenland/Svalbard
234 C2 Green Lane PA U.S.A.
146 F6 Greenlaw Scottish Borders, Scotland U.K.
146 E5 Greenloaning Perth and Kinross, Scotland U.K.
146 E6 Green Lowther hill Scotland U.K.
82 C3 Greenly Island S.A. Austr.
234 B3 Greenmount MD U.S.A.
233 G2 Green Mountains VT U.S.A.
146 D6 Greenock Inverclyde, Scotland U.K.
149 F3 Greenodd Cumbria, England U.K.
147 E2 Greenore Rep. of Ireland
87 B6 Greenough W.A. Austr.
87 B6 Greenough r. W.A. Austr.
235 D1 Green Pond NJ U.S.A.
233 G4 Greenport NY U.S.A.
241 L2 Green River UT U.S.A.
238 E3 Green River WY U.S.A.
231 C5 Greensboro AL U.S.A.
231 D5 Greensboro GA U.S.A.
234 C4 Greensboro MD U.S.A.
231 E4 Greensboro NC U.S.A.
230 C4 Greensburg IN U.S.A.
237 D4 Greensburg KS U.S.A.
230 C4 Greensburg KY U.S.A.
237 F6 Greensburg LA U.S.A.
232 D4 Greensburg PA U.S.A.
241 M4 Greens Peak NM U.S.A.
146 C4 Greenstone Point Scotland U.K.
226 E5 Greentown IN U.S.A.
234 C1 Greentown PA U.S.A.
236 F4 Greenup IL U.S.A.
232 B5 Greenup KY U.S.A.
85 F3 Greenvale Qld Austr.
233 F2 Green Valley Ont. Can.
241 L6 Green Valley AZ U.S.A.
222 D4 Greenville B.C. Can.
206 C5 Greenville Liberia
231 C6 Greenville AL U.S.A.
240 G1 Greenville CA U.S.A.
231 D6 Greenville FL U.S.A.
231 C5 Greenville GA U.S.A.
236 F4 Greenville IL U.S.A.
230 C4 Greenville KY U.S.A.
233 □I2 Greenville ME U.S.A.
226 E4 Greenville MI U.S.A.
237 F4 Greenville MO U.S.A.
237 F5 Greenville MS U.S.A.
231 E5 Greenville NC U.S.A.
233 H3 Greenville NH U.S.A.
236 G3 Greenville OH U.S.A.
232 C4 Greenville PA U.S.A.
231 D5 Greenville SC U.S.A.
237 D5 Greenville TX U.S.A.
232 D5 Greenville VA U.S.A.
150 C3 Greenway Pembrokeshire, Wales U.K.
Greenwich atoll Micronesia see Kapingamarangi
151 G3 Greenwich Greater London, England U.K.
235 E1 Greenwich CT U.S.A.
234 C3 Greenwich NJ U.S.A.
233 G3 Greenwich NY U.S.A.
232 B4 Greenwich OH U.S.A.
237 E5 Greenwood AR U.S.A.
234 C4 Greenwood DE U.S.A.
230 C4 Greenwood IN U.S.A.
237 F5 Greenwood MS U.S.A.
231 D5 Greenwood SC U.S.A.
226 B3 Greenwood WI U.S.A.
235 D1 Greenwood Lake NY U.S.A.
231 D5 Greer SC U.S.A.
148 C5 Greese r. Rep. of Ireland
168 C2 Greetsiel (Krummhörn) Ger.
250 D6 Gregório r. Brazil
84 D3 Gregory r. Qld Austr.
227 E4 Gregory MI U.S.A.
236 D3 Gregory SD U.S.A.
82 D2 Gregory, Lake salt flat S.A. Austr.
86 E4 Gregory, Lake salt flat W.A. Austr.
87 C5 Gregory, Lake salt flat W.A. Austr.
84 D3 Gregory Downs Qld Austr.
85 E3 Gregory Range hills Qld Austr.
86 D4 Gregory Range hills W.A. Austr.
178 E4 Greifenburg Austria
171 E4 Greifendorf Ger.
190 D1 Greifensee l. Switz.
169 D5 Greifenstein Ger.
170 E2 Greiffenberg Ger.
170 E1 Greifswald Ger.
170 E1 Greifswalder Bodden b. Ger.
179 F2 Grein Austria
171 D5 Greiz Ger.
168 F1 Gremersdorf Ger.
134 G1 Gremikha Rus. Fed.
134 L4 Gremyachinsk Rus. Fed.
137 J2 Gremyach'ye Rus. Fed.
142 D3 Grenå Denmark
237 F5 Grenada MS U.S.A.
247 □6 Grenada country West Indies
163 D5 Grenade France
163 B5 Grenade-sur-l'Adour France
157 F5 Grenant France
190 C1 Grenchen Switz.
83 G3 Grenfell N.S.W. Austr.
223 K5 Grenfell Sask. Can.
161 D3 Grenoble France
247 □6 Grenville Grenada
85 E1 Grenville, Cape Qld Austr.
Grenville Island Fiji see Rotuma
172 B4 Grenzach-Wyhlen Ger.
161 D5 Gréoux-les-Bains France
170 D1 Gresenhorst Ger.
238 B2 Gresham OR U.S.A.
95 F4 Gresik Jawa Timur Indon.
190 C3 Gressan Italy
161 D3 Gresse r. France
168 F2 Gresse Ger.
161 D4 Gresse-en-Vercors France
190 C3 Gressoney-la-Trinite Italy
179 G3 Gresten Austria
160 D3 Grésy-sur-Aix France
160 E3 Grésy-sur-Isère France
149 G3 Greta r. England U.K.
192 D2 Gretano r. Italy
146 E7 Gretna Dumfries and Galloway, Scotland U.K.
237 F6 Gretna LA U.S.A.
232 D6 Gretna VA U.S.A.
173 E2 Grettstadt Ger.
169 F4 Greußen Ger.
157 F4 Greux France
191 G5 Greve r. Italy
191 G5 Greve in Chianti Italy
164 C3 Grevelingen sea chan. Neth.
168 F2 Greven Mecklenburg-Vorpommern Ger.
169 C3 Greven Nordrhein-Westfalen Ger.
198 B1 Grevena Greece
165 E3 Grevenbicht Neth.
169 B4 Grevenbroich Ger.
165 F5 Grevenmacher Lux.
165 F5 Grevenmacher admin. dist. Lux.
170 C2 Grevesmühlen Ger.
225 J4 Grey r. Nfld. Can.
81 C5 Grey r. South I. N.Z.
84 D2 Grey, Cape N.T. Austr.
147 F2 Greyabbey Northern Ireland U.K.
238 E2 Greybull WY U.S.A.
238 E2 Greybull r. WY U.S.A.
222 C2 Grey Hunter Peak Y.T. Can.
215 G2 Greylingstad S. Africa
233 G3 Greylock, Mount MA U.S.A.
81 C5 Greymouth South I. N.Z.
83 E2 Grey Range hills Qld Austr.
87 B5 Grey's Plains W.A. Austr.
149 G3 Greystoke Cumbria, England U.K.
147 E3 Greystones Rep. of Ireland
214 B6 Greyton S. Africa
81 E4 Greytown North I. N.Z.
215 H3 Greytown S. Africa
165 D4 Grez-Doiceau Belgium
159 F4 Grez-en-Bouère France
191 G3 Grezzana Italy
146 B3 Griais Western Isles, Scotland U.K.
135 H6 Gribanovskiy Rus. Fed.
208 C2 Gribingui r. C.A.R.
240 G2 Gridley CA U.S.A.
226 C5 Gridley IL U.S.A.
171 C3 Grieben Ger.
183 I4 Griegos Spain
157 H4 Gries France
178 C3 Gries am Brenner Austria
172 C3 Griesbach Ger.
173 H3 Griesbach im Rottal Ger.
172 C2 Griesheim Ger.
179 E2 Grieskirchen Austria
171 F4 Grießen Ger.
173 G4 Griesstätt Ger.
179 F4 Griffen Austria
231 C5 Griffin GA U.S.A.
83 F3 Griffith N.S.W. Austr.
227 I3 Griffith Ont. Can.
232 C5 Griffithsville WV U.S.A.
Grigan i. N. Mariana Is see Agrihan
192 A5 Grighini, Monte hill Sardegna Italy
Grigioni canton Switz. see Graubünden
138 E4 Grigiškės Lith.
190 E3 Grigna mt. Italy
190 F3 Grigna r. Italy
161 C4 Grignan France
191 G2 Grigno Italy
191 G2 Grigno r. Italy
163 B4 Grignols France
160 C3 Grigny France
136 E4 Grigoriopol Moldova
183 F2 Grijota Spain
164 F1 Grijpskerk Neth.
161 C4 Grillon France
83 F5 Grim, Cape Tas. Austr.
193 I5 Grimaldi Italy
208 D3 Grimari C.A.R.
161 E5 Grimaud France
171 D4 Grimma Ger.
170 E1 Grimmen Ger.
179 E3 Grimming mt. Austria
149 J4 Grimoldby Lincolnshire, England U.K.
146 A4 Grimsay i. Scotland U.K.
227 H4 Grimsby Ont. Can.
149 I4 Grimsby North East Lincolnshire, England U.K.
140 □C2 Grímsey i. Iceland
222 G3 Grimshaw Alta Can.
142 C2 Grimstad Norway
151 H2 Grimston Norfolk, England U.K.
142 A2 Grindafjord Norway
141 J3 Grindaheim Norway
140 □B3 Grindavík Iceland
190 D2 Grindelwald Switz.
142 C4 Grindsted Denmark
227 F3 Grind Stone City MI U.S.A.
197 H3 Grindu Ialomiţa Romania
197 I3 Grindu Tulcea Romania
197 H2 Grinduşu, Vârful mt. Romania
139 I5 Grinevo Rus. Fed.
149 I4 Gringley on the Hill Nottinghamshire, England U.K.
236 E3 Grinnell IA U.S.A.
183 G4 Griñón Spain
178 B3 Grins Austria
197 G2 Grinţieş Romania
188 E2 Grintovec mt. Slovenia
178 C3 Grinzens Austria
183 I3 Grío r. Spain
Griomasaigh i. Scotland U.K. see Grimsay
215 G4 Griqualand East reg. S. Africa
214 D3 Griqualand West reg. S. Africa
214 D3 Griquatown S. Africa
Grischun canton Switz. see Graubünden
221 J2 Grise Fiord Nunavut Can.
186 B3 Grisén Spain
Grishino Ukr. see Krasnoarmiys'k
191 G3 Grisignano di Zocco Italy
156 B2 Gris Nez, Cap c. France
193 H5 Grisolia Italy
163 D5 Grisolles France
Grisons canton Switz. see Graubünden
143 H1 Grisslehamn Sweden
146 F3 Gritley Orkney, Scotland U.K.
137 J5 Grivenskaya Rus. Fed.
149 F3 Grizebeck Cumbria, England U.K.
222 F1 Grizzly Bear Mountain hill N.W.T. Can.
188 F3 Grmeč mts Bos.-Herz.
165 D3 Grobbendonk Belgium
173 F3 Gröbenzell Ger.
171 D4 Gröbers Ger.
138 C3 Grobiņa Latvia
215 G1 Groblersdal S. Africa
214 D3 Groblershoop S. Africa
179 E3 Gröbming Austria
171 C4 Gröbzig Ger.
196 E3 Grocka Srbija Yugo.
175 K4 Gródek Pol.
175 L2 Gródek Pol.
100 D3 Grodekovo Rus. Fed.
171 E4 Gröden Ger.
178 E3 Grödig Austria
171 E4 Gröditz Ger.
175 I2 Gródki Pol.
174 F5 Grodków Pol.
Grodnenskaya Oblast' admin. div. Belarus see Hrodzyenskaya Voblasts'
Grodnenskaya Vozvyshennost' hills Belarus see Hrodnyendskaye Wzvyshsha
Grodno Belarus see Hrodna
Grodno Oblast admin. div. Belarus see Hrodzyenskaya Voblasts'
175 H2 Grodziczno Pol.
174 G3 Grodziec Pol.
175 K3 Grodzisk Pol.
175 I3 Grodzisk Mazowiecki Pol.
174 E3 Grodzisk Wielkopolski Pol.
164 F2 Groenlo Neth.
215 H2 Groenvlei S. Africa
237 D6 Groesbeck TX U.S.A.
164 E3 Groesbeek Neth.
85 F3 Groganville Qld Austr.
169 E3 Grohnde (Emmerthal) Ger.
177 L6 Grohot, Vârful hill Romania
171 D4 Groitzsch Ger.
158 C4 Groix France
158 C4 Groix, Île de i. France
175 I4 Grójec Pol.
175 I2 Grom Pol.
174 D4 Gromadka Pol.
189 C7 Grombalia Tunisia
168 F1 Grömitz Ger.
175 I6 Gromnik Pol.
190 E3 Gromo Italy
168 D1 Grønå r. Denmark
169 E3 Gronau (Leine) Ger.
169 C3 Gronau (Westfalen) Ger.
193 I5 Grondo r. Italy
173 E4 Grönenbach Ger.
140 K2 Grong Norway
171 C4 Gröningen Ger.
164 F1 Groningen Neth.
164 F1 Groningen prov. Neth.
251 H3 Groningen Suriname
Grønland terr. N. America see Greenland
175 H1 Gronowo Markusy Pol.
143 F3 Grönskåra Sweden
237 C5 Groom TX U.S.A.
147 F2 Groomsport Northern Ireland U.K.
214 E5 Groot r. E. Cape S. Africa
214 B5 Groot r. W. Cape S. Africa
214 C5 Groot r. W. Cape S. Africa
214 C2 Groot-Aar Pan salt pan S. Africa
214 B5 Groot Berg r. S. Africa
215 E4 Groot Brak r. S. Africa
214 D6 Groot Brakrivier S. Africa
215 G2 Grootdraaidam dam S. Africa
214 C3 Grootdrink S. Africa
164 E2 Grootebroek Neth.
84 D2 Groote Eylandt i. N.T. Austr.
164 F1 Grootegast Neth.
212 C3 Grootfontein Namibia
212 C5 Groot Karas Berg plat. Namibia
213 F4 Groot Letaba r. S. Africa
215 F1 Groot Marico S. Africa
214 A3 Grootmis S. Africa
215 F1 Grootpan S. Africa
214 C5 Groot Swartberge mts S. Africa
215 G2 Grootvlei S. Africa
215 F5 Groot Winterberg mt. S. Africa
190 D3 Gropello Cairoli Italy
197 H3 Gropeni Romania
161 E5 Gros Bessillon hill France
160 C1 Grosbois-en-Montagne France
161 F3 Groscavallo Italy
190 F2 Grosio Italy
247 □3 Gros Islet St Lucia
247 □3 Gros-Morne Martinique
160 C2 Grosne r. France
178 B4 Grosotto Italy
247 □3 Gros Piton mt. St Lucia
173 E3 Großaitingen Ger.
169 E4 Großalmerode Ger.
171 C3 Groß Ammensleben Ger.
178 E3 Großarl Austria
169 F4 Großbartloff Ger.
171 E3 Großbeeren Ger.
168 C3 Groß Berßen Ger.
172 C2 Groß-Bieberau Ger.
169 F4 Großbodungen Ger.
171 D4 Großbothen Ger.
172 D3 Großbottwar Ger.
171 C5 Großbreitenbach Ger.
169 E3 Großburgwedel (Burgwedel) Ger.
169 F4 Großburschla Ger.
170 E3 Groß Dölln Ger.
171 F4 Großdubrau Ger.
172 C3 Große Enz r. Ger.
173 G3 Große Laaber r. Ger.
172 D3 Große Lauter r. Ger.
169 F3 Groß Elbe (Elbe) Ger.
172 C3 Grosselfingen Ger.
168 E2 Großenaspe Ger.
170 C1 Großenbrode Ger.
169 D5 Großen-Buseck Ger.
169 F4 Großenehrich Ger.
179 H2 Groß Engersdorf Austria
169 F4 Großengottern Ger.
171 E4 Großenhain Ger.
168 D3 Großenkneten Ger.
169 E5 Großenlüder Ger.
168 F2 Großensee Ger.
171 D5 Großenstein Ger.
168 E1 Großenwiehe Ger.
179 H2 Groß-Enzersdorf Austria

173 H2 Großer Arber mt. Ger.
169 F5 Großer Beerberg hill Ger.
179 F3 Grosser Bösenstein mt. Austria
169 F5 Großer Breitenberg hill Ger.
179 F3 Grosser Buchstein mt. Austria
172 B2 Großer Eyberg hill Ger.
169 F5 Großer Gleichberg hill Ger.
171 D5 Großer Kornberg hill Ger.
170 E2 Großer Landgraben r. Ger.
178 C3 Grosser Löffler mt. Austria
171 E4 Große Röder r. Ger.
176 C2 Großer Osser mt. Czech Rep./Ger.
168 F1 Großer Plöner See l. Ger.
179 F3 Grosser Priel mt. Austria
173 H3 Großer Rachel mt. Ger.
171 E3 Großer Selchower See l. Ger.
179 E4 Grosser Speikkofel mt. Austria
179 F4 Grosser Speikkogel mt. Austria
168 C2 Großes Meer l. Ger.
178 D3 Großes Wiesbachhorn mt. Austria
192 D2 Grosseto Italy
192 D2 Grosseto prov. Toscana Italy
192 A3 Grosseto-Prugna Corse France
173 G3 Große Vils r. Ger.
170 E2 Groß Fredenwalde Ger.
169 F4 Großfurra Ger.
170 C3 Groß Garz Ger.
172 C2 Groß-Gerau Ger.
179 F2 Groß-Gerungs Austria
169 E3 Groß Giesen Ger.
171 E3 Groß Glienicke Ger.
178 D3 Großglockner mt. Austria
173 G4 Großgmain Ger.
170 C2 Groß Godems Ger.
179 G2 Großgöttfritz Austria
168 F2 Groß Grönau Ger.
173 E2 Großhabersdorf Ger.
168 F2 Großhansdorf Ger.
179 H2 Großharras Austria
169 F3 Groß Heere (Heere) Ger.
171 F5 Großhennersdorf Ger.
171 C4 Großheringen Ger.
168 C3 Groß-Hesepe Ger.
172 D2 Großheubach Ger.
168 D3 Groß Ippener Ger.
173 G4 Großkarolinenfeld Ger.
171 C4 Großkayna Ger.
170 E1 Groß Kiesow Ger.
179 G4 Großklein Austria
171 D4 Großkorbetha Ger.
171 E3 Groß Köris Ger.
171 F4 Großkoschen Ger.
171 D3 Groß Kreutz Ger.
179 H2 Großkrut Austria
168 F1 Groß Kummerfeld Ger.
170 C2 Groß Laasch Ger.
169 F3 Groß Lafferde (Lahstedt) Ger.
173 E2 Großlangheim Ger.
171 D4 Großlehna Ger.
171 F3 Groß Leine Ger.
171 F3 Groß Leuthen Ger.
171 F3 Groß Lindow Ger.
169 B5 Großlittgen Ger.
169 F4 Großlohra Ger.
171 E4 Großmehlen Ger.
173 F3 Großmehring Ger.
170 E2 Groß Miltzow Ger.
170 D1 Groß Mohrdorf Ger.
171 C4 Großmonra Ger.
171 C4 Groß Mühlingen Ger.
171 E4 Großnaundorf Ger.
171 D4 Groß Naundorf Ger.
170 E2 Groß Nemerow Ger.
168 F3 Groß Oesingen Ger.
171 E5 Großolbersdorf Ger.
171 C4 Großörner Ger.
171 F4 Groß Oßnig Ger.
172 D2 Großostheim Ger.
179 H3 Großpetersdorf Austria
170 D2 Groß Plasten Ger.
171 C4 Groß Quenstedt Ger.
179 F3 Großraming Austria
171 F4 Großräschen Ger.
172 D2 Großrinderfeld Ger.
172 C2 Groß-Rohrheim Ger.
171 F4 Großröhrsdorf Ger.
171 C4 Groß Rosenburg Ger.
172 A2 Großrosseln Ger.
171 C4 Großrudestedt Ger.
179 H2 Großrußbach Austria
179 G4 Groß St Florian Austria
171 F4 Groß Särchen Ger.
171 F4 Groß Schacksdorf Ger.
171 E5 Großschirma Ger.
179 F2 Großschönau Austria
171 F5 Großschönau Ger.
170 E3 Groß Schönebeck Ger.
170 C3 Groß Schwechten Ger.
171 F4 Großschweidnitz Ger.
169 F3 Groß Schwülper (Schwülper) Ger.
179 G2 Groß-Siegharts Austria
168 E1 Großsolt Ger.
168 C3 Groß Stavern Ger.
171 D4 Großsteinberg Ger.
170 C2 Groß Stieten Ger.
171 D4 Großtreben Ger.
169 F3 Groß Twülpstedt Ger.
172 C2 Groß-Umstadt Ger.
178 D3 Großvenediger mt. Austria
172 D2 Großwallstadt Ger.
190 D1 Grosswangen Switz.
170 C2 Groß Warnow Ger.
169 F4 Großwechsungen Ger.
179 G2 Großweikersdorf Austria
170 D2 Groß Welle Ger.
168 E1 Groß Wittensee Ger.
170 D2 Groß Wokern Ger.
170 D3 Großwudicke Ger.
170 D2 Groß Wüstenfelde Ger.
170 E3 Groß Ziethen Ger.
172 C2 Groß-Zimmern Ger.
157 G4 Grostenquin France
188 E3 Grosuplje Slovenia
263 L1 Grosvenor Mountains Antarctica
238 E3 Gros Ventre Range mts WY U.S.A.
165 D3 Grote Nete r. Belgium
235 F1 Groton CT U.S.A.
233 E3 Groton NY U.S.A.
236 D2 Groton SD U.S.A.
193 E3 Grottaferrata Italy
195 G2 Grottaglie Italy
193 F2 Grottammare Italy
193 F1 Grottazzolina Italy
194 C5 Grotte Sicilia Italy
192 D2 Grotte di Castro Italy
195 F4 Grotteria Italy
232 D5 Grottoes VA U.S.A.
195 F2 Grottole Italy
222 G4 Grouard Mission Alta Can.
206 E5 Groumania Côte d'Ivoire
224 D3 Groundhog r. Ont. Can.
164 E1 Grouw Neth.
237 E4 Grove OK U.S.A.
232 B5 Grove City OH U.S.A.
232 C4 Grove City PA U.S.A.
231 C6 Grove Hill AL U.S.A.
141 K3 Grövelsjön Sweden
263 F2 Grove Mountains Antarctica
234 B1 Grover PA U.S.A.
240 G4 Grover Beach CA U.S.A.
233 H2 Groveton NH U.S.A.
237 E6 Groveton TX U.S.A.
234 D2 Groveville NJ U.S.A.
241 K5 Growler Mountains AZ U.S.A.
197 H4 Grozd'ovo Bulg.
129 D2 Groznyy Rus. Fed.
171 C5 Grub am Forst Ger.
142 B2 Grubbåfjellet mt. Norway
165 F3 Grubbenvorst Neth.
170 C1 Grube Ger.
188 F3 Grubišno Polje Croatia
174 G2 Gruczno Pol.
Grudovo Bulg. see Sredets
175 I2 Grudusk Pol.
174 G2 Grudziądz Pol.
190 D4 Grue r. Italy
157 G4 Gruey-lès-Surance France
190 C3 Grugliasco Italy
146 B6 Gruinart, Loch inlet Scotland U.K.
161 B5 Gruissan France
182 D1 Grullos Spain
197 H2 Grumăzeşti Romania
171 E4 Grumbach Ger.
193 H4 Grumento Nova Italy
195 F1 Grumo Appula Italy
142 E2 Grums Sweden
171 D5 Grüna Ger.
179 G2 Grünau Austria
179 E3 Grünau Austria
179 G3 Grünbach am Schneeberg Austria
169 D5 Grünberg Ger.
Grünberg Pol. see Zielona Góra
179 F3 Grünburg Austria
141 K3 Grundagssätern Sweden
141 K3 Grundforsen Sweden
179 E3 Grundlsee l. Austria
140 L3 Grundsuna Sweden
232 B6 Grundy VA U.S.A.
236 E3 Grundy Center IA U.S.A.
170 E3 Grüneberg Ger.
168 E2 Grünendeich Ger.
171 E4 Grünewald Ger.
171 E4 Grünewalde Ger.
171 E3 Grünheide Ger.
172 D4 Grünkraut Ger.
171 F3 Grunow Ger.
172 D2 Grünsfeld Ger.
172 C2 Grünstadt Ger.
160 B2 Grury France
174 G2 Gruta Pol.
146 □G2 Grutness Shetland, Scotland U.K.
237 C4 Gruver TX U.S.A.
190 C2 Gruyères Switz.
138 D3 Gruzdžiai Lith.
Gruzinskaya S.S.R. country Asia see Georgia
139 L5 Gryazi Rus. Fed.
139 L4 Gryaznoye Rus. Fed.
134 H4 Gryazovets Rus. Fed.
175 I6 Grybów Pol.
174 D2 Gryfice Pol.
174 C2 Gryfino Pol.
174 D4 Gryfów Śląski Pol.
174 F3 Grylewo Pol.
140 L1 Gryllefjord Norway
142 A2 Grytenuten hill Norway
143 G1 Gryttjom Sweden
259 □ Grytviken S. Georgia
175 I2 Gryźliny Pol.
174 G3 Grzegorzew Pol.
174 E2 Grzmiąca Pol.
174 G3 Grzymiszew Pol.
174 G2 Grzywna Pol.
179 E3 Gschwandt Austria
172 D3 Gschwend Ger.
190 C2 Gstaad Switz.
173 G4 Gstadt am Chiemsee Ger.
190 C2 Gsteig Switz.
117 F5 Gua Bihar India
191 G3 Guà r. Italy
242 □J7 Guabito Panama
246 C2 Guacanayabo, Golfo de b. Cuba
247 F5 Guacara Venez.
250 D3 Guacharía r. Col.
258 D2 Guachipas Arg.
257 G4 Guaçuí Brazil
185 G3 Guadahortuna Spain
185 H3 Guadahortuna r. Spain
184 D3 Guadaira r. Spain
184 E3 Guadairilla r. Spain
184 D2 Guadajira r. Spain
184 E3 Guadajoz Spain
185 F3 Guadajoz r. Spain
244 C3 Guadalajara Mex.
183 G4 Guadalajara Spain
183 H4 Guadalajara prov. Castilla - La Mancha Spain
187 B4 Guadalaviar r. Spain
184 E3 Guadalbacar r. Spain
185 G3 Guadalbullón r. Spain
78 □6 Guadalcanal i. Solomon Is
184 E2 Guadalcanal Spain
185 F3 Guadalcázar Spain
184 E2 Guadalefra r. Spain
185 G2 Guadalén r. Spain
185 H3 Guadalentín r. Spain
185 I3 Guadalentín r. Spain
184 D4 Guadalete r. Spain
185 F4 Guadalhorce r. Spain
185 G3 Guadalimar r. Spain
185 E3 Guadalmazán r. Spain
185 H2 Guadalmena r. Spain
185 F2 Guadalmez Spain
185 F2 Guadalmez r. Spain
186 C3 Guadalope r. Spain
185 D4 Guadalquivir r. Spain
216 □1c Guadalupe Graciosa Azores
254 E3 Guadalupe Brazil
245 E5 Guadalupe Guerrero Mex.
243 E3 Guadalupe Nuevo León Mex.
245 F4 Guadalupe Puebla Mex.
244 C2 Guadalupe Zacatecas Mex.
242 A2 Guadalupe i. Mex.
250 B6 Guadalupe Peru
185 E1 Guadalupe Spain
241 L5 Guadalupe AZ U.S.A.
240 G4 Guadalupe CA U.S.A.
237 D6 Guadalupe r. TX U.S.A.
237 D6 Guadalupe r. TX U.S.A.
184 E1 Guadalupe, Sierra de mts Spain
244 B1 Guadalupe Aguilera Mex.
239 F6 Guadalupe Bravos Mex.
237 B6 Guadalupe Peak TX U.S.A.
241 J5 Guadalupe Victoria Baja California Norte Mex.
244 B1 Guadalupe Victoria Durango Mex.
185 E3 Guadalvacarejo r. Spain
183 H4 Guadamajud r. Spain
185 E2 Guadamatilla r. Spain
184 E2 Guadamez r. Spain
183 F5 Guadamur Spain
183 F4 Guadarrama Spain
183 F5 Guadarrama r. Spain
183 F4 Guadarrama, Sierra de mts Spain
183 I5 Guadazaón r. Spain
247 □2 Guadeloupe terr. West Indies
247 □2 Guadeloupe Passage Caribbean Sea
184 D4 Guadiamar r. Spain
185 C3 Guadiana r. Port./Spain
185 G3 Guadiana Menor r. Spain
185 E4 Guadiaro r. Spain
185 E3 Guadiato r. Spain
183 H4 Guadiela r. Spain
183 E4 Guadiervas r. Spain
185 G3 Guadix Spain
259 B6 Guafo, Isla i. Chile
92 B3 Guagua Phil.
255 C9 Guaíba Brazil
250 B4 Guaillabamba r. Ecuador
246 C2 Guáimaro Cuba
250 D4 Guainia dept Col.
250 E4 Guainía r. Col./Venez.
251 F3 Guaiquinima, Cerro mt. Venez.
255 B8 Guaíra Brazil
256 C4 Guaira São Paulo Brazil
256 A5 Guairaçá Brazil
259 B6 Guaitecas, Islas is Chile
252 D2 Guajará Mirim Brazil
183 F5 Guajaraz r. Spain
185 G4 Guájar-Faraguit Spain
252 D1 Guajarraã Brazil
247 □1 Guajataca r. Puerto Rico
242 E3 Guaje, Llano de plain Mex.
250 C2 Guajira dept Col.
250 B5 Gualaceo Ecuador
240 F2 Gualala CA U.S.A.
243 H6 Gualán Guat.
250 B5 Gualaquiza Ecuador
193 E2 Gualdo Cattaneo Italy
191 H5 Gualdo Tadino Italy
261 H3 Gualeguay Arg.
261 H3 Gualeguay r. Arg.
261 H3 Gualeguaychu Arg.
259 D6 Gualicho, Salina salt flat Arg.
252 C4 Guallatiri vol. Chile
244 C2 Gualterio Mex.
191 F4 Gualtieri Italy
91 J4 Guam terr. N. Pacific Ocean
259 B7 Guamblin, Isla i. Chile
261 F5 Guamini Arg.
246 C2 Guamo Cuba
251 E3 Guampí, Sierra de mts Venez.
242 C3 Guamúchil Mex.
107 H4 Gu'an Hebei China
107 H5 Guan r. China
246 B2 Guanabacoa Cuba
242 □I7 Guanacaste, Cordillera de mts Costa Rica
242 D3 Guanacevi Mex.
261 F5 Guanaco, Cerro hill Arg.
246 A2 Guanahacabibes, Península de pen. Cuba
242 □I5 Guanaja Hond.
246 B2 Guanajay Cuba
244 D3 Guanajuato Mex.
244 D3 Guanajuato state Mex.
244 D3 Guanajuato, Sierra de mts Mex.
254 E5 Guanambi Brazil
250 B7 Guañape, Islas de is Peru
250 D2 Guanare Venez.
250 E2 Guanare Viejo r. Venez.
250 D2 Guanarito Venez.
250 D2 Guanarito r. Venez.
252 D3 Guanay Bol.
107 F4 Guandi Shan mt. Shanxi China
257 G3 Guandu r. Brazil
109 E3 Guandu Guangdong China
246 A2 Guane Cuba
108 C2 Guang'an Sichuan China
109 F3 Guangchang Jiangxi China
109 F2 Guangde Anhui China
109 E4 Guangdong prov. China
109 F2 Guangfeng Jiangxi China
109 E4 Guanghai Guangdong China
108 C2 Guanghan Sichuan China
Guanghua Hubei China see Laohekou
107 G4 Guangling Shanxi China
108 B3 Guangmao Shan mt. Yunnan China
Guangming Sichuan China see Xide
109 F2 Guangming Ding mt. Anhui China
108 C3 Guangnan Yunnan China
109 E4 Guangning Guangdong China
Guangning Liaoning China see Beining
107 H4 Guangrao Shandong China
109 E2 Guangshan Henan China
109 E2 Guangshui Hubei China
Guangxi aut. reg. China see Guangxi Zhuangzu Zizhiqu
108 D4 Guangxi Zhuangzu Zizhiqu aut. reg. China
108 C1 Guangyuan Sichuan China
109 F3 Guangze Fujian China
109 E4 Guangzhou Guangdong China
107 G4 Guangzong Hebei China
257 F3 Guanhães Brazil
257 F3 Guanhães r. Brazil
107 H5 Guanhe Kou r. mouth China
247 □1 Guánica Puerto Rico
251 F2 Guanipa r. Venez.
108 C3 Guanling Guizhou China
108 D2 Guanmian Shan mts China
108 D1 Guanpo Henan China
Guansuo Guizhou China see Guanling
260 B1 Guanta Chile
251 E2 Guanta Venez.
246 D2 Guantánamo Cuba
246 D3 Guantánamo Bay Naval Base military base Cuba
107 G4 Guantao Hebei China
Guanxian Sichuan China see Dujiangyan
109 D3 Guanyang Guangxi China
108 B2 Guanyinqiao Sichuan China
107 H5 Guanyun Jiangsu China
Guapay r. Santa Cruz Bol. see Grande
257 E4 Guapé Brazil
250 B4 Guapí Col.
256 C6 Guapiara Brazil
242 □J7 Guápiles Costa Rica
252 D3 Guaporé r. Bol./Brazil
255 C9 Guaporé Brazil
Guaporé state Brazil see Rondônia
252 C4 Guaqui Bol.
256 D4 Guará Brazil
254 D5 Guará r. Brazil
186 C2 Guara, Sierra de mts Spain
254 G3 Guarabira Brazil
257 F4 Guaraciaba Brazil
250 B5 Guaranda Ecuador
257 F4 Guarani Brazil
256 A6 Guaraniaçu Brazil
256 C4 Guarantã Brazil
257 G4 Guarapari Brazil
256 B6 Guarapuava Brazil
256 C6 Guaraqueçaba Brazil
256 B4 Guararapes Brazil
257 H2 Guaratinga Brazil
257 E5 Guaratinguetá Brazil
255 C8 Guaratuba Brazil
252 C3 Guarayos Bol.
193 F3 Guarcino Italy
182 C4 Guarda Port.
182 C4 Guarda admin. dist. Port.
Guardafui, Cape Somalia see Caseyr, Raas
185 H3 Guardal r. Spain
187 C6 Guardamar del Segura Spain
256 D2 Guarda Mor Brazil
195 F4 Guardavalle Italy
193 G2 Guardiagrele Italy
193 I4 Guardia Perticara Italy
193 I5 Guardia Piemontese Italy
193 G3 Guardia Sanframondi Italy
185 H4 Guardias Viejas Spain
186 E2 Guardiola de Bergueda Spain
183 F2 Guardo Spain
182 D3 Guardramiro Spain
182 C5 Guardunha, Serra de mts Port.
184 D2 Guareña Spain
183 E3 Guareña r. Spain
186 C2 Guarga r. Spain
253 E1 Guariba r. Brazil
250 E2 Guárico state Venez.
185 F4 Guaro Spain
185 G2 Guarrizas r. Spain
250 D3 Guarrojo r. Col.
185 G2 Guarromán Spain
256 D5 Guarujá Brazil
256 D5 Guarulhos Brazil
246 E5 Guasare r. Venez.
242 C3 Guasave Mex.
192 B5 Guasila Sardegna Italy
191 F4 Guastalla Italy
Guastatoya Guat. see El Progreso
117 G5 Guasuba r. India
243 H6 Guatemala country Central America
243 H6 Guatemala Guat.
267 M5 Guatemala Basin sea feature Pacific Ocean
Guatemala City Guat. see Guatemala
261 F3 Guatimozin Arg.
261 F5 Guatrache Arg.
250 D4 Guaviare dept Col.
250 E3 Guaviare r. Col.
256 D4 Guaxupé Brazil
246 C2 Guayabal Cuba
260 D2 Guayaguas, Sierra da mts Arg.
245 F2 Guayalejo r. Mex.
247 □1 Guayama Puerto Rico
247 □1 Guayanilla Puerto Rico
250 E3 Guayapo, Serranía mts Venez.
250 B5 Guayaquil Ecuador
250 A5 Guayaquil, Golfo de g. Ecuador
252 D2 Guayaramerín Bol.
250 A5 Guayas prov. Ecuador
242 C3 Guaymas Mex.
247 □1 Guaynabo Puerto Rico
261 H2 Guayquiraró r. Arg.
243 H6 Guazacapán Guat.
210 B2 Guba Eth.
120 D4 Gubadag Turkm.
134 L4 Gubakha Rus. Fed.
92 C3 Gubat Phil.
148 B3 Gubaveeny Rep. of Ireland
114 C3 Gubbi Karnataka India
191 H5 Gubbio Italy
129 E2 Gubden Rus. Fed.
171 F4 Guben Ger.
197 G4 Gŭbene Bulg.
175 J1 Guber r. Pol.
174 C4 Gubin Pol.
207 I3 Gubio Nigeria
135 G6 Gubkin Rus. Fed.
107 G4 Gucheng Hebei China
109 D1 Gucheng Hubei China
114 C4 Gudalur Tamil Nadu India
129 D2 Gudamaqris K'edi hills Georgia
186 C4 Gudar Spain
115 D2 Gudari Orissa India
129 B2 Gudaut'a Georgia
141 J3 Gudbrandsdalen val. Norway
142 D3 Gudenå r. Denmark
169 E4 Gudensberg Ger.
129 E2 Gudermes Rus. Fed.
168 E1 Guderup Denmark
143 F4 Gudhjem Bornholm Denmark
207 H4 Gudi Nigeria
114 D2 Gudivada Andhra Prad. India
114 C3 Gudiyattam Tamil Nadu India
142 D4 Gudme Denmark
157 F4 Gudmont-Villiers France
100 D4 Gudong r. China
168 F2 Gudow Ger.
123 E5 Gudri r. Pak.
126 D2 Güdül Turkey
114 C3 Gudur Andhra Prad. India
114 C3 Gudur Andhra Prad. India
100 E2 Gudzhal r. Rus. Fed.
225 G1 Guè, Rivière du r. Que. Can.
157 H5 Guebwiller France
206 C4 Guéckédou Guinea
158 D4 Guégon France
185 G3 Güéjar-Sierra Spain
204 C5 Guelb er Rîchât hill Maur.
208 B2 Guélengdeng Chad
205 G1 Guelma Alg.
189 A7 Guelma prov. Alg.
204 C3 Guelmine Morocco
224 D5 Guelph Ont. Can.
157 H4 Guémar France
158 E4 Guémené-Penfao France
158 C3 Guémené-sur-Scorff France
245 E2 Guémez Mex.
157 G3 Guénange France
207 F4 Guéné Benin
183 G1 Güeñes Spain
158 E4 Guenrouet France
206 B3 Guènt Paté Senegal
158 D4 Guer France
208 C2 Guéra pref. Chad
208 C2 Guéra, Massif du mts Chad
158 D4 Guérande France
205 G2 Guerara Alg.
204 E2 Guercif Morocco
202 D6 Guéréda Chad
162 D2 Guéret France
160 B1 Guérigny France
207 F4 Guérin-Kouka Togo
240 F2 Guerneville CA U.S.A.
Guernica Spain see Gernika-Lumo
158 D2 Guernsey terr. Channel Is
238 F3 Guernsey WY U.S.A.
206 C2 Guérou Maur.
184 C3 Guerreiros do Rio Port.
237 C6 Guerrero Coahuila Mex.
243 F3 Guerrero Tamaulipas Mex.
244 D5 Guerrero state Mex.
184 D2 Guerrero r. Spain
242 B3 Guerrero Negro Mex.
163 C6 Guerreys, Pic de mt. France
186 E2 Guerri de la Sal Spain
186 B2 Güesa Spain
163 A5 Guéthary France
160 C2 Gueugnon France
206 D5 Guéyo Côte d'Ivoire
Gufeng Fujian China see Pingnan
Gufu Hubei China see Xingshan
129 D3 Gugark' Armenia
210 C3 Gugē mt. Eth.
78 □3a Gugegwe i. Kwajalein Marshall Is
172 C2 Güglingen Ger.
193 G3 Guglionesi Italy
91 K3 Guguan i. N. Mariana Is
109 F2 Guhe Anhui China
122 D5 Gūh Kūh mt. Iran
170 D2 Gühlen-Glienicke Ger.
Guhuai Henan China see Pingyu
182 B5 Guia Port.
216 □3a Guía de Isora Tenerife Canary Is
182 D2 Guiana mt. Spain
264 F5 Guiana Basin sea feature N. Atlantic Ocean
250 E3 Guiana Highlands mts S. America
206 D5 Guibéroua Côte d'Ivoire
156 B4 Guichainville France
158 E4 Guichen France
82 D4 Guichen Bay S.A. Austr.
109 F2 Guichi Anhui China
245 G5 Guichicovi Mex.
261 I3 Guichón Uru.
158 C3 Guiclan France
207 G3 Guidan-Roumji Niger
208 C2 Guidari Chad
106 D5 Guide Qinghai China
158 C4 Guidel France
149 H2 Guide Post Northumberland, England U.K.
207 I4 Guider Cameroon
207 I4 Guidiguis Cameroon
206 B3 Guidimaka admin. reg. Maur.
108 C3 Guiding Guizhou China
191 F3 Guidizzolo Italy
109 E3 Guidong Hunan China
193 E3 Guidonia-Montecelio Italy
257 F4 Guidoval Brazil
206 B2 Guier, Lac de l. Senegal
160 D3 Guiers r. France
208 A5 Guietsou Gabon
108 D4 Guigang Guangxi China
191 F4 Guiglia Italy
206 D5 Guiglo Côte d'Ivoire
158 E4 Guignen France
156 C4 Guignes France
156 D3 Guignicourt France
213 G5 Guija Moz.
108 D4 Gui Jiang r. China
109 G2 Guiji Shan mts China
182 D4 Guijo de Coria Spain
182 D4 Guijo de Galisteo Spain
182 D4 Guijo de Granadilla Spain
182 E4 Guijuelo Spain
161 E4 Guil r. France
151 G3 Guildford Surrey, England U.K.
233 H2 Guildhall VT U.S.A.
146 E5 Guildtown Perth and Kinross, Scotland U.K.
158 B3 Guilers France
235 F1 Guilford CT U.S.A.
233 □I2 Guilford ME U.S.A.
161 C4 Guilherand France
Guilherme Capelo Angola see Cacongo
182 B3 Guilhofrei Port.
108 D3 Guilin Guangxi China
161 E4 Guillaumes France
184 D3 Guillena Spain
161 E4 Guillestre France
158 D3 Guilliers France
160 C1 Guillon France
163 B4 Guillos France
158 B4 Guilvinec France
216 □3a Güímar Tenerife Canary Is
254 D2 Guimarães Brazil
182 B3 Guimarães Port.
92 B4 Guimaras i. Phil.
107 H5 Guimeng Ding mt. Shandong China
207 F4 Guinagourou Benin
106 D5 Guinan Qinghai China
92 C4 Guindulman Phil.
206 C4 Guinea country Africa
207 G6 Guinea, Gulf of Africa
264 I5 Guinea Basin sea feature N. Atlantic Ocean
206 B4 Guinea-Bissau country Africa
Guinea-Conakry country Africa see Guinea
Guinea Ecuatorial country Africa see Equatorial Guinea
Guiné-Bissau country Africa see Guinea-Bissau
Guinée country Africa see Guinea
206 C4 Guinée-Forestière admin. reg. Guinea
206 B4 Guinée-Maritime admin. reg. Guinea
246 B2 Güines Cuba
156 B2 Guînes France
158 C3 Guingamp France
206 B3 Guinguinéo Senegal
158 B3 Guipavas France
108 D4 Guiping Guangxi China
158 E4 Guipry France
186 A1 Guipúzcoa prov. País Vasco Spain
246 B2 Güira de Melena Cuba
255 B6 Guiratinga Brazil
251 I3 Guisanbourg Fr. Guiana
183 E4 Guisando Spain
161 E4 Guisane r. France
149 H3 Guisborough Redcar and Cleveland, England U.K.
156 D3 Guiscard France
158 C3 Guiscriff France
156 D3 Guise France
149 H4 Guiseley West Yorkshire, England U.K.
Guishan Yunnan China see Xinping
158 B3 Guissény France
186 E3 Guissona Spain
151 H2 Guist Norfolk, England U.K.
182 C1 Guitiriz Spain
162 B3 Guîtres France
206 D5 Guitri Côte d'Ivoire
92 C4 Guiuan Phil.
140 N1 Guivi hill Fin.
Guixi Chongqing China see Dianjiang
108 C3 Guiyang Guizhou China
109 E3 Guiyang Hunan China
109 E3 Guiyang Hunan China
108 C3 Guizhou prov. China
109 D4 Guizi Guangdong China
163 A4 Gujan-Mestras France
116 C5 Gujarat state India
123 H3 Gujar Khan Pak.
207 H4 Gujba Nigeria
Gujerat state India see Gujarat
123 H3 Gujranwala Pak.
123 H3 Gujrat Pak.
129 D3 Gukarrich Armenia
Gukasyan Armenia see Ashots'k'
109 F3 Gukou Fujian China
135 G6 Gukovo Rus. Fed.
116 D2 Gulabgarh Jammu and Kashmir
120 D4 Gulabie Uzbek.
106 D4 Gulang Gansu China
83 G2 Gulargambone N.S.W. Austr.
199 E2 Gülbahçe Turkey
121 G4 Gul'bakhor Uzbek.
114 C2 Gulbarga Karnataka India
138 F3 Gulbene Latvia
Gul'cha Kyrg. see Gülchö
121 H4 Gülchö Kyrg.
129 B3 Gül dağı mt. Turkey
170 C1 Guldborg Denmark
126 D3 Gülek Turkey
Gulf of Chihli China see Bo Hai
237 F6 Gulfport MS U.S.A.
231 C6 Gulf Shores AL U.S.A.
83 G3 Gulgong N.S.W. Austr.
113 □1 Gulhi i. S. Male Maldives
100 B1 Gulian Heilong. China
108 C3 Gulin Sichuan China
121 G4 Gulistan Uzbek.
Guliston Uzbek. see Gulistan
170 C2 Gülitz Ger.
107 I1 Guliya Shan mt. Nei Mongol China
Gulja Xinjiang China see Yining
135 H7 Gul'kevichi Rus. Fed.
224 B3 Gull r. Ont. Can.
148 C3 Gulladuff Northern Ireland U.K.
146 F5 Gullane East Lothian, Scotland U.K.
223 I5 Gull Lake Sask. Can.
143 F2 Gullspång Sweden
199 F2 Güllü Uşak Turkey
199 E3 Güllübahçe Turkey
129 E3 Güllük Azer.
199 E3 Güllük Turkey
199 E3 Güllük Körfezi b. Turkey
116 C2 Gulmarg Jammu and Kashmir
126 D3 Gülnar Turkey
165 E4 Gulpen Neth.
170 D3 Gülper See l. Ger.
199 E2 Gülpınar Turkey
129 B2 Gulrip'shi Georgia
126 D3 Gülşehir Turkey
121 H3 Gul'shad Kazakh.
170 E2 Gültz Ger.
Gulü Henan China see Xincai
210 B4 Gulu Uganda
197 G4 Gŭlŭbovo Bulg.
85 G5 Guluguba Qld Austr.
207 I4 Gulumba Gana Nigeria
84 D1 Guluwuru Island N.T. Austr.
146 C5 Gulvain hill Scotland U.K.
211 C6 Gulwe Tanz.
197 G4 Gulyantsi Bulg.
170 D2 Gülzow Ger.
168 F2 Gülzow Ger.
Guma Xinjiang China see Pishan
123 G4 Gumal r. Pak.
212 D3 Gumare Botswana
Gumbinnen Rus. Fed. see Gusev
210 A3 Gumbiri mt. Sudan
122 C2 Gumdag Turkm.
207 H3 Gumel Nigeria
Gümgüm Turkey see Varto
183 G3 Gumiel de Hizán Spain
183 G3 Gumiel de Mercado Spain
117 F5 Gumla Bihar India
105 E2 Gumma pref. Japan
169 C4 Gummersbach Ger.
94 B1 Gumpang r. Indon.
169 F5 Gumpelstadt Ger.
170 D3 Gumtow Ger.
126 E2 Gümüşhane Turkey
129 A3 Gümüşhane prov. Turkey
199 E2 Gümüşsuyu Turkey
199 F1 Gümüşyaka Turkey
116 D4 Guna Madh. Prad. India
Gunan Chongqing China see Qijiang
177 I6 Gunaroš Vojvodina, Srbija Yugo.
210 C2 Guna Terara mt. Eth.
83 F3 Gunbar N.S.W. Austr.
123 G2 Gund r. Tajik.
83 G3 Gundagai N.S.W. Austr.
172 B3 Gundelfingen Ger.
173 E3 Gundelfingen an der Donau Ger.
172 D2 Gundelsheim Baden-Württemberg Ger.
173 E2 Gundelsheim Bayern Ger.
114 C3 Gunderi Karnataka India
157 H4 Gundershoffen France
114 D3 Gundlakamma r. India
114 C4 Gundlupet Karnataka India
126 D3 Gündoğmuş Turkey
Gundorovka Rus. Fed. see Donetsk
199 G2 Gündüzler Turkey
129 C4 Gündüzü Turkey
199 F2 Güneşli Turkey
199 F2 Güney Turkey
199 F2 Güney Turkey
126 E3 Güneydoğu Toroslar plat. Turkey
199 G2 Güneyköy Afyon Turkey
129 B3 Güneysu Turkey
128 A1 Güneyyurt Turkey
209 C6 Gungu Dem. Rep. Congo
209 B8 Gungue Angola
129 E2 Gunib Rus. Fed.
223 L4 Gunisao r. Man. Can.
188 G3 Gunja Croatia
206 A3 Gunjur Gambia
199 F2 Günlüce Turkey
Gunma pref. Japan see Gumma
140 L2 Gunnarn Sweden
140 M2 Gunnarsbyn Sweden
85 F3 Gunnawarra Qld Austr.
221 P3 Gunnbjørn Fjeld nunatak Greenland
83 G2 Gunnedah N.S.W. Austr.
149 I4 Gunness North Lincolnshire, England U.K.
83 G3 Gunning N.S.W. Austr.
150 C4 Gunnislake Cornwall, England U.K.
239 F4 Gunnison CO U.S.A.
241 L2 Gunnison UT U.S.A.
239 E4 Gunnison r. CO U.S.A.
241 L2 Gunnison Reservoir UT U.S.A.
84 B2 Gunn Point N.T. Austr.
84 D3 Gunpowder Creek r. Qld Austr.
234 B3 Gunpowder Falls r. MD U.S.A.
Güns Hungary see Kőszeg
114 C2 Gun Sangari Mahar. India
179 E2 Gunskirchen Austria
171 C4 Günstedt Ger.
Gunt r. Tajik. see Gund
114 C3 Guntakal Andhra Prad. India
169 F4 Güntersberge Ger.
172 C2 Guntersblum Ger.
179 H2 Guntersdorf Austria
172 D2 Güntersleben Ger.
231 C5 Guntersville AL U.S.A.
182 C2 Guntin de Pallares Spain
179 H2 Guntramsdorf Austria
114 D2 Guntur Andhra Prad. India
84 D3 Gununa Qld Austr.
94 B2 Gunungsitoli Indon.
94 B2 Gunungtua Sumatera Indon.
115 D2 Gunupur Orissa India
126 C3 Günyüzü Turkey
173 E3 Günz r. Ger.
Gunza Angola see Porto Amboim
173 E3 Günzburg Ger.
173 E2 Gunzenhausen Ger.
106 E4 Guochengyi Gansu China
109 E1 Guo He r. China
109 F1 Guo He r. China
Guoluezhen Henan China see Lingbao
109 F1 Guoyang Anhui China
Guozhen Shaanxi China see Baoji
116 C1 Gupis Jammu and Kashmir
197 H3 Gura Caliţei Romania
Guradu i. S. Male Maldives see Guraidhu
136 E4 Gura Galbenei Moldova
177 L5 Gurahonţ Romania
197 G2 Gura Humorului Romania
113 □1 Guraidhu i. S. Male Maldives
116 C2 Gurais Jammu and Kashmir
207 G4 Gurara r. Nigeria
177 L6 Gurasada Romania
197 G3 Gura Şuţii Romania
197 H3 Gura Teghii Romania
208 E4 Gurba r. Dem. Rep. Congo
107 G3 Gurban Obo Nei Mongol China
110 D2 Gurbantünggüt Shamo des. China
129 D4 Gürbulak Turkey
116 C2 Gurdaspur Punjab India
122 E5 Gurdim Iran
237 E5 Gurdon AR U.S.A.
Gurdzhaani Georgia see Gurjaani
199 E2 Güre Turkey
199 F2 Güre Turkey
Gurgan Iran see Gorgān
116 D3 Gurgaon Haryana India
202 E6 Gurgei, Jebel mt. Sudan
197 G2 Gurghiu r. Romania
197 G2 Gurghiului, Munţii mts Romania
254 E3 Gurgueia r. Brazil
116 B4 Gurha Rajasthan India
251 F3 Guri, Embalse de resr Venez.
256 C3 Gurinhatã Brazil
129 D3 Gurjaani Georgia
179 F4 Gurk Austria
179 F4 Gurk r. Austria
Gurlan Uzbek. see Gurlen
120 E4 Gurlen Uzbek.
114 C2 Gurmatkal Karnataka India
226 D4 Gurnee IL U.S.A.
150 D3 Gurnos Powys, Wales U.K.
213 G3 Guro Moz.
127 F3 Gürpınar Turkey
114 C3 Gurramkonda Andhra Prad. India
186 C2 Gurrea de Gállego Spain
199 F1 Gürsu Bursa Turkey
Gu-ru i. S. Male Maldives see Gulhi
Guru i. S. Male Maldives see Gulhi
213 H2 Gurué Moz.
126 E3 Gürün Turkey
251 I5 Gurupá Brazil
251 I5 Gurupa, Ilha Grande de i. Brazil
254 C4 Gurupi Brazil
254 C3 Gurupi, Serra do hills Brazil
116 C4 Guru Sikhar mt. Rajasthan India
213 F3 Guruve Zimbabwe
Guruwe Zimbabwe see Guruve
114 C2 Guruzala Andhra Prad. India
106 D3 Gurvan Sayan Uul mts Mongolia
Gur'yev Kazakh. see Atyrau
138 C4 Gur'yevsk Rus. Fed.
Gur'yevskaya Oblast' admin. div. Kazakh. see Atyrauskaya Oblast'
139 M4 Gus' r. Rus. Fed.
207 G3 Gusau Nigeria
170 C2 Gusborn Ger.
171 C3 Güsen Ger.
138 D4 Gusev Rus. Fed.
139 M4 Gusevskiy Rus. Fed.
101 B5 Gushan Liaoning China
123 E3 Gushgy Turkm.
123 E2 Gushgy r. Turkm.
109 E1 Gushi Henan China
207 E4 Gushiegu Ghana
102 □1 Gushikawa Japan
196 D4 Gusinje Crna Gora Yugo.
139 H4 Gusino Rus. Fed.
106 E1 Gusinoozersk Respublika Buryatiya Rus. Fed.
117 F5 Guskara W. Bengal India
139 M4 Gus'-Khrustal'nyy Rus. Fed.
170 F3 Gusow Ger.
192 A5 Guspini Sardegna Italy
190 F3 Gussago Italy
179 H3 Güssing Austria
190 F3 Gussola Italy
179 G3 Gußwerk Austria
140 □ Gustav Adolf Land reg. Svalbard
247 G3 Gustavia St Barthélémy West Indies
237 D7 Gustavo Díaz Ordaz Mex.
245 G5 Gustavo Diaz Ordaz Veracruz Mex.
143 H2 Gustavsberg Sweden
220 E4 Gustavus AK U.S.A.
140 □ Gustav V Land reg. Svalbard
171 C4 Güsten Ger.
172 A2 Gusterath Ger.
240 G3 Gustine CA U.S.A.
170 D2 Güstrow Ger.
102 □1 Gusukube Japan
172 C3 Gutach (Schwarzwaldbahn) Ger.
197 F2 Gutâiului, Munţii mts Romania
179 F2 Gutau Austria
146 □G1 Gutcher Shetland, Scotland U.K.
179 G3 Gutenstein Austria
171 E3 Güterfelde Ger.
171 C4 Güterglück Ger.
169 D4 Gütersloh Ger.
241 M5 Guthrie AZ U.S.A.
230 C4 Guthrie KY U.S.A.
237 D5 Guthrie OK U.S.A.
237 C5 Guthrie TX U.S.A.
236 E3 Guthrie Center IA U.S.A.
234 C2 Guthriesville PA U.S.A.
109 F3 Gutian Fujian China
109 F3 Gutian Fujian China
252 E4 Gutiérrez Bol.
245 H4 Gutiérrez Gómez Mex.
Guting Shandong China see Yutai
129 E3 Guton, Gora mt. Azer./Rus. Fed.
176 F5 Gutorfölde Hungary
170 D2 Gutow Ger.
190 D2 Guttannen Switz.
179 F4 Guttaring Austria
236 F3 Guttenberg IA U.S.A.
213 F3 Gutu Zimbabwe
170 E2 Gützkow Ger.
129 B4 Güveçli Turkey
140 L2 Guvertfjället mts Sweden
117 G4 Guwahati Assam India
127 F3 Guwēr Iraq
Guwlumayak Turkm. see Kuuli-Mayak
169 E4 Guxhagen Ger.
109 E3 Guxian Jiangxi China
251 G3 Guyana country S. America
Guyane Française terr. S. America see French Guiana
Guyang Hunan China see Guzhang
107 F3 Guyang Nei Mongol China
160 C2 Guye r. France
Guyi Guangxi China see Sanjiang
237 C4 Guymon OK U.S.A.
122 C4 Gūyom Iran
Guyong Fujian China see Jiangle
83 G2 Guyra N.S.W. Austr.
225 I4 Guysborough N.S. Can.
107 G3 Guyuan Hebei China
106 E5 Guyuan Ningxia China
121 F5 Guzar Uzbek.
129 F3 Güzdäk Azer.
128 B1 Güzeloluk Turkey
Güzelyurt Cyprus see Morfou
108 D2 Guzhang Hunan China
109 F1 Guzhen Anhui China
Guzhou Guizhou China see Rongjiang
242 D2 Guzmán, Lago de l. Mex.
138 C4 Gvardeysk Rus. Fed.
Gvardeyskoye Rus. Fed. see Elin-Yurt
137 K2 Gvazda Rus. Fed.
83 G2 Gwabegar N.S.W. Austr.
207 G4 Gwada Nigeria
207 G3 Gwadabawa Nigeria
123 E5 Gwadar Pak.
123 E5 Gwadar West Bay Pak.
Gwador Pak. see Gwadar
116 D4 Gwalior Madh. Prad. India
213 F4 Gwanda Zimbabwe
207 G4 Gwarzo Nigeria
150 D3 Gwaun-Cae-Gurwen Neath Port Talbot, Wales U.K.
213 E3 Gwayi r. Zimbabwe
174 E2 Gwda r. Pol.
147 C2 Gweebarra Bay Rep. of Ireland
147 C1 Gweedore Rep. of Ireland
Gwelo Zimbabwe see Gweru
213 F3 Gweru Zimbabwe
212 E4 Gweta Botswana
226 D2 Gwinn MI U.S.A.
236 D2 Gwinner ND U.S.A.
150 B4 Gwithian Cornwall, England U.K.
207 I4 Gwoza Nigeria
83 G2 Gwydir r. N.S.W. Austr.
150 C1 Gwynedd admin. div. Wales U.K.
150 D1 Gwytherin Conwy, Wales U.K.
160 D1 Gy France
111 F6 Gyaca Xizang China
Gya'gya Xizang China see Saga
Gyaijêpozhanggê Qinghai China see Zhidoi
111 F6 Gyai Qu r. Xizang China
108 A1 Gyairong Qinghai China
Gyaisi Sichuan China see Jiulong
177 I4 Gyál Hungary
199 E3 Gyali i. Greece
Gyamotang Xizang China see Dêngqên
Gyandzha Azer. see Gäncä
Gyangkar Xizang China see Dinngyê
111 D6 Gyangrang Xizang China
Gyangtse Xizang China see Gyangzê
111 E6 Gyangzê Xizang China
106 C5 Gyaring Qinghai China
111 E6 Gyaring Co l. China
106 C5 Gyaring Hu l. Qinghai China
176 G4 Gyarmat Hungary
198 D3 Gyaros i. Greece
Gyaurs Turkm. see Sakhra
Gydan, Khrebet mts Rus. Fed. see Kolymskiy, Khrebet
130 I2 Gydanskiy Poluostrov pen. Rus. Fed.
Gyêgu Qinghai China see Yushu
176 G5 Gyékényes Hungary
177 H4 Gyermely Hungary
156 E4 Gyé-sur-Seine France
Gyêwa Xizang China see Zabqung
168 E2 Gyhum Ger.
Gyigang Xizang China see Zayü
111 F6 Gyimda Xizang China
111 D6 Gyirong Xizang China
108 A2 Gyitang Xizang China
Gyixong Xizang China see Gonggar
111 F5 Gyiza Qinghai China
142 D4 Gyldenløveshøj hill Denmark
147 C5 Gyleen Rep. of Ireland
140 M2 Gyljen Sweden
85 H5 Gympie Qld Austr.
96 A3 Gyobingauk Myanmar
105 F2 Gyōda Japan
177 J5 Gyomaendrőd Hungary
177 G4 Gyömöre Hungary
177 I4 Gyömrő Hungary
177 I4 Gyöngyös Hungary
176 F4 Gyöngyös r. Hungary
177 G6 Gyöngyös r. Romania
177 I4 Gyöngyöshalász Hungary
177 I4 Gyöngyöspata Hungary
177 H5 Gyönk Hungary
177 G4 Győr Hungary
176 G4 Győr-Moson-Sopron county Hungary
177 G4 Győrság Hungary
Győrszentmárton Hungary see Pannonhalma
177 L4 Győrtelek Hungary
177 G4 Győrújbarát Hungary
177 G4 Győrújfalu Hungary
223 L5 Gypsumville Man. Can.
198 C3 Gytheio Greece
177 K5 Gyula Hungary
Gyulafehérvár Romania see Alba Iulia
177 L3 Gyulaháza Hungary
177 H5 Gyulaj Hungary
129 F3 Gyul'gerychay r. Rus. Fed.
Gyümai Qinghai China see Darlag
129 C3 Gyumri Armenia
197 H5 Gyurgen Bair hill Turkey
122 D2 Gyzylarbat Turkm.
139 J4 Gzhat' r. Rus. Fed.
Gzhatsk Rus. Fed. see Gagarin
175 I3 Gzy Pol.

H

117 G4 Ha Bhutan
138 E2 Haabneeme Estonia
165 D4 Haacht Belgium
179 F2 Haag Austria
179 E2 Haag am Hausruck Austria
173 F3 Haag an der Amper Ger.
173 G3 Haag in Oberbayern Ger.
140 □ Haakon VII Land reg. Svalbard
164 F2 Haaksbergen Neth.
165 D4 Haaltert Belgium
106 B1 Haanhöhiy Uul mts Mongolia
79 □2 Ha'ano i. Tonga
79 □2 Ha'apai Group is Tonga
134 D3 Haapajärvi Fin.
140 N2 Haapavesi Fin.
138 D2 Haapsalu Estonia
173 F3 Haar Ger.

Ha 'Arava *watercourse* Israel/Jordan *see* 'Arabah, Wādī al
173 H3 Haarbach Ger.
172 B2 Haardt *hills* Ger.
172 B2 Haardtkopf *hill* Ger.
164 D2 Haarlem Neth.
214 D5 Haarlem S. Africa
169 C4 Haarstrang *ridge* Ger.
81 B5 Haast *South I.* N.Z.
81 B5 Haast *r. South I.* N.Z.
84 B4 Haast Bluff *N.T.* Austr.
81 B6 Haast Range *mts South I.* N.Z.
164 D3 Haastrecht Neth.
123 F5 Hab *r.* Pak.
173 F4 Habach Ger.
110 D1 Habahe *Xinjiang* China
Habai Group *is* Tonga *see* Ha'apai Group
Habana Cuba *see* La Habana
173 G1 Habartov Czech Rep.
163 B5 Habas France
222 G3 Habay *Alta* Can.
165 E5 Habay-la-Neuve Belgium
124 D5 Ḩabbān Yemen
127 F4 Ḩabbānīyah, Hawr al *l.* Iraq
124 C4 Ḩabhab ash Shaykh, Ḩarrāt *lava field* Saudi Arabia
116 B3 Habicht *mt.* Austria
117 G4 Habiganj Bangl.
104 B4 Habikino Japan
128 B4 Ḩabīs, Wādī al *r.* Jordan
143 F3 Habo Sweden
177 I2 Habovka Slovakia
117 G5 Habra *W. Bengal* India
176 E2 Habry Czech Rep.
157 H5 Habsheim France
125 E4 Ḩabshīyah, Jabal *mts* Yemen
169 C5 Hachenburg Ger.
105 E2 Hachibuse-yama *mt.* Japan
104 D2 Hachimori-yama *mt.* Japan
102 J3 Hachinohe Japan
105 F3 Hachiōji Japan
199 F2 Hacıbekir Turkey
126 D3 Hacıbektaş Turkey
129 C4 Hachalit Turkey
Hacıköy Turkey *see* Çekerek
183 G3 Hacinas Spain
128 C1 Hacıpaşa Turkey
129 F4 Hacıqāhramanlı Azer.
129 F3 Hacı Zeynalabdin Azer.
82 D2 Hack, Mount *S.A.* Austr.
241 K4 Hackberry *AZ* U.S.A.
172 B2 Hackenheim Ger.
235 D2 Hackensack *NJ* U.S.A.
232 C5 Hacker Valley *WV* U.S.A.
147 E4 Hacketstown Rep. of Ireland
234 D2 Hackettstown *NJ* U.S.A.
151 G2 Hackleton *Northamptonshire,* England U.K.
151 I3 Hacklinge *Kent,* England U.K.
149 I3 Hackness *North Yorkshire,* England U.K.
234 C3 Hack Point *MD* U.S.A.
213 G4 Hacufera Moz.
175 J6 Hacçow Pol.
125 E3 Hadabat al Budū *plain* Saudi Arabia
114 B3 Hadagalli *Karnataka* India
169 D5 Hadamar Ger.
123 F4 Hada Mountains Afgh.
124 C3 Ḩadan, Ḩarrat *lava field* Saudi Arabia
105 F3 Hadano Japan
151 G3 Haddenham *Buckinghamshire,* England U.K.
146 F6 Haddington *East Lothian,* Scotland U.K.
151 I2 Haddiscoe *Norfolk,* England U.K.
234 C3 Haddonfield *NJ* U.S.A.
207 H3 Hadejia Nigeria
142 D1 Hadeland *reg.* Norway
128 B3 Ḩadera Israel
128 B3 Ḩadera *r.* Israel
142 D4 Haderslev Denmark
142 C3 Haderup Denmark
114 C2 Hadgaon *Mahar.* India
125 G3 Ḩadhah Saudi Arabia
125 E3 Ḩādh Banī Zaynān *des.* Saudi Arabia
113 D11 Hadhdhunmathi Atoll Maldives
Hadhramaut *reg.* Yemen *see* Ḩaḑramawt
125 F5 Ḩadīboh *Suquṭrā* Yemen
111 D4 Hadilik *Xinjiang* China
126 D3 Hadım Turkey
202 D5 Hadjer Momou *mt.* Chad
151 H2 Hadleigh *Suffolk,* England U.K.
150 E2 Hadley *Telford and Wrekin,* England U.K.
221 H2 Hadley Bay *Nunavut* Can.
235 F1 Hadlyme *CT* U.S.A.
171 C4 Hadmersleben Ger.
157 G4 Hadol France
125 E4 Ḩaḑramawt *governorate* Yemen
125 D5 Ḩaḑramawt *reg.* Yemen
Hadranum *Sicilia* Italy *see* Adrano
179 H2 Hadres Austria
Hadria Italy *see* Adria
149 G2 Hadrian's Wall *tourist site* England U.K.
Hadrumetum Tunisia *see* Sousse
129 E4 Hadrut Azer.
142 D1 Hadseløy *i.* Norway
140 H3 Hadsten Denmark
142 D3 Hadsund Denmark
137 G2 Hadyach Ukr.
102 □2 Haebaru Japan
261 I3 Haedo, Cuchilla de *hills* Uru.
101 E5 Haeju N. Korea
101 C5 Haeju-man *b.* N. Korea
165 E3 Haelen Neth.
240 □B7 Haena *HI* U.S.A.
101 C6 Haenam S. Korea
124 D1 Ḩafar al Bāṭin Saudi Arabia
223 J4 Hafford *Sask.* Can.
126 E3 Hafik Turkey
124 B2 Hafirat al 'Aydā Saudi Arabia
124 D2 Hafirat Nasah Saudi Arabia
125 F3 Ḩafit Oman
125 F2 Ḩafīt, Jabal *mt.* U.A.E.
123 H3 Hafizabad Pak.
117 H4 Haflong *Assam* India
140 □B2 Hafnarfjörður Iceland
179 G2 Hafnerbach Austria
129 F4 Hafitoni Azer.
140 □B2 Hafursfjörður *b.* Iceland
Haga Myanmar *see* Haka
203 G6 Hag Abdullah Sudan
215 G5 Haga-Haga S. Africa
179 H5 Haganj Croatia
227 G2 Hagar *Ont.* Can.
114 C3 Hagari *r.* India
203 H5 Hagar Nish Plateau Eritrea
78 □1 Hagåtña Guam
143 G3 Hagbyån *r.* Sweden
168 C2 Hage Ger.
171 D3 Hagelberg *hill* Ger.
169 C4 Hagen Ger.
91 J8 Hagen, Mount P.N.G.
169 C3 Hagen am Teutoburger Wald Ger.
172 C2 Hagenbach Ger.
169 E3 Hagenburg Ger.
168 D2 Hagen im Bremischen Ger.
170 C2 Hagenow Ger.
222 E4 Hagensborg *B.C.* Can.
171 F4 Hagenwerder Ger.
210 C2 Hāgere Hiywet Eth.
210 C3 Hāgere Selam Eth.
232 B6 Hagerhill *KY* U.S.A.
232 E5 Hagerstown *MD* U.S.A.
163 B5 Hagetaubin France
163 B5 Hagetmau France
143 E1 Hagfors Sweden
140 K3 Häggenäs Sweden
230 B2 Haggin, Mount *MT* U.S.A.
140 K3 Häggsjön Sweden
140 K3 Häggsjövik Sweden
103 E6 Hagi Japan
96 D2 Ha Giang Vietnam
97 E4 Ha Giao, Sông *r.* Vietnam
150 E2 Hagley *Herefordshire,* England U.K.
150 E2 Hagley *Worcestershire,* England U.K.
HaGolan *hills* Syria *see* Golan
157 G3 Hagondange France
147 B4 Hag's Head *hd* Rep. of Ireland
233 G3 Hague *NY* U.S.A.
157 H4 Haguenau France
217 □3a Hahaïa *Njazidja* Comoros
103 □3 Hahajima-rettō *is* Japan
169 F4 Hahausen Ger.
173 F2 Hahnbach Ger.
172 C2 Hähnlein Ger.
169 D5 Hahnstätten Ger.
176 F5 Hahót Hungary
107 H4 Hai *r.* China
211 C5 Hai Tanz.
109 G1 Hai'an *Jiangsu* China
172 D2 Haibach *Bayern* Ger.
173 F2 Haibach *Bayern* Ger.
105 E4 Haibara Japan
Haicheng *Guangdong* China *see* Haifeng
107 I3 Haicheng *Liaoning* China
Haicheng *Ningxia* China *see* Haiyuan
116 E4 Haidargarh *Uttar Prad.* India
172 F3 Haidenaab *r.* Ger.
179 F2 Haidershofen Austria
173 H3 Haidmühle Ger.
96 D2 Hai Dương Vietnam
Haifa Israel *see* Ḩefa
128 B3 Haifa, Bay of Israel
109 E4 Haifeng *Guangdong* China
87 E6 Haig *W.A.* Austr.
169 D5 Haiger Ger.
172 C3 Haigerloch Ger.
Haikakan *country* Asia *see* Armenia
Haikang *Guangdong* China *see* Leizhou
108 D4 Haikou *Hainan* China
124 C2 Ḩā'il Saudi Arabia
124 C2 Ḩā'il *prov.* Saudi Arabia
117 H4 Hailakandi *Assam* India
107 H1 Hailar *Nei Mongol* China
107 H1 Hailar *r.* China
238 D3 Hailey *ID* U.S.A.
224 E4 Haileybury *Ont.* Can.
100 D3 Hailin *Heilong.* China
Hailong *Jilin* China *see* Meihekou
151 H4 Hailsham *East Sussex,* England U.K.
100 C3 Hailun *Heilong.* China
140 N2 Hailuoto Fin.
109 G2 Haimen *Jiangsu* China
173 F3 Haimhausen Ger.
178 B3 Haiming Austria
173 G3 Haiming Ger.
169 F5 Haina Ger.
169 D4 Haina (Kloster) Ger.
108 D5 Hainan *i.* China
99 I8 Hainan *prov.* China
Hainan Strait China *see* Qiongzhou Haixia
165 D4 Hainaut *prov.* Belgium
179 H2 Hainburg an der Donau Austria
206 C5 Haindi Liberia
220 E4 Haines *AK* U.S.A.
221 J3 Haines City *FL* U.S.A.
222 B2 Haines Junction *Y.T.* Can.
233 D4 Hainesport *NJ* U.S.A.
222 B2 Haines Road Can./U.S.A.
179 G2 Hainfeld Austria
169 F4 Hainich *ridge* Ger.
171 E5 Hainichen Ger.
169 F4 Hainleite *ridge* Ger.
Haiphong Vietnam *see* Hai Phong
96 D2 Hai Phong Vietnam
106 E3 Haiqing *Heilong.* China
106 A2 Hairhan Namag *Nei Mongol* China
157 F4 Haironville France
172 C3 Haiterbach Ger.
246 D3 Haiti *country* West Indies
179 G2 Haitzendorf Austria
106 D4 Haiyan *Qinghai* China
109 G2 Haiyan *Zhejiang* China
Haiyang *Anhui* China *see* Xiuning
107 I4 Haiyang *Shandong* China
Haiyou *Zhejiang* China *see* Sanmen
106 E4 Haiyuan *Ningxia* China
107 H5 Haizhou Wan *b.* China
126 C3 Hāj Ali Qoli, Kavīr-e *salt l.* Iran
177 K4 Hajdú-Bihar *county* Hungary
177 K4 Hajdúböszörmény Hungary
177 K4 Hajdúdorog Hungary
177 K4 Hajdúhadház Hungary
177 K4 Hajdúnánás Hungary
177 K4 Hajdúsámson Hungary
177 K4 Hajdúszoboszló Hungary
177 K4 Hajdúszovát Hungary
125 F5 Ḩajhir *mt. Suquṭrā* Yemen
117 F4 Hajipur *Bihar* India
125 E2 Ḩajir *reg.* Saudi Arabia
124 C5 Ḩajjah Yemen
124 C4 Ḩajjah *governorate* Yemen
122 C4 Ḩājjīābād Iran
122 D4 Ḩājjīābād Iran
177 H4 Hajmáskér Hungary
175 L3 Hajnówka Pol.
117 G4 Hajo *Assam* India
177 I5 Hajós Hungary
124 C3 Ḩajrah Saudi Arabia
177 G3 Hájske Slovakia
96 A2 Haka Myanmar
240 □D9 Hakalau *HI* U.S.A.
129 E4 Häkäri *r.* Azer.
103 I5 Hakase-yama *mt.* Japan
81 C6 Hakataramea *South I.* N.Z.
81 C5 Hakatere *South I.* N.Z.
Hakatere *r. South I.* N.Z. *see* Ashburton
259 C6 Hakelhuincul, Altiplanicie de *plat.* Arg.
Haka Myanmar *see* Haka
128 B4 Hakippa, Har *hill* Israel
127 F3 Hakkâri Turkey
140 M2 Hakkas Sweden
104 B4 Hakken-zan *mt.* Japan
102 J3 Hakkōda-san *mt.* Japan
105 E4 Hakkō-san *hill* Japan
102 J4 Hakodate Japan
212 C4 Hakos Mountains Namibia
129 B4 Hakserver Turkey
104 C2 Hakui Japan
104 C2 Haku-san *vol.* Japan
Hal Belgium *see* Halle
123 G5 Hala Pak.
128 C2 Ḩalā', Jabal al *mt.* Jordan
128 C1 Ḩalab Syria
128 C1 Ḩalab *governorate* Syria
124 D3 Halabān Saudi Arabia
127 G4 Ḩalabja Iraq
Halach Turkm. *see* Khalach
243 H4 Halachó Mex.
100 C3 Halahai *Jilin* China
136 D3 Halahora de Sus Moldova
203 G4 Halaib Triangle *terr.* Egypt/Sudan
128 A4 Ḩalāl, Gebel *hill* Egypt
125 G4 Ḩalānīyāt, Juzur al *is* Oman
176 G4 Halászi Hungary
197 H2 Hălăuceşti Romania
143 F2 Hälaveden *hills* Sweden
240 □C8 Halawa *HI* U.S.A.
106 C1 Halban *Hövsgöl* Mongolia
171 E3 Halbe Ger.
179 G2 Halbenrain Austria
171 C4 Halberstadt Ger.
150 D4 Halberton *Devon,* England U.K.
173 E4 Halblech Ger.
179 H3 Halbturn Austria
92 B3 Halcon, Mount *Mindoro* Phil.
215 G4 Halcyon Drift S. Africa
142 D2 Halden Norway
171 D3 Haldensleben Ger.
173 E4 Haldenwang Ger.
117 G5 Haldi *r. W. Bengal* India
117 G5 Haldia *W. Bengal* India
116 D3 Haldwani *Uttar Prad.* India
149 G4 Hale *Greater Manchester,* England U.K.
227 F3 Hale *MI* U.S.A.
87 C5 Hale, Mount *hill W.A.* Austr.
129 C3 Halefoğlu Turkey
122 C5 Ḩāleh Iran
240 □ Haleiwa *HI* U.S.A.
165 E4 Halen Belgium
177 H2 Halenkov Czech Rep.
Haleparki Deresi *r.* Syria/Turkey *see* Quwayq, Nahr
151 I2 Hales *Norfolk,* England U.K.
150 E2 Halesowen *West Midlands,* England U.K.
151 I2 Halesworth *Suffolk,* England U.K.
234 B3 Halethorpe *MD* U.S.A.
149 G4 Halewood *Merseyside,* England U.K.
231 C5 Haleyville *AL* U.S.A.
125 G5 Half Assini Ghana
126 E3 Halfeti Turkey
173 G4 Halfing Ger.
81 B7 Halfmoon Bay Stewart I. N.Z.
240 F3 Half Moon Bay *CA* U.S.A.
82 C2 Half Moon Lake *salt flat S.A.* Austr.
222 F3 Halfway *r. B.C.* Can.
232 E5 Halfway *MD* U.S.A.
142 D2 Halfweg Neth
214 C4 Halfweg S. Africa
142 E1 Halgån *r.* Sweden
107 H2 Halhgol Mongolia
227 H3 Haliburton *Ont.* Can.
224 E4 Haliburton Highlands *hills Ont.* Can.
177 I3 Halič Slovakia
Halicarnassus Turkey *see* Bodrum
225 I4 Halifax *N.S.* Can.
149 H4 Halifax *West Yorkshire,* England U.K.
231 E4 Halifax *NC* U.S.A.
234 B2 Halifax *PA* U.S.A.
232 D6 Halifax *VA* U.S.A.
85 F3 Halifax, Mount *Qld* Austr.
85 F3 Halifax Bay *Qld* Austr.
138 D1 Halikko Fin.
129 B4 Halilçavuş Turkey
128 C2 Ḩalimah *mt.* Lebanon/Syria
82 B2 Halinor Lake *salt flat S.A.* Austr.
Haliut *Nei Mongol* China *see* Urad Zhongqi
114 B3 Haliyal *Karnataka* India
146 E3 Halkirk *Highland, Scotland* U.K.
150 D1 Halkyn *Flintshire,* Wales U.K.
Hall *atoll Gilbert Is* Kiribati *see* Maiana
143 H3 Hall *Gotland* Sweden
148 E2 Hall *East Renfrewshire,* Scotland U.K.
234 B4 Hall *MD* U.S.A.
140 L3 Halla Sweden
144 F2 Halladale *r.* Scotland U.K.
232 B4 Hallam *PA* U.S.A.
142 E3 Halland *county* Sweden
151 H4 Halland *East Sussex,* England U.K.
142 E3 Hallandsåsen *hills* Sweden
101 C6 Halla-san *mt.* S. Korea
221 J3 Hall Beach *Nunavut* Can.
173 F3 Hallbergmoos Ger.
165 D3 Halle *Antwerpen* Belgium
165 D4 Halle *Vlaams Brabant* Belgium
169 E4 Halle Ger.
171 C4 Halle *admin. reg. Sachsen-Anhalt* Ger.
171 C4 Halle (Saale) Ger.
169 D3 Halle (Westfalen) Ger.
143 F2 Hällefors Sweden
143 G2 Hälleforsnäs Sweden
178 E3 Hallein Austria
143 G2 Hällen *Jämtland* Sweden
143 G1 Hällen *Uppsala* Sweden
169 D4 Hallenberg Ger.
156 B3 Hallencourt France
171 C4 Halle-Neustadt Ger.
173 E2 Hallerndorf Ger.
263 L2 Hallett, Cape Antarctica
237 D6 Hallettsville *TX* U.S.A.
143 F2 Hällevikssrand Sweden
262 W1 Halley *research stn* Antarctica
262 X2 Hallgreen, Mount Antarctica
236 C2 Halliday *ND* U.S.A.
168 E1 Halligen *is* Ger.
142 C1 Hallingdal *val.* Norway
142 C1 Hallingdalselva *r.* Norway
143 G3 Hallingeberg Sweden
178 C3 Hall in Tirol Austria
266 F5 Hall Islands Micronesia
138 E2 Halliste *r.* Estonia
143 F1 Hällnäs Sweden
236 D1 Hallock *MN* U.S.A.
150 E2 Hallow *Worcestershire,* England U.K.
221 L3 Hall Peninsula *Nunavut* Can.
86 E2 Hall Point *W.A.* Austr.
234 B1 Halls *PA* U.S.A.
143 F2 Hallsberg Sweden
86 E3 Halls Creek *W.A.* Austr.
227 H3 Halls Lake *Ont.* Can.
173 E2 Hallstadt Ger.
179 E3 Hallstatt Austria
179 E3 Hallstätter See *l.* Austria
143 H1 Hallstavik Sweden
233 F4 Hallstead *PA* U.S.A.
147 E3 Halltown Rep. of Ireland
165 C4 Halluin Belgium
164 E1 Hallum Neth.
140 L3 Hällvik Sweden
140 K3 Hallviken Sweden
190 D1 Hallwiler See *l.* Switz.
150 C4 Hallworthy *Cornwall,* England U.K.
177 L5 Hălmăgel Romania
177 L5 Hălmagiu Romania
93 D2 Halmahera *i. Maluku* Indon.
93 D3 Halmahera Sea *Maluku* Indon.
177 L4 Halmășd Romania
197 F2 Halmeu Romania
142 E3 Halmstad Sweden
116 C5 Halol *Gujarat* India
188 E2 Haloze *reg.* Slovenia
142 D3 Hals Denmark
195 □ Hal Saflieni Hypogeum *tourist site* Malta
171 E5 Halsbrücke Ger.
169 C5 Halsenbach Ger.
Halsingborg Sweden *see* Helsingborg
151 H3 Halstead *Essex, England* U.K.
168 E2 Halstenbek Ger.
164 D3 Halsteren Neth.
157 G3 Halstroff France
140 N3 Halsua Fin.
106 B4 Haltang *r.* China
169 C3 Haltern Ger.
151 G3 Halton *Buckinghamshire,* England U.K.
149 G4 Halton *Lancashire,* England U.K.
149 G4 Halton *admin. div.* England U.K.
149 G3 Halton Gill *North Yorkshire,* England U.K.
149 G3 Haltwhistle *Northumberland,* England U.K.
116 B5 Halvad *Gujarat* India
169 C4 Halver Ger.
150 D4 Halwell *Devon, England* U.K.
136 C3 Halych Ukr.
137 G2 Halytsya Ukr.
176 B2 Halže Czech Rep.
157 G3 Ham France
146 □F1 Ham *Shetland, Scotland* U.K.
104 D4 Hamada Japan
206 C3 Hamâda Çafia *des.* Mali
204 D4 Hamada ed Douakel *plat.* Alg.
204 D5 Hamâda El Ḩaricha *des.* Mali
122 B3 Hamadān Iran
122 B3 Hamadān *prov.* Iran
202 B3 Ḩamādat Murzuq *plat.* Libya
204 D3 Hamada Tounassine *des.* Alg.
204 E3 Hamaguir Alg.
128 C2 Ḩamāh Syria
128 C2 Ḩamāh *governorate* Syria
104 B4 Hamāda Japan
217 □3a Hamalengo *mt. Njazidja* Comoros
104 D4 Hamamatsu Japan
104 D4 Hamana-ko *l.* Japan
184 E2 Hamapega *hill* Spain
141 J3 Hamar Norway
140 K1 Hamarøy Norway
140 K1 Hamarøy *i.* Norway
201 G5 Hamasien *prov.* Eritrea
203 G3 Hamâta, Gebel *mt.* Egypt
173 H3 Hambach France
114 D5 Hambantota Sri Lanka
168 F2 Hamberge Ger.
168 D2 Hambergen Ger.
151 G3 Hambleden *Buckinghamshire,* England U.K.
151 F4 Hamble-le-Rice *Hampshire,* England U.K.
149 G4 Hambleton *Lancashire,* England U.K.
232 D5 Hambleton *WV* U.S.A.
149 H3 Hambleton Hills *England* U.K.
172 C2 Hambrücken Ger.
168 E3 Hambühren Ger.
168 E2 Hamburg Ger.
168 E2 Hamburg *land* Ger.
215 F5 Hamburg S. Africa
237 F5 Hamburg *AR* U.S.A.
235 F1 Hamburg *CT* U.S.A.
236 E3 Hamburg *IA* U.S.A.
234 D1 Hamburg *NJ* U.S.A.
232 D3 Hamburg *NY* U.S.A.
234 C2 Hamburg *PA* U.S.A.
142 D2 Hamburgsund Sweden
158 E3 Hambye France
124 C4 Ḩamḑah Saudi Arabia
152 C3 Hamdallay Niger
124 C4 Ḩamdānah Saudi Arabia
233 G4 Hamden *CT* U.S.A.
199 E2 Hamdibey Turkey
128 B1 Hamdili Turkey
168 E1 Hamdorf Ger.
141 M3 Hämeenkangas *moorland* Fin.
138 E1 Hämeenkoski *Etelä-Suomi* Fin.
141 M3 Hämeenkoski *Länsi-Suomi* Fin.
141 N3 Hämeenkyrö Fin.
141 N3 Hämeenlinna Fin.
HaMelah, Yam *salt l.* Asia *see* Dead Sea
168 E3 Hämelhausen Ger.
87 B5 Hamelin *W.A.* Austr.
87 B5 Hamelin, Cape *W.A.* Austr.
87 B5 Hamelin Pool *b. W.A.* Austr.
169 E3 Hameln Ger.
171 C3 Hamersleben Ger.
86 C4 Hamersley *W.A.* Austr.
87 C6 Hamersley Lakes *salt flat W.A.* Austr.
86 C4 Hamersley Range *mts W.A.* Austr.
170 C3 Hämerten Ger.
101 C5 Hamhŭng N. Korea
106 B3 Hami *Xinjiang* China
122 B4 Ḩamid Iran
199 E1 Hamidiye Turkey
84 E4 Hamilton *Qld* Austr.
84 C5 Hamilton *S.A.* Austr.
231 □1 Hamilton Bermuda
224 E5 Hamilton *Ont.* Can.
Hamilton *r. Nfld.* Can. *see* Churchill
80 E2 Hamilton *North I.* N.Z.
146 D6 Hamilton *South Lanarkshire,* Scotland U.K.
231 C5 Hamilton *AL* U.S.A.
231 C5 Hamilton *GA* U.S.A.
230 B5 Hamilton *IL* U.S.A.
238 D2 Hamilton *MT* U.S.A.
235 D2 Hamilton *NJ* U.S.A.
233 F3 Hamilton *NY* U.S.A.
232 A5 Hamilton *OH* U.S.A.
237 D6 Hamilton *TX* U.S.A.
240 C3 Hamilton, Mount *CA* U.S.A.
241 J2 Hamilton, Mount *NV* U.S.A.
81 B6 Hamilton Burn *South I.* N.Z.
240 F2 Hamilton City *CA* U.S.A.
84 C4 Hamilton Downs *N.T.* Austr.
225 J2 Hamilton Inlet *Nfld.* Can.
233 F3 Hamilton Mountain *hill NY* U.S.A.
148 C3 Hamilton's Bawn *Northern Ireland* U.K.
141 N3 Hamina Fin.
116 D3 Hamirpur *Hima. Prad.* India
116 E4 Hamirpur *Uttar Prad.* India
Hamitabat Turkey *see* Isparta
231 E5 Hamlet *NC* U.S.A.
82 D3 Hamley Bridge *S.A.* Austr.
234 C1 Hamlin *PA* U.S.A.
237 C5 Hamlin *TX* U.S.A.
232 B5 Hamlin *WV* U.S.A.
169 C3 Hamm Ger.
172 B2 Hamm *Rheinland-Pfalz* Ger.
169 D4 Hamm *Nordrhein-Westfalen* Ger.
169 C5 Hamm (Sieg) Ger.
204 C3 Hammada du Drâa *plat.* Alg.
202 A2 Hammādat Tingharat *des.* Libya
168 E2 Hammah Ger.
127 F3 Ḩammām al 'Alīl Iraq
181 F5 Hammam Boughrara Alg.
189 C7 Hammamet Tunisia
205 H1 Hammamet, Golfe de *g.* Tunisia
189 C7 Hammam-Lif Tunisia
215 G1 Hammanskraal S. Africa
127 F4 Ḩammār, Hawr al *imp. l.* Iraq
141 L3 Hammarland *Åland* Fin.
215 H3 Hammarsdale S. Africa
140 L3 Hammarstrand Sweden
165 D3 Hamme Belgium
142 C3 Hammel Denmark
169 E5 Hammelburg Ger.
170 E2 Hammelspring Ger.
165 D4 Hamme-Mille Belgium
171 D5 Hammerbrücke Ger.
140 M3 Hammerdal Sweden
140 M1 Hammerfest Norway
151 F3 Hammerwich *Staffordshire,* England U.K.
169 B4 Hamminkeln Ger.
82 D3 Hammond *S.A.* Austr.
230 C3 Hammond *IN* U.S.A.
237 F6 Hammond *LA* U.S.A.
238 F2 Hammond *MT* U.S.A.
227 F3 Hammond Bay *MI* U.S.A.
232 E3 Hammondsport *NY* U.S.A.
234 D3 Hammonton *NJ* U.S.A.
146 □G1 Hamnavoe *Shetland,* Scotland U.K.
146 □G1 Hamnavoe *Shetland,* Scotland U.K.
146 □G1 Hamnavoe *Shetland,* Scotland U.K.
165 E4 Hamoir Belgium
165 E4 Hamois Belgium
165 E3 Hamont Belgium
234 C3 Hamorton *PA* U.S.A.
81 C6 Hampden *South I.* N.Z.
233 □I2 Hampden Highlands *ME* U.S.A.
232 D6 Hampden Sydney *VA* U.S.A.
114 C3 Hampi *Karnataka* India
140 M2 Hämpjäkk Sweden
157 G4 Hampont France
150 F4 Hampreston *Dorset,* England U.K.
151 F3 Hampshire *admin. div.* England U.K.
234 B3 Hampstead *MD* U.S.A.
225 H4 Hampton *N.B.* Can.
237 E5 Hampton *AR* U.S.A.
236 E3 Hampton *IA* U.S.A.
233 □H3 Hampton *NH* U.S.A.
230 D2 Hampton *NJ* U.S.A.
231 D5 Hampton *SC* U.S.A.
233 E6 Hampton *VA* U.S.A.
235 F2 Hampton Bays *NY* U.S.A.
87 E7 Hampton Tableland *reg. W.A.* Austr.
195 □ Hamrun Malta
238 E3 Hams Fork *r. WY* U.S.A.
157 G3 Ham-sous-Varsberg France
151 H3 Hamstreet *Kent, England* U.K.
165 D4 Ham-sur-Heure Belgium
96 D3 Ham Tān Vietnam
122 D5 Hāmūn-e Jaz Mūrīān *salt marsh* Iran
123 E4 Hāmūn Helmand *salt flat* Afgh./Iran
123 F4 Hamun-i-Lora *dry lake* Pak.
123 E4 Hamun-i-Mashkel *salt flat* Pak.
127 F3 Hamur Turkey
105 F3 Hamura Japan
Hamwic *Southampton, England* U.K. *see* Southampton
Hamza Uzbek. *see* Khamza
128 A1 Hamzalar Turkey
176 G2 Haná *r.* Czech Rep.
240 □C8 Hana *HI* U.S.A.
246 B2 Hanábana *r.* Cuba
129 C3 Hanak Turkey
Hanakpınar Turkey *see* Çınar
124 B2 Ḩanalc Saudi Arabia
240 □B7 Hanalei *HI* U.S.A.
102 J4 Hanamaki Japan
240 □B8 Hanamaulu *HI* U.S.A.
211 B6 Hanang *mt.* Tanz.
Hananui *hill Stewart I.* N.Z. *see* Anglem, Mount
240 □B8 Hanapepe *HI* U.S.A.
169 D5 Hanau Ger.
Hânceşti Moldova *see* Hînceşti
107 F5 Hancheng *Shaanxi* China
156 B4 Hanches France
109 E2 Hanchuan *Hubei* China
232 D5 Hancock *MD* U.S.A.
226 C2 Hancock *MI* U.S.A.
233 F4 Hancock *NY* U.S.A.
234 C3 Hancocks Bridge *NJ* U.S.A.
104 C4 Handa Japan
146 C3 Handa Island *Scotland* U.K.
107 G4 Handan *Hebei* China
168 E2 Handeloh Ger.
211 C6 Handeni Tanz.
168 E1 Handewitt Ger.
Handian *Shanxi* China *see* Changzhi
177 H3 Handlová Slovakia
168 F2 Handorf Ger.
168 C3 Handrup Ger.
105 F3 Haneda *airport* Japan
HaNegev *des.* Israel *see* Negev
168 E1 Hanerau-Hademarschen Ger.
Hanfeng *Chongqing* China *see* Kaixian
240 H3 Hanford *CA* U.S.A.
114 B3 Hangal *Karnataka* India
101 C5 Han-gang *r.* S. Korea
106 C1 Hangayn Nuruu *mts* Mongolia
Hangchow *Zhejiang* China *see* Hangzhou
Hangchuan *Fujian* China *see* Guangze
171 E3 Hangelsberg Ger.
Hanggin Houqi *Nei Mongol* China *see* Xamba
Hanggin Qi *Nei Mongol* China *see* Xin
Hangö Fin. *see* Hanko
107 H4 Hangu *Tianjin* China
123 G3 Hangu Pak.
109 G2 Hangzhou *Zhejiang* China
109 G2 Hangzhou Wan *b.* China
150 E3 Hanham *South Gloucestershire,* England U.K.
127 F3 Hani Turkey
125 E2 Ḩanīdh Saudi Arabia
199 F1 Hanife *r.* Turkey
177 K3 Haniska Slovakia
Hanjia *Chongqing* China *see* Pengshui
Hanjiang *Jiangsu* China *see* Yangzhou
109 F4 Han Jiang *r.* China
106 E4 Hanjiaoshui *Ningxia* China
140 N3 Hankasalmi Fin.
168 F3 Hankensbüttel Ger.
215 F5 Hankey S. Africa
141 M4 Hanko Fin.
199 G2 Hanköy Turkey
241 L2 Hanksville *UT* U.S.A.
116 D2 Hanle *Jammu and Kashmir*
223 J5 Hanley *Sask.* Can.
150 E2 Hanley Castle *Worcestershire,* England U.K.
81 D5 Hanmer Springs *South I.* N.Z.
85 F2 Hann *r. Qld* Austr.
86 E3 Hann *r. W.A.* Austr.
86 E2 Hann, Mount *hill W.A.* Austr.
223 I5 Hanna *Alta* Can.
175 L4 Hanna Pol.
241 M5 Hannagan Meadow *AZ* U.S.A.
236 F4 Hannibal *MO* U.S.A.
232 E3 Hannibal *NY* U.S.A.
232 C5 Hannibal *OH* U.S.A.
137 G3 Hannivka Ukr.
105 F3 Hannō Japan
157 F3 Hannonville-sous-les-Côtes France
169 E3 Hannover Ger.
169 E3 Hannover *admin. reg. Niedersachsen* Ger.
169 E4 Hannoversch Münden Ger.
84 C4 Hann Range *mts N.T.* Austr.
165 E4 Hannut Belgium
143 F4 Hanöbukten *b.* Sweden
Hanoi Vietnam *see* Ha Nôi
96 D2 Ha Nôi Vietnam
224 D4 Hanover *Ont.* Can.
Hanover Ger. *see* Hannover
246 □ Hanover *parish* Jamaica
215 E5 Hanover S. Africa
235 F1 Hanover *CT* U.S.A.
233 G3 Hanover *NH* U.S.A.
235 D2 Hanover *NJ* U.S.A.
234 B3 Hanover *PA* U.S.A.
232 E6 Hanover *VA* U.S.A.
259 B8 Hanover, Isla *i.* Chile
232 B6 Hanoverdale *PA* U.S.A.
214 E4 Hanover Road S. Africa
222 G3 Hansag *hill* Hungary
165 C3 Hansbeke Belgium
263 D2 Hansen Mountains Antarctica
170 C2 Hanshagen Ger.
109 D2 Hanshou *Hunan* China
109 E2 Han Shui *r.* China
116 D3 Hansi *Haryana* India
151 G2 Hanslope *Milton Keynes,* England U.K.
140 L1 Hansnes Norway
82 D2 Hanson, Lake *salt flat S.A.* Austr.
232 B6 Hansonville *VA* U.S.A.
168 F2 Hanstedt *Niedersachsen* Ger.
168 F2 Hanstedt *Niedersachsen* Ger.
142 C3 Hanstholm Denmark
107 H2 Han Sum *Nei Mongol* China
157 G4 Han-sur-Nied France
Hantengri Feng *mt.* Kazakh./Kyrg. *see* Khan-Tengri, Pik
177 H5 Hantos Hungary
138 F5 Hantsavichy Belarus
116 C4 Hanumana *Madh. Prad.* India
116 C3 Hanumangarh *Rajasthan* India
177 K2 Hanušovce nad Topľou Slovakia
176 F1 Hanušovice Czech Rep.
106 D1 Hanuy Gol *r.* Mongolia
158 B3 Hanvec France
83 F3 Hanwood *N.S.W.* Austr.
Hanyang *Hubei* China *see* Caidian
108 D1 Hanyin *Shaanxi* China
105 F2 Hanyū Japan
Hanyuan Gansu China *see* Xihe
108 B2 Hanyuan *Sichuan* China
108 C1 Hanzhong *Shaanxi* China
79 □3 Hao *atoll Arch. des Tuamotu* Fr. Polynesia
Haomen *Qinghai* China *see* Menyuan
117 G5 Haora *W. Bengal* India
185 E5 Haouz, Jebel el *hill* Morocco
140 N2 Haparanda Sweden
165 F3 Hapert Neth.
117 H4 Hapoli *Arun. Prad.* India
173 F2 Happburg Ger.
151 I2 Happisburgh *Norfolk,* England U.K.
241 L4 Happy Jack *AZ* U.S.A.
225 I2 Happy Valley - Goose Bay *Nfld.* Can.
164 E3 Haps Neth.
101 D4 Hapsu N. Korea
116 D3 Hapur *Uttar Prad.* India
126 D5 Ḩaql Saudi Arabia
210 D2 Hara Alol *mt.* Djibouti
124 C4 Ḩarad Yemen
128 B5 Ḩarad, Jabal al *mt.* Jordan
124 D3 Haradah Saudi Arabia
125 E3 Ḩaraḑh Saudi Arabia
138 G4 Haradok Belarus
138 G4 Haradotskaye Wzvyshsha *hills* Belarus
140 M2 Harads Sweden
138 F5 Haradzishcha Belarus
138 F5 Haradzyeya Belarus
117 E4 Haraiya *Uttar Prad.* India
124 C3 Ḩarajā Saudi Arabia
102 J5 Haramachi Japan
116 C2 Haramukh *mt.* Jammu and Kashmir
Haran Turkey *see* Harran
138 G4 Harany Belarus
123 H3 Harappa Road Pak.
213 F3 Harare Zimbabwe
215 E3 Ha Rasebi S. Africa
125 F4 Ḩarāsīs, Jiddat al *des.* Oman
175 K5 Harasiuki Pol.
122 C4 Harāt Iran
208 D2 Haraze-Mangueigne Chad
169 E4 Harbarnsen Ger.
206 C5 Harbel Liberia
100 C3 Harbin *Heilong.* China
171 C3 Harbke Ger.
151 I3 Harbledown *Kent, England* U.K.
123 F4 Harboi Hills Pak.
156 C3 Harbonnières France
227 F4 Harbor Beach *MI* U.S.A.
227 E4 Harbor Springs *MI* U.S.A.
225 K4 Harbour Breton *Nfld.* Can.
173 E3 Harburg (Schwaben) Ger.
151 F2 Harbury *Warwickshire,* England U.K.
241 K5 Harcuvar Mountains *AZ* U.S.A.
174 B3 Hard Austria
125 E4 Ḩardah, Wādī *r.* Yemen
116 D5 Harda Khas *Madh. Prad.* India
142 B1 Hardanger *reg.* Norway
142 A2 Hardangerfjorden *sea chan.* Norway
212 C5 Hardap *admin. reg.* Namibia
212 C5 Hardap Dam Namibia
141 I3 Hardbakke Norway
231 D5 Hardeeville *SC* U.S.A.
179 G2 Hardegg Austria
169 E4 Hardegsen Ger.
156 B2 Hardelot-Plage France
95 F1 Harden, Bukit *mt.* Indon.
172 D2 Hardenberg Neth.
164 E2 Harderwijk Neth.
87 C4 Hardey *r. W.A.* Austr.
172 D2 Hardheim Ger.
236 F4 Hardin *IL* U.S.A.
238 F2 Hardin *MT* U.S.A.
86 C4 Harding *r. W.A.* Austr.
215 G4 Harding S. Africa
234 D3 Harding Lakes *NJ* U.S.A.
87 C5 Harding Range *hills W.A.* Austr.
151 G2 Hardingstone *Northamptonshire, England* U.K.
164 D3 Hardinxveld-Giessendam Neth.
223 I4 Hardisty *Alta* Can.
116 E4 Hardoi *Uttar Prad.* India
172 C3 Hardt Ger.
Hardwar *Uttar Prad.* India *see* Haridwar
231 D5 Hardwick *GA* U.S.A.
232 G2 Hardwick *VT* U.S.A.
234 C1 Hardwood Ridge *PA* U.S.A.
237 F4 Hardy *AR* U.S.A.
82 D2 Hardy, Mount *North I.* N.Z. *see* Rangipoua
225 K3 Hare Bay *Nfld.* Can.
151 G3 Harefield *Greater London,* England U.K.
149 F2 Hare Hill *hill Scotland* U.K.
140 I3 Hareid Norway
165 C4 Harelbeke Belgium
164 F1 Haren Neth.
168 C3 Haren (Ems) Ger.
210 D2 Hārer Eth.
151 H3 Hare Street *Hertfordshire,* England U.K.
149 H4 Harewood *West Yorkshire,* England U.K.
128 B3 Harf el Mreffi *mt.* Lebanon
159 G2 Harfleur France
234 B3 Harford County *county MD* U.S.A.
107 H1 Hargant *Nei Mongol* China
Hargeisa Somalia *see* Hargeysa
172 B2 Hargesheim Ger.
210 E2 Hargeysa Somalia
197 G2 Harghita, Munţii *mts* Romania
197 G2 Harghita-Mădăraş, Vârful *mt.* Romania
203 H6 Hargigo Eritrea
165 E4 Hargimont Belgium
157 E2 Hargnies France
106 C4 Har Hu *l. Qinghai* China
216 □3c Haría *Lanzarote* Canary Is
126 E4 Harib Yemen
116 D3 Haridwar *Uttar Prad.* India
128 B4 Harif, Har *mt.* Israel
114 B3 Harihar *Karnataka* India
81 C5 Harihari *South I.* N.Z.
114 B3 Harihar pur *Karnataka* India
116 B5 Harij *Gujarat* India
138 D2 Hari kurk *sea chan.* Estonia
128 C1 Ḩārim Syria
104 A4 Harima-nada *b.* Japan
117 G5 Haringhat *r.* Bangl.
164 D3 Haringvliet *est.* Neth.
104 D2 Harinoki-dake *mt.* Japan
114 C4 Haripad *Kerala* India
123 H3 Haripur Pak.
128 C3 Ḩarīr, Wādī adh *r.* Syria
123 E3 Harī Rūd *r.* Afgh./Iran
141 K3 Härjåsjön Sweden
141 N3 Harjavalta Fin.
141 K3 Härjedalen *reg.* Sweden
176 F4 Harka Hungary
177 I5 Harkakötöny Hungary
140 M2 Hărkan *r.* Sweden
177 H6 Harkány Hungary
236 E3 Harlan *IA* U.S.A.
232 B6 Harlan *KY* U.S.A.
197 H2 Hârlău Romania
150 C2 Harlech *Gwynedd, Wales* U.K.
238 E1 Harlem *MT* U.S.A.
151 I2 Harleston *Norfolk, England* U.K.
234 C2 Harleysville *PA* U.S.A.
164 E1 Harlingen Neth.
237 D7 Harlingen *TX* U.S.A.
151 G3 Harlington *Bedfordshire,* England U.K.
151 H3 Harlow *Essex, England* U.K.
238 E2 Harlowton *MT* U.S.A.
156 D3 Harly France
232 B5 Harman *WV* U.S.A.
199 F2 Harmancık Turkey
129 B1 Harmanli Turkey
179 H2 Harmannsdorf Austria
234 B3 Harmans *MD* U.S.A.
164 D2 Harmelen Neth.
233 □I2 Harmony *ME* U.S.A.
226 A4 Harmony *MN* U.S.A.
234 C2 Harmony *NJ* U.S.A.
168 F1 Harmsdorf *Schleswig-Holstein* Ger.
168 F2 Harmsdorf *Schleswig-Holstein* Ger.
114 C3 Harnahalli *Karnataka* India
114 B2 Harnai *Mahar.* India
123 F4 Harnai Pak.
156 C2 Harnes France
238 C3 Harney Basin *OR* U.S.A.
238 C3 Harney Lake *OR* U.S.A.
140 L3 Härnösand Sweden
106 B1 Har Nuur *l.* Mongolia
183 H2 Haro Spain
232 B6 Harold *KY* U.S.A.
146 □H1 Haroldswick *Shetland,* Scotland U.K.
157 G4 Haroué France
114 B3 Harpanahalli *Karnataka* India
151 G3 Harpenden *Hertfordshire,* England U.K.
206 D5 Harper Liberia
237 D4 Harper *KS* U.S.A.
222 H3 Harper Creek *r. Alta* Can.
232 E5 Harpers Ferry *WV* U.S.A.
151 G2 Harpole *Northamptonshire,* England U.K.
168 D3 Harpstedt Ger.
Harqin Qi *Nei Mongol* China *see* Jinshan
Harqin Zuoqi Mongolzu Zizhixian *Liaoning* China *see* Dachengzi
241 K5 Harquahala Mountains *AZ* U.S.A.
116 D5 Harrai *Madh. Prad.* India
128 D1 Harran Turkey
124 C3 Ḩarrāt Kishb *lava field* Saudi Arabia
146 E2 Harray, Loch of *l.* Scotland U.K.
224 E3 Harricanaw *r. Ont./Que.* Can.
146 E5 Harrietfield *Perth and Kinross,* Scotland U.K.
151 H3 Harrietsham *Kent,* England U.K.
235 D1 Harriman *NY* U.S.A.
83 H2 Harrington *N.S.W.* Austr.
234 C4 Harrington *DE* U.S.A.
233 □J2 Harrington *ME* U.S.A.
225 J3 Harrington Harbour *Que.* Can.
146 B4 Harris *reg. Scotland* U.K.
82 C2 Harris, Lake *salt flat S.A.* Austr.
84 B5 Harris, Mount *N.T.* Austr.
146 A4 Harris, Sound of *sea chan.* Scotland U.K.
215 F2 Harrisburg S. Africa
237 F5 Harrisburg *AR* U.S.A.
237 F4 Harrisburg *IL* U.S.A.
236 C3 Harrisburg *NE* U.S.A.
232 B5 Harrisburg *OH* U.S.A.
227 I5 Harrisburg *PA* U.S.A.
168 E1 Harrislee Ger.
87 C7 Harrismith *W.A.* Austr.
215 G3 Harrismith S. Africa
81 B6 Harris Mountains *South I.* N.Z.
237 E5 Harrison *AR* U.S.A.
226 E3 Harrison *MI* U.S.A.
236 C3 Harrison *NE* U.S.A.
235 E2 Harrison *NY* U.S.A.
237 F6 Harrisonburg *LA* U.S.A.
232 D5 Harrisonburg *VA* U.S.A.
236 E4 Harrisonville *MO* U.S.A.
236 E4 Harrisonville *MO* U.S.A.
227 G4 Harriston *Ont.* Can.
227 F3 Harrisville *MI* U.S.A.
233 F2 Harrisville *NY* U.S.A.
232 C5 Harrisville *WV* U.S.A.
Harrodsville *North I.* N.Z. *see* Otorohanga
149 H4 Harrogate *North Yorkshire,* England U.K.
232 B6 Harrogate *TN* U.S.A.
227 I3 Harrowsmith *Ont.* Can.
141 K3 Harsa Sweden
106 C5 Har Sai Shan *mt. Qinghai* China
177 J4 Harsány Hungary
168 E2 Harsefeld Ger.
197 G3 Hârseşti Romania
168 F4 Harsewinkel Ger.
169 D4 Harsewinkel Ger.
122 A3 Harsin Iran
126 E2 Harşit *r.* Turkey
171 C4 Harsleben Ger.
197 H3 Hârşova Romania
140 L2 Harsprånget Sweden
140 L1 Harstad Norway
151 H2 Harston *Cambridgeshire,* England U.K.
116 D5 Harsud *Madh. Prad.* India
168 E3 Harsum Ger.
220 E3 Hart *r. Y.T.* Can.
226 D4 Hart *MI* U.S.A.
214 D3 Hartbees *watercourse* S. Africa
84 C3 Hart, Lake *salt flat S.A.* Austr.
86 E3 Hart, Mount *hill W.A.* Austr.
177 I5 Harta Hungary
107 I3 Hartao *Liaoning* China
215 F2 Hartbeesfontein S. Africa
215 F1 Hartbeespoort S. Africa
179 G3 Hartberg Austria
142 B1 Harteigan *mt.* Norway
168 F2 Hartenholm Ger.
156 D3 Hartennes-et-Taux France
172 D3 Hartenstein Ger.
149 G3 Harter Fell *hill England* U.K.
151 H3 Hartfield *East Sussex,* England U.K.
206 C5 Hartford Liberia
233 G4 Hartford *CT* U.S.A.
230 C4 Hartford *KY* U.S.A.
226 D4 Hartford *MI* U.S.A.
236 D3 Hartford *SD* U.S.A.
226 C4 Hartford *WI* U.S.A.
230 C3 Hartford City *IN* U.S.A.
171 D4 Hartha Ger.
172 C2 Harthausen Ger.
172 B4 Hartheim Ger.
149 F2 Harthill *North Lanarkshire,* Scotland U.K.
179 G3 Hârtibaciu *r.* Romania
178 C3 Hart im Zillertal Austria
236 D3 Hartington *NE* U.S.A.
179 E2 Hartkirchen Austria
225 H4 Hartland *N.B.* Can.
150 C4 Hartland *Devon, England* U.K.
233 □I2 Hartland *ME* U.S.A.
150 C4 Hartland Point *England* U.K.
150 E2 Hartlebury *Worcestershire,* England U.K.
149 H3 Hartlepool *Hartlepool,* England U.K.
149 H3 Hartlepool *admin. div.* England U.K.
234 A2 Hartleton *PA* U.S.A.
151 H3 Hartley *Kent, England* U.K.
237 C5 Hartley *TX* U.S.A.
Hartley Zimbabwe *see* Chegutu
222 D4 Hartley Bay *B.C.* Can.
151 G3 Hartley Wintney *Hampshire,* England U.K.
234 C3 Hartly *DE* U.S.A.
173 H2 Hartmanice Czech Rep.
169 E5 Hartmannsdorf Ger.
141 N3 Hartola Fin.
214 E3 Harts *r.* S. Africa
235 E□ Hartsdale *NY* U.S.A.
231 C5 Hartselle *AL* U.S.A.
173 E3 Härtsfeld *hills* Ger.
151 F2 Hartshill *Warwickshire,* England U.K.
151 F2 Hartshorne *Derbyshire,* England U.K.
237 E5 Hartshorne *OK* U.S.A.
84 C4 Harts Range *N.T.* Austr.
84 C4 Harts Range *mts N.T.* Austr.
231 D5 Hartsville *SC* U.S.A.
231 C4 Hartsville *TN* U.S.A.
215 F4 Hartswater S. Africa
237 E4 Hartville *MO* U.S.A.
232 C4 Hartville *OH* U.S.A.
151 G2 Hartwell *Northamptonshire,* England U.K.
231 D5 Hartwell *GA* U.S.A.
231 D5 Hartwell Reservoir *Georgia/S. Carolina* U.S.A.
114 C3 Harur *Tamil Nadu* India
106 B2 Har Us Nuur *l.* Mongolia
106 B1 Har Us Nuur *salt l.* Mongolia
106 E1 Haruuhin Gol *r.* Mongolia
226 C4 Harvard *IL* U.S.A.
239 F4 Harvard, Mount *CO* U.S.A.
87 B7 Harvey *W.A.* Austr.
225 H4 Harvey *N.B.* Can.
226 D2 Harvey *MI* U.S.A.
236 C2 Harvey *ND* U.S.A.
234 B1 Harveys Lake *PA* U.S.A.
151 F2 Harvington *Worcestershire,* England U.K.
151 F3 Harwell *Oxfordshire,* England U.K.
151 I3 Harwich *Essex, England* U.K.
233 H4 Harwich Port *MA* U.S.A.
151 E3 Harwinton *CT* U.S.A.
83 H2 Harwood *N.S.W.* Austr.
149 H4 Harworth *Nottinghamshire,* England U.K.
116 C3 Haryana *state* India
136 C1 Haryn' *r.* Belarus
Haryn' *r.* Ukr. *see* Horyn'
169 F4 Harz *hills* Ger.
171 C4 Harzgerode Ger.
129 E3 Hasan Dağı *mt.* Turkey
126 E3 Hasan Dağı *mts* Turkey
Hasan Guli Turkm. *see* Esenguly
127 F3 Hasankeyf Turkey
122 C5 Hasan Langī Iran
114 C3 Hasanparti *Andhra Prad.* India
199 F3 Hasanpaşa *Burdur* Turkey
122 A2 Ḩasan Sālārān Iran
114 C4 Hasanur *Tamil Nadu* India
128 E3 Hasbaiya Lebanon
128 B3 Hasbani *r.* Lebanon
126 E3 Hasbek Turkey
165 E4 Hasbergen Ger.
146 □H1 Hascosay *i. Scotland* U.K.
116 D3 Hasdo *r. Madh. Prad.* India
169 C3 Hase *r.* Ger.

168 E2 Haseldorf Ger.
168 C3 Haselünne Ger.
261 H2 Hasenkamp Arg.
169 F5 Hasenkopf hill Ger.
190 C1 Hasenmatt mt. Switz.
106 E2 Hashaat Mongolia
104 C3 Hashima Japan
104 B4 Hashimoto Japan
122 B3 Hashtgerd Iran
122 B2 Hashtpar Gīlān Iran
Hashtpar Gīlān Iran see Tālesh
122 A2 Hashtrud Iran
Hasić Bos.-Herz. see Srnice
123 H4 Hasilpur Pak.
237 D5 Haskell TX U.S.A.
129 C3 Hasköy Turkey
179 F2 Haslach an der Mühl Austria
172 C3 Haslach im Kinzigtal Ger.
149 H4 Hasland Derbyshire, England U.K.
143 F4 Hasle Bornholm Denmark
190 C1 Hasle Switz.
151 G3 Haslemere Surrey, England U.K.
142 D4 Haslev Denmark
149 G4 Haslingden Lancashire, England U.K.
168 E2 Hasloh Ger.
177 L5 Hășmaș Romania
197 G2 Hășmașul Mare mt. Romania
163 A5 Hasparren France
137 H5 Haspra Ukr.
129 C4 Hasretpınar Turkey
128 C1 Ḩaşş, Jabal al hills Syria
128 C1 Hassa Turkey
114 C3 Hassan Karnataka India
169 F5 Haßberge hills Ger.
168 E3 Haßbergen Ger.
168 E3 Hassel (Weser) Ger.
169 F4 Hasselfelde Ger.
165 E4 Hasselt Belgium
164 F2 Hasselt Neth.
169 E5 Haßfurt Ger.
204 B4 Hassi Aridal well Western Sahara
204 B5 Hassi Doumas well Western Sahara
205 G3 Hassi Messaoud Alg.
170 E2 Haßleben Ger.
171 C4 Haßleben Ger.
143 E3 Hässleholm Sweden
172 C2 Haßloch Ger.
172 D2 Haßmersheim Ger.
142 G1 Håstbo Sweden
169 E3 Haste Ger.
165 D4 Hastière-Lavaux Belgium
83 F4 Hastings Vic. Austr.
83 H2 Hastings r. N.S.W. Austr.
227 I3 Hastings Ont. Can.
80 F3 Hastings North I. N.Z.
151 H4 Hastings East Sussex, England U.K.
226 E4 Hastings MI U.S.A.
226 A3 Hastings MN U.S.A.
236 D3 Hastings NE U.S.A.
105 F3 Hasuda Japan
177 H2 Hat' Czech Rep.
177 L3 Hat' Ukr.
117 E4 Hata Uttar Prad. India
106 D2 Hatansuudal Mongolia
Hatay Turkey see Antakya
128 C1 Hatay prov. Turkey
234 C2 Hatboro PA U.S.A.
241 K3 Hatch UT U.S.A.
84 C4 Hatches Creek N.T. Austr.
237 F5 Hatchie r. TN U.S.A.
197 F3 Hațeg Romania
80 F3 Hatepe North I. N.Z.
102 □1 Hateruma-jima i. Japan
83 E3 Hatfield N.S.W. Austr.
151 G3 Hatfield Hertfordshire, England U.K.
149 I4 Hatfield South Yorkshire, England U.K.
234 C2 Hatfield PA U.S.A.
151 H3 Hatfield Broad Oak Essex, England U.K.
151 H3 Hatfield Peverel Essex, England U.K.
106 D1 Hatgal Mongolia
150 C4 Hatherleigh Devon, England U.K.
151 F2 Hathern Leicestershire, England U.K.
149 H4 Hathersage Derbyshire, England U.K.
116 D4 Hathras Uttar Prad. India
97 D5 Ha Tiên Vietnam
96 D3 Ha Tinh Vietnam
Hatisar Bhutan see Gelephu
250 D3 Hato Corozal Col.
247 E3 Hato Mayor Dom. Rep.
116 D5 Hat Piplia Madh. Prad. India
Hatra Iraq see Al Ḩaḑr
103 F6 Hatsukaichi Japan
116 D4 Hatta Madh. Prad. India
116 E5 Hatta Madh. Prad. India
83 E3 Hattah Vic. Austr.
164 F2 Hattem Neth.
173 E5 Hattenhofen Ger.
231 F5 Hatteras, Cape NC U.S.A.
264 E4 Hatteras Abyssal Plain sea feature S. Atlantic Ocean
169 D5 Hattersheim am Main Ger.
169 C5 Hattert Ger.
140 K2 Hattfjelldal Norway
115 D2 Hatti r. India
237 F6 Hattiesburg MS U.S.A.
169 C4 Hattingen Ger.
146 G4 Hatton Aberdeenshire, Scotland U.K.
151 F2 Hatton Derbyshire, England U.K.
95 G1 Hatton, Gunung hill Sabah Malaysia
169 F4 Hattorf am Harz Ger.
104 C4 Hattori-gawa r. Japan
97 B4 Hattras Passage Myanmar
168 E1 Hattstedt Ger.
141 N3 Hattula Fin.
177 I4 Hatvan Hungary
97 C6 Hat Yai Thai.
172 C3 Hatzenbühl Ger.
179 H4 Hatzendorf Austria
169 D5 Hatzfeld (Eder) Ger.
156 C2 Haubourdin France
210 E2 Haud reg. Eth.
172 B2 Hauenstein Ger.
142 B2 Hauge Norway
142 A2 Haugesund Norway
150 E2 Haughton Staffordshire, England U.K.
97 D5 Hâu Giang, Sông r. Vietnam
179 H2 Haugsdorf Austria
141 N3 Hauho Fin.
80 E3 Hauhungaroa mt. North I. N.Z.
80 E3 Hauhungaroa Range mts North I. N.Z.
140 N2 Haukipudas Fin.
140 O3 Haukivesi l. Fin.
141 N3 Haukivuori Fin.
164 F1 Haulerwijk Neth.
223 J4 Haultain r. Sask. Can.
80 F3 Haumoana North I. N.Z.
235 E2 Hauppauge NY U.S.A.
170 F3 Hauptgraben r. Ger.
215 F2 Hauptrus S. Africa
171 E4 Hauptspree r. Ger.
80 E2 Hauraki Gulf North I. N.Z.
81 A7 Hauroko, Lake South I. N.Z.
179 E3 Haus Austria
173 F4 Hausach Ger.
171 D4 Hausdorf Ger.
173 F2 Hausen Bayern Ger.
173 G3 Hausen Bayern Ger.
173 E2 Hausen bei Würzburg Ger.
172 B4 Hausen im Wiesental Ger.
172 C4 Häusern Ger.
179 F4 Hausham Ger.
138 E1 Hausjärvi Fin.
179 H2 Hausleiten Austria
179 G4 Hausmannstätten Austria
190 E2 Hausstock mt. Switz.
204 C3 Haut Atlas mts Morocco
Haut-Congo admin. reg. Dem. Rep. Congo see Orientale
157 G5 Haut-du-Them-Château-Lambert France
157 F5 Haute-Amance France
192 B2 Haute-Corse dept Corse France
160 D2 Hautecourt-Romanèche France
162 D3 Hautefort France
163 D5 Haute-Garonne dept Midi-Pyrénées France
206 C4 Haute-Guinée admin. reg. Guinea
208 D3 Haute-Kotto pref. C.A.R.
161 B3 Haute-Loire dept Auvergne France
160 E3 Hauteluce France
157 F4 Haute-Marne dept Champagne-Ardenne France
156 B3 Haute-Normandie admin. reg. France
225 G3 Hauterive Que. Can.
161 D3 Hauterives France
161 E4 Hautes-Alpes dept Provence-Alpes-Côte-d'Azur France
157 G5 Haute-Saône dept Franche-Comté France
157 F5 Haute-Saône, Plateau de France
160 E2 Haute-Savoie dept Rhône-Alpes France
165 F4 Hautes Fagnes moorland Belgium
163 C5 Hautes-Pyrénées dept Midi-Pyrénées France
162 B2 Hauteurs de la Gâtine reg. France
162 D3 Haute-Vienne dept Limousin France
160 D3 Hauteville-Lompnes France
156 D3 Hautevillers France
Haute-Volta country Africa see Burkina
165 E4 Haut-Fays Belgium
160 C2 Haut-Folin hill France
208 E3 Haut-Mbomou pref. C.A.R.
156 D2 Hautmont France
208 B5 Haut-Ogooué prov. Gabon
157 H5 Haut-Rhin dept Alsace France
159 I3 Hauts-de-Seine dept France
205 E2 Hauts Plateaux Alg.
Haut-Zaïre admin. reg. Dem. Rep. Congo see Orientale
240 □ Hauula HI U.S.A.
Hauvo Fin. see Nagu
81 E4 Hauwai South I. N.Z.
163 B5 Haux France
173 H3 Hauzenberg Ger.
Havana Cuba see La Habana
226 B5 Havana IL U.S.A.
151 G4 Havant Hampshire, England U.K.
197 H1 Havârna Romania
171 C3 Havel r. Ger.
165 E4 Havelange Belgium
170 D3 Havelberg Ger.
123 H4 Haveli Pak.
123 H3 Havelian Pak.
170 D3 Havelländisches Luch marsh Ger.
227 I3 Havelock Ont. Can.
81 D4 Havelock South I. N.Z.
81 C5 Havelock r. South I. N.Z.
Havelock Swaziland see Bulembu
231 E5 Havelock NC U.S.A.
84 C2 Havelock Falls N.T. Austr.
80 F3 Havelock North North I. N.Z.
164 F2 Havelte Neth.
237 D4 Haven KS U.S.A.
142 E1 Haverdal Sweden
150 C3 Haverfordwest Pembrokeshire, Wales U.K.
151 H2 Haverhill Suffolk, England U.K.
233 H3 Haverhill MA U.S.A.
114 B3 Haveri Karnataka India
169 F3 Haverlah Ger.
141 K3 Haverö Sweden
165 E4 Haversin Belgium
235 E1 Haverstraw NY U.S.A.
234 C3 Havertown PA U.S.A.
Havirna Romania see Havârna
177 H2 Havířov Czech Rep.
169 C4 Havixbeck Ger.
176 E2 Havlíčkův Brod Czech Rep.
140 N1 Havøysund Norway
177 J2 Havran mt. Slovakia
199 E2 Havran Turkey
199 F2 Havran r. Turkey
165 D4 Havré Belgium
238 E1 Havre MT U.S.A.
225 I4 Havre Aubert Que. Can.
234 B3 Havre de Grace MD U.S.A.
225 I3 Havre-St-Pierre Que. Can.
137 I3 Havrylivka Dnipropetrovs'ka Oblast' Ukr.
137 I3 Havrylivka Kharkivs'ka Oblast' Ukr.
136 D3 Havrylivtsi Ukr.
197 H5 Havsa Turkey
128 B1 Havutlu Turkey
126 D2 Havza Turkey
240 □D8 Hawaii i. HI U.S.A.
240 □D9 Hawaii state U.S.A.
266 H4 Hawaiian Islands N. Pacific Ocean
266 H4 Hawaiian Ridge sea feature N. Pacific Ocean
127 H5 Ḩawallī Kuwait
Hawar i. The Gulf see Ḩuwār
150 D1 Hawarden Flintshire, Wales U.K.
81 B6 Hawea, Lake South I. N.Z.
81 B6 Hawea Flat South I. N.Z.
80 E3 Hawera North I. N.Z.
149 G3 Hawes North Yorkshire, England U.K.
230 C4 Hawesville KY U.S.A.
240 □D8 Hawi HI U.S.A.
146 F6 Hawick Scottish Borders, Scotland U.K.
81 B6 Hawkdun Range mts South I. N.Z.
80 F3 Hawke Bay North I. N.Z.
82 D2 Hawker S.A. Austr.
82 E2 Hawkers Gate N.S.W. Austr.
225 J3 Hawke's Bay Nfld. Can.
80 F3 Hawke's Bay admin. reg. North I. N.Z.
233 F2 Hawkesbury Ont. Can.
150 E3 Hawkesbury South Gloucestershire, England U.K.
226 B4 Hawkeye IA U.S.A.
151 H3 Hawkhurst Kent, England U.K.
222 C3 Hawk Inlet AK U.S.A.
241 K3 Hawkins Peak UT U.S.A.
226 E1 Hawk Junction Ont. Can.
231 C5 Haw Knob mt. N. Carolina/Tennessee U.S.A.
246 C1 Hawksbill Cay i. Bahamas
233 □J2 Hawkshaw N.B. Can.
149 G3 Hawkshead Cumbria, England U.K.
238 F3 Hawk Springs WY U.S.A.
81 D5 Hawkswood South I. N.Z.
151 H3 Hawkwell Essex, England U.K.
85 G5 Hawkwood Qld Austr.
Hawlêr Iraq see Arbīl
151 G3 Hawley Hampshire, England U.K.
234 C1 Hawley PA U.S.A.
235 E1 Hawleyville CT U.S.A.
149 H3 Hawnby North Yorkshire, England U.K.
149 H4 Haworth West Yorkshire, England U.K.
125 E6 Ḩawrā' Yemen
128 B5 Ḩawşah hills Saudi Arabia
124 D3 Ḩawshah, Jibāl al mts Saudi Arabia
214 B6 Hawston S. Africa
235 D2 Hawthorne NJ U.S.A.
240 H2 Hawthorne NV U.S.A.
235 E1 Hawthorne NY U.S.A.
138 E5 Hawyz r. Belarus
151 H5 Haxby York, England U.K.
149 I4 Haxey North Lincolnshire, England U.K.
83 F3 Hay N.S.W. Austr.
222 H2 Hay r. Can.
226 B3 Hay r. WI U.S.A.
84 C4 Hay, Mount N.T. Austr.
102 J4 Hayachine-san mt. Japan
105 D1 Haya-gawa r. Japan
105 E3 Haya-kawa r. Japan
105 F3 Hayama Japan
157 G3 Hayange France
156 E2 Haybes France
137 I4 Haychur r. Ukr.
226 A3 Hay Creek MN U.S.A.
128 B4 Haydān, Wādī al r. Jordan
122 A2 Haydarābad Iran
199 G2 Haydarlı Turkey
199 E2 Haydaroba Turkey
241 L5 Hayden AZ U.S.A.
238 F3 Hayden CO U.S.A.
238 C2 Hayden ID U.S.A.
149 G4 Haydock Merseyside, England U.K.
149 G3 Haydon Bridge Northumberland, England U.K.
151 F3 Haydon Wick Swindon, England U.K.
223 M3 Hayes r. Man. Can.
221 I3 Hayes r. Nunavut Can.
236 C3 Hayes Center NE U.S.A.
84 B2 Hayes Creek N.T. Austr.
221 M2 Hayes Halvø pen. Greenland
231 D5 Hayesville NC U.S.A.
149 H4 Hayfield Derbyshire, England U.K.
226 A4 Hayfield MN U.S.A.
172 D3 Hayingen Ger.
125 G2 Ḩayl Oman
107 G2 Haylaastay Mongolia
150 B4 Hayle Cornwall, England U.K.
151 G4 Hayling Island England U.K.
125 G4 Haymā' Oman
126 D3 Haymana Turkey
85 G4 Hayman Island Qld Austr.
232 E5 Haymarket VA U.S.A.
138 G4 Hayna r. Belarus
237 E5 Haynesville LA U.S.A.
231 C5 Hayneville AL U.S.A.
150 D2 Hay-on-Wye Powys, Wales U.K.
Hayotboshi Toghi mt. Uzbek. see Khayatbashi, Gora
199 E1 Hayrabolu Turkey
129 B3 Hayrat Turkey
222 H2 Hay River N.W.T. Can.
222 H2 Hay River Reserve N.W.T. Can.
236 D4 Hays KS U.S.A.
238 E1 Hays MT U.S.A.
124 C5 Ḩays Yemen
202 B2 Hayshah, Sabkhat al salt pan Libya
232 B6 Haysi VA U.S.A.
262 N1 Hays Mountains Antarctica
236 C3 Hay Springs NE U.S.A.
237 D4 Haysville KS U.S.A.
136 E3 Haysyn Ukr.
236 D2 Hayti SD U.S.A.
149 G3 Hayton Cumbria, England U.K.
149 I4 Hayton East Riding of Yorkshire, England U.K.
136 E3 Hayvoron Ukr.
240 F3 Hayward CA U.S.A.
226 B2 Hayward WI U.S.A.
151 G4 Haywards Heath West Sussex, England U.K.
123 F3 Hazarajat reg. Afgh.
232 B6 Hazard KY U.S.A.
117 F5 Hazaribag Bihar India
117 E5 Hazaribagh Range mts Bihar India
122 D2 Hazār Masjed, Kūh-e mts Iran
156 C2 Hazebrouck France
149 G4 Hazel Grove Greater Manchester, England U.K.
226 C3 Hazelhurst WI U.S.A.
222 E4 Hazelton B.C. Can.
236 C2 Hazen ND U.S.A.
221 G2 Hazen Strait N.W.T./Nunavut Can.
231 D6 Hazlehurst GA U.S.A.
237 F6 Hazlehurst MS U.S.A.
151 G3 Hazlemere Buckinghamshire, England U.K.
235 D2 Hazlet NJ U.S.A.
234 C2 Hazleton PA U.S.A.
86 F4 Hazlett, Lake salt flat W.A. Austr.
177 K2 Hažlín Slovakia
176 B1 Hazlov Czech Rep.
Hazorasp Uzbek. see Khazarasp
129 F3 Häzrä Azer.
123 H3 Hazro Pak.
127 F3 Hazro Turkey
261 F4 H. Bouchard Arg.
151 H2 Heacham Norfolk, England U.K.
151 H3 Headcorn Kent, England U.K.
147 B3 Headford Rep. of Ireland
84 D4 Headingly Qld Austr.
151 G3 Headley Hampshire, England U.K.
82 B2 Head of Bight b. S.A. Austr.
146 D6 Heads of Ayr hd Scotland U.K.
226 C3 Heafford Junction WI U.S.A.
146 B4 Healabhal Bheag hill Scotland U.K.
240 F2 Healdsburg CA U.S.A.
237 D5 Healdton OK U.S.A.
83 F4 Healesville Vic. Austr.
149 I4 Healing North East Lincolnshire, England U.K.
232 D6 Healing Springs VA U.S.A.
149 H4 Heanor Derbyshire, England U.K.
150 C3 Heanton Punchardon Devon, England U.K.
265 I8 Heard Island Indian Ocean
237 D6 Hearne TX U.S.A.
224 D3 Hearst Ont. Can.
262 I2 Hearst Island Antarctica
236 C2 Heart r. ND U.S.A.
252 C3 Heath r. Bol./Peru
149 H4 Heath Derbyshire, England U.K.
83 F4 Heathcote Vic. Austr.
151 H4 Heathfield East Sussex, England U.K.
151 G3 Heathrow airport England U.K.
232 E6 Heathsville VA U.S.A.
237 E5 Heavener OK U.S.A.
237 D7 Hebbronville TX U.S.A.
234 B3 Hebbville MD U.S.A.
149 G4 Hebden Bridge West Yorkshire, England U.K.
107 G4 Hebei prov. China
83 F2 Hebel Qld Austr.
241 L4 Heber AZ U.S.A.
241 I5 Heber CA U.S.A.
241 L1 Heber City UT U.S.A.
237 E5 Heber Springs AR U.S.A.
173 G3 Hebertsfelden Ger.
173 F3 Hebertshausen Ger.
107 G5 Hebi Henan China
146 B5 Hebrides, Sea of the Scotland U.K.
225 I1 Hebron Nfld. Can.
235 F1 Hebron CT U.S.A.
226 D5 Hebron IN U.S.A.
233 F5 Hebron MD U.S.A.
236 C2 Hebron ND U.S.A.
236 D3 Hebron NE U.S.A.
128 B4 Hebron West Bank
Hebros r. Greece/Turkey see Evros
143 G2 Heby Sweden
222 D4 Hecate Strait B.C. Can.
243 H4 Hecelchakán Mex.
Hecheng Jiangxi China see Zixi
Hecheng Zhejiang China see Qingtian
108 D3 Hechi Guangxi China
172 C3 Hechingen Ger.
186 C2 Hecho Spain
165 E3 Hechtel Belgium
168 E2 Hechthausen Ger.
108 C2 Hechuan Chongqing China
Hechuan Jiangxi China see Yongxing
170 E3 Heckelberg Ger.
151 G2 Heckington Lincolnshire, England U.K.
171 C4 Hecklingen Ger.
234 C2 Hecktown PA U.S.A.
236 E2 Hector MN U.S.A.
81 E4 Hector, Mount North I. N.Z.
81 B6 Hector Mountain mts South I. N.Z.
246 □ Hector's River Jamaica
140 L2 Hedberg Sweden
172 C2 Heddesheim Ger.
Hede Jiangsu China see Sheyang
158 E3 Hédé France
141 K3 Hede Sweden
142 D2 Hedekas Sweden
164 E3 Hedel Neth.
143 F1 Hedemora Sweden
140 M2 Hedenäset Sweden
142 C4 Hedensted Denmark
169 F3 Hedersleben Ger.
171 C4 Hedersleben Ger.
176 G4 Hédervár Hungary
143 G1 Hedesunda Sweden
238 C2 He Devil Mountain ID U.S.A.
151 F4 Hedge End Hampshire, England U.K.
81 B7 Hedgehope South I. N.Z.
142 D1 Hedmark county Norway
149 I4 Hedon East Riding of Yorkshire, England U.K.
168 C3 Heede Ger.
164 E2 Heeg Neth.
169 C3 Heek Ger.
165 D4 Heel Neth.
168 E3 Heemsen Ger.
164 D2 Heemskerk Neth.
164 D2 Heemstede Neth.
165 D4 Heer Belgium
164 F2 Heerde Neth.
164 E2 Heerenveen Neth.
164 D2 Heerhugowaard Neth.
140 □ Heer Land reg. Svalbard
165 E4 Heerlen Neth.
165 E4 Heers Belgium
164 E3 Heesch Neth.
168 E2 Heeslingen Ger.
169 E3 Heeßen Ger.
164 E3 Heeswijk Neth.
164 F2 Heeten Neth.
165 E3 Heeze Neth.
128 B3 Ḩefa Israel
109 F2 Hefei Anhui China
108 D2 Hefeng Hubei China
231 C5 Heflin AL U.S.A.
100 D3 Hegang Heilong. China
114 C3 Heggadadevankote Karnataka India
141 J3 Heggenes Norway
234 B2 Hegins PA U.S.A.
176 G4 Hegyeshalom Hungary
179 H3 Hegykő Hungary
169 E4 Hehlen Ger.
Heidan r. Jordan see Haydān, Wādī al
171 C4 Heidberg hill Ger.
168 E1 Heide Ger.
173 F2 Heideck Ger.
172 C2 Heidelberg Ger.
215 G2 Heidelberg Gauteng S. Africa
214 C6 Heidelberg W. Cape S. Africa
169 E4 Heiden Ger.
190 E1 Heiden Switz.
168 E2 Heidenau Niedersachsen Ger.
171 E5 Heidenau Sachsen Ger.
173 E2 Heidenheim Ger.
173 E3 Heidenheim an der Brenz Ger.
179 G2 Heidenreichstein Austria
234 A3 Heidlersburg PA U.S.A.
102 J4 Hei-gawa r. Japan
169 E5 Heigenbrücken Ger.
149 H3 Heighington Darlington, England U.K.
149 I4 Heighington Lincolnshire, England U.K.
100 C2 Heihe Heilong. China
168 F1 Heikendorf Ger.
215 F2 Heilbron S. Africa
172 D2 Heilbronn Ger.
Heiligenbeil Rus. Fed. see Mamonovo
172 D4 Heiligenberg Ger.
170 C3 Heiligenfelde Ger.
170 D2 Heiligengrabe Ger.
168 F1 Heiligenhafen Ger.
169 E3 Heiligenhaus Ger.
179 G4 Heiligenkreuz am Waasen Austria
179 H4 Heiligenkreuz im Lafnitztal Austria
169 F4 Heiligenstadt Heilbad Ger.
173 F2 Heiligenstadt in Oberfranken Ger.
168 E2 Heiligenstedten Ger.
107 I2 Heilongjiang prov. China
100 E2 Heilong Jiang r. China/Rus. Fed. alt. Amur
164 D2 Heiloo Neth.
173 E2 Heilsbronn Ger.
157 E4 Heiltz-le-Maurupt France
Heilungkiang prov. China see Heilongjiang
140 □B3 Heimaey i. Iceland
172 B2 Heimbach Ger.
172 D2 Heimbuchenthal Ger.
169 F4 Heimburg Ger.
172 D4 Heimenkirch Ger.
173 G3 Heimertingen Ger.
179 G2 Heimschuh Austria
172 C3 Heimsheim Ger.
169 E4 Heinade Ger.
140 O3 Heinävesi Fin.
169 E4 Heinebach (Alheim) Ger.
171 F4 Heinersbrück Ger.
171 C3 Heinersdorf Ger.
173 F2 Heinersreuth Ger.
169 F3 Heiningen Ger.
165 C3 Heinkenszand Neth.
164 F2 Heino Neth.
141 N3 Heinola Fin.
Heinrichswalde Rus. Fed. see Slavsk
169 B4 Heinsberg Ger.
169 E4 Heinsen Ger.
97 B4 Heinz Bay Myanmar
97 B4 Heinze Islands Myanmar
107 I3 Heishan Liaoning China
107 H1 Heishantou Nei Mongol China
108 B1 Heishui Sichuan China
Heisker Islands Scotland U.K. see Monach Islands
168 E2 Heist Ger.
165 D3 Heist-op-den-Berg Belgium
128 A4 Heitân, Gebel hill Egypt
172 B4 Heitersheim Ger.
107 G4 Heituo Shan mt. Shanxi China
Hejaz reg. Saudi Arabia see Hijaz
107 H4 Hejian Hebei China
108 C2 Hejiang Sichuan China
109 D4 He Jiang r. China
107 F5 Hejin Shanxi China
110 D3 Hejing Xinjiang China
171 G5 Hejnice Czech Rep.
177 J4 Hejőbába Hungary
156 E2 Hekelgem Belgium
126 E3 Hekimhan Turkey
104 C4 Hekinan Japan
140 □C3 Hekla vol. Iceland
104 C3 Heko-san mt. Japan
106 D4 Hekou Gansu China
109 E2 Hekou Hubei China
Hekou Jiangxi China see Yanshan
Hekou Sichuan China see Yajiang
108 B4 Hekou Yunnan China
215 F1 Hekpoort S. Africa
143 H4 Hel Pol.
140 K3 Helagsfjället mt. Sweden
106 E4 Helan Shan mts China
165 E3 Helchteren Belgium
169 F5 Heldburg Ger.
173 G3 Heldenstein Ger.
171 C4 Heldrungen Ger.
185 E2 Helechal Spain
185 F1 Helechosa de los Montes Spain
197 H2 Helegiu Romania
117 H4 Helem Assam India
91 H6 Helen i. Palau
240 I3 Helen, Mount NV U.S.A.
238 D2 Helena MT U.S.A.
232 B4 Helena OH U.S.A.
113 □1 Helengeli i. N. Male Maldives
148 D3 Helen's Bay Northern Ireland U.K.
146 D5 Helensburgh Argyll and Bute, Scotland U.K.
84 C3 Helen Springs N.T. Austr.
80 E2 Helensville North I. N.Z.
179 F2 Helfenberg Austria
234 B2 Helfenstein PA U.S.A.
143 F4 Helge r. Sweden
142 D3 Helgenæs pen. Denmark
168 C1 Helgoland Ger.
168 C1 Helgoland i. Ger.
168 D1 Helgoländer Bucht b. Ger.
140 L3 Helgum Sweden
151 H2 Helhoughton Norfolk, England U.K.
Heligoland i. Ger. see Helgoland
Heligoland Bight b. Ger. see Helgoländer Bucht
Helixi Anhui China see Ningguo
Hellas country Europe see Greece
122 B4 Helleh r. Iran
164 F2 Hellendoorn Neth.
169 B5 Hellenthal Ger.
234 C2 Hellertown PA U.S.A.
164 D3 Hellevoetsluis Neth.
149 G3 Hellifield North Yorkshire, England U.K.
185 I2 Hellín Spain
151 H4 Hellingly East Sussex, England U.K.
Hell-Ville Madag. see Andoany
168 E2 Hellwege Ger.
240 G3 Helm CA U.S.A.
123 E4 Helmand prov. Afgh.
123 E4 Helmand r. Afgh.
Helmantica Spain see Salamanca
171 C5 Helmbrechts Ger.
171 C4 Helme r. Ger.
164 E3 Helmond Neth.
146 E3 Helmsdale Highland, Scotland U.K.
146 E3 Helmsdale r. Scotland U.K.
149 H3 Helmsley North Yorkshire, England U.K.
172 D2 Helmstadt Ger.
171 C3 Helmstedt Ger.
213 □K2 Helodrano Antongila b. Madag.
100 D4 Helong Jilin China
156 D2 Helpe r. France
241 L2 Helper UT U.S.A.
215 H3 Helpmekaar S. Africa
151 G2 Helpringham Lincolnshire, England U.K.
169 E3 Helpsen Ger.
170 E2 Helpter Berge hills Ger.
149 G4 Helsby Cheshire, England U.K.
168 E2 Helse Ger.
142 E3 Helsingborg Sweden
142 E3 Helsinge Denmark
Helsingfors Fin. see Helsinki
142 E3 Helsingør Denmark
141 N3 Helsinki Fin.
150 B4 Helston Cornwall, England U.K.
172 B2 Heltersberg Ger.
199 E2 Helvacı Turkey
149 F3 Helvellyn hill England U.K.
Helvetic Republic country Europe see Switzerland
164 E3 Helvoirt Neth.
203 F2 Helwân Egypt
156 D2 Hem France
173 F2 Hemau Ger.
Hembudu i. S. Male Maldives see Embudhu
151 G3 Hemel Hempstead Hertfordshire, England U.K.
169 C4 Hemer Ger.
240 I5 Hemet CA U.S.A.
173 E2 Hemhofen Ger.
236 C3 Hemingford NE U.S.A.
151 G2 Hemingford Grey Cambridgeshire, England U.K.
226 E1 Hemlo Ont. Can.
168 E1 Hemme Ger.
169 E3 Hemmingen Ger.
233 G2 Hemmingford Que. Can.
168 E1 Hemmingstedt Ger.
168 E2 Hemmoor Ger.
140 K2 Hemnesberget Norway
237 E6 Hemphill TX U.S.A.
151 I2 Hempnall Norfolk, England U.K.
151 H2 Hempstead Essex, England U.K.
235 E2 Hempstead NY U.S.A.
237 D6 Hempstead TX U.S.A.
172 C2 Hemsbach Ger.
168 E2 Hemsbünde Ger.
151 I2 Hemsby Norfolk, England U.K.
143 H3 Hemse Gotland Sweden
141 J3 Hemsedal Norway
141 J3 Hemsedal val. Norway
168 E2 Hemslingen Ger.
168 D3 Hemsloh Ger.
149 H4 Hemsworth West Yorkshire, England U.K.
150 D4 Hemyock Devon, England U.K.
106 D5 Henan Qinghai China
107 G5 Henan prov. China
142 D2 Henån Sweden
158 D3 Hénanbihen France
183 I3 Henar r. Spain
183 I5 Henarejos Spain
183 G4 Henares r. Spain
183 I5 Henares r. Spain
84 C5 Henbury N.T. Austr.
177 K4 Hencida Hungary
163 A5 Hendaye France
199 G1 Hendek Turkey
261 G5 Henderson Arg.
230 C4 Henderson KY U.S.A.
237 E6 Henderson LA U.S.A.
231 E4 Henderson NC U.S.A.
241 J3 Henderson NV U.S.A.
233 E3 Henderson NY U.S.A.
237 F5 Henderson TN U.S.A.
237 E5 Henderson TX U.S.A.
263 G2 Henderson Island Antarctica
267 K7 Henderson Island Pitcairn Is
231 D5 Hendersonville NC U.S.A.
231 C4 Hendersonville TN U.S.A.
Henderville atoll Gilbert Is Kiribati see Aranuka
151 G3 Hendon Greater London, England U.K.
122 C5 Hendorābī i. Iran
164 D3 Hendrik-Ido-Ambacht Neth.
215 H1 Hendriksdal S. Africa
215 G2 Hendrina S. Africa
Henegouwen prov. Belgium see Hainaut
151 G4 Henfield West Sussex, England U.K.
122 C5 Hengām, Jazīreh-ye i. Iran
109 G4 Hengch'un Taiwan
109 E3 Hengdong Hunan China
108 A2 Hengduan Shan mts Xizang China
164 F2 Hengelo Gelderland Neth.
164 F2 Hengelo Overijssel Neth.
173 H3 Hengersberg Ger.
164 F2 Hengevelde Neth.
190 D1 Henggart Switz.
Hengnan Hunan China see Hengyang
150 D3 Hengoed Caerphilly, Wales U.K.
100 D3 Hengshan Heilong. China
109 E3 Hengshan Hunan China
107 F4 Hengshan Shaanxi China
109 E3 Heng Shan mt. Hunan China
107 G4 Hengshui Hebei China
Hengshui Jiangxi China see Chongyi
108 D4 Hengxian Guangxi China
109 E3 Hengyang Hunan China
109 E3 Hengyang Hunan China
Hengzhou Guangxi China see Hengxian
137 H4 Heniches'k Ukr.
156 C2 Hénin-Beaumont France
Hénin-Liétard France see Hénin-Beaumont
81 C6 Henley South I. N.Z.
151 F2 Henley-in-Arden Warwickshire, England U.K.
151 G3 Henley-on-Thames Oxfordshire, England U.K.
151 G2 Henlow Bedfordshire, England U.K.
179 E3 Henndorf am Wallersee Austria
158 C4 Hennebont France
169 C5 Hennef (Sieg) Ger.
215 F2 Hennenman S. Africa
237 D4 Hennessey OK U.S.A.
157 G4 Hennezel France
171 E3 Hennickendorf Brandenburg Ger.
171 E3 Hennickendorf Brandenburg Ger.
170 E3 Hennigsdorf Berlin Ger.
233 H3 Henniker NH U.S.A.
168 E1 Hennstedt Ger.
172 B2 Hennweiler Ger.
162 E1 Henrichemont France
237 D5 Henrietta TX U.S.A.
241 L3 Henrieville UT U.S.A.
Henrique de Carvalho Angola see Saurimo
87 B4 Henry r. W.A. Austr.
226 C5 Henry IL U.S.A.
237 E5 Henryetta OK U.S.A.
262 T1 Henry Ice Rise Antarctica
Henryk Arctowski research stn Antarctica see Arctowski
174 F5 Henryków Pol.
175 I1 Henrykowo Pol.
241 L2 Henry Mountains UT U.S.A.
238 E3 Henrys Fork r. ID U.S.A.
227 G4 Hensall Ont. Can.
86 F3 Hensman, Mount hill W.A. Austr.
168 E2 Henstedt-Ulzburg Ger.
150 E4 Henstridge Somerset, England U.K.
107 F2 Hentiy prov. Mongolia
96 A3 Henzada Myanmar
Heping Guizhou China see Huishui
Heping Guizhou China see Yanhe
Hepo Guangdong China see Jiexi
165 E3 Heppen Belgium
172 C2 Heppenheim (Bergstraße) Ger.
238 C2 Heppner OR U.S.A.
168 E2 Hepstedt Ger.
Heptanesus is Greece see Ionioi Nisoi
108 D4 Hepu Guangxi China
108 B3 Heqing Yunnan China
107 F4 Hequ Shanxi China
Heraclea Turkey see Ereğli
Heraclea Pontica Turkey see Ereğli
Herakleion Kriti Greece see Irakleio
85 G3 Herald Cays atolls Coral Sea Is Terr. Austr.
244 C2 Herández Mex.
80 E3 Herangi hill North I. N.Z.
123 E3 Herāt Afgh.
123 E3 Herāt prov. Afgh.
113 □2 Herathera i. Addu Atoll Maldives
161 B5 Hérault dept Languedoc-Roussillon France
161 B5 Hérault r. France
161 C3 Herbasse r. France
159 H4 Herbault France
85 F3 Herbert r. Qld Austr.
223 J5 Herbert Sask. Can.
81 C6 Herbert South I. N.Z.
84 D4 Herbert Downs Qld Austr.
172 D3 Herbertingen Ger.
85 F3 Herberton Qld Austr.
214 C6 Herbertsdale S. Africa
147 C4 Herbertstown Rep. of Ireland
80 F4 Herbertville North I. N.Z.
87 E5 Herbert Wash salt flat W.A. Austr.
165 E5 Herbeumont Belgium
158 D4 Herbignac France
172 B3 Herbolzheim Ger.
169 D5 Herborn Ger.
173 E3 Herbrechtingen Ger.
169 F4 Herbsleben Ger.
169 E5 Herbstein Ger.
174 G5 Herby Pol.
183 H2 Herce Spain
Hercegfalva Hungary see Mezőfalva
177 H4 Herceghalom Hungary
196 D4 Herceg-Novi Crna Gora Yugo.
177 H6 Hercegszántó Hungary
256 B4 Herculândia Brazil
262 Q1 Hercules Dome ice feature Antarctica
169 C4 Herdecke Ger.
169 C5 Herdorf Ger.
177 M4 Hereclean Romania
242 □I7 Heredia Costa Rica
150 E2 Hereford Herefordshire, England U.K.
234 B3 Hereford MD U.S.A.
234 C2 Hereford PA U.S.A.
237 C5 Hereford TX U.S.A.
150 E2 Herefordshire admin. div. England U.K.
79 □3 Hérèhérétué atoll Arch. des Tuamotu Fr. Polynesia
80 D1 Herekino North I. N.Z.
185 G1 Herencia Spain
177 G4 Herend Hungary
165 D4 Herent Belgium
165 D3 Herentals Belgium
163 D5 Herenthout Belgium
161 B5 Hérépian France
169 D3 Herford Ger.
172 D4 Hergatz Ger.
Hergest Island Fr. Polynesia see Motu Iti
190 D2 Hergiswil Switz.
184 E1 Herguijuela Spain
158 E4 Héric France
160 E1 Héricourt France
159 G2 Héricourt-en-Caux France
160 E1 Hérimoncourt France
169 F5 Heringen (Werra) Ger.
170 C1 Heringsdorf Ger.
236 D4 Herington KS U.S.A.
81 B6 Heriot South I. N.Z.
146 F6 Heriot Scottish Borders, Scotland U.K.
127 G3 Heris Iran
190 E1 Herisau Switz.
160 A2 Hérisson France
262 S1 Heritage Range mts Antarctica
165 E4 Herk r. Belgium
165 E4 Herk-de-Stad Belgium
165 F3 Herkenbosch Neth.
233 F3 Herkimer NY U.S.A.
164 D3 Herkingen Neth.
107 F2 Herlen Mongolia
Herlen Gol r. China/Mongolia see Kerulen
107 H1 Herlen He r. China
169 F4 Herleshausen Ger.
240 G1 Herlong CA U.S.A.
158 D2 Herm i. Channel Is
163 A5 Herm France
179 F4 Hermagor Austria
136 E4 Hermanivka Ukr.
236 F4 Hermann MO U.S.A.
84 C4 Hermannsburg N.T. Austr.
168 F3 Hermannsburg Ger.
173 H2 Heřmanova Huť Czech Rep.
214 B6 Hermanus S. Africa
176 E2 Heřmanův Městec Czech Rep.
173 E3 Hermaringen Ger.
128 C2 Hermel Lebanon
160 A3 Herment France
172 B2 Hermersberg Ger.
215 G4 Hermes, Cape S. Africa
172 C3 Hermeskeil Ger.
83 F2 Hermidale N.S.W. Austr.
216 □3a Hermigua La Gomera Canary Is
182 D3 Hermisende Spain
238 C2 Hermiston OR U.S.A.
237 E4 Hermitage MO U.S.A.
232 C4 Hermitage PA U.S.A.
259 D9 Hermite, Islas is Chile
128 B3 Hermon, Mount Lebanon/Syria
Hermonthis Egypt see Armant
156 D3 Hermonville France
Hermopolis Magna Egypt see El Ashmunein
242 C2 Hermosillo Mex.
171 C5 Hermsdorf Ger.
177 J4 Hernád r. Hungary/Slovakia
177 J3 Hernádkak Hungary
253 G6 Hernandarias Para.
261 G3 Hernández Arg.
261 F3 Hernando Arg.
237 F5 Hernando MS U.S.A.
186 B1 Hernani Spain
183 F4 Hernansancho Spain
240 H3 Herndon CA U.S.A.
234 B2 Herndon PA U.S.A.
232 C6 Herndon WV U.S.A.
165 D4 Herne Belgium
169 C4 Herne Ger.
151 I3 Herne Bay Kent, England U.K.
142 C3 Herning Denmark
Heroica Nogales Mex. see Nogales
173 E2 Heroldsbach Ger.
173 F2 Heroldsberg Ger.
165 E4 Héron Belgium
226 D1 Heron Bay Ont. Can.
109 E2 Herong Hubei China
85 G4 Heron Island Qld Austr.
159 F2 Hérouville-St-Clair France
Herowābād Iran see Khalkhāl
179 H3 Herpenyő r. Hungary
169 F5 Herpf Ger.
258 F2 Herradura Arg.
244 D2 Herradura Mex.
183 G2 Herramélluri Spain
163 B5 Herré France
236 C2 Herreid SD U.S.A.
172 C3 Herrenberg Ger.
258 E3 Herrera Arg.
185 F3 Herrera Spain
186 B3 Herrera mt. Spain
185 E1 Herrera del Duque Spain
186 B3 Herrera de los Navarros Spain
183 F2 Herrera de Pisuerga Spain
183 I4 Herreria Spain
184 D1 Herreruela Spain
173 E2 Herrieden Ger.
236 F4 Herrin IL U.S.A.
172 B4 Herrischried Ger.
157 H4 Herrlisheim France
143 E2 Herrljunga Sweden
173 F4 Herrsching am Ammersee Ger.
143 H3 Herrvik Gotland Sweden
160 A1 Herry France
163 D5 Hers r. France
173 F2 Hersbruck Ger.
169 C5 Herschbach Ger.
169 C4 Herscheid Ger.
215 F4 Herschel S. Africa
172 B2 Herschweiler-Pettersheim Ger.
165 D3 Herselt Belgium
157 F3 Herserange France
227 I5 Hershey PA U.S.A.
261 G2 Hersilia Arg.
165 E4 Herstal Belgium
151 H4 Herstmonceux East Sussex, England U.K.
146 E3 Herston Orkney, Scotland U.K.
226 A3 Hertel WI U.S.A.
169 C4 Herten Ger.
151 G3 Hertford Hertfordshire, England U.K.
231 E4 Hertford NC U.S.A.
151 H3 Hertfordshire admin. div. England U.K.
136 D3 Hertsa Ukr.
215 E3 Hertzogville S. Africa
182 E4 Hervás Spain
165 E4 Herve Belgium
85 H5 Hervey Bay Qld Austr.
85 H5 Hervey Bay b. Qld Austr.
Hervey Island Cook Is see Manuae
267 I7 Hervey Islands Cook Is
164 E3 Herwijnen Neth.
172 C2 Herxheim bei Landau (Pfalz) Ger.
156 D5 Héry France
170 D3 Herzberg Brandenburg Ger.
171 E4 Herzberg Brandenburg Ger.
170 C2 Herzberg Mecklenburg-Vorpommern Ger.
169 F4 Herzberg am Harz Ger.
169 D4 Herzebrock-Clarholz Ger.
165 C4 Herzele Belgium
171 E3 Herzfelde Ger.
168 E2 Herzhorn Ger.
168 C3 Herzlake Ger.
128 B3 Herzliyya Israel
173 E2 Herzogenaurach Ger.
190 C1 Herzogenbuchsee Switz.
179 G2 Herzogenburg Austria
170 D2 Herzsprung Ger.
122 B3 Heşar Iran
156 C2 Hesdin France
168 C2 Hesel Ger.
108 D4 Heshan Guangxi China
109 E2 Heshengqiao Hubei China
107 F5 Heshui Gansu China
107 G4 Heshun Shanxi China
165 F5 Hespérange Lux.
240 I4 Hesperia CA U.S.A.
226 D4 Hesperia MI U.S.A.
222 E5 Hesquiat B.C. Can.
222 C2 Hess r. Y.T. Can.
173 E2 Heßdorf Ger.
Hesse land Ger. see Hessen
226 E2 Hessel MI U.S.A.
173 E2 Hesselberg hill Ger.
169 F3 Hessen Ger.
169 E5 Hessen land Ger.
172 C2 Heßheim Ger.
169 E4 Hessisch Lichtenau Ger.
169 E3 Hessisch Oldendorf Ger.
222 C2 Hess Mountains Y.T. Can.
169 F3 Hestern (Adenbüttel) Ger.
149 F4 Heswall Merseyside, England U.K.
96 D2 Het r. Laos
164 E3 Heteren Neth.
177 G5 Hetés Hungary
176 F5 Hetés hills Hungary
151 I2 Hethersett Norfolk, England U.K.
168 E2 Hetlingen Ger.
157 G3 Hettange-Grande France
172 C2 Hettenleidelheim Ger.
173 F3 Hettenshausen Ger.
172 D3 Hettingen Ger.
236 C2 Hettinger ND U.S.A.
149 G3 Hetton North Yorkshire, England U.K.
149 H3 Hetton-le-Hole Tyne and Wear, England U.K.
171 C4 Hettstedt Ger.
172 A2 Hetzerath Ger.
172 D3 Heubach Ger.
169 C4 Heubach r. Ger.
169 D5 Heuchelheim Ger.
156 C2 Heuchin France
169 F4 Heudeber Ger.
164 E3 Heukelum Neth.
Heung Kong Tsai H.K. China see Aberdeen
214 E3 Heuningneskloof S. Africa
215 F2 Heuningspruit S. Africa
165 E3 Heusden Belgium
164 E3 Heusden Neth.
169 D5 Heusenstamm Ger.
169 F5 Heustreu Ger.
172 A2 Heusweiler Ger.
233 F2 Heuvelton NY U.S.A.
177 J4 Heves Hungary
177 J4 Heves county Hungary
176 G5 Hévíz Hungary
177 I4 Hévizgyörk Hungary
176 F3 Hevlín Czech Rep.
Ḩevron West Bank see Hebron
235 D1 Hewitt NJ U.S.A.
232 E6 Hewlett VA U.S.A.
178 B3 Hexenkopf mt. Austria
149 G3 Hexham Northumberland, England U.K.
109 F2 Hexian Anhui China
109 D3 Hexian Guangxi China
Hexigten Qi Nei Mongol China see Jingpeng
106 D4 Hexipu Gansu China
151 H3 Hextable Kent, England U.K.
Heyang Hebei China see Nanhe
107 F5 Heyang Shaanxi China
151 H3 Heybridge Essex, England U.K.
Heydebreck Pol. see Kędzierzyn-Koźle
214 E4 Heydon S. Africa
169 E3 Heyen Ger.

Heyin Qinghai China see Guide
171 E4 Heynitz Ger.
160 D3 Heyrieux France
149 G3 Heysham Lancashire, England U.K.
215 H2 Heyshope Dam S. Africa
165 E3 Heythuysen Neth.
109 E4 Heyuan Guangdong China
82 E4 Heywood Vic. Austr.
149 G4 Heywood Greater Manchester, England U.K.
226 C5 Heyworth IL U.S.A.
107 G5 Heze Shandong China
108 C3 Hezhang Guizhou China
106 D5 Hezheng Gansu China
106 D5 Hezuozhen Gansu China
231 D7 Hialeah FL U.S.A.
Hiau i. Fr. Polynesia see Eiao
231 D5 Hiawassee GA U.S.A.
236 E4 Hiawatha KS U.S.A.
149 I4 Hibaldstow North Lincolnshire, England U.K.
215 H4 Hibberdene S. Africa
226 A2 Hibbing MN U.S.A.
83 F5 Hibbs, Point Tas. Austr.
86 D2 Hibernia Reef Ashmore & Cartier Is Austr.
237 F4 Hickman KY U.S.A.
231 D5 Hickory NC U.S.A.
234 C3 Hickory Hill PA U.S.A.
80 G2 Hicks Bay North I. N.Z.
235 E2 Hicksville NY U.S.A.
232 A4 Hicksville OH U.S.A.
237 D5 Hico TX U.S.A.
104 D3 Hida-gawa r. Japan
104 B5 Hidaka-gawa r. Japan
102 K2 Hidaka-sanmyaku mts Japan
104 C2 Hida-kōchi plat. Japan
243 F3 Hidalgo Coahuila Mex.
244 B1 Hidalgo Durango Mex.
245 E1 Hidalgo Tamaulipas Mex.
245 E3 Hidalgo state Mex.
242 D3 Hidalgo del Parral Mex.
177 H5 Hidas Hungary
104 D2 Hida-sanmyaku mts Japan
177 K3 Hidasnémeti Hungary
169 D3 Hiddenhausen Ger.
170 E1 Hiddensee Ger.
170 E1 Hiddensee i. Ger.
85 F3 Hidden Valley Qld Austr.
128 B1 Hıdırlı Turkey
197 F2 Hidişelu de Sus Romania
142 B2 Hidra i. Norway
256 C2 Hidrolândia Brazil
254 C5 Hidrolina Brazil
179 F3 Hieflau Austria
183 H3 Hiendelaencina Spain
78 □5 Hienghène New Caledonia
159 F4 Hière r. France
Hierosolyma Israel/West Bank see Jerusalem
183 G4 Hierro, Cabeza de mt. Spain
162 B3 Hiersac France
103 F6 Higashi-Hiroshima Japan
105 F2 Higashi-matsuyama Japan
105 F3 Higashimurayama Japan
102 J4 Higashine Japan
104 B4 Higashi-ōsaka Japan
103 D7 Higashi-suidō sea chan. Japan
105 D2 Higashi-yama mt. Japan
235 F1 Higganum CT U.S.A.
237 C4 Higgins TX U.S.A.
233 F3 Higgins Bay NY U.S.A.
214 D3 Higg's Hope S. Africa
151 H3 Higham Kent, England U.K.
151 G2 Higham Ferrers Northamptonshire, England U.K.
150 C4 Highampton Devon, England U.K.
High Atlas mts Morocco see Haut Atlas
149 G3 High Bentham North Yorkshire, England U.K.
146 D6 High Blantyre South Lanarkshire, Scotland U.K.
150 E3 Highbridge Somerset, England U.K.
234 D2 High Bridge NJ U.S.A.
151 F3 Highclere Hampshire, England U.K.
238 B3 High Desert OR U.S.A.
149 H3 High Etherley Durham, England U.K.
215 H4 Highflats S. Africa
151 H3 High Garrett Essex, England U.K.
246 □ Highgate Jamaica
151 H3 High Halden Kent, England U.K.
149 I3 High Hawsker North Yorkshire, England U.K.
149 G3 High Hesket Cumbria, England U.K.
237 E6 High Island TX U.S.A.
146 D4 Highland admin. div. Scotland U.K.
240 I4 Highland CA U.S.A.
234 B3 Highland MD U.S.A.
226 B2 Highland MN U.S.A.
235 E1 Highland NY U.S.A.
226 B4 Highland WI U.S.A.
234 B4 Highland Beach MD U.S.A.
235 E1 Highland Falls NY U.S.A.
234 D1 Highland Lake NY U.S.A.
235 D1 Highland Lakes NJ U.S.A.
226 D4 Highland Park IL U.S.A.
232 B3 Highland Park MI U.S.A.
235 D2 Highland Park NJ U.S.A.
240 H2 Highland Peak CA U.S.A.
241 J3 Highland Peak NV U.S.A.
235 E2 Highlands NJ U.S.A.
232 E6 Highland Springs VA U.S.A.
149 G4 High Legh Cheshire, England U.K.
222 G3 High Level Alta Can.
150 E2 Highley Shropshire, England U.K.
149 F3 High Lorton Cumbria, England U.K.
236 D2 Highmore SD U.S.A.
150 E3 Highnam Gloucestershire, England U.K.
149 H4 High Peak hill England U.K.
231 E5 High Point NC U.S.A.
234 D1 High Point hill NJ U.S.A.
222 G4 High Prairie Alta Can.
222 H5 High River Alta Can.
231 E7 High Rock Bahamas
83 F5 High Rocky Point Tas. Austr.
149 G3 High Seat hill England U.K.
231 D6 High Springs FL U.S.A.
High Tatras mts Pol./Slovakia see Tatry
235 D2 Hightstown NJ U.S.A.
151 F3 Highworth Swindon, England U.K.
151 G3 High Wycombe Buckinghamshire, England U.K.
242 D3 Higuera de Abuya Mex.
185 G3 Higuera de Arjona Spain
184 E2 Higuera de la Serena Spain
184 D3 Higuera de la Sierra Spain
184 D2 Higuera de Vargas Spain
184 D2 Higuera la Real Spain
247 □1 Higüero, Punta pt Puerto Rico
187 B6 Higueruela Spain
187 C5 Higueruelas Spain
247 E3 Higüey Dom. Rep.
105 F3 Higuri-gawa r. Japan
77 I3 Hihifo Tonga
210 E3 Hiiraan admin. reg. Somalia
138 D2 Hiiumaa i. Estonia
186 C3 Híjar Spain
94 C3 Hijau, Gunung mt. Indon.
124 B2 Hijaz reg. Saudi Arabia
105 E3 Hijiri-dake mt. Japan
92 C5 Hijo Phil.
183 H1 Hijuela r. Spain
105 E2 Hikabo-yama mt. Japan
103 E7 Hikari Japan
104 B5 Hiki-gawa r. Japan
241 J3 Hiko NV U.S.A.
104 C3 Hikone Japan
103 E7 Hiko-san mt. Japan
80 E1 Hikurangi North I. N.Z.
80 G2 Hikurangi mt. North I. N.Z.
129 F3 Hil Azer.
263 K1 Hilary Coast Antarctica
171 E5 Hilbersdorf Ger.
169 D5 Hilchenbach Ger.
241 K3 Hildale UT U.S.A.
169 F5 Hildburghausen Ger.
169 B4 Hilden Ger.
151 H3 Hildenborough Kent, England U.K.
169 F5 Hilders Ger.
149 I3 Hilderthorpe East Riding of Yorkshire, England U.K.
169 E3 Hildesheim Ger.
151 H2 Hilgay Norfolk, England U.K.
168 E3 Hilgermissen Ger.
173 F3 Hilgertshausen Ger.
117 G4 Hili Bangl.
168 C3 Hilkenbrook Ger.
87 B6 Hill r. W.A. Austr.
247 □4 Hillaby, Mount hill Barbados
Hillah Iraq see Al Ḥillah
214 C5 Hillandale S. Africa
232 B4 Hillard OH U.S.A.
236 D4 Hill City KS U.S.A.
236 C3 Hill City SD U.S.A.
241 M2 Hill Creek r. UT U.S.A.
234 B4 Hillcrest Heights MD U.S.A.
169 D3 Hille Ger.
164 D2 Hillegom Neth.
83 G3 Hill End N.S.W. Austr.
142 E4 Hillerød Denmark
81 D4 Hillersden South I. N.Z.
169 F3 Hillerse Ger.
143 E3 Hillerstorp Sweden
169 B5 Hillesheim Ger.
85 F3 Hillgrove Qld Austr.
227 F3 Hillman MI U.S.A.
87 C6 Hillman, Lake salt flat W.A. Austr.
236 F4 Hillsboro IL U.S.A.
236 F4 Hillsboro MO U.S.A.
236 D2 Hillsboro ND U.S.A.
233 H3 Hillsboro NH U.S.A.
239 F5 Hillsboro NM U.S.A.
232 B5 Hillsboro OH U.S.A.
238 B2 Hillsboro OR U.S.A.
237 D5 Hillsboro TX U.S.A.
226 B4 Hillsboro WI U.S.A.
247 □3 Hillsborough Grenada
147 E2 Hillsborough Northern Ireland U.K.
231 E4 Hillsborough NC U.S.A.
85 G4 Hillsborough, Cape Qld Austr.
169 C5 Hillscheid Ger.
226 E5 Hillsdale MI U.S.A.
233 G3 Hillsdale NY U.S.A.
227 I5 Hillsgrove PA U.S.A.
86 C4 Hillside W.A. Austr.
146 F5 Hillside Angus, Scotland U.K.
146 □G1 Hillside Shetland, Scotland U.K.
235 D2 Hillside NJ U.S.A.
224 C3 Hillsport Ont. Can.
83 F3 Hillston N.S.W. Austr.
232 C6 Hillsville VA U.S.A.
146 □G1 Hillswick Shetland, Scotland U.K.
147 E2 Hilltown Northern Ireland U.K.
240 □D9 Hilo HI U.S.A.
150 E3 Hilperton Wiltshire, England U.K.
173 F2 Hilpoltstein Ger.
157 H4 Hilsenheim France
169 D3 Hilter am Teutoburger Wald Ger.
84 D4 Hilton Qld Austr.
215 H3 Hilton S. Africa
151 F2 Hilton Derbyshire, England U.K.
232 E3 Hilton NY U.S.A.
227 F2 Hilton Beach Ont. Can.
231 D5 Hilton Head Island SC U.S.A.
173 F2 Hiltpoltstein Ger.
126 E3 Hilvan Turkey
164 E3 Hilvarenbeek Neth.
164 E2 Hilversum Neth.
172 C4 Hilzingen Ger.
116 D3 Himachal Pradesh state India
124 C2 Ḥimā Ḍarīyah, Jabal mt. Saudi Arabia
116 D2 Himalaya mts Asia
140 M2 Himanka Fin.
198 A1 Himarë Albania
80 E4 Himatangi North I. N.Z.
80 E4 Himatangi Beach North I. N.Z.
116 C5 Himatnagar Gujarat India
179 H2 Himberg Austria
168 F2 Himbergen Ger.
105 D1 Hime-gawa r. Japan
103 G6 Himeji Japan
102 J4 Himekami-dake mt. Japan
177 H5 Himesháza Hungary
215 G3 Himeville S. Africa
104 C2 Himi Japan
113 □1 Himmafushi i. N. Male Maldives
179 F4 Himmelberg Austria
142 C3 Himmelbjerget hill Denmark
168 E2 Himmelpforten Ger.
124 B5 Himora Eth.
128 C2 Ḥimṣ Syria
128 D2 Ḥimṣ governorate Syria
81 E4 Hinakura North I. N.Z.
92 C4 Hinatuan Phil.
136 E4 Hînceşti Moldova
246 D3 Hinche Haiti
85 F3 Hinchinbrook Island Qld Austr.
151 F2 Hinckley Leicestershire, England U.K.
226 C5 Hinckley IL U.S.A.
233 □I2 Hinckley ME U.S.A.
226 A2 Hinckley MN U.S.A.
241 K2 Hinckley UT U.S.A.
209 B6 Hinda Congo
111 B6 Hindan r. India
129 E3 Hindarx Azer.
116 D4 Hindaun Rajasthan India
173 E4 Hindelang Ger.
170 C3 Hindenburg Ger.
Hindenburg Pol. see Zabrze
149 I3 Hinderwell North Yorkshire, England U.K.
151 G3 Hindhead Surrey, England U.K.
149 G4 Hindley Greater Manchester, England U.K.
232 B6 Hindman KY U.S.A.
83 E4 Hindmarsh, Lake dry lake Vic. Austr.
117 F5 Hindola Orissa India
116 C4 Hindoli Rajasthan India
150 E3 Hindon Wiltshire, England U.K.
116 D5 Hindoria Madh. Prad. India
114 C3 Hindri r. India
81 C6 Hinds South I. N.Z.
142 D4 Hindsholm pen. Denmark
123 F3 Hindu Kush mts Afgh./Pak.
114 C3 Hindupur Andhra Prad. India
222 G3 Hines Creek Alta Can.
231 D6 Hinesville GA U.S.A.
116 D5 Hinganghat Mahar. India
151 H2 Hingham Norfolk, England U.K.
123 F5 Hingol r. Pak.
Hingol r. Pak. see Girdar Dhor
127 F3 Hınıs Turkey
234 B2 Hinkletown PA U.S.A.
140 □ Hinlopenstretet str. Svalbard
140 K1 Hinnøya i. Norway
105 F3 Hino Japan
92 B4 Hinobaan Phil.
104 C2 Hino-gawa r. Japan
104 C3 Hino-gawa r. Japan
182 D5 Hinojal Spain
184 D2 Hinojales Spain
185 H3 Hinojares Spain
185 F2 Hinojasas de Calatrava Spain
183 H3 Hinojedo mt. Spain
261 G5 Hinojo Arg.
184 D3 Hinojos Spain
183 I3 Hinojosa Spain
182 D4 Hinojosa de Duero Spain
186 C4 Hinojosa de Jarque Spain
185 E2 Hinojosa del Duque Spain
180 D2 Hinojosa de San Vicente Spain
233 G3 Hinsdale NH U.S.A.
168 C2 Hinte Ger.
178 C3 Hinteres Sonnenwendjoch mt. Austria
171 F5 Hinterhermsdorf Ger.
169 F5 Hinternah Ger.
190 E2 Hinterrhein Switz.
190 E2 Hinterrhein r. Switz.
173 H3 Hinterschmiding Ger.
170 F2 Hintersee Ger.
172 B2 Hinterweidenthal Ger.
172 C4 Hinterzarten Ger.
Hinthada Myanmar see Henzada
220 G4 Hinton Alta Can.
237 D5 Hinton OK U.S.A.
232 C6 Hinton WV U.S.A.
80 E2 Hinuera North I. N.Z.
190 D1 Hinwil Switz.
163 B5 Hinx France
Hiort i. Western Isles, Scotland U.K. see Hirta
178 C3 Hippach Austria
164 D2 Hippolytushoef Neth.
Hipponium Italy see Vibo Valentia
Hippo Regius Alg. see Annaba
Hippo Zarytus Tunisia see Bizerte
168 D2 Hipstedt Ger.
127 G3 Hirabit Dağ mt. Turkey
103 D7 Hirado Japan
150 D1 Hiraethog, Mynydd hills Wales U.K.
105 F1 Hiraga-take mt. Japan
104 B4 Hirakata Japan
117 E5 Hirakud Reservoir India
102 □1 Hirara Japan
103 F6 Hirata Japan
105 F3 Hiratsuka Japan
114 B3 Hirekerur Karnataka India
206 D5 Hiré-Watta Côte d'Ivoire
114 C3 Hiriyur Karnataka India
Hîrlău Romania see Hârlău
210 D2 Hīrna Eth.
137 I3 Hirnyk Donets'ka Oblast' Ukr.
175 M5 Hirnyk L'vivs'ka Oblast' Ukr.
102 J3 Hirosaki Japan
103 F6 Hiroshima Japan
103 F6 Hiroshima airport Japan
103 F6 Hiroshima pref. Japan
172 C3 Hirrlingen Ger.
173 F2 Hirschaid Ger.
173 F2 Hirschau Ger.
171 C5 Hirschberg Ger.
173 F4 Hirschberg mt. Ger.
Hirschberg Pol. see Jelenia Góra
173 G3 Hirschenstn mt. Ger.
171 E4 Hirschfeld Ger.
171 F5 Hirschfelde Ger.
172 C2 Hirschhorn (Neckar) Ger.
160 F1 Hirsingue France
137 H4 Hirsivka Ukr.
137 J3 Hirs'ke Ukr.
136 F3 Hirs'kyy Tikych r. Ukr.
156 E3 Hirson France
Hîrşova Romania see Hârşova
146 □ Hirta i. Western Isles, Scotland U.K.
179 H3 Hirtenberg Austria
142 C3 Hirtshals Denmark
105 F3 Hiruga-take mt. Japan
150 D3 Hirwaun Rhondda Cynon Taff, Wales U.K.
169 E5 Hirzenhain Ger.
104 C4 Hisai Japan
116 C3 Hisar Haryana India
199 F2 Hisarcık Turkey
Hisarköy Turkey see Domaniç
126 D2 Hisarönü Turkey
199 E3 Hisarönü Körfezi b. Turkey
123 G2 Hisor Tajik.
Hisor Tizmasi mts Tajik./Uzbek. see Gissar Range
Hispalis Spain see Sevilla
Hispania country Europe see Spain
246 D2 Hispaniola i. Caribbean Sea
Hissar Haryana India see Hisar
117 F4 Hisua Bihar India
127 F4 Hīt Iraq
103 E7 Hita Japan
183 G4 Hita Spain
105 G2 Hitachi Japan
105 G2 Hitachinaka Japan
105 G2 Hitachi-ōta Japan
113 □2 Hitaddu Addu Atoll Maldives
113 □2 Hitaddu i. Addu Atoll Maldives
151 G3 Hitchin Hertfordshire, England U.K.
Hithadhoo i. Addu Atoll Maldives see Hitaddu
103 E7 Hitoyoshi Japan
140 J3 Hitra i. Norway
178 A3 Hittisau Austria
170 C2 Hitzacker Ger.
179 G3 Hitzendorf Austria
173 F3 Hitzhofen Ger.
168 E2 Hitzhusen Ger.
190 D1 Hitzkirch Switz.
78 □5 Hiu i. Vanuatu
105 F2 Hiuchiga-take vol. Japan
79 □3 Hiva Oa i. Fr. Polynesia
222 F4 Hixon B.C. Can.
85 H4 Hixson Cay rf Qld Austr.
226 B3 Hixton WI U.S.A.
175 L5 Hiyche Ukr.
127 F3 Hizan Bitlis Turkey
142 D3 Hjallerup Denmark
143 F2 Hjälmaren l. Sweden
142 C2 Hjartdøld r. Norway
142 B2 Hjelmeland Norway
143 F2 Hjo Sweden
168 E1 Hjordkær Denmark
142 D3 Hjørring Denmark
142 D3 Hjuvik Sweden
96 B2 Hka, Nam r. Myanmar
96 B1 Hkakabo Razi mt. Myanmar
96 B2 Hkok r. Myanmar
96 B1 Hkring Bum mt. Myanmar
215 H3 Hlabisa S. Africa
96 B3 Hlaing r. Myanmar
Hlako Kangri mt. Xizang China see Lhagoi Kangri
215 H2 Hlatikulu Swaziland
176 F5 Hlebine Croatia
96 B3 Hlegu Myanmar
136 F2 Hlevakha Ukr.
136 E4 Hlinaia Moldova
177 H3 Hliník nad Hronom Slovakia
177 K3 Hlinné Slovakia
176 E2 Hlinsko Czech Rep.
197 H2 Hlipiceni Romania
191 J4 Hlm hill Croatia
137 G3 Hlobyne Ukr.
215 F3 Hlohlowane S. Africa
176 F3 Hlohovec Czech Rep.
177 G3 Hlohovec Slovakia
215 G3 Hlotse Lesotho
176 G2 Hlubočky Czech Rep.
176 D2 Hluboká nad Vltavou Czech Rep.
177 H2 Hlučín Czech Rep.
215 I3 Hluhluwe S. Africa
177 G3 Hluk Czech Rep.
137 G2 Hlukhiv Ukr.
136 E3 Hlukhivtsi Ukr.
138 G5 Hlusha Belarus
138 G5 Hlusk Belarus
136 C3 Hlyboka Ukr.
138 F4 Hlybokaye Belarus
136 D2 Hlynne Ukr.
137 G3 Hlyns'k Ukr.
136 C3 Hlynyany Ukr.
177 J2 Hniezdné Slovakia
177 J3 Hnilec r. Slovakia
136 E3 Hnivan' Ukr.
175 M6 Hnizdychiv Ukr.
136 C3 Hnizna r. Ukr.
177 I3 Hnúšťa Slovakia
136 C3 Hnyla Lypa r. Ukr.
137 I2 Hnylytsya Ukr.
136 F3 Hnylyy Tikych r. Ukr.
137 F4 Hnylyy Yelanets' r. Ukr.
207 F5 Ho Ghana
96 D2 Hoa Binh Vietnam
96 C2 Hoang Liên Sơn mts Vietnam
Hoang Sa is S. China Sea see Paracel Islands
83 F5 Hobart Tas. Austr.
237 D5 Hobart OK U.S.A.
237 C5 Hobbs NM U.S.A.
262 P1 Hobbs Coast Antarctica
129 B4 Höbek Dağı mt. Turkey
231 D7 Hobe Sound FL U.S.A.
215 F3 Hobhouse S. Africa
235 D2 Hoboken NJ U.S.A.
110 D2 Hoboksar Xinjiang China
177 G5 Hobol Hungary
142 D2 Hobøl Norway
107 G3 Hobor Nei Mongol China
Hobot Xar Qi Nei Mongol China see Xin Bulag
142 C3 Hobro Denmark
165 E5 Hobscheid Lux.
143 H3 Hoburg Gotland Sweden
210 F3 Hobyo Somalia
199 F2 Hocalar Turkey
178 D3 Hocharn mt. Austria
172 D2 Höchberg Ger.
179 F2 Hochbira hill Austria
168 E1 Hochdonn Ger.
172 D3 Hochdorf Ger.
190 D1 Hochdorf Switz.
172 C4 Höchenschwand Ger.
Hochfeiler mt. Austria/Italy see Gran Pilastro
179 E3 Hochfeind mt. Austria
157 H4 Hochfelden France
Hochgall mt. Austria/Italy see Collalto
173 G4 Hochgern mt. Ger.
179 E3 Hochgolling mt. Austria
169 F5 Höchheim Ger.
169 D5 Hochheim am Main Ger.
97 D5 Hô Chi Minh Vietnam
Ho Chi Minh City Vietnam see Hô Chi Minh
173 G4 Hochkalter mt. Ger.
178 E3 Hochkönig mt. Austria
179 F4 Hochobir mt. Austria
179 G3 Hochschwab mt. Austria
179 F3 Hochschwab mts Austria
172 B2 Hochspeyer Ger.
172 C2 Hochstadt (Pfalz) Ger.
173 E2 Höchstadt an der Aisch Ger.
173 E3 Höchstädt an der Donau Ger.
172 B2 Hochstetten-Dhaun Ger.
172 C2 Höchst im Odenwald Ger.
179 F3 Hochtor mt. Austria
178 C3 Hochunnutz mt. Austria
190 E2 Hochwang mt. Switz.
Hochwilde mt. Austria/Italy see L'Altissima
172 C2 Hockenheim Ger.
232 C5 Hocking r. OH U.S.A.
151 H3 Hockley Essex, England U.K.
151 F2 Hockley Heath West Midlands, England U.K.
175 K6 Hoczew Pol.
175 K6 Hoczewka r. Pol.
116 D4 Hodal Haryana India
177 L4 Hodász Hungary
104 C2 Hōdatsu-san hill Japan
210 F2 Hodda mt. Somalia
149 G4 Hodder r. England U.K.
151 G3 Hoddesdon Hertfordshire, England U.K.
Hodeidah Yemen see Al Ḥudaydah
177 J3 Hodejov Slovakia
168 E3 Hodenhagen Ger.
232 C5 Hodgesville WV U.S.A.
84 C2 Hodgson Downs N.T. Austr.
206 D2 Hodh Ech Chargui admin. reg. Maur.
206 C2 Hodh El Gharbi admin. reg. Maur.
177 J5 Hódmezővásárhely Hungary
205 G2 Hodna, Chott el salt l. Alg.
150 E2 Hodnet Shropshire, England U.K.
177 M4 Hodod Romania
179 H2 Hodonice Czech Rep.
176 G3 Hodonín Czech Rep.
197 G2 Hodoşa Romania
106 C1 Hödrögö Mongolia
215 G3 Hodsons Peak Lesotho
165 C3 Hoek Neth.
164 D3 Hoek van Holland Neth.
157 H4 Hœnheim France
165 E4 Hoensbroek Neth.
157 H4 Hœrdt France
100 D4 Hoeryŏng N. Korea
165 E4 Hoeselt Belgium
164 E2 Hoevelaken Neth.
164 D3 Hoeven Neth.
101 C5 Hoeyang N. Korea
171 C5 Hof Bayern Ger.
169 D5 Hof Rheinland-Pfalz Ger.
179 H3 Hof am Leithaberge Austria
178 E3 Hof bei Salzburg Austria
169 E5 Hofbieber Ger.
178 B3 Höfen Austria
168 F3 Höfer Ger.
233 G3 Hoffman Mountain NY U.S.A.
246 C1 Hoffman's Cay i. Bahamas
169 E4 Hofgeismar Ger.
169 D5 Hofheim am Taunus Ger.
169 F5 Hofheim in Unterfranken Ger.
173 H3 Hofkirchen Ger.
215 E4 Hofmeyr S. Africa
140 □D2 Höfn Iceland
143 G1 Hofors Sweden
140 □C2 Hofsjökull ice cap Iceland
103 E6 Hōfu Japan
Hofūf Saudi Arabia see Al Hufūf
142 E3 Höganäs Sweden
83 F4 Hogan Group is Tas. Austr.
233 F2 Hogansburg NY U.S.A.
85 F5 Hoganthulla Creek r. Qld Austr.
84 D4 Hogarth, Mount hill N.T. Austr.
222 C2 Hogg, Mount Y.T. Can.
205 G5 Hoggar plat. Alg.
143 G3 Högsby Sweden
143 F2 Högsjö Sweden
141 I3 Høgste Breakulen mt. Norway
149 J4 Hogsthorpe Lincolnshire, England U.K.
177 H5 Hőgyész Hungary
238 A2 Hoh r. WA U.S.A.
172 B3 Hohberg Ger.
171 D4 Hohburg Ger.
179 E4 Hohe Leier mt. Austria
178 E4 Hohe Leiten mt. Austria
173 E3 Hohen-Altheim Ger.
168 E2 Hohenaspe Ger.
173 H3 Hohenau Ger.
179 H2 Hohenau an der March Austria
179 G3 Hohenberg Austria
171 F4 Hohenbocka Ger.
179 H4 Hohenbrugg-Weinberg Austria
173 F3 Hohenbrunn Ger.
171 E4 Hohenbucko Ger.
173 F2 Hohenburg Ger.
171 C3 Hohendodeleben Ger.
170 E1 Hohendorf Ger.
169 F4 Hohenebra Ger.
179 G2 Hoheneich Austria
178 A3 Hohenems Austria
173 F2 Hohenfels Ger.
173 E4 Hohenfurch Ger.
170 D3 Hohengöhren Ger.
169 F3 Hohenhameln Ger.
173 F3 Hohenkammer Ger.
168 C2 Hohenkirchen Ger.
171 E4 Hohenleipisch Ger.
171 D5 Hohenleuben Ger.
173 F3 Hohenlinden Ger.
168 E2 Hohenlockstedt Ger.
172 D2 Hohenloher Ebene plain Ger.
170 E2 Hohenmocker Ger.
171 D4 Hohenmölsen Ger.
170 D3 Hohennauen Ger.
170 E3 Hohen Neuendorf Berlin Ger.
179 F3 Hohe Nock mt. Austria
169 E5 Hohenroda-Ransbach Ger.
169 F5 Hohenroth Ger.
170 F3 Hohensaaten Ger.
Hohensalza Pol. see Inowrocław
171 D3 Hohenseeden Ger.
171 D5 Hohenstein-Ernstthal Ger.
172 D3 Hohentengen Ger.
172 C4 Hohentengen am Hochrhein Ger.
173 G3 Hohenthann Ger.
171 D4 Hohenthurm Ger.
231 C5 Hohenwald TN U.S.A.
170 D2 Hohen Wangelin Ger.
173 F3 Hohenwart Ger.
173 G2 Hohenwarth Ger.
168 E1 Hohenwestedt Ger.
170 C3 Hohenwulsch Ger.
179 E2 Hohenzell Austria
179 E3 Hoher Dachstein mt. Austria
Hoh Ereg Nei Mongol China see Wuchuan
178 E3 Hoher Göll mt. Austria/Ger.
169 E5 Hohe Rhön mts Ger.
178 B3 Hoher Ifen mt. Austria/Ger.
178 D3 Hohe Salve mt. Austria
169 E4 Hohes Gras hill Ger.
169 F4 Hohes Kreuz Ger.
178 D3 Hohe Tauern mts Austria
165 F4 Hohe Venn moorland Belgium
190 C2 Hohgant mt. Switz.
Hohhot Nei Mongol China see Huhhot
172 C3 Hohloh hill Ger.
169 C5 Höhn Ger.
168 E1 Hohn Schleswig-Holstein Ger.
168 F3 Hohne Ger.
157 H4 Hohneck mt. France
168 F2 Hohnstorf (Elbe) Ger.
207 F5 Hohoe Ghana
137 G3 Hoholeve Ukr.
137 F2 Hoholiv Ukr.
137 H4 Hoholivka Ukr.
168 F1 Hohwacht (Ostsee) Ger.
111 E5 Hoh Xil Shan mts China
96 E4 Hôi An Vietnam
210 A4 Hoima Uganda
168 F2 Hoisdorf Ger.
236 D4 Hoisington KS U.S.A.
106 C4 Hoit Taria Qinghai China
117 H4 Hojai Assam India
Hojambaz Turkm. see Khodzhambaz
168 D1 Højer Denmark
103 F7 Hōjo Japan
96 C2 Hok r. Myanmar
143 E3 Hökensås hills Sweden
80 D1 Hokianga Harbour North I. N.Z.
105 G2 Hōki-gawa r. Japan
80 E4 Hokio Beach North I. N.Z.
81 C5 Hokitika South I. N.Z.
100 G4 Hokkaidō i. Japan
102 K2 Hokkaidō pref. Japan
142 C2 Hokksund Norway
122 D2 Hokmābād Iran
81 B7 Hokonui South I. N.Z.
81 B6 Hokonui Hills South I. N.Z.
129 D3 Hoktemberyan Armenia
105 E1 Hokura-gawa r. Japan
142 C1 Hol Buskerud Norway
140 L1 Hol Nordland Norway
177 J3 Hoľa mt. Slovakia
114 C3 Holalkere Karnataka India
137 G4 Hola Prystan' Ukr.
142 D4 Holbæk Denmark
215 H2 Holbank S. Africa
151 H2 Holbeach Lincolnshire, England U.K.
222 D5 Holberg B.C. Can.
168 E1 Holbøl Denmark
85 G3 Holborne Island Qld Austr.
83 F3 Holbrook N.S.W. Austr.
151 I3 Holbrook Suffolk, England U.K.
241 L4 Holbrook AZ U.S.A.
235 E2 Holbrook NY U.S.A.
226 B3 Holcombe WI U.S.A.
223 H4 Holden Alta Can.
149 G4 Holden Lancashire, England U.K.
241 K2 Holden UT U.S.A.
237 D5 Holdenville OK U.S.A.
149 I4 Holderness pen. England U.K.
168 D3 Holdorf Ger.
236 D3 Holdrege NE U.S.A.
168 G1 Holeby Denmark
114 C3 Hole Narsipur Karnataka India
177 G2 Holešov Czech Rep.
232 A4 Holgate OH U.S.A.
182 D5 Holguera Spain
246 C2 Holguín Cuba
176 G3 Holíč Slovakia
176 E1 Holice Czech Rep.
137 G2 Holinka Ukr.
141 K3 Höljes Sweden
179 H2 Hollabrunn Austria
169 C3 Hollage (Wallenhorst) Ger.
Holland country Europe see Netherlands
226 D4 Holland MI U.S.A.
232 D3 Holland NY U.S.A.
232 B4 Holland OH U.S.A.
237 F5 Hollandale MS U.S.A.
Hollandia Irian Jaya Indon. see Jayapura
151 I3 Holland-on-Sea Essex, England U.K.
164 F2 Hollandscheveld Neth.
146 F2 Hollandstoun Scotland U.K.
165 E5 Hollange Belgium
169 F3 Holle Ger.
171 C4 Holleben Ger.
173 F3 Hollenbach Ger.
168 F2 Hollenbek Ger.
179 G4 Hollenegg Austria
168 E2 Hollenstedt Ger.
179 F3 Hollenstein an der Ybbs Austria
232 D3 Holley NY U.S.A.
173 F2 Hollfeld Ger.
262 T2 Hollick-Kenyon Peninsula Antarctica
262 Q1 Hollick-Kenyon Plateau Antarctica
232 D4 Hollidaysburg PA U.S.A.
168 E1 Hollingstedt Ger.
151 H4 Hollington East Sussex, England U.K.
149 H4 Hollingworth Greater Manchester, England U.K.
222 C4 Hollis AK U.S.A.
237 D5 Hollis OK U.S.A.
240 G3 Hollister CA U.S.A.
177 K3 Hollóháza Hungary
141 N3 Hollola Fin.
164 E1 Hollum Neth.
227 F4 Holly MI U.S.A.
148 E2 Hollybush East Ayrshire, Scotland U.K.
150 E2 Hollybush Worcestershire, England U.K.
81 A6 Hollyford r. South I. N.Z.
235 D3 Holly Park NJ U.S.A.
237 F5 Holly Springs MS U.S.A.
147 E3 Hollywood Rep. of Ireland
231 D7 Hollywood FL U.S.A.
168 E2 Holm Ger.
136 E4 Hol'ma Ukr.
220 G2 Holman N.W.T. Can.
235 D2 Holmdel NJ U.S.A.
215 G2 Holmdene S. Africa
149 I4 Holme-on-Spalding-Moor East Riding of Yorkshire, England U.K.
235 E1 Holmes NY U.S.A.
149 G4 Holmes Chapel Cheshire, England U.K.
149 H4 Holmesfield Derbyshire, England U.K.
85 F3 Holmes Reef Coral Sea Is Terr. Austr.
142 D2 Holmestrand Norway
232 C4 Holmesville OH U.S.A.
149 H4 Holmfirth West Yorkshire, England U.K.
Holmgard Rus. Fed. see Velikiy Novgorod
140 M3 Holmsund Sweden
141 L3 Holmsveden Sweden
136 C2 Holoby Ukr.
177 L5 Holod Romania
197 F2 Holod r. Romania
136 C3 Holohory hills Ukr.
128 B3 Ḥolon Israel
86 E2 Holothuria Banks rf W.A. Austr.
173 H2 Holoubkov Czech Rep.
136 F3 Holovanivs'k Ukr.
136 B3 Holovets'ko Ukr.
137 G3 Holovkivka Ukr.
175 M4 Holovne Ukr.
136 E2 Holovyne Ukr.
85 E2 Holroyd r. Qld Austr.
142 E3 Holsljunga Sweden
215 G2 Holspruit r. S. Africa
168 D2 Holste Ger.
142 C3 Holstebro Denmark
142 C4 Holsted Denmark
190 C1 Hölstein Switz.
236 E3 Holstein IA U.S.A.
Holsteinsborg Greenland see Sisimiut
232 B6 Holston r. TN U.S.A.
150 C4 Holsworthy Devon, England U.K.
151 I2 Holt Norfolk, England U.K.
150 E3 Holt Wiltshire, England U.K.
150 E1 Holt Wrexham, Wales U.K.
226 E4 Holt MI U.S.A.
164 F2 Holten Neth.
168 C2 Holtgast Ger.
170 C2 Holthusen Ger.
168 C2 Holtland Ger.
236 E4 Holton KS U.S.A.
226 D4 Holton MI U.S.A.
149 I4 Holton le Clay Lincolnshire, England U.K.
168 C2 Holtrop (Großefehn) Ger.
168 E1 Holtsee Ger.
241 J5 Holtville CA U.S.A.
234 B3 Holtwood PA U.S.A.
240 □D9 Holualoa HI U.S.A.
137 H3 Holubivka Ukr.
164 E1 Holwerd Neth.
164 F1 Holwierde Neth.
147 D4 Holycross Rep. of Ireland
220 C3 Holy Cross AK U.S.A.
239 F4 Holy Cross, Mount of the CO U.S.A.
150 C1 Holyhead Isle of Anglesey, Wales U.K.
150 C1 Holyhead Bay Wales U.K.
149 H2 Holy Island England U.K.
146 C6 Holy Island Scotland U.K.
150 C1 Holy Island Wales U.K.
236 C3 Holyoke CO U.S.A.
233 G3 Holyoke MA U.S.A.
Holy See Europe see Vatican City
150 D1 Holywell Flintshire, Wales U.K.
147 D2 Holywell Northern Ireland U.K.
146 E6 Holywood Dumfries and Galloway, Scotland U.K.
147 F2 Holywood Northern Ireland U.K.
169 C5 Holzappel Ger.
171 E4 Holzdorf Ger.
169 E4 Holzen Ger.
172 D3 Holzgerlingen Ger.
171 D4 Holzhausen Ger.
169 C5 Holzhausen an der Haide Ger.
173 E3 Holzheim Bayern Ger.
173 E3 Holzheim Bayern Ger.
173 E3 Holzheim Bayern Ger.
169 D5 Holzheim Hessen Ger.
173 F4 Holzkirchen Ger.
169 E4 Holzminden Ger.
169 F4 Holzthaleben Ger.
171 D4 Holzweißig Ger.
169 C4 Holzwickede Ger.
210 B5 Homa Bay Kenya
96 A1 Homalin Myanmar
222 E5 Homathko r. B.C. Can.
Homāyūnshahr Iran see Khomeynīshahr
169 E4 Homberg (Efze) Ger.
169 D5 Homberg (Ohm) Ger.
156 C3 Hombleux France
206 E3 Hombori Mali
157 G3 Hombourg-Budange France
157 G3 Hombourg-Haut France
172 B2 Homburg Ger.
221 L3 Home Bay Nunavut Can.
157 F3 Homécourt France
85 F3 Home Hill Qld Austr.
86 □2 Home Island Cocos Is
182 B3 Homem r. Port.
220 C4 Homer AK U.S.A.
231 D5 Homer GA U.S.A.
237 E5 Homer LA U.S.A.
226 E4 Homer MI U.S.A.
233 E3 Homer NY U.S.A.
232 D4 Homer City PA U.S.A.
151 I2 Homersfield Suffolk, England U.K.
231 D6 Homerville GA U.S.A.
85 F4 Homestead Qld Austr.
231 D7 Homestead FL U.S.A.
234 C2 Hometown PA U.S.A.
234 C3 Homeville PA U.S.A.
81 E4 Homewood North I. N.Z.
231 C5 Homewood AL U.S.A.
140 J3 Hommelvik Norway
114 C2 Homnabad Karnataka India
197 H2 Homocea Romania
177 I5 Homokmégy Hungary
177 G5 Homokszentgyörgy Hungary
177 M4 Homoroade Romania
177 L3 Homorod r. Romania
Homs Libya see Al Khums
Homs Syria see Ḥimṣ
137 F1 Homyel' Belarus
Homyel Oblast admin. div. Belarus see Homyel'skaya Voblasts'
139 G5 Homyel'skaya Voblasts' admin. div. Belarus
232 C6 Honaker VA U.S.A.
Honan prov. China see Henan
240 □D9 Honaunau HI U.S.A.
114 C3 Honavalli Karnataka India
114 B3 Honavar Karnataka India
199 F3 Honaz Turkey
136 F2 Honcharivs'ke Ukr.
250 C3 Honda Col.
117 F5 Honda Orissa India
117 F5 Hondapa Orissa India
186 B1 Hondarribia Spain
214 E4 Hondeblaf r. S. Africa
214 A4 Hondeklipbaai S. Africa
243 H5 Hondo r. Belize/Mex.
103 E7 Hondo Japan
239 F5 Hondo NM U.S.A.
237 D6 Hondo TX U.S.A.
239 F5 Hondo r. NM U.S.A.
187 C6 Hondón de las Nieves Spain
187 C6 Hondón de los Frailes Spain
156 C2 Hondschoote France
246 A4 Honduras country Central America
242 □I5 Honduras, Gulf of Belize/Hond.
190 C3 Hône Italy
142 D1 Hønefoss Norway
232 E3 Honeoye Falls NY U.S.A.
234 C1 Honesdale PA U.S.A.
234 C2 Honey Brook PA U.S.A.
159 G2 Honfleur France
96 D2 Hong, Mouths of the Vietnam
96 D2 Hông, Sông r. Vietnam
109 E2 Hong'an Hubei China
101 C5 Hongch'ŏn S. Korea
96 D2 Hông Gai Vietnam
110 E4 Honggouzi Qinghai China
96 D1 Hongguo Guizhou China
109 E4 Honghai Wan b. China
108 B4 Honghe Yunnan China
109 E1 Hong He r. China
109 E2 Honghu Hubei China
Hongjialou Shandong China see Licheng
108 D3 Hongjiang Hunan China
Hongjiang Sichuan China see Wangcang
109 □ Hong Kong H.K. China
109 E4 Hong Kong special admin. reg. China
107 F4 Hongliu r. China
Hongliuwan Gansu China see Aksay
110 F3 Hongliuyuan Gansu China
97 D5 Hông Ngư Vietnam
Hongqiao Hunan China see Qidong
109 G2 Hongqiao airport China
Hongqizhen Hainan China see Tongshi
108 A2 Hongshan Yunnan China
108 D4 Hongshui He r. China
107 F4 Hongtong Shanxi China
225 H3 Honguedo, Détroit d' sea chan. Que. Can.
Hongwansi Gansu China see Sunan
101 C4 Hongwŏn N. Korea
108 B1 Hongyuan Sichuan China
109 F1 Hongze Jiangsu China
109 F1 Hongze Hu l. China
78 □6 Honiara Guadalcanal Solomon Is
150 D4 Honiton Devon, England U.K.
102 J4 Honjō Japan
105 F2 Honjō Japan
141 M3 Honkajoki Fin.
149 H4 Honley West Yorkshire, England U.K.
114 B3 Honnali Karnataka India
140 N1 Honningsvåg Norway
240 □D8 Honokaa HI U.S.A.
240 □C8 Honokahua HI U.S.A.
80 F2 Honokawa mt. North I. N.Z.
240 □ Honolulu HI U.S.A.
240 □ Honolulu County county HI U.S.A.
240 □D9 Honomu HI U.S.A.
226 D3 Honor MI U.S.A.
240 □ Honouliuli HI U.S.A.
174 B3 Hönow Ger.
183 H5 Honrubia Spain
183 G3 Honrubia de la Cuesta Spain
103 F6 Honshū i. Japan
183 H5 Hontacillas Spain
183 F3 Hontalbilla Spain
183 H5 Hontanaya Spain
163 B5 Hontanx France
177 H3 Hontianske Nemce Slovakia
183 G2 Hontoria de la Cantera Spain
183 G3 Hontoria del Pinar Spain
183 G3 Hontoria de Valdearados Spain
240 □D9 Honuapo HI U.S.A.
114 B2 Honwad Karnataka India
151 H3 Hoo Medway, England U.K.
238 B2 Hood, Mount vol. OR U.S.A.
222 C3 Hood Bay AK U.S.A.
Hood Island Islas Galápagos Ecuador see Española, Isla
87 C7 Hood Point W.A. Austr.
238 B2 Hood River OR U.S.A.
164 D2 Hoofddorp Neth.
168 D1 Hooge Ger.
165 D3 Hoogerheide Neth.
164 F2 Hoogersmilde Neth.
164 F2 Hoogeveen Neth.
164 F1 Hoogezand-Sappemeer Neth.
164 D3 Hooge Zwaluwe Neth.
164 F2 Hooghalen Neth.
Hooghly r. mouth India see Hugli
164 E2 Hoogkarspel Neth.
164 F3 Hoog-Keppel Neth.
164 F1 Hoogkerk Neth.
164 E2 Hoogland Neth.
168 B3 Hoogstede Ger.
165 D3 Hoogstraten Belgium
164 D3 Hoogvliet Neth.
149 I4 Hook East Riding of Yorkshire, England U.K.
151 G3 Hook Hampshire, England U.K.
237 C4 Hooker OK U.S.A.
151 F3 Hook Norton Oxfordshire, England U.K.
Hook of Holland Neth. see Hoek van Holland
85 H5 Hook Point Qld Austr.
85 G3 Hook Reef Qld Austr.
168 D2 Hooksiel Ger.
240 □C8 Hoolehua HI U.S.A.
220 E4 Hoonah AK U.S.A.
220 B3 Hooper Bay AK U.S.A.
226 D5 Hoopeston IL U.S.A.
215 E2 Hoopstad S. Africa
142 E4 Höör Sweden
164 E2 Hoorn Neth.
77 I3 Hoorn, Îles de is Wallis and Futuna Is
164 D3 Hoornaar Neth.
105 E3 Hōō-san mt. Japan
233 G3 Hoosick NY U.S.A.
241 J3 Hoover Dam AZ/NV U.S.A.
106 D2 Höövör Mongolia
140 □B2 Hóp lag. Iceland
127 F2 Hopa Turkey
234 D2 Hopatcong NJ U.S.A.
234 C1 Hop Bottom PA U.S.A.
222 F5 Hope B.C. Can.
81 D4 Hope South I. N.Z.
81 D5 Hope r. South I. N.Z.
150 D1 Hope Flintshire, Wales U.K.
237 E5 Hope AR U.S.A.
234 D2 Hope NJ U.S.A.
82 D2 Hope, Lake salt flat S.A. Austr.
87 D7 Hope, Lake salt flat W.A. Austr.
146 D3 Hope, Loch l. Scotland U.K.
246 □ Hope Bay Jamaica
225 I2 Hopedale Nfld. Can.
237 F6 Hopedale LA U.S.A.
214 B5 Hopefield S. Africa
Hopei prov. China see Hebei
243 H5 Hopelchén Mex.
146 E4 Hopeman Moray, Scotland U.K.
140 □ Hopen i. Svalbard
Hopes Advance Bay Que. Can. see Aupaluk
83 E3 Hopetoun Vic. Austr.
87 D7 Hopetoun W.A. Austr.
214 E3 Hopetown S. Africa
85 F2 Hope Vale Qld Austr.
233 H4 Hope Valley RI U.S.A.
234 D2 Hopewell NJ U.S.A.
232 E6 Hopewell VA U.S.A.
235 E1 Hopewell Junction NY U.S.A.
178 D3 Hopfgarten im Brixental Austria
83 E4 Hopkins r. Vic. Austr.
87 F5 Hopkins, Lake salt flat W.A. Austr.
230 C4 Hopkinsville KY U.S.A.
235 G1 Hopkinton RI U.S.A.
240 F2 Hopland CA U.S.A.
172 B2 Hoppstädten Ger.
169 C3 Hopsten Ger.
151 I2 Hopton Norfolk, England U.K.
151 H2 Hopton Suffolk, England U.K.
150 E2 Hoptonheath Shropshire, England U.K.
238 B2 Hoquiam WA U.S.A.
106 D5 Hor Qinghai China
136 F2 Hora Ukr.
129 E4 Horadiz Azer.
104 D4 Hōraiji-san hill Japan
151 H4 Horam East Sussex, England U.K.
127 F2 Horasan Turkey
176 C2 Horažďovice Czech Rep.
172 C3 Horb am Neckar Ger.
170 D1 Horbelev Denmark
151 G2 Horbling Lincolnshire, England U.K.
157 H4 Horbourg-Wihr France
178 A3 Hörbranz Austria
143 E4 Hörby Sweden
183 E3 Horcajo de las Torres Spain
185 F1 Horcajo de los Montes Spain
183 H5 Horcajo de Santiago Spain
183 E4 Horcajo Medianero Spain
183 G4 Horche Spain
185 F2 Horcón hill Spain
258 D2 Horcones r. Arg.
142 B1 Hordaland county Norway
169 F4 Hörden Ger.
151 F4 Hordle Hampshire, England U.K.
150 C2 Horeb Ceredigion, Wales U.K.
80 D1 Horeke North I. N.Z.
197 F3 Horezu Romania
173 E3 Horgau Ger.
190 D1 Horgen Switz.
172 D4 Horgenzell Ger.
106 C1 Horgo Mongolia
196 D2 Horgoš Vojvodina, Srbija Yugo.
136 B3 Horhany mts Ukr.
106 E3 Hörh Uul mts Mongolia
197 I3 Horia Romania
176 E1 Hořice Czech Rep.
226 C4 Horicon WI U.S.A.
107 F3 Horinger Nei Mongol China
179 H3 Horitschon Austria
106 D2 Horiult Mongolia
266 H7 Horizon Deep sea feature S. Pacific Ocean
171 F4 Horka Ger.
139 H4 Horki Belarus
151 G3 Horley Surrey, England U.K.
262 Q1 Horlick Mountains Antarctica
171 E4 Hörlitz Ger.
137 J3 Horlivka Ukr.
122 E4 Hormak Iran
247 □1 Hormigueros Puerto Rico
183 H2 Hormilla Spain
122 D5 Hormoz i. Iran
122 C5 Hormoz, Kūh-e mt. Iran
122 D5 Hormozgan prov. Iran
122 C5 Hormūd-e Bāgh Iran
122 D5 Hormuz, Strait of Iran/Oman
179 G2 Horn Austria
222 G2 Horn r. N.W.T. Can.
140 □B2 Horn c. Iceland
Horn, Cape Chile see Hornos, Cabo de
184 D2 Hornachos Spain
185 E3 Hornachuelos Spain
Hornád r. Hungary/Slovakia see Hernád

176 G3 Horná Potôň Slovakia
177 H3 Horná Štubňa Slovakia
140 L2 Hornavan l. Sweden
172 B2 Hornbach Ger.
169 D4 Horn-Bad Meinberg Ger.
237 E6 Hornbeck LA U.S.A.
172 C3 Hornberg Ger.
238 B3 Hornbrook CA U.S.A.
169 F3 Hornburg Ger.
149 G3 Hornby Lancashire, England U.K.
149 I4 Horncastle Lincolnshire, England U.K.
143 G1 Horndal Sweden
151 F4 Horndean Hampshire, England U.K.
Horne, Îles de is Wallis and Futuna Is see Hoorn, Îles de
168 E2 Horneburg Ger.
140 L3 Hörnefors Sweden
232 E3 Hornell NY U.S.A.
224 C3 Hornepayne Ont. Can.
235 D2 Hornerstown NJ U.S.A.
177 G3 Horné Saliby Slovakia
177 H2 Horné Srnie Slovakia
147 C1 Horn Head hd Rep. of Ireland
177 H2 Horní Bečva Czech Rep.
177 G2 Horní Benešov Czech Rep.
171 F5 Horní Beřkovice Czech Rep.
176 C2 Horní Bříza Czech Rep.
176 E2 Horní Cerekev Czech Rep.
176 C1 Horní Jiřetín Czech Rep.
242 C3 Hornillos Mex.
176 E2 Horní Moštěnice Czech Rep.
141 I3 Hornindal Norway
151 I2 Horning Norfolk, England U.K.
176 D3 Horní Planá Czech Rep.
171 F5 Horní Počaply Czech Rep.
172 C3 Hornisgrinde mt. Ger.
85 E1 Horn Island Qld Austr.
176 B1 Horní Slavkov Czech Rep.
176 D3 Horní Stropnice Czech Rep.
222 F2 Horn Mountains N.W.T. Can.
185 H2 Hornos Spain
259 D9 Hornos, Cabo de c. Chile
137 F1 Hornostayivka Chernihivs'ka Oblast' Ukr.
137 G4 Hornostayivka Khersons'ka Oblast' Ukr.
171 F4 Hornow Ger.
156 B3 Hornoy-le-Bourg France
222 D2 Horn Peak Y.T. Can.
83 G3 Hornsby N.S.W. Austr.
149 I4 Hornsea East Riding of Yorkshire, England U.K.
141 L3 Hornslandet pen. Sweden
142 D3 Hornslet Denmark
170 C2 Hornstorf Ger.
168 D1 Hörnum Ger.
177 L4 Horoatu Crasnei Romania
136 C3 Horodenka Ukr.
136 D2 Horodets' Ukr.
175 M5 Horodło Pol.
137 F2 Horodnya Ukr.
136 D2 Horodnytsya Ukr.
136 D3 Horodok Khmel'nyts'ka Oblast' Ukr.
136 B3 Horodok L'vivs'ka Oblast' Ukr.
137 F3 Horodyshche Cherkas'ka Oblast' Ukr.
137 F2 Horodyshche Chernihivs'ka Oblast' Ukr.
137 J3 Horodyshche Luhans'ka Oblast' Ukr.
136 C3 Horodyshche Ternopil's'ka Oblast' Ukr.
136 C2 Horokhiv Ukr.
137 I3 Horokhuvatka Ukr.
171 F5 Horoměřice Czech Rep.
177 L3 Horonda Ukr.
110 C3 Horo Shan mts China
102 K2 Horoshiri-dake mt. Japan
102 K1 Horoshiri-yama hill Japan
176 C2 Hořovice Czech Rep.
107 I3 Horqin Shadi reg. China
Horqin Youyi Qianqi Nei Mongol China see Ulanhot
Horqin Zuoyi Houqi Nei Mongol China see Ganjig
Horqin Zuoyi Zhongqi Nei Mongol China see Baokang
253 F5 Horqueta Para.
150 C4 Horrabridge Devon, England U.K.
170 C1 Horreby Denmark
142 E3 Horred Sweden
151 H2 Horringer Suffolk, England U.K.
87 B6 Horrocks W.A. Austr.
111 E6 Horru Xizang China
179 F2 Hörsching Austria
238 F3 Horse Creek r. WY U.S.A.
224 F2 Horsefly B.C. Can.
227 I4 Horseheads NY U.S.A.
149 H3 Horsehouse North Yorkshire, England U.K.
169 F4 Hörsel r. Ger.
147 C3 Horseleap Galway Rep. of Ireland
147 D3 Horseleap Westmeath Rep. of Ireland
142 C4 Horsens Denmark
84 C5 Horseshoe Bend N.T. Austr.
238 C3 Horseshoe Bend ID U.S.A.
241 L4 Horseshoe Reservoir AZ U.S.A.
264 H3 Horseshoe Seamounts sea feature N. Atlantic Ocean
151 I2 Horsford Norfolk, England U.K.
149 H4 Horsforth West Yorkshire, England U.K.
83 E4 Horsham Vic. Austr.
151 G3 Horsham West Sussex, England U.K.
234 C2 Horsham PA U.S.A.
136 E2 Horshchyk Ukr.
171 C3 Hörsingen Ger.
168 G1 Horslunde Denmark
151 H3 Horsmonden Kent, England U.K.
176 B2 Horšovský Týn Czech Rep.
169 E5 Horst hill Ger.
165 F3 Horst Neth.
168 E2 Horst (Holstein) Ger.
151 I2 Horstead Norfolk, England U.K.
168 E2 Horstedt Ger.
169 C3 Hörstel Ger.
169 C3 Horstmar Ger.
199 F3 Horsunlu Aydın Turkey
177 I4 Hort Hungary
216 □1c Horta Faial Azores
142 D1 Horten Norway
183 H3 Hortezuela Spain
183 G2 Hortigüela Spain
177 K4 Hortobágy Hungary
220 F3 Horton r. N.W.T. Can.
151 F4 Horton Heath Hampshire, England U.K.
149 G3 Horton in Ribblesdale North Yorkshire, England U.K.
168 E1 Horuphav Denmark
190 D1 Horw Switz.
149 G4 Horwich Greater Manchester, England U.K.
136 D2 Horyn' r. Ukr.
175 L5 Horyniec Pol.
175 L5 Horyszów Pol.
104 B4 Hōryūji tourist site Japan
210 C3 Hosa'ina Eth.
169 E5 Hösbach Ger.
114 C3 Hosdurga Karnataka India
95 F2 Hose, Pegunungan mts Sarawak Malaysia
171 F4 Hosena Ger.
169 E5 Hosenfeld Ger.
116 D5 Hoshangabad Madh. Prad. India
136 D2 Hoshcha Ukr.
116 C3 Hoshiarpur Punjab India
110 D1 Höshööt Mongolia
106 A1 Höshööt Mongolia
165 F4 Hosingen Lux.
199 E1 Hoşköy Turkey
114 C3 Hospet Karnataka India
163 C6 Hospice de France France
Hospitalet Cataluña Spain see L'Hospitalet de l'Infant
Hospitalet Cataluña Spain see L'Hospitalet de Llobregat
163 A5 Hosseger France
207 I4 Hossére Vokre mt. Cameroon
172 D4 Hoßkirch Ger.
177 K4 Hosszúpályi Hungary
176 G4 Hosszúpereszteg Hungary
186 F3 Hostalric Spain
Hostalrich Spain see Hostalric
259 C9 Hoste, Isla i. Chile
163 B4 Hostens France
176 F3 Hostěradice Czech Rep.
177 H3 Hostie Slovakia
176 E1 Hostinné Czech Rep.
176 D1 Hostivice Czech Rep.
171 F5 Hoštka Czech Rep.
176 C1 Hostomice Czech Rep.
173 G2 Hostouň Czech Rep.
168 E1 Hostrupskov Denmark
114 C3 Hosur Tamil Nadu India
140 K3 Hotagen r. Sweden
104 D2 Hotaka-dake mt. Japan
105 F2 Hotaka-yama mt. Japan
111 C4 Hotan Xinjiang China
214 D2 Hotazel S. Africa
235 E1 Hotchkissville CT U.S.A.
241 I2 Hot Creek r. NV U.S.A.
241 I2 Hot Creek Range mts NV U.S.A.
171 C3 Hötensleben Ger.
87 C7 Hotham r. W.A. Austr.
84 B2 Hotham, Cape N.T. Austr.
140 L2 Hoting Sweden
179 G4 Hotinja vas Slovenia
237 E5 Hot Springs AR U.S.A.
Hot Springs NM U.S.A. see Truth or Consequences
236 C3 Hot Springs SD U.S.A.
238 F3 Hot Sulphur Springs CO U.S.A.
222 G1 Hottah Lake N.W.T. Can.
212 B5 Hottentots Bay Namibia
165 E4 Hotton Belgium
78 □5 Houailu New Caledonia
156 C2 Houdain France
156 B4 Houdan France
157 F4 Houdelaincourt France
157 F4 Houécourt France
163 C4 Houeillès France
163 C5 Houeydets France
165 E4 Houffalize Belgium
85 F3 Houghton r. Qld Austr.
149 G3 Houghton Cumbria, England U.K.
226 C2 Houghton MI U.S.A.
232 D3 Houghton NY U.S.A.
226 E3 Houghton Lake MI U.S.A.
149 H3 Houghton le Spring Tyne and Wear, England U.K.
151 G3 Houghton Regis Bedfordshire, England U.K.
96 C2 Houie Moc, Phou mt. Laos
159 F2 Houlgate France
233 □J1 Houlton ME U.S.A.
107 F5 Houma Shanxi China
237 F6 Houma LA U.S.A.
109 E4 Houmen Guangdong China
205 H2 Houmt Souk Tunisia
206 E4 Houndé Burkina
146 F6 Houndslow Scottish Borders, Scotland U.K.
156 C2 Houplines France
146 C4 Hourn, Loch inlet Scotland U.K.
162 A3 Hourtin France
162 A3 Hourtin et de Carcans, Étang d' l. France
162 A3 Hourtin-Plage France
233 G3 Housatonic MA U.S.A.
235 E1 Housatonic r. CT U.S.A.
241 K2 House Range mts UT U.S.A.
149 G2 Housesteads tourist site England U.K.
222 E4 Houston B.C. Can.
234 C4 Houston DE U.S.A.
226 B4 Houston MN U.S.A.
237 F4 Houston MO U.S.A.
237 F5 Houston MS U.S.A.
237 E6 Houston TX U.S.A.
214 B6 Hout Bay S. Africa
164 E2 Houten Neth.
165 E3 Houthalen Belgium
165 B4 Houthulst Belgium
214 E4 Houtkraal S. Africa
87 B6 Houtman Abrolhos is W.A. Austr.
146 E3 Houton Orkney, Scotland U.K.
141 M3 Houtskär Fin.
214 D4 Houwater S. Africa
165 E4 Houyet Belgium
Houzhai Guangdong China see Nan'ao
142 D4 Hov Denmark
142 D1 Hov Norway
143 F2 Hova Sweden
106 D2 Hovd Hovd Mongolia
106 D2 Hovd Övörhangay Mongolia
106 B2 Hovd prov. Mongolia
142 C2 Hovdefjell hill Norway
106 B1 Hovd Gol r. Mongolia
151 G4 Hove Brighton and Hove, England U.K.
169 D4 Hövelhof Ger.
136 C3 Hoverla, Hora mt. Ukr.
151 I2 Hoveton Norfolk, England U.K.
122 B4 Hoveyzeh Iran
149 I3 Hovingham North Yorkshire, England U.K.
226 C2 Hovland MN U.S.A.
143 F3 Hovmantorp Sweden
129 G3 Hövsan Azer.
107 F3 Hövsgöl Mongolia
106 D1 Hövsgöl prov. Mongolia
106 D1 Hövsgöl Nuur l. Mongolia
137 G3 Hovtva Ukr.
137 G3 Hovtva r. Ukr.
124 C5 Howakil Bay Eritrea
202 E5 Howar, Wadi watercourse Sudan
85 H5 Howard Qld Austr.
237 D4 Howard KS U.S.A.
236 D2 Howard SD U.S.A.
226 D3 Howard WI U.S.A.
226 E4 Howard City MI U.S.A.
234 B3 Howard County county MD U.S.A.
149 H3 Howardian Hills England U.K.
84 C2 Howard Island N.T. Austr.
84 B2 Howard Springs N.T. Austr.
149 I4 Howden East Riding of Yorkshire, England U.K.
226 E5 Howe IN U.S.A.
83 G5 Howe, Cape Vic. Austr.
262 O1 Howe, Mount Antarctica
227 F4 Howell MI U.S.A.
146 F5 Howe of the Mearns reg. Scotland U.K.
236 C2 Howes SD U.S.A.
233 G2 Howick Que. Can.
215 H3 Howick S. Africa
82 D1 Howitt, Lake salt flat S.A. Austr.
233 □I2 Howland ME U.S.A.
77 I1 Howland Island N. Pacific Ocean
83 F3 Howlong N.S.W. Austr.
Howrah W. Bengal India see Haora
147 E3 Howth Rep. of Ireland
236 C4 Hoxie KS U.S.A.
169 E4 Höxter Ger.
110 D2 Hoxtolgay Xinjiang China
110 D3 Hoxud Xinjiang China
146 E3 Hoy i. Scotland U.K.
168 E3 Hoya Ger.
105 F3 Hōya Japan
185 I2 Hoya Gonzalo Spain
141 I3 Høyanger Norway
171 F4 Hoyerswerda Ger.
149 F4 Hoylake Merseyside, England U.K.
149 H4 Hoyland South Yorkshire, England U.K.
140 K2 Høylandet Norway
227 G1 Hoyle Ont. Can.
171 C4 Hoym Ger.
183 G4 Hoyo de Manzanares Spain
182 D4 Hoyos Spain
184 D5 Hoyos del Espino Spain
140 O3 Höytiäinen l. Fin.
183 E4 Hozat Turkey
185 E4 Hozgarganta r. Spain
104 B3 Hozu-gawa r. Japan
Hpa-an Myanmar see Pa-an
136 E3 Hrabove Ukr.
176 E1 Hradec Králové Czech Rep.
177 G2 Hradec nad Moravicí Czech Rep.
176 F2 Hradec nad Svitavou Czech Rep.
173 H2 Hrádek Czech Rep.
176 D1 Hrádek nad Nisou Czech Rep.
176 C2 Hradešice Czech Rep.
176 C1 Hradiště hill Czech Rep.
177 H3 Hradište Slovakia
137 G3 Hradyz'k Ukr.
138 G5 Hradzyanka Belarus
176 B1 Hranice Karlovarský kraj Czech Rep.
177 G2 Hranice Olomoucký kraj Czech Rep.
136 E2 Hranitne Ukr.
177 J3 Hranovnica Slovakia
188 G4 Hrasnica Bos.-Herz.
179 G4 Hrastnik Slovenia
140 □D2 Hraun slope Iceland
129 D3 Hrazdan Armenia
171 F5 Hrazený hill Czech Rep.
137 G2 Hrebinka Ukr.
136 F3 Hrebinky Ukr.
137 G1 Hrem"yach Ukr.
137 G4 Hreyhove Ukr.
177 J3 Hrhov Slovakia
175 L6 Hrimne Ukr.
177 I3 Hriňová Slovakia
136 E3 Hristovaia Moldova
171 E5 Hrob Czech Rep.
176 D3 Hrochoť Slovakia
176 E2 Hrochův Týnec Czech Rep.
138 D5 Hrodna Belarus
Hrodna Oblast admin. div. Belarus see Hrodzyenskaya Voblasts'
175 L2 Hrodyenskaye Wzvyshsha hills Belarus
138 E5 Hrodzyenskaya Voblasts' admin. div. Belarus
137 H4 Hromivka Ukr.
173 H2 Hromnice Czech Rep.
177 H4 Hron r. Slovakia
177 I3 Hronec Slovakia
176 F1 Hronov Czech Rep.
177 H3 Hronský Beňadik Slovakia
176 F2 Hrotovice Czech Rep.
171 D5 Hroznětín Czech Rep.
175 L5 Hrubieszów Pol.
175 M4 Hrudky Ukr.
137 H2 Hrun' Ukr.
137 H2 Hrun' r. Ukr.
137 I3 Hrushuvakha Ukr.
176 F3 Hrušky Czech Rep.
176 F3 Hrušovany nad Jevišovkou Czech Rep.
179 H1 Hrušovany u Brna Czech Rep.
177 I2 Hruštín Slovakia
175 K3 Hrusniew Pol.
Hrvatska country Europe see Croatia
188 F3 Hrvatska Kostajnica Croatia
Hrvatsko Grahovo Bos.-Herz. see Bosansko Grahovo
137 G2 Hryhorivka Chernihivs'ka Oblast' Ukr.
137 I3 Hryhorivka Dnipropetrovs'ka Oblast' Ukr.
137 G4 Hryhorivka Khersons'ka Oblast' Ukr.
136 D3 Hrymayliv Ukr.
136 C4 Hrynyava Ukr.
136 E3 Hryshkivtsi Ukr.
136 D3 Hrytsiv Ukr.
Hsiang Kang H.K. China see Hong Kong
96 B2 Hsi-hseng Myanmar
96 B2 Hsin, Nam r. Myanmar
Hsin-chia-p'o country Asia see Singapore
Hsin-chia-p'o Sing. see Singapore
109 G3 Hsinchu Taiwan
Hsinking Jilin China see Changchun
109 G4 Hsinying Taiwan
Hsi-sha Ch'un-tao is S. China Sea see Paracel Islands
109 G3 Hsüeh Shan mt. Taiwan
109 F3 Hua'an Fujian China
252 A2 Huacaibamba Peru
252 E2 Huacaraje Bol.
252 E5 Huacaya Bol.
109 E3 Huacheng Guangdong China
252 E3 Huachi Bol.
107 F4 Huachi Gansu China
252 A2 Huacho Peru
252 A2 Huachón Peru
100 D3 Huachuan Heilong. China
241 L6 Huachuca City AZ U.S.A.
260 C2 Huaco Arg.
252 A2 Huacrachuco Peru
107 G3 Huade Nei Mongol China
100 C4 Huadian Jilin China
109 E4 Huadu Guangdong China
Huafeng Fujian China see Hua'an
97 B4 Hua Hin Thai.
79 □3 Huahine i. Arch. de la Société Fr. Polynesia
107 G3 Huai'an Hebei China
109 F1 Huai'an Jiangsu China
109 F1 Huaibei Anhui China
109 E1 Huaibin Henan China
Huaicheng Guangdong China see Huaiji
Huaide Jilin China see Gongzhuling
Huaidian Henan China see Shenqiu
109 F1 Huai He r. China
109 D3 Huaihua Hunan China
109 E4 Huaiji Guangdong China
107 G3 Huailai Hebei China
96 C3 Huai Luang r. Thai.
109 F1 Huainan Anhui China
109 F2 Huaining Anhui China
107 G4 Huairen Shanxi China
107 H3 Huairou Beijing China
97 D4 Huai Samran r. Thai.
109 E1 Huaiyang Henan China
109 F1 Huaiyin Jiangsu China
109 F1 Huaiyin Jiangsu China
109 F1 Huaiyuan Anhui China
109 D4 Huaiyuan Guangxi China
245 F5 Huajuápan de León Mex.
243 F3 Hualahuises Mex.
241 K4 Hualapai Peak AZ U.S.A.
109 G4 Hualien Taiwan
252 B3 Hualla Peru
250 C6 Huallaga r. Peru
106 D4 Hualong Qinghai China
260 A5 Hualqui Chile
252 A1 Huamachuco Peru
245 F4 Huamantla Mex.
209 B8 Huambo Angola
209 B8 Huambo prov. Angola
100 B3 Huanan Heilong. China
250 B6 Huancabamba r. Peru
259 C6 Huancache, Sierra mts Arg.
252 B3 Huancapi Peru
252 B3 Huancavelica Peru
252 B3 Huancavelica dept Peru
252 B3 Huancayo Peru
Huancheng Gansu China see Huanxian
109 E3 Huangbei Jiangxi China
Huangcaoba Guizhou China see Xingyi
109 E1 Huangchuan Henan China
109 E2 Huanggang Hubei China
107 H4 Huang He r. China
107 H4 Huanghe Kou r. mouth China
107 H4 Huanghua Hebei China
109 G1 Huangjiajian Jiangsu China
107 F5 Huangling Shaanxi China
108 D5 Huangliu Hainan China
107 F5 Huanglong Shaanxi China
Huanglongsi Henan China see Kaifeng
109 F3 Huangmao Jian mt. Zhejiang China
109 E2 Huangmei Hubei China
100 C4 Huangnihe Jilin China
109 E2 Huangpi Hubei China
108 C3 Huangping Guizhou China
109 F3 Huangqi Fujian China
109 F2 Huangshan Anhui China
108 B1 Huangshengguan Sichuan China
109 E2 Huangshi Hubei China
106 D4 Huang Shui r. China
107 E4 Huangtu Gaoyuan plat. China
261 G5 Huanguelén Arg.
107 I4 Huangxian Shandong China
109 G3 Huangyan Zhejiang China
106 D4 Huangyuan Qinghai China
106 D4 Huangzhong Qinghai China
Huangzhou Hubei China see Huanggang
108 B3 Huaning Yunnan China
108 D3 Huanjiang Guangxi China
107 E4 Huan Jiang r. China
101 C4 Huanren Liaoning China
Huanshan Zhejiang China see Yuhuan
252 B3 Huanta Peru
107 H4 Huantai Shandong China
252 A2 Huánuco Peru
252 A2 Huánuco dept Peru
252 D4 Huanuni Bol.
244 C3 Huanusco Mex.
107 E4 Huanxian Gansu China
108 B3 Huaping Yunnan China
252 D4 Huari Bol.
252 A2 Huaral Peru
252 A2 Huaráz Peru
252 A2 Huari Peru
252 A2 Huarmey Peru
252 A3 Huarochirí Peru
109 E3 Huarong Hunan China
183 I2 Huarte-Araquil Spain
250 B5 Huasaga r. Peru
258 C3 Huasco Chile
107 F5 Hua Shan mt. Shaanxi China
106 C5 Huashixia Qinghai China
242 D3 Huatabampo Mex.
245 F4 Huatusco Mex.
245 E3 Huauchinango Mex.
252 A2 Huauru, Islas de is Peru
245 F4 Huautla Mex.
Huaxian Guangdong China see Huadu
107 G5 Huaxian Henan China
107 F5 Huaxian Shaanxi China
Huayang Anhui China see Jixi
252 A2 Huaylas Peru
Huayuan Hubei China see Xiaochang
108 D2 Huayuan Hunan China
Huazangsi Gansu China see Tianzhu
108 D4 Huazhaizi Gansu China
109 E4 Huazhou Guangdong China
245 F5 Huazolotitlán Mex.
222 B2 Hubbard, Mount Can./U.S.A.
109 E2 Hubei prov. China
114 B3 Hubli Karnataka India
177 I2 Hubová Slovakia
137 H3 Hubynykha Ukr.
101 C4 Huch'ang N. Korea
169 B4 Hückelhoven Ger.
169 C4 Hückeswagen Ger.
149 H4 Hucknall Nottinghamshire, England U.K.
156 B2 Hucqueliers France
175 L5 Huczwa r. Pol.
149 H4 Huddersfield West Yorkshire, England U.K.
169 D3 Hüde Ger.
168 D2 Hude (Oldenburg) Ger.
107 I1 Huder Nei Mongol China
197 H1 Hudeşti Romania
113 □1 Hudhuveli i. N. Male Maldives
141 L3 Hudiksvall Sweden
233 H3 Hudson MA U.S.A.
233 E5 Hudson MD U.S.A.
233 □I2 Hudson ME U.S.A.
227 E5 Hudson MI U.S.A.
233 H3 Hudson NH U.S.A.
233 G3 Hudson NY U.S.A.
226 A3 Hudson WI U.S.A.
233 G4 Hudson r. NY U.S.A.
Hudson, Baie d' sea Can. see Hudson Bay
259 B7 Hudson, Cerro mt. Chile
Hudson, Détroit d' str. Nunavut/Que. Can. see Hudson Strait
237 E4 Hudson, Lake OK U.S.A.
223 K4 Hudson Bay Sask. Can.
221 J4 Hudson Bay sea Can.
235 D2 Hudson County county NJ U.S.A.
233 G3 Hudson Falls NY U.S.A.
Hudson Island Tuvalu see Nanumanga
221 P2 Hudson Land reg. Greenland
262 R2 Hudson Mountains Antarctica
222 F3 Hudson's Hope B.C. Can.
221 L3 Hudson Strait Nunavut/Que. Can.
96 D3 Huê Vietnam
182 D4 Huebra r. Spain
183 I3 Huecha r. Spain
185 H4 Huécija Spain
197 F2 Huedin Romania
243 G6 Huehuetán Mex.
243 H6 Huehuetenango Guat.
244 E1 Huehueto, Cerro mt. Mex.
245 E4 Huejotzingo Mex.
244 D3 Huejuquilla Mex.
245 E3 Huejutla Mex.
185 G3 Huélago Spain
158 C3 Huelgoat France
185 G3 Huelma Spain
184 D3 Huelva Spain
184 D3 Huelva prov. Andalucía Spain
184 D3 Huelva r. Spain
183 H4 Huelves Spain
185 H3 Huéneja Spain
260 B2 Huentelauquén Chile
260 B5 Huépil Chile
260 A5 Huequén Chile
185 H4 Huércal de Almería Spain
185 I3 Huércal-Overa Spain
183 H2 Huércanos Spain
239 F4 Huerfano r. CO U.S.A.
183 I4 Huérguina Spain
183 G3 Huérmeces Spain
183 G2 Huerta del Rey Spain
183 G5 Huerta de Valdecarábanos Spain
183 H4 Huertahernando Spain
186 C3 Huerto Spain
183 H3 Huerva r. Spain
185 G3 Huesa Spain
186 C3 Huesa del Común Spain
186 C2 Huesca Spain
186 C2 Huesca prov. Aragón Spain
185 H3 Huéscar Spain
244 D4 Huetamo Mex.
183 H4 Huete Spain
185 F3 Huétor-Tájar Spain
245 E4 Hueyotlipan Mex.
231 C5 Hueytown AL U.S.A.
184 E3 Huezna r. Spain
172 C4 Hüfingen Ger.
146 □ Huftarøy i. Norway
209 B8 Humpata Angola
149 I4 Huggate East Riding of Yorkshire, England U.K.
85 F4 Hughenden Qld Austr.
261 G3 Hughes Arg.
82 B2 Hughes S.A. Austr.
223 K3 Hughes r. Man. Can.
233 E5 Hughesville MD U.S.A.
227 I5 Hughesville PA U.S.A.
240 G3 Hughson CA U.S.A.
150 □ Hugh Town Isles of Scilly, England U.K.
173 F4 Hüglfing Ger.
117 F5 Hugli r. mouth India
117 G5 Hugli-Chunchura W. Bengal India
236 C4 Hugo CO U.S.A.
237 E5 Hugo OK U.S.A.
236 C4 Hugoton KS U.S.A.
177 I3 Hugyag Hungary
Huhehot Nei Mongol China see Hohhot
107 F3 Huhhot Nei Mongol China
215 E2 Huhudi S. Africa
109 F3 Hui'an Fujian China
107 E4 Hui'anpu Ningxia China
80 F3 Huiarau Range mts North I. N.Z.
212 C5 Huib-Hoch Plateau Namibia
109 E3 Huichang Jiangxi China
245 E3 Huichapán Mex.
Huicheng Anhui China see Shexian
Huicheng Guangdong China see Huilai
101 C4 Huich'ŏn N. Korea
109 E4 Huidong Guangdong China
108 B3 Huidong Sichuan China
100 C4 Huifa r. China
107 H1 Huihe Nei Mongol China
165 D3 Huijbergen Neth.
109 E1 Huiji r. China
209 B8 Huíla Angola
209 B8 Huíla prov. Angola
250 C4 Huila dept Col.
250 C4 Huila, Nevado de vol. Col.
109 F4 Huilai Guangdong China
209 B8 Huíla Plateau Angola
108 B3 Huili Sichuan China
Huilongzhen Jiangsu China see Qidong
244 D4 Huimangaro Mex.
243 G5 Huimanguillo Mex.
107 H4 Huimin Shandong China
258 D1 Huinahuaca Arg.
252 C4 Huiñaimarca, Lago de l. Bol./Peru
100 C4 Huinan Jilin China
Huinan Shanghai China see Nanhui
260 E4 Huinca Renancó Arg.
106 E5 Huining Gansu China
173 E3 Huisheim Ger.
150 E3 Huish Episcopi Somerset, England U.K.
Huishi Gansu China see Huining
108 C3 Huishui Guizhou China
146 A4 Huisinis Western Isles, Scotland U.K.
159 G3 Huisne r. France
159 H4 Huisseau-sur-Cosson France
164 E3 Huissen Neth.
108 D3 Huitong Hunan China
141 M3 Huittinen Fin.
244 C2 Huitzila Mex.
245 F5 Huitzo Mex.
245 E5 Huitzuco Mex.
108 C1 Huixian Gansu China
107 G5 Huixian Henan China
243 G6 Huixtla Mex.
Huiyang Guangdong China see Huizhou
108 B3 Huize Yunnan China
164 E2 Huizen Neth.
109 E4 Huizhou Guangdong China
106 C1 Hujirt Arhangay Mongolia
106 D2 Hujirt Övörhangay Mongolia
106 E2 Hujirt Töv Mongolia
80 E4 Hukanui North I. N.Z.
81 C5 Hukarere South I. N.Z.
96 B1 Hukawng Valley Myanmar
109 F2 Hukou Jiangxi China
212 D4 Hukuntsi Botswana
100 C3 Hulan Heilong. China
100 C3 Hulan r. China
107 I2 Hulan Ergi Heilong. China
124 C2 Hulayfah Saudi Arabia
226 E2 Hulbert MI U.S.A.
232 B6 Hulen KY U.S.A.
Huliao Guangdong China see Dabu
100 E3 Hulin Heilong. China
176 G2 Hulín Czech Rep.
224 F4 Hull Que. Can.
Hull England U.K. see Kingston upon Hull
233 H3 Hull MA U.S.A.
150 E3 Hullavington Wiltshire, England U.K.
151 H3 Hullbridge Essex, England U.K.
169 D3 Hüllhorst Ger.
Hull Island Phoenix Is Kiribati see Orona
165 E4 Hulsberg Neth.
169 E3 Hülsede Ger.
165 D3 Hulshout Belgium
165 D3 Hulst Neth.
143 G3 Hulterstad Kalmar Sweden
143 F3 Hultsfred Sweden
107 F5 Hulu r. China
107 I3 Huludao Liaoning China
113 □1 Huluk i. N. Male Maldives
Hulumeedhoo i. Addu Atoll Maldives see Midu
Hulun Nei Mongol China see Hailar
Ḥulwān Egypt see Ḥelwān
137 I4 Hulyaypole Ukr.
100 C2 Huma Heilong. China
100 C2 Huma r. China
247 □1 Humacao Puerto Rico
253 E1 Humaitá Brazil
253 F6 Humaitá Para.
183 G4 Humanes de Mohernando Spain
215 E6 Humansdorp S. Africa
252 B3 Humay Peru
124 D2 Humayyān, Jabal hill Saudi Arabia
209 B9 Humbe Angola
209 B8 Humbe, Serra do mts Angola
149 J4 Humber, Mouth of the England U.K.
149 I4 Humberside airport England U.K.
149 I4 Humberston North East Lincolnshire, England U.K.
254 E2 Humberto de Campos Brazil
149 G2 Humbie East Lothian, Scotland U.K.
168 F1 Humble Denmark
261 G2 Humboldt Arg.
223 J4 Humboldt Sask. Can.
241 K4 Humboldt AZ U.S.A.
236 E3 Humboldt NE U.S.A.
240 H1 Humboldt NV U.S.A.
234 B2 Humboldt PA U.S.A.
237 F5 Humboldt TN U.S.A.
240 H1 Humboldt r. NV U.S.A.
78 □5 Humboldt, Mount New Caledonia
238 A3 Humboldt Bay CA U.S.A.
81 B6 Humboldt Mountain mts South I. N.Z.
240 H1 Humboldt Range mts NV U.S.A.
85 F5 Humburn Qld Austr.
261 G5 Humeda plain Arg.
177 G2 Humenec hill Czech Rep.
177 K3 Humenné Slovakia
83 F3 Hume Reservoir N.S.W. Austr.
157 F5 Humes-Jorquenay France
185 F3 Humilladero Spain
188 F3 Humka, Gora hill Croatia
164 F2 Hummelo Neth.
234 B2 Hummelstown PA U.S.A.
234 B2 Hummels Wharf PA U.S.A.
81 C6 Hummock hill South I. N.Z.
179 G4 Hum na Sutli Croatia
209 B8 Humpata Angola
Humphrey Island atoll Cook Is see Manihiki
240 H3 Humphreys, Mount CA U.S.A.
241 L4 Humphreys Peak AZ U.S.A.
176 E2 Humpolec Czech Rep.
141 M3 Humppila Fin.
84 B2 Humpty Doo N.T. Austr.
149 G2 Humshaugh Northumberland, England U.K.
107 I3 Hun r. China
202 B2 Hūn Libya
140 □B2 Húnaflói b. Iceland
109 E3 Hunan prov. China
100 D4 Hunchun Jilin China
100 D4 Hunchun r. China
177 J2 Huncovce Slovakia
171 D4 Hundeluft Ger.
173 G3 Hunderdorf Ger.
142 D4 Hundested Denmark
171 C3 Hundisburg Ger.
149 J4 Hundleby Lincolnshire, England U.K.
150 C3 Hundleton Pembrokeshire, Wales U.K.
141 J3 Hundorp Norway
232 C5 Hundred WV U.S.A.
171 D5 Hundshübel Ger.
168 D1 Hundslev Denmark
178 D3 Hundstein mt. Austria
197 F3 Hunedoara Romania
169 E5 Hünfeld Ger.
169 D5 Hünfelden-Kirberg Ger.
177 H4 Hungary country Europe
169 D5 Hungen Ger.
173 E3 Hungerberg hill Ger.
83 F2 Hungerford Qld Austr.
151 F3 Hungerford West Berkshire, England U.K.
106 B1 Hüngiy Gol r. Mongolia
101 C5 Hŭngnam N. Korea
147 B5 Hungry Hill hill Rep. of Ireland
114 C2 Hungund Karnataka India
96 D2 Hung Yên Vietnam
146 B4 Hunish, Rubha pt Scotland U.K.
Hunjiang Jilin China see Baishan
101 C4 Hun Jiang r. China
149 I3 Hunmanby North Yorkshire, England U.K.
142 D2 Hunnebostrand Sweden
165 E3 Hunsel Neth.
214 A2 Huns Mountains Namibia
157 H4 Hunspach France
151 H2 Hunstanton Norfolk, England U.K.
114 C3 Hunsur Karnataka India
227 G1 Hunta Ont. Can.
169 D2 Hunte r. Ger.
83 G3 Hunter r. N.S.W. Austr.
81 C6 Hunter South I. N.Z.
81 B6 Hunter r. South I. N.Z.
234 D2 Hunterdon County county NJ U.S.A.
117 F4 Hunterganj Bihar India
83 F5 Hunter Island Tas. Austr.
77 H4 Hunter Island S. Pacific Ocean
83 F5 Hunter Islands Tas. Austr.
81 A6 Hunter Mountains South I. N.Z.
146 D6 Hunter's Quay Argyll and Bute, Scotland U.K.
234 A2 Hunters Run PA U.S.A.
233 F2 Huntingdon Que. Can.
151 G2 Huntingdon Cambridgeshire, England U.K.
232 E4 Huntingdon PA U.S.A.
237 F4 Huntingdon TN U.S.A.
230 C3 Huntington IN U.S.A.
238 C2 Huntington OR U.S.A.
241 L2 Huntington UT U.S.A.
232 B5 Huntington WV U.S.A.
240 H5 Huntington Beach CA U.S.A.
241 J1 Huntington Creek r. NV U.S.A.
235 E2 Huntington Station NY U.S.A.
168 D3 Huntlosen Ger.
80 E2 Huntly North I. N.Z.
146 F4 Huntly Aberdeenshire, Scotland U.K.
238 F2 Hunt Mountain WY U.S.A.
82 D2 Hunt Peninsula S.A. Austr.
224 E4 Huntsville Ont. Can.
231 C5 Huntsville AL U.S.A.
237 E4 Huntsville AR U.S.A.
236 E4 Huntsville MO U.S.A.
237 E6 Huntsville TX U.S.A.
243 H4 Hunucmá Mex.
177 J5 Hunya Hungary
Hunyani r. Moz./Zimbabwe see Manyame
107 G4 Hunyuan Shanxi China
116 C1 Hunza Jammu and Kashmir
123 H3 Hunza r. Pak.
164 F1 Hunze r. Neth.
110 C2 Huocheng Xinjiang China
107 G5 Huojia Henan China
107 J2 Huolin r. China
100 C2 Huolongmen Heilong. China
Huolu Hebei China see Luquan
96 D3 Hương Thuy Vietnam
83 F5 Huonville Tas. Austr.
109 F1 Huoqiu Anhui China
109 F2 Huoshan Anhui China
109 F2 Huo Shan mt. Hubei China
Huoxian Shanxi China see Huozhou
107 F4 Huozhou Shanxi China
137 H3 Hupalivka Ukr.
Hupeh prov. China see Hubei
169 F4 Hüpstedt Ger.
Huras i. S. Male Maldives see Embudhu Finolhu
124 D2 Huraymilā Saudi Arabia
176 D2 Hurbanovo Slovakia
Hurd Island Gilbert Is Kiribati see Arorae
210 F2 Hurdiyo Somalia
107 I3 Hure Nei Mongol China
106 D1 Hüreemaral Mongolia
106 D2 Hürent Mongolia
Hure Qi Nei Mongol China see Hure
203 G3 Hurghada Egypt
210 C4 Huri mt. Kenya
160 A2 Huriel France
137 G3 Hurivka Ukr.
226 C1 Hurkett Ont. Can.
147 C4 Hurler's Cross Rep. of Ireland
233 F4 Hurley NY U.S.A.
226 B2 Hurley WI U.S.A.
226 D4 Hurlock MD U.S.A.
87 C7 Hurlstone, Lake salt flat W.A. Austr.
240 G3 Huron CA U.S.A.
232 B4 Huron OH U.S.A.
236 D2 Huron SD U.S.A.
227 F3 Huron, Lake Can./U.S.A.
226 C2 Huron Bay MI U.S.A.
227 E3 Huron Beach MI U.S.A.
226 B1 Huronian Ont. Can.
226 C2 Huron Mountains hills MI U.S.A.
241 K3 Hurricane UT U.S.A.
151 F3 Hursley Hampshire, England U.K.
151 F3 Hurstbourne Tarrant Hampshire, England U.K.
151 H3 Hurst Green East Sussex, England U.K.
151 G4 Hurstpierpoint West Sussex, England U.K.
260 B2 Hurtado r. Chile
183 H2 Hurteles Spain
169 B5 Hürth Ger.
231 C5 Hurtsboro AL U.S.A.
95 F2 Hurung, Gunung mt. Indon.
81 D5 Hurunui r. South I. N.Z.
142 C3 Hurup Denmark
168 E1 Hürup Ger.
149 H3 Hurworth-on-Tees Darlington, England U.K.
137 I4 Husarka Ukr.
177 K5 Husasău de Tinca Romania
140 □C2 Húsavík Iceland
151 F2 Husbands Bosworth Leicestershire, England U.K.
168 E1 Husby Ger.
143 G1 Husby Sweden
Huseyinabat Turkey see Alaca
Hüseyinli Turkey see Kızılırmak
Hushan Zhejiang China see Wuyi
Hushan Zhejiang China see Cixi
136 B2 Hushcha Ukr.
197 I2 Huşi Romania
176 G2 Huslenky Czech Rep.
137 H2 Huska r. Ukr.
143 F3 Huskvarna Sweden
220 C3 Huslia AK U.S.A.
Husn Jordan see Al Ḥiṣn
125 D4 Ḥuṣn Āl 'Abr Yemen
142 A2 Husnes Norway
144 J1 Husøy i. Norway
117 F4 Hussainabad Bihar India
176 F3 Hustopeče Czech Rep.
168 E3 Husum Niedersachsen Ger.
168 E1 Husum Schleswig-Holstein Ger.
140 L3 Husum Sweden
136 D3 Husyatyn Ukr.
175 K3 Huszlew Pol.
175 I4 Huta Pol.
106 D1 Hutag Mongolia
94 B2 Hutanopan Sumatera Indon.
124 C2 Hutaym, Harrat lava field Saudi Arabia
214 D4 Hutchinson S. Africa
236 D4 Hutchinson KS U.S.A.
236 E2 Hutchinson MN U.S.A.
241 L4 Hutch Mountain AZ U.S.A.
124 C4 Hūth Yemen
100 E3 Hutou Heilong. China
87 B6 Hutt r. W.A. Austr.
178 E3 Hüttau Austria
179 F4 Hüttenberg Austria
170 D2 Hüttenberg hill Ger.
169 D5 Hüttenberg-Hochelheim Ger.
169 F4 Hütterode Ger.
173 H3 Hutthurm Ger.
173 E3 Hüttlingen Ger.
149 J4 Huttoft Lincolnshire, England U.K.
150 E3 Hutton North Somerset, England U.K.
85 G5 Hutton, Mount hill Qld Austr.
149 I4 Hutton Cranswick East Riding of Yorkshire, England U.K.
87 D5 Hutton Range hills W.A. Austr.
149 H3 Hutton Rudby North Yorkshire, England U.K.
190 C1 Huttwil Switz.
110 D2 Hutubi Xinjiang China
110 D2 Hutubi He r. China
107 H4 Hutuo r. China
137 H2 Huty Ukr.
168 F2 Hützel Ger.
113 D11 Huvadhu Atoll Maldives
123 E5 Hüvār Iran
Hüvek Turkey see Bozova
168 C3 Hüven Ger.
122 D5 Hüvīān, Kūh-e mts Iran
125 E2 Huwār i. The Gulf
175 K6 Huwniki Pol.
109 E3 Huxi Jiangxi China
107 F5 Huxian Shaanxi China
86 E3 Huxley, Mount hill W.A. Austr.
81 B6 Huxley, Mount South I. N.Z.
165 E4 Huy Belgium
136 E2 Huyba r. Ukr.
149 G4 Huyton Merseyside, England U.K.
136 E2 Huyva r. Ukr.
109 G2 Huzhen Zhejiang China
109 G2 Huzhou Zhejiang China
106 D4 Huzhu Qinghai China
114 C2 Huzurnagar Andhra Prad. India
140 □B2 Hvammsfjörður inlet Iceland
140 □C2 Hvannadalshnúkur vol. Iceland
188 F4 Hvar Croatia
188 F4 Hvar i. Croatia
137 H3 Hvardiys'ke Ukr.
137 H5 Hvardiys'ke Ukr.
188 F4 Hvarski Kanal sea chan. Croatia
140 □B2 Hveragerði Iceland
142 C3 Hvide Sande Denmark
140 □B3 Hvíta r. Iceland
142 C2 Hvittingfoss Norway
136 C3 Hvizdets' Ukr.
137 G2 Hvyntove Ukr.
101 D4 Hwadae N. Korea
212 E3 Hwange Zimbabwe
Hwang Ho r. China see Huang He
101 C5 Hwangju N. Korea
213 F3 Hwedza Zimbabwe
Hwlffordd Pembrokeshire, Wales U.K. see Haverfordwest
104 B3 Hyakuriga-take hill Japan
233 H4 Hyannis MA U.S.A.
236 C3 Hyannis NE U.S.A.
106 B1 Hyargas Nuur salt l. Mongolia
234 B4 Hyattsville MD U.S.A.
222 C4 Hydaburg AK U.S.A.
81 C6 Hyde South I. N.Z.
149 G4 Hyde Greater Manchester, England U.K.
87 C7 Hyden W.A. Austr.
232 B6 Hyden KY U.S.A.
233 G2 Hyde Park VT U.S.A.
222 D4 Hyder AK U.S.A.
114 C2 Hyderabad Andhra Prad. India
123 G5 Hyderabad Pak.
Hydra i. Greece see Ydra
161 E5 Hyères France
161 E6 Hyères, Îles d' is France
101 D4 Hyesan N. Korea
222 D3 Hyland r. Y.T. Can.
83 H2 Hyland, Mount N.S.W. Austr.
84 B2 Hyland Bay N.T. Austr.
222 D3 Hyland Post B.C. Can.
141 I3 Hyllestad Norway
142 E3 Hyltebruk Sweden
157 G4 Hymont France
232 D5 Hyndman PA U.S.A.
238 D3 Hyndman Peak ID U.S.A.
146 B5 Hynish Argyll and Bute, Scotland U.K.
104 A3 Hyōgo pref. Japan
103 G6 Hyōno-sen mt. Japan
Hyrcania Iran see Gorgān
140 O2 Hyrynsalmi Fin.
238 F2 Hysham MT U.S.A.
222 G4 Hythe Alta Can.
151 F4 Hythe Hampshire, England U.K.
151 I3 Hythe Kent, England U.K.
103 E7 Hyūga Japan
141 N3 Hyvinkää Fin.
175 K6 Hyżne Pol.

I

97 E4 Ia A Dun r. Vietnam
256 C4 Iacanga Brazil
252 C2 Iaco r. Brazil
197 G2 Iacobeni Sibiu Romania
197 G2 Iacobeni Suceava Romania
256 B4 Iacri Brazil
254 E5 Iaçu Brazil
Iadera Croatia see Zadar
232 C6 Iaeger WV U.S.A.
213 □J4 Iakora Madag.
Ialbuzi Rus. Fed. see El'brus
136 C5 Ialomiţa r. Romania
197 H3 Ialomiţa r. Romania
197 H3 Ialomiţei, Balta marsh Romania
136 E4 Ialoveni Moldova
136 E4 Ialpug r. Moldova
197 H3 Ianca Romania
197 G3 Iancu Jianu Romania
129 C2 Ianet'i Georgia
257 F3 Iapu Brazil
197 F1 Iara r. Romania
251 F4 Iarauarune, Serra mts Brazil
147 B3 Iar Connaught reg. Rep. of Ireland
136 E4 Iargara Moldova
197 H2 Iaşi Romania
198 D1 Iasmos Greece
92 A3 Iba Phil.
207 F5 Ibadan Nigeria
250 C3 Ibagué Col.
184 E1 Ibahernando Spain
256 B5 Ibaiti Brazil
197 G2 Ibăneşti Romania
241 K1 Ibapah UT U.S.A.
196 E4 Ibar r. Yugo.
103 F6 Ibara Japan
104 B3 Ibaraki Japan
105 G2 Ibaraki pref. Japan
250 B4 Ibarra Ecuador
186 A1 Ibarra Spain
258 F2 Ibarreta Arg.
125 D4 Ibb Yemen
124 D5 Ibb governorate Yemen
169 C3 Ibbenbüren Ger.
183 I3 Ibdes Spain
198 A1 Ibë Albania
183 G2 Ibeas de Juarros Spain
258 F3 Iberá, Esteros del marsh Arg.
258 F3 Iberá, Lago l. Arg.
250 C6 Iberia Loreto Peru
252 C2 Iberia Madre de Dios Peru
257 F4 Ibertioga Brazil
224 G4 Iberville Que. Can.
225 F2 Iberville, Lac d' l. Que. Can.
140 L1 Ibestad Norway
94 B1 Ibi Sumatera Indon.
187 C6 Ibi Spain
256 D3 Ibiá Brazil
256 D3 Ibiaí Brazil
254 E2 Ibiapaba, Serra da hills Brazil
182 D1 Ibias r. Spain
255 F5 Ibicaraí Brazil
255 A9 Ibicuí r. Brazil

161 C4 Ibie r. France
104 C3 Ibi-gawa r. Japan
254 F4 Ibimirim Brazil
208 F4 Ibina r. Dem. Rep. Congo
256 B5 Ibiporã Brazil
256 C4 Ibirá Brazil
257 G3 Ibiraçu Brazil
254 E5 Ibitiara Brazil
256 C4 Ibitinga Brazil
256 D5 Ibiúna Brazil
Ibiza Spain see Eivissa
Ibiza i. Spain see Eivissa
194 D5 Iblei, Monti mts Sicilia Italy
163 B5 Ibos France
254 E5 Ibotirama Brazil
208 A5 Iboundji Gabon
208 A5 Iboundji, Mont hill Gabon
125 G3 Ibrā' Oman
Ibrala Turkey see Yeşildere
135 I5 Ibresi Rus. Fed.
125 G3 Ibrī Oman
185 G2 Ibros Spain
151 F2 Ibstock Leicestershire, England U.K.
104 C3 Ibuki-yama mt. Japan
103 E8 Ibusuki Japan
250 E5 Içá r. Brazil
252 B3 Ica Peru
252 B3 Ica dept Peru
250 E4 Içana r. Brazil
Icaria i. Greece see Ikaria
254 D2 Icatu Brazil
241 J3 Iceberg Canyon gorge NV U.S.A.
126 D3 İçel İel Turkey
128 A1 İçel prov. Turkey
221 Q3 Iceland country Europe
264 H2 Iceland Basin sea feature N. Atlantic Ocean
264 I1 Icelandic Plateau sea feature N. Atlantic Ocean
256 C4 Icem Brazil
117 F4 Ichak Bihar India
114 B2 Ichalkaranji Mahar. India
115 E2 Ichchapuram Andhra Prad. India
173 E3 Ichenhausen Ger.
172 B3 Ichenheim Ger.
105 G3 Ichihara Japan
105 F3 Ichikawa Japan
104 A4 Ichi-kawa r. Japan
105 E3 Ichikawadaimon Japan
252 D4 Ichilo r. Bol.
104 C3 Ichinomiya Aichi Japan
104 D4 Ichinomiya Aichi Japan
102 J4 Ichinoseki Japan
131 Q4 Ichinskiy, Vulkan vol. Rus. Fed.
Ichkeria aut. rep. Rus. Fed. see Chechenskaya Respublika
137 G2 Ichnya Ukr.
101 C5 Ich'ŏn N. Korea
101 C5 Ich'ŏn S. Korea
165 C3 Ichtegem Belgium
169 F5 Ichtershausen Ger.
199 F2 İcikler Turkey
173 F4 Icking Ger.
151 H4 Icklesham East Sussex, England U.K.
151 H2 Icklingham Suffolk, England U.K.
199 F3 İçmeler Turkey
254 F3 Icó Brazil
216 □3a Icod de Los Vinos Tenerife Canary Is
257 G4 Iconha Brazil
Iconium Turkey see Konya
Icosium Alg. see Alger
Iculisma France see Angoulême
İd Turkey see Narman
81 C6 Ida, Mount South I. N.Z.
237 E5 Idabel OK U.S.A.
236 E3 Ida Grove IA U.S.A.
207 G5 Idah Nigeria
238 D2 Idaho state U.S.A.
238 D3 Idaho City ID U.S.A.
238 D3 Idaho Falls ID U.S.A.
238 B2 Idanha OR U.S.A.
182 C5 Idanha-a-Nova Port.
116 C5 Idar Gujarat India
172 B2 Idar-Oberstein Ger.
81 B6 Ida Valley South I. N.Z.
142 D2 Idefjorden inlet Norway/Sweden
170 C3 Iden Ger.
106 C1 Ider Mongolia
106 D1 Ideriyn Gol r. Mongolia
170 C1 Idestrup Denmark
203 G3 Idfu Egypt
202 A3 Idhān Awbārī des. Libya
202 B3 Idhān Murzūq des. Libya
Idhra i. Greece see Ydra
Idi Amin Dada, Lake Dem. Rep. Congo/Uganda see Edward, Lake
186 A1 Idiazabal Spain
191 G4 Idice r. Italy
209 C6 Idiofa Dem. Rep. Congo
220 C3 Iditarod AK U.S.A.
140 M1 Idivuoma Sweden
203 F2 Idku Egypt
149 I4 Idle r. England U.K.
128 C2 Idlib Syria
128 C2 Idlib governorate Syria
151 F3 Idmiston Wiltshire, England U.K.
183 I2 Idocin Spain
177 J6 Iđoš Vojvodina, Srbija Yugo.
Idra i. Greece see Ydra
84 C5 Idracowra N.T. Austr.
141 K3 Idre Sweden
188 E2 Idrija Slovenia
188 D2 Idrijca r. Slovenia
138 G3 Idritsa Rus. Fed.
190 F3 Idro Italy
163 B5 Idron-Ousse-Sendets France
168 E1 Idstedt Ger.
169 D5 Idstein Ger.
114 C4 Idukki Kerala India
215 G5 Idutywa S. Africa
240 I5 Idyllwild CA U.S.A.
Idzhevan Armenia see Ijevan
102 □2 Ie Japan
138 E3 Iecava Latvia
138 D3 Iecava r. Latvia
102 □2 Ie-jima i. Japan
256 B5 Iepê Brazil
165 B4 Ieper Belgium
197 F2 Ier r. Romania
199 D4 Ierapetra Kriti Greece
211 C7 Ifakara Tanz.
91 J5 Ifalik atoll Micronesia
Ifaluk atoll Micronesia see Ifalik
213 □J4 Ifanadiana Madag.
213 □J4 Ifanirea Madag.
207 G5 Ife Nigeria
202 C6 Ifenat Chad
207 H2 Iferouâne Niger
205 G4 Ifetesene mt. Alg.
173 F4 Iffeldorf Ger.
158 D3 Iffendic France
172 C3 Iffezheim Ger.
85 E3 Iffley Qld Austr.
207 F2 Ifôghas, Adrar des hills Mali
207 G5 Ifon Nigeria
82 C2 Ifould Lake salt flat S.A. Austr.
204 D2 Ifrane Morocco
159 F2 Ifs France
169 F4 Ifta Ger.
179 F5 Ig Slovenia
207 G4 Igabi Nigeria
177 G5 Igal Hungary
196 D4 Igalo Crna Gora Yugo.
95 E2 Igan r. Sarawak Malaysia
210 B4 Iganga Uganda
177 H5 Igar Hungary
256 D4 Igarapava Brazil
254 D2 Igarape Açú Brazil
254 D3 Igarapé Grande Brazil
254 C2 Igarapé Miri Brazil
256 D5 Igaratá Brazil
130 J3 Igarka Rus. Fed.
253 G6 Igatimí Para.
114 B2 Igatpuri Mahar. India
207 G4 Igbeti Nigeria
207 F4 Igboho Nigeria
207 H5 Igbor Nigeria
127 G3 Iğdır Turkey
129 D4 Iğdır prov. Turkey
159 G3 Igé France
183 H2 Igea Spain
172 A2 Igel Ger.
173 F2 Igensdorf Ger.
172 D2 Igersheim Ger.
172 C2 Iggelheim Ger.
173 H3 Iggensbach Ger.
141 L3 Iggesund Sweden
197 F2 Ighiu Romania
190 E2 Igis Switz.
192 A5 Iglesias Sardegna Italy
192 A5 Iglesiente reg. Sardegna Italy
204 E3 Igli Alg.
173 E3 Igling Ger.
134 L5 Iglino Rus. Fed.
221 J3 Igloolik Nunavut Can.
Igluligaarjuk Nunavut Can. see Chesterfield Inlet
128 A5 'Igma, Gebel el plat. Egypt
224 B3 Ignace Ont. Can.
244 B1 Ignacio Allende Mex.
245 G4 Ignacio de la Llave Mex.
242 D2 Ignacio Zaragosa Mex.
138 F4 Ignalina Lith.
126 B2 İğneada Turkey
177 L5 Ignești Romania
157 G4 Igney France
160 D1 Ignon r. France
134 H4 Igodovo Rus. Fed.
211 A6 Igombe r. Tanz.
139 I4 Igorevskaya Rus. Fed.
160 C1 Igornay France
183 H1 Igorre Spain
198 B2 Igoumenitsa Greece
134 K4 Igra Rus. Fed.
182 B2 Igrexa Spain
182 B2 Igrexario Spain
186 C2 Igriés Spain
130 H3 Igrim Rus. Fed.
255 B8 Iguaçu r. Brazil
255 E5 Iguaí Brazil
250 C4 Iguaje, Mesa de hills Col.
245 E4 Iguala Mex.
186 E3 Igualada Spain
185 E4 Igualeja Spain
256 D6 Iguape Brazil
256 B5 Iguaraçu Brazil
257 E4 Iguarapé Brazil
257 E4 Iguatama Brazil
255 B7 Iguatemi Brazil
255 B7 Iguatemi r. Brazil
254 F3 Iguatu Brazil
182 D2 Igueña Spain
160 C2 Iguerande France
211 B6 Igunga Tanz.
207 G5 Iguobazuwa Nigeria
Iguvium Italy see Gubbio
213 □K2 Iharaña Madag.
176 G5 Iharosberény Hungary
114 B5 Ihavandhippolhu Atoll Maldives
107 E3 Ihbulag Mongolia
102 □1 Iheya-jima i. Japan
106 E2 Ihhayrhan Mongolia
207 G5 Ihiala Nigeria
177 J2 Ihľany Slovakia
168 C2 Ihlowerhörn (Ihlow) Ger.
136 E2 Ihnatpil' Ukr.
163 A5 Iholdy France
213 □J4 Ihosy Madag.
168 C2 Ihrhove Ger.
172 B3 Ihringen Ger.
173 F3 Ihrlerstein Ger.
199 G2 İhsaniye Turkey
106 E1 Ihsuuj Mongolia
107 I3 Ih Tal Nei Mongol China
105 D3 Iida Japan
102 I5 Iide-san mt. Japan
140 N2 Iijoki r. Fin.
140 N3 Iisalmi Fin.
138 F1 Iitti Fin.
105 E2 Iiyama Japan
103 E7 Iizuka Japan
207 F5 Ijebu-Ode Nigeria
129 D3 Ijevan Armenia
164 E1 IJlst Neth.
164 D2 IJmuiden Neth.
204 D5 Ijoubbâne des. Mali
164 E2 IJssel r. Neth.
164 E2 IJsselmeer l. Neth.
164 E2 IJsselmuiden Neth.
164 E2 IJsselstein Neth.
255 B9 Ijuí Brazil
253 G6 Ijuí r. Brazil
165 C3 IJzendijke Neth.
165 B3 IJzer r. Belgium alt. Yser (France)
Ikaahuk N.W.T. Can. see Sachs Harbour
141 M3 Ikaalinen Fin.
215 F1 Ikageleng S. Africa
215 F2 Ikageng S. Africa
213 □J3 Ikahavo hill Madag.
213 □J4 Ikalamavony Madag.
81 C5 Ikamatua South I. N.Z.
207 H5 Ikang Nigeria
207 H4 Ikara Nigeria
207 G5 Ikare Nigeria
199 E3 Ikaria i. Greece
104 B4 Ikaruga Japan
142 C3 Ikast Denmark
81 C6 Ikawai South I. N.Z.
80 F3 Ikawhenua Range mts North I. N.Z.
104 B3 Ikeda Japan
104 C4 Ikegoya-yama mt. Japan
207 F5 Ikeja Nigeria
208 D5 Ikela Dem. Rep. Congo
208 C4 Ikelemba r. Dem. Rep. Congo
207 G5 Ikem Nigeria
207 G5 Ikere Nigeria
Ikerre Nigeria see Ikere
176 F4 Ikervár Hungary
197 F4 Ikhtiman Bulg.
215 E3 Ikhutseng S. Africa
103 D7 Iki i. Japan
128 D1 İkiağiz Turkey
135 I7 Iki-Burul Rus. Fed.
207 G5 Ikire Nigeria
129 B3 İkizdere Turkey
207 H5 Ikom Nigeria
104 B4 Ikoma Japan
213 □J4 Ikongo Madag.
217 □3a Ikoni Njazidja Comoros
129 B1 Ikon-Khalk Rus. Fed.
213 □J3 Ikopa r. Madag.
137 J2 Ikorets r. Rus. Fed.
207 F5 Ikorodu Nigeria
207 G5 Ikot Ekpene Nigeria
205 H4 Ikouhaouene, Adrar mt. Alg.
177 G4 Ikrény Hungary
101 C6 Iksan S. Korea
211 B6 Ikungi Tanz.
211 B6 Ikungu Tanz.
136 C2 Ikva r. Ukr.
207 G4 Ila Nigeria
92 B2 Ilagan Phil.
114 C4 Ilaiyankudi Tamil Nadu India
213 □K3 Ilaka Atsinanana Madag.
122 A3 Īlām Iran
122 A3 Īlām prov. Iran
117 F4 Ilam Nepal
109 G3 Ilan Taiwan
174 C3 Ilanka r. Pol.
190 E2 Ilanz Switz.
137 H3 Ilarionove Ukr.
207 F5 Ilaro Nigeria
252 C4 Ilave Peru
175 H2 Iława Pol.
207 G5 Ilawe-Ekiti Nigeria
122 D4 Ilazārān, Kūh-e mt. Iran
106 C2 Il Bogd Uul mts Mongolia
192 B5 Ilbono Sardegna Italy
150 E4 Ilchester Somerset, England U.K.
Ile r. China/Kazakh. see Ili
223 J4 Île-à-la-Crosse Sask. Can.
209 D6 Ilebo Dem. Rep. Congo
156 C4 Île-de-France admin. reg. France
211 B7 Ileje Tanz.
120 C2 Ilek Kazakh.
120 C2 Ilek r. Rus. Fed.
137 H2 Ilek-Pen'kovka Rus. Fed.
147 B5 Ilen r. Rep. of Ireland
Ilerda prov. Cataluña Spain see Lérida
Île Royale i. N.S. Can. see Cape Breton Island
207 G5 Ilesa Nigeria
Ilesha Nigeria see Ilesa
207 F4 Ilesha Ibariba Nigeria
134 J5 Ilet' r. Rus. Fed.
134 H3 Ileza Rus. Fed.
169 F4 Ilfeld Ger.
223 M3 Ilford Man. Can.
151 H3 Ilford Greater London, England U.K.
85 F4 Ilfracombe Qld Austr.
150 C3 Ilfracombe Devon, England U.K.
126 D2 Ilgaz Turkey
126 C3 Ilgın Turkey
257 E5 Ilhabela Brazil
257 E5 Ilha Grande, Baía da b. Brazil
255 B7 Ilha Grande, Represa resr Brazil
256 B4 Ilha Solteíra, Represa resr Brazil
182 B4 Ílhavo Port.
255 F5 Ilhéus Brazil
121 I3 Ili r. China/Kazakh.
Ili Kazakh. see Kapchagay
197 F3 Ilia Romania
220 C4 Iliamna Lake AK U.S.A.
126 E3 İliç Turkey
129 B4 Ilıca Turkey
129 B4 Ilıca Turkey
121 G4 Il'ich Kazakh.
Il'ichevsk Azer. see Şärur
Il'ichevsk Ukr. see Illichivs'k
Ilici Spain see Elche
92 C4 Iligan Phil.
92 C4 Iligan Bay Phil.
Ili He r. China/Kazakh. see Ili
188 G4 Ilijaš Bos.-Herz.
221 P2 Ilimananngip Nunaa i. Greenland
131 L3 Ilimpeya r. Rus. Fed.
120 D2 Il'inka Kazakh.
121 K2 Il'inka Rus. Fed.
139 H4 Il'ino Rus. Fed.
134 K4 Il'inskiy Rus. Fed.
139 I1 Il'inskiy Rus. Fed.
100 G3 Il'inskiy Sakhalin Rus. Fed.
134 I3 Il'insko-Podomskoye Rus. Fed.
137 J4 Il'inskoye Rus. Fed.
139 J5 Il'inskoye Rus. Fed.
139 K3 Il'inskoye Rus. Fed.
139 L3 Il'inskoye Rus. Fed.
139 L3 Il'inskoye-Khovanskoye Rus. Fed.
Il'intsy Ukr. see Illintsi
233 F3 Ilion NY U.S.A.
188 E3 Ilirska Bistrica Slovenia
Ilium tourist site Turkey see Truva
138 F4 Iliya r. Belarus
Iliysk Kazakh. see Kapchagay
177 L3 Ilk Hungary
114 C3 Ilkal Karnataka India
151 F2 Ilkeston Derbyshire, England U.K.
149 H4 Ilkley West Yorkshire, England U.K.
157 H4 Ill r. France
183 H4 Illana Spain
92 B5 Illana Bay Phil.
260 B2 Illapel Chile
260 B2 Illapel r. Chile
185 H4 Illar Spain
191 G3 Illasi r. Italy
163 B4 Illats France
82 C1 Illbillee, Mount hill S.A. Austr.
158 E3 Ille r. France
158 E3 Ille-et-Vilaine dept Bretagne France
207 G3 Illéla Niger
207 G3 Illela Nigeria
173 D3 Iller r. Ger.
173 E3 Illerrieden Ger.
173 E3 Illertissen Ger.
183 G4 Illescas Spain
163 E6 Ille-sur-Têt France
136 F4 Illichivs'k Ukr.
156 B4 Illiers-Combray France
252 D4 Illimani, Nevado de mt. Bol.
172 C3 Illingen Baden-Württemberg Ger.
172 B2 Illingen Saarland Ger.
136 F4 Illinka Ukr.
226 B5 Illinois r. IL U.S.A.
236 F4 Illinois state U.S.A.
136 E3 Illintsi Ukr.
205 H4 Illizi Alg.
157 H4 Illkirch-Graffenstaden France
172 D4 Illmensee Ger.
179 H3 Illmitz Austria
185 G3 Íllora Spain
192 A4 Illorai Sardegna Italy
173 F2 Illschwang Ger.
183 I3 Illueca Spain
157 H5 Illzach France
171 C4 Ilm r. Ger.
173 F3 Ilm r. Ger.
87 E6 Ilma, Lake salt flat W.A. Austr.
124 D4 'Ilmān, Jabal al hill Saudi Arabia
139 H2 Il'men', Ozero l. Rus. Fed.
169 F5 Ilmenau Ger.
168 F2 Ilmenau r. Ger.
150 E4 Ilminster Somerset, England U.K.
136 B3 Il'nytsya Ukr.
252 C4 Ilo Peru
207 G5 Ilobu Nigeria
92 B4 Iloilo Phil.
140 O3 Ilomantsi Fin.
207 G4 Ilorin Nigeria
188 F3 Ilova r. Croatia
135 I6 Ilovatka Rus. Fed.
137 J4 Ilovays'k Ukr.
197 F5 Ilovica Macedonia
137 J2 Ilovka Rus. Fed.
135 H6 Ilovlya Rus. Fed.
135 H6 Ilovlya r. Rus. Fed.
175 I3 Iłów Pol.
174 D4 Iłowa Pol.
175 I2 Iłowo Osada Pol.
164 D2 Ilpendam Neth.
131 R3 Il'pyrskiy Rus. Fed.
Il'pyrskoye Rus. Fed. see Il'pyrskiy
141 L3 Ilsbo Sweden
169 F3 Ilse r. Ger.
169 F3 Ilsede Ger.
169 F4 Ilsenburg (Harz) Ger.
172 D2 Ilsfeld Ger.
172 D2 Ilshofen Ger.
150 D4 Ilsington Devon, England U.K.
137 J5 Il'skiy Rus. Fed.
138 F4 Ilūkste Latvia
221 M3 Ilulissat Greenland
Ilva i. Italy see Elba, Isola d'
138 F4 Il'ya Belarus
Il'yaly Turkm. see Gyaylanly
134 L3 Ilych r. Rus. Fed.
179 G3 Ilz Austria
173 H3 Ilz r. Ger.
175 J4 Iłża Pol.
175 J4 Iłżanka r. Pol.
103 F6 Imabari Japan
102 J3 Imabetsu Japan
251 G5 Imabú r. Brazil
105 F2 Imaichi Japan
213 H2 Imala Moz.
127 G5 Imām al Ḩamzah Iraq
126 D3 İmamoğlu Turkey
Iman Rus. Fed. see Dal'nerechensk
100 E3 Iman r. Rus. Fed.
121 G1 Imantau, Ozero l. Kazakh.
103 D7 Imari Japan
206 E3 Imasgo Burkina
Imassogo Burkina see Imasgo
251 F3 Imataca, Serranía de mts Venez.
141 O3 Imatra Fin.
250 B4 Imbabura prov. Ecuador
255 C9 Imbituba Brazil
256 B6 Imbituva Brazil
177 H4 Imeľ Slovakia
imeni 26 Bakinskikh Komissarov Azer. see 26 Bakı Komissarı
122 C2 imeni 26 Bakinskikh Komissarov Turkm.
134 H4 imeni Babushkina Rus. Fed.
123 E2 imeni C. A. Niyazova Turkm.
imeni Chapayevka Turkm. see imeni C. A. Niyazova
131 P3 imeni Gastello Rus. Fed.
imeni G. I. Petrovskogo Cherkas'ka Oblast' Ukr. see Horodyshche
139 M3 imeni Gor'kogo Rus. Fed.
imeni G. Ya. Sedova Ukr. see Syedove
137 H2 imeni Karla Libknekhta Rus. Fed.
imeni Khamzy Khakikmzade Uzbek. see Khamza
imeni Kirova Kazakh. see Kopbirlik
imeni Kirova Donets'ka Oblast' Ukr. see Kirove
imeni Kirova Donets'ka Oblast' Ukr. see Kirovs'k
imeni L. M. Kaganovicha Ukr. see Popasna
134 I4 imeni M. I. Kalinina Rus. Fed.
imeni Petra Stuchki Latvia see Aizkraukle
100 F1 imeni Poliny Osipenko Rus. Fed.
139 K2 imeni Zhelyabova Rus. Fed.
137 H3 Imeny Lenina, Ozero l. Ukr.
191 G2 Imèr Italy
194 D5 Imera r. Sicilia Italy
251 E4 Imeri, Serra mts Brazil
210 D3 Īmī Eth.
204 C3 Imi-n-Tanoute Morocco
204 B4 Imirikliy Labyad reg. Western Sahara
Imishli Azer. see İmişli
129 F4 İmişli Azer.
101 C5 Imjin-gang r. N. Korea/S. Korea
227 F4 Imlay City MI U.S.A.
169 F5 Immelborn Ger.
172 C4 Immendingen Ger.
169 E4 Immenhausen Ger.
173 F2 Immenreuth Ger.
172 D4 Immenstaad am Bodensee Ger.
173 E4 Immenstadt im Allgäu Ger.
149 I4 Immingham North East Lincolnshire, England U.K.
231 D7 Immokalee FL U.S.A.
207 G5 Imo state Nigeria
191 G4 Imola Italy
188 F4 Imotski Croatia
215 G3 Impendle S. Africa
254 D3 Imperatriz Brazil
190 D5 Imperia Italy
190 C4 Imperia prov. Liguria Italy
260 A6 Imperial r. Chile
252 A3 Imperial Peru
241 J5 Imperial CA U.S.A.
236 C3 Imperial NE U.S.A.
240 I5 Imperial Beach CA U.S.A.
86 C3 Imperieuse Reef W.A. Austr.
208 C4 Impfondo Congo
117 H4 Imphal Manipur India
160 B2 Imphy France
151 H2 Impington Cambridgeshire, England U.K.
191 G5 Impruneta Italy
177 I5 Imrehegy Hungary
199 D1 İmroz Çanakkale Turkey
İmroz i. Turkey see Gökçeada
İmrun Turkey see Pütürge
101 C6 Imsil S. Korea
178 B3 Imst Austria
242 C2 Imuris Mex.
180 E5 Imzouren Morocco
100 E2 In r. Rus. Fed.
105 D3 Ina Japan
174 C2 Ina r. Pol.
92 A4 Inagauan Phil.
104 B4 Ina-gawa r. Japan
147 B4 Inagh Rep. of Ireland
105 F3 Inagi Japan
254 F4 Inajá Brazil
253 H2 Inaja r. Brazil
252 C3 Inambari Peru
252 C3 Inambari r. Peru
177 K3 Ináncs Hungary
215 H3 Inanda S. Africa
81 C4 Inangahua Junction South I. N.Z.
252 C2 Iñapari Peru
140 N1 Inari Fin.
140 N1 Inarijärvi l. Fin.
140 N1 Inarijoki r. Fin./Norway
252 D2 Inauini r. Brazil
103 J5 Inawashiro-ko l. Japan
104 C3 Inazawa Japan
187 F5 Inca Spain
199 F3 İnceler Turkey
147 B4 Inch Kerry Rep. of Ireland
147 E4 Inch Wexford Rep. of Ireland
146 F5 Inchbare Angus, Scotland U.K.
81 C5 Inchbonnie South I. N.Z.
122 D2 Īncheh Iran
173 F3 Inchenhofen Ger.
156 B2 Incheville France
147 B5 Inchigeelagh Rep. of Ireland
210 C3 Īnch'īnī Terara mt. Eth.
146 D6 Inchinnan Renfrewshire, Scotland U.K.
204 B5 Inchiri admin. reg. Maur.
101 C5 Inch'ŏn S. Korea
213 G3 Inchope Moz.
146 E5 Inchture Perth and Kinross, Scotland U.K.
183 G2 Incinillas Spain
Incio Spain see A Cruz de Incio
Incirli Sakarya Turkey see Karasu
213 G5 Incomati r. Moz.
165 D4 Incourt Belgium
192 B3 Incudine, Monte mt. France
138 E3 Inčukalns Latvia
146 B6 Indaal, Loch b. Scotland U.K.
257 E3 Indaiá r. Brazil
256 A3 Indaiá Grande r. Brazil
256 D5 Indaiatuba Brazil
140 L3 Indalsälven r. Sweden
141 I3 Indalstø Norway
244 D4 Indaparapeo Mex.
116 D4 Indargarh Madh. Prad. India
116 D4 Indargarh Rajasthan India
210 C1 Inda Silasē Eth.
242 D3 Indé Mex.
Indefatigable Island Islas Galápagos Ecuador see Santa Cruz, Isla
240 H3 Independence CA U.S.A.
236 F3 Independence IA U.S.A.
237 E4 Independence KS U.S.A.
230 C4 Independence KY U.S.A.
226 A2 Independence MN U.S.A.
236 E4 Independence MO U.S.A.
232 C6 Independence VA U.S.A.
226 B3 Independence WI U.S.A.
238 C3 Independence Mountains NV U.S.A.
252 D4 Independencia Bol.
254 E3 Independência Brazil
245 F3 Independencia Mex.
197 H3 Independența Romania
197 I4 Independența Romania
197 H3 Independența Romania
107 I2 Inder Nei Mongol China
120 B2 Inderborskiy Kazakh.
114 C2 Indi Karnataka India
113 H6 India country Asia
226 D2 Indian r. MI U.S.A.
232 D4 Indiana PA U.S.A.
230 C3 Indiana state U.S.A.
264 P9 Indian-Antarctic Basin sea feature Southern Ocean
265 L8 Indian-Antarctic Ridge sea feature Southern Ocean
230 C4 Indianapolis IN U.S.A.
222 G3 Indian Cabins Alta Can.
Indian Desert India/Pak. see Thar Desert
232 B6 Indian Fields KY U.S.A.
225 J2 Indian Harbour Nfld. Can.
223 K5 Indian Head Sask. Can.
233 F3 Indian Lake NY U.S.A.
235 F1 Indian Neck CT U.S.A.
263 □G5 Indian Ocean OCEAN
236 E3 Indianola IA U.S.A.
237 F5 Indianola MS U.S.A.
256 D3 Indianópolis Brazil
241 K2 Indian Peak UT U.S.A.
226 E3 Indian River MI U.S.A.
241 J3 Indian Springs NV U.S.A.
241 L4 Indian Wells AZ U.S.A.
256 B2 Indiara Brazil
254 F4 Indiaroba Brazil
247 □1 Indiera Alta Puerto Rico
131 P2 Indigirka r. Rus. Fed.
196 E3 Inđija Vojvodina, Srbija Yugo.
242 □J7 Indio r. Nic.
241 I5 Indio CA U.S.A.
261 G6 Indio Rico Arg.
78 □6 Indispensable Strait Solomon Is
137 H5 Indol r. Ukr.
139 K1 Indomanka r. Rus. Fed.
90 D7 Indonesia country Asia
116 C5 Indore Madh. Prad. India
94 C3 Indragiri r. Indon.
95 E4 Indramayu Jawa Barat Indon.
Indrapura, Gunung vol. Indon. see Kerinci, Gunung
115 D2 Indravati r. India
159 H5 Indre dept Centre France
162 C1 Indre r. France
159 G4 Indre-et-Loire dept Centre France
82 C1 Indulkana S.A. Austr.
Indur Andhra Prad. India see Nizamabad
114 C2 Indurti Andhra Prad. India
116 E2 Indus r. China/Pak. alt. Shiquan He (China)
123 F5 Indus, Mouths of the Pak.
265 I3 Indus Cone sea feature Indian Ocean
215 F4 Indwe S. Africa
215 F5 Indwe r. S. Africa
197 H4 Indzhe Voyvoda Bulg.
126 D2 İnebolu Turkey
199 F1 İnegöl Turkey
93 B5 Inerie vol. Flores Indon.
197 E2 Ineu Arad Romania
177 L4 Ineu Bihor Romania
Inevi Turkey see Cihanbeyli
232 B6 Inez KY U.S.A.
204 C3 Inezgane Morocco
214 C6 Infanta, Cape S. Africa
Infantes Spain see Villanueva de los Infantes
245 G5 Inferior, Laguna lag. Mex.
253 E2 Infernao, Cachoeira waterfall Brazil
244 D4 Infiernillo, Presa resr Mex.
183 E1 Infiesto Spain
96 C2 Ing, Mae Nam r. Thai.
209 B6 Inga Dem. Rep. Congo
141 N3 Ingå Fin.
207 G2 Ingal Niger
240 G2 Ingalls, Mount CA U.S.A.
151 H3 Ingatestone Essex, England U.K.
172 D2 Ingelfingen Ger.
172 C2 Ingelheim am Rhein Ger.
165 C4 Ingelmunster Belgium
143 F3 Ingelstad Sweden
208 C5 Ingende Dem. Rep. Congo
258 E1 Ingeniero Guillermo Nueva Juárez Arg.
260 D6 Ingeniero Huergo Arg.
259 C6 Ingeniero Jacobacci Arg.
260 E4 Ingeniero Luiggi Arg.
261 H4 Ingeniero Maschwitz Arg.
261 H4 Ingeniero Otamendi Arg.
222 E3 Ingenika r. B.C. Can.
216 □3f Ingenio Gran Canaria Canary Is
252 B3 Ingenio r. Peru
224 D5 Ingersoll Ont. Can.
106 D1 Ingettolgoy Mongolia
85 F3 Ingham Qld Austr.
120 F5 Ingichka Uzbek.
183 H2 Inglares r. Spain
149 G3 Ingleborough hill England U.K.
149 H3 Ingleton Durham, England U.K.
149 G3 Ingleton North Yorkshire, England U.K.
149 G4 Inglewhite Lancashire, England U.K.
83 G2 Inglewood Qld Austr.
83 E4 Inglewood Vic. Austr.
80 E3 Inglewood North I. N.Z.
240 H5 Inglewood CA U.S.A.
149 G3 Inglewood Forest England U.K.
84 D2 Inglis Island N.T. Austr.
107 G1 Ingoda r. Rus. Fed.
96 B1 Ingoka Pum mt. Myanmar
172 D3 Ingoldingen Ger.
149 J4 Ingoldmells Lincolnshire, England U.K.
173 F3 Ingolstadt Ger.
82 C2 Ingomar S.A. Austr.
238 F2 Ingomar MT U.S.A.
225 I4 Ingonish N.S. Can.
117 G4 Ingraj Bazar W. Bengal India
146 G6 Ingram Northumberland, England U.K.
232 D6 Ingram VA U.S.A.
226 B3 Ingram WI U.S.A.
159 F4 Ingrandes Pays de la Loire France
159 G5 Ingrandes Poitou-Charentes France
252 E5 Ingre Bol.
156 B5 Ingré France
263 F2 Ingrid Christensen Coast Antarctica
158 C4 Inguiniel France
Ingul r. Ukr. see Inhul
Ingulets Ukr. see Inhulets'
Ingushetia aut. rep. Rus. Fed. see Ingushskaya Respublika
129 D2 Ingushskaya Respublika aut. rep. Rus. Fed.
215 I2 Ingwavuma S. Africa
Ingwavuma r. Swaziland see Ngwavuma
157 H4 Ingwiller France
213 G4 Inhambane Moz.
213 G4 Inhambane prov. Moz.
254 F4 Inhambupe Brazil
213 G3 Inhaminga Moz.
257 F3 Inhapim Brazil
213 G4 Inhassoro Moz.
205 F5 I-n-Hihaou, Adrar hills Alg.
199 G1 İnhisar Turkey
137 F4 Inhul r. Ukr.
137 G4 Inhulets' Ukr.
137 G4 Inhulets' r. Ukr.
256 C2 Inhumas Brazil
93 B5 Inielika vol. Flores Indon.
185 I1 Iniesta Spain
257 E3 Inimutaba Brazil
138 C1 Iniö Fin.
250 E4 Inírida r. Col.
Inis Rep. of Ireland see Ennis
Inis Córthaidh Rep. of Ireland see Enniscorthy
147 A3 Inishark i. Rep. of Ireland
147 A3 Inishbofin i. Rep. of Ireland
147 B3 Inisheer i. Rep. of Ireland
147 B3 Inishmaan i. Rep. of Ireland
147 B3 Inishmore i. Rep. of Ireland
147 C2 Inishmurray i. Rep. of Ireland
147 D1 Inishowen pen. Rep. of Ireland
147 E1 Inishowen Head hd Rep. of Ireland
147 D1 Inishtrahull i. Rep. of Ireland
147 D1 Inishtrahull Sound sea chan. Rep. of Ireland
147 A3 Inishturk i. Rep. of Ireland
107 H2 Injgan Sum Nei Mongol China
210 C2 Injibara Eth.
85 G5 Injune Qld Austr.
120 F3 Inkardar'ya Kazakh.
151 F2 Inkberrow Worcestershire, England U.K.
176 G5 Inke Hungary
85 E3 Inkerman Qld Austr.
137 G5 Inkerman Ukr.
222 C3 Inklin B.C. Can.
222 C3 Inklin r. B.C. Can.
81 D5 Inland Kaikoura Range mts South I. N.Z.
Inland Sea Japan see Seto-naikai
233 F3 Inlet NY U.S.A.
173 E5 Inn r. Europe
103 E7 Innai Japan
82 E1 Innamincka S.A. Austr.
140 K2 Inndyr Norway
146 D6 Innellan Argyll and Bute, Scotland U.K.
217 □2a Inner Islands Seychelles
146 E6 Innerleithen Scottish Borders, Scotland U.K.
173 H3 Innernzell Ger.
146 C4 Inner Sound sea chan. Scotland U.K.
190 D2 Innertkirchen Switz.
173 F3 Inning am Ammersee Ger.
85 F3 Innisfail Qld Austr.
222 H4 Innisfail Alta Can.
147 C5 Innishannon Rep. of Ireland
147 E2 Inniskeen Rep. of Ireland
100 D2 Innokent'yevka Rus. Fed.
103 F6 Innoshima Japan
178 C3 Innsbruck Austria
191 G1 Innsbruck airport Austria
224 E1 Innuksuak r. Que. Can.
147 A5 Inny r. Kerry Rep. of Ireland
147 D3 Inny r. Longford/Westmeath Rep. of Ireland
256 B3 Inocência Brazil
208 C5 Inongo Dem. Rep. Congo
199 G2 İnönü Turkey
Inoucdjouac Que. Can. see Inukjuak
177 H3 Inovec mt. Slovakia
175 I4 Inowłódz Pol.
174 G3 Inowrocław Pol.
129 C1 Inozemtsevo Rus. Fed.
252 D4 Inquisivi Bol.
190 C1 Ins Switz.
205 F4 In Salah Alg.
135 I5 Insar Rus. Fed.
146 F4 Insch Aberdeenshire, Scotland U.K.
87 B5 Inscription, Cape W.A. Austr.
96 B3 Insein Myanmar
174 D2 Ińsko Pol.
157 G4 Insming France
Insterburg Rus. Fed. see Chernyakhovsk
129 E3 İnstitut Azer.
138 C4 Instruch r. Rus. Fed.
197 H3 Însurăței Romania
213 E3 Insuza r. Zimbabwe
134 M2 Inta Rus. Fed.
261 F4 Intendente Alvear Arg.
199 E1 İntepe Turkey
Interamna Italy see Teramo
190 C2 Interlaken Switz.
226 A1 International Falls MN U.S.A.
197 H3 Întorsura Buzăului Romania
190 E3 Introbio Italy
250 C5 Intutu Peru
224 E1 Inukjuak Que. Can.
220 E3 Inuvik N.W.T. Can.
252 B2 Inuya r. Peru
104 C3 Inuyama Japan
134 L4 In'va r. Rus. Fed.
147 C2 Inver Rep. of Ireland
146 C4 Inveralligin Highland, Scotland U.K.
146 G4 Inverallochy Aberdeenshire, Scotland U.K.
147 B3 Inveran Rep. of Ireland
146 C5 Inveraray Argyll and Bute, Scotland U.K.
146 F5 Inverarity Angus, Scotland U.K.
146 D5 Inverarnan Argyll and Bute, Scotland U.K.
146 F5 Inverbervie Aberdeenshire, Scotland U.K.
81 B7 Invercargill South I. N.Z.
146 D6 Inverclyde admin. div. Scotland U.K.
83 G2 Inverell N.S.W. Austr.
146 E5 Inverey Aberdeenshire, Scotland U.K.
146 D4 Invergarry Highland, Scotland U.K.
146 D4 Invergordon Highland, Scotland U.K.
146 C5 Inverinan Argyll and Bute, Scotland U.K.
146 F5 Inverkeilor Angus, Scotland U.K.
146 E5 Inverkeithing Fife, Scotland U.K.
146 C3 Inverkirkaig Highland, Scotland U.K.
146 C4 Inverlael Highland, Scotland U.K.
85 E3 Inverleigh Qld Austr.
223 K5 Invermay Sask. Can.
146 D4 Invermoriston Highland, Scotland U.K.
225 I4 Inverness N.S. Can.
146 D4 Inverness Highland, Scotland U.K.
240 F2 Inverness CA U.S.A.
231 D6 Inverness FL U.S.A.
146 C5 Invernoaden Argyll and Bute, Scotland U.K.
146 D5 Inversnaid Stirling, Scotland U.K.
146 F4 Inverurie Aberdeenshire, Scotland U.K.
84 B3 Inverway N.T. Austr.
97 B4 Investigator Channel Myanmar
82 C3 Investigator Group is S.A. Austr.
265 K5 Investigator Ridge sea feature Indian Ocean
82 D3 Investigator Strait S.A. Austr.
232 D5 Inwood WV U.S.A.
215 G4 Inxu r. S. Africa
Inyanga Zimbabwe see Nyanga
213 G3 Inyangani mt. Zimbabwe
Inyati Zimbabwe see Nyathi
Inyazura Zimbabwe see Nyazura
240 I4 Inyokern CA U.S.A.
240 H3 Inyo Mountains CA U.S.A.
211 B6 Inyonga Tanz.
135 I5 Inza Rus. Fed.
173 G4 Inzell Ger.
120 D1 Inzer Rus. Fed.
134 L5 Inzer r. Rus. Fed.
135 H5 Inzhavino Rus. Fed.
178 C3 Inzing Austria
158 C4 Inzinzac-Lochrist France
198 B2 Ioannina Greece
198 B2 Ioanninon, Limni l. Greece
191 I2 Iôf di Montasio mt. Italy
103 □3 Iō-jima i. Japan
134 G2 Iokanga r. Rus. Fed.
237 E4 Iola KS U.S.A.
234 B1 Iola PA U.S.A.
226 C3 Iola WI U.S.A.
Iolotan' Turkm. see Yeloten
209 B9 Iona Angola
225 I4 Iona N.S. Can.
146 B5 Iona i. Scotland U.K.
146 B5 Iona Abbey tourist site Scotland U.K.
240 I2 Ione NV U.S.A.
238 C1 Ione WA U.S.A.
197 G3 Ionești Romania
226 E4 Ionia MI U.S.A.
Ionian Islands Greece see Ionioi Nisoi
198 A2 Ionian Sea Greece/Italy
Ionio prov. Puglia Italy see Taranto
198 A2 Ionioi Nisoi is Greece
Iori r. Azer. see Qabırrı
129 E3 Iori r. Georgia
198 D3 Ios Greece
199 D3 Ios i. Greece
Iō-tō i. Japan see Iō-jima
102 □1 Iō-Tori-jima i. Japan
206 A2 Iouîk Maur.
236 F3 Iowa r. IA U.S.A.
236 E3 Iowa state U.S.A.
236 F3 Iowa City IA U.S.A.
236 E3 Iowa Falls IA U.S.A.
104 C2 Iō-zan hill Japan
136 E1 Ipa r. Belarus
256 C2 Ipameri Brazil
257 G3 Ipanema Brazil
254 F4 Ipanema r. Brazil
252 B2 Iparía Peru
257 F3 Ipatinga Brazil
135 H7 Ipatovo Rus. Fed.
256 C5 Ipauçu Brazil
226 B5 Ipava IL U.S.A.
198 B2 Ipeiros admin. reg. Greece
177 H4 Ipeľ r. Slovakia
177 I3 Ipeľ r. Slovakia
215 E2 Ipelegeng S. Africa
177 H4 Ipeľská pahorkatina mts Slovakia
173 E2 Iphofen Ger.
256 C3 Ipiaçu Brazil
250 B4 Ipiales Col.
254 F5 Ipiaú Brazil
254 F5 Ipirá Brazil
256 B6 Ipiranga Brazil
Ípiros admin. reg. Greece see Ipeiros
78 □4a Ipis i. Chuuk Micronesia
252 B1 Ipixuna Brazil
252 B1 Ipixuna r. Amazonas Brazil
251 F6 Ipixuna r. Amazonas Brazil
94 C1 Ipoh Malaysia
177 H4 Ipoly r. Hungary/Slovakia
215 E3 Ipopeng S. Africa
256 B2 Iporá Brazil
256 C6 Iporanga Brazil
194 D6 Ippari r. Sicilia Italy
173 E2 Ippesheim Ger.
150 D4 Ipplepen Devon, England U.K.
208 D3 Ippy C.A.R.
199 E1 İpsala Turkey
173 E2 Ipsheim Ger.
149 H4 Ipstones Staffordshire, England U.K.
85 H5 Ipswich Qld Austr.
151 I2 Ipswich Suffolk, England U.K.
236 D2 Ipswich SD U.S.A.
254 E3 Ipu Brazil
256 C4 Ipuã Brazil
254 E3 Ipueiras Brazil
256 D5 Ipuiúna Brazil
254 E4 Ipupiara Brazil
139 H5 Iput' r. Rus. Fed.
137 F1 Iputs' r. Belarus
221 L3 Iqaluit Nunavut Can.
111 F4 Iqe He r. China
253 F3 Iquê r. Brazil
252 C5 Iquique Chile
Iquiri r. Brazil see Ituxi
250 C5 Iquitos Peru
102 □1 Irabu-jima i. Japan
251 H3 Iracoubo Fr. Guiana
104 C4 Irago-suidō str. Japan
255 B8 Irai Brazil
198 C1 Irakleia Greece
199 D3 Irakleia i. Greece
198 D4 Irakleio Kriti Greece
198 D4 Irakleiou, Kolpos b. Kriti Greece
Iráklia i. Greece see Irakleia
Iraklion Kriti Greece see Irakleio
254 E5 Iramaia Brazil
122 C4 Iran country Asia
95 F2 Iran, Pegunungan mts Indon.
156 D5 Irancy France
122 A2 Īrānshāh Iran
122 E5 Īrānshahr Iran
244 D3 Irapuato Mex.
127 F4 Iraq country Asia
205 G4 Irarrarene reg. Alg.
233 G2 Irasville VT U.S.A.
251 H5 Iratapuru r. Brazil
256 B6 Irati Brazil
183 I2 Irati r. Spain
177 K5 Iratoșu Romania
134 K2 Irayel' Rus. Fed.
242 □J7 Irazu, Volcán vol. Costa Rica
138 D3 Irbe r. Latvia
Irbes šaurums sea chan. Estonia/Latvia see Irbe Strait
138 D3 Irbe Strait Estonia/Latvia
Irbe väin sea chan. Estonia/Latvia see Irbe Strait
128 B3 Irbid Jordan
Irbil Iraq see Arbīl
130 H4 Irbit Rus. Fed.
151 G2 Irchester Northamptonshire, England U.K.
179 F3 Irdning Austria
137 F3 Irdyn' Ukr.
254 E4 Irecê Brazil
177 H5 Iregszemcse Hungary
183 H2 Iregua r. Spain
147 D3 Ireland, Republic of country Europe
235 D1 Ireland Corners NY U.S.A.
147 E3 Ireland's Eye i. Rep. of Ireland
134 L4 Iren' r. Rus. Fed.
81 A6 Irene, Mount South I. N.Z.
251 G4 Ireng r. Guyana/Venez.
256 A6 Iretama Brazil
129 D1 Irgakly Rus. Fed.
129 D3 Irganch'ai Georgia
199 F2 Irgıllı Turkey
120 E2 Irgiz Kazakh.
120 E2 Irgiz r. Kazakh.
192 B4 Irgoli Sardegna Italy
204 C3 Irherm Morocco
204 D3 Irhil M'Goun mt. Morocco
Iri S. Korea see Iksan
Irian Barat prov. Indon. see Irian Jaya
93 D3 Irian Jaya prov. Indon.
91 I7 Irian Jaya reg. Indon.
202 D6 Iriba Chad
251 G4 Iricoumé, Serra hills Brazil
122 A2 Īrī Dāgh mt. Iran
196 D3 Irig Vojvodina, Srbija Yugo.
92 B3 Iriga Phil.
160 C3 Irigny France
120 D2 Iriklinskiy Rus. Fed.
211 B6 Iringa Tanz.
211 B7 Iringa admin. reg. Tanz.
114 C4 Irinjalakuda Kerala India
102 □1 Iriomote-jima i. Japan
251 H5 Iriri r. Brazil
254 B4 Iriri Novo r. Brazil
Irish Free State country Europe see Ireland, Republic of
145 E5 Irish Sea Rep. of Ireland/U.K.
163 A5 Irissarry France
254 D2 Irituia Brazil
182 B2 Irixo Spain
137 J5 Irkliyevskaya Rus. Fed.
137 G3 Irkliyiv Ukr.
98 H1 Irkutsk Rus. Fed.
98 H1 Irkutskaya Oblast' admin. div. Rus. Fed.
Irkutsk Oblast admin. div. Rus. Fed. see Irkutskaya Oblast'
173 G3 Irlbach Ger.
223 I4 Irma Alta Can.
226 C3 Irma WI U.S.A.
126 D3 Irmak Turkey
264 G2 Irminger Basin sea feature N. Atlantic Ocean
194 D6 Irminio r. Sicilia Italy
231 D5 Irmo SC U.S.A.
164 E1 Irnsum Neth.
208 C2 Iro, Lac l. Chad
158 E3 Irodouër France
158 B3 Iroise, Mer d' g. France
82 D3 Iron Baron S.A. Austr.
227 F2 Iron Bridge Ont. Can.
150 E2 Ironbridge Telford and Wrekin, England U.K.
232 E3 Irondequoit NY U.S.A.
226 A2 Iron Junction MN U.S.A.
82 D3 Iron Knob S.A. Austr.
226 C3 Iron Mountain MI U.S.A.
241 K3 Iron Mountain mt. UT U.S.A.
147 C2 Iron Mountains hills Rep. of Ireland
226 C2 Iron River MI U.S.A.
226 B2 Iron River WI U.S.A.
237 F4 Ironton MO U.S.A.
232 B5 Ironton OH U.S.A.
226 B2 Ironwood MI U.S.A.
233 F2 Iroquois Ont. Can.
226 D5 Iroquois r. IN U.S.A.
224 D3 Iroquois Falls Ont. Can.
92 C3 Irosin Phil.
Irpen' Ukr. see Irpin'
136 F2 Irpin' Ukr.
136 F2 Irpin' r. Ukr.
125 D2 'Irq al Ḩarūrī des. Saudi Arabia
124 C2 Irq al Mazhūr des. Saudi Arabia
124 D2 'Irq ath Thāmām des. Saudi Arabia
124 D2 'Irq Banbān des. Saudi Arabia
125 D2 'Irq Jahām des. Saudi Arabia
124 C3 'Irq Subay des. Saudi Arabia

96 A3 Irrawaddy admin. div. Myanmar
96 A4 Irrawaddy r. Myanmar
96 A4 Irrawaddy, Mouths of the Myanmar
172 A2 Irrel Ger.
122 C1 Irsarybaba, Gory hills Turkm.
172 A2 Irsch Ger.
178 E4 Irschen Austria
173 F4 Irschenberg Ger.
173 E4 Irsee Ger.
136 E2 Irsha r. Ukr.
136 E2 Irshans'k Ukr.
136 B3 Irshava Ukr.
193 I4 Irsina Italy
143 G2 Irsta Sweden
149 G3 Irthing r. England U.K.
151 G2 Irthlingborough Northamptonshire, England U.K.
121 H1 Irtysh r. Kazakh./Rus. Fed.
121 H1 Irtyshsk Kazakh.
Irtyshskoye Kazakh. see Irtyshsk
183 H4 Irueste Spain
105 F3 Iruma Japan
105 F3 Iruma-gawa r. Japan
208 F4 Irumu Dem. Rep. Congo
186 B1 Irún Spain
Iruña Spain see Pamplona
252 D4 Irupana Bol.
186 B1 Irurita Spain
183 I2 Irurozqui Spain
Irurtzun Spain see Irurzun
183 I2 Irurzun Spain
146 D6 Irvine North Ayrshire, Scotland U.K.
240 I5 Irvine CA U.S.A.
232 B6 Irvine KY U.S.A.
85 F3 Irvinebank Qld Austr.
146 D6 Irvine Bay Scotland U.K.
147 D2 Irvinestown Northern Ireland U.K.
237 D5 Irving TX U.S.A.
87 B6 Irwin r. W.A. Austr.
231 D5 Irwinton GA U.S.A.
171 C3 Irxleben Ger.
207 G3 Isa Nigeria
85 G4 Isaac r. Qld Austr.
186 C2 Isaba Spain
236 C2 Isabel SD U.S.A.
92 B4 Isabela Negros Phil.
92 B5 Isabela Phil.
247 □1 Isabela Puerto Rico
250 □ Isabela, Isla i. Islas Galápagos Ecuador
242 □I6 Isabelia, Cordillera mts Nic.
226 B2 Isabella MN U.S.A.
86 E4 Isabella, Lake salt flat W.A. Austr.
247 □1 Isabel Segunda Puerto Rico
186 D2 Isábena r. Spain
199 F3 İsabey Turkey
129 C4 İsabey Dağı mt. Turkey
158 D4 Isac r. France
197 I3 Isaccea Romania
140 □B2 Ísafjarðardjúp est. Iceland
140 □B2 Ísafjörður Iceland
116 D4 Isagarh Madh. Prad. India
103 E7 Isahaya Japan
123 G3 Isà Khel Pak.
134 H2 Isakogorka Rus. Fed.
192 B4 Isalle r. Sardegna Italy
197 F3 Işalniţa Romania
250 D4 Isana r. Col.
207 G4 Isanlu Nigeria
205 G4 Isaouane-n-Tifernine des. Alg.
173 G3 Isar r. Ger.
191 G2 Isarco r. Italy
177 I4 Isaszeg Hungary
156 C2 Isbergues France
146 □G1 Isbister Shetland, Scotland U.K.
146 □H1 Isbister Shetland, Scotland U.K.
Isca Newport, Wales U.K. see Caerleon
183 F3 Íscar Spain
199 G2 İscehisar Turkey
157 F4 Isches France
178 B3 Ischgl Austria
193 F4 Ischia Italy
193 F4 Ischia, Isola d' i. Italy
193 H3 Ischitella Italy
86 E3 Isdell r. W.A. Austr.
156 C5 Isdes France
104 C4 Ise Japan
142 D4 Isefjord b. Denmark
105 F3 Isehara Japan
178 D4 Isel r. Austria
173 G3 Isen Ger.
173 G3 Isen r. Ger.
157 F4 Is-en-Bassigny France
134 K4 Isenbayevo Rus. Fed.
169 F3 Isenbüttel Ger.
190 F3 Iseo Italy
190 F3 Iseo, Lago d' l. Italy
161 D3 Isère dept Rhône-Alpes France
161 C4 Isère r. France
169 C4 Iserlohn Ger.
169 E3 Isernhagen Ger.
193 G3 Isernia Italy
193 G3 Isernia prov. Molise Italy
105 F2 Isesaki Japan
104 C4 Ise-wan b. Japan
207 F5 Iseyin Nigeria
Isfahan Iran see Eşfahān
121 G5 Isfana Kyrg.
123 G1 Isfara Tajik.
140 □ Isfjorden inlet Svalbard
129 D2 Ishcherskaya Rus. Fed.
134 L3 Isherim, Gora mt. Rus. Fed.
251 G4 Isherton Guyana
135 J5 Isheyevka Rus. Fed.
102 □1 Ishigaki-jima i. Japan
102 J2 Ishikari-gawa r. Japan
102 J2 Ishikari-wan b. Japan
104 C2 Ishikawa pref. Japan
121 G1 Ishim r. Kazakh./Rus. Fed.
130 H4 Ishim Rus. Fed.
120 D1 Ishimbay Rus. Fed.
102 J4 Ishinomaki Japan
105 G2 Ishioka Japan
103 F7 Ishizuchi-san mt. Japan
123 G2 Ishkoshim Tajik.
116 C1 Ishkuman Jammu and Kashmir
139 L3 Ishnya Rus. Fed.
226 D2 Ishpeming MI U.S.A.
Ishtikhon Uzbek. see Ishtykhan
121 F5 Ishtykhan Uzbek.
117 G4 Ishurdi Bangl.
252 D3 Isiboro r. Bol.
159 E3 Isigny-le-Buat France
159 E2 Isigny-sur-Mer France
199 G2 Işıklar Turkey
199 F2 Işıklı Turkey
192 B5 Isili Sardegna Italy
130 I4 Isil'kul' Rus. Fed.
250 B5 Isinliví Ecuador
215 H3 Isipingo S. Africa
208 E4 Isiro Dem. Rep. Congo
85 F5 Isisford Qld Austr.
179 F5 Iška r. Slovenia
134 K2 Iskateley Rus. Fed.
126 E3 İskenderun Turkey
126 D3 İskenderun Körfezi b. Turkey
126 D2 İskilip Turkey
Iski-Naukat Kyrg. see Eski-Nookat
130 J4 Iskitim Rus. Fed.
139 L4 Iskra Rus. Fed.
137 G3 Iskrivka Kirovohrads'ka Oblast' Ukr.
137 H3 Iskrivka Poltavs'ka Oblast' Ukr.
197 G4 Iskŭr r. Bulg.
210 F2 Iskushuban Somalia
222 D3 Iskut r. B.C. Can.
245 G4 Isla Mex.
146 E5 Isla r. Angus/Perth and Kinross, Scotland U.K.
184 C3 Isla Canela Spain
184 C3 Isla Cristina Spain
126 E3 İslahiye Turkey
129 B3 İslâhiye Turkey
Islamabad Jammu and Kashmir see Anantnag
123 H3 Islamabad Pak.
184 D3 Isla Mayor marsh Spain
184 D3 Isla Menor marsh Spain
123 G5 Islamkot Pak.
231 D7 Islamorada FL U.S.A.
117 F4 Islampur Bihar India
222 F2 Island r. N.W.T. Can.
Ísland country Europe see Iceland
233 □I1 Island Falls ME U.S.A.
82 D2 Island Lagoon salt flat S.A. Austr.
223 M4 Island Lake Man. Can.
223 M4 Island Lake l. Man. Can.
238 E2 Island Park ID U.S.A.
233 H2 Island Pond VT U.S.A.
80 E1 Islands, Bay of North I. N.Z.
181 H3 Islas Baleares aut. comm. Spain
261 F3 Isla Verde Arg.
146 B6 Islay i. Scotland U.K.
146 B6 Islay, Sound of sea chan. Scotland U.K.
197 G4 Islaz Romania
162 D3 Isle France
162 B4 Isle r. France
151 H2 Isleham Cambridgeshire, England U.K.
150 C1 Isle of Anglesey admin. div. Wales U.K.
148 E3 Isle of Man i. Irish Sea
146 D7 Isle of Whithorn Dumfries and Galloway, Scotland U.K.
151 F4 Isle of Wight admin. div. England U.K.
232 E6 Isle of Wight VA U.S.A.
156 E3 Isle-sur-Suippe France
Ismail Ukr. see Izmayil
203 G2 Ismâ'ilîya Egypt
128 A4 Ismâ'ilîya governorate Egypt
Ismailly Azer. see İsmayıllı
173 F3 Ismaning Ger.
129 F3 İsmayıllı Azer.
203 G3 Isna Egypt
182 C5 Isna Port.
194 D5 Isnello Sicilia Italy
173 E4 Isny im Allgäu Ger.
213 □J4 Isoanala Madag.
141 M3 Isojoki Fin.
211 B7 Isoka Zambia
140 M3 Isokyrö Fin.
161 F4 Isola France
161 F4 Isola 2000 France
192 B2 Isolaccio-di-Fiumorbo Corse France
193 F2 Isola del Gran Sasso d'Italia Italy
191 G3 Isola della Scala Italy
194 C4 Isola delle Femmine Sicilia Italy
193 F3 Isola del Liri Italy
195 G4 Isola di Capo Rizzuto Italy
158 C4 Isole r. France
190 D4 Isole del Cantone Italy
186 E2 Isona Spain
191 I3 Isonzo r. Italy
213 □J4 Isorana Madag.
190 F3 Isorella Italy
140 N2 Iso-Syöte hill Fin.
161 B4 Ispagnac France
Ispahan Iran see Eşfahān
199 G3 Isparta Turkey
199 G3 Isparta prov. Turkey
197 H4 Isperikh Bulg.
194 D6 Ispica Sicilia Italy
194 D6 Ispica r. Sicilia Italy
127 F2 İspir Turkey
Ispisar Tajik. see Khŭjand
163 A5 Ispoure France
190 D3 Ispra Italy
129 B1 Ispravnaya Rus. Fed.
172 C3 Ispringen Ger.
128 B3 Israel country Asia
256 B2 Israelândia Brazil
87 D7 Israelite Bay W.A. Austr.
Isra'īl country Asia see Israel
Issa Croatia see Vis
135 I5 Issa Rus. Fed.
138 G3 Issa r. Rus. Fed.
207 H5 Issanguele Cameroon
251 G3 Issano Guyana
161 C4 Issarlès France
169 B4 Isselburg Ger.
157 H5 Issenheim France
206 D5 Issia Côte d'Ivoire
163 C4 Issigeac France
190 C3 Issime Italy
127 G5 Issin tourist site Iraq
185 I2 Isso Spain
190 C3 Issogne Italy
160 B3 Issoire France
161 E5 Issole r. France
162 D2 Issoudun France
169 B4 Issum Ger.
211 B6 Issuna Tanz.
160 D1 Is-sur-Tille France
Issyk-Kul' Kyrg. see Balykchy
Issyk-Kul', Ozero salt l. Kyrg. see Ysyk-Köl
Issyk-Kul Oblast admin. div. Kyrg. see Ysyk-Köl
Issyk-Kul'skaya Oblast' admin. div. Kyrg. see Ysyk-Köl
160 B2 Issy-l'Évêque France
191 J4 Ist i. Croatia
139 K5 Ista r. Rus. Fed.
127 F4 Iştablāt tourist site Iraq
177 J3 Istállós-kő hill Hungary
185 F4 Istán Spain
199 F1 İstanbul Turkey
199 F1 İstanbul prov. Turkey
199 F1 İstanbul Boğazı str. Turkey
151 H3 Istead Rise Kent, England U.K.
174 G6 Istebna Pol.
177 I2 Istebné Slovakia
176 F5 Isten dombja hill Hungary
122 B3 Īstgāh-e Eznā Iran
198 C2 Istiaia Greece
123 H2 Istik r. Tajik.
129 D4 İstisu Azer.
250 B3 Istmina Col.
137 J2 Istobnoye Rus. Fed.
196 E4 Istok Kosovo, Srbija Yugo.
188 D3 Istra pen. Croatia
139 K4 Istra Rus. Fed.
161 C5 Istres France
Istria pen. Croatia see Istra
197 I3 Istria Romania
197 H3 Istriţa, Dealul hill Romania
163 A5 Isturits France
139 M4 Ist'ya r. Rus. Fed.
186 C2 Isuela r. Spain
183 I3 Isuela r. Spain
163 A6 Isuerre Spain
105 G3 Isumi-gawa r. Japan
117 G5 Iswaripur Bangl.
215 H2 Iswepe S. Africa
120 D1 Isyangulovo Rus. Fed.
121 I4 Isyk Kazakh.
254 F4 Itabaianinha Brazil
257 G4 Itabapoana r. Brazil
256 C5 Itaberá Brazil
254 E5 Itaberaba Brazil
256 C2 Itaberaí Brazil
257 F3 Itabira Brazil
257 F4 Itabirito Brazil
257 F5 Itaboraí Brazil
255 F5 Itabuna Brazil
254 C3 Itacaiuna r. Brazil
254 D4 Itacajá Brazil
257 F2 Itacambira Brazil
255 D5 Itacarambi Brazil
254 F5 Itacaré Brazil
253 H1 Itacayunas, Serra hills Brazil
251 G5 Itacoatiara Brazil
250 D6 Itacuaí r. Brazil
253 F6 Itacurubí del Rosario Para.
254 E5 Itaetê Brazil
Itagmatana Iran see Hamadān
257 H2 Itagmirim Brazil
257 G3 Itaguaçu Brazil
257 F5 Itaguaí Brazil
256 B5 Itaguajé Brazil
257 E4 Itaguara Brazil
256 C5 Itaí Brazil
254 E3 Itaim r. Brazil
255 C8 Itaiópolis Brazil
255 B8 Itaipu, Represa de resr Brazil
251 G6 Itaituba Brazil
256 B3 Itajá Brazil
255 C8 Itajaí Brazil
256 C4 Itajobi Brazil
257 E5 Itajubá Brazil
255 F5 Itajuipe Brazil
117 F5 Itaki Bihar India
Italia country Europe see Italy
188 E5 Italy country Europe
254 G3 Itamaracá, Ilha de i. Brazil
257 H2 Itamaraju Brazil
257 F2 Itamarandiba Brazil
257 G3 Itambacuri Brazil
257 G3 Itambacuri r. Brazil
255 E5 Itambé Brazil
257 F3 Itambé, Pico de mt. Brazil
104 B4 Itami Japan
104 B4 Itami airport Japan
112 H6 Itanagar Arun. Prad. India
254 D5 Itanguari r. Brazil
256 D6 Itanhaém Brazil
257 E5 Itanhandu Brazil
251 F6 Itanhauã r. Brazil
257 G2 Itanhém Brazil
257 H2 Itanhém r. Brazil
257 G3 Itanhomi Brazil
251 H4 Itany r. Fr. Guiana/Suriname
257 G2 Itaobím Brazil
257 F4 Itaocara Brazil
254 C5 Itapaci Brazil
254 F2 Itapagé Brazil
256 C3 Itapajipe Brazil
251 F6 Itaparaná r. Brazil
254 F4 Itaparica, Represa de resr Brazil
257 H1 Itapebi Brazil
257 E4 Itapecerica Brazil
257 G4 Itapemirim Brazil
257 G4 Itaperuna Brazil
255 E5 Itapetinga Brazil
256 C5 Itapetininga Brazil
256 C5 Itapeva Brazil
251 G5 Itapi r. Brazil
254 E4 Itapicuru Brazil
254 F4 Itapicuru r. Brazil
254 D3 Itapicuru, Serra de hills Brazil
254 D2 Itapicuru Mirim Brazil
254 F4 Itapicuru Mirim r. Brazil
254 F2 Itapipoca Brazil
256 D5 Itapira Brazil
251 G5 Itapiranga Brazil
256 B1 Itapirapuã Brazil
254 F3 Itapiúna Brazil
256 C4 Itápolis Brazil
254 F3 Itaporanga Paraíba Brazil
256 C5 Itaporanga São Paulo Brazil
255 C9 Itapuã Brazil
255 C5 Itapuranga Brazil
256 D5 Itaquaquecetuba Brazil
255 A9 Itaqui Brazil
257 G3 Itarana Brazil
257 G1 Itarantim Brazil
256 C6 Itararé Brazil
256 C5 Itararé r. Brazil
116 D5 Itarsi Madh. Prad. India
256 B3 Itarumã Brazil
140 O3 Itä-Suomi prov. Fin.
260 A5 Itata r. Chile
256 D5 Itatiba Brazil
256 C5 Itatinga Brazil
256 C2 Itauçu Brazil
254 E3 Itaueira r. Brazil
257 E4 Itaúna Brazil
257 H3 Itaúnas r. Brazil
198 C2 Itea Greece
183 F2 Itero de la Vega Spain
162 C2 Iteuil France
209 E8 Itezhi-Tezhi Dam Zambia
Ithaca Ionioi Nisoi Greece see Ithaki
Ithaca i. Greece see Ithaki
226 E4 Ithaca MI U.S.A.
232 E3 Ithaca NY U.S.A.
198 B2 Ithaki Ionioi Nisoi Greece
198 B2 Ithaki i. Greece
169 E3 Ith Hils ridge Ger.
211 B6 Itigi Tanz.
103 E7 Itihusa-yama mt. Japan
208 D4 Itimbiri r. Dem. Rep. Congo
257 G2 Itinga Brazil
255 B6 Itiquira Brazil
253 F4 Itiquira r. Brazil
256 D5 Itirapina Brazil
256 D4 Itirapuã Brazil
254 F4 Itiúba Brazil
254 F4 Itiúba, Serra de hills Brazil
258 E1 Itiyura r. Arg.
117 F4 Itkhari Bihar India
105 F4 Itō Japan
213 I2 Itoculo Moz.
105 D1 Itoigawa Japan
156 B3 Iton r. France
213 □J4 Itongafeno mt. Madag.
Iton-Qälla Rus. Fed. see Itum-Kale
185 G4 Itrabo Spain
193 F3 Itri Italy
217 □3a Itsikoudi Njazidja Comoros
103 E7 Itsuki Japan
103 F6 Itsukushima Shrine tourist site Japan
192 A4 Ittireddu Sardegna Italy
192 A4 Ittiri Sardegna Italy
165 D4 Ittre Belgium
256 D5 Itu Brazil
207 G5 Itu Nigeria
90 D4 Itu Abu Island S. China Sea
254 E5 Ituaçu Brazil
254 F5 Ituberá Brazil
252 C1 Itucumã r. Brazil
182 D4 Ituero de Azaba Spain
250 D6 Ituí r. Brazil
256 C3 Ituiutaba Brazil
256 C3 Itumbiara Brazil
129 D2 Itum-Kale Rus. Fed.
211 B7 Itungi Port Malawi
251 G3 Ituni Guyana
254 C3 Itupiranga Brazil
256 B3 Iturama Brazil
253 F6 Iturbe Para.
243 H5 Iturbide Campeche Mex.
245 E1 Iturbide Nuevo León Mex.
208 E4 Ituri r. Dem. Rep. Congo
99 Q3 Iturup, Ostrov i. Kuril'skiye O-va Rus. Fed.
257 E4 Itutinga Brazil
256 D4 Ituverava Brazil
252 D1 Ituxi r. Brazil
258 F2 Ituzaingo Arg.
Ityopia country Africa see Ethiopia
169 F6 Itz r. Ger.
168 E2 Itzehoe Ger.
168 F2 Itzstedt Ger.
194 D5 Iudica, Monte hill Sicilia Italy
237 F5 Iuka MS U.S.A.
131 T3 Iul'tin Rus. Fed.
213 H2 Iuluti Moz.
257 G4 Iúna Brazil
256 B6 Ivaí Brazil
256 A5 Ivaí r. Brazil
256 B6 Ivaiporã Brazil
213 □J4 Ivakoany mt. Madag.
140 N1 Ivalo Fin.
140 N1 Ivalojoki r. Fin.
176 F4 Iván Hungary
175 L6 Ivana Franka Ukr.
136 C1 Ivanava Belarus
176 F2 Ivančice Czech Rep.
188 F2 Ivanec Croatia
138 G2 Ivangorod Rus. Fed.
Ivangrad Crna Gora Yugo. see Berane
83 F3 Ivanhoe N.S.W. Austr.
86 F2 Ivanhoe W.A. Austr.
224 D3 Ivanhoe r. Ont. Can.
240 H3 Ivanhoe CA U.S.A.
236 D2 Ivanhoe MN U.S.A.
232 C6 Ivanhoe VA U.S.A.
188 F3 Ivanić-Grad Croatia
137 H2 Ivanino Rus. Fed.
139 M4 Ivanishchi Rus. Fed.
137 G4 Ivanivka Khersons'ka Oblast' Ukr.
137 H4 Ivanivka Khersons'ka Oblast' Ukr.
137 F3 Ivanivka Kyivs'ka Oblast' Ukr.
137 J3 Ivanivka Luhans'ka Oblast' Ukr.
136 F4 Ivanivka Odes'ka Oblast' Ukr.
177 L3 Ivanivka Zakarpats'ka Oblast' Ukr.
136 D3 Ivanivtsi Ukr.
196 E4 Ivanjica Srbija Yugo.
176 G3 Ivanka pri Dunaji Slovakia
136 E2 Ivankiv Ukr.
188 G3 Ivankovo Croatia
139 K4 Ivan'kovo Rus. Fed.
139 K3 Ivan'kovskoye Vodokhranilishche resr Rus. Fed.
100 E2 Ivankovtsy Rus. Fed.
136 C3 Ivano-Frankivs'k Ivano-Frankivs'ka Oblast' Ukr.
136 C3 Ivano-Frankivs'ka Oblast' admin. div. Ukr.
Ivano-Frankivs'k Oblast admin. div. Ukr. see Ivano-Frankivs'ka Oblast'
136 B3 Ivano-Frankove Ukr.
Ivano-Frankovsk Ivano-Frankivs'ka Oblast' Ukr. see Ivano-Frankivs'k
Ivano-Frankovskaya Oblast' admin. div. Ukr. see Ivano-Frankivs'ka Oblast'
Ivano-Frankovsk Oblast admin. div. Ukr. see Ivano-Frankivs'ka Oblast'
136 E3 Ivanopil' Ukr.
Ivanovka Kazakh. see Kokzhayyk
100 C2 Ivanovka Amurskaya Oblast' Rus. Fed.
120 C1 Ivanovka Orenburgskaya Oblast' Rus. Fed.
Ivanovo Belarus see Ivanava
197 G4 Ivanovo tourist site Bulg.
139 M3 Ivanovo Ivanovskaya Oblast' Rus. Fed.
139 K2 Ivanovo Tverskaya Oblast' Rus. Fed.
Ivanovo Oblast admin. div. Rus. Fed. see Ivanovskaya Oblast'
137 J5 Ivanovskaya Rus. Fed.
139 M3 Ivanovskaya Oblast' admin. div. Rus. Fed.
121 J2 Ivanovskiy Khrebet mts Kazakh.
137 H2 Ivanovskoye Kurskaya Oblast' Rus. Fed.
139 L3 Ivanovskoye Yaroslavskaya Oblast' Rus. Fed.
188 E2 Ivanšćica mts Croatia
197 H4 Ivanski Bulg.
120 B1 Ivanteyevka Rus. Fed.
Ivantsevichi Belarus see Ivatsevichy
136 C2 Ivanychi Ukr.
137 G2 Ivanytsya Ukr.
138 E5 Ivatsevichy Belarus
197 H5 Ivaylovgrad Bulg.
134 M3 Ivdel' Rus. Fed.
151 G3 Iver Buckinghamshire, England U.K.
147 B5 Iveragh reg. Rep. of Ireland
140 □ Iversenfjellet hill Svalbard
197 H3 Iveşti Romania
197 H2 Iveşti Romania
208 B5 Ivindo r. Gabon
151 G3 Ivinghoe Buckinghamshire, England U.K.
255 B7 Ivinheima Brazil
256 A5 Ivinheima r. Brazil
139 J1 Ivinskiy Razliv resr Rus. Fed.
Iviza i. Spain see Eivissa
137 I2 Ivnya Rus. Fed.
213 □J4 Ivohibe Madag.
256 B2 Ivolândia Brazil
232 E6 Ivor VA U.S.A.
Ivory Coast country Africa see Côte d'Ivoire
139 J5 Ivot Rus. Fed.
137 G2 Ivotka r. Ukr.
190 C3 Ivrea Italy
199 E2 İvrindi Turkey
129 D3 Ivris Zegani plat. Georgia
156 B4 Ivry-la-Bataille France
156 C4 Ivry-sur-Seine France
Ivugivik Que. Can. see Ivujivik
221 K3 Ivujivik Que. Can.
138 F5 Ivyanyets Belarus
150 D4 Ivybridge Devon, England U.K.
232 C5 Ivydale WV U.S.A.
151 H3 Iwade Kent, England U.K.
105 F2 Iwai Japan
105 G1 Iwaki Japan
102 J3 Iwaki-san vol. Japan
103 F6 Iwakuni Japan
104 C3 Iwakura Japan
102 J2 Iwamizawa Japan
95 F2 Iwan r. Indon.
175 J5 Iwaniska Pol.
102 J4 Iwanuma Japan
105 E2 Iwasuge-yama vol. Japan
105 D4 Iwata Japan
102 J4 Iwate pref. Japan
102 J4 Iwate-san vol. Japan
105 F3 Iwatsuki Japan
175 I6 Iwkowa Pol.
207 G5 Iwo Nigeria
Iwo Jima i. Japan see Iō-jima
138 E5 Iwye Belarus
245 G5 Ixaltepec Mex.
245 G5 Ixhuatán Mex.
245 F4 Ixhuatlán Mex.
252 C3 Ixiamas Bol.
245 E3 Ixmiquilpán Mex.
215 H4 Ixopo S. Africa
243 G5 Ixtacomitán Mex.
244 D5 Ixtapa Guerrero Mex.
244 B3 Ixtapa Jalisco Mex.
245 E4 Ixtapan de la Sal Mex.
245 E4 Ixtlahuaca Mex.
244 C3 Ixtlán Mex.
244 B3 Ixtlán Mex.
151 H2 Ixworth Suffolk, England U.K.
98 G1 Iya r. Rus. Fed.
211 B7 Iyayi Tanz.
129 B3 İyidere Turkey
İyirmi Altı Bakı Komissarı Azer. see 26 Bakı Komissarı
103 F7 Iyo Japan
103 F7 Iyomishima Japan
197 F2 Iza r. Romania
177 H4 Iža Slovakia
243 H6 Izabal, Lago de l. Guat.
183 G1 Izalde r. Spain
243 H4 Izamal Mex.
243 G6 Izapa tourist site Mex.
102 J2 Izari-dake mt. Japan
183 H2 Izarra Spain
197 G3 Izbăşeşti hill Romania
129 E2 Izberbash Rus. Fed.
175 L5 Izbica Pol.
174 G3 Izbica Kujawska Pol.
139 I4 Izdeshkovo Rus. Fed.
161 D3 Izeaux France
182 D3 Izeda Port.
165 C4 Izegem Belgium
122 B4 Īzeh Iran
102 □1 Izena-jima i. Japan
160 D2 Izernore France
161 D3 Izeron France
134 K4 Izhevsk Rus. Fed.
139 M4 Izhevskoye Rus. Fed.
134 K2 Izhma Respublika Komi Rus. Fed.
Izhma Respublika Komi Rus. Fed. see Sosnogorsk
134 K2 Izhma r. Rus. Fed.
125 G3 Izkī Oman
Izmail Ukr. see Izmayil
139 K5 Izmalkovo Rus. Fed.
136 E5 Izmayil Ukr.
Izmeny, Proliv sea chan. Japan/Rus. Fed. see Notsuke-suidō
199 E2 İzmir Turkey
199 E2 İzmir prov. Turkey
199 E2 İzmir Körfezi g. Turkey
İzmit Turkey see Kocaeli
199 F1 İzmit Körfezi b. Turkey
180 E5 Izmorene Morocco
185 F3 Iznájar Spain
185 G3 Iznalloz Spain
199 F1 İznik Turkey
199 F1 İznik Gölü l. Turkey
139 J4 Iznoski Rus. Fed.
Izobil'noye Rus. Fed. see Izobil'nyy
135 H7 Izobil'nyy Rus. Fed.
188 D3 Izola Slovenia
139 K3 Izoplit Rus. Fed.
253 E4 Izozog Bol.
128 C3 Izra' Syria
177 I5 Izsák Hungary
245 E4 Iztaccihuatl, Volcán vol. Mex.
197 G5 Iztochni Rodopi mts Bulg.
245 E4 Izúcar de Matamoros Mex.
105 E4 Izu-hantō pen. Japan
103 E7 Izumi Kagoshima Japan
104 B4 Izumi Ōsaka Japan
104 B4 Izumiōtsu Japan
104 B4 Izumisano Japan
103 F6 Izumo Japan
266 E3 Izu-Ogasawara Trench sea feature N. Pacific Ocean
105 F4 Izu-shotō is Japan
Izu-tobu vol. Japan see Amagi-san
100 D2 Izvestkovyy Rus. Fed.
197 G3 Izvoarele Giurgiu Romania
197 G3 Izvoarele Olt Romania
197 H3 Izvoarele Prahova Romania
197 G3 Izvoru Romania
136 D2 Izyaslav Ukr.
134 L2 Iz"yayu Rus. Fed.
137 I3 Izyum Ukr.

J

141 N3 Jaala Fin.
183 H4 Jabaga Spain
191 J4 Jabalanac Croatia
123 G3 Jabal as Sirāj Afgh.
185 H3 Jabalcón mt. Spain
185 F2 Jabalón r. Spain
187 B4 Jabaloyas Spain
116 D5 Jabalpur Madh. Prad. India
185 G2 Jabalquinto Spain
184 D1 Jabarriega hill Spain
124 C4 Jabbārah Fara Islands Saudi Arabia
165 C3 Jabbeke Belgium
128 C2 Jabbūl, Sabkhat al salt flat Syria
170 D2 Jabel Ger.
84 C2 Jabiru N.T. Austr.
128 B2 Jablah Syria
188 F4 Jablanica Bos.-Herz.
197 E4 Jablanica r. Yugo.
175 L4 Jabłoń Pol.
176 E1 Jablonec nad Nisou Czech Rep.
176 G3 Jablonica Slovakia
175 H6 Jabłonka Pol.
175 K3 Jabłonka Kościelna Pol.
175 I3 Jabłonna Pol.
175 K3 Jabłonna Lacka Pol.
175 K4 Jabłonna Pierwsza Pol.
176 D1 Jablonné v Podještědí Czech Rep.
175 H2 Jabłonowo Pomorskie Pol.
177 G2 Jablůnka Czech Rep.
177 H2 Jablunkov Czech Rep.
254 G4 Jaboatão Brazil
256 C4 Jaboticabal Brazil
257 F3 Jaboticatubas Brazil
161 C4 Jabron r. France
184 D3 Jabugo Spain
196 E3 Jabuka Vojvodina, Srbija Yugo.
186 C2 Jaca Spain
245 E3 Jacala Mex.
254 E4 Jacaré r. Brazil
251 F6 Jacaré r. Brazil
257 D5 Jacareí Brazil
256 C5 Jacarézinho Brazil
257 F4 Jaceaba Brazil
260 D2 Jáchal r. Arg.
173 F4 Jachen r. Ger.
173 F4 Jachenau Ger.
176 B1 Jáchymov Czech Rep.
255 B5 Jaciara Brazil
257 G2 Jacinto Brazil
261 F6 Jacinto Arauz Arg.
255 C9 Jacinto Machado Brazil
252 D2 Jaciparaná r. Brazil
85 F2 Jack r. Qld Austr.
226 D1 Jackfish Ont. Can.
233 □H2 Jackman ME U.S.A.
232 A6 Jacksboro TN U.S.A.
237 D5 Jacksboro TX U.S.A.
85 G5 Jackson Qld Austr.
231 C6 Jackson AL U.S.A.
240 G2 Jackson CA U.S.A.
231 D5 Jackson GA U.S.A.
232 B6 Jackson KY U.S.A.
226 E4 Jackson MI U.S.A.
236 E3 Jackson MN U.S.A.
237 F4 Jackson MO U.S.A.
237 F5 Jackson MS U.S.A.
231 E4 Jackson NC U.S.A.
232 B5 Jackson OH U.S.A.
237 F5 Jackson TN U.S.A.
226 C4 Jackson WI U.S.A.
238 E3 Jackson WY U.S.A.
262 T2 Jackson, Mount Antarctica
81 B5 Jackson Bay South I. N.Z.
81 B5 Jackson Bay b. South I. N.Z.
81 B5 Jackson Head hd South I. N.Z.
226 D3 Jacksonport WI U.S.A.
81 C5 Jacksons South I. N.Z.
225 J3 Jackson's Arm Nfld. Can.
231 C5 Jacksonville AL U.S.A.
237 E5 Jacksonville AR U.S.A.
231 D6 Jacksonville FL U.S.A.
236 F4 Jacksonville IL U.S.A.
234 B3 Jacksonville MD U.S.A.
231 E5 Jacksonville NC U.S.A.
232 B5 Jacksonville OH U.S.A.
237 E6 Jacksonville TX U.S.A.
231 D6 Jacksonville Beach FL U.S.A.
246 D3 Jacmel Haiti
123 G4 Jacobabad Pak.
254 E4 Jacobina Brazil
241 K3 Jacob Lake AZ U.S.A.
215 E3 Jacobsdal S. Africa
226 A2 Jacobson MN U.S.A.
81 B5 Jacobs River South I. N.Z.
234 B3 Jacobsville MD U.S.A.
234 B3 Jacobus PA U.S.A.
244 C4 Jacona Mex.
225 H3 Jacques-Cartier, Détroit de sea chan. Que. Can.
225 H3 Jacques Cartier, Mont mt. Que. Can.
Jacques Cartier Passage Que. Can. see Jacques-Cartier, Détroit de
225 H4 Jacquet River N.B. Can.
256 A3 Jacuba r. Brazil
256 D4 Jacuí Brazil
255 C9 Jacuí r. Brazil
254 F5 Jacuípe r. Brazil
250 D4 Jacumã r. Brazil
254 C3 Jacunda Brazil
251 I5 Jacundá r. Brazil
256 D6 Jacupiranga Brazil
250 D2 Jacura Venez.
188 G3 Jadar r. Bos.-Herz.
196 D3 Jadar r. Yugo.
114 C2 Jadcherla Andhra Prad. India
114 D2 Jaddangi Andhra Prad. India
168 D2 Jade r. Ger.
168 D2 Jade sea chan. Ger.
168 D2 Jadebusen b. Ger.
221 N3 J. A. D. Jensen Nunatakker nunataks Greenland
Jadotville Dem. Rep. Congo see Likasi
188 E3 Jadova r. Croatia
188 F3 Jadovnik mt. Bos.-Herz.
175 J3 Jadów Pol.
183 H4 Jadraque Spain
250 B6 Jaén Peru
92 B3 Jaen Phil.
185 G3 Jaén Spain
185 G2 Jaén prov. Andalucía Spain
142 A2 Jæren reg. Norway
122 B2 Ja'farābād Iran
Jaffa Israel see Tel Aviv-Yafo
82 D4 Jaffa, Cape S.A. Austr.
114 C4 Jaffna Sri Lanka
233 G3 Jaffrey NH U.S.A.
128 C4 Jafr, Qa' al imp. l. Jordan
116 D3 Jagadhri Haryana India
138 E2 Jägala r. Estonia
114 C3 Jagalur Karnataka India
114 D2 Jagdalpur Madh. Prad. India
107 J1 Jagdaqi Nei Mongol China
111 C7 Jagdishpur Uttar Prad. India
117 F4 Jagdispur Bihar India
179 G4 Jagerberg Austria
215 E3 Jagersfontein S. Africa
114 D2 Jaggayyapeta Andhra Prad. India
122 D5 Jaghīn Iran
196 E4 Jagodina Srbija Yugo.
Jagsamka Sichuan China see Luding
172 D2 Jagst r. Ger.
172 D2 Jagsthausen Ger.
173 E2 Jagstzell Ger.
114 C2 Jagtial Andhra Prad. India
256 B5 Jaguapitã Brazil
258 G4 Jaguarão r. Brazil/Uru.
258 G4 Jaguarão Uru.
254 E4 Jaguarari Brazil
254 F3 Jaguaretama Brazil
255 B9 Jaguari Brazil
256 C6 Jaguariaíva Brazil
254 F3 Jaguaribe Brazil
254 F5 Jaguaripe Brazil
254 F3 Jaguaruana Brazil
246 B2 Jagüey Grande Cuba
117 F4 Jahanabad Bihar India
122 B2 Jahān Dāgh mt. Iran
84 B1 Jahleel, Point N.T. Austr.
171 E4 Jahna r. Ger.
171 F3 Jahnsfelde Ger.
122 C4 Jahrom Iran
207 H3 Jahun Nigeria
254 E3 Jaicós Brazil
114 B2 Jaigarh Mahar. India
Jailolo Gilolo i. Maluku Indon. see Halmahera
106 D5 Jainca Qinghai China
117 H4 Jaintiapur Bangl.
116 C4 Jaipur Rajasthan India
117 G4 Jaipurhat Bangl.
116 E4 Jais Uttar Prad. India
116 B4 Jaisalmer Rajasthan India
116 E5 Jaisinghnagar Madh. Prad. India
116 C4 Jaitaran Rajasthan India
116 D5 Jaitgarh hill Mahar. India
116 D4 Jaitpur Uttar Prad. India
188 F3 Jajce Bos.-Herz.
Jajnagar state India see Orissa
176 F4 Ják Hungary
177 I5 Jakabszállás Hungary
94 D4 Jakarta Indon.
222 C2 Jakes Corner Y.T. Can.
116 B5 Jakhan Gujarat India
123 F4 Jakin mt. Afgh.
140 L2 Jäkkvik Sweden
116 C3 Jakliat Haryana India
Jakobshavn Greenland see Ilulissat
140 M3 Jakobstad Fin.
179 G5 Jakovlje Croatia
175 I3 Jaktorów Pol.
177 J2 Jakubany Slovakia
176 F3 Jakubov Slovakia
196 E5 Jakupica mts Macedonia
237 C5 Jal NM U.S.A.
244 B3 Jala Mex.
Jalaid Nei Mongol China see Inder
124 D2 Jalājil Saudi Arabia
123 G3 Jalālābād Afgh.
116 C3 Jalalabad Punjab India
116 D3 Jalalabad Uttar Prad. India
116 D4 Jalalabad Uttar Prad. India
121 H4 Jalal-Abad Kyrg.
121 H4 Jalal-Abad admin. div. Kyrg.
Jalal-Abad Oblast admin. div. Kyrg. see Jalal-Abad
116 C5 Jalalpur Gujarat India
117 E4 Jalalpur Uttar Prad. India
203 H2 Jalāmid, Ḩazm al ridge Saudi Arabia
125 G3 Ja'lān, Jabal mts Oman
187 B5 Jalance Spain
116 C3 Jalandhar Punjab India
94 □ Jalan Kayu Sing.
243 H6 Jalapa Guat.
243 G5 Jalapa Mex.
242 □I6 Jalapa Nic.
245 F4 Jalapa de Díaz Mex.
245 G5 Jalapa del Marqués Mex.
245 F4 Jalapa Enríquez Mex.
123 H3 Jalapur Pak.
123 G4 Jalapur Pirwala Pak.
140 M3 Jalasjärvi Fin.
116 D4 Jalaun Uttar Prad. India
127 G4 Jalawlā' Iraq
84 C2 Jalboi r. N.T. Austr.
244 B3 Jalcocotán Mex.
117 G4 Jaldhaka r. Bangl.
114 C2 Jaldrug Karnataka India
256 B4 Jales Brazil
116 D4 Jalesar Uttar Prad. India
117 F5 Jaleshwar Orissa India
116 C5 Jalgaon Mahar. India
165 E4 Jalhay Belgium
127 G5 Jalībah Iraq
160 B2 Jaligny-sur-Besbre France
207 H4 Jalingo Nigeria
244 B3 Jalisco Mex.
244 B4 Jalisco state Mex.
159 F4 Jallais France
114 B2 Jalna Mahar. India
78 □3b Jaloklab i. Majuro Marshall Is
187 C6 Jalón Spain
183 I3 Jalón r. Spain
183 H2 Jalón de Cameros Spain
116 C4 Jalor Rajasthan India
244 C3 Jalostotitlán Mex.
196 D3 Jalovik Srbija Yugo.
175 L2 Jałówka Pol.
244 C3 Jalpa Mex.
117 G4 Jalpaiguri W. Bengal India
245 E3 Jalpan Mex.
245 G5 Jaltepec r. Mex.
245 G5 Jaltipan Mex.
245 E3 Jaltocán Mex.
Jalūlā Iraq see Jalawlā'
122 E3 Jām r. Iran
250 A5 Jama Ecuador
246 D2 Jamaica Cuba
246 □ Jamaica country West Indies
246 D3 Jamaica Channel Haiti/Jamaica
117 G4 Jamalpur Bangl.
117 F4 Jamalpur Bihar India
251 G6 Jamanxim r. Brazil
245 F4 Jamapa r. Mex.
209 C8 Jamba Angola
94 C3 Jambi Sumatera Indon.
94 C3 Jambi prov. Indon.
215 H1 Jambila S. Africa
85 G5 Jambin Qld Austr.
116 C4 Jambo Rajasthan India
94 B1 Jamboaye r. Indon.
116 C5 Jambusar Gujarat India
114 C2 Jamekunte Andhra Prad. India
170 C2 Jameln Ger.
237 E4 James r. MO U.S.A.
236 D3 James r. N. Dakota/S. Dakota U.S.A.
232 E6 James r. VA U.S.A.
259 B7 James, Isla i. Chile
123 G5 Jamesabad Pak.
224 D2 James Bay Can.
235 D2 Jamesburg NJ U.S.A.
246 C1 James Cistern Eleuthera Bahamas
261 F3 James Craik Arg.
140 □ James I Land reg. Svalbard
James Island Islas Galápagos Ecuador see San Salvador, Isla
221 P2 Jameson Land reg. Greenland
87 E5 Jameson Range hills W.A. Austr.
81 B6 James Peak South I. N.Z.
84 C5 James Ranges mts N.T. Austr.
262 U2 James Ross Island Antarctica
221 I3 James Ross Strait Nunavut Can.
82 D3 Jamestown S.A. Austr.
Jamestown Ont. Can. see Wawa
147 D3 Jamestown Rep. of Ireland
215 F4 Jamestown S. Africa
216 □2b Jamestown St Helena
240 G3 Jamestown CA U.S.A.
230 C4 Jamestown KY U.S.A.
236 D2 Jamestown ND U.S.A.
232 D3 Jamestown NY U.S.A.
232 B5 Jamestown OH U.S.A.
232 C4 Jamestown PA U.S.A.
231 C4 Jamestown TN U.S.A.
157 F3 Jametz France
175 H2 Jamielnik Pol.
141 M3 Jämijärvi Fin.
185 G3 Jamilena Spain
234 C2 Jamison PA U.S.A.
143 F3 Jämjö Sweden
114 B2 Jamkhandi Karnataka India
114 B2 Jamkhed Mahar. India
114 C3 Jammalamadugu Andhra Prad. India
142 C3 Jammerbugten b. Denmark
116 C2 Jammu Jammu and Kashmir
116 D2 Jammu and Kashmir terr. Asia
116 B5 Jamnagar Gujarat India
116 C5 Jamner Mahar. India
116 D4 Jamni r. India
165 E5 Jamoigne Belgium
94 D4 Jampang Kulon Jawa Barat Indon.
123 G4 Jampur Pak.
141 N3 Jämsä Fin.
141 N3 Jämsänkoski Fin.
117 F5 Jamshedpur Bihar India
117 F5 Jamtara Bihar India
140 K3 Jämtland county Sweden
117 F4 Jamui Bihar India
95 G2 Jamuk, Gunung mt. Indon.
196 E3 Jamu Mare Romania
117 G5 Jamuna r. Bangl.
117 H4 Jamuna r. India
182 E2 Jamuz r. Spain
210 E4 Janaale Somalia
141 N3 Janakkala Fin.
116 E5 Janakpur Madh. Prad. India
117 F4 Janakpur Nepal
257 F1 Janaúba Brazil
251 I4 Janaucú, Ilha i. Brazil
177 L3 Jánd Hungary
256 B2 Jandaia Brazil
256 B5 Jandaia do Sul Brazil
129 D3 Jandari Georgia
173 H3 Jandelsbrunn Ger.
216 □3b Jandía hill Fuerteventura Canary Is
216 □3b Jandía, Península de pen. Fuerteventura Canary Is
116 C3 Jandiala Punjab India
250 D5 Jandiatuba r. Brazil
85 G5 Jandowae Qld Austr.
185 F2 Jándula r. Spain
185 G3 Jandulilla r. Spain
254 D5 Janeiro r. Brazil
240 G1 Janesville CA U.S.A.
226 C4 Janesville WI U.S.A.
122 D3 Jangal Iran
114 C2 Jangaon Andhra Prad. India
Jangeldi Uzbek. see Dzhangel'dy
117 G4 Jangipur W. Bengal India
Jangnga Turkm. see Dzhanga
111 D5 Jangngai Zangbo r. Xizang China
122 A2 Jānī Beyglū Iran
171 E3 Jänickendorf Ger.
174 G3 Janikowo Pol.
256 A6 Janiópolis Brazil
188 G3 Janja Bos.-Herz.
188 G3 Janja r. Bos.-Herz.
196 E4 Janjevo Kosovo, Srbija Yugo.
215 E2 Jan Kempdorp S. Africa
177 L4 Jánkmajtis Hungary
196 E4 Jankov Kamen mt. Yugo.
175 H3 Janków Pol.
174 F3 Jankowo Dolne Pol.
132 C2 Jan Mayen i. Arctic Ocean
138 E3 Jānmuiža Latvia
182 D4 Jaňona mt. Spain
177 I5 Jánoshalma Hungary
176 G4 Jánosháza Hungary
176 G4 Jánossomorja Hungary
173 H2 Janovice nad Úhlavou Czech Rep.
175 L2 Janów Pol.
175 H5 Janów Pol.
175 J4 Janowiec Pol.
175 I2 Janowiec Kościelny Pol.
174 F3 Janowiec Wielkopolski Pol.
175 K5 Janów Lubelski Pol.
175 I2 Janowo Pol.
175 L3 Janów Podlaski Pol.
223 I4 Jans Bay Sask. Can.
171 F4 Jänschwalde Ger.
214 E5 Jansenville S. Africa
255 D5 Januária Brazil
128 A5 Janûb Sînâ' governorate Egypt
156 B4 Janville France
114 C2 Janwada Karnataka India
123 E5 Janzar mt. Pak.
158 E4 Janzé France
116 C5 Jaora Madh. Prad. India
102 Japan country Asia
101 E5 Japan, Sea of N. Pacific Ocean
266 E3 Japan Basin sea feature Sea of Japan
266 E3 Japan Trench sea feature N. Pacific Ocean
129 E3 Jap'aridze Georgia
251 E5 Japurá r. Brazil
117 H4 Japvo Mount Nagaland India
183 I3 Jaraba Spain
246 E3 Jarabacoa Dom. Rep.
128 D1 Jarābulus Syria
174 F4 Jaraczewa Pol.
187 B5 Jarafuel Spain
256 C1 Jaraguá Brazil
255 C8 Jaraguá do Sul Brazil
255 B7 Jaraguari Brazil
182 E5 Jaraicejo Spain
182 E4 Jaraiz de la Vera Spain
183 G4 Jarama r. Spain
182 E4 Jarandilla de la Vera Spain
128 B3 Jarash Jordan
251 H5 Jarauçu r. Brazil
143 G1 Järbo Sweden
Jarboesville MD U.S.A. see Lexington Park
Jar-bulak Kazakh. see Kabanbay
175 L5 Jarczów Pol.
254 F3 Jardim Ceará Brazil
253 F5 Jardim Mato Grosso do Sul Brazil
185 H2 Jardín r. Spain
256 D4 Jardinópolis Brazil
162 A2 Jard-sur-Mer France
Jares r. Spain see Xares
106 D2 Jargalant Arhangay Mongolia
106 C2 Jargalant Bayanhongor Mongolia
106 A2 Jargalant Bayan-Ölgiy Mongolia
107 G2 Jargalant Dornod Mongolia
106 C2 Jargalant Govĭ-Altay Mongolia
Jargalant Hovd Mongolia see Hovd
106 E1 Jargalant Töv Mongolia
106 B2 Jargalant Hayrhan mt. Mongolia
107 F2 Jargalthaan Mongolia
156 C5 Jargeau France
251 I5 Jari r. Brazil
117 G4 Jaria Jhanjail Bangl.
170 E2 Jarmen Ger.
157 G4 Jarménil France
143 F1 Järna Dalarna Sweden
143 G2 Järna Stockholm Sweden
162 B3 Jarnac France
162 E2 Jarnages France
157 F3 Jarny France
175 K5 Jarocin Podkarpackie Pol.
174 F4 Jarocin Wielkopolskie Pol.
176 E1 Jaroměř Czech Rep.
176 E2 Jaroměřice nad Rokytnou Czech Rep.
176 F3 Jaroslavice Czech Rep.
175 K5 Jarosław Pol.
176 E2 Jarošov nad Nežárkou Czech Rep.
177 K2 Jarovnice Slovakia
140 K3 Järpen Sweden
168 E1 Jarplund-Weding Ger.
Jarqŭrghon Uzbek. see Dzharkurgan
84 C4 Jarra Jarra Range hills N.T. Austr.
232 E6 Jarratt VA U.S.A.
234 B3 Jarrettsville MD U.S.A.
149 H3 Jarrow Tyne and Wear, England U.K.
106 E4 Jartai Nei Mongol China
253 E2 Jarú Brazil

Jarud Nei Mongol China see Lubei
196 E4 Jarut mt. Yugo.
138 E2 Järvakandi Estonia
141 N3 Järvenpää Fin.
157 G4 Jarville-la-Malgrange France
75 I4 Jarvis Island terr. N. Pacific Ocean
140 K2 Järvsand Sweden
141 L3 Järvsö Sweden
117 E4 Jarwa Uttar Prad. India
159 F4 Jarzé France
116 B5 Jasdan Gujarat India
161 D5 Jas de Laure hill France
177 I3 Jasenie Slovakia
177 K3 Jasenov Slovakia
117 F5 Jashpurnagar Madh. Prad. India
174 D4 Jasień Pol.
174 F1 Jasień Pol.
175 J3 Jasienica Pol.
175 I4 Jasieniec Pol.
207 F5 Jasikan Ghana
175 J6 Jasiołka r. Pol.
175 K5 Jasionka Pol.
175 I5 Jasionna Pol.
175 L2 Jasionówka Pol.
122 D5 Jāsk Iran
122 D5 Jāsk-e Kohneh Iran
Jasliq Uzbek. see Zhaslyk
175 J6 Jasło Pol.
177 G3 Jaslovské Bohunice Slovakia
138 E4 Jašlūnai Lith.
170 E1 Jasmund pen. Ger.
262 T2 Jason Peninsula Antarctica
177 J3 Jasov Slovakia
177 H4 Jásová Slovakia
222 G4 Jasper Alta Can.
231 C5 Jasper AL U.S.A.
237 E4 Jasper AR U.S.A.
231 D6 Jasper FL U.S.A.
231 C5 Jasper GA U.S.A.
230 C4 Jasper IN U.S.A.
232 E3 Jasper NY U.S.A.
232 B5 Jasper OH U.S.A.
231 C5 Jasper TN U.S.A.
237 E6 Jasper TX U.S.A.
160 C3 Jassans-Riottier France
160 D2 Jasseron France
Jassy Romania see Iași
143 H4 Jastarnia Pol.
188 E3 Jastrebarsko Croatia
174 E2 Jastrowie Pol.
175 I4 Jastrząb Pol.
174 G1 Jastrzębia Góra Pol.
174 G6 Jastrzębie-Zdrój Pol.
175 K2 Jaświły Pol.
177 J4 Jászapáti Hungary
177 I4 Jászárokszállás Hungary
177 I4 Jászberény Hungary
177 I4 Jászboldogháza Hungary
177 I4 Jászfényszaru Hungary
177 J4 Jászkarajenő Hungary
177 J4 Jászkisér Hungary
177 J4 Jászladány Hungary
177 J4 Jász-Nagykun-Szolnok county Hungary
177 J4 Jászszentandrás Hungary
177 I5 Jászszentlászló Hungary
177 J4 Jásztelek Hungary
183 H1 Jata, Monte hill Spain
256 B2 Jataí Brazil
251 G5 Jatapu r. Brazil
185 G4 Jatar Spain
116 D4 Jatara Madh. Prad. India
123 G5 Jati Pak.
95 E4 Jatibarang Jawa Barat Indon.
246 C2 Jatibonico Cuba
Játiva Spain see Xátiva
95 E4 Jatiwangi Jawa Barat Indon.
194 C4 Jato r. Sicilia Italy
123 G4 Jatoi Pak.
141 L3 Jättendal Sweden
170 E2 Jatzke Ger.
170 E2 Jatznick Ger.
256 C5 Jaú Brazil
251 F5 Jaú r. Brazil
251 F5 Jauaperi r. Brazil
246 D2 Jauco Cuba
252 B2 Jauja Peru
186 C3 Jaulín Spain
245 E2 Jaumave Mex.
160 F2 Jaun Switz.
251 F6 Jauna r. Brazil
158 E5 Jaunay r. France
162 C2 Jaunay-Clan France
138 E3 Jaunjelgava Latvia
138 D3 Jaunmārupe Latvia
138 F3 Jaunpiebalga Latvia
138 D3 Jaunpils Latvia
117 E4 Jaunpur Uttar Prad. India
256 B2 Jaupaci Brazil
161 A5 Jaur r. France
261 H4 Jauregui Arg.
186 B2 Jaurrieta Spain
253 F4 Jauru r. Brazil
161 E4 Jausiers France
Java i. Indon. see Jawa
114 C3 Javadi Hills India
Javaés r. Tocantins Brazil see Formoso
254 C4 Javaés, Serra dos hills Brazil
129 C3 Javakhet'is K'edi hills Armenia/Georgia
187 C4 Javalambre mt. Spain
187 B4 Javalambre, Sierra de mts Spain
183 I4 Javalón mt. Spain
250 D6 Javari r. Brazil/Peru alt. Yavari
265 L5 Java Ridge sea feature Indian Ocean
107 G1 Javarthushuu Mongolia
95 E4 Java Sea Indon.
265 K5 Java Trench sea feature Indian Ocean
187 D6 Jávea Spain
170 C3 Jävenitz Ger.
185 F3 Javerero mt. Spain
162 C3 Javerlhac-et-la-Chapelle-St-Robert France
186 B2 Javier Spain
259 B7 Javier, Isla i. Chile
196 E4 Javor mts Yugo.
176 E2 Javořice hill Czech Rep.
177 I3 Javorie mt. Slovakia
196 D4 Javorje mt. Yugo.
176 G1 Javorník Czech Rep.
188 E2 Javornik mt. Slovenia
177 H2 Javorníky mts Slovakia
140 M2 Jävre Sweden
159 F3 Javron-les-Chapelles France
95 D5 Jawa i. Indon.
94 D4 Jawa Barat prov. Indon.
116 C4 Jawad Madh. Prad. India
116 B4 Jawai r. India
116 D3 Jawala Mukhi Hima. Prad. India
116 D5 Jawar Madh. Prad. India
95 E4 Jawa Tengah prov. Indon.
95 F4 Jawa Timur prov. Indon.
128 C1 Jawbān Bayk Syria
124 D5 Jawf, Wādī al watercourse Yemen
114 B2 Jawhar Mahar. India
210 E4 Jawhar Somalia
174 E4 Jawor Pol.
175 K6 Jawornik Polski Pol.
175 J4 Jawor Solecki Pol.
174 G6 Jaworze Pol.
175 H5 Jaworzno Pol.
175 H6 Jaworzyna mt. Pol.
174 E5 Jaworzyna Śląska Pol.
237 E4 Jay OK U.S.A.
91 I7 Jaya, Puncak mt. Indon.
114 B2 Jayakwadi Sagar l. India
250 B6 Jayanca Peru
117 G4 Jayanti W. Bengal India
91 J7 Jayapura Irian Jaya Indon.
185 G4 Jayena Spain
117 F4 Jaynagar Bihar India
117 G5 Jaynagar W. Bengal India
115 D2 Jaypur Orissa India
128 C3 Jayrūd Syria
237 C5 Jayton TX U.S.A.
247 □1 Jayuya Puerto Rico
162 C2 Jazeneuil France
125 F2 Jazīrat al Hamrā U.A.E.
128 B2 Jbail Lebanon
241 J4 Jean NV U.S.A.
237 F6 Jeanerette LA U.S.A.
222 F2 Jean Marie River N.W.T. Can.
122 D4 Jebāl Bārez, Kūh-e mts Iran
207 G4 Jebba Nigeria
196 E3 Jebel Romania
Jebel Turkm. see Dzhebel
210 A2 Jebel, Bahr el r. Sudan/Uganda alt. Abiad, Bahr el, conv. White Nile
203 F5 Jebel Abyad Plateau Sudan
Jebel Ali U.A.E. see Mina Jebel Ali
250 B6 Jeberos Peru
180 D5 Jebha Morocco
157 H4 Jebsheim France
146 F6 Jedburgh Scottish Borders, Scotland U.K.
124 B3 Jeddah Saudi Arabia
189 B7 Jedeida Tunisia
175 K4 Jedlanka Pol.
175 J6 Jedlicze Pol.
174 E5 Jedlina-Zdrój Pol.
175 J4 Jedlińsk Pol.
175 J4 Jedlnia-Letnisko Pol.
175 J2 Jednorożec Pol.
175 I5 Jędrzejów Pol.
184 E4 Jédula Spain
175 K2 Jedwabne Pol.
175 I2 Jedwabno Pol.
170 C2 Jeetze r. Ger.
231 D5 Jefferson GA U.S.A.
236 E3 Jefferson IA U.S.A.
232 C6 Jefferson NC U.S.A.
232 C4 Jefferson OH U.S.A.
237 E5 Jefferson TX U.S.A.
226 C4 Jefferson WI U.S.A.
238 E2 Jefferson r. MT U.S.A.
240 I2 Jefferson, Mount NV U.S.A.
238 B2 Jefferson, Mount vol. OR U.S.A.
236 E4 Jefferson City MO U.S.A.
232 E5 Jeffersonton VA U.S.A.
231 D5 Jeffersonville GA U.S.A.
230 C4 Jeffersonville IN U.S.A.
232 B6 Jeffersonville KY U.S.A.
232 B5 Jeffersonville OH U.S.A.
232 C6 Jeffrey WV U.S.A.
215 E6 Jeffrey's Bay S. Africa
207 G3 Jega Nigeria
163 C5 Jegun France
Jehanabad Bihar India see Jahanabad
168 D1 Jejsing Denmark
138 E3 Jēkabpils Latvia
174 F4 Jelcz-Laskowice Pol.
177 H3 Jelenec Slovakia
174 D5 Jelenia Góra Pol.
175 K1 Jeleniewo Pol.
175 H6 Jeleśnia Pol.
138 D3 Jelgava Latvia
177 G3 Jelka Slovakia
232 A6 Jellico TN U.S.A.
224 C3 Jellicoe Ont. Can.
80 E2 Jellicoe Channel North I. N.Z.
142 C4 Jelling Denmark
232 B4 Jelloway OH U.S.A.
168 F2 Jelmstorf Ger.
177 J3 Jelšava Slovakia
193 G3 Jelsi Italy
95 F5 Jember Jawa Timur Indon.
169 F3 Jembke Ger.
165 D4 Jemeppe Belgium
239 F5 Jemez Pueblo NM U.S.A.
168 C2 Jemgum Ger.
174 G5 Jemielnica Pol.
174 E4 Jemielno Pol.
110 D2 Jeminay (Topterek) Xinjiang China
207 H4 Jemma Bauchi Nigeria
207 H4 Jemma Kaduna Nigeria
176 E2 Jemnice Czech Rep.
171 C5 Jena Ger.
237 E6 Jena LA U.S.A.
178 C3 Jenbach Austria
205 H1 Jendouba Tunisia
189 B7 Jendouba admin. div. Tunisia
171 F5 Jeneč Czech Rep.
173 E4 Jengen Ger.
110 C3 Jengish Chokusu mt. China/Kyrg.
128 B3 Jenīn West Bank
232 C6 Jenkinjones WV U.S.A.
232 B6 Jenkins KY U.S.A.
234 D3 Jenkins NJ U.S.A.
234 C2 Jenkintown PA U.S.A.
Jenne Mali see Djenné
223 I5 Jenner Alta Can.
179 H4 Jennersdorf Austria
247 □2 Jennings Antigua and Barbuda
222 C3 Jennings r. B.C. Can.
237 E6 Jennings LA U.S.A.
223 L4 Jenpeg Man. Can.
241 M1 Jensen UT U.S.A.
95 E4 Jepara Jawa Tengah Indon.
83 E4 Jeparit Vic. Austr.
254 E5 Jequié Brazil
257 E2 Jequitaí Brazil
257 E2 Jequitaí r. Brazil
257 G2 Jequitinhonha Brazil
257 H1 Jequitinhonha r. Brazil
171 C3 Jerchel Ger.
244 D3 Jerécuaro Mex.
127 H5 Jereh Iran
246 D3 Jérémie Haiti
254 F4 Jeremoabo Brazil
244 C2 Jerez Mex.
244 C2 Jerez r. Mex.
184 D4 Jerez de la Frontera Spain
185 G3 Jerez del Marquesado Spain
184 D2 Jerez de los Caballeros Spain
140 L2 Jerfojaur Sweden
198 B2 Jergucat Albania
187 C5 Jérica Spain
85 F4 Jericho Qld Austr.
235 E2 Jericho NY U.S.A.
128 B4 Jericho West Bank
171 D3 Jerichow Ger.
205 H2 Jerid, Chott el salt l. Tunisia
83 F3 Jerilderie N.S.W. Austr.
174 E4 Jerka Pol.
129 D4 Jermuk Armenia
234 C1 Jermyn PA U.S.A.
241 K4 Jerome AZ U.S.A.
238 D3 Jerome ID U.S.A.
232 D4 Jerome PA U.S.A.
261 G2 Jeronimo Norte Arg.
87 C7 Jerramungup W.A. Austr.
168 F2 Jersbek Ger.
158 D2 Jersey terr. Channel Is
233 F4 Jersey City NJ U.S.A.
227 I5 Jersey Shore PA U.S.A.
236 F4 Jerseyville IL U.S.A.
182 E4 Jerte Spain
182 D5 Jerte r. Spain
254 E3 Jerumenha Brazil
128 B4 Jerusalem Israel/West Bank
80 E3 Jerusalem North I. N.Z.
83 G3 Jervis Bay Jervis Bay Austr.
83 G3 Jervis Bay b. Jervis Bay Austr.
83 G3 Jervis Bay Territory admin. div. Austr.
84 C4 Jervois Range hills N.T. Austr.
169 F3 Jerxheim Ger.
174 E4 Jerzmanowa Pol.
192 B5 Jerzu Sardegna Italy
169 E5 Jesberg Ger.
176 C1 Jesenice Středočeský kraj Czech Rep.
176 D2 Jesenice Středočeský kraj Czech Rep.
188 E2 Jesenice Slovenia
176 G1 Jeseník Czech Rep.
177 J3 Jesenské Slovakia
171 D3 Jeserig Brandenburg Ger.
171 D3 Jeserig Brandenburg Ger.
171 D4 Jesewitz Ger.
191 I5 Jesi Italy
222 F5 Jesmond B.C. Can.
191 H3 Jesolo Italy
Jesselton Sabah Malaysia see Kota Kinabalu
171 D4 Jessen Ger.
142 D1 Jessheim Norway
117 G5 Jessore Bangl.
234 B3 Jessup MD U.S.A.
168 E2 Jesteburg Ger.
176 D1 Ještěd mt. Czech Rep.
172 C4 Jestetten Ger.
231 D6 Jesup GA U.S.A.
245 G5 Jesús Carranza Mex.
261 E2 Jesús María Arg.
244 B3 Jesús María r. Mex.
116 B5 Jetalsar Gujarat India
Jethro tourist site Saudi Arabia see Maghā'ir Shu'ayb
236 D4 Jetmore KS U.S.A.
173 E3 Jettingen-Scheppach Ger.
173 F3 Jetzendorf Ger.
156 E2 Jeumont France
168 E1 Jevenstedt Ger.
168 C2 Jever Ger.
176 F2 Jevíčko Czech Rep.
176 F3 Jevišovice Czech Rep.
176 F3 Jevišovka r. Czech Rep.
142 D1 Jevnaker Norway
232 A4 Jewell OH U.S.A.
232 C6 Jewell Ridge VA U.S.A.
235 G1 Jewett City CT U.S.A.
Jewish Autonomous Oblast admin. div. Rus. Fed. see Yevreyskaya Avtonomnaya Oblast'
Jeyhun Turkm. see Dzheykhun
173 H2 Jezerní Stěna mt. Ger.
174 G2 Jeżewo Pol.
143 I4 Jeziorany Pol.
175 J3 Jeziorka r. Pol.
174 G4 Jeziorsko, Jezioro l. Pol.
175 K4 Jeziorzany Pol.
175 H4 Jeżów Pol.
175 K5 Jeżowe Pol.
128 B3 Jezzine Lebanon
116 C5 Jhabua Madh. Prad. India
117 F4 Jha Jha Bihar India
116 D3 Jhajjar Haryana India
116 C4 Jhajju Rajasthan India
123 F4 Jhal Pak.
117 G5 Jhalakati Bangl.
116 D4 Jhalawar Rajasthan India
117 F5 Jhalida W. Bengal India
116 D4 Jhalrapatan Rajasthan India
123 H4 Jhang Pak.
117 F4 Jhanjharpur Bihar India
116 D4 Jhansi Uttar Prad. India
111 F7 Jhanzi r. India
117 F5 Jhargram W. Bengal India
117 F5 Jharia Bihar India
117 F5 Jharsuguda Orissa India
123 G4 Jhatpat Pak.
116 C3 Jhelum r. India/Pak.
123 H3 Jhelum Pak.
Jhenaidaha Bangl. see Jhenida
117 G5 Jhenida Bangl.
168 C2 Jheringsfehn (Moormerland) Ger.
116 B5 Jhinjhuvada Gujarat India
117 F5 Jhinkpani Bihar India
123 G5 Jhudo Pak.
117 F4 Jhumritilaiya Bihar India
116 C3 Jhunjhunun Rajasthan India
116 E4 Jhusi Uttar Prad. India
108 C1 Jiachuan Sichuan China
Jiachuanzhen Sichuan China see Jiachuan
Jiading Jiangxi China see Xinfeng
109 G2 Jiading Shanghai China
109 E3 Jiahe Hunan China
108 B2 Jiajiang Sichuan China
108 C2 Jialing Jiang r. Sichuan China
Jialu Shaanxi China see Jiaxian
109 E1 Jialu r. China
100 D3 Jiamusi Heilong. China
109 E3 Ji'an Jiangxi China
109 E3 Ji'an Jiangxi China
101 C4 Ji'an Jilin China
Jianchang Jiangxi China see Nancheng
107 H3 Jianchang Liaoning China
108 A3 Jianchuan Yunnan China
Jiandaoyu Hubei China see Zigui
109 F2 Jiande Zhejiang China
108 C2 Jiang'an Sichuan China
Jiangbei Chongqing China see Yubei
108 B4 Jiangcheng Yunnan China
108 B3 Jiangchuan Yunnan China
109 D3 Jiangcun Hunan China
109 F1 Jiangdu Jiangsu China
108 C2 Jiange Sichuan China
108 C3 Jiangjiehe Guizhou China
108 C2 Jiangjin Chongqing China
106 A2 Jiangjunmiao Xinjiang China
106 C3 Jiangjuntai Gansu China
Jiangkou Guangdong China see Fengkai
108 D3 Jiangkou Guizhou China
108 C1 Jiangkou Shaanxi China
Jiangkou Sichuan China see Pingchang
109 F3 Jiangle Fujian China
Jiangling Hubei China see Jingzhou
108 C1 Jiangluozhen Gansu China
109 E4 Jiangmen Guangdong China
Jiangna Yunnan China see Yanshan
109 F2 Jiangning Jiangsu China
109 F2 Jiangshan Zhejiang China
Jiangsi Guizhou China see Dejiang
109 F1 Jiangsu prov. China
109 E3 Jiangxi prov. China
Jiangxia Hubei China see Wuchang
107 F5 Jiangxian Shanxi China
109 G1 Jiangyan Jiangsu China
109 G2 Jiangyin Jiangsu China
109 D3 Jiangyong Hunan China
108 C2 Jiangyou Sichuan China
109 F1 Jianhu Jiangsu China
109 D4 Jian Jiang r. China
Jianjun Shaanxi China see Yongshou
109 E2 Jianli Hubei China
109 F3 Jianning Fujian China
109 F3 Jian'ou Fujian China
107 H3 Jianping Liaoning China
107 H3 Jianping Liaoning China
108 A1 Jianshe Qinghai China
Jianshe Sichuan China see Baiyü
108 D2 Jianshi Hubei China
108 B4 Jianshui Yunnan China
108 C2 Jianxing Sichuan China
109 F3 Jianyang Fujian China
108 C2 Jianyang Sichuan China
108 B1 Jiaochang Sichuan China
Jiaochangba Sichuan China see Jiaochang
Jiaocheng Guangdong China see Jiaoling
107 G4 Jiaocheng Shanxi China
107 H4 Jiaohe Hebei China
100 C4 Jiaohe Jilin China
Jiaojiang Zhejiang China see Taizhou
107 F4 Jiaokou Shanxi China
Jiaokui Yunnan China see Yiliang
107 H4 Jiaolai r. China
107 I3 Jiaolai r. China
109 F3 Jiaoling Guangdong China
107 H5 Jiaonan Shandong China
109 F3 Jiaowei Fujian China
107 I4 Jiaozhou Shandong China
107 G5 Jiaozuo Henan China
100 C4 Jiapigou Jilin China
108 B3 Jiasa Yunnan China
Jiashan Anhui China see Mingguang
110 B4 Jiashi Xinjiang China
109 E1 Jiaxian Henan China
107 F4 Jiaxian Shaanxi China
107 H5 Jiaxiang Shandong China
109 G2 Jiaxing Zhejiang China
Jiayi Taiwan see Chiai
100 D2 Jiayin Heilong. China
109 E2 Jiayu Hubei China
106 C4 Jiayuguan Gansu China
109 F4 Jiazi Guangdong China
197 F2 Jibou Romania
Jībūtī country Africa see Djibouti
Jibuti Djibouti see Djibouti
245 E5 Jicayán Mex.
176 E1 Jičín Czech Rep.
Jiddah Saudi Arabia see Jeddah
100 D3 Jidong Heilong. China
140 L1 Jiehkkevarri mt. Norway
Jiehu Shandong China see Yinan
109 E4 Jieshi Guangdong China
109 E4 Jieshi Wan b. China
109 E1 Jieshou Anhui China
138 D4 Jiesia r. Lith.
140 N1 Iešjávri l. Norway
109 E4 Jiexi Guangdong China
107 F4 Jiexiu Shanxi China
109 F4 Jieyang Guangdong China
138 E4 Jieznas Lith.
207 H3 Jigawa state Nigeria
87 D4 Jiggalong W.A. Austr.
241 J1 Jiggs NV U.S.A.
246 C2 Jiguaní Cuba
108 B1 Jigzhi Qinghai China
176 E2 Jihlava Czech Rep.
176 F3 Jihlava r. Czech Rep.
176 E2 Jihlavský kraj admin. reg. Czech Rep.
205 G1 Jijel Alg.
197 I2 Jijia r. Romania
210 D2 Jijiga Eth.
187 C6 Jijona Spain
108 B2 Jiju Sichuan China
197 H3 Jilava Romania
176 E1 Jilemnice Czech Rep.
Jilf al Kabīr, Haḍabat al plat. Egypt see Gilf Kebir Plateau
123 G3 Jilga r. Afgh.
124 D2 Jilh al 'Ishār plain Saudi Arabia
210 D4 Jilib Somalia
100 C4 Jilin Jilin China
107 J3 Jilin prov. China
106 D4 Jiling Gansu China
100 C4 Jilin Handa Ling mts China
100 B2 Jiliu r. China
183 I3 Jiloca r. Spain
Jilong Taiwan see Chilung
245 E4 Jilotepec Mex.
176 D1 Jílové Czech Rep.
176 D2 Jílové u Prahy Czech Rep.
210 C3 Jīma Eth.
246 E3 Jimani Haiti
196 E3 Jimbolia Romania
Jimda Sichuan China see Zindo
185 G3 Jimena Spain
185 E4 Jimena de la Frontera Spain
242 D3 Jiménez Mex.
243 E2 Jiménez Mex.
245 E1 Jiménez Mex.
207 I4 Jimeta Nigeria
91 J7 Jimi r. P.N.G.
84 C2 Jim Jim Creek r. N.T. Austr.
107 I4 Jimo Shandong China
176 F2 Jimramov Czech Rep.
110 E3 Jimsar Xinjiang China
234 C2 Jim Thorpe PA U.S.A.
197 F3 Jina Romania
107 H4 Jinan Shandong China
Jin'an Sichuan China see Songpan
Jinbi Yunnan China see Dayao
176 C2 Jince Czech Rep.
106 D4 Jinchang Gansu China
107 G5 Jincheng Shanxi China
Jincheng Sichuan China see Leibo
Jincheng Sichuan China see Yilong
Jincheng Yunnan China see Wuding
Jinchengjiang Guangxi China see Hechi
Jinchuan Gansu China see Jinchang
Jinchuan Jiangxi China see Xingan
108 B2 Jinchuan Sichuan China
116 D3 Jind Haryana India
83 G4 Jindabyne N.S.W. Austr.
Jinding Yunnan China see Lanping
177 G1 Jindřichov Czech Rep.
176 E2 Jindřichův Hradec Czech Rep.
Jin'e Sichuan China see Longchang
106 C4 Jinfosi Gansu China
Jing Xinjiang China see Jinghe
107 F5 Jing r. China
Jing'an Guangdong China see Doumen
107 F4 Jingbian Shaanxi China
107 E5 Jingchuan Gansu China
109 F2 Jingde Anhui China
109 F2 Jingdezhen Jiangxi China
108 B3 Jingdong Yunnan China
109 E3 Jinggangshan Jiangxi China
109 E3 Jinggang Shan hill Jiangxi China
109 F2 Jinggongqiao Jiangxi China
108 B4 Jinggu Yunnan China
107 H4 Jinghai Tianjin China
110 C2 Jinghe Xinjiang China
108 B4 Jinghong Yunnan China
109 G1 Jingjiang Jiangsu China
107 G4 Jingle Shanxi China
109 E2 Jingmen Hubei China
106 E5 Jingning Gansu China
107 H3 Jingpeng Nei Mongol China
109 E2 Jingsha Hubei China
109 E2 Jingshan Hubei China
106 D4 Jingtai Gansu China
108 C4 Jingxi Guangxi China
109 F2 Jingxian Anhui China
Jingxian Hunan China see Jingzhou
Jingxin Yunnan China see Yongshan
108 C2 Jingyan Sichuan China
Jingyang Anhui China see Jingde
100 C4 Jingyu Jilin China
106 E4 Jingyuan Gansu China
109 E2 Jingzhou Hubei China
108 D3 Jingzhou Hunan China
Jinhe Yunnan China see Jinping
Jinhua Yunnan China see Jianchuan
109 F2 Jinhua Zhejiang China
107 G3 Jining Nei Mongol China
107 H5 Jining Shandong China
210 B4 Jinja Uganda
109 F3 Jinjiang Fujian China
Jinjiang Hainan China see Chengmai
108 B3 Jinjiang Yunnan China
108 D3 Jin Jiang r. China
109 E2 Jin Jiang r. China
210 C3 Jinka Eth.
108 B2 Jinkouhe Sichuan China
Jinmen Taiwan see Chinmen
108 B3 Jinning Yunnan China
242 □I6 Jinotega Nic.
242 □I7 Jinotepe Nic.
108 D3 Jinping Guizhou China
Jinping Yunnan China see Jingdong
108 B4 Jinping Yunnan China
Jinping Yunnan China see Qiubei
Jinsen S. Korea see Inch'ŏn
108 C3 Jinsha Guizhou China
112 J6 Jinsha Jiang r. China alt. Chang Jiang, alt. Tongtian He, alt. Zhi Qu, conv. Yangtze, long Yangtze Kiang
107 H3 Jinshan Nei Mongol China
109 G2 Jinshan Shanghai China
Jinshan Yunnan China see Lufeng
Jinshi Hunan China see Xinning
109 D2 Jinshi Hunan China
106 C4 Jinta Gansu China
109 F2 Jintan Jiangsu China
108 C2 Jintang Sichuan China
114 C2 Jintur Mahar. India
109 F3 Jinxi Jiangxi China
Jinxi Liaoning China see Lianshan
109 F3 Jin Xi r. China
109 F2 Jinxian Jiangxi China
Jinxian Liaoning China see Linhai
107 H5 Jinxiang Shandong China
109 G3 Jinxiang Zhejiang China
108 D3 Jinxiu Guangxi China
108 B3 Jinyang Sichuan China
Jinyuan Sichuan China see Dayi
109 G2 Jinyun Zhejiang China
109 E2 Jinzhai Anhui China
107 I3 Jinzhou Liaoning China
107 I4 Jinzhou Liaoning China
Jinzhu Sichuan China see Daocheng
104 D2 Jinzū-gawa r. Japan
253 E2 Ji-Paraná Brazil
253 E2 Jiparaná r. Brazil
250 A5 Jipijapa Ecuador
242 □H6 Jiquilisco El Salvador
244 C4 Jiquilpan de Juárez Mex.
245 H5 Jiquipilas Mex.
123 G2 Jirgatol Tajik.
117 H4 Jiri r. India
107 H2 Jirin Gol Nei Mongol China
176 C1 Jirkov Czech Rep.
171 F5 Jirny Czech Rep.
122 D4 Jīroft Iran
210 F3 Jirriiban Somalia
107 F5 Jishan Shanxi China
Jishi Qinghai China see Xunhua
108 D2 Jishou Hunan China
Jishui Jiangxi China see Yongfeng
128 C2 Jisr ash Shughūr Syria
176 D2 Jistebnice Czech Rep.
Jitian Guangdong China see Lianshan
94 C1 Jitra Malaysia
197 F4 Jiu r. Romania
106 E4 Jiudengkou Nei Mongol China
108 B2 Jiuding Shan mt. Sichuan China
109 E2 Jiugong Shan mt. Hubei China
109 E2 Jiujiang Jiangxi China
109 F2 Jiujiang Jiangxi China
Jiulian Yunnan China see Mojiang
109 E2 Jiuling Shan mts China
Jiulong H.K. China see Kowloon
108 B2 Jiulong Sichuan China
Jiulong Sichuan China see Yuechi
108 D3 Jiuqian Guizhou China
106 C4 Jiuquan Gansu China
100 C3 Jiutai Jilin China
109 F3 Jiuzhen Fujian China
123 E5 Jiwani Pak.
107 I1 Jiwen Nei Mongol China
109 F2 Jixi Anhui China
100 D3 Jixi Heilong. China
Jixian Hebei China see Jizhou
100 D3 Jixian Heilong. China
Jixian Henan China see Weihui
107 F4 Jixian Shanxi China
107 G5 Jiyuan Henan China
125 F4 Jiz, Wādī al r. Yemen
124 C4 Jīzān Saudi Arabia
124 C4 Jīzān prov. Saudi Arabia
176 D1 Jizera r. Czech Rep.
176 E1 Jizerské Hory mts Czech Rep.
107 G4 Jizhou Hebei China
105 F2 Jizō-dake mt. Japan
Jizzakh Uzbek. see Dzhizak
Jizzakh Wiloyati admin. div. Uzbek. see Dzhizakskaya Oblast'
255 C8 Joaçaba Brazil
170 E3 Joachimsthal Ger.
257 G2 Joaíma Brazil
206 A3 Joal-Fadiout Senegal
182 B3 Joane Port.
João Belo Moz. see Xai-Xai
João de Almeida Angola see Chibia
257 F3 João Monlevade Brazil
254 G3 João Pessoa Brazil
256 D2 João Pinheiro Brazil
257 E2 Joaquim Felício Brazil
258 D2 Joaquin V. González Arg.
160 B3 Job France
246 C2 Jobabo Cuba
116 C5 Jobat Madh. Prad. India
177 I4 Jobbágyi Hungary
247 □1 Jobos Puerto Rico
240 H2 Job Peak NV U.S.A.
178 D3 Jochberg Austria
171 D5 Jocketa Ger.
140 M2 Jockfall Sweden
172 C2 Jockgrim Ger.
244 C3 Jocotepec Mex.
245 E4 Jocotitlán, Volcán vol. Mex.
117 F5 Joda Orissa India
185 G3 Jódar Spain
116 C4 Jodhpur Rajasthan India
116 B5 Jodiya Gujarat India
165 D4 Jodoigne Belgium
225 K3 Joe Batt's Arm Nfld. Can.
140 O3 Joensuu Fin.
140 K2 Joesjö Sweden
105 E1 Jōetsu Japan
157 G3 Jœuf France
213 G4 Jofane Moz.
222 H5 Joffre, Mount Alta/B.C. Can.
104 D2 Jōganji-gawa r. Japan
117 F4 Jogbani Bihar India
138 F2 Jõgeva Estonia
122 D2 Joghatay, Kūh-ye hill Iran
117 G4 Jogighopa Assam India
116 D3 Jogindarnagar Hima. Prad. India
Jogjakarta Indon. see Yogyakarta
215 F2 Johannesburg S. Africa
240 I4 Johannesburg CA U.S.A.
171 D5 Johanngeorgenstadt Ger.
173 G3 Johanniskirchen Ger.
116 E5 Johilla r. Madh. Prad. India
86 F3 John, Mount hill W.A. Austr.
238 C2 John Day OR U.S.A.
238 B2 John Day r. OR U.S.A.
238 C2 John Day, Middle Fork r. OR U.S.A.
238 C2 John Day, North Fork r. OR U.S.A.
222 H3 John d'Or Prairie Alta Can.
233 G4 John F. Kennedy airport NY U.S.A.
222 D3 John Jay, Mount Alaska/B.C. Can./U.S.A.
222 F1 Johnny Hoe r. N.W.T. Can.
146 E3 John o'Groats Highland, Scotland U.K.
237 C4 Johnson KS U.S.A.
233 G2 Johnson VT U.S.A.
232 D4 Johnsonburg PA U.S.A.
227 J4 Johnson City NY U.S.A.
231 D4 Johnson City TN U.S.A.
237 D6 Johnson City TX U.S.A.
240 H4 Johnsondale CA U.S.A.
222 C2 Johnson's Crossing Y.T. Can.
231 E5 Johnsonville SC U.S.A.
150 C3 Johnston Pembrokeshire, Wales U.K.
231 D5 Johnston SC U.S.A.
87 D7 Johnston, Lake salt flat W.A. Austr.
Johnston and Sand Islands atoll N. Pacific Ocean see Johnston Atoll
75 H2 Johnston Atoll N. Pacific Ocean
146 D6 Johnstone Renfrewshire, Scotland U.K.
146 E6 Johnstonebridge Dumfries and Galloway, Scotland U.K.
87 C6 Johnston Range hills W.A. Austr.
147 D4 Johnstown Rep. of Ireland
233 F3 Johnstown NY U.S.A.
232 B4 Johnstown OH U.S.A.
232 D4 Johnstown PA U.S.A.
147 E3 Johnstown Bridge Rep. of Ireland
94 C2 Johor state Malaysia
94 □ Johor, Selat str. Malaysia/Sing.
94 □ Johor Bahru Malaysia
171 E5 Jöhstadt Ger.
138 F2 Jõhvi Estonia
156 D5 Joigny France
255 C8 Joinville Brazil
157 F4 Joinville France
262 U2 Joinville Island Antarctica
245 E4 Jojutla Mex.
138 E1 Jokela Fin.
221 P2 Jøkelbugten b. Greenland
141 M3 Jokioinen Fin.
140 L2 Jokkmokk Sweden
140 □B2 Jökulbunga hill Iceland
140 □B2 Jökulfirðir inlet Iceland
140 □D2 Jökulsá á Dál r. Iceland
140 □C2 Jökulsá á Fjöllum r. Iceland
191 G4 Jolanda di Savoia Italy
114 C3 Jolarpettai Tamil Nadu India
127 G3 Jolfa Iran
226 C5 Joliet IL U.S.A.
234 B2 Joliet PA U.S.A.
224 F4 Joliette Que. Can.
92 B5 Jolo Phil.
92 B5 Jolo i. Phil.
160 E3 Joly, Mont mt. France
138 B1 Jomala Åland Fin.
95 F4 Jombang Jawa Timur Indon.
108 A2 Jomda Xizang China
142 C2 Jomfruland i. Norway
105 F2 Jōmine-san mt. Japan
190 D1 Jona Switz.
122 C5 Jonāḥ Iran
232 B6 Jonancy KY U.S.A.
138 E4 Jonava Lith.
156 D3 Jonchery-sur-Vesle France
160 C2 Joncy France
142 B1 Jondal Norway
106 D5 Jonê Gansu China
104 D2 Jōnen-dake mt. Japan
237 F5 Jonesboro AR U.S.A.
237 F4 Jonesboro IL U.S.A.
226 E5 Jonesboro IN U.S.A.
237 E5 Jonesboro LA U.S.A.
233 □J2 Jonesboro ME U.S.A.
232 B6 Jonesboro TN U.S.A.
148 C3 Jonesborough Northern Ireland U.K.
232 D4 Jones Mills PA U.S.A.
262 R2 Jones Mountains Antarctica
233 □J2 Jonesport ME U.S.A.
221 J2 Jones Sound sea chan. Nunavut Can.
234 B2 Jonestown PA U.S.A.
237 F6 Jonesville LA U.S.A.
232 B6 Jonesville VA U.S.A.
210 B3 Jonglei state Sudan
175 I3 Joniec Pol.
138 E3 Joniškėlis Lith.
138 D3 Joniškis Lith.
117 E5 Jonk r. India
143 F3 Jönköping Sweden
143 F3 Jönköping county Sweden
175 I2 Jonkowo Pol.
225 G3 Jonquière Que. Can.
161 C4 Jonquières France
243 G5 Jonuta Mex.
162 B3 Jonzac France
237 E4 Joplin MO U.S.A.
245 E2 Jopoy Mex.
Joppa Israel see Tel Aviv-Yafo
234 B3 Joppatowne MD U.S.A.
195 E4 Joppolo Italy
116 D4 Jora Madh. Prad. India
186 C4 Jorcas Spain
128 C4 Jordan country Asia
128 B4 Jordan r. Asia
238 F2 Jordan MT U.S.A.
232 E3 Jordan NY U.S.A.
238 C3 Jordan r. OR U.S.A.
241 K1 Jordan r. UT U.S.A.
257 G1 Jordânia Brazil
161 A4 Jordanne r. France
175 H6 Jordanów Pol.
174 E5 Jordanów Śląski Pol.
238 C3 Jordan Valley OR U.S.A.
170 D2 Jördenstorf Ger.
142 D4 Jordløse Denmark
117 H4 Jorhat Assam India
129 D3 Jorjiashvili Georgia
168 E2 Jork Ger.
142 D3 Jörlanda Sweden
123 G2 Jorm Afgh.
140 K2 Jormvattnet Sweden
140 M2 Jörn Sweden
141 N3 Joroinen Fin.
142 B2 Jørpeland Norway
185 I1 Jorquera Spain
207 H4 Jos Nigeria
92 C5 Jose Abad Santos Phil.
254 B4 José Bispo r. Brazil
256 C4 José Bonifácio Brazil
245 F4 José Cardel Mex.
254 E3 José de Freitas Brazil
259 C7 José de San Martin Arg.
261 I3 José Enrique Rodó Uru.
171 G5 Josefův Důl Czech Rep.
244 A1 José López Portillo, Presa resr Mex.
244 C2 José Maria Morelos Mex.
92 B3 Jose Pañganiban Phil.
258 G4 José Pedro Varela Uru.
86 F2 Joseph Bonaparte Gulf W.A. Austr.
241 L4 Joseph City AZ U.S.A.
116 D3 Joshimath Uttar Prad. India
117 F5 Joshipur Orissa India
241 I4 Joshua Tree CA U.S.A.
156 B5 Josnes France
207 H4 Jos Plateau Nigeria
158 D4 Josselin France
171 D5 Jößnitz Ger.
141 I3 Jostedalsbreen glacier Norway
138 D4 Josvainiai Lith.
141 J3 Jotunheimen mts Norway
182 C3 Jou Port.
159 F3 Jouanne r. France
156 D4 Jouarre France
214 D5 Joubertina S. Africa
215 F2 Jouberton S. Africa
162 C1 Joué-lès-Tours France
158 E4 Joué-sur-Erdre France
160 A1 Jouet-sur-l'Aubois France
160 E2 Jougne France
128 B3 Joûnié Lebanon
161 D5 Jouques France
237 D6 Jourdanton TX U.S.A.
164 E2 Joure Neth.
162 C4 Journiac France
222 H4 Joussard Alta Can.
141 N3 Joutsa Fin.
141 O3 Joutseno Fin.
160 B1 Joux-la-Ville France
156 B4 Jouy France
157 G3 Jouy-aux-Arches France
156 C3 Jouy-le-Moutier France
156 B5 Jouy-le-Potier France
156 D3 Jouy-lès-Reims France
246 B2 Jovellanos Cuba
117 H4 Jowai Meghalaya India
123 F2 Jowzjān prov. Afgh.
222 C2 Joy, Mount Y.T. Can.
243 H6 Joya de Cerén tourist site El Salvador
147 B3 Joyce's Country reg. Rep. of Ireland
161 C4 Joyeuse France
104 B4 Jōyō Japan
160 B3 Joze France
175 J4 Józefów Pol.
175 L5 Józefów Pol.
175 J3 Józefów Pol.
215 I2 Jozini S. Africa
206 A2 Jreïda Maur.
250 E5 Juami r. Brazil
247 □1 Juana Díaz Puerto Rico
244 C1 Juan Aldama Mex.
107 G5 Juancheng Shandong China
222 E5 Juan de Fuca Strait Can./U.S.A.
213 □I3 Juan de Nova i. Indian Ocean
245 G4 Juan Díaz Covarrubias Mex.
252 □ Juan Fernández, Archipiélago is S. Pacific Ocean
Juan Fernández Islands S. Pacific Ocean see Juan Fernández, Archipiélago
245 G5 Juanita Mex.
252 A1 Juanjuí Peru
140 O3 Juankoski Fin.
161 F5 Juan-les-Pins France
261 I4 Juan L. Lacaze Uru.
261 H6 Juan N. Fernández Arg.
245 G4 Juan Rodriguez Clara Mex.
Juanshui Hubei China see Tongcheng
259 B7 Juan Stuven, Isla i. Chile
207 F5 Juapon Ghana
243 E3 Juaréz Mex.
245 F5 Juárez, Sierra mts Mex.
242 A1 Juárez, Sierra de mts Mex.
254 E4 Juàzeiro Brazil
254 F3 Juàzeiro do Norte Brazil
206 C5 Juazohn Liberia
Juba r. Somalia see Jubba
210 A3 Juba Sudan
124 D5 Juban Yemen
262 U2 Jubany research stn Antarctica
210 D5 Jubba r. Somalia
210 D4 Jubbada Dhexe admin. reg. Somalia
210 D4 Jubbada Hoose admin. reg. Somalia
Jubbulpore Madh. Prad. India see Jabalpur
168 E1 Jübek Ger.
87 E6 Jubilee Lake salt flat W.A. Austr.
159 F3 Jublains France
183 5 Júcar r. Spain
256 B1 Juçara Brazil
187 C5 Jucar-Turia, Canal r. Spain
254 F3 Jucas Brazil
169 B4 Jüchen Ger.
244 C3 Juchipila Mex.
244 C3 Juchipila r. Mex.
245 G5 Juchitán Mex.
175 L2 Juchnowiec Dolny Pol.
169 F5 Jüchsen Ger.
257 H2 Jucuruçu Brazil
257 H2 Jucuruçu r. Brazil
142 A2 Judaberg Norway
127 F5 Judaidat al Hamir Iraq
126 E4 Judaydah Syria
171 C5 Judenbach Ger.
179 F3 Judenburg Austria
183 H3 Judes mt. Spain
108 A3 Judian Yunnan China
238 E2 Judith r. MT U.S.A.
238 E2 Judith Gap MT U.S.A.
Juegang Jiangsu China see Rudong
185 G2 Juego de Bolos mt. Spain
142 D4 Juelsminde Denmark
183 I4 Juez mt. Spain
251 F5 Jufari r. Brazil
158 D3 Jugon-les-Lacs France
Jugoslavija country Europe see Yugoslavia
107 F4 Juh Nei Mongol China
169 E4 Jühnde Ger.
178 C3 Juifen mt. Austria
242 □I6 Juigalpa Nic.
159 F4 Juigné-sur-Loire France
162 D3 Juillac France
163 C5 Juillan France
156 C3 Juilly France
253 F2 Juína Brazil
253 F3 Juina r. Brazil
156 C4 Juine r. France
168 B2 Juist Ger.
168 C2 Juist i. Ger.
257 F4 Juiz de Fora Brazil
94 C3 Jujuhan r. Indon.
160 D2 Jujurieux France
258 D1 Jujuy prov. Arg.
140 M2 Jukkasjärvi Sweden
179 E2 Julbach Austria
173 G3 Julbach Ger.
236 C3 Julesburg CO U.S.A.
252 C4 Juli Peru
252 C3 Juliaca Peru
85 E4 Julia Creek Qld Austr.
85 E4 Julia Creek r. Qld Austr.
240 I5 Julian CA U.S.A.
164 D2 Julianadorp Neth.
Julian Alps mts Slovenia see Julijske Alpe
Julianatop mt. Indon. see Mandala, Puncak
251 G4 Juliana Top mt. Suriname
Julianehåb Greenland see Qaqortoq
147 E3 Julianstown Rep. of Ireland
169 B5 Jülich Ger.
160 C2 Julien, Mont hill France
160 C2 Juliénas France
188 D2 Julijske Alpe mts Slovenia
255 B9 Júlio de Castilhos Brazil
Juliomagus France see Angers
256 C5 Júlio Mesquita Brazil
84 D4 Julius, Lake Qld Austr.
234 D2 Juliustown NJ U.S.A.
158 E3 Jullouville France
Jullundur Punjab India see Jalandhar
251 E6 Juma r. Brazil
107 G4 Juma r. China
Juma Uzbek. see Dzhuma
108 A1 Jumanggoin Sichuan China
250 B6 Jumbilla Peru
161 B3 Jumeaux France
162 D3 Jumilhac-le-Grand France
187 B6 Jumilla Spain
116 E3 Jumla Nepal
168 C2 Jümme r. Ger.
Jumna r. India see Yamuna
226 B3 Jump r. WI U.S.A.
138 E3 Jumprava Latvia
116 B5 Junagadh Gujarat India
115 D2 Junagarh Orissa India
107 H5 Junan Shandong China
107 H2 Jun Bulen Nei Mongol China
260 B3 Juncal mt. Chile
182 B5 Juncal Port.
247 □1 Juncos Puerto Rico
186 D3 Juncosa Spain
237 D6 Junction TX U.S.A.
241 K2 Junction UT U.S.A.
84 C1 Junction Bay N.T. Austr.
236 D4 Junction City KS U.S.A.
238 B2 Junction City OR U.S.A.
85 E5 Jundah Qld Austr.
256 D5 Jundiaí Brazil
220 E4 Juneau AK U.S.A.
186 D3 Juneda Spain
83 F3 Junee N.S.W. Austr.
Jungar Qi Nei Mongol China see Shagedu
190 C2 Jungfrau mt. Switz.
110 D2 Junggar Pendi basin China
172 D3 Jungingen Ger.
165 F5 Junglinster Lux.
227 I5 Juniata r. PA U.S.A.
234 A2 Juniata County county PA U.S.A.
196 E4 Junik Kosovo, Srbija Yugo.
261 G4 Junín Arg.
260 C3 Junin Mendoza Arg.
252 A2 Junín Peru
252 B2 Junín dept Peru
232 D5 Junior WV U.S.A.
233 □J1 Juniper N.B. Can.
241 K4 Juniper Mountains AZ U.S.A.
240 G3 Junipero Serro Peak CA U.S.A.
156 E3 Juniville France
169 B5 Jünkerath Ger.
108 C2 Junlian Sichuan China
114 B2 Junnar Mahar. India
237 C6 Juno TX U.S.A.
140 M2 Junosuando Sweden
256 B4 Junqueirópolis Brazil
140 L3 Junsele Sweden
238 C3 Juntura OR U.S.A.
Junxi Fujian China see Datian
Junxian Hubei China see Danjiangkou
108 A1 Ju'nyung Sichuan China
Ju'nyunggoin Sichuan China see Ju'nyung
138 E4 Juodšiliai Lith.
138 E3 Juodupė Lith.
140 M2 Juoksengi Sweden
138 E4 Juosta r. Lith.
138 E4 Juozapinės kalnas hill Lith.
122 D4 Jūpār Iran
159 G4 Jupilles France
231 D7 Jupiter FL U.S.A.
165 E4 Juprelle Belgium
256 D6 Juquiá Brazil
256 D6 Juquiá r. Brazil
256 D5 Juquitiba Brazil
208 F2 Jur r. Sudan
160 D2 Jura dept Franche-Comté France
160 D3 Jura mts France/Switz.
138 D4 Jūra r. Lith.
190 C1 Jura canton Switz.
146 C5 Jura i. Scotland U.K.

146 C6 **Jura, Sound of** sea chan. Scotland U.K.
250 B3 **Juradó** Col.
257 F2 **Juramento** Brazil
163 B5 **Jurançon** France
256 A6 **Juranda** Brazil
138 D4 **Jurbarkas** Lith.
165 C4 **Jurbise** Belgium
170 C2 **Jürgenshagen** Ger.
170 D2 **Jürgenstorf** Ger.
86 D3 **Jurgurra** r. W.A. Austr.
107 I2 **Jurh** Nei Mongol China
111 E5 **Jurhen Ul Shan** mts China
138 E2 **Jüri** Estonia
87 B6 **Jurien** W.A. Austr.
87 B6 **Jurien Bay** W.A. Austr.
162 B3 **Jurignac** France
197 I3 **Jurilovca** Romania
251 G5 **Juriti Velho** Brazil
191 J4 **Jurjevo** Croatia
138 D3 **Jūrmala** Latvia
184 C2 **Juromenha** Port.
109 F2 **Jurong** Jiangsu China
94 □ **Jurong** Sing.
Jur pri Bratislave Slovakia see Svätý Jur
251 E5 **Juruá** Brazil
250 E5 **Juruá** r. Brazil
253 F3 **Juruena** Brazil
253 F1 **Juruena** r. Brazil
256 C5 **Jurumirim, Represa de** resr Brazil
253 G2 **Juruna** r. Brazil
252 C1 **Jurupari** r. Brazil
251 G5 **Juruti** Brazil
140 M3 **Jurva** Fin.
162 E4 **Jussac** France
157 F5 **Jussey** France
232 C6 **Justice** WV U.S.A.
261 F3 **Justiniano Posse** Arg.
260 E3 **Justo Daract** Arg.
177 G5 **Juta** Hungary
250 D6 **Jutaí** Brazil
250 E5 **Jutaí** r. Brazil
171 E4 **Jüterbog** Ger.
255 B7 **Juti** Brazil
243 H6 **Jutiapa** Guat.
242 □I6 **Jutiapa** Hond.
242 □I6 **Juticalpa** Hond.
Jutland pen. Denmark see Jylland
174 F4 **Jutrosin** Pol.
140 O3 **Juuka** Fin.
141 N3 **Juupajoki** Fin.
141 N3 **Juva** Fin.
244 D3 **Juventino Rosas** Mex.
159 E3 **Juvigné** France
159 E3 **Juvigny-le-Tertre** France
159 F3 **Juvigny-sous-Andaine** France
95 E4 **Juwana** Jawa Tengah Indon.
107 H5 **Juxian** Shandong China
107 H5 **Juye** Shandong China
122 D3 **Jūymand** Iran
122 C4 **Jūyom** Iran
157 E4 **Juzennecourt** France
163 C6 **Juzet-d'Izaut** France
Južnoukrajinsk Ukr. see Yuzhnoukrayinsk
212 E5 **Jwaneng** Botswana
142 D4 **Jyderup** Denmark
142 C3 **Jylland** pen. Denmark
121 I4 **Jyrgalang** Kyrg.
141 N3 **Jyväskylä** Fin.

K

116 D2 **K2** mt. China/Jammu and Kashmir
207 G4 **Ka** r. Nigeria
240 □ **Kaaawa** HI U.S.A.
Kaakhka Turkm. see **Kaka**
240 □ **Kaala** mt. HI U.S.A.
78 □5 **Kaala-Gomen** New Caledonia
215 H1 **Kaalrug** S. Africa
215 H1 **Kaapamuiden** S. Africa
Kaapstad S. Africa see **Cape Town**
141 M3 **Kaarina** Fin.
170 C2 **Kaarßen** Ger.
169 B4 **Kaarst** Ger.
206 C3 **Kaarta** reg. Mali
164 E3 **Kaatsheuvel** Neth.
140 O3 **Kaavi** Fin.
Kaba Xinjiang China see **Habahe**
121 K3 **Kaba** r. China/Kazakh.
177 K4 **Kaba** Hungary
123 E2 **Kabakly** Turkm.
129 C3 **Kabak Tepe** mt. Turkey
206 C4 **Kabala** Sierra Leone
211 A5 **Kabale** Uganda
Kabalega Falls National Park Uganda see **Murchison Falls National Park**
209 E6 **Kabalo** Dem. Rep. Congo
209 E6 **Kabambare** Dem. Rep. Congo
121 F1 **Kaban'** Kazakh.
121 J3 **Kabanbay** Kazakh.
94 B2 **Kabanjahe** Sumatera Indon.
120 B1 **Kabanovka** Rus. Fed.
Kabanye Ukr. see **Krasnorichens'ke**
79 □1 **Kabara** i. Fiji
137 I5 **Kabardinka** Rus. Fed.
Kabardino-Balkarskaya A.S.S.R. aut. rep. Rus. Fed. see **Kabardino-Balkarskaya Respublika**
129 C2 **Kabardino-Balkarskaya Respublika** aut. rep. Rus. Fed.
208 F5 **Kabare** Dem. Rep. Congo
Kabarega National Park Uganda see **Murchison Falls National Park**
92 B5 **Kabasalan** Phil.
105 G2 **Kaba-san** hill Japan
96 B3 **Kabaung** r. Myanmar
96 A2 **Kabaw Valley** Myanmar
207 G5 **Kabba** Nigeria
114 C3 **Kabbani** r. India
140 M2 **Kåbdalis** Sweden
177 G4 **Kab-hegy** hill Hungary
224 C3 **Kabinakagami** r. Ont. Can.
224 C3 **Kabinakagami Lake** Ont. Can.
209 E6 **Kabinda** Dem. Rep. Congo
128 B2 **Kabīr** r. Syria
122 A3 **Kabīrkūh** mts Iran
129 E4 **Käbirli** Azer.
123 G4 **Kabirwala** Pak.
116 D5 **Kabneshwar** Mahar. India
208 C3 **Kabo** C.A.R.
123 G2 **Kabodiyen** Tajik.
Kabodiyon Tajik. see **Kabodiyen**
209 E8 **Kabompo** Zambia
209 D8 **Kabompo** r. Zambia
209 E6 **Kabongo** Dem. Rep. Congo
207 F4 **Kabou** Togo
206 A3 **Kabrousse** Senegal
122 D2 **Kabūd Gonbad** Iran
122 B3 **Kabūd Rāhang** Iran
92 B2 **Kabugao** Phil.
123 G3 **Kābul** Afgh.
123 G3 **Kābul** prov. Afgh.
123 H3 **Kabul** r. Afgh.
209 F8 **Kabunda** Dem. Rep. Congo
105 F2 **Kabura-gawa** r. Japan
209 F8 **Kabwe** Zambia
120 E2 **Kabyrga** r. Kazakh.
196 E4 **Kačanik** Kosovo, Srbija Yugo.
137 G5 **Kacha** r. Ukr.
210 B4 **Kachagalau** mt. Kenya
Kachagani Georgia see **Qach'aghani**
123 E4 **Kacha Kuh** mts Iran/Pak.
135 I6 **Kachalinskaya** Rus. Fed.
116 B5 **Kachchh, Gulf of** Gujarat India
116 C4 **Kachhola** Rajasthan India
117 E4 **Kachhwa** Uttar Prad. India
207 G4 **Kachia** Nigeria
96 B1 **Kachin** state Myanmar
121 I1 **Kachiry** Kazakh.
211 A8 **Kacholola** Zambia
98 I1 **Kachug** Rus. Fed.
171 E5 **Kačice** Czech Rep.
127 F2 **Kaçkar Dağı** mt. Turkey
129 C4 **Kaçmaz** Turkey
167 H3 **Kaczawa** r. Pol.
174 E2 **Kaczory** Pol.
114 C4 **Kadaiyanallur** Tamil Nadu India
210 B4 **Kadam** mt. Uganda
176 C1 **Kadaň** Czech Rep.
123 F4 **Kadanai** r. Afgh./Pak.
97 B4 **Kadan Kyun** i. Myanmar
177 G5 **Kadarkút** Hungary
116 D4 **Kadaura** Uttar Prad. India
79 □1 **Kadavu** i. Fiji
79 □1a **Kadavu Passage** Fiji
107 H1 **Kadaya** Rus. Fed.
206 E5 **Kade** Ghana
87 E5 **Kadgo, Lake** salt flat W.A. Austr.
Kādhimain Iraq see **Al Kāẓimīyah**
116 C5 **Kadi** Gujarat India
206 D4 **Kadiana** Mali
114 C4 **Kadiapattanam** Tamil Nadu India
Kadijica mt. Bulg. see **Kadiytsa**
199 E1 **Kadıköy** Turkey
199 F1 **Kadıköy** Turkey
82 D3 **Kadina** S.A. Austr.
96 C3 **Kading** r. Laos
126 D3 **Kadınhanı** Turkey
206 D4 **Kadiolo** Mali
206 C4 **Kadiondola, Mount** Guinea
114 C3 **Kadiri** Andhra Prad. India
126 E3 **Kadirli** Turkey
Kadiyevka Ukr. see **Stakhanov**
197 F5 **Kadiytsa** mt. Bulg.
207 F5 **Kadjebi** Ghana
114 B4 **Kadmat** i. India
134 H4 **Kadnikov** Rus. Fed.
207 H5 **Kado** Nigeria
94 C1 **Kadok** Malaysia
236 C3 **Kadoka** SD U.S.A.
135 H5 **Kadom** Rus. Fed.
213 F3 **Kadoma** Zimbabwe
138 F2 **Kadrina** Estonia
208 F2 **Kadugli** Sudan
207 G4 **Kaduna** Nigeria
207 G4 **Kaduna** r. Nigeria
207 G4 **Kaduna** state Nigeria
114 C3 **Kadur** Karnataka India
108 A2 **Kadusam** mt. China/India
139 K2 **Kaduy** Rus. Fed.
134 H4 **Kadyy** Rus. Fed.
Kadzharan Armenia see **K'ajaran**
134 K2 **Kadzherom** Rus. Fed.
Kadzhi-Say Kyrg. see **Kajy-Say**
175 J2 **Kadzidło** Pol.
101 C5 **Kaechon** N. Korea
206 B2 **Kaédi** Maur.
207 I4 **Kaélé** Cameroon
240 □C8 **Kaeleku** HI U.S.A.
80 D1 **Kaeo** North I. N.Z.
168 E1 **Kær** Denmark
101 C5 **Kaesŏng** N. Korea
Kafa Ukr. see **Feodosiya**
209 D7 **Kafakumba** Dem. Rep. Congo
Kafan Armenia see **Kapan**
207 H4 **Kafanchan** Nigeria
215 F3 **Kafferrivier** S. Africa
207 H3 **Kaffin-Hausa** Nigeria
215 E3 **Kaffir** r. S. Africa
206 B3 **Kaffrine** Senegal
Kafirnigan Tajik. see **Kofarnihon**
206 D4 **Kafolo** Côte d'Ivoire
203 F2 **Kafr el Sheikh** Egypt
126 C5 **Kafr el Sheikh** governorate Egypt
210 B4 **Kafu** r. Uganda
209 F8 **Kafue** Zambia
209 F8 **Kafue** r. Zambia
104 C2 **Kaga** Japan
208 C3 **Kaga Bandoro** C.A.R.
137 J4 **Kagal'nik** Rus. Fed.
137 J4 **Kagal'nik** r. Rus. Fed.
135 H7 **Kagal'nitskaya** Rus. Fed.
120 F5 **Kagan** Uzbek.
106 D5 **Kagang** Qinghai China
Kaganovich Rus. Fed. see **Tovarkovskiy**
Kaganovichabad Tajik. see **Kolkhozobod**
Kaganovichi Pervyye Ukr. see **Polis'ke**
Kagarlyk Ukr. see **Kaharlyk**
103 G6 **Kagawa** pref. Japan
227 F3 **Kagawong** Ont. Can.
140 M2 **Kåge** Sweden
211 A5 **Kagera** admin. reg. Tanz.
127 F2 **Kağızman** Turkey
103 E8 **Kagoshima** Japan
102 □1 **Kagoshima** pref. Japan
Kagul Moldova see **Cahul**
240 □C8 **Kahakuloa** HI U.S.A.
240 □ **Kahaluu** HI U.S.A.
211 B5 **Kahama** Tanz.
136 F3 **Kaharlyk** Ukr.
95 F3 **Kahayan** r. Indon.
209 C6 **Kahemba** Dem. Rep. Congo
81 A6 **Kaherekoau Mountains** South I. N.Z.
169 D5 **Kahl** r. Ger.
171 C5 **Kahla** Ger.
169 E5 **Kahl am Main** Ger.
222 F3 **Kahntah** B.C. Can.
Kahnu Iran see **Kahnūj**
122 D5 **Kahnūj** Iran
80 D1 **Kahoe** North I. N.Z.
236 F3 **Kahoka** MO U.S.A.
240 □C8 **Kahoolawe** i. HI U.S.A.
130 D3 **Kahperusvaarat** mts Fin.
126 E3 **Kahramanmaraş** Turkey
123 G4 **Kahror** Pak.
126 E3 **Kahta** Turkey
240 □D8 **Kahua** HI U.S.A.
240 □ **Kahuku** HI U.S.A.
136 E5 **Kahul, Ozero** l. Ukr.
Kahulaui i. HI U.S.A. see **Kahoolawe**
240 □C8 **Kahului** HI U.S.A.
122 D4 **Kahūrak** Iran
80 D4 **Kahurangi Point** South I. N.Z.
123 H3 **Kahuta** Pak.
91 H8 **Kai, Kepulauan** is Indon.
210 A3 **Kaia** r. Sudan
80 D1 **Kaiaka** North I. N.Z.
207 F4 **Kaiama** Nigeria
81 D5 **Kaiapoi** South I. N.Z.
241 K3 **Kaibab** AZ U.S.A.
106 C4 **Kaibamardang** Qinghai China
91 H8 **Kai Besar** i. Indon.
241 L3 **Kaibito Plateau** AZ U.S.A.
78 □6 **Kaichui, Mount** Guadalcanal Solomon Is
110 D3 **Kaidu He** r. China
251 G3 **Kaieteur Falls** Guyana
107 G5 **Kaifeng** Henan China
107 G5 **Kaifeng** Henan China
80 D1 **Kaihu** North I. N.Z.
Kaihua Yunnan China see **Wenshan**
109 F2 **Kaihua** Zhejiang China
214 C3 **Kaiingveld** reg. S. Africa
108 C2 **Kaijiang** Sichuan China
91 H8 **Kai Kecil** i. Indon.
80 D1 **Kaikohe** North I. N.Z.
81 D5 **Kaikoura** South I. N.Z.
206 C4 **Kailahun** Sierra Leone
Kailas mt. Xizang China see **Kangrinboqê Feng**
Kailas Range mts Xizang China see **Gangdisê Shan**
108 C3 **Kaili** Guizhou China
107 I3 **Kailu** Nei Mongol China
240 □ **Kailua** HI U.S.A.
240 □D9 **Kailua Kona** HI U.S.A.
80 E2 **Kaimai** North I. N.Z.
80 E2 **Kaimai Range** hills North I. N.Z.
80 E3 **Kaimanawa Mountains** North I. N.Z.
108 A1 **Kaimar** Qinghai China
81 C5 **Kaimata** South I. N.Z.
116 D4 **Kaimganj** Uttar Prad. India
103 E8 **Kaimon-dake** hill Japan
116 E4 **Kaimur Range** hills India
138 D2 **Käina** Estonia
104 B4 **Kainan** Japan
Kainda Kyrg. see **Kayyngdy**
Kaindy Kyrg. see **Kayyngdy**
80 F3 **Kaingaroa Forest** North I. N.Z.
207 F3 **Kaingiwa** Nigeria
207 G4 **Kainji Reservoir** Nigeria
117 F5 **Kaintaragarh** Orissa India
140 M2 **Kainulasjärvi** Sweden
80 E2 **Kaipara Flats** North I. N.Z.
80 E2 **Kaipara Harbour** North I. N.Z.
241 L3 **Kaiparowits Plateau** UT U.S.A.
109 E4 **Kaiping** Guangdong China
Kaiping Yunnan China see **Dêqên**
Kaira Gujarat India see **Kheda**
80 F3 **Kairakau Beach** North I. N.Z.
116 D3 **Kairana** Uttar Prad. India
205 H2 **Kairouan** Tunisia
140 L1 **Kaisepakte** Sweden
172 B2 **Kaiserslautern** Ger.
263 F2 **Kaiser Wilhelm II Land** reg. Antarctica
100 D4 **Kaishantun** Jilin China
173 E3 **Kaisheim** Ger.
138 E4 **Kaišiadorys** Lith.
80 D1 **Kaitaia** North I. N.Z.
81 B7 **Kaitangata** South I. N.Z.
80 F3 **Kaitawa** North I. N.Z.
116 D5 **Kaitha** Madh. Prad. India
116 D3 **Kaithal** Haryana India
Kaitong Jilin China see **Tongyu**
140 M2 **Kaitum** Sweden
140 M2 **Kaitumälven** r. Sweden
240 □C8 **Kaiwi Channel** HI U.S.A.
108 D2 **Kaixian** Chongqing China
108 C3 **Kaiyang** Guizhou China
107 J3 **Kaiyuan** Liaoning China
108 B4 **Kaiyuan** Yunnan China
104 B4 **Kaizuka** Japan
140 N2 **Kajaani** Fin.
84 E4 **Kajabbi** Qld Austr.
94 C2 **Kajang** Malaysia
129 E4 **K'ajaran** Armenia
177 H5 **Kajdacs** Hungary
176 D3 **Kájov** Czech Rep.
122 A2 **Kaju** Iran
207 G4 **Kajuru** Nigeria
121 I4 **Kajy-Say** Kyrg.
122 D2 **Kaka** Turkm.
224 B3 **Kakabeka Falls** Ont. Can.
129 D3 **Kakabet'i** Georgia
92 C5 **Kakal** r. Phil.
214 C3 **Kakamas** S. Africa
210 B4 **Kakamega** Kenya
104 C3 **Kakamigahara** Japan
209 A6 **Kakamoéka** Congo
188 G3 **Kakanj** Bos.-Herz.
81 C6 **Kakanui Mountains** South I. N.Z.
80 E3 **Kakaramea** North I. N.Z.
80 E3 **Kakaramea** vol. North I. N.Z.
177 H5 **Kakasd** Hungary
206 C5 **Kakata** Liberia
80 E3 **Kakatahi** North I. N.Z.
117 H4 **Kakching** Manipur India
222 C3 **Kake** AK U.S.A.
105 E4 **Kakegawa** Japan
209 D6 **Kakenge** Dem. Rep. Congo
168 E2 **Kakenstorf** Ger.
170 C3 **Kakerbeck** Ger.
102 □1 **Kakeroma-jima** i. Japan
129 B2 **Kakhat'i** Georgia
129 D2 **Kakhet'is K'edi** hills Georgia
Kakhi Azer. see **Qax**
129 E2 **Kakhib** Rus. Fed.
137 G4 **Kakhovka** Ukr.
137 G4 **Kakhovs'ke Vodoskhovyshche** resr Ukr.
Kakhul Moldova see **Cahul**
122 B4 **Kākī** Iran
114 D2 **Kakinada** Andhra Prad. India
196 D4 **Kakinjës, Maja e** mt. Albania
222 G2 **Kakisa** N.W.T. Can.
222 G2 **Kakisa** r. N.W.T. Can.
104 A4 **Kakogawa** Japan
104 A4 **Kako-gawa** r. Japan
175 K4 **Kąkolewnica Wschodnia** Pol.
174 E4 **Kąkolewo** Pol.
116 D4 **Kakrala** Uttar Prad. India
206 B4 **Kakrima** r. Guinea
119 L1 **Kakshaal-Too** mts China/Kyrg.
220 D2 **Kaktovik** AK U.S.A.
177 I4 **Kakucs** Hungary
102 J5 **Kakuda** Japan
95 F2 **Kakus** r. Sarawak Malaysia
222 G4 **Kakwa** r. Alta Can.
188 E3 **Kal** hill Croatia
177 J4 **Kál** Hungary
211 A7 **Kala** Tanz.
205 H2 **Kalaâ Kebira** Tunisia
Kalaallit Nunaat terr. N. America see **Greenland**
123 G3 **Kalabagh** Pak.
Kalabak mt. Bulg./Greece see **Radomir**
Kalabáka Greece see **Kalampaka**
Kalabákion Greece see **Kalampaki**
114 C2 **Kalabgur** Andhra Prad. India
82 E2 **Kalabity** S.A. Austr.
209 D8 **Kalabo** Zambia
135 H6 **Kalach** Rus. Fed.
135 H6 **Kalach-na-Donu** Rus. Fed.
96 A2 **Kaladan** r. India/Myanmar
224 E4 **Kaladar** Ont. Can.
114 B2 **Kaladgi** Karnataka India
93 B3 **Kalaena** r. Indon.
212 D4 **Kalahari Desert** Africa
214 C1 **Kalahari Gemsbok National Park** S. Africa
240 □B8 **Kalaheo** HI U.S.A.
Kalaikhum Tajik. see **Qal'aikhum**
Kalai-Khumb Tajik. see **Qal'aikhum**
123 E3 **Kala-I-Mor** Turkm.
140 M2 **Kalajoki** Fin.
140 M2 **Kalajoki** r. Fin.
197 H4 **Kalakoch** hill Bulg.
207 F4 **Kalalé** Benin
116 D5 **Kalam** Mahar. India
Kalámai Greece see **Kalamata**
212 E4 **Kalamare** Botswana
198 C1 **Kalamaria** Greece
198 C3 **Kalamata** Greece
226 E4 **Kalamazoo** MI U.S.A.
226 D4 **Kalamazoo** r. MI U.S.A.
114 C2 **Kalamnuri** Mahar. India
198 B2 **Kalampaka** Greece
198 D1 **Kalampaki** Greece
206 C4 **Kalana** Mali
111 B6 **Kalanaur** Haryana India
116 C3 **Kalanaur** Punjab India
137 G4 **Kalanchak** Ukr.
Kalandula Angola see **Calandula**
210 B5 **Kalangala** Uganda
107 H1 **Kalanguy** Rus. Fed.
87 C6 **Kalannie** W.A. Austr.
116 C3 **Kalanwali** Haryana India
240 □D9 **Kalaoa** HI U.S.A.
92 C5 **Kalaong** Phil.
114 C4 **Kala Oya** r. Sri Lanka
240 □D9 **Kalapana** HI U.S.A.
Kalarash Moldova see **Călăraşi**
139 J3 **Kalashnikovo** Rus. Fed.
96 C3 **Kalasin** Thai.
Kalāt Iran see **Kabūd Gonbad**
123 F4 **Kalat** Pak.
122 D3 **Kalat, Kūh-e** mt. Iran
240 □C8 **Kalaupapa** HI U.S.A.
135 I7 **Kalaus** r. Rus. Fed.
116 B5 **Kalavad** Gujarat India
198 C2 **Kalavryta** Greece
125 G2 **Kalbā** U.A.E.
129 E3 **Kälbäcär** Azer.
87 B5 **Kalbarri** W.A. Austr.
214 B5 **Kalbaskraal** S. Africa
170 C3 **Kalbe (Milde)** Ger.
121 J2 **Kalbinskiy Khrebet** mts Kazakh.
173 F2 **Kalchreuth** Ger.
137 I4 **Kal'chyk** r. Ukr.
176 G4 **Káld** Hungary
128 B1 **Kaldırım** Turkey
120 C2 **Kaldygayty** r. Kazakh.
199 F3 **Kale** Denizli Turkey
129 A3 **Kale** Gümüşhane Turkey
129 A3 **Kale** r. Turkey
126 D2 **Kalecik** Turkey
169 F4 **Kalefeld** Ger.
122 B2 **Kaleh Sarai** Iran
209 E6 **Kalema** Dem. Rep. Congo
209 F6 **Kalémié** Dem. Rep. Congo
96 A2 **Kalemyo** Myanmar
188 G3 **Kalesija** Bos.-Herz.
174 G5 **Kalety** Pol.
140 O2 **Kalevala** Respublika Kareliya Rus. Fed.
96 A2 **Kalewa** Myanmar
146 F6 **Kale Water** r. Scotland U.K.
107 H1 **Kalga** Rus. Fed.
87 C7 **Kalgan** r. W.A. Austr.
Kalgan Hebei China see **Zhangjiakou**
114 B3 **Kalghatgi** Karnataka India
87 D6 **Kalgoorlie** W.A. Austr.
188 E3 **Kali** Croatia
116 E3 **Kali** r. India/Nepal
94 D4 **Kalianda** Sumatera Indon.
92 B4 **Kalibo** Phil.
232 A4 **Kalida** OH U.S.A.
117 F4 **Kali Gandaki** r. Nepal
114 C3 **Kaligiri** Andhra Prad. India
Kalikata W. Bengal India see **Calcutta**
139 L5 **Kalikino** Rus. Fed.
208 E5 **Kalima** Dem. Rep. Congo
95 E3 **Kalimantan** reg. Indon.
95 E2 **Kalimantan Barat** prov. Indon.
95 F3 **Kalimantan Selatan** prov. Indon.
95 F3 **Kalimantan Tengah** prov. Indon.
95 G2 **Kalimantan Timur** prov. Indon.
Kálimnos i. Greece see **Kalymnos**
117 G4 **Kalimpang** W. Bengal India
114 B3 **Kalinadi** r. India
116 E4 **Kali Nadi** r. India
115 E2 **Kalingapatnam** Andhra Prad. India
Kalinin Rus. Fed. see **Tver'**
Kalinin Turkm. see **Boldumsaz**
Kalininabad Tajik. see **Kalininobod**
138 C4 **Kaliningrad** Rus. Fed.
Kaliningrad Oblast admin. div. Rus. Fed. see **Kaliningradskaya Oblast'**
138 C4 **Kaliningradskaya Oblast'** admin. div. Rus. Fed.
138 B4 **Kaliningradskiy Zaliv** b. Rus. Fed.
129 D3 **Kalininkänd** Azer.
Kalinino Armenia see **Tashir**
134 H4 **Kalinino** Kostromskaya Oblast' Rus. Fed.
137 J5 **Kalinino** Krasnodarskiy Kray Rus. Fed.
121 H1 **Kalinino** Omskaya Oblast' Rus. Fed.
134 L4 **Kalinino** Permskaya Oblast' Rus. Fed.
123 G2 **Kalininobod** Tajik.
Kalininsk Moldova see **Cupcina**
135 I6 **Kalininsk** Rus. Fed.
135 G7 **Kalininskaya** Rus. Fed.
Kalininskaya Oblast' admin. div. Rus. Fed. see **Tverskaya Oblast'**
137 G4 **Kalinins'ke** Ukr.
116 C5 **Kalinjara** Rajasthan India
136 E1 **Kalinkavichy** Belarus
Kalinkovichi Belarus see **Kalinkavichy**
129 F4 **Kalinovka** Azer.
120 C2 **Kalinovka** Kazakh.
Kalinovka Vinnyts'ka Oblast' Ukr. see **Kalynivka**
129 D2 **Kalinovskaya** Rus. Fed.
174 G4 **Kalinowa** Pol.
175 K2 **Kalinowo** Pol.
210 F2 **Kalis** Somalia
95 F5 **Kalisat** Jawa Timur Indon.
Kalisch Pol. see **Kalisz**
114 C1 **Kali Sindh** r. India
174 G2 **Kaliska** Pol.
238 D1 **Kalispell** MT U.S.A.
176 D3 **Kaliště** hill Czech Rep.
174 G4 **Kalisz** Pol.
174 D2 **Kalisz Pomorski** Pol.
135 H6 **Kalitva** r. Rus. Fed.
140 M2 **Kalix** Sweden
140 M2 **Kalixälven** r. Sweden
116 D3 **Kalka** Haryana India
137 I4 **Kalka** r. Ukr.
199 F3 **Kalkan** Turkey
129 B3 **Kalkandere** Turkey
169 B4 **Kalkar** Ger.
84 B3 **Kalkaringi** N.T. Austr.
226 E3 **Kalkaska** MI U.S.A.
212 C4 **Kalkfeld** Namibia
170 C2 **Kalkhorst** Ger.
214 C3 **Kalkwerf** S. Africa
169 B5 **Kall** Ger.
114 C4 **Kallakkurichchi** Tamil Nadu India
140 L2 **Kallaktjåkkå** mt. Sweden
114 C2 **Kallam** Mahar. India
138 F2 **Kallaste** Estonia
140 N3 **Kallavesi** l. Fin.
140 K3 **Kållberget** Sweden
140 M2 **Kallfjärden** b. Sweden
179 E2 **Kallham** Austria
198 B2 **Kallifoni** Greece
143 F3 **Kallinge** Sweden
196 D5 **Kallmet i Madh** Albania
173 F2 **Kallmünz** Ger.
177 K4 **Kállósemjén** Hungary
140 K3 **Kallsjön** l. Sweden
114 C2 **Kallur** Karnataka India
177 K4 **Kálmánháza** Hungary
121 J1 **Kalmanka** Rus. Fed.
143 G3 **Kalmar** Sweden
143 G3 **Kalmar** county Sweden
143 G3 **Kalmarsund** sea chan. Sweden
172 C2 **Kalmit** hill Ger.
137 I4 **Kal'mius** r. Ukr.
165 D3 **Kalmthout** Belgium
114 D5 **Kalmunai** Sri Lanka
Kalmykia aut. rep. Rus. Fed. see **Kalmykiya - Khalm'g-Tangch, Respublika**
135 I7 **Kalmykiya - Khalm'g-Tangch, Respublika** aut. rep. Rus. Fed.
Kalmykovo Kazakh. see **Taypak**
Kalmytskaya Avtonomnaya Oblast' aut. rep. Rus. Fed. see **Kalmykiya - Khalm'g-Tangch, Respublika**
117 E5 **Kalnai** Madh. Prad. India
177 H3 **Kalná nad Hronom** Slovakia
138 D3 **Kalnciems** Latvia
117 G4 **Kalni** r. Bangl.
188 F2 **Kalnik** mts Croatia
199 D4 **Kalo Chorio** Kriti Greece
177 H5 **Kalocsa** Hungary
136 D2 **Kalodnaye** Belarus
116 C5 **Kalol** Gujarat India
116 C5 **Kalol** Gujarat India
209 E9 **Kalomo** Zambia
222 E4 **Kalone Peak** B.C. Can.
128 A2 **Kalopanagiotis** Cyprus
78 □6 **Kalourat, Mount** Malaita Solomon Is
122 A2 **Kalow** r. Iran
177 H5 **Káloz** Hungary
116 D3 **Kalpa** Hima. Prad. India
114 C4 **Kalpetta** Kerala India
116 D4 **Kalpi** Uttar Prad. India
110 B3 **Kalpin** Xinjiang China
Kalquduq Uzbek. see **Kulkuduk**
178 D3 **Kals am Großglockner** Austria
179 G4 **Kalsdorf bei Graz** Austria
122 D2 **Kāl-Shūr, Rūd-e** r. Iran
220 C3 **Kaltag** AK U.S.A.
134 K5 **Kaltasy** Rus. Fed.
190 E1 **Kaltbrunn** Switz.
178 C3 **Kaltenbach** Austria
168 E2 **Kaltenkirchen** Ger.
169 F5 **Kaltennordheim** Ger.
169 F5 **Kaltensundheim** Ger.
169 F5 **Kaltenwestheim** Ger.
84 B5 **Kaltukatjara** N.T. Austr.
207 H4 **Kaltungo** Nigeria
116 C3 **Kalu** Rajasthan India
114 B2 **Kalu** r. India
240 □C8 **Kaluaaha** HI U.S.A.
196 E3 **Kaluđerica** Srbija Yugo.
139 K4 **Kaluga** Rus. Fed.
Kaluga Oblast admin. div. Rus. Fed. see **Kaluzhskaya Oblast'**
137 G4 **Kaluha** Ukr.
95 F2 **Kalulong, Bukit** mt. Sarawak Malaysia
209 F8 **Kalulushi** Zambia
86 E2 **Kalumburu** W.A. Austr.
142 D4 **Kalundborg** Denmark
123 G3 **Kalur Kot** Pak.
136 C3 **Kalush** Ukr.
175 J3 **Kałuszyn** Pol.
114 C5 **Kalutara** Sri Lanka
139 J4 **Kaluzhskaya Oblast'** admin. div. Rus. Fed.
116 C5 **Kalvan** Mahar. India
138 D4 **Kalvarija** Lith.
138 E4 **Kalveliai** Lith.
134 C3 **Kälviä** Fin.
141 N3 **Kalvola** Fin.
114 C2 **Kalwakurti** Andhra Prad. India
179 F3 **Kalwang** Austria
175 H6 **Kalwaria Zebrzydowska** Pol.
134 L3 **Kal'ya** Rus. Fed.
114 B2 **Kalyan** Mahar. India
114 C3 **Kalyandurg** Andhra Prad. India
114 C2 **Kalyani** Karnataka India
115 D2 **Kalyansingapuram** Orissa India
139 K3 **Kalyazin** Rus. Fed.
199 E3 **Kalymnos** Greece
199 E3 **Kalymnos** i. Greece
136 F2 **Kalynivka** Kyivs'ka Oblast' Ukr.
137 H5 **Kalynivka** Respublika Krym Ukr.
136 E3 **Kalynivka** Vinnyts'ka Oblast' Ukr.
137 F2 **Kalyta** Ukr.
199 F3 **Kalythies** Notio Aigaio Greece
198 B2 **Kalyvia** Dytiki Ellas Greece
209 E5 **Kama** Dem. Rep. Congo
96 A3 **Kama** Myanmar
134 K4 **Kama** Rus. Fed.
134 K4 **Kama** r. Rus. Fed.
105 F3 **Kamagaya** Japan
102 J4 **Kamaishi** Japan
105 F3 **Kamakura** Japan
206 B4 **Kamakwie** Sierra Leone
114 C3 **Kamalapuram** Andhra Prad. India
123 H4 **Kamalia** Pak.
240 □C8 **Kamalo** HI U.S.A.
116 D4 **Kaman** Rajasthan India
126 D3 **Kaman** Turkey
105 E3 **Kamanashi-gawa** r. Japan
105 E3 **Kamanashi-yama** mt. Japan
214 D5 **Kamanassie** r. S. Africa
124 C5 **Kamaran** Yemen
124 C5 **Kamarān** i. Yemen
Kamaran Island Yemen see **Kamarān**
138 E3 **Kamarde** Latvia
114 C2 **Kamareddi** Andhra Prad. India
198 B2 **Kamares** Greece
129 D3 **Kämärli** Azer.
Kamarlu Armenia see **Artashat**
136 F2 **Kamaryn** Belarus
121 F5 **Kamashi** Uzbek.
213 E3 **Kamativi** Zimbabwe
207 F4 **Kamba** Nigeria
87 D6 **Kambalda** W.A. Austr.
114 C4 **Kambam** Tamil Nadu India
Kambara i. Fiji see **Kabara**
Kambara Japan see **Kanbara**
134 K4 **Kambarka** Rus. Fed.
206 B4 **Kambia** Sierra Leone
Kambo-san mt. N. Korea see **Kwanmo-bong**
209 E7 **Kambove** Dem. Rep. Congo
93 B3 **Kambuno, Bukit** mt. Indon.
197 H4 **Kamburovo** Bulg.
202 E2 **Kambūt** Libya
131 R4 **Kamchatka** r. Rus. Fed.
131 Q4 **Kamchatka, Poluostrov** pen. Rus. Fed.
266 G2 **Kamchatka Basin** sea feature Bering Sea
Kamchatka Peninsula Rus. Fed. see **Kamchatka, Poluostrov**
131 R4 **Kamchatskiy Proliv** str. Rus. Fed.
131 R4 **Kamchatskiy Zaliv** b. Rus. Fed.
197 H4 **Kamchiya** r. Bulg.
197 H4 **Kamchiyska Planina** hills Bulg.
214 D2 **Kamden** S. Africa
120 B1 **Kamelik** r. Rus. Fed.
197 G4 **Kamen** Bulg.
169 C4 **Kamen** Ger.
131 K3 **Kamen', Gory** mts Rus. Fed.
209 E6 **Kamende** Dem. Rep. Congo
176 D3 **Kamenec** mt. Czech Rep.
Kamenets-Podol'skiy Ukr. see **Kam"yanets'-Podil's'kyy**
177 J2 **Kamenica** Slovakia
197 F4 **Kamenica** Srbija Yugo.
176 E2 **Kamenice nad Lipou** Czech Rep.
171 F5 **Kamenický Šenov** Czech Rep.
177 H4 **Kameničná** Slovakia
177 H4 **Kamenín** Slovakia
126 A2 **Kamenitsa** mt. Bulg.
197 G4 **Kamenitsa** r. Bulg.
177 H6 **Kamenjak** hill Croatia
120 B2 **Kamenka** Kazakh.
Kamenka Moldova see **Camenca**
134 I2 **Kamenka** Arkhangel'skaya Oblast' Rus. Fed.
135 I5 **Kamenka** Penzenskaya Oblast' Rus. Fed.
100 F3 **Kamenka** Primorskiy Kray Rus. Fed.
135 G6 **Kamenka** Voronezhskaya Oblast' Rus. Fed.
Kamenka Ukr. see **Kam"yanka**
Kamenka-Bugskaya Ukr. see **Kam"yanka-Buz'ka**
Kamenka-Shevchenkovskaya Ukr. see **Kam"yanka**
Kamen'-Kashirskiy Ukr. see **Kamin'-Kashyrs'kyy**
Kamenka-Strumilovskaya Ukr. see **Kam"yanka-Buz'ka**
130 J4 **Kamen'-na-Obi** Rus. Fed.
134 G4 **Kamenniki** Rus. Fed.
138 G1 **Kamennogorsk** Rus. Fed.
129 B1 **Kamennomostskiy** Rus. Fed.
176 D2 **Kamenný Přívoz** Czech Rep.
176 D3 **Kamenný Újezd** Czech Rep.
197 H4 **Kameno** Bulg.
137 K4 **Kamenolomni** Rus. Fed.
Kamenongue Angola see **Camanongue**
100 E3 **Kamen'-Rybolov** Rus. Fed.
135 I6 **Kamenskiy** Rus. Fed.
131 R3 **Kamenskoye** Koryakskiy Avtonomnyy Okrug Rus. Fed.
139 L5 **Kamenskoye** Lipetskaya Oblast' Rus. Fed.
Kamenskoye Ukr. see **Dniprodzerzhyns'k**
135 H6 **Kamensk-Shakhtinskiy** Rus. Fed.
130 H4 **Kamensk-Ural'skiy** Rus. Fed.
171 F4 **Kamenz** Ger.
104 B3 **Kameoka** Japan
170 D3 **Kamern** Ger.
146 C6 **Kames** Argyll and Bute, Scotland U.K.
139 M3 **Kameshkovo** Rus. Fed.
111 B6 **Kamet** mt. Xizang China
104 C4 **Kameyama** Japan
196 D5 **Kamëz** Albania
238 C2 **Kamiah** ID U.S.A.
104 D2 **Kamichi** Japan
175 L4 **Kamień** Pol.
175 K5 **Kamień** Pol.
175 I6 **Kamienica** Pol.
174 E3 **Kamieniec** Pol.
174 E5 **Kamieniec Ząbkowicki** Pol.
174 F2 **Kamień Krajeński** Pol.
175 J4 **Kamienna** r. Pol.
174 E5 **Kamienna Gora** Pol.
174 F5 **Kamiennik** Pol.
174 C2 **Kamień Pomorski** Pol.
175 H4 **Kamieńsk** Pol.
170 F3 **Kamień Wielkie** Pol.
214 B4 **Kamiesberg** S. Africa
214 B4 **Kamiesberge** mts S. Africa
214 A4 **Kamieskroon** S. Africa
105 F3 **Kamifukuoka** Japan
84 E3 **Kamileroi** Qld Austr.
209 E7 **Kamina** Dem. Rep. Congo
136 C2 **Kamin'-Kashyrs'kyy** Ukr.
102 □1 **Kaminone-jima** i. Japan
102 J4 **Kaminoyama** Japan
188 E2 **Kaminške in Savinjske Alpe** mts Slovenia
139 M3 **Kaminskiy** Rus. Fed.
175 I3 **Kamion** Mazowieckie Pol.
175 I4 **Kamion** Mazowieckie Pol.
175 K4 **Kamionka** Pol.
199 E3 **Kamiros** Notio Aigaio Greece
209 F5 **Kamituga** Dem. Rep. Congo
121 G3 **Kamkaly** Kazakh.
117 F4 **Kamla** r. India
117 H4 **Kamla** r. India
222 F5 **Kamloops** B.C. Can.
173 E3 **Kammel** r. Ger.
214 E5 **Kammiebos** S. Africa
173 E3 **Kammlach** Ger.
104 C3 **Kammuri-yama** mt. Japan
188 E2 **Kamnik** Slovenia
129 D3 **Kamo** Armenia
80 E1 **Kamo** North I. N.Z.
105 G3 **Kamogawa** Japan
123 H4 **Kamoke** Pak.
179 G2 **Kamp** r. Austria
169 C5 **Kamp** Ger.
210 B4 **Kampala** Uganda
94 C2 **Kampar** r. Indon.
94 C1 **Kampar** Malaysia
138 D3 **Kamparkalns** hill Latvia
94 C2 **Kamparkiri** r. Indon.
168 D1 **Kampen** Ger.
164 E2 **Kampen** Neth.
209 E5 **Kampene** Dem. Rep. Congo
172 C3 **Kämpfelbach** Ger.
96 B3 **Kamphaeng Phet** Thai.
175 I3 **Kampinos** Pol.
114 C3 **Kampli** Karnataka India
169 B4 **Kamp-Lintfort** Ger.
97 D5 **Kâmpóng Cham** Cambodia
97 D4 **Kâmpóng Chhnăng** Cambodia
97 D4 **Kâmpóng Khleăng** Cambodia
Kâmpóng Saôm Cambodia see **Sihanoukville**
97 D5 **Kâmpóng Spoe** Cambodia
97 D4 **Kâmpóng Thum** Cambodia
97 D5 **Kâmpôt** Cambodia
206 E4 **Kampti** Burkina
Kampuchea country Asia see **Cambodia**
223 K5 **Kamsack** Sask. Can.
206 B4 **Kamsar** Guinea
171 C5 **Kamsdorf** Ger.
135 J5 **Kamskoye Ust'ye** Rus. Fed.
134 L4 **Kamskoye Vodokhranilishche** resr Rus. Fed.
116 E5 **Kamtha** Mahar. India
102 K2 **Kamui-dake** mt. Japan
210 B4 **Kamuli** Uganda
177 J5 **Kamut** Hungary
136 D2 **Kam"yane** Ukr.
137 H2 **Kam"yane** Ukr.
136 D3 **Kam"yanets'-Podil's'kyy** Ukr.
137 G3 **Kam"yanka** Ukr.
137 I3 **Kam"yanka** Ukr.
137 G3 **Kam"yanka** r. Ukr.
136 C2 **Kam"yanka-Buz'ka** Ukr.
137 H4 **Kam"yanka-Dniprovs'ka** Ukr.
136 E5 **Kam"yans'ke** Ukr.
137 H4 **Kam"yans'ke** Ukr.
138 D5 **Kamyanyets** Belarus
122 A3 **Kāmyārān** Iran
135 G7 **Kamyshevatskaya** Rus. Fed.
135 I6 **Kamyshin** Rus. Fed.
135 K5 **Kamyshla** Rus. Fed.
120 E3 **Kamyshlybash** Kazakh.
Kamyshnaya r. Rus. Fed./Ukr. see **Komyshna**
120 E2 **Kamysknoye** Kazakh.
Kamyslybas Kazakh. see **Kamyshlybash**
120 E3 **Kamyslybas, Ozero** l. Kazakh.
120 B3 **Kamyzyak** Rus. Fed.
125 G2 **Kamzar** Oman
131 K4 **Kan** r. Rus. Fed.
213 E3 **Kana** r. Zimbabwe
95 F2 **Kana, Bukit** mt. Sarawak Malaysia
224 E2 **Kanaaupscow** r. Que. Can.
241 K3 **Kanab** UT U.S.A.
241 K3 **Kanab Creek** r. AZ U.S.A.
220 A4 **Kanaga Island** AK U.S.A.
105 F3 **Kanagawa** pref. Japan
225 J2 **Kanairiktok** r. Nfld. Can.
114 C3 **Kanakapura** Karnataka India
179 E4 **Kanal** Slovenia
198 B2 **Kanallaki** Greece
140 K2 **Kanan** Sweden
215 F2 **Kanana** S. Africa
209 D6 **Kananga** Dem. Rep. Congo
Kanarak Orissa India see **Konarka**
241 K3 **Kanarraville** UT U.S.A.
134 I5 **Kanash** Rus. Fed.
232 B5 **Kanawha** r. WV U.S.A.
104 C2 **Kanazawa** Japan
96 A2 **Kanbalu** Myanmar
105 E3 **Kanbara** Japan
97 B4 **Kanchanaburi** Thai.
Kanchanjanga mt. India/Nepal see **Kangchenjunga**
114 C3 **Kanchipuram** Tamil Nadu India
175 K6 **Kańczuga** Pol.
123 F4 **Kand** mt. Pak.
123 F4 **Kandahār** Afgh.
123 F4 **Kandahār** prov. Afgh.
114 C2 **Kandahar** Mahar. India
140 P2 **Kandalaksha** Rus. Fed.
134 F2 **Kandalakshskiy Zaliv** g. Rus. Fed.
95 F3 **Kandangan** Kalimantan Selatan Indon.
138 D3 **Kandava** Latvia
Kandavu Passage Fiji see **Kadavu Passage**
207 F4 **Kandé** Togo
172 C2 **Kandel** Ger.
172 C3 **Kandel** mt. Ger.
170 E1 **Kandelin** Ger.
190 C2 **Kander** r. Switz.
172 B4 **Kandern** Ger.
190 C2 **Kandersteg** Switz.
123 G4 **Kandhkot** Pak.
207 F4 **Kandi** Benin
123 G5 **Kandiaro** Pak.
198 B2 **Kandila** Dytiki Ellas Greece
198 C3 **Kandila** Peloponnisos Greece
129 C4 **Kandil Dağı** mt. Turkey
129 B4 **Kandilli** Turkey
199 G1 **Kandıra** Turkey
116 B5 **Kandla** Gujarat India
113 □1 **Kandooma Fushi** i. S. Male Maldives
83 G3 **Kandos** N.S.W. Austr.
115 E1 **Kandra** Bihar India
213 □J3 **Kandreho** Madag.
117 E5 **Kandri** Madh. Prad. India
114 C3 **Kandukur** Andhra Prad. India
114 D5 **Kandy** Sri Lanka
120 D2 **Kandyagash** Kazakh.
232 D4 **Kane** PA U.S.A.
221 L2 **Kane Bassin** b. Greenland
202 B6 **Kanem** pref. Chad
240 □ **Kaneohe** HI U.S.A.
Kanev Ukr. see **Kaniv**
135 G7 **Kanevskaya** Rus. Fed.
206 B4 **Kanfarande** Guinea
212 D4 **Kang** Botswana
117 G5 **Kanga** r. Bangl.
221 M3 **Kangaatsiaq** Greenland
206 C4 **Kangaba** Mali
126 E3 **Kangal** Turkey
131 N3 **Kangalassy** Rus. Fed.
122 C5 **Kangān** Iran
94 C1 **Kangar** Malaysia
206 C4 **Kangaré** Mali
82 D3 **Kangaroo Island** S.A. Austr.
251 G3 **Kangaruma** Guyana
141 N3 **Kangasala** Fin.
140 O3 **Kangaslampi** Fin.
141 N3 **Kangasniemi** Fin.
122 A3 **Kangāvar** Iran
114 C4 **Kangayam** Tamil Nadu India
107 G3 **Kangbao** Hebei China
117 G4 **Kangchenjunga** mt. India/Nepal
108 B2 **Kangding** Sichuan China
95 F4 **Kangean, Kepulauan** is Indon.
210 B3 **Kangen** r. Sudan
221 M3 **Kangerlussuaq** Greenland
221 P2 **Kangertittivaq** sea chan. Greenland
101 C4 **Kanggye** N. Korea
221 P2 **Kangikajik** c. Greenland
225 H1 **Kangiqsualujjuaq** Que. Can.
221 K3 **Kangiqsujuaq** Que. Can.
221 K3 **Kangirsuk** Que. Can.
106 D5 **Kangle** Gansu China
Kangle Jiangxi China see **Wanzai**
108 A1 **Kanglong** Qinghai China
111 E6 **Kangmar** Xizang China
101 D5 **Kangnŭng** S. Korea
208 A4 **Kango** Gabon
140 M2 **Kangos** Sweden
107 I3 **Kangping** Liaoning China
116 D2 **Kangra** Hima. Prad. India
111 C6 **Kangrinboqê Feng** mt. Xizang China
Kangsangdobdê Xizang China see **Xainza**
111 F7 **Kangto** mt. China/India
111 D5 **Kangtog** Xizang China
108 C1 **Kangxian** Gansu China
96 A3 **Kangyidaung** Myanmar
116 D5 **Kanhan** r. India
117 E4 **Kanhar** r. Bihar India
114 C2 **Kanhargaon** Mahar. India
206 D4 **Kani** Côte d'Ivoire
104 D3 **Kani** Japan
96 A2 **Kani** Myanmar
209 E6 **Kaniama** Dem. Rep. Congo
123 G1 **Kanibadam** Tajik.
95 G1 **Kanibongan** Sabah Malaysia
81 C5 **Kaniere** South I. N.Z.
206 A3 **Kanifing** Gambia
113 □1 **Kanifinolhu** i. N. Male Maldives
114 C3 **Kanigiri** Andhra Prad. India
217 □3b **Kani-Kéli** Mayotte
120 F4 **Kanimekh** Uzbek.
134 I2 **Kanin, Poluostrov** pen. Rus. Fed.
134 H1 **Kanin Nos, Mys** c. Rus. Fed.
134 H2 **Kaninskiy Bereg** coastal area Rus. Fed.
178 A3 **Kanisfluh** mt. Austria
137 F3 **Kaniv** Ukr.
82 E4 **Kaniva** Vic. Austr.
117 E3 **Kanjiroba** mt. Nepal
196 E2 **Kanjiža** Vojvodina, Srbija Yugo.
141 M3 **Kankaanpää** Fin.
226 D5 **Kankakee** IL U.S.A.
226 C5 **Kankakee** r. IL U.S.A.
206 C4 **Kankan** Guinea
116 E5 **Kanker** Madh. Prad. India
114 D4 **Kankesanturai** Sri Lanka
207 G3 **Kankiya** Nigeria
206 C3 **Kankossa** Maur.
97 B5 **Kanmaw Kyun** i. Myanmar
103 F6 **Kanmuri-yama** mt. Japan
Kanmuri-yama mt. Japan see **Kammuri-yama**
116 C5 **Kannad** Mahar. India
105 F2 **Kanna-gawa** r. Japan
231 D5 **Kannapolis** NC U.S.A.
116 D4 **Kannauj** Uttar Prad. India
171 C4 **Kannawurf** Ger.
114 C4 **Kanniyakumari** Tamil Nadu India
116 D5 **Kannod** Madh. Prad. India
140 N3 **Kannonkoski** Fin.
Kannur Kerala India see **Cannanore**
140 M3 **Kannus** Fin.
207 H3 **Kano** Nigeria
207 H4 **Kano** r. Nigeria
207 H4 **Kano** state Nigeria
105 E3 **Kano-gawa** r. Japan
121 I2 **Kanonerka** Kazakh.
103 F6 **Kan-onji** Japan
116 C4 **Kanor** Rajasthan India
236 C4 **Kanorado** KS U.S.A.
241 K2 **Kanosh** UT U.S.A.
103 E8 **Kanoya** Japan
116 E4 **Kanpur** Uttar Prad. India
123 G4 **Kanpur** Pak.
104 B4 **Kansai** airport Japan
209 E8 **Kansanshi** Zambia
236 E4 **Kansas** r. KS U.S.A.
236 D4 **Kansas** state U.S.A.
236 E4 **Kansas City** KS U.S.A.
236 E4 **Kansas City** MO U.S.A.
131 K4 **Kansk** Rus. Fed.
Kansu prov. China see **Gansu**
210 B3 **Kanta** mt. Eth.
97 B6 **Kantang** Thai.
128 A2 **Kantara** hill Cyprus
97 D4 **Kantaralak** Thai.
129 B4 **Kantarkaya** Turkey
Kantavu i. Fiji see **Kadavu**
207 F3 **Kantchari** Burkina
135 G6 **Kantemirovka** Rus. Fed.
164 F1 **Kantens** Neth.
116 D3 **Kanth** Uttar Prad. India
117 F4 **Kanti** Bihar India
117 F5 **Kantilo** Orissa India
220 C3 **Kantishna** r. AK U.S.A.
111 A6 **Kantli** r. India
105 F3 **Kantō-heiya** plain Japan
77 I2 **Kanton** i. Phoenix Is Kiribati
Kan-Too, Pik mt. Kazakh./Kyrg. see **Khan-Tengri, Pik**
105 E3 **Kanto-sanchi** mts Japan
147 C4 **Kanturk** Rep. of Ireland
251 G4 **Kanuku Mountains** Guyana
105 F2 **Kanuma** Japan
114 C3 **Kanur** Andhra Prad. India
91 J8 **Kanuwe** r. P.N.G.
Kanyakubja Uttar Prad. India see **Kannauj**
215 H1 **KaNyamazane** S. Africa
212 E5 **Kanye** Botswana
207 G3 **Kao** Niger
79 □2 **Kao** i. Tonga
109 G4 **Kaohsiung** Taiwan
212 B3 **Kaokoveld** plat. Namibia
206 A3 **Kaolack** Senegal
209 E8 **Kaoma** Zambia
240 □B7 **Kapaa** HI U.S.A.
240 □D8 **Kapaau** HI U.S.A.
121 I3 **Kapal** Kazakh.
196 D4 **Kapa Moračka** mt. Yugo.
129 E4 **Kapan** Armenia
198 C2 **Kapareli** Greece
136 E1 **Kapatkyevichy** Belarus
211 A7 **Kapatu** Zambia
121 I4 **Kapchagay** Kazakh.
121 I4 **Kapchagayskoye Vodokhranilishche** resr Kazakh.
210 B4 **Kapchorwa** Uganda
164 C3 **Kapelle** Neth.
165 D3 **Kapellen** Belgium
143 H2 **Kapellskär** Sweden
Kapelskär Sweden see **Kapellskär**
210 B4 **Kapenguria** Kenya
179 G3 **Kapfenberg** Austria
179 G4 **Kapfenstein** Austria
199 E1 **Kapıdağı Yarımadası** pen. Turkey
117 G4 **Kapili** r. India
77 F1 **Kapingamarangi** atoll Micronesia
266 F5 **Kapingamarangi Rise** sea feature N. Pacific Ocean
199 G1 **Kapıorman Dağları** mts Turkey
209 F8 **Kapiri Mposhi** Zambia
123 G3 **Kāpīsā** prov. Afgh.
224 D2 **Kapiskau** r. Ont. Can.
137 F3 **Kapitanivka** Ukr.
81 E4 **Kapiti Island** North I. N.Z.
202 D6 **Kapka, Massif du** mts Chad
93 C3 **Kaplamada, Gunung** mt. Buru Indon.
122 C1 **Kaplankyr, Chink** hills Turkm./Uzbek.
176 D3 **Kaplice** Czech Rep.
97 B5 **Kapoe** Thai.
210 B3 **Kapoeta** Sudan
177 J4 **Kápolna** Hungary
80 E3 **Kaponga** North I. N.Z.
196 D2 **Kapos** r. Romania
177 G5 **Kaposfő** Hungary
177 H5 **Kaposszekcső** Hungary
177 G5 **Kaposvár** Hungary
172 B2 **Kappel** Ger.
179 F4 **Kappel am Krappfeld** Austria
172 B3 **Kappel-Grafenhausen** Ger.
168 E1 **Kappeln** Ger.
172 C3 **Kappelrodeck** Ger.
178 B3 **Kappl** Austria
116 D4 **Kapran** Rajasthan India

178 D3 Kaprun Austria
210 B4 Kapsabet Kenya
101 D4 Kapsan N. Korea
139 I2 Kapsha r. Rus. Fed.
Kapsukas Lith. see Marijampolė
117 H5 Kaptai Bangl.
107 H1 Kaptsegaytuy Rus. Fed.
136 E1 Kaptsevichy Belarus
95 E3 Kapuas r. Indon.
95 F3 Kapuas r. Indon.
95 F2 Kapuas Hulu, Pegunungan mts Indon./Malaysia
82 D3 Kapunda S.A. Austr.
116 C4 Kapuriya Rajasthan India
116 C3 Kapurthala Punjab India
177 K2 Kapušany Slovakia
224 D3 Kapuskasing Ont. Can.
224 D3 Kapuskasing r. Ont. Can.
135 I6 Kapustin Yar Rus. Fed.
137 F2 Kapustyntsi Kyivs'ka Oblast' Ukr.
137 H2 Kapustyntsi Sums'ka Oblast' Ukr.
209 F7 Kaputa Zambia
83 G2 Kaputar mt. N.S.W. Austr.
176 G4 Kapuvár Hungary
Kapydzhik, Gora mt. Armenia/Azer. see Qazangödağ
138 F5 Kapyl' Belarus
101 C5 Kap'yŏng S. Korea
111 F6 Ka Qu r. Xizang China
116 E4 Kara Uttar Prad. India
134 N1 Kara r. Rus. Fed.
207 F4 Kara Togo
199 F1 Kara r. Turkey
127 F3 Kara r. Turkey
199 E2 Karaağaç Balıkesir Turkey
126 D3 Karaali Turkey
Karaaul Vostochnyy Kazakhstan Kazakh. see Karaul
121 H4 Kara-Balta Kyrg.
139 L3 Karabanovo Rus. Fed.
121 H2 Karabas Kazakh.
Karabekaul Turkm. see Garabekevyul
129 B4 Karabey Turkey
199 E1 Karabiga Turkey
123 E2 Karabil', Vozvyshennost' hills Turkm.
129 B4 Karaboğa Dağları mts Turkey
122 C1 Kara-Bogaz-Gol, Proliv sea chan. Turkm.
122C1 Kara-Bogaz-Gol, Zaliv b. Turkm.
Karaboynak Turkm. see Atayab
129 E2 Karabudakhkent Rus. Fed.
126 D2 Karabük Turkey
121 I3 Karabulak Almatinskaya Oblast' Kazakh.
121 K3 Karabulak Vostochnyy Kazakhstan Kazakh.
129 D2 Karabulak Rus. Fed.
121 H2 Karabulakskaya Kazakh.
Karabura Xinjiang China see Yumin
199 F2 Karaburç İzmir Turkey
199 E2 Karaburun Turkey
120 E2 Karabutak Kazakh.
199 F1 Karacabey Turkey
199 E1 Karacakılavuz Turkey
126 C2 Karacaköy Turkey
127 E3 Karacalı Dağ mt. Turkey
128 A1 Karaçal Tepe mt. Turkey
199 F3 Karacasu Turkey
Karachay-Cherkess Republic aut. rep. Rus. Fed. see Karachayevo-Cherkesskaya Respublika
Karachayevo-Cherkesskaya A.S.S.R. aut. rep. Rus. Fed. see Karachayevo-Cherkesskaya Respublika
129 B2 Karachayevo-Cherkesskaya Respublika aut. rep. Rus. Fed.
129 B2 Karachayevsk Rus. Fed.
139 J5 Karachev Rus. Fed.
123 F5 Karachi Pak.
127 F3 Karaçoban Turkey
199 F3 Karaçulha Turkey
Karacurun Turkey see Hilvan
177 G5 Karád Hungary
114 B2 Karad Mahar. India
128 D1 Kara Dağ hill Turkey
199 E1 Kara Dağ hill Turkey
199 F1 Kara Dağ hills Turkey
126 D3 Kara Dağ mt. Turkey
121 H4 Kara-Darya r. Kyrg.
Kara-Dar'ya Uzbek. see Payshanba
Kara Deniz sea Asia/Europe see Black Sea
206 E4 Karaga Ghana
121 H2 Karaganda Kazakh.
121 H2 Karagandinskaya Oblast' admin. div. Kazakh.
129 D1 Karagas Rus. Fed.
121 I3 Karagash Kazakh.
134 K4 Karagay Rus. Fed.
121 H2 Karagayly Kazakh.
131 R4 Karaginskiy, Ostrov i. Rus. Fed.
120 B4 Karagiye, Vpadina depr. Kazakh.
129 B4 Karagöl Dağları mts Turkey
211 A5 Karagwe Tanz.
197 H5 Karahalil Turkey
199 F2 Karahallı Turkey
126 D3 Karahasanlı Turkey
199 F3 Karahisar Turkey
134 L5 Karaidel' Rus. Fed.
114 C4 Karaikal Pondicherry India
114 C4 Karaikkudi Tamil Nadu India
121 K3 Kara Irtysh r. Kazakh.
126 D3 Karaisalı Turkey
122 B3 Karaj Iran
Karak Jordan see Al Karak
Kara-Kala Turkm. see Garrygala
Karakalli Turkey see Özalp
120 D4 Karakalpakistan, Respublika aut. rep. Uzbek.
120 D3 Karakalpakiya Uzbek.
Karakalpakskaya Respublika aut. rep. Uzbek. see Karakalpakistan, Respublika
Karakalpakstan aut. rep. Uzbek. see Karakalpakistan, Respublika
120 F4 Karakatinskaya, Vpadina depr. Uzbek.
Karakax Xinjiang China see Moyu
111 C4 Karakax He r. China
111 C5 Karakax Shan mts Xinjiang China
129 C4 Karakaya r. Turkey
129 B4 Karakaya Tepe mt. Turkey
126 E3 Karakeçi Turkey
126 D3 Karakeçili Turkey
93 C1 Karakelong i. Indon.
Karaklis Armenia see Vanadzor
127 F3 Karakoçan Turkey
121 G1 Karakoga Kazakh.
120 C2 Karakol' Kazakh.
121 H4 Kara-Köl Kyrg.
121 I4 Karakol Kyrg.
Karaköprü Turkey see Karaçoban
123 H2 Karakoram mts Asia
116 D2 Karakoram Pass China/Jammu and Kashmir
210 C2 Kara K'orē Eth.
206 B3 Karakoro r. Mali/Maur.
Karaköse Turkey see Ağrı
128 B1 Karaköse Turkey
129 E2 Karakoysu r. Rus. Fed.
129 D4 Karakoyunlu Turkey
Karakubbud Ukr. see Komsomol's'ke
Kara-Kuga Kazakh. see Karakoga
Kara Kul' Kyrg. see Kara-Köl
120 E5 Karakul' Bukharskaya Oblast' Uzbek.
120 E5 Karakul' Bukharskaya Oblast' Uzbek.
Karakul', Ozero l. Tajik. see Qarokŭl
Kara-Kul'dzha Kyrg. see Kara-Kulja
134 K4 Karakulino Rus. Fed.
121 H4 Kara-Kulja Kyrg.
120 E1 Karakul'skoye Rus. Fed.
120 C3 Karakum, Peski des. Kazakh.
Karakum Desert Turkm. see Karakumy, Peski
123 E2 Karakumskiy Kanal canal Turkm.
122 E2 Karakumy, Peski des. Turkm.
127 F2 Karakurt Kars Turkey
199 E2 Karakurt Manisa Turkey
199 G2 Karakuş Dağı ridge Turkey
87 C5 Karalundi W.A. Austr.
93 A3 Karama r. Indon.
199 F2 Karaman Balıkesir Turkey
126 D3 Karaman Karaman Turkey
128 A1 Karaman prov. Turkey
199 F3 Karamanlı Turkey
110 D2 Karamay Xinjiang China
81 D4 Karamea South I. N.Z.
81 D4 Karamea r. South I. N.Z.
81 C4 Karamea Bight b. South I. N.Z.
199 G2 Karamıkkaracaören Turkey
111 D4 Karamiran Xinjiang China
111 D4 Karamiran He r. China
131 Q3 Karamken Rus. Fed.
199 F1 Karamürsel Turkey
138 G3 Karamyshevo Rus. Fed.
123 G2 Karan r. Afgh.
Karan state Myanmar see Kayin
177 I3 Karancsalja Hungary
177 I3 Karancskeszi Hungary
177 I3 Karancsság Hungary
206 A3 Karang Senegal
81 B5 Karangarua South I. N.Z.
95 F5 Karangasem Bali Indon.
95 E5 Karangbolong, Tanjung pt Indon.
93 C2 Karangetang vol. Indon.
208 B4 Karangoua r. Congo
116 D5 Karanja Mahar. India
114 C2 Karanja r. India
117 F5 Karanjia Orissa India
116 C3 Karanpura Rajasthan India
121 I1 Karaoba Kazakh.
199 E3 Karaova Turkey
121 H3 Karaoy Almatinskaya Oblast' Kazakh.
121 H3 Karaoy Almatinskaya Oblast' Kazakh.
197 H4 Karapelit Bulg.
126 D3 Karapınar Turkey
199 F2 Karapürçek Turkey
199 G1 Karapürçek Turkey
212 C5 Karas admin. reg. Namibia
214 A2 Karas mts Namibia
126 C2 Karaşar Turkey
111 C4 Karasay Xinjiang China
212 C6 Karasburg Namibia
Kara Sea Rus. Fed. see Karskoye More
139 L3 Karash Rus. Fed.
121 H2 Karashoky Kazakh.
188 G3 Karašica r. Croatia
177 H6 Karasica r. Hungary/Romania
137 H5 Karasivka r. Ukr.
140 N1 Kárášjohka Norway
140 N1 Kárášjohka r. Norway
Karasjok Norway see Kárášjohka
Karasjokka r. Norway see Kárášjohka
121 G1 Karasor, Ozero l. Kazakh.
Kara Strait Rus. Fed. see Karskiye Vorota, Proliv
120 E2 Karasu Kustanayskaya Oblast' Kazakh.
120 F1 Karasu Kustanayskaya Oblast' Kazakh.
121 H1 Karasu r. Kazakh.
128 C1 Karasu r. Syria/Turkey
Karasu Bitlis Turkey see Hizan
199 G1 Karasu Sakarya Turkey
127 F3 Karasu r. Turkey
Karasubazar Ukr. see Bilohirs'k
105 F2 Karasu-gawa r. Japan
121 I1 Karasuk Rus. Fed.
136 E5 Karasulak r. Ukr.
121 H4 Kara-Suu Kyrg.
136 C2 Karasyn Ukr.
122 E3 Karāt Iran
129 E2 Karata Rus. Fed.
121 K3 Karatan Kazakh.
126 D3 Karataş Turkey
128 C1 Karataş Turkey
199 F2 Karataş Manisa Turkey
121 G4 Karatau Kazakh.
121 F3 Karatau, Khrebet mts Kazakh.
114 C4 Karativu i. Sri Lanka
120 C2 Karatobe Kazakh.
120 D2 Karatogay Kazakh.
121 I3 Karatol r. Kazakh.
120 C3 Karaton Kazakh.
140 L2 Karats Sweden
103 D7 Karatsu Japan
106 A2 Karatünggü Xinjiang China
120 F2 Kara-Turgey r. Kazakh.
121 I2 Karaul Vostochnyy Kazakhstan Kazakh.
120 F5 Karaulbazar Uzbek.
116 D4 Karauli Rajasthan India
Karaulkel'dy Kazakh. see Bayganin
127 F2 Karaurgan Turkey
120 D4 Karauzyak Uzbek.
Karavan Kyrg. see Kerben
196 D5 Karavastasë, Gjiri i b. Albania
139 M3 Karavayevo Rus. Fed.
94 D4 Karawang Jawa Barat Indon.
Karaxahar r. China see Kaidu He
129 C4 Karayazı Turkey
128 C1 Karayılan Turkey
121 G2 Karazhal Kazakh.
120 D4 Karazhar Uzbek.
127 G4 Karbalā' Iraq
127 F4 Karbalā' governorate Iraq
169 D5 Karben Ger.
170 D2 Karbow-Vietlübbe Ger.
121 H2 Karbushevka Kazakh.
168 E1 Karby Ger.
177 J4 Karcag Hungary
177 K3 Karcsa Hungary
175 J3 Karczew Pol.
175 K4 Karczmiska Pol.
197 I4 Kardam Bulg.
199 E3 Kardamaina Notio Aigaio Greece
179 F1 Kardašova Řečice Czech Rep.
Kardeljevo Croatia see Ploče
169 C5 Karden Ger.
Kardhaámaina Notio Aigaio Greece see Kardamaina
Kardhítsa Greece see Karditsa
140 M2 Kardis Sweden
198 B2 Karditsa Greece
138 D2 Kärdla Estonia
177 J5 Kardos Hungary
179 H3 Kardos-ér r. Hungary
177 J5 Kardoskút Hungary
139 I4 Kardymovo Rus. Fed.
129 D2 Kardzhin Rus. Fed.
215 F3 Karee S. Africa
214 C4 Kareeberge mts S. Africa
214 E5 Kareedouw S. Africa
180 D5 Kareha, Jebel mt. Morocco
203 F5 Kareima Sudan
129 C3 K'areli Georgia
116 D5 Kareli Madh. Prad. India
Karelia aut. rep. Rus. Fed. see Kareliya, Respublika
138 F5 Karelichy Belarus
134 F3 Kareliya, Respublika aut. rep. Rus. Fed.
Karel'skaya A.S.S.R. aut. rep. Rus. Fed. see Kareliya, Respublika
134 F2 Karel'skiy Bereg coastal area Rus. Fed.
211 B6 Karema Dodoma Tanz.
211 A6 Karema Rukwa Tanz.
Karen state Myanmar see Kayin
99 K1 Karenga r. Rus. Fed.
116 D4 Karera Madh. Prad. India
140 M1 Karesuando Sweden
122 E5 Kārevāndar Iran
120 C2 Kargala Rus. Fed.
129 E2 Kargalinskaya Rus. Fed.
Kargalinski Rus. Fed. see Kargalinskaya
120 D2 Kargalinskoye Kazakh.
127 F3 Kargapazarı Dağları mts Turkey
Karghalik Xinjiang China see Yecheng
126 D2 Kargı Turkey
116 D2 Kargil Jammu and Kashmir
Kargilik Xinjiang China see Yecheng
128 B1 Kargıpınarı Turkey
134 G3 Kargopol' Rus. Fed.
174 D3 Kargowa Pol.
116 D4 Karhal Uttar Prad. India
143 G1 Karholmsbruk Sweden
207 H4 Kari Nigeria
204 D2 Karia Ba Mohammed Morocco
137 K1 Karian Rus. Fed.
213 F3 Kariba Zimbabwe
209 E9 Kariba, Lake resr Zambia/Zimbabwe
209 F9 Kariba Dam Zambia/Zimbabwe
102 I2 Kariba-yama vol. Japan
212 B4 Karibib Namibia
214 D5 Kariega r. S. Africa
80 D1 Karikari, Cape North I. N.Z.
95 E3 Karimata i. Indon.
95 E3 Karimata, Pulau-pulau is Indon.
95 E3 Karimata, Selat str. Indon.
117 H4 Karimganj Assam India
114 C2 Karimnagar Andhra Prad. India
95 E4 Karimunjawa, Pulau-pulau is Indon.
210 E2 Karin Somalia
141 M3 Karinainen Fin.
199 F3 Karınçalı Dağı mts Turkey
141 K3 Käringsjön Sweden
215 H1 Karino S. Africa
80 E2 Karioi hill North I. N.Z.
141 M3 Karis Fin.
211 A5 Karisimbi, Mont vol. Rwanda
Káristos Greece see Karystos
198 C1 Karitsa Greece
104 C4 Kariya Japan
Karjaa Fin. see Karis
138 D1 Karjalohja Fin.
116 C5 Karjan Gujarat India
114 B2 Karjat Mahar. India
117 F5 Karkai r. Bihar India
114 B3 Karkal Karnataka India
114 B2 Karkamb Mahar. India
214 A4 Karkams S. Africa
121 H2 Karkaralinsk Kazakh.
92 C5 Karkaralong, Kepulauan is Indon.
122 A4 Karkheh, Rūdkhāneh-ye r. Iran
137 G5 Karkinits'ka Zatoka g. Ukr.
141 N3 Karkkila Fin.
141 N3 Kärkölä Fin.
138 E2 Karksi-Nuia Estonia
106 B3 Karlik Shan mt. Xinjiang China
174 D1 Karlino Pol.
127 F3 Karlıova Turkey
137 H3 Karlivka Ukr.
129 C4 Karlıyayla Turkey
123 H2 Karl Marks, Qullai mt. Tajik.
Karl-Marx-Stadt Ger. see Chemnitz
Karlo-Libknekhtovsk Ukr. see Soledar
188 E3 Karlovac Croatia
176 B1 Karlovarský kraj admin. reg. Czech Rep.
176 G1 Karlovice Czech Rep.
Karlovka Ukr. see Karlivka
197 G4 Karlovo Bulg.
176 B1 Karlovy Vary Czech Rep.
172 C3 Karlsbad Ger.
141 K3 Karlsberg Sweden
143 F2 Karlsborg Sweden
170 E2 Karlsburg Ger.
Karlsburg Romania see Alba Iulia
172 C2 Karlsdorf-Neuthard Ger.
173 F3 Karlsfeld Ger.
170 E1 Karlshagen Ger.
143 F3 Karlshamn Sweden
168 E2 Karlshöfen Ger.
173 F3 Karlshuld Ger.
143 F2 Karlskoga Sweden
173 F3 Karlskron Ger.
143 F3 Karlskrona Sweden
172 C2 Karlsruhe Ger.
172 C3 Karlsruhe admin. reg. Baden-Württemberg Ger.
142 E2 Karlstad Sweden
236 D1 Karlstad MN U.S.A.
172 D2 Karlstadt Ger.
169 E5 Karlstein am Main Ger.
179 G2 Karlstein an der Thaya Austria
179 G2 Karlstetten Austria
220 C4 Karluk AK U.S.A.
139 H5 Karma Belarus
207 F3 Karma Niger
114 B2 Karmala Mahar. India
139 J4 Karmanovo Rus. Fed.
140 L2 Karmas Sweden
Karmir Armenia see Chambarak
Karmona Spain see Córdoba
142 A2 Karmøy i. Norway
120 F5 Karnabchul', Step' plain Uzbek.
117 H5 Karnafuli Reservoir Bangl.
116 D3 Karnal Haryana India
116 E3 Karnali r. Nepal
117 G5 Karnaphuli r. Bangl.
116 D3 Karnaprayag Uttar Prad. India
114 B3 Karnataka state India
137 H3 Karnaukhivka Ukr.
237 D6 Karnes City TX U.S.A.
174 D1 Karnice Pol.
175 I3 Karniewo Pol
178 D4 Karnische Alpen mts Austria
197 H4 Karnobat Bulg.
179 E4 Kärnten land Austria
213 F3 Karoi Zimbabwe
191 I3 Karojba Croatia
177 H2 Karolinka Czech Rep.
117 H4 Karong Manipur India
211 B7 Karonga Malawi
87 D6 Karonie W.A. Austr.
214 D5 Karoo National Park S. Africa
82 D3 Karoonda S.A. Austr.
123 G4 Karor Pak.
Káros i. Greece see Keros
199 E1 Karotis Greece
198 A2 Karousades Ionioi Nisoi Greece
170 D2 Karow Mecklenburg-Vorpommern Ger.
171 D3 Karow Sachsen-Anhalt Ger.
174 D5 Karpacz Pol.
128 B2 Karpasia pen. Cyprus
Karpas Peninsula Cyprus see Karpasia
199 E4 Karpathos Notio Aigaio Greece
199 E4 Karpathos i. Greece
199 E3 Karpathou, Steno sea chan. Greece
Karpaty mts Europe see Carpathian Mountains
198 B2 Karpenisi Greece
Karpilovka Homyel'skaya Voblasts' Belarus see Aktsyabrski
134 M4 Karpinsk Rus. Fed.
134 I2 Karpogory Rus. Fed.
199 E3 Karpuzlu Aydın Turkey
199 E1 Karpuzlu Edirne Turkey
136 F2 Karpylivka Chernihivs'ka Oblast' Ukr.
137 G2 Karpylivka Chernihivs'ka Oblast' Ukr.
136 D2 Karpylivka Rivnens'ka Oblast' Ukr.
86 C4 Karratha W.A. Austr.
170 C2 Karrenzin Ger.
215 F4 Karringmelkspruit S. Africa
Karroo plat. S. Africa see Great Karoo
123 E3 Karrukh Afgh.
127 F2 Kars Turkey
129 C3 Kars prov. Turkey
129 C3 Kars r. Turkey
121 F3 Karsakpay Kazakh.
140 N3 Kärsämäki Fin.
138 F3 Kārsava Latvia
171 C4 Karsdorf Ger.
120 F5 Karshi Uzbek.
120 F5 Karshinskaya Step' plain Uzbek.
129 B3 Karşıköy Turkey
174 F2 Karsin Pol.
199 F1 Karşıyaka Turkey
199 E2 Karşıyaka Turkey
117 G4 Karsiyang W. Bengal India
130 G3 Karskiye Vorota, Proliv str. Rus. Fed.
130 I2 Karskoye More sea Rus. Fed.
170 C2 Karstädt Ger.
170 C2 Karstädt Ger.
134 D3 Karstula Fin.
135 I5 Karsun Rus. Fed.
177 I4 Kartal Hungary
199 F1 Kartal Turkey
217 □3a Kartala vol. Njazidja Comoros
120 E1 Kartaly Rus. Fed.
116 C3 Kartarpur Punjab India
138 C4 Kartena Lith.
232 D4 Karthaus PA U.S.A.
129 D2 K'art'lis K'edi hills Georgia
Kartsa Rus. Fed. see Oktyabr'skoye
140 N3 Karttula Fin.
143 H4 Kartuzy Pol.
209 F8 Karubwe Zambia
102 J3 Karumai Japan
85 E3 Karumba Q'ld Austr.
122 B4 Karun, Kūh-e hill Iran
122 B4 Kārūn, Rūd-e r. Iran
114 C4 Karunagapalli Kerala India
140 M2 Karungi Sweden
86 E3 Karunjie W.A. Austr.
142 C3 Karup Denmark
142 C3 Karup r. Denmark
114 C4 Karur Tamil Nadu India
211 A5 Karuzi Burundi
114 C3 Karvetnagar Andhra Prad. India
141 M3 Karvia Fin.
177 H2 Karviná Czech Rep.
136 E2 Karvynivka Ukr.
114 B3 Karwar Karnataka India
116 E4 Karwi Uttar Prad. India
175 J2 Karwica Pol.
170 C2 Karwitz Ger.
198 B2 Karya Ionioi Nisoi Greece
Karyagino Azer. see Füzuli
99 J1 Karymskoye Rus. Fed.
120 C4 Karynzharyk, Peski des. Kazakh.
198 D2 Karystos Greece
199 F3 Kaş Turkey
114 B2 Kasa Mahar. India
Kasaba Turkey see Turgutlu
224 B2 Kasabonika Ont. Can.
104 D2 Kasaga-dake mt. Japan
104 D3 Kasagi-yama mt. Japan
209 C5 Kasai r. Dem. Rep. Congo
104 A4 Kasai Japan
209 D6 Kasai, Plateau du Dem. Rep. Congo
209 D6 Kasai Occidental admin. reg. Dem. Rep. Congo
209 E6 Kasai Oriental admin. reg. Dem. Rep. Congo
209 D7 Kasaji Dem. Rep. Congo
105 G2 Kasama Japan
211 A7 Kasama Zambia
104 C3 Kasamatsu Japan
120 F5 Kasan Uzbek.
212 E3 Kasane Botswana
211 A7 Kasanga Tanz.
209 B6 Kasangulu Dem. Rep. Congo
121 G4 Kasansay Uzbek.
114 B3 Kasaragod Kerala India
138 D2 Kasari r. Estonia
104 C4 Kasatori-yama hill Japan
223 K2 Kasba Lake Can.
204 D2 Kasba Tadla Morocco
103 E8 Kaseda Japan
176 C2 Kasejovice Czech Rep.
209 E8 Kasempa Zambia
171 C5 Kasendorf Ger.
209 F7 Kasenga Dem. Rep. Congo
210 A4 Kasese Uganda
Kasevo Rus. Fed. see Neftekamsk
116 D4 Kasganj Uttar Prad. India
Kasha Xizang China see Gonjo
224 B3 Kashabowie Ont. Can.
122 B3 Kāshān Iran
135 H6 Kashary Rus. Fed.
224 D2 Kashechewan Ont. Can.
Kashgar Xinjiang China see Kashi
110 B4 Kashi Xinjiang China
104 B4 Kashiba Japan
104 B4 Kashihara Japan
105 G3 Kashima Ibaraki Japan
103 E7 Kashima Saga Japan
105 G2 Kashima-nada b. Japan
104 D2 Kashimayaria-dake mt. Japan
139 K3 Kashin Rus. Fed.
139 K3 Kashinka r. Rus. Fed.
116 D3 Kashipur Uttar Prad. India
139 L4 Kashira Rus. Fed.
139 L4 Kashirka r. Rus. Fed.
137 J2 Kashirskoye Rus. Fed.
209 F8 Kashitu Zambia
105 F3 Kashiwa Japan
104 B4 Kashiwara Japan
103 I5 Kashiwazaki Japan
121 F5 Kashkadar'inskaya Oblast' admin. div. Uzbek.
123 F2 Kashkadar'ya r. Uzbek.
Kashkadarya Oblast admin. div. Uzbek. see Kashkadar'inskaya Oblast'
129 C2 Kashkhatau Kabardino-Balkarskaya Respublika Rus. Fed.
137 I4 Kashlahach r. Ukr.
122 D3 Kāshmar Iran
Kashmir terr. Asia see Jammu and Kashmir
116 C2 Kashmir, Vale of val. India
123 G4 Kashmor Pak.
209 E6 Kashyukulu Dem. Rep. Congo
Kasi Uttar Prad. India see Varanasi
117 E4 Kasia Uttar Prad. India
199 G3 Kasımlar Turkey
135 H5 Kasimov Rus. Fed.
179 H5 Kašina Croatia
177 I5 Kaskantyú Hungary
236 F4 Kaskaskia r. IL U.S.A.
223 N3 Kaskattama r. Man. Can.
121 I4 Kaskelen Kazakh.
141 M3 Kaskinen Fin.
Kas Klong i. Cambodia see Kŏng, Kaôh
Kaskö Fin. see Kaskinen
222 G5 Kaslo B.C. Can.
139 J4 Kasnya r. Rus. Fed.
209 E6 Kasongo Dem. Rep. Congo
209 C6 Kasongo-Lunda Dem. Rep. Congo
199 E4 Kasos i. Greece
176 C2 Kašperské Hory Czech Rep.
129 D3 Kaspi Georgia
Kaspīy Mangy Oypaty lowland Kazakh./Rus. Fed. see Prikaspiyskaya Nizmennost'
129 E2 Kaspiysk Rus. Fed.
Kaspiyskiy Rus. Fed. see Lagan'
Kaspiyskoye More sea Asia/Europe see Caspian Sea
139 H4 Kasplya Rus. Fed.
139 H4 Kasplya r. Rus. Fed.
116 C5 Kasrawad Madh. Prad. India
Kasrik Turkey see Gürpınar
129 E3 Kasristsqali Georgia
Kassa Slovakia see Košice
138 D2 Kassaare laht b. Estonia
203 H6 Kassala Sudan
203 G6 Kassala state Sudan
198 C1 Kassandra pen. Greece
198 C1 Kassandras, Kolpos b. Greece
198 C1 Kassandreia Greece
168 F1 Kasseedorf Ger.
169 E4 Kassel Ger.
169 E4 Kassel admin. reg. Hessen Ger.
205 H2 Kasserine Tunisia
226 A3 Kasson MN U.S.A.
126 D2 Kastamonu Turkey
169 C5 Kastellaun Ger.
198 C4 Kastelli Kriti Greece
199 D4 Kastelli Kriti Greece
Kastéllion Kriti Greece see Kastelli
Kastellorizon i. Greece see Megisti
165 D3 Kasterlee Belgium
173 F2 Kastl Bayern Ger.
173 G3 Kastl Bayern Ger.
168 F2 Kastorf Ger.
198 B1 Kastoria Greece
198 B1 Kastorias, Limni l. Greece
135 G6 Kastornoye Rus. Fed.
139 I5 Kastsyukovichy Belarus
139 H5 Kastsyukowka Belarus
104 C3 Kasugai Japan
105 F3 Kasukabe Japan
215 F5 Kasuka Road S. Africa
211 A6 Kasulu Tanz.
105 G2 Kasumiga-ura l. Japan
129 F3 Kasumkent Rus. Fed.
211 B8 Kasungu Malawi
123 H4 Kasur Pak.
177 J5 Kaszaper Hungary
207 H3 Katagum Nigeria
233 □I2 Katahdin, Mount ME U.S.A.
116 D2 Kataklik Jammu and Kashmir
210 B4 Katakwi Uganda
209 D6 Katanda Dem. Rep. Congo
209 E7 Katanga admin. reg. Dem. Rep. Congo
116 D5 Katangi Madh. Prad. India
116 D5 Katangi Madh. Prad. India
100 G2 Katangli Sakhalin Rus. Fed.
87 C7 Katanning W.A. Austr.
104 B4 Katano Japan
122 B2 Kata Pusht Iran
105 F2 Katashina-gawa r. Japan
198 B3 Katastari Ionioi Nisoi Greece
211 A6 Katavi National Park Tanz.
115 G5 Katchall i. Andaman & Nicobar Is India
207 F4 Katchamba Togo
209 C8 Katchiungo Angola
209 E6 Katea Dem. Rep. Congo
198 C1 Katerini Greece
136 F3 Katerynopil' Ukr.
147 E2 Katesbridge Northern Ireland U.K.
211 B6 Katesh Tanz.
220 E4 Kate's Needle mt. Alaska/B.C. Can./U.S.A.
211 B8 Katete Zambia
129 E3 Katex Azer.
117 E5 Katghora Madh. Prad. India
96 B1 Katha Myanmar
203 G2 Katherîna, Gebel mt. Egypt
84 C2 Katherine N.T. Austr.
84 B2 Katherine r. N.T. Austr.
116 C5 Kathi Mahar. India
116 B5 Kathiawar pen. Gujarat India
128 A4 Kathîb el Henu hill Egypt
215 G2 Kathlehong S. Africa
171 F4 Kathlow Ger.
117 F4 Kathmandu Nepal
214 D2 Kathu S. Africa
116 C2 Kathua Jammu and Kashmir
206 C3 Kati Mali
95 F2 Katibas r. Sarawak Malaysia
177 K4 Kati-ér r. Hungary
117 F4 Katihar Bihar India
80 E2 Katikati North I. N.Z.
215 F5 Kati-Kati S. Africa
212 E3 Katima Mulilo Namibia
206 D4 Katiola Côte d'Ivoire
Kā Tiritiri o te Moana mts South I. N.Z. see Southern Alps
136 E5 Katlabukh, Ozero l. Ukr.
169 F4 Katlenburg-Lindau Ger.
177 G3 Kátlovce Slovakia
111 D4 Katma Xinjiang China
Katmandu Nepal see Kathmandu
198 B2 Kato Achaïa Greece
198 B2 Katochi Greece
198 C3 Kato Doliana Peloponnisos Greece
198 B3 Kato Figaleia Greece
198 C3 Kato Glykovrysi Greece
116 D5 Katol Mahar. India
235 E1 Katonah NY U.S.A.
209 F8 Katondwe Zambia
198 C1 Kato Nevrokopi Greece
210 A4 Katonga r. Uganda
121 K2 Katon-Karagay Kazakh.
Katonqaraghay Kazakh. see Katon-Karagay
83 G3 Katoomba N.S.W. Austr.
93 B3 Katoposa, Gunung mt. Indon.
116 C5 Katosan Gujarat India
198 C2 Kato Tithorea Greece
Kåtotjåkka mt. Sweden see Godučohkka
176 C2 Katovice Czech Rep.
175 H5 Katowice Pol.
117 G5 Katoya W. Bengal India
116 C5 Katpur Gujarat India
199 F3 Katrancık Dağı mts Turkey
146 D5 Katrine, Loch l. Scotland U.K.
143 G2 Katrineholm Sweden
179 F2 Katsdorf Austria
198 B2 Katsikas Greece
207 G3 Katsina Nigeria
207 G4 Katsina state Nigeria
207 H5 Katsina-Ala Nigeria
105 F3 Katsura-gawa r. Japan
104 B4 Katsuragi-san hill Japan
105 G3 Katsuura Japan
104 C2 Katsuyama Japan
121 F5 Kattakurgan Uzbek.
86 E4 Kattamudda Well W.A. Austr.
Kattaqŭrghon Uzbek. see Kattakurgan
123 F3 Kattasang Hills Afgh.
142 D3 Kattegat str. Denmark/Sweden
140 L2 Kattisavan Sweden
Kattowitz Pol. see Katowice
114 C4 Kattuputtur Tamil Nadu India
211 B7 Katumbi Malawi
110 D1 Katun' r. Rus. Fed.
134 I4 Katunino Rus. Fed.
110 D1 Katunskiy Khrebet mts Rus. Fed.
Katwa W. Bengal India see Katoya
164 D2 Katwijk aan Zee Neth.
175 J2 Kąty Pol.
Katyk Ukr. see Shakhtars'k
177 I5 Katymár Hungary
174 E4 Kąty Wrocławskie Pol.
173 G2 Katzbach r. Ger.
179 H3 Katzelsdorf Austria
172 D2 Katzenbuckel hill Ger.
169 C5 Katzenelnbogen Ger.
171 C5 Katzhütte Ger.
172 B2 Katzweiler Ger.
240 □B7 Kauai i. HI U.S.A.
240 □B8 Kauai Channel HI U.S.A.
169 C5 Kaub Ger.
173 E4 Kaufbeuren Ger.
173 E3 Kaufering Ger.
237 D5 Kaufman TX U.S.A.
169 E4 Kaufungen Ger.
141 M3 Kauhajoki Fin.
140 M3 Kauhava Fin.
226 C3 Kaukauna WI U.S.A.
96 B1 Kaukkwè Hills Myanmar
240 □B8 Kaulakahi Channel HI U.S.A.
165 E3 Kaulille Belgium
171 C5 Kaulsdorf Ger.
80 E4 Kaumai North I. N.Z.
225 I1 Kaumajet Mountains Nfld. Can.
240 □B8 Kaumakani HI U.S.A.
240 □C8 Kaumalapau HI U.S.A.
240 □C8 Kaunakakai HI U.S.A.
138 D4 Kaunas Lith.
234 D1 Kauneonga Lake NY U.S.A.
117 G4 Kaunia Bangl.
140 M2 Kaunisvaara Sweden
138 E4 Kauno marios l. Lith.
81 C5 Kaupiri South I. N.Z.
240 □C8 Kaupo HI U.S.A.
207 G3 Kaura-Namoda Nigeria
Kaushany Moldova see Căușeni
140 M3 Kaustinen Fin.
165 F5 Kautenbach Lux.
140 M1 Kautokeino Norway
179 G2 Kautzen Austria
197 F5 Kavadarci Macedonia
196 D5 Kavajë Albania
199 E1 Kavak Çanakkale Turkey
126 E2 Kavak Samsun Turkey
199 E2 Kavak Dağı hill Turkey
199 F2 Kavaklıdere Turkey
199 F3 Kavaklıdere Turkey
198 D1 Kavala Greece
100 E3 Kavalerovo Rus. Fed.
114 D3 Kavali Andhra Prad. India
114 C4 Kavalpatnam Tamil Nadu India
122 C4 Kavār Iran
114 B4 Kavaratti Lakshadweep India
197 I4 Kavarna Bulg.
138 E4 Kavarskas Lith.
170 D2 Kavelstorf Ger.
206 B4 Kavendou, Mont mt. Guinea
114 C4 Kaveri r. India
114 C3 Kaveripatnam Tamil Nadu India
116 C5 Kavi Gujarat India
91 L7 Kavieng New Ireland P.N.G.
122 C3 Kavīr, Dasht-e des. Iran
122 C4 Kavīr-e Abarkuh des. Iran
122 D3 Kavīr-i-Namak salt flat Iran
129 C1 Kavkazskiy Rus. Fed.
175 L6 Kavs'ke Ukr.
251 H3 Kaw Fr. Guiana
104 C1 Kawachi-dake hill Japan
104 B4 Kawachi-nagano Japan
105 F3 Kawagoe Japan
105 F3 Kawaguchi Japan
240 □D8 Kawaihae HI U.S.A.
240 □B7 Kawaikini, Mount HI U.S.A.
240 □ Kawailoa Beach HI U.S.A.
80 E1 Kawakawa North I. N.Z.
209 F7 Kawambwa Zambia
104 B3 Kawanishi Japan
105 F2 Kawarazawa-gawa r. Japan
116 E5 Kawardha Madh. Prad. India
105 F3 Kawasaki Japan
225 H2 Kawawachikamach Que. Can.
80 F3 Kaweka mt. North I. N.Z.
80 F3 Kaweka Range mts North I. N.Z.
226 B1 Kawene Ont. Can.
80 F3 Kawerau North I. N.Z.
80 E3 Kawhia North I. N.Z.
80 E3 Kawhia Harbour North I. N.Z.
241 I3 Kawich Peak NV U.S.A.
241 I3 Kawich Range mts NV U.S.A.
96 B3 Kawkareik Myanmar
96 A2 Kawlin Myanmar
128 A4 Kawm Dafanah tourist site Egypt
Kawthoolei state Myanmar see Kayin
Kawthule state Myanmar see Kayin
Kaxgar Xinjiang China see Kashi
110 B4 Kaxgar He r. China
110 C3 Kax He r. China
111 C4 Kaxtax Shan mts China
206 E3 Kaya Burkina
129 C3 Kayaaltı Turkey
199 E2 Kayacı Dağı hill Turkey
126 E3 Kayadibi Turkey
105 E3 Kayaga-take mt. Japan
96 B3 Kayah state Myanmar
129 E2 Kayakent Rus. Fed.
211 A7 Kayambi Zambia
95 E3 Kayan r. Indon.
95 G2 Kayan r. Indon.
96 B3 Kayan Myanmar
211 A5 Kayanaza Burundi
92 □ Kayangel atoll Palau
114 C4 Kayankulam Kerala India
114 C2 Kayar Mahar. India
93 C2 Kayasa Halmahera Indon.
129 D1 Kayasula Rus. Fed.
238 F3 Kaycee WY U.S.A.
Kaydanovo Belarus see Dzyarzhynsk
241 L3 Kayenta AZ U.S.A.
209 B6 Kayes Congo
206 C3 Kayes Mali
206 C3 Kayes admin. reg. Mali
120 F2 Kayga Kazakh.
Kaygy Kazakh. see Kayga
96 B3 Kayin state Myanmar
165 F5 Kayl Lux.
199 F2 Kaymakçı İzmir Turkey
121 H1 Kaymanachikha Kazakh.
199 G2 Kaymaz Turkey
171 D5 Kayna Ger.
121 I2 Kaynar Kazakh.
126 E3 Kaynar Turkey
199 G1 Kaynarca Turkey
197 H5 Kaynarlı r. Turkey
199 G1 Kaynaşlı Turkey
Kayrakkum Tajik. see Qayroqqum
Kayrakkumskoye Vodokhranilishche resr Tajik. see Obanbori Qayroqqum
121 H2 Kayrakty Kazakh.
126 D3 Kayseri Turkey
157 H4 Kaysersberg France
94 D3 Kayuagung Sumatera Indon.
130 J3 Kayyerkan Rus. Fed.
121 H4 Kayyngdy Kyrg.
139 L5 Kazachka Rus. Fed.
131 O2 Kazach'ye Rus. Fed.
Kazakh Azer. see Qazax
Kazakhskaya S.S.R. country Asia see Kazakhstan
121 G2 Kazakhskiy Melkosopochnik plain Kazakh.
120 C4 Kazakhskiy Zaliv b. Kazakh.
120 J2 Kazakhstan country Asia
Kazakhstan Kazakh. see Aksay
139 L5 Kazaki Rus. Fed.
Kazakstan country Asia see Kazakhstan
120 E3 Kazalinsk Kazakh.
223 M2 Kazan r. Nunavut Can.
134 J5 Kazan' Rus. Fed.
129 C4 Kazan Turkey
126 D3 Kazancı Turkey
Kazandzhik Turkm. see Gazandzhyk
198 B2 Kazanje, Mal mt. Albania
134 J5 Kazanka r. Rus. Fed.
137 G4 Kazanka Ukr.
128 B1 Kazanlı Turkey
197 G4 Kazanlŭk Bulg.
139 L5 Kazanovka Rus. Fed.
175 J4 Kazanów Pol.
103 □3 Kazan-rettō is N. Pacific Ocean
135 H6 Kazanskaya Rus. Fed.
Kazatin Ukr. see Kozyatyn
120 D2 Kazatskiy Kazakh.
210 C1 Kaza Wenz r. Eth.
Kazbegi Georgia see Qazbegi
129 D2 Kazbek mt. Georgia/Rus. Fed.
199 E2 Kaz Dağı mts Turkey
122 B4 Kāzerūn Iran
121 G1 Kazgorodok Kazakh.
134 J3 Kazhim Rus. Fed.
123 E5 Kazhmak r. Pak.
Kazi Magomed Azer. see Qazımämmäd
175 I5 Kazimierza Wielka Pol.
174 G3 Kazimierz Biskupi Pol.
175 J4 Kazimierz Dolne Pol.
177 J3 Kazincbarcika Hungary
137 I2 Kazinka Belgorodskaya Oblast' Rus. Fed.
139 L5 Kazinka Lipetskaya Oblast' Rus. Fed.
139 L5 Kazinka Ryazanskaya Oblast' Rus. Fed.
137 K2 Kazinka Voronezhskaya Oblast' Rus. Fed.
138 E5 Kazlowshchyna Belarus
138 D4 Kazlų Rūda Lith.
174 E3 Kaźmierz Pol.
176 C2 Kaznějov Czech Rep.
105 F2 Kazo Japan
120 B2 Kaztalovka Kazakh.
209 D6 Kazumba Dem. Rep. Congo
209 E9 Kazungula Zambia
102 J3 Kazuno Japan
122 D2 Kazy Turkm.
121 G4 Kazygurt Yuzhnyy Kazakhstan Kazakh.
130 H3 Kazym r. Rus. Fed.
196 D4 Kçirë Albania
174 F3 Kcynia Pol.
176 C2 Kdyně Czech Rep.
198 D3 Kea i. Greece
240 □D9 Keaau HI U.S.A.
147 E2 Keady Northern Ireland U.K.
146 B5 Keal, Loch na b. Scotland U.K.
240 □C8 Kealaikahiki Channel HI U.S.A.
240 □D9 Kealakekua HI U.S.A.
240 □D9 Kealia HI U.S.A.
147 B5 Kealkill Rep. of Ireland
241 L4 Keams Canyon AZ U.S.A.
Kéamu i. Vanuatu see Anatom
235 D2 Keansburg NJ U.S.A.
147 F2 Kearney Northern Ireland U.K.
236 D3 Kearney NE U.S.A.
232 E5 Kearneysville WV U.S.A.
241 L5 Kearny AZ U.S.A.
235 D2 Kearny NJ U.S.A.
215 H3 Keate's Drift S. Africa
240 □D9 Keauhou HI U.S.A.
240 □C8 Keawakapu HI U.S.A.
126 E3 Keban Turkey
126 E3 Keban Barajı resr Turkey
207 F3 Kebbi state Nigeria
206 A3 Kébémèr Senegal
207 I4 Kébi r. Cameroon
205 H2 Kebili Tunisia
128 B2 Kebīr, Nahr al r. Lebanon/Syria
140 L2 Kebnekaise mt. Sweden
146 B3 Kebock Head hd Scotland U.K.
210 E3 K'ebrī Dehar Eth.
95 E4 Kebumen Jawa Tengah Indon.
177 I5 Kecel Hungary
210 C3 K'ech'a Terara mt. Eth.
222 E3 Kechika r. B.C. Can.
199 G3 Keçiborlu Turkey
177 I5 Kecskemét Hungary
94 C1 Kedah state Malaysia
138 D4 Kėdainiai Lith.
Kedairu Passage Fiji see Kadavu Passage
111 B6 Kedarnath Peak Uttar Prad. India
225 H4 Kedgwick N.B. Can.
109 E2 Kedian Hubei China
151 H2 Kedington Suffolk, England U.K.
95 F4 Kediri Jawa Timur Indon.
100 C3 Kedong Heilong. China
206 B3 Kédougou Senegal
134 K2 Kedva r. Rus. Fed.
174 G5 Kędzierzyn-Koźle Pol.
149 I4 Keelby Lincolnshire, England U.K.
222 E1 Keele r. Y.T. Can.
149 G4 Keele Staffordshire, England U.K.
222 D2 Keele Peak Y.T. Can.
240 I3 Keeler CA U.S.A.
Keeling Islands terr. Indian Ocean see Cocos Islands
Keelung Taiwan see Chilung
146 F5 Keen, Mount hill Scotland U.K.
147 D3 Keenagh Rep. of Ireland
240 H4 Keene CA U.S.A.
233 G3 Keene NH U.S.A.
232 C4 Keene OH U.S.A.
84 B2 Keep r. N.T. Austr.
165 D4 Keerbergen Belgium
215 F3 Keeromsberg mt. Free State S. Africa
214 B5 Keeromsberg mt. W. Cape S. Africa
85 E2 Keer-weer, Cape Qld Austr.
212 C5 Keetmanshoop Namibia
223 M5 Keewatin Ont. Can.
226 A2 Keewatin MN U.S.A.
Kefallinía i. Greece see Kefallonia
198 B2 Kefallonia i. Greece
199 E3 Kefalos Notio Aigaio Greece
Kefe Ukr. see Feodosiya
169 E5 Kefenrod Ger.
179 F2 Kefermarkt Austria
207 G4 Keffi Nigeria
199 G1 Kefken Kocaeli Turkey
140 □B2 Keflavík Iceland
114 D5 Kegalla Sri Lanka
Kegayli Uzbek. see Kegeyli
121 I4 Kegen Kazakh.
120 D4 Kegeyli Uzbek.
222 G3 Keg River Alta Can.
135 I7 Kegul'ta Rus. Fed.
138 E3 Kegums Latvia
151 F2 Kegworth Leicestershire, England U.K.
172 B3 Kehl Ger.
165 F5 Kehlen Lux.
138 E2 Kehra Estonia
169 C5 Kehrig Ger.
138 E2 Kehtna Estonia
137 H3 Kehychivka Ukr.
241 K3 Keibab Plateau AZ U.S.A.
149 H4 Keighley West Yorkshire, England U.K.
138 E2 Keila Estonia
138 E2 Keila r. Estonia
214 C3 Keimoes S. Africa
215 G5 Kei Mouth S. Africa
215 F5 Kei Road S. Africa
215 F5 Keiskama r. S. Africa
215 F5 Keiskammahoek S. Africa
146 E3 Keiss Highland, Scotland U.K.
207 G3 Keïta Niger
208 C2 Kéita, Bahr r. Chad
140 N3 Keitele Fin.
140 N3 Keitele l. Fin.
82 E4 Keith S.A. Austr.
146 F4 Keith Moray, Scotland U.K.
84 B1 Keith, Cape N.T. Austr.
222 F1 Keith Arm b. N.W.T. Can.
222 F4 Keithley Creek B.C. Can.
104 D2 Kekachi-yama mt. Japan
240 □B8 Kekaha HI U.S.A.
138 E3 Kekava Latvia
177 L3 Kékcse Hungary
81 D5 Kekerengu South I. N.Z.
177 J4 Kékes mt. Hungary
116 C4 Kekri Rajasthan India
Kёk-Tash Kyrg. see Kök-Tash
210 E3 K'elafo Eth.
114 B5 Kelai atoll Maldives
107 F4 Kelan Shanxi China
94 C2 Kelang Malaysia
94 C1 Kelantan r. Malaysia
94 C1 Kelantan state Malaysia
93 A4 Kelara r. Indon.
122 B2 Kelārdasht Iran
169 B5 Kelberg Ger.
171 C4 Kelbra (Kyffhäuser) Ger.
177 G2 Kelč Czech Rep.
198 B1 Këlcyrë Albania
129 C3 Kel Dağı mt. Turkey
177 I5 Kelebia Hungary
199 F3 Kelekçi Turkey
199 F2 Keles Turkey
121 G4 Keles Uzbek.
173 F3 Kelheim Ger.
205 H1 Kelibia Tunisia
123 F2 Kelif Turkm.
123 E2 Kelifskiy Uzboy marsh Turkm.
169 D5 Kelkheim (Taunus) Ger.
126 E2 Kelkit Turkey
126 E2 Kelkit r. Turkey
172 A2 Kell Ger.
81 A6 Kellard, Mount South I. N.Z.
146 E4 Kellas Moray, Scotland U.K.
138 F2 Kellavere hill Estonia
208 B5 Kéllé Congo
170 C1 Kellenhusen Ger.
87 C6 Kellerberrin W.A. Austr.
121 G1 Kellerovka Kazakh.
223 K5 Kelliher Sask. Can.
168 E2 Kellinghusen Ger.
173 E3 Kellmünz an der Iller Ger.
238 C2 Kellogg ID U.S.A.
147 A5 Kells Kerry Rep. of Ireland
147 D4 Kells Kilkenny Rep. of Ireland
147 E3 Kells Meath Rep. of Ireland
147 E2 Kells Northern Ireland U.K.
147 E2 Kells r. Northern Ireland U.K.
147 C3 Kellysgrove Rep. of Ireland
138 D4 Kelmė Lith.
136 D3 Kel'mentsi Ukr.
165 F4 Kelmis Belgium
208 B2 Kelo Chad
78 □6 Keloma i. Solomon Is
222 G5 Kelowna B.C. Can.
149 G4 Kelsall Cheshire, England U.K.
226 A2 Kelsey MN U.S.A.
240 F2 Kelseyville CA U.S.A.
81 B6 Kelso South I. N.Z.

146 F6 **Kelso** *Scottish Borders, Scotland* U.K.
241 J4 **Kelso** *CA* U.S.A.
238 B2 **Kelso** *WA* U.S.A.
169 D5 **Kelsterbach** Ger.
180 D5 **Kelti, Jebel** *mt.* Morocco
146 E5 **Kelty** *Fife, Scotland* U.K.
94 C2 **Keluang** Malaysia
151 H3 **Kelvedon** *Essex, England* U.K.
151 H3 **Kelvedon Hatch** *Essex, England* U.K.
223 K4 **Kelvington** *Sask.* Can.
123 H5 **Kelwara** *Rajasthan* India
134 F2 **Kem'** Rus. Fed.
134 F2 **Kem'** *r.* Rus. Fed.
139 K1 **Kema** *r.* Rus. Fed.
Ke Macina Mali *see* **Massina**
126 E3 **Kemah** Turkey
197 H5 **Kemal** Turkey
126 E3 **Kemaliye** Turkey
129 B3 **Kemalpaşa** Turkey
199 E2 **Kemalpaşa** Turkey
78 □6 **Kemalu** *i.* Solomon Is
222 E4 **Kemano** *B.C.* Can.
178 C3 **Kematen in Tirol** Austria
208 D3 **Kembé** C.A.R.
171 D4 **Kemberg** Ger.
234 C3 **Kemblesville** *PA* U.S.A.
210 C2 **Kembolcha** Eth.
157 H5 **Kembs** France
176 G4 **Kemeneshát** *hills* Hungary
176 G4 **Kemenesmagasi** Hungary
176 G4 **Kemenessömjén** Hungary
199 F3 **Kemer** *Antalya* Turkey
199 G3 **Kemer** *Antalya* Turkey
199 G3 **Kemer** *Burdur* Turkey
199 F3 **Kemer** *Muğla* Turkey
130 J4 **Kemerovo** Rus. Fed.
Kemerovo Oblast *admin. div.* Rus. Fed. *see* Kemerovskaya Oblast'
98 E1 **Kemerovskaya Oblast'** *admin. div.* Rus. Fed.
177 H6 **Kémes** Hungary
179 H3 **Kemeten** Austria
140 N2 **Kemi** Fin.
140 N2 **Kemijärvi** Fin.
140 N2 **Kemijoki** *r.* Fin.
121 H4 **Kemin** Kyrg.
140 N2 **Keminmaa** Fin.
Kemiö Fin. *see* **Kimito**
135 I5 **Kemlya** Rus. Fed.
165 B4 **Kemmel** Belgium
165 B4 **Kemmelberg** *hill* Belgium
238 E3 **Kemmerer** *WY* U.S.A.
173 E2 **Kemmern** Ger.
195 □ **Kemmuna** *i.* Malta
195 □ **Kemmunett** *i.* Malta
173 F2 **Kemnath** Ger.
146 F4 **Kemnay** *Aberdeenshire, Scotland* U.K.
170 E1 **Kemnitz** *Mecklenburg-Vorpommern* Ger.
171 F4 **Kemnitz** *Sachsen* Ger.
208 C3 **Kémo** *pref.* C.A.R.
134 M2 **Kempazh** *r.* Rus. Fed.
140 N2 **Kempele** Fin.
169 B4 **Kempen** Ger.
169 C5 **Kempenich** Ger.
263 D2 **Kemp Land** *reg.* Antarctica
262 U2 **Kemp Peninsula** Antarctica
246 C1 **Kemp's Bay** *Andros* Bahamas
83 H2 **Kempsey** *N.S.W.* Austr.
150 E2 **Kempsey** *Worcestershire, England* U.K.
151 G2 **Kempston** *Bedfordshire, England* U.K.
173 E4 **Kempten (Allgäu)** Ger.
83 F5 **Kempton** *Tas.* Austr.
215 G2 **Kempton Park** S. Africa
227 J3 **Kemptville** *Ont.* Can.
151 H3 **Kemsing** *Kent, England* U.K.
116 E4 **Ken** *r.* India
146 D7 **Ken, Loch** *l. Scotland* U.K.
227 H2 **Kenabeek** *Ont.* Can.
220 C3 **Kenai** *AK* U.S.A.
220 C4 **Kenai Mountains** *AK* U.S.A.
225 J2 **Kenamu** *r. Nfld.* Can.
210 B3 **Kenamuke Swamp** Sudan
231 E5 **Kenansville** *NC* U.S.A.
220 H4 **Kenaston** *Sask.* Can.
95 F2 **Kenawang, Bukit** *mt. Sarawak* Malaysia
232 D6 **Kenbridge** *VA* U.S.A.
95 E4 **Kendal** *Jawa Tengah* Indon.
215 G2 **Kendal** S. Africa
149 G3 **Kendal** *Cumbria, England* U.K.
83 H2 **Kendall** *N.S.W.* Austr.
85 E2 **Kendall** *r. Qld* Austr.
231 D7 **Kendall** *FL* U.S.A.
81 D4 **Kendall, Mount** *South I.* N.Z.
230 C3 **Kendallville** *IN* U.S.A.
93 B3 **Kendari** *Sulawesi Tenggara* Indon.
95 E3 **Kendawangan** *Kalimantan Barat* Indon.
95 E3 **Kendawangan** *r.* Indon.
177 J4 **Kenderes** Hungary
Kendhrikí Makedhonía *admin. reg.* Greece *see* Kentriki Makedonia
177 K3 **Kendice** Slovakia
117 F5 **Kendraparha** *Orissa* India
214 E5 **Kendrew** S. Africa
238 C2 **Kendrick** *ID* U.S.A.
241 L4 **Kendrick Peak** *AZ* U.S.A.
117 F5 **Kendujhargarh** *Orissa* India
121 H4 **Kendyktas** *mts* Kazakh.
120 C4 **Kendyrli-Kayasanskoye, Plato** *plat.* Kazakh.
83 G2 **Kenebri** *N.S.W.* Austr.
237 D6 **Kenedy** *TX* U.S.A.
215 G4 **Keneka** *r.* S. Africa
206 C5 **Kenema** Sierra Leone
95 E2 **Kenepai, Gunung** *mt.* Indon.
122 D1 **Keneurgench** Turkm.
177 K3 **Kenézlő** Hungary
150 D3 **Kenfig** *Bridgend, Wales* U.K.
209 C6 **Kenge** Dem. Rep. Congo
209 E7 **Kengere** Dem. Rep. Congo
140 M2 **Kengis** Sweden
96 B2 **Kengtung** Myanmar
177 J4 **Kengyet** Hungary
214 C3 **Kenhardt** S. Africa
234 C2 **Kenhorst** *PA* U.S.A.
206 C3 **Kéniéba** Mali
151 F2 **Kenilworth** *Warwickshire, England* U.K.
234 C2 **Kenilworth** *PA* U.S.A.
204 D2 **Kénitra** Morocco
107 H4 **Kenli** *Shandong* China
147 B5 **Kenmare** Rep. of Ireland
236 C1 **Kenmare** *ND* U.S.A.
147 A5 **Kenmare River** *inlet* Rep. of Ireland
146 E5 **Kenmore** *Perth and Kinross, Scotland* U.K.
232 D3 **Kenmore** *NY* U.S.A.
172 A2 **Kenn** Ger.
237 C5 **Kenna** *NM* U.S.A.
146 C6 **Kennacraig** *Argyll and Bute, Scotland* U.K.
236 D3 **Kennebec** *SD* U.S.A.
233 □I2 **Kennebec** *r. ME* U.S.A.
233 □H3 **Kennebunk** *ME* U.S.A.
233 □H3 **Kennebunkport** *ME* U.S.A.
85 F3 **Kennedy** *Qld* Austr.
85 F2 **Kennedy** *r. Qld* Austr.
Kennedy, Cape *FL* U.S.A. *see* Canaveral, Cape
87 B5 **Kennedy Range** *hills W.A.* Austr.
234 C3 **Kennedyville** *MD* U.S.A.
237 F6 **Kenner** *LA* U.S.A.
151 G3 **Kennet** *r. England* U.K.
146 F4 **Kennethmont** *Aberdeenshire, Scotland* U.K.
87 C4 **Kenneth Range** *hills W.A.* Austr.
237 F4 **Kennett** *MO* U.S.A.
234 C3 **Kennett Square** *PA* U.S.A.
238 C2 **Kennewick** *WA* U.S.A.
151 F3 **Kennington** *Oxfordshire, England* U.K.
146 E5 **Kennoway** *Fife, Scotland* U.K.
224 C3 **Kenogami** *r. Ont.* Can.
227 G1 **Kenogami Lake** *Ont.* Can.
222 C2 **Keno Hill** *Y.T.* Can.
223 M5 **Kenora** *Ont.* Can.
226 D4 **Kenosha** *WI* U.S.A.
232 B5 **Kenova** *WV* U.S.A.
146 B4 **Kensaleyre** *Highland, Scotland* U.K.
225 I4 **Kensington** *P.E.I.* Can.
235 F1 **Kensington** *CT* U.S.A.
151 G3 **Kensworth** *Bedfordshire, England* U.K.
151 H3 **Kent** *admin. div. England* U.K.
149 G3 **Kent** *r. England* U.K.
235 E1 **Kent** *CT* U.S.A.
232 C4 **Kent** *OH* U.S.A.
239 F6 **Kent** *TX* U.S.A.
232 C6 **Kent** *VA* U.S.A.
238 B2 **Kent** *WA* U.S.A.
234 C3 **Kent Acres** *DE* U.S.A.
215 G5 **Kentani** S. Africa
121 G4 **Kentau** Kazakh.
234 C3 **Kent County** *county DE* U.S.A.
234 B3 **Kent County** *county MD* U.S.A.
83 F4 **Kent Group** *is Tas.* Austr.
230 C3 **Kentland** *IN* U.S.A.
150 D4 **Kenton** *Devon, England* U.K.
234 C3 **Kenton** *DE* U.S.A.
226 C2 **Kenton** *MI* U.S.A.
232 B4 **Kenton** *OH* U.S.A.
215 F5 **Kenton-on-Sea** S. Africa
220 H3 **Kent Peninsula** *Nunavut* Can.
198 C1 **Kentriki Makedonia** *admin. reg.* Greece
232 A5 **Kentucky** *r. KY* U.S.A.
232 A6 **Kentucky** *state* U.S.A.
237 F6 **Kentwood** *LA* U.S.A.
226 E4 **Kentwood** *MI* U.S.A.
210 C4 **Kenya** *country* Africa
Kenya, Mount Kenya *see* Kirinyaga
176 G4 **Kenyeri** Hungary
94 C1 **Kenyir, Tasik** *resr* Malaysia
226 A3 **Kenyon** *MN* U.S.A.
129 C2 **Kenzhe** Rus. Fed.
172 B3 **Kenzingen** Ger.
240 □C8 **Keokea** *HI* U.S.A.
226 B5 **Keokuk** *IA* U.S.A.
236 F3 **Keosauqua** *IA* U.S.A.
231 D5 **Keowee, Lake** *resr SC* U.S.A.
94 C3 **Kepahiang** *Sumatera* Indon.
143 G4 **Kępice** Pol.
134 H2 **Kepina** *r.* Rus. Fed.
81 A6 **Kepler Mountains** *South I.* N.Z.
174 F4 **Kępno** Pol.
85 G4 **Keppel Bay** *Qld* Austr.
94 □ **Keppel Harbour** *sea chan.* Sing.
Keppel Island Tonga *see* **Tafahi**
199 F2 **Kepsut** Turkey
114 B4 **Kerala** *state* India
102 □1 **Kerama-rettō** *is* Japan
83 E3 **Kerang** *Vic.* Austr.
198 C3 **Keratea** Greece
86 C3 **Keraudren, Cape** *W.A.* Austr.
141 N3 **Kerava** Fin.
Kerbela Iraq *see* **Karbalā'**
121 G4 **Kerben** Kyrg.
100 F1 **Kerbi** *r.* Rus. Fed.
195 □ **Kercem** *Gozo* Malta
137 I5 **Kerch** Ukr.
134 K3 **Kerchem'ya** Rus. Fed.
134 L4 **Kerchevskiy** Rus. Fed.
177 J4 **Kerecsend** Hungary
177 I5 **Kerekegyháza** Hungary
91 K8 **Kerema** P.N.G.
222 G5 **Keremeos** *B.C.* Can.
203 H6 **Keren** Eritrea
122 A3 **Kerend** Iran
80 E2 **Kerepehi** *North I.* N.Z.
177 I4 **Kerepestarcsa** Hungary
139 H2 **Kerest'** *r.* Rus. Fed.
136 B3 **Kerets'ky** Ukr.
206 A3 **Kerewan** Gambia
122 D2 **Kergeli** Turkm.
265 I8 **Kerguélen, Îles** *is* Indian Ocean
Kerguelen Islands Indian Ocean *see* Kerguélen, Îles
265 I8 **Kerguelen Plateau** *sea feature* Indian Ocean
210 B5 **Kericho** Kenya
95 F2 **Kerihun** *mt.* Indon.
80 D1 **Kerikeri** *North I.* N.Z.
141 O3 **Kerimäki** Fin.
94 C3 **Kerinci, Gunung** *vol.* Indon.
Kerintji *vol.* Indon. *see* Kerinci, Gunung
Keriya *Xinjiang* China *see* Yutian
196 C2 **Kerka** *r.* Romania
164 E3 **Kerkdriel** Neth.
169 B4 **Kerken** Ger.
205 H2 **Kerkenah, Îles** *is* Tunisia
123 F2 **Kerki** Turkm.
123 F2 **Kerkichi** Turkm.
Kerkini Oros *mts* Bulg./Macedonia *see* **Belasica**
198 C1 **Kerkinitis, Limni** *l.* Greece
Kérkira *i.* Greece *see* **Kerkyra**
205 H1 **Kerkouane** *tourist site* Tunisia
165 F4 **Kerkrade** Neth.
164 E3 **Kerkwijk** Neth.
198 A2 **Kerkyra** *Ionioi Nisoi* Greece
198 A2 **Kerkyra** *i.* Greece
158 B3 **Kerlouan** France
203 F5 **Kerma** Sudan
77 I5 **Kermadec Islands** S. Pacific Ocean
266 H8 **Kermadec Trench** *sea feature* S. Pacific Ocean
122 D4 **Kermān** Iran
122 D4 **Kermān** *prov.* Iran
240 G3 **Kerman** *CA* U.S.A.
122 D4 **Kermān Desert** Iran
122 A3 **Kermānshāh** Iran
122 A3 **Kermānshāh** *prov.* Iran
Kermānshāhān *prov.* Iran *see* Kermānshāh
Kermine Uzbek. *see* **Navoi**
237 C6 **Kermit** *TX* U.S.A.
240 H4 **Kern** *r. CA* U.S.A.
240 H4 **Kern, South Fork** *r. CA* U.S.A.
158 C3 **Kernascléden** France
84 C5 **Kernot Range** *hills N.T.* Austr.
190 D2 **Kerns** Switz.
240 H4 **Kernville** *CA* U.S.A.
199 D3 **Keros** *i.* Greece
207 F4 **Kérou** Benin
206 C4 **Kérouané** Guinea
169 B5 **Kerpen** Ger.
263 K1 **Kerr, Cape** Antarctica
146 C5 **Kerrera** *i. Scotland* U.K.
223 I5 **Kerrobert** *Sask.* Can.
237 D6 **Kerrville** *TX* U.S.A.
147 B4 **Kerry** *county* Rep. of Ireland
147 B4 **Kerry Head** *hd* Rep. of Ireland
147 D1 **Kerrykeel** Rep. of Ireland
231 D5 **Kershaw** *SC* U.S.A.
149 G2 **Kershopefoot** *Cumbria, England* U.K.
171 C4 **Kerspleben** Ger.
143 G1 **Kerstinbo** Sweden
180 E5 **Kert, Oued** *r.* Morocco
142 D4 **Kerteminde** Denmark
177 K4 **Kertészsziget** Hungary
95 F4 **Kertosono** *Jawa Timur* Indon.
Kerulen *r.* China *see* **Herlen He**
107 G1 **Kerulen** *r.* China/Mongolia
114 B2 **Kerur** *Karnataka* India
139 L4 **Kerva** Rus. Fed.
158 C4 **Kervignac** France
128 A2 **Keryneia** Cyprus
205 E3 **Kerzaz** Alg.
190 C2 **Kerzers** Switz.
134 I4 **Kerzhenets** *r.* Rus. Fed.
224 E3 **Kesagami** *r. Ont.* Can.
141 O3 **Kesälahti** Fin.
199 E1 **Keşan** Turkey
126 E2 **Keşap** Turkey
197 G4 **Kesarevo** Bulg.
117 F4 **Kesariya** *Bihar* India
102 J4 **Kesennuma** Japan
151 I2 **Kesgrave** *Suffolk, England* U.K.
147 C2 **Kesh** Rep. of Ireland
147 D2 **Kesh** *Northern Ireland* U.K.
100 C2 **Keshan** *Heilong.* China
226 C3 **Keshena** *WI* U.S.A.
116 B5 **Keshod** *Gujarat* India
116 D4 **Keshorai Patan** *Rajasthan* India
127 H4 **Keshvar** Iran
126 D3 **Keskin** Turkey
139 K2 **Kes'ma** Rus. Fed.
199 G3 **Kesme** Turkey
139 K3 **Kesova Gora** Rus. Fed.
174 F2 **Kęsowo** Pol.
165 D3 **Kessel** Belgium
173 E3 **Kessel** *r.* Ger.
165 F3 **Kessel** Neth.
151 I2 **Kessingland** *Suffolk, England* U.K.
199 F1 **Kestel** *Bursa* Turkey
Kestel *Bursa* Turkey *see* **Gürsu**
215 G3 **Kestell** S. Africa
140 O2 **Kesten'ga** Rus. Fed.
140 N2 **Kestilä** Fin.
227 H3 **Keswick** *Ont.* Can.
149 F3 **Keswick** *Cumbria, England* U.K.
176 G5 **Keszthely** Hungary
130 J4 **Ket'** *r.* Rus. Fed.
207 F5 **Keta** Ghana
95 E3 **Ketapang** *Kalimantan Barat* Indon.
220 E4 **Ketchikan** *AK* U.S.A.
238 D3 **Ketchum** *ID* U.S.A.
177 K5 **Kétegyháza** Hungary
207 E5 **Kete Krachi** Ghana
176 G5 **Kéthely** Hungary
121 J4 **Ketmen', Khrebet** *mts* China/Kazakh.
207 F5 **Kétou** Benin
137 G4 **Ketrysanivka** Ukr.
143 I4 **Kętrzyn** Pol.
177 J5 **Kétsoprony** Hungary
207 I5 **Kétté** Cameroon
168 C3 **Kettenkamp** Ger.
151 G2 **Kettering** *Northamptonshire, England* U.K.
232 A5 **Kettering** *OH* U.S.A.
173 E3 **Kettershausen** Ger.
170 C1 **Kettinge** Denmark
222 G5 **Kettle** *r. B.C.* Can.
226 A3 **Kettle** *r. MN* U.S.A.
232 E4 **Kettle Creek** *r. PA* U.S.A.
238 C1 **Kettle Falls** *WA* U.S.A.
240 H3 **Kettleman City** *CA* U.S.A.
226 A2 **Kettle River** *MN* U.S.A.
238 C1 **Kettle River Range** *mts WA* U.S.A.
146 F2 **Kettletoft** *Orkney, Scotland* U.K.
149 G3 **Kettlewell** *North Yorkshire, England* U.K.
95 E2 **Ketungau** *r.* Indon.
175 H6 **Kęty** Pol.
171 E4 **Ketzerbach** *r.* Ger.
171 D3 **Ketzin** Ger.
232 E3 **Keuka** *NY* U.S.A.
169 F4 **Keula** Ger.
Keumgang, Mount N. Korea *see* **Kumgang-san**
Keumsang, Mount N. Korea *see* **Kumgang-san**
206 A2 **Keur Massène** Maur.
141 N3 **Keuruu** Fin.
179 F4 **Keutschach am See** Austria
169 B4 **Kevelaer** Ger.
177 K5 **Kevermes** Hungary
246 D2 **Kew** Turks and Caicos Is
226 C5 **Kewanee** *IL* U.S.A.
226 C4 **Kewaskum** *WI* U.S.A.
226 D3 **Kewaunee** *WI* U.S.A.
226 C2 **Keweenaw Bay** *MI* U.S.A.
226 C2 **Keweenaw Bay** *b. MI* U.S.A.
150 E3 **Kewstoke** *North Somerset, England* U.K.
147 C2 **Key, Lough** *l.* Rep. of Ireland
236 D3 **Keya Paha** *r. NE* U.S.A.
224 D4 **Key Harbour** *Ont.* Can.
110 C3 **Keyi** *Xinjiang* China
107 I1 **Keyihe** *Nei Mongol* China
149 I4 **Keyingham** *East Riding of Yorkshire, England* U.K.
231 D7 **Key Largo** *FL* U.S.A.
84 B2 **Keyling Inlet** *N.T.* Austr.
150 E3 **Keynsham** *Bath and North East Somerset, England* U.K.
232 D5 **Keyser** *WV* U.S.A.
232 D5 **Keysers Ridge** *MD* U.S.A.
241 L6 **Keystone Peak** *AZ* U.S.A.
232 D6 **Keysville** *VA* U.S.A.
236 E4 **Keytesville** *MO* U.S.A.
134 G2 **Keyvy, Vozvyshennost'** *hills* Rus. Fed.
231 D7 **Key West** *FL* U.S.A.
151 F2 **Keyworth** *Nottinghamshire, England* U.K.
134 K4 **Kez** Rus. Fed.
233 □H3 **Kezar Falls** *ME* U.S.A.
213 F4 **Kezi** Zimbabwe
177 J2 **Kežmarok** Slovakia
215 F2 **Kgakala** S. Africa
212 D5 **Kgalagadi** *admin. dist.* Botswana
212 E5 **Kgatleng** *admin. dist.* Botswana
215 F2 **Kgotsong** S. Africa
215 G3 **Kgubetswana** S. Africa
100 E2 **Khabarovsk** Rus. Fed.
100 E2 **Khabarovskiy Kray** *admin. div.* Rus. Fed.
Khabarovsk Kray *admin. div.* Rus. Fed. *see* Khabarovskiy Kray
121 I1 **Khabary** Rus. Fed.
129 B1 **Khabez** Rus. Fed.
Khabis Iran *see* **Shahdād**
124 C3 **Khabrā al'Arn** *salt pan* Saudi Arabia
128 D4 **Khabrah Sāfiyah** *hill* Saudi Arabia
118 E2 **Khābūr, Nahr al** *r.* Syria
Khachmas Azer. *see* **Xaçmaz**
116 C5 **Khachrod** *Madh. Prad.* India
125 G3 **Khadar, Jabal** *mt.* Oman
124 C4 **Khaḍārah** Saudi Arabia
129 A1 **Khadyzhensk** Rus. Fed.
129 E2 **Khadzhalmakhi** Rus. Fed.
197 F5 **Khadzhidimovo** Bulg.
136 F4 **Khadzhybeys'kyy Lyman** *l.* Ukr.
116 E4 **Khaga** *Uttar Prad.* India
117 F4 **Khagaria** *Bihar* India
117 F4 **Khagaul** *Bihar* India
117 G5 **Khagrachari** Bangl.
Khagrachchari Bangl. *see* Khagrachari
116 E5 **Khairagarh** *Madh. Prad.* India
111 B7 **Khairagarh** *Uttar Prad.* India
123 H4 **Khaïrpur** *Punjab* Pak.
123 G5 **Khairpur** *Sindh* Pak.
116 C5 **Khairwara** *Rajasthan* India
129 C2 **Khaishi** Georgia
122 B4 **Khāīz, Kūh-e** *mt.* Iran
123 F2 **Khaja du Koh** *hill* Afgh.
98 F1 **Khakasiya, Respublika** *aut. rep.* Rus. Fed.
Khakassia *aut. rep.* Rus. Fed. *see* **Khakasiya, Respublika**
Khakasskaya A.S.S.R. *aut. rep.* Rus. Fed. *see* Khakasiya, Respublika
129 D2 **Khakhalgi, Gora** *mt.* Rus. Fed.
212 D5 **Khakhea** Botswana
123 F2 **Khalach** Turkm.
129 E2 **Khalagork** *r.* Rus. Fed.
129 C2 **Khalatsa, Mt'a** Georgia/Rus. Fed.
116 D2 **Khalatse** Jammu and Kashmir
122 C3 **Khalidabad** Iran
123 F4 **Khalifat** *mt.* Pak.
117 E4 **Khalilabad** *Uttar Prad.* India
122 D3 **Khalilabad** Iran
120 D4 **Khalkabad** Uzbek.
122 B2 **Khalkhāl** Iran
Khálki *i.* Greece *see* **Chalki**
Khalkís Greece *see* **Chalkida**
115 E2 **Khallikot** *Orissa* India
134 N2 **Khal'mer-Yu** Rus. Fed.
138 G4 **Khalopyenichy** Belarus
Khalqobod Uzbek. *see* Khalkabad
Khalturin Rus. Fed. *see* **Orlov**
129 E2 **Khamamatyurt** Rus. Fed.
106 D1 **Khamar-Daban, Khrebet** *mts* Rus. Fed.
116 E5 **Khamaria** *Madh. Prad.* India
116 B5 **Khambhaliya** *Gujarat* India
116 C5 **Khambhat** *Gujarat* India
114 A2 **Khambhat, Gulf of** India
116 D5 **Khamgaon** *Mahar.* India
122 C5 **Khamīr** Iran
124 C4 **Khamir** Yemen
213 F4 **Khami Ruins National Monument** *tourist site* Zimbabwe
124 C4 **Khamis Mushayṭ** Saudi Arabia
114 D2 **Khammam** *Andhra Prad.* India
121 G4 **Khamza** Uzbek.
96 C3 **Khan, Nam** *r.* Laos
123 G2 **Khānābād** Afgh.
121 H4 **Khanabad** Uzbek.
127 F4 **Khān al Baghdādī** Iraq
127 G4 **Khān al Maḩāwīl** Iraq
114 B3 **Khanapur** *Karnataka* India
114 B2 **Khanapur** *Mahar.* India
122 A2 **Khānaqāh** Iran
127 G5 **Khān ar Raḩbah** Iraq
Khanbalik *Beijing* China *see* **Beijing**
83 G4 **Khancoban** *N.S.W.* Austr.
106 B1 **Khandagayty** Rus. Fed.
114 B2 **Khandala** *Mahar.* India
116 C4 **Khandela** *Rajasthan* India
116 D5 **Khandwa** *Madh. Prad.* India
131 O3 **Khandyga** Rus. Fed.
123 G4 **Khanewal** Pak.
123 G4 **Khangarh** Pak.
Khan Hung Vietnam *see* **Soc Trăng**
131 N4 **Khani** Rus. Fed.
Khaniá *Kriti* Greece *see* **Chania**
116 D4 **Khaniadhana** *Madh. Prad.* India
139 K4 **Khanino** Rus. Fed.
120 E4 **Khanka** Uzbek.
Khankendi Azer. *see* **Xankändi**
Khanki Uzbek. *see* **Khanka**
116 D3 **Khanna** *Punjab* India
205 G4 **Khannfoussa** *hill* Alg.
123 G4 **Khanpur** Pak.
Khān Ruḩābah Iraq *see* Khān ar Raḩbah
128 C2 **Khān Shaykhūn** Syria
129 A1 **Khanskaya** Rus. Fed.
121 J4 **Khan-Tengri, Pik** *mt.* Kazakh./Kyrg.
130 H3 **Khanty-Mansiysk** Rus. Fed.
134 M3 **Khanty-Mansiyskiy Avtonomnyy Okrug** *admin. div.* Rus. Fed.
Khanty-Mansy Autonomous Okrug *admin. div.* Rus. Fed. *see* Khanty-Mansiyskiy Avtonomnyy Okrug
128 B4 **Khān Yūnis** Gaza
97 B5 **Khao Chum Thong** Thai.
116 D5 **Khapa** *Madh. Prad.* India
107 G1 **Khapcheranga** Rus. Fed.
120 A3 **Kharabali** Rus. Fed.
129 C2 **Kharagauli** Georgia
116 B5 **Kharaghoda** *Gujarat* India
117 F4 **Kharagpur** *Bihar* India
117 F5 **Kharagpur** *W. Bengal* India
122 D2 **Kharakī** Iran
122 D5 **Khārān** *r.* Iran
123 F4 **Kharan** Pak.
Kharari *Rajasthan* India *see* Abu Road
114 B2 **Khardi** *Mahar.* India
127 G5 **Kharfiyah** Iraq
100 E1 **Kharga** *r.* Rus. Fed.
Kharga Oasis Egypt *see* **The Great Oasis**
116 D4 **Khargapur** *Madh. Prad.* India
122 B4 **Khārg Islands** Iran
116 C5 **Khargon** *Madh. Prad.* India
116 C4 **Khari** *r. Rajasthan* India
123 H3 **Kharian** Pak.
117 E5 **Khariar** *Orissa* India
128 A4 **Kharîm, Gebel** *hill* Egypt
116 E5 **Kharkhara** *r.* India
116 D3 **Kharkhauda** *Haryana* India
Kharkiv *r.* Rus. Fed./Ukr. *see* Khar'kov
137 I3 **Kharkiv** Ukr.
Kharkiv Oblast *admin. div.* Ukr. *see* **Kharkivs'ka Oblast'**
137 I3 **Kharkivs'ka Oblast'** *admin. div.* Ukr.
137 I2 **Khar'kov** *r.* Rus. Fed./Ukr.
Khar'kov Ukr. *see* **Kharkiv**
Kharkov Oblast *admin. div.* Ukr. *see* **Kharkivs'ka Oblast'**
Khar'kovskaya Oblast' *admin. div.* Ukr. *see* Kharkivs'ka Oblast'
122 C4 **Khār Kūh** *mt.* Iran
134 E3 **Kharlu** Rus. Fed.
197 G5 **Kharmanli** Bulg.
116 E5 **Kharora** *Madh. Prad.* India
134 H4 **Kharovsk** Rus. Fed.
122 B3 **Khar Rūd** *r.* Iran
117 F5 **Kharsawan** *Bihar* India
117 E5 **Kharsia** *Madh. Prad.* India
203 G6 **Khartoum** Sudan
203 G6 **Khartoum** *state* Sudan
203 G6 **Khartoum North** Sudan
137 J3 **Khartsyz'k** Ukr.
Kharuf, Ra's *mt.* Israel *see* Harif, Har
129 C2 **Khasan'ya** Rus. Fed.
122 D2 **Khasardag, Gora** *mt.* Turkm.
129 E2 **Khasav'yurt** Rus. Fed.
123 E4 **Khāsh** Iran
123 E4 **Khash Desert** Afgh.
210 B1 **Khashm el Girba Dam** Sudan
123 E4 **Khash Rūd** *r.* Afgh.
129 C3 **Khashuri** Georgia
117 G4 **Khasi Hills** *Meghalaya* India
197 G5 **Khaskovo** Bulg.
125 E2 **Khasm al Mu'ayqil** *hill* Saudi Arabia
124 B2 **Khatam, Jabal al** *hill* Saudi Arabia
131 L2 **Khatanga** Rus. Fed.
131 L2 **Khatanga** *r.* Rus. Fed.
Khatanga, Gulf of Rus. Fed. *see* **Khatangskiy Zaliv**
131 L2 **Khatangskiy Zaliv** *b.* Rus. Fed.
116 D5 **Khategaon** *Madh. Prad.* India
123 G2 **Khatlon** *admin. div.* Tajik.
Khatlon Oblast *admin. div.* Tajik. *see* **Khatlon**
125 G2 **Khatmat al Malāha** Oman
122 C4 **Khātūnābād** Iran
131 S3 **Khatyrka** Rus. Fed.
137 J2 **Khava** *r.* Rus. Fed.
121 G4 **Khavast** Uzbek.
116 B5 **Khavda** *Gujarat* India
125 G2 **Khawr Fakkan** U.A.E.
215 E4 **Khayamnandi** S. Africa
121 F4 **Khayatbashi, Gora** *mt.* Uzbek.
124 B2 **Khaybar** Saudi Arabia
121 G5 **Khaydarken** Kyrg.
214 B6 **Khayelitsha** S. Africa
120 E4 **Khazarasp** Uzbek.
129 E2 **Khebda** *Respublika Dagestan* Rus. Fed.
114 B2 **Khed** *Mahar.* India
114 B2 **Khed** *Mahar.* India
116 C5 **Kheda** *Gujarat* India
116 C4 **Khedbrahma** *Gujarat* India
Khefa Israel *see* **Ḩefa**
117 F5 **Khelari** *Bihar* India
141 O3 **Khelyulya** Rus. Fed.
180 D5 **Khemis Anjra** Morocco
180 D5 **Khemis Beni Arous** Morocco
205 F1 **Khemis Miliana** Alg.
204 D2 **Khemisset** Morocco
204 C2 **Khemis Zemamra** Morocco
96 D3 **Khemmarat** Thai.
205 G2 **Khenchela** Alg.
204 D2 **Khenifra** Morocco
116 C5 **Kheralu** *Gujarat* India
122 C4 **Kherāmeh** Iran
116 D4 **Kherli** *Rajasthan* India
122 B4 **Khersan** *r.* Iran
137 G4 **Kherson** Ukr.
Kherson Oblast *admin. div.* Ukr. *see* **Khersons'ka Oblast'**
137 G4 **Khersons'ka Oblast'** *admin. div.* Ukr.
Khersonskaya Oblast' *admin. div.* Ukr. *see* Khersons'ka Oblast'
122 B4 **Khesht** Iran
131 L2 **Kheta** *r.* Rus. Fed.
122 C2 **Khezerābād** Iran
97 C4 **Khiaw, Khao** *mt.* Thai.
124 D3 **Khidā, Jabal** *hill* Saudi Arabia
129 D3 **Khidist'avi** Georgia
116 D4 **Khilchipur** *Madh. Prad.* India
Khiliomódhion Greece *see* **Chiliomodi**
107 F1 **Khilok** Rus. Fed.
107 E1 **Khilok** *r.* Rus. Fed.
Khimadhítis, Límni *l.* Greece *see* **Cheimaditis, Limni**
139 K4 **Khimki** Rus. Fed.
100 D2 **Khingansk** Rus. Fed.
Khíos *i.* Greece *see* **Chios**
116 D5 **Khirkiya** *Madh. Prad.* India
197 G4 **Khisarya** Bulg.
139 I4 **Khislavichi** Rus. Fed.
129 E3 **Khiv** Rus. Fed.
120 E4 **Khiva** Uzbek.
Khiwa Uzbek. *see* **Khiva**
138 G1 **Khiytola** Rus. Fed.
139 L5 **Khlevnoye** Rus. Fed.
175 L5 **Khlivchany** Ukr.
97 C4 **Khlong, Mae** *r.* Thai.
97 C4 **Khlung** Thai.
139 L5 **Khmelinets** Rus. Fed.
137 G2 **Khmeliv** Ukr.
Khmel'nik Ukr. *see* **Khmil'nyk**
Khmel'nitskaya Oblast' *admin. div.* Ukr. *see* Khmel'nyts'ka Oblast'
Khmel'nitskiy Ukr. *see* Khmel'nyts'kyy
Khmelnitskiy Oblast *admin. div.* Ukr. *see* Khmel'nyts'ka Oblast'
136 D3 **Khmel'nyts'ka Oblast'** *admin. div.* Ukr.
136 D3 **Khmel'nyts'kyy** Ukr.
Khmelnytskyy Oblast *admin. div.* Ukr. *see* Khmel'nyts'ka Oblast'
137 F3 **Khmel'ove** Ukr.
Khmer Republic *country* Asia *see* **Cambodia**
180 D5 **Khmes, Jebel** *mt.* Morocco
136 D3 **Khmil'nyk** Ukr.
120 C2 **Khobda** Kazakh.
129 B2 **Khobi** *r.* Georgia
139 M5 **Khobotovo** Rus. Fed.
175 M5 **Khobultova** Ukr.
129 E4 **Khodā Āfarīn** Iran
136 C3 **Khodoriv** Ukr.
136 E2 **Khodorkiv** Ukr.
129 B1 **Khodz'** Rus. Fed.
Khodzhal, Gora *mt.* Georgia *see* **Khojali, Mt'a**
123 F2 **Khodzhambaz** Turkm.
119 J2 **Khodzhapir'yakh, Gora** *mt.* Uzbek.
Khodzhavend Azer. *see* Xocavänd
Khodzhent Tajik. *see* **Khŭjand**
120 D4 **Khodzheyli** Uzbek.
Khodzhorni Georgia *see* Khojorni
136 E5 **Khodzhyder** *r.* Ukr.
129 B2 **Khojali, Mt'a** Georgia
Khojand Tajik. *see* **Khŭjand**
129 D3 **Khojorni** Georgia
139 K2 **Khokhlovo** Rus. Fed.
135 G6 **Khokhol'skiy** Rus. Fed.
116 D5 **Kholapur** *Mahar.* India
137 J2 **Kholkhol-Trostyanka** Rus. Fed.
123 F2 **Kholm** Afgh.
Kholm Pol. *see* **Chełm**
139 H3 **Kholm** Rus. Fed.
177 L3 **Kholmets'** Ukr.
134 H2 **Kholmogory** Rus. Fed.
137 J5 **Kholmskiy** Rus. Fed.
137 G2 **Kholmy** Ukr.
139 I4 **Kholm-Zhirkovskiy** Rus. Fed.
Kholon Israel *see* **Ḩolon**
139 I2 **Kholova** *r.* Rus. Fed.
106 D1 **Kholtoson** Rus. Fed.
121 K2 **Kholzun, Khrebet** *mts* Kazakh./Rus. Fed.
122 B2 **Khoman** Iran
129 E4 **Khomārlū** Iran
212 C4 **Khomas** *admin. reg.* Namibia
212 B4 **Khomas Highland** *hills* Namibia
122 B3 **Khomeyn** Iran
122 B3 **Khomeynīshahr** Iran
136 D2 **Khomora** *r.* Ukr.
137 G2 **Khomutets'** Ukr.
137 H2 **Khomutovka** Rus. Fed.
139 K5 **Khomutovo** Rus. Fed.
Khong, Mae Nam *r.* Myanmar *see* **Salween**
129 C2 **Khoni** Georgia
122 C5 **Khonj** Iran
122 C5 **Khonj, Kūh-e** *mts* Iran
96 C3 **Khon Kaen** Thai.
Khonobod Uzbek. *see* Khanabad
Khonqa Uzbek. *see* **Khanka**
117 H4 **Khonsa** *Arun. Prad.* India
131 P3 **Khonuu** Rus. Fed.
135 H6 **Khoper** *r.* Rus. Fed.
100 E3 **Khor** Rus. Fed.
100 E3 **Khor** *r.* Rus. Fed.
Khóra Greece *see* **Chora**
122 D3 **Khorāsan** *prov.* Iran
96 C3 **Khorat Plateau** Thai.
Khorazm Wiloyati *admin. div.* Uzbek. *see* Khorezmskaya Oblast'
117 F5 **Khordha** *Orissa* India
Khorezm Oblast *admin. div.* Uzbek. *see* Khorezmskaya Oblast'
120 E4 **Khorezmskaya Oblast'** *admin. div.* Uzbek.
99 I1 **Khorinsk** Rus. Fed.
212 B4 **Khorixas** Namibia
122 B4 **Khormūj, Kūh-e** *mt.* Iran
Khorog Tajik. *see* **Khorugh**
100 E3 **Khorol** Rus. Fed.
137 G3 **Khorol** Ukr.
137 G3 **Khorol** *r.* Ukr.
121 I1 **Khorosheye** Rus. Fed.
136 C3 **Khorostkiv** Ukr.
122 B3 **Khorramābād** Iran
122 B2 **Khorram Darreh** Iran
122 B4 **Khorramshahr** Iran
123 G2 **Khorugh** Tajik.
137 G2 **Khoruzhivka** Ukr.
134 L2 **Khosedayu** *r.* Rus. Fed.
135 I7 **Khosheutovo** Rus. Fed.
122 B4 **Khosravī** Iran
122 B4 **Khosrowābād** Iran
129 A2 **Khosta** Rus. Fed.
Khotan *Xinjiang* China *see* Hotan
175 M4 **Khoteshiv** Ukr.
137 I3 **Khotimlya** *r.* Ukr.
137 H2 **Khotin'** Ukr.
139 K3 **Khot'kovo** Rus. Fed.
137 H2 **Khotmyzhsk** Rus. Fed.
139 I5 **Khotsimsk** Belarus
137 F3 **Khots'ky** Ukr.
136 D3 **Khotyn** Ukr.
139 J5 **Khotynets** Rus. Fed.
204 D2 **Khouribga** Morocco
123 G2 **Khovaling** Tajik.
117 G4 **Khowai** *Tripura* India
Khowos Uzbek. *see* **Khavast**
122 C3 **Khowrnag, Kūh-e** *mt.* Iran
123 G3 **Khowst** Afgh.
136 E2 **Khoyniki** Belarus
137 K2 **Khrenovoye** Rus. Fed.
137 G3 **Khrestyteleve** Ukr.
117 G4 **Khri** *r.* India
Khrisoúpolis Greece *see* Chrysoupoli
134 I3 **Khristoforovo** Rus. Fed.
131 P2 **Khroma** *r.* Rus. Fed.
120 D2 **Khromtau** Kazakh.
117 H4 **Khru** *r.* India
Khrushchev Ukr. *see* Svitlovods'k
100 E3 **Khrustalnyy** Rus. Fed.
137 G4 **Khrystoforivka** *Dnipropetrovs'ka Oblast'* Ukr.
137 G4 **Khrystoforivka** *Mykolayivs'ka Oblast'* Ukr.
136 E3 **Khrystynivka** Ukr.
215 G3 **Khubelu** *r.* Lesotho
129 E3 **Khuchni** Rus. Fed.
Khudat Azer. *see* **Xudat**
123 H4 **Khudian** Pak.
125 E4 **Khudrah, Wādī** *r.* Yemen
212 E4 **Khudumelapye** Botswana
Khudzhand Tajik. *see* **Khŭjand**
124 D3 **Khufaysah, Khashm al** *hill* Saudi Arabia
124 D2 **Khuff** Saudi Arabia
123 G1 **Khŭjand** Tajik.
Khŭjand *admin. div.* Tajik. *see* **Leninobod**
Khŭjayli Uzbek. *see* **Khodzheyli**
97 D4 **Khu Khan** Thai.
137 H2 **Khukhra** Ukr.
124 B3 **Khulays** Saudi Arabia
116 C5 **Khuldabad** *Mahar.* India
134 M2 **Khulga** *r.* Rus. Fed.
123 F2 **Khulm** *r.* Afgh.
117 G5 **Khulna** Bangl.
117 G5 **Khulna** *admin. div.* Bangl.
215 F2 **Khuma** S. Africa
129 D2 **Khumalag** Rus. Fed.
Khūnīnshahr Iran *see* Khorramshahr
116 C1 **Khunjerab Pass** China/Jammu and Kashmir
122 B3 **Khunsar** Iran
117 F5 **Khunti** *Bihar* India
129 E2 **Khunzakh** Rus. Fed.
139 M5 **Khupta** *r.* Rus. Fed.
122 D3 **Khur** *Khorāsan* Iran
122 D3 **Khūr** *Khorāsan* Iran
116 D4 **Khurai** *Madh. Prad.* India
125 E2 **Khurayṣ** Saudi Arabia
123 F3 **Khurd, Koh-i-** *mt.* Afgh.
116 D3 **Khurja** *Uttar Prad.* India
123 H3 **Khushab** Pak.
122 B2 **Khūshāvar** Iran
122 C2 **Khush Yailaq** *hill* Iran
136 B3 **Khust** Ukr.
116 E5 **Khutgaon** *Mahar.* India
135 H7 **Khutorskoy** Rus. Fed.
215 F2 **Khutsong** S. Africa
100 F2 **Khutu** *r.* Rus. Fed.
123 F5 **Khuzdar** Pak.
122 B4 **Khūzestān** *prov.* Iran
122 A2 **Khvājeh** Iran
120 B1 **Khvalynsk** Rus. Fed.
129 C2 **Khvanchkara** Georgia
139 J5 **Khvastovichi** Rus. Fed.
122 C3 **Khvor** Iran
122 B4 **Khvormūj** Iran
139 M5 **Khvorostyanka** *Lipetskaya Oblast'* Rus. Fed.
120 B1 **Khvorostyanka** *Samarskaya Oblast'* Rus. Fed.
122 A2 **Khvoy** Iran
139 J2 **Khvoynaya** Rus. Fed.
97 B4 **Khwae Noi** *r.* Thai.
123 F4 **Khwaja Amran** *mt.* Pak.
123 G2 **Khwaja-i-Ghar** Afgh.
123 G2 **Khwaja Muhammad Range** *mts* Afgh.
123 G3 **Khyber Pass** Afgh./Pak.
Khynchest' Moldova *see* Hînceşti
Khynchesty Moldova *see* Hînceşti
175 K6 **Khyriv** Ukr.
Khyrov Ukr. *see* **Khyriv**
Khyzy Azer. *see* **Xızı**
129 E2 **Khzanor** *r.* Rus. Fed.
83 G3 **Kiama** *N.S.W.* Austr.
92 C5 **Kiamba** Phil.
209 F6 **Kiambi** Dem. Rep. Congo
234 D1 **Kiamesha Lake** *NY* U.S.A.
237 E5 **Kiamichi** *r. OK* U.S.A.
Kiangsi *prov.* China *see* **Jiangxi**
Kiangsu *prov.* China *see* Jiangsu
198 C2 **Kiato** Greece
142 C3 **Kibæk** Denmark
211 C6 **Kibaha** Tanz.
210 A4 **Kibale** Uganda
208 F4 **Kibali** *r.* Dem. Rep. Congo
209 B5 **Kibangou** Congo
209 E7 **Kibara, Monts** *mts* Dem. Rep. Congo
211 B7 **Kibau** Tanz.
92 C5 **Kibawe** Phil.
211 C6 **Kibaya** Tanz.
211 C6 **Kiberege** Tanz.
210 A4 **Kiboga** Uganda
209 E5 **Kibombo** Dem. Rep. Congo
211 A5 **Kibondo** Tanz.
121 G4 **Kibray** Uzbek.
210 C3 **Kibre Mengist** Eth.
Kibris *country* Asia *see* **Cyprus**
211 A5 **Kibungo** Rwanda
211 A5 **Kibuye** Rwanda
211 A6 **Kibwesa** Tanz.
151 G2 **Kibworth Harcourt** *Leicestershire, England* U.K.
196 E5 **Kičevo** Macedonia
134 I4 **Kichmengskiy Gorodok** Rus. Fed.
129 E3 **Kiçik Dähnä** Azer.
207 F2 **Kidal** Mali
207 F2 **Kidal** *admin. reg.* Mali
150 E2 **Kidderminster** *Worcestershire, England* U.K.
215 F5 **Kidd's Beach** S. Africa
206 B3 **Kidira** Senegal
151 F3 **Kidlington** *Oxfordshire, England* U.K.
116 D2 **Kidmang** Jammu and Kashmir
80 F3 **Kidnappers, Cape** *North I.* N.Z.
179 G4 **Kidričevo** Slovenia
149 G4 **Kidsgrove** *Staffordshire, England* U.K.
211 C6 **Kidugallo** Tanz.
150 C3 **Kidwelly** *Carmarthenshire, Wales* U.K.
169 D5 **Kiedrich** Ger.
173 G4 **Kiefersfelden** Ger.
174 E3 **Kiekrz** Pol.
168 F1 **Kiel** Ger.
226 C4 **Kiel** *WI* U.S.A.
175 I5 **Kielce** Pol.
174 G4 **Kiełczygłów** Pol.
149 G2 **Kielder Water** *resr England* U.K.
165 D3 **Kieldrecht** Belgium
168 F1 **Kieler Bucht** *b.* Ger.
168 F1 **Kieler Förde** *g.* Ger.
206 E3 **Kiembara** Burkina
175 H3 **Kiemozia** Pol.
173 G3 **Kienberg** Ger.
209 E7 **Kienge** Dem. Rep. Congo
169 C4 **Kierspe** Ger.
169 F5 **Kieselbach** Ger.
78 □6 **Kieta** P.N.G.
174 G5 **Kietrz** Pol.
170 F3 **Kietz** Ger.
Kīev Kazakh. *see* **Kiyevka**
Kiev Ukr. *see* **Kyiv**
Kiev Oblast *admin. div.* Ukr. *see* **Kyivs'ka Oblast'**
206 C2 **Kiffa** Maur.
198 C2 **Kifisia** Greece
198 C2 **Kifisos** *r.* Greece
127 G4 **Kifrī** Iraq
211 A5 **Kigali** Rwanda
127 F3 **Kiğı** Turkey
225 I1 **Kiglapait Mountains** *Nfld.* Can.
206 D4 **Kignan** Mali
211 A6 **Kigoma** Tanz.
211 A6 **Kigoma** *admin. reg.* Tanz.
211 A6 **Kigosi** *r.* Tanz.
240 □C8 **Kihei** *HI* U.S.A.
80 E3 **Kihikihi** *North I.* N.Z.
141 M3 **Kihniö** Fin.
240 □D9 **Kiholo** *HI* U.S.A.
141 M3 **Kihti Skiftet** *sea chan.* Fin.
104 B5 **Kii-hantō** *pen.* Japan
140 O3 **Kiihtelysvaara** Fin.
121 H3 **Kiik** Kazakh.
138 D1 **Kiikala** Fin.
141 M3 **Kiikoinen** Fin.
140 N2 **Kiiminki** Fin.
104 B5 **Kii-sanchi** *mts* Japan
104 A5 **Kii-suidō** *sea chan.* Japan
175 I5 **Kije** Pol.
174 G2 **Kijewo Królewskie** Pol.
102 □1 **Kikai** Japan
102 □1 **Kikai-jima** *i.* Japan
138 G2 **Kikerino** Rus. Fed.
196 E3 **Kikinda** *Vojvodina, Srbija* Yugo.
Kikládhes *is* Greece *see* **Kyklades**
134 I4 **Kiknur** Rus. Fed.
175 H3 **Kikół** Pol.
209 E7 **Kikondja** Dem. Rep. Congo
91 J8 **Kikori** *r.* P.N.G.
103 E7 **Kikuchi** Japan
135 H6 **Kikvidze** Rus. Fed.
209 C6 **Kikwit** Dem. Rep. Congo
142 C2 **Kil** Norway
142 E2 **Kil** Sweden
143 G2 **Kilaån** *r.* Sweden
141 L3 **Kilafors** Sweden
114 C4 **Kilakkarai** *Tamil Nadu* India
122 C3 **Kīlan** Iran
240 □B7 **Kilauea** *HI* U.S.A.
240 □D9 **Kilauea Crater** *HI* U.S.A.
179 G2 **Kilb** Austria
147 B4 **Kilbaha** Rep. of Ireland
147 D3 **Kilbeggan** Rep. of Ireland
147 C4 **Kilbeheny** Rep. of Ireland
147 D3 **Kilberry** *Kildare* Rep. of Ireland
147 E3 **Kilberry** *Meath* Rep. of Ireland
146 C6 **Kilberry** *Argyll and Bute, Scotland* U.K.
148 E2 **Kilbirnie** *North Ayrshire, Scotland* U.K.
146 C6 **Kilbrannan Sound** *sea chan. Scotland* U.K.
147 E3 **Kilbride** *Meath* Rep. of Ireland
148 C4 **Kilbride** *Wicklow* Rep. of Ireland
147 E4 **Kilbride** *Wicklow* Rep. of Ireland
146 C5 **Kilbride** *Argyll and Bute, Scotland* U.K.
147 C5 **Kilbrittain** Rep. of Ireland
147 C2 **Kilcar** Rep. of Ireland
147 D3 **Kilcavan** Rep. of Ireland
172 C4 **Kilchberg** Switz.
137 H3 **Kil'chen'** *r.* Ukr.
146 C6 **Kilchenzie** *Argyll and Bute, Scotland* U.K.
146 B5 **Kilchoan** *Highland, Scotland* U.K.
146 C5 **Kilchrenan** *Argyll and Bute, Scotland* U.K.
101 D4 **Kilchu** N. Korea
147 E3 **Kilcock** Rep. of Ireland
147 C3 **Kilcoigan** Rep. of Ireland
147 C5 **Kilcolman** Rep. of Ireland
147 D4 **Kilcommon** Rep. of Ireland
147 C3 **Kilconnell** Rep. of Ireland
147 D2 **Kilconney** Rep. of Ireland
147 E3 **Kilcoole** Rep. of Ireland
147 D3 **Kilcormac** Rep. of Ireland
85 H5 **Kilcoy** *Qld* Austr.
146 D6 **Kilcreggan** *Argyll and Bute, Scotland* U.K.
147 C3 **Kilcrow** *r.* Rep. of Ireland
147 E3 **Kilcullen** Rep. of Ireland
147 E3 **Kildalkey** Rep. of Ireland
147 E3 **Kildare** Rep. of Ireland
147 E3 **Kildare** *county* Rep. of Ireland
140 P1 **Kil'dinstroy** Rus. Fed.
146 C6 **Kildonan** *North Ayrshire, Scotland* U.K.
213 F3 **Kildonan** Zimbabwe
147 C4 **Kildorrery** Rep. of Ireland
147 E2 **Kildress** *Northern Ireland* U.K.
134 I4 **Kilemary** Rus. Fed.
209 C6 **Kilembe** Dem. Rep. Congo
147 B4 **Kilfenora** Rep. of Ireland
146 C6 **Kilfinan** *Argyll and Bute, Scotland* U.K.
147 C4 **Kilfinnane** Rep. of Ireland
150 C3 **Kilgetty** *Pembrokeshire, Wales* U.K.
147 C3 **Kilglass** *Galway* Rep. of Ireland
147 C3 **Kilglass** *Roscommon* Rep. of Ireland
147 B4 **Kilgobnet** Rep. of Ireland
237 E5 **Kilgore** *TX* U.S.A.
84 C3 **Kilgour** *r. N.T.* Austr.
149 I3 **Kilham** *East Riding of Yorkshire, England* U.K.
149 G2 **Kilham** *Northumberland, England* U.K.
Kilia Ukr. *see* **Kiliya**
209 F5 **Kiliba** Dem. Rep. Congo
207 F4 **Kilibo** Benin
199 G3 **Kılıç** *Isparta* Turkey
129 B3 **Kılıçkaya** Turkey
211 C5 **Kilimanjaro** *admin. reg.* Tanz.
211 C5 **Kilimanjaro** *vol.* Tanz.
211 C5 **Kilimanjaro National Park** Tanz.
211 B6 **Kilimatinde** Tanz.
211 C6 **Kilindoni** Tanz.
138 E2 **Kilingi-Nõmme** Estonia
126 E3 **Kilis** Turkey
128 C1 **Kilis** *prov.* Turkey
136 E5 **Kiliya** Ukr.
148 C5 **Kilkea** Rep. of Ireland
147 B4 **Kilkee** Rep. of Ireland
147 F2 **Kilkeel** *Northern Ireland* U.K.
147 C3 **Kilkelly** Rep. of Ireland
147 D4 **Kilkenny** Rep. of Ireland
147 D4 **Kilkenny** *county* Rep. of Ireland
147 C3 **Kilkerrin** Rep. of Ireland
150 C4 **Kilkhampton** *Cornwall, England* U.K.
147 B4 **Kilkinlea** Rep. of Ireland
198 C1 **Kilkis** Greece
85 H5 **Kilkivan** *Qld* Austr.
147 E3 **Kill** *Kildare* Rep. of Ireland
147 D4 **Kill** *Waterford* Rep. of Ireland
147 B5 **Killabunane** Rep. of Ireland
148 B3 **Killadeas** *Northern Ireland* U.K.
147 B4 **Killadysert** Rep. of Ireland
148 C2 **Killagan Bridge** *Northern Ireland* U.K.
147 B2 **Killala** Rep. of Ireland
147 B2 **Killala Bay** Rep. of Ireland
147 C4 **Killaloe** Rep. of Ireland
227 I3 **Killaloe Station** *Ont.* Can.
223 I4 **Killam** *Alta* Can.
147 D4 **Killamerry** Rep. of Ireland
147 E4 **Killann** Rep. of Ireland
147 B4 **Killard** Rep. of Ireland
84 B3 **Killarney** *N.T.* Austr.
83 H2 **Killarney** *Qld* Austr.
224 D4 **Killarney** *Ont.* Can.
147 B4 **Killarney** Rep. of Ireland
147 B3 **Killarone** Rep. of Ireland
148 B4 **Killaskillen** Rep. of Ireland
147 C4 **Killavullen** Rep. of Ireland
147 C5 **Killeagh** *Cork* Rep. of Ireland
147 D5 **Killeagh** *Cork* Rep. of Ireland
146 C6 **Killean** *Argyll and Bute, Scotland* U.K.
147 B3 **Killeany** Rep. of Ireland
146 D5 **Killearn** *Stirling, Scotland* U.K.
237 D6 **Killeen** *TX* U.S.A.
147 D3 **Killeigh** Rep. of Ireland
147 D2 **Killen** *Northern Ireland* U.K.
147 E4 **Killerrig** Rep. of Ireland
147 D2 **Killeshandra** Rep. of Ireland
129 C3 **Killi Dağ** *mt.* Turkey
146 E5 **Killiecrankie** *Perth and Kinross, Scotland* U.K.
199 F2 **Killik** *Manisa* Turkey
147 B4 **Killimer** Rep. of Ireland
147 C3 **Killimor** Rep. of Ireland
146 D5 **Killin** *Stirling, Scotland* U.K.
147 B4 **Killinaboy** Rep. of Ireland
147 F2 **Killinchy** *Northern Ireland* U.K.
140 M2 **Killinge** Sweden
149 H2 **Killingworth** *Tyne and Wear, England* U.K.
235 F1 **Killingworth** *CT* U.S.A.
Killini *mt.* Greece *see* **Kyllini**
225 H1 **Killiniq** *Que.* Can.
147 B4 **Killorglin** Rep. of Ireland
147 E3 **Killough** Rep. of Ireland
147 F2 **Killough** *Northern Ireland* U.K.
148 B4 **Killucan** Rep. of Ireland
146 C5 **Killundine** *Highland, Scotland* U.K.
147 E4 **Killurin** Rep. of Ireland
147 C2 **Killybegs** Rep. of Ireland
147 D2 **Killyclogher** *Northern Ireland* U.K.
147 D3 **Killyconnan** Rep. of Ireland
147 D2 **Killygordon** Rep. of Ireland
147 E2 **Killylea** *Northern Ireland* U.K.
148 C4 **Kilmacanogue** Rep. of Ireland
148 E2 **Kilmacolm** *Inverclyde, Scotland* U.K.
147 D1 **Kilmacrenan** Rep. of Ireland
147 D4 **Kilmacthomas** Rep. of Ireland
147 D4 **Kilmaganny** Rep. of Ireland
147 B3 **Kilmaine** Rep. of Ireland
147 B4 **Kilmaley** Rep. of Ireland
146 C5 **Kilmalieu** *Highland, Scotland* U.K.
147 C4 **Kilmallock** Rep. of Ireland
146 B4 **Kilmaluag** *Highland, Scotland* U.K.
147 D4 **Kilmanagh** Rep. of Ireland
146 D6 **Kilmarnock** *East Ayrshire, Scotland* U.K.
233 E6 **Kilmarnock** *VA* U.S.A.
146 C5 **Kilmartin** *Argyll and Bute, Scotland* U.K.

148 E2 Kilmaurs East Ayrshire, Scotland U.K.
148 C4 Kilmeague Rep. of Ireland
147 B3 Kilmeena Rep. of Ireland
146 C5 Kilmelford Argyll and Bute, Scotland U.K.
134 J4 Kil'mez' Rus. Fed.
134 J4 Kil'mez' r. Rus. Fed.
150 D4 Kilmington Devon, England U.K.
147 C5 Kilmona Rep. of Ireland
83 F4 Kilmore Vic. Austr.
147 C4 Kilmore Clare Rep. of Ireland
147 E4 Kilmore Wexford Rep. of Ireland
147 E4 Kilmore Quay Rep. of Ireland
147 B4 Kilmorna Rep. of Ireland
146 C6 Kilmory Argyll and Bute, Scotland U.K.
146 B4 Kilmory Highland, Scotland U.K.
147 C4 Kilmurry Rep. of Ireland
148 C5 Kilmyshall Rep. of Ireland
147 D3 Kilnaleck Rep. of Ireland
147 E4 Kilnamanagh Rep. of Ireland
146 B5 Kilninian Argyll and Bute, Scotland U.K.
146 C5 Kilninver Argyll and Bute, Scotland U.K.
147 C3 Kilnock Rep. of Ireland
146 B5 Kiloran Argyll and Bute, Scotland U.K.
211 C6 Kilosa Tanz.
147 E4 Kilquiggin Rep. of Ireland
147 E2 Kilrea Northern Ireland U.K.
147 C2 Kilrean Rep. of Ireland
147 C3 Kilreekill Rep. of Ireland
147 B3 Kilronan Rep. of Ireland
147 D2 Kilross Donegal Rep. of Ireland
147 C4 Kilross Tipperary Rep. of Ireland
147 B4 Kilrush Rep. of Ireland
147 C3 Kilsallagh Rep. of Ireland
148 C4 Kilsaran Rep. of Ireland
147 E3 Kilskeer Rep. of Ireland
148 B3 Kilskeery Northern Ireland U.K.
146 D6 Kilsyth North Lanarkshire, Scotland U.K.
147 C3 Kiltartan Rep. of Ireland
147 E4 Kiltealy Rep. of Ireland
148 C4 Kilteel Rep. of Ireland
147 C3 Kiltimagh Rep. of Ireland
147 E4 Kiltogan Rep. of Ireland
147 C3 Kiltoom Rep. of Ireland
147 C3 Kiltullagh Rep. of Ireland
137 I4 Kil'tychchya r. Ukr.
148 A3 Kiltyclogher Rep. of Ireland
209 F7 Kilwa Dem. Rep. Congo
211 C7 Kilwa Kivinje Tanz.
211 C7 Kilwa Masoko Tanz.
147 F2 Kilwaughter Northern Ireland U.K.
146 D6 Kilwinning North Ayrshire, Scotland U.K.
147 C4 Kilworth Rep. of Ireland
Kilyazi Azer. see Giläzi
116 C5 Kim r. India
237 C4 Kim CO U.S.A.
211 C7 Kimambi Tanz.
82 D3 Kimba S.A. Austr.
236 C3 Kimball NE U.S.A.
232 B4 Kimball OH U.S.A.
91 L8 Kimbe New Britain P.N.G.
222 H5 Kimberley B.C. Can.
215 E3 Kimberley S. Africa
151 I2 Kimberley Norfolk, England U.K.
86 E3 Kimberley Downs W.A. Austr.
86 E3 Kimberley Plateau W.A. Austr.
87 C5 Kimberley Range hills W.A. Austr.
234 C2 Kimberton PA U.S.A.
151 G2 Kimbolton Cambridgeshire, England U.K.
101 D4 Kimch'aek N. Korea
101 D5 Kimch'ŏn S. Korea
101 D6 Kimhae S. Korea
Kími Greece see Kymi
141 M3 Kimito Fin.
105 F3 Kimitsu Japan
101 C6 Kimje S. Korea
221 L3 Kimmirut Nunavut Can.
198 D3 Kimolos i. Greece
209 B6 Kimongo Congo
139 L5 Kimovsk Tul'skaya Oblast' Rus. Fed.
206 D3 Kimparana Mali
232 B6 Kimper KY U.S.A.
209 B6 Kimpese Dem. Rep. Congo
102 I4 Kimpoku-san mt. Japan
151 G3 Kimpton Hertfordshire, England U.K.
139 K3 Kimry Rus. Fed.
222 E4 Kimsquit B.C. Can.
143 F2 Kimstad Sweden
209 B6 Kimvula Dem. Rep. Congo
95 G1 Kinabalu, Gunung mt. Sabah Malaysia
95 G1 Kinabatangan r. Sabah Malaysia
211 C6 Kinango Kenya
199 E3 Kinaros i. Greece
175 M6 Kinashiv Ukr.
222 G4 Kinbasket Lake B.C. Can.
146 E3 Kinbrace Highland, Scotland U.K.
223 J5 Kincaid Sask. Can.
224 D4 Kincardine Ont. Can.
149 F1 Kincardine Fife, Scotland U.K.
146 F4 Kincardine O'Neil Aberdeenshire, Scotland U.K.
96 B1 Kinchang Myanmar
222 D4 Kincolith B.C. Can.
146 E4 Kincraig Highland, Scotland U.K.
177 H4 Kincses Hungary
209 E7 Kinda Dem. Rep. Congo
209 B5 Kindamba Congo
96 A2 Kindat Myanmar
179 G3 Kindberg Austria
227 F4 Kinde MI U.S.A.
171 C4 Kindelbrück Ger.
237 E6 Kinder LA U.S.A.
169 C5 Kinderbeuern Ger.
164 D3 Kinderdijk Neth.
149 H4 Kinder Scout hill England U.K.
223 I5 Kindersley Sask. Can.
206 B4 Kindia Guinea
173 F3 Kinding Ger.
172 B2 Kindsbach Ger.
209 E5 Kindu Dem. Rep. Congo
135 J5 Kinel' Rus. Fed.
120 B1 Kinel'-Cherkasy Rus. Fed.
134 H4 Kineshma Rus. Fed.
151 F3 Kineton Gloucestershire, England U.K.
84 C1 King r. N.T. Austr.
84 C2 King r. N.T. Austr.
86 F2 King r. W.A. Austr.
87 D5 King, Lake salt flat W.A. Austr.
232 E6 King and QueenCourthouse VA U.S.A.
85 G5 Kingaroy Qld Austr.
147 C2 Kingarrow Rep. of Ireland
146 C6 Kingarth Argyll and Bute, Scotland U.K.
240 G3 King City CA U.S.A.
222 E5 Kingcome r. B.C. Can.
86 E2 King Edward r. W.A. Austr.
157 H5 Kingersheim France
233 □H2 Kingfield ME U.S.A.
237 D5 Kingfisher OK U.S.A.
232 E5 King George VA U.S.A.
259 E8 King George Bay Falkland Is
262 U2 King George Island Antarctica
King George Islands Arch. des Tuamotu Fr. Polynesia see Roi Georges, Îles du
87 C7 King George Sound b. W.A. Austr.
86 D4 King Hill hill W.A. Austr.
146 E5 Kinghorn Fife, Scotland U.K.
146 C4 Kingie r. Scotland U.K.
138 G2 Kingisepp Rus. Fed.
83 E4 King Island Tas. Austr.
King Island Myanmar see Kadan Kyun
Kingisseppa Estonia see Kuressaare
227 H1 King Kirkland Ont. Can.
263 F2 King Leopold and Queen Astrid Coast Antarctica
86 E3 King Leopold Ranges hills W.A. Austr.
241 J4 Kingman AZ U.S.A.
237 D4 Kingman KS U.S.A.
233 □I2 Kingman ME U.S.A.
75 I3 Kingman Reef N. Pacific Ocean
222 D3 King Mountain B.C. Can.
237 C6 King Mountain hill TX U.S.A.
234 C2 King of Prussia PA U.S.A.
82 C2 Kingoonya S.A. Austr.
262 S1 King Peak Antarctica
262 R2 King Peninsula Antarctica
147 D4 Kings r. Rep. of Ireland
240 G3 Kings r. CA U.S.A.
238 C3 Kings r. NV U.S.A.
146 F5 Kingsbarns Fife, Scotland U.K.
150 D4 Kingsbridge Devon, England U.K.
240 H3 Kingsburg CA U.S.A.
151 F2 Kingsbury Warwickshire, England U.K.
150 E4 Kingsbury Episcopi Somerset, England U.K.
84 B5 Kings Canyon N.T. Austr.
151 F3 Kingsclere Hampshire, England U.K.
82 D3 Kingscote S.A. Austr.
235 E2 Kings County county NY U.S.A.
147 E3 Kingscourt Rep. of Ireland
151 I3 Kingsdown Kent, England U.K.
80 E2 Kingseat North I. N.Z.
262 U2 King Sejong research stn Antarctica
226 C3 Kingsford MI U.S.A.
146 D5 Kingshouse Stirling, Scotland U.K.
150 D4 Kingskerswell Devon, England U.K.
231 D6 Kingsland GA U.S.A.
226 E5 Kingsland IN U.S.A.
151 G3 Kings Langley Hertfordshire, England U.K.
215 H2 Kingsley S. Africa
149 H4 Kingsley Staffordshire, England U.K.
226 E3 Kingsley MI U.S.A.
151 H2 King's Lynn Norfolk, England U.K.
77 H2 Kingsmill Group is Gilbert Is Kiribati
151 H3 Kingsnorth Kent, England U.K.
86 D3 King Sound b. W.A. Austr.
235 E2 Kings Park NY U.S.A.
238 E3 Kings Peak UT U.S.A.
232 B6 Kingsport TN U.S.A.
151 F2 King's Sutton Northamptonshire, England U.K.
150 D4 Kingsteignton Devon, England U.K.
150 E3 Kingsthorne Herefordshire, England U.K.
83 F5 Kingston Tas. Austr.
224 E4 Kingston Ont. Can.
246 □ Kingston Jamaica
81 B6 Kingston South I. N.Z.
146 E4 Kingston Moray, Scotland U.K.
233 H4 Kingston MA U.S.A.
236 E4 Kingston MO U.S.A.
233 F4 Kingston NY U.S.A.
232 B5 Kingston OH U.S.A.
234 C1 Kingston PA U.S.A.
231 C5 Kingston TN U.S.A.
232 C6 Kingston WV U.S.A.
151 F3 Kingston Bagpuize Oxfordshire, England U.K.
150 E2 Kingstone Herefordshire, England U.K.
241 J4 Kingston Peak CA U.S.A.
150 E3 Kingston Seymour North Somerset, England U.K.
82 D4 Kingston South East S.A. Austr.
149 I4 Kingston upon Hull Kingston upon Hull, England U.K.
149 I4 Kingston upon Hull admin. div. England U.K.
151 G3 Kingston upon Thames Greater London, England U.K.
247 □3 Kingstown St Vincent
231 E5 Kingstree SC U.S.A.
234 B3 Kingsville MD U.S.A.
237 D7 Kingsville TX U.S.A.
150 D4 Kingswear Devon, England U.K.
150 E3 Kingswood South Gloucestershire, England U.K.
151 G3 Kingswood Surrey, England U.K.
151 F3 King's Worthy Hampshire, England U.K.
150 D2 Kington Herefordshire, England U.K.
209 C6 Kingungi Dem. Rep. Congo
225 I1 Kingurutik r. Nfld. Can.
146 D4 Kingussie Highland, Scotland U.K.
232 E6 King William VA U.S.A.
221 I3 King William Island Nunavut Can.
Kingwilliamstown Rep. of Ireland see Ballydesmond
215 F5 King William's Town S. Africa
237 E6 Kingwood TX U.S.A.
232 D5 Kingwood WV U.S.A.
209 F7 Kiniama Dem. Rep. Congo
199 F3 Kınık Turkey
199 E2 Kınık Turkey
215 G4 Kinirapoort S. Africa
223 J4 Kinistino Sask. Can.
137 H4 Kinka r. Ukr.
209 B6 Kinkala Congo
80 E3 Kinleith North I. N.Z.
81 B6 Kinloch South I. N.Z.
146 B4 Kinloch Highland, Scotland U.K.
146 C3 Kinlochbervie Highland, Scotland U.K.
146 C5 Kinlocheil Highland, Scotland U.K.
146 C4 Kinlochewe Highland, Scotland U.K.
146 C4 Kinloch Hourn Highland, Scotland U.K.
146 D5 Kinlochleven Highland, Scotland U.K.
146 D5 Kinloch Rannoch Perth and Kinross, Scotland U.K.
146 E4 Kinloss Moray, Scotland U.K.
147 C2 Kinlough Rep. of Ireland
150 D1 Kinmel Bay Conwy, Wales U.K.
Kinmen Taiwan see Chinmen
227 H3 Kinmount Ont. Can.
142 E3 Kinna Sweden
147 B3 Kinnadoohy Rep. of Ireland
81 B5 Kinnaird, Mount South I. N.Z.
114 D2 Kinnarasani r. India
147 D3 Kinnegad Rep. of Ireland
235 D1 Kinnelon NJ U.S.A.
Kinneret, Yam l. Israel see Tiberias, Lake
147 D3 Kinnitty Rep. of Ireland
114 D4 Kinniyai Sri Lanka
140 N3 Kinnula Fin.
224 D2 Kinoje r. Ont. Can.
104 B4 Kino-kawa r. Japan
223 K3 Kinoosao Sask. Can.
Kinpoku-san mt. Japan see Kimpoku-san
165 E3 Kinrooi Belgium
215 G2 Kinross S. Africa
146 E5 Kinross Perth and Kinross, Scotland U.K.
147 C5 Kinsale Rep. of Ireland
232 E5 Kinsale VA U.S.A.
142 B1 Kinsarvik Norway
209 B6 Kinshasa Dem. Rep. Congo
209 C6 Kinshasa admin. reg. Dem. Rep. Congo
137 I4 Kins'ki Rozdory Ukr.
237 D4 Kinsley KS U.S.A.
232 C4 Kinsman OH U.S.A.
231 E5 Kinston NC U.S.A.
138 C4 Kintai Lith.
206 E4 Kintampo Ghana
151 F3 Kintbury West Berkshire, England U.K.
234 C2 Kintersville PA U.S.A.
84 B4 Kintore N.T. Austr.
146 F4 Kintore Aberdeenshire, Scotland U.K.
82 B1 Kintore, Mount S.A. Austr.
86 F4 Kintore Range hills N.T. Austr.
146 B6 Kintour Argyll and Bute, Scotland U.K.
146 C6 Kintyre pen. Scotland U.K.
96 A2 Kinu Myanmar
105 G3 Kinu-gawa r. Japan
105 F2 Kinunuma-yama mt. Japan
224 D2 Kinushseo r. Ont. Can.
222 H4 Kinuso Alta Can.
147 C3 Kinvara Rep. of Ireland
147 B3 Kinvarra Rep. of Ireland
150 E2 Kinver Staffordshire, England U.K.
114 C2 Kinwat Mahar. India
211 B6 Kinyangiri Tanz.
210 B4 Kinyeti mt. Sudan
172 B3 Kinzig r. Ger.
169 D5 Kinzig r. Ger.
211 B6 Kiomboi Tanz.
129 C2 Kion-Khokh, Gora mt. Rus. Fed.
227 H2 Kiosk Ont. Can.
239 F4 Kiowa CO U.S.A.
237 D4 Kiowa KS U.S.A.
238 F3 Kiowa Creek r. CO U.S.A.
240 □C3 Kipahulu HI U.S.A.
Kiparissía Greece see Kyparissia
134 G4 Kipelovo Rus. Fed.
138 G2 Kipen' Rus. Fed.
211 B7 Kipengere Range mts Tanz.
173 F3 Kipfenberg Ger.
211 A6 Kipili Tanz.
223 K5 Kipling Sask. Can.
Kipling Station Sask. Can. see Kipling
149 H4 Kippax West Yorkshire, England U.K.
190 C2 Kippel Switz.
146 D5 Kippen Stirling, Scotland U.K.
172 B3 Kippenheim Ger.
147 E3 Kippure hill Rep. of Ireland
121 J1 Kiprino Rus. Fed.
134 I4 Kipshenga Rus. Fed.
137 F2 Kipti Ukr.
233 F6 Kiptopeke VA U.S.A.
Kipungo Angola see Quipungo
209 E7 Kipushi Dem. Rep. Congo
209 F8 Kipushia Dem. Rep. Congo
117 E4 Kirakat Uttar Prad. India
78 □6 Kirakira San Cristobal Solomon Is
177 J3 Királd Hungary
177 G5 Királyegyháza Hungary
177 J5 Királyhegyes Hungary
199 E2 Kiran Dağları hills Turkey
114 D2 Kirandul Madh. Prad. India
206 C3 Kirané Mali
128 A1 Kıravga Turkey
138 G5 Kirawsk Belarus
199 F2 Kiraz Turkey
237 E6 Kirbyville TX U.S.A.
173 G4 Kirchanschöring Ger.
172 C2 Kirchardt Ger.
178 E4 Kirchbach Austria
179 G4 Kirchbach in Steiermark Austria
173 H3 Kirchberg Bayern Ger.
171 D5 Kirchberg Sachsen Ger.
190 C1 Kirchberg Bern Switz.
190 E1 Kirchberg Sankt Gallen Switz.
172 B2 Kirchberg (Hunsrück) Ger.
179 G2 Kirchberg am Wagram Austria
179 G2 Kirchberg am Walde Austria
179 G3 Kirchberg am Wechsel Austria
173 E3 Kirchberg an der Iller Ger.
172 D2 Kirchberg an der Jagst Ger.
179 G2 Kirchberg an der Pielach Austria
179 G4 Kirchberg an der Raab Austria
178 D3 Kirchberg in Tirol Austria
178 D3 Kirchbichl Austria
169 E4 Kirchbrak Ger.
170 C2 Kirchdorf Mecklenburg-Vorpommern Ger.
168 D3 Kirchdorf Niedersachsen Ger.
173 G3 Kirchdorf am Inn Ger.
173 F3 Kirchdorf an der Amper Ger.
179 F3 Kirchdorf an der Krems Austria
173 H3 Kirchdorf im Wald Ger.
178 D3 Kirchdorf in Tirol Austria
173 F2 Kirchehrenbach Ger.
169 C5 Kirchen (Sieg) Ger.
171 C5 Kirchenlamitz Ger.
173 F2 Kirchenpingarten Ger.
173 F2 Kirchensittenbach Ger.
172 D3 Kirchentellinsfurt Ger.
173 F2 Kirchenthumbach Ger.
169 D5 Kirchhain Ger.
169 F4 Kirchheilingen Ger.
172 D2 Kirchheim Bayern Ger.
169 E5 Kirchheim Hessen Ger.
172 D2 Kirchheim am Neckar Ger.
173 F3 Kirchheim bei München Ger.
172 C2 Kirchheim-Bolanden Ger.
173 E3 Kirchheim in Schwaben Ger.
172 D3 Kirchheim unter Teck Ger.
169 D4 Kirchhundem Ger.
170 C2 Kirch Jesar Ger.
169 F5 Kirchlauter Ger.
168 E3 Kirchlinteln Ger.
170 C2 Kirch Mulsow Ger.
169 E3 Kirchohsen (Emmerthal) Ger.
173 G3 Kirchroth Ger.
179 H3 Kirchschlag in der Buckligen Welt Austria
168 D3 Kirchseelte Ger.
168 E2 Kirchtimke Ger.
168 E2 Kirchwalsede Ger.
173 G3 Kirchweidach Ger.
168 D2 Kirchwistedt Ger.
169 F4 Kirchworbis Ger.
172 B4 Kirchzarten Ger.
172 D2 Kirchzell Ger.
129 C3 Kırdamı Turkey
131 L4 Kirensk Rus. Fed.
139 K5 Kireyevsk Rus. Fed.
Kirghizia country Asia see Kyrgyzstan
121 H4 Kirghiz Range mts Asia
120 C7 Kirgiz-Miyaki Rus. Fed.
Kirgizskaya S.S.R. country Asia see Kyrgyzstan
Kirgizskiy Khrebet mts Asia see Kirghiz Range
Kirgizstan country Asia see Kyrgyzstan
Kíria Greece see Kyria
Kiriákion Greece see Kyriaki
77 J2 Kiribati country Pacific Ocean
105 E2 Kiriga-mine mt. Japan
126 E3 Kırıkhan Turkey
126 D3 Kırıkkale Turkey
106 A2 Kirikkuduk Xinjiang China
80 E2 Kirikopuni North I. N.Z.
139 L2 Kirillov Rus. Fed.
Kirin Jilin China see Jilin
Kirin prov. China see Jilin
210 C5 Kirinyaga mt. Kenya
139 I2 Kirishi Rus. Fed.
103 E8 Kirishima-yama vol. Japan
267 I5 Kiritimati i. Kiribati
199 G2 Kırka Turkey
199 E2 Kırkağaç Turkey
146 E7 Kirkbean Dumfries and Galloway, Scotland U.K.
149 F3 Kirkbride Cumbria, England U.K.
122 A3 Kirk Bulāg Dāgi mt. Iran
149 H4 Kirkburton West Yorkshire, England U.K.
149 G4 Kirkby Merseyside, England U.K.
149 H4 Kirkby in Ashfield Nottinghamshire, England U.K.
149 G3 Kirkby Lonsdale Cumbria, England U.K.
149 H3 Kirkby Malzeard North Yorkshire, England U.K.
149 I3 Kirkbymoorside North Yorkshire, England U.K.
149 G3 Kirkby Stephen Cumbria, England U.K.
149 G3 Kirkby Thore Cumbria, England U.K.
146 E5 Kirkcaldy Fife, Scotland U.K.
146 C7 Kirkcolm Dumfries and Galloway, Scotland U.K.
146 E6 Kirkconnel Dumfries and Galloway, Scotland U.K.
146 D7 Kirkcowan Dumfries and Galloway, Scotland U.K.
147 F2 Kirkcubbin Northern Ireland U.K.
146 D7 Kirkcudbright Dumfries and Galloway, Scotland U.K.
148 E3 Kirkcudbright Bay Scotland U.K.
172 B2 Kirkel-Neuhäusel Ger.
142 E1 Kirkenær Norway
140 O1 Kirkenes Norway
227 H3 Kirkfield Ont. Can.
149 G4 Kirkham Lancashire, England U.K.
146 D7 Kirkinner Dumfries and Galloway, Scotland U.K.
146 D6 Kirkintilloch East Dunbartonshire, Scotland U.K.
141 N3 Kirkkonummi Fin.
241 K4 Kirkland AZ U.S.A.
226 C4 Kirkland IL U.S.A.
224 D3 Kirkland Lake Ont. Can.
129 A4 Kırklar Dağı mt. Turkey
129 B3 Kırklar Dağı mt. Turkey
126 B2 Kırklareli Turkey
199 E1 Kırklareli prov. Turkey
149 H3 Kirklevington Stockton-on-Tees, England U.K.
146 E6 Kirkliston Edinburgh, Scotland U.K.
81 C6 Kirkliston Range mts South I. N.Z.
148 E3 Kirk Michael Isle of Man
146 E5 Kirkmichael Perth and Kinross, Scotland U.K.
146 D6 Kirkmichael South Ayrshire, Scotland U.K.
146 E6 Kirkmuirhill South Lanarkshire, Scotland U.K.
149 G3 Kirkoswald Cumbria, England U.K.
146 D6 Kirkoswald South Ayrshire, Scotland U.K.
197 G5 Kirkovo Bulg.
129 B4 Kırköy Turkey
263 L1 Kirkpatrick, Mount Antarctica
146 E6 Kirkpatrick-Fleming Dumfries and Galloway, Scotland U.K.
149 H4 Kirk Sandall South Yorkshire, England U.K.
236 E3 Kirksville MO U.S.A.
148 D1 Kirkton Argyll and Bute, Scotland U.K.
146 F4 Kirkton of Durris Aberdeenshire, Scotland U.K.
146 F5 Kirkton of Menmuir Angus, Scotland U.K.
146 F4 Kirktown of Auchterless Aberdeenshire, Scotland U.K.
146 F4 Kirktown of Deskford Moray, Scotland U.K.
127 G4 Kirkūk Iraq
146 F3 Kirkwall Orkney, Scotland U.K.
215 E5 Kirkwood S. Africa
234 C3 Kirkwood DE U.S.A.
234 B3 Kirkwood PA U.S.A.
149 G2 Kirk Yetholm Scottish Borders, Scotland U.K.
Kirman Iran see Kermān
126 C2 Kırmır r. Turkey
129 A4 Kırmızıköprü Turkey
172 B2 Kirn Ger.
Kırobası Turkey see Mağara
Kirov Kazakh. see Balpyk Bi
Kirov Kyrg. see Kyzyl-Adyr
139 J4 Kirov Kaluzhskaya Oblast' Rus. Fed.
134 J4 Kirov Kirovskaya Oblast' Rus. Fed.
Kirova, Zaliv b. Azer. see Qızılağac Körfäzi
Kirovabad Azer. see Gäncä
Kirovabad Tajik. see Panj
Kirovakan Armenia see Vanadzor
137 I3 Kirove Donets'ka Oblast' Ukr.
137 G3 Kirove Kirovohrads'ka Oblast' Ukr.
137 H4 Kirove Zaporiz'ka Oblast' Ukr.
120 C2 Kirovo Kazakh.
Kirovo Donets'ka Oblast' Ukr. see Kirove
Kirovo Kirovohrads'ka Oblast' Ukr. see Kirovohrad
Kirovo Uzbek. see Besharyk
Kirov Oblast admin. div. Rus. Fed. see Kirovskaya Oblast'
134 J4 Kirovo-Chepetsk Rus. Fed.
Kirovo-Chepetskiy Rus. Fed. see Kirovo-Chepetsk
Kirovograd Kirovohrads'ka Oblast' Ukr. see Kirovohrad
Kirovograd Oblast admin. div. Ukr. see Kirovohrads'ka Oblast'
Kirovogradskaya Oblast' admin. div. Ukr. see Kirovohrads'ka Oblast'
137 G3 Kirovohrad Kirovohrads'ka Oblast' Ukr.
Kirovohrad Oblast admin. div. Ukr. see Kirovohrads'ka Oblast'
136 G3 Kirovohrads'ka Oblast' admin. div. Ukr.
129 F4 Kirovsk Azer.
139 H2 Kirovsk Leningradskaya Oblast' Rus. Fed.
134 F2 Kirovsk Murmanskaya Oblast' Rus. Fed.
Kirovsk Turkm. see Babadaykhan
137 I3 Kirovs'k Donets'ka Oblast' Ukr.
137 J3 Kirovs'k Ukr.
137 K4 Kirovskaya Rus. Fed.
134 J4 Kirovskaya Oblast' admin. div. Rus. Fed.
137 H3 Kirovs'ke Dnipropetrovs'ka Oblast' Ukr.
137 J3 Kirovs'ke Donets'ka Oblast' Ukr.
137 H5 Kirovs'ke Respublika Krym Ukr.
Kirovskiy Kazakh. see Balpyk Bi
137 I2 Kirovskiy Kurskaya Oblast' Rus. Fed.
100 E3 Kirovskiy Primorskiy Kray Rus. Fed.
Kirovskoye Kyrg. see Kyzyl-Adyr
Kirovskoye Dnipropetrovs'ka Oblast' Ukr. see Kirovs'ke
Kirovskoye Donets'ka Oblast' Ukr. see Kirovs'ke
Kirovskoye Respublika Krym Ukr. see Kirovs'ke
Kırpaşa pen. Cyprus see Karpasia
137 J5 Kirpili r. Rus. Fed.
137 J5 Kirpil'skaya Rus. Fed.
146 E5 Kirriemuir Angus, Scotland U.K.
134 K4 Kirs Rus. Fed.
135 H5 Kirsanov Rus. Fed.
172 B2 Kirschweiler Ger.
126 D3 Kırşehir Turkey
175 L1 Kiršna r. Lith.
207 F3 Kirtachi Niger
123 F5 Kirthar Range mts Pak.
151 F3 Kirtlington Oxfordshire, England U.K.
151 G2 Kirton Lincolnshire, England U.K.
151 I2 Kirton Suffolk, England U.K.
149 I4 Kirton in Lindsey North Lincolnshire, England U.K.
169 E5 Kirtorf Ger.
129 C2 Kirts'khi Georgia
140 M2 Kiruna Sweden
211 A5 Kirundo Burundi
262 X2 Kirwan Escarpment Antarctica
135 I5 Kirya Rus. Fed.
105 F2 Kiryū Japan
139 L3 Kirzhach Rus. Fed.
143 F3 Kisa Sweden
211 C6 Kisaki Tanz.
208 E4 Kisangani Dem. Rep. Congo
211 C6 Kisangire Tanz.
177 L3 Kisar Hungary
94 B2 Kisaran Sumatera Indon.
211 C6 Kisarawe Tanz.
105 F3 Kisarazu Japan
128 D1 Kısas Turkey
177 H4 Kisbér Hungary
98 E1 Kiselevsk Rus. Fed.
188 G4 Kiseljak Bos.-Herz.
139 I1 Kisel'nya Rus. Fed.
177 J3 Kisgyőr Hungary
117 F4 Kishanganj Bihar India
116 B4 Kishangarh Rajasthan India
116 C4 Kishangarh Rajasthan India
116 C2 Kishen Ganga r. India/Pak.
104 B4 Kishi-gawa r. Japan
Kishinev Moldova see Chişinău
Kishiözen r. Kazakh./Rus. Fed. see Malyy Uzen'
104 B4 Kishiwada Japan
121 H1 Kishkenekol' Kazakh.
117 G4 Kishorganj Bangl.
146 C4 Kishorn, Loch inlet Scotland U.K.
116 C2 Kishtwar Jammu and Kashmir
207 F4 Kisi Nigeria
175 H2 Kisielice Pol.
175 K2 Kisielnica Pol.
211 B6 Kisigo r. Tanz.
210 B5 Kisii Kenya
211 C6 Kisiju Tanz.
129 C3 Kısır Dağı mt. Turkey
220 A4 Kiska Island AK U.S.A.
141 M3 Kisko Fin.
177 J4 Kisköre Hungary
177 I5 Kiskőrös Hungary
177 I5 Kiskunfélegyháza Hungary
177 I5 Kiskunhalas Hungary
177 I4 Kiskunlacháza Hungary
177 I5 Kiskunmajsa Hungary
177 H5 Kisláng Hungary
177 K4 Kisléta Hungary
177 G4 Kislőd Hungary
129 C2 Kislovodsk Rus. Fed.
137 J4 Kislyakovskaya Rus. Fed.
210 D5 Kismaayo Somalia
177 K4 Kismarja Hungary
Kismayu Somalia see Kismaayo
104 C3 Kiso-gawa r. Japan
105 E3 Kiso-gawa r. Japan
211 A5 Kisoro Uganda
105 D3 Kiso-sanmyaku mts Japan
179 F4 Kisovec Slovenia
222 E4 Kispiox B.C. Can.
222 E4 Kispiox r. B.C. Can.
Kisseraing Island Myanmar see Kanmaw Kyun
206 C4 Kissidougou Guinea
231 D6 Kissimmee FL U.S.A.
231 D7 Kissimmee r. FL U.S.A.
173 E3 Kissing Ger.
172 D4 Kißlegg Ger.
202 E4 Kissu, Jebel mt. Sudan
177 I5 Kisszállás Hungary
172 D2 Kist Ger.
188 E4 Kistanje Croatia
177 I5 Kistelek Hungary
135 H5 Kistendey Rus. Fed.
Kistna r. India see Krishna
177 J3 Kistokaj Hungary
177 J4 Kisújszállás Hungary
103 F6 Kisuki Japan
210 B5 Kisumu Kenya
177 L3 Kisvárda Hungary
Kisykkamys Kazakh. see Dzhangala
174 F3 Kiszkowo Pol.
177 J5 Kiszombor Hungary
210 A3 Kit r. Sudan
206 C3 Kita Mali
121 F5 Kitab Uzbek.
104 C3 Kitagata Japan
105 G2 Kitaibaraki Japan
103 □3 Kita-Iō-jima vol. Kazan-rettō Japan
104 A4 Kitajima Japan
102 J4 Kitakami Japan
102 J4 Kitakami-gawa r. Japan
102 I5 Kitakata Japan
103 E7 Kita-Kyūshū Japan
210 B4 Kitale Kenya
102 K2 Kitami Japan
102 K1 Kitami-sanchi mts Japan
105 F2 Kitamoto Japan
104 B5 Kitayama-gawa r. Japan
236 C4 Kit Carson CO U.S.A.
224 D5 Kitchener Ont. Can.
224 E3 Kitchigama r. Que. Can.
140 O3 Kitee Fin.
210 B4 Kitgum Uganda
Kíthira i. Greece see Kythira
Kíthnos i. Greece see Kythnos
222 D4 Kitimat B.C. Can.
140 N2 Kitinen r. Fin.
222 D4 Kitkatla B.C. Can.
Kitob Uzbek. see Kitab
139 M3 Kitovo Rus. Fed.
222 D4 Kitsault B.C. Can.
223 I4 Kitscoty Alta Can.
136 C3 Kitsman' Ukr.
103 E7 Kitsuki Japan
232 D4 Kittanning PA U.S.A.
234 D2 Kittatinny Mountains hills NJ U.S.A.
233 □H3 Kittery ME U.S.A.
140 N2 Kittilä Fin.
105 G1 Kittoya-yama hill Fukushima Japan
179 I2 Kittsee Austria
114 B3 Kittur Karnataka India
231 F4 Kitty Hawk NC U.S.A.
211 C5 Kitui Kenya
211 C5 Kitumbeine vol. Tanz.
211 B6 Kitunda Tanz.
222 D4 Kitwanga B.C. Can.
209 F8 Kitwe Zambia
178 D3 Kitzbühel Austria
178 D3 Kitzbüheler Alpen mts Austria
178 D3 Kitzbüheler Horn mt. Austria
179 G4 Kitzeck im Sausal Austria
171 D4 Kitzen Ger.
173 E2 Kitzingen Ger.
171 D4 Kitzscher Ger.
178 D3 Kitzsteinhorn mt. Austria
175 H5 Kiucze Pol.
141 M3 Kiukainen Fin.
91 J8 Kiunga P.N.G.
140 N3 Kiuruvesi Fin.
140 N2 Kivalo ridge Fin.
198 C3 Kiveri Greece
139 K3 Kiverichi Rus. Fed.
136 C2 Kivertsi Ukr.
140 N3 Kivijärvi Fin.
143 F4 Kivik Sweden
138 F2 Kiviõli Estonia
137 I3 Kivsharivka Ukr.
208 F5 Kivu, Lake Dem. Rep. Congo/Rwanda
209 C7 Kiwaba N'zogi Angola
175 I1 Kiwity Pol.
Kiyev Ukr. see Kyiv
121 G2 Kiyevka Kazakh.
Kiyevskaya Oblast' admin. div. Ukr. see Kyivs'ka Oblast'
139 K4 Kiyevskiy Rus. Fed.
Kiyevskoye Vodokhranilishche resr Ukr. see Kyyivs'ke Vodoskhovyshche
197 I5 Kıyıköy Turkey
121 F2 Kiyma Kazakh.
105 G3 Kiyosumi-yama hill Japan
105 E1 Kiyotsu-gawa r. Japan
134 L4 Kizel Rus. Fed.
134 I3 Kizema Rus. Fed.
134 F3 Kizhi, Ostrov i. Rus. Fed.
199 G2 Kızık Afyon Turkey
128 A1 Kızılalan Turkey
199 F3 Kızılcadağ Turkey
199 F3 Kızılca Dağ mt. Turkey
126 D2 Kızılcahamam Turkey
199 G2 Kızılcaören Turkey
199 F2 Kızılca-söğüt Turkey
129 C4 Kızılcaziyaret Dağı mt. Turkey
128 B1 Kızıldağ mt. Turkey
128 A1 Kızıldağ mt. Turkey
126 E3 Kızıl Dağı mt. Turkey
126 D2 Kızılırmak Turkey
126 D2 Kızılırmak r. Turkey
199 G3 Kızılkaya Turkey
199 G2 Kızılören Turkey
126 D3 Kızılören Turkey
120 D1 Kizil'skoye Rus. Fed.
127 F3 Kızıltepe Turkey
128 A1 Kızılyaka Turkey
199 F3 Kızılyaka Turkey
129 E2 Kizil"yurt Rus. Fed.
128 B1 Kızkalesi Turkey
129 E2 Kizlyar Respublika Dagestan Rus. Fed.
129 D2 Kizlyar Respublika Severnaya Osetiya Rus. Fed.
134 J4 Kizner Rus. Fed.
104 B4 Kizu-gawa r. Japan
Kizyl-Arbat Turkm. see Gyzylarbat
123 F2 Kizylayak Turkm.
142 C3 Kjellerup Denmark
140 N1 Kjøllefjord Norway
140 L1 Kjøpsvik Norway
214 D5 Klaarstroom S. Africa
164 D3 Klaaswaal Neth.
176 C2 Klabava r. Czech Rep.
143 E1 Klacken hill Sweden
177 H3 Kľačno Slovakia
188 G3 Kladanj Bos.-Herz.
170 C3 Kläden Ger.
176 D1 Kladno Czech Rep.
197 F3 Kladovo Srbija Yugo.
176 B2 Kladruby Czech Rep.
179 F4 Klagenfurt Austria
191 J2 Klagenfurt airport Austria
241 M4 Klagetoh AZ U.S.A.
138 C4 Klaipėda Lith.
175 I6 Kłaj Pol.
177 H3 Kľak mt. Slovakia
177 I2 Kľak mt. Slovakia
Klaksvig Faroe Is see Klaksvík
144 D1 Klaksvík Faroe Is
238 A3 Klamath CA U.S.A.
238 A3 Klamath r. CA U.S.A.
238 B3 Klamath Falls OR U.S.A.
238 B3 Klamath Mountains CA U.S.A.
191 J3 Klana Croatia
Klang Malaysia see Kelang
168 D1 Klanxbüll Ger.
222 D3 Klappan r. B.C. Can.
142 E2 Klarälven r. Sweden
140 L3 Klärke Sweden
177 H3 Klasov Slovakia
142 E2 Klässbol Sweden
176 C1 Klášterec nad Ohří Czech Rep.
95 E4 Klaten Jawa Tengah Indon.
176 C2 Klatovy Czech Rep.
179 F3 Klaus an der Pyhrnbahn Austria
171 E3 Klausdorf Brandenburg Ger.
170 E1 Klausdorf Mecklenburg-Vorpommern Ger.
168 F1 Klausdorf Schleswig-Holstein Ger.
172 A2 Klausen Ger.
179 H2 Klausen Leopoldsdorf Austria
136 F2 Klavdiyevo-Tarasove Ukr.
214 B4 Klawer S. Africa
220 E4 Klawock AK U.S.A.
164 F2 Klazienaveen Neth.
206 C5 Kle Liberia
179 E4 Kleblach-Lind Austria
234 C2 Klecknersville PA U.S.A.
174 F3 Kłecko Pol.
174 G3 Kleczew Pol.
222 E5 Kleena Kleene B.C. Can.
214 C3 Kleinbegin S. Africa
168 C3 Klein Berßen Ger.
172 B2 Kleinblittersdorf Ger.
170 E2 Klein Bünzow Ger.
247 □10 Klein Curaçao i. Neth. Antilles
214 B4 Klein Doring r. S. Africa
171 E4 Kleine Elster r. Ger.
140 J3 Kleinegga mt. Norway
173 G3 Kleine Laaber r. Ger.
173 F3 Kleine Paar r. Ger.
170 E1 Kleiner Jasmunder Bodden b. Ger.
178 C3 Kleiner Solstein mt. Austria
171 F4 Kleine Spree r. Ger.
173 G3 Kleine Vils r. Ger.
234 B2 Kleinfeltersville PA U.S.A.
172 D2 Kleinheubach Ger.
171 C4 Kleinjena Ger.
171 D3 Klein Kreutz Ger.
171 E3 Kleinmachnow Ger.
214 B6 Kleinmond S. Africa
168 E2 Klein Nordende Ger.
172 D1 Kleinostheim Ger.
171 C4 Kleinpaschleben Ger.
172 D2 Kleinrinderfeld Ger.
214 C5 Klein Roggeveldberge mts S. Africa
168 F2 Klein Rönnau Ger.
179 F4 Klein Sankt Paul Austria
214 A3 Kleinsee S. Africa
214 C5 Klein Swartberg mt. S. Africa
215 F3 Klein-Vet r. S. Africa
172 D2 Kleinwallstadt Ger.
171 C3 Klein Wanzleben Ger.
169 F3 Kleinwinnigstedt (Winnigstedt) Ger.
198 C3 Kleitoria Greece
175 L3 Klejniki Pol.
188 F3 Klekovača mt. Bos.-Herz.
136 E3 Klembivka Ukr.
222 D4 Klemtu B.C. Can.
176 B2 Klenčí pod Čerchovem Czech Rep.
174 D4 Klenica Pol.
177 I3 Klenovec Slovakia
176 G2 Klenovice na Hané Czech Rep.
177 I3 Klenovský Vepor mt. Slovakia
175 L2 Kleosin Pol.
175 L2 Klepacze Pol.
137 K2 Klepovka Rus. Fed.
142 A2 Kleppe Norway
142 A1 Kleppestø Norway
174 D3 Klępsk Pol.
215 F2 Klerksdorp S. Africa
215 F2 Klerkskraal S. Africa
136 D2 Klesiv Ukr.
175 L3 Kleszczele Pol.
174 F3 Kleszczewo Pol.
175 H4 Kleszczów Pol.
139 I5 Kletnya Rus. Fed.
Kletsk Belarus see Klyetsk
135 H6 Kletskaya Rus. Fed.
Kletskiy Rus. Fed. see Kletskaya
171 E4 Klettwitz Ger.
136 C2 Klevan' Ukr.
169 B4 Kleve Ger.
137 G2 Kleven' r. Rus. Fed.
138 G5 Klichaw Belarus
107 H1 Klichka Rus. Fed.
171 D4 Klieken Ger.
215 E5 Klienpoort S. Africa
170 D3 Klietz Ger.
139 H5 Klimavichy Belarus
197 H4 Kliment Bulg.
177 H2 Klimkovice Czech Rep.
134 J4 Klimkovka Rus. Fed.
175 I5 Klimontów Pol.
175 J5 Klimontów Pol.
Klimovichi Belarus see Klimavichy
135 F5 Klimovo Rus. Fed.
139 K4 Klimovsk Rus. Fed.
140 K2 Klimpfjäll Sweden
139 K3 Klin Rus. Fed.
177 I2 Klin Slovakia
196 E4 Klina Kosovo, Srbija Yugo.
222 E5 Klinaklini r. B.C. Can.
92 C5 Kling Phil.
171 E5 Klingenberg Ger.
172 D2 Klingenberg am Main Ger.
171 D5 Klingenthal Ger.
234 B2 Klingerstown PA U.S.A.
95 E2 Klingkang, Banjaran mts Indon./Malaysia
170 D2 Klink Ger.
176 C1 Klínovec mt. Czech Rep.
139 K3 Klinsko-Dmitrovskaya Gryada ridge Rus. Fed.
143 H3 Klintehamn Gotland Sweden
120 B2 Klintsovka Rus. Fed.
139 I5 Klintsy Rus. Fed.
215 G2 Klip r. S. Africa
214 B6 Klipdale S. Africa
215 E5 Klipfontein S. Africa
168 E1 Kliplev Denmark
142 E3 Klippan Sweden
214 E5 Klipplaat S. Africa
214 B4 Kliprand S. Africa
215 H1 Klipskool S. Africa
188 F4 Klis Croatia
197 F4 Klisura Srbija Yugo.
142 C3 Klitmøller Denmark
Klitória Greece see Kleitoria
171 F4 Klitten Ger.
168 D1 Klixbüll Ger.
177 I6 Kljajićevo Vojvodina, Srbija Yugo.
188 F3 Ključ Bos.-Herz.
176 F3 Klobouky Czech Rep.
174 G5 Kłobuck Pol.
179 G4 Klöch Austria
175 J4 Kłoczew Pol.
170 G3 Kłodawa Pol.
174 G3 Kłodawa Pol.
174 E5 Kłodzko Pol.
142 D1 Kløfta Norway
175 H5 Kłomnice Pol.
174 G4 Kłonowa Pol.
138 E2 Klooga Estonia
164 F2 Kloosterhaar Neth.
165 D3 Kloosterzande Neth.
177 J3 Kloptaň mt. Slovakia
179 H5 Kloštar Ivanić Croatia
176 G6 Kloštar Podravski Croatia
170 E3 Klosterfelde Ger.
171 C4 Klosterhäseler Ger.
173 E3 Klosterlechfeld Ger.
171 C4 Klostermansfeld Ger.
179 H2 Klosterneuburg Austria
190 E2 Klosters Switz.
171 F4 Klosterwasser r. Ger.
171 E3 Kloster Zinna Ger.
172 C4 Kloten Switz.
169 C5 Klotten Ger.
170 C3 Klötze (Altmark) Ger.
222 B2 Kluane r. Y.T. Can.
Kluang Malaysia see Keluang
174 G5 Kluczbork Pol.
175 H5 Kluczewsko Pol.
Klukhori Rus. Fed. see Karachayevsk
175 H4 Kluki Pol.
175 K3 Klukowo Pol.
220 E4 Klukwan AK U.S.A.
164 D3 Klundert Neth.
95 F5 Klungkung Bali Indon.
123 G5 Klupro Pak.
168 C3 Kluse Ger.
175 K2 Klusy Pol.
170 C2 Klütz Ger.
175 I4 Klwów Pol.
138 G5 Klyava r. Belarus
135 K5 Klyavlino Rus. Fed.
139 M3 Klyaz'ma r. Rus. Fed.
138 F5 Klyetsk Belarus
137 H3 Klymivka Ukr.
137 G2 Klyshky Ukr.
131 R4 Klyuchevskaya, Sopka vol. Rus. Fed.
121 I1 Klyuchi Altayskiy Kray Rus. Fed.
131 R4 Klyuchi Kamchatskaya Oblast' Rus. Fed.
78 □6 Kmagha Sta Isabel Solomon Is
215 F4 Knapdaar S. Africa
81 B7 Knapdale South I. N.Z.
146 C6 Knapdale reg. Scotland U.K.
226 B3 Knapp Mound hill WI U.S.A.
142 E3 Knäred Sweden
149 H3 Knaresborough North Yorkshire, England U.K.
143 F1 Knästen hill Sweden
149 H3 Knayton North Yorkshire, England U.K.
151 G3 Knebworth Hertfordshire, England U.K.
168 F3 Knesebeck Ger.
165 C3 Knesselare Belgium
169 F6 Knetzgau Ger.
188 G3 Kneževi Vinogradi Croatia
177 H6 Kneževo Croatia
197 G4 Knezha Bulg.
171 G5 Kněžmost Czech Rep.
196 E4 Knić Srbija Yugo.
236 C2 Knife r. ND U.S.A.
226 B2 Knife River MN U.S.A.
150 D2 Knighton Powys, Wales U.K.
240 G2 Knights Landing CA U.S.A.
188 F3 Knin Croatia
143 F3 Knislinge Sweden
179 F3 Knittelfeld Austria
172 C2 Knittlingen Ger.
143 G2 Knivsta Sweden
176 D3 Knížecí stolec mt. Czech Rep.
197 G5 Knizhovnik Bulg.
197 F4 Knjaževac Srbija Yugo.
87 B6 Knobby Head hd W.A. Austr.
Knob Lake Nfld. Can. see Schefferville
86 F2 Knob Peak hill W.A. Austr.
147 B4 Knock Clare Rep. of Ireland
147 C3 Knock Mayo Rep. of Ireland
146 C5 Knock Argyll and Bute, Scotland U.K.
147 B5 Knockaboy hill Rep. of Ireland
147 B4 Knockacummer hill Rep. of Ireland
147 C2 Knockalongy hill Rep. of Ireland
147 B4 Knockalough Rep. of Ireland
148 C5 Knockananna Rep. of Ireland
148 C5 Knockanarrigan Rep. of Ireland
146 E4 Knockandhu Moray, Scotland U.K.
147 B4 Knockanefune hill Rep. of Ireland
146 D4 Knockban Highland, Scotland U.K.
147 E4 Knockbrandon Rep. of Ireland
147 E3 Knockbridge Rep. of Ireland
147 D4 Knockbrit Rep. of Ireland
147 C3 Knockcroghery Rep. of Ireland
146 F4 Knock Hill hill Scotland U.K.
147 C3 Knock International airport Rep. of Ireland
147 E1 Knocklayd hill Northern Ireland U.K.
147 C4 Knocklong Rep. of Ireland
147 C4 Knockmealdown Mountains hills Rep. of Ireland
147 B2 Knockmore Rep. of Ireland
147 C3 Knockmoyle Rep. of Ireland
147 B4 Knocknaboul Rep. of Ireland
148 C2 Knocknacarry Northern Ireland U.K.
147 B4 Knocknagree Rep. of Ireland
147 C4 Knocknaskagh hill Rep. of Ireland
147 C5 Knockraha Rep. of Ireland
147 C5 Knocks Rep. of Ireland
165 C3 Knokke-Heist Belgium
170 E2 Knorrendorf Ger.
198 D4 Knosos tourist site Greece
Knossós tourist site Greece see Knosos
149 H4 Knottingley West Yorkshire, England U.K.
151 F2 Knowle West Midlands, England U.K.
262 T2 Knowles, Cape Antarctica
233 □I1 Knowles Corner ME U.S.A.
233 G2 Knowlton Que. Can.
230 C3 Knox IN U.S.A.
232 D4 Knox PA U.S.A.
Knox Atoll Kiribati see Tarawa
226 A5 Knox City MO U.S.A.
263 G2 Knox Coast Antarctica
231 D5 Knoxville GA U.S.A.
236 E3 Knoxville IA U.S.A.
231 D5 Knoxville TN U.S.A.
146 C4 Knoydart mts Scotland U.K.
150 D2 Knucklas Powys, Wales U.K.
221 L2 Knud Rasmussen Land reg. Greenland
169 E4 Knüllwald-Remsfeld Ger.
174 G5 Knurów Pol.
149 G4 Knutsford Cheshire, England U.K.
134 I5 Knyaginino Rus. Fed.
138 F4 Knyahinin Belarus
137 G4 Knyaze-Hryhorivka Ukr.
175 M5 Knyazhe Ukr.
214 D6 Knysna S. Africa
175 K2 Knyszyn Pol.
100 F3 Ko, Gora mt. Rus. Fed.
208 F2 Koalib, Jebel mt. Sudan
211 C6 Koani Tanz.
Koartac Que. Can. see Quaqtaq

94 D3 **Koba** Indon.
179 E4 **Kobarid** Slovenia
103 E8 **Kobayashi** Japan
104 B4 **Kōbe** Japan
137 H3 **Kobelyaky** Ukr.
142 E4 **København** Denmark
142 E4 **København** *mun.* Denmark
206 C3 **Kobenni** Maur.
179 F3 **Kobenz** Austria
179 H3 **Kobersdorf** Austria
175 H4 **Kobiele Wielkie** Pol.
174 E5 **Kobierzyce** Pol.
174 G5 **Kobiór** Pol.
102 □1 **Kōbi-sho** *i.* Japan
169 C5 **Koblenz** Ger.
169 C5 **Koblenz** *admin. reg. Rheinland-Pfalz* Ger.
137 F4 **Kobleve** Ukr.
210 C1 **K'obo** Eth.
210 A4 **Koboko** Uganda
139 K2 **Kobozha** *r.* Rus. Fed.
134 J4 **Kobra** Rus. Fed.
Kobrin Belarus *see* **Kobryn**
91 H8 **Kobroör** *i.* Indon.
170 C2 **Kobrow** Ger.
136 C1 **Kobryn** Belarus
129 B3 **K'obulet'i** Georgia
105 E3 **Kobushiga-take** *mt.* Japan
131 N3 **Kobyay** Rus. Fed.
174 F4 **Kobyla Góra** Pol.
174 C2 **Kobylanka** Pol.
136 C3 **Kobylets'ka Polyana** Ukr.
176 F3 **Kobylí** Czech Rep.
174 F4 **Kobylin** Pol.
175 K2 **Kobylin-Borzymy** Pol.
175 J3 **Kobyłka** Pol.
174 F1 **Kobylnica** Pol.
175 I3 **Kobylniki** Pol.
199 F1 **Kocaafşar** *r.* Turkey
199 G1 **Kocaali** Turkey
199 G3 **Kocaaliler** Turkey
199 E2 **Kocaavşar** Turkey
199 F3 **Kocabaş** *Denizli* Turkey
199 F2 **Koca Dağ** *mt.* Turkey
199 F1 **Kocaeli** Turkey
199 F1 **Kocaeli** *prov.* Turkey
199 F1 **Kocaeli Yarımadası** *pen.* Turkey
129 C3 **Kocaköy** Turkey
197 F5 **Kočani** Macedonia
129 C4 **Kocapınar** Turkey
199 E3 **Koçarlı** Turkey
129 C4 **Kocasu** *r.* Turkey
199 F1 **Kocasu** *r.* Turkey
128 C1 **Kocatepe** Turkey
129 C4 **Koçbaşı Tepe** *mt.* Turkey
196 D3 **Koceljevo** *Srbija* Yugo.
188 E3 **Kočevje** Slovenia
101 C6 **Koch'ang** S. Korea
174 G5 **Kochanowice** Pol.
117 G4 **Koch Bihar** *W. Bengal* India
173 F4 **Kochel am See** Ger.
173 F4 **Kochelsee** *l.* Ger.
172 D2 **Kocher** *r.* Ger.
137 H3 **Kocherezhky** Ukr.
197 F4 **Kocherinovo** Bulg.
136 E2 **Kocheriv** Ukr.
137 I2 **Kochetovka** Rus. Fed.
134 K4 **Kochevo** Rus. Fed.
Kochi *Kerala* India *see* **Cochin**
103 F7 **Kōchi** Japan
103 F7 **Kōchi** *pref.* Japan
Koçhisar Turkey *see* **Kızıltepe**
120 E1 **Kochkar'** Rus. Fed.
121 H4 **Kochkor** Kyrg.
Kochkorka Kyrg. *see* **Kochkor**
135 I5 **Kochkurovo** Rus. Fed.
129 E1 **Kochubey** Rus. Fed.
129 B1 **Kochubeyevskoye** Rus. Fed.
198 D2 **Kochylas** *hill Sterea Ellas* Greece
175 K4 **Kock** Pol.
129 D3 **Koçkıran** Turkey
129 C3 **Koçköyü** Turkey
170 C3 **Köckte** Ger.
177 G3 **Kočovce** Slovakia
177 H4 **Kocs** Hungary
177 I4 **Kocsér** Hungary
177 H5 **Kocsola** Hungary
174 F2 **Koczała** Pol.
114 B3 **Kod** *Karnataka* India
114 C4 **Kodaikanal** *Tamil Nadu* India
105 F3 **Kodaira** Japan
102 □1 **Kodakara-jima** *i.* Japan
136 F2 **Kodaky** Ukr.
115 E2 **Kodala** *Orissa* India
117 F4 **Kodarma** *Bihar* India
175 L4 **Kodeń** Pol.
137 J2 **Kodentsovo** Rus. Fed.
171 F4 **Kodersdorf** Ger.
220 C4 **Kodiak** *AK* U.S.A.
220 C4 **Kodiak Island** *AK* U.S.A.
116 B5 **Kodinar** *Gujarat* India
134 G3 **Kodino** Rus. Fed.
138 C1 **Kodisjoki** Fin.
171 C5 **Köditz** Ger.
114 C4 **Kodiyakkarai** *Tamil Nadu* India
176 G4 **Kodó** *r.* Hungary
102 J3 **Kodomari** Japan
129 B2 **Kodori** *r.* Georgia
129 B2 **Kodoris K'edi** *hills* Georgia
136 E2 **Kodra** Ukr.
175 H4 **Kodrąb** Pol.
114 C3 **Kodumuru** *Andhra Prad.* India
136 E3 **Kodyma** Ukr.
136 F3 **Kodyma** *r.* Ukr.
197 G5 **Kodzhaele** *mt.* Bulg./Greece
Kodzhori Georgia *see* **Kojori**
214 D3 **Koegas** S. Africa
214 C3 **Koegrabie** S. Africa
164 F2 **Koekange** Neth.
165 B3 **Koekelare** Belgium
214 B4 **Koekenaap** S. Africa
212 C5 **Koës** Namibia
165 C3 **Koewacht** Neth.
241 K5 **Kofa Mountains** *AZ* U.S.A.
123 G2 **Kofarnihon** Tajik.
123 G2 **Kofarnihon** *r.* Tajik.
197 H5 **Kofçaz** Turkey
173 G3 **Köfering** Ger.
215 E3 **Koffiefontein** S. Africa
198 D4 **Kofinas, Oros** *mt. Kriti* Greece
179 G3 **Köflach** Austria
206 E5 **Koforidua** Ghana
105 E3 **Kōfu** Japan
105 F2 **Koga** Japan
197 I3 **Kogălniceanu** *airport* Romania
224 E1 **Kogaluc** *r. Que.* Can.
225 I1 **Kogaluk** *r. Nfld.* Can.
85 G5 **Kogan** *Qld* Austr.
105 F3 **Koganei** Japan
142 E4 **Køge** Denmark
142 E4 **Køge Bugt** *b.* Denmark
134 L3 **Kogel'** *r.* Rus. Fed.
207 G4 **Kogi** *state* Nigeria
Kogon Uzbek. *see* **Kagan**
123 G3 **Kohat** Pak.
138 E2 **Kohila** Estonia
117 H4 **Kohima** *Nagaland* India
78 □6 **Kohinggo** *i. New Georgia Is* Solomon Is
122 B4 **Kohkīlūyeh va Būyer Ahmadī** *prov.* Iran
173 G2 **Kohlberg** Ger.
168 D2 **Köhlen** Ger.
262 Q2 **Kohler Range** *mts* Antarctica
241 L4 **Kohls Ranch** *AZ* U.S.A.
138 F2 **Kohtla-Järve** Estonia
80 E2 **Kohukohunui** *hill North I.* N.Z.
81 C6 **Kohurau** *mt. South I.* N.Z.
136 E5 **Kohyl'nyk** *r.* Ukr.
222 A2 **Koidern** *Y.T.* Can.
222 A2 **Koidern Mountain** *Y.T.* Can.
Koidu Sierra Leone *see* **Sefadu**
214 A4 **Koiingnaas** S. Africa
114 C2 **Koilkonda** *Andhra Prad.* India
114 C3 **Koilkuntla** *Andhra Prad.* India
217 □3a **Koimbani** *Njazidja* Comoros
134 J3 **Koin** *r.* Rus. Fed.
127 G3 **Koi Sanjaq** Iraq
140 O3 **Koitere** *l.* Fin.
105 F3 **Koito-gawa** *r.* Japan
101 D6 **Kōje-do** *i.* S. Korea
176 G2 **Kojetín** Czech Rep.
87 C7 **Kojonup** *W.A.* Austr.
129 D3 **Kojori** Georgia
96 C2 **Kok** *r.* Thai.
177 I4 **Kóka** Hungary
233 □I2 **Kokadjo** *ME* U.S.A.
105 G3 **Kokai-gawa** *r.* Japan
120 F2 **Kokalaat** Kazakh.
121 G4 **Kokand** Uzbek.
Kokankishlak Uzbek. *see* **Pakhtaabad**
141 M4 **Kökar** *Åland* Fin.
138 C2 **Kökarsfjärden** *b.* Fin.
81 C5 **Kokatahi** *South I.* N.Z.
177 I3 **Kokava nad Rimavicou** Slovakia
123 G2 **Kokcha** *r.* Afgh.
Kokchetav Kazakh. *see* **Kokshetau**
141 M3 **Kokemäki** Fin.
138 G4 **Kokhanava** Belarus
139 M3 **Kokhma** Rus. Fed.
206 B3 **Koki** Senegal
121 H4 **Kök-Janggak** Kyrg.
140 M3 **Kokkola** Fin.
138 E3 **Koknese** Latvia
207 G4 **Koko** Nigeria
206 C3 **Kokofata** Mali
206 D5 **Kokolo-Pozo** Côte d'Ivoire
230 C3 **Kokomo** *IN* U.S.A.
139 J5 **Kokorevka** Rus. Fed.
139 K4 **Kokoshkino** Rus. Fed.
215 F2 **Kokosi** S. Africa
206 B4 **Kokou** *mt.* Guinea
121 J2 **Kokpekti** Kazakh.
179 F4 **Kokra** *r.* Slovenia
179 F4 **Kokrica** Slovenia
101 C5 **Koksan** N. Korea
121 G4 **Koksaray** Kazakh.
Kokshaal-Tau, Khrebet *mts* China/Kyrg. *see* **Kakshaal-Too**
134 I4 **Koksharka** Rus. Fed.
121 G1 **Kokshetau** Kazakh.
165 B3 **Koksijde** Belgium
225 G1 **Koksoak** *r. Que.* Can.
215 G4 **Kokstad** S. Africa
121 I3 **Koksu** *Almatinskaya Oblast'* Kazakh.
121 G4 **Koksu** *Yuzhnyy Kazakhstan* Kazakh.
121 I3 **Koktal** Kazakh.
121 H4 **Kök-Tash** Kyrg.
121 I3 **Kokterek** Kazakh.
Koktokay *Xinjiang* China *see* **Fuyun**
103 E8 **Kokubu** Japan
105 E3 **Kokushiga-take** *mt.* Japan
Kok-Yangak Kyrg. *see* **Kök-Janggak**
121 J2 **Kokzhayyk** Kazakh.
140 P1 **Kola** Rus. Fed.
140 P1 **Kola** *r.* Rus. Fed.
Kolab *r.* India *see* **Sabari**
117 F5 **Kolabira** *Orissa* India
123 F5 **Kolachi** *r.* Pak.
175 H4 **Kołacin** Pol.
175 L4 **Kołacze** Pol.
174 F3 **Kołaczkowo** Pol.
175 J6 **Kołaczyce** Pol.
117 F5 **Kolaghat** *W. Bengal* India
116 C2 **Kolahoi** *mt.* Jammu and Kashmir
206 C4 **Kolahun** Liberia
93 B4 **Kolaka** *Sulawesi Tenggara* Indon.
175 K2 **Kołaki Kościelne** Pol.
92 B4 **Kolambugan** Phil.
97 B6 **Ko Lanta** Thai.
Kola Peninsula Rus. Fed. *see* **Kol'skiy Poluostrov**
114 C3 **Kolar** *Karnataka* India
114 D2 **Kolar** *Madh. Prad.* India
116 D4 **Kolaras** *Madh. Prad.* India
114 C3 **Kolar Gold Fields** *Karnataka* India
140 M2 **Kolari** Fin.
Kolarovgrad Bulg. *see* **Shumen**
177 G4 **Kolárovo** Slovakia
140 K3 **Kolåsen** Sweden
196 D4 **Kolašin** *Crna Gora* Yugo.
116 C4 **Kolayat** *Rajasthan* India
143 G2 **Kolbäck** Sweden
170 F2 **Kołbacz** Pol.
174 C2 **Kołbaskowo** Pol.
Kolberg Pol. *see* **Kołobrzeg**
173 G4 **Kolbermoor** Ger.
175 J3 **Kołbiel** Pol.
142 D2 **Kolbotn** Norway
174 G1 **Kolbudy Górne** Pol.
175 J5 **Kolbuszowa** Pol.
139 L3 **Kol'chugino** Rus. Fed.
137 G5 **Kol'chuhyne** Ukr.
136 B3 **Kol'chyne** Ukr.
177 L3 **Kölcse** Hungary
174 F1 **Kołczygłowy** Pol.
206 B3 **Kolda** Senegal
199 E2 **Koldere** Turkey
142 C4 **Kolding** Denmark
240 □C8 **Kolekole** *mt. HI* U.S.A.
100 G1 **Kolendo** *Sakhalin* Rus. Fed.
140 M2 **Koler** Sweden
177 H5 **Kölesd** Hungary
134 J1 **Kolguyev, Ostrov** *i.* Rus. Fed.
117 F5 **Kolhan** *reg. Bihar* India
114 B2 **Kolhapur** *Mahar.* India
141 N3 **Kolho** Fin.
113 D11 **Kolhumadulu Atoll** Maldives
206 B3 **Koliba** *r.* Guinea/Guinea-Bissau
Kolikata *W. Bengal* India *see* **Calcutta**
140 N3 **Kolima** *l.* Fin.
176 E1 **Kolín** Czech Rep.
176 C2 **Kolinec** Czech Rep.
210 C3 **K'olīto** Eth.
173 E2 **Kolitzheim** Ger.
Kolkata *W. Bengal* India *see* **Calcutta**
177 H6 **Kölked** Hungary
Kolkhozabad *Khatlon* Tajik. *see* **Kolkhozobod**
123 G2 **Kolkhozobod** Tajik.
171 F4 **Kolkwitz** Ger.
136 C2 **Kolky** Ukr.
Kollam *Kerala* India *see* **Quilon**
173 H3 **Kollbach** *r.* Ger.
171 C4 **Kölleda** Ger.
114 C3 **Kollegal** *Karnataka* India
173 G2 **Kollnburg** Ger.
168 E2 **Kölln-Reisiek** Ger.
207 F3 **Kollo** Niger
164 F1 **Kollum** Neth.
168 E1 **Kollund** Denmark
169 B5 **Köln** Ger.
169 B5 **Köln** *admin. reg. Nordrhein-Westfalen* Ger.
169 C5 **Köln-Bonn** *airport* Ger.
175 L2 **Kolnica** Pol.
175 J2 **Kolno** *Podlaskie* Pol.
175 I2 **Kolno** *Warmińsko-Mazurskie* Pol.
209 B6 **Kolo** Dem. Rep. Congo
174 G3 **Koło** Pol.
211 B6 **Kolo** Tanz.
240 □B8 **Koloa** *HI* U.S.A.
139 M3 **Kolobovo** Rus. Fed.
143 F4 **Kołobrzeg** Pol.
171 E4 **Kolochau** Ger.
136 B3 **Kolochava** Ukr.
139 K2 **Kolodenskoye, Ozero** *l.* Rus. Fed.
137 J2 **Kolodeznyy** Rus. Fed.
136 C3 **Kolodne** Ukr.
134 I4 **Kologriv** Rus. Fed.
206 C3 **Kolokani** Mali
139 M3 **Koloksha** *r.* Rus. Fed.
137 H3 **Kolomak** Ukr.
137 H3 **Kolomak** *r.* Ukr.
78 □6 **Kolombangara** *i. New Georgia Is* Solomon Is
Kolomea Ukr. *see* **Kolomyya**
139 L4 **Kolomna** Rus. Fed.
Kołomyja Ukr. *see* **Kolomyya**
136 C3 **Kolomyya** Ukr.
206 D4 **Kolondiéba** Mali
93 B3 **Kolonedale** *Sulawesi Tengah* Indon.
78 □4b **Kolonia** *Pohnpei* Micronesia
196 D5 **Kolonjë** Albania
174 G5 **Kolonowskie** Pol.
137 H3 **Kolontayiv** Ukr.
139 J1 **Koloshma** *r.* Rus. Fed.
140 P1 **Kolozero, Ozero** *l.* Rus. Fed.
Kolozsvár Romania *see* **Cluj-Napoca**
139 K2 **Kolp'** *r.* Rus. Fed.
139 M4 **Kolp'** *r.* Rus. Fed.
130 J4 **Kolpashevo** Rus. Fed.
139 H2 **Kolpino** Rus. Fed.
135 G5 **Kolpny** Rus. Fed.
178 C3 **Kolsass** Austria
121 J4 **Kol'shat** Kazakh.
139 M3 **Kolshevo** Rus. Fed.
134 F2 **Kol'skiy Poluostrov** *pen.* Rus. Fed.
174 D4 **Kolsko** Pol.
143 F2 **Kolsva** Sweden
141 K3 **Kölsvallen** Sweden
177 H3 **Kolta** Slovakia
120 B1 **Koltubanovskiy** Rus. Fed.
196 E3 **Kolubara** *r.* Yugo.
Kölük Turkey *see* **Kahta**
203 I6 **Koluli** Eritrea
175 H4 **Koluszki** Pol.
121 G2 **Koluton** Kazakh.
134 L2 **Kolva** *r.* Rus. Fed.
134 L3 **Kolva** *r.* Rus. Fed.
140 J2 **Kolvereid** Norway
134 F2 **Kolvitskoye, Ozero** *l.* Rus. Fed.
209 E7 **Kolwezi** Dem. Rep. Congo
114 B2 **Kolya** *r.* India
139 L5 **Kolybel'skoye** Rus. Fed.
131 R3 **Kolyma** *r.* Rus. Fed.
Kolyma Lowland Rus. Fed. *see* **Kolymskaya Nizmennost'**
Kolyma Range *mts* Rus. Fed. *see* **Kolymskiy, Khrebet**
131 Q3 **Kolymskaya Nizmennost'** *lowland* Rus. Fed.
131 R3 **Kolymskiy, Khrebet** *mts* Rus. Fed.
131 P3 **Kolymskoye Vodokhranilische** *resr* Rus. Fed.
135 I5 **Kolyshley** Rus. Fed.
131 T3 **Kolyuchinskaya Guba** *b.* Rus. Fed.
121 J2 **Kolyvan'** Rus. Fed.
197 F4 **Kom** *mt.* Bulg.
177 K4 **Komádi** Hungary
105 F3 **Komae** Japan
105 D3 **Komaga-dake** *mt.* Japan
105 D3 **Komagane** Japan
105 F1 **Komaga-take** *mt.* Japan
102 J2 **Komaga-take** *vol.* Japan
214 A3 **Komaggas** S. Africa
214 A3 **Komaggas Mountains** S. Africa
104 C3 **Komaki** Japan
175 K6 **Komańcza** Pol.
100 F2 **Komandnaya, Gora** *mt.* Rus. Fed.
131 R4 **Komandorskiye Ostrova** *is* Rus. Fed.
139 J5 **Komarichi** Rus. Fed.
196 D4 **Komarnica** *r.* Yugo.
177 H4 **Komárno** Slovakia
136 B3 **Komarno** Ukr.
177 H4 **Komárom** Hungary
177 H4 **Komárom-Esztergom** *county* Hungary
176 C2 **Komárov** Czech Rep.
136 C2 **Komarove** Ukr.
138 G1 **Komarovo** Rus. Fed.
175 K4 **Komarówka Podlaska** Pol.
175 L5 **Komarów Osada** Pol.
215 H1 **Komati** *r.* Swaziland
215 H1 **Komatipoort** S. Africa
104 C2 **Komatsu** Japan
104 A4 **Komatsushima** Japan
212 C3 **Kombat** Namibia
206 E3 **Kombissiri** Burkina
Kombótion Greece *see* **Kompoti**
94 D3 **Komering** *r.* Indon.
215 F5 **Komga** S. Africa
134 J3 **Komi, Respublika** *aut. rep.* Rus. Fed.
Komi A.S.S.R. *aut. rep.* Rus. Fed. *see* **Komi, Respublika**
179 H4 **Komin** Croatia
Komintern Ukr. *see* **Marhanets'**
136 F4 **Kominternivs'ke** Ukr.
Komi-Permyak Autonomous Okrug *admin. div.* Rus. Fed. *see* **Komi-Permyatskiy Avtonomnyy Okrug**
134 K3 **Komi-Permyatskiy Avtonomnyy Okrug** *admin. div.* Rus. Fed.
188 F4 **Komiža** Croatia
177 H3 **Komjatice** Slovakia
177 I2 **Komjatná** Slovakia
214 B4 **Komkans** S. Africa
177 H5 **Komló** *Baranya* Hungary
177 J4 **Kömlő** *Heves* Hungary
214 D5 **Kommandokraal** S. Africa
214 B6 **Kommetjie** S. Africa
215 F3 **Kommissiepoort** S. Africa
Kommuna Turkm. *see* **Babadaykhan**
134 H4 **Kommunar** *Kostromskaya Oblast'* Rus. Fed.
139 H2 **Kommunar** *Leningradskaya Oblast'* Rus. Fed.
139 M3 **Kommunar** *Vladimirskaya Oblast'* Rus. Fed.
Kommunarsk Ukr. *see* **Alchevs'k**
Kommunizm, Qullai *mt.* Tajik. *see* **Garmo, Qullai**
Kommunizma, Pik *mt.* Tajik. *see* **Garmo, Qullai**
93 A5 **Komodo** *i.* Indon.
206 C4 **Komodou** Guinea
206 E5 **Komoé** *r.* Côte d'Ivoire
203 G3 **Kôm Ombo** Egypt
209 B5 **Komono** Congo
91 I8 **Komoran** *i.* Indon.
174 E3 **Komorniki** Pol.
177 L3 **Komoró** Hungary
105 E2 **Komoro** Japan
175 J3 **Komorowo** Pol.
174 G4 **Komorzno** Pol.
199 D1 **Komotini** Greece
137 G3 **Kompaniyivka** Ukr.
177 I5 **Kömpöc** Hungary
Kompong Cham Cambodia *see* **Kâmpóng Cham**
Kompong Chhnang Cambodia *see* **Kâmpóng Chhnăng**
Kompong Kleang Cambodia *see* **Kâmpóng Khleăng**
Kompong Som Cambodia *see* **Sihanoukville**
Kompong Speu Cambodia *see* **Kâmpóng Spoe**
Kompong Thom Cambodia *see* **Kâmpóng Thum**
198 B2 **Kompoti** Greece
174 F5 **Komprachcice** Pol.
Komrat Moldova *see* **Comrat**
214 C5 **Komsberg** *mt.* S. Africa
214 C5 **Komsberg** *mts* S. Africa
Komsomol Kazakh. *see* **Komsomolets**
Komsomol Turkm. *see* **Komsomol'sk**
120 E1 **Komsomolets** Kazakh.
131 K1 **Komsomolets, Ostrov** *i. Severnaya Zemlya* Rus. Fed.
139 M3 **Komsomol'sk** Rus. Fed.
123 E2 **Komsomol'sk** Turkm.
137 G3 **Komsomol's'k** Ukr.
137 J4 **Komsomol's'ke** Ukr.
137 I3 **Komsomol's'ke** Ukr.
131 S3 **Komsomol'skiy** Rus. Fed.
Komsomol'skiy Rus. Fed. *see* **Yugorsk**
129 E2 **Komsomol'skiy** Rus. Fed.
135 I7 **Komsomol'skiy** Rus. Fed.
135 I5 **Komsomol'skiy** *Respublika Mordoviya* Rus. Fed.
100 F2 **Komsomol'sk-na-Amure** Rus. Fed.
120 E2 **Komsomol'skoye** Kazakh.
197 G5 **Komuniga** Bulg.
128 C1 **Kömürçukuru** Turkey
127 F2 **Kömürlü** Turkey
137 G4 **Komyshany** Ukr.
137 J3 **Komyshna** *r.* Rus. Fed./Ukr.
137 G2 **Komyshnya** Ukr.
137 H4 **Komyshuvakha** Ukr.
137 F3 **Komyshuvate** Ukr.
137 I4 **Komysh-Zorya** Ukr.
117 E4 **Kon** *Uttar Prad.* India
128 B1 **Konacık** Turkey
115 D2 **Konada** *Andhra Prad.* India
129 C4 **Konakkuran** Turkey
139 K3 **Konakovo** Rus. Fed.
104 C3 **Kōnan** Japan
123 G3 **Konar** *prov.* Afgh.
Konarak *Orissa* India *see* **Konarka**
115 E2 **Konarka** *Orissa* India
175 K2 **Konarzyce** Pol.
174 F2 **Konarzyny** Pol.
116 D4 **Konch** *Uttar Prad.* India
139 J2 **Konchanskoye-Suvorovskoye** Rus. Fed.
134 F3 **Konchezero** Rus. Fed.
136 C1 **Konchytsy** Belarus
114 D2 **Kondagaon** *Madh. Prad.* India
129 E4 **Köndälänçay** *r.* Azer.
114 D2 **Kondapalle** *Andhra Prad.* India
114 D2 **Kondavid** *Andhra Prad.* India
87 C7 **Kondinin** *W.A.* Austr.
Kondinskoye *Khanty-Mansiyskiy Avtonomnyy Okrug* Rus. Fed. *see* **Oktyabr'skoye**
130 H3 **Kondinskoye** *Khanty-Mansiyskiy Avtonomnyy Okrug* Rus. Fed.
211 B6 **Kondoa** Tanz.
135 I5 **Kondol'** Rus. Fed.
129 D3 **Kondoli** Georgia
134 F3 **Kondopoga** Rus. Fed.
177 J5 **Kondoros** Hungary
174 E5 **Kondratowice** Pol.
139 J4 **Kondrovo** Rus. Fed.
123 G2 **Kondūz** Afgh.
123 G2 **Kondūz** *prov.* Afgh.
78 □5 **Koné** New Caledonia
197 F5 **Konečka Planina** *mts* Macedonia
Köneürgench Turkm. *see* **Keneurgench**
206 D4 **Kong** Côte d'Ivoire
97 C5 **Kōng, Kaôh** *i.* Cambodia
97 D4 **Kông, Tônlé** *r.* Cambodia
96 D4 **Kong, Xé** *r.* Laos
221 O3 **Kong Christian IX Land** *reg.* Greenland
221 P2 **Kong Christian X Land** *reg.* Greenland
142 C4 **Kongeå** *r.* Denmark
Kongelab *atoll* Marshall Is *see* **Rongelap**
142 E4 **Kongens Lyngby** Denmark
221 M3 **Kong Frederik IX Land** *reg.* Greenland
221 P2 **Kong Frederik VIII Land** *reg.* Greenland
221 N3 **Kong Frederik VI Kyst** *coastal area* Greenland
140 □ **Kong Karls Land** *is* Svalbard
95 G2 **Kong Kat** *hill* Indon.
95 G2 **Kongkemul** *mt.* Indon.
104 D2 **Kongōdo-san** *mt.* Japan
209 E6 **Kongolo** Dem. Rep. Congo
221 P2 **Kong Oscars Fjord** *inlet* Greenland
206 E3 **Kongoussi** Burkina
142 C2 **Kongsberg** Norway
140 □ **Kongsøya** *i.* Svalbard
142 E1 **Kongsvinger** Norway
110 A4 **Kongur Shan** *mt. Xinjiang* China
211 C6 **Kongwa** Tanz.
221 P2 **Kong Wilhelm Land** *reg.* Greenland
Konibodom Tajik. *see* **Kanibadam**
176 F2 **Konice** Czech Rep.
175 H5 **Koniecpol** Pol.
172 D2 **Königheim** Ger.
Königsberg Rus. Fed. *see* **Kaliningrad**
169 F5 **Königsberg in Bayern** Ger.
171 C3 **Königsborn** Ger.
173 E3 **Königsbronn** Ger.
171 E4 **Königsbrück** Ger.
173 E3 **Königsbrunn** Ger.
173 F4 **Königsdorf** Ger.
171 C5 **Königsee** Ger.
173 F2 **Königsfeld** Ger.
172 C3 **Königsfeld im Schwarzwald** Ger.
171 E3 **Königsgraben** *r.* Ger.
171 F4 **Königshain** Ger.
171 C4 **Königshofen** Ger.
Königshütte Pol. *see* **Chorzów**
169 F3 **Königslutter am Elm** Ger.
173 F3 **Königsmoos** Ger.
173 G4 **Königssee** Ger.
173 F2 **Königstein** Ger.
171 F5 **Königstein** Ger.
172 C2 **Königstuhl** *hill* Ger.
171 E5 **Königswalde** Ger.
171 F4 **Königswartha** Ger.
179 F2 **Königswiesen** Austria
169 C5 **Königswinter** Ger.
171 E3 **Königs Wusterhausen** Ger.
Konimekh Uzbek. *see* **Kanimekh**
174 G3 **Konin** Pol.
100 F1 **Konin** *r.* Rus. Fed.
198 B1 **Konitsa** Greece
171 C5 **Könitz** Ger.
190 C2 **Köniz** Switz.
188 F4 **Konj** *mt.* Bos.-Herz.
188 F4 **Konjic** Bos.-Herz.
188 G3 **Konjuh** *mts* Bos.-Herz.
140 M1 **Könkämäeno** *r.* Fin./Sweden
139 L5 **Kon'-Kolodez'** Rus. Fed.
206 E3 **Konna** Mali
232 C6 **Konnarock** *VA* U.S.A.
171 C4 **Könnern** Ger.
171 D5 **Konnersreuth** Ger.
140 N3 **Konnevesi** Fin.
137 F3 **Kononcha** Ukr.
206 E5 **Konongo** Ghana
137 G2 **Kononivka** Ukr.
177 I1 **Konopiska** Pol.
175 I2 **Konopki** Pol.
136 F4 **Konoplyane** Ukr.
134 H3 **Konosha** Rus. Fed.
105 F2 **Kōnosu** Japan
137 G2 **Konotop** Ukr.
110 E3 **Konqi He** *r.* China
171 C5 **Konradsreuth** Ger.
175 I4 **Końskie** Pol.
167 K3 **Końskowola** Pol.
210 C3 **Konso** Eth.
175 J3 **Konstancin-Jeziorna** Pol.
Konstantinograd Ukr. *see* **Krasnohrad**
100 C2 **Konstantinovka** Rus. Fed.
Konstantinovka *Donets'ka Oblast'* Ukr. *see* **Kostyantynivka**
Konstantinovka *Kharkivs'ka Oblast'* Ukr. *see* **Kostyantynivka**
Konstantinovka *Khersons'ka Oblast'* Ukr. *see* **Kostyantynivka**
Konstantinovka *Zaporiz'ka Oblast'* Ukr. *see* **Kostyantynivka**
139 L3 **Konstantinovo** Rus. Fed.
135 H7 **Konstantinovsk** Rus. Fed.
139 L3 **Konstantinovskiy** Rus. Fed.
176 B2 **Konstantinovy Lázně** Czech Rep.
175 L3 **Konstantynów** Pol.
175 H4 **Konstantynów Łódzki** Pol.
172 D4 **Konstanz** Ger.
207 G4 **Kontagora** Nigeria
140 O3 **Kontiolahti** Fin.
140 O2 **Kontiomäki** Fin.
97 D4 **Kon Tum** Vietnam
97 E4 **Kontum, Plateau du** Vietnam
Könugard Ukr. *see* **Kyiv**
199 G1 **Konuralp** *Bolu* Turkey
126 D3 **Konya** Turkey
177 K4 **Konyár** Hungary
121 H3 **Konyrat** *Karagandinskaya Oblast'* Kazakh.
121 I3 **Konyrolen** Kazakh.
137 H2 **Konyshevka** Rus. Fed.
120 C2 **Konystanu** Kazakh.
121 G1 **Konyukhovo** Kazakh.
172 A2 **Konz** Ger.
173 G2 **Konzell** Ger.
134 L4 **Konzhakovskiy Kamen', Gora** *mt.* Rus. Fed.
87 D6 **Kookynie** *W.A.* Austr.
86 D2 **Koolan Island** *W.A.* Austr.
87 C4 **Kooline** *W.A.* Austr.
84 D5 **Koolivoo, Lake** *salt flat Qld* Austr.
82 D2 **Koolkootinnie, Lake** *salt flat S.A.* Austr.
82 D3 **Koolunga** *S.A.* Austr.
87 C6 **Koolyanobbing** *W.A.* Austr.
83 F3 **Koondrook** *Vic.* Austr.
82 C2 **Koonibba** *S.A.* Austr.
214 C2 **Koopan-Suid** S. Africa
83 G3 **Koorawatha** *N.S.W.* Austr.
87 C6 **Koorda** *W.A.* Austr.
86 B4 **Koordarrie** *W.A.* Austr.
241 L2 **Koosharem** *UT* U.S.A.
238 C2 **Kooskia** *ID* U.S.A.
222 G5 **Kootenay** *r. B.C.* Can.
222 G5 **Kootenay Bay** *B.C.* Can.
222 G5 **Kootenay Lake** *B.C.* Can.
83 G2 **Kootingal** *N.S.W.* Austr.
214 C4 **Kootjieskolk** S. Africa
164 E2 **Kootwijkerbroek** Neth.
121 H4 **Kopa** Kazakh.
177 I2 **Kopa** *mt.* Slovakia
129 C4 **Kopal** Turkey
137 H4 **Kopani** Ukr.
135 I7 **Kopanovka** Rus. Fed.
137 J4 **Kopanskaya** Rus. Fed.
196 E4 **Kopaonik** *mts* Yugo.
114 B2 **Kopargaon** *Mahar.* India
136 D3 **Kopayhorod** Ukr.
121 I3 **Kopbirlik** Kazakh.
176 G3 **Kopčany** Slovakia
188 D3 **Koper** Slovenia
142 A2 **Kopervik** Norway
122 D2 **Kopet Dag** *mts* Iran/Turkm.
Kopet-Dag, Khrebet *mts* Iran/Turkm. *see* **Kopet Dag**
176 F4 **Kópháza** Hungary
174 F5 **Kopice** Pol.
176 E1 **Kopidlno** Czech Rep.
143 G2 **Köping** Sweden
196 D4 **Koplik** Albania
140 L3 **Köpmanholmen** Sweden
114 B3 **Koppa** *Karnataka* India
114 C3 **Koppal** *Karnataka* India
141 J3 **Koppang** Norway
196 D2 **Koppány** *r.* Romania
143 F2 **Kopparberg** Sweden
Kopparberg *county* Sweden *see* **Dalarna**
Koppeh Dāgh *mts* Iran/Turkm. *see* **Kopet Dag**
169 C5 **Köppel** *hill* Ger.
100 G2 **Koppi** *r.* Rus. Fed.
215 F2 **Koppies** S. Africa
214 C2 **Koppieskraal Pan** *salt pan* S. Africa
178 E3 **Koppl** Austria
188 F2 **Koprivnica** Croatia
126 C3 **Köprü** *r.* Turkey
199 F2 **Köprübaşı** *Manisa* Turkey
129 B3 **Köprübaşı** *Trabzon* Turkey
129 B4 **Köprüköy** Turkey
126 D3 **Köprülü** Turkey
175 J5 **Koprzywianka** *r.* Pol.
175 J5 **Koprzywnica** Pol.
215 F4 **Kopshorn** *mt.* S. Africa
165 F5 **Kopstal** Lux.
139 H4 **Koptsi** Belarus
138 E2 **Kõpu** *r.* Estonia
80 E2 **Kopu** *North I.* N.Z.
80 F3 **Kopuawhara** *North I.* N.Z.
136 C3 **Kopychyntsi** Ukr.
Kopyl' Belarus *see* **Kapyl'**
116 E4 **Kora** *Uttar Prad.* India
196 E5 **Korab** *mts* Albania/Macedonia
139 M5 **Korablino** Rus. Fed.
210 E3 **K'orahē** Eth.
111 D4 **Koramlik** *Xinjiang* China
188 E3 **Korana** *r.* Bos.-Herz./Croatia
114 C2 **Korangal** *Andhra Prad.* India
115 D2 **Koraput** *Orissa* India
Korat Thai. *see* **Nakhon Ratchasima**
114 C2 **Koratla** *Andhra Prad.* India
117 E5 **Korba** *Madh. Prad.* India
205 H1 **Korba** Tunisia
169 D4 **Korbach** Ger.
129 C2 **Korbouli** Georgia
94 C1 **Korbu, Gunung** *mt.* Malaysia
198 B1 **Korçë** Albania
121 J1 **Korchino** Rus. Fed.
136 D3 **Korchivka** Ukr.
170 C2 **Körchow** Ger.
136 D2 **Korchyk** *r.* Ukr.
188 F4 **Korčula** Croatia
188 F4 **Korčula** *i.* Croatia
188 F4 **Korčulanski Kanal** *sea chan.* Croatia
175 K3 **Korczew** Pol.
175 J6 **Korczyna** Pol.
121 H4 **Korday** *Zhambylskaya Oblast'* Kazakh.
172 A2 **Kordel** Ger.
136 E3 **Kordelivka** Ukr.
122 A3 **Kordestān** *prov.* Iran
127 H4 **Kord Khvord** Iran
122 C2 **Kord Kūy** Iran
134 L4 **Kordon** Rus. Fed.
101 C4 **Korea, North** *country* Asia
101 C5 **Korea, South** *country* Asia
101 C5 **Korea Bay** *g.* China/N. Korea
103 D6 **Korea Strait** Japan/S. Korea
114 B2 **Koregaon** *Mahar.* India
136 C3 **Korelychi** Ukr.
210 C1 **Korem** Eth.
137 I2 **Koren'** *r.* Rus. Fed.
137 H2 **Korenevo** Rus. Fed.
176 E1 **Kořenov** Czech Rep.
135 G7 **Korenovsk** Rus. Fed.
Korenovskaya Rus. Fed. *see* **Korenovsk**
206 C3 **Koréra-Koré** Mali
136 D2 **Korets'** Ukr.
131 R3 **Korf** Rus. Fed.
174 F5 **Korfantów** Pol.
199 F1 **Körfez** Turkey
262 T1 **Korff Ice Rise** Antarctica
100 E2 **Korfovskiy** Rus. Fed.
110 C2 **Korgas** *Xinjiang* China
140 K2 **Korgen** Norway
129 F3 **Korgöz** Azer.
199 G2 **Körhasan** Turkey
206 D4 **Korhogo** Côte d'Ivoire
206 C5 **Koribundu** Sierra Leone
116 B5 **Kori Creek** *inlet Gujarat* India
214 B5 **Koringberg** S. Africa
214 C5 **Koringplaas** S. Africa
80 E3 **Koriniti** *North I.* N.Z.
198 C1 **Korinos** Greece
142 D4 **Korinth** Denmark
198 C2 **Korinthiakos Kolpos** *sea chan.* Greece
198 C3 **Korinthos** Greece
177 G4 **Kőris-hegy** *hill* Hungary
Koritsa Albania *see* **Korçë**
103 J5 **Kōriyama** Japan
122 D2 **Korkī** Iran
130 H4 **Korkino** Rus. Fed.
131 Q3 **Korkodon** *r.* Rus. Fed.
199 G2 **Körküler** Turkey
199 G3 **Korkuteli** Turkey
110 D3 **Korla** *Xinjiang* China
169 E4 **Körle** Ger.
196 D4 **Korman** *mt.* Yugo.
176 F4 **Körmend** Hungary
175 L6 **Kornalovychi** Ukr.
188 E4 **Kornat** *i.* Croatia
169 F4 **Körner** Ger.
Korneshty Moldova *see* **Corneşti**
179 H2 **Korneuburg** Austria
121 H2 **Korneyevka** *Karagandinskaya Oblast'* Kazakh.
121 G1 **Korneyevka** *Severnyy Kazakhstan* Kazakh.
120 B2 **Korneyevka** Rus. Fed.
174 F3 **Kórnik** Pol.
121 J1 **Kornilovo** Rus. Fed.
Kornisi Georgia *see* **Qornisi**
172 D3 **Kornwestheim** Ger.
177 H4 **Környe** Hungary
136 E2 **Kornyn** Ukr.
206 D4 **Koro** Côte d'Ivoire
79 □1 **Koro** *i.* Fiji
93 B3 **Koro** *r.* Indon.
206 E3 **Koro** Mali
225 H1 **Koroc** *r. Que.* Can.
135 G6 **Korocha** Rus. Fed.
137 I2 **Korocha** *r.* Rus. Fed.
126 D2 **Köroğlu Dağları** *mts* Turkey
126 D2 **Köroğlu Tepesi** *mt.* Turkey
211 C6 **Korogwe** Tanz.
136 B3 **Koroleve** Ukr.
81 □3 **Koromiri** *i. Rarotonga* Cook Is
198 B3 **Koroni** Greece
198 C1 **Koronia, Limni** *l.* Greece
174 F2 **Koronowo** Pol.
137 G2 **Korop** Ukr.
198 C3 **Koropi** Greece
92 □ **Koror** Palau
196 E2 **Körös** *r.* Romania
177 I5 **Körös-ér** *r.* Hungary
177 K5 **Körösladány** Hungary
177 K4 **Körösszakál** Hungary
177 K5 **Köröstarcsa** Hungary
136 E2 **Korosten'** Ukr.
136 E2 **Korostyshiv** Ukr.
134 M1 **Korotaikha** *r.* Rus. Fed.
196 E4 **Korotnik** *mt.* Albania
135 G6 **Korotoyak** Rus. Fed.
Korovino Rus. Fed. *see* **Solntsevo**
79 □1a **Korovou** *Viti Levu* Fiji
137 G2 **Korovyntsi** Ukr.
139 L3 **Korozhechna** *r.* Rus. Fed.
172 A2 **Körperich** Ger.
141 N3 **Korpilahti** Fin.
140 M2 **Korpilombolo** Sweden
141 M3 **Korpo** Fin.
Korppoo Fin. *see* **Korpo**
129 E4 **Korrnidzor** Armenia
137 H4 **Korsak** *r.* Ukr.
100 G3 **Korsakov** *Sakhalin* Rus. Fed.
139 K5 **Korsakovo** Rus. Fed.
143 F3 **Korsberga** Sweden
137 K2 **Korshevo** Rus. Fed.
141 K3 **Korskrogen** Sweden
140 M3 **Korsnäs** Fin.
138 E1 **Korso** Fin.
142 D4 **Korsør** Denmark
137 F3 **Korsun'-Shevchenkivs'kyy** Ukr.
Korsun'-Shevchenkovskiy Ukr. *see* **Korsun'-Shevchenkivs'kyy**
143 I4 **Korsze** Pol.
136 C2 **Kortelisy** Ukr.
165 C3 **Kortemark** Belgium
140 M3 **Kortesjärvi** Fin.
165 E4 **Kortessem** Belgium
164 C3 **Kortgene** Neth.
203 F5 **Korti** Sudan
134 J3 **Kortkeros** Rus. Fed.
165 C4 **Kortrijk** Belgium
134 H4 **Kortsovo** Rus. Fed.
128 A1 **Korualan** Turkey
199 E2 **Korucu** Turkey
83 F4 **Korumburra** *Vic.* Austr.
116 D4 **Korwai** *Madh. Prad.* India
131 Q4 **Koryakskaya, Sopka** *vol.* Rus. Fed.
131 S3 **Koryakskiy Khrebet** *mts* Rus. Fed.
134 I3 **Koryazhma** Rus. Fed.
176 G2 **Koryčany** Czech Rep.
175 L2 **Korycin** Pol.
104 B4 **Kōryō** Japan
101 D6 **Koryŏng** S. Korea
175 J3 **Korytnica** Pol.
137 G2 **Koryukivka** Ukr.
175 I6 **Korzenna** Pol.
120 C2 **Korzhun** Kazakh.
199 E3 **Kos** *Notio Aigaio* Greece
199 E3 **Kos** *i.* Greece
134 K4 **Kosa** Rus. Fed.
134 K3 **Kosa** *r.* Rus. Fed.
136 F2 **Kosachivka** Ukr.
120 E2 **Kosagal** Kazakh.
104 D4 **Kosai** Japan
174 G1 **Kosakowo** Pol.
101 C5 **Kosan** N. Korea
138 E5 **Kosava** Belarus
139 K4 **Kosaya Gora** Rus. Fed.
120 C3 **Koschagyl** Kazakh.
173 F3 **Kösching** Ger.
179 F4 **Koschutnikturm** *mt.* Austria/Slovenia
174 E3 **Kościan** Pol.
174 G3 **Kościelec** Pol.
174 G4 **Kościelna Wieś** Pol.
143 G4 **Kościerzyna** Pol.
237 F5 **Kosciusko** *MS* U.S.A.
Kosciusko, Mount *N.S.W.* Austr. *see* **Kosciuszko, Mount**
83 G4 **Kosciuszko, Mount** *N.S.W.* Austr.
138 E2 **Kose** Estonia
129 A3 **Köse** Turkey
177 H2 **Košeca** Slovakia
128 A1 **Köseçobanlı** Turkey
129 C4 **Köse Dağı** *mt.* Turkey
126 E2 **Köse Dağı** *mt.* Turkey
199 E2 **Kösedere** Turkey
168 E1 **Kosel** Ger.
177 K4 **Kösély** *r.* Hungary
170 F1 **Koserow** Ger.
114 C2 **Kosgi** *Andhra Prad.* India
106 A1 **Kosh-Agach** Rus. Fed.
120 B2 **Koshankol'** Kazakh.
105 F3 **Koshigaya** Japan
103 D8 **Koshikijima-rettō** *is* Japan
103 D8 **Koshiki-kaikyō** *sea chan.* Japan
122 E3 **Koshkak** Iran
135 J5 **Koshki** Rus. Fed.
120 E4 **Koshkupyr** Uzbek.
136 D3 **Koshlyaky** Ukr.
137 H3 **Koshmanivka** Ukr.
105 E2 **Kōshoku** Japan
121 F4 **Koshrabad** Uzbek.
116 D4 **Kosi** *Uttar Prad.* India
116 D3 **Kosi** *r.* India
177 K3 **Košice** Slovakia
177 K3 **Košický Kraj** *admin. reg.* Slovakia
114 C3 **Kosigi** *Andhra Prad.* India
117 F4 **Kosi Reservoir** Nepal
120 D2 **Kos-Istek** Kazakh.
136 C3 **Kosiv** Ukr.
137 G3 **Kosivka** Ukr.
196 D4 **Kosjerić** *Srbija* Yugo.
199 F3 **Köşk** Turkey
Koski Fin. *see* **Hämeenkoski**
140 M2 **Koskullskulle** Sweden
134 J3 **Koslan** Rus. Fed.
Köslin Pol. *see* **Koszalin**
134 J2 **Kosma** *r.* Rus. Fed.
171 F5 **Kosmonosy** Czech Rep.
139 M3 **Kosmynino** Rus. Fed.
188 G3 **Košnica** *r.* Croatia
174 F2 **Kosobudy** Pol.
Koson Uzbek. *see* **Kasan**
101 D5 **Kosŏng** N. Korea
Kosonsoy Uzbek. *see* **Kasansay**
Kosova *prov.* Yugo. *see* **Kosovo**
196 E4 **Kosovo** *prov.* Yugo.
Kosovo-Metohija *prov.* Yugo. *see* **Kosovo**
196 E4 **Kosovo Polje** *Kosovo, Srbija* Yugo.
196 E4 **Kosovo Polje** *plain* Yugo.
197 E4 **Kosovska Kamenica** *Kosovo, Srbija* Yugo.
196 E4 **Kosovska Mitrovica** *Kosovo, Srbija* Yugo.
175 K3 **Kosów Lacki** Pol.
266 F5 **Kosrae** *atoll* Micronesia
128 B1 **Kösreli** Turkey
171 E4 **Koßdorf** Ger.
173 F2 **Kösseine** *hill* Ger.
178 D3 **Kössen** Austria
173 H3 **Kößlar** *r.* Ger.
206 D5 **Kossou, Lac de** *l.* Côte d'Ivoire
Kosta-Khetagurovo Rus. Fed. *see* **Nazran'**
120 E1 **Kostanay** Kazakh.
176 D2 **Kostelec nad Černými Lesy** Czech Rep.
171 F5 **Kostelec nad Labem** Czech Rep.
176 F1 **Kostelec nad Orlicí** Czech Rep.
197 F4 **Kostenets** Bulg.
215 F1 **Koster** S. Africa
139 L4 **Kosterevo** Rus. Fed.
203 G6 **Kosti** Sudan
179 H2 **Kostice** Czech Rep.
197 F4 **Kostinbrod** Bulg.
130 J3 **Kostino** Rus. Fed.
196 E3 **Kostolac** *Srbija* Yugo.
174 E4 **Kostomłoty** Pol.
140 O2 **Kostomuksha** Rus. Fed.
136 D2 **Kostopil'** Ukr.
Kostopol' Ukr. *see* **Kostopil'**
139 M3 **Kostroma** Rus. Fed.
134 H4 **Kostroma** *r.* Rus. Fed.
Kostroma Oblast *admin. div.* Rus. Fed. *see* **Kostromskaya Oblast'**
134 H4 **Kostromskaya Oblast'** *admin. div.* Rus. Fed.
174 C3 **Kostrzyn** *Lubuskie* Pol.
174 F3 **Kostrzyn** *Wielkopolskie* Pol.
175 K3 **Kostrzyń** *r.* Pol.
137 I3 **Kostyantynivka** *Donets'ka Oblast'* Ukr.
137 H3 **Kostyantynivka** *Kharkivs'ka Oblast'* Ukr.
137 G4 **Kostyantynivka** *Khersons'ka Oblast'* Ukr.
137 H4 **Kostyantynivka** *Zaporiz'ka Oblast'* Ukr.
Kostyukovichi Belarus *see* **Kastsyukovichy**
177 L3 **Kosyny** Ukr.
134 L2 **Kos'yu** *r.* Rus. Fed.
143 G4 **Koszalin** Pol.
174 G5 **Koszęcin** Pol.
176 F4 **Kőszeg** Hungary
179 H3 **Kőszegi-hegység** *hill* Hungary
175 I5 **Koszyce** Pol.
114 D3 **Kota** *Andhra Prad.* India
116 E5 **Kota** *Madh. Prad.* India
116 C4 **Kota** *Rajasthan* India
94 D4 **Kotaagung** *Sumatera* Indon.
Kota Baharu Malaysia *see* **Kota Bharu**
95 G3 **Kotabaru** *Kalimantan Selatan* Indon.
94 C1 **Kota Bharu** Malaysia
94 D4 **Kotabumi** *Sumatera* Indon.
123 G4 **Kot Addu** Pak.
95 G1 **Kota Kinabalu** *Sabah* Malaysia
93 C2 **Kotamobagu** *Sulawesi Utara* Indon.
222 E2 **Kotaneelee Range** *mts N.W.T./Y.T.* Can.
121 I3 **Kotanemel', Gora** *mt.* Kazakh.
94 C2 **Kotapinang** *Sumatera* Indon.
116 E4 **Kotar** *Madh. Prad.* India
116 C4 **Kotari** *r.* India
95 E2 **Kota Samarahan** *Sarawak* Malaysia
94 C2 **Kota Tinggi** Malaysia
117 G5 **Kotchandpur** Bangl.
222 F3 **Kotcho** *r. B.C.* Can.
123 G5 **Kot Diji** Pak.
116 D3 **Kotdwara** *Uttar Prad.* India
177 K5 **Kötegyán** Hungary
197 H4 **Kotel** Bulg.
177 J4 **Kötelek** Hungary
134 J4 **Kotel'nich** Rus. Fed.
135 H7 **Kotel'nikovo** Rus. Fed.
131 O2 **Kotel'nyy, Ostrov** *i. Novosibirskiye O-va* Rus. Fed.
170 E2 **Kotelow** Ger.
137 H2 **Kotel'va** Ukr.
80 F3 **Kotemaori** *North I.* N.Z.
115 D2 **Kotgar** *Orissa* India
116 D3 **Kotgarh** *Hima. Prad.* India
Kothagudem *Andhra Prad.* India *see* **Kottagudem**
171 C4 **Köthen (Anhalt)** Ger.
116 E4 **Kothi** *Madh. Prad.* India
206 B3 **Kotiari Naoude** Senegal
210 B4 **Kotido** Uganda
141 N3 **Kotka** Fin.
116 C3 **Kot Kapura** *Punjab* India
174 E4 **Kotla** Pol.
134 I3 **Kotlas** Rus. Fed.
123 H3 **Kotli** Pak.
220 B3 **Kotlik** *AK* U.S.A.
174 F4 **Kotlin** Pol.
175 J5 **Kotlina Sandomierska** *basin* Pol.
138 G2 **Kotly** Rus. Fed.
207 G4 **Koton-Karifi** Nigeria
196 D4 **Kotor** *Crna Gora* Yugo.
179 H4 **Kotoriba** Croatia
207 G3 **Kotorkoshi** Nigeria
139 L3 **Kotorosl'** *r.* Rus. Fed.
188 G3 **Kotorsko** Bos.-Herz.
188 F3 **Kotor Varoš** Bos.-Herz.
137 H3 **Kotovka** Ukr.
135 I6 **Kotovo** Rus. Fed.
Kotovsk Moldova *see* **Hînceşti**
135 H5 **Kotovsk** Rus. Fed.
136 E4 **Kotovs'k** Ukr.
116 D4 **Kot Putli** *Rajasthan* India
138 E5 **Kotra** *r.* Belarus
114 D2 **Kotri** *r.* India
123 G5 **Kotri** Pak.
178 E4 **Kötschach** Austria
114 D2 **Kottagudem** *Andhra Prad.* India
114 C4 **Kottayam** *Kerala* India
114 B4 **Kottayam** *Pondicherry* India
Kotte Sri Lanka *see* **Sri Jayewardenepura Kotte**
169 C5 **Kottenheim** Ger.
179 G2 **Kottes** Austria
179 F4 **Köttmannsdorf** Austria
208 D3 **Kotto** *r.* C.A.R.
114 C3 **Kotturu** *Karnataka* India
79 □2 **Kotu Group** *is* Tonga
175 K3 **Kotuń** Pol.
122 C2 **Koturdepe** Turkm.
131 L2 **Kotuy** *r.* Rus. Fed.
117 E5 **Kotwar Peak** *Madh. Prad.* India
Kotyuzhany Moldova *see* **Cotiujeni**
173 E3 **Kötz** Ger.
220 B3 **Kotzebue** *AK* U.S.A.
220 B3 **Kotzebue Sound** *sea chan. AK* U.S.A.
214 A3 **Kotzehoop** S. Africa
214 A4 **Kotzesrus** S. Africa
173 G2 **Kötzting** Ger.
208 D3 **Kouango** C.A.R.
206 C4 **Koubia** Guinea
166 A3 **Koudekerke** Neth.
206 E3 **Koudougou** Burkina
164 E2 **Koudum** Neth.
198 C1 **Koufalia** Greece
199 D3 **Koufonisi** *i.* Greece
214 E5 **Kouga** *r.* S. Africa
214 D5 **Kougaberge** *mts* S. Africa
208 B3 **Koui** C.A.R.
206 D5 **Kouibli** Côte d'Ivoire
209 A6 **Kouilou** *admin. reg.* Congo
206 D4 **Kouka** Burkina
208 C3 **Koukourou** *r.* C.A.R.
208 B5 **Koulamoutou** Gabon
206 D3 **Koulikoro** Mali
206 D3 **Koulikoro** *admin. reg.* Mali
207 I4 **Koum** Cameroon
208 C3 **Kouma** *r.* C.A.R.
78 □5 **Koumac** New Caledonia
85 G4 **Koumala** *Qld* Austr.
206 E4 **Koumbia** Burkina
206 B4 **Koumbia** Guinea
208 C2 **Koumra** Chad
206 B3 **Koundâra** Guinea
206 C3 **Koundian** Mali
206 D4 **Koundougou** Burkina
206 B3 **Koungheul** Senegal
217 □3b **Koungou** Mayotte
206 B3 **Kounkané** Senegal
121 H3 **Kounradskiy** *Karagandinskaya Oblast'* Kazakh.
Kounradskiy *Karagandinskaya Oblast'* Kazakh. *see* **Konyrat**
206 B4 **Kounsitél** Guinea
237 E6 **Kountze** *TX* U.S.A.
214 C5 **Koup** S. Africa
206 E3 **Koupéla** Burkina
Kouqian *Jilin* China *see* **Yongji**
217 □3a **Kourani** *Njazidja* Comoros
176 D2 **Kouřim** Czech Rep.
251 H3 **Kourou** Fr. Guiana
198 D1 **Kourou** *r.* Greece
206 C2 **Kouroudjél** Maur.
206 C4 **Kouroussa** Guinea
206 B3 **Koussanar** Senegal
206 C3 **Koussané** Mali
207 I3 **Kousséri** Cameroon
207 F4 **Koussountou** Togo
206 D3 **Koutiala** Mali
173 G2 **Kout na Šumav** Czech Rep.
206 D4 **Kouto** Côte d'Ivoire
198 C3 **Koutsopodi** *Peloponnisos* Greece
141 N3 **Kouvola** Fin.
208 C5 **Kouyou** *r.* Congo

196 E3 Kovačica Vojvodina, Srbija Yugo.
177 H5 Kővágószőlős Hungary
136 F3 Kovalivka Ukr.
134 B2 Kovallberget Sweden
177 H3 Kovarce Slovakia
176 C1 Kovářská Czech Rep.
137 F2 Kovchyn Ukr.
140 O2 Kovdor Rus. Fed.
136 C2 Kovel' Ukr.
134 H4 Kovernino Rus. Fed.
196 E3 Kovilj Vojvodina, Srbija Yugo.
114 C4 Kovilpatti Tamil Nadu India
196 E3 Kovin Vojvodina, Srbija Yugo.
Kovno Lith. see Kaunas
134 J2 Kovriga, Gora hill Rus. Fed.
139 M3 Kovrov Rus. Fed.
137 J3 Kovsuh r. Ukr.
137 H3 Kov"yahy Ukr.
135 H5 Kovylkino Rus. Fed.
139 K1 Kovzhskoye, Ozero l. Rus. Fed.
175 H3 Kowal Pol.
174 G4 Kowale Pol.
175 K1 Kowale Oleckie Pol.
174 G4 Kowale-Pańskie Pol.
174 G2 Kowalewo Pomorskie Pol.
85 E2 Kowanyama Qld Austr.
174 D5 Kowary Pol.
81 C5 Kowhitirangi South I. N.Z.
175 I4 Kowiesy Pol.
109 □ Kowloon H.K. China
109 □ Kowloon Peninsula H.K. China
206 C5 Koyama Guinea
199 F3 Köyceğiz Turkey
134 J3 Koygorodok Rus. Fed.
122 C1 Koymatdag, Gory hills Turkm.
197 G4 Koynare Bulg.
134 L3 Koyp, Gora mt. Rus. Fed.
220 C3 Koyukuk r. AK U.S.A.
126 E2 Koyulhisar Turkey
207 I4 Koza Cameroon
134 G4 Koza Rus. Fed.
137 I2 Kozacha Lopan' Ukr.
Kozağacı Turkey see Günyüzü
126 D3 Kozan Turkey
198 B1 Kozani Greece
188 F3 Kozara mts Bos.-Herz.
177 H5 Kozármisleny Hungary
137 F2 Kozarn Ukr.
177 H3 Kozárovce Slovakia
Kozarska Dubica Bos.-Herz. see Bosanska Dubica
137 G4 Kozats'ke Ukr.
137 G2 Kozats'ke Ukr.
137 F2 Kozelets' Ukr.
137 G3 Kozel'shchyna Ukr.
139 J4 Kozel'sk Rus. Fed.
120 E3 Kozhabakhy Kazakh.
136 E3 Kozhanka Ukr.
Kozhikode Kerala India see Calicut
134 L3 Kozhim-Iz, Gora mt. Rus. Fed.
136 D3 Kozhukliv Ukr.
134 L2 Kozhva Rus. Fed.
134 L2 Kozhva r. Rus. Fed.
134 L2 Kozhym r. Rus. Fed.
175 H5 Koziegłowy Pol.
174 C2 Kozielice Pol.
175 J4 Kozienice Pol.
137 H2 Koziyivka Ukr.
176 C2 Kožlany Czech Rep.
197 F4 Kozloduy Bulg.
177 H2 Kozlovice Czech Rep.
134 J5 Kozlovka Chuvashskaya Respublika Rus. Fed.
135 I5 Kozlovka Respublika Mordoviya Rus. Fed.
135 H6 Kozlovka Voronezhskaya Oblast' Rus. Fed.
137 K2 Kozlovka Voronezhskaya Oblast' Rus. Fed.
139 K3 Kozlovo Rus. Fed.
175 I5 Kozłów Pol.
175 I3 Kozłów Biskupi Pol.
175 I2 Kozłowo Pol.
126 C2 Kozlu Turkey
199 G3 Kozluca Turkey
188 G3 Kozluk Bos.-Herz.
174 F4 Koźmin Pol.
174 G4 Koźminek Pol.
134 I4 Koz'modem'yansk Rus. Fed.
121 G4 Kozmoldak Kazakh.
197 F4 Koznitsa mt. Bulg.
136 C3 Kozova Ukr.
175 K4 Kozubszczyzna Pol.
174 D4 Kożuchów Pol.
197 F5 Kožuf mts Greece/Macedonia
136 E3 Kozyatyn Ukr.
137 G2 Kozylivka Ukr.
136 F2 Kozyn Kyivs'ka Oblast' Ukr.
137 F3 Kozyn Kyivs'ka Oblast' Ukr.
199 E1 Kozyörük Turkey
137 F4 Kozyrka Ukr.
207 F5 Kpalimé Togo
207 E4 Kpandae Ghana
207 F5 Kpandu Ghana
207 F5 Kpedze Ghana
97 B5 Kra, Isthmus of Thai.
215 F4 Kraai r. S. Africa
214 E3 Kraankuil S. Africa
165 D3 Krabbendijke Neth.
97 B5 Krabi Thai.
97 B5 Kra Buri Thai.
97 D4 Krâchéh Cambodia
141 K3 Kräckelbäcken Sweden
170 F2 Krackow Ger.
139 J3 Kraftino, Ozero l. Rus. Fed.
171 C5 Kraftsdorf Ger.
95 E4 Kragan Jawa Tengah Indon.
142 C2 Kragerø Norway
164 E2 Kraggenburg Neth.
196 E3 Kragujevac Srbija Yugo.
173 G3 Kraiburg am Inn Ger.
172 C2 Kraichbach r. Ger.
173 F3 Krailling Ger.
174 F2 Krajenka Pol.
94 D4 Krakatau i. Indon.
Krakau Pol. see Kraków
136 B3 Krakovets' Ukr.
175 H5 Kraków Pol.
226 C3 Krakow WI U.S.A.
170 D2 Krakow am See Ger.
170 D2 Krakower See l. Ger.
175 G4 Krakowsko-Częstochowska, Wyżyna plat. Pol.
97 B5 Kra Lenya r. Myanmar
176 F1 Králíky Czech Rep.
188 E3 Kraljeviča Croatia
196 E4 Kraljevo Srbija Yugo.
177 G3 Kráľová, Vodná nádrž resr Slovakia
177 J3 Kráľova hoľa mt. Slovakia
177 G3 Kráľová nad Váhom Slovakia
177 G3 Kráľov Brod Slovakia
176 E1 Královéhradecký kraj admin. reg. Czech Rep.
176 C2 Kralovice Czech Rep.
177 K3 Kráľovský Chlmec Slovakia
176 D1 Kralupy nad Vltavou Czech Rep.
176 D2 Králův Dvůr Czech Rep.
174 F1 Kramarzyny Pol.
137 I3 Kramators'k Ukr.
140 L3 Kramfors Sweden
164 D3 Krammer est. Neth.
178 C3 Kramsach Austria
174 G3 Kramsk Pol.
169 B4 Kranenburg Ger.
198 C3 Kranidi Greece
188 E2 Kranj Slovenia
179 E4 Kranjska Gora Slovenia
215 G3 Kransfontein S. Africa
215 H3 Kranskop S. Africa
215 G2 Kranskop mt. S. Africa
173 F3 Kranzberg Ger.
188 E4 Krapanj Croatia
188 E2 Krapina Croatia
188 E2 Krapinske Toplice Croatia
174 F5 Krapkowice Pol.
179 E5 Kras plat. Slovenia
134 I3 Krasavino Rus. Fed.
137 G3 Krasenivka Ukr.
175 K6 Krasiczyn Pol.
Krasilov Ukr. see Krasyliv
Krasilovka Chernihivs'ka Oblast' Ukr. see Krasylivka
Krasilovka Zhytomyrs'ka Oblast' Ukr. see Krasylivka
175 L6 Krasiv Ukr.
136 C3 Krasiyiv Ukr.
100 D4 Kraskino Rus. Fed.
138 F4 Krāslava Latvia
176 B1 Kraslice Czech Rep.
137 J3 Krasna r. Ukr.
171 F5 Krásná Lípa Czech Rep.
139 H5 Krasnapollye Belarus
137 I4 Krasna Polyana Ukr.
136 F3 Krasna Slobidka Ukr.
138 E5 Krasnasyel'ski Belarus
139 H5 Krasnaya Gora Rus. Fed.
134 H5 Krasnaya Gorbatka Rus. Fed.
121 H2 Krasnaya Polyana Kazakh.
129 B2 Krasnaya Polyana Rus. Fed.
138 F5 Krasnaya Slabada Belarus
137 H2 Krasnaya Yaruga Rus. Fed.
139 K5 Krasnaya Zarya Rus. Fed.
175 I3 Krasne Mazowieckie Pol.
175 K5 Krasne Podkarpackie Pol.
137 F2 Krasne Chernihivs'ka Oblast' Ukr.
137 G2 Krasne Chernihivs'ka Oblast' Ukr.
136 C3 Krasne Ivano-Frankivs'ka Oblast' Ukr.
137 G4 Krasne Khersons'ka Oblast' Ukr.
136 C3 Krasne L'vivs'ka Oblast' Ukr.
136 D3 Krasne Ternopils'ka Oblast' Ukr.
136 E3 Krasne Vinnyts'ka Oblast' Ukr.
175 L5 Kraśniczyn Pol.
175 K5 Kraśnik Pol.
136 E4 Krasni Okny Ukr.
Krasnoarmeysk Kazakh. see Tayynsha
139 L3 Krasnoarmeysk Moskovskaya Oblast' Rus. Fed.
135 I6 Krasnoarmeysk Saratovskaya Oblast' Rus. Fed.
Krasnoarmeysk Ukr. see Krasnoarmiys'k
Krasnoarmeyskaya Rus. Fed. see Poltavskaya
131 S3 Krasnoarmeyskiy Chukotskiy Avtonomnyy Okrug Rus. Fed.
135 H7 Krasnoarmeyskiy Rostovskaya Oblast' Rus. Fed.
Krasnoarmeyskoye Rus. Fed. see Urus-Martan
137 I3 Krasnoarmiys'k Ukr.
134 I3 Krasnoborsk Rus. Fed.
175 L5 Krasnobród Pol.
135 G7 Krasnodar Rus. Fed.
Krasnodar Kray admin. div. Rus. Fed. see Krasnodarskiy Kray
129 A1 Krasnodarskiy Kray admin. div. Rus. Fed.
137 J3 Krasnodon Luhans'ka Oblast' Ukr.
137 J3 Krasnodon Luhans'ka Oblast' Ukr.
139 H2 Krasnofarfornyy Rus. Fed.
Krasnogorka Kazakh. see Ul'ken Sulutar
138 G3 Krasnogorodskoye Rus. Fed.
139 K4 Krasnogorsk Moskovskaya Oblast' Rus. Fed.
100 G2 Krasnogorsk Sakhalin Rus. Fed.
121 K1 Krasnogorskoye Altayskiy Kray Rus. Fed.
134 K4 Krasnogorskoye Udmurtskaya Respublika Rus. Fed.
Krasnograd Ukr. see Krasnohrad
Krasnogvardeysk Uzbek. see Bulungur
139 M3 Krasnogvardeyskiy Rus. Fed.
137 J2 Krasnogvardeyskoye Belgorodskaya Oblast' Rus. Fed.
137 J5 Krasnogvardeyskoye Respublika Adygeya Rus. Fed.
135 H7 Krasnogvardeyskoye Stavropol'skiy Kray Rus. Fed.
137 I3 Krasnohorivka Ukr.
137 H3 Krasnohrad Ukr.
137 H5 Krasnohvardiys'ke Ukr.
107 H1 Krasnokamensk Rus. Fed.
134 K4 Krasnokamsk Rus. Fed.
120 C2 Krasnokholm Rus. Fed.
Krasnokutsk Pavlodarskaya Oblast' Kazakh. see Aktogay
137 H2 Krasnokuts'k Ukr.
Krasnokutskoye Pavlodarskaya Oblast' Kazakh. see Aktogay
135 G6 Krasnolesnyy Rus. Fed.
138 D4 Krasnoles'ye Rus. Fed.
137 J2 Krasnolip'ye Rus. Fed.
139 J3 Krasnomayskiy Rus. Fed.
177 H2 Krásno nad Kysucou Slovakia
137 I3 Krasnopavlivka Ukr.
137 G5 Krasnoperekops'k Ukr.
136 E3 Krasnopil' Ukr.
136 F3 Krasnopilka Ukr.
137 H2 Krasnopillya Ukr.
175 L1 Krasnopol Pol.
100 E3 Krasnorechenskiy Rus. Fed.
Krasnorechenskoye Ukr. see Krasnorichens'ke
137 J3 Krasnorichens'ke Ukr.
130 J3 Krasnosel'kup Rus. Fed.
Krasnoselsk Armenia see Chambarak
121 J2 Krasnoshchekovo Rus. Fed.
175 J2 Krasnosielc Pol.
136 E3 Krasnosilka Vinnyts'ka Oblast' Ukr.
136 D3 Krasnosilka Zhytomyrs'ka Oblast' Ukr.
137 G3 Krasnosillya Ukr.
135 H5 Krasnoslobodsk Rus. Fed.
137 K1 Krasnosvobodnoye Rus. Fed.
130 H4 Krasnotur'insk Rus. Fed.
134 L4 Krasnoufimsk Rus. Fed.
120 D1 Krasnousol'skiy Rus. Fed.
134 L3 Krasnovishersk Rus. Fed.
Krasnovodsk Turkm. see Turkmenbashi
Krasnovodskaya Oblast' admin. div. Turkm. see Balkanskaya Oblast'
122 C2 Krasnovodskiy Zaliv b. Turkm.
122 C1 Krasnovodskoye Plato plat. Turkm.
120 C2 Krasnoyar Kazakh.
100 D2 Krasnoyarovo Rus. Fed.
131 K4 Krasnoyarsk Rus. Fed.
120 D2 Krasnoyarskiy Rus. Fed.
98 F1 Krasnoyarskiy Kray admin. div. Rus. Fed.
Krasnoyarsk Kray admin. div. Rus. Fed. see Krasnoyarskiy Kray
135 G6 Krasnoye Belgorodskaya Oblast' Rus. Fed.
137 J2 Krasnoye Belgorodskaya Oblast' Rus. Fed.
139 I5 Krasnoye Bryanskaya Oblast' Rus. Fed.
134 I4 Krasnoye Kirovskaya Oblast' Rus. Fed.
137 J4 Krasnoye Krasnodarskiy Kray Rus. Fed.
139 L5 Krasnoye Lipetskaya Oblast' Rus. Fed.
Krasnoye Respublika Kalmykiya - Khalm'g-Tangch Rus. Fed. see Ulan Erge
139 H4 Krasnoye Smolenskaya Oblast' Rus. Fed.
131 S3 Krasnoye, Ozero l. Rus. Fed.
139 M4 Krasnoye Ekho Rus. Fed.
139 M3 Krasnoye-na-Volge Rus. Fed.
139 L3 Krasnoye Plamya Rus. Fed.
139 J3 Krasnoye Znamya Rus. Fed.
136 C3 Krasnoyil's'k Ukr.
134 J3 Krasnozatonskiy Rus. Fed.
139 L3 Krasnozavodsk Rus. Fed.
138 D4 Krasnoznamensk Rus. Fed.
Krasnoznamenskiy Kazakh. see Krasnoznamenskoye
121 G2 Krasnoznamenskoye Kazakh.
137 G4 Krasnoznam"yanka Ukr.
175 L5 Krasnystaw Pol.
139 H4 Krasnyy Rus. Fed.
107 F1 Krasnyy Chikoy Rus. Fed.
134 I4 Krasnyye Baki Rus. Fed.
135 I7 Krasnyye Barrikady Rus. Fed.
139 L3 Krasnyye Tkachi Rus. Fed.
Krasnyy Kamyshanik Rus. Fed. see Komsomol'skiy
139 K2 Krasnyy Kholm Rus. Fed.
120 A2 Krasnyy Kut Rus. Fed.
137 J2 Krasnyy Liman Rus. Fed.
139 H3 Krasnyy Luch Rus. Fed.
137 J3 Krasnyy Luch Ukr.
137 I3 Krasnyy Lyman Ukr.
139 L3 Krasnyy Oktyabr' Rus. Fed.
139 M3 Krasnyy Profintern Rus. Fed.
137 K4 Krasnyy Sulin Rus. Fed.
135 I6 Krasnyy Tekstil'shchik Rus. Fed.
121 G1 Krasnyy Yar Kazakh.
120 B3 Krasnyy Yar Astrakhanskaya Oblast' Rus. Fed.
120 B1 Krasnyy Yar Samarskaya Oblast' Rus. Fed.
135 I6 Krasnyy Yar Volgogradskaya Oblast' Rus. Fed.
175 I5 Krasocin Pol.
136 E2 Krasyatychi Ukr.
136 D3 Krasyliv Ukr.
137 F2 Krasylivka Chernihivs'ka Oblast' Ukr.
136 E2 Krasylivka Zhytomyrs'ka Oblast' Ukr.
174 G4 Kraszewice Pol.
175 I1 Kraszewo Pol.
177 L3 Kraszna r. Hungary
Kratie Cambodia see Krâchéh
197 F4 Kratovo Macedonia
172 D3 Krauchenwies Ger.
138 F4 Krauja Latvia
262 X2 Kraul Mountains Antarctica
171 F4 Krauschwitz Ger.
172 D2 Krautheim Ger.
Krâvanh, Chuŏr Phnum mts Cambodia see Cardomom Range
177 H2 Kravaře Czech Rep.
129 E2 Kraynovka Rus. Fed.
171 F4 Kreba-Neudorf Ger.
169 F4 Krebeck Ger.
139 H2 Krechevitsy Rus. Fed.
169 B4 Krefeld Ger.
169 E4 Kreiensen Ger.
164 E2 Kreileroord Neth.
171 E5 Kreischa Ger.
138 E4 Krekenava Lith.
198 B2 Kremaston, Techniti Limni resr Greece
188 E3 Kremen mt. Croatia
Kremenchug Ukr. see Kremenchuk
137 G3 Kremenchuk Ukr.
137 G3 Kremenchuts'ka Vodoskhovyshche resr Ukr.
136 C2 Kremenets' Ukr.
139 K4 Kremenki Rus. Fed.
176 E2 Křemešník hill Czech Rep.
Kremges Ukr. see Svitlovods'k
137 J3 Kreminna Ukr.
136 C3 Kremintsi Ukr.
Kreml' Rus. Fed. see Solovetskiy
170 E3 Kremmen Ger.
238 F3 Kremmling CO U.S.A.
177 H3 Kremnica Slovakia
168 E2 Krempe Ger.
175 J6 Krempna Pol.
179 G2 Krems r. Austria
179 G2 Krems an der Donau Austria
179 F2 Kremsmünster Austria
176 D3 Křemže Czech Rep.
179 H2 Křepice Czech Rep.
137 J4 Krepkaya r. Rus. Fed./Ukr.
197 E3 Krepoljin Srbija Yugo.
234 C2 Kresgeville PA U.S.A.
171 F5 Křešice Czech Rep.
197 F5 Kresna Bulg.
172 D4 Kressbronn am Bodensee Ger.
131 T3 Kresta, Zaliv g. Rus. Fed.
198 B3 Krestena Greece
131 O3 Krest-Khal'dzhayy Rus. Fed.
139 I2 Kresttsy Rus. Fed.
138 C4 Kretinga Lith.
171 D4 Kretzschau Ger.
173 F4 Kreuth Ger.
169 B5 Kreuzau Ger.
178 E4 Kreuzeck mt. Austria
178 C3 Kreuzjoch mt. Austria
190 E1 Kreuzlingen Switz.
169 C5 Kreuztal Ger.
172 D2 Kreuzwertheim Ger.
207 H6 Kribi Cameroon
Krichev Belarus see Krychaw
197 G4 Krichim Bulg.
179 G3 Krieglach Austria
190 C1 Kriegstetten Switz.
215 G2 Kriel S. Africa
170 E2 Krien Ger.
190 D1 Kriens Switz.
138 C3 Krievukalns hill Latvia
198 B2 Krikellos Greece
Krikovo Moldova see Cricova
179 F5 Krim mt. Slovenia
208 B2 Krim-Krim Chad
164 D3 Krimpen aan de IJssel Neth.
176 E1 Křinec Czech Rep.
198 D1 Krinides Greece
Kripka r. Rus. Fed./Ukr. see Krepkaya
179 E3 Krippenstein mt. Austria
114 D2 Krishna r. India
114 D3 Krishna, Mouths of the India
114 C3 Krishnagiri Tamil Nadu India
117 G4 Krishnai r. India
117 G5 Krishnanagar W. Bengal India
114 C3 Krishnarajpet Karnataka India
143 G3 Kristdala Sweden
Kristiania Norway see Oslo
142 B2 Kristiansand Norway
143 F3 Kristianstad Sweden
140 I3 Kristiansund Norway
Kristiinankaupunki Fin. see Kristinestad
143 F2 Kristinehamn Sweden
141 M3 Kristinestad Fin.
Kristinopol' Ukr. see Chervonohrad
198 D4 Kriti admin. reg. Greece
198 D4 Kriti i. Greece
170 D1 Kritzmow Ger.
Kriulyany Moldova see Criuleni
139 L4 Kriusha Rus. Fed.
196 E4 Krivača mt. Yugo.
188 G3 Krivaja r. Bos.-Herz.
177 I6 Krivaja r. Yugo.
139 L4 Krivandino Rus. Fed.
197 F4 Kriva Palanka Macedonia
197 E4 Kriva Reka r. Macedonia
196 E5 Krivogaštani Macedonia
176 C2 Křivoklátská Vrchovina hills Czech Rep.
139 L5 Krivopolyan'ye Rus. Fed.
135 H6 Krivorozh'ye Rus. Fed.
134 F2 Krivoy Porog Rus. Fed.
Krivoy Rog Ukr. see Kryvyy Rih
176 F2 Křižanov Czech Rep.
188 F2 Križevci Croatia
188 G3 Krk mt. Bos.-Herz.
188 E3 Krk Croatia
188 E3 Krk i. Croatia
188 E4 Krka r. Croatia
188 E3 Krka r. Slovenia
176 E1 Krkonoše mts Czech Rep.
179 E4 Krn mt. Slovenia
196 E3 Krnjača Srbija Yugo.
177 G1 Krnov Czech Rep.
174 E4 Krobia Pol.
175 H5 Kroczyce Pol.
171 E4 Krögis Ger.
206 D5 Krohnwodoke Liberia
Krokeaí Greece see Krokees
198 C3 Krokees Greece
143 G2 Krokek Sweden
140 K3 Krokom Sweden
143 H4 Krokowa Pol.
140 J3 Krokstadøra Norway
137 G2 Krolevets' Ukr.
Królewska Huta Pol. see Chorzów
175 L2 Królowy Most Pol.
171 C5 Krölpa Ger.
215 E6 Krom r. S. Africa
139 J5 Kroma r. Rus. Fed.
215 G1 Kromdraai S. Africa
176 G2 Kroměříž Czech Rep.
164 D2 Krommenie Neth.
177 J3 Krompachy Slovakia
171 C5 Kromsdorf Ger.
139 J5 Kromy Rus. Fed.
171 C5 Kronach Ger.
172 C2 Kronau Ger.
169 D5 Kronberg im Taunus Ger.
142 C2 Kronfjell hill Norway
97 C5 Krŏng Kaôh Kŏng Cambodia
143 F3 Kronoberg county Sweden
140 M3 Kronoby Fin.
131 R4 Kronotskiy Zaliv b. Rus. Fed.
221 P1 Kronprins Christian Land reg. Greenland
221 O3 Kronprins Frederik Bjerge nunataks Greenland
168 D2 Kronprinzenkoog Ger.
168 F1 Kronshagen Ger.
138 G2 Kronshtadt Rus. Fed.
Kronstadt Romania see Brașov
Kronstadt Rus. Fed. see Kronshtadt
179 F2 Kronstorf Austria
215 F2 Kroonstad S. Africa
170 C1 Kröpelin Ger.
135 H7 Kropotkin Rus. Fed.
168 E1 Kropp Ger.
171 C4 Kroppenstedt Ger.
171 D4 Kropstädt Ger.
175 I6 Krościenko nad Dunajcem Pol.
170 E1 Kröslin Ger.
174 F4 Krośnice Pol.
175 H3 Krośniewice Pol.
175 J6 Krosno Pol.
174 D3 Krosno Odrzańskie Pol.
171 C5 Krossen Ger.
171 D4 Krostitz Ger.
174 E4 Krotoszyce Pol.
174 F4 Krotoszyn Pol.
179 G3 Krottendorf Austria
237 F6 Krotz Springs LA U.S.A.
176 F2 Krouna Czech Rep.
198 D4 Krousonas Kriti Greece
172 B2 Kröv Ger.
95 E4 Kroya Jawa Tengah Indon.
191 J3 Kršan Croatia
188 E3 Krško Slovenia
196 E4 Krstača mt. Yugo.
174 F3 Kruchowo Pol.
170 C3 Krüden Ger.
169 C5 Kruft Ger.
215 H1 Kruger National Park S. Africa
215 F2 Krugersdorp S. Africa
129 C1 Kruglolesskoye Rus. Fed.
Kruglyakov Rus. Fed. see Oktyabr'skiy
138 G4 Kruhlaye Belarus
94 C4 Krui Sumatera Indon.
214 C5 Kruidfontein S. Africa
165 D3 Kruiningen Neth.
215 E6 Kruisfontein S. Africa
165 C4 Kruishoutem Belgium
196 D5 Krujë Albania
175 L6 Krukenychi Ukr.
175 J1 Kruklanki Pol.
175 J2 Krukowo Pol.
179 H3 Krumbach Austria
173 E3 Krumbach (Schwaben) Ger.
196 E4 Krumë Albania
168 F2 Krummesse Ger.
197 G5 Krumovgrad Bulg.
171 C4 Krumpa (Geiseltal) Ger.
179 F4 Krumpendorf am Wörther See Austria
173 F4 Krün Ger.
Krungkao Thai. see Ayutthaya
Krung Thep Thai. see Bangkok
138 D3 Kruoja r. Lith.
Krupa Bos.-Herz. see Bosanska Krupa
Krupa na Uni Bos.-Herz. see Bosanska Krupa
196 D3 Krupanj Srbija Yugo.
175 L4 Krupe Pol.
177 I3 Krupina Slovakia
177 H3 Krupinica r. Slovakia
177 I3 Krupinská Planina plat. Slovakia
176 C1 Krupka Czech Rep.
138 G4 Krupki Belarus
137 G3 Krupodernytsi Ukr.
174 G5 Krupski Młyn Pol.
168 E1 Kruså Denmark
196 E4 Kruševac Srbija Yugo.
196 E5 Kruševo Macedonia
176 B1 Krušné Hory mts Czech Rep.
177 H3 Krušovce Slovakia
174 G3 Kruszwica Pol.
174 F1 Kruszyna Pomorskie Pol.
175 H5 Kruszyna Śląskie Pol.
137 J2 Krutchenskaya Baygora Rus. Fed.
139 K5 Krutoye Rus. Fed.
177 K2 Kružlov Slovakia
138 G4 Krybinka r. Belarus
139 H5 Krychaw Belarus
196 E4 Kryezi Albania
136 D2 Kryliv Ukr.
264 H4 Krylov Seamount sea feature N. Atlantic Ocean
137 J4 Krylovskaya Krasnodarskiy Kray Rus. Fed.
137 J4 Krylovskaya Krasnodarskiy Kray Rus. Fed.
175 M5 Kryłów Pol.
Krym' aut. rep. Ukr. see Krym, Respublika
Krym' pen. Ukr. see Kryms'kyy Pivostriv
137 H5 Krym, Respublika aut. rep. Ukr.
129 C1 Krymgireyevskoye Rus. Fed.
175 M4 Krymne Ukr.
135 G7 Krymsk Rus. Fed.
Krymskaya Rus. Fed. see Krymsk
137 J3 Kryms'ke Ukr.
137 H5 Kryms'ki Hori mts Ukr.
137 H5 Kryms'kyy Pivostriv pen. Ukr.
175 I6 Krynica Pol.
143 H4 Krynica Morska Pol.
174 F5 Krynka r. Pol.
137 J4 Krynka r. Ukr.
175 L2 Krynki Pol.
137 H3 Krynychky Dnipropetrovs'ka Oblast' Ukr.
137 F4 Krynychky Mykolayivs'ka Oblast' Ukr.
137 J3 Krynychna Ukr.
175 K2 Krypno Kościelne Pol.
171 E5 Kryry Czech Rep.
137 G2 Krysky Ukr.
Krystynopol Ukr. see Chervonohrad
198 D3 Krytiko Pelagos sea Greece
137 G3 Kryva Ruda Ukr.
136 E3 Kryvchunka Ukr.
136 F4 Kryve Ozero Ukr.
138 F4 Kryvichy Belarus
137 G4 Kryvyy Rih Ukr.
136 E3 Kryzhopil' Ukr.
174 G5 Krzanowice Pol.
175 K4 Krzczonów-Wójtostwo Pol.
174 D2 Krzęcin Pol.
174 G5 Krzepice Pol.
175 K3 Krzesk-Królowa Niwa Pol.
175 K5 Krzeszów Pol.
175 H5 Krzeszowice Pol.
174 D3 Krzeszyce Pol.
175 H5 Krzętów Pol.
175 L3 Krzna r. Pol.
175 K4 Krzna Południowa r. Pol.
174 G3 Krzymów Pol.
170 F3 Krzymów Pol.
175 I2 Krzynowłoga Mała Pol.
174 D4 Krzystkowice Pol.
175 K6 Krzywcza Pol.
175 K4 Krzywda Pol.
174 E4 Krzywiń Pol.
175 H3 Krzyżanów Pol.
174 G6 Krzyżanowice Pol.
174 E3 Krzyż Wielkopolski Pol.
129 D3 Ksani r. Georgia
205 F2 Ksar Chellala Alg.
205 F2 Ksar el Boukhari Alg.
205 F2 Ksar el Hirane Alg.
204 D2 Ksar el Kebir Morocco
Ksar-es-Souk Morocco see Er Rachidia
136 F2 Ksaverivka Ukr.
139 K5 Kshen' r. Rus. Fed.
135 G6 Kshenskiy Rus. Fed.
175 H2 Książki Pol.
175 I5 Książ Wielki Pol.
174 F3 Książ Wielkopolski Pol.
175 K5 Księżpol Pol.
122 C1 Kskyrbulak Yuzhnyy, Gora hill Turkm.
205 E2 Ksour, Monts des mts Alg.
205 H2 Ksour, Monts des mts Tunisia
205 H2 Ksour Essaf Tunisia
134 I4 Kstovo Rus. Fed.
125 D2 Kū', Jabal al hill Saudi Arabia
Kuaidamao Jilin China see Tonghua
95 F1 Kuala Belait Brunei
Kuala Dungun Malaysia see Dungun
94 C1 Kuala Kangsar Malaysia
95 F3 Kualakapuas Kalimantan Tengah Indon.
94 C1 Kuala Kerai Malaysia
95 G1 Kuala Kinabatangan r. mouth Sabah Malaysia
94 C2 Kuala Kubu Baharu Malaysia
94 C1 Kuala Lipis Malaysia
94 C2 Kuala Lumpur Malaysia
95 F3 Kualapembuang Kalimantan Tengah Indon.
94 C2 Kuala Pilah Malaysia
240 □C8 Kualapuu HI U.S.A.
94 B1 Kualasimpang Sumatera Indon.
94 C1 Kuala Terengganu Malaysia
94 C3 Kualatungal Sumatera Indon.
95 G1 Kuamut r. Sabah Malaysia
107 H3 Kuancheng Hebei China
101 C4 Kuandian Liaoning China
Kuangyuan Yunnan China see Yiliang
109 G4 Kuanshan Taiwan
94 C2 Kuantan Malaysia
80 E2 Kuaotuou North I. N.Z.
Kuba Azer. see Quba
129 C2 Kuba Rus. Fed.
129 E2 Kubachi Rus. Fed.
129 B1 Kuban' r. Rus. Fed.
129 A1 Kubanskaya Rus. Fed.
127 E4 Kubār Dayr az Zawr Syria
127 E4 Kubār Dayr az Zawr Syria
125 G3 Kubārah Oman
140 L3 Kubbe Sweden
177 J5 Kübekháza Hungary
134 G4 Kubenskoye, Ozero l. Rus. Fed.
Kuberle Rostovskaya Oblast' Rus. Fed. see Krasnoarmeyskiy
139 K4 Kubinka Rus. Fed.
190 E2 Küblis Switz.
136 E3 Kublych r. Ukr.
134 J5 Kubnya r. Rus. Fed.
197 H4 Kubrat Bulg.
139 L3 Kubrinsk Rus. Fed.
197 E3 Kučevo Srbija Yugo.
116 C4 Kuchaman Rajasthan India
172 D3 Kuchen Ger.
116 C4 Kuchera Rajasthan India
137 H2 Kucherivka Ukr.
95 E2 Kuching Sarawak Malaysia
102 □ Kuchino-shima i. Japan
178 E3 Kuchl Austria
136 E4 Kuchurhan r. Ukr.
Kucing Sarawak Malaysia see Kuching
175 H4 Kuciny Pol.
170 F2 Kückelsberg hill Ger.
198 A1 Kuçovë Albania
129 D4 Küçük Ağrı Dağı mt. Turkey
128 C1 Küçükdalyan Turkey
199 G3 Küçükköy Turkey
199 E2 Küçükköy Turkey
199 E2 Küçükkuyu anakkale Turkey
199 E1 Küçükmenderes r. Turkey
199 E3 Küçükmenderes r. Turkey
175 I2 Kuczbork-Osada Pol.
116 B5 Kuda Gujarat India
114 B2 Kudachi Karnataka India
113 □ Kuda Finolhu i. S. Male Maldives
114 B3 Kudal Mahar. India
113 □ Kudalhi i. N. Male Maldives
103 E7 Kudamatsu Japan
107 E1 Kudara-Somon Rus. Fed.
168 F2 Kuddewörde Ger.
138 G3 Kudev r. Rus. Fed.
138 D4 Kudirkos Naumiestis Lith.
114 C3 Kudligi Karnataka India
174 E5 Kudowa-Zdrój Pol.
114 B3 Kudremukh mt. Karnataka India
137 F4 Kudryavtsivka Ukr.
95 E4 Kudus Jawa Tengah Indon.
134 K4 Kudymkar Rus. Fed.
178 D3 Kufstein Austria
121 I3 Kugaly Kazakh.
134 I4 Kugesi Rus. Fed.
137 J4 Kugey Rus. Fed.
220 G3 Kugluktuk Nunavut Can.
137 J4 Kugo-Eya r. Rus. Fed.
135 H7 Kugul'ta Rus. Fed.
123 E5 Kūhak Iran
173 F3 Kühbach Ger.
170 D2 Kuhbier Ger.
122 D4 Kūhbonān Iran
122 A3 Kūhdasht Iran
170 C3 Kuhfelde Ger.
Kŭhi Piryakh mt. Tajik. see Pir'yakh, Gora
123 H2 Kŭhistoni Badakhshon aut. rep. Tajik.
170 C2 Kuhlen Ger.
140 O2 Kuhmo Fin.
141 N3 Kuhmoinen Fin.
169 F5 Kühndorf Ger.
122 C3 Kūhpāyeh Iran
122 D4 Kūhpāyeh mt. Iran
122 D5 Kūhrān, Kūh-e mt. Iran
122 B4 Kūhrang r. Iran
171 D4 Kühren Ger.
168 D2 Kührstedt Ger.
170 D2 Kuhs Ger.
168 D2 Kuhstedt Ger.
97 B4 Kui Buri Thai.
164 E2 Kuinre Neth.
109 E4 Kuitan Guangdong China
Kuitin Xinjiang China see Kuytun
209 C8 Kuito Angola
222 C3 Kuiu Island AK U.S.A.
140 N2 Kuivaniemi Fin.
138 F3 Kuja r. Latvia
174 G4 Kujakowice Dolne Pol.
117 F5 Kujang Orissa India
101 C5 Kujang N. Korea
174 G2 Kujawsko-Pomorskie prov. Pol.
102 J3 Kuji Japan
105 G2 Kuji-gawa r. Japan
105 G3 Kujikuri Japan
105 G3 Kujūkuri-hama coastal area Japan
103 E7 Kujū-san vol. Japan
122 B4 Kukālār, Kūh-e hill Iran
100 E2 Kukan Rus. Fed.
227 F1 Kukatush Ont. Can.
207 I3 Kukawa Nigeria
87 C7 Kukerin W.A. Austr.
196 E4 Kukës Albania
136 C2 Kukhits'ka Volya Ukr.
105 F2 Kuki Japan
174 F4 Kuklinów Pol.
179 H3 Kukmirn Austria
134 J4 Kukmor Rus. Fed.
134 G4 Kukoboy Rus. Fed.
138 F2 Kukruse Estonia
116 C5 Kukshi Madh. Prad. India
240 □D8 Kukuihaele HI U.S.A.
114 D2 Kukunuru Andhra Prad. India
95 F3 Kukusan, Gunung hill Indon.
134 L4 Kukushtan Rus. Fed.
122 C5 Kūl r. Iran
197 F4 Kula Bulg.
Kula r. Moldova see Cula
207 G5 Kula Nigeria
199 F2 Kula Turkey
196 D3 Kula Vojvodina, Srbija Yugo.
196 D4 Kula mt. Yugo.
94 B2 Kulabu, Gunung mt. Indon.
123 G4 Kulachi Pak.
120 B2 Kulagino Kazakh.
117 G3 Kula Kangri mt. Bhutan
210 C4 Kulal, Mount Kenya
123 F4 Kulao r. Pak.
131 O2 Kular Rus. Fed.
95 G2 Kulat, Gunung mt. Indon.
138 D4 Kulautuva Lith.
137 H2 Kul'baki Rus. Fed.
138 C3 Kuldīga Latvia
Kuldja Xinjiang China see Yining
100 D2 Kul'dur Rus. Fed.
120 E4 Kul'dzhuktau, Gory hills Uzbek.
135 H5 Kulebaki Rus. Fed.
199 G3 Kuleönü Turkey
137 J4 Kuleshovka Rus. Fed.
175 K2 Kulesze Pol.
175 K2 Kulesze Kościelne Pol.
84 C5 Kulgera N.T. Austr.
120 D1 Kulgunino Rus. Fed.
129 E2 Kuli Rus. Fed.
134 K4 Kuligi Rus. Fed.
134 I3 Kulikovo Arkhangel'skaya Oblast' Rus. Fed.
139 L5 Kulikovo Lipetskaya Oblast' Rus. Fed.
94 C1 Kulim Malaysia
87 C7 Kulin W.A. Austr.
114 C4 Kulittalai Tamil Nadu India
87 C6 Kulja W.A. Austr.
120 E4 Kulkuduk Uzbek.
141 M3 Kullaa Fin.
169 F4 Küllstedt Ger.
116 D3 Kullu Hima. Prad. India
173 F2 Kulmain Ger.
171 C5 Kulmbach Ger.
123 G2 Kŭlob Tajik.
139 I2 Kulotino Rus. Fed.
134 H3 Kuloy Rus. Fed.
134 H2 Kuloy r. Rus. Fed.
127 F3 Kulp Turkey
82 D3 Kulpara S.A. Austr.
234 B2 Kulpmont PA U.S.A.
120 C3 Kul'sary Kazakh.
172 D2 Külsheim Ger.
126 D3 Kulu Turkey
199 G3 Kulübe Tepe mt. Turkey
121 I1 Kulunda Rus. Fed.
121 I1 Kulunda r. Rus. Fed.
121 H1 Kulundinskaya Step' plain Kazakh./Rus. Fed.
121 I1 Kulundinskoye, Ozero salt l. Rus. Fed.
83 E3 Kulwin Vic. Austr.
Kulyab Tajik. see Kŭlob
136 C3 Kulykiv Ukr.
137 F2 Kulykivka Ukr.
129 E1 Kuma r. Rus. Fed.
140 O2 Kuma r. Rus. Fed.
105 F2 Kumagaya Japan
95 E3 Kumai, Teluk b. Indon.
120 D2 Kumak r. Rus. Fed.
199 G2 Kumalar Dağı mts Turkey
103 E7 Kumamoto Japan
103 E7 Kumamoto pref. Japan
104 C5 Kumano Japan
197 E4 Kumanovo Macedonia
81 C5 Kumara South I. N.Z.
81 C5 Kumara Junction South I. N.Z.
117 G5 Kumarkhali Bangl.
206 E5 Kumasi Ghana
215 G4 Ku-Mayima S. Africa
Kumayri Armenia see Gyumri
207 H5 Kumba Cameroon
199 E1 Kumbağ Turkey
114 C4 Kumbakonam Tamil Nadu India
179 G3 Kumberg Austria
199 G2 Kümbet Turkey
114 B2 Kumbharli Ghat mt. Mahar. India
114 B3 Kumbla Kerala India
207 H5 Kumbo Cameroon
138 D3 Kumbri Latvia
Kum-Dag Turkm. see Gumdag
124 D3 Kumdah Saudi Arabia
199 G2 Kumdanlı Isparta Turkey
102 □ Kume-jima i. Japan
134 J4 Kumeny Rus. Fed.
120 C1 Kumertau Rus. Fed.
101 C6 Kŭm-gang r. S. Korea
101 D5 Kumgang-san mt. N. Korea
117 G4 Kumguri Assam India
111 B6 Kumharsain Hima. Prad. India
173 G3 Kumhausen Ger.
116 D4 Kumher Rajasthan India
101 D6 Kŭmho-gang r. S. Korea
101 D5 Kumi S. Korea
210 B4 Kumi Uganda
202 B7 Kumishe Nigeria
199 E2 Kumkale Turkey
143 F2 Kumla Sweden
141 M3 Kumlinge Åland Fin.
128 C1 Kumlu Turkey
199 G3 Kumluca Turkey
170 C2 Kummer Ger.
170 D2 Kummerow Ger.
170 D2 Kummerower See l. Ger.
173 F2 Kümmersbruck Ger.
171 E3 Kummersdorf-Alexanderdorf Ger.
171 E3 Kummersdorf Gut Ger.
207 H4 Kumo Nigeria
96 B1 Kumon Range mts Myanmar
105 E3 Kumotori-yama mt. Japan
104 C4 Kumozu-gawa r. Japan
96 C3 Kumphawapi Thai.
140 N2 Kumputunturi hill Fin.
179 G4 Kumrovec Croatia
114 B3 Kumta Karnataka India
129 E2 Kumukh Rus. Fed.
Kumul Xinjiang China see Hami
117 E5 Kumund Orissa India
129 C3 Kumurdo Georgia
110 E3 Kümüx Xinjiang China
Kumylzhenskaya Rus. Fed. see Kumylzhenskiy
135 H6 Kumylzhenskiy Rus. Fed.
Kumyshtag, Pik mt. Kyrg. see Kyumyush-Tak, Pik
96 B3 Kun r. Myanmar
177 I5 Kunadacs Hungary
177 K5 Kunágota Hungary
87 D4 Kunanaggi Well W.A. Austr.
123 G3 Kunar r. Afgh.
100 H3 Kunashir, Ostrov i. Kuril'skiye O-va Rus. Fed.
Kunashirskiy Proliv sea chan. Japan/Rus. Fed. see Nemuro-kaikyō
177 I5 Kunbaja Hungary
177 I5 Kunbaracs Hungary
129 D1 Kun'bator Rus. Fed.
138 F2 Kunda Estonia
138 F2 Kunda r. Estonia
116 E4 Kunda Uttar Prad. India
209 C7 Kunda-dia-Baze Angola
114 B3 Kundapura Karnataka India
123 G3 Kundar r. Afgh./Pak.
95 G1 Kundat Sabah Malaysia
114 B3 Kundgol Karnataka India
123 G3 Kundian Pak.
178 C3 Kundl Austria
137 K4 Kundryuch'ya r. Rus. Fed./Ukr.
94 C2 Kundur i. Indon.
Kunduz Afgh. see Kondūz
209 B9 Kunene r. Angola/Namibia alt. Cunene
212 B3 Kunene admin. reg. Namibia
Künes Xinjiang China see Xinyuan
110 C3 Künes Chang Xinjiang China
110 C3 Künes He r. China
177 I5 Kunfehértó Hungary
142 D3 Kungälv Sweden
121 I4 Kungei Alatau mts Kazakh./Kyrg.
Kunggar Xizang China see Maizhokunggar
Küngöy Ala-Too mts Kazakh./Kyrg. see Kungei Alatau
120 D4 Kungrad Uzbek.
120 E4 Kungradkol' Uzbek.
143 G2 Kungsängen Sweden
142 E3 Kungsbacka Sweden
142 D2 Kungshamn Sweden
143 G2 Kungsör Sweden
Kungur mt. Xinjiang China see Kongur Shan
134 L4 Kungur Rus. Fed.
96 A3 Kungyangon Myanmar
177 J4 Kunhegyes Hungary
157 H4 Kunheim France
114 C2 Kuni r. India
174 E4 Kunice Pol.
Kunicha Moldova see Cunicea
Kunié i. New Caledonia see Pins, Île des
114 C3 Kunigai Karnataka India
104 C2 Kunimi-dake hill Japan
103 E7 Kunimi-dake mt. Japan
177 G2 Kunín Czech Rep.
95 E4 Kuningan Jawa Barat Indon.
174 G5 Kuniów Pol.
117 F5 Kunjabar Orissa India
234 C2 Kunkletown PA U.S.A.
116 B5 Kunlavav Gujarat India
117 G4 Kunlui r. India/Nepal
106 A4 Kunlun Shan mts China
177 J4 Kunmadaras Hungary
108 B3 Kunming Yunnan China
116 D4 Kuno r. India
176 G2 Kunovice Czech Rep.
175 J5 Kunów Pol.
174 F4 Kunowo Pol.
177 I4 Kunpeszér Hungary
170 C3 Kunrau Ger.
101 C6 Kunsan S. Korea
109 G2 Kunshan Jiangsu China
176 F2 Kunštát Czech Rep.
177 I5 Kunszállás Hungary
177 J5 Kunszentmárton Hungary
177 I4 Kunszentmiklós Hungary
86 F2 Kununurra W.A. Austr.
223 L2 Kunwak r. Nunavut Can.
116 D4 Kunwari r. India
139 H3 Kun'ya Rus. Fed.
139 H3 Kun'ya r. Rus. Fed.
Kunyang Henan China see Yexian
Kunyang Yunnan China see Jinning
Kunyang Zhejiang China see Pingyang
Kunya-Urgench Turkm. see Keneurgench
137 I3 Kun'ye Ukr.
176 E2 Kunžak Czech Rep.
169 E5 Künzell Ger.
172 D2 Künzelsau Ger.
171 C4 Künzels-Berg hill Ger.
173 H3 Künzing Ger.
109 G2 Kuocang Shan mts China
140 N3 Kuopio Fin.
141 N3 Kuorevesi Fin.
174 F5 Kup Pol.
188 F3 Kupa r. Croatia/Slovenia
93 B5 Kupang Timor Indon.
139 L3 Kupanskoye Rus. Fed.
117 F5 Kupari Orissa India
Kupchino Moldova see Cupcina
171 C5 Kupferberg Ger.
172 D2 Kupferzell Ger.
137 I2 Kupino Rus. Fed.
138 E4 Kupiškis Lith.
191 J3 Kupjak Croatia
199 F1 Küplü Turkey
172 C3 Kuppenheim Ger.
138 F3 Kuprava Latvia
222 C3 Kupreanof AK U.S.A.
220 E4 Kupreanof Island AK U.S.A.
171 C5 Küps Ger.
116 C2 Kupwara Jammu and Kashmir
137 I3 Kup"yans'k Ukr.
137 I3 Kup"yans'k-Vuzlovyy Ukr.
136 C2 Kupychiv Ukr.
110 C3 Kuqa Xinjiang China
129 E3 Kür Azer.
129 F4 Kür r. Azer.
127 G2 Kür r. Georgia
100 E2 Kur r. Rus. Fed.
129 D3 Kura r. Azer./Georgia
129 C2 Kura r. Rus. Fed.
129 C3 Kura r. Turkey
87 C5 Kurabuka r. W.A. Austr.
121 H4 Kuragaty Kazakh.
207 H4 Kuragwi Nigeria
104 D2 Kurai-yama mt. Japan
129 E3 Küräkçay r. Azer.
129 E3 Kurakh Rus. Fed.
137 I4 Kurakhove Ukr.
Kurakhovo Ukr. see Kurakhove
Kurakhovstroy Ukr. see Kurakhove
Kura kurk sea chan. Estonia/Latvia see Irbe Strait
104 B3 Kurama-yama hill Japan
85 F3 Kuranda Qld Austr.
120 D2 Kurashasayskiy Kazakh.
103 F6 Kurashiki Japan
116 E5 Kurasia Madh. Prad. India
86 E3 Kura Soak well W.A. Austr.
103 F6 Kurayoshi Japan
106 A1 Kurayskiy Khrebet mts Rus. Fed.
139 L3 Kurba Rus. Fed.
199 F1 Kurban Dağı mt. Turkey
137 J2 Kurbatovo Rus. Fed.
100 D2 Kurbin r. China
196 E2 Kurca r. Romania
129 E2 Kurchaloy Rus. Fed.
135 F6 Kurchatov Rus. Fed.
121 J2 Kurchum Kazakh.
121 J2 Kurchum r. Kazakh.
177 H5 Kurd Hungary
129 F3 Kürdämir Azer.
121 H4 Kurday Kazakh.
114 B2 Kurduvadi Mahar. India
197 G5 Kŭrdzhali Bulg.
129 B2 Kurdzhinovo Rus. Fed.
103 F6 Kure Japan
126 D2 Küre Turkey
75 G1 Kure Atoll HI U.S.A.
138 D2 Kuressaare Estonia
138 G2 Kureya r. Rus. Fed.
Kurgal'dzhino Kazakh. see Kurgal'dzhinskiy
121 G2 Kurgal'dzhinskiy Kazakh.
130 H4 Kurgan Rus. Fed.
135 H7 Kurganinsk Rus. Fed.
Kurgannaya Rus. Fed. see Kurganinsk
Kurgantyube Tajik. see Qŭrghonteppa
116 B4 Kuri Rajasthan India
77 H1 Kuria is Gilbert Is Kiribati
Kuria Muria Islands Oman see Ḥalāniyāt, Juzur al
84 E4 Kuridala Qld Austr.
117 G4 Kurigram Bangl.
140 M3 Kurikka Fin.
102 J4 Kurikoma-yama vol. Japan
266 E2 Kuril Basin sea feature Sea of Okhotsk
196 D4 Kurile, Mal mt. Albania
99 Q2 Kuril Islands Rus. Fed.
120 B2 Kurilovka Rus. Fed.
99 Q2 Kuril'sk Kuril'skiye O-va Rus. Fed.
Kuril'skiye Ostrova is Rus. Fed. see Kuril Islands
266 E3 Kuril Trench sea feature N. Pacific Ocean
176 F2 Kuřim Czech Rep.
129 A1 Kurinskaya Rus. Fed.
Kurkçü Turkey see Sarıkavak
139 L5 Kurkino Rus. Fed.
139 M4 Kurlovskiy Rus. Fed.
120 B1 Kurmanayevka Rus. Fed.
Kurmashkino Kazakh. see Kurchum
210 B2 Kurmuk Sudan
173 E2 Kürnach Ger.
172 C2 Kürnbach Ger.
136 E2 Kurne Ukr.
114 C3 Kurnool Andhra Prad. India
104 D2 Kurobe Japan
104 D2 Kurobe-gawa r. Japan
105 D2 Kurohime-yama mt. Japan
105 E1 Kurohume-yama hill Japan
102 J3 Kuroishi Japan
105 G2 Kuroiso Japan
203 F4 Kuror, Jebel mt. Sudan
171 E5 Kurort Bad Gottleuba Ger.
171 E5 Kurort-Berggießhübel Ger.
169 F5 Kurort Brotterode Ger.
171 D5 Kurort Oberwiesenthal Ger.
169 F5 Kurort Schmalkalden Ger.
169 F5 Kurort Steinbach-Hallenberg Ger.
137 H4 Kuroshany r. Ukr.
102 □ Kuro-shima i. Japan
104 C4 Kuroso-yama mt. Japan
100 C1 Kurovskiy Rus. Fed.
139 K4 Kurovskoy Rus. Fed.
139 L4 Kurovskoye Rus. Fed.

175 M6 Kurovychi Ukr.
81 C6 Kurow South I. N.Z.
175 K4 Kurów Pol.
175 H4 Kurowice Pol.
123 G3 Kurram r. Afgh./Pak.
83 G3 Kurri Kurri N.S.W. Austr.
129 C1 Kursavka Rus. Fed.
138 D3 Kuršėnai Lith.
124 C3 Kursh, Jabal hill Saudi Arabia
Kürshim Kazakh. see Kurchum
Kurshskiy Zaliv b. Lith./Rus. Fed. see Courland Lagoon
Kuršių marios b. Lith./Rus. Fed. see Courland Lagoon
135 G6 Kursk Rus. Fed.
129 D1 Kurskaya Rus. Fed.
135 G6 Kurskaya Oblast' admin. div. Rus. Fed.
Kurskiy Zaliv b. Lith./Rus. Fed. see Courland Lagoon
Kursk Oblast admin. div. Rus. Fed. see Kurskaya Oblast'
137 H2 Kurskoye Vodokhranilishche resr Rus. Fed.
196 E4 Kuršumlija Srbija Yugo.
126 D2 Kurşunlu Turkey
127 F3 Kurtalan Turkey
199 E1 Kurtbey Edirne Turkey
Kürti r. Kazakh. see Kurtty
240 □D9 Kurtistown HI U.S.A.
129 D3 K'urt'lari Georgia
128 B1 Kurtpınar Turkey
128 B1 Kurttepe Turkey
121 I3 Kurtty r. Kazakh.
Kurty r. Kazakh. see Kurtty
141 M3 Kuru Fin.
Kurú r. Greece see Kourou
117 F5 Kuru Bihar India
126 D2 Kurucaşile Turkey
116 E5 Kurud Madh. Prad. India
199 G1 Kurudere Turkey
116 D3 Kurukshetra Haryana India
110 D3 Kuruktag mts China
214 D2 Kuruman S. Africa
103 E7 Kurume Japan
99 J1 Kurumkan Rus. Fed.
210 B3 Kurun r. Sudan
114 B2 Kurundvad Mahar. India
114 D5 Kurunegala Sri Lanka
107 H1 Kurunzulay Rus. Fed.
115 D2 Kurupam Andhra Prad. India
203 F4 Kurush, Jebel hills Sudan
121 J2 Kur'ya Rus. Fed.
137 J3 Kuryachivka Ukr.
120 B4 Kuryk Kazakh.
137 H3 Kurylivka Ukr.
175 K5 Kuryłówka Pol.
175 H5 Kurzelów Pol.
175 I4 Kurzeszyn Pol.
175 H2 Kurzętnik Pol.
199 E3 Kuşadası Turkey
199 E3 Kuşadası Körfezi b. Turkey
Kusaie atoll Micronesia see Kosrae
128 C1 Kuşalanı Turkey
Kusary Azer. see Qusar
104 B3 Kusatsu Japan
172 B2 Kusel Ger.
170 C3 Kusey Ger.
116 C5 Kushalgarh Rajasthan India
139 K3 Kushalino Rus. Fed.
122 D3 Kūshank Iran
135 G7 Kushchevskaya Rus. Fed.
207 G4 Kusheriki Nigeria
104 C4 Kushida-gawa r. Japan
103 E8 Kushikino Japan
103 E8 Kushima Japan
102 L2 Kushiro Japan
Kushka Turkm. see Gushgy
120 F1 Kushmurun Kazakh.
120 F1 Kushmurun, Ozero salt l. Kazakh.
134 K5 Kushnarenkovo Rus. Fed.
114 C3 Kushtagi Karnataka India
117 G5 Kushtia Bangl.
137 H4 Kushuhum Ukr.
106 E4 Kushui r. China
120 B2 Kushum Kazakh.
120 B2 Kushum r. Kazakh.
128 A1 Kuskan Turkey
220 B3 Kuskokwim r. AK U.S.A.
220 B4 Kuskokwim Bay AK U.S.A.
220 C3 Kuskokwim Mountains AK U.S.A.
Kuşluyan Turkey see Gölköy
190 D1 Küsnacht Switz.
101 C5 Kusŏng N. Korea
102 L2 Kussharo-ko l. Japan
190 D1 Küssnacht Switz.
Kustanay Kazakh. see Kostanay
Kustanay Oblast admin. div. Kazakh. see Kustanayskaya Oblast'
120 E1 Kustanayskaya Oblast' admin. div. Kazakh.
141 M3 Kustavi Fin.
170 C3 Küsten Ger.
Küstence Romania see Constanța
172 D3 Kusterdingen Ger.
Kustia Bangl. see Kushtia
136 D3 Kustivtsi Ukr.
93 C2 Kusu Halmahera Indon.
104 C4 Kusu Japan
199 F2 Kuşu Kütahya Turkey
97 C5 Kut, Ko i. Thai.
94 B2 Kutacane Sumatera Indon.
199 F2 Kütahya Turkey
199 F2 Kütahya prov. Turkey
129 A1 Kutais Rus. Fed.
129 C2 K'ut'aisi Georgia
Kut-al-Imara Iraq see Al Kūt
129 E1 Kutan Rus. Fed.
Kutaraja Sumatera Indon. see Banda Aceh
80 F3 Kutarere North I. N.Z.
128 D4 Kutayfat Ţurayf vol. Saudi Arabia
Kutch, Gulf of Gujarat India see Kachchh, Gulf of
Kutch, Rann of marsh India see Rann of Kachchh
127 H4 Kūt-e Gapu tourist site Iran
168 E2 Kutenholz Ger.
137 J4 Kuteynykove Ukr.
188 F3 Kutina Croatia
188 F3 Kutjevo Croatia
215 F2 Kutloanong S. Africa
176 E2 Kutná Hora Czech Rep.
175 H3 Kutno Pol.
140 M1 Kuttainen Sweden
208 C5 Kutu Dem. Rep. Congo
202 E6 Kutum Sudan
Kutuzov Moldova see Ialoveni
176 G3 Kúty Slovakia
173 E3 Kutzenhausen Ger.
234 C2 Kutztown PA U.S.A.
220 G2 Kuujjua r. N.W.T. Can.
225 G1 Kuujjuaq Que. Can.
224 E2 Kuujjuarapik Que. Can.
122 C1 Kuuli-Mayak Turkm.
165 C4 Kuurne Belgium
138 E2 Kuusalu Estonia
140 O2 Kuusamo Fin.
141 N3 Kuusankoski Fin.
138 D1 Kuusjoki Fin.
138 F2 Kuutse mägi hill Estonia
134 K4 Kuva Rus. Fed.
120 D2 Kuvandyk Rus. Fed.
209 C8 Kuvango Angola
139 J3 Kuvshinovo Rus. Fed.
Kuwaé i. Vanuatu see Tongoa
127 G5 Kuwait country Asia
Kuwajleen atoll Marshall Is see Kwajalein
104 C3 Kuwana Japan
Küybyshev Kazakh. see Kuybyshevskiy
130 I4 Kuybyshev Novosibirskaya Oblast' Rus. Fed.
Kuybyshev Respublika Tatarstan Rus. Fed. see Bolgar
Kuybyshev Samarskaya Oblast' Rus. Fed. see Samara
137 I4 Kuybysheve Donets'ka Oblast' Ukr.
137 I4 Kuybysheve Zaporiz'ka Oblast' Ukr.
Kuybyshevka-Vostochnaya Rus. Fed. see Belogorsk
Kuybyshevo Kazakh. see Zhyngyldy
137 J4 Kuybyshevo Rus. Fed.
Kuybyshevskaya Oblast' admin. div. Rus. Fed. see Samarskaya Oblast'
121 F1 Kuybyshevskiy Kazakh.
135 J5 Kuybyshevskoye Vodokhranilishche resr Rus. Fed.
107 F4 Kuye r. China
134 K4 Kuyeda Rus. Fed.
121 H3 Kuygan Kazakh.
106 B3 Küysu Xinjiang China
110 D2 Kuytun Xinjiang China
110 C2 Kuytun He r. China
199 F3 Kuyucak Turkey
128 B1 Kuyuluk Turkey
251 G4 Kuyuwini r. Guyana
137 I3 Kuzemivka Ukr.
137 H2 Kuzemyn Ukr.
134 J4 Kuzhener Rus. Fed.
139 I3 Kuzhenkino Rus. Fed.
129 B1 Kuzhorskaya Rus. Fed.
138 D4 Kužiai Lith.
Kuzik'end Armenia see Garrnarrich
177 K3 Kuzmice Slovakia
175 K6 Kuźmina Pol.
139 H1 Kuz'molovskiy Rus. Fed.
138 G1 Kuznechnoye Rus. Fed.
120 A1 Kuznetsk Rus. Fed.
136 C2 Kuznetsovs'k Ukr.
174 G5 Kuźnia Raciborska Pol.
175 L2 Kuźnica Pol.
135 I5 Kuzovatovo Rus. Fed.
139 L5 Kuzovka Rus. Fed.
102 J3 Kuzumaki Japan
104 C2 Kuzuryū-gawa r. Japan
140 M1 Kvænangen sea chan. Norway
142 D4 Kværndrup Denmark
168 E1 Kværs Denmark
140 L1 Kvaløya i. Norway
140 M1 Kvaløya i. Norway
140 M1 Kvalsund Norway
Kvareli Georgia see Qvareli
120 D1 Kvarkeno Rus. Fed.
141 K3 Kvarnberg Sweden
188 E3 Kvarner g. Croatia
188 E3 Kvarnerić sea chan. Croatia
176 G2 Kvasice Czech Rep.
136 C3 Kvasy Ukr.
136 D2 Kvasyliv Ukr.
129 C3 K'veda Nasakirali Georgia
138 C4 Kvėdarna Lith.
129 D2 K'vemo Alvani Georgia
129 D3 K'vemo Bodbe Georgia
129 D3 K'vemo Bolnisi Georgia
140 L2 Kvikkjokk Sweden
143 F3 Kvillsfors Sweden
142 B2 Kvinesdal Norway
141 L3 Kvissleby Sweden
141 I3 Kvitanosi mt. Norway
141 I3 Kvitegga mt. Norway
142 C2 Kviteseid Norway
140 □ Kvitøya ice feature Svalbard
142 A2 Kvitsøy Norway
209 C5 Kwa r. Dem. Rep. Congo
165 E3 Kwaadmechelen Belgium
Kwabhaca S. Africa see Mount Frere
215 H2 KwaChibukhulu S. Africa
215 G2 KwaDela S. Africa
Kwadelen atoll Marshall Is see Kwajalein
215 G1 KwaGuqa S. Africa
78 □3a Kwajalein atoll Marshall Is
78 □3a Kwajalein i. Marshall Is
251 H3 Kwakoegron Suriname
251 G3 Kwakwani Guyana
215 F2 Kwakwatse S. Africa
211 C6 Kwale Kenya
207 G5 Kwale Nigeria
215 H3 KwaMashu S. Africa
215 I3 Kwa-Mbonambi S. Africa
206 E5 Kwame Danso Ghana
215 G1 KwaMhlanga S. Africa
211 B6 Kwa Mtoro Tanz.
Kwangchow Guangdong China see Guangzhou
101 C6 Kwangju S. Korea
209 C5 Kwango r. Dem. Rep. Congo
Kwangsi Chuang Autonomous Region aut. reg. China see Guangxi Zhuangzu Zizhiqu
Kwangtung prov. China see Guangdong
101 D4 Kwanmo-bong mt. N. Korea
215 E5 Kwanobuhle S. Africa
215 E5 KwaNojoli S. Africa
215 F5 Kwanonqubela S. Africa
215 E4 Kwanonzame S. Africa
Kwanza r. Angola see Cuanza
215 F5 Kwa-Pita S. Africa
207 F4 Kwara state Nigeria
215 H2 KwaThandeka S. Africa
215 F5 Kwatinidubu S. Africa
215 G2 KwaZamokhule S. Africa
214 E5 Kwazamukucinga S. Africa
215 E4 Kwazamuxolo S. Africa
215 G2 KwaZanele S. Africa
215 H3 Kwazulu-Natal prov. S. Africa
Kweichow prov. China see Guizhou
Kweiyang Guizhou China see Guiyang
213 F3 Kwekwe Zimbabwe
212 E4 Kweneng admin. dist. Botswana
209 C6 Kwenge r. Dem. Rep. Congo
224 D3 Kwetabohigan r. Ont. Can.
215 F4 Kwezi-Naledi S. Africa
174 G2 Kwidzyn Pol.
220 B4 Kwigillingok AK U.S.A.
174 E3 Kwilcz Pol.
209 C5 Kwilu r. Angola/Dem. Rep. Congo
87 B7 Kwinana W.A. Austr.
174 D4 Kwisa r. Pol.
251 G4 Kwitaro r. Guyana
91 H7 Kwoka mt. Indon.
208 E3 Kwoungo, Mont mt. C.A.R.
208 C2 Kyabé Chad
85 E5 Kyabra Qld Austr.
83 F4 Kyabram Vic. Austr.
96 A3 Kyaiklat Myanmar
96 B3 Kyaikto Myanmar
106 E1 Kyakhta Rus. Fed.
83 E3 Kyalite N.S.W. Austr.
82 C3 Kyancutta S.A. Austr.
96 A3 Kyangin Myanmar
96 B3 Kyaukhnyat Myanmar
96 A2 Kyaukpadaung Myanmar
96 A3 Kyaukpyu Myanmar
96 B2 Kyaukse Myanmar
96 B3 Kyauktan Myanmar
96 A3 Kyaunggon Myanmar
138 D4 Kybartai Lith.
83 G4 Kybeyan Range mts N.S.W. Austr.
82 E4 Kybybolite S.A. Austr.
96 D2 Ky Cung, Sông r. Vietnam
81 C6 Kyeburn South I. N.Z.
211 B7 Kyela Tanz.
116 D2 Kyelang Hima. Prad. India
206 E5 Kyeraa Ghana
121 H3 Kyeylbelen, Gora hill Kazakh.
96 B3 Kyidaunggan Myanmar
106 D4 Kyikug Qinghai China
207 E4 Kyinderi Ghana
136 F2 Kyiv Ukr.
136 F2 Kyivs'ka Oblast' admin. div. Ukr.
176 G2 Kyjov Czech Rep.
198 D3 Kyklades dept Greece
126 B3 Kyklades is Greece
223 I5 Kyle Sask. Can.
149 H3 Kyle r. England U.K.
146 C4 Kyleakin Highland, Scotland U.K.
146 C4 Kyle of Lochalsh Highland, Scotland U.K.
146 D3 Kyle of Tongue inlet Scotland U.K.
146 C4 Kylerhea Highland, Scotland U.K.
146 C6 Kyles of Bute sea chan. Scotland U.K.
146 B4 Kyles Scalpay Western Isles, Scotland U.K.
146 C3 Kylestrome Highland, Scotland U.K.
169 B6 Kyll r. Ger.
169 B5 Kyllburg Ger.
198 C3 Kyllini mt. Greece
141 M3 Kylmäkoski Fin.
198 D2 Kymi Greece
138 F1 Kymijoki r. Fin.
83 F4 Kyneton Vic. Austr.
142 E1 Kynna r. Norway
176 B1 Kynšperk nad Ohří Czech Rep.
85 E4 Kynuna Qld Austr.
210 B4 Kyoga, Lake Uganda
104 C2 Kyōga-dake mt. Japan
105 D3 Kyōga-dake mt. Japan
104 B3 Kyōga-misaki pt Japan
83 H2 Kyogle N.S.W. Austr.
85 F4 Kyong Qld Austr.
101 C5 Kyŏnggi-man b. S. Korea
101 D6 Kyŏngju S. Korea
96 A3 Kyonpyaw Myanmar
104 B4 Kyōto Japan
104 B3 Kyōto pref. Japan
102 J4 Kyōwa Japan
198 B3 Kyparissia Greece
198 B3 Kyparissiakos Kolpos b. Greece
Kypros country Asia see Cyprus
107 G1 Kyra Rus. Fed.
198 D2 Kyra Panagia i. Greece
Kyrenia Cyprus see Keryneia
Kyrenia Mountains Cyprus see Pentadaktylos Range
121 H4 Kyrgyzstan country Asia
136 E5 Kyrhyzh-Kytay r. Ukr.
198 D1 Kyria Greece
198 C2 Kyriaki Greece
170 D3 Kyritz Ger.
142 B2 Kyrkjenuten mt. Norway
140 J3 Kyrksæterøra Norway
136 E3 Kyrnasivka Ukr.
136 E5 Kyrnychky Ukr.
137 H2 Kyrykivka Ukr.
137 H4 Kyrylivka Ukr.
137 I3 Kyseli Ukr.
136 C3 Kyseliv Ukr.
137 F2 Kyselivka Ukr.
136 D2 Kyshyy Ukr.
177 H2 Kysucké Nové Mesto Slovakia
131 O3 Kytalyktakh Rus. Fed.
136 E5 Kytay, Ozero l. Ukr.
137 H3 Kytayhorod Ukr.
198 C3 Kythira i. Greece
198 D3 Kythnos i. Greece
128 A2 Kythrea Cyprus
121 G4 Kyumyush-Tak, Pik mt. Kyrg.
222 E5 Kyuquot B.C. Can.
Kyurdamir Azer. see Kürdämir
103 E8 Kyūshū i. Japan
266 E4 Kyushu-Palau Ridge sea feature N. Pacific Ocean
103 E7 Kyūshū-sanchi mts Japan
197 F4 Kyustendil Bulg.
96 B3 Kywebwe Myanmar
83 F3 Kywong N.S.W. Austr.
Kyyev Ukr. see Kyiv
Kyyiv Ukr. see Kyiv
136 F2 Kyyivs'ke Vodoskhovyshche resr Ukr.
140 N3 Kyyjärvi Fin.
120 C3 Kyzan Kazakh.
129 C2 Kyzburun Tretiy Rus. Fed.
120 D4 Kyzketken Uzbek.
Kyzyl Moldova see Ştefan Vodă
98 F1 Kyzyl Rus. Fed.
121 G4 Kyzyl-Adyr Kyrg.
121 I3 Kyzylagash Kazakh.
Kyzyl-Burun Azer. see Siyäzän
Kyzyl-Kiya Kyrg. see Kyzyl-Kyya
Kyzylkum, Peski des. Kazakh./Uzbek. see Kyzylkum Desert
120 F4 Kyzylkum Desert Kazakh./Uzbek.
121 H4 Kyzyl-Kyya Kyrg.
98 F1 Kyzyl-Mazhalyk Rus. Fed.
120 F3 Kyzylorda Kazakh.
Kyzyl-Orda Oblast admin. div. Kazakh. see Kzyl-Ordinskaya Oblast'
120 C4 Kyzylsay Kazakh.
121 I4 Kyzyl-Suu Kyrg.
121 G5 Kyzyl-Suu r. Kyrg.
121 H3 Kyzyltau Kazakh.
121 G2 Kyzylzhar Kazakh.
Kzyl-Dzhar Kazakh. see Kyzylzhar
Kzyl-Orda Kazakh. see Kyzylorda
120 E3 Kzyl-Ordinskaya Oblast' admin. div. Kazakh.
120 F3 Kzyl-Ordinskoye Vodokhranilishche resr Kazakh.
Kzyltu Kazakh. see Kishkenekol'

L

179 H2 Laa an der Thaya Austria
173 F2 Laaber Ger.
170 D2 Laage Ger.
138 E2 Laagri Estonia
182 D4 La Alberca Castilla y León Spain
187 B7 La Alberca Murcia Spain
183 H5 La Alberca de Záncara Spain
182 D4 La Alberguería de Argañán Spain
184 D2 La Albuera Spain
183 E4 La Aldehuela Spain
184 D3 La Algaba Spain
183 E4 La Aliseda de Tormes Spain
187 B7 La Aljorra Spain
183 H5 La Almarcha Spain
186 C3 La Almolda Spain
183 I3 La Almunia de Doña Godina Spain
260 E6 La Amarga, Lago l. Arg.
243 G6 La Angostura, Presa de resr Mex.
184 C3 La Antilla Spain
260 A6 La Araucania admin. reg. Chile
244 C2 La Ardilla, Cerro mt. Mex.
179 E3 Laarkirchen Austria
165 C3 Laarne Belgium
210 E2 Laascaanood Somalia
210 F2 Laasgoray Somalia
170 C2 Laaslich Ger.
251 F2 La Asunción Venez.
182 C5 La Atalaya de Santiago hill Spain
169 E3 Laatzen Ger.
190 E2 Laax Switz.
204 B4 Laâyoune Western Sahara
187 B7 La Azohía Spain
196 E4 Lab r. Yugo.
129 B1 Laba r. Rus. Fed.
242 E2 La Babia Mex.
159 F3 La Baconnière France
242 □I5 La Bahía, Islas de is Hond.
225 G3 La Baie Que. Can.
183 F4 Labajos Spain
224 E2 La Baleine, Grande Rivière de r. Que. Can.
224 E2 La Baleine, Petite Rivière de r. Que. Can.
225 H1 La Baleine, Rivière à r. Que. Can.
160 E3 La Balme-de-Sillingy France
258 D2 La Banda Arg.
244 B1 La Bandera, Cerro mt. Mex.
182 E2 La Bañeza Spain
Labao Guangxi China see Liujiang
244 C3 La Barca Mex.
238 E3 La Barge WY U.S.A.
158 D5 La Barre-de-Monts France
159 G3 La Barre-en-Ouche France
163 C5 La Barthe-de-Neste France
163 C5 Labarthe-Rivière France
79 □1 Labasa Vanua Levu Fiji
156 C2 La Bassée France
163 A5 La Bastide-Clairence France
163 D5 Labastide-d'Anjou France
163 B5 Labastide-d'Armangnac France
163 D5 La Bastide-de Bousignac France
163 D5 La Bastide-de-Sérou France
161 D5 La Bastide-des-Jourdans France
163 E4 La Bastide-l'Évêque France
163 D4 Labastide-Murat France
161 B4 La Bastide-Puylaurent France
161 A5 Labastide-Rouairoux France
163 D5 Labastide-St-Pierre France
163 D6 La Bastide-sur-l'Hers France
160 E3 La Bâthie France
161 E4 La Bâtie-Neuve France
217 □3b Labattoir Mayotte
163 B5 Labatut France
163 C5 Labatut-Rivière France
158 D4 La Baule-Escoublac France
159 G3 La Bazoche-Gouet France
159 G3 La Bazoge France
190 B2 L'Abbaye Switz.
176 D1 Labe r. Czech Rep. alt. Elbe (Germany)
206 B4 Labé Guinea
161 C4 La Bégude-de-Mazenc France
163 C5 Labéjan France
224 F4 Labelle Que. Can.
231 D7 La Belle FL U.S.A.
163 A5 Labenne France
161 E4 La Bérarde France
160 D1 Labergement-lès-Seurre France
161 E5 La Bernarde, Sommet de mt. France
158 D4 La Bernerie-en-Retz France
190 C2 La Berra mt. Switz.
173 G3 Laberweinting Ger.
222 F3 La Biche r. N.W.T. Can.
223 H4 La Biche, Lac l. Alta Can.
188 E3 Labin Croatia
129 B1 Labinsk Rus. Fed.
160 D3 La Biolle France
94 C2 Labis Malaysia
186 D3 La Bisbal de Falset Spain
186 E3 La Bisbal del Penedès Spain
186 G3 La Bisbal d'Empordà Spain
174 F3 Łabiszyn Pol.
161 C4 Lablachère France
261 F6 La Blanca Grande Laguna l. Arg.
92 B3 Labo Phil.
182 D1 La Bobia, Sierra de mts Spain
129 C2 Laboda, Gora mt. Georgia/Rus. Fed.
183 H3 La Bodera mt. Spain
168 F1 Laboe Ger.
156 B4 La Bonneville-sur-Iton France
261 F3 Laborde Arg.
177 K3 Laborec r. Slovakia
87 C5 Labouchere, Mount hill W.A. Austr.
158 E3 La Bouëxière France
163 B4 Labouheyre France
161 D5 La Bouilladisse France
261 F4 Laboulaye Arg.
160 A3 La Bourboule France
158 E3 La Boussac France
163 E5 Laboutarie France
183 E3 La Bóveda de Toro Spain
175 I6 Łabowa Pol.
225 I2 Labrador reg. Nfld. Can.
225 H2 Labrador City Nfld. Can.
221 M3 Labrador Sea Can./Greenland
Labrang Gansu China see Xiahe
250 C3 Labranzagrande Col.
252 D1 Lábrea Brazil
247 □7 La Brea Trin. and Tob.
163 B4 La Brède France
161 E4 La Bréole France
157 G4 La Bresse France
160 D3 La Bridoire France
163 B4 Labrit France
157 H4 La Broque France
158 E4 La Bruffière France
163 E5 Labruguière France
184 A1 Labrujeira Port.
159 F5 L'Absie France
95 F1 Labuan Malaysia
Labudalin Nei Mongol China see Ergun
244 C4 La Bufa, Cerro mt. Mex.
94 D4 Labuhan Jawa Barat Indon.
94 C2 Labuhanbilik Sumatera Indon.
94 B2 Labuhanruku Sumatera Indon.
161 D3 La Buisse France
95 G1 Labuk r. Sabah Malaysia
93 C3 Labuna Maluku Indon.
175 L5 Łabunie Pol.
156 C5 La Bussière France
96 A3 Labutta Myanmar
143 G1 Läby Sweden
82 C2 Labyrinth, Lake salt flat S.A. Austr.
130 H3 Labytnangi Rus. Fed.
196 D5 Laç Albania
202 B6 Lac pref. Chad
183 G4 La Cabrera Spain
182 D2 La Cabrera, Sierra de mts Spain
161 D5 La Cadière-d'Azur France
159 F5 La Caillère-St-Hilaire France
185 G3 Lacalahorra Spain
185 G1 La Calderina mt. Spain
185 G1 La Calderina, Sierra de mts Spain
260 E2 La Calera Arg.
216 □3a La Calera La Gomera Canary Is
260 B3 La Calera Chile
192 B4 La Caletta Sardegna Italy
225 I3 Lac Allard Que. Can.
La Calle Alg. see El Kala
161 A4 Lacalm France
161 C5 La Calmette France
183 E5 La Calzada de Oropesa Spain
185 E3 La Campana Spain
185 H4 La Cañada de San Urbano Spain
186 C4 La Cañada de Verich Spain
162 A4 Lacanau France
162 A3 Lacanau-Océan France
160 C1 Lacanche France
La Cañiza Spain see A Cañiza
161 B4 La Canourgue France
243 H5 Lacantún r. Mex.
156 D3 La Capelle France
161 A4 Lacapelle-Barrès France
163 D4 Lacapelle-Marival France
163 E4 Lacapelle-Viescamp France
184 D2 Lácara r. Spain
196 D3 Laćarak Vojvodina, Srbija Yugo.
182 D1 La Caridad Spain
261 F3 La Carlota Arg.
92 B4 La Carlota Phil.
185 F3 La Carlota Spain
185 G2 La Carolina Spain
163 A5 Lacarre France
161 A5 Lacaune France
161 A5 Lacaune, Monts de mts France
186 D4 La Cava Spain
183 G1 La Cavada Spain
161 B4 La Cavalerie France
163 D4 Lacave France
163 E5 Lacaze France
233 □I1 Lac-Baker N.B. Can.
Laccadive, Minicoy and Amindivi Islands union terr. India see Lakshadweep
114 B4 Laccadive Islands India
193 F4 Lacco Ameno Italy
223 L5 Lac du Bonnet Man. Can.
226 C3 Lac du Flambeau WI U.S.A.
149 I4 Laceby North East Lincolnshire, England U.K.
Lacedaemon Greece see Sparti
193 H3 Lacedonia Italy
242 □I6 La Ceiba Hond.
186 F3 La Cellera de Ter Spain
159 G4 La Celle-St-Avant France
156 C4 La Celle-St-Cloud France
La Cenia Spain see La Sènia
82 D4 Lacepede Bay S.A. Austr.
86 D3 Lacepede Islands W.A. Austr.
183 G2 La Cerca Spain
186 C4 La Cerollera Spain
191 F2 Laces Italy
225 G4 Lac-Etchemin Que. Can.
234 B1 Laceyville PA U.S.A.
233 □H1 Lac Frontière Que. Can.
134 G3 Lacha, Ozero l. Rus. Fed.
161 B3 La Chaise-Dieu France
158 E5 La Chaize-le-Vicomte France
161 E3 La Chambre France
160 A2 La Chapelaude France
157 F3 La Chapelle France
162 D3 La Chapelle-Aubareil France
157 G4 La Chapelle-aux-Bois France
162 D4 La Chapelle-aux-Saints France
160 E2 La Chapelle-d'Abondance France
159 F4 La Chapelle-d'Aligné France
159 F3 La Chapelle-d'Andaine France
159 I4 La Chapelle-d'Angillon France
158 E3 La Chapelle-des-Fougeretz France
158 D4 La-Chapelle-des-Marais France
161 E4 La Chapelle-en-Valgaudémar France
161 D4 La Chapelle-en-Vercors France
156 C4 La Chapelle-la-Reine France
161 B3 La Chapelle-Laurent France
160 B1 La Chapelle-St-André France
159 F5 La Chapelle-St-Laurent France
156 E4 La Chapelle-St-Luc France
156 B5 La Chapelle-St-Mesmin France
160 D1 La Chapelle-St-Quillain France
159 I4 La Chapelle-St-Ursin France
161 C4 Lachapelle-sous-Aubenas France
158 E4 La Chapelle-sur-Erdre France
160 B1 La Charité-sur-Loire France
159 G4 La Chartre-sur-le-Loir France
161 D3 La Chartreuse, Massif de mts France
162 B2 La Châtaigneraie France
162 D2 La Châtre France
162 D2 La Châtre-Langlin France
157 E5 La Chaume France
157 F3 Lachaussée, Étang de l. France
159 H4 La Chaussée-St-Victor France
156 E4 La Chaussée-sur-Marne France
190 B1 La Chaux-de-Fonds Switz.
160 D2 La Chaux-du-Dombief France
190 D1 Lachen Switz.
168 F3 Lachendorf Ger.
161 E5 Lachens, Montagne de mt. France
172 C2 Lachen-Speyerdorf Ger.
156 E3 La Cheppe France
158 E4 La Chevrolière France
158 D3 La Chèze France
227 F3 Lachine MI U.S.A.
83 E3 Lachlan r. N.S.W. Austr.
250 C5 La Chorrera Col.
242 □K7 La Chorrera Panama
175 K2 Lachowo Pol.
168 F3 Lachte r. Ger.
117 G4 Lachung Sikkim India
224 F4 Lachute Que. Can.
138 F4 Lāči Latvia
183 I4 La Cierva Spain
129 E4 Laçın Azer.
161 D5 La Ciotat France
183 F3 La Cisterniga Spain
244 B2 La Ciudad Mex.
175 H3 Łąck Pol.
148 B3 Lack Northern Ireland U.K.
232 D3 Lackawanna NY U.S.A.
234 C1 Lackawanna r. PA U.S.A.
234 C1 Lackawanna County county PA U.S.A.
234 D1 Lackawaxen r. PA U.S.A.
175 I6 Łącko Pol.
223 I4 Lac La Biche Alta Can.
Lac la Martre N.W.T. Can. see Wha Ti
160 C2 La Clayette France
160 E3 La Clusaz France
161 D4 La Cluse France
160 E2 La Cluse-et-Mijoux France
225 G4 Lac-Mégantic Que. Can.
258 D2 La Cocha Arg.
150 E3 Lacock Wiltshire, England U.K.
184 C1 La Codosera Spain
186 D3 La Cogulla mt. Spain
233 G2 Lacolle Que. Can.
161 F5 La Colle-sur-Loup France
245 E2 La Colmena, Sierra mts Mex.
242 C2 La Colorada Mex.
222 H4 Lacombe Alta Can.
226 C5 Lacon IL U.S.A.
183 G1 La Concha Spain
243 G5 La Concordia Mex.
161 E4 La Condamine-Châtelard France
192 B5 Laconi Sardegna Italy
233 H3 Laconia NH U.S.A.
260 C3 La Consulta Arg.
161 B5 La Coquillade hill France
162 C3 La Coquille France
223 I4 La Corey Alta Can.
227 I1 La Corne Que. Can.
185 E2 La Coronada Andalucía Spain
184 E2 La Coronada Extremadura Spain
La Coruña Spain see A Coruña
La Coruña prov. Galicia Spain see A Coruña
161 D5 Lacoste France
161 D3 La Côte-St-André France
162 A2 La-Couarde-sur-Mer France
162 C3 La Couronne France
163 D6 Lacourt France
162 E3 La Courtine France
156 B4 La Couture-Boussey France
161 B5 La Couvertoirade France
246 □ Lacovia Jamaica
163 B5 Lacq France
161 E5 La Crau France
162 B2 La Crèche France
226 B4 La Crescent MN U.S.A.
222 G3 La Crete Alta Can.
186 D4 La Creu de Santos hill Spain
261 G2 La Criolla Arg.
161 A4 Lacroix-Barrez France
159 E3 La Croixille France
156 C3 Lacroix-St-Ouen France
161 E5 La Croix-Valmer France
236 D4 La Crosse KS U.S.A.
232 D6 La Crosse VA U.S.A.
226 B4 La Crosse WI U.S.A.
163 E5 Lacrouzette France
258 F3 La Cruz Arg.
250 B4 La Cruz Col.
242 □I7 La Cruz Costa Rica
242 D4 La Cruz Sinaloa Mex.
245 E1 La Cruz Tamaulipas Mex.
242 □I6 La Cruz Nic.
244 D5 La Cruz, Cerro mt. Mex.
242 E2 La Cuesta Mex.
182 D3 La Culebra, Sierra de mts Spain
260 E2 La Cumbre Arg.
184 E1 La Cumbre Spain
183 H2 Lacunza Spain
236 E4 La Cygne KS U.S.A.
175 J4 Łączany Pol.
175 I5 Łączna Pol.
174 F5 Łącznik Pol.
175 K5 Łada r. Pol.
257 G2 Ladainha Brazil
116 D2 Ladakh Range mts India
137 G2 Ladan Ukr.
177 I4 Ladánybene Hungary
169 C3 Ladbergen Ger.
177 H2 Ladce Slovakia
226 C5 Ladd IL U.S.A.
174 F3 Lądek Pol.
174 E5 Lądek-Zdrój Pol.
168 E1 Ladelund Ger.
246 B2 La Demajagua Cuba
183 G2 La Demanda, Sierra de mts Spain
172 C2 Ladenburg Ger.
158 D2 La Déroute, Passage de str. Channel Is/France
247 □2 La Désirade i. Guadeloupe
146 C4 Ladhar Bheinn mt. Scotland U.K.
162 D3 Ladignac-le-Long France
217 □2a La Digue i. Inner Islands Seychelles
126 D2 Ladik Turkey
179 F4 Ladinger Spitz mt. Austria
163 E4 Ladinhac France
214 C5 Ladismith S. Africa
192 E3 Ladispoli Italy
123 E4 Lādīz Iran
116 C4 Ladnun Rajasthan India
182 C5 Ladoeiro Port.
190 B2 La Dôle mt. Switz.
156 C4 Ladon France
198 B3 Ladon r. Greece
108 D3 Ladong Guangxi China
139 H1 Ladozhskoye Ozero l. Rus. Fed.
182 C1 Ladra r. Spain
Ladrones terr. N. Pacific Ocean see Northern Mariana Islands
242 □J8 Ladrones, Islas is Panama
117 H4 Ladu mt. Arun. Prad. India
222 A2 Ladue r. Can./U.S.A.
138 C4 Ladushkin Rus. Fed.
134 F3 Ladva Rus. Fed.
134 F3 Ladva-Vetka Rus. Fed.
116 D3 Ladwa Haryana India
146 E5 Ladybank Fife, Scotland U.K.
83 G5 Lady Barron Tas. Austr.
215 F3 Ladybrand S. Africa
215 F4 Lady Frere S. Africa
215 F4 Lady Grey S. Africa
136 D3 Ladyhy Ukr.
148 E2 Lady Isle i. Scotland U.K.
146 F6 Ladykirk Scottish Borders, Scotland U.K.
146 F4 Ladysford Aberdeenshire, Scotland U.K.
222 F5 Ladysmith B.C. Can.
215 G3 Ladysmith S. Africa
226 B3 Ladysmith WI U.S.A.
121 G2 Ladyzhenka Kazakh.
136 E3 Ladyzhyn Ukr.
136 F3 Ladyzhynka Ukr.
175 H4 Ładzice Pol.
91 K8 Lae P.N.G.
261 G3 La Emilia Arg.
97 C4 Laem Ngop Thai.
187 C6 La Encina Spain
169 C3 Laer Ger.
183 E2 La Ercina Spain
141 I3 Lærdalsøyri Norway
192 A4 Laerru Sardegna Italy
La Escala Spain see L'Escala
142 D3 Læsø i. Denmark
142 D3 Læsø Rende sea chan. Denmark
253 E3 La Esperanza Bol.
216 □3a La Esperanza Tenerife Canary Is
242 □H6 La Esperanza Hond.
242 □I6 La Esperanza, Sierra de mts Hond.
182 D1 La Espina Spain
245 E3 La Estancia, Cerro mt. Mex.
183 E5 La Estrella Spain
260 E2 La Falda Arg.
161 D5 La Fare-les-Oliviers France
226 B4 La Farge WI U.S.A.
233 F2 La Fargeville NY U.S.A.
161 E5 La Farlède France
186 D3 La Fatarrella Spain
161 D4 La Faurie France
162 A2 La Faute-sur-Mer France
Lafayette Alg. see Bougaa
231 C5 Lafayette AL U.S.A.
240 F3 Lafayette CA U.S.A.
238 F4 Lafayette CO U.S.A.
231 C5 La Fayette GA U.S.A.
230 C3 Lafayette IN U.S.A.
237 E6 Lafayette LA U.S.A.
234 D1 Lafayette NJ U.S.A.
232 B5 Lafayette OH U.S.A.
231 C4 Lafayette TN U.S.A.
246 A2 Lafé Cuba
185 I1 La Felipa Spain
156 D3 La Fère France
158 E5 La Ferrière France
159 F3 La Ferrière-aux-Etangs France
227 H1 Laferté Que. Can.
222 G2 Laferte r. N.W.T. Can.
156 C4 La Ferté-Alais France
159 G3 La Ferté-Bernard France
159 G3 La Ferté-Frênel France
156 D4 La Ferté-Gaucher France
159 H4 La Ferté-Imbault France
156 D5 La Ferté-Loupière France
159 F3 La Ferté-Macé France
156 D3 La-Ferté-Milon France
156 B5 La Ferté-St-Aubin France
156 B5 La Ferté-St-Cyr France
156 D4 La Ferté-sous-Jouarre France
157 F5 Laferté-sur-Amance France
157 E4 Laferté-sur-Aube France
159 G3 La Férte-Vidame France
156 B5 La Ferté-Villeneuil France
207 H4 Lafia Nigeria
207 G4 Lafiagi Nigeria
163 C5 Lafitole France
224 E3 Laflamme r. Que. Can.
223 J5 Lafleche Sask. Can.
159 F4 La Flèche France
182 D1 La Florida Spain
162 A2 La Flotte France
179 H3 Lafnitz Austria
179 H4 Lafnitz r. Austria
78 □5 La Foa New Caledonia
232 A6 La Follette TN U.S.A.
226 E5 La Fontaine IN U.S.A.
159 G4 La Fontaine-St-Martin France
187 C6 La Font de la Figuera Spain
161 E4 La Font Sancte, Pic de mt. France
227 H2 Laforce Que. Can.
163 C4 La Force France
227 G2 Laforest Ont. Can.
158 C4 La Forêt-Fouesant France
159 F5 La Forêt-sur-Sèvre France
225 F2 Laforge Que. Can.
225 F2 Laforge r. Que. Can.
157 G4 La Forge France
186 D2 Lafortunada Spain
163 E4 La Fouillade France
160 C3 La Fouillouse France
237 F6 Lafourche, Bayou r. LA U.S.A.
161 E4 La Foux-d'Allos France
163 D4 Lafrançaise France
156 E3 La Francheville France
261 F2 La Francia Arg.
182 D4 La Fregeneda Spain
159 G3 La Fresnaye-sur-Chédouat France
157 H4 Lafrimbolle France
183 H4 La Frontera Spain
122 C5 Lāft Iran
182 D4 La Fuente de San Esteban Spain
186 E3 La Fuliola Spain
158 D4 La Gacilly France
186 D4 La Galera del Pla Spain
205 H1 La Galite, Canal de sea chan. Tunisia
258 E3 La Gallareta Arg.
256 D3 Lagamar Brazil
120 A3 Lagan' Rus. Fed.
143 E3 Lagan r. Sweden
147 F2 Lagan r. Northern Ireland U.K.
161 E5 La Garde France
161 C4 La Garde-Adhémar France
161 E5 La Garde-Freinet France
163 D5 Lagardelle-sur-Lèze France
182 C3 Lagarelhos Port.
182 C4 Lagares da Beira Port.
185 F2 La Garganta Spain
158 E5 La Garnache France
186 F3 La Garriga Spain
163 E5 Lagarrigue France
184 D2 La Garrovilla Spain
183 E5 Lagartera Spain
254 F4 Lagarto Brazil
256 A5 Lagarto, Serra do hills Brazil
159 E5 La Gaubretière France
148 C2 Lagavara Northern Ireland U.K.
206 B3 Lagbar Senegal
169 B3 Lage Niedersachsen Ger.
169 D4 Lage Nordrhein-Westfalen Ger.
165 E3 Lage Mierde Neth.
142 C1 Lågen r. Norway
142 D2 Lågen r. Norway
168 E2 Lägerdorf Ger.
146 C6 Lagg North Ayrshire, Scotland U.K.
146 D4 Laggan Highland, Scotland U.K.
146 D4 Laggan Highland, Scotland U.K.
146 D5 Laggan, Loch l. Scotland U.K.
148 C2 Laggan Bay Scotland U.K.
146 B5 Lagganulva Argyll and Bute, Scotland U.K.
147 C2 Laghey Rep. of Ireland
123 G3 Laghmān prov. Afgh.
205 F2 Laghouat Alg.
147 C3 Laghtgeorge Rep. of Ireland
174 E5 Łagiewniki Pol.
185 I1 La Gineta Spain
198 C1 Lagkadas Greece
158 E2 La Glacerie France
250 C2 La Gloria Col.
160 D3 Lagnieu France
156 C4 Lagny-sur-Marne France
193 I5 Lago Italy
Lago prov. Moz. see Niassa
216 □1b Lagoa São Miguel Azores
182 D3 Lagoa Bragança Port.
184 B3 Lagoa Faro Port.
182 D3 Lagoaça Port.
257 E4 Lagoa da Prata Brazil
257 E4 Lagoa Dourada Brazil
256 D3 Lagoa Formosa Brazil
257 F3 Lagoa Santa Brazil
255 C9 Lagoa Vermelha Brazil
254 D3 Lago da Pedra Brazil
129 E3 Lagodekhi Georgia
187 G5 Lago Menor Spain
216 □3a La Gomera i. Canary Is
243 H6 La Gomera Guat.
246 D3 La Gonâve, Île de i. Haiti
193 H4 Lagonegro Italy
92 B3 Lagonoy Gulf Phil.
84 D3 Lagoon Creek r. Qld Austr.
Lagoon Island atoll Arch. des Tuamotu Fr. Polynesia see Tematangi
163 B5 Lagor France
162 B3 Lagorce Aquitaine France
161 C4 Lagorce Rhône-Alpes France
262 O1 La Gorce Mountains Antarctica
162 A2 Lagord France
186 E3 La Gornal Spain
244 C3 Lagos r. Mex.
207 F5 Lagos Nigeria
207 F5 Lagos state Nigeria
184 B3 Lagos Port.
211 A6 Lagosa Tanz.
191 H4 Lagosanto Italy
244 D3 Lagos de Moreno Mex.
174 D3 Łagów Pol.
175 J5 Łagów Pol.
140 □ Lågøya i. Svalbard
183 H2 Lagrán Spain
184 D3 La Granada de Riotinto Spain
186 D3 La Granadella Spain
160 C3 La Grand-Croix France
224 E2 La Grande r. Que. Can.
238 C2 La Grande OR U.S.A.
224 E2 La Grande 2, Réservoir resr Que. Can.
224 F2 La Grande 3, Réservoir resr Que. Can.
224 F2 La Grande 4, Réservoir resr Que. Can.
161 E3 La Grande Casse, Pointe de mt. France
161 C4 La Grande-Combe France
161 C5 La Grande-Motte France
86 D3 Lagrange W.A. Austr.
240 G3 La Grange CA U.S.A.
231 C5 La Grange GA U.S.A.
230 C3 Lagrange IN U.S.A.
230 C4 La Grange KY U.S.A.
233 □I2 La Grange ME U.S.A.
237 D6 La Grange TX U.S.A.
86 D3 Lagrange Bay W.A. Austr.
235 E1 Lagrangeville NY U.S.A.
186 D3 La Granja d'Escarp Spain
185 E2 La Granjuela Spain
251 F3 La Gran Sabana plat. Venez.
161 A5 Lagrasse France
161 E3 La Grave France
163 D4 La Grésigne, Forêt de reg. France
190 C2 La Gruyère, Lac de l. Switz.
225 G4 La Guadeloupe Que. Can.
250 D2 La Guajira, Península de pen. Col.
216 □3a La Guancha Tenerife Canary Is
184 E2 La Guarda Spain
183 G5 La Guardia Castilla - La Mancha Spain
La Guardia Galicia Spain see A Guardia
183 H2 Laguardia Spain
185 G3 La Guardia de Jaén Spain
186 C2 Laguarta Spain
La Gudiña Spain see A Gudiña
162 D3 Laguenne France
163 D4 Laguépie France
158 E4 La Guerche-de-Bretagne France
160 A2 La Guerche-sur-l'Aubois France
158 D5 La Guérinière France
160 C2 La Guiche France
161 A4 Laguiole France
255 C9 Laguna Brazil
239 F5 Laguna NM U.S.A.
251 I5 Laguna, Ilha da i. Brazil
240 I5 Laguna Beach CA U.S.A.
182 E2 Laguna Dalga Spain
183 F3 Laguna de Duero Spain
182 E2 Laguna de Negrillos Spain
242 □J6 Laguna de Perlas Nic.
241 I5 Laguna Mountains CA U.S.A.
250 C6 Lagunas Peru
258 E2 Laguna Yema Arg.
191 G2 Lagundo Italy
182 E4 Lagunilla Spain
252 E4 Lagunillas Bol.
250 D2 Lagunillas Venez.
107 J1 Laha Heilong. China
184 E2 La Haba Spain
246 B2 La Habana Cuba
240 I5 La Habra CA U.S.A.
95 G1 Lahad Datu Sabah Malaysia
158 E2 La Hague, Cap de c. France
240 □C8 Lahaina HI U.S.A.
116 D4 Lahar Madh. Prad. India
147 B2 Lahardaun Rep. of Ireland
226 B5 La Harpe IL U.S.A.
116 E4 Laharpur Uttar Prad. India
234 C2 Lahaska PA U.S.A.
94 C3 Lahat Sumatera Indon.
158 E2 La Haye-du-Puits France
158 E3 La Haye-Pesnel France
168 C3 Lähden Ger.
260 B2 La Herradura Chile
185 H2 La Herrera Spain
159 G2 La Hève, Cap de c. France
157 F4 Laheycourt France
129 F3 Lahıc Azer.
187 B6 La Higuera Spain
124 D5 Laḩij Yemen
124 D5 Laḩij governorate Yemen
118 F2 Lāhījān Iran
147 B4 Lahinch Rep. of Ireland
182 E3 La Hiniesta Spain
136 C1 Lahishyn Belarus
168 C3 Lahn Ger.
169 C5 Lahn r. Ger.
169 D5 Lahnau Ger.
169 C5 Lahnstein Ger.
169 D5 Lahntal-Goßfelden Ger.
142 E3 Laholm Sweden
142 E3 Laholmsbukten b. Sweden
183 E4 La Horcajada Spain
123 H4 Lahore Pak.
183 G3 La Horra Spain
246 D3 La Hotte, Massif de mts Haiti
138 F4 Lahoysk Belarus
172 B3 Lahr (Schwarzwald) Ger.
141 N3 Lahti Fin.
250 A6 La Huaca Peru
244 D4 La Huacana Mex.
244 B4 La Huerta Mex.
260 D2 La Huerta, Sierra de mts Arg.
208 C2 Laï Chad

225 K3 **La Scie** *Nfld.* Can.
240 G4 **Las Cruces** *CA* U.S.A.
239 F5 **Las Cruces** *NM* U.S.A.
186 D2 **Lascuarre** Spain
183 F3 **La Seca** Spain
159 F4 **La Séguinière** France
246 E3 **La Selle** *mt.* Haiti
186 E3 **La Selva del Camp** Spain
163 E4 **La Selve** France
186 D4 **La Sènia** Spain
161 B5 **La Séranne, Montagne de** *ridge* France
260 B1 **La Serena** Chile
185 E2 **La Serena, Embalse de** *resr* Spain
160 D1 **La Serre, Massif de** *hills* France
243 E3 **Las Esperanças** Mex.
185 H3 **Las Estancias, Sierra de** *mts* Spain
161 D5 **La Seyne-sur-Mer** France
261 H5 **Las Flores** Arg.
244 C4 **Las Guacamayas** Mex.
123 E5 **Lāshār** *r.* Iran
223 I4 **Lashburn** *Sask.* Can.
260 C3 **Las Heras** Arg.
183 F5 **Las Herencias** Spain
261 E3 **Las Higueras** Arg.
123 F4 **Lashkar Gāh** Afgh.
260 A6 **Las Hortensias** Chile
175 H2 **Łasin** Pol.
245 F5 **La Sirena, Cerro** *mt.* Mex.
244 D3 **Las Jicamas** Mex.
261 F2 **Las Junturas** Arg.
175 H4 **Łask** Pol.
175 J4 **Łaskarzew** Pol.
173 G3 **Laskivtsi** Ukr.
179 G4 **Laško** Slovenia
175 I6 **Laskowa** Pol.
174 G2 **Laskowice** Pol.
185 G1 **Las Labores** Spain
260 B6 **Las Lajas** Arg.
260 B4 **Las Leñas** Arg.
250 A4 **Las Lomas** Peru
258 E2 **Las Lomitas** Arg.
183 H4 **Las Majadas** Spain
184 D3 **Las Marismas** *marsh* Spain
182 D2 **Las Médulas** *tourist site* *Castilla y León* Spain
185 H3 **Las Menas** Spain
250 E2 **Las Mercedes** Venez.
216 □3a **Las Mercedes, Monte de** *hill* *Tenerife* Canary Is
185 H1 **Las Mesas** Spain
243 H6 **Las Minas, Sierra de** *mts* Guat.
Las Mulatas *is* Panama *see* San Blas, Archipiélago de
245 E4 **Las Navajas, Cerro** *mt.* Mex.
185 E3 **Las Navas de la Concepción** Spain
183 F4 **Las Navas del Marqués** Spain
165 D4 **Lasne** Belgium
185 I4 **Las Negras** Spain
242 D3 **Las Nieves** Mex.
216 □3f **Las Nieves, Pico de** *mt.* *Gran Canaria* Canary Is
242 E3 **Las Nopaleras, Cerro** *mt.* Mex.
79 □3 **La Société, Archipel de** *is* Fr. Polynesia
185 G2 **La Solana** Spain
156 B2 **La Somme, Baie de** *b.* France
162 D2 **La Souterraine** France
174 G5 **Lasowice Małe** Pol.
258 F2 **Las Palmas** Arg.
216 □3f **Las Palmas de Gran Canaria** *Gran Canaria* Canary Is
244 D4 **Las Parotas** *r.* Mex.
185 H1 **Las Pedroñeras** Spain
261 F3 **Las Perdices** Arg.
242 □K7 **Las Perlas, Archipiélago de** *is* Panama
253 F4 **Las Petas** Bol.
190 E4 **La Spezia** Italy
190 E4 **La Spezia** *prov.* *Liguria* Italy
261 I4 **Las Piedras** Uru.
252 C3 **Las Piedras, Río de** *r.* Peru
193 H4 **La Spina, Monte** *mt.* Italy
192 A5 **Las Plassas** *Sardegna* Italy
186 D2 **Laspuña** Spain
123 H2 **Laspur** Pak.
261 G3 **Las Rosas** Arg.
187 D6 **Las Rotas** Spain
183 G4 **Las Rozas de Madrid** Spain
168 F2 **Lassahn** Ger.
260 D2 **Las Salinas, Pampa de** *salt pan* Arg.
170 E2 **Lassan** Ger.
257 E2 **Lassance** Brazil
159 F3 **Lassay-les-Châteaux** France
240 G1 **Lassen Peak** *vol.* *CA* U.S.A.
163 B5 **Lasseube** France
156 C3 **Lassigny** France
179 F3 **Lassing** Austria
179 G3 **Laßnitzhöhe** Austria
242 □J8 **Las Tablas** Panama
236 C4 **Last Chance** *CO* U.S.A.
191 G3 **Lastebasse** Italy
191 G2 **Lastè delle Sute** *mt.* Italy
258 D1 **Las Termas** Arg.
185 I3 **Las Terreras** Spain
187 B6 **Las Torres de Cotillas** Spain
260 C1 **Las Tórtolas, Cerro** *mt.* Chile
163 E5 **Lastours** France
208 B5 **Lastoursville** Gabon
188 F4 **Lastovo** *i.* Croatia
188 F4 **Lastovski Kanal** *sea chan.* Croatia
191 G5 **Lastra a Signa** Italy
183 F3 **Lastras de Cuéllar** Spain
242 B3 **Las Tres Vírgenes, Volcán** *vol.* Mex.
168 C3 **Lastrup** Ger.
246 C2 **Las Tunas** Cuba
159 G4 **La Suze-sur-Sarthe** France
242 D2 **Las Varas** *Chihuahua* Mex.
244 B3 **Las Varas** *Nayarit* Mex.
261 F2 **Las Varillas** Arg.
239 F5 **Las Vegas** *NM* U.S.A.
241 J3 **Las Vegas** *NV* U.S.A.
182 E4 **Las Veguillas** Spain
183 F5 **Las Ventas con Peña Aguilera** Spain
183 E4 **Las Ventas de San Julián** Spain
245 F4 **Las Vigas de Ramirez** Mex.
185 E1 **Las Villuercas** *mt.* Spain
252 C4 **Las Yaras** Peru
175 L5 **Łaszczów** Pol.
175 K5 **Laszki** Pol.
Lászlófalva Hungary *see* Szentkirály
225 J3 **La Tabatière** *Que.* Can.
250 B5 **Latacunga** Ecuador
258 B2 **Latady Island** Antarctica
162 C2 **La Tagnière** France
Latakia Syria *see* **Al Lādhiqīyah**
161 C3 **La Talaudière** France
159 F3 **La Tannière** France
227 H2 **Latchford** *Ont.* Can.
151 H3 **Latchingdon** *Essex, England* U.K.
79 □2 **Late** *i.* *Vava'u Gp* Tonga
117 F5 **Latehar** *Bihar* India
158 C4 **La Teignouse, Passage de** *str.* France
191 G2 **Latemar** *mt.* Italy
195 F2 **Laterza** Italy
163 A4 **La Teste** France
244 B3 **La Tetilla, Cerro** *mt.* Mex.
138 F3 **Latgales augstiene** *reg.* Latvia
87 C6 **Latham** *W.A.* Austr.
168 C3 **Lathen** Ger.
146 E3 **Latheron** *Highland, Scotland* U.K.
116 B5 **Lathi** *Gujarat* India
240 G3 **Lathrop** *CA* U.S.A.
190 B3 **La Thuile** Italy
162 C2 **Lathus** France
195 G2 **Latiano** Italy
140 L2 **Latikberg** Sweden
193 E3 **Latina** Italy
193 F3 **Latina** *prov.* *Lazio* Italy
191 I3 **Latisana** Italy
137 J2 **Latnaya** Rus. Fed.
195 F2 **Lato** *r.* Italy
260 E3 **La Toma** Arg.
176 E3 **Latorica** *r.* Slovakia
190 C2 **La Tornette** *mt.* Switz.
186 D2 **La Torre de Cabdella** Spain
251 E2 **La Tortuga, Isla** *i.* Venez.
136 B3 **Latorytsya** *r.* Ukr.
86 D3 **Latouche Treville, Cape** *W.A.* Austr.
162 C3 **La Tour-Blanche** France
161 D5 **La Tour-d'Aigues** France
160 A3 **La Tour-d'Auvergne** France
163 D6 **Latour-de-Carol** France
163 E6 **Latour-de-France** France
163 D5 **La Tour-du-Crieu** France
160 D3 **La Tour-du-Pin** France
160 E3 **La Tournette** *mt.* France
161 B5 **La Tour-sur-Orb** France
161 E3 **La Toussuire** France
175 J3 **Latowicz** Pol.
162 A2 **La Tranche-sur-Mer** France
163 D5 **Latrape** France
157 E5 **Latrecey-Ormoy-sur-Aube** France
162 A3 **La Tremblade** France
162 D2 **La Trimouille** France
242 □I6 **La Trinidad** Nic.
92 B2 **La Trinidad** Phil.
243 G5 **La Trinitaria** Mex.
161 F5 **La Trinité** France
247 □3 **La Trinité** Martinique
159 G3 **La Trinité-de-Réville** France
158 D3 **La Trinité-Porhoët** France
158 C4 **La Trinité-sur-Mer** France
83 F5 **Latrobe** *Tas.* Austr.
232 D4 **Latrobe** *PA* U.S.A.
161 D3 **La Tronche** France
193 I4 **Latronico** Italy
163 E4 **Latronquière** France
258 C3 **La Troya** *r.* Arg.
139 L2 **Latskoye** Rus. Fed.
Lattaquié Syria *see* Al Lādhiqīyah
193 I5 **Lattarico** Italy
Latte Island *Vava'u Gp* Tonga *see* Late
161 B5 **Lattes** France
164 F2 **Lattrop** Neth.
227 H2 **Latulipe** *Que.* Can.
225 F4 **La Tuque** *Que.* Can.
114 C2 **Latur** *Mahar.* India
158 D4 **La Turballe** France
138 D3 **Latvia** *country* Europe
Latvija *country* Europe *see* Latvia
Latviyskaya S.S.R. *country* Europe *see* **Latvia**
207 H4 **Lau** Nigeria
210 A3 **Lau** *r.* Sudan
117 F5 **Laua** *r.* *Madh. Prad.* India
169 D5 **Laubach** *Hessen* Ger.
169 C5 **Laubach** *Rheinland-Pfalz* Ger.
173 E3 **Lauben** *Bayern* Ger.
173 F4 **Lauben** *Bayern* Ger.
171 F4 **Laubusch** Ger.
171 C4 **Laucha (Unstrut)** Ger.
172 D3 **Lauchert** *r.* Ger.
171 E4 **Lauchhammer** Ger.
173 E3 **Lauchheim** Ger.
172 C3 **Lauchringen** Ger.
172 D2 **Lauda-Königshofen** Ger.
172 C2 **Laudenbach** Ger.
146 F6 **Lauder** *Scottish Borders, Scotland* U.K.
234 D3 **Lauderdale** *NJ* U.S.A.
161 C4 **Laudun** France
169 E3 **Lauenau** Ger.
168 F2 **Lauenbrück** Ger.
171 E2 **Lauenburg (Elbe)** Ger.
169 E4 **Lauenförde** Ger.
169 F5 **Lauer** *r.* Ger.
172 C3 **Lauf** Ger.
169 E5 **Laufach** Ger.
173 F2 **Lauf an der Pegnitz** Ger.
173 G4 **Laufen** Ger.
172 C1 **Laufen** Switz.
190 D1 **Laufenberg** Switz.
172 C4 **Laufenburg (Baden)** Ger.
221 L2 **Lauge Koch Kyst** *reg.* Greenland
150 C3 **Laugharne** *Carmarthenshire, Wales* U.K.
84 C4 **Laughlen, Mount** *N.T.* Austr.
239 F4 **Laughlin Peak** *NM* U.S.A.
174 C4 **Lauingen** Ger.
173 E3 **Lauingen (Donau)** Ger.
185 H4 **Laujar de Andarax** Spain
140 N3 **Laukaa** Fin.
138 D4 **Laukuva** Lith.
97 B5 **Laun** Thai.
163 D5 **Launac** France
227 H1 **Launay** *Que.* Can.
83 F5 **Launceston** *Tas.* Austr.
150 C4 **Launceston** *Cornwall, England* U.K.
147 B4 **Laune** *r.* Rep. of Ireland
97 B4 **Launglon Bok Islands** Myanmar
253 E3 **La Unión** Bol.
259 B6 **La Unión** Chile
250 B4 **La Unión** Col.
242 □I6 **La Unión** El Salvador
244 D5 **La Unión** Mex.
252 A2 **La Unión** *Huánuco* Peru
250 A6 **La Unión** *Piura* Peru
187 C7 **La Unión** Spain
161 E3 **Launois-sur-Vence** France
190 C2 **Laupen** Switz.
172 D3 **Laupheim** Ger.
92 B3 **Laur** Phil.
85 F2 **Laura** *Qld* Austr.
82 D3 **Laura** *S.A.* Austr.
163 E5 **Lauraguel** France
195 F4 **Laureana di Borrello** Italy
233 F5 **Laurel** *DE* U.S.A.
237 F6 **Laurel** *MS* U.S.A.
238 E2 **Laurel** *MT* U.S.A.
232 B4 **Laurel** *NE* U.S.A.
234 C2 **Laureldale** *PA* U.S.A.
232 D5 **Laurel Hill** *hills* *PA* U.S.A.
234 D4 **Laurel Springs** *NJ* U.S.A.
234 A2 **Laurelton** *PA* U.S.A.
146 F5 **Laurencekirk** *Aberdeenshire, Scotland* U.K.
147 C3 **Laurencetown** Rep. of Ireland
161 B5 **Laurens** France
236 E3 **Laurens** *IA* U.S.A.
231 D5 **Laurens** *SC* U.S.A.
193 H4 **Laurenzana** Italy
163 A5 **Laurhibar** *r.* France
116 E4 **Lauri** *Madh. Prad.* India
193 H4 **Lauria** Italy
262 V2 **Laurie Island** *S. Orkney Is* Antarctica
162 D2 **Laurière** France
146 D7 **Lauriston** *Dumfries and Galloway, Scotland* U.K.
83 H2 **Lauriston** *N.S.W.* Austr.
231 E5 **Laurinburg** *NC* U.S.A.
193 H4 **Laurino** Italy
161 D5 **Lauris** France
81 C5 **Lauriston** *South I.* N.Z.
226 C2 **Laurium** *MI* U.S.A.
194 D2 **Lauro** Italy
Lauru *i.* Solomon Is *see* Choiseul
190 B2 **Lausanne** Switz.
171 C4 **Lausehügel** *hill* Ger.
171 F4 **Lausitzer Gebirge** *hills* Ger.
171 E4 **Laußig** Ger.
171 E4 **Laußnitz** Ger.
161 C4 **Laussonne** France
163 C4 **Laussou** France
95 E1 **Laut** *i.* Indon.
95 E1 **Laut** *i.* Indon.
95 G3 **Laut** *i.* Indon.
171 F4 **Lauta** Ger.
260 A6 **Lautaro** Chile
259 B8 **Lautaro, Cerro** *vol.* Chile
172 C3 **Lautenbach** Ger.
157 I4 **Lauter** *r.* France/Ger.
171 D5 **Lauter** Ger.
178 A3 **Lauterach** Austria
173 F2 **Lauterach** *r.* Ger.
157 I4 **Lauterbourg** France
190 C2 **Lauterbrunnen** Switz.
172 D2 **Lauterecken** Ger.
173 F2 **Lauterhofen** Ger.
169 E5 **Lautersbach (Hessen)** Ger.
172 D3 **Lauterstein** Ger.
169 E5 **Lautertal** Ger.
95 F4 **Laut Kecil, Kepulauan** *is* Indon.
79 □1a **Lautoka** *Viti Levu* Fiji
163 E5 **Lautrec** France
140 J2 **Lauvsnes** Norway
163 D4 **Lauzerte** France
163 D4 **Lauzès** France
175 J1 **Lava** *r.* Rus. Fed.
234 C1 **Lava** *NY* U.S.A.
237 D6 **Lavaca** *r.* *TX* U.S.A.
190 E4 **Lavagna** Italy
190 E4 **Lavagne** *r.* Italy
224 F4 **Laval** *Que.* Can.
159 F3 **Laval** France
163 E5 **Lavalette** France
232 B5 **Lavalette** *WV* U.S.A.
161 D5 **La Valette-du-Var** France
191 G2 **La Valle** Italy
179 F4 **Lavamünd** Austria
161 E3 **La Vanoise, Massif de** *mts* France
186 E2 **Lavansa** *r.* Spain
160 D2 **Lavans-lès-St-Claude** France
179 F4 **Lavant** *r.* Austria/Slovenia
199 E1 **Lavara** Greece
163 C4 **Lavardac** France
163 C5 **Lavardens** France
260 D4 **La Varita, Pampa de** *plain* Arg.
122 C4 **Lāvar Meydān** *salt marsh* Iran
161 B3 **Lavaudieu** France
163 D5 **Lavaur** France
162 E2 **Lavaveix-les-Mines** France
240 G3 **Laveaga Peak** *CA* U.S.A.
183 E2 **La Vecilla** Spain
246 E3 **La Vega** Dom. Rep.
183 E2 **La Vega** *Cantabria* Spain
La Vega *Galicia* Spain *see* **A Veiga**
182 E1 **La Vega de Riosa** Spain
182 E1 **La Vega de Sariego** Spain
163 D6 **Lavelanet** France
182 E3 **La Vellés** Spain
193 H3 **Lavello** Italy
237 C6 **La Venada** *r.* Mex.
190 D3 **Lavena Ponte Tresa** Italy
151 H2 **Lavenham** *Suffolk, England* U.K.
190 D3 **Laveno** Italy
245 H5 **La Venta** *r.* Mex.
258 E5 **La Ventana, Sierra de** *mts* Arg.
156 C2 **Laventie** France
183 H4 **La Ventosa** Spain
195 F4 **La Verde** *r.* Italy
161 D5 **La Verdière** France
161 B4 **La Vernarède** France
237 D4 **Laverne** *OK* U.S.A.
160 D3 **La Verpillière** France
159 F5 **La Verrie** France
87 D6 **Laverton** *W.A.* Austr.
156 E3 **La Veuve** France
141 M3 **Lavia** Fin.
193 H4 **Laviano** Italy
242 E3 **La Víbora** Mex.
185 F3 **La Victoria** Spain
247 F5 **La Victoria** Venez.
181 □ **La Victoria de Acentejo** *Tenerife* Canary Is
183 G3 **La Vid** Spain
182 D5 **La Vid, Río de** *r.* Spain
227 G2 **Lavigne** *Ont.* Can.
192 C3 **La Villa** Italy
183 G5 **La Villa de Don Fadrique** Spain
156 B5 **La Ville-aux-Clercs** France
161 B4 **La Villedieu** France
161 C4 **Lavilledieu** France
162 C2 **La Villedieu-du-Clain** France
157 G5 **La Villedieu-en-Fontenette** France
258 D2 **La Viña** Arg.
238 E2 **Lavina** *MT* U.S.A.
193 E3 **Lavinio-Lido di Enea** Italy
261 G3 **La Violeta** Arg.
160 E1 **Laviron** France
191 G2 **Lavis** Italy
163 C5 **Lavit** France
157 G4 **La Vôge** *reg.* France
182 B4 **Lavos** Port.
161 C4 **La Voulte-sur-Rhône** France
161 B3 **Lavoûte-Chilhac** France
161 B3 **Lavoûte-sur-Loire** France
257 E4 **Lavras** Brazil
255 B9 **Lavras do Sul** Brazil
184 B2 **Lavre** Port.
184 B2 **Lavre** *r.* Port.
198 D3 **Lavrio** Greece
139 E5 **Lavrovo** Rus. Fed.
206 C5 **Lawa** *r.* Liberia
224 E3 **Lawagamau** *r.* *Ont.* Can.
116 E5 **Lawan** *Madh. Prad.* India
224 D2 **Lawashi** *r.* *Ont.* Can.
125 F5 **Lawdar** Yemen
263 H2 **Law Dome** *ice feature* Antarctica
146 D5 **Lawers** *Perth and Kinross, Scotland* U.K.
151 I3 **Lawford** *Essex, England* U.K.
95 F2 **Lawit, Gunung** *mt.* Indon./Malaysia
94 C1 **Lawit, Gunung** *mt.* Malaysia
226 A4 **Lawler** *IA* U.S.A.
86 E2 **Lawley** *r.* *W.A.* Austr.
234 B2 **Lawn** *PA* U.S.A.
84 D3 **Lawn Hill** *Qld* Austr.
84 D3 **Lawn Hill Creek** *r.* *Qld* Austr.
157 F3 **La Woëvre, Plaine de** *plain* France
157 H4 **La Wontzenau** France
206 E4 **Lawra** Ghana
81 B6 **Lawrence** *South I.* N.Z.
81 C5 **Lawrence** *South I.* N.Z.
236 E4 **Lawrence** *KS* U.S.A.
233 H3 **Lawrence** *MA* U.S.A.
231 C5 **Lawrenceburg** *TN* U.S.A.
233 □J2 **Lawrence Station** *N.B.* Can.
147 E2 **Lawrencetown** *Northern Ireland* U.K.
230 C4 **Lawrenceville** *IL* U.S.A.
234 D2 **Lawrenceville** *NJ* U.S.A.
232 E4 **Lawrenceville** *PA* U.S.A.
232 E6 **Lawrenceville** *VA* U.S.A.
87 D5 **Lawrence Wells, Mount** *hill* *W.A.* Austr.
175 K2 **Ławsk** Pol.
237 D5 **Lawton** *OK* U.S.A.
95 E4 **Lawu, Gunung** *vol.* Indon.
124 A1 **Lawz, Jabal al** *mt.* Saudi Arabia
143 F2 **Laxå** Sweden
182 B1 **Laxe** Spain
148 E3 **Laxey** *Isle of Man*
214 D2 **Laxey** S. Africa
146 C3 **Laxford Bridge** *Highland, Scotland* U.K.
222 D4 **Lax Kw'alaams** *B.C.* Can.
146 □G1 **Laxo** *Shetland, Scotland* U.K.
157 G4 **Laxou** France
143 G3 **Laxsjö** Sweden
143 F2 **Laxsjön** *l.* Sweden
162 A2 **Lay** *r.* France
134 I2 **Laya** *r.* Rus. Fed.
182 B2 **Layana** Spain
124 D3 **Laylā** Saudi Arabia
162 B1 **Layon** *r.* France
183 F5 **Layos** Spain
163 C4 **Layrac** France
75 H2 **Laysan Island** *HI* U.S.A.
234 D1 **Layton** *NJ* U.S.A.
240 F2 **Laytonville** *CA* U.S.A.
Layturi Georgia *see* **Lait'uri**
182 C2 **Laza** Spain
242 C4 **La Zacatosa, Picacho** *mt.* Mex.
183 H2 **Lazagurría** Spain
177 L5 **Lăzăreni** Romania
100 G1 **Lazarev** Rus. Fed.
196 E3 **Lazarevac** *Srbija* Yugo.
242 C4 **Lázaro, Sierra de San** *mts* Mex.
242 B2 **Lázaro Cárdenas** Mex.
244 C5 **Lázaro Cárdenas** Mex.
258 G4 **Lazcano** Uru.
138 D4 **Lazdijai** Lith.
193 E2 **Lazio** *admin. reg.* Italy
191 F3 **Lazise** Italy
175 J6 **Łaziska** Pol.
176 E1 **Lázně Bělohrad** Czech Rep.
176 B1 **Lázně Bohdaneč** Czech Rep.
176 E1 **Lázně Kynžvart** Czech Rep.
100 E4 **Lazo** *Primorskiy Kray* Rus. Fed.
131 O3 **Lazo** *Respublika Sakha (Yakutiya)* Rus. Fed.
149 G3 **Lazonby** *Cumbria, England* U.K.
Lazovsk Moldova *see* **Singerei**
177 L4 **Lazuri** Romania
177 L5 **Lazuri de Beiuș** Romania
137 G4 **Lazurne** Ukr.
175 H5 **Łazy** Pol.
212 D5 **Lazzaro, Monte** *hill* Italy
234 B2 **Leacock** *PA* U.S.A.
220 H5 **Lead** *SD* U.S.A.
146 E6 **Leadburn** *Midlothian, Scotland* U.K.
149 I4 **Leadenham** *Lincolnshire, England* U.K.
223 I5 **Leader** *Sask.* Can.
234 B3 **Leader Heights** *PA* U.S.A.
146 F6 **Leader Water** *r.* *Scotland* U.K.
149 H3 **Leadgate** *Durham, England* U.K.
146 E6 **Leadhills** *South Lanarkshire, Scotland* U.K.
83 G3 **Leadville** *N.S.W.* Austr.
239 F4 **Leadville** *CO* U.S.A.
237 F6 **Leaf** *r.* *MS* U.S.A.
Leaf Bay *Que.* Can. *see* Tasiujaq
223 K3 **Leaf Rapids** *Man.* Can.
262 Q2 **Leahy, Cape** Antarctica
86 E3 **Leake, Mount** *hill* *W.A.* Austr.
237 F6 **Leakesville** *MS* U.S.A.
237 D6 **Leakey** *TX* U.S.A.
Leaksville *NC* U.S.A. *see* **Eden**
86 C4 **Leal, Mount** *hill* *W.A.* Austr.
258 D2 **Leales** Arg.
224 D5 **Leamington** *Ont.* Can.
151 F2 **Leamington Spa, Royal** *Warwickshire, England* U.K.
109 E3 **Le'an** *Jiangxi* China
215 G2 **Leandra** S. Africa
261 G4 **Leandro N. Alem** Arg.
258 G2 **Leandro N. Alem** Arg.
147 B4 **Leane, Lough** *l.* Rep. of Ireland
213 □J2 **Leanja** Madag.
177 I4 **Leányfalu** Hungary
147 B5 **Leap** Rep. of Ireland
86 B4 **Learmonth** *W.A.* Austr.
149 I4 **Leasingham** *Lincolnshire, England* U.K.
151 G3 **Leatherhead** *Surrey, England* U.K.
165 D4 **L'Eau d'Heure** *l.* Belgium
165 D4 **L'Eau d'Heure** *r.* Belgium
Leava Wallis and Futuna Is *see* Sigave
149 I3 **Leavening** *North Yorkshire, England* U.K.
236 E4 **Leavenworth** *KS* U.S.A.
238 B2 **Leavenworth** *WA* U.S.A.
240 H2 **Leavitt Peak** *CA* U.S.A.
143 G4 **Łeba** Pol.
174 F1 **Łeba** *r.* Pol.
174 G1 **Łeba** *r.* Pol.
172 A2 **Lebach** Ger.
92 C5 **Lebak** Phil.
215 E2 **Lebaleng** S. Africa
208 A5 **Lébamba** Gabon
197 E4 **Lebane** *Srbija* Yugo.
128 B3 **Lebanon** *country* Asia
230 C3 **Lebanon** *IN* U.S.A.
236 D4 **Lebanon** *KS* U.S.A.
230 C4 **Lebanon** *KY* U.S.A.
237 E4 **Lebanon** *MO* U.S.A.
233 G3 **Lebanon** *NH* U.S.A.
234 D2 **Lebanon** *NJ* U.S.A.
232 A5 **Lebanon** *OH* U.S.A.
238 B2 **Lebanon** *OR* U.S.A.
227 I5 **Lebanon** *PA* U.S.A.
231 C4 **Lebanon** *TN* U.S.A.
232 B6 **Lebanon** *VA* U.S.A.
234 B2 **Lebanon County** *county* *PA* U.S.A.
157 G3 **Le Ban-St-Martin** France
123 E1 **Lebap** Turkm.
Lebap Oblast *admin. div.* Turkm. *see* Lebapskaya Oblast'
123 E2 **Lebapskaya Oblast'** *admin. div.* Turkm.
163 F6 **Le Barcarès** France
163 B4 **Le Barp** France
165 D3 **Lebbeke** Belgium
Lebda *tourist site* Libya *see* Leptis Magna
161 C4 **Le Béage** France
161 D5 **Le Beausset** France
240 H4 **Lebec** *CA* U.S.A.
159 G2 **Le Bec-Hellouin** France
Lebedin Ukr. *see* **Lebedyn**
139 L5 **Lebedyan'** Rus. Fed.
137 H2 **Lebedyn** Ukr.
224 E3 **Lebel-sur-Quévillon** *Que.* Can.
171 C4 **Lebendorf** Ger.
159 F5 **Le Bény-Bocage** France
176 G4 **Lébényemiklós** Hungary
163 F5 **Le Bez** France
156 B2 **Lebiez** France
162 E2 **Le Blot** France
162 C2 **Le Blanc** France
161 B4 **Le Bleymard** France
174 G1 **Łebno** Pol.
160 C3 **Le Bois-d'Oingt** France
162 A2 **Le Bois-Plage-en-Ré** France
Lebombberg *hills* Moz. *see* Lebombo Mountains
215 I2 **Lebombo Mountains** *hills* Moz.
215 I2 **Lebonang** S. Africa
161 F4 **Le Boréon** France
143 G4 **Lębork** Pol.
163 E6 **Le Boulou** France
159 F5 **Le Boupère** France
161 F4 **Le Bourg** France
161 E3 **Le Bourg-d'Oisans** France
160 D3 **Le Bourget-du-Lac** France
159 F3 **Le Bourgneuf-la-Forêt** France
163 B4 **Le Bouscat** France
161 B5 **Le Bousquet-d'Orb** France
215 F2 **Lebowakgomo** S. Africa
168 F1 **Lebrade** Ger.
160 C2 **Le Breuil** *Bourgogne* France
156 D4 **Le Breuil** *Champagne-Ardenne* France
160 E3 **Le Brévent** *mt.* France
184 D4 **Lebrija** Spain
179 G4 **Lebring-St Margarethen** Austria
163 C5 **Le Brouilh-Monbert** France
161 E4 **Le Brusquet** France
143 G4 **Łebsko, Jezioro** *lag.* Pol.
258 B5 **Lebu** Chile
182 C3 **Lebução** Port.
163 C4 **Le Bugue** France
161 B4 **Le Buisson** France
163 C4 **Le Buisson-de-Cadouin** France
171 F3 **Lebus** Ger.
171 E4 **Lebusa** Ger.
162 B2 **Le Busseau** France
137 H3 **Leb"yazhe** Ukr.
Lebyazh'ye *Kazakh.* *see* **Akku**
134 J4 **Lebyazh'ye** Rus. Fed.
139 O4 **Lebyazh'ye** Rus. Fed.
192 B3 **Leca da Palmeira** Port.
182 B3 **Leça do Bailio** Port.
Le Caire Egypt *see* **Cairo**
161 F5 **Le Cannet** France
161 E5 **Le Cannet-des-Maures** France
158 B3 **Le Cap** *c.* France
147 C3 **Lecarrow** Rep. of Ireland
156 E5 **Le Castellet** France
156 D5 **Le Cateau-Cambrésis** France
156 D2 **Le Catelet** France
161 B5 **Le Caylar** France
161 E4 **Le Cayrol** France
195 H2 **Lecce** Italy
195 H2 **Lecce** *prov.* *Puglia* Italy
190 E3 **Lecco** Italy
190 E3 **Lecco** *prov.* *Lombardia* Italy
190 E3 **Lecco, Lago di** *l.* Italy
236 E2 **Le Center** *MN* U.S.A.
186 C3 **Lécera** Spain
178 B3 **Lech** Austria
178 B3 **Lech** *r.* Austria/Ger.
198 B3 **Lechaina** Greece
161 C3 **Le Chambon-Feugerolles** France
161 C3 **Le Chambon-sur-Lignon** France
109 E3 **Lechang** *Guangdong* China
178 B3 **Lechaschau** Austria
190 B2 **Le Chasseron** *mt.* Switz.
162 A3 **Le Château-d'Oléron** France
162 E2 **Le Châtelard** France
159 F5 **Le Châtelet** France
156 C4 **Le Châtelet-en-Brie** France
173 E4 **Lechbruck** Ger.
156 E4 **Le Chêne** France
156 E3 **Le Chesne** France
160 E2 **Le Cheval Blanc** *mt.* France
161 E3 **Le Cheval Noir** *mt.* France
161 C4 **Le Cheylard** France
161 D3 **Le Cheylas** France
197 G2 **Lechința** Romania
197 G2 **Lechința** *r.* Romania
129 C2 **Lech'khumis K'edi** *hills* Georgia
151 F3 **Lechlade** *Gloucestershire, England* U.K.
178 B3 **Lechtaler Alpen** *mts* Austria
169 D3 **Lechtingen (Wallenhorst)** Ger.
186 C3 **Leciñena** Spain
168 D1 **Leck** Ger.
147 C2 **Leckaun** Rep. of Ireland
146 C4 **Leckmelm** *Highland, Scotland* U.K.
161 B5 **Le Clapier** France
184 B4 **Le Collet-de-Dèze** France
237 E6 **Lecompte** *LA* U.S.A.
158 B3 **Le Conquet** France
161 E3 **Le Corbier** France
160 C2 **Le Coteau** France
156 B3 **Le Coudray-St-Germer** France
158 E3 **Lécousse** France
156 B3 **Le Crès** France
160 C2 **Le Creusot** France
185 G4 **Lecrín** Spain
158 D4 **Le Croisic** France
156 B2 **Le Crotoy** France
163 C5 **Lectoure** France
186 B1 **Lecumberri** Spain
175 J4 **Łęczna** Pol.
175 H3 **Łęczyca** Pol.
174 F1 **Łęczyce** Pol.
168 C2 **Leda** *r.* Ger.
146 C5 **Ledaig** *Argyll and Bute, Scotland* U.K.
185 I1 **Ledaña** Spain
183 H4 **Ledanca** Spain
94 C2 **Ledang, Gunung** *mt.* Malaysia
188 F2 **Ledava** *r.* Slovenia
151 G3 **Ledburn** *Buckinghamshire, England* U.K.
150 E2 **Ledbury** *Herefordshire, England* U.K.
165 C4 **Lede** Belgium
163 C4 **Lède** *r.* France
176 E2 **Ledeč nad Sázavou** Czech Rep.
165 C4 **Ledegem** Belgium
134 I4 **Ledengskoye** Rus. Fed.
176 D3 **Ledenice** Czech Rep.
163 E4 **Ledergues** France
182 E3 **Ledesma** Spain
163 B5 **Ledeuix** France
161 B4 **Le Devès** *mt.* France
247 □3 **Le Diamant** Martinique
161 C5 **Lédignan** France
183 F2 **Ledigos** Spain
146 D3 **Ledmore** *Highland, Scotland* U.K.
134 F2 **Ledmozero** Rus. Fed.
177 H2 **Lednica** Slovakia
176 F3 **Lednice** Czech Rep.
108 D5 **Ledong** *Hainan* China
96 E3 **Ledong** *Hainan* China
160 B2 **Le Donjon** France
162 D2 **Le Dorat** France
Ledosus France *see* **Lezoux**
182 E4 **Ledrada** Spain
106 D4 **Ledu** *Qinghai* China
222 H4 **Leduc** *Alta* Can.
161 D4 **Le Duffre** *mt.* France
131 S3 **Ledyanaya, Gora** *mt.* Rus. Fed.
175 H5 **Łędziny** Pol.
147 C5 **Lee** *r.* Rep. of Ireland
149 G4 **Lee** *Lancashire, England* U.K.
233 G3 **Lee** *MA* U.S.A.
233 □I2 **Lee** *ME* U.S.A.
232 D4 **Leechburg** *PA* U.S.A.
149 H4 **Leeds** *West Yorkshire, England* U.K.
149 H4 **Leeds-Bradford** *airport* *England* U.K.
150 B4 **Leedstown** *Cornwall, England* U.K.
164 F1 **Leek** Neth.
149 G4 **Leek** *Staffordshire, England* U.K.
87 B6 **Leeman** *W.A.* Austr.
149 H3 **Leeming** *North Yorkshire, England* U.K.
150 C4 **Lee Moor** *Devon, England* U.K.
147 B3 **Leenane** Rep. of Ireland
165 C3 **Leende** Neth.
164 F1 **Leens** Neth.
151 F4 **Lee-on-the-Solent** *Hampshire, England* U.K.
232 D4 **Leeper** *PA* U.S.A.
168 C2 **Leer (Ostfriesland)** Ger.
164 E3 **Leerdam** Neth.
164 E2 **Leersum** Neth.
163 B6 **Lées-Athas** France
231 D6 **Leesburg** *FL* U.S.A.
231 C6 **Leesburg** *GA* U.S.A.
232 A5 **Leesburg** *KY* U.S.A.
234 D3 **Leesburg** *NJ* U.S.A.
232 B5 **Leesburg** *OH* U.S.A.
232 E5 **Leesburg** *VA* U.S.A.
169 E3 **Leese** Ger.
234 C2 **Leesport** *PA* U.S.A.
236 E4 **Lees Summit** *MO* U.S.A.
87 D5 **Lee Steere Range** *hills* *W.A.* Austr.
81 D5 **Leeston** *South I.* N.Z.
237 E6 **Leesville** *LA* U.S.A.
83 F3 **Leeton** *N.S.W.* Austr.
215 F2 **Leeudoringstad** S. Africa
214 C5 **Leeu-Gamka** S. Africa
215 F3 **Leeukop** *mt.* S. Africa
214 C5 **Leeuw** *r.* S. Africa
164 E1 **Leeuwarden** Neth.
87 B7 **Leeuwin, Cape** *W.A.* Austr.
240 H3 **Lee Vining** *CA* U.S.A.
247 F3 **Leeward Islands** Caribbean Sea
Leeward Islands *Arch. de la Société* Fr. Polynesia *see* Sous le Vent, Îles
170 C2 **Leezen** *Mecklenburg-Vorpommern* Ger.
168 F2 **Leezen** *Schleswig-Holstein* Ger.
158 B3 **Le Faou** France
158 C3 **Le Faouët** France
163 D5 **Le Fauga** France
197 G4 **Lefedzha** *r.* Bulg.
158 E5 **Le Fenouiller** France
156 C1 **Leffrinckoucke** France
128 A2 **Lefka** Cyprus
198 B2 **Lefkada** *Ionioi Nisoi* Greece
198 B2 **Lefkada** *i.* Greece
198 C4 **Lefka Ori** *mts* *Kriti* Greece
Lefkas *Ionioi Nisoi* Greece *see* Lefkada
Lefke Cyprus *see* **Lefka**
198 B2 **Lefkimmi** *Ionioi Nisoi* Greece
Lefkoşa Cyprus *see* **Lefkosia**
128 A2 **Lefkosia** Cyprus
163 C4 **Le Fleix** France
158 B3 **Le Folgoët** France
163 E5 **Leforest** France
156 C2 **Le Fossat** France
163 D5 **Le Fousseret** France
247 □3 **Le François** Martinique
225 G1 **Lefroy** *r.* *Que.* Can.
87 D6 **Lefroy, Lake** *salt flat* *W.A.* Austr.
161 E4 **Le Fugeret** France
159 E4 **Le Fuilet** France
175 J5 **Łęg** *r.* Pol.
78 □3a **Legan** *i.* *Kwajalein* Marshall Is
183 G4 **Leganés** Spain
183 H4 **Leganiel** Spain
224 C3 **Legarde** *r.* *Ont.* Can.
92 B3 **Legaspi** Phil.
173 E4 **Legau** Ger.
156 B4 **Le Gault-St-Denis** France
156 D4 **Le Gault-Soigny** France
186 A1 **Legazpia** Spain
170 C3 **Legde** Ger.
169 D3 **Legden** Ger.
158 E5 **Legé** France
163 A4 **Lège-Cap-Ferret** France
86 C4 **Legendre Island** *W.A.* Austr.
159 F3 **Le Genest-St-Isle** France
83 F5 **Legges Tor** *mt.* *Tas.* Austr.
240 F2 **Leggett** *CA* U.S.A.
147 D2 **Leggs** *Northern Ireland* U.K.
Leghorn Italy *see* **Livorno**
175 I3 **Legionowo** Pol.
165 E5 **Léglise** Belgium
191 G3 **Legnago** Italy
190 D3 **Legnano** Italy
174 E4 **Legnica** Pol.
174 E4 **Legnickie Pole** Pol.
190 E2 **Legnone, Monte** *mt.* Italy
162 C3 **Le Gond-Pontouvre** France
247 □2 **Le Gosier** Guadeloupe
174 G1 **Łęgowo** Pol.
179 H4 **Legrad** Croatia
240 G3 **Le Grand** *CA* U.S.A.
87 D7 **Le Grand, Cape** *W.A.* Austr.
160 E3 **Le Grand-Bornand** France
162 D2 **Le Grand-Bourg** France
161 E4 **Le Grand Coyer** *mt.* France
160 D2 **Le Grand Crêt d'Eau** *mt.* France
161 D3 **Le Grand-Lemps** France
159 G4 **Le Grand-Lucé** France
161 E4 **Le Grand Mont** *mt.* France
159 G5 **Le Grand-Pressigny** France
156 B3 **Le Grand-Quevilly** France
161 D3 **Le Grand-Serre** France
160 E2 **Le Grand Taureau** *mt.* France
161 D4 **Le Grand Veymont** *mt.* France
161 C5 **Le Grau-du-Roi** France
217 □1c **Le Gros Morne** *mt.* Réunion
159 G2 **Le Gros Theil** France
161 D3 **Le Gua** France
158 C3 **Léguer** *r.* France
163 D5 **Léguevin** France
84 B2 **Leguene** *N.T.* Austr.
182 B1 **Leguitiano** Spain
208 E4 **Legwe** *r.* Dem. Rep. Congo
116 D2 **Leh** Jammu and Kashmir
157 F5 **Le Haut du Sec** *hill* France
159 G2 **Le Havre** France
168 E1 **Lehe** Ger.
171 C5 **Lehesten** Ger.
241 L1 **Lehi** *UT* U.S.A.
234 C2 **Lehigh** *r.* *PA* U.S.A.
234 C2 **Lehigh County** *county* *PA* U.S.A.
234 C2 **Lehighton** *PA* U.S.A.
197 H3 **Lehliu-Gară** Romania
215 G4 **Lehlohonolo** S. Africa
261 G2 **Lehmann** Arg.
169 C5 **Lehmen** Ger.
168 F1 **Lehmkuhlen** Ger.
171 D5 **Lehndorf** Ger.
176 G3 **Lehnice** Slovakia
171 D3 **Lehnin** Ger.
170 E3 **Lehnitz** Ger.
157 H4 **Le Hohwald** France
158 D3 **Léhon** France
159 F3 **Le Horps** France
177 G3 **Lehota** Slovakia
163 B5 **Le Houga** France
173 E2 **Lehrberg** Ger.
169 F3 **Lehre** Ger.
169 E3 **Lehrte** Ger.
171 C2 **Lehsen** Ger.
140 M3 **Lehtimäki** Fin.
240 □A7 **Lehua** *i.* *HI* U.S.A.
212 D4 **Lehututu** Botswana
192 A4 **Lei** *Sardegna* Italy
123 G4 **Leiah** Pak.
172 D3 **Leibertingen** Ger.
173 G3 **Leiblfing** Ger.
179 G4 **Leibnitz** Austria
108 B2 **Leibo** *Sichuan* China
171 E3 **Leibsch** Ger.
151 F2 **Leicester** *Leicester, England* U.K.
151 F2 **Leicester** *admin. div.* *England* U.K.
151 G2 **Leicestershire** *admin. div.* *England* U.K.
84 D3 **Leichhardt** *r.* *Qld* Austr.
84 D3 **Leichhardt Falls** *Qld* Austr.
85 F4 **Leichhardt Range** *mts* *Qld* Austr.
169 C4 **Leichlingen (Rheinland)** Ger.
164 D2 **Leiden** Neth.
164 D2 **Leiderdorp** Neth.
164 D2 **Leidschendam** Neth.
165 C3 **Leie** *r.* Belgium
169 F3 **Leiferde** Ger.
82 D2 **Leigh** *North I.* N.Z.
149 G4 **Leigh** *Greater Manchester, England* U.K.
150 E2 **Leigh** *Worcestershire, England* U.K.
82 D2 **Leigh Creek** *S.A.* Austr.
147 E4 **Leighlinbridge** Rep. of Ireland
151 G3 **Leighton Buzzard** *Bedfordshire, England* U.K.
141 I3 **Leikanger** Norway
172 C2 **Leimen** Ger.
164 D2 **Leimuiden** Neth.
173 F2 **Leinburg** Ger.
169 E3 **Leine** *r.* Ger.
169 F4 **Leinefelde** Ger.
172 D3 **Leinfelden-Echterdingen** Ger.
190 C3 **Leini** Italy
172 D3 **Leinster** *W.A.* Austr.
147 E3 **Leinster** *reg.* Rep. of Ireland
147 E4 **Leinster, Mount** *hill* Rep. of Ireland
172 D3 **Leinzell** Ger.
183 H1 **Leioa** Spain
138 D4 **Leipalingis** Lith.
173 E2 **Leipheim** Ger.
140 M2 **Leipojärvi** Sweden
234 C3 **Leipsic** *DE* U.S.A.
232 B4 **Leipsic** *OH* U.S.A.
234 C3 **Leipsic** *r.* *DE* U.S.A.
199 E3 **Leipsoi** *i.* Greece
171 D4 **Leipzig** Ger.
171 D4 **Leipzig** *admin. reg.* *Sachsen* Ger.
171 D4 **Leipzig-Halle** *airport* Ger.
140 J3 **Leira** *Møre og Romsdal* Norway
141 J3 **Leira** *Oppland* Norway
182 B2 **Leirado** Spain
140 J2 **Leiranger** Norway
160 B3 **Leiranoux** *mt.* France
182 B5 **Leiria** Port.
182 B5 **Leiria** *admin. dist.* Port.
182 B2 **Leiro** Spain
182 B4 **Leirosa** Port.
142 A2 **Leirvik** Norway
108 D3 **Leishan** *Guizhou* China
109 E3 **Lei Shui** *r.* China
84 B4 **Leisler, Mount** *hill* *N.T.* Austr.
82 B2 **Leisler Hills** *S.A.* Austr.
171 D4 **Leisnig** Ger.
151 I2 **Leiston** *Suffolk, England* U.K.
230 C4 **Leitchfield** *KY* U.S.A.
149 F2 **Leith** *Edinburgh, Scotland* U.K.
81 D5 **Leithfield** *South I.* N.Z.
151 G3 **Leith Hill** *hill* *England* U.K.
147 C2 **Leitrim** *county* Rep. of Ireland
171 C4 **Leitzkau** Ger.
171 C3 **Leitzkau** Ger.
141 N3 **Leivonmäki** Fin.
172 A2 **Leiwen** Ger.
147 E3 **Leixlip** Rep. of Ireland
109 E3 **Leiyang** *Hunan* China
186 B1 **Leiza** Spain
108 E4 **Leizhou** *Guangdong* China
108 D4 **Leizhou Bandao** *pen.* China
143 F1 **Lejberget** *hill* Sweden
164 D3 **Lek** *r.* Neth.
140 J2 **Leka** Norway
140 J2 **Leka** *i.* Norway
208 B5 **Lékana** Congo
177 I3 **Lekárovce** Slovakia
175 H6 **Łękawica** Pol.
205 H1 **Le Kef** Tunisia
189 B8 **Le Kef** *admin. div.* Tunisia
183 H1 **Lekeitio** Spain
208 B5 **Lékéti** *r.* Congo
215 F5 **Lekfontein** S. Africa
Lekhainá Greece *see* **Lechaina**
206 C2 **Lekhcheb** Maur.
208 B5 **Lékila** Gabon
214 A3 **Lekkersing** S. Africa
174 C4 **Łęknica** Pol.
140 K1 **Lekoes** Norway
208 B5 **Lékoni** Gabon
209 B5 **Lékoumou** *admin. reg.* Congo
143 F1 **Leksand** Sweden
Leksʼuiri Georgia *see* **Lentekhi**
Leksura Georgia *see* **Lentekhi**
140 J3 **Leksvik** Norway
140 K2 **Lekvattnet** Sweden
226 C5 **Leland** *IL* U.S.A.
226 E3 **Leland** *MI* U.S.A.
237 F5 **Leland** *MS* U.S.A.
162 B2 **Le Langon** France
162 D3 **Le Lardin-St-Lazare** France
161 E4 **Le Lauzet-Ubaye** France
161 E5 **Le Lavandou** France
177 L3 **Leles** Slovakia
177 L6 **Lelese** Romania
163 B5 **Le Leuy** France
Leli *Guangxi* China *see* **Tianlin**
78 □6 **Leli** *i.* Solomon Is
175 H3 **Lelice** Pol.
188 G4 **Lelija** *mt.* Bos.-Herz.
107 H4 **Leling** *Shandong* China
159 F4 **Le Lion-d'Angers** France
175 J2 **Lelis** Pol.
175 I1 **Lelkowo** Pol.
190 B1 **Le Locle** Switz.
158 E4 **Le Loroux-Bottereau** France
247 □3 **Le Lorrain** Martinique
208 B4 **Lélouma** Guinea
159 F4 **Le Louroux-Béconnais** France
175 H5 **Lelów** Pol.
161 E5 **Le Luc** France
159 G4 **Le Lude** France
161 A3 **Le Luguet** *mt.* France
251 H3 **Lelydorp** Suriname
164 E2 **Lelystad** Neth.
259 D9 **Le Maire, Estrecho de** *sea chan.* Arg.
161 B4 **Le Malzieu-Ville** France
190 B2 **Léman, Lac** *l.* France/Switz.
159 G3 **Le Mans** France
247 □3 **Le Marin** Martinique
157 H5 **Le Markstein** France
236 D3 **Le Mars** *IA* U.S.A.
171 D5 **Lemberg** Ger.
161 C3 **Le Martinet** France
163 C4 **Le Mas-d'Agenais** France
163 D5 **Le Mas-d'Azil** France
163 E5 **Le Masnau-Massuguiès** France
161 B4 **Le Massegros** France
161 D5 **Le Mayet-de-Montagne** France
262 T2 **LeMay Range** *mts* Antarctica
159 F4 **Le May-sur-Èvre** France
179 E2 **Lembach im Mühlkreis** Austria
165 C3 **Lembeke** Belgium
157 H3 **Lemberg** France
172 B2 **Lemberg** Ger.
172 C3 **Lemberg** *mt.* Ger.
Lemberg Ukr. *see* **L'viv**
163 B5 **Lembeye** France
163 D4 **Lemboulas** *r.* France
163 C4 **Lembras** France
168 D3 **Lembruch** Ger.
94 B1 **Lembu, Gunung** *mt.* Indon.
Lemdiyya Alg. *see* **Médéa**
256 D5 **Leme** Brazil
164 F2 **Lemele** Neth.
164 F2 **Lemelerveld** Neth.
159 G3 **Le Mêle-sur-Sarthe** France
159 G3 **Le Merlerault** France
161 D4 **Le Merlu Rocher** *mt.* France
177 K3 **Lemešany** Slovakia
156 E4 **Le Mesnil-sur-Oger** France
128 A2 **Lemesos** Cyprus
169 D3 **Lemförde** Ger.
169 D3 **Lemgo** Ger.
238 D2 **Lemhi** *r.* *ID* U.S.A.
238 D2 **Lemhi Range** *mts* *ID* U.S.A.
141 N3 **Lemi** Fin.
221 L3 **Lemieux Islands** *Nunavut* Can.
141 M3 **Lemland** *Åland* Fin.
164 E2 **Lemmer** Neth.
236 C2 **Lemmon** *SD* U.S.A.
241 L5 **Lemmon, Mount** *AZ* U.S.A.
Lemnos *i.* Greece *see* **Limnos**
214 C5 **Lemoenshoek** S. Africa
159 F2 **Le Molay-Littry** France
160 E2 **Le Môle** *mt.* France
246 D3 **Le Môle St Nicolas** Haiti
190 C2 **Le Moleson** *mt.* Switz.
161 B4 **Le Monastier** France
161 B4 **Le Monastier-sur-Gazeille** France
240 H3 **Lemoncove** *CA* U.S.A.
161 E4 **Le Monêtier-les-Bains** France
240 I5 **Lemon Grove** *CA* U.S.A.
226 C5 **Lemont** *IL* U.S.A.
78 □5 **Le Mont-Dore** New Caledonia
161 B4 **Le Montet** France
158 E3 **Le Mont-St-Michel** *tourist site* France
240 H3 **Lemoore** *CA* U.S.A.
247 □3 **Le Morne Rouge** Martinique
161 B4 **Le Moure de la Gardille** *mt.* France
161 E4 **Le Mourre Froid** *mt.* France
141 M3 **Lempäälä** Fin.
160 B3 **Lempdes** *Auvergne* France
161 B3 **Lempdes** *Auvergne* France
96 A2 **Lemro** *r.* Myanmar
193 I3 **Le Murge** *hills* Italy
161 F5 **Le Muy** France
134 M2 **Lemva** *r.* Rus. Fed.
142 C3 **Lemvig** Denmark
168 E2 **Lemwerder** Ger.
147 D4 **Lemybrien** Rep. of Ireland
96 A3 **Lemyethna** Myanmar
134 L3 **Lem'yu** *r.* Rus. Fed.
142 D1 **Lena** Norway
182 B5 **Lena** *r.* Port.
98 **Lena** *r.* Rus. Fed.
226 C4 **Lena** *IL* U.S.A.
226 C3 **Lena** *WI* U.S.A.
179 G4 **Lenart** Slovenia
177 J6 **Lenauheim** Romania
162 C2 **Lencloître** France
256 C5 **Lençóis Paulista** Brazil
163 B4 **Lencouacq** France
178 E3 **Lend** Austria
208 F4 **Lenda** *r.* Dem. Rep. Congo
177 J2 **Lendak** Slovakia
188 F2 **Lendava** Slovenia
165 C4 **Lendelede** Belgium
191 G3 **Lendinara** Italy
179 E4 **Lendorf** Austria
176 C1 **Lenešice** Czech Rep.
159 G2 **Le Neubourg** France
178 E2 **Lengau** Austria
173 G3 **Lengdorf** Ger.
169 F3 **Lengede** Ger.
169 E3 **Lengefeld** Ger.
171 D5 **Lengenfeld** Ger.
169 F4 **Lengenfeld unterm Stein** Ger.
173 E4 **Lengenwang** Ger.
121 G4 **Lenger** Kazakh.
168 D3 **Lengerich** *Niedersachsen* Ger.
169 C3 **Lengerich** *Nordrhein-Westfalen* Ger.
173 F4 **Lenggries** Ger.
110 F4 **Lenghuzhen** *Qinghai* China
106 D4 **Lenglong Ling** *mts* China
190 C1 **Lengnau** Switz.
208 C5 **Lengoué** *r.* Congo
109 D3 **Lengshuijiang** *Hunan* China
109 D3 **Lengshuitan** *Hunan* China
177 G5 **Lengyeltóti** Hungary
151 H3 **Lenham** *Kent, England* U.K.
234 C2 **Lenhartsville** *PA* U.S.A.
143 F3 **Lenhovda** Sweden
192 A4 **Leni** *r.* *Sardegna* Italy
129 E3 **Lenin** Azer.
Lenin *Yuzhnyy Kazakhstan* Kazakh. *see* **Kazygurt**
123 G2 **Lenin** Tajik.
Lenin, Qullai *mt.* Kyrg./Tajik. *see* **Lenin Peak**
Lenina, Pik *mt.* Kyrg./Tajik. *see* **Lenin Peak**
Leninabad Tajik. *see* **Khŭjand**
120 D4 **Leninabad** Uzbek.
Leninabad Oblast *admin. div.* Tajik. *see* **Leninobod**
Leninakan Armenia *see* **Gyumri**
Lenin Atyndagy Choku *mt.* Kyrg./Tajik. *see* **Lenin Peak**
137 G4 **Lenine** *Mykolayivs'ka Oblast'* Ukr.
137 H5 **Lenine** *Respublika Krym* Ukr.
157 G4 **Léning** France
Leningori Georgia *see* Akhalgori
Leningrad Rus. Fed. *see* Sankt-Peterburg
Leningrad Tajik.
123 G2 **Leningrad Oblast** *admin. div.* Rus. Fed. *see* **Leningradskaya Oblast'**

135 G7 Leningradskaya Rus. Fed.
139 I2 Leningradskaya Oblast' admin. div. Rus. Fed.
131 S3 Leningradskiy Rus. Fed.
Leningradskiy Tajik. see Leningrad
137 F2 Leninivka Ukr.
129 E2 Leninkent Rus. Fed.
Lenino Respublika Krym Ukr. see Lenine
Leninobod Tajik. see Khŭjand
123 G2 Leninobod admin. div. Tajik.
Leninobod Uzbek. see Leninabad
Lenīnogor Kazakh. see Leninogorsk
121 J2 Leninogorsk Kazakh.
135 K5 Leninogorsk Rus. Fed.
121 H5 Lenin Peak Kyrg./Tajik.
121 G4 Leninpol' Kyrg.
135 I6 Leninsk Rus. Fed.
Leninsk Turkm. see Akdepe
Leninsk Uzbek. see Asaka
137 H4 Lenins'ke Ukr.
137 H5 Lenins'ke Ukr.
120 D2 Leninskiy Kazakh.
139 K4 Leninskiy Rus. Fed.
130 J4 Leninsk-Kuznetskiy Rus. Fed.
120 F1 Leninskoye Kustanayskaya Oblast' Kazakh.
Leninskoye Yuzhnyy Kazakhstan Kazakh. see Kazygurt
120 B2 Leninskoye Zapadnyy Kazakhstan Kazakh.
134 I4 Leninskoye Kirovskaya Oblast' Rus. Fed.
100 E3 Leninskoye Yevreyskaya Avtonomnaya Oblast' Rus. Fed.
163 B4 Le Nizan France
190 C2 Lenk Switz.
136 D3 Lenkivtsi Ukr.
Lenkoran' Azer. see Länkäran
86 E3 Lennard r. W.A. Austr.
169 E4 Lenne Ger.
169 C4 Lenne r. Ger.
169 D4 Lennestadt Ger.
172 D3 Lenningen Ger.
259 D9 Lennox, Isla i. Chile
146 D6 Lennoxtown East Dunbartonshire, Scotland U.K.
190 F3 Leno Italy
231 D5 Lenoir NC U.S.A.
231 C5 Lenoir City TN U.S.A.
190 B1 Le Noirmont Switz.
193 F3 Lenola Italy
232 B6 Lenore WV U.S.A.
156 D2 Le Nouvion-en-Thiérache France
233 G3 Lenox MA U.S.A.
165 C4 Lens Belgium
156 C2 Lens France
168 F1 Lensahn Ger.
131 M3 Lensk Rus. Fed.
160 D2 Lent France
164 E3 Lent Neth.
129 C2 Lentekhi Georgia
168 E2 Lentföhrden Ger.
176 F5 Lenti Hungary
191 H2 Lentiai Italy
173 F3 Lenting Ger.
195 E5 Lentini Sicilia Italy
195 E5 Lentini r. Sicilia Italy
Lentvaravas Lith. see Lentvaris
138 E4 Lentvaris Lith.
139 K2 Lent'yevo Rus. Fed.
240 I4 Lenwood CA U.S.A.
190 D1 Lenzburg Switz.
170 C2 Lenzen Ger.
179 E3 Lenzing Austria
172 C4 Lenzkirch Ger.
206 E4 Léo Burkina
191 F4 Leo r. Italy
179 G3 Leoben Austria
179 H2 Leobendorf Austria
179 H3 Leobersdorf Austria
Leodhais, Eilean i. Scotland U.K. see Lewis, Isle of
246 D3 Léogane Haiti
178 D3 Leogang Austria
163 B4 Léognan France
236 D2 Leola SD U.S.A.
150 E2 Leominster Herefordshire, England U.K.
233 H3 Leominster MA U.S.A.
163 A5 Léon France
244 D3 León Mex.
242 □I6 León Nic.
182 E2 León Spain
182 E2 León prov. Castilla y León Spain
236 E3 Leon IA U.S.A.
237 D6 Leon r. TX U.S.A.
182 D2 León, Montes de mts Spain
237 D5 Leonard TX U.S.A.
193 E3 Leonardo da Vinci airport Italy
232 E5 Leonardtown MD U.S.A.
212 C4 Leonardville Namibia
172 D3 Leonberg Ger.
161 D4 Léoncel France
Leondárion Greece see Leontari
179 F2 Leonding Austria
190 D2 Leone, Monte mt. Italy/Switz.
261 F3 Leones Arg.
193 E2 Leonessa Italy
194 D5 Leonforte Sicilia Italy
83 F4 Leongatha Vic. Austr.
192 D2 Leoni, Monte hill Italy
198 C3 Leonidi Greece
100 G2 Leonidovo Sakhalin Rus. Fed.
87 D6 Leonora W.A. Austr.
198 C2 Leontari Greece
86 E3 Leopold r. W.A. Austr.
232 C5 Leopold WV U.S.A.
86 E3 Leopold Downs W.A. Austr.
Léopold II, Lac l. Dem. Rep. Congo see Mai-Ndombe, Lac
257 F4 Leopoldina Brazil
256 C2 Leopoldo de Bulhões Brazil
165 E3 Leopoldsburg Belgium
179 H2 Leopoldsdorf im Marchfelde Austria
170 E2 Leopoldshagen Ger.
169 D3 Leopoldshöhe Ger.
Léopoldville Dem. Rep. Congo see Kinshasa
236 C4 Leoti KS U.S.A.
136 E4 Leova Moldova
223 J4 Leoville Sask. Can.
Leovo Moldova see Leova
158 C4 Le Palais France
162 D3 Le Palais-sur-Vienne France
158 E4 Le Pallet France
156 C2 Le Parcq France
163 C4 Le Passage France
156 D4 Le Pavillon-Ste-Julie France
184 C3 Lepe Spain
161 C3 Le Péage-de-Roussillon France
162 D2 Le Pêchereau France
Lepel' Belarus see Lyepyel'
158 E4 Le Pellerin France
198 B2 Lepenou Greece
161 D4 Le Périer France
163 E6 Le Perthus France
159 E3 Le Pertre France
156 B3 Le Petit-Quevilly France
215 E4 Lephoi S. Africa
162 B4 Le Pian-Médoc France
159 G3 Le Pin-au-Haras France
156 E4 L'Épine France
161 D4 L'Épine France
109 F2 Leping Jiangxi China
159 G3 Le Pin-la-Garenne France
162 C3 Le Pizou France
163 D5 Le Plan France
156 C3 Le Plessis-Belleville France
134 M3 Lep'lya r. Rus. Fed.
161 D4 Le Poët France
188 F2 Lepoglava Croatia
159 H5 Le Poinçonnet France
158 E5 Le Poiré-sur-Vie France
160 D3 Le Pont-de-Beauvoisin France
161 D3 Le Pont-de-Claix France
161 B4 Le Pont-de-Monvert France
161 C5 Le Pontet France
190 D2 Lepontine, Alpi mts Italy/Switz.
195 G2 Leporano Italy
163 A4 Le Porge France
163 A4 Le Porge-Océan France
156 B2 Le Portel France
196 E4 Leposavić Kosovo, Srbija Yugo.
161 B5 Le Pouget France
158 C4 Le Pouldu France
158 D4 Le Pouliguen France
161 C4 Le Pouzin France
140 N3 Leppävesi Fin.
140 N3 Leppävirta Fin.
161 E5 Le Pradet France
Lepsa Kazakh. see Lepsy
Lepsa r. Kazakh. see Lepsy
177 H4 Lepseny Hungary
Lepsi Kazakh. see Lepsinsk
121 J3 Lepsinsk Kazakh.
121 I3 Lepsy Kazakh.
121 I3 Lepsy r. Kazakh.
202 B1 Leptis Magna tourist site Libya
198 C1 Leptokarya Greece
156 B4 Le Puiset France
161 B3 Le-Puy-en-Velay France
159 F4 Le Puy-Notre-Dame France
161 D5 Le Puy-Ste-Réparade France
206 B2 Leqçeïba Maur.
156 D2 Le Quesnoy France
206 D4 Léraba r. Burkina/Côte d'Ivoire
156 C4 Le Raincy France
213 E4 Lerala Botswana
163 D6 Léran France
215 F3 Leratswana S. Africa
194 C5 Lercara Friddi Sicilia Italy
245 G4 Lerdo Mex.
208 B2 Léré Chad
160 A1 Léré France
206 D3 Léré Mali
207 H4 Lere Nigeria
158 B3 Le Relecq-Kerhuon France
182 B2 Lérez r. Spain
158 E3 Le Rheu France
190 E4 Lerici Italy
250 D5 Lérida Col.
Lérida Spain see Lleida
Lérida prov. Cataluña Spain see Lleida
129 F4 Lerik Azer.
183 I2 Lerín Spain
243 H5 Lerma Mex.
244 C3 Lerma r. Mex.
183 G2 Lerma Spain
245 E4 Lerma de Vilada Mex.
163 B4 Lerm-et Musset France
129 C1 Lermontov Rus. Fed.
100 E3 Lermontovka Rus. Fed.
Lermontovskiy Rus. Fed. see Lermontov
192 B4 Lerno, Monte mt. Sardegna Italy
160 E3 Le Roignais mt. France
199 E3 Leros i. Greece
163 E4 Le Rouget France
157 F4 Lérouville France
226 C5 Le Roy IL U.S.A.
226 A4 Le Roy MN U.S.A.
232 E3 Le Roy NY U.S.A.
234 B1 Leroy PA U.S.A.
161 B4 Le Rozier France
157 G4 Lerrain France
190 D4 Lerrone r. Italy
142 E3 Lerum Sweden
160 E1 Le Russey France
146 □G1 Lerwick Shetland, Scotland U.K.
163 C6 Lés Spain
190 D3 Lesa Italy
160 D3 Les Abrets France
247 □2 Les Abymes Guadeloupe
186 B1 Lesaca Spain
161 E5 Les Adrets-de-l'Estérel France
186 F3 Les Agudes mt. Spain
247 □3 Le St-Esprit Martinique
160 A1 Les Aix-d'Angillon France
160 A3 Les Ancizes-Comps France
156 B3 Les Andelys France
161 C5 Les Angles Languedoc-Roussillon France
163 E6 Les Angles Languedoc-Roussillon France
159 G3 Le Sap France
161 E5 Les Arcs Provence-Alpes-Côte-d'Azur France
160 E3 Les Arcs Rhône-Alpes France
159 F5 Les Aubiers France
161 E4 Le Sauze-Super-Sauze France
186 D3 Les Avellanes Spain
160 D3 Les Avenières France
161 B4 Les Bondons France
156 C5 Les Bordes France
163 D5 Les Bordes-sur-Arize France
186 D3 Les Borges Blanques Spain
186 E3 Les Borges del Camp Spain
Lesbos i. Greece see Lesvos
160 D2 Les Bouchoux France
149 H2 Lesbury Northumberland, England U.K.
163 D6 Les Cabannes France
186 G2 L'Escala Spain
161 E4 L'Escale France
163 E5 Les Cammazes France
163 B5 Lescar France
161 F5 L'Escarène France
160 E2 Les Carroz-d'Arâches France
186 D4 Les Cases d'Alcanar Spain
246 D3 Les Cayes Haiti
179 F4 Lesce Slovenia
159 F3 Les Coëvrons hills France
158 B4 Lesconil France
160 E3 Les Contamines-Montjoie France
160 E2 Les Cornettes de Bise mts France/Switz.
163 E5 Lescure-d'Albigeois France
161 E3 Les Deux-Alpes France
190 C2 Les Diablerets mts Switz.
208 D4 Lese r. Dem. Rep. Congo
195 F3 Lese r. Italy
161 D3 Les Échelles France
158 E2 Les Écréhou is Channel Is
162 B3 Les Églisottes-et-Chalaures France
161 E4 Le Seignus-d'Allos France
158 E4 Le Sel-de-Bretagne France
163 B4 Le Sen France
176 G5 Lesencetomaj Hungary
190 B2 Le Sentier Switz.
157 F3 Les Éparges France
159 F5 Les Epesses France
186 E2 Les Escaldes Andorra
225 G3 Les Escoumins Que. Can.
160 D2 Les Essards-Taignevaux France
158 E5 Les Essarts France
233 □I1 Les Étroits Que. Can.
186 E2 Le Seu d'Urgell Spain
163 D4 Les Eyzies-de-Tayac-Sireuil France
160 E1 Les Fins France
157 G4 Les Forges France
160 E2 Les Fourgs France
160 E2 Les Gets France
108 B2 Leshan Sichuan China
157 E3 Les Hautes-Rivières France
137 I2 Leshchinka r. Rus. Fed.
162 A2 Les Herbiers France
Leshou Hebei China see Xianxian
160 E3 Les Houches France
134 I2 Leshukonskoye Rus. Fed.
129 C2 Lesichine Georgia
156 C4 Lésigny France
190 E4 Lesima, Monte mt. Italy
193 H3 Lesina Italy
193 H3 Lesina, Lago di lag. Italy
161 E5 Les Issambres France
141 J3 Lesja Norway
143 F2 Lesjöfors Sweden
163 D4 Les Junies France
161 E3 Les Karellis France
129 C2 Lesken Rus. Fed.
Leskhimstroy Ukr. see Syeverodonets'k
175 K6 Lesko Pol.
197 E4 Leskovac Srbija Yugo.
198 B1 Leskovik Albania
263 F2 Leskov Island Antarctica
137 G3 Les'ky Ukr.
159 E5 Les Landes-Genusson France
162 C3 Les Lèches France
161 D5 Les Lecques France
146 E5 Leslie Fife, Scotland U.K.
226 E4 Leslie MI U.S.A.
158 E5 Les Lucs-sur-Boulogne France
146 E6 Lesmahagow South Lanarkshire, Scotland U.K.
160 D1 Les Maillys France
160 E3 Les Marches France
160 B3 Les Martres-de-Veyre France
161 B5 Les Matelles France
156 E3 Les Mazures France
225 H3 Les Méchins Que. Can.
161 D4 Les Mées France
161 E3 Les Menuires France
158 D3 Les Minquiers is Channel Is
161 E4 Les Monges mt. France
156 E4 Lesmont France
156 B4 Les Mureaux France
177 G2 Lešná Czech Rep.
174 D4 Leśna Pol.
175 L3 Leśna r. Pol.
158 B3 Lesneven France
174 G5 Leśnica Pol.
156 E4 Les Noës-près-Troyes France
134 K4 Lesnoy Kirovskaya Oblast' Rus. Fed.
Lesnoy Murmanskaya Oblast' Rus. Fed. see Umba
139 M4 Lesnoy Ryazanskaya Oblast' Rus. Fed.
139 J2 Lesnoye Rus. Fed.
134 K4 Lesnyye Polyany Rus. Fed.
100 G2 Lesogorsk Sakhalin Rus. Fed.
138 G1 Lesogorskiy Rus. Fed.
161 C4 Les Ollières-sur-Eyrieux France
100 E3 Lesopil'noye Rus. Fed.
161 E4 Les Orres France
131 K4 Lesosibirsk Rus. Fed.
215 G3 Lesotho country Africa
215 G3 Lesotho Highlands Water Scheme Lesotho
100 E3 Lesozavodsk Rus. Fed.
162 B3 Lesparre-Médoc France
162 B3 Les Peintures France
161 D5 Les Pennes-Mirabeau France
163 A5 Lesperon France
156 E3 Les Petites-Loges France
197 F2 Lespezi hill Romania
158 E2 Les Pieux France
161 B5 Lespignan France
186 D4 L'Espina mt. Spain
163 E5 Lespinassière France
161 A5 L'Espinouse, Monts de mts France
160 E2 Les Planches-en-Montagne France
186 E3 L'Espluga Calba Spain
186 E3 L'Espluga de Francolí Spain
162 B1 Les Ponts-de-Cé France
190 B1 Les Ponts-de-Martel Switz.
186 F2 Les Preses Spain
163 C5 Lespugue France
156 E5 Les Riceys France
159 F4 Les Rosiers France
160 E2 Les Rousses France
162 A2 Les Sables-d'Olonne France
161 C4 Les Salles-du-Gardon France
158 E2 Lessay France
165 D4 Lesse r. Belgium
247 F4 Lesser Antilles is Caribbean Sea
Lesser Caucasus mts Asia see Malyy Kavkaz
116 D3 Lesser Himalaya mts India/Nepal
Lesser Khingan Mountains China see Xiao Hinggan Ling
222 H4 Lesser Slave Lake Alta Can.
125 F2 Lesser Tunb i. The Gulf
156 D4 Les Sièges France
165 C4 Lessines Belgium
215 F3 Lessingskop mt. S. Africa
158 E4 Les Sorinières France
163 B5 Lestelle-Bétharram France
232 C6 Lester WV U.S.A.
161 B3 Les Ternes France
156 B3 Les Thilliers-en-Vexin France
161 E4 Les Thuiles France
140 N3 Lestijärvi Fin.
140 M2 Lestijoki r. Fin.
161 A4 Lestrade France
159 G4 Les Trois-Moutiers France
161 A4 Les Trucs d'Aubrac mt. France
86 E2 Lesueur Island W.A. Austr.
156 C4 Les Ulis France
95 F2 Lesung, Bukit mt. Indon.
187 C4 Les Useres Spain
161 C4 Les Vans France
161 B4 Les Vignes France
199 D2 Lesvos i. Greece
175 K4 Leszkowice Pol.
175 I3 Leszno Mazowieckie Pol.
174 E4 Leszno Wielkopolskie Pol.
174 D4 Leszno Górne Pol.
161 D3 Le Taillefer mt. France
186 C2 Le Taillon mt. Spain
159 F5 Le Tallud France
143 F2 Letälven r. Sweden
161 C4 Le Tanargue mt. France
177 K4 Létavértes Hungary
151 G3 Letchworth Hertfordshire, England U.K.
163 A4 Le Teich France
161 C4 Le Teil France
159 F3 Le Teilleul France
160 C1 Le Télégraphe hill France
163 B4 Le Temple France
161 E3 L'Étendard, Pic de mt. France
176 F5 Letenye Hungary
116 D4 Leteri Madh. Prad. India
215 F1 Lethabile S. Africa
96 A2 Letha Range mts Myanmar
222 H5 Lethbridge Alta Can.
225 K3 Lethbridge Nfld. Can.
168 D2 Lethe r. Ger.
159 G3 Le Theil France
158 E4 Le-Theil-de-Bretagne France
251 G4 Lethem Guyana
151 I2 Letheringsett Norfolk, England U.K.
157 G5 Le Thillot France
157 G4 Le Tholy France
161 E5 Le Thoronet France
93 C5 Leti, Kepulauan is Maluku Indon.
250 D6 Leticia Col.
107 H4 Leting Hebei China
193 G3 Letino Italy
214 D5 Letjiesbos S. Africa
177 H4 Letkés Hungary
212 E4 Letlhakane Botswana
212 E5 Letlhakeng Botswana
134 F2 Letnerechenskiy Rus. Fed.
191 H2 Le Tofane mt. Italy
195 E5 Letoianni Sicilia Italy
179 H1 Letonice Czech Rep.
156 B2 Le Touquet-Paris-Plage France
161 B5 Le Tour d'Arre hill France
161 D3 Le Touvet France
176 F2 Letovice Czech Rep.
96 A3 Letpadan Myanmar
156 B2 Le Tréport France
161 A4 Le Truel France
141 K3 Letsbo Sweden
170 F3 Letschin Ger.
215 E2 Letsopa S. Africa
Lette Island Vava'u Gp Tonga see Late
148 B3 Letterbreen Northern Ireland U.K.
147 B3 Lettercallow Rep. of Ireland
147 E5 Letterfinish Rep. of Ireland
147 B3 Letterfrack Rep. of Ireland
147 D2 Letterkenny Rep. of Ireland
150 C3 Letterston Pembrokeshire, Wales U.K.
185 H2 Letur Spain
163 E4 Le Tuzan France
136 D3 Letychiv Ukr.
Lëtzebuerg country Europe see Luxembourg
171 C3 Letzlingen Ger.
197 G3 Leu Romania
209 D7 Léua Angola
171 E4 Leuben Ger.
171 C4 Leubingen Ger.
163 E5 Leuc France
Leucas Ionioi Nisoi Greece see Lefkada
163 F6 Leucate France
146 F5 Leuchars Fife, Scotland U.K.
173 G2 Leuchtenberg Ger.
170 E3 Leuenberg Ger.
157 E5 Leuglay France
190 C2 Leuk Switz.
Leukas Ionioi Nisoi Greece see Lefkada
190 C2 Leukerbad Switz.
146 B3 Leumrabhagh Western Isles, Scotland U.K.
169 D5 Leun Ger.
241 L4 Leupp AZ U.S.A.
85 G4 Leura Qld Austr.
164 E2 Leusden Neth.
94 B2 Leuser, Gunung mt. Indon.
178 C3 Leutasch Austria
171 C5 Leutenberg Ger.
173 E2 Leutershausen Ger.
169 C5 Leutesdorf Ger.
173 E4 Leutkirch im Allgäu Ger.
165 D4 Leuven Belgium
165 C4 Leuze-en-Hainaut Belgium
198 C2 Levadeia Greece
161 E5 Le Val France
157 G5 Le Val-d'Ajol France
157 F5 Le Vallinot-Longeau-Percey France
158 E3 Le Val-St-Père France
198 A1 Levan Albania
241 L2 Levan UT U.S.A.
140 J3 Levanger Norway
190 D4 Levante, Riviera di coastal area Italy
190 E4 Levanto Italy
194 B5 Levanzo Sicilia Italy
194 B4 Levanzo, Isola di i. Sicilia Italy
129 E2 Levashi Rus. Fed.
247 □3 Le Vauclin Martinique
137 J2 Levaya Rossosh' Rus. Fed.
176 G4 Levél Hungary
237 C5 Levelland TX U.S.A.
81 C6 Levels South I. N.Z.
149 I4 Leven East Riding of Yorkshire, England U.K.
146 F5 Leven Fife, Scotland U.K.
146 C5 Leven, Loch inlet Scotland U.K.
146 E5 Leven, Loch l. Scotland U.K.
161 F5 Levens France
149 G3 Levens Cumbria, England U.K.
190 D2 Leventina, Valle val. Switz.
146 □G2 Levenwick Shetland, Scotland U.K.
86 D3 Lévêque, Cape W.A. Austr.
195 H2 Leverano Italy
146 A4 Leverburgh Western Isles, Scotland U.K.
162 A3 Le-Verdon-sur-Mer France
226 E3 Levering MI U.S.A.
169 B4 Leverkusen Ger.
163 D5 Le Vernet France
156 B4 Lèves France
159 I5 Levet France
161 A4 Lévézou mts France
177 H3 Levice Slovakia
191 G2 Levico Terme Italy
198 C3 Levidi Greece
192 B3 Levie Corse France
160 E2 Levier France
161 B5 Le Vigan France
163 D5 Lévignac France
163 C4 Lévignac-de-Guyanne France
163 A4 Lévignacq France
191 H5 Le Ville Italy
80 E4 Levin North I. N.Z.
225 G4 Lévis Que. Can.
199 E3 Levitha i. Greece
Levittown NJ U.S.A. see Willingboro
235 E2 Levittown NY U.S.A.
234 D2 Levittown PA U.S.A.
158 E3 Le-Vivier-sur-Mer France
197 H5 Levka Bulg.
Levkás i. Greece see Lefkada
Levkímmi Ionioi Nisoi Greece see Lefkimmi
177 J2 Levoča Slovakia
177 J2 Levočské vrchy mts Slovakia
162 D2 Levroux France
197 G4 Levski Bulg.
Levskigrad Bulg. see Karlovo
139 L5 Lev Tolstoy Rus. Fed.
79 □1a Levuka Ovalau Fiji
96 B3 Lewe Myanmar
151 H4 Lewes East Sussex, England U.K.
233 F5 Lewes DE U.S.A.
174 F5 Lewin Brzeski Pol.
241 M3 Lewis CO U.S.A.
237 D4 Lewis KS U.S.A.
238 B2 Lewis r. WA U.S.A.
146 B3 Lewis, Isle of i. Scotland U.K.
84 C4 Lewis, Lake salt flat N.T. Austr.
234 B2 Lewisberry PA U.S.A.
232 A5 Lewisburg OH U.S.A.
227 I5 Lewisburg PA U.S.A.
231 C5 Lewisburg TN U.S.A.
232 C6 Lewisburg WV U.S.A.
222 D3 Lewis Cass, Mount Alaska/B.C. Can./U.S.A.
225 J3 Lewis Hills hill Nfld. Can.
81 D5 Lewis Pass South I. N.Z.
225 K3 Lewisporte Nfld. Can.
86 F4 Lewis Range hills W.A. Austr.
238 D1 Lewis Range mts MT U.S.A.
231 C5 Lewis Smith, Lake AL U.S.A.
238 C2 Lewiston ID U.S.A.
233 □H2 Lewiston ME U.S.A.
227 E3 Lewiston MI U.S.A.
226 B4 Lewiston MN U.S.A.
232 D3 Lewiston NY U.S.A.
226 B5 Lewistown IL U.S.A.
226 B5 Lewistown MO U.S.A.
238 E2 Lewistown MT U.S.A.
232 E4 Lewistown PA U.S.A.
237 E5 Lewisville AR U.S.A.
232 C5 Lewisville OH U.S.A.
93 B5 Lewotobi, Gunung vol. Flores Indon.
231 D5 Lexington GA U.S.A.
226 C5 Lexington IL U.S.A.
230 C4 Lexington KY U.S.A.
227 F4 Lexington MI U.S.A.
236 E4 Lexington MO U.S.A.
237 F5 Lexington MS U.S.A.
231 D5 Lexington NC U.S.A.
236 D3 Lexington NE U.S.A.
232 B4 Lexington OH U.S.A.
231 D5 Lexington SC U.S.A.
237 F5 Lexington TN U.S.A.
232 D6 Lexington VA U.S.A.
232 E5 Lexington Park MD U.S.A.
149 H3 Leyburn North Yorkshire, England U.K.
Leyden Neth. see Leiden
108 C3 Leye Guangxi China
122 A2 Leyla Dāgh mt. Iran
149 G4 Leyland Lancashire, England U.K.
163 D4 Leyme France
151 H3 Leysdown-on-Sea Kent, England U.K.
190 C2 Leysin Switz.
92 C4 Leyte i. Phil.
92 C4 Leyte Gulf Phil.
190 C2 Leytron Switz.
163 D6 Lez r. France
183 H2 Leza r. Spain
175 K5 Leżajsk Pol.
161 C4 Lézan France
158 C3 Lézardrieux France
163 D5 Lézat-sur-Lèze France
162 B2 Lezay France
163 D5 Lèze r. France
196 D5 Lezhë Albania
108 C2 Lezhi Sichuan China
139 M3 Lezhnevo Rus. Fed.
161 A5 Lézignan-Corbières France
160 B3 Lezoux France
185 H2 Lezuza Spain
185 H1 Lezuza r. Spain
175 H4 Lgota Wielka Pol.
135 F6 L'gov Rus. Fed.
111 D6 Lhagoi Kangri mt. Xizang China
146 E4 Lhanbryde Moray, Scotland U.K.
111 F6 Lhari Xizang China
Lharigarbo Xizang China see Amdo
111 E6 Lhasa Xizang China
111 E6 Lhasa He r. China
108 A2 Lhatog Xizang China
156 C4 L'Hay-les-Roses France
111 D6 Lhazê Xizang China
179 F1 Lhenice Czech Rep.
163 D5 Lherm France
162 B2 L'Hermenault France
158 E3 L'Hermitage France
113 □1 Lhohifushi i. N. Male Maldives
94 B1 Lhokseumawe Sumatera Indon.
94 B1 Lhoksukon Sumatera Indon.
163 D4 L'Honor-de-Cos France
111 F6 Lhorong Xizang China
163 D4 L'Hospitalet France
186 D4 L'Hospitalet de l'Infant Cataluña Spain
186 F3 L'Hospitalet de Llobregat Cataluña Spain
161 B5 L'Hospitalet-du-Larzac France
163 D6 L'Hospitalet-près-l'Andorre France
186 D4 L'Hostal del Alls Spain
162 A2 L'Houmeau France
111 E6 Lhozhag Xizang China
160 D3 Lhuis France
159 F3 L'Huisserie France
156 E4 Lhuître France
111 F6 Lhünzê Xizang China
111 E6 Lhünzhub Xizang China
96 B3 Li, Mae r. Thai.
192 A2 Liamone r. Corse France
247 □2 Liamuiga, Mount vol. St Kitts and Nevis
109 F3 Liancheng Fujian China
Liancheng Guizhou China see Qinglong
Liancheng Yunnan China see Guangnan
156 C3 Liancourt France
101 D5 Liancourt Rocks i. N. Pacific Ocean
156 B2 Liane r. France
Lianfeng Fujian China see Liancheng
92 C4 Lianga Phil.
109 E2 Liangaz Hu l. China
107 G3 Liangcheng Nei Mongol China
108 C1 Liangdang Gansu China
108 D3 Liangfeng Guangxi China
108 A3 Lianghe Yunnan China
108 C1 Lianghekou Gansu China
108 B2 Lianghekou Sichuan China
Liangjiayoufang Shanxi China see Youyu
108 C2 Liangping Chongqing China
95 F2 Liangpran, Bukit mt. Indon.
Liangshan Chongqing China see Liangping
96 B1 Liang Shan mt. Myanmar
Liangshi Hunan China see Shaodong
94 C2 Liang Timur, Gunung mt. Malaysia
108 B3 Liangwang Shan mts Yunnan China
107 F4 Liangzhen Shaanxi China
Liangzhou Gansu China see Wuwei
Lianhe Chongqing China see Qianjiang
109 E3 Lianhua Jiangxi China
109 F3 Lianjiang Fujian China
108 D4 Lianjiang Guangdong China
Lianjiang Jiangxi China see Xingguo
109 E3 Lianjiangkou Guangdong China
108 C3 Lian Jiang r. China
109 E3 Liannan Guangdong China
198 C2 Lianokladi Sterea Ellas Greece
109 E3 Lianping Guangdong China
Lianran Yunnan China see Anning
109 E3 Lianshan Guangdong China
107 I3 Lianshan Liaoning China
Liantang Jiangxi China see Nanchang
109 D2 Liantuo Hubei China
Lianxian Guangdong China see Lianzhou
100 B1 Lianyin Heilong. China
109 D3 Lianyuan Hunan China
107 H5 Lianyungang Jiangsu China
109 E3 Lianzhou Guangdong China
Lianzhou Guangxi China see Hepu
100 D3 Lianzhushan Heilong. China
107 I3 Liao r. China
107 G4 Liaocheng Shandong China
107 I3 Liaodong Bandao pen. China
107 I3 Liaodong Wan b. China
106 B3 Liaodun Xinjiang China
106 B3 Liaodunzhan Xinjiang China
107 I3 Liaoning prov. China
107 I3 Liaoyang Liaoning China
100 C4 Liaoyuan Jilin China
107 I3 Liaozhong Liaoning China
198 A2 Liapades Ionioi Nisoi Greece
123 G3 Liaqatabad Pak.
222 F2 Liard r. Can.
222 F2 Liard Highway N.W.T. Can.
222 E2 Liard Plateau Y.T. Can.
222 E3 Liard River B.C. Can.
156 E3 Liart France
146 C4 Liathach mt. Scotland U.K.
143 F3 Liatorp Sweden
Liban country Asia see Lebanon
176 E1 Libáň Czech Rep.
128 C2 Liban, Jebel mts Lebanon
250 C3 Libano Col.
Libau Latvia see Liepāja
146 E6 Libberton South Lanarkshire, Scotland U.K.
238 D1 Libby MT U.S.A.
176 C1 Libčeves Czech Rep.
171 F5 Libčice nad Vltavou Czech Rep.
208 C4 Libenge Dem. Rep. Congo
175 I2 Liberadz Pol.
237 C4 Liberal KS U.S.A.
257 E5 Liberdade Brazil
252 C1 Liberdade r. Amazonas Brazil
254 B4 Liberdade r. Mato Grosso Brazil
176 E1 Liberec Czech Rep.
176 E1 Liberecký kraj admin. reg. Czech Rep.
206 C5 Liberia country Africa
242 □I7 Liberia Costa Rica
247 □2 Liberta Antigua and Barbuda
261 I4 Libertad Uru.
258 D1 Libertador General San Martin Arg.
215 F3 Libertase S. Africa
230 C4 Liberty IN U.S.A.
230 C4 Liberty KY U.S.A.
233 □I2 Liberty ME U.S.A.
236 E4 Liberty MO U.S.A.
233 F4 Liberty NY U.S.A.
234 A1 Liberty PA U.S.A.
237 E6 Liberty TX U.S.A.
232 A4 Liberty Center OH U.S.A.
226 D4 Libertyville IL U.S.A.
171 F5 Liběšice Czech Rep.
175 H5 Libiąż Pol.
176 E1 Libice nad Cidlinou Czech Rep.
165 E5 Libin Belgium
176 D3 Libín mt. Czech Rep.
176 G2 Libina Czech Rep.
92 B3 Libmanan Phil.
128 A4 Libni, Gebel hill Egypt
108 C3 Libo Guizhou China
171 F5 Libochovice Czech Rep.
215 G4 Libode S. Africa
198 B1 Libohovë Albania
171 F5 Libouchec Czech Rep.
163 B4 Libourne France
86 E4 Libral Well W.A. Austr.
165 E5 Libramont Belgium
196 E5 Librazhd Albania
242 C2 Libre, Sierra mts Mex.
245 F4 Libres Mex.
208 A4 Libreville Gabon
187 B7 Librilla Spain
187 B4 Libros Spain
92 C5 Libuganon r. Phil.
202 C3 Libya country Africa
202 E3 Libyan Desert Egypt/Libya
202 E2 Libyan Plateau Egypt
260 A4 Licantén Chile
194 C5 Licata Sicilia Italy
190 F4 Licciana Nardi Italy
127 F3 Lice Turkey
193 E2 Licenza Italy
183 G3 Liceras Spain
169 D5 Lich Ger.
Licheng Fujian China see Xianyou
Licheng Guangxi China see Lipu
107 H4 Licheng Shandong China
107 G4 Licheng Shanxi China
80 E3 Lichfield North I. N.Z.
151 F2 Lichfield Staffordshire, England U.K.
211 B8 Lichinga Moz.
177 G1 Lichnov Czech Rep.
174 G1 Lichnowy Pol.
171 C5 Lichte Ger.
172 C3 Lichtenau Baden-Württemberg Ger.
173 E2 Lichtenau Bayern Ger.
169 D4 Lichtenau Nordrhein-Westfalen Ger.
179 G2 Lichtenau im Waldviertel Austria
171 C5 Lichtenberg Bayern Ger.
171 E5 Lichtenberg Sachsen Ger.
215 F2 Lichtenburg S. Africa
171 C5 Lichtenfels Ger.
171 D5 Lichtenstein Ger.
164 F3 Lichtenvoorde Neth.
179 H3 Lichtenwörth Austria
170 E3 Lichterfelde Ger.
165 C3 Lichtervelde Belgium
108 D2 Lichuan Hubei China
109 F3 Lichuan Jiangxi China
213 H3 Liciro Moz.
232 A5 Licking r. KY U.S.A.
188 E3 Lički Osik Croatia
194 D5 Licodia Eubea Sicilia Italy
163 B5 Licq-Athérey France
156 B2 Licques France
Licun Shandong China see Laoshan
139 J2 Lid' r. Rus. Fed.
138 E5 Lida Belarus
142 E2 Lidan r. Sweden
149 G2 Liddel r. England/Scotland U.K.
215 F5 Liddleton S. Africa
177 H2 Lidečko Czech Rep.
142 E3 Lidhult Sweden
143 H2 Lidingö Sweden
142 E2 Lidköping Sweden
191 H3 Lido Italy
191 H4 Lido Adriano Italy
191 H4 Lido di Classe Italy
193 E3 Lido di Foce Verde Italy
191 H3 Lido di Jesolo Italy
195 F2 Lido di Metaponto Italy
193 E3 Lido di Ostia Italy
193 H3 Lido di Siponto Italy
191 H4 Lido di Spina Italy
140 K2 Lidsjöberg Sweden
175 H2 Lidzbark Pol.
143 I4 Lidzbark Warmiński Pol.
179 F2 Liebenau Austria
169 E4 Liebenau Hessen Ger.
168 E3 Liebenau Niedersachsen Ger.
215 G2 Liebenbergs Vlei r. S. Africa
169 F3 Liebenburg Ger.
179 F4 Liebenfels Austria
170 E3 Liebenwalde Ger.
171 F4 Lieberose Ger.
171 D4 Liebertwolkwitz Ger.
84 B4 Liebig, Mount N.T. Austr.
196 E3 Liebling Romania
179 G4 Lieboch Austria
171 E5 Liebstadt Ger.
172 D4 Liechtenstein country Europe
183 I2 Liédena Spain
165 E4 Liège Belgium
165 E4 Liège prov. Belgium
Liegnitz Pol. see Legnica
140 O3 Lieksa Fin.
138 E3 Lielupe r. Latvia
138 E3 Lielvārde Latvia
164 E3 Liempde Neth.
140 L3 Lien Sweden
164 E3 Lienden Neth.
169 C3 Lienen Ger.
178 D4 Lienz Austria
138 C3 Liepāja Latvia
Liepaya Latvia see Liepāja
170 E3 Liepe Ger.
170 E2 Liepen Ger.
170 F2 Liepgarten Ger.
165 D3 Lier Belgium
160 C1 Liernais France
165 E4 Lierneux Belgium
Lierre Belgium see Lier
177 I2 Liesek Slovakia
172 B2 Lieser Ger.
164 E3 Lieshout Neth.
178 F3 Liesing r. Austria
165 E3 Liessel Neth.
156 D3 Liesse-Notre-Dame France
190 C1 Liestal Switz.
177 H3 Liešťany Slovakia
138 D1 Lieto Fin.
185 I2 Liétor Spain
Lietuva country Europe see Lithuania
159 G2 Lieurey France
141 N3 Lievestuore Fin.
156 C2 Liévin France
224 F4 Lièvre r. Que. Can.
179 F3 Liezen Austria
148 C4 Liffey r. Rep. of Ireland
157 F4 Liffol-le-Grand France
147 D2 Lifford Rep. of Ireland
158 E3 Liffré France
259 C6 Lifi Mahuida mt. Arg.
78 □5 Lifou i. Î. Loyauté New Caledonia
150 C4 Lifton Devon, England U.K.
Lifu i. Î. Loyauté New Caledonia see Lifou
Lifudzin Rus. Fed. see Rudnyy
79 □2 Lifuka i. Tonga
92 B3 Ligao Phil.
163 C4 Ligardes France
138 E3 Līgatne Latvia
87 D6 Lightfoot Lake salt flat W.A. Austr.
83 F2 Lightning Ridge N.S.W. Austr.
234 B1 Lightstreet PA U.S.A.
179 G4 Ligist Austria
191 I3 Lignano Pineta Italy
191 I3 Lignano Sabbiadoro Italy
158 E4 Ligné France
158 E5 Ligneron r. France
165 F4 Ligneuville Belgium
159 I5 Lignières France
160 B3 Lignon r. France
161 C3 Lignon r. France
157 F4 Ligny-en-Barrois France
156 D5 Ligny-le-Châtel France
156 B5 Ligny-le-Ribault France
190 F4 Ligonchio Italy
213 H3 Ligonha r. Moz.
226 E5 Ligonier IN U.S.A.
232 D4 Ligonier PA U.S.A.
Ligoúrion Greece see Lygourio
175 H3 Ligowo Pol.
82 C3 Liguanea Island S.A. Austr.
159 G4 Ligueil France
162 C2 Ligugé France
242 C3 Ligui Mex.
Ligure, Mar sea France/Italy see Ligurian Sea
190 D4 Liguria admin. reg. Italy
188 B4 Ligurian Sea France/Italy
Ligurienne, Mer sea France/Italy see Ligurian Sea
241 J5 Ligurta AZ U.S.A.
142 C3 Lihme Denmark
85 G3 Lihou Reef and Cays Coral Sea Is Terr. Austr.
240 □B7 Lihue HI U.S.A.
138 D2 Lihula Estonia
Liivi laht b. Estonia/Latvia see Riga, Gulf of
185 H3 Lijar Spain
108 B3 Lijiang Yunnan China
Lijiang Yunnan China see Yuanjiang
96 E1 Li Jiang r. China
109 E2 Lijiazhai Henan China
96 C3 Lik, Nam r. Laos
188 E3 Lika reg. Croatia
122 B4 Likak Iran
209 E7 Likasi Dem. Rep. Congo
208 E4 Likati r. Dem. Rep. Congo
222 F4 Likely B.C. Can.
Likhachevo Ukr. see Pervomays'kyy
Likhachyovo Ukr. see Pervomays'kyy
139 J3 Likhoslavl' Rus. Fed.
137 K3 Likhovskoy Rus. Fed.
139 L4 Likino-Dulevo Rus. Fed.
116 E5 Likma Madh. Prad. India
208 C4 Likouala admin. reg. Congo
208 C5 Likouala r. Congo
208 C5 Likouala aux Herbes r. Congo
134 H4 Likurga Rus. Fed.
159 G4 L'Île-Bouchard France
192 A2 L'Île-Rousse Corse France
179 G2 Lilienfeld Austria
168 D2 Lilienthal Ger.
109 E3 Liling Hunan China
138 F1 Liljendal Fin.
123 H3 Lilla Pak.
142 E2 Lilla Edet Sweden
140 M2 Lilla Luleälven r. Sweden
140 L2 Lillblaiken hill Sweden
165 D3 Lille Belgium
156 D2 Lille France
142 C4 Lille Bælt sea chan. Denmark
159 G2 Lillebonne France
141 J3 Lillehammer Norway
156 C2 Lillers France
142 C2 Lillesand Norway
150 E2 Lilleshall Telford and Wrekin, England U.K.
142 D2 Lillestrøm Norway
226 E4 Lilley MI U.S.A.
87 E5 Lillian, Point hill W.A. Austr.
146 F6 Lilliesleaf Scottish Borders, Scotland U.K.
231 E5 Lillington NC U.S.A.
183 G5 Lillo Spain
222 F5 Lillooet B.C. Can.
222 F5 Lillooet r. B.C. Can.
222 F5 Lillooet Range mts B.C. Can.
208 E5 Lilo r. Dem. Rep. Congo
117 H4 Lilong Manipur India
211 B8 Lilongwe Malawi
92 B4 Liloy Phil.
226 C3 Lily WI U.S.A.
82 D3 Lilydale S.A. Austr.
83 F5 Lilydale Tas. Austr.
196 D4 Lim r. Yugo.
261 H4 Lima Arg.
191 F4 Lima r. Italy
253 F5 Lima Para.
252 A3 Lima Peru
252 A2 Lima dept Peru
226 B5 Lima IL U.S.A.
238 D2 Lima MT U.S.A.
232 E3 Lima NY U.S.A.
232 A4 Lima OH U.S.A.
257 F4 Lima Duarte Brazil
125 G2 Līmah Oman
120 A3 Liman Rus. Fed.
178 D4 Limana Italy
175 I6 Limanowa Pol.
260 B2 Limarí r. Chile
Limassol Cyprus see Lemesos
147 E1 Limavady Northern Ireland U.K.
260 D6 Limay r. Arg.
156 B3 Limay France
172 D2 Limbach Baden-Württemberg Ger.
172 A2 Limbach Saarland Ger.
171 D5 Limbach Sachsen Ger.
171 D5 Limbach-Oberfrohna Ger.
195 E4 Limbadi Italy
95 F1 Limbang r. Sarawak Malaysia
252 C3 Limbani Peru
138 E3 Limbaži Latvia
116 B5 Limbdi Gujarat India
207 H5 Limbe Cameroon
211 B8 Limbe Malawi
93 B2 Limboto Sulawesi Utara Indon.
165 E4 Limbourg Belgium
213 H3 Limbuè Moz.
84 B3 Limbunya N.T. Austr.
165 E3 Limburg prov. Belgium
165 E3 Limburg prov. Neth.
169 D5 Limburg an der Lahn Ger.
172 C2 Limburgerhof Ger.
214 D3 Lime Acres S. Africa
141 K3 Limedsforsen Sweden
81 B7 Limehills South I. N.Z.
256 D5 Limeira Brazil
149 F1 Limekilns Fife, Scotland U.K.
198 D1 Limenaria Anatoliki Makedonia kai Thraki Greece
147 C4 Limerick Rep. of Ireland
147 C4 Limerick county Rep. of Ireland
226 A4 Lime Springs IA U.S.A.
233 □J1 Limestone ME U.S.A.
142 C3 Limfjorden sea chan. Denmark
182 B3 Limia r. Spain
199 D4 Limin Chersonisou Kriti Greece
140 K2 Limingen Norway
233 □H3 Limington ME U.S.A.
140 N2 Liminka Fin.
142 E3 Limmared Sweden
164 D2 Limmen Neth.
84 D2 Limmen Bight b. N.T. Austr.
84 C2 Limmen Bight River r. N.T. Austr.
198 C2 Limni Greece
199 D2 Limnos i. Greece
254 G3 Limoeiro Brazil
233 F2 Limoges Ont. Can.
162 D3 Limoges France
163 D4 Limogne, Causse de hills France
163 D4 Limogne-en-Quercy France
242 □J7 Limón Costa Rica
242 □I6 Limón Hond.
236 C4 Limon CO U.S.A.
190 C4 Limone Piemonte Italy
160 C3 Limonest France
191 F3 Limone sul Garda Italy
184 D2 Limonetes r. Spain
126 D3 Limonlu Turkey
Limonum France see Poitiers
252 D3 Limoquije Bol.
193 G3 Limosano Italy
162 D3 Limousin admin. reg. France
162 D3 Limousin, Monts du hills France
162 D3 Limousin, Plateaux du France
163 E5 Limoux France
213 G5 Limpopo r. S. Africa/Zimbabwe
108 D3 Limu Guangxi China
209 D8 Limulunga Zambia
140 M2 Linaälven r. Sweden
140 O1 Linakhamari Rus. Fed.
Lin'an Yunnan China see Jianshui
109 F2 Lin'an Zhejiang China
92 A4 Linapacan Strait Phil.
162 D3 Linards France
260 B4 Linares Chile
243 F3 Linares Mex.
185 G2 Linares Spain
187 C4 Linares de Mora Spain
182 E4 Linares de Riofrío Spain
192 A5 Linas, Monte mt. Sardegna Italy
190 E3 Linate airport Italy
95 F2 Linau Balui plat. Sarawak Malaysia
108 B4 Lincang Yunnan China
165 E4 Lincent Belgium
Lincheng Hainan China see Lingao
Lincheng Hunan China see Huitong
109 F3 Linchuan Jiangxi China
262 R1 Linck Nunataks nunataks Antarctica
261 G4 Lincoln Arg.
81 D5 Lincoln South I. N.Z.
149 I4 Lincoln Lincolnshire, England U.K.
240 G2 Lincoln CA U.S.A.
234 C4 Lincoln DE U.S.A.
230 B3 Lincoln IL U.S.A.
236 D4 Lincoln KS U.S.A.
233 □I2 Lincoln ME U.S.A.
227 F3 Lincoln MI U.S.A.
236 D3 Lincoln NE U.S.A.
233 H2 Lincoln NH U.S.A.

234 B2 Lincoln PA U.S.A.
238 A2 Lincoln City OR U.S.A.
232 B4 Lincoln Park MI U.S.A.
221 N1 Lincoln Sea Can./Greenland
149 I4 Lincolnshire admin. div. England U.K.
149 I4 Lincolnshire Wolds hills England U.K.
231 D5 Lincolnton GA U.S.A.
234 C3 Lincoln University PA U.S.A.
235 D2 Lincroft NJ U.S.A.
254 E5 Linda, Serra hills Brazil
171 D3 Lindau Sachsen-Anhalt Ger.
168 E1 Lindau Schleswig-Holstein Ger.
172 D4 Lindau (Bodensee) Ger.
164 E2 Linde r. Neth.
168 F1 Lindelse Denmark
85 G4 Lindeman Group is Qld Austr.
222 H5 Linden Alta Can.
169 D5 Linden Hessen Ger.
168 E1 Linden Schleswig-Holstein Ger.
253 G3 Linden Guyana
231 C5 Linden AL U.S.A.
240 G2 Linden CA U.S.A.
232 B3 Linden MI U.S.A.
235 D2 Linden NJ U.S.A.
231 C5 Linden TN U.S.A.
237 E5 Linden TX U.S.A.
170 D2 Lindenberg Brandenburg Ger.
170 E3 Lindenberg Brandenburg Ger.
171 F3 Lindenberg Brandenburg Ger.
172 D4 Lindenberg im Allgäu Ger.
172 C2 Lindenfels Ger.
226 A2 Linden Grove MN U.S.A.
235 D3 Lindenwold NJ U.S.A.
168 C3 Lindern (Oldenburg) Ger.
143 F2 Lindesberg Sweden
142 B2 Lindesnes c. Norway
168 E1 Lindewitt Ger.
151 G3 Lindfield West Sussex, England U.K.
169 G3 Lindhorst Ger.
208 E4 Lindi r. Dem. Rep. Congo
211 C7 Lindi Tanz.
211 C7 Lindi admin. reg. Tanz.
107 J2 Lindian Heilong. China
Lindisfarne i. England U.K. see Holy Island
81 B6 Lindis Peak South I. N.Z.
169 C4 Lindlar Ger.
215 F2 Lindley S. Africa
256 D5 Lindóia Brazil
142 E3 Lindome Sweden
107 H3 Lindong Nei Mongol China
182 B3 Lindoso Port.
170 D3 Lindow Ger.
157 G4 Lindre, Étang de l. France
233 □J1 Lindsay N.B. Can.
224 E4 Lindsay Ont. Can.
240 H3 Lindsay CA U.S.A.
238 F2 Lindsay MT U.S.A.
87 D5 Lindsay Gordon Lagoon salt flat W.A. Austr.
236 D4 Lindsborg KS U.S.A.
143 G3 Lindsdal Sweden
232 C6 Lindside WV U.S.A.
170 C3 Lindstedt Ger.
Lindum Lincolnshire, England U.K. see Lincoln
168 E3 Lindwedel Ger.
176 C1 Líně Czech Rep.
234 B3 Lineboro MD U.S.A.
266 I5 Line Islands S. Pacific Ocean
234 C2 Line Lexington PA U.S.A.
107 F4 Linfen Shanxi China
234 C2 Linfield PA U.S.A.
151 H3 Linford Thurrock, England U.K.
146 C4 Ling r. Scotland U.K.
114 D2 Lingamparti Andhra Prad. India
108 D5 Lingao Hainan China
161 B4 Lingas, Montagne du mt. France
92 B2 Lingayen Phil.
92 B2 Lingayen Gulf Phil.
107 F5 Lingbao Henan China
109 F1 Lingbi Anhui China
Lingcheng Guangxi China see Lingshan
Lingcheng Hainan China see Lingshui
Lingcheng Shandong China see Lingxian
108 D3 Lingchuan Guangxi China
107 G5 Lingchuan Shanxi China
215 F5 Lingelethu S. Africa
215 F5 Lingelihle S. Africa
168 C3 Lingen (Ems) Ger.
178 A3 Lingenau Austria
172 C2 Lingenfeld Ger.
151 G3 Lingfield Surrey, England U.K.
94 D3 Lingga i. Indon.
94 D3 Lingga, Kepulauan is Indon.
92 C5 Lingig Phil.
238 F3 Lingle WY U.S.A.
234 B2 Linglestown PA U.S.A.
84 D3 Lingnoonganee Island Qld Austr.
157 H4 Lingolsheim France
107 G4 Lingqiu Shanxi China
108 D4 Lingshan Guangxi China
107 F4 Lingshi Shanxi China
108 D5 Lingshui Hainan China
114 D2 Lingsugur Karnataka India
107 E5 Lingtai Gansu China
195 E5 Linguaglossa Sicilia Italy
206 B3 Linguère Senegal
108 D3 Lingui Guangxi China
192 B2 Linguizzetta Corse France
151 I2 Lingwood Norfolk, England U.K.
Lingxi Hunan China see Yongshun
Lingxian Hunan China see Yanling
107 H4 Lingxian Shandong China
109 E2 Lingxiang Hubei China
107 H3 Lingyuan Liaoning China
108 C3 Lingyun Guangxi China
111 B5 Lingzi Thang Plains l. Aksai Chin
107 I3 Linhai Liaoning China
109 G2 Linhai Zhejiang China
257 G3 Linhares Brazil
182 C4 Linhares Port.
107 E3 Linhe Nei Mongol China
174 F1 Linia Pol.
81 B6 Linidis Valley South I. N.Z.
233 □H1 Linière Que. Can.
174 G1 Liniewo Pol.
Linjiang Fujian China see Shanghang
101 C4 Linjiang Jilin China
171 C2 Linkenheim-Hochstetten Ger.
143 F2 Linköping Sweden
100 D3 Linkou Heilong. China
146 E3 Linksness Orkney, Scotland U.K.
136 D3 Linkuva Lith.
109 D2 Linli Hunan China
146 E6 Linlithgow West Lothian, Scotland U.K.
107 G4 Linlü Shan mt. Henan China
Linmingguan Hebei China see Yongnian
236 F4 Linn MO U.S.A.
237 D7 Linn TX U.S.A.
240 F1 Linn, Mount CA U.S.A.
142 D2 Linnekleppen hill Norway
233 □J1 Linneus ME U.S.A.
146 C5 Linnhe, Loch inlet Scotland U.K.
169 B5 Linnich Ger.
189 D8 Linosa, Isola di i. Sicilia Italy
138 E5 Linova Belarus
170 D2 Linow Ger.
107 G4 Linqing Shandong China
Linru Henan China see Ruzhou
256 C4 Lins Brazil
168 E3 Linsburg Ger.
108 C2 Linshui Sichuan China
246 □ Linstead Jamaica
213 □J5 Linta r. Madag.
106 D5 Lintan Gansu China
106 D5 Lintao Gansu China
190 E1 Linth r. Switz.
190 E2 Linthal Switz.
171 D3 Linthe Ger.
234 B3 Linthicum Heights MD U.S.A.
168 D2 Lintig Ger.
80 E4 Linton North I. N.Z.
151 H2 Linton Cambridgeshire, England U.K.
236 C2 Linton ND U.S.A.
107 F5 Lintong Shaanxi China
170 D3 Linum Ger.
234 D3 Linwood NJ U.S.A.
109 E3 Linwu Hunan China
163 A5 Linxe France
107 H3 Linxi Nei Mongol China
106 D5 Linxia Gansu China
Linxian Henan China see Linzhou
107 F4 Linxian Shanxi China
109 E2 Linxiang Hunan China
212 E3 Linyanti r. Botswana/Namibia
212 D3 Linyanti Swamp Namibia
107 H4 Linyi Shandong China
107 H5 Linyi Shandong China
107 F5 Linyi Shanxi China
109 E1 Linying Henan China
186 D3 Linyola Spain
179 F2 Linz Austria
169 C5 Linz am Rhein Ger.
106 D4 Linze Gansu China
107 G4 Linzhou Henan China
186 B2 Linzoáin Spain
136 C2 Liobomlʼ Ukr.
213 H2 Lioma Moz.
161 B6 Lion, Golfe du g. France
246 □ Lionel Town Jamaica
193 H4 Lioni Italy
Lions, Gulf of France see Lion, Golfe du
222 F5 Lions Bay B.C. Can.
227 G3 Lion's Head Ont. Can.
159 F2 Lion-sur-Mer France
163 C4 Liorac-sur-Louyre France
202 B6 Lioua Chad
92 B3 Lipa Phil.
175 I2 Lipa Pol.
177 J2 Lipany Slovakia
194 D4 Lipari Isole Lipari Italy
194 D4 Lipari, Isola i. Isole Lipari Italy
194 D4 Lipari, Isole is Italy
136 D3 Lipcani Moldova
175 H4 Lipce Reymontowskie Pol.
140 O3 Liperi Fin.
139 L5 Lipetsk Rus. Fed.
139 L5 Lipetskaya Oblastʼ admin. div. Rus. Fed.
Lipetsk Oblast admin. div. Rus. Fed. see Lipetskaya Oblastʼ
252 D5 Lipez, Cordillera de mts Bol.
151 G3 Liphook Hampshire, England U.K.
174 C2 Lipiany Pol.
139 K1 Lipin Bor Rus. Fed.
108 D3 Liping Guizhou China
175 J6 Lipinki Pol.
174 D4 Lipinki Łużyckie Pol.
174 F2 Lipka Pol.
139 K5 Lipki Rus. Fed.
174 D3 Lipki Wielkie Pol.
196 E4 Lipljan Kosovo, Srbija Yugo.
139 I2 Lipnaya Gorka Rus. Fed.
175 H2 Lipnica Kujawsko-Pomorskie Pol.
174 F2 Lipnica Pomorskie Pol.
175 J5 Lipnik Pol.
175 H6 Lipnica Wielka Pol.
177 G2 Lipník nad Bečvou Czech Rep.
175 H3 Lipno Kujawsko-Pomorskie Pol.
174 E4 Lipno Wielkopolskie Pol.
163 B4 Lipostey France
197 E2 Lipova Romania
177 L6 Lipovei, Dealurile hills Romania
135 I6 Lipovka Volgogradskaya Oblastʼ Rus. Fed.
137 K2 Lipovka Voronezhskaya Oblastʼ Rus. Fed.
197 F3 Lipovu Romania
175 J2 Lipowiec Pol.
169 B4 Lippe r. Ger.
164 F1 Lippenhuizen Neth.
169 E4 Lippoldsberg (Wahlsburg) Ger.
169 D4 Lippstadt Ger.
237 C4 Lipscomb TX U.S.A.
175 L2 Lipsk Pol.
175 J4 Lipsko Pol.
Lipsoí i. Greece see Leipsoi
177 G2 Liptál Czech Rep.
207 F3 Liptougou Burkina
177 I2 Liptovská Kokava Slovakia
177 I2 Liptovská Mara, Vodná nádrž resr Slovakia
177 I3 Liptovská Osada Slovakia
177 J3 Liptovská Teplička Slovakia
177 I2 Liptovský Hrádok Slovakia
177 I2 Liptovský Mikuláš Slovakia
83 F4 Liptrap, Cape Vic. Austr.
108 D3 Lipu Guangxi China
195 G3 Lipuda r. Italy
174 F1 Lipusz Pol.
210 B4 Lira Uganda
159 E4 Liré France
193 F3 Liri r. Italy
210 A2 Liri, Jebel el mt. Sudan
190 E2 Liro r. Italy
196 E5 Lis Albania
197 G3 Lisa Romania
147 C3 Lisacul Rep. of Ireland
120 E1 Lisakovsk Kazakh.
208 D4 Lisala Dem. Rep. Congo
213 □J4 L'Isalo, Massif de mts Madag.
148 D3 Lisbane Northern Ireland U.K.
147 D2 Lisbellaw Northern Ireland U.K.
184 A2 Lisboa Port.
184 A1 Lisboa admin. dist. Port.
Lisbon Port. see Lisboa
226 C5 Lisbon IL U.S.A.
234 A3 Lisbon MD U.S.A.
233 □H2 Lisbon ME U.S.A.
236 D2 Lisbon ND U.S.A.
233 H2 Lisbon NH U.S.A.
232 C4 Lisbon OH U.S.A.
233 □H3 Lisbon Falls ME U.S.A.
147 E2 Lisburn Northern Ireland U.K.
147 B4 Liscannor Rep. of Ireland
147 B4 Liscannor Bay Rep. of Ireland
147 B3 Liscarney Rep. of Ireland
147 C4 Liscarroll Rep. of Ireland
192 B3 Liscia r. Sardegna Italy
192 B4 Liscoi r. Sardegna Italy
147 B3 Lisdoonvarna Rep. of Ireland
147 D3 Lisduff Rep. of Ireland
197 F5 Lisec mt. Macedonia
142 D3 Liseleje Denmark
147 C4 Lisgarode Rep. of Ireland
147 C5 Lisgoold Rep. of Ireland
Lishan Shaanxi China see Lintong
109 G3 Lishan Taiwan
136 E2 Lishchyn Ukr.
108 B3 Lishe Jiang r. Yunnan China
Lishi Jiangxi China see Dingnan
107 F4 Lishi Shanxi China
100 C4 Lishu Jilin China
109 F2 Lishui Jiangsu China
109 F2 Lishui Zhejiang China
108 D2 Li Shui r. China
175 J5 Lisia Góra Pol.
75 H2 Lisianski Island HI U.S.A.
Lisichansk Ukr. see Lysychansʼk
174 F5 Lisięcice Pol.
159 G2 Lisieux France
139 H1 Lisiy Nos Rus. Fed.
150 C4 Liskeard Cornwall, England U.K.
135 G6 Liski Rus. Fed.
177 I2 Lisková Slovakia
162 C3 Lisle France
147 E2 Lislea Northern Ireland U.K.
156 C3 L'Isle-Adam France
162 C3 L'Isle-d'Abeau France
163 C5 L'Isle-de-Noé France
162 C3 L'Isle-d'Espagnac France
163 C5 L'Isle-en-Dodon France
163 C4 L'Isle-Jourdain France
162 C2 L'Isle-Jourdain France
161 D5 L'Isle-sur-la-Sorgue France
160 E1 L'Isle-sur-le-Doubs France
160 C1 L'Isle-sur-Serein France
163 D5 Lisle-sur-Tarn France
83 H2 Lismore N.S.W. Austr.
81 C5 Lismore South I. N.Z.
147 D4 Lismore Rep. of Ireland
146 C5 Lismore i. Scotland U.K.
147 C4 Lisnagry Rep. of Ireland
147 D4 Lisnakill Rep. of Ireland
147 E2 Lisnamuck Northern Ireland U.K.
147 E2 Lisnarrick Northern Ireland U.K.
147 D2 Lisnaskea Northern Ireland U.K.
136 E4 Lisne Ukr.
160 D1 Lison r. France
176 D2 Lišov Czech Rep.
147 C5 Lispatrick Rep. of Ireland
147 A4 Lispole Rep. of Ireland
147 D4 Lisronagh Rep. of Ireland
148 B4 Lisryan Rep. of Ireland
128 D4 Liss mt. Saudi Arabia
151 G3 Liss Hampshire, England U.K.
Lissa Croatia see Vis
Lissa Wielkopolskie Pol. see Leszno
163 D4 Lissac-et-Mouret France
148 C3 Lissan Northern Ireland U.K.
164 D2 Lisse Neth.
147 B4 Lisselton Rep. of Ireland
169 B5 Lissendorf Ger.
142 E1 Lisskogsbrändan Sweden
190 E3 Lissone Italy
147 B4 Lissycasey Rep. of Ireland
168 D1 List Ger.
142 B2 Lista pen. Norway
143 E5 Listed Bornholm Denmark
263 K1 Lister, Mount Antarctica
147 D4 Listerlin Rep. of Ireland
148 D3 Listooder Northern Ireland U.K.
224 D5 Listowel Ont. Can.
147 B4 Listowel Rep. of Ireland
85 F5 Listowel Downs Qld Austr.
162 B3 Listrac-Médoc France
121 K2 Listvyaga, Khrebet mts Kazakh./Rus. Fed.
174 G4 Liswarta r. Pol.
151 E3 Liswerry Newport, Wales U.K.
175 H5 Liszki Pol.
174 F2 Liszkowo Pol.
140 K3 Lit Sweden
108 D4 Litang Guangxi China
108 B2 Litang Sichuan China
108 B2 Litang Qu r. Sichuan China
253 H4 Litani r. Fr. Guiana/Suriname
128 B3 Lītāni r. Lebanon
176 D2 Litavka r. Czech Rep.
240 G1 Litchfield CA U.S.A.
235 E1 Litchfield CT U.S.A.
236 F4 Litchfield IL U.S.A.
226 E4 Litchfield MI U.S.A.
226 A3 Litchfield MN U.S.A.
232 B4 Litchfield OH U.S.A.
234 E1 Litchfield County county CT U.S.A.
177 G4 Litér Hungary
163 A4 Lit-et-Mixe France
164 E3 Lith Neth.
149 G4 Litherland Merseyside, England U.K.
83 G3 Lithgow N.S.W. Austr.
138 D4 Lithuania country Europe
188 E2 Litija Slovenia
227 I5 Lititz PA U.S.A.
177 I3 Litke Hungary
198 C1 Litochoro Greece
176 D1 Litoměřice Czech Rep.
176 F2 Litomyšl Czech Rep.
184 B1 Litoral reg. Port.
176 G2 Litovel Czech Rep.
100 E2 Litovko Rus. Fed.
Litovskaya S.S.R. country Europe see Lithuania
179 G2 Litschau Austria
190 D1 Littau Switz.
237 E6 Little r. LA U.S.A.
237 E5 Little r. OK U.S.A.
237 D6 Little r. TX U.S.A.
231 E7 Little Abaco i. Bahamas
224 D3 Little Abitibi r. Ont. Can.
Little Aden Yemen see ʻAdan as Sughra
115 G4 Little Andaman i. Andaman & Nicobar Is India
Little Ararat mt. Turkey see Küçük Ağrı Dağı
236 D4 Little Arkansas r. KS U.S.A.
231 E7 Little Bahama Bank sea feature Bahamas
80 E2 Little Barrier i. North I. N.Z.
Little Belt sea chan. Denmark see Lille Bælt
238 E2 Little Belt Mountains MT U.S.A.
238 F2 Little Bighorn r. MT U.S.A.
Little Bitter Lake Egypt see Murrat el Sughra, Buheirat
236 D4 Little Blue r. KS U.S.A.
149 G4 Littleborough Greater Manchester, England U.K.
222 H5 Little Bow r. Alta Can.
222 H2 Little Buffalo r. N.W.T. Can.
246 B3 Little Cayman i. Cayman Is
223 M3 Little Churchill r. Man. Can.
151 I3 Little Clacton Essex, England U.K.
97 A4 Little Coco Island Cocos Is
241 L3 Little Colorado r. AZ U.S.A.
151 H4 Little Common East Sussex, England U.K.
234 C3 Little Creek DE U.S.A.
241 K3 Little Creek Peak UT U.S.A.
148 E2 Little Cumbrae i. Scotland U.K.
224 D4 Little Current Ont. Can.
224 C3 Little Current r. Ont. Can.
150 D4 Little Dart r. England U.K.
150 E3 Littledean Gloucestershire, England U.K.
151 H2 Little Downham Cambridgeshire, England U.K.
246 D2 Little Exuma i. Bahamas
236 E2 Little Falls MN U.S.A.
233 F3 Little Falls NY U.S.A.
146 D4 Littleferry Highland, Scotland U.K.
241 K3 Littlefield AZ U.S.A.
237 C5 Littlefield TX U.S.A.
215 F5 Little Fish r. S. Africa
226 A1 Little Fork MN U.S.A.
226 A1 Little Fork r. MN U.S.A.
222 F5 Little Fort B.C. Can.
Little Ganges atoll Cook Is see Rakahanga
234 C2 Little Gap PA U.S.A.
223 M4 Little Grand Rapids Man. Can.
151 G4 Littlehampton West Sussex, England U.K.
246 D2 Little Inagua Island Bahamas
232 C5 Little Kanawha r. WV U.S.A.
214 C5 Little Karoo plat. S. Africa
240 I4 Little Lake CA U.S.A.
146 C4 Little Loch Broom inlet Scotland U.K.
225 I3 Little Mecatina r. Newfoundland/Québec Can.
232 A5 Little Miami r. OH U.S.A.
146 E4 Littlemill Highland, Scotland U.K.
146 A4 Little Minch sea chan. Scotland U.K.
151 G3 Little Missenden Buckinghamshire, England U.K.
236 C2 Little Missouri r. ND U.S.A.
151 F3 Littlemore Oxfordshire, England U.K.
232 C5 Little Muskingum r. OH U.S.A.
115 G5 Little Nicobar i. Andaman & Nicobar Is India
151 I3 Little Oakley Essex, England U.K.
215 G1 Little Olifants r. S. Africa
151 H2 Little Ouse r. England U.K.
224 D1 Little Pic r. Ont. Can.
234 A1 Little Pine Creek r. PA U.S.A.
234 A3 Little Pipe Creek r. MD U.S.A.
151 H2 Littleport Cambridgeshire, England U.K.
238 F2 Little Powder r. MT U.S.A.
222 D2 Little Rancheria r. B.C. Can.
116 B5 Little Rann marsh Gujarat India
237 F5 Little Red r. AR U.S.A.
222 H3 Little Red River Alta Can.
81 D5 Little River South I. N.Z.
231 E5 Little River SC U.S.A.
237 E5 Little Rock AR U.S.A.
240 I4 Littlerock CA U.S.A.
87 C4 Little Sandy Desert W.A. Austr.
246 D1 Little San Salvador i. Bahamas
236 D3 Little Sioux r. IA U.S.A.
222 G4 Little Smoky Alta Can.
222 G4 Little Smoky r. Alta Can.
238 E3 Little Snake r. CO U.S.A.
151 H4 Littlestone-on-Sea Kent, England U.K.
234 A3 Littlestown PA U.S.A.
247 □5 Little Tobago i. Trin. and Tob.
148 B5 Littleton Rep. of Ireland
151 F3 Littleton Hampshire, England U.K.
226 B5 Littleton IL U.S.A.
233 H2 Littleton NH U.S.A.
232 C5 Littleton WV U.S.A.
226 E3 Little Traverse Bay MI U.S.A.
232 D3 Little Valley NY U.S.A.
236 F4 Little Wabash r. IL U.S.A.
81 D4 Little Wanganui South I. N.Z.
236 C3 Little White r. SD U.S.A.
237 D5 Little Wichita r. TX U.S.A.
238 E3 Little Wind r. WY U.S.A.
238 D3 Little Wood r. ID U.S.A.
Little Zab r. Iraq see Zāb aş Şaghīr, Nahr az
143 J1 Littoinen Fin.
207 H5 Littoral prov. Cameroon
211 B8 Litunde Moz.
176 C1 Litvínov Czech Rep.
136 E3 Lityn Ukr.
172 B3 Litzendorf Ger.
107 H3 Liu r. China
107 I3 Liu r. China
108 C1 Liuba Shaanxi China
96 E1 Liucheng Guangxi China
109 F2 Liucheng Zhejiang China
108 C3 Liuchong He r. Guizhou China
Liuchow Guangxi China see Liuzhou
107 I3 Liugu r. China
100 C4 Liuhe Jilin China
109 E2 Liujiachang Hubei China
108 D4 Liujiang Guangxi China
Liujiaxia Gansu China see Yongjing
Liulin Gansu China see Jonê
Liupai Guangxi China see Tianʼe
106 E5 Liupan Shan mts China
Liupanshui Guizhou China see Lupanshui
213 H2 Liupo Moz.
106 B3 Liushuquan Xinjiang China
209 D8 Liuwa Plain Zambia
109 E2 Liuyang Hunan China
109 E2 Liuyang He r. China
Liuzhangzhen Shanxi China see Yuanqu
108 D3 Liuzhou Guangxi China
177 K5 Livada Arad Romania
197 F2 Livada Satu Mare Romania
198 C1 Livadi Thessalia Greece
198 C1 Livadia Kentriki Makedonia Greece
100 E4 Livadiya Rus. Fed.
198 C2 Livanates Greece
138 F3 Līvāni Latvia
188 F3 Livanjsko Polje plain Bos.-Herz.
159 G2 Livarot France
138 D3 Līvbērze Latvia
137 J2 Livenka Rus. Fed.
191 H3 Livenza r. Italy
240 G2 Live Oak CA U.S.A.
231 D6 Live Oak FL U.S.A.
157 G4 Liverdun France
86 E3 Liveringa W.A. Austr.
240 G3 Livermore CA U.S.A.
239 F6 Livermore, Mount TX U.S.A.
233 □H2 Livermore Falls ME U.S.A.
163 D4 Livernon France
83 G3 Liverpool N.S.W. Austr.
84 C2 Liverpool r. N.T. Austr.
225 H4 Liverpool N.S. Can.
149 G4 Liverpool Merseyside, England U.K.
233 E3 Liverpool NY U.S.A.
234 B2 Liverpool PA U.S.A.
149 F4 Liverpool Bay England U.K.
83 G2 Liverpool Plains N.S.W. Austr.
83 G2 Liverpool Range mts N.S.W. Austr.
149 H4 Liversedge West Yorkshire, England U.K.
190 F2 Livigno Italy
243 H6 Livingston Guat.
146 E6 Livingston West Lothian, Scotland U.K.
237 F5 Livingston AL U.S.A.
240 G3 Livingston CA U.S.A.
232 A6 Livingston KY U.S.A.
237 F6 Livingston LA U.S.A.
238 E2 Livingston MT U.S.A.
231 C4 Livingston TN U.S.A.
237 E6 Livingston TX U.S.A.
237 E6 Livingston, Lake TX U.S.A.
209 E9 Livingstone Zambia
211 B7 Livingstone Mountains Tanz.
211 B7 Livingstonia Malawi
262 T2 Livingston Island Antarctica
233 F3 Livingston Manor NY U.S.A.
81 B6 Livingston Mountains South I. N.Z.
188 F4 Livno Bos.-Herz.
139 K5 Livny Rus. Fed.
140 O2 Livo r. Rus. Fed.
227 F4 Livonia MI U.S.A.
232 E3 Livonia NY U.S.A.
190 F5 Livorno Italy
190 F5 Livorno prov. Toscana Italy
190 D3 Livorno Ferraris Italy
160 B3 Livradois, Monts du mts France
216 □1b Livramento São Miguel Azores
254 E5 Livramento do Brumado Brazil
161 C4 Livron-sur-Drôme France
175 J3 Liw Pol.
129 G2 Liwā Oman
211 C7 Liwale Tanz.
175 J3 Liwiec r. Pol.
211 B8 Liwonde Malawi
Liwu Hebei China see Lixian
106 E5 Lixian Gansu China
107 G4 Lixian Hebei China
109 D2 Lixian Hunan China
108 B2 Lixian Sichuan China
109 F1 Lixin Anhui China
157 G3 Lixing-lès-St-Avold France
198 B2 Lixouri Ionioi Nisoi Greece
Lixus Morocco see Larache
198 B1 Liyadero Dytiki Makedonia Greece
109 F2 Liyang Jiangsu China
Liyuan Hunan China see Sangzhi
182 B5 Liz r. Port.
150 B5 Lizard Cornwall, England U.K.
254 D4 Lizarda Brazil
85 F2 Lizard Island Qld Austr.
150 B5 Lizard Point England U.K.
Lizarra Spain see Estella
183 H2 Lizarraga Spain
232 C5 Lizemores WV U.S.A.
137 J2 Lizinovka Rus. Fed.
108 B2 Liziping Sichuan China
162 C3 Lizonne r. France
156 D3 Lizy-sur-Ourcq France
195 H2 Lizzanello Italy
195 G2 Lizzano Italy
196 E3 Lig Srbija Yugo.
142 B2 Ljomsnuten mt. Norway
188 F3 Ljubija Bos.-Herz.
196 D4 Ljubišnja mts Yugo.
188 E2 Ljubljana Slovenia
179 F4 Ljubljana airport Slovenia
179 F4 Ljubljanica r. Slovenia
196 D3 Ljubovija Srbija Yugo.
188 F4 Ljubuški Bos.-Herz.
143 H3 Ljugarn Gotland Sweden
140 J3 Ljungå Sweden
141 L3 Ljungan r. Sweden
141 L3 Ljungaverk Sweden
143 E3 Ljungby Sweden
143 G3 Ljungbyholm Sweden
140 K3 Ljungdalen Sweden
143 F2 Ljungsbro Sweden
142 D2 Ljungskile Sweden
141 L3 Ljusdal Sweden
143 F2 Ljusfallshammar Sweden
142 E1 Ljusnan r. Sweden
141 L3 Ljusne r. Sweden
141 L3 Ljusne Sweden
188 F2 Ljutomer Slovenia
186 F3 Llagostera Spain
260 B6 Llaima, Volcán vol. Chile
261 G2 Llambí Campbell Arg.
150 C2 Llanaelhaearn Gwynedd, Wales U.K.
150 D2 Llanarmon Dyffryn Ceiriog Wrexham, Wales U.K.
150 C2 Llanarth Ceredigion, Wales U.K.
150 C3 Llanarthney Carmarthenshire, Wales U.K.
150 D1 Llanasa Flintshire, Wales U.K.
150 C2 Llanbadarn Fawr Ceredigion, Wales U.K.
150 C1 Llanbadrig Isle of Anglesey, Wales U.K.
Llanbedr Ceredigion, Wales U.K. see Lampeter
150 C2 Llanbedr Gwynedd, Wales U.K.
150 C2 Llanbedrog Gwynedd, Wales U.K.
150 C1 Llanberis Gwynedd, Wales U.K.
150 D2 Llanbister Powys, Wales U.K.
150 D2 Llanbrynmair Powys, Wales U.K.
186 G2 Llançà Spain
260 C4 Llancanelo, Salina salt flat Arg.
150 C2 Llandanwg Gwynedd, Wales U.K.
150 C3 Llanddarog Carmarthenshire, Wales U.K.
150 C1 Llanddeiniolen Gwynedd, Wales U.K.
150 D2 Llandderfel Gwynedd, Wales U.K.
150 C3 Llanddowror Carmarthenshire, Wales U.K.
150 D3 Llandeilo Carmarthenshire, Wales U.K.
150 E3 Llandinabo Herefordshire, England U.K.
150 D2 Llandinam Powys, Wales U.K.
150 C3 Llandissilio Pembrokeshire, Wales U.K.
150 D3 Llandovery Carmarthenshire, Wales U.K.
150 D2 Llandrillo Denbighshire, Wales U.K.
150 D2 Llandrindod Wells Powys, Wales U.K.
150 D1 Llandudno Conwy, Wales U.K.
150 C1 Llandwrog Gwynedd, Wales U.K.
150 C3 Llandybie Carmarthenshire, Wales U.K.
150 C2 Llandysul Ceredigion, Wales U.K.
150 C3 Llanegwad Carmarthenshire, Wales U.K.
150 C1 Llaneilian Isle of Anglesey, Wales U.K.
150 C3 Llanelli Carmarthenshire, Wales U.K.
150 D2 Llanelltyd Gwynedd, Wales U.K.
150 D3 Llanelly Monmouthshire, Wales U.K.
Llanelwy Denbighshire, Wales U.K. see St Asaph
150 C1 Llanerchymedd Isle of Anglesey, Wales U.K.
183 F1 Llanes Spain
150 C1 Llanfaelog Isle of Anglesey, Wales U.K.
150 D2 Llanfair Caereinion Powys, Wales U.K.
150 D1 Llanfairfechan Conwy, Wales U.K.
150 C1 Llanfairpwllgwyngyll Isle of Anglesey, Wales U.K.
150 D1 Llanfair Talhaiarn Conwy, Wales U.K.
150 C1 Llanfair-yn-Neubwll Isle of Anglesey, Wales U.K.
150 C2 Llanfarian Ceredigion, Wales U.K.
150 C2 Llanfihangel-ar-Arth Carmarthenshire, Wales U.K.
150 D2 Llanfyllin Powys, Wales U.K.
150 D1 Llanfynydd Flintshire, Wales U.K.
150 D2 Llangadfan Powys, Wales U.K.
150 D3 Llangadog Carmarthenshire, Wales U.K.
150 C1 Llangefni Isle of Anglesey, Wales U.K.
150 C2 Llangeler Carmarthenshire, Wales U.K.
150 C2 Llangelynin Gwynedd, Wales U.K.
150 C3 Llangendeirne Carmarthenshire, Wales U.K.
150 D1 Llangernyw Conwy, Wales U.K.
150 C1 Llangoed Isle of Anglesey, Wales U.K.
150 D2 Llangollen Denbighshire, Wales U.K.
150 C2 Llangranog Ceredigion, Wales U.K.
150 C1 Llangristiolus Isle of Anglesey, Wales U.K.
150 C3 Llangunnor Carmarthenshire, Wales U.K.
150 D2 Llangurig Powys, Wales U.K.
150 C3 Llangwm Pembrokeshire, Wales U.K.
150 D2 Llangynidr Powys, Wales U.K.
150 D3 Llanharan Rhondda Cynon Taff, Wales U.K.
150 D2 Llanidloes Powys, Wales U.K.
150 C2 Llanilar Ceredigion, Wales U.K.
150 D3 Llanishen Cardiff, Wales U.K.
150 D2 Llanllwchaiarn Powys, Wales U.K.
150 C1 Llanllyfni Gwynedd, Wales U.K.
150 C3 Llannon Carmarthenshire, Wales U.K.
150 C2 Llannor Wales U.K.
242 C2 Llano Mex.
237 D6 Llano TX U.S.A.
237 D6 Llano r. TX U.S.A.
237 C5 Llano Estacado plain New Mexico/Texas U.S.A.
150 C2 Llanon Ceredigion, Wales U.K.
250 D3 Llanos plain Col./Venez.
259 B6 Llanquihue, Lago l. Chile
150 D2 Llanrhaeadr-ym-Mochnant Powys, Wales U.K.
150 C3 Llanrhidian Swansea, Wales U.K.
150 C2 Llanrhystud Ceredigion, Wales U.K.
150 C1 Llanrug Gwynedd, Wales U.K.
150 D3 Llanrumney Cardiff, Wales U.K.
150 D1 Llanrwst Conwy, Wales U.K.
Llansá Spain see Llançà
150 D1 Llansanffraid Glan Conwy Conwy, Wales U.K.
150 D1 Llansannan Conwy, Wales U.K.
150 C2 Llansawel Carmarthenshire, Wales U.K.
Llansteffan Carmarthenshire, Wales U.K. see Llanstephan
150 C3 Llanstephan Carmarthenshire, Wales U.K.
150 D3 Llanthony Monmouthshire, Wales U.K.
150 D3 Llantilio Pertholey Monmouthshire, Wales U.K.
150 E3 Llantrisant Monmouthshire, Wales U.K.
150 D3 Llantrisant Rhondda Cynon Taff, Wales U.K.
150 D3 Llantwit Major Vale of Glamorgan, Wales U.K.
150 D2 Llanuwchllyn Gwynedd, Wales U.K.
150 D2 Llanwddyn Powys, Wales U.K.
150 C2 Llanwenog Ceredigion, Wales U.K.
150 C1 Llanwnda Gwynedd, Wales U.K.
150 D2 Llanwnog Powys, Wales U.K.
150 D3 Llanwrda Carmarthenshire, Wales U.K.
150 D2 Llanwrtyd Wells Powys, Wales U.K.
150 C2 Llanybydder Carmarthenshire, Wales U.K.
Llanymddyfri Carmarthenshire, Wales U.K. see Llandovery
150 C1 Llanynghenedl Isle of Anglesey, Wales U.K.
150 C2 Llanystumdwy Gwynedd, Wales U.K.
186 D3 Llardecans Spain
252 A2 Llata Peru
187 C5 Llauri Spain
186 E2 Llavorsí Spain
150 D1 Llay Wrexham, Wales U.K.
260 B3 Llay-Llay Chile
150 D2 Lledrod Ceredigion, Wales U.K.
186 D3 Lleida Spain
186 E2 Lleida prov. Cataluña Spain
184 D2 Llera Spain
245 E2 Llera de Canales Mex.
184 D2 Llerena Spain
150 C2 Lleyn Peninsula Wales U.K.
252 C4 Llica Bol.
187 C5 Llíria Spain
186 E2 Llivia Spain
186 E2 Llobregat r. Spain
186 E3 Llobregós r. Spain
183 H1 Llodio Spain
260 B3 Llolleo Chile
186 E3 Llorenç del Penedès Spain
186 F3 Lloret de Mar Spain
187 C5 Llosa de Ranes Spain
187 F5 Lloseta Spain
85 E2 Lloyd Bay Qld Austr.
222 E3 Lloyd George, Mount B.C. Can.
235 E2 Lloyd Harbor NY U.S.A.
223 I4 Lloydminster Alta Can.
187 G5 Llubí Spain
Lluchmayor Spain see Llucmajor
187 F5 Llucmajor Spain
252 C6 Llullaillaco, Volcán vol. Chile
150 D2 Llyswen Powys, Wales U.K.
174 G2 Lniano Pol.
165 B4 Lo Belgium
96 D2 Lô r. China/Vietnam
Lo i. Vanuatu see Loh
252 C5 Loa r. Chile
241 L2 Loa UT U.S.A.
95 G3 Loakulu Kalimantan Timur Indon.
256 A5 Loanda Brazil
146 E6 Loanhead Midlothian, Scotland U.K.
190 D4 Loano Italy
146 D6 Loans South Ayrshire, Scotland U.K.
186 C2 Loarre Spain
92 C4 Loay Phil.
139 J3 Lobʼ r. Rus. Fed.
175 M5 Lobachivka Ukr.
134 J4 Lobanʼ r. Rus. Fed.
139 L5 Lobanovo Rus. Fed.
185 F3 Lobatejo mt. Spain
212 E5 Lobatse Botswana
171 F4 Löbau Ger.
208 C3 Lobaye pref. C.A.R.
208 C4 Lobaye r. C.A.R.
161 F4 Lobbie, Cima delle mt. Italy
171 C4 Löbejün Ger.
171 D4 Löbenberg hill Ger.
186 B2 Lobera de Onsella Spain
261 H6 Lobería Arg.
174 D2 Łobez Pol.
78 □3b Lobikaere i. Majuro Marshall Is
164 F3 Lobith Neth.
209 B8 Lobito Angola
250 A6 Lobitos Peru
170 D1 Löbnitz Ger.
171 D4 Löbnitz Ger.
139 K3 Lobnya Rus. Fed.
180 C3 Lobón Spain
261 H4 Lobos Arg.
216 □3b Lobos i. Canary Is
185 H3 Lobos mt. Spain
250 A6 Lobos de Afuera, Islas is Peru
250 A6 Lobos de Tierra, Isla i. Peru
Lobositz Czech Rep. see Lovosice
137 H3 Loboykivka Ukr.
171 D4 Lobstädt Ger.
171 D3 Loburg Ger.
81 D5 Loburn South I. N.Z.
174 F2 Łobżenica Pol.
190 C3 Locana Italy
190 D2 Locarno Switz.
169 E3 Loccum (Rehburg-Loccum) Ger.
192 B5 Loceri Sardegna Italy
146 D5 Lochaber mts Scotland U.K.
146 C5 Lochailort Highland, Scotland U.K.
146 C5 Lochaline Highland, Scotland U.K.
227 E1 Lochalsh Ont. Can.
146 C7 Lochans Dumfries and Galloway, Scotland U.K.
146 E6 Locharbriggs Dumfries and Galloway, Scotland U.K.
178 A3 Lochau Austria
146 C5 Lochawe Argyll and Bute, Scotland U.K.
146 D5 Lochay r. Scotland U.K.
Loch Baghasdail Western Isles, Scotland U.K. see Lochboisdale
146 A4 Lochboisdale Western Isles, Scotland U.K.
146 C5 Lochbuie Argyll and Bute, Scotland U.K.
146 C4 Lochcarron Highland, Scotland U.K.
146 C5 Lochdon Argyll and Bute, Scotland U.K.
146 D5 Lochearnhead Stirling, Scotland U.K.
164 F2 Lochem Neth.
178 E2 Lochen Austria
146 D4 Lochend Highland, Scotland U.K.
162 C1 Loches France
Loch Garman Rep. of Ireland see Wexford
146 E5 Lochgelly Fife, Scotland U.K.
146 C5 Lochgilphead Argyll and Bute, Scotland U.K.
146 D5 Lochgoilhead Argyll and Bute, Scotland U.K.
81 B7 Lochiel South I. N.Z.
215 H2 Lochiel S. Africa
146 C3 Lochinver Highland, Scotland U.K.
146 E6 Lochmaben Dumfries and Galloway, Scotland U.K.
146 A4 Lochmaddy Western Isles, Scotland U.K.
146 E5 Lochnagar mt. Scotland U.K.
Loch nam Madadh Western Isles, Scotland U.K. see Lochmaddy
176 C2 Lochovice Czech Rep.
175 J3 Łochów Pol.
146 C6 Lochranza North Ayrshire, Scotland U.K.
165 C3 Lochristi Belgium
238 D2 Lochsa r. ID U.S.A.
146 A4 Loch Sgioport Western Isles, Scotland U.K.
146 D6 Lochwinnoch Renfrewshire, Scotland U.K.
146 D5 Lochy, Loch l. Scotland U.K.
82 C3 Lock S.A. Austr.
232 B5 Lockbourne OH U.S.A.
232 E3 Locke NY U.S.A.
240 G2 Lockeford CA U.S.A.
179 H3 Lockenhaus Austria
146 E6 Lockerbie Dumfries and Galloway, Scotland U.K.
86 B4 Locker Point W.A. Austr.
83 F3 Lockhart N.S.W. Austr.
237 D6 Lockhart TX U.S.A.
85 E2 Lockhart River Qld Austr.
232 E4 Lock Haven PA U.S.A.
150 E3 Locking North Somerset, England U.K.
170 F2 Löcknitz Ger.
170 C2 Löcknitz r. Ger.
232 D3 Lockport NY U.S.A.
151 F4 Locks Heath Hampshire, England U.K.
149 I3 Lockton North Yorkshire, England U.K.
158 C4 Locmaria France
158 B3 Locmaria-Plouzané France
158 D4 Locmariaquer France
158 D4 Locminé France
158 C4 Locmiquélic France
97 D5 Lôc Ninh Vietnam
158 C4 Locoal-Mendon France
193 H3 Locone r. Italy
195 G2 Locorotondo Italy
158 C3 Locquirec France
195 F4 Locri Italy
158 B3 Locronan France
158 B4 Loctudy France
192 B4 Loculi Sardegna Italy
252 C4 Locumba r. Peru
235 D2 Locust NJ U.S.A.
235 E2 Locust Valley NY U.S.A.
128 B4 Lod Israel
171 C4 Lödderitz Ger.
170 F1 Loddin Ger.
150 D4 Loddiswell Devon, England U.K.
83 E3 Loddon r. Vic. Austr.
151 I2 Loddon Norfolk, England U.K.
192 B4 Lodè Sardegna Italy
138 E3 Lode Latvia
176 D1 Loděnice Czech Rep.
171 C4 Lodersleben Ger.
161 B5 Lodève France
139 I1 Lodeynoye Pole Rus. Fed.
222 B3 Lodge, Mount Alaska/B.C. Can./U.S.A.
223 I5 Lodge Creek r. Can./U.S.A.
238 F2 Lodge Grass MT U.S.A.
236 C3 Lodgepole Creek r. WY U.S.A.
116 D5 Lodhikheda Madh. Prad. India
123 G4 Lodhran Pak.
190 E3 Lodi Italy
190 E3 Lodi prov. Lombardia Italy
240 G2 Lodi CA U.S.A.
235 D2 Lodi NJ U.S.A.
232 B4 Lodi OH U.S.A.
226 C4 Lodi WI U.S.A.
140 K2 Løding Norway
140 K1 Lødingen Norway
190 E3 Lodi Vecchio Italy
209 D5 Lodja Dem. Rep. Congo
Lodomeria Rus. Fed. see Vladimir
183 H2 Lodosa Spain
116 B5 Lodrani Gujarat India
210 B4 Lodwar Kenya
175 H6 Łodygowice Pol.
175 H4 Łódź Pol.
175 H4 Łódzkie prov. Pol.
183 G4 Loeches Spain
96 C3 Loei Thai.
164 F2 Loenen Gelderland Neth.
164 E2 Loenen Utrecht Neth.
215 E5 Loerie S. Africa
214 B4 Loeriesfontein S. Africa
169 C5 Löf Ger.
178 D3 Lofer Austria
172 C4 Löffingen Ger.
140 K1 Lofoten is Norway
141 K3 Lofsdalen Sweden
215 E4 Lofter S. Africa
149 I3 Loftus Redcar and Cleveland, England U.K.
87 C5 Lofty Range hills W.A. Austr.
135 H6 Log Rus. Fed.
207 F3 Loga Niger
214 E1 Logageng S. Africa
146 D6 Logan East Ayrshire, Scotland U.K.
236 E3 Logan IA U.S.A.
237 C5 Logan NM U.S.A.
232 B5 Logan OH U.S.A.
238 E3 Logan UT U.S.A.
232 C6 Logan WV U.S.A.
222 A2 Logan, Mount Y.T. Can.
238 B1 Logan, Mount WA U.S.A.
85 F4 Logan Creek r. Qld Austr.
236 D3 Logan Creek r. NE U.S.A.
241 J3 Logandale NV U.S.A.
222 F5 Logan Lake B.C. Can.
222 D2 Logan Mountains N.W.T./Y.T. Can.
230 C3 Logansport IN U.S.A.
237 E6 Logansport LA U.S.A.
234 B3 Loganville PA U.S.A.
188 E3 Logatec Slovenia
140 L2 Lögda Sweden
140 L3 Lögdeälven r. Sweden
209 B6 Loge r. Angola
150 E2 Loggerheads Staffordshire, England U.K.
142 B2 Logna r. Norway
158 E4 Logne r. France
208 B1 Logone r. Africa
207 I4 Logone Birni Cameroon
208 B2 Logone Occidental pref. Chad
208 C2 Logone Oriental pref. Chad
206 D5 Logoualé Côte d'Ivoire
197 F3 Logrești Romania
156 B4 Logron France
183 H2 Logroño Spain
185 E1 Logrosán Spain
142 C3 Løgstør Denmark
192 A4 Logudoro reg. Sardegna Italy
142 C4 Løgumkloster Denmark
78 □5 Loh i. Vanuatu
142 D4 Lohals Denmark
117 F4 Lohardaga Bihar India
116 C3 Loharu Haryana India
214 D3 Lohatlha S. Africa
116 C4 Lohawat Rajasthan India
173 H2 Lohberg Ger.
158 E4 Lohéac France
168 E1 Lohe-Rickelshof Ger.
169 E4 Lohfelden Ger.
Lohifushi i. N. Male Maldives see Lhohifushi
Lohil r. China/India see Zayü Qu
141 N3 Lohja Fin.
169 C5 Lohmar Ger.
170 E1 Lohme Ger.
170 D2 Lohmen Mecklenburg-Vorpommern Ger.
171 F5 Lohmen Sachsen Ger.
169 D5 Löhnberg Ger.
169 E3 Löhne Ger.
168 D3 Lohne (Oldenburg) Ger.
179 E2 Lohnsburg am Kobernaußerwald Austria
172 D2 Lohr r. Ger.
169 D5 Lohra Ger.
172 D2 Lohr am Main Ger.
174 F4 Lohsa Ger.
140 M2 Lohtaja Fin.
96 C2 Loi, Nam r. Myanmar
191 G4 Loiano Italy
173 G3 Loiching Ger.
159 F4 Loigné-sur-Mayenne France
156 B4 Loigny-la-Bataille France
96 B3 Loikaw Myanmar
96 B3 Loi Lan mt. Myanmar/Thai.
208 D5 Loile r. Dem. Rep. Congo
141 M3 Loimaa Fin.
138 D1 Loimaan kunta Fin.
138 D1 Loimijoki r. Fin.
156 C4 Loing r. France
96 B1 Loipyet Hills Myanmar
156 B5 Loir r. France
159 G4 Loir, Les Vaux du val. France
159 F4 Loiré France
160 C3 Loire dept Rhône-Alpes France
159 D4 Loire r. France
156 B5 Loire, Val de val. France
158 D4 Loire-Atlantique dept Pays de la Loire France
Loire-Inférieure dept Pays de la Loire France see Loire-Atlantique
160 C3 Loire-sur-Rhône France
156 C5 Loiret dept Centre France
156 B5 Loiret r. France
156 B5 Loir-et-Cher dept Centre France
192 B4 Loiri-Porto San Paolo Sardegna Italy
159 F3 Loiron France
173 F4 Loisach r. Ger.
96 B2 Loi Sang mt. Myanmar
160 C3 Loise r. France
157 F3 Loison r. France

96 B2 Loi Song mt. Myanmar
156 E4 Loisy-sur-Marne France
211 B5 Loita Plains Kenya
170 E2 Loitz Ger.
182 C3 Loivos Port.
182 C3 Loivos do Monte Port.
247 □1 Loiza Aldea Puerto Rico
250 B6 Loja Ecuador
250 B6 Loja prov. Ecuador
185 F3 Loja Spain
177 H3 Lok Slovakia
136 C2 Lokachi Ukr.
95 G1 Lokan r. Sabah Malaysia
179 E5 Lokavec Slovenia
129 F3 Lökbatan Azer.
177 I2 Lokca Slovakia
134 J3 Lokchim r. Rus. Fed.
165 D3 Lokeren Belgium
176 B1 Loket Czech Rep.
212 D5 Lokgwabe Botswana
137 G2 Lokhvytsya Ukr.
93 B3 Lokilalaki, Gunung mt. Indon.
142 C3 Løkken Denmark
140 J3 Løkken Norway
139 H3 Loknya Rus. Fed.
136 C2 Loknytsya Ukr.
207 G5 Lokoja Nigeria
208 C5 Lokolo r. Dem. Rep. Congo
208 C5 Lokoro r. Dem. Rep. Congo
208 C4 Lokosafa C.A.R.
177 K5 Lőkösháza Hungary
207 F5 Lokossa Benin
139 J5 Lokot' Rus. Fed.
138 E2 Loksa Estonia
209 B8 Lola Angola
206 C5 Lola Guinea
240 C2 Lola, Mount CA U.S.A.
136 C3 Lolishniy Shepit Ukr.
142 D4 Lolland i. Denmark
169 D5 Lollar Ger.
187 C6 L'Ollería Spain
211 B5 Lollondo Tanz.
238 D2 Lolo MT U.S.A.
93 C2 Loloda Utara, Kepulauan is Maluku Indon.
207 H6 Lolodorf Cameroon
260 B4 Lolol Chile
214 D2 Lolwane S. Africa
197 F4 Lom Bulg.
197 F4 Lom r. Bulg.
171 E5 Lom Czech Rep.
141 J3 Lom Norway
139 L3 Lom Rus. Fed.
241 M2 Loma CO U.S.A.
245 G4 Loma Bonita Mex.
260 C5 Loma del Jaguel Moro mt. Arg.
208 D4 Lomako r. Dem. Rep. Congo
240 I4 Loma Linda CA U.S.A.
209 E4 Lomami r. Dem. Rep. Congo
206 C4 Loma Mountains Sierra Leone
261 G5 Loma Negra Arg.
252 B3 Lomas Peru
262 T3 Lomas, Bahía de b. Chile
261 H4 Lomas de Zamora Arg.
Lomati r. S. Africa see Mlumati
175 L4 Łomazy Pol.
209 D8 Lomba r. Angola
216 □1b Lomba da Fazenda São Miguel Azores
216 □1b Lomba da Maia São Miguel Azores
251 H4 Lombarda, Serra hills Brazil
190 E3 Lombardia admin. reg. Italy
86 D3 Lombardina W.A. Austr.
163 E5 Lombers France
163 C5 Lombez France
95 G5 Lombok Lombok Indon.
95 G5 Lombok i. Indon.
95 F5 Lombok, Selat sea chan. Indon.
159 G3 Lombron France
207 F5 Lomé Togo
208 D5 Lomela r. Dem. Rep. Congo
190 D3 Lomello Italy
175 I3 Łomianki Pol.
207 I6 Lomié Cameroon
226 C4 Lomira WI U.S.A.
171 E4 Lommatzsch Ger.
156 C2 Lomme France
165 E3 Lommel Belgium
174 D3 Łomnica Pol.
176 F2 Lomnice Czech Rep.
176 D2 Lomnice r. Czech Rep.
179 F1 Lomnice nad Lužnicí Czech Rep.
176 E1 Lomnice nad Popelkou Czech Rep.
177 I2 Lomno mt. Slovakia
225 J3 Lomond Nfld. Can.
146 D5 Lomond, Loch l. Scotland U.K.
268 M1 Lomonosov Ridge sea feature Arctic Ocean
160 E1 Lomont hills France
138 G2 Lomoriosov Rus. Fed.
134 H2 Lomovoye Rus. Fed.
Lomphat Cambodia see Lumphăt
93 A4 Lompobattang, Gunung mt. Indon.
240 G4 Lompoc CA U.S.A.
96 C3 Lom Sak Thai.
140 L2 Lomsjö Sweden
175 K2 Łomża Pol.
114 C2 Lonar Mahar. India
190 F3 Lonato Italy
114 B2 Lonavale Mahar. India
176 G6 Lončarica Croatia
260 A6 Loncoche Chile
260 B6 Loncopue Arg.
117 G5 Londa Bangl.
114 B3 Londa Karnataka India
191 G5 Londa Italy
165 D4 Londerzeel Belgium
156 B3 Londinières France
Londinium Greater London, England U.K. see London
100 E2 Londoko Rus. Fed.
224 D5 London Ont. Can.
151 G3 London Greater London, England U.K.
232 A6 London KY U.S.A.
232 B5 London OH U.S.A.
152 London area map U.K.
151 H3 London City airport England U.K.
147 D2 Londonderry Northern Ireland U.K.
147 E2 Londonderry county Northern Ireland U.K.
233 G3 Londonderry VT U.S.A.
86 E2 Londonderry, Cape W.A. Austr.
259 C9 Londonderry, Isla i. Chile
258 D2 Londres Arg.
256 B5 Londrina Brazil
209 B8 Londuimbali Angola
235 E2 Lonelyville NY U.S.A.
240 H3 Lone Pine CA U.S.A.
156 B2 Long France
96 B3 Long Thai.
146 D5 Long, Loch inlet Argyll and Bute, Scotland U.K.
163 C6 Long, Pic mt. France
209 C8 Longa Angola
209 B7 Longa r. Bengo/Cuanza Sul Angola
209 C9 Longa r. Cuando Cubango Angola
198 B3 Longa Greece
131 S2 Longa, Proliv sea chan. Rus. Fed.
163 D5 Longages France
108 C4 Long'an Guangxi China
Long'an Sichuan China see Pingwu
191 G3 Longare Italy
186 B3 Longares Spain
191 H2 Longarone Italy
150 E3 Long Ashton North Somerset, England U.K.
260 B4 Longaví Chile
260 B4 Longaví r. Chile
260 B5 Longaví, Nevado de mt. Chile
81 C6 Longbeach South I. N.Z.
240 H5 Long Beach CA U.S.A.
235 E2 Long Beach NY U.S.A.
238 A2 Long Beach WA U.S.A.
151 G2 Long Bennington Lincolnshire, England U.K.
149 H2 Longbenton Tyne and Wear, England U.K.
233 G4 Long Branch NJ U.S.A.
150 E3 Longbridge Deverill Wiltshire, England U.K.
109 E3 Longbu Jiangxi China
151 F2 Long Buckby Northamptonshire, England U.K.
80 E4 Longburn North I. N.Z.
246 D2 Long Cay i. Bahamas
108 C2 Longchang Sichuan China
160 D2 Longchaumois France
Longcheng Anhui China see Xiaoxian
Longcheng Guangdong China see Longmen
Longcheng Jiangxi China see Pengze
Longcheng Yunnan China see Chenggong
109 E3 Longchuan Guangdong China
108 A3 Longchuan Yunnan China
Longchuan Yunnan China see Nanhua
108 A4 Longchuan Jiang r. China
151 F3 Long Compton Warwickshire, England U.K.
223 K5 Long Creek r. Sask. Can.
238 C2 Long Creek OR U.S.A.
151 F3 Long Crendon Buckinghamshire, England U.K.
151 F2 Longdon Staffordshire, England U.K.
151 F2 Long Eaton Derbyshire, England U.K.
160 D1 Longecourt-en-Plaine France
157 F4 Longeville-en-Barrois France
157 G3 Longeville-lès-St-Avold France
162 A2 Longeville-sur-Mer France
81 D5 Longfellow, Mount South I. N.Z.
147 D3 Longford Rep. of Ireland
147 D3 Longford county Rep. of Ireland
146 E5 Longforgan Perth and Kinross, Scotland U.K.
149 H2 Longframlington Northumberland, England U.K.
Longgang Chongqing China see Dazu
109 E4 Longgang Guangdong China
95 G2 Longgi r. Indon.
151 F3 Long Hanborough Oxfordshire, England U.K.
150 E3 Longhope Gloucestershire, England U.K.
146 E3 Longhope Orkney, Scotland U.K.
149 H2 Longhorsley Northumberland, England U.K.
149 H2 Longhoughton Northumberland, England U.K.
107 H3 Longhua Hebei China
109 D3 Longhui Hunan China
263 K1 Longhurst, Mount Antarctica
194 D4 Longi Sicilia Italy
262 U2 Longing, Cape Antarctica
95 F3 Longiram Kalimantan Timur Indon.
85 G4 Long Island Qld Austr.
246 D2 Long Island Bahamas
233 G4 Long Island NY U.S.A.
233 G4 Long Island Sound sea chan. CT/NY U.S.A.
151 F2 Long Itchington Warwickshire, England U.K.
107 I2 Longjiang Heilong. China
108 D3 Long Jiang r. China
Longjin Fujian China see Qingliu
Longjin Jiangxi China see Anyi
Longjuzhai Shaanxi China see Danfeng
107 I4 Longkou Shandong China
224 C3 Longlac Ont. Can.
233 F3 Long Lake NY U.S.A.
214 E3 Longlands S. Africa
151 F2 Long Lawford Warwickshire, England U.K.
108 C3 Longli Guizhou China
165 E5 Longlier Belgium
108 C3 Longlin Guangxi China
108 A3 Longling Yunnan China
146 F4 Longmanhill Aberdeenshire, Scotland U.K.
233 G3 Longmeadow MA U.S.A.
151 H2 Long Melford Suffolk, England U.K.
109 E4 Longmen Guangdong China
108 C1 Longmen Shan mts Sichuan China
108 C4 Longming Guangxi China
238 F3 Longmont CO U.S.A.
146 E4 Longmorn Moray, Scotland U.K.
109 E3 Longnan Jiangxi China
146 F6 Longniddry East Lothian, Scotland U.K.
159 G3 Longny-au-Perche France
193 I5 Longobardi Italy
195 F3 Longobucco Italy
184 C1 Longomel Port.
209 B8 Longonjo Angola
182 B2 Longos Vales Port.
260 B3 Longotoma Chile
Longping Guizhou China see Luodian
224 D5 Long Point Ont. Can.
227 G4 Long Point Bay Ont. Can.
234 D3 Longport NJ U.S.A.
236 E2 Long Prairie MN U.S.A.
156 B2 Longpré-les-Corps-Saints France
149 G3 Long Preston North Yorkshire, England U.K.
Longquan Guizhou China see Fenggang
Longquan Guizhou China see Danzhai
Longquan Yunnan China see Yimen
109 F2 Longquan Zhejiang China
109 G2 Longquan Xi r. China
225 J3 Long Range Mountains Nfld. Can.
225 J4 Long Range Mountains Nfld. Can.
162 B2 Longré France
85 F4 Longreach Qld Austr.
86 E2 Long Reef W.A. Austr.
108 B1 Longriba Sichuan China
149 G4 Longridge Lancashire, England U.K.
182 C4 Longroiva Port.
Longshan Guizhou China see Longli
108 D2 Longshan Hunan China
Longshan Yunnan China see Longling
108 D3 Longsheng Guangxi China
106 D4 Longshou Shan mts China
238 F3 Longs Peak CO U.S.A.
151 I2 Long Stratton Norfolk, England U.K.
151 H2 Long Sutton Lincolnshire, England U.K.
150 E3 Long Sutton Somerset, England U.K.
109 D2 Longtian Hunan China
85 F4 Longton Qld Austr.
149 G4 Longton Lancashire, England U.K.
150 E2 Longton Stoke-on-Trent, England U.K.
149 G2 Longtown Cumbria, England U.K.
156 C3 Longueau France
162 B1 Longué-Jumelles France
156 C2 Longuenesse France
225 H3 Longue-Pointe Que. Can.
233 G2 Longueuil Que. Can.
156 D4 Longueville France
156 B3 Longueville-sur-Scie France
157 F3 Longuyon France
240 F2 Longvale CA U.S.A.
241 L4 Long Valley AZ U.S.A.
234 D2 Long Valley NJ U.S.A.
160 D1 Longvic France
160 D1 Longvic airport France
222 H5 Longview Alta Can.
237 E5 Longview TX U.S.A.
238 B2 Longview WA U.S.A.
148 C4 Longwood Rep. of Ireland
157 F3 Longwy France
106 E5 Longxi Gansu China
Longxian Guangdong China see Wengyuan
106 E5 Longxian Shaanxi China
109 F3 Longxi Shan mt. Fujian China
Longxun Fujian China see Dehua
97 D5 Long Xuyên Vietnam
109 F3 Longyan Fujian China
107 G4 Longyao Hebei China
140 □ Longyearbyen Svalbard
100 C2 Longzhen Heilong. China
108 C4 Longzhou Guangxi China
Longzhouping Hubei China see Changyang
191 G3 Lonigo Italy
168 C3 Löningen Ger.
188 F3 Lonja r. Croatia
188 F3 Lonjsko Polje plain Croatia
159 F3 Lonlay-l'Abbaye France
164 F2 Lonneker Neth.
156 E3 Lonny France
237 F5 Lonoke AR U.S.A.
260 B6 Lonquimay, Volcán vol. Chile
163 B5 Lons France
143 F3 Lönsboda Sweden
140 K2 Lønsdalen val. Norway
160 D2 Lons-le-Saunier France
142 C3 Lønstrup Denmark
255 B7 Lontra r. Mato Grosso do Sul Brazil
254 C3 Lontra r. Tocantins Brazil
260 B4 Lontué Chile
165 F4 Lontzen Belgium
177 L3 Lónya Hungary
138 E2 Loo Estonia
92 B3 Looc Phil.
Loochoo Islands Japan see Nansei-shotō
226 E4 Looking Glass r. MI U.S.A.
240 H3 Lookout Mountain CA U.S.A.
85 F2 Lookout Point Qld Austr.
87 C7 Lookout Point W.A. Austr.
211 B5 Loolmalasin vol. crater Tanz.
86 E3 Looma W.A. Austr.
224 B3 Loon Ont. Can.
222 H3 Loon r. Alta Can.
87 E6 Loongana W.A. Austr.
223 I4 Loon Lake Sask. Can.
164 E3 Loon op Zand Neth.
156 C2 Loon-Plage France
147 B4 Loop Head hd Rep. of Ireland
156 D2 Loos France
179 G2 Loosdorf Austria
151 H3 Loose Kent, England U.K.
111 C4 Lop Xinjiang China
137 I3 Lopan r. Ukr.
139 J5 Lopandino Rus. Fed.
191 J4 Lopar Croatia
213 □J4 Lopary Madag.
Lopasnya Moskovskaya Oblast' Rus. Fed. see Chekhov
139 K4 Lopasnya r. Rus. Fed.
129 E2 Lopatin Rus. Fed.
100 G2 Lopatina, Gora mt. Sakhalin Rus. Fed.
120 A1 Lopatino Rus. Fed.
139 L4 Lopatinskiy Rus. Fed.
136 D3 Lopatnic Moldova
136 C2 Lopatyn Ukr.
139 I5 Lopazna Rus. Fed.
97 C4 Lop Buri Thai.
151 F3 Lopcombe Corner Wiltshire, England U.K.
158 B3 Loperhet France
78 □5 Lopévi i. Vanuatu
92 B3 Lopez Phil.
234 B1 Lopez PA U.S.A.
175 L4 Łopiennik Górny Pol.
192 A2 Lopigna Corse France
164 D3 Lopik Neth.
Lopnur Xinjiang China see Yuli
110 E3 Lop Nur salt l. China
208 C4 Lopori r. Dem. Rep. Congo
164 F1 Loppersum Neth.
140 M1 Lopphavet b. Norway
141 N3 Loppi Fin.
175 I5 Łopuszno Pol.
182 C2 Lor r. Spain
123 F4 Lora r. Afgh.
184 E3 Lora del Río Spain
232 B4 Lorain OH U.S.A.
226 B5 Loraine IL U.S.A.
123 G4 Loralai Pak.
123 G4 Loralai r. Pak.
183 G4 Loranca de Tajuña Spain
234 C2 Lorane PA U.S.A.
185 I3 Lorca Spain
172 D3 Lorch Baden-Württemberg Ger.
169 C5 Lorch Hessen Ger.
187 C6 Lorcha Spain
182 B3 Lordelo Port.
Lord Hood atoll Arch. des Tuamotu Fr. Polynesia see Marutea
Lord Howe Atoll Solomon Is see Ontong Java Atoll
82 □2 Lord Howe Island Austr.
266 F7 Lord Howe Rise sea feature S. Pacific Ocean
182 C4 Lordosa Port.
239 E5 Lordsburg NM U.S.A.
234 C1 Lords Valley PA U.S.A.
257 E5 Lorena Brazil
91 K7 Lorengau Admiralty Is P.N.G.
91 I8 Lorentz r. Indon.
245 F2 Lorenzo del Real Mex.
191 H3 Loreo Italy
122 B3 Lorestān prov. Iran
258 F2 Loreto Arg.
254 D3 Loreto Brazil
191 I5 Loreto Italy
242 C3 Loreto Mex.
253 F5 Loreto Para.
250 C5 Loreto dept Peru
92 C4 Loreto Phil.
193 F2 Loreto Aprutino Italy
226 B3 Loretta WI U.S.A.
161 E5 Lorgues France
210 C4 Lorian Swamp Kenya
250 C2 Lorica Col.
158 C4 Lorient France
182 C4 Loriga Port.
162 B3 Lorignac France
233 F2 L'Orignal Ont. Can.
187 C5 Loriguilla Spain
221 I3 Lorillard r. Nunavut Can.
177 I4 Lőrinci Hungary
238 F1 Loring MT U.S.A.
161 C4 Loriol-sur-Drôme France
160 B1 Lormes France
116 E5 Lormi Madh. Prad. India
163 B4 Lormont France
146 C5 Lorn, Firth of est. Scotland U.K.
85 F5 Lorne Qld Austr.
83 E4 Lorne Vic. Austr.
111 F6 Loro r. China
191 G5 Loro Ciuffenna Italy
206 E4 Loropéni Burkina
193 F1 Loro Piceno Italy
163 D5 Lorp-Sentaraille France
157 G4 Lorquin France
172 B4 Lörrach Ger.
157 G4 Lorrain, Plateau France
84 D3 Lorraine Qld Austr.
157 G4 Lorraine admin. reg. France
157 F4 Lorraine, Plaine plain France
156 C4 Lorrez-le-Bocage-Préaux France
156 C5 Lorris France
172 C2 Lorsch Ger.
87 D7 Lort r. W.A. Austr.
141 L3 Lörudden Sweden
168 C3 Lorup Ger.
206 B4 Los, Îles de is Guinea
183 G2 Losa r. Spain
182 D3 Losacino Spain
187 C5 Losa del Obispo Spain
116 C4 Losal Rajasthan India
242 E3 Los Alamitos, Sierra de mt. Mex.
240 G4 Los Alamos CA U.S.A.
239 F5 Los Alamos NM U.S.A.
187 C7 Los Alcázares Spain
187 B7 Los Algezares Spain
245 F4 Los Altos Mex.
260 B3 Los Andes Chile
260 A5 Los Angeles Chile
240 H4 Los Angeles CA U.S.A.
259 C7 Los Antiguos Arg.
246 B2 Los Arabos Cuba
183 H2 Los Arcos Spain
187 C6 Los Arenales del Sol Spain
183 H4 Losares mt. Spain
245 E5 Los Arroyos Mex.
240 G3 Los Banos CA U.S.A.
185 H2 Los Barreros mt. Spain
184 E4 Los Barrios Spain
182 E2 Los Barrios de Luna Spain
187 C7 Los Belones Spain
242 D2 Los Caballos Mesteños, Llano de plain Mex.
246 B2 Los Canarreos, Archipiélago de is Cuba
187 B7 Los Cantareros Spain
242 □I7 Los Chiles Costa Rica
259 B7 Los Chonos, Archipiélago de is Chile
260 E3 Los Condores Arg.
240 I5 Los Coronados, Islas is Mex.
183 F1 Los Corrales de Buelna Spain
186 B3 Loscos Spain
252 D3 Los Cusis Bol.
252 A6 Los Desventurados, Islas de is S. Pacific Ocean
Los Difuntos, Lago de l. Uru. see Negra, Lago
187 B7 Los Dolores Spain
259 D9 Los Estados, Isla de i. Arg.
135 H6 Losevo Rus. Fed.
185 I3 Los Gallardos Spain
245 E3 Los Gatos r. Mex.
240 G3 Los Gatos CA U.S.A.
260 E2 Los Gigantes, Cerro mt. Arg.
172 A2 Losheim Ger.
183 H5 Los Hinojosos Spain
175 K3 Łosice Pol.
188 E3 Lošinj i. Croatia
175 L3 Łosinka Pol.
246 C2 Los Jardines de la Reina, Archipiélago de is Cuba
258 E3 Los Juríes Arg.
215 G3 Loskop S. Africa
259 B5 Los Lagos Chile
259 B6 Los Lagos admin. reg. Chile
Loslau Pol. see Wodzisław Śląski
260 A6 Los Laureles Chile
260 D2 Los Llanos, Sierra de mts Arg.
216 □3d Los Llanos de Aridane La Palma Canary Is
239 F5 Los Lunas NM U.S.A.
187 B7 Los Maldonados Spain
187 B7 Los Martinez Spain
259 C6 Los Menucos Arg.
242 C3 Los Mochis Mex.
184 E3 Los Molares Spain
183 F4 Los Molinos Spain
240 F1 Los Molinos CA U.S.A.
260 B2 Los Molles r. Chile
242 □J7 Los Mosquitos, Golfo de b. Panama
245 F4 Los Naranjos Mex.
183 F5 Los Navalmorales Spain
183 F5 Los Navalucillos Spain
190 D2 Losone Switz.
175 I6 Łososina Dolna Pol.
246 B2 Los Palacios Cuba
184 E3 Los Palacios y Villafranca Spain
183 G1 Los Pandos Spain
260 C3 Los Paramillos, Sierra de mts Arg.
93 C5 Lospatos East Timor
260 C2 Los Patos, Río de r. Arg.
185 E2 Los Pedroches plat. Spain
187 B5 Los Pedrones Spain
185 G2 Los Pozuelos de Calatrava Spain
183 H3 Los Rábanos Spain
258 D2 Los Ralos Arg.
216 □3a Los Realejos Tenerife Canary Is
244 A1 Los Remedios r. Mex.
244 C4 Los Reyes Mex.
259 E6 Los Riachos, Islas de is Arg.
250 B5 Los Ríos prov. Ecuador
250 E2 Los Roques, Islas is Venez.
185 H3 Los Royos Spain
171 C4 Lossa r. Ger.
171 C4 Lossa (Finne) Ger.
182 E4 Los Santos Spain
184 D2 Los Santos de Maimona Spain
216 □3d Los Sauces La Palma Canary Is
260 A5 Los Sauces Chile
172 C3 Loßburg Ger.
163 B4 Losse France
164 F2 Losser Neth.
146 E4 Lossie r. Scotland U.K.
146 E4 Lossiemouth Moray, Scotland U.K.
216 □3a Los Silos Tenerife Canary Is
171 D5 Lößnitz Ger.
190 E2 Lostallo Switz.
250 D2 Los Taques Venez.
171 C3 Lostau Ger.
232 B6 Lost Creek KY U.S.A.
258 E3 Los Telares Arg.
244 C4 Los Tepames Mex.
250 E2 Los Teques Venez.
251 F2 Los Testigos is Venez.
240 H4 Lost Hills CA U.S.A.
149 G4 Lostock Gralam Cheshire, England U.K.
183 F1 Los Tojos Spain
185 F1 Los Torneros, Sierra de mts Spain
150 C4 Lostwithiel Cornwall, England U.K.
185 G3 Los Villares Spain
260 B2 Los Vilos Chile
183 G5 Los Yébenes Spain
137 F2 Losynivka Ukr.
163 D4 Lot dept Midi-Pyrénées France
161 A4 Lot r. France
258 B5 Lota Chile
141 J3 Løten Norway
163 C4 Lot-et-Garonne dept Aquitaine France
122 D2 Lotfābād Turkm.
146 F2 Loth Orkney, Scotland U.K.
215 H2 Lothair S. Africa
146 E3 Lothmore Highland, Scotland U.K.
210 B3 Lotikipi Plain Kenya
208 C5 Lotoi r. Dem. Rep. Congo
139 J3 Lotoshino Rus. Fed.
137 G4 Lotskyne Ukr.
Lot's Wife i. Japan see Sōfu-gan
140 O1 Lotta r. Fin./Rus. Fed. alt. Lutto
169 C3 Lotte Ger.
172 C4 Lottstetten Ger.
210 B3 Lotuke mt. Sudan
192 B5 Lotzorai Sardegna Italy
159 F4 Louailles France
96 C2 Louang Namtha Laos
96 C3 Louangphrabang Laos
108 B5 Louang Phrabang Range mts Laos/Thai.
158 C3 Louannec France
158 C3 Louargat France
209 B6 Loubomo Congo
171 G5 Loučeň Czech Rep.
176 C1 Loučná hill Czech Rep.
176 D3 Loučovice Czech Rep.
158 D3 Loudéac France
161 B3 Loudes France
109 D3 Loudi Hunan China
209 B6 Loudima Congo
231 C5 Loudon TN U.S.A.
232 B4 Loudonville OH U.S.A.
162 C1 Loudun France
159 F4 Loué France
160 D1 Loue r. France
209 B5 Louéssé r. Congo
206 A3 Louga Senegal
163 D5 Louge r. France
147 C1 Loughanure Rep. of Ireland
151 F2 Loughborough Leicestershire, England U.K.
147 E2 Loughbrickland Northern Ireland U.K.
147 B4 Lougher Rep. of Ireland
147 E2 Loughgall Northern Ireland U.K.
147 D3 Lough Gowna Rep. of Ireland
147 F2 Loughlinisland Northern Ireland U.K.
147 D4 Loughmoe Rep. of Ireland
150 C3 Loughor Swansea, Wales U.K.
150 C3 Loughor r. Wales U.K.
147 C3 Loughrea Rep. of Ireland
147 C2 Loughros More Bay Rep. of Ireland
151 H3 Loughton Essex, England U.K.
163 C4 Lougratte France
160 D2 Louhans France
232 B5 Louisa KY U.S.A.
232 E5 Louisa VA U.S.A.
225 J4 Louisbourg N.S. Can.
Louisburg N.S. Can. see Louisbourg
231 E4 Louisburg NC U.S.A.
Louis-Gentil Morocco see Youssoufia
91 L9 Louisiade Archipelago is P.N.G.
236 F4 Louisiana MO U.S.A.
237 F6 Louisiana state U.S.A.
213 F4 Louis Trichardt S. Africa
214 C3 Louisvale S. Africa
231 D5 Louisville GA U.S.A.
236 F4 Louisville IL U.S.A.
230 C4 Louisville KY U.S.A.
237 F5 Louisville MS U.S.A.
232 C4 Louisville OH U.S.A.
266 H8 Louisville Ridge sea feature S. Pacific Ocean
134 F2 Loukhi Rus. Fed.
208 C5 Loukoléla Congo
160 E1 Loulans France
162 B2 Loulay France
184 B3 Loulé Port.
206 D4 Loulouni Mali
207 H5 Loum Cameroon
176 C1 Louny Czech Rep.
161 F5 Loup r. France
236 D3 Loup r. NE U.S.A.
236 D3 Loup City NE U.S.A.
225 J3 Lourdes Nfld. Can.
163 B5 Lourdes France
226 A4 Lourdes IA U.S.A.
162 D2 Lourdoueix-St-Pierre France
Lourenço Marques Moz. see Maputo
184 A2 Loures Port.
182 B4 Louriçal Port.
184 A1 Lourinhã Port.
161 D5 Lourmarin France
198 B2 Louros Ipeiros Greece
182 B4 Lourosa Port.
156 C5 Loury France
182 B4 Lousã Port.
184 A2 Lousa Lisboa Port.
182 B4 Lousã, Serra da mts Port.
182 B3 Lousada Port.
214 D5 Louterwater S. Africa
83 F2 Louth N.S.W. Austr.
147 E3 Louth Rep. of Ireland
147 E3 Louth county Rep. of Ireland
149 I4 Louth Lincolnshire, England U.K.
198 C2 Loutra Aidipsou Greece
198 C3 Loutraki Greece
198 C1 Loutros Kentriki Makedonia Greece
Louvain Belgium see Leuven
165 E4 Louveigné Belgium
159 F3 Louverné France
163 B5 Louvie-Juzon France
156 B3 Louviers France
158 E3 Louvigné-de-Bais France
159 E3 Louvigné-du-Désert France
156 C3 Louvres France
156 D2 Louvroil France
214 E2 Louwna S. Africa
215 H2 Louwsburg S. Africa
156 E4 Louze France
140 M2 Lövånger Sweden
177 H4 Lovasberény Hungary
176 F5 Lovászi Hungary
177 G4 Lovászpatona Hungary
139 H2 Lovat' r. Rus. Fed.
140 K3 Lövberga Sweden
196 D3 Lovćenac Vojvodina, Srbija Yugo.
197 G4 Lovech Bulg.
238 F3 Loveland CO U.S.A.
233 □H2 Lovell ME U.S.A.
238 E2 Lovell WY U.S.A.
Lovello, Monte mt. Austria see Grosser Löffler
81 B7 Lovells Flat South I. N.Z.
240 H1 Lovelock NV U.S.A.
234 B1 Lovelton PA U.S.A.
165 C3 Lovendegem Belgium
190 F3 Lovere Italy
190 F2 Lovero Italy
232 C6 Lovers' Leap mt. VA U.S.A.
226 C4 Loves Park IL U.S.A.
141 N3 Loviisa Fin.
140 M2 Lovikka Sweden
232 D6 Lovingston VA U.S.A.
237 C5 Lovington NM U.S.A.
177 I3 Lovinobaňa Slovakia
141 K3 Lövnäsvallen Sweden
176 F4 Lövő Hungary
171 F5 Lovosice Czech Rep.
134 F1 Lovozero Rus. Fed.
188 E3 Lovran Croatia
179 G4 Lovrenc Slovenia
196 E3 Lovrin Romania
143 F1 Lövsjön Sweden
209 D6 Lóvua Lunda Norte Angola
209 D7 Lôvua Moxico Angola
227 J3 Low Que. Can.
208 E5 Lowa r. Dem. Rep. Congo
149 H4 Lowdham Nottinghamshire, England U.K.
226 D5 Lowell IN U.S.A.
233 H3 Lowell MA U.S.A.
226 E4 Lowell MI U.S.A.
238 B3 Lowell OR U.S.A.
233 G2 Lowell VT U.S.A.
233 □H2 Lowelltown ME U.S.A.
170 E3 Löwenberg Ger.
172 D2 Löwenstein Ger.
222 G5 Lower Arrow Lake B.C. Can.
Lower Austria land Austria see Niederösterreich
147 E2 Lower Ballinderry Northern Ireland U.K.
151 G3 Lower Beeding West Sussex, England U.K.
Lower California pen. Mex. see Baja California
150 E3 Lower Cam Gloucestershire, England U.K.
146 C4 Lower Diabaig Highland, Scotland U.K.
241 K4 Lower Granite Gorge AZ U.S.A.
81 E4 Lower Hutt North I. N.Z.
146 B5 Lower Kilchattan Argyll and Bute, Scotland U.K.
146 B6 Lower Killeyan Argyll and Bute, Scotland U.K.
222 C2 Lower Laberge Y.T. Can.
240 F2 Lower Lake CA U.S.A.
215 G3 Lower Loteni S. Africa
147 D2 Lower Lough Erne l. Northern Ireland U.K.
215 G4 Lower Pitseng S. Africa
222 D3 Lower Post B.C. Can.
215 H1 Lower Sabie S. Africa
Lower Saxony land Ger. see Niedersachsen
Lower Tunguska r. Rus. Fed. see Nizhnyaya Tunguska
151 I2 Lowestoft Suffolk, England U.K.
123 G3 Lowgar prov. Afgh.
149 H2 Lowick Northumberland, England U.K.
175 H3 Łowicz Pol.
Low Island Kiribati see Starbuck Island
232 D6 Lowmoor VA U.S.A.
83 F5 Low Rocky Point Tas. Austr.
151 I2 Low Street Norfolk, England U.K.
232 C5 Lowsville WV U.S.A.
146 E6 Lowther Hills Scotland U.K.
233 F3 Lowville NY U.S.A.
168 D2 Loxstedt Ger.
82 E3 Loxton S.A. Austr.
214 D4 Loxton S. Africa
146 D3 Loyal, Loch l. Scotland U.K.
227 I5 Loyalsock Creek r. PA U.S.A.
240 G2 Loyalton CA U.S.A.
234 B2 Loyalton PA U.S.A.
Loyalty Islands New Caledonia see Loyauté, Îles
Loyang Henan China see Luoyang
78 □5 Loyauté, Îles is New Caledonia
226 B4 Loyd WI U.S.A.
160 D3 Loyettes France
Loyev Belarus see Loyew
136 F2 Loyew Belarus
146 C4 Loyne, Loch l. Scotland U.K.
134 K4 Loyno Rus. Fed.
140 K2 Løypskardtinden mt. Norway
161 B4 Lozère dept Languedoc-Roussillon France
161 B4 Lozère, Mont mt. France
196 D3 Loznica Srbija Yugo.
197 H4 Loznitsa Bulg.
137 J3 Lozno-Oleksandrivka Ukr.
137 I2 Loznoye Rus. Fed.
176 G3 Lozorno Slovakia
137 H3 Lozova Kharkivs'ka Oblast' Ukr.
137 I3 Lozova Kharkivs'ka Oblast' Ukr.
Lozovaya Kazakh. see Lozovoye
Lozovaya Kharkivs'ka Oblast' Ukr. see Lozova
136 D3 Lozove Ukr.
137 I3 Lozoven'ka Ukr.
196 E3 Lozovik Srbija Yugo.
121 I1 Lozovoye Kazakh.
137 K2 Lozovoye Rus. Fed.
183 G4 Lozoya Spain
183 G4 Lozoya r. Spain
183 G4 Lozoyuela Spain
137 H4 Lozuvatka r. Ukr.
134 M3 Loz'va r. Rus. Fed.
191 H2 Lozzo di Cadore Italy
107 F4 Lu r. China
209 D7 Luacano Angola
209 D6 Luachimo r. Angola/Dem. Rep. Congo
208 C4 Lua Dekere r. Dem. Rep. Congo
213 H3 Luala r. Moz.
240 □ Lualualei HI U.S.A.
209 E8 Luampa r. Zambia
109 F2 Lu'an Anhui China
109 D1 Luanchuan Henan China
182 E1 Luanco Spain
209 B7 Luanda Angola
209 B7 Luanda prov. Angola
209 C7 Luando Angola
209 C7 Luando r. Angola
97 B5 Luang, Khao mt. Thai.
209 D8 Luanginga r. Zambia
78 □6 Luangiua i. Solomon Is
Luang Nam Tha Laos see Louang Namtha
Luang Prabang Laos see Louangphrabang
209 D8 Luanguinga r. Angola
209 F8 Luangwa Zambia
211 A8 Luangwa r. Zambia
106 B5 Luanhaizi Qinghai China
107 H4 Luan He r. China
107 H4 Luannan Hebei China
107 H3 Luanping Hebei China
209 F8 Luanshya Zambia
107 H4 Luanxian Hebei China
209 F7 Luanza Dem. Rep. Congo
Luanzhou Hebei China see Luanxian
Luao Angola see Luau
209 F7 Luapula prov. Zambia
182 D1 Luarca Spain
209 D7 Luashi Dem. Rep. Congo
211 C8 Luatize r. Moz.
209 D7 Luau Angola
207 H6 Luba Equat. Guinea
175 L5 Lubaczów Pol.
175 K5 Lubaczówka r. Pol.
209 C7 Lubalo Angola
174 D4 Lubań Pol.
138 F3 Lubāna Latvia
138 F3 Lubānas ezers l. Latvia
92 B3 Lubang Phil.
92 B3 Lubang i. Phil.
92 A3 Lubang Islands Phil.
209 B8 Lubango Angola
209 E6 Lubao Dem. Rep. Congo
171 D3 Lübars Ger.
175 K4 Lubartów Pol.
174 E3 Lubasz Pol.
175 H2 Lubawa Pol.
174 E5 Lubawka Pol.
169 D3 Lübbecke Ger.
165 D4 Lubbeek Belgium
171 E4 Lübben Ger.
171 E4 Lübbenau Ger.
237 C5 Lubbock TX U.S.A.
170 C3 Lübbow Ger.
233 □J2 Lubec ME U.S.A.
168 F2 Lübeck Ger.
232 C5 Lubeck WV U.S.A.
168 F1 Lübecker Bucht b. Ger.
209 E6 Lubefu Dem. Rep. Congo
107 I2 Lubei Nei Mongol China
177 I2 Ľubeľa Slovakia
175 K4 Lubelska, Wyżyna hills Pol.
175 K4 Lubelskie prov. Pol.
Lüben Dolnośląskie Pol. see Lubin
176 C1 Lubenec Czech Rep.
175 J6 Lubenia Pol.
177 J3 Lubeník Slovakia
120 C2 Lubenka Kazakh.
161 D5 Lubéron, Montagne du ridge France
162 D3 Lubersac France
170 C2 Lübesse Ger.
182 D2 Lubián Spain
174 G2 Łubianka Pol.
174 E4 Lubiąż Pol.
177 J2 Ľubica r. Slovakia
174 G2 Lubichowo Pol.
174 G2 Lubicz Dolny Pol.
175 H6 Lubień Pol.
175 G3 Lubienka r. Pol.
175 H3 Lubień Kujawski Pol.
174 G2 Lubiewo Pol.
174 E4 Lubin Dolnośląskie Pol.
167 H3 Lubiń Pol.
174 C3 Lubiszyn Pol.
175 K4 Lublin Pol.
174 G5 Lubliniec Pol.
170 E1 Lubmin Ger.
Lubnān country Asia see Lebanon
174 F2 Lubnia Pol.
174 G5 Łubniany Pol.
174 G4 Łubnice Pol.
175 J5 Łubnice Pol.
174 D3 Lubniewice Pol.
175 H3 Łubno Pol.
174 F1 Łubno Pol.
137 G2 Lubny Ukr.
215 H2 Lubombo admin. dist. Swaziland
175 I1 Lubomino Pol.
174 E3 Luboń Pol.
177 K2 Ľubotice Slovakia
177 J2 Ľubotín Slovakia
170 C2 Lübow Ger.
175 H2 Lubowidz Pol.
174 F3 Łubowo Pol.
174 G3 Lubraniec Pol.
185 H3 Lubrín Spain
174 D3 Lubrza Lubuskie Pol.
174 F5 Lubrza Opolskie Pol.
174 C4 Lubsko Pol.
170 C2 Lübstorf Ger.
174 G3 Lubstów Pol.
174 F5 Lubsza Pol.
174 C4 Lubsza r. Pol.
170 C2 Lübtheen Ger.
92 B2 Lubuagan Phil.
209 E7 Lubudi Dem. Rep. Congo
209 E7 Lubudi r. Dem. Rep. Congo
94 C3 Lubuklinggau Sumatera Indon.
94 B2 Lubukpakam Sumatera Indon.
94 C2 Lubuksikaping Sumatera Indon.
209 E7 Lubumbashi Dem. Rep. Congo
209 E8 Lubungu Zambia
174 D3 Lubuskie prov. Pol.
208 E5 Lubutu r. Dem. Rep. Congo
209 F7 Lubwe Zambia
176 B1 Luby Czech Rep.
175 L5 Lubycza Królewska Pol.
170 D2 Lübz Ger.
161 B4 Luc Languedoc-Roussillon France
163 E4 Luc Midi-Pyrénées France
185 H3 Lucainena de las Torres Spain
209 B7 Lucala Angola
227 G4 Lucan Ont. Can.
147 E3 Lucan Rep. of Ireland
196 E4 Lučani Srbija Yugo.
222 A2 Lucania, Mount Y.T. Can.
111 F4 Lücaoshan Qinghai China
209 D7 Lucapa Angola
185 H3 Lúcar Spain
185 H3 Lúcar mt. Spain
261 H2 Lucas r. Arg.
253 G3 Lucas Brazil
261 H3 Lucas González Arg.
232 B5 Lucasville OH U.S.A.
231 E7 Lucaya Bahamas
159 H4 Luçay-le-Mâle France
190 F5 Lucca Italy
190 F5 Lucca prov. Toscana Italy
236 D2 Lucca ND U.S.A.
194 C5 Lucca Sicula Sicilia Italy
192 B2 Lucciana Corse France
156 B4 Lucé France
246 □ Lucea Jamaica
146 D7 Luce Bay Scotland U.K.
237 F6 Lucedale MS U.S.A.
256 B4 Lucélia Brazil
92 B3 Lucena Phil.
185 F3 Lucena Spain
187 C4 Lucena r. Spain
186 B3 Lucena de Jalón Spain
187 C4 Lucena del Cid Spain
160 B2 Lucenay-lès-Aix France
160 C1 Lucenay-l'Évêque France
161 D4 Luc-en-Diois France
177 I3 Lučenec Slovakia
186 B3 Luceni Spain
193 H3 Lucera Italy
161 F5 Lucéram France
252 C3 Lucerna Peru
Lucerne Switz. see Luzern
240 F2 Lucerne CA U.S.A.
240 I4 Lucerne Valley CA U.S.A.
157 F4 Lucey France
177 I3 Lucfalva Hungary
100 E3 Luchegorsk Rus. Fed.
Lucheng Guangxi China see Luchuan
107 G4 Lucheng Shanxi China
Lucheng Sichuan China see Kangding
159 G4 Luché-Pringé France
211 C7 Lucheringo r. Moz.
156 C2 Lucheux France
139 L3 Luchki Rus. Fed.
139 H4 Luchosa r. Belarus
170 C3 Lüchow Ger.
108 D4 Luchuan Guangxi China
108 B4 Lüchun Yunnan China
156 C3 Luchy France
185 F2 Luciana Spain
175 H4 Luciąża r. Pol.
175 H3 Lucień Pol.
191 G5 Lucignano Italy
188 D3 Lucija Slovenia
182 D2 Lucillo de Somoza Spain
85 F3 Lucinda Qld Austr.
82 E4 Lucindale S.A. Austr.
93 C4 Lucipara, Kepulauan is Maluku Indon.
209 B8 Lucira Angola
193 G3 Lucito Italy
197 H3 Luciu Romania
Łuck Ukr. see Luts'k
226 A3 Luck WI U.S.A.
171 D4 Lucka Ger.
171 E4 Luckau Ger.
117 F4 Luckeesarai Bihar India
171 E3 Luckenwalde Ger.
215 E3 Luckhoff S. Africa
227 G4 Lucknow Ont. Can.
116 E4 Lucknow Uttar Prad. India
170 C3 Lückstedt Ger.
191 G2 Luco, Monte mt. Italy
193 F3 Luco dei Marsi Italy
162 A2 Luçon France
108 D2 Lücongpo Hubei China
163 B5 Lucq-de-Béarn France
159 F2 Luc-sur-Mer France
209 B6 Lucunga Angola
209 D8 Lucusse Angola
84 D4 Lucy Creek N.T. Austr.
160 B1 Lucy-le-Bois France
Lüda Liaoning China see Dalian
146 A4 Ludag Western Isles, Scotland U.K.
197 H4 Luda Kamchiya r. Bulg.
188 F2 Ludbreg Croatia
169 C4 Lüdenscheid Ger.
168 F3 Lüder Ger.
171 C3 Lüderitz Ger.
212 B5 Lüderitz Namibia
168 F2 Lüdersdorf Ger.
178 A3 Ludesch Austria
211 B7 Ludewa Tanz.
151 F3 Ludgershall Wiltshire, England U.K.
150 B4 Ludgvan Cornwall, England U.K.
116 C3 Ludhiana Punjab India
108 B3 Ludian Yunnan China
108 B2 Luding Sichuan China
169 C4 Lüdinghausen Ger.
226 D4 Ludington MI U.S.A.
235 E1 Ludingtonville NY U.S.A.
150 E2 Ludlow Shropshire, England U.K.
241 I4 Ludlow CA U.S.A.
233 G3 Ludlow VT U.S.A.
179 F4 Ludmannsdorf Austria
197 H4 Ludogorsko Plato plat. Bulg.
162 B4 Ludon-Médoc France
231 D6 Ludowici GA U.S.A.
157 G4 Ludres France
197 G2 Luduș Romania
143 F1 Ludvika Sweden
169 E5 Ludwigsau-Friedlos Ger.
172 D3 Ludwigsburg Ger.
171 G4 Ludwigsdorf Ger.
171 E3 Ludwigsfelde Ger.
172 D4 Ludwigshafen Ger.
172 C2 Ludwigshafen am Rhein Ger.
170 C2 Ludwigslust Ger.
Ludwigsort Rus. Fed. see Ladushkin
171 C5 Ludwigsstadt Ger.
175 K4 Ludwin Pol.
138 F3 Ludza Latvia
163 B4 Lüe France
209 D6 Luebo Dem. Rep. Congo
209 E5 Lueki r. Dem. Rep. Congo
182 D3 Luelmo Spain
209 C7 Luena Angola
209 E7 Luena Dem. Rep. Congo
209 F7 Luena Zambia
209 D8 Luena r. Zambia
209 D8 Luena Flats plain Zambia
209 D9 Luengue r. Angola
213 G3 Luenha r. Moz./Zimbabwe
169 E4 Lüerdissen Ger.
186 B2 Luesia Spain
108 C1 Lüeyang Shaanxi China
109 E4 Lufeng Guangdong China
Lufeng Hunan China see Xupu
108 B3 Lufeng Yunnan China
209 E7 Lufira r. Dem. Rep. Congo
237 E6 Lufkin TX U.S.A.
Lufu Yunnan China see Lunan
211 A7 Lufubu r. Zambia
196 E3 Lug r. Yugo.
138 G2 Luga Rus. Fed.
138 G2 Luga r. Rus. Fed.
190 D2 Lugano Switz.
190 D3 Lugano, Lago di l. Italy/Switz.
Lugano, Lake Italy/Switz. see Lugano, Lago di
Lugansk Ukr. see Luhans'k
Luganskaya Oblast' admin. div. Ukr. see Luhans'ka Oblast'
Lugansk Oblast admin. div. Ukr. see Luhans'ka Oblast'
78 □5 Luganville Vanuatu
177 L4 Lugașu de Jos Romania
171 D5 Lugau Ger.
169 E4 Lügde Ger.
Lugdunum France see Lyon

213 H3 Lugela Moz.
213 H3 Lugela r. Moz.
213 H1 Lugenda r. Moz.
150 E2 Lugg r. Wales U.K.
81 B6 Luggate South I. N.Z.
111 E6 Lugqudontsen mt. Xizang China
163 B4 Luglon France
193 E2 Lugnano in Teverina Italy
160 C2 Lugny France
160 C2 Lugny-lès-Charolles France
191 G4 Lugo Italy
182 C1 Lugo Spain
182 C2 Lugo prov. Galicia Spain
192 B2 Lugo-di-Nazza Corse France
197 E3 Lugoj Romania
182 E1 Lugones Spain
162 B4 Lugon-et-l'Île-du-Carnay France
163 B4 Lugos France
139 K3 Lugovaya Rus. Fed.
Lugovaya Proleyka Volgogradskaya Oblast' Rus. Fed. see Primorsk
121 H4 Lugovoy Kazakh.
121 H4 Lugovoye Kazakh.
160 E2 Lugrin France
185 G3 Lugros Spain
136 C2 Luha r. Ukr.
177 G2 Luhačovice Czech Rep.
137 J3 Luhan' r. Ukr.
137 J3 Luhanchyk r. Ukr.
141 N3 Luhanka Fin.
137 J3 Luhans'k Ukr.
137 J3 Luhans'ka Oblast' admin. div. Ukr.
Luhansk Oblast admin. div. Ukr. see Luhans'ka Oblast'
169 E3 Luhden Ger.
109 F1 Luhe Jiangsu China
168 F2 Luhe r. Ger.
173 G2 Luhe-Wildenau Ger.
107 H2 Luhin Sum Nei Mongol China
Luhit r. China/India see Zayü Qu
96 A1 Luhit r. India
170 E1 Lühmannsdorf Ger.
Luhua Sichuan China see Heishui
108 B2 Luhuo Sichuan China
136 E2 Luhyny Ukr.
209 D7 Luia Angola
209 D6 Luia r. Angola
213 G3 Luia r. Moz.
209 D9 Luiana Angola
209 D9 Luiana r. Angola
197 H3 Luica Romania
146 D4 Luichart, Loch l. Scotland U.K.
Luichow Peninsula China see Leizhou Bandao
Luik Belgium see Liège
208 D5 Luilaka r. Dem. Rep. Congo
Luimbale Angola see Londuimbali
Luimneach Rep. of Ireland see Limerick
146 C5 Luing i. Scotland U.K.
190 D3 Luino Italy
182 C2 Luintra Spain
209 D8 Luio r. Angola
140 N2 Luiro r. Fin.
156 B4 Luisant France
254 E2 Luís Correia Brazil
241 I5 Luís Echeverría Álvarez Mex.
254 F3 Luís Gomes Brazil
209 E7 Luishia Dem. Rep. Congo
242 D2 Luis L. León, Presa resr Mex.
244 C2 Luis Moya Mex.
262 V1 Luitpold Coast Antarctica
209 D6 Luiza Dem. Rep. Congo
209 E6 Luizi Dem. Rep. Congo
261 H4 Luján Arg.
261 H4 Luján r. Arg.
260 C3 Luján de Cuyo Arg.
109 F2 Lujiang Anhui China
137 G2 Luka Ukr.
177 G3 Lukáčovce Slovakia
176 F4 Lukácsháza Hungary
209 B6 Lukala Dem. Rep. Congo
209 E8 Lukanga Swamps Zambia
Lukapa Angola see Lucapa
188 G3 Lukavac Bos.-Herz.
175 L5 Lukawiec Pol.
87 F5 Luke, Mount hill W.A. Austr.
209 C5 Lukenie r. Dem. Rep. Congo
147 D4 Lukeswell Rep. of Ireland
241 K6 Lukeville AZ U.S.A.
134 H4 Lukh Rus. Fed.
134 H4 Lukh r. Rus. Fed.
139 L4 Lukhovitsy Rus. Fed.
197 G5 Lŭki Bulg.
136 C2 Lukiv Ukr.
109 □ Luk Keng H.K. China
208 C5 Lukolela Dem. Rep. Congo
Lukou Hunan China see Zhuzhou
188 G3 Lukovac r. Bos.-Herz.
198 A2 Lukovë Albania
197 G4 Lukovit Bulg.
139 J3 Lukovnikovo Rus. Fed.
175 K4 Łuków Pol.
175 K3 Łukowisko Pol.
135 I5 Lukoyanov Rus. Fed.
138 D4 Lukšiai Lith.
209 E6 Lukuga r. Dem. Rep. Congo
209 B6 Lukula Dem. Rep. Congo
211 C7 Lukuledi Tanz.
209 D8 Lukulu Zambia
209 F8 Lukusashi r. Zambia
136 B3 Luky Ukr.
209 D5 Lula r. Dem. Rep. Congo
192 B4 Lula Sardegna Italy
140 M2 Luleå Sweden
140 M2 Luleälven r. Sweden
199 E1 Lüleburgaz Turkey
258 D2 Lules Arg.
108 B3 Luliang Yunnan China
107 F4 Lüliang Shan mts China
107 D6 Luling TX U.S.A.
237 E6 Lullymore Rep. of Ireland
147 E3 Lulong Hebei China
109 H3 Lulonga r. Dem. Rep. Congo
208 C4 Lulonga r. Dem. Rep. Congo
208 D4 Lulu r. Dem. Rep. Congo
Luluabourg Dem. Rep. Congo see Kananga
111 D6 Lülung Xizang China
87 C5 Lulworth, Mount hill W.A. Austr.
111 D6 Lumachomo Xizang China
260 A6 Lumaco Chile
95 F5 Lumajang Jawa Timur Indon.
111 C5 Lumajangdong Co salt l. China
Lumbala Moxico Angola see Lumbala Kaquengue
Lumbala Moxico Angola see Lumbala N'guimbo
209 D8 Lumbala Kaquengue Angola
209 D8 Lumbala N'guimbo Angola
209 D9 Lumbe r. Zambia
235 E1 Lumber r. SC U.S.A.
231 E5 Lumberton NC U.S.A.
183 I2 Lumbier Spain
213 I2 Lumbo Moz.
183 D2 Lumbrales Spain
183 H2 Lumbreras Spain
156 C2 Lumbres France
117 H4 Lumding Assam India
211 B7 Lumecha Tanz.
190 F3 Lumezzane Italy
140 N2 Lumijoki Fin.
197 I3 Lumina Romania
257 E4 Luminárias Brazil
192 A2 Lumio Corse France
143 H3 Lummelunda Gotland Sweden
165 E4 Lummen Belgium
141 M3 Lumparland Åland Fin.
146 F4 Lumphanan Aberdeenshire, Scotland U.K.
97 D4 Lumphăt Cambodia
186 B3 Lumpiaque Spain
231 C5 Lumpkin GA U.S.A.
223 J5 Lumsden Sask. Can.
81 B6 Lumsden South I. N.Z.
95 F3 Lumut, Gunung mt. Indon.
106 E2 Lün Mongolia
92 B2 Luna Phil.
186 C2 Luna Spain
184 E4 Luna hill Spain
182 E2 Luna r. Spain
241 M5 Luna NM U.S.A.
156 C4 Lunain r. France
192 A5 Lunamatrona Sardegna Italy
108 B3 Lunan Yunnan China
227 F5 Luna Pier MI U.S.A.
161 B5 Lunas France
116 C5 Lunavada Gujarat India
124 B2 Lunayyir, Ḥarrāt lava field Saudi Arabia
177 L5 Lunca Bihor Romania
197 G4 Lunca Teleorman Romania
197 G2 Lunca Bradului Romania
177 L6 Lunca Cernii de Jos Romania
197 G2 Lunca Ilvei Romania
146 E5 Luncarty Perth and Kinross, Scotland U.K.
197 G3 Luncaviţa r. Romania
177 L5 Luncoiu de Jos Romania
142 E4 Lund Sweden
241 J2 Lund NV U.S.A.
241 K2 Lund UT U.S.A.
209 C7 Lunda Norte prov. Angola
223 L5 Lundar Man. Can.
209 D7 Lunda Sul prov. Angola
211 B8 Lundazi Zambia
222 H5 Lundbreck Alta Can.
168 F1 Lundby Denmark
142 C4 Lunde Denmark
168 E1 Lunden Ger.
Lundi r. Zimbabwe see Runde
146 F5 Lundin Links Fife, Scotland U.K.
226 C3 Lunds WI U.S.A.
150 C3 Lundy Island England U.K.
168 D2 Lune r. Ger.
149 G3 Lune r. England U.K.
169 B5 Lünebach Ger.
215 H2 Luneberg S. Africa
168 F2 Lüneburg Ger.
168 E2 Lüneburg admin. reg. Niedersachsen Ger.
161 C5 Lunel France
161 F3 Lunella, Punta mt. Italy
161 C5 Lunel-Viel France
169 C4 Lünen Ger.
231 D6 Lunenburg VA U.S.A.
159 I5 Lunery France
168 D2 Lunestedt Ger.
157 G4 Lunéville France
213 I2 Lunga Moz.
209 E8 Lunga r. Zambia
190 D2 Lungern Switz.
111 C6 Lunggar Xizang China
206 B4 Lungi Sierra Leone
Lunglei Mizoram India see Lunglei
117 H5 Lunglei Mizoram India
111 D6 Lungmari mt. Xizang China
147 E4 Lugnaquilla Mountain hill Rep. of Ireland
193 I5 Lungro Italy
209 D8 Lungué-Bungo r. Angola
209 D8 Lungwebungu r. Zambia
116 B4 Luni r. India
123 G4 Luni r. Pak.
Luninets Belarus see Luninyets
240 H2 Luning NV U.S.A.
135 I5 Lunino Rus. Fed.
136 D1 Luninyets Belarus
163 D5 L'Union France
116 C3 Lunkaransar Rajasthan India
116 C5 Lunkha Rajasthan India
123 H2 Lunkho mt. Afgh./Pak.
146 □G1 Lunna Ness hd Scotland U.K.
165 I3 Lünne Ger.
170 F3 Lunow Ger.
206 B4 Lunsar Sierra Leone
209 F8 Lunsemfwa r. Zambia
213 F5 Lunsklip S. Africa
110 D3 Luntai Xinjiang China
164 E2 Lunteren Neth.
198 B1 Lunxhërisë, Mali i ridge Albania
171 D5 Lunzenau Ger.
107 G5 Luo r. Henan China
107 F5 Luo r. Shaanxi China
100 D3 Luobei Heilong. China
110 E4 Luobuzhuang Xinjiang China
Luocheng Fujian China see Hui'an
106 C4 Luocheng Gansu China
108 D3 Luocheng Guangxi China
107 F5 Luochuan Shaanxi China
108 C3 Luodian Guizhou China
109 D4 Luoding Guangdong China
192 B3 Luogosanto Sardegna Italy
109 E1 Luohe Henan China
108 D4 Luo Jiang r. China
107 F5 Luonan Shaanxi China
107 F5 Luoning Henan China
108 C3 Luoping Yunnan China
141 N3 Luopioinen Fin.
109 E1 Luoshan Henan China
109 E2 Luotian Hubei China
140 M3 Luoto Fin.
Luoxiong Yunnan China see Luoping
Luoyang Guangdong China see Boluo
107 G5 Luoyang Henan China
Luoyang Zhejiang China see Taishun
109 F3 Luoyuan Fujian China
209 B6 Luozi Dem. Rep. Congo
100 D4 Luozigou Jilin China
211 B7 Lupa Market Tanz.
213 E3 Lupane Zimbabwe
108 C3 Lupanshui Guizhou China
95 E2 Lupar r. Sarawak Malaysia
143 G4 Łupawa r. Pol.
173 F2 Lupburg Ger.
184 C1 Lupe r. Port.
197 G2 Lupeni Harghita Romania
197 F3 Lupeni Hunedoara Romania
183 E2 Luperón Dom. Rep.
172 C3 Lupfen hill Ger.
176 C3 Lupiac France
211 B7 Lupilichi Moz.
186 C2 Lupiñén Spain
183 G3 Lupión Spain
209 C8 Lupire Angola
175 K6 Łupków Pol.
191 J3 Lupoglav Croatia
92 C5 Lupon Phil.
171 D4 Luppa Ger.
157 G4 Luppy France
241 M4 Lupton AZ U.S.A.
134 K3 Lup'ya r. Rus. Fed.
Luqiao Sichuan China see Luding
106 C5 Luqu Gansu China
Lu Qu r. China see Tao He
107 G4 Luquan Hebei China
108 B3 Luquan Yunnan China
185 F3 Luque Spain
209 C7 Luquembo Angola
247 □1 Luquillo Puerto Rico
192 B4 Luras Sardegna Italy
226 B5 Luray MO U.S.A.
232 D5 Luray VA U.S.A.
163 B5 Lurbe-St-Christau France
160 A2 Lurcy-Lévis France
157 G5 Lure France
161 D4 Lure, Montagne de mt. France
161 C4 Lure, Sommet de mt. France
211 C8 Lureco r. Moz.
209 C7 Luremo Angola
147 E2 Lurgan Northern Ireland U.K.
192 B2 Luri Corse France
210 A3 Luri r. Sudan
252 D4 Luribay Bol.
252 B3 Lurín Peru
Luring Xizang China see Gêrzê
213 I2 Lúrio Moz.
213 I2 Lúrio r. Moz.
140 K2 Lurøy Norway
161 F5 Lurs France
157 G4 Lury-sur-Arnon France
209 F8 Lusaka Zambia
209 F8 Lusaka prov. Zambia
209 D6 Lusambo Dem. Rep. Congo
209 E6 Lusangi Dem. Rep. Congo
194 D2 Lusciano Italy
223 I4 Luseland Sask. Can.
194 D3 Lusema San Giovanni Italy
86 E3 Lush, Mount hill W.A. Austr.
108 B2 Lushan Sichuan China
Lushar Qinghai China see Huangzhong
107 F5 Lushi Henan China
196 D5 Lushnjë Albania
211 C6 Lushoto Tanz.
108 A3 Lushui Yunnan China
107 I4 Lushunkou Liaoning China
109 G1 Lüsi Jiangsu China
95 E4 Lusi r. Indon.
162 C2 Lusignan France
160 B2 Lusigny France
156 E4 Lusigny-sur-Barse France
215 G4 Lusikisiki S. Africa
147 E3 Lusk Rep. of Ireland
238 F3 Lusk WY U.S.A.
161 D4 Lus-la-Croix-Haute France
Luso Angola see Luena
182 B4 Luso Port.
146 D5 Luss Argyll and Bute, Scotland U.K.
162 B4 Lussac France
162 C2 Lussac-les-Châteaux France
162 D2 Lussac-les-Églises France
148 D2 Lussa Loch l. Scotland U.K.
161 C4 Lussan France
168 F3 Lüßberg hill Ger.
168 F2 Lüssow Ger.
146 B4 Lusta Highland, Scotland U.K.
172 C2 Lustadt Ger.
190 E1 Lustenau Austria
215 H2 Lusushwana r. Swaziland
Lusutufu r. Africa see Usutu
175 H3 Luszyn Pol.
Lut, Bahrat salt l. Asia see Dead Sea
122 D4 Lut, Dasht-e des. Iran
191 G2 Lutago Italy
Lutai Tianjin China see Ninghe
168 F2 Lütau Ger.
256 B5 Lutécia Brazil
Lutetia France see Paris
122 D4 Lūt-e Zangī Aḥmad des. Iran
226 E3 Luther MI U.S.A.
237 D4 Luther OK U.S.A.
232 D4 Lutherstadt PA U.S.A.
171 D4 Lutherstadt Wittenberg Ger.
176 G2 Lutín Czech Rep.
168 F1 Lütjenburg Ger.
168 F2 Lütjensee Ger.
175 H3 Lutocin Pol.
175 H4 Lutomiersk Pol.
151 G3 Luton Luton, England U.K.
151 G3 Luton admin. div. England U.K.
95 F1 Lutong Sarawak Malaysia
213 F3 Lutope r. Zimbabwe
175 K6 Lutowiska Pol.
175 I1 Lutry Pol.
223 I2 Łutselk'e N.W.T. Can.
136 C2 Luts'k Ukr.
169 F4 Lutter am Barenberge Ger.
157 H5 Lutterbach France
151 F2 Lutterworth Leicestershire, England U.K.
214 D5 Luttig S. Africa
140 O1 Lutto r. Fin./Rus. Fed. alt. Lotta
209 D8 Lutuai Angola
137 J3 Lutuhyne Ukr.
137 G4 Lutuhyne Ukr.
174 F3 Lutynia r. Pol.
231 D6 Lutz FL U.S.A.
171 D4 Lützen Ger.
169 C5 Lutzerath Ger.
173 E3 Lutzingen Ger.
170 C2 Lützow Ger.
214 C4 Lutzputs S. Africa
171 D4 Lützschena Ger.
214 B4 Lutzville S. Africa
141 N3 Luumäki Fin.
210 D4 Luuq Somalia
231 C6 Luverne AL U.S.A.
236 D3 Luverne MN U.S.A.
141 M3 Luvia Fin.
209 E6 Luvua r. Dem. Rep. Congo
209 D8 Luvuei Angola
213 F4 Luvuvhu r. S. Africa
211 C7 Luwegu r. Tanz.
210 B4 Luwero Uganda
209 F7 Luwingu Zambia
93 B3 Luwuk Sulawesi Tengah Indon.
160 D1 Lux France
165 E4 Luxembourg prov. Belgium
165 F5 Luxembourg country Europe
165 F5 Luxembourg Lux.
165 F5 Luxembourg admin. dist. Lux.
Luxembourg country Europe see Luxembourg
226 D3 Luxemburg WI U.S.A.
163 A5 Luxe-Sumberraute France
157 G5 Luxeuil-les-Bains France
163 B4 Luxey France
108 D3 Luxi Hunan China
108 A3 Luxi Yunnan China
108 B3 Luxi Yunnan China
108 C2 Luxian Sichuan China
215 E4 Luxolweni S. Africa
Luxor Egypt see El Uqṣur
150 C4 Luxulyan Cornwall, England U.K.
163 A5 Luy r. France
Luyang Sichuan China see Lushan
163 B5 Luy de Béarn r. France
163 B5 Luy de France r. France
182 D2 Luyego de Somoza Spain
109 E1 Luyi Henan China
165 E3 Luyksgestel Neth.
159 G4 Luynes France
Luyuan Shaanxi China see Gaoling
216 □1c Luz Graciosa Azores
257 E3 Luz Brazil
184 C2 Luz Évora Port.
184 B3 Luz Faro Port.
184 C3 Luz Faro Port.
182 D3 Luz hill Port.
134 I3 Luza Rus. Fed.
134 I3 Luza r. Rus. Fed.
134 L2 Luza r. Rus. Fed.
183 H4 Luzaga Spain
156 C3 Luzarches France
163 B6 Luz-Ardiden France
176 F2 Luže Czech Rep.
163 D4 Luzech France
176 D1 Lužec nad Vltavou Czech Rep.
190 D2 Luzern Switz.
190 D2 Luzern canton Switz.
234 C1 Luzerne PA U.S.A.
234 B1 Luzerne County county PA U.S.A.
139 K4 Luzha r. Rus. Fed.
108 D3 Luzhai Guangxi China
Luzhang Yunnan China see Lushui
108 C3 Luzhi Guizhou China
108 C2 Luzhou Sichuan China
184 B3 Luzianes Port.
256 D2 Luziânia Brazil
176 D1 Lužické Hory mts Czech Rep.
254 D2 Luzilândia Brazil
174 G1 Luzino Pol.
183 F1 Luzmela Spain
176 C1 Lužná Czech Rep.
175 J6 Lużna Pol.
176 D2 Lužnice r. Czech Rep.
92 B3 Luzon i. Phil.
92 B2 Luzon Strait Phil.
163 C6 Luz-St-Sauveur France
160 B2 Luzy France
174 G4 Łużyca r. Pol.
191 F4 Luzzara Italy
193 I5 Luzzi Italy
136 D1 L'va r. Ukr.
136 C3 L'viv Ukr.
L'viv Oblast admin. div. Ukr. see L'vivs'ka Oblast'
136 C2 L'vivs'ka Oblast' admin. div. Ukr.
L'vov Ukr. see L'viv
Lvov Oblast admin. div. Ukr. see L'vivs'ka Oblast'
L'vovskaya Oblast' admin. div. Ukr. see L'vivs'ka Oblast'
139 K4 L'vovskiy Rus. Fed.
Lwów Ukr. see L'viv
174 E3 Lwówek Pol.
174 D4 Lwówek Śląski Pol.
136 D3 Lyadova r. Ukr.
138 G2 Lyady Rus. Fed.
138 F5 Lyakhavichy Belarus
Lyakhovichi Belarus see Lyakhavichy
131 P2 Lyakhovskiye Ostrova is Novosibirskiye O-va Rus. Fed.
81 A6 Lyall, Mount South I. N.Z.
Lyallpur Pak. see Faisalabad
121 F5 Lyal'mikar Uzbek.
135 I5 Lyambir' Rus. Fed.
134 L4 Lyamino Rus. Fed.
Lyangar Kashkadar'inskaya Oblast' Uzbek. see Langar
121 F4 Lyangar Navoiyskaya Oblast' Uzbek.
134 M3 Lyapin r. Rus. Fed.
137 G3 Lyashivka Ukr.
147 G3 Lyaskelya Rus. Fed.
197 G4 Lyaskovets Bulg.
138 E5 Lyasnaya Belarus
138 D5 Lyasnaya r. Belarus
175 L3 Lyasnaya Lyevaya r. Belarus
177 L3 Lybokhora Ukr.
146 E3 Lybster Highland, Scotland U.K.
175 M4 Lybytiv Ukr.
170 E2 Lychen Ger.
137 H3 Lychkove Ukr.
139 I3 Lychkovo Rus. Fed.
Lyck Pol. see Ełk
140 L2 Lycksele Sweden
234 A1 Lycoming County county PA U.S.A.
234 A1 Lycoming Creek r. PA U.S.A.
Lycopolis Egypt see Asyūţ
151 H4 Lydd Kent, England U.K.
Lydda Israel see Lod
262 W2 Lyddan Island Antarctica
213 F5 Lydenburg S. Africa
150 C4 Lydford Devon, England U.K.
150 E3 Lydney Gloucestershire, England U.K.
175 I3 Lydynia r. Pol.
136 E1 Lyeltsy Belarus
136 E2 Lyel'chytsy Belarus
240 H3 Lyell, Mount CA U.S.A.
84 B4 Lyell Brown, Mount hill N.T. Austr.
81 D4 Lyell Range mts South I. N.Z.
138 G4 Lyepyel' Belarus
198 C3 Lygourio Greece
137 I3 Lyhivka Ukr.
227 I5 Lykens PA U.S.A.
137 F2 Lykhachiv Ukr.
137 G3 Lykhivka Ukr.
139 I2 Lykoshino Rus. Fed.
214 E2 Lykso S. Africa
226 A4 Lyle MN U.S.A.
136 E5 Lyman Ukr.
238 E3 Lyman WY U.S.A.
137 I3 Lyman, Ozero l. Ukr.
136 E4 Lymans'ke Ukr.
150 E4 Lyme Bay England U.K.
150 E4 Lyme Regis Dorset, England U.K.
151 I3 Lyminge Kent, England U.K.
151 F4 Lymington Hampshire, England U.K.
149 G4 Lymm Warrington, England U.K.
151 I3 Lympne Kent, England U.K.
150 D4 Lympstone Devon, England U.K.
143 I4 Łyna r. Pol.
232 B6 Lynch KY U.S.A.
231 C5 Lynchburg TN U.S.A.
232 D6 Lynchburg VA U.S.A.
231 E5 Lynches r. SC U.S.A.
232 D6 Lynch Station VA U.S.A.
233 □H2 Lynchville ME U.S.A.
241 E3 Lynd r. Qld Austr.
238 B1 Lynden WA U.S.A.
85 F3 Lyndhurst Qld Austr.
82 D2 Lyndhurst S.A. Austr.
151 F4 Lyndhurst Hampshire, England U.K.
87 B4 Lyndon W.A. Austr.
87 B4 Lyndon r. W.A. Austr.
236 E4 Lyndon KS U.S.A.
226 C4 Lyndon Station WI U.S.A.
233 G2 Lyndonville NY U.S.A.
232 D2 Lyndonville VT U.S.A.
149 F3 Lyne r. England U.K.
151 F3 Lyneham Wiltshire, England U.K.
149 H2 Lynemouth Northumberland, England U.K.
146 E3 Lyness Orkney, Scotland U.K.
142 B2 Lyngdal Norway
140 M1 Lyngen sea chan. Norway
140 M1 Lyngseidet Norway
150 E4 Lynher r. England U.K.
86 D2 Lynher Reef W.A. Austr.
150 D3 Lynmouth Devon, England U.K.
Lynn Norfolk, England U.K. see King's Lynn
233 H3 Lynn MA U.S.A.
241 K2 Lynndyl UT U.S.A.
231 C6 Lynn Haven FL U.S.A.
223 K3 Lynn Lake Man. Can.
137 H2 Lynove Ukr.
137 G2 Lynovytsya Ukr.
87 B6 Lynton W.A. Austr.
150 D3 Lynton Devon, England U.K.
138 F4 Lyntupy Belarus
223 J2 Lynx Lake N.W.T. Can.
226 B4 Lynxville WI U.S.A.
160 C3 Lyon France
Lyon airport France see Satolas
146 E5 Lyon r. Scotland U.K.
146 D5 Lyon, Loch l. Scotland U.K.
233 G2 Lyon Mountain NY U.S.A.
160 C3 Lyonnais, Monts du hills France
82 C2 Lyons S.A. Austr.
87 B5 Lyons r. W.A. Austr.
Lyons France see Lyon
231 D5 Lyons GA U.S.A.
236 D4 Lyons KS U.S.A.
232 E3 Lyons NY U.S.A.
233 F3 Lyons Falls NY U.S.A.
156 B3 Lyons-la-Forêt France
235 E1 Lyons Plain CT U.S.A.
234 C2 Lyon Station PA U.S.A.
139 H2 Lyozna Belarus
136 C2 Lypa r. Ukr.
136 E2 Lypnyky Ukr.
137 G2 Lypova Dolyna Ukr.
137 G4 Lypovets' Ukr.
137 I2 Lyptsi Ukr.
156 D2 Lys r. France
190 C3 Lys r. Italy
168 F1 Lysabild Denmark
177 H2 Lysá Hora mt. Czech Rep.
137 F5 Lysa Hora Ukr.
176 E1 Lysá nad Labem Czech Rep.
177 H2 Lysá pod Makytou Slovakia
175 J2 Łyse Pol.
142 B2 Lysekammen mt. Norway
142 D2 Lysekil Sweden
142 D2 Lysekil Sweden
176 F2 Lysice Czech Rep.
198 B2 Lysimachia, Limni l. Greece
174 G5 Lysiel Pol.
134 I4 Lyskovo Rus. Fed.
174 G2 Łysomice Pol.
131 C1 Lyss Switz.
142 C4 Lystrup Denmark
134 L4 Lys'va Rus. Fed.
142 E1 Lysvik Sweden
136 E3 Lysyanka Ukr.
137 J3 Lysychans'k Ukr.
135 I6 Lysyye Gory Rus. Fed.
175 H4 Lyszkowice Pol.
150 E4 Lytchett Matravers Dorset, England U.K.
150 E4 Lytchett Minster Dorset, England U.K.
146 E3 Lyth Highland, Scotland U.K.
149 F4 Lytham St Anne's Lancashire, England U.K.
139 K4 Lytkarino Rus. Fed.
175 M5 Lytovezh Ukr.
81 D5 Lyttelton South I. N.Z.
81 D5 Lyttelton Harbour South I. N.Z.
222 F5 Lytton B.C. Can.
138 G5 Lyuban' Belarus
139 H2 Lyuban' Rus. Fed.
136 D3 Lyubar Ukr.
136 E3 Lyubashivka Ukr.
137 H1 Lyubazh Rus. Fed.
138 F5 Lyubcha Belarus
136 F2 Lyubech Ukr.
139 K4 Lyubertsy Rus. Fed.
136 C2 Lyubeshiv Ukr.
134 H4 Lyubim Rus. Fed.
197 H5 Lyubimets Bulg.
137 H2 Lyubimovka Rus. Fed.
138 E5 Lyubishchytsy Belarus
139 J2 Lyubitovo Rus. Fed.
175 I1 Lyublino Rus. Fed.
175 M4 Lyublynets' Ukr.
139 J5 Lyubokhna Rus. Fed.
175 M4 Lyubokhyny Ukr.
137 H2 Lyubotyn Ukr.
Lyubotin Ukr. see Lyubotyn
137 H3 Lyubotyn Ukr.
137 I4 Lyubymivka Ukr.
175 L6 Lyubyntsi Ukr.
139 I2 Lyubytino Rus. Fed.
139 J5 Lyudinovo Rus. Fed.
197 H4 Lyulyakovo Bulg.
134 I4 Lyunda r. Rus. Fed.
138 F5 Lyusina Belarus
134 L2 Lyzha r. Rus. Fed.
138 G3 Lža r. Latvia
138 G3 Lzha r. Rus. Fed.

M

96 B2 Ma r. Myanmar
96 C2 Ma, Nam r. Laos
96 D3 Ma, Sông r. Vietnam
113 □1 Maabadi i. N. Male Maldives
Maafushi i. S. Male Maldives see Mafushi
240 □C8 Maalaea HI U.S.A.
114 B5 Maalhosmadulu Atoll Maldives
147 B3 Maam Rep. of Ireland
Maamakundhoo i. N. Male Maldives see Makunudhoo
209 E9 Maamba Zambia
147 B3 Maam Cross Rep. of Ireland
207 H6 Ma'an Cameroon
128 B4 Ma'ān Jordan
140 N3 Maaninka Fin.
109 F2 Ma'anshan Anhui China
106 D1 Maanyt Bulgan Mongolia
107 E2 Maanyt Töv Mongolia
138 E2 Maardu Estonia
165 E3 Maarheeze Neth.
Maarianhamina Åland Fin. see Mariehamn
164 E2 Maarn Neth.
128 C2 Ma'arrat an Nu'mān Syria
164 E2 Maarssen Neth.
164 E2 Maarssenbroek Neth.
164 E2 Maartensdijk Neth.
164 D3 Maas r. Neth. alt. Meuse (Belgium/France)
147 C2 Maas Rep. of Ireland
165 E3 Maasbracht Neth.
165 F3 Maasbree Neth.
164 D3 Maasdam Neth.
165 E3 Maaseik Belgium
92 C4 Maasin Phil.
164 D3 Maasland Neth.
165 E4 Maasmechelen Belgium
164 D3 Maassluis Neth.
165 E4 Maastricht Neth.
83 F5 Maatsuyker Group is Tas. Austr.
Maba Guangdong China see Qujiang
109 F1 Maba Jiangsu China
215 F1 Mabaalstad North West S. Africa
215 F1 Mabaalstad North West S. Africa
92 B3 Mabalacat Phil.
208 A5 Mabanda Gabon
124 D5 Ma'bar Yemen
251 G2 Mabaruma Guyana
Mabating Yunnan China see Hongshan
82 C2 Mabel Creek S.A. Austr.
86 E3 Mabel Downs W.A. Austr.
224 B3 Mabella Ont. Can.
227 I3 Maberly Ont. Can.
108 B2 Mabian Sichuan China
149 I4 Mablethorpe Lincolnshire, England U.K.
160 C2 Mably France
215 G1 Mabopane S. Africa
225 I4 Mabou N.S. Can.
128 B4 Mabrak, Jabal mt. Jordan
214 E1 Mabule Botswana
212 D5 Mabutsane Botswana
259 B7 Macá, Monte mt. Chile
261 F5 Macachín Arg.
87 C5 Macadam Plains W.A. Austr.
84 B2 Macadam Range hills N.T. Austr.
257 G5 Macaé Brazil
185 H3 Macael Spain
254 G3 Macaíba Brazil
254 E5 Macajuba Brazil
254 B2 Macaloge Moz.
183 I3 Macamic Que. Can.
224 E3 Macamic Que. Can.
Macan, Kepulauan atolls Indon. see Taka'Bonerate, Kepulauan
186 F2 Maçanet de Cabrenys Spain
Macao Macau China see Macau
182 C5 Mação Port.
251 I4 Macapá Brazil
Macar Turkey see Gebiz
250 B6 Macará Ecuador
255 E5 Macarani Brazil
250 C4 Macarena, Cordillera mts Col.
251 E2 Macareo, Caño r. Venez.
83 E4 Macarthur Vic. Austr.
250 B5 Macas Ecuador
182 D3 Maçãs r. Port./Spain
Macassar Sulawesi Selatan Indon. see Ujung Pandang
Makassar Strait Indon. see Makassar Strait
187 C5 Macastre Spain
254 F3 Macau Brazil
109 E4 Macau Macau China
162 D3 Macau France
252 C2 Macaúba Brazil
254 E5 Macaúbas Brazil
77 I5 Macauley Island N.Z.
190 D2 Macagno Italy
213 G5 Macarretane Moz.
195 E5 Macchia r. Sicilia Italy
193 G3 Macchiagodena Italy
231 D6 Macclenny FL U.S.A.
149 G4 Macclesfield Cheshire, England U.K.
224 B3 Macdiarmid Ont. Can.
87 C4 Macdonald, Lake salt flat W.A. Austr.
84 B4 Macdonnell Ranges mts N.T. Austr.
146 F4 Macduff Aberdeenshire, Scotland U.K.
177 K5 Macea Romania
182 C2 Maceda Spain
182 D3 Macedo de Cavaleiros Port.
Macedon country Europe see Macedonia
197 E5 Macedonia country Europe
235 E1 Macedonia CT U.S.A.
254 F4 Maceió Brazil
182 C4 Maceira Guarda Port.
182 B5 Maceira Leiria Port.
206 C4 Macenta Guinea
191 I5 Macerata Italy
191 I5 Macerata prov. Marche Italy
191 H5 Macerata Feltria Italy
82 D3 Macfarlane, Lake salt flat S.A. Austr.
147 B5 Macgillycuddy's Reeks mts Rep. of Ireland
148 C3 MacGregor's Corner Northern Ireland U.K.
123 F4 Mach Pak.
257 G2 Machacalis Brazil
252 D4 Machacamarca Bol.
250 B5 Machachi Ecuador
253 E2 Machadinho r. Brazil
256 E4 Machado Brazil
215 H1 Machadodorp S. Africa
184 C2 Machados Port.
211 C5 Machakos Kenya
250 B5 Machala Ecuador
260 B4 Machali Chile
Machali Qinghai China see Madoi
213 G4 Machanga Moz.
253 E5 Machareti Bol.
210 B2 Machar Marshes Sudan
84 D5 Machattie, Lake salt flat Qld Austr.
156 E3 Machault France
Machaze Moz. see Chitobe
158 E5 Machecoul France
165 D4 Machelen Belgium
150 D3 Machen Caerphilly, Wales U.K.
109 E2 Macheng Hubei China
157 G3 Macheren France
114 C2 Macherla Andhra Prad. India
171 D4 Machern Ger.
185 F1 Machero mt. Spain
226 C4 Machesney Park IL U.S.A.
116 D3 Machhiwara Punjab India
116 E4 Machhlishahr Uttar Prad. India
233 □J2 Machias ME U.S.A.
232 D3 Machias NY U.S.A.
233 □I1 Machias r. ME U.S.A.
184 □ Machico Madeira
180 B4 Machida Japan
114 D2 Machilipatnam Andhra Prad. India
211 B8 Machinga Malawi
250 C2 Machiques Venez.
146 B6 Machir Bay Scotland U.K.
Machiwara Punjab India see Machhiwara
245 H4 Machona, Laguna lag. Mex.
146 C6 Machrihanish Argyll and Bute, Scotland U.K.
137 H3 Machukhy Ukr.
252 B3 Machupicchu tourist site Peru
252 D3 Machupo r. Bol.
150 D2 Machynlleth Powys, Wales U.K.
213 G5 Macia Moz.
Macias Nguema i. Equat. Guinea see Bioco
175 J4 Maciejowice Pol.
261 G3 Maciel Arg.
197 I3 Măcin Romania
192 B2 Macinaggio Corse France
83 G2 Macintyre r. N.S.W. Austr.
85 F5 Macintyre Brook r. Qld Austr.
252 B3 Macizo de Tocate mts Peru
241 M2 Mack CO U.S.A.
129 A3 Maçka Turkey
85 G4 Mackay Qld Austr.
223 I3 MacKay r. Alta Can.
238 D2 Mackay ID U.S.A.
86 F4 Mackay, Lake salt flat W.A. Austr.
223 I2 MacKay Lake N.W.T. Can.
262 O1 Mackay Mountains Antarctica
172 B2 Mackenbach Ger.
169 F4 Mackenrode Ger.
85 G4 Mackenzie r. Qld Austr.
222 F4 Mackenzie B.C. Can.
226 C1 Mackenzie Ont. Can.
222 E1 Mackenzie r. N.W.T. Can.
Mackenzie Guyana see Linden
Mackenzie atoll Micronesia see Ulithi
220 E3 Mackenzie Bay Y.T. Can.
222 G2 Mackenzie Highway N.W.T. Can.
221 G2 Mackenzie King Island N.W.T. Can.
222 C1 Mackenzie Mountains N.W.T./Y.T. Can.
Mackillop, Lake salt flat Qld Austr. see Yamma Yamma, Lake
226 E3 Mackinac Island MI U.S.A.
226 C5 Mackinaw r. IL U.S.A.
226 E3 Mackinaw City MI U.S.A.
223 I4 Macklin Sask. Can.
83 H2 Macksville N.S.W. Austr.
83 H2 Maclean N.S.W. Austr.
215 F5 Macleantown S. Africa
215 G4 Maclear S. Africa
83 H2 Macleay r. N.S.W. Austr.
MacLeod Alta Can. see Fort Macleod
87 B5 MacLeod, Lake imp. l. W.A. Austr.
222 C2 Macmillan r. Y.T. Can.
209 C6 Macocola Angola
185 B5 Macomb IL U.S.A.
192 A4 Macomer Sardegna Italy
211 D8 Macomia Moz.
160 C2 Mâcon France
231 D5 Macon GA U.S.A.
236 E4 Macon MO U.S.A.
237 F5 Macon MS U.S.A.
232 B5 Macon OH U.S.A.
237 F6 Macon, Bayou r. LA U.S.A.
235 D1 Macopin NJ U.S.A.
183 E4 Macotera Spain
213 G4 Macovane Moz.
Macpherson Robertson Land reg. Antarctica see Mac. Robertson Land
83 F2 Macquarie r. N.S.W. Austr.
83 F5 Macquarie r. Tas. Austr.
83 G3 Macquarie, Lake b. N.S.W. Austr.
83 F5 Macquarie Harbour Tas. Austr.
82 □3 Macquarie Island S. Pacific Ocean
83 F2 Macquarie Marshes N.S.W. Austr.
83 G3 Macquarie Mountain N.S.W. Austr.
266 F9 Macquarie Ridge sea feature S. Pacific Ocean
81 C6 Macraes Flat South I. N.Z.
263 E2 Mac. Robertson Land reg. Antarctica
147 C5 Macroom Rep. of Ireland
243 H5 Macuelizo Hond.
190 C3 Macugnaga Italy
196 E5 Macukull Albania
82 C1 Macumba S.A. Austr.
234 C2 Macungie PA U.S.A.
254 F4 Macururé Brazil
252 C3 Macusani Peru
245 G5 Macuspana Mex.
233 □I2 Macwahoc ME U.S.A.
177 K3 Mád Hungary
128 B4 Mādabā Jordan
215 H2 Madadeni S. Africa
213 □ Madagascar i. Africa
265 H6 Madagascar Basin sea feature Indian Ocean
265 G7 Madagascar Ridge sea feature Indian Ocean
207 I4 Madagali Nigeria
124 B2 Madā'in Şāliḩ Saudi Arabia
216 □1c Madalena Pico Azores
254 F3 Madalena Brazil
197 G5 Madan Bulg.
114 C3 Madanapalle Andhra Prad. India
91 K8 Madang P.N.G.
116 D4 Madanpur Uttar Prad. India
207 G3 Madaoua Niger
177 I5 Madaras Hungary
197 E2 Mădăraş Romania
117 G5 Madaripur Bangl.
207 G3 Madarounfa Niger
227 I3 Madawaska r. Ont. Can.
224 E4 Madawaska r. Ont. Can.
233 □I1 Madawaska ME U.S.A.
96 B2 Madaya Myanmar
192 B5 Maddalena Spiaggia Sardegna Italy
193 G3 Maddaloni Italy
116 E4 Madded Madh. Prad. India
114 C3 Maddur Karnataka India
164 D3 Made Neth.
251 G5 Madeira r. Brazil
184 □ Madeira terr. N. Atlantic Ocean
184 □ Madeira, Arquipélago da is N. Atlantic Ocean
Madeira, Arquipélago da terr. N. Atlantic Ocean see Madeira
184 □ Madeira, Ilha da i. Madeira
Madeira Islands N. Atlantic Ocean see Madeira, Arquipélago da
253 E2 Madeirinha r. Brazil
150 E2 Madeley Staffordshire, England U.K.
150 E2 Madeley Telford and Wrekin, England U.K.
236 E2 Madelia MN U.S.A.
126 E3 Maden Turkey
242 C2 Madera Mex.
185 H2 Madera r. Spain
240 G3 Madera CA U.S.A.
183 F3 Maderano r. Spain
178 B3 Maderanerspitze mt. Austria
183 G3 Maderuelo Spain
114 B3 Madgaon Goa India
116 B5 Madhapur Gujarat India
117 F4 Madhepura Bihar India
111 C7 Madhoganj Uttar Prad. India
117 F4 Madhubani Bihar India
114 C3 Madhugiri Karnataka India
116 D5 Madhya Pradesh state India
95 F2 Madi, Dataran Tinggi plat. Indon.
215 E2 Madibogo S. Africa
82 D2 Madigan Gulf salt flat S.A. Austr.
114 B3 Madikeri Karnataka India
237 D5 Madill OK U.S.A.
209 B6 Madimba Dem. Rep. Congo
206 D4 Madinani Côte d'Ivoire
124 D5 Madinat ash Sha'b Yemen
128 D2 Madinat ath Thawrah Syria
157 F4 Madine, Lac de l. France
209 A6 Madingo-Kayes Congo
209 B6 Madingou Congo
252 D3 Madini r. Bol.
163 B5 Madiran France
213 □J3 Madirovalo Madag.
231 C5 Madison AL U.S.A.
235 F1 Madison CT U.S.A.
231 D6 Madison FL U.S.A.
231 D5 Madison GA U.S.A.
230 C4 Madison IN U.S.A.
233 □I2 Madison ME U.S.A.
236 D3 Madison MN U.S.A.
236 D3 Madison NE U.S.A.
235 D2 Madison NJ U.S.A.
232 C4 Madison OH U.S.A.
236 D2 Madison SD U.S.A.
232 D5 Madison VA U.S.A.
226 C4 Madison WI U.S.A.
232 C5 Madison WV U.S.A.
238 E2 Madison r. MT U.S.A.
232 D6 Madison Heights VA U.S.A.
230 C4 Madisonville KY U.S.A.
231 C5 Madisonville TN U.S.A.
237 E6 Madisonville TX U.S.A.
95 E4 Madiun Jawa Timur Indon.
150 E2 Madley Herefordshire, England U.K.
87 D5 Madley, Mount hill W.A. Austr.
224 E4 Madoc Ont. Can.
177 H5 Madocsa Hungary
106 C5 Madoi Qinghai China
157 G4 Madon r. France
138 F3 Madona Latvia
194 C5 Madonie mts Sicilia Italy
234 B3 Madonna MD U.S.A.
191 F2 Madonna di Campiglio Italy
199 E2 Madra Dağı mts Turkey
124 B3 Madrakah Saudi Arabia
Madras Tamil Nadu India see Chennai
Madras state India see Tamil Nadu
238 B2 Madras OR U.S.A.
245 F1 Madre, Laguna lag. Mex.
237 D7 Madre, Laguna lag. TX U.S.A.
245 H5 Madre, Sierra mts Mex.
92 B2 Madre, Sierra mt. Phil.
Madre de Chiapas, Sierra m's Mex. see Madre, Sierra
257 E4 Madre de Deus de Minas Brazil
252 C2 Madre de Dios dept Peru
259 B8 Madre de Dios, Isla i. Chile
244 D4 Madre del Sur, Sierra mts Mex.
244 B1 Madre Occidental, Sierra mts Mex.
244 D1 Madre Oriental, Sierra mts Mex.
163 E6 Madrès, Pic de mt. France
92 C4 Madrid Phil.
183 G4 Madrid Spain
183 G4 Madrid aut. comm. Spain
92 B4 Madridejos Phil.
185 G1 Madridejos Spain
183 F3 Madrigal de las Altas Torres Spain
183 E4 Madrigal de la Vera Spain
183 G2 Madrigal del Monte Spain
184 E1 Madrigalejo Spain
185 I1 Madrigueras Spain
178 A4 Madrisahorn mt. Austria/Switz.
150 □ Madron Cornwall, England U.K.
184 E1 Madroñera Spain
185 G3 Madroño mt. Spain
246 B2 Madruga Cuba
113 □1 Madu i. S. Male Maldives
209 B6 Maduda Dem. Rep. Congo
115 D2 Madugula Andhra Prad. India
87 E6 Madura W.A. Austr.
95 F4 Madura i. Indon.
95 F4 Madura, Selat sea chan. Indon.
114 C4 Madurai Tamil Nadu India
114 C3 Madurantakam Tamil Nadu India
122 C4 Madvār, Kūh-e mt. Iran
116 E4 Madwas Madh. Prad. India
129 E2 Madzhalis Rus. Fed.
197 G5 Madzharovo Bulg.
213 F3 Madziwa Mine Zimbabwe
191 H2 Mae r. Italy
Maéwo i. Vanuatu see Émaé
105 F2 Maebashi Japan
96 B3 Mae Hong Son Thai.
158 C3 Maël-Carhaix France
142 C2 Mælefjell mt. Norway
186 D3 Maella Spain
183 F4 Maello Spain
150 C3 Maenclochog Pembrokeshire, Wales U.K.
150 D2 Maentwrog Gwynedd, Wales U.K.
193 F3 Maenza Italy
96 B3 Mae Ramat Thai.
96 B3 Mae Rim Thai.
197 F2 Măerişte Romania
96 B3 Mae Sariang Thai.
146 E3 Maes Howe tourist site Scotland U.K.
96 B3 Mae Sot Thai.
150 D3 Maesteg Bridgend, Wales U.K.
246 C3 Maestra, Sierra mts Cuba
185 E3 Maestre hill Spain
183 H2 Maestu Spain
96 B3 Mae Suai Thai.
213 □J3 Maevatanana Madag.
78 □5 Maéwo i. Vanuatu
223 K4 Mafeking Man. Can.
Mafeking S. Africa see Mafikeng
215 F3 Mafeteng Lesotho
83 F4 Maffra Vic. Austr.
211 C7 Mafia Channel Tanz.
211 C6 Mafia Island Tanz.
215 E1 Mafikeng S. Africa
211 B7 Mafinga Tanz.
255 C8 Mafra Brazil
184 A2 Mafra Port.
Mafraq Jordan see Al Mafraq
113 □1 Mafushi i. S. Male Maldives
215 H4 Magabeni S. Africa
184 E2 Magacela hill Spain
131 Q4 Magadan Rus. Fed.
161 B5 Magalas France
215 F1 Magaliesberg mts S. Africa
215 F1 Magaliesburg S. Africa
Magallanes Chile see Punta Arenas
92 B3 Magallanes Phil.
259 C9 Magallanes, Estrecho de sea chan. Chile
259 B9 Magallanes y Antártica Chilena admin. reg. Chile
183 I3 Magallón Spain
187 F5 Magalluf Spain
183 H3 Magaña Spain
147 F4 Maganey Rep. of Ireland
253 D4 Magaña Col.
126 D3 Mağara Turkey
129 C3 Mağara tourist site Turkey
128 A1 Mağara Dağı mt. Turkey

128 D1 Mağarali Turkey
129 F3 Magaramkent Rus. Fed.
207 H3 Magaria Niger
Magas Iran see Zābolī
92 B2 Magat r. Phil.
183 F3 Magaz Spain
237 E5 Magazine Mountain hill AR U.S.A.
194 C5 Magazzolo r. Sicilia Italy
206 C4 Magburaka Sierra Leone
100 C1 Magdagachi Rus. Fed.
171 C5 Magdala Ger.
261 I4 Magdalena Arg.
252 D3 Magdalena Bol.
250 C2 Magdalena dept Col.
250 C2 Magdalena r. Col.
242 C2 Magdalena Mex.
242 C2 Magdalena r. Mex.
239 F5 Magdalena NM U.S.A.
259 B7 Magdalena, Isla i. Chile
245 F4 Magdalena Cuayucatepec Mex.
Magdalena Island Fr. Polynesia see Fatu Hiva
95 G1 Magdalene, Gunung mt. Sabah Malaysia
171 C3 Magdeburg Ger.
171 C3 Magdeburg admin. reg. Sachsen-Anhalt Ger.
171 D3 Magdeburgerforth Ger.
85 G3 Magdelaine Cays atoll Coral Sea Is Terr. Austr.
237 F6 Magee MS U.S.A.
95 E4 Magelang Jawa Tengah Indon.
Magellan, Strait of Chile see Magallanes, Estrecho de
266 E4 Magellan Seamounts sea feature N. Pacific Ocean
190 D3 Magenta Italy
87 C7 Magenta, Lake salt flat W.A. Austr.
140 N1 Magerøya i. Norway
163 A5 Magescq France
177 L4 Măgeşti Romania
190 D2 Maggia Switz.
190 D2 Maggia r. Switz.
261 F3 Maggiolo Arg.
190 E4 Maggiorasca, Monte mt. Italy
190 D3 Maggiore, Lago l. Italy
Maggiore, Lake Italy see Maggiore, Lago
192 B4 Maggiore, Monte hill Sardegna Italy
193 G3 Maggiore, Monte mt. Italy
246 □ Maggotty Jamaica
203 F2 Maghâgha Egypt
128 B5 Maghā'ir Shu'ayb tourist site Saudi Arabia
206 B3 Maghama Maur.
147 B5 Maghanlawaun Rep. of Ireland
128 A4 Maghâra, Gebel hill Egypt
147 C2 Maghera Rep. of Ireland
147 E2 Maghera Northern Ireland U.K.
147 E2 Magherafelt Northern Ireland U.K.
148 C3 Magheralin Northern Ireland U.K.
147 D2 Magheramason Northern Ireland U.K.
147 E2 Maghery Northern Ireland U.K.
204 E2 Maghnia Alg.
149 G4 Maghull Merseyside, England U.K.
148 C2 Magilligan Northern Ireland U.K.
185 G3 Mágina mt. Spain
192 E1 Magione Italy
195 F3 Magisano Italy
Magitang Qinghai China see Jainca
188 G3 Maglaj Bos.-Herz.
160 E2 Magland France
197 F3 Maglavit Romania
193 F2 Magliano de'Marsi Italy
192 D2 Magliano in Toscana Italy
193 E2 Magliano Sabina Italy
195 H2 Maglie Italy
177 I4 Maglód Hungary
241 L5 Magma AZ U.S.A.
162 D2 Magnac-Laval France
162 C3 Magnac-sur-Touvre France
194 B6 Magna Grande hill Italy
195 E5 Magna Grande mt. Sicilia Italy
162 B2 Magné France
85 F3 Magnetic Island Qld Austr.
85 F3 Magnetic Passage Qld Austr.
134 F1 Magnetity Rus. Fed.
157 G4 Magnières France
139 J5 Magnitnyy Rus. Fed.
120 D1 Magnitogorsk Rus. Fed.
237 E5 Magnolia AR U.S.A.
234 C3 Magnolia DE U.S.A.
234 B3 Magnolia MD U.S.A.
237 F6 Magnolia MS U.S.A.
175 J4 Magnuszew Pol.
160 B2 Magny-Cours France
156 B3 Magny-en-Vexin France
100 G1 Mago Rus. Fed.
177 H5 Mágocs Hungary
177 J5 Mágocs-ér r. Hungary
213 F2 Màgoé Moz.
225 F4 Magog Que. Can.
192 A4 Magomadas Sardegna Italy
Magosa Cyprus see Ammochostos
209 E8 Magoye Zambia
245 F3 Magozal Mex.
225 H3 Magpie Que. Can.
224 C4 Magpie r. Ont. Can.
225 H3 Magpie r. Que. Can.
225 H3 Magpie-Ouest r. Que. Can.
190 E4 Magra r. Italy
222 H5 Magrath Alta Can.
187 C5 Magre r. Spain
240 I3 Magruder Mountain NV U.S.A.
206 B2 Magṭa' Laḥjar Maur.
211 B5 Magu Tanz.
108 C4 Maguan Yunnan China
213 G5 Magude Moz.
215 H2 Magudu S. Africa
182 C3 Magueija Port.
184 E2 Maguilla Spain
147 D2 Maguiresbridge Northern Ireland U.K.
207 I3 Magumeri Nigeria
233 □J2 Magundy N.B. Can.
117 G5 Magura Bangl.
177 H3 Magura mt. Slovakia
136 D4 Măgura, Dealul hill Moldova
197 F2 Măgura Mare, Vârful hill Romania
197 F3 Măgurii, Vârful mt. Romania
215 F5 Magwali S. Africa
Magway Myanmar see Magwe
Magway admin. div. Myanmar see Magwe
96 A2 Magwe Myanmar
96 A2 Magwe admin. div. Myanmar
177 K4 Magy Hungary
177 G5 Magyaratád Hungary
177 H6 Magyarbóly Hungary
Magyarkanizsa Vojvodina, Srbija Yugo. see Kanjiža
Magyar Köztársaság country Europe see Hungary
177 H5 Magyarszék Hungary
122 A2 Mahābād Iran
114 B2 Mahabaleshwar Mahar. India
116 F4 Mahabharat Range mts Nepal
213 □J4 Mahabo Madag.
114 B2 Mahad Mahar. India
210 E4 Mahaddayweyne Somalia
116 D5 Mahadeo Hills Madh. Prad. India
114 D2 Mahadeopur Andhra Prad. India
232 D4 Mahaffey PA U.S.A.
251 G3 Mahaicony Guyana
213 □J2 Mahajamba r. Madag.
116 C3 Mahajan Rajasthan India
213 □J2 Mahajanga Madag.
213 □J3 Mahajanga prov. Madag.
95 G3 Mahakam r. Indon.
213 E4 Mahalapye Botswana
211 A6 Mahale Mountain National Park Tanz.
213 □K2 Mahalevona Madag.
122 B3 Mahallāt Iran
116 D3 Maham Haryana India
122 D4 Māhān Iran
117 F5 Mahanadi r. India
213 □K3 Mahanoro Madag.
234 B2 Mahanoy City PA U.S.A.
234 B2 Mahanoy Creek r. PA U.S.A.
234 B2 Mahantango Creek r. PA U.S.A.
117 F4 Maharajganj Bihar India
116 E4 Maharajganj Uttar Prad. India
116 D4 Maharajpur Madh. Prad. India
114 B2 Maharashtra state India
122 C4 Mahārlū, Daryācheh-ye salt l. Iran
96 C3 Maha Sarakham Thai.
128 C4 Maḥaṭṭat Ḍab'ah Jordan
247 □2 Mahault, Baie b. Guadeloupe
213 □J2 Mahavavy r. Madag.
114 D4 Mahaweli Ganga r. Sri Lanka
213 □J3 Mahazoma Madag.
114 D2 Mahbubabad Andhra Prad. India
114 C2 Mahbubnagar Andhra Prad. India
124 C3 Mahd adh Dhahab Saudi Arabia
125 F2 Maḥḍah Oman
137 H3 Mahdalynivka Ukr.
205 F2 Mahdia Alg.
251 G3 Mahdia Guyana
205 H2 Mahdia Tunisia
114 B4 Mahe Pondicherry India
217 □2b Mahé i. Inner Islands Seychelles
217 □1b Mahébourg Mauritius
116 D3 Mahendragarh Haryana India
115 E2 Mahendragiri mt. Orissa India
211 C7 Mahenge Tanz.
81 C6 Maheno South I. N.Z.
175 L5 Maheriv Ukr.
116 C5 Mahesana Gujarat India
116 C5 Maheshwar Madh. Prad. India
125 F5 Maḥfirhīn Suquṭrā Yemen
116 D4 Mahgawan Madh. Prad. India
116 C5 Mahi r. Rajasthan India
80 F3 Mahia North I. N.Z.
80 F3 Mahia Peninsula North I. N.Z.
182 D3 Mahíde Spain
78 □6 Mahige Island Solomon Is
139 H5 Mahilyow Belarus
Mahilyow Oblast admin. div. Belarus see Mahilyowskaya Voblasts'
139 H5 Mahilyowskaya Voblasts' admin. div. Belarus
114 B2 Mahim Mahar. India
206 C3 Mahina Mali
140 K2 Mahkene mt. Sweden
215 H3 Mahlabatini S. Africa
96 A2 Mahlaing Myanmar
215 H2 Mahlangasi S. Africa
215 F3 Mahlatswetsa S. Africa
172 B3 Mahlberg Ger.
171 E3 Mahlow Ger.
170 C3 Mahlsdorf Ger.
171 C3 Mahlwinkel Ger.
116 E4 Mahmudabad Uttar Prad. India
122 C2 Mahmudabad Iran
123 G3 Maḥmūd-e 'Erāqī Afgh.
197 I3 Mahmudia Romania
199 E2 Mahmudiye anakkale Turkey
199 G2 Mahmudiye Eskişehir Turkey
128 A1 Mahmutlar Turkey
199 F1 Mahmutşevketpaşa Turkey
236 D2 Mahnomen MN U.S.A.
116 D4 Mahoba Uttar Prad. India
80 E3 Mahoenui North I. N.Z.
116 E4 Maholi Uttar Prad. India
186 □ Mahón Spain
225 H4 Mahone Bay N.S. Can.
235 E1 Mahopac NY U.S.A.
185 I1 Mahora Spain
206 D3 Mahou Mali
125 E4 Mahrāt, Wādī r. Yemen
116 D4 Mahrauni Uttar Prad. India
173 G2 Mähring Ger.
122 E3 Māhrūd Iran
Mahsana Gujarat India see Mahesana
111 F4 Mahuanggou Qinghai China
240 □D8 Mahukona HI U.S.A.
117 H4 Mahur Assam India
114 C2 Mahur Mahar. India
207 G4 Mahuta Nigeria
211 C7 Mahuta Tanz.
116 B5 Mahuva Gujarat India
116 D4 Mahwa Rajasthan India
197 H5 Mahya Dağı mt. Turkey
Mai i. Vanuatu see Émaé
78 □2 Maia American Samoa
216 □1b Maia São Miguel Azores
182 B3 Maia Port.
Maiaia Moz. see Nacala
186 D3 Maials Spain
77 H1 Maiana atoll Gilbert Is Kiribati
117 H4 Maibang Assam India
250 C2 Maicao Col.
224 E3 Maicasagi r. Que. Can.
224 E3 Maicasagi, Lac l. Que. Can.
160 E1 Maîche France
251 F6 Maici r. Brazil
251 H5 Maicuru r. Brazil
195 F4 Maida Italy
150 E3 Maiden Bradley Wiltshire, England U.K.
234 C2 Maiden Creek r. PA U.S.A.
151 G3 Maidenhead Windsor and Maidenhead, England U.K.
150 E4 Maiden Newton Dorset, England U.K.
226 A3 Maiden Rock WI U.S.A.
146 D6 Maidens South Ayrshire, Scotland U.K.
223 I4 Maidstone Sask. Can.
151 H3 Maidstone Kent, England U.K.
207 I4 Maiduguri Nigeria
190 E1 Maienfeld Switz.
195 F4 Maierato Italy
173 E4 Maierhöfen Ger.
197 G2 Maieru Romania
187 C6 Maigmó mt. Spain
156 C3 Maignelay-Montigny France
210 C3 Mai Gudo mt. Eth.
147 C4 Maigue r. Rep. of Ireland
116 E4 Maihar Madh. Prad. India
80 E3 Maihiihi North I. N.Z.
117 G5 Maijdi Bangl.
108 C1 Maiji Shan mt. Gansu China
116 E5 Maikala Range hills Madh. Prad. India
172 C2 Maikammer Ger.
208 E4 Maiko r. Dem. Rep. Congo
117 E5 Mailan Hill mt. Madh. Prad. India
116 E3 Mailani Uttar Prad. India
240 □ Maili HI U.S.A.
163 B4 Maillas France
156 B4 Maillebois France
162 B2 Maillezais France
160 B1 Mailly-la-Ville France
156 E4 Mailly-le-Camp France
156 C2 Mailly-Maillet France
123 H4 Mailsi Pak.
169 D5 Main r. Ger.
124 D4 Ma'īn tourist site Yemen
117 G4 Mainaguri W. Bengal India
172 D2 Mainaschaff Ger.
173 E2 Mainbernheim Ger.
225 K3 Main Brook Nfld. Can.
173 F3 Mainburg Ger.
114 C2 Maindargi Mahar. India
208 C5 Mai-Ndombe, Lac l. Dem. Rep. Congo
227 I4 Main Duck Island Ont. Can.
159 F4 Maine r. France
233 □I2 Maine state U.S.A.
233 □I3 Maine, Gulf of U.S.A.
159 F4 Maine-et-Loire dept Pays de la Loire France
250 C5 Mainé Hanari, Cerro hill Col.
207 I3 Maïné-Soroa Niger
96 B1 Maingkwan Myanmar
147 E3 Mainham Rep. of Ireland
172 D2 Mainhardt Ger.
92 C4 Mainit Phil.
108 A2 Mainkung Xizang China
146 E2 Mainland i. Orkney, Scotland U.K.
146 □G1 Mainland i. Shetland, Scotland U.K.
171 C5 Mainleus Ger.
111 F6 Mainling Xizang China
84 C2 Mainoru N.T. Austr.
84 C2 Mainoru r. N.T. Austr.
117 E5 Mainpat reg. Madh. Prad. India
116 D4 Mainpuri Uttar Prad. India
162 E2 Mainsat France
156 B4 Maintenon France
213 □J3 Maintirano Madag.
156 B4 Mainvilliers France
169 D5 Mainz Ger.
206 □ Maio i. Cape Verde
191 I5 Maiolati Spontini Italy
184 B1 Maior r. Port.
182 B4 Maiorca Port.
182 B5 Maiorga Port.
194 D2 Maiori Italy
260 B3 Maipó r. Chile
260 C4 Maipó, Volcán vol. Chile
261 I5 Maipú Arg.
260 C3 Maipú Arg.
260 B3 Maipú Chile
250 E2 Maiquetía Venez.
111 D6 Maiqu Zangbo r. Xizang China
190 C4 Maira r. Italy
184 E3 Mairena del Alcor Spain
254 E4 Mairi Brazil
256 D5 Mairiporã Brazil
256 C2 Mairipotaba Brazil
173 F3 Maisach Ger.
173 F3 Maisach r. Ger.
178 D3 Maishofen Austria
246 D2 Maisí Cuba
138 E4 Maišiagala Lith.
156 C4 Maisons-Laffitte France
179 G2 Maissau Austria
156 C4 Maisse France
165 E5 Maissin Belgium
Maitea i. Arch. de la Société Fr. Polynesia see Mehetia
173 G3 Maitenbeth Ger.
213 E4 Maitengwe Botswana
117 F5 Maithon Bihar India
83 G3 Maitland N.S.W. Austr.
82 D3 Maitland S.A. Austr.
86 C4 Maitland r. W.A. Austr.
95 G1 Maitland, Banjaran mts Sabah Malaysia
87 D5 Maitland, Lake salt flat W.A. Austr.
263 A2 Maitri research stn Antarctica
Maiwo i. Vanuatu see Maéwo
84 C2 Maiwok r. N.T. Austr.
84 B3 Maiyu, Mount hill N.T. Austr.
242 □J6 Maíz, Islas del is Nic.
111 E6 Maizhokunggar Xizang China
156 D4 Maizières-la-Grande-Paroisse France
157 G3 Maizières-lès-Metz France
104 B3 Maizuru Japan
184 E4 Majaceite r. Spain
183 G4 Majadahonda Spain
182 E5 Majadas de Tiétar Spain
196 D4 Maja Jezercë mt. Albania
114 C2 Majalgaon Mahar. India
251 F4 Majari r. Brazil
125 E5 Majdaḥah Yemen
175 J5 Majdan Królewski Pol.
175 L5 Majdan Niepryski Pol.
197 E3 Majdanpek Srbija Yugo.
257 F5 Majé Brazil
93 A3 Majene Sulawesi Selatan Indon.
188 G3 Majevica mts Bos.-Herz.
116 E4 Majhgawan Madh. Prad. India
116 D5 Majholi Madh. Prad. India
107 H4 Majia r. China
109 D4 Majiang Guangxi China
108 C3 Majiang Guizhou China
Majōl country N. Pacific Ocean see Marshall Islands
Majorca i. Spain see Mallorca
Mājro atoll Marshall Is see Majuro
177 H6 Majs Hungary
117 H4 Majuli Island India
Majunga Madag. see Mahajanga
78 □3b Majuro atoll Marshall Is
215 F3 Majwemasweu S. Africa
206 B3 Maka Senegal
209 B5 Makabana Congo
177 H4 Makád Hungary
240 □ Makaha HI U.S.A.
207 H6 Makak Cameroon
93 A3 Makale Sulawesi Selatan Indon.
117 F4 Makalu mt. China/Nepal
211 A6 Makamba Burundi
121 J3 Makanchi Kazakh.
211 B8 Makanjila Malawi
211 C6 Makanya Tanz.
208 C4 Makanza Dem. Rep. Congo
81 B7 Makarewa South I. N.Z.
207 I3 Makari Cameroon
Makari Mountain National Park Tanz. see Mahale Mountain National Park
136 E2 Makariv Ukr.
81 B6 Makarora r. South I. N.Z.
100 G2 Makarov Sakhalin Rus. Fed.
268 M1 Makarov Basin sea feature Arctic Ocean
136 B3 Makarove Ukr.
135 H5 Makarovo Rus. Fed.
188 F4 Makarska Croatia
134 J4 Makar'ye Rus. Fed.
134 H4 Makar'yev Rus. Fed.
Makassar Sulawesi Selatan Indon. see Ujung Pandang
93 A3 Makassar Strait Indon.
120 C3 Makat Kazakh.
215 I2 Makatini Flats lowland S. Africa
240 □C8 Makawao HI U.S.A.
213 □J4 Makay, Massif du mts Madag.
Makedonija country Europe see Macedonia
215 F3 Makeleketla S. Africa
79 □3 Makemo atoll Arch. des Tuamotu Fr. Polynesia
206 B4 Makeni Sierra Leone
211 B7 Makete Tanz.
Makeyevka Donets'ka Oblast' Ukr. see Makiyivka
212 E4 Makgadikgadi salt pan Botswana
129 E2 Makhachkala Rus. Fed.
215 F4 Makhaleng r. Lesotho
120 B3 Makhambet Kazakh.
124 C2 Makhāmīr, Jabal al hill Saudi Arabia
Makharadze Georgia see Ozurget'i
215 G3 Makheka mt. Lesotho
128 D2 Makhfar al Ḩammām Syria
129 D1 Makhmud-Mekteb Rus. Fed.
127 F4 Makhmūr Iraq
121 G1 Makhorovka Kazakh.
114 C2 Makhtal Andhra Prad. India
125 E4 Makhyah, Wādī r. Yemen
93 C2 Makian vol. Maluku Indon.
105 E2 Makihata-yama mt. Japan
81 C6 Makikihi South I. N.Z.
Makima atoll Arch. des Tuamotu Fr. Polynesia see Makemo
Makin atoll Kiribati see Butaritari
121 G1 Makinsk Kazakh.
Makira i. Solomon Is see San Cristobal
136 D3 Makiv Ukr.
137 F2 Makiyivka Chernihivs'ka Oblast' Ukr.
137 I3 Makiyivka Donets'ka Oblast' Ukr.
Makkah Saudi Arabia see Mecca
124 C3 Makkah prov. Saudi Arabia
225 J2 Makkovik Nfld. Can.
164 E1 Makkum Neth.
177 J5 Makó Hungary
251 G4 Makoa, Serra hills Brazil
79 □1 Makogai i. Fiji
208 B4 Makokou Gabon
215 F2 Makokskraal S. Africa
211 C7 Makonde Plateau Tanz.
Makongai i. Fiji see Makogai
211 B7 Makongolosi Tanz.
212 D5 Makopong Botswana
80 F4 Makotuku North I. N.Z.
208 B5 Makoua Congo
177 H2 Makov Slovakia
188 E3 Makovnik mt. Croatia
175 I4 Maków Pol.
174 F2 Mąkowarsko Pol.
175 J3 Maków Mazowiecki Pol.
175 H6 Maków Podhalański Pol.
198 C2 Makrakomi Greece
116 C4 Makrana Rajasthan India
Makran Coast Range mts Pak. see Talar-i-Band
198 D3 Makronisi i. Greece
198 C1 Makrygialos Kentriki Makedonia Greece
139 J3 Maksatikha Rus. Fed.
116 D5 Maksi Madh. Prad. India
100 F3 Maksimovka Rus. Fed.
116 D5 Maksudangarh Madh. Prad. India
174 G2 Maksymilianowo Pol.
122 A2 Mākū Iran
117 H4 Makum Assam India
211 B7 Makumbako Tanz.
209 D6 Makumbi Dem. Rep. Congo
Makundu i. N. Male Maldives see Makunudhoo
211 C6 Makunduchi Tanz.
109 F4 Makung Taiwan
211 C7 Makunguwiro Tanz.
113 □1 Makunudhoo i. N. Male Maldives
103 E8 Makurazaki Japan
207 H5 Makurdi Nigeria
80 E4 Makuri North I. N.Z.
215 E2 Makwassie S. Africa
117 G4 Mal W. Bengal India
252 A3 Mala Peru
Mala Rep. of Ireland see Mallow
Mala i. Solomon Is see Malaita
185 G3 Malá Spain
140 L2 Malå Sweden
92 C5 Malabang Phil.
114 B3 Malabar Coast India
137 H4 Mala Bilozerka Ukr.
207 H6 Malabo Equat. Guinea
177 I5 Mala Bosna Vojvodina, Srbija Yugo.
92 A4 Malabuñgan Phil.
Malaca Spain see Málaga
257 F2 Malacacheta Brazil
Malacca Malaysia see Melaka
Malacca state Malaysia see Melaka
94 B1 Malacca, Strait of Indon./Malaysia
176 G3 Malacky Slovakia
238 D3 Malad r. ID U.S.A.
238 D3 Malad City ID U.S.A.
137 G2 Mala Divytsya Ukr.
138 F4 Maladzyechna Belarus
177 H2 Malá Fatra mts Slovakia
185 F4 Málaga Spain
185 F4 Málaga prov. Andalucía Spain
234 C3 Malaga NJ U.S.A.
239 F5 Malaga NM U.S.A.
232 C5 Malaga OH U.S.A.
211 A6 Malagarasi r. Burundi/Tanz.
211 A6 Malagarasi Tanz.
185 G1 Malagón Spain
184 C3 Malagon r. Spain
147 E3 Malahide Rep. of Ireland
213 □J4 Malaimbandy Madag.
174 D2 Mała Ina r. Pol.
78 □6 Malaita i. Solomon Is
95 G5 Malaka mt. Sumbawa Indon.
210 A2 Malakal Sudan
114 D2 Malakanagiri Orissa India
188 E3 Mala Kapela mts Croatia
188 E3 Mala Kladuša Bos.-Herz.
78 □6 Malakobi Island Solomon Is
78 □5 Malakula i. Vanuatu
123 H3 Malakwal Pak.
191 G4 Malalbergo Italy
137 G4 Mala Lepetykha Ukr.
93 B3 Malamala Sulawesi Tenggara Indon.
191 H3 Malamocco Italy
136 C2 Mala Moshchanytsya Ukr.
157 F3 Malancourt France
95 F4 Malang Jawa Timur Indon.
Malange Angola see Malanje
209 C7 Malanje Angola
209 C7 Malanje prov. Angola
174 G4 Malanów Pol.
158 D4 Malansac France
207 F4 Malanville Benin
260 D2 Malanzán, Sierra de mts Arg.
137 H3 Mala Pereshchepyna Ukr.
114 C4 Malappuram Kerala India
143 G2 Mälaren l. Sweden
260 C4 Malargüe Arg.
224 E3 Malartic Que. Can.
136 C2 Malaryta Belarus
176 E1 Malá Skála Czech Rep.
222 E5 Malaspina Strait B.C. Can.
179 H4 Mala Subotica Croatia
137 H3 Mala Ternivka r. Ukr.
126 E3 Malatya Turkey
161 D4 Malaucène France
156 B3 Malaunay France
163 B5 Malaussanne France
116 C3 Malaut Punjab India
114 C3 Malavalli Karnataka India
136 F3 Mala Vil'shanka Ukr.
137 F3 Mala Vyska Ukr.
207 H3 Malawa Niger
174 F3 Mała Wełna r. Pol.
211 B7 Malawi country Africa
Malawi, Lake Africa see Nyasa, Lake
140 M3 Malax Fin.
Malaya pen. Malaysia see Malaysia, Semenanjung
129 E1 Malaya Areshevka Rus. Fed.
134 K2 Malaya Pera Rus. Fed.
139 I2 Malaya Vishera Rus. Fed.
92 C4 Malaybalay Phil.
122 B3 Malāyer Iran
156 D4 Malay-le-Grand France
85 G3 Malay Reef Coral Sea Is Terr. Austr.
94 C1 Malaysia country Asia
94 C2 Malaysia, Semenanjung pen. Malaysia
127 F3 Malazgirt Turkey
225 G4 Malbaie r. Que. Can.
207 G3 Malbaza Niger
84 E4 Malbon Qld Austr.
175 H1 Malbork Pol.
172 A2 Malborn Ger.
161 B4 Malbouzon France
160 E2 Malbuisson France
182 C4 Malcata, Serra de mts Port.
191 F3 Malcesine Italy
137 K3 Mal'chevskaya Rus. Fed.
170 D2 Malchin Ger.
170 D2 Malchiner See l. Ger.
170 D2 Malchow Ger.
177 K3 Malčice Slovakia
184 E2 Malcocinado Spain
87 D6 Malcolm W.A. Austr.
87 D7 Malcolm, Point W.A. Austr.
177 K2 Malcov Slovakia
174 E4 Malczyce Pol.
165 C3 Maldegem Belgium
164 E3 Malden Neth.
237 F4 Malden MO U.S.A.
267 I6 Malden Island Kiribati
186 D2 Malditos, Montes mts Spain
113 D10 Maldives country Indian Ocean
83 F4 Maldon Vic. Austr.
151 H3 Maldon Essex, England U.K.
258 G4 Maldonado Uru.
175 H2 Małdyty Pol.
217 □3a Male Njazidja Comoros
191 F2 Malè Italy
113 □1 Male N. Male Maldives
113 □1 Male Atoll Maldives
215 E3 Malebogo S. Africa
174 E1 Malechowo Pol.
114 C2 Malegaon Mahar. India
116 C5 Malegaon Mahar. India
183 I3 Maleján Spain
176 G3 Malé Karpaty hills Slovakia
122 E4 Malek Sīāh, Kūh-e mt. Afgh.
209 B6 Malele Dem. Rep. Congo
213 H2 Malema Moz.
161 D4 Malemort-du-Comtat France
162 D3 Malemort-sur-Corrèze France
168 F1 Malente Ger.
215 G1 Maleoskop S. Africa
143 F3 Målerås Sweden
116 C3 Maler Kotla Punjab India
190 D2 Malesco Italy
197 F5 Maleševske Planine mts Bulg./Macedonia
156 C4 Malesherbes France
198 C2 Malesina Greece
158 D4 Malestroit France
107 F1 Maleta Rus. Fed.
194 D5 Maletto Sicilia Italy
139 L5 Malevka Rus. Fed.
194 D4 Malfa Isole Lipari Italy
214 C6 Malgas S. Africa
173 G3 Malgersdorf Ger.
129 D2 Malgobek Rus. Fed.
140 L2 Malgomaj l. Sweden
186 F3 Malgrat de Mar Spain
254 E5 Malhada Brazil
182 D3 Malhadas Port.
124 D2 Malham Saudi Arabia
116 C4 Malhargarh Madh. Prad. India
238 C2 Malheur r. OR U.S.A.
206 D3 Mali country Africa
206 B3 Mali Guinea
199 D4 Malia Kriti Greece
107 E5 Malian r. China
215 G3 Malibamatso r. Lesotho
240 H4 Malibu CA U.S.A.
159 F4 Malicorne-sur-Sarthe France
156 D5 Maligny France
111 C7 Malihabad Uttar Prad. India
96 B1 Mali Hka r. Myanmar
177 I6 Mali Iđoš Vojvodina, Srbija Yugo.
161 E4 Malijai France
123 E4 Malik Naro mt. Pak.
97 B4 Mali Kyun i. Myanmar
93 B3 Malili Sulawesi Selatan Indon.
143 F3 Målilla Sweden
188 E3 Mali Lošinj Croatia
209 F6 Malimba, Monts mts Dem. Rep. Congo
175 L6 Mali Mokryany Ukr.
147 D1 Malin Rep. of Ireland
Malin Ukr. see Malyn
147 C2 Malin Beg Rep. of Ireland
211 D5 Malindi Kenya
177 I3 Málinec Slovakia
Malines Belgium see Mechelen
208 B5 Malinga Gabon
147 D1 Malin Head hd Rep. of Ireland
197 H2 Mălini Romania
147 C2 Malin More Rep. of Ireland
139 L4 Malino Rus. Fed.
93 B2 Malino, Gunung mt. Indon.
100 E3 Malinovka r. Rus. Fed.
121 I2 Malinovoye Ozero Altayskiy Kray Rus. Fed.
191 J3 Malinska Croatia
211 C7 Malinyi Tanz.
108 C4 Malipo Yunnan China
198 B1 Maliq Albania
188 E3 Mali Raginac mt. Croatia
92 C5 Malita Phil.
92 C4 Malitbog Phil.
116 B5 Maliya Gujarat India
137 G4 Maliyivka Ukr.
196 D3 Mali Zvornik Srbija Yugo.
129 C2 Malka Rus. Fed.
129 D2 Malka r. Rus. Fed.
114 B2 Malkapur Mahar. India
116 D5 Malkapur Mahar. India
199 E1 Malkara Turkey
138 F5 Mal'kavichy Belarus
175 K3 Małkinia Górna Pol.
197 H5 Malko Tŭrnovo Bulg.
83 G4 Mallacoota Vic. Austr.
83 G4 Mallacoota Inlet b. Vic. Austr.
146 C5 Mallaig Highland, Scotland U.K.
203 F3 Mallawi Egypt
140 M1 Mållejus hill Norway
161 D5 Mallemort France
183 I3 Mallén Spain
170 C2 Mallentin Ger.
190 E2 Mallero r. Italy
173 G3 Mallersdorf Ger.
191 F2 Malles Venosta Italy
255 C8 Mallét Brazil
Mallia Kriti Greece see Malia
170 C2 Mallìß Ger.
260 B4 Malloa Chile
187 F5 Mallorca i. Spain
147 C4 Mallow Rep. of Ireland
86 E4 Mallowa Well W.A. Austr.
150 D2 Mallwyd Gwynedd, Wales U.K.
140 J2 Malm Norway
123 E3 Malman Rūd r. Afgh.
140 M2 Malmberget Sweden
165 F4 Malmédy Belgium
214 B5 Malmesbury S. Africa
150 E3 Malmesbury Wiltshire, England U.K.
143 G2 Malmköping Sweden
142 E4 Malmö Sweden
142 E4 Malmö-Sturup airport Sweden
143 F2 Malmslätt Sweden
134 J4 Malmyzh Rus. Fed.
190 D3 Malnate Italy
191 G3 Malo Italy
78 □5 Malo i. Vanuatu
139 K5 Maloarkhangel'sk Rus. Fed.
196 E3 Malo Crniće Srbija Yugo.
175 I5 Małogoszcz Pol.
92 B3 Malolos Phil.
174 D4 Małomice Pol.
137 I3 Malomykhaylivka Ukr.
183 I3 Malón Spain
190 C3 Malone r. Italy
233 F2 Malone NY U.S.A.
108 B3 Malong Yunnan China
209 D7 Malonga Dem. Rep. Congo
190 F2 Malonno Italy
176 D3 Malonty Czech Rep.
175 I5 Małopolska, Wyżyna hills Pol.
175 I6 Małopolskie prov. Pol.
Malorita Belarus see Malaryta
134 G3 Maloshuyka Rus. Fed.
197 F3 Malovăț Romania
Malovata Moldova see Molovata
141 I3 Måløy Norway
139 K4 Maloyaroslavets Rus. Fed.
139 K2 Maloye Borisovo Rus. Fed.
175 I1 Maloye-Lugovoye Rus. Fed.
134 J2 Malozemel'skaya Tundra lowland Rus. Fed.
182 D4 Malpartida Port.
184 D1 Malpartida de Cáceres Spain
184 E2 Malpartida de la Serena Spain
182 D5 Malpartida de Plasencia Spain
149 G4 Malpas Cheshire, England U.K.
150 D3 Malpas Newport, Wales U.K.
216 □3e Malpaso mt. El Hierro Canary Is
267 N5 Malpelo, Isla de i. N. Pacific Ocean
182 B1 Malpica Spain
183 F5 Malpica de Tajo Spain
182 C5 Malpica do Tejo Port.
138 E3 Mālpils Latvia
114 C2 Malprabha r. India
116 C4 Malpura Rajasthan India
172 C3 Malsch Ger.
176 D3 Malše r. Czech Rep.
169 E4 Malsfeld Ger.
114 B2 Malsiras Mahar. India
179 E4 Malta Austria
189 E8 Malta country Europe
138 F3 Malta Latvia
138 F3 Malta r. Latvia
195 □ Malta i. Malta
182 C4 Malta Port.
238 D3 Malta ID U.S.A.
238 F1 Malta MT U.S.A.
212 C5 Maltahöhe Namibia
207 I3 Maltam Cameroon
149 H4 Maltby South Yorkshire, England U.K.
149 J4 Maltby le Marsh Lincolnshire, England U.K.
172 B3 Malterdingen Ger.
172 C4 Malters Switz.
149 I3 Malton North Yorkshire, England U.K.
183 I3 Maluenda Spain
Malukken is Indon. see Maluku
93 C3 Maluku is Indon.
93 D3 Maluku prov. Indon.
93 C2 Maluku, Kepulauan is Indon.
197 F2 Malului, Vârful hill Romania
207 G4 Malumfashi Nigeria
143 E1 Malung Sweden
175 H5 Maluszyn Pol.
215 G3 Maluti Mountains Lesotho
183 E3 Malva Spain
190 D2 Malvaglia Switz.
114 B2 Malvan Mahar. India
184 A2 Malveira Port.
Malvern Worcestershire, England U.K. see Great Malvern
237 E5 Malvern AR U.S.A.
232 C4 Malvern OH U.S.A.
150 E2 Malvern Link Worcestershire, England U.K.
Malvinas, Islas terr. S. Atlantic Ocean see Falkland Islands
171 F4 Malxe r. Ger.
177 H4 Malý Dunaj r. Slovakia
177 K3 Malý Horeš Slovakia
177 J3 Mályi Hungary
131 M3 Malykay Rus. Fed.
136 E2 Malyn Ukr.
137 I3 Malynivka Ukr.
136 D2 Malyns'k Ukr.
175 K2 Mały Płock Pol.
131 R3 Malyy Anyuy r. Rus. Fed.
177 L3 Malyy Bereznyy Ukr.
135 I7 Malyye Derbety Rus. Fed.
Malyye Kotyuzhany Moldova see Cotiujenii Mici
135 J5 Malyy Irgiz r. Rus. Fed.
129 C3 Malyy Kavkaz mts Asia
107 E1 Malyy Kunaley Rus. Fed.
136 D2 Malyy Stydyn Ukr.
120 B2 Malyy Uzen' r. Kazakh./Rus. Fed.
129 B1 Malyy Zelenchuk r. Rus. Fed.
131 P3 Mama r. Rus. Fed.
134 J5 Mamadysh Rus. Fed.
215 G2 Mamafubedu S. Africa
215 F3 Mamahabane S. Africa
79 □1 Mamanuca-i-Cake Group is Fiji
Mamanutha-i-Thake Group is Fiji see Mamanuca-i-Cake Group
80 D1 Mamaranui North I. N.Z.
235 E2 Mamaroneck NY U.S.A.
93 A3 Mamasa Sulawesi Selatan Indon.
254 D5 Mambai Brazil
92 C4 Mambajao Phil.
208 C4 Mambéré r. C.A.R.
208 B3 Mambéré-Kadéï pref. C.A.R.
208 C4 Mambili r. Congo
206 B4 Mambolo Sierra Leone
256 A6 Mamborê Brazil
183 G3 Mambrilla de Castejón Spain
92 B3 Mamburao Phil.
129 F2 Mamedkala Rus. Fed.
215 G1 Mamelodi S. Africa
159 G3 Mamers France
207 H5 Mamfé Cameroon
250 E5 Mamirauá, Reserve de Desenvolvimento Sustentável nature res. Brazil
160 E1 Mamirolle France
121 G1 Mamlyutka Kazakh.
173 F3 Mammendorf Ger.
173 G3 Mamming Ger.
195 F4 Mammola Italy
241 L5 Mammoth AZ U.S.A.
240 H3 Mammoth Lakes CA U.S.A.
192 B4 Mamoiada Sardegna Italy
192 B4 Mamone Sardegna Italy
138 B4 Mamonovo Rus. Fed.
121 J1 Mamontovo Rus. Fed.
234 D3 Mamora NJ U.S.A.
252 D2 Mamoré r. Bol./Brazil
206 B4 Mamou Guinea
217 □3b Mamoudzou Mayotte
Mamoutsou Mayotte see Mamoudzou
213 □J3 Mampikony Madag.
206 E5 Mampong Ghana
214 B5 Mamre S. Africa
175 J1 Mamry, Jezioro l. Pol.
93 A3 Mamuju Sulawesi Selatan Indon.
122 B3 Māmūnīyeh Iran
196 D5 Mamuras Albania
102 J4 Mamurogawa Japan
Mamutzu Mayotte see Mamoudzou
206 D5 Man Côte d'Ivoire
114 B2 Man r. India
232 C6 Man WV U.S.A.
251 H3 Mana Fr. Guiana
177 H3 Maňa Slovakia
240 □B7 Mana HI U.S.A.
250 B5 Manabí prov. Ecuador
250 C3 Manacacias r. Col.
251 F5 Manacapuru Brazil
187 G5 Manacor Spain
216 □1c Manadas São Jorge Azores
93 C2 Manado Sulawesi Utara Indon.
165 D4 Manage Belgium
242 □I6 Managua Nic.
242 □I6 Managua, Lago de l. Nic.
125 G3 Manaḥ Oman
80 E3 Manaia North I. N.Z.
213 □J4 Manakara Madag.
80 E4 Manakau North I. N.Z.
81 D5 Manakau mt. South I. N.Z.
124 C5 Manākhah Yemen
116 D2 Manali Hima. Prad. India
Manama Bahrain see Al Manāmah
114 C4 Manamadurai Tamil Nadu India
213 □J3 Manambaho r. Madag.
213 □J4 Manambondro Madag.
114 C4 Manamelkudi Tamil Nadu India
251 F2 Manamo, Caño r. Venez.
213 □J4 Mananantañana r. Madag.
213 □J4 Mananara r. Madag.
213 □K3 Mananara Avaratra Madag.
83 E3 Manangatang Vic. Austr.
84 D3 Manangoora N.T. Austr.
213 □K4 Mananjary Madag.
206 D4 Manankoro Mali
206 C3 Manantali, Lac de l. Mali
114 C4 Manantavadi Kerala India
78 □6 Manaoba Island Solomon Is
81 A6 Manapouri South I. N.Z.
81 A6 Manapouri, Lake South I. N.Z.
114 C4 Manapparai Tamil Nadu India
213 □J3 Manarantsandry Madag.
183 H1 Mañaria Spain
110 D2 Manas Xinjiang China
117 G4 Manas r. India
142 E1 Månäs Sweden
121 G4 Manas, Gora mt. Uzbek.
116 C4 Manasa Madh. Prad. India
110 D2 Manas He r. China
110 D2 Manas Hu l. China
129 E2 Manaskent Rus. Fed.
117 F3 Manaslu mt. Nepal
235 D2 Manasquan NJ U.S.A.
235 D2 Manasquan r. NJ U.S.A.
232 E5 Manassas VA U.S.A.
Manastir Macedonia see Bitola
177 L6 Mănăştiur Romania
247 □1 Manatí Puerto Rico
247 □1 Manati, Río Grande de r. Puerto Rico
Man-aung Kyun i. Myanmar see Cheduba Island
251 F5 Manaus Brazil
126 C3 Manavgat Turkey
226 C3 Manawa WI U.S.A.
116 C5 Manawar Madh. Prad. India
80 E2 Manawaru North I. N.Z.
80 E4 Manawatu r. North I. N.Z.
80 E3 Manawatu-Wanganui admin. reg. North I. N.Z.
92 C5 Manay Phil.
117 F5 Manbazar W. Bengal India
128 C1 Manbij Syria
149 J4 Manby Lincolnshire, England U.K.
226 E3 Mancelona MI U.S.A.
183 E4 Mancera de Abajo Spain
114 B2 Manchar Mahar. India
185 G3 Mancha Real Spain
158 E3 Manche dept Basse-Normandie France
246 □ Manchester parish Jamaica
149 G4 Manchester Greater Manchester, England U.K.
233 G4 Manchester CT U.S.A.
236 F3 Manchester IA U.S.A.
232 B6 Manchester KY U.S.A.
234 B3 Manchester MD U.S.A.
227 E4 Manchester MI U.S.A.
233 H3 Manchester NH U.S.A.
232 B5 Manchester OH U.S.A.
234 B2 Manchester PA U.S.A.
231 C5 Manchester TN U.S.A.
233 G3 Manchester VT U.S.A.
173 F3 Manching Ger.
246 □ Manchioneal Jamaica
184 D2 Manchita Spain
192 D2 Manciano Italy
163 C5 Manciet France
199 E2 Mancınık Dağı mts Turkey
239 E4 Mancos CO U.S.A.
241 M3 Mancos r. CO U.S.A.
122 B4 Mand, Rūd-e r. Iran
208 E2 Manda, Jebel mt. Sudan
213 □J4 Mandabe Madag.
256 A5 Mandaguaçu Brazil
256 B5 Mandaguari Brazil
116 B5 Mandal Gujarat India
116 C4 Mandal Rajasthan India
106 D1 Mandal Mongolia
142 B2 Mandal Norway
91 J7 Mandala, Puncak mt. Indon.
96 B2 Mandalay Myanmar
96 A2 Mandalay admin. div. Myanmar
Mandale Myanmar see Mandalay
Mandale admin. div. Myanmar see Mandalay
116 C4 Mandalgarh Rajasthan India
106 E2 Mandalgovĭ Mongolia
142 B2 Mandalselva r. Norway
107 G3 Mandalt Nei Mongol China
236 C2 Mandan ND U.S.A.
195 E4 Mandanici Sicilia Italy
92 B3 Mandaon Phil.
114 C4 Mandapam Tamil Nadu India
192 B5 Mandas Sardegna Italy
195 F3 Mandatoriccio Italy
116 B5 Mandav Hills Gujarat India
123 H4 Mandawa Rajasthan India
183 H4 Mandayona Spain
160 C2 Mandé, Mont de hill France
Mandeghughusu i. New Georgia Is Solomon Is see Simbo
172 B2 Mandelbachtal-Ormesheim Ger.
161 E5 Mandelieu-la-Napoule France
190 E3 Mandello del Lario Italy
182 B1 Mandeo r. Spain
210 D4 Mandera Kenya
241 K2 Manderfield UT U.S.A.
169 B5 Manderscheid Ger.
160 E1 Mandeure France
246 □ Mandeville Jamaica
81 B6 Mandeville South I. N.Z.
116 B4 Mandha Rajasthan India
Mandhoúdhíon Greece see Mantoudi
116 D3 Mandi Hima. Prad. India
206 D3 Mandiakui Mali
206 C4 Mandiana Guinea
123 H4 Mandi Burewala Pak.
Mandidzuzure Zimbabwe see Chimanimani
213 G3 Mandié Moz.
213 G2 Mandimba Moz.
208 A5 Mandji Gabon
116 E5 Mandla Madh. Prad. India
177 L3 Mándok Hungary
116 C4 Mandor Rajasthan India
86 D3 Mandora W.A. Austr.
84 B2 Mandorah N.T. Austr.
213 □J3 Mandoro Madag.
207 F4 Mandouri Togo
198 C2 Mandra Greece
213 □J5 Mandrare r. Madag.
Mandrenska r. Bulg. see Sredetska Reka
157 F4 Mandres-en-Barrois France
213 □K2 Mandritsara Madag.
213 □J4 Mandrosonoro Madag.
116 C4 Mandsaur Madh. Prad. India
161 C5 Manduel France
87 B7 Mandurah W.A. Austr.
195 G2 Manduria Italy
116 B5 Mandvi Gujarat India
116 C5 Mandvi Gujarat India
114 C3 Mandya Karnataka India
163 C5 Mane Midi-Pyrénées France
161 D5 Mane Provence-Alpes-Côte-d'Azur France
142 C2 Måne r. Norway
151 H2 Manea Cambridgeshire, England U.K.
169 F5 Manebach Ger.
116 B5 Manekwara Gujarat India
122 D2 Maneli Iran
116 E5 Manendragarh Madh. Prad. India
117 F4 Maner Bihar India
114 C2 Maner r. India
190 F3 Manerbio Italy
183 I2 Mañeru Spain
122 A3 Manesht Kūh mt. Iran
197 G3 Măneşti Romania
176 C2 Manětín Czech Rep.
136 C2 Manevychi Ukr.
203 F3 Manfalût Egypt
193 H3 Manfredonia Italy
193 I3 Manfredonia, Golfo di g. Italy
254 E5 Manga Brazil
206 E4 Manga Burkina
254 D4 Mangabeiras, Serra das hills Brazil
209 C6 Mangai Dem. Rep. Congo
81 □2 Mangaia i. Cook Is
80 E3 Mangakino North I. N.Z.
114 D2 Mangalagiri Andhra Prad. India
117 H4 Mangaldai Assam India
197 I4 Mangalia Romania
202 C6 Mangalmé Chad
114 B3 Mangalore Karnataka India
114 B2 Mangalvedha Mahar. India
81 D5 Mangamaunu South I. N.Z.
80 E3 Mangamingi North I. N.Z.
80 D1 Mangamuka North I. N.Z.
182 E3 Manganeses de la Lampreana Spain
182 E2 Manganeses de la Polvorosa Spain
80 D1 Manganui r. North I. N.Z.
114 B2 Mangaon Mahar. India
114 D2 Mangapet Andhra Prad. India
80 D4 Mangarakau South I. N.Z.
257 E5 Mangaratiba Brazil
79 □3 Mangareva i. Arch. des Tuamotu Fr. Polynesia
Mangareva Islands Arch. des Tuamotu Fr. Polynesia see Gambier, Îles
80 E4 Mangatainoka North I. N.Z.
80 E2 Mangatawhiri North I. N.Z.
215 F3 Mangaung S. Africa
116 E4 Mangawan Madh. Prad. India
80 E3 Mangaweka North I. N.Z.
80 F3 Mangaweka mt. North I. N.Z.
80 E2 Mangawhai North I. N.Z.
Mangde Chhu r. Bhutan see Trongsa Chhu
Ma'ngê Gansu China see Luqu
Mangea i. Cook Is see Mangaia
141 I3 Manger Norway
147 B5 Mangerton Mountain hill Rep. of Ireland
173 G4 Mangfall r. Ger.
173 F4 Mangfallgebirge mts Ger.
95 E3 Manggar Indon.
Mangghyshlaq Kazakh. see Mangistau
Mangghystaū Kazakh. see Mangistau
Mangghystaū Oblysy admin. div. Kazakh. see Mangistauskaya Oblast'
Mangghyt Uzbek. see Mangit
Manghit Uzbek. see Mangit
157 F3 Mangiennes France
120 B4 Mangistau Kazakh.
120 B3 Mangistau, Gory hills Kazakh.
120 C4 Mangistauskaya Oblast' admin. div. Kazakh.
120 E4 Mangit Uzbek.
95 F3 Mangkutup r. Indon.
129 D3 Manglisi Georgia
111 E4 Mangnai Qinghai China
211 B8 Mangochi Malawi
206 D4 Mangodara Burkina
213 □I4 Mangoky r. Toliara Madag.
213 □J4 Mangoky r. Toliara Madag.

93 C3 **Mangole** i. Indon.
114 B2 **Mangoli** Karnataka India
213 □I4 **Mangolovolo** Madag.
80 D1 **Mangonui** North I. N.Z.
213 □K3 **Mangoro** r. Madag.
150 E3 **Mangotsfield** South Gloucestershire, England U.K.
Mangqystaū Shyghanaghy b. Kazakh. see Mangyshlakskiy Zaliv
Mangra Qinghai China see Guinan
116 B5 **Mangral** Gujarat India
116 D4 **Mangrol** Rajasthan India
231 E7 **Mangrove Cay** i. Bahamas
116 D5 **Mangrul** Mahar. India
Mangshi Yunnan China see **Luxi**
182 C4 **Mangualde** Port.
258 G4 **Mangueira, Lago** l. Brazil
255 B8 **Mangueirinha** Brazil
205 H5 **Manguéni, Plateau du** Niger
100 B2 **Mangui** Nei Mongol China
Mangula Zimbabwe see Mhangura
242 □I6 **Mangulile** Hond.
237 D5 **Mangum** OK U.S.A.
254 D2 **Mangunça, Ilha** i. Brazil
107 G1 **Mangut** Rus. Fed.
Mangyshlak Kazakh. see Mangistau
120 B3 **Mangyshlak, Poluostrov** pen. Kazakh.
Mangyshlak Oblast admin. div. Kazakh. see Mangistauskaya Oblast'
Mangyshlakskaya Oblast' admin. div. Kazakh. see Mangistauskaya Oblast'
120 B3 **Mangyshlakskiy Zaliv** b. Kazakh.
Manhan Mongolia see **Tögrög**
179 G2 **Manhartsberg** hill Austria
236 D4 **Manhattan** KS U.S.A.
240 H5 **Manhattan Beach** CA U.S.A.
165 E4 **Manhay** Belgium
234 B2 **Manheim** PA U.S.A.
213 G5 **Manhica** Moz.
257 F4 **Manhuaçu** Brazil
257 G3 **Manhuaçu** r. Brazil
157 F3 **Manhuelles** France
257 G4 **Manhumirim** Brazil
250 C3 **Mani** Col.
198 C3 **Mani** pen. Greece
207 G3 **Mani** Nigeria
213 □J3 **Mania** r. Madag.
194 D5 **Maniace** Sicilia Italy
191 H2 **Maniago** Italy
198 B1 **Maniakoi** Greece
213 G3 **Manica** Moz.
213 G3 **Manica** prov. Moz.
213 G3 **Manicaland** prov. Zimbabwe
251 F6 **Manicoré** Brazil
251 F6 **Manicoré** r. Brazil
225 G3 **Manicouagan** Que. Can.
225 G3 **Manicouagan** r. Que. Can.
225 G3 **Manicouagan, Réservoir** resr Que. Can.
225 G3 **Manic Trois, Réservoir** resr Que. Can.
208 E5 **Maniema** admin. reg. Dem. Rep. Congo
125 E2 **Manīfah** Saudi Arabia
108 A2 **Maniganggo** Sichuan China
223 L5 **Manigotagan** Man. Can.
117 F4 **Manihari** Bihar India
79 □3 **Manihi** atoll Arch. des Tuamotu Fr. Polynesia
81 □2 **Manihiki** atoll Cook Is
221 M3 **Maniitsoq** Greenland
123 F5 **Maniji** r. Pak.
117 H5 **Manikchhari** Bangl.
117 G5 **Manikganj** Bangl.
Manikgarh Mahar. India see Rajura
116 E4 **Manikpur** Uttar Prad. India
92 B3 **Manila** Phil.
238 E3 **Manila** UT U.S.A.
92 B3 **Manila Bay** Phil.
83 G3 **Manildra** N.S.W. Austr.
83 G2 **Manilla** N.S.W. Austr.
185 E4 **Manilva** Spain
131 R3 **Manily** Rus. Fed.
84 C2 **Maningrida** N.T. Austr.
Manipur Manipur India see Imphal
117 H4 **Manipur** state India
96 A2 **Manipur** r. India/Myanmar
199 E2 **Manisa** Turkey
199 F2 **Manisa** prov. Turkey
187 C5 **Manises** Spain
254 B4 **Manissauá Missu** r. Brazil
226 D3 **Manistee** MI U.S.A.
226 D3 **Manistee** r. MI U.S.A.
226 D3 **Manistique** MI U.S.A.
223 L4 **Manitoba** prov. Can.
223 L5 **Manitoba, Lake** Man. Can.
223 L5 **Manitou** Man. Can.
225 H3 **Manitou** r. Que. Can.
232 E3 **Manitou Beach** NY U.S.A.
223 M5 **Manitou Falls** Ont. Can.
224 D4 **Manitoulin Island** Ont. Can.
224 C3 **Manitouwadge** Ont. Can.
227 G3 **Manitowaning** Ont. Can.
226 C2 **Manitowish Waters** WI U.S.A.
226 D3 **Manitowoc** WI U.S.A.
224 F4 **Maniwaki** Que. Can.
113 □1 **Maniyafushi** i. S. Male Maldives
250 C3 **Manizales** Col.
213 □J4 **Manja** Madag.
213 G5 **Manjacaze** Moz.
213 □J3 **Manjak** Madag.
114 B3 **Manjarabad** Karnataka India
114 C4 **Manjeri** Kerala India
101 C4 **Man Jiang** r. China
122 B2 **Manjil** Iran
87 C7 **Manjimup** W.A. Austr.
207 H5 **Manjo** Cameroon
114 C2 **Manjra** r. India
179 G2 **Mank** Austria
117 G4 **Mankachar** Assam India
Mankanza Dem. Rep. Congo see **Makanza**
236 D4 **Mankato** KS U.S.A.
236 E2 **Mankato** MN U.S.A.
136 F3 **Man'kivka** Ukr.
137 J3 **Man'kivka** Ukr.
136 E3 **Man'kivka** Ukr.
206 D4 **Mankono** Côte d'Ivoire
223 J5 **Mankota** Sask. Can.
160 C1 **Manlay** France
186 F3 **Manlleu** Spain
236 E3 **Manly** IA U.S.A.
116 C5 **Manmad** Mahar. India
84 C2 **Mann** r. N.T. Austr.
78 □3a **Mann** i. Kwajalein Marshall Is
84 B5 **Mann, Mount** N.T. Austr.
94 C4 **Manna** Sumatera Indon.
82 D3 **Mannahill** S.A. Austr.
114 C4 **Mannar** Sri Lanka
114 C4 **Mannar, Gulf of** India/Sri Lanka
114 C4 **Mannargudi** Tamil Nadu India
172 C4 **Männedorf** Switz.
179 H3 **Mannersdorf am Leithagebirge** Austria
179 H3 **Mannersdorf an der Rabnitz** Austria
114 D3 **Manneru** r. India
172 C2 **Mannheim** Ger.
Mannicolo Islands Solomon Is see **Vanikoro Islands**
222 G3 **Manning** Alta Can.
236 C2 **Manning** ND U.S.A.
231 D5 **Manning** SC U.S.A.
78 □6 **Manning Strait** Solomon Is
232 C5 **Mannington** WV U.S.A.
151 I3 **Manningtree** Essex, England U.K.
190 C2 **Männlifluh** mt. Switz.
84 B5 **Mann Ranges** mts S.A. Austr.
233 E3 **Mannsville** NY U.S.A.
192 A4 **Mannu** r. Sardegna Italy
192 A5 **Mannu** r. Sardegna Italy
192 B4 **Mannu** r. Sardegna Italy
192 B5 **Mannu** r. Sardegna Italy
192 A4 **Mannu, Monte** hill Sardegna Italy
223 I4 **Mannville** Alta Can.
206 C5 **Mano** r. Liberia/Sierra Leone
206 B5 **Mano** Sierra Leone
Man-of-War Rocks is HI U.S.A. see **Gardner Pinnacles**
111 B7 **Manoharpur** Rajasthan India
116 D4 **Manohar Thana** Rajasthan India
220 C4 **Manokotak** AK U.S.A.
186 G2 **Manol** r. Spain
197 H2 **Manoleasa** Romania
213 □K3 **Manompana** Madag.
209 E6 **Manono** Dem. Rep. Congo
150 C3 **Manorbier** Pembrokeshire, Wales U.K.
235 E2 **Manorhaven** NY U.S.A.
206 C5 **Mano River** Liberia
235 F2 **Manorville** NY U.S.A.
161 D5 **Manosque** France
174 E1 **Manowo** Pol.
101 C4 **Manp'o** N. Korea
116 C5 **Manpur** Madh. Prad. India
77 I2 **Manra** i. Phoenix Is Kiribati
186 E3 **Manresa** Spain
116 C5 **Mansa** Gujarat India
116 C3 **Mansa** Punjab India
209 F7 **Mansa** Zambia
206 B3 **Mansabá** Guinea-Bissau
206 B3 **Mansa Konko** Gambia
170 F3 **Manschnow** Ger.
123 H3 **Mansehra** Pak.
221 K3 **Mansel Island** Nunavut Can.
140 O2 **Mansel'kya** ridge Fin./Rus. Fed.
171 C4 **Mansfeld** Ger.
83 F4 **Mansfield** Vic. Austr.
149 H4 **Mansfield** Nottinghamshire, England U.K.
237 E5 **Mansfield** AR U.S.A.
237 E5 **Mansfield** LA U.S.A.
233 H3 **Mansfield** MA U.S.A.
232 B4 **Mansfield** OH U.S.A.
232 E4 **Mansfield** PA U.S.A.
233 G2 **Mansfield, Mount** VT U.S.A.
235 F1 **Mansfield Center** CT U.S.A.
149 H4 **Mansfield Woodhouse** Nottinghamshire, England U.K.
254 E4 **Mansidão** Brazil
183 H2 **Mansilla** Spain
183 E2 **Mansilla de las Mulas** Spain
162 C3 **Mansle** France
Manso r. Tocantins Brazil see Mortes, Rio das
192 A2 **Manso** Corse France
206 E5 **Manso-Nkwanta** Ghana
163 C4 **Mansonville** France
182 B4 **Mansores** Port.
150 E4 **Manston** Dorset, England U.K.
127 H5 **Manşūrī** Iran
126 D3 **Mansurlu** Turkey
250 A5 **Manta** Ecuador
92 A4 **Mantalingajan, Mount** Palawan Phil.
252 B3 **Mantaro** r. Peru
240 G3 **Manteca** CA U.S.A.
182 C4 **Manteigas** Port.
173 G2 **Mantel** Ger.
257 G3 **Mantena** Brazil
226 D5 **Manteno** IL U.S.A.
231 F5 **Manteo** NC U.S.A.
165 F5 **Manternach** Lux.
156 B4 **Mantes-la-Jolie** France
156 B4 **Mantes-la-Ville** France
114 C2 **Manthani** Andhra Prad. India
159 G4 **Manthelan** France
241 L2 **Manti** UT U.S.A.
257 D5 **Mantiqueira, Serra da** mts Brazil
160 D1 **Mantoche** France
235 D2 **Mantoloking** NJ U.S.A.
226 E3 **Manton** MI U.S.A.
198 C2 **Mantoudi** Greece
191 F3 **Mantova** Italy
191 F3 **Mantova** prov. Lombardia Italy
141 N3 **Mäntsälä** Fin.
141 N3 **Mänttä** Fin.
246 A2 **Mantua** Cuba
Mantua Italy see **Mantova**
234 C3 **Mantua** NJ U.S.A.
232 C4 **Mantua** OH U.S.A.
85 F5 **Mantuan Downs** Qld Austr.
134 I4 **Manturovo** Kostromskaya Oblast' Rus. Fed.
137 I2 **Manturovo** Kurskaya Oblast' Rus. Fed.
141 N3 **Mäntyharju** Fin.
Manu r. Bol. see **Mapiri**
252 C3 **Manú** r. Peru
81 □2 **Manuae** i. Cook Is
79 □3 **Manuae** atoll Arch. de la Société Fr. Polynesia
78 □2 **Manua Islands** American Samoa
215 G5 **Manubi** S. Africa
187 C5 **Manuel** Spain
254 C4 **Manuel Alves** r. Brazil
261 I4 **Manuel J. Cobo** Arg.
261 G3 **Manuel Ocampo** Arg.
256 B6 **Manuel Ribas** Brazil
259 B9 **Manuel Rodriguez, Isla** i. Chile
252 C2 **Manuel Urbano** Brazil
254 E5 **Manuel Vitorino** Brazil
122 D5 **Manūjān** Iran
92 B4 **Manukan** Phil.
80 E2 **Manukau** North I. N.Z.
80 E2 **Manukau Harbour** North I. N.Z.
147 B3 **Manulla** Rep. of Ireland
252 D2 **Manupari** r. Bol.
252 D2 **Manurimi** r. Bol.
252 D2 **Manuripi** r. Bol.
80 F3 **Manutuke** North I. N.Z.
114 C3 **Manvi** Karnataka India
234 D2 **Manville** NJ U.S.A.
114 C2 **Manwat** Mahar. India
237 E6 **Many** LA U.S.A.
213 F2 **Manyame** r. Moz./Zimbabwe
211 B5 **Manyara, Lake** salt l. Tanz.
199 E1 **Manyas** Turkey
197 F4 **Manyashki Vrŭkh** hill Bulg.
215 F3 **Manyatseng** S. Africa
223 I5 **Manyberries** Alta Can.
137 K4 **Manychskaya** Rus. Fed.
241 M3 **Many Farms** AZ U.S.A.
136 D3 **Manykivtsi** Ukr.
211 B6 **Manyoni** Tanz.
85 G5 **Many Peaks** Qld Austr.
87 C7 **Many Peaks, Mount** hill W.A. Austr.
162 C3 **Manzac-sur-Vern** France
128 A4 **Manzala, Bahra el** lag. Egypt
Manzala, Lake lag. Egypt see Manzala, Bahra el
182 D3 **Manzanal de Arriba** Spain
182 D2 **Manzanal del Puerto** Spain
185 G1 **Manzanares** Spain
183 G4 **Manzanares** r. Spain
183 G4 **Manzanares el Real** Spain
182 C2 **Manzaneda** Spain
182 C2 **Manzaneda, Cabeza de** mt. Spain
183 G2 **Manzanedo** Spain
183 G5 **Manzaneque** Spain
187 C4 **Manzanera** Spain
246 C2 **Manzanillo** Cuba
244 B4 **Manzanillo** Mex.
191 I3 **Manzano** Italy
209 F6 **Manzanza** Dem. Rep. Congo
122 B3 **Manzariyeh** Iran
160 A3 **Manzat** France
107 H1 **Manzhouli** Nei Mongol China
192 E2 **Manziana** Italy
160 C2 **Manziat** France
215 H2 **Manzini** Swaziland
215 H2 **Manzini** admin. dist. Swaziland
Manzovka Rus. Fed. see Sibirtsevo
202 B6 **Mao** Chad
246 E3 **Mao** Dom. Rep.
Maó Spain see **Mahón**
Mao, Nam r. Myanmar see Shweli
108 C3 **Maoba** Guizhou China
108 D2 **Maoba** Hubei China
109 E2 **Maocifan** Hubei China
108 B1 **Mao'ergai** Sichuan China
91 I7 **Maoke, Pegunungan** mts Indon.
215 F2 **Maokeng** S. Africa
101 B4 **Maokui Shan** mt. Liaoning China
106 D4 **Maomao Shan** mt. Gansu China
108 D4 **Maoming** Guangdong China
108 B3 **Maotou Shan** mt. Yunnan China
Maowen Sichuan China see Maoxian
108 B2 **Maoxian** Sichuan China
93 B3 **Mapane** Sulawesi Tengah Indon.
209 E9 **Mapanza** Zambia
243 G6 **Mapastepec** Mex.
215 E4 **Maphodi** S. Africa
91 I8 **Mapi** r. Indon.
250 E3 **Mapiche, Serranía** mts Venez.
242 E3 **Mapimí** Mex.
242 D3 **Mapimí, Bolsón de** des. Mex.
252 C3 **Mapiri** Bol.
252 D2 **Mapiri** r. Bol.
250 C4 **Mapirpán** Col.
80 E3 **Mapiu** North I. N.Z.
236 E3 **Maple** r. IA U.S.A.
226 E4 **Maple** r. MI U.S.A.
236 D2 **Maple** r. ND U.S.A.
236 D2 **Maple** r. ND U.S.A.
223 I5 **Maple Creek** Sask. Can.
241 M5 **Maple Peak** AZ U.S.A.
236 E3 **Mapleton** IA U.S.A.
241 L1 **Mapleton** UT U.S.A.
226 D3 **Maplewood** WI U.S.A.
266 G4 **Mapmakers Seamounts** sea feature N. Pacific Ocean
85 E1 **Mapoon** Qld Austr.
215 F3 **Mapoteng** Lesotho
114 B3 **Mapuca** Goa India
251 G5 **Mapuera** r. Brazil
215 H3 **Mapumulo** S. Africa
213 G5 **Maputo** Moz.
213 G5 **Maputo** prov. Moz.
213 G5 **Maputo** r. Moz./S. Africa
215 F3 **Maputsoe** Lesotho
Maqanshy Kazakh. see Makanchi
Maqat Kazakh. see **Makat**
106 D5 **Maqên** Qinghai China
106 C5 **Maqên Gangri** mt. Qinghai China
128 B5 **Maqla, Jabal al** mt. Saudi Arabia
204 C5 **Maqţeïr** reg. Maur.
108 B1 **Maqu** Gansu China
Ma Qu r. China see **Huang He**
111 D6 **Maquan He** r. Xizang China
183 F4 **Maqueda** Spain
209 B6 **Maquela do Zombo** Angola
259 C6 **Maquinchao** Arg.
236 F3 **Maquoketa** IA U.S.A.
236 F3 **Maquoketa** r. IA U.S.A.
142 C2 **Mår** r. Norway
123 F5 **Mar** r. Pak.
182 B3 **Mar** Port.
257 F5 **Mar, Serra do** mts Brazil
256 C6 **Mar, Serra do** mts Paraná Brazil
257 E5 **Mar, Serra do** mts Rio de Janeiro/São Paulo Brazil
255 C9 **Mar, Serra do** mts Rio Grande do Sul/Santa Catarina Brazil
251 G3 **Mara** Guyana
117 E5 **Mara** Madh. Prad. India
192 A4 **Mara** Sardegna Italy
211 B5 **Mara** admin. reg. Tanz.
246 E5 **Mara** Venez.
251 E5 **Maraã** Brazil
254 C3 **Maraba** Brazil
256 B5 **Marabá Paulista** Brazil
157 F5 **Marac** France
251 I5 **Maracá** r. Brazil
251 F4 **Maracá, Ilha** i. Brazil
251 I4 **Maracá, Ilha de** i. Brazil
256 B5 **Maracaí** Brazil
250 D2 **Maracaibo** Venez.
250 D2 **Maracaibo, Lago de** l. Venez.
Maracaibo, Lake Venez. see Maracaibo, Lago de
253 G5 **Maracaju** Brazil
253 G5 **Maracaju, Serra de** hills Brazil
192 B5 **Maracalagonis** Sardegna Italy
254 D2 **Maracanã** Brazil
251 H5 **Maracanaquará, Planalto** plat. Brazil
Maracanda Uzbek. see Samarkand
254 E5 **Maracás** Brazil
254 E5 **Maracás, Chapada de** hills Brazil
250 E2 **Maracay** Venez.
Maradhoo i. Addu Atoll Maldives see **Maradu**
207 G3 **Maradi** Niger
207 G3 **Maradi** dept Niger
113 □2 **Maradu** i. Addu Atoll Maldives
129 F3 **Maraga** Rus. Fed.
122 A2 **Marāgheh** Iran
254 G4 **Maragogi** Brazil
92 B3 **Maragondon** Phil.
124 D2 **Marah** Saudi Arabia
251 E4 **Marahuaca, Cerro** mt. Venez.
158 D5 **Marais breton** marsh France
236 E4 **Marais des Cygnes** r. KS U.S.A.
254 C2 **Marajó, Baía de** est. Brazil
251 I5 **Marajó, Ilha de** i. Brazil
77 H1 **Marakei** atoll Gilbert Is Kiribati
Maraki atoll Gilbert Is Kiribati see **Marakei**
114 C3 **Marakkanam** Tamil Nadu India
Maralaba i. Vanuatu see **Mere Lava**
210 C4 **Maralal** Kenya
Maralbashi Xinjiang China see Bachu
129 C3 **Maralik** Armenia
82 B2 **Maralinga** S.A. Austr.
Maralwexi Xinjiang China see Bachu
78 □6 **Maramasike** i. Solomon Is
Maramba Zambia see Livingstone
262 U2 **Marambio** research stn Antarctica
197 G2 **Maramureşului, Munţii** mts Romania
123 F4 **Maran** mt. Pak.
122 A3 **Marāna** Iraq
241 L5 **Marana** AZ U.S.A.
183 H3 **Maranchón** Spain
122 A2 **Marand** Iran
Marandellas Zimbabwe see Marondera
191 F4 **Maranello** Italy
157 G3 **Marange-Silvange** France
254 F2 **Maranguape** Brazil
254 C5 **Maranhão** r. Brazil
254 D3 **Maranhão** state Brazil
184 C1 **Maranhão** Port.
184 C1 **Maranhão, Barragem do** resr Port.
191 G4 **Marano** Italy
191 I3 **Marano, Laguna di** lag. Italy
85 G5 **Maranoa** r. Qld Austr.
194 D2 **Marano di Napoli** Italy
250 C6 **Marañón** r. Peru
191 F4 **Marano sul Panaro** Italy
162 B2 **Marans** France
157 E4 **Maranville** France
182 C3 **Marão** mt. Port.
182 B3 **Marão, Serra do** mts Port.
206 D5 **Maraoué** r. Côte d'Ivoire
78 □6 **Marapa** i. Solomon Is
254 D2 **Marapanim** Brazil
81 A6 **Mararoa** r. South I. N.Z.
Maraş Cyprus see **Varosia**
Maraş Turkey see Kahramanmaraş
197 H3 **Mărăşeşti** Romania
197 H3 **Mărașu** Romania
193 H5 **Maratea** Italy
184 B2 **Marateca** Port.
199 E3 **Marathokampos** Voreio Aigaio Greece
224 C3 **Marathon** Ont. Can.
Marathón Greece see Marathonas
231 D7 **Marathon** FL U.S.A.
233 E3 **Marathon** NY U.S.A.
237 C6 **Marathon** TX U.S.A.
226 C3 **Marathon** WI U.S.A.
198 C2 **Marathonas** Greece
251 E5 **Marauiá** r. Brazil
161 B5 **Maraussan** France
202 D1 **Marāwah** Libya
92 C4 **Marawi** Phil.
156 D4 **Maraye-en-Othe** France
129 F3 **Märäzä** Azer.
150 B4 **Marazion** Cornwall, England U.K.
171 E4 **Marbach** Ger.
190 C2 **Marbach** Switz.
172 D3 **Marbach am Neckar** Ger.
185 F4 **Marbella** Spain
185 F4 **Marbella, Ensenada de** b. Spain
86 C4 **Marble Bar** W.A. Austr.
241 L3 **Marble Canyon** AZ U.S.A.
213 F5 **Marble Hall** S. Africa
237 F4 **Marble Hill** MO U.S.A.
160 D2 **Marboz** France
215 H4 **Marburg** S. Africa
Marburg Slovenia see **Maribor**
169 D5 **Marburg an der Lahn** Ger.
177 L4 **Marca** Romania
176 G4 **Marcal** r. Hungary
176 G5 **Marcali** Hungary
176 G4 **Marcaltő** Hungary
191 I4 **Marčana** Croatia
194 B5 **Marcanzotta** r. Sicilia Italy
252 C3 **Marcapata** Peru
191 F3 **Marcaria** Italy
261 G2 **Marcelino Escalada** Arg.
193 E2 **Marcellina** Italy
226 E4 **Marcellus** MI U.S.A.
233 E3 **Marcellus** NY U.S.A.
177 H4 **Marcelová** Slovakia
162 B3 **Marcenais** France
161 A3 **Marcenat** France
179 H2 **March** r. Austria alt. **Morava (Europe)**
151 H2 **March** Cambridgeshire, England U.K.
214 C3 **Marchand** S. Africa
82 D3 **Marchant Hill** hill S.A. Austr.
191 H5 **Marche** admin. reg. Italy
165 E4 **Marche-en-Famenne** Belgium
179 H2 **Marchegg** Austria
185 E3 **Marchena** Spain
250 □ **Marchena, Isla** i. Islas Galápagos Ecuador
156 B5 **Marchenoir** France
163 B4 **Marcheprime** France
156 D2 **Marchiennes** France
260 B4 **Marchihue** Chile
165 E4 **Marchin** Belgium
84 D1 **Marchinbar Island** N.T. Austr.
151 F2 **Marchington** Staffordshire, England U.K.
261 F2 **Mar Chiquita, Lago** l. Arg.
261 I5 **Mar Chiquita, Lago** l. Arg.
179 F2 **Marchtrenk** Austria
150 E1 **Marchwiel** Wrexham, Wales U.K.
137 H2 **Marchykhyna Buda** Ukr.
163 C5 **Marciac** France
192 C2 **Marciana** Italy
192 C2 **Marciana Marina** Italy
193 G3 **Marcianise** Italy
191 G5 **Marciano della Chiana** Italy
138 F3 **Mārciena** Latvia
160 C2 **Marcigny** France
163 D4 **Marcilhac-sur-Célé** France
162 B3 **Marcillac** France
162 E3 **Marcillac-la-Croisille** France
163 E4 **Marcillac-Vallon** France
160 A2 **Marcillat-en-Combraille** France
159 H4 **Marcilly-en-Gault** France
156 C5 **Marcilly-en-Villette** France
156 D4 **Marcilly-le-Hayer** France
156 B4 **Marcilly-sur-Eure** France
175 I6 **Marcinkowice** Pol.
174 E5 **Marciszów** Pol.
156 B2 **Marck** France
157 H4 **Marckolsheim** France
182 B3 **Marco de Canaveses** Port.
156 D2 **Marcoing** France
253 F2 **Marcolino** r. Brazil
191 H3 **Marcòn** Italy
252 B3 **Marcona** Peru
191 H3 **Marco Polo** airport Italy
261 F3 **Marcos Juárez** Arg.
261 H4 **Marcos Paz** Arg.
161 E4 **Marcoux** France
156 D2 **Marcq-en-Barœul** France
233 G2 **Marcy, Mount** NY U.S.A.
129 G3 **Märdäkan** Azer.
123 H3 **Mardan** Pak.
136 E4 **Mardarivka** Ukr.
261 I5 **Mar de Ajó** Arg.
261 I5 **Mar del Plata** Arg.
150 E2 **Marden** Herefordshire, England U.K.
151 H3 **Marden** Kent, England U.K.
156 D3 **Mardeuil** France
86 B4 **Mardie** W.A. Austr.
127 F3 **Mardin** Turkey
140 L2 **Mårdsele** Sweden
140 M2 **Mårdudden** Sweden
106 D2 **Mardzad** Mongolia
160 C3 **Mare** r. France
78 □5 **Maré** i. Î. Loyauté New Caledonia
191 G2 **Marebbe** Italy
191 H4 **Marecchia** r. Italy
186 □ **Mare de Déu del Toro** hill Spain
146 C4 **Maree, Loch** l. Scotland U.K.
85 F3 **Mareeba** Qld Austr.
149 I4 **Mareham le Fen** Lincolnshire, England U.K.
192 C1 **Maremma** reg. Italy
206 C3 **Maréna** Mali
207 G2 **Marendet** Niger
236 E3 **Marengo** IA U.S.A.
226 C4 **Marengo** IL U.S.A.
226 B2 **Marengo** WI U.S.A.
226 C2 **Marenisco** MI U.S.A.
162 A3 **Marennes** France
195 F4 **Marepotamo** r. Italy
151 H4 **Maresfield** East Sussex, England U.K.
86 E2 **Maret Islands** W.A. Austr.
194 B5 **Marettimo** Sicilia Italy
194 B5 **Marettimo, Isola** i. Sicilia Italy
162 C3 **Mareuil** France
159 I5 **Mareuil-sur-Arnon** France
156 E3 **Mareuil-sur-Ay** France
162 A2 **Mareuil-sur-Lay-Dissais** France
139 I3 **Marevo** Rus. Fed.
160 D1 **Marey-sur-Tille** France
239 F6 **Marfa** TX U.S.A.
150 D3 **Margam** Neath Port Talbot, Wales U.K.
Marganets Kazakh. see **Zhezdy**
Marganets Ukr. see **Marhanets'**
Margao Goa India see Madgaon
86 E3 **Margaret** r. W.A. Austr.
86 C4 **Margaret, Mount** hill W.A. Austr.
222 E5 **Margaret Bay** B.C. Can.
87 B7 **Margaret River** W.A. Austr.
233 F3 **Margaretville** NY U.S.A.
251 F2 **Margarita, Isla de** i. Venez.
137 J4 **Margaritovo** Rus. Fed.
215 H4 **Margate** S. Africa
151 I3 **Margate** Kent, England U.K.
235 D3 **Margate City** NJ U.S.A.
197 F2 **Mărgău** Romania
162 B3 **Margaux** France
177 K3 **Margecany** Slovakia
156 E4 **Margerie-Hancourt** France
149 H4 **Margery Hill** hill England U.K.
172 D2 **Margetshöchheim** Ger.
117 H4 **Margherita** Assam India
193 I3 **Margherita di Savoia** Italy
208 F4 **Margherita Peak** Dem. Rep. Congo/Uganda
Marghilon Uzbek. see Margilan
197 F2 **Marghita** Romania
121 G4 **Margilan** Uzbek.
177 L6 **Margina** Romania
197 G2 **Marginea** Romania
156 C3 **Margny-lès-Compiègne** France
123 E4 **Margo, Dasht-i** des. Afgh.
190 C3 **Margone** Italy
174 F3 **Margonin** Pol.
92 B5 **Margosatubig** Phil.
165 E4 **Margraten** Neth.
222 F4 **Marguerite** B.C. Can.
Marguerite, Pic mt. Dem. Rep. Congo/Uganda see Margherita Peak
161 C5 **Marguerittes** France
157 F3 **Margut** France
127 G4 **Marhaj Khalīl** Iraq
151 H2 **Marham** Norfolk, England U.K.
127 F3 **Marhan Dāgh** hill Iraq
137 H4 **Marhanets'** Ukr.
205 E2 **Marhoum** Alg.
252 D1 **Mari** r. Brazil
255 B7 **Maria** r. Brazil
79 □3 **Maria** atoll Arch. des Tuamotu Fr. Polynesia
79 □3 **Maria** atoll Îs Australes Fr. Polynesia
185 H3 **María** Spain
179 G2 **Maria Anzbach** Austria
161 C4 **Mariac** France
252 C5 **María Elena** Chile
142 C3 **Mariager** Denmark
261 H5 **María Ignacia** Arg.
84 C2 **Maria Island** N.T. Austr.
83 G5 **Maria Island** Tas. Austr.
179 G3 **Maria Lankowitz** Austria
182 C4 **Marialva** Port.
85 G4 **Marian** Qld Austr.
257 F4 **Mariana** Brazil
183 H4 **Mariana** Spain
246 B2 **Marianao** Cuba
266 E4 **Mariana Ridge** sea feature N. Pacific Ocean
266 E5 **Mariana Trench** sea feature N. Pacific Ocean
117 H4 **Mariani** Assam India
Mariánica, Cordillera mts Spain see **Morena, Sierra**
237 F5 **Marianna** AR U.S.A.
231 C6 **Marianna** FL U.S.A.
143 F3 **Mariannelund** Sweden
190 E3 **Mariano Comense** Italy
258 F3 **Mariano Loza** Arg.
Mariano Machado Angola see Ganda
194 C5 **Marianopoli** Sicilia Italy
174 D2 **Marianowo** Pol.
176 B2 **Mariánské Lázně** Czech Rep.
179 E3 **Mariapfarr** Austria
250 D4 **Mariapirí, Mesa de** hills Col.
256 B4 **Mariápolis** Brazil
179 F4 **Maria Rain** Austria
238 E2 **Marias** r. MT U.S.A.
244 A3 **Marías, Islas** is Mex.
179 F4 **Maria Saal** Austria
261 G4 **María Teresa** Arg.
80 D1 **Maria van Diemen, Cape** North I. N.Z.
179 F4 **Maria Wörth** Austria
179 G3 **Mariazell** Austria
124 D5 **Ma'rib** Yemen
124 D5 **Ma'rib** governorate Yemen
226 D3 **Maribel** WI U.S.A.
142 D4 **Maribo** Denmark
188 E2 **Maribor** Slovenia
257 F5 **Maricá** Brazil
Marica r. Bulg. see **Maritsa**
247 □1 **Maricao** Puerto Rico
241 K5 **Maricopa** AZ U.S.A.
240 H4 **Maricopa** CA U.S.A.
241 K5 **Maricopa Mountains** AZ U.S.A.
Maricourt Que. Can. see Kangiqsujuaq
208 F3 **Maridi** Sudan
250 E5 **Marié** r. Brazil
262 P1 **Marie Byrd Land** reg. Antarctica
143 G2 **Mariefred** Sweden
247 □2 **Marie-Galante** i. Guadeloupe
141 L3 **Mariehamn** Åland Fin.
Mari El aut. rep. Rus. Fed. see **Mariy El, Respublika**
254 C5 **Mariembero** r. Brazil
165 D4 **Mariembourg** Belgium
Marienbad Czech Rep. see Mariánské Lázně
171 E5 **Marienberg** Ger.
Marienburg Pol. see **Malbork**
168 C2 **Marienhafe** Ger.
169 E3 **Marienhagen** Ger.
169 C4 **Marienheide** Ger.
169 F3 **Mariental** Ger.
212 C5 **Mariental** Namibia
232 D4 **Marienville** PA U.S.A.
Marienwerder Pol. see Kwidzyn
143 E2 **Mariestad** Sweden
224 E1 **Mariet** r. Que. Can.
231 C5 **Marietta** GA U.S.A.
232 C5 **Marietta** OH U.S.A.
237 D5 **Marietta** OK U.S.A.
234 B2 **Marietta** PA U.S.A.
233 G2 **Marieville** Que. Can.
207 G4 **Mariga** r. Nigeria
193 G4 **Marigliano** Italy
192 A2 **Marignana** Corse France
161 D5 **Marignane** France
159 G4 **Marigné-Laillé** France
160 E2 **Marignier** France
158 E2 **Marigny** France
156 D4 **Marigny-le-Châtel** France
160 B1 **Marigny-l'Église** France
247 □2 **Marigot** Dominica
247 G3 **Marigot** St Maarten West Indies
120 E1 **Mariinskoye** Rus. Fed.
138 D4 **Marijampolė** Lith.
215 F1 **Marikand** S. Africa
197 F5 **Marikostinovo** Bulg.
256 C5 **Marília** Brazil
86 C4 **Marillana** W.A. Austr.
256 A6 **Mariluz** Brazil
209 C7 **Marimba** Angola
182 B2 **Marín** Spain
240 G3 **Marina** CA U.S.A.
192 D2 **Marina di Alberese** Italy
195 F3 **Marina di Amendolara** Italy
192 A5 **Marina di Arbus** Sardegna Italy
193 H4 **Marina di Camerota** Italy
192 C2 **Marina di Campo** Italy
192 C1 **Marina di Castagneto Donoratico** Italy
190 F5 **Marina di Cecina** Italy
193 H3 **Marina di Chieuti** Italy
195 F2 **Marina di Ginosa** Italy
195 F4 **Marina di Gioiosa Ionica** Italy
192 C2 **Marina di Grosseto** Italy
195 H3 **Marina di Leuca** Italy
190 F4 **Marina di Massa** Italy
194 C5 **Marina di Palma** Sicilia Italy
195 G2 **Marina di Pulsano** Italy
194 D6 **Marina di Ragusa** Sicilia Italy
191 H4 **Marina di Ravenna** Italy
Mar'ina Gorka Belarus see Mar"ina Horka
138 G5 **Mar"ina Horka** Belarus
185 F3 **Marinaleda** Spain
193 F1 **Marina Palmense** Italy
191 H4 **Marina Romea** Italy
195 F3 **Marina Schiavonea** Italy
92 B3 **Marinduque** i. Phil.
227 F4 **Marine City** MI U.S.A.
194 B5 **Marinella** Sicilia Italy
194 C5 **Marineo** Sicilia Italy
156 B3 **Marines** France
187 C5 **Marines** Spain
226 D3 **Marinette** WI U.S.A.
256 B5 **Maringá** Brazil
208 C4 **Maringa** r. Dem. Rep. Congo
232 B4 **Maringo** OH U.S.A.
213 G3 **Maringué** Moz.
160 B3 **Maringues** France
182 B4 **Marinha das Ondas** Port.
182 B5 **Marinha Grande** Port.
184 B1 **Marinhais** Port.
182 B3 **Marinhas** Port.
191 J3 **Marinići** Croatia
129 C1 **Mar'in Kolodtsy** Rus. Fed.
193 E3 **Marino** Italy
Marino Alejandro Selkirk, Isla i. S. Pacific Ocean see Alejandro Selkirk, Isla
231 C5 **Marion** AL U.S.A.
237 F5 **Marion** AR U.S.A.
235 F1 **Marion** CT U.S.A.
237 F4 **Marion** IL U.S.A.
230 C3 **Marion** IN U.S.A.
236 D4 **Marion** KS U.S.A.
237 F4 **Marion** KY U.S.A.
226 E3 **Marion** MI U.S.A.
231 D5 **Marion** NC U.S.A.
232 B4 **Marion** OH U.S.A.
231 E5 **Marion** SC U.S.A.
232 C6 **Marion** VA U.S.A.
226 C3 **Marion** WI U.S.A.
82 D3 **Marion Bay** S.A. Austr.
84 D4 **Marion Downs** Qld Austr.
85 H3 **Marion Reef** Coral Sea Is Terr. Austr.
193 I3 **Mariotto** Italy
205 H5 **Mariou, Adrar** mt. Alg.
251 H4 **Maripasoula** Fr. Guiana
240 H3 **Mariposa** CA U.S.A.
240 G3 **Mariposa** r. CA U.S.A.
253 E5 **Mariscal Estigarribia** Para.
197 F2 **Mărişel** Romania
197 G2 **Mărişelu** Romania
161 E4 **Maritime Alps** mts France/Italy
Maritime Kray admin. div. Rus. Fed. see **Primorskiy Kray**
Maritsa Bulg. see Simeonovgrad
197 H5 **Maritsa** r. Bulg.
134 J4 **Mari-Turek** Rus. Fed.
137 I4 **Mariupol'** Ukr.
251 F2 **Mariusa, Isla** i. Venez.
127 G4 **Marīvān** Iran
134 J4 **Mariy El, Respublika** aut. rep. Rus. Fed.
Mariyskaya A.S.S.R. aut. rep. Rus. Fed. see Mariy El, Respublika
160 C2 **Marizy** France
183 G5 **Marjaliza** Spain
138 E2 **Märjamaa** Estonia
128 B3 **Marjayoûn** Lebanon
150 E3 **Mark** Somerset, England U.K.
210 E4 **Marka** Somalia
121 K2 **Markakol', Ozero** l. Kazakh.
206 D3 **Markala** Mali
108 A2 **Markam** Xizang China
129 D4 **Mārkān** Iran
114 C3 **Markapur** Andhra Prad. India
143 E3 **Markaryd** Sweden
122 B3 **Markazī** prov. Iran
227 G3 **Markdale** Ont. Can.
172 D4 **Markdorf** Ger.
164 F2 **Markelo** Neth.
213 F4 **Marken** S. Africa
164 E2 **Markermeer** l. Neth.
171 D5 **Markersdorf bei Burgstädt** Ger.
151 F2 **Market Bosworth** Leicestershire, England U.K.
151 G2 **Market Deeping** Lincolnshire, England U.K.
150 E2 **Market Drayton** Shropshire, England U.K.
151 G2 **Market Harborough** Leicestershire, England U.K.
147 E2 **Markethill** Northern Ireland U.K.
151 F3 **Market Lavington** Wiltshire, England U.K.
149 I4 **Market Rasen** Lincolnshire, England U.K.
149 H4 **Market Warsop** Nottinghamshire, England U.K.
149 I4 **Market Weighton** East Riding of Yorkshire, England U.K.
151 F2 **Markfield** Leicestershire, England U.K.
172 D3 **Markgröningen** Ger.
131 M3 **Markha** r. Rus. Fed.
224 E5 **Markham** Ont. Can.
263 K1 **Markham, Mount** Antarctica
121 H4 **Markhamet** Uzbek.
175 J3 **Marki** Pol.
137 J2 **Marki** Rus. Fed.
183 H1 **Markina-Xemein** Spain
146 E5 **Markinch** Fife, Scotland U.K.
171 E3 **Märkisch Buchholz** Ger.
110 B4 **Markit** Xinjiang China
140 M2 **Markitta** Sweden
137 J3 **Markivka** Ukr.
136 E3 **Markivka** r. Ukr.
171 D4 **Markkleeberg** Ger.
240 H2 **Markleeville** CA U.S.A.
232 D5 **Markleysburg** PA U.S.A.
173 G3 **Marklkofen** Ger.
168 E3 **Marklohe** Ger.
164 E2 **Marknesse** Neth.
171 D5 **Markneukirchen** Ger.
177 G4 **Márkó** Hungary
198 C3 **Markopoulo** Greece
208 C3 **Markounda** C.A.R.
179 H5 **Markovac Trojstveni** Croatia
131 S3 **Markovo** Chukotskiy Avtonomnyy Okrug Rus. Fed.
139 M3 **Markovo** Ivanovskaya Oblast' Rus. Fed.
137 H2 **Markovo** Kurskaya Oblast' Rus. Fed.
207 F3 **Markoye** Burkina
171 D4 **Markranstädt** Ger.
120 A2 **Marks** Rus. Fed.
237 F5 **Marks** MS U.S.A.
234 D2 **Marksboro** NJ U.S.A.
151 H3 **Marks Tey** Essex, England U.K.
169 F5 **Markshl** Ger.
237 E6 **Marksville** LA U.S.A.
179 H3 **Markt Allhau** Austria
173 E2 **Marktbergel** Ger.
173 E2 **Markt Berolzheim** Ger.
173 E2 **Markt Bibart** Ger.
173 E2 **Marktbreit** Ger.
173 E2 **Markt Erlbach** Ger.
179 G3 **Markt Hartmannsdorf** Austria
172 D2 **Marktheidenfeld** Ger.
173 F3 **Markt Indersdorf** Ger.
173 G3 **Marktl** Ger.
171 C5 **Marktleugast** Ger.
171 D5 **Marktleuthen** Ger.
173 E4 **Marktoberdorf** Ger.
173 E3 **Marktoffingen** Ger.
222 E5 **Marktosis** B.C. Can.
179 H3 **Markt Piesting** Austria
173 G1 **Marktredwitz** Ger.
173 E4 **Markt Rettenbach** Ger.
171 C5 **Marktrodach** Ger.
179 F2 **Markt St Florian** Austria
179 H3 **Markt St Martin** Austria
173 H4 **Marktschellenberg** Ger.
173 F3 **Markt Schwaben** Ger.
173 E2 **Marktseft** Ger.
173 E3 **Markt Wald** Ger.
175 K4 **Markuszów** Pol.
151 G3 **Markyate** Hertfordshire, England U.K.
169 C4 **Marl** Ger.
82 C1 **Marla** S.A. Austr.
87 C6 **Marlandy Hill** hill W.A. Austr.
234 C3 **Marlboro** NJ U.S.A.
235 D2 **Marlboro** NJ U.S.A.
235 E1 **Marlboro** NY U.S.A.
85 G4 **Marlborough** Qld Austr.
81 D4 **Marlborough** admin. reg. South I. N.Z.
151 F3 **Marlborough** Wiltshire, England U.K.
235 F1 **Marlborough** CT U.S.A.
233 H3 **Marlborough** MA U.S.A.
233 G3 **Marlborough** NH U.S.A.
151 F3 **Marlborough Downs** hills England U.K.
150 D4 **Marldon** Devon, England U.K.
156 D3 **Marle** France
191 G2 **Marlengo** Italy
157 H4 **Marlenheim** France
227 F4 **Marlette** MI U.S.A.
161 C3 **Marlhes** France
160 D2 **Marlieux** France
237 D6 **Marlin** TX U.S.A.
232 C5 **Marlinton** WV U.S.A.
171 C5 **Marlishausen** Ger.
83 G4 **Marlo** Vic. Austr.
170 D1 **Marlow** Ger.
151 G3 **Marlow** Buckinghamshire, England U.K.
234 D3 **Marlton** NJ U.S.A.
157 G3 **Marly** Lorraine France
156 D2 **Marly** Nord - Pas-de-Calais France
190 C2 **Marly** Switz.
156 C3 **Marly-la-Ville** France
114 B3 **Marmagao** Goa India
160 C2 **Marmagne** Bourgogne France
159 I4 **Marmagne** Centre France
163 C4 **Marmande** France
199 E1 **Marmara** Turkey
Marmara, Sea of g. Turkey see Marmara Denizi
199 E1 **Marmara Adası** i. Turkey
199 F1 **Marmara Denizi** g. Turkey
199 E1 **Marmaraereğlisi** Turkey
202 E2 **Marmarica** reg. Libya
199 F3 **Marmaris** Turkey
199 E2 **Marmaro** Voreio Aigaio Greece
236 C2 **Marmarth** ND U.S.A.
184 C2 **Marmelar** Port.
184 B1 **Marmeleira** Port.
184 B3 **Marmelete** Port.
251 F6 **Marmelos** r. Brazil
232 C5 **Marmet** WV U.S.A.
87 D6 **Marmion, Lake** salt l. W.A. Austr.
191 F3 **Marmirolo** Italy
191 G2 **Marmolada** mt. Italy
185 F2 **Marmolejo** Spain
190 C3 **Marmore** r. Italy
157 H4 **Marmoutier** France
160 D1 **Marnay** France
160 E2 **Marnaz** France
156 E3 **Marne** dept Champagne-Ardenne France
156 C4 **Marne** r. France
168 E2 **Marne** Ger.
157 F5 **Marne, Source de la** tourist site France
156 C4 **Marne-la-Vallée** France
129 D3 **Marneuli** Georgia
172 C2 **Marnheim** Ger.
150 E4 **Marnhull** Dorset, England U.K.
170 C2 **Marnitz** Ger.
83 E4 **Marnoo** Vic. Austr.
208 C2 **Maro** Chad
213 □K2 **Maroambihy** Madag.
213 □K2 **Maroantsetra** Madag.
257 H2 **Maroba** r. Brazil
194 D5 **Maroglio** r. Sicilia Italy
79 □3 **Marokau** atoll Arch. des Tuamotu Fr. Polynesia
80 E3 **Marokopa** North I. N.Z.
116 D2 **Marol** Jammu and Kashmir
213 □K4 **Marolambo** Madag.
169 F5 **Maroldsweisach** Ger.
159 G3 **Marolles-les-Braults** France
156 B3 **Maromme** France
213 □K2 **Maromokotro** mt. Madag.
213 F3 **Marondera** Zimbabwe
251 H3 **Maroni** r. Fr. Guiana
162 D3 **Maronne** r. France
85 H5 **Maroochydore** Qld Austr.
87 B4 **Maroonah** W.A. Austr.
239 F4 **Maroon Peak** CO U.S.A.
246 □ **Maroon Town** Jamaica
93 A4 **Maros** Sulawesi Selatan Indon.
93 A4 **Maros** r. Indon.
196 E2 **Maros** r. Romania
177 J5 **Maros-Körös Köze** plain Hungary
177 J5 **Maroslele** Hungary
191 G3 **Marostica** Italy
Marosvásárhely Romania see **Târgu Mureş**
79 □3 **Marotiri** is Îs Australes Fr. Polynesia
213 □K2 **Marotolana** Madag.
207 I4 **Maroua** Cameroon
158 D3 **Maroué** France
213 □J5 **Marovato** Madag.
213 □J3 **Marovoay** Mahajanga Madag.
213 □K3 **Marovoay** Toamasina Madag.
251 H3 **Marowijne** r. Suriname
172 B2 **Marpingen** Ger.
149 G4 **Marple** Greater Manchester, England U.K.
127 F4 **Marqādah** Syria
Marqaköl l. Kazakh. see Markakol', **Ozero**
108 B1 **Mar Qu** r. Sichuan China
215 F3 **Marquard** S. Africa
173 G4 **Marquartstein** Ger.
245 E5 **Marquelia** Mex.
Marquesas Islands Fr. Polynesia see Marquises, Îles
257 F5 **Marquês de Valença** Brazil
226 D2 **Marquette** MI U.S.A.
237 D6 **Marquez** TX U.S.A.
156 D2 **Marquion** France
156 B2 **Marquise** France
79 □3 **Marquises, Îles** is Fr. Polynesia
163 E6 **Marquixanes** France
83 E2 **Marra** N.S.W. Austr.
83 F2 **Marra** r. N.S.W. Austr.
202 E6 **Marra, Jebel** mt. Sudan
213 G5 **Marracuene** Moz.
191 G4 **Marradi** Italy
204 D3 **Marrakech** Morocco
Marrakesh Morocco see Marrakech
202 E6 **Marra Plateau** Sudan
83 F5 **Marrawah** Tas. Austr.
82 D2 **Marree** S.A. Austr.
237 F6 **Marrero** LA U.S.A.
213 G3 **Marromeu** Moz.
192 A5 **Marrubiu** Sardegna Italy
164 E1 **Marrum** Neth.
211 C8 **Marrupa** Moz.
82 C1 **Marryat** S.A. Austr.
161 A3 **Mars** r. France
232 C4 **Mars** PA U.S.A.
203 G3 **Marsa Alam** Egypt
202 C2 **Marsa al Burayqah** Libya
210 C4 **Marsabit** Kenya
160 B3 **Marsac-en-Livradois** France
158 E4 **Marsac-sur-Don** France
190 E4 **Marsaglia** Italy
157 G4 **Marsal** France
194 B5 **Marsala** Sicilia Italy
202 E2 **Marsa Matrûh** Egypt
160 C1 **Marsannay-la-Côte** France
161 C4 **Marsanne** France
206 B3 **Marsassoum** Senegal
195 □ **Marsaxlokk** Malta
169 D4 **Marsberg** Ger.
168 F2 **Marschacht** Ger.
193 E2 **Marsciano** Italy
83 F3 **Marsden** N.S.W. Austr.
223 I4 **Marsden** Sask. Can.
149 H4 **Marsden** West Yorkshire, England U.K.
164 D2 **Marsdiep** sea chan. Neth.
161 B5 **Marseillan** France
161 D5 **Marseille** France
Marseille airport France see **Provence**
156 B3 **Marseille-en-Beauvaisis** France
Marseilles France see Marseille
226 C5 **Marseilles** IL U.S.A.
140 K2 **Marsfjället** mt. Sweden
128 B5 **Marshah, Jabal** mt. Saudi Arabia
223 I4 **Marshall** Sask. Can.
237 E5 **Marshall** AR U.S.A.
230 C4 **Marshall** IL U.S.A.
226 E4 **Marshall** MI U.S.A.
236 E2 **Marshall** MN U.S.A.
236 E4 **Marshall** MO U.S.A.
231 D5 **Marshall** NC U.S.A.
237 E5 **Marshall** TX U.S.A.
232 E5 **Marshall** VA U.S.A.
266 F5 **Marshall Islands** country N. Pacific Ocean
234 C1 **Marshalls Creek** PA U.S.A.
234 C3 **Marshallton** DE U.S.A.
236 E3 **Marshalltown** IA U.S.A.
150 E3 **Marshfield** South Gloucestershire, England U.K.
237 E4 **Marshfield** MO U.S.A.
226 B3 **Marshfield** WI U.S.A.
231 E7 **Marsh Harbour** Bahamas
233 □J1 **Mars Hill** ME U.S.A.
222 C2 **Marsh Lake** Y.T. Can.
122 B2 **Marshūn** Iran
161 C5 **Marsillargues** France
238 C3 **Marsing** ID U.S.A.
149 H3 **Marske-by-the-Sea** Redcar and Cleveland, England U.K.
157 F3 **Mars-la-Tour** France
156 E4 **Marson** France
163 E5 **Marssac-sur-Tarn** France
143 G2 **Märsta** Sweden
142 D4 **Marstal** Denmark
190 E1 **Märstetten** Switz.
151 F3 **Marston** Oxfordshire, England U.K.
150 E4 **Marston Magna** Somerset, England U.K.
151 G2 **Marston Moretaine** Bedfordshire, England U.K.

78 □3a Marsugalt i. Kwajalein Marshall Is
117 F4 Marsyangdi r. Nepal
234 C4 Marsyhope r. MD U.S.A.
192 D2 Marta Italy
192 D2 Marta r. Italy
96 B3 Martaban Myanmar
96 B3 Martaban, Gulf of Myanmar
195 H2 Martano Italy
193 E2 Martano, Monte mt. Italy
95 F3 Martapura Kalimantan Selatan Indon.
94 D4 Martapura Sumatera Indon.
207 I3 Marte Nigeria
162 D4 Martel France
232 B4 Martel OH U.S.A.
162 D4 Martel, Causse de hills France
165 E5 Martelange Belgium
191 H3 Martellago Italy
191 F2 Martello Italy
177 J5 Mártély Hungary
224 E4 Marten River Ont. Can.
223 J4 Martensville Sask. Can.
187 C5 Martés mt. Spain
168 E3 Martfeld Ger.
177 J4 Martfű Hungary
151 I2 Martham Norfolk, England U.K.
233 H4 Martha's Vineyard i. MA U.S.A.
162 C3 Marthon France
246 C2 Martí Cuba
182 D4 Martiago Spain
191 I2 Martignacco Italy
163 B4 Martignas-sur-Jalles France
159 F4 Martigné-Briand France
158 E4 Martigné-Ferchaud France
159 F3 Martigné-sur-Mayenne France
190 C2 Martigny Switz.
160 C2 Martigny-le-Comte France
157 F4 Martigny-les-Bains France
157 F4 Martigny-les-Gerbonvaux France
183 F4 Martiherrero Spain
185 E5 Martil Morocco
163 B4 Martillac France
184 C3 Martim Longo Port.
182 E1 Martimporra Spain
Martim Vaz, Ilhas is S. Atlantic Ocean see Martin Vas, Ilhas
222 F2 Martin r. N.W.T. Can.
177 H2 Martin Slovakia
186 C3 Martín r. Spain
236 C3 Martin SD U.S.A.
195 G2 Martina Franca Italy
81 E4 Martinborough North I. N.Z.
182 B5 Martinchel Port.
185 F3 Martín de la Jara Spain
182 D4 Martín de Yeltes Spain
190 E3 Martinengo Italy
186 E2 Martinet Spain
245 F3 Martínez Mex.
240 F2 Martinez CA U.S.A.
231 D5 Martinez GA U.S.A.
241 J5 Martinez Lake AZ U.S.A.
169 F4 Martinfeld Ger.
182 B5 Martingança Port.
257 E3 Martinho Campos Brazil
247 □3 Martinique terr. West Indies
247 □2 Martinique Passage Dominica/Martinique
183 F3 Martín Muñoz de las Posadas Spain
198 C2 Martino Greece
256 B5 Martinópolis Brazil
262 Q2 Martin Peninsula Antarctica
179 G2 Martinsberg Austria
232 B4 Martinsburg OH U.S.A.
232 D4 Martinsburg PA U.S.A.
232 E5 Martinsburg WV U.S.A.
234 C2 Martins Creek PA U.S.A.
234 C1 Martins Creek r. PA U.S.A.
232 C4 Martins Ferry OH U.S.A.
193 F2 Martinsicuro Italy
147 C4 Martinstown Rep. of Ireland
230 C4 Martinsville IN U.S.A.
232 D6 Martinsville VA U.S.A.
264 H7 Martin Vas, Ilhas is S. Atlantic Ocean
Martin Vaz Islands S. Atlantic Ocean see Martin Vas, Ilhas
192 A4 Martis Sardegna Italy
159 H5 Martizay France
151 I2 Martlesham Suffolk, England U.K.
150 E2 Martley Worcestershire, England U.K.
150 E4 Martock Somerset, England U.K.
Martök Kazakh. see Martuk
80 E4 Marton North I. N.Z.
177 H4 Martonvásar Hungary
186 E3 Martorell Spain
185 G3 Martos Spain
163 D5 Martres-Tolosane France
141 M3 Marttila Fin.
120 D2 Martuk Kazakh.
129 D3 Martuni Armenia
129 C2 Martvili Georgia
137 G2 Martynivka Ukr.
136 E2 Martynovychi Ukr.
207 G3 Maru Nigeria
103 F6 Marugame Japan
183 F4 Marugán Spain
195 G2 Maruggio Italy
81 D4 Maruia r. South I. N.Z.
254 F4 Maruim Brazil
105 E2 Maruko Japan
83 G3 Marulan N.S.W. Austr.
261 F2 Marull Arg.
164 F1 Marum Neth.
78 □5 Marum, Mount vol. Vanuatu
122 B4 Mārūn r. Iran
104 C2 Maruoka Japan
175 J4 Maruszów Pol.
175 J5 Maruszów Pol.
79 □3 Marutea atoll Arch. des Tuamotu Fr. Polynesia
79 □3 Marutea atoll Arch. des Tuamotu Fr. Polynesia
104 A3 Maruyama-gawa r. Japan
184 C1 Marvão Port.
122 C4 Marvast Iran
122 C4 Marv Dasht Iran
161 B4 Marvejols France
87 C6 Marvel Loch W.A. Austr.
157 F3 Marville France
241 L2 Marvine, Mount UT U.S.A.
116 C4 Marwar Junction Rajasthan India
223 I4 Marwayne Alta Can.
173 E3 Marxheim Ger.
Marxwalde Ger. see Neuhardenberg
172 C3 Marxzell Ger.
84 B2 Mary r. N.T. Austr.
85 H5 Mary r. Qld Austr.
86 E3 Mary r. W.A. Austr.
123 E2 Mary Turkm.
175 M5 Mar"yanivka Ukr.
137 I4 Mar"yanivka Ukr.
136 D2 Mar"yanivka Ukr.
137 J5 Mar'yanskaya Rus. Fed.
Mary A.S.S.R. aut. rep. Rus. Fed. see Mariy El, Respublika
146 D4 Marybank Highland, Scotland U.K.
85 H5 Maryborough Qld Austr.
83 E4 Maryborough Vic. Austr.
214 D3 Marydale S. Africa
234 C3 Marydel MD U.S.A.
120 B1 Mar'yevka Rus. Fed.
146 □G1 Maryfield Shetland, Scotland U.K.
137 I4 Mar"yinka Ukr.
Maryino Rus. Fed. see Pristen'
137 H4 Mar"yivka Ukr.
146 F5 Marykirk Aberdeenshire, Scotland U.K.
234 B4 Maryland state U.S.A.
234 B3 Maryland Line MD U.S.A.
Mary Oblast admin. div. Turkm. see Maryyskaya Oblast'
146 E4 Marypark Moray, Scotland U.K.
149 F3 Maryport Cumbria, England U.K.
225 K2 Mary's Harbour Nfld. Can.
225 K4 Marystown Nfld. Can.
241 K2 Marysvale UT U.S.A.
83 F4 Marysville Vic. Austr.
225 H4 Marysville N.B. Can.
240 G2 Marysville CA U.S.A.
236 D4 Marysville KS U.S.A.
227 F4 Marysville MI U.S.A.
232 B4 Marysville OH U.S.A.
234 B2 Marysville PA U.S.A.
238 B1 Marysville WA U.S.A.
84 C5 Maryvale N.T. Austr.
85 F3 Maryvale Qld Austr.
236 E3 Maryville MO U.S.A.
231 D5 Maryville TN U.S.A.
146 F4 Marywell Aberdeenshire, Scotland U.K.
122 E2 Maryyskaya Oblast' admin. div. Turkm.
191 G4 Marzabotto Italy
256 C2 Marzagão Brazil
171 D3 Marzahna Ger.
171 D3 Marzahne Ger.
195 E6 Marzamemi Sicilia Italy
158 D4 Marzan France
191 G4 Marzeno r. Italy
173 F3 Marzling Ger.
160 B2 Marzy France
183 G2 Masa Spain
242 □I7 Masachapa Nic.
128 B4 Masada tourist site Israel
Más Afuera i. S. Pacific Ocean see Alejandro Selkirk, Isla
122 C4 Masāhūn, Kūh-e mt. Iran
211 B5 Masai Mara National Reserve nature res. Kenya
192 A5 Masainas Sardegna Italy
211 C6 Masai Steppe plain Tanz.
210 A5 Masaka Uganda
215 F4 Masakhane S. Africa
187 C5 Masalavés Spain
129 F4 Masallı Azer.
93 B3 Masamba Sulawesi Selatan Indon.
93 B3 Masamba mt. Indon.
101 D6 Masan S. Korea
137 H5 Masandra Ukr.
211 C7 Masasi Tanz.
Más á Tierra i. S. Pacific Ocean see Robinson Crusoe, Isla
253 E4 Masavi Bol.
242 □I7 Masaya Nic.
242 □I6 Masaya, Volcán vol. Nic.
92 B3 Masbate Phil.
92 B3 Masbate i. Phil.
163 E5 Mas-Cabardès France
195 E5 Mascali Sicilia Italy
195 E5 Mascalucia Sicilia Italy
205 F2 Mascara Alg.
183 G5 Mascaraque Spain
265 H6 Mascarene Basin sea feature Indian Ocean
265 H6 Mascarene Plain sea feature Indian Ocean
265 H5 Mascarene Ridge sea feature Indian Ocean
182 C3 Mascarenhas Port.
260 D2 Mascasín, Salina de salt pan Arg.
193 H4 Maschito Italy
163 D4 Masclat France
244 B3 Mascota Mex.
244 B3 Mascota r. Mex.
230 F2 Mascouche Que. Can.
186 C2 Mascún r. Spain
186 D4 Mas de Barberans Spain
186 C4 Mas de las Matas Spain
183 H4 Masegosa Spain
185 H2 Masegoso Spain
183 H4 Masegoso de Tajuña Spain
172 D3 Maselheim Ger.
210 B4 Maseno Kenya
190 D2 Masera Italy
178 D5 Maserada sul Piave Italy
215 F3 Maseru Lesotho
157 G5 Masevaux France
141 I3 Masfjorden Norway
163 D5 Mas-Grenier France
Mashaba Zimbabwe see Mashava
149 H3 Masham North Yorkshire, England U.K.
108 D4 Mashan Guangxi China
213 F4 Mashava Zimbabwe
116 D2 Masherbrum mt. Jammu and Kashmir
137 G1 Masheve Ukr.
122 D2 Mashhad Iran
116 C4 Mashi r. India
122 A2 Mashīrān Iran
137 H3 Mashivka Ukr.
123 E5 Mashket r. Pak.
123 E5 Māshkīd r. Iran
213 F3 Mashonaland Central prov. Zimbabwe
213 F3 Mashonaland East prov. Zimbabwe
213 F3 Mashonaland West prov. Zimbabwe
Mashtagi Azer. see Maştağa
242 C3 Masiáca Mex.
215 F4 Masibambane S. Africa
182 B2 Maside Spain
215 F3 Masilo S. Africa
209 C6 Masi-Manimba Dem. Rep. Congo
210 A4 Masindi Uganda
92 A3 Masinloc Phil.
190 E2 Masino r. Italy
214 D4 Masinyusane S. Africa
Masira, Gulf of Oman see Maşīrah, Khalīj
125 G3 Maşīrah, Jazīrat i. Oman
125 G4 Maşīrah, Khalīj b. Oman
Masira Island Oman see Maşīrah, Jazīrat
129 D3 Masis Armenia
252 B2 Masisea Peru
191 G4 Masi Torello Italy
93 D3 Masiwang r. Maluku Indon.
215 G3 Masjaing S. Africa
122 B4 Masjed Soleymān Iran
147 B3 Mask, Lough l. Rep. of Ireland
128 D1 Maskanah Syria
122 D5 Maskūtān Iran
163 B5 Maslacq France
177 K5 Maşloc Romania
137 I2 Maslova Pristan' Rus. Fed.
137 J2 Maslovka Rus. Fed.
175 H4 Masłowice Pol.
182 C1 Masma r. Spain
125 E5 Masna'ah Yemen
191 G2 Maso r. Italy
213 □K2 Masoala, Tanjona c. Madag.
226 E4 Mason MI U.S.A.
232 A5 Mason OH U.S.A.
237 D6 Mason TX U.S.A.
226 B2 Mason WI U.S.A.
232 B5 Mason WV U.S.A.
87 C5 Mason, Lake salt flat W.A. Austr.
236 E3 Mason City IA U.S.A.
226 C5 Mason City IL U.S.A.
190 D4 Masone Italy
81 D5 Masons Flat South I. N.Z.
232 D5 Masontown PA U.S.A.
232 D5 Masontown WV U.S.A.
Masqaţ Oman see Muscat
125 G3 Masqaţ governorate Oman
190 F4 Massa Italy
233 G3 Massachusetts state U.S.A.
233 H3 Massachusetts Bay MA U.S.A.
190 F5 Massaciuccoli, Lago di l. Italy
241 M1 Massadona CO U.S.A.
190 E4 Massa e Carrara prov. Toscana Italy
191 H4 Massa Fiscaglia Italy
195 G2 Massafra Italy
202 B6 Massaguet Chad
161 B4 Mas-St-Chély France
202 B6 Massakory Chad
191 G4 Massa Lombarda Italy
193 G4 Massa Lubrense Italy
187 C5 Massamagrell Spain
192 C1 Massa Marittimo Italy
193 E2 Massa Martana Italy
208 A5 Massana Gabon
213 G4 Massangena Moz.
209 C7 Massango Angola
213 G2 Massangulo Moz.
235 E2 Massapequa NY U.S.A.
190 F5 Massarosa Italy
163 D6 Massat France
203 H6 Massawa Eritrea
203 H5 Massawa Channel Eritrea
159 H4 Massay France
169 F5 Maßbach Ger.
171 E4 Massen Ger.
233 F2 Massena NY U.S.A.
208 C2 Massenya Chad
162 D3 Masseret France
195 G2 Masseria Risana hill Italy
222 C4 Masset B.C. Can.
163 C5 Masseube France
224 D4 Massey Ont. Can.
234 C3 Massey MD U.S.A.
161 B3 Massiac France
193 F3 Massico, Monte hill Italy
232 B5 Massieville OH U.S.A.
161 B3 Massif Central mts France
206 D4 Massigui Mali
Massilia France see Marseille
232 C4 Massillon OH U.S.A.
190 D4 Massimino Italy
206 D3 Massina Mali
173 G3 Massing Ger.
227 J3 Masson Que. Can.
192 C2 Massoncello, Monte hill Italy
263 G2 Masson Island Antarctica
156 C4 Massy France
129 F3 Maştağa Azer.
169 C5 Mastershausen Ger.
81 E4 Masterton North I. N.Z.
235 F2 Mastic NY U.S.A.
235 F2 Mastic Beach NY U.S.A.
246 C1 Mastic Point Andros Bahamas
144 J1 Mastrevik Norway
123 H2 Mastuj Pak.
123 F4 Mastung Pak.
124 B3 Mastūrah Saudi Arabia
138 E5 Masty Belarus
192 A5 Masua Sardegna Italy
103 E6 Masuda Japan
Masuku Gabon see Franceville
Masulipatam Andhra Prad. India see Machilipatnam
192 A5 Masullas Sardegna Italy
Masuna i. American Samoa see Tutuila
94 C3 Masurai, Bukit mt. Indon.
213 F4 Masvingo Zimbabwe
213 F4 Masvingo prov. Zimbabwe
211 B5 Maswe Tanz.
128 C2 Maşyāf Syria
136 B2 Masyevichy Belarus
174 C3 Maszewo Lubuskie Pol.
174 F1 Maszewo Pomorskie Pol.
174 D2 Maszewo Zachodniopomorskie Pol.
196 D5 Mat r. Albania
96 D3 Mat, Nam r. Laos
80 G2 Mata r. North I. N.Z.
251 E3 Mata, Serranía de mts Venez.
213 E3 Matabeleland North prov. Zimbabwe
213 F4 Matabeleland South prov. Zimbabwe
117 G4 Matabhanga W. Bengal India
183 G3 Matabuena Spain
184 D2 Matachel r. Spain
224 D4 Matachewan Ont. Can.
209 B6 Matadi Dem. Rep. Congo
237 C5 Matador TX U.S.A.
186 F3 Matagalls mt. Spain
242 □I5 Matagalpa Nic.
224 E3 Matagami Que. Can.
224 E3 Matagami, Lac l. Que. Can.
237 D6 Matagorda TX U.S.A.
254 F4 Mata Grande Brazil
80 E3 Matahiwi North I. N.Z.
Mataigou Ningxia China see Taole
80 F2 Matakana Island North I. N.Z.
81 D4 Matakitaki South I. N.Z.
209 B8 Matala Angola
184 D3 Matalascañas Spain
114 D5 Matale Sri Lanka
183 H3 Matalebreras Spain
214 E3 Mataleng S. Africa
124 C2 Maţāli', Jabal hill Saudi Arabia
183 E2 Matallana de Valmadrigal Spain
206 B3 Matam Senegal
183 H3 Matamala de Almazán Spain
80 E2 Matamata North I. N.Z.
214 C1 Mata-Mata S. Africa
80 F4 Matamau North I. N.Z.
207 H3 Matamey Niger
234 D1 Matamoras PA U.S.A.
242 E3 Matamoros Coahuila Mex.
243 F3 Matamoros Tamaulipas Mex.
183 F2 Matamorosa Spain
182 B5 Mata Mourisca Port.
211 C7 Matandu r. Tanz.
225 H3 Matane Que. Can.
213 □J4 Matanga Madag.
80 E2 Matangi North I. N.Z.
246 B2 Matanzas Cuba
256 C4 Matão Brazil
254 C4 Matão, Serra do hills Brazil
174 G5 Mata Panew r. Pol.
183 F2 Mataporquera Spain
183 F3 Matapozuelos Spain
260 A4 Mataquito r. Chile
114 D5 Matara Sri Lanka
198 B2 Mataragka Greece
95 G5 Mataram Lombok Indon.
Mataránga Greece see Mataragka
252 B4 Matarani Peru
84 C2 Mataranka N.T. Austr.
186 F3 Mataró Spain
80 E3 Mataroa North I. N.Z.
93 B3 Matarombea r. Indon.
186 D3 Matarraña r. Spain
196 E4 Mataruška Banja Srbija Yugo.
215 G4 Matatiele S. Africa
116 D4 Matatila Dam India
80 E3 Matau North I. N.Z.
81 B7 Mataura South I. N.Z.
81 B7 Mataura r. South I. N.Z.
77 I3 Matā'utu Wallis and Futuna Is
78 □2 Matavanu, Mount vol. Samoa
80 F3 Matawai North I. N.Z.
80 D1 Matawaia North I. N.Z.
235 D2 Matawan NJ U.S.A.
230 F2 Matawin r. Que. Can.
121 I3 Matay Kazakh.
253 E3 Mategua Bol.
244 D2 Matehuala Mex.
197 G2 Matei Romania
191 I5 Matelica Italy
247 □7 Matelot Trin. and Tob.
211 C7 Matemanga Tanz.
80 E3 Matemateaonga Range hills North I. N.Z.
213 G2 Matenge Moz.
195 F2 Matera Italy
193 I4 Matera prov. Basilicata Italy
193 G3 Matese, Monti del mts Italy
177 L4 Mátészalka Hungary
205 H1 Mateur Tunisia
257 E3 Mateus Leme Brazil
232 B6 Matewan WV U.S.A.
162 B3 Matha France
160 E1 Mathay France
224 D3 Matheson Ont. Can.
233 E6 Mathews VA U.S.A.
190 C3 Mathi Italy
232 D5 Mathias WV U.S.A.
113 □1 Mathidahura i. N. Male Maldives
237 D6 Mathis TX U.S.A.
83 F3 Mathoura N.S.W. Austr.
116 D4 Mathura Uttar Prad. India
92 C5 Mati Phil.
207 F3 Matiacoali Burkina
117 G4 Matiali W. Bengal India
109 E3 Matianxu Hunan China
123 G5 Matiari Pak.
257 F4 Matias Barbosa Brazil
254 E5 Matias Cardoso Brazil
245 G5 Matías Romero Mex.
213 I2 Matibane Moz.
158 D3 Matignon France
156 D3 Matigny France
225 H2 Matimekosh Que. Can.
195 H2 Matino Italy
108 B1 Matizi Sichuan China
214 C5 Matjiesfontein S. Africa
129 C2 Mat'khoji Georgia
117 G5 Matla r. India
123 G5 Matli Pak.
149 H4 Matlock Derbyshire, England U.K.
149 H4 Matlock Bath Derbyshire, England U.K.
215 F2 Matlwangtlwang S. Africa
251 E3 Mato r. Venez.
251 E3 Mato, Cerro mt. Venez.
232 C6 Matoaka WV U.S.A.
213 F4 Matobo Hills Zimbabwe
256 A2 Mato Grosso state Brazil
254 B5 Mato Grosso, Planalto do plat. Brazil
256 A4 Mato Grosso do Sul state Brazil
Matopo Hills Zimbabwe see Matobo Hills
252 D3 Matos r. Bol.
182 B3 Matosinhos Port.
Matou Guangxi China see Pingguo
160 C2 Matour France
257 E3 Matozinhos Brazil
177 I4 Mátra mts Hungary
177 J4 Matraballa Hungary
125 G3 Maţraḩ Oman
177 I3 Mátraterenye Hungary
177 I4 Mátraverebély Hungary
178 C3 Matrei am Brenner Austria
178 D3 Matrei in Osttirol Austria
214 B5 Matroosberg S. Africa
214 B5 Matroosberg mt. S. Africa
215 F1 Matrooster S. Africa
126 B5 Matrûh governorate Egypt
147 E3 Matry Rep. of Ireland
214 D3 Matsap S. Africa
129 A2 Matsesta Rus. Fed.
213 □J4 Matsiatra r. Madag.
104 B4 Matsubara Japan
105 F3 Matsuda Japan
105 F3 Matsudo Japan
103 F6 Matsue Japan
105 D2 Matsumoto Japan
104 C4 Matsusaka Japan
109 G3 Matsu Tao i. Taiwan
103 D7 Matsuura Japan
103 F7 Matsuyama Japan
190 E2 Matt Switz.
224 D3 Mattagami r. Ont. Can.
157 G4 Mattaincourt France
261 E4 Mattaldi Arg.
224 E4 Mattawa Ont. Can.
233 □I2 Mattawamkeag ME U.S.A.
190 C3 Matterhorn mt. Italy/Switz.
238 D3 Matterhorn mt. NV U.S.A.
179 H3 Mattersburg Austria
Matthew atoll Gilbert Is Kiribati see Marakei
77 H4 Matthew Island S. Pacific Ocean
231 D5 Matthews NC U.S.A.
210 C4 Matthews Peak Kenya
246 D2 Matthew Town Gt Inagua Bahamas
125 F3 Maţţī, Sabkhat salt pan Saudi Arabia
178 E2 Mattighofen Austria
193 I3 Mattinata Italy
151 I2 Mattishall Norfolk, England U.K.
235 F2 Mattituck NY U.S.A.
140 K3 Mattmar Sweden
104 C2 Mattō Japan
236 F4 Mattoon IL U.S.A.
178 E3 Mattsee Austria
178 E3 Mattsee l. Austria
141 K3 Mattsmyra Sweden
140 M2 Måttsund Sweden
Matturai Sri Lanka see Matara
252 A2 Matucana Peru
114 D5 Matugama Sri Lanka
79 □1 Matuku i. Fiji
191 J3 Matulji Croatia
209 C8 Matumbo Angola
Matun Afgh. see Khowst
251 F2 Maturín Venez.
183 H3 Matute mt. Spain
257 E3 Matutina Brazil
120 C1 Matveyevka Rus. Fed.
137 J4 Matveyev Kurgan Rus. Fed.
137 F4 Matviyivka Mykolayivs'ka Oblast' Ukr.
137 H4 Matviyivka Zaporiz'ka Oblast' Ukr.
215 F3 Matwabeng S. Africa
137 J1 Matyra r. Rus. Fed.
139 L5 Matyrskiy Rus. Fed.
139 L5 Matyrskoye Vodokhranilishche resr Rus. Fed.
116 D4 Mau Madh. Prad. India
116 E4 Mau Uttar Prad. India
117 E4 Mau Uttar Prad. India
213 H2 Maúa Moz.
116 E4 Mau Aimma Uttar Prad. India
186 D2 Maubermé, Pic de mt. France/Spain
156 E3 Maubert-Fontaine France
156 D2 Maubeuge France
115 G2 Maubin Myanmar
163 C5 Maubourguet France
162 A3 Maubuisson France
146 D6 Mauchline East Ayrshire, Scotland U.K.
146 F4 Maud Aberdeenshire, Scotland U.K.
87 B4 Maud, Point W.A. Austr.
116 E4 Maudaha Uttar Prad. India
83 F3 Maude N.S.W. Austr.
264 J10 Maud Seamount sea feature S. Atlantic Ocean
179 H2 Mauerbach Austria
178 E2 Mauerkirchen Austria
173 F3 Mauern Ger.
173 E4 Mauerstetten Ger.
251 G5 Maués r. Brazil
116 E4 Mauganj Madh. Prad. India
91 K2 Maug Islands N. Mariana Is
161 C5 Mauguio France
240 □C8 Maui i. HI U.S.A.
81 □2 Mauke i. Cook Is
172 C3 Maulbronn Ger.
157 H5 Maulburg Ger.
162 D3 Maulde r. France
151 G2 Maulden Bedfordshire, England U.K.
260 B4 Maule Chile
260 A4 Maule admin. reg. Chile
260 A4 Maule r. Chile
260 B5 Maule, Lago del l. Chile
162 B2 Mauléon France
163 C6 Mauléon-Barousse France
163 B5 Mauléon-d'Armagnac France
163 B5 Mauléon-Licharre France
159 F4 Maulévrier France
259 B6 Maullín Chile
117 G4 Maulvi Bazar Bangl.
147 B2 Maumakeogh hill Rep. of Ireland
80 E2 Maumaupaki hill North I. N.Z.
232 B4 Maumee OH U.S.A.
232 B4 Maumee r. OH U.S.A.
147 B3 Maumturk Mountains hills Rep. of Ireland
212 D3 Maun Botswana
247 □1 Maunabo Puerto Rico
240 □D9 Mauna Kea vol. HI U.S.A.
240 □C8 Mauna Loa HI U.S.A.
240 □D9 Mauna Loa vol. HI U.S.A.
213 E4 Maunatlala Botswana
80 F3 Maungaharuru Range mts North I. N.Z.
80 F3 Maungahaumi mt. North I. N.Z.
80 F3 Maungapohatu mt. North I. N.Z.
80 E3 Maungarau hill North I. N.Z.
80 F3 Maungataniwha mt. North I. N.Z.
80 E1 Maungatapere North I. N.Z.
80 E2 Maungaturoto North I. N.Z.
96 A2 Maungdaw Myanmar
97 B4 Maungmagan Islands Myanmar
79 □3 Maupihaa atoll Arch. de la Société Fr. Polynesia
238 B2 Maupin OR U.S.A.
142 D1 Maura Norway
116 D4 Mau Rampur Uttar Prad. India
116 E4 Maurawan Uttar Prad. India
158 E4 Maure-de-Bretagne France
163 E6 Maureillas-las-Illas France
162 C4 Maurens France
237 F6 Maurepas, Lake LA U.S.A.
161 E5 Maures, Massif des hills France
252 C4 Mauri r. Bol.
163 B4 Mauriac Aquitaine France
162 E3 Mauriac Auvergne France
Maurice country Indian Ocean see Mauritius
234 C3 Maurice r. NJ U.S.A.
82 B2 Maurice, Lake salt flat S.A. Austr.
234 D3 Mauricetown NJ U.S.A.
164 E3 Maurik Neth.
204 C6 Mauritania country Africa
Mauritanie country Africa see Mauritania
217 □1b Mauritius country Indian Ocean
193 G3 Mauro, Monte mt. Italy
158 D3 Mauron France
182 C3 Mauros mt. Spain
163 D4 Mauroux France
163 E4 Maurs France
163 E6 Maury France
234 B2 Mausdale PA U.S.A.
161 C5 Maussanne-les-Alpilles France
226 B4 Mauston WI U.S.A.
179 G2 Mautern an der Donau Austria
179 E3 Mauterndorf Austria
179 F3 Mautern in Steiermark Austria
173 H3 Mauth Ger.
179 F2 Mauthausen Austria
178 E4 Mauthen Austria
Mauti i. Cook Is see Mauke
157 F4 Mauvages France
161 C3 Mauves France
163 C5 Mauvezin France
162 B2 Mauzé-sur-le-Mignon France
251 E4 Mavaca r. Venez.
211 C8 Mavago Moz.
209 C9 Mavengue Angola
199 G3 Mavikent Turkey
209 D8 Mavinga Angola
232 B6 Mavisdale VA U.S.A.
213 G3 Mavita Moz.
193 F2 Mavone r. Italy
198 B1 Mavrodendri Dytiki Makedonia Greece
198 C1 Mavrothalassa Greece
215 F4 Mavuya S. Africa
95 F2 Mawa, Bukit mt. Indon.
124 D3 Māwān, Khashm hill Saudi Arabia
116 D3 Mawana Uttar Prad. India
209 C6 Mawanga Dem. Rep. Congo
109 F3 Mawei Fujian China
81 C5 Mawheraiti South I. N.Z.
Māwheranui r. South I. N.Z. see Grey
124 D5 Māwiyah Yemen
128 B4 Mawjib, Wādī al r. Jordan
96 A2 Mawlaik Myanmar
Mawlamyaing Myanmar see Moulmein
Mawlamyine Myanmar see Moulmein
150 B4 Mawnan Cornwall, England U.K.
117 G4 Mawphlang Meghalaya India
124 C2 Mawqaq Saudi Arabia
203 I6 Mawshij Yemen
263 E2 Mawson research stn Antarctica
263 E2 Mawson Coast Antarctica
263 E2 Mawson Escarpment Antarctica
263 K2 Mawson Peninsula Antarctica
97 B5 Maw Taung mt. Myanmar
124 C5 Mawza Yemen
236 C2 Max ND U.S.A.
234 C2 Maxatawny PA U.S.A.
158 D4 Maxent France
173 G2 Maxhütte-Haidhof Ger.
192 A5 Maxia, Punta mt. Sardegna Italy
182 C5 Maxieira Port.
261 G3 Máximo Paz Arg.
197 H3 Măxineni Romania
213 G4 Maxixe Moz.
140 M3 Maxmo Fin.
169 C5 Maxsain Ger.
233 F2 Maxville Ont. Can.
80 E3 Maxwell North I. N.Z.
85 E4 Maxwelton Qld Austr.
86 D3 May r. W.A. Austr.
146 F5 May, Isle of i. Scotland U.K.
131 O3 Maya r. Rus. Fed.
186 B1 Maya Spain
137 H3 Mayachka Ukr.
135 K5 Mayachnyy Rus. Fed.
246 D2 Mayaguana i. Bahamas
247 □1 Mayagüez Puerto Rico
207 G3 Mayahi Niger
120 C2 Mayak Rus. Fed.
Mayakovskiy Georgia see Baghdat'i
123 G2 Mayakovskogo mt. Tajik.
Mayakovskogo, Pik mt. Tajik. see Mayakovskogo
121 G4 Mayakum Kazakh.
136 E3 Mayaky Ukr.
Mayals Spain see Maials
209 B5 Mayama Congo
122 C2 Mayamey Iran
243 H5 Maya Mountains Belize/Guat.
108 D3 Mayang Hunan China
Mayaqum Kazakh. see Mayakum
146 E5 Mayar hill Scotland U.K.
246 D2 Mayarí Cuba
104 B4 Maya-san hill Japan
102 I4 Maya-san mt. Japan
238 E3 Maybell CO U.S.A.
232 C6 Maybeury WV U.S.A.
146 D6 Maybole South Ayrshire, Scotland U.K.
235 D1 Maybrook NY U.S.A.
210 C1 Maych'ew Eth.
123 G3 Maydā Shahr Afgh.
83 F5 Maydena Tas. Austr.
210 E2 Maydh Somalia
Maydos Turkey see Eceabat
169 C5 Mayen Ger.
159 F3 Mayenne France
159 F3 Mayenne dept Pays de la Loire France
159 F4 Mayenne r. France
241 K4 Mayer AZ U.S.A.
111 D5 Mayêr Kangri mt. Xizang China
237 F5 Mayersville MS U.S.A.
222 H4 Mayerthorpe Alta Can.
159 G4 Mayet France
125 D5 Mayfa'ah Yemen
81 C5 Mayfield South I. N.Z.
149 H4 Mayfield Staffordshire, England U.K.
237 F4 Mayfield KY U.S.A.
234 C1 Mayfield PA U.S.A.
241 L2 Mayfield UT U.S.A.
106 D2 Mayhan Mongolia
239 F5 Mayhill NM U.S.A.
100 D3 Mayi r. China
121 H2 Maykain Kazakh.
123 G2 Maykhura Tajik.
129 B1 Maykop Rus. Fed.
134 K4 Maykor Rus. Fed.
121 H4 Mayluu-Suu Kyrg.
Mayly-Say Kyrg. see Mayluu-Suu
121 K1 Mayma Rus. Fed.
121 G4 Maymak Kazakh.
96 B2 Maymyo Myanmar
98 F1 Mayna Respublika Khakasiya Rus. Fed.
135 I5 Mayna Ul'yanovskaya Oblast' Rus. Fed.
231 D4 Maynardville TN U.S.A.
114 B2 Mayni Mahar. India
227 I3 Maynooth Ont. Can.
147 E3 Maynooth Rep. of Ireland
222 C2 Mayo Y.T. Can.
239 E7 Mayo r. Mex.
252 A1 Mayo r. Peru
147 B3 Mayo Rep. of Ireland
147 B3 Mayo county Rep. of Ireland
231 D6 Mayo FL U.S.A.
234 B4 Mayo MD U.S.A.
207 I4 Mayo Alim Cameroon
207 I4 Mayo-Belwa Nigeria
147 E2 Mayobridge Northern Ireland U.K.
208 B2 Mayo-Kébbi pref. Chad
208 B5 Mayoko Congo
Mayo Landing Y.T. Can. see Mayo
92 B3 Mayon vol. Luzon Phil.
183 H4 Mayor r. Spain
183 I2 Mayor r. Spain
Mayor, Puig mt. Spain see Puig Major
261 F6 Mayor Buratovich Arg.
183 E2 Mayorga Spain
253 E4 Mayor Pablo Lagerenza Para.
217 □3b Mayotte terr. Africa
246 □ May Pen Jamaica
Mayqayyng Kazakh. see Maykain
247 □3 Mayreau i. St Vincent
161 C4 Mayres France
163 D5 Mayreville France
178 C3 Mayrhofen Austria
128 B4 Maysah, Tall al mt. Jordan
127 G5 Maysān governorate Iraq
169 C5 Mayschoß Ger.
175 I1 Mayskaya r. Rus. Fed.
137 I2 Mayskiy Belgorodskaya Oblast' Rus. Fed.
129 D2 Mayskiy Kabardino-Balkarskaya Respublika Rus. Fed.
134 K4 Mayskiy Permskaya Oblast' Rus. Fed.
137 K4 Mayskiy Rostovskaya Oblast' Rus. Fed.
121 I2 Mayskoye Kazakh.
234 D3 Mays Landing NJ U.S.A.
232 B5 Maysville KY U.S.A.
236 E4 Maysville MO U.S.A.
Maytag Xinjiang China see Dushanzi
96 A2 Mayu r. Myanmar
209 A5 Mayumba Gabon
114 C4 Mayuram Tamil Nadu India
227 F4 Mayville MI U.S.A.
236 D2 Mayville ND U.S.A.
232 D3 Mayville NY U.S.A.
236 C3 Maywood NE U.S.A.
131 O3 Mayya Rus. Fed.
261 F5 Maza Arg.
139 K2 Maza Rus. Fed.
209 E8 Mazabuka Zambia
Mazaca Turkey see Kayseri
Mazagan Morocco see El Jadida
251 I5 Mazagão Brazil
184 D3 Mazagón Spain
156 E3 Mazagran France
138 E3 Maza Jugla r. Latvia
186 D3 Mazaleón Spain
163 E5 Mazamet France
244 C4 Mazamitla Mex.
161 D4 Mazan France
250 C5 Mazán Peru
122 B2 Māzandarān prov. Iran
161 C4 Mazan-l'Abbaye France
244 D1 Mazapil Mex.
123 F3 Mazar, Koh-i- mt. Afgh.
194 B5 Mazara, Val di val. Sicilia Italy
194 B5 Mazara del Vallo Sicilia Italy
183 F5 Mazarambroz Spain
123 F2 Mazār-e Sharīf Afgh.
183 H4 Mazarete Spain
194 B5 Mazaro r. Sicilia Italy
187 B7 Mazarrón Spain
187 B7 Mazarrón, Golfo de b. Spain
110 B4 Mazartag mt. Xinjiang China
251 G3 Mazaruni r. Guyana
242 C2 Mazatán Mex.
245 F4 Mazateca, Sierra mts Mex.
243 H6 Mazatenango Guat.
244 A2 Mazatlán Mex.
241 L4 Mazatzal Peak AZ U.S.A.
159 F4 Mazé France
215 G5 Mazeepa Bay S. Africa
104 D3 Maze-gawa r. Japan
138 D3 Mažeikiai Lith.
234 B2 Mazeppa PA U.S.A.
163 D5 Mazères France
163 B5 Mazerolles France
161 C3 Mazet-St-Voy France
163 D4 Mazeyrolles France
129 A4 Mazgirt Turkey
199 E3 Mazı Turkey
138 F3 Mažiča r. Latvia
232 B5 Mazie KY U.S.A.
162 B2 Mazières-en-Gâtine France
216 □3d Mazo La Palma Canary Is
242 C2 Mazocahui Mex.
252 C4 Mazocruz Peru
Mazoe Zimbabwe see Mazowe
226 C4 Mazomanie WI U.S.A.
106 C3 Mazong Shan mt. Gansu China
106 B3 Mazong Shan mts China
213 F3 Mazowe Zimbabwe
213 G3 Mazowe r. Zimbabwe
175 I4 Mazowiecka reg. Pol.
175 J3 Mazowieckie prov. Pol.
138 E3 Mazsalaca Latvia
122 B3 Māzū Iran
175 I2 Mazurskie, Pojezierze reg. Pol.
136 E1 Mazyr Belarus
190 F3 Mazzano Italy
193 E2 Mazzano Romano Italy
194 D5 Mazzarino Sicilia Italy
194 D5 Mazzarrone Sicilia Italy
178 B4 Mazzo di Valtellina Italy
Mba Viti Levu Fiji see Ba
215 H2 Mbabane Swaziland
206 B3 Mbacké Senegal
208 C4 Mbaéré r. C.A.R.
206 B2 Mbagne Maur.
206 D5 Mbahiakro Côte d'Ivoire
208 C4 Mbaïki C.A.R.
211 A7 Mbala Zambia
207 I6 Mbalam Cameroon
210 B4 Mbale Uganda
207 H6 Mbalmayo Cameroon
207 H5 Mbam r. Cameroon
208 C5 Mbandaka Dem. Rep. Congo
207 H5 Mbandjok Cameroon
207 I6 Mbang Cameroon
207 H5 Mbanga Cameroon
78 □6 Mbanika i. Solomon Is
209 B6 M'banza Congo Angola
209 B6 Mbanza-Ngungu Dem. Rep. Congo
206 B3 Mbar Senegal
210 A5 Mbarara Uganda
208 D3 Mbari r. C.A.R.
211 C7 Mbarika Mountains Tanz.
215 I2 Mbaswana S. Africa
208 C4 Mbata C.A.R.
211 A7 Mbati Zambia
Mbatiki i. Fiji see Batiki
78 □6 Mbava i. New Georgia Is Solomon Is
207 I5 Mbé Cameroon
211 C7 Mbemkuru r. Tanz.
Mbengga i. Fiji see Beqa
207 H5 Mbengwi Cameroon
217 □3a Mbéni Njazidja Comoros
213 F4 Mberengwa Zimbabwe
209 F7 Mbereshi Zambia
211 B7 Mbeya Tanz.
211 B7 Mbeya admin. reg. Tanz.
207 I5 Mbi r. Cameroon
208 C3 Mbi r. C.A.R.
208 A5 Mbigou Gabon
196 D4 Mbilqethit, Maja e mt. Albania
208 B5 Mbinda Congo
211 B7 Mbinga Tanz.
207 H6 Mbini Equat. Guinea
207 H6 Mbini r. Equat. Guinea
78 □6 Mbita'ama Malaita Solomon Is
211 A7 Mbizi Mountains Tanz.
208 E3 Mboki C.A.R.
208 B4 Mbomo Congo
208 D3 Mbomou pref. C.A.R.
208 D3 Mbomou r. C.A.R./Dem. Rep. Congo
78 □6 Mborokua i. Solomon Is
207 H5 Mbouda Cameroon
206 A3 Mbour Senegal
206 B2 Mbout Maur.
211 B7 Mbozi Tanz.
208 C3 Mbrès C.A.R.
198 A1 Mbrostar Albania
209 D6 Mbuji-Mayi Dem. Rep. Congo
78 □6 Mbulo i. New Georgia Is Solomon Is
211 B5 Mbulu Tanz.
215 H2 Mbuluzana r. Swaziland
215 I2 Mbuluzi r. Swaziland
258 F3 Mburucuyá Arg.
225 H4 McAdam N.B. Can.
234 C2 McAdoo PA U.S.A.
234 D1 McAfee NJ U.S.A.
237 E5 McAlester OK U.S.A.
234 A2 McAlisterville PA U.S.A.
237 D7 McAllen TX U.S.A.
226 D3 McAllister WI U.S.A.
84 D2 McArthur r. N.T. Austr.
232 B5 McArthur OH U.S.A.
227 I3 McArthur Mills Ont. Can.
226 E3 McBain MI U.S.A.
222 F4 McBride B.C. Can.
238 C2 McCall ID U.S.A.
237 C6 McCamey TX U.S.A.
238 D3 McCammon ID U.S.A.
226 C3 McCaslin Mountain hill WI U.S.A.
263 K1 McClintock, Mount Antarctica
221 H2 McClintock Channel Nunavut Can.
86 E3 McClintock Range hills W.A. Austr.
84 C1 McCluer Island N.T. Austr.
232 B4 McClure OH U.S.A.
232 E4 McClure PA U.S.A.
220 G2 McClure Strait N.W.T. Can.
236 C2 McClusky ND U.S.A.
237 F6 McComb MS U.S.A.
232 B4 McComb OH U.S.A.
232 E5 McConnellsburg PA U.S.A.
232 C5 McConnelsville OH U.S.A.
236 C3 McCook NE U.S.A.
231 D5 McCormick SC U.S.A.
232 C6 McCoy VA U.S.A.
222 H2 McCrea r. N.W.T. Can.
223 L5 McCreary Man. Can.
241 J4 McCullough Range mts NV U.S.A.
232 B4 McCutchenville OH U.S.A.
222 D3 McDame B.C. Can.
238 C3 McDermitt NV U.S.A.
232 B5 McDermott OH U.S.A.
265 I8 McDonald Islands Indian Ocean
238 D2 McDonald Peak MT U.S.A.
231 C5 McDonough GA U.S.A.
241 L5 McDowell Peak AZ U.S.A.
234 B1 McEwensville PA U.S.A.
240 H4 McFarland CA U.S.A.
226 C4 McFarland WI U.S.A.
223 J3 McFarlane r. Sask. Can.
81 B5 McFarlane, Mount South I. N.Z.
241 J2 McGill NV U.S.A.
225 H4 McGivney N.B. Can.
220 C3 McGrath AK U.S.A.
226 A2 McGrath MN U.S.A.
222 F4 McGregor r. B.C. Can.
214 B5 McGregor S. Africa
226 A2 McGregor MN U.S.A.
227 G2 McGregor Bay Ont. Can.
85 E5 McGregor Range hills Qld Austr.
238 D2 McGuire, Mount ID U.S.A.
129 D2 Mchadijvari Georgia
204 D4 Mcherrah reg. Alg.
211 C7 Mchinga Tanz.
211 B8 Mchinji Malawi
85 E2 McIlwraith Range hills Qld Austr.
236 C2 McIntosh SD U.S.A.
86 D4 McKay Range hills W.A. Austr.
77 I2 McKean i. Phoenix Is Kiribati
232 A6 McKee KY U.S.A.
234 D3 McKee NJ U.S.A.
232 D4 McKeesport PA U.S.A.
232 C4 McKees Rocks PA U.S.A.
232 E6 McKenney VA U.S.A.
237 F4 McKenzie TN U.S.A.
238 B2 McKenzie r. OR U.S.A.
85 E4 McKinlay Qld Austr.
85 E4 McKinlay r. Qld Austr.
220 C3 McKinley, Mount AK U.S.A.
237 D5 McKinney TX U.S.A.
240 H4 McKittrick CA U.S.A.
236 C2 McLaughlin SD U.S.A.
226 C5 McLean IL U.S.A.
234 A4 McLean VA U.S.A.
236 F4 McLeansboro IL U.S.A.
222 G4 McLennan Alta Can.
222 H4 McLeod r. Alta Can.
222 F4 McLeod Lake B.C. Can.
238 B2 McMinnville OR U.S.A.
231 C5 McMinnville TN U.S.A.
263 L1 McMurdo research stn Antarctica
241 M4 McNary AZ U.S.A.
226 C3 McNaughton WI U.S.A.
McNaughton Lake B.C. Can. see Kinbasket Lake
241 M6 McNeal AZ U.S.A.
225 H2 McPhadyen r. Nfld. Can.
236 D4 McPherson KS U.S.A.
83 H2 McPherson Range mts N.S.W. Austr.
222 B2 McQuesten r. Y.T. Can.
231 D5 McRae GA U.S.A.
232 B6 McRoberts KY U.S.A.
234 A3 McSherrystown PA U.S.A.
220 G3 McTavish Arm b. N.W.T. Can.
232 E4 McVeytown PA U.S.A.
222 F1 McVicar Arm b. N.W.T. Can.
232 C5 McWhorter WV U.S.A.
139 I2 Mda r. Rus. Fed.
215 F5 Mdantsane S. Africa
205 G1 M'Daourouch Alg.
217 □3a Mde Njazidja Comoros
180 D5 Mdiq Morocco
241 J3 Mead, Lake resr NV U.S.A.
237 C4 Meade KS U.S.A.
220 C2 Meade r. AK U.S.A.
87 B5 Meadow W.A. Austr.
236 C2 Meadow SD U.S.A.
241 K2 Meadow UT U.S.A.
232 C6 Meadow Bridge WV U.S.A.
223 I4 Meadow Lake Sask. Can.
241 J3 Meadow Valley Wash r. NV U.S.A.
232 C6 Meadowview VA U.S.A.
237 F6 Meadville MS U.S.A.
232 C4 Meadville PA U.S.A.
227 G3 Meaford Ont. Can.
102 L2 Meaken vol. Japan
146 D4 Meal Fuar-mhonaidh hill Scotland U.K.
182 B4 Mealhada Port.
146 A3 Mealisval hill Scotland U.K.
146 D5 Meall Chuaich hill Scotland U.K.
146 D4 Meall Dubh hill Scotland U.K.
149 F3 Mealsgate Cumbria, England U.K.
225 J2 Mealy Mountains Nfld. Can.
192 B5 Meana Sardo Sardegna Italy
85 G5 Meandarra Qld Austr.
222 G3 Meander River Alta Can.
150 E3 Meare Somerset, England U.K.
151 F2 Mease r. England U.K.
151 F2 Measham Leicestershire, England U.K.
147 E3 Meath county Rep. of Ireland
160 A2 Meaulne France
156 C3 Méaulte France
156 C4 Meaux France
163 D4 Meauzac France
209 B6 Mebridege r. Angola
117 H3 Mebu Arun. Prad. India
213 G2 Mecanhelas Moz.
244 B3 Mecatán Mex.
124 B3 Mecca Saudi Arabia
241 I5 Mecca CA U.S.A.
232 C4 Mecca OH U.S.A.
233 □H2 Mechanic Falls ME U.S.A.
232 B4 Mechanicsburg OH U.S.A.
234 A2 Mechanicsburg PA U.S.A.
232 C6 Mechanicsburg VA U.S.A.
232 E6 Mechanicsville VA U.S.A.
233 G3 Mechanicville NY U.S.A.
210 D2 Mechāra Eth.
165 D3 Mechelen Belgium
165 E4 Mechelen Neth.
Mecherchar i. Palau see Eil Malk
205 E2 Mecheria Alg.
169 B5 Mechernich Ger.
135 H7 Mechetinskaya Rus. Fed.
202 B6 Mechiméré Chad
197 G4 Mechka r. Bulg.
168 F2 Mechtersen Ger.

169 F5 **Mechterstädt** Ger.
199 E1 **Mecidiye** *Edirne* Turkey
199 E2 **Mecidiye** *Manisa* Turkey
176 C2 **Měčín** Czech Rep.
185 G4 **Mecina-Bombarón** Spain
174 E4 **Męcinka** Pol.
126 D2 **Mecitözü** Turkey
172 D4 **Meckenbeuren** Ger.
169 C5 **Meckenheim** Ger.
172 C2 **Meckesheim** Ger.
170 C1 **Mecklenburger Bucht** *b.* Ger.
170 D2 **Mecklenburg-Vorpommern** *land* Ger.
Mecklenburg - West Pomerania *land* Ger. *see* Mecklenburg-Vorpommern
183 G4 **Meco** Spain
213 H2 **Meconta** Moz.
177 H5 **Mecsek** *mts* Hungary
177 H5 **Mecseknádasd** Hungary
213 I2 **Mecubúri** *r.* Moz.
213 I2 **Mecúfi** Moz.
211 C8 **Mecula** Moz.
86 D3 **Meda** *r.* *W.A.* Austr.
182 C4 **Meda** Port.
182 C2 **Meda** *mt.* Spain
114 C2 **Medak** *Andhra Prad.* India
94 B2 **Medan** *Sumatera* Indon.
261 F6 **Médanos** Arg.
226 D5 **Medaryville** *IN* U.S.A.
182 B3 **Medas** Port.
114 C2 **Medchal** *Andhra Prad.* India
172 B2 **Meddersheim** Ger.
164 F2 **Meddo** Neth.
190 D3 **Mede** Italy
205 F1 **Médéa** Alg.
169 D4 **Medebach** Ger.
257 G2 **Medeiros Neto** Brazil
182 C4 **Medelim** Port.
250 C3 **Medellín** Col.
184 E2 **Medellín** Spain
168 D2 **Medem** *r.* Ger.
164 E2 **Medemblik** Neth.
149 H4 **Meden** *r.* *England* U.K.
205 H2 **Medenine** Tunisia
Medenitsa Ukr. *see* Medenychi
136 B3 **Medenychi** Ukr.
124 C5 **Meder** Eritrea
206 B2 **Mederdra** Maur.
190 F4 **Medesano** Italy
233 G4 **Medford** *NY* U.S.A.
237 D4 **Medford** *OK* U.S.A.
238 B3 **Medford** *OR* U.S.A.
226 B3 **Medford** *WI* U.S.A.
234 D3 **Medford Lakes** *NJ* U.S.A.
197 I3 **Medgidia** Romania
197 J5 **Medgyesbodzás** Hungary
177 K5 **Medgyesegyháza** Hungary
113 □1 **Medhufinolhu** *i.* *N. Male* Maldives
234 C3 **Media** *PA* U.S.A.
186 C3 **Mediana** Spain
197 G2 **Mediaş** Romania
238 C2 **Medical Lake** *WA* U.S.A.
191 G4 **Medicina** Italy
238 F3 **Medicine Bow** *WY* U.S.A.
238 F3 **Medicine Bow** *r.* *WY* U.S.A.
238 F3 **Medicine Bow Mountains** *WY* U.S.A.
238 F3 **Medicine Bow Peak** *WY* U.S.A.
223 I5 **Medicine Hat** *Alta* Can.
237 D4 **Medicine Lodge** *KS* U.S.A.
257 G2 **Medina** Brazil
Medina Saudi Arabia *see* Al Madīnah
236 D2 **Medina** *ND* U.S.A.
232 D3 **Medina** *NY* U.S.A.
232 C4 **Medina** *OH* U.S.A.
237 D6 **Medina** *r.* *TX* U.S.A.
183 H3 **Medinaceli** Spain
184 D2 **Medina de las Torres** Spain
183 F3 **Medina del Campo** Spain
183 G2 **Medina de Pomar** Spain
183 E3 **Medina de Rioseco** Spain
206 B3 **Medina Gounas** Senegal
184 E4 **Medina-Sidonia** Spain
117 F5 **Medinipur** *W. Bengal* India
Mediolanum Italy *see* Milano
162 B3 **Médis** France
132 F7 **Mediterranean Sea**
161 B5 **Méditerranée** *airport* France
176 G2 **Medlov** Czech Rep.
120 D2 **Mednogorsk** Rus. Fed.
139 J3 **Mednoye** Rus. Fed.
131 R4 **Mednyy, Ostrov** *i.* Rus. Fed.
162 A3 **Médoc** *reg.* France
111 F6 **Mêdog** *Xizang* China
191 G4 **Medolla** Italy
236 D2 **Medora** *ND* U.S.A.
208 A4 **Médouneu** Gabon
260 D3 **Medrano** Arg.
175 I5 **Mędrzechów** Pol.
223 I4 **Medstead** *Sask.* Can.
151 F3 **Medstead** *Hampshire, England* U.K.
Medu Kongkar *Xizang* China *see* Maizhokunggar
191 I4 **Medulin** Croatia
191 H3 **Meduna** *r.* Italy
191 H2 **Meduno** Italy
Meduro *atoll* Marshall Is *see* Majuro
197 E4 **Medveda** *Srbija* Yugo.
134 I4 **Medvedevo** Rus. Fed.
136 H6 **Medveditsa** *r.* Rus. Fed.
188 E3 **Medvednica** *mts* Croatia
134 J4 **Medvedok** Rus. Fed.
137 J5 **Medvedovskaya** Rus. Fed.
138 D4 **Medvėgalio kalnis** *hill* Lith.
137 I2 **Medvenka** Rus. Fed.
134 F3 **Medvezh'yegorsk** Rus. Fed.
179 F4 **Medvode** Slovenia
151 H3 **Medway** *admin. div.* *England* U.K.
151 H3 **Medway** *r.* *England* U.K.
175 K6 **Medyka** Pol.
139 J4 **Medyn'** Rus. Fed.
136 D3 **Medzhybizh** Ukr.
177 K2 **Medzilaborce** Slovakia
86 E5 **Meekatharra** *W.A.* Austr.
164 F1 **Meeden** Neth.
169 F5 **Meeder** Ger.
87 C5 **Meekatharra** *W.A.* Austr.
238 F3 **Meeker** *CO* U.S.A.
232 B4 **Meeker** *OH* U.S.A.
240 G2 **Meeks Bay** *CA* U.S.A.
214 E5 **Meelberg** *mt.* S. Africa
147 C3 **Meelick** Rep. of Ireland
147 C2 **Meenacross** Rep. of Ireland
147 C2 **Meenanarwa** Rep. of Ireland
147 C2 **Meentullynagarn** Rep. of Ireland
165 D3 **Meer** Belgium
171 D5 **Meerane** Ger.
169 E3 **Meerbeck** Ger.
169 B4 **Meerbusch** Ger.
165 E3 **Meerhout** Belgium
164 D3 **Meerkerk** Neth.
165 D3 **Meerle** Belgium
164 F3 **Meerlo** Neth.
172 D4 **Meersburg** Ger.
165 E4 **Meerssen** Neth.
113 □1 **Meerufenfushi** *i.* *N. Male* Maldives
116 D3 **Meerut** *Uttar Prad.* India
163 A5 **Mées** France
238 E2 **Meeteetse** *WY* U.S.A.
Me'etia *i.* *Arch. de la Société* Fr. Polynesia *see* Mehetia
165 C3 **Meetkerke** Belgium
165 E3 **Meeuwen** Belgium
210 C3 **Mēga** Eth.
210 C3 **Mega Escarpment** Eth./Kenya
198 B2 **Megala Kalyvia** Greece
198 C1 **Megali Panagia** Greece
210 D3 **Megalo** Eth.
198 C1 **Megalopoli** Greece
198 C2 **Megara** Greece
164 E3 **Megen** Neth.
160 E3 **Megève** France
210 C2 **Megezez** *mt.* Eth.
117 G4 **Meghalaya** *state* India
117 G5 **Meghasani** *mt.* *Orissa* India
117 G5 **Meghna** *r.* Bangl.
129 E4 **Meghri** Armenia
Meghrut Armenia *see* Gugark'
130 I3 **Megion** Rus. Fed.
199 F3 **Megisti** *i.* Greece
139 J2 **Meglino, Ozero** *l.* Rus. Fed.
139 J1 **Megra** *r.* Rus. Fed.
Megri Armenia *see* Meghri
Megrut Armenia *see* Gugark'
197 F3 **Mehadica** Romania
165 E4 **Mehaigne** *r.* Belgium
140 N1 **Mehamn** Norway
123 F5 **Mehar** Pak.
87 C4 **Meharry, Mount** *W.A.* Austr.
Mehdia Tunisia *see* Mahdia
168 E2 **Mehe** *r.* Ger.
143 G1 **Mehedeby** Sweden
116 D5 **Mehekar** *Mahar.* India
117 G5 **Meherpur** Bangl.
232 D6 **Meherrin** *VA* U.S.A.
232 E6 **Meherrin** *r.* *VA* U.S.A.
79 □3 **Mehetia** *i.* *Arch. de la Société* Fr. Polynesia
116 C5 **Mehidpur** *Madh. Prad.* India
167 J5 **Méhkerék** Hungary
171 D5 **Mehltheuer** Ger.
236 F4 **Mehlville** *MO* U.S.A.
116 C5 **Mehmadabad** *Gujarat* India
117 E4 **Mehndawal** *Uttar Prad.* India
234 B1 **Mehoopany** *PA* U.S.A.
122 A2 **Mehrābān** Iran
169 B5 **Mehren** Ger.
172 A2 **Mehring** Ger.
179 E2 **Mehrnbach** Austria
172 D3 **Mehrstetten** Ger.
123 G3 **Mehtar Lām** Afgh.
162 E1 **Mehun-sur-Yèvre** France
256 C3 **Meia Ponte** *r.* Brazil
Meicheng *Anhui* China *see* Qianshan
Meicheng *Fujian* China *see* Minqing
109 D2 **Meichengzhen** *Hunan* China
150 C3 **Meidrim** *Carmarthenshire, Wales* U.K.
207 I5 **Meiganga** Cameroon
148 C3 **Meigh** *Northern Ireland* U.K.
146 E5 **Meigle** *Perth and Kinross, Scotland* U.K.
108 B2 **Meigu** *Sichuan* China
100 C4 **Meihekou** *Jilin* China
165 E3 **Meijel** Neth.
Meijiang *Jiangxi* China *see* Ningdu
109 E3 **Mei Jiang** *r.* China
109 E3 **Meikeng** *Guangdong* China
222 G3 **Meikle** *r.* *Alta* Can.
148 E1 **Meikle Bin** *hill* *Scotland* U.K.
148 D2 **Meikle Kilmory** *Argyll and Bute, Scotland* U.K.
146 E5 **Meikleour** *Perth and Kinross, Scotland* U.K.
146 F6 **Meikle Says Law** *hill* *Scotland* U.K.
96 A2 **Meiktila** Myanmar
190 D1 **Meilen** Switz.
163 B5 **Meilhan** France
163 C4 **Meilhan-sur-Garonne** France
Meilin *Jiangxi* China *see* Ganxian
158 E3 **Meillac** France
160 A2 **Meillant** France
160 E2 **Meillerie** France
222 E2 **Meilleur** *r.* *N.W.T.* Can.
Meilü *Guangdong* China *see* Wuchuan
182 C4 **Meimoa** Port.
190 D3 **Meina** Italy
169 F3 **Meine** Ger.
169 F3 **Meinersen** Ger.
169 C4 **Meinerzhagen** Ger.
178 A3 **Meiningen** Austria
169 F5 **Meiningen** Ger.
182 C1 **Meira** Spain
182 C1 **Meira, Serra de** *mts* Spain
190 D2 **Meiringen** Switz.
171 C4 **Meisdorf** Ger.
172 B2 **Meisenheim** Ger.
Meishan *Anhui* China *see* Jinzhai
108 B2 **Meishan** *Sichuan* China
171 E4 **Meißen** Ger.
168 E3 **Meißendorf** Ger.
172 E3 **Meißenheim** Ger.
222 D2 **Meister** *r.* *Y.T.* Can.
108 C3 **Meitan** *Guizhou* China
173 E3 **Meitingen** Ger.
165 E5 **Meix-devant-Virton** Belgium
100 D3 **Meixi** *Heilong.* China
Meixian *Guangdong* China *see* Meizhou
107 E5 **Meixian** *Shaanxi* China
Meixing *Sichuan* China *see* Xiaojin
109 F3 **Meizhou** *Guangdong* China
116 D4 **Mej** *r.* India
161 C4 **Méjan, Sommet de** *mt.* France
78 □3a **Mejatto** *i.* *Kwajalein* Marshall Is
161 B4 **Méjean, Causse** *plat.* France
189 B7 **Mejez el Bab** Tunisia
258 D3 **Mejicana** *mt.* Arg.
252 C5 **Mejillones** Chile
183 F4 **Mejorada** Spain
183 G4 **Mejorada del Campo** Spain
208 B4 **Mékambo** Gabon
196 G3 **Mekece** Turkey
210 C1 **Mek'elē** Eth.
206 A3 **Mékhé** Senegal
129 E2 **Mekhel'ta** Rus. Fed.
210 C2 **Meki** Eth.
179 F4 **Mekinje** Slovenia
207 F5 **Mekkaw** Nigeria
204 D2 **Meknès** Morocco
108 B4 **Mekong** *r.* Asia
alt. **Lancang Jiang**
97 D5 **Mekong, Mouths of the** Vietnam
191 H2 **Mel** Italy
208 D2 **Méla, Mont** *hill* C.A.R.
260 B4 **Melado** *r.* Chile
94 C2 **Melaka** Malaysia
94 C2 **Melaka** *state* Malaysia
193 H4 **Melandro** *r.* Italy
266 F6 **Melanesia** *is* Oceania
266 F5 **Melanesian Basin** *sea feature* Pacific Ocean
191 G3 **Melara** Italy
95 E2 **Melawi** *r.* Indon.
160 C2 **Melay** *Bourgogne* France
157 F5 **Melay** *Champagne-Ardenne* France
159 F4 **Melay** *Pays de la Loire* France
190 D4 **Melazzo** Italy
168 F2 **Melbeck** Ger.
151 H2 **Melbourn** *Cambridgeshire, England* U.K.
83 F4 **Melbourne** *Vic.* Austr.
151 F2 **Melbourne** *Derbyshire, England* U.K.
237 F4 **Melbourne** *AR* U.S.A.
231 D6 **Melbourne** *FL* U.S.A.
140 K1 **Melbu** Norway
146 □G1 **Melby** *Shetland, Scotland* U.K.
259 B7 **Melchor, Isla** *i.* Chile
243 H5 **Melchor de Mencos** Guat.
170 E3 **Melchow** Ger.
140 J3 **Meldal** Norway
191 H4 **Meldola** Italy
168 E1 **Meldorf** Ger.
232 B6 **Meldrum** *KY* U.S.A.
224 D4 **Meldrum Bay** *Ont.* Can.
190 D4 **Mele** Italy
139 K3 **Melech** *r.* Rus. Fed.
190 E3 **Melegnano** Italy
176 G4 **Meleg-víz** *r.* Hungary
Melekess Rus. Fed. *see* Dimitrovgrad
139 M3 **Melekhovo** Rus. Fed.
196 E3 **Melenci** *Vojvodina, Srbija* Yugo.
126 D3 **Melendiz Dağı** *mt.* Turkey
126 D3 **Melendugno** Italy
135 H5 **Melenki** Rus. Fed.
158 E3 **Melesse** France
Melet Turkey *see* Mesudiye
120 C1 **Meleuz** Rus. Fed.
225 G1 **Mélèzes, Rivière aux** *r.* Que. Can.
193 F3 **Melfa** *r.* Italy
233 F6 **Melfa** *VA* U.S.A.
208 C2 **Melfi** Chad
193 H4 **Melfi** Italy
223 J4 **Melfort** *Sask.* Can.
251 I5 **Melgaço** Brazil
182 B2 **Melgaço** Port.
183 G2 **Melgar** *r.* Spain
183 E2 **Melgar de Arriba** Spain
183 F2 **Melgar de Fernamental** Spain
182 D3 **Melgar de Tera** Spain
158 C4 **Melgven** France
140 J3 **Melhus** Norway
95 G1 **Meliau, Gunung** *mt.* *Sabah* Malaysia
165 F3 **Melick** Neth.
195 F4 **Melicucco** Italy
182 C2 **Melide** Spain
184 B2 **Melides** Port.
198 B3 **Meligalas** Greece
129 C3 **Melikköyü** Turkey
181 E5 **Melilla** N. Africa
195 E5 **Melilli** *Sicilia* Italy
259 B7 **Melimoyu, Monte** *mt.* Chile
81 B6 **Melina, Mount** *South I.* N.Z.
261 G3 **Melincué** Arg.
137 H3 **Melioratyvne** Ukr.
260 B6 **Melipeuco** Chile
260 B3 **Melipilla** Chile
157 G5 **Mélisey** France
164 C3 **Meliskerke** Neth.
195 G3 **Melissa** Italy
223 K5 **Melita** *Man.* Can.
Melitene Turkey *see* Malatya
198 B1 **Meliti** *Dytiki Makedonia* Greece
195 E5 **Melito** *r.* Italy
195 E5 **Melito di Porto Salvo** Italy
137 H4 **Melitopol'** Ukr.
179 G2 **Melk** Austria
179 G2 **Melk** *r.* Austria
215 E5 **Melk** *r.* S. Africa
214 B5 **Melkbosstrand** S. Africa
150 E3 **Melksham** *Wiltshire, England* U.K.
190 F3 **Mella** *r.* Italy
158 C4 **Mellac** France
140 L3 **Mellansel** Sweden
141 K3 **Mellansjö** Sweden
140 L2 **Mellanström** Sweden
178 A3 **Mellau** Austria
176 C3 **Melle** Belgium
162 B2 **Melle** France
169 D3 **Melle** Ger.
170 C2 **Mellen** Ger.
226 B2 **Mellen** *WI* U.S.A.
168 E3 **Mellendorf (Wedemark)** Ger.
171 E3 **Mellensee** Ger.
142 E2 **Mellerud** Sweden
236 D2 **Mellette** *SD* U.S.A.
Mellid Spain *see* Melide
195 □ **Mellieħa** Malta
168 F3 **Mellin** Ger.
171 C5 **Mellingen** Ger.
169 D3 **Mellinghausen** Ger.
259 B8 **Mellizo Sur, Cerro** *mt.* Chile
169 F5 **Mellrichstadt** Ger.
150 D3 **Melltte** *r.* *Wales* U.K.
78 □3a **Mellu** *i.* *Kwajalein* Marshall Is
168 D2 **Mellum** *i.* Ger.
149 G3 **Melmerby** *Cumbria, England* U.K.
215 H3 **Melmoth** S. Africa
176 D1 **Mělník** Czech Rep.
136 D3 **Mel'nytsya-Podil's'ka** Ukr.
258 G4 **Melo** Uru.
213 H2 **Meloco** Moz.
215 F2 **Meloding** S. Africa
182 B2 **Melón** Spain
207 H5 **Mélong** Cameroon
Melovoye Ukr. *see* Milove
220 C3 **Melozitna** *r.* *AK* U.S.A.
158 C4 **Melrand** France
182 B3 **Melres** Port.
205 G2 **Melrhir, Chott** *salt l.* Alg.
87 D5 **Melrose** *W.A.* Austr.
146 F6 **Melrose** *Scottish Borders, Scotland* U.K.
236 E2 **Melrose** *MN* U.S.A.
190 E1 **Mels** Switz.
169 E5 **Melsbach** Ger.
168 F1 **Melsdorf** Ger.
Melsetter Zimbabwe *see* Chimanimani
149 H3 **Melsonby** *North Yorkshire, England* U.K.
169 E4 **Melsungen** Ger.
Melta, Mount *Sabah* Malaysia *see* Meliau, Gunung
149 H4 **Meltham** *West Yorkshire, England* U.K.
83 F4 **Melton** *Vic.* Austr.
151 I2 **Melton** *Suffolk, England* U.K.
151 G2 **Melton Mowbray** *Leicestershire, England* U.K.
211 C8 **Meluco** Moz.
156 C4 **Melun** France
114 C4 **Melur** *Tamil Nadu* India
146 C4 **Melvaig** *Highland, Scotland* U.K.
146 E3 **Melvich** *Highland, Scotland* U.K.
223 K5 **Melville** *Sask.* Can.
85 F2 **Melville, Cape** *Qld* Austr.
84 D2 **Melville Bay** *N.T.* Austr.
Melville Bugt *b.* Greenland *see* Qimusseriarsuaq
84 B1 **Melville Island** *N.T.* Austr.
221 H2 **Melville Island** *N.W.T./Nunavut* Can.
221 J3 **Melville Peninsula** *Nunavut* Can.
226 C5 **Melvin** *IL* U.S.A.
147 C2 **Melvin, Lough** *l.* Rep. of Ireland/U.K.
177 I5 **Mélykút** Hungary
195 G4 **Melzo** Italy
198 A1 **Memaliaj** Albania
213 I2 **Memba** Moz.
91 I7 **Memberamo** *r.* Indon.
160 D1 **Membrey** France
185 G2 **Membrilla** Spain
182 C5 **Membrio** Spain
Memel Lith. *see* Klaipėda
215 G2 **Memel** S. Africa
138 E3 **Mēmele** *r.* Latvia
138 F4 **Memiakalnis** *hill* Lith.
173 E2 **Memmelsdorf** Ger.
173 E3 **Memmingen** Ger.
173 E4 **Memmingerberg** Ger.
156 E3 **Mémorial Américain** *hill* France
126 C5 **Memphis** *tourist site* Egypt
227 F4 **Memphis** *MI* U.S.A.
235 E5 **Memphis** *MO* U.S.A.
237 F5 **Memphis** *TN* U.S.A.
237 C5 **Memphis** *TX* U.S.A.
146 F4 **Memsie** *Aberdeenshire, Scotland* U.K.
102 K2 **Memuro-dake** *mt.* Japan
137 D2 **Mena** Ukr.
137 G2 **Mena** *r.* Ukr.
237 E5 **Mena** *AR* U.S.A.
213 □J4 **Menabe** *mts* Madag.
190 E2 **Menaggio** Italy
191 G3 **Menago** *r.* Italy
150 C1 **Menai Bridge** *Isle of Anglesey, Wales* U.K.
150 C1 **Menai Strait** *Wales* U.K.
207 F3 **Ménaka** Mali
164 E1 **Menaldum** Neth.
98 I8 **Mènam Khong** *r.* Laos/Thai.
213 □J5 **Menandra** *r.* Madag.
150 C1 **Menard** *TX* U.S.A.
156 B5 **Menars** France
156 F5 **Menasalbas** Spain
160 A2 **Menat** France
191 H4 **Menata** Italy
157 F4 **Menaucourt** France
158 G3 **Mencal** *mt.* Spain
116 E4 **Menchhapur** India
183 H1 **Mendaro** Spain
186 B1 **Mendaur** *mt.* Spain
183 H2 **Mendavia** Spain
95 F3 **Mendawai** *r.* Indon.
157 F4 **Mende** France
210 C3 **Mendebo Mountains** Eth.
203 H6 **Mendefera** Eritrea
268 M1 **Mendeleyev Ridge** *sea feature* Arctic Ocean
134 K5 **Mendeleyevsk** Rus. Fed.
169 C4 **Menden (Sauerland)** Ger.
237 F6 **Mendenhall** *MS* U.S.A.
199 E2 **Menderes** Turkey
243 F3 **Méndez** Mex.
245 E2 **Méndez** Mex.
92 B3 **Mendez-Nuñez** Phil.
234 D2 **Mendham** *NJ* U.S.A.
210 B2 **Mendī** Eth.
91 J8 **Mendi** P.N.G.
183 I2 **Mendigorría** Spain
150 E3 **Mendip Hills** *England* U.K.
163 B5 **Menditte** France
240 F2 **Mendocino** *CA* U.S.A.
238 A3 **Mendocino, Cape** *CA* U.S.A.
194 C5 **Mendola** *r.* *Sicilia* Italy
194 C5 **Mendola** *r.* *Sicilia* Italy
226 E4 **Mendon** *MI* U.S.A.
83 G2 **Mendooran** *N.S.W.* Austr.
240 G3 **Mendota** *CA* U.S.A.
226 C5 **Mendota** *IL* U.S.A.
260 C3 **Mendoza** Arg.
260 C4 **Mendoza** *prov.* Arg.
260 C3 **Mendoza** *r.* Arg.
190 D3 **Mendrisio** Switz.
87 D7 **Mends, Lake** *salt flat* *W.A.* Austr.
158 D3 **Ménéac** France
250 D2 **Mene de Mauroa** Venez.
190 E4 **Menegosa, Monte** *mt.* Italy
199 E2 **Menemen** Turkey
165 C4 **Menen** Belgium
161 D5 **Ménerbes** France
162 C3 **Ménesplet** France
160 C1 **Ménessaire** France
161 A3 **Menet** France
159 I4 **Menetou-Salon** France
158 C3 **Menez Bré** *hill* France
158 B3 **Menez Hom** *hill* France
194 B5 **Menfi** *Sicilia* Italy
108 B4 **Mengban** *Yunnan* China
109 F1 **Mengcheng** *Anhui* China
172 D3 **Mengen** Ger.
126 D2 **Mengen** Turkey
169 D5 **Mengerskirchen** Ger.
179 F4 **Mengeš** Slovenia
234 B3 **Menges Mills** *PA* U.S.A.
94 D4 **Menggala** *Sumatera* Indon.
108 B4 **Menghai** *Yunnan* China
185 G3 **Mengíbar** Spain
121 F1 **Mengisor, Ozero** *salt l.* Kazakh.
95 E2 **Mengkiang** *r.* Indon.
173 G3 **Mengkofen** Ger.
93 B3 **Mengkoka, Gunung** *mt.* Indon.
108 B4 **Mengla** *Yunnan* China
Menglang *Yunnan* China *see* Lancang
108 A4 **Menglian** *Yunnan* China
Menglie *Yunnan* China *see* Jiangcheng
Mengmeng *Yunnan* China *see* Shuangjiang
108 D3 **Mengshan** *Guangxi* China
Mengxian *Henan* China *see* Mengzhou
Mengyang *Sichuan* China *see* Mingshan
107 H5 **Mengyin** *Shandong* China
107 G5 **Mengzhou** *Henan* China
108 B4 **Mengzi** *Yunnan* China
150 C4 **Menheniot** *Cornwall, England* U.K.
162 B2 **Ménigoute** France
225 H2 **Menihek** *Nfld.* Can.
157 F4 **Ménil-la-Tour** France
157 G4 **Ménil-sur-Belvitte** France
Menin Belgium *see* Menen
179 H1 **Měnín** Czech Rep.
83 E3 **Menindee** *N.S.W.* Austr.
83 E3 **Menindee Lake** *N.S.W.* Austr.
82 D3 **Meningie** *S.A.* Austr.
147 B3 **Menlough** Rep. of Ireland
124 B5 **Menna** *r.* Eth.
156 C4 **Mennecy** France
156 F3 **Mennetou-sur-Cher** France
226 D3 **Menominee** *MI* U.S.A.
226 D3 **Menominee** *r.* *WI* U.S.A.
226 C4 **Menomonee Falls** *WI* U.S.A.
226 B3 **Menomonie** *WI* U.S.A.
209 C8 **Menongue** Angola
187 C7 **Menor, Mar** *lag.* Spain
186 □ **Menorca** *i.* Spain
160 B1 **Menou** France
161 D4 **Mens** France
162 C3 **Mensignac** France
168 C3 **Menslage** Ger.
149 H4 **Menston** *West Yorkshire, England* U.K.
Mentakab Malaysia *see* Mentekab
193 E2 **Mentana** Italy
92 A5 **Mentapok** *mt.* *Sabah* Malaysia
95 G2 **Mentarang** *r.* Indon.
94 B3 **Mentawai, Kepulauan** *is* Indon.
94 C3 **Mentawai, Selat** *sea chan.* Indon.
95 F3 **Mentaya** *r.* Indon.
182 C3 **Mente** *r.* Port./Spain
146 D5 **Menteith, Lake of** *Scotland* U.K.
94 C2 **Mentekab** Malaysia
87 B7 **Mentelle, Cape** *W.A.* Austr.
169 F4 **Menteroda** Ger.
199 F3 **Menteş** *Afyon* Turkey
160 E3 **Menthon-St-Bernard** France
184 C2 **Mentiras** *hill* Port.
185 H2 **Mentiras** *mt.* Spain
241 M4 **Mentmore** *NM* U.S.A.
94 D3 **Mentok** Indon.
161 F5 **Menton** France
237 C6 **Mentone** *TX* U.S.A.
232 C4 **Mentor** *OH* U.S.A.
183 F4 **Méntrida** Spain
95 F3 **Mentuba** *r.* Indon.
Menūfīya *governorate* Egypt *see* Minūfīya
95 G2 **Menyapa, Gunung** *mt.* Indon.
106 D4 **Menyuan** *Qinghai* China
107 F1 **Menza** *r.* Rus. Fed.
205 H1 **Menzel Bourguiba** Tunisia
134 K5 **Menzelinsk** Rus. Fed.
189 C7 **Menzel Temime** Tunisia
87 D6 **Menzies** *W.A.* Austr.
263 E2 **Menzies, Mount** Antarctica
190 D1 **Menznau** Switz.
159 H5 **Méobecq** France
191 H3 **Meolo** Italy
242 D2 **Meoqui** Mex.
161 D5 **Méounes-les-Montrieux** France
129 C3 **Mep'istsqaro, Mt'a** Georgia
211 B8 **Meponda** Moz.
164 F2 **Meppel** Neth.
168 C3 **Meppen** Ger.
215 G3 **Mepuleng** S. Africa
253 E3 **Mequéns** *r.* Brazil
186 D3 **Mequinenza** Spain
186 D3 **Mequinenza, Embalse de** *resr* Spain
226 D4 **Mequon** *WI* U.S.A.
156 B5 **Mer** France
190 E2 **Mera** *r.* Italy
94 D4 **Merak** *Jawa Barat* Indon.
140 J3 **Meråker** Norway
82 C2 **Meramangye, Lake** *salt flat* *S.A.* Austr.
236 F4 **Meramec** *r.* *MO* U.S.A.
191 G2 **Merano** Italy
95 E4 **Merapi, Gunung** *vol.* *Jawa* Indon.
95 F5 **Merapi, Gunung** *vol.* *Jawa* Indon.
94 C3 **Merapi, Gunung** *vol.* *Sumatera* Indon.
163 B5 **Méraq** France
251 F3 **Merari, Serra** *mt.* Brazil
225 K4 **Merasheen** *Nfld.* Can.
140 M2 **Merasjärvi** Sweden
190 E3 **Merate** Italy
212 E4 **Meratswe** *r.* Botswana
95 F3 **Meratus, Pegunungan** *mts* Indon.
91 J8 **Merauke** *Irian Jaya* Indon.
83 E3 **Merbein** *Vic.* Austr.
165 D4 **Merbes-le-Château** Belgium
Merca Somalia *see* Marka
186 □ **Mercadal** Spain
129 B4 **Mercan** Turkey
129 A4 **Mercan Dağları** *mts* Turkey
191 H5 **Mercatale** Italy
191 H5 **Mercatello sul Metauro** Italy
191 H5 **Mercatino Conca** Italy
193 G4 **Mercato San Severino** Italy
191 H5 **Mercato Saraceno** Italy
240 G3 **Merced** *CA* U.S.A.
240 G3 **Merced** *r.* *CA* U.S.A.
260 B2 **Mercedario, Cerro** *mt.* Arg.
261 H4 **Mercedes** *Buenos Aires* Arg.
258 F3 **Mercedes** *Corrientes* Arg.
260 E3 **Mercedes** *San Luis* Arg.
261 H3 **Mercedes** Uru.
233 □I2 **Mercer** *ME* U.S.A.
232 A4 **Mercer** *OH* U.S.A.
232 C4 **Mercer** *PA* U.S.A.
226 B2 **Mercer** *WI* U.S.A.
234 D2 **Mercer County** *county* *NJ* U.S.A.
232 E5 **Mercersburg** *PA* U.S.A.
234 D2 **Mercerville** *NJ* U.S.A.
257 F4 **Mercês** Brazil
173 E3 **Merching** Ger.
165 D4 **Merchtem** Belgium
128 B1 **Mercimek** Turkey
162 D3 **Mercœur** France
193 G4 **Mercogliano** Italy
163 D4 **Mercuès** France
160 C2 **Mercurey** France
160 E3 **Mercury** France
241 J3 **Mercury** *NV* U.S.A.
80 E2 **Mercury Bay** *North I.* N.Z.
80 E2 **Mercury Islands** *North I.* N.Z.
163 D6 **Mercus-Garrabet** France
Merdenik Turkey *see* Göle
172 B3 **Merdingen** Ger.
158 D3 **Merdrignac** France
165 C4 **Mere** Belgium
150 E3 **Mere** *Wiltshire, England* U.K.
159 I4 **Méreau** France
233 H3 **Meredith** *NH* U.S.A.
137 I3 **Merefa** Ukr.
78 □5 **Mere Lava** *i.* Vanuatu
165 C4 **Merelbeke** Belgium
80 E2 **Meremere** *North I.* N.Z.
140 M3 **Merenkurkku** *str.* Fin./Sweden
163 D6 **Mérens-les-Vals** France
156 C4 **Méréville** France
139 K2 **Merga** *r.* Rus. Fed.
202 E5 **Merga Oasis** Sudan
120 B2 **Mergenevo** Kazakh.
190 D3 **Mergozzo** Italy
97 B4 **Mergui** Myanmar
97 B5 **Mergui Archipelago** *is* Myanmar
192 B2 **Meria** *Corse* France
82 E3 **Meribah** *S.A.* Austr.
161 E3 **Méribel-les-Allues** France
Meriç *r.* Greece/Turkey *see* Evros
199 E1 **Meriç** Turkey
156 C2 **Méricourt** France
243 H4 **Mérida** Mex.
184 D2 **Mérida** Spain
250 D2 **Mérida** Venez.
250 D2 **Mérida** *state* Venez.
250 D3 **Mérida, Cordillera de** *mts* Venez.
151 F2 **Meriden** *West Midlands, England* U.K.
233 G4 **Meriden** *CT* U.S.A.
237 F5 **Meridian** *MS* U.S.A.
237 D6 **Meridian** *TX* U.S.A.
163 B4 **Mérignac** France
140 N2 **Merijärvi** Fin.
141 M3 **Merikarvia** Fin.
83 G4 **Merimbula** *N.S.W.* Austr.
176 E2 **Měřín** Czech Rep.
Merín, Laguna *l.* Brazil/Uru. *see* Mirim, Lagoa
160 A3 **Mérinchal** France
85 G4 **Merinda** *Qld* Austr.
161 D5 **Mérindol** France
215 F2 **Merindol** S. Africa
173 E3 **Mering** Ger.
207 I4 **Meringa** Nigeria
83 E3 **Meringur** *Vic.* Austr.
91 H6 **Merir** *i.* Palau
85 F5 **Merivale** *r.* *Qld* Austr.
177 L4 **Mérk** Hungary
121 H4 **Merke** Kazakh.
237 C5 **Merkel** *TX* U.S.A.
179 G4 **Merkendorf** Austria
172 E2 **Merkendorf** Ger.
138 E4 **Merkinė** Lith.
176 C2 **Merklín** Czech Rep.
172 D3 **Merklingen** Ger.
165 D3 **Merksplas** Belgium
175 M1 **Merkys** *r.* Lith.
191 G3 **Merlara** Italy
Merlav *i.* Vanuatu *see* Mere Lava
158 C4 **Merlevenez** France
162 E3 **Merlines** France
260 E3 **Merlo** Arg.
193 H3 **Merlo** *r.* Italy
85 E2 **Merluna** *Qld* Austr.
86 C3 **Mermaid Reef** *W.A.* Austr.
177 G5 **Mernye** Hungary
182 B1 **Mero** *r.* Spain
87 D6 **Merolia** *W.A.* Austr.
128 B3 **Meron, Har** *mt.* Israel
197 E4 **Merošina** *Srbija* Yugo.
203 F5 **Merowe** Sudan
87 C6 **Merredin** *W.A.* Austr.
157 F5 **Merrey** France
157 F5 **Merriam** *IN* U.S.A.
226 D5 **Merriam** *IN* U.S.A.
146 D6 **Merrick** *hill* *Scotland* U.K.
227 J3 **Merrickville** *Ont.* Can.
227 E4 **Merrill** *MI* U.S.A.
226 C3 **Merrill** *WI* U.S.A.
222 E5 **Merrill, Mount** *Y.T.* Can.
226 D5 **Merrillville** *IN* U.S.A.
230 C3 **Merrillville** *IN* U.S.A.
214 D4 **Merriman** S. Africa
236 C3 **Merriman** *NE* U.S.A.
150 E4 **Merriott** *Somerset, England* U.K.
222 F5 **Merritt** *B.C.* Can.
231 D6 **Merritt Island** *FL* U.S.A.
83 G3 **Merriwa** *N.S.W.* Austr.
83 G2 **Merrygoen** *N.S.W.* Austr.
203 I6 **Mersa Fatma** Eritrea
165 F5 **Mersch** Lux.
169 D5 **Merschbach** Ger.
192 D1 **Merse** *r.* Italy
151 H3 **Mersea Island** *England* U.K.
171 C4 **Merseburg (Saale)** Ger.
149 G4 **Mersey** *est.* *England* U.K.
149 F4 **Merseyside** *admin. div.* *England* U.K.
Mersin *İel* Turkey *see* İçel
126 E3 **Mersin** *Trabzon* Turkey
94 C2 **Mersing** Malaysia
95 F2 **Mersing, Bukit** *mt.* *Sarawak* Malaysia
156 B2 **Mers-les-Bains** France
138 D3 **Mērsrags** Latvia
116 C4 **Merta** *Rajasthan* India
116 C4 **Merta Road** *Rajasthan* India
165 F5 **Mertert** Lux.
172 A2 **Mertesdorf** Ger.
150 D3 **Merthyr Tydfil** *Merthyr Tydfil, Wales* U.K.
150 D3 **Merthyr Tydfil** *admin. div.* *Wales* U.K.
210 C4 **Merti** Kenya
173 E3 **Mertingen** Ger.
210 C4 **Merti Plateau** Kenya
169 C5 **Mertloch** Ger.
184 C3 **Mértola** Port.
237 C6 **Mertzon** *TX* U.S.A.
234 C2 **Mertztown** *PA* U.S.A.
157 H4 **Mertzwiller** France
156 C3 **Méru** France
210 C3 **Meru** Kenya
211 C5 **Meru** *vol.* Tanz.
182 B2 **Merufe** Port.
210 C4 **Meru National Park** Kenya
160 D2 **Mervans** France
162 B3 **Mervent** France
162 B2 **Mervent** France
215 F4 **Merweville** S. Africa
Merya Turkey *see* Veliköy
156 D4 **Méry-sur-Seine** France
169 C3 **Merzen** Ger.
126 D2 **Merzifon** Turkey
172 A2 **Merzig** Ger.
262 T2 **Merz Peninsula** Antarctica
215 G5 **Mesa** *r.* S. Africa
183 I3 **Mesa** *r.* Spain
241 L5 **Mesa** *AZ* U.S.A.
239 F5 **Mesa** *NM* U.S.A.
226 A2 **Mesabi Range** *hills* *MN* U.S.A.
195 G2 **Mesagne** Italy
158 E4 **Mésanger** France
182 C3 **Mesão Frio** Port.
198 D4 **Mesara, Ormos** *b.* *Kriti* Greece
169 D4 **Meschede** Ger.
162 B3 **Meschers-sur-Gironde** France
129 B3 **Mescit Dağları** *mts* Turkey
140 L2 **Meselefors** Sweden
78 □4a **Meseong** *i.* *Chuuk* Micronesia
156 D4 **Mesgrigny** France
134 J5 **Mesha** *r.* Rus. Fed.
139 J4 **Meshchovsk** Rus. Fed.
Meshed Iran *see* Mashhad
135 H6 **Meshkovskaya** Rus. Fed.
234 B1 **Meshoppen** *PA* U.S.A.
234 B1 **Meshoppen Creek** *r.* *PA* U.S.A.
226 E3 **Mesick** *MI* U.S.A.
188 F4 **Mesihovina** Bos.-Herz.
195 E4 **Mesima** *r.* Italy
198 C1 **Mesimeri** Greece
210 B3 **Meskhet'is K'edi** *hills* Georgia
159 F4 **Meslay-du-Maine** France
160 D2 **Mesnay** France
190 E2 **Mesocco** Switz.
191 H4 **Mesola** Italy
198 B2 **Mesolongi** Greece
Mesolongion Greece *see* Mesolongi
Mesón del Viente Spain *see* Mesón do Vento
182 B1 **Mesón do Vento** Spain
195 F3 **Mesoraca** Italy
172 D2 **Mespelbrunn** Ger.
158 D4 **Mesquer** France
257 F3 **Mesquita** Brazil
241 J3 **Mesquite** *NV* U.S.A.
237 D5 **Mesquite** *TX* U.S.A.
205 F2 **Messaad** Alg.
158 E4 **Messac** France
202 A3 **Messak Mellet** *hills* Libya
211 D7 **Messalo** *r.* Moz.
207 I6 **Messaména** Cameroon
Messana *Sicilia* Italy *see* Messina
165 E5 **Messancy** Belgium
163 A5 **Messanges** France
170 C3 **Meßdorf** Ger.
159 F3 **Messei** France
160 A3 **Messeix** France
184 B3 **Messejana** Port.
172 C2 **Messel** Ger.
195 E4 **Messina** *Sicilia* Italy
194 D5 **Messina** *prov.* *Sicilia* Italy
213 F4 **Messina** S. Africa
Messina, Strait of Italy *see* Messina, Stretta di
195 E4 **Messina, Stretta di** *str.* Italy
175 F3 **Messincourt** France
227 I2 **Messines** *Que.* Can.
169 C3 **Messingen** Ger.
149 I4 **Messingham** *North Lincolnshire, England* U.K.
198 C3 **Messini** Greece
198 C3 **Messiniakos Kolpos** *b.* Greece
172 D4 **Meßkirch** Ger.
140 K3 **Messlingen** Sweden
172 C3 **Meßstetten** Ger.
197 G5 **Mesta** *r.* Bulg.
Mesta *r.* Greece *see* Nestos
185 H2 **Mesta** *r.* Spain
185 F2 **Mestanza** Spain
176 E1 **Městec Králové** Czech Rep.
Mestghanem Alg. *see* Mostaganem
129 C2 **Mestia** Georgia
170 C2 **Mestlin** Ger.
171 G5 **Město Albrechtice** Czech Rep.
173 H2 **Město Touškov** Czech Rep.
191 H3 **Mestre** Italy
126 E2 **Mesudiye** Turkey
94 D4 **Mesuji** *r.* Indon.
160 A1 **Mesves-sur-Loire** France
156 C3 **Mesvres** France
160 C2 **Mesvrin** *r.* France
250 C4 **Meta** *dept* Col.
250 E3 **Meta** *r.* Col./Venez.
193 G4 **Meta** Italy
225 G3 **Métabetchouan** *Que.* Can.
160 E2 **Métabief** France
227 G2 **Metagama** *Ont.* Can.
221 I3 **Meta Incognita Peninsula** *Nunavut* Can.
237 F6 **Metairie** *LA* U.S.A.
197 F2 **Metaliferi, Munţii** *mts* Romania
191 F5 **Metallifere, Colline** *mts* Italy
139 H2 **Metallostroy** Rus. Fed.
226 C5 **Metamora** *IL* U.S.A.
258 D2 **Metán** Arg.
210 C2 **Metanara** Eth.
211 B8 **Metangula** Moz.
243 H6 **Metapan** El Salvador
191 I5 **Metauro** *r.* Italy
225 H4 **Meteghan** *N.S.* Can.
169 C3 **Metelen** Ger.
138 D4 **Metelys** *l.* Lith.
210 C3 **Metema** Eth.
198 B2 **Meteora** *tourist site* Greece
85 G5 **Meteor Creek** *r.* *Qld* Austr.
151 I2 **Metfield** *Suffolk, England* U.K.
149 I4 **Metheringham** *Lincolnshire, England* U.K.
146 F4 **Methlick** *Aberdeenshire, Scotland* U.K.
198 B3 **Methoni** Greece
233 H3 **Methuen** *MA* U.S.A.
86 E2 **Methuen, Mount** *hill* *W.A.* Austr.
81 C5 **Methven** *South I.* N.Z.
146 E5 **Methven** *Perth and Kinross, Scotland* U.K.
151 H2 **Methwold** *Norfolk, England* U.K.
188 F4 **Metković** Croatia
222 D4 **Metlakatla** *AK* U.S.A.
205 H2 **Metlaoui** Tunisia
188 E3 **Metlika** Slovenia
179 F4 **Metnitz** Austria
179 F4 **Metnitz** *r.* Austria
213 H2 **Metoro** Moz.
195 F4 **Metramo** *r.* Italy
94 D4 **Metro** *Sumatera* Indon.
237 F4 **Metropolis** *IL* U.S.A.
Metsada *tourist site* Israel *see* Masada
170 D2 **Metschow** Ger.
164 F1 **Metslawier** Neth.
198 B2 **Metsovo** Greece
172 D3 **Mettenberg** Ger.
172 A2 **Mettendorf** Ger.
173 G3 **Mettenheim** Ger.
231 D5 **Metter** *GA* U.S.A.
179 G4 **Mettersdorf am Saßbach** Austria
165 D4 **Mettet** Belgium
169 C3 **Mettingen** Ger.
172 A2 **Mettlach** Ger.
240 H4 **Mettler** *CA* U.S.A.
179 E2 **Mettmach** Austria
169 B4 **Mettmann** Ger.
159 G4 **Mettray** France
114 C4 **Mettuppalaiyam** *Tamil Nadu* India
114 C4 **Mettur** *Tamil Nadu* India
210 B2 **Metu** Eth.
235 D2 **Metuchen** *NJ* U.S.A.
176 E1 **Metuje** *r.* Czech Rep.
157 G3 **Metz** France
210 C3 **Metz** Kenya
157 H4 **Metzeral** France
157 G3 **Metzervisse** France
172 D3 **Metzingen** Ger.
245 E3 **Metzquititlán** Mex.
158 E3 **Meu** *r.* France
159 G5 **Meuble** France
94 B1 **Meulaboh** *Sumatera* Indon.
165 C4 **Meulebeke** Belgium
156 B5 **Meung-sur-Loire** France
160 C2 **Meursault** France
157 F4 **Meurthe** *r.* France
157 G4 **Meurthe-et-Moselle** *dept* *Lorraine* France
165 E4 **Meuse** *r.* Belgium/France
alt. **Maas (Neth.)**
157 F3 **Meuse** *dept* *Lorraine* France
171 D4 **Meuselwitz** Ger.
162 D3 **Meuzac** France
160 D2 **Meuzin** *r.* France
150 C4 **Mevagissey** *Cornwall, England* U.K.
108 B1 **Mêwa** *Sichuan* China
149 H4 **Mexborough** *South Yorkshire, England* U.K.
237 D6 **Mexia** *TX* U.S.A.
251 I4 **Mexiana, Ilha** *i.* Brazil
242 B1 **Mexicali** Mex.
241 M3 **Mexican Hat** *UT* U.S.A.
241 M3 **Mexican Water** *AZ* U.S.A.
242 B2 **Mexico** *country* Central America
245 E4 **México** Mex.
245 E4 **México** *state* Mex.
233 □H2 **Mexico** *ME* U.S.A.
236 F4 **Mexico** *MO* U.S.A.
233 E3 **Mexico** *NY* U.S.A.
229 G6 **Mexico, Gulf of** Mex./U.S.A.
Mexico City Mex. *see* México
184 B3 **Mexilhoeira Grande** Port.
160 D3 **Meximieux** France
148 E3 **Mey** *Highland, Scotland* U.K.
122 C3 **Meybod** Iran
170 D2 **Meyenburg** Ger.
222 C4 **Meyers Chuck** *AK* U.S.A.
232 D5 **Meyersdale** *PA* U.S.A.
215 G2 **Meyerton** S. Africa
161 D3 **Meylan** France
162 E3 **Meymac** France
123 F3 **Meymaneh** Afgh.
131 S3 **Meynypil'gyno** Rus. Fed.
161 D5 **Meyrargues** France
161 D5 **Meyreuil** France
161 E4 **Meyronnes** France
161 B4 **Meyrueis** France
162 D3 **Meyssac** France
161 C3 **Meysse** France
160 E3 **Meythet** France
160 C3 **Meyzieu** France
Mezada *tourist site* Israel *see* Masada
182 D4 **Mezas** *mt.* Spain
158 E4 **Mezcala** *r.* Mex.
243 G5 **Mezcalapa** *r.* Mex.
197 F4 **Mezdra** Bulg.
161 B5 **Mèze** France
161 E5 **Mézel** France
134 I2 **Mezen'** Rus. Fed.
134 I2 **Mezen'** *r.* Rus. Fed.
161 C4 **Mézenc, Mont** *mt.* France
134 H2 **Mezenskaya Guba** *b.* Rus. Fed.
160 D2 **Mézériat** France
139 H4 **Mezha** *r.* Rus. Fed.
98 E1 **Mezhdurechensk** *Kemerovskaya Oblast'* Rus. Fed.
134 J3 **Mezhdurechensk** *Respublika Komi* Rus. Fed.
130 H4 **Mezhdurechenskiy** Rus. Fed.
Mezhdurechnye Rus. Fed. *see* Shali
130 G2 **Mezhdusharskiy, Ostrov** *i.* *Novaya Zemlya* Rus. Fed.
137 I3 **Mezhova** Ukr.
120 D1 **Mezhozernyy** Rus. Fed.
137 H2 **Mezhyrich** Ukr.
176 C1 **Mezibořī** Czech Rep.
179 F4 **Mežica** Slovenia
159 F2 **Mézidon-Canon** France
159 H5 **Mézières-en-Brenne** France
162 C2 **Mézières-sur-Issoire** France
163 C4 **Mézilhac** France
156 D5 **Mézilles** France
176 F1 **Mezimĕstí** Czech Rep.
163 C4 **Mézin** France
139 M4 **Mezinovskiy** Rus. Fed.
182 C4 **Mezio** Port.
128 B1 **Mezitli** Turkey
177 K5 **Mezőberény** Hungary
177 J4 **Mezőcsát** Hungary
177 H5 **Mezőfalva** Hungary
177 K5 **Mezőgyán** Hungary
177 J5 **Mezőhegyes** Hungary
177 J4 **Mezőkeresztes** Hungary
177 H5 **Mezőkomárom** Hungary
177 J5 **Mezőkovácsháza** Hungary
177 J4 **Mezőkövesd** Hungary
177 G4 **Mezőörs** Hungary
163 A4 **Mézos** France
177 J4 **Mezőszemere** Hungary
177 H5 **Mezőszilas** Hungary
177 J4 **Mezőtárkány** Hungary
177 J5 **Mezőtúr** Hungary
186 C4 **Mezquita de Jarque** Spain
244 B2 **Mezquital** Mex.
244 B3 **Mezquital** *r.* Mex.
244 C2 **Mezquitic** Mex.
128 C1 **Mezraaköy** Turkey
191 F2 **Mezzana** Italy
190 E4 **Mezzanego** Italy
191 G2 **Mezzano** Italy
191 G2 **Mezzocorona** Italy
194 C5 **Mezzojuso** *Sicilia* Italy
190 E2 **Mezzoldo** Italy
191 G2 **Mezzolombardo** Italy
207 H6 **Mfou** Cameroon
209 B6 **Mfouati** Congo
211 A8 **Mfuwe** Zambia
100 G2 **Mgachi** *Sakhalin* Rus. Fed.
195 □ **Mġarr** *Gozo* Malta
195 □ **Mġarr** Malta
207 G5 **Mgbidi** Nigeria
139 I5 **Mglin** Rus. Fed.
215 G4 **Mgwali** *r.* S. Africa
213 F3 **Mhangura** Zimbabwe
184 E5 **Mharhar, Oued** *r.* Morocco
114 B2 **Mhasvad** *Mahar.* India
215 H2 **Mhlambanyatsi** Swaziland
215 H2 **Mhlume** Swaziland
215 G1 **Mhluzi** S. Africa
116 C5 **Mhow** *Medh. Prad.* India
107 H4 **Mi** *r.* China
96 A2 **Mi** *r.* Myanmar
146 B3 **Miabhaig** *Western Isles, Scotland* U.K.
245 E4 **Miacatlan** Mex.
175 L5 **Miączyn** Pol.
245 F5 **Miahuatlán** Mex.
184 E1 **Miajadas** Spain
156 C3 **Mialet** France
237 D4 **Miami** *AZ* U.S.A.
231 E7 **Miami** *FL* U.S.A.
237 E4 **Miami** *OK* U.S.A.
237 C5 **Miami** *TX* U.S.A.
231 D7 **Miami Beach** *FL* U.S.A.
232 A5 **Miamisburg** *OH* U.S.A.
106 C5 **Miancaowan** *Qinghai* China
123 H4 **Mian Channun** Pak.
107 F5 **Mianchi** *Henan* China
122 A2 **Miandowāb** Iran
213 □J3 **Miandrivazo** Madag.
107 I1 **Miandu He** *Nei Mongol* China
122 A2 **Mianeh** Iran
108 B2 **Mianning** *Sichuan* China
123 G3 **Mianwali** Pak.
108 C1 **Mianxian** *Shaanxi* China
Mianyang *Hubei* China *see* Xiantao
108 C2 **Mianyang** *Sichuan* China
108 C2 **Mianzhu** *Sichuan* China
107 I4 **Miaodao Qundao** *is* China
110 C2 **Miao'ergou** *Xinjiang* China
Miaogao *Zhejiang* China *see* Suichang
109 G3 **Miaoli** Taiwan
213 □J3 **Miarinarivo** Madag.
130 H4 **Miass** Rus. Fed.
174 F2 **Miasteczko Krajeńskie** Pol.
174 E1 **Miastko** Pol.
175 J4 **Miastków Kościelny** Pol.
175 J2 **Miastkowo** Pol.
105 D3 **Mibu-gawa** *r.* Japan
252 C5 **Mica, Cerro de** *mt.* Chile
222 G4 **Mica Creek** *B.C.* Can.
241 L5 **Mica Mountain** *AZ* U.S.A.
108 C1 **Micang Shan** *mts* China
177 K3 **Michalany** Slovakia
177 I3 **Michalová** Slovakia
177 K3 **Michalovce** Slovakia
175 I5 **Michałów** Pol.
175 J4 **Michałów Górny** Pol.
175 H5 **Michałowice** Pol.
175 F4 **Michałowice** Pol.
175 L2 **Michałowo** Pol.
223 I4 **Michel** *Sask.* Can.
171 C5 **Michelau in Oberfranken** Ger.
172 D2 **Michelbach an der Bilz** Ger.
179 F4 **Micheldorf** Austria
179 F3 **Micheldorf in Oberösterreich** Austria
172 D2 **Michelfeld** Ger.
220 D5 **Michelson, Mount** *AK* U.S.A.
172 D2 **Michelstadt** Ger.
171 E3 **Michendorf** Ger.
Micheng *Yunnan* China *see* Midu
247 E3 **Miches** Dom. Rep.
236 F2 **Michigan** *state* U.S.A.

226 D4 **Michigan, Lake** *MI/WI* U.S.A.
230 C3 **Michigan City** *IN* U.S.A.
208 B2 **Michika** Nigeria
226 C4 **Michipicoten Bay** *Ont.* Can.
224 C4 **Michipicoten River** *Ont.* Can.
244 C4 **Michoacán** *state* Mex.
175 K4 **Michów** Pol.
Michurin Bulg. *see* **Tsarevo**
135 H5 **Michurinsk** Rus. Fed.
149 G3 **Mickleton** *Durham, England* U.K.
151 F2 **Mickleton** *Gloucestershire, England* U.K.
242 □I6 **Mico** *r.* Nic.
247 □3 **Micoud** St Lucia
266 E5 **Micronesia** *is* Pacific Ocean
91 L6 **Micronesia, Federated States of** *country* N. Pacific Ocean
197 F2 **Micula** Romania
223 K5 **Midale** *Sask.* Can.
264 F4 **Mid-Atlantic Ridge** *sea feature* Atlantic Ocean
264 H8 **Mid-Atlantic Ridge** *sea feature* Atlantic Ocean
146 F2 **Midbea** *Orkney, Scotland* U.K.
165 E3 **Middelbeers** Neth.
164 C3 **Middelburg** Neth.
215 E4 **Middelburg** *E. Cape* S. Africa
215 G1 **Middelburg** *Mpumalanga* S. Africa
142 C4 **Middelfart** Denmark
164 D3 **Middelharnis** Neth.
165 B3 **Middelkerke** Belgium
214 C4 **Middelpos** S. Africa
164 F1 **Middelstum** Neth.
213 E5 **Middelwit** S. Africa
164 E2 **Middenmeer** Neth.
267 M5 **Middle America Trench** *sea feature* N. Pacific Ocean
115 G3 **Middle Andaman** *i. Andaman & Nicobar Is* India
Middle Atlas *mts* Morocco *see* **Moyen Atlas**
151 F3 **Middle Barton** *Oxfordshire, England* U.K.
225 J3 **Middle Bay** *Que.* Can.
233 H4 **Middleboro** *MA* U.S.A.
230 D4 **Middlebourne** *WV* U.S.A.
227 I5 **Middleburg** *PA* U.S.A.
232 E5 **Middleburg** *VA* U.S.A.
233 F3 **Middleburgh** *NY* U.S.A.
235 E1 **Middlebury** *CT* U.S.A.
226 E5 **Middlebury** *IN* U.S.A.
233 G2 **Middlebury** *VT* U.S.A.
237 C6 **Middle Concho** *r. TX* U.S.A.
Middle Congo *country* Africa *see* **Congo**
85 E3 **Middle Creek** *r. Qld* Austr.
234 C1 **Middle Creek** *r. PA* U.S.A.
235 F1 **Middlefield** *CT* U.S.A.
235 F1 **Middle Haddam** *CT* U.S.A.
149 H3 **Middleham** *North Yorkshire, England* U.K.
235 D1 **Middle Hope** *NY* U.S.A.
235 F2 **Middle Island** *NY* U.S.A.
236 D3 **Middle Loup** *r. NE* U.S.A.
150 E4 **Middlemarsh** *Dorset, England* U.K.
85 G4 **Middlemount** *Qld* Austr.
232 B5 **Middleport** *OH* U.S.A.
234 B2 **Middleport** *PA* U.S.A.
236 E3 **Middle Raccoon** *r. IA* U.S.A.
149 I4 **Middle Rasen** *Lincolnshire, England* U.K.
234 B3 **Middle River** *MD* U.S.A.
232 B6 **Middlesboro** *KY* U.S.A.
149 H3 **Middlesbrough** *Middlesbrough, England* U.K.
149 H3 **Middlesbrough** *admin. div. England* U.K.
232 E3 **Middlesex** *NY* U.S.A.
234 A2 **Middlesex** *PA* U.S.A.
235 F1 **Middlesex County** *county CT* U.S.A.
235 D2 **Middlesex County** *county NJ* U.S.A.
149 H3 **Middlesmoor** *North Yorkshire, England* U.K.
85 E4 **Middleton** *Qld* Austr.
225 H4 **Middleton** *N.S.* Can.
215 E5 **Middleton** S. Africa
149 G4 **Middleton** *Greater Manchester, England* U.K.
151 H2 **Middleton** *Norfolk, England* U.K.
232 A3 **Middleton** *MI* U.S.A.
226 C4 **Middleton** *WI* U.S.A.
151 F2 **Middleton Cheney** *Northamptonshire, England* U.K.
149 G3 **Middleton in Teesdale** *Durham, England* U.K.
151 G4 **Middleton-on-Sea** *West Sussex, England* U.K.
149 I4 **Middleton-on-the-Wolds** *East Riding of Yorkshire, England* U.K.
77 F4 **Middleton Reef** Austr.
151 F3 **Middleton Stoney** *Oxfordshire, England* U.K.
147 E2 **Middletown** *Northern Ireland* U.K.
240 F2 **Middletown** *CA* U.S.A.
235 F1 **Middletown** *CT* U.S.A.
234 C3 **Middletown** *DE* U.S.A.
232 E5 **Middletown** *MD* U.S.A.
235 D2 **Middletown** *NJ* U.S.A.
233 F4 **Middletown** *NY* U.S.A.
232 A5 **Middletown** *OH* U.S.A.
227 I5 **Middletown** *PA* U.S.A.
232 D5 **Middletown** *VA* U.S.A.
226 E4 **Middleville** *MI* U.S.A.
233 F3 **Middleville** *NY* U.S.A.
149 G4 **Middlewich** *Cheshire, England* U.K.
81 B6 **Mid Dome** *mt. South I.* N.Z.
204 D2 **Midelt** Morocco
80 E3 **Midhirst** *North I.* N.Z.
151 G4 **Midhurst** *West Sussex, England* U.K.
124 C4 **Mīdī** Yemen
163 E5 **Midi, Canal du** France
163 C6 **Midi de Bigorre, Pic du** *mt.* France
163 B6 **Midi d'Ossau, Pic du** *mt.* France
265 J5 **Mid-Indian Basin** *sea feature* Indian Ocean
265 I6 **Mid-Indian Ridge** *sea feature* Indian Ocean
161 A4 **Midi-Pyrénées** *admin. reg.* France
224 E4 **Midland** *Ont.* Can.
241 J5 **Midland** *CA* U.S.A.
227 E4 **Midland** *MI* U.S.A.
236 C2 **Midland** *SD* U.S.A.
237 C5 **Midland** *TX* U.S.A.
87 B6 **Midland Junction** *W.A.* Austr.
213 F3 **Midlands** *prov.* Zimbabwe
147 C5 **Midleton** Rep. of Ireland
146 E6 **Midlothian** *admin. div. Scotland* U.K.
237 D5 **Midlothian** *TX* U.S.A.
232 E6 **Midlothian** *VA* U.S.A.
168 D2 **Midlum** Ger.
227 G3 **Midmay** *Ont.* Can.
Midnapore *W. Bengal* India *see* **Medinipur**
213 □J4 **Midongy Atsimo** Madag.
103 E7 **Midori-gawa** *r.* Japan
163 B5 **Midou** *r.* France
163 B5 **Midouze** *r.* France
266 F4 **Mid-Pacific Mountains** *sea feature* N. Pacific Ocean
215 G1 **Midrand** S. Africa
92 C5 **Midsayap** Phil.
150 E3 **Midsomer Norton** *Bath and North East Somerset, England* U.K.
140 I3 **Midsund** Norway
108 B3 **Midu** *Yunnan* China
113 □2 **Midu** *i.* Addu Atoll Maldives
238 C2 **Midvale** *ID* U.S.A.
Midway Oman *see* **Thamarīt**
241 L1 **Midway** *UT* U.S.A.
75 H2 **Midway Islands** N. Pacific Ocean
87 D4 **Midway Well** *W.A.* Austr.
238 F3 **Midwest** *WY* U.S.A.
237 D5 **Midwest City** *OK* U.S.A.
164 G1 **Midwolda** Neth.
127 F3 **Midyat** Turkey
Midye Turkey *see* **Kıyıköy**
146 □G1 **Mid Yell** *Shetland, Scotland* U.K.
197 F4 **Midzhur** *mt.* Bulg./Yugo.
104 C4 **Mie** *pref.* Japan
175 I5 **Miechów** Pol.
177 L1 **Mieczka** *r.* Pol.
178 C3 **Mieders** Austria
183 I3 **Miedes** Spain
175 I3 **Miedziana Góra** Pol.
174 D3 **Miedzichowo** Pol.
175 K3 **Miedzna** *Mazowieckie* Pol.
175 H6 **Miedźna** Pol.
174 G5 **Miedźno** Pol.
174 E3 **Międzybórz** Pol.
174 D3 **Międzychód** Pol.
174 E5 **Międzylesie** Pol.
175 K4 **Międzyrzec Podlaski** Pol.
174 D3 **Międzyrzecz** Pol.
174 C2 **Międzyzdroje** Pol.
141 N3 **Miehikkälä** Fin.
169 C5 **Miehlen** Ger.
175 J6 **Miejsce Piastowe** Pol.
174 E4 **Miejska-Górka** Pol.
174 E4 **Miękinia** Pol.
163 C5 **Miélan** France
161 D4 **Miélandre, Montagne de** *mt.* France
175 J5 **Mielec** Pol.
174 F3 **Mieleszyn** Pol.
168 F1 **Mielkendorf** Ger.
175 I3 **Mielnik** Pol.
174 E1 **Mielno** Pol.
211 C7 **Miembwe** Tanz.
178 C3 **Mieming** Austria
175 G3 **Mień** *r.* Pol.
83 F5 **Miena** *Tas.* Austr.
209 F8 **Mienge** Zambia
183 G1 **Miera** *r.* Spain
197 G2 **Miercurea-Ciuc** Romania
182 E1 **Mieres** Spain
Mieres del Camín Spain *see* **Mieres**
Mieres del Camino Spain *see* **Mieres**
165 E3 **Mierlo** Neth.
175 E5 **Mieroszów** Pol.
163 D4 **Miers** France
244 D2 **Mier y Noriega** Mex.
175 I5 **Mierzawa** *r.* Pol.
143 H4 **Mierzeja Helska** *pen.* Pol.
143 H4 **Mierzeja Wiślana** *spit* Pol.
172 B2 **Miesau** Ger.
173 F4 **Miesbach** Ger.
174 F3 **Mieścisko** Pol.
172 B2 **Miesenbach** Ger.
210 D2 **Mī'ēso** Eth.
171 C3 **Mieste** Ger.
171 C3 **Miesterhorst** Ger.
171 C3 **Mieszków** Pol.
174 C3 **Mieszkowice** Pol.
172 D3 **Mietingen** Ger.
140 K3 **Mietoinen** Fin.
160 E2 **Mieussy** France
182 D3 **Mieza** Spain
232 B4 **Mifflin** *OH* U.S.A.
227 I5 **Mifflinburg** *PA* U.S.A.
232 E4 **Mifflintown** *PA* U.S.A.
234 B1 **Mifflinville** *PA* U.S.A.
106 B3 **Migang Shan** *mt. Gansu* China
215 E2 **Migdol** S. Africa
156 D5 **Migennes** France
191 G4 **Migliarino** Italy
191 G4 **Migliaro** Italy
195 F2 **Miglionica** Italy
162 C2 **Mignaloux-Beauvoir** France
193 F3 **Mignano Monte Lungo** Italy
192 D2 **Mignone** *r.* Italy
160 E2 **Mignovillard** France
225 H3 **Miguasha Park** *tourist site N.B.* Can.
245 F4 **Miguel Alemán** Mex.
245 F4 **Miguel Alemán, Presa** *resr* Mex.
254 E3 **Miguel Alves** Brazil
244 C1 **Miguel Auza** Mex.
254 E4 **Miguel Calmon** Brazil
245 F5 **Miguel de la Madrid, Presa** *resr* Mex.
183 G5 **Miguel Esteban** Spain
257 G4 **Miguel Pereira** Brazil
261 F5 **Miguel Riglos** Arg.
185 G2 **Migueltura** Spain
197 G3 **Mihăileşti** Romania
176 G5 **Mihálditi** Hungary
199 G1 **Mihalgazi** Turkey
126 C3 **Mihalıççık** Turkey
176 G4 **Mihályi** Hungary
103 F6 **Mihara** Japan
105 F4 **Mihara-yama** *vol.* Japan
Mihidjan *W. Bengal* India *see* **Chittaranjan**
117 F5 **Mihijam** *Bihar* India
169 F4 **Mihla** Ger.
183 F4 **Mijares** Spain
187 C4 **Mijares** *r.* Spain
175 F4 **Mijas** Spain
185 F4 **Mijas** *mt.* Spain
164 D2 **Mijdrecht** Neth.
105 F1 **Mijōga-take** *mt.* Japan
160 E2 **Mijoux** France
102 J2 **Mikasa** Japan
136 D1 **Mikashevichy** Belarus
177 K4 **Mikepércs** Hungary
138 F5 **Mikhanavichy** Belarus
Mikha Tskhakaia Georgia *see* **Senaki**
Mikhaykovskiy Rus. Fed. *see* **Prozorovo**
139 L4 **Mikhaylov** Rus. Fed.
Mikhaylovgrad Bulg. *see* **Montana**
121 I1 **Mikhaylovka** *Pavlodarskaya Oblast'* Kazakh.
Mikhaylovka *Zhambylskaya Oblast'* Kazakh. *see* **Sarykemer**
100 A2 **Mikhaylovka** *Chitinskaya Oblast'* Rus. Fed.
137 H1 **Mikhaylovka** *Kurskaya Oblast'* Rus. Fed.
100 E4 **Mikhaylovka** *Primorskiy Kray* Rus. Fed.
Mikhaylovka *Tul'skaya Oblast'* Rus. Fed. *see* **Kimovsk**
135 H6 **Mikhaylovka** *Volgogradskaya Oblast'* Rus. Fed.
197 F4 **Mikhaylovo** Bulg.
137 K3 **Mikhaylovo-Aleksandrovskiy** Rus. Fed.
121 I2 **Mikhaylovskiy** *Altayskiy Kray* Rus. Fed.
Mikhaylovskiy *Altayskiy Kray* Rus. Fed. *see* **Ust'-Kalmanka**
Mikhaylovskoye Ozero
Mikhaylovskoye Rus. Fed. *see* **Shpakovskoye**
263 F2 **Mikhaytov Island** Antarctica
139 K4 **Mikhnevo** Rus. Fed.
104 A4 **Miki** Japan
Mikines *tourist site* Greece *see* **Mycenae**
117 H4 **Mikir Hills** India
141 N3 **Mikkeli** Fin.
141 N3 **Mikkelin mlk** Fin.
222 H3 **Mikkwa** *r. Alta* Can.
179 G4 **Miklavž** Slovenia
174 F3 **Mikołajki** Pol.
175 H2 **Mikołajki Pomorskie** Pol.
174 G5 **Mikołów** Pol.
Mikonos *i.* Greece *see* **Mykonos**
174 G1 **Mikoszewo** Pol.
Mikoyan Armenia *see* **Yeghegnadzor**
Mikoyanovka Rus. Fed. *see* **Oktyabr'skiy**
198 C1 **Mikropoli** Greece
174 F4 **Mikstat** Pol.
171 F5 **Mikulášovice** Czech Rep.
176 G3 **Mikulov** Czech Rep.
176 G1 **Mikulovice** Czech Rep.
211 C6 **Mikumi** Tanz.
211 C6 **Mikumi National Park** Tanz.
134 J3 **Mikun'** Rus. Fed.
105 D3 **Mikuni-sanmyaku** *mts* Japan
105 E3 **Mikuni-yama** *mt.* Japan
205 G1 **Mila** Alg.
236 E2 **Milaca** *MN* U.S.A.
114 B5 **Miladhunmadulu Atoll** Maldives
254 F3 **Milagres** Brazil
250 B5 **Milagro** Ecuador
183 I2 **Milagro** Spain
183 G3 **Milagros** Spain
175 I1 **Miłakowo** Pol.
Milan Italy *see* **Milano**
227 F4 **Milan** *MI* U.S.A.
236 E3 **Milan** *MO* U.S.A.
232 B4 **Milan** *OH* U.S.A.
209 C7 **Milando** Angola
82 D3 **Milang** *S.A.* Austr.
213 G3 **Milange** Moz.
190 E3 **Milano** Italy
190 E3 **Milano** *prov. Lombardia* Italy
190 D3 **Milano (Malpensa)** *airport* Italy
191 H4 **Milano Marittima** Italy
Milanovce Slovakia *see* **Veľký Kýr**
175 K4 **Milanów** Pol.
175 I3 **Milanówek** Pol.
234 C1 **Milanville** *PA* U.S.A.
197 G2 **Milaş** Romania
199 G2 **Milas** Turkey
195 E4 **Milazzo** *Sicilia* Italy
236 D2 **Milbank** *SD* U.S.A.
150 E4 **Milborne Port** *Somerset, England* U.K.
150 E4 **Milborne St Andrew** *Dorset, England* U.K.
233 □J2 **Milbridge** *ME* U.S.A.
170 C3 **Milde** *r.* Ger.
151 H2 **Mildenhall** *Suffolk, England* U.K.
227 I5 **Mildred** *PA* U.S.A.
168 E1 **Mildstedt** Ger.
83 E3 **Mildura** *Vic.* Austr.
129 E3 **Mil Düzü** *lowland* Azer.
108 B3 **Mile** *Yunnan* China
210 D2 **Mīlē** Eth.
183 G3 **Milebush** *Northern Ireland* U.K.
151 H3 **Mile End** *Essex, England* U.K.
246 □ **Mile Gully** Jamaica
175 J3 **Milejczyce** Pol.
175 H1 **Milejewo** Pol.
175 K4 **Milejów** Pol.
194 C5 **Milena** *Sicilia* Italy
85 G5 **Miles** *Qld* Austr.
232 E4 **Milesburg** *PA* U.S.A.
238 F2 **Miles City** *MT* U.S.A.
176 C1 **Milešovka** *hill* Czech Rep.
147 D5 **Milestone** Rep. of Ireland
197 H2 **Miletin** *r.* Romania
195 F4 **Mileto** Italy
193 G3 **Miletto, Monte** *mt.* Italy
87 C5 **Mileura** *W.A.* Austr.
176 D2 **Milevsko** Czech Rep.
149 G2 **Milfield** *Northumberland, England* U.K.
184 B3 **Milfontes** Port.
147 C4 **Milford** *Cork* Rep. of Ireland
147 D1 **Milford** *Donegal* Rep. of Ireland
151 G3 **Milford** *Surrey, England* U.K.
235 E1 **Milford** *CT* U.S.A.
234 C4 **Milford** *DE* U.S.A.
226 D5 **Milford** *IL* U.S.A.
233 H3 **Milford** *MA* U.S.A.
234 B3 **Milford** *MD* U.S.A.
233 □I2 **Milford** *ME* U.S.A.
232 B3 **Milford** *MI* U.S.A.
236 D3 **Milford** *NE* U.S.A.
233 H3 **Milford** *NH* U.S.A.
235 C2 **Milford** *NJ* U.S.A.
234 D1 **Milford** *PA* U.S.A.
241 K2 **Milford** *UT* U.S.A.
232 E5 **Milford** *VA* U.S.A.
150 B3 **Milford Haven** *Pembrokeshire, Wales* U.K.
151 F4 **Milford on Sea** *Hampshire, England* U.K.
81 A6 **Milford Sound** *South I.* N.Z.
81 A6 **Milford Sound** *inlet South I.* N.Z.
234 C2 **Milford Square** *PA* U.S.A.
85 E3 **Milgarra** *Qld* Austr.
87 C5 **Milgun** *W.A.* Austr.
Milḥ, Baḥr al *l.* Iraq *see* **Razāzah, Buḥayrat ar**
182 D3 **Milhão** Port.
161 C5 **Milhaud** France
174 F4 **Milicz** Pol.
Milid Turkey *see* **Malatya**
84 B1 **Milikapiti** *N.T.* Austr.
87 C6 **Miling** *W.A.* Austr.
84 C2 **Milingimbi** *N.T.* Austr.
192 A4 **Milis** *Sardegna* Italy
194 D5 **Militello in Val di Catania** *Sicilia* Italy
158 B3 **Milizac** France
238 F1 **Milk** *r. MT* U.S.A.
203 F5 **Milk, Wadi el** *watercourse* Sudan
171 F4 **Milkel** Ger.
175 J2 **Miłki** Pol.
131 Q4 **Mil'kovo** Rus. Fed.
174 E4 **Miłkowice** Pol.
223 H5 **Milk River** *Alta* Can.
164 E3 **Mill** Neth.
85 F3 **Millaa Millaa** *Qld* Austr.
226 A5 **Millard** *MO* U.S.A.
183 I5 **Millares** Spain
161 B4 **Millau** France
160 C2 **Millay** France
232 D6 **Millboro** *VA* U.S.A.
227 H3 **Millbrook** *Ont.* Can.
150 C4 **Millbrook** *Cornwall, England* U.K.
231 C5 **Millbrook** *AL* U.S.A.
233 G4 **Millbrook** *NY* U.S.A.
146 E4 **Mill Buie** *hill Scotland* U.K.
238 B2 **Mill City** *OR* U.S.A.
232 D5 **Mill Creek** *WV* U.S.A.
240 F1 **Mill Creek** *r. CA* U.S.A.
234 B3 **Mill Creek** *r. PA* U.S.A.
235 F1 **Milldale** *CT* U.S.A.
231 D5 **Milledgeville** *GA* U.S.A.
226 C5 **Milledgeville** *IL* U.S.A.
226 E2 **Mille Lacs** *lakes MN* U.S.A.
224 B3 **Mille Lacs, Lac des** *l. Ont.* Can.
231 D5 **Millen** *GA* U.S.A.
214 D5 **Miller** S. Africa
236 D2 **Miller** *SD* U.S.A.
227 G3 **Miller Lake** *Ont.* Can.
135 H6 **Millerovo** Rus. Fed.
241 L6 **Miller Peak** *AZ* U.S.A.
227 I5 **Millersburg** *MI* U.S.A.
232 C4 **Millersburg** *OH* U.S.A.
227 I5 **Millersburg** *PA* U.S.A.
82 D2 **Millers Creek** *S.A.* Austr.
232 B6 **Millers Creek** *KY* U.S.A.
233 G3 **Millers Falls** *MA* U.S.A.
81 B6 **Millers Flat** *South I.* N.Z.
232 B5 **Millersport** *OH* U.S.A.
234 B2 **Millerstown** *PA* U.S.A.
234 B3 **Millersville** *MD* U.S.A.
234 B3 **Millersville** *PA* U.S.A.
233 G4 **Millerton** *NY* U.S.A.
161 E4 **Millevaches** France
162 D3 **Millevaches, Plateau de** France
147 E2 **Millford** *Northern Ireland* U.K.
232 E4 **Mill Hall** *PA* U.S.A.
235 D2 **Millhurst** *NJ* U.S.A.
82 E4 **Millicent** *S.A.* Austr.
157 F4 **Millières** France
164 F3 **Millingen aan de Rijn** Neth.
232 A3 **Millington** *MD* U.S.A.
227 F4 **Millington** *MI* U.S.A.
237 F5 **Millington** *TN* U.S.A.
233 □I2 **Millinocket** *ME* U.S.A.
252 C5 **Milliri, Cerro** *mt.* Bol.
263 G2 **Mill Island** Antarctica
147 F2 **Millisle** *Northern Ireland* U.K.
85 F4 **Millmerran** *Qld* Austr.
234 A2 **Millmont** *PA* U.S.A.
149 F3 **Millom** *Cumbria, England* U.K.
146 D6 **Millport** *North Ayrshire, Scotland* U.K.
234 D1 **Millrift** *PA* U.S.A.
232 E4 **Millsboro** *DE* U.S.A.
179 E4 **Millstatt** Austria
178 D4 **Millstätter See** *l.* Austria
226 B3 **Millston** *WI* U.S.A.
232 B6 **Millstone** *KY* U.S.A.
232 C5 **Millstone** *WV* U.S.A.
234 D2 **Millstone** *r. NJ* U.S.A.
86 C4 **Millstream** *W.A.* Austr.
147 B4 **Millstreet** Rep. of Ireland
225 F4 **Milltown** *N.B.* Can.
148 B3 **Milltown** *Cavan* Rep. of Ireland
147 C3 **Milltown** *Galway* Rep. of Ireland
147 B4 **Milltown** *Kerry* Rep. of Ireland
148 C4 **Milltown** *Kildare* Rep. of Ireland
146 F4 **Milltown** *Aberdeenshire, Scotland* U.K.
148 C3 **Milltown** *Northern Ireland* U.K.
238 D2 **Milltown** *MT* U.S.A.
226 A3 **Milltown** *WI* U.S.A.
147 B4 **Milltown Malbay** Rep. of Ireland
146 F4 **Milltown of Rothiemay** *Moray, Scotland* U.K.
85 E3 **Millungera** *Qld* Austr.
215 F1 **Millvale** S. Africa
240 F3 **Mill Valley** *CA* U.S.A.
233 □J1 **Millville** *N.B.* Can.
234 C3 **Millville** *NJ* U.S.A.
234 B1 **Millville** *PA* U.S.A.
235 E1 **Millwood** *NY* U.S.A.
237 E5 **Millwood Lake** *AR* U.S.A.
156 C4 **Milly-la-Forêt** France
160 C2 **Milly-Lamartine** France
87 C5 **Milly Milly** *W.A.* Austr.
183 I3 **Milmarcos** Spain
170 E2 **Milmersdorf** Ger.
165 E4 **Milmort** Belgium
146 E5 **Milnathort** *Perth and Kinross, Scotland* U.K.
Milne Land *i.* Greenland *see* **Ilimananngip Nunaa**
146 D6 **Milngavie** *East Dunbartonshire, Scotland* U.K.
149 G4 **Milnrow** *Greater Manchester, England* U.K.
149 G3 **Milnthorpe** *Cumbria, England* U.K.
206 C4 **Milo** *r.* Guinea
195 E5 **Milo** *Sicilia* Italy
233 □I2 **Milo** *ME* U.S.A.
160 E4 **Milogradovo** Rus. Fed.
240 □D9 **Milolii** *HI* U.S.A.
175 H2 **Miłomłyn** Pol.
174 G1 **Miłoradz** Pol.
198 D3 **Milos** *i.* Greece
139 L5 **Miloslavskoye** Rus. Fed.
174 F3 **Miłosław** Pol.
146 B4 **Milovaig** *Highland, Scotland* U.K.
137 K3 **Milove** Ukr.
171 F5 **Milovice** Czech Rep.
171 D3 **Milow** *Brandenburg* Ger.
170 C2 **Milow** *Mecklenburg-Vorpommern* Ger.
175 H6 **Milówka** Pol.
83 E2 **Milparinka** *N.S.W.* Austr.
240 G3 **Milpitas** *CA* U.S.A.
232 E4 **Milroy** *PA* U.S.A.
232 F5 **Miltach** Ger.
172 D2 **Miltenberg** Ger.
83 G3 **Milton** *N.S.W.* Austr.
227 H4 **Milton** *Ont.* Can.
81 B7 **Milton** *South I.* N.Z.
146 D4 **Milton** *Highland, Scotland* U.K.
146 E5 **Milton** *Perth and Kinross, Scotland* U.K.
233 F5 **Milton** *DE* U.S.A.
231 C6 **Milton** *FL* U.S.A.
233 □H3 **Milton** *NH* U.S.A.
235 F1 **Milton** *NY* U.S.A.
232 E5 **Milton** *PA* U.S.A.
234 B1 **Milton** *PA* U.S.A.
233 G2 **Milton** *VT* U.S.A.
232 B5 **Milton** *WV* U.S.A.
150 C4 **Milton Abbot** *Devon, England* U.K.
238 C2 **Milton-Freewater** *OR* U.S.A.
151 G2 **Milton Keynes** *Milton Keynes, England* U.K.
151 G2 **Milton Keynes** *admin. div. England* U.K.
170 E1 **Miltzow** Ger.
109 E2 **Miluo** *Hunan* China
227 G4 **Milverton** *Ont.* Can.
150 D3 **Milverton** *Somerset, England* U.K.
226 D4 **Milwaukee** *WI* U.S.A.
264 D4 **Milwaukee Deep** *sea feature* Caribbean Sea
120 E2 **Mily** Kazakh.
135 H6 **Milyutinskaya** Rus. Fed.
169 F5 **Milz** Ger.
163 B5 **Mimbaste** France
82 C1 **Mimili** *S.A.* Austr.
114 C4 **Mimisal** *Tamil Nadu* India
163 A4 **Mimizan** France
163 A4 **Mimizan-Plage** France
176 D1 **Mimoň** Czech Rep.
208 A5 **Mimongo** Gabon
257 G4 **Mimoso do Sul** Brazil
105 C3 **Mimuro-yama** *mt.* Japan
103 G6 **Mina** Mex.
240 H2 **Mina** *NV* U.S.A.
244 E4 **Mina, Nevado** *mt.* Peru
122 D5 **Mīnāb** Iran
122 D5 **Mīnāb** *r.* Iran
260 E2 **Mina Clavero** Arg.
184 C3 **Mina de São Domingos** Port.
223 L4 **Minago** *r. Man.* Can.
93 B2 **Minahasa, Semenanjung** *pen.* Indon.
Minahassa Peninsula Indon. *see* **Minahasa, Semenanjung**
125 F2 **Mina Jebel Ali** U.A.E.
Minaker *B.C.* Can. *see* **Prophet River**
223 M5 **Minaki** *Ont.* Can.
103 E7 **Minamata** Japan
84 C2 **Minamia** *N.T.* Austr.
105 F3 **Minamiashigara** Japan
104 C4 **Minamichita** Japan
104 B3 **Minami-gawa** *r.* Japan
103 □3 **Minami-lō-jima** *vol. Kazan-rettō* Japan
Min'an *Hunan* China *see* **Longshan**
146 C5 **Minard** *Argyll and Bute, Scotland* U.K.
81 B6 **Minaret Peaks** *South I.* N.Z.
246 C2 **Minas** Cuba
94 C2 **Minas** *Sumatera* Indon.
258 E3 **Minas** Uru.
127 H5 **Mīnā' Sa'ūd** Kuwait
225 H4 **Minas Channel** *N.S.* Can.
258 G3 **Minas de Corrales** Uru.
246 B2 **Minas de Matahambre** Cuba
184 D3 **Minas de Riotinto** Spain
256 D3 **Minas Gerais** *state* Brazil
257 F2 **Minas Novas** Brazil
185 I2 **Minateda** Spain
244 B4 **Minatitlán** Mex.
185 H1 **Minaya** Spain
96 A2 **Minbu** Myanmar
123 H4 **Minchinabad** Pak.
259 B6 **Minchinmávida** *vol.* Chile
146 E6 **Minch Moor** *hill Scotland* U.K.
195 F3 **Mincio** *r.* Italy
129 E4 **Mincivan** Azer.
92 C5 **Mindanao** *i.* Phil.
92 C5 **Mindanao** *r.* Phil.
82 E3 **Mindarie** *S.A.* Austr.
182 B5 **Minde** Port.
173 E3 **Mindel** *r.* Ger.
173 E3 **Mindelheim** Ger.
206 □ **Mindelo** Cape Verde
182 B3 **Mindelo** Port.
173 F3 **Mindelstetten** Ger.
227 H3 **Minden** *Ont.* Can.
169 D3 **Minden** Ger.
237 E5 **Minden** *LA* U.S.A.
236 D3 **Minden** *NE* U.S.A.
240 H2 **Minden** *NV* U.S.A.
227 F4 **Minden City** *MI* U.S.A.
165 D3 **Mindenhout** Belgium
184 B4 **Minderoo** *W.A.* Austr.
92 B3 **Mindoro** *i.* Phil.
92 A3 **Mindoro Strait** Phil.
209 B6 **Mindouli** Congo
177 J5 **Mindszent** Hungary
177 H5 **Mindszentgodisa** Hungary
257 E4 **Minduri** Brazil
120 D1 **Mindyak** Rus. Fed.
Mindzhivan Azer. *see* **Mincivan**
103 E6 **Mine** Japan
226 A1 **Mine Centre** *Ont.* Can.
147 D5 **Mine Head** Rep. of Ireland
150 D3 **Minehead** *Somerset, England* U.K.
124 A3 **Mineiga, Gebel** *mts* Egypt/Sudan
256 A2 **Mineiros** Brazil
194 D5 **Mineo** *Sicilia* Italy
235 E2 **Mineola** *NY* U.S.A.
237 E5 **Mineola** *TX* U.S.A.
235 I3 **Minera** *Wrexham, Wales* U.K.
232 E5 **Mineral** *VA* U.S.A.
129 C1 **Mineral'nyye Vody** Rus. Fed.
226 B4 **Mineral Point** *WI* U.S.A.
237 D5 **Mineral Wells** *TX* U.S.A.
232 C5 **Mineralwells** *WV* U.S.A.
191 G4 **Minerbio** Italy
232 B4 **Minersville** *PA* U.S.A.
241 K2 **Minersville** *UT* U.S.A.
Minerva *atoll* Arch. *des Tuamotu* Fr. Polynesia *see* **Reao**
232 C4 **Minerva** *OH* U.S.A.
193 H4 **Minervino Murge** Italy
161 A5 **Minervois, Monts du** *hills* France
172 C2 **Minfeld** Ger.
111 C4 **Minfeng** *Xinjiang* China
209 E7 **Minga** Dem. Rep. Congo
129 E3 **Mingäçevir** Azer.
129 E3 **Mingäçevir Su Anbarı** *resr* Azer.
208 D3 **Mingala** C.A.R.
225 H3 **Mingan** *Que.* Can.
225 I3 **Mingan, Îles de** *is Que.* Can.
193 H4 **Mingardo** *r.* Italy
82 E3 **Mingary** *S.A.* Austr.
Mingechaur Azer. *see* **Mingäçevir**
Mingechaurskoye Vodokhranilishche *resr* Azer. *see* **Mingäçevir Su Anbarı**
85 F3 **Mingela** *Qld* Austr.
87 B6 **Mingenew** *W.A.* Austr.
Mingfeng *Hubei* China *see* **Yuan'an**
109 E1 **Minggang** *Henan* China
109 F1 **Mingguang** *Anhui* China
96 A2 **Mingin** Myanmar
96 A2 **Mingin Range** *mts* Myanmar
121 H4 **Ming-Kush** Kyrg.
183 I5 **Minglanilla** Spain
232 C4 **Mingo Junction** *OH* U.S.A.
183 H4 **Mingorría** Spain
211 C7 **Mingoyo** Tanz.
Mingshan *Chongqing* China *see* **Fengdu**
108 B2 **Mingshan** *Sichuan* China
100 C3 **Mingshui** *Heilong.* China
146 A5 **Mingulay** *i. Scotland* U.K.
213 I2 **Minguri** Moz.
109 F3 **Mingxi** *Fujian* China
Mingzhou *Hebei* China *see* **Weixian**
Mingzhou *Shaanxi* China *see* **Suide**
Minhe *Jiangxi* China *see* **Jinxian**
112 J4 **Minhe** *Qinghai* China
96 A3 **Minhla** *Magwe* Myanmar
96 A3 **Minhla** *Pegu* Myanmar
109 F3 **Minhou** *Fujian* China
158 E3 **Miniac-Morvan** France
115 E3 **Minicoy** *i.* India
114 B4 **Minicoy** *i.* India
87 D6 **Minigwal, Lake** *salt flat W.A.* Austr.
179 H4 **Minihof-Liebau** Austria
138 C4 **Minija** *r.* Lith.
87 B4 **Minilya** *W.A.* Austr.
87 B4 **Minilya** *r. W.A.* Austr.
260 A5 **Mininco** Chile
206 D4 **Mininian** Côte d'Ivoire
183 H3 **Ministra** *mt.* Spain
183 H3 **Ministra, Sierra** *mts* Spain
223 K4 **Minitonas** *Man.* Can.
Minjian *Sichuan* China *see* **Mabian**
108 C2 **Min Jiang** *r. Sichuan* China
109 F3 **Min Jiang** *r.* China
84 C1 **Minjilang** *N.T.* Austr.
129 E4 **Minkänd** Azer.
Min-Kush Kyrg. *see* **Ming-Kush**
82 D3 **Minlaton** *S.A.* Austr.
106 D4 **Minle** *Gansu* China
207 G4 **Minna** Nigeria
263 L1 **Minna Bluff** *pt* Antarctica
102 □1 **Minna-shima** *i.* Japan
141 K3 **Minne** Sweden
236 D4 **Minneapolis** *KS* U.S.A.
226 A3 **Minneapolis** *MN* U.S.A.
223 L5 **Minnedosa** *Man.* Can.
232 D5 **Minnehaha Springs** *WV* U.S.A.
236 E4 **Minneola** *KS* U.S.A.
236 E2 **Minnesota** *r. MN* U.S.A.
236 E2 **Minnesota** *state* U.S.A.
226 B3 **Minnesota City** *MN* U.S.A.
236 D1 **Minnewaukan** *ND* U.S.A.
87 B4 **Minnie Creek** *W.A.* Austr.
146 D7 **Minnigaff** *Dumfries and Galloway, Scotland* U.K.
82 C3 **Minnipa** *S.A.* Austr.
184 C2 **Miño** Spain
182 B3 **Miño** *r.* Port./Spain
105 E3 **Minobu-san** *mt.* Japan
105 E4 **Minobu-sanchi** *mts* Japan
104 D3 **Minokamo** Japan
104 D3 **Mino-Mikawa-kōgen** *reg.* Japan
226 B2 **Minong** *WI* U.S.A.
226 C5 **Minonk** *IL* U.S.A.
104 B4 **Minoo** Japan
Minorca *i.* Spain *see* **Menorca**
160 C1 **Minot** France
236 C1 **Minot** *ND* U.S.A.
106 D4 **Minqin** *Gansu* China
109 F3 **Minqing** *Fujian* China
234 C3 **Minquadale** *DE* U.S.A.
107 G5 **Minquan** *Henan* China
168 C2 **Minsen** Ger.
108 B1 **Min Shan** *mts Sichuan* China
138 F5 **Minsk** Belarus
Minskaya Oblast *admin. div.* Belarus *see* **Minskaya Voblasts'**
138 F5 **Minskaya Voblasts'** *admin. div.* Belarus
175 J3 **Mińsk Mazowiecki** Pol.
Minsk Oblast *admin. div.* Belarus *see* **Minskaya Voblasts'**
151 H3 **Minster** *Kent, England* U.K.
151 I3 **Minster** *Kent, England* U.K.
232 A4 **Minster** *OH* U.S.A.
150 E2 **Minsterley** *Shropshire, England* U.K.
207 I5 **Minta** Cameroon
108 B1 **Mintang** *Qinghai* China
146 G4 **Mintlaw** *Aberdeenshire, Scotland* U.K.
225 H4 **Minto** *N.B.* Can.
Minto *atoll Arch. des Tuamotu* Fr. Polynesia *see* **Tenararo**
263 L2 **Minto, Mount** Antarctica
220 G2 **Minto Inlet** *N.W.T.* Can.
223 J5 **Minton** *Sask.* Can.
172 D3 **Mintraching** Ger.
239 F4 **Minturn** *CO* U.S.A.
Minturnae Italy *see* **Minturno**
193 F3 **Minturno** Italy
190 F4 **Minucciano** Italy
203 F2 **Minūf** Egypt
126 C5 **Minūfīya** *governorate* Egypt
98 F1 **Minusinsk** Rus. Fed.
190 D2 **Minusio** Switz.
108 A2 **Minutang** *Arun. Prad.* India
208 B4 **Minvoul** Gabon
106 E5 **Minxian** *Gansu* China
Minya Konka *mt. Sichuan* China *see* **Gongga Shan**
134 L5 **Minyar** Rus. Fed.
83 E4 **Minyip** *Vic.* Austr.
227 E3 **Mio** *MI* U.S.A.
196 E3 **Mionica** *Srbija* Yugo.
160 C3 **Mionnay** France
162 E3 **Mions** France
163 B4 **Mios** France
84 D5 **Mipia, Lake** *salt flat Qld* Austr.
106 B3 **Miquan** *Xinjiang* China
110 D3 **Miquan** *Xinjiang* China
224 E3 **Miquelon** *Que.* Can.
225 J4 **Miquelon** *i.* St Pierre and Miquelon
245 E2 **Miquihuana** Mex.
138 F5 **Mir** Belarus
250 B4 **Mira** *r.* Col.
191 H3 **Mira** Italy
182 B4 **Mira** Port.
182 B4 **Mira** Port.
183 I5 **Mira** Spain
184 B3 **Mira** *r.* Spain
161 D5 **Mirabeau** France
233 F2 **Mirabel** *Que.* Can.
182 D4 **Mirabel** France
182 D5 **Mirabel** Spain
257 E2 **Mirabela** Brazil
161 D4 **Mirabel-aux-Baronnies** France
194 D5 **Mirabella Imbaccari** *Sicilia* Italy
257 F4 **Miracema** Brazil
Miracema do Norte Brazil *see* **Miracema do Tocantins**
254 C4 **Miracema do Tocantins** Brazil
Mirada Hills *CA* U.S.A. *see* **La Mirada**
182 B5 **Mira de Aire** Port.
257 F4 **Miradouro** Brazil
163 C5 **Miradoux** France
250 C3 **Miraflores** Col.
183 G4 **Miraflores de la Sierra** Spain
257 F4 **Miraí** Brazil
114 B2 **Miraj** *Mahar.* India
261 I6 **Miramar** *Buenos Aires* Arg.
261 F2 **Miramar** *Córdoba* Arg.
191 H4 **Miramare** Italy
161 D5 **Miramas** France
162 B3 **Mirambeau** France
186 C4 **Mirambel** Spain
163 C4 **Miramont-de-Guyenne** France
163 B5 **Miramont-Sensacq** France
110 E4 **Miran** *Xinjiang* China
253 F5 **Miranda** Brazil
253 F4 **Miranda** *r.* Brazil
Miranda Moz. *see* **Macaloge**
240 F1 **Miranda** *CA* U.S.A.
250 E2 **Miranda** *state* Venez.
87 D5 **Miranda, Lake** *salt flat W.A.* Austr.
183 I2 **Miranda de Arga** Spain
183 H2 **Miranda de Ebro** Spain
182 E4 **Miranda del Castañar** Spain
182 B4 **Miranda do Corvo** Port.
182 D3 **Miranda do Douro** Port.
163 C5 **Mirande** France
182 C3 **Mirandela** Port.
184 D1 **Mirandilla** Spain
191 G4 **Mirandola** Italy
163 E4 **Mirandol-Bourgnounac** France
256 B4 **Mirandópolis** Brazil
191 H3 **Mirano** Italy
256 B5 **Mirante, Serra do** *hills* Brazil
256 B5 **Mirante do Paranapanema** Brazil
198 B1 **Miras** Albania
256 C4 **Mirassol** Brazil
182 D2 **Miravalles** *mt.* Spain
182 E5 **Miravete** *hill* Spain
Mir-Bashir Azer. *see* **Tärtär**
125 F4 **Mirbāṭ** Oman
129 F4 **Mircālal** Azer.
175 L5 **Mircze** Pol.
246 D3 **Mirebalais** Haiti
160 D1 **Mirebeau** *Bourgogne* France
162 C2 **Mirebeau** *Poitou-Charentes* France
157 G4 **Mirecourt** France
163 D5 **Miremont** France
179 G5 **Miren** Slovenia
163 E5 **Mirepoix** France
161 B5 **Mireval** France
117 F4 **Mirganj** *Bihar* India
Mirgorod Ukr. *see* **Myrhorod**
95 F1 **Miri** *Sarawak* Malaysia
123 E4 **Miri** *mt.* Pak.
207 H3 **Miria** Niger
114 C2 **Mirialguda** *Andhra Prad.* India
85 G5 **Miriam Vale** *Qld* Austr.
117 H4 **Miri Hills** India
258 G4 **Mirim, Lagoa** *l.* Brazil/Uru.
Mirina *Voreio Aigaio* Greece *see* **Myrina**
114 B3 **Mirjan** *Karnataka* India
122 D4 **Mīrjāveh** Iran
197 G4 **Mirkovo** Bulg.
188 D3 **Mirna** *r.* Croatia
179 G5 **Mirna** Slovenia
179 G5 **Mirna** *r.* Slovenia
263 G2 **Mirny** *research stn* Antarctica
134 H3 **Mirnyy** *Arkhangel'skaya Oblast'* Rus. Fed.
139 H5 **Mirnyy** *Bryanskaya Oblast'* Rus. Fed.
131 M3 **Mirnyy** *Respublika Sakha (Yakutiya)* Rus. Fed.
129 D1 **Mirnyy** *Stavropol'skiy Kray* Rus. Fed.
197 F3 **Miročhills** Yugo.
174 D4 **Mirocin Górny** Pol.
81 D5 **Miromiro** *mt. South I.* N.Z.
Mironovka *Kharkivs'ka Oblast'* Ukr. *see* **Myronivka**
Mironovka *Kyivs'ka Oblast'* Ukr. *see* **Myronivka**
179 H2 **Mirošov** Czech Rep.
174 F2 **Mirosławiec** Pol.
176 C2 **Mirošov** Czech Rep.
173 H2 **Mirotice** Czech Rep.
176 D2 **Mirovice** Czech Rep.
170 D2 **Mirow** Ger.
123 H3 **Mirpur** Pak.
123 G5 **Mirpur Batoro** Pak.
123 G5 **Mirpur Khas** Pak.
123 G5 **Mirpur Sakro** Pak.
222 H4 **Mirror** *Alta* Can.
110 D3 **Mirsali** *Xinjiang* China
175 K5 **Mirsk** Pol.
85 F4 **Mirtna** *Qld* Austr.
Mirtoan Sea Greece *see* **Mirtoö Pelagos**
195 F3 **Mirto Crosia** Italy
198 C3 **Mirtoö Pelagos** *sea* Greece
183 E4 **Miruela de los Infanzones** Spain
212 F2 **Miruro** Moz.
Miryalaguda *Andhra Prad.* India *see* **Mirialguda**
101 D6 **Miryang** S. Korea
Mirzachul Uzbek. *see* **Gulistan**
117 E4 **Mirzapur** *Uttar Prad.* India
175 J4 **Mirzec** Pol.
191 I5 **Misa** *r.* Italy
104 B4 **Misaki** Japan
191 H5 **Misano Adriatico** Italy
245 E4 **Misantla** Mex.
105 F3 **Misato** Japan
207 H4 **Misau** Nigeria
102 J3 **Misawa** Japan
177 K5 **Mişca** Romania
193 G3 **Miscano** *r.* Italy
179 H3 **Mischendorf** Austria
227 H2 **Misehkow** *r. Ont.* Can.
160 D1 **Miserey-Salines** France
116 C1 **Misgar** Jammu and Kashmir
214 D5 **Misgund** S. Africa
122 D3 **Mish, Kūh-e** *hill* Iran
224 C2 **Mishamattawa** *r. Ont.* Can.
100 D3 **Mishan** *Heilong.* China
226 D5 **Mishawaka** *IN* U.S.A.
139 L4 **Misheronskiy** Rus. Fed.
226 D3 **Mishicot** *WI* U.S.A.
105 E3 **Mishima** Japan
134 L5 **Mishkino** Rus. Fed.
124 D3 **Mishlah, Khashm** *hill* Saudi Arabia
117 H3 **Mishmi Hills** India
194 C4 **Misilmeri** *Sicilia* Italy
258 G2 **Misiones** *prov.* Arg.
124 C2 **Miskah** Saudi Arabia
177 I5 **Miske** Hungary
242 □J6 **Miskitos, Cayos** *is* Nic.
Miskitos, Costa de *coastal area* Nic. *see* **Costa de Mosquitos**
177 J3 **Miskolc** Hungary
179 G4 **Mislinja** Slovenia
188 E2 **Mislinja** *r.* Slovenia
124 C2 **Mismā, Jibāl al** *mts* Saudi Arabia
128 C3 **Mismā, Tall al** *hill* Jordan
161 D4 **Mison** France
93 D3 **Misoöl** *i. Irian Jaya* Indon.
234 C4 **Mispillion** *r. DE* U.S.A.
226 B2 **Misquah Hills** *MN* U.S.A.
235 G1 **Misquamicut** *RI* U.S.A.
Misr *country* Africa *see* **Egypt**
Misrakç Turkey *see* **Kurtalan**
202 B1 **Misrātah** Libya
116 E4 **Misrikh** *Uttar Prad.* India
227 E1 **Missanabie** *Ont.* Can.
193 I4 **Missanello** Italy
158 D4 **Missillac** France
224 D3 **Missinaibi** *r. Ont.* Can.
223 J4 **Missinipe** *Sask.* Can.
85 E2 **Mission** *r. Qld* Austr.
236 C3 **Mission** *SD* U.S.A.
237 D7 **Mission** *TX* U.S.A.
87 F3 **Mission Beach** *Qld* Austr.
240 I5 **Mission Viejo** *CA* U.S.A.
206 B3 **Missira** Senegal
224 C2 **Missisa** *r. Ont.* Can.
225 E3 **Missisicabi** *r. Que.* Can.
224 D3 **Missisagi** *r. Ont.* Can.
224 E5 **Mississauga** *Ont.* Can.
224 E4 **Mississippi** *Ont.* Can.
237 E6 **Mississippi** *r.* U.S.A.
237 F5 **Mississippi** *state* U.S.A.
237 F6 **Mississippi Delta** *LA* U.S.A.
237 F6 **Mississippi Sound** *sea chan. MS* U.S.A.
Missolonghi Greece *see* **Mesolongi**
238 D2 **Missoula** *MT* U.S.A.
204 E2 **Missour** Morocco
236 F4 **Missouri** *r.* U.S.A.
236 E4 **Missouri** *state* U.S.A.
236 E3 **Missouri Valley** *IA* U.S.A.
84 B3 **Mistake Creek** *N.T.* Austr.
85 F4 **Mistake Creek** *r. Qld* Austr.
225 I3 **Mistanipisipou** *r. Que.* Can.
225 F3 **Mistassibi** *r. Que.* Can.
225 F3 **Mistassini** *Que.* Can.
225 F3 **Mistassini** *r. Que.* Can.
225 F3 **Mistassini, Lac** *l. Que.* Can.
179 H2 **Mistelbach** Austria
173 F2 **Mistelgau** Ger.
195 E5 **Misterbianco** *Sicilia* Italy
149 I4 **Misterton** *Nottinghamshire, England* U.K.
224 F3 **Mistissini** *Que.* Can.
137 J3 **Mistky** Ukr.
261 F2 **Mistolar, Lago** *l.* Arg.
198 C3 **Mistras** *tourist site* Greece
194 D5 **Mistretta** *Sicilia* Italy
Misuratah Libya *see* **Mişrātah**
191 H2 **Misurina** Italy
140 K2 **Misvær** Norway
105 F3 **Mitaka** Japan
213 G2 **Mitande** Moz.
251 H4 **Mitaraca** *hill* Suriname
150 E3 **Mitcheldean** *Gloucestershire, England* U.K.
85 F5 **Mitchell** *Qld* Austr.
83 H2 **Mitchell** *r. N.S.W.* Austr.
85 E2 **Mitchell** *r. Qld* Austr.
83 F4 **Mitchell** *r. Vic.* Austr.
227 G4 **Mitchell** *Ont.* Can.
238 B2 **Mitchell** *OR* U.S.A.
236 D3 **Mitchell** *SD* U.S.A.
231 D5 **Mitchell, Mount** *NC* U.S.A.
Mitchell Island Cook Is *see* **Nassau**
Mitchell Island Tuvalu *see* **Nukulaelae**
84 B1 **Mitchell Point** *N.T.* Austr.
232 D5 **Mitchelltown** *VA* U.S.A.
147 C4 **Mitchelstown** Rep. of Ireland
203 F2 **Mit Ghamr** Egypt
116 B5 **Mithapur** *Gujarat* India
123 H3 **Mitha Tiwana** Pak.
123 G5 **Mithi** Pak.
Mithimna Greece *see* **Mithymna**
199 E2 **Mithymna** Greece
81 □2 **Mitiaro** *i.* Cook Is
Mitiaro *i.* Cook Is *see* **Mitiaro**
Mitilini *Voreio Aigaio* Greece *see* **Mytilini**
80 D2 **Mititai** *North I.* N.Z.
104 D4 **Mito** *Aichi* Japan
105 G3 **Mito** *Ibaraki* Japan
80 E4 **Mitre** *mt. North I.* N.Z.
77 H3 **Mitre Island** Solomon Is
81 A6 **Mitre Peak** *South I.* N.Z.
135 G6 **Mitrofanovka** Rus. Fed.
Mitrovica *Kosovo, Srbija* Yugo. *see* **Kosovska Mitrovica**
156 C4 **Mitry-Mory** France
217 □3a **Mitsamiouli** *Njazidja* Comoros
213 □J3 **Mitsinjo** Madag.
Mits'iwa Eritrea *see* **Massawa**
217 □3a **Mitsoudjé** *Njazidja* Comoros
105 F2 **Mitsukaidō** Japan
103 I5 **Mitsuke** Japan
104 D2 **Mitsumatarenge-dake** *mt.* Japan
83 G3 **Mitsutōge-yama** *mt.* Japan
83 G3 **Mittagong** *N.S.W.* Austr.
83 F4 **Mitta Mitta** *Vic.* Austr.
179 H3 **Mittelberg** Austria
173 E3 **Mittelberg** *hill* Ger.
172 D3 **Mittelbiberach** Ger.
173 E2 **Mittelfranken** *admin. reg.* Bayern Ger.
171 C4 **Mittelhausen** Ger.
169 E5 **Mittelkalbach** Ger.
169 E5 **Mittelsinn** Ger.
173 G4 **Mittelspitze** *mt.* Ger.
173 E4 **Mittenwald** Ger.
170 E2 **Mittenwalde** *Brandenburg* Ger.
171 E3 **Mittenwalde** *Brandenburg* Ger.
179 G3 **Mitterdorf im Mürztal** Austria
173 F5 **Mitterfels** Ger.
157 G4 **Mittersheim** France
178 D3 **Mittersill** Austria
173 G3 **Mitterskirchen** Ger.
173 G2 **Mitterteich** Ger.
Mittimatalik *Nunavut* Can. *see* **Pond Inlet**
171 D5 **Mittweida** Ger.
250 D4 **Mitú** Col.
250 D4 **Mituas** Col.
209 E7 **Mitumba, Chaîne des** *mts* Dem. Rep. Congo
208 F5 **Mitumba, Monts** *mts* Dem. Rep. Congo
209 E7 **Mitwaba** Dem. Rep. Congo
171 C5 **Mitwitz** Ger.
208 A4 **Mitzic** Gabon
Miughalaigh *i. Scotland* U.K. *see* **Mingulay**
105 F3 **Miura** Japan
105 F3 **Miura-hantō** *pen.* Japan
135 G7 **Mius** *r.* Rus. Fed.
137 J4 **Miusskiy Liman** *est.* Rus. Fed.
137 J3 **Miusyns'k** Ukr.
Mixian *Henan* China *see* **Xinmi**
245 E4 **Mixteco** *r.* Mex.
104 D2 **Miya-gawa** *r.* Japan
104 C4 **Miya-gawa** *r.* Japan
102 J4 **Miyagi** *pref.* Japan
102 J4 **Miyako** Japan
105 F3 **Miyake-jima** *i.* Japan
102 □1 **Miyako-jima** *i.* Japan
103 E8 **Miyakonojō** Japan
108 B2 **Miyaluo** *Sichuan* China
120 C2 **Miyaly** Kazakh.
Miyang *Yunnan* China *see* **Mile**
116 B5 **Miyani** *Gujarat* India
103 E8 **Miyanojō** Japan
102 □1 **Miyanoura-dake** *mt.* Japan
103 E8 **Miyazaki** Japan
103 E7 **Miyazaki** *pref.* Japan
104 B3 **Miyazu** Japan
108 B3 **Mi Yi** *Sichuan* China
103 F6 **Miyoshi** Japan
107 H3 **Miyun** *Beijing* China
210 B3 **Mizan Teferī** Eth.
Mizar Turkey *see* **Karakeçi**
147 B5 **Mizen Head** *hd Cork* Rep. of Ireland
147 E4 **Mizen Head** *hd Wicklow* Rep. of Ireland
136 B3 **Mizhhir"ya** Ukr.
107 F4 **Mizhi** *Shaanxi* China
197 H3 **Mizil** Romania
197 F4 **Miziya** Bulg.
136 D2 **Mizoch** Ukr.
195 F3 **Mizofato** *r.* Italy
Mizo Hills *state* India *see* **Mizoram**
117 H5 **Mizoram** *state* India
234 D3 **Mizpah** *NJ* U.S.A.
252 D4 **Mizque** Bol.
252 D4 **Mizque** *r.* Bol.
225 E3 **Mizugaki-yama** *mt.* Japan
105 F3 **Mizuho** Japan
104 D3 **Mizunami** Japan
105 F2 **Mizuno-gawa** *r.* Japan
102 J4 **Mizusawa** Japan
143 J5 **Mjölby** Sweden
142 C2 **Mjøndalen** Norway
142 D1 **Mjøsa** *l.* Norway
215 G4 **Mkambati** S. Africa
211 C6 **Mkata** Tanz.
211 C6 **Mkata Plain** Tanz.

215 H2 Mkhondvo r. Swaziland
211 C6 Mkoani Tanz.
211 C6 Mkokotoni Tanz.
211 C6 Mkomazi Tanz.
209 F8 Mkushi Zambia
215 I2 Mkuze S. Africa
215 I2 Mkuze r. S. Africa
176 D1 Mladá Boleslav Czech Rep.
176 D2 Mladá Vožice Czech Rep.
176 E1 Mladé Buky Czech Rep.
196 E3 Mladenovac Srbija Yugo.
197 E4 Mlado Nagoričane Macedonia
211 A6 Mlala Hills Tanz.
215 I2 Mlaula r. Swaziland
196 E3 Mlava r. Yugo.
175 I2 Mława Pol.
175 I3 Mławka r. Pol.
217 □3b Mlima Bénara mt. Mayotte
217 □3b Mlima Choungui mt. Mayotte
188 F4 Mljet i. Croatia
188 F4 Mljetski Kanal sea chan. Croatia
137 I2 Mlodat' r. Rus. Fed.
175 I3 Młodzieszyn Pol.
215 H1 Mlumati r. S. Africa
215 F4 Mlungisi S. Africa
175 H1 Mlynary Pol.
175 J3 Mlynarze Pol.
136 C2 Mlyniv Ukr.
175 M6 Mlynys'ka Ukr.
215 E1 Mmabatho S. Africa
213 E4 Mmadinare Botswana
176 D2 Mnichovice Czech Rep.
176 D1 Mnichovo Hradiště Czech Rep.
175 I5 Mnichów Pol.
175 I4 Mniów Pol.
177 J3 Mníšek nad Hnilcom Slovakia
175 J4 Mniszew Pol.
175 I4 Mniszków Pol.
215 H2 Mnjoli Dam Swaziland
100 F1 Mnogovershinnyy Rus. Fed.
141 I3 Mo Norway
252 B1 Moa r. Brazil
246 D2 Moa Cuba
93 D5 Moa i. Maluku Indon.
241 M2 Moab UT U.S.A.
208 A5 Moabi Gabon
252 C1 Moaco r. Brazil
91 J9 Moa Island Qld Austr.
79 □1 Moala i. Fiji
213 G5 Moamba Moz.
81 C5 Moana South I. N.Z.
182 B2 Moaña Spain
208 B5 Moanda Gabon
241 J3 Moapa NV U.S.A.
147 D3 Moate Rep. of Ireland
213 G3 Moatize Moz.
209 F6 Moba Dem. Rep. Congo
105 G3 Mobara Japan
208 D3 Mobaye C.A.R.
Mobayembongo Dem. Rep. Congo see Mobayi-Mbongo
208 D3 Mobayi-Mbongo Dem. Rep. Congo
149 G4 Mobberley Cheshire, England U.K.
236 E4 Moberly MO U.S.A.
222 F4 Moberly Lake B.C. Can.
226 E1 Mobert Ont. Can.
231 B6 Mobile AL U.S.A.
241 K5 Mobile AZ U.S.A.
237 F6 Mobile Bay AL U.S.A.
92 B3 Mobo Phil.
236 C2 Mobridge SD U.S.A.
Mobutu, Lake Dem. Rep. Congo/Uganda see Albert, Lake
Mobutu Sese Seko, Lake Dem. Rep. Congo/Uganda see Albert, Lake
246 E3 Moca Dom. Rep.
254 C2 Mocajuba Brazil
Moçambique country Africa see Mozambique
213 I2 Moçambique Moz.
Moçâmedes Angola see Namibe
234 B1 Mocanaqua PA U.S.A.
184 B1 Moçarria Port.
240 G3 Moccasin CA U.S.A.
232 B6 Moccasin Gap VA U.S.A.
183 G5 Mocejón Spain
177 G3 Močenok Slovakia
139 K4 Mocha r. Rus. Fed.
Mocha Yemen see Al Mukhā
258 B5 Mocha, Isla i. Chile
183 I3 Mochales Spain
175 H3 Mochowo Pol.
212 E5 Mochudi Botswana
174 E3 Mochy Pol.
211 D7 Mocimboa da Praia Moz.
211 C7 Mocímboa do Rovuma Moz.
197 G2 Mociu Romania
171 C3 Möckern Ger.
172 D2 Möckmühl Ger.
171 D4 Mockrehna Ger.
231 D5 Mocksville NC U.S.A.
185 G3 Moclín Spain
185 F4 Moclinejo Spain
182 C2 Moeć r. Brazil
250 B4 Mocoa Col.
256 D4 Mococa Brazil
261 I2 Mocoretá r. Arg.
242 D3 Mocorito Mex.
242 D2 Moctezuma Chihuahua Mex.
Moctezuma San Luis Potosí Mex.
242 C2 Moctezuma Sonora Mex.
245 E3 Moctezuma r. Mex.
239 E6 Moctezuma r. Mex.
213 H3 Mocuba Moz.
109 E4 Mocun Guangdong China
182 E3 Modane France
116 C5 Modasa Gujarat India
165 E4 Modave Belgium
150 D4 Modbury Devon, England U.K.
215 E3 Modder r. S. Africa
214 E3 Modderivier S. Africa
191 F4 Modena Italy
191 F4 Modena prov. Emilia-Romagna Italy
235 D1 Modena NY U.S.A.
234 C3 Modena PA U.S.A.
241 K3 Modena UT U.S.A.
157 H4 Moder r. France
240 G3 Modesto CA U.S.A.
194 D6 Modica Sicilia Italy
191 G4 Modigliana Italy
194 B5 Modione r. Sicilia Italy
175 K5 Modliborzyce Pol.
179 H2 Mödling Austria
175 I4 Modliszewice Pol.
192 A4 Modolo Sardegna Italy
172 F7 Modot Mongolia
176 G3 Modra Slovakia
188 G3 Modriča Bos.-Herz.
176 F2 Modřice Czech Rep.
179 F4 Mödringberg mt. Austria
177 I3 Modrý Kameň Slovakia
195 F1 Modugno Italy
83 F4 Moe Vic. Austr.
215 H3 Moebase Moz.
80 E2 Moehau hill North I. N.Z.
158 C4 Moëlan-sur-Mer France
150 D1 Moel Famau hill Wales U.K.
150 C1 Moelfre Isle of Anglesey, Wales U.K.
150 D2 Moel Sych hill Wales U.K.
141 J3 Moelv Norway
215 F3 Moemaneng S. Africa
Moen i. Chuuk Micronesia see Weno
140 L1 Moen Norway
191 G2 Moena Italy
251 H3 Moengo Suriname
241 L3 Moenkopi AZ U.S.A.
241 L4 Moenkopi Wash r. AZ U.S.A.
165 C3 Moerbeke Belgium
80 E1 Moerewa North I. N.Z.
164 E3 Moergestel Neth.
165 C3 Moerkerke Belgium
Moero, Lake Dem. Rep. Congo/Zambia see Mweru, Lake
169 B4 Moers Ger.
190 E2 Moesa r. Switz.
214 D2 Moeswal S. Africa
78 □6 Moetambe, Mount Choiseul Solomon Is
146 E6 Moffat Dumfries and Galloway, Scotland U.K.
182 D3 Mofreita Port.
177 L4 Moftin Romania
116 C3 Moga Punjab India
Mogadishu Somalia see Muqdisho
Mogador Morocco see Essaouira
182 D3 Mogadouro Port.
182 D3 Mogadouro, Serra de mts Port.
213 F4 Mogalakwena r. S. Africa
114 D2 Mogalturra Andhra Prad. India
102 I4 Mogami-gawa r. Japan
216 □3f Mogán Gran Canaria Canary Is
213 F5 Moganyaka S. Africa
96 B1 Mogaung Myanmar
147 C5 Mogeely Rep. of Ireland
170 D3 Mögelin Ger.
168 D1 Mogeltønder Denmark
179 H4 Mogersdorf Austria
191 I2 Moggio Udinese Italy
172 D3 Mögglingen Ger.
175 I4 Mogielnica Pol.
175 I6 Mogielnica mt. Pol.
256 D5 Mogi-Guaçu Brazil
196 E5 Mogila Macedonia
175 H6 Mogilany Pol.
Mogilev Belarus see Mahilyow
Mogilev Oblast admin. div. Belarus see Mahilyowskaya Voblasts'
Mogilev Podol'skiy Ukr. see Mohyliv Podil's'kyy
Mogilevskaya Oblast' admin. div. Belarus see Mahilyowskaya Voblasts'
174 E3 Mogilnica r. Pol.
174 F3 Mogilno Pol.
256 D5 Mogi-Mirim Brazil
213 I2 Mogincual Moz.
191 F4 Moglia Italy
191 I5 Mogliano Italy
191 H3 Mogliano Veneto Italy
172 D3 Möglingen Ger.
100 A1 Mogocha Rus. Fed.
139 K3 Mogocha r. Rus. Fed.
205 H1 Mogod mts Tunisia
213 E4 Mogoditshane Botswana
212 B4 Mogofores Port.
96 B2 Mogok Myanmar
241 L4 Mogollon Plateau AZ U.S.A.
185 G2 Mogón Spain
Mogontiacum Ger. see Mainz
192 A5 Mogorella Sardegna Italy
192 A5 Mogoro Sardegna Italy
192 A5 Mogoro r. Sardegna Italy
197 H2 Mogoşeşti Romania
175 I3 Mogowo Pol.
107 G1 Mogoytuy Rus. Fed.
208 B2 Mogroum Chad
184 D3 Moguer Spain
107 I2 Moguqi Nei Mongol China
215 F1 Mogwase S. Africa
177 I4 Mogyoród Hungary
177 H6 Mohács Hungary
80 F3 Mohaka r. North I. N.Z.
116 E5 Mohala Madh. Prad. India
215 F4 Mohale's Hoek Lesotho
236 C1 Mohall ND U.S.A.
Moḩammadābād Iran see Darreh Gaz
205 F2 Mohammadia Alg.
116 E3 Mohan r. India/Nepal
116 D4 Mohana Madh. Prad. India
117 G4 Mohanganj Bangl.
185 I2 Moharque Spain
241 J4 Mohave Mountains AZ U.S.A.
226 C2 Mohawk MI U.S.A.
233 G3 Mohawk r. NY U.S.A.
241 K5 Mohawk Mountains AZ U.S.A.
100 B1 Mohe Heilong. China
141 L3 Moheda Sweden
143 F3 Moheda Sweden
182 D4 Mohedas de Granadilla Spain
235 F1 Mohegan CT U.S.A.
235 E1 Mohegan Lake NY U.S.A.
Mohéli i. Comoros see Mwali
176 F2 Mohelnice Czech Rep.
176 F2 Mohelno Czech Rep.
123 G5 Mohenjo Daro tourist site Pak.
147 B4 Moher, Cliffs of Rep. of Ireland
184 B4 Mohernando Spain
147 D4 Mohill Rep. of Ireland
137 I4 Mohila Bel'mak, Hora hill Ukr.
147 D3 Mohill Rep. of Ireland
215 F2 Mohlakeng S. Africa
171 D4 Möhlau Ger.
169 C4 Möhne r. Ger.
234 B2 Mohnton PA U.S.A.
252 C3 Moho Peru
114 E2 Mohol Mahar. India
241 K4 Mohon Peak AZ U.S.A.
177 I4 Mohora Hungary
171 E5 Mohorn Ger.
217 □3a Mohoro Njazidja Comoros
211 C7 Mohoro Tanz.
173 E2 Möhrendorf Ger.
168 E1 Mohrkirch Ger.
234 C2 Mohrsville PA U.S.A.
136 D3 Mohyliv Podil's'kyy Ukr.
136 D2 Mohylyany Ukr.
142 B2 Moi Norway
186 F3 Moià Cataluña Spain
194 D1 Moiano Italy
146 C5 Moidart reg. Scotland U.K.
212 E4 Moijabana Botswana
182 C4 Moimenta da Beira Port.
159 E4 Moine r. France
157 H2 Moineville France
147 E4 Moinești Romania
160 C3 Moinkum des. Kazakh. see Moyynkum, Peski
Mointy Kazakh. see Moyynty
147 E2 Moira Northern Ireland U.K.
Moirai Kriti Greece see Moires
140 K2 Mo i Rana Norway
117 H4 Moirang Manipur India
161 D2 Moirans-en-Montagne France
163 C4 Moirax France
196 D4 Moires Kriti Greece
138 E2 Mõisaküla Estonia
182 E2 Moisburg Ger.
161 E3 Moisdon-la-Rivière France
197 G2 Moisei Romania
261 G2 Moisés Ville Arg.
225 H3 Moisie Que. Can.
225 H3 Moisie r. Que. Can.
156 C3 Moislains France
163 E2 Moissac France
161 E5 Moissac-Bellevue France
208 C2 Moïssala Chad
160 D1 Moissey France
192 B2 Moïta Corse France
182 B4 Moita Aveiro Port.
184 B2 Moita Setúbal Port.
187 C6 Moixent-Mogente Spain
183 E2 Mojácar Spain
183 F3 Mojados Spain
240 H4 Mojave CA U.S.A.
240 I4 Mojave r. CA U.S.A.
240 H4 Mojave Desert CA U.S.A.
108 B4 Mojiang Yunnan China
256 D5 Moji das Cruzes Brazil
256 C4 Moji-Guaçu r. Brazil
103 E7 Mojikō Japan
185 G2 Mojina mt. Spain
196 D4 Mojkovac Crna Gora Yugo.
252 D5 Mojo Bol.
210 C2 Mojo Eth.
95 F4 Mojokerto Jawa Timur Indon.
185 G3 Mojón Alto mt. Spain
183 H5 Mojón Alto mt. Spain
258 D2 Mojones, Cerro mt. Arg.
252 D3 Mojos, Llanos de plain Bol.
210 D3 Mojo Shet' r. Eth.
252 D3 Mojotoro Bol.
254 C2 Moju Brazil
102 G3 Mōka Japan
80 E3 Mokai North I. N.Z.
117 F4 Mokama Bihar India
209 F8 Mokambo Dem. Rep. Congo
80 E3 Mokau North I. N.Z.
80 E3 Mokau r. North I. N.Z.
208 B4 Mokéko Congo
240 G2 Mokelumne r. CA U.S.A.
215 G3 Mokhotlong Lesotho
139 K5 Mokhovoye Rus. Fed.
131 N3 Mokhsogollokh Rus. Fed.
136 D2 Mokiyivtsi Ukr.
205 H2 Moknine Tunisia
175 K3 Mokobody Pol.
Mokogai i. Fiji see Makogai
117 H4 Mokokchung Nagaland India
207 I4 Mokolo Cameroon
213 E4 Mokolo r. S. Africa
81 B7 Mokoreta South I. N.Z.
81 B7 Mokoreta hill South I. N.Z.
81 B7 Mokotua South I. N.Z.
101 C6 Mokp'o S. Korea
196 E4 Mokra Gora mts Yugo.
137 F3 Mokra Kalyhirka Ukr.
177 K3 Mokrance Slovakia
196 E3 Mokrin Vojvodina, Srbija Yugo.
137 I4 Mokri Yaly r. Ukr.
120 A2 Mokrous Rus. Fed.
135 H5 Moksha r. Rus. Fed.
135 I5 Mokshan Rus. Fed.
Mōktama Myanmar see Martaban
240 □ Mokuleia HI U.S.A.
Mokundurra Rajasthan India see Mukandwara
Mokvin Pershotravnevoye Ukr. see Mokvyn
136 D2 Mokvyn Ukr.
207 G4 Mokwa Nigeria
215 F2 Mokwallo S. Africa
165 E3 Mol Belgium
177 J6 Mol Vojvodina, Srbija Yugo.
195 G1 Mola di Bari Italy
163 D5 Molandier France
245 E3 Molango Mex.
198 C3 Molaoi Greece
190 D4 Molare Italy
188 E3 Molat i. Croatia
187 B6 Molatón mt. Spain
168 C3 Molbergen Ger.
179 F4 Mölbling Austria
150 D1 Mold Flintshire, Wales U.K.
177 J3 Moldava nad Bodvou Slovakia
Moldavia country Europe see Moldova
Moldavskaya S.S.R. country Europe see Moldova
140 I3 Molde Norway
140 K2 Moldjord Norway
136 E4 Moldova country Europe
197 H2 Moldova r. Romania
197 E3 Moldova Nouă Romania
197 G3 Moldoveanu, Vârful mt. Romania
197 G1 Moldovei, Podişul plat. Romania
136 D4 Moldovei Centrale, Podişul plat. Moldova
136 D3 Moldovei de Nord, Câmpia lowland Moldova
136 D3 Moldovei de Nord, Podişul plat. Moldova
136 E4 Moldovei de Sud, Câmpia plain Moldova
197 G2 Moldoviţa Romania
129 A2 Moldovka Rus. Fed.
150 D4 Mole r. England U.K.
103 A3 Mole Chaung r. Myanmar
182 B3 Moledo Viana do Castelo Port.
182 C3 Moledo Viseu Port.
182 B4 Molelos Port.
215 G2 Molen r. S. Africa
165 D4 Molenbeek-St-Jean Belgium
212 E5 Molepolole Botswana
149 I4 Molescroft East Riding of Yorkshire, England U.K.
156 E5 Molesmes France
138 E4 Molėtai Lith.
193 I3 Molfetta Italy
168 F1 Molfsee Ger.
143 F3 Molfsee Ger.
168 F1 Molfsee Ger.
163 D5 Molières France
163 C4 Molières France
161 C4 Molières-sur-Cèze France
163 A5 Moliets-et-Maa France
260 B4 Molina Chile
183 I4 Molina de Aragón Spain
187 B6 Molina de Segura Spain
191 F3 Molina di Ledro Italy
193 G3 Molinara Italy
182 D2 Molinaseca Spain
236 F3 Moline IL U.S.A.
237 D4 Moline KS U.S.A.
191 F3 Molinella Italy
161 E4 Molines-en-Queyras France
160 B2 Molinet France
160 B2 Molinges France
181 C3 Molinicos Spain
182 E3 Molini di Tures Italy
231 C6 Molino FL U.S.A.
234 B2 Molino PA U.S.A.
186 C2 Molino de Villobas Spain
186 C4 Molinos Spain
183 H5 Molins de Rei Spain
209 F7 Moliro Dem. Rep. Congo
193 G3 Molise admin. reg. Italy
193 H4 Moliterno Italy
163 E6 Molitg-les-Bains France
177 L5 Moliviş mt. Romania
171 D4 Molkau Ger.
143 E2 Molkom Sweden
178 E4 Möll r. Austria
122 B3 Mollā Bodāgh Iran
129 F3 Mollakänd Azer.
142 C4 Mollebjerg hill Denmark
117 H4 Mol Len mt. Nagaland India
170 E2 Möllenbeck Ger.
252 C4 Mollendo Peru
170 D2 Möllenhagen Ger.
87 C6 Mollerin, Lake salt flat W.A. Austr.
186 D3 Mollerussa Spain
186 F3 Molles France
186 F3 Mollet del Vallès Spain
163 D2 Molliens-Dreuil France
185 F3 Mollina Spain
160 E1 Mollis Switz.
170 F3 Mölln Austria
170 E2 Mölln Ger.
176 C1 Mölln Ger.
186 F2 Molló Spain
143 F2 Mölltorp Sweden
142 E3 Mölnlycke Sweden
137 I4 Molochans'k Ukr.
137 H4 Molochans'k Ukr.
137 H4 Molochna r. Ukr.
134 G4 Molochnoye Rus. Fed.
134 F1 Molochnyy Rus. Fed.
Molodechno Belarus see Maladzyechna
263 D2 Molodezhnaya research stn Antarctica
137 G3 Molodizhne Kirovohrads'ka Oblast' Ukr.
137 H5 Molodizhne Respublika Krym Ukr.
121 G1 Molodogvardeyskoye Kazakh.
139 I3 Molodoy Tud Rus. Fed.
139 K2 Mologa r. Rus. Fed.
240 □C8 Molokai i. HI U.S.A.
139 K2 Molokovo Rus. Fed.
134 J2 Moloma r. Rus. Fed.
184 B3 Molompize France
83 G3 Molong N.S.W. Austr.
212 D6 Molopo watercourse Botswana/S. Africa
198 C2 Molos Greece
Molotov Rus. Fed. see Perm'
Molotov Rus. Fed. see Oktyabr'skoye
Molotovsk Kyrg. see Kayyngdy
Molotovsk Arkhangel'skaya Oblast' Rus. Fed. see Severodvinsk
Molotovsk Kirovskaya Oblast' Rus. Fed. see Nolinsk
Molotovskaya Oblast' admin. div. Rus. Fed. see Permskaya Oblast'
207 I6 Moloundou Cameroon
136 E4 Molovata Moldova
160 B1 Molsheim France
169 F4 Molschleben Ger.
157 F4 Molsheim France
223 L5 Molson Man. Can.
215 F4 Molteno S. Africa
192 B2 Moltifao Corse France
Moluccas is Indon. see Maluku
93 C3 Molucca Sea Indon.
183 I5 Molungo mt. Spain
213 H2 Molumbo Moz.
191 F2 Molveno Italy
213 H3 Moma Moz.
83 E2 Momba N.S.W. Austr.
254 F3 Mombaça Brazil
190 D4 Mombaldone Italy
211 C5 Mombasa Kenya
184 B2 Mombeja Port.
183 E4 Mombeltrán Spain
190 D4 Mombercelli Italy
Mombetsu Japan see Monbetsu
208 C5 Mombonyo r. Dem. Rep. Congo
169 E5 Mömbris Ger.
256 A3 Mombuca, Serra da hills Brazil
182 D3 Mombuey Spain
197 G5 Momchilgrad Bulg.
226 D5 Momence IL U.S.A.
165 D4 Momignies Belgium
242 □16 Momotombo, Volcán vol. Nic.
250 C2 Mompós Col.
131 P3 Momskiy Khrebet mts Rus. Fed.
163 B5 Momuy France
142 E4 Møn i. Denmark
117 H4 Mon Nagaland India
96 B3 Mon state Myanmar
241 L2 Mona UT U.S.A.
232 C4 Monaca PA U.S.A.
182 E3 Monacia-d'Aullène Corse France
146 A4 Monach, Sound of sea chan. Scotland U.K.
185 G3 Monachil Spain
185 G3 Monachil r. Spain
146 A4 Monach Islands Scotland U.K.
192 B3 Monacia-d'Aullène Corse France
161 F5 Monaco country Europe
264 H4 Monaco Basin sea feature N. Atlantic Ocean
146 D4 Monadhliath Mountains Scotland U.K.
251 F2 Monagas state Venez.
147 E2 Monaghan Rep. of Ireland
147 E2 Monaghan county Rep. of Ireland
237 C6 Monahans TX U.S.A.
147 E4 Monamolin Rep. of Ireland
247 E3 Mona Passage Dom. Rep./Puerto Rico
213 I2 Monapo Moz.
209 C7 Mona Quimbundo Angola
146 C4 Monar, Loch l. Scotland U.K.
222 E5 Monarch Mountain B.C. Can.
222 G5 Monashee Mountains B.C. Can.
195 F4 Monasterace Italy
147 D3 Monasterevan Rep. of Ireland
183 H2 Monasterio de Suso tourist site Spain
128 A5 Monastery of St Catherine tourist site Egypt
128 A5 Monastery of St Anthony tourist site Egypt
128 A5 Monastery of St Paul tourist site Egypt
192 B5 Monastir Sardegna Italy
Monastir Macedonia see Bitola
205 H2 Monastir Tunisia
175 M6 Monastyrets' Ukr.
Monastyrishche Ukr. see Monastyrshche
139 H4 Monastyrshchina Rus. Fed.
136 E3 Monastyryshche Ukr.
136 C3 Monastyrys'ka Ukr.
207 H5 Monatélé Cameroon
81 C6 Monavale South I. N.Z.
79 □1a Monavatu mt. Viti Levu Fiji
147 D4 Monavullagh Mountains hills Rep. of Ireland
163 C4 Monbahus France
163 C4 Monbazillac France
163 D5 Monbéqui France
102 K1 Monbetsu Japan
163 D5 Monbrun France
187 C5 Moncada Spain
190 C3 Moncalieri Italy
190 D3 Moncalvo Italy
182 D2 Moncalvo mt. Spain
182 B2 Monção Port.
184 C3 Moncarapacho Port.
163 C4 Moncaut France
183 I3 Moncayo, Sierra del mts Spain
159 G4 Moncé-en-Belin France
157 G4 Moncel-sur-Seille France
190 D2 Mönch mt. Switz.
140 P2 Monchegorsk Rus. Fed.
164 E4 Mönchengladbach Ger.
179 H3 Mönchhof Austria
190 F4 Monchio delle Corti Italy
184 B3 Monchique Port.
184 B3 Monchique, Serra de mts Port.
173 E3 Mönchsdeggingen Ger.
231 D5 Moncks Corner SC U.S.A.
163 C4 Monclar France
163 D5 Monclar-de-Quercy France
243 E3 Monclova Mex.
187 C5 Moncófar Spain
158 D3 Moncontour Bretagne France
159 F5 Moncontour Poitou-Charentes France
159 F5 Moncoutant France
163 C4 Moncrabeau France
225 H4 Moncton N.B. Can.
185 F4 Monda Spain
255 B8 Mondaí Brazil
182 B2 Mondariz Spain
182 B2 Mondariz-Balneario Spain
163 D5 Mondavezan France
191 H5 Mondavio Italy
182 B4 Mondego r. Port.
182 B4 Mondego, Cabo c. Port.
183 G4 Mondéjar Spain
194 C4 Mondello Sicilia Italy
159 F2 Mondeville France
182 C3 Mondim de Basto Port.
215 H2 Mondlo S. Africa
202 B6 Mondo Chad
191 I5 Mondolfo Italy
182 C1 Mondoñedo Spain
165 F5 Mondorf-les-Bains Lux.
159 G4 Mondoubleau France
190 C4 Mondovi Italy
226 B3 Mondovi WI U.S.A.
161 C4 Mondragon France
183 H1 Mondragón Spain
193 F3 Mondragone Italy
179 E3 Mondsee Austria
179 E3 Mondsee l. Austria
211 C6 Monduli Tanz.
183 F5 Mondúver hill Spain
246 □ Moneague Jamaica
177 L5 Moneasa Romania
226 D5 Monee IL U.S.A.
147 C3 Moneen Rep. of Ireland
190 C3 Moneglia Italy
186 C3 Monegrillo Spain
163 B5 Monein France
232 D4 Monessen PA U.S.A.
183 G3 Monesterio Spain
161 D4 Monestier-de-Clermont France
163 E4 Monestiés France
227 J1 Monet Que. Can.
232 D6 Moneta VA U.S.A.
238 F3 Moneta WY U.S.A.
156 D5 Monéteau France
237 E4 Monett MO U.S.A.
147 D4 Moneygall Rep. of Ireland
146 B7 Moneyglass Northern Ireland U.K.
147 E2 Moneymore Northern Ireland U.K.
148 C3 Moneyneany Northern Ireland U.K.
148 D3 Moneyreagh Northern Ireland U.K.
191 I3 Monfalcone Italy
193 G4 Monfecorvino Rovella Italy
163 C4 Monflanquin France
250 D4 Monfort Col.
163 D5 Monfort France
184 C1 Monforte Port.
182 C2 Monforte Spain
182 C5 Monforte da Beira Port.
190 C4 Monforte d'Alba Italy
187 C6 Monforte del Cid Spain
186 C3 Monforte de Moyuela Spain
182 D4 Monfortinho Port.
184 B2 Monfurado hill Port.
256 D6 Mongaguá Brazil
208 C4 Mongala r. Dem. Rep. Congo
117 G4 Mongar Bhutan
234 D1 Mongaup r. NY U.S.A.
234 D1 Mongaup Valley NY U.S.A.
208 F4 Mongbwalu Dem. Rep. Congo
96 D2 Mông Cai Vietnam
87 C6 Mongers Lake salt flat W.A. Austr.
78 □6 Mongga New Georgia Is Solomon Is
191 G4 Monghidoro Italy
Monghyr Bihar India see Munger
202 C6 Mongo Chad
Mongó hill Spain see Montgó
106 D2 Mongolia country Asia
Mongolküre Xinjiang China see Zhaosu
Mongol Uls country Asia see Mongolia
207 H6 Mongomo Equat. Guinea
86 E2 Mongona, Mount hill W.A. Austr.
207 I3 Mongonu Nigeria
123 H3 Mongora Pak.
208 C3 Mongoumba C.A.R.
146 F5 Mongour hill Scotland U.K.
190 D3 Mongrando Italy
209 E8 Mongu Zambia
206 B2 Mônguel Maur.
191 H2 Monguelfo Italy
100 D2 Mönhbulag Mongolia
172 E3 Monheim Ger.
106 A2 Mönh Hayrhan Uul mt. Mongolia
146 E6 Moniaive Dumfries and Galloway, Scotland U.K.
226 C3 Monico WI U.S.A.
161 D4 Monieux France
146 F5 Monifieth Angus, Scotland U.K.
148 B4 Monilea Rep. of Ireland
250 C3 Moniquirá Col.
161 B4 Monistrol-d'Allier France
186 E3 Monistrol de Montserrat Spain
161 C3 Monistrol-sur-Loire France
240 I2 Monitor Mountain NV U.S.A.
240 I2 Monitor Range mts NV U.S.A.
257 E3 Monjolos Brazil
168 E1 Mönkeberg Ger.
211 B8 Monkey Bay Malawi
87 B5 Monkey Mia W.A. Austr.
161 F5 Monki Pol.
84 E5 Monkira Qld Austr.
150 C4 Monkokehampton Devon, England U.K.
208 D5 Monkoto Dem. Rep. Congo
151 H2 Monks Eleigh Suffolk, England U.K.
227 G4 Monkton Ont. Can.
234 B3 Monkton MD U.S.A.
187 C4 Monleón r. Spain
163 C5 Monléon-Magnoac France
150 E3 Monmouth Monmouthshire, Wales U.K.
240 H3 Monmouth CA U.S.A.
236 F3 Monmouth IL U.S.A.
235 D2 Monmouth County county NJ U.S.A.
234 D2 Monmouth Junction NJ U.S.A.
222 F5 Monmouth Mountain B.C. Can.
150 E3 Monmouthshire admin. div. Wales U.K.
159 G4 Monnaie France
232 B4 Monnett OH U.S.A.
164 E2 Monnickendam Neth.
150 E3 Monnow r. England/Wales U.K.
207 F4 Mono r. Togo
78 □6 Mono Island Solomon Is
177 K3 Monok Hungary
226 D5 Monon IN U.S.A.
226 B4 Monona IA U.S.A.
195 G2 Monopoli Italy
177 I4 Monor Hungary
232 D4 Monorgahela r. PA U.S.A.
177 K4 Monostorpályi Hungary
187 C6 Monóvar Spain
81 A6 Monowai, Lake South I. N.Z.
163 C4 Monpazier France
183 I2 Monreal Spain
185 H1 Monreal r. Spain
183 I3 Monreal del Campo Spain
194 C4 Monreale Sicilia Italy
146 D7 Monreith Dumfries and Galloway, Scotland U.K.
231 D5 Monroe GA U.S.A.
236 E3 Monroe IA U.S.A.
237 E5 Monroe LA U.S.A.
227 F5 Monroe MI U.S.A.
231 D5 Monroe NC U.S.A.
235 D1 Monroe NJ U.S.A.
235 D1 Monroe NY U.S.A.
241 K2 Monroe UT U.S.A.
232 D6 Monroe VA U.S.A.
238 B2 Monroe WA U.S.A.
226 C4 Monroe WI U.S.A.
236 F4 Monroe Center WI U.S.A.
236 E4 Monroe City MO U.S.A.
234 C1 Monroe County county PA U.S.A.
227 I5 Monroeton PA U.S.A.
231 C6 Monroeville AL U.S.A.
226 E5 Monroeville IN U.S.A.
234 C3 Monroeville NJ U.S.A.
232 B4 Monroeville OH U.S.A.
206 C5 Monrovia Liberia
182 D5 Monroy Spain
186 C4 Monroyo Spain
165 C4 Mons Belgium
161 A5 Mons Languedoc-Roussillon France
161 E5 Mons Provence-Alpes-Côte-d'Azur France
193 F2 Monsampolo del Tronto Italy
182 C4 Monsanto Port.
184 C2 Monsaraz Port.
169 B5 Monschau Ger.
162 C3 Monsec France
163 B5 Monségur France
163 C4 Monségur France
191 G3 Monselice Italy
163 C4 Monsempron-Libos France
156 D2 Mons-en-Barœul France
235 D1 Monsey NY U.S.A.
173 G3 Mönsheim Ger.
172 C2 Monsheim Rheinland-Pfalz Ger.
160 C2 Monsols France
233 □12 Monson ME U.S.A.
164 D2 Monster Neth.
143 G3 Mönsterås Sweden
191 F5 Monsummano Terme Italy
190 C4 Monta Italy
169 C5 Montabaur Ger.
187 C6 Montaberner Spain
160 D3 Montagnac France
161 B5 Montagnac France
191 G3 Montagnana Italy
162 B4 Montagne France
160 D1 Montagney France
161 B5 Montagnol France
160 D2 Montagny France
162 C3 Montagrier France
225 I4 Montague P.E.I. Can.
234 D1 Montague NJ U.S.A.
237 D5 Montague TX U.S.A.
87 C5 Montague Range hills W.A. Austr.
86 E2 Montague Sound b. W.A. Austr.
Montagu Island Vanuatu see Nguna
158 E5 Montaigu France
159 G4 Montaigu France
160 A2 Montaigut France
163 D5 Montaigut-sur-Save France
191 F5 Montaione Italy
95 F3 Montalat r. Indon.
186 C4 Montalbán Spain
185 F3 Montalbán de Córdoba Spain
194 E5 Montalbano Elicona Sicilia Italy
195 F2 Montalbano Jonico Italy
183 H5 Montalbo Spain
192 D1 Montalcino Italy
191 G5 Montale Italy
182 C3 Montalegre Port.
160 D3 Montalieu-Vercieu France
162 A3 Montalivet-les-Bains France
194 C5 Montallegro Sicilia Italy
195 E4 Montalto mt. Italy
193 F2 Montalto delle Marche Italy
192 D2 Montalto di Castro Italy
192 D2 Montalto Marina Italy
193 I5 Montalto Uffugo Italy
182 C5 Montalvão Port.
240 H4 Montalvo CA U.S.A.
182 E3 Montamarta Spain
197 F4 Montana Bulg.
190 C2 Montana Switz.
238 E2 Montana state U.S.A.
Montañana Spain see Puente de Montañana
242 □16 Montañas de Colón mts Hond.
184 D1 Montánchez hill Spain
184 D1 Montánchez, Sierra de mts Spain
234 B2 Montandon PA U.S.A.
187 C4 Montanejos Spain
163 B5 Montaner France
257 C3 Montanha Brazil
193 H4 Montano Antilia Italy
163 D5 Montans France
193 G3 Montaquila Italy
184 B1 Montargil Port.
156 C5 Montargis France
163 D5 Montastruc-la-Conseillère France
156 C3 Montataire France
163 D4 Montauban France
158 D3 Montauban-de-Bretagne France
163 E5 Montaud, Pic de mt. France
159 F3 Montaudin France
233 H4 Montauk NY U.S.A.
163 C4 Montauriol France
161 E5 Montauroux France
163 B5 Montaut Aquitaine France
163 B5 Montaut Aquitaine France
163 D5 Montaut Midi-Pyrénées France
163 D5 Montaut-les-Créneaux France
215 G3 Mont-aux-Sources mt. Lesotho
163 C4 Montayral France
193 G3 Montazzoli Italy
160 C1 Montbard France
160 D1 Montbarrey France
163 D5 Montbartier France
163 E4 Montbazens France
161 B5 Montbazin France
159 G4 Montbazon France
160 E1 Montbéliard France
160 D1 Montbenoît France
163 C5 Montbernard France
163 D4 Montbeton France
161 B5 Montblanc France
160 E3 Mont Blanc mt. France/Italy
186 E3 Montblanc Spain
Montblanch Spain see Montblanc
160 E3 Mont Blanc Tunnel France/Italy
161 C4 Montboucher-sur-Jaberon France
160 E1 Montbozon France
186 E3 Montbrió del Camp Spain
160 C3 Montbrison France
162 C3 Montbron France
163 D4 Montbrun France
161 D4 Montbrun-les-Bains France
232 C6 Montcalm WV U.S.A.
163 C4 Montcaret France
156 B2 Montcavrel France
160 C2 Montceau-les-Mines France
156 C2 Montcenis France
160 C2 Montchanin France
235 D2 Montclair NJ U.S.A.
163 D4 Montcornet France
156 C5 Montcresson France
163 D4 Montcuq France
156 E3 Montcy-Notre-Dame France
161 B5 Montdardier France
161 E4 Mont-Dauphin France
163 B5 Mont-de-Marsan France
156 C3 Montdidier France
160 A3 Mont-Dore France
261 F5 Monte, Lago del l. Arg.
193 H5 Montea mt. Italy
252 D4 Monteagudo Bol.
183 I3 Monteagudo Spain
183 I5 Monteagudo de las Salinas Spain
183 I5 Monteagudo de las Vicarías Spain
260 A5 Monte Aguila Chile
245 F5 Monte Albán tourist site Oaxaca Mex.
251 H5 Monte Alegre Brazil
256 B2 Monte Alegre r. Brazil
254 D5 Monte Alegre de Goiás Brazil
187 B6 Montealegre del Castillo Spain
256 C3 Monte Alegre de Minas Brazil
256 C4 Monte Alto Brazil
256 C4 Monte Aprazível Brazil
255 E5 Monte Azul Brazil
256 C4 Monte Azul Paulista Brazil
224 F4 Montebello Que. Can.
195 E5 Montebello Ionico Italy
86 B4 Montebello Islands W.A. Austr.
191 G3 Montebello Vicentino Italy
191 H3 Montebelluna Italy
158 E2 Montebourg France
190 E4 Montebruno Italy
261 F3 Monte Buey Arg.
191 H5 Montecalvo in Foglia Italy
258 G2 Montecarlo Arg.
161 F5 Monte-Carlo Monaco
256 D3 Monte Carmelo Brazil
261 I2 Monte Caseros Arg.
191 I5 Montecassiano Italy
193 E2 Monte Castello di Vibio Italy
193 E2 Montecastrilli Italy
191 F5 Montecatini Terme Italy
191 F5 Montecatini Val di Cecina Italy
191 H5 Montecchio Italy
190 F4 Montecchio Emilia Italy
191 G3 Montecchio Maggiore Italy
163 D5 Montech France
190 D3 Montechiaro d'Asti Italy
184 B3 Montechoro Port.
213 E4 Monte Christo S. Africa
193 G3 Montecilfone Italy
240 H4 Montecito CA U.S.A.
182 C5 Monte Claro Port.
182 B3 Monte Córdova Port.
193 G4 Montecorice Italy
193 I4 Monte Cotugna, Lago di l. Italy
191 H2 Montecreale Valcellina Italy
191 F4 Montecreto Italy
246 E3 Monte Cristi Dom. Rep.
250 A5 Montecristi Ecuador
253 E3 Monte Cristo Bol.
184 C1 Monte da Pedra Port.
184 B3 Monte da Rocha, Barragem do resr Port.
182 C2 Montederramo Spain
193 G4 Monte di Procida Italy
184 C2 Monte do Trigo Port.
184 B3 Monte Dourado Brazil
244 C2 Monte Escobedo Mex.
193 G4 Montefalcione Italy
193 E2 Montefalco Italy
193 G3 Montefalcone Italy
193 H3 Montefalcone di Val Fortore Italy
191 I5 Montefano Italy
191 H5 Montefelcino Italy
192 E2 Montefiascone Italy
193 F1 Montefiore dell'Aso Italy
191 F4 Montefiorino Italy
193 G4 Monteforte Irpino Italy
193 F2 Montefortino Italy
193 E2 Montefranco Italy
185 F3 Montefrío Spain
195 F2 Montegiordano Italy
193 F1 Montegiorgio Italy
246 □ Montego Bay Jamaica
246 □ Montego Bay b. Jamaica
184 C3 Monte Gordo Port.
191 I5 Montegranaro Italy
163 C5 Montégut-Arros France
261 G6 Monte Hermoso Arg.
182 D4 Montehermoso Spain
195 G2 Monteiasi Italy
163 D4 Monteils France
254 F3 Monteiro Brazil
185 E4 Montejaque Spain
185 G3 Montejícar Spain
84 B3 Montejinnie N.T. Austr.
183 G3 Montejo de la Sierra Spain
184 A1 Montejunto, Serra de hill Port.
191 H5 Montelabbate Italy
193 F3 Montelanico Italy
184 A2 Montelavar Port.
160 A3 Montel-de-Gelat France
193 H3 Monteleone di Puglia Italy
193 E2 Monteleone di Spoleto Italy
192 E2 Monteleone d'Orvieto Italy
192 A4 Monteleone Rocca Doria Sardegna Italy
193 E2 Monteleone Sabino Italy
194 C4 Montelepre Sicilia Italy
193 E2 Montelibretti Italy
161 D4 Montélier France
161 C4 Montélimar France
253 F5 Monte Lindo r. Para.
193 H4 Montella Italy
184 E3 Montellano Spain
226 C4 Montello WI U.S.A.
163 D5 Montels France
191 G5 Montelupo Fiorentino Italy
191 I5 Montelupone Italy
194 C5 Montemaggiore Belsito Sicilia Italy
261 F3 Monte Maíz Arg.
193 H4 Montemarano Italy
191 I5 Montemarciano Italy
185 H2 Montemayor r. Spain
185 F3 Montemayor Spain
259 D7 Montemayor, Meseta de plat. Arg.
183 F3 Montemayor de Pililla Spain
162 C3 Montemboeuf France
195 G2 Montemesola Italy
193 H3 Montemilone Italy
191 I5 Montemolín Spain
193 F2 Montemonaco Italy
243 F3 Montemorelos Mex.
184 B2 Montemor-o-Novo Port.
182 B4 Montemor-o-Velho Port.
191 G5 Montemurlo Italy
182 B3 Montemuro, Serra de mts Port.
193 H4 Montemurro Italy
159 F3 Montenay France
162 B3 Montendre France
Montenegro aut. rep. Yugo. see Crna Gora
183 H2 Montenegro de Cameros Spain
193 G3 Montenero di Bisaccia Italy
193 G2 Montenerodomo Italy
195 G2 Monteparano Italy
260 B2 Monte Patria Chile
247 E3 Monte Plata Dom. Rep.
191 I5 Monte Porzio Italy
193 F2 Monteprandone Italy
211 D8 Montepuez Moz.
211 D8 Montepuez r. Moz.
192 D1 Montepulciano Italy
258 E2 Monte Quemado Arg.
158 D4 Monterblanc France
191 H5 Montercchi Italy
182 B5 Monte Real Port.
193 F2 Montereale Italy
156 C4 Montereau-faut-Yonne France
182 B5 Monte Redondo Port.
191 G4 Monterenzio Italy
Monterey Nuevo León Mex. see Monterrey
240 G3 Monterey CA U.S.A.
232 D5 Monterey VA U.S.A.
240 F3 Monterey Bay CA U.S.A.
250 C2 Montería Col.
191 G5 Monteriggioni Italy
253 E4 Montero Bol.
193 G3 Monteroduni Italy
192 D2 Monte Romano Italy
195 G2 Monteroni d'Arbia Italy
195 H2 Monteroni di Lecce Italy
258 D2 Monteros Arg.
192 D2 Monterosi Italy
190 E4 Monterosso al Mare Italy
194 D6 Monterosso Almo Sicilia Italy
195 F4 Monterosso Calabro Italy
193 E2 Monterotondo Italy
192 C1 Monterotondo Marittimo Italy
187 C5 Monterreal Spain
241 J5 Monterrey Baja California Norte Mex.
243 E3 Monterrey Nuevo León Mex.
182 C2 Monterroso Spain
185 E2 Monterrubio de la Serena Spain
193 F1 Monterubbiano Italy
187 C6 Montesa Spain
254 D5 Montes Altos Brazil
193 F3 Monte San Biagio Italy
193 F3 Monte San Giovanni Campano Italy
238 B2 Montesano WA U.S.A.
195 H3 Montesano Salentino Italy
193 H4 Montesano sulla Marcellana Italy
191 G5 Monte San Savino Italy
191 H5 Monte Santa Maria Tiberina Italy
193 H3 Monte Sant'Angelo Italy
254 F4 Monte Santo Brazil
256 D4 Monte Santo de Minas Brazil
193 G3 Montesarchio Italy
195 F2 Montescaglioso Italy
257 F2 Montes Claros Brazil
183 F4 Montesclaros Spain
191 F5 Montescudaio Italy
191 F4 Montese Italy
193 G2 Montesilvano Italy
163 D4 Montesquieu France
163 D5 Montesquieu-Volvestre France
163 C5 Montesquiou France
163 D5 Montestruc-sur-Gers France
183 B3 Montes Velhos Port.
161 C4 Monteux France
194 B5 Montevago Sicilia Italy
191 G5 Montevarchi Italy
192 A5 Montevecchia Sardegna Italy
261 G2 Monte Vera Arg.
193 H3 Monteverde Italy
261 I4 Montevideo Uru.
261 I4 Montevideo dept Uru.
236 E2 Montevideo MN U.S.A.
184 B2 Montevil Port.
239 F4 Monte Vista CO U.S.A.
236 E3 Montezuma IA U.S.A.
237 C4 Montezuma KS U.S.A.
241 M3 Montezuma Creek UT U.S.A.
241 M3 Montezuma Creek r. CO U.S.A.
240 I3 Montezuma Peak NV U.S.A.
163 D4 Montfaucon Midi-Pyrénées France
159 E4 Montfaucon Pays de la Loire France
157 F3 Montfaucon-d'Argonne France
161 C3 Montfaucon-en-Velay France
163 C5 Montferran-Savès France
161 E5 Montferrat France
163 E5 Montferrier France
164 D2 Montfoort Neth.
163 B5 Montfort Aquitaine France
158 E3 Montfort Bretagne France
163 B5 Montfort-en-Chalosse France
156 B4 Montfort-l'Amaury France
159 G3 Montfort-le-Gesnois France
159 G2 Montfort-sur-Risle France
186 D3 Montgai Spain
163 C5 Montgaillard Midi-Pyrénées France
163 C5 Montgaillard Midi-Pyrénées France
163 D6 Montgaillard Midi-Pyrénées France
161 E4 Montgenèvre France
156 C4 Montgeron France
163 D5 Montgiscard France
159 H5 Montgivray France
187 D6 Montgó hill Spain
150 D2 Montgomery Powys, Wales U.K.
231 C5 Montgomery AL U.S.A.
235 D1 Montgomery NY U.S.A.
232 A5 Montgomery OH U.S.A.
227 I5 Montgomery PA U.S.A.
232 C5 Montgomery WV U.S.A.

236 F4 Montgomery City MO U.S.A.
234 A3 Montgomery County county MD U.S.A.
234 C2 Montgomery County county PA U.S.A.
86 D2 Montgomery Islands W.A. Austr.
162 B3 Montguyon France
156 E3 Monthermé France
190 B2 Monthey Switz.
156 E3 Monthois France
157 F4 Monthureux-sur-Saône France
192 B4 Monti Sardegna Italy
191 H3 Monticano r. Italy
190 E3 Monticelli d'Ongina Italy
192 A2 Monticello Corse France
237 F5 Monticello AR U.S.A.
231 D6 Monticello FL U.S.A.
231 D5 Monticello GA U.S.A.
236 F3 Monticello IL U.S.A.
230 C3 Monticello IN U.S.A.
230 C4 Monticello KY U.S.A.
233 □J1 Monticello ME U.S.A.
236 E2 Monticello MN U.S.A.
236 F3 Monticello MO U.S.A.
237 F6 Monticello MS U.S.A.
234 D1 Monticello NY U.S.A.
241 M3 Monticello UT U.S.A.
226 C4 Monticello WI U.S.A.
190 F3 Montichiari Italy
192 D1 Monticiano Italy
185 H2 Montiel Spain
261 H2 Montiel, Cuchilla de hills Arg.
159 H5 Montierchaume France
156 E4 Montier-en-Der France
192 D1 Montieri Italy
157 F4 Montiers-sur-Saulx France
162 D3 Montignac France
165 D4 Montignies-le-Tilleul Belgium
190 F4 Montignoso Italy
157 G4 Montigny France
156 D5 Montigny-la-Resle France
157 G3 Montigny-lès-Metz France
160 D1 Montigny-Mornay-Villeneuve-sur-Vingeanne France
157 E5 Montigny-sur-Aube France
184 B2 Montijo Port.
184 D2 Montijo Spain
185 F3 Montilla Spain
185 G3 Montillana Spain
163 E4 Montirat France
256 B2 Montividiu Brazil
159 G2 Montivilliers France
185 G2 Montizón Spain
185 G2 Montizón r. Spain
161 A4 Montjaux France
159 F3 Montjean France
159 F4 Montjean-sur-Loire France
225 G3 Mont-Joli Que. Can.
190 C3 Montjovet Italy
163 E5 Montlaur France
224 F4 Mont-Laurier Que. Can.
156 C4 Montlhéry France
162 B3 Montlieu-la-Garde France
225 H3 Mont Louis Que. Can.
163 E6 Mont-Louis France
159 G4 Montlouis-sur-Loire France
160 A2 Montluçon France
160 D3 Montluel France
221 K5 Montmagny Que. Can.
160 A2 Montmarault France
158 E3 Montmartin-sur-Mer France
157 F3 Montmédy France
160 E3 Montmélian France
160 C2 Montmerle-sur-Saône France
161 C4 Montmeyran France
161 E5 Montmeyan France
156 D4 Montmirail Champagne-Ardenne France
159 G3 Montmirail Pays de la Loire France
160 D1 Montmirey-le-Château France
162 C3 Montmoreau-St-Cybard France
226 D5 Montmorenci IN U.S.A.
230 G2 Montmorency Que. Can.
162 C2 Montmorillon France
161 D4 Montmorin France
160 D2 Montmorot France
156 D4 Montmort-Lucy France
186 F3 Montnegre de Llevant hill Spain
85 G5 Monto Qld Austr.
158 D4 Montoir-de-Bretagne France
159 G4 Montoire-sur-le-Loir France
156 D4 Montois slope France
161 C4 Montoison France
184 C2 Montoito Port.
163 E5 Montolieu France
183 I3 Montón Spain
191 H5 Montone Italy
191 H4 Montone r. Italy
193 E2 Montopoli di Sabina Italy
193 F2 Montorio al Vomano Italy
185 F2 Montoro Spain
185 G2 Montoro r. Spain
163 B5 Montory France
234 B1 Montour County county PA U.S.A.
232 E3 Montour Falls NY U.S.A.
159 F5 Montournais France
227 I5 Montoursville PA U.S.A.
246 □ Montpelier Jamaica
238 E3 Montpelier ID U.S.A.
226 E5 Montpelier IN U.S.A.
232 A4 Montpelier OH U.S.A.
233 G2 Montpelier VT U.S.A.
161 B5 Montpellier France
161 A4 Montpeyroux France
163 C4 Montpezat Aquitaine France
163 C5 Montpézat France
163 D4 Montpezat-de-Quercy France
161 C4 Montpezat-sous-Bauzon France
162 C3 Montpon-Ménestérol France
160 D2 Montpont-en-Bresse France
159 H4 Mont-près-Chambord France
Montreal Que. Can. see Montréal
224 F4 Montréal Que. Can.
224 C4 Montreal r. Ont. Can.
224 E4 Montreal r. Ont. Can.
160 C1 Montréal France
163 E5 Montréal France
163 C5 Montréal France
226 B2 Montreal WI U.S.A.
224 F4 Montréal-Dorval airport Que. Can.
160 D2 Montréal-la-Cluse France
223 J4 Montreal Lake Sask. Can.
224 F4 Montréal-Mirabel airport Que. Can.
224 C4 Montreal River Ont. Can.
163 E5 Montredon-Labessonnié France
161 C3 Montregard France
163 C5 Montréjeau France
159 H4 Montrésor France
192 A4 Montresta Sardegna Italy
160 D2 Montret France
156 C4 Montreuil Île-de-France France
156 B2 Montreuil Nord - Pas-de-Calais France
159 F4 Montreuil-Bellay France
159 F4 Montreuil-Juigné France
190 B2 Montreux Switz.
159 E4 Montrevault France
160 D2 Montrevel-en-Bresse France
159 H4 Montrichard France
163 D4 Montricoux France
160 E2 Montriond France
161 B4 Montrodat France
161 A5 Montrodre mt. France
186 D3 Mont-roig del Camp Spain
160 D2 Montrond France
160 C3 Montrond-les-Bains France
146 F5 Montrose Angus, Scotland U.K.
239 F4 Montrose CO U.S.A.
227 F4 Montrose MI U.S.A.
235 E1 Montrose NY U.S.A.
233 F4 Montrose PA U.S.A.
232 D5 Montrose WV U.S.A.
232 E5 Montross VA U.S.A.
187 C5 Montroy Spain
161 A4 Montrozier France
162 C1 Monts France
156 B3 Mont-St-Aignan France
160 C1 Mont-St-Jean France
157 F3 Mont-St-Martin France
158 E3 Mont-St-Michel, Baie du b. France
156 D5 Mont-St-Sulpice France
160 C2 Mont-St-Vincent France
163 E4 Montsalvy France
186 D3 Montsant r. Spain
160 C1 Montsauche-les-Settons France
163 C5 Montsaunès France
163 D6 Montségur France
186 F3 Montseny Spain
247 □2 Montserrat terr. West Indies
159 G4 Montsoreau France
163 B5 Montsoué France
160 D2 Mont-sous-Vaudrey France
159 G5 Monts-sur-Guesnes France
Mont St Michel tourist site France see Le Mont-St-Michel
159 F3 Montsûrs France
156 E4 Montsuzain France
187 F5 Montuïri Spain
242 □J8 Montuosa, Isla i. Panama
185 F3 Monturque Spain
232 D6 Montvale VA U.S.A.
163 D4 Montvalent France
156 B3 Montville France
235 F1 Montville CT U.S.A.
165 E4 Montzen Belgium
157 F3 Montzéville France
241 L3 Monument Valley reg. AZ U.S.A.
215 F2 Monyakeng S. Africa
96 A2 Monywa Myanmar
190 E3 Monza Italy
209 E9 Monze Zambia
Monze, Cape pt Pak. see Muari, Ras
172 B2 Monzelfeld Ger.
172 B2 Monzingen Ger.
252 A2 Monzón Peru
186 D3 Monzón Spain
183 F2 Monzón de Campos Spain
235 F1 Moodus CT U.S.A.
215 H3 Mooi r. Kwazulu-Natal S. Africa
215 F2 Mooi r. North West S. Africa
215 H3 Mooirivier S. Africa
164 E3 Mook Neth.
212 E4 Mookane Botswana
82 D2 Moolawatana S.A. Austr.
82 E2 Moomba S.A. Austr.
83 G2 Moomin Creek r. N.S.W. Austr.
82 C2 Moonaree S.A. Austr.
83 G2 Moonbi Range mts N.S.W. Austr.
147 D4 Mooncoin Rep. of Ireland
84 E5 Moonda Lake salt flat Qld Austr.
147 E4 Moone Rep. of Ireland
85 G5 Moonie Qld Austr.
83 G2 Moonie r. N.S.W./Qld Austr.
82 D3 Moonta S.A. Austr.
87 C6 Moora W.A. Austr.
85 E5 Mooraberree Qld Austr.
171 C5 Moorbad Lobenstein Ger.
238 F2 Moorcroft WY U.S.A.
168 C2 Moordorf (Südbrookmerland) Ger.
164 D3 Moordrecht Neth.
87 B6 Moore r. W.A. Austr.
238 E2 Moore MT U.S.A.
87 C6 Moore, Lake salt flat W.A. Austr.
79 □3a Moorea i. Fr. Polynesia
232 D5 Moorefield WV U.S.A.
231 D7 Moore Haven FL U.S.A.
149 I4 Moorends South Yorkshire, England U.K.
173 F3 Moorenweis Ger.
85 G3 Moore Reef Coral Sea Is Terr. Austr.
234 B2 Mooresburg PA U.S.A.
246 C1 Moores Island Bahamas
233 □J2 Moores Mills N.B. Can.
234 D3 Moorestown NJ U.S.A.
246 □ Moore Town Jamaica
148 C3 Moorfields Northern Ireland U.K.
146 E6 Moorfoot Hills Scotland U.K.
236 D2 Moorhead MN U.S.A.
83 E3 Moornanyah Lake imp. l. N.S.W. Austr.
82 E3 Moorook S.A. Austr.
84 C1 Mooroongga Island N.T. Austr.
83 F4 Mooroopna Vic. Austr.
240 H4 Moorpark CA U.S.A.
214 B5 Moorreesburg S. Africa
165 C4 Moorslede Belgium
168 C2 Moorweg Ger.
172 C4 Moos Baden-Württemberg Ger.
173 G3 Moos Bayern Ger.
173 G2 Moosbach Ger.
179 F4 Moosburg Austria
173 F3 Moosburg an der Isar Ger.
224 D3 Moose r. Ont. Can.
224 D3 Moose Factory Ont. Can.
233 □I2 Moosehead Lake ME U.S.A.
223 J5 Moose Jaw Sask. Can.
223 J5 Moose Jaw r. Sask. Can.
226 A2 Moose Lake MN U.S.A.
223 K5 Moose Mountain Creek r. Sask. Can.
224 D3 Moose River Ont. Can.
233 H2 Moosilauke, Mount NH U.S.A.
173 F3 Moosinning Ger.
179 G4 Mooskirchen Austria
223 K5 Moosomin Sask. Can.
224 D3 Moosonee Ont. Can.
173 G3 Moosthenning Ger.
213 F4 Mopane S. Africa
213 G3 Mopeia Moz.
Mopelia atoll Arch. de la Société Fr. Polynesia see Maupihaa
212 E4 Mopipi Botswana
206 D3 Mopti Mali
206 E3 Mopti admin. reg. Mali
252 C4 Moquegua Peru
252 C4 Moquegua dept Peru
261 H4 Moquehuá Arg.
177 H4 Mór Hungary
207 I4 Mora Cameroon
184 B2 Mora Port.
183 G5 Mora Spain
141 K3 Mora Sweden
226 A3 Mora MN U.S.A.
239 F5 Mora NM U.S.A.
239 F5 Mora r. NM U.S.A.
260 B4 Mora, Cerro mt. Arg./Chile
196 D4 Morača r. Yugo.
138 F5 Morach r. Belarus
123 F4 Morad r. Pak.
116 D3 Moradabad Uttar Prad. India
254 F3 Morada Nova Brazil
257 E3 Morada Nova de Minas Brazil
186 D3 Móra d'Ebre Spain
187 C4 Mora de Rubielos Spain
183 G3 Moradillo de Roa Spain
213 □J3 Morafenobe Madag.
175 H2 Morąg Pol.
177 I5 Mórahalom Hungary
182 D3 Morais Port.
186 D3 Móra la Nova Spain
185 G2 Moral de Calatrava Spain
259 B7 Moraleda, Canal sea chan. Chile
185 G3 Moraleda de Zafayona Spain
182 D4 Moraleja Spain
182 E3 Moraleja del Vino Spain
182 E3 Moraleja de Sayago Spain
242 □H6 Morales Guat.
185 H4 Morales r. Spain
182 E3 Morales del Vino Spain
183 E3 Morales de Toro Spain
182 E3 Morales de Valverde Spain
182 D3 Moralina Spain
114 C2 Moram Mahar. India
213 □K3 Moramanga Madag.
226 E3 Moran MI U.S.A.
238 E3 Moran WY U.S.A.
85 G4 Moranbah Qld Austr.
Morang Nepal see Biratnagar
117 H4 Moranhat Assam India
193 I5 Morano Calabro Italy
190 D3 Morano sul Po Italy
246 □ Morant Bay Jamaica
114 C3 Morappur Tamil Nadu India
146 C5 Morar Highland, Scotland U.K.
146 C5 Morar hills Scotland U.K.
146 C5 Morar, Loch l. Scotland U.K.
142 E3 Mörarp Sweden
182 D4 Morasverdes Spain
183 I3 Morata de Jalón Spain
183 G4 Morata de Tajuña Spain
185 I2 Moratalla Spain
114 C5 Moratuwa Sri Lanka
179 H2 Morava r. Europe alt. March (Austria)
179 H1 Moravany Czech Rep.
177 K3 Moravany Slovakia
213 □K2 Moravato Madag.
232 E3 Moravia NY U.S.A.
196 E4 Moravica r. Yugo.
197 E4 Moravica r. Yugo.
177 G2 Moravice r. Czech Rep.
177 H2 Morávka Czech Rep.
176 E3 Moravská Dyje r. Czech Rep.
179 I2 Moravská Nová Ves Czech Rep.
176 F2 Moravská Třebová Czech Rep.
176 E2 Moravské Budějovice Czech Rep.
177 H2 Moravskoslezské Beskydy mts Czech Rep.
176 G2 Moravský Beroun Czech Rep.
Moravský Ján Slovakia see Moravský Svätý Ján
176 G3 Moravský Písek Czech Rep.
176 G3 Moravský Svätý Ján Slovakia
87 B6 Morawa W.A. Austr.
175 I5 Morawica Pol.
146 E4 Moray admin. div. Scotland U.K.
85 F4 Moray Downs Qld Austr.
146 D4 Moray Firth b. Scotland U.K.
84 B2 Moray Range hills N.T. Austr.
172 B2 Morbach Ger.
190 E2 Morbegno Italy
116 B5 Morbi Gujarat India
160 E2 Morbier France
158 D4 Morbihan dept Bretagne France
179 H3 Mörbisch am See Austria
143 G3 Mörbylånga Kalmar Sweden
163 B4 Morcenx France
195 H3 Morciano di Leuca Italy
191 H5 Morciano di Romagna Italy
193 G3 Morcone Italy
100 B2 Mordaga Nei Mongol China
127 G3 Mor Dağı mt. Turkey
158 E3 Mordelles France
223 L5 Morden Man. Can.
199 E2 Mordoğan Turkey
Mordovia aut. rep. Rus. Fed. see Mordoviya, Respublika
135 I5 Mordoviya, Respublika aut. rep. Rus. Fed.
135 H5 Mordovo Rus. Fed.
Mordovskaya A.S.S.R. aut. rep. Rus. Fed. see Mordoviya, Respublika
139 L4 Mordves Rus. Fed.
Mordvinia aut. rep. Rus. Fed. see Mordoviya, Respublika
137 H4 Mordvynivka Ukr.
175 K3 Mordy Pol.
158 D4 Moréac France
184 C3 Moreanes Port.
236 C2 Moreau r. SD U.S.A.
236 C2 Moreau, South Fork r. SD U.S.A.
146 F6 Morebattle Scottish Borders, Scotland U.K.
149 G3 Morecambe Lancashire, England U.K.
149 F3 Morecambe Bay England U.K.
182 E1 Moreda Spain
183 H2 Moreda de Álava Spain
83 G2 Moree N.S.W. Austr.
156 B5 Morée France
232 B5 Morehead KY U.S.A.
231 E5 Morehead City NC U.S.A.
182 B3 Moreira do Rei Port.
116 D4 Morel r. India
190 D2 Mörel Switz.
244 D4 Morelia Mex.
85 E4 Morella Qld Austr.
186 C4 Morella Spain
194 D5 Morello r. Sicilia Italy
244 C2 Morelos Mex.
245 E4 Morelos state Mex.
116 D4 Morena Madh. Prad. India
184 D3 Morena, Sierra mts Spain
241 M5 Morenci AZ U.S.A.
227 E5 Morenci MI U.S.A.
197 G3 Moreni Romania
261 H4 Moreno Arg.
242 C2 Moreno Mex.
240 I5 Moreno Valley CA U.S.A.
183 H2 Morentín Spain
140 I3 Møre og Romsdal county Norway
253 F2 Morerú r. Brazil
182 E3 Moreruela de Tábara Spain
192 A4 Mores Sardegna Italy
149 F3 Moresby Cumbria, England U.K.
220 E4 Moresby, Mount B.C. Can.
222 C4 Moresby Island B.C. Can.
160 D3 Morestel France
85 H5 Moreton Bay Qld Austr.
150 D4 Moretonhampstead Devon, England U.K.
151 F3 Moreton-in-Marsh Gloucestershire, England U.K.
85 H5 Moreton Island Qld Austr.
150 E2 Moreton Say Shropshire, England U.K.
156 C4 Moret-sur-Loing France
190 C4 Moretta Italy
156 C3 Moreuil France
134 L1 Moreyu r. Rus. Fed.
160 E2 Morez France
150 C2 Morfa Nefyn Gwynedd, Wales U.K.
190 E4 Morfasso Italy
172 C2 Mörfelden Ger.
128 A2 Morfou Cyprus
128 A2 Morfou Bay Cyprus
140 N1 Morgam-Viibus hill Fin.
82 D3 Morgan S.A. Austr.
231 C6 Morgan GA U.S.A.
232 A5 Morgan KY U.S.A.
240 H3 Morgan, Mount CA U.S.A.
237 F6 Morgan City LA U.S.A.
230 C4 Morganfield KY U.S.A.
240 G3 Morgan Hill CA U.S.A.
231 D5 Morganton NC U.S.A.
230 C4 Morgantown KY U.S.A.
234 C2 Morgantown PA U.S.A.
232 D5 Morgantown WV U.S.A.
235 D2 Morganville NJ U.S.A.
158 E3 Morgat France
215 G2 Morgenzon S. Africa
190 E2 Morges Switz.
190 C3 Morgex Italy
157 G4 Morhange France
117 F4 Morhar r. India
106 A3 Mori Xinjiang China
191 F3 Mori Italy
105 D4 Mori Japan
241 J2 Moriah, Mount NV U.S.A.
239 F5 Moriarty NM U.S.A.
83 F2 Moriarty's Range hills Qld Austr.
206 C4 Moribaya Guinea
149 F3 Moricambe Bay England U.K.
222 E4 Moricetown B.C. Can.
250 D4 Morichal Col.
193 E2 Moricone Italy
156 C3 Morienval France
104 B4 Moriguchi Japan
215 F3 Morija Lesotho
207 G3 Moriki Nigeria
185 F3 Moriles Spain
Morin Dawa Nei Mongol China see Nirji
169 E4 Moringen Ger.
193 F3 Morino Italy
139 H3 Morino Rus. Fed.
102 J4 Morioka Japan
197 H2 Morişca r. Romania
83 G3 Morisset N.S.W. Austr.
146 D4 Moriston r. Scotland U.K.
171 E4 Moritzburg Ger.
104 C3 Moriyama Japan
102 J4 Moriyoshi-zan vol. Japan
140 M2 Morjärv Sweden
123 E4 Morjen r. Pak.
134 J4 Morki Rus. Fed.
139 K3 Morkiny Gory Rus. Fed.
163 B5 Morlaàs France
158 C3 Morlaix France
163 B5 Morlanne France
165 D4 Morlanwelz Belgium
172 C2 Mörlenbach Ger.
222 H5 Morley Alta Can.
157 F4 Morley France
149 H4 Morley West Yorkshire, England U.K.
193 I5 Mormanno Italy
156 C4 Mormant France
161 D4 Mormoiron France
Mormugao Goa India see Marmagao
160 C3 Mornand France
160 C3 Mornant France
161 C4 Mornas France
247 □2 Morne-à-l'Eau Guadeloupe
247 □2 Morne Constant hill Guadeloupe
247 □2 Morne Diablotin vol. Dominica
247 □2 Morne Macaque vol. Dominica
190 D4 Mornese Italy
85 E5 Morney Qld Austr.
259 B8 Mornington, Isla i. Chile
264 D9 Mornington Abyssal Plain sea feature S. Atlantic Ocean
84 D3 Mornington Island Qld Austr.
198 B2 Mornos r. Greece
173 F3 Mörnsheim Ger.
123 F5 Moro Pak.
238 B2 Moro OR U.S.A.
204 D3 Morocco country Africa
226 D5 Morocco IN U.S.A.
136 C2 Morochne Ukr.
237 E5 Moro Creek r. AR U.S.A.
211 C6 Morogoro Tanz.
211 C7 Morogoro admin. reg. Tanz.
92 B5 Moro Gulf Phil.
215 F3 Morojaneng S. Africa
214 D2 Morokweng S. Africa
244 D3 Moroleón Mex.
193 F3 Morolo Italy
213 □I4 Morombe Madag.
246 C2 Morón Cuba
106 D1 Mörön Mongolia
190 C1 Moron mt. Switz.
250 B5 Morona Ecuador
250 B6 Morona r. Peru
250 B5 Morona-Santiago prov. Ecuador
213 □J4 Morondava Madag.
183 H3 Morón de Almazán Spain
185 E3 Morón de la Frontera Spain
206 D4 Morondo Côte d'Ivoire
240 I4 Morongo Valley CA U.S.A.
217 □3a Moroni Njazidja Comoros
241 L2 Moroni UT U.S.A.
106 B5 Moron Us He r. Qinghai China
183 I3 Moros Spain
183 F3 Moros r. Spain
192 B2 Morosaglia Corse France
93 D2 Morotai i. Maluku Indon.
210 B4 Moroto Uganda
210 B4 Moroto, Mount Uganda
103 E7 Morotsuka Japan
196 D3 Morović Vojvodina, Srbija Yugo.
247 □1 Morovis Puerto Rico
81 A6 Morowai South I. N.Z.
139 H2 Morozova Rus. Fed.
137 J2 Morozovka Rus. Fed.
135 H6 Morozovsk Rus. Fed.
190 C4 Morozzo Italy
254 E4 Morpara Brazil
227 G4 Morpeth Ont. Can.
149 H2 Morpeth Northumberland, England U.K.
Morphou Cyprus see Morfou
256 C6 Morretes Brazil
232 A6 Morrill KY U.S.A.
236 C3 Morrill NE U.S.A.
237 E5 Morrilton AR U.S.A.
222 H5 Morrin Alta Can.
256 C2 Morrinhos Brazil
80 E2 Morrinsville North I. N.Z.
223 L5 Morris Man. Can.
226 C5 Morris IL U.S.A.
236 E2 Morris MN U.S.A.
227 I5 Morris PA U.S.A.
233 F2 Morrisburg Ont. Can.
234 D2 Morris County county NJ U.S.A.
221 O1 Morris Jesup, Kap c. Greenland
261 F3 Morrison Arg.
226 C5 Morrison IL U.S.A.
81 C6 Morrisons South I. N.Z.
235 D2 Morris Plains NJ U.S.A.
234 B1 Morris Run PA U.S.A.
150 D3 Morriston Swansea, Wales U.K.
241 K5 Morristown AZ U.S.A.
235 D2 Morristown NJ U.S.A.
233 F2 Morristown NY U.S.A.
231 D4 Morristown TN U.S.A.
233 F3 Morrisville NY U.S.A.
234 D2 Morrisville PA U.S.A.
233 G2 Morrisville VT U.S.A.
192 B3 Morro, Monte hill Sardegna Italy
256 C4 Morro Agudo Brazil
240 G4 Morro Bay CA U.S.A.
185 F2 Morro del Águila hill Spain
254 E4 Morro do Chapéu Brazil
257 G4 Morro do Coco Brazil
253 G2 Morro do Sinal hills Brazil
245 G5 Morro Mazatán Mex.
193 F2 Morrone, Monte mt. Italy
254 D2 Morros Brazil
191 I5 Morrovalle Italy
213 G3 Morrumbala Moz.
169 C5 Morsbach Ger.
172 C2 Morsberg hill Ger.
169 E4 Morschen Ger.
223 J5 Morse Sask. Can.
237 C4 Morse TX U.S.A.
226 B2 Morse WI U.S.A.
263 I2 Morse, Cape Antarctica
135 H5 Morshanka Rus. Fed.
Morshansk Rus. Fed. see Morshanka
136 B3 Morshyn Ukr.
116 D5 Morsi Mahar. India
171 C3 Morsleben Ger.
168 E3 Morsum Ger.
157 G4 Mortagne r. France
159 G3 Mortagne-au-Perche France
162 B3 Mortagne-sur-Gironde France
162 B1 Mortagne-sur-Sèvre France
182 B4 Mortágua Port.
159 F3 Mortain France
190 D3 Mortara Italy
160 D1 Morte r. France
160 E1 Morteau France
159 F3 Morteaux-Coulibœuf France
156 C3 Mortefontaine France
191 I3 Mortegliano Italy
150 C3 Mortehoe Devon, England U.K.
195 E4 Mortelle Sicilia Italy
261 G2 Morteros Arg.
257 E4 Mortes, Rio das r. Minas Gerais Brazil
254 C4 Mortes, Rio das r. Tocatins Brazil
215 E5 Mortimer S. Africa
151 F3 Mortimer West Berkshire, England U.K.
150 E2 Mortimer's Cross Herefordshire, England U.K.
223 J5 Mortlach Sask. Can.
83 E4 Mortlake Vic. Austr.
266 F5 Mortlock Islands Micronesia
Mortlock Islands P.N.G. see Tauu Islands
151 G2 Morton Lincolnshire, England U.K.
149 I4 Morton Lincolnshire, England U.K.
226 C5 Morton IL U.S.A.
237 C5 Morton TX U.S.A.
238 B2 Morton WA U.S.A.
159 G3 Mortrée France
178 D4 Mörtschach Austria
165 D3 Mortsel Belgium
83 F3 Morundah N.S.W. Austr.
210 B4 Morungole mt. Uganda
Moruroa atoll Arch. des Tuamotu Fr. Polynesia see Mururoa
83 G3 Moruya N.S.W. Austr.
160 B1 Morvan hills France
85 F5 Morven Qld Austr.
81 C6 Morven South I. N.Z.
146 E4 Morven hill Aberdeenshire, Scotland U.K.
146 E3 Morven hill Highland, Scotland U.K.
146 C5 Morvern reg. Scotland U.K.
Morvi Gujarat India see Morbi
150 E2 Morville Shropshire, England U.K.
83 F4 Morwell Vic. Austr.
150 C4 Morwenstow Cornwall, England U.K.
174 C3 Moryń Pol.
174 G2 Morzeszczyn Pol.
160 E2 Morzine France
139 J4 Mosal'sk Rus. Fed.
136 D3 Moşana Moldova
172 D2 Mosbach Ger.
149 H4 Mosborough South Yorkshire, England U.K.
238 F2 Mosby MT U.S.A.
184 A2 Moscavide Port.
191 G5 Moscia r. Italy
193 F2 Mosciano Sant'Angelo Italy
Moscow Rus. Fed. see Moskva
238 C2 Moscow ID U.S.A.
234 C1 Moscow PA U.S.A.
Moscow Oblast admin. div. Rus. Fed. see Moskovskaya Oblast'
171 D5 Mosel Ger.
169 C5 Mosel r. Ger.
232 E6 Moseley VA U.S.A.
157 G3 Moselle dept Lorraine France
157 G3 Moselle r. France
171 C3 Möser Ger.
240 I1 Moses, Mount NV U.S.A.
238 C2 Moses Lake WA U.S.A.
212 E4 Mosetse Botswana
81 C6 Mosgiel South I. N.Z.
232 D4 Moshannon PA U.S.A.
139 J2 Moshenskoye Rus. Fed.
227 E1 Mosher Ont. Can.
207 G4 Moshi r. Nigeria
211 C5 Moshi Tanz.
137 F3 Moshny Ukr.
174 E3 Mosina Pol.
226 C3 Mosinee WI U.S.A.
215 E2 Mosita S. Africa
140 K2 Mosjøen Norway
140 K2 Moskenesøy i. Norway
140 K2 Moskenestraumen sea chan. Norway
140 M1 Moskkugáisi mt. Norway
175 H5 Moskorzew Pol.
140 L2 Moskosel Sweden
139 L4 Moskovskaya Oblast' admin. div. Rus. Fed.
Moskovskiy Uzbek. see Shakhrikhan
137 J2 Moskovskoye Rus. Fed.
139 K4 Moskva Rus. Fed.
139 L4 Moskva r. Rus. Fed.
123 G2 Moskva Tajik.
177 G6 Moslavna Podravska Croatia
197 H2 Moşna Romania
177 K6 Moşniţa Nouă Romania
78 □5 Moso i. Vanuatu
191 G2 Moso in Passiria Italy
176 G4 Mosonmagyaróvár Hungary
188 F4 Mosor mts Croatia
177 H3 Mošovce Slovakia
137 I3 Mos'panove Ukr.
137 J4 Mospyne Ukr.
250 B4 Mosquera Col.
239 F5 Mosquero NM U.S.A.
187 C4 Mosqueruela Spain
142 D2 Moss Norway
208 C5 Mossaka Congo
Mossâmedes Angola see Namibe
256 B2 Mossâmedes Brazil
146 F4 Mossat Aberdeenshire, Scotland U.K.
81 B6 Mossburn South I. N.Z.
Mosselbaai S. Africa see Mossel Bay
214 D6 Mossel Bay S. Africa
209 B5 Mossendjo Congo
163 E6 Mosset France
83 F3 Mossgiel N.S.W. Austr.
215 G1 Mossiesdal S. Africa
172 D3 Mössingen Ger.
148 D3 Mossley Northern Ireland U.K.
85 F3 Mossman Qld Austr.
254 F3 Mossoró Brazil
147 E1 Moss-side Northern Ireland U.K.
146 E4 Mosstodloch Moray, Scotland U.K.
213 I2 Mossuril Moz.
83 G3 Moss Vale N.S.W. Austr.
223 K4 Mossy r. Sask. Can.
197 G5 Most Bulg.
176 C1 Most Czech Rep.
195 □ Mosta Malta
205 F2 Mostaganem Alg.
188 F4 Mostar Bos.-Herz.
255 C9 Mostardas Brazil
184 C3 Mosteiro Beja Port.
182 C5 Mosteiro Castelo Branco Port.
182 B2 Mosteiro Galicia Spain
182 C1 Mosteiro Galicia Spain
216 □1b Mosteiros São Miguel Azores
197 G3 Moşteni Romania
197 H3 Mostiştea r. Romania
175 I2 Mostkowo Pol.
183 G4 Móstoles Spain
223 I4 Mostoos Hills Sask. Can.
136 F4 Mostove Ukr.
129 B1 Mostovskoy Rus. Fed.
175 J3 Mostówka Pol.
Mosty Belarus see Masty
175 L4 Mosty Pol.
136 B3 Mostys'ka Ukr.
175 L6 Mostys'ka Druha Ukr.
Mosul Iraq see Al Mawşil
140 J3 Mosvik Norway
175 M4 Mosyr Ukr.
175 H4 Moszczenica Pol.
210 C2 Mot'a Eth.
78 □5 Mota i. Vanuatu
208 C4 Motaba r. Congo
185 H1 Mota del Cuervo Spain
183 E3 Mota del Marqués Spain
243 H6 Motagua r. Guat.
136 C1 Motal' Belarus
143 F2 Motala Sweden
78 □5 Mota Lava i. Vanuatu
174 F1 Motarzyno Pol.
197 H2 Moţca Romania
213 F5 Motetema S. Africa
116 D4 Moth Uttar Prad. India
146 E6 Motherwell North Lanarkshire, Scotland U.K.
214 D2 Mothibistat S. Africa
190 B2 Môtiers Switz.
117 F4 Motihari Bihar India
185 E2 Motilla hill Spain
183 I5 Motilla del Palancar Spain
143 E2 Motjärnshyttan Sweden
101 B4 Motlan Ling hill Liaoning China
213 F4 Motloutse r. Botswana
102 □2 Motobu Japan
212 D5 Motokwe Botswana
183 I4 Motos Spain
140 P1 Motovskiy Zaliv sea chan. Rus. Fed.
243 G6 Motozintla Mex.
185 G4 Motril Spain
197 F3 Motru Romania
197 F3 Motru r. Romania
215 F1 Motshikiri S. Africa
214 E3 Motswedimosa S. Africa
236 C2 Mott ND U.S.A.
193 H3 Motta Montecorvino Italy
195 E4 Motta San Giovanni Italy
190 D3 Motta Visconti Italy
169 E5 Motten Ger.
173 E3 Möttingen Ger.
195 G2 Mottola Italy
81 D4 Motueka South I. N.Z.
81 □1 Motu Fakataga i. Tokelau
Motuiti i. Fr. Polynesia see Motu Iti
79 □3 Motu Iti i. Fr. Polynesia
81 D5 Motukarara South I. N.Z.
243 H4 Motul Mex.
79 □3 Motu One atoll Arch. de la Société Fr. Polynesia
79 □3 Motu One i. Fr. Polynesia
81 D4 Motupiko South I. N.Z.
80 D4 Motupipi South I. N.Z.
80 D1 Motutangi North I. N.Z.
81 □3 Motutapu i. Rarotonga Cook Is
178 B3 Mötz Austria
142 D3 Mou Denmark
96 D3 Mouan, Nam r. Laos
207 H6 Mouanko Cameroon
161 E5 Mouans-Sartoux France
Mouaskar Alg. see Mascara
225 G3 Mouchalagane r. Que. Can.
159 E5 Mouchamps France
163 C5 Mouchan France
160 D2 Mouchard France
161 B4 Mouchet, Mont mt. France
246 E2 Mouchoir Bank sea feature Turks and Caicos Is
246 E2 Mouchoir Passage Turks and Caicos Is
182 C3 Mouçós Port.
108 B3 Mouding Yunnan China
206 B2 Moudjéria Maur.
190 B2 Moudon Switz.
161 F5 Mougins France
141 M3 Mouhijärvi Fin.
206 E4 Mouhoun r. Africa alt. Volta Noire, conv. Black Volta
208 A5 Mouila Gabon
159 F5 Mouilleron-en-Pareds France
83 F3 Moulamein N.S.W. Austr.
83 E3 Moulamein Creek r. N.S.W. Austr.
163 E4 Moularès France
Moulavibazar Bangl. see Maulvi Bazar
159 F3 Moulay France
247 □2 Moule Guadeloupe
209 A5 Moulèngui Binza Gabon
163 C4 Mouleydier France
159 G4 Mouliherne France
163 D5 Moulin-Neuf France
160 B2 Moulins France
160 B2 Moulins-Engilbert France
159 G3 Moulins-la-Marche France
163 D6 Moulis France
162 B3 Moulis-en-Médoc France
162 C2 Moulismes France
163 B5 Moulle de Jaut, Pic du mt. France
96 B3 Moulmein Myanmar
96 A3 Moulmeingyun Myanmar
204 E2 Moulouya, Oued r. Morocco
151 G4 Moulsecoomb Brighton and Hove, England U.K.
159 F2 Moult France
151 G2 Moulton Lincolnshire, England U.K.
151 G2 Moulton Northamptonshire, England U.K.
151 H2 Moulton Suffolk, England U.K.
231 C5 Moulton AL U.S.A.
262 P1 Moulton, Mount Antarctica
233 H3 Moultonborough NH U.S.A.
231 D6 Moultrie GA U.S.A.
Moumolu-Naunitu i. Solomon Is see San Jorge
237 F4 Mound City IL U.S.A.
236 E4 Mound City KS U.S.A.
236 E3 Mound City MO U.S.A.
236 C2 Mound City SD U.S.A.
208 C2 Moundou Chad
232 C5 Moundsville WV U.S.A.
231 C5 Moundville AL U.S.A.
161 E4 Mounier, Mont mt. France
116 C4 Mount Abu Rajasthan India
234 B2 Mount Aetna PA U.S.A.
239 F5 Mountainair NM U.S.A.
150 D3 Mountain Ash Rhondda Cynon Taff, Wales U.K.
231 C5 Mountain Brook AL U.S.A.
232 C6 Mountain City TN U.S.A.
237 E4 Mountain Grove MO U.S.A.
237 E4 Mountain Home AR U.S.A.
238 D3 Mountain Home ID U.S.A.
234 C1 Mountainhome PA U.S.A.
241 L1 Mountain Home UT U.S.A.
226 A2 Mountain Iron MN U.S.A.
232 D5 Mountain Lake Park MD U.S.A.
235 D2 Mountain Lakes NJ U.S.A.
241 J4 Mountain Pass CA U.S.A.
234 C1 Mountain Top PA U.S.A.
237 E5 Mountain View AR U.S.A.
240 F3 Mountain View CA U.S.A.
240 □D9 Mountain View HI U.S.A.
220 B3 Mountain Village AK U.S.A.
234 A3 Mount Airy MD U.S.A.
232 C6 Mount Airy NC U.S.A.
234 D2 Mount Arlington NJ U.S.A.
87 C5 Mount Augustus W.A. Austr.
215 G4 Mount Ayliff S. Africa
236 E3 Mount Ayr IA U.S.A.
240 I4 Mount Baldy CA U.S.A.
82 D3 Mount Barker S.A. Austr.
87 C7 Mount Barker W.A. Austr.
86 E3 Mount Barnett W.A. Austr.
83 F4 Mount Beauty Vic. Austr.
147 C3 Mount Bellew Rep. of Ireland
146 E6 Mountbenger Scottish Borders, Scotland U.K.
80 E4 Mount Bruce North I. N.Z.
227 G4 Mount Brydges Ont. Can.
85 F3 Mount Carbine Qld Austr.
230 C4 Mount Carmel IL U.S.A.
234 B2 Mount Carmel PA U.S.A.
232 B6 Mount Carmel TN U.S.A.
241 K3 Mount Carmel Junction UT U.S.A.
226 C4 Mount Carroll IL U.S.A.
84 C5 Mount Cavenagh N.T. Austr.
147 C2 Mountcharles Rep. of Ireland
87 C5 Mount Clere W.A. Austr.
147 B4 Mountcollins Rep. of Ireland
81 C5 Mount Cook South I. N.Z.
85 F4 Mount Coolon Qld Austr.
213 F3 Mount Darwin Zimbabwe
84 C4 Mount Denison N.T. Austr.
82 C2 Mount Eba S.A. Austr.
84 C5 Mount Ebenezer N.T. Austr.
222 C3 Mount Edgecumbe AK U.S.A.
237 E6 Mount Enterprise TX U.S.A.
226 E5 Mount Etna IN U.S.A.
148 B3 Mountfield Northern Ireland U.K.
215 G4 Mount Fletcher S. Africa
224 D5 Mount Forest Ont. Can.
215 G4 Mount Frere S. Africa
82 E4 Mount Gambier S.A. Austr.
85 F3 Mount Garnet Qld Austr.
232 B6 Mount Gay WV U.S.A.
232 B4 Mount Gilead OH U.S.A.
91 J8 Mount Hagen P.N.G.
148 B3 Mount Hamilton Northern Ireland U.K.
234 D3 Mount Holly NJ U.S.A.
234 A2 Mount Holly Springs PA U.S.A.
83 F3 Mount Hope N.S.W. Austr.
82 C3 Mount Hope S.A. Austr.
232 C6 Mount Hope WV U.S.A.
226 C4 Mount Horeb WI U.S.A.
86 E3 Mount House W.A. Austr.
85 E5 Mount Howitt Qld Austr.
81 C5 Mount Hutt South I. N.Z.
237 E5 Mount Ida AR U.S.A.
84 D4 Mount Isa Qld Austr.
232 D5 Mount Jackson VA U.S.A.
232 D4 Mount Jewett PA U.S.A.
147 D2 Mountjoy Northern Ireland U.K.
147 E2 Mountjoy Northern Ireland U.K.
234 B2 Mount Joy PA U.S.A.
87 D5 Mount Keith W.A. Austr.
210 C5 Mount Kenya National Park Kenya
235 E1 Mount Kisco NY U.S.A.
85 G4 Mount Larcom Qld Austr.
232 C4 Mount Lebanon PA U.S.A.
82 D3 Mount Lofty Range mts S.A. Austr.
227 G2 Mount MacDonald Ont. Can.
87 C6 Mount Magnet W.A. Austr.
83 E3 Mount Manara N.S.W. Austr.
80 F2 Mount Maunganui North I. N.Z.
147 D3 Mountmellick Rep. of Ireland
85 F3 Mount Molloy Qld Austr.
85 G4 Mount Morgan Qld Austr.
226 C4 Mount Morris IL U.S.A.
227 F4 Mount Morris MI U.S.A.
232 E3 Mount Morris NY U.S.A.
83 E2 Mount Murchison N.S.W. Austr.
232 C5 Mount Nebo WV U.S.A.
87 C4 Mount Newman W.A. Austr.
147 E2 Mount Norris Northern Ireland U.K.
147 D3 Mount Nugent Rep. of Ireland
232 A5 Mount Olivet KY U.S.A.
232 B5 Mount Orab OH U.S.A.
225 K4 Mount Pearl Nfld. Can.
234 C2 Mount Penn PA U.S.A.
85 G5 Mount Perry Qld Austr.
81 B6 Mount Pisa South I. N.Z.
82 D3 Mount Pleasant S.A. Austr.
225 H4 Mount Pleasant P.E.I. Can.
236 F3 Mount Pleasant IA U.S.A.
226 E4 Mount Pleasant MI U.S.A.
232 D4 Mount Pleasant PA U.S.A.
231 E5 Mount Pleasant SC U.S.A.
237 E5 Mount Pleasant TX U.S.A.
241 L2 Mount Pleasant UT U.S.A.
234 A2 Mount Pleasant Mills PA U.S.A.
234 C1 Mount Pocono PA U.S.A.
234 B4 Mount Rainier MD U.S.A.
147 D3 Mountrath Rep. of Ireland
81 D4 Mount Richmond Forest Park nature res. South I. N.Z.
214 E3 Mount Rupert S. Africa
234 D2 Mount Salem NJ U.S.A.
84 B3 Mount Sanford N.T. Austr.
150 B4 Mount's Bay England U.K.
147 C4 Mountshannon Rep. of Ireland
238 B3 Mount Shasta CA U.S.A.
81 C5 Mount Somers South I. N.Z.
151 F2 Mountsorrel Leicestershire, England U.K.
236 F4 Mount Sterling IL U.S.A.
232 B5 Mount Sterling KY U.S.A.
232 B5 Mount Sterling OH U.S.A.
214 E5 Mount Stewart S. Africa
232 D5 Mount Storm WV U.S.A.
85 F3 Mount Surprise Qld Austr.
84 C4 Mount Swan N.T. Austr.
147 C3 Mount Talbot Rep. of Ireland
232 E4 Mount Union PA U.S.A.
233 F3 Mount Upton NY U.S.A.
87 C5 Mount Vernon W.A. Austr.
237 F6 Mount Vernon AL U.S.A.
231 D5 Mount Vernon GA U.S.A.
236 F4 Mount Vernon IL U.S.A.
230 C4 Mount Vernon IN U.S.A.
232 A6 Mount Vernon KY U.S.A.
237 E4 Mount Vernon MO U.S.A.
235 E2 Mount Vernon NY U.S.A.
232 B4 Mount Vernon OH U.S.A.
237 E5 Mount Vernon TX U.S.A.
238 B1 Mount Vernon WA U.S.A.
234 B2 Mountville PA U.S.A.
84 C4 Mount Wedge N.T. Austr.
82 C3 Mount Wedge S.A. Austr.
82 C1 Mount Willoughby S.A. Austr.
234 B2 Mount Wolf PA U.S.A.
234 B4 Mount Zion MD U.S.A.
85 G5 Moura Qld Austr.
252 B1 Moura r. Brazil
184 C2 Moura Port.
184 C2 Mourão Port.
202 D5 Mourdi, Dépression du depr. Chad
206 D3 Mourdiah Mali
182 B3 Moure Port.
163 B5 Mourenx France
161 C5 Mouriès France
182 B4 Mourisca do Vouga Port.
182 B5 Mouriscas Port.
156 E3 Mourmelon-le-Grand France
148 B3 Mourne r. Northern Ireland U.K.
147 E2 Mourne Mountains hills Northern Ireland U.K.
161 E5 Mourre de Chanier mt. France
161 D5 Mourre Nègre mt. France
146 □G1 Mousa i. Scotland U.K.
165 C4 Mouscron Belgium
165 C4 Mouscron dept Belgium
208 C2 Mousgougou Chad
232 B6 Mousie KY U.S.A.
161 C5 Moussac France
161 A5 Moussan France
157 H4 Moussey France
202 C6 Moussoro Chad
163 E5 Moussoulens France
160 B1 Moussy France
158 C3 Moustéru France
163 B4 Moustey France
161 E5 Moustiers-Ste-Marie France
209 B5 Moutamba Congo
160 E2 Mouthe France
160 D2 Mouthier-en-Bresse France
160 E1 Mouthier-Haute-Pierre France
162 C3 Mouthiers-sur-Boëme France
232 C6 Mouth of Wilson VA U.S.A.
163 E6 Mouthoumet France
190 C1 Moutier Switz.
162 E2 Moutier-d'Ahun France
160 E3 Moûtiers France
162 A2 Moutiers-les-Mauxfaits France
179 H1 Moutnice Czech Rep.
207 I4 Moutourwa Cameroon
161 A5 Moux France
160 C1 Moux-en-Morvan France
156 C3 Mouy France
205 F4 Mouydir, Monts du plat. Alg.
209 B5 Mouyondzi Congo
198 B2 Mouzaki Greece
202 B6 Mouzarak Chad
157 F3 Mouzay France
157 F3 Mouzon France
157 F4 Mouzon r. France
242 C2 Movas Mex.
197 H3 Movila Miresii Romania
197 G3 Movileni Romania
147 D1 Moville Rep. of Ireland
85 G5 Mowbullan, Mount Qld Austr.
146 F5 Mowtie Aberdeenshire, Scotland U.K.
232 B5 Moxahala OH U.S.A.
246 C1 Moxey Town Andros Bahamas
209 C8 Moxico prov. Angola
147 B2 Moy r. Rep. of Ireland
146 D4 Moy Highland, Scotland U.K.
147 E2 Moy Northern Ireland U.K.
216 □3f Moya Gran Canaria Canary Is
217 □3 Moya Comoros
187 B5 Moya Castilla - La Mancha Spain
Moya Cataluña Spain see Moià
206 B4 Moyamba Sierra Leone
147 A3 Moyard Rep. of Ireland
147 B3 Moycullen Rep. of Ireland
156 D3 Moy-de-l'Aisne France
204 D2 Moyen Atlas mts Morocco
208 C2 Moyen-Chari pref. Chad
Moyen Congo country Africa see Congo
215 F4 Moyeni Lesotho
157 G4 Moyenmoutier France
206 B4 Moyenne-Guinée admin. reg. Guinea
156 B2 Moyenneville France
208 A5 Moyen-Ogooué prov. Gabon
147 E3 Moyer hill Rep. of Ireland
157 G3 Moyeuvre-Grande France
147 E2 Moygashel Northern Ireland U.K.
147 B2 Moylaw Rep. of Ireland
148 B4 Moylett Rep. of Ireland
147 C3 Moylough Rep. of Ireland
147 E3 Moynalty Rep. of Ireland
Moynaq Uzbek. see Muynak
147 D3 Moyne Rep. of Ireland
210 A4 Moyo Uganda
250 B6 Moyobamba Peru
148 C3 Moyola r. Northern Ireland U.K.
211 A6 Moyowosi r. Tanz.
140 K1 Møysalen mt. Norway
202 C6 Moyto Chad
111 B4 Moyu Xinjiang China
147 E3 Moyvalley Rep. of Ireland
148 B4 Moyvore Rep. of Ireland
148 B4 Moyvoughly Rep. of Ireland
121 H3 Moyynkum Kazakh.
121 F3 Moyynkum, Peski des. Kazakh.
121 H3 Moyynty Kazakh.
160 B3 Mozac France
213 G4 Mozambique country Africa
213 I4 Mozambique Channel Africa
265 G6 Mozambique Ridge sea feature Indian Ocean
182 E4 Mozárbez Spain
129 D2 Mozdok Rus. Fed.
122 E2 Mozdūrān Iran
232 B6 Mozelle KY U.S.A.

182 C4 **Mozelos** Port.
137 I3 **Mozh** r. Ukr.
138 G4 **Mozha** r. Belarus
139 K4 **Mozhaysk** Rus. Fed.
134 K4 **Mozhga** Rus. Fed.
108 A1 **Mozhong** Qinghai China
179 F4 **Mozirje** Slovenia
179 F4 **Mozirske Planine** mts Slovenia
137 G3 **Mozoliyivka** Ukr.
183 F3 **Mozoncillo** Spain
177 G5 **Mozsgó** Hungary
Mozyr' Belarus see **Mazyr**
206 A3 **Mpal** Senegal
211 A6 **Mpanda** Tanz.
215 H2 **Mpemvana** S. Africa
206 D3 **Mpessoba** Mali
215 G5 **Mpetu** S. Africa
210 B4 **Mpigi** Uganda
211 A7 **Mpika** Zambia
208 C3 **Mpoko** r. C.A.R.
215 H3 **Mpolweni** S. Africa
209 F7 **Mporokoso** Zambia
215 I3 **Mposa** S. Africa
208 C5 **Mpouya** Congo
211 A7 **Mpulungu** Zambia
215 H3 **Mpumalanga** S. Africa
215 G2 **Mpumalanga** prov. S. Africa
211 C6 **Mpwapwa** Tanz.
215 G4 **Mqanduli** S. Africa
Mqinvartsveri mt. Georgia/Rus. Fed. see **Kazbek**
175 J2 **Mrągowo** Pol.
173 G2 **Mrákov** Czech Rep.
135 L5 **Mrakovo** Rus. Fed.
Mrewa Zimbabwe see Murehwa
188 E3 **Mrežnica** r. Croatia
188 F3 **Mrkonjić-Grad** Bos.-Herz.
191 J3 **Mrkopalj** Croatia
174 F2 **Mrocza** Pol.
174 F4 **Mroczeń** Pol.
175 I4 **Mroczków** Pol.
175 H2 **Mroczno** Pol.
175 H4 **Mroga** r. Pol.
175 J3 **Mrozy** Pol.
137 F2 **Mryn** Ukr.
205 H2 **M'Saken** Tunisia
211 C6 **Msambweni** Kenya
211 C6 **Msata** Tanz.
174 E1 **Mścice** Pol.
176 D1 **Mšeno** Czech Rep.
138 G2 **Mshinskaya** Rus. Fed.
205 G2 **M'Sila** Alg.
139 J3 **Msta** Rus. Fed.
139 H2 **Msta** r. Rus. Fed.
Mstislavl' Belarus see Mstsislaw
175 H5 **Mstów** Pol.
139 H4 **Mstsislaw** Belarus
215 I2 **Msunduze** r. S. Africa
175 I6 **Mszana Dolna** Pol.
175 I4 **Mszczonów** Pol.
211 C7 **Mtama** Tanz.
210 B4 **Mtelo** Kenya
211 B6 **Mtera Reservoir** Tanz.
Mtoko Zimbabwe see **Mutoko**
215 H3 **Mtonjaneni** S. Africa
Mtorashanga Zimbabwe see Mutorashanga
217 □3b **Mtsamboro** Mayotte
217 □3b **Mtsangamouji** Mayotte
139 K5 **Mtsensk** Rus. Fed.
129 D3 **Mts'khet'a** Georgia
213 G6 **Mtubatuba** S. Africa
215 H3 **Mtunzini** S. Africa
211 D7 **Mtwara** Tanz.
211 C7 **Mtwara** admin. reg. Tanz.
96 A2 **Mu** r. Myanmar
184 B3 **Mu** hill Port.
211 C8 **Muaguide** Moz.
213 G2 **Mualadzi** Moz.
213 H3 **Mualama** Moz.
254 C2 **Muana** Brazil
209 B6 **Muanda** Dem. Rep. Congo
96 D3 **Muang Khammouan** Laos
97 D4 **Muang Không** Laos
96 D4 **Muang Khôngxédôn** Laos
97 B5 **Muang Luang** r. Thai.
96 C3 **Muang Pakxan** Laos
96 C3 **Muang Phôn-Hông** Laos
96 D4 **Muang Sam Sip** Thai.
96 C2 **Muang Sing** Laos
Muang Thai country Asia see Thailand
96 C3 **Muang Xaignabouri** Laos
213 G3 **Muanza** Moz.
94 C2 **Muar** Malaysia
94 C2 **Muar** r. Malaysia
94 C3 **Muarabeliti** Sumatera Indon.
94 C3 **Muarabungo** Sumatera Indon.
94 D4 **Muaradua** Sumatera Indon.
94 C3 **Muaraenim** Sumatera Indon.
94 C3 **Muaratebo** Sumatera Indon.
94 C3 **Muaratembesi** Sumatera Indon.
95 F3 **Muarateweh** Kalimantan Tengah Indon.
Muara Tuang Sarawak Malaysia see **Kota Samarahan**
123 F5 **Muari, Ras** pt Pak.
116 C3 **Muazzam** Punjab India
128 B5 **Mubārak, Jabal** mt. Jordan/Saudi Arabia
117 E4 **Mubarakpur** Uttar Prad. India
120 F5 **Mubarek** Uzbek.
210 A4 **Mubende** Uganda
207 I4 **Mubi** Nigeria
Muborak Uzbek. see **Mubarek**
209 B6 **Mucaba** Angola
251 F4 **Mucajaí** r. Brazil
251 F4 **Mucajaí, Serra do** mts Brazil
225 H1 **Mucalic** r. Que. Can.
213 F2 **Mucanha** r. Moz.
196 E4 **Mučanj** mt. Yugo.
86 D4 **Muccan** W.A. Austr.
193 F1 **Muccia** Italy
169 C5 **Much** Ger.
175 H6 **Mucharz** Pol.
87 B6 **Muchea** W.A. Austr.
171 C4 **Mücheln (Geiseltal)** Ger.
Mucheng Henan China see Wuzhi
211 A8 **Muchinga Escarpment** Zambia
253 E4 **Muchiri** Bol.
135 H6 **Muchkapskiy** Rus. Fed.
170 C2 **Muchow** Ger.
175 I6 **Muchówka** Pol.
108 B2 **Muchuan** Sichuan China
150 E2 **Much Wenlock** Shropshire, England U.K.
183 F3 **Mucientes** Spain
146 B5 **Muck** i. Scotland U.K.
171 F4 **Mücka** Ger.
85 G5 **Muckadilla** Qld Austr.
169 E5 **Mücke Große-Eichen** Ger.
169 E5 **Mücke-Nieder-Ohmen** Ger.
147 C1 **Muckish Mountain** hill Rep. of Ireland
146 □G1 **Muckle Roe** i. Scotland U.K.
250 D3 **Muco** r. Col.
211 D8 **Mucojo** Moz.
209 D7 **Muconda** Angola
195 F3 **Mucone** r. Italy
209 B9 **Mucope** Angola
177 H5 **Mucsi-hegy** hill Hungary
177 J3 **Múcsony** Hungary
213 H3 **Mucubela** Moz.
251 F5 **Mucucuaú** r. Brazil
251 E6 **Mucuim** r. Brazil
213 F3 **Mucumbura** Moz.
126 D3 **Mucur** Turkey
257 H3 **Mucuri** Brazil
257 H3 **Mucuri** r. Brazil
257 G3 **Mucurici** Brazil
216 □3b **Muda** hill Fuerteventura Canary Is
94 C1 **Muda** r. Malaysia
114 B3 **Mudabidri** Karnataka India
100 D3 **Mudanjiang** Heilong. China
100 D3 **Mudan Jiang** r. China
199 F1 **Mudanya** Turkey
172 D2 **Mudau** Ger.
128 C4 **Mudaysīsāt, Jabal al** hill Jordan
114 C2 **Muddebihal** Karnataka India
241 J3 **Muddy** r. NV U.S.A.
237 E5 **Muddy Boggy Creek** r. OK U.S.A.
234 B3 **Muddy Creek** r. PA U.S.A.
241 L2 **Muddy Creek** r. UT U.S.A.
241 J3 **Muddy Peak** NV U.S.A.
215 H3 **Muden** S. Africa
168 F3 **Müden (Aller)** Ger.
168 F3 **Müden (Örtze)** Ger.
169 C5 **Mudersbach** Ger.
114 C3 **Mudgal** Karnataka India
83 G3 **Mudgee** N.S.W. Austr.
114 B2 **Mudhol** Karnataka India
114 B3 **Mudigere** Karnataka India
223 J3 **Mudjatik** r. Sask. Can.
114 C2 **Mudkhed** Mahar. India
116 C3 **Mudki** Punjab India
96 B3 **Mudon** Myanmar
Mudraya country Africa see Egypt
210 E3 **Mudug** admin. reg. Somalia
199 G1 **Mudurnu** Turkey
199 G1 **Mudurnu** r. Turkey
134 G3 **Mud'yuga** Rus. Fed.
213 H2 **Muecate** Moz.
211 C7 **Mueda** Moz.
186 B3 **Muel** Spain
186 C4 **Muela de Arés** mt. Spain
183 G2 **Muela de Quintanilla** hill Spain
182 E3 **Muelas del Pan** Spain
86 E3 **Mueller Range** hills W.A. Austr.
245 G5 **Muerto, Mar** lag. Mex.
246 B1 **Muertos Cays** is Bahamas
147 D1 **Muff** Rep. of Ireland
203 G4 **Muftah** well Sudan
209 F8 **Mufulira** Zambia
209 E8 **Mufumbwe** Zambia
109 E2 **Mufu Shan** mts China
186 G2 **Muga** r. Spain
182 D3 **Muga de Sayago** Spain
129 F3 **Muğan** Azer.
129 F4 **Muğan Düzü** lowland Azer.
182 B1 **Mugardos** Spain
184 B1 **Muge** Port.
184 B1 **Muge** r. Port.
171 E4 **Mügeln** Ger.
171 E4 **Mügeln** Ger.
172 C3 **Muggensturm** Ger.
191 I3 **Muggia** Italy
Mughalbhin Pak. see **Jati**
117 E4 **Mughal Sarai** Uttar Prad. India
122 C3 **Mūghār** Iran
123 G2 **Mughsu** r. Tajik.
Mugia Spain see **Muxía**
209 F6 **Mugila, Monts** mts Dem. Rep. Congo
199 F3 **Muğla** Turkey
199 F3 **Muğla** prov. Turkey
120 D3 **Mugodzhary, Gory** mts Kazakh.
106 B5 **Mug Qu** r. Qinghai China
163 B5 **Mugron** France
211 C8 **Muguia** Moz.
116 E3 **Mugu Karnali** r. Nepal
211 B5 **Mugumu** Tanz.
106 A1 **Mugur-Aksy** Rus. Fed.
111 F5 **Mugxung** Qinghai China
Muhala Xinjiang China see Yutian
117 E4 **Muhammadabad** Uttar Prad. India
Muhammarah Iran see Khorramshahr
124 D3 **Muḩayriqah** Saudi Arabia
211 C6 **Muheza** Tanz.
172 C3 **Mühlacker** Ger.
171 D4 **Mühlanger** Ger.
170 E2 **Mühlbach** r. Ger.
171 E4 **Mühlberg** Ger.
169 F5 **Mühlberg** Ger.
173 G3 **Mühldorf am Inn** Ger.
179 F3 **Mühlen** Austria
170 D1 **Mühlen** hill Ger.
170 E3 **Mühlenbeck** Ger.
170 C2 **Mühlen-Eichsen** Ger.
172 C2 **Mühlhausen** Ger.
173 F2 **Mühlhausen** Ger.
169 F4 **Mühlhausen (Thüringen)** Ger.
169 D5 **Mühlheim am Main** Ger.
172 C3 **Mühlheim an der Donau** Ger.
263 A2 **Mühlig-Hofmann Mountains** Antarctica
172 D4 **Mühlingen** Ger.
171 C5 **Mühltroff** Ger.
140 N2 **Muhos** Fin.
128 C2 **Muḩradah** Syria
173 E2 **Muhr am See** Ger.
138 D2 **Muhu** i. Estonia
213 H2 **Muhula** Moz.
210 B3 **Mui** Eth.
164 E2 **Muiden** Neth.
156 B3 **Muids** France
209 D8 **Muié** Angola
Muineachán Rep. of Ireland see **Monaghan**
147 E4 **Muine Bheag** Rep. of Ireland
182 C3 **Muiños** Spain
226 E4 **Muir** MI U.S.A.
234 B2 **Muir** PA U.S.A.
146 F5 **Muirdrum** Angus, Scotland U.K.
146 E5 **Muirhead** Angus, Scotland U.K.
146 D6 **Muirkirk** East Ayrshire, Scotland U.K.
146 B3 **Muirneag** hill Scotland U.K.
146 F4 **Muir of Fowlis** Aberdeenshire, Scotland U.K.
146 D4 **Muir of Ord** Highland, Scotland U.K.
250 B4 **Muisne** Ecuador
213 H2 **Muite** Moz.
156 D3 **Muizon** France
95 F2 **Mujong** r. Sarawak Malaysia
101 C5 **Muju** S. Korea
Mukačevo Ukr. see **Mukacheve**
136 B3 **Mukacheve** Ukr.
Mukachevo Ukr. see Mukacheve
95 F2 **Mukah** r. Sarawak Malaysia
Mukalla Yemen see **Al Mukallā**
116 C4 **Mukandgarh** Rajasthan India
116 D4 **Mukandwara** Rajasthan India
102 J2 **Mu-kawa** r. Japan
96 D3 **Mukdahan** Thai.
Mukden Liaoning China see Shenyang
116 C3 **Mukerian** Punjab India
224 C2 **Muketei** r. Ont. Can.
175 M3 **Mukhavyets** r. Belarus
100 F2 **Mukhen** Rus. Fed.
107 F1 **Mukhorshibir'** Rus. Fed.
Mukhtuya Rus. Fed. see **Lensk**
87 C6 **Mukinbudin** W.A. Austr.
104 B4 **Mukō** Japan
94 C3 **Mukomuko** Sumatera Indon.
210 B4 **Mukono** Uganda
123 F2 **Mukry** Turkm.
Muksu r. Tajik. see **Mughsu**
116 C3 **Muktsar** Punjab India
209 F8 **Mukuku** Zambia
120 C3 **Mukur** Atyrauskaya Oblast' Kazakh.
121 J2 **Mukur** Vostochnyy Kazakhstan Kazakh.
223 L4 **Mukutawa** r. Man. Can.
226 C4 **Mukwonago** WI U.S.A.
116 D5 **Mul** Mahar. India
114 B2 **Mula** r. India
123 F4 **Mula** r. Pak.
187 B6 **Mula** Spain
185 I2 **Mula** r. Spain
113 D11 **Mulakatholhu Atoll** Maldives
Mulaku atoll Maldives see **Mulakatholhu Atoll**
100 D3 **Mulan** Heilong. China
92 B3 **Mulanay** Phil.
211 B8 **Mulanje** Malawi
213 G2 **Mulanje, Mount** Malawi
82 D2 **Mulapula, Lake** salt flat S.A. Austr.
190 E4 **Mulazzo** Italy
114 C3 **Mulbagal** Karnataka India
151 I2 **Mulbarton** Norfolk, England U.K.
116 D2 **Mulbekh** Jammu and Kashmir
146 E4 **Mulben** Moray, Scotland U.K.
237 E5 **Mulberry** AR U.S.A.
220 C3 **Mulchatna** r. AK U.S.A.
260 A5 **Mulchén** Chile
171 E5 **Mulda** Ger.
171 D4 **Mulde** r. Ger.
171 D4 **Muldenstein** Ger.
211 A5 **Muleba** Tanz.
238 F3 **Mule Creek** WY U.S.A.
242 B3 **Mulegé** Mex.
237 C5 **Muleshoe** TX U.S.A.
213 H3 **Mulevala** Moz.
172 D2 **Mulfingen** Ger.
86 C4 **Mulga Downs** W.A. Austr.
84 B5 **Mulga Park** N.T. Austr.
82 C2 **Mulgathing** S.A. Austr.
185 G3 **Mulhacén** mt. Spain
Mülhausen France see Mulhouse
169 B4 **Mülheim an der Ruhr** Ger.
169 C5 **Mülheim-Kärlich** Ger.
157 H5 **Mulhouse** France
108 B3 **Muli** Sichuan China
113 □2 **Mulikadu** i. Addu Atoll Maldives
100 D3 **Muling** Heilong. China
100 D3 **Muling** Heilong. China
100 E3 **Muling** r. China
146 C5 **Mull** i. Scotland U.K.
146 B5 **Mull, Sound of** sea chan. Scotland U.K.
122 B2 **Mulla Ali** Iran
148 C4 **Mullagh** Cavan Rep. of Ireland
147 B4 **Mullagh** Clare Rep. of Ireland
147 B3 **Mullagh** Mayo Rep. of Ireland
147 E3 **Mullagh** Meath Rep. of Ireland
147 B4 **Mullaghareirk** hill Rep. of Ireland
147 B4 **Mullaghareirk Mountains** hills Rep. of Ireland
147 D2 **Mullaghcarn** hill Northern Ireland U.K.
147 E3 **Mullaghcleevaun** hill Rep. of Ireland
147 D2 **Mullaghcloga** hill Northern Ireland U.K.
147 C2 **Mullaghmore** Rep. of Ireland
114 D4 **Mullaittivu** Sri Lanka
83 G2 **Mullaley** N.S.W. Austr.
147 E2 **Mullan** Rep. of Ireland
147 D2 **Mullan** Northern Ireland U.K.
146 C4 **Mullardoch, Loch** l. Scotland U.K.
147 F2 **Mullartown** Northern Ireland U.K.
236 C3 **Mullen** NE U.S.A.
83 F2 **Mullengudgery** N.S.W. Austr.
232 C6 **Mullens** WV U.S.A.
95 F2 **Muller, Pegunungan** mts Indon.
87 B6 **Mullewa** W.A. Austr.
172 B4 **Müllheim** Ger.
234 D3 **Mullica** r. NJ U.S.A.
234 C3 **Mullica Hill** NJ U.S.A.
147 D4 **Mullinavat** Rep. of Ireland
147 D3 **Mullingar** Rep. of Ireland
231 E5 **Mullins** SC U.S.A.
150 B4 **Mullion** Cornwall, England U.K.
83 G3 **Mullion Creek** N.S.W. Austr.
145 E4 **Mull of Galloway** c. Scotland U.K.
146 C6 **Mull of Kintyre** hd Scotland U.K.
146 B6 **Mull of Oa** hd Scotland U.K.
135 J5 **Mullovka** Rus. Fed.
171 F3 **Müllrose** Ger.
143 E3 **Mullsjö** Sweden
209 E9 **Mulobezi** Zambia
209 D9 **Mulonga Plain** Zambia
209 E6 **Mulongo** Dem. Rep. Congo
147 B3 **Mulrany** Rep. of Ireland
159 G4 **Mulsanne** France
116 D5 **Multai** Madh. Prad. India
123 G4 **Multan** Pak.
140 N3 **Multia** Fin.
95 F1 **Mulu, Gunung** mt. Sarawak Malaysia
114 C2 **Mulug** Andhra Prad. India
209 E7 **Mulumbe, Monts** mts Dem. Rep. Congo
122 E5 **Mūmān** Iran
114 B2 **Mumbai** Mahar. India
83 G3 **Mumbil** N.S.W. Austr.
209 B7 **Mumbondo** Angola
209 E8 **Mumbwa** Zambia
Muminabad Tajik. see Leningrad
Mŭ'minobod Tajik. see Leningrad
190 C1 **Mümliswil** Switz.
120 A3 **Mumra** Rus. Fed.
96 D4 **Mun, Mae Nam** r. Thai.
243 H4 **Muna** Mex.
131 N3 **Muna** r. Rus. Fed.
123 G5 **Munabao** Pak.
114 C2 **Munagala** Andhra Prad. India
103 E7 **Munakata** Japan
183 E4 **Muñana** Spain
120 C3 **Munayly** Kazakh.
120 C4 **Munayshy** Kazakh.
171 C5 **Münchberg** Ger.
171 F3 **Müncheberg** Ger.
173 F3 **München** Ger.
München airport Ger. see **Franz Josef Strauss**
171 C5 **Münchenbernsdorf** Ger.
190 C1 **Münchenbuchsee** Switz.
München-Gladbach Ger. see Mönchengladbach
169 D5 **Münchhausen** Ger.
222 E3 **Muncho Lake** B.C. Can.
101 C5 **Munch'ŏn** N. Korea
173 F3 **Münchsmünster** Ger.
173 E2 **Münchsteinach** Ger.
172 B2 **Münchweiler an der Rodalb** Ger.
190 E1 **Münchwilen** Switz.
230 C3 **Muncie** IN U.S.A.
84 D5 **Muncoonie West, Lake** salt flat Qld Austr.
227 I5 **Muncy** PA U.S.A.
234 B1 **Muncy Creek** r. PA U.S.A.
234 B1 **Muncy Valley** PA U.S.A.
183 H1 **Mundaka** Spain
207 H5 **Mundemba** Cameroon
178 E2 **Munderfing** Austria
172 D3 **Munderkingen** Ger.
151 I2 **Mundesley** Norfolk, England U.K.
151 H2 **Mundford** Norfolk, England U.K.
87 D4 **Mundiwindi** W.A. Austr.
85 E3 **Mundjura Creek** r. Qld Austr.
185 I2 **Mundo** r. Spain
157 H4 **Mundolshiem** France
254 E4 **Mundo Novo** Brazil
116 B5 **Mundra** Gujarat India
87 E6 **Mundrabilla** W.A. Austr.
241 L4 **Munds Park** AZ U.S.A.
85 G5 **Mundubbera** Qld Austr.
116 C4 **Mundwa** Rajasthan India
183 I3 **Munebrega** Spain
185 H1 **Munera** Spain
114 D2 **Muneru** r. India
230 C4 **Munfordville** KY U.S.A.
85 F5 **Mungallala** Qld Austr.
83 F2 **Mungallala Creek** r. Qld Austr.
85 F3 **Mungana** Qld Austr.
116 D4 **Mungaoli** Madh. Prad. India
213 G3 **Mungári** Moz.
116 E5 **Mungeli** Madh. Prad. India
117 F4 **Munger** Bihar India
227 F4 **Munger** MI U.S.A.
82 D2 **Mungeranie** S.A. Austr.
Mu Nggava i. Solomon Is see Rennell
183 H1 **Mungia** Spain
Mu Ngiki i. Solomon Is see Bellona
83 G2 **Mungindi** N.S.W. Austr.
117 G5 **Mungla** Bangl.
209 C7 **Mungo** Angola
147 C4 **Mungret** Rep. of Ireland
211 A7 **Mungwi** Zambia
101 C5 **Mun'gyŏng** S. Korea
209 B8 **Munhino** Angola
256 D5 **Munhoz** Brazil
Munich Ger. see **München**
183 E4 **Muñico** Spain
186 C3 **Muniesa** Spain
183 H2 **Munilla** Spain
226 D2 **Munising** MI U.S.A.
257 G4 **Muniz Freire** Brazil
Munkács Ukr. see **Mukacheve**
142 D2 **Munkedal** Sweden
140 K3 **Munkflohögen** Sweden
142 E2 **Munkfors** Sweden
106 D1 **Munku-Sardyk, Gora** mt. Mongolia/Rus. Fed.
165 C4 **Munkzwalm** Belgium
146 D4 **Munlochy** Highland, Scotland U.K.
169 F5 **Münnerstadt** Ger.
173 E3 **Munningen** Ger.
183 F4 **Muñogalindo** Spain
83 G5 **Munro, Mount** Tas. Austr.
117 G5 **Munshiganj** Bangl.
173 F4 **Münsing** Ger.
172 D3 **Münsingen** Ger.
190 C2 **Münsingen** Switz.
178 C3 **Münster** Austria
157 H4 **Munster** France
172 C2 **Münster** Ger.
168 F3 **Münster** Ger.
169 C4 **Münster** Ger.
169 C4 **Münster** admin. reg. Nordrhein-Westfalen Ger.
147 C4 **Munster** reg. Rep. of Ireland
190 D2 **Münster** Switz.
168 E2 **Münsterdorf** Ger.
173 E3 **Münsterhausen** Ger.
169 C5 **Münstermaifeld** Ger.
169 C3 **Münster-Osnabrück** airport Ger.
87 C6 **Muntadgin** W.A. Austr.
178 D3 **Muntanitz** mt. Austria
197 F2 **Muntele Mare, Vârful** mt. Romania
164 F1 **Muntendam** Neth.
197 H3 **Munteni** Romania
Munyal-Par sea feature India see **Bassas de Pedro Padua Bank**
213 F3 **Munyati** r. Zimbabwe
215 G4 **Munyu** S. Africa
169 D5 **Münzenberg** Ger.
179 E2 **Münzkirchen** Austria
140 M2 **Muodoslompolo** Sweden
140 M2 **Muonio** Fin.
140 M2 **Muonioälven** r. Fin./Sweden
140 M2 **Muonionalusta** Sweden
Muonionjoki r. Fin./Sweden see Muonioälven
190 D2 **Muotathal** Switz.
209 B9 **Mupa** Angola
213 F3 **Mupfure** r. Zimbabwe
107 I4 **Muping** Shandong China
124 D5 **Muqaybirah** Yemen
210 E4 **Muqdisho** Somalia
125 F4 **Muqshin, Wādī** r. Oman
129 F3 **Müqtädır** Azer.
257 G4 **Muqui** Brazil
Muqyr Atyrauskaya Oblast' Kazakh. see **Mukur**
179 H4 **Mur** r. Austria alt. **Mura (Croatia/Slovenia)**
179 H4 **Mura** r. Croatia/Slovenia alt. **Mur (Austria)**
173 G2 **Murach** r. Ger.
182 C5 **Muradal, Serra do** mts Port.
199 E2 **Muradiye** Manisa Turkey
127 F3 **Muradiye** Van Turkey
136 E3 **Murafa** r. Ukr.
102 I4 **Murakami** Japan
176 F5 **Murakeresztúr** Hungary
259 B8 **Murallón, Cerro** mt. Chile
211 A5 **Muramvya** Burundi
177 J3 **Muráň** Slovakia
177 J3 **Muráň** r. Slovakia
210 C5 **Muranga** Kenya
191 H3 **Murano** Italy
182 C1 **Muras** Spain
134 J4 **Murashi** Rus. Fed.
161 A5 **Murasson** France
176 F5 **Muraszemenye** Hungary
161 A3 **Murat** France
129 B4 **Murat** r. Turkey
127 E3 **Murat** r. Turkey
129 B4 **Muratgören** Turkey
199 E1 **Muratlı** Turkey
192 B2 **Murato** Corse France
161 A5 **Murat-sur-Vèbre** France
179 F3 **Murau** Austria
175 M3 **Murava** Belarus
192 B5 **Muravera** Sardegna Italy
102 J4 **Murayama** Japan
124 C2 **Murayr, Jabal** hill Saudi Arabia
190 D4 **Murazzano** Italy
157 H5 **Murbach** France
182 C3 **Murça** Port.
183 I2 **Murchante** Spain
170 E2 **Murchin** Ger.
83 F4 **Murchison** Vic. Austr.
87 B5 **Murchison** watercourse W.A. Austr.
81 D4 **Murchison** South I. N.Z.
263 L2 **Murchison, Mount** Antarctica
87 C5 **Murchison, Mount** hill W.A. Austr.
81 C5 **Murchison, Mount** South I. N.Z.
210 A4 **Murchison Falls National Park** Uganda
84 C4 **Murchison Range** hills N.T. Austr.
187 B7 **Murcia** Spain
185 I3 **Murcia** aut. comm. Spain
174 F3 **Murczyn** Pol.
161 A4 **Mur-de-Barrez** France
158 D3 **Mûr-de-Bretagne** France
234 C3 **Murderkill** r. DE U.S.A.
159 H4 **Mur-de-Sologne** France
236 C3 **Murdo** SD U.S.A.
225 H3 **Murdochville** Que. Can.
179 G4 **Mureck** Austria
199 E1 **Mürefte** Turkey
213 F3 **Murehwa** Zimbabwe
184 C2 **Mures** r. Port.
196 E2 **Mureș** r. Romania
163 D5 **Muret** France
Murewa Zimbabwe see Murehwa
140 K2 **Murfjället** mt. Norway
237 E5 **Murfreesboro** AR U.S.A.
231 E4 **Murfreesboro** NC U.S.A.
231 C5 **Murfreesboro** TN U.S.A.
172 C4 **Murg** Ger.
172 C3 **Murg** r. Ger.
123 H2 **Murgab** r. Tajik.
123 E2 **Murgap** Turkm.
123 E2 **Murgap** r. Turkm.
84 C1 **Murgenella Creek** r. N.T. Austr.
197 I2 **Murgeni** Romania
190 C1 **Murgenthal** Switz.
195 G2 **Murge Tarantine** hills Italy
123 E3 **Murghab** r. Afgh.
Murghob Turkm. see **Murgap**
Murghob r. Turkm. see **Murgap**
129 D3 **Murghuz Lerr** mt. Armenia
193 I4 **Murgia Sant'Elia** hill Italy
85 G5 **Murgon** Qld Austr.
87 C5 **Murgoo** W.A. Austr.
183 H2 **Murguía** Spain
129 B3 **Murgul** Turkey
106 C4 **Muri** Qinghai China
117 F5 **Muri** Bihar India
122 D2 **Mūrī** Iran
190 D1 **Muri** Aargau Switz.
190 C2 **Muri** Bern Switz.
95 E4 **Muria, Gunung** mt. Indon.
257 F4 **Muriaé** Brazil
182 D2 **Murias de Paredes** Spain
183 G1 **Muriedas** Spain
209 D7 **Muriege** Angola
102 K2 **Murii-dake** mt. Japan
226 C1 **Murillo** Ont. Can.
183 I2 **Murillo el Fruto** Spain
190 D3 **Murisengo** Italy
170 D2 **Müritz** l. Ger.
80 F3 **Muriwai** North I. N.Z.
140 M2 **Murjek** Sweden
148 B3 **Murley** Northern Ireland U.K.
192 D1 **Murlo** Italy
140 P1 **Murmansk** Rus. Fed.
140 P1 **Murmanskaya Oblast'** admin. div. Rus. Fed.
134 F1 **Murmanskiy Bereg** coastal area Rus. Fed.
Murmansk Oblast admin. div. Rus. Fed. see Murmanskaya Oblast'
140 P1 **Murmashi** Rus. Fed.
139 M4 **Murmino** Rus. Fed.
173 G4 **Murn** r. Ger.
173 F4 **Murnau am Staffelsee** Ger.
147 E4 **Murntown** Rep. of Ireland
182 B3 **Muro** Port.
187 G5 **Muro** Spain
187 G5 **Muro** r. Spain
187 C6 **Muro de Alcoy** Spain
160 A3 **Murol** France
195 H2 **Muro Leccese** Italy
193 H4 **Muro Lucano** Italy
134 H5 **Murom** Rus. Fed.
104 D2 **Muromagi-gawa** r. Japan
162 B2 **Muron** France
177 K5 **Murony** Hungary
102 J2 **Muroran** Japan
192 A4 **Muros** Sardegna Italy
182 D1 **Muros** Asturias Spain
182 A2 **Muros** Galicia Spain
103 G7 **Muroto** Japan
175 M5 **Murovane** Ukr.
136 D3 **Murovani Kurylivtsi** Ukr.
129 E3 **Murovdağ Silsiläsi** hills Azer.
174 F5 **Murów** Pol.
174 F3 **Murowana-Goślina** Pol.
238 C3 **Murphy** ID U.S.A.
231 D5 **Murphy** NC U.S.A.
240 G2 **Murphys** CA U.S.A.
83 F2 **Murra Murra** Qld Austr.
203 G2 **Murrat el Kubra, Buheirat** l. Egypt
128 A4 **Murrat el Sughra, Buheirat** l. Egypt
82 D3 **Murray** r. S.A. Austr.
87 B7 **Murray** r. W.A. Austr.
222 F3 **Murray** r. B.C. Can.
237 F4 **Murray** KY U.S.A.
91 J8 **Murray, Lake** P.N.G.
222 D2 **Murray, Mount** Y.T. Can.
82 D3 **Murray Bridge** S.A. Austr.
232 B5 **Murray City** OH U.S.A.
84 C4 **Murray Downs** N.T. Austr.
225 I4 **Murray Harbour** P.E.I. Can.
87 F5 **Murray Range** hills W.A. Austr.
214 D4 **Murraysburg** S. Africa
82 E3 **Murrayville** Vic. Austr.
123 H3 **Murree** Pak.
172 D3 **Murrhardt** Ger.
240 I5 **Murrieta** CA U.S.A.
83 G3 **Murringo** N.S.W. Austr.
147 B3 **Murrisk** reg. Rep. of Ireland
147 B3 **Murroogh** Rep. of Ireland
83 G3 **Murrumbateman** N.S.W. Austr.
83 E3 **Murrumbidgee** r. N.S.W. Austr.
213 H2 **Murrupula** Moz.
83 G2 **Murrurundi** N.S.W. Austr.
159 F4 **Mûrs-Erigné** France
117 G4 **Murshidabad** W. Bengal India
188 F2 **Murska Sobota** Slovenia
179 H4 **Mursko Središće** Croatia
116 D5 **Murtajapur** Mahar. India
185 G4 **Murtas** Spain
182 B4 **Murtede** Port.
190 C2 **Murten** Switz.
190 C2 **Murtensee** l. Switz.
188 E4 **Murter** Croatia
188 E4 **Murter** i. Croatia
83 E4 **Murtoa** Vic. Austr.
182 B4 **Murtosa** Port.
252 C2 **Muru** r. Brazil
114 B2 **Murud** Mahar. India
95 F2 **Murud, Gunung** mt. Indon.
183 H1 **Murueta** Spain
95 F3 **Murui** r. Indon.
95 F3 **Murung** r. Indon.
95 F3 **Murung** r. Indon.
120 F4 **Muruntau** Uzbek.
80 F3 **Murupara** North I. N.Z.
79 □3 **Mururoa** atoll Arch. des Tuamotu Fr. Polynesia
Murviedro Spain see **Sagunto**
161 B5 **Murviel-lès-Béziers** France
116 E5 **Murwara** Madh. Prad. India
83 H2 **Murwillumbah** N.S.W. Austr.
134 J4 **Murygino** Rus. Fed.
179 G3 **Mürz** r. Austria
202 B3 **Murzūq** Libya
174 D3 **Murzynowo** Pol.
179 G3 **Mürzzuschlag** Austria
127 F3 **Muş** Turkey
129 B4 **Muş** prov. Turkey
138 E3 **Mūša** r. Latvia/Lith.
124 A1 **Mûsa, Gebel** mt. Egypt
124 C5 **Musa Āli Terara** vol. Africa
117 F5 **Musabani** Bihar India
128 C1 **Musabeyli** Turkey
123 G4 **Musa Khel Bazar** Pak.
197 F4 **Musala** mt. Bulg.
128 B1 **Musalı** Turkey
101 D4 **Musan** N. Korea
125 G2 **Musandam** admin. reg. Oman
123 F3 **Musa Qala, Rūd-i** r. Afgh.
105 F3 **Musashino** Japan
Musay'īd Qatar see Umm Sa'id
124 D5 **Musaymir** Yemen
150 D4 **Musbury** Devon, England U.K.
125 G3 **Muscat** Oman
Muscat and Oman country Asia see **Oman**
236 F3 **Muscatine** IA U.S.A.
171 D4 **Muschwitz** Ger.
226 B4 **Muscoda** WI U.S.A.
234 C2 **Musconetcong** r. NJ U.S.A.
138 E4 **Musė** r. Lith.
192 A5 **Musei** Sardegna Italy
85 E2 **Musgrave** Qld Austr.
81 C5 **Musgrave, Mount** South I. N.Z.
225 K3 **Musgrave Harbour** Nfld. Can.
82 B1 **Musgrave Ranges** mts S.A. Austr.
209 C5 **Mushie** Dem. Rep. Congo
207 F5 **Mushin** Nigeria
137 G3 **Mushuryn Rig** Ukr.
114 C2 **Musi** r. India
94 D3 **Musi** r. Indon.
196 E5 **Musica** mt. Macedonia
241 K4 **Music Mountain** AZ U.S.A.
191 H3 **Musile di Piave** Italy
241 L2 **Musinia Peak** UT U.S.A.
222 F2 **Muskeg** r. N.W.T. Can.
233 H4 **Muskeget Channel** MA U.S.A.
226 D4 **Muskegon** MI U.S.A.
226 D4 **Muskegon** r. MI U.S.A.
226 D4 **Muskegon Heights** MI U.S.A.
222 G4 **Muskeg River** Alta Can.
232 C5 **Muskingum** r. OH U.S.A.
237 E5 **Muskogee** OK U.S.A.
227 H3 **Muskoka** Ont. Can.
222 F3 **Muskwa** r. B.C. Can.
Muslim-Croat Federation aut. div. Bos.-Herz. see Federacija Bosna i Hercegovina
134 K5 **Muslyumovo** Rus. Fed.
211 B5 **Musoma** Tanz.
191 I5 **Musone** r. Italy
225 I3 **Musquaro** Que. Can.
91 K7 **Mussau Island** P.N.G.
146 E6 **Musselburgh** East Lothian, Scotland U.K.
164 G2 **Musselkanaal** Neth.
238 F2 **Musselshell** r. MT U.S.A.
209 C7 **Mussende** Angola
209 B6 **Musserra** Angola
162 C3 **Mussidan** France
194 C5 **Mussomeli** Sicilia Italy
165 E5 **Musson** Belgium
116 D3 **Mussoorie** Uttar Prad. India
209 D8 **Mussuma** Angola
209 D8 **Mussuma** r. Angola
156 E5 **Mussy-sur-Seine** France
116 E4 **Mustafabad** Uttar Prad. India
199 F1 **Mustafakemalpaşa** Turkey
210 E3 **Mustahīl** Eth.
190 F2 **Müstair** Switz.
110 D2 **Mustau, Gora** mt. Xinjiang China
120 C2 **Mustayevo** Rus. Fed.
259 C7 **Musters, Lago** l. Arg.
247 □3 **Mustique** i. St Vincent
138 F3 **Mustjõgi** r. Estonia
138 E2 **Mustla** Estonia
138 F2 **Mustvee** Estonia
83 G3 **Muswellbrook** N.S.W. Austr.
175 I2 **Muszaki** Pol.
175 I6 **Muszyna** Pol.
203 F3 **Mut** Egypt
126 D3 **Mut** Turkey
179 G4 **Muta** Slovenia
209 E8 **Mutanda** Zambia
213 G3 **Mutare** Zimbabwe
124 D3 **Mutarjim, Khashm** hill Saudi Arabia
179 I2 **Mutěnice** Czech Rep.
146 E5 **Muthill** Perth and Kinross, Scotland U.K.
183 I2 **Mutilva Baja** Spain
Mutina Italy see **Modena**
93 C5 **Mutis, Gunung** mt. Timor Indon.
134 K2 **Mutnyy Materik** Rus. Fed.
213 G3 **Mutoko** Zimbabwe
82 E3 **Mutooroo** S.A. Austr.
213 F3 **Mutorashanga** Zimbabwe
193 G3 **Mutria, Monte** mt. Italy
217 □3 **Mutsamudu** Comoros
209 E7 **Mutshatsha** Dem. Rep. Congo
102 J3 **Mutsu** Japan
102 J3 **Mutsu-wan** b. Japan
85 F4 **Muttaburra** Qld Austr.
199 G2 **Muttalip** Turkey
178 B3 **Muttekopf** mt. Austria
190 C1 **Muttenz** Switz.
178 C3 **Mutters** Austria
172 C2 **Mutterstadt** Ger.
81 A7 **Muttonbird Islands** Stewart I. N.Z.
81 B7 **Muttonbird Islands** Stewart I. N.Z.
114 D3 **Muttukuru** Andhra Prad. India
114 C4 **Muttupet** Tamil Nadu India
213 H2 **Mutuali** Moz.
257 G3 **Mutum** Brazil
250 D6 **Mutum** r. Brazil
207 H4 **Mutum Biyu** Nigeria
254 C5 **Mutunópolis** Brazil
114 D4 **Mutur** Sri Lanka
187 C6 **Mutxamel** Spain
137 G2 **Mutyn** Ukr.
157 H4 **Mutzig** France
171 D4 **Mutzschen** Ger.
141 N3 **Muurame** Fin.
141 M3 **Muurla** Fin.
140 N2 **Muurola** Fin.
107 F4 **Mu Us Shamo** des. China
209 B7 **Muxaluando** Angola
129 E3 **Muxax** Azer.
Muxi Sichuan China see Muchuan
182 A1 **Muxía** Spain
209 B7 **Muxima** Angola
134 F3 **Muyezerskiy** Rus. Fed.
211 A5 **Muyinga** Burundi
120 D4 **Muynak** Uzbek.
Muynoq Uzbek. see **Muynak**
211 B7 **Muyombe** Zambia
207 H5 **Muyuka** Cameroon
209 E6 **Muyumba** Dem. Rep. Congo
121 G3 **Muyunkum, Peski** des. Kazakh.
121 H4 **Muyunkym** Kazakh.
108 D2 **Muyuping** Hubei China
123 H3 **Muzaffarabad** Pak.
123 G4 **Muzaffargarh** Pak.
116 D3 **Muzaffarnagar** Uttar Prad. India
117 F4 **Muzaffarpur** Bihar India
256 D4 **Muzambinho** Brazil
110 C3 **Muzat He** r. China
213 F2 **Muze** Moz.
158 D4 **Muzillac** France
250 C3 **Muzo** Col.
243 E3 **Múzquiz** Mex.
111 C5 **Muztag** mt. Xinjiang China
111 D4 **Muztag** mt. Xinjiang China
110 A4 **Muztagata** mt. Xinjiang China
Muztor Kyrg. see **Toktogul**
191 I3 **Muzzana del Turgnano** Italy
207 H6 **Mvangan** Cameroon
211 C6 **Mvomero** Tanz.
208 B4 **Mvoung** r. Gabon
217 □3a **Mvouni** Njazidja Comoros
209 B6 **Mvouti** Congo
213 F3 **Mvuma** Zimbabwe
217 □3 **Mwali** i. Comoros
211 C5 **Mwanga** Tanz.
211 B8 **Mwanza** Malawi
211 B5 **Mwanza** Tanz.
211 B5 **Mwanza** admin. reg. Tanz.
209 D6 **Mweka** Dem. Rep. Congo
209 F7 **Mwenda** Zambia
209 D6 **Mwene-Ditu** Dem. Rep. Congo
213 F4 **Mwenezi** Zimbabwe
213 F4 **Mwenezi** r. Zimbabwe
209 F7 **Mweru, Lake** Dem. Rep. Congo/Zambia
211 C7 **Mweru Plateau** Tanz.
209 E7 **Mwinilunga** Zambia
138 F4 **Myadzyel** Belarus
116 B4 **Myajlar** Rajasthan India
136 D2 **M"yakoty** Ukr.
96 A3 **Myanaung** Myanmar
96 A2 **Myanmar** country Asia
139 J4 **Myatlevo** Rus. Fed.
131 P3 **Myaundzha** Rus. Fed.
96 A3 **Myaungmya** Myanmar
146 E3 **Mybster** Highland, Scotland U.K.
198 C3 **Mycenae** tourist site Greece
Myeik Myanmar see **Mergui**
232 B5 **Myers** KY U.S.A.
234 B2 **Myerstown** PA U.S.A.
96 A2 **Myingyan** Myanmar
97 B4 **Myinmoletkat** mt. Myanmar
96 A2 **Myinmu** Myanmar
96 B1 **Myitkyina** Myanmar
96 B2 **Myittha** Myanmar
115 G1 **Myittha** r. Myanmar
177 G3 **Myjava** Slovakia
176 F3 **Myjava** r. Slovakia
137 G3 **Mykhaylivka** Cherkas'ka Oblast' Ukr.
137 I3 **Mykhaylivka** Kharkivs'ka Oblast' Ukr.
137 H3 **Mykhaylivka** Poltavs'ka Oblast' Ukr.
137 H4 **Mykhaylivka** Zaporiz'ka Oblast' Ukr.
137 H4 **Mykhaylivka** Zaporiz'ka Oblast' Ukr.
137 F2 **Mykhaylo-Kotsyubyns'ke** Ukr.
136 D2 **Mykhaylyuchka** Ukr.
136 B3 **Mykolayiv** L'vivs'ka Oblast' Ukr.
175 M5 **Mykolayiv** L'vivs'ka Oblast' Ukr.
137 G4 **Mykolayiv** Mykolayivs'ka Oblast' Ukr.
137 H4 **Mykolayivka** Dnipropetrovs'ka Oblast' Ukr.
137 I3 **Mykolayivka** Dnipropetrovs'ka Oblast' Ukr.
137 I3 **Mykolayivka** Donets'ka Oblast' Ukr.
137 H4 **Mykolayivka** Khersons'ka Oblast' Ukr.
136 F4 **Mykolayivka** Odes'ka Oblast' Ukr.
136 F5 **Mykolayivka** Odes'ka Oblast' Ukr.
137 I4 **Mykolayivka** Zaporiz'ka Oblast' Ukr.
136 E4 **Mykolayivka-Novorosiys'ka** Ukr.
Mykolayiv Oblast admin. div. Ukr. see **Mykolayivs'ka Oblast'**
137 G4 **Mykolayivs'ka Oblast'** admin. div. Ukr.
199 D3 **Mykonos** Notio Aigaio Greece
199 D3 **Mykonos** i. Greece
136 C3 **Mykulyntsi** Ukr.
134 J2 **Myla** r. Rus. Fed.
Mylae Sicilia Italy see **Milazzo**
Mylasa Turkey see **Milas**
171 D5 **Mylau** Ger.
138 F1 **Myllykoski** Fin.
150 B4 **Mylor** Cornwall, England U.K.
Mymensing Bangl. see Mymensingh
117 G4 **Mymensingh** Bangl.
138 C1 **Mynäjoki** r. Fin.
141 M3 **Mynämäki** Fin.
214 D4 **Mynfontein** S. Africa
105 E2 **Myōgi-san** mt. Japan
96 A2 **Myohaung** Myanmar
104 A4 **Myōken-yama** hill Japan
160 D1 **Myon** France
101 D4 **Myŏnggan** N. Korea
138 F4 **Myory** Belarus
103 J8 **Myozin-sho** i. Japan
140 □C3 **Mýrdalsjökull** ice cap Iceland
140 □C3 **Mýrdalssandur** sand area Iceland
140 K1 **Myre** Norway
140 M2 **Myrheden** Sweden
137 G3 **Myrhorod** Ukr.
198 D2 **Myrina** Voreio Aigaio Greece
137 G3 **Myrivs'ke** Ukr.
140 L1 **Myrlandshaugen** Norway
223 I4 **Myrnam** Alta Can.
137 I4 **Myrne** Donets'ka Oblast' Ukr.
137 G4 **Myrne** Khersons'ka Oblast' Ukr.
137 F2 **Myrne** Kyivs'ka Oblast' Ukr.
175 M5 **Myrne** Volyns'ka Oblast' Ukr.
137 H4 **Myrne** Zaporiz'ka Oblast' Ukr.
136 E4 **Myrnopillya** Ukr.
137 G5 **Myrnyy** Ukr.
137 I3 **Myronivka** Kharkivs'ka Oblast' Ukr.
136 F3 **Myronivka** Kyivs'ka Oblast' Ukr.
136 D2 **Myropil'** Ukr.
137 H2 **Myropillya** Ukr.
141 N3 **Myrskylä** Fin.
231 E5 **Myrtle Beach** SC U.S.A.
238 B3 **Myrtle Creek** OR U.S.A.
83 F4 **Myrtleford** Vic. Austr.
238 A3 **Myrtle Point** OR U.S.A.
121 G4 **Myrzakent** Kazakh.
142 D2 **Mysen** Norway
148 C5 **Myshall** Rep. of Ireland
138 E5 **Myshanka** r. Belarus
139 L3 **Myshkin** Rus. Fed.
Myshkino Rus. Fed. see Myshkin
137 I5 **Myskhako** Rus. Fed.
174 C3 **Mysla** r. Pol.
Mys Lazareva Rus. Fed. see Lazarev
175 H6 **Myślenice** Pol.
174 C3 **Myślibórz** Pol.
175 H2 **Myślice** Pol.
175 H5 **Mysłowice** Pol.
Myslowitz Pol. see **Mysłowice**
96 E4 **My Son** tourist site Vietnam
114 C3 **Mysore** Karnataka India
Mysore state India see Karnataka
Mysovsk Rus. Fed. see Babushkin
131 T3 **Mys Shmidta** Rus. Fed.
235 G1 **Mystic** CT U.S.A.
235 D3 **Mystic Islands** NJ U.S.A.
175 H1 **Myszewo** Pol.
175 H5 **Myszków** Pol.
175 J2 **Myszyniec** Pol.
134 H4 **Myt** Rus. Fed.
97 D5 **My Tho** Vietnam
Mytilene i. Greece see **Lesvos**
199 E2 **Mytilini** Voreio Aigaio Greece
199 E3 **Mytilinioi** Voreio Aigaio Greece
126 B3 **Mytilini Strait** Greece/Turkey
139 K4 **Mytishchi** Rus. Fed.
177 I3 **Mýtna** Slovakia
176 C2 **Mýto** Czech Rep.
241 L1 **Myton** UT U.S.A.
137 G3 **Mytrofanivka** Ukr.
140 □C2 **Mývatn** l. Iceland
140 □C2 **Mývatnsöræfi** lava field Iceland
136 C2 **Myzove** Ukr.
205 F2 **M'Zab Valley** tourist site Alg.
215 F4 **Mzamomhle** S. Africa
176 B2 **Mže** r. Czech Rep.
211 B7 **Mzimba** Malawi
213 F4 **Mzingwani** r. Zimbabwe
211 B7 **Mzuzu** Malawi
129 A2 **Mzymta** r. Rus. Fed.

N

96 C2 **Na, Nam** r. China/Vietnam
173 G2 **Naab** r. Ger.
164 D3 **Naaldwijk** Neth.
240 □D9 **Naalehu** HI U.S.A.
205 E2 **Naama** Alg.
141 M3 **Naantali** Fin.
164 E2 **Naarden** Neth.
179 F2 **Naarn im Machlande** Austria
147 E3 **Naas** Rep. of Ireland
214 A3 **Nababeep** S. Africa
Nabadwip W. Bengal India see Navadwip
182 B5 **Nabão** r. Port.
115 D2 **Nabarangapur** Orissa India
104 C4 **Nabari** Japan
104 C4 **Nabari-gawa** r. Japan
92 B4 **Nabas** Phil.
128 B3 **Nabatiyet et Tahta** Lebanon
87 D5 **Nabberu, Lake** salt flat W.A. Austr.
173 G2 **Nabburg** Ger.
211 C6 **Naberera** Tanz.
137 J2 **Naberezhnoye** Rus. Fed.
134 K5 **Naberezhnyye Chelny** Rus. Fed.
120 A2 **Naberezhnyy Uvekh** Rus. Fed.
205 H1 **Nabeul** Tunisia
189 C7 **Nabeul** admin. div. Tunisia
116 D3 **Nabha** Punjab India
129 E3 **Nābiağalı** Azer.
253 F5 **Nabileque** r. Brazil
117 F4 **Nabinagar** Bihar India
128 B3 **Nāblus** West Bank
206 E4 **Nabolo** Ghana
213 F5 **Naboomspruit** S. Africa
79 □1 **Nabouwalu** Vanua Levu Fiji
116 D2 **Nabra** r. India
177 L3 **Nábrád** Hungary
Nābulus West Bank see **Nāblus**
243 G5 **Nacajuca** Mex.
213 I2 **Nacala** Moz.
242 □I6 **Nacaome** Hond.
213 H2 **Nacaroa** Moz.
176 D2 **Načeradec** Czech Rep.
138 G4 **Nacha** r. Belarus
120 B3 **Nachalovo** Rus. Fed.
238 B2 **Naches** WA U.S.A.
211 C7 **Nachingwea** Tanz.
116 B4 **Nachna** Rajasthan India
176 F1 **Náchod** Czech Rep.
260 A5 **Nacimiento** Chile
185 H3 **Nacimiento** Spain
185 H4 **Nacimiento** r. Spain
170 D3 **Nackel** Ger.
172 C2 **Nackenheim** Ger.
237 E6 **Nacogdoches** TX U.S.A.
242 C2 **Nacozari de García** Mex.
175 I3 **Nacpolsk** Pol.
Nada Hainan China see Danzhou
222 C2 **Nadaleen** r. Y.T. Can.
176 F5 **Nádasd** Hungary
177 H4 **Nádasdladány** Hungary
116 D4 **Nadbai** Rajasthan India
151 F3 **Nadder** r. England U.K.
137 G4 **Naddnipryans'ke** Ukr.
Nådendal Fin. see **Naantali**
120 E1 **Nadezhdinka** Kazakh.
Nadezhdinskiy Kazakh. see Nadezhdinka
79 □1a **Nadi** Viti Levu Fiji
116 C5 **Nadiad** Gujarat India
196 E2 **Nădlac** Romania
204 E2 **Nador** Morocco
180 E5 **Nador** prov. Morocco
197 F3 **Nădrag** Romania
129 D2 **Nadterechnaya** Rus. Fed.
177 K4 **Nádudvar** Hungary
195 □ **Nadur** Gozo Malta
122 C3 **Nadūshan** Iran
136 C3 **Nadvirna** Ukr.
Nadvornaya Ukr. see **Nadvirna**
130 I3 **Nadym** Rus. Fed.
116 C4 **Naenwa** Rajasthan India
142 D4 **Næstved** Denmark
117 H5 **Naf** r. Bangl./Myanmar
128 B5 **Nafas, Râs el** mt. Egypt
190 E1 **Näfels** Switz.
149 I3 **Nafferton** East Riding of Yorkshire, England U.K.
128 B4 **Nafha, Har** hill Israel
198 B2 **Nafpaktos** Greece
198 C3 **Nafplio** Greece
Naft r. Iraq see **Āb Naft**
129 E3 **Naftalan** Azer.
124 D3 **Nafūd ad Daḩl** des. Saudi Arabia
124 C2 **Nafūd al 'Urayq** des. Saudi Arabia
124 D2 **Nafūd as Sirr** des. Saudi Arabia
124 C3 **Nafūd as Surrah** des. Saudi Arabia
124 D2 **Nafūd Qunayfidhah** des. Saudi Arabia
202 A2 **Nafūsah, Jabal** hills Libya
124 C2 **Nafy** Saudi Arabia
92 B3 **Naga** Phil.
224 C3 **Nagagami** r. Ont. Can.
104 C3 **Nagahama** Japan
117 H4 **Naga Hills** India

Naga Hills state India see Nagaland
102 J4 Nagai Japan
105 E3 Nagaizumi Japan
117 H4 Nagaland state India
83 F4 Nagambie Vic. Austr.
105 E2 Nagano Japan
105 D2 Nagano pref. Japan
103 I5 Nagaoka Japan
117 H4 Nagaon Assam India
Nagapatam Tamil Nadu India see Nagappattinam
114 C4 Nagappattinam Tamil Nadu India
117 G4 Nagar r. Bangl./India
116 D2 Nagar Hima. Prad. India
114 B3 Nagar Karnataka India
116 D4 Nagar Rajasthan India
104 C3 Nagara-gawa r. Japan
114 D2 Nagaram Andhra Prad. India
105 F3 Nagareyama Japan
114 C2 Nagar Karnul Andhra Prad. India
242 □I6 Nagarote Nic.
111 E6 Nagarzê Xizang China
103 D7 Nagasaki Japan
103 D7 Nagasaki pref. Japan
103 E6 Nagato Japan
116 C4 Nagaur Rajasthan India
115 D2 Nagavali r. India
116 C5 Nagda Madh. Prad. India
173 F2 Nagel Ger.
164 E2 Nagele Neth.
114 C4 Nagercoil Tamil Nadu India
203 G3 Nag' Hammâdi Egypt
116 D3 Nagina Uttar Prad. India
147 C4 Nagles Mountains hills Rep. of Ireland
175 I5 Nagłowice Pol.
116 E4 Nagod Madh. Prad. India
172 C3 Nagold Ger.
172 C3 Nagold r. Ger.
Nagong Chu r. China see Parlung Zangbo
183 I2 Nagore Spain
Nagorno-Karabakh aut. reg. Azer. see Dağlıq Qarabağ
Nagornyy Karabakh aut. reg. Azer. see Dağlıq Qarabağ
134 J4 Nagorsk Rus. Fed.
139 L3 Nagor'ye Rus. Fed.
191 F3 Nago-Torbole Italy
104 C3 Nagoya Japan
116 D5 Nagpur Mahar. India
111 F6 Nagqu Xizang China
111 F6 Nag Qu r. Xizang China
141 M3 Nagu Fin.
247 E3 Nagua Dom. Rep.
247 □1 Naguabo Puerto Rico
129 C1 Nagutskoye Rus. Fed.
176 G5 Nagyatád Hungary
177 G5 Nagybajom Hungary
177 J5 Nagybánhegyes Hungary
177 H5 Nagybaracska Hungary
Nagybecskerek Vojvodina, Srbija Yugo. see Zrenjanin
177 H5 Nagyberény Hungary
177 H5 Nagyberki Hungary
176 F4 Nagycenk Hungary
177 J4 Nagycsécs Hungary
177 K4 Nagycserkesz Hungary
177 L3 Nagydobos Hungary
177 H5 Nagydorog Hungary
177 L4 Nagyecsed Hungary
Nagyenyed Romania see Aiud
177 J4 Nagyfüged Hungary
177 K3 Nagyhalász Hungary
177 H6 Nagyharsány Hungary
177 K4 Nagyhegyes Hungary
177 H4 Nagyigmánd Hungary
177 J4 Nagyiván Hungary
177 K4 Nagykálló Hungary
177 K5 Nagykamarás Hungary
176 F5 Nagykanizsa Hungary
176 F5 Nagykapornak Hungary
177 H5 Nagykarácsony Hungary
177 I4 Nagykáta Hungary
177 K4 Nagykereki Hungary
177 H5 Nagykónyi Hungary
177 I4 Nagykőrös Hungary
177 H4 Nagykovácsi Hungary
177 J5 Nagylak Hungary
177 I3 Nagylóc Hungary
176 F4 Nagylózs Hungary
177 J5 Nagymágocs Hungary
177 H5 Nagymányok Hungary
177 H4 Nagymaros Hungary
177 K3 Nagy-Milic hill Hungary/Slovakia
177 H6 Nagynyárád Hungary
177 I4 Nagyoroszi Hungary
177 K4 Nagyrábé Hungary
176 G5 Nagyrécse Hungary
176 G4 Nagysimonyi Hungary
177 J5 Nagyszénás Hungary
177 G4 Nagyszentjános Hungary
177 H5 Nagyszokoly Hungary
177 I4 Nagytarcsa Hungary
177 J5 Nagytőke Hungary
Nagyvárad Romania see Oradea
177 L3 Nagyvarsány Hungary
177 G5 Nagyvázsony Hungary
177 H5 Nagyvenyim Hungary
102 □2 Naha Japan
116 D3 Nahan Hima. Prad. India
123 E5 Nahang r. Iran/Pak.
222 F2 Nahanni Butte N.W.T. Can.
222 F2 Nahanni Range mts N.W.T. Can.
128 B3 Nahariyya Israel
183 H4 Naharros Spain
122 B3 Nahāvand Iran
168 F2 Nahe Ger.
172 B2 Nahe r. Ger.
205 F4 N'Ahnet, Adrar mts Alg.
159 H4 Nahon r. France
124 B2 Nahr, Jabal hill Saudi Arabia
168 F2 Nahrendorf Ger.
244 D4 Nahuatzen Mex.
231 D6 Nahunta GA U.S.A.
92 B3 Naic Phil.
242 D3 Naica Mex.
117 G4 Naik Murad Bangl.
171 C5 Naila Ger.
163 D5 Nailloux France
150 E3 Nailsea North Somerset, England U.K.
150 E3 Nailsworth Gloucestershire, England U.K.
Naiman Qi Nei Mongol China see Daqin Tal
225 I1 Nain Nfld. Can.
116 E4 Naina Uttar Prad. India
116 D3 Naini Tal Uttar Prad. India
116 E5 Nainpur Madh. Prad. India
159 G5 Naintré France
79 □1 Nairai i. Fiji
146 E4 Nairn Highland, Scotland U.K.
146 E4 Nairn r. Scotland U.K.
227 G2 Nairn Centre Ont. Can.
211 C5 Nairobi Kenya
Naissus Srbija Yugo. see Niš
210 C5 Naivasha Kenya
157 F4 Naives-Rosières France
158 D4 Naizin France
100 C4 Naizishan Jilin China
163 D4 Najac France
122 B3 Najafābād Iran
246 C2 Najasa r. Cuba
124 C2 Najd reg. Saudi Arabia
183 H2 Nájera Spain
183 H2 Najerilla r. Spain
107 I1 Naji Nei Mongol China
116 D3 Najibabad Uttar Prad. India
183 H3 Nájima r. Spain
101 D4 Najin N. Korea
Najitun Nei Mongol China see Naji
125 E2 Najmah Saudi Arabia
124 D4 Najrān Saudi Arabia
124 D4 Najrān prov. Saudi Arabia
113 □1 Nakachchaafushi i. N. Male Maldives
105 G2 Naka-gawa r. Japan
103 G7 Naka-gawa r. Japan
102 □2 Nakagusuku Japan
Nakahchaafushi i. N. Male Maldives see Nakachchaafushi
103 E7 Nakama Japan
206 E4 Nakambé watercourse Burkina/Ghana alt. Nakanbe, alt. Volta Blanche, conv. White Volta
103 F7 Nakamura Japan
Nakanbé watercourse Burkina/Ghana see White Volta
105 E2 Nakano Japan
102 □1 Nakano-shima i. Japan
105 F1 Nakano-take mt. Japan
211 C7 Nakapanya Tanz.
210 B4 Nakasongola Uganda
Nakatchafushi i. N. Male Maldives see Nakachchaafushi
102 K1 Nakatonbetsu-chō hill Japan
103 E7 Nakatsu Japan
104 D3 Nakatsugawa Japan
105 E2 Nakatsu-gawa r. Japan
113 □1 Nakatuku Fushi i. N. Male Maldives
203 H5 Nakfa Eritrea
Nakhichevan' Azer. see Naxçıvan
Nakhichevan' aut. reg. Azer. see Naxçıvan
100 E4 Nakhodka Rus. Fed.
117 H4 Nakhola Assam India
97 C4 Nakhon Nayok Thai.
97 C4 Nakhon Pathom Thai.
96 D3 Nakhon Phanom Thai.
97 C4 Nakhon Ratchasima Thai.
96 C4 Nakhon Sawan Thai.
97 B5 Nakhon Si Thammarat Thai.
Nakhrachi Khanty-Mansiyskiy Avtonomnyy Okrug Rus. Fed. see Kondinskoye
116 B5 Nakhtarana Gujarat India
224 C3 Nakina Ont. Can.
222 C3 Nakina r. B.C. Can.
129 C2 Nakip'u Georgia
174 F1 Nakla Pol.
176 G2 Náklo Czech Rep.
175 H5 Nakło Pol.
179 F4 Naklo Slovenia
174 F2 Nakło nad Notecią Pol.
220 C4 Naknek AK U.S.A.
116 C3 Nakodar Punjab India
175 J1 Nakomiady Pol.
211 B7 Nakonde Zambia
138 D3 Nākotne Latvia
177 J6 Nakovo Vojvodina, Srbija Yugo.
207 E4 Nakpanduri Ghana
142 D4 Nakskov Denmark
140 K3 Näkten l. Sweden
101 D6 Naktong-gang r. S. Korea
210 C5 Nakuru Kenya
222 G5 Nakusp B.C. Can.
123 F5 Nal r. Pak.
107 E2 Nalayh Mongolia
172 A2 Nalbach Ger.
117 G4 Nalbari Assam India
129 C2 Nal'chik Rus. Fed.
183 H2 Nalda Spain
114 C2 Naldurg Mahar. India
175 K4 Nałęczów Pol.
177 J3 Nálepkovo Slovakia
206 E4 Nalerigu Ghana
114 C2 Nalgonda Andhra Prad. India
117 F4 Nalhati W. Bengal India
117 G4 Nalitabari Bangl.
116 D5 Nalkhera Madh. Prad. India
114 C3 Nallamala Hills India
162 A2 Nalliers France
199 G1 Nallıhan Turkey
121 G1 Nalobino Kazakh.
209 D8 Nalolo Zambia
182 D1 Nalón r. Spain
202 A2 Nālūt Libya
176 C2 Nalžovské Hory Czech Rep.
213 G5 Namaacha Moz.
209 B9 Namacunde Angola
213 H3 Namacurra Moz.
215 G2 Namahadi S. Africa
114 C4 Namakkal Tamil Nadu India
122 D4 Namakzar-e Shadad salt flat Iran
121 G4 Namangan Uzbek.
Namangan Oblast admin. div. Uzbek. see Namanganskaya Oblast'
121 G4 Namanganskaya Oblast' admin. div. Uzbek.
Namangan Wiloyati admin. div. Uzbek. see Namanganskaya Oblast'
211 A6 Namanyere Tanz.
213 H2 Namapa Moz.
212 C5 Namaqualand reg. Namibia
214 A3 Namaqualand reg. S. Africa
213 H2 Namarrói Moz.
117 H4 Nambol Manipur India
172 B2 Namborn Ger.
85 H5 Nambour Qld Austr.
Nambouwalu Vanua Levu Fiji see Nabouwalu
183 G5 Nambroca Spain
83 H2 Nambucca Heads N.S.W. Austr.
Namcha Barwa mt. Xizang China see Namjagbarwa Feng
117 F4 Namche Bazar Nepal
101 C5 Namch'ŏn N. Korea
140 K2 Namdalen val. Norway
140 J2 Namdalseid Norway
96 D2 Nam Đinh Vietnam
226 B3 Namekagon r. WI U.S.A.
Namen Belgium see Namur
104 D2 Namerikawa Japan
176 F2 Náměšť nad Oslavou Czech Rep.
177 I2 Námestovo Slovakia
213 H2 Nametil Moz.
101 C5 Nam-gang r. N. Korea
101 C6 Namhae-do i. S. Korea
213 H2 Namialo Moz.
212 B5 Namib Desert Namibia
209 B8 Namibe Angola
209 B8 Namibe prov. Angola
212 B4 Namibia country Africa
264 J8 Namibia Abyssal Plain sea feature N. Atlantic Ocean
213 H3 Namidobe Moz.
214 B3 Namies S. Africa
122 B2 Namīn Iran
211 B8 Namitete Malawi
111 F6 Namjagbarwa Feng mt. Xizang China
Namka Xizang China see Doilungdêqên
96 B2 Namlang r. Myanmar
111 E6 Namling Xizang China
96 C3 Nam Ngum Reservoir Laos
83 G2 Namoi r. N.S.W. Austr.
91 K5 Namonuito atoll Micronesia
222 G3 Nampa Alta Can.
116 E3 Nampa mt. Nepal
238 C3 Nampa ID U.S.A.
206 D3 Nampala Mali
101 C5 Namp'o N. Korea
213 H2 Nampula Moz.
213 H2 Nampula prov. Moz.
96 C3 Nam Pung Reservoir Thai.
117 H4 Namrup Assam India
117 H4 Namsi Arun. Prad. India
140 J2 Namsos Norway
140 K2 Namsskogan Norway
131 N3 Namtsy Rus. Fed.
96 B2 Namtu Myanmar
222 E5 Namu B.C. Can.
Namuka i. Tonga see Nomuka
213 H2 Namuli, Monte mt. Moz.
213 H2 Namuno Moz.
165 D4 Namur Belgium
165 D4 Namur prov. Belgium
209 E8 Namwala Zambia
101 C6 Namwŏn S. Korea
90 D4 Namyit Island S. China Sea
174 F4 Namysłów Pol.
96 C3 Nan Thai.
96 C4 Nan, Mae Nam r. Thai.
208 B3 Nana r. C.A.R.
177 H4 Nána Slovakia
208 C3 Nana Barya r. C.A.R./Chad
208 C3 Nana-Grébizi pref. C.A.R.
222 F5 Nanaimo B.C. Can.
240 □ Nanakuli HI U.S.A.
208 B3 Nana-Mambéré pref. C.A.R.
109 F3 Nan'an Fujian China
85 H5 Nanango Qld Austr.
109 F4 Nan'ao Guangdong China
Nan'ao Jiangxi China see Dayu
104 C1 Nanao Japan
104 C2 Nanatsuka Japan
250 C5 Nanay r. Peru
Nanbai Guizhou China see Zunyi
Nanbin Chongqing China see Shizhu
108 C2 Nanbu Sichuan China
260 B4 Nancagua Chile
159 I4 Nançay France
100 D3 Nancha Heilong. China
109 E2 Nanchang Jiangxi China
109 E2 Nanchang Jiangxi China
Nanchangshan Shandong China see Changdao
109 F3 Nancheng Jiangxi China
245 G4 Nanchital Mex.
108 C2 Nanchong Sichuan China
108 C2 Nanchuan Chongqing China
183 H2 Nanclares de la Oca Spain
222 E4 Nancut B.C. Can.
157 G4 Nancy France
116 E3 Nanda Devi mt. Uttar Prad. India
116 E3 Nanda Kot mt. Uttar Prad. India
108 C3 Nandan Guangxi China
114 C2 Nanded Mahar. India
Nander Mahar. India see Nanded
83 G2 Nandewar Range mts N.S.W. Austr.
116 C5 Nandgaon Mahar. India
114 D2 Nandigama Andhra Prad. India
114 C3 Nandikotkur Andhra Prad. India
108 A4 Nanding He r. Yunnan China
116 C5 Nandod Gujarat India
165 E4 Nandrin Belgium
108 D4 Nandu Jiang r. China
116 D5 Nandura Mahar. India
116 C5 Nandurbar Mahar. India
114 C3 Nandyal Andhra Prad. India
197 H3 Nănești Romania
109 D4 Nanfeng Guangdong China
109 F3 Nanfeng Jiangxi China
111 F6 Nang Xizang China
211 C7 Nangade Moz.
207 I5 Nanga Eboko Cameroon
95 E3 Nangahpinoh Kalimantan Barat Indon.
84 C2 Nangalala N.T. Austr.
116 C2 Nanga Parbat mt. Jammu and Kashmir
123 G3 Nangarhār prov. Afgh.
95 E3 Nangatayap Kalimantan Barat Indon.
156 D4 Nangis France
101 C4 Nangnim N. Korea
101 C4 Nangnim-sanmaek mts N. Korea
107 G4 Nangong Hebei China
108 A1 Nangqên Qinghai China
211 C7 Nangulangwa Tanz.
114 C4 Nanguneri Tamil Nadu India
107 G4 Nanhe Hebei China
110 F4 Nanhu Gansu China
108 B3 Nanhua Yunnan China
109 G2 Nanhui Shanghai China
221 J2 Nanisivik Nunavut Can.
114 C3 Nanjangud Karnataka India
108 B3 Nanjian Yunnan China
108 C1 Nanjiang Sichuan China
Nanjie Guangdong China see Guangning
109 F3 Nanjing Fujian China
109 F1 Nanjing Jiangsu China
108 A4 Nanka Jiang r. Yunnan China
109 E3 Nankang Jiangxi China
Nankang Jiangxi China see Xingzi
Nanking Jiangsu China see Nanjing
103 F7 Nankoku Japan
209 C9 Nankova Angola
108 A4 Nanlan He r. Yunnan China
78 □4b Nanlaud hill Pohnpei Micronesia
107 G4 Nanle Henan China
108 A4 Nanlei He r. Yunnan China
109 F2 Nanling Anhui China
109 D3 Nan Ling mts China
108 D4 Nanliu Jiang r. China
Nanlong Sichuan China see Nanbu
Nanma Shandong China see Yiyuan
Nanmulingzue Xizang China see Namling
87 C5 Nannine W.A. Austr.
108 D4 Nanning Guangxi China
87 B7 Nannup W.A. Austr.
96 C3 Na Noi Thai.
221 N3 Nanortalik Greenland
Nanouki atoll Gilbert Is Kiribati see Nonouti
Nanouti atoll Gilbert Is Kiribati see Nonouti
108 C3 Nanpan Jiang r. China
116 E4 Nanpara Uttar Prad. India
107 H4 Nanpi Hebei China
107 I3 Nanpiao Liaoning China
109 F3 Nanping Fujian China
108 C1 Nanping Sichuan China
Nanpu Fujian China see Pucheng
109 F3 Nanpu Xi r. China
Nanqiao Shanghai China see Fengxian
183 F1 Nansa r. Spain
104 C4 Nansei Japan
102 □ Nansei-shotō is Japan
268 B1 Nansen Basin sea feature Arctic Ocean
221 N1 Nansen Land reg. Greenland
221 I1 Nansen Sound sea chan. Nunavut Can.
90 E4 Nanshan Island S. China Sea
106 B3 Nanshankou Xinjiang China
Nansha Qundao is S. China Sea see Spratly Islands
211 B5 Nansio Tanz.
161 D5 Nans-les-Pins France
161 B4 Nant France
105 G2 Nantai-san hill Japan
105 F2 Nantai-san mt. Japan
150 D3 Nant Bran r. Wales U.K.
156 C4 Nanterre France
158 E4 Nantes France
162 A1 Nantes Atlantique airport France
156 C3 Nanteuil-le-Haudouin France
162 D2 Nantiat France
224 D5 Nanticoke Ont. Can.
233 F5 Nanticoke MD U.S.A.
234 B1 Nanticoke PA U.S.A.
233 F5 Nanticoke r. MD U.S.A.
104 C4 Nantō Japan
222 H5 Nanton Alta Can.
109 G1 Nantong Jiangsu China
109 G2 Nantong Jiangsu China
109 □ Nantou Guangdong China
109 G4 Nant'ou Taiwan
160 D2 Nantua France
233 H4 Nantucket MA U.S.A.
233 I4 Nantucket Island MA U.S.A.
233 H4 Nantucket Sound g. MA U.S.A.
211 C8 Nantulo Moz.
149 G4 Nantwich Cheshire, England U.K.
150 D3 Nantyglo Blaenau Gwent, Wales U.K.
232 D4 Nanty Glo PA U.S.A.
235 D1 Nanuet NY U.S.A.
Nanumaga i. Tuvalu see Nanumanga
77 H2 Nanumanga i. Tuvalu
77 H2 Nanumea i. Tuvalu
257 G2 Nanuque Brazil
93 C1 Nanusa, Kepulauan is Indon.
87 B4 Nanutarra Roadhouse W.A. Austr.
108 C2 Nanxi Sichuan China
109 E2 Nanxian Hunan China
109 E3 Nanxiong Guangdong China
109 G3 Nanyandang Shan mt. Zhejiang China
109 E1 Nanyang Henan China
102 J4 Nanyō Japan
210 C5 Nanyuki Kenya
107 J3 Nanzamu Liaoning China
109 D2 Nanzhang Hubei China
Nanzhao Fujian China see Zhao'an
109 E1 Nanzhao Henan China
108 C1 Nanzheng Shaanxi China
Nanzhou Hunan China see Nanxian
117 G4 Naogaon Bangl.
123 G5 Naokot Pak.
100 E3 Naoli r. China
122 E3 Naomid, Dasht-e des. Afgh./Iran
116 C2 Naoshera Jammu and Kashmir
198 C1 Naousa Kentriki Makedonia Greece
198 D3 Naousa Notio Aigaio Greece
240 F2 Napa CA U.S.A.
233 □J1 Napadogan N.B. Can.
213 H2 Napaha Moz.
220 C3 Napaimiut AK U.S.A.
210 B4 Napak mt. Uganda
220 G3 Napaktulik Lake Nunavut Can.
224 E4 Napanee Ont. Can.
235 D1 Napanoch NY U.S.A.
116 C4 Napasar Rajasthan India
220 B3 Napaskiak AK U.S.A.
226 C5 Naperville IL U.S.A.
190 C1 Napf mt. Switz.
80 F3 Napier North I. N.Z.
214 B6 Napier S. Africa
86 E2 Napier Broome Bay W.A. Austr.
263 D2 Napier Mountains Antarctica
84 C2 Napier Peninsula N.T. Austr.
86 E3 Napier Range hills W.A. Austr.
233 G2 Napierville Que. Can.
175 I2 Napiwoda Pol.
177 K4 Napkor Hungary
Naples Italy see Napoli
231 D7 Naples FL U.S.A.
233 □H3 Naples ME U.S.A.
232 E3 Naples NY U.S.A.
241 M1 Naples UT U.S.A.
108 C4 Napo Guangxi China
250 B5 Napo prov. Ecuador
250 C5 Napo r. Ecuador
194 B5 Napola Sicilia Italy
236 D2 Napoleon ND U.S.A.
232 A4 Napoleon OH U.S.A.
216 □2b Napoleon's Tomb tourist site St Helena
237 F6 Napoleonville LA U.S.A.
193 G4 Napoli Italy
193 G4 Napoli prov. Campania Italy
193 G4 Napoli, Golfo di b. Italy
261 F6 Naposta r. Arg.
226 E5 Nappanee IN U.S.A.
84 C4 Napperby N.T. Austr.
122 A2 Naqadeh Iran
128 A5 Naqb Malha mt. Egypt
124 D5 Naqūb Yemen
187 C5 Náquera Spain
104 B4 Nara Japan
104 B4 Nara pref. Japan
206 D3 Nara Mali
139 K4 Nara r. Rus. Fed.
138 F4 Narach Belarus
138 F4 Narach r. Belarus
82 E4 Naracoorte S.A. Austr.
83 F3 Naradhan N.S.W. Austr.
176 F4 Nárai Hungary
105 D2 Narai-gawa r. Japan
117 G5 Narail Bangl.
116 C4 Naraina Rajasthan India
107 G1 Naranbulag Dornod Mongolia
106 B1 Naranbulag Uvs Mongolia
250 B5 Naranjal Ecuador
247 □1 Naranjito Puerto Rico
245 F3 Naranjos Mex.
122 B3 Naraq Iran
115 E2 Narasannapeta Andhra Prad. India
114 D2 Narasapur Andhra Prad. India
114 D2 Narasaraopet Andhra Prad. India
105 G3 Narashino Japan
117 F5 Narasinghapur Orissa India
107 G1 Narasun Rus. Fed.
97 C6 Narathiwat Thai.
110 C3 Narat Shan mts China
237 C5 Nara Visa NM U.S.A.
117 G5 Narayanganj Bangl.
116 E5 Narayanganj Madh. Prad. India
114 B2 Narayangaon Mahar. India
114 C2 Narayanpet Andhra Prad. India
175 M6 Narayiv Ukr.
175 M6 Narayivka r. Ukr.
Narbada r. India see Narmada
150 C3 Narberth Pembrokeshire, Wales U.K.
Narbo France see Narbonne
192 A4 Narbolia Sardegna Italy
161 B5 Narbonne France
161 B5 Narbonne-Plage France
151 F2 Narborough Leicestershire, England U.K.
151 H2 Narborough Norfolk, England U.K.
Narborough Island Islas Galápagos Ecuador see Fernandina, Isla
192 A5 Narcao Sardegna Italy
182 D1 Narcea r. Spain
160 B1 Narcy France
122 C2 Nardin Iran
195 H2 Nardò Italy
123 G4 Narechi r. Pak.
114 B3 Naregal Karnataka India
87 C7 Narembeen W.A. Austr.
116 D3 Narendranagar Uttar Prad. India
264 E4 Nares Abyssal Plain sea feature S. Atlantic Ocean
264 E4 Nares Deep sea feature N. Atlantic Ocean
221 K2 Nares Strait Can./Greenland
87 E6 Naretha W.A. Austr.
175 L3 Narew Pol.
175 I3 Narew r. Pol.
175 L3 Narewka Pol.
175 L3 Narewka r. Pol.
123 F4 Nari r. Pak.
214 A4 Nariep S. Africa
129 F4 Närimanabad Azer.
129 F3 Närimankänd Azer.
120 A3 Narimanov Rus. Fed.
121 K2 Narimskiy Khrebet mts Kazakh.
126 E3 Narince Turkey
250 B4 Nariño dept Col.
105 G3 Narita Japan
105 G3 Narita airport Japan
140 M2 Narken Sweden
139 M4 Narma r. Rus. Fed.
116 C5 Narmada r. India
129 B3 Narman Turkey
116 D3 Narnaul Haryana India
193 E2 Narni Italy
Narnia Italy see Narni
194 C5 Naro Sicilia Italy
194 C5 Naro r. Sicilia Italy
134 M2 Narodnaya, Gora mt. Rus. Fed.
136 E2 Narodychi Ukr.
139 K4 Naro-Fominsk Rus. Fed.
211 B5 Narok Kenya
83 G4 Narooma N.S.W. Austr.
135 H5 Narovchat Rus. Fed.
136 E2 Narowlya Belarus
141 M3 Närpes Fin.
83 G2 Narrabri N.S.W. Austr.
233 H4 Narragansett Bay RI U.S.A.
83 F2 Narran r. N.S.W. Austr.
83 F3 Narrandera N.S.W. Austr.
83 F2 Narran Lake N.S.W. Austr.
87 C7 Narrogin W.A. Austr.
83 G3 Narromine N.S.W. Austr.
163 A5 Narrosse France
232 C6 Narrows VA U.S.A.
234 C1 Narrowsburg NY U.S.A.
114 C2 Narsapur Andhra Prad. India
221 N3 Narsaq Greenland
171 D4 Narsdorf Ger.
116 D5 Narsimhapur Madh. Prad. India
117 G5 Narsingdi Bangl.
116 D5 Narsinghgarh Madh. Prad. India
115 D2 Narsipatnam Andhra Prad. India
107 G3 Nart Nei Mongol China
106 E1 Nart Mongolia
179 H5 Narta Croatia
198 A1 Nartë Albania
129 C2 Nartkala Rus. Fed.
161 E5 Nartuby r. France
175 I3 Naruszewo Pol.
104 A4 Naruto Japan
138 G2 Narva Estonia
138 G2 Narva r. Estonia/Rus. Fed.
138 F2 Narva Bay Estonia/Rus. Fed.
92 B2 Narvacan Phil.
138 G2 Narva-Jõesuu Estonia
Narva laht b. Estonia/Rus. Fed. see Narva Bay
Narva Reservoir Estonia/Rus. Fed. see Narvskoye Vodokhranilishche
140 L1 Narvik Norway
Narvskiy Zaliv b. Estonia/Rus. Fed. see Narva Bay
138 G2 Narvskoye Vodokhranilishche resr Estonia/Rus. Fed.
116 D3 Narwana Haryana India
116 D4 Narwar Madh. Prad. India
84 C4 Narwietooma N.T. Austr.
134 K2 Nar'yan-Mar Rus. Fed.
121 H4 Naryn Kyrg.
121 H4 Naryn admin. div. Kyrg.
121 H4 Naryn r. Kyrg./Uzbek.
106 B1 Naryn Rus. Fed.
121 J4 Narynkol Kazakh.
Naryn Oblast admin. div. Kyrg. see Naryn
Narynqol Kazakh. see Narynkol
Narynskaya Oblast' admin. div. Kyrg. see Naryn
139 J5 Naryshkino Rus. Fed.
190 C4 Narzole Italy
140 L3 Näsåker Sweden
197 G2 Năsăud Romania
176 E2 Nasavrky Czech Rep.
161 B4 Nasbinals France
143 G3 Näsby Kalmar Sweden
81 C6 Naseby South I. N.Z.
116 C5 Nashik Mahar. India
226 A4 Nashua IA U.S.A.
233 H3 Nashua NH U.S.A.
237 E5 Nashville AR U.S.A.
231 D6 Nashville GA U.S.A.
236 F4 Nashville IL U.S.A.
231 E5 Nashville NC U.S.A.
232 B4 Nashville OH U.S.A.
234 B3 Nashville PA U.S.A.
231 C4 Nashville TN U.S.A.
226 A2 Nashwauk MN U.S.A.
188 G3 Našice Croatia
175 I3 Nasielsk Pol.
141 M3 Näsijärvi l. Fin.
Nasik Mahar. India see Nashik
Nasirabad Bangl. see Mymensingh
116 C4 Nasirabad Rajasthan India
123 G4 Nasirabad Pak.
225 I2 Naskaupi r. Nfld. Can.
117 F4 Nasmganj Bihar India
194 D4 Naso Sicilia Italy
194 D4 Naso r. Sicilia Italy
209 E7 Nasondoye Dem. Rep. Congo
226 B3 Nasonville WI U.S.A.
79 □1 Nasorolevu mt. Vanua Levu Fiji
Nasosnyy Azer. see Hacı Zeynalabdin
203 F2 Nasr Egypt
122 B3 Naşrābād Iran
122 D3 Naşrābād Iran
128 C3 Naşrānī, Jabal an mts Syria
Nasratabad Iran see Zābol
222 D4 Nass r. B.C. Can.
207 G4 Nassarawa Nigeria
207 H4 Nassarawa state Nigeria
85 E2 Nassau r. Qld Austr.
246 C1 Nassau Bahamas
81 □2 Nassau i. Cook Is
169 C5 Nassau Rheinland-Pfalz Ger.
171 E5 Nassau Sachsen Ger.
233 G3 Nassau NY U.S.A.
235 E2 Nassau County county NY U.S.A.
233 F6 Nassawadox VA U.S.A.
170 E3 Nassenheide Ger.
203 G4 Nasser, Lake resr Egypt
178 B3 Nassereith Austria
206 E4 Nassian Côte d'Ivoire
143 F3 Nässjö Sweden
165 E4 Nassogne Belgium
224 E1 Nastapoca r. Que. Can.
169 C5 Nastätten Ger.
138 E1 Nastola Fin.
105 F1 Nasu-dake vol. Japan
92 B3 Nasugbu Phil.
175 K4 Nasutów Pol.
139 H3 Nasva Rus. Fed.
139 H3 Nasva r. Rus. Fed.
141 L3 Nasviken Sweden
177 H4 Naszály Hungary
212 E4 Nata Botswana
254 G3 Natal Brazil
94 B2 Natal Sumatera Indon.
Natal prov. S. Africa see Kwazulu-Natal
265 G7 Natal Basin sea feature Indian Ocean
234 B2 Natalie PA U.S.A.
122 B3 Naţanz Iran
225 I3 Natashquan Que. Can.
225 I3 Natashquan r. Newfoundland/Québec Can.
81 □1 Na Taulaga i. Tokelau
237 F6 Natchez MS U.S.A.
237 E6 Natchitoches LA U.S.A.
149 G3 Nateby Cumbria, England U.K.
190 C2 Naters Switz.
83 F4 Nathalia Vic. Austr.
116 C3 Nathana Punjab India
84 C2 Nathan River N.T. Austr.
116 C4 Nathdwara Rajasthan India
140 □ Nathorst Land reg. Svalbard
207 F4 Natiaboani Burkina
240 I5 National City CA U.S.A.
80 E3 National Park North I. N.Z.
191 I3 Natisone r. Italy
207 F4 Natitingou Benin
257 G4 Natividade Rio de Janeiro Brazil
254 D4 Natividade Tocantins Brazil
222 D2 Natla r. N.W.T. Can.
96 A2 Natogyi Myanmar
117 G4 Nator Bangl.
102 J4 Natori Japan
211 C5 Natron, Lake salt l. Tanz.
105 G1 Natsui-gawa r. Japan
96 A3 Nattalin Myanmar
114 C4 Nattam Tamil Nadu India
96 B3 Nattaung mt. Myanmar
140 M2 Nattavaara Sweden
140 M2 Nattavaara by Sweden
179 E2 Natternback Austria
173 E3 Nattheim Ger.
137 I5 Natukhayevskaya Rus. Fed.
95 D1 Natuna, Kepulauan is Indon.
95 E1 Natuna Besar i. Indon.
232 D6 Natural Bridge VA U.S.A.
87 B7 Naturaliste, Cape W.A. Austr.
87 A5 Naturaliste Channel W.A. Austr.
265 L7 Naturaliste Plateau sea feature Indian Ocean
214 D5 Nature's Valley S. Africa
241 M2 Naturita CO U.S.A.
191 F2 Naturno Italy
Nau Tajik. see Nov
226 E2 Naubinway MI U.S.A.
163 E4 Naucelle France
162 E4 Naucelles France
178 B4 Nauders Austria
170 D3 Nauen Ger.
171 C4 Nauendorf Ger.
235 E1 Naugatuck CT U.S.A.
235 E1 Naugatuck r. CT U.S.A.
172 C2 Nauheim Ger.
162 A3 Naujac-sur-Mer France
92 B3 Naujan Phil.
138 D3 Naujoji Akmenė Lith.
116 C4 Naukh Rajasthan India
147 E3 Naul Rep. of Ireland
169 E4 Naumburg (Hessen) Ger.
171 C4 Naumburg (Saale) Ger.
171 E4 Naundorf Sachsen Ger.
171 E5 Naundorf Sachsen Ger.
169 C5 Nauroth Ger.
129 D2 Naurskaya Rus. Fed.
77 G2 Nauru i. Nauru
77 G2 Nauru country S. Pacific Ocean
123 G5 Naushahro Firoz Pak.
123 G5 Naushara Pak.
106 E1 Naushki Rus. Fed.
141 I3 Naustdal Norway
250 C6 Nauta Peru
Nautaca Uzbek. see Karshi
214 A2 Naute Dam Namibia
245 F3 Nautla Mex.
117 E4 Nautonwa Uttar Prad. India
226 B5 Nauvoo IL U.S.A.
208 E4 Nava r. Dem. Rep. Congo
183 E1 Nava Spain
Navabad Tajik. see Novobod
183 E4 Navacepeda de Tormes Spain
183 F4 Navacerreda Spain
185 G4 Navachica mt. Spain
182 E4 Navaconcejo Spain
183 F4 Nava de Arévalo Spain
183 F3 Nava de la Asunción Spain
183 E3 Nava del Rey Spain
183 E4 Nava de Sotrobal Spain
117 G5 Navadwip W. Bengal India
183 G3 Navafría Spain
183 F5 Navahermosa Spain
129 F3 Navahı Azer.
138 E5 Navahrudak Belarus
138 E5 Navahrudskaye Wzvyshsha hills Belarus
187 C5 Navajas Spain
239 F4 Navajo r. CO U.S.A.
241 L3 Navajo Mountain UT U.S.A.
183 E2 Navajos hill Spain
92 C4 Naval Phil.
186 D2 Naval Spain
183 F4 Navalagamella Spain
183 H3 Navalcaballo Spain
183 E4 Navalcán Spain
183 F4 Navalcarnero Spain
183 H3 Navalero Spain
183 F3 Navalmanzano Spain
183 F4 Navalmoral Spain
182 E5 Navalmoral de la Mata Spain
183 E4 Navalonguilla Spain
183 F4 Navalosa Spain
183 F4 Navalperal de Pinares Spain
185 F1 Navalpino Spain
183 F4 Navaluenga Spain
183 E5 Navalvillar de Ibor Spain
185 E1 Navalvillar de Pela Spain
183 F4 Navamorcuende Spain
147 E3 Navan Rep. of Ireland
Navangar Gujarat India see Jamnagar
138 G4 Navapolatsk Belarus
186 E3 Navarcles Spain
186 B2 Navardún Spain
131 S3 Navarin, Mys c. Rus. Fed.
259 D9 Navarino, Isla i. Chile
183 I2 Navarra aut. comm. Spain
83 E4 Navarre Vic. Austr.
Navarre aut. comm. Spain see Navarra
182 D4 Navarredonda de la Rinconada Spain
163 B5 Navarrenx France
187 C5 Navarrés Spain
183 H2 Navarrete Spain
261 H4 Navarro Arg.
240 F2 Navarro r. CA U.S.A.
186 E3 Navàs Spain
163 B6 Navasa Spain
185 F1 Navas de Estrena Spain
182 D5 Navas del Madroño Spain
183 F4 Navas del Rey Spain
183 F3 Navas de Oro Spain
185 G2 Navas de San Juan Spain
186 B2 Navaseués Spain
182 D4 Navasfrías Spain
134 H5 Navashino Rus. Fed.
237 D6 Navasota TX U.S.A.
237 D6 Navasota r. TX U.S.A.
246 D3 Navassa Island terr. West Indies
186 F2 Navata Spain
183 F4 Navatalgordo Spain
138 E5 Navayel'nya Belarus
190 F3 Nave Italy
184 B3 Nave Port.
182 C2 Navea r. Spain
182 D4 Nave de Haver Port.
148 C2 Nave Island Scotland U.K.
193 F2 Navelli Italy
160 E1 Navenne France
146 D3 Naver r. Scotland U.K.
146 D3 Naver, Loch l. Scotland U.K.
184 B3 Nave Redonda Port.
142 D2 Naverstad Sweden
162 D3 Naves France
186 E3 Navès Spain
139 K5 Navesnoye Rus. Fed.
138 E2 Navesti r. Estonia
185 E1 Navezuelas Spain
182 D1 Navia Spain
182 D1 Navia r. Spain
260 B3 Navidad Chile
237 D6 Navidad r. TX U.S.A.
247 E2 Navidad Bank sea feature Caribbean Sea
160 D2 Navilly France
255 B7 Naviraí Brazil
79 □1 Naviti i. Fiji
136 C2 Naviz Ukr.
139 J5 Navlya Rus. Fed.
139 J5 Navlya r. Rus. Fed.
197 I3 Năvodari Romania
120 F4 Navoi Uzbek.
120 E4 Navoiyskaya Oblast' admin. div. Uzbek.
242 C3 Navojoa Mex.
242 D3 Navolato Mex.
79 □1 Navotuvotu hill Vanua Levu Fiji
Navoy Oblast admin. div. Uzbek. see Navoiyskaya Oblast'
Návpaktos Greece see Nafpaktos
Návplion Greece see Nafplio
143 F3 Nävragöl Sweden
142 B2 Navrestad hill Norway
206 E4 Navrongo Ghana
Navşar Turkey see Şemdinli
116 C5 Navsari Gujarat India
116 C4 Nawa Rajasthan India
128 C3 Nawá Syria
117 G4 Nawabganj Bangl.
98 D6 Nawabganj Uttar Prad. India
111 C7 Nawabganj Uttar Prad. India
123 G5 Nawabshah Pak.
117 F4 Nawada Bihar India
116 C4 Nawalgarh Rajasthan India
111 B6 Nawashahr Punjab India
124 C3 Nawāşīf, Ḩarrāt lava field Saudi Arabia
96 B2 Nawnghkio Myanmar
96 B2 Nawngleng Myanmar
Nawoiy Uzbek. see Navoi
Nawoiy Wiloyati admin. div. Uzbek. see Navoiyskaya Oblast'
175 I6 Nawojowa Pol.
129 D4 Naxçıvan Azer.
129 D4 Naxçıvan aut. reg. Azer.
129 D4 Naxçıvançay r. Azer.
108 C2 Naxi Sichuan China
199 D3 Naxos Notio Aigaio Greece
199 D3 Naxos i. Greece
250 B4 Naya Col.
117 F5 Nayagarh Orissa India
244 B2 Nayarit state Mex.
122 D3 Nāy Band, Kūh-e mt. Iran
163 B5 Nay-Bourdettes France
108 C3 Nayong Guizhou China
102 K1 Nayoro Japan
114 C3 Nayudupeta Andhra Prad. India
254 E3 Nazare Brazil
182 A5 Nazaré Port.
242 E3 Nazareno Mex.
114 C4 Nazareth Tamil Nadu India
128 B3 Nazareth Israel
234 C2 Nazareth PA U.S.A.
256 C2 Nazário Brazil
242 D3 Nazas Mex.
242 D3 Nazas r. Mex.
252 B3 Nazca Peru
267 N7 Nazca Ridge sea feature S. Pacific Ocean
102 □1 Naze Japan
151 H3 Nazeing Essex, England U.K.
159 G4 Nazelles-Négron France
122 A2 Nāzīk Iran
199 F3 Nazilli Turkey
127 E3 Nazımiye Turkey
Nazinon r. Burkina/Ghana see Red Volta
117 H4 Nazira Assam India
117 G5 Nazir Hat Bangl.
129 E3 Näzirli Azer.
139 H2 Naziya Rus. Fed.
222 F4 Nazko B.C. Can.
222 F4 Nazko r. B.C. Can.
122 A2 Nāzlū r. Iran
129 D2 Nazran' Rus. Fed.
210 C2 Nazrēt Eth.
125 G3 Nazwá Oman
130 I4 Nazyvayevsk Rus. Fed.
206 B2 Nbâk Maur.
215 E5 Ncanaha S. Africa
209 F7 Nchelenge Zambia
Ncheu Malawi see Ntcheu
212 D4 Ncojane Botswana
215 F4 Ncora S. Africa
207 H6 Ncue Equat. Guinea
211 B6 Ndala Tanz.
209 B7 N'dalatando Angola
207 F4 Ndali Benin
208 D2 Ndélé C.A.R.
207 I5 Ndélélé Cameroon
208 A5 Ndendé Gabon
Ndende i. Santa Cruz Is Solomon Is see Ndeni
78 □6 Ndeni i. Santa Cruz Is Solomon Is
207 H5 Ndikiniméki Cameroon
206 B3 Ndioum Guènt Senegal
202 B6 Ndjamena Chad
N'Djamena Chad see Ndjamena
208 D3 Ndji r. C.A.R.
207 H5 Ndjim r. Cameroon
208 A5 Ndjolé Gabon
Ndjouani i. Comoros see Nzwani
206 B3 Ndofane Senegal
Ndoi i. Fiji see Doi
209 F8 Ndola Zambia
206 D4 Ndorola Burkina
210 C4 Ndoto mt. Kenya
208 A5 Ndougou Gabon
78 □6 Ndovele New Georgia Is Solomon Is
Nduke i. New Georgia Is Solomon Is see Kolombangara
211 C7 Ndumbwe Tanz.
215 I2 Ndumu S. Africa
215 H3 Ndwedwe S. Africa
162 B3 Né r. France
163 C6 Né, Mont mt. France
198 D4 Nea Alikarnassos Kriti Greece
198 C2 Nea Anchialos Greece
198 C1 Nea Apollonia Greece
198 C2 Nea Artaki Greece
85 F5 Neabul Creek r. Qld Austr.
198 C3 Nea Epidavros Greece
147 E2 Neagh, Lough l. Northern Ireland U.K.
238 A1 Neah Bay WA U.S.A.
197 G3 Neajlov r. Romania
198 C1 Nea Kallikrateia Greece
198 D1 Nea Karvali Greece
147 B3 Neale Rep. of Ireland
84 B5 Neale, Lake salt flat N.T. Austr.
198 C2 Nea Liosia Greece
198 C2 Nea Makri Greece
198 C1 Nea Moudania Greece
197 H2 Neamț r. Romania
198 D1 Nea Peramos Greece
198 B1 Neapoli Dytiki Makedonia Greece
199 D4 Neapoli Kriti Greece
198 C3 Neapoli Peloponnisos Greece
Neapolis Italy see Napoli
149 G3 Near Sawrey Cumbria, England U.K.
198 C1 Nea Santa Greece
150 D3 Neath Neath Port Talbot, Wales U.K.
150 D3 Neath r. Wales U.K.
150 D3 Neath Port Talbot admin. div. Wales U.K.
198 C1 Nea Zichni Greece
210 A4 Nebbi Uganda
168 D1 Nebel Ger.
173 E4 Nebelhorn mt. Ger.
110 C3 Nebesnaya, Gora mt. Xinjiang China
163 E6 Nébias France
83 F2 Nebine Creek r. Qld Austr.
122 C2 Nebitdag Turkm.
85 G4 Nebo Qld Austr.
241 L2 Nebo, Mount UT U.S.A.
139 I2 Nebolchi Rus. Fed.
171 C4 Nebra (Unstrut) Ger.
236 C3 Nebraska state U.S.A.
236 E3 Nebraska City NE U.S.A.
183 G3 Nebreda Spain
194 D5 Nebrodi, Monti mts Sicilia Italy
139 L3 Nebyloye Rus. Fed.
245 F3 Necaxa r. Mex.
226 B3 Necedah WI U.S.A.
176 E1 Nechanice Czech Rep.
137 F4 Nechayane Ukr.
237 E6 Neches r. TX U.S.A.
250 C2 Nechí r. Col.
185 G4 Nechite r. Spain
172 C2 Neckar r. Ger.
172 C2 Neckarbischofsheim Ger.
172 C2 Neckargemünd Ger.
172 C2 Neckarsteinach Ger.
172 D2 Neckarsulm Ger.
75 H2 Necker Island HI U.S.A.
261 H6 Necochea Arg.
250 B2 Necoclí Col.
151 H2 Necton Norfolk, England U.K.
182 B1 Neda Spain
136 F2 Nedanchychi Ukr.
198 B3 Nedas r. Greece
177 H2 Nedašov Czech Rep.
170 E2 Neddemin Ger.
197 G5 Nedelino Bulg.
188 F2 Nedelišće Croatia
Nederland country Europe see Netherlands
Nederlandse Antillen terr. West Indies see Netherlands Antilles
164 E2 Nederlangbroek Neth.
164 E3 Neder Rijn r. Neth.
170 C1 Neder Vindinge Denmark
165 E3 Nederweert Neth.
Nédha r. Greece see Nedas
171 D3 Nedlitz Ger.
136 D3 Nedoboyivtsi Ukr.
111 E6 Nêdong Xizang China
140 M1 Nedre Soppero Sweden
137 G2 Nedryhayliv Ukr.
142 A2 Nedstrandsfjorden sea chan. Norway
208 F4 Neduka r. Dem. Rep. Congo
176 F2 Nedvědice Czech Rep.
174 G5 Nędza Pol.
105 E2 Neeba-san mt. Japan
164 F2 Neede Neth.
233 H3 Needham MA U.S.A.
151 I2 Needham Market Suffolk, England U.K.
151 G2 Needingworth Cambridgeshire, England U.K.
241 J4 Needles CA U.S.A.
232 D5 Needmore PA U.S.A.
Neemuch Madh. Prad. India see Nimach
226 C3 Neenah WI U.S.A.
223 L5 Neepawa Man. Can.
165 F3 Neer Neth.
164 E3 Neerijnen Neth.
168 C2 Neermoor Ger.
165 E3 Neeroeteren Belgium
165 E3 Neerpelt Belgium
168 F2 Neetze Ger.
234 C2 Neffs PA U.S.A.
234 B2 Neffsville PA U.S.A.
205 G2 Nefta Tunisia
129 F4 Neftçala Azer.
129 G3 Neft Daşları Azer.
Neftechala Azer. see 26 Bakı Komissarı
Neftechala Azer. see Neftçala
129 A1 Neftegorsk Krasnodarskiy Kray Rus. Fed.
100 G1 Neftegorsk Sakhalin Rus. Fed.

206 C3 Niagassola Guinea
206 C4 Niagouelé, Mont du hill Guinea
206 D4 Niakaramandougou Côte d'Ivoire
207 F3 Niamey Niger
206 D3 Niamina Mali
207 F4 Niamtougou Togo
Nianbai Qinghai China see Ledu
206 C4 Niandan r. Guinea
206 C4 Niandankoro Guinea
211 C6 Niangandu Tanz.
208 E4 Niangara Dem. Rep. Congo
206 E3 Niangay, Lac l. Mali
206 D4 Niangoloko Burkina
237 E4 Niangua r. MO U.S.A.
Niangxi Hunan China see Xinshao
206 D4 Niankorodougou Burkina
235 F1 Niantic CT U.S.A.
107 I2 Nianzishan Heilong. China
209 B5 Niari admin. reg. Congo
94 B2 Nias i. Indon.
213 H2 Niassa prov. Moz.
Niassa, Lago l. Africa see Nyasa, Lake
Niaur i. Palau see Angaur
163 D6 Niaux France
190 E4 Nibbiano Italy
86 E4 Nibil Well W.A. Austr.
129 E3 Nic Azer.
195 G3 Nicà r. Italy
138 C3 Nīca Latvia
Nicaea Turkey see İznik
246 A4 Nicaragua country Central America
242 □I7 Nicaragua, Lago de l. Nic.
Nicaragua, Lake Nic. see Nicaragua, Lago de
246 D2 Nicaro Cuba
195 F4 Nicastro Italy
161 F5 Nice France
Nice airport France see Côte d'Azur
240 F2 Nice CA U.S.A.
Nicephorium Syria see Ar Raqqah
231 C6 Niceville FL U.S.A.
190 C3 Nichelino Italy
103 E8 Nichinan Japan
117 E4 Nichlaul Uttar Prad. India
246 B2 Nicholas Channel Bahamas/Cuba
230 C4 Nicholasville KY U.S.A.
246 C1 Nicholl's Town Andros Bahamas
233 E3 Nichols NY U.S.A.
86 F3 Nicholson W.A. Austr.
84 D3 Nicholson r. Qld Austr.
227 F2 Nicholson Ont. Can.
234 C1 Nicholson PA U.S.A.
87 C5 Nicholson Range hills W.A. Austr.
233 F2 Nicholville NY U.S.A.
179 I3 Nickelsdorf Austria
232 B6 Nickelsville VA U.S.A.
115 G4 Nicobar Islands Andaman & Nicobar Is India
197 I3 Nicolae Bălcescu Romania
243 H5 Nicolás Bravo Mex.
245 E4 Nicolás Romero Mex.
240 G2 Nicolaus CA U.S.A.
195 E5 Nicolosi Sicilia Italy
Nicomedia Turkey see Kocaeli
Nicopolis Bulg. see Nikopol
Nicosia Cyprus see Lefkosia
194 D5 Nicosia Sicilia Italy
195 E4 Nicotera Italy
242 □I7 Nicoya Costa Rica
242 □I7 Nicoya, Península de pen. Costa Rica
233 □J1 Nictau N.B. Can.
197 I3 Niculițel Romania
138 C4 Nida Lith.
175 I2 Nida r. Pol.
175 I5 Nida r. Pol.
114 D2 Nidadavole Andhra Prad. India
114 C2 Nidagunda Andhra Prad. India
190 C1 Nidau Switz.
149 H3 Nidd r. England U.K.
169 E5 Nidda Ger.
169 D5 Nidda r. Ger.
169 D5 Nidder r. Ger.
149 H3 Nidderdale val. England U.K.
142 C2 Nidelva r. Norway
190 D2 Nidwalden canton Switz.
197 E5 Nidže mt. Greece/Macedonia
175 I2 Nidzica Pol.
175 I5 Nidzica r. Pol.
164 F1 Niebert Neth.
184 D3 Niebla Spain
175 I3 Nieborów Pol.
168 D1 Niebüll Ger.
175 J6 Niebylec Pol.
174 F3 Niechanowo Pol.
175 H4 Niechcice Pol.
175 I2 Niechłonin Pol.
174 E4 Niechlów Pol.
157 G3 Nied r. France
157 G3 Nied Allemande r. France
169 E4 Niedenstein Ger.
173 G3 Niederaichbach Ger.
165 F5 Niederanven Lux.
169 E5 Niederaula Ger.
173 G3 Niederbayern admin. reg. Bayern Ger.
190 C1 Niederbipp Switz.
169 D5 Niederbrechen Ger.
172 C3 Niedereschach Ger.
179 E3 Niedere Tauern mts Austria
170 E3 Niederfinow Ger.
169 C5 Niederfischbach Ger.
169 E5 Nieder-Gemünden Ger.
171 D4 Niedergörsdorf Ger.
169 C5 Niederkassel Ger.
172 B2 Niederkirchen Ger.
169 B4 Niederkrüchten Ger.
168 C3 Niederlangen Ger.
171 E3 Niederlehme Ger.
171 C3 Niederndodeleben Ger.
178 D3 Niederndorf Austria
169 D5 Niederneisen Ger.
172 D2 Niedernhall Ger.
169 D5 Niedernhausen Ger.
178 D3 Niedernsill Austria
169 E3 Niedernwöhren Ger.
172 C2 Nieder-Olm Ger.
169 F4 Niederorschel Ger.
179 G2 Niederösterreich land Austria
169 E5 Nieder-Rodenbach Ger.
171 C4 Niederroßla Ger.
168 D3 Niedersachsen land Ger.
169 F4 Niedersachswerfen Ger.
169 D5 Niederselters Ger.
172 D2 Niederstetten Ger.
173 E3 Niederstotzingen Ger.
171 C4 Niedertrebra Ger.
190 E1 Niederurnen Switz.
173 G3 Niederviehbach Ger.
169 F5 Niederwerrn Ger.
171 E5 Niederwiesa Ger.
173 G3 Niederwinkling Ger.
172 B2 Niederwörresbach Ger.
169 C5 Niederzissen Ger.
175 K4 Niedrzwica Duża Pol.
175 K2 Niedźwiadna Pol.
175 I6 Niedźwiedź Pol.
207 H6 Niefang Equat. Guinea
172 C3 Niefern-Öschelbronn Ger.
175 J1 Niegocin, Jezioro l. Pol.
174 D4 Niegosławice Pol.
175 H5 Niegowa Pol.
171 C3 Niegripp Ger.
169 E4 Nieheim Ger.
164 F1 Niekerk Neth.
214 D3 Niekerkshoop S. Africa
175 I4 Niekłań Wielki Pol.
165 D3 Niel Belgium
175 L5 Nielisz Pol.
206 D4 Niellé Côte d'Ivoire
209 F6 Niemba Dem. Rep. Congo
171 D4 Niemberg Ger.
175 K4 Niemce Pol.
174 E5 Niemcza Pol.
171 D3 Niemegk Ger.
140 M2 Niemisel Sweden
174 F5 Niemodlin Pol.
174 G4 Niemysłów Pol.
206 D4 Niéna Mali
175 K5 Nienadówka Pol.
168 E1 Nienborstel Ger.
171 C4 Nienburg (Saale) Ger.
168 E3 Nienburg (Weser) Ger.
168 F3 Nienhagen Ger.
169 E3 Nienstädt Ger.
170 D1 Niepars Ger.
175 I5 Niepołomice Pol.
175 J3 Nieporęt Pol.
156 C2 Nieppe France
169 A4 Niers r. Ger.
172 C2 Nierstein Ger.
171 F4 Niesky Ger.
169 E4 Nieste Ger.
175 I4 Nieświń Pol.
174 G3 Nieszawa Pol.
175 J5 Nietulisko Duże Pol.
162 D3 Nieul France
162 A2 Nieul-le-Dolent France
162 A2 Nieul-sur-Mer France
251 H3 Nieuw Amsterdam Suriname
164 F3 Nieuw-Bergen Neth.
164 E2 Nieuwegein Neth.
164 D2 Nieuwe-Niedorp Neth.
164 F1 Nieuwe Pekela Neth.
164 D3 Nieuwerkerk Neth.
164 D3 Nieuwerkerk aan de IJssel Neth.
165 E4 Nieuwerkerken Belgium
164 G1 Nieuweschans Neth.
164 D3 Nieuwe-Tonge Neth.
164 F2 Nieuw-Heeten Neth.
164 D2 Nieuwkoop Neth.
164 F2 Nieuwlande Neth.
164 F2 Nieuwleusen Neth.
164 E2 Nieuw-Loosdrecht Neth.
164 E2 Nieuw-Milligen Neth.
165 D3 Nieuw-Namen Neth.
251 G3 Nieuw Nickerie Suriname
164 F1 Nieuwolda Neth.
214 B4 Nieuwoudtville S. Africa
165 B3 Nieuwpoort Belgium
164 D2 Nieuwveen Neth.
164 D2 Nieuw-Vennep Neth.
164 D3 Nieuw-Vossemeer Neth.
164 F2 Nieuw-Weerdinge Neth.
169 C5 Nievern Ger.
244 C2 Nieves Mex.
Nieves Galicia Spain see As Neves
160 B1 Nièvre dept Bourgogne France
160 B1 Nièvre r. France
160 B2 Nièvre de Champlemy r. France
175 K4 Niewęgłosz Pol.
126 D3 Niğde Turkey
215 G2 Nigel S. Africa
207 H2 Niger country Africa
207 G5 Niger r. Africa
207 G4 Niger state Nigeria
207 G5 Niger, Mouths of the Nigeria
206 C4 Niger, Source of the tourist site Guinea
264 J5 Niger Cone sea feature S. Atlantic Ocean
207 G4 Nigeria country Africa
146 D4 Nigg Bay Scotland U.K.
116 E3 Nighasan Uttar Prad. India
81 B6 Nightcaps South I. N.Z.
224 D3 Nighthawk Lake Ont. Can.
85 E2 Night Island Qld Austr.
182 B2 Nigrán Spain
198 C1 Nigrita Greece
244 D2 Nigromante Mex.
185 G4 Nigüelas Spain
138 E2 Nigula looduskaitseala nature res. Estonia
159 H5 Niherne France
Nihommatsu Japan see Nihonmatsu
Nihon country Asia see Japan
102 J5 Nihonmatsu Japan
102 I5 Niigata Japan
105 E1 Niigata pref. Japan
105 E2 Niigata-yake-yama vol. Japan
103 F7 Niihama Japan
240 □A8 Niihau i. HI U.S.A.
103 F6 Niimi Japan
102 I5 Niitsu Japan
185 H4 Níjar Spain
164 F2 Nijeveen Neth.
164 E2 Nijkerk Neth.
165 D3 Nijlen Belgium
164 E3 Nijmegen Neth.
164 F2 Nijverdal Neth.
198 C2 Nikaia Greece
140 O1 Nikel' Rus. Fed.
120 D2 Nikel'tau Kazakh.
121 J2 Nikitinka Kazakh.
137 J2 Nikitovka Rus. Fed.
140 L2 Nikkaluokta Sweden
207 F4 Nikki Benin
105 F2 Nikkō Japan
179 G3 Niklasdorf Austria
134 I4 Nikola Rus. Fed.
197 G4 Nikolaevo Bulg.
Nikolayev Mykolayivs'ka Oblast' Ukr. see Mykolayiv
121 F1 Nikolayevka Kazakh.
120 E1 Nikolayevka Chelyabinskaya Oblast' Rus. Fed.
100 E2 Nikolayevka Khabarovskiy Kray Rus. Fed.
137 J4 Nikolayevka Rostovskaya Oblast' Rus. Fed.
135 I5 Nikolayevka Ul'yanovskaya Oblast' Rus. Fed.
Nikolayev Oblast admin. div. Ukr. see Mykolayivs'ka Oblast'
135 I6 Nikolayevsk Rus. Fed.
Nikolayevskaya Oblast' admin. div. Ukr. see Mykolayivs'ka Oblast'
Nikolayevskiy Rus. Fed. see Nikolayevsk
100 G1 Nikolayevsk-na-Amure Rus. Fed.
Nikolayevskoye Respublika Adygeya Rus. Fed. see Krasnogvardeyskoye
135 I5 Nikol'sk Rus. Fed.
134 I4 Nikol'sk Rus. Fed.
Nikol'skaya Pestravka Rus. Fed. see Nikol'sk
Nikol'skiy Kazakh. see Satpayev
139 J1 Nikol'skiy Rus. Fed.
131 R4 Nikol'skoye Rus. Fed.
139 M3 Nikol'skoye Rus. Fed.
139 L5 Nikol'skoye Rus. Fed.
120 C1 Nikol'skoye Rus. Fed.
Nikol'skoye Rus. Fed. see Sheksna
139 K2 Nikol'skoye Rus. Fed.
197 G4 Nikopol Bulg.
137 H4 Nikopol' Ukr.
122 B2 Nīk Pey Iran
126 E2 Niksar Turkey
122 E5 Nīkshahr Iran
196 D4 Nikšić Crna Gora Yugo.
77 I2 Nikumaroro i. Phoenix Is Kiribati
77 H2 Nikunau i. Gilbert Is Kiribati
Nîl, Bahr el r. Africa see Nile
93 D4 Nila vol. Maluku Indon.
117 F5 Nilagiri Orissa India
114 C4 Nilakkottai Tamil Nadu India
114 C4 Nilambur Kerala India
241 J5 Niland CA U.S.A.
113 D11 Nilandhoo Atoll Maldives
114 C2 Nilanga Mahar. India
114 D4 Nilaveli Sri Lanka
203 F2 Nile r. Africa
203 G5 Nile state Sudan
226 D5 Niles MI U.S.A.
232 C4 Niles OH U.S.A.
114 B3 Nileswaram Kerala India
124 B5 Nili r. Eth.
140 M2 Nilivaara Sweden
110 C3 Nilka Xinjiang China
257 F5 Nilópolis Brazil
117 G4 Nilphamari Bangl.
140 O3 Nilsiä Fin.
199 F1 Nilüfer r. Turkey
157 G3 Nilvange France
142 C4 Nim Denmark
116 C4 Nimach Madh. Prad. India
116 C4 Nimaj Rajasthan India
100 E2 Niman r. Rus. Fed.
Nimba, Monts mts Africa see Nimba Mountains
116 C4 Nimbahera Rajasthan India
114 B2 Nimbal Karnataka India
206 C4 Nimba Mountains Africa
86 D4 Nimberra Well W.A. Austr.
Nimbhera Rajasthan India see Nimbahera
100 F1 Nimelen r. Rus. Fed.
161 C5 Nîmes France
191 I2 Nimis Italy
116 C4 Nimka Thana Rajasthan India
83 G4 Nimmitabel N.S.W. Austr.
222 E5 Nimpkish r. B.C. Can.
123 E4 Nīmrūz prov. Afgh.
116 D2 Nimu Jammu and Kashmir
Nimwegen Neth. see Nijmegen
78 □3a Ninai i. Kwajalein Marshall Is
127 F4 Nīnawá governorate Iraq
127 F3 Nīnawá tourist site Iraq
83 G2 Nindigully Qld Austr.
168 E1 Nindorf Ger.
114 B4 Nine Degree Channel India
Ninemile Bar Dumfries and Galloway, Scotland U.K. see Crocketford
83 E2 Nine Mile Lake salt flat N.S.W. Austr.
241 I2 Ninemile Peak NV U.S.A.
265 J7 Ninetyeast Ridge sea feature Indian Ocean
83 F4 Ninety Mile Beach Vic. Austr.
80 D1 Ninety Mile Beach North I. N.Z.
Nineveh tourist site Iraq see Nīnawá
151 H4 Ninfield East Sussex, England U.K.
100 D3 Ning'an Heilong. China
109 G2 Ningbo Zhejiang China
107 H3 Ningcheng Nei Mongol China
109 F3 Ningde Fujian China
109 E3 Ningdu Jiangxi China
Ning'er Yunnan China see Pu'er
109 F2 Ningguo Anhui China
109 G2 Ninghai Zhejiang China
107 H4 Ninghe Tianjin China
Ninghsia Hui Autonomous Region aut. reg. China see Ningxia Huizu Zizhiqu
109 F3 Ninghua Fujian China
207 H4 Ningi Nigeria
Ningjiang Jilin China see Songyuan
108 A2 Ningjing Shan mts Xizang China
108 B3 Ninglang Yunnan China
107 G5 Ningling Henan China
108 C4 Ningming Guangxi China
108 B3 Ningnan Sichuan China
108 C1 Ningqiang Shaanxi China
108 D1 Ningshan Shaanxi China
107 G4 Ningwu Shanxi China
Ningxia aut. reg. China see Ningxia Huizu Zizhiqu
106 E4 Ningxia Huizu Zizhiqu aut. reg. China
107 E5 Ningxian Gansu China
109 E2 Ningxiang Hunan China
107 H5 Ningyang Shandong China
109 D3 Ningyuan Hunan China
Ningzhou Yunnan China see Huaning
96 D2 Ninh Binh Vietnam
97 E4 Ninh Hoa Vietnam
260 A5 Ninhue Chile
91 J7 Ninigo Group is P.N.G.
102 J3 Ninohe Japan
129 C3 Ninotsminda Georgia
165 D4 Ninove Belgium
129 C1 Niny Rus. Fed.
253 G5 Nioaque Brazil
236 D3 Niobrara r. NE U.S.A.
208 C5 Nioki Dem. Rep. Congo
206 D3 Niono Mali
206 C3 Nioro Mali
206 B3 Nioro du Rip Senegal
162 B2 Niort France
114 B2 Nipani Karnataka India
260 A5 Ñipas Chile
223 J4 Nipawin Sask. Can.
116 C5 Niphad Mahar. India
224 B3 Nipigon Ont. Can.
236 F1 Nipigon r. Ont. Can.
224 B3 Nipigon, Lake Ont. Can.
227 H2 Nipissing Ont. Can.
224 E4 Nipissing, Lake Ont. Can.
240 G4 Nipomo CA U.S.A.
Nippon country Asia see Japan
Nippon Hai sea N. Pacific Ocean see Japan, Sea of
127 G4 Nippur tourist site Iraq
241 J4 Nipton CA U.S.A.
254 C5 Niquelândia Brazil
260 B5 Niquen Chile
246 C2 Niquero Cuba
122 A2 Nir Iran
114 B2 Nira r. India
105 E3 Nirasaki Japan
260 A4 Nirivilo Chile
107 J1 Nirji Nei Mongol China
114 C2 Nirmal Andhra Prad. India
117 F4 Nirmali Bihar India
114 C2 Nirmal Range hills India
197 E4 Niš Srbija Yugo.
182 C5 Nisa Port.
182 C5 Nisa r. Port.
124 D5 Nişāb Yemen
197 E4 Nišava r. Yugo.
146 F6 Nisbet Scottish Borders, Scotland U.K.
194 D5 Niscemi Sicilia Italy
Nīshāpūr Iran see Neyshābūr
138 G4 Nishcha r. Belarus
102 L2 Nishibetsu-gawa r. Japan
104 B4 Nishinomiya Japan
102 □1 Nishino-omote Japan
103 □3 Nishino-shima vol. Japan
104 D4 Nishio Japan
103 D7 Nishi-Sonogi-hantō pen. Japan
104 A4 Nishiwaki Japan
254 G3 Nísia Floresta Brazil
Nisibis Turkey see Nusaybin
103 E7 Nisi-mera Japan
Nísiros i. Greece see Nisyros
233 G3 Niskayuna NY U.S.A.
224 B1 Niskibi r. Ont. Can.
175 K5 Nisko Pol.
222 B2 Nisling r. Y.T. Can.
165 D4 Nismes Belgium
165 D4 Nismes, Forêt de for. Belgium
136 E4 Nisporeni Moldova
142 E3 Nissan r. Sweden
161 B5 Nissan-lez-Enserune France
104 D3 Nisshin Japan
194 D5 Nissoria Sicilia Italy
142 C3 Nissum Bredning b. Denmark
164 E3 Nistelrode Neth.
136 F4 Nistru r. Moldova alt. Dnister (Ukraine), conv. Dniester
136 E4 Nistrului Inferior, Cîmpia lowland Moldova
222 C2 Nisutlin r. Y.T. Can.
199 E3 Nisyros i. Greece
103 F6 Nita Japan
225 G2 Nitchequon Que. Can.
Nitendi i. Santa Cruz Is Solomon Is see Ndeni
257 F5 Niterói Brazil
146 E6 Nith r. Scotland U.K.
146 E6 Nithsdale val. Scotland U.K.
177 H3 Nitra Slovakia
177 H4 Nitra r. Slovakia
177 H3 Nitrianske Pravno Slovakia
177 H3 Nitriansky Kraj admin. reg. Slovakia
232 C5 Nitro WV U.S.A.
156 D5 Nitry France
142 D1 Nittedal Norway
172 A2 Nittel Ger.
173 G2 Nittenau Ger.
173 F2 Nittendorf Ger.
Niua i. Vanuatu see Aniwa
77 I3 Niuafo'ou i. Tonga
Niuafu i. Tonga see Niuafo'ou
77 I3 Niuatoputopu i. Tonga
110 F4 Niubiziliang Qinghai China
81 □4 Niue terr. S. Pacific Ocean
Niujing Yunnan China see Binchuan
77 H3 Niulakita i. Tuvalu
108 B3 Niulan Jiang r. Yunnan China
240 □D8 Niulii HI U.S.A.
Niushan Jiangsu China see Donghai
77 H2 Niutao i. Tuvalu
109 F2 Niutoushan Anhui China
107 I3 Niuzhuang Liaoning China
140 N3 Nivala Fin.
163 A5 Nive r. France
85 F5 Nive Downs Qld Austr.
165 D4 Nivelles Belgium
175 I1 Nivenskoye Rus. Fed.
158 D4 Nivillac France
156 C3 Nivillers France
160 D3 Nivolas-Vermelle France
140 P2 Nivskiy Rus. Fed.
116 C4 Niwai Rajasthan India
116 D4 Niwari Madh. Prad. India
116 E5 Niwas Madh. Prad. India
175 J5 Niwiska Pol.
157 F3 Nixéville-Blercourt France
Nixia Sichuan China see Sêrxu
240 H2 Nixon NV U.S.A.
Niya Xinjiang China see Minfeng
111 C4 Niya He r. China
129 F3 Niyazoba Azer.
95 E2 Niyut, Gunung mt. Indon.
105 F3 Niza Japan
114 C2 Nizamabad Andhra Prad. India
114 D3 Nizampatnam Andhra Prad. India
176 D2 Nižbor Czech Rep.
134 I4 Nizhegorodskaya Oblast' admin. div. Rus. Fed.
131 L4 Nizhneangarsk Rus. Fed.
137 I5 Nizhnebakanskiy Rus. Fed.
135 G6 Nizhnedevitsk Rus. Fed.
121 K1 Nizhnekamenka Rus. Fed.
134 J5 Nizhnekamsk Rus. Fed.
134 K5 Nizhnekamskoye Vodokhranilishche resr Rus. Fed.
98 G1 Nizhneudinsk Rus. Fed.
130 I3 Nizhnevartovsk Rus. Fed.
Nizhnevolzhsk Rus. Fed. see Narimanov
131 O2 Nizhneyansk Rus. Fed.
134 L4 Nizhni Irginski Rus. Fed.
135 I6 Nizhniy Baskunchak Rus. Fed.
129 C2 Nizhniy Chegem Rus. Fed.
135 H6 Nizhniy Chir Rus. Fed.
129 E2 Nizhniy Dzhengutay Rus. Fed.
Nizhniye Kresty Rus. Fed. see Cherskiy
Nizhniye Ustriki Pol. see Ustrzyki Dolne
137 J2 Nizhniy Karabut Rus. Fed.
137 K2 Nizhniy Kislyay Rus. Fed.
129 D2 Nizhniy Kurp Rus. Fed.
135 H5 Nizhniy Lomov Rus. Fed.
137 K2 Nizhniy Mamon Rus. Fed.
134 H4 Nizhniy Novgorod Rus. Fed.
Nizhniy Novgorod Oblast admin. div. Rus. Fed. see Nizhegorodskaya Oblast'
134 K3 Nizhniy Odes Rus. Fed.
137 J2 Nizhniy Ol'shan Rus. Fed.
130 G4 Nizhniy Tagil Rus. Fed.
107 G1 Nizhniy Tsasuchey Rus. Fed.
134 I4 Nizhniy Yenangsk Rus. Fed.
134 K3 Nizhnyaya Omra Rus. Fed.
140 P2 Nizhnyaya Pirenga, Ozero l. Rus. Fed.
131 K4 Nizhnyaya Poyma Rus. Fed.
121 I1 Nizhnyaya Suyetka Rus. Fed.
131 J3 Nizhnyaya Tunguska r. Rus. Fed.
130 G4 Nizhnyaya Tura Rus. Fed.
137 J2 Nizhnyaya Veduga Rus. Fed.
137 F2 Nizhyn Ukr.
175 I3 Nizina reg. Pol.
126 E3 Nizip Turkey
177 K2 Nízke Beskydy hills Slovakia
177 I3 Nízke Tatry mts Slovakia
100 E4 Nizmennyy, Mys pt Rus. Fed.
177 J3 Nižná Slaná Slovakia
177 K3 Nižný Hrušov Slovakia
177 K3 Nižný Žipov Slovakia
Nizwā Oman see Nazwá
Nizza France see Nice
195 E5 Nizza di Sicilia Sicilia Italy
190 D4 Nizza Monferrato Italy
217 □3a Njazidja i. Comoros
196 D4 Njegoš mts Yugo.
211 C7 Njinjo Tanz.
191 J3 Njivice Croatia
209 E9 Njoko r. Zambia
211 B7 Njombe Tanz.
211 B6 Njombe r. Tanz.
78 □6 Njoroveto New Georgia Is Solomon Is
141 L3 Njurundabommen Sweden
141 L3 Njutånger Sweden
207 H5 Nkambe Cameroon
215 H3 Nkandla S. Africa
211 A6 Nkasi Tanz.
206 E5 Nkawkaw Ghana
211 B7 Nkhata Bay Malawi
211 B8 Nkhotakota Malawi
207 H5 Nkongsamba Cameroon
206 E5 Nkoranza Ghana
207 I5 Nkoteng Cameroon
215 F4 Nkululeko S. Africa
210 A4 Nkusi r. Uganda
215 H3 Nkwalini S. Africa
207 F4 Nkwanta Ghana
215 F5 Nkwenkwezi S. Africa
96 B1 Nmai Hka r. Myanmar
117 I4 Noa Dihing r. India
163 B4 Noaillan France
156 C3 Noailles France
163 A6 Noain Spain
117 G5 Noakhali Bangl.
191 H3 Noale Italy
185 G3 Noalejo Spain
117 F5 Noamundi Bihar India
190 C3 Noasca Italy
220 B3 Noatak r. AK U.S.A.
148 C4 Nobber Rep. of Ireland
103 E7 Nobeoka Japan
171 D5 Nobitz Ger.
183 G5 Noblejas Spain
230 C3 Noblesville IN U.S.A.
215 F4 Nobokwe S. Africa
102 J2 Noboribetsu Japan
253 F3 Nobres Brazil
85 E5 Noccundra Qld Austr.
159 G3 Nocé France
191 G2 Noce r. Italy
193 H5 Noce r. Italy
182 D2 Noceda Spain
193 G4 Nocera Inferiore Italy
193 I5 Nocera Terinese Italy
193 E1 Nocera Umbra Italy
190 F4 Noceto Italy
244 C3 Nochistlán Mex.
195 G2 Noci Italy
175 M1 Nočia r. Belarus/Lith.
195 H2 Nociglia Italy
85 E5 Nockatunga Qld Austr.
237 D5 Nocona TX U.S.A.
105 F3 Noda Japan
236 E4 Nodaway r. MO U.S.A.
142 B2 Nodeland Norway
160 E1 Nods France
163 D5 Noé France
224 D4 Noelville Ont. Can.
214 C2 Noenieput S. Africa
193 I4 Noepoli Italy
168 F1 Noer Ger.
261 F3 Noetinger Arg.
156 C2 Nœux-les-Mines France
183 F5 Noez Spain
183 F5 Noez, Pico de mt. Spain
183 G2 Nofuentes Spain
242 C2 Nogales Mex.
184 D2 Nogales Spain
239 E6 Nogales AZ U.S.A.
191 G3 Nogara Italy
163 B5 Nogaro France
174 H1 Nogat r. Pol.
103 E7 Nōgata Japan
Nogaysk Ukr. see Prymors'ke
129 E1 Nogayskaya Step' reg. Rus. Fed.
120 C2 Nogayty Kazakh.
157 F4 Nogent France
159 G3 Nogent-le-Bernard France
156 B4 Nogent-le-Roi France
159 G3 Nogent-le-Rotrou France
156 E4 Nogent-sur-Aube France
156 C4 Nogent-sur-Marne France
156 C3 Nogent-sur-Oise France
156 D4 Nogent-sur-Seine France
156 C5 Nogent-sur-Vernisson France
131 K3 Noginsk Evenkiyskiy Avtonomnyy Okrug Rus. Fed.
139 L4 Noginsk Moskovskaya Oblast' Rus. Fed.
100 G2 Nogliki Sakhalin Rus. Fed.
85 G5 Nogo r. Qld Austr.
85 G4 Nogoa r. Qld Austr.
104 C3 Nōgōhaku-san mt. Japan
261 H3 Nogoyá Arg.
261 H3 Nogoya r. Arg.
177 I4 Nógrád Hungary
177 I4 Nógrád county Hungary
183 H3 Nograles Spain
104 D2 Noguchigorō-dake mt. Japan
182 D3 Nogueira, Serra de mts Port.
183 I4 Noguera Spain
186 D2 Noguera de Tor r. Spain
186 D2 Noguera Pallaresa r. Spain
186 D3 Noguera Ribagorçana r. Spain
163 B5 Noguères France
187 C4 Nogueruelas Spain
160 A1 Nohain r. France
159 H5 Nohant-Vic France
116 C3 Nohar Rajasthan India
172 B2 Nohfelden Ger.
163 D5 Nohic France
182 B2 Noia Galicia Spain
195 F1 Noicattaro Italy
160 E1 Noidans-lès-Vesoul France
163 C5 Noilhan France
161 B4 Noir, Causse plat. France
227 I3 Noire r. Que. Can.
163 E5 Noire, Montagne mts France
158 C3 Noires, Montagnes hills France
160 B3 Noirétable France
158 D5 Noirmoutier, Île de i. France
158 D4 Noirmoutier-en-l'Île France
157 G3 Noisseville France
183 G1 Noja Spain
232 E5 Nokesville VA U.S.A.
116 C4 Nokha Rajasthan India
122 E5 Nokhowch, Kūh-e mt. Iran
141 M3 Nokia Fin.
Nökis Uzbek. see Nukus
223 J5 Nokomis Sask. Can.
202 B6 Nokou Chad
117 G4 Nokrek Peak Meghalaya India
142 E3 Nol Sweden
208 C4 Nola C.A.R.
194 D2 Nola Italy
160 C2 Nolay France
190 D4 Noli Italy
231 D4 Nolichuky r. TN U.S.A.
134 J4 Nolinsk Kirovskaya Oblast' Rus. Fed.
214 D5 Noll S. Africa
183 F4 Nombela Spain
220 B3 Nome AK U.S.A.
157 G4 Nomeny France
157 G4 Nomexy France
Nomoi Islands Micronesia see Mortlock Islands
215 F4 Nomonde S. Africa
78 □4a Nomoneas is Chuuk Micronesia
106 E1 Nomto Rus. Fed.
79 □2 Nomuka i. Tonga
79 □2 Nomuka Group is Tonga
91 L5 Nomwin atoll Micronesia
134 H4 Nomzha Rus. Fed.
223 I2 Nonacho Lake N.W.T. Can.
156 B4 Nonancourt France
159 G3 Nonant-le-Pin France
191 G4 Nonantola Italy
186 D3 Nonaspe Spain
215 H3 Nondweni S. Africa
156 C3 Nonette r. France
100 C3 Nong'an Jilin China
97 C4 Nong Hong Thai.
Nonghui Sichuan China see Guang'an
96 C3 Nong Khai Thai.
215 H2 Nongoma S. Africa
117 G4 Nongstoin Meghalaya India
161 C4 Nonières France
172 B3 Nonnenweier Ger.
Nonni r. China see Nen Jiang
82 D3 Nonning S.A. Austr.
172 A2 Nonnweiler Ger.
255 B8 Nonoai Brazil
242 D3 Nonoava Mex.
77 H2 Nonouti atoll Gilbert Is Kiribati
101 C5 Nonsan S. Korea
97 C4 Nonthaburi Thai.
162 C3 Nontron France
192 B2 Nonza Corse France
214 E4 Nonzwakazi S. Africa
138 F2 Nõo Estonia
87 C5 Nookawarra W.A. Austr.
82 D1 Noolyeanna Lake salt flat S.A. Austr.
84 B2 Noonamah N.T. Austr.
87 C6 Noondie, Lake salt flat W.A. Austr.
86 E3 Noonkanbah W.A. Austr.
164 F1 Noordbergum Neth.
164 C3 Noordbeveland i. Neth.
164 E3 Noord-Brabant prov. Neth.
164 F1 Noordbroek-Uiterburen Neth.
164 D2 Noord-Holland prov. Neth.
215 H1 Noordkaap S. Africa
214 B5 Noordkuil S. Africa
164 E2 Noordoost Polder Neth.
164 D2 Noordwijk aan Zee Neth.
164 D2 Noordwijk-Binnen Neth.
164 D2 Noordwijkerhout Neth.
164 F2 Noordwolde Neth.
141 M3 Noormarkku Fin.
220 B3 Noorvik AK U.S.A.
85 H5 Noosa Heads Qld Austr.
164 D2 Nootdorp Neth.
245 F5 Nopala Mex.
245 F4 Nopaltepec Mex.
209 B6 Nóqui Angola
193 G2 Nora r. Italy
100 D2 Nora r. Rus. Fed.
143 F2 Nora Sweden
192 A4 Noragugume Sardegna Italy
123 G2 Norak Tajik.
Norakert Armenia see Baghramyan
92 C5 Norala Phil.
224 E3 Noranda Que. Can.
Nor-Bayazet Armenia see Kamo
143 F1 Norberg Sweden
193 F2 Norcia Italy
233 □I2 Norcross ME U.S.A.
207 I4 Nord prov. Cameroon
156 D2 Nord dept Nord - Pas-de-Calais France
140 □ Nordaustlandet i. Svalbard
142 C4 Nordborg Denmark
142 D4 Nordby Denmark
168 C2 Norddeich Ger.
168 D1 Norddorf Ger.
222 G4 Nordegg Alta Can.
168 C2 Norden Ger.
173 E3 Nordendorf Ger.
168 D2 Nordenham Ger.
131 K2 Nordenshel'da, Arkhipelag is Rus. Fed.
222 B2 Nordenskiold r. Y.T. Can.
140 □ Nordenskiøld Land reg. Svalbard
Nordenskjold Archipelago is Rus. Fed. see Nordenshel'da, Arkhipelag
168 D1 Norder Hever sea chan. Ger.
168 C2 Norderney Ger.
168 C2 Norderney i. Ger.
168 D1 Norderoogsand i. Ger.
168 F2 Norderstedt Ger.
216 □1b Nordeste São Miguel Azores
216 □1b Nordestinho São Miguel Azores
141 I3 Nordfjord reg. Norway
141 I3 Nordfjordeid Norway
168 D1 Nordfriesische Inseln is Ger.
168 D1 Nordfriesland reg. Ger.
171 C3 Nordgermersleben Ger.
171 C5 Nordhalben Ger.
168 E1 Nordhastedt Ger.
169 F4 Nordhausen Ger.
172 D2 Nordheim Ger.
168 D2 Nordholz Ger.
169 C3 Nordhorn Ger.
142 A2 Nordhuglo Norway
142 C3 Nordjylland county Denmark
Nord Kap c. Iceland see Horn
140 N1 Nordkapp c. Norway
169 C4 Nordkirchen Ger.
208 F5 Nord-Kivu admin. reg. Dem. Rep. Congo
140 L1 Nord-Kvaløy i. Norway
140 N1 Nordkynhalvøya i. Norway
140 K2 Nordland county Norway
168 D2 Nordleda Ger.
140 K2 Nordli Norway
173 E3 Nördlingen Ger.
140 L3 Nordmaling Sweden
207 H5 Nord-Ouest prov. Cameroon
156 C2 Nord - Pas-de-Calais admin. reg. France
169 C4 Nordrhein-Westfalen land Ger.
169 E3 Nordstemmen Ger.
168 D1 Nordstrand i. Ger.
140 K2 Nord-Trøndelag county Norway
140 □C2 Norðurland eystra constituency Iceland
140 □B2 Norðurland vestra constituency Iceland
140 J3 Nordvika Norway
169 C3 Nordwalde Ger.
147 E4 Nore r. Rep. of Ireland
163 E5 Nore, Pic de mt. France
Noreg country Europe see Norway
138 D4 Noreikiškės Lith.
182 E1 Noreña Spain
142 C1 Noresund Norway
151 H2 Norfolk admin. div. England U.K.
236 D3 Norfolk NE U.S.A.
233 F2 Norfolk NY U.S.A.
233 E6 Norfolk VA U.S.A.
82 □1 Norfolk Island terr. S. Pacific Ocean
266 G7 Norfolk Island Ridge sea feature Tasman Sea
164 F1 Norg Neth.
Norge country Europe see Norway
149 G2 Norham Northumberland, England U.K.
142 B1 Norheimsund Norway
244 D2 Noria de Ángeles Mex.
104 D2 Norikura-dake vol. Japan
130 J3 Noril'sk Rus. Fed.
Norkyung Xizang China see Bainang
227 H3 Norland Ont. Can.
193 E3 Norma Italy
234 C3 Norma NJ U.S.A.
226 C5 Normal IL U.S.A.
85 E3 Norman r. Qld Austr.
237 D5 Norman OK U.S.A.
231 D5 Norman, Lake resr NC U.S.A.
85 F2 Normanby r. Qld Austr.
80 E3 Normanby North I. N.Z.
85 G4 Normanby Range hills Qld Austr.
Normandes, Îles is English Chan. see Channel Islands
251 G4 Normandia Brazil
159 F3 Normandie reg. France
159 F3 Normandie, Collines de hills France
215 G2 Normandien S. Africa
Normandy reg. France see Normandie
85 E3 Normanton Qld Austr.
149 H4 Normanton West Yorkshire, England U.K.
82 D3 Normanville S.A. Austr.
222 E1 Norman Wells N.W.T. Can.
227 H1 Normétal Que. Can.
87 C7 Nornalup W.A. Austr.
160 E1 Noroy-le-Bourg France
223 K5 Norquay Sask. Can.
140 M2 Norra Bredåker Sweden
140 M3 Norra Gloppet b. Fin.
140 K2 Norråker Sweden
140 M3 Norra Kvarken str. Fin./Sweden
140 L2 Norrbotten county Sweden
142 C3 Nørreå r. Denmark
142 D4 Nørre Alslev Denmark
168 G1 Nørreballe Denmark
142 D4 Nørre Lyndelse Denmark
142 C4 Nørre Nebel Denmark
156 C2 Norrent-Fontes France
142 C4 Nørre Snede Denmark
140 M2 Norrfjärden Sweden
143 F3 Norrhult-Klavreström Sweden
234 C2 Norristown PA U.S.A.
143 G2 Norrköping Sweden
141 L3 Norrsundet Sweden
143 H2 Norrtälje Sweden
87 D7 Norseman W.A. Austr.
80 F4 Norsewood North I. N.Z.
140 L2 Norsjö Sweden
100 D1 Norsk Rus. Fed.
251 I4 Norte, Canal do sea chan. Brazil
253 F2 Norte, Serra do hills Brazil
250 C2 Norte de Santander dept Col.
216 □1c Norte Grande São Jorge Azores
253 F3 Nortelândia Brazil
169 E4 Nörten-Hardenberg Ger.
216 □1c Norte Pequeno São Jorge Azores
263 L2 North, Cape Antarctica
233 G3 North Adams MA U.S.A.
149 H3 Northallerton North Yorkshire, England U.K.
87 C6 Northam W.A. Austr.
150 C3 Northam Devon, England U.K.
218 North America continent
233 □J2 North Amity ME U.S.A.
87 B6 Northampton W.A. Austr.
151 G2 Northampton Northamptonshire, England U.K.
233 G3 Northampton MA U.S.A.
234 C2 Northampton PA U.S.A.
234 C2 Northampton County county PA U.S.A.
85 F5 Northampton Downs Qld Austr.
151 G2 Northamptonshire admin. div. England U.K.
115 G3 North Andaman i. Andaman & Nicobar Is India
232 E6 North Anna r. VA U.S.A.
233 □I2 North Anson ME U.S.A.
265 L5 North Australian Basin sea feature Indian Ocean
146 D6 North Ayrshire admin. div. Scotland U.K.
151 F4 North Baddesley Hampshire, England U.K.
232 B4 North Baltimore OH U.S.A.
223 I4 North Battleford Sask. Can.
224 E4 North Bay Ont. Can.
224 E1 North Belcher Islands Nunavut Can.
238 A3 North Bend OR U.S.A.
232 E4 North Bend PA U.S.A.
233 G3 North Bennington VT U.S.A.
235 D2 North Bergen NJ U.S.A.
146 F5 North Berwick East Lothian, Scotland U.K.
233 □H3 North Berwick ME U.S.A.
North Borneo state Malaysia see Sabah
237 D6 North Bosque r. TX U.S.A.
83 F2 North Bourke N.S.W. Austr.
227 F4 North Branch MI U.S.A.
226 A3 North Branch MN U.S.A.
234 D2 North Branch NJ U.S.A.
235 F1 North Branford CT U.S.A.
246 E2 North Caicos i. Turks and Caicos Is
237 E5 North Canadian r. OK U.S.A.
North Cape c. Norway see Nordkapp
80 D1 North Cape c. North I. N.Z.
259 □ North Cape c. S. Georgia
226 C4 North Cape WI U.S.A.
234 D4 North Cape May NJ U.S.A.
231 E4 North Carolina state U.S.A.
234 C2 North Catasauqua PA U.S.A.
149 I4 North Cave East Riding of Yorkshire, England U.K.
224 D4 North Channel lake channel Ont. Can.
146 B6 North Channel Northern Ireland/Scotland U.K.
231 E5 North Charleston SC U.S.A.
150 E3 North Cheriton Somerset, England U.K.
87 C7 Northcliffe W.A. Austr.
232 D3 North Collins NY U.S.A.
237 C6 North Concho r. TX U.S.A.
233 □H2 North Conway NH U.S.A.
North Cousin Islet i. Inner Islands Seychelles see Cousin
222 F5 North Cowichan B.C. Can.
149 H3 North Cowton North Yorkshire, England U.K.
233 G3 North Creek NY U.S.A.
236 C2 North Dakota state U.S.A.
151 G3 North Downs hills England U.K.
149 I4 North Duffield North Yorkshire, England U.K.
213 E4 North East admin. dist. Botswana
234 C3 North East MD U.S.A.
232 D3 North East PA U.S.A.
85 H4 North East Cay rf Coral Sea Is Terr. Austr.
210 D4 North-Eastern prov. Kenya
North-East Frontier Agency state India see Arunachal Pradesh
149 I4 North East Lincolnshire admin. div. England U.K.
267 I4 Northeast Pacific Basin sea feature Pacific Ocean
246 C1 Northeast Providence Channel Bahamas
240 I4 North Edwards CA U.S.A.
169 E4 Northeim Ger.
151 H2 North Elmham Norfolk, England U.K.
206 E4 Northern admin. reg. Ghana
211 B7 Northern admin. reg. Malawi
213 F4 Northern prov. S. Africa
206 C4 Northern prov. Sierra Leone
203 F4 Northern state Sudan
209 F7 Northern prov. Zambia
Northern Aegean admin. reg. Greece see Voreio Aigaio
123 H2 Northern Areas admin. div. Pak.
208 E2 Northern Bahr el Ghazal state Sudan
214 B3 Northern Cape prov. S. Africa
81 □2 Northern Cook Islands Cook Is
202 E5 Northern Darfur state Sudan
Northern Donets r. Rus. Fed. see Severskiy Donets
Northern Dvina r. Rus. Fed. see Severnaya Dvina
147 E2 Northern Ireland prov. U.K.
203 F6 Northern Kordofan state Sudan
77 I3 Northern Lau Group is Fiji
91 J3 Northern Mariana Islands terr. N. Pacific Ocean
Northern Pindus Mountains Greece see Voreia Pindos
Northern Rhodesia country Africa see Zambia
Northern Sporades is Greece see Voreioi Sporades
84 C3 Northern Territory admin. div. Austr.
Northern Transvaal prov. S. Africa see Northern
146 F5 North Esk r. Angus, Scotland U.K.
146 E6 North Esk r. Midlothian/Scottish Borders, Scotland U.K.
236 F4 North Fabius r. MO U.S.A.
149 I4 North Ferriby East Riding of Yorkshire, England U.K.
233 G3 Northfield MA U.S.A.
226 A3 Northfield MN U.S.A.
234 D3 Northfield NJ U.S.A.
233 G2 Northfield VT U.S.A.
226 B3 Northfield WI U.S.A.
151 H3 Northfleet Kent, England U.K.
235 F1 Northford CT U.S.A.
151 I3 North Foreland c. England U.K.
240 H3 North Fork CA U.S.A.
235 F1 North Franklin CT U.S.A.
224 D3 North French r. Ont. Can.
North Frisian Islands Ger. see Nordfriesische Inseln
268 T1 North Geomagnetic Pole Arctic Ocean
149 I3 North Grimston North Yorkshire, England U.K.
235 F1 North Haven CT U.S.A.
233 □J2 North Head N.B. Can.
233 G2 North Hero VT U.S.A.
240 G2 North Highlands CA U.S.A.
233 G3 North Hudson NY U.S.A.
149 I4 North Hykeham Lincolnshire, England U.K.
151 G2 Northill Bedfordshire, England U.K.
84 D2 North Island N.T. Austr.
87 B6 North Island W.A. Austr.
80 D3 North Island N.Z.
241 L4 North Jadito Canyon gorge AZ U.S.A.
226 D5 North Judson IN U.S.A.
North Kazakhstan Oblast admin. div. Kazakh. see Severnyy Kazakhstan
85 F2 North Kennedy r. Qld Austr.
146 D4 North Kessock Highland, Scotland U.K.
232 C4 North Kingsville OH U.S.A.
223 M3 North Knife r. Man. Can.
117 E4 North Koel r. Bihar India
241 L5 North Komelik AZ U.S.A.
117 H4 North Lakhimpur Assam India
146 E6 North Lanarkshire admin. div. Scotland U.K.
80 E1 Northland admin. reg. North I. N.Z.
North Land is Rus. Fed. see Severnaya Zemlya
241 J3 North Las Vegas NV U.S.A.
151 F3 Northleach Gloucestershire, England U.K.
226 D5 North Liberty IN U.S.A.
232 C4 North Lima OH U.S.A.
149 I4 North Lincolnshire admin. div. England U.K.
237 E5 North Little Rock AR U.S.A.
236 D3 North Loup r. NE U.S.A.
222 C2 North Macmillan r. Y.T. Can.
235 F1 North Madison CT U.S.A.
221 H2 North Magnetic Pole Nunavut Can.
113 □1 North Male Atoll Maldives
239 F4 North Mam Peak CO U.S.A.
226 E5 North Manchester IN U.S.A.
232 A5 North Middletown KY U.S.A.
150 D3 North Molton Devon, England U.K.
234 B1 North Mountain mts PA U.S.A.
86 B4 North Muiron Island W.A. Austr.
222 F2 North Nahanni r. N.W.T. Can.
227 G5 North Olmsted OH U.S.A.
236 E2 Northome MN U.S.A.
North Ossetia aut. rep. Rus. Fed. see Severnaya Osetiya, Respublika
240 H3 North Palisade mt. CA U.S.A.
236 C3 North Platte NE U.S.A.
236 C3 North Platte r. NE U.S.A.
87 B6 North Point W.A. Austr.
268 A1 North Pole Arctic Ocean
231 C5 Northport AL U.S.A.
231 D7 North Port FL U.S.A.
226 E3 Northport MI U.S.A.
149 F1 North Queensferry Fife, Scotland U.K.
North Rhine - Westphalia land Ger. see Nordrhein-Westfalen
241 K3 North Rim AZ U.S.A.
225 I4 North River Bridge N.S. Can.
146 □G1 North Roe Shetland, Scotland U.K.
North Rona i. Western Isles, Scotland U.K. see Rona

146 F2 North Ronaldsay i. Scotland U.K.
146 F2 North Ronaldsay Firth sea chan. Scotland U.K.
238 B2 North Santiam r. OR U.S.A.
222 J4 North Saskatchewan r. Alberta/Saskatchewan Can.
241 J2 North Schell Peak NV U.S.A.
144 H3 North Sea sea Europe
235 F2 North Sea NY U.S.A.
223 L3 North Seal r. Man. Can.
149 H2 North Shields Tyne and Wear, England U.K.
240 I2 North Shoshone Peak NV U.S.A.
North Siberian Lowland Rus. Fed. see Severo-Sibirskaya Nizmennost'
North Sinai governorate Egypt see Shamâl Sînâ'
220 D3 North Slope plain AK U.S.A.
149 J4 North Somercotes Lincolnshire, England U.K.
150 E3 North Somerset admin. div. England U.K.
147 B3 North Sound sea chan. Rep. of Ireland
85 H5 North Stradbroke Island Qld Austr.
233 H2 North Stratford NH U.S.A.
149 H2 North Sunderland Northumberland, England U.K.
80 E3 North Taranaki Bight b. North I. N.Z.
222 F5 North Thompson r. B.C. Can.
149 I4 North Thoresby Lincolnshire, England U.K.
151 F3 North Tidworth Wiltshire, England U.K.
146 A4 Northton Western Isles, Scotland U.K.
232 D3 North Tonawanda NY U.S.A.
233 G2 North Troy VT U.S.A.
233 H3 North Truro MA U.S.A.
149 G3 North Tyne r. England U.K.
146 G4 North Ugie r. Scotland U.K.
146 A4 North Uist i. Scotland U.K.
149 G2 Northumberland admin. div. England U.K.
234 B2 Northumberland PA U.S.A.
234 B2 Northumberland County county PA U.S.A.
85 G4 Northumberland Isles Qld Austr.
149 G2 Northumberland National Park England U.K.
225 H4 Northumberland Strait Can.
238 B3 North Umpqua r. OR U.S.A.
222 F5 North Vancouver B.C. Can.
233 F3 Northville NY U.S.A.
234 C2 North Wales PA U.S.A.
151 I2 North Walsham Norfolk, England U.K.
233 □H2 North Waterford ME U.S.A.
151 H3 North Weald Bassett Essex, England U.K.
215 E2 North West prov. S. Africa
264 F1 North West Atlantic Mid-Ocean Channel sea chan. N. Atlantic Ocean
86 B4 North West Cape W.A. Austr.
235 F1 North Westchester CT U.S.A.
209 D8 North-Western prov. Zambia
123 G3 North West Frontier prov. Pak.
266 F3 Northwest Pacific Basin sea feature N. Pacific Ocean
246 C1 Northwest Providence Channel Bahamas
225 J2 North West River Nfld. Can.
222 J2 Northwest Territories admin. div. Can.
149 G4 Northwich Cheshire, England U.K.
237 D5 North Wichita r. TX U.S.A.
234 D3 North Wildwood NJ U.S.A.
235 F1 North Windham CT U.S.A.
233 □H3 North Windham ME U.S.A.
268 N1 Northwind Ridge sea feature Arctic Ocean
149 H4 North Wingfield Derbyshire, England U.K.
151 F4 Northwood Isle of Wight, England U.K.
236 E3 Northwood IA U.S.A.
236 D2 Northwood ND U.S.A.
233 H3 Northwood NH U.S.A.
226 B3 Northwoods Beach WI U.S.A.
227 H4 North York Ont. Can.
149 I3 North York Moors moorland England U.K.
149 I3 North York Moors National Park England U.K.
149 H3 North Yorkshire admin. div. England U.K.
168 C2 Nortmoor Ger.
225 H4 Norton N.B. Can.
149 I3 Norton North Yorkshire, England U.K.
151 H2 Norton Suffolk, England U.K.
236 D4 Norton KS U.S.A.
232 B6 Norton VA U.S.A.
233 H2 Norton VT U.S.A.
213 F3 Norton Zimbabwe
149 H5 Norton Canes Staffordshire, England U.K.
Norton de Matos Angola see Balombo
150 D3 Norton Fitzwarren Somerset, England U.K.
226 D4 Norton Shores MI U.S.A.
220 B3 Norton Sound sea chan. AK U.S.A.
168 E1 Nortorf Ger.
168 C3 Nortrup Ger.
158 E4 Nort-sur-Erdre France
262 X2 Norvegia, Cape Antarctica
235 E1 Norwalk CT U.S.A.
232 B4 Norwalk OH U.S.A.
226 B4 Norwalk WI U.S.A.
235 E1 Norwalk r. CT U.S.A.
141 J3 Norway country Europe
233 □H2 Norway ME U.S.A.
227 I3 Norway Bay Que. Can.
223 L4 Norway House Man. Can.
264 I1 Norwegian Basin sea feature N. Atlantic Ocean
221 I2 Norwegian Bay Nunavut Can.
264 J1 Norwegian Sea N. Atlantic Ocean
227 G4 Norwich Ont. Can.
151 I2 Norwich Norfolk, England U.K.
233 G4 Norwich CT U.S.A.
233 F3 Norwich NY U.S.A.
146 □H1 Norwick Shetland, Scotland U.K.
233 H3 Norwood MA U.S.A.
231 D5 Norwood NC U.S.A.
233 F2 Norwood NY U.S.A.
232 A5 Norwood OH U.S.A.
92 B3 Norzagaray Phil.
102 J3 Noshiro Japan
137 F2 Nosivka Ukr.
136 D3 Noskivtsi Ukr.
214 C1 Nosop watercourse Africa alt. Nossob
Nosovka Ukr. see Nosivka
122 D4 Noşratābād Iran
146 □G1 Noss, Isle of i. Scotland U.K.
142 E2 Nossan r. Sweden
184 B2 Nossa Senhora da Boa Fé Port.
184 C1 Nossa Senhora da Graça de Póvoa e Meadas Port.
184 C2 Nossa Senhora da Graça do Divor Port.
184 C2 Nossa Senhora das Neves Port.
184 B2 Nossa Senhora da Torega Port.
184 C2 Nossa Senhora de Machede Port.
253 F3 Nossa Senhora do Livramento Brazil
216 □1b Nossa Senhora dos Remédios São Miguel Azores
142 E2 Nossebro Sweden
171 E4 Nossen Ger.
170 D2 Nossendorf Ger.
170 D2 Nossentiner Hütte Ger.
214 C2 Nossob watercourse Africa alt. Nosop
214 C1 Nossob Camp S. Africa
206 D3 Nossombougou Mali
213 □K4 Nosy Varika Madag.
176 G4 Noszlop Hungary
177 J4 Noszvaj Hungary
140 O1 Nota r. Fin./Rus. Fed.
225 I1 Notakwanon r. Nfld. Can.
193 F2 Notaresco Italy
241 K2 Notch Peak UT U.S.A.
174 D3 Noteć r. Pol.
198 B2 Notia Pindos mts Greece
222 G3 Notikewin r. Alta Can.
177 I4 Nőtincs Hungary
198 E3 Notio Aigaio admin. reg. Greece
Nótion Aiyaíon admin. reg. Greece see Notio Aigaio
198 C2 Notios Evvoïkos Kolpos sea chan. Greece
195 E6 Noto Sicilia Italy
195 E6 Noto, Golfo di g. Sicilia Italy
142 C2 Notodden Norway
104 C1 Noto-hantō pen. Japan
102 L1 Notoro-ko l. Japan
179 F5 Notranje Gorice Slovenia
225 G4 Notre Dame, Monts mts Que. Can.
225 K3 Notre Dame Bay Nfld. Can.
159 G2 Notre-Dame-de-Gravenchon France
Notre-Dame-de-Koartac Que. Can. see Quaqtaq
227 J3 Notre-Dame-de-la-Salette Que. Can.
158 D5 Notre-Dame-de-Monts France
158 E5 Notre-Dame-de-Riez France
162 C3 Notre-Dame-de-Sanilhac France
233 □H2 Notre-Dame-des-Bois Que. Can.
159 G4 Notre-Dame-d'Oé France
227 J2 Notre-Dame-du-Laus Que. Can.
227 H2 Notre-Dame-du-Nord Que. Can.
179 E4 Nötsch im Gailtal Austria
207 F5 Notsé Togo
102 L2 Notsuke-suidō sea chan. Japan/Rus. Fed.
227 G3 Nottawasaga Bay Ont. Can.
224 E3 Nottaway r. Que. Can.
168 E2 Nottensdorf Ger.
151 F2 Nottingham Nottingham, England U.K.
151 F2 Nottingham admin. div. England U.K.
234 B3 Nottingham PA U.S.A.
215 H3 Nottingham Road S. Africa
149 I4 Nottinghamshire admin. div. England U.K.
232 D6 Nottoway VA U.S.A.
232 E6 Nottoway r. VA U.S.A.
169 C4 Nottuln Ger.
223 J5 Notukeu Creek r. Sask. Can.
204 A5 Nouâdhibou Maur.
206 B2 Nouakchott Maur.
206 A2 Nouâmghâr Maur.
159 I4 Nouan-le-Fuzelier France
159 H4 Nouans-les-Fontaines France
157 F3 Nouart France
78 □5 Nouméa New Caledonia
207 H5 Noun r. Cameroon
206 E3 Nouna Burkina
215 E4 Noupoort S. Africa
Nouveau-Comptoir Que. Can. see Wemindji
Nouvelle Anvers Dem. Rep. Congo see Makanza
78 □5 Nouvelle Calédonie i. S. Pacific Ocean
Nouvelle Calédonie terr. S. Pacific Ocean see New Caledonia
Nouvelles Hébrides country S. Pacific Ocean see Vanuatu
156 B2 Nouvion France
158 E3 Nouvoitou France
159 G4 Nouzilly France
156 E3 Nouzonville France
123 G1 Nov Tajik.
176 F5 Nova Hungary
257 G4 Nova Almeida Brazil
254 C5 Nova América Brazil
256 A5 Nova Andradina Brazil
137 J3 Nova Astrakhan' Ukr.
256 C3 Nova Aurora Brazil
Novabad Tajik. see Novobod
Novabad Tajik. see Novobod
177 H3 Nová Baňa Slovakia
136 E2 Nova Borova Ukr.
176 E2 Nová Bystřice Czech Rep.
209 B6 Nova Caipemba Angola
256 A6 Nova Cantu Brazil
Nova Chaves Angola see Muconda
197 F3 Novaci Romania
196 E3 Nova Crnja Vojvodina, Srbija Yugo.
254 G3 Nova Cruz Brazil
177 H3 Nová Dubnica Slovakia
257 F3 Nova Era Brazil
Nova Esperança Angola see Buengas
256 A5 Nova Esperança Brazil
191 H5 Novafeltria Italy
Nova Freixa Moz. see Cuamba
257 F5 Nova Friburgo Brazil
Nova Gaia Angola see Cambundi-Catembo
Nova Goa Goa India see Panaji
213 G4 Nova Golegã Moz.
188 D3 Nova Gorica Slovenia
188 F3 Nova Gradiška Croatia
256 C4 Nova Granada Brazil
137 G3 Nova Haleshchyna Ukr.
257 F5 Nova Iguaçu Brazil
137 G4 Nova Kakhovka Ukr.
137 G4 Nova Kam"yanka Ukr.
177 H3 Nováky Slovakia
160 D3 Novalaise France
186 C2 Novales Spain
191 G2 Nova Levante Italy
257 F3 Nova Lima Brazil
Nova Lisboa Angola see Huambo
191 J4 Novalja Croatia
256 A5 Nova Londrina Brazil
177 J2 Nová Ľubovňa Slovakia
138 G4 Novalukoml' Belarus
213 G4 Nova Mambone Moz.
137 G4 Nova Mayachka Ukr.
137 F4 Nova Odesa Ukr.
176 E1 Nová Paka Czech Rep.
137 H3 Nova Parafiyivka Ukr.
196 E3 Nova Pazova Vojvodina, Srbija Yugo.
254 E4 Nova Pilão Arcado Brazil
256 D3 Nova Ponte Brazil
137 G3 Nova Praha Ukr.
190 D3 Novara Italy
190 D2 Novara prov. Piemonte Italy
195 E4 Novara di Sicilia Sicilia Italy
254 E4 Nova Remanso Brazil
256 D4 Nova Resende Brazil
171 D5 Nová Role Czech Rep.
254 D5 Nova Roma Brazil
254 E3 Nova Russas Brazil
225 H5 Nova Scotia prov. Can.
254 E4 Nova Sento Sé Brazil
257 E3 Nova Serrana Brazil
Nova Sintra Angola see Catabola
195 F2 Nova Siri Italy
137 H2 Nova Sloboda Ukr.
254 F4 Nova Soure Brazil
190 E2 Novate Mezzola Italy
240 F2 Novato CA U.S.A.
188 F3 Nova Topola Bos.-Herz.
134 I3 Novator Rus. Fed.
136 D3 Nova Ushytsya Ukr.
196 D4 Nova Varoš Srbija Yugo.
179 G1 Nová Včelnice Czech Rep.
257 G3 Nova Venécia Brazil
171 G5 Nová Ves I Czech Rep.
257 H2 Nova Viçosa Brazil
137 H3 Nova Vodolaha Ukr.
254 B5 Nova Xavantino Brazil
137 K2 Novaya Chigla Rus. Fed.
Novaya Kakhovka Ukr. see Nova Kakhovka
137 K2 Novaya Kalitva Rus. Fed.
120 B2 Novaya Kazanka Kazakh.
139 I1 Novaya Ladoga Rus. Fed.
Novaya Odessa Ukr. see Nova Odesa
Novaya Pismyanka Rus. Fed. see Leninogorsk
131 P2 Novaya Sibir', Ostrov i. Novosibirskiye O-va Rus. Fed.
137 J2 Novaya Usman' Rus. Fed.
Novaya Volodaga Ukr. see Nova Vodolaha
130 G2 Novaya Zemlya is Rus. Fed.
Novaya Zhizn Lipetskaya Oblast' Rus. Fed. see Kazinka
197 H4 Nova Zagora Bulg.
137 G4 Nova Zbur"yivka Ukr.
137 G3 Nove Ukr.
176 D3 Nové Hrady Czech Rep.
187 C6 Novelda Spain
191 F4 Novellara Italy
176 F1 Nové Město nad Metuj Czech Rep.
177 G3 Nové Mesto nad Váhom Slovakia
176 F2 Nové Město na Moravé Czech Rep.
175 K6 Nove Misto Ukr.
176 B6 Noventa di Piave Italy
191 G3 Noventa Vicentina Italy
161 C5 Noves France
183 F4 Novés Spain
171 D5 Nové Sedlo Czech Rep.
171 E5 Nové Strašecí Czech Rep.
177 H4 Nové Zámky Slovakia
Novgorod Rus. Fed. see Velikiy Novgorod
Novgorod Oblast admin. div. Rus. Fed. see Novgorodskaya Oblast'
Novgorod-Severskiy Ukr. see Novhorod-Sivers'kyy
139 I2 Novgorodskaya Oblast' admin. div. Rus. Fed.
Novgorod-Volynskiy Ukr. see Novohrad-Volyns'kyy
Novgradets Bulg. see Suvorovo
137 G3 Novhorodka Ukr.
137 G2 Novhorod-Sivers'kyy Ukr.
137 I3 Novhorods'ke Ukr.
227 F4 Novi MI U.S.A.
196 E3 Novi Bečej Vojvodina, Srbija Yugo.
136 E2 Novi Bilokorovychi Ukr.
137 F2 Novi Borovychi Ukr.
136 C2 Novi Chervyshcha Ukr.
121 J1 Novichikha Rus. Fed.
191 F4 Novi di Modena Italy
183 H3 Noviergas Spain
Novi Grad Bos.-Herz. see Bosanski Novi
191 I3 Novigrad Croatia
176 F5 Novigrad Podravski Croatia
197 F4 Novi Iskŭr Bulg.
177 J5 Novi Kneževac Vojvodina, Srbija Yugo.
100 G3 Novikovo Sakhalin Rus. Fed.
196 E3 Novi Kozarci Vojvodina, Srbija Yugo.
Novi Kritsim Bulg. see Stamboliyski
190 D4 Novi Ligure Italy
160 E1 Novillars France
165 D4 Noville Belgium
244 B2 Novillero Mex.
188 F2 Novi Marof Croatia
137 G2 Novi Mlyny Ukr.
156 E3 Novion-Porcien France
197 H4 Novi Pazar Bulg.
196 E4 Novi Pazar Srbija Yugo.
196 D3 Novi Sad Vojvodina, Srbija Yugo.
137 H3 Novi Sanzhary Ukr.
175 M6 Novi Strilyshcha Ukr.
188 F3 Novi Travnik Bos.-Herz.
188 E3 Novi Vinodolski Croatia
139 M3 Novki Rus. Fed.
100 G3 Novoaleksandropov Sakhalin Rus. Fed.
137 J2 Novoaleksandrovka Rus. Fed.
135 H7 Novoaleksandrovsk Rus. Fed.
Novoalekseyevka Kazakh. see Khobda
98 D1 Novoaltaysk Rus. Fed.
137 J4 Novoamvrosiyivs'ke Ukr.
135 H6 Novoanninskiy Rus. Fed.
251 F6 Novo Aripuanã Brazil
136 F3 Novoarkhanhel's'k Ukr.
137 J3 Novoaydar Ukr.
137 J4 Novoazovs'k Ukr.
137 J4 Novobataysk Rus. Fed.
137 J3 Novobelaya Rus. Fed.
196 E3 Novo Beograd Srbija Yugo.
137 J5 Novobeysugskaya Rus. Fed.
137 J3 Novobila Ukr.
123 G2 Novobod Tajik.
123 G2 Novobod Tajik.
Novobogatīnsk Kazakh. see Novobogatinskoye
120 B3 Novobogatinskoye Kazakh.
137 H4 Novobohdanivka Ukr.
137 J3 Novoborove Ukr.
100 D2 Novobureyskiy Rus. Fed.
134 I4 Novocheboksarsk Rus. Fed.
135 J5 Novocheremshansk Rus. Fed.
135 H7 Novocherkassk Rus. Fed.
257 G2 Novo Cruzeiro Brazil
137 H4 Novodanylivka Ukr.
137 J4 Novoderevyankovskaya Rus. Fed.
136 D3 Novodnistrovs'k Ukr.
121 H2 Novodolinka Kazakh.
137 I3 Novodonets'ke Ukr.
137 J3 Novodruzhes'k Ukr.
139 J4 Novodugino Rus. Fed.
134 H2 Novodvinsk Arkhangel'skaya Oblast' Rus. Fed.
Novoekonomicheskoye Ukr. see Dymytrov
136 E3 Novofastiv Ukr.
137 F4 Novofedorivka Ukr.
Novogroznenskiy Rus. Fed. see Oyskhara
Novogrudok Belarus see Navahrudak
139 K4 Novogurovskiy Rus. Fed.
255 C9 Novo Hamburgo Brazil
137 H4 Novohorivka Ukr.
256 C4 Novo Horizonte Brazil
137 G4 Novohradivka Ukr.
176 D3 Novohradské Hory mts Czech Rep.
136 D2 Novohrad-Volyns'kyy Ukr.
137 I3 Novohrodivka Ukr.
137 H4 Novohryhorivka Ukr.
137 H4 Novoivanivka Ukr.
129 D3 Novoivanovka Azer.
120 D1 Novokaolinovyy Rus. Fed.
129 E2 Novokayakent Rus. Fed.
Novokazalinsk Kazakh. see Ayteke Bi
135 H6 Novokhopersk Rus. Fed.
100 D2 Novokiyevskiy Uval Rus. Fed.
137 F4 Novokostyantynivka Ukr.
137 F3 Novokrasne Ukr.
137 J3 Novokrasnyanka Ukr.
135 H7 Novokubansk Rus. Fed.
Novokubanskiy Rus. Fed. see Novokubansk
120 B1 Novokuybyshevsk Rus. Fed.
130 J4 Novokuznetsk Rus. Fed.
137 G4 Novokyyivka Ukr.
129 E2 Novolakskoye Rus. Fed.
263 A2 Novolazarevskaya research stn Antarctica
137 J5 Novoleushkovskaya Rus. Fed.
Novolukoml' Belarus see Novalukoml'
139 L5 Novol'vovsk Rus. Fed.
137 J5 Novomalorossiyskaya Rus. Fed.
121 H2 Novomarkovka Kazakh.
137 H3 Novomar"yivka Ukr.
137 K2 Novomelovatka Rus. Fed.
188 E3 Novo Mesto Slovenia
139 L4 Novomichurinsk Rus. Fed.
135 G7 Novomikhaylovskiy Rus. Fed.
196 E3 Novo Miloševo Vojvodina, Srbija Yugo.
137 J4 Novominskaya Rus. Fed.
Novomirgorod Ukr. see Novomyrhorod
139 L4 Novomoskovsk Rus. Fed.
137 H3 Novomoskovs'k Ukr.
137 H4 Novomykhaylivka Ukr.
137 J3 Novomykil's'ke Ukr.
137 H3 Novomykolayivka Dnipropetrovs'ka Oblast' Ukr.
137 G4 Novomykolayivka Khersons'ka Oblast' Ukr.
137 H4 Novomykolayivka Khersons'ka Oblast' Ukr.
137 H4 Novomykolayivka Zaporiz'ka Oblast' Ukr.
137 F3 Novomyrhorod Ukr.
137 G4 Novonatalivka Ukr.
Novonazyvayevka Rus. Fed. see Nazyvayevsk
121 G4 Novonikolayevka Kazakh.
Novonikolayevsk Rus. Fed. see Novosibirsk
137 J5 Novonikolayevskaya Rus. Fed.
135 H6 Novonikolayevskiy Rus. Fed.
137 H4 Novooleksandrivka Ukr.
137 H4 Novooleksiyivka Ukr.
251 G5 Novo Olinda do Norte Brazil
177 I6 Novo Orahovo Vojvodina, Srbija Yugo.
254 E3 Novo Oriente Brazil
120 D2 Novoorsk Rus. Fed.
137 G2 Novoorzhyts'ke Ukr.
137 G5 Novoozerne Ukr.
136 E2 Novoozeryanka Ukr.
254 E3 Novo Parnarama Brazil
Novopashiyskiy Permskaya Oblast' Rus. Fed. see Gornozavodsk
137 I3 Novopavlivka Dnipropetrovs'ka Oblast' Ukr.
136 F4 Novopavlivka Mykolayivs'ka Oblast' Ukr.
107 F1 Novopavlovka Rus. Fed.
129 C2 Novopavlovsk Rus. Fed.
Novopavlovskaya Rus. Fed. see Novopavlovsk
137 H3 Novopetrivka Ukr.
137 H3 Novopidkryazh Ukr.
120 F1 Novopokrovka Kustanayskaya Oblast' Kazakh.
121 F1 Novopokrovka Severnyy Kazakhstan Kazakh.
121 J2 Novopokrovka Vostochnyy Kazakhstan Kazakh.
100 E3 Novopokrovka Primorskiy Kray Rus. Fed.
137 K1 Novopokrovka Tambovskaya Oblast' Rus. Fed.
137 H3 Novopokrovka Ukr.
135 H7 Novopokrovskaya Rus. Fed.
Novopolotsk Belarus see Navapolatsk
137 G4 Novopoltavka Mykolayivs'ka Oblast' Ukr.
137 I4 Novopoltavka Zaporiz'ka Oblast' Ukr.
137 J3 Novopskov Ukr.
Novo Redondo Angola see Sumbe
120 B2 Novorepnoye Rus. Fed.
135 G7 Novorossiysk Rus. Fed.
Novorossiyskiy Kazakh. see Novorossiyskoye
120 D2 Novorossiyskoye Kazakh.
137 J5 Novorozhdestvenskaya Rus. Fed.
121 F1 Novorybinka Kazakh.
138 G3 Novorzhev Rus. Fed.
136 E4 Novosamarka Ukr.
129 D3 Novosaratovka Azer.
171 E5 Novosedlice Czech Rep.
176 F3 Novosedly Czech Rep.
129 C1 Novoselitskoye Rus. Fed.
136 E4 Novoselivka Ukr.
137 G5 Novoselivs'ke Ukr.
197 F5 Novo Selo Macedonia
139 L3 Novoselovo Rus. Fed.
Novoselskoye Rus. Fed. see Achkhoy-Martan
138 G2 Novosel'ye Rus. Fed.
136 D3 Novoselytsya Ukr.
120 C1 Novosergiyevka Rus. Fed.
135 G7 Novoshakhtinsk Rus. Fed.
100 E3 Novoshakhtinskiy Rus. Fed.
137 J4 Novoshcherbinovskaya Rus. Fed.
135 J5 Novosheshminsk Rus. Fed.
130 J4 Novosibirsk Rus. Fed.
131 P2 Novosibirskiye Ostrova is Rus. Fed.
139 K5 Novosil' Rus. Fed.
137 J2 Novosil'skoye Rus. Fed.
137 G4 Novosofiyivka Ukr.
139 H3 Novosokol'niki Rus. Fed.
120 A1 Novospasskoye Rus. Fed.
137 J3 Novosvitlivka Ukr.
177 I2 Novoť Slovakia
137 J5 Novotitarovskaya Rus. Fed.
120 D2 Novotroitsk Rus. Fed.
Novotroitskoye Kazakh. see Tole Bi
137 I4 Novotroyits'ke Ukr.
137 H4 Novotroyits'ke Ukr.
137 H4 Novotroyits'ke Ukr.
Novoukrainka Kirovohrads'ka Oblast' Ukr. see Novoukrayinka
Novoukrainka Rivnens'ka Oblast' Ukr. see Novoukrayinka
137 F3 Novoukrayinka Kirovohrads'ka Oblast' Ukr.
136 C2 Novoukrayinka Rivnens'ka Oblast' Ukr.
120 D2 Novoural'sk Rus. Fed.
120 B2 Novouzensk Rus. Fed.
121 H1 Novovarshavka Rus. Fed.
137 H4 Novovasylivka Zaporiz'ka Oblast' Ukr.
137 I4 Novovasylivka Zaporiz'ka Oblast' Ukr.
136 C2 Novovolyns'k Ukr.
135 G6 Novovoronezh Rus. Fed.
Novovoronezhskiy Rus. Fed. see Novovoronezh
137 G4 Novovorontsovka Ukr.
137 G4 Novovoskresens'ke Ukr.
121 I4 Novovoznesenovka Kyrg.
137 H3 Novov"yazivs'ke Ukr.
136 B3 Novoyavorivs'ke Ukr.
139 L5 Novoye Dubovoye Rus. Fed.
121 J2 Novoyegor'yevskoye Rus. Fed.
139 M3 Novoye Leushino Rus. Fed.
139 K3 Novozavidovskiy Rus. Fed.
136 E3 Novozhyvotiv Ukr.
139 H5 Novozybkov Rus. Fed.
188 F3 Novska Croatia
176 D1 Nový Bor Czech Rep.
176 E1 Nový Bydžov Czech Rep.
156 E3 Novy-Chevrières France
Novyj Cholmogory Rus. Fed. see Arkhangel'sk
Novyj Holmogory Rus. Fed. see Arkhangel'sk
177 G2 Nový Jičín Czech Rep.
176 G2 Nový Malín Czech Rep.
Novyy Afon Georgia see Akhali Ap'oni
134 K2 Novyy Bor Rus. Fed.
Novyy Bug Ukr. see Novyy Buh
137 G4 Novyy Buh Ukr.
137 F2 Novyy Bykiv Ukr.
Novyy Donbass Ukr. see Dymytrov
Novyye Aneny Moldova see Anenii Noi
Novyye Belokorovichi Ukr. see Novi Bilokorovychi
120 A1 Novyye Burasy Rus. Fed.
Novyye Petushki Rus. Fed. see Petushki
Novyy Kholmogory Rus. Fed. see Arkhangel'sk
Novyy Margelan Uzbek. see Fergana
137 H3 Novyy Merchyk Ukr.
139 L3 Novyy Nekouz Rus. Fed.
135 G6 Novyy Oskol Rus. Fed.
136 C3 Novyy Rozdil Ukr.
137 G3 Novyystarodub Ukr.
137 J4 Novyy Svit Donets'ka Oblast' Ukr.
137 H5 Novyy Svit Respublika Krym Ukr.
129 E2 Novyy Terek r. Rus. Fed.
134 J4 Novyy Tor'yal Rus. Fed.
130 I3 Novyy Urengoy Rus. Fed.
100 E2 Novyy Urgal Rus. Fed.
Novyy Uzen' Kazakh. see Zhanaozen
175 M5 Novyy Vytkiv Ukr.
175 M6 Novyy Yarychiv Ukr.
134 K5 Novyy Zay Rus. Fed.
176 G3 Nový Život Slovakia
175 H4 Nowa Brzeźnica Pol.
175 L2 Nowa Chodorówka Pol.
175 J5 Nowa Dęba Pol.
174 G1 Nowa Karczma Pol.
174 E5 Nowa Ruda Pol.
175 K5 Nowa Sarzyna Pol.
175 J5 Nowa Słupia Pol.
174 D4 Nowa Sól Pol.
237 E4 Nowata OK U.S.A.
175 K2 Nowa Wieś Ełcka Pol.
174 F1 Nowa Wieś Lęborskie Pol.
174 G3 Nowa Wieś Wielka Pol.
175 J4 Nowa Wola Gołębiowska Pol.
122 B2 Nowdī Iran
174 G2 Nowe Pol.
175 I5 Nowe Brzesko Pol.
174 D4 Nowe Miasteczko Pol.
175 I3 Nowe Miasto Pol.
175 H2 Nowe Miasto Lubawskie Pol.
175 I4 Nowe Miasto nad Pilicą Pol.
147 B5 Nowen Hill hill Rep. of Ireland
175 H3 Nowe Ostrowy Pol.
175 K3 Nowe Piekuty Pol.
174 F4 Nowe Skalmierzyce Pol.
174 C2 Nowe Warpno Pol.
Nowgong Assam India see Nagaon
116 D4 Nowgong Madh. Prad. India
175 K2 Nowinka Pol.
122 C2 Now Kharegan Iran
175 K4 Nowodwór Pol.
174 D2 Nowogard Pol.
175 J2 Nowogród Pol.
174 D4 Nowogród Bobrzański Pol.
174 D3 Nowogródek Pomorski Pol.
174 D4 Nowogrodziec Pol.
238 F2 Nowood r. WY U.S.A.
Noworadomsk Pol. see Radomsko
175 L3 Nowosady Pol.
175 K6 Nowosielce Pol.
175 K5 Nowosielec Pol.
175 H4 Nowosolna Pol.
83 G3 Nowra N.S.W. Austr.
122 B2 Now Shahr Iran
123 H3 Nowshera Pak.
175 K3 Nowy Bartków Pol.
175 H3 Nowy Duninów Pol.
174 F2 Nowy Dwór Pol.
175 L2 Nowy Dwór Pol.
143 H4 Nowy Dwór Gdański Pol.
175 I3 Nowy Dwór Mazowiecki Pol.
175 I5 Nowy Korczyn Pol.
175 L5 Nowy Lubliniec Pol.
175 I6 Nowy Sącz Pol.
143 H4 Nowy Staw Pol.
175 I6 Nowy Targ Pol.
174 E3 Nowy Tomyśl Pol.
175 J6 Nowy Żmigród Pol.
227 I5 Noxen PA U.S.A.
96 D3 Noy, Xé r. Laos
Noya Cataluña Spain see L'Anoia
Noya Galicia Spain see Noia
130 I3 Noyabr'sk Rus. Fed.
158 D4 Noyal-Muzillac France
158 D4 Noyalo France
158 D3 Noyal-Pontivy France
159 G4 Noyant France
159 F4 Noyant-la-Plaine France
161 D3 Noyarey France
129 D3 Noyemberyan Armenia
159 F4 Noyen-sur-Sarthe France
156 D5 Noyers France
159 H4 Noyers-sur-Cher France
161 D4 Noyers-sur-Jabron France
114 C4 Noyil r. India
156 C3 Noyon France
158 E4 Nozay France
175 K6 Nozdrzec Pol.
160 E2 Nozeroy France
129 E2 Nozhay-Yurt Rus. Fed.
215 E4 Nozizwe S. Africa
178 B5 Nozza r. Italy
210 B4 Npitamaiong mt. Kenya
215 H4 Nqabeni S. Africa
215 F5 Nqamakwe S. Africa
215 H3 Nqutu S. Africa
211 A8 Nsalamu Zambia
211 B8 Nsanje Malawi
206 E5 Nsawam Ghana
207 H6 Nsoc Equat. Guinea
209 F7 Nsombo Zambia
207 G5 Nsukka Nigeria
209 E8 Ntambu Zambia
208 C5 Ntandembele Dem. Rep. Congo
211 B8 Ntcheu Malawi
211 B8 Ntchisi Malawi
207 H6 Ntem r. Cameroon
215 F2 Ntha S. Africa
215 G2 Nthorwane S. Africa
215 G4 Ntibane S. Africa
208 A4 Ntoum Gabon
217 □3a Ntsamouéni Njazidja Comoros
217 □3a Ntsoudjini Njazidja Comoros
207 H5 Ntui Cameroon
211 A5 Ntungamo Uganda
212 E4 Ntwetwe Pan salt pan Botswana
215 G4 Ntywenka S. Africa
159 F4 Nuaillé France
162 B2 Nuaillé-d'Aunis France
Nuanetsi r. Zimbabwe see Mwenezi
234 C1 Nuangola PA U.S.A.
203 F4 Nuba, Lake resr Sudan
210 A2 Nuba Mountains Sudan
168 E1 Nübbel Ger.
245 F5 Nube Flan, Cerro mt. Mex.
168 E1 Nübel Ger.
203 G4 Nubian Desert Sudan
140 M1 Nubivarri hill Norway
260 A5 Ñuble r. Chile
182 E1 Nubledo Spain
197 F2 Nucet Romania
241 M2 Nucla CO U.S.A.
171 D4 Nudersdorf Ger.
169 F5 Nüdlingen Ger.
139 K3 Nudol' Rus. Fed.
175 M4 Nudyzhe Ukr.
237 D7 Nueces r. TX U.S.A.
159 F5 Nueil-sur-Argent France
223 L2 Nueltin Lake Man./Nunavut Can.
165 E3 Nuenen Neth.
186 C2 Nueno Spain
187 E6 Nuestra Señora del Pilar Spain
183 F1 Nueva Spain
259 D9 Nueva, Isla i. Chile
250 C6 Nueva Alejandría Peru
242 □H6 Nueva Arcadia Hond.
185 F3 Nueva-Carteya Spain
237 D7 Nueva Ciudad Guerrero Mex.
251 E2 Nueva Esparta state Venez.
253 F5 Nueva Germania Para.
246 B2 Nueva Gerona Cuba
261 I4 Nueva Helvecia Uru.
260 A6 Nueva Imperial Chile
244 C4 Nueva Italia de Ruiz Mex.
184 D4 Nueva Jarilla Spain
250 B4 Nueva Loja Ecuador
242 □H6 Nueva Ocotepeque Hond.
261 H3 Nueva Palmira Uru.
243 E3 Nueva Rosita Mex.
243 H6 Nueva San Salvador El Salvador
245 E1 Nueva Villa de Padilla Mex.
Nueve de Julio Arg. see 9 de Julio
246 C2 Nuevitas Cuba
243 H4 Nuevo, Cayo i. Mex.
261 I3 Nuevo Berlín Uru.
242 D2 Nuevo Casas Grandes Mex.
242 D3 Nuevo Ideal Mex.
243 F3 Nuevo Laredo Mex.
241 J5 Nuevo León Mex.
244 E1 Nuevo León state Mex.
106 B1 Nuga Mongolia
210 F2 Nugaal admin. reg. Somalia
85 G5 Nuga Nuga, Lake Qld Austr.
81 B7 Nugget Point South I. N.Z.
192 B4 Nughedu di San Nicolò Sardegna Italy
139 K5 Nugr' r. Rus. Fed.
203 G3 Nugrus, Gebel mt. Egypt
114 C3 Nugu r. India
123 E5 Nuh, Ras pt Pak.
80 F3 Nuhaka North I. N.Z.
199 G2 Nuhköy Turkey
77 H2 Nui i. Tuvalu
Nui Con Voi r. Vietnam see Hông, Sông
159 F4 Nuillé-sur-Vicoin France
96 D4 Nui Ti On mt. Vietnam
156 E5 Nuits France
160 C1 Nuits-St-Georges France
108 A3 Nu Jiang r. China
Nu Jiang r. Myanmar see Salween
82 C3 Nukey Bluff hill S.A. Austr.
Nukha Azer. see Şäki
79 □2a Nuku'alofa Tongatapu Tonga
77 H2 Nukufetau i. Tuvalu
Nukuhiva i. Fr. Polynesia see Nuku Hiva
79 □3 Nuku Hiva i. Fr. Polynesia
77 H2 Nukulaelae i. Tuvalu
Nukulailai i. Tuvalu see Nukulaelae
Nukunau i. Gilbert Is Kiribati see Nikunau
Nukunono atoll Tokelau see Nukunonu
81 □1 Nukunonu atoll Tokelau
120 D4 Nukus Uzbek.
164 E3 Nuland Neth.
220 C3 Nulato AK U.S.A.
192 B4 Nule Sardegna Italy
187 C5 Nules Spain
86 D4 Nullagine W.A. Austr.
86 D4 Nullagine r. W.A. Austr.
82 B2 Nullarbor S.A. Austr.
82 B2 Nullarbor Plain S.A. Austr.
107 H3 Nulu'erhu Shan mts China
192 A4 Nulvi Sardegna Italy
83 F2 Numalla, Lake salt flat Qld Austr.
207 I4 Numan Nigeria
191 I5 Numana Italy
92 C4 Numancia Phil.
164 D3 Numansdorp Neth.
105 F2 Numata Japan
105 E3 Numazu Japan
215 H1 Numbi Gate S. Africa
84 C2 Numbulwar N.T. Austr.
142 C1 Numedal val. Norway
100 C3 Numin r. China
141 M3 Nummi Fin.
83 F4 Numurkah Vic. Austr.
221 N3 Nunap Isua c. Greenland
224 E1 Nunavik reg. Can.
223 L2 Nunavut admin. div. Can.
250 C3 Nunchía Col.
171 E4 Nünchritz Ger.
232 E3 Nunda NY U.S.A.
83 G2 Nundle N.S.W. Austr.
151 F2 Nuneaton Warwickshire, England U.K.
87 C6 Nungarin W.A. Austr.
107 H2 Nungnain Sum Nei Mongol China
213 H2 Nungo Moz.
220 B4 Nunivak Island AK U.S.A.
117 F5 Nunkapasi Orissa India
172 A2 Nunkirchen Ger.
116 D2 Nunkun mt. Jammu and Kashmir
131 T3 Nunligran Rus. Fed.
252 C3 Nuñoa Peru
182 D4 Nuñomoral Spain
171 E3 Nunsdorf Ger.
164 E2 Nunspeet Neth.
Nuojiang Sichuan China see Tongjiang
107 J1 Nuomin r. China
192 B4 Nuoro Sardegna Italy
192 B4 Nuoro prov. Sardegna Italy
78 □6 Nupani i. Santa Cruz Is Solomon Is
124 C2 Nuqrah Saudi Arabia
250 B3 Nuquí Col.
122 C2 Nur r. Iran
175 K3 Nur Pol.
121 G2 Nura r. Kazakh.
122 B4 Nūrâbâd Iran
192 B5 Nuragus Sardegna Italy
Nurakita i. Tuvalu see Niulakita
192 B5 Nurallao Sardegna Italy
192 B5 Nuraminis Sardegna Italy
120 F4 Nurata Uzbek.
121 F4 Nuratau, Khrebet mts Uzbek.
128 C1 Nurdağı Turkey
126 D3 Nur Dağları mts Turkey
190 E3 Nure r. Italy
192 A5 Nureci Sardegna Italy
Nurek Tajik. see Norak
Nurek Reservoir l. Tajik. see Obanbori Norak
Nurekskoye Vodokhranilishche l. Tajik. see Obanbori Norak
Nuremberg Ger. see Nürnberg
234 B2 Nuremberg PA U.S.A.
242 C2 Nuri Mex.
203 G5 Nuri Sudan
193 F2 Nuria, Monte mt. Italy
116 D2 Nurla Jammu and Kashmir
135 J5 Nurlat Rus. Fed.
134 J5 Nurlaty Rus. Fed.
140 O3 Nurmes Fin.
141 N3 Nurmijärvi Fin.
140 M3 Nurmo Fin.
173 F2 Nürnberg Ger.
148 C5 Nurney Carlow Rep. of Ireland
148 C4 Nurney Kildare Rep. of Ireland
Nurota Uzbek. see Nurata
123 G4 Nurpur Pak.
82 B2 Nurrai Lakes salt flat S.A. Austr.
192 B5 Nurri Sardegna Italy
83 F2 Nurri, Mount hill N.S.W. Austr.
140 K2 Nursfjellet mt. Norway
Nursia Italy see Norcia
172 D3 Nürtingen Ger.
175 K3 Nurzec r. Pol.
175 L3 Nurzec-Stacja Pol.
190 C3 Nus Italy
95 G5 Nusa Tenggara Barat prov. Indon.
93 B5 Nusa Tenggara Timur prov. Indon.
127 F3 Nusaybin Turkey
193 H4 Nusco Italy
93 D3 Nusela, Kepulauan is Irian Jaya Indon.
197 F2 Nuşfalău Romania
108 A3 Nu Shan mts China
123 F4 Nushki Pak.
172 C3 Nusplingen Ger.
179 F3 Nußbach Austria
173 G4 Nußdorf Ger.
173 G4 Nußdorf am Inn Ger.
178 D4 Nußdorf-Debant Austria
168 F2 Nusse Ger.
225 I1 Nutak Nfld. Can.
165 E4 Nuth Neth.
171 E3 Nuthe r. Ger.
151 G3 Nuthurst West Sussex, England U.K.
235 D2 Nutley NJ U.S.A.
241 M5 Nutrioso AZ U.S.A.
147 E2 Nutt's Corner Northern Ireland U.K.
84 C2 Nutwood Downs N.T. Austr.
221 M3 Nuuk Greenland
221 M2 Nuussuaq pen. Greenland
125 F2 Nuway Oman
214 B4 Nuwerus S. Africa
214 C5 Nuweveldberge mts S. Africa
192 A5 Nuxis Sardegna Italy
175 M4 Nuyno Ukr.
87 C7 Nuyts, Point W.A. Austr.
82 C3 Nuyts Archipelago is S.A. Austr.
178 A3 Nüziders Austria
114 D2 Nuzvid Andhra Prad. India
207 H5 Nwa Cameroon
212 E3 Nxai Pan National Park Botswana
95 F2 Nyaän, Bukit hill Indon.
87 C7 Nyabing W.A. Austr.
233 G4 Nyack NY U.S.A.
130 H3 Nyagan' Rus. Fed.
Nyagquka Sichuan China see Yajiang
Nyagrong Sichuan China see Xinlong
83 E3 Nyah West Vic. Austr.
111 E6 Nyainqêntanglha Feng mt. Xizang China
111 E6 Nyainqêntanglha Shan mts Xizang China
111 F5 Nyainrong Xizang China
215 F2 Nyakallong S. Africa
140 L3 Nyåker Sweden
Nyakh Rus. Fed. see Nyagan'
206 E5 Nyakrom Ghana
202 E6 Nyala Sudan
111 D6 Nyalam Xizang China
213 F3 Nyamandhiovu Zimbabwe
211 C7 Nyamtumbo Tanz.
Nyande Zimbabwe see Masvingo
134 H3 Nyandoma Rus. Fed.
134 G3 Nyandomskiy Vozvyshennost' hills Rus. Fed.
208 A5 Nyanga Congo
209 A5 Nyanga prov. Gabon
213 G3 Nyanga Zimbabwe
111 E6 Nyang Qu r. China
111 F6 Nyang Qu r. China
206 E4 Nyankpala Ghana
211 A5 Nyanza Rwanda
211 A6 Nyanza-Lac Burundi
95 G2 Nyapa, Gunung mt. Indon.
116 D3 Nyar r. India
176 G4 Nyárád Hungary
222 H2 Nyarling r. N.W.T. Can.
177 I5 Nyárlőrinc Hungary
177 I4 Nyársapát Hungary
211 A5 Nyarugumba Rwanda
211 B7 Nyasa, Lake Africa
Nyasaland country Africa see Malawi
138 F5 Nyasvizh Belarus
213 F3 Nyathi Zimbabwe
96 B3 Nyaunglebin Myanmar
96 A2 Nyaungu Myanmar
134 M3 Nyays r. Rus. Fed.
213 G3 Nyazura Zimbabwe
142 D4 Nyborg Denmark
140 O1 Nyborg Norway
140 M2 Nyborg Sweden
143 F3 Nybro Sweden
177 H2 Nýdek Czech Rep.
221 M1 Nyeboe Land reg. Greenland
138 F5 Nyeharelaye Belarus
111 E6 Nyêmo Xizang China
Nyenchen Tanglha Range mts Xizang China see Nyainqêntanglha Shan
210 C5 Nyeri Kenya
140 □ Ny-Friesland reg. Svalbard
143 F1 Nyhammar Sweden
111 D6 Nyima Xizang China
211 A8 Nyimba Zambia
111 F6 Nyingchi Xizang China
Nyinma Gansu China see Maqu
177 L4 Nyírábrány Hungary
177 K4 Nyíracsád Hungary
176 G4 Nyirád Hungary
177 K4 Nyíradony Hungary
177 L4 Nyírbátor Hungary
177 L4 Nyírbéltek Hungary
177 L4 Nyírbogát Hungary
177 K3 Nyírbogdány Hungary
177 L4 Nyírcsászári Hungary
177 K4 Nyíregyháza Hungary
177 K4 Nyírgelse Hungary
211 C5 Nyiri Desert Kenya
177 L4 Nyírlugos Hungary
177 K4 Nyírmártonfalva Hungary
177 K4 Nyírmihálydi Hungary
177 K3 Nyírtelek Hungary
177 K3 Nyírtét Hungary
177 K3 Nyírtura Hungary
210 C4 Nyiru, Mount Kenya
177 L4 Nyírvasvári Hungary
140 M3 Nykarleby Fin.
142 D4 Nykøbing Denmark
142 C3 Nykøbing Mors Denmark
142 D4 Nykøbing Sjælland Denmark
143 G2 Nyköping Sweden
143 F2 Nykroppa Sweden
143 G2 Nykvarn Sweden
134 B3 Nyland Sweden
213 F5 Nylstroom S. Africa
83 F3 Nymagee N.S.W. Austr.
83 H2 Nymboida N.S.W. Austr.
176 E1 Nymburk Czech Rep.
142 C4 Nymindegab Denmark
143 G2 Nynäshamn Sweden
83 F2 Nyngan N.S.W. Austr.
105 F2 Nyohō-san mt. Japan
159 F4 Nyoiseau France
215 G5 Nyokana S. Africa
138 D5 Nyoman r. Belarus/Lith.
138 E5 Nyomanskaya Nizina lowland Belarus
190 B2 Nyon Switz.
207 H6 Nyong r. Cameroon
161 D4 Nyons France
170 C1 Nyråd Denmark
176 C2 Nýřany Czech Rep.
134 L3 Nyrob Rus. Fed.
176 C2 Nýrsko Czech Rep.
174 F5 Nysa Pol.
174 F5 Nysa Kłodzka r. Pol.
Nysa Łużycka r. Ger./Pol. see Neiße
142 E2 Nysäter Sweden
140 K3 Nysätern Sweden
238 C3 Nyssa OR U.S.A.
Nystad Fin. see Uusikaupunki
142 D4 Nysted Denmark
105 E3 Nyūgasa-yama mt. Japan
134 I3 Nyuksenitsa Rus. Fed.
177 G4 Nyúl Hungary
209 F6 Nyunzu Dem. Rep. Congo
131 M3 Nyurba Rus. Fed.
129 E4 Nyuvadi Armenia
134 J3 Nyuvchim Rus. Fed.
131 M3 Nyuya Rus. Fed.
131 M3 Nyuya r. Rus. Fed.
175 M5 Nyvytsi Ukr.
136 B3 Nyzhankovychi Ukr.
137 H4 Nyzhni Sirohozy Ukr.
137 H4 Nyzhni Torhayi Ukr.
136 B3 Nyzhni Vorota Ukr.
136 B3 Nyzhniy Bystryy Ukr.
137 J3 Nyzhniy Nahol'chyk Ukr.
137 H5 Nyzhn'ohirs'kyy Ukr.
137 J3 Nyzhnya Dubanka Ukr.
137 H2 Nyzhnya Syrovatka Ukr.
137 H3 Nyzhnya Tersa r. Ukr.
177 M2 Nyzhnya Vysots'ke Ukr.
177 L2 Nyzhnya Yablun'ka Ukr.
137 H2 Nyzy Ukr.
209 A5 Nzambi Congo
208 F3 Nzara Sudan
206 C4 Nzébéla Guinea
211 B6 Nzega Tanz.
206 C5 Nzérékoré Guinea
209 B6 N'zeto Angola
206 D5 Nzi r. Côte d'Ivoire
206 D5 Nzo r. Côte d'Ivoire
210 B4 Nzoia r. Kenya
208 F4 Nzoro r. Dem. Rep. Congo
217 □3 Nzwani i. Comoros

O

236 D3 Oacoma SD U.S.A.
151 F2 Oadby Leicestershire, England U.K.
236 C2 Oahe, Lake SD U.S.A.
240 □ Oahu i. HI U.S.A.
Oaitupu i. Tuvalu see Vaitupu
82 E3 Oakbank S.A. Austr.
233 H4 Oak Bluffs MA U.S.A.
241 K2 Oak City UT U.S.A.
226 D4 Oak Creek WI U.S.A.
240 G3 Oakdale CA U.S.A.
235 F1 Oakdale CT U.S.A.
237 E6 Oakdale LA U.S.A.
235 E2 Oakdale NY U.S.A.
150 E2 Oakengates Telford and Wrekin, England U.K.
236 D2 Oakes ND U.S.A.
85 G5 Oakey Qld Austr.

232 D3 Oakfield NY U.S.A.
234 D2 Oakford PA U.S.A.
237 F5 Oak Grove LA U.S.A.
226 E3 Oak Grove MI U.S.A.
151 G2 Oakham Rutland, England U.K.
232 B4 Oak Harbor OH U.S.A.
238 B1 Oak Harbor WA U.S.A.
232 B5 Oak Hill OH U.S.A.
232 C6 Oak Hill WV U.S.A.
240 H3 Oakhurst CA U.S.A.
235 D2 Oakhurst NJ U.S.A.
240 G4 Oak Knolls CA U.S.A.
240 F3 Oakland CA U.S.A.
232 D5 Oakland MD U.S.A.
233 □I2 Oakland ME U.S.A.
236 D3 Oakland NE U.S.A.
235 D1 Oakland NJ U.S.A.
238 B3 Oakland OR U.S.A.
240 F3 Oakland airport CA U.S.A.
230 C4 Oakland City IN U.S.A.
83 F3 Oaklands N.S.W. Austr.
226 D5 Oak Lawn IL U.S.A.
151 G2 Oakley Bedfordshire, England U.K.
151 F3 Oakley Buckinghamshire, England U.K.
146 E5 Oakley Fife, Scotland U.K.
151 F3 Oakley Hampshire, England U.K.
236 C4 Oakley KS U.S.A.
227 E4 Oakley MI U.S.A.
232 D4 Oakmont PA U.S.A.
86 D4 Oakover r. W.A. Austr.
226 D5 Oak Park IL U.S.A.
235 D1 Oak Ridge NJ U.S.A.
238 B3 Oakridge OR U.S.A.
231 C4 Oak Ridge TN U.S.A.
234 C2 Oaks PA U.S.A.
234 D3 Oak Shade NJ U.S.A.
80 D3 Oakura North I. N.Z.
82 E3 Oakvale S.A. Austr.
240 H4 Oak View CA U.S.A.
224 E5 Oakville Ont. Can.
235 E1 Oakville CT U.S.A.
232 A4 Oakwood OH U.S.A.
232 A5 Oakwood OH U.S.A.
234 C3 Oakwood Beach NJ U.S.A.
81 C6 Oamaru South I. N.Z.
80 D3 Oaonui North I. N.Z.
81 D5 Oaro South I. N.Z.
105 F2 Ōashi-gawa r. Japan
240 I3 Oasis CA U.S.A.
238 D3 Oasis NV U.S.A.
197 F1 Oaşului, Munţii mts Romania
Oates Coast reg. Antarctica see Oates Land
263 K2 Oates Land reg. Antarctica
83 F5 Oatlands Tas. Austr.
214 E5 Oatlands S. Africa
245 F5 Oaxaca Mex.
245 F5 Oaxaca state Mex.
121 J1 Ob' r. Rus. Fed.
Ob, Gulf of sea chan. Rus. Fed. see Obskaya Guba
224 C3 Oba Ont. Can.
Oba i. Vanuatu see Aoba
Obaghan r. Kazakh. see Ubagan
104 B4 Obako-dake mt. Japan
128 A1 Obaköy Turkey
138 G4 Obal' Belarus
207 H5 Obala Cameroon
104 B3 Obama Japan
207 H5 Oban Nigeria
146 C5 Oban Argyll and Bute, Scotland U.K.
102 J4 Obanazawa Japan
123 G2 Obanbori Norak l. Tajik.
123 G1 Obanbori Qayroqqum resr Tajik.
207 H5 Oban Hills mt. Nigeria
182 D2 O Barco Spain
183 G2 Obarenes, Montes mts Spain
197 H2 Obârşeni, Dealul hill Romania
Obbia Somalia see Hobyo
140 M3 Obbola Sweden
197 G2 Obcina Feredeului ridge Romania
197 G2 Obcina Mare ridge Romania
197 G2 Obcina Mestecănişului ridge Romania
179 F3 Obdach Austria
164 D2 Obdam Neth.
Obdorsk Rus. Fed. see Salekhard
176 C2 Obecnice Czech Rep.
Óbecse Vojvodina, Srbija Yugo. see Bečej
222 G4 Obed Alta Can.
185 F2 Obejo Spain
129 A3 Öbektaş Turkey
138 E4 Obeliai Lith.
81 B6 Obelisk mt. South I. N.Z.
258 G2 Oberá Arg.
179 G3 Oberaich Austria
178 E3 Oberalm Austria
190 D2 Oberalpstock mt. Switz.
173 F4 Oberammergau Ger.
173 E2 Oberasbach Ger.
173 F4 Oberau Ger.
173 G4 Oberaudorf Ger.
169 E5 Oberaula Ger.
173 F4 Oberbayern admin. reg. Bayern Ger.
172 C2 Oberderdingen Ger.
173 F3 Oberding Ger.
169 F4 Oberdorla Ger.
178 D4 Oberdrauburg Austria
190 E1 Oberegg Switz.
169 F5 Oberelsbach Ger.
190 D1 Oberentfelden Switz.
172 D4 Oberessendorf Ger.
169 C5 Oberfell Ger.
171 C5 Oberfranken admin. reg. Bayern Ger.
169 F3 Oberg (Lahstedt) Ger.
190 C1 Obergösgen Switz.
179 G2 Ober-Grafendorf Austria
173 F3 Obergriesbach Ger.
173 E4 Obergünzburg Ger.
171 F4 Obergurig Ger.
179 G4 Oberhaag Austria
173 F3 Oberhaching Ger.
173 E2 Oberhaid Ger.
172 C3 Oberharmersbach Ger.
173 F3 Oberhausen Bayern Ger.
169 B4 Oberhausen Nordrhein-Westfalen Ger.
169 F5 Oberhof Ger.
190 C2 Oberhofen Switz.
178 C3 Oberhofen im Inntal Austria
157 H4 Oberhoffen-sur-Moder France
172 C3 Oberkirch Ger.
173 E3 Oberkochen Ger.
171 C5 Oberkotzau Ger.
168 C3 Oberlangen Ger.
171 F4 Oberlichtenau Ger.
178 D4 Oberlienz Austria
236 C4 Oberlin KS U.S.A.
237 E6 Oberlin LA U.S.A.
232 B4 Oberlin OH U.S.A.
172 D3 Obermarchtal Ger.
169 F5 Obermaßfeld-Grimmenthal Ger.
172 B2 Obermoschel Ger.
157 H4 Obernai France
179 E2 Obernberg am Inn Austria
172 D2 Obernburg am Main Ger.
173 E3 Oberndorf am Lech Ger.
172 C3 Oberndorf am Neckar Ger.
179 G2 Oberndorf an der Melk Austria
178 D3 Oberndorf bei Salzburg Austria
179 F2 Oberneukirchen Austria
169 F4 Obernfeld Ger.
172 C3 Obernheim Ger.
172 B2 Obernheim-Kirchenarnbach Ger.
169 E3 Obernkirchen Ger.
173 H3 Obernzell Ger.
173 E2 Obernzenn Ger.
171 F5 Oberoderwitz Ger.
172 C2 Ober-Olm Ger.
83 G3 Oberon N.S.W. Austr.
173 E4 Oberostendorf Ger.
179 E2 Oberösterreich land Austria
173 F2 Oberpfalz admin. reg. Bayern Ger.
173 G2 Oberpfälzer Wald mts Ger.
173 F3 Oberpframmern Ger.
179 H3 Oberpullendorf Austria
172 C2 Ober-Ramstadt Ger.
172 D4 Oberreute Ger.
172 B4 Oberried Ger.
173 E3 Oberrieden Ger.
190 E1 Oberriet Switz.
171 C4 Oberröblingen Ger.
172 C2 Ober-Roden Ger.
171 C4 Oberroßla Ger.
172 D2 Oberrot Ger.
172 B3 Oberrotweil Ger.
173 F3 Oberschleißheim Ger.
173 G3 Oberschneiding Ger.
171 E5 Oberschöna Ger.
179 H3 Oberschützen Austria
179 H2 Obersiebenbrunn Austria
190 D1 Obersiggenthal Switz.
169 E5 Obersinn Ger.
172 D2 Obersontheim Ger.
169 F4 Oberspier Ger.
172 D3 Oberstadion Ger.
173 E4 Oberstaufen Ger.
173 E4 Oberstdorf Ger.
172 D2 Oberstenfeld Ger.
173 G3 Obertaufkirchen Ger.
172 D4 Oberteuringen Ger.
172 B2 Oberthal Ger.
169 E5 Oberthulba Ger.
173 G3 Obertraubling Ger.
173 F2 Obertrubach Ger.
178 E3 Obertrum am See Austria
169 D5 Obertshausen Ger.
136 C3 Obertyn Ukr.
170 E2 Oberueckersee l. Ger.
169 D5 Oberursel (Taunus) Ger.
178 E4 Obervellach Austria
173 G2 Oberviechtach Ger.
190 D2 Oberwald Switz.
169 E4 Oberwälder Land reg. Ger.
179 H3 Oberwaltersdorf Austria
179 H3 Oberwart Austria
169 C5 Oberwesel Ger.
179 G2 Oberwölbling Austria
172 C3 Oberwolfach Ger.
179 F3 Oberwölz Austria
137 H2 Obesta r. Rus. Fed.
171 C4 Obhausen Ger.
93 C3 Obi i. Maluku Indon.
207 H4 Obi Nigeria
93 C3 Obi, Kepulauan is Maluku Indon.
251 H5 Óbidos Brazil
184 A1 Óbidos Port.
123 G2 Obigarm Tajik.
102 K2 Obihiro Japan
196 E4 Obilić Kosovo, Srbija Yugo.
135 I7 Obil'noye Rus. Fed.
173 G3 Obing Ger.
237 F4 Obion r. TN U.S.A.
250 D2 Obispos Venez.
261 F2 Obispo Trejo Arg.
105 F3 Obitsu-gawa r. Japan
162 D3 Objat France
174 F1 Objazda Pol.
175 M4 Oblapy Ukr.
179 E3 Öblarn Austria
135 H6 Oblivskaya Rus. Fed.
100 D2 Obluch'ye Rus. Fed.
139 K4 Obninsk Rus. Fed.
208 E3 Obo C.A.R.
214 C2 Obobogorap S. Africa
210 D2 Obock Djibouti
136 E3 Obodivka Ukr.
207 G5 Obolo Nigeria
182 C2 O Bolo Spain
137 G3 Obolon' Ukr.
186 C4 Obón Spain
95 F1 Obong, Gunung mt. Sarawak Malaysia
174 E3 Oborniki Pol.
174 E4 Oborniki Śląskie Pol.
135 G6 Oboyan' Rus. Fed.
134 H3 Obozerskiy Rus. Fed.
117 E4 Obra Uttar Prad. India
174 D3 Obra r. Pol.
196 E3 Obrenovac Srbija Yugo.
238 B3 O'Brien OR U.S.A.
172 D2 Obrigheim Ger.
172 C2 Obrigheim (Pfalz) Ger.
Obringa r. Switz. see Aare
176 C1 Obrnice Czech Rep.
197 I4 Obrochishte Bulg.
174 G3 Obrowo Pol.
126 D3 Obruk Turkey
175 J3 Obryte Pol.
174 E3 Obrzycko Pol.
82 C2 Observatory Hill hill S.A. Austr.
139 I4 Obsha r. Rus. Fed.
120 B2 Obshchiy Syrt hills Rus. Fed.
130 I3 Obskaya Guba sea chan. Rus. Fed.
175 K5 Obsza Pol.
137 G2 Obtove Ukr.
104 C3 Ōbu Japan
206 E5 Obuasi Ghana
207 H5 Obubra Nigeria
188 G3 Obudovac Bos.-Herz.
207 H5 Obudu Nigeria
136 F2 Obukhiv Ukr.
Obukhov Ukr. see Obukhiv
139 L4 Obukhovo Rus. Fed.
134 K4 Obva r. Rus. Fed.
190 D2 Obwalden canton Switz.
134 J3 Ob"yachevo Rus. Fed.
182 C1 O Cádabo Spain
231 D6 Ocala FL U.S.A.
242 E3 Ocampo Coahuila Mex.
244 D3 Ocampo Guanajuato Mex.
245 E2 Ocampo Tamaulipas Mex.
250 C2 Ocaña Col.
192 A3 Ocana Corse France
183 G5 Ocaña Spain
182 B2 O Castelo Spain
182 B2 O Castro Spain
191 G4 Occhiobello Italy
193 G3 Occhito, Lago di l. Italy
252 C4 Occidental, Cordillera mts Chile
250 B4 Occidental, Cordillera mts Col.
252 C4 Occidental, Cordillera mts Peru
190 D3 Occimiano Italy
232 E5 Occoquan VA U.S.A.
232 C6 Oceana WV U.S.A.
235 E2 Ocean Beach NY U.S.A.
233 F5 Ocean City MD U.S.A.
234 D3 Ocean City NJ U.S.A.
235 D3 Ocean County county NJ U.S.A.
222 E4 Ocean Falls B.C. Can.
235 D3 Ocean Gate NJ U.S.A.
235 D2 Ocean Grove NJ U.S.A.
Ocean Island Kiribati see Banaba
Ocean Island atoll HI U.S.A. see Kure Atoll
240 G4 Oceano CA U.S.A.
246 C1 Oceans Cay i. Bahamas
240 I5 Oceanside CA U.S.A.
237 F6 Ocean Springs MS U.S.A.
234 D3 Ocean View NJ U.S.A.
235 D3 Oceanville NJ U.S.A.
183 G3 Ocejón mt. Spain
78 □4a Ocha i. Chuuk Micronesia
186 B2 Ochagavía Spain
137 F4 Ochakiv Ukr.
129 B2 Och'amch'ire Georgia
134 K4 Ocher Rus. Fed.
136 E3 Ocheretnya Ukr.
137 H4 Ocheretuvate Ukr.
157 F4 Ochey France
146 E5 Ochil Hills Scotland U.K.
146 D6 Ochiltree East Ayrshire, Scotland U.K.
231 C6 Ochlockonee r. GA U.S.A.
175 H3 Ochnia r. Pol.
168 C2 Ocholt Ger.
246 □ Ocho Rios Jamaica
Ochrida, Lake Albania/Macedonia see Ohrid, Lake
173 E2 Ochsenfurt Ger.
172 D3 Ochsenhausen Ger.
169 C5 Ochtendung Ger.
198 D2 Ochthonia Greece
171 C3 Ochtmersleben Ger.
169 C3 Ochtrup Ger.
231 D6 Ocilla GA U.S.A.
141 L3 Ockelbo Sweden
168 D1 Ockholm Ger.
146 C5 Ockle Highland, Scotland U.K.
197 G2 Ocland Romania
231 D6 Ocmulgee r. GA U.S.A.
197 F2 Ocna Mureş Romania
197 G3 Ocna Sibiului Romania
136 D3 Ocniţa Moldova
197 G2 Ocolaşul Mare, Vârful mt. Romania
252 B4 Ocoña Peru
85 E4 O'Connell Creek r. Qld Austr.
226 C4 Oconomowoc WI U.S.A.
226 D3 Oconto WI U.S.A.
226 C3 Oconto Falls WI U.S.A.
182 B2 O Convento Spain
182 C2 O Corgo Spain
243 G6 Ocos Guat.
243 G5 Ocosingo Mex.
242 □I6 Ocotal Nic.
244 C3 Ocotlán Mex.
177 I3 Očová Slovakia
243 G5 Ocozocoautla Mex.
182 C5 Ocreza r. Port.
177 I4 Ócsa Hungary
177 H5 Öcsény Hungary
177 J5 Öcsöd Hungary
158 E2 Octeville France
159 G2 Octeville-sur-Mer France
October Revolution Island Severnaya Zemlya Rus. Fed. see Oktyabr'skoy Revolyutsii, Ostrov
234 B3 Octoraro Creek r. MD U.S.A.
242 □J8 Ocú Panama
213 H2 Ocua Moz.
245 E4 Ocuilan de Arteaga Mex.
252 D4 Ocurí Bol.
174 G2 Ocypel Pol.
206 E5 Oda Ghana
103 F6 Ōda Japan
203 H4 Oda, Jebel mt. Sudan
128 C1 Odabaşı Turkey
140 □C2 Ódáðahraun lava field Iceland
101 D4 Ŏdaejin N. Korea
104 C4 Ōdaigahara-zan mt. Japan
226 B2 Odanah WI U.S.A.
102 J3 Ōdate Japan
105 F3 Odawara Japan
142 B1 Odda Norway
142 D4 Odder Denmark
146 □H1 Oddsta Shetland, Scotland U.K.
184 C2 Odearce r. Port.
184 B3 Odeceixe Port.
223 L3 Odei r. Man. Can.
184 C3 Odeleite Port.
184 C3 Odeleite r. Port.
226 C5 Odell IL U.S.A.
184 B3 Odelouca r. Port.
173 F3 Odelzhausen Ger.
237 D7 Odem TX U.S.A.
184 B3 Odemira Port.
199 E2 Ödemiş Turkey
186 E3 Odena Spain
Ödenburg Hungary see Sopron
215 F2 Odendaalsrus S. Africa
143 F2 Odensbacken Sweden
142 D4 Odense Denmark
234 B3 Odenton MD U.S.A.
172 C2 Odenwald reg. Ger.
174 G6 Oder r. Ger. alt. Odra (Poland)
169 E4 Oder r. Ger./Pol.
170 F3 Oderberg Ger.
170 F1 Oderbucht b. Ger.
170 F2 Oderhaff b. Ger.
171 E3 Oderin Ger.
172 B2 Odernheim am Glan Ger.
191 H3 Oderzo Italy
136 F4 Odesa Ukr.
143 F2 Ödeshog Sweden
136 E4 Odes'ka Oblast' admin. div. Ukr.
Odessa Ukr. see Odesa
234 C3 Odessa DE U.S.A.
237 C6 Odessa TX U.S.A.
238 C2 Odessa WA U.S.A.
Odessa Oblast admin. div. Ukr. see Odes'ka Oblast'
Odesskaya Oblast' admin. div. Ukr. see Odes'ka Oblast'
121 H1 Odesskoye Rus. Fed.
Odessus Bulg. see Varna
158 B4 Odet r. France
184 B3 Odiáxere Port.
184 D3 Odiel r. Spain
206 D4 Odienné Côte d'Ivoire
151 G3 Odiham Hampshire, England U.K.
164 E2 Odijk Neth.
139 K4 Odintsovo Rus. Fed.
184 B2 Odivelas Beja Port.
184 A2 Odivelas Lisboa Port.
184 B2 Odivelas r. Port.
197 H3 Odobeşti Romania
197 H3 Odobeştilor, Măgura hill Romania
174 F4 Odolanów Pol.
171 F5 Odolena Voda Czech Rep.
159 F2 Odon r. France
183 I4 Odón Spain
164 F2 Odoorn Neth.
197 G2 Odorheiu Secuiesc Romania
139 K5 Odoyev Rus. Fed.
174 G6 Odra r. Pol. alt. Oder (Germany)
183 F2 Odra r. Spain
137 H4 Odradivka Ukr.
177 G2 Odry Czech Rep.
175 I4 Odrzywół Pol.
196 D3 Odžaci Vojvodina, Srbija Yugo.
213 G3 Odzi r. Zimbabwe
Oea Libya see Tripoli
169 F3 Oebisfelde Ger.
169 E4 Oedelsheim (Oberweser) Ger.
171 E5 Oederan Ger.
168 E2 Oederquart Ger.
163 A5 Œeyreluy France
164 E3 Oeffelt Neth.
164 D2 Oegstgeest Neth.
254 E3 Oeiras Brazil
184 A2 Oeiras Port.
184 C3 Oeiras r. Port.
169 D4 Oelde Ger.
168 E2 Oelixdorf Ger.
236 C3 Oelrichs SD U.S.A.
171 D5 Oelsnitz Sachsen Ger.
171 D5 Oelsnitz Sachsen Ger.
236 F3 Oelwein IA U.S.A.
164 F2 Oene Neth.
84 C2 Oenpelli N.T. Austr.
190 C1 Oensingen Switz.
168 E2 Oerel Ger.
168 F2 Oering Ger.
169 F5 Oerlenbach Ger.
169 D4 Oerlinghausen Ger.
Oesel i. Estonia see Hiiumaa
165 E5 Oesling hills Lux.
165 D3 Oesterdam barrage Neth.
171 C5 Oettersdorf Ger.
173 E3 Oettingen in Bayern Ger.
178 B3 Oetz Austria
168 F2 Oetzen Ger.
168 E1 Oeversee Ger.
104 B3 Ōe-yama hill Japan
127 F2 Of Turkey
238 F2 O'Fallon r. MT U.S.A.
193 I3 Ofanto r. Italy
193 F2 Ofena Italy
207 G4 Offa Nigeria
147 D3 Offaly county Rep. of Ireland
190 E3 Offanengo Italy
157 G5 Offemont France
169 D5 Offenbach am Main Ger.
172 C2 Offenbach an der Queich Ger.
173 G3 Offenberg Ger.
172 B3 Offenburg Ger.
140 K3 Offerdal Sweden
193 F2 Offida Italy
173 E3 Offingen Ger.
156 B3 Offranville France
140 L1 Ofotfjorden sea chan. Norway
172 D3 Ofterdingen Ger.
78 □2 Ofu i. American Samoa
102 J4 Ōfunato Japan
95 F2 Oga r. Indon.
102 I4 Oga Japan
105 F1 Oga-dake mt. Japan
210 E3 Ogadēn reg. Eth.
104 C3 Ōgaki Japan
236 C3 Ogallala NE U.S.A.
94 D3 Ogan r. Indon.
103 □3 Ogasawara-shotō is N. Pacific Ocean
105 E2 Ōga-tō mt. Japan
105 F2 Ogawa Japan
102 J3 Ogawara-ko l. Japan
Ogbomosho Nigeria see Ogbomoso
207 G4 Ogbomoso Nigeria
236 E3 Ogden IA U.S.A.
238 E3 Ogden UT U.S.A.
222 C3 Ogden, Mount B.C. Can.
234 D1 Ogdensburg NJ U.S.A.
233 F2 Ogdensburg NY U.S.A.
231 D6 Ogeechee r. GA U.S.A.
226 B3 Ogema WI U.S.A.
168 C2 Ogenbargen Ger.
156 E4 Oger France
163 B5 Ogeu-les-Bains France
157 G4 Ogéviller France
190 E3 Oggiono Italy
78 □6 Ogho Choiseul Solomon Is
224 C4 Ogidaki Ont. Can.
220 E3 Ogilvie r. Y.T. Can.
220 D3 Ogilvie Mountains Y.T. Can.
129 C4 Oğlaksuyu Turkey
122 C2 Oglanly Turkm.
192 B2 Ogliastro Corse France
190 F3 Oglio r. Italy
85 G4 Ogmore Qld Austr.
150 D3 Ogmore Vale of Glamorgan, Wales U.K.
150 D3 Ogmore Vale Bridgend, Wales U.K.
160 D1 Ognon r. France
Oğnut Turkey see Göynük
93 B2 Ogoamas, Gunung mt. Indon.
207 H5 Ogoja Nigeria
224 C3 Ogoki r. Ont. Can.
224 C3 Ogoki Lake Ont. Can.
208 A5 Ogooué r. Gabon
208 B5 Ogooué-Ivindo prov. Gabon
208 B5 Ogooué-Lolo prov. Gabon
208 A5 Ogooué-Maritime prov. Gabon
197 F4 Ogosta r. Bulg.
207 F5 Ogou r. Togo
87 C6 O'Grady, Lake salt flat W.A. Austr.
197 F5 Ogražden mts Bulg./Macedonia
Ograzhden mts Bulg./Macedonia see Ogražden
138 E3 Ogre Latvia
138 E3 Ogre r. Latvia
175 J3 Ogrodniki Pol.
175 H5 Ogrodzieniec Pol.
171 F4 Ogrosen Ger.
182 B2 O Grove Spain
139 L3 Ogudnevo Rus. Fed.
188 E3 Ogulin Croatia
207 F5 Ogun state Nigeria
233 □H3 Ogunquit ME U.S.A.
129 E3 Oğuz Azer.
177 K6 Ohaba Lungă Romania
207 G5 Ohafia Nigeria
81 A6 Ohai South I. N.Z.
80 E3 Ohakune North I. N.Z.
185 H3 Ohanes Spain
212 C3 Ohangwena admin. reg. Namibia
226 D5 O'Hare airport IL U.S.A.
80 E4 Ohau North I. N.Z.
81 C6 Ohau r. South I. N.Z.
80 E2 Ohaupo North I. N.Z.
Ohcejohka Fin. see Utsjoki
168 C2 Ohe r. Ger.
173 H3 Ohe r. Ger.
Ohétéroah i. Îs Australes Fr. Polynesia see Rurutu
165 E4 Ohey Belgium
260 B4 O'Higgins admin. reg. Chile
259 B8 O'Higgins, Lago l. Chile
80 E2 Ohinewai North I. N.Z.
226 C5 Ohio IL U.S.A.
236 F4 Ohio r. Ohio/West Virginia U.S.A.
232 B4 Ohio state U.S.A.
232 A4 Ohio City OH U.S.A.
262 Q1 Ohio Range mts Antarctica
235 D1 Ohioville NY U.S.A.
105 E3 Ōhito Japan
137 H3 Ohiyivka Ukr.
172 B3 Ohlsbach Ger.
179 E3 Ohlsdorf Austria
173 F4 Ohlstadt Ger.
169 D5 Ohm r. Ger.
138 F2 Õhne r. Estonia
169 C3 Ohne Ger.
172 C4 Öhningen Ger.
79 □2 'Ohonua Tonga
80 F2 Ohope North I. N.Z.
177 G3 Ohrady Slovakia
169 F5 Ohrdruf Ger.
176 D1 Ohře r. Czech Rep.
171 C3 Ohre r. Ger.
196 E5 Ohrid Macedonia
196 E5 Ohrid, Lake Albania/Macedonia
Ohridsko Ezero l. Albania/Macedonia see Ohrid, Lake
213 F5 Ohrigstad S. Africa
172 D2 Öhringen Ger.
Ohrit, Liqeni i l. Albania/Macedonia see Ohrid, Lake
169 F3 Ohrum Ger.
80 E3 Ohura North I. N.Z.
182 B4 Oiã Port.
251 I4 Oiapoque Brazil
251 I3 Oiapoque r. Brazil/Fr. Guiana
186 B1 Oiartzun Spain
146 D4 Oich r. Scotland U.K.
113 □1 Oidhuni i. S. Male Maldives
104 B3 Ōi-gawa r. Japan
105 E4 Ōi-gawa r. Japan
156 C2 Oignies France
160 D2 Oignin r. France
164 E3 Oijen Neth.
Oik Kazakh. see Uyuk
232 D4 Oil City PA U.S.A.
240 H4 Oildale CA U.S.A.
147 E4 Oilgate Rep. of Ireland
147 C2 Oily r. Rep. of Ireland
182 C3 Oímbra Spain
108 A2 Oi Qu r. Xizang China
102 J3 Oirase-gawa r. Japan
159 F5 Oiron France
164 E3 Oirschot Neth.
156 C3 Oise dept Picardie France
156 C4 Oise r. France
160 D1 Oiselay-et-Grachaux France
156 B3 Oisemont France
159 F3 Oisseau France
156 B3 Oissel France
164 E3 Oisterwijk Neth.
103 E7 Ōita Japan
103 E7 Ōita pref. Japan
182 B2 Oitavén r. Spain
198 C2 Oiti mt. Greece
197 H2 Oituz r. Romania
159 I4 Oizon France
104 C2 Oizuruga-dake mt. Japan
240 H4 Ojai CA U.S.A.
185 G2 Ojailén r. Spain
Ojalava i. Samoa see Upolu
138 F2 Ojamaa r. Estonia
141 K3 Öje Sweden
185 F4 Ojén Spain
104 B4 Ōji Japan
242 D2 Ojinaga Mex.
245 F4 Ojitlán Mex.
105 E1 Ojiya Japan
207 G5 Ojobo Nigeria
244 C2 Ojocaliente Mex.
239 F4 Ojo Caliente NM U.S.A.
258 C2 Ojos del Salado, Nevado mt. Arg./Chile
183 I4 Ojos Negros Spain
175 I3 Ojrzeń Pol.
207 H5 Oju Nigeria
141 K3 Öjung Sweden
207 G5 Oka Nigeria
139 M4 Oka r. Rus. Fed.
212 C4 Okahandja Namibia
Okahu b. South I. N.Z. see Jackson Bay
80 E3 Okahukura North I. N.Z.
80 D1 Okaihau North I. N.Z.
81 D5 Okains Bay Canterbury N.Z.
207 F4 Okaka Nigeria
212 C4 Okakarara Namibia
225 I1 Okak Islands Nfld. Can.
175 H2 Okalewo Pol.
222 G5 Okanagan Falls B.C. Can.
222 G5 Okanagan Lake B.C. Can.
238 C1 Okanogan WA U.S.A.
238 C1 Okanogan r. WA U.S.A.
177 K5 Okány Hungary
123 H4 Okara Pak.
80 D3 Okato North I. N.Z.
212 D3 Okavango r. Botswana/Namibia
212 C3 Okavango admin. reg. Namibia
212 D3 Okavango Delta swamp Botswana
103 E7 Ōkawa Japan
105 E2 Okaya Japan
103 F6 Okayama Japan
103 F6 Okayama pref. Japan
104 D4 Okazaki Japan
129 B3 Okçular Dağı mt. Turkey
231 D7 Okeechobee FL U.S.A.
231 D7 Okeechobee, Lake FL U.S.A.
237 D4 Okeene OK U.S.A.
105 F2 Okegawa Japan
150 C4 Okehampton Devon, England U.K.
207 F4 Oke-Iho Nigeria
237 D5 Okemah OK U.S.A.
150 C4 Okement r. England U.K.
207 G5 Okene Nigeria
169 F3 Oker r. Ger.
116 B5 Okha Gujarat India
100 G1 Okha Sakhalin Rus. Fed.
Okhadunga Nepal see Okhaldhunga
117 F4 Okhaldhunga Nepal
134 K4 Okhansk Rus. Fed.
131 P4 Okhotka r. Rus. Fed.
131 P4 Okhotsk Rus. Fed.
102 L1 Okhotsk, Sea of Japan/Rus. Fed.
Okhotskoye More sea Japan/Rus. Fed. see Okhotsk, Sea of
137 H4 Okhrimivka Ukr.
Okhthoniá Greece see Ochthonia
137 H2 Okhtyrka Ukr.
139 I3 Okhvat Rus. Fed.
214 A3 Okiep S. Africa
102 □2 Okinawa Japan
102 □2 Okinawa i. Japan
102 □1 Okinawa pref. Japan
Okinawa-guntō is Japan see Okinawa-shotō
102 □1 Okinawa-shotō is Japan
102 □1 Okinoerabu-jima i. Japan
103 F5 Oki-shotō is Japan
207 G5 Okitipupa Nigeria
96 A3 Okkan Myanmar
237 D5 Oklahoma state U.S.A.
237 D5 Oklahoma City OK U.S.A.
231 D6 Oklawaha r. FL U.S.A.
237 D5 Okmulgee OK U.S.A.
177 L3 Okna r. Slovakia
Oknitsa Moldova see Ocniţa
177 G4 Okoč Slovakia
207 H5 Okola Cameroon
237 F5 Okolona MS U.S.A.
232 A4 Okolona OH U.S.A.
208 B5 Okondja Gabon
174 E2 Okonek Pol.
175 L4 Okopy Pol.
177 G6 Okor r. Hungary
222 H5 Okotoks Alta Can.
139 I4 Okovskiy Les for. Rus. Fed.
208 B5 Okoyo Congo
121 J3 Okpety, Gora mt. Kazakh.
176 E2 Okříšky Czech Rep.
176 E2 Okrouhlice Czech Rep.
175 K4 Okrzeja Pol.
175 I5 Oksa Pol.
142 C4 Oksbøl Denmark
140 M1 Øksfjord Norway
134 G3 Oksovskiy Rus. Fed.
140 K2 Oksskolten mt. Norway
123 H2 Oksu r. Tajik.
Oktemberyan Armenia see Hoktemberyan
96 B3 Oktwin Myanmar
Oktyabr' Kazakh. see Kandyagash
121 I4 Oktyabr' Kazakh.
139 K3 Oktyabr' Rus. Fed.
Oktyabr'sk Kazakh. see Kandyagash
120 B1 Oktyabr'sk Rus. Fed.
Oktyabr'skaya Belarus see Aktsyabrskaya
137 J4 Oktyabr'skaya Rus. Fed.
Oktyabr'skiy Homyel'skaya Voblasts' Belarus see Aktsyabrski
Oktyabr'skiy Vitsyebskaya Voblasts' Belarus see Aktsyabrski
120 E1 Oktyabr'skiy Kazakh.
100 D1 Oktyabr'skiy Rus. Fed.
134 H3 Oktyabr'skiy Rus. Fed.
137 I2 Oktyabr'skiy Rus. Fed.
139 M3 Oktyabr'skiy Rus. Fed.
131 Q4 Oktyabr'skiy Rus. Fed.
137 J5 Oktyabr'skiy Rus. Fed.
Oktyabr'skiy Rus. Fed. see Takhtamukay
135 K5 Oktyabr'skiy Rus. Fed.
137 J4 Oktyabr'skiy Rus. Fed.
139 L4 Oktyabr'skiy Rus. Fed.
139 L5 Oktyabr'skiy Rus. Fed.
134 L4 Oktyabr'skiy Rus. Fed.
135 H7 Oktyabr'skiy Rus. Fed.
120 F1 Oktyabr'skoye Kazakh.
120 E1 Oktyabr'skoye Rus. Fed.
130 H3 Oktyabr'skoye Khanty-Mansiyskiy Avtonomnyy Okrug Rus. Fed.
139 L5 Oktyabr'skoye Rus. Fed.
120 C1 Oktyabr'skoye Rus. Fed.
129 D2 Oktyabr'skoye Rus. Fed.
131 K2 Oktyabr'skoy Revolyutsii, Ostrov i. Severnaya Zemlya Rus. Fed.
122 D1 Oktyah'sk Turkm.
188 F3 Okučani Croatia
103 E7 Ōkuchi Japan
139 I2 Okulovka Rus. Fed.
129 B2 Ok'umi Georgia
Okureshi Georgia see Oqureshi
81 B5 Okuru South I. N.Z.
104 D3 Oku-sangai-dake mt. Japan
102 I2 Okushiri-tō i. Japan
207 F4 Okuta Nigeria
131 Q4 Ola Rus. Fed.
237 E5 Ola AR U.S.A.
140 □B2 Ólafsvík Iceland
186 B2 Olague Spain
113 □1 Olahali i. N. Male Maldives
138 D3 Olaine Latvia
114 C3 Olakkur Tamil Nadu India
182 B5 Olalhas Port.
161 E4 Olan, Pic d' mt. France
240 H3 Olancha CA U.S.A.
240 H3 Olancha Peak CA U.S.A.
242 □I6 Olanchito Hond.
143 G3 Öland i. Sweden
161 A5 Olargues France
177 K5 Olari Romania
82 E3 Olary S.A. Austr.
177 K3 Olaszliszka Hungary
236 E4 Olathe KS U.S.A.
114 C4 Olavakod Kerala India
261 G5 Olavarría Arg.
183 I2 Olave Spain
140 □ Olav V Land reg. Svalbard
174 F5 Oława Pol.
183 H2 Olazagutía Spain
187 C4 Olba Spain
179 H3 Olbendorf Austria
171 E5 Olbernhau Ger.
171 F5 Olbersdorf Ger.
171 C4 Olbersleben Ger.
192 B4 Olbia Sardegna Italy
175 K5 Olbięcin Pol.
176 D2 Olbramovice Czech Rep.
177 K5 Olcea Romania
129 C3 Ölçek Turkey
173 F3 Olching Ger.
232 D3 Olcott NY U.S.A.
129 C3 Ölçülü Turkey
246 C2 Old Bahama Channel Bahamas/Cuba
151 F3 Old Basing Hampshire, England U.K.
114 D2 Old Bastar Madh. Prad. India
235 D2 Old Bridge NJ U.S.A.
150 E2 Oldbury West Midlands, England U.K.
147 D3 Oldcastle Rep. of Ireland
86 E3 Old Cherrabun W.A. Austr.
150 D1 Old Colwyn Conwy, Wales U.K.
85 E4 Old Cork Qld Austr.
220 E3 Old Crow Y.T. Can.
146 D6 Old Dailly South Ayrshire, Scotland U.K.
164 F2 Oldeberkoop Neth.
164 E1 Oldeboorn Neth.
164 E2 Oldebroek Neth.
164 F1 Oldehove Neth.
164 E2 Oldemarkt Neth.
168 D2 Oldenbrok Ger.
168 D2 Oldenburg Ger.
168 F1 Oldenburg in Holstein Ger.
168 E2 Oldendorf Ger.
168 F2 Oldendorf (Luhe) Ger.
168 D1 Oldenswort Ger.
164 F2 Oldenzaal Neth.
140 M1 Olderdalen Norway
151 I3 Old Felixstowe Suffolk, England U.K.
87 D7 Oldfield r. W.A. Austr.
233 F3 Old Forge NY U.S.A.
234 C1 Old Forge PA U.S.A.
232 B4 Old Fort OH U.S.A.
87 C5 Old Gidgee W.A. Austr.
149 G4 Oldham Greater Manchester, England U.K.
246 □ Old Harbour Jamaica
246 □ Old Harbour Bay Jamaica
147 C5 Old Head of Kinsale hd Rep. of Ireland
171 C4 Oldisleben Ger.
150 E3 Oldland South Gloucestershire, England U.K.
149 J4 Old Leake Lincolnshire, England U.K.
235 F1 Old Lyme CT U.S.A.
220 G5 Oldman r. Alta Can.
234 C3 Oldman's Creek r. NJ U.S.A.
146 F4 Oldmeldrum Aberdeenshire, Scotland U.K.
209 F8 Old Mkushi Zambia
215 G4 Old Morley S. Africa
235 G1 Old Mystic CT U.S.A.
233 □H3 Old Orchard Beach ME U.S.A.
225 K4 Old Perlican Nfld. Can.
240 H4 Old River CA U.S.A.
147 E4 Old Ross Rep. of Ireland
222 H5 Olds Alta Can.
235 F1 Old Saybrook CT U.S.A.
233 □H2 Old Speck Mountain ME U.S.A.
168 D1 Oldsum Ger.
147 E3 Oldtown Rep. of Ireland
149 G3 Old Town Cumbria, England U.K.
232 B5 Oldtown KY U.S.A.
233 □I2 Old Town ME U.S.A.
211 B5 Olduvai Gorge tourist site Tanz.
232 C4 Old Washington OH U.S.A.
234 D2 Oldwick NJ U.S.A.
241 J4 Old Woman Mountains CA U.S.A.
106 D1 Öldziyt Mongolia
232 D3 Olean NY U.S.A.
175 K1 Olecko Pol.
182 C5 Oledo Port.
190 D3 Oleggio Italy
182 C5 Oleiros Port.
131 N3 Olekma r. Rus. Fed.
131 N3 Olekminsk Rus. Fed.
137 G2 Oleksandrivka Chernihivs'ka Oblast' Ukr.
137 I3 Oleksandrivka Donets'ka Oblast' Ukr.
137 G3 Oleksandrivka Kirovohrads'ka Oblast' Ukr.
137 F4 Oleksandrivka Mykolayivs'ka Oblast' Ukr.
137 H4 Oleksandrivka Zaporiz'ka Oblast' Ukr.
Oleksandrivs'k Ukr. see Zaporizhzhya
137 G3 Oleksandriya Kirovohrads'ka Oblast' Ukr.
136 D2 Oleksandriya Rivnens'ka Oblast' Ukr.
137 I3 Oleksiyevo-Druzhkivka Ukr.
137 J3 Oleksiyivka Ukr.
165 D3 Olen Belgium
142 A2 Ølen Norway
134 F1 Olenegorsk Rus. Fed.
131 M3 Olenek Rus. Fed.
131 M2 Olenek r. Rus. Fed.
Ölengti r. Kazakh. see Olenti
139 I3 Olenino Rus. Fed.
137 I4 Olenivka Ukr.
Olenivs'ki Kar"yery Ukr. see Dokuchayevs'k
120 C2 Olenti r. Kazakh.
121 H1 Olenti r. Kazakh.
107 G1 Olentuy Rus. Fed.
Olenya Rus. Fed. see Olenegorsk
162 A3 Oléron, Île d' i. France
186 E3 Olesa de Montserrat Spain
Oleshky Ukr. see Tsyurupyns'k
137 F2 Oleshnya Chernihivs'ka Oblast' Ukr.
137 H2 Oleshnya Sums'ka Oblast' Ukr.
136 C3 Oles'ko Ukr.
174 F4 Oleśnica Pol.
175 J5 Oleśnica Pol.
175 I5 Olesno Małopolskie Pol.
174 G5 Olesno Opolskie Pol.
175 L5 Oleszyce Pol.
192 B2 Oletta Corse France
163 E6 Olette France
95 G5 Olet Tongo mt. Sumbawa Indon.
136 D2 Olevs'k Ukr.
234 C2 Oley PA U.S.A.
169 C4 Olfen Ger.
140 K2 Ølfjellet mt. Norway
100 E4 Ol'ga Rus. Fed.
224 E3 Olga, Lac l. Que. Can.
84 B5 Olga, Mount N.T. Austr.
140 □ Olgastretet str. Svalbard
190 E3 Olginate Italy
137 J5 Ol'ginskaya Rus. Fed.
137 J4 Ol'ginskaya Rus. Fed.
Olginskoye Rus. Fed. see Kochubeyevskoye
106 A1 Ölgiy Mongolia
146 E3 Olgrinmore Highland, Scotland U.K.
184 A1 Olhalvo Port.
184 C3 Olhão Port.
184 A1 Olho Marinho Port.
113 □1 Olhuveli i. S. Male Maldives
84 B5 Olia Chain mts N.T. Austr.
186 E2 Oliana Spain
183 G5 Olías del Rey Spain
188 E3 Olib i. Croatia
192 B4 Oliena Sardegna Italy
192 B4 Oliena r. Sardegna Italy
186 C3 Oliete Spain
212 C5 Olifants watercourse Namibia
214 B4 Olifants r. W. Cape S. Africa
214 C5 Olifants r. W. Cape S. Africa
213 F4 Olifants r. S. Africa
214 D2 Olifantshoek S. Africa
214 B5 Olifantsrivierberge mts S. Africa
193 G4 Oligastro Marina Italy
91 K5 Olimarao atoll Micronesia
Olimbos hill Cyprus see Olympos
Olimbos mt. Greece see Olympos
256 C4 Olímpia Brazil
245 E5 Olinalá Mex.
85 F1 Olinda Entrance sea chan. Qld Austr.
213 H3 Olinga Moz.
141 K3 Olingsjövallen Sweden
85 E4 Olio Qld Austr.
186 E3 Oliola Spain
Öli Qoltyq Sory dry lake Kazakh. see Sor Mertvyy Kultuk
Olisipo Port. see Lisboa
183 I2 Olite Spain
261 F3 Oliva Arg.
193 I5 Oliva r. Italy
187 C6 Oliva Spain
184 D2 Oliva hill Spain
258 C3 Oliva, Cordillera de mts Arg./Chile
184 D2 Oliva de la Frontera Spain
184 D2 Oliva de Mérida Spain
182 B3 Olival Port.
260 C2 Olivares, Cerro de mt. Arg./Chile
183 H5 Olivares de Júcar Spain
232 B5 Olive Hill KY U.S.A.
240 G2 Olivehurst CA U.S.A.
257 E4 Oliveira Brazil
182 B4 Oliveira de Azeméis Port.
182 B4 Oliveira de Frades Port.
182 B4 Oliveira do Bairro Port.
182 C4 Oliveira do Conde Port.
182 B3 Oliveira do Douro Port.
182 C4 Oliveira do Hospital Port.
254 E5 Oliveira dos Brejinhos Brazil
Olivença Moz. see Lupilichi
Olivença-a-Nova Angola see Capunda Cavilongo
193 H3 Olivento r. Italy
184 C2 Olivenza r. Port./Spain
184 C2 Olivenza Spain
222 G5 Oliver B.C. Can.
195 E4 Oliveri Sicilia Italy
261 G3 Oliveros Arg.
156 B5 Olivet France
226 E4 Olivet MI U.S.A.
236 D3 Olivet SD U.S.A.
193 H4 Oliveto Citra Italy
193 I4 Oliveto Lucano Italy
236 E2 Olivia MN U.S.A.
81 B6 Olivine Range mts South I. N.Z.
190 D2 Olivone Switz.
136 C3 Oliyiv Ukr.
177 K3 Olka r. Slovakia
210 C5 Ol Kalou Kenya
Ölkeyek r. Kazakh. see Ul'kayak
135 G6 Ol'khovatka Rus. Fed.
135 I6 Ol'khovka Rus. Fed.
175 H5 Olkusz Pol.
146 □G1 Ollaberry Shetland, Scotland U.K.
252 C3 Ollachea Peru
192 B5 Olla stu r. Sardegna Italy
149 H4 Ollerton Nottinghamshire, England U.K.
160 B3 Olliergues France
161 D5 Ollioules France
260 B2 Ollita, Cordillera de mts Arg./Chile
260 B2 Ollitas mt. Arg.
183 I2 Ollo Spain
192 B4 Ollolai Sardegna Italy
208 B5 Ollombo Congo
190 B2 Ollon Switz.
Olmaliq Uzbek. see Almalyk
183 G3 Olmedilla de Roa Spain
192 A4 Olmedo Sardegna Italy
183 F3 Olmedo Spain
192 B2 Olmeta-di-Tuda Corse France
192 A3 Olmeto Corse France
250 B6 Olmos Peru
183 F2 Olmos de Ojeda Spain
Olmütz Czech Rep. see Olomouc
151 G2 Olney Milton Keynes, England U.K.
236 F4 Olney IL U.S.A.
234 A3 Olney MD U.S.A.
237 D5 Olney TX U.S.A.
187 C5 Olocau Spain
186 C4 Olocau del Rey Spain
100 A2 Olochi Rus. Fed.
143 F3 Olofström Sweden
121 F1 Ol'oinka Kazakh.
225 I3 Olomane r. Que. Can.
176 G2 Olomouc Czech Rep.
176 G2 Olomoucký kraj admin. reg. Czech Rep.
190 E3 Olona r. Italy
139 I1 Olonets Rus. Fed.
139 I1 Olonetskaya Vozvyshennost' hills Rus. Fed.
92 B3 Olongapo Phil.
139 I1 Olonka r. Rus. Fed.
162 A2 Olonne-sur-Mer France
161 A5 Olonzac France
163 B5 Oloron-Ste-Marie France
78 □2 Olosega i. American Samoa
Olosenga i. American Samoa see Swains Island
186 F2 Olot Spain
Olot Uzbek. see Alat
171 D5 Oloví Czech Rep.
188 G3 Olovo Bos.-Herz.
107 G1 Olovyannaya Rus. Fed.
240 □C8 Olowalu HI U.S.A.
Oloy, Qatorkŭhi mts Asia see Alai Range
116 C5 Olpad Gujarat India
169 C4 Olpe Ger.
178 C3 Olperer mt. Austria
138 G5 Ol'sa r. Belarus
176 F2 Olšany Czech Rep.
176 G2 Olšany u Prostějova Czech Rep.
142 E2 Olsätter Sweden
177 G2 Olšava r. Czech Rep.
177 K3 Olšava r. Slovakia
169 D4 Olsberg Ger.
177 H2 Olše r. Czech Rep.
137 I2 Ol'shanka Rus. Fed.
137 F4 Ol'shans'ke Ukr.
164 F2 Olst Neth.
175 K3 Olszanka Mazowieckie Pol.
174 F5 Olszanka Opolskie Pol.
175 K6 Olszany Pol.
175 J2 Olszewka Pol.
175 J2 Olszewo-Borki Pol.
174 G3 Olszówka Pol.
175 H5 Olsztyn Śląskie Pol.
175 I2 Olsztyn Warmińsko-Mazurskie Pol.
175 I2 Olsztynek Pol.
175 L3 Olszyn Pol.
174 D4 Olszyna Pol.
197 G4 Olt r. Romania
260 D2 Olta Arg.
259 C6 Olte, Sierra de mts Arg.
190 C1 Olten Switz.
197 H3 Olteniţa Romania
197 G3 Olteţ r. Romania
197 H3 Oltina Romania
Oltinkŭl Uzbek. see Altynkul'
123 G1 Oltintopkan Tajik.
127 F2 Oltu Turkey
129 B3 Oltu r. Turkey
113 □1 Olugiri i. N. Male Maldives
129 C3 Oluklu Turkey
185 H3 Olula del Río Spain
129 C3 Olur Turkey
183 I3 Ólvega Spain
186 D2 Olvena Spain
185 E4 Olvera Spain
150 E3 Olveston South Gloucestershire, England U.K.
Ol'viopol' Ukr. see Pervomays'k
136 C2 Olyka Ukr.
139 L5 Olym r. Rus. Fed.
Olymbos hill Cyprus see Olympos
198 B3 Olympia tourist site Greece
238 B2 Olympia WA U.S.A.
128 A2 Olympos hill Cyprus
198 C1 Olympos mt. Greece
199 G3 Olympos tourist site Turkey
Olympus, Mount Greece see Olympos
238 B2 Olympus, Mount WA U.S.A.
137 J2 Olymskiy Rus. Fed.
234 C1 Olyphant PA U.S.A.
137 F2 Olyshivka Ukr.
131 R3 Olyutorskiy Rus. Fed.
131 R4 Olyutorskiy Zaliv b. Rus. Fed.
192 B4 Olzai Sardegna Italy
Olzheras Kemerovskaya Oblast' Rus. Fed. see Mezhdurechensk
111 C5 Oma Xizang China
134 I2 Oma r. Rus. Fed.
105 D2 Ōmachi Japan
102 J4 Ōmagari Japan
147 D2 Omagh Northern Ireland U.K.

105 F2 Ōta Japan
184 B1 Ota Port.
184 B1 Ota r. Port.
81 B6 Otago admin. reg. South I. N.Z.
81 C6 Otago Peninsula South I. N.Z.
Otahiti i. Fr. Polynesia see Tahiti
80 E3 Otairi North I. N.Z.
102 □1 O-take vol. Nansei-shotō Japan
102 □1 O-take vol. Nansei-shotō Japan
105 F3 Ōtake-san mt. Japan
80 E4 Otaki North I. N.Z.
81 B6 Otama South I. N.Z.
80 F3 Otamauri North I. N.Z.
121 H4 Otar Kazakh.
102 J2 Otaru Japan
176 G2 Otaslavice Czech Rep.
81 B7 Otatara South I. N.Z.
245 F4 Otatitlán Mex.
81 A7 Otautau South I. N.Z.
176 D2 Otava r. Czech Rep.
141 N3 Otava Fin.
250 B4 Otavalo Ecuador
212 C3 Otavi Namibia
105 G2 Ōtawara Japan
209 B9 Otchinjau Angola
Otdia atoll Marshall Is see Wotje
183 I2 Oteiza Spain
81 C6 Otekaieke South I. N.Z.
197 F3 Oțelu Roșu Romania
81 C6 Otematata South I. N.Z.
128 C1 Ötençay Turkey
138 F2 Otepää Estonia
138 F2 Otepää kõrgustik hills Estonia
140 L1 Oteren Norway
182 D3 Otero de Bodas Spain
183 F4 Otero de Herreros Spain
239 E7 Oteros r. Mex.
198 B1 Oteševo Macedonia
175 I5 Otfinów Pol.
151 H3 Otford Kent, England U.K.
106 C2 Otgon Tenger Uul mt. Mongolia
157 F3 Othain r. France
156 D4 Othe, Forêt d' for. France
238 C2 Othello WA U.S.A.
207 F4 Oti r. Ghana/Togo
177 G2 Otice Czech Rep.
172 C3 Ötigheim Ger.
215 H3 Otimati S. Africa
244 B1 Otinapa Mex.
81 C5 Otira South I. N.Z.
236 C3 Otis CO U.S.A.
172 C3 Ötisheim Ger.
234 D1 Otisville NY U.S.A.
185 G4 Otívar Spain
212 C4 Otjiwarongo Namibia
212 C4 Otjozondjupa admin. reg. Namibia
151 I2 Otley Suffolk, England U.K.
149 H4 Otley West Yorkshire, England U.K.
129 A4 Otlukbelı Erzincan Turkey
129 A4 Otlukbeli Dağları mts Turkey
174 F5 Otmuchów Pol.
179 H1 Otnice Czech Rep.
102 J2 Otobe-dake mt. Japan
188 E3 Otočac Croatia
Otog Qi Nei Mongol China see Ulan
188 G3 Otok Croatia
188 F3 Otoka Bos.-Herz.
80 F3 Otoko North I. N.Z.
207 F4 Otola Benin
80 E1 Otonga North I. N.Z.
210 A2 Otoro, Jebel mt. Sudan
80 E3 Otorohanga North I. N.Z.
174 E3 Otorowo Pol.
224 B3 Otoskwin r. Ont. Can.
103 □3 Otōto-jima i. Japan
120 B3 Otpan, Gora hill Kazakh.
Otpor Rus. Fed. see Zabaykal'sk
142 C2 Otra r. Norway
139 K5 Otradinskiy Rus. Fed.
129 B1 Otradnaya Rus. Fed.
139 H2 Otradnoye Leningradskaya Oblast' Rus. Fed.
Otradnoye Samarskaya Oblast' Rus. Fed. see Otradnyy
120 B1 Otradnyy Samarskaya Oblast' Rus. Fed.
195 H2 Otranto Italy
195 H2 Otranto, Strait of Albania/Italy
193 E2 Otricoli Italy
Otrogovo Saratovskaya Oblast' Rus. Fed. see Stepnoye
177 G2 Otrokovice Czech Rep.
131 S3 Otrozhnyy Rus. Fed.
226 E4 Otsego MI U.S.A.
104 B3 Ōtsu Japan
105 E3 Ōtsuki Japan
141 J3 Otta Norway
192 B4 Ottana Sardegna Italy
157 G3 Ottange France
224 F4 Ottawa Ont. Can.
224 F4 Ottawa r. Ont./Que. Can. alt. Outaouais, Rivière des
226 C5 Ottawa IL U.S.A.
236 E4 Ottawa KS U.S.A.
232 A4 Ottawa OH U.S.A.
224 D1 Ottawa Islands Nunavut Can.
171 E4 Ottendorf-Okrilla Ger.
172 B3 Ottenheim Ger.
172 C3 Ottenhöfen im Schwarzwald Ger.
179 G2 Ottenschlag Austria
179 F2 Ottensheim Austria
169 E4 Ottenstein Ger.
168 E2 Otter Ger.
150 D4 Otter r. England U.K.
172 B2 Otterbach Ger.
172 B2 Otterberg Ger.
149 G2 Otterburn Northumberland, England U.K.
146 C5 Otter Ferry Argyll and Bute, Scotland U.K.
173 F4 Otterfing Ger.
164 E2 Otterlo Neth.
168 D2 Otterndorf Ger.
224 D3 Otter Rapids Ont. Can.
168 E2 Ottersberg Ger.
142 E2 Otterstad Sweden
172 C3 Ottersweier Ger.
146 □G1 Otterswick Shetland, Scotland U.K.
142 D4 Otterup Denmark
171 D4 Otterwisch Ger.
150 C4 Ottery r. England U.K.
150 D4 Ottery St Mary Devon, England U.K.
177 G4 Öttevény Hungary
165 D4 Ottignies Belgium
157 H5 Ottmarsheim France
179 E2 Ottnang am Hausruck Austria
173 E4 Ottobeuren Ger.
173 F3 Ottobrunn Ger.
177 I5 Öttömös Hungary
190 E4 Ottone Italy
215 E2 Ottosdal S. Africa
215 E1 Ottoshoop S. Africa
169 E5 Ottrau Ger.
236 E3 Ottumwa IA U.S.A.
172 B2 Ottweiler Ger.
207 G5 Otukpa Nigeria
207 H5 Otukpo Nigeria
245 E4 Otumba Mex.
250 B6 Otuzco Peru
Otvazhniy Rus. Fed. see Zhigulevsk
232 B5 Otway OH U.S.A.
83 E4 Otway, Cape Vic. Austr.
83 E4 Otway Range mts Vic. Austr.
175 J3 Otwock Pol.
183 H1 Otxandio Spain
174 D4 Otyń Pol.
136 C3 Otyniya Ukr.
173 G3 Otzing Ger.
178 B4 Ötztaler Alpen mts Austria
96 C2 Ou, Nam r. Laos
207 H3 Ouacha Niger
237 F6 Ouachita r. AR U.S.A.
237 E5 Ouachita Mountains Arkansas/Oklahoma U.S.A.
228 H4 Ouachita Mountains AR/OK U.S.A.
208 D2 Ouadda C.A.R.
202 D6 Ouaddaï pref. Chad
206 B2 Ouâd Nâga Maur.
206 E3 Ouagadougou Burkina
206 E3 Ouahigouya Burkina
Ouahran Alg. see Oran
208 D3 Ouaka pref. C.A.R.
208 C3 Ouaka r. C.A.R.
206 D2 Oualâta Maur.
207 F4 Oualé r. Burkina
206 C3 Oualia Mali
207 F3 Ouallam Niger
251 I3 Ouanary Fr. Guiana
208 D2 Ouanda-Djailé C.A.R.
208 D3 Ouango C.A.R.
206 D4 Ouangolodougou Côte d'Ivoire
160 B1 Ouanne France
156 C5 Ouanne r. France
251 H4 Ouaqui Fr. Guiana
208 E3 Ouara r. C.A.R.
207 F4 Ouargaye Burkina
205 G3 Ouargla Alg.
204 C3 Ouarkziz, Jbel ridge Alg./Morocco
Ouarogou Burkina see Ouargaye
156 B4 Ouarville France
204 D3 Ouarzazate Morocco
207 F3 Ouatagouna Mali
Oubangui r. C.A.R./Dem. Rep. Congo see Ubangi
182 B4 Ouca Port.
160 D1 Ouche r. France
156 B5 Oucques France
164 D3 Oud-Beijerland Neth.
164 C3 Ouddorp Neth.
164 F1 Oudega Neth.
164 E2 Oudehaske Neth.
164 E2 Oudemirdum Neth.
165 C4 Oudenaarde Belgium
164 D3 Oudenbosch Neth.
165 C3 Oudenburg Belgium
164 G1 Oude Pekela Neth.
164 D2 Oude Rijn r. Neth.
164 D2 Ouderkerk aan de Amstel Neth.
164 D1 Oudeschild Neth.
164 D3 Oude-Tonge Neth.
164 D2 Oudewater Neth.
164 D3 Oud-Gastel Neth.
158 E4 Oudon France
159 F4 Oudon r. France
214 D5 Oudtshoorn S. Africa
165 D3 Oud-Turnhout Belgium
165 C3 Oudzele Belgium
204 D2 Oued Zem Morocco
78 □5 Ouégoa New Caledonia
206 D4 Ouéléssébougou Mali
207 F3 Ouella Niger
207 F5 Ouémé r. Benin
206 E4 Ouessa Burkina
158 A3 Ouessant, Île d' i. France
207 F4 Ouèssè Benin
208 C4 Ouésso Congo
207 H5 Ouest prov. Cameroon
204 D2 Ouezzane Morocco
165 E4 Ouffet Belgium
147 B3 Oughterard Rep. of Ireland
160 D1 Ougney France
104 A4 Ougo-gawa r. Japan
184 C1 Ouguela Port.
105 E2 Ougura-yama mt. Japan
208 C3 Ouham pref. C.A.R.
208 C2 Ouham r. C.A.R./Chad
208 C3 Ouham Pendé pref. C.A.R.
207 F5 Ouidah Benin
242 C3 Ouiriego Mex.
159 F2 Ouistreham France
204 E2 Oujda Morocco
206 B2 Oujeft Maur.
204 C3 Oulad Teïma Morocco
140 N2 Oulainen Fin.
156 D3 Oulchy-le-Château France
165 F4 Oulder Belgium
206 C3 Ould Yenjé Maur.
205 G2 Ouled Djellal Alg.
205 F2 Ouled Naïl, Monts des mts Alg.
160 C3 Oullins France
204 D2 Oulmès Morocco
151 I2 Oulton Suffolk, England U.K.
140 N2 Oulu Fin.
140 N2 Oulu prov. Fin.
140 N2 Oulujärvi l. Fin.
140 N2 Oulujoki r. Fin.
140 N2 Oulunsalo Fin.
190 B3 Oulx Italy
206 D5 Oumé Côte d'Ivoire
205 G2 Oum el Bouaghi Alg.
202 C6 Oum-Hadjer Chad
205 G4 Ounane, Djebel mt. Alg.
204 C3 Ounara Morocco
140 N2 Ounasjoki r. Fin.
151 G2 Oundle Northamptonshire, England U.K.
223 K5 Oungre Sask. Can.
165 E4 Oupeye Belgium
165 F5 Our r. Lux.
239 F4 Ouray CO U.S.A.
241 M1 Ouray UT U.S.A.
156 E4 Ource r. France
156 D3 Ourcq r. France
206 C4 Ouré Kaba Guinea
254 D2 Ourém Brazil
182 C2 Ourense Spain
182 C2 Ourense prov. Galicia Spain
254 E3 Ouricurí Brazil
256 C5 Ourinhos Brazil
184 B3 Ourique Port.
254 D4 Ouro r. Brazil
182 C1 Ouro r. Spain
257 F4 Ouro Branco Brazil
256 D5 Ouro Fino Brazil
182 C1 Ourol Spain
257 F4 Ouro Preto Brazil
160 B1 Ouroux-en-Morvan France
160 C2 Ouroux-sur-Saône France
165 E4 Ourthe r. Belgium
159 G2 Ourville-en-Caux France
151 H4 Ouse r. East Sussex, England U.K.
149 I4 Ouse r. England U.K.
163 D6 Oust France
158 D4 Oust r. France
184 B2 Outão Port.
224 F4 Outaouais, Rivière des r. Ont./Que. Can. alt. Ottawa
225 G3 Outardes r. Que. Can.
156 C4 Outarville France
204 E2 Outat Oulad el Haj Morocco
182 D3 Outeiro Bragança Port.
182 B3 Outeiro Viana do Castelo Port.
182 C1 Outeiro de Rei Spain
182 C3 Outeiro Seco Port.
214 D5 Outeniekwaberge mts S. Africa
146 A4 Outer Hebrides is Scotland U.K.
Outer Mongolia country Asia see Mongolia
240 H5 Outer Santa Barbara Channel CA U.S.A.
212 C4 Outjo Namibia
223 J5 Outlook Sask. Can.
134 E3 Outokumpu Fin.
182 C2 Outomuro Spain
81 C6 Outram South I. N.Z.
156 B2 Outreau France
146 □H1 Out Skerries is Scotland U.K.
151 H2 Outwell Norfolk, England U.K.
78 □5 Ouvéa i. Î. Loyauté New Caledonia
161 A5 Ouveillan France
161 C4 Ouvèze r. France
83 E3 Ouyen Vic. Austr.
151 G2 Ouzel r. England U.K.
156 B5 Ouzouer-le-Marché France
156 C5 Ouzouer-sur-Loire France
199 E1 Ova r. Turkey
192 B3 Ovace, Punta d' mt. Corse France
126 D3 Ovacık Turkey
126 E3 Ovacık Turkey
199 G3 Ovacık Dağı mt. Turkey
190 D4 Ovada Italy
199 E3 Ovaeymiri Turkey
199 F2 Ovakent İzmir Turkey
129 C4 Ovakışla Turkey
199 E3 Ovakışlacık Muğla Turkey
199 F3 Ovaköy Antalya Turkey
234 A1 Oval PA U.S.A.
79 □1a Ovalau i. Fiji
260 B2 Ovalle Chile
212 B3 Ovamboland reg. Namibia
208 B4 Ovan Gabon
182 B4 Ovar Port.
191 H2 Ovaro Italy
78 □6 Ovau i. Solomon Is
260 E3 Oveja mt. Arg.
168 D2 Ovelgönne Ger.
83 F4 Ovens r. Vic. Austr.
147 C5 Ovens Rep. of Ireland
169 C5 Overath Ger.
146 F2 Overbister Orkney, Scotland U.K.
164 G2 Overdinkel Neth.
140 J2 Overhalla Norway
165 D4 Overijse Belgium
164 F2 Overijssel prov. Neth.
140 M2 Överkalix Sweden
87 B5 Overlander Roadhouse W.A. Austr.
236 E4 Overland Park KS U.S.A.
234 B3 Overlea MD U.S.A.
164 E3 Overloon Neth.
260 B4 Overo, Volcán vol. Arg.
165 E3 Overpelt Belgium
151 F2 Overseal Derbyshire, England U.K.
151 F3 Overton Hampshire, England U.K.
150 E2 Overton Wrexham, Wales U.K.
241 J3 Overton NV U.S.A.
237 E5 Overton TX U.S.A.
140 M2 Övertorneå Sweden
146 E6 Overtown North Lanarkshire, Scotland U.K.
143 G3 Överum Sweden
140 K2 Överuman l. Sweden
164 D2 Overveen Neth.
151 F3 Over Wallop Hampshire, England U.K.
190 D2 Ovesca r. Italy
165 C3 Ovezande Neth.
236 C3 Ovid CO U.S.A.
226 E4 Ovid MI U.S.A.
232 E3 Ovid NY U.S.A.
136 F4 Ovidiopol' Ukr.
197 I3 Ovidiu Romania
182 E1 Oviedo Spain
182 D1 Oviedo prov. Asturias Spain
190 D4 Oviglio Italy
193 F2 Ovindoli Italy
139 K2 Ovinishchenskaya Vozvyshennost' hills Rus. Fed.
192 B4 Ovodda Sardegna Italy
Ovolau i. Fiji see Ovalau
107 G2 Ovoot Mongolia
106 D2 Övörhangay prov. Mongolia
141 I3 Øvre Årdal Norway
141 J3 Øvre Rendal Norway
140 M1 Övre Soppero Sweden
136 E2 Ovruch Ukr.
106 D2 Övt Mongolia
80 F4 Owahanga North I. N.Z.
81 B7 Owaka South I. N.Z.
226 B1 Owakonze Ont. Can.
208 B5 Owando Congo
Owa Rafa i. Solomon Is see Santa Ana
Owa Riki i. Solomon Is see Santa Catalina
104 C4 Owase Japan
237 E4 Owasso OK U.S.A.
236 E2 Owatonna MN U.S.A.
123 E3 Owbeh Afgh.
175 J4 Owczarnia Pol.
233 E3 Owego NY U.S.A.
147 D3 Owel, Lough l. Rep. of Ireland
172 D3 Owen Ger.
81 D4 Owen, Mount South I. N.Z.
207 G5 Owena Nigeria
147 C2 Owenbeg Rep. of Ireland
214 D3 Owendale S. Africa
147 B2 Owenduff r. Rep. of Ireland
210 B4 Owen Falls Dam Uganda
147 B2 Oweniny r. Rep. of Ireland
147 B2 Owenmore r. Rep. of Ireland
147 D2 Owenreagh r. Northern Ireland U.K.
81 D4 Owen River South I. N.Z.
240 I3 Owens r. CA U.S.A.
230 C4 Owensboro KY U.S.A.
224 D4 Owen Sound Ont. Can.
84 C4 Owen Springs N.T. Austr.
91 K8 Owen Stanley Range mts P.N.G.
236 F4 Owensville MO U.S.A.
232 A5 Owensville OH U.S.A.
230 C4 Owenton KY U.S.A.
207 G5 Owerri Nigeria
80 E3 Owhango North I. N.Z.
172 D4 Owingen Ger.
232 E5 Owings MD U.S.A.
234 B3 Owings Mills MD U.S.A.
232 B5 Owingsville KY U.S.A.
223 M3 Owl r. Man. Can.
238 E3 Owl Creek r. WY U.S.A.
233 □I2 Owls Head ME U.S.A.
Owminzatow Toghi hills Uzbek. see Auminzatau, Gory
207 G5 Owo Nigeria
227 E4 Owosso MI U.S.A.
168 E1 Owschlag Ger.
238 C3 Owyhee NV U.S.A.
238 C3 Owyhee r. OR U.S.A.
238 C3 Owyhee Mountains ID U.S.A.
238 C3 Owyhee North Fork r. ID U.S.A.
238 C3 Owyhee South Fork r. ID U.S.A.
252 B2 Oxapampa Peru
140 □C2 Öxarfjörður b. Iceland
223 K5 Oxbow Sask. Can.
236 C1 Ox Creek r. ND U.S.A.
143 G2 Oxelösund Sweden
149 H4 Oxenhope West Yorkshire, England U.K.
81 D5 Oxford South I. N.Z.
151 F3 Oxford Oxfordshire, England U.K.
235 E1 Oxford CT U.S.A.
233 H3 Oxford MA U.S.A.
233 □H2 Oxford ME U.S.A.
227 F4 Oxford MI U.S.A.
237 F5 Oxford MS U.S.A.
231 E4 Oxford NC U.S.A.
234 D2 Oxford NJ U.S.A.
233 F3 Oxford NY U.S.A.
232 A5 Oxford OH U.S.A.
234 C3 Oxford PA U.S.A.
226 C4 Oxford WI U.S.A.
85 G4 Oxford Downs Qld Austr.
223 M4 Oxford House Man. Can.
151 F3 Oxfordshire admin. div. England U.K.
142 E4 Oxie Sweden
243 H4 Oxkutzcab Mex.
83 F3 Oxley N.S.W. Austr.
83 G2 Oxleys Peak N.S.W. Austr.
Ox Mountains hills Rep. of Ireland see Slieve Gamph
240 H4 Oxnard CA U.S.A.
151 G3 Oxshott Surrey, England U.K.
151 H3 Oxted Surrey, England U.K.
146 F6 Oxton Scottish Borders, Scotland U.K.
227 H3 Oxtongue Lake Ont. Can.
Oxus r. Asia see Amudar'ya
198 D2 Oxylithos Greece
95 E2 Oya r. Sarawak Malaysia
140 K2 Øya Norway
104 C2 Oyabe Japan
104 D2 Oyabe-gawa r. Japan
105 F2 Oyama Japan
105 F3 Ō-yama mt. Japan
105 F4 Ō-yama vol. Japan
251 I3 Oyapock r. Brazil/Fr. Guiana
208 A4 Oyem Gabon
223 I5 Oyen Alta Can.
156 C2 Oye-Plage France
106 C1 Oygon Mongolia
146 D4 Oykel r. Scotland U.K.
146 D4 Oykel Bridge Highland, Scotland U.K.
173 E4 Oy-Mittelberg Ger.
208 B5 Oyo Congo
207 F5 Oyo Nigeria
207 F4 Oyo state Nigeria
252 A2 Oyón Peru
183 H2 Oyón Spain
160 D2 Oyonnax France
Oyoqquduq Uzbek. see Ayakkuduk
Oysangur Rus. Fed. see Oyskhara
129 E2 Oyskhara Rus. Fed.
214 E6 Oyster Bay S. Africa
235 E2 Oyster Bay NY U.S.A.
235 D3 Oyster Creek NJ U.S.A.
121 H4 Oytal Kazakh.
168 E2 Oyten Ger.
128 A1 Oyukludağı mt. Turkey
Oyyl Kazakh. see Uil
Oyyq Kazakh. see Uyuk
182 B1 Oza Spain
Ozaeta Spain see Ozeta
127 G3 Özalp Turkey
92 B4 Ozamiz Phil.
156 B4 Ozanne r. France
231 C6 Ozark AL U.S.A.
237 E5 Ozark AR U.S.A.
237 E4 Ozark MO U.S.A.
237 E4 Ozark Plateau MO U.S.A.
236 E4 Ozarks, Lake of the MO U.S.A.
175 J5 Ożarów Pol.
175 H5 Ożarowice Pol.
175 I3 Ożarów Mazowiecki Pol.
199 E3 Özbaşı Turkey
Ozbekiston country Asia see Uzbekistan
177 J3 Ózd Hungary
177 I3 Ožďany Slovakia
199 E3 Özdere Turkey
129 B4 Özdilek Turkey
Özen Kazakh. see Kyzylsay
139 J2 Ozerevo Rus. Fed.
136 E5 Ozerne Odes'ka Oblast' Ukr.
136 C2 Ozerne Volyns'ka Oblast' Ukr.
136 E2 Ozerne Zhytomyrs'ka Oblast' Ukr.
139 K4 Ozerninskoye Vodokhranilishche resr Rus. Fed.
131 Q4 Ozernovskiy Rus. Fed.
120 E1 Ozernoye Kustanayskaya Oblast' Kazakh.
120 B2 Ozernoye Rus. Fed.
Ozernyy Karagandinskaya Oblast' Kazakh. see Shashubay
Ozernyy Kustanayskaya Oblast' Kazakh. see Ozernoye
139 M3 Ozernyy Ivanovskaya Oblast' Rus. Fed.
120 E2 Ozernyy Orenburgskaya Oblast' Rus. Fed.
139 I4 Ozernyy Smolenskaya Oblast' Rus. Fed.
198 B2 Ozeros, Limni l. Greece
138 D4 Ozersk Rus. Fed.
100 G3 Ozerskiy Sakhalin Rus. Fed.
139 L4 Ozery Rus. Fed.
100 D2 Ozeryane Rus. Fed.
137 G2 Ozeryany Ukr.
183 H2 Ozeta Spain
121 H4 Özgön Kyrg.
139 L4 Ozherel'ye Rus. Fed.
131 Q3 Ozhogina r. Rus. Fed.
192 B4 Ozieri Sardegna Italy
174 G5 Ozimek Pol.
120 B2 Ozinki Rus. Fed.
156 C4 Ozoir-la-Ferrière France
138 D3 Ozolnieki Latvia
237 C6 Ozona TX U.S.A.
177 H5 Ozora Hungary
175 H4 Ozorków Pol.
207 G5 Ozoro Nigeria
103 F7 Ōzu Japan
245 E4 Ozumba de Alzate Mex.
129 C3 Ozurget'i Georgia
128 A1 Özyurt Dağı mts Turkey
175 M5 Ozyutychi Ukr.
191 G4 Ozzano dell'Emilia Italy
190 D3 Ozzano Monferrato Italy
P
206 E4 Pâ Burkina
165 E3 Paal Belgium
78 □5 Paama i. Vanuatu
221 N3 Paamiut Greenland
96 B3 Pa-an Myanmar
Paanopa i. Kiribati see Banaba
214 B5 Paarl S. Africa
78 □4a Paata i. Chuuk Micronesia
Paatsjoki r. Europe see Patsoyoki
240 □D8 Paauilo HI U.S.A.
Pabaigh i. Western Isles, Scotland U.K. see Pabbay
146 B3 Pabail Iarach Western Isles, Scotland U.K.
214 C3 Paballelo S. Africa
101 D4 P'abal-li N. Korea
146 A4 Pabbay i. Western Isles, Scotland U.K.
146 A5 Pabbay i. Western Isles, Scotland U.K.
244 C2 Pabeilón de Arteaga Mex.
175 H4 Pabianice Pol.
Pabianitz Pol. see Pabianice
192 A5 Pabillonis Sardegna Italy
245 E1 Pablillo r. Mex.
117 G4 Pabna Bangl.
179 F2 Pabneukirchen Austria
138 E4 Pabradė Lith.
123 F5 Pab Range mts Pak.
158 C3 Pabu France
252 D2 Pacaás, Serra dos hills Brazil
256 B4 Pacaembu Brazil
252 D2 Pacahuaras r. Bol.
254 F3 Pacajus Brazil
214 D6 Pacaltsdorp S. Africa
175 J5 Pacanów Pol.
Pacaraimã, Serra mts S. America see Pakaraima Mountains
250 B6 Pacasmayo Peru
254 F2 Pacatuba Brazil
250 C6 Pacaya r. Peru
243 H6 Pacaya, Volcán de vol. Guat.
158 E3 Pacé France
194 B5 Paceco Sicilia Italy
242 C2 Pacheco Mex.
135 H5 Pachelma Rus. Fed.
195 E6 Pachino Sicilia Italy
252 B2 Pachitea r. Peru
252 A1 Pachiza Peru
116 D5 Pachmarhi Madh. Prad. India
198 D1 Pachni Greece
116 D5 Pachor Madh. Prad. India
116 C5 Pachora Mahar. India
116 C4 Pachpadra Rajasthan India
245 E3 Pachuca Mex.
192 E1 Paciano Italy
240 F3 Pacifica CA U.S.A.
267 I9 Pacific-Antarctic Ridge sea feature Pacific Ocean
240 G3 Pacific Grove CA U.S.A.
266 Pacific Ocean
177 K3 Pácin Hungary
196 D3 Pačir Vojvodina, Srbija Yugo.
95 E5 Pacitan Jawa Timur Indon.
83 E2 Packsaddle N.S.W. Austr.
182 B3 Pacos de Ferreira Port.
176 E2 Pacov Czech Rep.
176 G5 Pacsa Hungary
257 E2 Pacuí r. Brazil
177 K2 Pacutová hill Slovakia
175 H3 Pacyna Pol.
156 B3 Pacy-sur-Eure France
174 F5 Paczków Pol.
92 C5 Padada Phil.
Padali Rus. Fed. see Amursk
116 C3 Padampur Rajasthan India
94 C3 Padang Sumatera Indon.
94 C3 Padangpanjang Sumatera Indon.
94 B2 Padangsidimpuan Sumatera Indon.
134 F3 Padany Rus. Fed.
95 F1 Padas r. Sabah Malaysia
141 N3 Padasjoki Fin.
122 B3 Padatha, Kūh-e mt. Iran
251 E5 Padauiri r. Brazil
168 E1 Padborg Denmark
151 G3 Padbury Buckinghamshire, England U.K.
252 D5 Padcaya Bol.
83 F3 Paddington N.S.W. Austr.
215 H4 Paddock S. Africa
151 H3 Paddock Wood Kent, England U.K.
177 J6 Padej Vojvodina, Srbija Yugo.
232 C5 Paden City WV U.S.A.
169 D4 Paderborn Ger.
184 B3 Paderne Faro Port.
182 B2 Paderne Viana do Castelo Port.
182 C2 Paderne de Allariz Spain
197 F3 Padeșu, Vârful mt. Romania
175 J5 Padew Narodowa Pol.
149 G4 Padiham Lancashire, England U.K.
252 D4 Padilla Bol.
197 H3 Padina Romania
196 E3 Padina Vojvodina, Srbija Yugo.
196 E3 Padinska Skela Srbija Yugo.
163 D4 Padirac France
Padma r. Bangl. see Ganges
114 C4 Padmanabhapuram Tamil Nadu India
116 E5 Padmapur Mahar. India
157 G4 Padoux France
191 G3 Padova Italy
191 G3 Padova prov. Veneto Italy
116 C5 Padra Gujarat India
117 F4 Padrauna Uttar Prad. India
184 D3 Padre Caro hill Spain
257 G2 Padre Paraíso Brazil
192 A4 Padria Sardegna Italy
192 A2 Padro, Monte mt. Corse France
182 B2 Padrón Spain
192 B4 Padru Sardegna Italy
150 C4 Padstow Cornwall, England U.K.
138 F4 Padsvillye Belarus
82 E4 Padthaway S.A. Austr.
115 D2 Padua Orissa India
Padua Italy see Padova
237 F4 Paducah KY U.S.A.
237 C5 Paducah TX U.S.A.
185 G3 Padul Spain
193 H4 Padula Italy
193 G3 Paduli Italy
116 D2 Padum Jammu and Kashmir
197 F2 Pădurea Craiului, Munții mts Romania
81 E4 Paekakariki North I. N.Z.
101 D4 Paekdu-san mt. China/N. Korea
81 B6 Paerau South I. N.Z.
80 E2 Paeroa North I. N.Z.
80 F3 Paeroa hill North I. N.Z.
190 C4 Paesana Italy
191 H3 Paese Italy
195 D2 Paestum tourist site Italy
92 B3 Paete Phil.
128 A2 Pafos Cyprus
128 A2 Pafos airport Cyprus
188 E3 Pag Croatia
188 E3 Pag i. Croatia
134 M2 Paga r. Rus. Fed.
95 D4 Pagadenbaru Jawa Barat Indon.
92 B5 Pagadian Phil.
Pagalu i. Equat. Guinea see Annobón
91 K3 Pagan i. N. Mariana Is
191 G2 Paganella mt. Italy
193 F2 Paganica Italy
192 D2 Paganico Italy
94 C3 Pagaralam Sumatera Indon.
198 C2 Pagasitikos Kolpos b. Greece
95 F3 Pagatan Kalimantan Selatan Indon.
241 L3 Page AZ U.S.A.
86 E3 Page, Mount hill W.A. Austr.
138 C4 Pagėgiai Lith.
259 □ Paget, Mount S. Georgia
85 H3 Paget Cay rf Coral Sea Is Terr. Austr.
151 G4 Pagham West Sussex, England U.K.
138 E4 Pagiriai Kėdainiai Lith.
138 E4 Pagiriai Vilnius Lith.
192 E2 Paglia r. Italy
193 G2 Paglieta Italy
157 G4 Pagny-sur-Moselle France
Pagon i. N. Mariana Is see Pagan
78 □2 Pago Pago American Samoa
239 F4 Pagosa Springs CO U.S.A.
207 F4 Pagouda Togo
Pagqên Qinghai China see Gadê
224 C3 Pagwachuan r. Ont. Can.
224 C3 Pagwa River Ont. Can.
240 □D9 Pahala HI U.S.A.
94 C2 Pahang r. Malaysia
94 C2 Pahang state Malaysia
117 G4 Paharpur tourist site Bangl.
123 G3 Paharpur Pak.
80 E4 Pahiatua North I. N.Z.
173 F4 Pähl Ger.
168 E1 Pahlen Ger.
116 C2 Pahlgam Jammu and Kashmir
240 □D9 Pahoa HI U.S.A.
231 D7 Pahokee FL U.S.A.
241 J3 Pahranagat Range mts NV U.S.A.
138 D5 Pahranichny Belarus
241 J3 Pahrump NV U.S.A.
116 D4 Pahuj r. India
240 I3 Pahute Mesa plat. NV U.S.A.
240 □C8 Paia HI U.S.A.
182 B4 Paião Port.
240 G3 Paicines CA U.S.A.
138 E2 Paide Estonia
150 D4 Paignton Torbay, England U.K.
80 E1 Paihia North I. N.Z.
250 B6 Paiján Peru
141 N3 Päijänne l. Fin.
207 G4 Paiko Nigeria
252 D4 Paila r. Bol.
260 A6 Pailahueque Chile
163 D5 Pailhès France
Pailing Zhejiang China see Chun'an
259 B6 Paillaco Chile
240 □C8 Pailolo Channel HI U.S.A.
158 D4 Paimbœuf France
141 M3 Paimio Fin.
158 C3 Paimpol France
158 D3 Paimpont France
94 C3 Painan Sumatera Indon.
114 C4 Painavu Kerala India
260 B3 Paine Chile
259 B8 Paine, Cerro mt. Chile
257 E3 Paineiras Brazil
226 C2 Painesdale MI U.S.A.
232 C4 Painesville OH U.S.A.
257 E4 Pains Brazil
150 E3 Painswick Gloucestershire, England U.K.
241 L3 Painted Desert AZ U.S.A.
173 F3 Painten Ger.
Paint Hills Que. Can. see Wemindji
237 D6 Paint Rock TX U.S.A.
232 B6 Paintsville KY U.S.A.
250 C3 Paipa Col.
116 E5 Pairi r. India
227 G3 Paisley Ont. Can.
146 D6 Paisley Renfrewshire, Scotland U.K.
183 H1 País Vasco aut. comm. Spain
78 □5 Païta New Caledonia
250 A6 Paita Peru
114 B2 Paithan Mahar. India
109 G2 Paitou Zhejiang China
182 B3 Paiva r. Port.
Paiva Couceiro Angola see Quipungo
109 E2 Paizhou Hubei China
140 M2 Pajala Sweden
250 A5 Pajan Ecuador
216 □3b Pájara Fuerteventura Canary Is
183 I5 Pajarón Spain
183 I5 Pajaroncillo Spain
174 G4 Pajęczno Pol.
176 F5 Páka Hungary
114 C3 Pakala Andhra Prad. India
Pakanbaru Sumatera Indon. see Pekanbaru
251 F4 Pakaraima Mountains S. America
117 F4 Pakaur Bihar India
80 D4 Pakawau South I. N.Z.
101 C5 Pakch'ŏn N. Korea
224 D4 Pakesley Ont. Can.
131 R3 Pakhachi Rus. Fed.
120 D2 Pakhar' Kazakh.
Pákhni Greece see Pachni
Pakhoi Guangxi China see Beihai
139 K4 Pakhomovo Rus. Fed.
121 H4 Pakhtaabad Uzbek.
123 F4 Pakistan country Asia
Paknampho Thai. see Nakhon Sawan
176 G5 Pakod Hungary
96 A2 Pakokku Myanmar
174 G3 Pakość Pol.
174 F4 Pakosław Pol.
188 E4 Pakoštane Croatia
80 D1 Pakotai North I. N.Z.
177 H4 Pákozd Hungary
123 H4 Pakpattan Pak.
97 C5 Pak Phanang Thai.
97 C6 Pak Phayun Thai.
188 F3 Pakra r. Croatia
188 F3 Pakrac Croatia
138 D4 Pakruojis Lith.
177 H5 Paks Hungary
Pakse Laos see Pakxé
109 □ Pak Tam Chung H.K. China
97 C4 Pak Thong Chai Thai.
123 G3 Paktīā prov. Afgh.
123 GH3 Paktīkā prov. Afgh.
95 F2 Paku r. Sarawak Malaysia
93 B3 Pakue Indon.
136 F2 Pakul' Ukr.
96 D4 Pakxé Laos
Pal Senegal see Mpal
208 B2 Pala Chad
94 D4 Palabuhanratu Jawa Barat Indon.
183 F3 Palacios de Goda Spain
183 G3 Palacios de la Sierra Spain
182 D2 Palacios del Sil Spain
182 D2 Palacios de Sanabria Spain
178 C4 Pala di San Martino mt. Italy
161 D3 Paladru, Lac de l. France
Palaestinia reg. Asia see Palestine
186 G3 Palafrugell Spain
195 F2 Palagianello Italy
195 G2 Palagiano Italy
194 D5 Palagonia Sicilia Italy
191 F5 Palaia Italy
198 C3 Palaia Fokaia Greece
198 C4 Palaiochora Kriti Greece
198 B2 Palairos Greece
156 C4 Palaiseau France
Palakkat Kerala India see Palghat
198 C2 Palamas Greece
186 G3 Palamós Spain
116 D2 Palam Pur Hima. Prad. India
116 C4 Palana Rajasthan India
131 Q4 Palana Rus. Fed.
92 B2 Palanan Phil.
187 C5 Palancia r. Spain
129 B4 Palandöken Dağları mts Turkey
116 E5 Palandur Mahar. India
138 C4 Palanga Lith.
122 E4 Palangān, Kūh-e mts Iran
161 A4 Palanges, Montagne des mts France
95 F3 Palangkaraya Kalimantan Tengah Indon.
114 C4 Palani Tamil Nadu India
116 C4 Palanpur Gujarat India
190 F4 Palanzano Italy
92 C3 Palapag Phil.
213 E4 Palapye Botswana
114 D3 Palar r. India
117 G4 Palasbari Assam India
182 C2 Palas de Rei Spain
138 G4 Palata r. Belarus
193 G3 Palata Italy
131 Q3 Palatka Rus. Fed.
231 D6 Palatka FL U.S.A.
192 B3 Palau Sardegna Italy
92 □ Palau country N. Pacific Ocean
92 A3 Palauig Phil.
91 H5 Palau Islands Palau
266 D5 Palau Trench sea feature N. Pacific Ocean
161 B5 Palavas-les-Flots France
97 B4 Palaw Myanmar
92 A4 Palawan i. Phil.
92 A4 Palawan Passage str. Phil.
266 C5 Palawan Trough sea feature N. Pacific Ocean
92 B3 Palayan Phil.
114 C4 Palayankottai Tamil Nadu India
183 F4 Palazuelos de Eresma Spain
194 C5 Palazzo Adriano Sicilia Italy
194 D5 Palazzolo Acreide Sicilia Italy
190 E3 Palazzolo sull'Oglio Italy
193 I4 Palazzo San Gervasio Italy
179 G4 Paldau Austria
138 E2 Paldiski Estonia
188 G4 Pale Bos.-Herz.
134 H4 Palekh Rus. Fed.
94 D3 Palembang Sumatera Indon.
259 C6 Palena Chile
193 G3 Palena Italy
183 F2 Palencia Spain
183 F2 Palencia prov. Castilla y León Spain
185 F3 Palenciana Spain
243 G5 Palenque Mex.
183 F2 Palenzuela Spain
194 C4 Palermo Sicilia Italy
194 C5 Palermo prov. Sicilia Italy
194 C4 Palermo, Golfo di b. Sicilia Italy
189 D6 Palermo Punta Raisi airport Sicilia Italy
128 B3 Palestine reg. Asia
237 E6 Palestine TX U.S.A.
193 E3 Palestrina Italy
177 H5 Pálfa Hungary
114 B2 Palghar Mahar. India
114 C4 Palghat Kerala India
87 B4 Palgrave, Mount hill W.A. Austr.
182 B4 Palhaça Port.
177 K3 Pálháza Hungary
255 C8 Palhoca Brazil
116 E5 Pali Madh. Prad. India
114 B2 Pali Mahar. India
116 C4 Pali Rajasthan India
193 F3 Paliano Italy
177 I5 Palić Vojvodina, Srbija Yugo.
78 □4b Palikir Pohnpei Micronesia
92 C5 Palimbang Phil.
160 C2 Palinges France
193 H4 Palinuro Italy
156 D4 Palis France
239 E4 Palisade CO U.S.A.
165 E5 Paliseul Belgium
116 B5 Palitana Gujarat India
138 D2 Palivere Estonia
195 F5 Palizzi Italy
140 L2 Palja hill Sweden
140 O2 Paljakka hill Fin.
141 N3 Pälkäne Fin.
114 C4 Palk Bay Sri Lanka
138 G3 Palkino Rus. Fed.
115 D2 Palkohda Andhra Prad. India
114 C3 Palkonda Range mts India
117 F5 Palkot Bihar India
177 H2 Palkovice Czech Rep.
114 C4 Palk Strait India/Sri Lanka
Palla Bianca mt. Austria/Italy see Weißkugel
114 C4 Palladani Tamil Nadu India
195 F3 Pallagorio Italy
252 B3 Pallapalla mt. Peru
184 D2 Pallarés Spain
186 E2 Pallaresa r. Spain
147 C4 Pallas Green Rep. of Ireland
147 C4 Pallaskenry Rep. of Ireland
120 A2 Pallasovka Rus. Fed.
114 D3 Pallavaram Tamil Nadu India
114 D2 Palleru r. India
173 G3 Palling Ger.
87 C7 Pallinup r. W.A. Austr.
210 B4 Pallisa Uganda
81 E4 Palliser, Cape North I. N.Z.
79 □3 Palliser, Îles is Arch. des Tuamotu Fr. Polynesia
81 E4 Palliser Bay North I. N.Z.
116 C3 Pallu Rajasthan India
158 E5 Palluau France
159 H5 Palluau-sur-Indre France
254 D5 Palma r. Brazil
211 D7 Palma Moz.
184 B2 Palma Port.
193 G4 Palma Campania Italy
185 E3 Palma del Río Spain
187 F5 Palma de Mallorca Spain
194 C5 Palma di Montechiaro Sicilia Italy
192 A4 Palmadula Sardegna Italy
114 C3 Palmaner Andhra Prad. India
191 I3 Palmanova Italy
187 F5 Palma Nova Spain
244 D2 Palma Pegada Mex.
244 D4 Palmar Chico Mex.
254 G4 Palmares Brazil
255 C9 Palmares do Sul Brazil
227 H1 Palmarolle Que. Can.
242 □J7 Palmar Sur Costa Rica
255 C8 Palmas Paraná Brazil
254 C4 Palmas Tocantins Brazil
246 D2 Palma Soriano Cuba
182 B4 Palmaz Port.
231 D7 Palm Bay FL U.S.A.
231 D6 Palm Coast FL U.S.A.
240 H4 Palmdale CA U.S.A.
241 I5 Palm Desert CA U.S.A.
256 C6 Palmeira Brazil
182 B3 Palmeira Port.
255 B8 Palmeira das Missões Brazil
254 F4 Palmeira dos Índios Brazil
254 E3 Palmeirais Brazil
254 D5 Palmeiras r. Brazil
256 C2 Palmeiras de Goiás Brazil
184 B2 Palmela Port.
262 T2 Palmer research stn Antarctica
85 E3 Palmer r. Qld Austr.
220 D3 Palmer AK U.S.A.
262 T2 Palmer Land reg. Antarctica
234 B4 Palmer Park MD U.S.A.
Palmerston N.T. Austr. see Darwin
84 B2 Palmerston N.T. Austr.
227 G4 Palmerston Ont. Can.
81 □2 Palmerston atoll Cook Is
81 C6 Palmerston South I. N.Z.
147 E3 Palmerston Rep. of Ireland
85 G4 Palmerston, Cape Qld Austr.
80 E4 Palmerston North North I. N.Z.
234 C2 Palmerton PA U.S.A.
85 F2 Palmerville Qld Austr.
231 D7 Palmetto FL U.S.A.
195 E4 Palmi Italy
245 E2 Palmillas Mex.
260 C3 Palmira Arg.
250 B4 Palmira Col.
246 B2 Palmira Cuba
256 A6 Palmital Paraná Brazil
256 B5 Palmital São Paulo Brazil
261 I3 Palmitas Uru.
Palmnicken Rus. Fed. see Yantarnyy
184 E4 Palmones r. Spain
177 I5 Pálmonostora Hungary
240 I5 Palm Springs CA U.S.A.
85 G5 Palm Tree Creek r. Qld Austr.
Palmyra Syria see Tadmur
236 F4 Palmyra MO U.S.A.
234 C2 Palmyra NJ U.S.A.
232 E3 Palmyra NY U.S.A.
227 I5 Palmyra PA U.S.A.
232 D6 Palmyra VA U.S.A.
75 I3 Palmyra Atoll N. Pacific Ocean
117 F5 Palmyras Point India
146 E7 Palnackie Dumfries and Galloway, Scotland U.K.
192 B3 Palneca Corse France
114 C4 Palni Hills India
92 C4 Palo Phil.
244 C3 Palo Alto Mex.
240 F3 Palo Alto CA U.S.A.
250 B3 Palo de las Letras Col.
195 F1 Palo del Colle Italy
252 C3 Palomani mt. Peru
186 C4 Palomar de Arroyos Spain
245 G5 Palomares Mex.
184 D3 Palomares del Río Spain
240 I5 Palomar Mountain CA U.S.A.
184 D2 Palomas Spain
193 G2 Palombaro Italy
194 E6 Palombieri r. Sicilia Italy
183 H4 Palomera Spain
186 B4 Palomera, Sierra mts Spain
183 H5 Palomeras del Campo Spain
184 D2 Palomilas r. Spain
193 H4 Palomonte Italy
191 G3 Palòn, Cima mt. Italy
114 D2 Paloncha Andhra Prad. India
237 D5 Palo Pinto TX U.S.A.
93 B3 Palopo Sulawesi Selatan Indon.
187 C7 Palos, Cabo de c. Spain
258 F2 Palo Santo Arg.
184 D3 Palos de la Frontera Spain
238 C2 Palouse r. WA U.S.A.
241 J5 Palo Verde CA U.S.A.
85 E5 Palparara Qld Austr.
186 G3 Pals Spain
116 C5 Palsana Gujarat India
140 N2 Paltamo Fin.
139 J5 Pal'tso Rus. Fed.
93 A3 Palu Sulawesi Tengah Indon.
93 A3 Palu r. Indon.
127 E3 Palu Turkey
92 B3 Paluan Phil.
195 F3 Paludi Italy
163 A5 Palue r. France
159 G2 Paluel France
191 I2 Paluzza Italy
123 F2 Pal'vart Turkm.
116 D3 Palwal Haryana India
Palwancha Andhra Prad. India see Paloncha
131 S3 Palyavaam r. Rus. Fed.
Palyeskaya Nizina marsh Belarus/Ukr. see Pripet Marshes
172 A2 Palzem Ger.
179 I2 Pama Austria
207 F4 Pama Burkina
208 C3 Pama r. C.A.R.
83 E3 Pamamaroo Lake N.S.W. Austr.
217 □3b Pamandzi Mayotte
95 D4 Pamanukan Jawa Barat Indon.
250 D5 Pamar Col.
129 D3 P'ambaki Lerrnashght'a mts Armenia
213 G4 Pambarra Moz.
83 G4 Pambula N.S.W. Austr.
179 G4 Pameče Slovenia
95 F4 Pamekasan Jawa Timur Indon.
95 D4 Pameungpeuk Jawa Barat Indon.
199 E2 Pamfylla Voreio Aigaio Greece
179 H3 Pamhagen Austria
174 E3 Pamiątkowo Pol.
114 C3 Pamidi Andhra Prad. India
163 D5 Pamiers France
123 H2 Pamir r. Afgh./Tajik.
121 H5 Pamir mts Asia
231 E5 Pamlico r. NC U.S.A.
231 E5 Pamlico Sound sea chan. NC U.S.A.
237 C5 Pampa TX U.S.A.
252 B3 Pampachiri Peru
258 E2 Pampa de Infierno Arg.
252 D4 Pampa Grande Bol.
93 B4 Pampanua Sulawesi Selatan Indon.
190 C4 Pamparato Italy
261 E5 Pampas reg. Arg.
252 B3 Pampas Peru
252 B3 Pampas r. Peru
163 E4 Pampelonne France
Pampeluna Spain see Pamplona
214 E2 Pampierstad S. Africa
182 B4 Pampilhosa Port.
182 C4 Pampilhosa da Serra Port.
183 G2 Pampliega Spain
232 D6 Pamplin VA U.S.A.
250 C3 Pamplona Col.
92 B4 Pamplona Phil.
183 I2 Pamplona Spain
170 C2 Pampow Ger.
162 B2 Pamproux France
199 E2 Pamukçu Turkey
199 G1 Pamukova Turkey
232 E6 Pamunkey r. VA U.S.A.
208 B5 Pana Gabon
236 F4 Pana IL U.S.A.
243 H4 Panabá Mex.

92 C5 Panabo Phil.
241 J3 Panaca NV U.S.A.
197 G2 Panaci Romania
116 E5 Panagar Madh. Prad. India
114 C2 Panagiri Andhra Prad. India
197 G4 Panagyurishte Bulg.
198 B2 Panaitolio Greece
114 B3 Panaji Goa India
246 B5 Panama country Central America
242 □K7 Panamá Panama
242 □K7 Panamá, Bahía de b. Panama
242 □K8 Panamá, Golfo de g. Panama
Panama, Gulf of Panama see Panamá, Golfo de
242 □K7 Panama Canal Panama
Panama City Panama see Panamá
231 C6 Panama City FL U.S.A.
240 I3 Panamint Range mts CA U.S.A.
240 I3 Panamint Valley CA U.S.A.
252 A2 Panao Peru
117 G4 Panar r. India
195 E4 Panarea, Isola i. Isole Lipari Italy
191 G4 Panaro r. Italy
95 F4 Panarukan Jawa Timur Indon.
163 C5 Panassac France
92 B4 Panay i. Phil.
92 B4 Panay Gulf Phil.
162 D3 Panazol France
215 H2 Panbult S. Africa
241 J2 Pancake Range mts NV U.S.A.
190 C4 Pancalieri Italy
257 G3 Pancas Brazil
196 E3 Pančevo Vojvodina, Srbija Yugo.
117 G4 Panchagarh Bangl.
137 F3 Pancheve Ukr.
109 G3 Panch'iao Taiwan
95 F2 Pancingapan, Bukit mt. Indon.
197 H3 Panciu Romania
183 G2 Pancorbo Spain
197 E2 Pâncota Romania
186 B4 Pancrudo Spain
186 B4 Pancrudo r. Spain
Pancsova Vojvodina, Srbija Yugo. see Pančevo
92 B4 Pandan Panay Phil.
92 C3 Pandan Phil.
116 E5 Pandaria Madh. Prad. India
114 C3 Pandavapura Karnataka India
94 D4 Pandeglang Jawa Barat Indon.
255 D5 Pandeiros r. Brazil
138 E3 Pandėlys Lith.
116 D5 Pandhana Madh. Prad. India
114 B2 Pandharpur Mahar. India
116 D5 Pandhurna Madh. Prad. India
82 D1 Pandie Pandie S.A. Austr.
190 E3 Pandino Italy
252 D2 Pando dept Bol.
261 J4 Pando Uru.
Pandokrátor hill Ionioi Nisoi Greece see Pantokratoras
232 B4 Pandora OH U.S.A.
85 F1 Pandora Entrance sea chan. Qld Austr.
142 C3 Pandrup Denmark
150 E3 Pandy Monmouthshire, Wales U.K.
177 G4 Pándzsa r. Hungary
Paneas Syria see Bāniyās
194 E5 Panebianco r. Sicilia Italy
253 E2 Panelas Brazil
183 F1 Panes Spain
138 E4 Panevėžys Lith.
Panfilov Kazakh. see Zharkent
135 H6 Panfilovo Rus. Fed.
137 F2 Panfyly Ukr.
100 C1 Pang r. China
96 B2 Pang, Nam r. Myanmar
79 □2 Pangai Tonga
114 C2 Pangal Andhra Prad. India
114 C2 Pangal Andhra Prad. India
95 E4 Pangandaran Jawa Barat Indon.
211 C6 Pangani Tanz.
211 C6 Pangani r. Tanz.
92 C3 Pañganiban Phil.
207 I5 Pangar r. Cameroon
151 F3 Pangbourne West Berkshire, England U.K.
157 G3 Pange France
78 □6 Panggoe Choiseul Solomon Is
123 H3 Pangi Range mts Pak.
93 A4 Pangkajene Sulawesi Selatan Indon.
95 E3 Pangkalanbuun Kalimantan Tengah Indon.
94 B1 Pangkalansusu Sumatera Indon.
94 C1 Pangkal Kalong Malaysia
94 D3 Pangkalpinang Indon.
223 J5 Pangman Sask. Can.
221 L3 Pangnirtung Nunavut Can.
209 B7 Pango Aluquém Angola
130 I3 Pangody Rus. Fed.
94 D4 Pangrango vol. Indon.
259 B5 Panguipulli Chile
241 K3 Panguitch UT U.S.A.
78 □6 Panguna P.N.G.
80 D1 Panguru North I. N.Z.
92 B5 Pangutaran Group is Phil.
237 C5 Panhandle TX U.S.A.
260 B4 Paniahue Chile
209 F6 Pania-Mwanga Dem. Rep. Congo
192 E1 Panicale Italy
78 □5 Panie, Mont mt. New Caledonia
260 B4 Panimávida Chile
116 C5 Pani Mines Gujarat India
135 H6 Panino Rus. Fed.
116 D3 Panipat Haryana India
160 C3 Panissières France
92 A4 Panitan Phil.
186 B3 Paniza Spain
139 H4 Panizowye Belarus
123 G2 Panj Tajik.
Panj r. Afgh./Tajik. see Pyandzh
123 F2 Panjakent Tajik.
Panjang i. Cocos Is see West Island
94 D4 Panjang Sumatera Indon.
163 B5 Panjas France
123 F5 Panjgur Pak.
116 C5 Panjhra r. India
Panjim Goa India see Panaji
107 I3 Panjin Liaoning China
123 G3 Panjkora r. Pak.
123 G4 Panjnad r. Pak.
140 O3 Pankakoski Fin.
168 F1 Panker Ger.
174 G5 Panki Pol.
139 H2 Pankovka Rus. Fed.
207 H4 Pankshin Nigeria
Panlian Sichuan China see Miyi
Panlong Henan China see Queshan
98 D7 Panna Madh. Prad. India
86 C4 Pannawonica W.A. Austr.
156 C4 Pannes France
193 H3 Panni Italy
165 E3 Panningen Neth.
177 G4 Pannonhalma Hungary
123 G5 Pano Aqil Pak.
184 B3 Panóias Port.
Panoplis Egypt see Akhmîm
256 B4 Panorama Brazil
Panormus Sicilia Italy see Palermo
114 C4 Panruti Tamil Nadu India
171 F4 Panschwitz-Kuckau Ger.
Panshan Liaoning China see Panjin
100 C4 Panshi Jilin China
Panshui Guizhou China see Pu'an
151 H3 Pant r. England U.K.
94 C3 Pantaicermin, Gunung mt. Indon.
253 F4 Pantanal de São Lourenço marsh Brazil
253 F4 Pantanal do Taquarí marsh Brazil
241 L6 Pantano AZ U.S.A.
93 C5 Pantar i. Indon.
137 G3 Pantayivka Ukr.
Pantelaria Sicilia Italy see Pantelleria
137 I3 Panteleymonivka Ukr.
194 A6 Pantelleria Sicilia Italy
194 B6 Pantelleria, Isola di i. Sicilia Italy
245 F3 Pantepec r. Mex.
Panticapaeum Ukr. see Kerch
186 C2 Panticosa Spain
183 G4 Pantoja Spain
198 A2 Pantokratoras hill Ionioi Nisoi Greece
86 F3 Panton r. W.A. Austr.
186 D3 Pantorrillas hill Spain
92 C5 Pantukan Phil.
150 D2 Pant-y-dwr Powys, Wales U.K.
245 E2 Pánuco Mex.
245 F2 Pánuco r. Mex.
114 B2 Panvel Mahar. India
116 D4 Panwari Uttar Prad. India
108 C3 Panxian Guizhou China
109 E4 Panyu Guangdong China
137 I3 Panyutyne Ukr.
108 B3 Panzhihua Sichuan China
209 C6 Panzi Dem. Rep. Congo
243 H6 Panzos Guat.
251 E2 Pao r. Venez.
254 F4 Pão de Açúcar Brazil
193 I5 Paola Italy
236 E4 Paola KS U.S.A.
230 C4 Paoli IN U.S.A.
234 C2 Paoli PA U.S.A.
192 B3 Paoloni, Serra hill Sardegna Italy
239 F4 Paonia CO U.S.A.
208 C3 Paoua C.A.R.
121 G4 Pap Uzbek.
176 G4 Pápa Hungary
240 □D9 Papa HI U.S.A.
193 H4 Papa, Monte del mt. Italy
240 □D9 Papaaloa HI U.S.A.
198 C3 Papadianika Greece
Papagaio r. Brazil see Sauêruiná
257 E3 Papagaios Brazil
245 E5 Papagayo r. Mex.
114 C3 Papagni r. India
240 □D9 Papaikou HI U.S.A.
80 E2 Papakura North I. N.Z.
245 G4 Papaloapan r. Mex.
80 F2 Papamoa Beach North I. N.Z.
114 C4 Papanasam Tamil Nadu India
114 C4 Papanasam Tamil Nadu India
245 F3 Papantla Mex.
250 C6 Papa Playa Peru
115 D2 Paparhahandi Orissa India
80 E2 Paparoa North I. N.Z.
81 C5 Paparoa Range mts South I. N.Z.
193 H5 Papasidero Italy
146 □G1 Papa Stour i. Scotland U.K.
146 F2 Papa Stronsay i. Scotland U.K.
177 G4 Pápateszér Hungary
80 E2 Papatoetoe North I. N.Z.
81 B7 Papatowai South I. N.Z.
146 F2 Papa Westray i. Scotland U.K.
Papay i. Scotland U.K. see Papa Westray
79 □3a Papeete Tahiti Fr. Polynesia
168 C2 Papenburg Ger.
170 D1 Papendorf Ger.
214 B4 Papendorp S. Africa
164 D3 Papendrecht Neth.
Paphos Cyprus see Pafos
Paphus Cyprus see Pafos
239 F6 Papigochic r. Mex.
197 G5 Papikio mt. Bulg./Greece
138 D3 Papilė Lith.
236 D3 Papillion NE U.S.A.
177 L2 Papín Slovakia
233 F2 Papineauville Que. Can.
197 H4 Papiya hill Bulg.
177 H4 Papkeszi Hungary
174 G2 Papowo Biskupie Pol.
173 E3 Pappenheim Ger.
175 K3 Paprotnia Pol.
146 B6 Paps of Jura hills Scotland U.K.
91 J8 Papua, Gulf of P.N.G.
78 □6 Papua New Guinea country Oceania
260 B3 Papudo Chile
96 B3 Papun Myanmar
84 B4 Papunya N.T. Austr.
151 G2 Papworth Everard Cambridgeshire, England U.K.
150 C4 Par Cornwall, England U.K.
257 E3 Pará r. Brazil
251 I5 Pará state Brazil
135 H5 Para r. Rus. Fed.
254 C2 Pará, Rio do r. Brazil
87 C4 Paraburdoo W.A. Austr.
177 I2 Paráč mt. Slovakia
92 B3 Paracale Phil.
257 F5 Paracambi Brazil
256 D2 Paracatu Brazil
256 D2 Paracatu r. Minas Gerais Brazil
257 E2 Paracatu r. Minas Gerais Brazil
90 D3 Paracel Islands S. China Sea
82 D2 Parachilna S.A. Austr.
123 G3 Parachinar Pak.
244 C4 Paracho Mex.
196 E4 Paraćin Srbija Yugo.
244 D3 Parácuaro Mex.
183 I5 Paracuellos Spain
254 F2 Paracuru Brazil
177 J4 Parád Hungary
182 C4 Parada Port.
182 C2 Parada Spain
182 B4 Parada de Ester Port.
182 C3 Parada de Pinhão Port.
183 E3 Parada de Rubiales Spain
185 E3 Paradas Spain
182 C3 Paradela Vila Real Port.
182 C3 Paradela Viseu Port.
182 C2 Paradela Spain
182 C3 Paradela de Guiães Port.
257 E3 Pará de Minas Brazil
224 E3 Paradis Que. Can.
225 J2 Paradise r. Nfld. Can.
251 G3 Paradise Guyana
240 G2 Paradise CA U.S.A.
226 E2 Paradise MI U.S.A.
241 J3 Paradise NV U.S.A.
222 H2 Paradise Gardens N.W.T. Can.
223 I4 Paradise Hill Sask. Can.
240 I2 Paradise Peak NV U.S.A.
225 J2 Paradise River Nfld. Can.
241 L5 Paradise Valley AZ U.S.A.
238 C3 Paradise Valley NV U.S.A.
117 F5 Paradwip Orissa India
175 I4 Paradyż Pol.
Paraetonium Egypt see Marsa Matrûh
137 G2 Parafiyivka Ukr.
138 F4 Paraf"yanava Belarus
254 D2 Paragominas Brazil
237 F4 Paragould AR U.S.A.
253 E3 Paragua r. Bol.
Paragua i. Phil. see Palawan
251 F3 Paragua r. Venez.
257 E4 Paraguaçu Brazil
256 B5 Paraguaçu Paulista Brazil
253 F5 Paraguai r. Brazil
246 E4 Paraguaná, Península de pen. Venez.
253 F6 Paraguarí Para.
258 F2 Paraguay r. Arg./Para.
253 F5 Paraguay country S. America
254 G3 Paraíba r. Brazil
254 F3 Paraíba state Brazil
257 F5 Paraíba do Sul Brazil
257 G4 Paraíba do Sul r. Brazil
257 E5 Paraibuna Brazil
Parainen Fin. see Pargas
243 G5 Paraíso Mex.
254 C4 Paraíso do Norte Brazil
257 E5 Paraisópolis Brazil
140 M2 Parakka Sweden
207 F4 Parakou Benin
82 D2 Parakylia S.A. Austr.
115 E2 Paralakhemundi Orissa India
198 C2 Paralia Greece
Paramagudi Tamil Nadu India see Paramakkudi
114 C4 Paramakkudi Tamil Nadu India
251 H3 Paramaribo Suriname
158 E3 Paramé France
250 C3 Paramillo mt. Col.
182 D3 Parâmio Port.
254 E5 Paramirim Brazil
254 E4 Paramirim r. Brazil
182 C2 Páramo hill Spain
182 D2 Páramo del Sil Spain
252 A2 Paramonga Peru
182 B4 Paramos Port.
235 D2 Paramus NJ U.S.A.
131 Q4 Paramushir, Ostrov i. Kuril'skiye O-va Rus. Fed.
198 B2 Paramythia Greece
261 G2 Paraná Arg.
254 D5 Paranã Brazil
254 C5 Paranã r. Brazil
256 B6 Paraná state Brazil
261 H4 Paraná r. S. America
261 H4 Paraná, Delta del Arg.
255 C8 Paranaguá Brazil
256 B3 Paranaíba Brazil
256 B4 Paranaíba r. Brazil
261 H3 Paraná Ibicuy r. Arg.
256 B3 Paranaiguara Brazil
253 F2 Paranaita r. Brazil
256 A5 Paranapanema r. Brazil
256 B6 Paranapiacaba, Serra mts Brazil
256 A5 Paranavaí Brazil
92 B5 Parang Phil.
114 D4 Parangi Aru r. Sri Lanka
114 C4 Parangipettai Tamil Nadu India
197 F3 Parângul Mare, Vârful mt. Romania
182 C4 Paranhos Port.
116 C5 Parantij Gujarat India
257 E3 Paraopeba Brazil
257 E3 Paraopeba r. Brazil
185 G3 Parapanda mt. Spain
93 C2 Parapara Halmahera Indon.
127 G4 Pārapāra Iraq
81 E4 Paraparaumu North I. N.Z.
256 B4 Parapuã Brazil
250 E3 Paraque, Cerro mt. Venez.
257 E5 Parati Brazil
254 E5 Paratinga Brazil
82 D3 Paratoo S.A. Austr.
127 G4 Parāū, Kūh-e mt. Iraq
254 C3 Parauapebas r. Brazil
251 H5 Parauaquara, Serra hill Brazil
251 G6 Parauari r. Brazil
129 E2 Paraulozen' r. Rus. Fed.
256 B2 Paraúna Brazil
160 C2 Paray-le-Monial France
116 D4 Parbati r. India
117 G4 Parbatipur Bangl.
114 C2 Parbhani Mahar. India
149 G4 Parbold Lancashire, England U.K.
247 □1 Parcelas Martorell Puerto Rico
187 C6 Parcent Spain
159 F4 Parcé-sur-Sarthe France
171 D3 Parchen Ger.
170 C2 Parchim Ger.
226 E4 Parchment MI U.S.A.
177 K3 Parchovany Slovakia
174 F1 Parchowo Pol.
175 J2 Parciaki Pol.
162 C3 Parcoul France
175 K4 Parczew Pol.
184 C2 Pardais Port.
226 C4 Pardeeville WI U.S.A.
163 B5 Pardies France
182 B4 Pardilhó Port.
197 I3 Pardina Romania
256 A4 Pardo r. Mato Grosso do Sul Brazil
255 F5 Pardo r. Bahia Brazil
255 D5 Pardo r. Minas Gerais Brazil
256 C4 Pardo r. São Paulo Brazil
256 C6 Pardo r. São Paulo Brazil
86 C4 Pardoo W.A. Austr.
176 E1 Pardubice Czech Rep.
176 F2 Pardubický kraj admin. reg. Czech Rep.
95 F4 Pare Jawa Timur Indon.
138 E5 Parechcha Belarus
111 B5 Pare Chu r. China
253 F3 Parecis r. Brazil
253 E2 Parecis, Serra dos hills Brazil
182 B3 Paredes Port.
182 B3 Paredes de Coura Port.
183 F2 Paredes de Nava Spain
260 B4 Paredones Chile
183 H4 Pareja Spain
161 A4 Pareloup, Lac de l. France
78 □4a Parem i. Chuuk Micronesia
81 E4 Paremata North I. N.Z.
78 □4b Parempei i. Pohnpei Micronesia
162 B4 Parempuyre France
114 B2 Parenda Mahar. India
224 F4 Parent Que. Can.
195 F3 Parenti Italy
163 A4 Parentis-en-Born France
81 C6 Pareora South I. N.Z.
93 A4 Parepare Sulawesi Selatan Indon.
260 E4 Parera Arg.
186 F3 Parets del Vallès Spain
171 C3 Parey Ger.
134 H4 Parfen'yevo Rus. Fed.
139 H3 Parfino Rus. Fed.
198 B2 Parga Greece
141 M3 Pargas Fin.
195 E4 Parghelia Italy
114 C2 Pargi Andhra Prad. India
157 E4 Pargny-sur-Saulx France
139 H1 Pargolovo Rus. Fed.
247 □2 Parham Antigua and Barbuda
252 D4 Paria Bol.
241 L3 Paria r. AZ/UT U.S.A.
247 □7 Paria, Gulf of Trin. and Tob./Venez.
251 F2 Paria, Península de pen. Venez.
94 C3 Pariaman Sumatera Indon.
241 K3 Paria Plateau AZ U.S.A.
244 C4 Paricutín, Volcán vol. Mex.
159 G4 Parigné-l'Évêque France
177 H5 Pári-hegy hill Hungary
141 O3 Parikkala Fin.
Parima r. Brazil see Uatatás
251 E4 Parima, Serra mts Brazil
250 C6 Parinari Peru
250 A6 Pariñas, Punta pt Peru
82 E3 Paringa S.A. Austr.
178 A5 Parino r. Italy
251 G5 Parintins Brazil
227 G4 Paris Ont. Can.
156 C4 Paris France
237 E5 Paris AR U.S.A.
238 E3 Paris ID U.S.A.
230 C4 Paris IL U.S.A.
232 A5 Paris KY U.S.A.
233 □H2 Paris ME U.S.A.
236 E4 Paris MO U.S.A.
237 F4 Paris TN U.S.A.
237 E5 Paris TX U.S.A.
153 Paris area map France
233 E3 Parish NY U.S.A.
163 D4 Parisot Midi-Pyrénées France
163 D5 Parisot Midi-Pyrénées France
120 E1 Parizh Rus. Fed.
236 D1 Park r. ND U.S.A.
140 M2 Parkajoki Sweden
114 C2 Parkal Andhra Prad. India
141 M3 Parkano Fin.
121 G4 Parkent Uzbek.
241 J4 Parker AZ U.S.A.
236 B4 Parker CO U.S.A.
236 D3 Parker SD U.S.A.
87 C7 Parker Range hills W.A. Austr.
232 C5 Parkersburg WV U.S.A.
83 G3 Parkes N.S.W. Austr.
234 C3 Parkesburg PA U.S.A.
226 B3 Park Falls WI U.S.A.
226 D5 Park Forest IL U.S.A.
Parkhar Tajik. see Farkhor
227 G4 Parkhill Ont. Can.
137 H2 Parkhomivka Ukr.
227 F2 Parkinson Ont. Can.
232 C4 Parkman OH U.S.A.
147 B5 Parknasilla Rep. of Ireland
236 E2 Park Rapids MN U.S.A.
233 F6 Parksley VA U.S.A.
173 G2 Parkstein Ger.
173 G3 Parkstetten Ger.
236 D3 Parkston SD U.S.A.
222 E5 Parksville B.C. Can.
116 D2 Parkutta Jammu and Kashmir
238 D3 Park Valley UT U.S.A.
234 B3 Parkville MD U.S.A.
183 G4 Parla Spain
Parlakimedi Orissa India see Paralakhemundi
115 E2 Parla Kimedi Orissa India
163 E4 Parlan France
114 C2 Parli Vaijnath Mahar. India
108 A2 Parlung Zangbo r. China
190 F4 Parma Italy
190 F4 Parma prov. Emilia-Romagna Italy
190 F4 Parma r. Italy
134 L2 Parma Rus. Fed.
238 C3 Parma ID U.S.A.
226 E4 Parma MI U.S.A.
232 C4 Parma OH U.S.A.
163 A5 Parme airport France
254 D4 Parnaguá Brazil
254 E2 Parnaíba Brazil
254 B4 Parnaíba r. Brazil
254 D4 Parnaibinha r. Brazil
254 E3 Parnarama Brazil
198 C2 Parnassos mt. Greece
81 D5 Parnassus South I. N.Z.
82 D3 Parndana S.A. Austr.
179 H3 Parndorf Austria
114 B2 Parner Mahar. India
198 C3 Parnon mts Greece
138 E2 Pärnu Estonia
138 E2 Pärnu r. Estonia
138 E2 Pärnu-Jaagupi Estonia
117 G4 Paro Bhutan
81 C5 Paroa South I. N.Z.
138 E1 Parola Fin.
156 D4 Paron France
Parona Turkey see Fındık
123 E3 Paropamisus mts Afgh.
93 A3 Paroreang, Bukit mt. Indon.
198 D3 Paros Notio Aigaio Greece
198 D3 Paros i. Greece
214 B5 Parow S. Africa
241 K3 Parowan UT U.S.A.
161 E4 Parpaillon mts France
82 E3 Parrakie S.A. Austr.
260 B5 Parral Chile
237 B7 Parral r. Mex.
83 G3 Parramatta N.S.W. Austr.
242 E3 Parras Mex.
150 D3 Parrett r. England U.K.
183 E4 Parrillas Spain
226 C3 Parrish WI U.S.A.
242 □I7 Parrita Costa Rica
225 H4 Parrsboro N.S. Can.
221 G2 Parry Channel Nunavut Can.
Parry Island Cook Is see Mauke
221 G2 Parry Islands Nunavut Can.
86 B4 Parry Range hills W.A. Austr.
224 D4 Parry Sound Ont. Can.
234 C2 Parryville PA U.S.A.
Pars prov. Iran see Fārs
117 F4 Parsa Bihar India
Parsa prov. Iran see Fārs
129 E4 Pārsābād Iran
168 F3 Parsau Ger.
173 F2 Parsberg Ger.
178 B3 Parseierspitze mt. Austria
174 D1 Parsęta r. Pol.
236 C2 Parshall ND U.S.A.
235 D2 Parsippany NJ U.S.A.
241 J2 Parsnip Peak NV U.S.A.
237 E4 Parsons KS U.S.A.
232 D5 Parsons WV U.S.A.
170 F3 Parstein Ger.
170 E3 Parsteiner See l. Ger.
114 B2 Partabgarh Mahar. India
114 D2 Partabpur Madh. Prad. India
117 E5 Partabpur Madh. Prad. India
185 H3 Partaloa Spain
194 B5 Partanna Sicilia Italy
140 L2 Pårte mt. Sweden
169 E5 Partenstein Ger.
162 B2 Parthenay France
192 A2 Partinello Corse France
149 G4 Partington Greater Manchester, England U.K.
194 C4 Partinico Sicilia Italy
100 E4 Partizansk Rus. Fed.
177 I2 Partizánska Ľupča Slovakia
177 H3 Partizánske Slovakia
149 J4 Partney Lincolnshire, England U.K.
149 F3 Parton Cumbria, England U.K.
224 D3 Partridge r. Ont. Can.
147 B3 Partry Rep. of Ireland
129 C2 P'arts'khanaqanevi Georgia
137 H4 Partyzany Ukr.
251 H5 Paru r. Brazil
251 E3 Parú, Serranía mts Venez.
251 G5 Paru de Oeste r. Brazil
114 C4 Parur Kerala India
137 F4 Parutyne Ukr.
123 G3 Parvān prov. Afgh.
122 D3 Parvāreh Iran
115 D2 Parvatipuram Andhra Prad. India
116 C4 Parvatsar Rajasthan India
111 C6 Paryang Xizang China
138 G5 Parychy Belarus
143 F3 Påryd Sweden
215 F2 Parys S. Africa
175 J4 Parysów Pol.
175 H4 Parzęczew Pol.
183 G1 Pas r. Spain
240 H4 Pasadena CA U.S.A.
234 B3 Pasadena MD U.S.A.
237 E6 Pasadena TX U.S.A.
186 B1 Pasai Donibane Spain
250 B5 Pasaje Ecuador
96 C4 Pa Sak, Mae Nam r. Thai.
129 C3 Paşalı Turkey
116 E5 Pasan Madh. Prad. India
129 D2 P'asanauri Georgia
127 I5 Pasargadae tourist site Iran
224 F3 Pascagama r. Que. Can.
237 F6 Pascagoula MS U.S.A.
237 F6 Pascagoula r. MS U.S.A.
227 I1 Pascalis Que. Can.
197 H2 Paşcani Romania
179 F2 Pasching Austria
252 B2 Pasco dept Peru
238 C2 Pasco WA U.S.A.
233 H4 Pascoag RI U.S.A.
257 H2 Pascoal, Monte hill Brazil
85 E2 Pascoe r. Qld Austr.
84 D3 Pascoe Inlet Qld Austr.
248 C5 Pascua, Isla de i. S. Pacific Ocean
92 B3 Pascual Phil.
156 C2 Pas-de-Calais dept Nord - Pas-de-Calais France
Pas de Calais str. France/U.K. see Dover, Strait of
156 C2 Pas-en-Artois France
170 F2 Pasewalk Ger.
139 I1 Pasha Rus. Fed.
139 I1 Pasha r. Rus. Fed.
137 J5 Pashkovskiy Rus. Fed.
191 I2 Pasiàn di Prato Italy
178 D5 Pasiano di Pordenone Italy
175 J3 Pasieki Pol.
92 B3 Pasig Phil.
117 H3 Pasighat Arun. Prad. India
127 F3 Pasinler Turkey
95 F5 Pasirian Jawa Timur Indon.
94 C1 Pasir Mas Malaysia
94 C2 Pasirpangarayan Sumatera Indon.
94 C1 Pasir Putih Malaysia
93 B4 Pasitelu, Pulau-pulau is Indon.
143 G3 Påskallavik Sweden
177 H2 Paskov Czech Rep.
123 E5 Paskūh Iran
143 H4 Pasłęk Pol.
143 H4 Pasłęka r. Pol.
87 D7 Pasley, Cape W.A. Austr.
188 E4 Pašman i. Croatia
123 E5 Pasni Pak.
245 F4 Paso del Macho Mex.
261 I1 Paso de los Libres Arg.
261 I3 Paso de los Toros Uru.
245 F4 Paso de Ovejas Mex.
253 F6 Paso de Patria Para.
259 C7 Paso Río Mayo Arg.
240 G4 Paso Robles CA U.S.A.
223 K4 Pasquia Hills Sask. Can.
123 H3 Pasrur Pak.
233 □I2 Passadumkeag ME U.S.A.
254 E3 Passagem Franca Brazil
147 C5 Passage West Rep. of Ireland
235 D2 Passaic NJ U.S.A.
235 D2 Passaic r. NJ U.S.A.
235 D1 Passaic County county NJ U.S.A.
179 G3 Passail Austria
159 F3 Passais France
217 □3b Passamaïnti Mayotte
257 E5 Passa Quatro Brazil
257 E4 Passa Tempo Brazil
173 H3 Passau Ger.
157 G5 Passavant-la-Rochère France
92 B4 Passi Phil.
192 E1 Passignano sul Trasimeno Italy
191 G2 Passirio r. Italy
255 B9 Passo Fundo Brazil
255 B9 Passo Real, Barragem resr Brazil
256 D4 Passos Brazil
170 F2 Passow Ger.
160 E3 Passy France
138 F4 Pastavy Belarus
250 B5 Pastaza prov. Ecuador
250 B6 Pastaza r. Peru
261 F4 Pasteur Arg.
250 B4 Pasto Col.
241 M3 Pastora Peak AZ U.S.A.
182 C1 Pastoriza Spain
244 D3 Pastor Ortiz Mex.
254 D3 Pastos Bons Brazil
183 H4 Pastrana Spain
116 C1 Pasu Jammu and Kashmir
92 B2 Pasuquin Phil.
Pasur Turkey see Kulp
95 F4 Pasuruan Jawa Timur Indon.
138 E3 Pasvalys Lith.
Pasvikelva r. Europe see Patsoyoki
175 I2 Pasym Pol.
174 E4 Paszowice Pol.
177 I4 Pásztó Hungary
252 C3 Pata Bol.
177 G3 Pata Slovakia
241 L6 Patagonia AZ U.S.A.
182 B5 Pataias Port.
Pataliputra Bihar India see Patna
Patan Gujarat India see Somnath
116 C5 Patan Gujarat India
116 D5 Patan Madh. Prad. India
114 B2 Patan Mahar. India
117 F4 Patan Nepal
114 C2 Patancheru Andhra Prad. India
123 F5 Patandar, Koh-i- mt. Pak.
207 G5 Patani Nigeria
116 D5 Patan Saongi Mahar. India
234 B3 Patapsco r. MD U.S.A.
234 B3 Patapsco, South Branch r. MD U.S.A.
116 D3 Pataudi Haryana India
Patavium Italy see Padova
156 B4 Patay France
83 E3 Patchewollock Vic. Austr.
235 E2 Patchogue NY U.S.A.
150 E3 Patchway South Gloucestershire, England U.K.
80 E3 Patea North I. N.Z.
Patea inlet South I. N.Z. see Doubtful Sound
80 E3 Patea r. North I. N.Z.
149 H3 Pateley Bridge North Yorkshire, England U.K.
215 E5 Patensie S. Africa
179 E4 Patergassen Austria
187 C5 Paterna Spain
184 D3 Paterna del Campo Spain
184 E4 Paterna de Rivera Spain
179 E4 Paternion Austria
193 H4 Paterno Basilicata Italy
194 D5 Paternò Sicilia Italy
193 H4 Paternopoli Italy
214 A5 Paternoster S. Africa
173 G2 Patersdorf Ger.
83 G3 Paterson N.S.W. Austr.
83 F2 Paterson r. Qld Austr.
215 E5 Paterson S. Africa
233 F4 Paterson NJ U.S.A.
86 D4 Paterson Range hills W.A. Austr.
117 E5 Pathalgaon Madh. Prad. India
114 C4 Pathanamthitta Kerala India
116 C2 Pathankot Punjab India
116 D5 Patharia Madh. Prad. India
Pathein Myanmar see Bassein
97 B5 Pathiu Thai.
114 C2 Pathri Mahar. India
97 C4 Pathum Thani Thai.
250 E5 Pati r. Brazil
116 C5 Pati Madh. Prad. India
95 E4 Pati Jawa Tengah Indon.
250 B4 Patía r. Col.
116 D3 Patiala Punjab India
247 □1 Patillas Puerto Rico
252 A2 Pativilca r. Peru
96 A1 Pātkai Bum mts India/Myanmar
111 D4 Patkaklik Xinjiang China
199 F3 Patlangıç Turkey
199 E3 Patmos i. Greece
117 F4 Patna Bihar India
146 D6 Patna East Ayrshire, Scotland U.K.
117 E5 Patnagarh Orissa India
127 F3 Patnos Turkey
174 G4 Pątnów Pol.
259 B7 Pato, Cerro mt. Chile
255 B8 Pato Branco Brazil
114 B2 Patoda Mahar. India
230 C4 Patoka r. IN U.S.A.
131 M4 Patomskoye Nagor'ye mts Rus. Fed.
198 A1 Patos Albania
254 F3 Patos Brazil
255 C9 Patos, Lagoa dos l. Brazil
256 D3 Patos de Minas Brazil
260 D2 Patquía Arg.
198 B2 Patra Greece
Patrae Greece see Patra
Pátrai Greece see Patra
198 B2 Patraïkos Kolpos b. Greece
Patras Greece see Patra
117 F5 Patrasaer W. Bengal India
117 F5 Patratu Bihar India
116 B5 Patri Gujarat India
195 E4 Patri r. Sicilia Italy
81 D4 Patriarch, Mount South I. N.Z.
193 F3 Patrica Italy
84 B4 Patricia, Mount hill N.T. Austr.
259 B8 Patricio Lynch, Isla i. Chile
232 C6 Patrick Springs VA U.S.A.
147 C4 Patrickswell Rep. of Ireland
192 B2 Patrimonio Corse France
149 J4 Patrington East Riding of Yorkshire, England U.K.
256 D3 Patrocínio Brazil
177 K3 Pátroha Hungary
178 C3 Patscherkofel mt. Austria
134 E1 Patsoyoki r. Europe
192 B4 Pattada Sardegna Italy
114 B2 Pattadakal tourist site Karnataka India
114 C4 Pattanapuram Kerala India
97 C6 Pattani Thai.
97 C6 Pattani r. Thai.
97 C4 Pattaya Thai.
233 □I2 Patten ME U.S.A.
234 C2 Pattenburg NJ U.S.A.
169 E3 Pattensen Ger.
149 G3 Patterdale Cumbria, England U.K.
240 G3 Patterson CA U.S.A.
237 F6 Patterson LA U.S.A.
235 E1 Patterson NY U.S.A.
232 D5 Patterson r. WV U.S.A.
222 C1 Patterson, Mount Y.T. Can.
240 H3 Patterson Mountain CA U.S.A.
116 E4 Patti Uttar Prad. India
194 D4 Patti Sicilia Italy
140 N2 Pattijoki Fin.
114 C3 Pattikonda Andhra Prad. India
150 E2 Pattingham Staffordshire, England U.K.
114 C4 Pattukkottai Tamil Nadu India
222 D3 Pattullo, Mount B.C. Can.
254 F3 Patu Brazil
117 G5 Patuakhali Bangl.
223 J4 Patuanak Sask. Can.
242 □I6 Patuca r. Hond.
197 F3 Pătulele Romania
116 D5 Patur Mahar. India
165 C4 Pâturages Belgium
80 E3 Patutu mt. North I. N.Z.
232 E5 Patuxent r. MD U.S.A.
262 S1 Patuxent Range mts Antarctica
177 H4 Páty Hungary
244 D4 Pátzcuaro Mex.
244 D4 Patzcuaro, Laguna de l. Mex.
163 B5 Pau France
Pau airport France see Pyrénées
252 B3 Paucarbamba Peru
252 B2 Paucartambo Peru
Paucartambo r. Peru see Yavero
253 H1 Pau d'Arco r. Brazil
179 G2 Paudorf Austria
117 G4 Pauhunri mt. Sikkim China/India
163 C5 Pauilhac France
162 B3 Pauillac France
252 D1 Pauini Brazil
252 D1 Pauiní r. Brazil
251 F5 Pauini r. Brazil
96 A2 Pauk Myanmar
182 C4 Paul Port.
191 I2 Paularo Italy
220 F3 Paulatuk N.W.T. Can.
241 K4 Paulden AZ U.S.A.
237 F5 Paulding MS U.S.A.
232 A4 Paulding OH U.S.A.
161 A3 Paulhac France
161 B4 Paulhac-en-Margeride France
161 B3 Paulhaguet France
161 B5 Paulhan France
256 B4 Paulicéia Brazil
192 A4 Paulilatino Sardegna Italy
170 D3 Paulinenaue Ger.
163 E5 Paulinet France
234 C2 Paulins Kill r. NJ U.S.A.
Paulis Dem. Rep. Congo see Isiro
197 E2 Păuliș Romania
254 G3 Paulista Brazil
254 E4 Paulistana Brazil
236 E3 Paullina IA U.S.A.
254 F4 Paulo Afonso Brazil
256 C4 Paulo de Faria Brazil
215 H2 Paulpietersburg S. Africa
186 D4 Paüls dels Ports Spain
237 D5 Pauls Valley OK U.S.A.
150 E3 Paulton Bath and North East Somerset, England U.K.
158 E5 Paulx France
Paum i. Vanuatu see Paama
Paumotu, Îles is Fr. Polynesia see Tuamotu, Archipel des
197 H2 Păunești Romania
96 A3 Paungde Myanmar
116 D5 Pauni Mahar. India
234 C1 Paupack PA U.S.A.
116 D3 Pauri Uttar Prad. India
171 D5 Pausa Ger.
250 D3 Pauto r. Col.
140 L2 Pauträsk Sweden
156 E3 Pauvres France
240 □C8 Pauwela HI U.S.A.
114 C3 Pavagada Karnataka India
257 G2 Pavão Brazil
122 A3 Pāveh Iran
139 L5 Pavelets Rus. Fed.
190 E3 Pavia Italy
190 E3 Pavia prov. Lombardia Italy
184 B2 Pavia Port.
182 B4 Pavia r. Port.
191 I3 Pavia di Udine Italy
187 C5 Pavías Spain
163 C5 Pavie France
232 D3 Pavilion NY U.S.A.
156 A3 Pavilly France
138 C3 Pāvilosta Latvia
134 I4 Pavino Rus. Fed.
138 D4 Pavištyčio kalnas hill Lith.
175 M4 Pavitstsye Belarus
197 G4 Pavlikeni Bulg.
136 E4 Pavlivka Odes'ka Oblast' Ukr.
137 H2 Pavlivka Sums'ka Oblast' Ukr.
136 C2 Pavlivka Volyns'ka Oblast' Ukr.
121 I1 Pavlodar Kazakh.
Pavlodar Oblast admin. div. Kazakh. see Pavlodarskaya Oblast'
Pavlodar Oblysy admin. div. Kazakh. see Pavlodarskaya Oblast'
121 I1 Pavlodarskaya Oblast' admin. div. Kazakh.
220 B4 Pavlof Volcano AK U.S.A.
Pavlograd Ukr. see Pavlohrad
121 H1 Pavlogradka Rus. Fed.
137 H3 Pavlohrad Ukr.
137 H4 Pavlopillya Ukr.
177 L3 Pavlovce nad Uhom Slovakia
121 H2 Pavlovka Akmolinskaya Oblast' Kazakh.
120 E1 Pavlovka Kustanayskaya Oblast' Kazakh.
134 L5 Pavlovka Respublika Bashkortostan Rus. Fed.
120 A1 Pavlovka Ul'yanovskaya Oblast' Rus. Fed.
134 H5 Pavlovo Rus. Fed.
121 J1 Pavlovsk Altayskiy Kray Rus. Fed.
139 H2 Pavlovsk Leningradskaya Oblast' Rus. Fed.
135 H6 Pavlovsk Voronezhskaya Oblast' Rus. Fed.
135 G7 Pavlovskaya Rus. Fed.
120 E1 Pavlovskiy Kazakh.
139 L4 Pavlovskiy Posad Rus. Fed.
137 G3 Pavlysh Ukr.
191 F4 Pavullo nel Frignano Italy
78 □6 Pavuvu i. Solomon Is
116 E4 Pawai Madh. Prad. India
95 E3 Pawan r. Indon.
80 D1 Pawarenga North I. N.Z.
116 E3 Pawayan Uttar Prad. India
235 G1 Pawcatuck CT U.S.A.
171 D3 Päwesin Ger.
237 D4 Pawhuska OK U.S.A.
235 E1 Pawling NY U.S.A.
174 F2 Pawłówek Pol.
174 G6 Pawłowice Pol.
174 E4 Pawłowice Pol.
174 G5 Pawłowiczki Pol.
96 B3 Pawn r. Myanmar
237 D4 Pawnee OK U.S.A.
236 D4 Pawnee r. KS U.S.A.
236 D3 Pawnee City NE U.S.A.
174 G5 Pawonków Pol.
226 E4 Paw Paw MI U.S.A.
232 D5 Paw Paw WV U.S.A.
233 H4 Pawtucket RI U.S.A.
182 C2 Paxaro mt. Spain
234 B2 Paxinos PA U.S.A.
198 B2 Paxoi i. Greece
220 D3 Paxson AK U.S.A.
146 F6 Paxton Scottish Borders, Scotland U.K.
226 C5 Paxton IL U.S.A.
236 C3 Paxton NE U.S.A.
234 B2 Paxtonia PA U.S.A.
234 A2 Paxtonville PA U.S.A.
94 C3 Payakumbuh Sumatera Indon.
114 B3 Payaswani r. India
179 G3 Payerbach Austria
190 B2 Payerne Switz.
238 C2 Payette ID U.S.A.
238 C2 Payette r. ID U.S.A.
134 M1 Pay-Khoy, Khrebet hills Rus. Fed.
184 C3 Paymogo Spain
Payne Que. Can. see Kangirsuk
232 A4 Payne OH U.S.A.
240 G1 Paynes Creek CA U.S.A.
87 C6 Payne's Find W.A. Austr.
83 F4 Paynesville Vic. Austr.
236 E2 Paynesville MN U.S.A.
163 D4 Payrac France
163 E5 Payrin-Augmontel France
261 H3 Paysandú Uru.
261 I3 Paysandú dept Uru.
162 A1 Pays de la Loire admin. reg. France
163 E6 Pays de Sault reg. France
121 F4 Payshanba Uzbek.
241 L4 Payson AZ U.S.A.
260 C5 Payún, Altiplanicie del plat. Arg.
260 C5 Payún, Cerro vol. Arg.
134 N2 Payyer, Gora mt. Rus. Fed.
162 D3 Payzac France
Payzawat Xinjiang China see Jiashi
254 C4 Paz, Rio da r. Brazil
127 F2 Pazar Turkey
126 E3 Pazarcık Turkey
197 G4 Pazardzhik Bulg.
199 E2 Pazarköy Turkey
199 F2 Pazarlar Turkey
199 F2 Pazaryeri Turkey
129 B3 Pazaryolu Turkey
250 D3 Paz de Ariporo Col.
250 C3 Paz de Rio Col.
188 D3 Pazin Croatia
163 E6 Paziols France
182 B1 Pazo de Irixoa Spain
182 B2 Pazos Spain
139 H2 Pchevzha r. Rus. Fed.
175 H6 Pcim Pol.
197 E5 Pčinja r. Macedonia
256 A5 Peabiru Brazil
236 D4 Peabody KS U.S.A.
233 H3 Peabody MA U.S.A.
222 I3 Peace r. Alta/B.C. Can.
231 D7 Peace r. FL U.S.A.
151 G4 Peacehaven East Sussex, England U.K.
223 H3 Peace Point Alta Can.
222 G3 Peace River Alta Can.
232 C6 Peach Creek WV U.S.A.
222 G5 Peachland B.C. Can.
241 K4 Peach Springs AZ U.S.A.
87 D7 Peak Charles hill W.A. Austr.
149 H4 Peak District National Park England U.K.
233 □I1 Peaked Mountain hill ME U.S.A.
83 G3 Peak Hill N.S.W. Austr.
87 C5 Peak Hill W.A. Austr.
240 H4 Peak Mountain CA U.S.A.
85 G4 Peak Range hills Qld Austr.
185 G3 Peal de Becerro Spain
241 M2 Peale, Mount UT U.S.A.
241 M6 Pearce AZ U.S.A.
84 B2 Pearce Point N.T. Austr.
232 C6 Pearisburg VA U.S.A.
226 C1 Pearl Ont. Can.
237 F6 Pearl r. MS U.S.A.
75 H1 Pearl and Hermes Atoll HI U.S.A.
240 □ Pearl City HI U.S.A.
Pearl River r. China see Zhu Jiang
235 D1 Pearl River NY U.S.A.
237 D6 Pearsall TX U.S.A.
231 D6 Pearson GA U.S.A.
226 C3 Pearson WI U.S.A.
82 C3 Pearson Islands S.A. Austr.
215 E5 Pearston S. Africa
221 I2 Peary Channel Nunavut Can.
221 O1 Peary Land reg. Greenland
237 D5 Pease r. TX U.S.A.
150 E3 Peasedown St John Bath and North East Somerset, England U.K.
158 D4 Péaule France
86 C4 Peawah r. W.A. Austr.
224 C2 Peawanuck Ont. Can.
213 H3 Pebane Moz.
250 D5 Pebas Peru
161 B3 Pébrac France
196 E4 Peć Kosovo, Srbija Yugo.
237 D6 Pecan Bayou r. TX U.S.A.
257 F3 Peçanha Brazil
237 E6 Pecan Island LA U.S.A.
256 C6 Peças, Ilha das i. Brazil
226 C4 Pecatonica IL U.S.A.
190 D2 Peccia Switz.
191 F5 Peccioli Italy
177 I4 Pécel Hungary
140 O1 Pecha r. Rus. Fed.
140 O1 Pechenga Rus. Fed.
140 O1 Pechenga r. Rus. Fed.
137 I3 Pechenihy Ukr.
137 I3 Pecheniz'ke Vodoskhovyshche resr Ukr.
139 L4 Pecherniki Rus. Fed.
139 I4 Pechersk Rus. Fed.
185 H4 Pechina Spain
134 L2 Pechora Rus. Fed.
134 K1 Pechora r. Rus. Fed.
Pechora Sea Rus. Fed. see Pechorskoye More
134 K1 Pechorskaya Guba b. Rus. Fed.
134 K1 Pechorskoye More sea Rus. Fed.
138 F3 Pechory Rus. Fed.
196 E2 Pecica Romania
197 I4 Pecineaga Romania
227 F4 Peck MI U.S.A.
234 C1 Pecks Pond PA U.S.A.
176 E1 Pečky Czech Rep.
174 E4 Pęcław Pol.
192 C2 Pecora r. Italy
237 C6 Pecos TX U.S.A.
237 C6 Pecos r. New Mexico/Texas U.S.A.
165 C4 Pecq Belgium
177 H5 Pécs Hungary
177 H5 Pécsvárad Hungary
174 G4 Pęczniew Pol.
193 F1 Pedaso Italy
114 C2 Peddavagu r. India
114 C2 Pedda Vagu r. India
83 F5 Pedder, Lake Tas. Austr.
215 F5 Peddie S. Africa
138 F3 Pededze r. Latvia
250 A4 Pedernales Ecuador
246 E3 Pedernales Haiti
239 F6 Pedernales Mex.
237 D6 Pedernales r. TX U.S.A.
251 F2 Pedernales Venez.
256 C5 Pederneiras Brazil
191 G3 Pederobba Italy
140 M3 Pedersöre Fin.
138 F2 Pedja r. Estonia
257 G1 Pedra Azul Brazil
206 □ Pedra Badejo São Tiago Cape Verde
182 B3 Pedrada mt. Port.
182 C2 Pedrafita do Cebreiro Spain
182 B3 Pedra Furada Port.
183 F3 Pedrajas de San Esteban Spain
187 C5 Pedralba Spain
182 D2 Pedralba de la Pradería Spain
254 C5 Pedra Preta, Serra da mts Brazil
254 B3 Pedras r. Amazonas Brazil
254 D5 Pedras r. Bahia Brazil
250 D2 Pedregal Venez.
187 D6 Pedreguer Spain
256 D4 Pedregulho Brazil
254 D3 Pedreiras Maranhão Brazil
256 D5 Pedreiras São Paulo Brazil
185 F3 Pedrera Spain
186 F3 Pedres hill Spain
242 E3 Pedriceña Mex.
234 C3 Pedricktown NJ U.S.A.
183 G3 Pedro r. Spain
185 F3 Pedro Abad Spain
254 C4 Pedro Afonso Brazil
254 F3 Pedro Avelino Brazil
246 C3 Pedro Bank sea feature Jamaica
256 D6 Pedro Barros Brazil
183 F4 Pedro Bernardo Spain
246 C3 Pedro Cays is Jamaica
185 F2 Pedroche Spain
250 D4 Pedro Chico Col.
252 C5 Pedro de Valdivia Chile
244 D3 Pedro Escobedo Mex.
184 C2 Pedrógão Port.
182 C4 Pedrógão Port.
182 B5 Pedrógão Port.
182 B5 Pedrógão Grande Port.
182 B5 Pedrógão Pequeno Port.
255 B6 Pedro Gomes Brazil
184 E1 Pedro Gómez mt. Spain
250 E4 Pedro II, Ilha reg. Brazil/Venez.
253 G5 Pedro Juan Caballero Para.
257 E3 Pedro Leopoldo Brazil
254 E3 Pedroll Brazil
185 G3 Pedro-Martínez Spain
185 H1 Pedro Muñoz Spain
258 G3 Pedro Osório Brazil
183 G1 Pedrosa Spain
183 F2 Pedrosa del Príncipe Spain
182 E4 Pedrosillo de los Aires Spain
182 B3 Pedroso Port.
183 H2 Pedroso Spain
256 D6 Pedro Toledo Brazil
163 D6 Pédrous, Pic mt. France
182 B2 Pedrouzos Spain

192 A4 **Pedruso, Monte** hill Sardegna Italy
82 E3 **Peebinga** S.A. Austr.
146 E6 **Peebles** Scottish Borders, Scotland U.K.
232 B5 **Peebles** OH U.S.A.
86 B4 **Peedamulla** W.A. Austr.
231 E5 **Pee Dee** r. SC U.S.A.
233 G4 **Peekskill** NY U.S.A.
220 E3 **Peel** r. Y.T. Can.
148 E3 **Peel** Isle of Man
81 C5 **Peel, Mount** South I. N.Z.
87 B7 **Peel Inlet** W.A. Austr.
170 E2 **Peene** r. Ger.
170 E1 **Peenemünde** Ger.
165 E3 **Peer** Belgium
82 D1 **Peera Peera Poolanna Lake** salt flat S.A. Austr.
222 H3 **Peerless Lake** Alta Can.
222 G4 **Peers** Alta Can.
182 C4 **Pega** Port.
161 B5 **Pégairolles-de-l'Escalette** France
81 D5 **Pegasus Bay** South I. N.Z.
171 D4 **Pegau** Ger.
179 G3 **Peggau** Austria
190 D4 **Pegli** Italy
193 H4 **Peglio** r. Italy
173 F2 **Pegnitz** Ger.
173 E2 **Pegnitz** r. Ger.
184 B1 **Pego** Port.
187 C6 **Pego** Spain
184 B2 **Pego do Altar, Barragem do** resr Port.
184 B2 **Pegões** Port.
174 E4 **Pęgów** Pol.
96 B3 **Pegu** Myanmar
96 A3 **Pegu** admin. div. Myanmar
187 F5 **Peguera** Spain
96 A3 **Pegu Yoma** mts Myanmar
151 I3 **Pegwell Bay** England U.K.
199 E1 **Pehlivanköy** Turkey
207 F4 **Péhonko** Benin
116 D3 **Pehowa** Haryana India
261 G4 **Pehuajó** Arg.
109 G4 **Peikang** Taiwan
158 D4 **Peillac** France
161 F5 **Peille** France
146 B4 **Peinchorran** Highland, Scotland U.K.
169 F3 **Peine** Ger.
259 B8 **Peineta, Cerro** mt. Arg.
116 C5 **Peint** Mahar. India
191 F2 **Peio** Italy
161 D4 **Peipin** France
Peipsi järv l. Estonia/Rus. Fed. see **Peipus, Lake**
138 F2 **Peipus, Lake** Estonia/Rus. Fed.
161 F5 **Peïra-Cava** France
198 C3 **Peiraias** Greece
160 E3 **Peisey-Nancroix** France
Pei Shan mts China see **Bei Shan**
171 C4 **Peißen** Ger.
171 D4 **Peißen** Ger.
173 F4 **Peißenberg** Ger.
173 E4 **Peiting** Ger.
171 F4 **Peitz** Ger.
254 C5 **Peixe** Brazil
256 C2 **Peixe** r. Goiás Brazil
254 C5 **Peixe** r. Goiás Brazil
256 B4 **Peixe** r. São Paulo Brazil
256 A2 **Peixe, Rio do** r. Brazil
257 F5 **Peixes** r. Brazil
253 F2 **Peixes** r. Brazil
107 H5 **Peixian** Jiangsu China
Peixian Jiangsu China see **Pizhou**
256 D4 **Peixoto, Represa** resr Brazil
254 B4 **Peixoto de Azevedo** Brazil
253 G2 **Peixoto de Azevedo** r. Brazil
164 F1 **Peize** Neth.
Peje Kosovo, Srbija Yugo. see **Peć**
197 E3 **Pek** r. Yugo.
215 F3 **Peka** Lesotho
95 E4 **Pekalongan** Jawa Tengah Indon.
94 C2 **Pekanbaru** Sumatera Indon.
225 H2 **Pékans, Rivière aux** r. Que. Can.
207 F5 **Peki** Ghana
226 C5 **Pekin** IL U.S.A.
Peking Beijing China see **Beijing**
94 C2 **Pelabuhan Kelang** Malaysia
259 C7 **Pelada, Pampa** hills Arg.
187 B5 **Pelado** mt. Spain
189 D8 **Pelagie, Isole** is Sicilia Italy
191 G5 **Pelago** Italy
196 E5 **Pelagonija** plain Macedonia
183 F4 **Pelahustán** Spain
95 F3 **Pelaihari** Kalimantan Selatan Indon.
260 B4 **Pelarco** Chile
182 B5 **Pelariga** Port.
182 D4 **Pelarrodríguez** Spain
198 C2 **Pelasgia** Greece
Pelasyía Greece see **Pelasgia**
161 E4 **Pelat, Mont** mt. France
215 G3 **Pelatsoeu** mt. Lesotho
78 □6 **Pelau** i. Solomon Is
174 D2 **Pełczyce** Pol.
197 F3 **Peleaga, Vârful** mt. Romania
183 E3 **Peleagonzalo** Spain
247 □3 **Pelée, Montagne** vol. Martinique
224 D5 **Pelee Island** Ont. Can.
224 D5 **Pelee Point** Ont. Can.
92 □ **Peleliu** i. Palau
134 J3 **Peles** Rus. Fed.
176 E2 **Pelhřimov** Czech Rep.
220 E4 **Pelican** AK U.S.A.
85 E3 **Pelican Creek** r. Qld Austr.
226 C3 **Pelican Lake** WI U.S.A.
223 K4 **Pelican Narrows** Sask. Can.
185 G3 **Peligros** Spain
136 D4 **Pelinia** Moldova
161 D5 **Pélissanne** France
196 E5 **Pelister** mt. Macedonia
188 F4 **Pelješac** pen. Croatia
140 N2 **Pelkosenniemi** Fin.
214 B3 **Pella** S. Africa
226 A1 **Pelland** MN U.S.A.
195 E4 **Pellaro** Italy
231 C5 **Pell City** AL U.S.A.
261 F5 **Pellegrini** Arg.
260 D6 **Pellegrini, Lago** l. Arg.
190 E4 **Pellegrino Parmense** Italy
163 C4 **Pellegrue** France
177 H5 **Pellérd** Hungary
191 H3 **Pellestrina** Italy
159 H5 **Pellevoisin** France
190 C4 **Pellice** r. Italy
178 B4 **Pellizzano** Italy
140 M2 **Pello** Fin.
226 E3 **Pellston** MI U.S.A.
260 A4 **Pelluhue** Chile
168 D1 **Pellworm** i. Ger.
222 B2 **Pelly** r. Y.T. Can.
221 J3 **Pelly Bay** Nunavut Can.
222 B2 **Pelly Crossing** Y.T. Can.
222 C2 **Pelly Mountains** Y.T. Can.
169 B5 **Pelm** Ger.
178 D4 **Pelmo, Monte** mt. Italy
185 E1 **Peloche** Spain
Peloponnese admin. reg. Greece see **Peloponnisos**
Peloponnesus admin. reg. Greece see **Peloponnisos**
198 C3 **Peloponnisos** admin. reg. Greece
195 D5 **Peloritani, Monti** mts Sicilia Italy
258 G3 **Pelotas** Brazil
255 C8 **Pelotas, Rio das** r. Brazil
197 G4 **Pelovo** Bulg.
174 G2 **Pelplin** Pol.
151 F2 **Pelsall** West Midlands, England U.K.
87 B6 **Pelsart Group** is W.A. Austr.
170 E2 **Pelsin** Ger.
128 A4 **Pelusium** tourist site Egypt
Pelusium, Bay of Egypt see **Tîna, Khalîg el**
161 C3 **Pélussin** France
161 E4 **Pelvoux** France
161 E4 **Pelvoux, Massif du** mts France
161 E4 **Pelvoux, Mont** mt. France
177 J4 **Pély** Hungary
150 C4 **Pelynt** Cornwall, England U.K.
227 F2 **Pemache** r. Ont. Can.
95 E4 **Pemalang** Jawa Tengah Indon.
95 E2 **Pemangkat** Kalimantan Barat Indon.
94 B2 **Pematangsiantar** Sumatera Indon.
213 I2 **Pemba** Moz.
209 E9 **Pemba** Zambia
211 C6 **Pemba Channel** Tanz.
211 C6 **Pemba Island** Tanz.
211 C6 **Pemba North** admin. reg. Tanz.
211 C6 **Pemba South** admin. reg. Tanz.
87 B7 **Pemberton** W.A. Austr.
222 F5 **Pemberton** B.C. Can.
234 D3 **Pemberton** NJ U.S.A.
222 H4 **Pembina** r. Alta Can.
236 D1 **Pembina** ND U.S.A.
236 D1 **Pembina** r. ND U.S.A.
226 D3 **Pembine** WI U.S.A.
150 C3 **Pembrey** Carmarthenshire, Wales U.K.
150 E2 **Pembridge** Herefordshire, England U.K.
224 E4 **Pembroke** Ont. Can.
150 C3 **Pembroke** Pembrokeshire, Wales U.K.
231 D5 **Pembroke** GA U.S.A.
233 □J2 **Pembroke** ME U.S.A.
81 A6 **Pembroke, Mount** South I. N.Z.
150 C3 **Pembroke Dock** Pembrokeshire, Wales U.K.
231 D7 **Pembroke Pines** FL U.S.A.
150 C3 **Pembrokeshire** admin. div. Wales U.K.
150 B3 **Pembrokeshire Coast National Park** Wales U.K.
151 H3 **Pembury** Kent, England U.K.
260 B5 **Pemehue, Cordillera de** mts Chile
173 G2 **Pemfling** Ger.
260 A5 **Pemuco** Chile
114 B2 **Pen** Mahar. India
96 A2 **Pen** r. Myanmar
137 H2 **Pena** r. Rus. Fed.
183 G3 **Peña Cabollera** mt. Spain
185 G3 **Peña Cambrón** mt. Spain
183 H2 **Peñacerrada** Spain
183 F1 **Peña Cerredo** mt. Spain
186 C2 **Peña Collarada** mt. Spain
183 E2 **Peña Corada** mt. Spain
182 B4 **Penacova** Port.
182 D4 **Peña de Francia** mt. Spain
183 I2 **Peña de Izaga** mt. Spain
183 G1 **Peña del Aro** mt. Spain
186 C2 **Peña de Oroel** mt. Spain
182 B3 **Penafiel** Port.
183 F3 **Peñafiel** Spain
185 E3 **Peñaflor** Spain
183 F3 **Peñaflor de Hornija** Spain
187 C4 **Peñagolosa** mt. Spain
183 H1 **Peña Gorbea** mt. Spain
183 G1 **Penagos** Spain
183 F1 **Peña Labra, Sierra de** mts Spain
183 G4 **Peñalara** mt. Spain
186 C3 **Peñalba** Spain
182 D2 **Peñalba de Santiago** tourist site Spain
183 H4 **Peñalén** Spain
150 C3 **Penally** Pembrokeshire, Wales U.K.
185 E2 **Peñalsordo** Spain
182 C4 **Penalva do Castelo** Port.
182 C4 **Penamacor** Port.
Penambo Range mts Sarawak Malaysia see **Tama Abu, Banjaran**
182 D3 **Peña Mira** mt. Spain
182 D2 **Peña Negra** mt. Spain
245 E2 **Peña Nevada, Cerro** mt. Mex.
Penang state Malaysia see **Pinang**
256 B4 **Penápolis** Brazil
183 F1 **Peña Prieta** mt. Spain
183 E4 **Peñaranda de Bracamonte** Spain
183 G3 **Peñaranda de Duero** Spain
234 C2 **Pen Argyl** PA U.S.A.
83 E3 **Penarie** N.S.W. Austr.
186 C4 **Peñarroya** mt. Spain
185 E2 **Peñarroya-Pueblonuevo** Spain
185 H2 **Peñarrubia** Spain
150 D3 **Penarth** Vale of Glamorgan, Wales U.K.
182 E1 **Peñas, Cabo de** c. Spain
259 B7 **Penas, Golfo de** g. Chile
183 F1 **Peña Santa** mt. Spain
185 H2 **Peñascosa** Spain
185 I2 **Peñas de San Pedro** Spain
182 D1 **Peña Treisa** mt. Spain
182 E1 **Peña Ubiña** mt. Spain
182 E3 **Peñausende** Spain
184 D2 **Peña Utrera** hill Spain
150 C2 **Penbryn** Ceredigion, Wales U.K.
177 I4 **Penc** Hungary
150 C2 **Pencader** Carmarthenshire, Wales U.K.
146 F6 **Pencaitland** East Lothian, Scotland U.K.
116 D5 **Pench** r. India
Pencheng Jiangxi China see **Ruichang**
263 F2 **Penck, Cape** Antarctica
150 D3 **Pencoed** Bridgend, Wales U.K.
208 C3 **Pendé** r. C.A.R.
150 □ **Pendeen** Cornwall, England U.K.
206 B4 **Pendembu** Sierra Leone
236 D3 **Pender** NE U.S.A.
86 D3 **Pender Bay** W.A. Austr.
199 F1 **Pendik** Turkey
182 C4 **Pendilhe** Port.
150 C3 **Pendine** Carmarthenshire, Wales U.K.
149 G4 **Pendle Hill** hill England U.K.
238 C2 **Pendleton** OR U.S.A.
222 E4 **Pendleton Bay** B.C. Can.
94 C3 **Pendopo** Sumatera Indon.
238 C1 **Pend Oreille** r. WA U.S.A.
238 C1 **Pend Oreille Lake** ID U.S.A.
116 E5 **Pendra** Madh. Prad. India
114 B2 **Penduv** Mahar. India
Pendzhikent Tajik. see **Panjakent**
184 C3 **Penedo Gordo** Port.
182 C4 **Penedono** Port.
182 B4 **Penela** Port.
207 F4 **Pénessoulou** Benin
158 D4 **Pénestin** France
177 L4 **Penészlek** Hungary
227 H3 **Penetanguishene** Ont. Can.
232 D4 **Penfield** PA U.S.A.
Penfro Pembrokeshire, Wales U.K. see **Pembroke**
108 C2 **Peng'an** Sichuan China
114 C2 **Penganga** r. India
209 E6 **Penge** Dem. Rep. Congo
109 F4 **P'enghu Ch'üntao** is Taiwan
P'enghu Liehtao is Taiwan see **P'enghu Ch'üntao**
226 A2 **Pengilly** MN U.S.A.
107 I4 **Penglai** Shandong China
108 B2 **Pengshan** Sichuan China
108 D2 **Pengshui** Chongqing China
108 C2 **Pengxi** Sichuan China
Pengxian Sichuan China see **Pengzhou**
109 F2 **Pengze** Jiangxi China
108 B2 **Pengzhou** Sichuan China
255 C8 **Penha** Brazil
182 C4 **Penha Garcia** Port.
213 G3 **Penhalonga** Zimbabwe
182 B5 **Penhascoso** Port.
232 D6 **Penhook** VA U.S.A.
184 A1 **Peniche** Port.
146 E6 **Penicuik** Midlothian, Scotland U.K.
171 D5 **Penig** Ger.
134 F3 **Peninga** Rus. Fed.
Peninsular Malaysia Malaysia see **Malaysia, Semenanjung**
146 C6 **Peninver** Argyll and Bute, Scotland U.K.
187 D4 **Peñíscola** Spain
149 H4 **Penistone** South Yorkshire, England U.K.
254 D4 **Penitente, Serra do** hills Brazil
207 H5 **Penja** Cameroon
244 D3 **Penjamo** Mex.
127 G4 **Pēnjwīn** Iraq
149 G4 **Penketh** Warrington, England U.K.
150 E2 **Penkridge** Staffordshire, England U.K.
170 F2 **Penkun** Ger.
150 E2 **Penley** Wrexham, Wales U.K.
156 B3 **Penly** France
158 B4 **Penmarch** France
158 B4 **Penmarch, Pointe de** pt France
Penn PA U.S.A. see **Penn Hills**
193 E2 **Penna in Teverina** Italy
163 E5 **Pennautier** France
163 D4 **Penne** France
193 F2 **Penne** Italy
163 C4 **Penne-d'Agenais** France
263 L2 **Pennell Coast** Antarctica
114 D3 **Penner** r. India
82 D3 **Penneshaw** S.A. Austr.
233 □J2 **Pennfield** N.B. Can.
232 D4 **Penn Hills** PA U.S.A.
160 F3 **Pennine, Alpi** mts Italy/Switz.
Pennine Alps mts Italy/Switz. see **Pennine, Alpi**
149 G3 **Pennines** hills England U.K.
215 H4 **Pennington** S. Africa
234 D2 **Pennington** NJ U.S.A.
232 B6 **Pennington Gap** VA U.S.A.
193 E1 **Pennino, Monte** mt. Italy
232 C5 **Pennsboro** WV U.S.A.
234 C2 **Pennsburg** PA U.S.A.
234 A2 **Penns Creek** PA U.S.A.
234 B2 **Penns Creek** r. PA U.S.A.
234 C3 **Penns Grove** NJ U.S.A.
234 C3 **Pennsville** NJ U.S.A.
227 H5 **Pennsylvania** state U.S.A.
232 E3 **Penn Yan** NY U.S.A.
146 B5 **Pennyghael** Argyll and Bute, Scotland U.K.
221 L3 **Penny Icecap** Nunavut Can.
263 K1 **Penny Point** Antarctica
234 D3 **Penny Pot** NJ U.S.A.
139 I3 **Peno** Rus. Fed.
233 □I2 **Penobscot** r. ME U.S.A.
82 E4 **Penola** S.A. Austr.
242 D3 **Peñón Blanco** Mex.
82 C2 **Penong** S.A. Austr.
242 □J7 **Penonomé** Panama
150 C2 **Penrhiw-pal** Ceredigion, Wales U.K.
81 □2 **Penrhyn** atoll Cook Is
267 I6 **Penrhyn Basin** sea feature Pacific Ocean
150 D1 **Penrhyn Bay** Conwy, Wales U.K.
150 C2 **Penrhyndeudraeth** Gwynedd, Wales U.K.
83 G3 **Penrith** N.S.W. Austr.
149 G3 **Penrith** Cumbria, England U.K.
150 B4 **Penryn** Cornwall, England U.K.
231 C6 **Pensacola** FL U.S.A.
262 T1 **Pensacola Mountains** Antarctica
253 E3 **Pensamiento** Bol.
122 B2 **Pensär** Azer.
226 D3 **Pensaukee** WI U.S.A.
83 E4 **Penshurst** Vic. Austr.
150 C4 **Pensilva** Cornwall, England U.K.
128 A2 **Pentadaktylos Range** mts Cyprus
192 B2 **Penta-di-Casinca** Corse France
115 D2 **Pentakota** Andhra Prad. India
86 E2 **Pentecost** r. W.A. Austr.
78 □5 **Pentecost Island** Vanuatu
225 H3 **Pentecôte** r. Que. Can.
Pentecôte, Île i. Vanuatu see **Pentecost Island**
197 H3 **Penteleu, Vârful** mt. Romania
222 G5 **Penticton** B.C. Can.
150 C1 **Pentir** Gwynedd, Wales U.K.
85 F4 **Pentland** Qld Austr.
146 E3 **Pentland Firth** sea chan. Scotland U.K.
146 E6 **Pentland Hills** Scotland U.K.
173 G3 **Pentling** Ger.
150 C1 **Pentraeth** Isle of Anglesey, Wales U.K.
150 D1 **Pentrefoelas** Conwy, Wales U.K.
226 D4 **Pentwater** MI U.S.A.
114 C3 **Penukonda** Andhra Prad. India
158 C3 **Penvénan** France
96 B3 **Penwegon** Myanmar
149 G4 **Penwortham** Lancashire, England U.K.
137 H2 **Peny** Rus. Fed.
150 D2 **Penybont** Powys, Wales U.K.
Pen-y-Bont ar Ogwr Bridgend, Wales U.K. see **Bridgend**
150 D2 **Pen-y-bont-fawr** Powys, Wales U.K.
150 D3 **Pen-y-fai** Bridgend, Wales U.K.
150 D2 **Penygadair** hill Wales U.K.
149 G3 **Pen-y-Ghent** hill England U.K.
150 C1 **Penygroes** Gwynedd, Wales U.K.
93 C4 **Penyu, Kepulauan** is Maluku Indon.
150 D3 **Penywaun** Rhondda Cynon Taff, Wales U.K.
135 I5 **Penza** Rus. Fed.
150 □ **Penzance** Cornwall, England U.K.
Penza Oblast admin. div. Rus. Fed. see **Penzenskaya Oblast'**
173 F4 **Penzberg** Ger.
135 I5 **Penzenskaya Oblast'** admin. div. Rus. Fed.
131 R3 **Penzhinskaya Guba** b. Rus. Fed.
173 E3 **Penzing** Ger.
170 E2 **Penzlin** Ger.
161 E4 **Péone** France
238 E1 **Peoples Creek** r. MT U.S.A.
241 K5 **Peoria** AZ U.S.A.
226 C5 **Peoria** IL U.S.A.
226 C5 **Peoria Heights** IL U.S.A.
240 □D9 **Pepeekeo** HI U.S.A.
206 B4 **Pepel** Sierra Leone
170 C1 **Pepelow** Ger.
161 A5 **Pépieux** France
165 D4 **Pepingen** Belgium
165 E4 **Pepinster** Belgium
174 F4 **Pępowo** Pol.
215 G3 **Pepworth** S. Africa
196 D5 **Pëqin** Albania
235 D2 **Pequannock** NJ U.S.A.
182 D2 **Peque** Spain
234 B3 **Pequea** PA U.S.A.
234 B3 **Pequea Creek** r. PA U.S.A.
234 C2 **Pequest** r. NJ U.S.A.
257 E3 **Pequi** Brazil
177 G4 **Pér** Hungary
184 B3 **Pêra** Port.
198 C2 **Perachora** Peloponnisos Greece
85 E2 **Pera Head** hd Qld Austr.
182 C5 **Perais** Port.
94 C1 **Perak** r. Malaysia
94 C1 **Perak** state Malaysia
186 G2 **Peralada** Spain
183 E5 **Peraleda de la Mata** Spain
184 E2 **Peraleda del Zaucejo** Spain
186 B4 **Peralejos** Spain
186 C4 **Perales del Alfambra** Spain
182 D4 **Perales del Puerto** Spain
183 I2 **Peralta** Spain
186 C3 **Peralta de Alcofea** Spain
186 D3 **Peralta de la Sal** Spain
186 C2 **Peraltilla** Spain
184 C3 **Peralva** Port.
183 H4 **Peralveche** Spain
198 D4 **Perama** Kriti Greece
114 C4 **Perambalur** Tamil Nadu India
186 E2 **Peramola** Spain
184 C3 **Peramora** r. Spain
178 D4 **Perarolo di Cadore** Italy
225 H3 **Percé** Que. Can.
159 G3 **Perche, Collines du** hills France
179 H2 **Perchtoldsdorf** Austria
86 E4 **Percival Lakes** salt flat W.A. Austr.
158 E3 **Percy** France
233 H2 **Percy** NH U.S.A.
85 G4 **Percy Isles** Qld Austr.
192 B5 **Perdasdefogu** Sardegna Italy
192 A5 **Perdaxius** Sardegna Italy
215 G2 **Perdekop** S. Africa
254 D4 **Perdida** r. Brazil
261 H5 **Perdido** r. Arg.
253 F5 **Perdido** r. Brazil
186 D2 **Perdido, Monte** mt. Spain
193 H4 **Perdifumo** Italy
186 C3 **Perdiguera** Spain
186 D2 **Perdiguère, Pic** mt. France/Spain
198 B2 **Perdika** Greece
234 B2 **Perdix** PA U.S.A.
256 D3 **Perdizes** Brazil
257 E4 **Perdões** Brazil
185 H3 **Perea** mt. Spain
136 D2 **Perebrody** Ukr.
136 B3 **Perechyn** Ukr.
182 D3 **Peredo** Port.
130 H3 **Peregrebnoye** Rus. Fed.
177 J5 **Peregu Mare** Romania
136 C3 **Perehins'ke** Ukr.
250 C3 **Pereira** Col.
256 B4 **Pereira Barreto** Brazil
Pereira de Eça Angola see **Ondjiva**
184 B3 **Pereiras** Port.
254 F3 **Pereiro** Brazil
180 C4 **Pereiro** Port.
182 C1 **Pereiro** Spain
182 C2 **Pereiro de Aguiar** Spain
183 I3 **Perejiles** r. Spain
139 H2 **Perekhoda** r. Rus. Fed.
137 G2 **Perekopivka** Ukr.
137 K2 **Pereleshinskiy** Rus. Fed.
120 B2 **Perelyub** Rus. Fed.
226 D4 **Pere Marquette** r. MI U.S.A.
120 B2 **Peremetnoye** Kazakh.
137 F2 **Peremoha** Ukr.
139 K4 **Peremyshl'** Rus. Fed.
136 C3 **Peremyshlyany** Ukr.
252 B2 **Perené** r. Peru
87 C6 **Perenjori** W.A. Austr.
182 E3 **Pereruela** Spain
136 E4 **Peresecina** Moldova
137 H3 **Pereshchepyne** Ukr.
139 L3 **Pereslavl'-Zalesskiy** Rus. Fed.
175 M5 **Perespa** Ukr.
179 H3 **Pereszteg** Hungary
191 G5 **Peretola** airport Italy
197 G3 **Peretu** Romania
137 J3 **Pereval's'k** Ukr.
137 G2 **Perevid** r. Ukr.
120 C2 **Perevolotskiy** Rus. Fed.
134 I5 **Perevoz** Rus. Fed.
100 E3 **Pereyaslavka** Rus. Fed.
Pereyaslav-Khmel'nitskiy Ukr. see **Pereyaslav-Khmel'nyts'kyy**
137 F2 **Pereyaslav-Khmel'nyts'kyy** Ukr.
261 G3 **Pérez** Arg.
192 A4 **Perfugas** Sardegna Italy
179 F2 **Perg** Austria
261 G3 **Pergamino** Arg.
191 G5 **Pergine Valdarno** Italy
191 G2 **Pergine Valsugana** Italy
191 H5 **Pergola** Italy
140 N3 **Perho** Fin.
196 E2 **Periam** Romania
185 F4 **Periana** Spain
244 C4 **Peribán de Ramos** Mex.
225 F3 **Péribonca** r. Que. Can.
258 D2 **Perico** Arg.
244 B2 **Pericos** Nayarit Mex.
242 D3 **Pericos** Sinaloa Mex.
241 L5 **Peridot** AZ U.S.A.
197 H2 **Perieni** Romania
158 E2 **Périers** France
162 A2 **Périgny** France
162 C3 **Périgueux** France
250 C2 **Perija, Sierra de** mts Venez.
182 E3 **Perilla de Castro** Spain
177 K3 **Perín-Chym** Slovakia
94 C1 **Peringat** Malaysia
197 I3 **Periprava** Romania
197 H3 **Perișoru** Romania
198 C2 **Peristera** i. Greece
198 C2 **Peristerio** Greece
129 A4 **Peri Suyu** r. Turkey
259 C7 **Perito Moreno** Arg.
114 C4 **Perivar** r. India
198 B2 **Perivoli** Ionioi Nisoi Greece
198 D4 **Perivolia** Kriti Greece
177 J4 **Perje** r. Hungary
234 C2 **Perkasie** PA U.S.A.
177 H4 **Perkáta** Hungary
234 C2 **Perkiomen Creek** r. PA U.S.A.
172 A2 **Perl** Ger.
242 □J6 **Perlas, Laguna de** lag. Nic.
242 □J6 **Perlas, Punta de** pt Nic.
173 G2 **Perlbach** r. Ger.
170 C2 **Perleberg** Ger.
175 K3 **Perlejewo** Pol.
173 H3 **Perlesreut** Ger.
137 J2 **Perlevka** Rus. Fed.
94 C1 **Perlis** state Malaysia
175 J1 **Perły** Pol.
134 L4 **Perm'** Rus. Fed.
134 I4 **Permas** Rus. Fed.
198 B1 **Përmet** Albania
Perm Oblast admin. div. Rus. Fed. see **Permskaya Oblast'**
134 L4 **Permskaya Oblast'** admin. div. Rus. Fed.
188 E3 **Permuda** i. Croatia
138 F1 **Pernå** Fin.
Pernambuco Brazil see **Recife**
254 F4 **Pernambuco** state Brazil
264 H6 **Pernambuco Abyssal Plain** sea feature S. Atlantic Ocean
160 C1 **Pernand-Vergelesses** France
176 C2 **Pernarec** Czech Rep.
82 D2 **Pernatty Lagoon** salt flat S.A. Austr.
179 G3 **Pernegg an der Mur** Austria
114 B3 **Pernem** Goa India
179 H2 **Pernersdorf** Austria
184 B1 **Pernes** Port.
161 D5 **Pernes-les-Fontaines** France
198 D1 **Perni** Greece
197 F4 **Pernik** Bulg.
141 M3 **Perniö** Fin.
179 G3 **Pernitz** Austria
Pernov Estonia see **Pärnu**
190 E3 **Pero** Italy
184 B2 **Peroguarda** Port.
161 B5 **Pérols** France
160 D2 **Péron** France
87 B5 **Peron, Cape** W.A. Austr.
87 B7 **Peron, Point** W.A. Austr.
84 B2 **Peron Islands** N.T. Austr.
160 D2 **Péronnas** France
156 C3 **Péronne** France
87 B5 **Peron Peninsula** W.A. Austr.
190 C4 **Perosa Argentina** Italy
245 F4 **Perote** Mex.
160 D3 **Pérouges** France
182 C4 **Pero Viseu** Port.
163 E6 **Perpignan** France
260 A6 **Perquenco** Chile
260 B4 **Perquilauquén** r. Chile
150 B4 **Perranporth** Cornwall, England U.K.
150 B4 **Perranzabuloe** Cornwall, England U.K.
160 C2 **Perrecy-les-Forges** France
Perrégaux Alg. see **Mohammadia**
160 C2 **Perreux** France
160 D2 **Perrigny** France
240 I5 **Perris** CA U.S.A.
157 F5 **Perrogney-les-Fontaines** France
154 C2 **Perros-Guirec** France
226 E2 **Perry** Ont. Can.
231 D6 **Perry** FL U.S.A.
231 D5 **Perry** GA U.S.A.
236 E3 **Perry** IA U.S.A.
233 □J2 **Perry** ME U.S.A.
227 E4 **Perry** MI U.S.A.
237 D4 **Perry** OK U.S.A.
234 A2 **Perry County** county PA U.S.A.
234 B3 **Perry Hall** MD U.S.A.
234 B3 **Perryman** MD U.S.A.
263 G2 **Perrymennyy, Cape** Antarctica
232 B4 **Perrysburg** OH U.S.A.
237 C4 **Perryton** TX U.S.A.
237 E5 **Perryville** AR U.S.A.
234 B3 **Perryville** MD U.S.A.
163 E4 **Pers** France
156 C3 **Persan** France
129 C2 **P'ersat'i** Georgia
179 G2 **Persenbeug** Austria
122 C4 **Persepolis** tourist site Iran
253 E3 **Perseverancia** Bol.
143 G2 **Pershagen** Sweden
Pershnotravnevoye Ukr. see **Pershotravens'k**
150 E2 **Pershore** Worcestershire, England U.K.
137 I3 **Pershotravens'k** Ukr.
137 I4 **Pershotravneve** Donets'ka Oblast' Ukr.
136 E2 **Pershotravneve** Zhytomyrs'ka Oblast' Ukr.
Pershotravnevoye Ukr. see **Mokvyn**
Persia country Asia see **Iran**
Persian Gulf Asia see **The Gulf**
Persis prov. Iran see **Fārs**
143 G3 **Persnäs** Kalmar Sweden
142 E3 **Perstorp** Sweden
126 E3 **Pertek** Turkey
83 F5 **Perth** Tas. Austr.
87 B6 **Perth** W.A. Austr.
224 E4 **Perth** Ont. Can.
146 E5 **Perth** Perth and Kinross, Scotland U.K.
235 D2 **Perth Amboy** NJ U.S.A.
146 D5 **Perth and Kinross** admin. div. Scotland U.K.
225 H4 **Perth-Andover** N.B. Can.
265 L6 **Perth Basin** sea feature Indian Ocean
156 E3 **Perthes** Champagne-Ardenne France
156 C4 **Perthes** Île-de-France France
141 M3 **Pertteli** Fin.
161 D5 **Pertuis** France
162 A2 **Pertuis Breton** sea chan. France
162 A2 **Pertuis d'Antioche** sea chan. France
141 N3 **Pertunmaa** Fin.
186 C2 **Pertusa** Spain
192 B3 **Pertusato, Capo** c. Corse France
Peru atoll Gilbert Is Kiribati see **Beru**
252 B2 **Peru** country S. America
226 C5 **Peru** IL U.S.A.
230 C3 **Peru** IN U.S.A.
233 G2 **Peru** NY U.S.A.
267 M7 **Peru Basin** sea feature S. Pacific Ocean
171 E5 **Peruc** Czech Rep.
267 N6 **Peru-Chile Trench** sea feature S. Pacific Ocean
193 E1 **Perugia** Italy
191 H5 **Perugia** prov. Umbria Italy
258 F3 **Perugorría** Arg.
256 D6 **Peruíbe** Brazil
114 C3 **Peruru** Andhra Prad. India
197 G4 **Perushtitsa** Bulg.
Perusia Italy see **Perugia**
165 C4 **Péruwelz** Belgium
159 G3 **Pervenchères** France
165 B3 **Pervijze** Belgium
137 H1 **Pervoavgustovskiy** Rus. Fed.
136 E4 **Pervomaisc** Moldova
121 H4 **Pervomay** Kyrg.
135 H5 **Pervomaysk** Rus. Fed.
137 J3 **Pervomays'k** Ukr.
136 F3 **Pervomays'k** Ukr.
137 G4 **Pervomays'ke** Ukr.
137 G5 **Pervomays'ke** Ukr.
121 J2 **Pervomayskiy** Kazakh.
Pervomayskiy Kyrg. see **Pervomay**
Pervomayskiy Arkhangel'skaya Oblast' Rus. Fed. see **Novodvinsk**
120 C2 **Pervomayskiy** Orenburgskaya Oblast' Rus. Fed.
139 I4 **Pervomayskiy** Smolenskaya Oblast' Rus. Fed.
139 M5 **Pervomayskiy** Tambovskaya Oblast' Rus. Fed.
139 K4 **Pervomayskiy** Tul'skaya Oblast' Rus. Fed.
Pervomayskoye Kyrg. see **Pervomay**
137 I3 **Pervomays'kyy** Ukr.
165 D4 **Perwez** Belgium
139 J2 **Pes'** Rus. Fed.
139 J2 **Pes'** r. Rus. Fed.
191 G5 **Pesa** r. Italy
183 G2 **Pesadas de Burgos** Spain
95 E3 **Pesaguan** r. Indon.
191 H5 **Pesaro** Italy
191 H5 **Pesaro e Urbino** prov. Marche Italy
240 F3 **Pescadero** CA U.S.A.
Pescadores is Taiwan see **P'enghu Ch'üntao**
190 F5 **Pescaglia** Italy
191 F3 **Pescantina** Italy
193 G2 **Pescara** Italy
193 F2 **Pescara** prov. Abruzzo Italy
193 G2 **Pescara** r. Italy
197 E3 **Pescari** Romania
193 F3 **Pescasseroli** Italy
160 B3 **Peschadoires** France
135 H7 **Peschanokopskoye** Rus. Fed.
Peschanoye Rus. Fed. see **Yashkul'**
193 I3 **Peschici** Italy
191 F5 **Pescia** Italy
193 F2 **Pescina** Italy
193 G3 **Pescocostanzo** Italy
193 G3 **Pescolanciano** Italy
193 H4 **Pescopagano** Italy
193 G3 **Pescopennataro** Italy
193 F2 **Pescorocchiano** Italy
193 G3 **Pesco Sannita** Italy
242 □J8 **Pesé** Panama
190 B2 **Peseux** Switz.
134 I2 **Pesha** r. Rus. Fed.
123 G3 **Peshawar** Pak.
196 E5 **Peshkopi** Albania
137 J4 **Peshkovo** Rus. Fed.
197 G4 **Peshtera** Bulg.
226 D3 **Peshtigo** WI U.S.A.
226 D3 **Peshtigo** r. WI U.S.A.
190 C4 **Pesio** r. Italy
121 F1 **Peski** Kazakh.
139 L4 **Peski** Moskovskaya Oblast' Rus. Fed.
135 H6 **Peski** Voronezhskaya Oblast' Rus. Fed.
134 K4 **Peskovka** Rus. Fed.
160 D1 **Pesmes** France
188 E2 **Pesnica** Slovenia
139 L2 **Pesochnoye** Rus. Fed.
182 C3 **Peso da Régua** Port.
242 □I6 **Pespire** Hond.
254 F4 **Pesqueira** Brazil
183 F3 **Pesquera de Duero** Spain
163 B4 **Pessac** France
163 C5 **Pessan** France
164 F2 **Pesse** Neth.
170 D3 **Pessin** Ger.
177 I4 **Pest** county Hungary
139 J2 **Pestovo** Rus. Fed.
120 B1 **Pestravka** Rus. Fed.
134 H4 **Pestyaki** Rus. Fed.
183 F1 **Pesués** Spain
244 C5 **Petacalco, Bahía de** b. Mex.
193 G2 **Petacciato** Italy
128 B3 **Petah Tiqwa** Israel
141 N3 **Petäjävesi** Fin.
198 B3 **Petalidi** Greece
198 D2 **Petalioi** i. Greece
198 D2 **Petalion, Kolpos** sea chan. Greece
240 F2 **Petaluma** CA U.S.A.
165 E5 **Pétange** Lux.
250 E2 **Petare** Venez.
198 B2 **Petas** Greece
244 D5 **Petatlán** Mex.
211 A8 **Petauke** Zambia
227 I3 **Petawawa** Ont. Can.
179 H4 **Peteranec** Croatia
224 D3 **Peterbell** Ont. Can.
82 D3 **Peterborough** S.A. Austr.
83 E4 **Peterborough** Vic. Austr.
224 E4 **Peterborough** Ont. Can.
151 G2 **Peterborough** Peterborough, England U.K.
151 G2 **Peterborough** admin. div. England U.K.
233 H3 **Peterborough** NH U.S.A.
146 F4 **Peterculter** Aberdeen, Scotland U.K.
146 G4 **Peterhead** Aberdeenshire, Scotland U.K.
177 I4 **Péteri** Hungary
262 R2 **Peter I Island** Antarctica
Peter I Øy i. Antarctica see **Peter I Island**
149 H3 **Peterlee** Durham, England U.K.
221 P2 **Petermann Bjerg** nunatak Greenland
84 B5 **Petermann Ranges** mts N.T. Austr.
260 B4 **Peteroa, Volcán** vol. Chile
173 E2 **Petersaurach** Ger.
169 E5 **Petersberg** Ger.
215 E5 **Petersburg** S. Africa
220 E4 **Petersburg** AK U.S.A.
236 F4 **Petersburg** IL U.S.A.
230 C4 **Petersburg** IN U.S.A.
234 D3 **Petersburg** NJ U.S.A.
233 G3 **Petersburg** NY U.S.A.
232 C4 **Petersburg** OH U.S.A.
232 E6 **Petersburg** VA U.S.A.
232 D5 **Petersburg** WV U.S.A.
173 F3 **Petersdorf** Ger.
170 C1 **Petersdorf auf Fehmarn** Ger.
151 G3 **Petersfield** Hampshire, England U.K.
171 F3 **Petershagen** Brandenburg Ger.
169 D3 **Petershagen** Nordrhein-Westfalen Ger.
173 F3 **Petershausen** Ger.
232 C6 **Peterstown** WV U.S.A.
220 C3 **Petersville** AK U.S.A.
147 C3 **Peterswell** Rep. of Ireland
Pétervárad Vojvodina, Srbija Yugo. see **Petrovaradin**
177 J3 **Pétervására** Hungary
Peterwardein Vojvodina, Srbija Yugo. see **Petrovaradin**
114 B2 **Peth** Mahar. India
195 F3 **Petilia Policastro** Italy
186 B2 **Petilla de Aragón** Spain
182 C2 **Petín** Spain
Petit Atlas mts Morocco see **Anti Atlas**
225 H4 **Petitcodiac** N.B. Can.
159 H2 **Petit-Couronne** France
162 D2 **Petite Creuse** r. France
163 B4 **Petite Leyre** r. France
157 G3 **Petite-Rosselle** France
159 I4 **Petite Sauldre** r. France
217 □3b **Petite Terre** i. Mayotte
246 D3 **Petit-Goâve** Haiti
Petitjean Morocco see **Sidi Kacem**
159 E5 **Petit Lay** r. France
158 E4 **Petit Maine** r. France
158 E4 **Petit-Mars** France
Petit Mécatina r. Newfoundland/Québec Can. see **Little Mecatina**
157 G4 **Petitmont** France
156 D4 **Petit Morin** r. France
160 D2 **Petit-Noir** France
222 F2 **Petitot** r. Alta/B.C. Can.
161 C5 **Petit Rhône** r. France
171 E4 **Petkus** Ger.
116 C5 **Petlad** Gujarat India
245 F4 **Petlalcingo** Mex.
116 C5 **Petlawad** Madh. Prad. India
177 L3 **Petneháza** Hungary
243 H4 **Peto** Mex.
177 I4 **Petőfibánya** Hungary
177 I5 **Petőfiszállás** Hungary
260 B3 **Petorca** Chile
226 E3 **Petoskey** MI U.S.A.
128 B4 **Petra** tourist site Jordan
187 G5 **Petra** Spain
195 E4 **Petrace** r. Italy
194 D5 **Petralia-Soprana** Sicilia Italy
194 D5 **Petralia-Sottana** Sicilia Italy
262 P1 **Petras, Mount** Antarctica
227 I4 **Petre, Point** Ont. Can.
Petrel Spain see **Petrer**
193 F3 **Petrella, Monte** mt. Italy
193 F2 **Petrella Salto** Italy
193 G3 **Petrella Tifernina** Italy
187 C6 **Petrer** Spain
177 L4 **Petrești** Romania
192 A3 **Petreto-Bicchisano** Corse France
191 H5 **Petriano** Italy
197 F5 **Petrich** Bulg.
188 G3 **Petrijevci** Croatia
Petrikau Pol. see **Piotrków Trybunalski**
Petrikov Belarus see **Pyetrykaw**
197 F3 **Petrila** Romania
188 F3 **Petrinja** Croatia
177 L5 **Petriș** Romania
193 F1 **Petritoli** Italy
137 H4 **Petrivka** Khersons'ka Oblast' Ukr.
136 F4 **Petrivka** Odes'ka Oblast' Ukr.
137 I4 **Petrivs'ke** Ukr.
137 G3 **Petrivtsi** Ukr.
258 C3 **Petro, Cerro de** mt. Chile
Petroaleksandrovsk Uzbek. see **Turtkul'**
138 G2 **Petrodvorets** Rus. Fed.
Petrograd Rus. Fed. see **Sankt-Peterburg**
Petrokov Pol. see **Piotrków Trybunalski**
Petrokrepost' Rus. Fed. see **Shlissel'burg**
185 I2 **Pétrola** Spain
254 F4 **Petrolândia** Brazil
227 F4 **Petrolia** Ont. Can.
240 E1 **Petrolia** CA U.S.A.
254 E4 **Petrolina** Brazil
256 C2 **Petrolina de Goiás** Brazil
Petromaryevka Ukr. see **Pervomays'k**
198 B1 **Petron, Limni** l. Greece
195 F3 **Petronà** Italy
Petropavl Kazakh. see **Petropavlovsk**
137 I3 **Petropavlivka** Ukr.
121 J3 **Petropavlovka** Kazakh.
106 E1 **Petropavlovka** Respublika Buryatiya Rus. Fed.
135 H6 **Petropavlovka** Voronezhskaya Oblast' Rus. Fed.
121 G1 **Petropavlovsk** Kazakh.
Petropavlovsk Rus. Fed. see **Petropavlovsk-Kamchatskiy**
131 Q4 **Petropavlovsk-Kamchatskiy** Rus. Fed.
121 K1 **Petropavlovskoye** Rus. Fed.
257 F5 **Petrópolis** Brazil
197 F3 **Petroșani** Romania
194 B5 **Petrosino** Sicilia Italy
176 G3 **Petrov** Czech Rep.
Petrovac Bos.-Herz. see **Bosanski Petrovac**
196 E3 **Petrovac** Srbija Yugo.
177 K3 **Petrovany** Slovakia
196 D3 **Petrovaradin** Vojvodina, Srbija Yugo.
137 G3 **Petrove** Ukr.
176 D2 **Petrovice** Czech Rep.
121 G1 **Petrovka** Kazakh.
120 A1 **Petrovsk** Rus. Fed.
135 G7 **Petrovskaya** Rus. Fed.
137 J3 **Petrovs'ke** Ukr.
139 M3 **Petrovskiy** Rus. Fed.
Petrovskoye Stavropol'skiy Kray Rus. Fed. see **Svetlograd**
139 M5 **Petrovskoye** Tambovskaya Oblast' Rus. Fed.
139 L3 **Petrovskoye** Yaroslavskaya Oblast' Rus. Fed.
107 F1 **Petrovsk-Zabaykal'skiy** Rus. Fed.
135 I6 **Petrov Val** Rus. Fed.
134 F3 **Petrozavodsk** Rus. Fed.
197 G2 **Petru Rareș** Romania
215 E3 **Petrusburg** S. Africa
136 D4 **Petrușeni** Moldova
215 G2 **Petrus Steyn** S. Africa
214 E4 **Petrusville** S. Africa
177 H2 **Petřvald** Czech Rep.
137 H3 **Petrykivka** Ukr.
Petsamo Rus. Fed. see **Pechenga**
215 G2 **Petsana** S. Africa
Pettau Slovenia see **Ptuj**
164 D2 **Petten** Neth.
173 G2 **Pettendorf** Ger.
147 D2 **Pettigo** Northern Ireland U.K.
195 F3 **Pettinascura, Monte** mt. Italy
194 D5 **Pettineo** Sicilia Italy
173 G4 **Petting** Ger.
178 B3 **Pettneu am Arlberg** Austria
193 F3 **Pettorano sul Gizio** Italy
191 G2 **Pettorina** r. Italy
130 H4 **Petukhovo** Rus. Fed.
139 L4 **Petushki** Rus. Fed.
151 G4 **Petworth** West Sussex, England U.K.
178 D4 **Petzeck** mt. Austria
179 E2 **Peuerbach** Austria
94 B1 **Peuetsagu, Gunung** vol. Indon.
162 B3 **Peujard** France
260 B4 **Peumo** Chile
94 B1 **Peureula** Sumatera Indon.
131 S3 **Pevek** Rus. Fed.
151 H4 **Pevensey** East Sussex, England U.K.
190 C4 **Peveragno** Italy
151 F3 **Pewsey** Wiltshire, England U.K.
151 F3 **Pewsey, Vale of** val. England U.K.
168 C2 **Pewsum (Krummhörn)** Ger.
157 G4 **Pexonne** France
161 E5 **Peymeinade** France
161 B5 **Peyne** r. France
161 D5 **Peynier** France
161 D5 **Peypin** France
162 D3 **Peyrat-le-Château** France
163 A5 **Peyrehorade** France
161 B4 **Peyreleau** France
162 E3 **Peyrelevade** France
190 C5 **Peyrevieille, Mont** mt. Italy
161 A5 **Peyriac-de-Mer** France
163 E5 **Peyriac-Minervois** France
160 D3 **Peyrieu** France
161 D3 **Peyrins** France
161 D5 **Peyrolles-en-Provence** France
161 D4 **Peyruis** France
163 C5 **Peyrusse-Grande** France
163 E4 **Peyrusse-le-Roc** France
134 I2 **Peza** r. Rus. Fed.
161 B5 **Pézenas** France
174 D2 **Pęzino** Pol.
176 G3 **Pezinok** Slovakia
163 C4 **Pezuls** France
173 G3 **Pfaffenberg** Ger.
171 F3 **Pfaffendorf** Ger.
173 E3 **Pfaffenhausen** Ger.
173 F3 **Pfaffenhofen an der Ilm** Ger.
173 E3 **Pfaffenhofen an der Roth** Ger.
157 H4 **Pfaffenhoffen** France
172 B4 **Pfaffenweiler** Ger.
190 D1 **Pfäffikon** Schwyz Switz.
190 D1 **Pfäffikon** Zürich Switz.
173 G3 **Pfaffing** Ger.
172 B2 **Pfälzer Wald** hills Ger.
169 C5 **Pfalzfeld** Ger.
172 C3 **Pfalzgrafenweiler** Ger.
173 G3 **Pfarrkirchen** Ger.
169 F5 **Pfarrweisach** Ger.
178 E3 **Pfarrwerfen** Austria
173 G3 **Pfatter** Ger.
172 D2 **Pfedelbach** Ger.
173 F3 **Pfeffenhausen** Ger.
178 B3 **Pflach** Austria
178 C3 **Pfons** Austria
173 F3 **Pförring** Ger.
173 E4 **Pforzen** Ger.
172 C3 **Pforzheim** Ger.
173 G2 **Pfreimd** Ger.
173 G2 **Pfreimd** r. Ger.
172 D3 **Pfronstetten** Ger.
173 E4 **Pfronten** Ger.
172 D4 **Pfullendorf** Ger.
172 D3 **Pfullingen** Ger.
178 B4 **Pfunds** Austria
172 C2 **Pfungstadt** Ger.
190 D1 **Pfyn** Switz.
116 C3 **Phagwara** Punjab India
215 F3 **Phahameng** Free State S. Africa
213 F5 **Phahameng** Northern S. Africa
213 F4 **Phalaborwa** S. Africa
123 H3 **Phalia** Pak.
116 C4 **Phalodi** Rajasthan India
157 H4 **Phalsbourg** France
116 B4 **Phalsund** Rajasthan India
114 B2 **Phaltan** Mahar. India
117 G4 **Phalut Peak** India/Nepal
97 C5 **Phangan, Ko** i. Thai.
97 B5 **Phangnga** Thai.
97 E5 **Phan Rang** Vietnam
97 E5 **Phan Ri** Vietnam
97 E5 **Phan Thiêt** Vietnam
116 D4 **Phaphund** Uttar Prad. India
148 C2 **Pharis** Northern Ireland U.K.
96 D2 **Phat Diêm** Vietnam
97 C6 **Phatthalung** Thai.
96 B3 **Phayao** Thai.
117 H4 **Phek** Nagaland India
84 C2 **Phelp** r. N.T. Austr.
232 E3 **Phelps** NY U.S.A.
226 C2 **Phelps** WI U.S.A.
96 C3 **Phen** Thai.
232 D6 **Phenix** VA U.S.A.
231 C5 **Phenix City** AL U.S.A.
97 B4 **Phet Buri** Thai.
96 C3 **Phetchabun** Thai.
96 C3 **Phichit** Thai.
Philadelphia Jordan see **'Ammān**
214 B5 **Philadelphia** S. Africa
Philadelphia Turkey see **Alașehir**
237 F5 **Philadelphia** MS U.S.A.
233 F2 **Philadelphia** NY U.S.A.
234 C3 **Philadelphia** PA U.S.A.
234 C3 **Philadelphia County** county PA U.S.A.
203 G4 **Philae** tourist site Egypt
Philip atoll Arch. des Tuamotu Fr. Polynesia see **Makemo**
236 C2 **Philip** SD U.S.A.
Philip Atoll Micronesia see **Sorol**
Philippeville Alg. see **Skikda**
165 D4 **Philippeville** Belgium
232 C5 **Philippi** WV U.S.A.
84 D5 **Philippi, Lake** salt flat Qld Austr.
165 C3 **Philippine** Neth.
266 D4 **Philippine Basin** sea feature N. Pacific Ocean
92 B3 **Philippines** country Asia
90 F3 **Philippine Sea** N. Pacific Ocean
266 D4 **Philippine Trench** sea feature N. Pacific Ocean
215 E4 **Philippolis** S. Africa
215 E4 **Philippolis Road** S. Africa
Philippopolis Bulg. see **Plovdiv**
172 C2 **Philippsburg** Ger.
173 H3 **Philippsreut** Ger.
169 F5 **Philippsthal (Werra)** Ger.
247 G3 **Philipsburg** St Maarten Neth. Antilles
238 D2 **Philipsburg** MT U.S.A.
232 D4 **Philipsburg** PA U.S.A.
164 D3 **Philipsdam** barrage Neth.
220 D3 **Philip Smith Mountains** AK U.S.A.
214 E4 **Philipstown** S. Africa
83 F4 **Phillip Island** Vic. Austr.
87 D7 **Phillips** r. W.A. Austr.
233 □H2 **Phillips** ME U.S.A.
226 B3 **Phillips** WI U.S.A.
222 E5 **Phillips Arm** B.C. Can.
236 D4 **Phillipsburg** KS U.S.A.
234 C2 **Phillipsburg** NJ U.S.A.
82 C2 **Phillipson, Lake** salt flat S.A. Austr.
86 E3 **Phillips Range** hills W.A. Austr.
232 D4 **Phillipston** PA U.S.A.
233 G3 **Philmont** NY U.S.A.
Philomelium Turkey see **Akșehir**
96 D4 **Phimun Mangsahan** Thai.
215 F2 **Phiritona** S. Africa
96 C3 **Phitsanulok** Thai.
226 C3 **Phlox** WI U.S.A.

Phnom Penh Cambodia see Phnom Pénh
97 D5 Phnom Pénh Cambodia
233 F3 Phoenicia NY U.S.A.
241 K5 Phoenix AZ U.S.A.
233 E3 Phoenix NY U.S.A.
Phoenix Island Phoenix Is Kiribati see Rawaki
77 I2 Phoenix Islands Kiribati
234 C2 Phoenixville PA U.S.A.
215 G2 Phola S. Africa
215 F2 Phomolong S. Africa
96 C4 Phon Thai.
96 D3 Phong Nha Vietnam
96 C2 Phôngsali Laos
Phong Saly Laos see Phôngsali
83 E4 Phoques Bay Tas. Austr.
84 E4 Phosphate Hill Qld Austr.
96 C3 Phou San mt. Laos
96 C3 Phrae Thai.
Phra Nakhon Si Ayutthaya Thai. see Ayutthaya
96 B3 Phrao Thai.
97 B5 Phra Saeng Thai.
Phu Cuong Vietnam see Thu Dâu Môt
96 D2 Phuc Yên Vietnam
117 G4 Phuentsholing Bhutan
97 B6 Phuket Thai.
97 B6 Phuket, Ko i. Thai.
117 F5 Phulabani Orissa India
116 E4 Phulpur Uttar Prad. India
96 D2 Phu Ly Vietnam
97 D5 Phumĭ Chhuk Cambodia
97 D4 Phumĭ Kâmpóng Trâlach Cambodia
97 D4 Phumĭ Mlu Prey Cambodia
97 C4 Phumĭ Prâmaôy Cambodia
97 C4 Phumĭ Sâmraông Cambodia
Phuntsholing Bhutan see Phuentsholing
96 C2 Phu Phac Mo mt. Vietnam
97 D4 Phu Quôc, Đao i. Vietnam
215 G3 Phuthaditjhaba S. Africa
96 D2 Phư Tho Vietnam
Phu Vinh Vietnam see Tra Vinh
163 E6 Pia France
95 F2 Piabung, Gunung mt. Indon.
256 B4 Piacatu Brazil
190 E3 Piacenza Italy
190 E4 Piacenza prov. Emilia-Romagna Italy
190 F3 Piadena Italy
224 E2 Piagochioui r. Que. Can.
261 G3 Piamonte Arg.
83 G2 Pian r. N.S.W. Austr.
192 A2 Piana Corse France
190 D4 Piana Crixia Italy
194 C5 Piana degli Albanesi Sicilia Italy
194 D5 Piana di Catania plain Sicilia Italy
192 D2 Piancastagnaio Italy
191 H5 Piandimeleto Italy
192 B4 Pianedda, M. sa hill Sardegna Italy
193 G2 Pianella Italy
190 E4 Pianello Val Tidone Italy
83 E3 Piangil Vic. Austr.
107 F4 Pianguan Shanxi China
191 G4 Piano del Voglio Italy
191 G4 Pianoro Italy
192 C2 Pianosa Italy
193 G2 Pianosa Italy
192 B3 Pianotolli-Caldarello Corse France
192 D2 Piansano Italy
184 C2 Pias Port.
175 J3 Piaseczno Pol.
175 K4 Piaski Lubelskie Pol.
174 F4 Piaski Wielkopolskie Pol.
254 F4 Piassabussu Brazil
175 I3 Piastów Pol.
254 E5 Piatã Brazil
175 H3 Piątek Pol.
175 K2 Piątnica Poduchowna Pol.
197 G4 Piatra Romania
197 H2 Piatra Neamţ Romania
197 G3 Piatra Olt Romania
197 H2 Piatra Şoimului Romania
163 C6 Piau-Engaly France
254 E3 Piauí r. Brazil
254 E3 Piauí state Brazil
254 E4 Piauí, Serra de hills Brazil
191 H3 Piave r. Italy
244 A2 Piaxtla r. Mex.
190 F4 Piazza al Serchio Italy
194 D5 Piazza Armerina Sicilia Italy
190 E3 Piazza Brembana Italy
190 E3 Piazzatorre Italy
190 F2 Piazzi, Cima de' mt. Italy
191 G3 Piazzola sul Brenta Italy
210 B2 Pibor r. Sudan
210 B3 Pibor Post Sudan
163 D5 Pibrac France
224 C3 Pic r. Ont. Can.
252 C5 Pica Chile
241 L5 Picacho AZ U.S.A.
242 B2 Picachos, Cerro dos mt. Mex.
187 B5 Picaracho mt. Spain
156 C3 Picardie admin. reg. France
156 B3 Picardie reg. France
Picardy reg. France see Picardie
187 C5 Picassent Spain
158 E2 Picauville France
237 F6 Picayune MS U.S.A.
191 G2 Picco della Croce mt. Italy
258 D1 Pichanal Arg.
170 C2 Picher Ger.
260 A4 Pichilemu Chile
236 C3 Pichilingue Mex.
250 B5 Pichincha prov. Ecuador
179 E2 Pichl bei Wels Austria
116 D4 Pichor Madh. Prad. India
243 G5 Pichucalco Mex.
232 C5 Pickens WV U.S.A.
227 H4 Pickering Ont. Can.
149 I3 Pickering North Yorkshire, England U.K.
149 I3 Pickering, Vale of val. England U.K.
227 E2 Pickford MI U.S.A.
224 B3 Pickle Lake Ont. Can.
216 □1c Pico i. Azores
216 □1c Pico mt. Pico Azores
193 F3 Pico Italy
192 B5 Picocca r. Sardegna Italy
216 □1c Pico Gorda vol. Faial Azores
185 F1 Picón Spain
255 C5 Picos Brazil
250 B6 Picota Peru
259 D7 Pico Truncado Arg.
156 C3 Picquigny France
226 D1 Pic River Ont. Can.
83 G3 Picton N.S.W. Austr.
224 E5 Picton Ont. Can.
81 E4 Picton South I. N.Z.
83 F5 Picton, Mount Tas. Austr.
225 I4 Pictou N.S. Can.
222 H5 Picture Butte Alta Can.
234 B1 Picture Rocks PA U.S.A.
255 F3 Picuí Brazil
260 C6 Picún Leufú r. Arg.
175 M5 Pidbrezzya Ukr.
175 L6 Pidbuzh Ukr.
Piddle r. England U.K. see Trent
150 E4 Piddletrenthide Dorset, England U.K.
136 C3 Pidhaytsi Ukr.
136 F3 Pidhorodna Ukr.
137 H3 Pidhorodne Ukr.
175 L6 Pidhorodtsi Ukr.
173 G4 Piding Ger.
217 □3a Pidjani Njazidja Comoros
136 C3 Pidkamin' Ukr.
137 B6 Pidlisne Ukr.
114 D5 Pidurutalagala mt. Sri Lanka
136 D3 Pidvolochys'k Ukr.
136 F3 Pidvysoke Ukr.
174 G3 Piechcin Pol.
174 D5 Piechowice Pol.
175 J2 Piecki Pol.
216 □1c Piedade Pico Azores
256 D5 Piedade Brazil
184 B3 Piedade, Ponta da pt Port.
192 B2 Piedicorte-di-Gaggio Corse France
192 B2 Piedicroce Corse France
195 E5 Piedimonte Etneo Sicilia Italy
193 G3 Piedimonte Matese Italy
190 D2 Piedimulera Italy
Piedmont admin. reg. Italy see Piemonte
231 C5 Piedmont AL U.S.A.
237 F4 Piedmont MO U.S.A.
232 C4 Piedmont OH U.S.A.
183 I3 Piedra r. Spain
185 F1 Piedrabuena Spain
259 C6 Piedra de Aguila Arg.
245 F5 Piedra de Olla, Cerro mt. Mex.
Piedrafita Spain see Pedrafita do Cebreiro
182 D2 Piedrafita de Babia Spain
183 E4 Piedrahita Spain
183 F4 Piedralaves Spain
182 D5 Piedras Albas Spain
182 E1 Piedras Blancas Spain
240 G4 Piedras Blancas Point CA U.S.A.
243 H5 Piedras Negras Guat.
243 E2 Piedras Negras Coahuila Mex.
245 F4 Piedras Negras Veracruz Mex.
192 E2 Piegaro Italy
162 C3 Piégut-Pluviers France
174 G5 Piekary Śląskie Pol.
170 E1 Piekberg hill Ger.
175 I5 Piekoszów Pol.
140 N3 Pieksämäki Fin.
207 E3 Piela Burkina
179 G2 Pielach r. Austria
140 N3 Pielavesi Fin.
174 D4 Pielgrzymka Pol.
140 O3 Pielinen l. Fin.
190 C4 Piemonte admin. reg. Italy
215 G1 Pienaarsrivier S. Africa
143 I4 Pieniężno Pol.
157 F3 Piennes France
174 F3 Pieńsk Pol.
192 D1 Pienza Italy
186 E3 Piera Spain
236 D3 Pierce NE U.S.A.
223 I4 Pierceland Sask. Can.
226 E5 Pierceton IN U.S.A.
198 C1 Pieria mts Greece
146 F2 Pierowall Orkney, Scotland U.K.
236 C2 Pierre SD U.S.A.
237 F6 Pierre, Bayou r. MS U.S.A.
237 E6 Pierre Bayou r. LA U.S.A.
162 D3 Pierre-Buffière France
161 D4 Pierre-Châtel France
160 D2 Pierre-de-Bresse France
161 E5 Pierrefeu-du-Var France
163 B6 Pierrefitte-Nestalas France
157 F4 Pierrefitte-sur-Aire France
160 B2 Pierrefitte-sur-Loire France
156 C3 Pierrefonds France
160 E1 Pierrefontaine-les-Varans France
161 A4 Pierrefort France
161 C4 Pierrelatte France
157 F3 Pierrepont France
156 B4 Pierres France
160 B3 Pierre-sur-Haute mt. France
161 D5 Pierrevert France
247 □7 Pierreville Trin. and Tob.
156 D3 Pierry France
164 D3 Piershil Neth.
175 I5 Pierzchnica Pol.
171 C5 Piesau Ger.
178 D3 Piesendorf Austria
172 A2 Piesport Ger.
179 G3 Piešťany Slovakia
175 I1 Pieszkowo Pol.
174 E5 Pieszyce Pol.
215 H3 Pietermaritzburg S. Africa
Pietersaari Fin. see Jakobstad
213 F4 Pietersburg S. Africa
214 E2 Piet Plessis S. Africa
193 G3 Pietrabbondante Italy
193 G3 Pietracatella Italy
192 B3 Pietracorbara Corse France
192 B2 Pietra-di-Verde Corse France
193 H4 Pietragalla Italy
192 B2 Pietralba Corse France
190 D4 Pietra Ligure Italy
191 H5 Pietralunga Italy
193 G3 Pietramelara Italy
193 H3 Pietramontecorvino Italy
194 D5 Pietraperzia Sicilia Italy
190 C4 Pietraporzio Italy
190 F5 Pietrasanta Italy
193 G4 Pietrastornina Italy
193 G3 Pietravairano Italy
193 G3 Pietrelcina Italy
215 H2 Piet Retief S. Africa
177 L5 Pietroasa Bihor Romania
177 L6 Pietroasa Timiș Romania
192 A3 Pietrosella Corse France
197 G2 Pietrosu, Vârful mt. Romania
197 G2 Pietrosu, Vârful mt. Romania
174 G5 Pietrowice Wielkie Pol.
191 H2 Pieve d'Alpago Italy
190 D3 Pieve del Cairo Italy
178 B5 Pieve di Bono Italy
191 H3 Pieve di Cadore Italy
191 G4 Pieve di Cento Italy
191 H3 Pieve di Soligo Italy
190 C4 Pieve di Teco Italy
191 F4 Pievepelago Italy
190 F5 Pieve Santo Stefano Italy
193 F1 Pieve Torina Italy
190 D2 Pieve Vergonte Italy
156 D4 Piffonds France
224 B3 Pigeon r. Can./U.S.A.
227 F4 Pigeon MI U.S.A.
227 C2 Pigeon River MN U.S.A.
232 D6 Pigg r. VA U.S.A.
237 F4 Piggott AR U.S.A.
215 H1 Pigg's Peak Swaziland
193 F3 Piglio Italy
190 C5 Pigna Italy
161 B5 Pignans France
193 F5 Pignataro Interamna Italy
194 D1 Pignataro Maggiore Italy
193 H4 Pignola Italy
198 B2 Pigon, Limni l. Greece
261 F5 Pigüé Arg.
245 E3 Piguicas mt. Mex.
80 E3 Piha North I. N.Z.
80 D2 Pihama North I. N.Z.
116 E4 Pihani Uttar Prad. India
109 F1 Pi He r. China
Pihkva järv l. Estonia/Rus. Fed. see Pskov, Lake
141 O3 Pihlajavesi l. Fin.
141 M3 Pihlava Fin.
140 N3 Pihtipudas Fin.
244 C4 Pihuamo Mex.
138 D1 Piikkiö Fin.
140 N2 Piippola Fin.
78 □4a Piis-Panewu i. Chuuk Micronesia
Piji Sichuan China see Puge
243 G6 Pijijiapan Mex.
164 D2 Pijnacker Neth.
139 J2 Pikalevo Rus. Fed.
232 F6 Pike NY U.S.A.
232 C5 Pike WV U.S.A.
227 G3 Pike Bay Ont. Can.
234 C1 Pike County county PA U.S.A.
91 K5 Pikelot i. Micronesia
239 F4 Pikes Peak CO U.S.A.
232 B5 Pikesville MD U.S.A.
214 B5 Piketberg S. Africa
232 B6 Piketon OH U.S.A.
232 B5 Pikeville KY U.S.A.
231 C5 Pikeville TN U.S.A.
Pikirakatahi mt. South I. N.Z. see Earnslaw, Mount
107 I4 Pikou Liaoning China
208 C4 Pikounda Congo
261 H5 Pila Arg.
191 H4 Pila Italy
174 E2 Piła Pol.
187 B6 Pila mt. Spain
258 F2 Pilagá r. Arg.
116 C3 Pilani Rajasthan India
261 H4 Pilar Buenos Aires Arg.
261 F2 Pilar Córdoba Arg.
261 G2 Pilar Santa Fé Arg.
258 F2 Pilar Para.
92 C4 Pilar Phil.
254 C5 Pilar de Goiás Brazil
187 C7 Pilar de la Horadada Spain
256 D5 Pilar do Sul Brazil
183 D3 Pilas Spain
161 C3 Pilat, Mont mt. France
175 J4 Pilawa Pol.
174 E2 Piława r. Pol.
174 E5 Piława Górna Pol.
252 D5 Pilaya r. Bol.
253 F6 Pilcomayo r. Bol./Para.
Pilenkovo Georgia see Gant'iadi
114 C3 Piler Andhra Prad. India
187 C6 Piles Spain
Pili Notio Aigaio Greece see Pyli
92 B3 Pili Phil.
252 D5 Pili, Cerro mt. Chile
138 E4 Pilikalnis hill Lith.
116 C3 Pilibangan Rajasthan India
116 D3 Pilibhit Uttar Prad. India
175 H5 Pilica Pol.
175 J4 Pilica r. Pol.
Pilipinas country Asia see Philippines
177 I4 Pilis Hungary
177 H4 Pilis hill Hungary
177 H4 Piliscsév Hungary
177 H4 Pilisszentiván Hungary
177 H4 Pilisszentkereszt Hungary
177 H4 Pilisvörösvár Hungary
149 F3 Pillar hill England U.K.
Pillau Rus. Fed. see Baltiysk
83 G2 Pilliga N.S.W. Austr.
149 G4 Pilling Lancashire, England U.K.
261 G3 Pillo, Isla del i. Arg.
234 B2 Pillow PA U.S.A.
134 I5 Pil'na Rus. Fed.
137 I2 Pil'na r. Ukr.
150 E3 Pilning South Gloucestershire, England U.K.
256 D2 Pilões, Serra dos mts Brazil
246 C3 Pilón Cuba
183 E1 Piloña r. Spain
Pilos Greece see Pylos
Piloto Juan Fernández i. S. Pacific Ocean see Alejandro Selkirk, Isla
240 I2 Pilot Peak NV U.S.A.
220 C4 Pilot Point AK U.S.A.
238 C2 Pilot Rock OR U.S.A.
220 B3 Pilot Station AK U.S.A.
237 F6 Pilottown LA U.S.A.
173 F2 Pilsach Ger.
Pilsen Czech Rep. see Plzeň
226 D3 Pilsen WI U.S.A.
175 H6 Pilsko mt. Pol.
173 G3 Pilsting Ger.
138 C3 Piltene Latvia
177 K5 Pilu Romania
96 B3 Pilu, Nam r. Myanmar
138 D4 Pilviškiai Lith.
175 J6 Pilzno Pol.
241 M5 Pima AZ U.S.A.
253 E2 Pimenta Bueno Brazil
192 B5 Pimentel Sardegna Italy
116 C5 Pimpalner Mahar. India
150 E4 Pimperne Dorset, England U.K.
116 B5 Pimpri Gujarat India
116 D2 Pin r. India
96 A2 Pin r. Myanmar
136 D1 Pina r. Belarus
186 C3 Pina Spain
187 C4 Pina mt. Spain
241 K6 Pinacate, Cerro del mt. Mex.
183 F3 Piña de Esgueva Spain
116 D4 Pinahat Uttar Prad. India
241 L5 Pinaleno Mountains AZ U.S.A.
92 B3 Pinamalayan Phil.
261 I5 Pinamar Arg.
Pinang Malaysia see George Town
94 C1 Pinang i. Malaysia
94 C1 Pinang state Malaysia
185 E4 Pinar mt. Spain
187 G5 Pinar, Cap des c. Spain
126 E3 Pınarbaşı Turkey
246 B2 Pinar del Río Cuba
126 B2 Pınarhisar Turkey
129 A4 Pınarlar Turkey
129 C4 Pınarlı Turkey
250 B5 Piñas Ecuador
190 C4 Pinasca Italy
90 F3 Pinatubo, Mt vol. Phil.
177 H5 Pincehely Hungary
151 G2 Pinchbeck Lincolnshire, England U.K.
222 H5 Pincher Creek Alta Can.
236 F4 Pinckneyville IL U.S.A.
159 F3 Pinçon, Mont hill France
227 F4 Pinconning MI U.S.A.
Pîncota Romania see Pâncota
175 I5 Pińczów Pol.
257 E5 Pindamonhangaba Brazil
87 D6 Pindar W.A. Austr.
116 D3 Pindar r. India
254 D2 Pindaré r. Brazil
254 D2 Pindaré Mirim Brazil
123 H3 Pind Dadan Khan Pak.
Pindhos Óros mts Greece see Pindos
123 H4 Pindi Bhattian Pak.
123 H3 Pindi Gheb Pak.
198 B2 Pindos mts Greece
Pindus Mountains Greece see Pindos
116 C4 Pindwara Rajasthan India
226 E3 Pine r. MI U.S.A.
226 E4 Pine r. MI U.S.A.
226 B4 Pine r. WI U.S.A.
226 C3 Pine r. WI U.S.A.
237 E5 Pine Bluff AR U.S.A.
238 F3 Pine Bluffs WY U.S.A.
235 D1 Pine Bush NY U.S.A.
226 A3 Pine City MN U.S.A.
84 B2 Pine Creek N.T. Austr.
232 E4 Pine Creek r. PA U.S.A.
240 G2 Pinecrest CA U.S.A.
183 H3 Pineda de Cigüela Spain
183 G2 Pineda de la Sierra Spain
186 F3 Pineda de Mar Spain
238 E3 Pinedale WY U.S.A.
223 L5 Pine Dock Man. Can.
223 L5 Pine Falls Man. Can.
134 F2 Pinega Rus. Fed.
134 H2 Pinega r. Rus. Fed.
87 B5 Pinegrove W.A. Austr.
232 A5 Pine Grove KY U.S.A.
234 C3 Pine Grove PA U.S.A.
227 I5 Pine Grove PA U.S.A.
232 C5 Pine Grove WV U.S.A.
84 C4 Pine Hill N.T. Austr.
234 D3 Pine Hill NJ U.S.A.
240 I4 Pine Hills CA U.S.A.
231 D6 Pine Hills FL U.S.A.
223 J4 Pinehouse Lake Sask. Can.
234 B3 Pinehurst MD U.S.A.
224 B2 Pineimuta r. Ont. Can.
198 C2 Pineios r. Greece
226 A3 Pine Island MN U.S.A.
235 D1 Pine Island NY U.S.A.
262 R1 Pine Island Glacier Antarctica
182 D3 Pinela Port.
237 E6 Pineland TX U.S.A.
183 F3 Piñel de Abajo Spain
81 B6 Pinelheugh mt. South I. N.Z.
231 D7 Pinellas Park FL U.S.A.
240 G4 Pine Mountain CA U.S.A.
222 H2 Pine Point N.W.T. Can.
240 H3 Pineridge CA U.S.A.
236 C3 Pine Ridge SD U.S.A.
190 C4 Pinerolo Italy
Pines, Isle of i. Cuba see La Juventud, Isla de
Pines, Isle of i. New Caledonia see Pins, Île des
193 G2 Pineto Italy
241 M4 Pinetop AZ U.S.A.
215 H3 Pinetown S. Africa
163 C4 Pineuilh France
227 I4 Pine Valley NY U.S.A.
232 B6 Pineville KY U.S.A.
237 E6 Pineville LA U.S.A.
234 C2 Pineville PA U.S.A.
232 C6 Pineville WV U.S.A.
156 E4 Piney France
96 C4 Ping, Mae Nam r. Thai.
116 C1 Pingal Jammu and Kashmir
106 D4 Ping'an Qinghai China
Ping'anyi Qinghai China see Ping'an
87 C7 Pingaring W.A. Austr.
108 C3 Pingba Guizhou China
108 B4 Pingbian Yunnan China
108 C2 Pingchang Sichuan China
107 G4 Pingding Shanxi China
Pingdingbu Hebei China see Guyuan
109 E1 Pingdingshan Henan China
Pingdong Taiwan see P'ingtung
Pingdu Jiangxi China see Anfu
107 H4 Pingdu Shandong China
87 C7 Pingelly W.A. Austr.
179 H3 Pinggau Austria
107 H3 Pinggu Beijing China
108 C4 Pingguo Guangxi China
109 E4 Pinghai Guangdong China
109 F3 Pinghe Fujian China
Pinghu Guizhou China see Pingtang
109 G2 Pinghu Zhejiang China
109 E2 Pingjiang Hunan China
108 D3 Pingle Guangxi China
108 D1 Pingli Shaanxi China
106 E5 Pingliang Gansu China
107 F5 Pinglu Shanxi China
106 E4 Pingluo Ningxia China
Pingma Guangxi China see Tiandong
109 F3 Pingnan Fujian China
109 D4 Pingnan Guangxi China
107 H3 Pingquan Hebei China
87 C7 Pingrup W.A. Austr.
Pingshan Guangdong China see Huidong
107 G4 Pingshan Hebei China
108 C2 Pingshan Sichuan China
Pingshan Yunnan China see Luquan
109 E3 Pingshi Guangdong China
Pingshu Hebei China see Daicheng
109 F3 Pingtan Fujian China
108 C3 Pingtang Guizhou China
109 G4 P'ingtung Taiwan
108 C1 Pingwu Sichuan China
Pingxi Guizhou China see Yuping
Pingxiang Gansu China see Tongwei
108 C4 Pingxiang Guangxi China
109 E3 Pingxiang Jiangxi China
107 J1 Pingyang Heilong. China
109 G3 Pingyang Zhejiang China
107 G4 Pingyao Shanxi China
107 H5 Pingyi Shandong China
107 H4 Pingyin Shandong China
109 E1 Pingyu Henan China
109 E3 Pingyuan Guangdong China
107 H4 Pingyuan Shandong China
Pingyuan Yunnan China see Yingjiang
108 B4 Pingyuanjie Yunnan China
108 D3 Pingzhai Guizhou China
256 D5 Pinhal Brazil
184 B2 Pinhal Novo Port.
182 C3 Pinhão Port.
254 D2 Pinheiro Brazil
182 D3 Pinheiro Porto Port.
184 B2 Pinheiro Setúbal Port.
258 G3 Pinheiro Machado Brazil
257 G3 Pinheiros Brazil
182 C4 Pinhel Port.
150 D4 Pinhoe Devon, England U.K.
251 E5 Pinhuã r. Brazil
185 H2 Pinilla r. Spain
183 I4 Pinilla de Molina Spain
183 E3 Pinilla de Toro Spain
Piniós r. Greece see Pineios
87 B7 Pinjarra W.A. Austr.
87 D6 Pinjin W.A. Austr.
179 H3 Pinkafeld Austria
84 B2 Pinkerton Range hills N.T. Austr.
222 F3 Pink Mountain B.C. Can.
81 D4 Pinnacle mt. South I. N.Z.
232 D5 Pinnacle hill VA/WV U.S.A.
82 E3 Pinnaroo S.A. Austr.
168 E2 Pinnau r. Ger.
168 E2 Pinneberg Ger.
171 F4 Pinnow Ger.
192 B2 Pino Corse France
182 D3 Pino Spain
183 F2 Pino del Río Spain
183 D3 Pinofranqueado Spain
95 E3 Pinoh r. Indon.
161 B3 Pinols France
182 B2 Piñor Spain
244 D2 Pinos Mex.
186 E3 Pinós hill Spain
Pinos, Isla de i. Cuba see La Juventud, Isla de
240 H4 Pinos, Mount CA U.S.A.
187 B6 Pinoso Spain
183 H4 Pinos mt. Spain
185 G3 Pinos-Puente Spain
245 E5 Pinotepa Nacional Mex.
93 A3 Pinrang Sulawesi Selatan Indon.
78 □5 Pins, Île des i. New Caledonia
163 D4 Pinsac France
179 D2 Pinsdorf Austria
136 D1 Pinsk Belarus
183 I2 Pinsoro Spain
250 □ Pinta, Isla i. Islas Galápagos Ecuador
241 K5 Pinta, Sierra hill AZ U.S.A.
186 B2 Pintano Spain
183 G4 Pinto Spain
241 K3 Pintura UT U.S.A.
192 B4 Pinu, Monte hill Sardegna Italy
146 D6 Pinwherry South Ayrshire, Scotland U.K.
191 H2 Pinzano al Tagliamento Italy
182 C4 Pinzio Port.
191 F2 Pinzolo Italy
191 H5 Piobbico Italy
241 J3 Pioche NV U.S.A.
78 □6 Pio Island Solomon Is
254 E3 Pio IX Brazil
161 C4 Piolenc France
190 E3 Pioltello Italy
192 E3 Piomba r. Italy
192 C2 Piombino Italy
191 G3 Piombino Dese Italy
232 A4 Pioneer OH U.S.A.
138 C4 Pionerskiy Kaliningradskaya Oblast' Rus. Fed.
130 H3 Pionerskiy Khanty-Mansiyskiy Avtonomnyy Okrug Rus. Fed.
175 J4 Pionki Pol.
160 A2 Pionsat France
80 E3 Piopio North I. N.Z.
Piopiotahi inlet South I. N.Z. see Milford Sound
193 E1 Pioraco Italy
251 F5 Piorini r. Brazil
251 F5 Piorini, Lago l. Brazil
190 C4 Piossasco Italy
174 G3 Piotrków Kujawski Pol.
175 H4 Piotrków Trybunalski Pol.
191 H3 Piove di Sacco Italy
191 H3 Piovene Rocchette Italy
190 E2 Piovera r. Italy
122 E5 Pip Iran
100 D4 Pipa Dingzi mt. China
116 C4 Pipar Rajasthan India
116 C4 Pipar Road Rajasthan India
240 I3 Piper Peak NV U.S.A.
234 C2 Pipersville PA U.S.A.
223 K5 Pipestone Man. Can.
224 B2 Pipestone r. Ont. Can.
236 D3 Pipestone MN U.S.A.
197 H2 Pipirig Romania
80 E3 Pipiriki North I. N.Z.
116 D3 Pipli Haryana India
225 G3 Pipmuacan, Réservoir resr Que. Can.
158 E4 Pipriac France
Piqan Xinjiang China see Shanshan
110 C3 Piqanlik Xinjiang China
232 A4 Piqua OH U.S.A.
163 C5 Piqué r. France
254 F3 Piquet Carneiro Brazil
257 E5 Piquete Brazil
253 G4 Piquiri r. Mato Grosso do Sul Brazil
256 A6 Piquiri r. Paraná Brazil
177 L4 Pir Romania
256 C1 Piracanjuba Brazil
256 C1 Piracanjuba r. Brazil
256 D5 Piracicaba Brazil
257 E3 Piracicaba r. Minas Gerais Brazil
256 C5 Piracicaba r. São Paulo Brazil
256 D4 Piraçununga Brazil
254 E2 Piracuruca Brazil
Piraeus Greece see Peiraias
256 C6 Piraí do Sul Brazil
Piráievs Greece see Peiraias
194 D4 Piraino Sicilia Italy
256 C5 Piraju Brazil
256 C3 Pirajuba Brazil
256 C4 Pirajuí Brazil
129 G3 Pirallahı Adası Azer.
191 I3 Piran Slovenia
258 F2 Pirané Arg.
257 F4 Piranga Brazil
257 F4 Piranga r. Brazil
257 E5 Piranguinho Brazil
254 F4 Piranhas Alagoas Brazil
256 B2 Piranhas Goiás Brazil
256 B2 Piranhas r. Goiás Brazil
254 F3 Piranhas r. Rio Grande do Norte Brazil
254 D2 Pirapemas Brazil
257 F4 Pirapetinga Brazil
256 A5 Pirapó r. Brazil
257 E2 Pirapora Brazil
256 B5 Pirapozinho Brazil
256 C6 Piraquara Brazil
258 G3 Piratini Brazil
256 C5 Piratininga Brazil
116 D4 Pirawa Rajasthan India
151 G3 Pirbright Surrey, England U.K.
Pirchevan Azer. see Zängilan
256 C1 Pirenópolis Brazil
256 C2 Pires do Rio Brazil
117 G4 Pirganj Bangl.
Pirgos Greece see Pyrgos
197 G4 Pirgovo Bulg.
158 D4 Piriac-sur-Mer France
80 E3 Piriaka North I. N.Z.
258 G4 Piriápolis Uru.
177 L4 Piricse Hungary
197 F5 Pirin mts Bulg.
Pirineos mts Europe see Pyrenees
254 E3 Piripiri Brazil
138 E2 Pirita r. Estonia
250 D2 Piritu Venez.
179 G3 Pirka Austria
141 M3 Pirkkala Fin.
Pirlerkondu Turkey see Taşkent
172 B2 Pirmasens Ger.
114 C4 Pirmed Kerala India
171 E5 Pirna Ger.
146 C6 Pirnmill North Ayrshire, Scotland U.K.
117 G5 Pirojpur Bangl.
183 F3 Pirón r. Spain
80 E2 Pirongia North I. N.Z.
80 E2 Pirongia vol. North I. N.Z.
139 I2 Piros, Ozero l. Rus. Fed.
197 F4 Pirot Srbija Yugo.
261 G5 Pirovano Arg.
117 F4 Pirpainti Bihar India
116 C2 Pir Panjal Range mts India/Pak.
127 F3 Pirrasit Dağ hill Turkey
129 F4 Pirsaat Azer.
129 F3 Pirsaatçay r. Azer.
177 I5 Pirtó Hungary
140 L2 Pirttivuopio Sweden
123 G2 Pir'yakh, Gora mt. Tajik.
Piryatin Ukr. see Pyryatyn
Piryetós Greece see Pyrgetos
Piryion Voreio Aigaio Greece see Pyrgi
190 F5 Pisa Italy
191 F5 Pisa prov. Toscana Italy
175 J2 Pisa r. Pol.
252 C3 Pisac Peru
Pisae Italy see Pisa
78 □4a Pisamwe i. Chuuk Micronesia
162 B3 Pisany France
78 □4a Pisar i. Chuuk Micronesia
81 B6 Pisa Range mts South I. N.Z.
Pisaurum Italy see Pesaro
235 D2 Piscataway NJ U.S.A.
179 G3 Pischelsdorf in der Steiermark Austria
177 K6 Pischia Romania
193 H4 Pisciotta Italy
252 A3 Pisco Peru
252 A3 Pisco r. Peru
177 L4 Piscolt Romania
176 D2 Písek Czech Rep.
81 A6 Pisgah, Mount South I. N.Z.
81 C6 Pisgah, Mount South I. N.Z.
Pisha Sichuan China see Ningnan
111 B4 Pishan Xinjiang China
136 B2 Pishcha Ukr.
136 E3 Pishchana Ukr.
137 F3 Pishchane Ukr.
136 E3 Pishchanka Ukr.
123 E5 Pishin Iran
123 F4 Pishin Pak.
123 F4 Pishin Lora r. Pak.
Pishpek Kyrg. see Bishkek
175 I3 Pisia r. Pol.
241 K5 Pisinimo AZ U.S.A.
78 □4a Pisininn i. Chuuk Micronesia
Piskent Uzbek. see Pskent
136 E2 Piskivka Ukr.
137 I3 Pisky Kharkivs'ka Oblast' Ukr.
137 J3 Pisky Luhans'ka Oblast' Ukr.
240 G4 Pismo Beach CA U.S.A.
253 E3 Piso Firme Bol.
190 E3 Pisogne Italy
138 C4 Pissa r. Rus. Fed.
258 C2 Pissis, Cerro mt. Arg.
163 B4 Pissos France
140 O2 Pista r. Rus. Fed.
243 H4 Pisté Mex.
195 F2 Pisticci Italy
191 F5 Pistoia Italy
191 F5 Pistoia prov. Toscana Italy
Pistoriae Italy see Pistoia
139 M3 Pistsovo Rus. Fed.
183 F3 Pisuerga r. Spain
175 J2 Pisz Pol.
175 L4 Piszczac Pol.
238 B3 Pit r. CA U.S.A.
206 B4 Pita Guinea
225 H2 Pitaga Nfld. Can.
243 H5 Pital Mex.
250 B4 Pitalito Col.
256 B6 Pitanga Brazil
256 C4 Pitangueiras Brazil
257 E3 Pitangui Brazil
83 E3 Pitarpunga Lake imp. l. N.S.W. Austr.
186 C4 Pitarque Spain
267 K7 Pitcairn Island S. Pacific Ocean
206 B3 Pitche Guinea-Bissau
140 M2 Piteå Sweden
140 M2 Piteälven r. Sweden
191 F4 Piteglio Italy
135 H5 Pitelino Rus. Fed.
128 F2 Piterka Rus. Fed.
197 G3 Pitești Romania
87 B6 Pithara W.A. Austr.
156 C4 Pithiviers France
116 E3 Pithoragarh Uttar Prad. India
192 D2 Pitigliano Italy
183 I2 Pitillas Spain
242 B2 Pitiquito Mex.
134 E3 Pitkyaranta Rus. Fed.
146 E5 Pitlochry Perth and Kinross, Scotland U.K.
234 C3 Pitman NJ U.S.A.
146 F4 Pitmedden Aberdeenshire, Scotland U.K.
150 D4 Pitminster Somerset, England U.K.
207 I4 Pitoa Cameroon
188 F3 Pitomača Croatia
217 □1c Piton de la Fournaise vol. Réunion
217 □1c Piton des Neiges mt. Réunion
Pitong Sichuan China see Pixian
156 B3 Pitres France
185 G4 Pitres Spain
260 A6 Pitrufquén Chile
179 G4 Pitschgau Austria
151 G3 Pitstone Buckinghamshire, England U.K.
Pitsunda Georgia see Bichvint'a
151 F3 Pitt Hampshire, England U.K.
165 C4 Pittem Belgium
179 H3 Pitten Austria
146 D4 Pittentrail Highland, Scotland U.K.
146 F5 Pittenweem Fife, Scotland U.K.
222 D4 Pitt Island B.C. Can.
80 □ Pitt Island Chatham Is S. Pacific Ocean
Pitt Islands Solomon Is see Vanikoro Islands
237 F5 Pittsboro MS U.S.A.
231 E5 Pittsboro NC U.S.A.
240 G2 Pittsburg CA U.S.A.
237 E4 Pittsburg KS U.S.A.
233 H2 Pittsburg NH U.S.A.
237 E5 Pittsburg TX U.S.A.
232 D4 Pittsburgh PA U.S.A.
236 F4 Pittsfield IL U.S.A.
233 G3 Pittsfield MA U.S.A.
233 □I2 Pittsfield ME U.S.A.
233 H3 Pittsfield NH U.S.A.
233 G3 Pittsfield VT U.S.A.
234 C1 Pittston PA U.S.A.
233 □I2 Pittston Farm ME U.S.A.
226 B3 Pittsville WI U.S.A.
85 G5 Pittsworth Qld Austr.
177 J5 Pitvaros Hungary
254 C4 Pium Brazil
257 E4 Piumhí Brazil
250 A6 Piura Peru
250 A6 Piura dept Peru
138 F3 Piusa r. Estonia
241 J4 Piute Mountains CA U.S.A.
240 H4 Piute Peak CA U.S.A.
224 D3 Pivabiska r. Ont. Can.
136 F4 Pivdennyy Buh r. Ukr.
250 C2 Pivijay Col.
188 E3 Pivka Slovenia
191 J3 Pivka r. Slovenia
175 I6 Piwniczna Pol.
Pixariá mt. Greece see Pyxaria
108 B2 Pixian Sichuan China
240 H4 Pixley CA U.S.A.
243 H5 Pixoyal Mex.
252 C4 Pizacoma Peru
185 F4 Pizarra Spain
190 E2 Piz Bernina mt. Italy/Switz.
178 C4 Piz Boè mt. Italy
178 B4 Piz Buin mt. Austria/Switz.
190 E2 Piz d'Anarosa mt. Switz.
190 E2 Piz Duan mt. Switz.
190 E2 Piz Ela mt. Switz.
134 J4 Pizhanka Rus. Fed.
207 G4 Pizhi Nigeria
134 I4 Pizhma Rus. Fed.
134 J4 Pizhma r. Rus. Fed.
134 K2 Pizhma r. Rus. Fed.
107 H5 Pizhou Jiangsu China
190 E2 Piz Kesch mt. Switz.
190 D2 Piz Medel mt. Switz.
190 E2 Pizol mt. Switz.
190 E2 Piz Pisoc mt. Switz.
190 E2 Piz Platta mt. Switz.
190 E2 Piz Varuna mt. Italy/Switz.
190 E3 Pizzighettone Italy
195 F4 Pizzo Italy
190 E3 Pizzo Arera mt. Italy
194 C5 Pizzo Cangialoso mt. Sicilia Italy
194 D5 Pizzo Carbonara mt. Sicilia Italy
190 F3 Pizzo della Presolana mt. Italy
190 F2 Pizzo di Coca mt. Italy
193 G3 Pizzoferrato Italy
193 F1 Pizzoli Italy
190 D2 Pizzo Rotondo mt. Switz.
194 C5 Pizzo Telegrafo hill Sicilia Italy
193 E2 Pizzuto, Monte mt. Italy
170 D2 Plaaz Ger.
158 B3 Plabennec France
225 K4 Placentia Nfld. Can.
Placentia Italy see Piacenza
225 K4 Placentia Bay Nfld. Can.
92 B4 Placer Masbate Phil.
92 C4 Placer Mindanao Phil.
240 G2 Placerville CA U.S.A.
239 E4 Placerville CO U.S.A.
246 C2 Placetas Cuba
252 D2 Plácido de Castro Brazil
260 B3 Placilla Chile
190 C2 Plaffeien Switz.
169 C5 Plaidt Ger.
159 I4 Plaimpied-Givaudins France
237 E5 Plain Dealing LA U.S.A.
157 H4 Plainfaing France
235 G1 Plainfield CT U.S.A.
230 C4 Plainfield IN U.S.A.
235 D2 Plainfield NJ U.S.A.
233 G2 Plainfield VT U.S.A.
226 C3 Plainfield WI U.S.A.
237 C4 Plains KS U.S.A.
237 C5 Plains TX U.S.A.
234 D2 Plainsboro NJ U.S.A.
158 D3 Plaintel France
226 A3 Plainview MN U.S.A.
236 D3 Plainview NE U.S.A.
235 E2 Plainview NY U.S.A.
237 C5 Plainview TX U.S.A.
235 F1 Plainville CT U.S.A.
236 D4 Plainville KS U.S.A.
226 E4 Plainwell MI U.S.A.
165 C5 Plaisance Belgium
247 D3 Plaisance Haiti
163 D5 Plaisance-du-Touch France
156 B4 Plaisir France
233 H3 Plaistow NH U.S.A.
94 D3 Plaju Sumatera Indon.
95 G5 Plampang Sumbawa Indon.
176 B2 Planá Czech Rep.
246 D2 Plana Cays is Bahamas
240 G3 Planada CA U.S.A.
256 D1 Planaltina Brazil
176 C1 Plaňany Czech Rep.
157 G5 Plancher-Bas France
157 G5 Plancher-les-Mines France
158 D3 Plancoët France
156 D4 Plancy-l'Abbaye France
244 D3 Plan de Ayala Mex.
161 D4 Plan-de-Baux France
161 D5 Plan-de-Cuques France
161 E5 Plan-de-la-Tour France
196 E3 Plandište Vojvodina, Srbija Yugo.
161 C5 Plan-d'Orgon France
171 D3 Plane r. Ger.
173 F3 Planegg Ger.
163 E6 Planès France
176 C2 Plánice Czech Rep.
191 J3 Planik mt. Croatia
173 F2 Plankenfels Ger.
236 D3 Plankinton SD U.S.A.
226 C5 Plano IL U.S.A.
237 D5 Plano TX U.S.A.
261 I1 Plano Alto Brazil
178 B3 Plansee l. Austria
163 D5 Plantaurel, Montagnes du hills France
231 D7 Plant City FL U.S.A.
235 F1 Plantsville CT U.S.A.
256 C4 Planura Brazil
237 F6 Plaquemine LA U.S.A.
182 D4 Plasencia Spain
186 C2 Plasencia del Monte Spain
175 L2 Płaska Pol.
188 E3 Plaški Croatia
196 E1 Plasnica Macedonia
135 K5 Plast Rus. Fed.
241 J5 Plaster City CA U.S.A.
225 H4 Plaster Rock N.B. Can.
215 H1 Plaston S. Africa
177 H3 Plášťovce Slovakia
100 F3 Plastun Rus. Fed.
129 A2 Plastunka Rus. Fed.
137 J5 Plastunovskaya Rus. Fed.
176 C2 Plasy Czech Rep.
192 A4 Platamona Lido Sardegna Italy
198 C2 Platamonas Greece
194 C5 Platani r. Sicilia Italy
195 F3 Platania Italy
198 B3 Platanos Greece
214 B4 Platbakkies S. Africa
215 G3 Platberg mt. S. Africa
170 C2 Plate Ger.
207 G4 Plateau state Nigeria
208 B5 Plateaux admin. reg. Congo
168 F3 Platendorf (Sassenburg) Ger.
214 C5 Plathuis S. Africa
195 F4 Plati Italy
196 D3 Platičevo Vojvodina, Srbija Yugo.
Platikambos Greece see Platykampos
240 F1 Platina CA U.S.A.
220 B4 Platinum AK U.S.A.
137 J5 Platnirovskaya Rus. Fed.
250 C2 Plato Col.
215 G2 Platrand S. Africa
236 E4 Platte r. MO U.S.A.
236 E3 Platte r. NE U.S.A.
236 E4 Platte City MO U.S.A.
217 □2 Platte Island Seychelles
235 D1 Plattekill NY U.S.A.
179 F2 Plattenberg hill Austria
238 F3 Platteville CO U.S.A.
236 F3 Platteville WI U.S.A.
173 G3 Plattling Ger.
233 G2 Plattsburgh NY U.S.A.
236 E3 Plattsmouth NE U.S.A.
198 C1 Platy Greece
198 C2 Platykampos Greece
170 D2 Plau Ger.
169 F5 Plaue Ger.
171 D5 Plauen Ger.
170 D2 Plauer See l. Ger.
136 D2 Plav r. Ukr.
196 D4 Plav Crna Gora Yugo.
139 K5 Plava r. Rus. Fed.
179 I2 Plavecký Štvrtok Slovakia
138 E3 Pļaviņas Latvia
137 K1 Plavitsa r. Rus. Fed.
139 K5 Plavsk Rus. Fed.
216 □3c Playa Blanca Lanzarote Canary Is
184 D3 Playa de Castilla coastal area Spain
247 □1 Playa de Fajardo Puerto Rico
216 □3a Playa de las Americas Tenerife Canary Is
181 □ Playa del Inglés Gran Canaria Canary Is
261 I4 Playa Pascual Uru.
250 A5 Playas Ecuador
245 H5 Playas r. Mex.
244 D4 Playa Vicente Mex.
97 E4 Play Cu Vietnam
242 C3 Playón Mex.
162 D3 Plazac France
185 F2 Plaza del Judío mt. Spain
260 C6 Plaza Huincul Arg.
175 L5 Płazów Pol.
233 □J2 Pleasant, Mount hill N.B. Can.
234 C2 Pleasant Corners PA U.S.A.
235 D2 Pleasant Grove NJ U.S.A.
241 L1 Pleasant Grove UT U.S.A.
240 F3 Pleasant Hill CA U.S.A.
232 A4 Pleasant Hill OH U.S.A.
240 G3 Pleasanton CA U.S.A.
237 D6 Pleasanton TX U.S.A.
81 C6 Pleasant Point South I. N.Z.
235 E1 Pleasant Valley NY U.S.A.
234 C3 Pleasantville DE U.S.A.
234 D3 Pleasantville NJ U.S.A.
235 E1 Pleasantville NY U.S.A.
234 B3 Pleasant Hill PA U.S.A.
149 H4 Pleasley Derbyshire, England U.K.
235 F1 Pleasure Beach CT U.S.A.
234 B3 Pleasureville PA U.S.A.
162 E3 Pleaux France
173 F2 Plech Ger.
176 C3 Plechý mt. Czech Rep.
175 H3 Plecka Dąbrowa Pol.
158 D3 Plédran France
158 D3 Pléhédel France
158 E3 Pleine-Fougères France
173 E2 Pleinfeld Ger.
173 G3 Pleiskirchen Ger.
171 D5 Pleißa Ger.
171 D4 Pleiße r. Ger.
137 J1 Plekhanovo Rus. Fed.
158 D3 Plélan-le-Grand France
158 D3 Plélan-le-Petit France
158 D3 Plélo France
158 D3 Plémet France
158 D3 Plénée-Jugon France
158 D3 Pléneuf-Val-André France
80 F2 Plenty, Bay of g. North I. N.Z.
238 F1 Plentywood MT U.S.A.
183 H1 Plentzia Spain
158 D3 Plérin France
139 M3 Ples Rus. Fed.
179 G3 Pleschkogel mt. Austria
158 D4 Plescop France
177 L5 Pleșcuța Romania
134 H3 Plesetsk Rus. Fed.
120 C1 Pleshanovo Rus. Fed.
Pleshchenitsy Belarus see Pyeshchanitsy
139 L3 Pleshcheyevo, Ozero l. Rus. Fed.
177 J3 Plešivec Slovakia
179 F4 Plešivec mt. Slovenia
158 D3 Pleslin-Trigavou France
176 B1 Plesná Czech Rep.
169 F5 Pleß hill Ger.
171 E4 Plessa Ger.
158 E4 Plessé France
158 C3 Plestin-les-Grèves France
174 F4 Pleszew Pol.
137 F3 Pletenyy Tashlyk Ukr.
188 F3 Pleternica Croatia
169 C4 Plettenberg Ger.
214 D6 Plettenberg Bay S. Africa
178 D3 Pletzen mt. Austria
158 C3 Pleubian France
158 D3 Pleudihen-sur-Rance France
159 G5 Pleumartin France
158 D3 Pleumeur-Bodou France
156 D4 Pleurs France
158 D3 Pleurtuit France
158 B4 Pleuven France
197 G4 Pleven Bulg.
Plevna Bulg. see Pleven
177 H2 Plevník-Drienové Slovakia
158 C3 Pleyben France
158 D3 Pleyber-Christ France
173 G2 Pleystein Ger.
187 B7 Pliego Spain
173 F3 Pliening Ger.
95 F2 Pliěran r. Sarawak Malaysia
177 I3 Pliešovce Slovakia
163 C5 Plieux France
191 F2 Plima r. Italy
174 C3 Pliszka r. Pol.
188 E3 Plješevica mts Croatia
196 D4 Pljevlja Crna Gora Yugo.
192 B4 Ploaghe Sardegna Italy
158 B4 Plobannalec France
157 H4 Plobsheim France
188 F4 Ploče Croatia
172 D3 Plochingen Ger.
175 K1 Płociczno Pol.
175 H3 Płock Pol.
146 C4 Plockton Highland, Scotland U.K.
188 F4 Pločno mt. Bos.-Herz.
139 H1 Plodovoye Rus. Fed.
158 C4 Ploemeur France
158 D4 Ploëren France
158 D4 Ploërmel France
Ploești Romania see Ploiești
158 D3 Plœuc-sur-Lié France
158 B4 Plogastel-St-Germain France
158 B4 Plogonnec France
170 E1 Plogshagen Ger.
197 H3 Ploiești Romania
199 E5 Plomari Voreio Aigaio Greece
161 A3 Plomb du Cantal mt. France
157 G5 Plombières-les-Bains France
158 B4 Plomelin France
158 B4 Plomeur France
158 C3 Plomodiern France
168 F1 Plön Ger.
158 B4 Plonéour-Lanvern France
158 C3 Plonévez-du-Faou France
158 B4 Plonévez-Porzay France
174 C2 Płonia r. Pol.
175 I2 Płonka r. Pol.
175 J3 Płońsk Pol.
197 F2 Plopiș Romania
175 H1 Płoskinia Pol.
139 H3 Ploskosh' Rus. Fed.
Ploskoye Rus. Fed. see Stanovoye
175 I2 Płośnica Pol.
173 G2 Plößberg Ger.
174 D2 Płoty Pol.
171 D3 Plötzin Ger.
171 C3 Plötzky Ger.
158 C3 Plouagat France
158 C3 Plouaret France
158 B3 Plouarzel France
158 C3 Plouay France
158 D3 Ploubalay France

222 E5 Port McNeill B.C. Can.
225 H3 Port-Menier Que. Can.
246 □ Port Morant Jamaica
246 □ Portmore Jamaica
91 K8 Port Moresby P.N.G.
156 B3 Port-Mort France
147 F2 Portmuck Northern Ireland U.K.
85 E1 Port Musgrave b. Qld Austr.
146 C5 Portnacroish Argyll and Bute, Scotland U.K.
146 B3 Portnaguran Western Isles, Scotland U.K.
146 B6 Portnahaven Argyll and Bute, Scotland U.K.
146 B4 Portnalong Highland, Scotland U.K.
Port nan Giúran Western Isles, Scotland U.K. see Portnaguran
146 A4 Port nan Long Western Isles, Scotland U.K.
158 D4 Port-Navalo France
237 E6 Port Neches TX U.S.A.
82 D3 Port Neill S.A. Austr.
246 D2 Port Nelson Rum Cay Bahamas
225 G3 Portneuf r. Que. Can.
238 D3 Portneuf r. ID U.S.A.
146 B3 Port Nis Western Isles, Scotland U.K.
82 D3 Port Noarlunga S.A. Austr.
214 A3 Port Nolloth S. Africa
147 C2 Portnoo Rep. of Ireland
234 C3 Port Norris NJ U.S.A.
Port-Nouveau-Québec Que. Can. see Kangiqsualujjuaq
254 E2 Porto Brazil
192 A2 Porto Corse France
182 B3 Porto Port.
182 B3 Porto admin. dist. Port.
182 D2 Porto Spain
255 C9 Porto Alegre Brazil
Porto Alexandre Angola see Tombua
184 B2 Porto Alto Port.
209 B7 Porto Amboim Angola
Porto Amélia Moz. see Pemba
192 C2 Porto Azzurro Italy
81 C6 Portobello South I. N.Z.
255 C8 Porto Belo Brazil
192 A5 Porto Botte Sardegna Italy
182 B2 Portobravo Spain
254 G4 Porto Cavlo Brazil
192 B3 Porto Cervo Sardegna Italy
195 G2 Porto Cesareo Italy
187 G5 Porto Colom Spain
184 B3 Porto Covo da Bandeira Port.
187 G5 Porto Cristo Spain
184 □ Porto da Cruz Madeira
254 F4 Porto da Fôlha Brazil
182 B5 Porto de Mós Port.
251 H5 Porto de Moz Brazil
182 C1 Porto do Barqueiro Spain
253 F2 Porto dos Gaúchos Óbidos Brazil
182 A2 Porto do Son Spain
194 C5 Porto Empedocle Sicilia Italy
192 D2 Porto Ercole Italy
253 F3 Porto Esperidião Brazil
256 D5 Porto Feliz Brazil
192 C2 Portoferraio Italy
256 D4 Porto Ferreira Brazil
190 E4 Portofino Italy
257 F4 Porto Firme Brazil
146 D5 Port of Menteith Stirling, Scotland U.K.
254 D3 Porto Franco Brazil
247 □7 Port of Spain Trin. and Tob.
191 H4 Porto Garibaldi Italy
191 H3 Portogruaro Italy
206 □ Porto Inglês Cape Verde
216 □1a Porto Judeu Terceira Azores
240 G2 Portola CA U.S.A.
194 D4 Porto Levante Isole Lipari Italy
191 H3 Porto Levante Veneto Italy
255 B8 Porto Luceno Brazil
191 G4 Portomaggiore Italy
182 C2 Portomarín Spain
184 □ Porto Moniz Madeira
253 F5 Porto Murtinho Brazil
254 C4 Porto Nacional Brazil
207 F5 Porto-Novo Benin
206 □ Porto Novo Cape Verde
Porto Novo Tamil Nadu India see Parangipettai
194 B5 Porto Palo Sicilia Italy
189 E7 Portopalo di Capo Passero Sicilia Italy
192 A6 Porto Pino Sardegna Italy
256 A4 Porto Primavera, Represa resr Brazil
231 D6 Port Orange FL U.S.A.
238 B2 Port Orchard WA U.S.A.
191 I5 Porto Recanati Italy
238 A3 Port Orford OR U.S.A.
209 B6 Porto Rico Angola
192 B3 Porto Rotondo Sardegna Italy
191 I3 Portorož Slovenia
191 I5 Porto San Giorgio Italy
192 B4 Porto San Paolo Sardegna Italy
251 I5 Porto Santana Brazil
191 I5 Porto Sant'Elpidio Italy
184 □ Porto Santo Madeira
184 □ Porto Santo, Ilha de i. Madeira
192 D2 Porto Santo Stefano Italy
192 A5 Portoscuso Sardegna Italy
257 H2 Porto Seguro Brazil
191 H4 Porto Tolle Italy
192 A4 Porto Torres Sardegna Italy
255 C8 Porto União Brazil
192 B3 Porto-Vecchio Corse France
252 E2 Porto Velho Brazil
190 E4 Portovenere Italy
250 A5 Portoviejo Ecuador
146 C7 Portpatrick Dumfries and Galloway, Scotland U.K.
234 C3 Port Penn DE U.S.A.
227 H3 Port Perry Ont. Can.
83 F4 Port Phillip Bay Vic. Austr.
82 D3 Port Pirie S.A. Austr.
Port Radium N.W.T. Can. see Echo Bay
147 E3 Portrane Rep. of Ireland
150 B4 Portreath Cornwall, England U.K.
146 B4 Portree Highland, Scotland U.K.
222 E5 Port Renfrew B.C. Can.
225 K3 Port Rexton Nfld. Can.
147 C4 Portroe Rep. of Ireland
84 C2 Port Roper b. N.T. Austr.
227 G4 Port Rowan Ont. Can.
246 □ Port Royal Jamaica
232 E5 Port Royal VA U.S.A.
147 E1 Portrush Northern Ireland U.K.
Port Said Egypt see Bûr Sa'îd
163 C4 Port-Ste-Foy-et-Ponchapt France
163 C4 Port-Ste-Marie France
231 C6 Port St Joe FL U.S.A.
215 G4 Port St Johns S. Africa
161 C5 Port-St-Louis-du-Rhône France
231 D7 Port Saint Lucie City FL U.S.A.
148 E3 Port St Mary Isle of Man
158 E4 Port-St-Père France
158 B3 Portsall France
147 D1 Portsalon Rep. of Ireland
227 F4 Port Sanilac MI U.S.A.
179 F4 Pörtschach am Wörther See Austria
186 D4 Ports de Beseit mts Spain
227 H3 Port Severn Ont. Can.
215 H4 Port Shepstone S. Africa
Port Simpson B.C. Can. see Lax Kw'alaams
247 □2 Portsmouth Dominica
151 F4 Portsmouth Portsmouth, England U.K.
151 F4 Portsmouth admin. div. England U.K.
233 □H3 Portsmouth NH U.S.A.
232 B5 Portsmouth OH U.S.A.
233 E6 Portsmouth VA U.S.A.
146 F4 Portsoy Aberdeenshire, Scotland U.K.
Port Stanley Falkland Is see Stanley
83 H3 Port Stephens b. N.S.W. Austr.
147 E1 Portstewart Northern Ireland U.K.
203 H5 Port Sudan Sudan
237 F6 Port Sulphur LA U.S.A.
157 G5 Port-sur-Saône France
Port Swettenham Malaysia see Pelabuhan Kelang
150 D3 Port Talbot Neath Port Talbot, Wales U.K.
238 B1 Port Townsend WA U.S.A.
234 B2 Port Trevorton PA U.S.A.
180 C3 Portugal country Europe
183 G1 Portugalete Spain
Portugália Angola see Chitato
250 D2 Portuguesa state Venez.
Portuguese East Africa country Africa see Mozambique
Portuguese Guinea country Africa see Guinea-Bissau
Portuguese Timor terr. Asia see East Timor
Portuguese West Africa country Africa see Angola
147 C3 Portumna Rep. of Ireland
Portus Herculis Monoeci country Europe see Monaco
182 B3 Portuzelo Port.
163 F6 Port-Vendres France
82 D3 Port Victoria S.A. Austr.
78 □5 Port Vila Vanuatu
232 D3 Portville NY U.S.A.
82 D3 Port Vincent S.A. Austr.
140 P1 Port Vladimir Rus. Fed.
80 E2 Port Waikato North I. N.Z.
82 D3 Port Wakefield S.A. Austr.
86 E2 Port Warrender W.A. Austr.
235 E2 Port Washington NY U.S.A.
226 D4 Port Washington WI U.S.A.
146 D7 Port William Dumfries and Galloway, Scotland U.K.
226 B2 Port Wing WI U.S.A.
114 C3 Porumamilla Andhra Prad. India
246 □ Porus Jamaica
139 H3 Porus'ya r. Rus. Fed.
252 C2 Porvenir Pando Bol.
253 E3 Porvenir Santa Cruz Bol.
259 C9 Porvenir Chile
141 N3 Porvoo Fin.
138 E1 Porvoonjoki r. Fin.
101 C5 Poryŏng S. Korea
175 J3 Porządzie Pol.
185 F1 Porzuna Spain
192 B4 Posada Sardegna Italy
192 B4 Posada r. Sardegna Italy
182 E1 Posada de Llanera Spain
183 F1 Posada de Valdeón Spain
258 G2 Posadas Arg.
185 E3 Posadas Spain
137 G4 Posad-Pokrovs'ke Ukr.
190 F2 Poschiavo Switz.
Poseidonia tourist site Italy see Paestum
Posen Pol. see Poznań
227 F3 Posen MI U.S.A.
170 E1 Poseritz Ger.
186 D2 Posets mt. Spain
134 G4 Poshekhon'ye Rus. Fed.
Poshekon'ye-Volodarsk Rus. Fed. see Poshekhon'ye
122 D4 Poshteh-ye Chaqvīr hill Iran
122 A3 Posht-e Kūh mts Iran
122 B2 Posht Kūh hill Iran
137 G5 Poshtove Ukr.
178 C5 Posina r. Italy
173 G2 Pösing Ger.
140 O2 Posio Fin.
193 G4 Positano Italy
Poskam Xinjiang China see Zepu
235 F1 Posnet CT U.S.A.
93 B3 Poso Sulawesi Tengah Indon.
93 B3 Poso r. Indon.
127 F2 Posof Turkey
129 C3 Posof r. Turkey
250 A5 Posorja Ecuador
121 J1 Pospelikha Rus. Fed.
178 C5 Possagno Italy
254 D5 Posse Brazil
171 E5 Possendorf Ger.
157 E4 Possesse France
263 L2 Possession Islands Antarctica
171 C5 Pößneck Ger.
237 C5 Post TX U.S.A.
193 F2 Posta Italy
197 H3 Poşta Câlnău Romania
Poşta Cîlnău Romania see Poşta Câlnău
191 G2 Postal Italy
193 H3 Posta Piana Italy
173 G3 Postau Ger.
Postavy Belarus see Pastavy
173 F2 Postbauer-Heng Ger.
215 E5 Post Chalmers S. Africa
Poste-de-la-Baleine Que. Can. see Kuujjuarapik
165 F3 Posterholt Neth.
214 D3 Postmasburg S. Africa
173 G3 Postmünster Ger.
188 E3 Postojna Slovenia
175 J3 Postoliska Pol.
176 C1 Postoloprty Czech Rep.
174 C3 Postomia r. Pol.
174 E1 Postomino Pol.
241 J4 Poston AZ U.S.A.
225 J2 Postville Nfld. Can.
226 B4 Postville IA U.S.A.
Postysheve Ukr. see Krasnoarmiys'k
188 F4 Posušje Bos.-Herz.
175 I4 Poświętne Pol.
175 J3 Poświętne Pol.
175 K3 Poświętne Pol.
100 D4 Pos'yet Rus. Fed.
236 C3 Potato Creek SD U.S.A.
215 F2 Potchefstroom S. Africa
197 G3 Potcoava Romania
257 G2 Poté Brazil
237 E5 Poteau OK U.S.A.
114 D2 Potegaon Mahar. India
174 F1 Potęgowo Pol.
Potentia Italy see Potenza
193 H4 Potenza Italy
193 H4 Potenza prov. Basilicata Italy
191 I5 Potenza r. Italy
191 I5 Potenza Picena Italy
81 A7 Poteriteri, Lake South I. N.Z.
183 F1 Potes Spain
214 E4 Potfontein S. Africa
213 F5 Potgietersrus S. Africa
254 E3 Poti r. Brazil
129 B2 P'ot'i Georgia
159 F3 Potigny France
114 D2 Potikal Madh. Prad. India
255 F5 Potiraguá Brazil
207 H4 Potiskum Nigeria
136 E2 Potiyivka Ukr.
238 C2 Potlatch ID U.S.A.
175 K5 Potok Górny Pol.
175 H5 Potok Złoty Pol.
232 E5 Potomac MD U.S.A.
232 E5 Potomac r. MD/VA U.S.A.
232 D5 Potomac, South Branch r. WV U.S.A.
232 D5 Potomac, South Fork South Branch r. WV U.S.A.
93 C5 Potomana, Gunung mt. Indon.
206 C5 Potoru Sierra Leone
252 D4 Potosí Bol.
252 D5 Potosí dept Bol.
230 B4 Potosi MO U.S.A.
241 J4 Potosi Mountain NV U.S.A.
92 B4 Pototan Phil.
258 C2 Potrerillos Chile
242 □I6 Potrerillos Hond.
245 F3 Potrero del Llano Mex.
250 B6 Potro r. Peru
171 E3 Potsdam Ger.
233 F2 Potsdam NY U.S.A.
177 G2 Potštát Czech Rep.
78 □5 Pott, Île i. New Caledonia
115 D2 Pottangi Orissa India
179 H3 Pottendorf Austria
179 H3 Pottenstein Austria
173 F2 Pottenstein Ger.
236 C3 Potter NE U.S.A.
150 E3 Potterne Wiltshire, England U.K.
151 G3 Potters Bar Hertfordshire, England U.K.
240 F2 Potter Valley CA U.S.A.
232 A3 Potterville MI U.S.A.
173 F3 Pöttmes Ger.
151 G2 Potton Bedfordshire, England U.K.
179 H3 Pöttsching Austria
234 B1 Potts Grove PA U.S.A.
234 C2 Pottstown PA U.S.A.
234 B2 Pottsville PA U.S.A.
137 J2 Potudan' r. Rus. Fed.
175 I4 Potworów Pol.
172 B2 Potzberg hill Ger.
158 E4 Pouancé France
222 F4 Pouce Coupe B.C. Can.
225 K4 Pouch Cove Nfld. Can.
233 G4 Poughkeepsie NY U.S.A.
235 E1 Poughquag NY U.S.A.
160 B1 Pougny France
160 B1 Pougues-les-Eaux France
156 E4 Pougy France
160 D1 Pouilley-les-Vignes France
163 B5 Pouillon France
160 C1 Pouilly-en-Auxois France
160 C2 Pouilly-sous-Charlieu France
160 A1 Pouilly-sur-Loire France
160 D1 Pouilly-sur-Saône France
159 H4 Poulaines France
158 B4 Pouldreuzic France
160 C2 Poule-les-Écharmeaux France
147 B5 Poulgorm Bridge Rep. of Ireland
159 H5 Pouligny-St-Pierre France
158 C3 Poullaouen France
147 D4 Poulnamucky Rep. of Ireland
233 G3 Poultney VT U.S.A.
149 G4 Poulton-le-Fylde Lancashire, England U.K.
207 H6 Pouma Cameroon
232 B6 Pound VA U.S.A.
214 E4 Poupan S. Africa
163 C5 Poupas France
160 D2 Poupet, Mont hill France
161 D5 Pourcieux France
80 F4 Pourerere North I. N.Z.
156 D5 Pourrain France
160 E3 Pourri, Mont mt. France
161 D5 Pourrières France
182 C4 Pousada Port.
182 B3 Pousadela Port.
257 E5 Pouso Alegre Brazil
182 B5 Pousos Port.
161 B5 Poussan France
157 G4 Poussay France
97 C4 Poŭthĭsăt Cambodia
80 E2 Pouto North I. N.Z.
157 G4 Pouxeux France
96 C3 Pouy, Nam r. Laos
163 C5 Pouyastruc France
163 B5 Pouydesseaux France
163 D5 Pouy-de-Touges France
162 B2 Pouzauges France
159 G4 Pouzay France
139 K3 Povarovo Rus. Fed.
177 H2 Považská Bystrica Slovakia
177 G3 Považský Inovec mts Slovakia
139 J3 Poved' r. Rus. Fed.
185 H2 Povedilla Spain
134 F3 Povenets Rus. Fed.
80 F3 Poverty Bay North I. N.Z.
191 F4 Poviglio Italy
196 D3 Povlen mt. Yugo.
216 □1b Povoação São Miguel Azores
182 B3 Póvoa de Lanhoso Port.
184 C2 Póvoa de São Miguel Port.
182 B3 Póvoa de Varzim Port.
182 C4 Póvoa do Concelho Port.
191 I2 Povoletto Italy
135 H6 Povorino Rus. Fed.
136 C2 Povors'k Ukr.
171 F5 Povrly Czech Rep.
240 I5 Poway CA U.S.A.
149 H2 Powburn Northumberland, England U.K.
238 F2 Powder r. MT U.S.A.
238 C2 Powder r. OR U.S.A.
238 F3 Powder, South Fork r. WY U.S.A.
238 F3 Powder River WY U.S.A.
234 B1 Powell PA U.S.A.
238 E2 Powell WY U.S.A.
232 B6 Powell r. TN/VA U.S.A.
241 L3 Powell, Lake resr UT U.S.A.
240 H2 Powell Mountain NV U.S.A.
222 E5 Powell River B.C. Can.
226 D3 Powers MI U.S.A.
147 C3 Power's Cross Rep. of Ireland
237 F4 Powhatan AR U.S.A.
232 E6 Powhatan VA U.S.A.
232 C5 Powhatan Point OH U.S.A.
150 E2 Powick Worcestershire, England U.K.
174 F3 Powidz Pol.
146 E5 Powmill Perth and Kinross, Scotland U.K.
108 A1 Powo Sichuan China
Pöwrize Turkm. see Firyuza
150 D2 Powys admin. div. Wales U.K.
255 B5 Poxoréu Brazil
78 □5 Poya New Caledonia
183 E4 Poyales del Hoyo Spain
Poyang Jiangxi China see Boyang
109 F2 Poyang Hu l. China
100 D2 Poyarkovo Rus. Fed.
183 H4 Poyatos Spain
226 C4 Poynette WI U.S.A.
149 G4 Poynton Cheshire, England U.K.
147 E2 Poyntz Pass Northern Ireland U.K.
185 H3 Poyo, Cerro mt. Spain
199 E2 Poyrazcık İzmir Turkey
179 H2 Poysdorf Austria
141 M3 Pöytyä Fin.
183 G2 Poza de la Sal Spain
183 F3 Pozaldez Spain
126 D3 Pozantı Turkey
196 E3 Požarevac Srbija Yugo.
245 F3 Poza Rica Mex.
177 K3 Pozdišovce Slovakia
188 F3 Požega Croatia
196 E4 Požega Srbija Yugo.
175 J1 Pozezdrze Pol.
139 H3 Pozhnya Rus. Fed.
134 L4 Pozhva Rus. Fed.
177 G2 Pozlovice Czech Rep.
174 E3 Poznań Pol.
185 H3 Pozo Alcón Spain
183 E3 Pozoantiguo Spain
185 F2 Pozoblanco Spain
185 I2 Pozo Cañada Spain
253 F5 Pozo Colorado Para.
183 G4 Pozo de Guadalajara Spain
258 E2 Pozo del Tigre Arg.
258 D2 Pozo Hondo Arg.
185 I2 Pozohondo Spain
185 I1 Pozo-Lorente Spain
183 I4 Pozondón Spain
179 H1 Pozořice Czech Rep.
183 H5 Pozorrubio Spain
Pozsony Slovakia see Bratislava
185 H2 Pozuelo Spain
183 G4 Pozuelo de Alarcón Spain
183 I3 Pozuelo de Aragón Spain
182 E2 Pozuelo del Páramo Spain
183 G4 Pozuelo del Rey Spain
182 D4 Pozuelo de Zarzón Spain
185 F2 Pozuelos de Calatrava Spain
252 B2 Pozuzo Peru
191 G2 Pozza di Fasso Italy
194 D6 Pozzallo Sicilia Italy
190 D4 Pozzolo Formigaro Italy
192 A4 Pozzomaggiore Sardegna Italy
193 G4 Pozzuoli Italy
178 E5 Pozzuolo del Friuli Italy
206 E5 Pra r. Ghana
139 M4 Pra r. Rus. Fed.
94 D3 Prabumulih Sumatera Indon.
175 H2 Prabuty Pol.
176 D2 Prachatice Czech Rep.
115 E2 Prachi r. India
97 C4 Prachin Buri Thai.
169 C5 Pracht Ger.
97 B5 Prachuap Khiri Khan Thai.
173 G2 Prackenbach Ger.
182 C1 Pradairo mt. Spain
183 F2 Prádanos de Ojeda Spain
176 G1 Praděd mt. Czech Rep.
183 H2 Pradejón Spain
161 B4 Pradelles France
163 E5 Pradelles-en-Val France
183 G3 Prádena Spain
250 B4 Pradera Col.
163 E6 Prades Languedoc-Roussillon France
163 D6 Prades Midi-Pyrénées France
161 A4 Prades-d'Aubrac France
183 H2 Pradillo Spain
163 D4 Pradines France
257 H2 Prado Brazil
182 B3 Prado Port.
183 E2 Prado de la Guzpeña Spain
184 E4 Prado del Rey Spain
183 G2 Pradoluengo Spain
161 E4 Prads-Haute-Bléone France
Praeneste Italy see Palestrina
142 E4 Præstø Denmark
190 B3 Pragelato Italy
179 G4 Pragersko Slovenia
178 D3 Prägraten Austria
Prague Czech Rep. see Praha
176 D1 Praha Czech Rep.
176 D1 Praha admin. reg. Czech Rep.
176 C2 Praha hill Czech Rep.
162 B2 Prahecq France
197 H3 Prahova r. Romania
216 □1c Praia Graciosa Azores
206 □ Praia São Tiago Cape Verde
193 H5 Praia a Mare Italy
182 B4 Praia da Barra Port.
184 B3 Praia da Rocha Port.
182 B4 Praia da Tocha Port.
182 B4 Praia de Esmoriz Port.
182 B4 Praia de Mira Port.
216 □1c Praia do Almoxarife Faial Azores
216 □1c Praia do Norte Faial Azores
256 D6 Praia Grande Brazil
194 D2 Praiano Italy
184 B2 Praias do Sado Port.
216 □1c Prainha Pico Azores
251 H5 Prainha Brazil
85 F4 Prairie Qld Austr.
226 A2 Prairie r. MN U.S.A.
238 C2 Prairie City OR U.S.A.
237 C5 Prairie Dog Town Fork r. TX U.S.A.
226 B4 Prairie du Chien WI U.S.A.
223 K4 Prairie River Sask. Can.
97 C4 Prakhon Chai Thai.
177 J3 Prakovce Slovakia
161 E3 Pralognan-la-Vanoise France
161 E4 Pra-Loup France
179 E2 Pram r. Austria
198 B2 Pramanta Greece
179 E2 Prambachkirchen Austria
207 F5 Prampram Ghana
97 C4 Pran r. Thai.
97 B4 Pran Buri Thai.
206 E5 Prang Ghana
114 C2 Pranhita r. India
179 F3 Prankerhöhe mt. Austria
94 B2 Prapat Sumatera Indon.
177 H3 Prašice Slovakia
129 D1 Praskoveya Rus. Fed.
176 G2 Přáslavice Czech Rep.
157 F5 Praslay France
217 □2a Praslin i. Inner Islands Seychelles
247 □3 Praslin Bay St Lucia
174 G4 Praszka Pol.
256 C3 Prata Brazil
256 A3 Prata r. Goiás Brazil
256 C3 Prata r. Minas Gerais Brazil
256 D2 Prata r. Minas Gerais Brazil
191 H3 Prata di Pordenone Italy
116 C4 Pratapgarh Rajasthan India
171 D4 Pratau Ger.
186 D4 Prat de Comte Spain
Prat de Llobregat Spain see El Prat de Llobregat
186 D3 Pratdip Spain
193 G3 Pratella Italy
Prathes Thai country Asia see Thailand
256 D3 Pratinha Brazil
191 G5 Prato Italy
191 G5 Prato prov. Toscana Italy
191 F2 Prato allo Stelvio Italy
193 F2 Pratola Peligna Italy
194 D2 Pratola Serra Italy
191 G5 Pratovecchio Italy
186 F2 Prats de Lluçanes Spain
163 E6 Prats-de-Mollo-la-Preste France
237 D4 Pratt KS U.S.A.
190 C1 Pratteln Switz.
231 C5 Prattville AL U.S.A.
157 F5 Prauthoy France
114 B2 Pravara r. India
197 H4 Pravda Bulg.
138 C4 Pravdinsk Rus. Fed.
137 G4 Pravdyne Ukr.
182 D1 Pravia Spain
95 G5 Praya Lombok Indon.
163 D4 Prayssac France
163 C4 Prayssas France
160 E3 Praz-sur-Arly France
97 D4 Preah, Prêk r. Cambodia
97 D4 Preăh Vihear Cambodia
233 E3 Preble NY U.S.A.
179 G4 Prebold Slovenia
163 B4 Préchac France
163 B5 Préchacq-les-Bains France
139 I4 Prechistoye Smolenskaya Oblast' Rus. Fed.
134 H4 Prechistoye Yaroslavskaya Oblast' Rus. Fed.
193 F2 Preci Italy
159 F4 Précigné France
177 H2 Prečín Slovakia
160 C1 Précy-sous-Thil France
191 G4 Predappio Italy
191 G2 Predazzo Italy
197 G3 Predeal Romania
179 G4 Preding Austria
179 E3 Predlitz Austria
190 D4 Predosa Italy
223 K5 Preeceville Sask. Can.
159 F3 Pré-en-Pail France
150 E2 Prees Shropshire, England U.K.
149 G4 Preesall Lancashire, England U.K.
168 F1 Preetz Ger.
158 D4 Préfailles France
191 H3 Preganziòl Italy
179 F2 Pregarten Austria
138 C4 Pregolya r. Rus. Fed.
179 G4 Pregrada Croatia
129 B2 Pregradnaya Rus. Fed.
163 B4 Preignac France
163 C5 Preignan France
138 F3 Preiļi Latvia
179 F4 Preitenegg Austria
163 E5 Preixan France
196 D4 Prekornica mts Yugo.
223 I5 Prelate Sask. Can.
179 H2 Prellenkirchen Austria
179 H4 Prelog Croatia
176 E1 Přelouč Czech Rep.
83 G2 Premer N.S.W. Austr.
160 B1 Prémery France
190 D2 Premia Italy
186 F3 Premià de Mar Spain
191 G5 Premilcuore Italy
160 A2 Prémilhat France
170 D3 Premnitz Ger.
156 D3 Prémontré France
190 D2 Premosello Chiovenda Italy
136 E4 Prenistrului, Dealurile hills Moldova
188 F4 Prenj mts Bos.-Herz.
226 B3 Prentice WI U.S.A.
237 F6 Prentiss MS U.S.A.
170 E2 Prenzlau Ger.
100 E4 Preobrazheniye Rus. Fed.
137 H4 Preobrazhenka Ukr.
129 C1 Preobrazhenskoye Rus. Fed.
97 A4 Preparis Island Cocos Is
96 A4 Preparis North Channel Cocos Is
97 A4 Preparis South Channel Cocos Is
160 B2 Préporché France
176 G2 Přerov Czech Rep.
182 B5 Presa Port.
161 C4 Présailles France
160 E3 Pre-St-Didier Italy
191 F2 Presanella, Cima mt. Italy
Prescelly Mts hills Wales U.K. see Preseli, Mynydd
149 G4 Prescot Merseyside, England U.K.
224 F4 Prescott Ont. Can.
237 E5 Prescott AR U.S.A.
241 K4 Prescott AZ U.S.A.
226 A3 Prescott WI U.S.A.
241 K4 Prescott Valley AZ U.S.A.
150 C3 Preseli, Mynydd hills Wales U.K.
197 E4 Preševo Srbija Yugo.
236 C3 Presho SD U.S.A.
195 H3 Presicce Italy
258 F2 Presidencia Roca Arg.
258 E2 Presidencia Roque Sáenz Peña Arg.
256 C5 Presidente Alves Brazil
256 B5 Presidente Bernardes Brazil
258 F2 Presidente de la Plaza Arg.
254 D3 Presidente Dutra Brazil
262 U2 Presidente Eduardo Frei research stn Antarctica
256 A4 Presidente Epitácio Brazil
Presidente Juan Perón prov. Arg. see Chaco
257 E3 Presidente Juscelino Brazil
256 D3 Presidente Olegário Brazil
256 B5 Presidente Prudente Brazil
256 B4 Presidente Venceslau Brazil
244 A2 Presidio r. Mex.
239 F6 Presidio TX U.S.A.
Preslav Bulg. see Veliki Preslav
121 F1 Presnovka Kazakh.
177 K3 Prešov Slovakia
177 K2 Prešovský Kraj admin. reg. Slovakia
198 B1 Prespa, Lake Europe
Prespansko Ezero l. Europe see Prespa, Lake
Prespës, Liqeni i l. Europe see Prespa, Lake
233 □I1 Presque Isle ME U.S.A.
227 F3 Presque Isle MI U.S.A.
226 C2 Presque Isle WI U.S.A.
162 C2 Pressac France
173 F2 Pressath Ger.
179 H2 Pressbaum Austria
Pressburg Slovakia see Bratislava
171 C5 Presseck Ger.
171 D4 Pressel Ger.
171 C5 Pressig Ger.
150 D1 Prestatyn Denbighshire, Wales U.K.
149 G4 Prestbury Cheshire, England U.K.
150 E3 Prestbury Gloucestershire, England U.K.
206 E5 Prestea Ghana
150 D2 Presteigne Powys, Wales U.K.
176 C2 Přeštice Czech Rep.
150 E4 Preston Dorset, England U.K.
149 I4 Preston East Riding of Yorkshire, England U.K.
149 G4 Preston Lancashire, England U.K.
146 F6 Preston Scottish Borders, Scotland U.K.
231 C5 Preston GA U.S.A.
238 E3 Preston ID U.S.A.
233 F5 Preston MD U.S.A.
226 A4 Preston MN U.S.A.
237 E4 Preston MO U.S.A.
86 C4 Preston, Cape W.A. Austr.
149 G2 Prestonpans East Lothian, Scotland U.K.
232 B6 Prestonsburg KY U.S.A.
149 G4 Prestwich Greater Manchester, England U.K.
146 D6 Prestwick South Ayrshire, Scotland U.K.
251 E5 Preto r. Amazonas Brazil
251 F5 Preto r. Amazonas Brazil
254 E4 Preto r. Bahia Brazil
256 B3 Preto r. Goiás Brazil
256 D2 Preto r. Minas Gerais Brazil
253 E2 Preto r. Rondônia Brazil
256 C4 Preto r. São Paulo Brazil
215 G1 Pretoria S. Africa
Pretoria-Witwatersrand-Vereeniging prov. S. Africa see Gauteng
171 D4 Prettin Ger.
173 F2 Pretzfeld Ger.
170 C3 Pretzier Ger.
171 D4 Pretzsch Ger.
171 E5 Pretzschendorf Ger.
159 G5 Preuilly-sur-Claise France
Preussisch-Eylau Rus. Fed. see Bagrationovsk
169 D3 Preußisch Oldendorf Ger.
Preußisch Stargard Pol. see Starogard Gdański
179 F4 Prevalje Slovenia
161 B4 Prévenchères France
162 E2 Préveranges France
198 B2 Preveza Greece
97 D5 Prey Vêng Cambodia
157 F4 Prez-sous-Lafauche France
178 C5 Priaforà, Monte mt. Italy
100 E2 Priamurskiy Yevreyskaya Avtonomnaya Oblast' Rus. Fed.
120 E3 Priaral'skiye Karakumy, Peski des. Kazakh.
182 D2 Priaranza del Bierzo Spain
107 H1 Priargunsk Rus. Fed.
137 J5 Priazovskaya Rus. Fed.
137 H4 Priazovskaya Vozvyshennost' hills Ukr.
177 H4 Pribeta Slovakia
176 F3 Přibice Czech Rep.
220 A4 Pribilof Islands AK U.S.A.
188 F3 Pribinić Bos.-Herz.
179 H4 Pribislavec Croatia
196 D4 Priboj Srbija Yugo.
177 H2 Příbor Czech Rep.
170 D2 Priborn Ger.
176 D2 Příbram Czech Rep.
175 I1 Pribrezhnoye Rus. Fed.
176 E2 Přibyslav Czech Rep.
84 B2 Price r. N.T. Austr.
225 G3 Price Que. Can.
232 D6 Price NC U.S.A.
241 L2 Price UT U.S.A.
241 L2 Price r. UT U.S.A.
237 F6 Prichard AL U.S.A.
232 B5 Prichard WV U.S.A.
137 G4 Prichernomorskaya Nizmennost' lowland Ukr.
173 E2 Prichsenstadt Ger.
183 H4 Priego Spain
185 F3 Priego de Córdoba Spain
138 C3 Priekule Latvia
138 C4 Priekulė Lith.
138 E3 Priekuļi Latvia
138 D4 Prienai Lith.
173 G4 Prien am Chiemsee Ger.
171 E3 Prieros Ger.
214 D3 Prieska S. Africa
171 D4 Prießnitz Ger.
171 C4 Prießnitz Ger.
171 E4 Priestewitz Ger.
246 □ Priestman's River Jamaica
185 F4 Prieta, Sierra mt. Spain
185 G2 Prieto hill Spain
177 H3 Prievidza Slovakia
188 F3 Prijedor Bos.-Herz.
196 D4 Prijepolje Srbija Yugo.
120 A3 Prikaspiyskaya Nizmennost' lowland Kazakh./Rus. Fed.
206 E5 Prikro Côte d'Ivoire
137 J5 Prikubanskaya Nizmennost' lowland Rus. Fed.
197 E5 Prilep Macedonia
Priluki Ukr. see Pryluky
176 B2 Přimda Czech Rep.
254 E2 Primeira Cruz Brazil
261 F2 Primero r. Arg.
246 C2 Primero de Enero Cuba
236 E3 Primghar IA U.S.A.
191 G3 Primolano Italy
175 I1 Primorsk Kaliningradskaya Oblast' Rus. Fed.
138 G1 Primorsk Leningradskaya Oblast' Rus. Fed.
135 I6 Primorsk Volgogradskaya Oblast' Rus. Fed.
Primorsk Ukr. see Prymors'k
100 D4 Primorskiy Rus. Fed.
100 E3 Primorskiy Kray admin. div. Rus. Fed.
135 G7 Primorsko-Akhtarsk Rus. Fed.
Primorskoye Ukr. see Prymors'ke
222 B2 Primrose r. Y.T. Can.
172 A2 Prims r. Ger.
223 J4 Prince Albert Sask. Can.
214 D5 Prince Albert S. Africa
263 K1 Prince Albert Mountains Antarctica
220 G2 Prince Albert Peninsula N.W.T. Can.
214 C5 Prince Albert Road S. Africa
220 G2 Prince Albert Sound sea chan. N.W.T. Can.
214 B5 Prince Alfred Hamlet S. Africa
221 K3 Prince Charles Island Nunavut Can.
263 E2 Prince Charles Mountains Antarctica
225 I4 Prince Edward Island prov. Can.
265 G8 Prince Edward Islands Indian Ocean
232 E5 Prince Frederick MD U.S.A.
86 E2 Prince Frederick Harbour W.A. Austr.
222 F4 Prince George B.C. Can.
234 B4 Prince George's County county MD U.S.A.
221 H2 Prince Gustaf Adolf Sea Nunavut Can.
263 C2 Prince Harald Coast Antarctica
85 E1 Prince of Wales Island Qld Austr.
221 I2 Prince of Wales Island Nunavut Can.
220 E4 Prince of Wales Island AK U.S.A.
220 G2 Prince of Wales Strait N.W.T. Can.
220 G2 Prince Patrick Island N.W.T. Can.
86 E2 Prince Regent r. W.A. Austr.
221 I2 Prince Regent Inlet sea chan. Nunavut Can.
222 D4 Prince Rupert B.C. Can.
151 G3 Princes Risborough Buckinghamshire, England U.K.
233 F5 Princess Anne MD U.S.A.
263 A2 Princess Astrid Coast Antarctica
85 E2 Princess Charlotte Bay Qld Austr.
263 F2 Princess Elizabeth Land reg. Antarctica
86 E2 Princess May Range hills W.A. Austr.
81 A6 Princess Mountains South I. N.Z.
263 B2 Princess Ragnhild Coast Antarctica
87 D5 Princess Range hills W.A. Austr.
222 D4 Princess Royal Island B.C. Can.
247 □7 Prince's Town Trin. and Tob.
151 F2 Princethorpe Warwickshire, England U.K.
222 F5 Princeton B.C. Can.
240 F2 Princeton CA U.S.A.
226 C5 Princeton IL U.S.A.
230 C4 Princeton IN U.S.A.
230 C4 Princeton KY U.S.A.
233 □J2 Princeton ME U.S.A.
236 E3 Princeton MO U.S.A.
234 D2 Princeton NJ U.S.A.
226 C4 Princeton WI U.S.A.
232 C6 Princeton WV U.S.A.
234 D2 Princeton Junction NJ U.S.A.
150 D4 Princetown Devon, England U.K.
233 □J2 Prince William N.B. Can.
220 D3 Prince William Sound b. AK U.S.A.
207 G6 Príncipe i. São Tomé and Príncipe
238 B2 Prineville OR U.S.A.
164 D3 Prinsenbeek Neth.
Prins Harald Kyst coastal area Antarctica see Prince Harald Coast
140 □ Prins Karls Forland i. Svalbard
242 □J6 Prinzapolca Nic.
168 D3 Prinzhöfte Ger.
195 E5 Priolo Gargallo Sicilia Italy
183 F2 Prioro Spain
Priozernyy Kazakh. see Tugyl
139 H1 Priozersk Rus. Fed.
Priozyorsk Rus. Fed. see Priozersk
136 F2 Pripet r. Belarus/Ukr. alt. Pryp"yat' (Ukraine), alt. Prypyats' (Belarus)
136 C2 Pripet Marshes Belarus/Ukr.
134 L2 Pripolyarnyy Ural mts Rus. Fed.
197 H2 Priponeşti Romania
197 H2 Prisăcani Romania
188 F3 Priseka hill Croatia
176 E1 Příšovice Czech Rep.
162 D2 Prissac France
160 C2 Prissé France
Pristan' Przheval'sk Kyrg. see Przheval'sk Pristany
137 I2 Pristen' Rus. Fed.
196 E4 Priština Kosovo, Srbija Yugo.
116 D4 Prithvipur Madh. Prad. India
173 E3 Prittriching Ger.
171 D3 Pritzerbe Ger.
170 C2 Pritzier Ger.
170 D2 Pritzwalk Ger.
161 C4 Privas France
193 F3 Priverno Italy
188 E3 Privlaka Croatia
139 J4 Privokzal'nyy Rus. Fed.
137 J4 Privol'naya Rus. Fed.
139 M3 Privolzhsk Rus. Fed.
135 I6 Privolzhskaya Vozvyshennost' hills Rus. Fed.
135 I6 Privolzhskiy Rus. Fed.
120 B1 Privolzh'ye Rus. Fed.
135 H7 Priyutnoye Rus. Fed.
196 E4 Prizren Kosovo, Srbija Yugo.
194 C5 Prizzi Sicilia Italy
188 F3 Prnjavor Bos.-Herz.
182 D1 Proaza Spain
182 D2 Proba Spain
197 F4 Probištip Macedonia
95 F4 Probolinggo Jawa Timur Indon.
168 F1 Probsteierhagen Ger.
171 C5 Probstzella Ger.
150 C4 Probus Cornwall, England U.K.
192 D2 Proceno Italy
174 E4 Prochowice Pol.
193 G4 Procida Italy
226 A2 Proctor MN U.S.A.
233 G3 Proctor VT U.S.A.
232 B5 Proctorville OH U.S.A.
114 C3 Proddatur Andhra Prad. India
182 C5 Proença-a-Nova Port.
182 C4 Proença-a-Velha Port.
171 D4 Profen Ger.
251 H3 Professor van Blommestein Meer resr Suriname
165 D4 Profondeville Belgium
191 F3 Progno r. Italy
261 G2 Progreso Arg.
242 □I6 Progreso Hond.
243 E3 Progreso Coahuila Mex.
245 E3 Progreso Hidalgo Mex.
243 H4 Progreso Yucatán Mex.
244 C2 Progreso Zacatecas Mex.
100 D2 Progress Rus. Fed.
170 E1 Prohn Ger.
238 B3 Project City CA U.S.A.
175 I1 Prokhladnaya r. Rus. Fed.
129 D2 Prokhladnyy Rus. Fed.
137 I2 Prokhorovka Rus. Fed.
137 G2 Prokhory Ukr.
196 D4 Prokletije mts Albania/Yugo.
198 C2 Prokopi Sterea Ellas Greece
130 J4 Prokop'yevsk Rus. Fed.
197 E4 Prokuplje Srbija Yugo.
139 H2 Proletariy Rus. Fed.
135 H7 Proletarsk Rus. Fed.
Proletarskaya Rus. Fed. see Proletarsk
137 H2 Proletarskiy Rus. Fed.
Prome Myanmar see Pyè
256 C4 Promissão Brazil
256 C4 Promissão, Represa resr Brazil
175 I4 Promna Pol.
193 H3 Promontorio del Gargano plat. Italy
234 C1 Prompton PA U.S.A.
134 H4 Pronino Rus. Fed.
169 B5 Pronsfeld Ger.
139 L4 Pronsk Rus. Fed.
168 F2 Pronstorf Ger.
139 H5 Pronya r. Belarus
222 F3 Prophet r. B.C. Can.
222 F3 Prophet River B.C. Can.
226 C5 Prophetstown IL U.S.A.
254 F4 Propriá Brazil
192 A3 Propriano Corse France
129 E1 Prorva r. Rus. Fed.
120 F1 Proryvnoye Rus. Fed.
176 F2 Proseč Czech Rep.
171 E4 Prösen Ger.
146 F5 Prosen Water r. Scotland U.K.
85 G4 Proserpine Qld Austr.
Proskurov Ukr. see Khmel'nyts'kyy
199 D1 Proskynites Anatoliki Makedonia kai Thraki Greece
174 F3 Prosna r. Pol.
198 C1 Prosotsani Greece
235 F1 Prospect CT U.S.A.
233 F3 Prospect NY U.S.A.
232 B4 Prospect OH U.S.A.
238 B3 Prospect OR U.S.A.
232 C4 Prospect PA U.S.A.
235 D2 Prospect Plains NJ U.S.A.
92 C4 Prosperidad Phil.
148 C4 Prosperous Rep. of Ireland
238 C2 Prosser WA U.S.A.
176 G2 Prostějov Czech Rep.
175 K2 Prostki Pol.
85 G5 Proston Qld Austr.
137 H3 Prosyane Ukr.
174 F5 Prószków Pol.
175 I5 Proszowice Pol.
175 I5 Proszówki Pol.
214 C6 Protem S. Africa
176 F2 Protivanov Czech Rep.
176 D2 Protivín Czech Rep.
137 I5 Protoka r. Rus. Fed.
137 I3 Protopopivka Ukr.
136 F2 Protsiv Ukr.
139 K4 Protva Rus. Fed.
139 K4 Protva r. Rus. Fed.
139 K4 Protvino Rus. Fed.
170 E3 Prötzel Ger.
197 H4 Provadiya Bulg.
184 B3 Provença Port.
161 D5 Provence airport France
161 E5 Provence-Alpes-Côte-d'Azur admin. reg. France
157 H4 Provenchères-sur-Fave France
Providence MD U.S.A. see Annapolis
233 H4 Providence RI U.S.A.
81 A7 Providence, Cape South I. N.Z.
217 □2 Providence Atoll Seychelles
227 F3 Providence Bay Ont. Can.
246 B4 Providencia, Isla de i. Caribbean Sea
253 E2 Providência, Serra de hills Brazil
246 D2 Providenciales Island Turks and Caicos Is
131 T3 Provideniya Rus. Fed.
85 E2 Providential Channel Qld Austr.
233 H3 Provincetown MA U.S.A.
156 D4 Provins France
241 L1 Provo UT U.S.A.
223 I4 Provost Alta Can.
188 F4 Prozor Bos.-Herz.
139 K2 Prozorovo Rus. Fed.
196 E5 Prrenjas Albania
206 E4 Pru r. Ghana
134 K3 Prub r. Rus. Fed.
175 K6 Pruchnik Pol.
256 B6 Prudentópolis Brazil
149 H3 Prudhoe Northumberland, England U.K.
220 D2 Prudhoe Bay AK U.S.A.
85 G4 Prudhoe Island Qld Austr.
174 F5 Prudnik Pol.
137 I2 Prudyanka Ukr.
177 K3 Prügy Hungary
171 F5 Průhonice Czech Rep.
169 B5 Prüm Ger.
169 B6 Prüm r. Ger.
185 E4 Pruna Spain
197 G3 Prundeni Romania
197 H3 Prundu Romania
197 G2 Prundu Bârgăului Romania
Prundu Bîrgăului Romania see Prundu Bârgăului
192 B2 Prunelli-di-Fiumorbo Corse France
163 E4 Prunet France
161 E4 Prunières France
159 H4 Pruniers-en-Sologne France
232 C5 Pruntytown WV U.S.A.
Prusa Turkey see Bursa
179 H2 Prušánky Czech Rep.
Prushkov Pol. see Pruszków
174 E4 Prusice Pol.
177 G2 Prusinovice Czech Rep.
174 G2 Pruszcz Pol.
143 H4 Pruszcz Gdański Pol.
175 I3 Pruszków Pol.
136 E5 Prut r. Europe
173 G4 Prutting Ger.
178 B3 Prutz Austria
138 E5 Pruzhany Belarus
177 H2 Pružina Slovakia
179 E5 Prvačina Slovenia
188 E3 Prvić i. Croatia
137 H2 Pryamitsyno Rus. Fed.
137 H4 Pryazovs'ke Ukr.
137 I2 Prykolotne Ukr.
137 G2 Pryluky Ukr.
137 I4 Prymors'k Ukr.
Prymors'ke Ukr. see Sartana
137 G4 Prymors'ke Ukr.
136 E5 Prymors'ke Ukr.
137 H4 Prymors'ke Ukr.
137 H5 Prymors'kyy Ukr.
237 E4 Pryor OK U.S.A.
136 F2 Pryp"yat' Ukr.
136 F2 Pryp"yat' r. Ukr. alt. Prypyats' (Belarus), conv. Pripet
136 E2 Prypyats' r. Belarus alt. Pryp"yat' (Ukraine), conv. Pripet
137 J3 Pryvillya Ukr.
137 G4 Pryvil'ne Ukr.
136 C2 Pryvitne Ukr.
137 G3 Pryyutivka Ukr.
175 I2 Przasnysz Pol.
174 F2 Przechlewo Pol.
175 H5 Przeciszów Pol.
175 J5 Przecław Pol.
175 H4 Przedbórz Pol.
174 G3 Przedecz Pol.
174 D2 Przelewice Pol.
174 D4 Przemków Pol.
177 I1 Przemsza r. Pol.
175 K6 Przemyśl Pol.
175 K1 Przerośl Pol.
175 K3 Przesmyki Pol.
175 L5 Przewale Pol.
175 L4 Przewłoka Pol.
174 F5 Przeworno Pol.
175 K5 Przeworsk Pol.
174 C4 Przewóz Pol.
175 K3 Przeździatka Pol.
175 I2 Przezdzięk Wielki Pol.
175 H2 Przezmark Pol.
Przheval'sk Kyrg. see Karakol
139 H4 Przheval'skoye Smolenskaya Oblast' Rus. Fed.
121 I4 Przheval'sk Pristany Kyrg.
174 G1 Przodkowo Pol.
174 C2 Przybiernów Pol.
175 I3 Przyborowice Pol.
174 G3 Przybranowo Pol.
174 F4 Przygodzice Pol.
174 G4 Przykona Pol.
175 H5 Przyrów Pol.
175 J5 Przyrwa r. Pol.
174 G5 Przystajń Pol.
175 I4 Przysucha Pol.
174 D3 Przytoczna Pol.
175 K4 Przytoczno Pol.
175 K2 Przytuły Pol.
175 I4 Przytyk Pol.

174 G1 Przywidz Pol.
198 C2 Psachna Greece
Psakhná Greece see Psachna
199 D2 Psara i. Greece
129 E1 Psebay Rus. Fed.
129 D2 Psedakh Rus. Fed.
129 A1 Psekups r. Rus. Fed.
Psel r. Rus. Fed./Ukr. see Ps'ol
137 I2 Pselets Rus. Fed.
199 E3 Pserimos i. Greece
137 J5 Pshada Rus. Fed.
129 A1 Pshekha r. Rus. Fed.
129 A1 Pshish r. Rus. Fed.
121 G4 Pskent Uzbek.
138 G3 Pskov Rus. Fed.
138 F2 Pskov, Lake Estonia/Rus. Fed.
138 G3 Pskova r. Rus. Fed.
Pskov Oblast admin. div. Rus. Fed. see Pskovskaya Oblast'
138 G3 Pskovskaya Oblast' admin. div. Rus. Fed.
Pskovskoye Ozero l. Estonia/Rus. Fed. see Pskov, Lake
137 H2 Ps'ol r. Rus. Fed./Ukr.
188 F3 Psunj mts Croatia
174 D3 Pszczew Pol.
174 G1 Pszczółki Pol.
174 G6 Pszczyna Pol.
139 L5 Ptan' r. Rus. Fed.
198 C2 Pteleos Thessalia Greece
198 B1 Ptolemaïda Greece
Ptolemais Israel see 'Akko
138 G5 Ptsich r. Belarus
188 E2 Ptuj Slovenia
179 G4 Ptujsko jezero l. Slovenia
136 C2 Ptycha Ukr.
107 E5 Pu r. China
94 C3 Pu r. Indon.
240 □D9 Puako HI U.S.A.
261 F5 Puán Arg.
108 C3 Pu'an Guizhou China
Pu'an Sichuan China see Jiange
96 E2 Pubei Guangxi China
160 E2 Publier France
250 B6 Pucacaca Peru
250 C5 Pucacuro r. Peru
252 B2 Pucallpa Peru
252 C3 Pucara Peru
252 C4 Pucarani Bol.
Pucarevo Bos.-Herz. see Novi Travnik
250 D5 Puca Urco Peru
178 E3 Puch bei Hallein Austria
179 G3 Puchberg am Schneeberg Austria
109 F3 Pucheng Fujian China
107 F5 Pucheng Shaanxi China
134 H4 Puchezh Rus. Fed.
173 F3 Puchheim Ger.
101 C5 Puch'ŏn S. Korea
177 H2 Púchov Slovakia
197 G3 Pucioasa Romania
143 H4 Puck Pol.
143 H4 Pucka, Zatoka b. Pol.
147 C4 Puckaun Rep. of Ireland
87 C5 Puckford, Mount hill W.A. Austr.
187 C5 Puçol Spain
260 B6 Pucón Chile
122 C3 Pūdanū Iran
140 N2 Pudasjärvi Fin.
150 E4 Puddletown Dorset, England U.K.
169 C5 Puderbach Ger.
215 E2 Pudimoe S. Africa
108 C3 Puding Guizhou China
109 G2 Pudong airport China
134 G3 Pudozh Rus. Fed.
149 H4 Pudsey West Yorkshire, England U.K.
Puduchcheri Pondicherry India see Pondicherry
114 C4 Pudukkottai Tamil Nadu India
245 F3 Puebillo Mex.
241 J5 Puebla Baja California Norte Mex.
245 E4 Puebla Puebla Mex.
245 E4 Puebla state Mex.
186 C3 Puebla de Albortón Spain
185 E2 Puebla de Alcocer Spain
186 C3 Puebla de Alfindén Spain
183 H5 Puebla de Almenara Spain
183 G4 Puebla de Beleña Spain
186 D4 Puebla de Benifasar Spain
182 C2 Puebla de Brollón Spain
185 H3 Puebla de Don Fadrique Spain
185 F1 Puebla de Don Rodrigo Spain
184 C3 Puebla de Guzmán Spain
184 D2 Puebla de la Calzada Spain
184 D2 Puebla de la Reina Spain
182 B2 Puebla del Caramiñal Spain
183 E1 Puebla de Lillo Spain
184 D2 Puebla del Maestre Spain
185 H2 Puebla del Príncipe Spain
184 D2 Puebla del Prior Spain
184 D1 Puebla de Obando Spain
182 D2 Puebla de Sanabria Spain
184 D2 Puebla de Sancho Pérez Spain
Puebla de San Julián Spain see Puebla de San Xulián
187 B4 Puebla de San Miguel Spain
182 C2 Puebla de San Xulián Spain
182 C2 Puebla de Trives Spain
182 D4 Puebla de Yeltes Spain
Puebla de Zaragoza Puebla Mex. see Puebla
239 F4 Pueblo CO U.S.A.
261 H2 Pueblo Arrúa Arg.
261 F3 Pueblo Italiano Arg.
242 □I6 Pueblo Nuevo Nic.
245 F2 Pueblo Viejo, Laguna de lag. Mex.
242 C3 Pueblo Yaqui Mex.
161 A4 Puech del Pal mt. France
163 E4 Puech de Rouet hill France
260 B3 Puente Alto Chile
Puenteareas Spain see Ponteareas
Puente Caldelas Spain see Ponte Caldelas
182 D2 Puente de Domingo Flórez Spain
185 H2 Puente de Génave Spain
245 E4 Puente de Ixtla Mex.
182 E4 Puente del Congosto Spain
186 D2 Puente de Montañana Spain
183 F1 Puente de San Miguel Spain
185 F3 Puente-Genil Spain
183 I2 Puente la Reina Spain
183 F1 Puentenansa Spain
Puentes de García Rodríguez Spain see As Pontes de García Rodríguez
250 D2 Puente Torres Venez.
183 G1 Puente Viesgo Spain
108 B4 Pu'er Yunnan China
252 C3 Puerto Acosta Bol.
259 B7 Puerto Aisén Chile
253 E3 Puerto Alegre Bol.
250 B6 Puerto America Peru
243 F6 Puerto Ángel Mex.
245 F6 Puerto Angel Mex.
253 F6 Puerto Antequera Para.
245 H6 Puerto Arista Mex.
242 □J7 Puerto Armuelles Panama
250 B4 Puerto Asís Col.
250 E3 Puerto Ayacucho Venez.
250 □ Puerto Baquerizo Moreno Islas Galápagos Ecuador
242 □H6 Puerto Barrios Guat.
258 F2 Puerto Bermejo Arg.
250 C3 Puerto Berrío Col.
250 D2 Puerto Cabello Venez.
242 □J6 Puerto Cabezas Nic.
242 □J6 Puerto Cabo Gracias á Dios Nic.
250 E3 Puerto Carreño Col.
253 F5 Puerto Casado Para.
250 B6 Puerto Chicama Peru
259 B7 Puerto Cisnes Chile
250 D5 Puerto Córdoba Col.
242 □I6 Puerto Cortés Hond.
242 C3 Puerto Cortés Mex.
250 D2 Puerto Cumarebo Venez.
182 E4 Puerto de Béjar Spain
Puerto de Cabras Fuerteventura Canary Is see Puerto del Rosario
216 □3a Puerto de la Cruz Tenerife Canary Is
Puerto de la Selva Spain see El Port de la Selva
216 □3b Puerto del Rosario Fuerteventura Canary Is
Puerto del Son Spain see Porto do Son
187 B7 Puerto de Mazarrón Spain
243 I4 Puerto de Morelos Mex.
Puerto de Pollensa Spain see Port de Pollença
185 E1 Puerto de San Vicente Spain
Puerto de Sóller Spain see Port de Sóller
245 F6 Puerto Escondido Mex.
250 B5 Puerto Francisco de Orellana Ecuador
253 E3 Puerto Frey Bol.
252 D4 Puerto Grether Bol.
252 B2 Puerto Inca Peru
250 E4 Puerto Inírida Col.
253 F4 Puerto Isabel Bol.
242 □I7 Puerto Jesus Costa Rica
243 I4 Puerto Juáres Mex.
247 F5 Puerto La Cruz Venez.
185 G1 Puerto Lápice Spain
186 D2 Puértolas Spain
242 □J6 Puerto Lempira Hond.
185 F2 Puertollano Spain
250 C3 Puerto Lopéz Col.
185 I3 Puerto Lumbreras Spain
243 G6 Puerto Madero Mex.
259 D6 Puerto Madryn Arg.
252 C3 Puerto Maldonado Peru
252 D4 Puerto Mamoré Bol.
246 C2 Puerto Manatí Cuba
250 A6 Puerto Máncora Peru
253 F5 Puerto María Auxiliadora Para.
Puertomarín Spain see Portomarín
Puerto México Mex. see Coatzacoalcos
253 F5 Puerto Mihanovich Para.
187 C4 Puertomingalvo Spain
250 E3 Puerto Miranda Venez.
259 B6 Puerto Montt Chile
242 □I6 Puerto Morazán Nic.
250 B7 Puerto Morín Peru
259 B8 Puerto Natáles Chile
250 D3 Puerto Nuevo Col.
246 C2 Puerto Padre Cuba
250 E3 Puerto Páez Venez.
252 D3 Puerto Pando Bol.
242 B2 Puerto Peñasco Mex.
253 F5 Puerto Pinasco Para.
251 E2 Puerto Píritu Venez.
246 E3 Puerto Plata Dom. Rep.
252 B2 Puerto Portillo Peru
252 B2 Puerto Prado Peru
Puerto Presidente Stroessner Para. see Ciudad del Este
92 A4 Puerto Princesa Phil.
242 □I7 Puerto Quepos Costa Rica
184 D4 Puerto Real Spain
258 G2 Puerto Rico Arg.
252 D2 Puerto Rico Bol.
247 □1 Puerto Rico terr. West Indies
264 E4 Puerto Rico Trench sea feature Caribbean Sea
259 B5 Puerto Saavedra Chile
Puerto Sama Cuba see Samá
242 □I6 Puerto Sandino Nic.
259 C8 Puerto Santa Cruz Arg.
253 F5 Puerto Sastre Para.
253 E3 Puerto Saucedo Bol.
Puertos de Beceite mts Spain see Ports de Beseit
182 D4 Puerto Seguro Spain
184 E4 Puerto Serrano Spain
250 D5 Puerto Socorro Peru
Puerto Somoza Nic. see Puerto Sandino
253 F4 Puerto Suárez Bol.
252 A2 Puerto Supe Peru
252 C3 Puerto Tahuantisuyo Peru
250 B4 Puerto Tejado Col.
250 B5 Puerto Tunigrama Peru
244 B3 Puerto Vallarta Mex.
259 B6 Puerto Varas Chile
252 B2 Puerto Victoria Peru
253 E3 Puerto Villazon Bol.
183 I2 Pueyo Spain
120 B1 Pugachev Rus. Fed.
134 K4 Pugachevo Rus. Fed.
116 C3 Pugal Rajasthan India
108 B3 Puge Sichuan China
161 E5 Puget-sur-Argens France
161 E5 Puget-Théniers France
161 E5 Puget-Ville France
234 C2 Pughtown PA U.S.A.
193 H3 Puglia admin. reg. Italy
193 E2 Puglia r. Italy
162 B3 Pugnac France
193 I3 Pugnochiuso Italy
225 I4 Pugwash N.S. Can.
80 F3 Puha North I. N.Z.
122 C5 Pūhāl-e Khamīr, Kūh-e mts Iran
Puhiwaero c. Stewart I. N.Z. see South West Cape
138 F2 Puhja Estonia
197 F3 Pui Romania
161 A5 Puichéric France
197 H3 Puiești Romania
187 C5 Puig Spain
186 E2 Puigcerdà Spain
186 F3 Puig d'Arques hill Spain
181 H1 Puig de Comanegra mt. Spain
186 E2 Puig de les Morreres mt. Spain
187 G5 Puig de Sant Salvador hill Spain
187 F5 Puig des Galatzó mt. Spain
187 F5 Puig Major mt. Spain
186 F2 Puigmal mt. France/Spain
186 E2 Puig Pedrós mt. Spain
186 E3 Puig-reig Spain
186 D3 Puigverd de Lleida Spain
161 E5 Puimoisson France
156 C4 Puiseaux France
156 C2 Puisieux France
163 B4 Puisseguin France
161 B5 Puisserguier France
156 E4 Puits r. France
163 E6 Puivert France
161 C4 Pujaut France
206 C5 Pujehun Sierra Leone
Puji Shaanxi China see Wugong
109 F2 Pujiang Zhejiang China
163 C5 Pujo France
163 B4 Pujols Aquitaine France
163 C4 Pujols Aquitaine France
81 C6 Pukaki, Lake South I. N.Z.
177 H3 Pukanec Slovakia
81 □2 Pukapuka atoll Cook Is
79 □3 Pukapuka i. Arch. des Tuamotu Fr. Polynesia
79 □3 Pukarua atoll Arch. des Tuamotu Fr. Polynesia
226 E1 Pukaskwa r. Ont. Can.
223 K4 Pukatawagan Man. Can.
101 C4 Pukchin N. Korea
101 D4 Pukch'ŏng N. Korea
196 D4 Pukë Albania
80 G2 Pukeamaru hill North I. N.Z.
80 E3 Pukearuhe North I. N.Z.
80 F3 Pukehoi North I. N.Z.
80 E2 Pukekohe North I. N.Z.
80 D1 Pukenui North I. N.Z.
80 E3 Pukeokahu North I. N.Z.
81 C6 Pukerangi South I. N.Z.
81 B7 Pukerau South I. N.Z.
80 E3 Pukeroa North I. N.Z.
81 E4 Pukerua Bay North I. N.Z.
81 D5 Puketeraki Range mts South I. N.Z.
80 F3 Puketitiri North I. N.Z.
80 F2 Puketoetoe mt. North I. N.Z.
80 F4 Puketoi Range hills North I. N.Z.
80 E3 Puketutu North I. N.Z.
81 C6 Pukeuri Junction South I. N.Z.
141 N3 Pukkila Fin.
134 H3 Puksoozero Rus. Fed.
101 C4 Puksubaek-san mt. N. Korea
Pula Xizang China see Nyingchi
188 D3 Pula Croatia
191 I4 Pula airport Croatia
192 B5 Pula Sardegna Italy
252 D5 Pulacayo Bol.
107 I4 Pulandian Liaoning China
92 C5 Pulangi r. Phil.
91 K5 Pulap atoll Micronesia
252 C6 Pular, Cerro mt. Chile
233 E3 Pulaski NY U.S.A.
231 C5 Pulaski TN U.S.A.
232 C6 Pulaski VA U.S.A.
226 C3 Pulaski WI U.S.A.
91 I8 Pulau r. Indon.
Pulau Pinang state Malaysia see Pinang
175 J4 Puławy Pol.
151 G4 Pulborough West Sussex, England U.K.
191 I2 Pulfero Italy
183 F5 Pulgar Spain
169 B4 Pulheim Ger.
114 D3 Pulicat Tamil Nadu India
114 D3 Pulicat Lake inlet India
160 C2 Puligny-Montrachet France
114 C3 Pulivendla Andhra Prad. India
179 G2 Pulkau Austria
179 H2 Pulkau r. Austria
140 N2 Pulkkila Fin.
173 F3 Pullach in Isartal Ger.
238 C2 Pullman WA U.S.A.
91 H6 Pulo Anna i. Palau
92 B2 Pulog, Mount Luzon Phil.
140 P1 Pulozero Rus. Fed.
185 I3 Pulpí Spain
195 G2 Pulsano Italy
171 E4 Pulsen Ger.
171 F4 Pulsnitz Ger.
171 E4 Pulsnitz r. Ger.
175 J3 Pułtusk Pol.
86 □2 Pulu Capelok i. Cocos Is
127 E3 Pülümür Turkey
86 □2 Pulu Pandang i. Cocos Is
91 K5 Pulusuk atoll Micronesia
91 K5 Puluwat atoll Micronesia
157 H5 Pulversheim France
211 B6 Puma Tanz.
260 B4 Pumanque Chile
Pumiao Guangxi China see Yongning
238 F2 Pumpkin Creek r. MT U.S.A.
150 D2 Pumsaint Carmarthenshire, Wales U.K.
250 A5 Puná, Isla i. Ecuador
258 D2 Puna de Atacama plat. Arg.
81 C5 Punakaiki South I. N.Z.
117 G4 Punakha Bhutan
240 □D9 Punaluu HI U.S.A.
79 □3a Punaruu r. Tahiti Fr. Polynesia
191 J3 Punat Croatia
252 D4 Punata Bol.
123 H3 Punch Pak.
222 F4 Punchaw B.C. Can.
213 F4 Punda Maria S. Africa
116 D3 Pundri Haryana India
114 B2 Pune Mahar. India
114 C3 Punganuru Andhra Prad. India
209 B7 Pungo Andango Angola
101 D4 P'ungsan N. Korea
213 G3 Púnguè r. Moz.
191 F2 Puni r. Italy
208 E5 Punia Dem. Rep. Congo
109 F4 Puning Guangdong China
260 B2 Punitaqui Chile
116 C3 Punjab state India
123 G4 Punjab prov. Pak.
141 O3 Punkaharju Fin.
252 C3 Puno Peru
252 C3 Puno dept Peru
117 F4 Punpun r. India
175 L1 Puńsk Pol.
247 □1 Punta, Cerro de mt. Puerto Rico
192 C2 Punta Ala Italy
261 F6 Punta Alta Arg.
259 C9 Punta Arenas Chile
192 B4 Punta Balestrieri mt. Sardegna Italy
252 C4 Punta de Bombón Peru
242 □H5 Punta Gorda Belize
216 □3d Puntagorda La Palma Canary Is
231 D7 Punta Gorda FL U.S.A.
191 J4 Punta Križa Croatia
216 □3d Puntallana La Palma Canary Is
192 A5 Punta Mumullonis hill Sardegna Italy
242 □I7 Puntarenas Costa Rica
191 H3 Punta Sabbioni Italy
247 □1 Punta Santiago Puerto Rico
252 D5 Puntas Negras, Cerro mt. Chile
184 D3 Punta Umbría Spain
250 D2 Punto Fijo Venez.
186 C2 Puntón de Guara mt. Spain
232 D4 Punxsutawney PA U.S.A.
140 N2 Puolanka Fin.
140 M2 Puoltikasvaara Sweden
109 E2 Puqi Hubei China
252 B3 Puquio Peru
130 I3 Pur r. Rus. Fed.
116 E3 Puranpur Uttar Prad. India
91 J8 Purari r. P.N.G.
179 H3 Purbach am Neusiedler See Austria
95 E4 Purbalingga Jawa Tengah Indon.
150 E4 Purbeck, Isle of pen. England U.K.
237 D5 Purcell OK U.S.A.
222 G5 Purcell Mountains B.C. Can.
232 E5 Purcellville VA U.S.A.
185 H3 Purchena Spain
185 G3 Purchil Spain
258 B5 Purén Chile
244 C4 Purépero Mex.
151 H3 Purfleet Thurrock, England U.K.
237 C4 Purgatoire r. CO U.S.A.
173 E3 Pürgen Ger.
179 G2 Purgstall an der Erlauf Austria
209 B6 Puri Angola
115 E2 Puri Orissa India
244 B4 Purificación Mex.
245 E2 Purificación r. Mex.
150 E3 Puriton Somerset, England U.K.
179 H2 Purkersdorf Austria
151 G3 Purley Greater London, England U.K.
151 F3 Purley on Thames West Berkshire, England U.K.
164 D2 Purmerend Neth.
114 C2 Purna Mahar. India
114 C2 Purna r. Mahar. India
116 D5 Purna r. Mahar. India
117 G4 Purnabhaba r. India
82 B1 Purndu Saltpan salt flat S.A. Austr.
Purnea Bihar India see Purnia
117 F4 Purnia Bihar India
259 B6 Purranque Chile
Pursat Cambodia see Poŭthĭsăt
151 F3 Purton Wiltshire, England U.K.
221 K3 Purtuniq Que. Can.
244 D3 Puruandíro Mex.
244 D4 Puruarán Mex.
250 D5 Puruê r. Brazil
183 I3 Purujosa Spain
117 F5 Puruliya W. Bengal India
185 G3 Purullena Spain
251 F5 Purus r. Peru
141 O3 Puruvesi l. Fin.
237 F6 Purvis MS U.S.A.
197 G4 Pŭrvomay Bulg.
116 E4 Purwa Uttar Prad. India
94 D4 Purwakarta Jawa Barat Indon.
95 E4 Purwareja Jawa Tengah Indon.
95 E4 Purwodadi Jawa Tengah Indon.
95 E4 Purwokerto Jawa Tengah Indon.
101 D4 Puryŏng N. Korea
114 C2 Pus r. India
183 F5 Pusa r. Spain
114 C2 Pusad Mahar. India
101 D6 Pusan S. Korea
173 E2 Puschendorf Ger.
171 F4 Puschwitz Ger.
136 F2 Pushcha-Vodytsya Ukr.
139 K4 Pushchino Rus. Fed.
134 I3 Pushemskiy Rus. Fed.
116 C4 Pushkar Rajasthan India
139 H2 Pushkin Rus. Fed.
Pushkino Azer. see Biläsuvar
120 A2 Pushkino Rus. Fed.
100 G3 Pushkinskaya, Gora mt. Sakhalin Rus. Fed.
138 G3 Pushkinskiye Gory Rus. Fed.
186 C2 Pusilibro mt. Spain
177 K4 Püspökladány Hungary
138 F2 Püssi Estonia
177 H2 Pustá Polom Czech Rep.
191 G2 Pusteria, Val val. Italy
177 G3 Pusté Úľany Slovakia
196 D4 Pusti Lisac mt. Yugo.
176 G2 Pustiměř Czech Rep.
136 B3 Pustomyty Ukr.
138 G3 Pustoshka Rus. Fed.
136 F3 Pustovity Ukr.
138 D1 Pusula Fin.
117 G5 Pusur r. Bangl.
175 L2 Puszcza Augustowska for. Pol.
175 I4 Puszcza Mariańska Pol.
174 D3 Puszcza Natecka for. Pol.
174 E3 Puszczykowo Pol.
177 G5 Pusztakovácsi Hungary
177 I5 Pusztamérges Hungary
177 I4 Pusztamonostor Hungary
177 I5 Pusztaszer Hungary
177 I4 Pusztavacs Hungary
177 H4 Pusztavám Hungary
260 B3 Putaendo Chile
159 F3 Putanges-Pont-Écrepin France
80 E3 Putaruru North I. N.Z.
170 E1 Putbus Ger.
Puteoli Italy see Pozzuoli
80 F3 Putere North I. N.Z.
134 L2 Puteyets Rus. Fed.
Puthein Myanmar see Bassein
109 F3 Putian Fujian China
192 A4 Putifigari Sardegna Italy
195 G2 Putignano Italy
134 I4 Putilovo Rus. Fed.
252 C3 Putina Peru
Puting Jiangxi China see De'an
245 F5 Putla Mex.
170 D2 Putlitz Ger.
197 H3 Putna r. Romania
233 H4 Putnam CT U.S.A.
235 E1 Putnam County county NY U.S.A.
235 E1 Putnam Valley NY U.S.A.
233 G3 Putney VT U.S.A.
177 J3 Putnok Hungary
131 K3 Putorana, Gory mts Rus. Fed.
94 C2 Putrajaya Malaysia
252 C4 Putre Chile
214 C3 Putsonderwater S. Africa
114 C4 Puttalam Sri Lanka
114 C4 Puttalam Lagoon Sri Lanka
165 D3 Putte Belgium
165 D3 Putte Neth.
157 G3 Puttelange-aux-Lacs France
164 E2 Putten Neth.
170 C1 Puttgarden Ger.
172 A2 Püttlingen Ger.
114 B3 Puttur Karnataka India
260 A4 Putú Chile
250 C4 Putumayo dept Col.
250 D5 Putumayo r. Col.
101 B7 Putuo Zhejiang China
126 E3 Pütürge Turkey
95 F2 Putusibau Kalimantan Barat Indon.
135 H5 Putyatino Rus. Fed.
136 C4 Putyla Ukr.
136 E2 Putylovychi Ukr.
137 G2 Putyvl' Ukr.
170 E2 Putzar Ger.
171 F4 Putzkau Ger.
240 □D9 Puuanahulu HI U.S.A.
240 □C8 Puukolii HI U.S.A.
141 N3 Puula l. Fin.
141 O3 Puumala Fin.
165 D3 Puurs Belgium
240 □A8 Puuwai HI U.S.A.
221 K3 Puvurnituq Que. Can.
107 F4 Puxian Shanxi China
238 B2 Puyallup WA U.S.A.
107 G5 Puyang Henan China
Puyang Zhejiang China see Pujiang
163 D4 Puybrun France
163 C5 Puycasquier France
159 F5 Puy Crapaud hill France
160 B3 Puy-de-Dôme dept Auvergne France
160 A3 Puy de Dôme mt. France
163 D5 Puy de Faucher hill France
161 D4 Puy de la Gagère mt. France
160 B3 Puy de Montoncel mt. France
160 A3 Puy de Sancy mt. France
162 D2 Puy des Trois-Cornes hill France
163 E5 Puygouzon France
161 A3 Puy Griou mt. France
161 E3 Puy Gris mt. France
160 B3 Puy-Guillaume France
163 D4 Puylaroque France
163 E5 Puylaurens France
163 D4 Puy-l'Évêque France
161 A3 Puy Mary mt. France
163 C5 Puymaurin France
163 C4 Puymirol France
162 C3 Puymoyen France
250 B5 Puyo Ecuador
163 B5 Puyôo France
161 E4 Puy-St-Vincent France
Puzol Spain see Puçol
177 H4 Puztaszabolcs Hungary
211 C6 Pwani admin. reg. Tanz.
209 F7 Pweto Dem. Rep. Congo
150 C2 Pwllheli Gwynedd, Wales U.K.
134 F3 Pyal'ma Rus. Fed.
96 A4 Pyamalaw r. Myanmar
123 G2 Pyandzh r. Afgh./Tajik.
Pyandzh Khatlon Tajik. see Dusti
Pyandzh Khatlon Tajik. see Panj
Pyanskiy Perevoz Rus. Fed. see Perevoz
140 O2 Pyaozero, Ozero l. Rus. Fed.
140 O2 Pyaozerskiy Rus. Fed.
96 A3 Pyapon Myanmar
130 J2 Pyasina r. Rus. Fed.
197 G4 Pyasŭchnik r. Bulg.
129 C1 Pyatigorsk Rus. Fed.
Pyatikhatka Ukr. see P"yatykhatka
Pyatikhatki Ukr. see P"yatykhatky
Pyatimar Kazakh. see Pyatimarskoye
120 B2 Pyatimarskoye Kazakh.
136 E2 P"yatka Ukr.
137 I2 Pyatnitskoye Rus. Fed.
139 K4 Pyatovskiy Rus. Fed.
137 H5 P"yatykhatka Ukr.
137 G3 P"yatykhatky Ukr.
96 B3 Pyaunglaung r. Myanmar
96 B2 Pyawbwe Myanmar
139 J1 Pyazhelka Rus. Fed.
134 K4 Pychas Rus. Fed.
96 A3 Pyè Myanmar
81 B7 Pye, Mount hill South I. N.Z.
138 E5 Pyershamayski Belarus
80 F2 Pyes Pa North I. N.Z.
136 E1 Pyetrykaw Belarus
140 N2 Pyhäjoki Fin.
140 N2 Pyhäjoki r. Fin.
140 N2 Pyhäntä Fin.
141 M3 Pyhäranta Fin.
140 N3 Pyhäsalmi Fin.
140 O3 Pyhäselkä Fin.
140 O3 Pyhäselkä l. Fin.
179 G2 Pyhra Austria
141 N3 Pyhtää Fin.
Pyin Myanmar see Pyè
96 B3 Pyinmana Myanmar
163 A4 Pyla-sur-Mer France
150 D3 Pyle Bridgend, Wales U.K.
199 E3 Pyli Notio Aigaio Greece
198 B2 Pyli Thessalia Greece
140 N3 Pylkönmäki Fin.
198 B3 Pylos Greece
136 D2 Pylypovychi Ukr.
101 C5 Pyŏksŏng N. Korea
101 C4 Pyŏktong N. Korea
101 C5 P'yŏnggang N. Korea
101 C5 P'yŏngsong N. Korea
101 C5 P'yŏngt'aek S. Korea
101 C5 P'yŏngyang N. Korea
178 D3 Pyramidenspitze mt. Austria
83 F4 Pyramid Hill Vic. Austr.
87 D7 Pyramid Lake salt flat W.A. Austr.
240 H1 Pyramid Lake NV U.S.A.
240 H2 Pyramid Range mts NV U.S.A.
173 F2 Pyrbaum Ger.
Pyrénées mts Europe see Pyrenees
186 F2 Pyrenees mts Europe
163 B5 Pyrénées airport France
163 B5 Pyrénées-Atlantiques dept Aquitaine France
163 E6 Pyrénées-Orientales dept Languedoc-Roussillon France
198 C2 Pyrgetos Greece
199 D2 Pyrgi Voreio Aigaio Greece
198 B3 Pyrgos Greece
136 E2 Pyrizhky Ukr.
137 G3 Pyrohy Ukr.
86 C4 Pyrton, Mount hill W.A. Austr.
137 G2 Pyryatyn Ukr.
174 C2 Pyrzyce Pol.
134 I4 Pyshchug Rus. Fed.
174 G5 Pyskowice Pol.
137 H3 Pys'menne Ukr.
174 G4 Pyszna r. Pol.
175 K5 Pysznica Pol.
138 F3 Pytalovo Rus. Fed.
96 B3 Pyu Myanmar
198 C2 Pyxaria mt. Greece

Q

126 E4 Qaa Lebanon
129 E3 Qäbälä Azer.
Qabanbay Kazakh. see Kabanbay
128 B3 Qabātiya West Bank
125 F3 Qābil Oman
129 E3 Qabırrı r. Azer.
Qabka Xizang China see Xaitongmoin
Qabqa Qinghai China see Gonghe
125 E4 Qabr Hūd Oman
Qabyrgha r. Kazakh. see Kabyrga
Qacentina Alg. see Constantine
129 D3 Qach'aghani Georgia
215 G4 Qacha's Nek Lesotho
129 F3 Qäçräş Azer.
122 D2 Qadamgāli Iran
124 B3 Qaḑīmah Saudi Arabia
127 G4 Qādir Karam Iraq
125 F5 Qādub Suquţrā Yemen
122 B4 Qā'emīyeh Iran
198 B1 Qafzez Kolonjë Albania
107 H1 Qagan Nei Mongol China
107 G3 Qagan Nur Nei Mongol China
107 G3 Qagan Nur Nei Mongol China
107 G3 Qagan Teg Nei Mongol China
Qagan Us Qinghai China see Dulan
106 C4 Qagan Us He r. China
108 A1 Qagca Sichuan China
Qagchêng Sichuan China see Xiangcheng
Qahar Youyi Houqi Nei Mongol China see Bayan Qagan
Qahar Youyi Qianqi Nei Mongol China see Togrog Ul
Qahar Youyi Zhongqi Nei Mongol China see Hobor
124 D4 Qahr, Jibāl al hills Saudi Arabia
129 E4 Qährämanlı Azer.
Qahremānshahr Iran see Kermānshāh
106 C4 Qaidam He r. China
111 F4 Qaidam Pendi basin China
123 F2 Qaisar r. Afgh.
123 F3 Qaisar, Koh-i- mt. Afgh.
195 □ Qala Gozo Malta
215 G2 Qalabotjha S. Africa
203 G6 Qala'en Nahl Sudan
123 G2 Qal'aikhum Tajik.
Qalamshia Georgia see Gant'iadi
125 F5 Qalansīyah Suquţrā Yemen
123 F3 Qalāt Afgh.
128 C2 Qal'at al Ḩişn tourist site Syria
128 B2 Qal'at al Marqab tourist site Syria
124 B2 Qal'at al Mu'aẓẓam Saudi Arabia
124 C3 Qal'at Bīshah Saudi Arabia
128 D2 Qal'at Muqaybirah, Jabal mt. Syria
127 G5 Qal'at Şāliḩ Iraq
Qalbī Zhotasy mts Kazakh. see Kalbinskiy Khrebet
122 A2 Qal'eh Dāgh mt. Iran
123 E3 Qal 'eh-ye Now Afgh.
125 G3 Qalhāt Oman
128 B3 Qalqīlya West Bank
Qalqutan Kazakh. see Koluton
203 F2 Qalyûb Qalyûbîya Egypt
126 C5 Qalyûbîya governorate Egypt
Qamanittuaq Nunavut Can. see Baker Lake
125 F4 Qamar, Ghubbat al b. Yemen
125 F4 Qamar, Jabal al mts Oman
129 E3 Qämärvan Azer.
Qamashi Uzbek. see Kamashi
108 A2 Qamdo Xizang China
79 □1 Qamea i. Fiji
202 C2 Qamīnis Libya
122 B3 Qamşar Iran
Qamystybas Kazakh. see Kamyshlybash
Qandahar Afgh. see Kandahār
210 F2 Qandala Somalia
122 A2 Qandaranbashi mt. Iran
Qandyaghash Kazakh. see Kandyagash
Qapal Kazakh. see Kapal
122 C2 Qapan Iran
110 C3 Qapqal Xinjiang China
Qapshagay Kazakh. see Kapchagay
Qapshagay Bögeni resr Kazakh. see Kapchagayskoye Vodokhranilishche
221 N3 Qaqortoq Greenland
125 F4 Qarā', Jabal al mts Oman
Qara Āghach r. Iran see Mand, Rūd-e
128 B3 Qaraaoun Lebanon
129 E3 Qarabağ Silsiläsi hills Azer.
129 D4 Qarabağ Yaylası plat. Armenia/Azer.
Qarabas Kazakh. see Karabas
Qarabulaq Almatinskaya Oblast' Kazakh. see Karabulak
Qarabutaq Kazakh. see Karabutak
129 F4 Qaraçala Azer.
Qara Ertis r. China/Kazakh. see Ertix He
Qaraghandy Kazakh. see Karaganda
Qaraghandy Oblysy admin. div. Kazakh. see Karagandinskaya Oblast'
Qaraghayly Kazakh. see Karagayly
124 D4 Qārah, Jabal al hill Saudi Arabia
Qaraköl Kazakh. see Karakol'
129 F3 Qaramäryam Azer.
122 A2 Qaranqu r. Iran
Qaraoy Almatinskaya Oblast' Kazakh. see Karaoy
Qara Özek Uzbek. see Karauzyak
Qaraqalpaqstan Respublikasy aut. rep. Uzbek. see Karakalpakistan, Respublika
Qaraqum des. Kazakh. see Karakum, Peski
Qaraqum des. Turkm. see Karakumy, Peski
Qarasor Köli l. Kazakh. see Karasor, Ozero
129 F3 Qarasu Azer.
129 E3 Qarasu r. Azer.
129 E4 Qarasu r. Azer.
Qarasū Kustanayskaya Oblast' Kazakh. see Karasu
Qara Şū Chāy r. Syria/Turkey see Karasu
123 F3 Qara Tarai mt. Afgh.
Qarataū Kazakh. see Karatau
Qarataū Zhotasy mts Kazakh. see Karatau, Khrebet
Qaratöbe Kazakh. see Karatobe
Qaratoghay Kazakh. see Karatogay
Qaraton Kazakh. see Karaton
Qaraūyl Vostochnyy Kazakhstan Kazakh. see Karaul
129 E3 Qarayeri Azer.
Qarazhal Kazakh. see Karazhal
210 F2 Qardho Somalia
122 B3 Qareh Chāy r. Iran
122 A2 Qareh Dāgh mt. Iran
122 A2 Qareh Dāsh, Kūh-e mt. Iran
122 A2 Qareh Sū r. Iran
129 D4 Qareh Ẕīā' od Dīn Iran
106 B4 Qarhan Qinghai China
Qarkilik Xinjiang China see Ruoqiang
124 C3 Qarnayt, Jabal hill Saudi Arabia
203 G2 Qarn el Kabsh, Gebel mt. Egypt
123 H2 Qarokŭl l. Tajik.
Qarqan Xinjiang China see Qiemo
110 D4 Qarqan He r. China
Qarqaraly Kazakh. see Karkaralinsk
129 E4 Qarqarçay r. Azer.
110 D3 Qarqi Xinjiang China
120 C5 Qārqi Iran
123 F2 Qarqīn Afgh.
Qarsaqbay Kazakh. see Karsakpay
Qarshi Uzbek. see Karshi
Qarshi Chŭli plain Uzbek. see Karshinskaya Step'
128 B2 Qartaba Lebanon
127 H5 Qārūh, Jazīrat i. Kuwait
125 D2 Qaryat al Ulyā Saudi Arabia
122 C2 Qāsam, Kūh-e mt. Iran
122 D3 Qasamī Iran
123 E3 Qasa Murg mts Afgh.
117 F4 Qasba Bihar India
Qashqadaryo r. Uzbek. see Kashkadar'ya
Qashqadaryo Wiloyati admin. div. Uzbek. see Kashkadar'inskaya Oblast'
221 M3 Qasigiannguit Greenland
Qaskelen Kazakh. see Kaskelen
107 F3 Qasq Nei Mongol China
128 B4 Qaşr ad Dayr, Jabal mt. Jordan
128 C2 Qasr al Ḩayr tourist site Syria
128 C4 Qaşr 'Amrah tourist site Jordan
127 H5 Qaşr aş Şabīyah Kuwait
128 C3 Qaşr Burqu' tourist site Jordan
122 E5 Qaşr-e-Qand Iran
202 E3 Qasr Farafra Egypt
124 D3 Qaşr Ḩimām Saudi Arabia
124 D5 Qa'tabah Yemen
128 C3 Qaţanā Syria
125 E2 Qatar country Asia
119 H5 Qatār, Jabal hill Oman
122 D2 Qatlish Iran
202 E2 Qattâra, Râs esc. Egypt
202 E2 Qattâra Depression Egypt
Qaţţārah, Munkhafaḑ al depr. Egypt see Qattâra Depression
129 E3 Qax Azer.
122 D3 Qāyen Iran
Qayghy Kazakh. see Kayga
Qaynar Kazakh. see Kaynar
Qayraqty Kazakh. see Kayrakty
123 G1 Qayroqqum Tajik.
129 E3 Qaysa Georgia
128 C4 Qaysīyah, Qa' al imp. l. Jordan
127 F4 Qayyārah Iraq
Qazaly Kazakh. see Kazalinsk
129 E4 Qazangödağ mt. Armenia/Azer.
Qazaq Shyghanaghy b. Kazakh. see Kazakhskiy Zaliv
Qazaqstan country Asia see Kazakhstan
129 D3 Qazax Azer.
129 D2 Qazbegi Georgia
123 G5 Qazi Ahmad Pak.
129 F3 Qazımämmäd Azer.
122 B2 Qazvīn Iran
122 B2 Qazvīn prov. Iran
Qazyqurt Yuzhnyy Kazakhstan Kazakh. see Kazygurt
106 D3 Qeh Nei Mongol China
79 □1 Qelelevu i. Fiji
198 B1 Qelqëzës, Mali i mt. Albania
203 G3 Qena Egypt
124 A2 Qena governorate Egypt
221 M3 Qeqertarsuaq Greenland
221 M3 Qeqertarsuaq i. Greenland
221 M3 Qeqertarsuup Tunua b. Greenland
122 D5 Qeshm Iran
122 D5 Qeshm i. Iran
122 B2 Qeydār Iran
122 C5 Qeys i. Iran
122 B2 Qezel Owzan, Rūdkhāneh-ye r. Iran
129 D4 Qezel Qeshlāq Iran
107 G5 Qi r. China
107 E5 Qian r. China
107 H4 Qian'an Hebei China
107 J2 Qian'an Jilin China
108 D3 Qiancheng Hunan China
107 H5 Qiang r. China
Qian Gorlos Jilin China see Qianguozhen
100 C3 Qianguozhen Jilin China
108 D2 Qianjiang Chongqing China
109 E2 Qianjiang Hubei China
100 E3 Qianjin Heilong. China
108 B2 Qianning Sichuan China
109 F2 Qianshan Anhui China
107 I3 Qian Shan mts China
264 R4 Qiansuo Zhejiang China
108 B2 Qianwei Sichuan China
108 C3 Qianxi Guizhou China
107 H3 Qianxi Hebei China
107 F5 Qianxian Shaanxi China
108 D3 Qianyang Hunan China
107 E5 Qianyang Shaanxi China
109 F2 Qianyang Zhejiang China
Qianyou Shaanxi China see Zhashui
108 B3 Qiaojia Yunnan China
Qiaoshan Shaanxi China see Huangling
Qiaotou Qinghai China see Datong
108 B3 Qiaotou Yunnan China
Qiaowa Sichuan China see Muli
106 C3 Qiaowan Gansu China
Qiaozhuang Sichuan China see Qingchuan
124 D2 Qibā' Saudi Arabia
215 F3 Qibing S. Africa
Qibray Uzbek. see Kibray
109 E2 Qichun Hubei China
109 E3 Qidong Hunan China
109 G2 Qidong Jiangsu China
111 D4 Qiemo Xinjiang China
107 H4 Qihe Shandong China
108 C2 Qijiang Chongqing China
221 L3 Qikiqtarjuaq Nunavut Can.
Qili Anhui China see Shitai
106 D4 Qilian Qinghai China
106 C4 Qilian Shan mts China
106 C4 Qilian Shan mts China
Qīma Kazakh. see Kiyma
111 E4 Qimantag mts China
109 F2 Qimen Anhui China
221 L2 Qimusseriarsuaq b. Greenland
107 G5 Qin r. China
Qinā Egypt see Qena
125 E4 Qināb, Wādī r. Yemen
106 E5 Qin'an Gansu China
Qincheng Jiangxi China see Nanfeng
100 B4 Qing r. China
100 C3 Qing'an Heilong. China
Qingcheng Gansu China see Qingyang
101 B4 Qingchengzi Liaoning China
108 C1 Qingchuan Sichuan China
107 I4 Qingdao Shandong China
100 C3 Qinggang Heilong. China
Qinggil Xinjiang China see Qinghe
108 D2 Qingguandu Hunan China
106 C4 Qinghai prov. China
106 D4 Qinghai Hu salt l. Qinghai China
106 C4 Qinghai Nanshan mts China
107 G4 Qinghe Hebei China
106 A2 Qinghe Xinjiang China
Qinghua Henan China see Bo'ai
107 F4 Qingjian Shaanxi China
Qingjiang Jiangsu China see Huaiyin
Qingjiang Jiangxi China see Zhangshu
108 D2 Qing Jiang r. China
Qingkou Jiangsu China see Ganyu
109 F3 Qingliu Fujian China
108 C3 Qinglong Guizhou China
107 H3 Qinglong Hebei China
107 H4 Qinglong r. China
109 G2 Qingpu Shanghai China
Qingquan Hubei China see Xishui
Qingshan Heilong. China see Dedu
108 B2 Qingshen Sichuan China
106 D4 Qingshizui Qinghai China
106 E5 Qingshui Gansu China
107 F4 Qingshuihe Nei Mongol China
108 A1 Qingshuihe Qinghai China
109 G2 Qingtian Zhejiang China
106 E4 Qingtongxia Ningxia China
107 H4 Qingxian Hebei China
107 G4 Qingxu Shanxi China
109 F2 Qingyang Anhui China
107 E4 Qingyang Gansu China
Qingyang Jiangsu China see Sihong
Qingyuan Gansu China see Weiyuan
109 E4 Qingyuan Guangdong China
Qingyuan Guangxi China see Yizhou
100 C4 Qingyuan Liaoning China
Qingyuan Shanxi China see Qingxu
109 F3 Qingyuan Zhejiang China
107 H4 Qingyun Shandong China
111 D5 Qing Zang Gaoyuan plat. Xizang China
108 C3 Qingzhen Guizhou China
Qingzhou Hebei China see Qingxian
109 D2 Qingzhou Hubei China
107 H4 Qingzhou Shandong China
107 H4 Qinhuangdao Hebei China
Qinjiang Jiangxi China see Shicheng
108 C1 Qin Ling mts China
107 G5 Qinshui Shanxi China
Qinting Jiangxi China see Lianhua
107 G4 Qinxian Shanxi China
107 G5 Qinyang Henan China
107 G4 Qinyuan Shanxi China
108 D4 Qinzhou Guangxi China
108 D5 Qionghai Hainan China
Qiongjiexue Xizang China see Qonggyai
108 B2 Qionglai Sichuan China
108 B2 Qionglai Shan mts Sichuan China
108 D5 Qiongshan Hainan China
Qiongxi Sichuan China see Hongyuan
108 D5 Qiongzhong Hainan China
108 D5 Qiongzhou Haixia str. China
107 I2 Qiqihar Heilong. China
122 C4 Qīr Iran
111 C4 Qira Xinjiang China
129 E4 Qırmızı Bazar Azer.
129 F4 Qırmızkänd Azer.
128 B4 Qiryat Gat Israel
128 B3 Qiryat Shemona Israel
Qishan Anhui China see Qimen
107 E5 Qishan Shaanxi China
125 E5 Qishn Yemen
128 B3 Qishon r. Israel
124 C3 Qishrān Island Saudi Arabia
126 E5 Qitab ash Shāmah vol. crater Saudi Arabia
110 E3 Qitai Xinjiang China
100 D3 Qitaihe Heilong. China
125 F4 Qitbīt, Wādī r. Oman
108 C3 Qiubei Yunnan China
109 E2 Qiujin Jiangxi China
107 I4 Qixia Shandong China
107 G5 Qixian Henan China
107 G5 Qixian Henan China
107 G4 Qixian Shanxi China
100 E3 Qixing r. China
109 D3 Qiyang Hunan China
129 F4 Qızılağac Körfäzi b. Azer.
129 F3 Qızıldaş Azer.
Qizqetkan Uzbek. see Kyzketken
215 G5 Qoboqobo S. Africa
129 F3 Qobustan Azer.
Qoghaly Kazakh. see Kugaly
Qogir Feng mt. China/Jammu and Kashmir see K2
122 A2 Qojūr Iran
215 G5 Qolora Mouth S. Africa
122 B3 Qom Iran
122 B3 Qom prov. Iran
Qomdo Xizang China see Qumdo
122 B3 Qomishēh Iran
Qomolangma Feng mt. China/Nepal see Everest, Mount
129 F3 Qonaqkänd Azer.
111 E6 Qonggyai Xizang China
107 F3 Qongj Nei Mongol China
Qongrat Uzbek. see Kungrad
Qongyrat Karagandinskaya Oblast' Kazakh. see Kounradskiy
Qongyrat Karagandinskaya Oblast' Kazakh. see Konyrat
Qongyröleng Kazakh. see Konyrolen
Qonystanū Kazakh. see Konystanu
Qoqek Xinjiang China see Tacheng
215 F4 Qoqodala S. Africa
Qoradaryo r. Kyrg. see Kara-Darya
Qoraghaty Kazakh. see Kuragaty
Qoraqalpoghiston Uzbek. see Karakalpakiya
Qoraqalpoghiston Respublikasi aut. rep. Uzbek. see Karakalpakistan, Respublika
Qoraŭzak Uzbek. see Karauzyak
Qorday Kazakh. see Kurday
Qorghalzhyn Kazakh. see Kurgal'dzhinskiy
128 C2 Qornet es Saouda mt. Lebanon
129 C2 Qornisi Georgia
Qorowulbozor Uzbek. see Karaulbazar
122 A3 Qorveh Iran
127 F3 Qosh Tepe Iraq
129 E3 Qoşqarçay r. Azer.
Qosshaghyl Kazakh. see Koschagyl
Qostanay Kazakh. see Kostanay
Qostanay Oblysy admin. div. Kazakh. see Kustanayskaya Oblast'
122 D5 Qoţbābād Iran
122 A2 Qoţūr Iran
128 C2 Qoubaiyat Lebanon
129 D3 Qovlar Azer.

182 D4 Quadrazais Port.
193 G3 Quadri Italy
146 E5 Quaich r. Scotland U.K.
240 I4 Quail Mountains CA U.S.A.
87 C7 Quairading W.A. Austr.
168 C3 Quakenbrück Ger.
235 F1 Quaker Hill CT U.S.A.
234 D2 Quakertown NJ U.S.A.
234 C2 Quakertown PA U.S.A.
234 B2 Qualake PA U.S.A.
193 G4 Qualiano Italy
83 E3 Quambatook Vic. Austr.
83 F2 Quambone N.S.W. Austr.
84 E4 Quamby Qld Austr.
237 D5 Quanah TX U.S.A.
107 F5 Quanbao Shan mt. Henan China
Quan Dao Hoang Sa is S. China Sea see Paracel Islands
Quan Dao Truong Sa is S. China Sea see Spratly Islands
96 E4 Quang Ngai Vietnam
96 D3 Quang Tri Vietnam
96 D2 Quang Yen Vietnam
109 E1 Quan He r. China
Quanjiang Jiangxi China see Suichuan
Quan Long Vietnam see Ca Mau
109 E3 Quannan Jiangxi China
Quan Phu Quoc i. Vietnam see Phu Quôc, Đao
109 F3 Quanshang Fujian China
150 D3 Quantock Hills England U.K.
Quanwan H.K. China see Tsuen Wan
109 F3 Quanzhou Fujian China
109 D3 Quanzhou Guangxi China
223 K5 Qu'Appelle Sask. Can.
223 K5 Qu'Appelle r. Man./Sask. Can.
221 L3 Quaqtaq Que. Can.
255 A9 Quaraí Brazil
261 I2 Quaraí r. Brazil
165 C4 Quaregnon Belgium
190 D4 Quargnento Italy
142 C4 Quarnbek Ger.
190 D3 Quarona Italy
191 F5 Quarrata Italy
160 B1 Quarré-les-Tombes France
81 B7 Quarry Hills South I. N.Z.
234 B3 Quarryville PA U.S.A.
184 B3 Quarteira Port.
187 C5 Quartell Spain
190 E1 Quarten Switz.
192 B5 Quartu Sant'Elena Sardegna Italy
241 I3 Quartzite Mountain NV U.S.A.
241 J5 Quartzsite AZ U.S.A.
124 D4 Quaryat al Faw tourist site Saudi Arabia
256 B5 Quatá Brazil
247 □3 Quatre, Isle á i. St Vincent
156 E3 Quatre-Champs France
187 C6 Quatretonda Spain
216 □1a Quatro Ribeiras Terceira Azores
129 F3 Quba Azer.
129 E4 Qubadlı Azer.
129 F3 Qubalıbalaoğlan Azer.
122 D2 Quchan Iran
215 H3 Qudeni S. Africa
129 F3 Qudıyalçay r. Azer.
83 G3 Queanbeyan A.C.T. Austr.
225 G4 Québec Que. Can.
225 F2 Québec prov. Can.
256 D3 Quebra Anzol r. Brazil
261 I3 Quebracho Uru.
247 □1 Quebradillas Puerto Rico
150 E3 Quedgeley Gloucestershire, England U.K.
171 C4 Quedlinburg Ger.
Queen Adelaide Islands Chile see La Reina Adelaida, Archipiélago de
128 B4 Queen Alia airport 'Ammān Jordan
234 C4 Queen Anne MD U.S.A.
234 B3 Queen Anne's County county MD U.S.A.
222 E5 Queen Bess, Mount B.C. Can.
151 H3 Queenborough Kent, England U.K.
222 C4 Queen Charlotte B.C. Can.
259 E8 Queen Charlotte Bay Falkland Is
222 C4 Queen Charlotte Islands B.C. Can.
222 D5 Queen Charlotte Sound sea chan. B.C. Can.
222 E5 Queen Charlotte Strait B.C. Can.
226 A5 Queen City MO U.S.A.
241 L5 Queen Creek AZ U.S.A.
221 H2 Queen Elizabeth Islands N.W.T./Nunavut Can.
263 K1 Queen Elizabeth Range mts Antarctica
263 C2 Queen Fabiola Mountains Antarctica
222 B2 Queen Mary, Mount Y.T. Can.
263 G2 Queen Mary Land reg. Antarctica
221 H3 Queen Maud Gulf Nunavut Can.
263 A2 Queen Maud Land reg. Antarctica
262 O1 Queen Maud Mountains Antarctica
215 H3 Queensburgh S. Africa
149 H4 Queensbury West Yorkshire, England U.K.
84 B2 Queens Channel N.T. Austr.
221 I2 Queens Channel Nunavut Can.
83 F4 Queenscliff Vic. Austr.
235 E2 Queens County county NY U.S.A.
85 F4 Queensland state Austr.
83 F5 Queenstown Tas. Austr.
81 B6 Queenstown South I. N.Z.
Queenstown Rep. of Ireland see Cóbh
215 F4 Queenstown S. Africa
234 B4 Queenstown MD U.S.A.
238 A2 Queets WA U.S.A.
261 H3 Queguay Grande r. Uru.
160 E3 Queige France
254 F4 Queimadas Brazil
182 C4 Queiriga Port.
256 B4 Queiroz Brazil
183 H2 Quel Spain
209 C7 Quela Angola
159 F4 Quelaines-St-Gault France
213 H3 Quelimane Moz.
244 A2 Quelite Mex.
260 A5 Quella Chile
171 D4 Quellendorf Ger.
259 B6 Quellón Chile
Quelpart Island S. Korea see Cheju-do
257 E5 Queluz Brazil
184 A2 Queluz Port.
183 G3 Quemada Spain
256 D6 Quemada Grande, Ilha i. Brazil
239 E5 Quemado NM U.S.A.
209 D8 Quembo r. Angola
259 B6 Quemchi Chile
Quemoy i. Taiwan see Chinmen Tao
261 F5 Quemú-Quemú Arg.
156 B2 Quend France
169 C3 Quendorf Ger.
171 C4 Quenstedt Ger.
185 G3 Quéntar Spain
234 B2 Quentin PA U.S.A.
114 B3 Quepem Goa India
Que Que Zimbabwe see Kwekwe
261 H6 Quequén Grande r. Arg.
186 F2 Queralbs Spain
190 F5 Quercianella Italy
184 C3 Querença Port.
256 A5 Querência do Norte Brazil
244 D4 Queréndaro Mex.
169 F3 Querenhorst Ger.
244 D3 Querétaro Mex.
245 E3 Querétaro state Mex.
171 C4 Querfurt Ger.
163 E6 Quérigut France
168 E1 Quern Ger.
169 D3 Quernheim Ger.
149 G3 Quernmore Lancashire, England U.K.
191 G3 Quero Italy
183 G5 Quero Spain
242 C2 Querobabi Mex.
186 E3 Querol Spain
158 E2 Querqueville France
156 C3 Querrieu France
157 G5 Quers France
187 C5 Quesa Spain
185 G3 Quesada Spain
185 G3 Quesada r. Spain
109 E1 Queshan Henan China
222 F4 Quesnel B.C. Can.
222 F4 Quesnel r. B.C. Can.
156 D2 Quesnoy-sur-Deûle France
158 D3 Quessoy France
156 D3 Quessy France
158 D4 Questembert France
252 D5 Quetena de Lipez r. Bol.
160 D1 Quetigny France
123 F4 Quetta Pak.
158 E2 Quettehou France
158 E3 Quettreville-sur-Sienne France
245 E5 Quetzala r. Mex.
260 B5 Queuco Chile
259 B5 Queule Chile
156 C3 Quevauvillers France
158 C4 Quéven France
158 D3 Quévert France
162 B3 Queyrac France
163 E4 Quézac France
243 H6 Quezaltenango Guat.
243 H6 Quezaltepeque El Salvador
92 B4 Quezon Negros Phil.
92 A4 Quezon Palawan Phil.
92 B3 Quezon City Phil.
107 H5 Qufu Shandong China
111 E6 Qugayatang Xizang China
182 B4 Quiaios Port.
209 B7 Quibala Angola
209 B7 Quibaxe Angola
250 B3 Quibdó Col.
158 C4 Quiberon France
158 C4 Quiberon, Baie de b. France
158 C4 Quiberon, Presqu'île de pen. France
168 E2 Quickborn Ger.
209 B7 Quiculungo Angola
157 H3 Quierschied Ger.
156 D3 Quierzy France
156 D2 Quiévrechain France
260 A5 Quilaco Chile
114 B4 Quilandi Kerala India
252 B4 Quilca Peru
209 B7 Quilenda Angola
209 B8 Quilengues Angola
190 D4 Quiliano Italy
260 B3 Quilimarí Chile
260 E2 Quilino Arg.
252 D4 Quillacollo Bol.
163 E6 Quillan France
260 A5 Quillon Chile
260 B3 Quillota Chile
261 H4 Quilmes Arg.
209 B7 Quilombo dos Dembos Angola
114 C4 Quilon Kerala India
85 F5 Quilpie Qld Austr.
260 B3 Quilpué Chile
213 H3 Quilua Moz.
209 C6 Quimbele Angola
252 D4 Quime Bol.
244 B2 Quimichis Mex.
258 E2 Quimilí Arg.
158 B4 Quimper France
158 C4 Quimperlé France
147 C4 Quin Rep. of Ireland
146 C3 Quinag hill Scotland U.K.
238 A2 Quinault r. WA U.S.A.
252 C3 Quince Mil Peru
190 C3 Quincinetto Italy
240 G2 Quincy CA U.S.A.
231 C6 Quincy FL U.S.A.
230 B4 Quincy IL U.S.A.
233 H3 Quincy MA U.S.A.
226 E5 Quincy MI U.S.A.
232 B4 Quincy OH U.S.A.
156 C4 Quincy-Voisins France
250 C3 Quindio dept Col.
260 E3 Quines Arg.
158 E2 Quinéville France
213 I2 Quinga Moz.
160 D1 Quingey France
220 B4 Quinhagak AK U.S.A.
206 B4 Quinhámel Guinea-Bissau
97 E4 Qui Nhon Vietnam
251 E3 Quinigua, Cerro mts Venez.
238 C3 Quinn r. NV U.S.A.
241 J3 Quinn Canyon Range mts NV U.S.A.
232 C6 Quinnimont WV U.S.A.
161 E5 Quinson France
160 A2 Quinssaines France
184 C3 Quintã hill Port.
184 B2 Quinta do Anjo Port.
256 B5 Quintana Brazil
184 E2 Quintana de la Serena Spain
182 D2 Quintana del Castillo Spain
183 G2 Quintana del Pino Spain
183 F2 Quintana del Puente Spain
183 E2 Quintana de Rueda Spain
183 G2 Quintanapalla Spain
183 G5 Quintanar de la Orden Spain
183 G3 Quintanar de la Sierra Spain
185 I1 Quintanar del Rey Spain
183 H3 Quintana Redonda Spain
243 H5 Quintana Roo state Mex.
182 D3 Quintanilha Port.
Quintanilla de Abajo Spain see Quintanilla de Omesimo
183 F3 Quintanilla de Omesimo Spain
182 B4 Quintãs Port.
161 C3 Quintenas France
236 C4 Quinter KS U.S.A.
260 B3 Quintero Chile
158 D3 Quintin France
260 E4 Quinto r. Arg.
186 C3 Quinto Spain
190 D2 Quinto Switz.
234 C3 Quinton NJ U.S.A.
209 B6 Quinzau Angola
211 D7 Quionga Moz.
254 G4 Quipapá Brazil
185 I2 Quipar r. Spain
209 B8 Quipungo Angola
252 D3 Quiquive r. Bol.
242 □H6 Quiriguá tourist site Guat.
260 A5 Quirihue Chile
209 C7 Quirima Angola
83 G2 Quirindi N.S.W. Austr.
256 B3 Quirinópolis Brazil
252 D4 Quiroga Bol.
244 D4 Quiroga Mex.
182 C2 Quiroga Spain
182 E2 Quiruelas de Vidriales Spain
183 F4 Quismondo Spain
161 C5 Quissac France
257 G5 Quissamã Brazil
211 D8 Quissanga Moz.
209 C7 Quitapa Angola
211 D7 Quiterajo Moz.
256 B4 Quitéria r. Brazil
Quitexe Angola see Dange
258 E2 Quitilipi Arg.
231 D6 Quitman GA U.S.A.
237 F5 Quitman MS U.S.A.
237 E5 Quitman TX U.S.A.
250 B5 Quito Ecuador
156 A3 Quittebeuf France
254 F3 Quixadá Brazil
213 I2 Quixaxe Moz.
254 F3 Quixeramobim Brazil
209 B7 Quixinge Angola
109 E3 Qujiang Guangdong China
Qujiang Sichuan China see Quxian
108 C2 Qu Jiang r. China
108 B3 Qujing Yunnan China
215 G5 Quko S. Africa
Quljuqtow Toghi hills Uzbek. see Kul'dzhuktau, Gory
Qulsary Kazakh. see Kul'sary
126 C5 Qulûsana Egypt
106 B5 Qumar He r. China
106 B5 Qumarheyan Qinghai China
106 B5 Qumarlêb Qinghai China
215 G4 Qumbu S. Africa
111 F6 Qumdo Xizang China
215 F5 Qumrha S. Africa
202 D2 Qunayyin, Sabkhat al salt marsh Libya
Qŭnghirot Uzbek. see Kungrad
108 A2 Qu'nyido Xizang China
223 M1 Quoich r. Nunavut Can.
146 C4 Quoich, Loch l. Scotland U.K.
147 F2 Quoile r. Northern Ireland U.K.
84 B2 Quoin Island N.T. Austr.
111 C5 Quong Muztag mt. Xinjiang/Xizang China
82 D3 Quorn S.A. Austr.
212 E4 Quoxo r. Botswana
Quqên Sichuan China see Jinchuan
Qŭqon Uzbek. see Kokand
125 G3 Qurayat Oman
128 C5 Qurayyah tourist site Saudi Arabia
123 G2 Qŭrghonteppa Tajik.
129 E3 Qurmuxçay r. Azer.
203 G3 Qus Egypt
129 F3 Qusar Azer.
129 F3 Qusarçay r. Azer.
125 E5 Quşay'ir Saudi Arabia
203 G3 Quseir Egypt
Qushan Sichuan China see Beichuan
122 A2 Qūshchī Iran
Qŭshkŭpir Uzbek. see Koshkupyr
Qŭshrabot Uzbek. see Koshrabad
Qusmuryn Kazakh. see Kushmurun
Qusmuryn Köli salt l. Kazakh. see Kushmurun, Ozero
111 F6 Qusum Xizang China
Quthing Lesotho see Moyeni
215 F4 Quthing r. Lesotho
124 C2 Quţn, Jabal hill Saudi Arabia
124 C4 Qutū' Island Saudi Arabia
128 C2 Quwayq, Nahr r. Syria/Turkey
125 F4 Qū' Wishām reg. Oman
106 E4 Quwu Shan mts China
Quxar Xizang China see Lhazê
108 C2 Quxian Sichuan China
111 E6 Qüxü Xizang China
Quyang Hunan China see Jingzhou
Quyghan Kazakh. see Kuygan
227 I3 Quyon Que. Can.
129 E3 Quzanlı Azer.
107 G4 Quzhou Hebei China
109 F2 Quzhou Zhejiang China
107 E4 Quzi Gansu China
129 D3 Qvareli Georgia
129 C2 Qvirila r. Georgia
Qyteti Stalin Albania see Kuçovë
Qyzan Kazakh. see Kyzan
Qyzylaghash Kazakh. see Kyzylagash
Qyzylorda Kazakh. see Kyzylorda
Qyzylorda Oblysy admin. div. Kazakh. see Kzyl-Ordinskaya Oblast'
Qyzyltaū Kazakh. see Kyzyltau
Qyzyltū Kazakh. see Kishkenekol'
Qyzylzhar Kazakh. see Kyzylzhar

R

179 E2 Raab Austria
179 H4 Raab r. Austria
Raab Hungary see Győr
179 G2 Raabs an der Thaya Austria
140 N2 Raahe Fin.
140 O3 Rääkkylä Fin.
164 F2 Raalte Neth.
164 D3 Raamsdonksveer Neth.
124 C2 Ra'an, Khashm ar hill Saudi Arabia
146 B4 Raasay i. Scotland U.K.
146 B4 Raasay, Sound of sea chan. Scotland U.K.
138 E2 Raasiku Estonia
188 E3 Rab i. Croatia
176 G4 Rába r. Hungary
95 G5 Raba Sumbawa Indon.
175 I5 Raba r. Pol.
191 J3 Rabac Croatia
182 B4 Rabaçal Port.
182 C4 Rabaçal Port.
182 C3 Rabaçal r. Port./Spain
182 C1 Rábade Spain
177 L5 Răbăgani Romania
176 F4 Rábahidvég Hungary
203 G6 Rabak Sudan
176 G4 Rábakecöl Hungary
182 D3 Rabanales Spain
176 F4 Rábapaty Hungary
176 G4 Rábapordány Hungary
163 D5 Rabastens France
163 C5 Rabastens-de-Bigorre France
Rabat Gozo Malta see Victoria
195 □ Rabat Malta
204 D2 Rabat Morocco
91 L7 Rabaul New Britain P.N.G.
175 H6 Raba Wyżna Pol.
Rabbath Ammon Jordan see 'Ammān
191 H4 Rabbi r. Italy
191 F2 Rabbies r. Italy
222 E3 Rabbit r. B.C. Can.
84 B4 Rabbit Flat N.T. Austr.
222 F2 Rabbitskin r. N.W.T. Can.
177 G4 Rábca r. Hungary
177 I2 Rabča Slovakia
177 I2 Rabčice Slovakia
171 E5 Rabenau Ger.
179 G2 Rabenstein an der Pielach Austria
170 C2 Raben Steinfeld Ger.
79 □1 Rabi i. Fiji
124 B3 Rābigh Saudi Arabia
243 H6 Rabinal Guat.
174 D2 Rąbino Pol.
190 E2 Rabiusa r. Switz.
175 H6 Rabka Pol.
169 F3 Räbke Ger.
Rabkob Madh. Prad. India see Dharmjaygarh
117 G5 Rabnabad Islands Bangl.
Râbniţa Moldova see Rîbniţa
216 □1b Rabo de Peixe São Miguel Azores
122 D4 Rābor Iran
191 H3 Raboso r. Italy
204 B5 Rabt Sbayta des. Western Sahara
202 D3 Rabyānah, Ramlat des. Libya
196 E3 Rača Srbija Yugo.
195 H3 Racale Italy
177 H4 Rácalmás Hungary
194 C5 Racalmuto Sicilia Italy
193 I4 Racanello r. Italy
191 I2 Raccolana r. Italy
190 C4 Racconigi Italy
246 D2 Raccoon Cay i. Bahamas
234 C3 Raccoon Creek r. NJ U.S.A.
232 B5 Raccoon Creek r. OH U.S.A.
194 D4 Raccuia Sicilia Italy
179 G4 Rače Slovenia
225 K4 Race, Cape Nfld. Can.
237 F6 Raceland LA U.S.A.
128 B3 Rachaïya Lebanon
237 D7 Rachal TX U.S.A.
175 L5 Rachanie Pol.
157 F4 Rachecourt-sur-Marne France
241 J3 Rachel NV U.S.A.
97 D5 Rach Gia Vietnam
129 C2 Rachis K'edi hills Georgia
174 F2 Raciąż Pol.
175 I3 Raciąż Pol.
175 I3 Raciążnica r. Pol.
174 G5 Racibórz Pol.
175 I6 Raciechowice Pol.
226 D4 Racine WI U.S.A.
232 C5 Racine WV U.S.A.
197 G2 Râciu Romania
177 H4 Ráckeve Hungary
146 E3 Rackwick Orkney, Scotland U.K.
171 D4 Rackwitz Ger.
175 I5 Racławice Pol.
197 G2 Racoş Romania
197 H3 Racoviţa Romania
177 K6 Racoviţa Romania
175 K2 Raczki Podlaskie Pol.
175 I2 Rączki Pol.
124 D5 Radā' Yemen
260 A6 Radal Chile
138 F4 Radashkovichy Belarus
197 G2 Rădăuţi Romania
176 C2 Radbuza r. Czech Rep.
139 K3 Radchenko Rus. Fed.
137 K3 Radchenskoye Rus. Fed.
230 C4 Radcliff KY U.S.A.
149 G4 Radcliffe Greater Manchester, England U.K.
151 F2 Radcliffe on Trent Nottinghamshire, England U.K.
194 D5 Raddusa Sicilia Italy
142 D2 Rade Norway
171 E4 Radeberg Ger.
171 E4 Radebeul Ger.
171 E4 Radeburg Ger.
179 G4 Radeče Slovenia
171 D4 Radefeld Ger.
171 D4 Radegast Ger.
136 C2 Radekhiv Ukr.
179 H4 Radenci Slovenia
137 G4 Radens'k Ukr.
170 D3 Radensleben Ger.
179 E4 Radenthein Austria
169 C4 Radevormwald Ger.
174 D1 Radew r. Pol.
178 C3 Radfeld Austria
232 C6 Radford VA U.S.A.
84 B1 Radford Point N.T. Austr.
151 F2 Radford Semele Warwickshire, England U.K.
116 B5 Radhanpur Gujarat India
171 F4 Radibor Ger.
192 D2 Radicofani Italy
191 G5 Radicondoli Italy
193 H3 Radicosa r. Italy
171 D4 Radis Ger.
120 A1 Radishchevo Rus. Fed.
224 E2 Radisson Que. Can.
223 J4 Radisson Sask. Can.
226 B3 Radisson WI U.S.A.
139 J5 Raditsa-Krylovka Rus. Fed.
222 G5 Radium Hot Springs B.C. Can.
179 G4 Radizelj Slovenia
137 I2 Rad'kovka Rus. Fed.
174 E5 Radków Pol.
175 H5 Radków Pol.
151 G3 Radlett Hertfordshire, England U.K.
262 R1 Radlinski, Mount Antarctica
179 G4 Radlje ob Dravi Slovenia
175 I5 Radłów Pol.
174 G5 Radłów Pol.
197 G4 Radnevo Bulg.
176 C2 Radnice Czech Rep.
177 J6 Radojevo Vojvodina, Srbija Yugo.
172 C4 Radolfzell am Bodensee Ger.
175 J4 Radom Pol.
175 H2 Radomin Pol.
197 F4 Radomir Bulg.
197 F5 Radomir mt. Bulg./Greece
175 J4 Radomka r. Pol.
177 K2 Radomka r. Slovakia
137 G2 Radomka Ukr.
175 J4 Radomska, Równina plain Pol.
175 H4 Radomsko Pol.
136 E2 Radomyshl' Ukr.
175 J5 Radomyśl nad Sanem Pol.
175 J5 Radomyśl Wielki Pol.
176 C1 Radonice Czech Rep.
Radoshkovichi Belarus see Radashkovichy
177 G3 Radošina Slovakia
176 G3 Radošovce Slovakia
175 I4 Radoszyce Pol.
197 H5 Radovets Bulg.
197 F5 Radoviš Macedonia
139 L4 Radovitskiy Rus. Fed.
188 E2 Radovljica Slovenia
174 D2 Radowo Małe Pol.
144 J1 Radøy i. Norway
179 E3 Radstadt Austria
150 E3 Radstock Bath and North East Somerset, England U.K.
82 C3 Radstock, Cape S.A. Austr.
197 H2 Răducăneni Romania
136 F2 Radul' Ukr.
138 E4 Radun' Belarus
143 H4 Radunia r. Pol.
137 G4 Radushne Ukr.
138 D4 Radviliškis Lith.
124 B2 Radwā, Jabal mt. Saudi Arabia
174 D4 Radwanice Pol.
175 K6 Radymno Pol.
136 C2 Radyvyliv Ukr.
175 I3 Radzanów Pol.
175 I4 Radzice Duże Pol.
174 F2 Radzicz Pol.
175 J1 Radzieje Pol.
174 G3 Radziejów Pol.
175 I6 Radziejowa mt. Pol.
175 I3 Radziejowice Pol.
175 I5 Radziemice Pol.
175 K2 Radziłów Pol.
177 I3 Radzovce Slovakia
175 J3 Radzymin Pol.
174 G2 Radzyń Chełminski Pol.
175 K4 Radzyń Podlaski Pol.
116 E4 Rae Bareli Uttar Prad. India
222 G2 Rae-Edzo N.W.T. Can.
231 E5 Raeford NC U.S.A.
222 G1 Rae Lakes N.W.T. Can.
165 F4 Raeren Belgium
169 B4 Raesfeld Ger.
87 D6 Raeside, Lake salt flat W.A. Austr.
80 D1 Raetea hill North I. N.Z.
80 E3 Raetihi North I. N.Z.
127 E5 Rāf hill Saudi Arabia
260 A5 Rafael Chile
261 G2 Rafaela Arg.
246 D2 Rafael Freyre Cuba
245 F4 Rafael J Garcia Mex.
Rafah Gaza see Rafiah
208 D3 Rafaï C.A.R.
136 D2 Rafalivka Ukr.
187 C5 Rafelbunyol Spain
194 C5 Raffadali Sicilia Italy
146 E4 Rafford Moray, Scotland U.K.
147 F2 Raffrey Northern Ireland U.K.
127 F5 Rafhā' Saudi Arabia
128 B4 Rafiah Gaza
198 D2 Rafina Greece
147 C3 Raford r. Rep. of Ireland
122 C4 Rafsanjān Iran
238 D3 Raft r. Idaho/Nevada U.S.A.
183 E4 Rágama Spain
138 E3 Ragana Latvia
195 F3 Raganello r. Italy
92 C5 Ragang, Mount vol. Mindanao Phil.
92 B3 Ragay Gulf Phil.
170 D2 Rägelin Ger.
87 D7 Ragged, Mount hill W.A. Austr.
246 D2 Ragged Island Bahamas
116 D4 Raghogarh Madh. Prad. India
80 E2 Raglan North I. N.Z.
150 E3 Raglan Monmouthshire, Wales U.K.
179 G4 Ragnitz Austria
171 D3 Ragösen Ger.
225 G3 Ragueneau Que. Can.
171 D4 Raguhn Ger.
Ragusa Croatia see Dubrovnik
194 D6 Ragusa Sicilia Italy
194 D6 Ragusa prov. Sicilia Italy
117 H4 Raha Assam India
93 B4 Raha Sulawesi Tenggara Indon.
139 H5 Rahachow Belarus
203 G6 Rahad r. Sudan
Rahaeng Thai. see Tak
124 C3 Rahaţ, Harrat lava field Saudi Arabia
116 D5 Rahatgaon Madh. Prad. India
169 D3 Rahden Ger.
114 B2 Rahimatpur Mahar. India
123 G4 Rahimyar Khan Pak.
157 G5 Rahin r. France
122 B3 Rāhjerd Iran
80 D3 Rahotu North I. N.Z.
260 B6 Rahue mt. Chile
114 B2 Rahuri Mahar. India
193 F2 Raiano Italy
79 □3 Raiatea i. Arch. de la Société Fr. Polynesia
114 C2 Raichur Karnataka India
117 G4 Raiganj W. Bengal India
117 E5 Raigarh Madh. Prad. India
114 D2 Raigarh Orissa India
116 C3 Raikot Punjab India
241 J2 Railroad Valley NV U.S.A.
117 G5 Raimangal r. Bangl.
173 E3 Rain Bayern Ger.
173 G3 Rain Bayern Ger.
179 F2 Rainbach im Mühlkreis Austria
83 E3 Rainbow Vic. Austr.
85 H5 Rainbow Beach Qld Austr.
222 G3 Rainbow Lake Alta Can.
85 F1 Raine Entrance sea chan. Qld Austr.
85 F1 Raine Island Qld Austr.
232 C6 Rainelle WV U.S.A.
149 G4 Rainford Merseyside, England U.K.
123 G4 Raini r. Pak.
238 B2 Rainier, Mount vol. WA U.S.A.
149 G4 Rainow Cheshire, England U.K.
149 H4 Rainworth Nottinghamshire, England U.K.
236 E1 Rainy r. MN U.S.A.
223 M5 Rainy Lake Ont. Can.
223 M5 Rainy River Ont. Can.
117 G5 Raipur Bangl.
116 E5 Raipur Madh. Prad. India
116 C4 Raipur Rajasthan India
117 F5 Raipur W. Bengal India
117 F5 Rairangpur Orissa India
78 □3b Rairik i. Majuro Marshall Is
182 C2 Rairiz de Veiga Spain
Rairoa atoll Arch. des Tuamotu Fr. Polynesia see Rangiroa
168 F1 Raisdorf Ger.
116 D5 Raisen Madh. Prad. India
116 C3 Raisinghnagar Rajasthan India
141 M3 Raisio Fin.
156 D2 Raismes France
116 D5 Raitalai Madh. Prad. India
173 F2 Raitenbuch Ger.
226 C1 Raith Ont. Can.
81 D4 Rai Valley South I. N.Z.
79 □3 Raivavae i. Îs Australes Fr. Polynesia
123 H4 Raiwind Pak.
138 F2 Raja Estonia
93 D3 Rajaampat, Kepulauan is Irian Jaya Indon.
94 D4 Rajabasa, Gunung vol. Indon.
117 F5 Rajagangapur Orissa India
114 D2 Rajahmundry Andhra Prad. India
116 C3 Rajaldesar Rajasthan India
138 E1 Rajamäki Fin.
114 C3 Rajampet Andhra Prad. India
95 E2 Rajang r. Sarawak Malaysia
123 G4 Rajanpur Pak.
114 C4 Rajapalaiyam Tamil Nadu India
114 B2 Rajapur Mahar. India
116 C4 Rajasthan state India
117 F4 Rajauli Bihar India
117 G5 Rajbari Bangl.
176 F2 Rájec Czech Rep.
177 H2 Rajec Slovakia
177 H2 Rajecká Lesná Slovakia
116 D4 Rajgarh Madh. Prad. India
114 B2 Rajgarh Mahar. India
116 C3 Rajgarh Rajasthan India
116 D4 Rajgarh Rajasthan India
117 F4 Rajgir Bihar India
175 K2 Rajgród Pol.
179 H1 Rajhrad Czech Rep.
176 F2 Rajhradice Czech Rep.
116 E5 Rajim Madh. Prad. India
197 E4 Rajince Srbija Yugo.
176 G3 Rajka Hungary
116 B5 Rajkot Gujarat India
117 F4 Rajmahal Bihar India
117 F4 Rajmahal Hills India
116 E5 Raj Nandgaon Madh. Prad. India
116 C5 Rajpipla Gujarat India
116 C5 Rajpur Madh. Prad. India
116 D3 Rajpura Punjab India
Rajputana Agency state India see Rajasthan
116 C4 Rajsamand Rajasthan India
117 G4 Rajshahi Bangl.
117 G4 Rajshahi admin. div. Bangl.
128 C1 Rājū Syria
116 B5 Rajula Gujarat India
116 D5 Rajur Mahar. India
114 C2 Rajura Mahar. India
Rajura Mahar. India see Ahmadpur
111 D6 Raka Xizang China
177 J3 Rakaca r. Hungary
81 □2 Rakahanga atoll Cook Is
Rakahuri r. South I. N.Z. see Ashley
210 A5 Rakai Uganda
81 D5 Rakaia South I. N.Z.
81 D5 Rakaia r. South I. N.Z.
177 K3 Rakamaz Hungary
125 E2 Rakan, Ra's pt Qatar
116 C1 Rakaposhi mt. Jammu and Kashmir
Raka Zangbo r. Xizang China see Dogxung Zangbo
81 A7 Rakeahua, Mount hill Stewart I. N.Z.
179 F5 Rakek Slovenia
Rakhaing state Myanmar see Arakan
Rakhine state Myanmar see Arakan
136 C3 Rakhiv Ukr.
137 G4 Rakhmanivka Ukr.
123 E5 Rakhshan r. Pak.
79 □1a Rakiraki Viti Levu Fiji
197 G4 Rakitnitsa r. Bulg.
135 F6 Rakitnoye Belgorodskaya Oblast' Rus. Fed.
100 E3 Rakitnoye Primorskiy Kray Rus. Fed.
Rakiura i. N.Z. see Stewart Island
138 F2 Rakke Estonia
142 D2 Rakkestad Norway
123 G4 Rakni r. Pak.
177 J4 Rákóczifalva Hungary
177 J4 Rákócziújfalu Hungary
174 E3 Rakoniewice Pol.
177 L3 Rakoshyn Ukr.
177 H2 Raková Slovakia
197 F4 Rakovitsa Bulg.
176 C1 Rakovnická Pahorkatina hills Czech Rep.
176 C1 Rakovník Czech Rep.
197 G4 Rakovski Bulg.
170 E1 Rakow Ger.
175 J5 Raków Pol.
175 K5 Rakszawa Pol.
138 F2 Rakvere Estonia
176 F3 Rakvice Czech Rep.
237 F5 Raleigh MS U.S.A.
231 E5 Raleigh NC U.S.A.
172 A2 Ralingen Ger.
226 D2 Ralph MI U.S.A.
223 I5 Ralston Alta Can.
227 I5 Ralston PA U.S.A.
113 □1 Raluara Giri i. N. Male Maldives
222 F2 Ram r. N.W.T. Can.
128 B3 Rama Israel
242 □I6 Rama Nic.
136 C2 Rama r. Ukr.
194 D5 Ramacca Sicilia Italy
260 B3 Ramada, Cerro de la mt. San Juan Arg.
225 I1 Ramah Nfld. Can.
183 G1 Ramales de la Victoria Spain
184 A1 Ramalhal Port.
254 D5 Ramalho, Serra do hills Brazil
128 B4 Ramallah West Bank
261 G3 Ramallo Arg.
114 C3 Ramanagaram Karnataka India
114 C4 Ramanathapuram Tamil Nadu India
117 E5 Ramanuj Ganj Madh. Prad. India
235 D2 Ramapo r. NJ U.S.A.
215 E1 Ramatlabama S. Africa
161 E5 Ramatuelle France
114 C2 Ramayampet Andhra Prad. India
140 K1 Ramberg Norway
157 G4 Rambervillers France
170 E1 Rambin Ger.
187 B6 Rambla del Judío r. Spain
187 B6 Rambla del Moro r. Spain
156 B4 Rambouillet France
156 B4 Rambouillet, Forêt de for. France
165 E5 Rambrouch Lux.
157 F4 Rambucourt France
114 B3 Ramdurg Karnataka India
150 C4 Rame Cornwall, England U.K.
147 D1 Ramelton Rep. of Ireland
139 L4 Ramenskoye Rus. Fed.
156 E4 Ramerupt France
81 C5 Rameses, Mount South I. N.Z.
139 K3 Rameshki Rus. Fed.
114 C4 Rameswaram Tamil Nadu India
111 B7 Ramganga r. India
117 G5 Ramgarh Bangl.
117 F5 Ramgarh Bihar India
116 B4 Ramgarh Rajasthan India
116 C4 Ramgarh Rajasthan India
116 D4 Ramgarh Rajasthan India
122 B4 Rāmhormoz Iran
165 D4 Ramillies Belgium
84 C2 Ramingining N.T. Austr.
179 E3 Ramingstein Austria
216 □1a Raminho Terceira Azores
182 C2 Ramirás Spain
Ramitan Uzbek. see Romitan
128 B4 Ramla Israel
125 F3 Ramlat al Ghāfah des. Saudi Arabia
125 G3 Ramlat al Wahībah des. Oman
125 F4 Ramlat Amilḩayt des. Oman
124 D4 Ramlat Dahm des. Saudi Arabia/Yemen
128 B5 Ramm, Jabal mts Jordan
172 B2 Rammelsbach Ger.
171 F4 Rammenau Ger.
173 E3 Rammingen Ger.
215 F2 Rammulotsi S. Africa
Ramnad Tamil Nadu India see Ramanathapuram
116 E4 Ramnagar Madh. Prad. India
116 D3 Ramnagar Uttar Prad. India
116 C2 Ramnagar Jammu and Kashmir
143 G2 Ramnäs Sweden
142 D2 Ramnes Norway
197 H3 Râmnicul Sărat r. Romania
197 H3 Râmnicu Sărat Romania
197 G3 Râmnicu Vâlcea Romania
213 E4 Ramokgwebane Botswana
137 J2 Ramon' Rus. Fed.
240 I5 Ramona CA U.S.A.
157 G5 Ramonchamp France
244 C1 Ramón Corona Mex.
163 D5 Ramonville-St-Agne France
227 G1 Ramore Ont. Can.
237 B7 Ramos r. Mex.
243 E3 Ramos Arizpe Mex.
190 F2 Ramosch Switz.
212 E5 Ramotswa Botswana
107 G1 Rampart of Genghis Khan tourist site Asia
149 F3 Rampside Cumbria, England U.K.
111 B6 Rampur Hima. Prad. India
116 D3 Rampur Uttar Prad. India
116 D3 Rampur Uttar Prad. India
116 C4 Rampura Madh. Prad. India
Rampur Boalia Bangl. see Rajshahi
117 F4 Rampur Hat W. Bengal India
96 A3 Ramree Island Myanmar
179 E3 Ramsau am Dachstein Austria
173 G4 Ramsau bei Berchtesgaden Ger.
178 C3 Ramsau im Zillertal Austria
143 F2 Ramsberg Sweden
149 G4 Ramsbottom Greater Manchester, England U.K.
151 F3 Ramsbury Wiltshire, England U.K.
140 L3 Ramsele Sweden
172 C4 Ramsen Switz.
227 F2 Ramsey Ont. Can.
148 E3 Ramsey Isle of Man
151 G2 Ramsey Cambridgeshire, England U.K.
235 D1 Ramsey NJ U.S.A.
148 E3 Ramsey Bay Isle of Man
150 B3 Ramsey Island Wales U.K.
151 G2 Ramsey St Mary's Cambridgeshire, England U.K.
215 H4 Ramsgate S. Africa
151 I3 Ramsgate Kent, England U.K.
117 G4 Ramshai Hat W. Bengal India
122 B4 Rāmshir Iran
117 H3 Ramsing mt. Arun. Prad. India
141 K3 Ramsjö Sweden
168 C2 Ramsloh (Saterland) Ger.
172 B2 Ramstein Ger.
116 D5 Ramtek Mahar. India
117 H5 Ramu Bangl.
91 J7 Ramu r. P.N.G.
140 K3 Ramundberget Sweden
140 L3 Ramvik Sweden
138 E4 Ramygala Lith.
250 D4 Rana, Cerro hill Col.
182 D1 Rañadoiro, Sierra de mts Spain
117 G5 Ranaghat W. Bengal India
Ranai i. HI U.S.A. see Lanai
116 C4 Rana Pratap Sagar resr India
116 C5 Ranapur Madh. Prad. India
142 D1 Rånåsfoss Norway
260 B4 Rancagua Chile
165 D4 Rance Belgium
158 D3 Rance r. France
161 A5 Rance r. France
256 B5 Rancharia Brazil
222 D2 Rancheria Y.T. Can.
222 D2 Rancheria r. Y.T. Can.
238 F2 Ranchester WY U.S.A.
117 F5 Ranchi Bihar India
240 G2 Rancho Cordova CA U.S.A.
261 H4 Ranchos Arg.
239 F4 Ranchos de Taos NM U.S.A.
259 B6 Ranco, Lago l. Chile
234 D3 Rancocas Creek, North Branch r. NJ U.S.A.
234 D3 Rancocas Woods NJ U.S.A.
83 F3 Rand N.S.W. Austr.
232 C5 Rand WV U.S.A.
215 H3 Randalhurst S. Africa
234 B3 Randallstown MD U.S.A.
147 E2 Randalstown Northern Ireland U.K.
160 B2 Randan France
194 D5 Randazzo Sicilia Italy
215 F2 Randburg S. Africa
179 F2 Randegg Austria
142 D3 Randers Denmark
172 D2 Randersacker Ger.
215 F2 Randfontein S. Africa
233 H3 Randolph MA U.S.A.
233 □I2 Randolph ME U.S.A.
232 D3 Randolph NY U.S.A.
238 E3 Randolph UT U.S.A.
233 G3 Randolph VT U.S.A.
159 G3 Randonnai France
170 F2 Randow r. Ger.
240 I4 Randsburg CA U.S.A.
141 K3 Randsjö Sweden
215 G2 Randvaal S. Africa
140 M2 Råneå Sweden
159 F3 Rânes France
81 C6 Ranfurly South I. N.Z.
117 H4 Ranga r. India
97 C6 Rangae Thai.
117 H5 Rangamati Bangl.
117 H4 Rangapara North Assam India
233 □H2 Rangeley ME U.S.A.
241 M1 Rangely CO U.S.A.
172 C3 Rangendingen Ger.
224 D4 Ranger Lake Ont. Can.
178 D4 Rangersdorf Austria
116 E5 Rangi Mahar. India
117 G4 Rangia Patharughat Assam India
Rangiauria i. Chatham Is S. Pacific Ocean see Pitt Island
81 D5 Rangiora South I. N.Z.
80 F2 Rangipoua mt. North I. N.Z.
79 □3 Rangiroa atoll Arch. des Tuamotu Fr. Polynesia
80 F3 Rangitaiki North I. N.Z.
80 F2 Rangitaiki r. North I. N.Z.
81 C6 Rangitata South I. N.Z.
81 C6 Rangitata r. South I. N.Z.
80 E4 Rangitikei r. North I. N.Z.
80 E3 Rangiwaea Junction North I. N.Z.
80 E3 Rangiwahia North I. N.Z.
94 D4 Rangkasbitung Jawa Barat Indon.
Rangke Sichuan China see Zamtang
Rangôn Myanmar see Yangôn
Rangôn admin. div. Myanmar see Yangôn
Rangoon Myanmar see Yangôn
Rangoon admin. div. Myanmar see Yangôn
96 B3 Rangoon r. Myanmar
117 G4 Rangpur Bangl.
94 C2 Rangsang i. Indon.
171 E3 Rangsdorf Ger.
182 C4 Ranhados Port.
116 C4 Rani Rajasthan India
116 C3 Rania Haryana India
114 B3 Ranibennur Karnataka India
226 A1 Ranier City MN U.S.A.
117 F5 Raniganj W. Bengal India
117 E5 Ranijula Peak Madh. Prad. India
116 D3 Ranikhet Uttar Prad. India
123 G5 Ranipur Pak.
171 C5 Ranis Ger.
116 C4 Raniwara Rajasthan India
175 J5 Ranizów Pol.
237 C6 Rankin TX U.S.A.
223 M2 Rankin Inlet Nunavut Can.
83 F3 Rankin's Springs N.S.W. Austr.
Rankovićevo Srbija Yugo. see Kraljevo
178 A3 Rankweil Austria
85 G5 Rannes Qld Austr.
120 C2 Ranneye Rus. Fed.
146 D5 Rannoch, Loch l. Scotland U.K.
146 D5 Rannoch Moor moorland Scotland U.K.
146 D5 Rannoch Station Perth and Kinross, Scotland U.K.
116 B4 Rann of Kachchh marsh India
207 H4 Rano Nigeria
78 □6 Rano, Mount New Georgia Is Solomon Is
213 □J3 Ranobe r. Madag.
213 □K3 Ranomafana Madag.
213 □J4 Ranomena Madag.
97 B5 Ranong Thai.
78 □6 Ranongga i. New Georgia Is Solomon Is
213 □J5 Ranopiso Madag.
97 C6 Ranot Thai.
139 M4 Ranova r. Rus. Fed.
116 B5 Ranpur Gujarat India
169 C5 Ransbach-Baumbach Ger.
142 E1 Ransby Sweden
149 H4 Ranskill Nottinghamshire, England U.K.
226 C5 Ransom IL U.S.A.
234 C1 Ransom PA U.S.A.
165 D3 Ranst Belgium
213 □K2 Rantabe Madag.
141 O3 Rantasalmi Fin.
95 F3 Rantau Kalimantan Selatan Indon.
94 C2 Rantau i. Indon.
94 B2 Rantauprapat Sumatera Indon.
93 B3 Rantemario, Gunung mt. Indon.
179 F3 Ranten Austria
93 A3 Rantepao Sulawesi Selatan Indon.
226 C5 Rantoul IL U.S.A.
168 E1 Rantrum Ger.
139 J3 Rantsevo Rus. Fed.
140 N2 Rantsila Fin.
168 D1 Rantum Ger.
140 N2 Ranua Fin.
142 C3 Ranum Denmark
196 D5 Ranxë Albania
127 G3 Rānya Iraq
96 D3 Rao Go mt. Laos/Vietnam
100 E3 Raohe Heilong. China
157 G4 Raon-l'Étape France
191 G3 Raossi Italy
77 I4 Raoul Island N.Z.
79 □3 Rapa i. Îs Australes Fr. Polynesia
140 L2 Rapaälven r. Sweden
Rapa-iti i. Îs Australes Fr. Polynesia see Rapa
190 E4 Rapallo Italy
116 B5 Rapar Gujarat India
116 D3 Rapar Punjab India
260 B3 Rapel r. Chile
148 B4 Rapemills Rep. of Ireland
147 D2 Raphoe Rep. of Ireland
232 E5 Rapidan r. VA U.S.A.
82 D3 Rapid Bay S.A. Austr.
236 C2 Rapid City SD U.S.A.
227 H2 Rapide-Deux Que. Can.
227 H2 Rapide-Sept Que. Can.
193 F3 Rapido r. Italy
226 D3 Rapid River MI U.S.A.
138 F2 Räpina Estonia
252 D2 Rapirrān r. Brazil
138 E2 Rapla Estonia
191 G5 Rapolano Terme Italy
193 H4 Rapolla Italy
184 B1 Raposa Port.
176 G1 Rapotín Czech Rep.
182 C4 Rapoula do Côa Port.
232 E6 Rappahannock r. VA U.S.A.
93 A3 Rappang Sulawesi Selatan Indon.
169 F4 Rappbodetalstausee resr Ger.
172 C4 Rapperswil Switz.
179 G2 Rappottenstein Austria
116 E4 Rapti r. India
252 D3 Rapulo r. Bol.
114 C3 Rapur Andhra Prad. India
116 B5 Rapur Gujarat India
Raqqa Syria see Ar Raqqah
233 F2 Raquette r. NY U.S.A.
84 D1 Raragala Island N.T. Austr.
156 C3 Raray France
234 D2 Raritan, South Branch r. NJ U.S.A.
79 □3 Raroia atoll Arch. des Tuamotu Fr. Polynesia
190 C2 Raron Switz.
81 □3 Rarotonga i. Cook Is
116 C4 Ras Rajasthan India
191 J3 Raša Croatia
188 E3 Raša r. Croatia
125 G4 Ra's ad Daqm Oman
125 G3 Ra's al Ḩadd Oman
125 F2 Ras al Khaimah U.A.E.
Ra's al Khaymah U.A.E. see Ras al Khaimah
124 C3 Raşan, Jabal hill Saudi Arabia
183 G4 Rascafría Spain
Râşcani Moldova see Rîşcani
171 D5 Raschau Ger.
210 C1 Ras Dashen mt. Eth.
169 E5 Rasdorf Ger.
138 D4 Raseiniai Lith.
206 D2 Râs el Mâ Mali
113 □1 Rasfaree i. N. Male Maldives
203 G2 Râs Ghârib Egypt
106 A2 Rashaant Bayan-Ölgiy Mongolia
106 E2 Rashaant Dundgovĭ Mongolia
210 A2 Rashad Sudan
147 E2 Rasharkin Northern Ireland U.K.
147 D2 Rashedoge Rep. of Ireland
203 F2 Rashîd Egypt
137 G2 Rashivka Ukr.
215 F1 Rashoop S. Africa
122 B2 Rasht Iran
196 E4 Rasina r. Yugo.
183 G1 Rasines Spain
141 K3 Råsjö Sweden
123 E5 Rāsk Balūchestān va Sīstān Iran
196 E4 Raška Srbija Yugo.
111 A4 Raskam mts China
123 F4 Ras Koh mt. Pak.
123 F4 Raskoh mts Pak.
177 H2 Raškovice Czech Rep.
177 K2 Raslavice Slovakia

221 I3 Rasmussen Basin sea feature Nunavut Can.
197 G3 Râşnov Romania
206 □ Raso i. Cape Verde
254 F4 Raso da Catarina hills Brazil
87 E6 Rason Lake salt flat W.A. Austr.
138 G4 Rasony Belarus
197 H3 Rasova Romania
197 F4 Rasovo Bulg.
171 G5 Raspenava Czech Rep.
186 D3 Rasquera Spain
117 E4 Rasra Uttar Prad. India
124 B2 Ra's Sāq, Jabal hill Saudi Arabia
125 G3 Ra's Şirāb Oman
189 C7 Rass Jebel Tunisia
135 H5 Rasskazovo Rus. Fed.
197 F4 Rast Romania
139 H5 Rasta r. Belarus
125 E2 Ras Tannūrah Saudi Arabia
172 C3 Rastatt Ger.
168 C3 Rastdorf Ger.
142 C3 Råsted Denmark
168 D2 Rastede Ger.
171 C4 Rastenberg Ger.
179 G2 Rastenfeld Austria
178 C3 Rastkogel mt. Austria
Rastorguyevo Rus. Fed. see Vidnoye
170 C2 Rastow Ger.
183 E3 Rasueros Spain
174 F4 Raszków Pol.
137 I2 Rat' r. Rus. Fed.
80 E3 Rata North I. N.Z.
Ratae Leicester, England U.K. see Leicester
94 D4 Ratai, Gunung mt. Indon.
138 F5 Ratamka Belarus
215 G2 Ratanda S. Africa
116 C4 Ratangarh Madh. Prad. India
116 C3 Ratangarh Rajasthan India
116 C5 Ratanpur Gujarat India
116 E5 Ratanpur Madh. Prad. India
141 K3 Rätansbyn Sweden
97 B4 Rat Buri Thai.
139 L5 Ratchino Lipetskaya Oblast' Rus. Fed.
120 C1 Ratchino Orenburgskaya Oblast' Rus. Fed.
168 F2 Ratekau Ger.
214 B4 Ratelfontein S. Africa
182 B3 Rates Port.
116 D4 Rath Uttar Prad. India
148 B4 Rath Rep. of Ireland
147 E3 Rathangan Rep. of Ireland
147 C3 Rathcabban Rep. of Ireland
147 D3 Rathconrath Rep. of Ireland
147 C4 Rathcool Rep. of Ireland
147 E3 Rathcoole Rep. of Ireland
147 C4 Rathcormack Rep. of Ireland
148 C5 Rathdangan Rep. of Ireland
147 D4 Rathdowney Rep. of Ireland
147 E4 Rathdrum Rep. of Ireland
96 A2 Rathedaung Myanmar
170 D3 Rathenow Ger.
150 A1 Rathfarnham Rep. of Ireland
147 E2 Rathfriland Northern Ireland U.K.
146 E5 Rathillet Fife, Scotland U.K.
147 C4 Rathkeale Rep. of Ireland
147 D4 Rathkeevin Rep. of Ireland
147 B2 Rathlackan Rep. of Ireland
147 B2 Rathlee Rep. of Ireland
147 E1 Rathlin Island Northern Ireland U.K.
147 C4 Rathluirc Rep. of Ireland
147 E3 Rathmolyon Rep. of Ireland
147 B4 Rathmore Rep. of Ireland
147 D1 Rathmullan Rep. of Ireland
147 E4 Rathnew Rep. of Ireland
146 E6 Ratho Edinburgh, Scotland U.K.
147 D3 Rathowen Rep. of Ireland
Ratibor Pol. see Racibórz
169 B4 Ratingen Ger.
Ratisbon Ger. see Regensburg
188 E2 Ratitovec mt. Slovenia
116 C3 Ratiya Haryana India
177 K3 Rátka Hungary
116 C5 Ratlam Madh. Prad. India
114 B2 Ratnagiri Mahar. India
114 D5 Ratnapura Sri Lanka
136 C2 Ratne Ukr.
Ratno Ukr. see Ratne
148 C4 Ratoath Rep. of Ireland
123 G5 Rato Dero Pak.
239 F4 Raton NM U.S.A.
169 F5 Rattelsdorf Ger.
179 G3 Ratten Austria
146 E5 Rattray Perth and Kinross, Scotland U.K.
141 K3 Rättvik Sweden
222 C3 Ratz, Mount B.C. Can.
168 F2 Ratzeburg Ger.
168 F2 Ratzeburger See l. Ger.
171 C3 Rätzlingen Ger.
94 C2 Raub Malaysia
169 C5 Raubach Ger.
173 G4 Raubling Ger.
261 H5 Rauch Arg.
234 A1 Rauchtown PA U.S.A.
157 E3 Raucourt-et-Flaba France
140 N2 Raudanjoki r. Fin.
197 F3 Râu de Mori Romania
127 G5 Raudhatain Kuwait
138 E2 Raudna r. Estonia
138 D4 Raudondvaris Lith.
171 F3 Rauen Ger.
172 C2 Rauenberg Ger.
171 C5 Rauenstein Ger.
173 E2 Rauhe Ebrach r. Ger.
80 F2 Raukokore North I. N.Z.
80 G2 Raukumara mt. North I. N.Z.
80 F3 Raukumara Range mts North I. N.Z.
117 E5 Raul r. India
161 A4 Raulhac France
257 F4 Raul Soares Brazil
141 M3 Rauma Fin.
81 E4 Raumati North I. N.Z.
138 E3 Rauna Latvia
151 G2 Raunds Northamptonshire, England U.K.
80 E3 Raurimu North I. N.Z.
178 D3 Rauris Austria
117 F5 Raurkela Orissa India
Rauschen Kaliningradskaya Oblast' Rus. Fed. see Svetlogorsk
169 D5 Rauschenberg Ger.
102 L1 Rausu-dake mt. Japan
136 E4 Răut r. Moldova
191 H2 Raut, Monte mt. Italy
140 N3 Rautalampi Fin.
140 O3 Rautavaara Fin.
171 D5 Rautenkranz Ger.
141 O3 Rautjärvi Fin.
Rauza Mahar. India see Khuldabad
163 E4 Rauzan France
79 □3 Ravahéré atoll Arch. des Tuamotu Fr. Polynesia
238 E2 Ravalli MT U.S.A.
122 A3 Ravānsar Iran
194 C5 Ravanusa Sicilia Italy
122 E4 Rāvar Iran
136 B2 Rava-Rus'ka Ukr.
193 G4 Ravello Italy
165 D3 Ravels Belgium
179 G2 Ravelsbach Austria
143 F3 Rävemåla Sweden
233 G3 Ravena NY U.S.A.
149 F3 Ravenglass Cumbria, England U.K.
191 H4 Ravenna Italy
191 H4 Ravenna prov. Emilia-Romagna Italy
236 D3 Ravenna NE U.S.A.
232 C4 Ravenna OH U.S.A.
234 C2 Raven Rock NJ U.S.A.
172 D4 Ravensburg Ger.
148 C3 Ravensdale Rep. of Ireland
85 F3 Ravenshoe Qld Austr.
164 E3 Ravenstein Neth.
87 D7 Ravensthorpe W.A. Austr.
149 G3 Ravenstonedale Cumbria, England U.K.
85 F4 Ravenswood Qld Austr.
232 C5 Ravenswood WV U.S.A.
116 D5 Raver Mahar. India
123 G4 Ravi r. Pak.
156 E5 Ravières France
234 B2 Ravine PA U.S.A.
188 E3 Ravna Gora Croatia
188 F3 Ravna Gora hill Croatia
179 G4 Ravne Slovenia
179 F4 Ravne na Koroškem Slovenia
123 E2 Ravnina Turkm.
120 D4 Ravshan Uzbek.
168 E1 Ravsted Denmark
127 F4 Rāwah Iraq
77 I2 Rawaki i. Phoenix Is Kiribati
123 H3 Rawala Kot Pak.
123 H3 Rawalpindi Pak.
175 I4 Rawa Mazowiecka Pol.
127 G3 Rawāndiz Iraq
94 C3 Rawas r. Indon.
116 C3 Rawatsar Rajasthan India
149 I4 Rawcliffe East Riding of Yorkshire, England U.K.
149 H4 Rawcliffe York, England U.K.
124 D5 Rawdah Yemen
174 E4 Rawicz Pol.
175 I4 Rawka r. Pol.
87 E6 Rawlinna W.A. Austr.
238 F3 Rawlins WY U.S.A.
87 E5 Rawlinson, Mount hill W.A. Austr.
87 F5 Rawlinson Range hills W.A. Austr.
149 H4 Rawmarsh South Yorkshire, England U.K.
Rawnina Turkm. see Ravnina
261 G4 Rawson Buenos Aires Arg.
259 D6 Rawson Chubut Arg.
262 N1 Rawson Mountains Antarctica
214 B5 Rawsonville S. Africa
149 G4 Rawtenstall Lancashire, England U.K.
117 F4 Raxaul Bihar India
226 A1 Ray MN U.S.A.
95 E3 Raya, Bukit mt. Kalimantan Indon.
95 F3 Raya, Bukit mt. Kalimantan Indon.
114 C3 Rayachoti Andhra Prad. India
114 C3 Rayadurg Andhra Prad. India
115 D2 Rayagarha Orissa India
128 C3 Rayak Lebanon
100 D2 Raychikhinsk Rus. Fed.
139 K2 Rayda Rus. Fed.
124 D5 Raydah Yemen
122 D4 Rāyen Iran
240 H4 Rayes Peak CA U.S.A.
120 C1 Rayevskiy Rus. Fed.
137 F3 Rayhorod Ukr.
137 J3 Rayhorodka Ukr.
137 I3 Rayhorodok Ukr.
151 H3 Rayleigh Essex, England U.K.
222 H5 Raymond Alta Can.
233 H3 Raymond NH U.S.A.
238 B2 Raymond WA U.S.A.
83 G3 Raymond Terrace N.S.W. Austr.
237 D7 Raymondville TX U.S.A.
223 J5 Raymore Sask. Can.
117 F5 Rayna W. Bengal India
151 H3 Rayne Essex, England U.K.
161 E5 Rayol-Canadel-sur-Mer France
245 E3 Rayón Mex.
243 E3 Rayones Mex.
97 C4 Rayong Thai.
125 F4 Raysūt Oman
215 G1 Rayton S. Africa
237 F5 Rayville LA U.S.A.
124 B3 Rayyis Saudi Arabia
158 B3 Raz, Pointe du pt France
162 C3 Razac-sur-l'Isle France
115 D2 Razam Andhra Prad. India
122 B3 Razan Iran
197 E4 Ražanj Srbija Yugo.
127 F4 Razāzah, Buḩayrat ar l. Iraq
Razdan Armenia see Hrazdan
Razdel'naya Ukr. see Rozdil'na
100 D4 Razdol'noye Rus. Fed.
122 B3 Razeh Iran
162 D2 Razès France
197 H4 Razgrad Bulg.
111 E6 Razhêng Zangbo r. Xizang China
197 I3 Razim, Lacul lag. Romania
197 F5 Razlog Bulg.
138 F3 Rāznas l. Latvia
177 H3 Ráztočno Slovakia
137 I2 Razumnoye Rus. Fed.
Raz"yezd 3km Rus. Fed. see Novyy Urgal
162 A2 Ré, Île de i. France
150 E2 Rea Brook r. England U.K.
246 □ Reading Jamaica
151 G3 Reading Reading, England U.K.
151 G3 Reading admin. div. England U.K.
226 E5 Reading MI U.S.A.
232 A5 Reading OH U.S.A.
234 C2 Reading PA U.S.A.
234 D2 Readington NJ U.S.A.
233 G3 Readsboro VT U.S.A.
226 B4 Readstown WI U.S.A.
147 E3 Reaghstown Rep. of Ireland
215 F1 Reagile S. Africa
254 F4 Real r. Brazil
182 B1 Real Spain
260 D4 Real de Padre Arg.
195 G2 Reale, Canale r. Italy
185 E4 Reales mt. Spain
261 E4 Realicó Arg.
163 E5 Réalmont France
194 C5 Realmonte Sicilia Italy
163 D4 Réalville France
234 B2 Reamstown PA U.S.A.
97 C4 Reăng Kesei Cambodia
79 □3 Reao atoll Arch. des Tuamotu Fr. Polynesia
Reate Italy see Rieti
163 C4 Réaup France
234 D2 Reaville NJ U.S.A.
146 E3 Reay Highland, Scotland U.K.
156 D4 Rebais France
140 L1 Rebbenesøy i. Norway
87 D6 Rebecca, Lake salt flat W.A. Austr.
165 D4 Rebecq Belgium
163 B5 Rébénacq France
163 E6 Rébenty r. France
Rebiana Sand Sea des. Libya see Rabyānah, Ramlat
185 F2 Rebollera mt. Spain
183 G3 Rebollo Spain
183 H3 Rebollosa de Jadraque Spain
182 C3 Rebordelo Port.
182 B1 Rebordelo Spain
121 J1 Rebrikha Rus. Fed.
194 D1 Recale Italy
191 I5 Recanati Italy
197 E3 Recaş Romania
183 G4 Recas Spain
190 E4 Recco Italy
136 E4 Recea Moldova
147 B3 Recess Rep. of Ireland
157 E5 Recey-sur-Ource France
87 D7 Recherche, Archipelago of the is W.A. Austr.
157 G4 Réchicourt-le-Château France
Rechitsa Homyel'skaya Voblasts' Belarus see Rechytsa
170 D2 Rechlin Ger.
123 H4 Rechna Doab lowland Pak.
179 H3 Rechnitz Austria
165 F4 Recht Belgium
172 D2 Rechtenbach Ger.
168 C2 Rechtsupweg Ger.
136 D2 Rechytsa Brestskaya Voblasts' Belarus
136 F1 Rechytsa Homyel'skaya Voblasts' Belarus
179 G4 Rečica Slovenia
254 G4 Recife Brazil
169 C3 Recke Ger.
190 D2 Reckingen Switz.
169 C4 Recklinghausen Ger.
170 D1 Recknitz r. Ger.
191 G3 Recoaro Terme Italy
258 F3 Reconquista Arg.
161 D4 Recoubeau-Jansac France
161 A4 Recoules-Prévinquières France
257 F4 Recreio Brazil
258 D3 Recreo Catamarca Arg.
261 G2 Recreo Santa Fé Arg.
177 J4 Recsk Hungary
232 B5 Rectorville KY U.S.A.
183 H3 Recuerda Spain
174 D2 Recz Pol.
175 H4 Ręczno Pol.
85 E3 Red r. Qld Austr.
222 E3 Red r. B.C. Can.
223 L5 Red r. Can./U.S.A.
237 F6 Red r. U.S.A.
237 D5 Red, North Fork r. OK U.S.A.
174 G1 Reda Pol.
174 G1 Reda r. Pol.
165 E5 Redange Lux.
235 D2 Red Bank NJ U.S.A.
231 C5 Red Bank TN U.S.A.
Red Basin Sichuan China see Sichuan Pendi
225 J3 Red Bay Nfld. Can.
87 C5 Red Bluff hill W.A. Austr.
240 F1 Red Bluff CA U.S.A.
151 G3 Redbourn Hertfordshire, England U.K.
241 K4 Red Butte mt. AZ U.S.A.
149 H3 Redcar Redcar and Cleveland, England U.K.
149 H3 Redcar and Cleveland admin. div. England U.K.
148 B2 Redcastle Rep. of Ireland
223 I5 Redcliff Alta Can.
226 B2 Red Cliff WI U.S.A.
213 F3 Redcliff Zimbabwe
150 E3 Redcliff Bay North Somerset, England U.K.
85 H5 Redcliffe Qld Austr.
87 D6 Redcliffe, Mount hill W.A. Austr.
83 E3 Red Cliffs Vic. Austr.
236 D3 Red Cloud NE U.S.A.
147 E4 Redcross Rep. of Ireland
222 H4 Red Deer Alta Can.
222 I5 Red Deer r. Alberta/Saskatchewan Can.
223 K4 Red Deer r. Man./Sask. Can.
170 C1 Reddelich Ger.
215 F3 Reddersburg S. Africa
238 B3 Redding CA U.S.A.
235 E1 Redding CT U.S.A.
235 E1 Redding Ridge CT U.S.A.
151 F2 Redditch Worcestershire, England U.K.
149 G2 Rede r. England U.K.
222 H3 Red Earth Creek Alta Can.
170 C2 Redefin Ger.
214 B5 Redelinghuys S. Africa
254 C3 Redenção Brazil
254 D4 Redenção Brazil
158 C4 Rédené France
161 C5 Redessan France
205 H2 Redeyef Tunisia
236 D2 Redfield SD U.S.A.
146 F5 Redford Angus, Scotland U.K.
222 B2 Red Granite Mountain Y.T. Can.
82 D3 Redhill S.A. Austr.
151 G3 Redhill Surrey, England U.K.
234 C2 Red Hill PA U.S.A.
147 D2 Redhills Rep. of Ireland
237 D4 Red Hills KS U.S.A.
233 G4 Red Hook NY U.S.A.
176 F5 Rédics Hungary
157 H4 Réding France
Redingen Lux. see Redange
182 B4 Redinha Port.
230 C3 Redkey IN U.S.A.
139 K3 Redkino Rus. Fed.
222 G2 Redknife r. N.W.T. Can.
223 M5 Red Lake Ont. Can.
241 K4 Red Lake AZ U.S.A.
236 E2 Red Lake MN U.S.A.
236 D2 Red Lake r. MN U.S.A.
236 D2 Red Lake Falls MN U.S.A.
236 E1 Red Lakes MN U.S.A.
240 I4 Redlands CA U.S.A.
234 D3 Red Lion NJ U.S.A.
234 B3 Red Lion PA U.S.A.
238 E2 Red Lodge MT U.S.A.
151 F4 Redlynch Wiltshire, England U.K.
238 B2 Redmond OR U.S.A.
241 L2 Redmond UT U.S.A.
173 E2 Rednitz r. Ger.
173 F2 Rednitzhembach Ger.
236 E3 Red Oak IA U.S.A.
235 E1 Red Oaks Mill NY U.S.A.
158 D4 Redon France
182 B2 Redondela Spain
182 C3 Redondelo Port.
184 C2 Redondo Port.
240 H5 Redondo Beach CA U.S.A.
238 D2 Red Peak MT U.S.A.
146 C4 Redpoint Highland, Scotland U.K.
Red River r. Vietnam see Hông, Sông
Red River, Mouths of the Vietnam see Hong, Mouths of the
224 B3 Red Rock Ont. Can.
241 L5 Red Rock AZ U.S.A.
227 I5 Red Rock PA U.S.A.
238 D2 Red Rock r. MT U.S.A.
87 E7 Red Rocks Point W.A. Austr.
150 C3 Red Roses Carmarthenshire, Wales U.K.
150 B4 Redruth Cornwall, England U.K.
124 A2 Red Sea Africa/Asia
203 G5 Red Sea state Sudan
222 F4 Redstone B.C. Can.
222 E1 Redstone r. N.W.T. Can.
227 G1 Redstone r. Ont. Can.
206 E4 Red Volta r. Burkina/Ghana
238 F1 Redwater r. MT U.S.A.
240 F1 Redway CA U.S.A.
236 C3 Red Willow Creek r. NE U.S.A.
225 J2 Red Wine r. Nfld. Can.
226 A3 Red Wing MN U.S.A.
171 C5 Redwitz an der Rodach Ger.
240 F3 Redwood City CA U.S.A.
236 E2 Redwood Falls MN U.S.A.
240 F2 Redwood Valley CA U.S.A.
175 H5 Rędziny Pol.
147 D3 Ree, Lough l. Rep. of Ireland
226 E4 Reed City MI U.S.A.
240 H3 Reedley CA U.S.A.
226 C4 Reedsburg WI U.S.A.
238 A3 Reedsport OR U.S.A.
232 C5 Reedsville OH U.S.A.
232 E4 Reedsville PA U.S.A.
233 E6 Reedville VA U.S.A.
232 C5 Reedy WV U.S.A.
81 C5 Reefton South I. N.Z.
147 C4 Reens Rep. of Ireland
151 I2 Reepham Norfolk, England U.K.
169 B4 Rees Ger.
227 F4 Reese MI U.S.A.
240 I1 Reese r. NV U.S.A.
168 E2 Reeßum Ger.
170 C2 Reetz Brandenburg Ger.
171 D3 Reetz Brandenburg Ger.
164 D2 Reeuwijksebrug Neth.
126 E3 Refahiye Turkey
182 B3 Refóios do Lima Port.
237 F5 Reform AL U.S.A.
243 G5 Reforma Mex.
234 B3 Refton PA U.S.A.
237 D6 Refugio TX U.S.A.
174 D1 Rega r. Pol.
182 B3 Regadas Port.
194 D5 Regalbuto Sicilia Italy
186 C3 Regallo r. Spain
179 E3 Regau Austria
173 H3 Regen Ger.
173 G2 Regen r. Ger.
173 G2 Regensburg Ger.
190 D1 Regensdorf Switz.
173 G2 Regenstauf Ger.
256 B5 Regente Feijó Brazil
205 F4 Reggane Alg.
164 F2 Regge r. Neth.
191 G5 Reggello Italy
Reggio Calabria Italy see Reggio di Calabria
Reggio Emilia-Romagna Italy see Reggio nell'Emilia
195 E4 Reggio di Calabria Calabria Italy
195 F4 Reggio di Calabria prov. Calabria Italy
Reggio Emilia Emilia-Romagna Italy see Reggio nell'Emilia
191 F4 Reggio nell'Emilia Emilia-Romagna Italy
191 F4 Reggio nell'Emilia prov. Emilia-Romagna Italy
197 G2 Reghin Romania
186 A1 Regil Spain
175 I3 Regimin Pol.
223 J5 Regina Sask. Can.
251 H3 Régina Fr. Guiana
256 D6 Registro Brazil
Regium Lepidum Emilia-Romagna Italy see Reggio nell'Emilia
171 D5 Regnitzlosau Ger.
160 C3 Régny France
182 B2 Reguengo Spain
184 C2 Reguengos de Monsaraz Port.
158 D4 Réguiny France
171 D5 Rehau Ger.
169 E3 Rehburg (Rehburg-Loccum) Ger.
168 D3 Rehden Ger.
116 D5 Rehli Madh. Prad. India
173 E3 Rehling Ger.
172 A2 Rehlingen-Siersburg Ger.
171 E5 Řehlovice Czech Rep.
170 C2 Rehna Ger.
212 C4 Rehoboth Namibia
233 F5 Rehoboth Bay DE U.S.A.
233 F5 Rehoboth Beach DE U.S.A.
157 F3 Réhon France
128 B4 Rehovot Israel
Reïbell Alg. see Ksar Chellala
171 D4 Reibitz Ger.
173 E2 Reiche Ebrach r. Ger.
172 C2 Reichelsheim (Odenwald) Ger.
169 D5 Reichelsheim (Wetterau) Ger.
172 D4 Reichenau Ger.
179 G3 Reichenau an der Rax Austria
172 C2 Reichenbach Hessen Ger.
171 D5 Reichenbach Sachsen Ger.
190 C2 Reichenbach Switz.
171 F4 Reichenbach (Oberlausitz) Ger.
172 D2 Reichenberg Ger.
179 F3 Reichenfels Austria
169 F4 Reichensachsen (Wehretal) Ger.
173 F2 Reichenschwand Ger.
178 D3 Reichenspitze mt. Austria
179 F2 Reichenthal Austria
173 F3 Reichertshausen Ger.
173 G3 Reichertsheim Ger.
173 F3 Reichertshofen Ger.
173 E4 Reichling Ger.
171 C5 Reichmannsdorf Ger.
172 D2 Reicholzheim Ger.
179 F3 Reichraming Austria
157 H4 Reichshoffen France
157 H4 Reichstett France
87 F6 Reid W.A. Austr.
190 C1 Reiden Switz.
146 C4 Reidh, Rubha pt Scotland U.K.
231 D5 Reidsville GA U.S.A.
231 E4 Reidsville NC U.S.A.
182 D4 Reigada Port.
151 G3 Reigate Surrey, England U.K.
162 B3 Reignac France
160 E2 Reignier France
169 C5 Reil Ger.
241 L5 Reiley Peak AZ U.S.A.
163 D4 Reilhaguet France
172 C2 Reilingen Ger.
161 D5 Reillanne France
183 I5 Reillo Spain
156 E3 Reims France
184 E2 Reina Spain
190 D1 Reinach Aargau Switz.
190 C1 Reinach Basselland Switz.
142 B2 Reinaknuten hill Norway
168 F2 Reinbek Ger.
170 E1 Reinberg Ger.
223 K4 Reindeer r. Sask. Can.
223 K3 Reindeer Lake Man./Sask. Can.
140 K2 Reine Norway
232 C5 Reinersville OH U.S.A.
141 J3 Reineskarvet mt. Norway
168 F2 Reinfeld (Holstein) Ger.
80 D1 Reinga, Cape North I. N.Z.
172 C2 Reinheim Ger.
234 B2 Reinholds PA U.S.A.
183 F2 Reinosa Spain
160 C2 Reins r. France
171 D4 Reinsdorf Sachsen-Anhalt Ger.
171 C4 Reinsdorf Thüringen Ger.
172 A2 Reinsfeld Ger.
142 B2 Reinsnosi mt. Norway
140 □B2 Reiphólsfjöll hill Iceland
Reirson Island atoll Cook Is see Rakahanga
173 G3 Reisbach Ger.
173 G3 Reischach Ger.
140 N3 Reisjärvi Fin.
169 D5 Reiskirchen Ger.
234 B3 Reisterstown MD U.S.A.
194 D5 Reitano Sicilia Italy
164 F1 Reitdiep r. Neth.
173 G4 Reit im Winkl Ger.
215 G2 Reitz S. Africa
215 F2 Reitzburg S. Africa
138 E2 Reiu r. Estonia
214 E2 Reivilo S. Africa
143 F2 Rejmyre Sweden
175 L4 Rejowiec Pol.
175 L4 Rejowiec Fabryczny Pol.
179 H4 Reka Croatia
191 J3 Reka r. Slovenia
114 D2 Rekapalle Andhra Prad. India
169 C4 Reken Ger.
164 F2 Rekken Neth.
175 M5 Reklynets' Ukr.
196 E4 Rekovac Srbija Yugo.
175 M6 Rekshyn Ukr.
142 C1 Reksjåeggi mt. Norway
138 D4 Rekyvos ežeras l. Lith.
223 I2 Reliance N.W.T. Can.
184 B3 Relíquias Port.
205 F2 Relizane Alg.
187 C6 Relleu Spain
115 D2 Relli Andhra Prad. India
168 E2 Rellingen Ger.
216 □1b Relva São Miguel Azores
177 I5 Rém Hungary
169 C5 Remagen Ger.
159 G3 Rémalard France
82 D3 Remarkable, Mount hill S.A. Austr.
95 E4 Rembang Jawa Tengah Indon.
157 F4 Rembercourt-Sommaisne France
171 C5 Remda Ger.
216 □1b Remédios São Miguel Azores
246 C2 Remedios Cuba
205 H3 Remel el Abiod des. Tunisia
168 C2 Remels (Uplengen) Ger.
236 E2 Remer MN U.S.A.
122 D5 Remeshk Iran
177 L5 Remetea Romania
177 K6 Remetea Mare Romania
197 F2 Remeţi Romania
179 H4 Remetinec Croatia
Remi France see Reims
165 F5 Remich Lux.
165 E4 Remicourt Belgium
157 E3 Remilly-Aillicourt France
232 E5 Remington VA U.S.A.
251 H3 Rémire Fr. Guiana
217 □2 Rémire i. Seychelles
157 G4 Remiremont France
169 F3 Remlingen Ger.
238 B1 Remmel Mountain WA U.S.A.
186 B3 Remolinos Spain
157 G4 Remoncourt France
135 H7 Remontnoye Rus. Fed.
165 E4 Remouchamps Belgium
161 C5 Remoulins France
170 D2 Remplin Ger.
171 C5 Remptendorf Ger.
172 D3 Rems r. Ger.
169 C4 Remscheid Ger.
178 B4 Remulo r. Italy
158 D4 Remungol France
226 E4 Remus MI U.S.A.
161 D4 Rémuzat France
141 J3 Rena Norway
141 J3 Rena r. Norway
184 E1 Rena Spain
227 F1 Renabie Ont. Can.
161 D3 Renage France
260 A5 Renaico Chile
160 B2 Renaison France
Renaix Belgium see Ronse
114 C2 Renapur Mahar. India
159 E4 Renazé France
172 C3 Renchen Ger.
Rende Yunnan China see Xundian
193 I5 Rende Italy
78 □6 Rendova i. New Georgia Is Solomon Is
168 E1 Rendsburg Ger.
183 G1 Renedo Cantabria Spain
183 F3 Renedo Castilla y León Spain
183 F2 Renedo de la Vega Spain
190 B2 Renens Switz.
164 C3 Renesse Neth.
225 K4 Renews Nfld. Can.
224 E4 Renfrew Ont. Can.
146 D6 Renfrew Renfrewshire, Scotland U.K.
146 D6 Renfrewshire admin. div. Scotland U.K.
94 C3 Rengat Sumatera Indon.
260 B4 Rengo Chile
169 C5 Rengsdorf Ger.
169 E4 Rengshausen (Knüllwald) Ger.
108 D1 Ren He r. China
109 E2 Renheji Henan China
Renhou Hebei China see Tangxian
109 E3 Renhua Guangdong China
108 C3 Renhuai Guizhou China
136 E5 Reni Ukr.
232 C6 Renick WV U.S.A.
114 C3 Renigunta Andhra Prad. India
146 B4 Renish Point Scotland U.K.
168 C3 Renkenberge Ger.
138 E1 Renko Fin.
164 E3 Renkum Neth.
Renland reg. Greenland see Tuttut Nunaat
82 E3 Renmark S.A. Austr.
194 D6 Renna r. Sicilia Italy
169 F3 Rennau Ger.
78 □6 Rennell i. Solomon Is
169 D5 Rennerod Ger.
84 C3 Renner Springs N.T. Austr.
173 F3 Rennertshofen Ger.
158 E3 Rennes France
158 E3 Rennes, Bassin de basin France
163 E6 Rennes-les-Bains France
142 A2 Rennesøy i. Norway
223 M5 Rennie Man. Can.
172 C3 Renningen Ger.
149 H2 Rennington Northumberland, England U.K.
179 E3 Rennweg Austria
191 H4 Reno r. Italy
226 B4 Reno MN U.S.A.
240 H2 Reno NV U.S.A.
191 G2 Renòn Italy
192 B2 Rénoso, Monte mt. Corse France
215 F2 Renoster r. S. Africa
214 D5 Renosterkop S. Africa
215 F2 Renosterspruit S. Africa
232 E4 Renovo PA U.S.A.
107 H4 Renqiu Hebei China
168 E1 Rens Denmark
108 C2 Renshou Sichuan China
174 F5 Reńska Wieś Pol.
174 G5 Reńska Wieś Pol.
230 C3 Rensselaer IN U.S.A.
233 G3 Rensselaer NY U.S.A.
164 E2 Renswoude Neth.
186 B1 Rentería Spain
140 L2 Rentjärn Sweden
238 B2 Renton WA U.S.A.
169 F5 Rentweinsdorf Ger.
117 E4 Renukut Uttar Prad. India
156 E3 Renwez France
81 D4 Renwick South I. N.Z.
139 K2 Renya r. Rus. Fed.
170 C2 Renzow Ger.
206 E3 Réo Burkina
176 F4 Répce r. Hungary
176 G4 Répcelak Hungary
213 G4 Repembe r. Moz.
175 K3 Repki Pol.
160 C2 Replonges France
140 N1 Repokaira reg. Fin.
80 F3 Reporoa North I. N.Z.
141 M3 Reposaari Fin.
170 D1 Reppelin Ger.
168 F2 Reppenstedt Ger.
232 B4 Republic OH U.S.A.
238 C1 Republic WA U.S.A.
236 D4 Republican r. NE U.S.A.
236 C3 Republican, South Fork r. NE U.S.A.
188 F3 Republika Srpska aut. div. Bos.-Herz.
85 G4 Repulse Bay b. Qld Austr.
221 J3 Repulse Bay Nunavut Can.
135 G6 Rep'yevka Rus. Fed.
182 D2 Requejo Spain
250 C6 Requena Peru
187 B5 Requena Spain
260 B4 Requinoa Chile
163 E4 Réquista France
254 E3 Reriutaba Brazil
127 F3 Reşadiye Turkey
Reşadiye Turkey see Yeniçağa
126 E2 Reşadiye Turkey
199 E3 Reşadiye Yarımadası pen. Turkey
94 D4 Resag, Gunung mt. Indon.
191 G3 Resana Italy
197 E3 Resava r. Yugo.
197 E3 Resavica Srbija Yugo.
146 F5 Rescobie Angus, Scotland U.K.
196 E5 Resen Macedonia
257 E5 Resende Brazil
182 C3 Resende Port.
256 B6 Reserva Brazil
239 E5 Reserve NM U.S.A.
139 K3 Reshetnikovo Rus. Fed.
137 H3 Reshetylivka Ukr.
109 D2 Reshi Hunan China
234 C1 Resica Falls PA U.S.A.
258 F2 Resistencia Arg.
197 E3 Reşiţa Romania
174 D2 Resko Pol.
221 I2 Resolute Bay Nunavut Can.
221 L3 Resolution Island Nunavut Can.
81 A6 Resolution Island South I. N.Z.
150 D3 Resolven Neath Port Talbot, Wales U.K.
183 G1 Respaldiza Spain
183 F2 Respenda de la Peña Spain
257 G3 Resplendor Brazil
139 J4 Ressa r. Rus. Fed.
215 H1 Ressango Garcia S. Africa
139 J5 Resseta r. Rus. Fed.
156 C3 Ressons-sur-Matz France
196 E5 Restelica Kosovo, Srbija Yugo.
233 □J1 Restigouche r. N.B. Can.
255 B9 Restinga Seca Brazil
Resülayn Turkey see Ceylanpınar
194 D5 Resuttano Sicilia Italy
137 G2 Ret' r. Ukr.
243 H6 Retalhuleu Guat.
184 E2 Retamal Spain
182 C5 Retaxo Port.
149 I4 Retford Nottinghamshire, England U.K.
156 E3 Rethel France
168 E3 Rethem (Aller) Ger.
Réthimnon Kriti Greece see Rethymno
156 C3 Rethondes France
198 D4 Rethymno Kriti Greece
165 E3 Retie Belgium
183 G4 Retiendas Spain
158 E4 Retiers France
184 D2 Retín r. Spain
260 B5 Retiro Chile
182 D4 Retortillo Spain
183 F2 Retortillo tourist site Spain
183 H3 Retortillo de Soria Spain
161 C3 Retournac France
85 E5 Retreat Qld Austr.
177 I4 Rétság Hungary
173 E4 Rettenberg Ger.
186 B4 Retuerta mt. Spain
185 F1 Retuerta del Bullaque Spain
179 G2 Retz Austria
171 D3 Reuden Sachsen-Anhalt Ger.
171 D4 Reuden Sachsen-Anhalt Ger.
159 I4 Reuilly France
217 □1c Réunion terr. Indian Ocean
169 F5 Reurieth Ger.
186 E3 Reus Spain
165 E3 Reusel Neth.
165 E3 Reusel r. Neth.
190 D1 Reuss r. Switz.
173 G3 Reut Ger.
Reut r. Moldova see Răut
137 H2 Reut r. Rus. Fed.
172 B3 Reute Ger.
136 D4 Reuţel Moldova
170 D2 Reuterstadt Stavenhagen Ger.
173 G2 Reuth bei Erbendorf Ger.
172 D3 Reutlingen Ger.
139 K4 Reutov Rus. Fed.
178 B3 Reutte Austria
165 F3 Reuver Neth.
Reval Estonia see Tallinn
134 F2 Revda Rus. Fed.
241 I3 Reveille Peak NV U.S.A.
Revel Estonia see Tallinn
163 E5 Revel France
117 F4 Revelganj Bihar India
190 C4 Revello Italy
222 G5 Revelstoke B.C. Can.
250 A6 Reventazón Peru
234 C2 Revere PA U.S.A.
160 D3 Revermont reg. France
161 D4 Revest-du-Bion France
177 G5 Révfülöp Hungary
197 H3 Reviga Romania
197 H3 Reviga r. Romania
157 E4 Revigny-sur-Ornain France
183 F2 Revilla de Collazos Spain
183 G2 Revilla del Campo Spain
228 D7 Revillagigedo, Islas is Mex.
220 E4 Revillagigedo Island AK U.S.A.
156 E3 Revin France
191 H3 Revine-Lago Italy
139 J5 Revna r. Rus. Fed.
176 D2 Řevnice Czech Rep.
176 C1 Řevničov Czech Rep.
191 G2 Revò Italy
185 H2 Revolcadores mt. Spain
Revolyutsii, Pik mt. Tajik. see Revolyutsiya, Qullai
123 H2 Revolyutsiya, Qullai mt. Tajik.
177 J3 Revúca Slovakia
213 G3 Revuè r. Moz.
139 K4 Revyakino Rus. Fed.
116 E4 Rewa Madh. Prad. India
81 E4 Rewa hill North I. N.Z.
174 D1 Rewal Pol.
116 D3 Rewari Haryana India
262 S2 Rex, Mount Antarctica
238 E3 Rexburg ID U.S.A.
225 H4 Rexton N.B. Can.
242 □K7 Rey, Isla del i. Panama
136 E2 Reya Ukr.
207 I4 Rey Bouba Cameroon
151 I2 Reydon Suffolk, England U.K.
252 D3 Reyes Bol.
240 F2 Reyes, Point CA U.S.A.
128 C1 Reyhanlı Turkey
140 □B3 Reykjanes constituency Iceland
264 G2 Reykjanes Ridge sea feature N. Atlantic Ocean
140 □B3 Reykjanestá pt Iceland
140 □B2 Reykjavík Iceland
84 B2 Reynolds r. N.T. Austr.
232 B5 Reynoldsburg OH U.S.A.
84 C4 Reynolds Range mts N.T. Austr.
243 F3 Reynosa Mex.
160 C3 Reyrieux France
160 C2 Reyssouze r. France
122 B3 Rezā, Kūh-e hill Iran
Rezā'īyeh Iran see Orūmīyeh
Rezā'īyeh, Daryācheh-ye salt l. Iran see Orūmīyeh, Daryācheh-ye
158 E4 Rezé France
138 F3 Rēzekne Latvia
138 F3 Rēzekne r. Latvia
176 G5 Rezi Hungary
136 E4 Rezina Moldova
188 E3 Rezinjski vrh mt. Slovenia
197 I5 Rezovska Reka r. Bulg./Turkey
Rezvāndeh Iran see Rezvānshahr
122 B2 Rezvānshahr Iran
190 F3 Rezzato Italy
190 C4 Rezzo Italy
190 E4 Rezzoaglio Italy
197 F3 Rgotina Srbija Yugo.
168 E2 Rhade Ger.
190 E1 Rhätikon mts Switz.
172 B2 Rhaunen Ger.
150 D2 Rhayader Powys, Wales U.K.
169 D4 Rheda-Wiedenbrück Ger.
169 B4 Rhede Ger.
168 C2 Rhede (Ems) Ger.
169 E3 Rheden Ger.
234 B2 Rheems PA U.S.A.
Rhegium Calabria Italy see Reggio di Calabria
150 C2 Rheidol r. Wales U.K.
Rheims France see Reims
172 A1 Rhein r. Ger. alt. Rhin (France), conv. Rhine
172 B3 Rheinau Ger.
169 B5 Rheinbach Ger.
169 B4 Rheinberg Ger.
172 B2 Rheinböllen Ger.
169 C5 Rheinbreitbach Ger.
169 C5 Rheinbrohl Ger.
169 C3 Rheine Ger.
190 E1 Rheineck Switz.
190 C1 Rheinfelden Switz.
172 B4 Rheinfelden (Baden) Ger.
172 B2 Rheinhessen-Pfalz admin. reg. Rheinland-Pfalz Ger.
169 B5 Rheinisches Schiefergebirge hills Ger.
169 C6 Rheinland-Pfalz land Ger.
169 B4 Rhein-Ruhr airport Ger.
170 D2 Rheinsberg Ger.
172 C3 Rheinstetten Ger.
190 E2 Rheinwaldhorn mt. Switz.
172 C2 Rheinzabern Ger.
190 C3 Rhêmes-Notre-Dame Italy
190 C3 Rhêmes-St-Georges Italy
164 E3 Rhenen Neth.
169 C5 Rhens Ger.
146 D3 Rhiconich Highland, Scotland U.K.
160 F1 Rhin r. France alt. Rhein (Germany), conv. Rhine
170 D2 Rhin r. Ger.
157 H4 Rhinau France
157 G1 Rhine r. France alt. Rhein (Germany), alt. Rhin (France)
233 G4 Rhinebeck NY U.S.A.
226 C3 Rhinelander WI U.S.A.
Rhineland-Palatinate land Ger. see Rheinland-Pfalz
170 D3 Rhinluch marsh Ger.
146 D6 Rhinns of Kells hills Scotland U.K.
210 A4 Rhino Camp Uganda
170 D3 Rhinow Ger.
170 D3 Rhinowes Berge hills Ger.
165 D4 Rhisnes Belgium
190 E3 Rho Italy
147 D3 Rhode Rep. of Ireland
233 H4 Rhode Island state U.S.A.
169 E4 Rhoden (Diemelstadt) Ger.
Rhodes Notio Aigaio Greece see Rodos
Rhodes i. Greece see Rodos
Rhodesia country Africa see Zimbabwe
238 D2 Rhodes Peak ID U.S.A.
197 F5 Rhodope Mountains Bulg./Greece
Rhodus i. Greece see Rodos
169 E5 Rhön mts Ger.
150 D3 Rhondda reg. Wales U.K.
150 D3 Rhondda Cynon Taff admin. div. Wales U.K.
160 C3 Rhône dept Rhône-Alpes France
161 C5 Rhône r. France/Switz.
161 D3 Rhône-Alpes admin. reg. France
150 D3 Rhoose Vale of Glamorgan, Wales U.K.
173 G4 Rhordorf Ger.
150 D3 Rhos Neath Port Talbot, Wales U.K.
150 D1 Rhosllanerchrugog Wrexham, Wales U.K.
150 D1 Rhôs-on-Sea Conwy, Wales U.K.
150 C3 Rhossili Swansea, Wales U.K.
148 E1 Rhu Argyll and Bute, Scotland U.K.
150 D1 Rhuddlan Denbighshire, Wales U.K.
161 A3 Rhue r. France
169 F4 Rhumspringe Ger.
Rhuthun Denbighshire, Wales U.K. see Ruthin
Rhydaman Carmarthenshire, Wales U.K. see Ammanford
150 D1 Rhyl Denbighshire, Wales U.K.
150 D3 Rhymney Caerphilly, Wales U.K.
146 F4 Rhynie Aberdeenshire, Scotland U.K.
207 H6 Riaba Equat. Guinea
195 F4 Riace Italy
254 D3 Riachão Brazil
254 D4 Riachão das Neves Brazil
254 E5 Riacho de Santana Brazil
257 F1 Riacho dos Machados Brazil
183 G3 Riaguas r. Spain
158 E4 Riaillé France
182 B2 Rial Spain
186 E2 Rialb de Noguera Spain
255 C5 Rialma Brazil
Rialp Spain see Rialb de Noguera
240 I4 Rialto CA U.S.A.
Rianjo Spain see Rianxo
193 E2 Riano Italy
183 F2 Riaño Spain
253 H3 Rianópolis Brazil
161 D5 Rians France
183 G5 Riansáres r. Spain
158 C4 Riantec France
182 B2 Rianxo Spain
116 C2 Riasi Jammu and Kashmir
94 C2 Riau prov. Indon.
94 D2 Riau, Kepulauan is Indon.
190 C2 Riaz Switz.
183 G3 Riaza Spain
183 G3 Riaza r. Spain
183 G1 Riba Spain
182 B2 Ribadavia Spain
182 D2 Ribadelago Spain
182 C1 Ribadeo Spain
183 H4 Riba de Saelices Spain
183 E1 Ribadesella Spain
183 I2 Ribaforada Spain
183 H2 Ribafrecha Spain
186 D3 Riba-roja d'Ebre Spain
Ribas de Fresser Spain see Ribes de Freser
255 B7 Ribas do Rio Pardo Brazil
213 H2 Ribáuè Moz.
169 F3 Ribbesbüttel Ger.
149 G4 Ribble r. England U.K.
149 G3 Ribblesdale val. England U.K.
142 C4 Ribe Denmark
142 C4 Ribe county Denmark
157 H4 Ribeauvillé France
156 C3 Ribécourt-Dreslincourt France
256 C6 Ribeira Brazil
256 D6 Ribeira r. Brazil
184 □ Ribeira Brava Madeira
184 □ Ribeira da Janela Madeira
182 C3 Ribeira de Pena Port.
216 □1b Ribeira Grande São Miguel Azores
182 B3 Ribeirão Port.
256 C6 Ribeirão Branco Brazil
257 E3 Ribeirão das Neves Brazil
256 B5 Ribeirão do Pinhal Brazil
256 D4 Ribeirão Preto Brazil
216 □1c Ribeiras Pico Azores
216 □1c Ribeira Seca São Jorge Azores
216 □1b Ribeira Seca São Miguel Azores
216 □1c Ribeirinha Faial Azores
216 □1c Ribeirinha Pico Azores
216 □1a Ribeirinha Terceira Azores
156 D3 Ribemont France
194 C5 Ribera Sicilia Italy
162 C3 Ribérac France
184 D2 Ribera del Fresno Spain
252 D2 Riberalta Bol.
187 C4 Ribesalbes Spain
186 F2 Ribes de Freser Spain
161 D4 Ribiers France
177 L5 Ribiţa Romania
188 E3 Ribnica Slovenia
136 E4 Rîbniţa Moldova
170 D1 Ribnitz-Damgarten Ger.
197 F5 Ribnovo Bulg.
183 G3 Ribota Spain
195 E4 Ricadi Italy
179 H1 Říčany Czech Rep.
176 D2 Říčany Czech Rep.
149 I3 Riccal r. England U.K.
193 G3 Riccia Italy
191 H5 Riccio Italy
191 H4 Riccione Italy
190 E4 Riccò del Golfo di Spezia Italy
241 J4 Rice CA U.S.A.
232 D6 Rice VA U.S.A.
226 B3 Rice Lake WI U.S.A.
226 A4 Riceville IA U.S.A.
232 B6 Riceville KY U.S.A.
157 G4 Richardménil France
215 I3 Richards Bay S. Africa
223 I3 Richardson r. Alta Can.
220 E3 Richardson Mountains N.W.T. Can.
81 B6 Richardson Mountains South I. N.Z.
206 B2 Richard Toll Senegal
234 C2 Richboro PA U.S.A.
233 G2 Richelieu Que. Can.
162 C1 Richelieu France
234 A2 Richfield PA U.S.A.
241 K2 Richfield UT U.S.A.
233 F3 Richfield Springs NY U.S.A.
233 E3 Richford NY U.S.A.
233 G2 Richford VT U.S.A.
240 H4 Richgrove CA U.S.A.
147 E2 Richhill Northern Ireland U.K.
225 H4 Richibucto N.B. Can.
223 I4 Rich Lake Alta Can.
234 D3 Richland NJ U.S.A.
234 B2 Richland PA U.S.A.
238 C2 Richland WA U.S.A.
226 B4 Richland Center WI U.S.A.
232 C6 Richlands VA U.S.A.
234 C2 Richlandtown PA U.S.A.
83 G3 Richmond N.S.W. Austr.
85 E4 Richmond Qld Austr.
227 J3 Richmond Ont. Can.
225 F4 Richmond Que. Can.
81 D4 Richmond South I. N.Z.
215 H3 Richmond Kwazulu-Natal S. Africa
214 D4 Richmond N. Cape S. Africa
149 H3 Richmond North Yorkshire, England U.K.
240 F3 Richmond CA U.S.A.
226 C4 Richmond IL U.S.A.
230 C4 Richmond IN U.S.A.
232 A6 Richmond KY U.S.A.
233 □I2 Richmond ME U.S.A.
227 F4 Richmond MI U.S.A.
237 E6 Richmond TX U.S.A.
232 E6 Richmond VA U.S.A.
233 G2 Richmond VT U.S.A.
81 D4 Richmond, Mount South I. N.Z.
235 D2 Richmond County county NY U.S.A.
232 B5 Richmond Dale OH U.S.A.
224 E5 Richmond Hill Ont. Can.
231 D6 Richmond Hill GA U.S.A.
247 □3 Richmond Peak St Vincent
83 H2 Richmond Range hills N.S.W. Austr.
81 D4 Richmond Range mts South I. N.Z.
233 F3 Richmondville NY U.S.A.
170 D1 Richtenberg Ger.
172 C4 Richterswil Switz.
237 F6 Richton MS U.S.A.
240 G2 Richvale CA U.S.A.
232 B4 Richwood OH U.S.A.

232 C5 **Richwood** *WV* U.S.A.
193 H4 **Ricigliano** Italy
172 B4 **Rickenbach** Ger.
151 H2 **Rickinghall** *Suffolk, England* U.K.
140 M2 **Rickleån** *r.* Sweden
168 F1 **Rickling** Ger.
151 G3 **Rickmansworth** *Hertfordshire, England* U.K.
183 I3 **Ricla** Spain
182 E3 **Ricobayo, Embalse de** *resr* Spain
Ricomagus France *see* **Riom**
177 K3 **Ricse** Hungary
263 E2 **Riddell Nunataks** *nunataks* Antarctica
Ridder Kazakh. *see* **Leninogorsk**
164 D3 **Ridderkerk** Neth.
190 C2 **Riddes** Switz.
232 D4 **Riddlesburg** *PA* U.S.A.
227 J3 **Rideau** *r. Ont.* Can.
234 B3 **Riderwood** *MD* U.S.A.
224 C3 **Ridge** *r. Ont.* Can.
235 F2 **Ridge** *NY* U.S.A.
240 I4 **Ridgecrest** *CA* U.S.A.
235 E1 **Ridgefield** *CT* U.S.A.
235 D2 **Ridgefield** *NJ* U.S.A.
237 F5 **Ridgeland** *MS* U.S.A.
231 D5 **Ridgeland** *SC* U.S.A.
226 B3 **Ridgeland** *WI* U.S.A.
234 C4 **Ridgely** *MD* U.S.A.
227 G4 **Ridgetown** *Ont.* Can.
226 B4 **Ridgeway** *IA* U.S.A.
235 D2 **Ridgeway** *NJ* U.S.A.
232 D6 **Ridgeway** *VA* U.S.A.
235 D2 **Ridgewood** *NJ* U.S.A.
232 D4 **Ridgway** *PA* U.S.A.
177 I6 **Riđica** *Vojvodina, Srbija* Yugo.
146 G7 **Riding Mill** *Northumberland, England* U.K.
86 C4 **Ridley** *r. W.A.* Austr.
215 F2 **Riebeeckstad** S. Africa
214 B5 **Riebeek-Kasteel** S. Africa
215 F5 **Riebeek-Oos** S. Africa
214 B5 **Riebeek Wes** S. Africa
158 C4 **Riec-sur-Belon** France
173 F3 **Ried** Ger.
190 D2 **Ried** Switz.
173 E4 **Riedbergerhorn** *mt.* Ger.
168 D3 **Riede** Ger.
173 F2 **Rieden** Ger.
173 F3 **Riedenburg** Ger.
173 G4 **Riedering** Ger.
179 E2 **Ried im Innkreis** Austria
178 B3 **Ried im Oberinntal** Austria
178 C3 **Ried im Zillertal** Austria
179 F2 **Ried in der Riedmark** Austria
157 H5 **Riedisheim** France
172 D3 **Riedlingen** Ger.
172 A2 **Riegelsberg** Ger.
179 G3 **Riegersburg** Austria
234 C2 **Rieglelsville** *PA* U.S.A.
182 E2 **Riego de la Vega** Spain
190 C1 **Riehen** Switz.
215 F1 **Riekertsdam** S. Africa
172 C4 **Rielasingen-Worblingen** Ger.
182 E2 **Riello** Spain
183 F5 **Rielves** Spain
165 E4 **Riemst** Belgium
169 E5 **Rieneck** Ger.
177 L5 **Rieni** Romania
191 G2 **Rienza** *r.* Italy
140 M1 **Rieppesgai'sa** *mt.* Norway
168 F1 **Riepsdorf** Ger.
186 E3 **Riera de Rajadell** *r.* Spain
171 E4 **Riesa** Ger.
259 B9 **Riesco, Isla** *i.* Chile
168 E1 **Rieseby** Ger.
194 D5 **Riesi** *Sicilia* Italy
169 D3 **Rieste** Ger.
171 C4 **Riestedt** Ger.
214 D3 **Riet** *r.* S. Africa
138 C4 **Rietavas** Lith.
169 D4 **Rietberg** Ger.
214 D5 **Rietbron** S. Africa
214 C2 **Rietfontein** S. Africa
170 F2 **Rieth** Ger.
165 E3 **Riethoven** Neth.
214 C6 **Riethuiskraal** S. Africa
193 E2 **Rieti** Italy
193 E2 **Rieti** *prov. Lazio* Italy
215 G2 **Rietkuil** S. Africa
214 B4 **Rietpoort** S. Africa
171 F4 **Rietschen** Ger.
215 H3 **Rietvlei** S. Africa
178 C3 **Rietz** Austria
163 D5 **Rieumes** France
163 E4 **Rieupeyroux** France
161 B4 **Rieutort-de-Randon** France
158 D4 **Rieux** *Bretagne* France
163 D5 **Rieux** *Midi-Pyrénées* France
163 E5 **Rieux-Minervois** France
161 E5 **Riez** France
128 C3 **Rifā'ī, Tall** *mt.* Jordan/Syria
256 D4 **Rifaina** Brazil
Rifeng *Jiangxi* China *see* **Lichuan**
178 E3 **Rifflkopf** *mt.* Austria
191 G2 **Rifiano** Italy
239 F4 **Rifle** *CO* U.S.A.
210 B4 **Rift Valley** *prov.* Kenya
111 F6 **Riga** *Arun. Prad.* India
138 E3 **Rīga** Latvia
138 D3 **Riga, Gulf of** Estonia/Latvia
207 G4 **Rigacikun** Nigeria
122 D4 **Rīgān** Iran
Rīgas jūras līcis *b.* Estonia/Latvia *see* **Riga, Gulf of**
233 F2 **Rigaud** *Que.* Can.
161 E5 **Rigaud** France
238 E3 **Rigby** *ID* U.S.A.
238 C2 **Riggins** *ID* U.S.A.
160 F2 **Riggisberg** Switz.
190 D1 **Rigi** *mts* Switz.
190 E3 **Riglio** *r.* Italy
163 E4 **Rignac** France
193 E2 **Rignano Flaminio** Italy
193 H3 **Rignano Garganico** Italy
191 G5 **Rignano sull'Arno** Italy
156 D4 **Rigny-le-Ferron** France
160 C2 **Rigny-sur-Arroux** France
159 G4 **Rigny-Ussé** France
225 J2 **Rigolet** *Nfld.* Can.
202 B6 **Rig-Rig** Chad
146 E6 **Rigside** *South Lanarkshire, Scotland* U.K.
183 I2 **Riguel** *r.* Spain
124 B4 **Rīh, Gezirat er** *i.* Sudan
113 □1 **Rihiveli** *i. S. Male* Maldives
Riia laht *b.* Estonia/Latvia *see* **Riga, Gulf of**
141 N3 **Riihimäki** Fin.
138 E2 **Riisipere** Estonia
207 G4 **Rijau** Nigeria
188 E3 **Riječki Zaliv** *b.* Croatia
188 E3 **Rijeka** Croatia
191 J3 **Rijeka** *airport* Croatia
164 D3 **Rijen** Neth.
165 D3 **Rijkevorsel** Belgium
164 D2 **Rijnsaterwoude** Neth.
164 D2 **Rijnsburg** Neth.
164 D3 **Rijsbergen** Neth.
164 F2 **Rijssen** Neth.
164 D2 **Rijswijk** Neth.
136 B3 **Rika** *r.* Ukr.
140 L1 **Riksgränsen** Sweden
102 J4 **Rikuzen-takata** Japan
197 F4 **Rila** Bulg.
197 F4 **Rila** *mts* Bulg.
238 C3 **Riley** *OR* U.S.A.
232 D5 **Rileyville** *VA* U.S.A.
162 D3 **Rilhac-Rancon** France
165 D3 **Rilland** Neth.
159 G4 **Rillé** France
160 C3 **Rillieux-la-Pape** France
241 L5 **Rillito** *AZ* U.S.A.
186 C4 **Rillo** Spain
183 I4 **Rillo de Gallo** Spain
156 E3 **Rilly-la-Montagne** France
79 □3 **Rimatara** *i. Îs Australes* Fr. Polynesia
Rimatera *i. Îs Australes* Fr. Polynesia *see* **Rimatara**
157 F4 **Rimaucourt** France
177 J3 **Rimava** *r.* Slovakia
177 J3 **Rimavská Seč** Slovakia
177 J3 **Rimavská Sobota** Slovakia
173 G2 **Rimbach** *Bayern* Ger.
172 C2 **Rimbach** *Hessen* Ger.
222 H4 **Rimbey** *Alta* Can.
143 H2 **Rimbo** Sweden
232 D4 **Rimersburg** *PA* U.S.A.
197 F2 **Rimetea** Romania
143 F2 **Rimforsa** Sweden
191 H4 **Rimini** Italy
191 H4 **Rimini** *prov. Emilia-Romagna* Italy
Rîmnicu Sărat Romania *see* **Râmnicu Sărat**
Rîmnicu Vîlcea Romania *see* **Râmnicu Vâlcea**
156 E3 **Rimogne** France
163 D6 **Rimont** France
225 G3 **Rimouski** *Que.* Can.
172 D2 **Rimpar** Ger.
173 G4 **Rimsting** Ger.
111 E6 **Rinbung** *Xizang* China
93 A5 **Rinca** *i.* Indon.
256 C4 **Rincão** Brazil
173 H3 **Rinchnach** Ger.
Rincon Morocco *see* **Mdiq**
247 □1 **Rincón** Puerto Rico
252 D6 **Rincón, Cerro del** *mt.* Chile
245 F4 **Rinconada** Mex.
260 C4 **Rincón del Atuel** Arg.
185 F4 **Rincón de la Victoria** Spain
261 I3 **Rincón del Bonete, Lago Artificial de** *resr* Uru.
244 C2 **Rincón de Romos** Mex.
183 I2 **Rincón de Soto** Spain
116 E4 **Rind** *r.* India
138 C3 **Rinda** *r.* Latvia
140 J3 **Rindal** Norway
198 D3 **Rineia** *i.* Greece
194 D4 **Rinella** *Isole Lipari* Italy
232 C6 **Riner** *VA* U.S.A.
83 F5 **Ringarooma Bay** *Tas.* Austr.
143 G2 **Ringarum** Sweden
116 C4 **Ringas** *Rajasthan* India
147 C5 **Ringaskiddy** Rep. of Ireland
142 D4 **Ringe** Denmark
168 B3 **Ringe** Ger.
141 J3 **Ringebu** Norway
190 E2 **Ringelspitz** *mt.* Switz.
170 E2 **Ringenwalde** Ger.
231 C5 **Ringgold** *GA* U.S.A.
207 H3 **Ringim** Nigeria
142 C3 **Ringkøbing** Denmark
142 C3 **Ringkøbing** *county* Denmark
142 C4 **Ringkøbing Fjord** *lag.* Denmark
151 I2 **Ringland** *Norfolk, England* U.K.
171 C4 **Ringleben** Ger.
151 H4 **Ringmer** *East Sussex, England* U.K.
234 D2 **Ringoes** *NJ* U.S.A.
148 C2 **Ringsend** *Northern Ireland* U.K.
142 D4 **Ringsted** Denmark
140 L1 **Ringvassøy** *i.* Norway
147 D4 **Ringville** Rep. of Ireland
151 F4 **Ringwood** *Hampshire, England* U.K.
233 F4 **Ringwood** *NJ* U.S.A.
Rinía *i.* Greece *see* **Rineia**
168 E1 **Rinkenæs** Denmark
146 E4 **Rinloan** *Aberdeenshire, Scotland* U.K.
178 C3 **Rinn** Austria
146 C7 **Rinns of Galloway** *pen. Scotland* U.K.
146 B6 **Rinns of Islay** *pen. Scotland* U.K.
256 B4 **Rinópolis** Brazil
169 E3 **Rinteln** Ger.
196 C3 **Rinya** *r.* Romania
226 C4 **Rio** *WI* U.S.A.
255 C8 **Rio Azul** Brazil
250 B5 **Riobamba** Ecuador
257 G3 **Rio Bananal** Brazil
239 F4 **Rio Blanco** *CO* U.S.A.
257 F5 **Rio Bonito** Brazil
252 D2 **Rio Branco** Brazil
Rio Branco *state* Brazil *see* **Roraima**
256 C6 **Rio Branco do Sul** Brazil
255 B7 **Rio Brilhante** Brazil
259 B6 **Río Bueno** Chile
246 □ **Rio Bueno** Jamaica
182 B3 **Rio Caldo** Port.
251 F2 **Río Caribe** Venez.
257 F4 **Rio Casca** Brazil
260 E2 **Río Ceballos** Arg.
257 E5 **Rio Claro** *Rio de Janeiro* Brazil
256 D5 **Rio Claro** *São Paulo* Brazil
247 □7 **Rio Claro** Trin. and Tob.
261 E6 **Río Colorado** Arg.
260 E3 **Río Cuarto** Arg.
257 F5 **Rio de Janeiro** Brazil
257 F4 **Rio de Janeiro** *state* Brazil
238 A3 **Rio Dell** *CA* U.S.A.
182 C4 **Rio de Mel** Port.
184 B3 **Rio de Moinhos** *Beja* Port.
184 C2 **Rio de Moinhos** *Évora* Port.
184 B2 **Rio de Moinhos** *Setúbal* Port.
182 D3 **Rio de Onor** Port.
204 A5 **Río de Oro, Bahía de** *b.* Western Sahara
187 B4 **Ríodeva** *r.* Spain
191 G2 **Rio di Pusteria** Italy
257 F4 **Rio Doce** Brazil
255 C8 **Rio do Sul** Brazil
182 C3 **Rio Douro** Port.
254 G4 **Rio Formoso** Brazil
183 F4 **Riofrío** Spain
182 D3 **Riofrío de Aliste** Spain
183 G3 **Riofrío de Riaza** Spain
259 C8 **Río Gallegos** Arg.
185 F4 **Ríogordo** Spain
259 D9 **Río Grande** Arg.
258 G4 **Rio Grande** Brazil
246 □ **Rio Grande** *r.* Jamaica
245 F6 **Río Grande** Mex.
244 C2 **Río Grande** Mex.
242 F3 **Rio Grande** *r.* Mex./U.S.A. *alt.* **Bravo del Norte, Río**
247 □1 **Rio Grande** Puerto Rico
234 D3 **Rio Grande** *NJ* U.S.A.
258 C2 **Río Grande, Salar de** *salt flat* Arg.
237 D7 **Rio Grande City** *TX* U.S.A.
254 F3 **Rio Grande do Norte** *state* Brazil
255 B9 **Rio Grande do Sul** *state* Brazil
264 G8 **Rio Grande Rise** *sea feature* S. Atlantic Ocean
250 C2 **Ríohacha** Col.
258 D2 **Río Hondo, Embalse** *resr* Arg.
250 B6 **Rioja** Peru
185 H4 **Rioja** Spain
243 H4 **Río Lagartos** Mex.
254 G4 **Rio Largo** Brazil
192 A5 **Riola Sardo** *Sardegna* Italy
182 D5 **Riolobos** Spain
191 G4 **Riolo Terme** Italy
161 A5 **Riols** France
160 B3 **Riom** France
190 E4 **Riomaggiore** Italy
184 B1 **Rio Maior** Port.
192 C2 **Rio Marina** Italy
182 B3 **Rio Mau** Port.
161 A3 **Riom-ès-Montagnes** France
246 □ **Rio Minho** *r.* Jamaica
163 B5 **Rion-des-Landes** France
260 D6 **Río Negro** *prov.* Arg.
255 C8 **Rio Negro** Brazil
259 B6 **Río Negro** Chile
261 I3 **Río Negro** *dept* Uru.
182 D2 **Rionegro del Puente** Spain
193 H4 **Rionero in Vulture** Italy
193 G3 **Rionero Sannitico** Italy
129 B2 **Rioni** *r.* Georgia
257 F4 **Rio Novo** Brazil
257 G4 **Rio Novo do Sul** Brazil
163 B4 **Rions** France
181 E3 **Riópar** Spain
255 E5 **Rio Pardo de Minas** Brazil
257 F4 **Rio Pomba** Brazil
257 F5 **Rio Preto** Brazil
256 D2 **Rio Preto, Serra do** *hills* Brazil
261 F2 **Río Primero** Arg.
239 F5 **Rio Rancho** *NM* U.S.A.
160 C2 **Riorges** France
241 L6 **Rio Rico** *AZ* U.S.A.
182 C3 **Ríos** Spain
182 E2 **Rioseco de Tapia** Spain
261 F2 **Río Segundo** Arg.
250 B3 **Ríosucio** Col.
254 G3 **Rio Tinto** Brazil
182 C3 **Rio Torto** Port.
92 A4 **Rio Tuba** Phil.
256 B2 **Rio Verde** Brazil
250 B4 **Rioverde** Ecuador
190 C4 **Rioverde** *r.* Italy
245 E3 **Río Verde** Mex.
255 B6 **Rio Verde de Mato Grosso** Brazil
257 F3 **Rio Vermelho** Brazil
240 G2 **Rio Vista** *CA* U.S.A.
160 E1 **Rioz** France
250 E5 **Riozinho** *r. Amazonas* Brazil
253 F4 **Riozinho** *r. Mato Grosso do Sul* Brazil
190 B3 **Ripa** *r.* Italy
196 E3 **Ripanj** *Srbija* Yugo.
191 F5 **Riparbella** Italy
193 F2 **Ripatransone** Italy
140 M2 **Ripats** Sweden
191 I5 **Ripe** Italy
193 F3 **Ripi** Italy
193 H4 **Ripiti** *r.* Italy
137 F2 **Ripky** Ukr.
149 H4 **Ripley** *Derbyshire, England* U.K.
149 H3 **Ripley** *North Yorkshire, England* U.K.
237 F5 **Ripley** *MS* U.S.A.
232 D3 **Ripley** *NY* U.S.A.
232 B5 **Ripley** *OH* U.S.A.
237 F5 **Ripley** *TN* U.S.A.
232 C5 **Ripley** *WV* U.S.A.
186 F2 **Ripoll** Spain
149 H3 **Ripon** *North Yorkshire, England* U.K.
240 G3 **Ripon** *CA* U.S.A.
226 C4 **Ripon** *WI* U.S.A.
195 E5 **Riposto** *Sicilia* Italy
150 E2 **Ripple** *Worcestershire, England* U.K.
149 H4 **Ripponden** *West Yorkshire, England* U.K.
164 E3 **Rips** Neth.
157 H4 **Riquewihr** France
123 H3 **Risalpur** Pak.
128 A4 **Risân 'Aneiza** *hill* Egypt
250 C3 **Risaralda** *dept* Col.
141 K3 **Risarven** Sweden
140 K2 **Risbäck** Sweden
150 D3 **Risca** *Caerphilly, Wales* U.K.
136 D4 **Rîşcani** Moldova
163 B5 **Riscle** France
260 C4 **Risco Plateado** *mt.* Arg.
140 K2 **Risede** Sweden
116 D3 **Rishikesh** *Uttar Prad.* India
100 G3 **Rishiri-zan** *vol.* Japan
128 B4 **Rishon Le Ẕiyyon** Israel
149 G4 **Rishton** *Lancashire, England* U.K.
230 C4 **Rising Sun** *IN* U.S.A.
234 B3 **Rising Sun** *MD* U.S.A.
159 G2 **Risle** *r.* France
Rîşnov Romania *see* **Râşnov**
237 E5 **Rison** *AR* U.S.A.
142 C2 **Risør** Norway
156 C4 **Ris-Orangis** France
160 E2 **Risoux, Mont** *mt.* France
172 D3 **Riß** *r.* Ger.
140 J3 **Rissa** Norway
160 E2 **Risse** *r.* France
80 F3 **Rissington** *North I.* N.Z.
141 N3 **Ristiina** Fin.
140 O2 **Ristijärvi** Fin.
168 D1 **Risum-Lindholm** Ger.
95 F2 **Ritan** *r.* Indon.
138 E3 **Rītausma** Latvia
214 E3 **Ritchie** S. Africa
115 G3 **Ritchie's Archipelago** *is Andaman & Nicobar Is* India
209 C9 **Rito** Angola
262 X2 **Ritscher Upland** *mts* Antarctica
140 L2 **Ritsem** Sweden
240 H3 **Ritter, Mount** *CA* U.S.A.
168 D2 **Ritterhude** Ger.
169 B5 **Rittersdorf** Ger.
171 D5 **Rittersgrün** Ger.
183 H3 **Rituerto** *r.* Spain
138 F3 **Rītupe** *r.* Latvia
238 C2 **Ritzville** *WA* U.S.A.
186 E3 **Riudoms** Spain
136 E3 **Riv** *r.* Ukr.
138 C3 **Rīva** *r.* Latvia
159 F2 **Riva Bella** France
261 F4 **Rivadavia** *Buenos Aires* Arg.
260 C3 **Rivadavia** *Mendoza* Arg.
191 F3 **Riva del Garda** Italy
178 B5 **Riva di Solto** Italy
191 H2 **Riva di Tures** Italy
140 □ **Rivalensundet** *str.* Svalbard
190 C5 **Riva Ligure** Italy
190 E4 **Rivanazzano** Italy
239 F6 **Riva Palacio** Mex.
190 D4 **Rivardo Ligure** Italy
190 C3 **Rivarolo Canavese** Italy
190 F3 **Rivarolo Mantovano** Italy
242 □I7 **Rivas** Nic.
183 G4 **Rivas-Vaciamadrid** Spain
160 C3 **Rive-de-Gier** France
162 A2 **Rivedoux-Plage** France
193 H4 **Rivello** Italy
261 F5 **Rivera** Arg.
255 B9 **Rivera** Uru.
206 C5 **River Cess** Liberia
240 H3 **Riverdale** *CA* U.S.A.
226 A3 **River Falls** *WI* U.S.A.
233 G4 **Riverhead** *NY* U.S.A.
223 J5 **Riverhurst** *Sask.* Can.
87 D6 **Riverina** *W.A.* Austr.
83 F3 **Riverina** *reg. N.S.W.* Austr.
207 G5 **Rivers** *state* Nigeria
81 B6 **Riversdale** *South I.* N.Z.
214 C6 **Riversdale** S. Africa
81 F4 **Riversdale Beach** *North I.* N.Z.
81 C6 **Riverside** *South I.* N.Z.
215 G4 **Riverside** S. Africa
240 I5 **Riverside** *CA* U.S.A.
234 D2 **Riverside** *NJ* U.S.A.
234 B2 **Riverside** *PA* U.S.A.
222 E5 **Rivers Inlet** *B.C.* Can.
84 D3 **Riversleigh** *Qld* Austr.
147 C2 **Riverstown** *Sligo* Rep. of Ireland
147 D3 **Riverstown** *Tipperary* Rep. of Ireland
223 L5 **Riverton** *Man.* Can.
81 B7 **Riverton** *South I.* N.Z.
214 E3 **Riverton** S. Africa
234 C2 **Riverton** *NJ* U.S.A.
241 L1 **Riverton** *UT* U.S.A.
232 D5 **Riverton** *VA* U.S.A.
238 E3 **Riverton** *WY* U.S.A.
225 H4 **Riverview** *N.B.* Can.
215 I3 **River View** S. Africa
235 D2 **Riverwood** *NJ* U.S.A.
156 C3 **Rivery** France
161 D3 **Rives** France
163 E6 **Rivesaltes** France
232 C5 **Rivesville** *WV* U.S.A.
234 B3 **Riviera Beach** *MD* U.S.A.
235 D2 **Riviera Beach** *NJ* U.S.A.
225 H3 **Rivière-au-Renard** *Que.* Can.
225 G4 **Rivière Bleue** *Que.* Can.
225 G4 **Rivière-du-Loup** *Que.* Can.
225 H3 **Riviere-Pentecote** *Que.* Can.
225 H3 **Riviere-Pigou** *Que.* Can.
247 □3 **Rivière-Pilote** Martinique
247 □3 **Rivière-Salée** Martinique
161 B4 **Rivière-sur-Tarn** France
214 B6 **Riviersonderend** S. Africa
191 I3 **Rivignano** Italy
137 F3 **Rivne** *Kirovohrads'ka Oblast'* Ukr.
136 D2 **Rivne** *Rivnens'ka Oblast'* Ukr.
136 D3 **Rivne** *Vinnyts'ka Oblast'* Ukr.
136 D2 **Rivnens'ka Oblast'** *admin. div.* Ukr.
Rivne Oblast *admin. div.* Ukr. *see* **Rivnens'ka Oblast'**
193 E2 **Rivodutri** Italy
190 C3 **Rivoli** Italy
215 H1 **Rivulets** S. Africa
209 D9 **Rivungo** Angola
81 D4 **Riwaka** *South I.* N.Z.
112 I5 **Riwoqê** *Xizang* China
165 D4 **Rixensart** Belgium
157 H5 **Rixheim** France
124 D2 **Riyadh** Saudi Arabia
92 B3 **Rizal** Phil.
127 F2 **Rize** Turkey
129 B3 **Rize** *prov.* Turkey
107 H5 **Rizhao** *Shandong* China
107 H5 **Rizhao** *Shandong* China
Rizokarpaso Cyprus *see* **Rizokarpason**
128 B2 **Rizokarpason** Cyprus
198 C2 **Rizomylos** Greece
192 A3 **Rizzanese** *r. Corse* France
195 E4 **Rizziconi** Italy
194 D5 **Rizzuto** *r. Sicilia* Italy
195 G4 **Rizzuto, Capo** *c.* Italy
142 C2 **Rjukan** Norway
142 B2 **Rjuvbrokkene** *mt.* Norway
206 B2 **Rkîz** Maur.
191 G4 **Ro** Italy
142 D1 **Roa** Norway
183 G3 **Roa** Spain
82 □2 **Roach Island** *Lord Howe I.* Austr.
151 G2 **Roade** *Northamptonshire, England* U.K.
147 B3 **Roadford** Rep. of Ireland
232 B5 **Roads** *OH* U.S.A.
146 E3 **Roadside** *Highland, Scotland* U.K.
247 F3 **Road Town** Virgin Is (U.K.)
163 B4 **Roaillan** France
140 J2 **Roan** Norway
241 M2 **Roan Cliffs** *ridge UT* U.S.A.
146 F6 **Roan Fell** *hill Scotland* U.K.
160 C2 **Roannais** *reg.* France
160 C2 **Roanne** France
231 C5 **Roanoke** *AL* U.S.A.
226 C5 **Roanoke** *IL* U.S.A.
232 D6 **Roanoke** *VA* U.S.A.
232 E6 **Roanoke** *r. NC* U.S.A.
231 E4 **Roanoke Rapids** *NC* U.S.A.
241 M2 **Roan Plateau** *UT* U.S.A.
234 B1 **Roaring Branch** *PA* U.S.A.
190 F2 **Roasco** *r.* Italy
242 □I5 **Roatán** Hond.
150 D3 **Roath** *Cardiff, Wales* U.K.
134 C3 **Röbäck** Sweden
123 E4 **Robat** *r.* Afgh.
122 D4 **Robāṭ** Iran
122 C4 **Robāṭ-e Shahr-e Bābak** Iran
122 D2 **Robāṭ-e Ṭoroq** Iran
122 B3 **Robāṭ Karīm** Iran
222 G4 **Robb** *Alta* Can.
214 B5 **Robben Island** S. Africa
231 D5 **Robbinsville** *NC* U.S.A.
234 D2 **Robbinsville** *NJ* U.S.A.
190 D3 **Robbio** Italy
82 D4 **Robe** *S.A.* Austr.
86 B4 **Robe** *r. W.A.* Austr.
210 C3 **Robē** Eth.
147 B3 **Robe** *r.* Rep. of Ireland
82 E2 **Robe, Mount** *hill N.S.W.* Austr.
190 F3 **Robecco d'Oglio** Italy
170 D2 **Röbel** Ger.
157 F4 **Robert-Espagne** France
237 C6 **Robert Lee** *TX* U.S.A.
146 F6 **Roberton** *Scottish Borders, Scotland* U.K.
146 E6 **Roberton** *South Lanarkshire, Scotland* U.K.
238 D3 **Roberts** *ID* U.S.A.
83 H2 **Roberts, Mount** *Qld* Austr.
232 C5 **Robertsburg** *WV* U.S.A.
263 K2 **Roberts Butte** *mt.* Antarctica
241 I2 **Roberts Creek Mountain** *NV* U.S.A.
140 M2 **Robertsfors** Sweden
117 E4 **Robertsganj** *Uttar Prad.* India
85 E3 **Robertson** *r. Qld* Austr.
214 B5 **Robertson** S. Africa
262 U2 **Robertson Island** Antarctica
87 D4 **Robertson Range** *hills W.A.* Austr.
206 C5 **Robertsport** Liberia
82 D3 **Robertstown** *S.A.* Austr.
Robert Williams Angola *see* **Caála**
225 F3 **Roberval** *Que.* Can.
234 B2 **Robesonia** *PA* U.S.A.
161 C4 **Robiac** France
149 I3 **Robin Hood's Bay** *North Yorkshire, England* U.K.
84 D3 **Robinson** *r. N.T.* Austr.
86 E3 **Robinson** *r. W.A.* Austr.
222 C2 **Robinson** *Y.T.* Can.
230 C4 **Robinson** *IL* U.S.A.
232 A5 **Robinson** *KY* U.S.A.
85 G5 **Robinson Creek** *r. Qld* Austr.
252 □ **Robinson Crusoe, Isla** *i.* S. Pacific Ocean
87 C5 **Robinson Range** *hills W.A.* Austr.
84 D3 **Robinson River** *N.T.* Austr.
83 E3 **Robinvale** *Vic.* Austr.
161 D5 **Robion** France
185 H2 **Robledo** Spain
183 F4 **Robledo de Chavela** Spain
183 F5 **Robledo del Mazo** Spain
182 E5 **Robledollano** Spain
183 E2 **Robles de la Valcueva** Spain
250 C2 **Robles La Paz** Col.
223 K5 **Roblin** *Man.* Can.
171 C4 **Röblingen am See** Ger.
182 E4 **Robliza de Cojos** Spain
253 F4 **Robore** Bol.
183 G3 **Robregordo** Spain
186 C3 **Robres** Spain
183 H2 **Robres del Castillo** Spain
78 □6 **Rob Roy** *i.* Solomon Is
223 I5 **Robsart** *Sask.* Can.
222 G4 **Robson, Mount** *B.C.* Can.
237 D7 **Robstown** *TX* U.S.A.
237 C5 **Roby** *TX* U.S.A.
184 A2 **Roca, Cabo da** *c.* Port.
Roçadas Angola *see* **Xangongo**
186 E3 **Rocafort de Queralt** Spain
163 D4 **Rocamadour** France
250 □ **Roca Redonda** *i. Islas Galápagos* Ecuador
242 B3 **Rocas Alijos** *is* Mex.
195 H2 **Roca Vecchia** Italy
161 E5 **Rocbaron** France
190 F3 **Roccabianca** Italy
194 C5 **Rocca Busambra** *mt. Sicilia* Italy
193 H4 **Roccadaspide** Italy
193 F3 **Rocca d'Evandro** Italy
193 F2 **Rocca di Cambio** Italy
193 F2 **Rocca di Mezzo** Italy
195 F3 **Rocca di Neto** Italy
193 E3 **Rocca di Papa** Italy
190 E3 **Roccafranca** Italy
193 H4 **Roccagloriosa** Italy
195 F2 **Rocca Imperiale** Italy
190 C4 **Rocca la Meia** *mt.* Italy
192 D2 **Roccalbegna** Italy
195 E5 **Roccalumera** *Sicilia* Italy
193 G3 **Roccamandolfi** Italy
193 E3 **Rocca Massima** Italy
194 C5 **Roccamena** *Sicilia* Italy
193 F3 **Roccamonfina** Italy
193 G2 **Roccamontepiano** Italy
193 I4 **Roccanova** Italy
194 C5 **Roccapalumba** *Sicilia* Italy
193 F3 **Rocca Pia** Italy
193 G3 **Roccaraso** Italy
191 G4 **Rocca San Casciano** Italy
193 G2 **Rocca San Giovanni** Italy
193 F3 **Roccasecca** Italy
193 F3 **Roccasecca dei Volsci** Italy
193 E2 **Rocca Sinibalda** Italy
192 D1 **Roccastrada** Italy
190 C4 **Roccavione** Italy
195 F4 **Roccella Ionica** Italy
193 H3 **Rocchetta Sant'Antonio** Italy
186 F2 **Roc de France** *mt.* France/Spain
161 A5 **Roc de Layre** *mt.* France
161 A5 **Roc de Montalet** *mt.* France
160 E2 **Roc d'Enfer** *mt.* France
158 C3 **Roc de Toullaëron** *hill* France
151 F2 **Rocester** *Staffordshire, England* U.K.
258 G4 **Rocha** Uru.
149 G4 **Rochdale** *Greater Manchester, England* U.K.
150 C4 **Roche** *Cornwall, England* U.K.
161 E3 **Roche Bernaude** *mt.* France/Italy
161 E4 **Rochebrune, Grand Pic de** *mt.* France
162 C3 **Rochechouart** France
159 G4 **Rochecorbon** France
161 D3 **Roche de Méaudre** *mt.* France
162 D3 **Roche de Vic** *hill* France
255 B6 **Rochedo** Brazil
165 E4 **Rochefort** Belgium
162 B3 **Rochefort** France
158 D4 **Rochefort-en-Terre** France
160 A3 **Rochefort-Montagne** France
160 D1 **Rochefort-sur-Nenon** France
134 H3 **Rochegda** Rus. Fed.
161 C4 **Rochegude** France
165 E5 **Rochehaut** Belgium
161 C3 **Roche-la-Molière** France
160 E1 **Roche-lez-Beaupré** France
226 C5 **Rochelle** *IL* U.S.A.
161 C4 **Rochemaure** France
157 F4 **Roches-Bettaincourt** France
158 E5 **Rocheservière** France
83 F4 **Rochester** *Vic.* Austr.
151 H3 **Rochester** *Medway, England* U.K.
149 G2 **Rochester** *Northumberland, England* U.K.
230 C3 **Rochester** *IN* U.S.A.
227 F4 **Rochester** *MI* U.S.A.
226 A3 **Rochester** *MN* U.S.A.
233 □H3 **Rochester** *NH* U.S.A.
232 E3 **Rochester** *NY* U.S.A.
147 D4 **Rochestown** Rep. of Ireland
157 F5 **Rochetaillée** France
151 H3 **Rochford** *Essex, England* U.K.
147 D3 **Rochfortbridge** Rep. of Ireland
156 D2 **Rochin** France
171 D4 **Rochlitz** Ger.
158 C3 **Roc'h Trévezel** *hill* France
184 D3 **Rociana del Condado** Spain
184 D4 **Rocina** *r.* Spain
222 E2 **Rock** *r. Y.T.* Can.
150 E2 **Rock** *Worcestershire, England* U.K.
226 D2 **Rock** *MI* U.S.A.
236 D3 **Rock** *r. IA* U.S.A.
226 B5 **Rock** *r. IL* U.S.A.
144 □ **Rockall** *i.* N. Atlantic Ocean
264 H2 **Rockall Bank** *sea feature* N. Atlantic Ocean
81 B6 **Rock and Pillar Range** *mts South I.* N.Z.
164 D3 **Rockanje** Neth.
222 E5 **Rock Bay** *B.C.* Can.
146 E7 **Rockcliffe** *Dumfries and Galloway, Scotland* U.K.
147 D2 **Rockcorry** Rep. of Ireland
232 C4 **Rock Creek** *OH* U.S.A.
238 F1 **Rock Creek** *r. MT* U.S.A.
234 A3 **Rock Creek** *r. PA* U.S.A.
234 B3 **Rockdale** *MD* U.S.A.
237 D6 **Rockdale** *TX* U.S.A.
262 O1 **Rockefeller Plateau** Antarctica
169 D5 **Rockenberg** Ger.
172 B2 **Rockenhausen** Ger.
235 F1 **Rockfall** *CT* U.S.A.
231 C5 **Rockford** *AL* U.S.A.
226 C4 **Rockford** *IL* U.S.A.
226 E4 **Rockford** *MI* U.S.A.
232 A4 **Rockford** *OH* U.S.A.
223 J5 **Rockglen** *Sask.* Can.
234 B2 **Rock Glen** *PA* U.S.A.
234 B3 **Rock Hall** *MD* U.S.A.
85 G4 **Rockhampton** *Qld* Austr.
84 C3 **Rockhampton Downs** *N.T.* Austr.
226 C1 **Rock Harbor** *MI* U.S.A.
147 C4 **Rockhill** Rep. of Ireland
234 D1 **Rock Hill** *NY* U.S.A.
231 D5 **Rock Hill** *SC* U.S.A.
87 B7 **Rockingham** *W.A.* Austr.
151 G2 **Rockingham** *Northamptonshire, England* U.K.
231 E5 **Rockingham** *NC* U.S.A.
85 F3 **Rockingham Bay** *Qld* Austr.
151 G2 **Rockingham Forest** *England* U.K.
233 G2 **Rock Island** *Que.* Can.
236 F3 **Rock Island** *IL* U.S.A.
236 D1 **Rocklake** *ND* U.S.A.
233 F2 **Rockland** *Ont.* Can.
233 H3 **Rockland** *MA* U.S.A.
233 □I2 **Rockland** *ME* U.S.A.
226 C2 **Rockland** *MI* U.S.A.
235 D1 **Rockland County** *county NY* U.S.A.
87 C4 **Rocklea** *W.A.* Austr.
240 G2 **Rocklin** *CA* U.S.A.
171 D4 **Röcknitz** Ger.
241 M3 **Rock Point** *AZ* U.S.A.
230 C4 **Rockport** *IN* U.S.A.
233 H3 **Rockport** *MA* U.S.A.
237 D7 **Rockport** *TX* U.S.A.
238 B1 **Rockport** *WA* U.S.A.
232 C5 **Rockport** *WV* U.S.A.
236 D3 **Rock Rapids** *IA* U.S.A.
238 F3 **Rock River** *WY* U.S.A.
246 C1 **Rock Sound** *Eleuthera* Bahamas
238 F2 **Rock Springs** *MT* U.S.A.
237 C6 **Rocksprings** *TX* U.S.A.
238 E3 **Rock Springs** *WY* U.S.A.
251 G3 **Rockstone** Guyana
226 C4 **Rockton** *IL* U.S.A.
230 C4 **Rockville** *IN* U.S.A.
234 A3 **Rockville** *MD* U.S.A.
235 G1 **Rockville** *RI* U.S.A.
235 E2 **Rockville Centre** *NY* U.S.A.
237 D5 **Rockwall** *TX* U.S.A.
236 E3 **Rockwell City** *IA* U.S.A.
150 D4 **Rockwell Green** *Somerset, England* U.K.
233 □I2 **Rockwood** *ME* U.S.A.
227 F4 **Rockwood** *MI* U.S.A.
232 D5 **Rockwood** *PA* U.S.A.
222 H5 **Rockyford** *Alta* Can.
236 C4 **Rocky Ford** *CO* U.S.A.
87 C7 **Rocky Gully** *W.A.* Austr.
225 J3 **Rocky Harbour** *Nfld.* Can.
235 F1 **Rocky Hill** *CT* U.S.A.
232 B5 **Rocky Hill** *OH* U.S.A.
222 G3 **Rocky Lane** *Alta* Can.
231 E5 **Rocky Mount** *NC* U.S.A.
232 D6 **Rocky Mount** *VA* U.S.A.
222 H4 **Rocky Mountain House** *Alta* Can.
228 E2 **Rocky Mountains** *CO* U.S.A.
156 D3 **Rocourt-St-Martin** France
156 E3 **Rocroi** France
171 C5 **Rodach** *r.* Ger.
169 F5 **Rodach** *r.* Ger.
169 F5 **Rodach bei Coburg** Ger.
186 E3 **Roda de Berà** Spain
186 F3 **Roda de Ter** Spain
172 B2 **Rodalben** Ger.
168 E2 **Rodau** *r.* Ger.
142 C1 **Rodberg** Norway
150 E3 **Rodborough** *Gloucestershire, England* U.K.
168 G1 **Rødby** Denmark
142 D4 **Rødbyhavn** Denmark
225 K3 **Roddickton** *Nfld.* Can.
142 C4 **Rødding** *Sønderjylland* Denmark
142 C3 **Rødding** *Viborg* Denmark
215 G4 **Rode** S. Africa
143 F3 **Rödeby** Sweden
149 G4 **Rode Heath** *Cheshire, England* U.K.
182 C2 **Rodeiro** Spain
142 C4 **Rødekro** Denmark
146 B4 **Rodel** *Western Isles, Scotland* U.K.
186 C2 **Rodellar** Spain
161 A4 **Rodelle** France
164 F1 **Roden** Neth.
150 E2 **Roden** *r. England* U.K.
183 I4 **Ródenas** Spain
168 D2 **Rodenkirchen (Stadland)** Ger.
171 C5 **Rödental** Ger.
260 C2 **Rodeo** Arg.
242 D3 **Rodeo** Mex.
239 E6 **Rodeo** *NM* U.S.A.
87 C5 **Roderick** *r. W.A.* Austr.
168 E3 **Rodewald** Ger.
171 D5 **Rodewisch** Ger.
161 A4 **Rodez** France
169 D5 **Rodheim-Bieber** Ger.
Rodholívos Greece *see* **Rodolivos**
Rodhópolis Greece *see* **Rodopoli**
Ródhos *i.* Greece *see* **Rodos**
Rodi *i.* Greece *see* **Rodos**
179 E4 **Rodica** *mt.* Slovenia
193 H3 **Rodi Garganico** Italy
173 G2 **Roding** Ger.
121 J1 **Rodino** Rus. Fed.
137 J4 **Rodionovo-Nesvetayskaya** Rus. Fed.
143 G1 **Rödjebro** Sweden
171 D4 **Rodleben** Ger.
197 G2 **Rodna** Romania
197 G2 **Rodnei, Munții** *mts* Romania
80 E2 **Rodney, Cape** *North I.* N.Z.
150 E3 **Rodney Stoke** *Somerset, England* U.K.
234 C3 **Rodney Village** *DE* U.S.A.
Rodnichek Rus. Fed. *see* **Rodnichok**
135 H6 **Rodnichok** Rus. Fed.
137 G3 **Rodnykivka** Ukr.
120 D2 **Rodnykovka** Kazakh.
242 A2 **Rodolfo Sanchez Toboada** Mex.
198 C1 **Rodolivos** Greece
196 D5 **Rodonit, Kepi i** *pt* Albania
Rodopi Planina *mts* Bulg./Greece *see* **Rhodope Mountains**
198 C1 **Rodopoli** Greece
199 F3 **Rodos** *Notio Aigaio* Greece
199 F3 **Rodos** *i.* Greece
186 F3 **Rodós** *mt.* Spain
Rodosto Turkey *see* **Tekirdağ**
182 C1 **Rodrigas** Spain
217 □1a **Rodrigues Island** Mauritius
261 I4 **Rodriguez** Uru.
86 E2 **Roe** *r. W.A.* Austr.
148 C2 **Roe** *r. Northern Ireland* U.K.
234 D2 **Roebling** *NJ* U.S.A.
86 C4 **Roebourne** *W.A.* Austr.
86 D3 **Roebuck Bay** *W.A.* Austr.
213 F5 **Roedtan** S. Africa
191 G2 **Roèn, Monte** *mt.* Italy
87 E6 **Roe Plains** *W.A.* Austr.
165 E3 **Roermond** Neth.
165 B4 **Roesbrugge-Haringe** Belgium
165 C4 **Roeselare** Belgium
221 J3 **Roes Welcome Sound** *sea chan. Nunavut* Can.
169 B5 **Roetgen** Ger.
193 H4 **Rofrano** Italy
Rogachev Belarus *see* **Rahachow**
137 J2 **Rogachevka** Rus. Fed.
139 K3 **Rogachevo** Rus. Fed.
252 D3 **Rogagua, Laguna** *l.* Bol.
142 B2 **Rogaland** *county* Norway
188 E2 **Rogaška Slatina** Slovenia
174 F4 **Rogaszyce** Pol.
151 G3 **Rogate** *West Sussex, England* U.K.
179 G4 **Rogatec** Slovenia
188 G4 **Rogatica** Bos.-Herz.
Rogatin Ukr. *see* **Rohatyn**
171 C3 **Rogätz** Ger.
222 G5 **Rogers** *B.C.* Can.
237 E4 **Rogers** *AR* U.S.A.
232 C6 **Rogers, Mount** *VA* U.S.A.
227 F3 **Rogers City** *MI* U.S.A.
238 D3 **Rogerson** *ID* U.S.A.
232 B6 **Rogersville** *TN* U.S.A.
224 E2 **Roggan** *r. Que.* Can.
165 E3 **Roggel** Neth.
173 E3 **Roggenburg** Ger.
170 C2 **Roggendorf** Ger.
170 D2 **Roggentin** Ger.
267 N8 **Roggeveen Basin** *sea feature* S. Pacific Ocean
214 C5 **Roggeveld** *plat.* S. Africa
214 C5 **Roggeveldberge** *esc.* S. Africa
193 I5 **Roggiano Gravina** Italy
Roghadal *Western Isles, Scotland* U.K. *see* **Rodel**
195 E4 **Roghudi** Italy
184 B3 **Rogil** Port.
192 B2 **Rogliano** *Corse* France
195 F3 **Rogliano** Italy
191 F5 **Roglio** *r.* Italy
161 D5 **Rognac** France
140 K2 **Rognan** Norway
139 I5 **Rognedino** Rus. Fed.
161 D5 **Rognes** France
168 F2 **Rögnitz** *r.* Ger.
157 F4 **Rognon** *r.* France
161 C5 **Rognonas** France
190 B4 **Rognosa, Punta** *mt.* Italy
137 J2 **Rogovatoye** Rus. Fed.
137 J5 **Rogovskaya** Rus. Fed.
175 H4 **Rogów** Pol.
174 F3 **Rogowo** *Kujawsko-Pomorskie* Pol.
175 H3 **Rogowo** *Kujawsko-Pomorskie* Pol.
174 E4 **Rogoźnica** Pol.
175 K3 **Rogoźniczka** Pol.
174 G2 **Rogóźno** Pol.
174 F3 **Rogoźno** Pol.
141 L3 **Rogsta** Sweden
238 A3 **Rogue** *r. OR* U.S.A.
78 □3b **Roguron** *i. Majuro* Marshall Is
175 J3 **Roguszyn** Pol.
114 B2 **Roha** *Mahar.* India
136 D2 **Rohachiv** Ukr.
158 D3 **Rohan** France
137 I3 **Rohan'** Ukr.
176 G3 **Rohatec** Czech Rep.
136 C3 **Rohatyn** Ukr.
137 F2 **Rohizky** Ukr.
173 E3 **Röhlingen** Ger.
170 C2 **Rohlsdorf** *Brandenburg* Ger.
170 D2 **Rohlsdorf** *Brandenburg* Ger.
240 F2 **Rohnert Park** *CA* U.S.A.
177 L3 **Rohod** Hungary
176 G3 **Rohovce** Slovakia
179 H2 **Rohrau** Austria
173 F3 **Rohrbach** Ger.
179 E2 **Rohrbach in Oberösterreich** Austria
157 H3 **Rohrbach-lès-Bitche** France
170 C3 **Rohrberg** Ger.
123 G5 **Rohri** Pak.
173 F3 **Rohr in Niederbayern** Ger.
173 F3 **Röhrmoos** Ger.
173 H3 **Röhrnbach** Ger.
168 E3 **Rohrsen** Ger.
116 D3 **Rohtak** *Haryana* India
96 C3 **Roi Et** Thai.
161 C3 **Roiffieux** France
79 □3 **Roi Georges, Îles du** *is Arch. des Tuamotu* Fr. Polynesia
78 □3a **Roi-Namur** *i. Kwajalein* Marshall Is
141 N3 **Roine** *l.* Fin.
117 H3 **Roing** *Arun. Prad.* India
146 C5 **Rois-Bheinn** *hill Scotland* U.K.
156 D3 **Roisel** France
156 C4 **Roissy-en-Brie** France
183 F1 **Roiz** Spain
138 D3 **Roja** Latvia
187 C6 **Rojales** Spain
261 G4 **Rojas** Arg.
142 E1 **Röjdåfors** Sweden
174 G3 **Rojewo** Pol.
123 G4 **Rojhan** Pak.
247 □1 **Rojo, Cabo** Puerto Rico
247 □1 **Rojo, Cabo** *c.* Puerto Rico
252 D3 **Rojo Aguado, Laguna** *l.* Bol.
94 C2 **Rokan** *r.* Indon.
85 E2 **Rokeby** *Qld* Austr.
175 H4 **Rokiciny** Pol.
175 K6 **Rokietnica** *Podkarpackie* Pol.
174 E3 **Rokietnica** *Wielkopolskie* Pol.
138 E4 **Rokiškis** Lith.
175 L3 **Rokitno** Pol.
140 M2 **Roknäs** Sweden
177 H3 **Rokoš** *mt.* Slovakia
105 E2 **Rokuriga-hara** *plain* Japan
176 C2 **Rokycany** Czech Rep.
136 C2 **Rokyni** Ukr.
176 F2 **Rokytná** *r.* Czech Rep.
136 F3 **Rokytne** *Kyivs'ka Oblast'* Ukr.
136 D2 **Rokytne** *Rivnens'ka Oblast'* Ukr.
176 G2 **Rokytnice** Czech Rep.
111 E5 **Rola Kangri** *mt. Xizang* China
157 F5 **Rolampont** France
256 B5 **Rolândia** Brazil
261 G3 **Roldan** Arg.
164 F2 **Rolde** Neth.
253 E2 **Rolim de Moura** Brazil
241 K5 **Roll** *AZ* U.S.A.
236 F4 **Rolla** *MO* U.S.A.
236 D1 **Rolla** *ND* U.S.A.
142 C1 **Rollag** Norway
182 E4 **Rollán** Spain
190 B2 **Rolle** Switz.
151 I2 **Rollesby** *Norfolk, England* U.K.
85 G5 **Rolleston** *Qld* Austr.
81 D5 **Rolleston** *South I.* N.Z.
81 C5 **Rolleston, Mount** *South I.* N.Z.
81 C5 **Rolleston Range** *mts South I.* N.Z.
227 H2 **Rollet** *Que.* Can.
246 D2 **Rolleville** *Gt Exuma* Bahamas
237 F5 **Rolling Fork** *MS* U.S.A.
238 D2 **Rollins** *MT* U.S.A.
233 □H3 **Rollinsford** *NH* U.S.A.
206 E3 **Rollo** Burkina
227 I2 **Rolphton** *Ont.* Can.
162 C2 **Rom** France
170 C2 **Rom** Ger.
210 B4 **Rom** *mt.* Uganda
85 G5 **Roma** *Qld* Austr.
193 E3 **Roma** Italy
193 E2 **Roma** *prov. Lazio* Italy
215 F3 **Roma** Lesotho
197 H2 **Roma** Romania
143 H3 **Roma** *Gotland* Sweden
237 D7 **Roma** *TX* U.S.A.
190 D3 **Romagnano Sesia** Italy
158 E3 **Romagné** France
81 B7 **Romahapa** *South I.* N.Z.
225 I3 **Romaine** *r. Que.* Can.
190 B2 **Romainmôtier** Switz.
197 H2 **Roman** Romania
151 H3 **Roman** *r. England* U.K.
192 A4 **Romana** *Sardegna* Italy
197 F3 **Română, Câmpia** *plain* Romania
197 F3 **Romanaților, Câmpia** *plain* Romania
149 H3 **Romanby** *North Yorkshire, England* U.K.
161 D3 **Romanche** *r.* France
264 H6 **Romanche Gap** *sea feature* S. Atlantic Ocean
234 B4 **Romancoke** *MD* U.S.A.
160 C2 **Romanèche-Thorins** France
197 G2 **Romania** *country* Europe
183 H3 **Romanillos de Atienza** Spain
175 M6 **Romaniv** Ukr.
137 H5 **Roman-Kosh** *mt.* Ukr.
146 E6 **Romannobridge** *Scottish Borders, Scotland* U.K.
191 G3 **Romano d'Ezzelino** Italy
190 E3 **Romano di Lombardia** Italy
183 H4 **Romanones** Spain
Romanovka Moldova *see* **Basarabeasca**
99 J1 **Romanovka** *Respublika Buryatiya* Rus. Fed.
135 H6 **Romanovka** *Saratovskaya Oblast'* Rus. Fed.
121 J1 **Romanovo** Rus. Fed.
190 E1 **Romanshorn** Switz.
161 D3 **Romans-sur-Isère** France
158 E3 **Romazy** France
157 G3 **Rombas** France
195 F4 **Rombiolo** Italy
92 B3 **Romblon** Phil.
Rombo, Ilhéus do *is* Cape Verde *see* **Secos, Ilhéus**
Rome Italy *see* **Roma**
231 C5 **Rome** *GA* U.S.A.
226 C5 **Rome** *IL* U.S.A.
233 □I2 **Rome** *ME* U.S.A.
233 F3 **Rome** *NY* U.S.A.
160 C2 **Rome Château, Mont de** *hill* France
226 E5 **Rome City** *IN* U.S.A.
184 B1 **Romeira** Port.
137 G2 **Romen** *r.* Ukr.
239 F4 **Romeo** *CO* U.S.A.
227 F4 **Romeo** *MI* U.S.A.
172 D3 **Römerstein** *hill* Ger.
182 C3 **Romeu** Port.
151 H3 **Romford** *Greater London, England* U.K.
169 F5 **Römhild** Ger.
158 E3 **Romillé** France
156 B3 **Romilly-sur-Andelle** France
156 D4 **Romilly-sur-Seine** France
244 D3 **Romita** Mex.
120 F5 **Romitan** Uzbek.
169 B4 **Rommerskirchen** Ger.
232 D5 **Romney** *WV* U.S.A.
151 H3 **Romney Marsh** *reg. England* U.K.
137 G2 **Romny** Ukr.
142 C4 **Rømø** *i.* Denmark
137 G3 **Romodan** Ukr.
135 I5 **Romodanovo** Rus. Fed.
190 B2 **Romont** Switz.
78 □4a **Romonum** *i. Chuuk* Micronesia
162 D1 **Romorantin-Lanthenay** France
94 C2 **Rompin** *r.* Malaysia
169 E5 **Romrod** Ger.
151 F4 **Romsey** *Hampshire, England* U.K.
142 D2 **Rømskog** Norway
150 E2 **Romsley** *Worcestershire, England* U.K.
95 G5 **Romu** *mt. Sumbawa* Indon.
197 G2 **Romuli** Romania
227 F4 **Romulus** *MI* U.S.A.
114 B3 **Ron** *Karnataka* India
146 C4 **Rona** *i. Highland, Scotland* U.K.
146 C2 **Rona** *i. Western Isles, Scotland* U.K.
Ronaigh *i. Scotland* U.K. *see* **Ronay**
146 □G1 **Ronas Hill** *hill Scotland* U.K.
146 A4 **Ronay** *i. Scotland* U.K.
191 H3 **Roncade** Italy
256 A6 **Roncador** Brazil
254 B5 **Roncador, Serra do** *hills* Brazil
246 B4 **Roncador Cay** *i.* Caribbean Sea
78 □6 **Roncador Reef** Solomon Is
186 C2 **Roncal** Spain
178 C4 **Roncegno** Italy
162 A3 **Ronce-les-Bains** France
186 B1 **Roncesvalles** Spain
232 C6 **Ronceverte** *WV* U.S.A.
157 G5 **Ronchamp** France
191 I3 **Ronchi dei Legionari** Italy
192 E2 **Ronciglione** Italy
191 H4 **Ronco** *r.* Italy
190 C3 **Ronco Canavese** Italy
191 F3 **Roncone** Italy
190 D4 **Ronco Scrivia** Italy
156 D2 **Roncq** France
185 E4 **Ronda** Spain
185 E4 **Ronda, Serranía de** *mts* Spain
142 D3 **Rønde** Denmark
190 C3 **Rondissone** Italy
256 A5 **Rondon** Brazil
250 D3 **Rondón** Col.
252 E2 **Rondônia** *state* Brazil
255 B6 **Rondonópolis** Brazil
98 C4 **Rondu** Jammu and Kashmir
108 D3 **Rong'an** *Guangxi* China
108 A2 **Rongbaca** *Sichuan* China
108 C2 **Rongchang** *Chongqing* China
Rongcheng *Anhui* China *see* **Qingyang**
Rongcheng *Guangxi* China *see* **Rongxian**
Rongcheng *Hubei* China *see* **Jianli**
107 I4 **Rongcheng** *Shandong* China
111 E6 **Rong Chu** *r.* China
266 G6 **Rongelap** *atoll* Marshall Is
108 D3 **Rongjiang** *Guizhou* China
Rongjiang *Jiangxi* China *see* **Nankang**
108 D4 **Rong Jiang** *r.* China
Rongjiawan *Hunan* China *see* **Yueyang**
96 A2 **Rongklang Range** *mts* Myanmar
Rongmei *Hubei* China *see* **Hefeng**
108 D3 **Rongshui** *Guangxi* China
Rongwo *Qinghai* China *see* **Tongren**
108 D4 **Rongxian** *Guangxi* China
108 C2 **Rongxian** *Sichuan* China
Rongzhag *Sichuan* China *see* **Danba**
Rönlap *atoll* Marshall Is *see* **Rongelap**
143 F4 **Rønne** *Bornholm* Denmark
171 D5 **Ronneburg** Ger.
143 F3 **Ronneby** Sweden
262 S2 **Ronne Entrance** *str.* Antarctica
169 E3 **Ronnenberg** Ger.
140 K3 **Rönnöfors** Sweden
86 C4 **Ronsard Island** *W.A.* Austr.
173 E4 **Ronsberg** Ger.
165 C4 **Ronse** Belgium
169 E5 **Ronshausen** Ger.
254 B5 **Ronuro** *r.* Brazil

147 C3 Rooaun Rep. of Ireland
215 G2 Roodebank S. Africa
164 F1 Roodeschool Neth.
215 G3 Rooiberg mt. Free State S. Africa
214 C5 Rooiberg mt. W. Cape S. Africa
215 G1 Rooikraal S. Africa
215 F2 Rooiwal S. Africa
147 B3 Roonah Quay Rep. of Ireland
164 E1 Roordahuizum Neth.
116 D3 Roorkee Uttar Prad. India
215 G3 Roosboom S. Africa
164 D3 Roosendaal Neth.
241 L5 Roosevelt AZ U.S.A.
235 D2 Roosevelt NJ U.S.A.
241 M1 Roosevelt UT U.S.A.
222 E3 Roosevelt, Mount B.C. Can.
235 D3 Roosevelt City NJ U.S.A.
262 N1 Roosevelt Island Antarctica
147 D3 Roosky Leitrim Rep. of Ireland
147 C3 Roosky Mayo Rep. of Ireland
215 G1 Roossenekal S. Africa
222 F2 Root r. N.W.T. Can.
226 B4 Root r. MN U.S.A.
175 J6 Ropa Pol.
175 J6 Ropa r. Pol.
138 E3 Ropaži Latvia
175 J5 Ropczyce Pol.
84 C2 Roper r. N.T. Austr.
84 C2 Roper Bar N.T. Austr.
85 G4 Roper Creek r. Qld Austr.
182 E2 Roperuelos del Páramo Spain
84 C2 Roper Valley N.T. Austr.
175 K6 Ropienka Pol.
178 B3 Roppen Austria
161 F4 Roquebillière France
161 B5 Roquebrun France
161 F5 Roquebrune-Cap-Martin France
161 E5 Roquebrune-sur-Argens France
163 C4 Roquecor France
163 E5 Roquecourbe France
216 □3d Roque de los Muchachos vol. La Palma Canary Is
163 B4 Roquefort France
161 A5 Roquefort-sur-Soulzon France
161 C4 Roquemaure France
261 H4 Roque Pérez Arg.
161 F5 Roquesteron France
186 D4 Roquetas Spain
185 H4 Roquetas de Mar Spain
161 D5 Roquevaire France
251 F4 Roraima state Brazil
251 F3 Roraima, Mount Guyana
116 C3 Rori Punjab India
140 J3 Røros Norway
190 E1 Rorschach Switz.
142 D4 Rørvig Denmark
140 J2 Rørvik Norway
175 M2 Ros' Belarus
138 E5 Ros' r. Belarus
136 F3 Ros' r. Ukr.
191 G3 Rosà Italy
190 C3 Rosa, Monte mt. Italy/Switz.
190 C2 Rosablanche mt. Switz.
216 □1c Rosais São Jorge Azores
184 C3 Rosal de la Frontera Spain
238 C2 Rosalia WA U.S.A.
246 B3 Rosalind Bank sea feature Caribbean Sea
240 H4 Rosamond CA U.S.A.
256 A5 Rosana Brazil
178 B3 Rosanna r. Austria
161 D4 Rosans France
147 D1 Rosapenna Rep. of Ireland
261 G3 Rosario Arg.
254 D2 Rosário Brazil
242 B2 Rosario Baja California Norte Mex.
244 B2 Rosario Sinaloa Mex.
242 C3 Rosario Sonora Mex.
253 F6 Rosario Para.
92 B2 Rosario Luzon Phil.
92 B3 Rosario Luzon Phil.
184 B3 Rosário Port.
261 I4 Rosario Uru.
250 C2 Rosario Venez.
258 D2 Rosario de la Frontera Arg.
258 D2 Rosario de Lerma Arg.
261 H3 Rosario del Tala Arg.
255 B9 Rosário do Sul Brazil
253 F3 Rosário Oeste Brazil
242 A1 Rosarito Baja California Norte Mex.
242 B2 Rosarito Baja California Norte Mex.
242 C3 Rosarito Baja California Sur Mex.
195 E4 Rosarno Italy
Rosas Spain see Roses
Rosas, Golfe de b. Spain see Roses, Golf de
137 F3 Rosava r. Ukr.
250 B4 Rosa Zárate Ecuador
169 D5 Rosbach vor der Höhe Ger.
147 C2 Rosbeg Rep. of Ireland
147 E4 Rosbercon Rep. of Ireland
158 B3 Roscanvel France
168 F3 Rosche Ger.
179 G2 Röschitz Austria
175 H3 Rościszewo Pol.
226 C4 Roscoe IL U.S.A.
158 C3 Roscoff France
147 C3 Roscommon Rep. of Ireland
147 C3 Roscommon county Rep. of Ireland
226 E3 Roscommon MI U.S.A.
147 D4 Roscrea Rep. of Ireland
169 E4 Rosdorf Ger.
84 C2 Rose r. N.T. Austr.
193 I5 Rose Italy
240 H2 Rose, Mount NV U.S.A.
247 □2 Roseau Dominica
236 E1 Roseau MN U.S.A.
236 D1 Roseau r. MN U.S.A.
149 H3 Roseberry Topping hill England U.K.
84 D5 Roseberth Qld Austr.
83 F5 Rosebery Tas. Austr.
225 J4 Rose Blanche Nfld. Can.
222 H5 Rosebud r. Alta Can.
238 F2 Rosebud MT U.S.A.
238 F2 Rosebud Creek r. MT U.S.A.
238 B3 Roseburg OR U.S.A.
227 E3 Rose City MI U.S.A.
226 A4 Rose Creek MN U.S.A.
85 G5 Rosedale Qld Austr.
83 F4 Rosedale Vic. Austr.
234 B3 Rosedale MD U.S.A.
237 F5 Rosedale MS U.S.A.
149 I3 Rosedale Abbey North Yorkshire, England U.K.
214 D5 Rosedene S. Africa
165 D4 Rosée Belgium
179 F4 Rosegg Austria
246 □ Rose Hall Jamaica
146 D4 Rosehall Highland, Scotland U.K.
146 F4 Rosehearty Aberdeenshire, Scotland U.K.
210 B2 Roseires Reservoir Sudan
75 H4 Rose Island American Samoa
231 □2 Rose Island Bahamas
186 D4 Rosell Spain
235 D2 Roselle NJ U.S.A.
146 D4 Rosemarkie Highland, Scotland U.K.
86 C4 Rosemary Island W.A. Austr.
147 D3 Rosenallis Rep. of Ireland
237 E6 Rosenberg TX U.S.A.
142 B2 Rosendal Norway
215 F3 Rosendal S. Africa
226 C4 Rosendale WI U.S.A.
172 C3 Rosenfeld Ger.
168 E2 Rosengarten Ger.
234 C3 Rosenhayn NJ U.S.A.
173 G4 Rosenheim Ger.
179 E4 Rosennock mt. Austria
170 E2 Rosenow Ger.
179 F4 Rosental val. Austria
169 D5 Rosenthal Ger.
241 M5 Rose Peak AZ U.S.A.
143 G2 Roserberg Sweden
186 G2 Roses Spain
186 G2 Roses, Golf de b. Spain
234 C2 Roseto PA U.S.A.
195 F3 Roseto Capo Spulico Italy
193 G2 Roseto degli Abruzzi Italy
193 H3 Roseto Valfortore Italy
223 J5 Rosetown Sask. Can.
Rosetta Egypt see Rashîd
85 F4 Rosetta Creek r. Qld Austr.
223 K4 Rose Valley Sask. Can.
240 G2 Roseville CA U.S.A.
236 F3 Roseville IL U.S.A.
227 F4 Roseville MI U.S.A.
232 B5 Roseville OH U.S.A.
146 E6 Rosewell Midlothian, Scotland U.K.
85 H5 Rosewood Qld Austr.
232 B4 Rosewood OH U.S.A.
139 L4 Roshal' Rus. Fed.
138 G1 Roshchino Rus. Fed.
157 H4 Rosheim France
226 C3 Rosholt WI U.S.A.
212 C5 Rosh Pinah Namibia
146 C5 Roshven Highland, Scotland U.K.
177 L5 Roșia Romania
176 F2 Rosice Czech Rep.
161 B3 Rosières France
156 C3 Rosières-en-Santerre France
156 E4 Rosières-près-Troyes France
190 F5 Rosignano Marittimo Italy
86 B4 Rosily Island W.A. Austr.
177 H2 Rosina Slovakia
197 H3 Roșiori Romania
197 G3 Roșiori de Vede Romania
197 H4 Rositsa Bulg.
197 G4 Rositsa r. Bulg.
171 D4 Rositz Ger.
146 B4 Roskhill Highland, Scotland U.K.
142 E4 Roskilde Denmark
142 E4 Roskilde county Denmark
174 E3 Rosko Pol.
198 A1 Roskovec Albania
171 D3 Roskow Ger.
241 L5 Roskruge Mountains AZ U.S.A.
171 C5 Röslau Ger.
171 D5 Röslau r. Ger.
139 I5 Roslavl' Rus. Fed.
146 E6 Roslin Midlothian, Scotland U.K.
140 P1 Roslyakovo Rus. Fed.
134 I4 Roslyatino Rus. Fed.
164 E3 Rosmalen Neth.
182 C5 Rosmaninhal Port.
215 E4 Rosmead S. Africa
147 B3 Rosmuck Rep. of Ireland
174 E1 Rosnowo Pol.
191 H3 Rosolina Italy
191 H3 Rosolina Mare Italy
194 D6 Rosolini Sicilia Italy
197 E5 Rosoman Macedonia
156 D4 Rosoy France
178 D3 Röspitze mt. Austria/Italy
158 C4 Rosporden France
169 C5 Rösrath Ger.
83 F5 Ross Tas. Austr.
222 C2 Ross r. Y.T. Can.
81 C5 Ross South I. N.Z.
81 E4 Ross, Mount hill North I. N.Z.
195 F3 Rossano Italy
191 G3 Rossano Veneto Italy
182 B3 Rossas Port.
147 B3 Rossaveel Rep. of Ireland
173 G3 Roßbach Ger.
171 C4 Roßbach Ger.
225 H2 Ross Bay Junction Nfld. Can.
147 B5 Rossbrin Rep. of Ireland
147 B3 Rosscahill Rep. of Ireland
147 B5 Ross Carbery Rep. of Ireland
147 C2 Rosscor Northern Ireland U.K.
262 N2 Ross Dependency Antarctica
172 C2 Roßdorf Ger.
186 D3 Rosselló Spain
191 F4 Rossenno r. Italy
147 C1 Rosses Bay Rep. of Ireland
147 C2 Rosses Point Rep. of Ireland
150 E1 Rossett Wrexham, Wales U.K.
173 E4 Roßhaupten Ger.
263 M1 Ross Ice Shelf Antarctica
190 D4 Rossiglione Italy
165 E5 Rossignol Belgium
169 E3 Rössing (Nordstemmen) Ger.
149 H4 Rossington South Yorkshire, England U.K.
147 C2 Rossinver Rep. of Ireland
184 B1 Rossio ao Sul do Tejo Port.
263 L1 Ross Island Antarctica
87 D7 Rossiter Bay W.A. Austr.
Rossiyskaya Sovetskaya Federativnaya Sotsialisticheskaya Respublika country Asia/Europe see Russian Federation
171 C4 Roßla Ger.
222 G5 Rossland B.C. Can.
147 E4 Rosslare Rep. of Ireland
147 E4 Rosslare Harbour Rep. of Ireland
147 E4 Rosslare Point Rep. of Ireland
171 D4 Roßlau Ger.
147 D2 Rosslea Northern Ireland U.K.
171 C4 Roßleben Ger.
179 F3 Roßleithen Austria
227 I3 Rossmore Ont. Can.
147 C2 Rossnowlagh Rep. of Ireland
206 B2 Rosso Maur.
140 L3 Rossön Sweden
150 E3 Ross-on-Wye Herefordshire, England U.K.
Rossony Belarus see Rasony
135 G6 Rossosh' Rus. Fed.
175 L4 Rossosz Pol.
174 G4 Rossoszyca Pol.
215 F4 Rossouw S. Africa
170 D2 Rossow Ger.
226 D1 Rossport Ont. Can.
84 C4 Ross River N.T. Austr.
222 C2 Ross River Y.T. Can.
263 L1 Ross Sea Antarctica
173 E2 Roßtal Ger.
164 E3 Rossum Neth.
140 K2 Røssvatnet l. Norway
226 B4 Rossville IA U.S.A.
226 D5 Rossville IL U.S.A.
226 D5 Rossville IN U.S.A.
234 B2 Rossville PA U.S.A.
171 E4 Roßwein Ger.
222 D4 Rosswood B.C. Can.
127 G3 Rōst Iraq
140 K2 Røst Norway
136 F3 Rostabytsya r. Ukr.
123 G2 Rostāq Afgh.
122 C4 Rostāq Iran
174 E3 Rostarzewo Pol.
140 K2 Røsthavet sea chan. Norway
223 J4 Rosthern Sask. Can.
170 D1 Rostock Ger.
140 M1 Rostonsölkä ridge Sweden
139 L3 Rostov Rus. Fed.
135 G7 Rostov-na-Donu Rus. Fed.
Rostov Oblast admin. div. Rus. Fed. see Rostovskaya Oblast'
Rostov-on-Don Rus. Fed. see Rostov-na-Donu
135 H7 Rostovskaya Oblast' admin. div. Rus. Fed.
215 E2 Rostrataville S. Africa
158 C3 Rostrenen France
147 E2 Rostrevor Northern Ireland U.K.
147 B3 Rosturk Rep. of Ireland
140 K2 Røsvik Norway
140 M2 Rosvik Sweden
231 C5 Roswell GA U.S.A.
239 F5 Roswell NM U.S.A.
177 J5 Röszke Hungary
172 D3 Rot r. Ger.
91 K4 Rota i. N. Mariana Is
184 D4 Rota Spain
172 D4 Rotach r. Ger.
193 I5 Rota Greca Italy
173 E2 Rot am See Ger.
173 E3 Rot an der Rot Ger.
171 D5 Rotava Czech Rep.
Rotch Island Gilbert Is Kiribati see Tamana
93 B5 Rote i. Indon.
193 G3 Rotello Italy
168 E2 Rotenburg (Wümme) Ger.
169 E4 Rotenburg an der Fulda Ger.
171 C5 Roter Main r. Ger.
178 A3 Rote Wand mt. Austria
Rot-Front Ukr. see Dobropillya
173 F2 Roth Ger.
173 E3 Roth r. Ger.
173 F2 Roth r. Ger.
171 D4 Rötha Ger.
169 D5 Rothaargebirge hills Ger.
149 H2 Rothbury Northumberland, England U.K.
149 H2 Rothbury Forest England U.K.
173 F2 Röthenbach an der Pegnitz Ger.
172 C2 Rothenberg Ger.
172 D2 Rothenbuch Ger.
171 C4 Rothenburg Ger.
171 F4 Rothenburg (Oberlausitz) Ger.
173 E2 Rothenburg ob der Tauber Ger.
158 E3 Rothéneuf France
172 D2 Rothenfels Ger.
171 C5 Rothenstein Ger.
151 G4 Rother r. England U.K.
262 T2 Rothera research stn Antarctica
151 H3 Rotherfield East Sussex, England U.K.
81 D5 Rotherham South I. N.Z.
149 H4 Rotherham South Yorkshire, England U.K.
146 E4 Rothes Moray, Scotland U.K.
146 C6 Rothesay Argyll and Bute, Scotland U.K.
165 E4 Rotheux-Rimière Belgium
146 F2 Rothiesholm Orkney, Scotland U.K.
173 E2 Röthlein Ger.
172 B4 Rothrist Switz.
226 C3 Rothschild WI U.S.A.
262 T2 Rothschild Island Antarctica
234 B2 Rothsville PA U.S.A.
151 G2 Rothwell Northamptonshire, England U.K.
149 H4 Rothwell West Yorkshire, England U.K.
169 E4 Rothwesten (Fuldatal) Ger.
Roti i. Indon. see Rote
83 F3 Roto N.S.W. Austr.
80 F3 Rotoiti, Lake North I. N.Z.
81 D4 Rotoiti, Lake South I. N.Z.
Rotomagus France see Rouen
81 C5 Rotomanu South I. N.Z.
193 I5 Rotonda Italy
195 F2 Rotondella Italy
192 B2 Rotondo, Monte mt. Corse France
81 D4 Rotoroa, Lake South I. N.Z.
80 F3 Rotorua North I. N.Z.
80 F3 Rotorua, Lake North I. N.Z.
165 D4 Rotselaar Belgium
178 D4 Rotsteinberg mt. Austria
173 E4 Rott Ger.
173 H3 Rott r. Ger.
171 D4 Rotta Ger.
173 F4 Rottach-Egern Ger.
173 G4 Rott am Inn Ger.
157 G4 Rotte r. France
172 D3 Rottenacker Ger.
173 E2 Röttenbach Bayern Ger.
173 F2 Röttenbach Bayern Ger.
171 C5 Rottenbach Thüringen Ger.
173 E4 Rottenbuch Ger.
172 C3 Rottenburg am Neckar Ger.
173 G3 Rottenburg an der Laaber Ger.
173 E2 Rottendorf Ger.
179 F3 Rottenmann Austria
164 D3 Rotterdam Neth.
233 G3 Rotterdam NY U.S.A.
164 F1 Rottevalle Neth.
173 H3 Rotthalmünster Ger.
151 G4 Rottingdean Brighton and Hove, England U.K.
172 D2 Röttingham Ger.
169 F4 Rottleberode Ger.
142 E2 Rottnan r. Sweden
87 B7 Rottnest Island W.A. Austr.
190 E3 Rottofreno Italy
172 C3 Rottweil Ger.
77 H3 Rotuma i. Fiji
197 G4 Rotunda Romania
140 K3 Rötviken Sweden
173 F4 Rotwand mt. Ger.
173 G2 Rötz Ger.
158 E4 Rouans France
156 D2 Roubaix France
161 C4 Roubion r. France
186 E2 Rouch, Mont mt. France/Spain
176 F2 Rouchovany Czech Rep.
176 D1 Roudnice nad Labem Czech Rep.
156 B3 Rouen France
157 H5 Rouffach France
162 E3 Rouffiac France
162 C3 Rouffignac France
158 E4 Rougé France
160 E1 Rougemont France
157 G5 Rougemont-le-Château France
81 B6 Rough Ridge South I. N.Z.
151 I2 Roughton Norfolk, England U.K.
147 B5 Roughty r. Rep. of Ireland
162 C3 Rougnac France
162 B3 Rouillac France
162 C2 Rouillé France
161 B5 Roujan France
160 E1 Roulans France
Roulers Belgium see Roeselare
232 D4 Roulette PA U.S.A.
Roumania country Europe see Romania
162 C3 Roumazières-Loubert France
161 E5 Roumoules France
232 B4 Roundhead OH U.S.A.
149 H3 Round Hill hill England U.K.
83 H2 Round Mountain mt. N.S.W. Austr.
240 I2 Round Mountain NV U.S.A.
241 M3 Round Rock AZ U.S.A.
237 D6 Round Rock TX U.S.A.
147 B3 Roundstone Rep. of Ireland
234 B2 Round Top hill PA U.S.A.
238 E2 Roundup MT U.S.A.
151 F3 Roundway Wiltshire, England U.K.
148 C4 Roundwood Rep. of Ireland
251 H3 Roura Fr. Guiana
190 C3 Roure Italy
146 E2 Rousay i. Scotland U.K.
233 G2 Rouses Point NY U.S.A.
176 F2 Rousínov Czech Rep.
148 B3 Rousky Northern Ireland U.K.
161 D5 Rousset France
161 D5 Roussillon Provence-Alpes-Côte-d'Azur France
155 G4 Roussillon Rhône-Alpes France
161 C4 Rousson France
159 G2 Routot France
164 F2 Rouveen Neth.
159 F3 Rouvre r. France
156 C2 Rouvroy France
156 E3 Rouvroy-sur-Audry France
215 F4 Rouxville S. Africa
160 B1 Rouy France
224 E3 Rouyn Que. Can.
Rouyuan Gansu China see Huachi
Rouyuanchengzi Gansu China see Huachi
140 N2 Rovaniemi Fin.
190 D3 Rovasenda r. Italy
190 F3 Rovato Italy
190 E4 Rovegno Italy
135 G6 Roven'ki Rus. Fed.
Rovenki Ukr. see Roven'ky
137 J3 Roven'ky Ukr.
Rovenskaya Oblast' admin. div. Ukr. see Rivnens'ka Oblast'
191 F3 Roverbella Italy
190 E2 Roveredo Switz.
191 G3 Rovereto Italy
170 D1 Rövershagen Ger.
193 E2 Roviano Italy
191 G3 Rovigo Italy
191 G3 Rovigo prov. Veneto Italy
197 F3 Rovinari Romania
188 D3 Rovinj Croatia
176 G3 Rovinka Slovakia
179 H5 Rovišće Croatia
Rovno Rivnens'ka Oblast' Ukr. see Rivne
Rovno Oblast admin. div. Ukr. see Rivnens'ka Oblast'
120 A2 Rovnoye Rus. Fed.
150 E3 Rowde Wiltshire, England U.K.
83 G2 Rowena N.S.W. Austr.
234 D1 Rowland PA U.S.A.
232 D5 Rowlesburg WV U.S.A.
86 C3 Rowley Shoals sea feature W.A. Austr.
Równe Rivnens'ka Oblast' Ukr. see Rivne
174 E4 Rów Polski r. Pol.
232 B4 Rowsburg OH U.S.A.
92 B2 Roxas Luzon Phil.
92 B4 Roxas Mindanao Phil.
92 B3 Roxas Mindoro Phil.
92 A4 Roxas Palawan Phil.
92 B4 Roxas Panay Phil.
231 E4 Roxboro NC U.S.A.
84 D4 Roxborough Downs Qld Austr.
81 B6 Roxburgh South I. N.Z.
Roxburgh Island Cook Is see Rarotonga
235 E1 Roxbury CT U.S.A.
235 E1 Roxbury Falls CT U.S.A.
82 D2 Roxby Downs S.A. Austr.
184 B3 Roxo r. Port.
184 B3 Roxo, Barragem do resr Port.
151 G2 Roxton Bedfordshire, England U.K.
146 D5 Roy r. Scotland U.K.
238 E2 Roy MT U.S.A.
239 F4 Roy NM U.S.A.
161 F5 Roya r. France/Italy
226 D5 Royal Center IN U.S.A.
117 F4 Royal Chitwan National Park Nepal
226 C1 Royale, Isle i. MI U.S.A.
227 F4 Royal Oak MI U.S.A.
263 K1 Royal Society Range mts Antarctica
234 B2 Royalton PA U.S.A.
226 C3 Royalton WI U.S.A.
162 A3 Royan France
160 B3 Royat France
161 D3 Roybon France
151 H2 Roydon Norfolk, England U.K.
151 I2 Roydon Norfolk, England U.K.
156 C3 Roye France
162 D3 Royère-de-Vassivière France
234 C2 Royersford PA U.S.A.
86 C4 Roy Hill W.A. Austr.
137 F2 Royishche Ukr.
151 G2 Royston Hertfordshire, England U.K.
149 H4 Royston South Yorkshire, England U.K.
149 G4 Royton Greater Manchester, England U.K.
183 I4 Royuela Spain
196 E4 Rožaje Crna Gora Yugo.
183 H5 Rozalén del Monte Spain
175 J3 Różan Pol.
196 D3 Rožanj hill Yugo.
156 C4 Rozay-en-Brie France
176 E1 Rožďalovice Czech Rep.
175 M6 Rozdil Ukr.
136 F4 Rozdil'na Ukr.
137 G5 Rozdol'ne Ukr.
137 H3 Rozdory Ukr.
174 F4 Rozdrażew Pol.
164 D3 Rozenburg Neth.
164 E2 Rozendaal Neth.
121 G2 Rozhdestvenka Kazakh.
139 K3 Rozhdestveno Tverskaya Oblast' Rus. Fed.
139 K3 Rozhdestveno Yaroslavskaya Oblast' Rus. Fed.
134 I4 Rozhdestvenskoye Rus. Fed.
139 I3 Rozhdestvo Rus. Fed.
137 G2 Rozhnivka Ukr.
136 F2 Rozhny Ukr.
136 C3 Rozhnyativ Ukr.
136 C2 Rozhyshche Ukr.
197 G4 Rozino Bulg.
137 I4 Rozivka Ukr.
176 C2 Rožmitál pod Třemšínem Czech Rep.
177 J3 Rožňava Slovakia
174 G3 Rożniatów Pol.
177 H2 Rožnov pod Radhoštěm Czech Rep.
175 I6 Rożnów Pol.
174 E3 Roznowo Pol.
175 J2 Rozoga r. Pol.
175 J2 Rozogi Pol.
156 E3 Rozoy-sur-Serre France
175 H4 Rozprza Pol.
175 I6 Roztoka Wielka Pol.
171 E5 Roztoky Středočeský kraj Czech Rep.
171 F5 Roztoky Středočeský kraj Czech Rep.
190 E3 Rozzano Italy
196 D5 Rrëshen Albania
196 D5 Rrogozhinë Albania
135 H5 Rtishchevo Rus. Fed.
182 B1 Ru Spain
182 C4 Rua Port.
150 D2 Ruabon Wrexham, Wales U.K.
211 B6 Ruaha National Park Tanz.
80 F4 Ruahine Range mts North I. N.Z.
80 E1 Ruakaka North I. N.Z.
147 C4 Ruan Rep. of Ireland
Ruanda country Africa see Rwanda
80 E3 Ruapehu, Mount vol. North I. N.Z.
81 B7 Ruapuke Island South I. N.Z.
150 E3 Ruardean Gloucestershire, England U.K.
80 E1 Ruatangata North I. N.Z.
81 C5 Ruatapu South I. N.Z.
80 G2 Ruatoria North I. N.Z.
159 G4 Ruaudin France
139 H4 Ruba Belarus
124 D4 Rub' al Khālī des. Saudi Arabia
177 H4 Rúbaň Slovakia
148 D3 Rubane Northern Ireland U.K.
137 H4 Rubanivka Ukr.
191 G3 Rubano Italy
125 E2 Rubaydā reg. Saudi Arabia
183 G1 Rubayo Spain
211 C6 Rubeho Mountains Tanz.
169 F4 Rübeland Ger.
257 F2 Rubelita Brazil
183 G2 Rubena Spain
171 E5 Rübenau Ger.
Rubezhnoye Ukr. see Rubizhne
Rubha an t-Siumpain hd Scotland U.K. see Tiumpan Head
Rubha Robhanais hd Scotland U.K. see Butt of Lewis
208 E4 Rubi r. Dem. Rep. Congo
186 F3 Rubí Spain
182 D2 Rubiá Spain
256 B4 Rubiácea Brazil
240 G2 Rubicon r. CA U.S.A.
191 H4 Rubicone r. Italy
183 F3 Rubí de Bracamonte Spain
186 B4 Rubielos de la Cérida Spain
187 C4 Rubielos de Mora Spain
191 F4 Rubiera Italy
257 G2 Rubim Brazil
183 G3 Rubio mt. Spain
137 J3 Rubizhne Ukr.
170 E2 Rubkow Ger.
183 G2 Rublacedo de Abajo Spain
211 A5 Rubondo National Park Tanz.
137 I3 Rubtsi Ukr.
121 J2 Rubtsovsk Rus. Fed.
124 C4 Rubūț, Jabal ar hill Saudi Arabia
220 C3 Ruby AK U.S.A.
81 D4 Ruby Bay South I. N.Z.
238 D3 Ruby Dome mt. NV U.S.A.
136 D2 Rubyel' Belarus
241 J1 Ruby Mountains NV U.S.A.
241 K3 Rubys Inn UT U.S.A.
85 F4 Rubyvale Qld Austr.
241 J1 Ruby Valley NV U.S.A.
197 G3 Rucăr Romania
Rucheng Guangdong China see Ruyuan
109 E3 Rucheng Hunan China
137 G2 Ruchky Ukr.
175 J2 Ruciane-Nida Pol.
171 E4 Rückersdorf Ger.
232 D5 Ruckersville VA U.S.A.
164 D3 Rucphen Neth.
174 G4 Ruda Pol.
177 J3 Rudabánya Hungary
175 L4 Ruda-Huta Pol.
175 I4 Ruda Maleniecka Pol.
175 L5 Ruda Różaniecka Pol.
117 E4 Rudarpur Uttar Prad. India
174 G5 Ruda Śląska Pol.
116 E4 Rudauli Uttar Prad. India
122 B2 Rūdbār Iran
165 C3 Ruddervoorde Belgium
151 F2 Ruddington Nottinghamshire, England U.K.
173 F3 Rudelzhausen Ger.
179 F4 Ruden Austria
172 D3 Rudersberg Ger.
179 H3 Rudersdorf Austria
171 E3 Rüdersdorf Berlin Ger.
169 F4 Rüdershausen Ger.
173 H3 Ruderting Ger.
136 E3 Rude Selo Ukr.
172 B2 Rüdesheim Ger.
172 B2 Rüdesheim am Rhein Ger.
151 G3 Rudgwick West Sussex, England U.K.
138 E4 Rūdiškės Lith.
169 F5 Rudisleben Ger.
137 G2 Rudivka Ukr.
175 K3 Rudka Pol.
175 L4 Rudka r. Pol.
142 D4 Rudkøbing Denmark
175 L6 Rudky Ukr.
171 F5 Rudná Czech Rep.
174 E4 Rudna Pol.
197 F3 Rudna Glava Srbija Yugo.
174 E4 Rudna Wielka Pol.
100 E3 Rudnaya Pristan' Rus. Fed.
100 E4 Rudnaya Pristan' Rus. Fed.
136 B3 Rudne Ukr.
121 I3 Rudnichnyy Kazakh.
134 K4 Rudnichnyy Rus. Fed.
175 K5 Rudnik Podkarpackie Pol.
174 G5 Rudnik Śląskie Pol.
174 G4 Rudniki Pol.
Rudnik Ingichka Uzbek. see Ingichka
170 E3 Rüdnitz Ger.
139 H4 Rudnya Smolenskaya Oblast' Rus. Fed.
135 I6 Rudnya Volgogradskaya Oblast' Rus. Fed.
136 D2 Rudnya-Ivanivs'ka Ukr.
175 L6 Rudnyky Ukr.
136 E3 Rudnytsya Ukr.
120 E1 Rudnyy Kazakh.
100 E3 Rudnyy Rus. Fed.
Rudolf, Lake salt l. Eth./Kenya see Turkana, Lake
179 F2 Rudolfov Czech Rep.
171 C5 Rudolstadt Ger.
109 G1 Rudong Jiangsu China
197 G5 Rudozem Bulg.
122 B2 Rūdsar Iran
149 I3 Rudston East Riding of Yorkshire, England U.K.
226 E2 Rudyard MI U.S.A.
174 F5 Rudziczka Pol.
138 F5 Rudzyensk Belarus
156 B2 Rue France
184 E1 Ruecas r. Spain
183 F3 Rueda Spain
156 C4 Rueil-Malmaison France
227 G2 Ruel Ont. Can.
Ruen mt. Macedonia see Rujen
183 F1 Ruente Spain
213 G3 Ruenya r. Zimbabwe
178 C3 Ruetz r. Austria
203 G6 Rufa'a Sudan
195 H3 Ruffano Italy
159 H5 Ruffec Centre France
162 C2 Ruffec Poitou-Charentes France
160 D1 Ruffey-lès-Echirey France
160 D2 Ruffey-sur-Seille France
158 D4 Ruffiac France
160 D2 Ruffieu France
160 D3 Ruffieux France
149 G4 Rufford Lancashire, England U.K.
211 C7 Rufiji r. Tanz.
191 G5 Rufina Italy
261 F4 Rufino Arg.
206 A3 Rufisque Senegal
209 F8 Rufunsa Zambia
109 G1 Rugao Jiangsu China
170 C2 Rugberg hill Ger.
151 F2 Rugby Warwickshire, England U.K.
236 C1 Rugby ND U.S.A.
151 F2 Rugeley Staffordshire, England U.K.
170 E1 Rügen i. Ger.
222 E5 Rugged Mountain B.C. Can.
173 E2 Rügland Ger.
159 G3 Rugles France
169 F3 Rühen Ger.
211 A5 Ruhengeri Rwanda
169 F5 Ruhla Ger.
171 E4 Ruhland Ger.
173 G3 Ruhmannsfelden Ger.
170 C2 Rühn Ger.
173 G4 Ruhpolding Ger.
169 B4 Ruhr r. Ger.
173 H3 Ruhstorf an der Rott Ger.
211 B7 Ruhudji r. Tanz.
109 G3 Rui'an Zhejiang China
109 E2 Ruichang Jiangxi China
185 H2 Ruidera Spain
239 F6 Ruidosa TX U.S.A.
239 F5 Ruidoso NM U.S.A.
109 E3 Ruijin Jiangxi China
108 A3 Ruili Yunnan China
192 A5 Ruinas Sardegna Italy
164 F2 Ruinen Neth.
164 F2 Ruinerwold Neth.
211 C7 Ruipa Tanz.
165 C3 Ruiselede Belgium
182 B3 Ruivães Port.
184 □ Ruivo, Pico mt. Madeira
244 B3 Ruiz Mex.
197 F4 Ruj mt. Bulg.
138 E3 Rūja r. Latvia
174 E4 Ruja Pol.
128 C3 Rujaylah, Ḩarrat ar lava field Jordan
197 F4 Rujen mt. Macedonia
138 E3 Rūjiena Latvia
Ruk is Micronesia see Chuuk
129 F2 Rukel' Rus. Fed.
129 B2 Rukhi Georgia
208 C4 Ruki r. Dem. Rep. Congo
210 A5 Rukungiri Uganda
211 A6 Rukwa admin. reg. Tanz.
211 B7 Rukwa, Lake Tanz.
141 K3 Rulbo Sweden
125 G2 Rūl Ḑadnah U.A.E.
237 F5 Ruleville MS U.S.A.
86 E2 Rulhieres, Cape W.A. Austr.
Rulin Hunan China see Chengbu
169 D3 Rulle (Wallenhorst) Ger.
168 F2 Rullstorf Ger.
160 C2 Rully France
Rulong Sichuan China see Xinlong
172 C2 Rülzheim Ger.
178 C3 Rum Austria
176 F4 Rum Hungary
122 D3 Rūm Iran
146 B5 Rum i. Scotland U.K.
236 E2 Rum r. MN U.S.A.
Rum, Jebel mts Jordan see Ramm, Jabal
146 B5 Rum, Sound of sea chan. Scotland U.K.
207 G3 Ruma Nigeria
196 D3 Ruma Vojvodina, Srbija Yugo.
125 D2 Rumāh Saudi Arabia
210 B5 Ruma National Park Kenya
Rumania country Europe see Romania
208 F3 Rumbek Sudan
185 G2 Rumblar r. Spain
176 D1 Rumburk Czech Rep.
246 D2 Rum Cay i. Bahamas
165 F5 Rumelange Lux.
165 C4 Rumes Belgium
233 □H2 Rumford ME U.S.A.
143 H4 Rumia Pol.
156 E3 Rumigny France
160 D3 Rumilly France
84 B2 Rum Jungle N.T. Austr.
124 C2 Rummān, Jabal ar mts Saudi Arabia
128 D3 Rummānā hill Syria
150 D3 Rumney Cardiff, Wales U.K.
102 J2 Rumoi Japan
211 A5 Rumonge Burundi
157 F4 Rumont France
211 B7 Rumphi Malawi
235 E2 Rumson NJ U.S.A.
165 D3 Rumst Belgium
85 F3 Rumula Qld Austr.
184 A1 Runa Port.
109 E1 Runan Henan China
81 C5 Runanga South I. N.Z.
80 F2 Runaway, Cape North I. N.Z.
246 □ Runaway Bay Jamaica
149 G4 Runcorn Halton, England U.K.
197 F3 Runcu Romania
177 L6 Runcu r. Romania
213 G4 Runde r. Zimbabwe
212 C3 Rundu Namibia
140 L3 Rundvik Sweden
97 C5 Rŭng, Kaôh i. Cambodia
95 F3 Rungan r. Indon.
208 E4 Rungu Dem. Rep. Congo
211 B6 Rungwa Tanz.
211 A6 Rungwa r. Tanz.
109 F1 Runheji Anhui China
Runing Henan China see Runan
169 D5 Runkel Ger.
240 I4 Running Springs CA U.S.A.
87 D4 Runton Range hills W.A. Austr.
151 H3 Runwell Essex, England U.K.
78 □4a Ruo i. Chuuk Micronesia
141 O3 Ruokolahti Fin.
161 C4 Ruoms France
110 E4 Ruoqiang Xinjiang China
110 E4 Ruoqiang He r. China
193 H4 Ruoti Italy
141 N3 Ruotsinpyhtää Fin.
141 N3 Ruovesi Fin.
117 H4 Rupa Arun. Prad. India
94 C2 Rupat i. Indon.
197 G2 Rupea Romania
224 E3 Rupert r. Que. Can.
238 D3 Rupert ID U.S.A.
232 C6 Rupert WV U.S.A.
262 O1 Rupert Coast Antarctica
85 E4 Rupert Creek r. Qld Austr.
116 C4 Rupnagar Rajasthan India
170 D3 Ruppiner See l. Ger.
179 G2 Ruprechtshofen Austria
157 G5 Rupt-sur-Moselle France
232 C6 Rural Retreat VA U.S.A.
252 D3 Rurrenabaque Bol.
79 □3 Rurutu i. Îs Australes Fr. Polynesia
197 F2 Rus Romania
185 G2 Rus Spain
185 H1 Rus r. Spain
Rusaddir N. Africa see Melilla
137 G2 Rusanivka Ukr.
213 G3 Rusape Zimbabwe
197 F3 Rusca Montană Romania
Ruschuk Bulg. see Ruse
197 G2 Ruscova Romania
197 G4 Ruse Bulg.
179 G4 Ruše Slovenia
117 F4 Rusera Bihar India
197 H3 Rușețu Romania
147 E3 Rush Rep. of Ireland
151 F2 Rushall West Midlands, England U.K.
107 I4 Rushan Shandong China
Rushan Tajik. see Rushon
236 C4 Rush Creek r. CO U.S.A.
151 G2 Rushden Northamptonshire, England U.K.
226 B4 Rushford MN U.S.A.
213 G3 Rushinga Zimbabwe
232 E6 Rushmere VA U.S.A.
151 I2 Rushmere St Andrew Suffolk, England U.K.
123 G2 Rushon Tajik.
106 E5 Rushui r. China
236 F3 Rushville IL U.S.A.
230 C4 Rushville IN U.S.A.
236 C3 Rushville NE U.S.A.
232 B5 Rushville OH U.S.A.
83 F4 Rushworth Vic. Austr.
174 G4 Rusiec Pol.
175 I4 Rusinów Pol.
237 E6 Rusk TX U.S.A.
140 L2 Ruskele Sweden
196 D3 Ruski Krstur Vojvodina, Srbija Yugo.
231 D7 Ruskin FL U.S.A.
149 I4 Ruskington Lincolnshire, England U.K.
137 I2 Rus'ki Tyshky Ukr.
177 J6 Rusko Selo Vojvodina, Srbija Yugo.
177 K3 Ruskov Slovakia
138 C4 Rusnė Lith.
197 H4 Rusokastro Bulg.
136 E3 Rusova r. Ukr.
150 E3 Ruspidge Gloucestershire, England U.K.
254 F3 Russas Brazil
223 K5 Russell Man. Can.
233 F2 Russell Ont. Can.
80 E1 Russell North I. N.Z.
236 D4 Russell KS U.S.A.
232 D4 Russell PA U.S.A.
78 □6 Russell Islands Solomon Is
231 C5 Russellville AL U.S.A.
237 E5 Russellville AR U.S.A.
230 C4 Russellville KY U.S.A.
232 B5 Russellville OH U.S.A.
234 C3 Russellville PA U.S.A.
172 C1 Rüsselsheim Ger.
191 H4 Russi Italy
Russia country Asia/Europe see Russian Federation
130 F4 Russian Federation country Asia/Europe
Russian Soviet Federal Socialist Republic country Asia/Europe see Russian Federation
121 H1 Russkaya-Polyana Rus. Fed.
135 H6 Russkaya Zhuravka Rus. Fed.
139 K5 Russkiy Brod Rus. Fed.
120 A1 Russkiy Kameshkir Rus. Fed.
179 H3 Rust Austria
129 D3 Rüstäm Äliyev Azer.
129 D3 Rust'avi Georgia
232 D6 Rustburg VA U.S.A.
215 G1 Rust de Winter S. Africa
129 C4 Rüstemgedik Turkey
215 F1 Rustenburg S. Africa
142 B2 Rustfjellheii mt. Norway
215 F2 Rustig S. Africa
151 G4 Rustington West Sussex, England U.K.
237 E5 Ruston LA U.S.A.
161 D5 Rustrel France
190 D1 Ruswil Switz.
174 D4 Ruszów Pol.
139 K4 Rut' r. Rus. Fed.
192 B2 Rutali Corse France
211 A5 Rutana Burundi
Rutanzige, Lake Dem. Rep. Congo/Uganda see Edward, Lake
185 F3 Rute Spain
172 C3 Rutesheim Ger.
241 J2 Ruth NV U.S.A.
169 D4 Rüthen Ger.
Ruthenia admin. div. Ukr. see Zakarpats'ka Oblast'
235 D2 Rutherford NJ U.S.A.
231 D5 Rutherfordton NC U.S.A.
83 F4 Rutherglen Vic. Austr.
227 H2 Rutherglen Ont. Can.
146 D6 Rutherglen South Lanarkshire, Scotland U.K.
232 E6 Ruther Glen VA U.S.A.
150 D1 Ruthin Denbighshire, Wales U.K.
190 D1 Rüti Switz.
195 G1 Rutigliano Italy
193 H4 Rutino Italy
134 I4 Rutka r. Rus. Fed.
175 K1 Rutka-Tartak Pol.
175 K2 Rutki-Kossaki Pol.
151 G2 Rutland admin. div. England U.K.
233 G3 Rutland VT U.S.A.
85 E2 Rutland Plains Qld Austr.
151 G2 Rutland Water resr England U.K.
232 B6 Rutledge TN U.S.A.
111 B5 Rutog Xizang China
164 E2 Rutten Neth.
227 G2 Rutter Ont. Can.
129 E3 Rutul Rus. Fed.
140 N2 Ruukki Fin.
164 F2 Ruurlo Neth.
193 H4 Ruvo del Monte Italy
193 I3 Ruvo di Puglia Italy
Ruvu Tanz. see Pangani
211 D7 Ruvuma r. Moz./Tanz.
211 C7 Ruvuma admin. reg. Tanz.
125 F2 Ruweis U.A.E.
208 F5 Ruwenzori mts Dem. Rep. Congo/Uganda
160 D3 Ruy France
213 G3 Ruya r. Zimbabwe
211 A5 Ruyigi Burundi
161 B3 Ruynes-en-Margeride France
150 E2 Ruyton-XI-Towns Shropshire, England U.K.
109 E3 Ruyuan Guangdong China
139 K4 Ruza Rus. Fed.
121 F1 Ruzayevka Kazakh.
135 I5 Ruzayevka Rus. Fed.
138 E5 Ruzhany Belarus
107 G5 Ruzhou Henan China
136 E3 Ruzhyn Ukr.
177 I2 Ružomberok Slovakia
177 I5 Ruzsa Hungary
211 A5 Rwanda country Africa
142 C3 Ry Denmark
142 C3 Ryå r. Denmark
122 C2 Ryābād Iran
137 H2 Ryabyna Ukr.
81 B7 Ryal Bush South I. N.Z.
81 C5 Ryall, Mount South I. N.Z.
146 C6 Ryan, Loch b. Scotland U.K.
137 H3 Ryas'ke Ukr.
137 F4 Ryasnopil' Ukr.
139 L4 Ryazan' Rus. Fed.
Ryazan Oblast admin. div. Rus. Fed. see Ryazanskaya Oblast'
139 L4 Ryazanovskiy Rus. Fed.
137 J5 Ryazanskaya Rus. Fed.
139 M4 Ryazanskaya Oblast' admin. div. Rus. Fed.
139 L3 Ryazantsevo Rus. Fed.
139 M5 Ryazhsk Rus. Fed.
121 J3 Rybache Kazakh.
140 P1 Rybachiy, Poluostrov pen. Rus. Fed.
Rybach'ye Kyrg. see Balykchy
177 H3 Rybany Slovakia
139 L2 Rybinsk Rus. Fed.
139 L2 Rybinskoye Vodokhranilishche resr Rus. Fed.
176 E1 Rybitví Czech Rep.
174 G5 Rybnik Pol.
Rybnitsa Moldova see Rîbnița
175 I3 Rybno Mazowieckie Pol.
175 H2 Rybno Warmińsko-Mazurskie Pol.
175 J2 Rybno Warmińsko-Mazurskie Pol.
139 L4 Rybnoye Rus. Fed.
175 L3 Ryboły Pol.
134 F3 Rybreka Rus. Fed.
175 H2 Rychliki Pol.
176 F1 Rychnov nad Kněžnou Czech Rep.
171 G5 Rychnov u Jablonce nad Nisou Czech Rep.
175 I2 Rychnowo Pol.
174 F4 Rychtal Pol.
174 G3 Rychwał Pol.
170 E1 Ryck r. Ger.
222 G4 Rycroft Alta Can.
175 J4 Ryczywół Pol.
174 E3 Ryczywół Pol.
143 F3 Ryd Sweden
262 S2 Rydberg Peninsula Antarctica
151 F4 Ryde Isle of Wight, England U.K.
136 C3 Rydomyl' Ukr.
174 G5 Rydułtowy Pol.
174 E4 Rydzyna Pol.
151 H4 Rye East Sussex, England U.K.
149 I3 Rye r. England U.K.
235 E2 Rye NY U.S.A.
151 H4 Rye Bay England U.K.
233 □H3 Rye Beach NH U.S.A.
238 E2 Ryegate MT U.S.A.
240 H1 Rye Patch Reservoir NV U.S.A.
159 F2 Ryes France
175 J6 Ryglice Pol.
151 G2 Ryhall Rutland, England U.K.
174 G2 Ryjewo Pol.
136 D2 Rykhal's'ke Ukr.
175 J4 Ryki Pol.
Rykovo Ukr. see Yenakiyeve
175 M5 Rykovychi Ukr.
135 F6 Ryl'sk Rus. Fed.
83 G3 Rylstone N.S.W. Austr.
175 J6 Rymanów Pol.
176 G2 Rýmařov Czech Rep.
141 M3 Rymättylä Fin.
143 I4 Ryn Pol.
174 F2 Rynarzewo Pol.
120 B3 Ryn-Peski des. Kazakh.
174 G2 Ryńsk Pol.
105 E2 Ryōgami-san mt. Japan
104 C3 Ryōhaku-sanchi mts Japan
Ryojun Liaoning China see Lushunkou
102 I4 Ryōtsu Japan
104 C3 Ryōzen-zan mt. Japan
175 H2 Rypin Pol.
Ryshkany Moldova see Rîşcani
168 C2 Rysum (Krummhörn) Ger.
177 J2 Rysy mt. Pol.
174 F2 Rytel Pol.
143 F4 Rytterknægten hill Bornholm Denmark
138 E1 Ryttylä Fin.
175 J5 Rytwiany Pol.
104 C3 Ryūga-dake mt. Japan
105 G3 Ryūgasaki Japan
Ryukyu Islands Japan see Nansei-shotō
Ryūkyū-rettō is Japan see Nansei-shotō
266 D4 Ryukyu Trench sea feature N. Pacific Ocean
105 E3 Ryūsō-san mt. Japan
139 H4 Ryzhikovo Rus. Fed.
136 F3 Ryzyne Ukr.
175 J3 Rządza r. Pol.
175 H4 Rząśnia Pol.
175 J3 Rząśnik Pol.
188 G4 Rzav r. Bos.-Herz.
174 F2 Rzeczenica Pol.
174 G4 Rzeczyca Łódzkie Pol.
175 I4 Rzeczyca Łódzkie Pol.
175 I2 Rzęgnowo Pol.
175 H4 Rzejowice Pol.
175 J2 Rzekuń Pol.
175 J6 Rzepiennik Strzyżewski Pol.
174 C3 Rzepin Pol.
175 H5 Rzerzęczyce Pol.
175 K5 Rzeszów Pol.
175 H4 Rzgów Pol.
174 G3 Rzgów Pierwszy Pol.
135 H5 Rzhaksa Rus. Fed.
139 I5 Rzhanitsa Rus. Fed.
139 H5 Rzhawka r. Belarus
139 J3 Rzhev Rus. Fed.
137 F3 Rzhyshchiv Ukr.
175 I4 Rzuców Pol.

S

122 D3 Sa'ābād Iran
122 C4 Sa'ādatābād Iran
214 C4 Saaifontein S. Africa
170 D1 Saal Ger.
173 H4 Saalach r. Ger.
173 F3 Saal an der Donau Ger.
169 F5 Saal an der Saale Ger.
172 C2 Saalbach r. Ger.
178 D3 Saalbach-Hinterglemm Austria
171 C5 Saalburg Ger.
173 G4 Saaldorf Ger.
171 C4 Saale r. Ger.
157 H4 Saales France
171 C5 Saalfeld Ger.
178 D3 Saalfelden am Steinernen Meer Austria

156 A3 Saâne r. France
190 C2 Saane r. Switz.
190 C2 Saanen Switz.
222 F5 Saanich B.C. Can.
Saar land Ger. see Saarland
172 A2 Saar r. Ger.
172 A2 Saarbrücken Ger.
172 A2 Saarburg Ger.
138 D2 Saaremaa i. Estonia
140 N2 Saarenkylä Fin.
141 O3 Saari Fin.
140 N3 Saarijärvi Fin.
172 A2 Saarland land Ger.
172 A2 Saarlouis Ger.
172 A2 Saarwellingen Ger.
190 E2 Saas Switz.
190 C2 Saas Fee Switz.
190 C2 Saas Grund Switz.
190 C2 Saastal val. Switz.
129 F4 Saatlı Azer.
Saatly Azer. see Saatlı
261 F5 Saavedra Arg.
247 G3 Saba i. Neth. Antilles
128 C3 Sab' Ābār Syria
169 E4 Sababurg Ger.
196 D3 Šabac Srbija Yugo.
186 F3 Sabadell Spain
206 C4 Sabadou Baranama Guinea
104 C3 Sabae Japan
95 G1 Sabah state Malaysia
211 D5 Sabaki r. Kenya
93 A4 Sabalana, Kepulauan is Indon.
116 D4 Sabalgarh Madh. Prad. India
242 □I6 Sabamagrande Hond.
246 B2 Sabana, Archipiélago de is Cuba
247 E3 Sabana de la Mar Dom. Rep.
247 □1 Sabana Grande Puerto Rico
250 C2 Sabanalarga Col.
246 E3 Sabaneta Dom. Rep.
94 A1 Sabang Indon.
126 D2 Şabanözü Turkey
197 H2 Săbăoani Romania
257 F3 Sabará Brazil
163 D5 Sabarat France
114 D2 Sabari r. India
116 C5 Sabarmati r. Gujarat India
128 B3 Sabastiya West Bank
193 G3 Sabato r. Italy
193 F3 Sabaudia Italy
252 C4 Sabaya Bol.
129 B2 Sabazho Georgia
190 F4 Sabbionetta Italy
214 D4 Sabelo S. Africa
210 C4 Sabena Desert Kenya
183 E2 Sabero Spain
202 B3 Sabhā Libya
116 B5 Sabhrai Gujarat India
116 D3 Sabi r. India
Sabi r. Moz./Zimbabwe see Save
215 I1 Sabie r. Moz./S. Africa
213 F5 Sabie S. Africa
138 D3 Sabile Latvia
232 B5 Sabina OH U.S.A.
186 C2 Sabiñánigo Spain
185 H4 Sabinar, Punta del mt. Spain
243 E3 Sabinas Mex.
237 C7 Sabinas r. Coahuila Mex.
237 D7 Sabinas r. Nuevo León Mex.
243 E3 Sabinas Hidalgo Mex.
237 E6 Sabine r. Louisiana/Texas U.S.A.
140 □ Sabine Land reg. Svalbard
237 E6 Sabine Pass TX U.S.A.
193 E2 Sabini, Monti mts Italy
257 F3 Sabinópolis Brazil
177 K2 Sabinov Slovakia
185 G2 Sabiote Spain
129 F3 Sabir Azer.
129 F3 Sabirabad Azer.
92 B3 Sablayan Phil.
225 H5 Sable, Cape N.S. Can.
231 D7 Sable, Cape FL U.S.A.
78 □5 Sable, Île de i. New Caledonia
225 G2 Sable, Rivière du r. Que. Can.
225 J5 Sable Island N.S. Can.
227 F2 Sables, River aux r. Ont. Can.
158 D3 Sables-d'Or-les-Pins France
159 F4 Sablé-sur-Sarthe France
161 D4 Sablet France
161 C4 Sablières France
129 C1 Sablinskoye Rus. Fed.
161 C3 Sablons France
254 F3 Saboeiro Brazil
184 B3 Sabóia Port.
207 H3 Sabon Kafi Niger
182 C3 Sabor r. Port.
206 E3 Sabou Burkina
163 B4 Sabres France
263 H2 Sabrina Coast Antarctica
182 C3 Sabrosa Port.
129 D2 Sabue Georgia
182 C4 Sabugal Port.
184 B2 Sabugueiro Évora Port.
182 C4 Sabugueiro Guarda Port.
129 F3 Sabunçu Azer.
199 G2 Sabuncu Kütahya Turkey
105 E2 Saburyū-yama mt. Japan
124 C4 Şabyā Saudi Arabia
Sabzawar Afgh. see Shīndand
122 D2 Sabzevār Iran
Sabzvārān Iran see Jīroft
197 G2 Saca, Vârful mt. Romania
187 F5 Sa Cabaneta Spain
252 D4 Sacaca Bol.
177 L4 Săcădat Romania
177 K6 Săcălaz Romania
233 F3 Sacandaga r. NY U.S.A.
187 C5 Sacañet Spain
261 F2 Sacanta Arg.
177 L4 Săcăşeni Romania
241 L5 Sacaton AZ U.S.A.
184 A2 Sacavém Port.
190 C4 Saccarel, Mont mt. France/Italy
236 E3 Sac City IA U.S.A.
193 F3 Sacco r. Italy
183 H4 Sacecorbo Spain
183 H4 Sacedón Spain
197 G3 Săcele Romania
197 I3 Săcele Romania
197 G3 Săceni Romania
185 F2 Saceruela Spain
223 N4 Sachigo r. Ont. Can.
116 C5 Sachin Gujarat India
129 C2 Sach'khere Georgia
101 D6 Sach'on S. Korea
190 D2 Sachseln Switz.
171 E4 Sachsen land Ger.
171 C3 Sachsen-Anhalt land Ger.
173 E2 Sachsen bei Ansbach Ger.
169 D4 Sachsenberg (Lichtenfels) Ger.
169 F5 Sachsenbrunn Ger.
179 E4 Sachsenburg Austria
169 E3 Sachsenhagen Ger.
169 E4 Sachsenhausen (Waldeck) Ger.
172 D3 Sachsenheim Ger.
220 F2 Sachs Harbour N.W.T. Can.
191 H3 Sacile Italy
Sacirsuyu r. Syria/Turkey see Sājūr, Nahr
233 E3 Sackets Harbor NY U.S.A.
169 D5 Sackpfeife hill Ger.
225 H4 Sackville N.B. Can.
233 □H3 Saco ME U.S.A.
238 F1 Saco MT U.S.A.
177 K6 Sacoşu Turcesc Romania
160 D1 Sacquenay France
183 G3 Sacramenia Spain
256 D3 Sacramento Brazil
240 G2 Sacramento CA U.S.A.
240 G2 Sacramento r. CA U.S.A.
252 A1 Sacramento, Pampa del plain Peru
239 F5 Sacramento Mountains NM U.S.A.
240 F1 Sacramento Valley CA U.S.A.
253 F3 Sacre r. Brazil
149 H3 Sacriston Durham, England U.K.
193 E2 Sacrofano Italy
197 F2 Săcueni Romania
177 L5 Săcuieu Romania
253 F3 Sacuriuiná r. Brazil
217 □3b Sada Mayotte
215 F5 Sada S. Africa
182 B1 Sada Spain
183 I2 Sádaba Spain
116 D4 Sadabad Uttar Prad. India
122 B4 Sa'dābād Iran
Sá da Bandeira Angola see Lubango
163 A6 Sada de Sangüesa Spain
124 C4 Şa'dah Yemen
124 C4 Şa'dah governorate Yemen
192 B5 Sadali Sardegna Italy
93 A3 Sadang r. Indon.
211 C6 Sadani Tanz.
97 C6 Sadao Thai.
125 E5 Şadārah Yemen
129 D4 Sădārāk Azer.
114 C2 Sadaseopet Andhra Prad. India
146 C6 Saddell Argyll and Bute, Scotland U.K.
Saddleback hill England U.K. see Blencathra
237 C5 Saddleback Mesa mt. NM U.S.A.
85 F2 Saddle Hill hill Qld Austr.
81 D4 Saddle Hill mt. South I. N.Z.
Saddle Island Vanuatu see Mota Lava
115 G3 Saddle Peak hill Andaman & Nicobar Is India
97 D5 Sa Đec Vietnam
125 F4 Sadḩ Oman
116 D3 Sadhaura Haryana India
123 G4 Sadiqabad Pak.
129 D3 Sadıqlı Azer.
127 G4 Sa'dīyah, Hawr as imp. l. Iraq
213 □K2 Sadjoavato Madag.
122 D2 Sad-Kharv Iran
174 F2 Sadki Pol.
175 I4 Sadkowice Pol.
174 G2 Sadlinki Pol.
184 B2 Sado r. Port.
102 I5 Sadoga-shima i. Japan
127 G2 Sadon Rus. Fed.
95 E2 Sadong r. Sarawak Malaysia
192 B4 Sa Donna, Pico mt. Sardegna Italy
137 H5 Sadove Ukr.
135 I7 Sadovoye Respublika Kalmykiya - Khalm'g-Tangch Rus. Fed.
137 K2 Sadovoye Voronezhskaya Oblast' Rus. Fed.
175 J5 Sadowie Pol.
175 J3 Sadowne Pol.
187 F5 Sa Dragonera i. Spain
116 C4 Sadri Rajasthan India
234 C3 Sadsburyville PA U.S.A.
171 F5 Sadská Czech Rep.
116 C3 Sadulshahar Rajasthan India
124 D2 Sādūs Saudi Arabia
142 D3 Sæby Denmark
168 D1 Sæd Denmark
232 C4 Saegertown PA U.S.A.
183 H5 Saelices Spain
183 H4 Saelices de la Sal Spain
183 E2 Saelices del Rio Spain
183 E2 Saelices de Mayorga Spain
Saena Julia Italy see Siena
169 C3 Saerbeck Ger.
165 E5 Saeul Lux.
Safad Israel see Ẕefat
206 E3 Safané Burkina
184 C2 Safara Port.
Šafárikovo Slovakia see Tornaľa
123 G2 Safed Khirs mts Afgh.
123 F3 Safed Koh mts Afgh.
142 E2 Säffle Sweden
241 M5 Safford AZ U.S.A.
158 E4 Saffré France
151 H2 Saffron Walden Essex, England U.K.
Safi Jordan see Aş Şāfī
204 C2 Safi Morocco
122 D2 Safiabad Iran
122 B2 Safīd r. Iran
122 E4 Safidabeh Iran
122 C4 Safīdār, Kūh-e mt. Iran
122 B3 Safid Dasht Iran
Safīd Kūh mts Afgh. see Paropamisus
257 G3 Safiras, Serra das mts Brazil
128 C2 Şāfītā Syria
134 F1 Safonovo Murmanskaya Oblast' Rus. Fed.
139 I4 Safonovo Smolenskaya Oblast' Rus. Fed.
124 C2 Safrā' al Asyāḩ esc. Saudi Arabia
124 D2 Safrā' as Sark esc. Saudi Arabia
126 D2 Safranbolu Turkey
127 G5 Safwān Iraq
177 L4 Sâg Romania
196 E3 Şag Romania
111 D6 Šaga Xizang China
103 E7 Saga Japan
103 E7 Saga pref. Japan
120 F2 Saga Kazakh.
102 J4 Sagae Japan
96 A2 Sagaing Myanmar
96 A2 Sagaing admin. div. Myanmar
192 A4 Sagama Sardegna Italy
105 F3 Sagamihara Japan
105 F4 Sagami-nada g. Japan
105 F3 Sagami-wan b. Japan
232 D4 Sagamore PA U.S.A.
207 F5 Sagamu Nigeria
97 B4 Saganthit Kyun i. Myanmar
114 B3 Sagar Karnataka India
114 C2 Sagar Karnataka India
116 D5 Sagar Madh. Prad. India
170 E1 Sagard Ger.
Sagaredzho Georgia see Sagarejo
129 D3 Sagarejo Georgia
117 G5 Sagaria Bangl.
117 G5 Sagar Island India
Sagarmatha mt. China/Nepal see Everest, Mount
117 F4 Sagarmatha National Park Nepal
117 F4 Sagauli Bihar India
220 D2 Sagavanirktok r. AK U.S.A.
168 D3 Sage Ger.
238 E3 Sage WY U.S.A.
238 E1 Sage Creek r. MT U.S.A.
143 F1 Sågen Sweden
147 E3 Saggart Rep. of Ireland
128 B4 Saggi, Har mt. Israel
235 F2 Sag Harbor NY U.S.A.
Saghyz Kazakh. see Sagiz
114 C3 Sagileru r. India
227 F4 Saginaw MI U.S.A.
226 A2 Saginaw MN U.S.A.
227 F4 Saginaw Bay MI U.S.A.
199 F2 Sağırlar Turkey
193 F2 Sagittario r. Italy
120 C2 Sagiz Kazakh.
Sagiz r. Kazakh. see Sagyz
199 E1 Sağlamtaş Turkey
129 F4 Şağlasär Azer.
206 C5 Sagleipie Liberia
Saglouc Que. Can. see Salluit
192 A2 Sagone Corse France
185 H3 Sagra mt. Spain
260 B4 Sagrada Familia Chile
184 B3 Sagres Port.
184 B4 Sagres, Ponta de pt Port.
96 A2 Sagu Myanmar
177 K5 Şagu Romania
239 F4 Saguache CO U.S.A.
239 F4 Saguache Creek r. CO U.S.A.
246 D2 Sagua de Tánamo Cuba
246 B2 Sagua la Grande Cuba
225 G3 Saguenay r. Que. Can.
Sagunt Spain see Sagunto
187 C5 Sagunto Spain
Saguntum Spain see Sagunto
137 J2 Saguny Rus. Fed.
142 A2 Sagvåg Norway
116 C5 Sagwara Rajasthan India
160 D2 Sagy France
120 C3 Sagyz r. Kazakh.
128 C4 Saḩāb Jordan
116 D3 Sahabab Uttar Prad. India
122 B2 Şahağac Azer.
245 E4 Sahagún Mex.
183 E2 Sahagún Spain
141 N3 Sahalahti Fin.
151 H2 Saham Toney Norfolk, England U.K.
122 A2 Sahand, Kūh-e mt. Iran
129 C3 Sahandöken Turkey
204 G6 Sahara des. Africa
203 F3 Şaḩara el Gharbîya des. Egypt
203 G3 Şaḩara el Sharqîya des. Egypt
Saharan Atlas mts Alg. see Atlas Saharien
116 D3 Saharanpur Uttar Prad. India
86 D4 Sahara Well W.A. Austr.
117 F4 Saharsa Bihar India
116 D3 Sahaswan Uttar Prad. India
122 C3 Sahat, Kūh-e hill Iran
117 F4 Sahatwar Uttar Prad. India
213 □K4 Sahavato Madag.
129 D4 Şahbuz Azer.
129 D3 Şahdağ Silsiläsi hills Armenia/Azer.
124 B4 Sahel prov. Eritrea
117 F4 Sahibganj Bihar India
123 H4 Sahiwal Punjab Pak.
123 H4 Sahiwal Punjab Pak.
122 D3 Sahlābād Iran
124 C3 Sahl Rakbah plain Saudi Arabia
125 G2 Şaḩm Oman
122 A3 Şaḩneh Iran
127 G5 Şaḩrā al Ḩijārah reg. Iraq
Sahu Qinghai China see Zadoi
242 C2 Sahuaripa Mex.
241 L6 Sahuarita AZ U.S.A.
244 C3 Sahuayo Mex.
186 D2 Sahún Spain
161 D4 Sahune France
137 G3 Sahunivka Ukr.
129 B4 Şahvelet Dağları mts Turkey
177 H3 Šahy Slovakia
Sahyadri mts India see Western Ghats
116 C5 Sahyadriparvat Range hills India
128 C2 Şahyūn tourist site Syria
116 E4 Sai r. India
97 C6 Sai Buri Thai.
97 C6 Sai Buri r. Thai.
205 F2 Saïda Alg.
128 B3 Saïda Lebanon
97 C4 Sai Dao Tai, Khao mt. Thai.
181 E5 Saïdia Morocco
117 G4 Saidpur Bangl.
117 E4 Saidpur Uttar Prad. India
123 H3 Saidu Pak.
104 C2 Sai-gawa r. Japan
105 E2 Sai-gawa r. Japan
146 A4 Saighdinis Western Isles, Scotland U.K.
162 E3 Saignes France
161 D5 Saignon France
Saigon Vietnam see Hô Chi Minh
117 H5 Saiha Mizoram India
107 G3 Saihan Tal Nei Mongol China
106 D3 Saihan Toroi Nei Mongol China
103 F7 Saijō Japan
103 E7 Saiki Japan
116 C5 Sailana Madh. Prad. India
163 E6 Saillagouse-Llo France
161 D4 Saillans France
162 C3 Saillat-sur-Vienne France
160 B3 Sail-sous-Couzan France
141 O3 Saimaa l. Fin.
141 O3 Saimaankanava r. Fin.
126 E3 Saimbeyli Turkey
244 C2 Sain Alto Mex.
160 B2 Saincaize-Meauce France
122 A2 Sa'īndezh Iran
Sa'īn Qal'eh Iran see Sa'īndezh
156 D3 Sains-Richaumont France
236 F4 Saint r. IL U.S.A.
146 F6 St Abbs Scottish Borders, Scotland U.K.
146 F6 St Abb's Head hd Scotland U.K.
156 C2 St-Acheul France
161 A5 St-Affrique France
161 A4 St-Affrique, Causse de plat. France
160 B2 St-Agnan France
160 C1 St-Agnan France
161 D4 St-Agnan-en-Vercors France
162 B3 St-Agnant France
162 D2 St-Agnant-de-Versillat France
150 B4 St Agnes Cornwall, England U.K.
150 □ St Agnes i. England U.K.
161 C3 St-Agrève France
162 D1 St-Aignan France
159 E4 St-Aignan-sur-Roë France
162 B3 St-Aigulin France
160 C2 St-Albain France
158 D3 St-Alban France
161 C3 St-Alban-d'Ay France
160 D3 St-Alban-Leysse France
225 K4 St Alban's Nfld. Can.
151 G3 St Albans Hertfordshire, England U.K.
233 G2 St Albans VT U.S.A.
232 C5 St Albans WV U.S.A.
150 E4 St Alban's Head hd England U.K.
161 B4 St-Alban-sur-Limagnole France
222 H4 St Albert Alta Can.
St Aldhelm's Head hd England U.K. see St Alban's Head
159 F2 St-Amand France
160 B1 St-Amand-en-Puisaye France
156 D2 St-Amand-les-Eaux France
159 H4 St-Amand-Longpré France
160 A2 St-Amand-Montrond France
156 E4 St-Amand-sur-Fion France
161 B4 St-Amans France
161 A4 St-Amans-des-Cots France
163 E5 St-Amans-Soult France
162 C3 St-Amant-de-Boixe France
160 B3 St-Amant-Roche-Savine France
160 B3 St-Amant-Tallende France
157 H5 St-Amarin France
225 G3 St-Ambroise Que. Can.
161 C4 St-Ambroix France
160 D2 St-Amour France
161 C5 St-Andiol France
163 E6 St-André France
161 F5 St-André France
St-André, Cap pt Madag. see Vilanandro, Tanjona
160 C3 St-André-de-Corcy France
161 C4 St-André-de-Cruzières France
162 B4 St-André-de-Cubzac France
156 B4 St-André-de-l'Eure France
161 E4 St-André-d'Embrun France
161 B5 St-André-de-Sangonis France
163 A5 St-André-de-Seignanx France
161 B4 St-André-de-Valborgne France
160 B1 St-André-en-Morvan France
160 D3 St-André-le-Gaz France
161 E5 St-André-les-Alpes France
156 E4 St-André-les-Vergers France
246 □ St Andrew parish Jamaica
233 □J2 St Andrews N.B. Can.
81 C6 St Andrews South I. N.Z.
146 F5 St Andrews Fife, Scotland U.K.
162 E3 St-Angel France
246 □ St Ann parish Jamaica
158 D2 St Anne Channel Is
226 D5 Saint Anne IL U.S.A.
246 □ St Ann's Bay Jamaica
150 B3 St Ann's Head hd Wales U.K.
226 A4 St Ansgar IA U.S.A.
160 B3 St-Anthème France
225 K3 St Anthony Nfld. Can.
238 E3 Saint Anthony ID U.S.A.
163 D4 St-Antonin-Noble-Val France
159 H5 St-Août France
160 D1 St-Apollinaire France
161 B3 St-Arcons-d'Allier France
83 E4 St Arnaud Vic. Austr.
81 D4 St Arnaud South I. N.Z.
81 D5 St Arnaud Range mts South I. N.Z.
156 B4 St-Arnoult-en-Yvelines France
150 D1 St Asaph Denbighshire, Wales U.K.
84 B1 St Asaph Bay N.T. Austr.
162 C3 St-Astier France
163 C4 St-Astier France
150 D3 St Athan Vale of Glamorgan, Wales U.K.
161 E5 St-Auban France
161 D4 St-Auban-sur-l'Ouvèze France
160 D1 St-Aubin France
156 D5 St-Aubin-Château-Neuf France
158 E3 St-Aubin-d'Aubigné France
158 E3 St-Aubin-du-Cormier France
156 B3 St-Aubin-lès-Elbeuf France
159 F2 St-Aubin-sur-Mer France
225 J3 St-Augustin Que. Can.
225 J3 St Augustin r. Newfoundland/Québec Can.
231 D6 St Augustine FL U.S.A.
162 C3 St-Aulaye France
150 C4 St Austell Cornwall, England U.K.
150 C4 St Austell Bay England U.K.
158 D4 St-Avé France
159 G4 St-Avertin France
157 G3 St-Avold France
156 B5 St-Ay France
161 E5 St-Aygulf France
160 D3 St-Baldoph France
225 J3 St Barbe Nfld. Can.
225 F4 St-Barthélémi Que. Can.
247 G3 St Barthélémy i. West Indies
163 D6 St-Barthélemy, Pic de mt. France
163 C4 St-Barthélemy-d'Agenais France
159 F4 St-Barthélemy-d'Anjou France
162 C3 St-Barthélemy-de-Bellegarde France
161 C3 St-Barthélemy-de-Vals France
81 B6 St Bathans South I. N.Z.
81 B6 St Bathans, Mount South I. N.Z.
161 B5 St-Bauzille-de-Putois France
163 C6 St-Béat France
161 A4 St-Beauzély France
149 F3 St Bees Cumbria, England U.K.
149 F3 St Bees Head hd England U.K.
160 B1 St-Benin-d'Azy France
163 E5 St-Benoît France
162 C2 St-Benoît France
217 □1c St-Benoit Réunion
163 E4 St-Benoît-de-Carmaux France
162 D2 St-Benoît-du-Sault France
156 C5 St-Benoît-sur-Loire France
81 D5 St Bernard mt. South I. N.Z.
160 D3 St-Béron France
159 F3 St-Berthevin France
163 C5 St-Bertrand-de-Comminges France
190 B1 St-Blaise Switz.
157 H4 St-Blaise-la-Roche France
157 F4 St-Blin-Semilly France
160 C2 St-Boil France
162 C2 St-Bonnet-de-Bellac France
160 C2 St-Bonnet-de-Joux France
160 C2 St-Bonnet-des-Bruyères France
161 E4 St-Bonnet-en-Champsaur France
161 C3 St-Bonnet-le-Château France
161 C3 St-Bonnet-le-Froid France
162 B3 St-Bonnet-sur-Gironde France
160 C1 St-Brancher France
159 G4 St-Branchs France
158 D2 St Brelade Channel Is
158 D4 St-Brevin-les-Pins France
158 D3 St-Briac-sur-Mer France
150 E3 St Briavels Gloucestershire, England U.K.
156 E3 St-Brice-Courcelles France
158 E3 St-Brice-en-Coglès France
150 B3 St Brides Pembrokeshire, Wales U.K.
150 B3 St Bride's Bay Wales U.K.
150 D3 St Brides Major Vale of Glamorgan, Wales U.K.
158 D3 St-Brieuc France
158 D3 St-Brieuc, Baie de b. France
156 D5 St-Bris-le-Vineux France
160 C1 St-Brisson France
157 E5 St-Broing-les-Moines France
158 E3 St-Broladre France
150 □ St Buryan Cornwall, England U.K.
159 G4 St-Calais France
161 D5 St-Cannat France
158 D3 St-Cast-le-Guildo France
224 E5 St Catharines Ont. Can.
246 □ St Catherine parish Jamaica
247 □6 St Catherine, Mount hill Grenada
225 K4 St Catherine's Nfld. Can.
151 F4 St Catherine's Point England U.K.
163 D4 St-Céré France
190 B2 St-Cergue Switz.
160 E2 St-Cergues France
162 E3 St-Cernin France
233 G2 St-Césaire Que. Can.
161 E4 St-Chaffrey France
163 D4 St-Chamarand France
161 D5 St-Chamas France
161 C3 St-Chamond France
161 C5 St-Chaptes France
227 G2 St Charles Ont. Can.
238 E3 Saint Charles ID U.S.A.
232 E5 St Charles MD U.S.A.
227 E4 Saint Charles MI U.S.A.
226 A4 St Charles MN U.S.A.
236 F4 St Charles MO U.S.A.
160 D3 St-Chef France
161 B4 St-Chély-d'Apcher France
161 A4 St-Chély-d'Aubrac France
161 A5 St-Chinian France
161 D4 St-Christol France
161 C4 St-Christol-lès-Alès France
162 B3 St-Christoly-de-Blaye France
162 B3 St-Christoly-Médoc France
160 F3 St-Christophe Italy
158 E5 St-Christophe-du-Ligneron France
159 H4 St-Christophe-en-Bazelle France
160 C2 St-Christophe-en-Brionnais France
St Christopher i. St Kitts and Nevis see St Kitts
St Christopher and Nevis country West Indies see St Kitts and Nevis
162 B3 St-Ciers-sur-Gironde France
163 B5 St-Circq-Chalosse France
161 C4 St-Cirgues-en-Montagne France
163 D4 St-Cirq-Lapopie France
224 D5 St Clair r. Can./U.S.A.
227 F4 St Clair MI U.S.A.
234 B2 St Clair PA U.S.A.
227 F4 St Clair, Lake Can./U.S.A.
161 C3 St-Clair-du-Rhône France
156 B3 St-Clair-sur-Epte France
159 E2 St-Clair-sur-l'Elle France
232 C4 St Clairsville OH U.S.A.
163 C5 St-Clar France
162 C3 St-Claud France
160 D2 St-Claude France
150 C3 St Clears Carmarthenshire, Wales U.K.
158 D2 St Clement Channel Is
156 D4 St-Clément France
162 D3 St-Clément France
157 G4 St-Clément France
161 B5 St-Clément de-Rivière France
231 D6 Saint Cloud FL U.S.A.
236 E2 St Cloud MN U.S.A.
225 G3 St-Coeur-de-Marie Que. Can.
150 C4 St Columb Major Cornwall, England U.K.
146 G4 St Combs Aberdeenshire, Scotland U.K.
163 E4 St-Constant France
159 G3 St-Cosme-en-Vairais France
162 C3 St-Crépin-de-Richemont France
221 L5 St Croix r. Can./U.S.A.
226 A3 St Croix r. WI U.S.A.
226 A3 St Croix Falls WI U.S.A.
247 F3 St Croix Island Virgin Is (U.S.A.)
163 D4 St-Cyprien France
163 F6 St-Cyprien France
163 D4 St-Cyprien France
156 C4 St-Cyr-l'École France
162 C1 St-Cyr-sur-Loire France
161 D5 St-Cyr-sur-Mer France
156 D4 St-Cyr-sur-Morin France
161 E4 St-Dalmas-le-Selvage France
225 G4 St-Damien-de-Buckland Que. Can.
241 L6 St David AZ U.S.A.
226 B5 St David IL U.S.A.
150 B3 St David's Pembrokeshire, Wales U.K.
150 B3 St David's Head hd Wales U.K.
150 B4 St Day Cornwall, England U.K.
156 C4 St-Denis France
163 E5 St-Denis France
217 □1c St-Denis Réunion
159 F4 St-Denis-d'Anjou France
159 F3 St-Denis-de-Gastines France
162 D2 St-Denis-de-Jouhet France
162 A2 St-Denis-d'Oléron France
159 F3 St-Denis-d'Orques France
St-Denis-du-Sig Alg. see Sig
160 D3 St-Denis-en-Bugey France
160 D2 St-Denis-lès-Bourg France
150 C4 St Dennis Cornwall, England U.K.
158 D3 St-Denoual France
160 C2 St-Désert France
161 C3 St-Didier-en-Velay France
160 C2 St-Didier-sur-Chalaronne France
160 B3 St-Didier-sur-Rochefort France
157 G4 St-Dié France
160 B3 St-Dier-d'Auvergne France
157 E4 St-Dizier France
162 D2 St-Dizier-Leyrenne France
150 C2 St Dogmaels Pembrokeshire, Wales U.K.
158 D4 St-Dolay France
158 E3 St-Domineuc France
St-Domingue country West Indies see Haiti
161 C3 St-Donat-sur-l'Herbasse France
159 I4 St-Doulchard France
159 G2 Ste-Adresse France
162 C4 Ste-Alvère France
223 L5 Sainte Anne Man. Can.
247 □2 Ste-Anne Guadeloupe
158 D4 Ste-Anne-d'Auray France
225 G4 Ste-Anne-de-Beaupré Que. Can.
233 □I1 Ste-Anne-de-Madawaska N.B. Can.
225 G3 Ste-Anne-de-Portneuf Que. Can.
225 H3 Ste-Anne-des-Monts Que. Can.
227 J2 Ste-Anne-du-Lac Que. Can.
163 C4 Ste-Bazeille France
233 □H1 Ste-Camille-de-Lellis Que. Can.
161 C4 Ste-Cécile-les-Vignes France
160 D2 Ste-Croix France
161 D4 Ste-Croix France
190 B2 Ste-Croix Switz.
161 E5 Ste-Croix, Lac de l. France
163 D5 Ste-Croix-Volvestre France
224 F4 Ste-Émélie-de-l'Énergie Que. Can.
163 B5 Ste-Engrâce France
161 B4 Ste-Énimie France
161 A4 Ste-Eulalie d'Olt France
163 A4 Ste-Eulalie-en-Born France
162 D2 Ste-Feyre France
161 B3 Ste-Florine France
162 D3 Ste-Fortunade France
163 D5 Ste-Foy-de-Peyrolières France
163 C4 Ste-Foy-la-Grande France
160 C3 Ste-Foy-l'Argentière France
160 C3 Ste-Foy-lès-Lyon France
160 E3 Ste-Foy-Tarentaise France
159 G3 Ste-Gauburge-Ste-Colombe France
162 A2 Ste-Gemme-la-Plaine France
156 C3 Ste-Geneviève France
236 F4 Sainte Genevieve MO U.S.A.
161 A4 Ste-Geneviève-sur-Argence France
161 D3 St-Égrève France
162 B4 Ste-Hélène France
162 A2 Ste-Hermine France
233 □H1 Ste-Justine Que. Can.
233 □I1 St-Éleuthère Que. Can.
222 A2 St Elias Mountains Y.T. Can.
251 H3 St Élie Fr. Guiana
163 C4 Ste-Livrade-sur-Lot France
163 D5 St-Élix-le-Château France
163 C5 St-Élix-Theux France
246 □ St Elizabeth parish Jamaica
159 I4 Ste-Lizaigne France
160 A2 St-Éloy-les-Mines France
192 B3 Ste-Lucie-de-Tallano Corse France
225 H3 Sainte Marguerite r. Que. Can.
157 G4 Ste-Marguerite France
225 G4 Ste-Marie Que. Can.
161 A4 Ste-Marie France
163 F6 Ste-Marie France
247 □3 Ste-Marie Martinique
Ste-Marie, Cap c. Madag. see Vohimena, Tanjona
Sainte-Marie, Île i. Madag. see Boraha, Nosy
157 H4 Ste-Marie-aux-Mines France
163 C4 Ste-Maure-de-Peyriac France
162 C1 Ste-Maure-de-Touraine France
161 E5 Ste-Maxime France
157 E3 Ste-Menehould France
158 E2 Ste-Mère-Église France
160 C2 St-Émiland France
163 B4 St-Émilion France
150 C4 St Endellion Cornwall, England U.K.
150 C4 St Enoder Cornwall, England U.K.
162 D3 Ste-Orse France
158 E4 Ste-Pazanne France
159 F5 Ste-Radegonde France
156 D3 St Erme-Outre-et-Ramecourt France
247 □2 Ste-Rose Guadeloupe
Ste-Rose-du-Dégelé Que. Can. see Dégelis
223 L5 Sainte Rose du Lac Man. Can.
150 B4 St Erth Cornwall, England U.K.
162 B3 Saintes France
247 □2 Saintes, Îles des is Guadeloupe
160 C1 Ste-Sabine France
156 E4 Ste-Savine France
Ste-Scholastique Que. Can. see Mirabel
162 E2 Ste-Sévère-sur-Indre France
161 C3 Ste-Sigolène France
163 A5 St-Esteben France
162 B3 St-Estèphe France
163 E6 St-Estève France
159 F3 Ste-Suzanne France
233 G2 Ste-Thérèse Que. Can.
161 C3 St-Étienne France
162 E4 St-Étienne-Cantalès France
163 A5 St-Étienne-de-Baïgorry France
161 D3 St-Étienne-de-Crossey France
161 C4 St-Étienne-de-Fontbellon France
162 D2 St-Étienne-de-Fursac France
161 B4 St-Étienne-de-Lugdarès France
158 E4 St-Étienne-de-Montluc France
161 D3 St-Étienne-de-St-Geoirs France
161 E4 St-Étienne-de-Tinée France
163 D4 St-Étienne-de-Tulmont France
160 D2 St-Étienne-du-Bois France
156 B3 St-Étienne-du-Rouvray France
161 D4 St-Étienne-en-Dévoluy France
161 D4 St-Étienne-les-Orgues France
157 G4 St-Étienne-lès-Remiremont France
161 B4 St-Étienne-Vallée-Française France
161 D5 Ste-Tulle France
233 F2 St Eugene Ont. Can.
233 □I1 St-Eusèbe Que. Can.
233 G2 St-Eustache Que. Can.
247 □2 St Eustatius i. Neth. Antilles
158 B4 St-Évarzec France
156 D5 Ste-Vertu France
161 D5 Ste-Victoire, Montagne mt. France
225 G3 St-Fabien Que. Can.
215 H4 St Faith's S. Africa
160 B1 St-Fargeau France
225 F3 St-Félicien Que. Can.
161 C3 St-Félicien France
227 H1 St-Félix-de-Dalquier Que. Can.
163 D5 St-Félix-Lauragais France
146 G4 St Fergus Aberdeenshire, Scotland U.K.
163 C4 St-Ferme France
147 F2 Saintfield Northern Ireland U.K.
146 D5 St Fillans Perth and Kinross, Scotland U.K.
157 G4 St-Firmin France
161 E4 St-Firmin France
156 D4 St-Flavy France
192 B2 St-Florent Corse France
162 A2 St-Florent-des-Bois France
156 D4 St-Florentin France
159 E4 St-Florent-le-Vieil France
162 E2 St-Florent-sur-Cher France
161 B3 St-Flour France
159 H5 St-Flovier France
160 C3 St-Fons France
162 B3 St-Fort-sur-Gironde France
163 C5 St-Frajou France
237 F6 St Francesville LA U.S.A.
233 □I1 St Francis r. Can./U.S.A.
236 C4 Saint Francis KS U.S.A.
233 □I1 St Francis ME U.S.A.
237 F5 St Francis r. Arkansas/Missouri U.S.A.
215 E6 St Francis Bay S. Africa
82 C3 St Francis Isles S.A. Austr.
225 F4 St-François r. Que. Can.
247 □2 St-François Guadeloupe
217 □2 St François i. Seychelles
161 E3 St-François-Longchamp France
161 C4 St-Front France
162 C3 St-Front-de-Pradoux France
159 E5 St-Fulgent France
160 C3 St-Galmier France
159 G2 St-Gatien-des-Bois France
163 C5 St-Gaudens France
162 D2 St-Gaultier France
233 □H2 St-Gédéon Que. Can.
163 B5 St-Gein France
161 B5 St-Gély-du-Fesc France
165 D4 St-Genesius-Rode Belgium
161 C3 St-Genest-Malifaux France
160 C2 St-Gengoux-le-National France
161 C5 St-Geniès-de-Malgoirès France
161 E4 St-Geniez France
161 A4 St-Geniez-d'Olt France
162 B3 St-Genis-de-Saintonge France
163 E6 St-Génis-des-Fontaines France
160 C3 St-Genis-Laval France
160 E2 St-Genis-Pouilly France
160 D3 St-Genix-sur-Guiers France
150 C4 St Gennys Cornwall, England U.K.
159 H5 St-Genou France
161 D3 St-Geoire-en-Valdaine France
83 G2 St George Qld Austr.
85 F3 St George r. Qld Austr.
225 H4 St George N.B. Can.
220 B4 St George AK U.S.A.
231 D5 St George SC U.S.A.
241 K3 St George UT U.S.A.
83 G3 St George Head hd A.C.T. Austr.
86 E3 St George Range hills W.A. Austr.
225 J3 St George's Nfld. Can.
225 G4 St-Georges Que. Can.
251 I4 St-Georges Fr. Guiana
247 □6 St George's Grenada
234 C3 St Georges DE U.S.A.
225 J3 St George's Bay Nfld. Can.
225 I4 St George's Bay N.S. Can.
159 F3 St-Georges-Buttavent France
147 E5 St George's Channel Rep. of Ireland/U.K.
161 B3 St-Georges-d'Aurac France
161 D3 St-Georges-de-Commiers France
162 B3 St-Georges-de-Didonne France
161 A4 St-Georges-de-Luzençon France
160 A3 St-Georges-de-Mons France
158 E5 St-Georges-de-Montaigu France
160 C2 St-Georges-de-Reneins France
159 F3 St-Georges-des-Groseillers France
160 D3 St-Georges-d'Espéranche France
162 A3 St-Georges-d'Oléron France
159 G2 St-Georges-du-Vièvre France
160 B3 St-Georges-en-Couzan France
159 G5 St-Georges-lès-Baillargeaux France
156 D5 St-Georges-sur-Baulche France
159 H4 St-Georges-sur-Cher France
156 B4 St-Georges-sur-Eure France
159 F4 St-Georges-sur-Loire France
163 A5 St-Geours-de-Maremne France
160 B2 St-Gérand-le-Puy France
226 C3 St Germain WI U.S.A.
160 B2 St-Germain-Chassenay France
161 B4 St-Germain-de-Calberte France
159 G3 St-Germain-de-la-Coudre France
160 B2 St-Germain-des-Fossés France
162 B3 St-Germain-d'Esteuil France
163 D4 St-Germain-du-Bel-Air France
160 D2 St-Germain-du-Bois France
159 G3 St-Germain-du-Corbeis France
160 C2 St-Germain-du-Plain France
162 E1 St-Germain-du-Puy France
161 B4 St-Germain-du-Teil France
156 C4 St-Germain-en-Laye France
160 C3 St-Germain-Laval France
161 B3 St-Germain-Lembron France
162 D3 St-Germain-les-Belles France
160 B2 St-Germain-Lespinasse France
162 D3 St-Germain-les-Vergnes France
161 B3 St-Germain-l'Herm France
150 C4 St Germans Cornwall, England U.K.
163 B5 St-Germé France
156 B3 St-Germer-de-Fly France
158 D5 St-Gervais France
161 D3 St-Gervais France
160 A2 St-Gervais-d'Auvergne France
159 H4 St-Gervais-la-Forêt France
160 E3 St-Gervais-les-Bains France
159 G5 St-Gervais-les-Trois-Clochers France
161 B5 St-Gervais-sur-Mare France
163 D4 St-Géry France
165 C4 St-Ghislain Belgium
158 D4 St-Gildas-de-Rhuys France
158 D4 St-Gildas-des-Bois France
161 C5 St-Gilles France
158 E5 St-Gilles-Croix-de-Vie France
160 E2 St-Gingolph France
163 D6 St-Girons France
163 A5 St-Girons-Plage France
156 D3 St-Gobain France
St Gotthard Pass pass Switz. see San Gottardo, Passo del
158 E3 St-Grégoire France
158 B4 St-Guénolé France
161 B5 St-Guilhem-le-Désert France
160 B2 St-Haon-le-Châtel France
160 C3 St-Héand France
226 E3 St Helen MI U.S.A.
216 □2b St Helena terr. S. Atlantic Ocean
240 F2 St Helena CA U.S.A.
214 B5 St Helena Bay S. Africa
83 G5 St Helens Tas. Austr.
149 G4 St Helens Merseyside, England U.K.
238 B2 St Helens OR U.S.A.
238 B2 St Helens, Mount vol. WA U.S.A.
83 G5 St Helens Point Tas. Austr.
158 D2 St Helier Channel Is
158 E4 St-Herblain France
163 E5 St-Hilaire France
156 E3 St-Hilaire-au-Temple France
161 C4 St-Hilaire-de-Brethmas France
158 E4 St-Hilaire-de-Loulay France
163 C4 St-Hilaire-de-Lusignan France
158 E5 St-Hilaire-de-Riez France
162 B2 St-Hilaire-des-Loges France
162 B3 St-Hilaire-de-Villefranche France
159 E3 St-Hilaire-du-Harcouët France
161 D3 St-Hilaire-du-Rosier France
160 B2 St-Hilaire-Fontaine France
156 E3 St-Hilaire-le-Grand France
159 F4 St-Hilaire-St-Florent France
157 H4 St-Hippolyte France
160 E1 St-Hippolyte France
161 B5 St-Hippolyte-du-Fort France
117 F5 Sainthiya W. Bengal India
161 E4 St-Honorat, Mont mt. France
160 B2 St-Honoré-les-Bains France
161 C3 St-Hostien France
165 E4 St-Hubert Belgium
225 F4 St-Hyacinthe Que. Can.
226 E3 St Ignace MI U.S.A.
190 B1 St-Imier Switz.
150 C3 St Ishmael Carmarthenshire, Wales U.K.
161 D3 St-Ismier France
150 C4 St Ive Cornwall, England U.K.
151 G2 St Ives Cambridgeshire, England U.K.
150 □ St Ives Cornwall, England U.K.
161 A5 St-Izaire France
233 □I1 St-Jacques N.B. Can.
St Jacques, Cap Vietnam see Vung Tau
224 E3 St-Jacques-de-Dupuy Que. Can.
158 E3 St-Jacques-de-la-Lande France
158 D3 St-Jacut-de-la-Mer France
158 E3 St-James France
246 □ St James parish Jamaica
226 E3 St James MI U.S.A.
236 E3 St James MN U.S.A.
236 F4 St James MO U.S.A.
235 E2 St James NY U.S.A.
225 H3 St-Jean r. Que. Can.
225 H3 St-Jean r. Que. Can.
163 D5 St-Jean France
251 H3 St Jean Fr. Guiana
225 F3 St-Jean, Lac l. Que. Can.
158 D4 St-Jean-Brévelay France
161 F5 St-Jean-Cap-Ferrat France
St-Jean-d'Acre Israel see 'Akko
162 B3 St-Jean-d'Angély France
159 G3 St-Jean-d'Assé France
160 D3 St-Jean-de-Bournay France
156 B5 St-Jean-de-Braye France
159 E2 St-Jean-de-Daye France
156 B5 St-Jean-de-la-Ruelle France
160 D1 St-Jean-de-Losne France
163 A5 St-Jean-de-Luz France
161 C4 St-Jean-de-Mauréjols-et-Avéjan France
161 E3 St-Jean-de-Maurienne France
158 D5 St-Jean-de-Monts France
161 C3 St-Jean-de-Muzols France
225 G4 St-Jean-de-Port-Joli Que. Can.
159 G5 St-Jean-de-Sauves France
160 E3 St-Jean-de-Sixt France
161 B5 St-Jean-de-Védas France
163 B4 St-Jean-d'Illac France
161 B4 St-Jean-du-Bruel France
163 D5 St-Jean-du-Falga France
161 B4 St-Jean-du-Gard France
161 D3 St-Jean-en-Royans France
163 A5 St-Jean-Pied-de-Port France
163 C5 St-Jean-Poutge France
160 C3 St-Jean-Soleymieux France
159 F3 St-Jean-sur-Erve France
160 D2 St-Jean-sur-Reyssouze France
225 F4 St-Jean-sur-Richelieu Que. Can.
160 E2 St-Jeoire France
224 F4 St-Jérôme Que. Can.
161 C3 St-Jeure-d'Ay France
161 C3 St-Jeures France
158 D4 St-Joachim France
238 C2 St Joe r. ID U.S.A.
225 H4 Saint John N.B. Can.
158 D2 St John Channel Is
206 C5 St John r. Liberia
236 D4 St John KS U.S.A.
233 □J2 St John r. ME U.S.A.
247 F3 St John Island Virgin Is (U.S.A.)
247 □2 St John's Antigua and Barbuda
225 K4 St John's Nfld. Can.
241 M4 St Johns AZ U.S.A.
226 E4 St Johns MI U.S.A.
232 A4 St Johns OH U.S.A.
231 D6 St Johns r. FL U.S.A.
233 G2 St Johnsbury VT U.S.A.
148 B3 St Johnstown Rep. of Ireland
146 D6 St John's Town of Dalry Dumfries and Galloway, Scotland U.K.
233 F3 St Johnsville NY U.S.A.
158 E2 St-Jores France
160 E3 St-Jorioz France
165 C3 St-Joris Belgium
163 D5 St-Jory France
162 C3 St-Jory-de-Chalais France
247 □3 St-Joseph Martinique
237 F6 St Joseph LA U.S.A.
226 D4 St Joseph MI U.S.A.
236 E4 St Joseph MO U.S.A.
226 D4 St Joseph r. MI U.S.A.
226 E5 St Joseph r. MI U.S.A.
224 B3 St Joseph, Lake Ont. Can.
St-Joseph-d'Alma Que. Can. see Alma
158 E3 St-Jouan-des-Guérets France
159 G2 St-Jouin-Bruneval France
159 F5 St-Jouin-de-Marnes France
224 F4 St Jovité Que. Can.
163 E5 St-Juéry France
St Julian's Malta see San Ġiljan
160 D2 St-Julien France
163 D5 St-Julien France
162 B3 St-Julien-Beychevelle France
161 C4 St-Julien-Boutières France
160 C2 St-Julien-de-Civry France
154 D3 St-Julien-de-Concelles France
158 E4 St-Julien-de-Vouvantes France
156 D4 St-Julien-du-Sault France
161 E5 St-Julien-du-Verdon France
161 D4 St-Julien-en-Beauchêne France
163 A4 St-Julien-en-Born France
160 E2 St-Julien-en-Genevois France
161 D4 St-Julien-en-Quint France
162 C2 St-Julien-l'Ars France
161 C4 St-Julien-les-Rosiers France
156 E4 St-Julien-les-Villas France
160 D2 St-Julien-sur-Reyssouze France
162 C3 St-Junien France
161 C4 St-Just France
150 □ St Just Cornwall, England U.K.
156 C3 St-Just-en-Chaussée France
160 B3 St-Just-en-Chevalet France
163 A5 St-Just-Ibarre France
163 B5 St-Justin France
150 B4 St Just in Roseland Cornwall, England U.K.
160 C3 St-Just-la-Pendue France
162 A3 St-Just-Luzac France
156 D4 St-Just-Sauvage France
160 C3 St-Just-St-Rambert France
150 B4 St Keverne Cornwall, England U.K.
146 □ St Kilda i. Scotland U.K.
247 □2 St Kitts i. St Kitts and Nevis
247 □2 St Kitts and Nevis country West Indies
159 F4 St-Lambert-des-Levées France
159 F4 St-Lambert-du-Lattay France
163 C5 St-Lary France
163 C6 St-Lary-Soulan France

St-Laurent, Golfe du g. Que. Can. see St Lawrence, Gulf of
156 C2 St-Laurent-Blangy France
163 B5 St-Laurent-Bretagne France
161 C5 St-Laurent-d'Aigouze France
161 C4 St-Laurent-de-Carnols France
186 F2 St-Laurent-de-Cerdans France
160 C3 St-Laurent-de-Chamousset France
161 A5 St-Laurent-de-la-Cabrerisse France
163 E6 St-Laurent-de-la-Salanque France
163 C5 St-Laurent-de-Neste France
251 H3 St-Laurent-du-Maroni Fr. Guiana
161 D3 St-Laurent-du-Pont France
161 F5 St-Laurent-du-Var France
161 E4 St-Laurent-du-Verdon France
159 G2 St-Laurent-en-Caux France
160 D2 St-Laurent-en-Grandvaux France
161 B4 St-Laurent-les-Bains France
162 B3 St-Laurent-Médoc France
156 B5 St-Laurent-Nouan France
162 C3 St-Laurent-sur-Gorre France
157 F3 St-Laurent-sur-Othain France
159 F5 St-Laurent-sur-Sèvre France
85 G4 St Lawrence Qld Austr.
225 K4 St Lawrence Nfld. Can.
225 G3 St Lawrence inlet Que. Can.
234 C2 St Lawrence PA U.S.A.
225 I3 St Lawrence, Gulf of Que. Can.
220 B3 St Lawrence Island AK U.S.A.
224 F4 St Lawrence Seaway sea chan. Can./U.S.A.
223 K5 St Lazare Man. Can.
165 E5 St-Léger Belgium
160 B1 St-Léger-de-Fougeret France
160 B2 St-Léger-des-Vignes France
156 B4 St-Léger-en-Yvelines France
160 C2 St-Léger-sous-Beuvray France
160 C2 St-Léger-sur-Dheune France
225 H4 St-Léonard N.B. Can.
225 F4 St-Léonard Que. Can.
157 G4 St-Léonard France
232 E5 St Leonard MD U.S.A.
162 D3 St-Léonard-de-Noblat France
151 F4 St Leonards Dorset, England U.K.
162 C3 St-Léon-sur-l'Isle France
156 C3 St-Leu-d'Esserent France
225 K2 St Lewis Nfld. Can.
225 J2 St Lewis r. Nfld. Can.
163 D5 St-Lizier France
159 E2 St-Lô France
163 A5 St-Lon-les-Mines France
160 D2 St-Lothian France
163 B4 St-Loubès France
160 F1 St-Louis France
247 □2 St-Louis Guadeloupe
206 A2 St-Louis Senegal
226 E4 St Louis MI U.S.A.
236 F4 St Louis MO U.S.A.
226 A2 St Louis r. MN U.S.A.
246 D3 St-Louis du Nord Haiti
157 H4 St-Louis-lès-Bitche France
161 B5 St-Loup, Pic hill France
160 C2 St-Loup-de-la-Salle France
156 D4 St-Loup-de-Naud France
159 F5 St-Loup-Lamairé France
157 G5 St-Loup-sur-Semouse France
156 B4 St-Lubin-des-Joncherets France
158 E4 St-Luce-sur-Loire France
247 □3 St Lucia country West Indies
215 I3 St Lucia, Lake S. Africa
215 I3 St Lucia Estuary S. Africa
St Luke's Island Myanmar see Zadetkale Kyun
158 D3 St-Lunaire France
160 D2 St-Lupicin France
156 E4 St-Lyé France
163 D5 St-Lys France
163 B4 St-Macaire France
162 B1 St-Macaire-en-Mauges France
163 B4 St-Magne France
163 B4 St-Magne-de-Castillon France
146 □G1 St Magnus Bay Scotland U.K.
161 D5 St-Maime France
162 B2 St-Maixent-l'École France
158 D3 St-Malo France
158 D3 St-Malo, Golfe de g. France
158 E2 St-Malo-de-la-Lande France
161 C5 St-Mamert-du-Gard France
163 E4 St-Mamet-la-Salvetat France
161 D5 St-Mandrier-sur-Mer France
246 D3 St Marc Haiti
160 C2 St-Marcel France
162 D2 St-Marcel France
156 B3 St-Marcel France
161 C4 St-Marcel-d'Ardèche France
161 C3 St-Marcel-lès-Annonay France
161 C4 St-Marcel-lès-Sauzet France
161 C4 St-Marcel-lès-Valence France
161 D3 St-Marcellin France
163 C5 St-Marcet France
156 E5 St-Marc-sur-Seine France
156 D4 St-Mards-en-Othe France
151 I3 St Margaret's at Cliffe Kent, England U.K.
146 F3 St Margaret's Hope Orkney, Scotland U.K.
238 C2 Saint Maries ID U.S.A.
St Mark's S. Africa see Cofimvaba
215 F5 St Marks E. Cape S. Africa
163 E6 St-Marsal France
159 G4 St-Mars-d'Outillé France
158 E4 St-Mars-du-Désert France
159 G3 St-Mars-la-Brière France
158 E4 St-Mars-la-Jaille France
161 B4 St-Martial France
163 D4 St-Martial-de-Nabirat France
162 C3 St-Martial-de-Valette France
158 D2 St Martin Channel Is
158 D2 St Martin Channel Is
161 D5 St-Martin France
247 G3 St Martin i. West Indies
156 B2 St-Martin-Boulogne France
156 D3 St-Martin-d'Ablois France
163 A5 St-Martin-d'Arrossa France
159 I4 St-Martin-d'Auxigny France
161 E3 St-Martin-de-Belleville France
161 D5 St-Martin-de-Castillon France
161 C5 St-Martin-de-Crau France
161 B4 St-Martin-de-Fugères France
158 E3 St-Martin-de-Landelles France
161 B5 St-Martin-de-Londres France
161 E4 St-Martin-d'Entraunes France
162 A2 St-Martin-de-Ré France
159 F2 St-Martin-des-Besaces France
158 E3 St-Martin-des-Champs France
158 C3 St-Martin-des-Champs France
163 A5 St-Martin-de-Seignanx France
161 C4 St-Martin-de-Valamas France
161 C4 St-Martin-de-Valgalgues France
161 D3 St-Martin-d'Hères France
163 B5 St-Martin-d'Oney France
160 D2 St-Martin-du-Frêne France
160 D2 St-Martin-du-Mont France
161 F5 St-Martin-du-Var France
160 D2 St-Martin-en-Bresse France
160 C3 St-Martin-en-Haut France
160 C3 St-Martin-la-Plaine France
159 G4 St-Martin-le-Beau France
150 D2 St Martin's Shropshire, England U.K.
150 □ St Martin's i. England U.K.
156 D5 St-Martin-sur-Ouanne France
162 E3 St-Martin-Valmeroux France
161 F4 St-Martin-Vésubie France
163 C5 St-Martory France
222 F5 St Mary r. B.C. Can.
246 □ St Mary parish Jamaica
81 B6 St Mary, Mount South I. N.Z.
151 F3 St Mary Bourne Hampshire, England U.K.
151 H3 St Mary in the Marsh Kent, England U.K.
82 D2 St Mary Peak S.A. Austr.
83 G5 St Marys Tas. Austr.
227 G4 St Mary's Ont. Can.
146 F3 St Mary's Orkney, Scotland U.K.
150 □ St Mary's i. England U.K.
236 D4 Saint Marys KS U.S.A.
232 A4 St Marys OH U.S.A.
232 D4 St Marys PA U.S.A.
232 C5 St Marys WV U.S.A.
236 G3 St Marys r. OH U.S.A.
225 K4 St Mary's Bay b. Nfld. Can.
151 H3 St Mary's Bay Kent, England U.K.
232 E5 St Marys City MD U.S.A.
227 H1 St-Mathieu Que. Can.
162 C3 St-Mathieu France
158 B3 St-Mathieu, Pointe de pt France
162 A2 St-Mathurin France
220 A3 St Matthew Island AK U.S.A.
231 D5 Saint Matthews SC U.S.A.
159 H5 St-Maur France
156 C4 St-Maur-des-Fossés France
224 F4 St Maurice r. Que. Can.
190 B2 St-Maurice Switz.
160 C3 St-Maurice-de-Beynost France
161 C3 St-Maurice-de-Lignon France
162 C3 St-Maurice-des-Lions France
162 D2 St-Maurice-la-Souterraine France
161 C3 St-Maurice-l'Exil France
161 B5 St-Maurice-Navacelles France
163 C4 St-Maurin France
150 B4 St Mawes Cornwall England U.K.
157 G4 St-Max France
156 B2 St-Maxent France
156 C3 St-Maximin France
161 D5 St-Maximin-la-Ste-Baume France
162 C3 St-Méard-de-Drône France
162 B3 St-Médard-de-Guizières France
163 B4 St-Médard-en-Jalles France
158 D3 St-Méen-le-Grand France
158 E3 St-Méloir-des-Ondes France
162 B3 St-Même-les-Carrières France
156 E4 St-Memmie France
157 E3 St-Menges France
160 B2 St-Menoux France
150 C4 St Merryn Cornwall, England U.K.
162 D3 St-Mesmin France
156 D4 St-Mesmin France
159 F5 St-Mesmin France
163 C4 St-Mézard France
233 E5 St Michaels MD U.S.A.
150 □ St Michael's Mount tourist site England U.K.
163 C5 St-Michel France
156 E3 St-Michel France
162 C3 St-Michel France
158 C3 St-Michel, Montagne hill France
158 D4 St-Michel-Chef-Chef France
163 B4 St-Michel-de-Castelnau France
161 E3 St-Michel-de-Maurienne France
224 F4 St-Michel-des-Saints Que. Can.
158 C3 St-Michel-en-Grève France
162 A2 St-Michel-en-l'Herm France
159 F5 St-Michel-Mont-Mercure France
157 G4 St-Michel-sur-Meurthe France
157 F4 St-Mihiel France
146 F5 St Monans Fife, Scotland U.K.
163 B5 St-Mont France
161 C4 St-Montant France
157 G4 St-Nabord France
163 D5 St-Nauphary France
158 D4 St-Nazaire France
St-Nazaire, Étang de lag. France see Canet, Étang de
161 D3 St-Nazaire-en-Royans France
161 D4 St-Nazaire-le-Désert France
160 A3 St-Nectaire France
151 G2 St Neots Cambridgeshire, England U.K.
St Nicolas Belgium see Sint Niklaas
156 C2 St-Nicolas France
165 F5 St-Nicolas, Mont hill Lux.
156 B3 St-Nicolas-d'Aliermont France
163 D4 St-Nicolas-de-la-Grave France
157 G4 St-Nicolas-de-Port France
158 D4 St-Nicolas-de-Redon France
158 C3 St-Nicolas-du-Pélem France
190 C2 St Niklaus Switz.
146 □G2 St Ninian's Isle i. Scotland U.K.
158 D4 St-Nolff France
164 E3 St-Oedenrode Neth.
156 C2 St-Omer France
163 D5 St-Orens-de-Gameville France
163 C5 St-Ost France
151 I3 St Osyth Essex, England U.K.
158 D2 St Ouen Channel Is
156 B5 St-Ouen France
156 C2 St-Ouen France
159 F3 St-Ouen-des-Toits France
156 E4 St-Ouen-Domprot France
150 E3 St Owen's Cross Herefordshire, England U.K.
225 G4 St-Pacôme Que. Can.
158 E3 St-Pair-sur-Mer France
163 A5 St-Palais France
162 A3 St-Palais-sur-Mer France
161 B3 St-Pal-de-Chalancon France
161 C3 St-Pal-de-Mons France
233 □I1 St-Pamphile Que. Can.
160 C2 St-Pantaléon France
163 D4 St-Pantaléon France
162 D3 St-Pantaléon-de-Larche France
163 E5 St-Papoul France
162 D2 St-Pardoux, Lac de l. France
163 C4 St-Pardoux-Isaac France
162 C3 St-Pardoux-la-Rivière France
232 B4 St Paris OH U.S.A.
160 B2 St-Parize-le-Châtel France
156 E4 St-Parres-lès-Vaudes France
225 G4 St Pascal Que. Can.
159 G3 St-Paterne France
159 G4 St-Paterne-Racan France
223 I4 St Paul Alta Can.
225 J3 St Paul r. Newfoundland/Québec Can.
161 E4 St-Paul France
St Paul atoll Arch. des Tuamotu Fr. Polynesia see Héréhérétué
206 C5 St Paul r. Liberia
217 □1c St Paul Réunion
226 A3 St Paul MN U.S.A.
236 D3 St Paul NE U.S.A.
232 B6 St Paul VA U.S.A.
265 J7 St Paul, Île i. Indian Ocean
163 D5 St-Paul-Cap-de-Joux France
163 E6 St-Paul-de-Fenouillet France
163 D6 St-Paul-de-Jarrat France
162 E4 St-Paul-des-Landes France
163 C4 St-Paul-d'Espis France
163 A4 St-Paul-en-Born France
161 E5 St-Paul-en-Forêt France
161 B5 St-Paul-et-Valmalle France
161 B3 St-Paulien France
161 C4 St-Paul-le-Jeune France
163 A5 St-Paul-lès-Dax France
161 D5 St-Paul-lès-Durance France
161 D3 St-Paul-lès-Romans France
161 C4 St-Paul-Trois-Châteaux France
163 B5 St-Pé-de-Bigorre France
163 A5 St-Pée-sur-Nivelle France
161 C4 St-Péray France
160 B1 St-Père France
158 D4 St-Père-en-Retz France
236 E2 St Peter MN U.S.A.
St Peter and St Paul Rocks is N. Atlantic Ocean see São Pedro e São Paulo
158 D2 St Peter in the Wood Channel Is
158 D2 St Peter Port Channel Is
225 I4 St Peter's N.S. Can.
225 I4 St Peters P.E.I. Can.
151 I3 St Peter's Kent, England U.K.
231 D7 St Petersburg FL U.S.A.
156 D4 St-Phal France
158 E5 St-Philbert-de-Bouaine France
158 E4 St-Philbert-de-Grand-Lieu France
161 D5 St-Pierre mt. France
160 F3 St-Pierre Italy
247 □3 St-Pierre Martinique
217 □1c St-Pierre Réunion
217 □2 St Pierre i. Seychelles
225 K4 St-Pierre St Pierre and Miquelon
225 J4 St Pierre and Miquelon terr. N. America
160 E3 St-Pierre-d'Albigny France
161 E3 St-Pierre-d'Allevard France
163 B4 St-Pierre-d'Aurillac France
161 D3 St-Pierre-de-Chartreuse France
162 C3 St-Pierre-de-Chignac France
162 C3 St-Pierre-de-Côle France
161 B5 St-Pierre-de-la-Fage France
159 G5 St-Pierre-de-Maillé France
158 E3 St-Pierre-de-Plesguen France
162 C1 St-Pierre-des-Corps France
159 F4 St-Pierre-des-Échaubrognes France
159 E3 St-Pierre-des-Landes France
159 F3 St-Pierre-des-Nids France
163 E5 St-Pierre-de-Trivisy France
163 A5 St-Pierre-d'Irube France
162 A3 St-Pierre-d'Oléron France
159 F5 St-Pierre-du-Chemin France
163 B5 St-Pierre-du-Mont France
158 E2 St-Pierre-Église France
160 E2 St-Pierre-en-Faucigny France
159 G2 St-Pierre-en-Port France
159 E3 St-Pierre-la-Cour France
160 B2 St-Pierre-le-Moûtier France
156 B3 St-Pierre-lès-Elbeuf France
156 C4 St-Pierre-lès-Nemours France
158 C4 St-Pierre-Quiberon France
159 F2 St-Pierre-sur-Dives France
161 C4 St-Pierreville France
163 C5 St-Plancard France
159 E3 St-Pois France
159 E4 St-Poix France
158 C3 St-Pol-de-Léon France
156 C1 St-Pol-sur-Mer France
156 C2 St-Pol-sur-Ternoise France
163 D4 St-Pompont France
161 E4 St-Pons France
161 A5 St-Pons-de-Thomières France
162 B3 St-Porchaire France
163 D4 St-Porquier France
160 B2 St-Pourçain-sur-Sioule France
190 B2 St-Prex Switz.
160 C3 St-Priest France
160 A3 St-Priest-de-Champs France
160 B3 St-Priest-Laprugne France
162 D3 St-Priest-Taurion France
162 E3 St-Privat France
161 B4 St-Privat-d'Allier France
161 C4 St-Privat-des-Vieux France
160 B2 St-Prix France
161 C4 St-Prix France
163 D4 St-Projet France
233 □H1 St-Prosper Que. Can.
163 C5 St-Puy France
225 H4 St Quentin N.B. Can.
156 D3 St-Quentin France
161 C4 St-Quentin-la-Poterie France
161 D3 St-Quentin-sur-Isère France
157 H4 St-Quirin France
161 C3 St-Rambert-d'Albon France
160 D3 St-Rambert-en-Bugey France
161 E5 St-Raphaël France
238 D2 Saint Regis MT U.S.A.
233 F2 St Regis r. NY U.S.A.
233 F2 St Regis Falls NY U.S.A.
161 C4 St-Remèze France
233 G2 St-Rémi Que. Can.
160 C2 St-Rémy France
161 C5 St-Rémy-de-Provence France
156 E4 St-Remy-en-Bouzemont-St-Genest-et-Isson France
156 B4 St-Rémy-sur-Avre France
160 B3 St-Rémy-sur-Durolle France
158 B3 St-Renan France
160 B1 St-Révérien France
190 C3 St-Rhemy Italy
160 C2 St-Rigaud, Mont mt. France
156 B2 St-Riquier France
159 G2 St-Romain-de-Colbosc France
160 D3 St-Romain-de-Jalionas France
160 C3 St-Romain-en-Gal France
160 C3 St-Romain-le-Puy France
160 C2 St-Romain-sous-Versigny France
159 H4 St-Romain-sur-Cher France
161 D3 St-Romans France
161 A4 St-Rome-de-Cernon France
161 A4 St-Rome-de-Tarn France
156 B3 St-Saëns France
158 D2 St Sampson Channel Is
163 E4 St-Santin France
162 E2 St-Saturnin France
161 D5 St-Saturnin-lès-Apt France
162 C3 St-Saud-Lacoussière France
160 B1 St-Saulge France
160 A3 St-Sauves-d'Auvergne France
158 B3 St-Sauveur France
157 G5 St-Sauveur France
161 C4 St-Sauveur-de-Montagut France
224 F4 St-Sauveur-des-Monts Que. Can.
160 B1 St-Sauveur-en-Puisaye France
161 D4 St-Sauveur-Gouvernet France
158 E2 St-Sauveur-Lendelin France
158 E2 St-Sauveur-le-Vicomte France
161 F4 St-Sauveur-sur-Tinée France
163 C5 St-Sauvy France
162 B3 St-Savin France
162 C2 St-Savin France
162 B3 St-Savinien France
158 D2 St Saviour Channel Is
233 □H2 St-Sébastien Que. Can.
156 B3 St-Sébastien-de-Morsent France
158 E4 St-Sébastien-sur-Loire France
160 C1 St-Seine-l'Abbaye France
163 B4 St-Selve France
161 C4 St-Semin France
161 A5 St-Sernin-sur-Rance France
156 D4 St-Sérotin France
163 B5 St-Sever France
159 E3 St-Sever-Calvados France
225 G4 St Siméon Que. Can.
161 D3 St-Siméon-de-Bressieux France
162 E4 St-Simon France
156 D3 St-Simon France
160 E2 St-Sorlin, Mont de mt. France
161 E3 St-Sorlin-d'Arves France
156 C3 St-Soupplets France
233 □J2 St Stephen N.B. Can.
150 C4 St Stephen Cornwall, England U.K.
231 E5 St Stephen SC U.S.A.
163 D5 St-Sulpice France
162 A3 St-Sulpice-de-Royan France
158 E4 St-Sulpice-des-Landes France
162 D2 St-Sulpice-Laurière France
162 D2 St-Sulpice-le-Guérétois France
162 E3 St-Sulpice-les-Champs France
162 D2 St-Sulpice-les-Feuilles France
163 D5 St-Sulpice-sur-Lèze France
159 G3 St-Sulpice-sur-Risle France
159 F2 St-Sylvain France
159 F4 St-Sylvain-d'Anjou France
163 C4 St-Sylvestre-sur-Lot France
163 B4 St-Symphorien France
160 C3 St-Symphorien-de-Lay France
160 C3 St-Symphorien-d'Ozon France
160 C3 St-Symphorien-sur-Coise France
150 C4 St Teath Cornwall, England U.K.
222 C3 St Terese AK U.S.A.
158 C3 St-Thégonnec France
233 □H2 St-Théophile Que. Can.
223 M4 St Theresa Point Man. Can.
161 B5 St-Thibéry France
157 F4 St-Thiébault France
224 D5 St Thomas Ont. Can.
246 □ St Thomas parish Jamaica
247 F3 St Thomas Island Virgin Is (U.S.A.)
158 C4 St-Thurien France
225 G4 St-Tite-des-Caps Que. Can.
160 D2 St-Trivier-de-Courtes France
160 C2 St-Trivier-sur-Moignans France
162 A3 St-Trojan-les-Bains France
St Trond Belgium see Sint Truiden
161 E5 St-Tropez France
163 D5 St-Urcisse France
161 B4 St-Urcize France
161 C3 St-Uze France
158 E2 St-Vaast-la-Hougue France
156 D4 St-Valérien France
159 G2 St-Valery-en-Caux France
156 B2 St-Valery-sur-Somme France
160 C2 St-Vallier France
161 C3 St-Vallier France
161 E5 St-Vallier-de-Thiey France
159 F5 St-Varent France
162 D2 St-Vaury France
161 E4 St-Véran France
161 C3 St-Victor France
161 D5 St-Victoret France
161 C4 St-Victor-la-Coste France
159 F2 St-Vigor-le-Grand France
190 C3 St-Vincent Italy
236 D1 St Vincent MN U.S.A.
247 □3 St Vincent i. West Indies
St-Vincent, Cap pt Madag. see Ankaboa, Tanjona
83 F5 St Vincent, Cape Tas. Austr.
St Vincent, Cape Port. see São Vicente, Cabo de
82 D3 St Vincent, Gulf S.A. Austr.
247 □3 St Vincent and the Grenadines i. West Indies
162 C3 St-Vincent-de-Connezac France
163 B5 St-Vincent-de-Paul France
163 A5 St-Vincent-de-Tyrosse France
231 C6 St Vincent Island FL U.S.A.
161 E4 St-Vincent-les-Forts France
247 □3 St Vincent Passage St Lucia/St Vincent
160 D1 St-Vit France
163 C4 St-Vite France
162 A3 St-Vivien-de-Médoc France
223 I4 St Walburg Sask. Can.
227 G4 St Williams Ont. Can.
162 A2 St-Xandre France
160 C2 St-Yan France
163 D5 St-Ybars France
160 B2 St-Yorre France
162 D3 St-Yrieix-la-Perche France
162 C3 St-Yrieix-sur-Charente France
158 C4 St-Yvy France
161 D5 St-Zacharie France
156 B4 Sainville France
116 E3 Saipal mt. Nepal
91 K3 Saipan i. N. Mariana Is
158 E2 Saire r. France
163 B5 Saison r. France
163 E5 Saissac France
105 E3 Saitama pref. Japan
Saiteli Turkey see Kadınhanı
103 E7 Saito Japan
140 M1 Saivomuotka Sweden
163 E5 Saïx France
252 C4 Sajama, Nevado mt. Bol.
197 F4 Šajince Srbija Yugo.
124 D2 Sājir Saudi Arabia
175 J1 Sajna r. Pol.
177 J4 Sajó r. Hungary
177 J3 Sajóhidvég Hungary
177 J3 Sajókaza Hungary
177 J3 Sajópetri Hungary
177 J3 Sajószentpéter Hungary
177 K4 Sajószöged Hungary
177 J3 Sajóvámos Hungary
128 D1 Sājūr, Nahr r. Syria/Turkey
210 C2 Saka Eth.
105 F3 Sakado Japan
105 F2 Sakai Gumma Japan
104 B4 Sakai Ōsaka Japan
103 F6 Sakaide Japan
103 F6 Sakaiminato Japan
127 F5 Sakākah Saudi Arabia
236 C2 Sakakawea, Lake ND U.S.A.
224 F2 Sakami Que. Can.
224 E2 Sakami r. Que. Can.
105 F3 Sakami-gawa r. Japan
224 E2 Sakami Lake Que. Can.
209 F8 Sakania Dem. Rep. Congo
197 H5 Sakar mts Bulg.
123 E2 Sakar Turkm.
213 □J4 Sakaraha Madag.
123 E2 Sakar-Chaga Turkm.
Sakartvelo country Asia see Georgia
199 G1 Sakarya Turkey
199 G1 Sakarya prov. Turkey
199 G1 Sakarya r. Turkey
206 D5 Sakassou Côte d'Ivoire
102 I4 Sakata Japan
101 C4 Sakchu N. Korea
121 H2 Saken Seyfullin Kazakh.
97 C4 Sa Keo r. Thai.
207 F5 Sakété Benin
100 G2 Sakhalin i. Rus. Fed.
Sakhalin Oblast admin. div. Rus. Fed. see Sakhalinskaya Oblast'
100 G2 Sakhalinskaya Oblast' admin. div. Rus. Fed.
100 G1 Sakhalinskiy Zaliv b. Sakhalin Rus. Fed.
139 K3 Sakharovo Rus. Fed.
215 H1 Sakhelwe S. Africa
215 G2 Sakhile S. Africa
136 D3 Sakhnivtsi Ukr.
137 H3 Sakhnovshchyna Ukr.
122 D2 Sakhra Turkm.
122 B2 Sakht-Sar Iran
129 E3 Şäki Azer.
207 F4 Saki Nigeria
Saki Ukr. see Saky
138 D4 Šakiai Lith.
189 B7 Sakiet Sidi Youssef Tunisia
123 F4 Sakir mt. Pak.
102 □1 Sakishima-shotō is Japan
114 B3 Sakleshpur Karnataka India
120 C2 Sakmara Rus. Fed.
116 D5 Sakoli Mahar. India
96 D3 Sakon Nakhon Thai.
233 H4 Sakonnet r. RI U.S.A.
123 G5 Sakrand Pak.
214 C4 Sakrivier S. Africa
120 E3 Saksaul'skiy Kazakh.
Saksaul'skoye Kazakh. see Saksaul'skiy
140 J3 Sakshaug Norway
170 C1 Sakskøbing Denmark
117 E5 Sakti Madh. Prad. India
138 E2 Saku Estonia
105 E2 Saku Japan
105 G3 Sakura Japan
105 G2 Sakura-gawa r. Japan
104 B4 Sakurai Japan
103 E8 Sakura-jima vol. Japan
137 G5 Saky Ukr.
141 M3 Säkylä Fin.
206 □ Sal i. Cape Verde
135 H7 Sal r. Rus. Fed.
138 E3 Sala Latvia
177 G3 Šaľa Slovakia
143 G2 Sala Sweden
93 B3 Salabangka, Kepulauan is Indon.
224 F4 Salaberry-de-Valleyfield Que. Can.
138 E3 Salaca r. Latvia
197 F2 Sălacea Romania
138 E3 Salacgrīva Latvia
193 H4 Sala Consilina Italy
186 E2 Salada r. Spain
258 C2 Salada, Bahía b. Chile
242 B1 Salada, Laguna salt l. Mex.
258 F3 Saladas Arg.
261 H4 Saladillo Arg.
261 H4 Saladillo r. Buenos Aires Arg.
261 F3 Saladillo r. Córdoba Arg.
261 G2 Saladillo r. Santa Fé Arg.
258 E3 Saladillo r. Santiago del Estero Arg.
260 D5 Salado r. Arg.
261 I4 Salado r. Buenos Aires Arg.
258 F2 Salado r. Formosa Arg.
258 C3 Salado r. La Rioja Arg.
259 D6 Salado r. Río Negro Arg.
261 G3 Salado r. Santa Fé Arg.
246 C2 Salado r. Cuba
245 E3 Salado r. Hidalgo/México Mex.
245 F5 Salado r. Oaxaca/Puebla Mex.
243 F3 Salado r. Mex.
184 D4 Salado r. Andalucía Spain
184 E4 Salado r. Andalucía Spain
185 F3 Salado r. Andalucía Spain
185 F3 Salado r. Andalucía Spain
206 C4 Saladou Guinea
206 E4 Salaga Ghana
162 D3 Salagnac France
161 B5 Salagou, Lac du l. France
128 D3 Şalāḩ, Tall hill Jordan
127 F4 Şalāḩ ad Dīn governorate Iraq
127 G3 Salahuddin Iraq
161 C3 Salaise-sur-Sanne France
177 M4 Sălaj county Romania
212 E4 Salajwe Botswana
125 G3 Salakh, Jabal mt. Oman
202 C6 Salal Chad
125 F4 Şalālah Oman
243 H6 Salamá Guat.
242 □I6 Salamá Hond.
260 B2 Salamanca Chile
244 D3 Salamanca Mex.
182 E4 Salamanca Spain
182 D4 Salamanca prov. Castilla y León Spain
232 D3 Salamanca NY U.S.A.
Salamantica Spain see Salamanca
208 D2 Salamat pref. Chad
208 C2 Salamat, Bahr r. Chad
122 A3 Salāmatābād Iran
198 C3 Salamina Greece
198 C3 Salamina i. Greece
128 A2 Salamis tourist site Cyprus
Salamís i. Greece see Salamina
128 C2 Salamīyah Syria
226 E5 Salamonie r. IN U.S.A.
117 F5 Salandi r. India
193 I4 Salandra Italy
138 C3 Salantai Lith.
216 □1c Salão Faial Azores
194 B5 Salaparuta Sicilia Italy
107 F3 Salaqi Nei Mongol China
185 F3 Salar Spain
197 F2 Sălard Romania
186 D2 Salardu Spain
250 B6 Salas Peru
182 D1 Salas Spain
197 F3 Salaš Srbija Yugo.
183 G2 Salas de los Infantes Spain
138 E3 Salaspils Latvia
163 C5 Salat r. France
95 E4 Salatiga Jawa Tengah Indon.
162 B4 Salaunes France
134 K4 Salaush Rus. Fed.
197 G2 Sălăuța r. Romania
120 C1 Salavat Rus. Fed.
252 A2 Salaverry Peru
93 D3 Salawati i. Irian Jaya Indon.
92 C4 Salay Phil.
116 B5 Salaya Gujarat India
93 B4 Salayar i. Indon.
267 L7 Sala y Gómez, Isla i. S. Pacific Ocean
Salazar Angola see N'dalatando
261 F5 Salazar Arg.
186 B2 Salazar r. Spain
190 B3 Salbertrand Italy
162 E1 Salbris France
252 B3 Salccantay, Cerro mt. Peru
246 E3 Salcedo Dom. Rep.
173 G3 Salching Ger.
138 E4 Šalčia r. Lith.
197 H3 Sălciile Romania
138 E4 Šalčininkai Lith.
197 H3 Sălcioara Romania
150 D4 Salcombe Devon, England U.K.
Saldae Alg. see Bejaïa
183 F2 Saldaña Spain
214 A5 Saldanha S. Africa
173 H3 Saldenburg Ger.
183 I4 Saldón Spain
183 H3 Salduero Spain
261 G6 Saldungaray Arg.
191 F2 Saldura r. Italy
138 D3 Saldus Latvia
83 F4 Sale Vic. Austr.
86 E3 Sale r. W.A. Austr.
190 D4 Sale Italy
96 A2 Sale Myanmar
149 G4 Sale Greater Manchester, England U.K.
163 C6 Saléchan France
95 G5 Saleh, Teluk b. Sumbawa Indon.
122 B3 Şāleḩābād Iran
122 A3 Şāleḩābād Iran
151 H4 Salehurst East Sussex, England U.K.
130 H3 Salekhard Rus. Fed.
172 D4 Salem Baden-Württemberg Ger.
168 F2 Salem Schleswig-Holstein Ger.
114 C4 Salem Tamil Nadu India
215 F5 Salem S. Africa
237 F4 Salem AR U.S.A.
236 F4 Salem IL U.S.A.
230 C4 Salem IN U.S.A.
233 H3 Salem MA U.S.A.
237 F4 Salem MO U.S.A.
234 C3 Salem NJ U.S.A.
233 G3 Salem NY U.S.A.
232 C4 Salem OH U.S.A.
238 B2 Salem OR U.S.A.
236 D3 Salem SD U.S.A.
241 L1 Salem UT U.S.A.
232 C6 Salem VA U.S.A.
232 C5 Salem WV U.S.A.
234 C3 Salem r. NJ U.S.A.
234 C3 Salem County county NJ U.S.A.
194 B5 Salemi Sicilia Italy
141 K3 Sälen Sweden
146 C5 Salen Argyll and Bute, Scotland U.K.
146 C5 Salen Highland, Scotland U.K.
161 E5 Salernes France
193 G4 Salerno Italy
193 H4 Salerno prov. Campania Italy
193 G4 Salerno, Golfo di g. Italy
Salernum Italy see Salerno
162 E3 Salers France
256 D4 Sales Oliveira Brazil
257 E5 Salesópolis Brazil
161 B4 Salettes France
156 C3 Saleux France
149 G4 Salford Greater Manchester, England U.K.
151 G3 Salfords Surrey, England U.K.
254 F4 Salgado Brazil
254 F3 Salgado r. Brazil
177 I3 Salgótarján Hungary
254 F4 Salgueiro Brazil
182 C5 Salgueiro Port.
182 C3 Salgueiros Port.
151 I2 Salhouse Norfolk, England U.K.
142 A1 Salhus Norway
137 H5 Salhyr r. Ukr.
195 G2 Salice Salentino Italy
190 D4 Saliceto Italy
194 D5 Salici, Monte mt. Sicilia Italy
239 F4 Salida CO U.S.A.
138 D3 Saliena Latvia
163 B5 Salies-de-Béarn France
163 C5 Salies-du-Salat France
162 D4 Salignac-Eyvignes France
199 F2 Salihli Turkey
138 F5 Salihorsk Belarus
206 B3 Salikénié Senegal
186 B3 Salillas de Jalón Spain
211 B8 Salima Malawi
236 D4 Salina KS U.S.A.
241 L2 Salina UT U.S.A.
194 D4 Salina, Isola i. Isole Lipari Italy
245 G5 Salina Cruz Mex.
257 F2 Salinas Brazil
250 A5 Salinas Ecuador
244 D2 Salinas Mex.
237 D7 Salinas r. Mex.
247 □1 Salinas Puerto Rico
182 E1 Salinas Asturias Spain
187 C6 Salinas Valencia Spain
240 G3 Salinas CA U.S.A.
240 G3 Salinas r. CA U.S.A.
183 H2 Salinas de Añana Spain
252 D4 Salinas de Garci Mendoza Bol.
183 I4 Salinas del Manzano Spain
183 I2 Salinas de Pamplona Spain
183 F2 Salinas de Pisuerga Spain
186 D2 Salinas de Sín Spain
239 F5 Salinas Peak NM U.S.A.
161 C5 Salin-de-Giraud France
161 C4 Salindres France
193 G2 Saline r. Italy
149 F1 Saline Fife, Scotland U.K.
227 F4 Saline MI U.S.A.
237 E5 Saline r. AR U.S.A.
236 D4 Saline r. KS U.S.A.
191 F5 Saline di Volterra Italy
193 F2 Salinello r. Italy
240 I3 Saline Valley depr. CA U.S.A.
232 C4 Salineville OH U.S.A.
96 A2 Salingyi Myanmar
254 D2 Salinópolis Brazil
162 E3 Salins France
160 D2 Salins-les-Bains France
184 B3 Salir Port.
151 F3 Salisbury Wiltshire, England U.K.
233 F5 Salisbury MD U.S.A.
231 D5 Salisbury NC U.S.A.
232 D5 Salisbury PA U.S.A.
Salisbury Zimbabwe see Harare
235 D1 Salisbury Mills NY U.S.A.
151 E3 Salisbury Plain England U.K.
197 F3 Săliște Romania
197 G2 Săliștea de Sus Romania
194 C5 Salito r. Sicilia Italy
244 C2 Salitral de Carrera Mex.
254 E4 Salitre r. Brazil
177 H4 Salka Slovakia
128 C3 Şalkhad Syria
117 F5 Salki r. India
128 C1 Salkım Turkey
136 E3 Sal'kove Ukr.
140 O2 Salla Fin.
234 A1 Salladasburg PA U.S.A.
160 E3 Sallanches France
186 E3 Sallent Spain
186 C2 Sallent de Gállego Spain
163 B4 Salles France
161 A4 Salles-Curan France
162 B3 Salles-d'Angles France
161 B5 Salles-d'Aude France
163 E4 Salles-la-Source France
163 D5 Salles-sur-l'Hers France
171 E4 Sallgast Ger.
179 G2 Sallingberg Austria
147 E3 Sallins Rep. of Ireland
261 F5 Salliqueló Arg.
237 E5 Sallisaw OK U.S.A.
221 K3 Salluit Que. Can.
116 E3 Sallyana Nepal
147 C4 Sallypark Rep. of Ireland
165 E4 Salm r. Belgium
128 C2 Salmá Syria
122 A2 Salmās Iran
183 H4 Salmerón Spain
183 H4 Salmeroncillos de Abajo Spain
134 E3 Salmi Rus. Fed.
222 G5 Salmo B.C. Can.
238 D2 Salmon ID U.S.A.
235 F1 Salmon r. CT U.S.A.
238 C2 Salmon r. ID U.S.A.
238 D2 Salmon, Middle Fork r. ID U.S.A.
222 G5 Salmon Arm B.C. Can.
238 D3 Salmon Falls Creek r. Idaho/Nevada U.S.A.
87 D7 Salmon Gums W.A. Austr.
Salmonhurst N.B. Can. see New Denmark
238 D2 Salmon River Mountains ID U.S.A.
183 E4 Salmoral Spain
172 A2 Salmtal Ger.
141 M3 Salo Fin.
191 F3 Salò Italy
185 H2 Salobre Spain
185 G4 Salobreña Spain
140 N2 Saloinen Fin.
241 K5 Salome AZ U.S.A.
156 E4 Salon France
160 D1 Salon r. France
116 E4 Salon Uttar Prad. India
161 D5 Salon-de-Provence France
208 D5 Salonga r. Dem. Rep. Congo
Salonica Greece see Thessaloniki
Salonika Greece see Thessaloniki
197 E2 Salonta Romania
Salop admin. div. England U.K. see Shropshire
182 C5 Salor r. Spain
186 E2 Salòria, Pic de mt. Spain
184 C1 Salorino Spain
160 C2 Salornay-sur-Guye France
191 G2 Salorno Italy
186 E3 Salou Spain
186 E3 Salou, Cap de c. Spain
156 C3 Salouël France
141 N3 Salpausselkä reg. Fin.
128 C1 Salqīn Syria
147 B3 Salruck Rep. of Ireland
260 E2 Salsacate Arg.
186 D4 Salsadella Spain
163 E6 Salses-le-Château France
135 H7 Sal'sk Rus. Fed.
194 C5 Salso r. Sicilia Italy
194 D5 Salso r. Sicilia Italy
193 H3 Salsola r. Italy
190 E4 Salsomaggiore Terme Italy
Salt Jordan see As Salţ
186 F3 Salt Spain
241 K5 Salt r. AZ U.S.A.
236 F4 Salt r. MO U.S.A.
238 E3 Salt r. WY U.S.A.
258 D2 Salta Arg.
258 D2 Salta prov. Arg.
235 E2 Saltaire NY U.S.A.
191 H5 Saltara Italy
150 C4 Saltash Cornwall, England U.K.
149 I3 Saltburn-by-the-Sea Redcar and Cleveland, England U.K.
146 D6 Saltcoats North Ayrshire, Scotland U.K.
232 B5 Salt Creek r. OH U.S.A.
151 G4 Saltdean Brighton and Hove, England U.K.
147 E4 Saltee Islands Rep. of Ireland
184 D3 Salteras Spain
222 E5 Saltery Bay B.C. Can.
140 K2 Saltfjorden sea chan. Norway
239 F6 Salt Flat TX U.S.A.
150 E3 Saltford Bath and North East Somerset, England U.K.
237 D4 Salt Fork r. KS U.S.A.
237 D4 Salt Fork Arkansas r. KS U.S.A.
237 C5 Salt Fork Brazos r. TX U.S.A.
237 D5 Salt Fork Red r. OK U.S.A.
147 B3 Salthill Rep. of Ireland
243 E3 Saltillo Mex.
Salt Island Vanuatu see Loh
214 E3 Salt Lake S. Africa
238 E3 Salt Lake City UT U.S.A.
232 B5 Salt Lick KY U.S.A.
150 E1 Saltney Flintshire, Wales U.K.
261 G4 Salto Arg.
256 D5 Salto Brazil
193 E2 Salto r. Italy
182 C3 Salto Port.
261 I2 Salto Uru.
261 I2 Salto dept Uru.
257 H2 Salto da Divisa Brazil
243 G5 Salto de Agua Mex.
253 G6 Salto del Guaíra Para.
261 G3 Salto Grande Arg.
256 C5 Salto Grande Brazil
241 I5 Salton City CA U.S.A.
241 J5 Salton Sea salt l. CA U.S.A.
206 E5 Saltpond Ghana
223 H2 Salt River N.W.T. Can.
Saltrou Haiti see Belle-Anse
143 H2 Saltsjöbaden Sweden
141 M3 Saltvik Åland Fin.
232 C6 Saltville VA U.S.A.
231 D5 Saluda SC U.S.A.
232 E6 Saluda VA U.S.A.
231 D5 Saluda r. SC U.S.A.
191 H5 Saludecio Italy
190 D3 Saluggia Italy
202 E2 Salûm, Gulf of Egypt
116 C4 Salumbar Rajasthan India
122 D2 Saluq, Kūh-e mt. Iran
115 D2 Salur Andhra Prad. India
190 D3 Salussola Italy
190 C4 Saluzzo Italy
183 I4 Salvacañete Spain
184 C3 Salvada Port.
254 F5 Salvador Brazil
Salvador country Central America see El Salvador
182 C4 Salvador Port.
258 E1 Salvador Mazza Arg.
163 D5 Salvagnac France
184 D2 Salvaleón Spain
254 C2 Salvaterra Brazil
184 B1 Salvaterra de Magos Port.
182 D5 Salvaterra do Extremo Port.
244 D3 Salvatierra Mex.
183 H2 Salvatierra Spain
184 D2 Salvatierra de los Barros Spain
184 D1 Salvatierra de Santiago Spain
241 L2 Salvation Creek r. UT U.S.A.
195 H3 Salve Italy
163 D4 Salviac France
125 E2 Salwah Saudi Arabia
125 E2 Salwah, Dawḩat b. Qatar/Saudi Arabia
Salween r. China see Nu Jiang
96 B3 Salween r. Myanmar
129 C4 Salyamaç Turkey
129 F4 Salyan Azer.
Sal'yany Azer. see Salyan
232 B6 Salyersville KY U.S.A.
179 F3 Salza r. Austria
178 D2 Salzach r. Austria/Ger.
179 E3 Salza-Stausee resr Austria
169 C3 Salzbergen Ger.
178 E3 Salzburg Austria
178 E3 Salzburg land Austria
169 F3 Salzgitter Ger.
168 F2 Salzhausen Ger.
169 E3 Salzhemmendorf Ger.
169 D4 Salzkotten Ger.
171 C4 Salzmünde Ger.
170 C3 Salzwedel Ger.
173 H3 Salzweg Ger.
116 B4 Sam Rajasthan India
96 D3 Sam, Nam r. Laos/Vietnam
246 D2 Samá Cuba
174 E3 Sama r. Pol.
Šamac Bos.-Herz. see Bosanski Šamac
125 G3 Şamad Oman
163 B5 Samadet France
106 B1 Samagaltay Rus. Fed.
252 E4 Samaipata Bol.
242 D2 Samalayuca Mex.
92 B5 Samales Group is Phil.
114 D2 Samalkot Andhra Prad. India
203 F2 Samâlût Egypt
247 E3 Samaná Dom. Rep.
116 D3 Samana Punjab India
246 D2 Samana Cay i. Bahamas
Samanala mt. Sri Lanka see Sri Pada
126 D3 Samandağı Turkey
123 F2 Samangān prov. Afgh.
250 B4 Samaniego Col.
199 F1 Samanlı Dağları mts Turkey
203 F2 Samannûd Egypt
225 F3 Samaqua r. Que. Can.
Samar Kazakh. see Samarskoye
92 C4 Samar i. Phil.
120 B1 Samara Samarskaya Oblast' Rus. Fed.
120 B1 Samara r. Rus. Fed.
137 H3 Samara r. Ukr.
Samarahan Sarawak Malaysia see Sri Aman
Samara Oblast admin. div. Rus. Fed. see Samarskaya Oblast'
190 D3 Samarate Italy
100 F3 Samarga Rus. Fed.
95 G3 Samarinda Kalimantan Timur Indon.
100 E3 Samarka Rus. Fed.
121 F5 Samarkand Uzbek.
123 G2 Samarkand, Pik mt. Tajik.
Samarkand Oblast admin. div. Uzbek. see Samarkandskaya Oblast'
121 F5 Samarkandskaya Oblast' admin. div. Uzbek.
Samarobriva France see Amiens
Samarqand Uzbek. see Samarkand
Samarqand, Qullai mt. Tajik. see Samarkand, Pik
Samarqand Wiloyati admin. div. Uzbek. see Samarkandskaya Oblast'
127 F4 Sāmarrā' Iraq
92 C4 Samar Sea g. Phil.
120 B1 Samarskaya Oblast' admin. div. Rus. Fed.
121 J2 Samarskoye Kazakh.
137 J4 Samarskoye Rus. Fed.
136 C2 Samary Ukr.
123 G4 Samasata Pak.
192 A5 Samassi Sardegna Italy
117 F4 Samastipur Bihar India
163 C5 Samatan France
192 B5 Samatzai Sardegna Italy
129 F3 Şamaxı Azer.
209 E6 Samba Dem. Rep. Congo
95 F3 Samba r. Indon.
116 C2 Samba Jammu and Kashmir
209 B7 Samba Cajú Angola
182 D3 Sambade Port.
254 D3 Sambaiba Brazil
206 B3 Sambaïlo Guinea
95 G2 Sambaliung mts Indon.
117 E5 Sambalpur Orissa India
95 E2 Sambas Kalimantan Barat Indon.
Sambat Ukr. see Kyiv
177 L5 Sâmbăta Romania
213 □K2 Sambava Madag.
137 J4 Sambek Rostovskaya Oblast' Rus. Fed.
137 J4 Sambek Rostovskaya Oblast' Rus. Fed.
Sambe-san vol. Japan see Sanbe-san
116 D3 Sambhal Uttar Prad. India
116 C4 Sambhar Rajasthan India
193 I6 Sambiase Italy
136 B3 Sambir Ukr.
93 A3 Sambo Sulawesi Selatan Indon.
183 F3 Samboal Spain
95 G3 Samboja Kalimantan Timur Indon.
Sambor Ukr. see Sambir
261 I4 Samborombón r. Arg.
261 I4 Samborombón, Bahía b. Arg.
175 J5 Samborzec Pol.
165 D4 Sambre r. Belgium/France
194 C5 Sambuca di Sicilia Sicilia Italy
191 G4 Sambuca Pistoiese Italy
161 F4 Sambuco Italy
194 D5 Sambughetti, Monte mt. Sicilia Italy
101 D5 Samch'ŏk S. Korea
Samch'ŏnp'o S. Korea see Sach'on
118 E2 Samdi Dag mt. Turkey
190 E2 Samedan Switz.
182 C4 Sameiro Port.
156 B2 Samer France
169 C3 Samern Ger.
129 C2 Samerts'khle, Mt'a Georgia
183 E1 Sames Spain
139 M3 Samet' Rus. Fed.
209 F7 Samfya Zambia
136 E3 Samhorodok Kyivs'ka Oblast' Ukr.
136 E3 Samhorodok Vinnyts'ka Oblast' Ukr.
116 B5 Sami Gujarat India
182 D3 Samil Port.
124 C2 Samīrah Saudi Arabia
182 D3 Samir de los Caños Spain
250 C6 Samiria r. Peru
Samirum Iran see Yazd-e Khvāst
129 D2 Samkhret' Oset'i aut. reg. Georgia

129 E3 **Şämkir** Azer.
129 E3 **Şämkirçay** *r.* Azer.
128 C1 **Şamköy** Turkey
199 E2 **Şamlı** Turkey
195 F2 **Sammichele di Bari** Italy
190 F2 **Samnaun** Switz.
Sam Neua Laos *see* **Xam Hua**
182 B2 **Samo** *r.* Spain
78 □2 **Samoa** *country* S. Pacific Ocean
266 H7 **Samoa Basin** *sea feature* Pacific Ocean
Samoa i Sisifo *country* S. Pacific Ocean *see* **Samoa**
188 E3 **Samobor** Croatia
179 G5 **Samoborska Gora** *hills* Croatia
134 H3 **Samoded** Rus. Fed.
160 E2 **Samoëns** France
191 G4 **Samoggia** *r.* Italy
197 F4 **Samokov** Bulg.
190 E2 **Samolaco** Italy
136 D3 **Samoluskivtsi** Ukr.
184 B2 **Samora Correia** Port.
176 G3 **Šamorín** Slovakia
199 E3 **Samos** *Voreio Aigaio* Greece
199 E3 **Samos** *i.* Greece
182 C2 **Samos** Spain
Samothrace *i.* Greece *see* Samothraki
199 D1 **Samothraki** *i.* Greece
197 G4 **Samovodene** Bulg.
135 H6 **Samoylovka** Rus. Fed.
206 E5 **Sampa** Côte d'Ivoire
260 E3 **Sampacho** Arg.
95 F4 **Sampang** *Jawa Timur* Indon.
186 C3 **Samper de Calanda** Spain
190 C4 **Sampeyre** Italy
194 D6 **Sampieri** *Sicilia* Italy
157 F4 **Sampigny** France
95 F3 **Sampit** *Kalimantan Tengah* Indon.
95 F3 **Sampit** *r.* Indon.
95 F3 **Sampit, Teluk** *b.* Indon.
135 H5 **Sampur** Rus. Fed.
209 E7 **Sampwe** Dem. Rep. Congo
237 E6 **Sam Rayburn Reservoir** *TX* U.S.A.
206 E5 **Samreboe** Ghana
138 G2 **Samro, Ozero** *l.* Rus. Fed.
Samrong Cambodia *see* **Phumĭ Sâmraông**
111 C6 **Samsang** *Xizang* China
96 C2 **Sam Sao, Phou** *mts* Laos/Vietnam
142 D4 **Samsø** *i.* Denmark
142 D4 **Samsø Bælt** *sea chan.* Denmark
96 D3 **Sâm Sơn** Vietnam
177 L4 **Şamşud** Romania
126 E2 **Samsun** Turkey
171 C3 **Samswegen** Ger.
121 I4 **Samsy** Kazakh.
170 E1 **Samtens** Ger.
116 D4 **Samthar** *Uttar Prad.* India
129 C2 **Samtredia** Georgia
84 C3 **Samuel, Mount** *hill N.T.* Austr.
192 A5 **Samugheo** *Sardegna* Italy
97 C5 **Samui, Ko** *i.* Thai.
105 F3 **Samukawa** Japan
123 H4 **Samundri** Pak.
129 F3 **Samur** Azer.
129 F3 **Samur** *r.* Azer./Rus. Fed.
Samutlu Turkey *see* **Temelli**
97 C4 **Samut Prakan** Thai.
97 C4 **Samut Sakhon** Thai.
97 C4 **Samut Songkhram** Thai.
206 D3 **San** Mali
175 J5 **San** *r.* Pol.
97 D4 **San, Tônlé** *r.* Cambodia
188 F3 **Sana** *r.* Bos.-Herz.
124 D5 **Şan'ā'** Yemen
124 C5 **Şan'ā'** *governorate* Yemen
210 E2 **Sanaag** *admin. reg.* Somalia
183 I2 **San Adrián** Spain
262 X2 **Sanae** *research stn* Antarctica
207 H6 **Sanaga** *r.* Cameroon
San Agostín *FL* U.S.A. *see* **St Augustine**
260 E2 **San Agustín** Arg.
250 B4 **San Agustín** Col.
92 C5 **San Agustin, Cape** Phil.
183 G4 **San Agustín de Guadalix** Spain
146 B6 **Sanaigmore** *Argyll and Bute, Scotland* U.K.
124 D3 **Sanām** Saudi Arabia
182 B2 **San Amaro** Spain
252 A6 **San Ambrosio** *i.* S. Pacific Ocean
122 A3 **Sanandaj** Iran
206 D3 **Sanando** Mali
240 G2 **San Andreas** *CA* U.S.A.
177 K6 **Sânandrei** Romania
252 D3 **San Andrés** Bol.
250 C3 **San Andrés** Col.
92 C3 **San Andres** Phil.
246 B4 **San Andrés, Isla de** *i.* Caribbean Sea
261 H4 **San Andrés de Giles** Arg.
182 E2 **San Andrés del Rabanedo** Spain
244 C4 **San Andrés Ixtlán** Mex.
239 F5 **San Andres Mountains** *NM* U.S.A.
245 G4 **San Andrés Tuxtla** Mex.
237 C6 **San Angelo** *TX* U.S.A.
206 D3 **Sanankoroba** Mali
240 F3 **San Anselmo** *CA* U.S.A.
182 D1 **San Antolín de Ibias** Spain
182 B2 **San Antoniño** Spain
258 D3 **San Antonio** Arg.
242 □H5 **San Antonio** Belize
252 D3 **San Antonio** Bol.
260 B3 **San Antonio** Chile
92 B3 **San Antonio** Phil.
187 B5 **San Antonio** Spain
239 F5 **San Antonio** *NM* U.S.A.
237 D6 **San Antonio** *TX* U.S.A.
240 G4 **San Antonio** *r. CA* U.S.A.
237 D6 **San Antonio** *r. TX* U.S.A.
240 I4 **San Antonio, Mount** *CA* U.S.A.
187 E6 **San Antonio Abad** Spain
261 H4 **San Antonio de Areco** Arg.
258 D2 **San Antonio de los Cobres** Arg.
242 □I6 **San Antonio de Oriente** Hond.
207 G7 **San Antonio de Palé** Equat. Guinea
259 D6 **San Antonio Oeste** Arg.
161 D5 **Sanary-sur-Mer** France
183 H2 **San Asensio** Spain
78 □4a **Sanat** *i. Chuuk* Micronesia
234 C2 **Sanatoga** *PA* U.S.A.
260 D2 **San Augustín de Valle Fértil** Arg.
237 E6 **San Augustine** *TX* U.S.A.
116 D5 **Sanawad** *Madh. Prad.* India
244 D2 **San Bartolo** Mex.
216 □3c **San Bartolomé** *Lanzarote* Canary Is
183 F5 **San Bartolomé de las Abiertas** Spain
184 C3 **San Bartolomé de la Torre** Spain
183 F4 **San Bartolomé de Pinares** Spain
216 □3f **San Bartolomé de Tirajana** *Gran Canaria* Canary Is
193 H3 **San Bartolomeo in Galdo** Italy
245 E4 **San Bartolo Morelos** Mex.
245 E3 **San Bartolo Tutotepec** Mex.
260 E3 **San Basilio** Arg.
192 B5 **San Basilio** *Sardegna* Italy
San Baudillo de Llobregat Spain *see* Sant Boix de Llobregat
193 F2 **San Benedetto del Tronto** Italy
191 F3 **San Benedetto Po** Italy
243 H5 **San Benito** Guat.
185 F2 **San Benito** Spain
237 D7 **San Benito** *TX* U.S.A.
240 G3 **San Benito** *r. CA* U.S.A.
184 C2 **San Benito de la Contienda** Spain
240 G3 **San Benito Mountain** *CA* U.S.A.
240 I4 **San Bernardino** *CA* U.S.A.
190 E2 **San Bernardino, Passo di** *pass* Switz.
241 I4 **San Bernardino Mountains** *CA* U.S.A.
260 B3 **San Bernardo** Chile
242 D3 **San Bernardo** Mex.
103 F6 **Sanbe-san** *vol.* Japan
191 H3 **San Biagio di Callalta** Italy
194 C5 **San Biago Platani** *Sicilia* Italy
244 B3 **San Blas** *Nayarit* Mex.
242 C3 **San Blas** *Sinaloa* Mex.
242 □K7 **San Blas, Archipiélago de** *is* Panama
242 □K7 **San Blas, Cordillera de** *mts* Panama
191 G3 **San Bonifacio** Italy
252 D3 **San Borja** Bol.
236 E3 **Sanborn** *IA* U.S.A.
233 □H3 **Sanbornville** *NH* U.S.A.
243 E3 **San Buenaventura** Mex.
213 G3 **Sança** Moz.
191 H2 **San Candido** Italy
186 C3 **San Caprasio** *hill* Spain
260 C3 **San Carlos** *Mendoza* Arg.
258 D2 **San Carlos** *Salta* Arg.
260 B5 **San Carlos** Chile
San Carlos Equat. Guinea *see* Luba
243 E2 **San Carlos** *Coahuila* Mex.
245 E1 **San Carlos** *Tamaulipas* Mex.
242 □I7 **San Carlos** Nic.
253 F5 **San Carlos** Para.
253 F5 **San Carlos** *r.* Para.
92 B3 **San Carlos** *Luzon* Phil.
92 B4 **San Carlos** *Negros* Phil.
258 G4 **San Carlos** Uru.
241 L5 **San Carlos** *AZ* U.S.A.
250 E3 **San Carlos** *Apure* Venez.
250 D2 **San Carlos** *Cojedes* Venez.
261 G2 **San Carlos Centro** Arg.
259 C6 **San Carlos de Bariloche** Arg.
261 G5 **San Carlos de Bolívar** Arg.
San Carlos de la Rápita Spain *see* **Sant Carles de la Ràpita**
185 G2 **San Carlos del Valle** Spain
250 D2 **San Carlos del Zulia** Venez.
261 G2 **San Carlos Sur** Arg.
192 D2 **San Casciano dei Bagni** Italy
191 G5 **San Casciano in Val di Pesa** Italy
195 H2 **San Cataldo** *Puglia* Italy
194 C5 **San Cataldo** *Sicilia* Italy
261 H6 **San Cayetano** Arg.
182 E3 **San Cebrián de Castro** Spain
187 F5 **Sancellas** Spain
San Celoni Spain *see* Sant Celoni
160 A1 **Sancergues** France
160 A1 **Sancerre** France
160 A1 **Sancerrois, Collines du** *hills* France
195 H2 **San Cesario di Lecce** Italy
160 E1 **Sancey-le-Grand** France
Sanchahe *Jilin* China *see* **Fuyu**
108 C3 **Sancha He** *r. Guizhou* China
156 B4 **Sancheville** France
245 H4 **Sánchez Magallanes** Mex.
116 D5 **Sanchi** *Madh. Prad.* India
183 F4 **Sanchidrián** Spain
96 C2 **San Chien Pau** *mt.* Laos
193 I4 **San Chirico Nuovo** Italy
193 I4 **San Chirico Raparo** Italy
116 B4 **Sanchor** *Rajasthan* India
107 F4 **Sanchuan** *r.* China
134 I4 **Sanchursk** Rus. Fed.
182 C2 **San Cibrán das Viñas** Spain
194 C5 **San Cipirello** *Sicilia* Italy
193 G4 **San Cipriano d'Aversa** Italy
245 E3 **San Ciro de Acosta** Mex.
260 B4 **San Clemente** Chile
185 H1 **San Clemente** Spain
240 I5 **San Clemente** *CA* U.S.A.
261 I5 **San Clemente del Tuyú** Arg.
240 H5 **San Clemente Island** *CA* U.S.A.
182 C2 **San Clodio** Spain
160 A2 **Sancoins** France
258 F2 **San Cosme** Arg.
182 C1 **San Cosme** Spain
193 I4 **San Costantino Albanese** Italy
191 I5 **San Costanzo** Italy
261 G2 **San Cristóbal** Arg.
252 D5 **San Cristóbal** Bol.
253 E3 **San Cristóbal** Bol.
246 E3 **San Cristóbal** Dom. Rep.
78 □6 **San Cristobal** *i.* Solomon Is
250 C3 **San Cristóbal** Venez.
250 □ **San Cristóbal, Isla** *i. Islas Galápagos* Ecuador
242 □I6 **San Cristóbal, Volcán** *vol.* Nic.
San Cristóbal de Cea *Galicia* Spain *see* **Cea**
182 E2 **San Cristóbal de Entreviñas** Spain
216 □3a **San Cristóbal de la Laguna** *Tenerife* Canary Is
243 G5 **San Cristóbal de las Casas** Mex.
183 F3 **San Cristóbal de la Vega** Spain
193 H4 **San Croce, Monte** *mt.* Italy
261 F3 **Sancti Spiritu** Arg.
246 C2 **Sancti Spíritus** Cuba
246 C2 **Sancti Spíritus** *prov.* Cuba
182 D4 **Sancti-Spíritus** Spain
185 E2 **Sancti-Spiritus** Spain
157 F3 **Sancy** France
142 B2 **Sand** Norway
215 F3 **Sand** *r. Free State* S. Africa
213 F4 **Sand** *r. Northern* S. Africa
104 B4 **Sanda** Japan
146 C6 **Sanda Island** *Scotland* U.K.
95 G1 **Sandakan** *Sabah* Malaysia
117 G4 **Sandakphu Peak** *Sikkim* India
190 D4 **San Damiano d'Asti** Italy
190 C4 **San Damiano Macra** Italy
169 F6 **Sand am Main** Ger.
141 I3 **Sandane** Norway
178 E4 **San Daniele del Friuli** Italy
190 F3 **San Daniele Po** Italy
197 F5 **Sandanski** Bulg.
Sandaohezi *Xinjiang* China *see* Shawan
206 C3 **Sandaré** Mali
170 D3 **Sandau** Ger.
146 F2 **Sanday** *i. Scotland* U.K.
146 F2 **Sanday Sound** *sea chan. Scotland* U.K.
172 D2 **Sandbach** *r.* Ger.
149 G4 **Sandbach** *Cheshire, England* U.K.
169 F5 **Sandberg** Ger.
214 B5 **Sandberg** S. Africa
168 G1 **Sandby** Denmark
140 K2 **Sanddøla** *r.* Norway
168 D2 **Sande** Ger.
141 I3 **Sande** *Sogn og Fjordane* Norway
142 D2 **Sande** *Vestfold* Norway
182 B3 **Sande** Port.
142 D2 **Sandefjord** Norway
142 D2 **Sandefjord (Torp)** *airport* Norway
142 A2 **Sandeid** Norway
195 F3 **San Demetrio Corone** Italy
193 F2 **San Demetrio ne Vestini** Italy
263 D2 **Sandercock Nunataks** *nunataks* Antarctica
241 M4 **Sanders** *AZ* U.S.A.
171 D4 **Sandersdorf** Ger.
169 E4 **Sandershausen (Niestetal)** Ger.
171 C4 **Sandersleben** Ger.
237 C6 **Sanderson** *TX* U.S.A.
231 D5 **Sandersville** *GA* U.S.A.
168 F2 **Sandesneben** Ger.
86 D3 **Sandfire Roadhouse** *W.A.* Austr.
142 B2 **Sandfloeggi** *mt.* Norway
232 C5 **Sand Fork** *WV* U.S.A.
146 F2 **Sandgarth** *Orkney, Scotland* U.K.
172 C2 **Sandhausen** Ger.
146 D7 **Sandhead** *Dumfries and Galloway, Scotland* U.K.
236 D2 **Sand Hill** *r. MN* U.S.A.
236 C3 **Sand Hills** *NE* U.S.A.
140 K2 **Sandhornøy** *i.* Norway
151 G3 **Sandhurst** *Bracknell Forest, England* U.K.
116 E4 **Sandi** *Uttar Prad.* India
252 C3 **Sandia** Peru
182 C2 **Sandiás** Spain
244 D3 **San Diego** Mex.
240 I5 **San Diego** *CA* U.S.A.
237 D7 **San Diego** *TX* U.S.A.
242 C2 **San Diego, Sierra** *mts* Mex.
199 G2 **Sandıklı** Turkey
116 E4 **Sandila** *Uttar Prad.* India
156 C5 **Sandillon** France
87 B5 **Sandiman, Mount** *hill W.A.* Austr.
134 L2 **Sandivey** *r.* Rus. Fed.
170 E3 **Sandkrug** Ger.
179 F2 **Sandl** Austria
224 C4 **Sand Lake** *Ont.* Can.
142 A2 **Sandnes** Norway
146 □G1 **Sandness** *Shetland, Scotland* U.K.
140 K2 **Sandnessjøen** Norway
Sandø *i.* Faroe Is *see* **Sandoy**
182 D4 **Sando** Spain
209 D7 **Sandoa** Dem. Rep. Congo
175 J5 **Sandomierz** Pol.
197 G2 **Sândominic** Romania
250 B4 **Sandoná** Col.
195 G2 **San Donaci** Italy
191 H3 **San Donà di Piave** Italy
195 H2 **San Donato di Lecce** Italy
193 I5 **San Donato di Ninea** Italy
190 E3 **San Donato Milanese** Italy
193 F3 **San Donato Val di Comino** Italy
177 J5 **Sándorfalva** Hungary
139 K2 **Sandovo** Rus. Fed.
263 G2 **Sandow, Mount** Antarctica
96 A3 **Sandoway** Myanmar
151 F4 **Sandown** *Isle of Wight, England* U.K.
144 D1 **Sandoy** *i.* Faroe Is
140 I3 **Sandøy** Norway
150 C4 **Sandplace** *Cornwall, England* U.K.
238 C1 **Sandpoint** *ID* U.S.A.
146 A5 **Sandray** *i. Scotland* U.K.
151 G3 **Sandridge** *Hertfordshire, England* U.K.
84 D5 **Sandringham** *Qld* Austr.
215 H2 **Sand River Reservoir** Swaziland
140 L2 **Sandsele** Sweden
149 I3 **Sandsend** *North Yorkshire, England* U.K.
222 D4 **Sandspit** *B.C.* Can.
237 D4 **Sand Springs** *OK* U.S.A.
215 F2 **Sandspruit** *r.* S. Africa
168 D2 **Sandstedt** Ger.
232 E6 **Sandston** *VA* U.S.A.
87 C5 **Sandstone** *W.A.* Austr.
226 A2 **Sandstone** *MN* U.S.A.
241 K5 **Sand Tank Mountains** *AZ* U.S.A.
215 G2 **Sandton** S. Africa
234 C2 **Sandts Eddy** *PA* U.S.A.
108 C3 **Sandu** *Guizhou* China
109 E3 **Sandu** *Hunan* China
114 C3 **Sandur** *Karnataka* India
227 F4 **Sandusky** *MI* U.S.A.
232 B4 **Sandusky** *OH* U.S.A.
142 D2 **Sandvika** Norway
143 G1 **Sandviken** Sweden
214 E5 **Sandvlakte** S. Africa
151 I3 **Sandwich** *Kent, England* U.K.
233 H4 **Sandwich** *MA* U.S.A.
Sandwich Island Vanuatu *see* **Éfaté**
Sandwich Islands N. Pacific Ocean *see* **Hawaiian Islands**
117 G5 **Sandwip** Bangl.
151 G2 **Sandy** *Bedfordshire, England* U.K.
238 E3 **Sandy** *UT* U.S.A.
233 □I2 **Sandy** *r. ME* U.S.A.
223 K4 **Sandy Bay** *Sask.* Can.
246 □ **Sandy Bay** Jamaica
87 D7 **Sandy Bight** *b. W.A.* Austr.
85 H5 **Sandy Cape** *Qld* Austr.
83 F5 **Sandy Cape** *Tas.* Austr.
84 D3 **Sandy Creek** *r. Qld* Austr.
235 E1 **Sandy Hook** *CT* U.S.A.
232 B5 **Sandy Hook** *KY* U.S.A.
86 D2 **Sandy Island** *W.A.* Austr.
123 E2 **Sandykachi** Turkm.
Sandykly Gumy *des.* Turkm. *see* **Sundukli, Peski**
222 H4 **Sandy Lake** *Alta* Can.
223 M4 **Sandy Lake** *Ont.* Can.
231 C5 **Sandy Springs** *GA* U.S.A.
232 C5 **Sandyville** *WV* U.S.A.
160 D2 **Sâne** *r.* France
165 E5 **Sanem** Lux.
182 E2 **San Emiliano** Spain
253 F6 **San Estanislao** Para.
245 F4 **San Esteban Cuautempan** Mex.
183 G3 **San Esteban de Gormaz** Spain
182 E4 **San Esteban de la Sierra** Spain
260 B5 **San Fabián de Alico** Chile
193 H4 **San Fele** Italy
193 G3 **San Felice a Cancello** Italy
193 F3 **San Felice Circeo** Italy
182 D4 **San Felices de los Gallegos** Spain
191 G4 **San Felice sul Panaro** Italy
260 B3 **San Felipe** Chile
242 B2 **San Felipe** *Baja California Norte* Mex.
242 D3 **San Felipe** *Chihuahua* Mex.
244 D3 **San Felipe** *Guanajuato* Mex.
183 I4 **San Felipe** *mt.* Spain
250 D2 **San Felipe** Venez.
San Feliú de Guíxols Spain *see* **Sant Feliu de Guíxols**
San Feliú de Pallarols Spain *see* **Sant Feliu de Palterols**
San Feliú Sasssera Spain *see* Sant Feliu Sasserra
252 A6 **San Félix, Isla** *i.* S. Pacific Ocean
195 E4 **San Ferdinando** Italy
193 I3 **San Ferdinando di Puglia** Italy
261 H4 **San Fernando** Arg.
260 B4 **San Fernando** Chile
242 B2 **San Fernando** *Baja California Norte* Mex.
243 F3 **San Fernando** *Tamaulipas* Mex.
92 B2 **San Fernando** *Luzon* Phil.
92 B3 **San Fernando** *Luzon* Phil.
184 D4 **San Fernando** Spain
247 □7 **San Fernando** Trin. and Tob.
240 H4 **San Fernando** *CA* U.S.A.
250 E3 **San Fernando de Apure** Venez.
250 E3 **San Fernando de Atabapo** Venez.
183 G4 **San Fernando de Henares** Spain
193 I5 **San Fili** Italy
195 E4 **San Filippo del Mela** *Sicilia* Italy
182 C3 **Sanfins do Douro** Port.
87 B5 **Sanford** *r. W.A.* Austr.
231 D6 **Sanford** *FL* U.S.A.
233 □H3 **Sanford** *ME* U.S.A.
226 E4 **Sanford** *MI* U.S.A.
231 E5 **Sanford** *NC* U.S.A.
261 F2 **San Francisco** Arg.
252 D3 **San Francisco** Bol.
242 B2 **San Francisco** Mex.
240 F3 **San Francisco** *CA* U.S.A.
239 E5 **San Francisco** *r. NM* U.S.A.
240 F3 **San Francisco Bay** *inlet CA* U.S.A.
245 F6 **San Francisco Cozoaltepec** Mex.
258 E3 **San Francisco del Chañar** Arg.
260 D3 **San Francisco del Monte de Oro** Arg.
242 D3 **San Francisco del Oro** Mex.
244 D3 **San Francisco del Rincón** Mex.
246 E3 **San Francisco de Macorís** Dom. Rep.
260 B3 **San Francisco de Mostazal** Chile
259 D8 **San Francisco de Paula, Cabo** *c.* Arg.
242 □H6 **San Francisco Gotera** El Salvador
187 E6 **San Francisco Javier** Spain
194 D4 **San Fratello** *Sicilia* Italy
190 C4 **Sanfront** Italy
250 B4 **San Gabriel** Ecuador
245 F4 **San Gabriel Chilac** Mex.
240 H4 **San Gabriel Mountains** *CA* U.S.A.
Sangachaly Azer. *see* **Sanqaçal**
94 D3 **Sangaigerong** *Sumatera* Indon.
108 A2 **Sa'ngain** *Xizang* China
182 B4 **Sangalhos** Port.
252 A3 **San Gallan, Isla** *i.* Peru
114 C3 **Sangam** *Andhra Prad.* India
114 B2 **Sangameshwar** *Mahar.* India
114 B2 **Sangamner** *Mahar.* India
236 F3 **Sangamon** *r. IL* U.S.A.
123 F3 **Sangan, Koh-i-** *mt.* Afgh.
123 G4 **Sangar** *r.* Pak.
131 N3 **Sangar** Rus. Fed.
183 F4 **Sangarcía** Spain
206 B4 **Sangaréa** Guinea
114 C2 **Sangareddi** *Andhra Prad.* India
206 B4 **Sangarédi** Guinea
116 C3 **Sangaria** *Rajasthan* India
95 G3 **Sangasanga** *Kalimantan Timur* Indon.
Sangasso Mali *see* **Zangasso**
156 B2 **Sangatte** France
192 A5 **San Gavino Monreale** *Sardegna* Italy
250 B5 **Sangay, Volcán** *vol.* Ecuador
141 K3 **Sångbäcken** Sweden
122 D3 **Sang Bast** Iran
92 B5 **Sangboy Islands** Phil.
93 A5 **Sangeang** *i.* Indon.
106 E3 **Sangejing** *Nei Mongol* China
193 E2 **San Gemini** Italy
261 G3 **San Genaro** Arg.
Sangenjo Spain *see* **Sanxenxo**
197 G2 **Sângeorgiu de Pădure** Romania
197 G2 **Sângeorz-Băi** Romania
197 G2 **Sânger** Romania
240 H3 **Sanger** *CA* U.S.A.
Sângera Moldova *see* **Sîngera**
Sângerei Moldova *see* **Sîngerei**
233 F3 **Sangerfield** *NY* U.S.A.
171 C4 **Sangerhausen** Ger.
247 □1 **San Germán** Puerto Rico
161 F4 **San Germano Chisone** Italy
107 G3 **Sanggan** *r.* China
108 B1 **Sanggarmai** *Sichuan* China
95 E2 **Sanggau** *Kalimantan Barat* Indon.
207 F4 **Sangha** Burkina
208 B4 **Sangha** *admin. reg.* Congo
208 C5 **Sangha** *r.* Congo
208 C4 **Sangha-Mbaéré** *pref.* C.A.R.
123 G5 **Sanghar** Pak.
191 G2 **San Giacomo, Cima** *mt.* Italy
250 C3 **San Gil** Col.
106 B1 **Sangilen, Nagor'ye** *mts* Rus. Fed.
195 □ **San Ġiljan** Malta
191 G5 **San Gimignano** Italy
183 I4 **San Ginés** *mt.* Spain
193 F1 **San Ginesio** Italy
193 F3 **San Giorgio a Liri** Italy
191 H2 **San Giorgio della Richinvelda** Italy
191 I3 **San Giorgio di Nogaro** Italy
191 G4 **San Giorgio di Piano** Italy
195 G2 **San Giorgio Ionico** Italy
193 G3 **San Giorgio la Molara** Italy
195 F2 **San Giorgio Lucano** Italy
193 H4 **San Giovanni a Piro** Italy
190 E3 **San Giovanni Bianco** Italy
192 D1 **San Giovanni d'Asso** Italy
194 C5 **San Giovanni Gemini** *Sicilia* Italy
193 F3 **San Giovanni Incarico** Italy
190 F3 **San Giovanni in Croce** Italy
195 F3 **San Giovanni in Fiore** Italy
191 G4 **San Giovanni in Persiceto** Italy
191 G3 **San Giovanni Lupatoto** Italy
193 H3 **San Giovanni Rotondo** Italy
192 A5 **San Giovanni Suegiu** *Sardegna* Italy
193 G2 **San Giovanni Teatino** Italy
191 G5 **San Giovanni Valdarno** Italy
116 C5 **Sangir** *Mahar.* India
93 C2 **Sangir** *i.* Indon.
93 C2 **Sangir, Kepulauan** *is* Indon.
190 F5 **San Giuliano Terme** Italy
194 C5 **San Giuseppe Jato** *Sicilia* Italy
194 D2 **San Giuseppe Vesuviano** Italy
191 H5 **San Giustino** Italy
106 E2 **Sangiyn Dalay** Mongolia
101 D5 **Sangju** S. Korea
93 A4 **Sangkarang, Kepulauan** *is* Indon.
97 C4 **Sângke, Stœng** *r.* Cambodia
95 G2 **Sangkulirang** *Kalimantan Timur* Indon.
123 H4 **Sangla** Pak.
114 B2 **Sangli** *Mahar.* India
207 H6 **Sangmélima** Cameroon
116 D4 **Sangod** *Rajasthan* India
191 G5 **San Godenzo** Italy
114 B2 **Sangole** *Mahar.* India
187 B7 **Sangonera** *r.* Spain
240 I4 **San Gorgonio Mountain** *CA* U.S.A.
190 D2 **San Gottardo, Passo del** *pass* Switz.
Sangpi *Sichuan* China *see* Xiangcheng
108 A2 **Sang Qu** *r. Xizang* China
239 F4 **Sangre de Cristo Range** *mts CO* U.S.A.
261 F4 **San Gregorio** Arg.
260 B5 **San Gregorio** Chile
258 G4 **San Gregorio de Polanca** Uru.
193 H4 **San Gregorio Magno** Italy
193 G3 **San Gregorio Matese** Italy
247 □7 **Sangre Grande** Trin. and Tob.
183 F5 **Sangrera** *r.* Spain
111 F6 **Sangri** *Xizang* China
193 G2 **Sangro** *r.* Italy
116 C3 **Sangrur** *Punjab* India
111 D6 **Sangsang** *Xizang* China
117 G5 **Sangu** *r.* Bangl.
222 H4 **Sangudo** *Alta* Can.
253 F2 **Sangue** *r.* Brazil
183 I2 **Sangüesa** Spain
190 E3 **San Guiliano Milanese** Italy
186 E3 **San Guim de Freixenet** Spain
163 A4 **Sanguinet** France
191 G3 **Sanguinetto** Italy
Sangyuan *Hebei* China *see* Wuqiao
108 D2 **Sangzhi** *Hunan* China
206 D4 **Sanhala** Côte d'Ivoire
Sanhe *Guizhou* China *see* Sandu
107 I1 **Sanhe** *Nei Mongol* China
109 F2 **Sanhezhen** *Anhui* China
San Hilario Sacalm Spain *see* Sant Hilari Sacalm
203 F2 **Sanhûr** Egypt
243 H5 **San Ignacio** Belize
252 D3 **San Ignacio** *Beni* Bol.
252 E4 **San Ignacio** *Santa Cruz* Bol.
253 E4 **San Ignacio** *Santa Cruz* Bol.
253 F6 **San Ignacio** Para.
250 B6 **San Ignacio** Peru
224 E1 **Sanikiluaq** *Nunavut* Can.
183 G4 **San Ildefonso** Spain
197 F2 **Sanislău** Romania
170 D1 **Sanitz** Ger.
250 C2 **San Jacinto** Col.
92 B3 **San Jacinto** Phil.
240 I5 **San Jacinto** *CA* U.S.A.
240 I5 **San Jacinto Peak** *CA* U.S.A.
117 F5 **Sanjai** *r. Bihar* India
261 H2 **San Jaime** Arg.
261 H2 **San Javier** Arg.
252 D3 **San Javier** *Beni* Bol.
253 E4 **San Javier** *Santa Cruz* Bol.
187 C7 **San Javier** Spain
261 H3 **San Javier** Uru.
260 B4 **San Javier de Loncomilla** Chile
123 G4 **Sanjawi** Pak.
244 D5 **San Jerónimo** Mex.
Sanjiang *Guangdong* China *see* Liannan
108 D3 **Sanjiang** *Guangxi* China
Sanjiang *Guizhou* China *see* **Jinping**
Sanjiaocheng *Qinghai* China *see* **Haiyan**
108 D2 **Sanjiaoping** *Hunan* China
109 G2 **Sanjie** *Zhejiang* China
103 I5 **Sanjō** Japan
252 D3 **San Joaquín** Bol.
253 F6 **San Joaquin** Para.
240 G3 **San Joaquin** *CA* U.S.A.
240 G2 **San Joaquin** *r. CA* U.S.A.
240 G3 **San Joaquin Valley** *CA* U.S.A.
237 C5 **San Jon** *NM* U.S.A.
261 G2 **San Jorge** Arg.
78 □6 **San Jorge** *i.* Solomon Is
186 D4 **San Jorge** Spain
259 D7 **San Jorge, Golfo de** *g.* Arg.
San Jorge, Golfo de *g.* Spain *see* **Sant Jordi, Golf de**
184 C2 **San Jorge de Alor** Spain
242 □I7 **San José** Costa Rica
243 H6 **San José** Guat.
92 B3 **San Jose** *Luzon* Phil.
92 B3 **San Jose** *Mindoro* Phil.
92 B3 **San Jose** *Mindoro* Phil.
185 H4 **San José** Spain
187 E6 **San José** Spain
261 I4 **San José** *dept* Uru.
261 I4 **San José** *r.* Uru.
240 G3 **San Jose** *CA* U.S.A.
239 F5 **San Jose** *NM* U.S.A.
261 I2 **San José, Cuchilla de** *hills* Uru.
260 C3 **San José, Volcán** *vol.* Chile
242 D2 **San José de Bavicora** Mex.
92 B4 **San Jose de Buenavista** Phil.
253 E4 **San José de Chiquitos** Bol.
242 C3 **San José de Comondú** Mex.
261 H2 **San José de Feliciano** Arg.
244 C2 **San Jose de Gracia** *Aguascalientes* Mex.
242 B3 **San José de Gracia** Mex.
244 C4 **San José de Gracia** Mex.
242 C2 **San José de Gracia** Mex.
247 F5 **San José de Guaribe** Venez.
260 C2 **San José de Jáchal** Arg.
242 C3 **San Joséde la Brecha** Mex.
261 F2 **San José de la Dormida** Arg.
259 B5 **San José de la Mariquina** Chile
242 C4 **San José del Cabo** Mex.
250 C4 **San José del Guaviare** Col.
245 F5 **San José del Progreso** Mex.
184 E4 **San José del Valle** Spain
260 B3 **San José de Maipó** Chile
261 I4 **San José de Mayo** Uru.
246 E3 **San José de Ocoa** Dom. Rep.
250 D3 **San José de Ocuné** Col.
239 E6 **San José de Primas** Mex.
244 D1 **San José de Raíces** Mex.
244 D3 **San José Iturbide** Mex.
260 C2 **San Juan** Arg.
260 C2 **San Juan** *prov.* Arg.
250 B3 **San Juan** *r.* Col.
242 □J7 **San Juan** *r.* Costa Rica/Nic.
246 B2 **San Juan** *mt.* Cuba
246 E3 **San Juan** Dom. Rep.
242 D3 **San Juan** Mex.
244 C3 **San Juan** *r. Jalisco* Mex.
245 G4 **San Juan** *r. Veracruz* Mex.
252 B3 **San Juan** Peru
92 C4 **San Juan** *Leyte* Phil.
92 C4 **San Juan** *Mindanao* Phil.
247 □1 **San Juan** Puerto Rico
184 D2 **San Juan** *r.* Spain
240 G4 **San Juan** *r. CA* U.S.A.
241 L3 **San Juan** *r. UT* U.S.A.
253 F6 **San Juan Bautista** Para.
252 □ **San Juan Bautista** S. Pacific Ocean
187 E5 **San Juan Bautista** Spain
240 G3 **San Juan Bautista** *CA* U.S.A.
245 F4 **San Juan Bautista Tuxtepec** Mex.
240 I5 **San Juan Capistrano** *CA* U.S.A.
242 □I6 **San Juancito** Hond.
187 C6 **San Juan de Alicante** Spain
184 D3 **San Juan de Aznalfarache** Spain
244 C1 **San Juan de Guadalupe** Mex.
259 B6 **San Juan dela Costa** Chile
245 E4 **San Juan de las Huertas** Mex.
242 □J7 **San Juan del Norte** Nic.
242 □J7 **San Juan del Norte, Bahía de** *b.* Nic.
244 C3 **San Juan de los Lagos** Mex.
250 E2 **San Juan de los Morros** Venez.
184 D3 **San Juan del Puerto** Spain
242 D3 **San Juan del Río** Mex.
245 E3 **San Juan del Río** Mex.
242 □I7 **San Juan del Sur** Nic.
245 G5 **San Juan Evangelista** Mex.
245 F4 **San Juan Ixcaquixtla** Mex.
239 F4 **San Juan Mountains** *CO* U.S.A.
246 B2 **San Juan y Martínez** Cuba
259 D8 **San Julián** Arg.
244 C3 **San Julian** Mex.
186 C4 **San Just** *mt.* Spain
261 G2 **San Justo** Arg.
182 D2 **San Justo de la Vega** Spain
206 C4 **Sankanbiaiwa** *mt.* Sierra Leone
206 C4 **Sankarani** *r.* Côte d'Ivoire/Guinea
114 C4 **Sankarankovil** *Tamil Nadu* India
114 B2 **Sankeshwar** *Karnataka* India
117 F5 **Sankh** *r. Bihar* India
122 D2 **Sankhāş** Iran
Sankosh *r.* Bhutan *see* Sunkosh Chhu
116 E5 **Sankra** *Madh. Prad.* India
116 B4 **Sankra** *Rajasthan* India
179 G3 **Sankt Aegyd am Neuwalde** Austria
179 F4 **Sankt Andrä** Austria
179 H3 **Sankt Andrä am Zicksee** Austria
169 F4 **Sankt Andreasberg** Ger.
179 G4 **Sankt Anna am Aigen** Austria
178 B3 **Sankt Anton am Arlberg** Austria
179 G3 **Sankt Anton an der Jeßnitz** Austria
169 C5 **Sankt Augustin** Ger.
172 C4 **Sankt Blasien** Ger.
171 D5 **Sankt Egidien** Ger.
179 F3 **Sankt Gallen** Austria
190 E1 **Sankt Gallen** Switz.
190 E1 **Sankt Gallen** *canton* Switz.
178 A3 **Sankt Gallenkirch** Austria
171 C5 **Sankt Gangloff** Ger.
179 F4 **Sankt Georgen am Längsee** Austria
179 F2 **Sankt Georgen am Walde** Austria
179 F2 **Sankt Georgen an der Gusen** Austria
179 E3 **Sankt Georgen im Attergau** Austria
179 F4 **Sankt Georgen im Lavanttal** Austria
172 C3 **Sankt Georgen im Schwarzwald** Ger.
179 E3 **Sankt Gilgen** Austria
169 C5 **Sankt Goar** Ger.
169 C5 **Sankt Goarshausen** Ger.
Sankt Gotthard Hungary *see* Szentgotthárd
172 B2 **Sankt Ingbert** Ger.
179 F4 **Sankt Jakob im Rosental** Austria
179 G3 **Sankt Jakob im Walde** Austria
178 D4 **Sankt Jakob in Defereggen** Austria
178 E3 **Sankt Johann im Pongau** Austria
179 G4 **Sankt Johann im Saggautal** Austria
178 D3 **Sankt Johann in Tirol** Austria
172 B2 **Sankt Julian** Ger.
179 F4 **Sankt Kanzian am Klopeiner See** Austria
179 F3 **Sankt Lambrecht** Austria
179 G2 **Sankt Leonhard am Forst** Austria
179 G2 **Sankt Leonhard am Hornerwald** Austria
178 B3 **Sankt Leonhard im Pitztal** Austria
179 E3 **Sankt Lorenz** Austria
179 G3 **Sankt Lorenzen im Mürztal** Austria
179 F3 **Sankt Lorenzen ob Murau** Austria
179 G3 **Sankt Marein im Mürztal** Austria
179 F4 **Sankt Margareten im Rosental** Austria
168 E2 **Sankt Margarethen** Ger.
179 G3 **Sankt Margarethen an der Raab** Austria
179 F3 **Sankt Margarethen bei Knittelfeld** Austria
179 H3 **Sankt Margarethen im Burgenland** Austria
172 C3 **Sankt Märgen** Ger.
179 F2 **Sankt Marien** Austria
179 E2 **Sankt Marienkirchen an der Polsenz** Austria
179 F2 **Sankt Martin** *Niederösterreich* Austria
179 E3 **Sankt Martin** *Salzburg* Austria
179 H4 **Sankt Martin an der Raab** Austria
179 F2 **Sankt Martin im Mühlkreis** Austria
179 G4 **Sankt Martin im Sulmtal** Austria
179 H3 **Sankt Michael im Burgenland** Austria
179 E3 **Sankt Michael im Lungau** Austria
179 G3 **Sankt Michael in Obersteiermark** Austria
168 E2 **Sankt Michaelisdonn** Ger.
190 E2 **Sankt Moritz** Switz.
179 G4 **Sankt Nikolai im Saustal** Austria
179 F2 **Sankt Oswald bei Freistadt** Austria
173 H3 **Sankt Oswald-Riedlhütte** Ger.
178 D2 **Sankt Pantaleon** Austria
179 F4 **Sankt Paul im Lavanttal** Austria
172 C3 **Sankt Peter** Ger.
178 E2 **Sankt Peter am Hart** Austria
179 F3 **Sankt Peter am Kammersberg** Austria
179 G4 **Sankt Peter am Ottersbach** Austria
139 H2 **Sankt-Peterburg** Rus. Fed.
179 G3 **Sankt Peter-Freienstein** Austria
179 G4 **Sankt Peter im Sulmtal** Austria
179 F2 **Sankt Peter in der Au** Austria
168 D1 **Sankt Peter-Ording** Ger.
Sankt Petersburg Rus. Fed. *see* **Sankt-Peterburg**
179 G2 **Sankt Pölten** Austria
179 G3 **Sankt Ruprecht an der Raab** Austria
179 F4 **Sankt Stefan** Austria
179 E4 **Sankt Stefan im Gailtal** Austria
179 G4 **Sankt Stefan im Rosental** Austria
179 F3 **Sankt Stefan ob Leoben** Austria
179 G4 **Sankt Stefan ob Stainz** Austria
178 D3 **Sankt Ulrich am Pillersee** Austria
179 F2 **Sankt Ulrich bei Steyr** Austria
179 F4 **Sankt Urban** Austria
179 F2 **Sankt Valentin** Austria
179 G4 **Sankt Veit am Vogau** Austria
179 F4 **Sankt Veit an der Glan** Austria
179 G2 **Sankt Veit an der Gölsen** Austria
178 E3 **Sankt Veit im Pongau** Austria
172 B2 **Sankt Wendel** Ger.
173 G3 **Sankt Wolfgang** Ger.
179 E3 **Sankt Wolfgang im Salzkammergut** Austria
209 D6 **Sankuru** *r.* Dem. Rep. Congo
253 F5 **San Lázaro** Para.
191 G4 **San Lazzaro di Savena** Italy
240 F3 **San Leandro** *CA* U.S.A.
191 H5 **San Leo** Italy
194 C5 **San Leonardo** *r. Sicilia* Italy
183 G3 **San Leonardo de Yagüe** Spain
191 G2 **San Leonardo in Passiria** Italy
126 E3 **Şanlıurfa** Turkey
128 D1 **Şanlıurfa** *prov.* Turkey
258 F3 **San Lorenzo** *Corrientes* Arg.
261 G3 **San Lorenzo** *Santa Fé* Arg.
252 D3 **San Lorenzo** *Beni* Bol.
252 D5 **San Lorenzo** *Tarija* Bol.
250 B4 **San Lorenzo** Ecuador
195 E5 **San Lorenzo** Italy
242 D2 **San Lorenzo** Mex.
252 C2 **San Lorenzo** Peru
183 H2 **San Lorenzo** *mt.* Spain
259 B7 **San Lorenzo, Cerro** *mt.* Arg./Chile
252 A3 **San Lorenzo, Isla** *i.* Peru
190 C5 **San Lorenzo al Mare** Italy
193 I5 **San Lorenzo Bellizzi** Italy
185 G2 **San Lorenzo de Calatrava** Spain
183 F4 **San Lorenzo de El Escorial** Spain
183 H5 **San Lorenzo de la Parrilla** Spain
San Lorenzo de Morunys Spain *see* Sant Llorenç de Morunys
191 G2 **San Lorenzo di Sebato** Italy
191 H5 **San Lorenzo in Campo** Italy
192 D2 **San Lorenzo Nuovo** Italy
195 F4 **San Luca** Italy
184 D4 **Sanlúcar de Barrameda** Spain
184 C3 **Sanlúcar de Guadiana** Spain
184 D3 **Sanlúcar la Mayor** Spain
252 D5 **San Lucas** Bol.
242 C4 **San Lucas** Mex.
250 C3 **San Lucas, Serranía de** *mts* Col.
193 I5 **San Lucido** Italy
260 D3 **San Luis** Arg.
260 D3 **San Luis** *prov.* Arg.
246 D2 **San Luis** Cuba
243 H5 **San Luis** Guat.
244 D5 **San Luis** Mex.
186 □ **San Luis** Spain
241 J5 **San Luis** *AZ* U.S.A.
241 L5 **San Luis** *AZ* U.S.A.
239 F4 **San Luis** *CO* U.S.A.
260 D3 **San Luis, Sierra de** *mts* Arg.
244 D3 **San Luis de la Paz** Mex.
258 F2 **San Luis del Palmar** Arg.
240 G4 **San Luis Obispo** *CA* U.S.A.
240 G4 **San Luis Obispo Bay** *CA* U.S.A.
242 □H6 **San Luis Pajón** Hond.
244 D2 **San Luis Potosí** Mex.
244 D2 **San Luis Potosí** *state* Mex.
242 B1 **San Luis Río Colorado** Mex.
192 A5 **Sanluri** *Sardegna* Italy
191 H2 **San Maddalena Vallalta** Italy
182 C2 **San Mamede, Serra do** *mts* Spain
183 F2 **San Mamés de Campos** Spain
193 I5 **San Mango d'Aquino** Italy
261 H5 **San Manuel** Arg.
241 L5 **San Manuel** *AZ* U.S.A.
191 I5 **San Marcello** Italy
191 F4 **San Marcello Pistoiese** Italy
193 I5 **San Marco Argentano** Italy
194 D4 **San Marco d'Alunzio** *Sicilia* Italy
193 G3 **San Marco dei Cavoti** Italy
193 H3 **San Marco in Lamis** Italy
250 C2 **San Marcos** Col.
243 H6 **San Marcos** Guat.
242 □I6 **San Marcos** Hond.
245 E5 **San Marcos** Mex.
252 A1 **San Marcos** Peru
182 B1 **San Marcos** Spain
240 I5 **San Marcos** *CA* U.S.A.
237 D6 **San Marcos** *TX* U.S.A.
237 D6 **San Marcos** *r. TX* U.S.A.
191 H5 **San Marino** *country* Europe
191 H5 **San Marino** San Marino
262 T2 **San Martín** *research stn* Antarctica
260 C3 **San Martín** Arg.
253 E3 **San Martín** *r.* Bol.
252 A1 **San Martín** *dept* Peru
177 K4 **Sânmartin** Romania
186 A1 **San Martín** Spain
259 B8 **San Martín, Lago** *l.* Arg./Chile
245 G4 **San Martín, Volcán** *vol.* Mex.
183 G4 **San Martín de la Vega** Spain
183 E4 **San Martín de la Vega del Alberche** Spain
259 C6 **San Martín de los Andes** Arg.
183 E4 **San Martin del Pimpollar** Spain
183 F5 **San Martín de Montalbán** Spain
183 F5 **San Martín de Pusa** Spain
183 I2 **San Martin de Unx** Spain
183 F4 **San Martín de Valdeiglesias** Spain
191 G3 **San Martino Buon Albergo** Italy
191 G2 **San Martino di Castrozza** Italy
192 B2 **San-Martino-di-Lota** *Corse* France
191 G3 **San Martino di Lupari** Italy
191 G3 **San Martino di Venezze** Italy
191 G2 **San Martino in Badia** Italy
191 G2 **San Martino in Passiria** Italy
193 H3 **San Martino in Pensilis** Italy
San Mateo Spain *see* Sant Mateu
240 F3 **San Mateo** *CA* U.S.A.
186 C3 **San Mateo de Gállego** Spain
243 H6 **San Mateo Ixtatán** Guat.
253 F4 **San Matías** Bol.
259 D6 **San Matías, Golfo** *g.* Arg.
194 D5 **San Mauro Castelverde** *Sicilia* Italy
193 I4 **San Mauro Forte** Italy
191 H4 **San Mauro Pascoli** Italy
190 C3 **San Mauro Torinese** Italy
109 G2 **Sanmen** *Zhejiang* China
193 H3 **San Menaio** Italy
109 G2 **Sanmen Wan** *b.* China
107 F5 **Sanmenxia** *Henan* China
191 H3 **San Michele al Tagliamento** Italy
190 C4 **San Michele Mondovì** Italy
195 G2 **San Michele Salentino** Italy
258 F3 **San Miguel** Arg.
253 E4 **San Miguel** Bol.
252 E3 **San Miguel** *r.* Bol.
250 C4 **San Miguel** *r.* Col.
242 □H6 **San Miguel** El Salvador
244 B2 **San Miguel** Mex.
252 B3 **San Miguel** Peru
92 B3 **San Miguel** Phil.
San Miguel Spain *see* Sant Miquel
187 D4 **San Miguel** *r.* Spain
240 G4 **San Miguel** *CA* U.S.A.
239 E4 **San Miguel** *r. CO* U.S.A.
216 □3a **San Miguel de Abona** *Tenerife* Canary Is
244 D3 **San Miguel de Allende** Mex.
183 F3 **San Miguel de Arroyo** Spain
183 G3 **San Miguel de Bernuy** Spain
244 B1 **San Miguel de Cruces** Mex.
242 C2 **San Miguel de Horcasitas** *r.* Mex.
252 D3 **San Miguel de Huachi** Bol.
261 H4 **San Miguel del Monte** Arg.
187 C7 **San Miguel de Salinas** Spain
258 D2 **San Miguel de Tucumán** Arg.
254 C5 **San Miguel do Araguaia** Brazil
244 C3 **San Miguel el Alto** Mex.
240 G4 **San Miguel Island** *CA* U.S.A.
92 A5 **San Miguel Islands** Phil.
242 □K7 **San Miguelito** Panama
244 D3 **San Miguel Octopan** Mex.
245 F5 **San Miguel Sola de Vega** Mex.
183 G2 **San Millán** *mt.* Spain
183 H2 **San Millán de la Cogolla** Spain
109 F3 **Sanming** *Fujian* China
191 F5 **San Miniato** Italy
175 J5 **Sanna** *r.* Pol.
92 B3 **San Narciso** Phil.
215 F3 **Sannaspos** S. Africa
190 D3 **Sannazzaro de'Burgondi** Italy
114 B3 **Sanndatti** *Karnataka* India
Sanndraigh *i. Scotland* U.K. *see* Sandray
195 F2 **Sannicandro di Bari** Italy
193 H3 **Sannicandro Garganico** Italy
195 H2 **Sannicola** Italy
195 F3 **San Nicola dell'Alto** Italy
192 B2 **San-Nicolao** *Corse* France
260 A5 **San Nicolás** Chile
244 B4 **San Nicolás** *r.* Mex.
92 B2 **San Nicolas** Phil.
244 D3 **San Nicolás de los Agustinos** Mex.
261 G3 **San Nicolás de los Arroyos** Arg.
184 E2 **San Nicolás del Puerto** Spain
216 □3f **San Nicolás de Tolentino** *Gran Canaria* Canary Is
239 C5 **San Nicolas Island** *CA* U.S.A.
196 E2 **Sânnicolau Mare** Romania
191 G4 **San Nicolò** Italy
192 A5 **San Nicolò d'Arcidano** *Sardegna* Italy
192 B5 **San Nicolò Gerrei** *Sardegna* Italy
215 E2 **Sannieshof** S. Africa
175 H3 **Sanniki** Pol.
193 G3 **Sannio, Monti del** *mts* Italy
206 C5 **Sanniquellie** Liberia
105 F2 **Sano** Japan
258 D3 **Sañogasta, Sierra de** *mts* Arg.
175 K6 **Sanok** Pol.
250 C2 **San Onofre** Col.
252 D5 **San Pablo** *Potosí* Bol.
253 E3 **San Pablo** *Santa Cruz* Bol.
253 E3 **San Pablo** *r.* Bol.
245 E3 **San Pablo** Mex.
92 B3 **San Pablo** Phil.
240 F3 **San Pablo** *CA* U.S.A.
183 F5 **San Pablo de los Montes** Spain
San Pablo de Manta Ecuador *see* **Manta**
191 G2 **San Pancrazio** Italy
195 G2 **San Pancrazio Salentino** Italy
193 H3 **San Paolo di Civitate** Italy
261 H3 **San Pedro** *Buenos Aires* Arg.
258 D2 **San Pedro** *Catamarca* Arg.
260 E2 **San Pedro** *Córdoba* Arg.
258 D2 **San Pedro** *Jujuy* Arg.
258 G2 **San Pedro** *Misiones* Arg.
243 I5 **San Pedro** Belize
252 D3 **San Pedro** *Beni* Bol.
253 E4 **San Pedro** *Santa Cruz* Bol.
252 D4 **San Pedro** *r.* Bol.
260 B3 **San Pedro** *Santiago* Chile
260 B3 **San Pedro** *Valparaíso* Chile
206 D5 **San-Pédro** Côte d'Ivoire
246 C2 **San Pedro** *r.* Cuba
242 C4 **San Pedro** Mex.
239 F6 **San Pedro** *r. Chihuahua* Mex.
244 B3 **San Pedro** *r. Nayarit* Mex.
253 F6 **San Pedro** Para.
92 B3 **San Pedro** Phil.
185 H2 **San Pedro** Spain
241 L5 **San Pedro** *watercourse AZ* U.S.A.
184 C1 **San Pedro, Sierra de** *mts* Spain
244 D3 **San Pedro Almoloyan** Mex.
245 F5 **San Pedro Apóstol** Mex.
243 H6 **San Pedro Carchá** Guat.
240 H5 **San Pedro Channel** *CA* U.S.A.
185 F4 **San Pedro de Alcántara** Spain
250 D3 **San Pedro de Arimena** Col.
252 C5 **San Pedro de Atacama** Chile
182 D2 **San Pedro de Ceque** Spain
239 E6 **San Pedro de la Cueva** Mex.
183 F4 **San Pedro del Arroyo** Spain
242 E3 **San Pedro de las Colonias** Mex.
183 E3 **San Pedro de Latarce** Spain
250 B6 **San Pedro de Lloc** Peru
253 F6 **San Pedro del Paraná** Para.
187 C7 **San Pedro del Pinatar** Spain
183 G1 **San Pedro del Romeral** Spain
247 E3 **San Pedro de Macoris** Dom. Rep.
182 E4 **San Pedro de Rozados** Spain
242 C2 **San Pedro el Saucito** Mex.
183 H2 **San Pedro Manrique** Spain
242 □H6 **San Pedro Sula** Hond.
177 J5 **Sânpetru Mare** Romania

Sardica Bulg. see Sofiya
176 G3 Šardice Czech Rep.
250 C2 Sardinata Col.
Sardinia i. Italy see Sardegna
185 G2 Sardinilla r. Spain
237 F5 Sardis MS U.S.A.
232 C5 Sardis WV U.S.A.
182 B5 Sardoal Port.
163 A5 Sare France
140 L2 Sarektjåkkå mt. Sweden
95 F3 Sarempaka, Gunung mt. Indon.
187 F5 S'Arenal Islas Baleares Spain
191 G2 Sarentino Italy
123 F2 Sar-e Pol Afgh.
123 F2 Sar-e Pol prov. Afgh.
127 G4 Sar-e Pol-e Žahāb Iran
Sar Eskandar Iran see Hashtrud
190 C3 Sareva r. Italy
123 H2 Sarez, Kŭli l. Tajik.
Sarezskoye Ozero l. Tajik. see Sarez, Kŭli
190 E1 Sargans Switz.
264 E4 Sargasso Sea Atlantic Ocean
123 H3 Sargodha Pak.
208 C2 Sarh Chad
206 D4 Sarhala Côte d'Ivoire
204 D3 Sarhro, Jbel mt. Morocco
122 C2 Sārī Iran
199 E4 Saria i. Notio Aigaio Greece
199 G1 Sarıcakaya Turkey
129 B4 Sarıcan Turkey
197 I3 Sarichioi Romania
129 C4 Sarıçiçek Dağı mt. Turkey
192 A2 Sari-d'Orcino Corse France
182 E2 Sariegos Spain
91 K3 Sarigan i. N. Mariana Is
129 B3 Sarıgöl Turkey
199 F2 Sarıgöl Turkey
199 G3 Sarıidris Turkey
127 F2 Sarıkamış Turkey
128 A1 Sarıkavak Turkey
95 E2 Sarikei Sarawak Malaysia
199 E3 Sarıkemer Turkey
199 E1 Sarıköy Turkey
Sarikŭl, Qatorkŭhi mts China/Tajik. see Sarykol Range
116 D4 Sarila Uttar Prad. India
85 G4 Sarina Qld Austr.
186 C3 Sariñena Spain
Sarıoğlan Turkey see Belören
129 C4 Sarıpınar Turkey
122 C2 Sārī Qamīsh Iran
Sariqamish Kuli salt l. Turkm./Uzbek. see Sarykamyshkoye Ozero
202 C4 Sarīr Tibesti des. Libya
202 D3 Sarir Water Wells Field Libya
117 G4 Sarishabari Bangl.
129 B3 Sarısu Turkey
129 F3 Sarısu Gölü l. Azer.
237 D7 Sarita TX U.S.A.
128 A1 Sarıveliler Turkey
101 C5 Sariwŏn N. Korea
129 E4 Sarıxanlı Azer.
129 G1 Sarıyar Turkey
199 F1 Sarıyer Turkey
126 E3 Sarız Turkey
158 D2 Sark i. Channel Is
177 K5 Sarkad Hungary
177 K5 Sarkadkeresztúr Hungary
121 I3 Sarkand Kazakh.
116 B4 Sarkari Tala Rajasthan India
177 H4 Sárkeresztes Hungary
177 H4 Sárkeresztúr Hungary
126 C3 Şarkikaraağaç Turkey
141 M3 Särkisalo Fin.
126 E3 Şarkışla Turkey
199 E1 Şarköy Turkey
123 F4 Sarlath Range mts Afgh./Pak.
163 D4 Sarlat-la-Canéda France
179 E2 Sarleinsbach Austria
162 C3 Sarliac-sur-l'Isle France
129 C2 Sarmakovo Rus. Fed.
134 K5 Sarmanovo Rus. Fed.
197 F2 Sărmășag Romania
197 G2 Sărmașu Romania
195 F2 Sarmento r. Italy
259 C7 Sarmiento Arg.
141 K3 Särna Sweden
182 C5 Sarnadas do Ródão Port.
175 K3 Sarnaki Pol.
193 F1 Sarnano Italy
122 A3 Sarneh Iran
190 D2 Sarnen Switz.
Sarni Madh. Prad. India see Amla
224 D5 Sarnia Ont. Can.
190 E3 Sarnico Italy
193 G4 Sarno Italy
174 E4 Sarnowa Pol.
136 D2 Sarny Ukr.
139 J2 Sarogozha r. Rus. Fed.
94 C3 Sarolangun Sumatera Indon.
102 K1 Saroma-ko l. Japan
226 B3 Sarona WI U.S.A.
198 C3 Saronikos Kolpos g. Greece
190 E3 Saronno Italy
177 H4 Sárosd Hungary
199 E1 Saros Körfezi b. Turkey
177 K3 Sárospatak Hungary
116 C4 Sarotra Gujarat India
135 H5 Sarova Rus. Fed.
177 H3 Šarovce Slovakia
170 E2 Sarow Ger.
123 G3 Sarowbī Afgh.
Sarpan i. N. Mariana Is see Rota
196 E5 Šar Planina mts Macedonia/Yugo.
142 D2 Sarpsborg Norway
Sarqant Kazakh. see Sarkand
183 G2 Sarracín Spain
186 E3 Sarral Spain
157 H4 Sarralbe France
163 B5 Sarrance France
162 C6 Sarrancolin France
182 C3 Sarraquinhos Port.
161 C3 Sarras France
157 H3 Sarre r. France
190 C3 Sarre Italy
151 I3 Sarre Kent, England U.K.
Sarreal Spain see Sarral
182 C2 Sarreaus Spain
157 H4 Sarre Blanche r. France
157 H4 Sarrebourg France
157 H4 Sarreguemines France
177 K4 Sárrétudvari Hungary
157 H4 Sarre-Union France
182 C2 Sarria Spain
186 F2 Sarrià de Ter Spain
161 C4 Sarrians France
187 C4 Sarrión Spain
206 D3 Sarro Mali
186 D3 Sarroca de Segre Spain
192 B5 Sarròch Sardegna Italy
177 H3 Sárród Hungary
192 A2 Sarrola-Carcopino Corse France
163 B5 Sarron France
156 E4 Sarry France
134 L4 Sars Rus. Fed.
191 H5 Sarsina Italy
162 E3 Sarssonne r. France
169 E3 Sarstedt Ger.
177 H5 Sárszentágota Hungary
177 H5 Sárszentmihály Hungary
165 E4 Sart Belgium
183 H2 Sartaguda Spain
137 I4 Sartana Ukr.
192 D2 Sarteano Italy
192 A3 Sartène Corse France
159 G4 Sarthe dept Pays de la Loire France
159 F4 Sarthe r. France
129 D3 Sart'ichala Georgia
158 E3 Sartilly France
Sartu Heilong. China see Daqing
177 J4 Sárud Hungary
122 B3 Sarud, Rūdkhāneh-ye r. Iran
102 K2 Saru-gawa r. Japan
199 E2 Saruhanlı Turkey
192 B4 Sarule Sardegna Italy
125 F3 Saruna r. Pak.
116 C3 Sarupsar Rajasthan India
129 D4 Şärur Azer.
123 E4 Saru Tara tourist site Afgh.
122 A3 Sarvābād Iran
Sarvani Georgia see Marneuli
176 F4 Sárvár Hungary
122 C4 Sarvestān Iran
186 C2 Sarvisé Spain
196 D2 Sárvíz r. Romania
116 C4 Sarwar Rajasthan India
114 B2 Sarya r. India
121 G4 Saryagach Kazakh.
138 F4 Sar"yanka r. Belarus/Latvia
Sarydhaz r. Kyrg. see Sary-Jaz
Sarydzhas Kazakh. see Saryzhaz
Sarygamysh Köli salt l. Turkm./Uzbek. see Sarykamyshkoye Ozero
Sary-Ishikotrau, Peski des. Kazakh. see Saryyesik-Atyrau, Peski
121 I4 Sary-Jaz r. Kyrg.
120 C3 Sarykamys Kazakh.
122 D1 Sarykamyshkoye Ozero salt l. Turkm./Uzbek.
121 G4 Sarykemer Zhambylskaya Oblast' Kazakh.
121 H2 Sarykiyak Kazakh.
123 H2 Sarykol Range mts China/Tajik.
121 I3 Saryozek Kazakh.
Saryqamys Kazakh. see Sarykamys
121 H3 Saryshagan Kazakh.
121 H5 Sary-Tash Kyrg.
121 I4 Saryter, Gora mt. Kyrg.
120 B2 Saryumir Kazakh.
121 H3 Saryyesik-Atyrau, Peski des. Kazakh.
Saryzhal Kazakh. see Sarzhal
121 I4 Saryzhaz Kazakh.
190 E4 Sarzana Italy
158 D4 Sarzeau France
182 C5 Sarzedas Port.
121 I2 Sarzhal Kazakh.
241 L6 Sasabe AZ U.S.A.
183 F2 Sasamón Spain
78 □6 Sasamungga Choiseul Solomon Is
117 F4 Sasaram Bihar India
78 □6 Sasari, Mount Sta Isabel Solomon Is
172 B3 Sasbach Baden-Württemberg Ger.
172 C3 Sasbach Baden-Württemberg Ger.
172 C3 Sasbachwalden Ger.
137 G2 Saschnivka Ukr.
177 H5 Sásd Hungary
103 D7 Sasebo Japan
137 G3 Sasivka Ukr.
223 J4 Saskatchewan prov. Can.
223 K4 Saskatchewan r. Man./Sask. Can.
223 J4 Saskatoon Sask. Can.
131 M2 Saskylakh Rus. Fed.
242 □16 Saslaya mt. Nic.
136 E1 Sasnovy Bor Belarus
215 F2 Sasolburg S. Africa
135 H5 Sasovo Rus. Fed.
222 H2 Sass r. N.W.T. Can.
234 C3 Sassafras MD U.S.A.
206 D5 Sassandra Côte d'Ivoire
206 D5 Sassandra r. Côte d'Ivoire
193 H4 Sassano Italy
192 A4 Sassari Sardegna Italy
192 A4 Sassari prov. Sardegna Italy
190 D4 Sassello Italy
170 E1 Sassen Ger.
161 D3 Sassenage France
169 D4 Sassenberg Ger.
164 D2 Sassenheim Neth.
192 C1 Sassetta Italy
170 E1 Sassnitz Ger.
191 H5 Sassocorvaro Italy
190 E2 Sasso della Paglia mt. Switz.
191 G4 Sasso di Castro mt. Italy
191 H5 Sassoferrato Italy
191 G2 Sasso Lungo mt. Italy
191 G4 Sasso Marconi Italy
191 G2 Sass Rigais mt. Italy
206 C5 Sass Town Liberia
191 F4 Sassuolo Italy
186 C3 Sástago Spain
176 G3 Šaštín-Stráže Slovakia
121 G4 Sastobe Kazakh.
261 G2 Sastre Arg.
114 B2 Sasvad Mahar. India
165 C3 Sas Van Gent Neth.
137 F4 Sasyk r. Ukr.
121 J3 Sasykkol', Ozero l. Kazakh.
135 I7 Sasykoli Rus. Fed.
Sasyqköl l. Kazakh. see Sasykkol', Ozero
206 C3 Satadougou Mali
Satahual i. Micronesia see Satawal
206 D5 Satama-Sokoura Côte d'Ivoire
116 C5 Satana Mahar. India
136 D3 Sataniv Ukr.
182 C4 Satão Port.
114 B2 Satara Mahar. India
213 F5 Satara S. Africa
91 K5 Satawal i. Micronesia
Sätbaev Kazakh. see Satpayev
196 E3 Satchinez Romania
143 F1 Säter Sweden
239 F7 Satevo r. Mex.
240 H4 Saticoy CA U.S.A.
231 D6 Satilla r. GA U.S.A.
161 C3 Satillieu France
135 H5 Satinka Rus. Fed.
252 B2 Satipo Peru
206 D4 Satiri Burkina
Satırlar Turkey see Yeşilova
130 G4 Satka Rus. Fed.
117 H5 Satkania Bangl.
129 C3 Sat'khe Georgia
117 G5 Satkhira Bangl.
Satluj r. India/Pak. see Sutlej
114 C2 Satmala Range hills India
116 E4 Satna Madh. Prad. India
160 D3 Satolas airport France
177 K3 Sátoraljaújhely Hungary
188 E3 Satorina mt. Croatia
170 C2 Satow Ger.
121 F3 Satpayev Kazakh.
116 C5 Satpura Range mts India
193 H4 Satriano di Lucania Italy
138 D4 Šatrijos kalnis hill Lith.
168 E1 Satrup Ger.
103 E8 Satsuma-hantō pen. Japan
102 K2 Satsunai-gawa r. Japan
97 C4 Sattahip Thai.
105 F2 Satte Japan
178 A3 Satteins Austria
173 E2 Satteldorf Ger.
114 D2 Sattenapalle Andhra Prad. India
116 D2 Satti Jammu and Kashmir
179 F2 Sattledt Austria
197 F2 Satu Mare Romania
177 L4 Satu Mare county Romania
97 C6 Satun Thai.
102 □1 Satunan-shotō is Japan
261 F2 Saturnino M. Laspiur Arg.
116 D5 Satwas Madh. Prad. India
142 B2 Sauanuten mt. Norway
163 A5 Saubusse France
177 L4 Săuca Romania
183 H3 Saúca Spain
163 B4 Saucats France
261 H2 Sauce Arg.
261 G6 Sauce r. Arg.
241 K5 Sauceda Mountains AZ U.S.A.
261 H2 Sauce de Luna Arg.
242 D2 Saucillo Mex.
161 B5 Sauclières France
142 B2 Sauda Norway
121 G4 Saudakent Kazakh.
140 □C2 Sauðárkrókur Iceland
118 E5 Saudi Arabia country Asia
138 E2 Saue Estonia
168 E2 Sauensiek Ger.
157 I4 Sauer r. France
173 F4 Sauerlach Ger.
253 F3 Sauêruiná r. Brazil
92 C5 Saug r. Phil.
138 E2 Sauga r. Estonia
226 D4 Saugatuck MI U.S.A.
224 D4 Saugeen r. Ont. Can.
233 G3 Saugerties NY U.S.A.
149 G4 Saughall Cheshire, England U.K.
163 B4 Saugnacq-et-Muret France
161 B4 Saugues France
Sāūjbolāgh Iran see Mahābād
258 D2 Saujil Arg.
162 B3 Saujon France
236 E2 Sauk Center MN U.S.A.
226 C4 Sauk City WI U.S.A.
251 H4 Saul Fr. Guiana
147 F2 Saul Northern Ireland U.K.
142 C2 Sauland Norway
161 C4 Saulce-sur-Rhône France
157 G4 Saulcy-sur-Meurthe France
172 D4 Sauldorf Ger.
162 D1 Sauldre r. France
172 D3 Saulgau Ger.
162 C2 Saulgé France
173 F4 Saulgrub Ger.
172 C2 Saulheim Ger.
160 C1 Saulieu France
138 E3 Saulkrasti Latvia
161 D4 Sault France
163 B5 Sault-de-Navailles France
156 E3 Sault-lès-Rethel France
224 C4 Sault Sainte Marie Ont. Can.
227 E2 Sault Ste Marie MI U.S.A.
157 G5 Saulx France
157 E4 Saulx r. France
157 G5 Saulxures-sur-Moselotte France
160 A2 Saulzais-le-Potier France
121 G1 Saumalkol' Kazakh.
85 H4 Saumarez Reef Coral Sea Is Terr. Austr.
163 A4 Saumos France
162 B1 Saumur France
84 B2 Saunders, Mount hill N.T. Austr.
262 O1 Saunders Coast Antarctica
150 C3 Saundersfoot Pembrokeshire, Wales U.K.
226 C5 Saunemin IL U.S.A.
233 F3 Sauquoit NY U.S.A.
121 K3 Saur, Khrebet mts China/Kazakh.
163 D6 Saurat France
138 E3 Saurieši Latvia
209 D7 Saurimo Angola
191 H2 Sauris Italy
193 I4 Sauro r. Italy
240 F3 Sausalito CA U.S.A.
116 D5 Sausar Madh. Prad. India
161 D5 Sausset-les-Pins France
160 C1 Saussy France
209 C7 Sautar Angola
178 B3 Sautens Austria
163 B4 Sauternes France
247 □6 Sauteurs Grenada
158 E4 Sautron France
163 B5 Sauvagnon France
161 B5 Sauve France
161 B4 Sauveterre, Causse de plat. France
163 B5 Sauveterre-de-Béarn France
163 B4 Sauveterre-de-Guyenne France
163 E4 Sauveterre-de Rouergue France
163 D4 Sauveterre-la-Lémance France
162 D3 Sauviat-sur-Vige France
160 B2 Sauvigny-les-Bois France
141 M3 Sauvo Fin.
164 F1 Sauwerd Neth.
160 B3 Sauxillanges France
260 A4 Sauzal Maule Chile
260 B4 Sauzal O'Higgins Chile
163 D4 Sauzet France
162 C2 Sauzé-Vaussais France
158 C4 Sauzon France
167 J6 Sava r. Europe
242 □16 Savá Hond.
195 G2 Sava Italy
234 B3 Savage MD U.S.A.
83 F5 Savage River Tas. Austr.
78 □2 Savai'i i. Samoa
135 H6 Savala r. Rus. Fed.
207 F5 Savalou Benin
Savanat Iran see Eşţahbān
225 G3 Savane r. Que. Can.
213 G3 Savane Moz.
236 F3 Savanna IL U.S.A.
231 D5 Savannah GA U.S.A.
236 E4 Savannah MO U.S.A.
232 B4 Savannah OH U.S.A.
237 F5 Savannah TN U.S.A.
231 D5 Savannah r. Georgia/S. Carolina U.S.A.
246 C1 Savannah Sound Eleuthera Bahamas
96 D3 Savannakhét Laos
246 □ Savanna-la-Mar Jamaica
226 B1 Savanne Ont. Can.
224 B3 Savant Lake Ont. Can.
Savantvadi Mahar. India see Vadi
114 B3 Savanur Karnataka India
140 M3 Sävar Sweden
197 F2 Săvârşin Romania
140 M2 Sävast Sweden
199 E2 Savaştepe Turkey
207 F4 Savè Benin
163 D5 Save r. France
213 G4 Save Moz.
213 G4 Save r. Moz./Zimbabwe
122 B3 Sāveh Iran
195 F3 Savelli Italy
206 E4 Savelugu Ghana
191 G4 Savena r. Italy
158 E4 Savenay France
197 H2 Săveni Romania
163 D5 Saverdun France
157 H4 Saverne France
156 D4 Savières France
190 C4 Savigliano Italy
162 C3 Savignac-les-Églises France
193 H3 Savignano Irpino Italy
191 H4 Savignano sul Rubicone Italy
159 G3 Savigné-l'Évêque France
160 C3 Savigneux France
160 A1 Savigny-en-Sancerre France
160 C1 Savigny-lès-Beaune France
159 G4 Savigny-sur-Braye France
156 C4 Savigny-sur-Orge France
161 E4 Savines-le-Lac France
197 H2 Săvineşti Romania
188 E2 Savinja r. Slovenia
139 M3 Savino Rus. Fed.
134 H3 Savinskiy Rus. Fed.
191 H4 Savio r. Italy
141 N3 Savitaipale Fin.
114 B2 Savitri r. India
143 G2 Sävja Sweden
199 G3 Savköy Isparta Turkey
196 D4 Šavnik Crna Gora Yugo.
78 □6 Savo i. Solomon Is
190 E2 Savognin Switz.
193 H4 Savoia di Lucania Italy
160 E3 Savoie dept Rhône-Alpes France
160 E2 Savoie reg. France
156 E5 Savoisy France
190 D4 Savona Italy
190 D4 Savona prov. Liguria Italy
193 F3 Savone r. Italy
141 O3 Savonlinna Fin.
140 O3 Savonranta Fin.
220 A3 Savoonga AK U.S.A.
Savoy reg. France see Savoie
136 F3 Savran' Ukr.
136 F3 Savranka r. Ukr.
127 F2 Şavşat Turkey
143 F3 Sävsjö Sweden
93 B5 Savu i. Indon.
140 O2 Savukoski Fin.
127 F3 Savur Turkey
79 □1 Savusavu Vanua Levu Fiji
212 E3 Savute r. Botswana
193 I5 Savuto r. Italy
137 G2 Savynky Ukr.
137 I3 Savyntsi Ukr.
94 C3 Sawahlunto Sumatera Indon.
116 D4 Sawai Madhopur Rajasthan India
79 □1 Sawaleke Fiji
96 B3 Sawankhalok Thai.
116 C4 Sawar Rajasthan India
105 G3 Sawara Japan
239 F4 Sawatch Range mts CO U.S.A.
151 H3 Sawbridgeworth Hertfordshire, England U.K.
202 B2 Sawdā', Jabal as hills Libya
147 D2 Sawel Mountain hill Northern Ireland U.K.
175 L4 Sawin Pol.
125 G4 Şawqirah, Dawḩat b. Oman
Şawqirah Bay Oman see Şawqirah, Dawḩat
151 H2 Sawston Cambridgeshire, England U.K.
83 H2 Sawtell N.S.W. Austr.
226 B2 Sawtooth Mountains hills MN U.S.A.
238 B1 Sawtooth Range mts WA U.S.A.
151 G2 Sawtry Cambridgeshire, England U.K.
Sawu i. Indon. see Savu
93 B5 Sawu Sea Indon.
187 C6 Sax Spain
146 □H1 Saxa Vord hill Scotland U.K.
85 E3 Saxby r. Qld Austr.
179 F2 Saxen Austria
149 I4 Saxilby Lincolnshire, England U.K.
222 D4 Saxman AK U.S.A.
151 I2 Saxmundham Suffolk, England U.K.
140 K2 Saxnäs Sweden
190 C2 Saxon Switz.
Saxony land Ger. see Sachsen
Saxony-Anhalt land Ger. see Sachsen-Anhalt
151 I2 Saxthorpe Norfolk, England U.K.
232 A6 Saxton KY U.S.A.
232 D4 Saxton PA U.S.A.
206 D3 Say Mali
207 F3 Say Niger
Sayabouri Laos see Muang Xaignabouri
121 I3 Sayak Kazakh.
114 C4 Sayalkudi Tamil Nadu India
105 F3 Sayama Japan
252 A2 Sayán Peru
98 F1 Sayano-Shushenskoye Vodokhranilishche resr Rus. Fed.
Sayaq Kazakh. see Sayak
123 E2 Sayat Turkm.
183 H4 Sayatón Spain
171 E5 Sayda Ger.
Sayda Lebanon see Saïda
162 B4 Saye r. France
128 B1 Saygeçit Turkey
125 G3 Sayḩ al Aḩmar reg. Oman
125 E5 Sayḩūt Yemen
108 B3 Sayingpan Yunnan China
120 A2 Saykhin Kazakh.
210 D2 Sāylac Somalia
Saylan country Asia see Sri Lanka
234 C2 Saylorsburg PA U.S.A.
107 F2 Saynshand Mongolia
106 B2 Sayn-Ust Mongolia
186 B1 Sayoa mt. Spain
Sayot Turkm. see Sayat
Say-Ötesh Kazakh. see Say-Utes
Sayqyn Kazakh. see Saykhin
121 G4 Sayramskiy, Pik mt. Uzbek.
237 D5 Sayre OK U.S.A.
227 I5 Sayre PA U.S.A.
235 D2 Sayreville NJ U.S.A.
244 C4 Sayula Jalisco Mex.
245 G5 Sayula Veracruz Mex.
125 E4 Say'ūn Yemen
120 C3 Say-Utes Kazakh.
235 E2 Sayville NY U.S.A.
222 E5 Sayward B.C. Can.
Sayyod Turkm. see Sayat
198 A1 Sazan i. Albania
176 D2 Sázava r. Czech Rep.
134 L4 Sazhino Rus. Fed.
137 I2 Sazhnoye Rus. Fed.
139 J2 Sazonovo Rus. Fed.
Saztöbe Kazakh. see Sastobe
205 E3 Sbaa Alg.
205 H2 Sbeitla Tunisia
87 D7 Scaddan W.A. Austr.
158 C3 Scaër France
193 G2 Scafa Italy
149 F3 Scafell Pike hill England U.K.
234 B3 Scaggsville MD U.S.A.
194 D5 Scala, Monte della hill Sicilia Italy
146 B5 Scalasaig Argyll and Bute, Scotland U.K.
149 I3 Scalby North Yorkshire, England U.K.
149 F2 Scald Law hill Scotland U.K.
193 H5 Scalea Italy
195 E4 Scaletta Zanclea Sicilia Italy
146 □G1 Scalloway Shetland, Scotland U.K.
Scalpaigh, Eilean i. Western Isles, Scotland U.K. see Scalpay
146 C4 Scalpay i. Highland, Scotland U.K.
146 B4 Scalpay i. Western Isles, Scotland U.K.
147 D1 Scalp Mountain hill Rep. of Ireland
147 E2 Scalva Northern Ireland U.K.
83 G5 Scamander Tas. Austr.
220 B3 Scammon Bay AK U.S.A.
149 I4 Scampton Lincolnshire, England U.K.
195 F3 Scandale Italy
191 F4 Scandiano Italy
191 G5 Scandicci Italy
193 E2 Scandriglia Italy
193 F3 Scanno Italy
192 A4 Scano di Montiferro Sardegna Italy
192 D2 Scansano Italy
197 H3 Scânteia Romania
195 F2 Scanzano Jonico Italy
146 F3 Scapa Orkney, Scotland U.K.
146 E3 Scapa Flow inlet Scotland U.K.
146 E3 Scaraben hill Scotland U.K.
146 C5 Scarba i. Scotland U.K.
224 E5 Scarborough Ont. Can.
247 □5 Scarborough Trin. and Tob.
149 I3 Scarborough North Yorkshire, England U.K.
232 C6 Scarbro WV U.S.A.
191 H4 Scardovari Italy
81 D5 Scargill South I. N.Z.
146 B5 Scarinish Argyll and Bute, Scotland U.K.
149 G4 Scarisbrick Lancashire, England U.K.
234 C2 Scarlets Mill PA U.S.A.
192 C2 Scarlino Italy
146 A3 Scarp i. Scotland U.K.
Scarpanto i. Greece see Karpathos
156 D2 Scarpe r. France
191 G5 Scarperia Italy
147 C4 Scarriff Rep. of Ireland
235 E1 Scarsdale NY U.S.A.
194 A6 Scauri Sicilia Italy
179 H4 Ščavnica r. Slovenia
193 G2 Scerni Italy
157 F5 Scey-sur-Saône-et-St-Albin France
172 D2 Schaafheim Ger.
168 E1 Schaalby Ger.
168 F2 Schaale r. Ger.
168 F2 Schaalsee l. Ger.
172 D4 Schaan Liechtenstein
164 E2 Schaarsbergen Neth.
168 E1 Schacht-Audorf Ger.
234 B2 Schaefferstown PA U.S.A.
165 D4 Schaerbeek Belgium
165 F4 Schaesberg Neth.
190 D1 Schaffhausen Switz.
190 D1 Schaffhausen canton Switz.
168 E1 Schafflund Ger.
168 E1 Schafstedt Ger.
173 F4 Schäftlarn Ger.
164 D2 Schagen Neth.
164 D2 Schagerbrug Neth.
164 E3 Schaijk Neth.
178 E2 Schalchen Austria
171 C5 Schalkau Ger.
164 F2 Schalkhaar Neth.
169 C4 Schalksmühle Ger.
172 B4 Schallstadt Ger.
190 E1 Schänis Switz.
169 C3 Schapen Ger.
170 E1 Schaprode Ger.
168 F1 Scharbeutz Ger.
179 E2 Schardenberg Austria
179 E2 Schärding Austria
178 E3 Schareck mt. Austria
164 C3 Scharendijke Neth.
178 C3 Scharfreiter mt. Austria/Ger.
171 F3 Scharmützelsee l. Ger.
168 F2 Scharnebeck Ger.
164 E1 Scharnegoutum Neth.
178 C3 Scharnitz Austria
179 E3 Scharnstein Austria
168 C2 Scharrel (Oldenburg) Ger.
169 B5 Scharteberg hill Ger.
164 E2 Scharwoude Neth.
168 F1 Schashagen Ger.
179 H3 Schattendorf Austria
226 C4 Schaumburg IL U.S.A.
173 E2 Schebheim Ger.
173 G4 Schechen Ger.
169 E4 Scheden Ger.
164 F1 Scheemda Neth.
172 D3 Scheer Ger.
168 E2 Scheeßel Ger.
178 E3 Scheffau am Tennengebirge Austria
178 D3 Scheffau am Wilden Kaiser Austria
225 H2 Schefferville Nfld. Can.
172 D2 Schefflenz Ger.
191 H5 Scheggia e Pascelupo Italy
193 E2 Scheggino Italy
179 G2 Scheibbs Austria
179 H3 Scheiblingkirchen Austria
172 D4 Scheidegg Ger.
179 F3 Scheifling Austria
173 E2 Scheinfeld Ger.
172 D3 Schelklingen Ger.
241 J2 Schell Creek Range mts NV U.S.A.
165 D3 Schelle Belgium
169 F3 Schellerten Ger.
168 F1 Schellhorn Ger.
232 D4 Schellsburg PA U.S.A.
240 F2 Schellville CA U.S.A.
172 D3 Schemmerhofen Ger.
233 G3 Schenectady NY U.S.A.
168 E1 Schenefeld Schleswig-Holstein Ger.
168 E2 Schenefeld Schleswig-Holstein Ger.
179 F2 Schenkenfelden Austria
172 C3 Schenkenzell Ger.
169 E5 Schenklengsfeld Ger.
169 B4 Schermbeck Ger.
171 C3 Schermen Ger.
164 D2 Schermerhorn Neth.
169 F4 Schernberg Ger.
173 F3 Schernfeld Ger.
165 D4 Scherpenheuvel Belgium
164 E2 Scherpenzeel Neth.
237 D6 Schertz TX U.S.A.
157 H4 Scherwiller France
190 E1 Scherzingen Switz.
178 A3 Schesaplana mt. Austria/Switz.
173 F2 Scheßlitz Ger.
173 F3 Scheyern Ger.
191 H2 Schiara, Monte mt. Italy
193 G3 Schiavi di Abruzzo Italy
164 D3 Schiedam Neth.
169 E4 Schieder-Schwalenberg Ger.
179 F4 Schiefling am See Austria
146 D5 Schiehallion mt. Scotland U.K.
165 F5 Schieren Lux.
169 F4 Schierke Ger.
173 G3 Schierling Ger.
164 F1 Schiermonnikoog Neth.
164 F1 Schiermonnikoog i. Neth.
190 E2 Schiers Switz.
168 D2 Schiffdorf Ger.
172 C2 Schifferstadt Ger.
165 F5 Schifflange Lux.
172 B2 Schiffweiler Ger.
164 E3 Schijndel Neth.
165 D3 Schilde Belgium
168 F2 Schilde r. Ger.
170 E3 Schildow Ger.
164 F1 Schildwolde-Hellum Neth.
172 A2 Schillingen Ger.
173 E2 Schillingsfürst Ger.
190 F2 Schilpario Italy
172 C3 Schiltach Ger.
173 F3 Schiltberg Ger.
157 H4 Schiltigheim France
198 C2 Schimatari Greece
165 E4 Schinnen Neth.
165 E4 Schinveld Neth.
191 G3 Schio Italy
164 F2 Schipbeek r. Neth.
164 D2 Schiphol airport Neth.
171 E4 Schipkau Ger.
157 H4 Schirmeck France
173 G2 Schirmitz Ger.
171 D5 Schirnding Ger.
197 H2 Schitu Duca Romania
171 D4 Schkeuditz Ger.
171 C4 Schkölen Ger.
171 D4 Schköna Ger.
171 C4 Schkopau Ger.
171 E4 Schlabendorf Ger.
169 F3 Schladen Ger.
179 E3 Schladming Austria
168 F2 Schlagsdorf Ger.
169 D4 Schlangen Ger.
169 D5 Schlangenbad Ger.
171 C3 Schlanstedt Ger.
173 G4 Schleching Ger.
168 F1 Schlei r. Ger.
169 B5 Schleiden Ger.
171 F4 Schleife Ger.
190 D1 Schleitheim Switz.
171 C5 Schleiz Ger.
171 D5 Schlema Ger.
171 E3 Schlepzig Ger.
Schlesien reg. Europe see Silesia
168 E1 Schleswig Ger.
168 E1 Schleswig-Holstein land Ger.
171 D5 Schlettau Ger.
169 F5 Schleusingen Ger.
171 E4 Schlieben Ger.
172 B4 Schliengen Ger.
172 D4 Schlier Ger.
179 F3 Schlierbach Austria
190 D1 Schlieren Switz.
173 F4 Schliersee Ger.
178 A3 Schlins Austria
178 C3 Schlitters Austria
169 E5 Schlitz Ger.
169 D4 Schloß Holte-Stukenbrock Ger.
190 C2 Schlosswil Switz.
169 F4 Schlotheim Ger.
172 C4 Schluchsee Ger.
172 C4 Schluchsee l. Ger.
169 E5 Schlüchtern Ger.
Schlüsselburg Rus. Fed. see Shlissel'burg
173 E2 Schlüsselfeld Ger.
168 E2 Schmalfeld Ger.
169 D4 Schmallenberg Ger.
172 A2 Schmelz Ger.
173 G2 Schmidgaden Ger.
173 F2 Schmidmühlen Ger.
214 E3 Schmidtsdrif S. Africa
171 E5 Schmiedeberg Ger.
178 D3 Schmittenhöhe mt. Austria
170 F2 Schmölln Ger.
171 D5 Schmölln Ger.
173 F2 Schnabelwaid Ger.
170 C2 Schnackenburg Ger.
173 G3 Schnaitsee Ger.
173 F2 Schnaittach Ger.
173 G2 Schnaittenbach Ger.
190 D1 Schnebelhorn mt. Switz.
234 C2 Schnecksville PA U.S.A.
171 D5 Schneeberg Ger.
168 F3 Schnega Ger.
Schneidemühl Pol. see Piła
171 C4 Schneidlingen Ger.
173 G4 Schneizlreuth Ger.
173 E2 Schnelldorf Ger.
168 E2 Schneverdingen Ger.
172 D3 Schnürpflingen Ger.
168 E1 Schobüll Ger.
247 □3 Schœlcher Martinique
165 F4 Schoenberg Belgium
226 C3 Schofield WI U.S.A.
233 F3 Schoharie NY U.S.A.
164 E2 Schokland tourist site Flevoland Neth.
168 D3 Scholen Ger.
149 H4 Scholes West Yorkshire, England U.K.
170 D3 Schollene Ger.
169 E5 Schöllkrippen Ger.
173 H3 Schöllnach Ger.
215 E4 Schombee S. Africa
172 C3 Schömberg Ger.
172 C3 Schömberg Ger.
172 D3 Schönaich Ger.
172 C2 Schönau Ger.
173 G3 Schönau Ger.
173 G4 Schönau am Königssee Ger.
172 B4 Schönau im Schwarzwald Ger.
179 G2 Schönbach Austria
173 H3 Schönberg Ger.
170 D3 Schönberg Ger.
168 F2 Schönberg Ger.
168 F2 Schönberg Ger.
168 F1 Schönberg (Holstein) Ger.
179 G2 Schönberg am Kamp Austria
168 F1 Schönbergerstrand Ger.
178 C3 Schönberg im Stubaital Austria
171 E4 Schönborn Ger.
169 F5 Schönbrunn Ger.
171 C4 Schönburg Ger.
169 E5 Schondra Ger.
170 D2 Schönebeck Ger.
171 C3 Schönebeck (Elbe) Ger.
171 D5 Schöneck Ger.
169 B5 Schönecken Ger.
171 E3 Schönefeld Ger.
171 E3 Schönefeld airport Ger.
171 E3 Schöneiche Berlin Ger.
172 B2 Schönenberg-Kübelberg Ger.
170 E2 Schönermark Ger.
170 F2 Schönermark Ger.
171 E4 Schönewalde Ger.
168 F3 Schönewörde Ger.
171 E4 Schönfeld Ger.
173 E4 Schongau Ger.
170 D3 Schönhausen Ger.
171 D5 Schönheide Ger.
169 F3 Schöningen Ger.
168 F1 Schönkirchen Ger.
173 G2 Schönsee Ger.
169 F4 Schönstedt Ger.
172 D2 Schöntal Ger.
173 G2 Schönthal Ger.
169 F5 Schonungen Ger.
171 D5 Schönwald Ger.
170 E3 Schönwalde Ger.
170 E3 Schönwalde Ger.
171 E4 Schönwalde Ger.
168 F1 Schönwalde am Bungsberg Ger.
178 B3 Schönwies Austria
226 E4 Schoolcraft MI U.S.A.
165 C3 Schoondijke Neth.
164 F2 Schoonebeek Neth.
164 D3 Schoonhoven Neth.
164 F2 Schoonoord Neth.
164 D2 Schoorl Neth.
172 B4 Schopfheim Ger.
179 G2 Schöpfl hill Austria
173 E2 Schopfloch Ger.
169 F3 Schöppenstedt Ger.
169 C3 Schöppingen Ger.
170 E3 Schorfheide reg. Ger.
179 E3 Schörfling am Attersee Austria
172 D3 Schorndorf Baden-Württemberg Ger.
173 G2 Schorndorf Bayern Ger.
168 C2 Schortens Ger.
165 D3 Schoten Belgium
169 E5 Schotten Ger.
83 G5 Schouten Island Tas. Austr.
234 B1 Schrader r. PA U.S.A.
172 C3 Schramberg Ger.
178 C3 Schrankogel mt. Austria
171 C4 Schraplau Ger.
169 E5 Schrecksbach Ger.
224 C3 Schreiber Ont. Can.
179 G2 Schrems Austria
170 D3 Schrepkow Ger.
172 C2 Schriesheim Ger.
173 F3 Schrobenhausen Ger.
179 F3 Schröder Austria
233 G3 Schroon Lake NY U.S.A.
Schröttersburg Pol. see Płock
172 D2 Schrozberg Ger.
178 A3 Schruns Austria
190 D1 Schübelbach Switz.
168 E1 Schuby Ger.
169 F4 Schulenberg im Oberharz Ger.
237 D6 Schulenburg TX U.S.A.
223 I5 Schuler Alta Can.
147 B5 Schull Rep. of Ireland
170 F3 Schulzendorf Ger.
171 E3 Schulzendorf bei Eichwalde Ger.
190 D2 Schüpfheim Switz.
172 D3 Schurwald for. Ger.
240 H2 Schurz NV U.S.A.
172 D4 Schussen r. Ger.
172 B3 Schutter r. Ger.
173 F3 Schutter r. Ger.
172 B3 Schuttertal Ger.
172 B3 Schutterwald Ger.
169 C3 Schüttorf Ger.
236 D3 Schuyler NE U.S.A.
233 F3 Schuyler Lake NY U.S.A.
233 G3 Schuylerville NY U.S.A.
234 C3 Schuylkill r. PA U.S.A.
234 B2 Schuylkill County county PA U.S.A.
227 I5 Schuylkill Haven PA U.S.A.
170 D2 Schwaan Ger.
173 F2 Schwabach Ger.
173 E3 Schwaben admin. reg. Bayern Ger.
172 C4 Schwäbische Alb mts Ger.
172 D3 Schwäbisch Gmünd Ger.
172 D2 Schwäbisch Hall Ger.
173 E3 Schwabmünchen Ger.
168 E1 Schwabstedt Ger.
168 D3 Schwaförden Ger.
173 F2 Schwaig bei Nürnberg Ger.
172 D2 Schwaigern Ger.
172 A2 Schwalbach Ger.
169 F5 Schwallungen Ger.
169 E4 Schwalm r. Ger.
169 E5 Schwalmstadt-Treysa Ger.
169 E5 Schwalmstadt-Ziegenhain Ger.
179 G4 Schwanberg Austria
190 E1 Schwanden Switz.
173 G2 Schwandorf Ger.
170 E3 Schwanebeck Brandenburg Ger.
171 C4 Schwanebeck Sachsen-Anhalt Ger.
179 E2 Schwanenstadt Austria
95 F3 Schwaner, Pegunungan mts Indon.
168 D2 Schwanewede Ger.
173 E4 Schwangau Ger.
168 F2 Schwanheide Ger.
173 F2 Schwanstetten Ger.
168 E3 Schwarme Ger.
168 E3 Schwarmstedt Ger.
263 D2 Schwartz Range mts Antarctica
170 D2 Schwarz Ger.
169 F5 Schwarza Ger.
172 C4 Schwarza r. Ger.
171 C5 Schwarza r. Ger.
178 A3 Schwarzach Austria
173 G3 Schwarzach Ger.
173 F3 Schwarzach r. Ger.
173 G2 Schwarzach r. Ger.
178 E3 Schwarzach im Pongau Austria
171 D4 Schwarze Elster r. Ger.
173 G3 Schwarze Laber r. Ger.
179 G2 Schwarzenau Austria
179 H3 Schwarzenbach Austria
171 C5 Schwarzenbach am Wald Ger.
171 C5 Schwarzenbach an der Saale Ger.
168 F2 Schwarzenbek Ger.
171 D5 Schwarzenberg Ger.
169 E5 Schwarzenborn Ger.
173 F2 Schwarzenbruck Ger.
190 C2 Schwarzenburg Switz.
173 G2 Schwarzenfeld Ger.
178 C3 Schwarzenstein mt. Austria/Italy
171 F4 Schwarze Pumpe Ger.
173 G2 Schwarzer Bach r. Ger.
169 B5 Schwarzer Mann hill Ger.
173 G2 Schwarzer Regen r. Ger.
171 F4 Schwarzer Schöps r. Ger.
171 E4 Schwarzheide Ger.
173 G2 Schwarzhofen Ger.
178 C3 Schwarzhorn mt. Austria
190 D2 Schwarzhorn mt. Switz.
212 C5 Schwarzrand mts Namibia
173 G2 Schwarzriegel mt. Ger.
172 C4 Schwarzwald mts Ger.
178 C3 Schwaz Austria
179 H2 Schwechat Austria
168 F1 Schwedeneck Ger.
170 F2 Schwedt an der Oder Ger.
172 C2 Schwegenheim Ger.
168 D2 Schwei (Stadland) Ger.
168 D2 Schweiburg Ger.
172 A2 Schweich Ger.
172 B2 Schweigen-Rechtenbach Ger.
157 H4 Schweighouse-sur-Moder France
169 F5 Schweina Ger.
169 F5 Schweinfurt Ger.
171 E4 Schweinitz Ger.
170 D2 Schweinrich Ger.
173 F3 Schweitenkirchen Ger.
Schweiz country Europe see Switzerland
215 E2 Schweizer-Reneke S. Africa
169 C4 Schwelm Ger.
178 C3 Schwendau Austria
172 D3 Schwendi Ger.
172 C3 Schwenningen Baden-Württemberg Ger.
172 C3 Schwenningen Baden-Württemberg Ger.
171 E4 Schwepnitz Ger.
170 C2 Schwerin Ger.
170 C2 Schweriner See l. Ger.
168 E3 Schweringen Ger.
179 F2 Schwertberg Austria
169 C4 Schwerte Ger.
172 C2 Schwetzingen Ger.
170 E2 Schwichtenberg Ger.
172 D3 Schwieberdingen Ger.
171 F3 Schwielochsee l. Ger.
170 C3 Schwiesau Ger.
173 G3 Schwindegg Ger.
168 E2 Schwinge r. Ger.
170 D2 Schwinkendorf Ger.
178 D3 Schwoich Austria
172 B4 Schwörstadt Ger.
190 D1 Schwyz Switz.
190 D1 Schwyz canton Switz.
194 C5 Sciacca Sicilia Italy
194 D6 Scicli Sicilia Italy
156 B3 Scie r. France
160 E2 Sciez France
195 F3 Scigliano Italy
195 E4 Scilla Italy
Scilly, Île atoll Arch. de la Société Fr. Polynesia see Manuae
150 □ Scilly, Isles of England U.K.
174 E4 Ścinawa Pol.
174 E5 Ścinawka r. Pol.
232 C4 Scio OH U.S.A.
160 E2 Scionzier France
234 C2 Sciota PA U.S.A.
232 B5 Scioto r. OH U.S.A.
241 K2 Scipio UT U.S.A.
150 C3 Scleddau Pembrokeshire, Wales U.K.
238 F1 Scobey MT U.S.A.
Scodra Albania see Shkodër
194 D6 Scoglitti Sicilia Italy
195 D4 Scolaticci Isole Lipari Italy
151 I2 Scole Norfolk, England U.K.
191 F4 Scoltenna r. Italy
83 G3 Scone N.S.W. Austr.
146 B4 Sconser Highland, Scotland U.K.
190 D3 Scopello Italy
193 F2 Scoppito Italy
159 G5 Scorbé-Clairvaux France
194 D5 Scordia Sicilia Italy
221 P2 Scoresby Land reg. Greenland
Scoresby Sund sea chan. Greenland see Kangertittivaq
158 C4 Scorff r. France
197 G3 Scorniceşti Romania
87 E7 Scorpion Bight b. W.A. Austr.
195 H2 Scorrano Italy
149 H3 Scorton North Yorkshire, England U.K.
191 H3 Scorzè Italy
148 C3 Scotch Corner Rep. of Ireland
149 H3 Scotch Corner North Yorkshire, England U.K.
235 D2 Scotch Plains NJ U.S.A.
264 F9 Scotia Ridge sea feature S. Atlantic Ocean
227 G4 Scotland Ont. Can.
146 E4 Scotland admin. div. U.K.
233 E5 Scotland MD U.S.A.
234 C1 Scotrun PA U.S.A.
147 D2 Scotshouse Rep. of Ireland
225 G4 Scotstown Que. Can.
84 B2 Scott, Cape N.T. Austr.
237 D5 Scott, Mount hill OK U.S.A.
263 L1 Scott Base research stn Antarctica
215 H4 Scottburgh S. Africa
236 C4 Scott City KS U.S.A.
263 K1 Scott Coast Antarctica
149 I4 Scotter Lincolnshire, England U.K.
146 F6 Scottish Borders admin. div. Scotland U.K.
263 L2 Scott Island Antarctica
263 D2 Scott Mountains Antarctica
149 H3 Scotton North Yorkshire, England U.K.
151 I2 Scottow Norfolk, England U.K.
86 D2 Scott Reef W.A. Austr.
236 C3 Scottsbluff NE U.S.A.
231 C5 Scottsboro AL U.S.A.
230 C4 Scottsburg IN U.S.A.
83 F5 Scottsdale Tas. Austr.
241 L5 Scottsdale AZ U.S.A.
230 C4 Scottsville KY U.S.A.
232 D6 Scottsville VA U.S.A.
226 D4 Scottville MI U.S.A.
146 C3 Scourie Highland, Scotland U.K.
146 □G2 Scousburgh Shetland, Scotland U.K.
146 E3 Scrabster Highland, Scotland U.K.
234 C1 Scranton PA U.S.A.
147 B3 Screeb Rep. of Ireland
147 D3 Screggan Rep. of Ireland
147 C2 Scribbagh Northern Ireland U.K.
146 B5 Scridain, Loch inlet Scotland U.K.
190 D3 Scrivia r. Italy
149 I4 Scunthorpe North Lincolnshire, England U.K.
190 F2 Scuol Switz.
Scupi Macedonia see Skopje
193 F2 Scurcola Marsicana Italy
Scutari Albania see Shkodër
196 D4 Scutari, Lake Albania/Yugo.
232 E6 Seaboard NC U.S.A.
234 C3 Seabrook NJ U.S.A.
87 C6 Seabrook, Lake salt flat W.A. Austr.
197 G3 Seaca Romania
151 H4 Seaford East Sussex, England U.K.
233 F5 Seaford DE U.S.A.
227 G4 Seaforth Ont. Can.
246 □ Seaforth Jamaica
146 B4 Seaforth, Loch inlet Scotland U.K.
149 H3 Seaham Durham, England U.K.
149 H2 Seahouses Northumberland, England U.K.
234 D3 Sea Isle City NJ U.S.A.
223 M3 Seal r. Man. Can.
83 E3 Sea Lake Vic. Austr.
246 E2 Seal Cays is Turks and Caicos Is
233 □J2 Seal Cove N.B. Can.
225 J3 Seal Cove Nfld. Can.
237 D6 Sealy TX U.S.A.
232 B5 Seaman OH U.S.A.

241 J3 Seaman Range mts NV U.S.A.
149 I3 Seamer North Yorkshire, England U.K.
148 E2 Seamill North Ayrshire, Scotland U.K.
182 B3 Seara Port.
241 J4 Searchlight NV U.S.A.
237 F5 Searcy AR U.S.A.
233 □I2 Searsport ME U.S.A.
149 F3 Seascale Cumbria, England U.K.
240 G3 Seaside CA U.S.A.
238 B2 Seaside OR U.S.A.
235 D3 Seaside Park NJ U.S.A.
149 F3 Seaton Cumbria, England U.K.
150 D4 Seaton Devon, England U.K.
149 H2 Seaton Delaval Northumberland, England U.K.
149 H2 Seaton Sluice Northumberland, England U.K.
238 B2 Seattle WA U.S.A.
222 B2 Seattle, Mount Can./U.S.A.
215 E6 Sea View S. Africa
151 F4 Seaview Isle of Wight, England U.K.
85 F3 Seaview Range mts Qld Austr.
234 D3 Seaville NJ U.S.A.
81 D5 Seaward Kaikoura Range mts South I. N.Z.
242 □I6 Sebaco Nic.
182 B4 Sebal Port.
Sebastea Turkey see Sivas
231 D7 Sebastian FL U.S.A.
261 F2 Sebastián Elcano Arg.
242 B2 Sebastián Vizcaíno, Bahía b. Mex.
233 □I2 Sebasticook r. ME U.S.A.
Sebastopol Ukr. see Sevastopol'
240 F2 Sebastopol CA U.S.A.
95 G1 Sebatik i. Indon.
95 E3 Sebayan, Bukit mt. Indon.
161 A4 Sébazac-Concourès France
207 F3 Sebba Burkina
142 C3 Sebbersund Denmark
205 E2 Sebdou Alg.
206 C3 Sébékoro Mali
126 C2 Seben Turkey
Sebenico Croatia see Šibenik
Sebennytos Egypt see Samannûd
197 F3 Sebeș Romania
197 F2 Sebeș r. Romania
177 J5 Sebes-Körös r. Hungary
227 F4 Sebewaing MI U.S.A.
138 G3 Sebezh Rus. Fed.
126 E2 Şebinkarahisar Turkey
197 F2 Sebiș Romania
139 K2 Sebla r. Rus. Fed.
94 C3 Seblat, Gunung mt. Indon.
171 F5 Sebnitz Ger.
233 □I2 Seboeis ME U.S.A.
232 E6 Sebrell VA U.S.A.
231 D7 Sebring FL U.S.A.
135 H6 Sebrovo Rus. Fed.
95 G3 Sebuku i. Indon.
95 G1 Sebuku r. Indon.
260 D5 Seca, Pampa plain Arg.
196 E3 Sečanj Vojvodina, Srbija Yugo.
182 B4 Secarias Port.
177 K6 Secaș Romania
197 F2 Secaș r. Romania
242 □J8 Secas, Islas is Panama
191 G3 Secchia r. Italy
175 H5 Secemin Pol.
222 F5 Sechelt B.C. Can.
135 I5 Sechenovo Rus. Fed.
250 A6 Sechura Peru
250 A6 Sechura, Bahía de b. Peru
172 D2 Seckach Ger.
179 F3 Seckau Austria
156 D2 Seclin France
186 D4 Seco r. Spain
203 F4 Second Cataract rapids Sudan
162 B2 Secondigny France
241 L4 Second Mesa AZ U.S.A.
234 B2 Second Mountain ridge PA U.S.A.
85 E2 Second Three Mile Opening sea chan. Qld Austr.
206 □ Secos, Ilhéus is Cape Verde
177 K3 Sečovce Slovakia
81 A6 Secretary Island South I. N.Z.
215 G2 Secunda S. Africa
114 C2 Secunderabad Andhra Prad. India
252 D3 Sécure r. Bol.
177 J5 Secusigiu Romania
138 E3 Seda Latvia
138 E3 Seda r. Latvia
138 D3 Seda Lith.
184 C1 Seda Port.
184 B2 Seda r. Port.
236 E4 Sedalia MO U.S.A.
114 C2 Sedam Karnataka India
82 D3 Sedan S.A. Austr.
157 E3 Sedan France
237 D4 Sedan KS U.S.A.
85 E3 Sedan Dip Qld Austr.
183 G2 Sedano Spain
149 G3 Sedbergh Cumbria, England U.K.
81 E4 Seddon South I. N.Z.
81 C4 Seddonville South I. N.Z.
122 C4 Sedeh Fārs Iran
122 D3 Sedeh Khorāsan Iran
161 D4 Séderon France
149 H3 Sedgefield Durham, England U.K.
223 I4 Sedgewick Alta Can.
150 E2 Sedgley West Midlands, England U.K.
233 □I2 Sedgwick ME U.S.A.
206 B3 Sédhiou Senegal
191 H2 Sedico Italy
192 A4 Sedilo Sardegna Italy
192 A4 Sedini Sardegna Italy
176 G6 Sedlarica Croatia
176 D2 Sedlčany Czech Rep.
176 D2 Sedlec Prčice Czech Rep.
Sedlets Pol. see Siedlce
177 K3 Sedlice Slovakia
171 F4 Sedlitz Ger.
171 F5 Sedlo hill Czech Rep.
136 C2 Sedlyshche Ukr.
241 L4 Sedona AZ U.S.A.
Sedovo Ukr. see Syedove
205 G1 Sédrata Alg.
190 E3 Sedrina Italy
138 D4 Šeduva Lith.
175 H4 Sędziejowice Pol.
174 G3 Sędzin Pol.
175 I5 Sędziszów Pol.
175 J5 Sędziszów Małopolski Pol.
178 B3 See Austria
159 E3 Sée r. France
172 C3 Seebach Baden-Württemberg Ger.
169 F5 Seebach Thüringen Ger.
170 F2 Seebad Ahlbeck Ger.
170 F2 Seebad Bansin Ger.
170 F2 Seebad Heringsdorf Ger.
169 F5 Seebergen Ger.
179 E4 Seeboden Austria
173 G4 Seebruck Ger.
169 F4 Seeburg Ger.
168 F1 Seedorf Schleswig-Holstein Ger.
168 F2 Seedorf Schleswig-Holstein Ger.
173 F3 Seefeld Bayern Ger.
170 E3 Seefeld Brandenburg Ger.
168 D2 Seefeld (Stadland) Ger.
178 C3 Seefeld in Tirol Austria
147 D4 Seefin hill Rep. of Ireland
173 E4 Seeg Ger.
171 D4 Seegrehna Ger.
170 E2 Seehausen Brandenburg Ger.
171 C3 Seehausen Sachsen-Anhalt Ger.
170 C3 Seehausen (Altmark) Ger.
173 F4 Seehausen am Staffelsee Ger.
172 C2 Seeheim-Jugenheim Ger.
178 E3 Seekirchen am Wallersee Austria
214 D5 Seekoegat S. Africa
215 E4 Seekoei r. S. Africa
172 B3 Seelbach Ger.
241 J5 Seeley CA U.S.A.
262 R1 Seelig, Mount Antarctica
171 D5 Seelingstädt Ger.
170 F3 Seelow Ger.
169 E3 Seelze Ger.
Seenu Atoll Maldives see Addu Atoll
173 G4 Seeon Ger.
190 D1 Seerücken val. Switz.
159 G3 Sées France
169 F4 Seesen Ger.
173 F4 Seeshaupt Ger.
168 F2 Seevetal Ger.
179 E3 Seewalchen am Attersee Austria
160 E3 Séez France
206 C4 Sefadu Sierra Leone
199 E2 Seferihisar Turkey
206 C3 Séféto Mali
122 B3 Sefīd, Kūh-e mt. Iran
213 E4 Sefophe Botswana
204 D2 Sefrou Morocco
81 C5 Sefton, Mount South I. N.Z.
206 C3 Ségala Mali
141 J3 Segalstad Norway
95 G1 Segama r. Sabah Malaysia
94 C2 Segamat Malaysia
180 E5 Segangane Morocco
197 F3 Şegarcea Romania
207 F4 Ségbana Benin
176 G5 Segesd Hungary
134 F3 Segezha Rus. Fed.
192 D2 Seggiano Italy
158 C3 Séglien France
193 F3 Segni Italy
Segontia Gwynedd, Wales U.K. see Caernarfon
Segontium Gwynedd, Wales U.K. see Caernarfon
162 B3 Segonzac France
187 C5 Segorbe Spain
206 D3 Ségou Mali
206 D3 Ségou admin. reg. Mali
250 C3 Segovia Col.
Segovia r. Hond./Nic. see Coco
183 F4 Segovia Spain
183 F3 Segovia prov. Castilla y León Spain
134 F3 Segozerskoye, Ozero resr Rus. Fed.
159 F4 Segré France
186 D3 Segre r. Spain
159 G3 Ségrie France
206 D5 Séguéla Côte d'Ivoire
206 D4 Séguélon Côte d'Ivoire
206 E3 Séguénéga Burkina
261 G3 Seguí Arg.
237 D6 Seguin TX U.S.A.
261 F2 Segundo r. Arg.
161 A4 Ségur France
182 D5 Segura Port.
185 I2 Segura r. Spain
185 H3 Segura, Sierra de mts Spain
185 H2 Segura de la Sierra Spain
184 D2 Segura de León Spain
186 C4 Segura de los Baños Spain
183 F4 Segurilla Spain
212 D4 Sehithwa Botswana
169 F3 Sehlde Ger.
169 E3 Sehnde Ger.
116 D5 Sehore Madh. Prad. India
123 F5 Sehwan Pak.
182 C4 Seia Port.
236 C4 Seibert CO U.S.A.
158 E4 Seiche r. France
159 F4 Seiches-sur-le-Loir France
179 G3 Seiersberg Austria
140 J2 Seierstad Norway
171 F5 Seifhennersdorf Ger.
150 E2 Seighford Staffordshire, England U.K.
161 A4 Seigne, Mont mt. France
225 G3 Seignelay r. Que. Can.
156 D5 Seignelay France
190 B1 Seignelégier Switz.
163 A5 Seignosse France
96 A2 Seikpyu Myanmar
146 C5 Seil i. Scotland U.K.
140 M1 Seiland i. Norway
162 D3 Seilhac France
237 D4 Seiling OK U.S.A.
161 E5 Seillans France
160 C2 Seille r. France
157 G3 Seille r. France
165 E4 Seilles Belgium
138 D4 Šeimena r. Lith.
140 M3 Seinäjoki Fin.
224 B3 Seine r. Ont. Can.
156 A3 Seine r. France
159 F2 Seine, Baie de b. France
160 C1 Seine, Sources de la tourist site France
156 D4 Seine, Val de val. France
156 D4 Seine-et-Marne dept Île-de-France France
Seine-Inférieure dept Haute-Normandie France see Seine-Maritime
156 A3 Seine-Maritime dept Haute-Normandie France
159 I3 Seine-St-Denis dept France
197 F2 Seini Romania
173 E2 Seinsheim Ger.
186 D2 Seira Spain
163 C5 Seissan France
179 F2 Seitenstetten Austria
177 J5 Şeitin Romania
163 D6 Seix France
184 □ Seixal Madeira
184 A2 Seixal Port.
182 B3 Seixas Port.
184 B3 Seixe r. Port.
182 C4 Seixo da Beira Port.
142 D4 Sejerby Denmark
142 D4 Sejerø i. Denmark
142 D4 Sejerø Bugt b. Denmark
175 L1 Sejny Pol.
94 C3 Sekayu Sumatera Indon.
177 K3 Sekčov r. Slovakia
Seke Sichuan China see Sêrtar
209 B6 Seke-Banza Dem. Rep. Congo
104 C3 Seki Japan
199 F3 Seki Turkey
199 F3 Seki r. Turkey
102 □1 Sekibi-sho i. Japan
94 D4 Sekicau, Gunung vol. Indon.
104 C2 Sekidō-san hill Japan
206 E5 Sekondi Ghana
210 C1 Sek'ot'a Eth.
175 J6 Sękowa Pol.
Sekseüil Kazakh. see Saksaul'skiy
123 E4 Sekūheh Iran
Şela Rus. Fed. see Shali
94 C3 Selagan r. Indon.
238 B2 Selah WA U.S.A.
94 C2 Selangor state Malaysia
192 B5 Selargius Sardegna Italy
94 C2 Selatpanjang Sumatera Indon.
150 D2 Selattyn Shropshire, England U.K.
220 B3 Selawik AK U.S.A.
183 G1 Selaya Spain
171 D5 Selb Ger.
178 D3 Selbhorn mt. Austria
171 C5 Selbitz Ger.
140 J3 Selbu Norway
149 H4 Selby North Yorkshire, England U.K.
236 C2 Selby SD U.S.A.
233 F5 Selbyville DE U.S.A.
191 J3 Selce Croatia
199 E3 Selçuk Turkey
236 C4 Selden KS U.S.A.
220 C4 Seldovia AK U.S.A.
193 G4 Sele r. Italy
213 E4 Selebi-Phikwe Botswana
Selebi-Pikwe Botswana see Selebi-Phikwe
197 E5 Selečka Planina mts Macedonia
192 B5 Selegas Sardegna Italy
192 B4 S'Elema r. Sardegna Italy
100 D1 Selemdzha r. Rus. Fed.
199 F2 Selendi Turkey
106 E1 Selenduma Rus. Fed.
106 E1 Selenga r. Rus. Fed.
106 E1 Selenge prov. Mongolia
106 E1 Selenge Mörön r. Mongolia
198 A1 Selenicë Albania
168 F1 Selent Ger.
168 F1 Selenter See l. Ger.
157 H4 Sélestat France
121 H1 Seletinskoye Kazakh.
Selety r. Kazakh. see Sileti
Seletyteniz, Oz. salt l. Kazakh. see Siletiteniz, Ozero
Seleucia Turkey see Silifke
Seleucia Pieria Turkey see Samandağı
177 K5 Seleuș Romania
138 G1 Seleznevo Rus. Fed.
140 □B3 Selfoss Iceland
236 C2 Selfridge ND U.S.A.
206 B3 Sélibabi Maur.
Selidovo Ukr. see Selydove
169 D5 Seligenstadt Ger.
139 I3 Seliger, Ozero l. Rus. Fed.
241 K4 Seligman AZ U.S.A.
129 C3 Selim Turkey
203 F4 Selîma Oasis Sudan
199 E3 Selimiye Turkey
206 C4 Sélingué, Lac de l. Mali
206 C3 Selinnkegni Mali
198 C2 Selinous r. Greece
234 B2 Selinsgrove PA U.S.A.
139 I3 Selishche Rus. Fed.
135 H5 Selishchi Rus. Fed.
120 A3 Selitrennoye Rus. Fed.
139 I3 Selizharovo Rus. Fed.
141 I3 Selje Norway
142 C2 Seljord Norway
171 C4 Selke r. Ger.
223 L5 Selkirk Man. Can.
145 F6 Selkirk Scottish Borders, Scotland U.K.
222 G4 Selkirk Mountains B.C. Can.
Şelkovski Rus. Fed. see Shelkovskaya
187 C6 Sella Spain
183 E1 Sella r. Spain
149 F3 Sellafield Cumbria, England U.K.
146 □G1 Sellafirth Shetland, Scotland U.K.
193 E2 Sellano Italy
234 C2 Sellersville PA U.S.A.
162 D1 Selles-St-Denis France
159 H4 Selles-sur-Cher France
85 F4 Sellheim r. Qld Austr.
195 F4 Sellia Marina Italy
160 D2 Sellières France
151 H3 Sellindge Kent, England U.K.
164 G2 Sellingen Neth.
Sellore Island Myanmar see Saganthit Kyun
178 C3 Sellrain Austria
241 L6 Sells AZ U.S.A.
177 G6 Sellye Hungary
169 C4 Selm Ger.
231 C5 Selma AL U.S.A.
240 H3 Selma CA U.S.A.
237 F5 Selmer TN U.S.A.
184 C2 Selmes Port.
182 D2 Selmo r. Spain
168 F2 Selmsdorf Ger.
156 B5 Selommes France
95 G5 Selong Lombok Indon.
160 D1 Selongey France
161 E4 Selonnet France
215 G1 Selonsrivier S. Africa
206 C4 Sélouma Guinea
222 C2 Selous, Mount Y.T. Can.
170 C2 Selow Ger.
122 E4 Selseleh-ye Pīr Shūrān mts Iran
151 G4 Selsey West Sussex, England U.K.
151 G4 Selsey Bill hd England U.K.
168 E2 Selsingen Ger.
169 C5 Selters (Westerwald) Ger.
139 J5 Sel'tso Rus. Fed.
134 K4 Selty Rus. Fed.
157 I4 Seltz France
Selukwe Zimbabwe see Shurugwi
159 E3 Sélune r. France
195 G2 Selva Italy
187 F5 Selva Spain
186 B2 Selva mt. Spain
191 G2 Selva dei Molini Italy
191 G3 Selva di Progno Italy
178 C4 Selva di Val Gardena Italy
204 B3 Selvagens, Ilhas is Madeira
127 G3 Selvānā Iran
260 A6 Selva Obscura Chile
250 D6 Selvas reg. Brazil
191 G3 Selvazzano Dentro Italy
190 E3 Selvino Italy
238 D2 Selway r. ID U.S.A.
223 J2 Selwyn Lake N.W.T./Sask. Can.
222 D1 Selwyn Mountains N.W.T./Y.T. Can.
84 C4 Selwyn Range hills Qld Austr.
136 C4 Selyatyn Ukr.
137 I3 Selydove Ukr.
172 C2 Selz r. Ger.
179 F3 Selzthal Austria
163 E5 Sémalens France
198 A1 Seman r. Albania
95 E4 Semarang Jawa Tengah Indon.
161 B3 Sembadel France
95 G2 Sembakung r. Indon.
208 B4 Sembé Congo
159 G4 Semblançay France
190 C2 Sembrancher Switz.
127 G3 Şemdinli Turkey
163 C5 Séméac France
160 B2 Sémelay France
Semendire Srbija Yugo. see Smederevo
197 F3 Semenic, Vârful mt. Romania
137 G1 Semenivka Chernihivs'ka Oblast' Ukr.
137 I3 Semenivka Kharkivs'ka Oblast' Ukr.
137 F2 Semenivka Kyivs'ka Oblast' Ukr.
137 G3 Semenivka Poltavs'ka Oblast' Ukr.
120 C1 Semenkino Rus. Fed.
137 K2 Semeno-Aleksandrovka Rus. Fed.
134 I4 Semenov Rus. Fed.
Semenovka Chernihivs'ka Oblast' Ukr. see Semenivka
94 F5 Semeru, Gunung vol. Indon.
Semey Kazakh. see Semipalatinsk
124 B5 Semhar prov. Eritrea
137 J4 Semibalki Rus. Fed.
139 L3 Semibratovo Rus. Fed.
182 B4 Semide Port.
137 J2 Semidesyatnoye Rus. Fed.
134 H4 Semigorodnyaya Rus. Fed.
135 H7 Semikarakorsk Rus. Fed.
135 G6 Semiluki Rus. Fed.
176 E1 Semily Czech Rep.
195 E4 Seminara Italy
160 D2 Semine r. France
237 C5 Seminole TX U.S.A.
121 K2 Seminskiy Khrebet mts Rus. Fed.
120 F1 Semiozernoye Kazakh.
121 J2 Semipalatinsk Kazakh.
121 F1 Semipolka Kazakh.
92 B4 Semirara Islands Phil.
95 E2 Semitau Kalimantan Barat Indon.
121 I2 Semiyarka Kazakh.
121 H2 Semizbuga Kazakh.
Semizbughy Kazakh. see Semizbuga
139 L3 Semkhoz Rus. Fed.
Sem Kolodezey Respublika Krym Ukr. see Lenine
196 E2 Semlac Romania
139 I4 Semlevo Rus. Fed.
208 F4 Semliki r. Dem. Rep. Congo/Uganda
170 D1 Semlow Ger.
169 F3 Semmenstedt Ger.
122 C3 Semnān Iran
122 B3 Semnān prov. Iran
106 D4 Sêmnyi Qinghai China
165 D5 Semois r. Belgium
165 D5 Semois, Vallée de la val. Belgium/France
157 F4 Semoutiers-Montsaon France
190 D1 Sempach Switz.
179 E5 Šempeter Slovenia
192 D2 Semproniano Italy
173 F3 Sempt r. Ger.
179 G3 Semriach Austria
139 I5 Semtsy Rus. Fed.
160 C1 Semur-en-Auxois France
160 C2 Semur-en-Brionnais France
162 B3 Semussac France
Semyonovskoye Arkhangel'skaya Oblast' Rus. Fed. see Bereznik
Semyonovskoye Kostromskaya Oblast' Rus. Fed. see Ostrovskoye
97 D4 Sên, Stœng r. Cambodia
252 D2 Sena Bol.
177 K3 Seňa Slovakia
186 C3 Sena Spain
256 C2 Senador Canedo Brazil
254 F3 Senador Pompeu Brazil
203 H6 Senafe Eritrea
191 G2 Senaiga r. Italy
129 C2 Senaki Georgia
191 F2 Senales Italy
192 B4 Senalonga, Punta mt. Sardegna Italy
252 C2 Sena Madureira Brazil
209 D9 Senanga Zambia
156 B3 Senarpont France
161 D5 Sénas France
237 F5 Senatobia MS U.S.A.
Sencelles Spain see Sancellas
137 G2 Sencha Ukr.
179 F4 Šenčur Slovenia
103 E8 Sendai Kagoshima Japan
102 J4 Sendai Miyagi Japan
103 E8 Sendai-gawa r. Japan
215 F2 Sendelingsfontein S. Africa
173 E3 Senden Bayern Ger.
169 C4 Senden Nordrhein-Westfalen Ger.
169 C4 Sendenhorst Ger.
182 D3 Sendim Bragança Port.
182 B3 Sendim Porto Port.
Sêndo Xizang China see Chido
197 H3 Şendreni Romania
158 D4 Séné France
206 E5 Sene r. Ghana
176 G3 Senec Slovakia
226 C5 Seneca IL U.S.A.
236 D4 Seneca KS U.S.A.
238 C2 Seneca OR U.S.A.
232 D4 Seneca PA U.S.A.
232 D5 Seneca Rocks WV U.S.A.
165 D4 Seneffe Belgium
206 B3 Senegal country Africa
206 A2 Sénégal r. Maur./Senegal
192 A4 Seneghe Sardegna Italy
215 F3 Senekal S. Africa
185 H3 Senes Spain
192 B4 Senes, Monte hill Sardegna Italy
226 E2 Seney MI U.S.A.
161 E5 Senez France
179 G2 Senftenberg Austria
171 F4 Senftenberg Ger.
211 B8 Senga Malawi
116 D4 Sengar r. India
173 F2 Sengenthal Ger.
211 B5 Sengerema Tanz.
256 C6 Sengés Brazil
135 J5 Sengiley Rus. Fed.
Sengirli, Mys pt Kazakh. see Syngyrli, Mys
163 C6 Sengouagnet France
259 C7 Senguerr r. Arg.
213 F3 Sengwa r. Zimbabwe
124 B5 Senhit prov. Eritrea
184 C1 Senhora do Rosário Port.
254 E4 Senhor do Bonfim Brazil
176 G3 Senica Slovakia
176 G2 Senice na Hané Czech Rep.
191 I5 Senigallia Italy
191 H4 Senio r. Italy
199 G2 Senirkent Turkey
192 A5 Senis Sardegna Italy
193 I4 Senise Italy
188 E3 Senj Croatia
140 L1 Senja i. Norway
104 B4 Senjōga-dake mt. Japan
105 E3 Senjōga-dake mt. Japan
127 F2 Şenkaya Turkey
206 C4 Senko Guinea
209 E9 Senkobo Zambia
137 I3 Sen'kove Ukr.
128 C1 Şenköy Turkey
116 D2 Senku Jammu and Kashmir
214 D1 Senlac S. Africa
100 D4 Senlin Shan mt. Jilin China
156 C3 Senlis France
97 D4 Senmonorom Cambodia
104 B4 Sennan Japan
203 G6 Sennar Sudan
203 G6 Sennar state Sudan
192 A4 Sennariolo Sardegna Italy
160 C2 Sennecey-le-Grand France
160 D1 Sennecey-lès-Dijon France
150 □ Sennen Cornwall, England U.K.
224 E3 Senneterre Que. Can.
171 C4 Sennewitz Ger.
Senno Belarus see Syanno
105 E2 Sennokura-yama mt. Japan
192 A4 Sennori Sardegna Italy
190 E1 Sennwald Switz.
150 D3 Sennybridge Powys, Wales U.K.
156 B4 Senonches France
157 G4 Senones France
192 B5 Senorbì Sardegna Italy
163 D5 Senouillac France
161 B3 Senouire r. France
179 G4 Senovo Slovenia
215 F4 Senqu r. Lesotho
156 D4 Sens France
158 E3 Sens-de-Bretagne France
156 D2 Sensée r. France
242 □H6 Sensuntepeque El Salvador
196 E3 Senta Vojvodina, Srbija Yugo.
163 C6 Sentein France
163 D6 Sentenac-d'Oust France
186 D2 Senterada Spain
179 G4 Šentilj Slovenia
241 K5 Sentinel AZ U.S.A.
193 G3 Sentinella, Colle della hill Italy
222 F4 Sentinel Peak B.C. Can.
262 S1 Sentinel Range mts Antarctica
Sentinum Italy see Sassoferrato
179 G5 Šentjernej Slovenia
179 G4 Šentjur pri Celju Slovenia
94 □ Sentosa i. Sing.
157 E3 Senuc France
177 K4 Sényő Hungary
129 B3 Şenyurt Erzurum Turkey
127 F3 Şenyurt Turkey
171 E3 Senzig Ger.
Seo de Urgell Spain see Le Seu d'Urgell
190 D1 Seon Switz.
116 E5 Seonath r. India
116 D4 Seondha Madh. Prad. India
116 D5 Seoni Madh. Prad. India
116 D5 Seoni Chhapara Madh. Prad. India
116 D5 Seoni-Malwa Madh. Prad. India
Seoul S. Korea see Sŏul
163 C4 Séoune r. France
86 D4 Separation Well W.A. Austr.
122 A3 Separ Shāhābād Iran
252 D1 Sepatini r. Brazil
257 E5 Sepetiba, Baía de b. Brazil
91 J7 Sepik r. P.N.G.
95 F2 Seping r. Sarawak Malaysia
193 G3 Sepino Italy
101 C5 Sep'o N. Korea
174 F2 Sępólno Krajeńskie Pol.
117 H4 Sepon Assam India
253 F3 Sepotuba r. Brazil
117 H4 Seppa Arun. Prad. India
160 F1 Seppois-le-Bas France
197 E2 Şepreuș Romania
161 D5 Septèmes-les-Vallons France
156 B4 Septeuil France
163 D4 Septfonds France
225 H3 Sept-Îles Que. Can.
160 D2 Septmoncel France
182 D4 Sepulcro-Hilario Spain
183 G3 Sepúlveda Spain
94 D4 Seputih r. Indon.
191 H2 Sequàls Italy
231 C5 Sequatchie r. TN U.S.A.
182 D4 Sequeros Spain
183 E3 Sequillo r. Spain
124 B5 Serae prov. Eritrea
129 B4 Şerafettin Dağları mts Turkey
135 H6 Serafimovich Rus. Fed.
156 E3 Seraincourt France
165 E4 Seraing Belgium
Sêraitang Qinghai China see Baima
93 D3 Seram i. Maluku Indon.
93 D3 Seram Sea Indon.
160 D3 Séran r. France
94 D4 Serang Jawa Barat Indon.
161 E5 Séranon France
95 E2 Serasan, Selat sea chan. Indon.
190 F5 Seravezza Italy
128 A5 Serbâl, Gebel mt. Egypt
Serbia aut. rep. Yugo. see Srbija
136 D3 Serbynivtsi Ukr.
111 F6 Sêrca Xizang China
191 F5 Serchio r. Italy
192 B5 Serdiana Sardegna Italy
Serdica Bulg. see Sofiya
135 I5 Serdoba r. Rus. Fed.
135 I5 Serdobsk Rus. Fed.
121 J2 Serebryansk Kazakh.
139 L4 Serebryanyye Prudy Rus. Fed.
177 G3 Sereď Slovakia
139 M3 Sereda Rus. Fed.
139 J4 Seredeyskiy Rus. Fed.
138 G2 Seredka Rus. Fed.
136 F4 Seredniy Kuyal'nyk r. Ukr.
206 C4 Sérédou Guinea
137 H1 Seredyna-Buda Rus. Fed.
136 B3 Seredyne Ukr.
126 D3 Şereflikoçhisar Turkey
177 H4 Seregélyes Hungary
190 E3 Seregno Italy
162 D3 Séreilhac France
156 D5 Serein r. France
94 C2 Seremban Malaysia
211 B5 Serengeti National Park Tanz.
211 B5 Serengeti Plain Tanz.
209 F8 Serenje Zambia
158 D4 Sérent France
210 B4 Serere Uganda
136 C3 Seret r. Ukr.
134 H5 Serezha r. Rus. Fed.
139 H3 Serezha r. Rus. Fed.
178 B3 Serfaus Austria
134 L4 Ser'ga Rus. Fed.
134 I5 Sergach Rus. Fed.
107 F2 Sergelen Mongolia
197 H5 Sergen Turkey
121 G2 Sergeyevka Akmolinskaya Oblast' Kazakh.
121 F1 Sergeyevka Severnyy Kazakhstan Kazakh.
137 J2 Sergeyevka Rus. Fed.
156 D4 Sergines France
130 H3 Sergino Rus. Fed.
254 F4 Sergipe state Brazil
139 L3 Sergiyev Posad Rus. Fed.
135 J5 Sergiyevsk Rus. Fed.
Sergiyevskiy Rus. Fed. see Fakel
190 E3 Sergnano Italy
Sergo Ukr. see Stakhanov
129 E2 Sergokala Rus. Fed.
137 G2 Serhiyivka Chernihivs'ka Oblast' Ukr.
137 H4 Serhiyivka Khersons'ka Oblast' Ukr.
136 F4 Serhiyivka Odes'ka Oblast' Ukr.
95 F1 Seria Brunei
190 E3 Seriate Italy
156 B3 Sérifontaine France
198 D3 Serifos i. Greece
161 B5 Sérignan France
161 C4 Sérignan-du-Comtat France
225 G2 Sérigny r. Que. Can.
199 G3 Serik Turkey
190 E3 Serina Italy
213 □J3 Sèrinama Madag.
251 I6 Seringa, Serra da hills Brazil
86 D2 Seringapatam Reef W.A. Austr.
199 F3 Serinhisar Turkey
129 B4 Serinova Turkey
128 C1 Serinyol Turkey
190 E3 Serio r. Italy
Sêrkang Xizang China see Nyainrong
136 C2 Serkhiv Ukr.
205 G5 Serkout mt. Alg.
Serle atoll Arch. des Tuamotu Fr. Polynesia see Pukarua
156 C4 Sermaises France
157 E4 Sermaize-les-Bains France
192 B2 Sermano Corse France
197 F5 Sermenin Macedonia
191 G4 Sermide Italy
160 B2 Sermoise-sur-Loire France
193 F3 Sermoneta Italy
160 C2 Sermoyer France
182 C4 Sernancelhe Port.
177 L3 Serne r. Ukr.
175 K4 Serniki Pol.
171 D4 Serno Ger.
135 J5 Sernovodsk Rus. Fed.
134 J4 Sernur Rus. Fed.
136 D2 Sernyky Ukr.
174 G2 Serock Kujawsko-Pomorskie Pol.
175 J3 Serock Mazowieckie Pol.
261 G3 Serodino Arg.
185 H3 Serón Spain
183 H3 Serón de Nájima Spain
164 C3 Serooskerke Neth.
186 D3 Seròs Spain
130 H4 Serov Rus. Fed.
212 E4 Serowe Botswana
184 C3 Serpa Port.
Serpa Pinto Angola see Menongue
225 G3 Serpent r. Que. Can.
87 B7 Serpentine r. W.A. Austr.
82 B2 Serpentine Lakes salt flat S.A. Austr.
247 G5 Serpent's Mouth sea chan. Trin. and Tob./Venez.
182 B4 Serpins Port.
187 C6 Serpis r. Spain
136 E4 Serpneve Ukr.
139 K4 Serpukhov Rus. Fed.
157 F5 Serqueux France
159 G2 Serquigny France
257 G4 Serra Brazil
192 A4 Serra r. Sardegna Italy
187 C5 Serra Spain
193 H3 Serracapriola Italy
183 F3 Serrada Spain
191 I5 Serra de'Conti Italy
182 B2 Serra de Outes Spain
216 □1a Serra de Santa Barbara vol. Terceira Azores
194 C5 Serradifalco Sicilia Italy
192 A3 Serra-di-Ferro Corse France
182 D5 Serradilla Spain
182 D4 Serradilla del Arroyo Spain
257 G2 Serra dos Aimorés Brazil
256 D3 Serra do Salitre Brazil
Sérrai Greece see Serres
192 A5 Serramanna Sardegna Italy
191 F4 Serramazzoni Italy
256 D4 Serrana Brazil
246 C4 Serranilla Bank sea feature Caribbean Sea
183 F4 Serranillos Spain
256 A3 Serranópolis Brazil
190 D4 Serra Riccò Italy
195 F4 Serra San Bruno Italy
191 I5 Serra San Quirico Italy
254 F3 Serra Talhada Brazil
191 H5 Serravalle San Marino
193 E1 Serravalle di Chienti Italy
190 D4 Serravalle Scrivia Italy
156 D3 Serre r. France
193 H4 Serre Italy
161 E4 Serre-Chevalier France
182 E5 Serrejón Spain
192 A5 Serrenti Sardegna Italy
Serrera, Pic de la mt. Andorra see Serrère, Pic de
186 E2 Serrère, Pic de mt. Andorra
161 D4 Serres France
198 C1 Serres Greece
163 B5 Serres-Castet France
216 □1a Serreta Terceira Azores
192 B5 Serri Sardegna Italy
192 A2 Serriera Corse France
160 D3 Serrière-de-Briord France
161 C3 Serrières France
172 A2 Serrig Ger.
254 F4 Serrinha Brazil
254 F3 Serrita Brazil
257 F3 Sêrro Brazil
183 E4 Serrota mt. Spain
162 C3 Sers France
195 F3 Sersale Italy
182 B5 Sertã Port.
254 F4 Sertânia Brazil
256 B5 Sertanópolis Brazil
256 A3 Sertão de Camapuã reg. Brazil
256 D4 Sertãozinho Brazil
108 B1 Sêrtar Sichuan China
139 H1 Sertolovo Rus. Fed.
93 D4 Serua vol. Maluku Indon.
213 E4 Serule Botswana
95 F3 Seruyan r. Indon.
138 F4 Servach r. Belarus
157 G5 Servance France
161 B4 Serverette France
198 C1 Servia Greece
161 B5 Servian France
193 F1 Servigliano Italy
186 D4 Servol r. Spain
158 E3 Servon-sur-Vilaine France
160 E3 Servoz France
108 A1 Sêrxu Sichuan China
156 E3 Sery France
186 C3 Sesa Spain
95 G2 Sesayap r. Indon.
227 G1 Sesekinika Ont. Can.
Sesel country Indian Ocean see Seychelles
183 G4 Seseña Spain
212 B3 Sesfontein Namibia
114 C3 Seshachalam Hills India
209 E9 Sesheke Zambia
190 D3 Sesia r. Italy
184 A2 Sesimbra Port.
183 H2 Sesma Spain
209 D8 Sessa Angola
193 F3 Sessa Aurunca Italy
193 H4 Sessa Cilento Italy
187 G5 Ses Salines Spain
190 D3 Sessera r. Italy
169 F5 Seßlach Ger.
190 E4 Sesta Godano Italy
183 H1 Sestao Spain
191 H5 Sestino Italy
191 H2 Sesto Italy
191 H3 Sesto al Reghena Italy
190 D3 Sesto Calende Italy
193 G3 Sesto Campano Italy
191 G5 Sesto Fiorentino Italy
191 F4 Sestola Italy
190 E3 Sesto San Giovanni Italy
139 K3 Sestra r. Rus. Fed.
190 B4 Sestriere Italy
190 E4 Sestri Levante Italy
138 G1 Sestroretsk Rus. Fed.
188 E3 Sestrunj i. Croatia
192 B5 Sestu Sardegna Italy
138 D4 Šešupė r. Lith./Rus. Fed.
188 F3 Sesvete Croatia
186 D3 Set r. Spain
96 D4 Set, Phou mt. Laos
235 E2 Setauket NY U.S.A.
161 B5 Sète France
256 D6 Sete Barras Brazil
138 E4 Šetekšna r. Lith.
257 E3 Sete Lagoas Brazil
185 E4 Setenil Spain
140 L1 Setermoen Norway
142 B2 Setesdal val. Norway
102 □1 Seteuchi Japan
168 F2 Seth Ger.
Seti Georgia see Mestia
116 E3 Seti r. Nepal
117 F4 Seti r. Nepal
Setia Italy see Sezze
205 G1 Sétif Alg.
183 I4 Setiles Spain
203 G6 Setit r. Africa
104 D3 Seto Japan
103 F7 Seto-naikai sea Japan
191 G4 Setta r. Italy
204 D2 Settat Morocco
208 A5 Setté Cama Gabon
192 B5 Sette Fratelli, Monte dei mt. Sardegna Italy
190 D4 Settepani, Monte mt. Italy
190 C3 Settimo Torinese Italy
190 C3 Settimo Vittone Italy
149 G3 Settle North Yorkshire, England U.K.
84 D3 Settlement Creek r. Qld Austr.
216 □2c Settlement of Edinburgh Tristan da Cunha S. Atlantic Ocean
257 F2 Setúbal r. Brazil
184 B2 Setúbal Port.
184 B2 Setúbal admin. dist. Port.
184 A2 Setúbal, Baía de b. Port.
257 F2 Setubinha Brazil
Seu i. Vanuatu see Hiu
173 F2 Seubersdorf in der Oberpfalz Ger.
162 B3 Seudre r. France
162 B3 Seugne r. France
192 B5 Seui Sardegna Italy
157 F4 Seuil-d'Argonne France
223 M5 Seul, Lac l. Ont. Can.
169 F4 Seulingen Ger.
159 F2 Seulles r. France
192 B5 Seulo Sardegna Italy
160 D1 Seurre France
137 H1 Sev r. Rus. Fed.
186 F3 Seva Spain
129 D3 Sevan Armenia
Sevan, Lake Armenia see Sevana Lich
Sevan, Ozero l. Armenia see Sevana Lich
129 D3 Sevana Lich l. Armenia
137 G5 Sevastopol' Ukr.
149 I3 Seven r. England U.K.
Seven Islands Que. Can. see Sept-Îles
87 C4 Seven Mile Creek r. W.A. Austr.
215 H3 Sevenoaks S. Africa
151 H3 Sevenoaks Kent, England U.K.
150 D3 Seven Sisters Neath Port Talbot, Wales U.K.
85 G5 Seventeen Seventy Qld Austr.
Seventy Mile House B.C. Can. see 70 Mile House
165 F3 Sevenum Neth.
234 B3 Seven Valleys PA U.S.A.
182 C3 Sever Port.
161 B4 Sévérac-le-Château France
182 B4 Sever do Vouga Port.
139 L4 Severka r. Rus. Fed.
83 G2 Severn r. N.S.W. Austr.
224 C2 Severn r. Ont. Can.
81 D5 Severn mt. South I. N.Z.
214 D2 Severn S. Africa
150 E3 Severn r. England/Wales U.K.
234 B3 Severn MD U.S.A.
232 E6 Severn NC U.S.A.
234 B4 Severn r. MD U.S.A.
234 B3 Severna Park MD U.S.A.
134 H2 Severnaya Dvina r. Rus. Fed.
134 L3 Severnaya Mylva r. Rus. Fed.
129 D2 Severnaya Osetiya, Respublika aut. rep. Rus. Fed.
130 H3 Severnaya Sos'va r. Rus. Fed.
131 L1 Severnaya Zemlya is Rus. Fed.
150 E3 Severn Beach South Gloucestershire, England U.K.
135 K5 Severnoye Rus. Fed.
137 I2 Severnyy Belgorodskaya Oblast' Rus. Fed.
139 K3 Severnyy Moskovskaya Oblast' Rus. Fed.
134 N2 Severnyy Respublika Komi Rus. Fed.
175 H1 Severnyy, Mys pt Rus. Fed.
131 S3 Severnyy Anyuyskiy Khrebet mts Rus. Fed.
120 D3 Severnyy Chink Ustyurta esc. Kazakh.
121 G1 Severnyy Kazakhstan admin. div. Kazakh.
134 K4 Severnyy Kommunar Rus. Fed.
Severnyy Suchan Rus. Fed. see Uglekamensk
134 L3 Severnyy Ural mts Rus. Fed.
99 I1 Severobaykal'sk Rus. Fed.
131 M4 Severo-Baykalskoye Nagor'ye mts Rus. Fed.
110 D1 Severo-Chuyskiy Khrebet mts Rus. Fed.
Severodonetsk Ukr. see Syeverodonets'k
134 G2 Severodvinsk Arkhangel'skaya Oblast' Rus. Fed.
Severo-Kazakhstanskaya Oblast' admin. div. Kazakh. see Severnyy Kazakhstan
131 Q4 Severo-Kuril'sk Kuril'skiye O-va Rus. Fed.
140 P1 Severomorsk Rus. Fed.
134 G3 Severoonezhsk Rus. Fed.
Severo-Osetinskaya A.S.S.R. aut. rep. Rus. Fed. see Severnaya Osetiya, Respublika
131 L2 Severo-Sibirskaya Nizmennost' lowland Rus. Fed.
134 L3 Severoural'sk Rus. Fed.
131 K3 Severo-Yeniseyskiy Rus. Fed.
139 L4 Severo-Zadonsk Rus. Fed.
Seversk Ukr. see Sivers'k
135 G7 Severskaya Rus. Fed.
135 H7 Severskiy Donets r. Rus. Fed.
Severskiy Donets r. Ukr. see Sivers'kyy Donets'
158 E2 Sèves r. France
155 I4 Seveso Italy
190 E3 Seveso r. Italy
179 F1 Ševětín Czech Rep.
241 K2 Sevier UT U.S.A.
241 K2 Sevier r. UT U.S.A.
231 D5 Sevierville TN U.S.A.
158 D3 Sévignac France
163 B5 Sévignacq France
156 E3 Sévigny-Waleppe France
250 C3 Sevilla Col.
184 E3 Sevilla Spain
184 E3 Sevilla prov. Andalucía Spain
183 F4 Sevilla la Nueva Spain
Seville Spain see Sevilla
183 F5 Sevilleja de la Jara Spain
197 G4 Sevlievo Bulg.
Sevlyush Ukr. see Vynohradiv
188 E2 Sevnica Slovenia
196 D4 Sevojno Srbija Yugo.
162 A1 Sèvre Nantaise r. France
162 A2 Sèvre Niortaise r. France
160 E3 Sévrier France
160 D2 Sevron r. France
137 H1 Sevsk Rus. Fed.
114 B2 Sewand r. India
116 C3 Sewani Haryana India
220 D3 Seward AK U.S.A.
226 C4 Seward IL U.S.A.
236 D3 Seward NE U.S.A.
232 D4 Seward PA U.S.A.
262 T2 Seward Mountains Antarctica
220 B3 Seward Peninsula AK U.S.A.
260 B4 Sewell Chile
234 C3 Sewell NJ U.S.A.
222 C4 Sewell Inlet B.C. Can.
172 B3 Sexau Ger.
Sexi Spain see Almuñécar
222 G4 Sexsmith Alta Can.
242 D3 Sextín r. Mex.
123 E3 Seyah Band Koh mts Afgh.
243 H5 Seybaplaya Mex.
217 □2 Seychelles country Indian Ocean
163 C4 Seyches France
171 D4 Seyda Ger.
199 G2 Seydi r. Turkey
123 E2 Seydi Turkm.
126 C3 Seydişehir Turkey
158 E2 Seye r. France
Seyhan Turkey see Adana
126 D3 Seyhan r. Turkey
199 G2 Seyitgazi Turkey
199 F2 Seyitömer Turkey
137 I2 Seym Rus. Fed.
137 H2 Seym r. Rus. Fed./Ukr.
131 Q3 Seymchan Rus. Fed.
199 F1 Seymen Turkey
83 F4 Seymour Vic. Austr.
215 F5 Seymour S. Africa
235 E1 Seymour CT U.S.A.
230 C4 Seymour IN U.S.A.
237 D5 Seymour TX U.S.A.
84 C5 Seymour Range mts N.T. Austr.
161 E4 Seyne France
161 C4 Seynes France
160 E3 Seynod France
Seypan i. N. Mariana Is see Saipan
160 D3 Seyssel France
163 D5 Seysses France
160 C3 Seysseuel France
161 D3 Seyssins France
197 H5 Seytan r. Turkey
188 D3 Sežana Slovenia
156 D4 Sézanne France
215 H4 Sezela S. Africa
139 J4 Sezha r. Rus. Fed.
176 D2 Sezimovo Ústí Czech Rep.
193 F3 Sezze Italy
197 G3 Sfântu Gheorghe Romania
197 I3 Sfântu Gheorghe Romania
205 H2 Sfax Tunisia
198 C1 Sfendami Greece
198 C1 Sfikia, Limni resr Greece
Sfîntu Gheorghe Romania see Sfântu Gheorghe
Sgiersch Pol. see Zgierz
146 B3 Sgiogarstaigh Western Isles, Scotland U.K.
146 C4 Sgorr Ruadh hill Scotland U.K.
164 D3 's-Gravendeel Neth.
164 D2 's-Gravenhage Neth.
165 C3 's-Gravenpolder Neth.
165 E4 's-Gravenvoeren Belgium
164 D3 's-Gravenzande Neth.
193 F3 Sgurgola Italy
146 C4 Sgurr a'Chaorachain mt. Scotland U.K.
146 D4 Sgurr a'Choire Ghlais mt. Scotland U.K.
146 B4 Sgurr Alasdair hill Scotland U.K.
146 D4 Sgurr a'Mhuilinn hill Scotland U.K.
146 C5 Sgurr Dhomhnuill hill Scotland U.K.
146 C4 Sgurr Fhuaran mt. Scotland U.K.
146 C4 Sgurr Mor mt. Scotland U.K.
146 C4 Sgurr na Ciche mt. Scotland U.K.
107 G4 Sha r. China
107 F5 Shaanxi prov. China
Shaartuz Tajik. see Shahrtuz
Shaba admin. reg. Dem. Rep. Congo see Katanga
Shabani Zimbabwe see Zvishavane
Shabbaz Uzbek. see Beruni
210 E4 Shabeellaha Dhexe admin. reg. Somalia
210 D4 Shabeellaha Hoose admin. reg. Somalia
135 G7 Shabel'sk Rus. Fed.
122 A2 Shabestar Iran
197 I4 Shabla Bulg.
139 J5 Shablykino Rus. Fed.
208 E5 Shabunda Dem. Rep. Congo
124 D5 Shabwah Yemen
124 D5 Shabwah governorate Yemen
110 B4 Shache Xinjiang China
Shacheng Hebei China see Huailai
263 L1 Shackleton Coast Antarctica
262 V1 Shackleton Range mts Antarctica
123 F5 Shadadkot Pak.
108 D2 Shadaogou Hubei China
232 B5 Shade OH U.S.A.
122 B4 Shādegān Iran
234 C1 Shades Glen PA U.S.A.
130 H4 Shadrinsk Rus. Fed.
232 D5 Shadwell VA U.S.A.
238 B3 Shady Grove OR U.S.A.
234 B4 Shady Side MD U.S.A.
232 C6 Shady Spring WV U.S.A.
263 K2 Shafer Peak Antarctica
122 D2 Shafi'abad Iran
120 F4 Shafirkan Uzbek.
120 C1 Shafranovo Rus. Fed.
Shafrikan Uzbek. see Shafirkan
240 H4 Shafter CA U.S.A.

149 J4 **Sibsey** *Lincolnshire, England* U.K.
95 E2 **Sibu** *Sarawak* Malaysia
92 B5 **Sibuco** Phil.
92 B5 **Sibuguey** *r.* Phil.
92 B5 **Sibuguey Bay** Phil.
208 C3 **Sibut** C.A.R.
92 B3 **Sibuyan** *i.* Phil.
197 F2 **Sic** Romania
222 G5 **Sicamous** *B.C.* Can.
92 B2 **Sicapoo** *mt. Luzon* Phil.
252 D4 **Sicasica** Bol.
92 B4 **Sicayac** Phil.
Sicca Veneria Tunisia *see* **Le Kef**
Sicheng *Guangxi* China *see* **Lingyun**
97 B5 **Sichon** Thai.
108 B2 **Sichuan** *prov.* China
108 C2 **Sichuan Pendi** *basin Sichuan* China
194 D5 **Sicilia** *admin. reg.* Italy
194 D4 **Sicilia** *i.* Italy
194 B5 **Sicilian Channel** Italy/Tunisia
Sicily *i.* Italy *see* **Sicilia**
174 E4 **Siciny** Pol.
234 D3 **Sicklerville** *NJ* U.S.A.
169 F3 **Sickte** Ger.
252 C3 **Sicuani** Peru
177 K5 **Şicula** Romania
194 C5 **Siculiana** *Sicilia* Italy
177 I3 **Šid** Slovakia
196 D3 **Šid** *Vojvodina, Srbija* Yugo.
150 D4 **Sidbury** *Devon, England* U.K.
164 F1 **Siddeburen** Neth.
116 C5 **Siddhapur** *Gujarat* India
Siddharthanagar Nepal *see* **Bhairawa**
114 C2 **Siddipet** *Andhra Prad.* India
140 L3 **Sidensjö** Sweden
206 D4 **Sidéradougou** Burkina
195 F4 **Siderno** Italy
214 D5 **Sidesaviwa** S. Africa
150 D4 **Sidford** *Devon, England* U.K.
116 E4 **Sidhauli** *Uttar Prad.* India
116 E4 **Sidhi** *Madh. Prad.* India
Sidhirókastron Greece *see* **Sidirokastro**
Sidhpur *Gujarat* India *see* **Siddhapur**
205 F2 **Sidi Aïssa** Alg.
202 E2 **Sidi Barrani** Egypt
205 E2 **Sidi Bel Abbès** Alg.
204 C2 **Sidi Bennour** Morocco
Sidi Bou Sa'id Tunisia *see* **Sidi Bouzid**
205 H2 **Sidi Bouzid** Tunisia
204 C3 **Sidi Ifni** Morocco
204 D2 **Sidi Kacem** Morocco
94 B2 **Sidikalang** *Sumatera* Indon.
205 G2 **Sidi Khaled** Alg.
204 B5 **Sidi Mhamed** *well* Western Sahara
205 G2 **Sidi Okba** Alg.
198 C1 **Sidirokastro** Greece
204 C2 **Sidi-Smaïl** Morocco
146 E5 **Sidlaw Hills** *Scotland* U.K.
151 H4 **Sidley** *East Sussex, England* U.K.
262 P1 **Sidley, Mount** Antarctica
150 D4 **Sidmouth** *Devon, England* U.K.
85 E2 **Sidmouth, Cape** *Qld* Austr.
226 C2 **Sidnaw** *MI* U.S.A.
222 F5 **Sidney** *B.C.* Can.
236 E3 **Sidney** *IA* U.S.A.
238 F2 **Sidney** *MT* U.S.A.
236 C3 **Sidney** *NE* U.S.A.
233 F3 **Sidney** *NY* U.S.A.
232 A4 **Sidney** *OH* U.S.A.
231 D5 **Sidney Lanier, Lake** *GA* U.S.A.
214 E3 **Sidney-on-Vaal** S. Africa
206 D4 **Sido** Mali
95 F4 **Sidoarjo** *Jawa Timur* Indon.
163 E5 **Sidobre** *reg.* France
Sidon Lebanon *see* **Saïda**
134 H4 **Sidorovo** Rus. Fed.
175 L2 **Sidra** *r.* Pol.
255 B7 **Sidrolândia** Brazil
215 H2 **Sidvokodvo** Swaziland
215 G4 **Sidwadweni** S. Africa
121 G4 **Sidzhak** Uzbek.
174 F5 **Sidzina** Pol.
140 M1 **Siebejokka** *r.* Norway
164 F3 **Siebengewald** Neth.
171 E4 **Siebenlehn** Ger.
174 D4 **Siecieborzyce** Pol.
175 J4 **Sieciechów** Pol.
168 D3 **Siedenburg** Ger.
175 J5 **Siedlanka** Pol.
175 K3 **Siedlce** Pol.
174 E3 **Siedlec** Pol.
174 D4 **Siedlisko** *Lubuskie* Pol.
174 E3 **Siedlisko** *Wielkopolskie* Pol.
175 L4 **Siedliszcze** *Lubelskie* Pol.
175 L4 **Siedliszcze** *Lubelskie* Pol.
169 C5 **Sieg** *r.* Ger.
169 C5 **Siegburg** Ger.
169 D5 **Siegen** Ger.
173 F3 **Siegenburg** Ger.
179 H3 **Siegendorf im Burgenland** Austria
179 H3 **Sieggraben** Austria
179 H2 **Sieghartskirchen** Austria
173 G4 **Siegsdorf** Ger.
168 F2 **Siek** Ger.
171 G4 **Siekierczyn** Pol.
175 L4 **Sielec** Pol.
177 I3 **Sielnica** Slovakia
171 F4 **Sielow** Ger.
175 L3 **Siemianówka** Pol.
175 L3 **Siemianówka, Jezioro** *l.* Pol.
175 K3 **Siemiatycze** Pol.
175 K4 **Siemień** Pol.
174 G4 **Siemkowice** Pol.
97 C4 **Siĕmréab** Cambodia
Siem Reap Cambodia *see* **Siĕmréab**
174 D1 **Siemyśl** Pol.
Si'en *Guangxi* China *see* **Huanjiang**
191 G5 **Siena** Italy
191 G5 **Siena** *prov. Toscana* Italy
175 K5 **Sieniawa** Pol.
158 E2 **Sienne** *r.* France
175 J3 **Siennica** Pol.
175 J4 **Sienno** Pol.
175 H6 **Siepraw** Pol.
174 G4 **Sieradz** Pol.
174 G5 **Sieraków** Pol.
174 E3 **Sieraków** Pol.
175 H3 **Sierakówek** Pol.
174 F1 **Sierakowice** Pol.
157 G3 **Sierck-les-Bains** France
157 H5 **Sierentz** France
168 F1 **Sierksdorf** Ger.
179 H2 **Sierndorf** Austria
179 F2 **Sierning** Austria
174 F4 **Sieroszewice** Pol.
175 H3 **Sierpc** Pol.
175 H3 **Sierpienica** *r.* Pol.
239 F6 **Sierra Blanca** *TX* U.S.A.
261 G5 **Sierra Chica** Arg.
184 D1 **Sierra de Fuentes** Spain
Sierra del Gistral *mts* Spain *see* **Xistral, Serra do**
186 C2 **Sierra de Luna** Spain
185 F3 **Sierra de Yeguas** Spain
187 D4 **Sierra Engarcerán** Spain
259 D6 **Sierra Grande** Arg.
206 C4 **Sierra Leone** *country* Africa
264 H5 **Sierra Leone Basin** *sea feature* N. Atlantic Ocean
264 H5 **Sierra Leone Rise** *sea feature* N. Atlantic Ocean
240 G4 **Sierra Madre Mountains** *CA* U.S.A.
242 E3 **Sierra Mojada** Mex.
240 G2 **Sierraville** *CA* U.S.A.
241 L6 **Sierra Vista** *AZ* U.S.A.
190 C2 **Sierre** Switz.
185 H3 **Sierro** Spain
185 H3 **Sierro** *r.* Spain
171 C4 **Siersleben** Ger.
138 D4 **Siesartis** *r.* Lith.
138 E4 **Siesartis** *r.* Lith.
187 C5 **Siete Aguas** Spain
183 E3 **Siete Iglesias de Trabancos** Spain
170 D2 **Sietow** Ger.
197 G2 **Şieu** Romania
197 G2 **Şieu** *r.* Romania
191 G5 **Sieve** *r.* Italy
170 D3 **Sieversdorf** Ger.
168 E1 **Sieverstedt** Ger.
140 N3 **Sievi** Fin.
175 H5 **Siewierz** Pol.
108 C4 **Sifang Ling** *mts* China
206 D5 **Sifié** Côte d'Ivoire
198 D3 **Sifnos** *i.* Greece
205 E2 **Sig** Alg.
139 I3 **Sig, Ozero** *l.* Rus. Fed.
79 □1a **Sigatoka** *Viti Levu* Fiji
77 I3 **Sigave** Wallis and Futuna Is
161 A5 **Sigean** France
170 C2 **Siggelkow** Ger.
149 I4 **Sigglesthorne** *East Riding of Yorkshire, England* U.K.
221 M2 **Sigguup Nunaa** *pen.* Greenland
197 F2 **Sighetu Marmaţiei** Romania
197 G2 **Sighişoara** Romania
191 H5 **Sigillo** Italy
114 D5 **Sigiriya** Sri Lanka
129 F3 **Sığırlı** Azer.
94 A1 **Sigli** *Sumatera* Indon.
140 □C2 **Siglufjörður** Iceland
92 B4 **Sigma** Phil.
172 D3 **Sigmaringen** Ger.
172 D3 **Sigmaringendorf** Ger.
179 G2 **Sigmundsherberg** Austria
191 G5 **Signa** Italy
173 G2 **Signalberg** *hill* Ger.
165 F4 **Signal de Botrange** *hill* Belgium
161 D5 **Signal de la Ste-Baume** *mt.* France
161 B4 **Signal de Mailhebiau** *mt.* France
161 B4 **Signal de Randon** *mt.* France
160 C3 **Signal de St-André** *hill* France
162 D2 **Signal de Sauvagnac** *hill* France
162 D3 **Signal du Pic** *hill* France
159 F3 **Signal du Viviers** *hill* France
241 J5 **Signal Peak** *AZ* U.S.A.
190 C2 **Signau** Switz.
161 D5 **Signes** France
156 E3 **Signy-l'Abbaye** France
156 E3 **Signy-le-Petit** France
215 G4 **Sigoga** S. Africa
162 B3 **Sigogne** France
163 C4 **Sigoulès** France
236 E3 **Sigourney** *IA* U.S.A.
264 C4 **Sigsbee Deep** *sea feature* G. of Mexico
143 G2 **Sigtuna** Sweden
243 I6 **Siguatepeque** Hond.
182 B2 **Sigüeiro** Spain
183 H3 **Sigüenza** Spain
163 D6 **Siguer** *r.* France
186 B2 **Sigües** Spain
206 C4 **Siguiri** Guinea
138 E3 **Sigulda** Latvia
241 L2 **Sigurd** *UT* U.S.A.
97 C5 **Sihanoukville** Cambodia
116 E5 **Sihawa** *Madh. Prad.* India
177 I2 **Sihelné** Slovakia
109 F1 **Sihong** *Jiangsu* China
116 E5 **Sihora** *Madh. Prad.* India
116 D5 **Sihora** *Mahar.* India
Sihou *Shandong* China *see* **Changdao**
252 A2 **Sihuas** Peru
109 E4 **Sihui** *Guangdong* China
141 M3 **Siikainen** Fin.
140 N2 **Siikajoki** Fin.
140 N2 **Siikajoki** *r.* Fin.
140 N3 **Siilinjärvi** Fin.
127 F3 **Siirt** Turkey
78 □4a **Siis** *i. Chuuk* Micronesia
Sijjak Uzbek. *see* **Sidzhak**
165 C3 **Sijsele** Belgium
94 C3 **Sijunjung** *Sumatera* Indon.
116 B5 **Sika** *Gujarat* India
Sikaka Saudi Arabia *see* **Sakākah**
116 D4 **Sikandra Rao** *Uttar Prad.* India
222 F3 **Sikanni Chief** *B.C.* Can.
222 F3 **Sikanni Chief** *r. B.C.* Can.
116 C4 **Sikar** *Rajasthan* India
123 G3 **Sikaram** *mt.* Afgh.
206 D4 **Sikasso** Mali
206 D4 **Sikasso** *admin. reg.* Mali
198 C1 **Sikea** *Kentriki Makedonia* Greece
Sikéa Greece *see* **Sykea**
177 H4 **Sikenica** *r.* Slovakia
237 F4 **Sikeston** *MO* U.S.A.
177 H5 **Sik-hegy** *hill* Hungary
100 E4 **Sikhote-Alin'** *mts* Rus. Fed.
198 D3 **Sikinos** *i.* Greece
188 G3 **Sikirevci** Croatia
117 G4 **Sikkim** *state* India
177 H6 **Siklós** Hungary
175 H3 **Sikórz** Pol.
140 L2 **Siksjö** Sweden
117 F4 **Sikta** *Bihar* India
Sikuaishi *Liaoning* China *see* **Changhai**
182 C2 **Sil** *r.* Spain
92 C4 **Silago** Phil.
138 D4 **Šilalė** Lith.
191 F2 **Silandro** Italy
192 A4 **Silanus** *Sardegna* Italy
244 D3 **Silao** Mex.
237 F6 **Silas** *AL* U.S.A.
94 A1 **Silawaih Agam** *vol.* Indon.
92 B4 **Silay** Phil.
188 E3 **Silba** *i.* Croatia
168 E2 **Silberberg** *hill* Ger.
168 E1 **Silberstedt** Ger.
117 H4 **Silchar** *Assam* India
191 H3 **Sile** *r.* Italy
199 F1 **Şile** Turkey
151 F2 **Sileby** *Leicestershire, England* U.K.
149 F3 **Silecroft** *Cumbria, England* U.K.
138 F4 **Silene** Latvia
190 D2 **Silenen** Switz.
165 D4 **Silenrieux** Belgium
231 E5 **Siler City** *NC* U.S.A.
114 D2 **Sileru** *r.* India
185 H2 **Siles** Spain
174 E4 **Silesia** *reg.* Europe
Sileti Kazakh. *see* **Seletinskoye**
121 H1 **Sileti** *r.* Kazakh.
121 H1 **Siletiteniz, Ozero** *salt l.* Kazakh.
158 C3 **Silfiac** France
Silgadi Nepal *see* **Silgarhi**
116 E3 **Silgarhi** Nepal
117 H4 **Silghat** *Assam* India
217 □2a **Silhouette** *i. Inner Islands* Seychelles
205 H1 **Siliana** Tunisia
189 B8 **Siliana** *admin. div.* Tunisia
126 D3 **Silifke** Turkey
192 A4 **Siligo** *Sardegna* Italy
Siliguri *W. Bengal* India *see* **Shiliguri**
177 K5 **Şilindia** Romania
111 E6 **Siling Co** *salt l.* China
116 D4 **Silipur** *Madh. Prad.* India
192 A5 **Siliqua** *Sardegna* Italy
192 A4 **Silis** *r. Sardegna* Italy
78 □2 **Silisili, Mount** Samoa
Silistat Turkey *see* **Bozkır**
197 G3 **Siliştea** Romania
197 G3 **Siliştea Nouă** Romania
197 H3 **Silistra** Bulg.
Silistria Bulg. *see* **Silistra**
199 F1 **Silivri** Turkey
142 C2 **Siljan** Norway
141 K3 **Siljan** *l.* Sweden
143 F1 **Siljansnäs** Sweden
142 C3 **Silkeborg** Denmark
85 F3 **Silkwood** *Qld* Austr.
234 B1 **Silkworth** *PA* U.S.A.
178 C3 **Sill** *r.* Austria
187 C5 **Silla** Spain
138 F2 **Sillamäe** Estonia
190 F4 **Sillano** Italy
161 E5 **Sillans-la-Cascade** France
191 G4 **Sillaro** *r.* Italy
126 D3 **Sille** Turkey
182 B2 **Silleda** Spain
159 F3 **Sillé-le-Guillaume** France
156 E3 **Sillery** France
117 F5 **Silli** *Bihar* India
178 D4 **Sillian** Austria
116 C5 **Sillod** *Mahar.* India
149 F3 **Silloth** *Cumbria, England* U.K.
237 E4 **Siloam Springs** *AR* U.S.A.
215 H2 **Silobela** S. Africa
184 D3 **Silos de Calañas** Spain
134 M2 **Silovayakha** *r.* Rus. Fed.
186 F3 **Sils** Spain
190 E2 **Sils** Switz.
237 E6 **Silsbee** *TX* U.S.A.
149 H4 **Silsden** *West Yorkshire, England* U.K.
169 F4 **Silstedt** Ger.
138 F1 **Siltakylä** Fin.
123 E5 **Silūp** *r.* Iran
138 C4 **Šilutė** Lith.
215 H3 **Silutshana** S. Africa
257 F5 **Silva Jardim** Brazil
127 F3 **Silvan** Turkey
256 C2 **Silvânia** Brazil
190 E2 **Silvaplana** Switz.
182 B3 **Silvares** *Braga* Port.
182 C4 **Silvares** *Castelo Branco* Port.
116 C5 **Silvassa** *Dadra* India
184 B2 **Silveiras** Port.
143 G3 **Silverån** *r.* Sweden
247 E2 **Silver Bank** *sea feature* Turks and Caicos Is
246 E2 **Silver Bank Passage** Turks and Caicos Is
226 B2 **Silver Bay** *MN* U.S.A.
222 B2 **Silver City** *Y.T.* Can.
239 E5 **Silver City** *NM* U.S.A.
240 H2 **Silver City** *NV* U.S.A.
232 D3 **Silver Creek** *NY* U.S.A.
241 L4 **Silver Creek** *r. AZ* U.S.A.
80 E2 **Silverdale** *North I.* N.Z.
149 G3 **Silverdale** *Lancashire, England* U.K.
234 C2 **Silverdale** *PA* U.S.A.
151 H3 **Silver End** *Essex, England* U.K.
80 E3 **Silverhope** *North I.* N.Z.
226 C1 **Silver Islet** *Ont.* Can.
238 B3 **Silver Lake** *OR* U.S.A.
226 C3 **Silver Lake** *WI* U.S.A.
147 C4 **Silvermine Mountains** *hills* Rep. of Ireland
147 C4 **Silvermines** Rep. of Ireland
240 I3 **Silver Peak Range** *mts NV* U.S.A.
234 B4 **Silver Spring** *MD* U.S.A.
240 H2 **Silver Springs** *NV* U.S.A.
151 F2 **Silverstone** *Northamptonshire, England* U.K.
214 D3 **Silver Streams** S. Africa
222 E5 **Silverthrone Mountain** *B.C.* Can.
233 B1 **Silvertip Mountain** *B.C.* Can.
82 E2 **Silverton** *N.S.W.* Austr.
222 G5 **Silverton** *B.C.* Can.
150 D4 **Silverton** *Devon, England* U.K.
239 F4 **Silverton** *CO* U.S.A.
235 D2 **Silverton** *NJ* U.S.A.
237 C5 **Silverton** *TX* U.S.A.
227 F3 **Silver Water** *Ont.* Can.
251 G5 **Silves** Brazil
184 B3 **Silves** Port.
193 G2 **Silvi** Italy
250 B4 **Silvia** Col.
238 C3 **Silvies** *r. OR* U.S.A.
243 H5 **Silvituc** Mex.
190 F2 **Silvretta Gruppe** *mts* Switz.
178 B4 **Silvrettahorn** *mt.* Austria
129 F3 **Şilyan** Azer.
178 B3 **Silz** Austria
134 L5 **Sim** Rus. Fed.
134 L5 **Sim** *r.* Rus. Fed.
217 □3 **Sima** Comoros
139 L3 **Sima** Rus. Fed.
192 A5 **Simala** *Sardegna* Italy
183 F3 **Simancas** Spain
177 K5 **Şimand** Romania
160 C2 **Simandre** France
136 E2 **Simanichy** Belarus
198 C1 **Simantra** Greece
108 B4 **Simao** *Yunnan* China
254 F4 **Simão Dias** Brazil
127 G4 **Şīmareh, Rūdkhāneh-ye** *r.* Iran
117 F4 **Simaria** *Bihar* India
116 E4 **Simaria** *Madh. Prad.* India
187 C5 **Simat de la Valdigna** Spain
199 F2 **Simav** Turkey
199 F2 **Simav Dağları** *mts* Turkey
192 A5 **Simaxis** *Sardegna* Italy
173 G3 **Simbach** Ger.
173 H3 **Simbach am Inn** Ger.
195 F4 **Simbario** Italy
Simbirsk Rus. Fed. *see* **Ul'yanovsk**
78 □6 **Simbo** *i. New Georgia Is* Solomon Is
193 F3 **Simbruini, Monti** *mts* Italy
224 D5 **Simcoe** *Ont.* Can.
224 E4 **Simcoe, Lake** *Ont.* Can.
117 F5 **Simdega** *Bihar* India
141 L3 **Simeå** Sweden
203 H6 **Simēn Mountains** Eth.
197 G4 **Simeonovgrad** Bulg.
195 F4 **Simeri** *r.* Italy
197 F3 **Simeria** Romania
195 F4 **Simeri-Crichi** Italy
194 E5 **Simeto** *r. Sicilia* Italy
94 B2 **Simeuluë** *i.* Indon.
137 H5 **Simferopol'** Ukr.
Sími *i.* Greece *see* **Symi**
177 L4 **Şimian** Romania
161 D5 **Simiane-la-Rotonde** France
178 B4 **Similaun** *mt.* Austria/Italy
177 J2 **Siminy** *mt.* Slovakia
197 F5 **Simitli** Bulg.
240 H4 **Simi Valley** *CA* U.S.A.
Simla *Hima. Prad.* India *see* **Shimla**
239 F4 **Simla** *CO* U.S.A.
142 E3 **Simlångsdalen** Sweden
197 F2 **Şimleu Silvaniei** Romania
190 C2 **Simme** *r.* Switz.
173 F2 **Simmelsdorf** Ger.
169 B5 **Simmerath** Ger.
172 B2 **Simmern (Hunsrück)** Ger.
237 F6 **Simmesport** *LA* U.S.A.
246 D2 **Simm's** *Long I.* Bahamas
238 E2 **Simms** *MT* U.S.A.
138 D4 **Simnas** Lith.
140 N2 **Simo** Fin.
222 G4 **Simonette** *r. Alta* Can.
223 K4 **Simonhouse** *Man.* Can.
177 K3 **Šimonka** *mt.* Slovakia
232 C4 **Simons** *OH* U.S.A.
150 D3 **Simonsbath** *Somerset, England* U.K.
168 D1 **Simonsberg** Ger.
214 B6 **Simon's Town** S. Africa
164 F1 **Simonszand** *i.* Neth.
177 H5 **Simontornya** Hungary
222 E5 **Simoom Sound** *B.C.* Can.
Simoon Sound *B.C.* Can. *see* **Simoom Sound**
163 C5 **Simorre** France
94 D3 **Simpang** *Sumatera* Indon.
165 E4 **Simpelveld** Neth.
254 E3 **Simplício Mendes** Brazil
190 D2 **Simplon** Switz.
190 D2 **Simplon Pass** Switz.
223 J5 **Simpson** *Sask.* Can.
238 E1 **Simpson** *MT* U.S.A.
234 C1 **Simpson** *PA* U.S.A.
84 D5 **Simpson Desert** *N.T.* Austr.
87 E5 **Simpson Hill** *hill W.A.* Austr.
240 I2 **Simpson Park Mountains** *NV* U.S.A.
234 B3 **Simpsonville** *MD* U.S.A.
231 D5 **Simpsonville** *SC* U.S.A.
143 F4 **Simrishamn** Sweden
131 Q5 **Simushir, Ostrov** *i. Kuril'skiye O-va* Rus. Fed.
114 E2 **Sina** *r.* India
Sīnā', Shibh Jazīrat *pen.* Egypt *see* **Sinai**
94 E2 **Sinabang** Indon.
179 G3 **Sinabelkirchen** Austria
94 E2 **Sinabung** *vol.* Indon.
203 G2 **Sinai** *pen.* Egypt
156 E3 **Sinai, Mont** *hill* France
197 G3 **Sinaia** Romania
Sinai al Janûbîya *governorate* Egypt *see* **Janûb Sînâ'**
Sinai ash Shamâlîya *governorate* Egypt *see* **Shamâl Sînâ'**
97 B4 **Si Nakarin Reservoir** Thai.
244 A2 **Sinaloa** *state* Mex.
191 G5 **Sinalunga** Italy
Sinancha Rus. Fed. *see* **Cheremshany**
101 C5 **Sinanju** N. Korea
198 A2 **Sinarades** *Ionioi Nisoi* Greece
187 B5 **Sinarcas** Spain
209 E9 **Sinazongwe** Zambia
96 A3 **Sinbaungwe** Myanmar
96 A2 **Sinbyugyun** Myanmar
126 E3 **Sincan** Turkey
199 G2 **Sincanlı** Turkey
250 C2 **Sincé** Col.
250 C2 **Sincelejo** Col.
156 D3 **Sinceny** France
Sinchu Taiwan *see* **T'aoyüan**
222 F4 **Sinclair Mills** *B.C.* Can.
146 E3 **Sinclair's Bay** *Scotland* U.K.
254 E5 **Sincora, Serra do** *hills* Brazil
116 D4 **Sind** *r.* India
Sind *prov.* Pak. *see* **Sindh**
100 F2 **Sinda** Rus. Fed.
142 D3 **Sindal** Denmark
92 B4 **Sindañgan** Phil.
94 D4 **Sindangbarang** *Jawa Barat* Indon.
208 A5 **Sindara** Gabon
116 B4 **Sindari** *Rajasthan* India
172 C3 **Sindelfingen** Ger.
114 C2 **Sindgi** *Karnataka* India
123 G5 **Sindh** *prov.* Pak.
114 C3 **Sindhnur** *Karnataka* India
Síndhos Greece *see* **Sindos**
117 F4 **Sindhuli Garhi** Nepal
Sindhulimadi Nepal *see* **Sindhuli Garhi**
138 E2 **Sindi** Estonia
116 D5 **Sindi** *Mahar.* India
192 A4 **Sindia** *Sardegna* Italy
199 F2 **Sındırgı** Turkey
114 C2 **Sindkhed** *Mahar.* India
116 C5 **Sindkheda** *Mahar.* India
Sîndominic Romania *see* **Sândominic**
134 J3 **Sindor** Rus. Fed.
198 C1 **Sindos** Greece
206 D4 **Sindou** Burkina
114 C2 **Sindphana** *r.* India
117 F5 **Sindri** *Bihar* India
123 G4 **Sind Sagar Doab** *lowland* Pak.
134 J4 **Sinegor'ye** Rus. Fed.
199 E1 **Sinekçi** Turkey
193 G2 **Sinello** *r.* Italy
Sinel'nikovo Ukr. *see* **Synel'nykove**
207 F4 **Sinendé** Benin
184 B3 **Sines** Port.
184 B3 **Sines, Cabo de** *c.* Port.
187 G5 **Sineu** Spain
139 J5 **Sinezerki** Rus. Fed.
206 D5 **Sinfra** Côte d'Ivoire
203 G6 **Singa** Sudan
116 E3 **Singahi** *Uttar Prad.* India
217 □3a **Singani** *Njazidja* Comoros
94 D2 **Singapore** *country* Asia
94 □ **Singapore** Sing.
94 □ **Singapore, Strait of** Indon./Sing.
Singapura *country* Asia *see* **Singapore**
Singapura Sing. *see* **Singapore**
95 F5 **Singaraja** *Bali* Indon.
114 D2 **Singareni** *Andhra Prad.* India
Singatoka *Viti Levu* Fiji *see* **Sigatoka**
Singave Wallis and Futuna Is *see* **Sigave**
97 C4 **Sing Buri** Thai.
172 C4 **Singen (Hohentwiel)** Ger.
Sîngeorgiu de Pădure Romania *see* **Sângeorgiu de Pădure**
Sîngeorz-Băi Romania *see* **Sângeorz-Băi**
136 E4 **Sîngera** Moldova
136 E4 **Sîngerei** Moldova
110 E3 **Singgimtay** *Xinjiang* China
227 G3 **Singhampton** *Ont.* Can.
169 C5 **Singhofen** Ger.
211 B6 **Singida** Tanz.
211 B6 **Singida** *admin. reg.* Tanz.
Singidunum *Srbija* Yugo. *see* **Beograd**
Singim *Xinjiang* China *see* **Singgimtay**
93 B4 **Singkang** *Sulawesi Selatan* Indon.
95 E2 **Singkawang** *Kalimantan Barat* Indon.
94 D3 **Singkep** *i.* Indon.
94 B2 **Singkil** *Sumatera* Indon.
83 G3 **Singleton** *N.S.W.* Austr.
84 C4 **Singleton** *N.T.* Austr.
84 B4 **Singleton, Mount** *hill N.T.* Austr.
87 C6 **Singleton, Mount** *hill W.A.* Austr.
116 C4 **Singoli** *Madh. Prad.* India
Singora Thai. *see* **Songkhla**
Sin'gosan N. Korea *see* **Kosan**
117 G4 **Singra** *Assam* India
96 A2 **Singu** Myanmar
245 E4 **Singuilucan** Mex.
197 G3 **Singureni** Romania
101 C5 **Sin'gye** N. Korea
124 D4 **Sinḩ, Jabal** *hill* Saudi Arabia
Sinhala *country* Asia *see* **Sri Lanka**
101 C4 **Sinhŭng** N. Korea
192 A5 **Sini** *Sardegna* Italy
178 C4 **Sinigo** *r.* Italy
92 B3 **Siniloan** Phil.
Sining *Qinghai* China *see* **Xining**
93 A3 **Sinio, Gunung** *mt.* Indon.
192 B4 **Siniscola** *Sardegna* Italy
197 G5 **Sini Vrŭkh** *mt.* Bulg.
137 J2 **Siniye Lipyagi** Rus. Fed.
120 E2 **Siniy-Shikhan** Rus. Fed.
188 F4 **Sinj** Croatia
93 B4 **Sinjai** *Sulawesi Selatan* Indon.
127 F3 **Sinjār** Iraq
127 F3 **Sinjār, Jabal** *mt.* Iraq
203 H5 **Sinkat** Sudan
Sinkiang *aut. reg.* China *see* **Xinjiang Uygur Zizhiqu**
Sinkiang Uighur Autonomous Region *aut. reg.* China *see* **Xinjiang Uygur Zizhiqu**
147 C3 **Sinking** *r.* Rep. of Ireland
232 B5 **Sinking Spring** *OH* U.S.A.
136 D1 **Sinkyevichy** Belarus
183 F3 **Sinlabajos** Spain
156 D2 **Sin-le-Noble** France
Sînmartin Romania *see* **Sânmartin**
169 D5 **Sinn** Ger.
169 E5 **Sinn** *r.* Ger.
192 B5 **Sinnai** *Sardegna* Italy
251 H3 **Sinnamary** Fr. Guiana
114 B2 **Sinnar** *Mahar.* India
128 A5 **Sinn Bishr, Gebel** *hill* Egypt
137 H2 **Sinne** Ukr.
Sinneh Iran *see* **Sanandaj**
232 D4 **Sinnemahoning** *PA* U.S.A.
193 I4 **Sinni** *r.* Italy
Sînnicolau Mare Romania *see* **Sânnicolau Mare**
Sinoia Zimbabwe *see* **Chinhoyi**
197 I3 **Sinoie, Lacul** *lag.* Romania
253 G2 **Sinop** Brazil
126 D2 **Sinop** Turkey
Sinope Turkey *see* **Sinop**
195 E4 **Sinopoli** Italy
101 C4 **Sinp'a** N. Korea
Sînpetru Mare Romania *see* **Sânpetru Mare**
101 D4 **Sinp'o** N. Korea
101 C5 **Sinp'yŏng** N. Korea
172 C4 **Sins** Switz.
101 C5 **Sinsang** N. Korea
172 C2 **Sinsheim** Ger.
95 E2 **Sintang** *Kalimantan Barat* Indon.
164 D3 **Sint Annaland** Neth.
164 E1 **Sint Annaparochie** Neth.
164 E3 **Sint Anthonis** Neth.
247 □10 **Sint Christoffelberg** *hill Curaçao* Neth. Antilles
177 K5 **Sintea Mare** Romania
177 L4 **Şinteu** Romania
165 D3 **Sint Gillis-Waas** Belgium
165 E3 **Sint Huibrechts-Lille** Belgium
164 E1 **Sint Jacobiparochie** Neth.
165 D3 **Sint Jansteen** Neth.
165 D3 **Sint Katelijne-Waver** Belgium
165 C3 **Sint Laureins** Belgium
165 D3 **Sint Lenaarts** Belgium
247 G3 **Sint Maarten** *i.* Neth. Antilles
164 D3 **Sint Maartensdijk** Neth.
165 C3 **Sint Margriete** Belgium
165 C4 **Sint Maria-Lierde** Belgium
165 C3 **Sint Martens-Latem** Belgium
247 □9 **Sint Nicolaas** Aruba
164 E2 **Sint Nicolaasga** Neth.
165 D3 **Sint Niklaas** Belgium
237 D6 **Sinton** *TX* U.S.A.
164 D2 **Sint Pancras** Neth.
164 D3 **Sint Philipsland** Neth.
165 D4 **Sint Pieters-Leeuw** Belgium
184 A2 **Sintra** Port.
191 G4 **Sintria** *r.* Italy
139 K3 **Sintsovo** Rus. Fed.
165 E4 **Sint Truiden** Belgium
165 F4 **Sint Vith** Belgium
250 C2 **Sinú** *r.* Col.
101 C4 **Sinŭiju** N. Korea
138 G3 **Sinyaya** *r.* Rus. Fed.
172 C3 **Sinzheim** Ger.
169 C5 **Sinzig** Ger.
173 G3 **Sinzing** Ger.
177 H5 **Sió** *r.* Romania
186 D3 **Sió** *r.* Spain
177 H5 **Sióagárd** Hungary
92 B5 **Siocon** Phil.
177 H5 **Siófok** Hungary
209 D9 **Sioma** Zambia
190 C2 **Sion** Switz.
146 C3 **Sionascaig, Loch** *l. Scotland* U.K.
147 D2 **Sion Mills** *Northern Ireland* U.K.
160 B2 **Sioule** *r.* France
236 D3 **Sioux Center** *IA* U.S.A.
236 D3 **Sioux City** *IA* U.S.A.
236 D3 **Sioux Falls** *SD* U.S.A.
224 B3 **Sioux Lookout** *Ont.* Can.
243 H6 **Sipacate** Guat.
92 B4 **Sipalay** Phil.
247 □7 **Siparia** Trin. and Tob.
Siphaqeni S. Africa *see* **Flagstaff**
100 C4 **Siping** *Jilin* China
223 L4 **Sipiwesk** *Man.* Can.
262 P2 **Siple, Mount** Antarctica
262 N1 **Siple Coast** Antarctica
262 P2 **Siple Island** Antarctica
Sipolilo Zimbabwe *see* **Guruve**
197 H2 **Şipote** Romania
188 F3 **Šipovo** Bos.-Herz.
172 D4 **Sipplingen** Ger.
237 F5 **Sipsey** *r. AL* U.S.A.
125 F5 **Siqirah** *Suquṭrā* Yemen
256 C5 **Siqueira Campos** Brazil
242 □I6 **Siquia** *r.* Nic.
92 B4 **Siquijor** Phil.
92 B4 **Siquijor** *i.* Phil.
123 G6 **Sir** *r.* Pak.
114 C3 **Sira** *Karnataka* India
142 B2 **Sira** *r.* Norway
161 E4 **Sirac** *mt.* France
97 C4 **Si Racha** Thai.
195 E5 **Siracusa** *Sicilia* Italy
195 E5 **Siracusa** *prov. Sicilia* Italy
117 G4 **Sirajganj** Bangl.
222 F4 **Sir Alexander, Mount** *B.C.* Can.
162 E4 **Siran** France
126 E2 **Şiran** Turkey
116 E4 **Sirathu** *Uttar Prad.* India
207 F3 **Sirba** *r.* Burkina/Niger
Sircilla *Andhra Prad.* India *see* **Sirsilla**
Sirdaryo *r.* Asia *see* **Syrdar'ya**
Sirdaryo Uzbek. *see* **Syrdar'ya**
Sirdaryo Wiloyati *admin. div.* Uzbek. *see* **Syrdar'inskaya Oblast'**
Sirdingka *Xizang* China *see* **Lhari**
210 C2 **Sīrē** *Oromia* Eth.
210 C2 **Sīrē** *Oromia* Eth.
84 D2 **Sir Edward Pellew Group** *is N.T.* Austr.
226 A3 **Siren** *WI* U.S.A.
193 F2 **Sirente, Monte** *mt.* Italy
197 H2 **Siret** Romania
197 I3 **Siret** *r.* Romania
Siret *r.* Ukr. *see* **Seret**
86 E2 **Sir Graham Moore Islands** *W.A.* Austr.
128 C4 **Sirḩān, Wādī as** *watercourse* Jordan/Saudi Arabia
116 D3 **Sirhind** *Punjab* India
197 E2 **Şiria** Romania
122 D5 **Sīrīk** Iran
142 C2 **Sirikjerka** *hill* Norway
Sirína *i.* Greece *see* **Syrna**
123 G4 **Siritoi** *r.* Pak.
222 E2 **Sir James MacBrien, Mount** *N.W.T.* Can.
122 C4 **Sīrjān** *Kermān* Iran
122 C4 **Sīrjān** *salt flat* Iran
116 D3 **Sirmaur** *Hima. Prad.* India
191 F3 **Sirmione** Italy
Sirmium *Vojvodina, Srbija* Yugo. *see* **Sremska Mitrovica**
116 E4 **Sirmour** *Madh. Prad.* India
Sirmur *Hima. Prad.* India *see* **Sirmaur**
190 E1 **Sirnach** Switz.
127 F3 **Şırnak** Turkey
179 F4 **Širnitz** Austria
160 E2 **Sirod** France
116 C4 **Sirohi** *Rajasthan* India
177 J4 **Sirok** Hungary
177 J2 **Široké** Slovakia
191 I5 **Sirolo** Italy
114 D2 **Sironcha** *Mahar.* India
116 D4 **Sironj** *Madh. Prad.* India
191 G2 **Siròr** Italy
Síros *i.* Greece *see* **Syros**
204 D3 **Siroua, Jbel** *mt.* Morocco
114 C2 **Sirpur** *Andhra Prad.* India
240 H4 **Sirretta Peak** *CA* U.S.A.
122 C5 **Sīrrī, Jazīreh-ye** *i.* Iran
116 C3 **Sirsa** *Haryana* India
222 G5 **Sir Sandford, Mount** *B.C.* Can.
114 B3 **Sirsi** *Karnataka* India
116 D3 **Sirsi** *Uttar Prad.* India
114 C2 **Sirsilla** *Andhra Prad.* India
Sirte Libya *see* **Surt**
Sirte, Gulf of Libya *see* **Surt, Khalīj**
82 B1 **Sir Thomas, Mount** *hill S.A.* Austr.
185 E2 **Siruela** Spain
114 C3 **Siruguppa** *Karnataka* India
239 E6 **Sirupa** *r.* Mex.
114 B2 **Sirur** *Karnataka* India
114 B2 **Sirur** *Mahar.* India
127 F3 **Şirvan** Turkey
129 E3 **Şirvan Düzü** *lowland* Azer.
129 F3 **Şirvanovka** Azer.
114 C3 **Sirvel** *Andhra Prad.* India
175 K1 **Širvinta** *r.* Lith.
138 E4 **Širvintos** Lith.
127 G4 **Sīrwān** *r.* Iraq
222 G4 **Sir Wilfrid Laurier, Mount** *B.C.* Can.
85 E2 **Sir William Thompson Range** *hills Qld* Austr.
122 D3 **Siryan** Iran
Sis Turkey *see* **Kozan**
188 F3 **Sisak** Croatia
96 D4 **Sisaket** Thai.
243 H4 **Sisal** Mex.
185 H1 **Sisante** Spain
Siscia Croatia *see* **Sisak**
192 B2 **Sisco** *Corse* France
214 D2 **Sishen** S. Africa
129 E4 **Sisian** Armenia
206 E4 **Sisili** *r.* Burkina/Ghana
221 M3 **Sisimiut** Greenland
97 C4 **Sisŏphŏn** Cambodia
240 G4 **Sisquoc** *r. CA* U.S.A.
190 C1 **Sissach** Switz.
236 D2 **Sisseton** *SD* U.S.A.
206 E4 **Sissili** *r.* Burkina
156 D3 **Sissonne** France
232 C5 **Sissonville** *WV* U.S.A.
177 K5 **Şiştarovăţ** Romania
226 D3 **Sister Bay** *WI* U.S.A.
161 D4 **Sisteron** France
238 B2 **Sisters** *OR* U.S.A.
232 C5 **Sistersville** *WV* U.S.A.
193 F3 **Sisto** *r.* Italy
178 C3 **Sistrans** Austria
139 K2 **Sit'** *r.* Rus. Fed.
117 F4 **Sitamarhi** *Bihar* India
116 C5 **Sitamau** *Madh. Prad.* India
175 L5 **Sitaniec** Pol.
116 E4 **Sitapur** *Uttar Prad.* India
176 F2 **Šitbořice** Czech Rep.
199 E4 **Siteia** *Kriti* Greece
215 H2 **Siteki** Swaziland
186 E3 **Sitges** Spain
198 C1 **Sithonia** *pen.* Greece
Sitía *Kriti* Greece *see* **Siteia**
106 B3 **Sitian** *Xinjiang* China
108 C3 **Siting** *Guizhou* China
254 D5 **Sítio da Abadia** Brazil
254 E5 **Sítio do Mato** Brazil
111 D7 **Sitka** *Bihar* India
220 E4 **Sitka** *AK* U.S.A.
175 I5 **Sitkówka-Nowiny** Pol.
196 E4 **Sitnica** *r.* Yugo.
177 H3 **Sitno** *mt.* Slovakia
138 G3 **Sitnya** *r.* Rus. Fed.
202 E2 **Sitra** *oasis* Egypt
96 B3 **Sittang** *r.* Myanmar
165 E4 **Sittard** Neth.
Sittaung *r.* Myanmar *see* **Sittang**
168 E2 **Sittensen** Ger.
172 D4 **Sitter** *r.* Ger.
179 F4 **Sittersdorf** Austria
215 F5 **Sittingbourne** S. Africa
151 H3 **Sittingbourne** *Kent, England* U.K.
Sittoung *r.* Myanmar *see* **Sittang**
96 A2 **Sittwe** Myanmar
95 F4 **Situbondo** *Jawa Timur* Indon.
171 C5 **Sitzendorf** Ger.
179 G2 **Sitzendorf an der Schmida** Austria
171 D4 **Sitzenroda** Ger.
242 □I6 **Siuna** Nic.
141 N3 **Siuntio** Fin.
192 B5 **Siurgus Donigala** *Sardegna* Italy
117 F5 **Siuri** *W. Bengal* India
134 K4 **Siva** Rus. Fed.
177 I6 **Sivac** *Vojvodina, Srbija* Yugo.
114 C4 **Sivaganga** *Tamil Nadu* India
114 C4 **Sivakasi** *Tamil Nadu* India
100 C1 **Sivaki** Rus. Fed.
122 C4 **Sivand** Iran
126 E3 **Sivas** Turkey
199 F2 **Sivaslı** Turkey
206 B3 **Sivé** Maur.
126 E3 **Siverek** Turkey
137 J3 **Sivers'k** Ukr.
139 H2 **Siverskiy** Rus. Fed.
Sivers'kyy Donets' *r.* Rus. Fed. *see* **Severskiy Donets**
137 J3 **Sivers'kyy Donets'** *r.* Ukr.
175 M6 **Sivka-Voynylivs'ka** Ukr.
134 M2 **Sivomaskinskiy** Rus. Fed.
126 E3 **Sivrice** Turkey
126 C3 **Sivrihisar** Turkey
165 D4 **Sivry** Belgium
157 F3 **Sivry-sur-Meuse** France
215 G2 **Sivukile** S. Africa
202 E2 **Siwa** Egypt
116 D3 **Siwalik Range** *mts* India/Nepal
117 F4 **Siwan** *Bihar* India
116 C4 **Siwana** *Rajasthan* India
202 E2 **Siwa Oasis** Egypt
129 E3 **Şıxarx** Azer.
161 D5 **Six-Fours-les-Plages** France
109 F1 **Sixian** *Anhui* China
226 E4 **Six Lakes** *MI* U.S.A.
147 C4 **Sixmilebridge** Rep. of Ireland
147 D2 **Sixmilecross** *Northern Ireland* U.K.
160 E2 **Sixt-Fer-à-Cheval** France
215 G1 **Siyabuswa** S. Africa
Siyang *Guangxi* China *see* **Shangsi**
109 F1 **Siyang** *Jiangsu* China
215 G2 **Siyathemba** S. Africa
215 H1 **Siyathuthuka** S. Africa
129 F3 **Siyäzän** Azer.
107 F3 **Siyitang** *Nei Mongol* China
184 A1 **Sizandro** *r.* Port.
Siziwang Qi *Nei Mongol* China *see* **Ulan Hua**
158 B3 **Sizun** France
134 K2 **Sizyabsk** Rus. Fed.
142 D4 **Sjælland** *i.* Denmark
196 E4 **Sjenica** *Srbija* Yugo.
143 E4 **Sjöbo** Sweden
140 I3 **Sjøholt** Norway
140 K2 **Sjona** *sea chan.* Norway
140 K2 **Sjoutnäset** Sweden
140 L1 **Sjøvegan** Norway
140 M2 **Sjulsmark** Sweden
140 □ **Sjuøyane** *is* Svalbard
140 K3 **Skäckerfjällen** *mts* Sweden
137 G4 **Skadovs'k** Ukr.
142 D4 **Skælsør** Denmark
142 C4 **Skærbæk** Denmark
221 Q2 **Skærfjorden** *inlet* Greenland
140 □C3 **Skaftárós** *r. mouth* Iceland
140 □C2 **Skagafjörður** *inlet* Iceland
140 □B2 **Skagaheiði** *reg.* Iceland
142 D3 **Skagen** Denmark
143 F2 **Skagern** *l.* Sweden
142 C3 **Skagerrak** *str.* Denmark/Norway
238 B1 **Skagit** *r. WA* U.S.A.
222 F5 **Skagit Mountain** *B.C.* Can.
220 E4 **Skagway** *AK* U.S.A.
138 E4 **Skaidiškės** Lith.
146 E2 **Skaill** *Orkney, Scotland* U.K.
146 F3 **Skaill** *Orkney, Scotland* U.K.
199 E3 **Skala** *Notio Aigaio* Greece
198 C3 **Skala** *Peloponnisos* Greece
175 H5 **Skała** Pol.
140 L1 **Skaland** Norway
136 D3 **Skala-Podil's'ka** Ukr.
171 F5 **Skalice** Czech Rep.
129 B1 **Skalistyy Khrebet** *reg.* Rus. Fed.
177 H2 **Skalité** Slovakia
140 K2 **Skalmodal** Sweden
176 B1 **Skalná** Czech Rep.
142 C3 **Skals** *r.* Denmark
142 C3 **Skanderborg** Denmark
142 E4 **Skåne** *county* Sweden
232 E3 **Skaneateles** *NY* U.S.A.
140 L2 **Skansholm** Sweden
174 D3 **Skąpe** Pol.
142 E2 **Skara** Sweden
146 E2 **Skara Brae** *tourist site Scotland* U.K.
Skardarsko Jezero *l.* Albania/Yugo. *see* **Scutari, Lake**
85 E1 **Skardon** *r. Qld* Austr.
116 C2 **Skardu** Jammu and Kashmir
142 B2 **Skåreheia** *mt.* Norway
142 D3 **Skärhamn** Sweden
142 D1 **Skarnes** Norway
143 G1 **Skärplinge** Sweden
141 K3 **Skärsjövålen** Sweden
141 J3 **Skarstind** *mt.* Norway
174 G1 **Skarszewy** Pol.
141 J3 **Skarvedalseggen** *mt.* Norway
140 L2 **Skarvsjöby** Sweden
175 J4 **Skaryszew** Pol.
136 D3 **Skarzhyntsi** Ukr.
175 I4 **Skarżysko-Kamienna** Pol.
142 E1 **Skasberget** *hill* Norway
138 D4 **Skaudvilė** Lith.
140 M2 **Skaulo** Sweden
142 C3 **Skave** Denmark
146 □H1 **Skaw** *Shetland, Scotland* U.K.
175 H5 **Skawa** *r.* Pol.
175 H6 **Skawina** Pol.
143 H2 **Skebobruk** Sweden
143 F2 **Skeda udde** Sweden
222 D4 **Skeena** *r. B.C.* Can.
222 D3 **Skeena Mountains** *B.C.* Can.
149 J4 **Skegness** *Lincolnshire, England* U.K.
140 □C3 **Skeiðarársandur** *sand area* Iceland
146 □G1 **Skeld** *Shetland, Scotland* U.K.
168 E1 **Skelde** Denmark
140 M2 **Skellefteå** Sweden
140 M2 **Skellefteälven** *r.* Sweden
140 M2 **Skelleftebukten** *b.* Sweden
140 M2 **Skelleftehamn** Sweden
149 G4 **Skelmersdale** *Lancashire, England* U.K.
146 D6 **Skelmorlie** *North Ayrshire, Scotland* U.K.
149 I3 **Skelton** *Redcar and Cleveland, England* U.K.
150 E3 **Skenfrith** *Monmouthshire, Wales* U.K.
175 H3 **Skępe** Pol.
141 L3 **Skeppshamn** Sweden
214 D3 **Skerpioenpunt** S. Africa
146 D3 **Skerray** *Highland, Scotland* U.K.
147 E3 **Skerries** Rep. of Ireland
150 D3 **Sketty** *Swansea, Wales* U.K.
136 B3 **Skhidni Beskydy** *mts* Pol./Ukr.
136 B3 **Skhidni Karpaty** *mts* Ukr.
175 L6 **Skhidnytsya** Ukr.
Skhimatárion Greece *see* **Schimatari**
142 D2 **Ski** Norway
198 C2 **Skiathos** Greece
198 C2 **Skiathos** *i.* Greece
147 B5 **Skibbereen** Rep. of Ireland
138 E5 **Skidal'** Belarus
149 F3 **Skiddaw** *hill England* U.K.
222 D4 **Skidegate Mission** *B.C.* Can.
Skidel' Belarus *see* **Skidal'**
234 B3 **Skidmore** *MD* U.S.A.
142 C2 **Skien** Norway
175 L5 **Skierbieszów** Pol.
175 I4 **Skierniewice** Pol.
205 G1 **Skikda** Alg.
143 F2 **Skinnskatteberg** Sweden
116 D2 **Skio** Jammu and Kashmir
146 C6 **Skipness** *Argyll and Bute, Scotland* U.K.
234 C2 **Skippack** *PA* U.S.A.
149 I4 **Skipsea** *East Riding of Yorkshire, England* U.K.
214 C6 **Skipskop** S. Africa
83 E4 **Skipton** *Vic.* Austr.
149 G4 **Skipton** *North Yorkshire, England* U.K.
234 B4 **Skipton** *MD* U.S.A.
Skíros *i.* Greece *see* **Skyros**
142 C3 **Skive** Denmark
175 K3 **Skiwy Duże** Pol.
140 □C2 **Skjálfandafljót** *r.* Iceland
140 □C2 **Skjálfandi** *b.* Iceland
140 K2 **Skjelatinden** *mt.* Norway
142 D1 **Skjellinhovde** *hill* Norway
142 B1 **Skjemmene** *mt.* Norway
142 B2 **Skjerkeknuten** *hill* Norway
142 C4 **Skjern** Denmark
142 C4 **Skjern** *r.* Denmark
140 M1 **Skjervøy** Norway
Skobelev Uzbek. *see* **Fergana**
121 H5 **Skobeleva, Pik** *mt.* Kyrg.
179 E5 **Skocjanske Jame** *tourist site* Slovenia
174 G6 **Skoczów** Pol.
215 E6 **Skoenmakerskop** S. Africa
188 E2 **Škofja Loka** Slovenia
179 F5 **Škofljica** Slovenia
141 L3 **Skog** Sweden
143 F3 **Skoghult** Sweden
150 B3 **Skokholm Island** *Wales* U.K.
174 F3 **Skoki** Pol.
226 D4 **Skokie** *IL* U.S.A.
136 B3 **Skole** Ukr.
143 F2 **Sköllersta** Sweden
175 J6 **Skołyszyn** Pol.
150 B3 **Skomer Island** *Wales* U.K.
174 G4 **Skomlin** Pol.
215 F2 **Skoonspruit** *r.* S. Africa
198 C2 **Skopelos** Greece
198 C2 **Skopelos** *i.* Greece
198 D2 **Skopia** *hill Voreio Aigaio* Greece
139 L5 **Skopin** Rus. Fed.
196 E5 **Skopje** Macedonia
Skoplje Macedonia *see* **Skopje**
174 G2 **Skórcz** Pol.
135 G6 **Skorodnoye** Rus. Fed.
174 F5 **Skorogoszcz** Pol.
174 F5 **Skoroszyce** Pol.
144 J1 **Skorpa** *i.* Norway
142 C3 **Skørping** Denmark
175 K3 **Skórzec** Pol.
198 C1 **Skotoussa** Greece
142 E2 **Skotterud** Norway
198 C1 **Skoutari** Greece
199 E2 **Skoutaros** *Voreio Aigaio* Greece
143 E2 **Skövde** Sweden
100 B1 **Skovorodino** Rus. Fed.
233 □I2 **Skowhegan** *ME* U.S.A.
142 C2 **Skrimfjell** *hill* Norway
138 E3 **Skrīveri** Latvia
188 D2 **Škrlatica** *mt.* Slovenia
175 J2 **Skroda** *r.* Pol.
140 M2 **Skröven** Sweden
138 D3 **Skrunda** Latvia
175 H3 **Skrwa** *r.* Pol.
175 H2 **Skrwilno** Pol.
174 E2 **Skrzatusz** Pol.
175 G6 **Skrzyczne** *mt.* Pol.
175 I4 **Skrzyńsko** Pol.
175 J6 **Skrzyszów** Pol.
142 A2 **Skudeneshavn** Norway
144 D1 **Skúgvoy** *i.* Faroe Is
215 F1 **Skuinsdrif** S. Africa
222 C2 **Skukum, Mount** *Y.T.* Can.
213 F5 **Skukuza** S. Africa
241 I3 **Skull Peak** *NV* U.S.A.
241 K4 **Skull Valley** *AZ* U.S.A.
174 G3 **Skulsk** Pol.
143 G2 **Skultuna** Sweden
236 F3 **Skunk** *r. IA* U.S.A.
138 C3 **Skuodas** Lith.
139 K4 **Skuratovskiy** Rus. Fed.
142 E4 **Skurup** Sweden
197 F4 **Skŭt** *r.* Bulg.
143 G1 **Skutskär** Sweden
175 M6 **Skvaryava** Ukr.
136 E3 **Skvyra** Ukr.
174 D3 **Skwierzyna** Pol.
177 H3 **Skýcov** Slovakia
198 C1 **Skydra** *Kentriki Makedonia* Greece
146 B4 **Skye** *i. Scotland* U.K.
142 B2 **Skykula** *hill* Norway
198 D2 **Skyros** *Sterea Ellas* Greece
198 D2 **Skyros** *i.* Greece
234 C1 **Skytop** *PA* U.S.A.
262 S1 **Skytrain Ice Rise** Antarctica
175 I5 **Słaboszów** Pol.
234 B2 **Slabtown** *PA* U.S.A.
234 D2 **Slack Woods** *NJ* U.S.A.
Sládečkovce Slovakia *see* **Močenok**
144 D1 **Slættaratindur** *hill* Faroe Is
142 D4 **Slagelse** Denmark
164 F2 **Slagharen** Neth.
140 L2 **Slagnäs** Sweden
149 G4 **Slaidburn** *Lancashire, England* U.K.
146 E6 **Slamannan** *Falkirk, Scotland* U.K.
95 E4 **Slamet, Gunung** *vol.* Indon.
177 J3 **Slaná** *r.* Slovakia
147 E3 **Slane** Rep. of Ireland
177 K3 **Slanec** Slovakia
147 E4 **Slaney** *r.* Rep. of Ireland
197 G3 **Slănic** Romania
197 H3 **Slănic** *r.* Romania
197 H2 **Slănic Moldova** Romania
177 K3 **Slanské Vrchy** *mts* Slovakia
138 G2 **Slantsy** Rus. Fed.
176 D1 **Slaný** Czech Rep.
176 F2 **Šlapanice** Czech Rep.
85 F3 **Slashers Reefs** *Qld* Austr.
Śląsk *reg.* Europe *see* **Silesia**
175 G5 **Śląska, Wyżyna** *hills* Pol.
174 G5 **Śląskie** *prov.* Pol.
234 C2 **Slateford** *PA* U.S.A.
235 D1 **Slate Hill** *NY* U.S.A.
188 F3 **Slatina** Croatia
197 G3 **Slatina** Romania
177 I3 **Slatina** *r.* Slovakia
197 F3 **Slatina-Timiş** Romania
234 C2 **Slatington** *PA* U.S.A.
176 G2 **Slatinice** Czech Rep.
232 C5 **Slaty Fork** *WV* U.S.A.
137 I2 **Slatyne** Ukr.
222 H2 **Slave** *r. Alta/N.W.T.* Can.
207 F5 **Slave Coast** Africa
222 H4 **Slave Lake** *Alta* Can.
Slavgorod Belarus *see* **Slawharad**
121 I1 **Slavgorod** Rus. Fed.
Slavgorod *Dnipropetrovs'ka Oblast'* Ukr. *see* **Slavhorod**

137 H3 Slavhorod Dnipropetrovs'ka Oblast' Ukr.
137 H2 Slavhorod Sums'ka Oblast' Ukr.
177 G2 Slavičín Czech Rep.
197 F4 Slavinja Srbija Yugo.
138 G3 Slavkovichi Rus. Fed.
176 B1 Slavkovský Les hill Czech Rep.
176 F2 Slavkov u Brna Czech Rep.
191 I3 Slavnik mt. Slovenia
176 E3 Slavonice Czech Rep.
Slavonska Požega Croatia see Požega
188 G3 Slavonski Brod Croatia
177 J3 Slavošovce Slovakia
138 C4 Slavsk Rus. Fed.
136 D2 Slavuta Ukr.
136 F2 Slavutych Ukr.
Slavyanka Kazakh. see Myrzakent
100 D4 Slavyanka Rus. Fed.
197 G4 Slavyanovo Bulg.
Slavyansk Ukr. see Slov"yans'k
Slavyanskaya Rus. Fed. see Slavyansk-na-Kubani
135 G7 Slavyansk-na-Kubani Rus. Fed.
174 E4 Sława Pol.
175 L4 Sławatycze Pol.
174 F2 Sławęcin Pol.
139 H5 Slawharad Belarus
143 G4 Sławno Pol.
174 D2 Sławoborze Pol.
236 E3 Slayton MN U.S.A.
149 I4 Slea r. England U.K.
149 I4 Sleaford Lincolnshire, England U.K.
82 C3 Sleaford Bay S.A. Austr.
146 C4 Sleat pen. Scotland U.K.
146 C4 Sleat, Sound of sea chan. Scotland U.K.
149 I3 Sledmere East Riding of Yorkshire, England U.K.
164 F2 Sleen Neth.
164 D3 Sleeuwijk Neth.
149 I3 Sleights North Yorkshire, England U.K.
95 E4 Sleman Indon.
175 H6 Ślemień Pol.
129 D2 Sleptsovskaya Rus. Fed.
174 G3 Ślesin Pol.
174 E5 Ślęża hill Pol.
174 E4 Ślęża r. Pol.
Slezsko reg. Europe see Silesia
177 I3 Sliač Slovakia
241 M2 Slick Rock CO U.S.A.
237 F6 Slidell LA U.S.A.
233 F4 Slide Mountain NY U.S.A.
141 J3 Slidre Norway
164 D3 Sliedrecht Neth.
195 □ Sliema Malta
147 A4 Slievanea hill Rep. of Ireland
147 D2 Slieve Anierin hill Rep. of Ireland
147 D4 Slieveardagh Hills Rep. of Ireland
147 C3 Slieve Aughty Mountains hills Rep. of Ireland
147 D2 Slieve Beagh hill Rep. of Ireland/U.K.
147 C4 Slieve Bernagh hills Rep. of Ireland
147 D4 Slieve Bloom Mountains hills Rep. of Ireland
147 B4 Slievecallan hill Rep. of Ireland
147 B2 Slieve Car hill Rep. of Ireland
147 F2 Slieve Donard hill Northern Ireland U.K.
147 C4 Slievefelim Mountains hills Rep. of Ireland
148 C3 Slieve Gallion hill Northern Ireland U.K.
147 B3 Slieve Gamph hills Rep. of Ireland
147 C4 Slievekimalta hill Rep. of Ireland
147 D2 Slievekirk hill Northern Ireland U.K.
147 A4 Slieve Mish Mountains hills Rep. of Ireland
147 A5 Slieve Miskish Mountains hills Rep. of Ireland
147 D2 Slievenakilla hill Rep. of Ireland
147 D4 Slievenamon hill Rep. of Ireland
148 B3 Slieve Rushen hill Northern Ireland U.K.
147 C2 Slieve Snaght hill Donegal Rep. of Ireland
147 D1 Slieve Snaght hill Donegal Rep. of Ireland
146 B4 Sligachan Highland, Scotland U.K.
Sligeach Rep. of Ireland see Sligo
147 C2 Sligo Rep. of Ireland
147 C2 Sligo county Rep. of Ireland
232 D4 Sligo PA U.S.A.
147 C2 Sligo Bay Rep. of Ireland
175 K2 Ślina r. Pol.
151 G3 Slinfold West Sussex, England U.K.
164 F2 Slinge r. Neth.
146 C4 Slioch hill Scotland U.K.
137 G3 Sliporid r. Ukr.
232 C4 Slippery Rock PA U.S.A.
143 H3 Slite Gotland Sweden
197 H4 Sliven Bulg.
197 F4 Slivnitsa Bulg.
197 H4 Slivo Pole Bulg.
174 G2 Śliwice Pol.
188 E3 Sljeme mt. Croatia
241 J4 Sloan NV U.S.A.
240 G2 Sloat CA U.S.A.
235 D1 Sloatsburg NY U.S.A.
136 E4 Slobidka Ukr.
Sloboda Respublika Komi Rus. Fed. see Ezhva
Sloboda Smolenskaya Oblast' Rus. Fed. see Przheval'skoye
135 H6 Sloboda Voronezhskaya Oblast' Rus. Fed.
137 G2 Sloboda Ukr.
134 J4 Slobodskoy Rus. Fed.
Slobodzeya Moldova see Slobozia
136 E4 Slobozia Moldova
197 H3 Slobozia Romania
197 H3 Slobozia Bradului Romania
222 G5 Slocan B.C. Can.
164 F1 Slochteren Neth.
175 I5 Słomniki Pol.
138 E5 Slonim Belarus
137 I2 Slonovka Rus. Fed.
174 C3 Słońsk Pol.
164 D2 Slootdorp Neth.
164 E2 Sloten Neth.
151 G3 Slough Slough, England U.K.
151 G3 Slough admin. div. England U.K.
176 F2 Sloupnice Czech Rep.
177 I3 Slovakia country Europe
136 E2 Slovechna r. Ukr.
136 E2 Slovechne Ukr.
188 E2 Slovenia country Europe
Slovenija country Europe see Slovenia
188 E2 Slovenj Gradec Slovenia
188 E2 Slovenska Bistrica Slovenia
177 J2 Slovenská Ves Slovakia
188 E2 Slovenske Gorice hills Slovenia
179 G4 Slovenske Konjice Slovenia
177 K3 Slovenské Nové Mesto Slovakia
177 I3 Slovenské Rudohorie mts Slovakia
Slovensko country Europe see Slovakia
177 J3 Slovenský kras mts Slovakia
177 J3 Slovinky Slovakia
175 M6 Slovita Ukr.
137 I3 Slov"yanka Ukr.
137 I3 Slov"yanohirs'k Ukr.
137 J3 Slov"yanoserbs'k Ukr.
137 I3 Slov"yans'k Ukr.
136 E2 Slovyechna r. Belarus
175 H4 Słowik Pol.
174 C3 Słubice Pol.
175 H3 Słubice Pol.
138 F5 Sluch r. Belarus
136 D2 Sluch r. Ukr.
191 F2 Sluderno Italy
134 J4 Sludka Rus. Fed.
165 C3 Sluis Neth.
165 C3 Sluiskil Neth.
176 D1 Šluknov Czech Rep.
176 G2 Slunečná hill Czech Rep.
188 E3 Slunj Croatia
174 F3 Słupca Pol.
175 J5 Słupcza Pol.
175 H4 Słupia Pol.
175 H5 Słupia Pol.
175 I4 Słupia Pol.
143 G4 Słupia r. Pol.
175 H3 Słupno Pol.
143 G4 Słupsk Pol.
140 L2 Slussfors Sweden
174 G4 Słuszków Pol.
138 F5 Slutsk Belarus
138 D4 Šlyna r. Lith.
98 H1 Slyudyanka Rus. Fed.
237 E5 Smackover AR U.S.A.
162 A2 Smagne r. France
146 F6 Smailholm Scottish Borders, Scotland U.K.
143 F3 Småland reg. Sweden
142 D4 Smålandsfarvandet sea chan. Denmark
142 E3 Smålandsstenar Sweden
151 F2 Smalley Derbyshire, England U.K.
225 H2 Smallwood Reservoir Nfld. Can.
138 G4 Smalyavichy Belarus
175 I4 Smardzewice Pol.
138 F4 Smarhon' Belarus
179 G4 Šmarje pri Jelšah Slovenia
179 G4 Šmartno Slovenia
162 C2 Smarves France
223 J4 Smeaton Sask. Can.
171 F5 Smečno Czech Rep.
176 D1 Smědá r. Czech Rep.
143 G3 Smedby Sweden
196 E3 Smederevo Srbija Yugo.
196 E3 Smederevska Palanka Srbija Yugo.
197 H3 Smeeni Romania
151 H3 Smeeth Kent, England U.K.
Smela Ukr. see Smila
232 D4 Smethport PA U.S.A.
151 F2 Smethwick West Midlands, England U.K.
174 G2 Smętowo Graniczne Pol.
176 E1 Smidary Czech Rep.
175 M4 Smidyn Ukr.
174 E3 Śmigiel Pol.
137 F3 Smila Ukr.
138 G5 Smilavichy Belarus
164 F2 Smilde Neth.
137 G2 Smile Ukr.
136 D2 Smilka r. Ukr.
138 E3 Smiltene Latvia
138 D3 Smiltiņu kalns hill Latvia
176 E1 Smiřice Czech Rep.
121 G1 Smirnovo Kazakh.
Smirnovskiy Kazakh. see Smirnovo
100 G2 Smirnykh Sakhalin Rus. Fed.
222 H4 Smith Alta Can.
238 E2 Smith r. MT U.S.A.
232 D6 Smith r. VA U.S.A.
220 F3 Smith Arm b. N.W.T. Can.
147 D2 Smithborough Rep. of Ireland
236 D4 Smith Center KS U.S.A.
222 E4 Smithers B.C. Can.
222 E4 Smithers Landing B.C. Can.
215 F4 Smithfield S. Africa
231 E5 Smithfield NC U.S.A.
238 E3 Smithfield UT U.S.A.
232 E6 Smithfield VA U.S.A.
262 Q1 Smith Glacier Antarctica
262 T2 Smith Island Antarctica
237 F4 Smithland KY U.S.A.
84 B1 Smith Point N.T. Austr.
222 E3 Smith River B.C. Can.
232 E5 Smithsburg MD U.S.A.
224 E4 Smiths Falls Ont. Can.
83 F5 Smithton Tas. Austr.
83 H2 Smithtown N.S.W. Austr.
235 E2 Smithtown NY U.S.A.
235 D3 Smithville NJ U.S.A.
237 E5 Smithville OK U.S.A.
231 C5 Smithville TN U.S.A.
232 C5 Smithville WV U.S.A.
214 E5 Smitskraal S. Africa
177 J3 Smižany Slovakia
140 □D2 Smjörfjöll mts Iceland
240 H1 Smoke Creek Desert NV U.S.A.
222 G3 Smoky r. Alta Can.
82 C3 Smoky Bay S.A. Austr.
82 C3 Smoky Bay b. S.A. Austr.
83 H2 Smoky Cape N.S.W. Austr.
224 D3 Smoky Falls Ont. Can.
236 D4 Smoky Hill r. KS U.S.A.
236 C4 Smoky Hill, North Fork r. KS U.S.A.
228 G3 Smoky Hills KS U.S.A.
223 H4 Smoky Lake Alta Can.
140 I3 Smøla i. Norway
174 F1 Smołdzino Pol.
120 B2 Smolenka Rus. Fed.
139 I4 Smolensk Rus. Fed.
139 I4 Smolenskaya Oblast' admin. div. Rus. Fed.
Smolensk Oblast admin. div. Rus. Fed. see Smolenskaya Oblast'
139 I4 Smolensko-Moskovskaya Vozvyshennost' hills Rus. Fed.
121 K1 Smolenskoye Rus. Fed.
Smolevichi Belarus see Smalyavichy
174 F4 Smolice Pol.
198 B1 Smolikas mt. Greece
137 F3 Smoline Ukr.
142 E2 Smolmark Sweden
177 J3 Smolník Slovakia
197 G5 Smolyan Bulg.
100 E4 Smolyoninovo Rus. Fed.
224 D3 Smooth Rock Falls Ont. Can.
Smorgon' Belarus see Smarhon'
139 I5 Smotrova Buda Rus. Fed.
136 D3 Smotrych Ukr.
176 G1 Smrk mt. Czech Rep.
171 G5 Smrk mt. Czech Rep.
137 F2 Smyach Ukr.
197 H4 Smyadovo Bulg.
142 E4 Smygehamn Sweden
136 C2 Smyha Ukr.
175 I4 Smyków Pol.
262 S2 Smyley Island Antarctica
Smyrna Turkey see İzmir
234 C3 Smyrna DE U.S.A.
231 C5 Smyrna GA U.S.A.
231 C5 Smyrna TN U.S.A.
234 C3 Smyrna r. DE U.S.A.
233 □I1 Smyrna Mills ME U.S.A.
Smyth Island atoll Marshall Is see Majuro
140 □D2 Snæfell mt. Iceland
148 E3 Snaefell hill Isle of Man
140 □B2 Snæfellsjökull ice cap Iceland
140 □B2 Snæfellsnes pen. Iceland
222 A2 Snag Y.T. Can.
149 I3 Snainton North Yorkshire, England U.K.
149 H4 Snaith East Riding of Yorkshire, England U.K.
236 C3 Snake r. NE U.S.A.
238 C2 Snake r. U.S.A.
84 B2 Snake Creek r. N.T. Austr.
241 J2 Snake Range mts NV U.S.A.
222 F3 Snake River B.C. Can.
238 D3 Snake River Plain ID U.S.A.
222 G2 Snare r. N.W.T. Can.
Snare Lakes N.W.T. Can. see Wekweti
77 G6 Snares Islands N.Z.
140 K2 Snåsa Norway
232 B6 Sneedville TN U.S.A.
164 E1 Sneek Neth.
147 B5 Sneem Rep. of Ireland
214 B5 Sneeuberg mt. S. Africa
214 E4 Sneeuberge mts S. Africa
Snegurovka Ukr. see Tetiyiv
240 G3 Snelling CA U.S.A.
151 H2 Snettisham Norfolk, England U.K.
139 K5 Snezhed' r. Rus. Fed.
130 J3 Snezhnogorsk Rus. Fed.
Snezhnoye Ukr. see Snizhne
176 E1 Sněžka mt. Czech Rep.
188 E3 Snežnik mt. Slovenia
175 J2 Śniadowo Pol.
175 J2 Śniardwy, Jezioro l. Pol.
Sniečkus Lith. see Visaginas
Sniežka mt. Czech Rep. see Sněžka
174 E5 Śnieżnik mt. Pol.
137 G4 Snihurivka Ukr.
177 L3 Snina Slovakia
151 F2 Snitterfield Warwickshire, England U.K.
137 G2 Snityn Ukr.
137 J3 Snizhne Ukr.
146 B4 Snizort, Loch b. Scotland U.K.
141 J3 Snøhetta mt. Norway
238 B2 Snohomish WA U.S.A.
142 B2 Snønuten mt. Norway
139 I5 Snopot' r. Rus. Fed.
137 F2 Snov r. Ukr.
137 I2 Snova r. Rus. Fed.
139 L5 Snova r. Rus. Fed.
Snovsk Ukr. see Shchors
138 F5 Snow Belarus
222 G5 Snowcrest Mountain B.C. Can.
81 B6 Snowdon mt. South I. N.Z.
150 C1 Snowdon mt. Wales U.K.
150 D2 Snowdonia National Park Wales U.K.
Snowdrift N.W.T. Can. see Łutselk'e
223 I2 Snowdrift r. N.W.T. Can.
241 L4 Snowflake AZ U.S.A.
233 F5 Snow Hill MD U.S.A.
231 E5 Snow Hill NC U.S.A.
223 K4 Snow Lake Man. Can.
82 D3 Snowtown S.A. Austr.
238 D3 Snowville UT U.S.A.
83 G4 Snowy r. N.S.W./Vic. Austr.
233 F3 Snowy Mountain NY U.S.A.
83 F4 Snowy Mountains N.S.W. Austr.
246 D2 Snug Corner Acklins I. Bahamas
225 K2 Snug Harbour Nfld. Can.
227 G3 Snug Harbour Ont. Can.
136 C3 Snyatyn Ukr.
237 D5 Snyder OK U.S.A.
237 C5 Snyder TX U.S.A.
234 A2 Snyder County county PA U.S.A.
234 C2 Snyders PA U.S.A.
136 E3 Snyvoda r. Ukr.
Soaigh i. Western Isles, Scotland U.K. see Soay
182 B3 Soajo Port.
81 A6 Soaker, Mount South I. N.Z.
213 □J3 Soalala Madag.
182 B3 Soalhães Port.
182 C4 Soalheira Port.
213 □J4 Soamanonga Madag.
190 C3 Soana r. Italy
213 □K3 Soanierana-Ivongo Madag.
191 H5 Soara r. Italy
191 G3 Soave Italy
213 □J3 Soavinandriana Madag.
146 B4 Soay i. Highland, Scotland U.K.
146 □ Soay i. Western Isles, Scotland U.K.
136 E3 Sob r. Ukr.
207 H4 Soba Nigeria
101 C6 Sobaek-sanmaek mts S. Korea
210 A2 Sobat r. Sudan
105 E3 Sobatsubu-yama mt. Japan
182 C2 Sober Spain
172 B2 Sobernheim Ger.
176 D2 Soběslav Czech Rep.
91 J7 Sobger r. Indon.
139 M4 Sobinka Rus. Fed.
139 L4 Sobolevo Rus. Fed.
175 J4 Sobolew Pol.
103 E7 Sobo-san mt. Japan
175 H3 Sobota Pol.
176 G1 Sobotín Czech Rep.
176 G3 Sobotište Slovakia
176 E1 Sobotka Czech Rep.
174 E5 Sobótka Pol.
175 J5 Sobótka Pol.
174 F4 Sobótka Pol.
174 G1 Sobowidz Pol.
182 D2 Sobradelo Spain
256 D1 Sobradinho Brazil
182 B1 Sobrado Galicia Spain
182 B2 Sobrado Galicia Spain
254 E2 Sobral Brazil
182 B4 Sobral Port.
184 C2 Sobral da Adiça Port.
184 A1 Sobral de Monte Agraço Port.
182 C4 Sobral do Campo Port.
177 L3 Sobrance Slovakia
182 B3 Sobreira Port.
182 C5 Sobreira Formosa Port.
168 F1 Søby Denmark
137 G2 Sobych Ukr.
Soča r. Italy see Isonzo
188 D3 Soča r. Slovenia
191 H2 Socchieve Italy
175 I3 Sochaczew Pol.
129 A2 Sochi Rus. Fed.
175 I3 Sochocin Pol.
101 C5 Söch'ŏn S. Korea
198 C1 Sochos Greece
Society Islands Fr. Polynesia see La Société, Archipel de
177 K5 Socodor Romania
196 E3 Socol Romania
177 L4 Socond Romania
Soconusco, Sierra de mts Mex. see Madre, Sierra
256 D5 Socorro Brazil
250 C3 Socorro Col.
239 F5 Socorro NM U.S.A.
228 D7 Socorro, Isla i. Mex.
250 B6 Socota Peru
Socotra i. Yemen see Suquṭrā
185 I2 Socovos Spain
97 D5 Soc Trăng Vietnam
185 H1 Socuéllamos Spain
140 N2 Sodankylä Fin.
111 B5 Soda Plains Aksai Chin
238 E3 Soda Springs ID U.S.A.
105 F3 Sodegaura Japan
143 G3 Söderåkra Sweden
143 F1 Söderbärke Sweden
143 H1 Söderboda Sweden
143 G1 Söderfors Sweden
141 L3 Söderhamn Sweden
143 G2 Söderköping Sweden
143 G2 Södermanland county Sweden
168 F2 Soderstorf Ger.
143 G2 Södertälje Sweden
203 F6 Sodiri Sudan
214 D4 Sodium S. Africa
210 C3 Sodo Eth.
140 M3 Södra Gloppet b. Fin.
141 L3 Södra Kvarken str. Fin./Sweden
143 F3 Södra Vi Sweden
232 E3 Sodus NY U.S.A.
214 A4 Soebatsfontein S. Africa
213 F4 Soekmekaar S. Africa
Soerabaia Jawa Timur Indon. see Surabaya
165 E3 Soerendonk Neth.
169 D4 Soest Ger.
164 E2 Soest Neth.
168 C2 Soeste r. Ger.
198 C2 Sofades Greece
83 G3 Sofala N.S.W. Austr.
213 G4 Sofala Moz.
213 G3 Sofala prov. Moz.
Sofia Bulg. see Sofiya
213 □J2 Sofia r. Madag.
198 C3 Sofiko Greece
197 F4 Sofiya Bulg.
Sofiyevka Ukr. see Vil'nyans'k
137 G3 Sofiyivka Ukr.
100 E1 Sofiysk Khabarovskiy Kray Rus. Fed.
100 F2 Sofiysk Khabarovskiy Kray Rus. Fed.
139 K3 Sofrino Rus. Fed.
177 K5 Şofronea Romania
128 A1 Softa Kalesi tourist site Turkey
103 J9 Sōfu-gan i. Japan
111 F6 Sog Xizang China
250 C3 Sogamoso Col.
129 A3 Soğanlı Dağları mts Turkey
110 D3 Sogat Xinjiang China
100 E2 Sogda Rus. Fed.
168 C3 Sögel Ger.
142 B2 Søgne Norway
141 I3 Sognefjorden inlet Norway
141 I3 Sogn og Fjordane county Norway
92 C4 Sogod Phil.
129 D4 Soğuksu Turkey
199 G1 Söğüt Turkey
199 F3 Söğüt Dağı mts Turkey
129 B4 Söğütlü Turkey
101 C6 Sögwip'o S. Korea
203 F3 Sohâg Egypt
116 D5 Sohagpur Madh. Prad. India
151 H2 Soham Cambridgeshire, England U.K.
123 G3 Sohan r. Pak.
Sohar Oman see Şuḩār
165 E4 Soheit-Tinlot Belgium
117 E5 Sohela Orissa India
171 F4 Sohland am Rotstein Ger.
169 F3 Söhlde Ger.
116 D3 Sohna Haryana India
97 B4 Sohng Gwe, Khao hill Myanmar/Thai.
172 B2 Sohren Ger.
156 E2 Soignes, Forêt de for. Belgium
165 D4 Soignies Belgium
108 A2 Soila Xizang China
177 L5 Şoimi Romania
160 D1 Soing France
159 H4 Soings-en-Sologne France
140 N3 Soini Fin.
157 E2 Soire-le-Château France
169 E5 Soisberg hill Ger.
156 D3 Soissons France
156 D4 Soizy-aux-Bois France
103 F6 Sōja Japan
116 C4 Sojat Rajasthan India
116 C4 Sojat Road Rajasthan India
175 K5 Sójkowa Pol.
179 H4 Söjtör Hungary
135 J5 Sok r. Rus. Fed.
105 F3 Sōka Japan
136 C2 Sokal' Ukr.
101 D5 Sokch'o S. Korea
199 E3 Söke Turkey
209 E7 Sokele Dem. Rep. Congo
107 F1 Sokhondo, Gora mt. Rus. Fed.
106 E1 Sokhor, Gora mt. Rus. Fed.
Sokhós Greece see Sochos
129 B2 Sokhumi Georgia
129 B2 Sokhumi-Babushara airport Georgia
Sokiryany Ukr. see Sokyryany
103 D6 Sökkuram Grotto tourist site S. Korea
197 E4 Sokobanja Srbija Yugo.
207 F4 Sokodé Togo
100 G3 Sokol Sakhalin Rus. Fed.
134 H4 Sokol Vologod. Obl. Rus. Fed.
188 G4 Sokolac Bos.-Herz.
175 L2 Sokolany Pol.
136 F3 Sokolivka Cherkas'ka Oblast' Ukr.
175 M5 Sokolivka L'vivs'ka Oblast' Ukr.
175 L2 Sokółka Pol.
175 K1 Sokółki Pol.
179 H1 Sokolnice Czech Rep.
139 L4 Sokol'niki Rus. Fed.
139 J3 Sokol'niki Rus. Fed.
206 D3 Sokolo Mali
137 H4 Sokolohirne Ukr.
176 B1 Sokolov Czech Rep.
137 H3 Sokolova Balka Ukr.
179 H4 Sokolovac Croatia
121 G1 Sokolovka Kazakh.
121 K1 Sokolovo Rus. Fed.
137 J4 Sokolovo-Kundryuchenskiy Rus. Fed.
175 K5 Sokołów Małopolski Pol.
175 K3 Sokołow Podlaski Pol.
134 H4 Sokol'skoye Rus. Fed.
175 K3 Sokoły Pol.
206 A3 Sokone Senegal
177 G4 Sokorópátka Hungary
140 O1 Sokosti hill Fin.
207 G3 Sokoto Nigeria
207 G4 Sokoto r. Nigeria
207 G3 Sokoto state Nigeria
206 C4 Sokourala Guinea
136 D3 Sokyryany Ukr.
175 K5 Sól Pol.
246 C2 Sola Cuba
175 H6 Soła r. Pol.
Sola i. Tonga see Ata
116 D3 Solan Hima. Prad. India
240 I5 Solana Beach CA U.S.A.
184 D2 Solana de los Barros Spain
185 F2 Solana del Pino Spain
183 F4 Solana de Rioalmar Spain
142 C1 Sølandsfjellet mt. Norway
92 B2 Solano Phil.
114 B2 Solapur Mahar. India
195 E5 Solarino Sicilia Italy
192 B3 Solaro Corse France
192 A5 Solarussa Sardegna Italy
146 A4 Solas Western Isles, Scotland U.K.
140 L3 Solberg Sweden
143 F3 Solberga Sweden
197 G2 Solca Romania
177 H3 Solčany Slovakia
191 F2 Solda Italy
191 F2 Solda r. Italy
136 E4 Şoldăneşti Moldova
129 C1 Soldato-Aleksandrovskoye Rus. Fed.
129 C2 Soldatskaya Rus. Fed.
178 C4 Sölden Austria
186 E2 Soldeu Andorra
233 □I1 Soldier Pond ME U.S.A.
220 C3 Soldotna AK U.S.A.
174 G2 Solec Kujawski Pol.
175 I5 Solec-Zdrój Pol.
246 D5 Soledad Col.
240 G3 Soledad CA U.S.A.
245 F4 Soledad de Doblado Mex.
244 D2 Soledad Diez Gutierrez Mex.
255 B9 Soledade Brazil
137 J3 Soledar Ukr.
192 B5 Soleminis Sardegna Italy
141 J3 Sølen mt. Norway
135 H7 Solenoye Rus. Fed.
192 B3 Solenzara Corse France
206 D3 Solenzo Burkina
191 G3 Solesino Italy
156 D2 Solesmes Nord - Pas-de-Calais France
159 F4 Solesmes Pays de la Loire France
195 H2 Soleto Italy
163 B4 Solférino France
191 F3 Solferino Italy
140 K2 Solfjellsjøen Norway
134 H3 Solginskiy Rus. Fed.
127 F3 Solhan Turkey
191 F4 Soliera Italy
134 H4 Soligalich Rus. Fed.
162 D3 Solignac France
190 E4 Solignano Italy
191 H3 Soligo r. Italy
Soligorsk Belarus see Salihorsk
151 F2 Solihull West Midlands, England U.K.
134 L4 Solikamsk Rus. Fed.
120 C2 Sol'-Iletsk Rus. Fed.
189 C7 Soliman Tunisia
175 K6 Solina Pol.
169 C4 Solingen Ger.
175 K6 Solinka r. Pol.
175 K6 Solińskie, Jezioro l. Pol.
250 C4 Solita Col.
81 A6 Solitary, Mount South I. N.Z.
186 E3 Solivella Spain
Sol-Karmala Rus. Fed. see Severnoye
178 D3 Söll Austria
192 A3 Sollacaro Corse France
142 E2 Sollebrunn Sweden
140 L3 Sollefteå Sweden
179 H3 Sollenau Austria
143 G2 Sollentuna Sweden
187 F5 Sóller Spain
141 K3 Sollerön Sweden
168 G1 Søllested Denmark
171 D4 Söllichau Ger.
161 E5 Solliès-Pont France
161 E5 Solliès-Ville France
169 E4 Solling hills Ger.
169 F3 Söllingen Ger.
169 F4 Sollstedt Ger.
169 D5 Solms Ger.
139 K3 Solnechnogorsk Rus. Fed.
100 F2 Solnechnyy Khabarovskiy Kray Rus. Fed.
Solnechnyy Khabarovskiy Kray Rus. Fed. see Gornyy
176 F1 Solnice Czech Rep.
137 I2 Solntsevo Rus. Fed.
93 B3 Solo r. Indon.
95 F4 Solo r. Indon.
136 D3 Solobkivtsi Ukr.
193 G4 Solofra Italy
94 C3 Solok Sumatera Indon.
136 C2 Solokiya r. Ukr.
243 H6 Sololá Guat.
129 D1 Solomenskoye Rus. Fed.
163 C5 Solomiac France
136 D3 Solomna Ukr.
241 M5 Solomon AZ U.S.A.
236 D4 Solomon r. KS U.S.A.
236 D4 Solomon, North Fork r. KS U.S.A.
236 D4 Solomon, South Fork r. KS U.S.A.
78 □6 Solomon Islands country S. Pacific Ocean
91 L8 Solomon Sea P.N.G./Solomon Is
107 I2 Solon Nei Mongol China
233 □I2 Solon ME U.S.A.
137 H4 Solona r. Ukr.
137 I3 Solona r. Ukr.
137 H3 Solone Ukr.
121 K2 Soloneshnoye Rus. Fed.
226 B2 Solon Springs WI U.S.A.
194 D1 Solopaca Italy
93 B5 Solor, Kepulauan is Indon.
183 G1 Solórzano Spain
183 F4 Solosancho Spain
139 L4 Solotcha Rus. Fed.
190 C1 Solothurn Switz.
190 C1 Solothurn canton Switz.
136 C3 Solotvyn Ukr.
134 F2 Solovetskiy Rus. Fed.
134 F2 Solovetskiye Ostrova is Rus. Fed.
134 I4 Solovetskoye Rus. Fed.
136 E2 Soloviyivka Ukr.
107 G1 Solov'yevsk Mongolia
100 C1 Solov'yevsk Rus. Fed.
186 E3 Solsona Spain
177 I5 Solt Hungary
188 F4 Šolta i. Croatia
122 D2 Soltānābād Iran
122 B3 Soltānābād Iran
129 E4 Soltanlı Azer.
168 E3 Soltau Ger.
168 F3 Soltendieck Ger.
121 K1 Solton Rus. Fed.
139 H2 Sol'tsy Rus. Fed.
Soltüstik Qazaqstan Oblysy admin. div. Kazakh. see Severnyy Kazakhstan
177 I5 Soltvadkert Hungary
177 I5 Soltzentimre Hungary
196 E5 Solunska Glava mt. Macedonia
160 C2 Solutré-Pouilly France
150 B3 Solva Pembrokeshire, Wales U.K.
150 B3 Solva r. Wales U.K.
240 G4 Solvang CA U.S.A.
233 E3 Solvay NY U.S.A.
143 F3 Sölvesborg Sweden
134 I3 Sol'vychegodsk Rus. Fed.
146 E7 Solway Firth est. Scotland U.K.
209 E8 Solwezi Zambia
102 J5 Sōma Japan
199 E2 Soma Turkey
156 D2 Somain France
210 D3 Somali admin. reg. Eth.
210 E4 Somalia country Africa
265 H5 Somali Basin sea feature Indian Ocean
Somali Republic country Africa see Somalia
207 E5 Somanya Ghana
95 G2 Sombang, Gunung mt. Indon.
177 H5 Somberek Hungary
160 C1 Sombernon France
209 D7 Sombo Angola
196 D3 Sombor Vojvodina, Srbija Yugo.
169 E5 Somborn Ger.
165 D4 Sombreffe Belgium
244 C2 Sombrerete Mex.
259 C9 Sombrero Chile
115 G5 Sombrero Channel Andaman & Nicobar Is India
197 F2 Şomcuţa Mare Romania
116 C4 Somdari Rajasthan India
234 C3 Somerdale NJ U.S.A.
165 E3 Someren Neth.
141 M3 Somero Fin.
150 E3 Somerset admin. div. England U.K.
230 C4 Somerset KY U.S.A.
233 H4 Somerset MA U.S.A.
226 E4 Somerset MI U.S.A.
232 B5 Somerset OH U.S.A.
232 D5 Somerset PA U.S.A.
234 D2 Somerset County county NJ U.S.A.
215 E5 Somerset East S. Africa
221 I2 Somerset Island Nunavut Can.
214 B6 Somerset West S. Africa
151 H2 Somersham Cambridgeshire, England U.K.
234 D3 Somers Point NJ U.S.A.
233 □H3 Somersworth NH U.S.A.
150 E3 Somerton Somerset, England U.K.
241 J5 Somerton AZ U.S.A.
138 F2 Sõmeru Estonia
234 D2 Somerville NJ U.S.A.
237 F5 Somerville TN U.S.A.
197 F2 Someş r. Romania
197 F2 Someşan, Podişul plat. Romania
197 F2 Someşu Cald r. Romania
197 F2 Someşul Mare r. Romania
197 F2 Someşului, Câmpia plain Romania
197 F2 Someşu Mic r. Romania
233 □I2 Somesville ME U.S.A.
175 J3 Somianka Pol.
139 J2 Somino Rus. Fed.
215 I3 Somkele S. Africa
176 G4 Somlóvásárhely Hungary
191 F3 Sommacampagna Italy
190 D3 Somma Lombardo Italy
190 C4 Sommariva del Bosco Italy
194 C5 Sommatino Sicilia Italy
156 C3 Somme dept Picardie France
160 B2 Somme r. France
165 A4 Somme r. France
157 F3 Sommedieue France
165 E4 Somme-Leuze Belgium
143 F2 Sommen Sweden
143 F2 Sommen l. Sweden
156 E3 Sommepy-Tahure France
171 C4 Sömmerda Ger.
170 E3 Sommerfeld Ger.
171 C3 Sommersdorf Ger.
156 E3 Somme-Soude r. France
156 E4 Sommesous France
156 E3 Somme-Suippe France
157 E4 Sommevoire France
161 C5 Sommières France
162 C2 Sommières-du-Clain France
116 B5 Somnath Gujarat India
176 G5 Somogy county Hungary
177 G5 Somogyapáti Hungary
177 G5 Somogyjád Hungary
177 G5 Somogysárd Hungary
176 G5 Somogyszentpál Hungary
176 G5 Somogyszob Hungary
226 C5 Somonauk IL U.S.A.
174 G1 Somonino Pol.
185 H3 Somontín Spain
79 □1 Somosomo Taveuni Fiji
242 □I6 Somotillo Nic.
242 □I6 Somoto Nic.
137 J2 Somovo Rus. Fed.
115 E2 Sompeta Andhra Prad. India
174 G3 Sompolno Pol.
151 G4 Sompting West Sussex, England U.K.
156 E4 Sompuis France
197 E3 Šomrda hill Yugo.
259 D6 Somuncurá, Mesa Volcánica de plat. Arg.
114 B3 Somvarpet Karnataka India
165 D4 Somzée Belgium
117 F4 Son r. India
164 E3 Son Neth.
142 D2 Son Norway
191 F3 Sona Italy
242 □J8 Soná Panama
175 I3 Sona r. Pol.
Sonag Qinghai China see Zêkog
117 H4 Sonai r. India
117 H4 Sonai r. India
117 E5 Sonakhan Madh. Prad. India
116 D5 Sonala Mahar. India
121 G2 Sonaly Kazakh.
117 F5 Sonamukhi W. Bengal India
117 E5 Sonapur Orissa India
117 H4 Sonari Assam India
190 C1 Sonceboz Switz.
101 C5 Sŏnch'ŏn N. Korea
183 G2 Soncillo Spain
190 E3 Soncino Italy
190 F2 Sondalo Italy
142 C4 Sønderå r. Denmark
142 C4 Sønderborg Denmark
142 C4 Sønderjylland county Denmark
142 C4 Sønder Omme Denmark
169 F4 Sondershausen Ger.
142 D4 Søndersø Denmark
142 C3 Sønderup Denmark
Søndre Strømfjord Greenland see Kangerlussuaq
190 E2 Sondrio Italy
190 E2 Sondrio prov. Lombardia Italy
187 C5 Soneja Spain
114 C2 Sonepet Mahar. India
234 B1 Sonestown PA U.S.A.
207 I4 Song Nigeria
116 B5 Songad Gujarat India
Songbai Hubei China see Shennongjia
109 E2 Songbu Hubei China
97 E4 Sông Cau Vietnam
Songcheng Fujian China see Xiapu
97 D5 Sông Co Chiên r. mouth Vietnam
211 B7 Songea Tanz.
156 B3 Songeons France
101 C4 Sŏnggan N. Korea
97 D5 Sông Ham Luông r. mouth Vietnam
100 E3 Songhua Jiang r. China
Songjiachuan Shaanxi China see Wubu
100 D4 Songjiang Jilin China
109 G2 Songjiang Shanghai China
101 C4 Songjianghe Jilin China
Sŏngjin N. Korea see Kimch'aek
108 C2 Songkan Guizhou China
97 C6 Songkhla Thai.
96 D3 Song Khram, Mae Nam r. Thai.
121 H4 Songköl l. Kyrg.
107 I2 Songling Nei Mongol China
107 H3 Song Ling mts China
Songmai Sichuan China see Dêrong
108 B3 Songming Yunnan China
101 C5 Sŏngnam S. Korea
101 C5 Songnim N. Korea
209 B6 Songo Angola
213 G2 Songo Moz.
Songololo Dem. Rep. Congo see Mbanza-Ngungu
209 B6 Songololo Dem. Rep. Congo
108 B1 Songpan Sichuan China
117 G4 Songsak Meghalaya India
101 C6 Sŏngsan S. Korea
Songshan Guizhou China see Ziyun
107 G5 Song Shan mt. Henan China
108 D2 Songtao Guizhou China
109 F3 Songxi Fujian China
107 G5 Songxian Henan China
Songyang Yunnan China see Songming
Songyuan Fujian China see Songxi
100 C3 Songyuan Jilin China
109 D2 Songzi Hubei China
117 E5 Sonhat Madh. Prad. India
Sonid Youqi Nei Mongol China see Saihan Tal
Sonid Zuoqi Nei Mongol China see Mandalt
182 C3 Sonim Port.
116 D3 Sonipat Haryana India
116 D5 Sonkach Madh. Prad. India
134 D3 Sonkajärvi Fin.
Sonkël', Ozero l. Kyrg. see Songköl
139 K3 Sonkovo Rus. Fed.
96 C2 Sơn La Vietnam
123 F5 Sonmiani Bay Pak.
178 D3 Sonnblick mt. Austria
171 C5 Sonneberg Ger.
169 F5 Sonneborn Ger.
171 C5 Sonnefeld Ger.
178 D3 Sonnenjoch mt. Austria
171 E4 Sonnewalde Ger.
151 G3 Sonning Common Oxfordshire, England U.K.
193 F3 Sonnino Italy
179 F3 Sonntagberg Austria
257 E2 Sono r. Minas Gerais Brazil
254 C4 Sono r. Tocantins Brazil
241 L6 Sonoita AZ U.S.A.
240 F2 Sonoma CA U.S.A.
215 F1 Sonop S. Africa
242 C2 Sonora r. Mex.
242 C2 Sonora state Mex.
240 G3 Sonora CA U.S.A.
237 C6 Sonora TX U.S.A.
240 H2 Sonora Peak CA U.S.A.
122 A3 Sonqor Iran
183 G5 Sonseca Spain
187 G5 Son Servera Spain
175 I3 Sońsk Pol.
250 C3 Sonsón Col.
243 H6 Sonsonate El Salvador
91 H5 Sonsorol Islands Palau
214 D2 Sonstraal S. Africa
96 D2 Sơn Tây Vietnam
173 E3 Sontheim Ger.
173 E3 Sontheim an der Brenz Ger.
173 E4 Sonthofen Ger.
169 E4 Sontra Ger.
215 G4 Sonwabile S. Africa
Soochow Jiangsu China see Suzhou
138 E2 Soodla r. Estonia
Soomaaliya country Africa see Somalia
163 A5 Soorts-Hossegor France
261 I2 Sopas r. Uru.
186 D2 Sopeira Spain
231 D5 Soperton GA U.S.A.
161 F5 Sophia-Antipolis France
196 E5 Sopište Macedonia
197 G4 Sopot Bulg.
143 H4 Sopot Pol.
196 E3 Sopot Srbija Yugo.
108 A5 Sop Prap Thai.
176 F4 Sopron Hungary
176 F4 Sopronkövesd Hungary
183 G1 Sopuerta Spain
116 C2 Sopur Jammu and Kashmir
93 C2 Soputan, Gunung vol. Indon.
78 □4a Sopweru i. Chuuk Micronesia
111 F5 Soq Qu r. Xizang China
163 E5 Sor r. France
184 B2 Sôr r. Port.
182 C1 Sor r. Spain
193 F3 Sora Italy
179 F4 Sora r. Slovenia
114 B3 Sorab Karnataka India
191 G2 Soraga Italy
190 F4 Soragna Italy
141 L3 Söråker Sweden
101 D5 Sŏrak-san mt. S. Korea
192 D2 Sorano Italy
191 H2 Sorapis mt. Italy
252 C3 Sorata Bol.
142 B2 Sør-Audnedal Norway
185 H3 Sorbas Spain
183 G4 Sorbe r. Spain
146 D7 Sorbie Dumfries and Galloway, Scotland U.K.
190 F4 Sorbolo Italy
157 F4 Sorcy-St-Martin France
163 A5 Sorde-l'Abbaye France
163 B4 Sore France
163 E6 Sorède France
221 K5 Sorel Que. Can.
83 F5 Sorell Tas. Austr.
128 B4 Soreq r. Israel
190 E3 Soresina Italy
163 E5 Sorèze France
169 F4 Sorge Ger.
168 E1 Sorge r. Ger.
162 C3 Sorges France
192 B4 Sorgono Sardegna Italy
161 C4 Sorgues France
161 A5 Sorgues r. France
128 B1 Sorgun İçel Turkey
126 D3 Sorgun Yozgat Turkey
128 B1 Sorgun r. Turkey
183 H3 Soria Spain
183 H3 Soria prov. Castilla y León Spain
261 H3 Soriano Uru.
261 I3 Soriano dept Uru.
195 F4 Soriano Calabro Italy
193 E2 Soriano nel Cimino Italy
182 E4 Sorihuela Spain
185 G2 Sorihuela del Gaudalimar Spain
94 B2 Sorikmarapi vol. Indon.
146 B5 Sorisdale Argyll and Bute, Scotland U.K.
140 □ Sørkapp Land reg. Svalbard
120 C3 Sor Kaydak dry lake Kazakh.
122 C3 Sorkh, Kūh-e mts Iran
122 C3 Sorkheh Iran
128 A1 Sorkun Turkey
175 J2 Sorkwity Pol.
140 K2 Sørland Norway
120 C3 Sor Mertvyy Kultuk dry lake Kazakh.
140 M3 Sörmjöle Sweden
156 E3 Sormonne r. France
148 E2 Sorn East Ayrshire, Scotland U.K.
162 E3 Sornac France
172 B4 Sorne r. Switz.
142 D4 Sorø Denmark
117 F5 Soro Orissa India
194 D5 Soro, Monte mt. Sicilia Italy
136 E3 Soroca Moldova
256 D5 Sorocaba Brazil
120 C1 Sorochinsk Rus. Fed.
Soroki Moldova see Soroca
121 K1 Sorokino Rus. Fed.
Sorokino Luhans'ka Oblast' Ukr. see Krasnodon
91 J5 Sorol atoll Micronesia
93 D3 Sorong Irian Jaya Indon.
138 G3 Sorot' r. Rus. Fed.
210 B4 Soroti Uganda
140 M1 Sørøya i. Norway
140 M1 Sørøysundet sea chan. Norway
Sorp Turkey see Reşadiye
192 A4 Sorradile Sardegna Italy
184 B1 Sorraia r. Port.
140 L1 Sørreisa Norway
193 G4 Sorrento Italy
140 N3 Sorsakoski Fin.
140 O2 Sorsatunturi hill Fin.
140 L2 Sorsele Sweden
192 A4 Sorso Sardegna Italy
92 C3 Sorsogon Phil.
186 E2 Sort Spain
141 O3 Sortavala Rus. Fed.
182 C4 Sortelha Port.
195 E5 Sortino Sicilia Italy
140 K1 Sortland Norway
140 J3 Sør-Trøndelag county Norway
143 G2 Sorunda Sweden
168 E1 Sörup Ger.
Sõrve väin sea chan. Estonia/Latvia see Irbe Strait
185 G4 Sorvilán Spain
163 C4 Sos France
101 C5 Sŏsan S. Korea
143 E3 Sösdala Sweden
186 B2 Sos del Rey Católico Spain
139 J4 Sosenskiy Rus. Fed.
186 D3 Soses Spain
215 G1 Soshanguve S. Africa
175 M4 Soshychne Ukr.
194 C5 Sosio r. Sicilia Italy
139 J5 Soskovo Rus. Fed.
177 H4 Sóskút Hungary
139 L5 Sosna r. Rus. Fed.
260 C4 Sosneado mt. Arg.
174 F4 Sośnie Pol.
136 C2 Sosnivka L'vivs'ka Oblast' Ukr.
137 G2 Sosnivka Sums'ka Oblast' Ukr.
136 C2 Sosnivka Ternopils'ka Oblast' Ukr.
174 F2 Sośno Pol.
134 K3 Sosnogorsk Respublika Komi Rus. Fed.
136 D2 Sosnove Ukr.
121 I2 Sosnovka Kazakh.
134 I3 Sosnovka Arkhangel'skaya Oblast' Rus. Fed.
135 H5 Sosnovka Tambovskaya Oblast' Rus. Fed.
139 K2 Sosnovka Vologod. Obl. Rus. Fed.
139 H1 Sosnovo Rus. Fed.
135 I5 Sosnovoborsk Rus. Fed.
99 J1 Sosnovo-Ozerskoye Rus. Fed.
134 F2 Sosnovyy Rus. Fed.
Sosnovyy Bor Belarus see Sasnovy Bor
138 G2 Sosnovyy Bor Rus. Fed.
175 L4 Sosnowica Pol.
175 H5 Sosnowiec Pol.
Sosnowitz Pol. see Sosnowiec
175 L4 Sosnówka Pol.
137 G2 Sosnytsya Ukr.
161 F5 Sospel France
163 C6 Sost France
179 G4 Šoštanj Slovenia
130 H4 Sos'va Rus. Fed.
137 J4 Sosyka r. Rus. Fed.
207 F4 Sota r. Benin
260 B2 Sotaquí Chile
252 D2 Sotério r. Brazil
184 D3 Sotiel Coronada Spain
184 E2 Sotillo r. Spain
183 F4 Sotillo de la Adrada Spain
183 H3 Sotillo del Rincón Spain
140 O2 Sotkamo Fin.
260 E2 Soto Arg.
182 D1 Soto Spain
182 E2 Soto de la Vega Spain
183 G4 Soto del Real Spain
182 E1 Soto de Ribera Spain
245 E2 Soto la Marina Mex.
245 F2 Soto La Marina r. Mex.
183 G2 Sotopalacios Spain
183 H4 Sotos Spain
182 D4 Sotoserrano Spain
207 F4 Sotouboua Togo
182 E2 Soto y Amio Spain
183 F1 Sotres Spain
183 F2 Sotresgudo Spain
182 E1 Sotrondio Spain
Sotsgorodok Donets'ka Oblast' Ukr. see Hirnyk
192 B3 Sotta Corse France
156 B3 Sotteville-lès-Rouen France
194 D5 Sotto di Troina r. Sicilia Italy
191 H3 Sottomarina Italy
168 E2 Sottrum Ger.
141 M3 Sottunga Åland Fin.
185 H1 Sotuélamos Spain
243 H4 Sotuta Mex.
156 E3 Souain-Perthes-lès-Hurlus France
163 E5 Soual France
208 B4 Souanké Congo
161 B5 Soubès France
206 D5 Soubré Côte d'Ivoire
156 D4 Soucy France
198 D4 Souda Kriti Greece
84 D4 Soudan N.T. Austr.
158 E4 Soudan France
234 C2 Souderton PA U.S.A.
Soúdha Kriti Greece see Souda
163 C5 Soueich France
163 D6 Soueix France
159 I4 Souesmes France
157 H4 Soufflenheim France
199 E1 Soufli Greece
247 □2 Soufrière vol. Guadeloupe
247 □3 Soufrière St Lucia

247 D3 Soufrière vol. St Vincent
247 D3 Soufrière Hills Montserrat
206 B4 Souguéta Guinea
183 D4 Souillac France
157 F3 Souilly France
205 G1 Souk Ahras Alg.
189 A7 Souk Ahras prov. Alg.
204 D2 Souk el Arbaâ du Rharb Morocco
180 D5 Souk el Had el Rharbia Morocco
180 C5 Souk Khemis du Sahel Morocco
180 D5 Souk Tleta Taghramet Morocco
180 D5 Souk-Tnine-de-Sidi-el-Yamani Morocco
101 C5 Sŏul S. Korea
162 A3 Soulac-sur-Mer France
156 E4 Soulaines-Dhuys France
163 D6 Soulan France
163 E6 Soulatgé France
159 F3 Soulgé-sur-Ouette France
158 E5 Soullans France
158 E2 Soulles r. France
157 H4 Soultz-sous-Forêts France
165 E4 Soumagne Belgium
163 B5 Soumoulou France
235 F2 Sound Beach NY U.S.A.
223 I4 Sounding Creek r. Alta Can.
156 C4 Souppes-sur-Loing France
163 B5 Souprosse France
128 B3 Soûr Lebanon
159 F3 Sourdeval France
254 C2 Soure Brazil
182 B4 Soure Port.
223 K5 Souris Man. Can.
225 I4 Souris P.E.I. Can.
223 L5 Souris r. Sask. Can.
Souriya country Asia see Syria
163 E6 Sournia France
182 C4 Souro Pires Port.
198 C2 Sourpi Greece
156 B4 Sours France
163 C5 Sourzac France
254 F3 Sousa Brazil
182 B3 Sousa r. Port.
Sousa Lara Angola see Bocoio
163 E4 Sousceyrac France
184 C2 Sousel Port.
182 B4 Souselas Port.
79 D3 Sous le Vent, Îles is Arch. de la Société Fr. Polynesia
205 H2 Sousse Tunisia
163 A5 Soustons France
214 B4 Sout r. S. Africa
234 B4 South r. MD U.S.A.
South Africa country Africa see South Africa, Republic of
212 E6 South Africa, Republic of country Africa
84 C2 South Alligator r. N.T. Austr.
151 F2 Southam Warwickshire, England U.K.
235 D2 South Amboy NJ U.S.A.
248 South America continent
224 D4 Southampton Ont. Can.
151 F4 Southampton Southampton, England U.K.
151 F4 Southampton admin. div. England U.K.
233 G4 Southampton NY U.S.A.
223 O1 Southampton Island Nunavut Can.
151 F4 Southampton Water est. England U.K.
115 G4 South Andaman i. Andaman & Nicobar Is India
232 E6 South Anna r. VA U.S.A.
149 H4 South Anston South Yorkshire, England U.K.
235 D2 Southard NJ U.S.A.
82 C2 South Australia state Austr.
265 L7 South Australian Basin sea feature Indian Ocean
237 F5 Southaven MS U.S.A.
146 D6 South Ayrshire admin. div. Scotland U.K.
239 F5 South Baldy mt. NM U.S.A.
149 H3 South Bank Redcar and Cleveland, England U.K.
231 D7 South Bay FL U.S.A.
224 D4 South Baymouth Ont. Can.
230 C3 South Bend IN U.S.A.
238 B2 South Bend WA U.S.A.
151 H3 South Benfleet Essex, England U.K.
151 H3 Southborough Kent, England U.K.
232 D6 South Boston VA U.S.A.
150 D4 South Brent Devon, England U.K.
81 D5 Southbridge South I. N.Z.
233 G3 Southbridge MA U.S.A.
225 J3 South Brook Nfld. Can.
215 H4 Southbroom S. Africa
233 G2 South Burlington VT U.S.A.
81 C6 Southburn South I. N.Z.
235 E1 Southbury CT U.S.A.
234 C1 South Canaan PA U.S.A.
231 D5 South Carolina state U.S.A.
149 I4 South Cave East Riding of Yorkshire, England U.K.
151 F3 South Cerney Gloucestershire, England U.K.
150 E4 South Chard Somerset, England U.K.
232 B5 South Charleston OH U.S.A.
232 C5 South Charleston WV U.S.A.
90 E4 South China Sea N. Pacific Ocean
South Coast Town Qld Austr. see Gold Coast
236 C2 South Dakota state U.S.A.
146 F6 Southdean Scottish Borders, Scotland U.K.
233 G3 South Deerfield MA U.S.A.
234 D3 South Dennis NJ U.S.A.
151 G4 South Downs hills England U.K.
83 F5 South East Cape Tas. Austr.
265 J7 Southeast Indian Ridge sea feature Indian Ocean
87 D7 South East Isles W.A. Austr.
267 L10 Southeast Pacific Basin sea feature S. Pacific Ocean
234 D3 South Egg Harbor NJ U.S.A.
223 K3 Southend Sask. Can.
146 C6 Southend Argyll and Bute, Scotland U.K.
151 H3 Southend admin. div. England U.K.
151 H3 Southend-on-Sea Southend, England U.K.
210 C3 Southern admin. reg. Eth.
211 B8 Southern admin. reg. Malawi
206 B5 Southern prov. Sierra Leone
209 E9 Southern prov. Zambia
Southern Aegean admin. reg. Greece see Notio Aigaio
81 C5 Southern Alps mts South I. N.Z.
81 D2 Southern Cook Islands Cook Is
87 C3 Southern Cross W.A. Austr.
208 E2 Southern Darfur state Sudan
223 L3 Southern Indian Lake Man. Can.
208 F2 Southern Kordofan state Sudan
77 I3 Southern Lau Group is Fiji
262 F3 Southern Ocean OCEAN
231 E5 Southern Pines NC U.S.A.
Southern Rhodesia country Africa see Zimbabwe
146 D6 Southern Uplands hills Scotland U.K.
Southern Urals mts Rus. Fed. see Yuzhnyy Ural
151 H2 Southery Norfolk, England U.K.
146 F5 South Esk r. Angus, Scotland U.K.
86 E3 South Esk Tableland reg. W.A. Austr.
223 J5 Southey Sask. Can.
215 F4 Southeyville S. Africa
236 F4 South Fabius r. MO U.S.A.
232 B3 Southfield MI U.S.A.
235 F1 Southfields NY U.S.A.
266 G7 South Fiji Basin sea feature S. Pacific Ocean
151 I3 South Foreland pt England U.K.
240 F1 South Fork CA U.S.A.
239 F4 South Fork CO U.S.A.
234 D4 South Fork PA U.S.A.
222 E5 Southgate r. B.C. Can.
151 G3 Southgate Greater London, England U.K.
263 H1 South Geomagnetic Pole (1995) Antarctica
264 G9 South Georgia terr. S. Atlantic Ocean
249 G7 South Georgia and South Sandwich Islands terr. S. Atlantic Ocean
234 C1 South Gibson PA U.S.A.
226 C1 South Gillies Ont. Can.
235 F1 South Glastonbury CT U.S.A.
150 E3 South Gloucestershire admin. div. England U.K.
236 E4 South Grand r. MO U.S.A.
151 G4 South Harting West Sussex, England U.K.
226 D4 South Haven MI U.S.A.
80 E2 South Head North I. N.Z.
233 G2 South Hero VT U.S.A.
149 H3 South Hetton Durham, England U.K.
232 D6 South Hill VA U.S.A.
266 E3 South Honshu Ridge sea feature N. Pacific Ocean
223 L3 South Indian Lake Man. Can.
235 F1 Southington CT U.S.A.
86 D2 South Island Cocos Is
81 D6 South Island N.Z.
210 C4 South Island National Park Kenya
223 M5 South Junction Man. Can.
South Kazakhstan Oblast admin. div. Kazakh. see Yuzhnyy Kazakhstan
149 I4 South Kelsey Lincolnshire, England U.K.
149 H4 South Kirkby West Yorkshire, England U.K.
117 F5 South Koel r. Bihar India
240 G2 South Lake Tahoe CA U.S.A.
146 E6 South Lanarkshire admin. div. Scotland U.K.
81 A6 Southland admin. reg. South I. N.Z.
151 H2 South Lopham Norfolk, England U.K.
236 D3 South Loup r. NE U.S.A.
235 F1 South Lyme CT U.S.A.
222 C2 South Macmillan r. Y.T. Can.
263 J2 South Magnetic Pole (1995) Antarctica
113 D1 South Male Atoll Maldives
151 H3 Southminster Essex, England U.K.
150 D3 South Molton Devon, England U.K.
234 A3 South Mountains hills PA U.S.A.
86 B4 South Muiron Island W.A. Austr.
222 D1 South Nahanni r. N.W.T. Can.
146 D1 South Nesting Bay Scotland U.K.
233 F3 South New Berlin NY U.S.A.
151 H3 South Ockendon Thurrock, England U.K.
235 F1 Southold NY U.S.A.
264 G10 South Orkney Islands S. Atlantic Ocean
South Ossetia aut. reg. Georgia see Samkhret' Oset'i
151 G3 South Oxhey Hertfordshire, England U.K.
233 H2 South Paris ME U.S.A.
87 B5 South Passage W.A. Austr.
231 D6 South Patrick Shores FL U.S.A.
150 E4 South Petherton Somerset, England U.K.
235 D2 South Plainfield NJ U.S.A.
236 C3 South Platte r. CO U.S.A.
262 T1 South Pole Antarctica
224 D3 South Porcupine Ont. Can.
85 H5 Southport Qld Austr.
83 F5 Southport Tas. Austr.
149 F4 Southport Merseyside, England U.K.
235 E1 Southport CT U.S.A.
231 E5 Southport NC U.S.A.
227 I4 Southport NY U.S.A.
233 H3 South Portland ME U.S.A.
149 F2 South Queensferry Edinburgh, Scotland U.K.
227 H3 South River Ont. Can.
South Rona i. Highland, Scotland U.K. see Rona
146 F3 South Ronaldsay i. Scotland U.K.
233 G3 South Royalton VT U.S.A.
226 A3 South Saint Paul MN U.S.A.
264 H9 South Sandwich Islands S. Atlantic Ocean
264 H9 South Sandwich Trench sea feature S. Atlantic Ocean
240 F3 South San Francisco CA U.S.A.
223 J4 South Saskatchewan r. Alberta/Saskatchewan Can.
223 L3 South Seal r. Man. Can.
262 U2 South Shetland Islands Antarctica
264 E10 South Shetland Trough sea feature S. Atlantic Ocean
149 H2 South Shields Tyne and Wear, England U.K.
South Sinai governorate Egypt see Janūb Sīnā'
149 I4 South Skirlaugh East Riding of Yorkshire, England U.K.
236 E3 South Skunk r. IA U.S.A.
266 F6 South Solomon Trench sea feature Pacific Ocean
234 C1 South Sterling PA U.S.A.
234 C2 South Tamaqua PA U.S.A.
80 E3 South Taranaki Bight b. North I. N.Z.
265 N8 South Tasman Rise sea feature Southern Ocean
241 L2 South Tent mt. UT U.S.A.
235 D3 South Toms River NJ U.S.A.
116 E4 South Tons r. India
241 L5 South Tucson AZ U.S.A.
149 G3 South Tyne r. England U.K.
South Tyrol prov. Trentino - Alto Adige Italy see Bolzano
146 A4 South Uist i. Scotland U.K.
238 B3 South Umpqua r. OR U.S.A.
146 E3 South Walls pen. Scotland U.K.
151 G4 Southwater West Sussex, England U.K.
149 I4 Southwell Nottinghamshire, England U.K.
84 D3 South Wellesley Islands Qld Austr.
South-West Africa country Africa see Namibia
83 F5 South West Cape Tas. Austr.
81 A7 South West Cape Stewart I. N.Z.
85 H4 South West Cay rf Coral Sea Is Terr. Austr.
233 I2 Southwest Harbor ME U.S.A.
265 G7 Southwest Indian Ridge sea feature Indian Ocean
85 G3 South West Island Coral Sea Is Terr. Austr.
267 I8 Southwest Pacific Basin sea feature S. Pacific Ocean
Southwest Peru Ridge sea feature S. Pacific Ocean see Nazca Ridge
83 H2 South West Rocks N.S.W. Austr.
226 E5 South Whitley IN U.S.A.
237 D5 South Wichita r. TX U.S.A.
150 E3 Southwick Wiltshire, England U.K.
232 B6 South Williamson KY U.S.A.
227 I5 South Williamsport PA U.S.A.
233 G3 South Windham ME U.S.A.
151 I2 Southwold Suffolk, England U.K.
151 H3 South Woodham Ferrers Essex, England U.K.
151 H2 South Wootton Norfolk, England U.K.
149 H4 South Yorkshire admin. div. England U.K.
232 B5 South Zanesville OH U.S.A.
182 D4 Souto Guarda Port.
182 B5 Souto Santarém Port.
182 C2 Souto Spain
182 C4 Souto da Casa Port.
213 F3 Soutpan S. Africa
213 F4 Soutpansberg mts S. Africa
204 B5 Soutouf, Adrar mts Western Sahara
160 B2 Souvigny France
142 B1 Sovanuten mt. Norway
197 G2 Sovata Romania
197 H2 Soveja Romania
195 F4 Soverato Italy
192 B2 Soveria Corse France
195 F3 Soveria Mannelli Italy
123 G2 Sovet Tajik.
Sovetabad Uzbek. see Khanabad
Sovetashen Armenia see Zangakatun
136 C4 Sovetsk Kaliningradskaya Oblast' Rus. Fed.
134 J4 Sovetsk Kirovskaya Oblast' Rus. Fed.
139 K5 Sovetsk Tul'skaya Oblast' Rus. Fed.
129 B1 Sovetskaya Krasnodarskiy Kray Rus. Fed.
129 D1 Sovetskaya Stavropol'skiy Kray Rus. Fed.
100 G2 Sovetskaya Gavan' Rus. Fed.
130 H3 Sovetskiy Khanty-Mansiyskiy Avtonomnyy Okrug Rus. Fed.
138 G1 Sovetskiy Leningradskaya Oblast' Rus. Fed.
134 N2 Sovetskiy Respublika Komi Rus. Fed.
134 J4 Sovetskiy Respublika Mariy El Rus. Fed.
Sovetskiy Tajik. see Sovet
137 J2 Sovetskoye Belgorodskaya Oblast' Rus. Fed.
Sovetskoye Chechenskaya Respublika Rus. Fed. see Shatoy
Sovetskoye Kabardino-Balkarskaya Respublika Rus. Fed. see Kashkhatau
Sovetskoye Respublika Dagestan Rus. Fed. see Khebda
120 A2 Sovetskoye Saratovskaya Oblast' Rus. Fed.
Sovetskoye Stavropol'skiy Kray Rus. Fed. see Zelenokumsk
188 F4 Soviči Bos.-Herz.
195 E5 Sovicille Italy
137 H5 Sovyets'kyy Ukr.
212 E4 Sowa Botswana
108 A2 Sowa Sichuan China
212 E4 Sowa Pan salt pan Botswana
149 H3 Sowerby North Yorkshire, England U.K.
149 H4 Sowerby Bridge West Yorkshire, England U.K.
215 F2 Soweto S. Africa
Sōya-kaikyō str. Japan/Rus. Fed. see La Pérouse Strait
243 G5 Soyaló Mex.
134 I2 Soyana r. Rus. Fed.
162 C3 Soyaux France
160 E1 Soye France
173 G3 Soyen Ger.
Soylan Armenia see Vayk'
134 J2 Soyma r. Rus. Fed.
209 B6 Soyo Angola
161 C4 Soyons France
Sozaq Kazakh. see Suzak
139 H5 Sozh r. Europe
134 K4 Sozimskiy Rus. Fed.
198 F1 Sozopol Bulg.
165 E4 Spa Belgium
262 T2 Spaatz Island Antarctica
172 B2 Spabrücken Ger.
195 E6 Spadafora Sicilia Italy
168 C3 Spahnharrenstätte Ger.
172 C3 Spaichingen Ger.
180 E2 Spain country Europe
Spalato Croatia see Split
Spalatum Croatia see Split
82 D3 Spalding S.A. Austr.
149 I5 Spalding Lincolnshire, England U.K.
176 G2 Spálené Poříčí Czech Rep.
173 E2 Spalt Ger.
169 E4 Spangenberg Ger.
150 D3 Span Head hill England U.K.
225 K4 Spaniard's Bay Nfld. Can.
224 D4 Spanish Ont. Can.
224 D4 Spanish r. Ont. Can.
241 L1 Spanish Fork UT U.S.A.
Spanish Guinea country Africa see Equatorial Guinea
Spanish Netherlands country Europe see Belgium
145 C5 Spanish Point Rep. of Ireland
Spanish Sahara terr. Africa see Western Sahara
246 Spanish Town Jamaica
246 C1 Spanish Wells Eleuthera Bahamas
170 E2 Spantekow Ger.
194 B4 Sparagio, Monte mt. Sicilia Italy
193 G5 Sparanise Italy
240 H2 Sparks NV U.S.A.
232 B3 Sparlingville MI U.S.A.
234 D1 Sparrow Bush NY U.S.A.
Sparta Greece see Sparti
195 E4 Spartà Sicilia Italy
231 D5 Sparta GA U.S.A.
226 E4 Sparta MI U.S.A.
232 C6 Sparta NC U.S.A.
234 D1 Sparta NJ U.S.A.
231 C5 Sparta TN U.S.A.
226 B4 Sparta WI U.S.A.
231 D5 Spartanburg SC U.S.A.
232 D4 Spartansburg PA U.S.A.
198 C3 Sparti Greece
193 F6 Spartivento, Capo c. Italy
222 H5 Sparwood B.C. Can.
139 J4 Spas-Demensk Rus. Fed.
137 H3 Spas'ke Ukr.
139 M4 Spas-Klepiki Rus. Fed.
137 I3 Spas'ko-Mykhaylivka Ukr.
137 G3 Spasove Ukr.
100 E3 Spassk-Dal'niy Rus. Fed.
139 M4 Spassk-Ryazanskiy Rus. Fed.
169 C5 Spay Ger.
146 D5 Spean Bridge Highland, Scotland U.K.
236 C2 Spearfish SD U.S.A.
237 C4 Spearman TX U.S.A.
195 H3 Specchia Italy
233 F3 Speculator NY U.S.A.
151 F3 Speen West Berkshire, England U.K.
190 E1 Speer mt. Switz.
223 J4 Speers Sask. Can.
172 A2 Speicher Ger.
173 F2 Speichersdorf Ger.
247 D4 Speightstown Barbados
179 G3 Speikkogel mt. Austria
211 B5 Speke Gulf Tanz.
169 C3 Spelle Ger.
193 E2 Spello Italy
146 C5 Spelve, Loch inlet Scotland U.K.
Spence Bay Nunavut Can. see Taloyoak
236 E3 Spencer IA U.S.A.
238 D3 Spencer ID U.S.A.
230 C4 Spencer IN U.S.A.
233 H3 Spencer MA U.S.A.
236 D3 Spencer NE U.S.A.
233 E3 Spencer NY U.S.A.
232 C6 Spencer VA U.S.A.
232 C5 Spencer WV U.S.A.
82 D3 Spencer, Cape S.A. Austr.
212 B5 Spencer Bay Namibia
82 D3 Spencer Gulf est. S.A. Austr.
86 E3 Spencer Range hills N.T. Austr.
222 F5 Spences Bridge B.C. Can.
169 D3 Spenge Ger.
149 H3 Spennymoor Durham, England U.K.
81 D5 Spenser Mountains South I. N.Z.
198 C2 Spercheios r. Greece
171 E3 Sperenberg Ger.
Sperkhiós r. Greece see Spercheios
194 D5 Sperlinga Sicilia Italy
193 F3 Sperlonga Italy
197 G2 Spermezeu Romania
147 D2 Sperrin Mountains hills Northern Ireland U.K.
232 D5 Sperryville VA U.S.A.
169 E6 Spessart reg. Ger.
Spétsai i. Greece see Spetses
198 C3 Spetses Greece
198 C3 Spetses i. Greece
146 E4 Spey r. Scotland U.K.
146 E4 Spey Bay Moray, Scotland U.K.
172 C2 Speyer Ger.
158 C3 Spézet France
193 I5 Spezzano Albanese Italy
Spice Islands Indon. see Maluku
175 K4 Spiczyn Pol.
147 B3 Spiddal Rep. of Ireland
173 H3 Spiegelau Ger.
168 C2 Spiekeroog Ger.
168 C2 Spiekeroog i. Ger.
179 F3 Spielberg bei Knittelfeld Austria
179 G4 Spielfeld Austria
172 B2 Spiesen-Elversberg Ger.
190 C2 Spiez Switz.
190 D4 Spigno Monferrato Italy
193 F3 Spigno Saturnia Italy
164 F1 Spijk Neth.
164 C3 Spijkenisse Neth.
191 G4 Spilamberto Italy
193 G2 Spilimbergo Italy
195 E4 Spilinga Italy
149 J4 Spilsby Lincolnshire, England U.K.
193 I4 Spinazzola Italy
157 F3 Spincourt France
191 H3 Spinea Italy
193 F2 Spinetoli Italy
234 C2 Spinnerstown PA U.S.A.
193 H4 Spinoso Italy
177 L4 Spinuș Romania
236 E3 Spirit Lake IA U.S.A.
238 C1 Spirit Lake ID U.S.A.
223 J4 Spiritwood Sask. Can.
139 J3 Spirovo Rus. Fed.
176 G6 Špišić-Bukovica Croatia
177 J3 Spišská Belá Slovakia
177 J3 Spišská Nová Ves Slovakia
177 J2 Spišská Stará Ves Slovakia
177 J3 Spišské Podhradie Slovakia
177 J3 Spišské Vlachy Slovakia
177 J2 Spišský Štvrtok Slovakia
129 D3 Spitak Armenia
179 G3 Spital am Pyhrn Austria
179 G3 Spital am Semmering Austria
116 D3 Spiti r. India
86 C4 Spit Point W.A. Austr.
140 Spitsbergen i. Svalbard
214 D5 Spitskop mt. S. Africa
213 D5 Spitskopvlei S. Africa
179 F4 Spittal an der Drau Austria
146 E5 Spittal of Glenshee Perth and Kinross, Scotland U.K.
179 G2 Spitz Austria
Spitzbergen i. Svalbard see Spitsbergen
178 D4 Spitzkofel mt. Austria
190 E2 Spitzmeilen mt. Switz.
137 J3 Spivakivka Ukr.
151 I2 Spixworth Norfolk, England U.K.
142 C3 Spjald Denmark
188 F4 Split Croatia
223 L3 Split Lake Man. Can.
190 E2 Splügen Switz.
136 I3 Spodakhy Ukr.
136 E3 Spodnja Idrija Slovenia
179 G4 Spodnje Hoče Slovenia
168 F1 Spodsbjerg Denmark
149 H4 Spofforth North Yorkshire, England U.K.
238 C2 Spokane WA U.S.A.
238 C2 Spokane r. WA U.S.A.
129 B1 Spokoynaya Rus. Fed.
191 H2 Spöl r. Italy
Spoletium Italy see Spoleto
193 E2 Spoleto Italy
193 G2 Spoltore Italy
191 F2 Spondigna Italy
165 E4 Spontin Belgium
226 B5 Spoon r. IL U.S.A.
226 B3 Spooner WI U.S.A.
171 D4 Spora Ger.
170 C2 Spornitz Ger.
234 B2 Sporting Hill PA U.S.A.
190 E3 Spotorno Italy
235 D2 Spotswood NJ U.S.A.
232 E5 Spotsylvania VA U.S.A.
238 F3 Spotted Horse WY U.S.A.
227 F2 Spragge Ont. Can.
238 B3 Sprague r. OR U.S.A.
172 D3 Spraitbach Ger.
222 F4 Spranger, Mount B.C. Can.
90 D5 Spratly Island S. China Sea
90 D5 Spratly Islands S. China Sea
238 C2 Spray OR U.S.A.
226 C3 Spread Eagle WI U.S.A.
188 G3 Spreča r. Bos.-Herz.
171 E3 Spree r. Ger.
171 E3 Spreenhagen Ger.
172 C4 Spreitenbach Switz.
171 F4 Spremberg Ger.
172 B2 Sprendlingen Ger.
193 E3 Spresiano Italy
190 E2 Spriana Italy
165 E4 Sprimont Belgium
237 E4 Spring r. MO U.S.A.
227 F3 Spring Bay Ont. Can.
214 A3 Springbok S. Africa
234 C2 Spring City PA U.S.A.
241 L2 Spring City UT U.S.A.
84 D3 Spring Creek r. N.T. Austr.
236 C3 Spring Creek r. NE U.S.A.
225 K3 Springdale Nfld. Can.
237 E4 Springdale AR U.S.A.
169 E3 Springe Ger.
239 F4 Springer NM U.S.A.
241 M4 Springerville AZ U.S.A.
81 C5 Springfield South I. N.Z.
147 D2 Springfield Northern Ireland U.K.
237 C4 Springfield CO U.S.A.
231 D5 Springfield GA U.S.A.
238 D3 Springfield ID U.S.A.
226 B4 Springfield IL U.S.A.
232 F3 Springfield KY U.S.A.
233 G3 Springfield MA U.S.A.
236 D3 Springfield MN U.S.A.
236 E4 Springfield MO U.S.A.
232 B5 Springfield OH U.S.A.
238 B3 Springfield OR U.S.A.
234 C3 Springfield PA U.S.A.
231 C4 Springfield TN U.S.A.
233 G2 Springfield VT U.S.A.
232 D5 Springfield WV U.S.A.
215 E4 Springfontein S. Africa
251 G3 Spring Garden Guyana
235 D1 Spring Glen NY U.S.A.
234 B2 Spring Glen PA U.S.A.
241 J2 Spring Glen UT U.S.A.
226 B4 Spring Green WI U.S.A.
226 A3 Spring Grove MN U.S.A.
234 B3 Spring Grove PA U.S.A.
232 E6 Spring Grove VA U.S.A.
225 H4 Springhill N.S. Can.
231 D6 Spring Hill FL U.S.A.
146 D6 Springholm Dumfries and Galloway, Scotland U.K.
222 F5 Springhouse B.C. Can.
226 D4 Spring Lake MI U.S.A.
235 D2 Spring Lake Heights NJ U.S.A.
241 J3 Spring Mountains NV U.S.A.
226 E4 Springport MI U.S.A.
215 G3 Springs S. Africa
233 F3 Springs NY U.S.A.
81 D5 Springs Junction South I. N.Z.
85 G5 Springsure Qld Austr.
226 A3 Springvale WI U.S.A.
215 F5 Spring Valley S. Africa
240 I5 Spring Valley CA U.S.A.
226 A4 Spring Valley MN U.S.A.
235 D1 Spring Valley NY U.S.A.
226 A3 Spring Valley WI U.S.A.
236 D3 Springview NE U.S.A.
240 H3 Springville CA U.S.A.
232 D3 Springville NY U.S.A.
234 C1 Springville PA U.S.A.
241 L1 Springville UT U.S.A.
232 E3 Springwater NY U.S.A.
149 I4 Sproatley East Riding of Yorkshire, England U.K.
169 C4 Sprockhövel Ger.
151 I2 Sprowston Norfolk, England U.K.
222 H4 Spruce Grove Alta Can.
232 D5 Spruce Knob mt. WV U.S.A.
241 M2 Spruce Mountain CO U.S.A.
241 J1 Spruce Mountain NV U.S.A.
164 D3 Sprundel Neth.
234 B3 Spry PA U.S.A.
149 J4 Spurn Head hd England U.K.
220 C5 Spurr, Mount vol. AK U.S.A.
222 F5 Spuzzum B.C. Can.
175 J2 Spychowo Pol.
222 F5 Squamish B.C. Can.
222 F5 Squamish r. B.C. Can.
191 G3 Squaranto r. Italy
195 F4 Squillace Italy
195 F4 Squillace, Golfo di g. Italy
195 H2 Squinzano Italy
232 C6 Squire WV U.S.A.
87 E5 Squires, Mount hill W.A. Austr.
95 E4 Sragen Jawa Tengah Indon.
188 F3 Srbac Bos.-Herz.
196 E4 Srbica Kosovo, Srbija Yugo.
Srbija aut. rep. Yugo.
Srbinje Bos.-Herz. see Foča
Srbobran Bos.-Herz. see Donji Vakuf
196 D3 Srbobran Vojvodina, Srbija Yugo.
197 H3 Srebărna tourist site Bulg.
188 G3 Srebrenica Bos.-Herz.
197 H4 Sredets Burgas Bulg.
Sredets Grad Sofiya Bulg. see Sofiya
197 H4 Sredetska Reka r. Bulg.
131 Q4 Sredinnyy Khrebet mts Rus. Fed.
179 H4 Središče Slovenia
197 H4 Sredishte Bulg.
197 F4 Sredna Gora mts Bulg.
100 C2 Srednebelaya Rus. Fed.
131 Q3 Srednekolymsk Rus. Fed.
139 K4 Sredne-Russkaya Vozvyshennost' hills Rus. Fed.
131 M3 Sredne-Sibirskoye Ploskogor'ye plat. Rus. Fed.
137 J2 Sredniy Ikorets Rus. Fed.
197 G4 Srednogorie Bulg.
135 I6 Srednyaya Akhtuba Rus. Fed.
174 F3 Śrem Pol.
196 D3 Sremska Mitrovica Vojvodina, Srbija Yugo.
97 D4 Srêpôk, Tônlé r. Cambodia
99 K1 Sretensk Rus. Fed.
95 E2 Sri Aman Sarawak Malaysia
137 G2 Sribne Ukr.
115 E3 Sriharikota Island India
113 G4 Sri Jayewardenepura Kotte Sri Lanka
115 E2 Srikakulam Andhra Prad. India
114 C3 Sri Kalahasti Andhra Prad. India
114 D5 Sri Lanka country Asia
116 C4 Sri Madhopur Rajasthan India
116 G4 Srimangal Bangl.
116 D3 Srinagar Uttar Prad. India
116 C2 Srinagar Jammu and Kashmir India
114 B3 Sringeri Karnataka India
114 D5 Sri Pada mt. Sri Lanka
114 C4 Srirangam Tamil Nadu India
114 C2 Srisailam Andhra Prad. India
114 C4 Srivaikuntam Tamil Nadu India
114 B2 Srivardhan Mahar. India
114 C4 Srivilliputtur Tamil Nadu India
188 F3 Srnetica mts Bos.-Herz.
188 G3 Srnice Bos.-Herz.
175 J1 Srockowo Pol.
174 E4 Środa Śląska Pol.
174 F3 Środa Wielkopolska Pol.
146 D4 Sron a'Choire Ghairbh hill Scotland U.K.
121 K1 Srostki Rus. Fed.
196 E3 Srpska Crnja Vojvodina, Srbija Yugo.
Srpska Kostajnica Bos.-Herz. see Bosanska Kostajnica
Srpski Brod Bos.-Herz. see Bosanski Brod
196 E3 Srpski Itebej Vojvodina, Srbija Yugo.
115 D2 Srungavarapukota Andhra Prad. India
139 L5 Sselki Rus. Fed.
214 C2 Staansaam S. Africa
85 E3 Staaten r. Qld Austr.
179 H2 Staatz Austria
165 D3 Stabroek Belgium
Stabroek Guyana see Georgetown
176 C2 Stachy Czech Rep.
146 C3 Stac Pollaidh hill Scotland U.K.
Stac Polly hill Scotland U.K. see Stac Pollaidh
226 A3 Stacy MN U.S.A.
226 A4 Stacyville IA U.S.A.
168 E2 Stade Ger.
173 G4 Stadelhorn mt. Ger.
165 C4 Staden Belgium
168 F3 Stadensen Ger.
151 F3 Stadhampton Oxfordshire, England U.K.
146 A4 Stadhlaigearraidh Western Isles, Scotland U.K.
179 E2 Stadl-Paura Austria
164 F2 Stadskanaal Neth.
169 E5 Stadtallendorf Ger.
173 E3 Stadtbergen Ger.
169 E3 Stadthagen Ger.
171 C5 Stadtilm Ger.
169 B5 Stadtkyll Ger.
169 F5 Stadtlauringen Ger.
169 F5 Stadtlengsfeld Ger.
169 B4 Stadtlohn Ger.
169 E4 Stadtoldendorf Ger.
172 D2 Stadtprozelten Ger.
171 C5 Stadtroda Ger.
179 H3 Stadtschlaining Austria
171 C5 Stadtsteinach Ger.
168 D1 Stadum Ger.
190 D1 Stäfa Switz.
146 B5 Staffa i. Scotland U.K.
173 E2 Staffelberg hill Ger.
157 H5 Staffelfelden France
169 F5 Staffelstein Ger.
168 E3 Staffhorst Ger.
146 B4 Staffin Highland, Scotland U.K.
191 I5 Staffolo Italy
190 E3 Staffora r. Italy
150 E2 Stafford Staffordshire, England U.K.
232 E5 Stafford VA U.S.A.
246 C1 Stafford Creek Andros Bahamas
150 E2 Staffordshire admin. div. England U.K.
215 G4 Stafford's Post S. Africa
233 G4 Stafford Springs CT U.S.A.
174 H2 Stăhlavy Czech Rep.
171 E3 Stahnsdorf Ger.
138 E3 Staicele Latvia
172 D3 Staig Ger.
193 H3 Staina r. Italy
179 H3 Stainach Austria
149 H3 Staindrop Durham, England U.K.
151 G3 Staines Surrey, England U.K.
149 G3 Stainforth North Yorkshire, England U.K.
149 H4 Stainforth South Yorkshire, England U.K.
149 I3 Staintondale North Yorkshire, England U.K.
157 F4 Stainville France
179 G4 Stainz Austria
195 F5 Staiti Italy
177 I4 Stakčín Slovakia
146 D6 Stake, Hill of hill Scotland U.K.
137 J3 Stakhanov Ukr.
Stakhanovo Rus. Fed. see Zhukovskiy
150 E4 Stalbridge Dorset, England U.K.
190 C2 Stalden Switz.
151 I2 Stalham Norfolk, England U.K.
222 E3 Stalin, Mount B.C. Can.
Stalinabad Tajik. see Dushanbe
Stalingrad Rus. Fed. see Volgograd
Stalingradskaya Oblast' admin. div. Rus. Fed. see Volgogradskaya Oblast'
Staliniri Georgia see Ts'khinvali
Stalino Ukr. see Donets'k
Stalino Uzbek. see Shakhrikhan
Stalinogorsk Rus. Fed. see Novomoskovsk
Stalinogród Pol. see Katowice
Stalinsk Rus. Fed. see Novokuznetsk
178 E4 Stall Austria
143 G2 Stallarholmen Sweden
179 G3 Stallhofen Austria
149 G3 Stalling Busk North Yorkshire, England U.K.
173 G2 Stallwang Ger.
175 K5 Stalowa Wola Pol.
197 H3 Stălpu Romania
149 G4 Stalybridge Greater Manchester, England U.K.
197 G4 Stamboliyski Bulg.
85 E4 Stamford Qld Austr.
151 G2 Stamford Lincolnshire, England U.K.
233 G4 Stamford CT U.S.A.
233 F3 Stamford NY U.S.A.
237 D5 Stamford TX U.S.A.
149 I4 Stamford Bridge East Riding of Yorkshire, England U.K.
149 H2 Stamfordham Northumberland, England U.K.
171 C5 Stammbach Ger.
173 F3 Stammham Ger.
Stampalia i. Greece see Astypalaia
212 C5 Stampriet Namibia
178 B3 Stams Austria
173 G2 Stamsried Ger.
140 K1 Stamsund Norway
147 E3 Stamullen Rep. of Ireland
232 D5 Stanardsville VA U.S.A.
236 E3 Stanberry MO U.S.A.
222 H5 Standard Alta Can.
164 D3 Standdaarbuiten Neth.
215 G2 Standerton S. Africa
149 G4 Standish Greater Manchester, England U.K.
227 F4 Standish MI U.S.A.
151 H3 Standon Hertfordshire, England U.K.
148 F2 Stane North Lanarkshire, Scotland U.K.
197 G3 Stănești Romania
241 L5 Stanfield AZ U.S.A.
214 B6 Stanford S. Africa
230 C4 Stanford KY U.S.A.
238 E2 Stanford MT U.S.A.
151 H3 Stanford-le-Hope Thurrock, England U.K.
143 H3 Stånga Gotland Sweden
143 G3 Stångån r. Sweden
193 H4 St'Angelo a Fasanella Italy
193 H4 St'Angelo dei Lombardi Italy
140 O1 Stangenestind hill Norway
215 H3 Stanger S. Africa
151 H2 Stanhoe Norfolk, England U.K.
149 G3 Stanhope Durham, England U.K.
234 D2 Stanhope NJ U.S.A.
197 I2 Stănilești Romania
175 K4 Stanin Pol.
196 D3 Stanišić Vojvodina, Srbija Yugo.
Stanislav Ivano-Frankivs'ka Oblast' Ukr. see Ivano-Frankivs'k
137 G4 Stanislav Khersons'ka Oblast' Ukr.
175 M5 Stanislavchyk Ukr.
175 J3 Stanisławów Pol.
197 G2 Stânișoarei, Munții mts Romania
Stanke Dimitrov Bulg. see Dupnitsa
176 C2 Staňkov Czech Rep.
83 F5 Stanley Tas. Austr.
233 J1 Stanley N.B. Can.
109 Stanley H.K. China
259 F8 Stanley Falkland Is
149 H3 Stanley Durham, England U.K.
146 E5 Stanley Perth and Kinross, Scotland U.K.
238 D2 Stanley ID U.S.A.
236 C1 Stanley ND U.S.A.
232 D5 Stanley VA U.S.A.
226 B3 Stanley WI U.S.A.
84 B4 Stanley, Mount hill N.T. Austr.
83 F5 Stanley, Mount hill Tas. Austr.
Stanley, Mount Dem. Rep. Congo/Uganda see Margherita Peak
Stanleyville Dem. Rep. Congo see Kisangani
Stann Creek Belize see Dangriga
149 H2 Stannington Northumberland, England U.K.
198 B2 Stanos Greece
139 L5 Stanovaya Ryasa r. Rus. Fed.
139 L5 Stanovoye Rus. Fed.
131 M4 Stanovoye Nagor'ye mts Rus. Fed.
131 N4 Stanovoy Khrebet mts Rus. Fed.
139 K5 Stanovoy Kolodez' Rus. Fed.
178 C3 Stans Austria
190 D2 Stans Switz.
82 D3 Stansbury S.A. Austr.
86 F4 Stansmore Range hills W.A. Austr.
151 H3 Stansted airport England U.K.
151 H3 Stansted Mountfitchet Essex, England U.K.
83 G2 Stanthorpe Qld Austr.
151 H2 Stanton Suffolk, England U.K.
234 C3 Stanton DE U.S.A.
232 B6 Stanton KY U.S.A.
226 E4 Stanton MI U.S.A.
236 C2 Stanton ND U.S.A.
236 D3 Stanton NE U.S.A.
237 C5 Stanton TX U.S.A.
139 K5 Stantsiya Skuratovo Rus. Fed.
Stantsiya-Yakkabag Uzbek. see Yakkabag
151 H3 Stanway Essex, England U.K.
139 I3 Stanychno-Luhans'ke Ukr.
179 G3 Stanz im Mürztal Austria
168 F2 Stapel Ger.
169 F4 Stapelburg Ger.
168 F2 Stapelfeld Ger.
164 F2 Staphorst Neth.
151 F2 Stapleford Nottinghamshire, England U.K.
151 H3 Staplehurst Kent, England U.K.
236 E2 Staples MN U.S.A.
236 C3 Stapleton NE U.S.A.
175 I4 Stąporków Pol.
85 F3 Star r. Qld Austr.
139 J5 Star' Rus. Fed.
137 F2 Stara Basan' Ukr.
177 H2 Stará Bystrica Slovakia
175 M4 Stara Chortoryya Ukr.
175 J4 Starachowice Pol.
176 D2 Stará Huť Czech Rep.
174 G2 Stara Kiszewa Pol.
175 J4 Stara Kornica Pol.
136 E2 Stara Kotel'nya Ukr.
174 E2 Stara Łubianka Pol.
177 J2 Stará Ľubovňa Slovakia
177 I6 Stara Moravica Vojvodina, Srbija Yugo.
176 E1 Stará Paka Czech Rep.
196 E3 Stara Pazova Vojvodina, Srbija Yugo.
197 F4 Stara Planina mts Bulg./Yugo.
179 H5 Stara Ploščica Croatia
175 K5 Stara Sil' Ukr.
136 D3 Stara Ushytsya Ukr.
136 C2 Stara Vyzhivka Ukr.
175 K5 Stara Wieś Pol.
Staraya Barda Altayskiy Kray Rus. Fed. see Krasnogorskoye
137 K2 Staraya Chigla Rus. Fed.
137 J2 Staraya Kalitva Rus. Fed.
120 A1 Staraya Kulatka Rus. Fed.
120 A2 Staraya Poltavka Rus. Fed.
139 H3 Staraya Russa Rus. Fed.
139 J3 Staraya Toropa Rus. Fed.
135 J5 Staraya Tumba Rus. Fed.
197 G4 Stara Zagora Bulg.
136 C3 Stara Zhadova Ukr.
267 I6 Starbuck Island Kiribati
137 I4 Starchenkove Ukr.
197 H3 Starchiojd Romania
237 F5 Star City AR U.S.A.
226 D5 Star City IN U.S.A.
150 D4 Starcross Devon, England U.K.
174 G5 Stare Budkowice Pol.
179 G1 Stařeč Czech Rep.
174 C2 Stare Czarnowo Pol.
174 D2 Stare Dąbrowa Pol.
175 K2 Stare Dolistowo Pol.
175 K3 Stare Hołowczyce Pol.
171 F5 Staré Křečany Czech Rep.
174 D3 Stare Kurowo Pol.
176 F1 Staré Město Czech Rep.
174 G3 Stare Miasto Pol.
175 H1 Stare Pole Pol.
136 C3 Stare Selo Ukr.
174 E4 Stare Strącze Pol.
Stargard in Pommern Pol. see Stargard Szczeciński
174 D2 Stargard Szczeciński Pol.
175 M4 Stari Koshary Ukr.
136 F2 Stari Petrivtsi Ukr.
196 E4 Stari Ras and Sopoćani tourist site Yugo.
139 J3 Staritsa Rus. Fed.
231 D6 Starke FL U.S.A.
171 D5 Starkenberg Ger.
232 D6 Starkey VA U.S.A.
237 F5 Starkville MS U.S.A.
233 F2 Star Lake NY U.S.A.
173 F4 Starnberg Ger.
173 F4 Starnberger See l. Ger.
110 C1 Staroaleyskoye Rus. Fed.
Starobel'sk Ukr. see Starobil's'k
137 J4 Starobesheve Ukr.
137 J3 Starobil's'k Ukr.
137 J3 Starobohdanivka Ukr.
138 F5 Starobyn Belarus
137 J4 Staroderevyankovskaya Rus. Fed.
139 I5 Starodub Rus. Fed.
174 G2 Starogard Gdański Pol.
Starokonstantinov Ukr. see Starokostyantyniv
136 D3 Starokostyantyniv Ukr.
136 E4 Starokozache Ukr.
137 J5 Staroleushkovskaya Rus. Fed.
135 G7 Starominskaya Rus. Fed.
137 I4 Staromlynivka Ukr.
137 J5 Staronizhestebliyevskaya Rus. Fed.
197 H4 Staro Oryakhovo Bulg.
137 I2 Starooskol'skoye Vodokhranilishche resr Rus. Fed.
197 G4 Starosel Bulg.
197 H4 Staro Selo Bulg.
139 M5 Staroseslavino Rus. Fed.
135 G7 Staroshcherbinovskaya Rus. Fed.
120 D1 Starosubkhangulovo Rus. Fed.
137 I5 Starotitarovskaya Rus. Fed.
137 H3 Starovirivka Ukr.
175 H4 Starowa Góra Pol.
134 H4 Staroye Rus. Fed.
135 I5 Staroye Drozhzhanoye Rus. Fed.
139 K3 Staroye Melkovo Rus. Fed.
135 H5 Staroyur'yevo Rus. Fed.
139 L4 Starozhilovo Rus. Fed.
175 H3 Starożreby Pol.
240 H1 Star Peak NV U.S.A.
193 H4 St'Arsenio Italy
150 D4 Start Bay England U.K.
149 H3 Startforth Durham, England U.K.
Starve Island Kiribati see Starbuck Island
175 H2 Stary Dzierzgoń Pol.
177 L1 Stary Dzików Pol.
177 G2 Starý Jičín Czech Rep.
174 D4 Stary Kisielin Pol.
175 H3 Stary Kobrzyniec Pol.
175 K5 Stary Majdan Pol.
176 G2 Starý Plzenec Czech Rep.
175 I6 Stary Sącz Pol.
177 J2 Starý Smokovec Slovakia
175 J3 Stary Szelków Pol.
175 H2 Stary Targ Pol.
177 H3 Starý Tekov Slovakia
137 I2 Starytsya Ukr.
175 K4 Stary Uścimów Pol.
138 G5 Staryya Darohi Belarus
136 C2 Staryy Chortoryys'k Ukr.
Staryye Dorogi Belarus see Staryya Darohi
137 I4 Staryy Krym Donets'ka Oblast' Ukr.
137 H5 Staryy Krym Respublika Krym Ukr.
129 C2 Staryy Lesken Rus. Fed.
130 I3 Staryy Nadym Rus. Fed.
136 C3 Staryy Oleksynets' Ukr.
137 I2 Staryy Oskol Rus. Fed.
136 D3 Staryy Ostropil' Ukr.
Staryy Salavan Rus. Fed. see Novocheremshansk
137 I2 Staryy Saltiv Ukr.
136 B3 Staryy Sambir Ukr.
Staryy Sambor Ukr. see Staryy Sambir
129 E2 Staryy Terek r. Rus. Fed.
129 D2 Staryy Urukh Rus. Fed.
174 G1 Starzyno Pol.
171 C4 Staßfurt Ger.
175 J5 Staszów Pol.
232 E4 State College PA U.S.A.
237 F6 State Line MS U.S.A.
Staten Island Arg. see Los Estados, Isla de
235 D2 Staten Island NY U.S.A.
231 D5 Statenville GA U.S.A.
231 D5 Statesboro GA U.S.A.
231 D5 Statesville NC U.S.A.
142 C2 Stathelle Norway
235 D2 Statue of Liberty tourist site NJ U.S.A.
179 G2 Statzberg hill Austria
179 G2 Statzendorf Austria
196 E4 Stăuceni Moldova
171 E4 Stauchitz Ger.
172 B4 Staufen im Breisgau Ger.
173 E3 Staufersberg hill Ger.
150 E3 Staunton Gloucestershire, England U.K.
232 D5 Staunton VA U.S.A.
171 E4 Staupitz Ger.
142 A2 Stavanger Norway
81 C5 Staveley South I. N.Z.
149 H4 Staveley Derbyshire, England U.K.
165 E4 Stavelot Belgium
164 D3 Stavenisse Neth.
142 D2 Stavern Norway
197 G4 Stavertsi Bulg.
136 E3 Stavkove Ukr.
136 I3 Stavne Ukr.
164 E2 Stavoren Neth.
135 H7 Stavropol' Rus. Fed.
Stavropol' Kray admin. div. Rus. Fed. see Stavropol'skiy Kray
Stavropol'-na-Volge Rus. Fed. see Tol'yatti
135 H7 Stavropol'skaya Vozvyshennost' hills Rus. Fed.
129 C1 Stavropol'skiy Kray admin. div. Rus. Fed.
198 C1 Stavros Kentriki Makedonia Greece
198 C1 Stavros Kentriki Makedonia Greece
198 D1 Stavroupoli Anatoliki Makedonia kai Thraki Greece
83 E4 Stawell Vic. Austr.

85 E4 **Stawell** *r. Qld* Austr.
175 I2 **Stawiguda** Pol.
175 K2 **Stawiski** Pol.
174 G4 **Stawiszyn** Pol.
149 I3 **Staxton** *North Yorkshire, England* U.K.
136 F2 **Stayky** Ukr.
227 G3 **Stayner** *Ont.* Can.
238 B2 **Stayton** *OR* U.S.A.
215 G3 **Steadville** S. Africa
240 H2 **Steamboat** *NV* U.S.A.
238 F3 **Steamboat Springs** *CO* U.S.A.
175 I2 **Stębark** Pol.
220 B3 **Stebbins** *AK* U.S.A.
137 F3 **Stebliv** Ukr.
175 L6 **Stebnyk** Ukr.
195 F4 **Steccato** Italy
176 D2 **Štěchovice** Czech Rep.
170 D3 **Stechow** Ger.
190 D1 **Steckborn** Switz.
168 C2 **Stedesdorf** Ger.
171 C4 **Stedten** Ger.
164 F1 **Stedum** Neth.
214 E2 **Steekdorings** S. Africa
224 C3 **Steel** *r. Ont.* Can.
236 D2 **Steele** *ND* U.S.A.
262 T2 **Steele Island** Antarctica
234 B2 **Steelton** *PA* U.S.A.
236 F4 **Steelville** *MO* U.S.A.
222 G3 **Steen** *r. Alta* Can.
164 D3 **Steenbergen** Neth.
164 F2 **Steenderen** Neth.
215 H1 **Steenkampsberge** *mts* S. Africa
222 G3 **Steen River** *Alta* Can.
238 C3 **Steens Mountain** *OR* U.S.A.
156 C2 **Steenvoorde** France
164 F2 **Steenwijk** Neth.
149 J4 **Steeping** *r. England* U.K.
151 G3 **Steeple Claydon** *Buckinghamshire, England* U.K.
87 B5 **Steep Point** *W.A.* Austr.
149 H4 **Steeton** *West Yorkshire, England* U.K.
176 G3 **Štefanov** Slovakia
198 C2 **Stefanoviki** Greece
221 H2 **Stefansson Island** *Nunavut* Can.
136 E4 **Ştefan Vodă** Moldova
197 H3 **Ştefan Vodă** Romania
190 C2 **Steffisburg** Switz.
139 L5 **Stegalovka** Rus. Fed.
173 E2 **Stegaurath** Ger.
142 E4 **Stege** Denmark
171 C3 **Stegelitz** Ger.
179 H3 **Stegersbach** Austria
164 F2 **Steggerda** Neth.
Stegi Swaziland *see* **Siteki**
175 H1 **Stegny** Pol.
197 F2 **Ştei** Romania
179 G3 **Steiermark** *land* Austria
173 E2 **Steigerwald** *mts* Ger.
215 H2 **Steilrand** S. Africa
168 E3 **Steimbke** Ger.
173 F2 **Stein** Ger.
165 E4 **Stein** Neth.
172 B4 **Stein** Switz.
172 C4 **Steina** *r.* Ger.
172 C3 **Steinach** *Baden-Württemberg* Ger.
173 G3 **Steinach** *Bayern* Ger.
171 C5 **Steinach** *Thüringen* Ger.
178 C3 **Steinach am Brenner** Austria
179 G2 **Steinakirchen am Forst** Austria
190 D1 **Stein am Rhein** Switz.
168 D2 **Steinau** Ger.
169 E5 **Steinau an der Straße** Ger.
223 L5 **Steinbach** *Man.* Can.
171 E5 **Steinbach** Ger.
169 D5 **Steinbach (Taunus)** Ger.
179 E3 **Steinbach am Attersee** Austria
171 C5 **Steinbach am Wald** Ger.
179 F3 **Steinbach an der Steyr** Austria
173 G2 **Steinberg** *Bayern* Ger.
168 E1 **Steinberg** *Schleswig-Holstein* Ger.
168 E1 **Steinbergkirche** Ger.
168 F2 **Steinburg** Ger.
179 F4 **Steindorf am Ossiacher See** Austria
172 B4 **Steinen** Ger.
178 E4 **Steinfeld** Austria
172 D2 **Steinfeld** *Bayern* Ger.
172 C2 **Steinfeld** *Rheinland-Pfalz* Ger.
168 D3 **Steinfeld (Oldenburg)** Ger.
165 E5 **Steinfort** Lux.
169 C3 **Steinfurt** Ger.
173 E4 **Steingaden** Ger.
170 D1 **Steinhagen** *Mecklenburg-Vorpommern* Ger.
169 D3 **Steinhagen** *Nordrhein-Westfalen* Ger.
171 C5 **Steinheid** Ger.
169 E4 **Steinheim** Ger.
173 E3 **Steinheim am Albuch** Ger.
172 D3 **Steinheim an der Murr** Ger.
171 F3 **Steinhöfel** Ger.
173 G3 **Steinhöring** Ger.
168 F3 **Steinhorst** *Niedersachsen* Ger.
168 F2 **Steinhorst** *Schleswig-Holstein* Ger.
171 F4 **Steinigtwolmsdorf** Ger.
168 E2 **Steinkirchen** Ger.
140 J2 **Steinkjer** Norway
169 D5 **Steinkopf** *hill* Ger.
214 A3 **Steinkopf** S. Africa
171 F3 **Steinsdorf** Ger.
173 E2 **Steinsfeld** Ger.
142 A1 **Steinsland** Norway
172 B2 **Steinwenden** Ger.
171 C5 **Steinwiesen** Ger.
172 C4 **Steißlingen** Ger.
214 D4 **Stekaar** S. Africa
165 D3 **Stekene** Belgium
191 G5 **Stella** *r.* Italy
191 I3 **Stella** *r.* Italy
215 E2 **Stella** S. Africa
168 F2 **Stelle** Ger.
214 B5 **Stellenbosch** S. Africa
164 D3 **Stellendam** Neth.
192 B2 **Stello, Monte** *mt. Corse* France
168 E2 **Stemmen** Ger.
169 D3 **Stemshorn** Ger.
174 E5 **Stěnava** *r.* Pol.
157 F3 **Stenay** France
143 G3 **Stenbo** Sweden
170 C3 **Stendal** Ger.
138 D3 **Stende** Latvia
143 G2 **Stenhamra** Sweden
146 E5 **Stenhousemuir** *Falkirk, Scotland* U.K.
191 F2 **Stenico** Italy
142 E4 **Stenløse** Denmark
146 □G1 **Stenness** *Shetland, Scotland* U.K.
146 E2 **Stenness, Loch of** *l. Scotland* U.K.
173 H2 **Štěnovice** Czech Rep.
142 E4 **Stensved** Denmark
146 F6 **Stenton** *East Lothian, Scotland* U.K.
140 L2 **Stenudden** Sweden
142 D2 **Stenungsund** Sweden
175 M5 **Stenyatyn** Ukr.
136 C2 **Stenzharychi** Ukr.
Steornabhagh *Western Isles, Scotland* U.K. *see* **Stornoway**
136 D2 **Stepan'** Ukr.
Stepanakert Azer. *see* **Xankändi**
129 D3 **Step'anavan** Armenia
136 D2 **Stepanivka** *Khmel'nyts'ka Oblast'* Ukr.
137 H2 **Stepanivka** *Sums'ka Oblast'* Ukr.
137 H4 **Stepanivka Persha** Ukr.
120 D2 **Stepanovka** Kazakh.
147 E3 **Stepaside** Rep. of Ireland
168 F2 **Stepenitz** *r.* Ger.
173 G4 **Stephanskirchen** Ger.
173 G3 **Stephansposching** Ger.
236 D1 **Stephen** *MN* U.S.A.
80 D4 **Stephens, Cape** *South I.* N.Z.
234 D2 **Stephensburg** *NJ* U.S.A.
232 D5 **Stephens City** *VA* U.S.A.
83 E2 **Stephens Creek** *N.S.W.* Austr.
226 D3 **Stephenson** *MI* U.S.A.
262 T2 **Stephenson, Mount** Antarctica
225 J3 **Stephenville** *Nfld.* Can.
237 D5 **Stephenville** *TX* U.S.A.
137 J5 **Stepnaya** Rus. Fed.
137 G1 **Stepne** Ukr.
235 E1 **Stepney** *CT* U.S.A.
174 C2 **Stepnica** Pol.
121 H1 **Stepnogorsk** Kazakh.
137 H4 **Stepnohirs'k** Ukr.
Stepnoy Rus. Fed. *see* **Elista**
120 E1 **Stepnoye** *Chelyabinskaya Oblast'* Rus. Fed.
120 A2 **Stepnoye** *Saratovskaya Oblast'* Rus. Fed.
129 D1 **Stepnoye** *Stavropol'skiy Kray* Rus. Fed.
121 G1 **Stepnyak** Kazakh.
196 E3 **Stepojevac** *Srbija* Yugo.
175 K3 **Sterdyń** Pol.
198 C2 **Sterea Ellas** *admin. reg.* Greece
215 F4 **Sterkspruit** S. Africa
215 F4 **Sterkstroom** S. Africa
175 J1 **Sterławki-Wielkie** Pol.
120 C1 **Sterlibashevo** Rus. Fed.
214 C4 **Sterling** S. Africa
236 C3 **Sterling** *CO* U.S.A.
235 G1 **Sterling** *CT* U.S.A.
226 C5 **Sterling** *IL* U.S.A.
236 D4 **Sterling** *KS* U.S.A.
227 E3 **Sterling** *MI* U.S.A.
236 C2 **Sterling** *ND* U.S.A.
241 L2 **Sterling** *UT* U.S.A.
237 C6 **Sterling City** *TX* U.S.A.
227 F4 **Sterling Heights** *MI* U.S.A.
120 C1 **Sterlitamak** Rus. Fed.
170 C2 **Sternberg** Ger.
176 G2 **Šternberk** Czech Rep.
168 E1 **Sterup** Ger.
157 F5 **Stes-Geosmes** France
161 C5 **Stes Maries, Golfe des** *b.* France
161 C5 **Stes-Maries-de-la-Mer** France
174 E3 **Stęszew** Pol.
176 D1 **Štětí** Czech Rep.
137 G3 **Stetsivka** Ukr.
137 H2 **Stets'kivka** Ukr.
172 D3 **Stetten am kalten Markt** Ger.
Stettin Pol. *see* **Szczecin**
Stettiner Haff *b.* Ger. *see* **Oderhaff**
238 D1 **Stettler** *Alta* Can.
232 C4 **Steubenville** *OH* U.S.A.
179 F4 **Steuerberg** Austria
171 D4 **Steutz** Ger.
151 G3 **Stevenage** *Hertfordshire, England* U.K.
80 D4 **Stevens, Mount** *South I.* N.Z.
238 B2 **Stevenson** *WA* U.S.A.
226 C3 **Stevens Point** *WI* U.S.A.
146 D6 **Stevenston** *North Ayrshire, Scotland* U.K.
220 D3 **Stevens Village** *AK* U.S.A.
234 B4 **Stevensville** *MD* U.S.A.
226 D4 **Stevensville** *MI* U.S.A.
227 I5 **Stevensville** *PA* U.S.A.
262 O1 **Steventon Island** Antarctica
85 E2 **Stewart** *r. Qld* Austr.
222 D4 **Stewart** *B.C.* Can.
222 B2 **Stewart** *r. Y.T.* Can.
240 L5 **Stewart** *NV* U.S.A.
84 C1 **Stewart, Cape** *N.T.* Austr.
259 C9 **Stewart, Isla** *i.* Chile
222 B2 **Stewart Crossing** *Y.T.* Can.
81 A7 **Stewart Island** N.Z.
78 □6 **Stewart Islands** Solomon Is
146 D6 **Stewarton** *East Ayrshire, Scotland* U.K.
240 F2 **Stewarts Point** *CA* U.S.A.
147 E2 **Stewartstown** *Northern Ireland* U.K.
234 B3 **Stewartstown** *PA* U.S.A.
246 □ **Stewart Town** Jamaica
223 J5 **Stewart Valley** *Sask.* Can.
226 A4 **Stewartville** *MN* U.S.A.
225 I4 **Stewiacke** *N.S.* Can.
168 E3 **Steyerberg** Ger.
151 G4 **Steyning** *West Sussex, England* U.K.
215 F2 **Steynrus** S. Africa
215 E4 **Steynsburg** S. Africa
179 F2 **Steyr** Austria
179 F3 **Steyr** *r.* Austria
179 F2 **Steyregg** Austria
214 E5 **Steytlerville** S. Africa
175 J4 **Stężyca** Pol.
174 F1 **Stężyca** Pol.
191 G5 **Stia** Italy
177 H3 **Štiavnické Vrchy** *mts* Slovakia
177 H2 **Štiavnik** Slovakia
150 C4 **Stibb Cross** *Devon, England* U.K.
149 G2 **Stichill** *Scottish Borders, Scotland* U.K.
149 J4 **Stickney** *Lincolnshire, England* U.K.
169 F4 **Stiege** Ger.
164 E1 **Stiens** Neth.
191 G4 **Stienta** Italy
Stif Alg. *see* **Sétif**
237 E5 **Stigler** *OK* U.S.A.
193 I4 **Stigliano** Italy
195 F4 **Stignano** Italy
143 G2 **Stigtomta** Sweden
222 C3 **Stikine** *r. B.C.* Can.
222 D3 **Stikine Plateau** *B.C.* Can.
142 D2 **Stikkvasskollen** *hill* Norway
214 C6 **Stilbaai** S. Africa
226 C3 **Stiles** *WI* U.S.A.
215 F2 **Stilfontein** S. Africa
Stilís Greece *see* **Stylida**
149 H3 **Stillington** *North Yorkshire, England* U.K.
234 B3 **Still Pond** *MD* U.S.A.
226 A3 **Stillwater** *MN* U.S.A.
237 D4 **Stillwater** *OK* U.S.A.
238 E2 **Stillwater** *r. MT* U.S.A.
240 H2 **Stillwater Range** *mts NV* U.S.A.
195 F4 **Stilo** Italy
195 F4 **Stilo, Punta** *pt* Italy
188 F4 **Štilt** *mt.* Bos.-Herz.
151 G2 **Stilton** *Cambridgeshire, England* U.K.
237 E5 **Stilwell** *OK* U.S.A.
196 E4 **Štimlje** *Kosovo, Srbija* Yugo.
173 E2 **Stimpfach** Ger.
263 E2 **Stinear, Mount** Antarctica
237 C5 **Stinnett** *TX* U.S.A.
192 A4 **Stintino** *Sardegna* Italy
193 H4 **Stio** Italy
197 F5 **Štip** Macedonia
188 E3 **Stipanov Grič** *mt.* Croatia
157 G3 **Stiring-Wendel** France
84 C4 **Stirling** *N.T.* Austr.
227 I3 **Stirling** *Ont.* Can.
146 E5 **Stirling** *Stirling, Scotland* U.K.
146 D5 **Stirling** *admin. div. Scotland* U.K.
235 D2 **Stirling** *NJ* U.S.A.
87 C6 **Stirling, Mount** *hill W.A.* Austr.
84 B3 **Stirling Creek** *r. N.T.* Austr.
82 D3 **Stirling North** *S.A.* Austr.
87 C7 **Stirling Range** *mts W.A.* Austr.
190 F4 **Stirone** *r.* Italy
232 B6 **Stirrat** *WV* U.S.A.
150 B4 **Stithians** *Cornwall, England* U.K.
177 J3 **Štítnik** Slovakia
227 J3 **Stittsville** *Ont.* Can.
176 F2 **Štíty** Czech Rep.
191 G3 **Stizzon** *r.* Italy
140 M1 **Stjernøya** *i.* Norway
140 J3 **Stjørdalshalsen** Norway
146 D5 **Stob Choire Claurigh** *mt. Scotland* U.K.
146 D5 **Stob Ghabhar** *mt. Scotland* U.K.
175 J6 **Stobnica** *r.* Pol.
174 F5 **Stobrawa** *r.* Pol.
176 C1 **Stochov** Czech Rep.
151 H3 **Stock** *Essex, England* U.K.
157 G4 **Stock, Étang du** *l.* France
172 D4 **Stockach** Ger.
151 F3 **Stockbridge** *Hampshire, England* U.K.
227 E4 **Stockbridge** *MI* U.S.A.
168 F2 **Stockelsdorf** Ger.
179 E4 **Stockenboi** Austria
179 H2 **Stockerau** Austria
234 C2 **Stockertown** *PA* U.S.A.
171 C5 **Stockheim** Ger.
143 H2 **Stockholm** Sweden
143 G2 **Stockholm** *county* Sweden
233 □I1 **Stockholm** *ME* U.S.A.
235 D1 **Stockholm** *NJ* U.S.A.
190 C2 **Stockhorn** *mt.* Switz.
83 F3 **Stockinbingal** *N.S.W.* Austr.
179 G4 **Stocking** Austria
149 G4 **Stockport** *Greater Manchester, England* U.K.
149 H4 **Stocksbridge** *South Yorkshire, England* U.K.
168 E3 **Stöckse** Ger.
149 H3 **Stocksfield** *Northumberland, England* U.K.
264 G6 **Stocks Seamount** *sea feature* S. Atlantic Ocean
172 D2 **Stockstadt am Main** Ger.
172 C2 **Stockstadt am Rhein** Ger.
240 G3 **Stockton** *CA* U.S.A.
226 B4 **Stockton** *IL* U.S.A.
236 D4 **Stockton** *KS* U.S.A.
237 E4 **Stockton** *MO* U.S.A.
234 D2 **Stockton** *NJ* U.S.A.
241 K1 **Stockton** *UT* U.S.A.
149 G4 **Stockton Heath** *Warrington, England* U.K.
149 H3 **Stockton-on-Tees** *Stockton-on-Tees, England* U.K.
149 H3 **Stockton-on-Tees** *admin. div. England* U.K.
237 C6 **Stockton Plateau** *TX* U.S.A.
233 □I2 **Stockton Springs** *ME* U.S.A.
236 C3 **Stockville** *NE* U.S.A.
175 J4 **Stoczek Łukowski** Pol.
175 J3 **Stoczek-Osada** Pol.
176 C2 **Stod** Czech Rep.
141 L3 **Stöde** Sweden
139 I4 **Stodolishche** Rus. Fed.
97 D4 **Stœng Trêng** Cambodia
146 C3 **Stoer** *Highland, Scotland* U.K.
215 G1 **Stoffberg** S. Africa
196 E5 **Stogovo Planina** *mts* Macedonia
150 D3 **Stogursey** *Somerset, England* U.K.
151 G2 **Stoke Albany** *Northamptonshire, England* U.K.
151 I2 **Stoke Ash** *Suffolk, England* U.K.
151 H3 **Stoke-by-Nayland** *Suffolk, England* U.K.
151 I2 **Stoke Holy Cross** *Norfolk, England* U.K.
151 G3 **Stoke Mandeville** *Buckinghamshire, England* U.K.
151 G3 **Stokenchurch** *Buckinghamshire, England* U.K.
150 D4 **Stokenham** *Devon, England* U.K.
149 G4 **Stoke-on-Trent** *Stoke-on-Trent, England* U.K.
149 G4 **Stoke-on-Trent** *admin. div. England* U.K.
151 G3 **Stoke Poges** *Buckinghamshire, England* U.K.
150 E2 **Stoke Prior** *Worcestershire, England* U.K.
81 E4 **Stokes, Mount** *South I.* N.Z.
150 E2 **Stokesay** *Shropshire, England* U.K.
87 D7 **Stokes Inlet** *W.A.* Austr.
149 H3 **Stokesley** *North Yorkshire, England* U.K.
83 E5 **Stokes Point** *Tas.* Austr.
84 B3 **Stokes Range** *hills N.T.* Austr.
150 D4 **Stoke St Mary** *Somerset, England* U.K.
150 E4 **Stoke sub Hamdon** *Somerset, England* U.K.
81 E4 **Stokes Valley** *North I.* N.Z.
136 C2 **Stokhid** *r.* Ukr.
168 G1 **Stokkemarke** Denmark
140 K1 **Stokmarknes** Norway
176 E2 **Štoky** Czech Rep.
179 E4 **Stol** *mt.* Slovenia
197 F3 **Stol** *mt.* Yugo.
188 F4 **Stolac** Bos.-Herz.
169 F4 **Stolberg (Harz) Kurort** Ger.
169 B5 **Stolberg (Rheinland)** Ger.
121 K2 **Stolboukha** Kazakh.
Stolbtsy Belarus *see* **Stowbtsy**
174 F2 **Stołczno** Pol.
177 J3 **Stolica** *mt.* Slovakia
188 G3 **Stolice** *hill* Bos.-Herz.
136 D2 **Stolin** Belarus
171 D5 **Stollberg** Ger.
168 D2 **Stollhamm (Butjadingen)** Ger.
174 G2 **Stolno** Pol.
Stolp Pol. *see* **Słupsk**
170 F3 **Stolpe** *Brandenburg* Ger.
168 F1 **Stolpe** *Schleswig-Holstein* Ger.
171 F4 **Stolpen** Ger.
164 D3 **Stolwijk** Neth.
169 E3 **Stolzenau** Ger.
214 A5 **Stompneusbaai** S. Africa
150 E3 **Stone** *Gloucestershire, England* U.K.
151 H3 **Stone** *Kent, England* U.K.
150 E2 **Stone** *Staffordshire, England* U.K.
232 C4 **Stoneboro** *PA* U.S.A.
224 E4 **Stonecliffe** *Ont.* Can.
236 C3 **Stoneham** *CO* U.S.A.
234 D3 **Stone Harbor** *NJ* U.S.A.
146 F5 **Stonehaven** *Aberdeenshire, Scotland* U.K.
85 E5 **Stonehenge** *Qld* Austr.
151 F3 **Stonehenge** *tourist site England* U.K.
150 E3 **Stonehouse** *Gloucestershire, England* U.K.
146 E6 **Stonehouse** *South Lanarkshire, Scotland* U.K.
226 B3 **Stone Lake** *WI* U.S.A.
233 F4 **Stone Ridge** *NY* U.S.A.
232 D6 **Stoneville** *NC* U.S.A.
223 L5 **Stonewall** *Man.* Can.
237 D5 **Stonewall** *OK* U.S.A.
227 H4 **Stoney Creek** *Ont.* Can.
234 C2 **Stoney Creek Mills** *PA* U.S.A.
147 D4 **Stoneyford** Rep. of Ireland
146 D7 **Stoneykirk** *Dumfries and Galloway, Scotland* U.K.
227 F4 **Stoney Point** *Ont.* Can.
215 G4 **Stoneyride** S. Africa
235 G1 **Stonington** *CT* U.S.A.
233 □I2 **Stonington** *ME* U.S.A.
146 □G2 **Stonybreck** *Shetland, Scotland* U.K.
235 E2 **Stony Brook** *NY* U.S.A.
234 B3 **Stony Brook** *PA* U.S.A.
235 F1 **Stony Creek** *CT* U.S.A.
232 E6 **Stony Creek** *VA* U.S.A.
222 H4 **Stony Plain** *Alta* Can.
223 J3 **Stony Rapids** *Sask.* Can.
151 G2 **Stony Stratford** *Milton Keynes, England* U.K.
179 H3 **Stoob** Austria
224 D2 **Stooping** *r. Ont.* Can.
175 J1 **Stopki** Pol.
175 I5 **Stopnica** Pol.
168 E2 **Stör** *r.* Ger.
142 C3 **Stora** *r.* Denmark
143 F2 **Storå** Sweden
143 G3 **Stora Alvaret** *i.* Sweden
141 K3 **Storbäcken** Sweden
141 J3 **Storbekkfjellet** *mt.* Norway
141 K3 **Storbo** Sweden
142 A2 **Stord** *i.* Norway
140 I3 **Stordal** Norway
141 J3 **Store** *mt.* Norway
179 G4 **Štore** Slovenia
142 D4 **Store Bælt** *sea chan.* Denmark
142 A1 **Storebø** Norway
170 D1 **Store Damme** Denmark
142 E4 **Store Heddinge** Denmark
141 J3 **Store Jukleeggi** *mt.* Norway
140 M1 **Store Lenangstind** *mt.* Norway
140 J3 **Støren** Norway
142 B2 **Store Nup** *mt.* Norway
168 F1 **Store Rise** Denmark
142 A1 **Store Sotra** *i.* Norway
140 □ **Storfjorden** *sea chan.* Svalbard
143 F2 **Storfors** Sweden
140 K2 **Storforshei** Norway
140 K2 **Storjola** Sweden
142 B2 **Storkarshei** *hill* Norway
221 H2 **Storkerson Peninsula** *Nunavut* Can.
171 E3 **Storkow** Ger.
83 F5 **Storm Bay** *Tas.* Austr.
215 F4 **Stormberg** S. Africa
215 F4 **Stormberg** *mt.* S. Africa
215 F4 **Stormberg** *r.* S. Africa
215 F4 **Stormberge** *mts* S. Africa
236 E3 **Storm Lake** *IA* U.S.A.
214 D5 **Stormsrivier** S. Africa
193 H3 **Stornara** Italy
193 H3 **Stornarella** Italy
146 B3 **Stornoway** *Western Isles, Scotland* U.K.
191 F3 **Storo** Italy
140 □ **Storøya** *i.* Svalbard
134 K3 **Storozhevsk** Rus. Fed.
136 C3 **Storozhynets'** Ukr.
151 G4 **Storrington** *West Sussex, England* U.K.
142 C2 **Stor-Roan** *mt.* Norway
233 G4 **Storrs** *CT* U.S.A.
140 L2 **Storseleby** Sweden
143 G1 **Storsjön** *l.* Sweden
143 G2 **Storsjön** *l.* Sweden
140 K3 **Storsjön** *l.* Sweden
140 J3 **Storskarhø** *mt.* Norway
140 K2 **Storskog** Sweden
140 M1 **Storslett** Norway
142 D4 **Storstrøm** *county* Denmark
140 M2 **Storsund** Sweden
151 H3 **Stort** *r. England* U.K.
164 E1 **Stortemelk** *sea chan.* Neth.
140 L2 **Storuman** Sweden
140 L2 **Storuman** *l.* Sweden
140 K3 **Storvigelen** *mt.* Norway
143 G1 **Storvik** Sweden
142 D3 **Storvorde** Denmark
143 G2 **Storvreta** Sweden
238 F2 **Story** *WY* U.S.A.
259 B8 **Stosch, Isla** *i.* Chile
171 C4 **Stößen** Ger.
151 G2 **Stotfold** *Bedfordshire, England* U.K.
173 E4 **Stötten am Auerberg** Ger.
171 C4 **Stotternheim** Ger.
234 B2 **Stouchsburg** *PA* U.S.A.
223 K5 **Stoughton** *Sask.* Can.
165 E4 **Stoumont** Belgium
97 D4 **Stoŭng, Stœng** *r.* Cambodia
150 F4 **Stour** *r. Dorset, England* U.K.
151 I3 **Stour** *r. Essex/Suffolk, England* U.K.
151 I3 **Stour** *r. Kent, England* U.K.
151 F2 **Stour** *r. Oxfordshire/Warwickshire, England* U.K.
150 E2 **Stourbridge** *West Midlands, England* U.K.
150 E2 **Stourport-on-Severn** *Worcestershire, England* U.K.
146 F6 **Stow** *Scottish Borders, Scotland* U.K.
138 F5 **Stowbtsy** Belarus
234 C2 **Stowe** *PA* U.S.A.
174 F1 **Stowięcino** Pol.
151 H2 **Stowmarket** *Suffolk, England* U.K.
151 F3 **Stow-on-the-Wold** *Gloucestershire, England* U.K.
136 C2 **Stoyaniv** Ukr.
100 D1 **Stoyba** Rus. Fed.
175 K1 **Stożne** Pol.
191 H3 **Stra** Italy
171 D4 **Straach** Ger.
215 F1 **Straatsdrif** S. Africa
147 D2 **Strabane** *Northern Ireland* U.K.
175 L3 **Strabla** Pol.
146 F4 **Strachan** *Aberdeenshire, Scotland* U.K.
146 C5 **Strachur** *Argyll and Bute, Scotland* U.K.
168 C2 **Strackholt (Großefehn)** Ger.
147 D3 **Stradbally** Rep. of Ireland
151 I2 **Stradbroke** *Suffolk, England* U.K.
190 E3 **Stradella** Italy
179 G4 **Straden** Austria
151 H2 **Stradishall** *Suffolk, England* U.K.
147 D3 **Stradone** Rep. of Ireland
151 H2 **Stradsett** *Norfolk, England* U.K.
169 B4 **Straelen** Ger.
83 F5 **Strahan** *Tas.* Austr.
241 L3 **Straight Cliffs** *ridge UT* U.S.A.
165 E5 **Straimont** Belgium
176 C2 **Strakonice** Czech Rep.
197 H4 **Straldzha** Bulg.
179 G3 **Strallegg** Austria
146 E5 **Straloch** *Perth and Kinross, Scotland* U.K.
170 E1 **Stralsund** Ger.
190 C3 **Strambino** Italy
165 E3 **Stramproy** Neth.
214 B6 **Strand** S. Africa
140 I3 **Stranda** Norway
168 F1 **Strande** Ger.
147 C2 **Strandhill** Rep. of Ireland
231 E7 **Strangers Cay** *i.* Bahamas
147 F2 **Strangford** *Northern Ireland* U.K.
147 F2 **Strangford Lough** *inlet Northern Ireland* U.K.
143 G2 **Strängnäs** Sweden
193 F3 **Strangolagalli** Italy
84 C2 **Strangways** *r. N.T.* Austr.
84 C4 **Strangways Range** *mts N.T.* Austr.
177 G3 **Strání** Czech Rep.
147 E1 **Stranocum** *Northern Ireland* U.K.
147 D2 **Stranorlar** Rep. of Ireland
146 C7 **Stranraer** *Dumfries and Galloway, Scotland* U.K.
194 B5 **Strasatti** *Sicilia* Italy
157 H4 **Strasbourg** France
170 E2 **Strasburg** Ger.
232 C4 **Strasburg** *OH* U.S.A.
234 B3 **Strasburg** *PA* U.S.A.
232 D5 **Strasburg** *VA* U.S.A.
136 E4 **Strășeni** Moldova
Strasheny Moldova *see* **Strășeni**
173 H2 **Strašice** Czech Rep.
172 D3 **Straßberg** Ger.
171 C4 **Straßberg** Ger.
179 F4 **Straßburg** Austria
Strassburg France *see* **Strasbourg**
165 F5 **Strassen** Lux.
179 G3 **Straßengel** Austria
169 C5 **Straßenhaus** Ger.
179 H2 **Strasshof an der Norbahn** Austria
173 G3 **Straßkirchen** Ger.
178 E3 **Straßwalchen** Austria
151 F3 **Stratfield Mortimer** *West Berkshire, England* U.K.
224 D5 **Stratford** *Ont.* Can.
80 E3 **Stratford** *North I.* N.Z.
147 E4 **Stratford** Rep. of Ireland
240 H3 **Stratford** *CA* U.S.A.
235 E1 **Stratford** *CT* U.S.A.
237 C4 **Stratford** *TX* U.S.A.
226 B3 **Stratford** *WI* U.S.A.
151 F2 **Stratford-upon-Avon** *Warwickshire, England* U.K.
82 D3 **Strathalbyn** *S.A.* Austr.
146 D6 **Strathaven** *South Lanarkshire, Scotland* U.K.
148 E2 **Strathblane** *Stirling, Scotland* U.K.
146 F4 **Strathbogie** *reg. Scotland* U.K.
146 D4 **Strathcarron** *val. Scotland* U.K.
263 G2 **Strathcona, Mount** Antarctica
146 D4 **Strathconon** *val. Scotland* U.K.
146 D4 **Strath Dearn** *val. Scotland* U.K.
146 E4 **Strathdon** *Aberdeenshire, Scotland* U.K.
146 D5 **Strath Earn** *val. Scotland* U.K.
146 D3 **Strath Fleet** *val. Scotland* U.K.
146 D4 **Strathglass** *val. Scotland* U.K.
83 F5 **Strathgordon** *Tas.* Austr.
146 E3 **Strath Halladale** *val. Scotland* U.K.
222 H5 **Strathmore** *Alta* Can.
146 D3 **Strathmore** *r. Scotland* U.K.
240 H3 **Strathmore** *CA* U.S.A.
222 F4 **Strathnaver** *B.C.* Can.
146 D3 **Strathnaver** *val. Scotland* U.K.
146 E3 **Strath of Kildonan** *val. Scotland* U.K.
146 D4 **Strathpeffer** *Highland, Scotland* U.K.
227 G4 **Strathroy** *Ont.* Can.
146 E4 **Strathspey** *val. Scotland* U.K.
146 E5 **Strath Tay** *val. Scotland* U.K.
146 E3 **Strathy** *Highland, Scotland* U.K.
146 D3 **Strathy Point** *Scotland* U.K.
146 D5 **Strathyre** *Stirling, Scotland* U.K.
198 C1 **Stratoni** *Kentriki Makedonia* Greece
199 F3 **Stratonıkeıa** *tourist site* Turkey
198 B2 **Stratos** *Dytiki Ellas* Greece
150 C4 **Stratton** *Cornwall, England* U.K.
233 □H2 **Stratton** *ME* U.S.A.
233 G3 **Stratton Mountain** *VT* U.S.A.
151 F3 **Stratton St Margaret** *Swindon, England* U.K.
173 G3 **Straubing** Ger.
140 K1 **Straume** Norway
140 □B2 **Straumnes** *pt* Iceland
171 F4 **Straupitz** Ger.
170 E3 **Strausberg** Ger.
169 F4 **Straußfurt** Ger.
234 B2 **Strausstown** *PA* U.S.A.
241 L4 **Strawberry** *AZ* U.S.A.
238 C2 **Strawberry Mountain** *OR* U.S.A.
175 I5 **Strawczyn** Pol.
226 C5 **Strawn** *IL* U.S.A.
197 F4 **Straža** *mt.* Macedonia
197 G4 **Strazhitsa** Bulg.
176 D2 **Stráž nad Nežárkou** Czech Rep.
171 G5 **Stráž nad Nisou** Czech Rep.
179 E2 **Strážný** Czech Rep.
176 C2 **Strážov** Czech Rep.
177 H3 **Strážov** *mt.* Slovakia
171 F5 **Stráž pod Ralskem** Czech Rep.
177 K3 **Strážske** Slovakia
82 C3 **Streaky Bay** *S.A.* Austr.
82 C3 **Streaky Bay** *b. S.A.* Austr.
147 D3 **Streamstown** Rep. of Ireland
151 F3 **Streatley** *West Berkshire, England* U.K.
226 C5 **Streator** *IL* U.S.A.
176 D2 **Středočeský Kraj** *admin. reg.* Czech Rep.
168 D2 **Streek** Ger.
150 E3 **Street** *Somerset, England* U.K.
197 F3 **Strehaia** Romania
171 E4 **Strehla** Ger.
197 F3 **Strei** *r.* Romania
87 D6 **Streich Mound** *hill W.A.* Austr.
177 H4 **Strekov** Slovakia
176 C2 **Střela** *r.* Czech Rep.
197 G4 **Strelcha** Bulg.
137 I2 **Streletskoye** Rus. Fed.
176 F2 **Střelice** Czech Rep.
137 J2 **Strelitsa** Rus. Fed.
86 C4 **Strelley** *W.A.* Austr.
86 C4 **Strelley** *r. W.A.* Austr.
134 G2 **Strel'na** *r.* Rus. Fed.
179 H3 **Strem** Austria
191 F2 **Strembo** Italy
171 D3 **Stremme** *r.* Ger.
136 E2 **Stremyhorod** Ukr.
138 E3 **Strenči** Latvia
179 F2 **Strengberg** Austria
178 B3 **Strengen** Austria
149 H3 **Strensall** *York, England* U.K.
175 M5 **Streptiv** Ukr.
190 D3 **Stresa** Italy
149 G4 **Stretford** *Greater Manchester, England* U.K.
151 H2 **Stretham** *Cambridgeshire, England* U.K.
151 F2 **Stretton** *Staffordshire, England* U.K.
169 F5 **Streu** *r.* Ger.
169 F5 **Streufdorf** Ger.
144 D1 **Streymoy** *i.* Faroe Is
130 I3 **Strezhevoy** Rus. Fed.
176 B2 **Stříbro** Czech Rep.
146 F4 **Strichen** *Aberdeenshire, Scotland* U.K.
91 J8 **Strickland** *r.* P.N.G.
191 G2 **Strigno** Italy
179 H4 **Štrigova** Croatia
164 D3 **Strijen** Neth.
176 E2 **Strimilov** Czech Rep.
198 C1 **Strimonas** *r.* Greece
Strimonikón Greece *see* **Strymoniko**
148 D2 **Striven, Loch** *inlet Scotland* U.K.
188 G3 **Strizivojna** Croatia
179 G5 **Strmec** Croatia
169 F4 **Ströbeck** Ger.
179 E3 **Strobl** Austria
259 E6 **Stroeder** Arg.
173 F3 **Strogen** *r.* Ger.
137 G4 **Strohanivka** Ukr.
168 D3 **Ströhen** Ger.
136 E4 **Stroiești** Moldova
137 I2 **Stroitel'** Rus. Fed.
147 C3 **Strokestown** Rep. of Ireland
170 E2 **Strom** *r.* Ger.
146 E3 **Stroma, Island of** *Scotland* U.K.
141 L3 **Strömbacka** Sweden
172 B2 **Stromberg** Ger.
195 E4 **Stromboli, Isola** *i. Isole Lipari* Italy
146 C4 **Stromeferry** *Highland, Scotland* U.K.
259 □ **Stromness** S. Georgia
146 E3 **Stromness** *Orkney, Scotland* U.K.
141 L3 **Strömsbruk** Sweden
236 D3 **Stromsburg** *NE* U.S.A.
142 D2 **Strömstad** Sweden
140 K3 **Strömsund** Sweden
193 E2 **Stroncone** Italy
190 F3 **Strone** *r.* Italy
146 D6 **Strone** *Argyll and Bute, Scotland* U.K.
237 E5 **Strong** *AR* U.S.A.
195 G3 **Strongoli** Italy
232 C4 **Strongsville** *OH* U.S.A.
174 E5 **Stronie Śląskie** Pol.
146 F2 **Stronsay** *i. Scotland* U.K.
146 F2 **Stronsay Firth** *sea chan. Scotland* U.K.
179 H2 **Stronsdorf** Austria
146 C5 **Strontian** *Highland, Scotland* U.K.
177 K2 **Stropkov** Slovakia
176 D3 **Stropnice** *r.* Czech Rep.
190 D3 **Stroppiana** Italy
190 C4 **Stroppo** Italy
150 E3 **Stroud** *Gloucestershire, England* U.K.
83 G3 **Stroud Road** *N.S.W.* Austr.
234 C2 **Stroudsburg** *PA* U.S.A.
Stroyentsy Moldova *see* **Stroiești**
175 H6 **Stróża** Pol.
168 C2 **Strücklingen (Saterland)** Ger.
142 C3 **Struer** Denmark
196 E5 **Struga** Macedonia
174 F3 **Struga** *r.* Pol.
138 G2 **Strugi-Krasnyye** Rus. Fed.
214 C6 **Struis Bay** S. Africa
147 D2 **Strule** *r. Northern Ireland* U.K.
173 E2 **Strullendorf** Ger.
197 F5 **Struma** *r.* Bulg.
150 B2 **Strumble Head** *hd Wales* U.K.
198 C1 **Strumeshnitsa** *r.* Bulg.
197 F5 **Strumica** Macedonia
197 F5 **Strumica** *r.* Macedonia
174 G6 **Strumień** Pol.
177 L3 **Strumkivka** Ukr.
139 L3 **Strunino** Rus. Fed.
179 F1 **Strunkovice nad Blanicí** Czech Rep.
169 F4 **Struth** Ger.
232 C4 **Struthers** *OH* U.S.A.
197 G4 **Stryama** *r.* Bulg.
214 D3 **Strydenburg** S. Africa
215 E2 **Strydpoort** S. Africa
175 H4 **Stryków** Pol.
198 C1 **Strymoniko** Greece
141 I3 **Stryn** Norway
136 C3 **Strypa** *r.* Ukr.
136 F4 **Stryukove** Ukr.
136 B3 **Stryy** Ukr.
136 C3 **Stryy** *r.* Ukr.
136 E3 **Stryzhavka** Ukr.
174 F3 **Strzałkowo** Pol.
174 G5 **Strzebień** Pol.
175 I3 **Strzegocin** Pol.
174 E5 **Strzegom** Pol.
174 E5 **Strzegomka** *r.* Pol.
175 I3 **Strzegowo-Osada** Pol.
175 H3 **Strzelce** Pol.
174 D3 **Strzelce Krajeńskie** Pol.
174 G5 **Strzelce Opolskie** Pol.
175 H4 **Strzelce Wielkie** Pol.
84 C4 **Strzelecki, Mount** *hill N.T.* Austr.
174 F5 **Strzeleczki** Pol.
174 F5 **Strzelin** Pol.
174 G3 **Strzelno** Pol.
174 G1 **Strzepcz** Pol.
175 J6 **Strzyżów** Pol.
136 D1 **Stsvina** *r.* Belarus
85 G5 **Stuart** *r. Qld* Austr.
231 D7 **Stuart** *FL* U.S.A.
236 E3 **Stuart** *IA* U.S.A.
236 D3 **Stuart** *NE* U.S.A.
232 C6 **Stuart** *VA* U.S.A.
84 C4 **Stuart Bluff Range** *mts N.T.* Austr.
146 F4 **Stuartfield** *Aberdeenshire, Scotland* U.K.
81 A6 **Stuart Mountains** *South I.* N.Z.
82 C2 **Stuart Range** *hills S.A.* Austr.
232 D5 **Stuarts Draft** *VA* U.S.A.
178 C3 **Stubaier Alpen** *mts* Austria
168 E1 **Stubbæk** Denmark
170 D1 **Stubbekøbing** Denmark
168 D2 **Stubben** Ger.
151 F4 **Stubbington** *Hampshire, England* U.K.
179 G3 **Stubenberg** Austria
196 E4 **Stubica** *Srbija* Yugo.
196 E3 **Stubline** *Srbija* Yugo.
175 K6 **Stubno** Pol.
Stuchka Latvia *see* **Aizkraukle**
Stučka Latvia *see* **Aizkraukle**
176 E2 **Studená** Czech Rep.
136 E3 **Studena** Ukr.
179 E2 **Studená Vltava** *r.* Czech Rep.
196 E4 **Studenica** *tourist site* Yugo.
170 D3 **Stüdenitz** Ger.
177 H2 **Studénka** Czech Rep.
136 D2 **Studenytsya** *r.* Ukr.
151 G3 **Studham** *Bedfordshire, England* U.K.
81 C6 **Studholme Junction** *South I.* N.Z.
176 G3 **Studienka** Slovakia
214 E5 **Studis** S. Africa
151 F4 **Studland** *Dorset, England* U.K.
151 F2 **Studley** *Warwickshire, England* U.K.
143 G2 **Studsvik** Sweden
134 B3 **Studsviken** Sweden
237 C6 **Study Butte** *TX* U.S.A.
174 F1 **Studzienice** Pol.
140 K3 **Stugun** Sweden
178 D3 **Stuhlfelden** Austria
172 C4 **Stühlingen** Ger.
136 F2 **Stuhna** *r.* Ukr.
168 D2 **Stuhr** Ger.
171 E3 **Stülpe** Ger.
197 G2 **Stulpicani** Romania
178 C3 **Stumm** Austria
Stung Treng Cambodia *see* **Stœng Trêng**
223 M4 **Stupart** *r. Man.* Can.
176 G3 **Stupava** Slovakia
139 L4 **Stupino** Rus. Fed.
175 I2 **Stupsk** Pol.
190 D3 **Stura** *r.* Italy
190 C3 **Stura di Ala** *r.* Italy
190 C4 **Stura di Demonte** *r.* Italy
161 F3 **Stura di Val Grande** *r.* Italy
190 C3 **Stura di Viù** *r.* Italy
263 K2 **Sturge Island** Antarctica
224 E4 **Sturgeon** *r. Ont.* Can.
223 J4 **Sturgeon** *r. Sask.* Can.
226 D3 **Sturgeon** *r. MI* U.S.A.
226 D3 **Sturgeon Bay** *WI* U.S.A.
226 E3 **Sturgeon Bay** *b. MI* U.S.A.
224 E4 **Sturgeon Falls** *Ont.* Can.
230 C4 **Sturgis** *KY* U.S.A.
226 E5 **Sturgis** *MI* U.S.A.
236 C2 **Sturgis** *SD* U.S.A.
190 E4 **Sturla** *r.* Italy
188 E3 **Šturlić** Bos.-Herz.
150 E4 **Sturminster Newton** *Dorset, England* U.K.
177 H4 **Štúrovo** Slovakia
151 I3 **Sturry** *Kent, England* U.K.
83 E2 **Sturt, Mount** *hill N.S.W.* Austr.
82 D3 **Sturt Bay** *S.A.* Austr.
86 F3 **Sturt Creek** *W.A.* Austr.
226 D4 **Sturtevant** *WI* U.S.A.
84 C3 **Sturt Plain** *N.T.* Austr.
82 E2 **Sturt Stony Desert** *Qld* Austr.
157 H3 **Sturzelbronn** France
215 F5 **Stutterheim** S. Africa
172 D3 **Stuttgart** Ger.
172 D2 **Stuttgart** *admin. reg. Baden-Württemberg* Ger.
237 F5 **Stuttgart** *AR* U.S.A.
Stutthof Pol. *see* **Sztutowo**
169 F5 **Stützerbach** Ger.
136 D2 **Stvyha** *r.* Ukr.
140 □B2 **Stykkishólmur** Iceland
137 I4 **Styla** Ukr.
198 C2 **Stylida** Greece
136 D1 **Styr** *r.* Belarus/Ukr.
Styria *land* Austria *see* **Steiermark**
257 G3 **Suaçuí Grande** *r.* Brazil
203 H5 **Suakin** Sudan
203 H5 **Suakin Archipelago** *is* Sudan
164 F1 **Suameer** Neth.
183 F1 **Suances** Spain
109 G3 **Suao** Taiwan
242 C2 **Suaqui Grande** Mex.
203 H5 **Suara, Mount** Eritrea
138 E4 **Subačius** Lith.
95 D4 **Subang** *Jawa Barat* Indon.
111 F7 **Subansiri** *r.* India
117 F5 **Subarnarekha** *r. W. Bengal* India
199 F1 **Subaşı** Turkey
199 E2 **Subaşı** Turkey
193 E1 **Subasio, Monte** *mt.* Italy
138 E3 **Subate** Latvia
191 G5 **Subbiano** Italy
197 G2 **Subcetate** Romania
110 F4 **Subei** *Gansu* China
Subeita *tourist site* Israel *see* **Shivta**
179 E2 **Suben** Austria
193 F3 **Subiaco** Italy
174 G1 **Subkowy** Pol.
237 C4 **Sublette** *KS* U.S.A.
196 D2 **Subotica** *Vojvodina, Srbija* Yugo.
203 I6 **Subucle** *mt.* Eritrea
177 H2 **Sučany** Slovakia
162 D3 **Suc-au-May** *hill* France
234 D2 **Succasunna** *NJ* U.S.A.
190 F4 **Succiso, Alpi di** *mts* Italy
197 H2 **Suceava** Romania
197 G2 **Suceava** *r.* Romania
158 E4 **Sucé-sur-Erdre** France
175 H6 **Sucha Beskidzka** Pol.
175 H1 **Suchacz** Pol.
177 G3 **Suchá Loz** Czech Rep.
174 D2 **Suchań** Pol.
Suchan Rus. Fed. *see* **Partizansk**
100 E4 **Suchan** *r.* Rus. Fed.
176 E2 **Suchdol** Czech Rep.
176 D3 **Suchdol nad Lužnicí** Czech Rep.
175 I4 **Suchedniów** Pol.
190 B2 **Suchet, Mont** *mt.* Switz.
244 C2 **Suchil** Mex.
175 L2 **Suchowola** Pol.
175 K3 **Suchożebry** Pol.
187 C7 **Sucina** Spain
250 B3 **Sucio** *r.* Col.
197 G2 **Suciu de Sus** Romania
147 C3 **Suck** *r.* Rep. of Ireland
227 G2 **Sucker Creek Landing** *Ont.* Can.
170 C2 **Suckow** Ger.
252 D4 **Sucre** Bol.
250 C2 **Sucre** *dept* Col.
251 F2 **Sucre** *state* Venez.
250 B5 **Sucumbíos** *prov.* Ecuador
251 G6 **Sucunduri** *r.* Brazil
256 B4 **Sucuriú** *r.* Brazil
Suczawa Romania *see* **Suceava**
207 H6 **Sud** *prov.* Cameroon
233 G2 **Sud, Rivière du** *r. Que.* Can.
139 K2 **Suda** Rus. Fed.
139 K2 **Suda** *r.* Rus. Fed.
137 H5 **Sudak** Ukr.
203 F6 **Sudan** *country* Africa
134 H4 **Suday** Rus. Fed.
120 C1 **Sud'bodarovka** Rus. Fed.
224 D4 **Sudbury** *Ont.* Can.
151 F2 **Sudbury** *Derbyshire, England* U.K.
151 H2 **Sudbury** *Suffolk, England* U.K.
210 A3 **Sudd** *swamp* Sudan
169 C3 **Suddendorf** Ger.
251 G3 **Suddie** Guyana
168 F2 **Sude** *r.* Ger.
168 D1 **Süden** Ger.
168 E1 **Süderbrarup** Ger.
168 F3 **Suderburg** Ger.
168 F2 **Südergellersen** Ger.
168 E1 **Süderhastedt** Ger.
168 D1 **Süderlügum** Ger.
168 D1 **Süderoogsand** *i.* Ger.
168 E1 **Süderstapel** Ger.
Sudetenland *mts* Czech Rep./Pol. *see* **Sudety**
174 D5 **Sudety** *mts* Czech Rep./Pol.
139 J5 **Sudimir** Rus. Fed.
139 M3 **Sudislavl'** Rus. Fed.
209 F5 **Sud-Kivu** *admin. reg.* Dem. Rep. Congo
234 C3 **Sudlersville** *MD* U.S.A.
169 B4 **Südlohn** Ger.
139 M4 **Sudogda** Rus. Fed.
139 M3 **Sudogda** *r.* Rus. Fed.
176 G3 **Sudoměřice** Czech Rep.
138 G3 **Sudomskiye Vysoty** *hills* Rus. Fed.
139 I5 **Sudost'** *r.* Rus. Fed.
207 H5 **Sud-Ouest** *prov.* Cameroon
136 B3 **Sudova Vyshnya** Ukr.
203 G2 **Sudr** Egypt
Südtirol *prov. Trentino - Alto Adige* Italy *see* **Bolzano**
140 □B2 **Suðurland** *constituency* Iceland
130 A3 **Suðuroy** *i.* Faroe Is
144 D1 **Suðuroy** *i.* Faroe Is
168 D3 **Sudwalde** Ger.
137 H2 **Sudzha** Rus. Fed.
137 H2 **Sudzha** *r.* Rus. Fed.
187 C5 **Sueca** Spain
197 G4 **Sŭedinenie** Bulg.
192 B5 **Suelli** *Sardegna* Italy
156 B5 **Suèvres** France
Suez Egypt *see* **El Suweis**
203 G2 **Suez, Gulf of** Egypt
203 G2 **Suez Canal** Egypt
124 C3 **Şufaynah** Saudi Arabia
235 D1 **Suffern** *NY* U.S.A.
151 H2 **Suffolk** *admin. div. England* U.K.
232 E6 **Suffolk** *VA* U.S.A.
235 F2 **Suffolk County** *county NY* U.S.A.
122 A2 **Sūfiān** Iran
129 C2 **Sugan, Gora** *mt.* Rus. Fed.
226 C4 **Sugar** *r. WI* U.S.A.
226 C3 **Sugarbush Hill** *hill WI* U.S.A.
232 B5 **Sugar Grove** *OH* U.S.A.
235 D1 **Sugar Loaf** *NY* U.S.A.
147 B5 **Sugarloaf Mountain** *hill* Rep. of Ireland
233 □H2 **Sugarloaf Mountain** *ME* U.S.A.
83 H3 **Sugarloaf Point** *N.S.W.* Austr.
234 C1 **Sugar Notch** *PA* U.S.A.
234 B1 **Sugar Run** *PA* U.S.A.
173 E2 **Sugenheim** Ger.
Süget *Xinjiang* China *see* **Sogat**
95 G1 **Sugut** *r. Sabah* Malaysia
197 G4 **Suhaia** Romania
106 E4 **Suhait** *Nei Mongol* China
Sūhāj Egypt *see* **Sohâg**
125 G2 **Şuḩār** Oman
197 H1 **Suharău** Romania
106 E1 **Sühbaatar** Mongolia
107 G2 **Sühbaatar** *prov.* Mongolia
179 F5 **Suhi vrh** *mt.* Slovenia
169 F5 **Suhl** Ger.
168 F3 **Suhlendorf** Ger.
188 F3 **Suhopolje** Croatia
172 C4 **Suhr** Switz.
125 F3 **Suhūl al Kidan** *plain* Saudi Arabia
206 E5 **Suhum** Ghana
199 G2 **Şuhut** Turkey
254 B4 **Suiá Missur** *r.* Brazil
Sui'an *Fujian* China *see* **Zhangpu**
100 D3 **Suibin** *Heilong.* China
109 F2 **Suichang** *Zhejiang* China
Suicheng *Fujian* China *see* **Jianning**
Suicheng *Guangdong* China *see* **Suixi**
109 E3 **Suichuan** *Jiangxi* China
Suid-Afrika *country* Africa *see* **South Africa, Republic of**
107 F4 **Suide** *Shaanxi* China
182 B2 **Suido, Serra do** *mts* Spain
100 D4 **Suifen** *r.* China
100 D3 **Suifenhe** *Heilong.* China
116 B4 **Suigam** *Gujarat* India
100 C3 **Suihua** *Heilong.* China
108 B2 **Suijiang** *Yunnan* China
100 C3 **Suileng** *Heilong.* China
160 B1 **Suilly-la-Tour** France
146 C3 **Suilven** *hill Scotland* U.K.
108 D3 **Suining** *Hunan* China
109 F1 **Suining** *Jiangsu* China
108 C2 **Suining** *Sichuan* China
252 D5 **Suipacha** Bol.
109 E1 **Suiping** *Henan* China
156 D3 **Suippe** *r.* France
156 E3 **Suippes** France
147 D4 **Suir** *r.* Rep. of Ireland
Suisse *country* Europe *see* **Switzerland**
104 B4 **Suita** Japan
234 B4 **Suitland** *MD* U.S.A.
109 F1 **Suixi** *Anhui* China
108 D4 **Suixi** *Guangdong* China
107 G5 **Suixian** *Henan* China
Suixian *Hubei* China *see* **Suizhou**
108 C3 **Suiyang** *Guizhou* China
Suizhai *Henan* China *see* **Xiancheng**
107 I3 **Suizhong** *Liaoning* China
109 E2 **Suizhou** *Hubei* China
116 C4 **Sujangarh** *Rajasthan* India
123 G5 **Sujawal** Pak.
Suk *atoll* Micronesia *see* **Pulusuk**
94 D4 **Sukabumi** *Jawa Barat* Indon.
95 E3 **Sukadana** *Kalimantan Barat* Indon.
94 D4 **Sukadana** *Sumatera* Indon.
105 G1 **Sukagawa** Japan
Sukarnapura *Irian Jaya* Indon. *see* **Jayapura**
Sukarno, Puntjak *mt.* Indon. *see* **Jaya, Puncak**
116 D4 **Suket** *Rajasthan* India
140 N3 **Sukeva** Fin.
139 J4 **Sukhinichi** Rus. Fed.
137 I4 **Sukhi Yaly** *r.* Ukr.
175 M6 **Sukhodil** Ukr.
139 L5 **Sukhodol'skiy** Rus. Fed.
139 J4 **Sukhodrev** *r.* Rus. Fed.
Sukhoivanovka Ukr. *see* **Stepnohirs'k**
134 I3 **Sukhona** *r.* Rus. Fed.
96 B3 **Sukhothai** Thai.
139 J3 **Sukhoverkovo** Rus. Fed.
Sukhumi Georgia *see* **Sokhumi**
Sukhum-Kale Georgia *see* **Sokhumi**
137 I3 **Sukhyy Torets'** *r.* Ukr.
137 F4 **Sukhyy Yelanets'** Ukr.
Sukkertoppen Greenland *see* **Maniitsoq**
134 F3 **Sukkozero** Rus. Fed.
123 G5 **Sukkur** Pak.
114 D2 **Sukma** *Madh. Prad.* India
177 H5 **Sükösd** Hungary
170 C2 **Sukow** Ger.
100 F3 **Sukpay** *r.* Rus. Fed.
116 C4 **Sukri** *r.* India
116 C4 **Sukri** *r.* India
139 K3 **Sukromny** Rus. Fed.
134 L4 **Suksun** Rus. Fed.
117 E5 **Suktel** *r.* India
103 F7 **Sukumo** Japan

T

250 B3 Tadó Col.
225 G3 Tadoussac Que. Can.
114 C3 Tadpatri Andhra Prad. India
205 H4 Tadrart hills Alg.
202 A3 Tadrart Acacus tourist site Libya
114 C2 Tadwale Mahar. India
Tadzhikskaya S.S.R. country Asia see Tajikistan
138 D2 Taebla Estonia
Taech'ŏn S. Korea see Poryŏng
101 C5 Taedong-gang r. N. Korea
101 D6 Taegu S. Korea
101 C5 Taejŏn S. Korea
101 C6 Taejŏng S. Korea
101 D5 T'aepaek S. Korea
150 C3 Taf r. Wales U.K.
77 I3 Tafahi i. Tonga
183 I2 Tafalla Spain
215 E4 Tafelberg S. Africa
214 C5 Tafelberg mt. S. Africa
251 G4 Tafelberg mt. Suriname
190 C2 Tafers Switz.
150 D3 Taffs Well Cardiff, Wales U.K.
Tafila Jordan see Aṭ Ṭafīlah
206 D4 Tafiré Côte d'Ivoire
258 D2 Tafí Viejo Arg.
204 C3 Tafraoute Morocco
122 B3 Tafresh Iran
240 H4 Taft CA U.S.A.
123 E4 Taftān, Kūh-e mt. Iran
128 C2 Taftanāz Syria
234 C1 Tafton PA U.S.A.
186 F2 Taga mt. Spain
102 J4 Tagajō Japan
135 G7 Taganrog Rus. Fed.
137 J4 Taganrog, Gulf of Rus. Fed./Ukr.
Taganrogskiy Zaliv b. Rus. Fed./Ukr. see Taganrog, Gulf of
206 C2 Tagant admin. reg. Maur.
122 D2 Tagarev, Gora mt. Iran/Turkm.
103 E7 Tagawa Japan
135 I5 Tagay Rus. Fed.
92 B4 Tagbilaran Phil.
111 C5 Tagchagpu Ri mt. Xizang China
Tagdempt Alg. see Tiaret
190 C5 Taggia Italy
206 E3 Taghin-Dassouri Burkina
Ţâghira Moldova see Ţighira
222 C2 Tagish Y.T. Can.
193 F2 Tagliacozzo Italy
191 I3 Tagliamento r. Italy
192 B2 Taglio-Isolaccio Corse France
156 E3 Tagnon France
92 C4 Tagoloan r. Phil.
122 D1 Tagta Turkm.
123 E3 Tagtabazar Turkm.
256 C1 Taguatinga Minas Gerais Brazil
254 D5 Taguatinga Tocantins Brazil
92 B2 Tagudin Phil.
77 F3 Tagula Island P.N.G.
92 C5 Tagum Phil.
184 B1 Tagus r. Port./Spain alt. Tajo (Spain), alt. Tejo (Portugal)
107 J2 Taha Heilong. China
222 G5 Tahaetkun Mountain B.C. Can.
185 H3 Tahal Spain
94 C1 Tahan, Gunung mt. Malaysia
204 D3 Tahanaoute Morocco
79 □3 Tahanea atoll Arch. des Tuamotu Fr. Polynesia
Tahanroz'ka Zatoka b. Rus. Fed./Ukr. see Taganrog, Gulf of
205 G5 Tahat, Mont mt. Alg.
Tahaurawe i. HI U.S.A. see Kahoolawe
100 C1 Tahe Heilong. China
80 D1 Taheke North I. N.Z.
147 B5 Tahilla Rep. of Ireland
106 C2 Tahilt Mongolia
79 □3a Tahiti i. Fr. Polynesia
177 I4 Tahitótfalu Hungary
123 E4 Tahlab r. Iran/Pak.
123 E4 Tahlab, Dasht-i plain Pak.
237 E5 Tahlequah OK U.S.A.
222 D3 Tahltan B.C. Can.
240 G2 Tahoe City CA U.S.A.
240 G2 Tahoe Vista CA U.S.A.
237 C5 Tahoka TX U.S.A.
80 E3 Tahora North I. N.Z.
80 F3 Tahorakuri North I. N.Z.
207 G3 Tahoua Niger
207 G3 Tahoua dept Niger
122 D4 Tahrūd Iran
122 D4 Tahrūd r. Iran
222 E5 Tahsis B.C. Can.
203 F3 Tahta Egypt
199 F2 Tahtaköprü Bursa Turkey
199 G3 Tahtali Dağ mt. Turkey
222 E4 Tahtsa Peak B.C. Can.
252 D2 Tahuamanú r. Bol.
252 C2 Tahuamanú Peru
79 □3 Tahuata i. Fr. Polynesia
93 C2 Tahuna Sulawesi Utara Indon.
206 D5 Taï Côte d'Ivoire
107 I3 Tai'an Liaoning China
107 H4 Tai'an Shandong China
107 E5 Taibai Shaanxi China
108 C1 Taibai Shan mt. Shaanxi China
Taibei Taiwan see T'aipei
185 H2 Taibilla r. Spain
191 H2 Taibòn Agordino Italy
Taibus Qi Nei Mongol China see Baochang
109 G3 T'aichung Taiwan
Taidong Taiwan see T'aitung
81 C7 Taieri r. South I. N.Z.
81 C6 Taieri Ridge South I. N.Z.
Taigong Guizhou China see Taijiang
107 G4 Taigu Shanxi China
107 G4 Taihang Shan mts China
107 G4 Taihang Shan mts China
80 E3 Taihape North I. N.Z.
109 E1 Taihe Anhui China
109 E3 Taihe Jiangxi China
Taihe Sichuan China see Shehong
Taihezhen Sichuan China see Shehong
109 F2 Taihu Anhui China
108 D3 Taijiang Guizhou China
107 J2 Taikang Heilong. China
107 G5 Taikang Henan China
96 A3 Taikkyi Myanmar
104 B3 Taiko-yama hill Japan
107 I2 Tailai Heilong. China
82 D3 Tailem Bend S.A. Austr.
Tailuge Taiwan see T'ailuko
109 G3 T'ailuko Taiwan
206 E4 Tain r. Ghana
146 D4 Tain Highland, Scotland U.K.
109 G4 T'ainan Taiwan
160 B1 Taingy France
161 C3 Tain-l'Hermitage France
157 G4 Taintrux France
109 □ Tai O H.K. China
191 G2 Taio Italy
257 F1 Taiobeiras Brazil
80 D1 Taipa North I. N.Z.
141 O3 Taipalsaari Fin.
109 G3 T'aipei Taiwan
Taiping Guangdong China see Shixing
109 E4 Taiping Guangdong China
Taiping Guangxi China see Chongzuo
108 D4 Taiping Guangxi China
94 C1 Taiping Malaysia
107 I2 Taiping Ling mt. Nei Mongol China
109 □ Tai Po H.K. China
254 G3 Taipu Brazil
107 G5 Taiqian Henan China
102 □1 Taira-jima i. Japan
Tairbeart Western Isles, Scotland U.K. see Tarbert
80 E2 Tairua North I. N.Z.
122 A3 Tairuq Iran
94 C4 Tais Sumatera Indon.
102 K2 Taisetsu-zan mts Japan
105 F2 Taishaku-san mt. Japan
109 E4 Taishan Guangdong China
109 F3 Taishun Zhejiang China
179 E2 Taiskirchen im Innkreis Austria
156 E3 Taissy France
81 D5 Taitanu South I. N.Z.
259 B7 Taitao, Península de pen. Chile
210 B4 Taiti mt. Kenya
109 G4 T'aitung Taiwan
140 O2 Taivalkoski Fin.
140 N1 Taivaskero hill Fin.
141 M3 Taivassalo Fin.
109 G4 Taiwan country Asia
Taiwan Haixia str. China/Taiwan see Taiwan Strait
Taiwan Shan mts Taiwan see Chungyang Shanmo
109 F4 Taiwan Strait China/Taiwan
Taixian Jiangsu China see Jiangyan
109 G1 Taixing Jiangsu China
Taÿetos Óros mts Greece see Taygetos
107 G4 Taiyuan Shanxi China
107 F4 Taiyue Shan mts China
160 C2 Taizé France
111 F6 Taizhao Xizang China
Taizhong Taiwan see T'aichung
109 F1 Taizhou Jiangsu China
109 G2 Taizhou Zhejiang China
109 G2 Taizhou Wan b. China
101 C4 Taizi r. China
124 C5 Ta'izz Yemen
124 C5 Ta'izz governorate Yemen
243 H6 Tajamulco, Volcán de vol. Guat.
95 D3 Tajem, Gunung hill Indon.
205 H2 Tajerouine Tunisia
123 G2 Tajikistan country Asia
104 D3 Tajimi Japan
116 D4 Taj Mahal tourist site Uttar Prad. India
180 C3 Tajo r. Spain alt. Tejo (Portugal), conv. Tagus
127 H4 Tajrīsh Iran
252 D5 Tajsara, Cordillera de mts Bol.
183 G4 Tajuña r. Spain
96 B3 Tak Thai.
122 A2 Takāb Iran
93 B4 Taka'Bonerate, Kepulauan atolls Indon.
176 G4 Takácsi Hungary
105 G2 Takahagi Japan
104 C4 Takahama Japan
104 D2 Takahara-gawa r. Japan
103 F6 Takahashi Japan
262 Q1 Takahe, Mount Antarctica
104 B4 Takaishi Japan
81 D4 Takaka South I. N.Z.
116 D5 Takal Madh. Prad. India
103 G6 Takamatsu Japan
104 C4 Takami-yama mt. Japan
104 D2 Takaoka Japan
80 F4 Takapau North I. N.Z.
80 G3 Takapau North I. N.Z.
80 E2 Takapuna North I. N.Z.
102 □1 Takara-jima i. Japan
104 A4 Takasago Japan
105 F2 Takasaki Japan
104 C2 Takashōzu-yama mt. Japan
105 E2 Takasuma-yama mt. Japan
105 G2 Takasuzu-san hill Ibaraki Japan
212 E5 Takatokwane Botswana
104 B4 Takatsuki Japan
103 F7 Takatsuki-yama mt. Japan
251 G4 Takatu r. Brazil/Guyana
104 D2 Takayama Japan
97 C6 Tak Bai Thai.
104 C3 Takefu Japan
103 F6 Takehara Japan
151 H3 Takeley Essex, England U.K.
94 B1 Takengon Sumatera Indon.
Takeo Cambodia see Takêv
103 E7 Takeo Japan
Take-shima i. N. Pacific Ocean see Liancourt Rocks
122 B2 Takestān Iran
103 E7 Taketa Japan
104 C4 Taketoyo Japan
97 D5 Takêv Cambodia
123 G2 Takhar prov. Afgh.
116 E5 Takhatpur Madh. Prad. India
181 G5 Takhemaret Alg.
Takhiatash Uzbek. see Gulabie
222 C2 Takhini r. Y.T. Can.
222 C2 Takhini Hotspring Y.T. Can.
96 C4 Ta Khli Thai.
97 D5 Ta Khmau Cambodia
135 H7 Takhta Rus. Fed.
Takhta Turkm. see Tagta
Takhta-Bazar Turkm. see Tagtabazar
121 F1 Takhtabrod Kazakh.
120 E4 Takhtakupyr Uzbek.
137 J5 Takhtamukay Rus. Fed.
Takhtamukayskiy Rus. Fed. see Takhtamukay
122 B3 Takht Apān, Kūh-e mt. Iran
127 I5 Takht-e Jamshīd tourist site Iran
123 G4 Takht-i-Sulaiman mt. Pak.
122 B2 Takht-i-Suleiman mt. Iran
207 H3 Takiéta Niger
Takijuq Lake Nunavut Can. see Napaktulik Lake
102 J2 Takikawa Japan
81 A6 Takitimu Mountains South I. N.Z.
129 F4 Täklä Azer.
222 E4 Takla Landing B.C. Can.
Takla Makan des. China see Taklimakan Shamo
Taklimakan Desert China see Taklimakan Shamo
110 C4 Taklimakan Shamo des. China
123 G2 Takob Tajik.
206 E5 Takoradi Ghana
111 F6 Takpa Shiri mt. Xizang China
177 I4 Taksony Hungary
177 K4 Takta r. Hungary
177 K3 Taktaharkány Hungary
177 K3 Taktakenéz Hungary
222 C3 Taku B.C. Can.
220 E4 Taku r. Can./U.S.A.
103 E7 Taku Japan
78 □6 Takuan, Mount P.N.G.
97 B5 Takua Pa Thai.
97 B5 Takua Thung Thai.
207 H5 Takum Nigeria
81 □2 Takutea i. Cook Is
78 □6 Takwa Malaita Solomon Is
116 C5 Tal Madh. Prad. India
244 C3 Tala Mex.
258 G4 Tala Uru.
138 G4 Talachyn Belarus
123 H3 Talagang Pak.
260 B3 Talagante Chile
187 E6 Talaiassa, Serra hill Spain
161 A5 Talairan France
162 A3 Talais France
116 C5 Talaja Gujarat India
100 E2 Talakan Rus. Fed.
116 B5 Talala Gujarat India
137 G2 Talalayivka Ukr.
242 □J7 Talamanca, Cordillera de mts Costa Rica
183 I3 Talamantes Spain
190 E2 Talamona Italy
192 D2 Talamone Italy
192 B4 Talana Sardegna Italy
100 D2 Talandzha Rus. Fed.
94 C3 Talang, Gunung vol. Indon.
94 D3 Talangbetutu Sumatera Indon.
160 D1 Talant France
117 H4 Talap Assam India
250 A6 Talara Peru
123 E5 Talar-i-Band mts Pak.
185 E1 Talarrubias Spain
121 G3 Talas r. Kazakh./Kyrg.
121 H4 Talas Kyrg.
121 G4 Talas admin. div. Kyrg.
121 G4 Talas Ala-Too mts Kyrg.
139 I4 Talashkino Rus. Fed.
Talas Oblast admin. div. Kyrg. see Talas
Talas Range mts Kyrg. see Talas Ala-Too
Talasskaya Oblast' admin. div. Kyrg. see Talas
Talasskiy Alatau, Khrebet mts Kyrg. see Talas Ala-Too
128 B4 Tal'at al Jamā'ah, Rujm mt. Jordan
207 G3 Talata-Mafara Nigeria
128 C2 Ţal 'at Mūsá mt. Lebanon/Syria
93 C1 Talaud, Kepulauan is Indon.
182 D5 Talaván Spain
183 F5 Talavera de la Reina Spain
184 D2 Talavera la Real Spain
84 E3 Talawanta Qld Austr.
131 Q3 Talaya Rus. Fed.
92 C5 Talayan Phil.
187 B7 Talayón hill Spain
182 E5 Talayuela Spain
187 B5 Talayuelas Spain
183 H5 Talayuelo mt. Spain
116 D4 Talbehat Uttar Prad. India
87 E5 Talbot, Mount hill W.A. Austr.
234 B4 Talbot County county MD U.S.A.
231 C5 Talbotton GA U.S.A.
83 G3 Talbragar r. N.S.W. Austr.
260 B4 Talca Chile
258 B5 Talcahuano Chile
117 F5 Talcher Orissa India
100 C1 Taldan Rus. Fed.
139 K3 Taldom Rus. Fed.
121 I3 Taldykorgan Kazakh.
Taldy-Kurgan Kazakh. see Taldykorgan
Taldyqorghan Kazakh. see Taldykorgan
Taldysu Kyrg. see Taldy-Suu
121 I4 Taldy-Suu Kyrg.
114 B2 Talegaon Mahar. India
114 C1 Talegaon Mahar. India
122 B3 Taleh Zang Iran
116 D5 Talen Madh. Prad. India
163 B4 Talence France
215 G5 Taleni S. Africa
158 E3 Talensac France
187 C5 Tales Spain
122 B2 Tālesh Gīlān Iran
Tālesh Gīlān Iran see Hashtpar
139 K2 Talets, Ozero l. Rus. Fed.
86 C4 Talga r. W.A. Austr.
121 I4 Talgar Kazakh.
121 I4 Talgar, Pik mt. Kazakh.
150 C2 Talgarreg Ceredigion, Wales U.K.
150 D3 Talgarth Powys, Wales U.K.
182 B4 Talhadas Port.
124 C4 Ţalḩah Saudi Arabia
82 C3 Talia S.A. Austr.
93 C3 Taliabu i. Indon.
161 E4 Taliard France
92 C4 Talibon Phil.
150 D2 Taliesin Ceredigion, Wales U.K.
184 C2 Táliga Spain
114 C2 Talikota Karnataka India
120 F5 Talimardzhan Uzbek.
129 C3 T'alin Armenia
204 D3 Taliouine Morocco
114 B3 Taliparamba Kerala India
92 B4 Talisay Phil.
92 C4 Talisayan Phil.
129 F4 Talış Dağları mts Azer./Iran
146 B4 Talisker Highland, Scotland U.K.
134 I4 Talitsa Rus. Fed.
137 K1 Talitskiy Chamlyk Rus. Fed.
95 G5 Taliwang Sumbawa Indon.
168 F2 Talkau Ger.
191 G5 Talla Italy
82 C2 Tallacootra, Lake salt flat S.A. Austr.
146 C4 Talladale Highland, Scotland U.K.
231 C5 Talladega AL U.S.A.
127 F3 Tall 'Afar Iraq
147 E3 Tallaght Rep. of Ireland
231 C6 Tallahassee FL U.S.A.
83 F4 Tallangatta Vic. Austr.
147 E3 Tallanstown Rep. of Ireland
231 C5 Tallapoosa r. AL U.S.A.
231 C5 Tallassee AL U.S.A.
127 F3 Tall Baydar Syria
163 A5 Taller France
87 B6 Tallering Peak hill W.A. Austr.
234 C3 Talleyville DE U.S.A.
138 E2 Tallinn Estonia
128 C2 Tall Kalakh Syria
127 F3 Tall Kayf Iraq
127 F3 Tall Kūjik Syria
232 C4 Tallmadge OH U.S.A.
160 E3 Talloires France
192 B2 Tallone Corse France
182 B2 Tallós Spain
147 C4 Tallow Rep. of Ireland
237 F5 Tallulah LA U.S.A.
Tallymerjen Uzbek. see Talimardzhan
197 G3 Tălmaciu Romania
234 B2 Talmage PA U.S.A.
160 D1 Talmay France
146 D3 Talmine Highland, Scotland U.K.
162 B3 Talmont France
162 A2 Talmont-St-Hilaire France
136 F3 Tal'ne Ukr.
Tal'noye Ukr. see Tal'ne
116 C5 Talod Gujarat India
116 C5 Taloda Mahar. India
208 F2 Talodi Sudan
237 D4 Taloga OK U.S.A.
123 F5 Taloi Range mts Pak.
123 G2 Tāloqān Afgh.
192 B4 Talora r. Sardegna Italy
263 K2 Talos Dome ice feature Antarctica
96 C2 Ta Loung San mt. Laos
137 G3 Talova Balka Ukr.
135 H6 Talovaya Rus. Fed.
129 E1 Talovka Rus. Fed.
221 I3 Taloyoak Nunavut Can.
244 B3 Talpa Mex.
195 G2 Talsano Italy
106 C2 Talshand Mongolia
138 D3 Talsi Latvia
258 C2 Taltal Chile
223 H2 Taltson r. N.W.T. Can.
94 B2 Talu Sumatera Indon.
93 B2 Taludaa Sulawesi Utara Indon.
191 G2 Talvera r. Italy
83 G2 Talwood Qld Austr.
135 H6 Taly Rus. Fed.
136 F3 Tal'yanky Ukr.
83 E3 Talyawalka r. N.S.W. Austr.
Talyshskiye Gory mts Azer./Iran see Talış Dağları
105 F3 Tama Japan
183 F1 Tama Spain
95 F2 Tama Abu, Banjaran mts Sarawak Malaysia
Tamabo Range mts Sarawak Malaysia see Tama Abu, Banjaran
105 F3 Tama-gawa r. Japan
102 □2 Tamagusuku Japan
96 B1 Tamai, Nam r. Myanmar
183 G3 Tamajón Spain
87 B5 Tamala W.A. Austr.
135 H5 Tamala Rus. Fed.
250 C2 Tamalameque Col.
206 E4 Tamale Ghana
182 D4 Tamames Spain
103 E7 Tamana Japan
77 H2 Tamana i. Gilbert Is Kiribati
204 C3 Tamanar Morocco
206 D3 Tamani Mali
103 F6 Tamano Japan
205 G5 Tamanrasset Alg.
234 C2 Tamaqua PA U.S.A.
117 F5 Tamar Bihar India
Tamar Syria see Tadmur
150 C4 Tamar r. England U.K.
186 D3 Tamarite de Litera Spain
252 C4 Tamarugal, Pampa de plain Chile
177 H5 Tamási Hungary
197 H2 Tamaşi Romania
Tamatave Madag. see Toamasina
245 E2 Tamaulipas state Mex.
245 E2 Tamaulipas, Sierra de mts Mex.
242 D3 Tamazula Durango Mex.
244 C4 Tamazula Jalisco Mex.
245 E3 Tamazunchale Mex.
210 B4 Tambach Kenya
169 F5 Tambach-Dietharz Ger.
206 B3 Tambacounda Senegal
104 B3 Tamba-kōchi plat. Japan
213 G3 Tambara Moz.
83 G2 Tambar Springs N.S.W. Austr.
256 D4 Tambau Brazil
207 G3 Tambawel Nigeria
94 D2 Tambelan, Kepulauan is Indon.
87 C7 Tambellup W.A. Austr.
260 C3 Tambillo, Cerro mt. Arg.
85 F5 Tambo Qld Austr.
83 F4 Tambo r. Vic. Austr.
252 C4 Tambo r. Peru
252 B3 Tambobamba Peru
252 A3 Tambo de Mora Peru
250 A6 Tambo Grande Peru
213 □I3 Tambohorano Madag.
252 C3 Tambopata r. Peru
95 G5 Tambora, Gunung vol. Sumbawa Indon.
254 E3 Tamboril Brazil
250 C5 Tamboryacu r. Peru
135 H5 Tambov Rus. Fed.
100 D2 Tambovka Rus. Fed.
Tambov Oblast admin. div. Rus. Fed. see Tambovskaya Oblast'
135 H5 Tambovskaya Oblast' admin. div. Rus. Fed.
182 B2 Tambre r. Spain
95 G1 Tambunan, Bukit hill Sabah Malaysia
208 E3 Tambura Sudan
95 G1 Tambuyukon, Gunung mt. Sabah Malaysia
206 C2 Tâmchekkeţ Maur.
120 D2 Tamdy Kazakh.
120 F4 Tamdybulak Uzbek.
120 F4 Tamdytau, Gory hills Uzbek.
250 D3 Tame Col.
182 B3 Tâmega r. Port.
Tamenghest Alg. see Tamanrasset
117 H4 Tamenglong Manipur India
Tamerlanovka Kazakh. see Temirlanovka
207 G2 Tamesna reg. Niger
207 H2 Tamgak, Adrar mt. Niger
206 B3 Tamguée, Massif du mt. Guinea
116 D5 Tamia Madh. Prad. India
245 F3 Tamiahua Mex.
245 F3 Tamiahua, Laguna de lag. Mex.
94 B1 Tamiang r. Indon.
114 C4 Tamil Nadu state India
234 C1 Tamiment PA U.S.A.
190 E2 Tamins Switz.
106 D2 Tamirin Gol r. Mongolia
196 E3 Tamiš r. Yugo.
254 B5 Tamitatoala r. Brazil
203 F2 Tâmîya Egypt
124 C2 Tamīyah, Jabal hill Saudi Arabia
204 E2 Tamlelt, Plaine de plain Morocco
117 F5 Tamluk W. Bengal India
172 D3 Tamm Ger.
193 G3 Tammaro r. Italy
223 K1 Tammarvi r. Nunavut Can.
138 D1 Tammela Fin.
168 D1 Tammensiel Ger.
Tammerfors Fin. see Tampere
Tammisaari Fin. see Ekenäs
196 E3 Tamnava r. Yugo.
160 B1 Tamnay-en-Bazois France
182 C1 Támoga r. Spain
231 D7 Tampa FL U.S.A.
231 D7 Tampa Bay FL U.S.A.
141 M3 Tampere Fin.
245 F2 Tampico Mex.
124 D3 Tamrah Saudi Arabia
138 F2 Tamsalu Estonia
250 C6 Tamshiyacu Peru
179 E3 Tamsweg Austria
245 E3 Tamuín Mex.
117 F4 Tamur r. Nepal
185 F2 Tamurejo Spain
83 G2 Tamworth N.S.W. Austr.
149 H5 Tamworth Staffordshire, England U.K.
Tana r. Fin./Norway see Tenojoki
210 D5 Tana r. Kenya
Tana Madag. see Antananarivo
Tana i. Vanuatu see Tanna
Tana, Lake Eth. see T'ana Hāyk'
103 G7 Tanabe Japan
256 C4 Tanabi Brazil
140 O1 Tana Bru Norway
140 O1 Tanafjorden inlet Norway
220 A4 Tanaga Island AK U.S.A.
193 H4 Tanagro r. Italy
210 C2 T'ana Hāyk' l. Eth.
95 G3 Tanahgrogot Kalimantan Timur Indon.
94 B3 Tanahmasa i. Indon.
116 E3 Tanakpur Uttar Prad. India
93 A3 Tanambung Sulawesi Selatan Indon.
84 B3 Tanami N.T. Austr.
84 B3 Tanami Desert N.T. Austr.
97 D5 Tân An Vietnam
220 C3 Tanana AK U.S.A.
Tananarive Madag. see Antananarivo
213 □I4 Tanandava Madag.
190 D3 Tanaro r. Italy
150 D2 Tanat r. Wales U.K.
92 C4 Tanauan Phil.
192 B4 Tanaunella Sardegna Italy
Tanba-kōchi plat. Japan see Tamba-kōchi
85 E5 Tanbar Qld Austr.
159 G2 Tancarville France
Tancheng Fujian China see Pingtan
107 H5 Tancheng Shandong China
101 D4 Tanch'ŏn N. Korea
244 C4 Tancítario, Cerro de mt. Mex.
245 H5 Tancochapa r. Mex.
206 E5 Tanda Côte d'Ivoire
116 D3 Tanda Uttar Prad. India
117 E4 Tanda Uttar Prad. India
141 K3 Tandådalen Sweden
92 C4 Tandag Phil.
197 H3 Ţăndărei Romania
209 C9 Tandaué Angola
173 F3 Tandern Ger.
116 D2 Tandi Hima. Prad. India
261 H5 Tandil Arg.
261 H5 Tandil, Sierra del hills Arg.
208 C2 Tandjilé pref. Chad
123 G5 Tando Adam Pak.
123 G5 Tando Alahyar Pak.
123 G5 Tando Bago Pak.
123 G5 Tando Muhammmad Khan Pak.
83 E3 Tandou Lake imp. l. N.S.W. Austr.
147 E2 Tandragee Northern Ireland U.K.
141 K3 Tandsjöborg Sweden
116 E5 Tandula r. India
114 C2 Tandur Andhra Prad. India
114 C2 Tandur Andhra Prad. India
80 F3 Taneatua North I. N.Z.
102 □1 Tanega-shima i. Japan
96 B3 Tanen Taunggyi mts Thai.
175 K5 Tanew r. Pol.
234 A3 Taneytown MD U.S.A.
205 E5 Tanezrouft reg. Alg./Mali
205 E5 Tanezrouft Tan-Ahenet reg. Alg.
128 D3 Ţanf, Jabal aţ hill Syria
148 B4 Tang Rep. of Ireland
107 F1 Tanga Rus. Fed.
211 C6 Tanga Tanz.
211 C6 Tanga admin. reg. Tanz.
80 E2 Tangaehe North I. N.Z.
117 G4 Tangail Bangl.
213 □J4 Tangainony Madag.
114 D5 Tangalla Sri Lanka
244 C4 Tangamandapio Mex.
244 C4 Tangancícuaro de Arista Mex.
Tanganyika country Africa see Tanzania
211 A6 Tanganyika, Lake Africa
122 C2 Tangar Iran
255 C8 Tangará Brazil
78 □6 Tangarare Guadalcanal Solomon Is
114 C4 Tangasseri Kerala India
108 B3 Tangdan Yunnan China
Tangdukou Hunan China see Shaoyang
122 C2 Tangeli Iran
263 D2 Tange Promontory hd Antarctica
204 D2 Tanger Morocco
180 D5 Tanger prov. Morocco
94 D4 Tangerang Jawa Barat Indon.
171 C3 Tangerhütte Ger.
170 C3 Tangermünde Ger.
108 B1 Tanggor Sichuan China
107 H4 Tanggu Tianjin China
Tanggulashan Qinghai China see Tuotuoheyan
111 E5 Tanggula Shan mt. Qinghai China
111 E5 Tanggula Shan mts Xizang China
109 E1 Tanghe Henan China
109 E1 Tang He r. China
123 G3 Tangi Pak.
Tangier Morocco see Tanger
80 E4 Tangimoana North I. N.Z.
93 B3 Tangkelemboko, Gunung mt. Indon.
94 D4 Tangkittebak, Gunung mt. Indon.
96 A1 Tangla Assam India
108 A1 Tanglag Qinghai China
111 F6 Tangmai Xizang China
85 F4 Tangorin Qld Austr.
111 D6 Tangra Yumco salt l. China
107 H4 Tangshan Hebei China
168 F2 Tangstedt Ger.
96 B2 Tangte mt. Myanmar
92 B4 Tangub Mindanao Phil.
92 B4 Tangub Negros Phil.
207 F4 Tanguieta Benin
108 D3 Tangwan Hunan China
100 D3 Tangwang r. China
100 D2 Tangwanghe Heilong. China
107 G4 Tangxian Hebei China
109 E2 Tangxianzhen Hubei China
108 D2 Tangyan He r. China
107 G5 Tangyin Henan China
100 D3 Tangyuan Heilong. China
254 E5 Tanhaçu Brazil
108 A2 Taniantaweng Shan mts Xizang China
105 E2 Tanigawa-dake mt. Japan
91 H8 Tanimbar, Kepulauan is Indon.
160 E2 Taninges France
Taninthari Myanmar see Tenasserim
Tanintharyi Myanmar see Tenasserim
Tanintharyi admin. div. Myanmar see Tenasserim
Taninthayi Myanmar see Tenasserim
Tanjah Morocco see Tanger
92 B4 Tanjay Phil.
Tanjore Tamil Nadu India see Thanjavur
95 F3 Tanjung Kalimantan Selatan Indon.
94 B2 Tanjungbalai Sumatera Indon.
94 D4 Tanjungkarang-Telukbetung Sumatera Indon.
95 D3 Tanjungpandan Indon.
94 D2 Tanjungpinang Indon.
94 B2 Tanjungpura Sumatera Indon.
94 D3 Tanjungraja Sumatera Indon.
95 G2 Tanjungredeb Kalimantan Timur Indon.
95 G2 Tanjungselor Kalimantan Timur Indon.
123 G3 Tank Pak.
116 B5 Tankara Gujarat India
116 C5 Tankhala Gujarat India
106 E1 Tankhoy Rus. Fed.
116 D2 Tankse Jammu and Kashmir
117 F4 Tankuhi Uttar Prad. India
214 B5 Tankwa r. S. Africa
156 E5 Tanlay France
96 A3 Tanlwe r. Myanmar
173 G3 Tann Ger.
169 F5 Tann (Rhon) Ger.
171 C5 Tanna Ger.
78 □5 Tanna i. Vanuatu
146 F5 Tannadice Angus, Scotland U.K.
141 K3 Tännäs Sweden
160 B1 Tannay Bourgogne France
157 E3 Tannay Champagne-Ardenne France
169 F4 Tanne Ger.
Tannenberg Pol. see Stębark
222 G5 Tanner, Mount B.C. Can.
161 E5 Tanneron France
234 C1 Tannersville PA U.S.A.
173 G2 Tännesberg Ger.
173 E3 Tannhausen Ger.
178 B3 Tannheim Austria
173 E4 Tannheim Ger.
142 D3 Tannis Bugt b. Denmark
Tannoa i. Vanuatu see Tongoa
171 C5 Tannroda Ger.
85 G4 Tannum Sands Qld Austr.
106 A1 Tannu-Ola, Khrebet mts Rus. Fed.
Tannu Tuva aut. rep. Rus. Fed. see Tyva, Respublika
92 B4 Tañon Strait Phil.
116 B4 Tanot Rajasthan India
207 H3 Tanout Niger
245 E3 Tanquian Mex.
117 E4 Tansen Nepal
109 G3 Tanshui Taiwan
206 D3 Tansilla Burkina
149 H4 Tansley Derbyshire, England U.K.
203 F2 Tanta Egypt
96 B3 Tantabin Myanmar
204 C3 Tan-Tan Morocco
82 E4 Tantanoola S.A. Austr.
157 G4 Tantonville France
170 F2 Tantow Ger.
245 E3 Tantoyuca Mex.
116 D4 Tantpur Uttar Prad. India
107 I2 Tantu Jilin China
128 B3 Tantura Israel
114 D2 Tanuku Andhra Prad. India
105 F2 Tanuma Japan
84 C3 Tanumbirini N.T. Austr.
142 D2 Tanumshede Sweden
176 E1 Tanvald Czech Rep.
96 E2 Tanxu Guangxi China
137 J3 Tanyushivka Ukr.
211 B6 Tanzania country Africa
222 D3 Tanzilla r. B.C. Can.
Tao'an Jilin China see Taonan
Taobh Tuath Western Isles, Scotland U.K. see Northton
Taocheng Fujian China see Yongchun
Taocheng Guangdong China see Daxin
107 I2 Tao'er r. China
106 D5 Tao He r. China
Taohong Hunan China see Longhui
Taohuaping Hunan China see Longhui
109 E2 Taojiang Hunan China
Taolanaro Madag. see Tôlañaro
106 E4 Taole Ningxia China
107 I2 Taonan Jilin China
195 E5 Taormina Sicilia Italy
239 F4 Taos NM U.S.A.
204 D2 Taounate Morocco
204 E2 Taourirt Morocco
109 F3 Taoxi Fujian China
Taoyang Gansu China see Lintao
109 D2 Taoyuan Hunan China
109 G3 T'aoyüan Taiwan
Taozhou Anhui China see Guangde
138 E2 Tapa Estonia
243 G6 Tapachula Mex.
251 H5 Tapajós r. Brazil
94 B2 Tapaktuan Sumatera Indon.
244 C4 Tapalpa Mex.
261 G5 Tapalqué Arg.
Tapan Turkey see Mansurlu
251 H3 Tapanahoni r. Suriname
245 G5 Tapanatepec Mex.
251 H5 Tapara, Serra do hills Brazil
251 E6 Tapauá Brazil
251 E6 Tapauá r. Brazil
81 D4 Tapawera South I. N.Z.
255 B9 Tapera Brazil
254 F5 Taperoá Brazil
255 C9 Tapes Brazil
206 C5 Tapeta Liberia
173 E3 Tapfheim Ger.
116 C5 Tapi r. India
182 D1 Tapia de Casariego Spain
Tapiau Rus. Fed. see Gvardeysk
250 C6 Tapiche r. Peru
177 J4 Tápió r. Hungary
177 I4 Tápióbicske Hungary
256 D2 Tapiocanga, Chapada do hills Brazil
177 I4 Tápiógyörgye Hungary
177 I4 Tápióság Hungary
177 I4 Tápiószecső Hungary
177 I4 Tápiószele Hungary
177 I4 Tápiószőlős Hungary
256 D3 Tapira Minas Gerais Brazil
256 A5 Tapira Paraná Brazil
256 D5 Tapiraí Brazil
253 H2 Tapirapé r. Brazil
251 E4 Tapirapecó, Sierra mts Brazil/Venez.
94 C1 Tapis mt. Malaysia
176 F4 Táplánszentkereszt Hungary
176 G5 Tapolca Hungary
146 F4 Tap o' Noth hill Scotland U.K.
232 E6 Tappahannock VA U.S.A.
116 D3 Tappal Uttar Prad. India
235 E1 Tappan NY U.S.A.
122 B3 Tappeh, Kūh-e hill Iran
129 E3 Tap Qaraqoyunlu Azer.
Taprobane country Asia see Sri Lanka
176 G5 Tapsony Hungary
81 D4 Tapuaenuku mt. South I. N.Z.
92 B5 Tapul Phil.
92 B5 Tapul Group is Phil.
94 B2 Tapulonanjing mt. Indon.
94 C2 Tapung r. Indon.
Taputeouea atoll Gilbert Is Kiribati see Tabiteuea
124 D5 Taqar mt. Yemen
127 G4 Ţaqţaq Iraq
255 C9 Taquara Brazil
256 A1 Taquaral, Serra do hills Brazil
253 F4 Taquarí r. Brazil
256 C4 Taquaritinga Brazil
256 C5 Taquarituba Brazil
256 A4 Taquaruçu r. Brazil
177 I4 Tar Hungary
147 D4 Tar r. Rep. of Ireland
85 G5 Tara Qld Austr.
196 D4 Tara r. Bos.-Herz./Yugo.
147 E3 Tara, Hill of hill Rep. of Ireland
207 H4 Taraba r. Nigeria
207 H4 Taraba state Nigeria
256 B5 Tarabaí Brazil
252 D4 Tarabuco Bol.
Ţarābulus Libya see Tripoli
183 G4 Taracena Spain
136 E5 Taraclia Moldova
80 F3 Taradale North I. N.Z.
161 E5 Taradeau France
Taraíra r. Brazil see Traíra
252 E5 Tarairí Bol.
95 G2 Tarakan Kalimantan Timur Indon.
199 G1 Taraklı Turkey
Tarakliya Moldova see Taraclia
83 G3 Taralga N.S.W. Austr.
102 □1 Tarama-jima i. Japan
182 C1 Taramundi Spain
116 D5 Tarana Madh. Prad. India
116 C3 Taranagar Rajasthan India
80 D3 Taranaki admin. reg. North I. N.Z.
80 E3 Taranaki, Mount vol. North I. N.Z.
183 G4 Tarancón Spain
114 C4 Tarangambadi Tamil Nadu India
211 C6 Tarangire National Park Tanz.
Tarangul l. Kazakh. see Tarankol', Ozero
121 G1 Tarankol', Ozero l. Kazakh.
120 E1 Taranovskoye Kazakh.
146 A4 Taransay i. Scotland U.K.
195 G2 Taranto Italy
195 G2 Taranto prov. Puglia Italy
195 G2 Taranto, Golfo di g. Italy
176 G5 Tarany Hungary
252 C4 Tarapacá admin. reg. Chile
250 D5 Tarapacá Col.
250 B6 Tarapoto Peru
160 C3 Tarare France
261 I4 Tarariras Uru.
81 E4 Tararua Range mts North I. N.Z.
Tarasaigh i. Scotland U.K. see Taransay
161 C5 Tarascon France
163 D6 Tarascon-sur-Ariège France
136 D3 Tarashany Ukr.
136 F3 Tarashcha Ukr.
122 D3 Tarasht Iran
137 G4 Tarasivka Khersons'ka Oblast' Ukr.
137 J3 Tarasivka Luhans'ka Oblast' Ukr.
135 H6 Tarasovskiy Rus. Fed.
205 H4 Tarat Alg.
252 C4 Tarata Peru
252 C2 Tarauacá Brazil
250 D6 Tarauacá r. Brazil
192 A3 Taravo r. Corse France
77 H1 Tarawa atoll Kiribati
80 F3 Tarawera North I. N.Z.
80 F3 Tarawera, Lake North I. N.Z.
80 F3 Tarawera, Mount North I. N.Z.
121 G4 Taraz Zhambylskaya Oblast' Kazakh.
183 I3 Tarazona Spain
185 I1 Tarazona de la Mancha Spain
121 J3 Tarbagatay Kazakh.
107 E1 Tarbagatay Rus. Fed.
121 J3 Tarbagatay, Khrebet mts Kazakh.
187 C6 Tárbena Spain
147 B4 Tarbert Rep. of Ireland
146 C6 Tarbert Argyll and Bute, Scotland U.K.
146 C6 Tarbert Argyll and Bute, Scotland U.K.
146 B4 Tarbert Western Isles, Scotland U.K.
146 B6 Tarbert, Loch inlet Scotland U.K.
163 C5 Tarbes France
146 D5 Tarbet Argyll and Bute, Scotland U.K.
146 D6 Tarbolton South Ayrshire, Scotland U.K.
231 E5 Tarboro NC U.S.A.
177 L5 Tărcaia Romania
177 K3 Tarcal Hungary
177 L4 Tarcea Romania
191 I2 Tarcento Italy
82 C2 Tarcoola S.A. Austr.
83 F2 Tarcoon N.S.W. Austr.
197 F3 Ţarcului, Munţii mts Romania
83 F3 Tarcutta N.S.W. Austr.
175 I4 Tarczyn Pol.
158 E3 Tard r. France
183 G2 Tardajos Spain
183 H3 Tardelcuende Spain
162 E2 Tardes r. France
163 B5 Tardets-Sorholus France
186 C3 Tardienta Spain
162 C3 Tardoire r. France
100 F2 Tardoki-Yani, Gora mt. Rus. Fed.
83 H2 Taree N.S.W. Austr.
83 E2 Tarella N.S.W. Austr.
140 M2 Tärendö Sweden
Tarentum Italy see Taranto
244 D4 Taretán Mex.
124 C4 Ţarfā, Ra's aţ pt Saudi Arabia
204 B4 Tarfaya Morocco
146 F5 Tarfside Angus, Scotland U.K.
Targan Kazakh. see Targyn
163 B4 Targon France
197 G3 Târgovişte Romania
174 F3 Targowa Górka Pol.
197 H3 Târgu Bujor Romania
197 F3 Târgu Cărbuneşti Romania
197 H2 Târgu Frumos Romania
204 D2 Targuist Morocco
197 F3 Târgu Jiu Romania
197 F2 Târgu Lăpuş Romania
197 G2 Târgu Mureş Romania
197 H2 Târgu Neamţ Romania
197 H2 Târgu Ocna Romania
197 H2 Târgu Secuiesc Romania
121 J2 Targyn Kazakh.
122 A3 Tarhān Iran
177 K5 Tarhos Hungary
202 B1 Tarhūnah Libya
125 F2 Tarif U.A.E.
184 E4 Tarifa Spain
252 D5 Tarija Bol.
252 D5 Tarija dept Bol.
114 B3 Tarikere Karnataka India
91 I7 Tariku r. Indon.
125 E4 Tarīm Yemen
Tarim Basin China see Tarim Pendi
211 B5 Tarime Tanz.
110 D3 Tarim He r. China
110 D3 Tarim Liuchang Xinjiang China
244 D3 Tarimoro Mex.
110 C4 Tarim Pendi basin China
123 F3 Tarīn Kowt Afgh.
91 I7 Taritatu r. Indon.
177 H4 Tarján Hungary
215 E5 Tarka r. S. Africa
177 G4 Tárkány Hungary
215 F5 Tarkastad S. Africa
129 E2 Tarki Rus. Fed.
236 E3 Tarkio MO U.S.A.
130 I3 Tarko-Sale Rus. Fed.
206 E5 Tarkwa Ghana
92 B3 Tarlac Phil.
92 B2 Tarlac r. Phil.
149 G4 Tarleton Lancashire, England U.K.
232 B5 Tarlton OH U.S.A.
142 C4 Tarm Denmark
252 B2 Tarma Peru
168 E2 Tarmstedt Ger.
163 E5 Tarn dept Midi-Pyrénées France
161 A4 Tarn r. France
177 I4 Tarna r. Hungary
140 K2 Tärnaby Sweden
123 F4 Tarnak r. Afgh.
177 J3 Tarnalelesz Hungary
177 J4 Tarnaméra Hungary
177 J4 Tarnaőrs Hungary
177 J4 Tarnaszentmiklós Hungary
197 F2 Târnava Mare r. Romania
197 F2 Târnava Mică r. Romania
197 G2 Târnăveni Romania
175 K5 Tarnawa Duża Pol.
175 L5 Tarnawatka Pol.
163 D4 Tarn-et-Garonne dept Midi-Pyrénées France
175 K6 Tarnica mt. Pol.
175 J5 Tarnobrzeg Pol.
175 K5 Tarnogród Pol.
134 H3 Tarnogskiy Gorodok Rus. Fed.
177 H4 Tárnok Hungary
Tarnopol Ukr. see Ternopil'
163 A5 Tarnos France
175 L5 Tarnoszyn Pol.
177 K5 Târnova Romania
197 F3 Târnova Romania
170 D2 Tarnow Ger.
175 I5 Tarnów Pol.
175 J6 Tarnowiec Pol.
Tarnowitz Pol. see Tarnowskie Góry
174 E2 Tarnówka Pol.
174 E3 Tarnowo Podgórne Pol.
174 G5 Tarnów Opolski Pol.
174 G5 Tarnowskie Góry Pol.
190 F4 Taro r. Italy
137 H3 Taroms'ke Ukr.
163 B5 Taron-Sadirac-Viellenave France
85 G5 Taroom Qld Austr.
105 F2 Tarō-san mt. Japan
182 C3 Tarouca Port.
204 C3 Taroudannt Morocco
182 B3 Tarouquela Port.
168 E1 Tarp Ger.
177 L3 Tarpa Hungary
117 G5 Tarpasa Bangl.
84 D3 Tarpaulin Swamp N.T. Austr.
82 E4 Tarpeena S.A. Austr.
231 D6 Tarpon Springs FL U.S.A.
149 G4 Tarporley Cheshire, England U.K.
246 C1 Tarpum Bay Eleuthera Bahamas
192 D2 Tarquinia Italy
192 D2 Tarquinia Lido Italy
Tarquinii Italy see Tarquinia
84 C3 Tarrabool Lake salt flat N.T. Austr.
Tarracina Italy see Terracina
Tarraco Spain see Tarragona
186 E3 Tarragona Spain
186 D3 Tarragona prov. Cataluña Spain
83 F5 Tarraleah Tas. Austr.
83 F3 Tarran Hills hill N.S.W. Austr.
81 B6 Tarras South I. N.Z.
Tarrasa Spain see Terrassa
186 E3 Tàrrega Spain
146 E4 Tarrel Highland, Scotland U.K.
178 B3 Tarrenz Austria
182 B1 Tarrio Spain
186 E3 Tarroja de Segarra Spain
Tarrong Xizang China see Nyêmo
235 E1 Tarrytown NY U.S.A.
193 I5 Tarsia Italy
202 C4 Tarso Ahon mt. Chad
202 C4 Tarso Emissi mt. Chad
202 C4 Tarso Kobour mt. Chad
126 D3 Tarsus Turkey
128 B1 Tarsus r. Turkey
258 E1 Tartagal Salta Arg.
258 F3 Tartagal Santa Fé Arg.
175 M5 Tartakiv Ukr.
129 E3 Tärtär Azer.
129 E3 Tärtär r. Azer.
129 E3 Tärtär r. Azer.
191 H3 Tartaro r. Italy
163 B5 Tartas France
138 F2 Tartu Estonia
128 B2 Ţarţūs Syria
128 C2 Ţarţūs governorate Syria
104 C3 Tarui Japan
Tarumae-san vol. Japan see Shikotsu
257 G3 Tarumirim Brazil
103 E8 Tarumizu Japan
129 E1 Tarumovka Rus. Fed.
96 B1 Tarung Hka r. Myanmar
139 K4 Tarusa Rus. Fed.
139 K4 Tarusa r. Rus. Fed.
94 B2 Tarutung Sumatera Indon.
136 E4 Tarutyne Ukr.
146 F4 Tarves Aberdeenshire, Scotland U.K.
149 G4 Tarvin Cheshire, England U.K.
191 I2 Tarvisio Italy
Tarvisium Italy see Treviso
195 □ Tarxien Malta
122 D4 Tarz Iran
120 F3 Tasbuget Kazakh.
224 E3 Taschereau Que. Can.
222 F5 Taseko Mountain B.C. Can.
114 B2 Tasgaon Mahar. India
129 A3 Taşgeçit Turkey
137 H3 Tashan' r. Ukr.
Tashauz Turkm. see Dashkhovuz
Tashauzskaya Oblast' admin. div. Turkm. see Dashkhovuzskaya Oblast'
136 E5 Tashbunar r. Ukr.
Tashi Chho Bhutan see Thimphu
Tashigang Bhutan see Trashigang
Tashino Rus. Fed. see Pervomaysk
129 D3 Tashir Armenia
121 G4 Tashkent Uzbek.
Tashkent Oblast admin. div. Uzbek. see Tashkentskaya Oblast'
121 G4 Tashkentskaya Oblast' admin. div. Uzbek.

123 E2 Tashkepri Turkm.
121 H4 Tash-Kömür Kyrg.
Tash-Kumyr Kyrg. see Tash-Kömür
120 C2 Tashla Rus. Fed.
137 F3 Tashlyk Ukr.
Tāshqurghān Afgh. see Kholm
Tasiilaq Greenland see Ammassalik
95 E4 Tasikmalaya Jawa Barat Indon.
168 F1 Tåsinge i. Denmark
225 G1 Tasiujaq Que. Can.
140 K2 Tåsjö Sweden
128 A1 Taşkale Turkey
128 A1 Taşkent Turkey
207 H3 Tasker Niger
121 J3 Taskesken Kazakh.
129 B3 Taşkıran Turkey
126 D2 Taşköprü Turkey
127 F3 Taşlıçay Turkey
129 C3 Taşlıoğul Turkey
81 D4 Tasman South I. N.Z.
81 D4 Tasman admin. reg. South I. N.Z.
81 C6 Tasman r. South I. N.Z.
81 C5 Tasman, Mount South I. N.Z.
266 F8 Tasman Abyssal Plain sea feature Austr.
265 O7 Tasman Basin sea feature Tasman Sea
81 D4 Tasman Bay South I. N.Z.
83 F5 Tasman Head hd Tas. Austr.
83 F5 Tasmania state Austr.
81 D4 Tasman Mountains South I. N.Z.
83 G5 Tasman Peninsula Tas. Austr.
77 H6 Tasman Sea S. Pacific Ocean
197 F2 Tăşnad Romania
126 E2 Taşova Turkey
177 I4 Tass Hungary
148 C3 Tassagh Northern Ireland U.K.
207 G2 Tassara Niger
160 C1 Tasselot, Mont hill France
205 G5 Tassili du Hoggar plat. Alg.
205 G4 Tassili n'Ajjer plat. Alg.
160 C3 Tassin-la-Demi-Lune France
142 E4 Tåstrup Denmark
121 G3 Tasty Kazakh.
121 F2 Tasty-Taldy Kazakh.
222 C4 Tasu B.C. Can.
128 A1 Taşucu Turkey
177 G5 Taszár Hungary
177 H4 Tát Hungary
177 H4 Tata Hungary
204 D3 Tata Morocco
177 H4 Tatabánya Hungary
177 I5 Tataháza Hungary
245 G4 Tatahuicapan Mex.
225 I4 Tatamagouche N.S. Can.
93 C5 Tata Mailau, Gunung mt. East Timor
78 □6 Tatamba Sta Isabel Solomon Is
117 F5 Tatanagar Bihar India
205 H2 Tataouine Tunisia
136 E5 Tatarbunary Ukr.
138 G5 Tatarka Belarus
137 H3 Tatarka r. Ukr.
199 G2 Tatarlı Turkey
128 C1 Tatarlı Turkey
116 D4 Tatarpur Rajasthan India
130 I4 Tatarsk Rus. Fed.
Tatarskaya A.S.S.R. aut. rep. Rus. Fed. see Tatarstan, Respublika
100 G2 Tatarskiy Proliv str. Rus. Fed.
134 J5 Tatarstan, Respublika aut. rep. Rus. Fed.
Tatar Strait Rus. Fed. see Tatarskiy Proliv
177 I4 Tatárszentgyörgy Hungary
197 H2 Tătăruşi Romania
122 A2 Tatavi r. Iran
85 E3 Tate r. Qld Austr.
105 F2 Tatebayashi Japan
105 E2 Tateshina-yama mt. Japan
105 F4 Tateyama Chiba Japan
104 D2 Tateyama Toyama Japan
104 D2 Tate-yama vol. Japan
124 C4 Tathlīth Saudi Arabia
83 G4 Tathra N.S.W. Austr.
213 E4 Tati Botswana
168 D1 Tating Ger.
120 A2 Tatishchevo Rus. Fed.
96 B2 Tatkon Myanmar
222 E5 Tatla Lake B.C. Can.
222 E5 Tatlayoko Lake B.C. Can.
110 D4 Tatlikbulak Xinjiang China
Tatra Mountains Pol./Slovakia see Tatry
111 D4 Tatrang Xinjiang China
175 H6 Tatry mts Pol./Slovakia
222 B3 Tatshenshini r. B.C. Can.
135 H6 Tatsinskiy Rus. Fed.
103 G6 Tatsuno Hyōgo Japan
105 D3 Tatsuno Nagano Japan
123 F5 Tatta Pak.
149 I4 Tattershall Lincolnshire, England U.K.
121 H4 Tatti Kazakh.
Tatty Kazakh. see Tatti
80 E3 Tatu hill North I. N.Z.
256 D5 Tatuí Brazil
222 E4 Tatuk Mountain B.C. Can.
138 E3 Tatula r. Lith.
237 C5 Tatum NM U.S.A.
237 E5 Tatum TX U.S.A.
127 F3 Tatvan Turkey
78 □2 Tau i. American Samoa
142 A2 Tau Norway
254 E3 Taua Brazil
257 E5 Taubaté Brazil
171 E4 Taubenheim Ger.
172 D2 Tauber r. Ger.
172 D2 Tauberbischofsheim Ger.
171 D4 Taucha Ger.
171 F3 Tauche Ger.
120 B3 Tauchik Kazakh.
171 F4 Tauer Ger.
173 F3 Taufkirchen Bayern Ger.
173 G3 Taufkirchen Bayern Ger.
173 G3 Taufkirchen (Vils) Ger.
169 E5 Taufstein hill Ger.
80 F3 Tauhara mt. North I. N.Z.
80 E2 Tauhoa North I. N.Z.
251 G4 Tauini r. Brazil
121 H3 Taukum, Peski des. Kazakh.
158 C3 Taulé France
161 C4 Taulignan France
80 E3 Taumarunui North I. N.Z.
215 E2 Taung S. Africa
96 A2 Taungdwingyi Myanmar
96 B2 Taunggyi Myanmar
96 B3 Taungnyo Range mts Myanmar
96 A2 Taungtha Myanmar
96 A3 Taunqup Myanmar
123 G4 Taunsa Pak.
150 D3 Taunton Somerset, England U.K.
233 H4 Taunton MA U.S.A.
169 C5 Taunus hills Ger.
80 E2 Taupiri North I. N.Z.
179 F3 Tauplitz Austria
80 F3 Taupo North I. N.Z.
80 E3 Taupo, Lake North I. N.Z.
138 D4 Tauragė Lith.
138 C4 Tauralaukis Lith.
80 F2 Tauranga North I. N.Z.
Taurasia Italy see Torino
224 F4 Taureau, Réservoir resr Que. Can.
195 F4 Taurianova Italy
80 E1 Taurikura North I. N.Z.
162 D3 Taurion r. France
195 H3 Taurisano Italy
Tauriuiná r. Mato Grosso Brazil see Verde
80 D1 Tauroa Point North I. N.Z.
Taurus Mountains Turkey see Toros Dağları
Taūshyq Kazakh. see Tauchik
186 B3 Tauste Spain
177 K5 Tăuţ Romania
163 E6 Tautavel France
158 E2 Taute r. France
171 C5 Tautenhain Ger.
177 L4 Tăuteu Romania
77 F2 Tauu Islands P.N.G.
160 A3 Tauves France
80 G3 Tauwhareparae North I. N.Z.
131 Q4 Tauyskaya Guba g. Rus. Fed.
Tauz Azer. see Tovuz
192 A2 Tavaco Corse France
191 I2 Tavagnacco Italy
196 D2 Tavankut Vojvodina, Srbija Yugo.
190 C1 Tavannes Switz.
159 G4 Tavant France
231 D6 Tavares FL U.S.A.
191 G5 Tavarnelle Val di Pesa Italy
199 F3 Tavas Turkey
Tavastehus Fin. see Hämeenlinna
160 D1 Tavaux France
130 H4 Tavda Rus. Fed.
182 B4 Taveiro Port.
161 C4 Tavel France
140 M2 Tavelsjö Sweden
151 I2 Taverham Norfolk, England U.K.
195 F3 Taverna Italy
160 C1 Tavernay France
192 E1 Tavernelle Italy
161 E5 Tavernes France
187 C5 Tavernes de la Valldigna Spain
150 C3 Tavernspite Pembrokeshire, Wales U.K.
156 C3 Taverny France
190 E4 Taverone r. Italy
186 F3 Tavertet Spain
79 □1 Taveuni i. Fiji
198 C3 Tavgetos mts Greece
195 H3 Taviano Italy
192 B2 Tavignano r. Corse France
193 H3 Taviolere plain Italy
184 C3 Tavira Port.
184 C3 Tavira, Ilha de i. Port.
227 G4 Tavistock Ont. Can.
150 C4 Tavistock Devon, England U.K.
193 G2 Tavo r. Italy
182 C3 Távora r. Spain
97 B4 Tavoy Myanmar
97 B4 Tavoy b. Myanmar
Tavoy Island Myanmar see Mali Kyun
121 J2 Tavricheskoye Kazakh.
Tavrīl Kazakh. see Tavricheskoye
137 G4 Tavriys'k Ukr.
199 F2 Tavşanlı Turkey
79 □1 Tavuki Kadavu Fiji
191 H5 Tavullia Italy
129 D3 Tavush r. Armenia
150 C4 Tavy r. England U.K.
150 C3 Taw r. England U.K.
81 E4 Tawa North I. N.Z.
117 G4 Tawang Arun. Prad. India
104 B4 Tawaramoto Japan
227 F3 Tawas City MI U.S.A.
95 G1 Tawau Sabah Malaysia
Tawè Myanmar see Tavoy
150 D3 Tawe r. Wales U.K.
172 A2 Tawern Ger.
80 F3 Tawhiuau mt. North I. N.Z.
116 C2 Tawi r. India
109 G4 Tawu Taiwan
245 E4 Taxco Mex.
178 D3 Taxenbach Austria
111 A4 Taxkorgan Xinjiang China
222 C2 Tay r. Y.T. Can.
146 E5 Tay r. Scotland U.K.
146 E5 Tay, Firth of est. Scotland U.K.
87 D7 Tay, Lake salt flat W.A. Austr.
146 D5 Tay, Loch l. Scotland U.K.
252 A2 Tayabamba Peru
92 B3 Tayabas Bay Phil.
210 E3 Tayeeglow Somalia
130 J4 Tayga Rus. Fed.
146 C6 Tayinloan Argyll and Bute, Scotland U.K.
136 F4 Tayirove Ukr.
222 F3 Taylor B.C. Can.
241 L4 Taylor AZ U.S.A.
236 D3 Taylor NE U.S.A.
234 C1 Taylor PA U.S.A.
237 D6 Taylor TX U.S.A.
239 F4 Taylor r. CO U.S.A.
81 C5 Taylor, Mount South I. N.Z.
239 F5 Taylor, Mount NM U.S.A.
234 C3 Taylors Bridge DE U.S.A.
148 B4 Taylor's Cross Rep. of Ireland
230 C4 Taylorsville KY U.S.A.
234 A3 Taylorsville MD U.S.A.
231 D5 Taylorsville NC U.S.A.
235 D2 Taylortown NJ U.S.A.
236 F4 Taylorville IL U.S.A.
124 B2 Taymā' Saudi Arabia
233 □J1 Taymouth N.B. Can.
131 K3 Taymura r. Rus. Fed.
131 L2 Taymyr, Ozero l. Rus. Fed.
131 J2 Taymyr, Poluostrov pen. Rus. Fed.
Taymyr Peninsula Rus. Fed. see Taymyr, Poluostrov
97 D5 Tây Ninh Vietnam
146 C5 Taynuilt Argyll and Bute, Scotland U.K.
120 B2 Taypak Kazakh.
Taypaq Kazakh. see Taypak
146 F5 Tayport Fife, Scotland U.K.
131 K4 Tayshet Rus. Fed.
120 C2 Taysoygan, Peski des. Kazakh.
Tayspun tourist site Iraq see Ctesiphon
199 F2 Taytan Turkey
92 B3 Taytay Luzon Phil.
92 A4 Taytay Palawan Phil.
95 E4 Tayu Jawa Tengah Indon.
100 C2 Tayuan Heilong. China
148 D1 Tayvallich Argyll and Bute, Scotland U.K.
122 E3 Tayyebād Iran
121 G1 Tayynsha Kazakh.
130 I3 Taz r. Rus. Fed.
204 E2 Taza Morocco
Taza-Bazar Uzbek. see Shumanay
216 □3d Tazacorte La Palma Canary Is
129 E3 Täzäkänd Azer.
127 G4 Tāza Khurmātū Iraq
102 J4 Tazawa-ko l. Japan
122 A2 Tazeh Kand Azer.
129 E4 Tāzeh Kand-e Angūt Iran
204 D3 Tazenakht Morocco
232 B6 Tazewell TN U.S.A.
232 C6 Tazewell VA U.S.A.
223 I2 Tazin r. N.W.T./Sask. Can.
202 D3 Tazirbu Water Wells Field Libya
177 I5 Tázlár Hungary
197 H2 Tazlău Romania
197 H2 Tazlău r. Romania
183 E1 Tazones Spain
205 E5 Tazouikert hill Mali
130 I3 Tazovskiy Rus. Fed.
204 D3 Tazzarine Morocco
Tbessa Alg. see Tébessa
129 D3 T'bilisi Georgia
135 H7 Tbilisskaya Rus. Fed.
207 I5 Tchabal Gangdaba mt. Cameroon
207 I5 Tchabal Mbabo mt. Cameroon
Tchad country Africa see Chad
207 F4 Tchamba Togo
207 F4 Tchaourou Benin
207 F5 Tchetti Benin
208 A5 Tchibanga Gabon
202 B4 Tchigaï, Plateau du Niger
209 C8 Tchikala-Tcholohanga Angola
209 B8 Tchindjenje Angola
207 G3 Tchin-Tabaradene Niger
207 I4 Tcholliré Cameroon
143 H4 Tczew Pol.
97 D4 Te, Prêk r. Cambodia
250 E5 Tea r. Brazil
182 B2 Tea r. Spain
244 B2 Teacapán Mex.
87 D5 Teague, Lake salt flat W.A. Austr.
81 A6 Te Anau South I. N.Z.
81 A6 Te Anau, Lake South I. N.Z.
235 D2 Teaneck NJ U.S.A.
80 E3 Te Anga North I. N.Z.
193 G3 Teano Italy
Teanum Sidicinum Italy see Teano
243 G5 Teapa Mex.
80 G2 Te Araroa North I. N.Z.
196 E4 Tearce Macedonia
80 E2 Te Aroha North I. N.Z.
80 E2 Te Aroha, Mount hill North I. N.Z.
Teate Italy see Chieti
80 E3 Te Awamutu North I. N.Z.
185 F4 Teba Spain
183 H5 Tebar Spain
207 G3 Tébarat Niger
149 G3 Tebay Cumbria, England U.K.
129 B2 Teberda Rus. Fed.
129 B2 Teberda r. Rus. Fed.
205 H2 Tébessa Alg.
205 H2 Tébessa, Monts de mts Alg.
253 F6 Tebicuary r. Para.
94 B2 Tebingtinggi Sumatera Indon.
94 C3 Tebingtinggi Sumatera Indon.
94 C3 Tebo r. Indon.
185 B7 Tébourba Tunisia
185 B7 Téboursouk Tunisia
129 D2 Tebulos Mt'a Georgia/Rus. Fed.
244 C4 Tecalitlán Mex.
245 E4 Tecamac Mex.
245 F4 Tecamachalco Mex.
245 F4 Tecamachalco Nogales Mex.
242 A1 Tecate Mex.
123 B1 Tece Turkey
163 F6 Tech r. France
206 E5 Techiman Ghana
197 I3 Techirghiol Romania
259 C6 Tecka Arg.
259 C6 Tecka r. Arg.
142 E4 Teckomatorp Sweden
243 H4 Tecoh Mex.
245 F3 Tecolutla Mex.
244 C4 Tecomán Mex.
241 I4 Tecopa CA U.S.A.
242 C2 Tecoripa Mex.
244 D5 Técpan Mex.
244 D5 Tecpan r. Mex.
244 B2 Tecuala Mex.
197 H3 Tecuci Romania
227 F5 Tecumseh MI U.S.A.
236 D3 Tecumseh NE U.S.A.
104 C2 Tedori-gawa r. Japan
122 E2 Tedzhen Turkm.
123 E2 Tedzhen r. Turkm.
122 E2 Tedzhenstroy Turkm.
241 M3 Teec Nos Pos AZ U.S.A.
106 D1 Teel Mongolia
110 E1 Teeli Rus. Fed.
147 D2 Teemore Northern Ireland U.K.
147 A5 Teeranearagh Rep. of Ireland
149 H3 Tees r. England U.K.
149 G3 Teesdale val. England U.K.
149 H3 Teesside airport England U.K.
227 G3 Teeswater Ont. Can.
148 C4 Teevurcher Rep. of Ireland
81 □1 Te Fakanava i. Tokelau
251 E5 Tefé r. Brazil
251 E5 Tefé, Lago l. Brazil
205 G4 Tefedest mts Alg.
199 F3 Tefenni Turkey
95 E4 Tegal Jawa Tengah Indon.
170 E3 Tegel airport Ger.
165 F3 Tegelen Neth.
173 G2 Tegernheim Ger.
173 F4 Tegernsee Ger.
193 H4 Teggiano Italy
207 G4 Tegina Nigeria
177 K4 Téglás Hungary
190 F2 Teglio Italy
191 H2 Tegnàs r. Italy
78 □5 Tégua i. Vanuatu
242 □16 Tegucigalpa Hond.
216 □3a Tegueste Tenerife Canary Is
216 □3c Teguise Lanzarote Canary Is
240 H4 Tehachapi CA U.S.A.
80 E2 Te Hana North I. N.Z.
80 E3 Te Hauke North I. N.Z.
Teheran Iran see Tehrān
206 E4 Téhini Côte d'Ivoire
122 B3 Tehrān Iran
122 B3 Tehrān prov. Iran
Tehri Madh. Prad. India see Tikamgarh
116 D3 Tehri Uttar Prad. India
245 F4 Tehuacán Mex.
245 G5 Tehuantepec r. Mex.
243 G5 Tehuantepec, Golfo de g. Mex.
Tehuantepec, Gulf of Mex. see Tehuantepec, Golfo de
245 G5 Tehuantepec, Istmo de isth. Mex.
267 M5 Tehuantepec Ridge sea feature N. Pacific Ocean
245 E4 Tehuitzingo Mex.
171 G4 Teicha Ger.
171 D5 Teichwolframsdorf Ger.
216 □3a Teide, Pico del vol. Tenerife Canary Is
150 C2 Teifi r. Wales U.K.
150 D4 Teign r. England U.K.
150 D4 Teignmouth Devon, England U.K.
158 E4 Teillay France
163 E5 Teillet France
173 G4 Teisendorf Ger.
173 H2 Teisnach Ger.
161 A4 Teissières-lès-Bouliès France
169 F4 Teistungen Ger.
211 C5 Teita Hills Kenya
245 F5 Teitipac Mex.
197 G3 Teiu Romania
197 F2 Teiuş Romania
254 F3 Teixeira Brazil
Teixeira da Silva Angola see Bailundo
Teixeira de Sousa Angola see Luau
257 F4 Teixeiras Brazil
256 B3 Teixeira Soares Brazil
182 B1 Teixeiro Spain
182 C4 Teixoso Port.
182 C3 Teja r. Port.
183 I4 Tejadillos Spain
183 H3 Tejado Spain
95 F5 Tejakula Bali Indon.
245 F4 Tejar Mex.
216 □3f Tejeda Gran Canaria Canary Is
182 E4 Tejeda de Tiétar Spain
Tejen Turkm. see Tedzhen
117 G5 Tejgaon Bangl.
184 B2 Tejo r. Port. alt. Tajo (Spain), conv. Tagus
244 D4 Tejupilco Mex.
80 F2 Te Kaha North I. N.Z.
80 D1 Te Kao North I. N.Z.
81 C6 Tekapo r. South I. N.Z.
81 C5 Tekapo, Lake South I. N.Z.
117 F4 Tekari Bihar India
105 E3 Tekari-dake mt. Japan
80 E2 Te Kauwhata North I. N.Z.
243 H4 Tekax Mex.
121 G4 Teke Kazakh.
197 H5 Teke r. Turkey
121 H1 Teke, Ozero salt l. Kazakh.
128 B1 Tekebaşı Turkey
121 I3 Tekeli Kazakh.
110 C3 Tekes Xinjiang China
121 J4 Tekes Kazakh.
110 C3 Tekes He r. China
203 H6 Tekezē Wenz r. Eritrea/Eth.
111 C4 Tekiliktag mt. Xinjiang China
199 E1 Tekirdağ Turkey
199 E1 Tekirdağ prov. Turkey
199 G3 Tekirova Turkey
115 E2 Tekkali Andhra Prad. India
129 A3 Tekke Turkey
127 F3 Tekman Turkey
117 H5 Teknaf Bangl.
129 B3 Tekneciler Turkey
81 D5 Tekoa, Mount South I. N.Z.
226 E4 Tekonsha MI U.S.A.
80 D2 Te Kopuru North I. N.Z.
81 □3 Te Kou hill Rarotonga Cook Is
80 E2 Te Kowhai North I. N.Z.
128 D1 Tektek Dağlari hills Turkey
80 E3 Te Kuiti North I. N.Z.
117 E5 Tel r. India
242 □16 Tela Hond.
81 □1 Te Lafu i. Tokelau
81 □1 Te Lafu i. Tokelau
205 E2 Télagh Alg.
175 K3 Telaki Pol.
Telanaipura Sumatera Indon. see Jambi
207 F2 Télataï Mali
175 L5 Telatyn Pol.
129 D3 T'elavi Georgia
128 B3 Tel Aviv-Yafo Israel
176 E2 Telč Czech Rep.
243 H4 Telchac Puerto Mex.
139 K5 Tel'ch'ye Rus. Fed.
197 G2 Telciu Romania
168 F2 Teldau Ger.
216 □3f Telde Gran Canaria Canary Is
208 D4 Tele r. Dem. Rep. Congo
206 E2 Télé, Lac l. Mali
197 G3 Teleajen r. Romania
196 D3 Telečka Vojvodina, Srbija Yugo.
222 D3 Telegraph Creek B.C. Can.
177 J5 Telekgerendás Hungary
Telekhany Belarus see Tsyelyakhany
256 B6 Telêmaco Borba Brazil
142 C2 Telemark county Norway
260 E5 Telén Arg.
95 G2 Telen r. Indon.
Teleneshty Moldova see Teleneşti
136 E4 Teleneşti Moldova
197 G4 Teleorman r. Romania
205 G4 Telertheba, Djebel mt. Alg.
240 I3 Telescope Peak CA U.S.A.
193 G3 Telese Italy
253 F1 Teles Pires r. Brazil
129 E2 Teletl' Rus. Fed.
86 D4 Telfer Mining Centre W.A. Austr.
150 E2 Telford Telford and Wrekin, England U.K.
234 C2 Telford PA U.S.A.
150 E2 Telford and Wrekin admin. div. England U.K.
178 C3 Telfs Austria
177 J3 Telgárt Slovakia
158 B3 Telgruc-sur-Mer France
169 C4 Telgte Ger.
182 C4 Telhado Port.
206 B4 Télimélé Guinea
245 F5 Telixtlahuaca Mex.
202 E6 Teljo, Jebel mt. Sudan
222 E4 Telkwa B.C. Can.
157 F3 Tellancourt France
194 E6 Tellaro r. Sicilia Italy
Tell Atlas mts Alg. see Atlas Tellien
220 B3 Teller AK U.S.A.
Tell es-Sultan West Bank see Jericho
114 B4 Tellicherry Pondicherry India
165 E4 Tellin Belgium
168 E1 Tellingstedt Ger.
129 B3 Telli Tepe mt. Turkey
136 F4 Tellodar Ukr.
127 G5 Telloh Iraq
239 F4 Telluride CO U.S.A.
137 J4 Tel'manove Ukr.
Tel'mansk Turkm. see Gubadag
128 B3 Tel Megiddo tourist site Israel
179 H1 Telnice Czech Rep.
159 G4 Teloché France
182 C3 Telões Port.
245 E4 Teloloapán Mex.
Telo Martius France see Toulon
81 □1 Te Loto i. Tokelau
134 L3 Tel'pos-Iz, Gora mt. Rus. Fed.
138 D4 Telšiai Lith.
192 B4 Telti Sardegna Italy
171 E3 Teltow Ger.
94 C1 Teluk Anson Malaysia
Telukbajur Sumatera Indon. see Telukbayur
94 C3 Telukbayur Sumatera Indon.
Telukbetung Sumatera Indon. see Tanjungkarang-Telukbetung
94 B2 Telukdalam Indon.
Teluk Intan Malaysia see Teluk Anson
207 F5 Tema Ghana
227 H2 Temagami Ont. Can.
81 □3 Te Manga hill Rarotonga Cook Is
95 E4 Temanggung Jawa Tengah Indon.
80 E3 Te Mapou hill North I. N.Z.
245 F4 Temascal Mex.
80 E2 Te Mata North I. N.Z.
79 □3 Tematangi atoll Arch. des Tuamotu Fr. Polynesia
243 H4 Temax Mex.
215 G1 Temba S. Africa
91 I7 Tembagapura Irian Jaya Indon.
215 I2 Tembe r. Moz.
131 K3 Tembenchi r. Rus. Fed.
94 C3 Tembesi r. Indon.
94 C3 Tembilahan Sumatera Indon.
215 G2 Tembisa S. Africa
183 G5 Tembleque Spain
209 C6 Tembo Aluma Angola
Tembué Moz. see Chifunde
215 G4 Tembuland reg. S. Africa
150 E2 Teme r. England U.K.
240 I5 Temecula CA U.S.A.
126 D3 Temelli Turkey
106 C1 Temenchula, Gora mt. Rus. Fed.
94 C1 Temengor, Tasik resr Malaysia
179 G5 Temenica r. Slovenia
196 D3 Temerin Vojvodina, Srbija Yugo.
94 C2 Temerloh Malaysia
94 C1 Temiang, Bukit mt. Malaysia
120 D2 Temir Aktyubinskaya Oblast' Kazakh.
Temir Yuzhnyy Kazakhstan Kazakh. see Tumur
Temirlan Kazakh. see Temirlanovka
121 G4 Temirlanovka Kazakh.
121 H2 Temirtau Kazakh.
225 F3 Témiscamie r. Que. Can.
224 E4 Temiscaming Que. Can.
139 J4 Temkino Rus. Fed.
83 F5 Temma Tas. Austr.
140 N2 Temmes Fin.
135 H5 Temnikov Rus. Fed.
192 A4 Temo r. Sardegna Italy
79 □3 Temoe atoll Arch. des Tuamotu Fr. Polynesia
83 F3 Temora N.S.W. Austr.
241 L5 Tempe AZ U.S.A.
84 C5 Tempe Downs N.T. Austr.
171 E3 Tempelhof airport Ger.
192 B4 Tempio Pausania Sardegna Italy
226 E3 Temple MI U.S.A.
234 C2 Temple PA U.S.A.
237 D6 Temple TX U.S.A.
150 C2 Temple Bar Ceredigion, Wales U.K.
147 C4 Templederry Rep. of Ireland
151 I3 Temple Ewell Kent, England U.K.
147 B4 Templeglentan Rep. of Ireland
147 D4 Templemore Rep. of Ireland
147 B5 Templenoe Rep. of Ireland
147 E2 Templepatrick Northern Ireland U.K.
149 G3 Temple Sowerby Cumbria, England U.K.
81 D5 Templeton South I. N.Z.
150 C3 Templeton Pembrokeshire, Wales U.K.
240 G4 Templeton CA U.S.A.
147 D4 Templetuohy Rep. of Ireland
156 D2 Templeuve France
170 E2 Templin Ger.
147 D2 Tempo Northern Ireland U.K.
245 E3 Tempoal Mex.
245 E3 Tempoal r. Mex.
209 C8 Tempué Angola
135 G7 Temryuk Rus. Fed.
135 G7 Temryukskiy Zaliv b. Rus. Fed.
165 D3 Temse Belgium
197 F4 Temska Srbija Yugo.
190 F2 Temù Italy
260 A6 Temuco Chile
81 C6 Temuka South I. N.Z.
Temuli Sichuan China see Butuo
78 □4b Temwen i. Pohnpei Micronesia
78 □4b Temwetemwensekir hill Pohnpei Micronesia
120 D1 Temyasovo Rus. Fed.
250 B5 Tena Ecuador
243 H4 Tenabo Mex.
240 I1 Tenabo, Mount NV U.S.A.
206 E3 Ténado Burkina
235 E2 Tenafly NJ U.S.A.
138 D1 Tenala Fin.
114 D2 Tenali Andhra Prad. India
228 G7 Tenancingo Mex.
245 E4 Tenango Mex.
79 □3 Tenarunga atoll Arch. des Tuamotu Fr. Polynesia
97 B4 Tenasserim Myanmar
97 B4 Tenasserim admin. div. Myanmar
97 B4 Tenasserim r. Myanmar
160 D3 Tenay France
164 F1 Ten Boer Neth.
150 E2 Tenbury Wells Worcestershire, England U.K.
150 C3 Tenby Pembrokeshire, Wales U.K.
227 F2 Tenby Bay Ont. Can.
161 C3 Tence France
210 D2 Tendaho Eth.
155 H4 Tende France
115 G4 Ten Degree Channel Andaman & Nicobar Is India
203 F6 Tendelti Sudan
206 B2 Te-n-Dghâmcha, Sebkhet salt marsh Maur.
183 H4 Tendilla Spain
102 J4 Tendō Japan
204 E2 Tendrara Morocco
190 B2 Tendre, Mont mt. Switz.
159 H5 Tendu France
116 D5 Tendukheda Madh. Prad. India
129 C4 Tendürek Dağı mt. Turkey
206 C4 Téné r. Guinea
206 D3 Ténenkou Mali
138 C4 Tenenys r. Lith.
207 H1 Ténéré du Tafassâsset des. Niger
216 □3a Tenerife i. Canary Is
205 F1 Ténès Alg.
197 H4 Tenevo Bulg.
96 B3 Teng, Nam r. Myanmar
95 G4 Tengah, Kepulauan is Indon.
Tengcheng Guangxi China see Tengxian
108 A3 Tengchong Yunnan China
120 C4 Tenge Kazakh.
177 H5 Tengelic Hungary
172 C4 Tengen Ger.
95 G3 Tenggarong Kalimantan Timur Indon.
106 E4 Tengger Shamo des. Nei Mongol China
121 G2 Tengiz, Ozero salt l. Kazakh.
206 D4 Tengréla Côte d'Ivoire
135 H5 Ten'gushevo Rus. Fed.
108 D4 Tengxian Guangxi China
Tengxian Shandong China see Tengzhou
107 H5 Tengzhou Shandong China
161 E4 Ténibre, Mont mt. France/Italy
Teniente Jubany research stn Antarctica see Jubany
231 D6 Tenille FL U.S.A.
172 B3 Teningen Ger.
206 A2 Te-n-Ioubrar, Sebkhet salt marsh Maur.
177 J4 Tenk Hungary
114 C4 Tenkasi Tamil Nadu India
209 E7 Tenke Dem. Rep. Congo
131 P2 Tenkeli Rus. Fed.
134 J5 Ten'ki Rus. Fed.
206 E4 Tenkodogo Burkina
87 D5 Ten Mile Lake salt flat W.A. Austr.
191 I5 Tenna r. Italy
84 C3 Tennant Creek N.T. Austr.
172 C3 Tennenbronn Ger.
235 D2 Tennent NJ U.S.A.
237 F4 Tennessee r. U.S.A.
232 A6 Tennessee state U.S.A.
165 E4 Tenneville Belgium
140 L1 Tennevoll Norway
140 K2 Tennholmfjorden sea chan. Norway
140 O2 Tenniöjoki r. Fin./Rus. Fed.
260 B4 Teno Chile
260 B4 Teno r. Chile
245 F4 Tenochtitlán Mex.
140 O1 Tenojoki r. Fin./Norway
243 H5 Tenosique Mex.
104 B4 Tenri Japan
105 D4 Tenryū Japan
105 D4 Tenryū-gawa r. Japan
238 F2 Ten Sleep WY U.S.A.
93 B3 Tenteno Sulawesi Tengah Indon.
151 H3 Tenterden Kent, England U.K.
83 H2 Tenterfield N.S.W. Austr.
93 B2 Tentolomatinan, Gunung mt. Indon.
184 D2 Tentudia mt. Spain
182 B4 Tentúgal Port.
158 E4 Tenu r. France
177 G4 Tényő Hungary
244 C3 Teocaltiche Mex.
245 F4 Teocelo Mex.
261 G4 Teodelina Arg.
256 A5 Teodoro Sampaio Brazil
260 A6 Teodoro Schmidt Chile
257 G2 Teófilo Otôni Brazil
136 D3 Teofipol' Ukr.
116 E4 Teonthar Madh. Prad. India
243 G5 Teopisca Mex.
193 H4 Teora Italy
245 E4 Teotihuacán tourist site Mex.
245 F5 Teotitlán del Valle Mex.
206 E5 Tepa Ghana
242 C2 Tepache Mex.
80 D1 Te Paki North I. N.Z.
244 C4 Tepalcatepec Mex.
244 C4 Tepalcatepec r. Mex.
245 E3 Tepatepec Mex.
244 C3 Tepatitlán Mex.
177 K4 Tépe Hungary
245 F4 Tepeaca Mex.
245 E4 Tepeapulco Mex.
199 F1 Tepecik Turkey
242 D3 Tepehuanes Mex.
245 E4 Tepeji Mex.
Tepeköy Turkey see Karakoçan
198 B1 Tepelenë Albania
245 F5 Tepelmeme de Morelos Mex.
176 B2 Tepelská Vrchovina hills Czech Rep.
251 F4 Tepequem, Serra mts Brazil
244 D3 Tepetates Mex.
244 B3 Tepic Mex.
81 C5 Te Pirita South I. N.Z.
176 B2 Teplá Czech Rep.
176 B1 Teplá r. Czech Rep.
176 C3 Teplá Vltava r. Czech Rep.
134 L4 Teplaya Gora Rus. Fed.
137 J3 Teple Ukr.
129 D2 Tepli, Gora mt. Rus. Fed.
176 C1 Teplice Czech Rep.
177 J3 Teplička Slovakia
139 L5 Teploye Lipetskaya Oblast' Rus. Fed.
139 K5 Teploye Tul'skaya Oblast' Rus. Fed.
136 E3 Teplyk Ukr.
245 E4 Tepoztlan Mex.
193 E3 Teppia r. Italy
80 F2 Te Puke North I. N.Z.
80 F2 Te Puna North I. N.Z.
244 C3 Tequila Mex.
244 C3 Tequila, Volcán de vol. Mex.
245 G5 Tequisistlán Mex.
245 G5 Tequisistlán r. Mex.
245 E3 Tequisquiapán Mex.
245 F4 Tequixquitla Mex.
245 F4 Tequixtépec Mex.
186 G2 Ter r. Spain
207 F3 Téra Niger
184 B2 Tera r. Port.
182 E3 Tera r. Spain
164 D2 Ter Aar Neth.
80 E2 Te Rahu North I. N.Z.
116 D2 Teram Kangri mt. China/Jammu and Kashmir
193 F2 Teramo Italy
193 F2 Teramo prov. Abruzzo Italy
83 E4 Terang Vic. Austr.
80 E2 Te Rapa North I. N.Z.
164 G2 Ter Apel Neth.
123 G4 Teratani r. Pak.
175 L5 Teratyn Pol.
81 E4 Terawhiti, Cape North I. N.Z.
164 F3 Terborg-Silvolde Neth.
139 L5 Terbuny Rus. Fed.
Tercan Erzincan Turkey see Otlukbelı
127 F3 Tercan Erzincan Turkey
216 □1a Terceira i. Azores
261 F3 Tercero r. Arg.
163 A5 Tercis-les-Bains France
190 E3 Terdoppio r. Italy
139 J5 Tereben' Rus. Fed.
177 L4 Terebeşti Romania
136 B3 Tereblya r. Ukr.
136 C3 Terebovlya Ukr.
197 F3 Teregova Romania
Terek r. Georgia see Tergi
129 D2 Terek Rus. Fed.
127 G2 Terek r. Rus. Fed.
106 B1 Tere-Khol' Rus. Fed.
129 D1 Terekli-Mekteb Rus. Fed.
121 G4 Terek-Say Kyrg.
110 D1 Terektinskiy Khrebet mts Rus. Fed.
121 K2 Terekty Vostochnyy Kazakhstan Kazakh.
177 J6 Teremia Mare Romania
184 C2 Terena Port.
135 J5 Teren'ga Rus. Fed.
94 C1 Terengganu r. Malaysia
94 C1 Terengganu state Malaysia
Terengözek Kazakh. see Terenozek
255 B7 Terenos Brazil
120 F3 Terenozek Kazakh.
120 D2 Terensay Rus. Fed.
147 E3 Terenure Rep. of Ireland
Teren-Uzyak Kazakh. see Terenozek
256 B6 Teresa Cristina Brazil
187 B5 Teresa de Cofrentes Spain
120 A2 Tereshka r. Rus. Fed.
175 I3 Teresin Pol.
254 E3 Teresina Brazil
250 D4 Teresita Col.
257 F5 Teresópolis Brazil
175 L3 Terespol Pol.
136 B3 Teresva Ukr.
136 B4 Teresva r. Ukr.
175 K5 Tereszpol-Zaorenda Pol.
176 D1 Terezín Czech Rep.
136 F3 Terezyne Ukr.
178 C3 Terfens Austria
184 C3 Terges r. Port.
Tergeste Italy see Trieste
129 D2 Tergi r. Georgia
156 D3 Tergnier France
191 H3 Tergola r. Italy
192 A4 Tergu Sardegna Italy
164 D3 Terheijden Neth.
134 F1 Teriberka Rus. Fed.
121 F2 Terisakkan r. Kazakh.
175 K6 Terka Pol.
191 G2 Terlano Italy
237 C6 Terlingua Creek r. TX U.S.A.
193 I3 Terlizzi Italy
203 I6 Terma, Ras pt Eritrea
136 E2 Termakhivka Ukr.
126 E2 Terme Turkey
193 H5 Terme Luigiane Italy
186 D3 Térmens Spain
163 E5 Termes France
121 F5 Termez Uzbek.
161 E3 Termignon France
87 D7 Termination Island W.A. Austr.
156 B4 Terminiers France
194 C5 Termini Imerese Sicilia Italy
194 C4 Termini Imerese, Golfo di b. Sicilia Italy
193 E2 Terminillo, Monte mt. Italy
243 H5 Términos, Laguna de lag. Mex.
207 H2 Termit, Massif de hill Niger
Termiz Uzbek. see Termez
193 G3 Termoli Italy
147 D1 Termon Rep. of Ireland
Termonde Belgium see Dendermonde
148 C4 Termonfeckin Rep. of Ireland
150 E2 Tern r. England U.K.
137 H2 Tern r. Ukr.
164 E1 Ternaard Neth.
93 C2 Ternate Maluku Indon.
179 F3 Ternberg Austria
165 C3 Terneuzen Neth.
100 F3 Terney Rus. Fed.
193 E2 Terni Italy
193 E2 Terni prov. Umbria Italy
160 C2 Ternin r. France
179 H3 Ternitz Austria
137 I3 Ternivka Dnipropetrovs'ka Oblast' Ukr.
137 G4 Ternivka Mykolayivs'ka Oblast' Ukr.
136 E3 Ternivka Vinnyts'ka Oblast' Ukr.
156 C2 Ternoise r. France
136 C3 Ternopil' Ukr.
Ternopil Oblast admin. div. Ukr. see Ternopils'ka Oblast'
136 C3 Ternopils'ka Oblast' admin. div. Ukr.
Ternopol' Ukr. see Ternopil'
Ternopol Oblast admin. div. Ukr. see Ternopils'ka Oblast'
Ternopol'skaya Oblast' admin. div. Ukr. see Ternopils'ka Oblast'
135 H6 Ternovka Rus. Fed.
Ternovka Dnipropetrovs'ka Oblast' Ukr. see Ternivka
137 I4 Ternuvate Ukr.
137 I3 Terny Donets'ka Oblast' Ukr.
137 G2 Terny Sums'ka Oblast' Ukr.
216 □3f Teror Gran Canaria Canary Is
82 D3 Terowie S.A. Austr.
100 G2 Terpeniya, Zaliv g. Sakhalin Rus. Fed.
232 D5 Terra Alta WV U.S.A.
240 H4 Terra Bella CA U.S.A.
256 A5 Terra Boa Brazil
257 F2 Terra Branca Brazil
222 D4 Terrace B.C. Can.
224 C3 Terrace Bay Ont. Can.
216 □1a Terra Chã Terceira Azores
193 F3 Terracina Italy
193 F3 Terracina, Golfo di b. Italy
Terradas Spain see Terrades
186 F2 Terrades Spain
214 D1 Terra Firma S. Africa
140 K2 Terråk Norway
192 A5 Terralba Sardegna Italy
195 F3 Terranova da Sibari Italy
193 I5 Terranova di Pollino Italy
191 G5 Terranuova Bracciolini Italy
256 A5 Terra Rica Brazil
182 B3 Terras do Bouro Port.
194 C4 Terrasini Sicilia Italy
186 F3 Terrassa Spain
162 D3 Terrasson-la-Villedieu France
163 C5 Terraube France
195 F3 Terravecchia Italy
Terre Adélie reg. Antarctica see Adélie Land
247 □2 Terre de Bas i. Guadeloupe
247 □2 Terre de Haut i. Guadeloupe
230 C4 Terre Haute IN U.S.A.
234 B2 Terre Hill PA U.S.A.
237 D5 Terrell TX U.S.A.
157 F5 Terre-Natale France
245 F4 Terrenate Mex.
225 K4 Terrenceville Nfld. Can.
160 C1 Terre Plaine plain France
Terres Australes et Antarctiques Françaises terr. Indian Ocean see French Southern and Antarctic Lands
191 F5 Terricciola Italy
183 I4 Terriente Spain
185 E4 Terril mt. Spain
148 B4 Terrin Rep. of Ireland
185 H2 Terrinches Spain
149 I3 Terrington North Yorkshire, England U.K.
151 H2 Terrington St Clement Norfolk, England U.K.
157 G5 Territoire de Belfort dept Franche-Comté France
163 D4 Terrou France
184 A2 Terrugem Lisboa Port.
184 C2 Terrugem Portalegre Port.
238 F2 Terry MT U.S.A.
235 E1 Terryville CT U.S.A.
235 E2 Terryville NY U.S.A.
135 I6 Tersa r. Rus. Fed.
Tersakkan r. Kazakh. see Terisakkan
164 E1 Terschelling i. Neth.
Terskey Alatau, Khrebet mts Kyrg. see Terskey Ala-Too
121 I4 Terskey Ala-Too mts Kyrg.
134 G2 Terskiy Bereg coastal area Rus. Fed.
137 H4 Tersyanka Ukr.
192 B5 Tertenia Sardegna Italy
Terter Azer. see Tärtär
156 D3 Tertry France
187 B4 Teruel Spain
183 4 Teruel prov. Aragón Spain
138 E1 Tervakoski Fin.
197 H4 Tervel Bulg.
159 F5 Terves France
140 N3 Tervo Fin.
140 N2 Tervola Fin.
139 K3 Teryayevo Rus. Fed.
177 H4 Tés Hungary
191 H2 Tesa r. Italy
188 F3 Tešanj Bos.-Herz.
163 D4 Tescou r. France
245 G4 Tesechoacán r. Mex.
177 G3 Tešedíkovo Slovakia
203 H6 Teseney Eritrea
191 G2 Tesero Italy
135 H5 Tesha r. Rus. Fed.
207 E5 Teshi Ghana
102 K2 Teshio-dake mt. Japan
102 J1 Teshio-gawa r. Japan
102 J1 Teshio-sanchi mts Japan
197 E4 Tešica Srbija Yugo.
191 G2 Tesimo Italy
191 G3 Tesina r. Italy
244 C3 Tesistán Mex.
106 B1 Tesiyn Gol r. Mongolia
188 F3 Teslić Bos.-Herz.
222 C2 Teslin Y.T. Can.
222 C2 Teslin r. Y.T. Can.
197 G3 Teslui r. Romania
182 E3 Teso Santo hill Spain
255 B6 Tesouro Brazil
139 H2 Tesovo-Netyl'skiy Rus. Fed.
139 H2 Tesovskiy Rus. Fed.
168 F2 Tespe Ger.
207 G3 Tessaoua Niger
159 F3 Tessé-la-Madeleine France
165 E3 Tessenderlo Belgium
170 D1 Tessin Ger.
Tessin canton Switz. see Ticino
162 B3 Tesson France
159 E3 Tessy-sur-Vire France
151 F4 Test r. England U.K.
193 I3 Testa del Gargano Italy
194 D6 Testa dell'Acqua Sicilia Italy
182 B2 Testeiro, Montes de mts Spain
165 D3 Testelt Belgium
183 G5 Testillos r. Spain
205 H1 Testour Tunisia
163 F6 Têt r. France
177 G4 Tét Hungary
225 H4 Tetagouche r. N.B. Can.
150 E3 Tetbury Gloucestershire, England U.K.
177 L4 Teţchea Romania
213 G3 Tete Moz.
213 G2 Tete prov. Moz.
161 E4 Tête de l'Enchastraye mt. France/Italy
161 E4 Tête de l'Estrop mt. France
161 E4 Tête de Soulaure mt. France
190 B4 Tête des Toillies mt. Italy
222 G4 Tête Jaune Cache B.C. Can.
80 F3 Te Teko North I. N.Z.
245 E4 Tetela de Volcán Mex.
78 □6 Tetepare i. New Georgia Is Solomon Is
164 D3 Teteringen Neth.
136 F2 Teteriv r. Ukr.
170 D2 Teterow Ger.
177 K4 Tetétlen Hungary
197 G4 Teteven Bulg.
149 I4 Tetford Lincolnshire, England U.K.
192 B4 Teti Sardegna Italy
Tetiyev Ukr. see Tetiyiv
136 E3 Tetiyiv Ukr.
137 H2 Tetkino Rus. Fed.
149 I4 Tetney Lincolnshire, England U.K.
238 E2 Teton r. MT U.S.A.
204 D2 Tétouan Morocco
180 D5 Tétouan prov. Morocco
196 E4 Tetovo Macedonia
116 B5 Tetpur Gujarat India
171 C5 Tettau Ger.
168 C2 Tettens Ger.
172 D4 Tettnang Ger.
Tetuán Morocco see Tétouan
79 □3a Tetufera mt. Tahiti Fr. Polynesia
Tetyukhe Rus. Fed. see Dal'negorsk
Tetyukhe-Pristan' Rus. Fed. see Rudnaya Pristan'
135 J5 Tetyushi Rus. Fed.
173 G2 Teublitz Ger.
171 D4 Teuchern Ger.
Teuchezhsk Rus. Fed. see Adygeysk
258 E2 Teuco r. Arg.
190 E1 Teufen Switz.
192 A6 Teulada Sardegna Italy
187 D6 Teulada Spain
244 C3 Teul de González Ortega Mex.
93 D4 Teun vol. Maluku Indon.
94 A1 Teunom r. Indon.
173 G2 Teunz Ger.
171 E3 Teupitz Ger.
171 C5 Teuschnitz Ger.
169 D3 Teutoburger Wald hills Ger.
171 C4 Teutschenthal Ger.
141 M3 Teuva Fin.
177 H5 Tevel Hungary
191 H5 Tevere r. Italy
193 E1 Teverone r. Italy
128 B3 Teverya Israel
81 B6 Teviot South I. N.Z.
215 E4 Teviot S. Africa
146 F6 Teviot r. Scotland U.K.
146 F6 Teviotdale val. Scotland U.K.
146 F6 Teviothead Scottish Borders, Scotland U.K.
81 A7 Te Waewae South I. N.Z.
81 A7 Te Waewae Bay South I. N.Z.
Te Waiponamu i. N.Z. see South Island
85 H5 Tewantin Qld Austr.
95 F3 Teweh r. Indon.
80 E3 Te Wera North I. N.Z.
80 F3 Te Wera North I. N.Z.
80 F3 Te Whaiti North I. N.Z.
81 E4 Te Wharau North I. N.Z.
150 E3 Tewkesbury Gloucestershire, England U.K.
138 E5 Tewli Belarus
106 D5 Têwo Gansu China
146 B6 Texa i. Scotland U.K.
237 E5 Texarkana AR U.S.A.
237 E5 Texarkana TX U.S.A.
83 G2 Texas Qld Austr.
237 D6 Texas state U.S.A.
237 E6 Texas City TX U.S.A.
245 E4 Texcoco Mex.
164 D1 Texel i. Neth.
237 C4 Texhoma OK U.S.A.
245 G5 Texistepec Mex.
245 E4 Texmelucan Mex.
237 D5 Texoma, Lake Oklahoma/Texas U.S.A.
215 F3 Teyateyaneng Lesotho
162 C3 Teyjat France
139 M3 Teykovo Rus. Fed.
151 H3 Teynham Kent, England U.K.
163 D4 Teyssieu France
160 C2 Teyssonne r. France
134 H4 Teza r. Rus. Fed.
215 I3 Teza S. Africa
245 F4 Teziutlán Mex.
245 F4 Tezonapa Mex.
245 E3 Tezontepec Mex.
117 H4 Tezpur Assam India
117 I4 Tezu Arun. Prad. India
96 C2 Tha, Nam r. Laos
223 M2 Tha-anne r. Nunavut Can.
215 G3 Thabana-Ntlenyana mt. Lesotho
215 F3 Thaba Nchu S. Africa
215 H2 Thabankulu mt. S. Africa
213 E6 Thaba Putsoa mt. Lesotho
215 F4 Thaba Putsoa mts S. Africa
215 G3 Thaba-Tseka Lesotho
213 E5 Thabazimbi S. Africa
96 C3 Tha Bo Laos

215 F2 Thabong S. Africa
161 E3 Thabor, Mont mt. France
96 A3 Thade r. Myanmar
124 D2 Thādiq Saudi Arabia
Tha Hin Thai. see Lop Buri
96 D2 Thai Binh Vietnam
96 C3 Thailand country Asia
97 C5 Thailand, Gulf of Asia
97 B5 Thai Muang Thai.
96 D2 Thai Nguyên Vietnam
125 E2 Thaj Saudi Arabia
117 G4 Thakurgaon Bangl.
116 E5 Thakurtola Madh. Prad. India
169 F5 Thal Ger.
123 G3 Thal Pak.
205 H2 Thala Tunisia
97 B5 Thalang Thai.
Thalassery Pondicherry India see Tellicherry
173 F2 Thalbach r. Ger.
123 G4 Thal Desert Pak.
171 C4 Thale (Harz) Ger.
172 B2 Thaleischweiler-Fröschen Ger.
97 C6 Thale Luang lag. Thai.
172 A2 Thalfang Ger.
178 E3 Thalgau Austria
171 D4 Thalheim Ger.
179 F2 Thalheim bei Wels Austria
Thaliparamba Kerala India see Taliparamba
83 G2 Thallon Qld Austr.
171 D4 Thallwitz Ger.
173 F2 Thalmässing Bayern Ger.
173 G3 Thalmassing Bayern Ger.
190 D1 Thalwil Switz.
212 E5 Thamaga Botswana
124 D5 Thamar, Jabal mt. Yemen
125 F4 Thamarīt Oman
151 G3 Thame Oxfordshire, England U.K.
151 F3 Thame r. England U.K.
227 F4 Thames r. Ont. Can.
80 E2 Thames North I. N.Z.
151 H3 Thames est. England U.K.
151 H3 Thames r. England U.K.
235 F1 Thames r. CT U.S.A.
80 E2 Thames, Firth of b. North I. N.Z.
Thamesdown admin. div. England U.K. see Swindon
227 G4 Thamesford Ont. Can.
227 G4 Thamesville Ont. Can.
169 F4 Thamsbrück Ger.
125 E4 Thamūd Yemen
Thamugadi tourist site Alg. see Timgad
Thana Mahar. India see Thane
116 D4 Thana Ghazi Rajasthan India
96 B3 Thanatpin Myanmar
96 B4 Thanbyuzayat Myanmar
116 C5 Thandla Madh. Prad. India
Thandwè Myanmar see Sandoway
114 B2 Thane Mahar. India
151 I3 Thanet, Isle of pen. England U.K.
116 B5 Thangadh Gujarat India
86 D3 Thangoo W.A. Austr.
85 G5 Thangool Qld Austr.
96 D3 Thanh Hoa Vietnam
114 C4 Thanjavur Tamil Nadu India
Thanlwin r. Myanmar see Salween
157 H5 Thann France
173 E3 Thannhausen Ger.
123 F5 Thano Bula Khan Pak.
212 D3 Thaoge r. Botswana
157 G4 Thaon-les-Vosges France
97 B5 Thap Put Thai.
97 B5 Thap Sakae Thai.
116 B5 Thara Gujarat India
116 B4 Tharad Gujarat India
171 E5 Tharandt Ger.
164 E2 't Harde Neth.
116 B4 Thar Desert India/Pak.
85 E5 Thargomindah Qld Austr.
96 A3 Tharrawaddy Myanmar
184 C3 Tharsis Spain
127 F4 Tharthār, Buḩayrat ath l. Iraq
125 F3 Tharwānīyyah U.A.E.
198 D1 Thasos Anatoliki Makedonia kai Thraki Greece
198 D1 Thasos i. Greece
151 F3 Thatcham West Berkshire, England U.K.
241 M5 Thatcher AZ U.S.A.
198 B1 Thatë, Mali i mt. Albania
96 D2 Thât Khê Vietnam
96 B3 Thaton Myanmar
161 B5 Thau, Bassin de lag. France
160 A2 Thaumiers France
96 A1 Thaungdut Myanmar
96 B3 Thaungyin r. Myanmar/Thai.
178 C3 Thaur Austria
96 D3 Tha Uthen Thai.
128 B5 Thawr, Jabal mt. Jordan
151 H3 Thaxted Essex, England U.K.
179 G2 Thaya Austria
179 G2 Thaya r. Austria/Czech Rep.
96 A3 Thayetmyo Myanmar
190 D1 Thayngen Switz.
96 B2 Thazi Myanmar
241 K5 Theba AZ U.S.A.
Thebae tourist site Egypt see Thebes
229 K6 The Bahamas country West Indies
203 G3 Thebes tourist site Egypt
Thebes Greece see Thiva
246 C1 The Bluff Eleuthera Bahamas
151 I2 The Broads nat. park England U.K.
149 G3 The Calf hill England U.K.
85 H1 The Calvados Chain is P.N.G.
149 G2 The Cheviot hill England U.K.
246 □ The Cockpit Country hills Jamaica
82 D3 The Coorong inlet S.A. Austr.
148 C4 The Curragh lowland Rep. of Ireland
238 B2 The Dalles OR U.S.A.
236 C3 Thedford NE U.S.A.
148 C3 The Diamond Northern Ireland U.K.
168 E3 Thedinghausen Ger.
84 D1 The English Company's Islands N.T. Austr.
83 G3 The Entrance N.S.W. Austr.
151 G2 The Fens reg. England U.K.
206 A3 The Gambia country Africa
146 D6 The Glenkens val. Scotland U.K.
84 B4 The Granites hill N.T. Austr.
203 F3 The Great Oasis Egypt
247 □3 The Grenadines is St Vincent
125 E1 The Gulf Asia
The Hague Neth. see 's-Gravenhage
147 E4 The Harrow Rep. of Ireland
215 G5 The Haven S. Africa
214 D4 The Horseshoe mt. S. Africa
81 C6 The Hunters Hills South I. N.Z.
159 I4 Theillay France
171 D4 Theißen Ger.
158 D4 Theix France
81 A6 The Key South I. N.Z.
223 L1 Thelon r. N.W.T./Nunavut Can.
150 E2 The Long Mynd hills England U.K.
148 C3 The Loup Northern Ireland U.K.
85 F3 The Lynd Junction Qld Austr.
146 D7 The Machars reg. Scotland U.K.
169 F5 Themar Ger.
214 E5 Thembalesizwe S. Africa
215 G2 Thembalihle S. Africa
146 B3 The Minch sea chan. Scotland U.K.
163 D4 Thémines France
150 D3 The Mumbles Swansea, Wales U.K.
159 H5 Thenay France
The Naze c. Norway see Lindesnes
151 F4 The Needles stack England U.K.
159 F5 Thénezay France
116 D5 Theni Madh. Prad. India
205 F2 Theniet El Had Alg.
162 D3 Thenon France
146 F2 The North Sound sea chan. Scotland U.K.
84 B4 Theo, Mount hill N.T. Austr.
146 B6 The Oa pen. Scotland U.K.
85 G5 Theodore Qld Austr.
223 K5 Theodore Sask. Can.
253 E1 Theodore Roosevelt r. Brazil
Theodosia Ukr. see Feodosiya
149 F3 The Old Man of Coniston hill England U.K.
159 I4 Théols r. France
161 E5 Théoule-sur-Mer France
147 B4 The Paps hill Rep. of Ireland
223 K4 The Pas Man. Can.
147 D4 The Pike Rep. of Ireland
Thera i. Greece see Thira
156 C3 Thérain r. France
81 B6 The Remarkables mts South I. N.Z.
169 F5 Theres Ger.
233 F2 Theresa NY U.S.A.
85 G4 Theresa Creek r. Qld Austr.
198 C1 Thermaïkos Kolpos g. Greece
198 C1 Thermi Kentriki Makedonia Greece
198 B2 Thermo Greece
Thérmon Greece see Thermo
238 E3 Thermopolis WY U.S.A.
83 F3 The Rock N.S.W. Austr.
185 □ The Rock hill Gibraltar
156 C2 Thérouanne France
86 □1 The Settlement Christmas I.
147 E2 The Sheddings Northern Ireland U.K.
The Slot sea chan. Solomon Is see New Georgia Sound
146 □F1 The Sneug hill Scotland U.K.
151 F4 The Solent str. England U.K.
198 B2 Thesprotiko Greece
198 B2 Thessalia admin. reg. Greece
224 D4 Thessalon Ont. Can.
Thessalonica Greece see Thessaloniki
198 C1 Thessaloniki Greece
Thessaly admin. reg. Greece see Thessalia
151 H3 The Stocks Kent, England U.K.
146 B4 The Storr hill Scotland U.K.
151 H2 Thet r. England U.K.
92 A4 The Teeth mt. Palawan Phil.
148 D3 The Temple Northern Ireland U.K.
87 D6 The Terraces hills W.A. Austr.
151 H2 Thetford Norfolk, England U.K.
225 G4 Thetford Mines Que. Can.
81 C5 The Thumbs mt. South I. N.Z.
96 A4 Thetkethaung r. Myanmar
96 B1 The Triangle mts Myanmar
146 D5 The Trossachs hills Scotland U.K.
82 C2 The Twins S.A. Austr.
96 D3 Theun r. Laos
215 F3 Theunissen S. Africa
165 E4 Theux Belgium
Theva-i-Ra rf Fiji see Ceva-i-Ra
247 G3 The Valley Anguilla
82 C3 Thevenard S.A. Austr.
86 B4 Thevenard Island W.A. Austr.
Theveste Alg. see Tébessa
151 H2 The Wash b. England U.K.
151 H3 The Weald reg. England U.K.
237 E6 The Woodlands TX U.S.A.
The Wrekin admin. div. England U.K. see Telford and Wrekin
163 B5 Thèze France
161 D4 Thèze France
Thíamis r. Greece see Thyamis
157 F4 Thiaucourt-Regniéville France
159 G2 Thiberville France
156 E4 Thibie France
237 F6 Thibodaux LA U.S.A.
223 L4 Thicket Portage Man. Can.
156 E4 Thiéblemont-Farémont France
236 D1 Thief River Falls MN U.S.A.
Thiel Neth. see Tiel
190 B2 Thielle r. Switz.
235 D1 Thiells NY U.S.A.
262 R1 Thiel Mountains Antarctica
238 B3 Thielsen, Mount OR U.S.A.
Thielt Belgium see Tielt
191 G3 Thiene Italy
173 E3 Thierhaupten Ger.
190 B2 Thierrens Switz.
160 B3 Thiers France
178 D3 Thiersee Austria
171 D5 Thiersheim Ger.
157 F3 Thierville-sur-Meuse France
206 A3 Thiès Senegal
192 A4 Thiesi Sardegna Italy
170 E1 Thießow Ger.
161 A3 Thiézac France
211 C5 Thika Kenya
Thikombia i. Fiji see Cikobia
114 B5 Thiladhunmathee Atoll Maldives
206 B3 Thilogne Senegal
Thimbu Bhutan see Thimphu
156 B4 Thimert-Gâtelles France
117 G4 Thimphu Bhutan
140 □B2 Thingvallavatn (Þingvallavatn) l. Iceland
140 □B2 Thingvellir (Þingvellir) Iceland
156 E3 Thin-le-Moutier France
78 □5 Thio New Caledonia
157 G3 Thionville France
199 D3 Thira Greece
199 D3 Thira i. Greece
203 F5 Third Cataract rapids Sudan
159 G3 Thiron Gardais France
156 B4 Thironne r. France
149 H3 Thirsk North Yorkshire, England U.K.
87 D7 Thirsty, Mount hill W.A. Austr.
Thiruvananthapuram Kerala India see Trivandrum
114 C4 Thiruvarur Tamil Nadu India
Thiruvattiyur Tamil Nadu India see Tiruvottiyur
160 E1 Thise France
142 C3 Thisted Denmark
140 □D2 Thistilfjörður (Þistilfjörður) b. Iceland
222 B2 Thistle Creek Y.T. Can.
82 D3 Thistle Island S.A. Austr.
198 C2 Thiva Greece
Thívai Greece see Thiva
156 B4 Thivars France
162 C3 Thiviers France
160 C2 Thizy France
140 □C2 Thjórsá (Þjórsá) r. Iceland
223 M2 Thlewiaza r. Nunavut Can.
223 I2 Thoa r. N.W.T. Can.
161 E4 Thoard France
96 B3 Thoen Thai.
96 C3 Thoeng Thai.
213 F4 Thohoyandou S. Africa
160 D2 Thoirette France
156 B4 Thoiry Île-de-France France
160 D2 Thoiry Rhône-Alpes France
160 C2 Thoissey France
160 C1 Thoisy-la-Berchère France
164 D3 Tholen Neth.
164 D3 Tholen i. Neth.
172 B2 Tholey Ger.
156 D4 Tholon r. France
87 C5 Thomas r. W.A. Austr.
84 D5 Thomas, Lake salt flat S.A. Austr.
168 F2 Thomasburg Ger.
240 I5 Thomas Mountain CA U.S.A.
235 E1 Thomaston CT U.S.A.
231 C5 Thomaston GA U.S.A.
233 □I2 Thomaston ME U.S.A.
233 □J2 Thomaston Corner N.B. Can.
147 D4 Thomastown Rep. of Ireland
231 C6 Thomasville AL U.S.A.
231 D6 Thomasville GA U.S.A.
231 D5 Thomasville NC U.S.A.
165 F4 Thommen Belgium
246 E3 Thomonde Haiti
223 L4 Thompson Man. Can.
222 F5 Thompson r. B.C. Can.
226 D3 Thompson MI U.S.A.
241 M2 Thompson UT U.S.A.
236 E4 Thompson r. MO U.S.A.
238 D2 Thompson Falls MT U.S.A.
239 F5 Thompson Peak NM U.S.A.
222 E5 Thompson Sound B.C. Can.
234 A2 Thompsontown PA U.S.A.
233 G4 Thompsonville CT U.S.A.
231 D5 Thomson GA U.S.A.
226 B5 Thomson IL U.S.A.
81 B6 Thomson Mountains South I. N.Z.
97 C4 Thon Buri Thai.
160 E3 Thônes France
96 B3 Thongwa Myanmar
157 F4 Thonnance-lès-Joinville France
160 E2 Thonon-les-Bains France
161 E4 Thorame-Basse France
161 E4 Thorame-Haute France
161 B4 Thoras France
163 E5 Thoré r. France
239 E5 Thoreau NM U.S.A.
159 G4 Thoré-la-Rochette France
161 E5 Thorenc France
160 E3 Thorens-Glières France
222 H4 Thorhild Alta Can.
156 D4 Thorigny-sur-Oreuse France
140 □C2 Thórisvatn (Þórisvatn) l. Iceland
179 G3 Thörl Austria
165 E3 Thorn Neth.
Thorn Pol. see Toruń
149 H3 Thornaby-on-Tees Stockton-on-Tees, England U.K.
226 E4 Thornapple r. MI U.S.A.
81 B7 Thornbury South I. N.Z.
150 E3 Thornbury South Gloucestershire, England U.K.
227 H2 Thorne Ont. Can.
149 I4 Thorne South Yorkshire, England U.K.
240 H2 Thorne NV U.S.A.
222 C4 Thorne Bay AK U.S.A.
151 G2 Thorney Peterborough, England U.K.
149 I4 Thorngumbald East Riding of Yorkshire, England U.K.
146 E6 Thornhill Dumfries and Galloway, Scotland U.K.
148 E1 Thornhill Stirling, Scotland U.K.
234 C1 Thornhurst PA U.S.A.
149 H3 Thornley Durham, England U.K.
84 D3 Thornton r. Qld Austr.
146 E5 Thornton Fife, Scotland U.K.
149 G4 Thornton Lancashire, England U.K.
226 C3 Thornton WI U.S.A.
149 I3 Thornton Dale North Yorkshire, England U.K.
235 E1 Thornwood NY U.S.A.
227 H4 Thorold Ont. Can.
226 B3 Thorp WI U.S.A.
81 D4 Thorpe South I. N.Z.
151 I3 Thorpe-le-Soken Essex, England U.K.
151 I2 Thorpe Market Norfolk, England U.K.
151 I2 Thorpeness Suffolk, England U.K.
151 I2 Thorpe St Andrew Norfolk, England U.K.
222 H4 Thorsby Alta Can.
Thorshavn Faroe Is see Tórshavn
Thorshavnfjella reg. Antarctica see Thorshavnheiane
263 B2 Thorshavnheiane reg. Antarctica
140 □C2 Thorvaldsfell (Þorvaldsfell) vol. Iceland
215 F3 Thota-ea-Moli Lesotho
159 F4 Thouarcé France
158 E4 Thouaré-sur-Loire France
162 B2 Thouars France
117 H4 Thoubal Manipur India
162 B1 Thouet r. France
86 C4 Thouin, Cape pt W.A. Austr.
156 C3 Thourotte France
Thourout Belgium see Torhout
227 I3 Thousand Islands Can./U.S.A.
241 L2 Thousand Lake Mountain UT U.S.A.
240 H4 Thousand Oaks CA U.S.A.
241 I5 Thousand Palms CA U.S.A.
232 B6 Thousandsticks KY U.S.A.
198 D1 Thrakiko Pelagos sea Greece
151 G2 Thrapston Northamptonshire, England U.K.
83 G4 Thredbo N.S.W. Austr.
234 D2 Three Bridges NJ U.S.A.
238 E2 Three Forks MT U.S.A.
108 D2 Three Gorges Project resr China
83 F5 Three Hummock Island Tas. Austr.
80 D1 Three Kings Islands North I. N.Z.
226 C3 Three Lakes WI U.S.A.
226 D5 Three Oaks MI U.S.A.
241 L5 Three Points AZ U.S.A.
240 H3 Three Rivers CA U.S.A.
226 E5 Three Rivers MI U.S.A.
237 D6 Three Rivers TX U.S.A.
214 D4 Three Sisters S. Africa
238 B2 Three Sisters mt. OR U.S.A.
78 □6 Three Sisters Islands Solomon Is
87 B6 Three Springs W.A. Austr.
149 F3 Threlkeld Cumbria, England U.K.
149 G3 Threshfield North Yorkshire, England U.K.
Thrissur Kerala India see Trichur
237 D5 Throckmorton TX U.S.A.
234 C1 Throop PA U.S.A.
149 H2 Thropton Northumberland, England U.K.
87 E5 Throssell, Lake salt flat W.A. Austr.
86 D4 Throssel Range hills W.A. Austr.
146 E3 Thrumster Highland, Scotland U.K.
150 E3 Thrupp Gloucestershire, England U.K.
149 H4 Thrybergh South Yorkshire, England U.K.
97 D5 Thu Dâu Môt Vietnam
83 G3 Thuddungra N.S.W. Austr.
163 E6 Thuès-entre-Valls France
161 C4 Thueyts France
165 D4 Thuin Belgium
169 C3 Thuine Ger.
163 E6 Thuir France
128 D2 Thulaythawāt Gharbī, Jabal hill Syria
169 E5 Thulba r. Ger.
213 F4 Thuli r. Zimbabwe
Thulusdhoo N. Male Maldives see Thulusdhu
113 □1 Thulusdhu N. Male Maldives
171 D5 Thum Ger.
190 C2 Thun Switz.
85 E5 Thunda Qld Austr.
87 C6 Thundelarra W.A. Austr.
224 B3 Thunder Bay Ont. Can.
224 B3 Thunder Bay b. Ont. Can.
227 F3 Thunder Bay b. MI U.S.A.
223 J5 Thunder Creek r. Sask. Can.
246 B3 Thunder Knoll sea feature Caribbean Sea
151 H3 Thundersley Essex, England U.K.
190 C2 Thuner See l. Switz.
172 D2 Thüngen Ger.
172 D2 Thüngersheim Ger.
97 B5 Thung Song Thai.
97 B6 Thung Wa Thai.
157 H4 Thur r. France
190 D1 Thur r. Switz.
80 E4 Thuraua North I. N.Z.
149 H4 Thurcroft South Yorkshire, England U.K.
159 G5 Thuré France
160 B3 Thuret France
160 D2 Thurey France
190 E1 Thurgau canton Switz.
178 A3 Thüringen Austria
169 F4 Thüringen land Ger.
171 C4 Thüringer Becken reg. Ger.
169 F5 Thüringer Wald mts Ger.
Thuringia land Ger. see Thüringen
Thuringian Forest mts Ger. see Thüringer Wald
160 C3 Thurins France
170 D2 Thürkow Ger.
151 G2 Thurlby Lincolnshire, England U.K.
147 D4 Thurles Rep. of Ireland
171 D5 Thurm Ger.
173 H3 Thurmansbang Ger.
232 E5 Thurmont MD U.S.A.
171 C5 Thurnau Ger.
149 H4 Thurnscoe South Yorkshire, England U.K.
151 H3 Thurrock admin. div. England U.K.
149 F3 Thursby Cumbria, England U.K.
85 E1 Thursday Island Qld Austr.
233 F2 Thurso Que. Can.
146 E3 Thurso Highland, Scotland U.K.
146 E3 Thurso r. Scotland U.K.
151 H2 Thurston Suffolk, England U.K.
262 R2 Thurston Island Antarctica
Thurston Peninsula i. Antarctica see Thurston Island
151 I2 Thurton Norfolk, England U.K.
159 F3 Thury-Harcourt France
190 E2 Thusis Switz.
169 E3 Thüster Berg hill Ger.
160 D3 Thusy France
149 G3 Thwaite North Yorkshire, England U.K.
198 B2 Thyamis r. Greece
Thyatira Turkey see Akhisar
142 C3 Thyborøn Denmark
160 E2 Thyez France
85 E5 Thylungra Qld Austr.
211 B8 Thyolo Malawi
206 E4 Thyou Boulkiemde Burkina
Thyou Yatenga Burkina see Tiou
173 H3 Thyrnau Ger.
Thysville Dem. Rep. Congo see Mbanza-Ngungu
122 D5 Tīāb Iran
252 C4 Tiahuanaco Bol.
192 B4 Tiana Sardegna Italy
106 C3 Tiancang Gansu China
109 F1 Tianchang Anhui China
Tiancheng Hubei China see Chongyang
Tianchi Sichuan China see Lezhi
108 C4 Tiandeng Guangxi China
Tiandiba Sichuan China see Jinyang
108 C4 Tiandong Guangxi China
108 C3 Tian'e Guangxi China
129 D2 T'ianet'i Georgia
109 F2 Tianfanjie Jiangxi China
254 E2 Tianguá Brazil
107 H4 Tianjin Tianjin China
107 H4 Tianjin mun. China
106 C4 Tianjun Qinghai China
108 C3 Tianlin Guangxi China
109 E2 Tianmen Hubei China
100 D4 Tianqiaoling Jilin China
108 B2 Tianquan Sichuan China
107 I3 Tianshan Nei Mongol China
Tian Shan mts China/Kyrg. see Tien Shan
101 C4 Tianshifu Liaoning China
106 E5 Tianshui Gansu China
110 F3 Tianshuijing Gansu China
109 G2 Tiantai Zhejiang China
107 H3 Tiantaiyong Nei Mongol China
Tiantang Anhui China see Yuexi
108 C4 Tianyang Guangxi China
Tianyi Nei Mongol China see Ningcheng
Tianzhen Shandong China see Gaoqing
107 G3 Tianzhen Shanxi China
Tianzhou Guangxi China see Tianyang
106 D4 Tianzhu Gansu China
108 D3 Tianzhu Guizhou China
205 F2 Tiaret Alg.
85 H5 Tiaro Qld Austr.
216 □3c Tías Lanzarote Canary Is
206 D5 Tiassalé Côte d'Ivoire
256 B6 Tibagi Brazil
256 B5 Tibagi r. Brazil
Tibaji r. Brazil see Tibagi
127 F4 Tibal, Wādī watercourse Iraq
250 C3 Tibaná Col.
207 I5 Tibati Cameroon
123 G4 Tibba Pak.
146 E5 Tibbermore Perth and Kinross, Scotland U.K.
206 C4 Tibé, Pic de mt. Guinea
Tiber r. Italy see Tevere
Tiberias Israel see Teverya
128 B3 Tiberias, Lake Israel
202 C4 Tibesti mts Chad
Tibet, Plateau of Xizang China see Qing Zang Gaoyuan
187 C6 Tibi Spain
207 G3 Tibiri Niger
197 G2 Tibleş, Vârful mt. Romania
177 J4 Tiboldaróc Hungary
83 E2 Tibooburra N.S.W. Austr.
177 L4 Tiborszállás Hungary
117 E3 Tibrikot Nepal
143 F2 Tibro Sweden
149 H4 Tibshelf Derbyshire, England U.K.
Tibur Italy see Tivoli
242 B2 Tiburón, Isla i. Mex.
151 H3 Ticehurst East Sussex, England U.K.
197 H4 Ticha r. Bulg.
197 F4 Tichak mt. Bulg.
Tichau Pol. see Tychy
227 I3 Tichborne Ont. Can.
225 F3 Tichégami r. Que. Can.
206 C2 Tîchît Maur.
190 E3 Ticino r. Italy/Switz.
190 D2 Ticino canton Switz.
Ticinum Italy see Pavia
149 H4 Tickhill South Yorkshire, England U.K.
197 F3 Ţicleni Romania
233 G3 Ticonderoga NY U.S.A.
243 H4 Ticul Mex.
Ticumbia i. Fiji see Cikobia
143 E2 Tidaholm Sweden
143 F2 Tidan Sweden
143 E2 Tidan r. Sweden
168 F3 Tiddische Ger.
150 E3 Tidenham Gloucestershire, England U.K.
149 H4 Tideswell Derbyshire, England U.K.
205 F4 Tidikelt, Plaine du plain Alg.
232 D4 Tidioute PA U.S.A.
206 C2 Tidjikja Maur.
190 E3 Tidone r. Italy
163 A6 Tiebas Spain
206 D5 Tiébissou Côte d'Ivoire
183 E3 Tiedra Spain
107 I3 Tiefa Liaoning China
173 G2 Tiefenbach Bayern Ger.
173 G3 Tiefenbach Bayern Ger.
173 H3 Tiefenbach Bayern Ger.
172 C3 Tiefenbronn Ger.
190 E2 Tiefencastel Switz.
170 E3 Tiefensee Ger.
164 E3 Tiel Neth.
206 B3 Tiel Senegal
165 D3 Tielen Belgium
100 C3 Tieli Heilong. China
107 I3 Tieling Liaoning China
165 C4 Tielt Belgium
206 D4 Tiémé Côte d'Ivoire
165 D4 Tienen Belgium
172 C4 Tiengen Ger.
110 B3 Tien Shan mts China/Kyrg.
Tien Shan Oblast admin. div. Kyrg. see Naryn
Tientsin Tianjin China see Tianjin
Tientsin mun. China see Tianjin
191 F4 Tiepido r. Italy
159 F4 Tiercé France
215 F3 Tierfontein S. Africa
183 I3 Tierga Spain
143 G1 Tierp Sweden
258 C2 Tierra Amarilla Chile
239 F4 Tierra Amarilla NM U.S.A.
245 F4 Tierra Blanca Mex.
245 E5 Tierra Colorada Mex.
259 D9 Tierra del Fuego prov. Arg.
259 C9 Tierra del Fuego, Isla Grande de i. Arg./Chile
184 C3 Tierra Llana de Huelva plain Spain
183 I4 Tierzo Spain
185 E3 Tiesa hill Spain
179 G4 Tieschen Austria
182 E5 Tiétar r. Spain
183 E4 Tiétar, Valle de val. Spain
256 D5 Tietê Brazil
256 B4 Tietê r. Brazil
164 E1 Tietjerk Neth.
82 C1 Tieyon S.A. Austr.
159 E4 Tiffauges France
232 B4 Tiffin OH U.S.A.
Tiflis Georgia see T'bilisi
231 D6 Tifton GA U.S.A.
78 □5 Tiga i. Î. Loyauté New Caledonia
215 F2 Tigane S. Africa
197 G4 Tigăneşti Romania
94 C3 Tigapuluh, Pegunungan mts Indon.
136 E5 Tigheciului, Dealurile hills Moldova
136 E4 Tighina Moldova
136 D4 Ţighira Moldova
146 C6 Tighnabruaich Argyll and Bute, Scotland U.K.
121 J2 Tigiretskiy Khrebet mts Kazakh./Rus. Fed.
117 F5 Tigiria Orissa India
191 F3 Tignale Italy
207 I5 Tignère Cameroon
160 E3 Tignes France
225 H4 Tignish P.E.I. Can.
139 H2 Tigoda r. Rus. Fed.
Tigranocerta Turkey see Siirt
210 C1 Tigray admin. reg. Eth.
261 H4 Tigre Arg.
250 C6 Tigre r. Ecuador/Peru
245 F2 Tigre r. Mex.
245 E2 Tigre, Cerro del mt. Mex.
260 C2 Tigre, Sierra mts Arg.
127 F3 Tigris r. Turkey alt. Dicle (Turkey), alt. Dijlah, Nahr (Iraq/Syria)
206 B2 Tiguent Maur.
204 C4 Tiguesmat hills Maur.
207 G2 Tiguidit, Falaise de esc. Niger
156 C5 Tigy France
203 G2 Tīh, Gebel el plat. Egypt
124 C4 Tihāmah reg. Saudi Arabia
177 G5 Tihany Hungary
252 D3 Tijamuchi r. Bol.
116 D4 Tijara Rajasthan India
216 □3d Tijarafe La Palma Canary Is
164 E1 Tijnje Neth.
185 H3 Tíjola Spain
242 A1 Tijuana Mex.
255 C8 Tijucas Brazil
256 B3 Tijuco r. Brazil
Tika i. Î. Loyauté New Caledonia see Tiga
243 H5 Tikal tourist site Guat.
116 D4 Tikamgarh Madh. Prad. India
110 D3 Tikanlik Xinjiang China
137 J2 Tikhaya Sosna r. Rus. Fed.
Tikherón Greece see Tykhero
139 L2 Tikhmenevo Rus. Fed.
139 K4 Tikhonova Pustyn' Rus. Fed.
135 H7 Tikhoretsk Rus. Fed.
139 I2 Tikhvin Rus. Fed.
139 I2 Tikhvinka r. Rus. Fed.
139 I2 Tikhvinskaya Gryada ridge Rus. Fed.
267 K7 Tiki Basin sea feature Pacific Ocean
80 G2 Tikitiki North I. N.Z.
140 N3 Tikkakoski Fin.
138 E1 Tikkurila Fin.
80 F3 Tikokino North I. N.Z.
77 G3 Tikopia i. Solomon Is
127 F4 Tikrīt Iraq
131 N2 Tiksi Rus. Fed.
Tikumbia i. Fiji see Cikobia
215 E2 Tikwana S. Africa
116 E3 Tila r. Nepal
122 C2 Tilavar Iran
128 C1 Tilbeşar Ovasi plain Turkey
85 F5 Tilbooroo Qld Austr.
164 E3 Tilburg Neth.
227 F4 Tilbury Ont. Can.
151 H3 Tilbury Thurrock, England U.K.
258 D1 Tilcara Arg.
82 E2 Tilcha S.A. Austr.
160 D1 Til-Châtel France
237 D6 Tilden TX U.S.A.
197 F2 Tileagd Romania
151 F3 Tilehurst Reading, England U.K.
207 G3 Tilemsès Niger
207 F2 Tîlemsi, Vallée du watercourse Mali
233 E5 Tilghman MD U.S.A.
163 B5 Tilh France
116 D4 Tilhar Uttar Prad. India
Tiligulo-Berezanka Ukr. see Berezanka
Tilimsen Alg. see Tlemcen
260 E3 Tilisarao Arg.
149 G2 Till r. England U.K.
207 F3 Tillabéri Niger
207 F3 Tillabéri dept Niger
163 C5 Tillac France
238 B2 Tillamook OR U.S.A.
160 D1 Tille r. France
171 C4 Tilleda (Kyffhäuser) Ger.
223 I5 Tilley Alta Can.
207 G2 Tillia Niger
146 E5 Tillicoultry Clackmannanshire, Scotland U.K.
156 B4 Tillières-sur-Avre France
156 E3 Tilloy-et-Bellay France
224 D5 Tillsonburg Ont. Can.
146 F4 Tillyfourie Aberdeenshire, Scotland U.K.
159 F2 Tilly-sur-Seulles France
Tilogne Senegal see Thilogne
199 E3 Tilos i. Greece
83 F2 Tilpa N.S.W. Austr.
138 F3 Tilsa r. Latvia
Tilsit Kaliningradskaya Oblast' Rus. Fed. see Sovetsk
149 G4 Tilston Cheshire, England U.K.
146 E5 Tilt r. Scotland U.K.
260 B3 Tiltil Chile
233 H3 Tilton NH U.S.A.
93 B3 Tilu, Bukit mt. Indon.
135 G6 Tim Rus. Fed.
137 I1 Tim r. Rus. Fed.
203 F3 Tima Egypt
148 B5 Timahoe Rep. of Ireland
253 F5 Timane r. Para.
216 □3c Timanfaya hill Lanzarote Canary Is
134 J2 Timanskiy Kryazh ridge Rus. Fed.
127 F3 Timar Turkey
81 C6 Timaru South I. N.Z.
120 B1 Timashevo Rus. Fed.
135 G7 Timashevsk Rus. Fed.
Timashevskaya Rus. Fed. see Timashevsk
191 I2 Timau Italy
Timbákion Kriti Greece see Tympaki
254 G3 Timbaúba Brazil
206 C2 Timbedgha Maur.
84 B2 Timber Creek N.T. Austr.
236 C2 Timber Lake SD U.S.A.
241 I3 Timber Mountain NV U.S.A.
232 D5 Timberville VA U.S.A.
250 B4 Timbiquí Col.
206 C4 Timbo Guinea
83 E4 Timboon Vic. Austr.
Timbuktu Mali see Tombouctou
179 E2 Timelkam Austria
206 E2 Timétrine reg. Mali
205 G2 Timgad tourist site Alg.
205 F3 Timimoun Alg.
121 F1 Timiryazev Kazakh.
121 F1 Timiryazevo Kazakh.
177 K6 Timiş county Romania
197 E3 Timiş r. Romania
196 E3 Timişoara Romania
196 E3 Timişului, Câmpia plain Romania
168 F2 Timmendorfer Strand Ger.
224 D3 Timmins Ont. Can.
226 B3 Timms Hill hill WI U.S.A.
Timoé atoll Arch. des Tuamotu Fr. Polynesia see Temoe
197 F3 Timok r. Yugo.
139 K2 Timokhino Rus. Fed.
147 C5 Timoleague Rep. of Ireland
254 E3 Timon Brazil
192 D2 Timone r. Italy
234 B3 Timonium MD U.S.A.
93 C5 Timor i. Indon.
76 C3 Timor Sea Austr./Indon.
Timor Timur terr. Asia see East Timor
257 F3 Timóteo Brazil
205 E3 Timoudi Alg.
87 D5 Timperley Range hills W.A. Austr.
141 L3 Timrå Sweden
150 E3 Timsbury Bath and North East Somerset, England U.K.
146 A3 Timsgearraidh Western Isles, Scotland U.K.
134 K3 Timshor r. Rus. Fed.
Timur Yuzhnyy Kazakhstan Kazakh. see Tumur
116 D5 Timurni Muafi Madh. Prad. India
124 C2 Tīn, Jabal hill Saudi Arabia
191 G2 Tina r. Italy
215 G4 Tina r. S. Africa
128 A4 Tîna, Khalîg el b. Egypt
148 C5 Tinahely Rep. of Ireland
183 H4 Tinajas Spain
216 □3c Tinajo Lanzarote Canary Is
182 C5 Tinalhas Port.
177 K5 Tinca Romania
85 H5 Tin Can Bay Qld Austr.
159 F3 Tinchebray France
114 C3 Tindivanam Tamil Nadu India
204 C4 Tindouf Alg.
144 D1 Tindur hill Faroe Is
161 F5 Tinée r. France
182 D1 Tineo Spain
204 D3 Tinerhir Morocco
151 F3 Tingewick Buckinghamshire, England U.K.
94 D2 Tinggi i. Malaysia
206 C4 Tingi Mountains Sierra Leone
Tingis Morocco see Tanger
109 F3 Ting Jiang r. China
142 C4 Tinglev Denmark
Tingrela Côte d'Ivoire see Tengréla
143 F3 Tingsryd Sweden
143 H3 Tingstäde Gotland Sweden
244 C4 Tinguindín Mex.
260 B4 Tinguiririca Chile
260 B4 Tinguiririca, Volcán vol. Chile
142 B2 Tingvatn Norway
140 J3 Tingvoll Norway
146 E2 Tingwall Orkney, Scotland U.K.
146 □G1 Tingwall Shetland, Scotland U.K.
Tingzhou Fujian China see Changting
254 F5 Tinharé, Ilha de i. Brazil
182 C3 Tinhela r. Port.
91 K4 Tinian i. N. Mariana Is
Tini Heke is N.Z. see Snares Islands
80 F3 Tiniroto North I. N.Z.
188 G3 Tinja r. Bos.-Herz.
95 F1 Tinjar r. Sarawak Malaysia
206 C4 Tinkisso r. Guinea
137 G3 Tin'ky Ukr.
81 D5 Tinline, Mount South I. N.Z.
205 H5 Ti-n-Merzouga des. Alg.
142 C2 Tinne r. Norway
Tinnelvelly Tamil Nadu India see Tirunelveli
177 H4 Tinnye Hungary
258 D3 Tinogasta Arg.
198 D3 Tinos Notio Aigaio Greece
198 D3 Tinos i. Greece
185 F3 Tiñosa mt. Spain
183 F4 Tiñosillos Spain
156 D3 Tinqueux France
205 G3 Tinrhert, Plateau du Alg.
117 H4 Tinsukia Assam India
222 E4 Tintagel B.C. Can.
150 C4 Tintagel Cornwall, England U.K.
206 C2 Ţînţâne Maur.
205 F4 Tintejert, Adrar mt. Alg.
158 E3 Tinténiac France
150 E3 Tintern Parva Monmouthshire, Wales U.K.
165 E5 Tintigny Belgium
258 E2 Tintina Arg.
82 E3 Tintinara S.A. Austr.
184 D3 Tinto r. Spain
149 F2 Tinto hill Scotland U.K.
81 F4 Tinui North I. N.Z.
236 C1 Tioga ND U.S.A.
232 E4 Tioga PA U.S.A.
232 E3 Tioga r. PA U.S.A.
234 A1 Tioga County county PA U.S.A.
94 D2 Tioman i. Malaysia
227 F1 Tionaga Ont. Can.
191 G3 Tione r. Italy
191 F2 Tione di Trento Italy
232 D4 Tionesta PA U.S.A.
206 C3 Tioribougou Mali
206 E3 Tiou Burkina
233 F3 Tioughnioga r. NY U.S.A.
205 F1 Tipasa Alg.
242 □I6 Tipitapa Nic.
226 C3 Tipler WI U.S.A.
230 C3 Tippecanoe r. IN U.S.A.
147 C4 Tipperary Rep. of Ireland
147 D4 Tipperary county Rep. of Ireland
240 H3 Tipton CA U.S.A.
236 F3 Tipton IA U.S.A.
236 E4 Tipton MO U.S.A.
241 J4 Tipton, Mount AZ U.S.A.
237 F4 Tiptonville TN U.S.A.
232 C6 Tiptop VA U.S.A.
224 C3 Tip Top Hill hill Ont. Can.
151 H3 Tiptree Essex, England U.K.
114 C3 Tiptur Karnataka India
252 C3 Tipuani Bol.
250 D4 Tiquié r. Brazil
243 H6 Tiquisate Guat.
254 D3 Tiracambu, Serra do hills Brazil
122 B3 Tīrān Iran
Tirana Albania see Tiranë
196 D5 Tiranë Albania
161 B3 Tiranges France
190 F2 Tirano Italy
117 H4 Tirap Arun. Prad. India
124 C2 Tirāq, Jibāl al hills Saudi Arabia
82 D1 Tirari Desert S.A. Austr.
136 E4 Tiraspol Moldova
80 E2 Tirau North I. N.Z.
80 F4 Tiraumea North I. N.Z.
199 E2 Tire Turkey
177 L4 Tiream Romania
146 B5 Tiree i. Scotland U.K.
146 B4 Tirga Mor hill Scotland U.K.
183 H2 Tirgo Spain
Tîrgovişte Romania see Târgovişte
Tîrgu Bujor Romania see Târgu Bujor
Tîrgu Cărbuneşti Romania see Târgu Cărbuneşti
Tîrgu Frumos Romania see Târgu Frumos
Tîrgu Jiu Romania see Târgu Jiu
Tîrgu Lăpuş Romania see Târgu Lăpuş
Tîrgu Mureş Romania see Târgu Mureş
Tîrgu Neamţ Romania see Târgu Neamţ
Tîrgu Ocna Romania see Târgu Ocna
Tîrgu Secuiesc Romania see Târgu Secuiesc
123 G2 Tirich Mir mt. Pak.
185 H2 Tiriez Spain
186 D4 Tirig Spain
195 F4 Tiriolo Italy
204 C5 Tiris Zemmour admin. reg. Maur.
138 D3 Tirkšliai Lith.
Tirlemont Belgium see Tienen
120 D1 Tirlyanskiy Rus. Fed.
114 C2 Tirna r. India
Tîrnăveni Romania see Târnăveni
Tírnavos Greece see Tyrnavos
Tîrnova Romania see Târnova
185 E2 Tiro hill Spain
116 D5 Tirodi Madh. Prad. India
178 C3 Tirol land Austria
183 H2 Tirón r. Spain
80 E2 Tironia North I. N.Z.
257 E3 Tiros Brazil
171 D5 Tirpersdorf Ger.
190 F5 Tirrenia Italy
Tirreno, Mare sea France/Italy see Tyrrhenian Sea
173 G2 Tirschenreuth Ger.
192 A5 Tirso r. Sardegna Italy
142 D3 Tirstrup Denmark
185 F2 Tirteafuera Spain
185 F2 Tirteafuera r. Spain
114 B3 Tirthahalli Karnataka India
114 C4 Tiruchchendur Tamil Nadu India
114 C4 Tiruchchirappalli Tamil Nadu India
114 C4 Tiruchengodu Tamil Nadu India
114 C4 Tirukkoyilur Tamil Nadu India
114 C4 Tirumangalam Tamil Nadu India
114 C4 Tirunelveli Tamil Nadu India
252 B1 Tiruntán Peru
114 C3 Tirupati Andhra Prad. India
114 C3 Tiruppattur Tamil Nadu India
114 C4 Tiruppattur Tamil Nadu India
114 C4 Tiruppur Tamil Nadu India
114 C3 Tiruttani Andhra Prad. India
114 C4 Tirutturaippundi Tamil Nadu India
114 C3 Tiruvallur Tamil Nadu India
114 C3 Tiruvannamalai Tamil Nadu India
114 C3 Tiruvettipuram Tamil Nadu India
114 D3 Tiruvottiyur Tamil Nadu India
86 E4 Tiru Well W.A. Austr.
198 C3 Tiryns tourist site Greece
138 F3 Tirza r. Latvia
197 E4 Tisa r. Yugo. alt. Tisza (Hungary), alt. Tysa (Ukraine)
114 C4 Tisaiyanvilai Tamil Nadu India
197 H3 Tisău Romania
150 E3 Tisbury Wiltshire, England U.K.
223 J4 Tisdale Sask. Can.
237 D5 Tishomingo OK U.S.A.
171 F5 Tišice Czech Rep.
205 H5 Tiska, Mont mt. Alg.
176 F2 Tišnov Czech Rep.
177 I3 Tisovec Slovakia
205 F2 Tissemsilt Alg.
192 A4 Tissi Sardegna Italy
117 G4 Tista r. India
177 J5 Tisza r. Hungary alt. Tisa (Yugoslavia), alt. Tysa (Ukraine)
177 I5 Tiszaalpár Hungary
177 L3 Tiszabecs Hungary
177 L3 Tiszabezdéd Hungary
177 J4 Tiszabő Hungary
177 J4 Tiszabura Hungary
177 K4 Tiszacsege Hungary
177 J4 Tiszaderzs Hungary
177 K3 Tiszadob Hungary
177 K3 Tiszaeszlár Hungary
177 J5 Tiszaföldvár Hungary
177 J4 Tiszafüred Hungary
177 J4 Tiszaigar Hungary
177 J4 Tiszajenő Hungary
177 K3 Tiszakarád Hungary
177 J5 Tiszakécske Hungary
177 L3 Tiszakerecseny Hungary
177 J4 Tiszakeszi Hungary
177 K3 Tiszalök Hungary
177 K3 Tiszalúc Hungary
177 K3 Tiszanagyfalu Hungary
177 J4 Tiszanána Hungary
177 J4 Tiszaörs Hungary
177 J4 Tiszapüspöki Hungary
177 J4 Tiszaroff Hungary
177 J5 Tiszasas Hungary
177 L3 Tiszaszentmárton Hungary
177 J5 Tiszasziget Hungary
177 K3 Tiszatelek Hungary
177 J4 Tiszatenyő Hungary
177 J5 Tiszaug Hungary
177 K4 Tiszaújváros Hungary
177 K4 Tiszavasvári Hungary
117 H4 Titabar Assam India
187 B5 Titaguas Spain
263 K1 Titan Dome ice feature Antarctica
206 E3 Titao Burkina
198 C2 Titarisios r. Greece
131 N2 Tit-Ary Rus. Fed.
Titawin Morocco see Tétouan
206 B4 Tite Guinea-Bissau
196 E3 Titel Vojvodina, Srbija Yugo.
193 G3 Titerno r. Italy
123 H3 Tithwal Pak.
252 C3 Titicaca, Lago l. Bol./Peru
Titicaca, Lake Bol./Peru see Titicaca, Lago
235 E1 Titicus CT U.S.A.
172 C4 Titisee Ger.
Tititea mt. South I. N.Z. see Aspiring, Mount
117 E5 Titlagarh Orissa India
190 D2 Titlis mt. Switz.
193 H4 Tito Italy
Titograd Crna Gora Yugo. see Podgorica
188 E3 Titova Korenica Croatia
Titova Mitrovica Kosovo, Srbija Yugo. see Kosovska Mitrovica
188 F3 Titov Drvar Bos.-Herz.
140 O1 Titovka r. Rus. Fed.
Titovo Užice Srbija Yugo. see Užice
Titovo Velenje Slovenia see Velenje
Titov Veles Macedonia see Veles
Titov Vrbas Vojvodina, Srbija Yugo. see Vrbas
84 C4 Ti Tree N.T. Austr.
227 F4 Tittabawassee r. MI U.S.A.
173 F3 Titting Ger.
173 H3 Tittling Ger.
173 G3 Tittmoning Ger.
197 G3 Titu Romania
183 G4 Titulcia Spain
231 D6 Titusville FL U.S.A.
232 D4 Titusville PA U.S.A.
146 B3 Tiumpan Head hd Scotland U.K.
116 C4 Tivari Rajasthan India
196 D4 Tivat Crna Gora Yugo.
186 D4 Tivenis Spain
227 G3 Tiverton Ont. Can.
150 D4 Tiverton Devon, England U.K.
Tivisa Spain see Tivissa
186 D3 Tivissa Spain
193 E3 Tivoli Italy
125 G3 Ţīwī Oman
243 H4 Tixkokob Mex.
245 E5 Tixtla Mex.
210 C2 Tiya tourist site Eth.
244 C3 Tizapán el Alto Mex.
243 H4 Tizimín Mex.
205 G1 Tizi Ouzou Alg.
111 B4 Tiznap He r. China
204 C3 Tiznit Morocco
192 A3 Tizzano Corse France
143 F2 Tjällmo Sweden
140 L2 Tjåmotis Sweden
215 H1 Tjaneni Swaziland
140 L2 Tjappsåive Sweden
140 K2 Tjärmyrberget Sweden
140 M2 Tjautas Sweden
144 J1 Tjeldstø Norway
Tjirebon Jawa Barat Indon. see Cirebon
Tjolotjo Zimbabwe see Tsholotsho
142 D2 Tjøme Norway
142 D2 Tjörn i. Sweden
140 □C2 Tjörnes pen. Iceland
Tjumen' Rus. Fed. see Tyumen'
Tkibuli Georgia see Tqibuli
Tkvarcheli Georgia see Tqvarch'eli

245 F5 Tlacolula Mex.
245 G4 Tlacotalpán Mex.
245 E4 Tlacotenco Mex.
244 D5 Tlacotepec, Cerro mt. Mex.
245 E4 Tlahuapan Mex.
244 C3 Tlajomulco Mex.
245 F4 Tlalchichuca Mex.
245 F4 Tlalixcoyan Mex.
245 E4 Tlalmanalco Mex.
245 E4 Tlalnepantla Mex.
245 E4 Tlálpan Mex.
245 D4 Tlalpujahua Mex.
244 C3 Tlaltenango de Sánchez Román Mex.
245 E5 Tlapa Mex.
245 F4 Tlapacoyan Mex.
245 E4 Tlapaneco r. Mex.
244 D4 Tlapehuala Mex.
244 C3 Tlaquepaque Mex.
245 E4 Tlaxcala Mex.
245 E4 Tlaxcala state Mex.
245 E4 Tlaxco Mex.
245 F5 Tlaxiaco Mex.
222 D4 Tlell B.C. Can.
205 E2 Tlemcen Alg.
174 G2 Tleń Pol.
180 D5 Tleta Rissana Morocco
215 F2 Tlhabologang S. Africa
214 D3 Tlhakalatlou S. Africa
214 E2 Tlhakgameng S. Africa
215 G3 Tlholong S. Africa
177 H3 Tlmače Slovakia
215 E5 Tlokweng Botswana
175 H3 Tluchowo Pol.
173 H2 Tlučná Czech Rep.
136 D3 Tlumach Ukr.
174 F6 Tlumačov Czech Rep.
175 J3 Tłuszcz Pol.
129 E2 Tlyarata Rus. Fed.
137 J5 Tlyustenkhabl' Rus. Fed.
139 J3 T'ma r. Rus. Fed.
204 B5 Tmeïmîchât Maur.
97 D5 Tnaôt, Prêk r. Cambodia
136 D2 Tnya r. Ukr.
96 B3 To r. Myanmar
246 D2 Toa r. Cuba
247 □¹ Toa Alta Puerto Rico
146 □G2 Toab Shetland, Scotland U.K.
247 □¹ Toa Baja Puerto Rico
222 E3 Toad r. B.C. Can.
222 E3 Toad River B.C. Can.
177 I4 Tóalmás Hungary
213 □K3 Toamasina Madag.
213 □K3 Toamasina prov. Madag.
147 C5 Toames Rep. of Ireland
241 J1 Toana mts NV U.S.A.
191 F4 Toano Italy
232 E6 Toano VA U.S.A.
232 C6 Toast NC U.S.A.
80 F3 Toatoa North I. N.Z.
260 E5 Toay Arg.
103 A2 Toba Xizang China
169 F4 Toba Ger.
104 C4 Toba Japan
94 B2 Toba, Danau l. Indon.
Toba, Lake Indon. see Toba, Danau
123 F4 Toba and Kakar Ranges mts Pak.
247 □⁵ Tobago i. Trin. and Tob.
215 F4 Tobane Botswana
185 I2 Tobarra Spain
123 H4 Toba Tek Singh Pak.
179 G4 Tobelbad Austria
147 E2 Tobermore Northern Ireland U.K.
84 D4 Tobermory N.T. Austr.
85 E5 Tobermory Qld Austr.
224 D4 Tobermory Ont. Can.
146 B5 Tobermory Argyll and Bute, Scotland U.K.
146 C5 Toberonochy Argyll and Bute, Scotland U.K.
91 H6 Tobi i. Palau
254 F4 Tobias Barreto Brazil
86 E4 Tobin, Lake salt flat W.A. Austr.
240 I1 Tobin, Mount NV U.S.A.
225 H4 Tobique r. N.B. Can.
94 D3 Toboali Indon.
120 E1 Tobol Kazakh.
120 F1 Tobol r. Kazakh./Rus. Fed.
130 H4 Tobol'sk Rus. Fed.
78 □⁶ Tobona Island Solomon Is
92 B4 Toboso Phil.
Tobruk Libya see Tubruq
234 C1 Tobyhanna PA U.S.A.
Tobyl Kazakh. see Tobol
Tobyl r. Kazakh./Rus. Fed. see Tobol
134 J2 Tobysh r. Rus. Fed.
252 A2 Tocache Nuevo Peru
162 C3 Tocane-St-Apre France
254 D3 Tocantinópolis Brazil
251 G6 Tocantins r. Pará Brazil
251 I5 Tocantins r. Brazil
254 C4 Tocantins state Brazil
231 D5 Toccoa GA U.S.A.
193 E2 Tocco da Casauria Italy
190 D3 Toce r. Italy
182 E4 Tocha Port.
123 G3 Tochi r. Pak.
105 F2 Tochigi Japan
105 F2 Tochigi pref. Japan
103 I5 Tochio Japan
142 D2 Töcksfors Sweden
185 G3 Tocón Spain
252 C5 Toconao Chile
252 C5 Tocopilla Chile
252 D5 Tocorpuri, Cerros de mts Bol./Chile
83 F3 Tocumwal N.S.W. Austr.
175 K3 Toczna r. Pol.
203 G3 Tôd Egypt
222 G5 Tod, Mount B.C. Can.
105 F3 Toda Japan
116 D4 Toda Bhim Rajasthan India
116 C4 Toda Rai Singh Rajasthan India
261 G4 Todd Arg.
151 G3 Toddington Bedfordshire, England U.K.
151 F3 Toddington Gloucestershire, England U.K.
233 □J1 Todd Mountain hill N.B. Can.
87 E5 Todd Range hills W.A. Austr.
235 E1 Toddville NY U.S.A.
168 F2 Todesfelde Ger.
193 E2 Todi Italy
190 D2 Todi mt. Switz.
149 G4 Todmorden West Yorkshire, England U.K.
257 G2 Todos os Santos r. Brazil
252 D4 Todos Santos Bol.
244 C4 Todos Santos Mex.
172 B4 Todtmoos Ger.
172 B4 Todtnau Ger.
146 A4 Toe Head hd Scotland U.K.
96 B4 Toe Jaga, Khao hill Thai.
182 C2 Toén Spain
226 E3 Toéni Burkina
81 B7 Toetoes Bay South I. N.Z.
222 H4 Tofield Alta Can.
222 E5 Tofino B.C. Can.
146 □G Toft Shetland, Scotland U.K.
226 D2 Tofte MN U.S.A.
167 C4 Toftlund Denmark
79 □² Tofua i. Tonga
232 D6 Toga VA U.S.A.
78 □⁵ Toga i. Vanuatu
105 G3 Tōgane Japan
120 G3 Togdheer admin. reg. Somalia
147 E5 Togher Cork Rep. of Ireland
147 E3 Togher Louth Rep. of Ireland
147 D3 Togher Offaly Rep. of Ireland
220 B4 Togiak AK U.S.A.
93 B3 Togian, Kepulauan is Indon.
173 G3 Töging am Inn Ger.
Togliatti Rus. Fed. see Tol'yatti
207 F4 Togo country Africa
229 E2 Togo MN U.S.A.
111 E4 Tograsay He r. China
106 B2 Tögrög Mongolia
107 G3 Togrog Ul Nei Mongol China
149 H2 Togston Northumberland, England U.K.
107 F3 Togtoh Nei Mongol China
130 J4 Toguchin Rus. Fed.
113 B4 Tohana Haryana India
241 M4 Tohatchi NM U.S.A.
95 F2 Tohenbatu mt. Sarawak Malaysia
140 O3 Tohmajärvi Fin.
140 N3 Toholampi Fin.
106 E3 Tohom Nei Mongol China
107 F2 Tōhōm Mongolia
207 F5 Tohoun Togo
111 E6 Toiba Xizang China
141 M3 Toijala Fin.
190 D4 Toirano Italy
141 N3 Toivakka Fin.
240 I2 Toiyabe Range mts NV U.S.A.
Tojikiston country Asia see Tajikistan
120 C1 Tok r. Rus. Fed.
220 D3 Tok AK U.S.A.
102 K2 Tokachi-gawa r. Japan
104 C3 Tōkai Japan
177 K3 Tokaj Hungary
93 B3 Tokala, Gunung mt. Indon.
105 E1 Tōkamachi Japan
81 B7 Tokanui South I. N.Z.
203 H5 Tokar Sudan
81 C6 Tokarahi South I. N.Z.
102 □¹ Tokara-rettō is Japan
121 H2 Tokarevka Kazakh.
135 H6 Tokarevka Rus. Fed.
175 I5 Tokarnia Pol.
102 □¹ Tokashiki-jima i. Japan
126 E2 Tokat Turkey
80 D2 Tokatoka North I. N.Z.
137 K2 Tokay r. Rus. Fed.
101 C5 Tŏkch'ŏn N. Korea
Tokdo i. N. Pacific Ocean see Liancourt Rocks
81 □¹ Tokelau terr. S. Pacific Ocean
T'okhluja Armenia see Drakhtik
Tokhtamysh Tajik. see Tükhtamish
82 B1 Tokio Qld Austr.
104 D3 Toki Japan
104 C3 Toki-gawa r. Japan
Tokkuztara Xinjiang China see Gongliu
137 H4 Tokmachka r. Ukr.
121 H4 Tokmak Kyrg.
137 H4 Tokmak Ukr.
Tokmok Kyrg. see Tokmak
177 H4 Tokod Hungary
80 G3 Tokomaru Bay North I. N.Z.
104 C4 Tokoname Japan
80 E3 Tokoroa North I. N.Z.
102 L2 Tokoro-gawa r. Japan
105 F3 Tokorozawa Japan
206 C4 Tokounou Guinea
215 G2 Tokoza S. Africa
Toksu Xinjiang China see Xinhe
110 E3 Toksun Xinjiang China
Tok-tō i. N. Pacific Ocean see Liancourt Rocks
121 H4 Toktogul Kyrg.
Toktogul'skoye Vodokhranilishche resr Kyrg. see Toktogul Suu Saktagychy
121 H4 Toktogul Suu Saktagychy resr Kyrg.
Tokto-ri i. N. Pacific Ocean see Liancourt Rocks
77 I3 Toku i. Tonga
102 □¹ Tokunoshima Japan
102 □¹ Toku-no-shima i. Japan
100 E1 Tokur Rus. Fed.
104 A4 Tokushima Japan
103 G7 Tokushima pref. Japan
103 E6 Tokuyama Japan
Tokwe r. Zimbabwe see Tugwi
105 F3 Tōkyō Japan
105 F3 Tōkyō mun. Japan
105 F3 Tōkyō-wan b. Japan
78 □⁴ᵃ Tol i. Chuuk Micronesia
80 G3 Tolaga Bay North I. N.Z.
213 □J5 Tôlañaro Madag.
258 D2 Tolar, Cerro mt. Arg.
146 B3 Tolastadh Ùr Western Isles, Scotland U.K.
183 F4 Tolbaños Spain
137 G5 Tolbazy Rus. Fed.
164 F1 Tolbert Neth.
106 A1 Tolbo Mongolia
Tolbukhin Bulg. see Dobrich
139 M3 Tolbukhino Rus. Fed.
262 T1 Tolchin, Mount Antarctica
177 K3 Tolcsva Hungary
121 H4 Tole Bi Kazakh.
255 B8 Toledo Brazil
183 F5 Toledo Spain
183 F5 Toledo prov. Castilla - La Mancha Spain
236 E3 Toledo IA U.S.A.
236 F4 Toledo IL U.S.A.
232 B4 Toledo OH U.S.A.
238 B2 Toledo OR U.S.A.
183 F5 Toledo, Montes de mts Spain
237 E6 Toledo Bend Reservoir Louisiana/Texas U.S.A.
191 I5 Tolentino Italy
Toletum Spain see Toledo
192 D2 Tolfa Italy
85 F3 Tolga Qld Austr.
141 J3 Tolga Norway
110 C2 Toli Xinjiang China
213 □J4 Toliara Madag.
213 □J4 Toliara prov. Madag.
250 C4 Tolima dept Col.
Toling Xizang China see Zanda
93 B2 Tolitoli Sulawesi Tengah Indon.
168 E1 Tolk Ger.
143 H4 Tolkmicko Pol.
164 D2 Tollebeek Neth.
170 E2 Tollense r. Ger.
170 E2 Tollensesee l. Ger.
151 H3 Tollesbury Essex, England U.K.
151 H3 Tolleshunt D'Arcy Essex, England U.K.
241 K5 Tolleson AZ U.S.A.
Tollimarjon Uzbek. see Talimardzhan
193 G2 Tollo Italy
142 D4 Tølløse Denmark
130 G2 Tolmachevo Rus. Fed.
191 I2 Tolmezzo Italy
188 D2 Tolmin Slovenia
177 I5 Tolna Hungary
177 H5 Tolna county Hungary
177 H5 Tolnai-hegyhát hills Hungary
177 H5 Tolnanémedi Hungary
242 □6 Toloa Creek Hond.
Tolochin Belarus see Talachyn
Tolosa France see Toulouse
184 C1 Tolosa Spain
186 A1 Tolosa Spain
185 F4 Tolox Spain
227 F3 Tolsmaville Ont. Can.
146 B3 Tolsta Head hd Scotland U.K.
259 B5 Toltén Chile
250 C3 Tolú Col.
245 E4 Toluca Mex.
186 D2 Tolva Spain
193 I4 Tolve Italy
193 I4 Tolve r. Italy
135 J5 Tol'yatti Rus. Fed.
121 H2 Tolybay Kazakh.
163 C4 Tolzac r. France
100 C2 Tom' r. Rus. Fed.
206 E3 Toma Burkina
226 B4 Tomah WI U.S.A.
226 C3 Tomahawk WI U.S.A.
137 J4 Tomakivka r. Ukr.
102 J2 Tomakomai Japan
227 F2 Tomales CA U.S.A.
79 □¹ᵃ Tomanivi mt. Viti Levu Fiji
182 B5 Tomar Port.
100 G3 Tomari Sakhalin Rus. Fed.
126 E2 Tomarza Turkey
198 B2 Tomaros mt. Greece
137 I2 Tomarovka Rus. Fed.
126 D3 Tomarza Turkey
252 D4 Tomás Barron Bol.
261 I2 Tomás Gomensoro Uru.
136 D2 Tomashgrod Rivnens'ka Oblast' Ukr.
136 D2 Tomashorod Rivnens'ka Oblast' Ukr.
136 E3 Tomashpil' Ukr.
176 G3 Tomášov Slovakia
177 I3 Tomášovce Slovakia
175 J5 Tomaszów Lubelski Pol.
175 I4 Tomaszów Mazowiecki Pol.
116 E4 Tomatin Highland, Scotland U.K.
244 B4 Tomatlán Mex.
252 D5 Tomave Bol.
256 C5 Tomazina Brazil
254 E4 Tombador, Serra do hills Bahia Brazil
253 F3 Tombador, Serra do hills Mato Grosso Brazil
153 C4 Tombebœf France
231 C6 Tombigbee r. AL U.S.A.
215 G4 Tombo S. Africa
209 B6 Tomboco Angola
257 F4 Tombos Brazil
203 E2 Tombouctou Mali
203 E2 Tombouctou admin. reg. Mali
241 L6 Tombstone AZ U.S.A.
240 I2 Tombua Angola
213 E4 Tom Burke S. Africa
Tamdybuloq Uzbek. see Tamdybulak
Tomditow Toghi hills Uzbek. see Tamdytau, Gory
258 B5 Tomé Chile
143 E4 Tomelilla Sweden
185 G1 Tomelloso Spain
121 F4 Tomenaryk Kazakh.
177 L5 Tomeşti Romania
177 L6 Tomeşti Romania
Tomi Romania see Constanţa
175 H6 Tomice Pol.
104 C4 Tomigusuku Japan
227 H2 Tomiko Ont. Can.
252 D4 Tomina Bol.
205 B3 Tominé r. Guinea
83 G3 Tomingley N.S.W. Austr.
93 B3 Tomini, Teluk g. Indon.
206 D3 Tominian Mali
146 E4 Tomintoul Moray, Scotland U.K.
105 E2 Tomioka Japan
188 F4 Tomislavgrad Bos.-Herz.
235 E1 Tomkins Cove NY U.S.A.
87 E2 Tomkinson Ranges mts S.A. Austr.
131 N4 Tommot Rus. Fed.
146 E4 Tomnavoulin Moray, Scotland U.K.
250 C3 Tomo r. Col.
198 B1 Tomorit, Maja e mt. Albania
111 E4 Tomorlog Qinghai China
107 G3 Tomortei Nei Mongol China
177 I5 Tompa Hungary
86 C4 Tom Price W.A. Austr.
235 D3 Toms r. NJ U.S.A.
130 J4 Tomsk Rus. Fed.
235 D3 Toms River NJ U.S.A.
143 F5 Tomtabacken hill Sweden
131 P3 Tomtor Rus. Fed.
128 B1 Tömük Turkey
102 K2 Tomuraushi-yama mt. Japan
Tomur Feng mt. China/Kyrg. see Jengish Chokusu
129 E1 Tomuzlovka r. Rus. Fed.
220 E3 Tom White, Mount AK U.S.A.
186 E3 Tona Spain
102 I1 Tonaki-jima i. Japan
245 E5 Tonala Mex.
244 C3 Tonalá Jalisco Mex.
104 C2 Tonami Japan
250 E5 Tonantins Brazil
192 B4 Tonara Sardegna Italy
238 C1 Tonasket WA U.S.A.
251 H3 Tonate Fr. Guiana
235 E3 Tonawanda NY U.S.A.
244 C4 Tonaya Mex.
Tonb-e Bozorg, Jazireh-ye i. The Gulf see Greater Tunb
Tonb-e Küchek, Jazireh-ye i. The Gulf see Lesser Tunb
151 H3 Tonbridge Kent, England U.K.
182 E4 Tonda Port.
104 E4 Tondabayashi Japan
93 C2 Tondano Sulawesi Utara Indon.
182 E4 Tondela Port.
142 C4 Tønder Denmark
114 C4 Tondi Tamil Nadu India
150 E3 Tone r. England U.K.
105 G3 Tone-gawa r. Japan
262 Q1 Toney Mount Antarctica
191 G3 Tonezza del Cimone Italy
207 H5 Tonga Cameroon
79 □² Tonga country S. Pacific Ocean
215 H3 Tongaat S. Africa
109 F3 Tong'an Fujian China
80 E3 Tongaporutu North I. N.Z.
Tongareva atoll Cook Is see Penrhyn
80 E3 Tongariro vol. North I. N.Z.
79 □²ᵃ Tongatapu i. Tonga
79 □²ᵃ Tongatapu Group is Tonga
266 H7 Tonga Trench sea feature S. Pacific Ocean
109 E1 Tongbai Henan China
109 E1 Tongbai Shan mts China
109 E2 Tongcheng Anhui China
109 E2 Tongcheng Hubei China
Tongcheng Shandong China see Dong'e
101 C5 T'ongch'ŏn N. Korea
107 F5 Tongchuan Shaanxi China
Tongchuan Sichuan China see Santai
108 D3 Tongdao Hunan China
106 D5 Tongde Qinghai China
101 C5 Tongduch'ŏn S. Korea
165 E4 Tongeren Belgium
109 E2 Tonggu Jiangxi China
109 F2 Tongguan Shaanxi China
105 E1 Tonghae S. Korea
108 D3 Tonghai Yunnan China
100 D3 Tonghe Heilong. China
101 C4 Tonghua Jilin China
101 C4 Tonghua Jilin China
Tongjiang Jiangxi see Tungi
100 E3 Tongjiang Heilong. China
108 C2 Tongjiang Sichuan China
100 C3 Tongken r. China
96 E2 Tongking, Gulf of China/Vietnam
146 D7 Tongland Dumfries and Galloway, Scotland U.K.
Tongle Guangxi China see Leye
107 I3 Tongliao Nei Mongol China
109 F2 Tongling Anhui China
109 F2 Tongling Anhui China
109 F2 Tonglu Zhejiang China
103 D6 Tongnae S. Korea
83 E2 Tongo N.S.W. Austr.
78 □⁵ Tongoa i. Vanuatu
213 □J4 Tongobory Madag.
260 B2 Tongoi, Bahía b. Chile
83 E2 Tongo Lake salt flat N.S.W. Austr.
260 B2 Tongoy Chile
Tongquan Yunnan China see Malong
108 D3 Tongren Guizhou China
106 D5 Tongren Qinghai China
Tongres Belgium see Tongeren
Tongsa Bhutan see Trongsa
Tongshan Jiangsu China see Xuzhou
108 D5 Tongshi Hainan China
108 A1 Tongtian He r. China
alt. Chang Jiang,
alt. Jinsha Jiang,
alt. Zhi Qu,
conv. Yangtze,
long Yangtze Kiang
146 D3 Tongue Highland, Scotland U.K.
238 F2 Tongue r. MT U.S.A.
Tongue of Arabat spit Ukr. see Arabats'ka Strilka, Kosa
246 C1 Tongue of the Ocean sea chan. Bahamas
106 E5 Tongwei Gansu China
107 H4 Tongxian Beijing China
109 G2 Tongxiang Zhejiang China
106 E4 Tongxin Ningxia China
101 D6 T'ongyŏng S. Korea
107 I2 Tongyu Jilin China
Tongzhou Beijing China see Tongxian
108 C2 Tongzi Guizhou China
Tonhil Mongolia see Dzüyl
226 C5 Tonica IL U.S.A.
244 C4 Tonila Mex.
208 F3 Tonj Sudan
116 C4 Tonk Rajasthan India
122 B2 Tonkābon Iran
237 D4 Tonkawa OK U.S.A.
134 I4 Tonkino Rus. Fed.
97 D4 Tonle Repou r. Laos
97 C4 Tonle Sab l. Cambodia
Tonle Sap l. Cambodia see Tônlé Sab
150 D3 Tonna Neath Port Talbot, Wales U.K.
162 B3 Tonnay-Boutonne France
162 B3 Tonnay-Charente France
163 C4 Tonneins France
156 D5 Tonnerre France
168 D1 Tönning Ger.
102 J4 Tōno Japan
78 □⁴ᵃ Tonoas i. Chuuk Micronesia
241 K5 Tonopah AZ U.S.A.
240 I2 Tonopah NV U.S.A.
111 B6 Tons r. India
142 D2 Tønsberg Norway
139 K2 Tonshalovo Rus. Fed.
182 B2 Tonstad Norway
260 C2 Tontal, Sierra mts Arg.
214 C4 Tontelbos S. Africa
245 F4 Tonto r. Mex.
241 L5 Tonto Basin AZ U.S.A.
150 D3 Tonyrefail Rhondda Cynon Taff, Wales U.K.
82 B2 Toobeah Qld Austr.
206 C5 Toobli Liberia
87 C6 Toodyay W.A. Austr.
241 K1 Tooele UT U.S.A.
85 H5 Toogoolawah Qld Austr.
83 E3 Tooleybuc N.S.W. Austr.
82 C3 Tooligie S.A. Austr.
83 G4 Tooma r. N.S.W. Austr.
147 E2 Toomebridge Northern Ireland U.K.
85 F5 Toompine Qld Austr.
83 F4 Toora Vic. Austr.
83 G2 Tooraweenah N.S.W. Austr.
214 E5 Toorberg mt. S. Africa
147 B5 Toormore Rep. of Ireland
85 G5 Toowoomba Qld Austr.
210 F2 Tooxin Somalia
139 K2 Topa r. Rus. Fed.
197 G3 Topana Romania
185 G3 Topares Spain
176 D1 Topchikha Rus. Fed.
171 E3 Topchin Ger.
137 H3 Topchyne Ukr.
149 H3 Topcliffe North Yorkshire, England U.K.
129 B4 Topçu Dağı mt. Turkey
129 C4 Top Dağı mt. Turkey
228 B4 Topeka KS U.S.A.
171 C5 Töpen Ger.
242 D3 Topia Mex.
193 E2 Topino r. Italy
130 J4 Topki Rus. Fed.
177 K3 Topľa r. Slovakia
93 C3 Toplana, Gunung mt. Seram Indon.
222 E4 Topley B.C. Can.
222 E4 Topley Landing B.C. Can.
196 E4 Toplica r. Yugo.
197 G2 Toplița Romania
177 L6 Toplița Romania
171 D3 Toplitz Ger.
216 □¹ᶜ Topo São Jorge Azores
241 J4 Topock AZ U.S.A.
177 H3 Topoľčany Slovakia
177 H3 Topoľčianky Slovakia
174 G3 Topólka Pol.
177 G2 Topolná Czech Rep.
174 G2 Topolnitsa r. Bulg.
197 G4 Topolobampo Mex.
242 C3 Topolobampo Mex.
197 I3 Topoloveni Romania
197 G3 Topolog r. Romania
177 K6 Topolovățu Mare Romania
197 G3 Topoloveni Romania
197 G4 Topolovgrad Bulg.
179 G4 Topolšica Slovenia
177 J2 Toporec Slovakia
136 D2 Topory Ukr.
136 E2 Toporyshche Ukr.
134 F2 Topozero, Ozero l. Rus. Fed.
238 B2 Toppenish WA U.S.A.
197 I3 Topraisar Romania
129 C4 Toprakkale Ağrı Turkey
129 D3 Toprakkale Osmaniye Turkey
233 □J2 Topsfield ME U.S.A.
150 D4 Topsham Devon, England U.K.
128 B4 Toptepe Turkey
251 H4 Topton PA U.S.A.
80 E2 Topuni North I. N.Z.
252 C4 Toquepala Peru
186 E3 Torà de Riubreós Spain
129 F3 Torağay Dağı hill Azer.
183 F3 Toral de los Guzmanes Spain
182 D2 Toral de los Vados Spain
Toraman Turkey see Halilçavuş
193 I5 Torano Castello Italy
252 C4 Torata Peru
182 A1 Torbali Turkey
184 D2 Tor Baldak mt. Afgh.
123 F4 Torbalı Turkey
127 H4 Torbat-e Heydarīyeh Iran
122 E3 Torbat-e Jām Iran
150 D4 Torbay admin. div. England U.K.
87 C7 Torbay Bay W.A. Austr.
135 H5 Torbeyevo Rus. Fed.
223 K4 Torch r. Sask. Can.
110 C4 Torchiarolo Italy
193 H5 Torchiarolo Italy
195 H2 Torchiarolo Italy
139 M3 Torchino Rus. Fed.
136 C2 Torchyn Ukr.
183 F5 Torcón r. Spain
162 F5 Torcy France
158 B3 Torcy-le-Petit France
177 H4 Tordas Hungary
183 E3 Tordehumos Spain
135 F3 Tordera Spain
136 F3 Tordesillas Spain
133 I4 Tordesilos Spain
193 F2 Tordino r. Italy
140 M2 Töre Sweden
146 D4 Tore Highland, Scotland U.K.
142 D3 Töreboda Sweden
170 C1 Toreby Denmark
142 E3 Torekov Sweden
142 E3 Torekov Sweden
185 E3 Torellano Spain
140 □ Torell Land reg. Svalbard
174 F2 Torelló Spain
164 F2 Torenberg hill Neth.
162 D2 Toreno Spain
80 F3 Tore North I. N.Z.
139 F3 Torey Rus. Fed.
106 E1 Torey Rus. Fed.
137 J3 Torez Ukr.
150 D3 Torfaen admin. div. Wales U.K.
Torga i. Vanuatu see Toga
171 D4 Torgau Ger.
170 F2 Torgelow Ger.
Torghay Kustanayskaya Oblast' Kazakh. see Turgay
193 E2 Torgiano Italy
120 A2 Torgun r. Rus. Fed.
143 F3 Torhamn Sweden
165 C3 Torhout Belgium
136 C2 Torhovytsya Ukr.
117 F5 Tori Bihar India
210 A3 Tori r. Sudan
103 G3 Toride Japan
159 F2 Torigni-sur-Vire France
183 F3 Torija Spain
105 E2 Torikabuto-yama mt. Japan
190 C3 Torino Italy
190 C3 Torino prov. Piemonte Italy
193 G2 Torino di Sangro Italy
103 J8 Tori-shima i. Japan
210 B3 Torit Sudan
193 F2 Toritto Italy
256 A2 Torixoreu Brazil
122 A2 Torkamān Iran
139 H2 Torkovichi Rus. Fed.
186 C2 Torla Spain
86 D3 Torment, Point W.A. Austr.
182 D3 Tormes r. Spain
187 B4 Tormón Spain
146 C6 Tormore North Ayrshire, Scotland U.K.
183 F4 Tornadizos de Ávila Spain
222 H5 Tornado Mountain Alta/B.C. Can.
183 E5 Tornajuelos mt. Spain
177 J3 Tornaľa Slovakia
183 F4 Tornavacas Spain
149 4 Torne r. England U.K.
Torneå Fin. see Tornio
140 N2 Torneälven r. Sweden
140 L1 Torneträsk Sweden
140 L1 Torneträsk l. Sweden
Torngat, Monts mts Newfoundland/Québec Can. see Torngat Mountains
225 H1 Torngat Mountains Newfoundland/Québec Can.
196 D4 Tornik mt. Yugo.
140 N2 Tornio Fin.
177 I6 Tornjoš Vojvodina, Srbija Yugo.
190 E3 Torno Italy
183 I4 Tornos Spain
170 E2 Tornow Ger.
261 F6 Tornquist Arg.
177 L3 Tornyospálca Hungary
207 H4 Toro Nigeria
183 E3 Toro Spain
244 D1 Toro, Pico del mt. Mex.
207 F3 Torodi Niger
177 H4 Törökbálint Hungary
177 J4 Törökszentmiklós Hungary
224 E5 Toronto Ont. Can.
232 C4 Toronto OH U.S.A.
179 H3 Torony Hungary
139 H3 Toropatsa Rus. Fed.
139 H3 Toropets Rus. Fed.
210 B4 Tororo Uganda
126 D3 Toros Dağları mts Turkey
192 B4 Torpè Sardegna Italy
146 F4 Torphins Aberdeenshire, Scotland U.K.
150 C4 Torpoint Cornwall, England U.K.
83 F4 Torquay Vic. Austr.
150 D4 Torquay Torbay, England U.K.
183 F2 Torquemada Spain
147 E1 Torr Northern Ireland U.K.
185 G1 Torralba de Calatrava Spain
192 A4 Torralba Sardegna Italy
183 F4 Torralba Spain
186 C3 Torralba de Aragón Spain
183 H3 Torralba de El Burgo Spain
183 E5 Torralba de Oropesa Spain
191 E3 Torralba de Sisones Spain
240 H5 Torrance CA U.S.A.
184 B2 Torrão Port.
182 C4 Torre mt. Port.
193 G4 Torre Annunziata Italy
187 B4 Torrebaja Spain
183 E2 Torreblacos Spain
187 D4 Torreblanca Spain
242 B1 Torre Blanco, Cerro mt. Mex.
185 G3 Torreblascopedro Spain
193 G3 Torrebruna Italy
183 F4 Torrecaballeros Spain
185 F2 Torrecampo Spain
195 G2 Torre Canne Italy
185 G3 Torre-Cardela Spain
185 F4 Torrecilla mt. Spain
183 F5 Torrecilla de la Jara Spain
183 E5 Torrecilla de la Orden Spain
186 B4 Torrecilla del Rebollar Spain
183 H2 Torrecilla en Cameros Spain
182 E5 Torrecillas de la Tiesa Spain
193 G3 Torrecuso Italy
184 B2 Torre da Gadanha Port.
184 C1 Torre das Vargens Port.
186 E2 Torre de Cadí mt. Spain
182 C3 Torre de Dona Chama Port.
182 B4 Torredeita Port.
183 G4 Torre de Juan Abad Spain
182 D2 Torre del Bierzo Spain
183 G4 Torre del Burgo Spain
185 F4 Torre del Campo Spain
193 E4 Torre del Greco Italy
185 E4 Torre del Mar Spain
183 F3 Torredembarra Spain
184 D2 Torre de Miguel Sesmero Spain
182 C3 Torre de Moncorvo Port.
193 F2 Torre de'Passeri Italy
183 F3 Torredonjimeno Spain
182 C4 Torre do Terrenho Port.
182 D3 Torregamones Spain
186 D3 Torregrossa Spain
183 F3 Torreiglesias Spain
182 B4 Torreira Port.
185 F3 Torrejoncillo Spain
183 H4 Torrejoncillo del Rey Spain
183 F4 Torrejón de Ardoz Spain
183 G4 Torrejón del Rey Spain
182 E5 Torrejón el Rubio Spain
186 B4 Torrelacarcel Spain
183 G4 Torrelaguna Spain
183 F3 Torrelapaja Spain
183 F1 Torrelavega Spain
183 I3 Torrellas Spain
186 E3 Torrelles de Foix Spain
186 C3 Torrelobatón Spain
183 G3 Torrelodones Spain
193 H3 Torremaggiore Italy
187 C6 Torremanzanas Spain
182 D2 Torremayor Spain
184 D2 Torremegía Spain
193 H3 Torre Mileto Italy
184 D1 Torremocha Spain
185 F4 Torremolinos Spain
187 D4 Torrenostra Spain
82 D2 Torrens, Lake salt flat S.A. Austr.
85 F4 Torrens Creek Qld Austr.
187 C5 Torrent Spain
Torrente Spain see Torrent
186 D3 Torrente de Cinca Spain
185 G2 Torrenueva Spain
195 E5 Torre Nuovo Scalo Italy
242 E3 Torreón Mex.
185 G3 Torreorgaz Spain
184 D1 Torreorgaz Spain
193 H4 Torre Orsaia Italy
187 C7 Torre-Pacheco Spain
185 F3 Torreparedones hill Spain
190 C4 Torre Pellice Italy
185 G2 Torreperogil Spain
255 C9 Torres Brazil
185 G3 Torres Spain
183 G3 Torres Spain
185 G3 Torres Spain
183 G3 Torresandino Spain
195 H3 Torre San Giovanni Italy
193 G2 Torre Santa Susanna Italy
195 G2 Torres de Albánchez Spain
185 H2 Torres de Albánchez Spain
186 B3 Torres de Berrellén Spain
183 G4 Torres de la Alameda Spain
182 E3 Torres del Carrizal Spain
183 E2 Torres de Segre Spain
186 D3 Torres de Segre Spain
78 □⁵ Torres Islands Vanuatu
182 E3 Torresmenudas Spain
184 E3 Torres Novas Port.
76 E2 Torres Strait Qld Austr.
184 A1 Torres Vedras Port.
187 E5 Torreta, Sierra hill Spain
193 H4 Torretta, Monte mt. Italy
186 C4 Torrevelilla Spain
187 C6 Torrevieja Spain
193 F5 Torrevecchia Teatina Italy
193 F3 Torrice Italy
195 G2 Torricella Italy
193 E2 Torricella in Sabina Italy
193 G2 Torricella Peligna Italy
193 F2 Torricella Sicura Italy
190 D2 Torricella Taverne Switz.
183 E5 Torrico Spain
134 D1 Torrico de San Pedro hill Spain
191 F3 Torri del Benaco Italy
150 D4 Torridge r. England U.K.
146 C4 Torridon Highland, Scotland U.K.
146 C4 Torridon, Loch b. Scotland U.K.
190 E4 Torriglia Italy
193 E2 Torri in Sabina Italy
187 C4 Torrijas Spain
183 I3 Torrijo Spain
183 F5 Torrijos Spain
146 B4 Torrin Highland, Scotland U.K.
233 G4 Torrington CT U.S.A.
238 F3 Torrington WY U.S.A.
256 C5 Torrinha Brazil
192 D1 Torrita di Siena Italy
184 B2 Torroal Port.
186 G2 Torroella de Montgrí Spain
140 K3 Torrön l. Sweden
185 G4 Torrox Spain
183 H5 Torrubia del Campo Spain
183 H3 Torrubia de Soria Spain
117 G4 Torsa Chhu r. Bhutan
141 D3 Torsåker Sweden
142 D3 Torsås Sweden
167 D3 Torsåker Sweden
142 B1 Torsby Sweden
143 G2 Torshälla Sweden
144 □ Tórshavn Faroe Is
171 I4 Törtel Hungary
241 I5 Tortilla Flat AZ U.S.A.
Törtköl Uzbek. see Turtkul'
194 C5 Torto r. Sicilia Italy
247 F3 Tortola i. Virgin Is (U.K.)
183 H5 Tórtola de Henares Spain
183 F3 Tórtoles de Esgueva Spain
192 B5 Tortoli Sardegna Italy
197 I3 Tortomanu Romania
190 D4 Tortona Italy
193 H5 Tortora Italy
193 F2 Tortoreto Italy
194 D4 Tortorici Sicilia Italy
186 D4 Tortosa Spain
182 C4 Tortozendo Port.
183 I4 Tortuera Spain
245 E2 Tortuga, Laguna l. Mex.
261 G3 Tortugas Arg.
127 F2 Tortum Turkey
122 C3 Torud Iran
126 E2 Torul Turkey
174 G2 Toruń Pol.
138 E2 Tõrva Estonia
193 E3 Tor Vaianica Italy
149 F3 Torver Cumbria, England U.K.
185 G4 Torvizcón Spain
141 I3 Torvløysa mt. Norway
140 L2 Torvsjö Sweden
147 C1 Tory Island Rep. of Ireland
177 J2 Torysa Slovakia
177 K3 Torysa r. Slovakia
147 C1 Tory Sound sea chan. Rep. of Ireland
139 J3 Torzhok Rus. Fed.
174 D3 Torzym Pol.
103 F7 Tosa Japan
191 F2 Tosa, Cima mt. Italy
103 F7 Tosashimizu Japan
103 F7 Tosa-wan b. Japan
214 D1 Tosca S. Africa
146 C4 Toscaig Highland, Scotland U.K.
191 G5 Toscana admin. reg. Italy
192 B1 Toscano, Arcipelago is Italy
191 F3 Toscolano-Maderno Italy
102 J3 Tōshima-yama mt. Japan
Toshkent Uzbek. see Tashkent
Toshkent Wiloyati admin. div. Uzbek. see Tashkentskaya Oblast'
139 H2 Tosno Rus. Fed.
106 C1 Tosontsengel Mongolia
190 D1 Töss r. Switz.
186 F3 Tossa Spain
186 E3 Tossal de la Baltasana mt. Spain
186 E2 Tossal de l'Orri mt. Spain
163 A5 Tosse France
191 F4 Tossicia Italy
149 G3 Tosside Lancashire, England U.K.
258 E3 Tostado Arg.
168 E2 Tostedt Ger.
126 E2 Tosu Japan
126 E2 Tosya Turkey
177 J4 Tószeg Hungary
174 G5 Toszek Pol.
185 G4 Totana Spain
114 D5 Totapola mt. Sri Lanka
81 C6 Totara South I. N.Z.
80 D4 Totaranui South I. N.Z.
172 B3 Totenkopf hill Ger.
156 B3 Tôtes France
78 □⁴ᵃ Totiw i. Chuuk Micronesia
151 F4 Totland Isle of Wight, England U.K.
134 F4 Tot'ma Rus. Fed.
150 D4 Totnes Devon, England U.K.
251 G3 Totness Suriname
134 H4 Totomitsa Rus. Fed.
243 H6 Totonicapán Guat.
261 G3 Totoras Arg.
206 C5 Totota Liberia
244 C3 Totatlán Mex.
79 □¹ Totoya i. Fiji
120 C1 Totskoye Rus. Fed.
104 B5 Totsu-kawa r. Japan
176 F5 Tótszentmárton Hungary
176 F5 Tótszerdahely Hungary
151 F4 Totton Hampshire, England U.K.
103 G6 Tottori Japan
103 F6 Tottori pref. Japan
177 G4 Tótvázsony Hungary
206 D4 Touba Côte d'Ivoire
206 B3 Touba Senegal
204 D2 Toubkal, Jbel mt. Morocco
207 I5 Touboro Cameroon
182 C3 Touça Port.
163 C5 Touch r. France
238 C2 Touchet r. WA U.S.A.
156 D5 Toucy France
106 E4 Toudaohu Nei Mongol China
164 D4 Touffailles France
206 E3 Tougan Burkina
163 C5 Touget France
205 G2 Touggourt Alg.
206 E3 Tougouri Burkina
206 C4 Tougué Guinea
78 □⁵ Touho New Caledonia
206 C3 Touil Maur.
163 C3 Toukoto Mali
207 F4 Toukountouna Benin
164 F4 Toul France
206 C5 Toulépleu Côte d'Ivoire
206 E3 Toulfé Burkina
109 G4 Touliu Taiwan
225 G3 Toulnustouc r. Que. Can.
161 D5 Toulon France
226 C5 Toulon IL U.S.A.
160 B2 Toulon-sur-Allier France
160 B2 Toulon-sur-Arroux France
163 E6 Toulouges France
163 D5 Toulouse France
206 D5 Toumodi Côte d'Ivoire
206 D4 Touna Mali
207 I4 Toungo Nigeria
96 B3 Toungoo Myanmar
108 D3 Toupai Guangxi China
159 G2 Touques France
159 G2 Touques r. France
206 D5 Toura, Monts mt. Côte d'Ivoire
159 G4 Touraine, Val de val. France
182 B2 Toural Spain
Tourane Vietnam see Đa Nẵng
158 C3 Tourch France
156 D2 Tourcoing France
161 F5 Tourette-sur-Loup France
182 B1 Touriñán, Cabo c. Spain
158 F5 Tourlaville France
147 B3 Tourmakeady Rep. of Ireland
160 C3 Tour Matagrin hill France
165 C4 Tournai Belgium
161 F4 Tournairet, Mont mt. France
156 C4 Tournan-en-Brie France
252 C4 Tournavista Peru
163 C5 Tournay France
163 D5 Tournecoupe France
162 D5 Tournefeuille France
163 C4 Tournon-d'Agenais France
159 G5 Tournon-St-Martin France
161 C3 Tournon-sur-Rhône France
160 C2 Tournus France
156 B3 Tourny France
182 C4 Touro Spain
254 G3 Touros Brazil
159 G3 Tourouvre France
159 G3 Tourteville-Levens France
162 C1 Tours France
165 G3 Tourtein France
162 D3 Tourtoirac France
161 D5 Tourves France
156 B4 Toury France
206 B4 Toussiana Burkina
202 C4 Toussidé, Pic mt. Chad
208 D2 Toussoro, Mont mt. C.A.R.
100 C3 Toutai Heilong. China
184 C2 Toutalga r. Port.
158 E5 Touvois France
215 G4 Touws r. S. Africa
214 D5 Touwsrivier S. Africa
176 B1 Toužim Czech Rep.
106 E2 Töv prov. Mongolia
176 G2 Tovačov Czech Rep.
250 D2 Tovar Venez.
139 J4 Tovarkovo Rus. Fed.
139 I5 Tovarkovskiy Rus. Fed.
177 K3 Tovarné Slovakia
188 G3 Tovarnik Croatia
151 G2 Tove r. England U.K.
136 C3 Tovste Ukr.
129 D3 Tovuz Azer.
Towuzqay r. Armenia see Tavush
235 D2 Towaco NJ U.S.A.
102 J3 Towada Japan
102 J3 Towada-ko l. Japan
80 E1 Towai North I. N.Z.
131 B3 Towak Mountain hill AK U.S.A.
227 I5 Towanda PA U.S.A.
234 B1 Towanda Creek r. PA U.S.A.
241 M3 Towaoc CO U.S.A.
151 G2 Towcester Northamptonshire, England U.K.
147 C5 Tower Rep. of Ireland
226 A2 Tower MN U.S.A.
234 B2 Tower City PA U.S.A.
Tower Island Islas Galápagos Ecuador see Genovesa, Isla
81 A7 Tower Peak South I. N.Z.
149 H3 Tow Law Durham, England U.K.
234 D4 Town Bank NJ U.S.A.
236 C1 Towner ND U.S.A.
146 E7 Townhead of Greenlaw Dumfries and Galloway, Scotland U.K.
146 E5 Townhill Fife, Scotland U.K.
84 C2 Towns r. N.T. Austr.
234 C3 Townsend DE U.S.A.
233 H3 Townsend MA U.S.A.
238 E2 Townsend MT U.S.A.
85 G4 Townshend Island Qld Austr.
85 F3 Townsville Qld Austr.
93 B3 Towori, Teluk b. Indon.
234 B3 Towson MD U.S.A.
150 D1 Towyn Conwy, Wales U.K.
Towyn Gwynedd, Wales U.K. see Tywyn
110 C3 Toxkan He r. China
240 H1 Toy NV U.S.A.
237 C6 Toyah TX U.S.A.
104 D2 Toyama Japan
104 D2 Toyama pref. Japan
104 D2 Toyama-wan b. Japan
136 C2 Toykut Ukr.
103 F7 Tōyō Japan
104 C3 Toyoake Japan
103 D7 Toyohashi Japan
104 D4 Toyokawa Japan
104 D4 Toyo-kawa r. Japan
104 B4 Toyonaka Japan
104 A3 Toyooka Japan
102 I5 Toyosaka Japan
105 D2 Toyoshina Japan
104 D3 Toyota Japan
140 M3 Töysä Fin.
121 G4 Toytepa Uzbek.
Tozal del Orri mt. Spain see Tossal de l'Orri
Tozanli Turkey see Almus
111 C5 Tozê Kangri mt. Xizang China
205 H2 Tozeur Tunisia
129 E3 Tqibuli Georgia
129 C2 Tqibuli Georgia
129 B2 Tqvarch'eli Georgia
182 C1 Trabada Spain
182 D3 Trabanca Spain
182 D3 Trabazos Spain
194 C5 Trabia Sicilia Italy
174 G1 Trąbki Wielkie Pol.
128 B2 Trâblous Lebanon
179 F3 Traboch Austria
197 F5 Trabotivište Macedonia
127 E2 Trabzon Turkey
127 E2 Trabzon prov. Turkey
194 B6 Tracino Sicilia Italy
233 □J2 Tracy N.B. Can.
240 G3 Tracy CA U.S.A.
236 E2 Tracy MN U.S.A.
160 A1 Tracy-sur-Loire France
190 D3 Tradate Italy
169 D4 Traddelkopf hill Ger.
226 A3 Trade Lake WI U.S.A.
237 F4 Tradewater r. KY U.S.A.
224 B3 Trading r. Ont. Can.
140 K2 Trænfjorden sea chan. Norway
236 E3 Traer IA U.S.A.
184 D4 Trafalgar, Cabo c. Spain
222 D2 Traffic Mountain Y.T. Can.
183 I4 Tragacete Spain
185 H2 Tragoncillo mt. Spain
179 F2 Tragwein Austria
197 G4 Traian Romania
177 L6 Traian Vuia Romania
183 I4 Traid Spain
260 A6 Traiguén Chile
186 D4 Traiguera Spain
222 G5 Trail B.C. Can.
237 D5 Trail OK U.S.A.
173 F3 Train Ger.
156 D4 Trainel France
234 C3 Trainer PA U.S.A.
155 C5 Trainou France
254 F4 Traipu Brazil
250 D5 Traíra r. Brazil
256 D2 Trairas r. Brazil
254 F2 Trairi Brazil
179 G2 Traisen Austria
179 G2 Traisen r. Austria
179 H2 Traiskirchen Austria
179 G2 Traismauer Austria
173 G2 Traitsching Ger.
257 F5 Trajano de Morais Brazil
Trajectum Neth. see Utrecht
214 D5 Traka r. S. Africa
138 E4 Trakai Lith.
134 J3 Trakt Rus. Fed.
147 B4 Tralee Rep. of Ireland
147 B4 Tralee Bay Rep. of Ireland
Trá Lí Rep. of Ireland see Tralee
183 I4 Tramacastilla Spain
192 A4 Tramariglio Sardegna Italy
187 B4 Tramacastiel Spain
192 A4 Tramatza Sardegna Italy
191 G4 Tramazzo r. Italy
172 B4 Tramelan Switz.
163 C6 Tramezaïgues France
Trá Mhór Rep. of Ireland see Tramore
232 B6 Trammel VA U.S.A.
191 H2 Tramonti di Sopra Italy
178 D4 Tramonti di Sotto Italy
147 D4 Tramore Rep. of Ireland
187 F5 Tramuntana, Serra de mts Spain
193 H4 Tramutola Italy
143 F2 Tranås Sweden
142 D3 Tranbjerg Denmark
182 C4 Trancoso Port.
142 D4 Tranebjerg Denmark
143 E3 Tranemo Sweden
146 F6 Tranent East Lothian, Scotland U.K.
97 B6 Trang Thai.
91 H8 Trangan i. Indon.
83 G3 Trangie N.S.W. Austr.
193 I3 Trani Italy
156 E4 Trannes France
258 G3 Tranqueras Uru.
260 B3 Tranquilla Chile
158 E3 Trans France
262 K2 Transantarctic Mountains Antarctica
223 H5 Trans Canada Highway Can.
Transcarpathian Oblast admin. div. Ukr. see Zakarpats'ka Oblast'
223 L5 Transcona Man. Can.
161 E5 Trans-en-Provence France
245 E4 Transfiguracion Mex.
197 G2 Transilvaniei, Podişul plat. Romania
141 K3 Transtrand Sweden
Transylvanian Alps mts Romania see Carpaţii Meridionali
Transylvanian Basin plat. Romania see Transilvaniei, Podişul
146 E3 Trantlemore Highland, Scotland U.K.
194 B4 Trapani Sicilia Italy
194 B5 Trapani prov. Sicilia Italy
Trapezus Turkey see Trabzon
234 C2 Trappe PA U.S.A.
168 F1 Trappenkamp Ger.
238 D2 Trapper Peak MT U.S.A.
156 C4 Trappes France
255 B9 Trapua r. Brazil
83 F4 Traralgon Vic. Austr.
172 B2 Trarbach Ger.
143 E3 Traryd Sweden
206 B2 Trarza admin. reg. Maur.
193 F3 Trasacco Italy
197 F2 Trascăului, Munţii mts Romania
117 G4 Trashigang Bhutan
192 E1 Trasimeno, Lago l. Italy
182 C2 Trasmiras Spain
192 D2 Trasubbie r. Italy

97 C4 Trat Thai.
192 A5 Tratalias Sardegna Italy
179 F2 Traun Austria
179 F2 Traun r. Austria
173 G3 Traun r. Ger.
173 G4 Traunreut Ger.
179 E3 Traunsee l. Austria
179 G2 Traunstein Austria
173 G4 Traunstein Ger.
179 H2 Trautmannsdorf an der Leitha Austria
190 F3 Travagliato Italy
182 B4 Travanca do Mondego Port.
182 B4 Travassô Port.
182 C4 Travassós de Cima Port.
168 F2 Trave r. Ger.
83 E3 Travellers Lake imp. l. N.S.W. Austr.
168 F2 Travemünde Ger.
168 F2 Travenbrück Ger.
190 B2 Travers Switz.
81 D5 Travers, Mount South I. N.Z.
226 E3 Traverse City MI U.S.A.
190 F4 Traversetolo Italy
260 D4 Travesia Puntana des. Arg.
260 D3 Travesia Tunuyán des. Arg.
191 G2 Travignolo r. Italy
97 D5 Tra Vinh Vietnam
188 F3 Travnik Bos.-Herz.
192 B3 Travo r. Corse France
190 E4 Travo Italy
150 D2 Trawsfynydd Gwynedd, Wales U.K.
87 C6 Trayning W.A. Austr.
188 E2 Trbovlje Slovenia
147 B3 Trean Rep. of Ireland
246 □ Treasure Beach Jamaica
78 □6 Treasury Islands Solomon Is
177 G3 Trebatice Slovakia
171 F3 Trebatsch Ger.
190 E3 Trebbia r. Italy
171 E3 Trebbin Ger.
170 C3 Trebel Ger.
170 E2 Trebel r. Ger.
171 D4 Treben Ger.
176 C1 Třebenice Czech Rep.
170 E2 Trebenow Ger.
163 E5 Trèbes France
179 E4 Trebesing Austria
158 C3 Trébeurden France
176 E2 Třebíč Czech Rep.
188 G4 Trebinje Bos.-Herz.
195 F3 Trebisacce Italy
188 F4 Trebišnjica r. Bos.-Herz.
177 K3 Trebišov Slovakia
171 D4 Trebitz Ger.
188 F4 Trebižat r. Bos.-Herz.
Trebizond Turkey see Trabzon
188 E3 Trebnje Slovenia
182 C2 Trebolle Spain
176 D2 Třeboň Czech Rep.
85 F3 Trebonne Qld Austr.
158 B3 Tréboul France
171 D4 Trebsen Ger.
184 D4 Trebujena Spain
172 C2 Trebur Ger.
150 D3 Trecastle Powys, Wales U.K.
190 D3 Trecate Italy
193 H4 Trecchina Italy
191 G3 Trecenta Italy
150 D3 Tredegar Blaenau Gwent, Wales U.K.
151 F2 Tredington Warwickshire, England U.K.
191 G4 Tredozio Italy
148 B3 Treehoo Rep. of Ireland
168 E1 Treene r. Ger.
Trefaldwyn Powys, Wales U.K. see Montgomery
150 D2 Trefeglwys Powys, Wales U.K.
179 E4 Treffen Austria
158 B4 Treffiagat France
160 D2 Treffort-Cuisiat France
169 F4 Treffurt Ger.
Treffynnon Flintshire, Wales U.K. see Holywell
150 D1 Trefriw Conwy, Wales U.K.
Trefynwy Monmouthshire, Wales U.K. see Monmouth
150 D2 Tregaron Ceredigion, Wales U.K.
158 C3 Trégastel France
191 G3 Tregnago Italy
226 B3 Trego WI U.S.A.
150 C4 Tregony Cornwall, England U.K.
85 G3 Tregosse Islets and Reefs Coral Sea Is Terr. Austr.
260 A5 Treguaco Chile
158 D3 Trégueux France
158 C3 Tréguier France
158 C4 Trégunc France
150 D2 Tregynon Powys, Wales U.K.
140 L3 Trehörningsjö Sweden
168 E1 Treia Ger.
191 I5 Treia Italy
146 D5 Treig, Loch l. Scotland U.K.
162 D3 Treignac France
160 B1 Treigny France
Treinta de Agosto Arg. see 30 de Agosto
258 G4 Treinta y Tres Uru.
169 C5 Treis Ger.
246 □ Trelawney parish Jamaica
159 F4 Trélazé France
150 C3 Trelech Carmarthenshire, Wales U.K.
259 D6 Trelew Arg.
162 C3 Trélissac France
158 D3 Trélivan France
142 E4 Trelleborg Sweden
162 E3 Trélon France
197 F4 Trem mt. Yugo.
150 C2 Tremadog Gwynedd, Wales U.K.
150 C2 Tremadog Bay Wales U.K.
224 F4 Tremblant, Mont hill Que. Can.
158 E3 Tremblay France
156 B4 Tremblay-les-Villages France
184 D3 Tremedal de Tormes Spain
165 D4 Tremelo Belgium
159 F4 Trémentines France
184 B1 Tremês Port.
158 D3 Tréméven France
190 E3 Tremezzo Italy
193 H2 Tremiti, Isole is Italy
158 D3 Tremlya r. Belarus
163 C4 Trémolat France
227 I5 Tremont PA U.S.A.
238 D3 Tremonton UT U.S.A.
176 C2 Třemošná Czech Rep.
176 E2 Třemošnice Czech Rep.
161 E4 Trémouilles France
186 D2 Tremp Spain
226 B3 Trempealeau r. WI U.S.A.
168 E2 Trendelburg Ger.
150 B4 Trenance Cornwall, England U.K.
226 D2 Trenary MI U.S.A.
225 F4 Trenche r. Que. Can.
177 H3 Trenčianska Turná Slovakia
177 G3 Trenčianske Stankovce Slovakia
177 H3 Trenčianske Teplice Slovakia
177 H3 Trenčiansky Kraj admin. reg. Slovakia
177 H3 Trenčín Slovakia
169 E4 Trendelburg Ger.
261 E4 Trenel Arg.
95 E5 Trengganu Jawa Timur Indon.
Trengganu state Malaysia see Terengganu
261 F4 Trenque Lauquén Arg.
163 B4 Trensacq France
170 E1 Trent Ger.
Trent Italy see Trento
149 I4 Trent r. Dorset, England U.K.
150 E4 Trent r. England U.K.
163 C4 Trentels France
191 G2 Trentino - Alto Adige admin. reg. Italy
191 G2 Trento Italy
191 G2 Trento prov. Trentino - Alto Adige Italy
193 G4 Trentola-Ducenta Italy
224 E4 Trenton Ont. Can.
231 D6 Trenton FL U.S.A.
231 C5 Trenton GA U.S.A.
236 E3 Trenton MO U.S.A.
231 E5 Trenton NC U.S.A.
236 C3 Trenton NE U.S.A.
234 D2 Trenton NJ U.S.A.
237 F5 Trenton TN U.S.A.
156 B4 Tréon France
150 D3 Treorchy Rhondda Cynon Taff, Wales U.K.
84 B1 Trepang Bay N.T. Austr.
225 K4 Trepassey Nfld. Can.
171 F3 Treppeln Ger.
160 D3 Trept France
195 H2 Trepuzzi Italy
190 D2 Trequanda Italy
190 D2 Tresa r. Italy
261 F4 Tres Algarrobas Arg.
190 E4 Tresana Italy
261 G6 Tres Arroyos Arg.
256 B6 Três Bicos Brazil
234 C2 Tresckow PA U.S.A.
161 D4 Trescléoux France
150 □ Tresco i. England U.K.
257 E4 Três Corações Brazil
190 E3 Trescore Balneario Italy
190 F2 Tresenda Italy
250 C4 Tres Esquinas Col.
Tres Forcas, Cabo c. Morocco see Trois Fourches, Cap des
146 B5 Treshnish Isles Scotland U.K.
191 G4 Tresigallo Italy
190 F2 Tre Signori, Corno dei mt. Italy
256 B4 Três Irmãos, Represa resr Brazil
258 E2 Tres Isletas Arg.
196 E4 Treska r. Macedonia
256 B4 Três Lagoas Brazil
261 F5 Tres Lomas Arg.
183 F1 Tres Mares, Pico mt. Spain
257 E3 Três Marias Brazil
257 E3 Três Marias, Represa resr Brazil
259 B7 Tres Montes, Península pen. Chile
192 A4 Tresnuraghes Sardegna Italy
183 G2 Trespaderne Spain
245 E5 Tres Palos Mex.
239 F6 Tres Picachos, Sierra mts Mex.
259 C6 Tres Picos mt. Arg.
245 E5 Tres Picos Mex.
261 G6 Tres Picos, Cerro mt. Arg.
245 H5 Tres Picos, Cerro mt. Mex.
239 F4 Tres Piedras NM U.S.A.
240 G3 Tres Pinos CA U.S.A.
257 E4 Três Pontas Brazil
256 C6 Três Pontões, Pico mt. Brazil
260 C3 Tres Porteñas Arg.
256 D3 Três Ranchos Brazil
256 D3 Tres Rios Brazil
146 E5 Tressait Perth and Kinross, Scotland U.K.
160 D3 Tresserve France
176 F2 Třešť Czech Rep.
193 G3 Treste r. Italy
245 F4 Tres Valles Mex.
245 G4 Tres Zapotes tourist site Mex.
150 D3 Tretower Powys, Wales U.K.
161 D5 Trets France
173 E3 Treuchtlingen Ger.
171 D5 Treuen Ger.
171 D3 Treuenbrietzen Ger.
142 C2 Treungen Norway
158 D3 Trévé France
183 G4 Trevélez Spain
185 G4 Trevélez r. Spain
259 C6 Trevelín Arg.
157 F4 Tréveray France
161 B4 Trèves France
Treves Ger. see Trier
193 E2 Trevi Italy
193 G3 Treviana Spain
183 G2 Trévières France
190 E3 Treviglio Italy
192 E2 Trevignano Romano Italy
160 E1 Trévillers France
183 H2 Treviño Spain
191 H3 Treviso Italy
191 H3 Treviso airport Italy
191 H3 Treviso prov. Veneto Italy
182 C3 Trevões Port.
234 B2 Trevorton PA U.S.A.
234 D2 Trevose PA U.S.A.
150 B4 Trevose Head hd England U.K.
160 C3 Trévoux France
234 C2 Trexlertown PA U.S.A.
160 B2 Trézelles France
197 F4 Trgovište Srbija Yugo.
176 D3 Trhové Sviny Czech Rep.
177 K3 Trhovište Slovakia
83 F5 Triabunna Tas. Austr.
162 C3 Triacastela Spain
162 A2 Triaize France
84 D2 Trial Bay N.T. Austr.
129 D3 T'rialet'i Georgia
129 C3 T'rialet'is K'edi hills Georgia
Triánda Notio Aigaio Greece see Trianta
232 E5 Triangle VA U.S.A.
199 F3 Trianta Notio Aigaio Greece
123 G3 Tribal Areas admin. div. Pak.
177 H3 Tribeč mts Slovakia
158 E2 Tribehou France
172 C3 Triberg im Schwarzwald Ger.
100 G1 Tri Brata, Gora hill Sakhalin Rus. Fed.
170 D1 Tribsees Ger.
85 F3 Tribulation, Cape Qld Austr.
236 C4 Tribune KS U.S.A.
193 I4 Tricarico Italy
195 H3 Tricase Italy
191 I2 Tricesimo Italy
191 H2 Trichiana Italy
Trichinopoly Tamil Nadu India see Tiruchchirappalli
198 B2 Trichonida, Limni l. Greece
114 C4 Trichur Kerala India
156 C3 Tricot France
83 F3 Trida N.S.W. Austr.
Tridentum Italy see Trento
171 D5 Triebel r. Ger.
179 F3 Trieben Austria
171 D5 Triebes Ger.
156 B3 Trie-Château France
192 B2 Triei Sardegna Italy
190 B4 Triengen Switz.
172 C4 Trier Ger.
172 A2 Trier admin. reg. Rheinland-Pfalz Ger.
169 B5 Trier admin. reg. Rheinland-Pfalz Ger.
172 A2 Trierweiler Ger.
191 I3 Trieste Italy
191 I3 Trieste prov. Friuli - Venezia Giulia Italy
Trieste, Golfo di g. Europe see Trieste, Gulf of
188 D3 Trieste, Gulf of Europe
191 I3 Trieste-Ronchi dei Legionari airport Italy
163 C5 Trie-sur-Baïse France
157 F3 Trieux France
158 C3 Trieux r. France
173 H3 Triftern Ger.
184 C2 Trigaches Port.
161 E5 Trigance France
195 F1 Triggiano Italy
179 E4 Triglav mt. Slovenia
170 D2 Triglitz Ger.
158 D4 Trignac France
193 G2 Trigno r. Italy
216 □1c Trigo, Monte hill São Jorge Azores
161 C5 Triguères France
184 C3 Trigueros Spain
183 F3 Trigueros del Valle Spain
198 B2 Trikala Greece
Trikkala Greece see Trikala
91 I7 Trikora, Puncak mt. Indon.
198 C2 Trikorfa mt. Greece
188 F4 Trilj Croatia
147 D2 Trillick Northern Ireland U.K.
183 H4 Trillo Spain
156 C4 Trilport France
147 E3 Trim Rep. of Ireland
149 H3 Trimdon Durham, England U.K.
151 I3 Trimley St Mary Suffolk, England U.K.
190 E2 Trimmis Switz.
86 B4 Trimouille Island W.A. Austr.
150 C3 Trimsaran Carmarthenshire, Wales U.K.
114 D4 Trincomalee Sri Lanka
256 C2 Trindade Brazil
184 C3 Trindade Beja Port.
182 C3 Trindade Bragança Port.
264 H7 Trindade, Ilha da i. S. Atlantic Ocean
177 H2 Třinec Czech Rep.
151 G3 Tring Hertfordshire, England U.K.
198 B2 Tringia mt. Greece
252 D3 Trinidad Bol.
246 C2 Trinidad Cuba
245 G5 Trinidad r. Mex.
247 □7 Trinidad i. Trin. and Tob.
261 I3 Trinidad Uru.
239 F4 Trinidad CO U.S.A.
261 G6 Trinidad, Isla i. Arg.
247 G5 Trinidad and Tobago country West Indies
192 A4 Trinità d'Agultu Sardegna Italy
193 I3 Trinitapoli Italy
237 E6 Trinity TX U.S.A.
238 B3 Trinity r. CA U.S.A.
237 E6 Trinity r. TX U.S.A.
237 D5 Trinity, West Fork r. OK U.S.A.
85 F3 Trinity Bay Qld Austr.
225 K4 Trinity Bay Nfld. Can.
240 H1 Trinity Range mts NV U.S.A.
190 D3 Trino Italy
178 C3 Trins Austria
182 C4 Trinta Port.
232 B4 Trinway OH U.S.A.
170 D1 Trinwillershagen Ger.
183 F2 Triollo Spain
193 H3 Triolo r. Italy
195 F3 Trionto r. Italy
190 C5 Triora Italy
94 B2 Tripa r. Indon.
170 C2 Tripkau Ger.
198 C3 Tripoli Greece
Tripoli Lebanon see Trâblous
202 B1 Tripoli Libya
Trípolis Greece see Tripoli
Tripolis Lebanon see Trâblous
202 B2 Tripolitania reg. Libya
172 B2 Trippstadt Ger.
171 C5 Triptis Ger.
114 C4 Tripunittura Kerala India
117 G5 Tripura state India
178 B3 Trisanna r. Austria
178 D4 Tristach Austria
216 □2c Tristan da Cunha i. S. Atlantic Ocean
206 B4 Tristao, Îles is Guinea
178 E4 Tristenspitze mt. Austria
116 D3 Trisul mt. Uttar Prad. India
225 K3 Triton Nfld. Can.
168 F2 Trittenheim Ger.
254 F3 Triunfo Brazil
114 C4 Trivandrum Kerala India
193 G3 Trivento Italy
190 D3 Triverο Italy
193 F3 Triversa r. Italy
193 H4 Trivigno Italy
161 A3 Trizac France
177 G2 Trnava Czech Rep.
177 G3 Trnava Slovakia
177 H3 Trnavá Hora Slovakia
177 G3 Trnavský Kraj admin. reg. Slovakia
179 H4 Trnovec Bartolovečki Croatia
179 E5 Trnovski gozd mts Slovenia
159 F2 Troarn France
171 E4 Tröbitz Ger.
172 D3 Trochtelfingen Ger.
222 H5 Trochu Alta Can.
141 I3 Trödje Sweden
182 B3 Trofa Port.
179 G3 Trofaiach Austria
140 K2 Trofors Norway
188 F3 Trogir Croatia
178 E4 Trogkofel mt. Austria/Italy
188 F4 Troglav mt. Croatia
142 D2 Trogstad Norway
193 H3 Troia Italy
184 B2 Tróia Port.
194 D5 Troina Sicilia Italy
194 D5 Troina r. Sicilia Italy
169 C5 Troisdorf Ger.
157 H4 Troisfontaines France
204 E2 Trois Fourches, Cap des c. Morocco
225 G3 Trois-Pistoles Que. Can.
165 E4 Trois-Ponts Belgium
225 F4 Trois-Rivières Que. Can.
247 □2 Trois-Rivières Guadeloupe
163 D6 Trois Seigneurs, Pic des mt. France
156 C3 Troissereux France
160 B2 Trois-Vèvres France
165 F4 Troisvierges Lux.
139 M4 Troitsa Rus. Fed.
120 E1 Troitsk Chelyabinskaya Oblast' Rus. Fed.
139 K4 Troitsk Moskovskaya Oblast' Rus. Fed.
137 I2 Troitskiy Belgorodskaya Oblast' Rus. Fed.
Troitskiy Moskovskaya Oblast' Rus. Fed. see Troitsk
134 L3 Troitsko-Pechorsk Rus. Fed.
121 K1 Troitskoye Altayskiy Kray Rus. Fed.
100 F2 Troitskoye Khabarovskiy Kray Rus. Fed.
120 C1 Troitskoye Orenburgskaya Oblast' Rus. Fed.
120 D1 Troitskoye Respublika Bashkortostan Rus. Fed.
135 I7 Troitskoye Respublika Kalmykiya - Khalm'g-Tangch Rus. Fed.
246 □ Troja Jamaica
174 G5 Troja r. Pol.
142 E2 Trollhättan Sweden
251 G5 Trombetas r. Brazil
217 □1 Tromelin, Île i. Indian Ocean
Tromelin Island Micronesia see Fais
190 D3 Tromello Italy
260 B5 Tromen, Volcán vol. Arg.
146 D4 Tromie r. Scotland U.K.
215 E4 Trompsburg S. Africa
140 L1 Troms county Norway
140 L1 Tromsø Norway
240 I4 Trona CA U.S.A.
259 C6 Tronador, Monte mt. Arg.
161 A4 Tronçais, Forêt de for. France
182 C3 Tronco Port.
244 C2 Troncoso Mex.
140 J3 Trondheim Norway
140 J3 Trondheimsfjorden sea chan. Norway
150 D4 Troney r. England U.K.
117 G4 Trongsa Bhutan
117 G4 Trongsa Chhu r. Bhutan
193 F2 Tronto r. Italy
157 F4 Tronville-en-Barrois France
190 D3 Tronzano Vercellese Italy
159 G4 Troo France
128 A2 Troödos, Mount Cyprus
128 A2 Troödos Mountains Cyprus
146 D6 Troon South Ayrshire, Scotland U.K.
198 B3 Tropaia Greece
251 G6 Tropas r. Brazil
254 F2 Tropea Italy
254 D5 Tropeiros, Serra dos hills Brazil
241 K3 Tropic UT U.S.A.
147 D2 Trory Northern Ireland U.K.
139 J5 Trosna Rus. Fed.
171 D4 Trossin Ger.
172 C3 Trossingen Ger.
139 I5 Trostan' Rus. Fed.
147 E1 Trostan hill Northern Ireland U.K.
171 E4 Tröstau Ger.
173 G3 Trostberg Ger.
137 H2 Trostyanets' Ukr.
136 E3 Trostyanets' Ukr.
136 C2 Trostyanets' Ukr.
146 B4 Trotternish hills Scotland U.K.
197 H2 Troțuș r. Romania
122 E3 Trout r. B.C. Can.
222 G2 Trout r. N.W.T. Can.
151 E4 Troutbeck Cumbria, England U.K.
227 H3 Trout Creek Ont. Can.
226 C2 Trout Creek MI U.S.A.
232 C6 Trout Dale VA U.S.A.
222 H3 Trout Lake Alta Can.
222 F2 Trout Lake N.W.T. Can.
222 F2 Trout Lake l. N.W.T. Can.
223 M5 Trout Lake l. Ont. Can.
226 E2 Trout Lake MI U.S.A.
225 J3 Trout River Nfld. Can.
227 I5 Trout Run PA U.S.A.
232 D6 Troutville VA U.S.A.
159 G2 Trouville-sur-Mer France
159 I4 Trouy France
182 B5 Troviscal Port.
150 E3 Trowbridge Wiltshire, England U.K.
83 F5 Trowutta Tas. Austr.
Troy tourist site Turkey see Truva
231 C6 Troy AL U.S.A.
236 E4 Troy KS U.S.A.
227 F4 Troy MI U.S.A.
236 F4 Troy MO U.S.A.
238 D1 Troy MT U.S.A.
231 E5 Troy NC U.S.A.
233 G3 Troy NH U.S.A.
233 G3 Troy NY U.S.A.
232 A4 Troy OH U.S.A.
227 I5 Troy PA U.S.A.
197 G4 Troyan Bulg.
136 E2 Troyaniv Ukr.
136 F3 Troyanka Ukr.
139 L5 Troyekurovo Lipetskaya Oblast' Rus. Fed.
139 L5 Troyekurovo Lipetskaya Oblast' Rus. Fed.
156 E4 Troyes France
137 J3 Troyits'ke Ukr.
136 F4 Troyits'ke Ukr.
137 G4 Troyits'ko-Safonove Ukr.
157 F3 Troyon France
241 J2 Troy Peak NV U.S.A.
176 G2 Tršice Czech Rep.
179 E5 Trstelj hill Slovenia
177 I2 Trstená Slovakia
196 E4 Trstenik Srbija Yugo.
177 G3 Trstice Slovakia
176 G3 Trstín Slovakia
84 D1 Truant Island N.T. Austr.
139 I5 Trubchevsk Rus. Fed.
139 L5 Trubetchino Rus. Fed.
182 E1 Trubia Spain
182 E1 Trubia r. Spain
137 F2 Trubizh r. Ukr.
161 B4 Truc de la Garde mt. France
Truc Giang Vietnam see Bên Tre
182 D2 Truchas Spain
157 H4 Truchtersheim France
Trucial Coast country Asia see United Arab Emirates
Trucial States country Asia see United Arab Emirates
240 C2 Truckee CA U.S.A.
120 A3 Trudfront Rus. Fed.
Trudovoy Kazakh. see Kuybyshevskiy
Trudovoy Rus. Fed. see Yusta
100 E4 Trudovoye Rus. Fed.
139 K5 Trudy r. Rus. Fed.
84 B4 Truer Range hills N.T. Austr.
184 D2 Trujillanos Spain
242 □16 Trujillo Hond.
252 A2 Trujillo Peru
184 E1 Trujillo Spain
250 D2 Trujillo Venez.
250 D2 Trujillo state Venez.
Trujillo, Monte mt. Dom. Rep. see Duarte, Pico
247 □1 Trujillo Alto Puerto Rico
Truk is Micronesia see Chuuk
172 B2 Trulben Ger.
150 D4 Trull Somerset, England U.K.
237 F5 Trumann AR U.S.A.
232 E3 Trumansburg NY U.S.A.
235 E1 Trumbull CT U.S.A.
241 K3 Trumbull, Mount AZ U.S.A.
151 H2 Trumpington Cambridgeshire, England U.K.
197 F4 Trŭn Bulg.
159 G3 Trun France
190 D2 Trun Switz.
197 F4 Trŭna mt. Bulg.
83 F3 Trundle N.S.W. Austr.
Trung Sa is S. China Sea see Spratly Islands
225 I4 Truro N.S. Can.
150 B4 Truro Cornwall, England U.K.
95 F1 Trusan r. Sarawak Malaysia
197 H2 Trușești Romania
169 F5 Trusetal Ger.
196 D5 Trush Albania
137 G3 Trushivtsi Ukr.
135 G4 Truskavets' Ukr.
136 C2 Truskmore hill Rep. of Ireland
95 G1 Trus Madi, Gunung mt. Sabah Malaysia
197 G4 Trustenik Bulg.
222 F3 Trutch B.C. Can.
222 F3 Trutch Creek r. B.C. Can.
239 F5 Truth or Consequences NM U.S.A.
176 E1 Trutnov Czech Rep.
199 E2 Truva tourist site Turkey
161 A4 Truyère r. France
139 J2 Truzhenik Rus. Fed.
197 G4 Tryavna Bulg.
198 B3 Tryfos Dytiki Ellas Greece
168 F1 Tryggelev Denmark
163 F4 Tryncza Pol.
236 C3 Tryon NE U.S.A.
141 K3 Trysil Norway
141 K3 Trysilelva r. Norway
141 K3 Trysilfjellet mt. Norway
138 D3 Tryškiai Lith.
188 F3 Tržac Bos.-Herz.
175 J3 Trzcianka Mazowieckie Pol.
174 E2 Trzcianka Wielkopolskie Pol.
175 K2 Trzcianne Pol.
174 D3 Trzciel Pol.
174 C4 Trzcinica Pol.
174 D3 Trzcińsko-Zdrój Pol.
174 C4 Trzebiel Pol.
174 F1 Trzebielino Pol.
175 K4 Trzebieszów Pol.
174 C2 Trzebież Pol.
174 F3 Trzebinia Pol.
174 F5 Trzebnica Pol.
175 K5 Trzebownisko Pol.
174 E4 Trzemeszno Pol.
174 E3 Trzemeszno Pol.
175 L3 Trzeszczany Pol.
174 F5 Trzeszcza Pol.
175 J6 Trześniów Pol.
175 J5 Trześniówka r. Pol.
175 L5 Trzeszczany Pierwsze Pol.
188 E2 Tržič Slovenia
179 F4 Trzin Slovenia
174 C3 Trzciński-Zdrój Pol.
175 H5 Trzyciąż Pol.
175 K5 Trzydnik Duży Pol.
106 A1 Tsagaannuur Bayan-Ölgiy Mongolia
107 H2 Tsagaannuur Dornod Mongolia
106 B2 Tsagaan Nuur salt l. Mongolia
Tsagaan-Ulul Hövsgöl Mongolia see Sharga
135 I7 Tsagan Aman Rus. Fed.
135 I7 Tsagan-Nur Rus. Fed.
129 C2 Ts'ageri Georgia
Tsaidam Basin China see Qaidam Pendi
140 M1 Tsåktso mt. Sweden
129 C2 Tsalenjikha Georgia
142 K2 Tsangatjåkka mt. Sweden
213 □J3 Tsaramandroso Madag.
213 □J3 Tsaratanana Madag.
213 □K2 Tsaratanana, Massif du mts Madag.
197 H4 Tsarevo Bulg.
Tsaribrod Srbija Yugo. see Dimitrovgrad
197 G4 Tsarimir Bulg.
Tsaritsyn Rus. Fed. see Volgograd
137 H3 Tsarychanka Ukr.
215 G4 Tsatsana mt. S. Africa
211 G4 Tsavo East National Park Kenya
211 C5 Tsavo West National Park Kenya
215 F4 Tsazo S. Africa
178 A3 Tschagguns Austria
168 E3 Tschernitz Ger.
171 D2 Tschernitz Ger.
106 B2 Tseel Mongolia
Tsefat Israel see Ẕefat
135 H7 Tselina Rus. Fed.
121 K1 Tselinnoye Rus. Fed.
120 E2 Tselinnyy Rus. Fed.
Tselinograd Kazakh. see Astana
Tselinogradskaya Oblast' admin. div. Kazakh. see Akmolinskaya Oblast'
Tsementnyy Rus. Fed. see Fokino
106 D1 Tsengel Mongolia
134 J4 Tsentral'nyy Rus. Fed.
Tsentral'nyy Rus. Fed. see Radovitskiy
139 L5 Tsentral'nyy Rus. Fed.
197 F4 Tserovo Bulg.
106 B2 Tsetsegnuur Mongolia
106 D2 Tsetserleg Arhangay Mongolia
Tsetserleg Hövsgöl Mongolia see Halban
207 F5 Tsévié Togo
212 D5 Tsabong Botswana
Tshad country Africa see Chad
209 B6 Tshela Dem. Rep. Congo
213 E4 Tshesebe Botswana
209 D6 Tshibala Dem. Rep. Congo
209 D6 Tshikapa Dem. Rep. Congo
209 D6 Tshikapa r. Dem. Rep. Congo
209 D6 Tshilenge Dem. Rep. Congo
209 D6 Tshimbulu Dem. Rep. Congo
215 F2 Tshing S. Africa
213 F4 Tshipise S. Africa
209 D6 Tshiumbe r. Angola/Dem. Rep. Congo
209 E6 Tshofa Dem. Rep. Congo
213 F5 Tshokwane S. Africa
213 E3 Tsholotsho Zimbabwe
212 D4 Tshootsha Botswana
208 D5 Tshuapa r. Dem. Rep. Congo
213 □J3 Tsiazonano mt. Madag.
197 F4 Tsibritsa r. Bulg.
220 E3 Tsiigehtchic N.W.T. Can.
134 J2 Tsil'ma r. Rus. Fed.
135 H7 Tsimlyansk Rus. Fed.
135 H7 Tsimlyanskoye Vodokhranilishche resr Rus. Fed.
Tsinan Shandong China see Jinan
214 D2 Tsineng S. Africa
Tsingtai prov. China see Qinghai
217 □3b Tsingoni Mayotte
Tsingtao Shandong China see Qingdao
Tsining Nei Mongol China see Jining
213 □J3 Tsinjomay mt. Madag.
213 □J5 Tsiombe Madag.
213 □J3 Tsiroanomandidy Madag.
Tsiteli Tskaro Georgia see Dedop'listsqaro
Tsitsihar Heilong. China see Qiqihar
222 E4 Tsitsutl Peak B.C. Can.
129 B2 Ts'ivi r. Georgia
129 D3 Ts'ivi, Mt'a Georgia
134 I5 Tsivil'sk Rus. Fed.
Tskhakaia Georgia see Senaki
Tskhaltubo Georgia see Tsqaltubo
129 C2 Ts'khinvali Georgia
129 D3 Ts'khneti Georgia
139 E5 Tsna r. Belarus
135 H5 Tsna r. Rus. Fed.
139 J3 Tsna r. Rus. Fed.
139 L4 Tsna r. Rus. Fed.
129 D3 Tsnori Georgia
212 D3 Tsodilo Hills Botswana
116 D2 Tsokr Chumo l. Jammu and Kashmir
215 G4 Tsolo S. Africa
215 F5 Tsomo S. Africa
215 F5 Tsomo r. S. Africa
116 D2 Tso Morari Lake Jammu and Kashmir
139 K5 Tson r. Rus. Fed.
Tsona Xizang China see Cona
199 D1 Tsopan hill Greece
198 B1 Tsotili Dytiki Makedonia Greece
129 D3 Tsovinar Armenia
129 C2 Tsqaltubo Georgia
104 C4 Tsu Japan
103 I5 Tsubame Japan
105 G2 Tsuchiura Japan
109 □ Tsuen Wan H.K. China
102 J3 Tsugarū-kaikyō str. Japan
Tsugaru Strait Japan see Tsugarū-kaikyō
105 G2 Tsukuba Japan
103 E7 Tsukumi Japan
106 E2 Tsul-Ulaan Mongolia
136 C2 Tsuman' Ukr.
212 B4 Tsumeb Namibia
212 B3 Tsumkwe Namibia
129 E2 Tsurib Rus. Fed.
105 E3 Tsuru Japan
104 C3 Tsuruga Japan
104 D2 Tsurugi-dake mt. Japan
103 G7 Tsurugi-san mt. Japan
Tsurukhaytuy Rus. Fed. see Priargunsk
102 I4 Tsuruoka Japan
104 C3 Tsushima Japan
Tsushima-kaikyō str. Japan/S. Korea see Korea Strait
103 G6 Tsuyama Japan
197 F5 Tsvetino Bulg.
137 F3 Tsvitkove Ukr.
137 G3 Tsvitne Ukr.
215 E3 Tswaraganang S. Africa
215 E2 Tswelelang S. Africa
136 E3 Tsybuliv Ukr.
138 E5 Tsyelyakhany Belarus
137 F1 Tsyerakhowka Belarus
Tsygira Moldova see Ţighira
175 N4 Tsyr r. Ukr.
137 G4 Tsyurupyns'k Ukr.
Tthenaagoo N.W.T. Can. see Nahanni Butte
182 C3 Tua r. Port.
80 E2 Tuakau North I. N.Z.
147 C3 Tuam Rep. of Ireland
81 D4 Tuamarina South I. N.Z.
147 C4 Tuamgraney Rep. of Ireland
79 □3 Tuamotu, Archipel des is Fr. Polynesia
Tuamotu Islands Fr. Polynesia see Tuamotu, Archipel des
81 B7 Tuapeka Mouth South I. N.Z.
135 F2 Tuapse Rus. Fed.
94 □ Tuas Sing.
81 A7 Tuatapere South I. N.Z.
146 B5 Tuath, Loch sea chan. Scotland U.K.
Tuath, Loch a' b. Scotland U.K. see Broad Bay
241 L3 Tuba City AZ U.S.A.
95 F4 Tuban Jawa Timur Indon.
255 C9 Tubarão Brazil
128 B3 Tūbās West Bank
92 A4 Tubbataha Reefs Phil.
147 C2 Tubbercurry Rep. of Ireland
147 F2 Tubbergen Neth.
148 B5 Tubbrid Rep. of Ireland
183 G2 Tubilla del Agua Spain
172 D3 Tübingen Ger.
172 D3 Tübingen admin. reg. Baden-Württemberg Ger.
120 D1 Tubinskiy Rus. Fed.
165 D4 Tubize Belgium
206 C5 Tubmanburg Liberia
207 G4 Tubo r. Nigeria
92 B4 Tubod Phil.
79 F5 Tubre Italy
202 D1 Tubruq Libya
95 G2 Tubu r. Indon.
79 □3 Tubuai i. Îs Australes Fr. Polynesia
242 C2 Tubutama Mex.
238 C2 Tucannon r. WA U.S.A.
254 F4 Tucano Brazil
260 B5 Tucapel Chile
253 F4 Tucavaca Bol.
253 F4 Tucavaca r. Bol.
163 C6 Tuc de les Carants mt. Spain
163 E6 Tuchan France
172 D3 Tüchen Ger.
171 D3 Tuchheim Ger.
222 D2 Tuchitua Y.T. Can.
139 K4 Tuchkovo Rus. Fed.
171 E5 Tuchlovice Czech Rep.
222 F3 Tuchodi r. B.C. Can.
174 F2 Tuchola Pol.
174 F1 Tuchomie Pol.
175 J6 Tuchów Pol.
175 K4 Tuchowicz Pol.
136 D2 Tuchyn Ukr.
234 D3 Tuckahoe NJ U.S.A.
235 F2 Tuckahoe NY U.S.A.
234 D3 Tuckahoe r. NJ U.S.A.
234 C4 Tuckahoe Creek r. MD U.S.A.
87 C5 Tuckanarra W.A. Austr.
235 D3 Tuckerton NJ U.S.A.
234 C2 Tuckerton PA U.S.A.
Tucopia i. Solomon Is see Tikopia
157 F3 Tucquegnieux France
241 L5 Tucson AZ U.S.A.
241 L5 Tucson Mountains AZ U.S.A.
225 H1 Tuctuc r. Que. Can.
Tucumán prov. Arg. see San Miguel de Tucumán
258 D2 Tucumán prov. Arg.
237 C5 Tucumcari NM U.S.A.
251 F2 Tucupita Venez.
251 I5 Tucuruí Brazil
251 I6 Tucuruí, Represa resr Brazil
175 L4 Tuczna Pol.
174 E2 Tuczno Pol.
142 D4 Tudeå r. Denmark
183 I2 Tudela Spain
183 F3 Tudela de Duero Spain
Tuder Italy see Todi
197 H2 Tudora Romania
197 H3 Tudor Vladimirescu Romania
139 I3 Tudovka r. Rus. Fed.
150 C2 Tudweiliog Gwynedd, Wales U.K.
187 B5 Tuejar Spain
182 C3 Tuela r. Port.
109 □ Tuen Mun H.K. China
191 G2 Tuenno Italy
117 H4 Tuensang Nagaland India
251 I5 Tueré r. Brazil
182 E2 Tuerto r. Spain
125 E2 Ţufayḩ Saudi Arabia
159 G3 Tuffé France
267 J2 Tufts Abyssal Plain sea feature N. Pacific Ocean
Tuga i. Vanuatu see Tégua
215 H3 Tugela r. S. Africa
215 H3 Tugela Ferry S. Africa
Tūghyl Kazakh. see Tugyl
108 B3 Tuguancun Yunnan China
92 B2 Tuguegarao Phil.
213 F4 Tugwi r. Zimbabwe
121 K3 Tugyl Kazakh.
107 H4 Tuhai r. China
182 B2 Tui Spain
252 D3 Tuichi r. Bol.
192 A5 Tuili Sardegna Italy
115 F5 Tuilianpui r. Bangl./India
216 □3b Tuineje Fuerteventura Canary Is
Tujiabu Jiangxi China see Yongxiu
120 D1 Tukan Rus. Fed.
93 B4 Tukangbesi, Kepulauan is Indon.
136 B3 Tukhol'ka Ukr.
123 H2 Tŭkhtamish Tajik.
81 F3 Tukituki r. North I. N.Z.
202 D1 Tükrah Libya
220 E3 Tuktoyaktuk N.W.T. Can.
138 D3 Tukums Latvia
95 E3 Tukung, Bukit mt. Indon.
100 C1 Tukuringra, Khrebet mts Rus. Fed.
129 D1 Tukuy-Mekteb Rus. Fed.
121 B7 Tukuyu Tanz.
192 A4 Tula Sardegna Italy
245 E3 Tula Hidalgo Mex.
245 E2 Tula Tamaulipas Mex.
245 E3 Tula r. Mex.
139 K4 Tula Rus. Fed.
Tulach Mhór Rep. of Ireland see Tullamore
78 □6 Tulaghi Solomon Is
111 F4 Tulagt Ar Gol r. China
106 C4 Tulai Qinghai China
106 C4 Tulai Nanshan mts China
106 C4 Tulai Shan mts China
263 D2 Tula Mountains Antarctica
245 E3 Tulancingo Mex.
94 D4 Tulangbawang r. Indon.
Tula Oblast admin. div. Rus. Fed. see Tul'skaya Oblast'
240 H3 Tulare CA U.S.A.
239 F5 Tularosa NM U.S.A.
114 D2 Tulasi mt. Madh. Prad./Orissa India
168 F3 Tülau Ger.
175 I2 Tulawki Pol.
214 B5 Tulbagh S. Africa
179 H2 Tulbing Austria
177 K5 Tulca Romania
250 B4 Tulcán Ecuador
174 F3 Tulce Pol.
197 I3 Tulcea Romania
Tul'chin Ukr. see Tul'chyn
136 E3 Tul'chyn Ukr.
240 H3 Tule r. CA U.S.A.
Tulear Madag. see Toliara
238 B3 Tulelake CA U.S.A.
161 C4 Tulette France
176 F5 Tulfes r. Hungary
178 C3 Tulfes Austria
197 G2 Tulgheș Romania
237 C5 Tulia TX U.S.A.
107 I1 Tulihe Nei Mongol China
174 G3 Tuliszków Pol.
222 E1 Tulit'a N.W.T. Can.
116 C2 Tuljapur Mahar. India
128 B3 Ţūlkarm West Bank
147 C4 Tulla Rep. of Ireland
147 C2 Tullaghan Rep. of Ireland
231 C5 Tullahoma TN U.S.A.
147 D3 Tullamore Rep. of Ireland
83 F3 Tullamore N.S.W. Austr.
147 D3 Tullamore Rep. of Ireland
148 B5 Tullaroan Rep. of Ireland
162 D3 Tulle France
83 F3 Tullibigeal N.S.W. Austr.
161 D3 Tullins France
179 H2 Tulln Austria
179 H2 Tullnerbach Austria
147 E4 Tullow Rep. of Ireland
85 F3 Tully Qld Austr.
147 D2 Tully Northern Ireland U.K.
147 D2 Tully Northern Ireland U.K.
147 E3 Tullyallen Rep. of Ireland
147 E2 Tullybrack hill Northern Ireland U.K.
147 E4 Tullycanna Rep. of Ireland
147 E2 Tullyhogue Northern Ireland U.K.
234 D2 Tullytown PA U.S.A.
147 D2 Tullyvin Rep. of Ireland
147 D2 Tullyvoos Rep. of Ireland
197 H3 Tulnici Romania
140 P1 Tuloma r. Rus. Fed.
175 I3 Tułowice Pol.
174 F5 Tułowice Pol.
237 E4 Tulsa OK U.S.A.
222 C3 Tulsequah B.C. Can.
116 E3 Tulsipur Nepal
147 C3 Tulsk Rep. of Ireland
139 K5 Tul'skaya Oblast' admin. div. Rus. Fed.
129 B1 Tul'skiy Rus. Fed.
137 G2 Tul'skoye Kazakh.
250 B3 Tuluá Col.
197 I3 Tulucești Romania
220 B3 Tuluksak AK U.S.A.
128 C3 Tulúl al Ashāqif hills Jordan
243 I4 Tulum tourist site Mex.
260 C2 Tulum, Valle de val. Arg.
98 H1 Tulun Rus. Fed.
95 E5 Tulungagung Jawa Timur Indon.
Tulusdu N. Male Maldives see Thulusdhu
251 F4 Tulu-Tuloi, Serra hills Brazil
210 B2 Tulu Welel mt. Eth.
134 K4 Tulva r. Rus. Fed.
137 G2 Tulyholove Ukr.
242 □16 Tuma r. Nic.
139 M4 Tuma Rus. Fed.
250 B4 Tumaco Col.
215 F4 Tumahole S. Africa
111 E5 Tumain Xizang China
120 B3 Tumak Rus. Fed.
Tuman-gang r. Asia see Tumen Jiang
Tumannaya r. Asia see Tumen Jiang
134 F1 Tumannyy Rus. Fed.
139 J4 Tumanovo Rus. Fed.
131 S3 Tumanskiy Rus. Fed.
Tumasik Sing. see Singapore
251 G3 Tumatumari Guyana
143 G2 Tumba Sweden
92 C5 Tumbao Phil.
83 G3 Tumbarumba N.S.W. Austr.
250 A5 Tumbes Peru
250 A5 Tumbes dept Peru
222 F4 Tumbler Ridge B.C. Can.
82 D3 Tumby Bay S.A. Austr.
140 O2 Tumcha r. Fin./Rus. Fed.
Tumd Youqi Nei Mongol China see Salaqi
Tumd Zuoqi Nei Mongol China see Qasq
100 D4 Tumen Jilin China
108 D1 Tumen Shaanxi China
100 D4 Tumen Jiang r. Asia
251 F3 Tumereng Guyana
257 G3 Tumiritinga Brazil
114 C3 Tumkur Karnataka India
146 E5 Tummel, Loch l. Scotland U.K.
146 D5 Tummel Bridge Perth and Kinross, Scotland U.K.
202 B4 Tummo, Mountains of Libya/Niger
100 G2 Tumnin r. Rus. Fed.
97 C4 Tumpôr, Phnum mt. Cambodia
93 B3 Tumpu, Gunung mt. Indon.
93 B3 Tumputiga, Gunung mt. Indon.
116 D5 Tumsar Mahar. India
206 E4 Tumu Ghana
251 G4 Tumucumaque, Serra hills Brazil
115 D2 Tumudibandh Orissa India
183 D5 Tumuja r. Spain
252 D3 Tumupasa Bol.
121 G4 Tumur Yuzhnyy Kazakhstan Kazakh.
252 D5 Tumusla Bol.
83 G3 Tumut N.S.W. Austr.
134 K5 Tumutuk Rus. Fed.
110 C3 Tumxuk Xinjiang China
206 E4 Tuna Ghana
247 □1 Tuna, Punta pt Puerto Rico
143 F1 Tuna-Hästberg Sweden
247 □7 Tunapuna Trin. and Tob.
246 C2 Tunas de Zaza Cuba
Ţunb al Kubrá i. The Gulf see Greater Tunb
Ţunb aş Şughrá i. The Gulf see Lesser Tunb
151 H3 Tunbridge Wells, Royal Kent, England U.K.
199 F2 Tunçbilek Turkey
126 E3 Tunceli Turkey
129 A4 Tunceli prov. Turkey
108 D5 Tunchang Hainan China
129 C3 Tunçoluk Turkey
83 H3 Tuncurry N.S.W. Austr.
116 E4 Tundla Uttar Prad. India
211 B7 Tunduma Tanz.
207 H4 Tundun-Wada Nigeria
211 C7 Tunduru Tanz.
197 H5 Tundzha r. Bulg.
142 E4 Tune Denmark
Tunes Tunisia see Tunis
207 H4 Tunga Nigeria
146 B3 Tunga Western Isles, Scotland U.K.
114 C3 Tungabhadra r. India
92 B5 Tungawan Phil.
Tungdor Xizang China see Mainling
117 G5 Tungi Bangl.
140 □C2 Tungnaá r. Iceland
100 G1 Tungor Sakhalin Rus. Fed.
222 D2 Tungsten N.W.T. Can.
95 F2 Tungun, Bukit mt. Indon.
115 D2 Tuni Andhra Prad. India
237 F5 Tunica MS U.S.A.
172 C3 Tuningen Ger.
227 G1 Tunis Ont. Can.
205 H1 Tunis Tunisia
205 H1 Tunis, Golfe de g. Tunisia
205 H2 Tunisia country Africa
250 C3 Tunja Col.
234 C1 Tunkhannock PA U.S.A.
107 G4 Tunliu Shanxi China
226 B3 Tunnel City WI U.S.A.
232 D5 Tunnelton WV U.S.A.
139 M3 Tunoshna Rus. Fed.
151 I2 Tunstall Suffolk, England U.K.
173 G4 Tuntenhausen Ger.
225 H1 Tunulic r. Que. Can.
220 B3 Tununak AK U.S.A.
260 C3 Tunuyán Arg.
260 D4 Tunuyán r. Arg.
Tunxi Anhui China see Huangshan
177 L4 Tunyogmatolcs Hungary
Tuodian Yunnan China see Shuangbai
109 F1 Tuo He r. China
Tuojiang Hunan China see Fenghuang
Tuojiang Hunan China see Shuikou
108 C2 Tuo Jiang r. Sichuan China
240 G3 Tuolumne CA U.S.A.
240 G3 Tuolumne r. CA U.S.A.
240 H3 Tuolumne Meadows CA U.S.A.
192 D1 Tuoma r. Italy
108 C3 Tuoniang Jiang r. Guangxi China
Tuoputieke Xinjiang China see Jeminay (Topterek)
191 H5 Tuoro sul Trasimeno Italy
111 F5 Tuotuo He r. China
106 B5 Tuotuoheyan Qinghai China
121 I4 Tüp Kyrg.
256 B4 Tupã Brazil
256 C3 Tupaciguara Brazil
Tupai i. Fr. Polynesia see Motu Iti
255 B9 Tupanciretã Brazil
237 F5 Tupelo MS U.S.A.
176 G2 Tupesy Czech Rep.
251 G5 Tupinambarana, Ilha i. Brazil
256 B4 Tupi Paulista Brazil
252 D5 Tupiza Bol.
174 C4 Tuplice Pol.
222 F4 Tupper B.C. Can.
233 F2 Tupper Lake NY U.S.A.
Tüpqaraghan Tübegi pen. Kazakh. see Mangyshlak, Poluostrov
260 C3 Tupungato Arg.
260 C3 Tupungato, Cerro mt. Arg./Chile
107 I2 Tuquan Nei Mongol China
250 B4 Túquerres Col.
197 F1 Tur r. Romania
111 D4 Tura Xinjiang China
177 I4 Tura Hungary
117 G4 Tura Meghalaya India
131 L3 Tura Rus. Fed.
124 C3 Turabah Saudi Arabia
251 E3 Turagua, Serranía mt. Venez.
80 E4 Turakina North I. N.Z.
80 E4 Turakina r. North I. N.Z.
100 D2 Turana, Khrebet mts Rus. Fed.
80 E3 Turangi North I. N.Z.
120 D5 Turan Lowland Asia
193 E2 Turano r. Italy
Turanskaya Nizmennost' lowland Asia see Turan Lowland
121 G4 Tura-Ryskulova Kazakh.
136 D1 Turaw Belarus
138 E2 Turba Estonia
250 C2 Turbaco Col.
175 I6 Turbacz mt. Pol.
123 E5 Turbat Pak.
190 D1 Turbenthal Switz.
244 D3 Turbio r. Mex.
250 B2 Turbo Col.
234 B1 Turbotville PA U.S.A.
178 E3 Türchlwand mt. Austria
182 E2 Turcia Spain
177 H3 Turčianske Teplice Slovakia
157 H4 Turckheim France
197 F2 Turda Romania
160 C3 Turdine r. France
87 C4 Turee Creek r. W.A. Austr.
183 F3 Turégano Spain

174 G3 Turek Pol.
138 E1 Turenki Fin.
174 E3 Turew Pol.
Turfan Xinjiang China see Turpan
Turfan Depression China see Turpan Pendi
121 H2 Turgay Akmolinskaya Oblast' Kazakh.
120 E2 Turgay Kustanayskaya Oblast' Kazakh.
120 E3 Turgay r. Kazakh.
120 E2 Turgayskaya Dolina val. Kazakh.
120 E2 Turgayskaya Stolovaya Strana reg. Kazakh.
106 A1 Türgen Uul mt. Mongolia
106 A1 Türgen Uul mt. Mongolia
224 E3 Turgeon r. Ont./Que. Can.
197 H4 Tŭrgovishte Bulg.
126 C3 Turgut Konya Turkey
199 F3 Turgut Muğla Turkey
199 E2 Turgutalp Turkey
199 E2 Turgutlu Turkey
199 E3 Turgutreis Turkey
126 E2 Turhal Turkey
138 E2 Türi Estonia
195 G2 Turi Italy
187 C5 Turia r. Spain
254 D2 Turiaçu Brazil
254 D2 Turiaçu r. Brazil
177 H2 Turie Slovakia
177 H3 Turiec r. Slovakia
223 H5 Turin Alta Can.
Turin Italy see Torino
130 H4 Turinsk Rus. Fed.
187 C5 Turís Spain
136 C2 Turiya r. Ukr.
136 C2 Turiys'k Ukr.
176 G5 Türje Hungary
99 I1 Turka Rus. Fed.
136 B3 Turka Ukr.
210 B4 Turkana, Lake salt l. Eth./Kenya
199 E1 Türkeli Turkey
173 F3 Türkenfeld Ger.
121 G4 Turkestan Kazakh.
123 F2 Turkestan Range mts Asia
177 J4 Túrkeve Hungary
126 D3 Turkey country Asia
232 B6 Turkey KY U.S.A.
236 F3 Turkey r. IA U.S.A.
86 F3 Turkey Creek W.A. Austr.
173 E3 Türkheim Ger.
135 H6 Turki Rus. Fed.
Türkistan Kazakh. see Turkestan
122 C1 Turkmenbashi Turkm.
199 G2 Türkmen Dağı mt. Turkey
123 E2 Turkmengala Turkm.
122 D1 Turkmenistan country Asia
Turkmeniya country Asia see Turkmenistan
Turkmen-Kala Turkm. see Turkmengala
Türkmenostan country Asia see Turkmenistan
Turkmenskaya S.S.R. country Asia see Turkmenistan
126 E3 Türkoğlu Turkey
246 E2 Turks and Caicos Islands terr. West Indies
246 E2 Turks Island Passage Turks and Caicos Is
246 E2 Turks Islands Turks and Caicos Is
141 M3 Turku Fin.
183 G5 Turleque Spain
240 G3 Turlock CA U.S.A.
147 B3 Turlough Clare Rep. of Ireland
147 B3 Turlough Mayo Rep. of Ireland
257 F2 Turmalina Brazil
222 E3 Turnagain r. B.C. Can.
80 F4 Turnagain, Cape North I. N.Z.
129 A3 Turnalı Turkey
177 J3 Turňa nad Bodvou Slovakia
179 G3 Turnau Austria
146 D6 Turnberry South Ayrshire, Scotland U.K.
81 B6 Turnbull, Mount South I. N.Z.
241 L5 Turnbull, Mount AZ U.S.A.
86 C4 Turner r. W.A. Austr.
227 F3 Turner MI U.S.A.
86 F3 Turner River W.A. Austr.
151 G3 Turners Hill West Sussex, England U.K.
206 B5 Turner's Peninsula Sierra Leone
222 H5 Turner Valley Alta Can.
165 D3 Turnhout Belgium
179 H4 Turnišče Slovenia
179 G3 Türnitz Austria
223 I3 Turnor Lake Sask. Can.
176 E1 Turnov Czech Rep.
Tŭrnovo Bulg. see Veliko Tŭrnovo
197 G4 Turnu Măgurele Romania
Turnu Severin Romania see Drobeta - Turnu Severin
175 K5 Turobin Pol.
83 G3 Turon r. N.S.W. Austr.
185 F4 Turón r. Spain
Turones France see Tours
188 E3 Turopolje plain Croatia
175 J2 Turośl Pol.
175 J2 Turośl Pol.
134 H4 Turovets Rus. Fed.
175 K4 Turów Pol.
110 E3 Turpan Xinjiang China
110 E3 Turpan Pendi depr. China
110 E3 Turpan Zhan Xinjiang China
184 B1 Turquel Port.
185 I3 Turre Spain
242 □J7 Turrialba Costa Rica
161 E4 Turriers France
146 F4 Turriff Aberdeenshire, Scotland U.K.
Turris Libisonis Sardegna Italy see Porto Torres
195 F2 Tursi Italy
197 F2 Turt Romania
120 E4 Turtkul' Uzbek.
223 I4 Turtleford Sask. Can.
85 G3 Turtle Island Coral Sea Is Terr. Austr.
Turtle Island Fiji see Vatoa
92 A5 Turtle Islands Phil.
206 B5 Turtle Islands Sierra Leone
226 A3 Turtle Lake WI U.S.A.
130 J3 Turukhansk Rus. Fed.
177 M4 Turulung Romania
251 G4 Turuna r. Brazil
136 F4 Turunchuk r. Ukr.
128 B1 Turunçlu Turkey
199 G3 Turunçova Turkey
114 C3 Turuvanur Karnataka India
256 B2 Turvelândia Brazil
255 C9 Turvo Brazil
256 B2 Turvo r. Goiás Brazil
256 C3 Turvo r. São Paulo Brazil
256 C5 Turvo r. São Paulo Brazil
177 L3 Tur"ya r. Ukr.
177 L3 Tur"ya-Bystra Ukr.
129 E3 Türyançay Azer.
129 E3 Türyançay r. Azer.
177 L3 Tur"ya-Polyana Ukr.
136 B3 Tur"ye Ukr.
177 L3 Tur"yi Remety Ukr.
136 C2 Turynka Ukr.
175 I2 Turza Wielka Pol.
177 H2 Turzovka Slovakia
122 D2 Ţūs Iran
185 H2 Tús r. Spain
194 D5 Tusa Sicilia Italy
194 D4 Tusa r. Sicilia Italy
241 K4 Tusayan AZ U.S.A.
231 C5 Tuscaloosa AL U.S.A.
192 D2 Tuscania Italy
Tuscany admin. reg. Italy see Toscana
232 C4 Tuscarawas r. OH U.S.A.
234 B2 Tuscarora PA U.S.A.
232 E4 Tuscarora Mountains hills PA U.S.A.
236 F4 Tuscola IL U.S.A.
237 D5 Tuscola TX U.S.A.
231 C5 Tuscumbia AL U.S.A.
236 E4 Tuscumbia MO U.S.A.
137 I2 Tuskar' r. Rus. Fed.
231 C5 Tuskegee AL U.S.A.
173 E3 Tussenhausen Ger.
232 D4 Tussey Mountains hills PA U.S.A.
173 G3 Tüßling Ger.
226 E3 Tustin MI U.S.A.
175 J5 Tuszów Narodowy Pol.
175 J5 Tuszyma Pol.
175 H4 Tuszyn Pol.
127 F3 Tutak Turkey
139 L3 Tutayev Rus. Fed.
151 F2 Tutbury Staffordshire, England U.K.
Tutera Spain see Tudela
114 C4 Tuticorin Tamil Nadu India
95 F2 Tutoh r. Sarawak Malaysia
95 F1 Tutong Brunei
197 H2 Tutova r. Romania
170 E2 Tutow Ger.
197 H3 Tutrakan Bulg.
150 E3 Tutshill Gloucestershire, England U.K.
234 D1 Tuttles Corner NJ U.S.A.
172 C4 Tuttlingen Ger.
221 P2 Tuttut Nunaat reg. Greenland
211 B6 Tutubu Tanz.
78 □2 Tutuila i. American Samoa
80 E1 Tutukaka North I. N.Z.
213 E4 Tutume Botswana
252 C4 Tutupaca, Volcán vol. Peru
81 E4 Tuturumuri North I. N.Z.
245 F5 Tututepec Mex.
173 F4 Tutzing Ger.
170 E2 Tützpatz Ger.
106 E1 Tuul Gol r. Mongolia
138 E1 Tuulos Fin.
101 C4 Tuun-bong mt. N. Korea
140 O3 Tuupovaara Fin.
140 O3 Tuusniemi Fin.
141 N3 Tuusula Fin.
Tuva aut. rep. Rus. Fed. see Tyva, Respublika
77 H2 Tuvalu country S. Pacific Ocean
77 I4 Tuvana-i-Colo i. Fiji
77 I4 Tuvana-i-Ra i. Fiji
Tuvana-i-Tholo i. Fiji see Tuvana-i-Colo
142 D3 Tuve Sweden
262 S2 Tuve, Mount Antarctica
Tuvinskaya A.S.S.R. aut. rep. Rus. Fed. see Tyva, Respublika
121 I4 Tuvuk Kazakh.
95 G2 Tuwau r. Indon.
124 D2 Tuwayq, Jabal hills Saudi Arabia
124 D3 Tuwayq, Jabal mts Saudi Arabia
128 B5 Ţuwayyil al Ḩājj mt. Jordan
128 C4 Ţuwayyil ash Shiḩāq mt. Jordan
124 B3 Tuwwal Saudi Arabia
235 D1 Tuxedo Park NY U.S.A.
178 C3 Tuxer Gebirge mts Austria
149 I4 Tuxford Nottinghamshire, England U.K.
244 C4 Tuxpan Jalisco Mex.
244 B3 Tuxpan Nayarit Mex.
245 F3 Tuxpan Veracruz Mex.
243 G5 Tuxtla Gutiérrez Mex.
Túy Spain see Tui
247 F5 Tuy r. Venez.
96 D2 Tuyên Quang Vietnam
97 E4 Tuy Hoa Vietnam
135 K5 Tuymazy Rus. Fed.
122 B3 Tūysarkān Iran
Tŭytepa Uzbek. see Toytepa
Tuz, Lake salt l. Turkey see Tuz Gölü
244 D4 Tuzantla r. Mex.
126 D3 Tuz Gölü salt l. Turkey
197 G4 Tŭzha Bulg.
134 I4 Tuzha Rus. Fed.
196 D4 Tuzi Crna Gora Yugo.
127 G4 Tuz Khurmātū Iraq
188 G3 Tuzla Bos.-Herz.
197 I3 Tuzla Romania
126 D3 Tuzla Turkey
127 F3 Tuzla r. Turkey
135 H7 Tuzlov r. Rus. Fed.
129 C3 Tuzluca Turkey
179 H4 Tužno Croatia
96 A1 Tuzu r. Myanmar
142 E3 Tvååker Sweden
140 L2 Tvärålund Sweden
176 F2 Tvarožná Czech Rep.
142 C2 Tvedestrand Norway
142 A1 Tveitakvitingen mt. Norway
139 J3 Tver' Rus. Fed.
Tver Oblast admin. div. Rus. Fed. see Tverskaya Oblast'
129 A1 Tverskaya Rus. Fed.
139 J3 Tverskaya Oblast' admin. div. Rus. Fed.
139 J3 Tvertsa r. Rus. Fed.
144 D1 Tvøroyri Faroe Is
179 H2 Tvrdonice Czech Rep.
177 I2 Tvrdošín Slovakia
197 G4 Tvŭrditsa Bulg.
240 G2 Twain Harte CA U.S.A.
174 F4 Twardogóra Pol.
146 E2 Twatt Orkney, Scotland U.K.
227 I3 Tweed Ont. Can.
149 G2 Tweed r. England/Scotland U.K.
146 E6 Tweeddale val. Scotland U.K.
164 F2 Tweede Exloërmond Neth.
83 H2 Tweed Heads N.S.W. Austr.
223 I4 Tweedie Alta Can.
149 G2 Tweedmouth Northumberland, England U.K.
146 E6 Tweedsmuir Scottish Borders, Scotland U.K.
214 B5 Tweefontein S. Africa
215 G2 Tweeling S. Africa
215 F3 Tweespruit S. Africa
164 F2 Twello Neth.
241 I4 Twentynine Palms CA U.S.A.
225 K3 Twillingate Nfld. Can.
240 G2 Twin Bridges CA U.S.A.
238 D2 Twin Bridges MT U.S.A.
225 H2 Twin Falls Nfld. Can.
238 D3 Twin Falls ID U.S.A.
86 E4 Twin Heads hill W.A. Austr.
234 D1 Twin Lakes PA U.S.A.
233 H2 Twin Mountain NH U.S.A.
240 G2 Twin Peak CA U.S.A.
87 C7 Twin Peaks hill W.A. Austr.
232 C4 Twinsburg OH U.S.A.
238 B1 Twisp WA U.S.A.
168 C3 Twist Ger.
169 D4 Twiste (Twistetal) Ger.
168 D3 Twistringen Ger.
222 D1 Twitya r. N.W.T. Can.
81 C6 Twizel South I. N.Z.
237 C4 Two Butte Creek r. CO U.S.A.
226 B2 Two Harbors MN U.S.A.
223 I4 Two Hills Alta Can.
148 B5 Twomileborris Rep. of Ireland
147 D3 Two Mile Bridge Rep. of Ireland
226 D3 Two Rivers WI U.S.A.
174 G5 Tworóg Pol.
151 F3 Twyford Hampshire, England U.K.
151 G3 Twyford Wokingham, England U.K.
146 D7 Twynholm Dumfries and Galloway, Scotland U.K.
Tyachev Ukr. see Tyachiv
136 B3 Tyachiv Ukr.
137 G4 Tyahynka Ukr.
Tyan' Shan' mts China/Kyrg. see Tien Shan
Tyanshanskaya Oblast' admin. div. Kyrg. see Naryn
96 A2 Tyao r. India/Myanmar
137 G3 Tyasmyn r. Ukr.
102 M1 Tyatya, Vulkan vol. Rus. Fed.
174 E2 Tychowo Pol.
174 G5 Tychy Pol.
175 K6 Tyczyn Pol.
140 J3 Tydal Norway
148 B3 Tydavnet Rep. of Ireland
Tyddewi Pembrokeshire, Wales U.K. see St David's
232 D5 Tygart Valley WV U.S.A.
100 C1 Tygda Rus. Fed.
100 C1 Tygda r. Rus. Fed.
147 E2 Tyholland Rep. of Ireland
199 E1 Tykhero Greece
137 G2 Tykhonovychi Ukr.
175 K2 Tykocin Pol.
175 J6 Tylawa Pol.
237 E5 Tyler TX U.S.A.
237 F6 Tylertown MS U.S.A.
136 F4 Tylihul r. Ukr.
100 G2 Tym' r. Sakhalin Rus. Fed.
175 I6 Tymbark Pol.
137 G3 Tymchenky Ukr.
137 J3 Tymonove Ukr.
137 H4 Tymoshivka Ukr.
100 G2 Tymovskoye Sakhalin Rus. Fed.
198 D4 Tympaki Kriti Greece
164 F1 Tynaarlo Neth.
148 C3 Tynan Northern Ireland U.K.
131 N4 Tynda Rus. Fed.
236 D3 Tyndall SD U.S.A.
Tyndinskiy Rus. Fed. see Tynda
146 D5 Tyndrum Stirling, Scotland U.K.
146 F5 Tyne r. Scotland U.K.
149 H3 Tyne and Wear admin. div. England U.K.
176 E1 Týnec nad Labem Czech Rep
176 D2 Týnec nad Sázavou Czech Rep.
149 H2 Tynemouth Tyne and Wear, England U.K.
233 H3 Tyngsboro MA U.S.A.
143 E1 Tyngsjö Sweden
176 F1 Týniště nad Orlicí Czech Rep.
136 F3 Tynivka Ukr.
176 D2 Týn nad Vltavou Czech Rep.
136 D2 Tynne Ukr.
141 J3 Tynset Norway
Tyr Lebanon see Soûr
Tyras Ukr. see Bilhorod-Dnistrovs'kyy
175 K6 Tyrawa Wołoska Pol.
Tyre Lebanon see Soûr
262 S1 Tyree, Mount Antarctica
148 D3 Tyrella Northern Ireland U.K.
143 H2 Tyresö Sweden
173 G3 Tyrlaching Ger.
100 E2 Tyrma Rus. Fed.
100 D2 Tyrma r. Rus. Fed.
140 N2 Tyrnävä Fin.
198 C2 Tyrnavos Greece
129 C2 Tyrnyauz Rus. Fed.
Tyrol land Austria see Tirol
147 D2 Tyrone county Northern Ireland U.K.
239 E5 Tyrone NM U.S.A.
232 D4 Tyrone PA U.S.A.
83 E3 Tyrrell r. Vic. Austr.
83 E3 Tyrrell, Lake dry lake Vic. Austr.
147 D3 Tyrrellspass Rep. of Ireland
189 C5 Tyrrhenian Sea France/Italy
Tyrus Lebanon see Soûr
136 E3 Tysa r. Ukr. alt. Tisa (Yugoslavia), alt. Tisza (Hungary)
136 C3 Tysmenytsya Ukr.
142 A2 Tysnesøy i. Norway
142 A1 Tysse Norway
142 B1 Tyssedal Norway
175 L5 Tyszowce Pol.
150 D3 Tythegston Bridgend, Wales U.K.
138 D4 Tytuvėnai Lith.
129 E2 Tyube Rus. Fed.
129 E1 Tyub-Karagan, Poluostrov pen. Kazakh.
130 I4 Tyukalinsk Rus. Fed.
120 B3 Tyulen'i, Ostrova is Kazakh.
129 E1 Tyuleniy, Ostrov i. Rus. Fed.
120 D1 Tyul'gan Rus. Fed.
134 J4 Tyul'kino Rus. Fed.
130 H4 Tyumen' Rus. Fed.
Tyumen'-Aryk Kazakh. see Tomenaryk
121 J1 Tyumentsevo Rus. Fed.
131 N3 Tyung r. Rus. Fed.
Tyup Kyrg. see Tüp
106 C1 Tyva, Respublika aut. rep. Rus. Fed.
136 E3 Tyvriv Ukr.
174 C2 Tywa r. Pol.
150 C4 Tywardreath Cornwall, England U.K.
150 C3 Tywi r. Wales U.K.
150 C2 Tywyn Gwynedd, Wales U.K.
213 F4 Tzaneen S. Africa
243 H4 Tzucacab Mex.
164 E1 Tzummarum Neth.

U

Uaco Congo Angola see Waku-Kungo
79 □3 Ua Huka i. Fr. Polynesia
250 D4 Uainambi Brazil
Ualan atoll Micronesia see Kosrae
Üälīkhanov Kazakh. see Valikhanovo
79 □3 Ua Pou i. Fr. Polynesia
Ua Pu i. Fr. Polynesia see Ua Pou
251 E5 Uarini Brazil
87 B4 Uaroo W.A. Austr.
251 E3 Uasadi-jidi, Sierra mts Venez.
251 F4 Uatatás r. Brazil
251 G5 Uatumã r. Brazil
254 F4 Uauá Brazil
250 E5 Uaupés Brazil
250 E4 Uaupés r. Brazil
243 H5 Uaxactún Guat.
196 E3 Ub Srbija Yugo.
257 F4 Ubá Brazil
121 J2 Uba r. Kazakh.
169 E5 Übach-Palenberg Ger.
120 F1 Ubagan r. Kazakh.
257 E2 Ubaí Brazil
254 F5 Ubaitaba Brazil
124 C5 'Ubāl Yemen
120 C4 Ubal Karabaur hills Uzbek.
120 C4 Ubal Muzbel' hills Kazakh.
208 C5 Ubangi r. C.A.R./Dem. Rep. Congo
Ubangi-Shari country Africa see Central African Republic
257 F3 Ubaporanga Brazil
136 E1 Ubarts r. Belarus
250 C3 Ubate Col.
257 E5 Ubatuba Brazil
123 G4 Ubauro Pak.
161 E4 Ubaye r. France
103 E7 Ube Japan
185 G2 Úbeda Spain
256 D3 Uberaba Brazil
256 C4 Uberaba r. Brazil
172 A2 Überherrn Ger.
256 C3 Uberlândia Brazil
172 D4 Überlingen Ger.
173 G4 Übersee Ger.
183 H1 Ubidea Spain
256 A5 Ubiratã Brazil
227 F4 Ubly MI U.S.A.
137 I2 Ublya r. Rus. Fed.
96 C3 Ubolratna Reservoir Thai.
215 I2 Ubombo S. Africa
96 D4 Ubon Ratchathani Thai.
136 D2 Ubort' r. Ukr.
161 E5 Ubraye France
185 E4 Ubrique Spain
172 C2 Ubstadt-Weiher Ger.
208 E5 Ubundu Dem. Rep. Congo
261 F3 Ucacha Arg.
129 E3 Ucar Azer.
252 B2 Ucayali dept Peru
250 C5 Ucayali r. Peru
192 A2 Ucciani Corse France
165 D4 Uccle Belgium
183 G4 Uceda Spain
161 C4 Ucel France
183 G3 Ucero Spain
183 G3 Ucero r. Spain
123 G4 Uch Pak.
182 B3 Ucha Port.
123 E2 Uch-Adzhi Turkm.
Üchajy Turkm. see Uch-Adzhi
122 B2 Ūchān Iran
121 J3 Ucharal Kazakh.
161 C4 Uchaux France
105 E2 Uchimura-gawa r. Japan
104 C2 Uchinada Japan
102 J2 Uchiura-wan b. Japan
252 A2 Uchiza Peru
160 C2 Uchizy France
129 C2 Uchkeken Rus. Fed.
120 E4 Uchkuduk Uzbek.
121 F5 Uchkyay Uzbek.
Uchquduq Uzbek. see Uchkuduk
120 D4 Uchsay Uzbek.
Uchsoy Uzbek. see Uchsay
169 D3 Uchte Ger.
170 C3 Uchte r. Ger.
169 F5 Üchtelhausen Ger.
123 F5 Uchto r. Pak.
170 C3 Uchtspringe Ger.
131 O4 Uchur r. Rus. Fed.
183 F2 Ucieza r. Spain
157 G3 Uckange France
170 F1 Ückeritz Ger.
151 H4 Uckfield East Sussex, England U.K.
121 F4 Uckkulach Uzbek.
171 E4 Uckro Ger.
183 H5 Uclés Spain
222 E5 Ucluelet B.C. Can.
128 A1 Üçpınar Turkey
238 F2 Ucross WY U.S.A.
100 E1 Uda r. Rus. Fed.
137 I3 Uda r. Ukr.
129 D3 Udabno, Mt'a hill Georgia
135 I7 Udachnoye Rus. Fed.
131 M3 Udachnyy Rus. Fed.
114 C4 Udagamandalam Tamil Nadu India
116 C4 Udaipur Rajasthan India
116 C4 Udaipur Rajasthan India
117 G5 Udaipur Tripura India
116 D5 Udaipura Madh. Prad. India
175 L4 Udal r. Pol.
117 H4 Udalguri Assam India
174 E4 Udanin Pol.
117 E5 Udanti r. India/Myanmar
129 C1 Udarnyy Rus. Fed.
177 K3 Udava r. Slovakia
177 K3 Udavské Slovakia
137 G2 Uday r. Ukr.
114 C3 Udayagiri Andhra Prad. India
143 E1 Uddeholm Sweden
164 E2 Uddel Neth.
142 D2 Uddevalla Sweden
148 E2 Uddingston South Lanarkshire, Scotland U.K.
146 E6 Uddington South Lanarkshire, Scotland U.K.
140 L2 Uddjaure l. Sweden
129 C3 Ude Georgia
164 E3 Uden Neth.
164 E3 Udenhout Neth.
169 F4 Uder Ger.
178 C3 Uderns Austria
169 B5 Üdersdorf Ger.
114 C2 Udgir Mahar. India
Udhagamandalam Tamil Nadu India see Udagamandalam
116 C2 Udhampur Jammu and Kashmir
177 H2 Udiča Slovakia
134 I3 Udimskiy Rus. Fed.
191 I2 Udine Italy
191 H2 Udine prov. Friuli - Venezia Giulia Italy
Udmalaippettai Tamil Nadu India see Udumalaippettai
Udmurtia aut. rep. Rus. Fed. see Udmurtskaya Respublika
Udmurtskaya A.S.S.R. aut. rep. Rus. Fed. see Udmurtskaya Respublika
134 K4 Udmurtskaya Respublika aut. rep. Rus. Fed.
129 B1 Udobnaya Rus. Fed.
131 M4 Udokan, Khrebet mts Rus. Fed.
139 J3 Udomlya Rus. Fed.
96 C3 Udon Thani Thai.
174 F1 Udorpie Pol.
78 □4a Udot i. Chuuk Micronesia
175 L5 Udrycze Pol.
114 C4 Udumalaippettai Tamil Nadu India
114 B3 Udupi Karnataka India
137 I2 Udy Ukr.
Udzharma Georgia see Ujarma
Udzhary Azer. see Ucar
Uéa i. Î. Loyauté New Caledonia see Ouvéa
171 E4 Uebigau Ger.
170 F2 Uecker r. Ger.
170 F2 Ueckermünde Ger.
105 E2 Ueda Japan
173 E2 Uehlfeld Ger.
169 F3 Uehrde Ger.
93 B3 Uekuli Sulawesi Tengah Indon.
208 D3 Uele r. Dem. Rep. Congo
131 U3 Uelen Rus. Fed.
131 T3 Uel'kal' Rus. Fed.
169 B3 Uelsen Ger.
168 F3 Uelzen Ger.
104 C4 Ueno Japan
208 E4 Uere r. Dem. Rep. Congo
190 C2 Uetendorf Switz.
168 E2 Uetersen Ger.
172 D2 Uettingen Ger.
169 F3 Uetze Ger.
134 K5 Ufa Rus. Fed.
134 L5 Ufa r. Rus. Fed.
150 D4 Uffculme Devon, England U.K.
173 E2 Uffenheim Ger.
173 F4 Uffing am Staffelsee Ger.
193 H3 Ufita r. Italy
169 F4 Uftrungen Ger.
134 I3 Uftyuga r. Rus. Fed.
138 D3 Ugāle Latvia
211 A6 Ugalla r. Tanz.
210 B4 Uganda country Africa
188 F3 Ugar r. Bos.-Herz.
183 H1 Ugarana Spain
150 D4 Ugborough Devon, England U.K.
168 E1 Uge Denmark
195 H3 Ugento Italy
142 A1 Uggdal Norway
142 D3 Uggerby r. Denmark
195 H2 Uggiano la Chiesa Italy
207 G5 Ughelli Nigeria
215 G4 Ugie S. Africa
Ugi Island Solomon Is see Uki Island
185 G4 Ugíjar Spain
160 E3 Ugine France
100 G2 Uglegorsk Sakhalin Rus. Fed.
100 E4 Uglekamensk Rus. Fed.
134 L4 Ugleural'skiy Rus. Fed.
139 L3 Uglich Rus. Fed.
188 E3 Ugljan i. Croatia
139 I2 Uglovka Rus. Fed.
100 D2 Uglovoye Amurskaya Oblast' Rus. Fed.
100 E4 Uglovoye Primorskiy Kray Rus. Fed.
121 J2 Uglovskoye Rus. Fed.
177 G4 Ugod Hungary
Ugodskiy Zavod Rus. Fed. see Zhukovo
131 P3 Ugol'noye Rus. Fed.
Ugolnyy Chukotskiy Avtonomnyy Okrug Rus. Fed. see Beringovskiy
129 C2 Ugol'nyy Rus. Fed.
131 S3 Ugol'nyye Kopi Rus. Fed.
139 J4 Ugra Rus. Fed.
139 K4 Ugra r. Rus. Fed.
197 G4 Ugŭrchin Bulg.
130 I3 Ugut Rus. Fed.
177 K3 Uh r. Slovakia
Uharte-Arakil Spain see Huarte-Araquil
179 H2 Uherčice Czech Rep.
175 L4 Uherka r. Pol.
176 G2 Uherské Hradiště Czech Rep.
177 G2 Uherský Brod Czech Rep.
172 D3 Uhingen Ger.
176 C2 Úhlava r. Czech Rep.
172 D4 Uhldingen Ger.
176 E2 Uhlířské Janovice Czech Rep.
171 C5 Uhlstädt Ger.
136 B2 Uhniv Ukr.
232 C4 Uhrichsville OH U.S.A.
177 H3 Uhrovec Slovakia
137 H2 Uhroyidy Ukr.
171 C3 Uhrsleben Ger.
171 F4 Uhyst Ger.
254 E4 Uibaí Brazil
Uibhist a' Deas i. Scotland U.K. see South Uist
Uibhist a' Tuath i. Scotland U.K. see North Uist
171 C4 Uichteritz Ger.
146 B4 Uig Highland, Scotland U.K.
209 B6 Uíge Angola
209 B6 Uíge prov. Angola
101 C5 Ŭijŏngbu S. Korea
101 C4 Ŭiju N. Korea
120 C2 Uil Kazakh.
120 C2 Uil r. Kazakh.
129 C2 Uilpata, Gora mt. Rus. Fed.
140 O3 Uimaharju Fin.
241 K3 Uinkaret Plateau AZ U.S.A.
134 L4 Uinskoye Rus. Fed.
238 E3 Uinta r. CO U.S.A.
238 E3 Uinta Mountains UT U.S.A.
215 E5 Uitenhage S. Africa
164 D2 Uitgeest Neth.
164 D2 Uithoorn Neth.
164 F1 Uithuizen Neth.
164 F1 Uithuizermeeden Neth.
214 B3 Uitkyk S. Africa
214 C2 Uitsakpan salt pan S. Africa
214 B5 Uitspankraal S. Africa
177 J6 Uivar Romania
129 D3 Ujarma Georgia
175 H4 Ujazd Łódzkie Pol.
174 G5 Ujazd Opolskie Pol.
177 G2 Újezd Czech Rep.
176 F2 Újezd u Brna Czech Rep.
177 K4 Újfehértó Hungary
116 D4 Ujhani Uttar Prad. India
177 I4 Újhartyán Hungary
104 B4 Uji Japan
104 B4 Uji-gawa r. Japan
Ujiyamada Japan see Ise
116 C5 Ujjain Madh. Prad. India
177 L3 Újkenéz Hungary
176 F4 Újkér Hungary
177 K5 Újkígyós Hungary
177 K4 Újléta Hungary
177 H6 Újpetre Hungary
174 E2 Ujście Pol.
175 H6 Ujsoły Pol.
177 K5 Újszalonta Hungary
177 J4 Újszász Hungary
177 J5 Újszentiván Hungary
177 K4 Újszentmargita Hungary
177 I4 Újszilvás Hungary
177 K4 Újtikos Hungary
176 F5 Újudvar Hungary
93 A4 Ujung Pandang Sulawesi Selatan Indon.
Újvidék Vojvodina, Srbija Yugo. see Novi Sad
207 G4 Ukata Nigeria
102 □1 Uke-jima i. Japan
127 F4 Ukhaydir tourist site Iraq
124 D4 Ukhdūd tourist site Saudi Arabia
135 H5 Ukholovo Rus. Fed.
175 M4 Ukhovets'k Ukr.
117 H4 Ukhrul Manipur India
Ukhta Respublika Kareliya Rus. Fed. see Kalevala
134 K3 Ukhta Respublika Komi Rus. Fed.
134 K3 Ukhta r. Rus. Fed.
83 H2 Uki N.S.W. Austr.
240 F2 Ukiah CA U.S.A.
238 C2 Ukiah OR U.S.A.
78 □6 Uki Island Solomon Is
174 D2 Ukleja r. Pol.
138 E4 Ukmergė Lith.
136 F3 Ukraine country Europe
121 J2 Ukrainka Vostochnyy Kazakhstan Kazakh.
121 J2 Ukrainka Vostochnyy Kazakhstan Kazakh.
Ukrainka Ukr. see Ukrayinka
Ukrainskaya S.S.R. country Europe see Ukraine
Ukrainskoye Ukr. see Ukrayins'ke
Ukrayina country Europe see Ukraine
136 F2 Ukrayinka Ukr.
137 G2 Ukrayins'ke Ukr.
188 F3 Ukrina r. Bos.-Herz.
209 B7 Uku Angola
209 B8 Ukuma Angola
111 B6 Ul r. India
138 G4 Ula Belarus
138 G4 Ula r. Belarus
175 M1 Ūla r. Lith.
199 F3 Ula Turkey
106 E2 Ulaanbaatar Mongolia
106 E2 Ulaanbaatar mun. Mongolia
107 F2 Ulaan-Ereg Mongolia
106 B1 Ulaangom Mongolia
106 E2 Ulaanhudag Mongolia
106 D2 Ulaan-Uul Mongolia
107 F2 Ulaan-Uul Mongolia
83 G3 Ulan N.S.W. Austr.
107 F4 Ulan Nei Mongol China
106 C4 Ulan Qinghai China
Ulan Bator Mongolia see Ulaanbaatar
121 G3 Ulanbel' Kazakh.
135 I7 Ulan Erge Respublika Kalmykiya - Khalm'g-Tangch Rus. Fed.
Ulanhad Nei Mongol China see Chifeng
107 I2 Ulanhot Nei Mongol China
107 F3 Ulan Hua Nei Mongol China
136 E3 Ulaniv Ukr.
135 I7 Ulan-Khol Rus. Fed.
175 K4 Ulan-Majorat Pol.
137 H2 Ulanove Ukr.
175 K5 Ulanów Pol.
106 D3 Ulan Tohoi Nei Mongol China
98 I1 Ulan-Ude Rus. Fed.
260 D2 Ulapes Arg.
126 E3 Ulaş Turkey
199 E1 Ulaş Turkey
192 B5 Ulassai Sardegna Italy
78 □6 Ulawa Island Solomon Is
121 J2 Ul'ba Kazakh.
Ülbi Kazakh. see Ul'ba
138 E3 Ulbroka Latvia
146 E3 Ulbster Highland, Scotland U.K.
149 I4 Ulceby North Lincolnshire, England U.K.
101 D5 Ulchin S. Korea
196 D5 Ulcinj Crna Gora Yugo.
214 E3 Ulco S. Africa
142 C4 Uldum Denmark
107 F1 Uldz Mongolia
107 G1 Uldz r. Mongolia
Uleåborg Fin. see Oulu
142 C2 Ulefoss Norway
185 H3 Uleila del Campo Spain
138 F2 Ülenurme Estonia
107 G1 Ulety Rus. Fed.
175 K4 Ułęż Pol.
142 C3 Ulfborg Denmark
Ulflingen Lux. see Troisvierges
164 F3 Ulft Neth.
107 H2 Ulgain Gol r. China
149 H2 Ulgham Northumberland, England U.K.
114 B2 Ulhasnagar Mahar. India
175 L5 Ulhówek Pol.
107 H2 Uliastai Nei Mongol China
106 C2 Uliastay Mongolia
Uliatea i. Arch. de la Société Fr. Polynesia see Raiatea
177 L3 Ulič Slovakia
165 D3 Ulicoten Neth.
Ulie atoll Micronesia see Woleai
78 □3b Uliga i. Majuro Marshall Is
208 E5 Ulindi r. Dem. Rep. Congo
134 F1 Ulita r. Rus. Fed.
91 I4 Ulithi atoll Micronesia
Uljanovsk Rus. Fed. see Ul'yanovsk
120 E2 Ul'kayak r. Kazakh.
Ülkenözen r. Kazakh./Rus. Fed. see Bol'shoy Uzen'
121 H4 Ul'ken Sulutar Kazakh.
Ülken Vladīmīrovka Kazakh. see Bol'shaya Vladimirovka
182 B2 Ulla r. Spain
83 G3 Ulladulla N.S.W. Austr.
146 C4 Ullapool Highland, Scotland U.K.
142 E3 Ullared Sweden
140 M2 Ullatti Sweden
186 D4 Ulldecona Spain
186 D3 Ulldemolins Spain
142 D4 Ullerslev Denmark
177 I5 Üllés Hungary
149 H4 Ulleskelf North Yorkshire, England U.K.
262 S1 Ullmer, Mount Antarctica
252 C4 Ulloma Bol.
140 L1 Ullsfjorden sea chan. Norway
129 F2 Ulluchay r. Rus. Fed.
101 D5 Ullŭng-do i. S. Korea
172 D3 Ulm Ger.
100 D2 Ul'ma r. Rus. Fed.
169 E5 Ulmbach Ger.
184 B1 Ulme r. Port.
169 B5 Ulmen Ger.
197 H3 Ulmeni Călărași Romania
197 F2 Ulmeni Maramureș Romania
188 G4 Ulog Bos.-Herz.
213 G2 Ulongue Moz.
82 D1 Uloowaranie, Lake salt flat S.A. Austr.
149 F3 Ulpha Cumbria, England U.K.
142 E3 Ulricehamn Sweden
179 E2 Ulrichsberg Austria
169 E5 Ulrichstein Ger.
164 F1 Ulrum Neth.
101 D6 Ulsan S. Korea
146 □G1 Ulsta Shetland, Scotland U.K.
142 D3 Ulsted Denmark
140 I3 Ulsteinvik Norway
147 D2 Ulster reg. Rep. of Ireland/U.K.
227 I5 Ulster PA U.S.A.
235 D1 Ulster County county NY U.S.A.
83 E3 Ultima Vic. Austr.
252 B1 Ultraoriental, Cordillera mts Peru
242 □I6 Ulua r. Hond.
129 B3 Ulubağ Turkey
199 F2 Ulubey Turkey
199 G2 Uluborlu Turkey
199 F1 Uludağ mt. Turkey
94 C2 Ulu Kali, Gunung mt. Malaysia
126 D3 Ulukışla Turkey
199 G2 Uluköy Turkey
215 H3 Ulundi S. Africa
110 D2 Ulungur He r. China
110 D2 Ulungur Hu l. China
240 □C8 Ulupalakua HI U.S.A.
Uluqsaqtuuq N.W.T. Can. see Holman
84 B5 Uluru hill N.T. Austr.
199 F2 Ulus Dağı mt. Turkey
Ulutau Kazakh. see Ulytau
121 F3 Ulutau, Gory mts Kazakh.
146 B5 Ulva i. Scotland U.K.
Ulvéah i. Vanuatu see Lopévi
142 A2 Ulvenåso mt. Norway
164 D3 Ulvenhout Neth.
149 F3 Ulverston Cumbria, England U.K.
83 F5 Ulverstone Tas. Austr.
142 B1 Ulvik Norway
141 L3 Ulvsjön Sweden
139 K2 Ul'yanikha Rus. Fed.
137 F4 Ulyanivka Mykolayivs'ka Oblast' Ukr.
137 H2 Ulyanivka Sums'ka Oblast' Ukr.
Ūl'yanov Kazakh. see Ul'yanovskiy
139 H2 Ul'yanovka Rus. Fed.
136 F3 Ul'yanovka Ukr.
139 J5 Ul'yanovo Rus. Fed.
121 G4 Ul'yanovo Uzbek.
135 J5 Ul'yanovsk Rus. Fed.
135 I5 Ul'yanovskaya Oblast' admin. div. Rus. Fed.
121 H2 Ul'yanovskiy Kazakh.
Ulyanovsk Oblast admin. div. Rus. Fed. see Ul'yanovskaya Oblast'
Ul'yanovskoye Kazakh. see Ul'yanovskiy
107 H1 Ulyatuy Rus. Fed.
237 C4 Ulysses KS U.S.A.
232 B6 Ulysses KY U.S.A.
121 F2 Ulytau Kazakh.
120 E2 Uly-Zhylanshyk r. Kazakh.
183 I2 Ulzama r. Spain
100 E1 Uma Rus. Fed.
188 D3 Umag Croatia
252 D4 Umala Bol.
'Umān country Asia see Oman
243 H4 Umán Mex.
78 □4a Uman i. Chuuk Micronesia
136 F3 Uman' Ukr.
258 C3 Umango, Cerro mt. Arg.
116 E5 Umaria Madh. Prad. India
114 C2 Umarkhed Mahar. India
114 D2 Umarkot Orissa India
123 G5 Umarkot Pak.
82 D1 Umaroona, Lake salt flat S.A. Austr.
116 C5 Umarpada Gujarat India
238 C2 Umatilla OR U.S.A.
92 C4 Umayan r. Phil.
134 F2 Umba Murmanskaya Oblast' Rus. Fed.
84 D2 Umbakumba N.T. Austr.
84 C5 Umbeara N.T. Austr.
150 D4 Umberleigh Devon, England U.K.
191 H5 Umbertide Italy
81 B6 Umbrella Mountains South I. N.Z.
191 H5 Umbria admin. reg. Italy
195 F3 Umbriatico Italy
215 H3 Umdloti Beach S. Africa
213 F3 Ume r. Zimbabwe
140 M3 Umeå Sweden
140 M3 Umeälven r. Sweden
135 H5 Umet Rus. Fed.
215 I3 Umfolozi r. S. Africa
140 K2 Umfors Sweden
Umfuli r. Zimbabwe see Mupfure
215 H4 Umgababa S. Africa
215 H3 Umgeni r. S. Africa
125 D1 Umgharah Kuwait
215 H3 Umhali S. Africa
178 B3 Umhausen Austria
215 H3 Umhlanga S. Africa
182 B2 Umia r. Spain
105 D1 Umi-gawa r. Japan
240 □D9 Umikoa HI U.S.A.
220 H3 Umingmaktok Nunavut Can.
120 B4 Umirzak Kazakh.
224 E1 Umiujaq Que. Can.
172 B3 Umkirch Ger.
215 H4 Umkomaas S. Africa
215 H4 Umkomaas r. S. Africa
215 H3 Umlazi S. Africa
127 G5 Umma tourist site Iraq
128 B3 Umm ad Daraj, Jabal mt. Jordan
124 B3 Umm al Birak Saudi Arabia
128 B5 Umm al Hashīm, Jabal mt. Jordan
Umm al Qaywayn U.A.E. see Umm al Qaiwain
125 F2 Umm al Qaiwain U.A.E.
125 F3 Umm as Samīm salt flat Oman
125 E2 Umm Bāb Qatar
172 D3 Ummendorf Ger.
124 B2 Umm Lajj Saudi Arabia
128 B5 Umm Mafrûd, Gebel mt. Egypt
124 B3 Umm Mukhbār, Jabal hill Saudi Arabia
128 D5 Umm Nukhaylah hill Saudi Arabia
203 F6 Umm Ruwaba Sudan
202 E2 Umm Sa'ad Libya
125 E2 Umm Sa'id Qatar
128 B5 Umm Saysabān, Jabal mt. Jordan
128 A5 Umm Shomar, Gebel mt. Egypt
128 A5 Umm Tinâssib, Gebel mt. Egypt
128 D4 Umm Wa'āl hill Saudi Arabia
128 A5 Umm Zanatir mt. Egypt
220 B4 Umnak Island AK U.S.A.
238 A3 Umpqua r. OR U.S.A.
199 G2 Umraniye Turkey
116 D5 Umred Mahar. India
114 B1 Umreth Gujarat India
Umtali Zimbabwe see Mutare
215 H4 Umtamvuna r. S. Africa
215 G4 Umtata S. Africa
215 G4 Umtata r. S. Africa
215 H4 Umtentweni S. Africa
207 G5 Umuahia Nigeria
256 A5 Umuarama Brazil
129 E3 Umudlu Azer.
129 B3 Umudum Turkey
199 E1 Umurbey Turkey
199 F2 Umurlar Turkey
80 E4 Umutoi North I. N.Z.
215 H3 Umvoti r. S. Africa
Umvuma Zimbabwe see Mvuma
215 G4 Umzimhlava r. S. Africa
215 G4 Umzimkulu S. Africa
215 H4 Umzimkulu r. S. Africa
215 G4 Umzimvubu r. S. Africa
Umzingwani r. Zimbabwe see Mzingwani
215 H4 Umzinto S. Africa
215 H4 Umzumbe S. Africa
188 F3 Una r. Bos.-Herz./Croatia
255 F5 Una Brazil
254 G4 Una r. Brazil
116 D3 Una Hima. Prad. India
183 I4 Uña Spain
81 D5 Una, Mount South I. N.Z.
128 C5 'Unāb, Jabal al hill Jordan
188 F3 Unac r. Bos.-Herz.
182 D2 Uña de Quintana Spain
233 F3 Unadilla NY U.S.A.
233 F3 Unadilla r. NY U.S.A.
256 D2 Unaí Brazil
220 B3 Unalakleet AK U.S.A.
220 B4 Unalaska AK U.S.A.
220 B4 Unalaska Island AK U.S.A.
211 B8 Unango Moz.
176 F3 Únanov Czech Rep.
146 C3 Unapool Highland, Scotland U.K.
136 F2 Unava r. Ukr.
124 C2 'Unayzah Saudi Arabia
126 E4 'Unayzah, Jabal hill Iraq
186 B2 Uncastillo Spain
116 E4 Unchahra Madh. Prad. India
241 M2 Uncompahgre Plateau CO U.S.A.
215 G3 Underberg S. Africa
83 E3 Underbool Vic. Austr.
140 K3 Undersåker Sweden
236 C2 Underwood ND U.S.A.
172 D3 Undingen Ger.
135 J5 Undory Rus. Fed.
163 A6 Undués de Lerda Spain
150 E3 Undy Monmouthshire, Wales U.K.
139 I5 Unecha Rus. Fed.
139 H5 Unecha r. Rus. Fed.
251 E5 Uneiuxi r. Brazil
83 F3 Ungarie N.S.W. Austr.
82 D3 Ungarra S.A. Austr.
Ungava, Baie d' b. Que. Can. see Ungava Bay
221 K3 Ungava, Péninsule d' pen. Que. Can.
225 H1 Ungava Bay Que. Can.
Ungava Peninsula Que. Can. see Ungava, Péninsule d'
Ungeny Moldova see Ungheni
173 E3 Ungerhausen Ger.
100 D4 Unggi N. Korea
136 D4 Ungheni Moldova
197 G2 Ungheni Romania
Unguja North admin. reg. Tanz. see Zanzibar North
Unguja South admin. reg. Tanz. see Zanzibar South
Unguja West admin. reg. Tanz. see Zanzibar West
197 G2 Ungurași Romania
122 D2 Unguz, Solonchakovyye Vpadiny salt flat Turkm.
Üngüz Angyrsyndaky Garagum des. Turkm. see Zaunguzskiye Karakumy
Ungvár Ukr. see Uzhhorod
211 D5 Ungwana Bay Kenya
182 C4 Unhais da Serra Port.
182 C4 Unhais-o-Velho Port.
171 F5 Unhošt' Czech Rep.
134 J4 Uni Rus. Fed.
254 E3 União Brazil
255 C8 União da Vitória Brazil
254 G4 União dos Palmares Brazil
116 D4 Uniara Rajasthan India
176 G2 Uničov Czech Rep.
174 G4 Uniejów Pol.
161 C3 Unieux France
188 E3 Unije i. Croatia
220 B4 Unimak Island AK U.S.A.
176 G3 Unín Slovakia
251 F5 Unini r. Brazil
252 B2 Unini Peru
260 E4 Unión Arg.
253 F6 Unión Para.
233 □I2 Union ME U.S.A.
236 F4 Union MO U.S.A.
235 D2 Union NJ U.S.A.
238 C2 Union OR U.S.A.
231 D5 Union SC U.S.A.
232 C6 Union WV U.S.A.
259 E5 Unión, Bahía b. Arg.
241 K4 Union, Mount AZ U.S.A.
235 D2 Union Beach NJ U.S.A.
234 A3 Union Bridge MD U.S.A.
232 A4 Union City OH U.S.A.
232 D4 Union City PA U.S.A.
237 F4 Union City TN U.S.A.
235 D2 Union County county NJ U.S.A.
234 A2 Union County county PA U.S.A.
214 D5 Uniondale S. Africa
234 C1 Union Dale PA U.S.A.
246 B2 Unión de Reyes Cuba
244 B4 Unión de Tula Mex.
147 B5 Unionhall Rep. of Ireland
245 G5 Unión Hidalgo Mex.
247 □3 Union Island St Vincent
231 C5 Union Springs AL U.S.A.
232 E3 Union Springs NY U.S.A.
231 C5 Uniontown AL U.S.A.
232 D5 Uniontown PA U.S.A.
235 F1 Unionville CT U.S.A.
227 F4 Unionville MI U.S.A.
236 E3 Unionville MO U.S.A.
240 H1 Unionville NV U.S.A.
234 D1 Unionville NY U.S.A.
234 C3 Unionville PA U.S.A.
232 E5 Unionville VA U.S.A.
174 G2 Unisław Pol.
125 F3 United Arab Emirates country Asia
United Arab Republic country Africa see Egypt
145 G4 United Kingdom country Europe
United Provinces state India see Uttar Pradesh
228 G3 United States of America country N. America
221 L1 United States Range mts Nunavut Can.
191 H4 Uniti r. Italy
223 I4 Unity Sask. Can.
238 C2 Unity OR U.S.A.
234 B1 Unityville PA U.S.A.
116 C5 Unjha Gujarat India
169 C5 Unkel Ger.
178 D3 Unken Austria
172 D3 Unlingen Ger.
169 C4 Unna Ger.
116 E4 Unnao Uttar Prad. India
169 C5 Unnau Ger.
101 C5 Ŭnp'a N. Korea
261 E2 Unquillo Arg.
101 C4 Unsan P'yŏngan-bukto N. Korea
101 C5 Ŭnsan P'yŏngan-namdo N. Korea
129 C4 Ünseli Turkey
146 □H1 Unst i. Scotland U.K.
149 H4 Unstone Derbyshire, England U.K.
171 C4 Unstrut r. Ger.
117 E4 Untari Bihar India
197 H2 Unţeni Romania
190 D1 Unterägeri Switz.
173 F4 Unterammergau Ger.
169 E5 Unterbreizbach Ger.
173 E4 Unterdießen Ger.
173 G3 Unterdietfurt Ger.

169 E5 Unterfranken admin. reg. Bayern Ger.
173 H3 Untergriesbach Ger.
173 F3 Unterhaching Ger.
178 C3 Unter Inn Thal val. Austria
190 D1 Unterkulm Switz.
179 H4 Unterlamm Austria
168 F3 Unterlüß Ger.
169 F5 Untermaßfeld Ger.
173 E3 Untermeitingen Ger.
169 F5 Untermerzbach Ger.
172 D2 Untermünkheim Ger.
173 G3 Unterneukirchen Ger.
173 E2 Unterpleichfeld Ger.
173 G3 Unterreit Ger.
190 D2 Unterschächen Switz.
173 F3 Unterschleißheim Ger.
173 E3 Unterschneidheim Ger.
169 F5 Untersiemau Ger.
171 C5 Untersteinach Ger.
173 E4 Unterthingau Ger.
170 E2 Unterueckersee l. Ger.
179 F2 Unterweißenbach Austria
171 C5 Unterwellenborn Ger.
173 G4 Unterwössen Ger.
129 E2 Untsukul' Rus. Fed.
251 E4 Unturán, Sierra de mts Venez.
222 D3 Unuk r. Can./U.S.A.
106 A5 Unuli Horog Qinghai China
156 B4 Unverre France
134 L3 Un'ya r. Rus. Fed.
134 I4 Unzha Rus. Fed.
183 I2 Unzue Spain
102 □1 Uoturi-shima i. Japan
104 D2 Uozu Japan
176 E1 Úpa r. Czech Rep.
139 K4 Upa r. Rus. Fed.
241 L1 Upalco UT U.S.A.
117 F5 Upar Ghat reg. Madh. Prad. India
151 F3 Upavon Wiltshire, England U.K.
221 M2 Upernavik Greenland
168 C2 Upgant-Schott Ger.
92 C5 Upi Phil.
250 C3 Upía r. Col.
176 F1 Úpice Czech Rep.
214 C3 Upington S. Africa
141 N3 Upinniemi Fin.
240 I4 Upland CA U.S.A.
116 B5 Upleta Gujarat India
150 E4 Uplyme Devon, England U.K.
80 E3 Upokongaro North I. N.Z.
78 □2 Upolu i. Samoa
129 B1 Upornaya Rus. Fed.
232 B4 Upper Arlington OH U.S.A.
222 G5 Upper Arrow Lake B.C. Can.
Upper Austria land Austria see Oberösterreich
234 C2 Upper Black Eddy PA U.S.A.
146 E3 Upper Camster Highland, Scotland U.K.
150 D2 Upper Chapel Powys, Wales U.K.
Upper Chindwin Myanmar see Mawlaik
151 F3 Upper Clatford Hampshire, England U.K.
234 B3 Upper Crossroads MD U.S.A.
234 C3 Upper Darby PA U.S.A.
206 E4 Upper East admin. reg. Ghana
222 F4 Upper Fraser B.C. Can.
151 F3 Upper Heyford Oxfordshire, England U.K.
81 E4 Upper Hutt North I. N.Z.
226 B4 Upper Iowa r. IA U.S.A.
233 □J1 Upper Kent N.B. Can.
238 B3 Upper Klamath Lake OR U.S.A.
146 E4 Upper Knockando Moray, Scotland U.K.
147 E2 Upperlands Northern Ireland U.K.
222 D2 Upper Liard Y.T. Can.
147 D2 Upper Lough Erne l. Northern Ireland U.K.
234 B4 Upper Marlboro MD U.S.A.
210 B2 Upper Nile state Sudan
235 E1 Upper Nyack NY U.S.A.
232 B4 Upper Sandusky OH U.S.A.
Upper Seal Lake Que. Can. see Iberville, Lac d'
81 D4 Upper Takaka South I. N.Z.
151 F2 Upper Tean Staffordshire, England U.K.
Upper Tunguska r. Rus. Fed. see Angara
Upper Volta country Africa see Burkina
114 B3 Uppinangadi Karnataka India
151 G2 Uppingham Rutland, England U.K.
143 G2 Uppland reg. Sweden
143 G1 Upplanda Sweden
143 G2 Upplands-Väsby Sweden
143 G2 Uppsala Sweden
143 G1 Uppsala county Sweden
224 B3 Upsala Ont. Can.
116 D2 Upshi Jammu and Kashmir
226 B2 Upson WI U.S.A.
85 F3 Upstart Bay Qld Austr.
150 E4 Upton Dorset, England U.K.
233 H3 Upton MA U.S.A.
150 E3 Upton St Leonards Gloucestershire, England U.K.
150 E2 Upton upon Severn Worcestershire, England U.K.
80 E1 Upua North I. N.Z.
128 C2 'Uqayribāt Syria
124 C2 'Uqlat aş Şuqūr Saudi Arabia
Uqturpan Xinjiang China see Wushi
127 G5 Ur tourist site Iraq
Urad Qianqi Nei Mongol China see Xishanzui
107 F3 Urad Zhongqi Nei Mongol China
146 □G1 Urafirth Shetland, Scotland U.K.
190 E3 Urago d'Oglio Italy
140 P1 Ura-Guba Rus. Fed.
256 B5 Uraí Brazil
176 F4 Uraiújfalu Hungary
114 C4 Urakam Kerala India
83 F3 Ural hill N.S.W. Austr.
120 B3 Ural r. Kazakh./Rus. Fed.
83 G2 Uralla N.S.W. Austr.
Ural Mountains Rus. Fed. see Ural'skiy Khrebet
120 B2 Ural'sk Kazakh.
Ural'skaya Oblast' admin. div. Kazakh. see Zapadnyy Kazakhstan
Ural'skiye Gory mts Rus. Fed. see Ural'skiy Khrebet
134 L2 Ural'skiy Khrebet mts Rus. Fed.
211 B6 Urambo Tanz.
114 B2 Uran Mahar. India
83 F3 Urana N.S.W. Austr.
83 F3 Urana, Lake N.S.W. Austr.
84 D4 Urandangi Qld Austr.
254 E5 Urandi Brazil
223 I3 Uranium City Sask. Can.
83 F3 Uranquity N.S.W. Austr.
84 C2 Urapunga N.T. Austr.
84 C4 Urapuntja N.T. Austr.
251 F4 Uraricoera r. Brazil
Urartu country Asia see Armenia
192 A5 Uras Sardegna Italy
Ura-Tyube Tajik. see Üroteppa
114 C3 Uravakonda Andhra Prad. India
241 M2 Uravan CO U.S.A.
105 F3 Urawa Japan
130 H3 Uray Rus. Fed.
105 F3 Urayasu Japan
125 E2 Uray'irah Saudi Arabia
124 D2 'Urayq ad Duḩūl des. Saudi Arabia
124 D2 'Urayq Sāqān des. Saudi Arabia
174 E4 Uraz Pol.
135 I5 Urazovka Rus. Fed.
135 G6 Urazovo Rus. Fed.
169 C5 Urbach Ger.
236 F3 Urbana IL U.S.A.
226 E5 Urbana IN U.S.A.
232 B4 Urbana OH U.S.A.
191 H5 Urbania Italy
254 E2 Urbano Santos Brazil
169 C5 Urbar Ger.
190 D4 Urbe Italy
183 G2 Urbel r. Spain
83 H2 Urbenville N.S.W. Austr.
172 C2 Urberach Ger.
191 H5 Urbino Italy
Urbinum Italy see Urbino
183 H2 Urbión mt. Spain
191 I5 Urbisaglia Italy
160 B2 Urbise France
Urbs Vetus Italy see Orvieto
176 G2 Určice Czech Rep.
252 C3 Urcos Peru
163 A5 Urcuit France
185 G1 Urda Spain
261 G5 Urdampolleta Arg.
186 B1 Urdax Spain
Ur'devarri hill Fin./Norway see Urtivaara
261 H3 Urdinarrain Arg.
134 J3 Urdoma Rus. Fed.
172 C4 Urdorf Switz.
163 B6 Urdos France
106 D2 Urd Tamir Gol r. Mongolia
183 H1 Urduliz Spain
121 J3 Urdzhar Kazakh.
149 H3 Ure r. England U.K.
138 F5 Urechcha Belarus
197 H2 Urechești Romania
134 I4 Uren' Rus. Fed.
130 I3 Urengoy Rus. Fed.
142 B2 Urenosi mt. Norway
80 E3 Urenui North I. N.Z.
78 □5 Uréparapara i. Vanuatu
163 A5 Urepel France
164 F1 Ureterp Neth.
Urfa Turkey see Şanlıurfa
169 B5 Urft r. Ger.
Urga Mongolia see Ulaanbaatar
100 E2 Urgal r. Rus. Fed.
Urganch Uzbek. see Urgench
199 E2 Urganlı Turkey
120 E4 Urgench Uzbek.
126 D3 Ürgüp Turkey
121 F5 Urgut Uzbek.
110 D2 Urho Xinjiang China
192 A4 Uri Sardegna Italy
116 C2 Uri Jammu and Kashmir
190 D2 Uri canton Switz.
81 C5 Uriah, Mount South I. N.Z.
250 C2 Uribia Col.
146 F4 Urie r. Scotland U.K.
157 G4 Uriménil France
244 C4 Uripitijuata, Cerro mt. Mex.
239 F7 Urique r. Mex.
190 D2 Uri-Rotstock mt. Switz.
83 E2 Urisino N.S.W. Austr.
120 F1 Uritskiy Kazakh.
137 J1 Uritskoye Rus. Fed.
210 C1 Urī Wenz r. Eth.
141 M3 Urjala Fin.
164 E2 Urk Neth.
100 C1 Urkan Rus. Fed.
100 C1 Urkan r. Rus. Fed.
129 E2 Urkarakh Rus. Fed.
177 G4 Úrkút Hungary
199 E2 Urla Turkey
197 H3 Urlați Romania
147 D4 Urlingford Rep. of Ireland
197 G4 Urlui r. Romania
107 E1 Urluk Rus. Fed.
134 I5 Urmary Rus. Fed.
123 G2 Urmetan Tajik.
100 E2 Urmi r. Rus. Fed.
Urmia Iran see Orūmīyeh
Urmia, Lake salt l. Iran see Orūmīyeh, Daryācheh-ye
157 H2 Urmitz Ger.
149 G4 Urmston Greater Manchester, England U.K.
190 E1 Urnäsch Switz.
186 A1 Urola r. Spain
207 G5 Uromi Nigeria
196 E4 Uroševac Kosovo, Srbija Yugo.
123 G2 Ŭroteppa Tajik.
137 H5 Urozhayne Ukr.
129 D2 Urozhaynoye Rus. Fed.
183 H2 Urquilla, Sierra de mts Spain
184 C1 Urra Port.
186 C3 Urrea de Gaén Spain
186 B3 Urrea de Jalón Spain
163 A6 Urriés Spain
182 C3 Urros Port.
183 I2 Urroz Spain
163 A5 Urrugne France
Ursat'yevskaya Uzbek. see Khavast
173 E3 Ursberg Ger.
173 F2 Ursensollen Ger.
139 M4 Urshel'skiy Rus. Fed.
245 E2 Úrsulo Galván Mex.
245 F4 Ursulo Galván Mex.
163 A5 Ursuya, Mont hill France
175 L4 Urszulin Pol.
163 A5 Urt France
190 C1 Urtenen Switz.
140 M1 Urtivaara hill Fin./Norway
242 C3 Uruáchic Mex.
254 C5 Uruaçu Brazil
253 H3 Uruana Brazil
239 C6 Uruapan Baja California Norte Mex.
244 C4 Uruapan Michoacán Mex.
252 B3 Urubamba Peru
251 E5 Urubaxi r. Brazil
251 G5 Urubu r. Brazil
256 B4 Urubupungá, Salto do waterfall Brazil
251 G5 Urucara Brazil
251 F6 Urucu r. Brazil
254 D3 Uruçuí Brazil
254 D4 Uruçuí, Serra do hills Brazil
257 E2 Urucuia r. Brazil
254 D3 Uruçui Preto r. Brazil
251 G5 Urucurituba Brazil
183 E3 Urueña Spain
255 B8 Uruguai r. Brazil alt. Uruguay (Arg./Uru.)
258 F3 Uruguaiana Brazil
261 H3 Uruguay r. Arg./Uru. alt. Uruguai (Brazil)
258 G4 Uruguay country S. America
Uruk tourist site Iraq see Erech
129 D2 Urukh r. Rus. Fed.
92 □ Urukthapel i. Palau
Urumchi Xinjiang China see Ürümqi
110 D3 Ürümqi Xinjiang China
Urundi country Africa see Burundi
83 H2 Urunga N.S.W. Austr.
129 B2 Urup Rus. Fed.
129 B1 Urup r. Rus. Fed.
131 Q5 Urup, Ostrov i. Kuril'skiye O-va Rus. Fed.
253 E2 Urupá r. Brazil
256 C4 Urupês Brazil
Urupskaya Krasnodarskiy Kray Rus. Fed. see Sovetskaya
124 D4 'Urūq al Awārik des. Saudi Arabia
125 F3 'Urūq ash Shaybah des. Saudi Arabia
193 H3 Ururi Italy
100 B1 Urusha Rus. Fed.
100 B1 Urusha r. Rus. Fed.
129 D2 Urus-Martan Rus. Fed.
135 K5 Urussu Rus. Fed.
256 C2 Urutaí Brazil
80 E3 Uruti North I. N.Z.
211 A6 Uruwira Tanz.
129 C2 Urvan' Rus. Fed.
158 E2 Urville Nacqueville France
121 K2 Uryl' Kazakh.
102 J2 Uryū-gawa r. Japan
100 B1 Uryumkan r. Rus. Fed.
135 H6 Uryupinsk Rus. Fed.
184 B3 Urza hill Port.
175 K5 Urzędów Pol.
216 □1c Urzelina São Jorge Azores
Ürzhar Kazakh. see Urdzhar
134 J4 Urzhum Rus. Fed.
197 H3 Urziceni Ialomița Romania
177 L4 Urziceni Satu Mare Romania
137 I4 Urzuf Ukr.
192 B4 Urzulei Sardegna Italy
160 B1 Urzy France
138 G5 Usa r. Belarus
103 E7 Usa Japan
120 B1 Usa r. Rus. Fed.
134 L2 Usa r. Rus. Fed.
184 D2 Usagre Spain
199 F2 Uşak Turkey
199 F2 Uşak prov. Turkey
212 B4 Usakos Namibia
211 C6 Usambara Mountains Tanz.
263 K2 Usarp Mountains Antarctica
259 F8 Usborne, Mount hill Falkland Is
196 E4 Ušće Srbija Yugo.
169 E4 Uschlag (Staufenberg) Ger.
175 J6 Uście Gorlickie Pol.
175 I5 Uście Solne Pol.
190 E4 Uscio Italy
170 E2 Usedom Ger.
170 F2 Usedom i. Ger.
87 B5 Useless Loop W.A. Austr.
192 A5 Usellus Sardegna Italy
124 B3 Usfān Saudi Arabia
138 E5 Usha r. Belarus
138 G5 Usha r. Belarus
Ushachi Belarus see Ushachy
138 G4 Ushachy Belarus
121 J2 Ushanovo Kazakh.
Ushant i. France see Ouessant, Île d'
Üsharal Kazakh. see Ucharal
121 G4 Usharal Zhambylskaya Oblast' Kazakh.
149 H3 Ushaw Moor Durham, England U.K.
124 D2 Ushayqir Saudi Arabia
124 C3 'Ushayrah Saudi Arabia
129 C2 Ushba, Mt'a Georgia
138 G4 Ushcha r. Rus. Fed.
139 H5 Ushcherp'ye Rus. Fed.
103 E7 Ushibuka Japan
105 G2 Ushiku Japan
104 B5 Ushimawashi-yama mt. Japan
121 I3 Ushtobe Kazakh.
Ush-Tyube Kazakh. see Ushtobe
259 C9 Ushuaia Arg.
136 D3 Ushytsya r. Ukr.
169 D5 Usingen Ger.
192 A4 Usini Sardegna Italy
134 L2 Usinsk Rus. Fed.
150 E3 Usk Monmouthshire, Wales U.K.
150 E3 Usk r. Wales U.K.
117 E4 Uska Uttar Prad. India
138 F5 Uskhodni Belarus
Uskoplje Bos.-Herz. see Gornji Vakuf
199 F1 Üsküdar Turkey
197 H5 Üsküp Turkey
169 E4 Uslar Ger.
176 C2 Úslava r. Czech Rep.
139 L5 Usman' Rus. Fed.
139 L5 Usman' r. Rus. Fed.
121 F5 Usmat Uzbek.
Usmet Uzbek. see Usmat
183 E5 Uso r. Spain
134 J3 Usogorsk Rus. Fed.
211 B6 Usoke Tanz.
134 L4 Usol'ye Rus. Fed.
98 H1 Usol'ye-Sibirskoye Rus. Fed.
188 G3 Usora r. Bos.-Herz.
176 G2 Úsov Czech Rep.
137 H1 Usozha r. Rus. Fed.
137 H1 Usozha r. Rus. Fed.
260 C3 Uspallata Arg.
137 I4 Uspenivka Ukr.
121 I1 Uspenka Kazakh.
137 G3 Uspenka Kirovohrads'ka Oblast' Ukr.
137 G2 Uspenka Sums'ka Oblast' Ukr.
121 H2 Uspenskiy Kazakh.
135 H7 Uspenskoye Rus. Fed.
134 H4 Uspen'ye Rus. Fed.
164 F1 Usquert Neth.
192 B5 Ussana Sardegna Italy
192 B5 Ussassai Sardegna Italy
161 F3 Usseglio Italy
161 A3 Ussel Auvergne France
162 E3 Ussel Limousin France
160 D3 Usses r. France
162 C2 Usson-du-Poitou France
161 B3 Usson-en-Forez France
100 E2 Ussuri r. Rus. Fed.
100 D4 Ussuriysk Rus. Fed.
134 I4 Usta r. Rus. Fed.
Ust'-Abakanskoye Rus. Fed. see Abakan
134 I3 Ust'-Alekseyevo Rus. Fed.
123 G4 Usta Muhammad Pak.
163 A5 Ustaritz France
Ust'-Balyk Rus. Fed. see Nefteyugansk
99 I1 Ust'-Barguzin Rus. Fed.
135 H7 Ust'-Donetskiy Rus. Fed.
129 B1 Ust'-Dzheguta Rus. Fed.
Ust'-Dzhegutinskaya Rus. Fed. see Ust'-Dzheguta
176 C1 Ústecký kraj admin. reg. Czech Rep.
176 D1 Úštěk Czech Rep.
190 D1 Uster Switz.
194 C4 Ustica Sicilia Italy
194 C4 Ustica, Isola di i. Sicilia Italy
131 L4 Ust'-Ilimsk Rus. Fed.
131 L4 Ust'-Ilimskiy Vodokhrinilishche resr Rus. Fed.
107 G1 Ust'-Ilya Rus. Fed.
176 D1 Ústí nad Labem Czech Rep.
176 F2 Ústí nad Orlicí Czech Rep.
Ustinov Rus. Fed. see Izhevsk
Ustirt plat. Kazakh./Uzbek. see Ustyurt Plateau
143 G4 Ustka Pol.
121 J1 Ust'-Kalmanka Rus. Fed.
131 R4 Ust'-Kamchatsk Rus. Fed.
121 J2 Ust'-Kamenogorsk Kazakh.
110 D1 Ust'-Kan Rus. Fed.
100 A1 Ust'-Karsk Rus. Fed.
110 D1 Ust'-Koksa Rus. Fed.
134 K3 Ust'-Kulom Rus. Fed.
131 L4 Ust'-Kut Rus. Fed.
131 O2 Ust'-Kuyga Rus. Fed.
135 G7 Ust'-Labinsk Rus. Fed.
Ust'-Labinskaya Rus. Fed. see Ust'-Labinsk
131 O3 Ust'-Maya Rus. Fed.
Ust'-Mongunay Rus. Fed. see Primorskiy
131 P3 Ust'-Nera Rus. Fed.
131 M2 Ust'-Olenek Rus. Fed.
131 P3 Ust'-Omchug Rus. Fed.
98 H1 Ust'-Ordynskiy Rus. Fed.
98 H1 Ust'-Ordynskiy Buryatskiy Avtonomnyy Okrug admin. div. Rus. Fed.
163 D6 Ustou France
197 H4 Ustrem Bulg.
174 G6 Ustroń Pol.
174 D1 Ustronie Morskie Pol.
175 K6 Ustrzyki Dolne Pol.
134 H3 Ust'-Shonosha Rus. Fed.
134 K2 Ust'-Tsil'ma Rus. Fed.
110 D1 Ust'-Ulagan Rus. Fed.
100 E2 Ust'-Umalta Rus. Fed.
134 L2 Ust'-Usa Rus. Fed.
120 E1 Ust'-Uyskoye Kazakh.
134 H3 Ust'-Vayen'ga Rus. Fed.
134 H3 Ust'ya r. Rus. Fed.
134 G4 Ust'ye Rus. Fed.
134 H4 Ust'ye Rus. Fed.
139 L3 Ust'ye r. Rus. Fed.
139 J2 Ust'ye-Kirovskoye Rus. Fed.
136 C2 Ustyluh Ukr.
137 G4 Ustynivka Ukr.
Ustyurt, Plato plat. Kazakh./Uzbek. see Ustyurt Plateau
120 D4 Ustyurt Plateau Kazakh./Uzbek.
Ustyurt Platosi plat. Kazakh./Uzbek. see Ustyurt Plateau
139 J2 Ustyutskoye Rus. Fed.
139 K2 Ustyuzhna Rus. Fed.
110 D2 Usu Xinjiang China
103 E7 Usuki Japan
242 □H6 Usulután El Salvador
243 G5 Usumacinta r. Guat./Mex.
Usumbura Burundi see Bujumbura
95 F2 Usun Apau, Dataran Tinggi plat. Sarawak Malaysia
186 A1 Usurbil Spain
175 H6 Úšust mt. Pol.
215 I2 Usutu r. Africa
134 L4 Us'va Rus. Fed.
139 H4 Usvyaty Rus. Fed.
138 G4 Usvyeyka r. Belarus
175 I6 Uszew Pol.
177 H5 Uszód Hungary
175 I5 Uszwica r. Pol.
192 A5 Uta Sardegna Italy
241 L2 Utah state U.S.A.
140 N2 Utajärvi Fin.
168 C2 Utarp Ger.
Utashinai Kuril'skiye O-va Rus. Fed. see Yuzhno-Kuril'sk
125 E2 Utayyiq Saudi Arabia
186 C3 Utebo Spain
237 C5 Ute Creek r. NM U.S.A.
161 F5 Utelle France
209 D9 Utembo r. Angola
138 E4 Utena Lith.
168 D1 Utersum Ger.
211 C7 Utete Tanz.
96 C4 Uthai Thani Thai.
123 F5 Uthal Pak.
169 F4 Uthleben Ger.
168 D2 Uthlede Ger.
227 F4 Utica MI U.S.A.
237 F5 Utica MS U.S.A.
233 F3 Utica NY U.S.A.
232 B4 Utica OH U.S.A.
187 B5 Utiel Spain
242 □I5 Utila Hond.
254 E5 Utinga r. Brazil
215 E2 Utlwanang S. Africa
103 E7 Uto Japan
84 C4 Utopia N.T. Austr.
175 I3 Utrata r. Pol.
116 E4 Utraula Uttar Prad. India
164 E2 Utrecht Neth.
164 E2 Utrecht prov. Neth.
215 H2 Utrecht S. Africa
184 E3 Utrera Spain
186 C4 Utrillas Spain
177 I6 Utrine Vojvodina, Srbija Yugo.
138 G3 Utroya r. Rus. Fed.
142 A2 Utsira Norway
140 N1 Utsjoki Fin.
105 D3 Utsugi-dake mt. Japan
105 F2 Utsunomiya Japan
135 I7 Utta Rus. Fed.
96 C3 Uttaradit Thai.
116 D3 Uttarkashi Uttar Prad. India
116 D4 Uttar Pradesh state India
178 E2 Uttendorf Oberösterreich Austria
178 D3 Uttendorf Salzburg Austria
173 F2 Uttenreuth Ger.
172 D3 Uttenweiler Ger.
168 G1 Utterslev Denmark
173 F3 Utting am Ammersee Ger.
151 F2 Uttoxeter Staffordshire, England U.K.
Utu Xinjiang China see Miao'ergou
247 □1 Utuado Puerto Rico
110 D2 Utubulak Xinjiang China
78 □6 Utupua i. Solomon Is
120 C2 Utva r. Kazakh.
170 E2 Utzedel Ger.
221 M2 Uummannaq Greenland
Uummannarsuaq c. Greenland see Nunap Isua
140 N3 Uurainen Fin.
106 D1 Üür Gol r. Mongolia
Uusikaarlepyy Fin. see Nykarleby
141 M3 Uusikaupunki Fin.
212 B3 Uutapi Namibia
250 D4 Uva r. Col.
134 K4 Uva Rus. Fed.
196 D4 Uvac r. Bos.-Herz./Yugo.
237 D6 Uvalde TX U.S.A.
176 D1 Úvaly Czech Rep.
139 H5 Uvaravichy Belarus
139 J4 Uvarovka Rus. Fed.
135 H6 Uvarovo Rus. Fed.
Uvéa i. Î. Loyauté New Caledonia see Ouvéa
120 E1 Uvel'ka r. Rus. Fed.
139 J2 Uver' r. Rus. Fed.
161 E4 Uvernet-Fours France
211 A6 Uvinza Tanz.
209 F5 Uvira Dem. Rep. Congo
139 M3 Uvod' r. Rus. Fed.
215 H4 Uvongo S. Africa
106 B1 Uvs prov. Mongolia
106 B1 Uvs Nuur salt l. Mongolia
103 F7 Uwajima Japan
124 B2 'Uwayriḑ, Ḩarrat al lava field Saudi Arabia
202 E4 Uweinat, Jebel mt. Sudan
227 H3 Uxbridge Ont. Can.
151 G3 Uxbridge Greater London, England U.K.
160 C2 Uxeau France
169 B5 Üxheim Ger.
107 F4 Uxin Ju Nei Mongol China
Uxin Qi Nei Mongol China see Dabqig
243 H4 Uxmal tourist site Mex.
245 G5 Uxpanapa r. Mex.
110 D3 Uxxaktal Xinjiang China
120 E1 Uy r. Rus. Fed.
131 K4 Uyar Rus. Fed.
106 E2 Üydzin Mongolia
146 □H1 Uyea i. Scotland U.K.
146 □H1 Uyeasound Shetland, Scotland U.K.
207 G5 Uyo Nigeria
106 B2 Üyönch Mongolia
106 A2 Üyönch Gol r. China
120 E1 Uyskoye Rus. Fed.
96 A1 Uyu Chaung r. Myanmar
121 G4 Uyuk Kazakh.
125 E2 Uyun Saudi Arabia
252 D5 Uyuni, Salar de salt flat Bol.
163 A4 Uza France
120 A1 Uza r. Rus. Fed.
127 G4 'Uzaym, Nahr al r. Iraq
120 E4 Uzbekistan country Asia
Ŭzbekiston country Asia see Uzbekistan
Uzbekskaya S.S.R. country Asia see Uzbekistan
Uzbek S.S.R. country Asia see Uzbekistan
138 F5 Uzda Belarus
158 D3 Uzel France
Uzen' Kazakh. see Kyzylsay
121 I4 Uzengyu-Kuush, Gora mt. China/Kyrg.
161 C4 Uzer France
162 D3 Uzerche France
161 C4 Uzès France
Uzgen Kyrg. see Özgön
136 B3 Uzh r. Ukr.
136 F2 Uzh r. Ukr.
139 I4 Uzha r. Rus. Fed.
Uzhgorod Ukr. see Uzhhorod
136 B3 Uzhhorod Ukr.
136 B3 Uzhok Ukr.
Užhorod Ukr. see Uzhhorod
196 D4 Užice Srbija Yugo.
139 L5 Uzlovaya Rus. Fed.
134 H4 Uzola r. Rus. Fed.
129 A4 Üzümlü Turkey
199 F3 Üzümlü Turkey
121 G5 Uzun Uzbek.
121 I4 Uzunagach Almatinskaya Oblast' Kazakh.
121 I4 Uzunagach Almatinskaya Oblast' Kazakh.
110 D2 Uzunbulak Xinjiang China
128 A1 Uzuncaburç Turkey
129 B3 Uzundere Turkey
129 B3 Uzungöl Turkey
199 E1 Uzunköprü Turkey
129 F4 Uzuntäpä Azer.
138 D4 Užventis Lith.
136 F3 Uzyn Ukr.
Uzynaghash Almatinskaya Oblast' Kazakh. see Uzunagach
120 E3 Uzynkair Kazakh.

V

113 □1 Vaadhu i. S. Male Maldives
113 □1 Vaagali i. S. Male Maldives
134 D3 Vaajakoski Fin.
215 D3 Vaal r. S. Africa
140 N2 Vaala Fin.
215 G2 Vaal Dam S. Africa
168 E2 Vaale Ger.
215 G1 Vaalplass S. Africa
165 F4 Vaals Neth.
165 F4 Vaalserberg hill Neth.
213 F5 Vaalwater S. Africa
159 G4 Vaas France
140 M3 Vaasa Fin.
164 E2 Vaassen Neth.
113 □1 Vaataru i. N. Male Maldives
138 E4 Vabalninkas Lith.
138 G5 Vabich r. Belarus
120 F4 Vabkent Uzbek.
139 I5 Vablya r. Rus. Fed.
163 E5 Vabre France
161 A5 Vabres-l'Abbaye France
177 I4 Vác Hungary
195 F4 Vacale r. Italy
257 E4 Vacaré r. Brazil
255 C9 Vacaria Brazil
257 F2 Vacaria r. Minas Gerais Brazil
255 B7 Vacaria r. Mato Grosso do Sul Brazil
240 G2 Vacaville CA U.S.A.
161 C5 Vaccarès, Étang de lag. France
195 F3 Vaccarizzo Albanese Italy
169 F5 Vacha Ger.
134 H5 Vacha Rus. Fed.
177 I4 Váchartyán Hungary
160 E2 Vacheresse France
129 E2 Vachi Rus. Fed.
143 F3 Väckelsång Sweden
173 H2 Vacov Czech Rep.
161 C4 Vacqueyras France
197 H2 Văculești Romania
134 I5 Vad Rus. Fed.
135 H5 Vad r. Rus. Fed.
114 B2 Vada Mahar. India
138 D3 Vadakste r. Latvia/Lith.
197 G4 Vădăstrița Romania
142 C4 Vadehavet sea chan. Denmark
197 H3 Vădeni Romania
136 E4 Vădeni, Dealul hill Moldova
114 B3 Vadi Mahar. India
135 H5 Vadinsk Rus. Fed.
183 G3 Vadocondes Spain
116 C5 Vadodara Gujarat India
190 D4 Vado Ligure Italy
140 O1 Vadsø Norway
143 F2 Vadstena Sweden
197 F2 Vadu Crișului Romania
172 D4 Vaduz Liechtenstein
170 C1 Væggerløse Denmark
140 K2 Værøy i. Norway
134 H3 Vaga r. Rus. Fed.
141 J3 Vågåmo Norway
188 E3 Vaganski Vrh mt. Croatia
144 D1 Vágar i. Faroe Is
114 D2 Vagavaram Andhra Prad. India
143 F3 Vaggeryd Sweden
78 □6 Vaghena i. Solomon Is
198 C2 Vagia Sterea Ellas Greece
191 G5 Vaglia Italy
193 H4 Vaglio Basilicata Italy
190 F4 Vagli Sotto Italy
157 G4 Vagney France
143 G2 Vagnhärad Sweden
182 B4 Vagos Port.
140 L2 Vägsele Sweden
140 L1 Vågsfjorden sea chan. Norway
177 H4 Váh r. Slovakia
140 M3 Vähäkyrö Fin.
169 E4 Vahlbruch Ger.
259 □ Vahsel, Cape S. Georgia
141 M3 Vahto Fin.
77 H2 Vaiaku Tuvalu
184 C1 Vaiamonte Port.
191 G5 Vaiano Italy
138 E2 Vaida Estonia
237 F5 Vaiden MS U.S.A.
114 C4 Vaigai r. India
159 F3 Vaiges France
172 C3 Vaihingen an der Enz Ger.
114 B2 Vaijapur Mahar. India
114 C4 Vaikam Kerala India
138 F2 Väike Emajõgi r. Estonia
138 F2 Väike-Maarja Estonia
140 L2 Vaikijaur Sweden
236 B4 Vail CO U.S.A.
146 □G1 Vaila i. Scotland U.K.
156 D3 Vailly-sur-Aisne France
160 A1 Vailly-sur-Sauldre France
235 D1 Vails Gate NY U.S.A.
138 F3 Väimela Estonia
138 C3 Vaiņode Latvia
114 C4 Vaippar r. India
157 F4 Vair r. France
193 G3 Vairano Patenora Italy
193 G3 Vairano Scalo Italy
161 E5 Vaire r. France
116 C3 Vairowal Punjab India
182 B4 Vais Port.
161 D4 Vaison-la-Romaine France
163 D4 Vaïssac France
77 H2 Vaitupu i. Tuvalu
160 E1 Vaivre-et-Montoille France
177 L4 Vaja Hungary
Vajrakarur Andhra Prad. India see Kanur
177 G6 Vajszló Hungary
177 H5 Vajta Hungary
208 D2 Vakaga pref. C.A.R.
208 D2 Vakaga r. C.A.R.
137 J3 Vakhrusheve Ukr.
123 G2 Vakhsh Tajik.
123 G2 Vakhsh r. Tajik.
Vakhshstroy Tajik. see Vakhsh
134 I4 Vakhtan Rus. Fed.
142 A1 Vaksdal Norway
197 E4 Vaksince Macedonia
177 H4 Vál Hungary
140 K3 Vålådalen Sweden
182 B2 Valadares Port.
182 C1 Valadouro mts Spain
190 C2 Valais canton Switz.
177 K3 Valaliky Slovakia
134 K4 Valamaz Rus. Fed.
197 F5 Valandovo Macedonia
159 F4 Valanjou France
183 I2 Valareña Spain
177 I3 Valaská Slovakia
177 G2 Valašská Polanka Czech Rep.
177 H2 Valašské Klobouky Czech Rep.
177 G2 Valašské Meziříčí Czech Rep.
227 J2 Val-Barrette Que. Can.
161 E4 Valberg France
143 G1 Valbo Sweden
187 C4 Valbona Spain
190 F2 Valbondione Italy
161 D4 Valbonnais France
161 F5 Valbonne France
183 F3 Valbuena de Duero Spain
177 H2 Valča Slovakia
197 G3 Vâlcănești Romania
197 F3 Vâlcanului, Munții mts Romania
177 L4 Valcău de Jos Romania
161 E3 Val-Cenis France
259 D6 Valcheta Arg.
186 D3 Valcuerna r. Spain
191 G3 Valdagno Italy
160 E1 Valdahon France
Valdai Hills Rus. Fed. see Valdayskaya Vozvyshennost'
191 H2 Valdaora Italy
183 F2 Valdavia r. Spain
139 I3 Valday Rus. Fed.
139 I3 Valdayskaya Vozvyshennost' hills Rus. Fed.
139 I2 Valdayskoye, Ozero l. Rus. Fed.
186 C3 Valdealgorfa Spain
185 F2 Valdeazogues r. Spain
161 F4 Valdeblore France
185 E1 Valdecaballeros Spain
182 E5 Valdecañas, Embalse de resr Spain
182 E5 Valdecañas de Tajo Spain
183 E4 Valdecarros Spain
183 F2 Valdecebollas mt. Spain
183 G1 Valdecilla Spain
183 I4 Valdecuenca Spain
184 D1 Valdefuentes Spain
185 I1 Valdeganga Spain
183 F2 Valdeginate r. Spain
182 E4 Valdelacasa Spain
183 E5 Valdelacasa de Tajo Spain
184 D3 Valdelamusa Spain
186 C4 Valdelinares Spain
183 I4 Valdellosa mt. Spain
185 F2 Valdemanco del Esteras Spain
159 I3 Val-de-Marne dept France
138 D3 Valdemārpils Latvia
143 G2 Valdemarsvik Sweden
183 I4 Valdemeca Spain
184 D2 Valdemedé r. Spain
183 I5 Valdemembra r. Spain
157 F4 Val-de-Meuse France
183 F4 Valdemorillo Spain
183 G4 Valdemoro Spain
183 I4 Valdemoro-Sierra Spain
183 G4 Valdenoches Spain
261 I4 Valdense Uru.
182 D4 Valdeobispo Spain
185 G2 Valdepeñas Spain
185 G3 Valdepeñas de Jaén Spain
183 E2 Valdepiélago Spain
183 E3 Valderaduey r. Spain
183 E2 Valderas Spain
156 B3 Val-de-Reuil France
194 B4 Valderice Sicilia Italy
163 E4 Valderiès France
186 D4 Valderrobes Spain
183 F2 Valderrueda Spain
226 D3 Valders WI U.S.A.
261 G4 Valdés Arg.
259 E6 Valdés, Península pen. Arg.
183 F4 Val de Santo Domingo Spain
227 J3 Val-des-Bois Que. Can.
183 F3 Valdestillas Spain
186 D4 Valdetormo Spain
184 D2 Valdetorres Spain
183 E5 Valdeverdeja Spain
182 E2 Valdevimbre Spain
250 B4 Valdez Ecuador
220 D3 Valdez AK U.S.A.
Valdgeym Ukr. see Dobropillya
190 F2 Valdidentro Italy
183 F4 Valdihuelo mt. Spain
183 G4 Valdilecha Spain
161 E3 Val-d'Isère France
190 F2 Valdisotto Italy
259 B5 Valdivia Chile
250 C3 Valdivia Col.
162 C2 Valdivienne France
158 E3 Val-d'Izé France
191 G3 Valdobbiadene Italy
157 G5 Valdoie France
156 C3 Val-d'Oise dept Île-de-France France
224 E3 Val-d'Or Que. Can.
183 G3 Valdosa mt. Spain
231 D6 Valdosta GA U.S.A.
141 J3 Valdres val. Norway
161 D4 Valdrôme France
183 E2 Valdunquillo Spain
158 D2 Vale Channel Is
129 C3 Vale Georgia
238 C2 Vale OR U.S.A.
197 F2 Valea lui Mihai Romania
197 G2 Valea Lungă Romania
197 G3 Valea Lungă Romania
184 C3 Vale da Rosa Port.
184 B1 Vale das Mós Port.
184 C3 Vale de Açor Port.
184 C1 Vale de Açor Port.
182 B4 Vale de Cambra Port.
184 B1 Vale de Cavalos Port.
182 D4 Vale de Espinho Port.
182 C4 Vale de Estrela Port.
184 B1 Vale de Figueira Port.
184 B2 Vale de Guiso Port.
182 C4 Vale de Prazeres Port.
184 B2 Vale de Reis Port.
182 C3 Vale de Salgueiro Port.
184 B1 Vale de Santarém Port.
184 C3 Vale de Vargo Port.
184 C2 Vale do Pereiro Port.
184 C1 Vale do Peso Port.
182 B4 Válega Port.
191 F3 Valeggio sul Mincio Italy
222 G4 Valemount B.C. Can.
254 F5 Valença Brazil
182 B2 Valença Port.
254 E3 Valença do Piauí Brazil
162 D1 Valençay France
163 C4 Valence Midi-Pyrénées France
161 C4 Valence Rhône-Alpes France
163 E4 Valence-d'Albigeois France
163 C5 Valence-sur-Baïse France
187 C5 Valencia Spain
187 C5 Valencia aut. comm. Spain
187 C5 Valencia prov. Valencia Spain
250 E2 Valencia Venez.
187 D5 Valencia, Golfo de g. Spain
184 C1 Valencia de Alcántara Spain
182 E2 Valencia de Don Juan Spain
184 D2 Valencia de las Torres Spain
184 C2 Valencia del Mombuey Spain
184 D2 Valencia del Ventoso Spain
147 A5 Valencia Island Rep. of Ireland
Valenciana, Comunidad aut. comm. Spain see Valencia
156 D2 Valenciennes France
197 H3 Vălenii de Munte Romania
161 D5 Valensole France
161 E5 Valensole, Plateau de France
192 D2 Valentano Italy
245 F4 Valente Díaz y La Loma Mex.
Valentia Spain see Valencia
160 E1 Valentigney France
100 E4 Valentin Rus. Fed.
163 C5 Valentine France
236 C3 Valentine NE U.S.A.
239 F6 Valentine TX U.S.A.
190 D3 Valenza Italy
195 F1 Valenzano Italy
92 B3 Valenzuela Phil.
185 F3 Valenzuela Spain
185 G2 Valenzuela de Calatrava Spain
150 D3 Vale of Glamorgan admin. div. Wales U.K.
142 D1 Våler Norway
250 D2 Valera Venez.
183 H5 Valera de Arriba Spain
161 D4 Valernes France
184 C3 Vales Mortos Port.
193 E1 Valfabbrica Italy
186 C3 Valfarta Spain
157 G4 Valfroicourt France
190 F2 Valfurva Italy
138 F3 Valga Estonia
Valga Spain see Ponte Valga
138 E2 Valgejõgi r. Estonia
161 C4 Valgorge France
190 C3 Valgrisenche Italy
194 D5 Valguarnera Caropepe Sicilia Italy
235 E1 Valhalla NY U.S.A.
182 C4 Valhelhas Port.
183 I4 Valhermoso Spain
163 D6 Valier, Mont mt. France
121 G1 Valikhanovo Kazakh.
256 D5 Valinhos Brazil
186 E2 Valira r. Andorra/Spain
196 D3 Valjevo Srbija Yugo.
186 D4 Valjunquera Spain
138 F3 Valka Latvia
141 N3 Valkeakoski Fin.
165 E4 Valkenburg Limburg Neth.
164 D2 Valkenburg Zuid-Holland Neth.
165 E3 Valkenswaard Neth.
138 F1 Valko Fin.
177 I4 Valkó Hungary
Valkoni Fin. see Valko
137 H3 Valky Ukr.
263 C1 Valkyrie Dome ice feature Antarctica
116 B5 Vallabhipur Gujarat India
161 C5 Vallabrègues France
187 C6 Vallada Spain
243 H4 Valladolid Mex.
183 F3 Valladolid Spain
183 F3 Valladolid prov. Castilla y León Spain
187 B7 Valladolises Spain
177 L4 Vállaj Hungary
161 F5 Vallauris France
146 A4 Vallay i. Scotland U.K.
140 I3 Valldal Norway
187 C4 Vall d'Alba Spain
187 F5 Valldemossa Spain
187 C5 Vall de Uxó Spain
250 B4 Valle dept Col.
142 B2 Valle Norway
183 F1 Valle Spain
193 F2 Valle Castellana Italy
193 F3 Vallecorsa Italy
190 C3 Valle d'Aosta admin. reg. Italy
185 F4 Valle de Abdalajís Spain
244 D4 Valle de Bravo Mex.
184 E2 Valle de la Serena Spain
184 D2 Valle de Matamoros Spain
184 D2 Valle de Santa Ana Spain
244 D3 Valle de Santiago Mex.
191 H2 Valle di Cadore Italy
194 C5 Valledolmo Sicilia Italy
192 A4 Valledoria Sardegna Italy
250 C2 Valledupar Col.
217 □2a Vallée de Mai tourist site Seychelles
225 G4 Vallée-Jonction Que. Can.
260 C2 Valle Fértil, Sierra de mts Arg.
252 D4 Valle Grande Bol.
216 □3a Vallehermoso La Gomera Canary Is
243 F3 Valle Hermoso Mex.
160 D2 Valleiry France
240 F2 Vallejo CA U.S.A.
194 C5 Vallelunga Pratameno Sicilia Italy
190 D3 Valle Mosso Italy
140 L3 Vallen Sweden
245 F5 Valle Nacional Mex.
258 C3 Vallenar Chile
187 B4 Vallenca Spain
169 C5 Vallendar Ger.
156 E4 Vallentigny France
143 H2 Vallentuna Sweden
161 B4 Valleraugue France
192 A5 Vallermosa Sardegna Italy
193 F3 Vallerotonda Italy
216 □3f Valleseco Gran Canaria Canary Is
158 E4 Vallet France
195 □ Valletta Malta
223 L5 Valley r. Man. Can.
173 F4 Valley Ger.
150 C1 Valley Isle of Anglesey, Wales U.K.
240 I5 Valley Center CA U.S.A.
236 D2 Valley City ND U.S.A.
238 B3 Valley Falls OR U.S.A.
234 C2 Valley Forge PA U.S.A.
232 C5 Valley Head WV U.S.A.
147 E3 Valleymount Rep. of Ireland
203 G3 Valley of The Kings tourist site Egypt
240 G2 Valley Springs CA U.S.A.
230 C4 Valley Station KY U.S.A.
235 E2 Valley Stream NY U.S.A.
222 G4 Valleyview Alta Can.
234 B2 Valley View PA U.S.A.
186 E3 Vallfogona de Riucorb Spain
162 E3 Vallières France
186 E3 Vallmoll Spain
193 H4 Vallo della Lucania Italy
161 E3 Valloire France
160 A2 Vallon-en-Sully France
161 C4 Vallon-Pont-d'Arc France
190 B2 Vallorbe Switz.
160 E2 Vallorcine France
161 E4 Vallouise France
186 E3 Valls Spain
141 L3 Vallsta Sweden
190 E3 Valmadrera Italy
186 C3 Valmadrid Spain
223 J5 Val Marie Sask. Can.
Valmaseda Spain see Balmaseda
185 F2 Valmayor r. Spain
138 E3 Valmiera Latvia
183 F4 Valmojado Spain
159 G2 Valmont France
193 E3 Valmontone Italy
161 E3 Valmorel France
156 E3 Valmy France
183 G1 Valnera mt. Spain
158 E2 Valognes France
Valona Albania see Vlorë
184 C1 Valongo Portalegre Port.
182 B3 Valongo Porto Port.
185 G4 Válor Spain
183 F3 Valoria la Buena Spain
138 F4 Valozhyn Belarus
182 C3 Valpaços Port.
186 C2 Valpalmas Spain
224 E3 Val-Paradis Que. Can.
114 C4 Valparai Tamil Nadu India
256 B4 Valparaíso Brazil
260 B3 Valparaíso Chile
260 B3 Valparaíso admin. reg. Chile
244 C2 Valparaíso Mex.
243 I2 Valparaiso FL U.S.A.
230 C3 Valparaiso IN U.S.A.
160 F3 Valpelline Italy
190 C3 Valpelline val. Italy
190 C3 Valperga Italy
114 B3 Valpoi Goa India
188 G3 Valpovo Croatia
161 B5 Valras-Plage France
161 C4 Valréas France
185 F1 Valronquillo hill Spain
161 B5 Valros France
215 F2 Vals r. S. Africa
190 E2 Vals Switz.
116 C5 Valsad Gujarat India
190 C3 Valsavarenche Italy
170 C1 Vålse Denmark
183 F3 Valseca Spain
216 □3f Valsequillo Gran Canaria Canary Is
185 E2 Valsequillo Spain
160 D2 Valserine r. France
195 F2 Valsinni Italy
140 K2 Valsjöbyn Sweden
161 C4 Vals-les-Bains France
215 E2 Valspan S. Africa
215 G3 Valsrivier S. Africa
191 G3 Valstagna Italy
191 G2 Valsura r. Italy
160 C1 Val-Suzon France
161 E3 Val-Thorens France
176 F3 Valtice Czech Rep.
183 G3 Valtiendas Spain
183 I2 Valtierra Spain
140 O3 Valtimo Fin.
193 E1 Valtopina Italy
198 B2 Valtou mts Greece
190 C3 Valtournenche Italy
Valua i. Vanuatu see Mota Lava
161 A3 Valuéjols France
137 J2 Valuy r. Rus. Fed.
135 H7 Valuyevka Rus. Fed.
135 G6 Valuyki Rus. Fed.
129 F3 Välväläçay r. Azer.
216 □3e Valverde El Hierro Canary Is
Valverde Dom. Rep. see Mao
184 D2 Valverde de Burguillos Spain
183 H5 Valverde de Júcar Spain
184 D3 Valverde del Camino Spain
184 D2 Valverde de Leganés Spain
182 D4 Valverde del Fresno Spain
184 E2 Valverde de Llerena Spain
183 G3 Valverde de los Arroyos Spain
184 D2 Valverde de Mérida Spain
197 F2 Vama Satu Mare Romania
197 G2 Vama Suceava Romania
176 F1 Vamberk Czech Rep.
97 D5 Vam Co Dông r. Vietnam
97 D5 Vam Co Tay r. Vietnam
142 C4 Vamdrup Denmark
141 M3 Vammala Fin.
177 I4 Vámosgyörk Hungary
177 H4 Vámosmikola Hungary
177 K4 Vámospércs Hungary
177 K3 Vámosújfalu Hungary
141 M3 Vampula Fin.
115 E2 Vamsadhara r. India
127 F3 Van Turkey
129 C4 Van prov. Turkey
Van, Lake salt l. Turkey see Van Gölü
129 D3 Vanadzor Armenia
141 K3 Vanån r. Sweden
197 I3 Vânători Romania
197 G2 Vânători Romania
156 E4 Vanault-les-Dames France
131 L3 Vanavara Rus. Fed.

237 E5 Van Buren AR U.S.A.
226 E5 Van Buren IN U.S.A.
233 □J1 Van Buren ME U.S.A.
237 F4 Van Buren MO U.S.A.
Van Buren OH U.S.A. see Kettering
233 □J2 Vanceboro ME U.S.A.
232 B5 Vanceburg KY U.S.A.
Vanch Tajik. see Vanj
Vanchskiy Khrebet mts Tajik. see Vanj, Qatorkŭhi
232 B6 Vancleve KY U.S.A.
235 E1 Van Cortlandtville NY U.S.A.
222 F5 Vancouver B.C. Can.
238 B2 Vancouver WA U.S.A.
87 C7 Vancouver, Cape W.A. Austr.
222 B2 Vancouver, Mount Can./U.S.A.
222 E5 Vancouver Island B.C. Can.
177 K4 Váncsod Hungary
Vanda Fin. see Vantaa
236 F4 Vandalia IL U.S.A.
232 A5 Vandalia OH U.S.A.
129 E3 Vandam Azer.
178 A3 Vandans Austria
114 C3 Vandavasi Tamil Nadu India
186 D3 Vandellós Spain
160 B2 Vandenesse France
160 C1 Vandenesse-en-Auxois France
215 F2 Vanderbijlpark S. Africa
226 E3 Vanderbilt MI U.S.A.
232 D4 Vandergrift PA U.S.A.
222 E4 Vanderhoof B.C. Can.
84 D2 Vanderlin Island N.T. Austr.
84 B1 Van Diemen, Cape N.T. Austr.
84 D3 Van Diemen, Cape Qld Austr.
84 C1 Van Diemen Gulf N.T. Austr.
Van Diemen's Land state Austr. see Tasmania
234 C1 Vandling PA U.S.A.
157 G4 Vandœvre-lès-Nancy France
191 G2 Vandoies Italy
138 E2 Vändra Estonia
193 G3 Vandra r. Italy
215 G2 Vandyksdrif S. Africa
Väner, Lake Sweden see Vänern
142 E2 Vänern l. Sweden
142 E2 Vänersborg Sweden
183 F2 Vañes Spain
262 T2 Vang, Mount Antarctica
211 C6 Vanga Kenya
213 □J4 Vangaindrano Madag.
138 E3 Vangaži Latvia
129 E3 Vängli Azer.
127 F3 Van Gölü salt l. Turkey
140 L1 Vangsvik Norway
223 J5 Vanguard Sask. Can.
78 □6 Vangunu i. New Georgia Is Solomon Is
78 □6 Vangunu, Mount New Georgia Is Solomon Is
239 F6 Van Horn TX U.S.A.
129 C2 Vani Georgia
224 F4 Vanier Ont. Can.
78 □6 Vanikoro Islands Solomon Is
190 C2 Vanil Noir mt. Switz.
91 J7 Vanimo P.N.G.
100 G2 Vanino Rus. Fed.
114 C3 Vaniyambadi Tamil Nadu India
123 G2 Vanj Tajik.
123 G2 Vanj, Qatorkŭhi mts Tajik.
140 L2 Vänjaurträsk Sweden
197 F3 Vânju Mare Romania
131 T3 Vankarem Rus. Fed.
233 F2 Vankleek Hill Ont. Can.
232 B4 Vanlue OH U.S.A.
140 □ Van Mijenfjorden inlet Svalbard
140 L1 Vanna i. Norway
140 L3 Vännäs Sweden
156 D4 Vanne r. France
158 D4 Vannes France
Vannovka Kazakh. see Tura-Ryskulova
140 L1 Vanntindan mt. Norway
191 G3 Vanoi r. Italy
215 G3 Van Reenen S. Africa
91 I7 Van Rees, Pegunungan mts Indon.
214 B4 Vanrhynsdorp S. Africa
85 E3 Vanrook Qld Austr.
85 E3 Vanrook Creek r. Qld Austr.
116 C5 Vansada Gujarat India
232 B6 Vansant VA U.S.A.
143 F1 Vansbro Sweden
142 B2 Vanse Norway
86 E2 Vansittart Bay W.A. Austr.
215 F3 Vanstadensrus S. Africa
141 N3 Vantaa Fin.
138 E1 Vantaa r. Fin.
87 D5 Van Truer Tableland reg. W.A. Austr.
215 H3 Vant's Drift S. Africa
77 I3 Vanua Balavu i. Fiji
78 □5 Vanua Lava i. Vanuatu
79 □1 Vanua Levu i. Fiji
Vanua Mbalavu i. Fiji see Vanua Balavu
78 □5 Vanuatu country S. Pacific Ocean
Vanua Valavo i. Fiji see Vanua Balavu
156 E5 Vanvey France
236 G3 Van Wert OH U.S.A.
214 C5 Van Wyksdorp S. Africa
214 C4 Vanwyksvlei S. Africa
177 I4 Vanyarc Hungary
190 D3 Vanzone Italy
214 D2 Van Zylsrus S. Africa
78 □5 Vao New Caledonia
163 D4 Vaour France
176 G1 Vápenná Czech Rep.
136 E3 Vapnyarka Ukr.
184 C3 Vaqueiros Port.
161 E5 Var dept Provence-Alpes-Côte-d'Azur France
161 F5 Var r. France
190 E4 Vara r. Italy
142 E2 Vara Sweden
114 C3 Varada r. India
185 H1 Vara del Rey Spain
246 B2 Varadero Cuba
159 E4 Varades France
177 L5 Vărădia de Mureș Romania
161 D5 Varages France
116 B5 Varahi Gujarat India
163 D4 Varaire France
190 C4 Varaita r. Italy
138 F3 Varakļāni Latvia
177 H5 Varalja Hungary
190 D3 Varallo Italy
122 B3 Varāmīn Iran
117 E4 Varanasi Uttar Prad. India
134 L1 Varandey Rus. Fed.
140 O1 Varangerfjorden sea chan. Norway
140 O1 Varangerhalvøya pen. Norway
193 H3 Varano, Lago di lag. Italy
190 E4 Varano de'Melegari Italy
138 F4 Varapayeva Belarus
185 F2 Varas r. Spain
188 F2 Varaždin Croatia
179 H4 Varaždinske Toplice Croatia
190 D4 Varazze Italy
142 E3 Varberg Sweden
177 J3 Varbó Hungary
161 D3 Varces France
177 L5 Vârciorog Romania
198 B2 Varda Greece
123 G3 Vardak prov. Afgh.
114 C2 Vardannapet Andhra Prad. India
196 F5 Vardar r. Macedonia
142 C4 Varde Denmark
142 C4 Varde r. Denmark
129 D3 Vardenis Armenia
129 D3 Vardenisi Lerr mt. Armenia
129 D4 Vardenisi Lerrnashght'a mts Armenia
129 D3 Vardisubani Georgia
141 M3 Vårdö Åland Fin.
140 O1 Vardø Norway
177 H5 Várdomb Hungary
138 D3 Varduva r. Lith.
139 L3 Varegovo Rus. Fed.
168 D2 Varel Ger.
206 A3 Varela Guinea-Bissau
138 E4 Varėna Lith.
138 E4 Varėnė r. Lith.
156 A3 Varengeville-sur-Mer France
137 I5 Varenikovskaya Rus. Fed.
156 B3 Varenne r. France
156 C5 Varennes-Changy France
157 F3 Varennes-en-Argonne France
160 D2 Varennes-St-Sauveur France
160 B2 Varennes-sur-Allier France
160 B1 Varennes-Vauzelles France
137 J4 Varenovka Rus. Fed.
188 G3 Vareš Bos.-Herz.
190 D3 Varese Italy
190 D3 Varese prov. Lombardia Italy
190 E4 Varese Ligure Italy
162 D3 Varetz France
100 E3 Varfolomeyevka Rus. Fed.
177 L5 Vârfurașu, Vârful mt. Romania
177 L5 Vârfurile Romania
142 E2 Vårgårda Sweden
254 F4 Vargem r. Brazil
257 G4 Vargem Alta Brazil
254 E2 Vargem Grande Brazil
256 D4 Vargem Grande do Sul Brazil
257 E4 Varginha Brazil
142 A2 Varhaug Norway
177 J5 Variaș Romania
163 D5 Varilhes France
177 H2 Varín Slovakia
Varkana Iran see Gorgān
140 N3 Varkaus Fin.
169 E4 Varlosen (Niemetal) Ger.
142 E2 Värmland county Sweden
142 E2 Värmland reg. Sweden
197 H4 Varna Bulg.
114 B2 Varna r. India
191 G2 Varna Italy
120 E1 Varna Rus. Fed.
143 F3 Värnamo Sweden
142 E1 Värnäs Sweden
134 I4 Varnavino Rus. Fed.
138 D4 Varniai Lith.
Várnjárg pen. Norway see Varangerhalvøya
176 D1 Varnsdorf Czech Rep.
231 D5 Varnville SC U.S.A.
177 I5 Városföld Hungary
Varosha Cyprus see Varosia
128 A2 Varosia Cyprus
188 F3 Varoška Rijeka Bos.-Herz.
177 G4 Városlőd Hungary
140 N3 Varpaisjärvi Fin.
177 H4 Várpalota Hungary
168 D3 Varrel Ger.
162 C3 Vars Poitou-Charentes France
161 E4 Vars Provence-Alpes-Côte-d'Azur France
197 G2 Vărșag Romania
199 G3 Varsak Turkey
196 E2 Vărșand Romania
177 I3 Varsány Hungary
190 E4 Varsi Italy
164 F3 Varsseveld Neth.
143 G2 Vårsta Sweden
Vartashen Azer. see Oğuz
142 D2 Varteig Norway
198 B3 Vartholomio Greece
127 F3 Varto Turkey
197 F3 Vârtop Romania
129 C2 Varts'ikhe Georgia
140 O3 Värtsilä Fin.
137 G2 Varva Ukr.
137 I2 Varvarivka Kharkivs'ka Oblast' Ukr.
136 D2 Varvarivka Khmel'nyts'ka Oblast' Ukr.
137 J2 Varvarovka Rus. Fed.
177 L3 Vary Ukr.
136 C2 Varyazh Ukr.
254 F3 Várzea Alegre Brazil
257 E2 Várzea da Palma Brazil
254 E3 Várzea Grande Brazil
190 E4 Varzi Italy
190 D2 Varzo Italy
160 B1 Varzy France
176 F4 Vas county Hungary
Vasa Fin. see Vaasa
254 F4 Vasa Barris r. Brazil
177 I4 Vasad Hungary
114 B2 Vasai Mahar. India
138 E2 Vasalemma Estonia
138 E2 Vasalemma r. Estonia
193 E2 Vasanello Italy
177 H5 Vásárosdombó Hungary
177 L3 Vásárosnamény Hungary
184 C3 Vascão r. Port.
197 F2 Vașcău Romania
134 I2 Vashka r. Rus. Fed.
136 C3 Vashkivtsi Ukr.
Vasht Iran see Khāsh
198 C1 Vasilika Greece
Vasilkov Ukr. see Vasyl'kiv
Vasilkovka Ukr. see Vasyl'kivka
134 I4 Vasil'sursk Rus. Fed.
136 E1 Vasilyevichy Belarus
135 H6 Vasil'yevka Rus. Fed.
139 J3 Vasil'yevskiy Mokh Rus. Fed.
136 E2 Vas'kovychi Ukr.
177 H5 Vaskút Hungary
162 B2 Vasles France
197 H2 Vaslui Romania
177 K3 Vasmegyer Hungary
227 F4 Vassar MI U.S.A.
141 K3 Vassbo Sweden
161 D4 Vassieux-en-Vercors France
162 D3 Vassivière, Lac de l. France
176 F4 Vas-Soproni-síkság hills Hungary
257 F5 Vassouras Brazil
159 F3 Vassy France
176 F4 Vasszécseny Hungary
Vastan Turkey see Gevaș
140 L3 Västana Sweden
138 D1 Västanfjärd Fin.
140 L2 Västansjö Sweden
143 G2 Västerås Sweden
140 K2 Västerbotten county Sweden
141 K3 Västerdalälven r. Sweden
140 L2 Västerfjäll Sweden
143 H2 Västerhaninge Sweden
140 L3 Västernorrland county Sweden
143 G3 Västervik Sweden
143 F2 Västmanland county Sweden
193 G2 Vasto Italy
168 F2 Vastorf Ger.
142 E2 Västra Ämtervik Sweden
142 E2 Västra Götaland county Sweden
140 M3 Västra Kvarken sea chan. Sweden
140 L2 Västra Ormsjö Sweden
176 F4 Vasvár Hungary
137 G3 Vasylivka Kirovohrads'ka Oblast' Ukr.
137 H2 Vasylivka Sums'ka Oblast' Ukr.
137 H4 Vasylivka Zaporiz'ka Oblast' Ukr.
136 F2 Vasyl'kiv Ukr.
137 I3 Vasyl'kivka Ukr.
175 M6 Vasyuchyn Ukr.
137 G3 Vasyutyntsi Ukr.
177 G4 Vaszar Hungary
177 L5 Vața de Jos Romania
162 D1 Vatan France
143 H3 Väte Gotland Sweden
Vaté i. Vanuatu see Éfaté
146 B4 Vaternish Point Scotland U.K.
146 A5 Vatersay i. Scotland U.K.
173 F3 Vaterstetten Ger.
Vathi Ionioi Nisoi Greece see Ithaki
Vathí Greece see Vathy
199 E3 Vathy Greece
193 E3 Vatican City Europe
195 E4 Vaticano, Capo c. Italy
Vaticano, Città del Europe see Vatican City
78 □6 Vatilau i. Solomon Is
Vatiu i. Cook Is see Atiu
140 □C2 Vatnajökull ice cap Iceland
140 I3 Vatne Norway
77 I3 Vatoa i. Fiji
213 □K3 Vatomandry Madag.
197 G2 Vatra Dornei Romania
177 J4 Vatta Hungary
Vätter, Lake Sweden see Vättern
143 F2 Vättern l. Sweden
143 G1 Vattholma Sweden
141 L3 Vattrång Sweden
79 □1a Vatukoula Viti Levu Fiji
79 □1 Vatulele i. Fiji
159 F2 Vaubadon France
157 F4 Vaubecourt France
156 D4 Vauchassis France
160 B1 Vauclaix France
161 D4 Vaucluse dept Provence-Alpes-Côte-d'Azur France
161 D5 Vaucluse, Monts de mts France
160 D1 Vauconcourt-Nervezain France
157 F4 Vaucouleurs France
190 B2 Vaud canton Switz.
157 G4 Vaudémont France
156 D4 Vaudeurs France
84 B4 Vaughan Springs N.T. Austr.
239 F5 Vaughn NM U.S.A.
160 C3 Vaugneray France
160 B1 Vault-de-Lugny France
160 C3 Vaulx-en-Velin France
160 D3 Vaulx-Milieu France
250 D4 Vaupés dept Col.
250 D4 Vaupés r. Col.
224 E2 Vauquelin r. Que. Can.
161 D5 Vauvenargues France
161 C5 Vauvert France
157 G5 Vauvillers France
157 F3 Vaux-devant-Damloup France
223 H5 Vauxhall Alta Can.
156 C4 Vaux-le-Pénil France
162 A3 Vaux-sur-Mer France
165 E5 Vaux-sur-Sûre Belgium
116 B4 Vav Gujarat India
213 □K3 Vavatenina Madag.
77 I3 Vava'u i. Tonga
79 □2 Vava'u Group is Tonga
157 F4 Vavincourt France
Vavitao i. Îs Australes Fr. Polynesia see Raivavae
206 D5 Vavoua Côte d'Ivoire
134 J4 Vavozh Rus. Fed.
114 D4 Vavuniya Sri Lanka
138 E5 Vawkavysk Belarus
138 E5 Vawkavyskaye Wzvyshsha hills Belarus
143 H2 Vaxholm Sweden
143 F3 Växjö Sweden
114 C3 Vayalpad Andhra Prad. India
Vayenga Rus. Fed. see Severomorsk
130 G2 Vaygach, Ostrov i. Rus. Fed.
114 C4 Vayittiri Kerala India
129 D4 Vayk' Armenia
162 D4 Vayrac France
162 C3 Vayres France
256 D2 Vazante Brazil
Vazáš Sweden see Vittangi
129 D3 Vazashen Armenia
177 I2 Važec Slovakia
139 J1 Vazhinka r. Rus. Fed.
129 D3 Vaziani Georgia
213 □J3 Vazobe mt. Madag.
139 J4 Vazuza r. Rus. Fed.
139 J4 Vazuzskoye Vodokhranilishche resr Rus. Fed.
176 D3 Včelná Czech Rep.
Veaikevárri Sweden see Svappavaara
160 C3 Veauche France
142 E4 Veberöd Sweden
140 M2 Vebomark Sweden
161 B4 Vebron France
190 F5 Vecchiano Italy
177 K3 Vechec Slovakia
169 F3 Vechelde Ger.
164 F2 Vecht r. Neth. alt. Vechte (Germany)
168 D3 Vechta Ger.
169 B3 Vechte r. Ger. alt. Vecht (Neth.)
182 E4 Vecinos Spain
169 F4 Veckenstedt Ger.
169 E4 Veckerhagen (Reinhardshagen) Ger.
177 I4 Vecsés Hungary
176 E2 Vectec hill Czech Rep.
138 E3 Vecumnieki Latvia
Vedana Rus. Fed. see Vedeno
114 C4 Vedaranniyam Tamil Nadu India
114 C4 Vedasandur Tamil Nadu India
142 E3 Veddige Sweden
197 G3 Vedea Argeș Romania
197 G4 Vedea Giurgiu Romania
197 G4 Vedea r. Romania
191 H3 Vedelago Italy
161 C5 Vedène France
129 E2 Vedeno Rus. Fed.
143 F2 Vedevåg Sweden
129 D4 Vedi Armenia
261 G4 Vedia Arg.
134 F3 Vedlozero Rus. Fed.
137 J3 Vedmezha r. Ukr.
182 B2 Vedra Spain
161 B3 Védrines-St-Loup France
136 F1 Vedrych r. Belarus
137 J2 Veduga r. Rus. Fed.
164 F1 Veendam Neth.
164 E2 Veenendaal Neth.
164 F1 Veenhuizen Neth.
168 C2 Veenhusen Ger.
164 F2 Veenoord Neth.
164 E1 Veenwouden Neth.
164 C3 Veere Neth.
168 E2 Veerse r. Ger.
140 K2 Vefsnfjord sea chan. Norway
140 J2 Vega i. Norway
237 C5 Vega TX U.S.A.
247 □1 Vega Alta Puerto Rico
247 □1 Vega Baja Puerto Rico
182 E2 Vegacervera Spain
182 D2 Vega de Espinareda Spain
182 C1 Vegadeo Spain
183 G1 Vega de Pas Spain
216 □3f Vega de San Mateo Gran Canaria Canary Is
182 E3 Vega de Tirados Spain
182 D2 Vega de Valcarce Spain
183 E3 Vega de Valdetronco Spain
183 G3 Veganzones Spain
182 D2 Vegarienza Spain
142 C2 Vegarshei Norway
183 E2 Vegas del Condado Spain
183 F4 Vegas de Matute Spain
164 E3 Veghel Neth.
195 G2 Veglie Italy
198 B1 Vegoritis, Limni l. Greece
159 F4 Vègre r. France
223 H4 Vegreville Alta Can.
252 A2 Végueta Peru
138 F1 Vehkalahti Fin.
170 D2 Vehlow Ger.
141 M3 Vehmaa Fin.
123 G4 Vehoa r. Pak.
159 G4 Veigné France
160 E2 Veigy-Foncenex France
169 F5 Veilsdorf Ger.
Veinticinco de Mayo Buenos Aires Arg. see 25 de Mayo
Veinticinco de Mayo La Pampa Arg. see 25 de Mayo
Veinticinco de Mayo Mendoza Arg. see 25 de Mayo
Veinticinco de Mayo Uru. see 25 de Mayo
184 C2 Veiros Port.
138 D4 Veisiejis Lith.
173 E2 Veitsbronn Ger.
179 G3 Veitsch Austria
179 G3 Veitsch mt. Austria
172 D2 Veitshöchheim Ger.
140 N2 Veitsiluoto Fin.
138 C4 Veiviržas r. Lith.
192 E2 Vejano Italy
142 C4 Vejen Denmark
184 E4 Vejer de la Frontera Spain
142 C4 Vejle Denmark
142 C4 Vejle county Denmark
173 H2 Vejprnice Czech Rep.
176 C1 Vejprty Czech Rep.
120 E5 Vekil'bazar Turkm.
116 C5 Velachha Gujarat India
183 F5 Velada Spain
188 F4 Vela Luka Croatia
183 H3 Velamazán Spain
216 □1c Velas São Jorge Azores
258 D3 Velasco, Sierra de mts Arg.
113 □1 Velassary i. S. Male Maldives
161 D5 Velaux France
258 G4 Velázquez Uru.
169 C4 Velbert Ger.
173 F2 Velburg Ger.
214 E5 Velddrif S. Africa
165 C3 Veldegem Belgium
173 F2 Velden Bayern Ger.
173 G3 Velden Bayern Ger.
165 F3 Velden Neth.
179 F4 Velden am Wörther See Austria
165 E3 Veldhoven Neth.
114 C3 Veldurti Andhra Prad. India
188 E3 Velebit mts Croatia
188 E3 Velebitski Kanal sea chan. Croatia
185 H3 Velefique Spain
197 H4 Veleka r. Bulg.
169 B4 Velen Ger.
177 H4 Velence Hungary
188 E2 Velenje Slovenia
197 E5 Veles Macedonia
196 D5 Velës, Mali i mt. Albania
176 D3 Velešín Czech Rep.
185 G3 Veleta, Pico mt. Spain
188 F4 Velež mts Bos.-Herz.
250 C3 Vélez Col.
185 H3 Vélez-Blanco Spain
185 G4 Vélez de Benaudalla Spain
185 F4 Vélez-Málaga Spain
185 H3 Vélez-Rubio Spain
170 D1 Velgast Ger.
256 D3 Velhas r. Minas Gerais Brazil
257 E2 Velhas r. Minas Gerais Brazil
Velibaba Turkey see Aras
135 I7 Velichayevskoye Rus. Fed.
136 C3 Velika Berezovytsya Ukr.
196 E4 Velika Drenova Srbija Yugo.
188 F3 Velika Gorica Croatia
136 C2 Velika Hlusha Ukr.
188 E3 Velika Kapela mts Croatia
188 E3 Velika Kladuša Bos.-Herz.
188 F3 Velika Mlaka Croatia
176 G6 Velika Pisanica Croatia
196 E3 Velika Plana Srbija Yugo.
179 F4 Velika Rogatec mt. Slovenia
134 J4 Velikaya Rus. Fed.
134 J4 Velikaya r. Rus. Fed.
131 S3 Velikaya r. Rus. Fed.
138 G3 Velikaya r. Rus. Fed.
134 F3 Velikaya Guba Rus. Fed.
100 F3 Velikaya Kema Rus. Fed.
Velikaya Novoselka Ukr. see Velyka Novosilka
188 F4 Veliki Drvenik i. Croatia
176 G6 Veliki Grđevac Croatia
196 E4 Veliki Jastrebac mts Yugo.
136 C3 Veliki Kunynets' Ukr.
197 H4 Veliki Preslav Bulg.
188 E3 Veliki Risnjak mt. Croatia
197 E4 Veliki Šiljegovac Srbija Yugo.
197 F4 Veliki Strešer mt. Yugo.
196 E3 Veliki Šturac mt. Yugo.
139 H3 Velikiye Luki Rus. Fed.
137 F2 Velikiy Lystven Ukr.
136 B3 Velikiy Lyubin' Ukr.
139 H2 Velikiy Novgorod Rus. Fed.
134 I3 Velikiy Ustyug Rus. Fed.
137 K2 Velikoarkhangel'skoye Rus. Fed.
139 M4 Velikodvorskiy Rus. Fed.
137 I2 Velikomikhaylovka Rus. Fed.
114 C3 Velikonda Range hills India
139 I3 Velikooktyabr'skiy Rus. Fed.
176 F6 Veliko Trojstvo Croatia
197 G4 Veliko Tŭrnovo Bulg.
129 C3 Veliköy Turkey
139 K2 Velikoye Vologod. Obl. Rus. Fed.
139 L3 Velikoye Yaroslavskaya Oblast' Rus. Fed.
139 M4 Velikoye, Ozero l. Rus. Fed.
186 D3 Velilla de Cinca Spain
186 C3 Velilla de Ebro Spain
Velilla de Guardo Spain see Velilla del Río Carrión
183 F2 Velilla del Río Carrión Spain
185 G3 Velillas r. Spain
188 E3 Veli Lošinj Croatia
196 D4 Velimlje Crna Gora Yugo.
163 C4 Vélines France
206 B3 Vélingara Senegal
197 G4 Velingrad Bulg.
193 E2 Velino r. Italy
193 F2 Velino, Monte mt. Italy
139 H4 Velizh Rus. Fed.
176 F2 Velká Bíteš Czech Rep.
176 D1 Velká Dobrá Czech Rep.
177 K2 Veľká Domaša, Vodná nádrž resr Slovakia
177 H3 Veľká Fatra mts Slovakia
176 G2 Velká Haná r. Czech Rep.
173 G2 Velká Hleďsebe Czech Rep.
177 G3 Velká Javořina hill Czech Rep./Slovakia
177 K2 Veľká Javořina mt. Slovakia
177 H3 Veľká Lehota Slovakia
177 H2 Veľká Lúka mt. Slovakia
177 H2 Velká Polom Czech Rep.
Veľká Rača mt. Pol./Slovakia see Wielka Racza
176 F3 Velké Bílovice Czech Rep.
171 F5 Velké Březno Czech Rep.
177 L3 Veľké Kapušany Slovakia
177 H2 Velké Karlovice Czech Rep.
179 I2 Veľké Leváre Slovakia
176 G1 Velké Losiny Czech Rep.
177 H3 Veľké Lovce Slovakia
177 H4 Veľké Ludince Slovakia
176 F2 Velké Meziříčí Czech Rep.
176 F3 Velké Němčice Czech Rep.
176 F3 Velké Pavlovice Czech Rep.
177 G3 Veľké Rípňany Slovakia
177 L3 Veľké Trakany Slovakia
177 H3 Veľké Uherce Slovakia
138 C1 Velkua Fin.
177 J3 Veľký Blh Slovakia
177 H3 Veľký Ďur Slovakia
177 H2 Veľký Javorník mt. Slovakia
177 I2 Veľký Kriváň mt. Slovakia
177 I3 Veľký Krtíš Slovakia
177 H3 Veľký Kýr Slovakia
177 G3 Veľký Lopeník hill Czech Rep.
177 G4 Veľký Meder Slovakia
177 K2 Veľký Šariš Slovakia
177 H3 Veľký Tribeč hill Slovakia
176 G2 Velký Týnec Czech Rep.
176 B2 Velký Zvon hill Czech Rep.
179 F4 Vellach r. Austria
168 F2 Vellahn Ger.
78 □6 Vella Lavella i. New Georgia Is Solomon Is
114 C4 Vellar r. India
172 D2 Vellberg Ger.
193 E3 Velletri Italy
160 E1 Vellevans France
160 D1 Vellexon-Queutrey-et-Vaudey France
142 E4 Vellinge Sweden
183 H4 Vellisca Spain
169 E4 Vellmar Ger.
114 C3 Vellore Tamil Nadu India
186 D2 Vellos r. Spain
131 K3 Vel'mo r. Rus. Fed.
198 C3 Velo Peloponnisos Greece
157 F3 Velosnes France
165 E4 Velp r. Belgium
164 E3 Velp Neth.
169 F3 Velpke Ger.
134 H3 Vel'sk Rus. Fed.
Velsuna Italy see Orvieto
170 E3 Velten Ger.
169 F3 Veltheim (Ohe) Ger.
176 D1 Veltrusy Czech Rep.
191 G2 Velturno Italy
164 E2 Veluwemeer l. Neth.
236 C1 Velva ND U.S.A.
176 D1 Velvary Czech Rep.
198 C1 Velvendos Greece
139 I3 Vel'ye, Ozero l. Rus. Fed.
137 G3 Velyka Andrusivka Ukr.
137 I3 Velyka Babka Ukr.
137 G3 Velyka Bahachka Ukr.
137 H4 Velyka Bilozerka Ukr.
137 H4 Velyka Bilozerka r. Ukr.
137 G3 Velyka Burimka Ukr.
136 F2 Velyka Dymerka Ukr.
175 L6 Velyka Horozhanna Ukr.
136 E3 Velyka Kisnytsya Ukr.
137 I3 Velyka Komyshuvakha Ukr.
177 M3 Velyka Kopanya Ukr.
137 F4 Velyka Korenykha Ukr.
137 G4 Velyka Kostromka Ukr.
137 G4 Velyka Lepetykha Ukr.
136 E4 Velyka Mykhaylivka Ukr.
137 I4 Velyka Novosilka Ukr.
137 G4 Velyka Oleksandrivka Ukr.
137 H2 Velyka Pysarivka Ukr.
137 H3 Velyka Rublivka Ukr.
136 D2 Velyka Tsvilya Ukr.
137 F3 Velyka Vys' r. Ukr.
137 F3 Velyka Vyska Ukr.
137 H4 Velyka Znam"yanka Ukr.
177 L3 Velyki Kom"yaty Ukr.
137 G4 Velyki Kopani Ukr.
136 E3 Velyki Korovyntsi Ukr.
137 G3 Velyki Krynky Ukr.
177 L3 Velyki Luchky Ukr.
136 C2 Velyki Mosty Ukr.
137 G2 Velyki Sorochyntsi Ukr.
137 G3 Velykiy Khutir Ukr.
136 F4 Velykiy Kuyal'nyk r. Ukr.
137 G2 Velykiy Sambir Ukr.
136 F4 Velykodolyns'ke Ukr.
137 I4 Velykomykhaylivka Ukr.
137 H3 Velykooleksandrivka Ukr.
137 F4 Velykoserbulivka Ukr.
136 B3 Velykyy Bereznyy Ukr.
137 I2 Velykyy Burluk Ukr.
136 C4 Velykyy Bychkiv Ukr.
Velykyy Tokmak Ukr. see Tokmak
134 K3 Vel'yu r. Rus. Fed.
114 C2 Vemalwada Andhra Prad. India
264 J8 Vema Seamount sea feature S. Atlantic Ocean
265 I5 Vema Trench sea feature Indian Ocean
177 H5 Véménd Hungary
100 G3 Vemor'ye Sakhalin Rus. Fed.
114 C3 Vempalle Andhra Prad. India
192 B2 Venaco Corse France
245 E3 Venados r. Mex.
261 G3 Venado Tuerto Arg.
193 G3 Venafro Italy
251 F3 Venamo r. Guyana/Venez.
251 F3 Venamo, Cerro mt. Venez.
158 E5 Venansault France
160 C1 Venarey-les-Laumes France
190 C3 Venaria Italy
193 F2 Venarotta Italy
161 F4 Venasca Italy
161 F5 Vence France
256 C5 Venceslau Bráz Brazil
138 E4 Venciūnai Lith.
191 G3 Venda, Monte hill Italy
184 A2 Venda do Pinheiro Port.
257 G4 Venda Nova Brazil
182 C3 Venda Nova, Barragem de resr Port.
161 B5 Vendargues France
184 B2 Vendas de Azeitão Port.
184 B2 Vendas Novas Port.
160 B2 Vendat France
162 A3 Vendays-Montalivet France
158 E5 Vendée dept Pays de la Loire France
162 B2 Vendée r. France
157 H4 Vendenheim France
159 G5 Vendeuvre-du-Poitou France
156 E4 Vendeuvre-sur-Barse France
184 C2 Vendinha Port.
159 H5 Vendœuvres France
156 B5 Vendôme France
184 D2 Vendoval r. Spain
Vendrell Spain see El Vendrell
136 D3 Vendychany Ukr.
244 D2 Venegas Mex.
161 D5 Venelles France
163 E5 Vénès France
191 H3 Veneta, Laguna lag. Italy
Venetia Italy see Venezia
191 G3 Veneto admin. reg. Italy
139 L4 Venev Rus. Fed.
191 H3 Venezia Italy
191 H3 Venezia prov. Veneto Italy
Venezia, Golfo di g. Europe see Venice, Gulf of
251 E3 Venezuela country S. America
250 D2 Venezuela, Golfo de g. Venez.
264 E4 Venezuelan Basin sea feature S. Atlantic Ocean
114 B3 Vengurla Mahar. India
164 E2 Venhuizen Neth.
182 E3 Venialbo Spain
220 C4 Veniaminof Volcano AK U.S.A.
Venice Italy see Venezia
231 D7 Venice FL U.S.A.
237 F6 Venice LA U.S.A.
188 D3 Venice, Gulf of Europe
190 E2 Venina r. Italy
160 C3 Vénissieux France
156 D3 Venizel France
141 K3 Venjan Sweden
114 C3 Venkatagiri Andhra Prad. India
114 D2 Venkatapuram Andhra Prad. India
165 F3 Venlo Neth.
142 B2 Vennesla Norway
193 H4 Venosa Italy
193 H3 Venosa r. Italy
191 F2 Venosta, Val val. Italy
156 D5 Venoy France
164 E3 Venray Neth.
79 □3 Vent, Îles du is Arch. de la Société Fr. Polynesia
138 D3 Venta r. Latvia/Lith.
138 D3 Venta Lith.
161 D5 Ventabren France
161 F5 Ventabren, Mont mt. France
183 F3 Venta de Baños Spain
182 E1 Venta de las Ranas Spain
185 F2 Venta del Charco Spain
187 B5 Venta del Moro Spain
185 G2 Venta de los Santos Spain
182 D1 Venta Nueva Spain
185 G3 Ventas de Huelma Spain
185 F4 Ventas de Zafarraya Spain
161 D4 Ventavon France
215 F3 Ventersburg S. Africa
215 F2 Ventersdorp S. Africa
215 F2 Venterskroon S. Africa
215 E4 Venterstad S. Africa
161 B4 Venteuges France
190 C5 Ventimiglia Italy
192 B3 Ventiseri Corse France
259 C6 Ventisquero mt. Arg.
151 F4 Ventnor Isle of Wight, England U.K.
235 D3 Ventnor City NJ U.S.A.
193 F4 Ventotene, Isola i. Italy
161 D4 Ventoux, Mont mt. France
170 C2 Ventschow Ger.
138 C3 Ventspils Latvia
251 E3 Ventuari r. Venez.
240 H4 Ventura CA U.S.A.
83 F4 Venus Bay Vic. Austr.
Venusia Italy see Venosa
244 C4 Venustiano Mex.
245 F3 Venustiano Carranza Puebla Mex.
243 E3 Venustiano Carranza, Presa resr Mex.
192 B2 Venzolasca Corse France
191 I2 Venzone Italy
176 F4 Vép Hungary
137 H2 Vepryk Ukr.
139 J1 Vepsovskaya Vozvyshennost' hills Rus. Fed.
258 E3 Vera Arg.
185 I3 Vera Spain
256 C5 Vera Cruz Brazil
245 F4 Veracruz Mex.
Vera Cruz Mex. see Veracruz
245 F3 Veracruz state Mex.
184 C2 Vera Cruz Port.
234 C2 Vera Cruz PA U.S.A.
186 B1 Vera de Bidasoa Spain
186 C2 Veral r. Spain
255 C9 Veranópolis Brazil
116 B5 Veraval Gujarat India
136 C2 Verba Rivnens'ka Oblast' Ukr.
136 C2 Verba Volyns'ka Oblast' Ukr.
190 D3 Verbania Italy
235 E1 Verbank NY U.S.A.
190 D2 Verbano-Cusio-Ossola prov. Piemonte Italy
156 C3 Verberie France
193 H5 Verbicaro Italy
190 C2 Verbier Switz.
139 K3 Verbilki Rus. Fed.
137 G3 Verblyuzhka Ukr.
137 H4 Verbove Ukr.
136 C3 Verbovets' Ukr.
135 H5 Verbovskiy Rus. Fed.
190 E2 Verceia Italy
190 D3 Vercelli Italy
190 D3 Vercelli prov. Piemonte Italy
160 E1 Vercel-Villedieu-le-Camp France
170 D2 Verchen Ger.
161 D4 Vercors reg. France
Vercovicium tourist site England U.K. see Housesteads
179 F5 Verd Slovenia
139 M5 Verda r. Rus. Fed.
161 E4 Verdaches France
140 J3 Verdalsøra Norway
259 D6 Verde r. Arg.
256 B3 Verde r. Goiás Brazil
256 D3 Verde r. Goiás/Minas Gerais Brazil
256 B4 Verde r. Mato Grosso do Sul Brazil
256 B3 Verde r. Minas Gerais Brazil
256 C3 Verde r. Minas Gerais Brazil
257 E4 Verde r. Minas Gerais Brazil
254 E4 Verde r. Bahia Brazil
253 F3 Verde r. Mato Grosso Brazil
253 G2 Verde r. Mato Grosso Brazil
244 C3 Verde r. Aguascalientes/Jalisco Mex.
242 D3 Verde r. Chihuahua/Durango Mex.
245 E5 Verde r. Guerrero/Oaxaca Mex.
245 F6 Verde r. Oaxaca Mex.
245 E3 Verde r. San Luis Potosí Mex.
253 F5 Verde r. Para.
185 G3 Verde r. Spain
185 G4 Verde r. Spain
241 L5 Verde r. AZ U.S.A.
Verde, Cabo c. Senegal see Vert, Cap
261 F6 Verde, Península pen. Arg.
257 F1 Verde Grande r. Brazil
168 E3 Verden (Aller) Ger.
254 E5 Verde Pequeno r. Brazil
240 H2 Verdi NV U.S.A.
237 E5 Verdigris r. KS U.S.A.
198 B2 Verdikoussa Greece
256 B2 Verdinho r. Brazil
256 B3 Verdinho, Serra do mts Brazil
161 D5 Verdon r. France
182 B2 Verdugo r. Spain
157 F3 Verdun France
163 D5 Verdun-sur-Garonne France
160 D2 Verdun-sur-le-Doubs France
194 C5 Verdura r. Sicilia Italy
215 F2 Vereeniging S. Africa
137 G3 Veremiyivka Ukr.
215 G1 Verena S. Africa
177 I4 Veresegyház Hungary
134 K4 Vereshchagino Rus. Fed.
137 F2 Veresoch Ukr.
139 K3 Verestovo, Ozero l. Rus. Fed.
139 K4 Vereya Rus. Fed.
163 D4 Verfeil Midi-Pyrénées France
163 D5 Verfeil Midi-Pyrénées France
Vergara Spain see Bergara
258 G4 Vergara Uru.
191 G4 Vergato Italy
157 G4 Vergaville France
187 D6 Vergel Spain
214 E1 Vergeleë S. Africa
233 G2 Vergennes VT U.S.A.
186 G2 Verges Spain
161 C5 Vergèze France
191 H5 Verghereto Italy
156 D5 Vergigny France
198 C1 Vergina Greece
161 B3 Vergongheon France
162 C3 Vergt France
137 G3 Verhuny Cherkas'ka Oblast' Ukr.
137 G3 Verhuny Poltavs'ka Oblast' Ukr.
Véria Greece see Veroia
182 C3 Verín Spain
172 D3 Veringenstadt Ger.
Verin T'alin Armenia see T'alin
256 C3 Veríssimo Brazil
Veríssimo Sarmento Angola see Camissombo
215 F3 Verkeerdevlei S. Africa
137 H3 Verkhivtseve Ukr.
120 D1 Verkhne-Avzyan Rus. Fed.
137 I5 Verkhnebakanskiy Rus. Fed.
121 J2 Verkhne-berezovskiy Kazakh.
Verkhnedneprovsk Ukr. see Verkhn'odniprovs'k
139 I4 Verkhnedneprovskiy Rus. Fed.
130 J3 Verkhneimbatsk Rus. Fed.
134 L2 Verkhnekolvinsk Rus. Fed.
139 J4 Verkhneruzskoye Vodokhranilishche resr Rus. Fed.
134 I4 Verkhnespasskoye Rus. Fed.
140 O1 Verkhnetulomskiy Rus. Fed.
140 O1 Verkhnetulomskoye Vodokhranilishche resr Rus. Fed.
137 J2 Verkhneturovo Rus. Fed.
120 D1 Verkhneural'sk Rus. Fed.
131 N3 Verkhnevilyuysk Rus. Fed.
139 I3 Verkhnevolzhskoye Vodokhranilishche resr Rus. Fed.
134 K5 Verkhneyarkeyevo Rus. Fed.
131 Q3 Verkhniy At-Uryakh Rus. Fed.
135 I6 Verkhniy Baskunchak Rus. Fed.
137 I3 Verkhniy Byshkyn Ukr.
129 D2 Verkhniye Achaluki Rus. Fed.
Verkhniye Kholokhory Moldova see Halahora de Sus
129 D2 Verkhniy Fiagdon Rus. Fed.
Verkhniy Karabulag Georgia see Zemo Qarabulakhi
139 L5 Verkhniy Lomovets Rus. Fed.
135 H6 Verkhniy Mamon Rus. Fed.
Verkhniy Naur Rus. Fed. see Lakkha-Nevre
137 H4 Verkhniy Rohachyk Ukr.
107 F1 Verkhniy Shergol'dzhin Rus. Fed.
134 K4 Verkhniy Tatyshly Rus. Fed.
137 I4 Verkhniytokmak Ukr.
137 H3 Verkhn'odniprovs'k Ukr.
136 F3 Verkhnyachka Ukr.
175 M6 Verkhnya Lypytsya Ukr.
137 H2 Verkhnya Syrovatka Ukr.
137 H3 Verkhnya Tersa r. Ukr.
136 B3 Verkhnya Vysots'ke Ukr.
177 L3 Verkhnya Vyznytsya Ukr.
129 C2 Verkhnyaya Balkariya Rus. Fed.
177 L2 Verkhnya Yablun'ka Ukr.
137 I2 Verkhnyaya Grayvoronka Rus. Fed.
134 M2 Verkhnyaya Inta Rus. Fed.
135 G6 Verkhnyaya Khava Rus. Fed.
129 C2 Verkhnyaya Mara Rus. Fed.
131 K2 Verkhnyaya Taymyra r. Rus. Fed.
129 B2 Verkhnyaya Teberda Rus. Fed.
137 K2 Verkhnyaya Tishanka Rus. Fed.
137 K2 Verkhnyaya Toyda Rus. Fed.
134 I3 Verkhnyaya Toyma Rus. Fed.
139 K3 Verkhnyaya Troitsa Rus. Fed.
Verkhnyaya Tunguska r. Rus. Fed. see Angara
136 B3 Verkhnye Syn'ovydne Ukr.
134 J4 Verkhoshizhem'ye Rus. Fed.
139 N1 Verkhovazh'ye Rus. Fed.
Verkhovina Ukr. see Verkhovyna
139 K5 Verkhov'ye Rus. Fed.
136 C3 Verkhovyna Ukr.
131 N2 Verkhoyanskiy Khrebet mts Rus. Fed.
121 J2 Verkhuba Kazakh.
138 E4 Verknė r. Lith.
215 G2 Verkykerskop S. Africa
169 D4 Verl Ger.
165 E4 Verlaine Belgium
214 C6 Vermaaklikheid S. Africa
156 D3 Vermand France
256 B5 Vermelha, Serra hills Brazil
253 H3 Vermelho r. Mato Grosso Brazil
254 C3 Vermelho r. Pará Brazil
254 D3 Vermelho r. Tocantins Brazil
156 D5 Vermenton France
197 E3 Vermeș Romania
191 F2 Vermiglio Italy
223 I4 Vermilion Alta Can.
232 B4 Vermilion OH U.S.A.
226 C5 Vermilion r. IL U.S.A.
241 K3 Vermilion Cliffs esc. AZ U.S.A.
241 K3 Vermilion Cliffs esc. UT U.S.A.
226 A2 Vermilion Range hills MN U.S.A.
236 D3 Vermillion SD U.S.A.
236 D3 Vermillion r. SD U.S.A.
236 D3 Vermillion, East Fork r. SD U.S.A.
223 M5 Vermillion Bay Ont. Can.
230 F2 Vermillon r. Que. Can.
182 D4 Vermiosa Port.
182 B5 Vermoil Port.
233 G2 Vermont state U.S.A.
262 T2 Vernadsky research stn Antarctica
163 D6 Vernajoul France
238 E3 Vernal UT U.S.A.
190 C4 Vernante Italy
159 G4 Vernantes France
190 C2 Vernayaz Switz.
159 F4 Vern-d'Anjou France
224 D4 Verner Ont. Can.
176 D1 Verneřice Czech Rep.
163 D5 Vernet France
163 E6 Vernet-les-Bains France
159 G3 Verneuil-sur-Avre France
162 D3 Verneuil-sur-Vienne France
214 C3 Verneuk Pan salt pan S. Africa
190 B2 Vernier Switz.
191 G4 Vernio Italy
163 D5 Verniolle France
195 H2 Vernole Italy
222 G5 Vernon B.C. Can.
156 B3 Vernon France
237 F5 Vernon AL U.S.A.
230 C4 Vernon IN U.S.A.
235 D1 Vernon NJ U.S.A.
237 D5 Vernon TX U.S.A.
241 K1 Vernon UT U.S.A.
87 C5 Vernon, Mount hill W.A. Austr.
84 B2 Vernon Islands N.T. Austr.
156 B4 Vernouillet France
161 C4 Vernoux-en-Vivarais France
234 D2 Vernoy NJ U.S.A.
100 D2 Vernoye Rus. Fed.
158 E3 Vern-sur-Seiche France
157 G3 Verny France
Vernyy Kazakh. see Almaty
192 A2 Vero Corse France
186 D3 Vero r. Spain
231 D7 Vero Beach FL U.S.A.
177 I4 Verőcemaros Hungary
198 C1 Veroia Greece
190 F3 Verolanuova Italy
193 F3 Veroli Italy
156 D4 Véron France
191 F3 Verona Italy
191 G3 Verona prov. Veneto Italy
232 D5 Verona VA U.S.A.
226 C4 Verona WI U.S.A.
261 I4 Verónica Arg.
160 C2 Verosvres France
177 J4 Verpelét Hungary
235 E1 Verplanck NY U.S.A.
82 D3 Verran S.A. Austr.
190 C3 Verres Italy
162 C2 Verrières France
193 G3 Verrino r. Italy
190 D4 Versa r. Italy
190 E3 Versa r. Italy
191 I3 Versa r. Italy
156 C4 Versailles France
230 C4 Versailles IN U.S.A.
230 C4 Versailles KY U.S.A.
236 E4 Versailles MO U.S.A.
232 A4 Versailles OH U.S.A.
252 E3 Versalles Bol.
Versec Vojvodina, Srbija Yugo. see Vršac
138 E4 Verseka r. Lith.
160 D2 Vers-en-Montage France
169 D3 Versmold Ger.
190 B2 Versoix Switz.
161 A5 Versols-et-Lapeyre France
159 F2 Verson France
161 C5 Vers-Pont-du-Gard France
163 B4 Vert France
163 D4 Vert r. France
206 A3 Vert, Cap c. Senegal
160 B3 Vertaizon France
162 C3 Verteillac France
254 C4 Vertentes r. Brazil
177 H4 Vértesacsa Hungary
177 H4 Vértesboglár Hungary
163 C4 Verteuil-d'Agenais France
162 C3 Verteuil-sur-Charente France
162 B3 Vertheuil France
246 C2 Vertientes Cuba
137 F2 Vertiyivka Ukr.
156 B2 Verton France
191 F2 Vertona, Cima mt. Italy
158 E4 Vertou France
156 E4 Vertus France
191 H5 Verucchio Italy
215 H3 Verulam S. Africa
Verulamium Hertfordshire, England U.K. see St Albans
165 E4 Verviers Belgium
156 D3 Vervins France
Verwoerdburg S. Africa see Centurion
223 J5 Verwood Sask. Can.
151 F4 Verwood Dorset, England U.K.
Veryína Greece see Vergina
159 F4 Verzée r. France
156 E3 Verzenay France
195 F3 Verzino Italy
190 C4 Verzuolo Italy
156 E3 Verzy France
140 N3 Vesanto Fin.
192 B2 Vescovato Corse France
190 F3 Vescovato Italy
165 E4 Vesdre r. Belgium
176 G5 Vése Hungary
137 H4 Vesele Ukr.
197 G4 Veselina r. Bulg.
176 D2 Veselí nad Lužnicí Czech Rep.
176 G3 Veselí nad Moravou Czech Rep.
136 E2 Veselivka Ukr.
137 J4 Veselo-Voznesenka Rus. Fed.
121 J2 Veseloyarsk Rus. Fed.
137 J2 Veseloye Rus. Fed.
137 F2 Veselynivka Ukr.
137 F4 Veselynove Ukr.
135 H7 Veselyy Rus. Fed.
120 F1 Veselyy Podol Kazakh.
156 B4 Vesgre r. France
135 H6 Veshenskaya Rus. Fed.
190 D4 Vesime Italy
156 D3 Vesle r. France
134 K3 Veslyana r. Rus. Fed.
Vesontio France see Besançon
160 E1 Vesoul France
190 D3 Vespolate Italy
165 E3 Vessem Neth.
142 B2 Vest-Agder county Norway
140 K1 Vesterålen is Norway
140 K1 Vesterålsfjorden sea chan. Norway
168 G1 Vesterby Denmark
168 E1 Vester Sottrup Denmark
140 □B2 Vestfirðir constituency Iceland
142 C2 Vestfjorddalen val. Norway
140 K2 Vestfjorden sea chan. Norway
142 D2 Vestfold county Norway
263 F2 Vestfold Hills Antarctica
140 □ Vestfonna ice cap Svalbard
144 D1 Vestmanna Faroe Is
140 □B3 Vestmannaeyjar is Iceland
140 I3 Vestnes Norway
190 F3 Vestone Italy
142 D4 Vestsjælland county Denmark
140 □B2 Vesturland constituency Iceland
140 K1 Vestvågøy i. Norway
161 F5 Vésubie r. France
193 G4 Vesuvio vol. Italy
Vesuvius vol. Italy see Vesuvio
139 K2 Ves'yegonsk Rus. Fed.
176 G4 Veszkény Hungary
177 G4 Veszprém Hungary
176 G4 Veszprém county Hungary
177 G4 Veszprémvarsány Hungary
177 K5 Vésztő Hungary
215 E2 Vet r. S. Africa
79 □1 Vetauua i. Fiji
140 M3 Veteli Fin.
223 I4 Veteran Alta Can.
196 D3 Veternik Vojvodina, Srbija Yugo.
156 B3 Vétheuil France
177 L4 Vetiș Romania
143 F3 Vetlanda Sweden

134 I4 **Vetluga** Rus. Fed.
134 I4 **Vetluga** *r.* Rus. Fed.
130 F4 **Vetluzhskiy** *Kostromskaya Oblast'* Rus. Fed.
134 I4 **Vetluzhskiy** *Nizhegorodskaya Oblast'* Rus. Fed.
136 C2 **Vetly** Ukr.
139 I5 **Vet'ma** *r.* Rus. Fed.
197 H4 **Vetovo** Bulg.
192 E2 **Vetralla** Italy
197 H4 **Vetren** Bulg.
197 I2 **Vetrişoaia** Romania
176 D3 **Větřní** Czech Rep.
171 F4 **Vetschau** Ger.
140 M2 **Vettasjärvi** Sweden
169 C5 **Vettelschoß** Ger.
190 F4 **Vetto** Italy
193 F2 **Vettore, Monte** *mt.* Italy
159 G4 **Veude** *r.* France
159 G2 **Veules-les-Roses** France
159 G2 **Veulettes-sur-Mer** France
165 B3 **Veurne** Belgium
230 C4 **Vevay** *IN* U.S.A.
210 B3 **Veveno** *r.* Sudan
190 B2 **Vevey** Switz.
190 C2 **Vex** Switz.
135 G6 **Veydelevka** Rus. Fed.
160 C2 **Veyle** *r.* France
161 D4 **Veynes** France
160 B2 **Veynon** *r.* France
241 K3 **Veyo** *UT* U.S.A.
160 B3 **Veyre-Monton** France
160 E3 **Veyrier-du-Lac** France
122 B4 **Veys** Iran
138 C4 **Vėžaičiai** Lith.
160 B1 **Vézelay** France
157 G4 **Vézelise** France
161 C4 **Vézénobres** France
162 C4 **Vézère** *r.* France
197 G4 **Vezhen** *mt.* Bulg.
159 F4 **Vezins** France
161 A4 **Vézins-de-Lévézou** France
199 F1 **Vezirhan** Turkey
126 D2 **Vezirköprü** Turkey
157 G4 **Vezouze** *r.* France
190 F2 **Vezza d'Oglio** Italy
178 C4 **Vezzana, Cima della** *mt.* Italy
192 B2 **Vezzani** *Corse* France
191 G2 **Vezzano** Italy
206 C5 **Via** *r.* Liberia
252 C4 **Viacha** Bol.
191 F4 **Viadana** Italy
182 C3 **Viade de Baixo** Port.
161 F5 **Vial, Mont** *mt.* France
161 A4 **Viala du Tarn** France
Vialar Alg. *see* **Tissemsilt**
161 B4 **Vialas** France
261 G2 **Viale** Arg.
255 C9 **Viamao** Brazil
209 B7 **Viana** Angola
257 G4 **Viana** *Espírito Santo* Brazil
254 D2 **Viana** *Maranhão* Brazil
183 H2 **Viana** Spain
183 F3 **Viana de Cega** Spain
Viana del Bollo Spain *see* **Viana do Bolo**
184 C2 **Viana do Alentejo** Port.
182 C2 **Viana do Bolo** Spain
182 B3 **Viana do Castelo** Port.
182 B3 **Viana do Castelo** *admin. dist.* Port.
165 F5 **Vianden** Lux.
161 A5 **Viane** France
164 E3 **Vianen** Neth.
96 C3 **Viangchan** Laos
163 C4 **Vianne** France
182 B1 **Viaño Pequeno** Spain
256 C2 **Vianópolis** Brazil
185 H2 **Vianos** Spain
184 E3 **Viar** *r.* Spain
190 F5 **Viareggio** Italy
156 C3 **Viarmes** France
161 B5 **Vias** France
182 B3 **Viatodos** Port.
185 H4 **Viator** Spain
163 D4 **Viaur** *r.* France
163 E4 **Viazac** France
193 H4 **Vibonati** Italy
185 F3 **Víboras** *r.* Spain
142 C3 **Viborg** Denmark
142 C3 **Viborg** *county* Denmark
Viborg Rus. Fed. *see* **Vyborg**
195 F4 **Vibo Valentia** Italy
195 F4 **Vibo Valentia** *prov.* *Calabria* Italy
159 G3 **Vibraye** France
186 F3 **Vic** Spain
242 C3 **Vicam** Mex.
185 H4 **Vícar** Spain
194 C5 **Vicari** *Sicilia* Italy
148 B4 **Vicarstown** Rep. of Ireland
191 G5 **Vicchio** Italy
163 D6 **Vicdessos** France
163 D6 **Vicdessos** *r.* France
Viçe Turkey *see* **Fındıklı**
Vicecomodoro Marambio *research stn* Antarctica *see* **Marambio**
182 C1 **Vicedo** Spain
163 C5 **Vic-en-Bigorre** France
240 H5 **Vicente, Point** *CA* U.S.A.
242 A2 **Vicente Guerrero** *Baja California Norte* Mex.
245 H4 **Vicente Guerrero** *Tabasco* Mex.
245 E4 **Vicente Guerrero** *Tlaxcala* Mex.
245 F4 **Vicente y Camalote** Mex.
191 G3 **Vicenza** Italy
191 G3 **Vicenza** *prov.* *Veneto* Italy
163 C5 **Vic-Fezensac** France
Vich Spain *see* **Vic**
250 D3 **Vichada** *dept* Col.
250 E3 **Vichada** *r.* Col.
258 G3 **Vichadero** Uru.
134 H4 **Vichuga** Rus. Fed.
260 A4 **Vichuquén** Chile
160 B2 **Vichy** France
237 D4 **Vici** *OK* U.S.A.
186 C2 **Vicién** Spain
149 F3 **Vickerstown** *Cumbria, England* U.K.
241 K5 **Vicksburg** *AZ* U.S.A.
226 E4 **Vicksburg** *MI* U.S.A.
237 F5 **Vicksburg** *MS* U.S.A.
234 B2 **Vicksburg** *PA* U.S.A.
160 B3 **Vic-le-Comte** France
192 A2 **Vico** *Corse* France
192 E2 **Vico, Lago di** *l.* Italy
193 H3 **Vico del Gargano** Italy
193 G4 **Vico Equense** Italy
190 C4 **Vicoforte** Italy
193 F3 **Vico nel Lazio** Italy
254 F4 **Viçosa** Brazil
257 F4 **Viçosa** Brazil
193 E2 **Vicovaro** Italy
197 G2 **Vicovu de Sus** Romania
159 I5 **Vicq-Exemplet** France
162 D3 **Vicq-sur-Breuilh** France
156 D3 **Vic-sur-Aisne** France
161 A4 **Vic-sur-Cère** France
157 G4 **Vic-sur-Seille** France
263 C2 **Victor, Mount** Antarctica
168 C2 **Victorbur (Südbrookmerland)** Ger.
82 D3 **Victor Harbor** *S.A.* Austr.
261 G3 **Victoria** Arg.
261 H3 **Victoria** *r.* Arg.
84 B2 **Victoria** *r.* *N.T.* Austr.
83 F4 **Victoria** *state* Austr.
Victoria Cameroon *see* **Limbe**
222 F5 **Victoria** *B.C.* Can.
260 A6 **Victoria** Chile
247 □6 **Victoria** Grenada
242 □I6 **Victoria** Hond.
Victoria Malaysia *see* **Labuan**
195 □ **Victoria** *Gozo* Malta
92 B3 **Victoria** Phil.
197 H3 **Victoria** *Brăila* Romania
197 G3 **Victoria** *Braşov* Romania
217 □2b **Victoria** *Mahé* Seychelles
237 D6 **Victoria** *TX* U.S.A.
232 D6 **Victoria** *VA* U.S.A.
259 B7 **Victoria, Isla** *i.* Chile
82 E3 **Victoria, Lake** *N.S.W.* Austr.
Victoria, Mount *Viti Levu* Fiji *see* **Tomanivi**
96 A2 **Victoria, Mount** Myanmar
81 D5 **Victoria, Mount** *South I.* N.Z.
91 K8 **Victoria, Mount** P.N.G.
221 K2 **Victoria and Albert Mountains** *Nunavut* Can.
209 E9 **Victoria Falls** *waterfall* Zambia/Zimbabwe
212 E3 **Victoria Falls** Zimbabwe
220 H2 **Victoria Island** *N.W.T./Nunavut* Can.
263 K2 **Victoria Land** *coastal area* Antarctica
109 □ **Victoria Peak** *hill H.K.* China
81 D5 **Victoria Range** *mts* *South I.* N.Z.
84 B2 **Victoria River** *N.T.* Austr.
84 B3 **Victoria River Downs** *N.T.* Austr.
80 D1 **Victoria Valley** *North I.* N.Z.
225 G4 **Victoriaville** *Que.* Can.
214 D4 **Victoria West** S. Africa
260 E5 **Victorica** Arg.
240 I4 **Victorville** *CA* U.S.A.
177 K6 **Victor Vlad Delamarina** Romania
232 E3 **Victory** *NY* U.S.A.
84 C5 **Victory Downs** *N.T.* Austr.
260 B2 **Vicuña** Chile
260 E3 **Vicuña Mackenna** Arg.
182 C3 **Vidago** Port.
184 A1 **Vidais** Port.
237 F6 **Vidalia** *LA* U.S.A.
241 J4 **Vidal Junction** *CA* U.S.A.
186 B2 **Vidángoz** Spain
161 E5 **Vidauban** France
192 A4 **Viddalba** *Sardegna* Italy
142 C3 **Videbæk** Denmark
255 C8 **Videira** Brazil
261 G2 **Videla** Arg.
197 G3 **Videle** Romania
182 C4 **Videmonte** Port.
197 F4 **Viden** *mt.* Bulg.
175 K1 **Vidgiriu kalnas** *hill* Lith.
184 C2 **Vidigueira** Port.
197 G4 **Vidima** *r.* Bulg.
197 F4 **Vidin** Bulg.
177 I3 **Vidiná** Slovakia
116 D5 **Vidisha** *Madh. Prad.* India
146 □G1 **Vidlin** *Shetland, Scotland* U.K.
139 I1 **Vidlitsa** Rus. Fed.
176 G1 **Vidnava** Czech Rep.
139 K4 **Vidnoye** Rus. Fed.
161 C5 **Vidourle** *r.* France
188 F4 **Vidova Gora** *hill* Croatia
179 H4 **Vidovec** Croatia
177 L5 **Vidra** Romania
Vidreras Spain *see* **Vidrieres**
186 F3 **Vidrieres** Spain
140 M2 **Vidsel** Sweden
138 D4 **Vidukle** Lith.
188 G4 **Viduša** *mts* Bos.-Herz.
138 E3 **Vidzemes centrālā augstiene** *hills* Latvia
138 F4 **Vidzy** Belarus
158 E5 **Vie** *r.* France
159 F2 **Vie** *r.* France
173 G2 **Viechtach** Ger.
175 M1 **Viečiūnai** Lith.
215 G4 **Viedgesville** S. Africa
259 E6 **Viedma** Arg.
259 B8 **Viedma, Lago** *l.* Arg.
179 F2 **Viehberg** *mt.* Austria
158 E5 **Vieillevigne** France
182 B5 **Vieira de Leiria** Port.
182 B3 **Vieira do Minho** Port.
244 B2 **Viejo** *r.* Mex.
242 B2 **Viejo, Cerro** *mt.* Mex.
138 D3 **Viekšniai** Lith.
170 C2 **Vielank** Ger.
186 D2 **Vielha** Spain
163 B5 **Viella** France
Viella Spain *see* **Vielha**
163 C6 **Vielle-Aure** France
161 B3 **Vielle-Brioude** France
163 A5 **Vielle-St-Girons** France
163 E5 **Vielmur-sur-Agout** France
165 E4 **Vielsalm** Belgium
160 D1 **Vielverge** France
169 F4 **Vienenburg** Ger.
Vienna Austria *see* **Wien**
231 D5 **Vienna** *GA* U.S.A.
237 F4 **Vienna** *IL* U.S.A.
233 F5 **Vienna** *MD* U.S.A.
236 F4 **Vienna** *MO* U.S.A.
234 D2 **Vienna** *NJ* U.S.A.
232 C5 **Vienna** *WV* U.S.A.
160 C3 **Vienne** France
159 G5 **Vienne** *dept* *Poitou-Charentes* France
162 C1 **Vienne** *r.* France
157 E3 **Vienne-le-Château** France
Vientiane Laos *see* **Viangchan**
260 B5 **Viento, Cordillera del** *mts* Arg.
247 □1 **Vieques** *i.* Puerto Rico
157 E4 **Vière** *r.* France
170 F2 **Viereck** Ger.
140 N3 **Vieremä** Fin.
173 E2 **Viereth-Trunstadt** Ger.
173 F3 **Vierkirchen** Ger.
164 E3 **Vierlingsbeek** Neth.
169 F5 **Viernau** Ger.
172 C2 **Viernheim** Ger.
170 F2 **Vierraden** Ger.
169 B4 **Viersen** Ger.
159 F2 **Vierville-sur-Mer** France
190 D1 **Vierwaldstätter See** *l.* Switz.
162 E1 **Vierzon** France
242 E3 **Viesca** Mex.
170 D2 **Viesecke** Ger.
171 C5 **Vieselbach** Ger.
138 E3 **Viesīte** Latvia
193 I3 **Vieste** Italy
140 L2 **Vietas** Sweden
96 D3 **Vietnam** *country* Asia
Viet Nam *country* Asia *see* **Vietnam**
193 H4 **Vietri di Potenza** Italy
193 G4 **Vietri sul Mare** Italy
96 D2 **Việt Tri** Vietnam
163 A5 **Vieux-Boucau-les-Bains** France
247 □2 **Vieux Bourg** Guadeloupe
161 E4 **Vieux Chaillol** *mt.* France
160 E1 **Vieux-Charmont** France
156 D2 **Vieux-Condé** France
225 J3 **Vieux-Fort** *Que.* Can.
247 □3 **Vieux Fort** St Lucia
247 □2 **Vieux Habitants** Guadeloupe
138 E4 **Vievis** Lith.
148 E2 **Viewpark** *North Lanarkshire, Scotland* U.K.
161 D3 **Vif** France
138 E2 **Vigala** *r.* Estonia
92 B2 **Vigan** Phil.
191 G4 **Vigarano Mainarda** Italy
191 F3 **Vigasio** Italy
178 E3 **Vigaun** Austria
162 D3 **Vigeois** France
190 D3 **Vigevano** Italy
192 A3 **Viggianello** *Corse* France
193 I5 **Viggianello** Italy
193 H4 **Viggiano** Italy
190 D3 **Viggiù** Italy
254 C2 **Vigia** Brazil
184 B3 **Vigia** *hill* Port.
243 I5 **Vigía Chico** Mex.
177 I3 **Vígľaš** Slovakia
193 F3 **Viglio, Monte** *mt.* Italy
156 C2 **Vignacourt** France
190 D3 **Vignale Monferrato** Italy
193 E2 **Vignanello** Italy
163 B6 **Vignemale** *mt.* France
157 F4 **Vigneulles-les-Hattonchâtel** France
160 D2 **Vignoble** *reg.* France
191 G4 **Vignola** Italy
192 B3 **Vignola** *r.* *Sardegna* Italy
192 B3 **Vignola Mare l'Agnata** *Sardegna* Italy
157 F4 **Vignory** France
156 B3 **Vigny** France
182 B2 **Vigo** Spain
191 H2 **Vigo di Cadore** Italy
178 C4 **Vigo di Fassa** Italy
190 C4 **Vigone** Italy
191 G3 **Vigonza** Italy
191 F2 **Vigo Rendena** Italy
86 C4 **Vigors, Mount** *W.A.* Austr.
142 C3 **Vigsø Bugt** *b.* Denmark
190 D4 **Viguzzolo** Italy
157 G3 **Vigy** France
140 N2 **Vihanti** Fin.
123 H4 **Vihari** Pak.
162 B1 **Vihiers** France
177 L3 **Vihorlat** *mt.* Slovakia
177 K3 **Vihorlatské vrchy** *mts* Slovakia
138 D2 **Vihterpalu** *r.* Estonia
141 N3 **Vihti** Fin.
141 M3 **Viiala** Fin.
177 L4 **Viile Satu Mare** Romania
Viipuri Rus. Fed. *see* **Vyborg**
177 L4 **Viişoara** Romania
140 N3 **Viitasaari** Fin.
116 C3 **Vijainagar** *Rajasthan* India
116 C5 **Vijapur** *Gujarat* India
114 B2 **Vijayadurg** *Mahar.* India
Vijayanagar *Karnataka* India *see* **Hampi**
114 C4 **Vijayapati** *Tamil Nadu* India
114 D2 **Vijayawada** *Andhra Prad.* India
140 K2 **Vik** Norway
114 C2 **Vikarabad** *Andhra Prad.* India
143 G2 **Vikbolandet** *pen.* Sweden
142 A2 **Vikedal** Norway
142 C2 **Vikersund** Norway
142 A2 **Vikevåg** Norway
139 H4 **Vikhra** *r.* Rus. Fed.
197 F5 **Vikhren** *mt.* Bulg.
223 I4 **Viking** *Alta* Can.
140 J2 **Vikna** *i.* Norway
141 I3 **Vikøyri** Norway
Viktorovka Kazakh. *see* **Taranovskoye**
171 C4 **Viktorshöhe** *hill* Ger.
182 B3 **Vila** Spain
Vila Vanuatu *see* **Port Vila**
Vila Alferes Chamusca Moz. *see* **Guija**
184 C2 **Vila Alva** Port.
Vila Arriaga Angola *see* **Bibala**
250 D5 **Vila Bittencourt** Brazil
182 D4 **Vila Boa** Port.
184 C2 **Vila Boim** Port.
Vila Bugaço Angola *see* **Camanongue**
Vila Cabral Moz. *see* **Lichinga**
182 B3 **Vila Caiz** Port.
252 D4 **Vilacaya** Bol.
182 B3 **Vila Chã** Port.
182 C4 **Vila Chã de Sá** Port.
182 B3 **Vila Chão do Marão** Port.
Vila Coutinho Moz. *see* **Ulongue**
182 C4 **Vila Cova à Coelheira** Port.
182 B3 **Vila Cova da Lixa** Port.
186 E2 **Vilada** Spain
182 C1 **Vila da Igrexa** Spain
186 G2 **Viladamat** Spain
Vila da Ponte Angola *see* **Kuvango**
182 C3 **Vila da Ponte** Port.
216 □1a **Vila da Praia da Vitória** *Terceira* Azores
206 □ **Vila da Ribeira Brava** Cape Verde
Vila de Aljustrel Angola *see* **Cangamba**
Vila de Almoster Angola *see* **Chiange**
186 F3 **Viladecans** Spain
182 B2 **Vila de Cruces** Spain
Vila de João Belo Moz. *see* **Xai-Xai**
Vila de Junqueiro Moz. *see* **Gurué**
Vilademat Spain *see* **Viladamat**
182 B5 **Vila de Rei** Port.
206 □ **Vila de Sal Rei** Cape Verde
213 G3 **Vila de Sena** Moz.
Vila de Trego Morais Moz. *see* **Chókwé**
184 B3 **Vila do Bispo** Port.
182 B3 **Vila do Conde** Port.
206 □ **Vila do Tarrafal** *São Tiago* Cape Verde
186 F3 **Viladrau** Spain
184 C2 **Vila Fernando** Port.
216 □3a **Vilaflor** *Tenerife* Canary Is
182 C3 **Vila Flor** Port.
Vila Fontes Moz. *see* **Caia**
182 C4 **Vila Franca das Naves** Port.
186 E3 **Vilafranca del Penedès** Spain
184 B2 **Vila Franca de Xira** Port.
216 □1b **Vila Franca do Campo** *São Miguel* Azores
182 B2 **Vilagarcía de Arousa** Spain
Vila Gouveia Moz. *see* **Catandica**
158 D4 **Vilaine** *r.* France
186 G2 **Vilajüiga** Spain
138 F3 **Viļaka** Latvia
182 C1 **Vilalba** Spain
186 F2 **Vilallonga** Spain
Vila Luísa Moz. *see* **Marracuene**
Vila Marechal Carmona Angola *see* **Uíge**
182 C2 **Vilamartín de Valdeorras** Spain
187 C5 **Vilamarxant** Spain
260 A5 **Vila Mercedes** Chile
Vila Miranda Moz. *see* **Macaloge**
184 B1 **Vila Moreira** Port.
184 B3 **Vilamoura** Port.
213 □J3 **Vilanandro, Tanjona** *pt* Madag.
186 F2 **Vilanant** Spain
213 G4 **Vilanculos** Moz.
138 F3 **Viļāni** Latvia
184 A2 **Vila Nogueira de Azeitão** Port.
Vila Nova Angola *see* **Tchikala-Tcholohanga**
216 □1a **Vila Nova** *Terceira* Azores
184 B2 **Vila Nova da Baronia** Port.
187 D4 **Vilanova d'Alcolea** Spain
186 D3 **Vilanova d'Aplicat** Spain
182 B4 **Vila Nova de Anços** Port.
182 B2 **Vilanova de Arousa** Spain
Vilanova de Castelló Spain *see* Villanueva de Castellón
182 B3 **Vila Nova de Cerveira** Port.
182 B3 **Vila Nova de Famalicão** Port.
182 C3 **Vila Nova de Foz Coa** Port.
182 B3 **Vila Nova de Gaia** Port.
186 E3 **Vilanova de l'Aguda** Spain
182 C1 **Vilanova de Lourenzá** Spain
186 E3 **Vilanova de Meià** Spain
182 B5 **Vila Nova de Ourém** Port.
182 C4 **Vila Nova de Paiva** Port.
182 B4 **Vila Nova de Poiares** Port.
184 C3 **Vila Nova de São Bento** Port.
Vila Nova do Seles Angola *see* **Uku**
186 E3 **Vilanova i la Geltrú** Spain
206 □ **Vila Nova Sintra** Cape Verde
Vila Paiva de Andrada Moz. *see* **Gorongosa**
Vila Pery Moz. *see* **Chimoio**
182 C4 **Vila Pouca da Beira** Port.
182 C3 **Vila Pouca de Aguiar** Port.
182 B3 **Vila Praia de Âncora** Port.
182 C3 **Vilarandelo** Port.
182 C2 **Vilarchao** Spain
182 B3 **Vilar da Veiga** Port.
182 B3 **Vilar de Andorinho** Port.
182 C2 **Vilar de Barrio** Spain
182 C2 **Vilar de Santos** Spain
182 C3 **Vilardevós** Spain
182 C3 **Vila Real** Port.
182 C3 **Vila Real** *admin. dist.* Port.
187 C5 **Vila-real de los Infantes** Spain
184 C3 **Vila Real de Santo António** Port.
182 C3 **Vilarelho da Raia** Port.
182 D4 **Vilar Formoso** Port.
182 C3 **Vilarinho da Castanheira** Port.
182 B4 **Vilarinho do Bairro** Port.
182 C2 **Vilariño de Conso** Spain
186 E3 **Vila-rodona** Spain
184 C2 **Vila Ruiva** Port.
Vilas *i.* *S. Male* Maldives *see* **Velassary**
Vila Salazar Angola *see* **N'dalatando**
129 F4 **Viläşçay** *r.* Azer.
182 B3 **Vila Seca** Port.
186 E3 **Vilaseca de Solcina** Spain
Vila Teixeira de Sousa Angola *see* **Luau**
114 C4 **Vilavankod** *Tamil Nadu* India
257 G4 **Vila Velha** Brazil
182 C5 **Vila Velha de Ródão** Port.
182 B3 **Vila Verde** *Braga* Port.
182 B4 **Vila Verde** *Coimbra* Port.
182 C3 **Vila Verde** *Vila Real* Port.
182 C3 **Vila Verde da Raia** Port.
184 C3 **Vila Verde de Ficalho** Port.
184 C2 **Vila Viçosa** Port.
252 B3 **Vilcabamba, Cordillera** *mts* Peru
252 C3 **Vilcanota, Cordillera de** *mts* Peru
136 E2 **Vil'cha** Ukr.
185 G2 **Vilches** Spain
260 A6 **Vilcun** Chile
134 I3 **Viled'** *r.* Rus. Fed.
Vileyka Belarus *see* **Vilyeyka**
134 J3 **Vil'gort** Rus. Fed.
140 L2 **Vilhelmina** Sweden
253 E3 **Vilhena** Brazil
Viligili *i.* *N. Male* Maldives *see* **Villingli**
137 G5 **Viline** Ukr.
113 □1 **Vilingli** *i.* *N. Male* Maldives
138 E4 **Viliya** *r.* Belarus/Lith.
136 D2 **Viliya** *r.* Ukr.
138 E2 **Viljandi** Estonia
214 B6 **Viljoenshof** S. Africa
215 F2 **Viljoenskroon** S. Africa
138 D4 **Vilkaviškis** Lith.
137 J3 **Vil'khova** *r.* Ukr.
138 D4 **Vilkija** Lith.
252 D5 **Villa Abecia** Bol.
260 C2 **Villa Aberastain** Arg.
189 D5 **Villa Adriana** *tourist site* Italy
242 D2 **Villa Ahumada** Mex.
261 F6 **Villa Alba** Arg.
260 B4 **Villa Alegre** Chile
260 B3 **Villa Alemana** Chile
246 E3 **Villa Altagracia** Dom. Rep.
258 F3 **Villa Ana** Arg.
258 E2 **Villa Angela** Arg.
261 G3 **Villa Angelica** Arg.
244 D3 **Villa Apaseo El Alto** Mex.
261 F6 **Villa Atlantica** Arg.
260 D4 **Villa Atuel** Arg.
245 F3 **Villa Ávila Camacho** Mex.
245 G4 **Villa Azueta** Mex.
191 G3 **Villa Bartolomea** Italy
194 C4 **Villabate** *Sicilia* Italy
Villa Bens Morocco *see* **Tarfaya**
258 E2 **Villa Berthet** Arg.
184 C3 **Villablanca** Spain
182 D2 **Villablino** Spain
186 A1 **Villabona** Spain
183 E3 **Villabrágima** Spain
183 E3 **Villabuena del Puente** Spain
162 D3 **Villac** France
261 G4 **Villa Cañás** Arg.
183 G5 **Villacañas** Spain
190 F3 **Villa Carcina** Italy
186 □ **Villacarlos** Spain
260 E2 **Villa Carlos Paz** Arg.
185 G2 **Villacarrillo** Spain
195 G2 **Villa Castelli** Italy
183 F4 **Villacastín** Spain
179 E4 **Villach** Austria
192 A5 **Villacidro** *Sardegna* Italy
183 H3 **Villaciervos** Spain
Villa Cisneros Western Sahara *see* **Ad Dakhla**
Villa Cisneros, Ría de *b.* Western Sahara *see* **Río de Oro, Bahía de**
243 G6 **Villa Comaltitlán** Mex.
261 F2 **Villa Concepción del Tío** Arg.
183 G4 **Villaconejos** Spain
183 H4 **Villaconejos de Trabaque** Spain
261 G3 **Villa Constitución** Arg.
Villa Constitución Mex. *see* **Ciudad Constitución**
244 C3 **Villa Corona** Mex.
260 E2 **Villa Cura Brochero** Arg.
261 G3 **Villada** Arg.
183 F2 **Villada** Spain
190 E3 **Villa d'Almè** Italy
244 C4 **Villa de Álvarez** Mex.
244 C2 **Villa de Cos** Mex.
183 F4 **Villa del Prado** Spain
244 D3 **Villa del Pueblito** Mex.
185 F3 **Villa del Río** Spain
261 F2 **Villa del Rosario** Arg.
182 D3 **Villadepera** Spain
187 B5 **Villa de Ves** Spain
261 G3 **Villa Diego** Arg.
183 F2 **Villadiego** Spain
260 E2 **Villa Dolores** Arg.
261 H3 **Villa Domínguez** Arg.
191 G3 **Villadose** Italy
190 D2 **Villadossola** Italy
186 B3 **Villadoz** Spain
260 C6 **Villa El Chocón** Arg.
183 F2 **Villaeles de Valdavia** Spain
261 H3 **Villa Elisa** Arg.
261 G3 **Villa Eloisa** Arg.
244 D4 **Villa Escalante** Mex.
183 H5 **Villaescusa de Haro** Spain
183 G2 **Villaescusa la Sombría** Spain
182 E3 **Villafáfila** Spain
187 C4 **Villafamés** Spain
183 I3 **Villafeliche** Spain
243 G5 **Villa Flores** Mex.
183 E3 **Villaflores** Spain
253 F6 **Villa Florida** Para.
183 I2 **Villafranca** Spain
190 D4 **Villafranca d'Asti** Italy
187 G5 **Villafranca de Bonany** Spain
185 F3 **Villafranca de Córdoba** Spain
186 C3 **Villafranca de Ebro** Spain
182 D2 **Villafranca del Bierzo** Spain
186 B4 **Villafranca del Campo** Spain
186 C4 **Villafranca del Cid** Spain
184 D2 **Villafranca de los Barros** Spain
185 G1 **Villafranca de los Caballeros** Spain
Villafranca del Penedès Spain *see* **Vilafranca del Penedès**
191 F3 **Villafranca di Verona** Italy
190 E4 **Villafranca in Lunigiana** Italy
183 G2 **Villafranca-Montes de Oca** Spain
195 E4 **Villafranca Tirrena** *Sicilia* Italy
191 F3 **Villafranca Veronese** *airport* Italy
184 D3 **Villafranco del Guadalquivir** Spain
194 C5 **Villafrati** *Sicilia* Italy
183 E3 **Villafrechos** Spain
183 G3 **Villafruela** Spain
183 F3 **Villafuerte** Spain
Villagarcía de Arosa Spain *see* **Vilagarcía de Arousa**
183 E3 **Villagarcía de Campos** Spain
184 D2 **Villagarcía de la Torre** Spain
185 I1 **Villagarcía del Llano** Spain
261 I5 **Villa Gesell** Arg.
195 F3 **Villagio Mancuso** Italy
184 D2 **Villagonzalo** Spain
261 G3 **Villa Governador Gálvez** Arg.
245 E1 **Villagrán** Mex.
192 B5 **Villagrande Strisaili** *Sardegna* Italy
261 H2 **Villaguay** Arg.
258 F3 **Villa Guillermina** Arg.
185 F2 **Villaharta** Spain
253 F6 **Villa Hayes** Para.
243 G5 **Villahermosa** Mex.
185 H2 **Villahermosa** Spain
187 C4 **Villahermosa del Río** Spain
261 H2 **Villa Hernandarias** Arg.
183 F2 **Villaherreros** Spain
244 B3 **Villa Hidalgo** *Nayarit* Mex.
239 E6 **Villa Hidalgo** Mex.
183 G2 **Villahizán** Spain
183 G2 **Villahoz** Spain
260 E4 **Villa Huidobro** Arg.
156 E5 **Villaines-en-Duesmois** France
159 F3 **Villaines-la-Juhel** France
159 F4 **Villaines-sous-Malicorne** France
242 C3 **Villa Insurgentes** Mex.
261 F6 **Villa Iris** Arg.
187 C6 **Villajoyosa** Spain
244 B3 **Villa Juárez** Mex.
244 D2 **Villa Juárez** Mex.
191 G3 **Villa Lagarina** Italy
193 F3 **Villalago** Italy
183 E3 **Villalar de los Comuneros** Spain
193 F3 **Villa Latina** Italy
245 G4 **Villa La Venta** Mex.
245 F3 **Villa Lázaro Cárdenas** Mex.
194 C5 **Villalba** *Sicilia* Italy
247 □1 **Villalba** Puerto Rico
183 G3 **Villalba de Duero** Spain
183 F2 **Villalba de Guardo** Spain
184 D3 **Villalba del Alcor** Spain
183 H4 **Villalba de la Sierra** Spain
183 F3 **Villalba de los Alcores** Spain
184 D2 **Villalba de los Barros** Spain
183 H4 **Villalba del Rey** Spain
186 D3 **Villalba dels Arcs** Spain
183 H2 **Villalba de Rioja** Spain
182 D3 **Villalcampo** Spain
183 F2 **Villalcázar de Sirga** Spain
243 E3 **Villaldama** Mex.
183 I3 **Villalengua** Spain
185 H1 **Villalgordo del Júcar** Spain
183 H5 **Villalgordo del Marquesado** Spain
193 G3 **Villa Literno** Italy
183 E3 **Villalobos** Spain
183 E2 **Villalón de Campos** Spain
259 E5 **Villálonga** Arg.
187 C6 **Villalonga** Spain
183 E3 **Villalpando** Spain
185 I1 **Villalpardo** Spain
183 G4 **Villaluenga de la Sagra** Spain
183 F2 **Villalumbroso** Spain
185 I1 **Villamalea** Spain
182 E2 **Villamañán** Spain
182 E2 **Villamandos** Spain
185 H2 **Villamanrique** Spain
184 D3 **Villamanrique de la Condesa** Spain
183 F4 **Villamanta** Spain
192 A5 **Villamar** *Sardegna* Italy
Villamarchante Spain *see* **Vilamarxant**
261 F3 **Villa María** Arg.
261 G2 **Villa María** Arg.
261 H2 **Villa María Grande** Arg.
252 D5 **Villa Martín** Bol.
184 E4 **Villamartín** Spain
183 F2 **Villamartín de Campos** Spain
192 A5 **Villamassargia** *Sardegna* Italy
182 E4 **Villamayor** Spain
185 F2 **Villamayor de Calatrava** Spain
183 E3 **Villamayor de Campos** Spain
183 H5 **Villamayor de Santiago** Spain
183 F2 **Villamayor de Treviño** Spain
162 C3 **Villamblard** France
183 F2 **Villamediana** Spain
183 H2 **Villamediana de Iregua** Spain
182 D2 **Villamejil** Spain
184 E1 **Villamesías** Spain
182 D4 **Villamiel** Spain
190 F4 **Villa Minozzo** Italy
252 E5 **Villa Montes** Bol.
182 E3 **Villamor de los Escuderos** Spain
244 D3 **Villa Morelos** Mex.
183 G5 **Villamuelas** Spain
183 F3 **Villamuriel de Cerrato** Spain
163 B4 **Villandraut** France
195 G2 **Villanova** Italy
190 D4 **Villanova d'Albenga** Italy
190 C4 **Villanova d'Asti** Italy
193 H3 **Villanova del Battista** Italy
192 B5 **Villanovafranca** *Sardegna* Italy
192 A4 **Villanova Monteleone** *Sardegna* Italy
192 A5 **Villanova Truschedu** *Sardegna* Italy
192 B5 **Villanova Tulo** *Sardegna* Italy
190 E3 **Villanterio** Italy
186 C2 **Villanúa** Spain
183 F3 **Villanubla** Spain
261 F3 **Villa Nueva** Arg.
250 C2 **Villanueva** Col.
244 C2 **Villanueva** Mex.
Villanueva Spain *see* Vilanova de Lourenzá
183 H5 **Villanueva de Alcardete** Spain
Villanueva de Alcolea Spain *see* Vilanova d'Alcolea
183 H4 **Villanueva de Alcorón** Spain
185 F3 **Villanueva de Algaidas** Spain
183 G2 **Villanueva de Argaño** Spain
Villanueva de Arosa Spain *see* Vilanova de Arousa
183 G5 **Villanueva de Bogas** Spain
183 H2 **Villanueva de Cameros** Spain
187 C5 **Villanueva de Castellón** Spain
185 F2 **Villanueva de Córdoba** Spain
186 C3 **Villanueva de Gállego** Spain
183 F4 **Villanueva de Gómez** Spain
183 G4 **Villanueva de la Cañada** Spain
185 F4 **Villanueva de la Concepción** Spain
185 H2 **Villanueva de la Fuente** Spain
185 I1 **Villanueva de la Jara** Spain
185 G2 **Villanueva de la Reina** Spain
185 G2 **Villanueva del Arzobispo** Spain
184 C3 **Villanueva de las Cruces** Spain
184 E2 **Villanueva de la Serena** Spain
182 D4 **Villanueva de la Sierra** Spain
185 G3 **Villanueva de las Torres** Spain
183 E4 **Villanueva de la Vera** Spain
183 E3 **Villanueva del Campo** Spain
185 F2 **Villanueva del Duque** Spain
184 C2 **Villanueva del Fresno** Spain
184 C3 **Villanueva de los Castillejos** Spain
185 H2 **Villanueva de los Infantes** Spain
185 E2 **Villanueva del Rey** Spain
187 B6 **Villanueva del Río Segura** Spain
184 E3 **Villanueva del Río y Minas** Spain
185 F4 **Villanueva del Rosario** Spain
185 F3 **Villanueva del Trabuco** Spain
185 G2 **Villanueva de San Carlos** Spain
185 E3 **Villanueva de San Juan** Spain
185 F3 **Villanueva de Tapia** Spain
183 G2 **Villanueva de Valdegovia** Spain
Villanueva-y-Geltrú Spain *see* Vilanova i la Geltrú
183 F2 **Villanuño de Valdavia** Spain
177 H6 **Villány** Hungary
177 H6 **Villányi-hegység** *ridge* Hungary
258 F3 **Villa Ocampo** Arg.
242 D3 **Villa Ocampo** Mex.
258 E3 **Villa Ojo de Agua** Arg.
Villa O. Pereyra Mex. *see* **Villa Orestes Pereyra**
191 I3 **Villa Opicina** Italy
242 D3 **Villa Orestes Pereyra** Mex.
252 D4 **Villa Oropeza** Bol.
185 H2 **Villapalacios** Spain
192 A5 **Villaperuccio** *Sardegna* Italy
195 F3 **Villapiana** Italy
195 F3 **Villapiana Lido** Italy
191 G4 **Villa Poma** Italy
160 B2 **Villapourçon** France
260 B4 **Villa Prat** Chile
192 B5 **Villaputzu** *Sardegna* Italy
182 E2 **Villaquejida** Spain
182 E2 **Villaquilambre** Spain
252 D4 **Villar** Bol.
182 E3 **Villaralbo** Spain
185 F2 **Villaralto** Spain
261 G3 **Villa Ramírez** Arg.
183 G2 **Villarcayo** Spain
161 E3 **Villar-d'Arêne** France
161 D3 **Villard-Bonnot** France
161 D3 **Villard-de-Lans** France
185 I2 **Villar de Chinchilla** Spain
182 D4 **Villar de Ciervo** Spain
182 D3 **Villardeciervos** Spain
183 E3 **Villardefrades** Spain
187 C5 **Villar del Arzobispo** Spain
182 D4 **Villar de la Yegua** Spain
182 D3 **Villar del Buey** Spain
183 I4 **Villar del Cobo** Spain
183 I5 **Villar del Humo** Spain
182 D2 **Villar de los Barrios** Spain
186 B3 **Villar de los Navarros** Spain
183 E5 **Villar del Pedroso** Spain
184 D1 **Villar del Rey** Spain
183 I4 **Villar del Salz** Spain
183 H4 **Villar de Olalla** Spain
182 D3 **Villar de Peralonso** Spain
184 E1 **Villar de Rena** Spain
183 H2 **Villar de Torre** Spain
185 F3 **Villardompardo** Spain
Villareal Spain *see* Vila-real de los Infantes
Villareal de los Infantes Spain *see* **Vila-real de los Infantes**
261 F3 **Villa Reducción** Arg.
260 D6 **Villa Regina** Arg.
183 H5 **Villarejo de Fuentes** Spain
183 F5 **Villarejo de Montalbán** Spain
182 E2 **Villarejo de Orbigo** Spain
183 G4 **Villarejo de Salvanés** Spain
191 F2 **Villa Rendena** Italy
183 E2 **Villarente** Spain
182 E3 **Villares de la Reina** Spain
185 G3 **Villargordo** Spain
182 D3 **Villarino de los Aires** Spain
186 C4 **Villarluengo** Spain
194 D5 **Villarosa** *Sicilia* Italy
186 B4 **Villarquemado** Spain
183 F2 **Villarramiel** Spain
186 B3 **Villarreal de Huerva** Spain
260 A6 **Villarrica** Chile
253 F6 **Villarrica** Para.
260 A6 **Villarrica, Lago** *l.* Chile
182 E3 **Villarrín de Campos** Spain
185 H1 **Villarrobledo** Spain
185 H2 **Villarrodrigo** Spain
183 H2 **Villarroya** Spain
186 C4 **Villarroya de los Pinares** Spain
185 G1 **Villarrubia de los Ojos** Spain
183 G5 **Villarrubia de Santiago** Spain
183 H5 **Villarrubio** Spain
162 C3 **Villars** *Aquitaine* France
161 C3 **Villars** *Rhône-Alpes* France
161 E4 **Villar-St-Pancrace** France
183 H5 **Villars del Saz** Spain
160 E1 **Villars-lès-Blamont** France
160 D3 **Villars-les-Dombes** France
161 F5 **Villars-sur-Var** France
185 I1 **Villarta** Spain
185 F1 **Villarta de los Montes** Spain
185 G1 **Villarta de San Juan** Spain
234 D3 **Villas** *NJ* U.S.A.
192 B5 **Villasalto** *Sardegna* Italy
180 E1 **Villasana de Mena** Spain
183 F2 **Villasandino** Spain
195 E4 **Villa San Giovanni** Italy
261 H3 **Villa San José** Arg.
Villa Sanjurjo Morocco *see* **Al Hoceima**
258 D3 **Villa San Martin** Arg.
193 G3 **Villa Santa Maria** Italy
260 C2 **Villa Santa Rosa** Arg.
183 G1 **Villasante de Montija** Spain
191 H2 **Villa Santina** Italy
183 F2 **Villasarracino** Spain
163 E5 **Villasavary** France
183 H3 **Villasayas** Spain
182 D3 **Villasbuenas** Spain
182 D3 **Villasdardo** Spain
182 D2 **Villaseca de Laciana** Spain
183 G5 **Villaseca de la Sagra** Spain
182 D3 **Villaseco de los Gamitos** Spain
182 D3 **Villaseco de los Reyes** Spain
182 E3 **Villaseco del Pan** Spain
183 G5 **Villasequilla de Yepes** Spain
252 D4 **Villa Serrano** Bol.
192 B5 **Villasimius** *Sardegna* Italy
195 E5 **Villasmundo** *Sicilia* Italy
192 A5 **Villasor** *Sardegna* Italy
192 A5 **Villaspeciosa** *Sardegna* Italy
182 D4 **Villasrubias** Spain
187 B4 **Villastar** Spain
183 G2 **Villasur de Herreros** Spain
183 G5 **Villatobas** Spain
183 E4 **Villatoro** Spain
187 B5 **Villatoya** Spain
261 E2 **Villa Tulumba** Arg.
183 E2 **Villaturiel** Spain
183 F2 **Villaumbrales** Spain
258 C3 **Villa Unión** Arg.
243 E2 **Villa Unión** Mex.
244 B2 **Villa Unión** Mex.
244 A2 **Villa Unión** Mex.
192 A5 **Villaurbana** *Sardegna* Italy
260 E4 **Villa Valeria** Arg.
193 F3 **Villavallelonga** Italy
246 E3 **Villa Vasquez** Dom. Rep.
183 H2 **Villavelayo** Spain
192 A5 **Villa Verde** *Sardegna* Italy
185 H2 **Villaverde de Guadalimar** Spain
184 E3 **Villaverde del Río** Spain
187 A5 **Villaverde y Pasaconsol** Spain
190 D4 **Villavernia** Italy
250 C3 **Villavicencio** Col.
183 E1 **Villaviciosa de Asturias** Spain
185 E2 **Villaviciosa de Córdoba** Spain
183 G4 **Villaviciosa de Odón** Spain
187 C5 **Villavieja** Spain
183 G3 **Villavieja del Lozoya** Spain
182 D4 **Villavieja de Yeltes** Spain
252 D4 **Villa Viscarra** Bol.
183 F3 **Villaviudas** Spain
182 D1 **Villayón** Spain
183 F2 **Villazanzo de Valderaduey** Spain
252 D5 **Villazon** Bol.
157 H4 **Villé** France
160 D3 **Villebois** France
162 C3 **Villebois-Lavalette** France
163 D5 **Villebrumier** France
163 C5 **Villecomtal-sur-Arros** France
160 D1 **Villecomte** France
161 E5 **Villecroze** France
161 A5 **Villedaigne** France
244 D3 **Ville de Reyes** Mex.
159 E4 **Villedieu-la-Blouère** France
158 E3 **Villedieu-les-Poêles** France
159 H5 **Villedieu-sur-Indre** France
192 B2 **Ville-di-Pietrabugno** *Corse* France
159 G4 **Villedômer** France
156 D3 **Ville-en-Tardenois** France
162 C2 **Villefagnan** France
160 D3 **Villefontaine** France
161 B4 **Villefort** France
156 D5 **Villefranche** *Bourgogne* France
163 C5 **Villefranche** *Midi-Pyrénées* France
163 E5 **Villefranche-d'Albigeois** France
160 A2 **Villefranche-d'Allier** France
163 E6 **Villefranche-de-Conflent** France
163 D5 **Villefranche-de-Lauragais** France
162 C4 **Villefranche-de-Lonchat** France
161 A4 **Villefranche-de-Panat** France
163 E4 **Villefranche-de-Rouergue** France
163 D4 **Villefranche-du-Périgord** France
159 H4 **Villefranche-sur-Cher** France
161 F5 **Villefranche-sur-Mer** France
160 C3 **Villefranche-sur-Saône** France
163 A5 **Villefranque** France
183 F2 **Villegas** Spain
244 C2 **Ville Juarez** Mex.
187 B4 **Villel** Spain
161 D5 **Villelaure** France
156 C5 **Villemandeur** France
227 H2 **Ville-Marie** *Que.* Can.
Ville-Marie *Que.* Can. *see* **Montréal**
156 D4 **Villemaur-sur-Vanne** France
227 H1 **Villemontel** *Que.* Can.
156 E4 **Villemorien** France
163 E5 **Villemoustaussou** France
163 D5 **Villemur-sur-Tarn** France
187 C6 **Villena** Spain
156 D4 **Villenauxe-la-Grande** France
163 B4 **Villenave-d'Ornon** France
163 E4 **Villeneuve** *Midi-Pyrénées* France
161 D5 **Villeneuve** *Provence-Alpes-Côte-d'Azur* France
160 C2 **Villeneuve** *Rhône-Alpes* France
190 B2 **Villeneuve** Switz.
156 D4 **Villeneuve-au-Chemin** France
161 B3 **Villeneuve-d'Allier** France
156 D2 **Villeneuve-d'Ascq** France
161 C4 **Villeneuve-de-Berg** France
163 B5 **Villeneuve-de-Marsan** France
163 C5 **Villeneuve-de-Rivière** France
163 D6 **Villeneuve-d'Olmes** France
163 D5 **Villeneuve-du-Paréage** France
156 D4 **Villeneuve-la-Guyard** France
156 D4 **Villeneuve-l'Archevêque** France
161 C5 **Villeneuve-lès-Avignon** France
161 B5 **Villeneuve-lès-Béziers** France
161 B5 **Villeneuve-lès-Maguelonne** France
161 F5 **Villeneuve-Loubet** France
156 D3 **Villeneuve-St-Germain** France
160 B2 **Villeneuve-sur-Allier** France
163 C4 **Villeneuve-sur-Lot** France
156 D4 **Villeneuve-sur-Yonne** France
163 D5 **Villeneuve-Tolosane** France
163 D5 **Villenouvelle** France
163 E5 **Villepinte** France
237 E6 **Ville Platte** *LA* U.S.A.
159 G2 **Villequier** France
161 A4 **Villercomtal** France
163 C4 **Villeréal** France
160 C3 **Villerest** France
183 F3 **Villerías** Spain
161 A5 **Villerouge-Termenès** France
159 F2 **Villers-Bocage** France
156 C3 **Villers-Bocage** France
156 C3 **Villers-Bretonneux** France
156 C3 **Villers-Carbonnel** France
156 D3 **Villers-Cotterêts** France
156 A3 **Villers-Écalles** France
157 E3 **Villers-en-Argonne** France
160 E1 **Villersexel** France
160 D1 **Villers-Farlay** France
165 E4 **Villers-le-Bouillet** Belgium
160 E1 **Villers-le-lac** France
157 G4 **Villers-lès-Nancy** France
156 D2 **Villers-Outréaux** France
165 B5 **Villers-St-Paul** France
156 E3 **Villers-Semeuse** France
190 C2 **Villers-sur-Glâne** Switz.
159 F2 **Villers-sur-Mer** France
157 F3 **Villers-sur-Meuse** France
157 F3 **Villerupt** France
159 G2 **Villerville** France
156 E4 **Villery** France
156 E4 **Villeseneux** France
161 D4 **Villes-sur-Auzon** France
157 E3 **Ville-sur-Tourbe** France
193 F3 **Villetta Barrea** Italy
160 D3 **Villette-d'Anthon** France
160 C3 **Villeurbanne** France
161 B5 **Villeveyrac** France
161 C3 **Villevocance** France
260 C2 **Villicun, Sierra** *mts* Arg.
160 C2 **Villié-Morgon** France
215 G2 **Villiers** S. Africa
159 F4 **Villiers-Charlemagne** France
214 B5 **Villiersdorp** S. Africa
157 E4 **Villiers-en-Lieu** France
162 B2 **Villiers-en-Plaine** France
156 C3 **Villiers-le-Bel** France
157 F4 **Villiers-le-Sec** France
156 D5 **Villiers-St-Benoît** France
156 D4 **Villiers-St-Georges** France
147 D4 **Villierstown** Rep. of Ireland
160 D3 **Villieu-Loyes-Mollon** France
172 C3 **Villingen** Ger.
172 C3 **Villingendorf** Ger.
113 □1 **Villingli** *i.* *N. Male* Maldives
169 D5 **Villmar** Ger.
183 F2 **Villoldo** Spain
183 I5 **Villora** Spain
183 I5 **Villora** *r.* Spain
191 H3 **Villorba** Italy
183 E4 **Villoria** Spain
183 E3 **Villoruela** Spain
157 F4 **Villotte-sur-Aire** France
Villupuram *Tamil Nadu* India *see* **Viluppuram**
177 K3 **Vilmány** Hungary
223 I4 **Vilna** *Alta* Can.
Vilna Lith. *see* **Vilnius**
138 E4 **Vilnius** Lith.
137 H3 **Vil'nohirs'k** Ukr.
137 H4 **Vil'nyans'k** Ukr.
186 F3 **Viloví d'Onyar** Spain
141 N3 **Vilppula** Fin.
178 B3 **Vils** Austria
173 F2 **Vils** *r.* Ger.
173 H3 **Vils** *r.* Ger.
138 C2 **Vilsandi** *i.* Estonia
173 G3 **Vilsbiburg** Ger.
173 F2 **Vilseck** Ger.
137 F3 **Vil'shana** Ukr.
137 G2 **Vil'shana** Ukr.
137 I3 **Vil'shana** Ukr.
136 F3 **Vil'shanka** Ukr.
136 E3 **Vil'shanka** Ukr.
136 E2 **Vil'shanka** Ukr.
173 H3 **Vilshofen** Ger.
142 C3 **Vilsund Vest** Denmark
114 C4 **Viluppuram** *Tamil Nadu* India
182 D3 **Vilvestre** Spain
165 D4 **Vilvoorde** Belgium
138 F4 **Vilyeyka** Belarus
131 N3 **Vilyuy** *r.* Rus. Fed.
131 M3 **Vilyuyskoye Vodokhranilishche** *resr* Rus. Fed.
209 F8 **Vimbe** *mt.* Zambia
186 E3 **Vimbodi** Spain
184 A1 **Vimeiro** Port.
190 E3 **Vimercate** Italy
182 A1 **Vimianzo** Spain
184 C2 **Vimieiro** Port.
182 D3 **Vimioso** Port.
143 F3 **Vimmerby** Sweden
156 C5 **Vimory** France
159 G3 **Vimoutiers** France
140 M3 **Vimpeli** Fin.
176 C2 **Vimperk** Czech Rep.
207 I5 **Vina** *r.* Cameroon
240 F2 **Vina** *CA* U.S.A.
186 C3 **Vinaceite** Spain
260 B3 **Viña del Mar** Chile
190 C4 **Vinadio** Italy
186 D3 **Vinaixa** Spain
246 B2 **Viñales Valley** *tourist site* *Pinar del Río* Cuba
233 □I2 **Vinalhaven** *ME* U.S.A.
187 C6 **Vinalopó** *r.* Spain
171 F5 **Vinařice** Czech Rep.
78 □6 **Vinarori, Mount** *New Georgia Is* Solomon Is
186 D4 **Vinaròs** Spain
Vinaroz Spain *see* **Vinaròs**
161 B5 **Vinassan** France
161 D3 **Vinay** France
245 F3 **Vinazco** *r.* Mex.
163 E6 **Vinça** France
230 C4 **Vincennes** *IN* U.S.A.
234 D3 **Vincentown** *NJ* U.S.A.
250 B5 **Vinces** *r.* Ecuador
157 G4 **Vincey** France
193 G3 **Vinchiaturo** Italy
258 C3 **Vinchina** Arg.
252 B3 **Vinchos** Peru
191 F5 **Vinci** Italy
168 F1 **Vindeballe** Denmark
140 L3 **Vindelälven** *r.* Sweden
140 L2 **Vindeln** Sweden
142 C3 **Vinderup** Denmark
116 C5 **Vindhya Range** *hills* *Madh. Prad.* India
Vindobona Austria *see* **Wien**
186 D3 **Vinebre** Spain
234 C3 **Vineland** *NJ* U.S.A.
159 H4 **Vineuil** *Centre* France
159 H5 **Vineuil** *Centre* France
215 F4 **Vineyard** S. Africa
196 E2 **Vinga** Romania
196 E2 **Vingăi, Câmpia** *plain* Romania
143 F2 **Vingåker** Sweden
160 D1 **Vingeanne** *r.* France
163 E6 **Vingrau** France
96 D3 **Vinh** Vietnam
182 D3 **Vinhais** Port.
182 D3 **Vinhas** Port.
97 D5 **Vinh Long** Vietnam
96 D2 **Vinh Yên** Vietnam
179 H4 **Vinica** Croatia
197 F5 **Vinica** Macedonia
177 I3 **Vinica** Slovakia
176 G3 **Viničné** Slovakia
179 H1 **Viničné Šumice** Czech Rep.
183 H2 **Viniegra de Arriba** Spain
237 E4 **Vinita** *OK* U.S.A.
116 B5 **Vinjhan** *Gujarat* India
Vînju Mare Romania *see* **Vânju Mare**
136 D3 **Vin'kivtsi** Ukr.
188 G3 **Vinkovci** Croatia
Vinland *i.* *Nfld.* Can. *see* **Newfoundland**

177 K3 Vinné Slovakia
138 F2 Vinni Estonia
172 B2 Vinningen Ger.
Vinnitsa Ukr. see Vinnytsya
Vinnitsa Oblast admin. div. Ukr. see Vinnyts'ka Oblast'
Vinnitskaya Oblast' admin. div. Ukr. see Vinnyts'ka Oblast'
139 J1 Vinnitsy Rus. Fed.
136 D3 Vinnyts'ka Oblast' admin. div. Ukr.
136 E3 Vinnytsya Ukr.
Vinnytsya Oblast admin. div. Ukr. see Vinnyts'ka Oblast'
177 H3 Vinodol Slovakia
Vinogradov Ukr. see Vynohradiv
177 G3 Vinohrady nad Váhom Slovakia
161 D5 Vinon-sur-Verdon France
161 D4 Vinsobres France
262 S1 Vinson Massif mt. Antarctica
141 J3 Vinstra Norway
92 B2 Vintar Phil.
235 E3 Vinton IA U.S.A.
183 G4 Viñuelas Spain
183 H3 Vinuesa Spain
114 C2 Vinukonda Andhra Prad. India
209 B5 Vinza Congo
170 C3 Vinzelberg Ger.
168 E1 Viöl Ger.
160 C3 Violay France
161 C4 Violès France
Violeta Cuba see Primero de Enero
161 B5 Viols-le-Fort France
214 A3 Vioolsdrif S. Africa
156 C3 Viosne r. France
179 E5 Vipava Slovenia
179 E5 Vipava r. Slovenia
211 B8 Viphya Mountains Malawi
191 G2 Vipiteno Italy
170 D2 Vipperow Ger.
183 E3 Vir i. Croatia
179 F4 Vir Slovenia
92 C3 Virac Phil.
256 C4 Viradouro Brazil
116 C5 Viramgam Gujarat India
127 E3 Viranşehir Turkey
114 B3 Virarajendrapet Karnataka India
163 C4 Virazeil France
138 D3 Vircava r. Latvia/Lith.
86 C4 Virchow, Mount hill W.A. Austr.
223 K5 Virden Man. Can.
159 F3 Vire France
159 E2 Vire r. France
209 B8 Virei Angola
156 E2 Vireux-Molhain France
156 E2 Vireux-Wallerand France
156 E4 Virey-sous-Bar France
197 E2 Vîrful Highiş hill Romania
257 F2 Virgem da Lapa Brazil
178 D3 Virgen Austria
232 D6 Virgilina VA U.S.A.
241 J3 Virgin r. AZ U.S.A.
227 H1 Virginatown Ont. Can.
247 F3 Virgin Gorda i. Virgin Is (U.K.)
147 D3 Virginia Rep. of Ireland
215 F3 Virginia S. Africa
226 A2 Virginia MN U.S.A.
232 D6 Virginia state U.S.A.
233 F6 Virginia Beach VA U.S.A.
238 E2 Virginia City MT U.S.A.
240 H2 Virginia City NV U.S.A.
151 G3 Virginia Water Surrey, England U.K.
247 F3 Virgin Islands (U.K.) terr. West Indies
247 F3 Virgin Islands (U.S.A.) terr. West Indies
241 J3 Virgin Mountains AZ U.S.A.
257 F3 Virginópolis Brazil
160 D2 Viriat France
160 D3 Virieu France
160 D3 Virieu-le-Grand France
160 C3 Virigneux France
160 D3 Virignin France
161 D3 Viriville France
188 F2 Virje Croatia
138 E1 Virkkala Fin.
97 D4 Virôchey Cambodia
165 D4 Viroin r. Belgium
141 N3 Virolahti Fin.
226 B4 Viroqua WI U.S.A.
188 F3 Virovitica Croatia
141 M3 Virrat Fin.
143 F3 Virserum Sweden
165 E5 Virton Belgium
252 A2 Virú Peru
114 C4 Virudunagar Tamil Nadu India
138 D3 Virvytė r. Lith.
160 D2 Viry Franche-Comté France
160 E2 Viry Rhône-Alpes France
156 D3 Viry-Noureuil France
188 F4 Vis Croatia
188 F4 Vis i. Croatia
138 F4 Visaginas Lith.
Visakhapatnam Andhra Prad. India see Vishakhapatnam
240 H3 Visalia CA U.S.A.
161 C4 Visan France
197 H3 Vişani Romania
114 B2 Visapur Mahar. India
116 B5 Visavadar Gujarat India
92 B4 Visayan Sea Phil.
168 D3 Visbek Ger.
168 D1 Visby Denmark
143 H3 Visby Gotland Sweden
257 F4 Visconde do Rio Branco Brazil
221 G2 Viscount Melville Sound sea chan. N.W.T./Nunavut Can.
165 E4 Visé Belgium
188 G4 Višegrad Bos.-Herz.
191 H4 Viserba Italy
254 D2 Viseu Brazil
182 C4 Viseu Port.
182 C4 Viseu admin. dist. Port.
197 G2 Vişeu r. Romania
197 G2 Vişeu de Sus Romania
191 J3 Viševica mt. Croatia
115 D2 Vishakhapatnam Andhra Prad. India
197 H5 Vishegrad hill Bulg.
134 K3 Vishera r. Rus. Fed.
134 L4 Vishera r. Rus. Fed.
139 H2 Vishera r. Rus. Fed.
121 H2 Vishnevka Kazakh.
135 H5 Vishnevoye Rus. Fed.
Vishnevoye Dnipropetrovs'ka Oblast' Ukr. see Vyshneve
186 B4 Visiedo Spain
197 G3 Vişina Romania
143 F2 Visingsö i. Sweden
142 E3 Viskan r. Sweden
138 F3 Viški Latvia
188 F4 Viški Kanal sea chan. Croatia
143 F3 Vislanda Sweden
116 C5 Visnagar Gujarat India
171 G5 Višňová Czech Rep.
176 F3 Višňové Czech Rep.
177 H2 Višňové Slovakia
190 C4 Viso, Monte mt. Italy
185 G2 Viso del Marqués Spain
188 G4 Visoko Bos.-Herz.
190 D4 Visone Italy
177 J4 Visonta Hungary
190 C2 Visp Switz.
215 E4 Visrivier S. Africa
161 B3 Vissac-Auteyrac France
114 D2 Vissannapeta Andhra Prad. India
143 F3 Visselfjärda Sweden
168 E3 Visselhövede Ger.
193 F2 Visso Italy
190 C2 Vissoie Switz.
240 I5 Vista CA U.S.A.
235 E1 Vista NY U.S.A.
187 C4 Vistabella del Maestrazgo Spain
260 C3 Vista Flores Arg.
Vistula r. Pol. see Wisła
137 G4 Visun' r. Ukr.
177 J4 Visznek Hungary
197 G4 Vit r. Bulg.
250 E3 Vita r. Col.
194 B5 Vita Sicilia Italy
196 D4 Vitao mt. Yugo.
177 J3 Vít'az Slovakia
Vitebsk Belarus see Vitsyebsk
Vitebskaya Oblast' admin. div. Belarus see Vitsyebskaya Voblasts'
Vitebsk Oblast admin. div. Belarus see Vitsyebskaya Voblasts'
192 E2 Viterbo Italy
192 D2 Viterbo prov. Lazio Italy
157 G4 Viterne France
188 F3 Vitez Bos.-Herz.
252 D5 Vitichi Bol.
182 D3 Vitigudino Spain
79 □1a Viti Levu i. Fiji
99 K1 Vitim r. Rus. Fed.
99 J1 Vitimskoye Ploskogor'ye plat. Rus. Fed.
196 E4 Vitina Kosovo, Srbija Yugo.
179 G2 Vitis Austria
177 G2 Vítkov Czech Rep.
179 H3 Vitnyéd Hungary
197 E5 Vitolište Macedonia
196 E4 Vitomirica Kosovo, Srbija Yugo.
252 C4 Vitor Peru
252 B4 Vitor r. Peru
192 E2 Vitorchiano Italy
257 G4 Vitória Brazil
Vitoria Spain see Vitoria-Gasteiz
183 H2 Vitoria airport Spain
255 E5 Vitória da Conquista Brazil
183 H2 Vitoria-Gasteiz Spain
264 G7 Vitória Seamount sea feature S. Atlantic Ocean
195 G3 Vitravo r. Italy
158 E3 Vitré France
157 F5 Vitrey-sur-Mance France
161 D5 Vitrolles France
156 C2 Vitry-en-Artois France
156 E4 Vitry-en-Perthois France
156 E4 Vitry-la-Ville France
156 E4 Vitry-le-François France
160 B2 Vitry-sur-Loire France
156 C4 Vitry-sur-Seine France
136 E2 Vits' r. Belarus
139 H4 Vitsyebsk Belarus
138 G4 Vitsyebskaya Voblasts' admin. div. Belarus
140 M2 Vittangi Sweden
160 C1 Vitteaux France
157 F4 Vittel France
194 D6 Vittoria Sicilia Italy
191 H3 Vittorio Veneto Italy
193 G3 Vitulazio Italy
137 I5 Vityazevo Rus. Fed.
171 C4 Vitzenburg Ger.
187 C5 Viuda r. Spain
160 E2 Viuz-en-Sallaz France
161 C4 Vivarais, Monts du mts France
192 B2 Vivario Corse France
137 J3 Vivcharove Ukr.
182 C1 Viveiro Spain
186 C4 Vivel del Río Martín Spain
187 C5 Viver Spain
Vivero Spain see Viveiro
161 B3 Viverols France
185 H2 Viveros Spain
237 E5 Vivian LA U.S.A.
157 E3 Vivier-au-Court France
161 C4 Viviers France
163 E4 Viviez France
161 C5 Viv-le-Fesq France
213 F4 Vivo S. Africa
179 F4 Vivodnik mt. Slovenia
162 C2 Vivonne France
156 E5 Vix Bourgogne France
162 B2 Vix Pays de la Loire France
137 H3 Viys'kove Ukr.
136 D3 Viytivtsi Ukr.
Vizagapatam Andhra Prad. India see Vishakhapatnam
242 B3 Vizcaíno, Desierto de des. Mex.
242 B3 Vizcaíno, Sierra mts Mex.
183 H1 Vizcaya prov. País Vasco Spain
126 B2 Vize Turkey
160 C3 Vizézy r. France
134 I2 Vizhas r. Rus. Fed.
175 L6 Vizhomlya Ukr.
115 D2 Vizianagaram Andhra Prad. India
161 D3 Vizille France
134 J3 Vizinga Rus. Fed.
197 H3 Viziru Romania
177 G2 Vizovice Czech Rep.
177 I3 Vizslás Hungary
177 K3 Vizsoly Hungary
194 D5 Vizzini Sicilia Italy
198 A1 Vjosë r. Albania
165 D4 Vlaams Brabant prov. Belgium
164 D3 Vlaardingen Neth.
179 E1 Vlachovo Březí Czech Rep.
177 L5 Vlădeasa, Munţii mts Romania
197 F2 Vlădeasa, Vârful mt. Romania
197 F4 Vladičin Han Srbija Yugo.
129 D2 Vladikavkaz Rus. Fed.
139 M3 Vladimir Rus. Fed.
177 K5 Vladimirescu Romania
100 E4 Vladimiro-Aleksandrovskoye Rus. Fed.
Vladimir Oblast admin. div. Rus. Fed. see Vladimirskaya Oblast'
120 F1 Vladimirovka Kazakh.
129 D1 Vladimirovka Rus. Fed.
197 F4 Vladimirovo Bulg.
Vladimirovskiy Kazakh. see Vladimirovka
139 M4 Vladimirskaya Oblast' admin. div. Rus. Fed.
Vladimir-Volynskiy Ukr. see Volodymyr-Volyns'kyy
176 E2 Vladislav Czech Rep.
100 D4 Vladivostok Rus. Fed.
134 G4 Vladychnoye Rus. Fed.
164 G1 Vlagtwedde Neth.
197 G2 Vlăhiţa Romania
197 E4 Vlajna mt. Yugo.
188 G3 Vlasenica Bos.-Herz.
196 D3 Vlašić Planina mts Yugo.
176 D2 Vlašim Czech Rep.
137 G3 Vlasivka Ukr.
197 F4 Vlasotince Srbija Yugo.
Vlasova-Ayuta Rus. Fed. see Ayutinskiy
139 L4 Vlasovo Rus. Fed.
177 G3 Vlčany Slovakia
164 F2 Vledder Neth.
214 C5 Vleiland S. Africa
164 E2 Vleuten Neth.
164 D1 Vlieland i. Neth.
164 E3 Vlijmen Neth.
165 C3 Vlissingen Neth.
198 A1 Vlorë Albania
198 A1 Vlorës, Gjiri i b. Albania
169 D3 Vlotho Ger.
Vlotslavsk Pol. see Włocławek
176 D1 Vltava r. Czech Rep.
179 F4 Vnanje Gorice Slovenia
139 K2 Vnina r. Rus. Fed.
171 D4 Vockerode Ger.
179 E2 Vöcklabruck Austria
179 E2 Vöcklamarkt Austria
177 G3 Voderady Slovakia
191 J3 Vodice Istra Croatia
188 E4 Vodice Šibenik Croatia
134 G3 Vodlozero, Ozero l. Rus. Fed.
176 D2 Vodňany Czech Rep.
188 D3 Vodnjan Croatia
Vodopyanovo Lipetskaya Oblast' Rus. Fed. see Donskoye
146 □G1 Voe Shetland, Scotland U.K.
215 E5 Voël r. S. Africa
169 B4 Voerde (Niederrhein) Ger.
165 E4 Voerendaal Neth.
142 D3 Voerså Denmark
207 F5 Vogan Togo
164 D2 Vogelenzang Neth.
157 H4 Vogelgrun France
Vogelkop Peninsula Indon. see Doberai, Jazirah
207 H4 Vogel Peak Nigeria
170 E2 Vogelsang Ger.
169 D5 Vogelsberg hills Ger.
171 E3 Vogelsdorf Ger.
157 H4 Vogelsheim France
172 B2 Vogelweh Ger.
190 E4 Voghera Italy
191 G4 Voghiera Italy
129 E4 Voghji r. Armenia
188 G4 Vogošća Bos.-Herz.
172 D4 Vogt Ger.
173 G4 Vogtareuth Ger.
161 C4 Vogüé France
78 □5 Voh New Caledonia
173 F3 Vohburg an der Donau Ger.
Vohémar Madag. see Iharaña
173 G2 Vohenstrauß Ger.
Vohibinany Madag. see Ampasimanolotra
213 □J4 Vohilava Fianarantsoa Madag.
213 □K4 Vohilava Fianarantsoa Madag.
Vohimarina Madag. see Iharaña
213 □J5 Vohimena, Tanjona c. Madag.
213 □J4 Vohipeno Madag.
213 □K4 Vohitrandriana Madag.
169 D4 Vöhl Ger.
138 E2 Võhma Estonia
172 C3 Vöhrenbach Ger.
172 C3 Vöhringen Ger.
173 E3 Vöhringen Ger.
211 C5 Voi Kenya
157 F4 Void-Vacon France
171 C4 Voigtstedt Ger.
157 E4 Voillecomte France
197 F3 Voineasa Romania
197 H2 Voineşti Romania
206 C4 Voinjama Liberia
161 D3 Voiron France
156 B4 Voise r. France
160 D2 Voiteur France
179 G3 Voitsberg Austria
177 K3 Vojčice Slovakia
142 C4 Vojens Denmark
Vojnice Slovakia see Bátorove Kosihy
179 G4 Vojnik Slovenia
196 D3 Vojvodina prov. Yugo.
138 F2 Voka Estonia
177 H6 Vokány Hungary
134 I4 Vokhma Rus. Fed.
207 I4 Voko Cameroon
134 K3 Vol' r. Rus. Fed.
176 C3 Volary Czech Rep.
Volaterrae Italy see Volterra
238 F2 Volborg MT U.S.A.
258 D1 Volcán Arg.
252 D5 Volcán, Cerro vol. Bol.
260 B2 Volcán, Cerro del vol. Chile
261 H5 Volcán, Sierra del hills Arg.
Volcano Bay Japan see Uchiura-wan
240 □D9 Volcano House HI U.S.A.
Volcano Islands N. Pacific Ocean see Kazan-rettō
Volchansk Ukr. see Vovchans'k
139 H5 Volchas r. Belarus
121 J1 Volchikha Rus. Fed.
139 J3 Volchina r. Rus. Fed.
141 I3 Volda Norway
173 H2 Volduchy Czech Rep.
164 E2 Volendam Neth.
232 D6 Volens VA U.S.A.
139 L3 Volga Rus. Fed.
139 L3 Volga r. Rus. Fed.
Volga Upland hills Rus. Fed. see Privolzhskaya Vozvyshennost'
135 H7 Volgodonsk Rus. Fed.
135 I6 Volgograd Rus. Fed.
Volgograd Oblast admin. div. Rus. Fed. see Volgogradskaya Oblast'
135 I6 Volgogradskaya Oblast' admin. div. Rus. Fed.
135 I6 Volgogradskoye Vodokhranilishche resr Rus. Fed.
139 M3 Volgorechensk Rus. Fed.
Volhynia admin. div. Ukr. see Volyns'ka Oblast'
136 E4 Volintiri Moldova
173 E2 Volkach Ger.
173 E2 Volkach r. Ger.
179 F4 Völkermarkt Austria
172 C4 Volkertshausen Ger.
190 D1 Volketswil Switz.
139 I2 Volkhov Rus. Fed.
139 I1 Volkhov r. Rus. Fed.
139 I1 Volkhovskaya Guba b. Rus. Fed.
139 H2 Volkhovskiy Rus. Fed.
172 A2 Völklingen Ger.
169 E4 Volkmarsen Ger.
Volkovysk Belarus see Vawkavysk
Volkovyskiye Vysoty hills Belarus see Vawkavyskaye Wzvyshsha
215 G2 Volksrust S. Africa
171 C4 Volkstedt Ger.
168 C2 Völlen Ger.
164 E2 Vollenhove Neth.
168 D2 Vollersode Ger.
160 B3 Vollore-Montagne France
157 H3 Volmunster France
160 C1 Volnay France
Vol'nogorsk Ukr. see Vil'nohirs'k
100 D4 Vol'no-Nadezhdinskoye Rus. Fed.
137 I4 Volnovakha Ukr.
121 G1 Vol'noye Rus. Fed.
Vol'nyansk Ukr. see Vil'nyans'k
100 E2 Volochayevka-Vtoraya Rus. Fed.
Volochisk Ukr. see Volochys'k
136 D3 Volochys'k Ukr.
136 E3 Volodarka Ukr.
137 I4 Volodars'ke Ukr.
120 B3 Volodarskiy Rus. Fed.
Volodarskoye Kazakh. see Saumalkol'
136 E2 Volodars'k-Volyns'kyy Ukr.
136 D2 Volodymyrets' Ukr.
137 G4 Volodymyrivka Ukr.
136 C2 Volodymyr-Volyns'kyy Ukr.
134 G4 Vologda Rus. Fed.
Vologda Oblast admin. div. Rus. Fed. see Vologodskaya Oblast'
157 G4 Vologne r. France
139 M2 Vologodskaya Oblast' admin. div. Rus. Fed.
137 I3 Volokhiv Yar Ukr.
139 J3 Volokolamsk Rus. Fed.
135 G6 Volokonovka Rus. Fed.
161 E4 Volonne France
214 D3 Volop S. Africa
198 C2 Volos Greece
175 L6 Voloshcha Ukr.
137 J3 Voloshino Rus. Fed.
134 H3 Voloshka Rus. Fed.
137 I3 Volos'ka Balakliya Ukr.
137 I3 Volos'ka Balakliyka r. Ukr.
138 G2 Volosovo Rus. Fed.
177 L3 Volosyanka Ukr.
139 H3 Volot Rus. Fed.
137 J2 Volotovo Rus. Fed.
136 B3 Volovets' Ukr.
135 G5 Volovo Lipetskaya Oblast' Rus. Fed.
139 L5 Volovo Tul'skaya Oblast' Rus. Fed.
177 J3 Volovské vrchy mts Slovakia
Volozhin Belarus see Valozhyn
178 D5 Volpago del Mòntello Italy
190 D4 Volpedo Italy
190 C3 Volpiano Italy
171 C3 Völpke Ger.
178 C3 Völs Austria
170 E2 Völschow Ger.
192 D2 Volsini, Monti mts Italy
Volsinii Italy see Orvieto
120 A1 Vol'sk Rus. Fed.
214 D5 Volstruisleegte S. Africa
207 F5 Volta admin. reg. Ghana
207 F5 Volta r. Ghana
207 F5 Volta, Lake resr Ghana
Volta Blanche r. Africa see White Volta
86 E2 Voltaire, Cape W.A. Austr.
Volta Noire r. Africa see Black Volta
257 E5 Volta Redonda Brazil
Volta Rouge r. Burkina/Ghana see Nazinon
191 F5 Volterra Italy
169 C3 Voltlage Ger.
183 F3 Voltoya r. Spain
193 H3 Volturara Appula Italy
194 D2 Volturara Irpina Italy
193 H3 Volturino Italy
193 H4 Volturino, Monte mt. Italy
193 F3 Volturno r. Italy
204 D2 Volubilis tourist site Morocco
197 H3 Voluntari Romania
235 G1 Voluntown CT U.S.A.
198 C1 Volvi, Limni l. Greece
160 B3 Volvic France
161 D5 Volx France
137 J2 Volya Rus. Fed.
134 M3 Vol'ya r. Rus. Fed.
175 L6 Volya Arlamivs'ka Ukr.
176 C2 Volyně Czech Rep.
176 C2 Volyňka r. Czech Rep.
137 G2 Volynka Ukr.
Volyn Oblast admin. div. Ukr. see Volyns'ka Oblast'
136 C2 Volyns'ka Oblast' admin. div. Ukr.
Volynskaya Oblast' admin. div. Ukr. see Volyns'ka Oblast'
136 D3 Volytsya Ukr.
136 D3 Volytsya Druha Ukr.
134 J5 Volzhsk Rus. Fed.
120 B1 Volzhskiy Samarskaya Oblast' Rus. Fed.
135 I6 Volzhskiy Volgogradskaya Oblast' Rus. Fed.
193 G2 Vomano r. Italy
178 C3 Vomp Austria
78 □6 Vonavona i. New Georgia Is Solomon Is
223 J4 Vonda Sask. Can.
134 I4 Vondanka Rus. Fed.
213 □J4 Vondrozo Madag.
160 D1 Vonges France
198 B2 Vonitsa Greece
160 C2 Vonnas France
114 C3 Vontimitta Andhra Prad. India
176 G5 Vonyarcvashegy Hungary
164 D2 Voorburg Neth.
233 G3 Voorheesville NY U.S.A.
164 D2 Voorschoten Neth.
164 F2 Voorst Neth.
164 E2 Voorthuizen Neth.
138 D2 Voosi kurk sea chan. Estonia
139 I4 Vop' r. Rus. Fed.
140 □D2 Vopnafjörður b. Iceland
140 M3 Vörå Fin.
179 F3 Voralm mt. Austria
138 E4 Voranava Belarus
178 A3 Vorarlberg land Austria
179 E2 Vorchdorf Austria
164 F2 Vorden Neth.
179 F3 Vordernberg Austria
190 E1 Vorderrhein r. Switz.
142 D4 Vordingborg Denmark
169 F3 Vordorf Ger.
196 D5 Vorë Albania
198 B1 Voreia Pindos mts Greece
199 D2 Voreio Aigaio admin. reg. Greece
198 C2 Voreioi Sporades is Greece
198 C2 Voreios Evvoïkos Kolpos sea chan. Greece
161 D3 Voreppe France
161 B3 Vorey France
139 I5 Vorga Rus. Fed.
134 M2 Vorgashor Rus. Fed.
Voríai Sporádhes is Greece see Voreioi Sporades
Voría Píndhos mts Greece see Voreia Pindos
264 J1 Voring Plateau sea feature N. Atlantic Ocean
117 H3 Vorjing mt. Arun. Prad. India
134 N2 Vorkuta Rus. Fed.
142 D1 Vorma r. Norway
138 D2 Vormsi i. Estonia
139 L5 Vorob'yevka Rus. Fed.
135 H6 Vorob'yevka Rus. Fed.
130 J3 Vorogovo Rus. Fed.
136 C3 Vorokhta Ukr.
197 H2 Vorona Romania
135 H6 Vorona r. Rus. Fed.
135 G6 Voronezh Rus. Fed.
139 L5 Voronezh r. Rus. Fed.
Voronezh Oblast admin. div. Rus. Fed. see Voronezhskaya Oblast'
135 H6 Voronezhskaya Oblast' admin. div. Rus. Fed.
137 G2 Voronizh Ukr.
137 G2 Voron'ky Ukr.
136 D2 Voronky Rivnens'ka Oblast' Ukr.
139 I1 Voronov, Mys pt Rus. Fed.
139 K4 Voronovo Rus. Fed.
136 E3 Voronovytsya Ukr.
121 J2 Vorontsovka Kazakh.
135 H6 Vorontsovka Rus. Fed.
Vorontsovo-Aleksandrovskoye Stavropol'skiy Kray Rus. Fed. see Zelenokumsk
136 C3 Voronyaky hills Ukr.
134 H4 Voron'ye Rus. Fed.
Voroshilov Rus. Fed. see Ussuriysk
Voroshilovgrad Ukr. see Luhans'k
Voroshilovsk Rus. Fed. see Stavropol'
Voroshilovsk Ukr. see Alchevs'k
129 E4 Vorotan r. Iran
134 I4 Vorotynets Rus. Fed.
139 K4 Vorotynsk Rus. Fed.
129 C1 Vorovskolesskaya Rus. Fed.
137 H2 Vorozhba Sums'ka Oblast' Ukr.
137 H2 Vorozhba Sums'ka Oblast' Ukr.
263 B2 Vorposten Peak Antarctica
173 F2 Vorra Ger.
179 G3 Vorsau Austria
165 D3 Vorselaar Belgium
135 F6 Vorskla r. Rus. Fed.
137 H2 Vorsklitsa r. Rus. Fed./Ukr.
165 E3 Vorst Belgium
214 D1 Vorstershoop S. Africa
177 L5 Vorţa Romania
263 B2 Vørterkaka Nunatak mt. Antarctica
138 E2 Võrtsjärv l. Estonia
138 F3 Võru Estonia
168 E2 Vorwerk Ger.
139 J4 Vorya r. Rus. Fed.
136 F2 Vorzel' Ukr.
214 D4 Vosburg S. Africa
123 G2 Vose Tajik.
179 H2 Vösendorf Austria
157 G4 Vosges dept Lorraine France
157 G5 Vosges mts France
139 L3 Voshchazhnikovo Rus. Fed.
129 D3 Voskevan Armenia
139 L4 Voskresensk Rus. Fed.
137 G4 Voskresens'ke Ukr.
139 L5 Voskresenskoye Lipetskaya Oblast' Rus. Fed.
134 I4 Voskresenskoye Nizhegorodskaya Oblast' Rus. Fed.
120 D1 Voskresenskoye Respublika Bashkortostan Rus. Fed.
139 K4 Voskresenskoye Tul'skaya Oblast' Rus. Fed.
139 K2 Voskresenskoye Vologod. Obl. Rus. Fed.
160 C1 Vosne-Romanée France
141 I3 Voss Norway
165 D3 Vosselaar Belgium
Vostochno-Kazakhstanskaya Oblast' admin. div. Kazakh. see Vostochnyy Kazakhstan
Vostochno-Kounradskiy Kazakh. see Shygys Konyrat
100 G2 Vostochno-Sakhalinskiy Gory mts Sakhalin Rus. Fed.
134 K4 Vostochnyy Rus. Fed.
120 D4 Vostochnyy Chink Ustyurta esc. Uzbek.
121 K2 Vostochnyy Kazakhstan admin. div. Kazakh.
98 F1 Vostochnyy Sayan mts Rus. Fed.
100 E3 Vostok Primorskiy Kray Rus. Fed.
Vostok Sakhalin Rus. Fed. see Neftegorsk
176 D2 Votice Czech Rep.
134 K4 Votkinsk Rus. Fed.
134 K4 Votkinskoye Vodokhranilishche resr Rus. Fed.
142 C1 Votna r. Norway
256 D5 Votorantim Brazil
139 I4 Votrya r. Rus. Fed.
256 C4 Votuporanga Brazil
162 E2 Voueize r. France
Vouga Angola see Cunhinga
182 B4 Vouga r. Port.
160 C1 Vougeot France
162 B2 Vouillé France
162 C2 Vouillé France
198 C3 Voula Greece
156 E5 Voulaines-les-Templiers France
156 C4 Voulx France
162 C2 Vouneuil-sous-Biard France
159 G5 Vouneuil-sur-Vienne France
198 B1 Vourinos mt. Greece
160 B1 Voutenay-sur-Cure France
162 D3 Voutezac France
162 B2 Vouvant France
159 G4 Vouvray France
190 B2 Vouvry Switz.
182 B4 Vouzela Port.
156 E3 Vouziers France
156 C5 Vouzon France
137 H3 Vovcha r. Ukr.
137 I2 Vovcha r. Ukr.
137 I2 Vovchans'k Ukr.
137 G2 Vovchyk Ukr.
156 B4 Voves France
136 D3 Vovk r. Ukr.
136 D2 Vovkoshiv Ukr.
136 D3 Vovkovyntsi Ukr.
208 E3 Vovodo r. C.A.R.
141 K3 Voxna Sweden
141 L3 Voxnan r. Sweden
134 J4 Voya r. Rus. Fed.
137 F3 Voyevods'ke Ukr.
175 M6 Voynyliv Ukr.
Vöyri Fin. see Vörå
134 K3 Voyvozh Rus. Fed.
78 □6 Voza Choiseul Solomon Is
139 K3 Vozdvizhenskoye Rus. Fed.
139 L4 Vozha r. Rus. Fed.
134 G3 Vozhe, Ozero l. Rus. Fed.
134 H3 Vozhega Rus. Fed.
183 I3 Vozmediano Spain
121 G1 Voznesenka Kazakh.
137 F4 Voznesens'k Ukr.
129 D2 Voznesenskaya Ingushskaya Respublika Rus. Fed.
129 B1 Voznesenskaya Krasnodarskiy Kray Rus. Fed.
137 F4 Voznesens'ke Ukr.
135 H5 Voznesenskoye Rus. Fed.
139 M3 Voznesen'ye Rus. Fed.
139 J1 Voznesen'ye Rus. Fed.
137 G4 Vozsiyats'ke Ukr.
121 G1 Vozvyshenka Kazakh.
Vozvyshenskiy Kazakh. see Vozvyshenka
100 D2 Vozzhayevka Rus. Fed.
142 C3 Vrå Denmark
197 G4 Vrabevo Bulg.
177 H3 Vráble Slovakia
198 B3 Vrachionas hill Ionioi Nisoi Greece
198 B2 Vrachnaiika Greece
142 C2 Vrådal Norway
136 F4 Vradiyivka Ukr.
Vrakhiónas Óros hill Ionioi Nisoi Greece see Vrachionas
Vrakhnaíika Greece see Vrachnaiika
188 F4 Vran mt. Bos.-Herz.
197 H4 Vrana r. Bulg.
100 E4 Vrangel' Rus. Fed.
100 F1 Vrangelya, Mys pt Rus. Fed.
131 T2 Vrangelya, Ostrov i. Rus. Fed.
188 G3 Vranjak Bos.-Herz.
197 E4 Vranje Srbija Yugo.
197 F4 Vranjska Banja Srbija Yugo.
179 H2 Vranovice Czech Rep.
177 K3 Vranov nad Topľou Slovakia
196 E5 Vrapčište Macedonia
197 F4 Vratarnica Srbija Yugo.
197 F4 Vratsa Bulg.
188 F3 Vrbanja r. Bos.-Herz.
188 F3 Vrbas r. Bos.-Herz.
196 D3 Vrbas Vojvodina, Srbija Yugo.
176 G1 Vrbno pod Pradědem Czech Rep.
177 J2 Vrbov Slovakia
176 G3 Vrbovce Slovakia
177 G3 Vrbové Slovakia
188 F3 Vrbovec Croatia
188 E3 Vrbovsko Croatia
176 E1 Vrchlabí Czech Rep.
157 F4 Vrécourt France
215 G2 Vrede S. Africa
215 F2 Vredefort S. Africa
169 B3 Vreden Ger.
214 A5 Vredenburg S. Africa
214 B4 Vredendal S. Africa
251 G3 Vreed-en-Hoop Guyana
164 E2 Vreeland Neth.
168 C3 Vrees Ger.
182 C3 Vreia de Jales Port.
196 E4 Vrela Kosovo, Srbija Yugo.
179 F5 Vremščica mt. Slovenia
165 D5 Vresse Belgium
188 E3 Vrhnika Slovenia
114 C4 Vriddhachalam Tamil Nadu India
164 F1 Vries Neth.
164 F2 Vriezenveen Neth.
143 F3 Vrigstad Sweden
160 A1 Vrille r. France
111 B7 Vrindavan Uttar Prad. India
156 E3 Vrizy France
196 E4 Vrnjačka Banja Srbija Yugo.
156 B2 Vron France
164 F2 Vroomshoop Neth.
176 C1 Vroutek Czech Rep.
164 C3 Vrouwenpolder Neth.
196 D5 Vrrin Albania
196 E3 Vršac Vojvodina, Srbija Yugo.
191 I3 Vrsar Croatia
179 E5 Vrtojba Slovenia
215 E2 Vryburg S. Africa
215 H2 Vryheid S. Africa
173 H2 Všeruby Czech Rep.
171 F5 Všetaty Czech Rep.
177 G2 Vsetín Czech Rep.
139 H1 Vsevolozhsk Rus. Fed.
137 H3 Vshyva r. Ukr.
177 H3 Vtáčnik mt. Slovakia
177 H3 Vtáčnik mts Slovakia
160 D2 Vuache, Montagne de mt. France
79 □1 Vuaqava i. Fiji
197 G5 Vŭcha r. Bulg.
188 G3 Vučica r. Croatia
196 E4 Vučitrn Kosovo, Srbija Yugo.
197 E4 Vučje Srbija Yugo.
164 E3 Vught Neth.
137 I4 Vuhledar Ukr.
137 J3 Vuhlehirs'k Ukr.
188 G3 Vuka r. Croatia
188 G3 Vukovar Croatia
134 L3 Vuktyl' Rus. Fed.
215 G2 Vukuzakhe S. Africa
222 H5 Vulcan Alta Can.
197 F3 Vulcan Romania
136 E5 Vulcăneşti Moldova
194 D4 Vulcano, Isola i. Isole Lipari Italy
197 F4 Vŭlchedrŭm Bulg.
197 H4 Vŭlchidol Bulg.
193 H3 Vulgano r. Italy
Vulkaneshty Moldova see Vulcăneşti
193 H4 Vulture, Monte mt. Italy
241 K5 Vulture Mountains AZ U.S.A.
97 D5 Vung Tau Vietnam
138 F1 Vuohijärvi Fin.
140 O2 Vuokatti Fin.
138 H1 Vuoksa r. Rus. Fed.
138 G1 Vuoksi r. Fin.
140 N2 Vuolijoki Fin.
140 M2 Vuollerim Sweden
197 H4 Vŭrbitsa Bulg.
197 G3 Vurpăr Romania
197 F4 Vŭrshets Bulg.
197 H2 Vutcani Romania
114 D2 Vuyyuru Andhra Prad. India
179 G4 Vuzenica Slovenia
136 C2 Vuzlove L'vivs'ka Oblast' Ukr.
136 B3 Vuzlove Zakarpats'ka Oblast' Ukr.
138 F4 Vuzlyanka r. Belarus
120 E1 Vvedenka Kazakh.
139 M3 Vveden'ye Rus. Fed.
211 B7 Vwawa Tanz.
175 M2 Vyalikaya Byerastavitsa Belarus
139 H2 Vyal'ye, Ozero l. Rus. Fed.
116 C5 Vyara Gujarat India
Vyarkhowye Belarus see Ruba
Vyatka Kirovskaya Oblast' Rus. Fed. see Kirov
134 J5 Vyatka r. Rus. Fed.
134 J4 Vyatskiye Polyany Rus. Fed.
100 E3 Vyazemskiy Rus. Fed.
139 J4 Vyaz'ma Rus. Fed.
139 J4 Vyaz'ma r. Rus. Fed.
134 H4 Vyazniki Rus. Fed.
120 A1 Vyazovka Saratovskaya Oblast' Rus. Fed.
135 H6 Vyazovka Volgogradskaya Oblast' Rus. Fed.
137 I2 Vyazovoye Rus. Fed.
138 G1 Vyborg Rus. Fed.
138 G1 Vyborgskiy Zaliv b. Rus. Fed.
134 I3 Vychegda r. Rus. Fed.
134 I3 Vychegodskiy Rus. Fed.
177 I2 Východná Slovakia
175 N4 Vyderta Ukr.
175 M4 Vydranytsya Ukr.
106 E1 Vydrino Rus. Fed.
175 M4 Vydrychi Ukr.
138 F4 Vyerkhnyadzvinsk Belarus
139 H5 Vyetka Belarus
138 G4 Vyetryna Belarus
139 J5 Vygonichi Rus. Fed.
134 F3 Vygozero, Ozero l. Rus. Fed.
177 H3 Vyhne Slovakia
135 H5 Vyksa Rus. Fed.
160 E1 Vy-lès-Lure France
136 E5 Vylkove Ukr.
136 B3 Vylok Ukr.
134 J3 Vym' r. Rus. Fed.
136 C3 Vynnyky Ukr.
136 B3 Vynohradiv Ukr.
137 F4 Vynohradne Ukr.
137 G4 Vynohradove Khersons'ka Oblast' Ukr.
137 G5 Vynohradove Respublika Krym Ukr.
139 I3 Vypolzovo Rus. Fed.
137 G2 Vyrishal'ne Ukr.
139 H2 Vyritsa Rus. Fed.
137 H2 Vyry Ukr.
135 G7 Vyselki Rus. Fed.
136 F2 Vyshcha Dubechnya Ukr.
137 I3 Vyshche Solone Ukr.
137 H4 Vyshchetarasivka Ukr.
139 M4 Vyshgorod Rus. Fed.
136 F2 Vyshhorod Ukr.
136 B3 Vyshka Ukr.
139 H5 Vyshkov Rus. Fed.
136 B3 Vyshkove Ukr.
137 G3 Vyshneve Dnipropetrovs'ka Oblast' Ukr.
136 F2 Vyshneve Kyivs'ka Oblast' Ukr.
139 J3 Vyshnevolotskaya Gryada ridge Rus. Fed.
139 J3 Vyshnevolotskoye Vodokhranilishche resr Rus. Fed.
137 I1 Vyshneye-Ol'shanoye Rus. Fed.
175 N4 Vyshniv Ukr.
136 C3 Vyshnivets' Ukr.
139 J3 Vyshniy-Volochek Rus. Fed.
136 B3 Vyshnya r. Ukr.
137 G3 Vyshnyaky Ukr.
176 G2 Vyškov Czech Rep.
176 D3 Vysoká mt. Czech Rep.
176 G3 Vysoká hill Slovakia
136 E2 Vysoka Pich Ukr.
176 F3 Vysoká pri Morave Slovakia
138 D5 Vysokaye Belarus
176 F2 Vysoké Mýto Czech Rep.
139 K4 Vysokinichi Rus. Fed.
137 H3 Vysokopillya Kharkivs'ka Oblast' Ukr.
137 G4 Vysokopillya Khersons'ka Oblast' Ukr.
139 K3 Vysokovsk Rus. Fed.
Vysokoye Belarus see Vysokaye
139 J3 Vysokoye Rus. Fed.
138 G1 Vysotsk Rus. Fed.
136 D2 Vysots'k Ukr.
179 F2 Vyšší Brod Czech Rep.
136 E2 Vystupovychi Ukr.
139 K1 Vytegra Rus. Fed.
134 I3 Vyya r. Rus. Fed.
136 C2 Vyzhivka r. Ukr.
136 C3 Vyzhnytsya Ukr.
138 E4 Vyžuona r. Lith.
175 I1 Vzmor'ye Rus. Fed.

W

206 E4 Wa Ghana
168 E1 Waabs Ger.
210 D4 Waajid Somalia
169 F4 Waake Ger.
173 F4 Waakirchen Ger.
173 E4 Waal Ger.
164 D3 Waal r. Neth.
165 E3 Waalre Neth.
164 E3 Waalwijk Neth.
164 D2 Waarland Neth.
165 C3 Waarschoot Belgium
165 D3 Waasmunster Belgium
91 J8 Wabag P.N.G.
224 B3 Wabakimi Lake Ont. Can.
222 H4 Wabamun Alta Can.
222 H3 Wabasca r. Alta Can.
222 H4 Wabasca-Desmarais Alta Can.
230 C3 Wabash IN U.S.A.
232 A4 Wabash OH U.S.A.
236 F4 Wabash r. IN U.S.A.
226 A3 Wabasha MN U.S.A.
224 C3 Wabassi r. Ont. Can.
210 D3 Wabē Gestro r. Eth.
210 D3 Wabē Mena r. Eth.
226 C3 Wabeno WI U.S.A.
169 E4 Wabern Ger.
210 E3 Wabē Shebelē Wenz r. Eth.
223 L4 Wabowden Man. Can.
174 G2 Wąbrzeźno Pol.
109 F1 Wabu Anhui China
225 H2 Wabush Nfld. Can.
231 E5 Waccamaw r. SC U.S.A.
233 F6 Wachapreague VA U.S.A.
172 C2 Wachenheim an der Weinstraße Ger.
170 D3 Wachow Ger.
165 C3 Wachtebeke Belgium
169 E5 Wächtersbach Ger.
168 E1 Wacken Ger.
173 G2 Wackersdorf Ger.
225 H3 Waco Que. Can.
237 D6 Waco TX U.S.A.
226 A3 Wacouta MN U.S.A.
202 E6 Wad Banda Sudan
202 B2 Waddān, Jabal hills Libya
164 D1 Waddeneilanden is Neth.
Wadden Islands Neth. see Waddeneilanden
164 D2 Waddenzee sea chan. Neth.
151 G3 Waddesdon Buckinghamshire, England U.K.
168 F2 Waddeweitz Ger.
82 D3 Waddikee S.A. Austr.
149 I4 Waddington Lincolnshire, England U.K.
222 E5 Waddington, Mount B.C. Can.
147 E4 Waddingtown Rep. of Ireland
164 D2 Waddinxveen Neth.
85 H5 Waddy Point Qld Austr.
150 C4 Wadebridge Cornwall, England U.K.
223 K5 Wadena Sask. Can.
236 E2 Wadena MN U.S.A.
190 D1 Wädenswil Switz.
172 A2 Wadern Ger.
169 D4 Wadersloh Ger.
231 D5 Wadesboro NC U.S.A.
84 B2 Wadeye N.T. Austr.
114 B2 Wadgaon Mahar. India
116 D5 Wadgaon Mahar. India
172 A2 Wadgassen Ger.
151 H3 Wadhurst East Sussex, England U.K.
116 B5 Wadhwan Gujarat India
Wadhwan Gujarat India see Surendranagar
114 C2 Wadi Karnataka India
109 E1 Wadian Henan China
128 B4 Wādī as Sīr Jordan
203 F4 Wadi Halfa Sudan
128 B4 Wādī Mūsá Jordan
234 D3 Wading r. NJ U.S.A.
235 F2 Wading River NY U.S.A.
175 H4 Wadlew Pol.
203 G6 Wad Medani Sudan
102 □1 Wadomari Japan
175 H6 Wadowice Pol.
175 J5 Wadowice Górne Pol.
240 H2 Wadsworth NV U.S.A.
232 C4 Wadsworth OH U.S.A.
Wadu i. S. Male Maldives see Vaadhu
214 C6 Waenhuiskrans S. Africa
262 P1 Waesche, Mount Antarctica
107 I4 Wafangdian Liaoning China
102 J4 Waga-gawa r. Japan
116 C3 Wagah Punjab India
174 G3 Waganiec Pol.
168 D3 Wagenfeld Ger.
168 F3 Wagenhoff Ger.
164 E3 Wageningen Neth.
251 G3 Wageningen Suriname
221 J3 Wager Bay Nunavut Can.
83 F3 Wagga Wagga N.S.W. Austr.
172 C2 Waghäusel Ger.
87 C7 Wagin W.A. Austr.
173 G4 Waging am See Ger.
173 G4 Waginger See l. Ger.
222 D4 Waglisla B.C. Can.
254 E5 Wagner Brazil
236 D3 Wagner SD U.S.A.
237 E4 Wagoner OK U.S.A.
239 F4 Wagon Mound NM U.S.A.
178 E3 Wagrain Austria
174 F3 Wągrowiec Pol.
123 H3 Wah Pak.
207 F5 Wahala Togo
208 F2 Wahda state Sudan
240 □ Wahiawa HI U.S.A.
169 E4 Wahlhausen Ger.
171 E4 Wahlsdorf Ger.
168 F2 Wahlstedt Ger.
236 D3 Wahoo NE U.S.A.
236 D2 Wahpeton ND U.S.A.
Wahran Alg. see Oran
168 F3 Wahrenholz Ger.
241 K2 Wah Wah Mountains UT U.S.A.
114 B2 Wai Mahar. India
240 □C8 Waiakoa HI U.S.A.
240 □B8 Waialeale, Mount HI U.S.A.
240 □ Waialee HI U.S.A.
240 □ Waialua HI U.S.A.
240 □ Waianae HI U.S.A.
80 G2 Waiapu r. North I. N.Z.
80 F4 Waiaruhe North I. N.Z.
81 D5 Waiau South I. N.Z.
80 F3 Waiau r. North I. N.Z.
81 A7 Waiau r. South I. N.Z.
81 D5 Waiau r. South I. N.Z.
172 D3 Waiblingen Ger.
172 C2 Waibstadt Ger.
173 G2 Waidhaus Ger.
173 F3 Waidhofen Ger.
179 G2 Waidhofen an der Thaya Austria
179 F3 Waidhofen an der Ybbs Austria
93 D3 Waigeo i. Irian Jaya Indon.
173 E2 Waigolshausen Ger.
81 C6 Waihao Downs South I. N.Z.
80 D1 Waiharara North I. N.Z.
80 E2 Waiharoa North I. N.Z.
80 E2 Waiheke Island North I. N.Z.
80 E2 Waihi North I. N.Z.
80 E2 Waihi Beach North I. N.Z.
80 E2 Waihou r. North I. N.Z.
80 F3 Waihua North I. N.Z.
81 B6 Waikaia South I. N.Z.
81 B6 Waikaia r. South I. N.Z.
81 B6 Waikaka South I. N.Z.
81 E4 Waikanae North I. N.Z.
240 □ Waikane HI U.S.A.
240 □C8 Waikapu HI U.S.A.
80 E2 Waikare, Lake North I. N.Z.
80 F3 Waikaremoana, Lake North I. N.Z.
80 E2 Waikaretu North I. N.Z.
81 D5 Waikari South I. N.Z.
80 E2 Waikato admin. reg. North I. N.Z.
80 E2 Waikato r. North I. N.Z.
81 B7 Waikawa South I. N.Z.
80 E3 Waikeria North I. N.Z.
82 D3 Waikerie S.A. Austr.
240 □D9 Waikii HI U.S.A.
80 F3 Waikirikiri North I. N.Z.
81 B7 Waikoikoi South I. N.Z.
80 F3 Waikokopa North I. N.Z.
81 C6 Waikouaiti South I. N.Z.
240 □B7 Wailua HI U.S.A.
240 □C8 Wailua HI U.S.A.
240 □C8 Wailuku HI U.S.A.
81 B7 Waimahaka South I. N.Z.
81 D5 Waimakariri r. South I. N.Z.
80 F3 Waimana North I. N.Z.
240 □ Waimanalo HI U.S.A.
81 C4 Waimangaroa South I. N.Z.
80 F3 Waimarama North I. N.Z.
81 C4 Waimarie South I. N.Z.
81 C6 Waimate South I. N.Z.
80 D1 Waimatenui North I. N.Z.
80 E2 Waimauku North I. N.Z.
240 □B8 Waimea HI U.S.A.
240 □D8 Waimea HI U.S.A.
240 □ Waimea HI U.S.A.
165 F4 Waimes Belgium
173 E3 Wain Ger.
232 D3 Wainfleet Ont. Can.
149 J4 Wainfleet All Saints Lincolnshire, England U.K.
114 C2 Wainganga r. India
81 E4 Waingawa North I. N.Z.
150 C4 Wainhouse Corner Cornwall, England U.K.
223 I4 Wainwright Alta Can.
220 C2 Wainwright AK U.S.A.
80 F3 Waioeka r. North I. N.Z.
80 E1 Waiotira North I. N.Z.
80 E3 Waiouru North I. N.Z.
80 E2 Waipa r. North I. N.Z.
81 B7 Waipahi South I. N.Z.
240 □ Waipahu HI U.S.A.
80 F3 Waipaoa r. North I. N.Z.
81 D5 Waipara South I. N.Z.
80 F3 Waipawa North I. N.Z.
80 E2 Waipipi North I. N.Z.
80 E1 Waipu North I. N.Z.
80 F3 Waipukurau North I. N.Z.
80 F3 Wairakei North I. N.Z.
81 E4 Wairarapa, Lake North I. N.Z.
81 E4 Wairau r. South I. N.Z.
81 D4 Wairau Valley South I. N.Z.
80 F3 Wairoa North I. N.Z.
80 E2 Wairoa r. North I. N.Z.
80 F3 Wairoa r. North I. N.Z.
173 F2 Waischenfeld Ger.
109 F2 Waishe Zhejiang China
80 F3 Waitahanui North I. N.Z.
81 B6 Waitahuna South I. N.Z.
80 E2 Waitakaruru North I. N.Z.
81 C6 Waitaki South I. N.Z.
81 C6 Waitaki r. South I. N.Z.
80 □ Waitangi Chatham Is S. Pacific Ocean
81 C5 Waitangitaona r. South I. N.Z.
80 E3 Waitara North I. N.Z.
81 C6 Waitati South I. N.Z.
84 C4 Waite River N.T. Austr.
80 E2 Waitoa North I. N.Z.
80 E3 Waitomo Caves North I. N.Z.
80 E3 Waitotara North I. N.Z.
80 E3 Waitotari r. North I. N.Z.
238 C2 Waitsburg WA U.S.A.
80 E2 Waiuku North I. N.Z.
81 B7 Waiwera South South I. N.Z.
109 F3 Waiyang Fujian China
79 □1 Waiyevu Taveuni Fiji
179 E2 Waizenkirchen Austria
103 H5 Wajima Japan

210 D4 Wajir Kenya
81 D4 Wakapuaka South I. N.Z.
104 B3 Wakasa-wan b. Japan
81 B6 Wakatipu, Lake South I. N.Z.
223 J4 Wakaw Sask. Can.
79 □1 Wakaya i. Fiji
104 B4 Wakayama Japan
104 B5 Wakayama pref. Japan
75 F2 Wake Atoll N. Pacific Ocean
236 D4 WaKeeney KS U.S.A.
227 J3 Wakefield Que. Can.
246 □ Wakefield Jamaica
81 D4 Wakefield South I. N.Z.
149 H4 Wakefield West Yorkshire, England U.K.
226 C2 Wakefield MI U.S.A.
232 B5 Wakefield OH U.S.A.
234 B3 Wakefield PA U.S.A.
233 H4 Wakefield RI U.S.A.
232 E6 Wakefield VA U.S.A.
Wakeham Que. Can. see Kangiqsujuaq
Wake Island N. Pacific Ocean see Wake Atoll
96 A3 Wakema Myanmar
102 J1 Wakkanai Japan
215 H2 Wakkerstroom S. Africa
83 F3 Wakool N.S.W. Austr.
83 E3 Wakool r. N.S.W. Austr.
209 B7 Waku-Kungo Angola
224 D3 Wakwayowkastic r. Ont. Can.
114 C3 Walajapet Tamil Nadu India
171 C3 Walbeck Ger.
151 I2 Walberswick Suffolk, England U.K.
174 E5 Wałbrzych Pol.
169 E4 Walburg Ger.
83 G2 Walcha N.S.W. Austr.
173 F4 Walchensee l. Ger.
178 D3 Walchsee Austria
168 C3 Walchum Ger.
238 F3 Walcott WY U.S.A.
165 D4 Walcourt Belgium
174 E2 Wałcz Pol.
172 D4 Wald Baden-Württemberg Ger.
173 G2 Wald Bayern Ger.
172 C4 Wald Switz.
173 C2 Waldachtal Ger.
179 F2 Waldaist r. Austria
172 B2 Waldböckelheim Ger.
169 C5 Waldbreitbach Ger.
169 C5 Waldbröl Ger.
172 D2 Waldbrunn Ger.
169 D5 Waldbrunn-Lahr Ger.
172 D4 Waldburg Ger.
87 C5 Waldburg Range mts W.A. Austr.
171 E4 Walddrehna Ger.
169 E4 Waldeck Ger.
179 H3 Waldegg Austria
235 D1 Walden NY U.S.A.
172 D3 Waldenbuch Ger.
172 D2 Waldenburg Baden-Württemberg Ger.
171 D5 Waldenburg Sachsen Ger.
Waldenburg Pol. see Wałbrzych
190 C1 Waldenburg Switz.
173 G2 Walderbach Ger.
173 G2 Waldershof Ger.
151 H3 Walderslade Medway, England U.K.
172 B2 Waldfischbach-Burgalben Ger.
179 G2 Waldhausen Austria
179 F2 Waldhausen im Strudengau Austria
171 E4 Waldheim Ger.
179 F2 Walding Austria
169 E4 Waldkappel Ger.
173 B3 Waldkirch Ger.
173 H3 Waldkirchen Ger.
173 G3 Waldkraiburg Ger.
172 C2 Wald-Michelbach Ger.
172 B2 Waldmohr Ger.
173 G2 Waldmünchen Ger.
231 D6 Waldo FL U.S.A.
226 D4 Waldo WI U.S.A.
233 □I2 Waldoboro ME U.S.A.
150 C4 Waldon r. England U.K.
232 E5 Waldorf MD U.S.A.
174 G2 Waldowo-Szlacheckie Pol.
238 A2 Waldport OR U.S.A.
172 A2 Waldrach Ger.
237 E5 Waldron AR U.S.A.
226 E5 Waldron MI U.S.A.
263 H2 Waldron, Cape Antarctica
171 D5 Waldsassen Ger.
172 C4 Waldshut Ger.
190 E1 Waldstatt Switz.
172 D3 Waldstetten Baden-Württemberg Ger.
173 E3 Waldstetten Bayern Ger.
173 G2 Waldthurn Ger.
87 C6 Walebing W.A. Austr.
108 B2 Walêg Sichuan China
190 E1 Walenstadt Switz.
150 D2 Wales admin. div. U.K.
206 E4 Walewale Ghana
165 F5 Walferdange Lux.
83 G2 Walgett N.S.W. Austr.
262 Q1 Walgreen Coast Antarctica
226 D4 Walhalla MI U.S.A.
236 D1 Walhalla ND U.S.A.
231 D5 Walhalla SC U.S.A.
87 B6 Walkaway W.A. Austr.
170 D2 Walkendorf Ger.
169 F4 Walkenried Ger.
84 C2 Walker r. N.T. Austr.
226 E4 Walker MI U.S.A.
236 E2 Walker MN U.S.A.
240 H2 Walker r. NV U.S.A.
237 E7 Walker Cay i. Bahamas
85 E3 Walker Creek r. Qld Austr.
240 H2 Walker Lake NV U.S.A.
262 R2 Walker Mountains Antarctica
232 E5 Walkersville MD U.S.A.
232 C5 Walkersville WV U.S.A.
227 G3 Walkerton Ont. Can.
226 D5 Walkerton IN U.S.A.
235 D1 Walker Valley NY U.S.A.
236 C2 Wall SD U.S.A.
87 C4 Wall, Mount hill W.A. Austr.
87 B6 Wallabi Group is W.A. Austr.
85 E2 Wallaby Island Qld Austr.
238 C2 Wallace ID U.S.A.
231 E5 Wallace NC U.S.A.
236 C3 Wallace NE U.S.A.
232 B6 Wallace VA U.S.A.
224 D5 Wallaceburg Ont. Can.
81 B7 Wallacetown South I. N.Z.
86 D3 Wallal Downs W.A. Austr.
87 C6 Wallambin, Lake salt flat W.A. Austr.
83 G2 Wallangarra Qld Austr.
82 D3 Wallaroo S.A. Austr.
149 F4 Wallasey Merseyside, England U.K.
85 G5 Wallaville Qld Austr.
238 C2 Walla Walla WA U.S.A.
172 C2 Walldorf Baden-Württemberg Ger.
172 C1 Walldorf Hessen Ger.
169 F5 Walldorf Thüringen Ger.
172 D2 Walldürn Ger.
214 D4 Wallekraal S. Africa
83 G3 Wallendbeen N.S.W. Austr.
171 C5 Wallenfels Ger.
190 E1 Wallensee l. Switz.
173 G3 Wallerfing Ger.
179 H3 Wallern im Burgenland Austria
173 G3 Wallersdorf Ger.
173 E3 Wallersee l. Austria
173 E3 Wallerstein Ger.
173 F4 Wallgau Ger.
172 E2 Wallhausen Baden-Württemberg Ger.
172 B2 Wallhausen Rheinland-Pfalz Ger.
80 F4 Wallingford North I. N.Z.
151 F3 Wallingford Oxfordshire, England U.K.
235 F1 Wallingford CT U.S.A.
233 G3 Wallingford VT U.S.A.
Wallis canton Switz. see Valais
77 I3 Wallis, Îles is Wallis and Futuna Is
77 I3 Wallis and Futuna Islands terr. S. Pacific Ocean
172 C4 Wallisellen Switz.
Wallis et Futuna, Îles terr. S. Pacific Ocean see Wallis and Futuna Islands
Wallis Islands Wallis and Futuna Is see Wallis, Îles
235 D1 Wallkill NY U.S.A.
235 E1 Wallkill r. NY U.S.A.
238 C2 Wallowa OR U.S.A.
238 C2 Wallowa Mountains OR U.S.A.
146 □G1 Walls Shetland, Scotland U.K.
168 E1 Wallsbüll Ger.
149 H3 Wallsend Tyne and Wear, England U.K.
170 C3 Wallstawe Ger.
169 D5 Walluf Ger.
238 C2 Wallula WA U.S.A.
85 G5 Wallumbilla Qld Austr.
149 F3 Walney, Isle of i. England U.K.
226 C5 Walnut IL U.S.A.
232 E4 Walnut Bottom PA U.S.A.
240 F3 Walnut Creek CA U.S.A.
236 D4 Walnut Creek r. KS U.S.A.
240 G2 Walnut Grove CA U.S.A.
234 C2 Walnutport PA U.S.A.
237 F4 Walnut Ridge AR U.S.A.
173 F3 Walpertskirchen Ger.
87 C7 Walpole W.A. Austr.
233 G3 Walpole NH U.S.A.
78 □5 Walpole, Île i. New Caledonia
175 J2 Wałpusza r. Pol.
178 D3 Wals Austria
151 F2 Walsall West Midlands, England U.K.
173 E2 Walsdorf Ger.
239 F4 Walsenburg CO U.S.A.
85 E3 Walsh r. Qld Austr.
237 C4 Walsh CO U.S.A.
170 D3 Walsleben Ger.
151 H2 Walsoken Cambridgeshire, England U.K.
168 E3 Walsrode Ger.
175 H1 Wałsza r. Pol.
115 D2 Waltair Andhra Prad. India
173 E4 Waltenhofen Ger.
231 D5 Walterboro SC U.S.A.
237 D5 Walters OK U.S.A.
169 F5 Waltershausen Ger.
83 F2 Walter's Range hills Qld Austr.
237 F5 Walthall MS U.S.A.
227 I3 Waltham Que. Can.
149 I4 Waltham North East Lincolnshire, England U.K.
233 H3 Waltham MA U.S.A.
233 □I2 Waltham ME U.S.A.
151 H3 Waltham Abbey Essex, England U.K.
151 G2 Waltham on the Wolds Leicestershire, England U.K.
173 F3 Walting Ger.
226 D5 Walton IN U.S.A.
235 D1 Walton NY U.S.A.
232 C5 Walton WV U.S.A.
149 G4 Walton-le-Dale Lancashire, England U.K.
151 G3 Walton-on-Thames Surrey, England U.K.
151 I3 Walton-on-the-Naze Essex, England U.K.
Walvisbaai Namibia see Walvis Bay
212 B4 Walvis Bay Namibia
212 B4 Walvis Bay b. Namibia
264 I8 Walvis Ridge sea feature S. Atlantic Ocean
87 C6 Walyahmoing hill W.A. Austr.
208 E4 Wamba Dem. Rep. Congo
209 C5 Wamba r. Dem. Rep. Congo
207 G3 Wamba Nigeria
183 F3 Wamba Spain
236 D4 Wamego KS U.S.A.
211 C6 Wami r. Tanz.
238 F3 Wamsutter WY U.S.A.
83 F2 Wanaaring N.S.W. Austr.
81 B6 Wanaka South I. N.Z.
81 B6 Wanaka, Lake South I. N.Z.
235 D2 Wanamassa NJ U.S.A.
234 B1 Wanamie PA U.S.A.
109 E3 Wan'an Jiangxi China
235 E2 Wanaque NJ U.S.A.
83 E3 Wanbi S.A. Austr.
108 B3 Wanbi Yunnan China
231 F5 Wanchese NC U.S.A.
256 G2 Wanda Arg.
100 E3 Wanda Shan mts China
223 H4 Wandering River Alta Can.
169 F5 Wandersleben Ger.
168 E1 Wanderup Ger.
108 A3 Wanding Yunnan China
Wandingzhen Yunnan China see Wanding
Wandiwash Tamil Nadu India see Vandavasi
81 D5 Wandle Downs South I. N.Z.
170 E3 Wandlitz Ger.
85 G5 Wandoan Qld Austr.
151 G3 Wandsworth Greater London, England U.K.
179 G2 Wang Austria
96 B3 Wang, Mae Nam r. Thai.
80 E3 Wanganui North I. N.Z.
80 E3 Wanganui r. North I. N.Z.
81 C5 Wanganui r. South I. N.Z.
83 F4 Wangaratta Vic. Austr.
82 C3 Wangary S.A. Austr.
108 C1 Wangcang Sichuan China
109 E2 Wangcheng Hunan China
Wangda Xizang China see Zogang
107 G4 Wangdu Hebei China
117 G4 Wangdue Phodrang Bhutan
169 E4 Wangelnstedt Ger.
168 C2 Wangels Ger.
190 C1 Wangen Switz.
172 D4 Wangen im Allgäu Ger.
168 C2 Wangerooge Ger.
168 C2 Wangerooge i. Ger.
93 B5 Wanggamet, Gunung mt. Sumba Indon.
106 C4 Wang Gaxun Qinghai China
Wanggezhuang Shandong China see Jiaonan
190 D1 Wangi Switz.
109 F2 Wangjiang Anhui China
100 C3 Wangkui Heilong. China
Wang Mai Khon Thai. see Sawankhalok
108 D4 Wangmao Guangxi China
108 C3 Wangmo Guizhou China
Wangolodougou Côte d'Ivoire see Ouangolodougou
100 D4 Wangqing Jilin China
Wangying Jiangsu China see Huaiyin
108 C1 Wangziguan Gansu China
222 G4 Wanham Alta Can.
251 H3 Wanhatti Suriname
208 E4 Wanie-Rukula Dem. Rep. Congo
116 B5 Wankaner Gujarat India
168 F1 Wankendorf Ger.
Wankie Zimbabwe see Hwange
210 E4 Wanlaweyn Somalia
168 D2 Wanna Ger.
87 F6 Wanna Lakes salt flat W.A. Austr.
87 B6 Wanneroo W.A. Austr.
109 F2 Wannian Jiangxi China
108 D5 Wanning Hainan China
164 E3 Wanroij Neth.
107 F5 Wanrong Shanxi China
108 D3 Wanshan Guizhou China
171 C4 Wansleben am See Ger.
80 F4 Wanstead North I. N.Z.
151 F3 Wantage Oxfordshire, England U.K.
235 E2 Wantagh NY U.S.A.
227 G2 Wanup Ont. Can.
108 D2 Wanxian Chongqing China
108 D2 Wanxian Chongqing China
108 D1 Wanyuan Sichuan China
109 E3 Wanzai Jiangxi China
165 E4 Wanze Belgium
Wanzhi Anhui China see Wuhu
232 A4 Wapakoneta OH U.S.A.
164 F2 Wapenveld Neth.
175 H2 Wapiersk Pol.
222 G4 Wapiti r. Alta Can.
175 I2 Waplewo Pol.
174 F3 Wapno Pol.
235 E1 Wappinger Creek r. NY U.S.A.
235 E1 Wappingers Falls NY U.S.A.
236 F3 Wapsipinicon r. IA U.S.A.
108 B1 Waqên Sichuan China
232 C6 War WV U.S.A.
208 F2 Warab Sudan
208 F2 Warab state Sudan
105 F3 Warabi Japan
123 F5 Warah Pak.
114 C2 Warangal Andhra Prad. India
116 E5 Waraseoni Madh. Prad. India
83 F5 Waratah Tas. Austr.
169 F3 Warberg Ger.
151 G2 Warboys Cambridgeshire, England U.K.
85 E5 Warbreccan Qld Austr.
222 H4 Warburg Alta Can.
169 E4 Warburg Ger.
83 F4 Warburton Vic. Austr.
87 E5 Warburton W.A. Austr.
82 D1 Warburton watercourse S.A. Austr.
215 F2 Warburton S. Africa
87 E5 Warburton Range hills W.A. Austr.
165 E4 Warche r. Belgium
149 G3 Warcop Cumbria, England U.K.
157 F3 Warcq France
81 E4 Ward South I. N.Z.
262 T2 Ward, Mount Antarctica
81 A6 Ward, Mount South I. N.Z.
81 B5 Ward, Mount South I. N.Z.
82 D3 Wardang Island S.A. Austr.
215 G2 Warden S. Africa
168 D2 Wardenburg Ger.
116 D5 Wardha Mahar. India
114 C2 Wardha r. India
146 E3 Ward Hill hill Scotland U.K.
151 E2 Wardington Oxfordshire, England U.K.
146 □G1 Ward of Bressay hill Scotland U.K.
170 D2 Wardow Ger.
149 G3 Ward's Stone hill England U.K.
222 E3 Ware B.C. Can.
151 G3 Ware Hertfordshire, England U.K.
233 G3 Ware MA U.S.A.
165 C4 Waregem Belgium
150 E4 Wareham Dorset, England U.K.
233 H4 Wareham MA U.S.A.
165 E4 Waremme Belgium
170 D2 Waren Ger.
169 C4 Warendorf Ger.
164 F1 Warffum Neth.
164 E1 Warga Neth.
Wargili i. S. Male Maldives see Vaagali
85 G4 Warginburra Peninsula Qld Austr.
Wargla Alg. see Ouargla
151 G3 Wargrave Wokingham, England U.K.
83 G2 Warialda N.S.W. Austr.
170 C2 Warin Ger.
96 D4 Warin Chamrap Thai.
147 E2 Waringstown Northern Ireland U.K.
149 G2 Wark Northumberland, England U.K.
175 J4 Warka Pol.
80 E2 Warkworth North I. N.Z.
149 H2 Warkworth Northumberland, England U.K.
Warli Sichuan China see Walêg
151 G3 Warlingham Surrey, England U.K.
156 C2 Warloy-Baillon France
174 G2 Warlubie Pol.
223 I4 Warman Sask. Can.
212 C6 Warmbad Namibia
173 F2 Warmensteinach Ger.
156 E3 Warmeriville France
143 I4 Warmia reg. Pol.
151 F2 Warmington Warwickshire, England U.K.
175 I2 Warmińsko-Mazurskie prov. Pol.
150 E3 Warminster Wiltshire, England U.K.
234 C2 Warminster PA U.S.A.
164 D2 Warmond Neth.
169 D3 Warmsen Ger.
241 I2 Warm Springs NV U.S.A.
232 D5 Warm Springs VA U.S.A.
214 C5 Warmwaterberg S. Africa
170 D2 Warnemünde Ger.
223 H5 Warner Alta Can.
233 H3 Warner NH U.S.A.
238 B3 Warner Mountains CA U.S.A.
231 D5 Warner Robins GA U.S.A.
240 I5 Warner Springs CA U.S.A.
253 E4 Warnes Bol.
165 B4 Warneton Belgium
173 F4 Warngau Ger.
151 G3 Warnham West Sussex, England U.K.
174 C2 Warnice Pol.
170 C2 Warnow Ger.
170 D1 Warnow r. Ger.
164 F2 Warnsveld Neth.
114 C2 Warona Mahar. India
87 B7 Waroona W.A. Austr.
116 D5 Warora Mahar. India
168 E3 Warpe Ger.
85 G5 Warra Qld Austr.
83 E4 Warracknabeal Vic. Austr.
83 G4 Warragamba Reservoir N.S.W. Austr.
83 F4 Warragul Vic. Austr.
82 D2 Warrakalanna, Lake salt flat S.A. Austr.
82 C3 Warramboo S.A. Austr.
87 C6 Warramboo hill W.A. Austr.
83 F2 Warrambool r. N.S.W. Austr.
82 D1 Warrandirinna, Lake salt flat S.A. Austr.
83 E4 Warrayure Vic. Austr.
84 D4 Warrawagine W.A. Austr.
83 F2 Warrego r. N.S.W./Qld Austr.
85 F5 Warrego Range hills Qld Austr.
83 F2 Warren N.S.W. Austr.
87 B7 Warren r. W.A. Austr.
227 G2 Warren Ont. Can.
237 E5 Warren AR U.S.A.
226 C4 Warren IL U.S.A.
226 E5 Warren IN U.S.A.
227 F4 Warren MI U.S.A.
227 D2 Warren MN U.S.A.
232 C4 Warren OH U.S.A.
232 A4 Warren PA U.S.A.
234 D2 Warren County county NJ U.S.A.
235 D3 Warren Grove NJ U.S.A.
Warren Hastings Island Palau see Merir
147 E2 Warrenpoint Northern Ireland U.K.
226 B3 Warrens WI U.S.A.
236 E4 Warrensburg MO U.S.A.
233 G2 Warrensburg NY U.S.A.
234 B1 Warrensville PA U.S.A.
215 E3 Warrenton S. Africa
231 D5 Warrenton GA U.S.A.
236 F4 Warrenton MO U.S.A.
238 B2 Warrenton OR U.S.A.
232 E5 Warrenton VA U.S.A.
207 G5 Warri Nigeria
87 C6 Warriedar hill W.A. Austr.
81 C6 Warrington South I. N.Z.
149 G4 Warrington Warrington, England U.K.
149 G4 Warrington admin. div. England U.K.
231 C6 Warrington FL U.S.A.
83 E4 Warrnambool Vic. Austr.
82 A3 Warrow S.A. Austr.
84 C1 Warruwi N.T. Austr.
Warsaw Pol. see Warszawa
226 B5 Warsaw IL U.S.A.
230 C3 Warsaw IN U.S.A.
232 A6 Warsaw KY U.S.A.
236 E4 Warsaw MO U.S.A.
232 D3 Warsaw NY U.S.A.
232 E6 Warsaw VA U.S.A.
179 F3 Warscheneck mt. Austria
210 E4 Warsheikh Somalia
169 C4 Warsingsfehn Ger.
149 H4 Warslow Staffordshire, England U.K.
169 D4 Warstein Ger.
175 J3 Warszawa Pol.
174 G4 Warta Pol.
174 C3 Warta r. Pol.
174 D4 Warta Bolesławiecka Pol.
179 F3 Wartberg an der Krems Austria
231 C4 Wartburg TN U.S.A.
171 B5 Wartburg Schloß tourist site Thüringen Ger.
173 F3 Wartenberg Ger.
169 E5 Wartenberg-Angersbach Ger.
172 D3 Wartenhausen Ger.
170 F2 Wartin Ger.
175 H4 Wartkowice Pol.
169 E5 Wartmannsroth Ger.
149 G3 Warton Lancashire, England U.K.
116 D5 Warud Mahar. India
83 H2 Warwick Qld Austr.
151 F2 Warwick Warwickshire, England U.K.
234 C3 Warwick MD U.S.A.
235 D1 Warwick NY U.S.A.
233 H4 Warwick RI U.S.A.
149 G3 Warwick Bridge Cumbria, England U.K.
84 D2 Warwick Channel N.T. Austr.
151 F2 Warwickshire admin. div. England U.K.
108 B2 Warzhong Sichuan China
222 H5 Wasa B.C. Can.
207 G4 Wasagu Nigeria
227 G3 Wasaga Beach Ont. Can.
241 L2 Wasatch Range mts UT U.S.A.
215 H3 Wasbank S. Africa
168 E1 Wasbek Ger.
146 E2 Wasbister Orkney, Scotland U.K.
169 F3 Wasbüttel Ger.
223 J5 Wascana Creek r. Sask. Can.
235 D1 Wäschenbeuren Ger.
240 H4 Wasco CA U.S.A.
226 B2 Wascott WI U.S.A.
236 E2 Waseca MN U.S.A.
175 J3 Wąsewo Pol.
226 C5 Washburn IL U.S.A.
233 □I1 Washburn ME U.S.A.
236 C2 Washburn ND U.S.A.
232 B6 Washburn TN U.S.A.
226 B2 Washburn WI U.S.A.
104 C3 Washiga-take mt. Japan
116 D5 Washim Mahar. India
225 F3 Washimeska r. Que. Can.
149 H3 Washington Tyne and Wear, England U.K.
235 E1 Washington CT U.S.A.
234 C3 Washington DC U.S.A.
231 D5 Washington GA U.S.A.
236 F3 Washington IA U.S.A.
226 C5 Washington IL U.S.A.
230 C4 Washington IN U.S.A.
236 D4 Washington KS U.S.A.
232 B5 Washington KY U.S.A.
231 E5 Washington NC U.S.A.
233 G3 Washington NH U.S.A.
235 D2 Washington NJ U.S.A.
234 D2 Washington PA U.S.A.
241 K3 Washington UT U.S.A.
232 D5 Washington VA U.S.A.
238 B2 Washington state U.S.A.
263 L2 Washington, Cape Antarctica
233 H2 Washington, Mount NH U.S.A.
232 B5 Washington Court House OH U.S.A.
234 D2 Washington Crossing NJ U.S.A.
235 E1 Washington Depot CT U.S.A.
234 A3 Washington Grove MD U.S.A.
226 D3 Washington Island WI U.S.A.
221 L2 Washington Land reg. Greenland
235 D1 Washingtonville NY U.S.A.
234 B1 Washingtonville PA U.S.A.
237 D5 Washita r. OK U.S.A.
225 H3 Washkutucna WA U.S.A.
156 E3 Wasigny France
175 L2 Wasilków Pol.
221 D3 Wasilla AK U.S.A.
127 G4 Wāsiṭ governorate Iraq
127 G4 Wāsiṭ tourist site Iraq
224 E3 Waskaganish Que. Can.
222 H4 Waskatenau Alta Can.
174 E4 Wąsosz Pol.
175 K2 Wąsosz Pol.
175 J3 Wąsowo Pol.
242 □I6 Waspán Nic.
163 D4 Waspik Neth.
149 H3 Wass North Yorkshire, England U.K.
206 B3 Wassadou Senegal
165 E4 Wasseiges Belgium
157 H4 Wasselonne France
164 D2 Wassen Switz.
164 D2 Wassenaar Neth.
169 B4 Wassenberg Ger.
172 D3 Wasseralfingen Ger.
173 G3 Wasserburg am Inn Ger.
169 E5 Wasserkuppe hill Ger.
169 F4 Wasserleben Ger.
172 A2 Wasserliesch Ger.
169 F4 Wasserlosen Ger.
172 D2 Wassertrüdingen Ger.
172 D2 Wassigny France
206 B4 Wassou Guinea
240 H2 Wassuk Range mts NV U.S.A.
157 E4 Wassy France
96 C4 Wat, Nam r. Laos
93 B4 Watampone Sulawesi Selatan Indon.
93 A4 Watansoppeng Sulawesi Selatan Indon.
105 F2 Watarase-gawa r. Japan
232 B6 Watauga r. TN U.S.A.
150 E3 Watchet Somerset, England U.K.
149 G3 Watchgate Cumbria, England U.K.
Watenstadt-Salzgitter Ger. see Salzgitter
151 H2 Waterbeach Cambridgeshire, England U.K.
233 G4 Waterbury CT U.S.A.
233 G2 Waterbury VT U.S.A.
246 C2 Water Cays i. Bahamas
227 H4 Waterdown Ont. Can.
231 D5 Wateree r. SC U.S.A.
221 D3 Waterfall AK U.S.A.
142 C4 Waterford Rep. of Ireland
147 D4 Waterford county Rep. of Ireland
215 E5 Waterford S. Africa
240 G3 Waterford CA U.S.A.
235 F1 Waterford CT U.S.A.
232 D4 Waterford PA U.S.A.
226 C4 Waterford WI U.S.A.
234 D3 Waterford Works NJ U.S.A.
223 J4 Waterhen r. Sask. Can.
84 C2 Waterhouse r. N.T. Austr.
84 C5 Waterhouse Range mts N.T. Austr.
164 D2 Wateringen Neth.
165 C4 Waterland-Oudeman Belgium
82 D2 Waterloo N.T. Austr.
165 D4 Waterloo Belgium
224 D5 Waterloo Ont. Can.
206 B4 Waterloo Sierra Leone
226 E3 Waterloo IA U.S.A.
226 E3 Waterloo IL U.S.A.
234 B4 Waterloo MD U.S.A.
232 E3 Waterloo NY U.S.A.
226 C4 Waterloo WI U.S.A.
151 F4 Waterlooville Hampshire, England U.K.
226 C5 Waterman IL U.S.A.
227 F4 Watermill NY U.S.A.
149 F2 Water of Leith r. Scotland U.K.
149 F2 Water of Tulla r. Scotland U.K.
151 F2 Water Orton Warwickshire, England U.K.
213 F4 Waterpoort S. Africa
147 D2 Waterside Northern Ireland U.K.
226 C2 Watersmeet MI U.S.A.
222 H5 Waterton Park Alta Can.
235 E1 Watertown CT U.S.A.
233 F3 Watertown NY U.S.A.
236 D2 Watertown SD U.S.A.
226 C4 Watertown WI U.S.A.
215 F2 Waterval r. S. Africa
215 I2 Waterval-Boven S. Africa
82 D3 Watervale S.A. Austr.
237 F5 Water Valley MS U.S.A.
147 A5 Waterville Rep. of Ireland
233 □I2 Waterville ME U.S.A.
232 B4 Waterville OH U.S.A.
238 B2 Waterville WA U.S.A.
233 G3 Watervliet NY U.S.A.
95 E4 Wates Indon.
227 G4 Watford Ont. Can.
151 G3 Watford Hertfordshire, England U.K.
236 C2 Watford City ND U.S.A.
223 K3 Wathaman r. Sask. Can.
87 C6 Watheroo W.A. Austr.
222 G4 Watino Alta Can.
232 E3 Watkins Glen NY U.S.A.
231 D5 Watkinsville GA U.S.A.
Watling Island Bahamas see San Salvador
151 F3 Watlington Oxfordshire, England U.K.
237 D5 Watonga OK U.S.A.
93 D2 Watowato, Bukit mt. Halmahera Indon.
223 J5 Watrous Sask. Can.
239 F5 Watrous NM U.S.A.
208 F4 Watsa Dem. Rep. Congo
226 D5 Watseka IL U.S.A.
85 E2 Watson r. Qld Austr.
223 J4 Watson Sask. Can.
262 P1 Watson Escarpment Antarctica
222 D2 Watson Lake Y.T. Can.
234 B1 Watsontown PA U.S.A.
240 G3 Watsonville CA U.S.A.
87 E5 Watt, Mount hill W.A. Austr.
156 C2 Watten France
146 E2 Watten Highland, Scotland U.K.
168 F1 Wattenbek Ger.
178 C3 Wattens Austria
190 C2 Wattenwil Switz.
156 E2 Wattignies-la-Victoire France
147 D2 Wattlebridge Northern Ireland U.K.
170 D2 Wattmannshagen Ger.
151 H2 Watton Norfolk, England U.K.
151 G3 Watton-at-Stone Hertfordshire, England U.K.
156 D2 Wattrelos France
231 C5 Watts Bar Lake resr TN U.S.A.
232 D3 Wattsburg PA U.S.A.
190 E1 Wattwil Switz.
93 B3 Watuwila, Bukit mt. Indon.
169 D5 Watzenborn-Steinberg Ger.
208 E3 Wau Sudan
83 H2 Wauchope N.S.W. Austr.
84 C4 Wauchope N.T. Austr.
231 D7 Wauchula FL U.S.A.
93 A3 Waukara, Gunung mt. Indon.
86 D4 Waukarlycarly, Lake salt flat W.A. Austr.
226 C4 Waukau WI U.S.A.
226 D4 Waukegan IL U.S.A.
226 C4 Waukesha WI U.S.A.
226 B4 Waukon IA U.S.A.
226 C3 Waunakee WI U.S.A.
236 C3 Wauneta NE U.S.A.
226 C3 Waupaca WI U.S.A.
226 C4 Waupun WI U.S.A.
235 G1 Wauregan CT U.S.A.
237 D5 Waurika OK U.S.A.
226 C3 Wausau WI U.S.A.
226 D3 Wausaukee WI U.S.A.
232 A4 Wauseon OH U.S.A.
226 C3 Wautoma WI U.S.A.
84 B3 Wave Hill N.T. Austr.
151 I2 Waveney r. England U.K.
80 E3 Waverley North I. N.Z.
236 E3 Waverly IA U.S.A.
232 E3 Waverly NY U.S.A.
232 B5 Waverly OH U.S.A.
231 C4 Waverly TN U.S.A.
232 E6 Waverly VA U.S.A.
165 D4 Wavre Belgium
156 C2 Wavrin France
96 B3 Waw Myanmar
224 C4 Wawa Ont. Can.
207 G4 Wawa Nigeria
224 E3 Wawagosic r. Que. Can.
235 D1 Wawarsing NY U.S.A.
174 F5 Wąwelno Pol.
91 J8 Wawoi r. P.N.G.
175 K4 Wąwolnica Pol.
174 D3 Wawrów Pol.
175 I5 Wawrzeńczyce Pol.
237 D5 Waxahachie TX U.S.A.
169 B5 Waxweiler Ger.
110 D4 Waxxari Xinjiang China
87 D5 Way, Lake salt flat W.A. Austr.
79 □1a Waya i. Fiji
Wayaobu Shaanxi China see Zichang
231 D6 Waycross GA U.S.A.
232 B6 Wayland KY U.S.A.
226 E4 Wayland MI U.S.A.
226 B5 Wayland MO U.S.A.
232 E3 Wayland NY U.S.A.
227 F4 Wayne MI U.S.A.
236 D3 Wayne NE U.S.A.
235 D2 Wayne NJ U.S.A.
234 C2 Wayne PA U.S.A.
232 B5 Wayne WV U.S.A.
234 C1 Wayne County county PA U.S.A.
231 D5 Waynesboro GA U.S.A.
237 F6 Waynesboro MS U.S.A.
234 B3 Waynesboro PA U.S.A.
231 C5 Waynesboro TN U.S.A.
232 D5 Waynesboro VA U.S.A.
232 C5 Waynesburg PA U.S.A.
237 E4 Waynesville MO U.S.A.
231 D5 Waynesville NC U.S.A.
237 D4 Waynoka OK U.S.A.
207 I4 Waza Cameroon
156 D2 Waziers France
123 H3 Wazirabad Pak.
174 G2 Wda r. Pol.
Wdig Pembrokeshire, Wales U.K. see Goodwick
78 □5 Wé Î. Loyauté New Caledonia
149 H3 Wear r. England U.K.
233 H3 Weare NH U.S.A.
80 D3 Wearyan r. N.T. Austr.
85 F2 Weary Bay Qld Austr.
237 D5 Weatherford OK U.S.A.
237 D5 Weatherford TX U.S.A.
234 C2 Weatherly PA U.S.A.
149 G4 Weaverham Cheshire, England U.K.
238 B3 Weaverville CA U.S.A.
86 F4 Webb, Mount hill W.A. Austr.
224 D4 Webbwood Ont. Can.
224 C2 Webequie Ont. Can.
80 F4 Weber North I. N.Z.
238 D3 Weber r. UT U.S.A.
222 D4 Weber, Mount B.C. Can.
265 M5 Weber Basin sea feature Indon.
210 D4 Webi Shabeelle r. Somalia
233 H3 Webster MA U.S.A.
234 B3 Webster MD U.S.A.
236 D2 Webster SD U.S.A.
226 A3 Webster WI U.S.A.
236 E3 Webster City IA U.S.A.
232 C5 Webster Springs WV U.S.A.
165 D3 Wechelderzande Belgium
172 D3 Wechmar Ger.
222 H3 Wecho r. N.W.T. Can.
171 D4 Wechselburg Ger.
164 F3 Wedde Neth.
164 G1 Weddel Neth.
262 V2 Weddell Abyssal Plain sea feature Southern Ocean
259 E8 Weddell Island Falkland Is
263 W2 Weddell Sea Antarctica
83 E4 Wedderburn Vic. Austr.
81 C6 Wedderburn South I. N.Z.
168 E1 Weddingstedt Ger.
169 F4 Weddel (Holstein) Ger.
140 □ Wedel Jarlsberg Land reg. Svalbard
222 F5 Wedge Mountain B.C. Can.
150 E3 Wedmore Somerset, England U.K.
150 E2 Wednesbury West Midlands, England U.K.
231 C5 Wedowee AL U.S.A.
238 B3 Weed CA U.S.A.
168 F2 Weede Ger.
151 F2 Weedon Bec Northamptonshire, England U.K.
234 D3 Weedsville PA U.S.A.
232 D3 Weedsville PA U.S.A.
165 D3 Weelde Belgium
83 G2 Weemelah N.S.W. Austr.
215 H3 Weenen S. Africa
168 C2 Weener Ger.
178 C3 Weerberg Austria
164 F2 Weerselo Neth.
165 E3 Weert Neth.
168 E1 Wees Ger.
190 E1 Weesen Switz.
164 E2 Weesp Neth.
83 F2 Weethalle N.S.W. Austr.
83 G2 Wee Waa N.S.W. Austr.
169 B4 Weeze Ger.
171 C3 Wefferlingen Ger.
169 B4 Wegberg Ger.
214 C3 Wegdraai S. Africa
171 C4 Wegeleben Ger.
171 C3 Wegenstedt Ger.
172 C4 Weggis Switz.
174 D4 Węgliniec Pol.
175 J1 Węgorzewo Pol.
174 D2 Węgorzyno Pol.
175 K3 Węgrów Pol.
175 I3 Węgrzynowo Pol.
173 H3 Wegscheid Ger.
168 C2 Wehdel Ger.
164 F1 Wehe-den Hoorn Neth.
164 F3 Wehl Neth.
Wehlau Rus. Fed. see Znamensk
172 B4 Wehr Ger.
169 B4 Wehrbleck Ger.
169 D5 Wehrheim Ger.
173 E3 Wehringen Ger.
107 G4 Wei r. Henan China
107 F5 Wei r. Shaanxi China
107 H4 Wei r. Shandong China
169 C5 Weibern Ger.
172 D2 Weibersbrunn Ger.
107 H3 Weichang Hebei China
173 F3 Weichering Ger.
173 F5 Weichs Ger.
171 D5 Weida Ger.
171 D5 Weida r. Ger.
173 E2 Weidenbach Ger.
173 F2 Weidenberg Ger.
173 G2 Weiden in der Oberpfalz Ger.
172 D2 Weidenstetten Ger.
172 C2 Weidenthal Ger.
173 G2 Weiding Ger.
Weidongmen Heilong. China see Qianjin
172 B2 Weiersbach Ger.
108 C1 Weifang Shandong China
171 F4 Weigersdorf Ger.
234 B3 Weiglestown PA U.S.A.
107 I4 Weihai Shandong China
173 E2 Weihenzell Ger.
173 G2 Weiherhammer Ger.
173 E2 Weihmichl Ger.
107 G5 Weihui Henan China
179 H2 Weikendorf Austria
172 D2 Weikersheim Ger.
173 E3 Weil Ger.
172 B4 Weil am Rhein Ger.
172 C2 Weilbach Ger.
172 D2 Weilburg Ger.
169 D5 Weilburg Ger.
172 C3 Weil der Stadt Ger.
178 A3 Weiler Austria
172 D2 Weiler Ger.
172 E2 Weilerbach Ger.
172 B2 Weilerbach Ger.
169 B5 Weilerswist Ger.
172 C4 Weilheim Ger.
172 D3 Weilheim an der Teck Ger.
173 F4 Weilheim in Oberbayern Ger.
83 F2 Weilmoringle N.S.W. Austr.
169 D5 Weilmünster Ger.
171 C5 Weimar Ger.
169 E4 Weimar (Ahnatal) Ger.
107 F5 Weinan Shaanxi China
169 D5 Weinbach Ger.
171 E4 Weinböhla Ger.
190 E1 Weinfelden Switz.
172 D4 Weingarten Ger.
172 C2 Weingarten (Baden) Ger.
172 C2 Weinheim Ger.
108 C3 Weining Guizhou China
172 D3 Weinsberg Ger.
172 B2 Weinsheim Rheinland-Pfalz Ger.
169 B5 Weinsheim Rheinland-Pfalz Ger.
173 E2 Weinstadt Ger.
85 E2 Weipa Qld Austr.
Weiqu Shaanxi China see Chang'an
83 G2 Weir r. Qld Austr.
87 C5 Weiragoo Range hills W.A. Austr.
223 M3 Weir River Man. Can.
232 C4 Weirton WV U.S.A.
171 D5 Weischlitz Ger.
146 □G1 Weisdale Shetland, Scotland U.K.
170 C2 Weisen Ger.
173 E2 Weisendorf Ger.
238 C2 Weiser ID U.S.A.
238 C2 Weiser r. ID U.S.A.
107 H5 Weishan Shandong China
108 B3 Weishan Yunnan China
107 G5 Weishi Henan China
172 A2 Weiskirchen Ger.
171 C5 Weismain Ger.
173 F4 Weißach r. Ger.
171 F4 Weiße Elster r. Ger.
173 F4 Weiße Laber r. Ger.
178 B3 Weißenbach am Lech Austria
171 F4 Weißenberg Ger.
169 F4 Weißenborn Ger.
171 E5 Weißenborn Ger.
169 F4 Weißenborn-Lüderode Ger.
173 E2 Weißenbrunn Ger.
173 F3 Weißenburg in Bayern Ger.
171 C4 Weißenfels Ger.
173 E2 Weißenhorn Ger.
172 D4 Weißensberg Ger.
172 C4 Weißensee Ger.
171 C5 Weißensee Ger.
179 E4 Weißenstein Austria
169 C5 Weißenthurm Ger.
173 C5 Weißer Main r. Ger.
173 F3 Weißer Regen r. Ger.
173 F4 Weißer Schöps r. Ger.
190 C2 Weisshorn mt. Switz.
171 E4 Weißig Ger.
171 F4 Weißkeißel Ger.
179 F2 Weißkirchen an der Traun Austria
179 F3 Weißkirchen in Steiermark Austria
171 F4 Weißkollm Ger.
178 B4 Weißkugel mt. Austria/Italy
190 D2 Weissmies mt. Switz.
212 C5 Weissrand Mountains Namibia
171 F4 Weißwasser Ger.
179 F2 Weistrach Austria
165 F4 Weiswampach Lux.
172 B3 Weisweil Ger.
179 F4 Weitbruch France
169 F5 Weitefeld Ger.
179 G2 Weiten Austria
179 G4 Weitendorf Austria
170 E1 Weitenhagen Ger.
171 F4 Weitensfeld Austria
179 F4 Weiterfeld Austria
172 C2 Weiterstadt Ger.
164 G1 Weiteveen Neth.
173 E4 Weitnau Ger.
179 F2 Weitra Austria
173 E4 Weitramsdorf Ger.
171 E4 Weixdorf Ger.
108 A3 Weixi Yunnan China
107 G4 Weixian Hebei China
108 C3 Weixin Yunnan China
106 B3 Weiya Xinjiang China
106 E5 Weiyuan Gansu China
Weiyuan Qinghai China see Huzhu
Weiyuan Sichuan China see Jinggu
108 B4 Weiyuan Jiang r. Yunnan China
179 G3 Weiz Austria
Weizhou Sichuan China see Wenchuan
107 I3 Weizi Liaoning China
143 H4 Wejherowo Pol.
223 L4 Wekusko Man. Can.
222 H1 Wekweti N.W.T. Can.
175 H2 Wel r. Pol.
82 C1 Welbourn Hill S.A. Austr.
232 C6 Welch WV U.S.A.
233 □H2 Weld ME U.S.A.
87 D6 Weld, Mount hill W.A. Austr.
173 E3 Welden Ger.
210 C2 Weldiya Eth.
151 G2 Weldon Northamptonshire, England U.K.
87 C5 Weld Range hills W.A. Austr.
165 E4 Welkenraedt Belgium
210 C2 Welk'īt'ē Eth.
215 F2 Welkom S. Africa
164 F3 Well Neth.
227 H4 Welland Ont. Can.
151 G2 Welland r. England U.K.
227 H4 Welland Canal Ont. Can.
171 D4 Wellaune Ger.
168 E2 Welle Ger.
165 E4 Wellen Belgium
172 C3 Wellendingen Ger.
151 F2 Wellesbourne Warwickshire, England U.K.
227 G4 Wellesley Ont. Can.
84 D3 Wellesley Islands Qld Austr.
233 H4 Wellfleet MA U.S.A.
173 F3 Wellheim Ger.
165 E4 Wellin Belgium
169 C5 Welling Ger.
151 G2 Wellingborough Northamptonshire, England U.K.
83 G3 Wellington N.S.W. Austr.
82 D3 Wellington S.A. Austr.
227 I4 Wellington Ont. Can.
81 E4 Wellington North I. N.Z.
81 E4 Wellington admin. reg. North I. N.Z.
214 B5 Wellington S. Africa
150 D4 Wellington Somerset, England U.K.
150 E2 Wellington Telford and Wrekin, England U.K.
238 F3 Wellington CO U.S.A.
237 D4 Wellington KS U.S.A.
240 H2 Wellington NV U.S.A.
232 B4 Wellington OH U.S.A.
237 C5 Wellington TX U.S.A.
241 L2 Wellington UT U.S.A.
259 B8 Wellington, Isla i. Chile
147 E4 Wellington Bridge Rep. of Ireland
84 C2 Wellington Range hills N.T. Austr.
87 D5 Wellington Range hills W.A. Austr.
222 F4 Wells B.C. Can.
150 E3 Wells Somerset, England U.K.
238 D3 Wells NV U.S.A.
87 D5 Wells, Lake salt flat W.A. Austr.
232 E4 Wellsboro PA U.S.A.
232 C4 Wellsburg WV U.S.A.
80 E2 Wellsford North I. N.Z.
151 H2 Wells-next-the-Sea Norfolk, England U.K.
226 E3 Wellston MI U.S.A.
232 E3 Wellsville NY U.S.A.
232 C4 Wellsville OH U.S.A.
234 B2 Wellsville PA U.S.A.
241 J5 Wellton AZ U.S.A.
174 E3 Welna r. Pol.
151 F2 Welney Norfolk, England U.K.
175 L4 Wełnianka r. Pol.
240 □D9 Weloka HI U.S.A.
179 F2 Wels Austria
172 A2 Welschbillig Ger.
170 F2 Welse r. Ger.
150 G3 Welsh Newton Herefordshire, England U.K.
150 D2 Welshpool Powys, Wales U.K.
172 E2 Welsickendorf Ger.
170 E3 Welsickendorf Ger.
171 G4 Welsleben Ger.
149 I4 Welton Lincolnshire, England U.K.
169 C4 Welver Ger.
Welwitschia Namibia see Khorixas
151 G3 Welwyn Hertfordshire, England U.K.
151 G3 Welwyn Garden City Hertfordshire, England U.K.
172 D3 Welzheim Ger.
172 D3 Welzheimer Wald hills Ger.
171 F4 Welzow Ger.
150 E2 Wem Shropshire, England U.K.
150 D3 Wembdon Somerset, England U.K.
211 B6 Wembere r. Tanz.
215 G3 Wembesi S. Africa
222 G4 Wembley Alta Can.
173 E3 Wemding Ger.
164 D3 Wemeldinge Neth.
210 D3 Wemel Shet' r. Eth.
224 E2 Wemindji Que. Can.
146 D6 Wemyss Bay Inverclyde, Scotland U.K.
246 C1 Wemyss Bight Eleuthera Bahamas
107 H5 Wen r. China
251 F3 Wenamu r. Guyana/Venez.
238 B2 Wenatchee WA U.S.A.
238 B2 Wenatchee Mountains WA U.S.A.
108 D5 Wenchang Hainan China
Wenchang Sichuan China see Zitong
109 G3 Wencheng Zhejiang China
206 E5 Wenchi Ghana
210 C2 Wench'it Shet' r. Eth.
Wenchow Zhejiang China see Wenzhou
108 B2 Wenchuan Sichuan China
169 F3 Wendeburg Ger.
172 C2 Wendelsheim Ger.
173 G4 Wendelstein Ger.
173 F4 Wendelstein mt. Ger.
169 C5 Wenden Ger.
Wenden Latvia see Cēsis
241 K5 Wenden AZ U.S.A.
109 G3 Wendeng Shandong China
151 H2 Wendens Ambo Essex, England U.K.
168 F2 Wendisch Evern Ger.
170 D2 Wendisch Priborn Ger.
171 F3 Wendisch Rietz Ger.
172 D3 Wendlingen am Neckar Ger.
210 C3 Wendo Eth.
206 B4 Wêndou Mbôrou Guinea
151 G3 Wendover Buckinghamshire, England U.K.
238 D3 Wendover UT U.S.A.
150 B4 Wendron Cornwall, England U.K.
165 C3 Wenduine Belgium
Wenfeng Jiangxi China see Yongfeng
190 C2 Wengen Switz.
169 C3 Wengsel (Isterberg) Ger.
108 A2 Wengshui Yunnan China
109 E3 Wengyuan Guangdong China
Wenhua Yunnan China see Weishan
Wenjiang Sichuan China see Gaoxian
109 E3 Wenjiashi Jiangxi China
Wenlan Yunnan China see Mengzi
Wenlin Sichuan China see Renshou
109 G2 Wenling Zhejiang China
85 E2 Wenlock r. Qld Austr.
150 E2 Wenlock Edge ridge England U.K.
250 □ Wenman, Isla i. Islas Galápagos Ecuador
169 D4 Wenne r. Ger.
169 E3 Wennigsen (Deister) Ger.
149 G3 Wenning r. England U.K.
168 D1 Wenningstedt Ger.
178 B3 Wenns Austria
78 □4a Weno Chuuk Micronesia
78 □4a Weno i. Chuuk Micronesia
226 C5 Wenona IL U.S.A.
233 F5 Wenona MD U.S.A.
Wenping Yunnan China see Ludian
108 D2 Wenquan Chongqing China
108 C2 Wenquan Guizhou China
Wenquan Hubei China see Yingshan
106 C5 Wenquan Qinghai China
110 C3 Wenquan Xinjiang China
109 E2 Wenquanzhen Hubei China
108 C4 Wenshan Yunnan China
108 C2 Wenshui Guizhou China
149 H3 Wensley North Yorkshire, England U.K.
149 G3 Wensleydale val. England U.K.
110 C3 Wensu Xinjiang China

151 I2 Wensum r. England U.K.
149 I4 Went r. England U.K.
168 F2 Wentorf Ger.
168 F2 Wentorf bei Hamburg Ger.
83 E3 Wentworth N.S.W. Austr.
231 E4 Wentworth NC U.S.A.
233 H3 Wentworth NH U.S.A.
226 B2 Wentworth WI U.S.A.
107 F3 Wenxi Shanxi China
108 C1 Wenxian Gansu China
107 F4 Wenyu r. China
173 G2 Wenzenbach Ger.
109 G3 Wenzhou Zhejiang China
171 D3 Wenzlow Ger.
150 E2 Weobley Herefordshire, England U.K.
215 F3 Wepener S. Africa
165 D4 Wépion Belgium
116 D4 Wer Rajasthan India
172 D2 Werbach Ger.
170 E3 Werbellin Ger.
171 F4 Werben Ger.
170 C1 Werben (Elbe) Ger.
171 E4 Werbig Ger.
175 L5 Werbkowice Pol.
165 E4 Werbomont Belgium
212 D5 Werda Botswana
171 D5 Werdau Ger.
210 E3 Werder Eth.
171 D3 Werder Brandenburg Ger.
170 E2 Werder Mecklenburg-Vorpommern Ger.
169 C4 Werdohl Ger.
168 C2 Werdum Ger.
151 H2 Wereham Norfolk, England U.K.
178 E3 Werfen Austria
169 C4 Werl Ger.
168 C3 Werlte Ger.
169 C4 Wermelskirchen Ger.
171 D4 Wermsdorf Ger.
168 E5 Wern r. Ger.
172 D3 Wernau Ger.
179 E4 Wernberg Austria
173 G2 Wernberg-Köblitz Ger.
179 G4 Werndorf Austria
169 C4 Werne Ger.
171 B5 Werneck Ger.
171 E3 Werneuchen Ger.
169 F4 Wernigerode Ger.
169 F5 Wernshausen Ger.
168 C3 Werpeloh Ger.
169 E4 Werra r. Ger.
169 D3 Werre r. Ger.
82 E3 Werrimull Vic. Austr.
83 G2 Werris Creek N.S.W. Austr.
173 E4 Wertach Ger.
173 E3 Wertach r. Ger.
172 D2 Wertheim Ger.
172 C4 Werthenstein Switz.
169 F4 Werther Ger.
169 D3 Werther (Westfalen) Ger.
173 E3 Wertingen Ger.
164 E2 Wervershoof Neth.
165 C4 Wervik Belgium
169 B4 Wesel Ger.
170 D2 Wesenberg Ger.
168 F3 Wesendorf Ger.
164 F2 Wesepe Neth.
169 D2 Weser r. Ger.
168 D2 Weser sea chan. Ger.
168 C3 Weser-Ems admin. reg. Niedersachsen Ger.
169 D3 Wesergebirge hills Ger.
236 C4 Weskan KS U.S.A.
237 D7 Weslaco TX U.S.A.
215 F5 Wesley S. Africa
233 □J2 Wesley ME U.S.A.
225 K3 Wesleyville Nfld. Can.
232 C3 Wesleyville PA U.S.A.
175 J3 Wesoła Pol.
84 D1 Wessel, Cape N.T. Austr.
168 D1 Wesselburen Ger.
169 B5 Wesseling Ger.
84 D1 Wessel Islands N.T. Austr.
168 E1 Wessen Ger.
215 E2 Wesselsbron S. Africa
214 D2 Wesselsvlei S. Africa
215 G2 Wesselton S. Africa
165 E3 Wessem Neth.
235 D2 Wessington Springs SD U.S.A.
173 F3 Weßling Ger.
173 F4 Wessobrunn Ger.
234 B4 West r. MD U.S.A.
82 C3 Westall, Point S.A. Austr.
84 C2 West Alligator r. N.T. Austr.
226 C4 West Allis WI U.S.A.
262 P1 West Antarctica reg. Antarctica
235 D3 West Atlantic City NJ U.S.A.
149 H3 West Auckland Durham, England U.K.
265 K6 West Australian Basin sea feature Indian Ocean
235 E2 West Babylon NY U.S.A.
84 B2 West Baines r. N.T. Austr.
116 B5 West Banas r. India
128 B4 West Bank terr. Asia
225 J2 West Bay Nfld. Can.
246 B3 West Bay Cayman Is
226 C4 West Bend WI U.S.A.
117 F5 West Bengal state India
151 H3 West Bergholt Essex, England U.K.
151 F3 West Berkshire admin. div. England U.K.
234 D3 West Berlin NJ U.S.A.
232 B5 Westboro OH U.S.A.
227 E3 West Branch MI U.S.A.
151 F2 West Bridgford Nottinghamshire, England U.K.
151 F2 West Bromwich West Midlands, England U.K.
235 F1 Westbrook CT U.S.A.
233 □H3 Westbrook ME U.S.A.
234 D1 Westbrookville NY U.S.A.
233 H2 West Burke VT U.S.A.
83 F5 Westbury Tas. Austr.
150 E3 Westbury Wiltshire, England U.K.
226 B4 Westby WI U.S.A.
246 D2 West Caicos i. Turks and Caicos Is
146 E6 West Calder West Lothian, Scotland U.K.
234 B2 West Cameron PA U.S.A.
81 A6 West Cape South I. N.Z.
87 C7 West Cape Howe W.A. Austr.
234 D4 West Cape May NJ U.S.A.
266 E5 West Caroline Basin sea feature N. Pacific Ocean
234 C3 West Chester PA U.S.A.
235 E1 Westchester County county NY U.S.A.
239 F4 Westcliffe CO U.S.A.
81 C5 West Coast admin. reg. South I. N.Z.
150 E4 West Coker Somerset, England U.K.
226 A3 West Concord MN U.S.A.
151 G3 Westcott Surrey, England U.K.
235 D3 West Creek NJ U.S.A.
81 B6 West Dome mt. South I. N.Z.
165 C3 Westdorpe Neth.
227 F3 West Duck Island Ont. Can.
146 D6 West Dunbartonshire admin. div. Scotland U.K.
231 E7 West End Bahamas
233 F3 West End NY U.S.A.
165 B3 Westende Belgium
178 D3 Westendorf Austria
164 F2 Westenholte Neth.
168 E1 Westensee Ger.
168 F3 Westerbeck (Sassenburg) Ger.
214 D3 Westerberg S. Africa
164 F2 Westerbork Neth.
169 C5 Westerburg Ger.
146 E3 Westerdale Highland, Scotland U.K.
171 C4 Westeregeln Ger.
168 C2 Westerende-Kirchloog (Ihlow) Ger.
81 C5 Westerfield South I. N.Z.
151 G4 Westergate West Sussex, England U.K.
168 F2 Westergellersen Ger.
164 F2 Westerhaar Neth.
151 H3 Westerham Kent, England U.K.
171 C4 Westerhausen Ger.
172 D3 Westerheim Baden-Württemberg Ger.
173 E3 Westerheim Bayern Ger.
168 C2 Westerholt Ger.
168 E2 Westerhorn Ger.
165 E3 Westerhoven Neth.
168 D1 Westerland Ger.
165 D3 Westerlo Belgium
235 G1 Westerly RI U.S.A.
206 E5 Western admin. reg. Ghana
209 D8 Western prov. Zambia
206 B4 Western Area admin. div. Sierra Leone
87 D5 Western Australia state Austr.
208 E3 Western Bahr el Ghazal state Sudan
214 C5 Western Cape prov. S. Africa
202 D6 Western Darfur state Sudan
Western Dvina r. Europe see Zapadnaya Dvina
208 F3 Western Equatoria state Sudan
114 B3 Western Ghats mts India
146 B3 Western Isles admin. div. Scotland U.K.
208 F2 Western Kordofan state Sudan
Western Lesser Sunda Islands prov. Indon. see Nusa Tenggara Barat
83 F4 Western Port b. Vic. Austr.
Western Province prov. Zambia see Copperbelt
204 D3 Western Sahara terr. Africa
Western Samoa country S. Pacific Ocean see Samoa
Western Sayan Mountains reg. Rus. Fed. see Zapadnyy Sayan
168 E1 Wester-Ohrstedt Ger.
146 E6 Wester Parkgate Dumfries and Galloway, Scotland U.K.
146 C4 Wester Ross reg. Scotland U.K.
155 C3 Westerschelde est. Neth.
168 C2 Westerstede Ger.
172 D3 Westerstetten Ger.
232 B4 Westerville OH U.S.A.
164 E3 Westervoort Neth.
169 C5 Westerwald hills Ger.
171 E4 Westewitz Ger.
259 E8 West Falkland i. Falkland Is
236 D2 West Fargo ND U.S.A.
91 K5 West Fayu atoll Micronesia
149 I4 West Fen reg. Lincolnshire, England U.K.
151 H4 Westfield East Sussex, England U.K.
233 G3 Westfield MA U.S.A.
233 □J1 Westfield ME U.S.A.
235 D2 Westfield NJ U.S.A.
232 D3 Westfield NY U.S.A.
232 E4 Westfield PA U.S.A.
226 C4 Westfield WI U.S.A.
West Flanders prov. Belgium see West-Vlaanderen
233 □I2 West Forks ME U.S.A.
235 D2 West Freehold NJ U.S.A.
West Frisian Islands Neth. see Waddeneilanden
164 F1 Westgat sea chan. Neth.
85 F5 Westgate Qld Austr.
149 G3 Westgate Durham, England U.K.
238 D1 West Glacier MT U.S.A.
151 G4 West Grinstead West Sussex, England U.K.
234 C3 West Grove PA U.S.A.
151 F2 West Haddon Northamptonshire, England U.K.
232 B5 West Hamlin WV U.S.A.
235 F2 Westhampton NY U.S.A.
150 E3 West Harptree Bath and North East Somerset, England U.K.
235 F1 West Hartford CT U.S.A.
173 E3 Westhausen Ger.
235 F1 West Haven CT U.S.A.
235 E1 West Haverstraw NY U.S.A.
234 C2 West Hazleton PA U.S.A.
146 F4 Westhill Aberdeenshire, Scotland U.K.
172 C2 Westhofen Ger.
157 H4 Westhoffen France
236 C1 Westhope ND U.S.A.
263 F2 West Ice Shelf Antarctica
247 F2 West Indies N. America
146 □H1 Westing Shetland, Scotland U.K.
West Irian prov. Indon. see Irian Jaya
84 D2 West Island N.T. Austr.
86 □2 West Island Cocos Is
235 E2 West Islip NY U.S.A.
232 B5 West Jefferson OH U.S.A.
164 C3 Westkapelle Neth.
West Kazakhstan Oblast admin. div. Kazakh. see Zapadnyy Kazakhstan
146 D6 West Kilbride North Ayrshire, Scotland U.K.
233 H4 West Kingston RI U.S.A.
149 F4 West Kirby Merseyside, England U.K.
149 I3 West Knapton North Yorkshire, England U.K.
230 C3 West Lafayette IN U.S.A.
85 E4 Westland Qld Austr.
232 B3 Westland MI U.S.A.
78 □3b West Landing i. Majuro Marshall Is
151 F3 West Lavington Wiltshire, England U.K.
234 C2 West Lawn PA U.S.A.
215 F2 Westleigh S. Africa
151 I2 Westleton Suffolk, England U.K.
232 B6 West Liberty KY U.S.A.
232 B4 West Liberty OH U.S.A.
146 E6 West Linton Scottish Borders, Scotland U.K.
146 C6 West Loch Tarbert inlet Scotland U.K.
222 H4 Westlock Alta Can.
150 C4 West Looe Cornwall, England U.K.
224 D5 West Lorne Ont. Can.
146 E6 West Lothian admin. div. Scotland U.K.
150 E4 West Lulworth Dorset, England U.K.
209 E8 West Lunga r. Zambia
West Malaysia pen. Malaysia see Malaysia, Semenanjung
165 D3 Westmalle Belgium
151 H3 West Malling Kent, England U.K.
Westman Islands Iceland see Vestmannaeyjar
85 G5 Westmar Qld Austr.
266 E4 West Mariana Basin sea feature Pacific Ocean
147 D3 Westmeath county Rep. of Ireland
237 F5 West Memphis AR U.S.A.
151 F3 West Meon Hampshire, England U.K.
80 E3 Westmere North I. N.Z.
151 H3 West Mersea Essex, England U.K.
151 F2 West Midlands admin. div. England U.K.
235 D1 West Milford NJ U.S.A.
227 F5 West Millgrove OH U.S.A.
232 A5 West Milton OH U.S.A.
234 B1 West Milton PA U.S.A.
234 B3 Westminster MD U.S.A.
150 D3 West Monkton Somerset, England U.K.
237 E5 West Monroe LA U.S.A.
151 F4 West Moors Dorset, England U.K.
84 D3 Westmoreland Qld Austr.
236 D4 Westmoreland KS U.S.A.
246 □ Westmoreland Jamaica
241 J5 Westmorland CA U.S.A.
234 B1 West Nanticoke PA U.S.A.
146 E2 Westness Orkney, Scotland U.K.
149 F3 Westnewton Cumbria, England U.K.
213 F4 West Nicholson Zimbabwe
237 D6 West Nueces r. TX U.S.A.
235 E1 West Nyack NY U.S.A.
81 C6 Weston South I. N.Z.
150 E4 Weston Dorset, England U.K.
150 E2 Weston Staffordshire, England U.K.
235 E1 Weston CT U.S.A.
232 B4 Weston OH U.S.A.
232 C5 Weston WV U.S.A.
215 F2 Westonaria S. Africa
150 E3 Weston-super-Mare North Somerset, England U.K.
150 E3 Westonzoyland Somerset, England U.K.
233 F5 Westover MD U.S.A.
231 D7 West Palm Beach FL U.S.A.
West Papua prov. Indon. see Irian Jaya
237 F4 West Plains MO U.S.A.
83 F5 West Point pt. Tas. Austr.
240 G2 West Point CA U.S.A.
226 D5 Westpoint IN U.S.A.
237 F5 West Point MS U.S.A.
236 D3 West Point NE U.S.A.
233 G4 West Point NY U.S.A.
232 C4 West Point OH U.S.A.
232 E6 West Point VA U.S.A.
231 C5 West Point Lake resr Alabama/Georgia U.S.A.
227 I3 Westport Ont. Can.
81 C4 Westport South I. N.Z.
147 B3 Westport Rep. of Ireland
240 F2 Westport CA U.S.A.
235 E1 Westport CT U.S.A.
233 G2 Westport NY U.S.A.
147 B3 Westport Quay Rep. of Ireland
149 H3 West Rainton Durham, England U.K.
223 K4 Westray Man. Can.
146 E2 Westray i. Scotland U.K.
146 E2 Westray Firth sea chan. Scotland U.K.
235 E1 West Redding CT U.S.A.
224 D4 Westree Ont. Can.
222 F4 West Road r. B.C. Can.
146 F6 Westruther Scottish Borders, Scotland U.K.
233 G3 West Rutland VT U.S.A.
240 C2 West Sacramento CA U.S.A.
232 B4 West Salem OH U.S.A.
227 H4 West Seneca NY U.S.A.
West Siberian Plain Rus. Fed. see Zapadno-Sibirskaya Ravnina
83 F4 West Sister Island Tas. Austr.
151 I2 West Somerton Norfolk, England U.K.
233 H2 West Stewartstown NH U.S.A.
151 G4 West Sussex admin. div. England U.K.
164 E1 West-Terschelling Neth.
233 G2 West Topsham VT U.S.A.
151 G4 West Town Hampshire, England U.K.
234 D1 Westtown NY U.S.A.
226 B4 West Union IA U.S.A.
232 B5 West Union OH U.S.A.
232 C5 West Union WV U.S.A.
238 E3 West Valley City UT U.S.A.
226 D5 Westville IN U.S.A.
237 E5 Westville OK U.S.A.
232 C5 West Virginia state U.S.A.
165 B4 West-Vlaanderen prov. Belgium
240 H2 West Walker r. NV U.S.A.
150 C3 Westward Ho! Devon, England U.K.
151 E5 West Wellow Hampshire, England U.K.
146 E5 West Wemyss Fife, Scotland U.K.
149 J5 West Winch Norfolk, England U.K.
85 G4 Westwood Qld Austr.
240 C1 Westwood CA U.S.A.
235 D2 Westwood NJ U.S.A.
83 F3 West Wyalong N.S.W. Austr.
151 G3 West Wycombe Buckinghamshire, England U.K.
146 □G1 West Yell Shetland, Scotland U.K.
238 E2 West Yellowstone MT U.S.A.
234 E3 West York PA U.S.A.
149 G4 West Yorkshire admin. div. England U.K.
164 D2 Westzaan Neth.
93 G4 Wetar i. Maluku Indon.
93 G5 Wetar, Selat sea chan. Indon.
222 H4 Wetaskiwin Alta Can.
211 C3 Wete Tanz.
171 C4 Wethau Ger.
149 G3 Wetheral Cumbria, England U.K.
149 H4 Wetherby West Yorkshire, England U.K.
235 F1 Wethersfield CT U.S.A.
175 K6 Wetlina Pol.
226 D2 Wetmore MI U.S.A.
168 D3 Wetschen Ger.
169 D5 Wetter r. Ger.
169 D5 Wetter (Hessen) Ger.
169 C4 Wetter (Ruhr) Ger.
165 C3 Wetteren Belgium
171 C4 Wetterzeube Ger.
171 C4 Wettin Ger.
190 D1 Wettingen Switz.
169 C3 Wettringen Ger.
169 C3 Wettrup Ger.
173 F3 Wettstetten Ger.
231 C5 Wetumpka AL U.S.A.
190 D1 Wetzikon Switz.
169 D5 Wetzlar Ger.
165 C4 Wevelgem Belgium
231 C6 Wewahitchka FL U.S.A.
91 J7 Wewak P.N.G.
168 E2 Wewelsfleth Ger.
237 D5 Wewoka OK U.S.A.
147 E4 Wexford Rep. of Ireland
147 E4 Wexford county Rep. of Ireland
147 E4 Wexford Bay Rep. of Ireland
223 J4 Weyakwin Sask. Can.
173 F4 Weyarn Ger.
226 C3 Weyauwega WI U.S.A.
151 G3 Weybridge Surrey, England U.K.
223 K5 Weyburn Sask. Can.
169 C5 Weyerbusch Ger.
179 F3 Weyer Markt Austria
157 H4 Weyersheim France
169 F3 Weyhausen Ger.
168 D3 Weyhe Ger.
225 H4 Weymouth N.S. Can.
150 E4 Weymouth Dorset, England U.K.
233 H3 Weymouth MA U.S.A.
234 D3 Weymouth NJ U.S.A.
85 E2 Weymouth, Cape Qld Austr.
164 F2 Wezep Neth.
80 F3 Whakaki North I. N.Z.
80 E3 Whakamaru North I. N.Z.
80 F3 Whakapunake hill North I. N.Z.
Whakaraupō inlet South I. N.Z. see Lyttelton Harbour
80 F2 Whakatane North I. N.Z.
Whakatipu Kā Tuka r. South I. N.Z. see Hollyford
83 G2 Whalan Creek r. N.S.W. Austr.
Whale r. Que. Can. see La Baleine, Rivière à
222 C3 Whale Bay AK U.S.A.
246 C1 Whale Cay i. Bahamas
223 M2 Whale Cove Nunavut Can.
222 C3 Whale Pass AK U.S.A.
149 H4 Whaley Bridge Derbyshire, England U.K.
232 E6 Whaleyville VA U.S.A.
146 □H1 Whalsay i. Scotland U.K.
149 H2 Whalton Northumberland, England U.K.
80 E4 Whangaehu r. North I. N.Z.
80 E2 Whangamata North I. N.Z.
81 D4 Whangamoa South I. N.Z.
80 E3 Whangamomona North I. N.Z.
80 E2 Whangaparaoa North I. N.Z.
80 G3 Whangara North I. N.Z.
80 E1 Whangarei North I. N.Z.
151 G2 Whaplode Lincolnshire, England U.K.
224 E2 Whapmagoostui Que. Can.
81 E4 Wharanui South I. N.Z.
81 F4 Whareama North I. N.Z.
149 H4 Wharfe r. England U.K.
227 F2 Wharncliffe Ont. Can.
232 C6 Wharncliffe WV U.S.A.
234 D2 Wharton NJ U.S.A.
237 D6 Wharton TX U.S.A.
81 C5 Whataroa South I. N.Z.
222 G2 Wha Ti N.W.T. Can.
146 D7 Whauphill Dumfries and Galloway, Scotland U.K.
240 G2 Wheatland CA U.S.A.
238 F3 Wheatland WY U.S.A.
227 F4 Wheatley Ont. Can.
226 C5 Wheaton IL U.S.A.
236 D2 Wheaton MN U.S.A.
150 E2 Wheaton Aston Staffordshire, England U.K.
234 A3 Wheaton-Glenmont MD U.S.A.
150 D3 Wheddon Cross Somerset, England U.K.
237 C5 Wheeler TX U.S.A.
226 B3 Wheeler WI U.S.A.
231 C5 Wheeler Lake resr AL U.S.A.
239 F4 Wheeler Peak NM U.S.A.
241 J2 Wheeler Peak NV U.S.A.
232 B5 Wheelersburg OH U.S.A.
240 H4 Wheeler Springs CA U.S.A.
232 C4 Wheeling WV U.S.A.
261 G3 Wheelwright Arg.
149 G3 Whernside hill England U.K.
151 F3 Wherwell Hampshire, England U.K.
149 H3 Whickham Tyne and Wear, England U.K.
150 D4 Whiddon Down Devon, England U.K.
147 B5 Whiddy Island Rep. of Ireland
86 C4 Whim Creek W.A. Austr.
150 D4 Whimple Devon, England U.K.
82 B1 Whinham, Mount S.A. Austr.
235 D2 Whippany NJ U.S.A.
240 F2 Whispering Pines CA U.S.A.
222 F5 Whistler B.C. Can.
225 K4 Whitbourne Nfld. Can.
146 E6 Whitburn West Lothian, Scotland U.K.
227 H4 Whitby Ont. Can.
149 I3 Whitby North Yorkshire, England U.K.
151 G3 Whitchurch Buckinghamshire, England U.K.
150 D3 Whitchurch Cardiff, Wales U.K.
151 F3 Whitchurch Hampshire, England U.K.
150 E2 Whitchurch Shropshire, England U.K.
227 H4 Whitchurch-Stouffville Ont. Can.
81 C5 Whitcombe, Mount South I. N.Z.
224 C3 White r. Ont. Can.
222 B2 White r. Can./U.S.A.
229 H4 White r. AR U.S.A.
237 E5 White r. AR U.S.A.
241 M1 White r. CO U.S.A.
230 C4 White r. IN U.S.A.
226 D4 White r. MI U.S.A.
241 J3 White r. NV U.S.A.
236 D3 White r. SD U.S.A.
233 G3 White r. VT U.S.A.
226 B2 White r. WI U.S.A.
230 C4 White, East Fork r. IN U.S.A.
84 B4 White, Lake salt flat N.T. Austr.
237 E4 White, North Fork r. MO U.S.A.
149 G2 Whiteadder Water r. Scotland U.K.
225 J3 White Bay Nfld. Can.
236 C2 White Butte mt. ND U.S.A.
241 L3 White Canyon UT U.S.A.
147 C5 Whitechurch Cork Rep. of Ireland
147 D4 Whitechurch Waterford Rep. of Ireland
83 E2 White Cliffs N.S.W. Austr.
226 E4 White Cloud MI U.S.A.
81 B6 Whitecoomb mt. South I. N.Z.
146 E6 White Coomb hill Scotland U.K.
222 H4 Whitecourt Alta Can.
146 E6 Whitecraig East Lothian, Scotland U.K.
147 E2 Whitecross Northern Ireland U.K.
234 B1 White Deer PA U.S.A.
233 G2 Whiteface Mountain NY U.S.A.
233 H2 Whitefield NH U.S.A.
227 G2 Whitefish Ont. Can.
222 E1 Whitefish r. N.W.T. Can.
238 D1 Whitefish MT U.S.A.
226 D3 Whitefish r. MI U.S.A.
226 D3 Whitefish Bay WI U.S.A.
223 J2 Whitefish Lake N.W.T. Can.
234 B3 Whiteford MD U.S.A.
147 C4 Whitegate Clare Rep. of Ireland
147 C5 Whitegate Cork Rep. of Ireland
147 B5 White Hall Rep. of Ireland
147 D4 Whitehall Rep. of Ireland
146 F2 Whitehall Orkney, Scotland U.K.
236 F4 White Hall IL U.S.A.
234 B3 White Hall MD U.S.A.
226 D4 Whitehall MI U.S.A.
238 D2 Whitehall MT U.S.A.
233 G3 Whitehall NY U.S.A.
232 B5 Whitehall OH U.S.A.
234 B1 White Hall PA U.S.A.
234 C2 Whitehall PA U.S.A.
226 B3 Whitehall WI U.S.A.
149 F3 Whitehaven Cumbria, England U.K.
234 C1 White Haven PA U.S.A.
147 F2 Whitehead Northern Ireland U.K.
225 I4 White Hill hill N.S. Can.
151 G3 Whitehill Hampshire, England U.K.
146 F4 Whitehills Aberdeenshire, Scotland U.K.
222 C2 Whitehorse Y.T. Can.
234 D2 White Horse NJ U.S.A.
151 F3 White Horse, Vale of val. England U.K.
234 D2 Whitehouse NJ U.S.A.
234 D2 Whitehouse Station NJ U.S.A.
263 D2 White Island Antarctica
215 F5 White Kei r. S. Africa
87 D5 White Lake salt flat W.A. Austr.
234 D1 White Lake NY U.S.A.
83 F5 Whitemark Tas. Austr.
234 C1 White Mills PA U.S.A.
240 H3 White Mountain Peak CA U.S.A.
233 H2 White Mountains NH U.S.A.
228 G1 Whitemouth r. Man. Can.
203 G6 White Nile state Sudan
203 G6 White Nile r. Sudan/Uganda alt. Abiad, Bahr el, alt. Jebel, Bahr el
203 G6 White Nile Dam Sudan
212 C4 White Nossob watercourse Namibia
232 B6 White Oak KY U.S.A.
226 E5 White Pigeon MI U.S.A.
226 C2 White Pine MI U.S.A.
241 J2 White Pine Range mts NV U.S.A.
235 E1 White Plains NY U.S.A.
146 F4 Whiterashes Aberdeenshire, Scotland U.K.
224 C3 White River Ont. Can.
241 M5 Whiteriver AZ U.S.A.
236 C3 White River SD U.S.A.
233 G3 White River Junction VT U.S.A.
241 J2 White River Valley NV U.S.A.
241 J2 White Rock Peak NV U.S.A.
White Russia country Europe see Belarus
238 B2 White Salmon WA U.S.A.
222 H2 Whitesand r. Alta/N.W.T. Can.
223 K5 Whitesand r. Sask. Can.
235 D3 Whitesboro NJ U.S.A.
233 F3 Whitesboro NY U.S.A.
232 B6 Whitesburg KY U.S.A.
White Sea Rus. Fed. see Beloye More
233 E6 White Stone VA U.S.A.
238 E2 White Sulphur Springs MT U.S.A.
232 C6 White Sulphur Springs WV U.S.A.
234 C1 Whites Valley PA U.S.A.
232 C6 Whitesville WV U.S.A.
215 H3 White Umfolozi r. S. Africa
231 E5 Whiteville NC U.S.A.
206 E4 White Volta watercourse Burkina/Ghana alt. Nakambé, alt. Nakanbe, alt. Volta Blanche
206 E4 White Volta r. Ghana
240 I5 White Water CA U.S.A.
241 M2 Whitewater CO U.S.A.
226 C4 Whitewater WI U.S.A.
239 E5 Whitewater Baldy mt. NM U.S.A.
82 B2 White Well S.A. Austr.
236 C4 White Woman Creek r. KS U.S.A.
85 E4 Whitewood Qld Austr.
223 K5 Whitewood Sask. Can.
83 F4 Whitfield Vic. Austr.
151 I3 Whitfield Kent, England U.K.
150 D1 Whitford Flintshire, Wales U.K.
146 D7 Whithorn Dumfries and Galloway, Scotland U.K.
80 E2 Whitianga North I. N.Z.
233 □J2 Whiting ME U.S.A.
235 D3 Whiting NJ U.S.A.
226 C3 Whiting WI U.S.A.
146 C6 Whiting Bay North Ayrshire, Scotland U.K.
150 C3 Whitland Carmarthenshire, Wales U.K.
149 H2 Whitley Bay Tyne and Wear, England U.K.
231 C4 Whitley City KY U.S.A.
234 C3 Whitman Square NJ U.S.A.
231 D5 Whitmire SC U.S.A.
215 G4 Whitmore S. Africa
262 Q1 Whitmore Mountains Antarctica
151 F2 Whitnash Warwickshire, England U.K.
227 H3 Whitney Ont. Can.
240 H3 Whitney, Mount CA U.S.A.
233 F3 Whitney Point NY U.S.A.
150 C4 Whitsand Bay England U.K.
151 I3 Whitstable Kent, England U.K.
85 G4 Whitsunday Group is Qld Austr.
85 G4 Whitsunday Island Qld Austr.
85 G4 Whitsunday Passage Qld Austr.
Whitsun Island Vanuatu see Pentecost Island
227 F3 Whittemore MI U.S.A.
240 H5 Whittier CA U.S.A.
149 H2 Whittingham Northumberland, England U.K.
150 D2 Whittington Shropshire, England U.K.
83 F4 Whittlesea Vic. Austr.
215 F5 Whittlesea S. Africa
151 G2 Whittlesey Cambridgeshire, England U.K.
226 B3 Whittlesey WI U.S.A.
226 B3 Whittlesey, Mount hill WI U.S.A.
83 F3 Whitton N.S.W. Austr.
149 G4 Whitworth Lancashire, England U.K.
223 J2 Wholdaia Lake N.W.T. Can.
241 K5 Why AZ U.S.A.
82 D3 Whyalla S.A. Austr.
Whydah Benin see Ouidah
96 B3 Wiang Pa Pao Thai.
96 C3 Wiang Sa Thai.
175 K6 Wiar r. Pol.
175 J2 Wiartel Pol.
224 D4 Wiarton Ont. Can.
206 E4 Wiasi Ghana
174 F3 Wiatrowo Pol.
206 E5 Wiawso Ghana
146 A4 Wiay i. Scotland U.K.
174 F5 Wiązów Pol.
238 F2 Wibaux MT U.S.A.
165 C3 Wichelen Belgium
237 D4 Wichita KS U.S.A.
237 D5 Wichita r. TX U.S.A.
237 D5 Wichita Falls TX U.S.A.
237 D5 Wichita Mountains OK U.S.A.
146 E3 Wick Highland, Scotland U.K.
150 E3 Wick South Gloucestershire, England U.K.
150 D3 Wick Vale of Glamorgan, Wales U.K.
151 G4 Wick West Sussex, England U.K.
146 E3 Wick r. Scotland U.K.
169 C4 Wickede airport Ger.
169 C4 Wickede (Ruhr) Ger.
241 K5 Wickenburg AZ U.S.A.
87 C7 Wickepin W.A. Austr.
237 E5 Wickes AR U.S.A.
151 H3 Wickford Essex, England U.K.
86 C4 Wickham W.A. Austr.
84 B3 Wickham r. N.T. Austr.
151 F4 Wickham Hampshire, England U.K.
83 E4 Wickham, Cape Tas. Austr.
84 B3 Wickham, Mount hill N.T. Austr.
151 I2 Wickham Market Suffolk, England U.K.
237 F4 Wickliffe KY U.S.A.
147 E4 Wicklow Rep. of Ireland
147 E3 Wicklow county Rep. of Ireland
147 F3 Wicklow Head hd Rep. of Ireland
147 E4 Wicklow Mountains Rep. of Ireland
174 F1 Wicko Pol.
150 E3 Wickwar South Gloucestershire, England U.K.
234 B2 Wiconisco PA U.S.A.
234 B2 Wiconisco Creek r. PA U.S.A.
174 F4 Widawa r. Pol.
175 G4 Widawka r. Pol.
85 H5 Wide Bay Qld Austr.
150 D4 Widecombe in the Moor Devon, England U.K.
146 E2 Wide Firth sea chan. Scotland U.K.
263 B2 Widerøe, Mount Antarctica
151 H3 Widford Hertfordshire, England U.K.
87 D6 Widgiemooltha W.A. Austr.
93 D3 Widi, Kepulauan is Maluku Indon.
190 E1 Widnau Switz.
149 G4 Widnes Halton, England U.K.
174 C2 Widuchowa Pol.
174 F2 Więcbork Pol.
170 D1 Wieck am Darß Ger.
175 I2 Wieczfnia Kościelna Pol.
169 C5 Wied r. Ger.
169 F4 Wieda Ger.
171 D5 Wiederau Ger.
171 D4 Wiederitzsch Ger.
171 F4 Wiednitz Ger.
168 D2 Wiefelstede Ger.
171 C4 Wiehe Ger.
169 D3 Wiehengebirge hills Ger.
169 C5 Wiehl Ger.
170 E1 Wiek Ger.
174 G5 Większyce Pol.
175 I2 Wielbark Pol.
174 E3 Wieleń Pol.
173 F4 Wielenbach Ger.
175 H3 Wielgie Pol.
174 E3 Wielichowo Pol.
175 I6 Wieliczka Pol.
175 K2 Wieliczki Pol.
174 G2 Wielka Nieszawka Pol.
177 H2 Wielka Racza mt. Pol./Slovakia
175 K6 Wielka Rawka mt. Pol.
174 E5 Wielka Sowa mt. Pol.
175 L5 Wielkie Oczy Pol.
174 G1 Wielki Klincz Pol.
174 F3 Wielkopolskie prov. Pol.
175 J6 Wielopole Skrzyńskie Pol.
174 G5 Wielowieś Pol.
165 C4 Wielsbeke Belgium
174 G4 Wieluń Pol.
168 E2 Wiemersdorf Ger.
179 H2 Wien Austria
179 H2 Wien land Austria
179 H2 Wiener Neudorf Austria
179 H3 Wiener Neustadt Austria
168 F3 Wienhausen Ger.
175 I4 Wieniawa Pol.
174 G3 Wieniec Pol.
179 G2 Wiensberg mt. Austria
170 C3 Wiepke Ger.
175 H6 Wieprz Pol.
175 J4 Wieprz r. Pol.
143 G4 Wieprza r. Pol.
175 K3 Wiercień Duży Pol.
164 F2 Wierden Neth.
168 F3 Wieren Ger.
164 D2 Wieringermeer Polder Neth.
164 E2 Wieringerwerf Neth.
172 C3 Wiernsheim Ger.
174 G4 Wieruszów Pol.
175 L4 Wierzbica Lubelskie Pol.
175 J4 Wierzbica Mazowieckie Pol.
174 F4 Wierzbica Górna Pol.
174 G3 Wierzbinek Pol.
174 F5 Wierzbnik Pol.
175 L2 Wierzchlesie Pol.
174 G4 Wierzchosławice Pol.
175 I5 Wierzchosławice Pol.
174 F2 Wierzchowo Pol.
174 G1 Wierzchucino Pol.
174 G2 Wierzyca r. Pol.
179 G4 Wies Austria
173 E4 Wies Ger.
171 D5 Wiesa Ger.
173 G2 Wiesau Ger.
169 D5 Wiesbaden Ger.
172 B4 Wiese r. Ger.
179 G2 Wieselburg Austria
179 H3 Wiesen Austria
169 E5 Wiesen Ger.
190 E2 Wiesen Switz.
171 F3 Wiesenau Ger.
171 D3 Wiesenburg Ger.
173 G2 Wiesenfelden Ger.
172 D3 Wiesensteig Ger.
173 G2 Wiesent Ger.
173 F2 Wiesent r. Ger.
173 F2 Wiesenthau Ger.
173 E2 Wiesentheid Ger.
173 F2 Wiesenttal Ger.
178 C3 Wiesing Austria
168 E2 Wiesle r. Ger.
172 C2 Wiesloch Ger.
179 H3 Wiesmath Austria
168 C2 Wiesmoor Ger.
234 C2 Wiessport PA U.S.A.
168 C3 Wietmarschen Ger.
175 I5 Wietrzychowice Pol.
168 E3 Wietze Ger.
169 E3 Wietze r. Ger.
168 E3 Wietzen Ger.
168 E3 Wietzendorf Ger.
143 H4 Wieżyca hill Pol.
149 G4 Wigan Greater Manchester, England U.K.
173 E4 Wiggensbach Ger.
237 F6 Wiggins MS U.S.A.
145 G6 Wight, Isle of i. England U.K.
150 E2 Wigmore Herefordshire, England U.K.
151 F2 Wigston Leicestershire, England U.K.
149 F3 Wigton Cumbria, England U.K.
146 D7 Wigtown Dumfries and Galloway, Scotland U.K.
146 D7 Wigtown Bay Scotland U.K.
164 E3 Wijchen Neth.
140 □ Wijdefjorden inlet Svalbard
174 E4 Wijewo Pol.
164 F2 Wijhe Neth.
164 D2 Wijk aan Zee Neth.
164 E3 Wijk bij Duurstede Neth.
164 E3 Wijk en Aalburg Neth.
165 D3 Wijnegem Belgium
164 F1 Wijnjewoude Neth.
241 K4 Wikieup AZ U.S.A.
210 C1 Wik'ro Eth.
227 G3 Wikwemikong Ont. Can.
190 E1 Wil Switz.
175 H6 Wilamowice Pol.
236 D3 Wilber NE U.S.A.
81 C5 Wilberforce r. South I. N.Z.
84 D1 Wilberforce, Cape N.T. Austr.
238 C2 Wilbur WA U.S.A.
173 E2 Wilburgstetten Ger.
237 E5 Wilburton OK U.S.A.
83 E2 Wilcannia N.S.W. Austr.
232 D4 Wilcox PA U.S.A.
Wilczek Land i. Zemlya Frantsa-Iosifa Rus. Fed. see Zemlya Vil'cheka
175 H1 Wilczęta Pol.
174 G3 Wilczogóra Pol.
174 G3 Wilczyn Pol.
171 E3 Wildau Ger.
172 C3 Wildbad im Schwarzwald Ger.
172 C3 Wildberg Baden-Württemberg Ger.
170 D3 Wildberg Brandenburg Ger.
170 E2 Wildberg Mecklenburg-Vorpommern Ger.
240 I2 Wildcat Peak NV U.S.A.
215 G4 Wild Coast S. Africa
169 F5 Wildeck-Obersuhl Ger.
169 F5 Wildeck-Richelsdorf Ger.
169 F4 Wildemann Ger.
179 H2 Wildendürnbach Austria
171 D5 Wildenfels Ger.
214 D5 Wilderness S. Africa
232 E5 Wilderness VA U.S.A.
168 D3 Wildeshausen Ger.
169 E5 Wildflecken Ger.
226 C1 Wild Goose Ont. Can.
222 G4 Wildhay r. Alta Can.
190 C2 Wildhorn mt. Switz.
239 F6 Wild Horse Draw r. TX U.S.A.
236 C3 Wild Horse Hill mt. NE U.S.A.
179 G4 Wildon Austria
173 E4 Wildpoldsried Ger.
236 D2 Wild Rice r. MN U.S.A.
236 D2 Wild Rice r. ND U.S.A.
178 D3 Wildseeloder mt. Austria
178 D2 Wildshut Austria
178 B4 Wildspitze mt. Austria
222 H4 Wildwood Alta Can.
231 D6 Wildwood FL U.S.A.
234 D4 Wildwood NJ U.S.A.
234 D4 Wildwood Crest NJ U.S.A.
236 C4 Wiley CO U.S.A.
232 D5 Wiley Ford WV U.S.A.
175 J4 Wilga Pol.
175 J4 Wilga r. Pol.
215 G2 Wilge r. Free State S. Africa
215 G1 Wilge r. Gauteng/Mpumalanga S. Africa
82 C2 Wilgena S.A. Austr.
91 J8 Wilhelm, Mount P.N.G.
251 G4 Wilhelmina Gebergte mts Suriname
140 □ Wilhelmøya i. Svalbard
Wilhelm-Pieck-Stadt Ger. see Guben
179 G2 Wilhelmsburg Austria
170 E2 Wilhelmsburg Ger.
172 D4 Wilhelmsdorf Ger.
168 D2 Wilhelmshaven Ger.
171 C5 Wilhelmsthal Ger.
179 F2 Wilhering Austria
173 E2 Wilhermsdorf Ger.
113 □2 Wilingili i. Addu Atoll Maldives
171 D5 Wilkau-Haßlau Ger.
234 C1 Wilkes-Barre PA U.S.A.
231 D4 Wilkesboro NC U.S.A.
263 I2 Wilkes Coast Antarctica
263 I2 Wilkes Land reg. Antarctica
223 I4 Wilkie Sask. Can.
232 D4 Wilkinsburg PA U.S.A.
262 T2 Wilkins Coast Antarctica
82 C2 Wilkinson Lakes salt flat S.A. Austr.
147 E3 Wilkinstown Rep. of Ireland
175 K4 Wilkołaz Pierwszy Pol.
175 J4 Wilków Pol.
174 F4 Wilków Pol.
222 D3 Will, Mount B.C. Can.
238 B2 Willamette r. OR U.S.A.
150 D4 Willand Devon, England U.K.
239 F5 Willard NM U.S.A.
232 B4 Willard OH U.S.A.
233 F5 Willards MD U.S.A.
149 F4 Willaston Cheshire, England U.K.
241 M5 Willcox AZ U.S.A.
169 E4 Willebadessen Ger.
165 D3 Willebroek Belgium
164 D3 Willemstad Neth.
247 □10 Willemstad Curaçao Neth. Antilles
84 B2 Willeroo N.T. Austr.
223 I3 William r. Sask. Can.
83 E4 William, Mount Vic. Austr.
87 B4 Williambury W.A. Austr.
82 D2 William Creek S.A. Austr.
87 C7 Williams W.A. Austr.
85 E4 Williams r. Qld Austr.
87 C7 Williams r. W.A. Austr.
241 K4 Williams AZ U.S.A.
240 F2 Williams CA U.S.A.
236 E3 Williamsburg IA U.S.A.
232 A6 Williamsburg KY U.S.A.
226 E3 Williamsburg MI U.S.A.
232 A5 Williamsburg OH U.S.A.
232 D4 Williamsburg PA U.S.A.
232 E6 Williamsburg VA U.S.A.
246 C1 Williams Island Bahamas
222 F4 Williams Lake B.C. Can.
232 E3 Williamson NY U.S.A.
232 B6 Williamson WV U.S.A.
230 C3 Williamsport IN U.S.A.
232 B5 Williamsport OH U.S.A.
227 I5 Williamsport PA U.S.A.
227 E4 Williamston MI U.S.A.
231 E5 Williamston NC U.S.A.
233 G3 Williamstown MA U.S.A.
234 D3 Williamstown NJ U.S.A.
233 F3 Williamstown NY U.S.A.
234 B2 Williamstown PA U.S.A.
232 C5 Williamstown WV U.S.A.
169 B4 Willich Ger.
233 G4 Willimantic CT U.S.A.
235 F1 Willimantic r. CT U.S.A.
234 D2 Willingboro NJ U.S.A.
151 H4 Willingdon East Sussex, England U.K.
169 D4 Willingen (Upland) Ger.
151 H2 Willingham Cambridgeshire, England U.K.
Willingili i. N. Male Maldives see Villingli
Willingili i. N. Male Maldives see Vilingli
169 E5 Willingshausen Ger.
151 F2 Willington Derbyshire, England U.K.
190 D1 Willisau Switz.
85 G3 Willis Group atolls Coral Sea Is Terr. Austr.
259 □ Willis Islands S. Georgia
214 C4 Williston S. Africa
231 D6 Williston FL U.S.A.
236 C1 Williston ND U.S.A.
231 D5 Williston SC U.S.A.
222 F4 Williston Lake B.C. Can.
150 D3 Williton Somerset, England U.K.
240 F2 Willits CA U.S.A.
236 E2 Willmar MN U.S.A.
149 J4 Willoughby Lincolnshire, England U.K.
232 C4 Willoughby OH U.S.A.
233 G2 Willoughby, Lake VT U.S.A.
222 F4 Willow r. B.C. Can.
241 J4 Willow Beach AZ U.S.A.
223 J5 Willow Bunch Sask. Can.
222 H5 Willow Creek r. Alta Can.
238 B3 Willow Creek CA U.S.A.
238 B2 Willow Creek r. OR U.S.A.
241 M1 Willow Creek r. UT U.S.A.
234 C3 Willow Grove DE U.S.A.
234 C2 Willow Grove PA U.S.A.
232 E4 Willow Hill PA U.S.A.
222 F2 Willowlake r. N.W.T. Can.
214 D5 Willowmore S. Africa
84 C4 Willowra N.T. Austr.
240 F2 Willows CA U.S.A.
237 F4 Willow Springs MO U.S.A.
234 B3 Willow Street PA U.S.A.
215 G5 Willowvale S. Africa
86 F4 Wills, Lake salt flat W.A. Austr.
172 B3 Willstätt Ger.
82 D3 Willunga S.A. Austr.
231 C6 Wilma FL U.S.A.
170 E2 Wilmersdorf Brandenburg Ger.
171 F4 Wilmersdorf Brandenburg Ger.
82 D3 Wilmington S.A. Austr.
234 C3 Wilmington DE U.S.A.
231 E5 Wilmington NC U.S.A.
232 B5 Wilmington OH U.S.A.
233 G3 Wilmington VT U.S.A.
231 D5 Wilmington Island GA U.S.A.
149 G4 Wilmslow Cheshire, England U.K.
164 D2 Wilnis Neth.
Wilno Lith. see Vilnius
169 D5 Wilnsdorf Ger.
164 F2 Wilp Neth.
171 E4 Wilsdruff Ger.
168 E2 Wilseder Berg hill Ger.
170 E2 Wilsickow Ger.
86 F3 Wilson r. W.A. Austr.
Wilson atoll Micronesia see Ifalik
236 D4 Wilson KS U.S.A.
226 B4 Wilson MN U.S.A.
231 E5 Wilson NC U.S.A.
232 D3 Wilson NY U.S.A.
234 C2 Wilson PA U.S.A.
239 F4 Wilson, Mount CO U.S.A.
241 J2 Wilson, Mount NV U.S.A.
238 B2 Wilson, Mount OR U.S.A.
263 K2 Wilson Hills Antarctica
240 H3 Wilsonia CA U.S.A.
232 E6 Wilsons VA U.S.A.
83 F4 Wilson's Promontory pen. Vic. Austr.
168 E2 Wilstedt Ger.
168 E2 Wilster Ger.
168 B3 Wilsum Ger.
179 H2 Wiltersdorf Austria
171 F4 Wilthen Ger.
172 A2 Wiltingen Ger.
84 C2 Wilton r. N.T. Austr.
151 F3 Wilton Wiltshire, England U.K.
235 E1 Wilton CT U.S.A.
233 □H2 Wilton ME U.S.A.
236 C2 Wilton ND U.S.A.
233 H3 Wilton NH U.S.A.
150 F3 Wiltshire admin. div. England U.K.
165 E5 Wiltz Lux.
87 D5 Wiluna W.A. Austr.
80 F4 Wimbledon North I. N.Z.
151 H2 Wimblington Cambridgeshire, England U.K.
151 F4 Wimborne Minster Dorset, England U.K.
156 B2 Wimereux France
171 C4 Wimmelburg Ger.
83 E4 Wimmera r. Vic. Austr.
190 C2 Wimmis Switz.
179 H3 Wimpassing Austria
Wina r. Cameroon see Vina
230 C3 Winamac IN U.S.A.
215 F3 Winburg S. Africa
214 D2 Wincanton S. Africa
150 E3 Wincanton Somerset, England U.K.
151 F3 Winchcombe Gloucestershire, England U.K.
151 H4 Winchelsea East Sussex, England U.K.
233 G3 Winchendon MA U.S.A.
172 A2 Wincheringen Ger.
233 F2 Winchester Ont. Can.
81 C6 Winchester South I. N.Z.
151 F3 Winchester Hampshire, England U.K.
236 F4 Winchester IL U.S.A.
230 C3 Winchester IN U.S.A.
232 A6 Winchester KY U.S.A.
233 G3 Winchester NH U.S.A.
231 C5 Winchester TN U.S.A.
232 D5 Winchester VA U.S.A.
165 E4 Wincrange Lux.
220 E3 Wind r. Y.T. Can.
238 E3 Wind r. WY U.S.A.
175 J1 Winda Pol.
82 D2 Windabout, Lake salt flat S.A. Austr.
173 F3 Windach Ger.
Windau Latvia see Ventspils
232 D4 Windber PA U.S.A.
168 E1 Windeby Ger.
231 D5 Winder GA U.S.A.
149 G3 Windermere Cumbria, England U.K.
149 G3 Windermere l. England U.K.
172 B2 Windesheim Ger.
234 C2 Windgap PA U.S.A.
169 C5 Windhagen Ger.
222 C3 Windham AK U.S.A.
235 F1 Windham CT U.S.A.
232 C4 Windham OH U.S.A.
169 F4 Windhausen Ger.
212 C4 Windhoek Namibia
221 I4 Windigo r. Ont. Can.
179 G2 Windigsteig Austria
173 G2 Windischeschenbach Ger.
179 F3 Windischgarsten Austria

X

Xinhua Yunnan China see Funing
06 D4 Xinhuacun Gansu China
08 D3 Xinhuang Hunan China
07 H3 Xinhui Nei Mongol China
06 D4 Xining Qinghai China
07 G4 Xinji Hebei China
Xinji Henan China see Xinxian
109 E2 Xinjian Jiangxi China
107 F5 Xinjiang Shanxi China
Xinjiang aut. reg. China see Xinjiang Uygur Zizhiqu
109 F2 Xin Jiang r. China
Xinjiangkou Hubei China see Songzi
106 A3 Xinjiang Uygur Zizhiqu aut. reg. China
Xinjie Yunnan China see Yuanyang
Xinjin Liaoning China see Pulandian
108 B2 Xinjin Sichuan China
Xinjing Guangxi China see Jingxi
107 I3 Xinkai r. China
Xinling Hubei China see Badong
108 B2 Xinlong Sichuan China
107 G5 Xinmi Henan China
Xinmian Sichuan China see Shimian
107 I3 Xinmin Liaoning China
Xinning Gansu China see Ningxian
Xinning Guangxi China see Fusui
108 D3 Xinning Hunan China
Xinning Jiangxi China see Wuning
Xinning Sichuan China see Kaijiang
108 B3 Xinping Yunnan China
100 D2 Xinqing Heilong. China
109 F3 Xinquan Fujian China
Xinshan Jiangxi China see Anyuan
109 D3 Xinshao Hunan China
Xinshi Hubei China see Jingshan
Xinshiba Sichuan China see Ganluo
107 H5 Xintai Shandong China
109 E2 Xintanpu Hubei China
109 E3 Xintian Hunan China
109 E2 Xinxian Henan China
107 G5 Xinxiang Henan China
109 E4 Xinxing Guangdong China
109 E1 Xinyang Henan China
109 G1 Xinyang Gang r. China
109 E1 Xinye Henan China
107 H5 Xinye r. China
109 D4 Xinyi Guangdong China
107 H5 Xinyi Jiangsu China
Xinying Taiwan see Hsinying
109 E3 Xinyu Jiangxi China
Xinyuan Qinghai China see Tianjun
110 C3 Xinyuan Xinjiang China
107 I1 Xinzhangfang Nei Mongol China
107 G5 Xinzheng Henan China
Xinzhou Guangxi China see Longlin
Xinzhou Guizhou China see Huangping
109 E2 Xinzhou Hubei China
107 G4 Xinzhou Shanxi China
Xinzhu Taiwan see Hsinchu
182 C2 Xinzo de Limia Spain
Xiongshan Fujian China see Zhenghe
Xiongzhou Guangdong China see Nanxiong
252 D2 Xipamanu r. Bol./Brazil
109 D1 Xiping Henan China
109 E1 Xiping Henan China
106 D5 Xiqing Shan mts China
254 E4 Xique Xique Brazil
129 F3 Xırdalan Azer.
187 C5 Xirivella Spain
198 C2 Xiro hill Greece
199 E3 Xirokampo Greece
250 E6 Xiruá r. Brazil
Xisa Yunnan China see Xichou
107 F3 Xishanzui Nei Mongol China
Xisha Qundao is S. China Sea see Paracel Islands
108 C2 Xishui Guizhou China
109 E2 Xishui Hubei China
182 C1 Xistral, Serra do mts Spain
206 B4 Xitole Guinea-Bissau
Xiucaiwan Chongqing China see Fengdu
Xiugu Jiangxi China see Jinxi
Xi Ujimqin Qi Nei Mongol China see Bayan Ul Hot
109 F2 Xiuning Anhui China
108 D2 Xiushan Chongqing China
Xiushan Yunnan China see Tonghai
109 E2 Xiushui Jiangxi China
109 E2 Xiu Shui r. China
108 C3 Xiuwen Guizhou China
107 G5 Xiuwu Henan China
107 I3 Xiuyan Liaoning China
Xiuyan Shaanxi China see Qingjian
108 D4 Xiuying Hainan China
Xiwanzi Hebei China see Chongli
108 A1 Xiwu Qinghai China
111 D6 Xixabangma Feng mt. Xizang China
109 D1 Xixia Henan China
109 E1 Xixian Henan China
107 F4 Xixian Shanxi China
108 C1 Xixiang Shaanxi China
Xixón Spain see Gijón
107 G4 Xiyang Shanxi China
108 C3 Xiyang Jiang r. Yunnan China
Xizang aut. reg. China see Xizang Zizhiqu
Xizang Gaoyuan plat. Xizang China see Qing Zang Gaoyuan
108 A2 Xizang Zizhiqu aut. reg. China
129 F3 Xızı Azer.
210 E2 Xjis Somalia
129 E4 Xocalı Azer.
129 E4 Xocavänd Azer.
245 E3 Xochiatipan Mex.
245 E4 Xochicalco tourist site Mex.
245 E4 Xochimilco Mex.
245 E5 Xochistlahuaca Mex.
Xoi Xizang China see Qūxü
215 F5 Xolobe S. Africa
129 F4 Xol Qarabucaq Azer.
97 D5 Xom An Lôc Vietnam
97 D5 Xom Duc Hanh Vietnam
245 E4 Xonacatlán Mex.
Xonrupt France see Xonrupt-Longemer
157 G4 Xonrupt-Longemer France
110 E4 Xorkol Xinjiang China
129 E3 Xosrov Azer.
182 C1 Xove Spain
Xuancheng Anhui China see Xuanzhou
108 D2 Xuan'en Hubei China
108 C2 Xuanhan Sichuan China
107 G3 Xuanhua Hebei China
97 D5 Xuân Lôc Vietnam
108 C3 Xuanwei Yunnan China
109 F2 Xuanzhou Anhui China
182 B2 Xubín Spain
109 E1 Xuchang Henan China
99 J5 Xuchang Henan China
Xucheng Guangdong China see Xuwen
129 F3 Xudat Azer.
210 D3 Xuddur Somalia
Xueba Xizang China see Sangri
Xuefeng Fujian China see Mingxi
108 D3 Xuefeng Shan mts China
107 F5 Xuehua Shan hill Shanxi China
108 A3 Xue Shan mts Yunnan China
107 H5 Xugou Jiangsu China
Xuguit Qi Nei Mongol China see Yakeshi
Xujiang Jiangxi China see Guangchang
Xulun Hobot Qagan Qi Nei Mongol China see Qagan Nur
Xulun Hoh Qi Nei Mongol China see Dund Hot
100 D2 Xun r. China
108 B3 Xundian Yunnan China
111 F6 Xung Qu r. Xizang China
111 D6 Xungru Xizang China
100 C2 Xunhe Heilong. China
108 D1 Xun He r. China
106 D5 Xunhua Qinghai China
108 D4 Xun Jiang r. China
100 D2 Xunke Heilong. China
182 C2 Xunqueira de Ambía Spain
109 E3 Xunwu Jiangxi China
107 G5 Xunxian Henan China
108 D1 Xunyang Shaanxi China
107 F5 Xunyi Shaanxi China
108 D3 Xupu Hunan China
107 G4 Xushui Hebei China
108 D4 Xuwen Guangdong China
Xuyang Sichuan China see Rongxian
109 F1 Xuyi Jiangsu China
108 C2 Xuyong Sichuan China
107 H5 Xuzhou Jiangsu China
199 D1 Xylagani Greece
198 C2 Xylokastro Greece
198 C1 Xylopoli Greece

Y

85 G4 Yaamba Qld Austr.
108 B2 Ya'an Sichuan China
83 E3 Yaapeet Vic. Austr.
Yabanabat Turkey see Kızılcahamam
207 H5 Yabassi Cameroon
78 □3a Yabbenohr i. Kwajalein Marshall Is
210 C3 Yabēlo Eth.
197 G4 Yablanitsa Bulg.
197 H4 Yablanovo Bulg.
137 J2 Yablochnoye Rus. Fed.
137 K1 Yablonovets Rus. Fed.
137 J5 Yablonovskiy Rus. Fed.
107 F1 Yablonovyy Khrebet mts Rus. Fed.
136 C3 Yabluniv Ukr.
137 F3 Yablunivka Ukr.
207 G3 Yabo Nigeria
106 D4 Yabrai Shan mts China
106 D4 Yabrai Yanchang Nei Mongol China
128 C3 Yabrūd Syria
247 □1 Yabucoa Puerto Rico
100 D3 Yabuli Heilong. China
136 E2 Yabunets' Ukr.
Yacha Hainan China see Baisha
108 D5 Yacheng Hainan China
108 C3 Yachi He r. China
105 G3 Yachiyo Chiba Japan
105 F2 Yachiyo Ibaraki Japan
83 F4 Yackandandah Vic. Austr.
252 E5 Yacuiba Bol.
114 C2 Yadgir Karnataka India
114 C3 Yadiki Andhra Prad. India
231 D5 Yadkin r. NC U.S.A.
231 D4 Yadkinville NC U.S.A.
111 E7 Yadong Xizang China
134 I5 Yadrin Rus. Fed.
79 □1 Yadua i. Fiji
Yafa Israel see Tel Aviv-Yafo
202 B1 Yafran Libya
206 E4 Yagaba Ghana
Yagaing state Myanmar see Arakan
199 E2 Yağcılı Turkey
Yağda Turkey see Erdemli
264 E9 Yaghan Basin sea feature S. Atlantic Ocean
128 B1 Yağızlar Turkey
129 C3 Yağlıca Dağı mt. Turkey
122 C2 Yagman Turkm.
129 C4 Yağmurlu r. Turkey
139 K2 Yagnitsa Rus. Fed.
197 G4 Yagoda Bulg.
120 A2 Yagodnaya Polyana Rus. Fed.
131 P3 Yagodnoye Rus. Fed.
Yagotin Ukr. see Yahotyn
207 I4 Yagoua Cameroon
111 C6 Yagra Xizang China
106 B5 Yagradagzê Shan mt. Qinghai China
246 C2 Yaguajay Cuba
Yaguarón r. Brazil/Uru. see Jaguarão
250 D5 Yaguas r. Peru
97 C6 Yaha Thai.
104 C4 Yahagi-gawa r. Japan
222 G5 Yahk B.C. Can.
136 E4 Yahorlyk r. Ukr.
137 F2 Yahotyn Ukr.
244 C3 Yahualica Mex.
118 D2 Yahyalı Turkey
97 B4 Yai, Khao hill Thai.
105 F2 Yaita Japan
216 □3c Yaiza Lanzarote Canary Is
105 E4 Yaizu Japan
108 B2 Yajiang Sichuan China
128 C1 Yakacık Turkey
128 B1 Yakapınar Turkey
104 D2 Yake-dake vol. Japan
107 I1 Yakeshi Nei Mongol China
136 D3 Yakhivtsi Ukr.
137 G2 Yakhnyky Ukr.
139 K3 Yakhroma Rus. Fed.
238 B2 Yakima WA U.S.A.
238 C2 Yakima r. WA U.S.A.
121 F5 Yakkabag Uzbek.
206 E3 Yako Burkina
197 F4 Yakoruda Bulg.
137 I3 Yakovenkove Ukr.
100 E3 Yakovlevka Rus. Fed.
137 I2 Yakovlevo Rus. Fed.
134 K4 Yakshur-Bod'ya Rus. Fed.
102 □1 Yaku-shima i. Japan
220 E4 Yakutat AK U.S.A.
131 N3 Yakutsk Rus. Fed.
137 H4 Yakymivka Ukr.
97 C6 Yala Thai.
199 F1 Yalakdere Turkey
129 F3 Yalama Azer.
128 A1 Yalan Dünya Mağarası tourist site Turkey
81 D5 Yaldhurst South I. N.Z.
222 F5 Yale B.C. Can.
227 F4 Yale MI U.S.A.
206 E3 Yalgo Burkina
87 C6 Yalgoo W.A. Austr.
199 E3 Yalıkavak Turkey
197 I5 Yalıköy Turkey
208 D3 Yalinga C.A.R.
138 G5 Yalizava Belarus
246 □ Yallahs Jamaica
85 F5 Yalleroi Qld Austr.
87 B7 Yallingup W.A. Austr.
83 F4 Yallourn Vic. Austr.
129 C3 Yalnızçam Dağları mts Turkey
237 F5 Yalobusha r. MS U.S.A.
Yalogo Burkina see Yalgo
208 C3 Yaloké C.A.R.
108 B3 Yalong Jiang r. Sichuan China
199 F1 Yalova Turkey
197 I5 Yalova prov. Turkey
Yaloven' Moldova see Ialoveni
136 E5 Yalpuh, Ozero l. Ukr.
Yalpukh r. Moldova see Ialpug
137 I4 Yalta Donets'ka Oblast' Ukr.
137 H5 Yalta Respublika Krym Ukr.
136 D3 Yaltushkiv Ukr.
107 I2 Yalu Jiang r. China
101 C4 Yalu Jiang r. China/N. Korea
130 H4 Yalutorovsk Rus. Fed.
199 G2 Yalvaç Turkey
Yama Ukr. see Sivers'k
103 E7 Yamaga Japan
102 J3 Yamagata Iwate Japan
102 J4 Yamagata Yamagata Japan
102 I4 Yamagata pref. Japan
103 E6 Yamaguchi Japan
103 E6 Yamaguchi pref. Japan
105 F3 Yamakita Japan
130 H2 Yamal, Poluostrov pen. Rus. Fed.
Yamal Peninsula Rus. Fed. see Yamal, Poluostrov
104 C2 Yamanaka Japan
105 E3 Yamanashi Japan
105 E3 Yamanashi pref. Japan
Yamankhalinka Kazakh. see Makhambet
105 E2 Yamanouchi Japan
107 F1 Yamarovka Rus. Fed.
105 F3 Yamato Kanagawa Japan
102 □1 Yamato Nansei-shotō Japan
104 B4 Yamato-kōriyama Japan
104 B4 Yamatotakada Japan
83 H2 Yamba N.S.W. Austr.
83 E4 Yambacoona Tas. Austr.
84 B2 Yambarran Range hills N.T. Austr.
208 B2 Yamba Tchangsou Chad
206 B4 Yambéring Guinea
250 D4 Yambi, Mesa de hills Col.
208 F3 Yambio Sudan
197 H4 Yambol Bulg.
250 B6 Yambrasbamba Peru
91 H8 Yamdena i. Indon.
103 E7 Yame Japan
96 B2 Yamethin Myanmar
105 G2 Yamizo-san mt. Japan
114 B2 Yamkanmardi Karnataka India
Yamkhad Syria see Ḥalab
138 G2 Yamm Rus. Fed.
85 E5 Yamma Yamma, Lake salt flat Qld Austr.
137 H2 Yamne Ukr.
206 D5 Yamoussoukro Côte d'Ivoire
137 F3 Yampil' Cherkas'ka Oblast' Ukr.
136 D3 Yampil' Khmel'nyts'ka Oblast' Ukr.
137 G2 Yampil' Sums'ka Oblast' Ukr.
136 E3 Yampil' Vinnyts'ka Oblast' Ukr.
Yampol' Cherkas'ka Oblast' Ukr. see Yampil'
Yampol' Khmel'nyts'ka Oblast' Ukr. see Yampil'
Yampol' Sums'ka Oblast' Ukr. see Yampil'
Yampol' Vinnyts'ka Oblast' Ukr. see Yampil'
116 E4 Yamuna r. India
116 D3 Yamunanagar Haryana India
111 E6 Yamzho Yumco l. China
107 F4 Yan r. China
207 H4 Yana Nigeria
131 O2 Yana r. Rus. Fed.
82 E4 Yanac Vic. Austr.
103 F7 Yanadani Japan
103 F7 Yanai Japan
114 D2 Yanam Andhra Prad. India
107 F4 Yan'an Shaanxi China
252 C3 Yanaoca Peru
Yanaon Andhra Prad. India see Yanam
134 K4 Yanaul Rus. Fed.
139 H4 Yanavichy Belarus
108 B3 Yanbian Sichuan China
124 B2 Yanbu' al Baḥr Saudi Arabia
124 B2 Yanbu' an Nakhl reg. Saudi Arabia
231 E4 Yanceyville NC U.S.A.
107 F4 Yanchang Shaanxi China
109 G1 Yancheng Jiangsu China
Yancheng Shandong China see Qihe
Yancheng Sichuan China see Jingyan
87 B6 Yanchep W.A. Austr.
107 E4 Yanchi Ningxia China
107 F4 Yanchuan Shaanxi China
137 I4 Yanchur r. Ukr.
83 F3 Yanco N.S.W. Austr.
83 F3 Yanco Creek r. N.S.W. Austr.
83 E2 Yanco Glen N.S.W. Austr.
Yandao Sichuan China see Yingjing
110 E4 Yandaxkak Xinjiang China
87 C5 Yandil W.A. Austr.
85 H5 Yandina Qld Austr.
96 A3 Yandoon Myanmar
Yandua i. Fiji see Yadua
106 B3 Yandun Xinjiang China
139 I1 Yanega Rus. Fed.
206 C4 Yanfolila Mali
107 G3 Yang r. China
208 E4 Yangambi Dem. Rep. Congo
111 F6 Ya'ngamdo Xizang China
111 F6 Ya'ngamdo Xizang China
206 D3 Yangasso Mali
111 E6 Yangbajain Xizang China
108 A3 Yangbi Yunnan China
Yangcheng Guangdong China see Yangshan
107 G5 Yangcheng Shanxi China
Yangchuan Guizhou China see Suiyang
109 D4 Yangchun Guangdong China
109 E4 Yangcun Guangdong China
Yangcun Tianjin China see Wuqing
101 C5 Yangdok N. Korea
107 G3 Yanggao Shanxi China
107 G4 Yanggu Shandong China
Yanghe Ningxia China see Yongning
120 E4 Yangiaryk Uzbek.
121 F4 Yangikishlak Uzbek.
120 F5 Yangi-Nishan Uzbek.
123 G2 Yangi Qal'eh Afgh.
120 F4 Yangirabad Uzbek.
121 G4 Yangiyul' Uzbek.
109 D4 Yangjiang Guangdong China
96 B3 Yangôn Myanmar
115 H2 Yangôn admin. div. Myanmar
109 D2 Yangping Hubei China
107 G4 Yangquan Shanxi China
109 E3 Yangshan Guangdong China
108 D3 Yangshuo Guangxi China
96 C3 Yang Talat Thai.
108 B3 Yangtouyan Yunnan China
108 A1 Yangtze r. China
alt. Chang Jiang,
alt. Jinsha Jiang,
alt. Tongtian He,
alt. Zhi Qu,
long Yangtze Kiang
Yangtze, Mouth of the China see Changjiang Kou
Yangtze Kiang r. China see Yangtze
183 H2 Yanguas Spain
109 D4 Yangxi Guangdong China
108 C1 Yangxian Shaanxi China
101 D5 Yangyang S. Korea
107 G3 Yangyuan Hebei China
109 F1 Yangzhou Jiangsu China
108 D2 Yanhe Guizhou China
82 C3 Yaninee, Lake salt flat S.A. Austr.
134 F3 Yanishpole Rus. Fed.
100 D4 Yanji Jilin China
107 G5 Yanjin Henan China
108 C2 Yanjin Yunnan China
Yanjing Sichuan China see Yanyuan
108 A2 Yanjing Xizang China
Yanjing Yunnan China see Yanjin
Yankou Sichuan China see Wusheng
236 D3 Yankton SD U.S.A.
129 C1 Yankul' Rus. Fed.
129 C1 Yankul' r. Rus. Fed.
107 G5 Yanling Henan China
109 E3 Yanling Hunan China
Yannina Greece see Ioannina
131 P2 Yano-Indigirskaya Nizmennost' lowland Rus. Fed.
114 D4 Yan Oya r. Sri Lanka
110 D3 Yanqi Xinjiang China
107 G3 Yanqing Beijing China
125 G3 Yanqul Oman
87 B4 Yanrey r. W.A. Austr.
107 H4 Yanshan Hebei China
109 F2 Yanshan Jiangxi China
108 C4 Yanshan Yunnan China
107 H3 Yan Shan mts China
107 G5 Yanshi Henan China
111 F5 Yanshiping Qinghai China
100 D3 Yanshou Heilong. China
131 O2 Yanskiy Zaliv g. Rus. Fed.
83 F2 Yantabulla N.S.W. Austr.
122 B2 Yantagh Iran
107 I4 Yantai Shandong China
259 B6 Yántales, Cerro mt. Chile
138 B4 Yantarnyy Rus. Fed.
235 F1 Yantic r. CT U.S.A.
108 C2 Yanting Sichuan China
100 C4 Yantongshan Jilin China
109 G2 Yantou Zhejiang China
197 G4 Yantra r. Bulg.
124 C3 Yanūfī, Jabal al hill Saudi Arabia
Yany-Kurgan Kazakh. see Zhanakorgan
108 B3 Yanyuan Sichuan China
107 H5 Yanzhou Shandong China
104 B4 Yao Japan
108 B3 Yao'an Yunnan China
Yaodu Anhui China see Dongzhi
109 F2 Yaoli Jiangxi China
207 H6 Yaoundé Cameroon
107 F5 Yaoxian Shaanxi China
107 F4 Yaozhen Shaanxi China
91 I5 Yap i. Micronesia
252 D3 Yapacani r. Bol.
258 F3 Yapeyú Arg.
235 F2 Yaphank NY U.S.A.
85 E3 Yappar r. Qld Austr.
151 G4 Yapton West Sussex, England U.K.
266 E5 Yap Trench sea feature N. Pacific Ocean
251 G4 Yapukarri Guyana
242 C3 Yaqui r. Mex.
134 K4 Yar Rus. Fed.
246 C2 Yara Cuba
250 D2 Yaracuy state Venez.
85 F5 Yaraka Qld Austr.
Yarangüme Turkey see Tavas
134 I4 Yaransk Rus. Fed.
82 C3 Yardea S.A. Austr.
129 F4 Yardımlı Azer.
234 D2 Yardley PA U.S.A.
234 D2 Yardville NJ U.S.A.
Yardymly Azer. see Yardımlı
151 I2 Yare r. England U.K.
134 K3 Yarega Rus. Fed.
136 C3 Yaremcha Ukr.
77 G2 Yaren Nauru
134 J3 Yarenga r. Rus. Fed.
134 J3 Yarensk Rus. Fed.
137 G3 Yares'ky Ukr.
Yargara Moldova see Iargara
250 C5 Yari r. Col.
104 D2 Yariga-take mt. Japan
124 D5 Yarīm Yemen
Yarımca Turkey see Körfez
247 E5 Yaritagua Venez.
Yarkand Xinjiang China see Shache
Yarkant Xinjiang China see Shache
111 B4 Yarkant He r. China
227 I3 Yarker Ont. Can.
123 H2 Yarkhun r. Pak.
87 F6 Yarle Lakes salt flat S.A. Austr.
197 F4 Yarlovo Bulg.
111 E7 Yarlung Zangbo r. China
alt. Dihang (India),
conv. Brahmaputra
149 H3 Yarm Stockton-on-Tees, England U.K.
136 D3 Yarmolyntsi Ukr.
225 H5 Yarmouth N.S. Can.
151 F4 Yarmouth Isle of Wight, England U.K.
Yarmouth Norfolk, England U.K. see Great Yarmouth
233 □H3 Yarmouth ME U.S.A.
128 B3 Yarmūk r. Asia
241 K4 Yarnell AZ U.S.A.
151 F3 Yarnton Oxfordshire, England U.K.
137 G2 Yaroshivka Ukr.
137 G2 Yaroslavets' Ukr.
139 L3 Yaroslavl' Rus. Fed.
Yaroslavl Oblast admin. div. Rus. Fed. see Yaroslavskaya Oblast'
129 B1 Yaroslavskaya Rus. Fed.
139 L3 Yaroslavskaya Oblast' admin. div. Rus. Fed.
100 E3 Yaroslavskiy Rus. Fed.
128 B3 Yarqon r. Israel
85 E2 Yarraden Qld Austr.
83 F4 Yarra Junction Vic. Austr.
86 B4 Yarraloola W.A. Austr.
83 F4 Yarram Vic. Austr.
85 G5 Yarraman Qld Austr.
83 F4 Yarrawonga Vic. Austr.
87 B6 Yarra Yarra Lakes salt flat W.A. Austr.
86 D4 Yarrie W.A. Austr.
85 F5 Yarronvale Qld Austr.
85 F4 Yarrowmere Qld Austr.
139 I4 Yartsevo Rus. Fed.
111 D6 Yaru r. China
250 C3 Yarumal Col.
108 A2 Yarwa Sichuan China
108 A2 Yarzhong Xizang China
Yaş Romania see Iaşi
115 E1 Yasai r. W. Bengal India
79 □1 Yasawa i. Fiji
79 □1 Yasawa Group is Fiji
136 C3 Yasen' Ukr.
137 J4 Yaseni r. Rus. Fed.
197 H4 Yasenkovo Bulg.
135 G7 Yasenskaya Rus. Fed.
135 H7 Yashalta Rus. Fed.
207 G3 Yashi Nigeria
207 F4 Yashikera Nigeria
135 K5 Yashkino Rus. Fed.
135 I7 Yashkul' Rus. Fed.
116 C1 Yasin Jammu and Kashmir
Yasinovataya Ukr. see Yasynuvata
136 C3 Yasinya Ukr.
197 H4 Yasna Polyana Bulg.
139 K4 Yasnogorsk Rus. Fed.
137 I3 Yasnohirka Ukr.
136 F2 Yasnohorodka Ukr.
120 D2 Yasnyy Rus. Fed.
96 D4 Yasothon Thai.
83 G3 Yass N.S.W. Austr.
83 G3 Yass r. N.S.W. Austr.
199 F3 Yassıhüyük Denizli Turkey
137 H2 Yastrubyne Ukr.
104 C3 Yasu Japan
103 F6 Yasugi Japan
122 B4 Yāsūj Iran
77 G3 Yasur vol. Vanuatu
136 D1 Yasyel'da r. Belarus
137 I3 Yasynuvata Ukr.
252 D2 Yata r. Bol.
208 D2 Yata r. C.A.R.
199 F3 Yatağan Turkey
211 C5 Yata Plateau Kenya
78 □5 Yaté New Caledonia
150 E3 Yate South Gloucestershire, England U.K.
151 G3 Yateley Hampshire, England U.K.
222 H2 Yates r. Alta/N.W.T. Can.
237 E4 Yates Center KS U.S.A.
Yatou Shandong China see Rongcheng
187 C5 Yatova Spain
136 F3 Yatran' r. Ukr.
105 E3 Yatsuga-take vol. Japan
103 E7 Yatsushiro Japan
103 E7 Yatsushiro-kai b. Japan
128 B4 Yaṭṭa West Bank
150 E3 Yatton North Somerset, England U.K.
252 B3 Yauca Peru
252 B3 Yauca r. Peru
247 □1 Yauco Puerto Rico
252 A2 Yauli Peru
250 D5 Yauna Maloca Col.
252 C3 Yauri Peru
245 E4 Yautepec Mex.
252 B3 Yauyos Peru
Yavan Tajik. see Yovon
250 D6 Yavari r. Brazil/Peru alt. Javari
242 C3 Yávaros Mex.
116 D5 Yavatmal Mahar. India
252 B3 Yavero r. Peru
251 E3 Yaví, Cerro mt. Venez.
137 G4 Yavkyne Ukr.
121 G1 Yavlenka Kazakh.
175 L6 Yavora Ukr.
136 C3 Yavoriv Ivano-Frankivs'ka Oblast' Ukr.
136 B3 Yavoriv L'vivs'ka Oblast' Ukr.
140 O1 Yavr r. Fin./Rus. Fed.
128 C1 Yavuzlu Turkey
104 B4 Yawata Japan
103 F7 Yawatahama Japan
111 C4 Yawatongguz He r. China
111 C4 Yawatongguzlangar Xinjiang China
96 A2 Yaw Chaung r. Myanmar
243 H5 Yaxchilan tourist site Guat.
Yaxian Hainan China see Sanya
151 G2 Yaxley Cambridgeshire, England U.K.
129 B4 Yaygın Turkey
129 A4 Yaylabaşı Turkey
128 C2 Yayladağı Hatay Turkey
129 B4 Yayladere Turkey
129 C4 Yayladüzü Turkey
134 L4 Yayva Rus. Fed.
96 A2 Yazagyo Myanmar
122 C4 Yazd Iran
122 C4 Yazd prov. Iran
122 C4 Yazd-e Khvāst Iran
Yazgulemskiy Khrebet mts Tajik. see Yazgulom, Qatorkŭhi
123 G2 Yazgulom, Qatorkŭhi mts Tajik.
139 I2 Yazhelbitsy Rus. Fed.
126 E3 Yazıhan Malatya Turkey
199 F3 Yazıkent Turkey
199 G3 Yazır Turkey
237 F5 Yazoo r. MS U.S.A.
237 F5 Yazoo City MS U.S.A.
134 L3 Yaz'va r. Rus. Fed.
Y Bala Gwynedd, Wales U.K. see Bala
179 G2 Ybbs r. Austria
179 G2 Ybbs an der Donau Austria
179 F3 Ybbsitz Austria
253 F6 Ybycui Para.
163 B4 Ychoux France
162 E3 Ydes France
142 C4 Yding Skovhøj hill Denmark
198 C3 Ydra Greece
198 C3 Ydra i. Greece
Y Drenewydd Powys, Wales U.K. see Newtown
96 B4 Ye Myanmar
96 B4 Ye r. Myanmar
149 H4 Yeadon West Yorkshire, England U.K.
150 D4 Yealmpton Devon, England U.K.
Yebaishou Liaoning China see Jianping
121 G4 Yebekshi Kazakh.
183 H4 Yebra Spain
186 C2 Yebra de Basa Spain
111 B4 Yecheng Xinjiang China
187 B6 Yecla Spain
182 D4 Yecla de Yeltes Spain
242 C2 Yécora Mex.
114 C3 Yedatore Karnataka India
Yedintsy Moldova see Edineţ
129 B4 Yedisu Turkey
128 B2 Yeditepe Turkey
139 I3 Yedrovo Rus. Fed.
86 D3 Yeeda River W.A. Austr.
231 D7 Yeehaw Junction FL U.S.A.
82 C3 Yeelanna S.A. Austr.
139 J2 Yefimovskiy Rus. Fed.
139 L5 Yefremov Rus. Fed.
Yêgainnyin Qinghai China see Henan
129 D4 Yeghegis r. Armenia
129 D4 Yeghegnadzor Armenia
129 D3 Yeghvard Armenia
121 I2 Yegindybulak Kazakh.
135 H7 Yegorlyk r. Rus. Fed.
135 H7 Yegorlykskaya Rus. Fed.
139 L4 Yegor'yevsk Rus. Fed.
185 F2 Yeguas r. Spain
207 F4 Yégué Togo
210 A3 Yei r. Sudan
109 E2 Yeji Anhui China
206 E4 Yeji Ghana
Yejiaji Anhui China see Yeji
130 H4 Yekaterinburg Rus. Fed.
Yekaterinodar Rus. Fed. see Krasnodar
Yekaterinoslav Ukr. see Dnipropetrovs'k
100 D2 Yekaterinoslavka Rus. Fed.
137 J4 Yekaterinovka Rostovskaya Oblast' Rus. Fed.
135 I5 Yekaterinovka Saratovskaya Oblast' Rus. Fed.
Yekaterinovskaya Krasnodarskiy Kray Rus. Fed. see Krylovskaya
129 D2 Yekatorinogradskaya Rus. Fed.
Yekhegnadzor Armenia see Yeghegnadzor
139 I4 Yekimovichi Rus. Fed.
208 D4 Yekokora r. Dem. Rep. Congo
100 E2 Yelabuga Khabarovskiy Kray Rus. Fed.
134 J5 Yelabuga Respublika Tatarstan Rus. Fed.
135 H6 Yelan' Rus. Fed.
135 H6 Yelan' r. Rus. Fed.
135 H6 Yelan' r. Rus. Fed.
137 F4 Yelanets' Ukr.
83 G2 Yelarbon Qld Austr.
135 H5 Yelat'ma Rus. Fed.
199 F2 Yeleğen Turkey
Yelenovka Ukr. see Zoryns'k
Yelenovskiye Kar'yery Ukr. see Dokuchayevs'k
139 J5 Yelenskiy Rus. Fed.
139 L5 Yelets Rus. Fed.
134 N2 Yeletskiy Rus. Fed.
139 I2 Yeligovo Rus. Fed.
206 C3 Yélimané Mali
139 L4 Yelino Rus. Fed.
Yelizavetgrad Kirovohrads'ka Oblast' Ukr. see Kirovohrad
137 J4 Yelizavetovka Rostovskaya Oblast' Rus. Fed.
137 K2 Yelizavetovka Voronezhskaya Oblast' Rus. Fed.
131 Q4 Yelizovo Rus. Fed.
135 J5 Yelkhovka Rus. Fed.
146 □G1 Yell i. Scotland U.K.
114 D2 Yellandu Andhra Prad. India
114 B3 Yellapur Karnataka India
114 C2 Yellareddi Andhra Prad. India
226 B4 Yellow r. WI U.S.A.
87 C6 Yellowdine W.A. Austr.
234 D2 Yellow Frame NJ U.S.A.
234 C2 Yellow House PA U.S.A.
222 H2 Yellowknife N.W.T. Can.
222 H2 Yellowknife r. N.W.T. Can.
83 F3 Yellow Mountain hill N.S.W. Austr.
Yellow River r. China see Huang He
266 D3 Yellow Sea N. Pacific Ocean
232 B5 Yellow Springs OH U.S.A.
236 C2 Yellowstone r. MT U.S.A.
146 □G1 Yell Sound str. Scotland U.K.
237 E4 Yellville AR U.S.A.
238 B2 Yelm WA U.S.A.
185 H2 Yelmo mt. Spain
135 H5 Yel'niki Rus. Fed.
139 I4 Yel'nya Rus. Fed.
123 E2 Yeloten Turkm.
134 K4 Yelovo Rus. Fed.
129 D4 Yelp'in Armenia
136 E2 Yel'sk Belarus
182 D4 Yeltes r. Spain
242 □I6 Yelucá mt. Nic.
134 J3 Yelva r. Rus. Fed.
137 I4 Yelyseyivka Ukr.
137 G3 Yelyzavethradka Ukr.
106 C4 Yematan Qinghai China
183 I5 Yémeda Spain
124 D5 Yemen country Asia
136 D2 Yemil'chyne Ukr.
Yemişenbükü Turkey see Taşova
Yemmiganur Andhra Prad. India see Emmiganuru
134 H3 Yemtsa Rus. Fed.
134 J3 Yemva Respublika Komi Rus. Fed.
207 G5 Yenagoa Nigeria
137 J3 Yenakiyeve Ukr.
Yenakiyevo Ukr. see Yenakiyeve
96 A2 Yenangyaung Myanmar
96 D2 Yên Bai Vietnam
83 F3 Yenda N.S.W. Austr.
207 E4 Yendi Ghana
Yêndum Xizang China see Zhag'yab
208 D5 Yenge r. Dem. Rep. Congo
206 C4 Yengema Sierra Leone
110 B4 Yengisar Xinjiang China
110 D3 Yengisar Xinjiang China
129 B4 Yenibaşlar Turkey
135 F8 Yeniçağa Turkey
199 E2 Yenice Çanakkale Turkey
128 B1 Yenice İçel Turkey
199 F1 Yeniceköy Bursa Turkey
126 D3 Yeniceoba Turkey
199 E1 Yeniçiftlik Çanakkale Turkey
199 E1 Yeniçiftlik Turkey
129 B4 Yenidal Turkey
199 F3 Yenidere r. Turkey
199 E2 Yenifoça Turkey
Yenihan Turkey see Yıldızeli
199 E3 Yenihisar Turkey
Yenije-i-Vardar Greece see Giannitsa
129 F3 Yenikänd Azer.
199 E2 Yeniköy İzmir Turkey
199 F2 Yeniköy Turkey
199 F2 Yeniköy Turkey
199 E1 Yenimuhacirköy Edirne Turkey
199 F3 Yenipazar Aydın Turkey
199 G1 Yenipazar Bilecik Turkey
199 E2 Yenişakran Turkey
Yeniséa Greece see Genisea
Yenişehir Greece see Larisa
199 F1 Yenişehir Turkey
98 Yenisey r. Rus. Fed.
131 K4 Yeniseysk Rus. Fed.
131 K4 Yeniseyskiy Kryazh ridge Rus. Fed.
106 C5 Yeniugou Qinghai China
Yeniyol Turkey see Borçka
160 D3 Yenne France
135 I7 Yenotayevka Rus. Fed.
150 D4 Yeo r. England U.K.
116 C5 Yeola Mahar. India
87 E5 Yeo Lake salt flat W.A. Austr.
Yeotmal Mahar. India see Yavatmal
83 G3 Yeoval N.S.W. Austr.
150 E4 Yeovil Somerset, England U.K.
150 E3 Yeovilton Somerset, England U.K.
Yeo Yeo r. N.S.W. Austr. see Bland
183 G5 Yepes Spain
139 L5 Yepifan' Rus. Fed.
85 G4 Yeppoon Qld Austr.
Yerakaroú Greece see Gerakarou
135 H5 Yerakhtur Rus. Fed.
Yerákion Greece see Geraki
Yeraliyev Kazakh. see Kuryk
131 L3 Yerbogachen Rus. Fed.
114 C4 Yercaud Tamil Nadu India
121 H2 Yerementau, Gory hills Kazakh.
129 D3 Yerevan Armenia
121 H2 Yereymentau Kazakh.
114 C2 Yergara Karnataka India
135 I7 Yergeni hills Rus. Fed.
Yergoğu Romania see Giurgiu
Yeriḥo West Bank see Jericho
87 D6 Yerilla W.A. Austr.
240 H2 Yerington NV U.S.A.
199 F3 Yerkesik Muğla Turkey
128 A1 Yerköprü Mağarası tourist site Turkey
126 D3 Yerköy Turkey
114 B2 Yerla r. India
Yermak Pavlodarskaya Oblast' Kazakh. see Aksu
Yermentau Kazakh. see Yereymentau
135 H5 Yermish' Rus. Fed.
242 D3 Yermo Mex.
240 I4 Yermo CA U.S.A.
139 M3 Yermolino Rus. Fed.
100 B1 Yerofey Pavlovich Rus. Fed.
128 B4 Yeroham Israel
Yeropótamos r. Kriti Greece see Geropotamos
156 B4 Yerre r. France
156 C4 Yerres r. France
134 K2 Yersa r. Rus. Fed.
164 D3 Yerseke Neth.
139 I5 Yershichi Rus. Fed.
120 B2 Yershov Rus. Fed.
139 M1 Yertsevo Rus. Fed.
252 A2 Yerupaja mt. Peru
Yerushalayim Israel/West Bank see Jerusalem
120 A2 Yeruslan r. Rus. Fed.
159 G2 Yerville France
137 K2 Yeryshevka Rus. Fed.
Yerzhar Uzbek. see Gagarin
186 B2 Yesa Spain
Yeshera Georgia see Eshera
121 F2 Yesil' Kazakh.
128 C1 Yeşil Turkey
199 F3 Yeşildere Turkey
128 C1 Yeşildere Turkey
128 A1 Yeşildere Turkey
126 D3 Yeşilhisar Turkey
126 E2 Yeşilırmak r. Turkey
128 C1 Yeşilkent Turkey
199 F2 Yeşilköy Kütahya Turkey
199 F3 Yeşilova Turkey
Yeşilova Yozgat Turkey see Sorgun
199 G3 Yeşilyayla Turkey
199 F2 Yeşilyurt Manisa Turkey
199 F3 Yeşilyuva Turkey
146 E2 Yesnaby Orkney, Scotland U.K.
260 B4 Yeso, Cerro mt. Chile
129 C1 Yessentuki Rus. Fed.
129 C1 Yessentukskaya Rus. Fed.
131 L3 Yessey Rus. Fed.
185 H2 Yeste Spain
150 C4 Yes Tor hill England U.K.
185 H2 Yetas de Abajo Spain
Yêtatang Xizang China see Baqên
83 G2 Yetman N.S.W. Austr.
96 A2 Yeu Myanmar
158 D5 Yeu, Île d' i. France
Yevdokimovskoye Stavropol'skiy Kray Rus. Fed. see Krasnogvardeyskoye
Yevlakh Azer. see Yevlax
129 E3 Yevlax Azer.
137 G5 Yevpatoriya Ukr.
160 A1 Yèvre r. France
100 E2 Yevreyskaya Avtonomnaya Oblast' admin. div. Rus. Fed.
137 J3 Yevsuh r. Ukr.
109 E1 Yexian Henan China
Yexian Shandong China see Laizhou
121 I4 Yeygen'yevka Kazakh.
135 G7 Yeysk Rus. Fed.
137 J4 Yeyskoye Ukreplenie Rus. Fed.
110 D3 Yeyungou Xinjiang China
Yezhou Hubei China see Jianshi
134 I2 Yezhuga r. Rus. Fed.
Yezo i. Japan see Hokkaidō
138 G4 Yezyaryshcha Belarus
Y Fenni Monmouthshire, Wales U.K. see Abergavenny
158 D3 Yffiniac France
Y Fflint Flintshire, Wales U.K. see Flint
163 B5 Ygos-St-Saturnin France
160 A2 Ygrande France
107 G5 Yi r. Henan China
107 H5 Yi r. Shandong China
261 I3 Yí r. Uru.
Yialí i. Greece see Gyali
128 A4 Yi'allaq, Gebel mt. Egypt
Yialousa Cyprus see Aigialousa
100 C3 Yi'an Heilong. China
Yiannitsá Greece see Giannitsa
108 C2 Yibin Sichuan China
108 C2 Yibin Sichuan China
109 D2 Yichang Hubei China
109 E2 Yicheng Hubei China
107 F5 Yicheng Shanxi China
107 G5 Yichuan Henan China
107 F5 Yichuan Shaanxi China
100 D3 Yichun Heilong. China
109 E3 Yichun Jiangxi China
Yidu Shandong China see Qingzhou
108 A2 Yidun Sichuan China
109 E2 Yifeng Jiangxi China
Yiggêtang Qinghai China see Qumarlêb
199 G1 Yığılca Turkey
128 C1 Yiğityolu Turkey
109 F3 Yihuang Jiangxi China
Yijiang Jiangxi China see Yiyang
107 F5 Yijun Shaanxi China
107 J1 Yilaha Heilong. China
100 D3 Yilan Heilong. China
Yilan Taiwan see Ilan
129 B3 Yıldırım Turkey
126 B2 Yıldız Dağları mts Turkey
126 E3 Yıldızeli Turkey
108 B3 Yiliang Yunnan China
108 C3 Yiliang Yunnan China
87 C7 Yilliminning W.A. Austr.
100 C3 Yilong Heilong. China
108 C2 Yilong Sichuan China
Yilong Yunnan China see Shiping
107 H3 Yimatu r. China
96 C1 Yimen Yunnan China
100 D3 Yimianpo Heilong. China
107 H1 Yimin r. China
107 H5 Yinan Shandong China
Yincheng Jiangxi China see Dexing
106 E4 Yinchuan Ningxia China
87 D6 Yindarlgooda, Lake salt flat W.A. Austr.
109 E2 Yingcheng Hubei China
109 E3 Yingde Guangdong China
Yinggen Hainan China see Qiongzhong
109 F1 Ying He r. China
108 A3 Yingjiang Yunnan China
108 B2 Yingjing Sichuan China
Yingkou Liaoning China see Dashiqiao
107 I3 Yingkou Liaoning China
109 E2 Yingshan Hubei China
108 C2 Yingshan Sichuan China
109 F1 Yingshang Anhui China
109 F2 Yingtan Jiangxi China
Yingtaoyuan Henan China see Fanxian
207 H5 Yingui Cameroon
107 G4 Yingxian Shanxi China
Yining Jiangxi China see Xiushui
110 C3 Yining Xinjiang China
108 D3 Yinjiang Guizhou China
109 E3 Yinkeng Jiangxi China
100 C3 Yinma r. China
96 A2 Yinmabin Myanmar
107 F3 Yin Shan mts China
Yinxian Zhejiang China see Ningbo
Yiófiros r. Kriti Greece see Giofyros
111 F6 Yi'ong Zangbo r. Xizang China
Yioúra i. Greece see Gioura
108 B3 Yipinglang Yunnan China
199 G2 Yıprak Turkey
Yiquan Guizhou China see Meitan
257 E5 Yira Chapeu, Monte mt. Brazil
210 C3 Yirga Alem Eth.
210 C3 Yirga Ch'efē Eth.
84 D2 Yirrkala N.T. Austr.
Yirshi Nei Mongol China see Yirxie
107 H2 Yirxie Nei Mongol China
Yisa Yunnan China see Honghe
Yishan Guangxi China see Yizhou
Yishan Jiangsu China see Guanyun
107 H4 Yi Shan mt. Shandong China
107 H5 Yishui Shandong China
Yíthion Greece see Gytheio
Yitiaoshan Gansu China see Jingtai
100 C4 Yitong Jilin China
100 C3 Yitong r. China
96 B2 Yi Tu, Nam r. Myanmar
107 I1 Yitulihe Nei Mongol China
106 B3 Yiwanquan Xinjiang China
106 B3 Yiwu Xinjiang China
109 F2 Yixian Anhui China
107 G4 Yixian Hebei China
107 I3 Yixian Liaoning China
109 F2 Yixing Jiangsu China
107 H3 Yixun r. China
109 E2 Yiyang Hunan China
109 F2 Yiyang Jiangxi China
107 H4 Yiyuan Shandong China
109 E3 Yizhang Hunan China
109 F1 Yizheng Jiangsu China
108 D3 Yizhou Guangxi China
Yizhou Hebei China see Yixian
Yizhou Liaoning China see Yixian
Yizra'el country Asia see Israel
141 O3 Ylämaa Fin.
141 M3 Yläne Fin.
140 M3 Ylihärmä Fin.
140 N2 Yli-Ii Fin.
140 N2 Ylikiiminki Fin.
140 M3 Ylistaro Fin.
140 M2 Ylitornio Fin.
140 N2 Ylivieska Fin.
140 N2 Ylläs hill Fin.
150 D2 Y Llethr hill Wales U.K.
141 M3 Ylöjärvi Fin.
221 P2 Ymer Nunatak Greenland
156 B4 Ymonville France
131 O3 Ynykchanskiy Rus. Fed.
Ynys Môn i. Wales U.K. see Anglesey
237 D6 Yoakum TX U.S.A.
207 H4 Yobe state Nigeria
102 J2 Yobetsu-dake vol. Japan
104 B4 Yodo-gawa r. Japan
234 B3 Yoe PA U.S.A.
259 C9 Yogan, Cerro mt. Chile
95 E4 Yogyakarta Indon.
95 E5 Yogyakarta admin. dist. Indon.
102 J2 Yoichi-dake mt. Japan
242 □I6 Yojoa, Lago de l. Hond.
101 C5 Yŏju S. Korea
207 I6 Yokadouma Cameroon
104 C3 Yōkaichi Japan
105 G3 Yōkaichiba Japan
102 □1 Yokate-jima i. Japan
104 C4 Yokkaichi Japan
207 I5 Yoko Cameroon
105 F3 Yokohama Japan
105 F3 Yokosuka Japan
102 J4 Yokote Japan
102 J3 Yokotsu-dake mt. Japan
207 I4 Yola Nigeria
240 G2 Yolo CA U.S.A.
Yolöten Turkm. see Yeloten
96 C4 Yom, Mae Nam r. Thai.
105 G1 Yomogida-dake hill Fukushima Japan
206 C5 Yomou Guinea
129 A3 Yomra Turkey
162 A2 Yon r. France
103 F6 Yonago Japan
102 □1 Yonaguni-jima i. Japan
101 C5 Yŏnan N. Korea
102 J3 Yoneshiro-gawa r. Japan
105 E1 Yone-yama hill Japan
102 J5 Yonezawa Japan
82 D3 Yongala S.A. Austr.
101 C6 Yŏng-am S. Korea
Yong'an Chongqing China see Fengjie
109 F3 Yong'an Fujian China
Yongbei Yunnan China see Yongsheng
106 D4 Yongchang Gansu China
109 F1 Yongcheng Henan China
101 D6 Yŏngch'ŏn S. Korea
108 C2 Yongchuan Chongqing China
109 F3 Yongchun Fujian China
108 A3 Yongde Yunnan China
106 D4 Yongdeng Gansu China
109 F3 Yongding Fujian China
Yongding Yunnan China see Fumin

Yongding Yunnan China see Yongren
107 H4 **Yongding** r. China
109 E3 **Yongfeng** Jiangxi China
Yongfeng Jiangxi China see Guangfeng
108 D3 **Yongfu** Guangxi China
101 C6 **Yŏnggwang** S. Korea
107 F4 **Yonghe** Shanxi China
101 C5 **Yŏnghŭng** N. Korea
100 C4 **Yongji** Jilin China
109 G2 **Yongjia** Zhejiang China
106 D5 **Yongjing** Gansu China
Yongjing Guizhou China see Xifeng
Yongjing Liaoning China see Xifeng
101 D5 **Yŏngju** S. Korea
109 G2 **Yongkang** Zhejiang China
Yongle Shaanxi China see Zhen'an
Yongle Sichuan China see Nanping
101 C4 **Yongling** Liaoning China
107 G4 **Yongnian** Hebei China
108 D4 **Yongning** Guangxi China
Yongning Jiangxi China see Tonggu
106 E4 **Yongning** Ningxia China
Yongning Sichuan China see Xuyong
108 A3 **Yongping** Yunnan China
Yongqing Gansu China see Qingshui
108 B3 **Yongren** Yunnan China
101 C6 **Yŏngsan-gang** r. S. Korea
108 B2 **Yongshan** Yunnan China
108 B3 **Yongsheng** Yunnan China
107 F5 **Yongshou** Shaanxi China
108 D2 **Yongshun** Hunan China
109 F3 **Yongtai** Fujian China
101 D5 **Yŏngwol** S. Korea
Yongxi Guizhou China see Nayong
109 E3 **Yongxing** Hunan China
109 E3 **Yongxing** Jiangxi China
109 E2 **Yongxiu** Jiangxi China
109 D3 **Yongzhou** Hunan China
233 G4 **Yonkers** NY U.S.A.
156 D5 **Yonne** dept Bourgogne France
156 C4 **Yonne** r. France
250 C3 **Yopal** Col.
110 B4 **Yopurga** Xinjiang China
116 C2 **Yordu** Jammu and Kashmir
87 C6 **York** W.A. Austr.
227 H4 **York** Ont. Can.
223 M4 **York** r. Man. Can.
149 H4 **York** York, England U.K.
149 H4 **York** admin. div. England U.K.
237 F5 **York** AL U.S.A.
236 D3 **York** NE U.S.A.
234 B3 **York** PA U.S.A.
231 D5 **York** SC U.S.A.
85 E1 **York, Cape** Qld Austr.
149 H3 **York, Vale of** val. England U.K.
234 B3 **York County** county PA U.S.A.
85 E2 **York Downs** Qld Austr.
82 D3 **Yorke Peninsula** S.A. Austr.
82 D3 **Yorketown** S.A. Austr.
234 B2 **York Haven** PA U.S.A.
149 G3 **Yorkshire Dales National Park** England U.K.
149 I4 **Yorkshire Wolds** hills England U.K.
234 A2 **York Springs** PA U.S.A.
223 K5 **Yorkton** Sask. Can.
232 E6 **Yorktown** VA U.S.A.
235 E1 **Yorktown Heights** NY U.S.A.
242 □I6 **Yoro** Hond.
104 C3 **Yōrō** Japan
102 □1 **Yoro-jima** i. Japan
102 □1 **Yoron-tō** i. Japan
106 E1 **Yöröö Gol** r. Mongolia
206 D3 **Yorosso** Mali
240 H3 **Yosemite Village** CA U.S.A.
105 E4 **Yoshida** Japan
103 G6 **Yoshii-gawa** r. Japan
104 B4 **Yoshino-gawa** r. Japan
103 G6 **Yoshino-gawa** r. Japan
134 I4 **Yoshkar-Ola** Rus. Fed.
253 E4 **Yotau** Bol.
102 J2 **Yōtei-zan** mt. Japan
105 G3 **Yotsukaidō** Japan
222 E5 **Youbou** B.C. Can.
111 E4 **Youdunzi** Qinghai China
147 D5 **Youghal** Rep. of Ireland
147 C5 **Youghal Bay** Rep. of Ireland
108 D4 **You Jiang** r. China
149 H4 **Youlgreave** Derbyshire, England U.K.
83 G3 **Young** N.S.W. Austr.
87 D7 **Young** r. W.A. Austr.
261 I3 **Young** Uru.
241 L4 **Young** AZ U.S.A.
82 D2 **Younghusband, Lake** salt flat S.A. Austr.
82 D3 **Younghusband Peninsula** S.A. Austr.
263 K2 **Young Island** Antarctica
81 B6 **Young Range** mts South I. N.Z.
223 I5 **Youngstown** Alta Can.
232 C4 **Youngstown** OH U.S.A.
232 D4 **Youngsville** PA U.S.A.
240 F2 **Yountville** CA U.S.A.
111 E4 **Youshashan** Qinghai China
108 D2 **You Shui** r. China
204 C2 **Youssoufia** Morocco
206 D3 **Youvarou** Mali
109 F3 **Youxi** Fujian China
109 E3 **Youxian** Hunan China
108 D2 **Youyang** Chongqing China
100 D3 **Youyi** Heilong. China
110 D1 **Youyi Feng** mt. China/Rus. Fed.
107 G4 **Youyu** Shanxi China
123 G2 **Yovon** Tajik.
87 C5 **Yowereena Hill** hill W.A. Austr.
151 F2 **Yoxall** Staffordshire, England U.K.
151 I2 **Yoxford** Suffolk, England U.K.
126 D3 **Yozgat** Turkey
253 G5 **Ypé-Jhú** Para.
159 G2 **Yport** France
Ypres Belgium see **Ieper**
227 F4 **Ypsilanti** MI U.S.A.
238 B3 **Yreka** CA U.S.A.
Yrghyz Kazakh. see **Irgiz**
Yr Wyddfa mt. Wales U.K. see **Snowdon**
Yr Wyddgrug Flintshire, Wales U.K. see **Mold**
150 D2 **Ysbyty Ystwyth** Ceredigion, Wales U.K.
156 C2 **Yser** r. France alt. **IJzer (Belgium)**
164 E3 **Ysselsteyn** Neth.
161 C3 **Yssingeaux** France
143 E4 **Ystad** Sweden
150 D3 **Ystalyfera** Neath Port Talbot, Wales U.K.
150 D1 **Ystrad** r. Wales U.K.
150 D3 **Ystradgynlais** Powys, Wales U.K.
150 C2 **Ystwyth** r. Wales U.K.
Ysyk-Köl Kyrg. see **Balykchy**
121 I4 **Ysyk-Köl** admin. div. Kyrg.
121 I4 **Ysyk-Köl** salt l. Kyrg.
146 F4 **Ythan** r. Scotland U.K.
Y Trallwng Powys, Wales U.K. see **Welshpool**
Ytre Vinje Norway see **Åmot**
131 O3 **Ytyk-Kyuyel'** Rus. Fed.
107 G4 **Yu** r. China
109 D2 **Yuan'an** Hubei China
108 D3 **Yuanbao Shan** mt. Guangxi China
109 E2 **Yuanjiang** Hunan China
108 B4 **Yuanjiang** Yunnan China
108 D2 **Yuan Jiang** r. Hunan China
108 B4 **Yuan Jiang** r. Yunnan China
Yuanjiazhuang Shaanxi China see **Foping**
109 G3 **Yüanli** Taiwan
107 I1 **Yuanlin** Nei Mongol China
108 D2 **Yuanling** Hunan China
Yuanma Yunnan China see Yuanmou
108 B3 **Yuanmou** Yunnan China
107 G4 **Yuanping** Shanxi China
107 F5 **Yuanqu** Shanxi China
Yuanquan Gansu China see Anxi
Yuanshan Guangdong China see **Lianping**
106 C4 **Yuanshanzi** Gansu China
108 B4 **Yuanyang** Yunnan China
240 G2 **Yuba City** CA U.S.A.
102 J2 **Yūbari** Japan
102 K2 **Yūbari-dake** mt. Japan
102 K2 **Yūbari-sanchi** mts Japan
108 C2 **Yubei** Chongqing China
102 K1 **Yūbetsu-gawa** r. Japan
121 J2 **Yubileynyy** Kazakh.
240 I4 **Yucaipa** CA U.S.A.
243 H5 **Yucatán** pen. Mex.
243 H4 **Yucatán** state Mex.
243 I4 **Yucatan Channel** Cuba/Mex.
241 J4 **Yucca** AZ U.S.A.
241 I3 **Yucca Lake** NV U.S.A.
241 I4 **Yucca Valley** CA U.S.A.
129 B4 **Yücetepe** Turkey
Yucheng Guangdong China see Yunan
107 G5 **Yucheng** Henan China
107 H4 **Yucheng** Shandong China
107 G4 **Yuci** Shanxi China
134 J5 **Yudino** Respublika Tatarstan Rus. Fed.
134 G4 **Yudino** Yaroslavskaya Oblast' Rus. Fed.
100 B1 **Yudi Shan** mt. China
131 O4 **Yudoma** r. Rus. Fed.
109 E3 **Yudu** Jiangxi China
Yuecheng Sichuan China see Yuexi
108 C2 **Yuechi** Sichuan China
Yuelai Heilong. China see Huachuan
84 B4 **Yuendumu** N.T. Austr.
109 □ **Yuen Long** H.K. China
109 G2 **Yueqing** Zhejiang China
109 F2 **Yuexi** Anhui China
108 B2 **Yuexi** Sichuan China
109 E2 **Yueyang** Hunan China
109 E2 **Yueyang** Hunan China
Yueyang Sichuan China see Anyue
134 L4 **Yug** Rus. Fed.
134 I3 **Yug** r. Rus. Fed.
109 F2 **Yugan** Jiangxi China
128 A1 **Yuğluk Dağı** mts Turkey
134 K4 **Yugo-Kamskiy** Rus. Fed.
Yugo-Osetinskaya Avtonomnaya Oblast' aut. reg. Georgia see **Samkhret' Oset'i**
130 H3 **Yugorsk** Rus. Fed.
134 M1 **Yugorskiy Poluostrov** pen. Rus. Fed.
196 E3 **Yugoslavia** country Europe
109 G2 **Yuhang** Zhejiang China
Yuhu Yunnan China see Eryuan
109 G2 **Yuhuan** Zhejiang China
107 H4 **Yuhuang Ding** mt. Shandong China
105 E3 **Yui** Japan
87 C5 **Yuin** W.A. Austr.
109 F2 **Yujiang** Jiangxi China
108 D4 **Yu Jiang** r. China
Yujin Sichuan China see Qianwei
131 Q3 **Yukagirskoye Ploskogor'ye** plat. Rus. Fed.
134 K4 **Yukamenskoye** Rus. Fed.
199 E2 **Yukarıbey** Turkey
129 C3 **Yukarıgündeş** Turkey
129 C3 **Yukarıkaragüney** Turkey
199 G2 **Yukarı Sakarya Ovaları** plain Turkey
129 C3 **Yukarısarıkamış** Turkey
126 D3 **Yukarısarıkaya** Turkey
135 J5 **Yukhmachi** Rus. Fed.
139 J4 **Yukhnov** Rus. Fed.
209 C5 **Yuki** Dem. Rep. Congo
105 F2 **Yūki** Japan
220 B3 **Yukon** r. Can./U.S.A.
222 B2 **Yukon Crossing** Y.T. Can.
222 C2 **Yukon Territory** admin. div. Can.
127 G3 **Yüksekova** Turkey
103 E7 **Yukuhashi** Japan
84 B5 **Yulara** N.T. Austr.
120 D1 **Yuldybayevo** Rus. Fed.
86 C4 **Yule** r. W.A. Austr.
85 G5 **Yuleba** Qld Austr.
231 D6 **Yulee** FL U.S.A.
110 D3 **Yuli** Xinjiang China
109 G4 **Yüli** Taiwan
108 D4 **Yulin** Guangxi China
107 F4 **Yulin** Shaanxi China
108 B3 **Yulongxue Shan** mt. Yunnan China
241 J5 **Yuma** AZ U.S.A.
236 C3 **Yuma** CO U.S.A.
241 J5 **Yuma Desert** AZ U.S.A.
120 D1 **Yumaguzino** Rus. Fed.
260 A5 **Yumbel** Chile
250 B4 **Yumbo** Col.
106 C4 **Yumen** Gansu China
106 C3 **Yumenzhen** Gansu China
110 C2 **Yumin** Xinjiang China
106 C2 **Yumt Uul** mt. Mongolia
128 B1 **Yumurtalık** Turkey
87 B6 **Yuna** W.A. Austr.
246 E3 **Yuna** r. Dom. Rep.
126 C3 **Yunak** Turkey
137 H2 **Yunakivka** Ukr.
109 D4 **Yunan** Guangdong China
107 G5 **Yuncheng** Shandong China
107 F5 **Yuncheng** Shanxi China
87 D6 **Yundamindera** W.A. Austr.
109 E4 **Yunfu** Guangdong China
252 D4 **Yungas** reg. Bol.
252 C4 **Yungayo** Peru
108 B3 **Yun Gui Gaoyuan** plat. Yunnan China
Yunhe Jiangsu China see Pizhou
Yunhe Yunnan China see Heqing
109 F2 **Yunhe** Zhejiang China
Yunjinghong Yunnan China see Jinghong
108 D4 **Yunkai Dashan** mts China
Yunling Fujian China see Yunxiao
108 A3 **Yun Ling** mts Yunnan China
108 A3 **Yunlong** Yunnan China
109 E2 **Yunmeng** Hubei China
109 E3 **Yunmenling** Jiangxi China
108 B3 **Yunnan** prov. China
137 J3 **Yunokomunarivs'k** Ukr.
185 F4 **Yunquera** Spain
183 G4 **Yunquera de Henares** Spain
109 E2 **Yun Shui** r. China
82 D3 **Yunta** S.A. Austr.
128 A1 **Yunt Dağı** mt. Turkey
199 F2 **Yunuslar** Turkey
108 D1 **Yunxi** Hubei China
Yunxi Sichuan China see Yanting
108 D1 **Yunxian** Hubei China
108 B3 **Yunxian** Yunnan China
109 F4 **Yunxiao** Fujian China
134 M2 **Yun'yakha** r. Rus. Fed.
108 D2 **Yunyang** Chongqing China
109 E1 **Yunyang** Henan China
Yupin Yunnan China see Pingbian
Yuping Guizhou China see **Libo**
108 D3 **Yuping** Guizhou China
108 C3 **Yuqing** Guizhou China
252 D5 **Yura** Bol.
252 D5 **Yura** r. Bol.
250 B6 **Yuracyacu** Peru
104 B3 **Yura-gawa** r. Japan
102 J2 **Yūrappu-dake** mt. Japan
138 E4 **Yuratsishki** Belarus
137 I3 **Yurchenkove** Ukr.
128 B1 **Yürekli** Turkey
130 J4 **Yurga** Rus. Fed.
250 B6 **Yurimaguas** Peru
134 I4 **Yurino** Rus. Fed.
244 D3 **Yuriria** Mex.
244 D3 **Yuriria, Laguna** l. Mex.
129 E1 **Yurkovka** Rus. Fed.
134 K4 **Yurla** Rus. Fed.
137 I5 **Yurovka** Rus. Fed.
199 E1 **Yürük** Turkey
111 C4 **Yurungkax He** r. China
134 J4 **Yur'ya** Rus. Fed.
134 K2 **Yur'yakha** r. Rus. Fed.
Yuryev Estonia see **Tartu**
134 H4 **Yur'yevets** Rus. Fed.
139 M3 **Yur'yevets** Rus. Fed.
139 L3 **Yur'yev-Pol'skiy** Rus. Fed.
137 I3 **Yur"yivka** Ukr.
137 I4 **Yur"yivka** Ukr.
242 □I6 **Yuscarán** Hond.
109 F3 **Yushan** Fujian China
109 F2 **Yushan** Jiangxi China
109 G4 **Yü Shan** mt. Taiwan
107 G4 **Yushe** Shanxi China
134 F2 **Yushkozero** Rus. Fed.
100 C3 **Yushu** Jilin China
108 A1 **Yushu** Qinghai China
110 D3 **Yushugou** Xinjiang China
134 J4 **Yushut** r. Rus. Fed.
Yushuwan Hunan China see Huaihua
135 I7 **Yusta** Rus. Fed.
127 F2 **Yusufeli** Turkey
134 K4 **Yus'va** Rus. Fed.
Yuta West Bank see **Yaṭṭa**
107 H5 **Yutai** Shandong China
135 K5 **Yutaza** Rus. Fed.
107 H4 **Yutian** Hebei China
111 C4 **Yutian** Xinjiang China
253 F6 **Yuty** Para.
157 G3 **Yutz** France
199 F3 **Yuva** Turkey
102 □1 **Yuwan-dake** mt. Nansei-shotō Japan
106 E4 **Yuwang** Ningxia China
129 D3 **Yuxarı Salahlı** Azer.
129 E3 **Yuxarı Tala** Azer.
Yuxi Guizhou China see Daozhen
109 D2 **Yuxi** Hubei China
108 B3 **Yuxi** Yunnan China
108 D2 **Yuxiakou** Hubei China
107 G4 **Yuxian** Hebei China
107 G4 **Yuxian** Shanxi China
109 F2 **Yuxikou** Anhui China
109 D2 **Yuyangguan** Hubei China
109 G2 **Yuyao** Zhejiang China
Yuyue Hubei China see **Jiayu**
102 J4 **Yuzawa** Japan
129 D3 **Yüzbaşılar** Turkey
134 H4 **Yuzha** Rus. Fed.
137 F4 **Yuzhne** Ukr.
Yuzhno-Kazakhstanskaya Oblast' admin. div. Kazakh. see Yuzhnyy Kazakhstan
99 Q3 **Yuzhno-Kuril'sk** Kuril'skiye O-va Rus. Fed.
131 M4 **Yuzhno-Muyskiy Khrebet** mts Rus. Fed.
100 G3 **Yuzhno-Sakhalinsk** Sakhalin Rus. Fed.
129 D1 **Yuzhno-Sukhokumsk** Rus. Fed.
135 E7 **Yuzhnoukrayinsk** Ukr.
120 E1 **Yuzhnoural'sk** Rus. Fed.
121 J1 **Yuzhnyy** Altayskiy Kray Rus. Fed.
Yuzhnyy Respublika Kalmykiya - Khalm'g-Tangch Rus. Fed. see **Adyk**
135 H7 **Yuzhnyy** Rostovskaya Oblast' Rus. Fed.
121 K2 **Yuzhnyy Altay, Khrebet** mts Kazakh.
Yuzhnyy Bug r. Ukr. see **Pivdennyy Buh**
121 G4 **Yuzhnyy Kazakhstan** admin. div. Kazakh.
120 D1 **Yuzhnyy Ural** mts Rus. Fed.
106 E5 **Yuzhong** Gansu China
Yuzhou Hebei China see **Yuxian**
107 G5 **Yuzhou** Henan China
Yuzovka Ukr. see **Donets'k**
104 A4 **Yuzuruha-yama** hill Japan
158 D3 **Yvel** r. France
156 B4 **Yvelines** dept Île-de-France France
190 B2 **Yverdon** Switz.
159 G2 **Yvetot** France
158 D3 **Yvignac** France
165 D4 **Yvoir** Belgium
160 E2 **Yvoire** France
190 B2 **Yvonand** Switz.
122 D1 **Ylanly** Turkm.
214 B5 **Yzerfontein** S. Africa
160 B2 **Yzeure** France
159 G5 **Yzeures-sur-Creuse** France

Z

204 E2 **Za, Oued** r. Morocco
245 F5 **Zaachila** Mex.
214 D5 **Zaaimansdal** S. Africa
121 G5 **Zaamin** Uzbek.
165 C3 **Zaamslag** Neth.
164 D2 **Zaandam** Neth.
164 D2 **Zaandijk** Neth.
197 H3 **Zăbala** r. Romania
196 E3 **Žabalj** Vojvodina, Srbija Yugo.
127 F3 **Zāb al Kabīr, Nahr az** r. Iraq
127 F4 **Zāb aş Şaghīr, Nahr az** r. Iraq
107 H1 **Zabaykal'sk** Rus. Fed.
195 □ **Żabbar** Malta
176 F2 **Žabčice** Czech Rep.
122 A3 **Zab-e Kuchek** r. Iran
171 E4 **Zabeltitz-Treugeböhla** Ger.
175 I3 **Żabia Wola** Pol.
124 C5 **Zabīd** Yemen
175 J2 **Zabiele** Pol.
175 J3 **Ząbki** Pol.
174 E5 **Ząbkowice Śląskie** Pol.
175 L4 **Zabłocie** Pol.
175 L2 **Zabłudów** Pol.
179 H5 **Žabno** Croatia
175 I5 **Żabno** Pol.
188 E2 **Zabok** Croatia
177 H2 **Žabokreky** Slovakia
123 F3 **Zābol** prov. Afgh.
123 E4 **Zābol** Iran
123 E5 **Zābolī** Iran
136 C3 **Zabolotiv** Ukr.
136 C2 **Zabolottya** Ukr.
139 J2 **Zabor'ye** Rus. Fed.
170 F2 **Żabów** Pol.
111 D6 **Zabqung** Xizang China
197 E2 **Zăbrani** Romania
129 F3 **Zabrat** Azer.
206 E4 **Zabré** Burkina
176 F2 **Zábřeh** Czech Rep.
174 G5 **Zabrze** Pol.
136 E2 **Zabuyannya** Ukr.
136 B2 **Zabuzhzhya** Ukr.
207 F4 **Zabzugu** Ghana
243 H6 **Zacapa** Guat.
245 F4 **Zacapoaxtla** Mex.
244 D4 **Zacapu** Mex.
254 C4 **Zacarias** r. Brazil
244 C2 **Zacatecas** Mex.
244 C2 **Zacatecas** state Mex.
242 □H6 **Zacatecoluca** El Salvador
245 E4 **Zacatepec** Morelos Mex.
245 F5 **Zacatepec** Oaxaca Mex.
245 F4 **Zacatlán** Mex.
120 B2 **Zachagansk** Kazakh.
198 B3 **Zacharo** Greece
174 F2 **Zacharzyn** Pol.
173 H3 **Zachenberg** Ger.
137 H3 **Zachepylivka** Ukr.
174 D2 **Zachodniopomorskie** prov. Pol.
244 C3 **Zacoalco** Mex.
244 B3 **Zacualpan** Mex.
Zacynthus i. Greece see Zakynthos
188 E3 **Zadar** Croatia
188 E3 **Zadarski Kanal** sea chan. Croatia
97 B5 **Zadetkale Kyun** i. Myanmar
111 F5 **Zadoi** Qinghai China
139 L5 **Zadonsk** Rus. Fed.
183 H2 **Zadorra** r. Spain
177 G2 **Zádveřice** Czech Rep.
203 G2 **Za'farâna** Egypt
185 F4 **Zafarraya** Spain
123 H3 **Zafarwal** Pak.
195 E5 **Zafferana Etnea** Sicilia Italy
184 D2 **Zafra** Spain
183 H5 **Zafra de Záncara** Spain
183 I4 **Zafrilla** Spain
204 C3 **Zag** Morocco
174 D4 **Żagań** Pol.
138 D3 **Žagarė** Lith.
193 E3 **Zagarolo** Italy
203 F2 **Zagazig** Egypt
129 D3 **Zages** Georgia
122 B3 **Zāgheh** Iran
205 H1 **Zaghouan** Tunisia
189 C7 **Zaghouan** admin. div. Tunisia
175 I5 **Zagnańsk** Pol.
197 H3 **Zagon** Romania
198 C2 **Zagora** Greece
204 D3 **Zagora** Morocco
188 E2 **Zagorje ob Savi** Slovenia
174 F3 **Zagórów** Pol.
Zagorsk Rus. Fed. see Sergiyev Posad
175 K6 **Zagórz** Pol.
185 F3 **Zagra** Spain
197 G5 **Zagrazhden** Bulg.
188 E3 **Zagreb** Croatia
174 D4 **Zagrodno** Pol.
122 A3 **Zagros, Kūhhā-ye** mts Iran
Zagros Mountains Iran see Zagros, Kūhhā-ye
197 E3 **Žagubica** Srbija Yugo.
Zagunao Sichuan China see Lixian
111 E6 **Za'gya Zangbo** r. Xizang China
177 J4 **Zagyva** r. Hungary
177 J4 **Zagyvarékas** Hungary
136 E2 **Zahal'tsi** Ukr.
185 E4 **Zahara** Spain
184 E4 **Zahara de los Atunes** Spain
125 E4 **Zahawn, Wādī** r. Yemen
122 E4 **Zāhedān** Iran
122 C4 **Zāhedān** Iran
184 D2 **Zahinos** Spain
128 B3 **Zahlé** Lebanon
Zähmet Turkm. see **Zakhmet**
171 D4 **Zahna** Ger.
177 L3 **Záhony** Hungary
177 G2 **Záhorovice** Czech Rep.
176 F3 **Záhorská Ves** Slovakia
124 C4 **Zahrān** Saudi Arabia
186 D3 **Zaidín** Spain
124 D3 **Zā'in, Jabal** hill Saudi Arabia
122 C3 **Zaindeh** r. Iran
Zainlha Sichuan China see Xiaojin
Zaire country Africa see **Congo, Democratic Republic of**
209 B6 **Zaire** prov. Angola
Zaïre r. Congo/Dem. Rep. Congo see **Congo**
196 E5 **Zajas** Macedonia
197 F4 **Zaječar** Srbija Yugo.
173 H2 **Zaječov** Czech Rep.
213 F4 **Zaka** Zimbabwe
106 D1 **Zakamensk** Rus. Fed.
176 F5 **Zákány** Hungary
177 I5 **Zákányszek** Hungary
136 B3 **Zakarpats'ka Oblast'** admin. div. Ukr.
Zakarpatskaya Oblast' admin. div. Ukr. see **Zakarpats'ka Oblast'**
Zakataly Azer. see **Zaqatala**
Zakháro Greece see **Zacharo**
139 L4 **Zakharovo** Rus. Fed.
136 C2 **Zakhidnyy Buh** r. Ukr.
123 E2 **Zakhmet** Turkm.
127 F3 **Zākhō** Iraq
Zakhodnyaya Dzvina r. Europe see **Zapadnaya Dvina**
122 A2 **Zakī, Kūh-e** mt. Iran
Zákinthos i. Greece see Zakynthos
175 I6 **Zakliczyn** Pol.
175 K5 **Zaklików** Pol.
175 H6 **Zakopane** Pol.
175 K5 **Zakrzew** Lubelskie Pol.
175 J4 **Zakrzew** Mazowieckie Pol.
174 G3 **Zakrzewo** Kujawsko-Pomorskie Pol.
174 F2 **Zakrzewo** Wielkopolskie Pol.
175 K5 **Zakrzówek-Osada** Pol.
176 D1 **Zákupy** Czech Rep.
222 F5 **Zakwaski, Mount** B.C. Can.
198 B3 **Zakynthos** Ionioi Nisoi Greece
198 B3 **Zakynthos** i. Greece
209 B6 **Zala** Angola
176 F5 **Zala** county Hungary
196 C2 **Zala** r. Romania
176 G5 **Zalaapáti** Hungary
176 F5 **Zalaegerszeg** Hungary
176 F5 **Zalai-domsag** hills Hungary
176 G5 **Zalakaros** Hungary
176 G5 **Zalakomár** Hungary
176 F5 **Zalalövő** Hungary
184 E2 **Zalamea de la Serena** Spain
184 D3 **Zalamea la Real** Spain
207 H4 **Zalanga** Nigeria
107 I2 **Zalantun** Nei Mongol China
176 G5 **Zalaszántó** Hungary
176 F5 **Zalaszentbalázs** Hungary
176 G5 **Zalaszentgrót** Hungary
176 F5 **Zalaszentiván** Hungary
176 F5 **Zalaszentmihály** Hungary
197 F2 **Zalău** Romania
177 L4 **Zalău** r. Romania
176 G5 **Zalavár** Hungary
175 J4 **Załazy** Pol.
188 E2 **Žalec** Slovenia
139 K5 **Zalegoshch'** Rus. Fed.
174 F3 **Zalesie** Kujawsko-Pomorskie Pol.
175 L3 **Zalesie** Lubelskie Pol.
232 B5 **Zaleski** OH U.S.A.
139 K2 **Zales'ye** Rus. Fed.
175 H2 **Zalewo** Pol.
174 C2 **Zalew Szczeciński** b. Pol.
143 H4 **Zalew Wiślany** b. Pol.
124 C3 **Zalim** Saudi Arabia
136 C3 **Zalishchyky** Ukr.
136 C3 **Zalissya** Ukr.
137 I4 **Zaliznychne** Ukr.
137 G4 **Zaliznyy Port** Ukr.
136 C3 **Zaliztsi** Ukr.
183 G1 **Zalla** Spain
124 B2 **Zalmā, Jabal az** mt. Saudi Arabia
174 F2 **Żalno** Pol.
164 E3 **Zaltbommel** Neth.
139 H3 **Zaluch'ye** Rus. Fed.
129 C2 **Zalukokoazhe** Rus. Fed.
175 M2 **Zal'vyanka** r. Belarus
177 L5 **Zam** Romania
105 F3 **Zama** Japan
222 G3 **Zama City** Alta Can.
125 D4 **Zamakh** Saudi Arabia
215 G2 **Zamani** S. Africa
126 D3 **Zamanti** r. Turkey
177 G5 **Zamárdi** Hungary
174 F2 **Zamarte** Pol.
92 B3 **Zambales Mountains** Phil.
176 F1 **Žamberk** Czech Rep.
209 D7 **Zambeze** r. Angola alt. **Zambezi**
209 D8 **Zambezi** r. Africa alt. **Zambeze (Angola)**
209 D8 **Zambezi** Zambia
213 H3 **Zambézia** prov. Moz.
209 E8 **Zambia** country Africa
92 B5 **Zamboanga** Phil.
92 B5 **Zamboanga Peninsula** Phil.
92 B4 **Zamboanguita** Phil.
183 H2 **Zambrana** Spain
175 K3 **Zambrów** Pol.
184 A2 **Zambujal de Cima** Port.
184 B3 **Zambujeira do Mar** Port.
207 G3 **Zamfara** state Nigeria
204 B4 **Zamlat Amagraj** hills Western Sahara
177 H4 **Zámoly** Hungary
250 B6 **Zamora** Ecuador
250 B5 **Zamora** r. Ecuador
182 E3 **Zamora** Spain
182 E3 **Zamora** prov. Castilla y León Spain
244 C4 **Zamora de Hidalgo** Mex.
175 L5 **Zamość** Pol.
175 J2 **Zamość** Pol.
Zamost'ye Pol. see **Zamość**
129 C3 **Zamp Dağı** mt. Turkey
178 B3 **Zams** Austria
108 B1 **Zamtang** Sichuan China
251 F3 **Zamuro, Sierra del** mts Venez.
208 B5 **Zanaga** Congo
245 G5 **Zanatepec** Mex.
183 G5 **Záncara** r. Spain
Zancle Sicilia Italy see **Messina**
111 B6 **Zanda** Xizang China
251 H3 **Zanderij** Suriname
165 D3 **Zandhoven** Belgium
171 F5 **Žandov** Czech Rep.
165 D3 **Zandvliet** Belgium
164 D2 **Zandvoort** Neth.
232 B5 **Zanesville** OH U.S.A.
129 D4 **Zangakutan** Armenia
206 D3 **Zangasso** Mali
Zangelan Azer. see **Zängilan**
129 D4 **Zangezuri Lerrnashght'a** mts Armenia/Azer.
129 E4 **Zängilan** Azer.
116 D2 **Zangla** Jammu and Kashmir
111 D5 **Zangsêr Kangri** mt. Xizang China
107 G4 **Zanhuang** Hebei China
174 F3 **Zaniemyśl** Pol.
122 B2 **Zanjān** Iran
122 B2 **Zanjān** prov. Iran
127 G3 **Zanjān Rūd** r. Iran
125 F2 **Zannah, Jabal az** hill U.A.E.
87 D6 **Zanthus** W.A. Austr.
206 D4 **Zantiébougou** Mali
211 C6 **Zanzibar** Tanz.
211 C6 **Zanzibar Channel** Tanz.
211 C6 **Zanzibar Island** Tanz.
211 C6 **Zanzibar North** admin. reg. Tanz.
211 C6 **Zanzibar South** admin. reg. Tanz.
211 C6 **Zanzibar West** admin. reg. Tanz.
139 K4 **Zaokskiy** Rus. Fed.
189 C7 **Zaonia Mornag** Tunisia
183 H4 **Zaorejas** Spain
109 E2 **Zaoshi** Hubei China
109 E3 **Zaoshi** Hunan China
109 E1 **Zaoyang** Hubei China
109 E1 **Zaoyangzhan** Hubei China
102 J4 **Zaō-zan** vol. Japan
137 G5 **Zaozerne** Ukr.
131 K4 **Zaozernyy** Rus. Fed.
139 L3 **Zaozer'ye** Rus. Fed.
107 H5 **Zaozhuang** Shandong China
127 F3 **Zap** r. Turkey
196 E4 **Zapadna Morava** r. Yugo.
139 H4 **Zapadnaya Dvina** r. Europe alt. **Daugava (Latvia)**, alt. **Zakhodnyaya Dzvina**, conv. **Western Dvina**
139 I3 **Zapadnaya Dvina** Rus. Fed.
197 F5 **Zapadni Rodopi** mts Bulg.
Zapadno-Kazakhstanskaya Oblast' admin. div. Kazakh. see **Zapadnyy Kazakhstan**
100 G2 **Zapadno-Sakhalinskiy Khrebet** mts Rus. Fed.
Zapadno-Sibirskaya Nizmennost' plain Rus. Fed. see **Zapadno-Sibirskaya Ravnina**
130 J3 **Zapadno-Sibirskaya Ravnina** plain Rus. Fed.
121 H4 **Zapadnyy Alamedin, Pik** mt. Kyrg.
120 C4 **Zapadnyy Chink Ustyurta** esc. Kazakh.
120 B2 **Zapadnyy Kazakhstan** admin. div. Kazakh.
98 E1 **Zapadnyy Sayan** reg. Rus. Fed.
136 D3 **Zapadyntsi** Ukr.
260 B6 **Zapala** Arg.
260 B3 **Zapallar** Chile
175 K5 **Zapałów** Pol.
183 E3 **Zapardiel** r. Spain
237 D7 **Zapata** TX U.S.A.
246 B2 **Zapata, Península de** pen. Cuba
250 C3 **Zapatoca** Col.
184 D2 **Zapatón** r. Spain
169 F5 **Zapfendorf** Ger.
138 G2 **Zaplyus'ye** Rus. Fed.
197 H2 **Zăpodeni** Romania
174 G4 **Zapolice** Pol.
140 O1 **Zapolyarnyy** Murmanskaya Oblast' Rus. Fed.
134 M2 **Zapolyarnyy** Respublika Komi Rus. Fed.
139 K2 **Zapol'ye** Rus. Fed.
244 C3 **Zapopan** Mex.
137 H4 **Zaporizhzhya** Ukr.
Zaporizhzhya Oblast admin. div. Ukr. see **Zaporiz'ka Oblast'**
137 H4 **Zaporiz'ka Oblast'** admin. div. Ukr.
Zaporozhskaya Oblast' admin. div. Ukr. see **Zaporiz'ka Oblast'**
Zaporozh'ye Ukr. see **Zaporizhzhya**
Zaporozhye Oblast admin. div. Ukr. see **Zaporiz'ka Oblast'**
244 C4 **Zapotiltic** Mex.
244 C3 **Zapotlanejo** Mex.
171 C4 **Zappendorf** Ger.
193 H3 **Zapponeta** Italy
188 E3 **Zaprešić** Croatia
139 K3 **Zaprudnya** Rus. Fed.
175 M6 **Zapytiv** Ukr.
129 E3 **Zaqatala** Azer.
111 F5 **Zaqên** Qinghai China
108 A2 **Za Qu** r. Qinghai China
111 E5 **Zaqungngomar** mt. Xizang China
Zara Croatia see **Zadar**
126 E3 **Zara** Turkey
120 F4 **Zarafshan** Uzbek.
123 G2 **Zarafshon** Tajik.
123 G2 **Zarafshon** r. Tajik.
Zarafshon Uzbek. see **Zarafshan**
Zarafshon r. Uzbek. see **Zeravshan**
123 F2 **Zarafshon, Qatorkŭhi** mts Tajik.
250 C3 **Zaragoza** Col.
243 E2 **Zaragoza** Coahuila Mex.
245 F4 **Zaragoza** Puebla Mex.
186 C3 **Zaragoza** Spain
183 I3 **Zaragoza** prov. Aragón Spain
186 C4 **Zaragozana** mt. Spain
122 D4 **Zarand** Kermān Iran
122 B3 **Zarand** Markazī Iran
177 K5 **Zărand** Romania
197 F2 **Zarandului, Munții** hills Romania
123 E4 **Zaranj** Afgh.
138 F4 **Zarasai** Lith.
183 H1 **Zaratamo** Spain
183 F3 **Zaratán** Spain
261 H4 **Zárate** Arg.
186 A1 **Zarautz** Spain
139 L4 **Zaraysk** Rus. Fed.
251 E2 **Zaraza** Venez.
121 G4 **Zarbdar** Uzbek.
185 I3 **Zarcilla de Ramos** Spain
129 E3 **Zärdab** Azer.
175 J2 **Zaręby** Pol.
175 K3 **Zaręby-Kościelne** Pol.
134 E2 **Zarechensk** Rus. Fed.
139 L5 **Zarechnyy** Rus. Fed.
123 F4 **Zargun** mt. Pak.
207 G4 **Zaria** Nigeria
Zariaspa Afgh. see **Balkh**
177 L3 **Zaricheve** Ukr.
136 D2 **Zarichne** Ukr.
122 A2 **Zarīneh Rūd** r. Iran
175 H5 **Żarki** Pol.
197 G3 **Zărnești** Romania
177 H3 **Žarnovica** Slovakia
175 I4 **Żarnów** Pol.
175 H5 **Żarnowiec** Pol.
174 E5 **Żarów** Pol.
168 F2 **Zarpen** Ger.
Zarqā' Jordan see **Az Zarqā'**
128 B3 **Zarqā', Nahr az** r. Jordan
122 C4 **Zarqān** Iran
129 F3 **Zärqava** Azer.
165 B3 **Zarren** Belgium
168 F2 **Zarrentin** Ger.
175 K6 **Zarszyn** Pol.
139 I2 **Zarubino** Novgorodskaya Oblast' Rus. Fed.
100 D4 **Zarubino** Primorskiy Kray Rus. Fed.
105 E3 **Zaruga-dake** mt. Japan
174 D4 **Żary** Pol.
185 E2 **Zarza Capilla** Spain
184 D2 **Zarza de Alange** Spain
182 D4 **Zarza de Granadilla** Spain
183 G4 **Zarza de Tajo** Spain
185 I3 **Zarzadilla de Totana** Spain
250 B3 **Zarzal** Col.
182 D5 **Zarza la Mayor** Spain
175 K6 **Zarzecze** Pol.
205 H2 **Zarzis** Tunisia
183 F4 **Zarzuela del Monte** Spain
183 F3 **Zarzuela del Pinar** Spain
182 B1 **Zas** Spain
121 J2 **Zashchita** Kazakh.
116 D2 **Zaskar** r. India
116 D2 **Zaskar Mountains** India
177 I2 **Žaškov** Slovakia
138 F4 **Zaslawye** Belarus
176 E2 **Zásmuky** Czech Rep.
137 J2 **Zasosna** Rus. Fed.
175 J5 **Zasów** Pol.
129 B1 **Zassovskaya** Rus. Fed.
136 C3 **Zastavna** Ukr.
215 F4 **Zastron** S. Africa
176 C1 **Žatec** Czech Rep.
129 D1 **Zaterechnyy** Rus. Fed.
120 E1 **Zatobol'sk** Kazakh.
136 F4 **Zatoka** Ukr.
177 G1 **Zátor** Czech Rep.
175 H6 **Zator** Pol.
175 J3 **Zatory** Pol.
136 C2 **Zaturtsi** Ukr.
136 E4 **Zatyshshya** Ukr.
122 D1 **Zaunguzskiye Karakumy** des. Turkm.
245 F4 **Zautla** Mex.
177 M2 **Zavadka** Ukr.
177 I3 **Závadka nad Hronom** Slovakia
263 F2 **Zavadovskiy Island** Antarctica
261 G3 **Zavalla** Arg.
237 E6 **Zavalla** TX U.S.A.
136 F3 **Zavallya** Ukr.
122 C3 **Zavareh** Iran
190 E4 **Zavattarello** Italy
165 D4 **Zaventem** Belgium
135 H7 **Zavetnoye** Rus. Fed.
100 G2 **Zavety Il'icha** Rus. Fed.
188 G3 **Zavidoviči** Bos.-Herz.
Zavitaya Rus. Fed. see **Zavitinsk**
100 D2 **Zavitinsk** Rus. Fed.
176 G3 **Závod** Slovakia
175 M5 **Zavods'ke** Ukr.
136 C3 **Zavods'ke** Ukr.
121 K1 **Zavodskoy** Altayskiy Kray Rus. Fed.
Zavodskoy Respublika Mordoviya Rus. Fed. see Komsomol'skiy
129 D2 **Zavodskoy** Respublika Severnaya Osetiya Rus. Fed.
134 H4 **Zavolzhsk** Rus. Fed.
Zavolzh'ye Rus. Fed. see Zavolzhsk
137 F2 **Zavorychi** Ukr.
121 J1 **Zav'yalovo** Rus. Fed.
175 L6 **Zavydovychi** Ukr.
106 D4 **Zawa** Qinghai China
175 H4 **Zawada** Łódzkie Pol.
175 L5 **Zawada** Lubelskie Pol.
174 D4 **Zawada** Lubuskie Pol.
174 F5 **Zawada** Opolskie Pol.
175 H5 **Zawada** Śląskie Pol.
175 K2 **Zawady** Pol.
174 G5 **Zawadzkie** Pol.
96 B2 **Zawgyi** r. Myanmar
175 J5 **Zawichost** Pol.
174 D4 **Zawidów** Pol.
175 H3 **Zawidz Kościelny** Pol.
175 H5 **Zawiercie** Pol.
128 C2 **Zāwīyah, Jabal az** hills Syria
125 F3 **Zawlīyah, Jiddat az** plain Oman
175 H6 **Zawoja** Pol.
174 F4 **Zawonia** Pol.
134 J5 **Zay** r. Rus. Fed.
179 H2 **Zaya** r. Austria
129 D3 **Zäyäm** Azer.
129 D3 **Zäyämçay** r. Azer.
121 K3 **Zaysan** Kazakh.
Zaysan, Lake Kazakh. see Zaysan, Ozero
121 J2 **Zaysan, Ozero** l. Kazakh.
137 J3 **Zaytseve** Ukr.
108 A2 **Zayü** Xizang China
108 A2 **Zayü** Xizang China
129 C2 **Zayukovo** Rus. Fed.
108 A2 **Zayü Qu** r. China/India
177 I2 **Zázrivá** Slovakia
136 C3 **Zbarazh** Ukr.
174 D3 **Zbąszyn** Pol.
174 D3 **Zbąszynek** Pol.
175 H2 **Zbiczno** Pol.
174 G4 **Zbiersk** Pol.
173 H2 **Zbiroh** Czech Rep.
174 G2 **Zblewo** Pol.
175 I5 **Zbludowice** Pol.
175 J2 **Zbójna** Pol.
175 H2 **Zbójno** Pol.
196 D4 **Zborište** mt. Yugo.
136 C3 **Zboriv** Ukr.
177 K2 **Zborov** Slovakia
174 F6 **Zborovice** Czech Rep.
179 H1 **Zbraslav** Czech Rep.
176 E2 **Zbraslavice** Czech Rep.
136 D3 **Zbruch** r. Ukr.
176 C2 **Zbůch** Czech Rep.
175 K3 **Zbuczyn Poduchowny** Pol.
179 H1 **Zbýšov** Czech Rep.
176 G5 **Ždala** Croatia
179 I1 **Ždánice** Czech Rep.
176 F2 **Ždánický Les** for. Czech Rep.
171 G5 **Žďár** Czech Rep.
176 E2 **Žďár nad Sázavou** Czech Rep.
176 E2 **Žďárské Vrchy** hills Czech Rep.
177 J2 **Ždiar** Slovakia
176 C2 **Zdíkov** Czech Rep.
176 E2 **Ždírec nad Doubravou** Czech Rep.
136 D2 **Zdolbuniv** Ukr.
Zdolbunov Ukr. see **Zdolbuniv**
176 G2 **Zdounky** Czech Rep.
174 G4 **Zduńska Wola** Pol.
175 H3 **Zduny** Łódzkie Pol.
174 F4 **Zduny** Wielkopolskie Pol.
136 F2 **Zdvyzh** r. Ukr.
175 J6 **Zdynia** Pol.
174 G4 **Zdziechowice** Opolskie Pol.
175 K5 **Zdziechowice** Podkarpackie Pol.
174 G5 **Zdzieszowice** Pol.
175 K5 **Zdziłowice** Pol.
Zealand i. Denmark see Sjælland
259 C7 **Zeballos** mt. Arg.
222 E5 **Zeballos** B.C. Can.
127 G3 **Zēbār** Iraq
195 □ **Żebbuġ** Gozo Malta
195 □ **Żebbuġ** Malta
174 G5 **Zębowice** Pol.
173 H2 **Žebrák** Czech Rep.
182 C5 **Zebreira** Port.
174 D4 **Zebrzydowa** Pol.
174 G6 **Zebrzydowice Dolne** Pol.
231 C5 **Zebulon** GA U.S.A.
232 B6 **Zebulon** KY U.S.A.
231 E5 **Zebulon** NC U.S.A.
170 D2 **Zechlin Dorf** Ger.
170 D2 **Zechlinerhütte** Ger.
164 F3 **Zeddam** Neth.
192 A5 **Zeddiani** Sardegna Italy
165 C3 **Zedelgem** Belgium
179 E3 **Zederhaus** Austria
177 I6 **Žednik** Vojvodina, Srbija Yugo.
165 C3 **Zeebrugge** Belgium
83 F5 **Zeehan** Tas. Austr.
164 E3 **Zeeland** Neth.
164 C3 **Zeeland** prov. Neth.
226 D4 **Zeeland** MI U.S.A.
215 F1 **Zeerust** S. Africa
171 E3 **Zeesen** Ger.
164 E2 **Zeewolde** Neth.
128 B3 **Zefat** Israel
186 A2 **Zegama** Spain
175 I6 **Żegiestów** Pol.
175 I6 **Żegocina** Pol.
175 J3 **Zegrzyńskie, Jezioro** l. Pol.
170 E3 **Zehdenick** Ger.
170 D2 **Zehna** Ger.
171 E4 **Zehren** Ger.
84 C4 **Zeil, Mount** N.T. Austr.
169 F5 **Zeil am Main** Ger.
173 G3 **Zeilarn** Ger.
138 E3 **Žeimelis** Lith.
179 H2 **Zeiselmauer** Austria
164 E2 **Zeist** Neth.
171 E4 **Zeithain** Ger.
173 G2 **Zeitlarn** Ger.
169 E5 **Zeitlofs** Ger.
171 D4 **Zeitz** Ger.
195 □ **Żejtun** Malta
106 D5 **Zêkog** Qinghai China
Zela Turkey see **Zile**
174 G4 **Żelazków** Pol.
165 D3 **Zele** Belgium
175 I4 **Żelechlinek** Pol.
175 J4 **Żelechów** Pol.
136 D3 **Zelena** Chernivets'ka Oblast' Ukr.
136 C3 **Zelena** Ivano-Frankivs'ka Oblast' Ukr.
136 C3 **Zelena** Ivano-Frankivs'ka Oblast' Ukr.
188 F4 **Zelena Gora** mt. Bos.-Herz.
176 G2 **Zelená Hora** tourist site Czech Rep.
121 H1 **Zelenaya Roshcha** Kazakh.
129 B2 **Zelenchukskaya** Rus. Fed.
171 F5 **Zeleneč** Czech Rep.
177 G3 **Zeleneč** Slovakia
188 G4 **Zelengora** mts Bos.-Herz.
137 G4 **Zelenivka** Ukr.
134 I3 **Zelennik** Rus. Fed.
140 P2 **Zelenoborskiy** Rus. Fed.
134 J5 **Zelenodol'sk** Rus. Fed.
137 G4 **Zelenodol's'k** Ukr.
138 G1 **Zelenogorsk** Rus. Fed.
139 K3 **Zelenograd** Rus. Fed.
138 C4 **Zelenogradsk** Rus. Fed.
136 F4 **Zelenohirs'ke** Ukr.
129 C1 **Zelenokumsk** Stavropol'skiy Kray Rus. Fed.
134 I4 **Zelentsovo** Rus. Fed.
121 G2 **Zelenyy Gay** Kazakh.
179 H1 **Želešice** Czech Rep.
176 E2 **Želetava** Czech Rep.
176 C2 **Železná Ruda** Czech Rep.
176 E2 **Železné Hory** hills Czech Rep.
179 F4 **Železniki** Slovenia
176 E1 **Železný Brod** Czech Rep.
164 F2 **Zelhem** Neth.
232 C4 **Zelienople** PA U.S.A.
177 H3 **Želiezovce** Slovakia
188 F3 **Zelina** Croatia
106 C4 **Zelinggou** Qinghai China
196 E5 **Želino** Macedonia
176 E2 **Želivka** r. Czech Rep.
196 E4 **Željin** mt. Yugo.
175 K3 **Żelków-Kolonia** Pol.
171 C5 **Zell** Ger.
169 C5 **Zell (Mosel)** Ger.
169 F5 **Zella-Mehlis** Ger.
172 C3 **Zell am Harmersbach** Ger.
178 D3 **Zell am See** Austria
178 C3 **Zell am Ziller** Austria
179 E2 **Zell an der Pram** Austria
179 G2 **Zellerndorf** Austria
172 D4 **Zellersee** l. Ger.
172 B4 **Zell im Wiesental** Ger.
172 D2 **Zellingen** Ger.
177 I3 **Želovce** Slovakia
175 H4 **Zelów** Pol.
172 B2 **Zeltingen-Rachtig** Ger.
179 F3 **Zeltweg** Austria
138 E5 **Zel'va** Belarus
165 C3 **Zelzate** Belgium
138 C4 **Žemaičių Naumiestis** Lith.
177 H3 **Žemberovce** Slovakia
198 B1 **Zemblak** Korçë Albania
175 K3 **Zembrów** Pol.
175 H6 **Zembrzyce** Pol.
108 B1 **Zêmdasam** Sichuan China
197 F4 **Zemen** Bulg.
197 H2 **Zemeș** Romania
135 H5 **Zemetchino** Rus. Fed.
177 G4 **Zemianska Olča** Slovakia
208 E3 **Zémio** C.A.R.
170 E2 **Zemitz** Ger.
130 F1 **Zemlya Aleksandry** i. Zemlya Frantsa-Iosifa Rus. Fed.
130 G2 **Zemlya Frantsa-Iosifa** is Rus. Fed.
130 F1 **Zemlya Georga** i. Zemlya Frantsa-Iosifa Rus. Fed.
137 J2 **Zemlyansk** Rus. Fed.
130 H1 **Zemlya Vil'cheka** i. Zemlya Frantsa-Iosifa Rus. Fed.
172 A2 **Zemmer** Ger.
129 B2 **Zemo Barghebi** Georgia
129 C3 **Zemo Khveduret'i** Georgia
129 D3 **Zemo Qarabulakhi** Georgia
177 L3 **Zemplénagárd** Hungary
177 K3 **Zempléni-hegység** hills Hungary
177 L3 **Zemplínska širava** l. Slovakia
177 K3 **Zemplínska Teplica** Slovakia
177 L3 **Zemplínske Hámre** Slovakia
245 E4 **Zempoala** Hidalgo Mex.
245 F4 **Zempoala** Veracruz Mex.
245 G5 **Zempoaltépetl, Nudo de** mt. Mex.
165 D4 **Zemst** Belgium
139 I3 **Zemtsy** Rus. Fed.
196 E3 **Zemun** Srbija Yugo.
108 A1 **Zênda** Sichuan China
109 E4 **Zengcheng** Guangdong China
100 D4 **Zengfeng Shan** mt. China
177 H5 **Zengő** hill Hungary
188 F3 **Zenica** Bos.-Herz.
173 E2 **Zenn** r. Ger.
150 □ **Zennor** Cornwall, England U.K.
Zenta Vojvodina, Srbija Yugo. see **Senta**
103 F6 **Zentsūji** Japan
205 F2 **Zenzach** Alg.
188 G3 **Žepče** Bos.-Herz.
170 E3 **Zepernick** Ger.
240 H2 **Zephyr Cove** NV U.S.A.
231 D6 **Zephyrhills** FL U.S.A.
111 B4 **Zepu** Xinjiang China
210 A2 **Zeraf, Bahr el** r. Sudan
Zeravshan Tajik. see **Zarafshon**
Zeravshan r. Tajik. see Zarafshon
121 E5 **Zeravshan** r. Uzbek.
Zeravshanskiy Khrebet mts Tajik. see **Zarafshon, Qatorkŭhi**
171 D4 **Zerbst** Ger.
121 G1 **Zerenda** Kazakh.
172 A2 **Zerf** Ger.
205 G2 **Zeribet el Oued** Alg.
177 K5 **Zerind** Romania
174 F3 **Żerków** Pol.
190 C2 **Zermatt** Switz.
190 F2 **Zernez** Switz.
168 F2 **Zernien** Ger.
170 D3 **Zernitz** Ger.
135 H7 **Zernograd** Rus. Fed.
Zernovoy Rus. Fed. see Zernograd
191 H3 **Zero** r. Italy
170 E3 **Zerpenschleuse** Ger.
170 F2 **Zerrenthin** Ger.
Zestafoni Georgia see Zestap'oni
129 C2 **Zestap'oni** Georgia
186 A1 **Zestoa** Spain
196 D4 **Zeta** r. Yugo.
111 E6 **Zêtang** Xizang China
197 G2 **Zetea** Romania
168 C2 **Zetel** Ger.
171 C5 **Zeulenroda** Ger.
171 E3 **Zeuthen** Ger.
168 E2 **Zeven** Ger.
164 F3 **Zevenaar** Neth.
164 D3 **Zevenbergen** Neth.
164 F1 **Zevenhuizen** Neth.
198 C3 **Zevgolatio** Greece
191 G3 **Zevio** Italy
100 C1 **Zeya** Rus. Fed.
100 C2 **Zeya** r. Rus. Fed.
122 C4 **Zeydābād** Iran
122 D2 **Zeydar** Iran
122 D4 **Zeynalābād** Iran
100 D2 **Zeysko-Bureinskaya Vpadina** depr. Rus. Fed.
100 C1 **Zeyskoye Vodokhranilishche** resr Rus. Fed.
199 E2 **Zeytindağ** Turkey
198 B1 **Zezë, Maja e** mt. Albania

182 B5 Zêzere r. Port.
128 B2 Zgharta Lebanon
175 H4 Zgierz Pol.
175 I6 Zgłobice Pol.
179 F4 Zgornje Bitnje Slovenia
179 G4 Zgornji Duplek Slovenia
174 D4 Zgorzelec Pol.
136 D3 Zguriţa Moldova
111 D6 Zhabdün Xizang China
136 C1 Zhabinka Belarus
136 E3 Zhabokrychka Ukr.
Zhabye Ukr. see Verkhovyna
136 E2 Zhad'ky Ukr.
137 G1 Zhadove Ukr.
Zhaggo Sichuan China see Luhuo
108 A1 Zhaglag Sichuan China
108 A2 Zhag'yab Xizang China
120 E2 Zhailma Kazakh.
121 F2 Zhaksy Kazakh.
121 G2 Zhaksy-Kon watercourse Kazakh.
120 E3 Zhaksykylysh, Ozero salt l. Kazakh.
Zhalaghash Kazakh. see Dzhalagash
121 I4 Zhalanash Almatinskaya Oblast' Kazakh.
Zhalanash Kustanayskaya Oblast' Kazakh. see Damdy
Zhalgyztöbe Kazakh. see Zhangiztobe
120 B2 Zhalpaktal Kazakh.
Zhalpaqtal Kazakh. see Zhalpaktal
121 G2 Zhaltyr Kazakh.
138 E5 Zhaludok Belarus
120 E2 Zhamanakkol', Ozero salt l. Kazakh.
121 G3 Zhambyl Karagandinskaya Oblast' Kazakh.
Zhambyl Zhambylskaya Oblast' Kazakh. see Taraz
Zhambyl Oblast admin. div. Kazakh. see Zhambylskaya Oblast'
121 H3 Zhambylskaya Oblast' admin. div. Kazakh.
121 J3 Zhameuka Kazakh.
Zhamo Xizang China see Bomi
100 D2 Zhan r. China
121 F4 Zhanakorgan Kazakh.
120 E3 Zhanakurylys Kazakh.
111 E6 Zhanang Xizang China
121 H3 Zhanaortalyk Kazakh.
120 C4 Zhanaozen Kazakh.
121 I4 Zhanatala Kazakh.
121 G4 Zhanatas Kazakh.
120 B3 Zhanbay Kazakh.
100 C2 Zhanbei Heilong. China
107 G4 Zhang r. China
Zhangaözen Kazakh. see Zhanaozen
Zhangaqazaly Kazakh. see Ayteke Bi
Zhanga Qazan Kazakh. see Novaya Kazanka
Zhangaqorghan Kazakh. see Zhanakorgan
Zhangatas Kazakh. see Zhanatas
107 G3 Zhangbei Hebei China
Zhangcheng Fujian China see Yongtai
109 F1 Zhangcunpu Anhui China
Zhangde Henan China see Anyang
Zhangdian Shandong China see Zibo
Zhanggu Sichuan China see Danba
100 D3 Zhangguangcai Ling mts China
Zhanghua Taiwan see Changhua
121 J2 Zhangiztobe Kazakh.
Zhangjiajie Hunan China see Dayong
107 G3 Zhangjiakou Hebei China
Zhangjiapan Shaanxi China see Jingbian
108 B1 Zhangla Sichuan China
109 F1 Zhanglou Anhui China
109 F3 Zhangping Fujian China
109 F3 Zhangpu Fujian China
107 H4 Zhangqiu Shandong China
109 E2 Zhangshu Jiangxi China
107 H4 Zhangwei Xinhe r. China
107 I3 Zhangwu Liaoning China
106 E5 Zhangxian Gansu China
106 D4 Zhangye Gansu China
109 F3 Zhangzhou Fujian China
107 G4 Zhangzi Shanxi China
Zhanhe Heilong. China see Zhanbei
107 H4 Zhanhua Shandong China
Zhanibek Kazakh. see Dzhanybek
108 D4 Zhanjiang Guangdong China
Zhansügirov Kazakh. see Dzhansugurov
120 C3 Zhanterek Kazakh.
108 B3 Zhanyi Yunnan China
109 F4 Zhao'an Fujian China
100 C3 Zhaodong Heilong. China
Zhaoge Henan China see Qixian
108 B2 Zhaojue Sichuan China
109 E2 Zhaoliqiao Hubei China
108 D3 Zhaoping Guangxi China
109 E4 Zhaoqing Guangdong China
Zhaoren Shaanxi China see Changwu
110 C3 Zhaosu Xinjiang China
107 I3 Zhaosutai r. China
108 B3 Zhaotong Yunnan China
107 G4 Zhaoxian Hebei China
100 C3 Zhaoyuan Heilong. China
107 I4 Zhaoyuan Shandong China
Zhaozhen Sichuan China see Jintang
Zhaozhou Hebei China see Zhaoxian
100 C3 Zhaozhou Heilong. China
109 D4 Zhapo Guangdong China
Zhaqsy Kazakh. see Zhaksy
136 E3 Zhar r. Ukr.
Zharbulak Kazakh. see Kabanbay
111 D6 Zhari Namco salt l. China
120 D3 Zharkamys Kazakh.
121 J3 Zharkent Kazakh.
139 I4 Zharkovskiy Rus. Fed.
121 J2 Zharma Kazakh.
120 C3 Zharmysh Kazakh.
Zharyk Kazakh. see Saken Seyfullin
136 F3 Zhashkiv Ukr.
Zhashkov Ukr. see Zhashkiv
108 D1 Zhashui Shaanxi China
120 D4 Zhaslyk Uzbek.
Zhaxi Yunnan China see Weixin
108 A2 Zhaxizê Xizang China
121 G2 Zhayrem Kazakh.
108 A2 Zhayü Xizang China
Zhayylma Kazakh. see Zhailma
Zhayyq r. Kazakh./Rus. Fed. see Ural
137 H3 Zhdanivka Ukr.
Zhdanov Ukr. see Mariupol'
121 G4 Zhdanovo Kazakh.
Zhdanovsk Azer. see Beyläqan
137 G2 Zhdany Ukr.
Zhdenevo Ukr. see Zhdeniyevo
136 B3 Zhdeniyevo Ukr.
107 G5 Zhecheng Henan China
Zhedao Yunnan China see Lianghe
108 B2 Zhêhor Sichuan China
109 G2 Zhejiang prov. China
109 E4 Zhelang Guangdong China
138 F2 Zhelcha r. Rus. Fed.
121 H1 Zhelezinka Kazakh.
138 C4 Zheleznodorozhnyy Kaliningradskaya Oblast' Rus. Fed.
Zheleznodorozhnyy Respublika Komi Rus. Fed. see Yemva
Zheleznodorozhnyy Uzbek. see Kungrad
139 J5 Zheleznogorsk Rus. Fed.
129 C1 Zheleznovodsk Rus. Fed.
Zhelou Guizhou China see Ceheng
121 H3 Zheltorangy Kazakh.
Zheltyye Vody Ukr. see Zhovti Vody
137 H5 Zhelyabovka Ukr.
197 H4 Zhelyu Voyvoda Bulg.
Zhem Kazakh. see Emba
117 G4 Zhemgang Bhutan
108 D1 Zhen'an Shaanxi China
108 C1 Zhenba Shaanxi China
108 C3 Zhenfeng Guizhou China
108 C2 Zheng'an Guizhou China
107 G4 Zhengding Hebei China
109 F3 Zhenghe Fujian China
Zhengjiakou Hebei China see Gucheng
Zhengjiatun Jilin China see Shuangliao
Zhengkou Hebei China see Gucheng
Zhenglan Qi Nei Mongol China see Dund Hot
107 F5 Zhengning Gansu China
Zhengxiangbai Qi Nei Mongol China see Qagan Nur
109 E1 Zhengyang Henan China
107 G5 Zhengzhou Henan China
109 G2 Zhenhai Zhejiang China
109 F1 Zhenjiang Jiangsu China
108 B1 Zhenjiangguan Sichuan China
108 A4 Zhenkang Yunnan China
107 I2 Zhenlai Jilin China
108 C3 Zhenning Guizhou China
108 D2 Zhenping Shaanxi China
Zhenwudong Shaanxi China see Ansai
107 I2 Zhenxi Jilin China
108 C3 Zhenxiong Yunnan China
Zhenyang Henan China see Zhengyang
107 E5 Zhenyuan Gansu China
108 D3 Zhenyuan Guizhou China
108 B4 Zhenyuan Yunnan China
108 D2 Zhenziling Hubei China
135 H6 Zherdevka Rus. Fed.
136 D3 Zherdya Ukr.
137 J3 Zherebets' r. Ukr.
136 E2 Zheriv r. Ukr.
136 E2 Zheriv r. Ukr.
109 F3 Zherong Fujian China
134 J3 Zheshart Rus. Fed.
Zhetibay Kazakh. see Zhetybay
Zhetikara Kazakh. see Zhitikara
Zhetisay Kazakh. see Zhetysay
120 C4 Zhetybay Kazakh.
121 G4 Zhetysay Kazakh.
121 F2 Zhezdy Kazakh.
121 F3 Zhezkazgan Karagandinskaya Oblast' Kazakh.
121 F3 Zhezkazgan Karagandinskaya Oblast' Kazakh.
Zhezqazghan Karagandinskaya Oblast' Kazakh. see Zhezkazgan
Zhicheng Zhejiang China see Changxing
107 F4 Zhidan Shaanxi China
111 F5 Zhidoi Qinghai China
131 N3 Zhigansk Rus. Fed.
120 B1 Zhigulevsk Rus. Fed.
111 E6 Zhigung Xizang China
108 D3 Zhijiang Hunan China
108 C3 Zhijin Guizhou China
139 L4 Zhilevo Rus. Fed.
Zhilong Guangdong China see Yangxi
Zhilyanka Kazakh. see Kargalinskoye
Zhi Qu r. China see Yangtze
135 I6 Zhirnovsk Rus. Fed.
Zhirnovskiy Rus. Fed. see Zhirnovsk
Zhirnoye Rus. Fed. see Zhirnovsk
139 I5 Zhiryatino Rus. Fed.
Zhitarovo Bulg. see Vetren
120 E1 Zhitikara Kazakh.
Zhitkovichi Belarus see Zhytkavichy
135 I6 Zhitkur Rus. Fed.
198 A1 Zhitom Berat Albania
Zhitomir Ukr. see Zhytomyr
Zhitomir Oblast admin. div. Ukr. see Zhytomyrs'ka Oblast'
Zhitomirskaya Oblast' admin. div. Ukr. see Zhytomyrs'ka Oblast'
127 G4 Zhivār Iran
139 J5 Zhizdra Rus. Fed.
139 K4 Zhizdra r. Rus. Fed.
139 H3 Zhizhitsa Rus. Fed.
139 H3 Zhizhitskoye, Ozero l. Rus. Fed.
139 H5 Zhlobin Belarus
Zhmerinka Ukr. see Zhmerynka
136 E3 Zhmerynka Ukr.
123 G4 Zhob Pak.
123 G3 Zhob r. Pak.
138 G4 Zhodzina Belarus
Zholkva Ukr. see Zhovkva
121 G2 Zholymbet Kazakh.
Zhong'an Yunnan China see Fuyuan
109 E4 Zhongba Guangdong China
Zhongba Sichuan China see Jiangyou
Zhongcheng Sichuan China see Xingwen
Zhongcheng Yunnan China see Suijiang
108 A3 Zhongdian Yunnan China
Zhongduo Chongqing China see Youyang
Zhongguo country Asia see China
Zhongguo Renmin Gongheguo country Asia see China
Zhonghe Chongqing China see Xiushan
107 G5 Zhongmou Henan China
106 E4 Zhongning Ningxia China
Zhongping Yunnan China see Huize
263 F2 Zhongshan research stn Antarctica
109 E4 Zhongshan Guangdong China
109 D3 Zhongshan Guangxi China
Zhongshan Guizhou China see Lupanshui
Zhongshu Yunnan China see Luxi
Zhongshu Yunnan China see Luliang
Zhongtai Gansu China see Lingtai
107 F5 Zhongtiao Shan mts China
106 E4 Zhongwei Ningxia China
108 D2 Zhongxian Chongqing China
109 E3 Zhongxin Guangdong China
Zhongxin Yunnan China see Zhongdian
Zhongxin Yunnan China see Huaping
Zhongxing Jiangsu China see Siyang
109 F2 Zhongxingji Anhui China
107 F4 Zhongyang Shanxi China
108 B3 Zhongyicun Yunnan China
109 G2 Zhongze Zhejiang China
108 C1 Zhongzhai Gansu China
Zhongzhou Chongqing China see Zhongxian
175 L4 Zhorany Ukr.
137 G3 Zhorte Ukr.
137 G2 Zhortneve Ukr.
Zhosaly Kzyl-Ordinskaya Oblast' Kazakh. see Dzhusaly
121 I2 Zhosaly Pavlodarskaya Oblast' Kazakh.
108 C2 Zhou He r. China
Zhoujiaping Shaanxi China see Nenzheng
109 E1 Zhoukou Henan China
Zhoukou Sichuan China see Peng'an
109 F3 Zhouning Fujian China
109 G2 Zhoushan Zhejiang China
109 G2 Zhoushan Dao i. China
109 G2 Zhoushan Qundao is China
107 F5 Zhouzhi Shaanxi China
136 B2 Zhovkva Ukr.
137 G4 Zhovta r. Ukr.
136 F4 Zhovten' Ukr.
137 G3 Zhovti Vody Ukr.
137 I3 Zhovtneve Kharkivs'ka Oblast' Ukr.
137 H3 Zhovtneve Poltavs'ka Oblast' Ukr.
137 H2 Zhovtneve Sums'ka Oblast' Ukr.
175 M5 Zhovtneve Volyns'ka Oblast' Ukr.
120 E2 Zhualy Kazakh.
107 I4 Zhuanghe Liaoning China
106 E5 Zhuanglang Gansu China
121 G3 Zhuantobe Kazakh.
108 A1 Zhubgyügoin Qinghai China
136 D2 Zhubrovychi Ukr.
107 H5 Zhucheng Shandong China
Zhudong Taiwan see Chutung
108 C1 Zhugqu Gansu China
109 E4 Zhuhai Guangdong China
Zhuji Henan China see Shangqiu
109 G2 Zhuji Zhejiang China
107 F4 Zhujia Chuan r. China
109 E4 Zhu Jiang r. China
Zhujing Shanghai China see Jinshan
109 E4 Zhukeng Guangdong China
139 I3 Zhukopa r. Rus. Fed.
139 I5 Zhukovka Rus. Fed.
139 K4 Zhukovo Rus. Fed.
139 L4 Zhukovskiy Rus. Fed.
136 F2 Zhukyn Ukr.
107 G4 Zhulong r. China
109 E1 Zhumadian Henan China
120 B3 Zhumysker Kazakh.
107 G3 Zhuolu Hebei China
Zhuoyang Henan China see Suiping
107 G4 Zhuozhang r. China
107 H4 Zhuozhou Hebei China
107 G3 Zhuozi Nei Mongol China
Zhuozishan Nei Mongol China see Zhuozi
121 G2 Zhuravlevka Kazakh.
136 C3 Zhuravno Ukr.
137 J5 Zhuravskaya Rus. Fed.
137 F2 Zhurivka Ukr.
120 D2 Zhuryn Kazakh.
121 H3 Zhusandala, Step' plain Kazakh.
108 D1 Zhushan Hubei China
Zhushan Hubei China see Xuan'en
108 D1 Zhuxi Hubei China
Zhuyang Sichuan China see Dazhu
109 E3 Zhuzhou Hunan China
109 E3 Zhuzhou Hunan China
175 M5 Zhvyrka Ukr.
136 C3 Zhydachiv Ukr.
120 C2 Zhympity Kazakh.
120 B3 Zhyngyldy Kazakh.
175 M4 Zhyrychi Ukr.
136 D1 Zhytkavichy Belarus
136 E2 Zhytomyr Ukr.
Zhytomyr Oblast admin. div. Ukr. see Zhytomyrs'ka Oblast'
136 D2 Zhytomyrs'ka Oblast' admin. div. Ukr.
136 E3 Zhyvka r. Ukr.
138 E5 Zhyzhma r. Belarus
107 H4 Zi r. China
206 C4 Ziama mt. Guinea
122 D2 Ziarat Iran
177 H3 Žiar nad Hronom Slovakia
127 F3 Zībār Iraq
190 F3 Zibello Italy
107 H4 Zibo Shandong China
184 B1 Zibreira Port.
192 B3 Zicavo Corse France
107 F4 Zichang Shaanxi China
Zicheng Guangdong China see Zijin
173 H2 Žichovice Czech Rep.
170 C2 Zickhusen Ger.
137 I3 Zid'ky Ukr.
174 F5 Ziębice Pol.
170 C2 Ziegendorf Ger.
171 C5 Ziegenrück Ger.
171 E4 Ziegra Ger.
Ziel, Mount N.T. Austr. see Zeil, Mount
175 L4 Zielawa r. Pol.
171 C3 Zielitz Ger.
175 I3 Zielkowice Pol.
175 H2 Zielona Pol.
174 F2 Zielona Chocina Pol.
174 D4 Zielona Góra Pol.
175 J3 Zielonka Pol.
175 H2 Zieluń Pol.
138 D3 Ziemelkursas augstiene hills Latvia
173 E3 Ziemetshausen Ger.
169 E4 Zierenberg Ger.
164 C3 Zierikzee Neth.
179 G2 Ziersdorf Austria
170 C2 Zierzow Ger.
171 D3 Ziesar Ger.
203 F2 Ziftá Egypt
96 A3 Zigon Myanmar
108 C2 Zigong Sichuan China
108 D2 Zigui Hubei China
206 A3 Ziguinchor Senegal
138 F3 Žīguri Latvia
176 C1 Žihle Czech Rep.
244 D5 Zihuatanejo Mex.
109 E4 Zijin Guangdong China
164 F2 Zijpenberg hill Neth.
Ziketan Qinghai China see Xinghai
139 J5 Zikeyevo Rus. Fed.
128 B3 Zikhron Ya'aqov Israel
120 D1 Zilair Rus. Fed.
138 E3 Zilaiskalns Latvia
126 D2 Zile Turkey
135 L5 Zilim r. Rus. Fed.
177 H2 Žilina Slovakia
177 I2 Žilinský Kraj admin. reg. Slovakia
178 C3 Ziller r. Austria
178 C3 Zillertal val. Austria
178 C3 Zillertaler Alpen mts Austria
190 E2 Zillis Switz.
169 F4 Zilly Ger.
171 F3 Ziltendorf Ger.
138 G3 Zilupe Latvia
98 H1 Zima Rus. Fed.
177 K5 Zimandu Nou Romania
245 E3 Zimapán Mex.
245 F5 Zimatlán Mex.
209 E9 Zimba Zambia
213 F4 Zimbabwe country Africa
Zimbabwe tourist site Zimbabwe see Great Zimbabwe National Monument
122 A3 Zīmkān, Rūdkhāneh-ye r. Iran
Zimmerbude Kaliningradskaya Oblast' Rus. Fed. see Svetlyy
172 C3 Zimmern ob Rottweil Ger.
169 E4 Zimmersrode (Neuental) Ger.
206 C5 Zimmi Sierra Leone
197 G4 Zimnicea Romania
134 G2 Zimniy Bereg coastal area Rus. Fed.
135 H7 Zimovniki Rus. Fed.
245 G5 Zinapa r. Mex.
207 H3 Zinder Niger
207 H3 Zinder dept Niger
108 B2 Zindo Sichuan China
207 H4 Zing Nigeria
170 D1 Zingst reg. Ger.
206 E3 Ziniaré Burkina
106 E4 Zinihu Nei Mongol China
124 D5 Zinjibār Yemen
137 H2 Zin'kiv Ukr.
173 H2 Zinkovy Czech Rep.
215 H3 Zinkwazi Beach S. Africa
170 E1 Zinnowitz Ger.
Zinoyevsk Kirovohrads'ka Oblast' Ukr. see Kirovohrad
206 D3 Zinzana Mali
226 D4 Zion IL U.S.A.
234 C3 Zion MD U.S.A.
234 B2 Zion Grove PA U.S.A.
108 A1 Ziqudukou Qinghai China
122 C2 Zirab Iran
179 F3 Zirbitzkogel mt. Austria
177 G4 Zirc Hungary
170 F2 Zirchow Ger.
129 C4 Zirekli Turkey
179 F4 Žiri Slovenia
188 E4 Žirje i. Croatia
238 F3 Zirkel, Mount CO U.S.A.
178 C3 Zirl Austria
173 E2 Zirndorf Ger.
117 H4 Ziro Arun. Prad. India
179 G1 Žirovnice Czech Rep.
109 E2 Zi Shui r. China
179 H2 Zistersdorf Austria
244 D4 Zitácuaro Mex.
177 H4 Žitava r. Slovakia
196 E3 Žitište Vojvodina, Srbija Yugo.
254 D2 Zitiua r. Brazil
Zito Xizang China see Lhorong
108 C2 Zitong Sichuan China
197 E4 Žitorsda Srbija Yugo.
171 F5 Zittau Ger.
178 A3 Zitterklapfen mt. Austria
171 D3 Zitz Ger.
188 G3 Živinice Bos.-Herz.
210 C2 Ziway Häyk' l. Eth.
109 F3 Zixi Jiangxi China
109 E3 Zixing Hunan China
107 H4 Ziya r. China
120 D2 Ziyanchurino Rus. Fed.
Ziyang Jiangxi China see Wuyuan
108 D1 Ziyang Shaanxi China
108 C2 Ziyang Sichuan China
128 B1 Ziyaret Dağı hill Turkey
129 A3 Ziyaret Dağı mt. Turkey
108 D3 Ziyuan Guangxi China
108 C3 Ziyun Guizhou China
190 E2 Zizers Switz.
108 C2 Zizhong Sichuan China
107 F4 Zizhou Shaanxi China
179 H4 Zlatar Croatia
196 D4 Zlatar mts Yugo.
179 H4 Zlatar-Bistrica Croatia
177 H3 Zlatá Studňa mt. Slovakia
176 G1 Zlaté Hory Czech Rep.
177 H3 Zlaté Moravce Slovakia
197 F3 Zlaten Rog Bulg.
196 D4 Zlatibor mts Yugo.
196 E3 Zlatica r. Yugo.
197 F2 Zlatna Romania
197 G5 Zlatograd Bulg.
130 G4 Zlatoust Rus. Fed.
100 E1 Zlatoustovsk Rus. Fed.
177 J3 Zlatý Stôl mt. Slovakia
174 G2 Zławieś Wielka Pol.
136 D2 Zlazne Ukr.
177 G2 Zlín Czech Rep.
177 G2 Zlínský kraj admin. reg. Czech Rep.
202 B1 Zlīţan Libya
176 D2 Zliv Czech Rep.
174 E2 Złocieniec Pol.
174 G4 Złoczew Pol.
171 F5 Zlonice Czech Rep.
175 I4 Złota Pol.
174 G3 Złotniki Kujawskie Pol.
174 D4 Złotoryja Pol.
174 F2 Złotów Pol.
174 E5 Złoty Stak Pol.
176 C1 Žlutice Czech Rep.
135 E5 Zlynka Rus. Fed.
137 F3 Zlynka Ukr.
121 J2 Zmeinogorsk Rus. Fed.
174 E4 Żmigród Pol.
191 I3 Žminj Croatia
Zmiyev Ukr. see Zmiyiv
139 K5 Zmiyevka Rus. Fed.
137 I3 Zmiyiv Ukr.
137 G4 Zmiyivka Ukr.
175 L4 Żmudź Pol.
121 I2 Znamenka Kazakh.
121 I1 Znamenka Altayskiy Kray Rus. Fed.
139 J5 Znamenka Orlovskaya Oblast' Rus. Fed.
Znamenka Ukr. see Znam"yanka
175 J1 Znamensk Rus. Fed.
139 J5 Znamenskoye Rus. Fed.
137 G3 Znam"yanka Ukr.
137 G3 Znam"yanka Druha Ukr.
Znauri Georgia see Qornisi
174 F3 Żnin Pol.
137 G1 Znobivka r. Ukr.
137 G1 Znob Novhorods'ke Ukr.
176 F3 Znojmo Czech Rep.
190 E4 Zoagli Italy
214 C5 Zoar S. Africa
213 G2 Zóbuè Moz.
129 C2 Zodi Georgia
Zodi-Qornisi Georgia see Zodi
164 E3 Zoelen Neth.
165 D3 Zoersel Belgium
207 H6 Zoetéle Cameroon
164 D2 Zoetermeer Neth.
164 D2 Zoeterwoude Neth.
190 C1 Zofingen Switz.
Zogainrawar Qinghai China see Huashixia
108 A2 Zogang Xizang China
190 E3 Zogno Italy
108 A1 Zogqên Sichuan China
198 C3 Zografos Greece
176 F3 Zohor Slovakia
122 B4 Zohreh r. Iran
108 B1 Zoigê Sichuan China
215 F5 Zola S. Africa
191 G4 Zola Predosa Italy
165 E3 Zolder Belgium
191 H2 Zoldo Alto Italy
129 C1 Zolka r. Rus. Fed.
175 K5 Żółkiewka-Osada Pol.
170 C2 Zölkow Ger.
190 C1 Zollikofen Switz.
190 D1 Zollikon Switz.
173 F3 Zolling Ger.
Zolochev Kharkivs'ka Oblast' Ukr. see Zolochiv
Zolochev L'vivs'ka Oblast' Ukr. see Zolochiv
137 H2 Zolochiv Kharkivs'ka Oblast' Ukr.
136 C3 Zolochiv L'vivs'ka Oblast' Ukr.
136 C3 Zolota Lypa r. Ukr.
100 C1 Zolotaya Gora Rus. Fed.
137 J3 Zolote Ukr.
175 K6 Zolotkovychi Ukr.
136 C3 Zolotnyky Ukr.
137 G3 Zolotonosha Ukr.
Zolotoye Ukr. see Zolote
135 G5 Zolotukhino Rus. Fed.
136 C3 Zolotyy Potik Ukr.
175 K5 Żołynia Pol.
213 J4 Zomandao r. Madag.
177 H5 Zomba Hungary
211 B8 Zomba Malawi
Zombor Vojvodina, Srbija Yugo. see Sombor
165 C3 Zomergem Belgium
Zomin Uzbek. see Zaamin
Zongga Xizang China see Gyirong
208 C3 Zongo Dem. Rep. Congo
245 F4 Zongolica Mex.
126 C2 Zonguldak Turkey
199 G1 Zonguldak prov. Turkey
109 F2 Zongyang Anhui China
165 E4 Zonhoven Belgium
165 B4 Zonnebeke Belgium
122 A2 Zonūz Iran
192 B3 Zonza Corse France
174 F5 Żórawina Pol.
171 D4 Zörbig Ger.
129 C4 Zor Dağ mt. Turkey
169 F4 Zorge Ger.
206 E3 Zorgho Burkina
Zorgo Burkina see Zorgho
Zorinsk Ukr. see Zoryns'k
184 E1 Zorita Spain
183 F4 Zorita r. Spain
186 C4 Zorita del Maestrazgo Spain
197 H2 Zorleni Romania
197 E3 Zorlenţu Mare Romania
157 I4 Zorn r. France
173 F3 Zorneding Ger.
172 C2 Zornheim Ger.
197 H4 Zornitsa Bulg.
250 A5 Zorritos Peru
174 G5 Żory Pol.
137 J3 Zoryns'k Ukr.
206 C5 Zorzor Liberia
171 E3 Zossen Ger.
165 C4 Zottegem Belgium
206 C5 Zouan-Hounien Côte d'Ivoire
107 H5 Zoucheng Shandong China
204 B5 Zouérat Maur.
106 C4 Zoulang Nanshan mts China
107 H4 Zouping Shandong China
109 D2 Zoushi Hunan China
164 F1 Zoutkamp Neth.
165 E4 Zoutleeuw Belgium
Zouxian Shandong China see Zoucheng
179 G4 Zreče Slovenia
196 E3 Zrenjanin Vojvodina, Srbija Yugo.
188 E3 Zrmanja r. Croatia
173 H2 Zruč Czech Rep.
176 E2 Zruč nad Sázavou Czech Rep.
177 K5 Zsadány Hungary
177 K4 Zsáka Hungary
177 H4 Zsámbék Hungary
177 I4 Zsámbok Hungary
177 I5 Zsana Hungary
171 E5 Zschaitz Ger.
171 E5 Zschopau Ger.
171 E4 Zschopau r. Ger.
171 D4 Zschortau Ger.
177 G5 Zselic hills Hungary
251 E3 Zuata r. Venez.
183 H3 Zuazo de Cuartango Spain
124 C5 Zubayr, Jazā'ir az i. Yemen
177 I2 Zuberec Slovakia
180 E4 Zubia Spain
183 H1 Zubiaur Spain
190 D3 Zubiena Italy
186 B1 Zubieta Spain
183 I2 Zubiri Spain
135 H5 Zubova Polyana Rus. Fed.
135 J5 Zubovka Rus. Fed.
136 B3 Zubra r. Ukr.
139 J3 Zubtsov Rus. Fed.
187 C4 Zucaina Spain
190 D2 Zucchero, Monte mt. Switz.
172 B4 Zuchwil Switz.
178 C4 Zuckerhütl mt. Austria
183 H2 Zudaire Spain
170 E1 Zudar Ger.
206 D5 Zuénoula Côte d'Ivoire
186 C3 Zuera Spain
125 F4 Zufār admin. reg. Oman
184 D3 Zufre Spain
190 D1 Zug Switz.
190 D1 Zug canton Switz.
186 B1 Zugarramurdi Spain
129 B2 Zugdidi Georgia
190 D1 Zuger See l. Switz.
178 B3 Zugspitze mt. Austria/Ger.
207 G4 Zugu Nigeria
185 F3 Zuheros Spain
137 J3 Zuhres Ukr.
164 D3 Zuid-Beijerland Neth.
Zuider Zee l. Neth. see IJsselmeer
164 D3 Zuid-Holland prov. Neth.
164 F1 Zuidhorn Neth.
164 D3 Zuidland Neth.
164 F1 Zuidlaren Neth.
164 F2 Zuidwolde Neth.
165 C3 Zuienkerke Belgium
Zuitai Gansu China see Kangxian
Zuitaizi Gansu China see Kangxian
Zuitou Shaanxi China see Taibai
185 H3 Zújar Spain
185 E1 Zújar r. Spain
175 L4 Żuków Pol.
174 D4 Żukowice Pol.
143 H4 Żukowo Pol.
250 D2 Zulia state Venez.
176 G1 Žulová Czech Rep.
169 B5 Zülpich Ger.
165 C4 Zulte Belgium
186 A1 Zumaia Spain
186 A1 Zumarraga Spain
250 B6 Zumba Ecuador
179 G5 Žumberačka Gora mts Croatia
213 F2 Zumbo Moz.
226 A3 Zumbro r. MN U.S.A.
226 A3 Zumbrota MN U.S.A.
185 H2 Zumeta r. Spain
245 E4 Zumpahuacán Mex.
245 E4 Zumpango Mex.
245 E5 Zumpango del Río Mex.
165 D3 Zundert Neth.
207 G4 Zungeru Nigeria
195 E4 Zungri Italy
107 H3 Zunhua Hebei China
241 M4 Zuni NM U.S.A.
239 E5 Zuni Mountains NM U.S.A.
108 C3 Zunyi Guizhou China
108 C3 Zunyi Guizhou China
183 I2 Zunzarren Spain
96 E2 Zuo Jiang r. China/Vietnam
107 G4 Zuoquan Shanxi China
107 G4 Zuoyun Shanxi China
190 E2 Zuoz Switz.
188 G3 Županja Croatia
196 E4 Žur Kosovo, Srbija Yugo.
185 H3 Zurgena Spain
190 D1 Zürich Switz.
190 D1 Zürich canton Switz.
190 D1 Zürichsee l. Switz.
129 E3 Zurnabad Azer.
179 I3 Zurndorf Austria
197 H4 Zurnevo Bulg.
175 H2 Żuromin Pol.
170 C2 Zurow Ger.
195 Żurrieq Malta
207 G4 Zuru Nigeria
190 D1 Zurzach Switz.
Zurzuna Turkey see Çıldır
173 E3 Zusam r. Ger.
139 K5 Zusha r. Rus. Fed.
105 F3 Zushi Japan
173 E3 Zusmarshausen Ger.
170 C2 Züsow Ger.
170 E2 Züssow Ger.
165 E4 Zutendaal Belgium
164 F2 Zutphen Neth.
202 B1 Zuwārah Libya
137 H5 Zuya r. Ukr.
156 C1 Zuydcoote France
134 J4 Zuyevka Rus. Fed.
179 F5 Žužemberk Slovenia
186 A1 Zuzurkil Spain
196 E4 Zvečan Kosovo, Srbija Yugo.
138 E3 Zvejniekciems Latvia
139 K4 Zvenigorod Rus. Fed.
Zvenigorodka Ukr. see Zvenyhorodka
136 F3 Zvenyhorodka Ukr.
137 K3 Zverevo Rus. Fed.
197 F4 Zverino Bulg.
120 F1 Zverinogolovskoye Rus. Fed.
198 B1 Zvezdë Albania
188 G3 Zvijezda mts Bos.-Herz.
213 F4 Zvishavane Zimbabwe
177 I3 Zvolen Slovakia
197 F4 Zvonce Srbija Yugo.
188 G3 Zvornik Bos.-Herz.
175 M5 Zvynyache Ukr.
164 F1 Zwaagwesteinde Neth.
179 G4 Zwaring Austria
214 C4 Zwarkop S. Africa
164 F2 Zwartsluis Neth.
206 C5 Zwedru Liberia
164 F2 Zweeloo Neth.
172 B2 Zweibrücken Ger.
190 C2 Zweisimmen Switz.
214 B5 Zweletemba S. Africa
215 F5 Zwelitsha S. Africa
171 D4 Zwenkau Ger.
179 G2 Zwentendorf an der Donau Austria
171 E4 Zwethau Ger.
179 G2 Zwettl Austria
179 F1 Zwettl r. Austria
165 C4 Zwevegem Belgium
165 C3 Zwevezele Belgium
171 D5 Zwickau Ger.
171 D5 Zwickauer Mulde r. Ger.
172 D3 Zwiefalten Ger.
174 D3 Zwierzyn Pol.
175 K5 Zwierzyniec Pol.
173 H2 Zwiesel Ger.
173 G4 Zwiesel mt. Ger.
165 D3 Zwijndrecht Belgium
164 D3 Zwijndrecht Neth.
190 C1 Zwingen Switz.
172 C3 Zwingenberg Ger.
168 D2 Zwischenahner Meer l. Ger.
178 A3 Zwischenwasser Austria
171 D4 Zwochau Ger.
175 J4 Zwoleń Pol.
164 F2 Zwolle Neth.
171 D5 Zwönitz Ger.
171 D5 Zwota Ger.
175 H3 Żychlin Pol.
174 F3 Żydowo Pol.
174 G4 Zygry Pol.
175 M5 Zymne Ukr.
Zymogor'ye Ukr. see Zymohir"ya
137 J3 Zymohir"ya Ukr.
175 I3 Żyrardów Pol.
Zyryan Kazakh. see Zyryanovsk
131 Q3 Zyryanka Rus. Fed.
121 K2 Zyryanovsk Kazakh.
175 K4 Żyrzyn Pol.
175 K1 Żytkiejmy Pol.
175 H5 Żytno Pol.
175 H6 Żywiec Pol.
174 F5 Żywocice Pol.

ACKNOWLEDGEMENTS

MAPS AND DATA

Maps designed and created by
HarperCollins Cartographic, Glasgow

Additional work by:
Alan Collinson Design, Llandudno, UK
Cosmographics, Watford,
Dave Edwards Cartography, North Berwick
Lovell Johns Ltd, Long Hanborough, UK

Design: One O'Clock Gun Design Consultants Ltd, Edinburgh

Data acknowledgements
Plate 121: Antarctic Digital Database (versions 1 and 2), © Scientific Committee on Antarctic Research (SCAR), Cambridge (1993, 1998)
Bathymetric data: The GEBCO Digital Atlas published by the British Oceanographic Data Centre on behalf of IOC and IHO, 1994

The mapping in this atlas is available in digital form from Bartholomew Mapping Services. For details and information visit
www.bartholomewmaps.com
or contact
Bartholomew Mapping Services
Tel: +44 (01) 141 306 3344
Fax: +44 (01) 141 306 3104
E-mail:bartholomew@harpercollins.co.uk

The publishers would like to thank all National Survey Departments, Road, Rail and National Park authorities, Statistical Offices and national place name committees throughout the World for their valuable assistance, and in particular the following:

Antarctic Place-Names Committee, FCO, London, UK

Australian Surveying & Land Information Group, Belconnen, Australia

Automobile Association of South Africa, Johannesburg, Republic of South Africa

British Antarctic Survey, Cambridge, UK

BP Amoco PLC, London, UK

British Geological Survey, Keyworth, Nottingham, UK

Chief Directorate: Surveys and Mapping, Mowbray, Republic of South Africa

Commission de toponymie du Québec, Québec, Canada

Defence Geographic and Imagery Intelligence Agency, Geographic Information Group, Tolworth, UK

Federal Survey Division, Lagos, Nigeria

Food and Agriculture Organization of the United Nations, Rome, Italy

Foreign and Commonwealth Office, London, UK

Mr P J M Geelan, London, UK

General Directorate of Highways, Ankara, Turkey

Hydrographic Office, Ministry of Defence, Taunton, UK

Institut Géographique National, Brussels, Belgium

Institut Géographique National, Paris, France

Instituto Brasileiro de Geografia e Estatistica, Rio de Janeiro, Brazil

Instituto Geográfico Nacional, Lima, Peru

Instituto Geográfico Nacional, Madrid, Spain

Instituto Portugués de Cartografia e Cadastro, Lisbon, Portugal

International Atomic Energy Agency, Vienna, Austria

International Boundary Research Unit, University of Durham, UK

International Hydrographic Organization, Monaco

International Union for the Conservation of Nature, Gland, Switzerland and Cambridge, UK

Kort- og Matrikelstyrelsen, Copenhagen, Denmark

Land Information New Zealand, Wellington, New Zealand

Lands and Surveys Department, Kampala, Uganda

H A G Lewis OBE

National Geographic Society, Washington DC, USA

National Library of Scotland, Edinburgh, UK

National Mapping and Resources Information Authority (NAMRIA), Manila, Philippines

National Oceanic and Atmospheric Administration, USA

Permanent Committee on Geographical Names, London, UK

Royal Geographical Society, London, UK

Royal Scottish Geographical Society, Glasgow, UK

Scientific Committee on Antarctic Research, Cambridge, UK

Scott Polar Research Institute, Cambridge, UK

Scottish Office Development Department, Edinburgh, UK

SNCF French Railways, London, UK

Statens Kartverket, Hønefoss, Norway

Survey Department, Singapore

Survey of India, Dehra Dun, India

Survey of Israel, Tel Aviv, Israel

Survey of Kenya, Nairobi, Kenya

Surveyor General, Harare, Zimbabwe

Surveyor General, Ministry of Lands and Natural Resources, Lusaka, Zambia

Surveys and Mapping Branch, Natural Resources, Ottawa, Canada

Surveys and Mapping Division, Dar-es-Salaam, Tanzania

Terralink New Zealand Ltd, Wellington, New Zealand

The Meteorological Office, Bracknell, Berkshire, UK

The National Imagery and Mapping Agency (NIMA), Bethesda, Maryland, USA

The Stationery Office, London, UK

The United States Board on Geographic Names, Washington DC, USA

The United States Department of State, Washington DC, USA

The United States Geological Survey, Earth Science Information Center, Reston, Virginia, USA

United Nations, specialized agencies, New York, USA

Marcel Vârlan, University 'Al. I. Cuza', Iași, Romania

IMAGES AND PHOTOS

pages 8–19
Remote Sensing Applications Consultants Ltd, 4 Mansfield Park, Medstead, Alton, Hants, GU34 5PZ, UK

pages 20–21
NRSC Ltd/Science Photo Library

pages 22–23
The Sun: Jisas/Lockheed/Science Photo Library
Mercury: NASA/Science Photo Library
Venus: NASA/Science Photo Library
Earth: Photo Library International/Science Photo Library
Mars: US Geological Survey/Science Photo Library
Jupiter: NASA/Science Photo Library
Saturn: Space Telescope ScienceInstitute/NASA/ Science Photo Library
Uranus: NASA/Science Photo Library
Neptune: NASA/Science Photo Library
Pluto and Charon: Space Telescope Science Institute/ NASA/Science Photo Library

pages 24–25
Kobe earthquake: Axiom Photographic Agency Ltd
Kilauea volcano: Soames Summerhays/Science Photo Library

pages 26–27
1: WHF Smith, US National Oceanic and Atmospheric Administration (NOAA), USA
2: A McDonald and C Wunsch, USA
4: NASA/JPL, USA
5: L Talley, USA

pages 28–29
Hurricane Floyd: National Climatic Data Centre (NCDC), National Oceanic and Atmospheric Administration (NOAA), USA

pages 30–31
2: Earth Satellite Corporation/Science Photo Library
3: CNES 1989 Distribution SPOT Image/Science Photo Library

page 41
TeleGeography Inc, Washington D.C., USA
www.telegeography.com

pages 42–43
1: © British Museum, London, UK
2: The British Library, London, UK
3: Hereford Cathedral/Bridgeman Art Library
4: E T Archive/Bibliothèque National, Paris
5: E T Archive/The British Library
6: The British Library, London, UK
7 and 8: Reproduced by permission of the Trustees of the National Library of Scotland, Edinburgh, UK
9: Derived from data collected in Parry, R.B. and Perkins, C.R. (2000) World Mapping Today. Edition 2. London:Bowker Saur

pages 44–45
1, 2, and 3: National Maritime Museum, Greenwich, London, UK
4: CNES, 1994 Distribution SPOT Image/Science Photo Library
6: Alan Collinson Design, Llandudno, UK

pages 46–47
Elbrus: Giles Pittman
Kilimanjaro and Mt McKinley: Tony Stone Images Ltd
Vinson Massif: B. Storey/British Antarctic Survey
Puncak Jaya: Alpine Ascents International Inc.
Everest: Simon Fraser/Science Photo Library
Cerro Aconcagua: Andes Press Agency
Continental images: Mountain High Maps™ Copyright © 1993 Digital Wisdom Inc

pages 48–49
Volga: CNES, 1996 Distribution SPOT Image/Science Photo Library
Nile: Earth Satellite Corporation/Science Photo Library
Chang Jiang (Yangtze): Earth Satellite Corporation/ Science Photo Library
Mississippi-Missouri: NASA/Science Photo Library
Amazon (Amazonas): Earth Satellite Corporation/ Science Photo Library

220-221
222-223
224-225
226-227
Chicago
226
NORTH AMERICA
218-219
240-241
San Francisco
239
New York
235
234-235
Washington
235
232-233
Los Angeles
239
242-243
238-239
Bermuda
231
246-2
236-237
New Providence
231
230-231
244-245
Mexico
245
228-229
242
KEY TO MAP PAGES
228-229
1:9 000 000 and smaller
244-245
1:2 000 000 - 1:4 000 000
246-247
1:5 000 000 - 1:8 000 000
234-235
1:1 000 000 - 1:2 000 000
Inset maps of islands and cities are named.